WORLD POPULATION AND PRODUCTION
TRENDS AND OUTLOOK

PRINTED IN THE UNITED STATES OF AMERICA BY

THE LORD BALTIMORE PRESS, BALTIMORE, MARYLAND

WORLD POPULATION AND PRODUCTION

TRENDS AND OUTLOOK

WORLD

POPULATION AND

PRODUCTION

TRENDS AND OUTLOOK

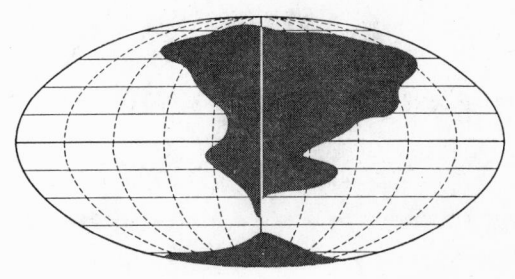

W. S. Woytinsky AND *E. S. Woytinsky*

THE TWENTIETH CENTURY FUND

NEW YORK · 1953

PRINTED IN THE UNITED STATES OF AMERICA BY

THE LORD BALTIMORE PRESS, BALTIMORE, MARYLAND

FOREWORD

THIS BOOK — together with a volume now in progress on world trade, transportation and government to be published in 1954 — represents an effort to put between the covers of two manageable volumes what amounts to a statistical picture of the collective resources, as well as the economic performance and promise of the full array of the nations of the world. The authors, Mr. and Mrs. W. S. Woytinsky, have hoped and planned for many years past to prepare a broad survey such as this. Their joint background and training — years of residence and study in the United States and European countries, a knowledge of several languages and extensive travel in both industrialized and underdeveloped countries — have made them exceptionally able to carry out a study of this tremendous range. They are its sole authors and have prepared it without the help of research contributors or collaborators.

As the project took definite shape, the Rockefeller Foundation became interested in its usefulness and promise and agreed to aid in financing it through a grant administered by the Johns Hopkins University. The Fund joined with the Foundation in underwriting the preparation of the study and agreed, also, to take responsibility for its publication. An advisory committee, composed of Dr. Robert Crane and Dr. Fritz Machlup of the Johns Hopkins University and Dr. J. Frederic Dewhurst of the Twentieth Century Fund, aided materially in the administration of the project.

The Fund was led to undertake the publication of the study partly because of the wide usefulness of a similarly conceived stocktaking of the American economy which the Fund published in 1947 under the title *America's Needs and Resources*. This report, which is now being completely revised and brought up to date, is a record of past production in each of the major areas of the American economy, the resources, both human and material, available to meet the needs and demands of the people, and the probable course of future developments. Mr. and Mrs. Woytinsky's study is, in effect, a "Needs and Resources" of the entire world.

The present volume is the result of more than five years of intensive work by the authors. They bear joint responsibility for the outline of the study and every detail in carrying it into effect. Mrs. Woytinsky is primarily responsible for the sections in the present volume on agriculture (Chapters 14–20), mining (Chapters 22–24) and manufacturing (Chapters 27–31); Mr. Woytinsky, for the sections on population (Chapters 1–7), world needs and resources (Chapters 8–13) and a few chapters in other sections (Chapters 21, 25 and 26).

In a period when, more than ever before in history, all parts of the world are the direct and vital concern of every other part, this and the forthcoming volume should give the public the detailed factual basis for dealing with the multitude of problems with which the world is now beset. The Fund hopes that the panorama of the world's economy as a whole — its achievements, but even more its potentials — which these books unfold may give the reader confidence and courage to face the dangerous years ahead.

The Fund has been glad to cooperate with the Rockefeller Foundation and the Johns Hopkins University in carrying this important project through to its completion. Our appreciation also goes in full measure to the indefatigable authors, who have mastered an immense and intractable mass of factual material and made it useful and understandable to the general public which needs it so much.

EVANS CLARK, *Executive Director*
The Twentieth Century Fund

330 WEST 42D STREET
NEW YORK 36, NEW YORK
JUNE 1, 1953

ACKNOWLEDGMENTS

THE AUTHORS are deeply indebted to Dr. Joseph Willits of the Rockefeller Foundation for his confidence in the feasibility of their plan for this study; to the Johns Hopkins University under whose auspices the Rockefeller grant was administered and to the Twentieth Century Fund for carrying out the publication of the study in its present form. The authors also wish to express here their deep gratitude to the members of an Advisory Committee for the project — Dr. Robert Crane and Dr. Fritz Machlup of the Johns Hopkins University, and Dr. J. Frederic Dewhurst of the Twentieth Century Fund.

While the authors had no contributors or collaborators in their work, they had the generous aid of many experts. We fully appreciate how much we are indebted to them for their criticisms and suggestions.

We also acknowledge with deep gratitude the assistance of various governmental and international agencies, particularly the United States Departments of Agriculture and the Interior, the Economic Cooperation Administration's missions abroad and the Secretariat of the United Nations. During our study trip in Europe, covering the United Kingdom, France, Scandinavia, the Low Countries, Switzerland, Western Germany and Italy, we received the generous cooperation of many individuals and agencies — too numerous to mention here by name.

To the following persons goes our grateful appreciation for having read different parts of the manuscript and given comments and suggestions on questions pertaining to their special interest and experience:

Francis L. Adams, Federal Power Commission
Harry D. Angney, Federal Reserve Bank, Boston
A. W. Anderson, Department of the Interior
Olav F. Anderson, Department of Agriculture
Wilhelm Anderson, Department of Agriculture
Solomon Barkin, Textile Workers Union of America
Claudius Bennett, Federal Power Commission
Dorothy Brady, Department of Labor
George F. Carter, Johns Hopkins University
Leroy S. Christey, Department of the Interior
Robert E. De Luccia, Federal Power Commission
J. Frederic Dewhurst, Twentieth Century Fund
W. Duane Evans, Department of Labor
Solomon Fabricant, National Bureau of Economic Research
Marcus Goldstein, Public Health Service
Leo Grebler, Columbia University
A. B. Kinzel, Union Carbide and Carbon Research Laboratories
Eugene M. Kulischer, Library of Congress
Simon Kuznets, University of Pennsylvania
W. H. Larrimer, Department of Agriculture
Nicholas Luango, Department of State

Allen F. Matthews, The President's Materials Policy Commission
Lowell B. Moon, Bureau of Mines
Frank W. Notestein, Princeton University
Elmer W. Pehrson, Bureau of Mines
Clarence E. Pike, Department of Agriculture
Joseph Pogue, Chase National Bank, New York
Clarence M. Purves, Department of Agriculture
Leonard S. Rosenfeld, Public Health Service
Barkev Sanders, Social Security Administration
Walter L. Slifer, Bituminous Coal Institute
M. W. Terry, Department of the Interior
Frank L. Weaver, Federal Power Commission
Lincoln Work, Consulting Engineer, New York

Our warm appreciation also goes to Mary Ross Gannett for her unsparing efforts in editing this study.

We recognize with gratitude the work of the Twentieth Century Fund in handling the difficult task of publishing a volume of this size and scope. Our deep appreciation goes to Evans Clark, the Executive Director, for his many constructive suggestions and to the Fund staff as a group for the tremendous amount of effort entailed in preparing the manuscript for the printer. Acknowledgment is also given to I. J. Starworth for his competent and careful work in drawing and preparing most of the maps and charts included as illustrative material in the book. A further word of credit is due to Minn Radner who prepared the index.

In a study of this scope, with its vast amount of detail, covering world-wide problems and some of the most controversial issues of our time, we are aware that errors are unavoidable. We accept full responsibility for possible mistakes and inconsistencies that may have occurred during the long course of preparing the original draft of the manuscript and revising it in the light of new sources of statistical data that became available before the book was published. We have, however, tried to make use of the most reliable sources of information at our disposal and have employed them to the best of our ability.

W. S. WOYTINSKY
E. S. WOYTINSKY

CONTENTS

PART I

MAN AND HIS ENVIRONMENT

PART II

WORLD NEEDS AND RESOURCES

PART III

AGRICULTURE

PART V

MANUFACTURES

TABLES

PART I. MAN AND HIS ENVIRONMENT

CHAPTER 1. THE EARTH

CHAPTER 2. PEOPLES OF THE WORLD

CHAPTER 6. HEALTH

Chapter 10. Natural Resources

Chapter 11. Human Resources

PART III. AGRICULTURE

CHAPTER 14. AGRICULTURE IN THE WORLD ECONOMY

CHAPTER 15. LAND, FARMS AND FARMING

Chapter 16. Food Crops

CHAPTER 17. TECHNICAL CROPS

CHAPTER 18. LIVESTOCK AND ANIMAL PRODUCTS

PART V. MANUFACTURES
CHAPTER 26. MANUFACTURES IN THE WORLD ECONOMY

CHAPTER 29. THE IRON AND STEEL INDUSTRY

CHAPTER 30. THE MACHINERY AND TRANSPORTATION EQUIPMENT INDUSTRIES

FIGURES

PART I. MAN AND HIS ENVIRONMENT

CHAPTER 1. THE EARTH

CHAPTER 2. PEOPLES OF THE WORLD

PART II. WORLD NEEDS AND RESOURCES

CHAPTER 8. CONSUMER NEEDS AND OUTLAYS

CHAPTER 9. CONSUMPTION AND STANDARDS OF LIVING

CHAPTER 10. NATURAL RESOURCES

PART IV. ENERGY AND MINING

CHAPTER 21. MINING IN THE WORLD ECONOMY

CHAPTER 22. METALLIC AND NONMETALLIC MINERALS

CHAPTER 23. COAL

CHAPTER 24. PETROLEUM AND NATURAL GAS

CHAPTER 25. THE ECONOMICS OF ENERGY AND POWER

PART V. MANUFACTURES

CHAPTER 26. MANUFACTURES IN THE WORLD ECONOMY

CHAPTER 27. THE FOOD, DRINK AND TOBACCO INDUSTRIES

CHAPTER 28. THE TEXTILE INDUSTRY

Chapter 29. The Iron and Steel Industry

Chapter 30. The Machinery and Transportation Equipment Industries

CHAPTER 31. THE CHEMICAL INDUSTRY

INTRODUCTION

THE PURPOSE of this study is to outline world economic forces and trends during the fateful era in which mechanized economy, originated on the two coasts of the North Atlantic, is becoming the universal civilization of mankind. A long and winding road has brought the world to this turn, and the turn itself is marked by violent clashes — revolutions, wars, disintegration of old empires and the rise of new.

BACKGROUND: THE TECHNICAL REVOLUTION

As long as the mechanized economy was a monopoly of a few nations, it gave them tremendous advantage over the rest of mankind. The world economy of the nineteenth century was like a pyramid, with a broad foundation and narrow top: at the base, hundreds of millions of poverty-stricken men and women, mostly illiterate, haunted by disease, many condemned in advance to premature death; at the top the industrialized nations with steadily rising standards of life, declining mortality, increasing expectation of life.

The gap between the have and have-not nations was the most characteristic feature of this system. Its transformation began when modern methods of agriculture, mining, manufacturing and transportation began to invade the underdeveloped regions. The spread of industrialism over the world has not brought equality and freedom from want to the awakening nations, but it has given them hope of a better life. They feel — or believe — that improvement is within their reach. Thus to the technological and economic dynamism of the industrial, prosperous nations is added the political dynamism in the traditionally underdeveloped, slumbering areas.

The new economic techniques challenge the patriarchal, semifeudal patterns of life that prevail in these areas. The foundations and landmarks of the primitive subsistence economy, old customs and social institutions inherited from time immemorial are disappearing in fires blazing in all parts of the world. The process is long — even now, more people live under the conditions of a subsistence economy than in the areas dominated by mechanized civilization. One civilization is on its way out; the other is advancing.

The economic transformation of the world implies far-reaching social and political changes. Whether violent or orderly, they are revolutionary in the sense of a complete and irrevocable break with the past. Such are the land reforms — or land revolutions — sweeping the underdeveloped areas of the world.

Some changes are bound to bring disillusionment to the people. Their desires are growing more rapidly than the means at their disposal. Moreover, along with obsolete customs and institutions, the new mechanized civilization is destroying traditions that made life worth living.[1]

---

1. In his genial and lively *Strange Lands and Friendly People,* William O. Douglas describes such customs among the most backward tribes in the Near East. A traveler can readily observe similar patterns among the peoples in the tropical highlands of Central America.

The progress of mechanized civilization is the central topic of this study. We have tried to describe, measure and explain this development but have not attempted to appraise it.

The expansion of mechanized civilization has destroyed the foundation of international relationships that existed in the nineteenth century — the domination by the industrial countries of colonial and semicolonial areas in Middle and South America, Asia, Africa and Oceania. A new pattern of division of labor and international cooperation must be found to assure stability to the world which emerges from the clashes of our time. To be acceptable to the peoples that are entering — or re-entering — the historical scene, the new system of international relations must promise them equality of opportunity with their former masters. They will settle for nothing less. Equal opportunity, however, does not mean equality of wealth and income. The latter will depend on how the awakening peoples utilize the new economic and political tools being placed in their hands. Their first steps along the new road in the new environment are discussed, described and analyzed in the following pages.

The Mechanized Economy

Recent economic changes are characterized by steadily increasing momentum. The mechanized economy born some two centuries ago has been growing ever since at a continuously increasing rate. The beginning was slow, from the timid, not too successful experiments with the steam engine in the second half of the eighteenth century, to the huge but poorly equipped mills and rudimentary railways in the first half of the nineteenth. Even in the most progressive countries, the economic system of the middle of the past century was a clumsy, slowly moving affair without very bright promise for the future — wooden sailing vessels on the oceans, horse and buggy transportation on land, kerosene lights on the streets and in homes, cities scattered like islands amid borderless expanses of primitive farming.

Contrary to the prophetic vision of Adam Smith, most scholars of that time believed that the capitalistic system of production had only limited possibilities. So slow were the changes that many keen observers failed to notice them. Thus, the capitalism which Karl Marx described was an economy without railroads, practically without iron — a stock exchange with cotton mills clustered around it.

The economic world portrayed at about the same time by Friedrich List was more modern. It was planning railroads and beginning to build them. List brought his dynamic concept of an industrial system to slumbering provincial Germany from the United States, where he had witnessed the revolutionary impact of the new means of transportation on business. Contrary to Marx who, as an economist, never ceased to write about the industrial system as it had existed after the Napoleonic wars, List was fascinated by the new technological trends. But how old fashioned even his world looks to the modern reader!

Technological Progress

Acceleration of technological and economic progress came simultaneously on both sides of the Atlantic in the second half of the nineteenth century, especially the latter part of this period. The quickening came with electricity, steel and petroleum; with the steamship that linked nations, with railways that crossed the continents and linked towns and villages to the thoroughfares. The last two or three decades of the nineteenth century brought more technological and economic changes to the nations of the West than the preceding hundred and twenty or thirty years. So stupendous was the progress that by the end of the century some students, in America as well as in Europe, believed that the industrial system had reached maturity — that every conceivable machine had been invented and put in action, all necessary railroads had been built, all major projects of urbanization completed. The speed of progress was bound to decrease.

Actually what they had seen was only the prologue to an explosive economic expansion. Unprecedented progress began after the turn of the century with the penetration of applied sciences into all fields of human activity. Inventions and discoveries followed in close succession. Cars and trucks appeared on the roads, calling to life a new system of highways. Airplanes rose in the sky and found their way into areas hitherto inaccessible by highway and railroad. Scientific agriculture came to the aid of the farmer. New, man-made materials invaded the markets. The complete story of the role of chemistry and electronics in the modern economy cannot be told within the compass of this work, but the study outlines the main developments in each field of economic activity.

The "Know-how" Formula

What has happened in the past three decades, since World War I, has been more than acceleration of the former long-range trend. The problems of struggle against hunger and want and of prosperity and economic progress have been reduced to a simple formula: *know-how*. People have discovered that skill and organization rather than accumulated wealth are the clues to economic progress, and this has been the most revolutionary discovery of our time. The tree of knowledge has been shown to the have-not peoples and there are no cherubim with flaming swords to keep them away from it.

The turn in our economic thinking and the growing emphasis on know-how as the basis of prosperity implies recognition of the supremacy of the searching, alert, flexible and free human mind and of the unlimited possibilities beyond the visible horizons of our knowledge of today. Moreover, while accumulated wealth is the possession of a few, economic and technical know-how is widespread in modern society, belonging to all and denied to none.

Indeed, the facility with which it can be transferred characterizes modern mechanized civilization. Air transportation epitomizes this. A plane can land almost anywhere and in a short time it can bring all the accessories of an efficient airfield to a selected site at a crossing of caravan trails, on a tiny island or in an oasis surrounded by bare desert. A country too rugged and too poor to build railroads and highways can have a network of airfields. The radio penetrates the wilderness ahead of the telephone and telegraph, indeed ahead of the elementary school. A hydroelectric station can be built in a region too remote from modern civilization to use a steam engine fed by coal. Modern technology spreads as widely as gaseous matter released from a container.

Natural Resources

The technological progress initiated in the modern industrialized countries and now spreading to the remotest corners of the world is the answer to questions on the carrying capacity of our planet, the depletion of its natural resources and the pressure of overpopulation. In some limited areas, scarcity of land and other natural resources, combined with a rapidly growing density of population, have doubtless produced a Malthusian situation — poverty due largely to overpopulation. Such a situation is particularly disturbing on some islands in each hemisphere — for example, in Puerto Rico, Japan and Indonesia. This is a local phenomenon, however, similar to another source of poverty — technological unemployment in certain professions in particular areas.

But overpopulation is no more responsible for poverty in a large part of the world than technological progress is to blame for mass unemployment during a depression. This question is examined in detail in the following pages. No evidence has been found of a general tendency of mankind to outgrow available resources. There is evidence, however, that the short-sighted destructive exploitation of land, forests and other resources characteristic of the ruthless nineteenth century, is being brought under control in recent times. The present phase of economic history is characterized by reclamation of the soil, irrigation of deserts, drainage of swamps, flood control, conquest of malaria and other environmental diseases, protection of cattle and plants against parasites and diseases.

Long-Range Economic Trends

This description of the present phase of our civilization may impress the reader as too optimistic. The authors are aware of the other side of the picture: of the contradictions within the modern industrial system; of the gap between technological progress and other aspects of civilization; of international tensions and the imminent danger of a new world war. These issues are not within the scope of this study. Its purpose is to outline long-range and recent trends in the world's economic structure — a broad but still limited task that provides a background for the discussion of other problems.

The trends in world economy are presented by topic rather than by country. The elucidation of particular subjects, however, is not the final aim of the study but mainly a medium for giving an over-all picture of the world. This objective has determined the selection of single topics: the space given to each depends not on its importance alone but on its relation to the whole picture.

A study of economic trends in the world requires a broad historical approach to each topic. Our economic civilization is both older and younger than most people believe. Its roots penetrate deep into the past, but most of our machines and technical methods and many of our raw materials were unknown to the generations just before us.

Modern technology is heavily concentrated in the two North Atlantic regions. The United States leads in many fields; never before has a single nation controlled so large a percentage of the world's industrial capacity. The incomparable industrial plant of the country, however, has been built on the foundation of a rich inheritance from the

Old World. The United States itself is an emanation of European culture, and its superlative techniques in agriculture, mining, manufacturing and transportation rest largely on ingenious practical adaptations of theoretical ideas originated in a dozen old countries. Although the immediate concern of this study is the present and the future rather than the past, it stresses the international genealogy of many modern inventions and occasionally refers to times as remote as those of the Bible and ancient Greece. Apart from tracing the historical roots of modern economy, such references are designed to emphasize the dynamism of the modern economy in contrast to the slowness of economic progress in the preceding millenniums.

A historical approach is particularly necessary in considering the unique position of the United States in world economics and politics. So rapid and so radical have been the changes that the present generation has been unexpectedly catapulted into the center of unfamiliar events and problems. How did the country reach this position? What are the foundations of its economic power? What are its responsibilities? A survey of historical development will aid the reader in his search for answers to these and related questions.

SCOPE OF THE STUDY

Volume One

Because of the broad scope of this survey, it is advisable to publish it in two volumes. The present volume, consisting of five parts, covers matters related to population, patterns of economic civilization and production. Some indication of the topics included in each part is given in the summary that follows.

Part I. Man and His Environment. Population problems, in a broad sense of the term, are dealt with in this section. Geographical statistics are given; a survey of the distribution of the people of the world includes data on trends in growth of population, prevalence of races, languages and religions. Migration, and the development and role of cities are considered next. The changing patterns of natality and mortality are outlined; health patterns, and the progress in the struggle against disease are described. Part I concludes with a venture in forecasting future world population.

Part II. World Needs and Resources. Human desires and the means of their satisfaction are analyzed in the chapters on consumer needs, and consumption and standards of living. Resources at the disposal of mankind are examined under two headings: natural resources and human resources. The two following chapters survey the distribution of economic activities and wealth in the world.

Part III. Agriculture. Agriculture's role in the world economy is here considered; such fundamental agricultural problems as soil depletion, reclamation and conservation; patterns of farming and land ownership; the struggle for land; and the main aspects of modern agricultural technology are then explored. In the chapters that follow, agricultural production is studied in detail: food crops, technical crops, and livestock and animal products. The survey of agriculture proper is supplemented by additional chapters on forests and forest products, and on fisheries.

Part IV. Energy and Mining. The introductory chapter, mining in the world economy, indicates the value of world mineral output and distribution. Subsequent chapters examine production in metallic and nonmetallic minerals, coal, and petroleum and natural gas. A concluding chapter discusses the economics of energy and power.

Part V. Manufactures. The final section presents an over-all survey of manufactures in the world economy, and contains detailed descriptions of five leading industrial divisions: (1) food, drink and tobacco industries; (2) textiles; (3) iron and steel; (4) machinery and transportation equipment; and (5) the chemical industry.

Volume Two

The second volume of the study, to be completed in 1953, will deal with international trade and investments; land, water and air transportation; political organization of the world; colonialism; public finance; and international cooperation.

Each volume is planned for continuous reading or for reference use — each part, and each chapter, separately. Repetition, unavoidable in such a plan, has been reduced so far as possible by cross references.

STATISTICAL AND TABULAR METHODS

World economic trends do not all incline in the same direction, nor do they move at the same pace. Some are waning as others are becoming increasingly important. The component trends that make up the over-all pattern of development must be weighted, and this is a task for statistics. This consideration has determined the character of the study; synthetic and interpretative in purpose, it is largely statistical in form. It not only makes extensive use of statistics but is also intended to serve as an introduction to the realm of international statistics.

Statistical tables on the following pages are designed for laymen. They are accompanied by methodological explanations that would be omitted in a more technical publication, but the technician will miss the customary array of footnotes.

This omission is intentional. In a ten-column table that covers some fifty countries, only a few figures are strictly comparable and each line, each column and almost each figure calls for a footnote.[2] Such paraphernalia, however, would appear as unbearable pedantry to the general reader. Moreover, after having read — or skipped — all the footnotes the reader would learn not much more than that the figures differ from one another in concept, method of computation and the exact date to which they refer and are to be used with caution. Since this warning applies to almost all international tables, it can be given directly, here and now, without repetitious footnotes.

This study makes a point of presenting statistics in the simplest possible form, with illustrative charts and brief analytical summaries in the text but with a minimum of technical detail. The reader interested in omitted details is referred to the original sources.

World Totals and Averages

The pages that follow contain frequent references to world totals and national and regional averages — for population; births and deaths; acreage and harvest; output of

---

2. The United Nations *Demographic Yearbook, 1951* contains tables with more than one hundred footnotes and one requires a hundred and fifty-six, although footnotes are used with discrimination and restraint.

mineral fuels and metals; consumption of food; raw materials and energy; national income and so on. Most of these data are presented in the conventional form: population with precision to the nearest thousand or million; birth and death rates to one tenth of one per cent per 1,000 inhabitants; output of metals to one thousand tons; per capita consumption to one tenth of a pound; per capita national income to the dollar. These precise figures should not be taken too seriously, however, for most of the data have a considerable margin of error.

In fact, more or less reliable and detailed current population statistics are available for only two dozen countries, with an aggregate population of less than 600 million, about a fourth of mankind. Even these data are not strictly comparable because of significant differences in methods of enumeration and classification. For an area embracing another fourth of the world's population, including India and large parts of South America, statistics are less abundant. For the rest of the world — notably China, the Near and Far East, the USSR and a large part of Africa — statistical information is extremely meager.

When the precise number of inhabitants in an area is unknown, its other statistics become doubtful. When a country with rudimentary school and public health services reports a death rate lower than that of the most progressive countries, this rate reflects the inadequacy of the country's statistics rather than the enviable health of its inhabitants. Such death rates, however, belong in the picture of world health statistics and cannot be denied a place in international surveys.

The reader is cautioned that international surveys covering a large number of countries are not selective and contain figures of unequal reliability; inclusion of a figure in the survey does not mean its endorsement by the authors.

This observation applies also to economic statistics. Official data on the acreage and yield of various grains and livestock, on mineral and industrial production, on national income, consumption and so on are based largely on estimates and extrapolation of small samples. They always contain an appreciable margin of error, and these errors are not always distributed at random; there may be a definite tendency toward understatement or overstatement in certain series.

Despite these limitations in international statistics, they are the only available tool for quantitative appraisal of the divergent trends in world affairs, indeed, the cornerstone of any exploration in the field of world economy. Their indisputable service is to give the reader a sense of magnitude and relative values.

Life Behind the Iron Curtain

The United Nations and its specialized agencies have made serious attempts to develop modern statistical reporting throughout the world and to increase the comparability of national statistics. The Kremlin has met these efforts with a resolute veto and a statistical blackout in the areas under its control. Besides boycotting the inquiries of the United Nations, the Kremlin is flooding the world with reports of its own which contravene all principles of modern statistics. These reports are usually indexes of production computed in an unknown way and related to an unknown base.

There is no way to segregate truth from falsehood in these communications, but their purpose is obvious. Some of them have scarcely more than accidental similarity to the statistics used by the Soviet authorities in the economic planning and operation of their industrial plant and are concocted as instruments of propaganda at home and abroad. Moreover, most of the Soviet statistics are presented in such a form as to be effective as propaganda without revealing the facts of life behind the Iron Curtain.

Apart from the lack of more or less trustworthy statistics, it is difficult to discuss the economy of the USSR in an economic survey of the world because of the basic differences between totalitarian and free economies.

The incentive in the free economy is profit, but the producer cannot make a profit unless he sells his product and cannot sell the product unless it incites or satisfies demand and meets the needs of consumers. Thus, the enterprise system is ultimately oriented toward satisfaction of people's needs. In a totalitarian state, on the contrary, all economic activities are subordinated to the interests of the party or clique that controls the government. The perpetuation and expansion of its power become the ultimate goals of the national economy and determine production plans. The remaining surpluses are used for private consumption and are distributed among various groups of the population according to political expediency.

This economic system, although perfectly logical when observed according to the scale of values of the totalitarian state, seems full of contradictions from the Western viewpoint. It combines an extremely low level of living and real wages with a formidable heavy industry. In contrast to the free economy, it permits only insignificant improvement — or no improvement at all — in civilian consumption while its munitions industries are among the most dynamic and efficient in the world.

It is noteworthy that the repercussions of World War II on the economic system of the USSR have conformed to its militaristic nature. The vast conquests in the west have brought little improvement to the working population in the USSR but have put at the disposal of the Soviet the arsenals of Skoda, the munitions factories of Eastern Germany and an army of Czech and German technicians who were the brains of the war industry under Hitler. The duality of the Soviet economy is clearly revealed by the ranking of the USSR among other nations: close to the bottom in per capita consumption and close to the top in capacity of iron and steel mills.

Estimates and Projections

Despite the limitations of international statistics, they permit certain generalizations and projections. The writer must judge how far he should go in this direction. The only rigid rule is that he must warn the reader when he shifts from the thin ice of official statistics to the still thinner ice of extrapolation. In the pages that follow the reader will find warning signs wherever they seem appropriate.

This study includes numerous estimates of the distribution of world population by language and religion; the size of the world's labor force and its distribution by continent and industry; the value of world output and so on.

All these estimates are, of course, open to criticism and are presented as rough approximations. They cannot be more precise than the statistics on which they are based. The projections ventured here and there require an additional reservation: they express simply the opinion of the authors on the probable course of events, on the hypothesis that recent trends will continue.

International Tables

A major problem in arranging international statistical tables is the order in which individual countries are listed. The Statistical Office of the United Nations lists the continents and broad geographic regions *alphabetically* — from Africa to Oceania and the USSR — and arranges the countries alphabetically within each division: first, sovereign countries by the first letter of their English name; then colonies and possessions grouped by the first letter of the name of the colonial power and, within each group, by the first letter of their name.[3]

This system is very convenient for reference, for the reader knows where to find the area in which he is interested. The weak point of the system, however, is that each area is handled as an unrelated unit, like names in a telephone directory.

The purpose of the present study calls for a different arrangement. Alphabetical order is incompatible with the approach to national data as elements of the world picture, illustrative of the pattern and trends prevailing in different parts of our planet. Most of our tables are therefore arranged *geographically,* following the outline shown on the key maps used as end papers and in the table on page lxviii.

This arrangement has certain weaknesses. The geographic principle, from north to south and from west to east, cannot always be followed consistently; the starting point for each continent must be selected arbitrarily; and the whole arrangement is less clear than the alphabetical order. It is recognized also that tables arranged in this way may seem confusing to the reader accustomed to the alphabetical system.

Essentially, the two arrangements are analogous to the two patterns used by the United States Bureau of the Census in its arrangement of state statistics. Some of its tables are arranged alphabetically, running from Alabama to Wyoming; in others the states are arranged by geographic division, from New England to the Pacific. The latter pattern is followed in most of the tables in this study.

In some analytical tables, however, countries are arrayed by a definite statistical feature, for example, by increasing birth or death rates, per capita income and so on.

Units of Measurement

Most statistics in this study are expressed in the units used in the United States: acres, short and long tons, pounds, dollars. Metric units have been used, however, in some of the United Nations series which are continued in their current publications. The conversion factor is given under most of these tables.

Foreign currency units appear in historical surveys for single countries where the conversion of original data into dollars would have introduced a new source of uncertainty and erratic fluctuations.

---

3. The complete list begins with Africa, from Egypt to the Union of South Africa; next comes an array of African colonies, from Belgian Congo and France's Algeria to the United Kingdom's Zanzibar; this is followed by a third alphabetical listing of trust territories, from the Cameroons to Togoland; and, finally, a fourth list of military governments, condominiums and so on. Similarly, the list for North America begins with independent nations, from Canada, Costa Rica and Cuba to the United States; next, non-self-governing territories are listed, from Denmark's Greenland to the United States' Virgin Islands. The same procedure is used for other continents.

ARRANGEMENT OF COUNTRIES AND AREAS, BY CONTINENT [a]

NORTH AMERICA

1. United States
2. Alaska
3. Canada
4. Newfoundland
5. Greenland

MIDDLE AMERICA

1. Mexico
2. Guatemala
3. El Salvador
4. Honduras
5. Nicaragua
6. Costa Rica
7. Panama

8. Cuba
9. Jamaica
10. Haiti
11. Dominican Republic
12. Puerto Rico

SOUTH AMERICA

1. Venezuela
2. Colombia
3. Ecuador

4. Brazil
5. Peru
6. Bolivia
7. Paraguay

8. Chile
9. Uruguay
10. Argentina

EUROPE

1. United Kingdom
2. Ireland
3. France
4. Luxembourg
5. Belgium
6. Netherlands
7. Denmark
8. Sweden
9. Norway
10. Finland

11. Germany
12. Poland
13. Czechoslovakia

14. Switzerland
15. Austria
16. Hungary

17. Portugal
18. Spain
19. Italy
20. Yugoslavia
21. Romania
22. Bulgaria
23. Albania
24. Greece

USSR

ASIA

1. China
2. Mongolia
3. Korea
4. Japan
5. Taiwan (Formosa)
6. Hong Kong

7. Turkey
8. Cyprus
9. Lebanon
10. Israel

11. Syria
12. Jordan
13. Saudi Arabia
14. Bahrein Islands
15. Kuwait
16. Iraq
17. Iran
18. Afghanistan
19. Pakistan

20. India
21. Jammu and Kashmir
22. Nepal
23. Bhutan
24. Burma

25. Thailand
26. Indochina

27. Ceylon
28. Federation of Malaya
29. Singapore
30. Indonesia
31. Borneo
32. Philippines
33. New Guinea

AFRICA

1. Morocco
2. Algeria
3. Tunisia

4. Libya
5. Egypt
6. Sudan
7. Ethiopia
8. Somaliland

9. West Africa
10. Equatorial Africa
11. Congo

12. Liberia
13. Gold Coast
14. Nigeria
15. Cameroons

16. Kenya
17. Uganda
18. Ruanda-Urundi
19. Tanganyika
20. Nyasaland
21. Mozambique
22. Madagascar

23. Angola
24. Northern Rhodesia
25. Southern Rhodesia

26. South-West Africa
27. Bechuanaland
28. Union of South Africa

OCEANIA

1. Australia
2. New Zealand
3. Hawaii
4. New Guinea

a. Order numbers are the same as in the end-paper maps.

Symbols

A dash (—) in the table columns means zero or less than half the smallest unit recorded in the respective column.

Dots (. . .) indicate "no information available" or "unknown."

The footnote "preliminary data" is used in some cases for recent years and shows that final data are expected to appear in the near future. This note is omitted when statistics for more or less remote years are used.

Maps and Their Use

The purpose of this survey has determined the choice of its standard world map. Neither a map showing the hemispheres as two circles nor the Mercator projection could be used, since both give a false picture of the spatial interrelation of the different parts of the world.[4]

The same objection is valid in relation to the popular equal-area projections, such as Goode's homolosine projection and its modifications. Excellent for portraying single continents, they fail to represent the world as a continuity. For similar reasons, the authors could not use Van der Grinten's projection, which shows the Americas in the middle of the world, with Europe, Africa and the western parts of the USSR and Asia (including India) to the right, and eastern Asia (including another part of the USSR, China, Indochina and Indonesia) and Australia to the left.

The projection developed by Dr. Erwin Raisz best meets the requirements of this study. Dr. Raisz describes his map as the "armadillo projection" and stresses its realism, rather than its theoretical perfection. Like all continuous maps of the world, it admits deviations from the principle of equal areas, but its main distortions are confined to the Pacific Ocean and polar regions, while the shape and relative location of all continents except Australia are preserved fairly well.[5] (See map on page lxx.) The great advantage of this map is that it shows the world as two huge masses of land on both sides of the Atlantic, brings the North Atlantic regions into sharp focus and presents Europe in the middle of the conflicting forces of the West and the East.

Distorted Maps

Among other graphic devices, this study uses *distorted maps* on which continents, geographic regions and countries are drawn to the scale of population, income or some other characteristic. The method is not new, but a feature that distinguishes these distorted maps from the usual ones requires explanation.

Since a distorted map shows some areas on a larger scale than others, it cannot locate countries and regions at the correct longitudes and latitudes. It would be logical, therefore, to draw distorted maps without the network of meridians and parallels. Such a map would look like a diagram, however, and would not suggest clearly

---

4. A few official maps, however, based on the Mercator projection are reproduced. They serve to stress certain features of world economics that can be successfully represented in this way despite the distortion of the regions close to the poles.

5. In the arrangement of continents, this map has a vague resemblance to the Mollweide equal-area elliptical projection, but ingeniously avoids some of its distortions and makes more economical use of the space, permitting a larger scale in presenting continents on a given-size page.

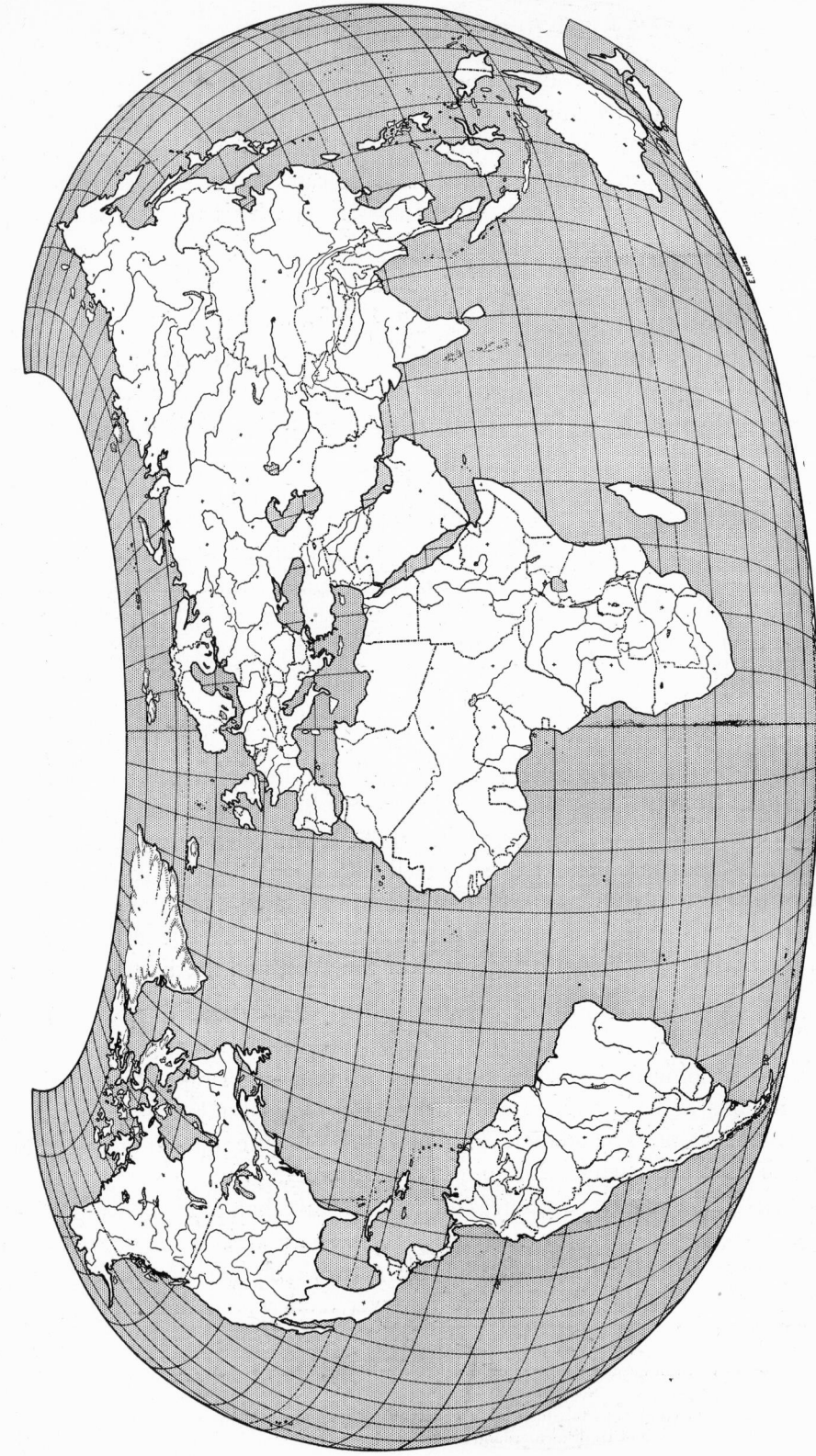

KEY MAP: OUTLINE OF CONTINENTS ACCORDING TO THE PROJECTION OF ERWIN RAISZ

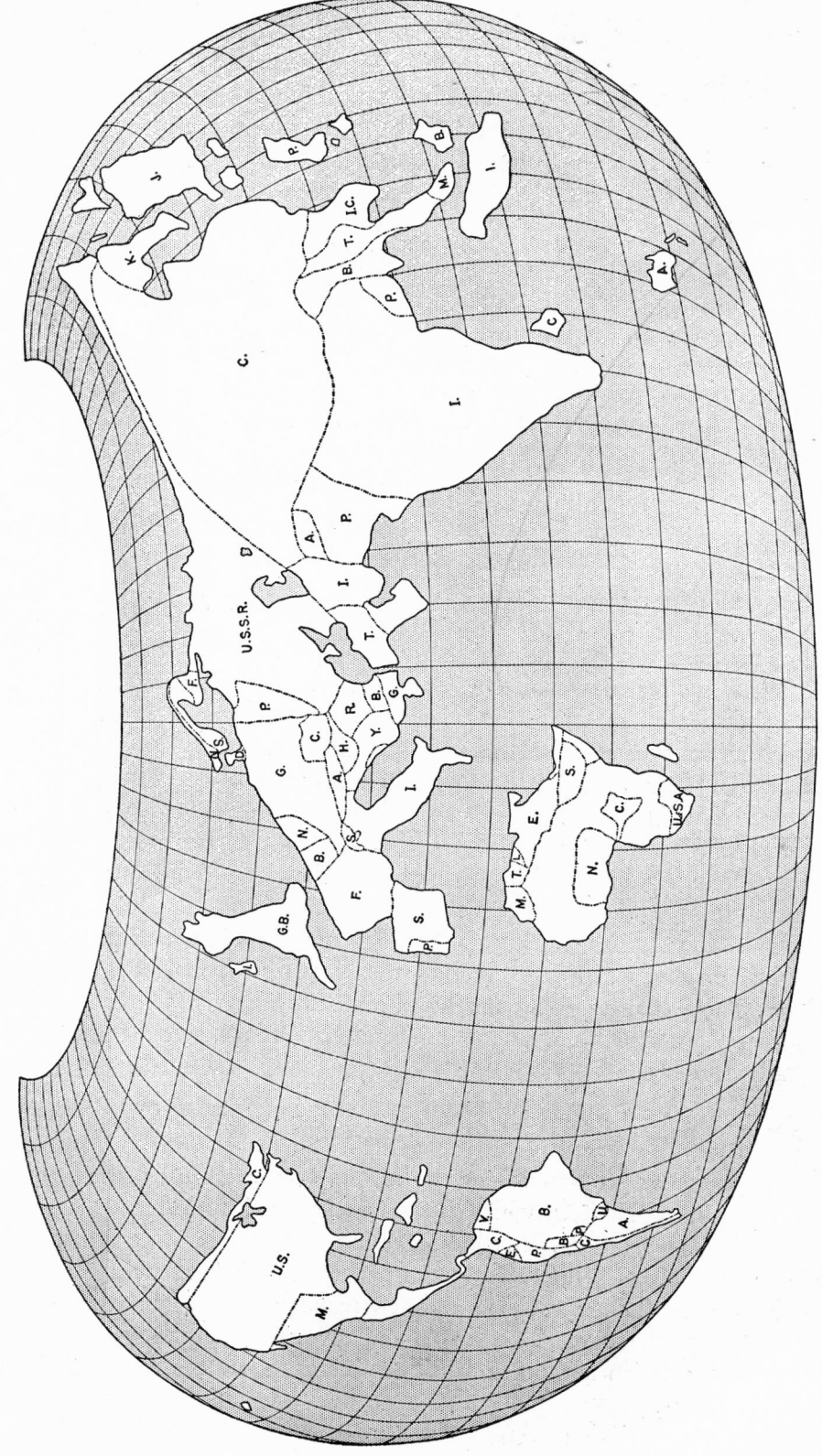

KEY MAP: CONTINENTS AND SELECTED COUNTRIES ON THE SCALE OF THEIR POPULATION, AROUND 1950

enough the spatial relationships of each region to the rest of the world. It seems preferable, therefore, to project the distorted continents and countries against the background of our planet, with the conventional network of longitudes and latitudes. (See map on page lxxi.) The justification for this unorthodox course is that all maps of this type try to picture the relative location of different areas. Once this principle is accepted, why not draw the distorted map of the world in a form reminiscent of maps of the conventional type?

SOURCES AND REFERENCES

Because the broad scope of this volume makes exhaustive discussion of each subject impossible, the reader's attention is directed to the lists of sources at the end of the book. A separate list has been prepared for each chapter; the numbers in these lists correspond to the boldface source number given in the footnotes. Only publications used in the study are listed. Although the lists do not meet all the requirements of a selected bibliography, they should be a helpful guide to the reader.

Many of the international tables are based on publications of the United Nations and its agencies — the Economic Commission for Europe, the Food and Agriculture Organization and its forestry and fishery divisions, the International Labor Organization, the World Health Organization and others. Statistical series of these agencies are not all of the same quality, and some of them are subject to frequent revisions. Occasionally these sources may contradict one another. All in all, however, publications of the United Nations contain the largest and most systematic collection of international statistics ever assembled by any organization.

There is a special reason for using this source in the present study. Most of the tables are carried through 1950 and a few through 1951, while others could not be carried further than 1949. Wherever a table for recent years is derived from the United Nations, its continuation can be found in the current publications of the agency cited as the source.

During the printing of this volume, some tables were revised in accordance with the most recent information, which had become available after the manuscript was sent to the printer. These changes could not be introduced, however, into some of the figures and maps. This explains occasional minor discrepancies between them and the respective statistical tables.

Geographic Names

In the transcription of geographic names the study follows the nomenclature established by the United Nations, which is, in most cases, identical with *Webster's Geographical Dictionary* (1949). In tables covering a period in which a country's name has been changed, only the recently established name is listed as, for example, Thailand, Iran, Jordan, Indonesia. When the new name appears only at the end of a long period covered by the survey, both the old and new names are shown, as in Russia (USSR). Names of Russian authors and titles of books follow the transliteration of the Library of Congress.

PART I

MAN AND HIS ENVIRONMENT

Chapter 1

THE EARTH

Each civilization has a world of its own, a world that embraces all the land and water known to the men who belong to it. What is beyond their knowledge is another world.

Our World

The frontiers of our world have been widening since our civilization began. The world of Herodotus, clustered around the Mediterranean and the Black Sea, later became the nucleus of the Roman world. The world of the Middle Ages, expanding further toward all points of the compass, included the Balkans, Scandinavia and eastern Europe. On the eve of modern times, the Caribbean and the seacoast of America became part of the European world. Through the twenty centuries from Herodotus to Columbus, however, other worlds continued to exist outside the world of European civilization.

Now our world has broadened, until it is neither European nor American, neither Atlantic nor Pacific, but *global*. Men of our civilization have yet to explore uncharted spaces beyond the polar circles and in the middle of South America, Africa, Asia and Australia, but there are no unknown worlds there. Mapping these areas is merely a matter of time.

Our present world is almost as broad as our planet, and expansion beyond these limits may be in the offing. It is this global world we think of when we speak of the needs and resources, hopes and fears of mankind.

The community of nations that we have in mind in speaking of world economy, world trade and world politics is much narrower. It is limited to the regions tied to one another by exchange of goods, services or ideas, by mutual friendship or mutual suspicion. Most of what we call world politics and economics directly involves only a part of mankind and is dominated by a few great powers. The small nations, however, often play an important part in the clash between the big rivals.

This narrower world of international politics and economics changes continually. Never has it changed so rapidly as since the beginning of the twentieth century. Revolutions and wars are at once the cause, the result and the manifestation of these changes, which are proceeding with increasing speed. Split between divergent interests and conflicting ideologies, full of confusion, mankind still faces the eternal problems of food and shelter, peace and security, freedom and justice.

The stage on which the historical drama of mankind is enacted is the Earth, with its continents and oceans, mountains and rivers, sunshine and rain. This study begins, therefore, with a brief description of our globe in its relation to the distribution, character and activities of men.

Land and Water

The surface of the globe comprises 197 million square miles. The division of this area between land and water cannot be measured precisely for lack of exact information on the coast line of the Antarctic region, and innumerable oceanic islands and fringing seas.

At a rough approximation, land constitutes slightly over 29 per cent of the total surface of the earth and water, nearly 71 per cent. In this estimate, land (about 57.4 million square miles) includes the continents and islands and their lakes and rivers, while the water area (about 139.6 million square miles) is made up of the oceans and the enclosed and fringing seas. Without inland waters the land area represents nearer 28 per cent of the surface of the globe.

In the Northern Hemisphere slightly more than 60 per cent of the earth's surface is under water, in the Southern over 80 per cent. In each hemisphere the distribution of land and water differs greatly at different latitudes. Between 70° N and 60° N more than 70 per cent of the surface of the earth emerges from the ocean; between 60° and 40°, over 50 per cent; along the equator and between 20° N and 30° S, land represents, on the average, 20 to 25 per cent, and toward 60° S the proportion is still less.[1] (See

1. **13**, p. 27.

Figure 1.) Moreover, much of what we call land is covered by the permanent ice cap, as in Antarctica, Greenland and many polar islands.

LAND

CONTINENTS

In physical geography continents are described as large continuous masses of land, but the delimitation is more or less arbitrary. Asia and Europe are traditionally regarded as two continents, although they are a single continuous land mass. North and South America could similarly be regarded as a single continent. Most people, however, think of six continents: Europe, Asia, Africa and Australia in the Eastern Hemisphere, North America and South America in the Western.

Classifying Islands

Islands are classified as belonging to a continent, not always the nearest. Most of the islands in the Pacific, the eastern part of New Guinea, New Zealand and Tasmania are grouped with Australia as parts of Oceania, while the islands between India and Australia (including the Philippines, Java, Sumatra, Borneo, Celebes and the western part of New Guinea) are considered as belonging to Asia.[2]

Classifying the USSR

This classification of the continents proves unsatisfactory in modern political and economic geography. The main stumbling block is the USSR, which is partly in Europe and partly in Asia and represents a sizable part of the area and population of both continents. Soviet statistics, however, make no distinction between the European and Asiatic parts of the Union,[3] and it is therefore impossible to allocate the share of the USSR in the world economy to continents. In discussing economic and political matters, it seems preferable to use a classification based

partly on political boundaries: Europe without the European part of the USSR, Asia without the Asiatic part of the USSR, and the USSR as a quasi-continental unit between them.

Classifying Countries South of the Rio Grande

In the Western Hemisphere, likewise, it is sometimes preferable to group countries by similarity in political institutions and economic structure rather than merely by geographic proximity. In a statistical total for all North American countries from Canada to Panama, the United States outweighs countries south of the Rio Grande, which are very different from the United States in language, tradition, race, politics and economy. It is advisable, therefore, to consider as a separate group Mexico, the five republics of Central America (Guatemala, El Salvador, Honduras, Nicaragua and Costa Rica), Panama, British Honduras and the Caribbean islands (Cuba, Haiti and the Dominican Republic). Some publications of the United Nations designate this group of countries as "Mexico and the Caribbean"; another frequently used term is "Middle America."

Classifying the Polar Regions

In a classification of countries by continent, the Arctic islands are usually divided among North America (Canadian islands and Greenland), Europe (Lofoten Islands) and the USSR (Novaya Zemlya), while Antarctica is classified as a separate unit, along with other continental and quasi-continental areas. (See Table 1 and Figure 2.)

Earlier Concepts of Continents

Our view of this world and its continents is very different from that of European scholars centuries ago, when the Antarctic region and Australia were practically unknown, northern Asia was unexplored, and the Western Hemisphere had merely begun to emerge on the horizon, first as land somewhere west and south of the Caribbean islands, and half a century later, as a New World with Brazil, or America, in the middle of a vast continent and vague expanses to the north, in the general direction of Japan and India. (See Figure 3.) As late as the beginning of the eighteenth century, Europeans viewed the Western Hemisphere merely as a maze of European plantations and dominions. (See Figure 4.) In *A New Survey of the Globe,*

---

2. In this classification, used by the United Nations, New Guinea is split between the two continents along the boundary between the Dutch and Australian possessions.

3. Some provinces (republics) of the Soviet Union are situated fully in Europe, others fully in Asia, but the largest province (the RSFSR, or Russia proper) stretches from the Gulf of Finland to the Pacific Ocean, so that administrative borders cannot be adjusted to the hypothetical division line between the two continents.

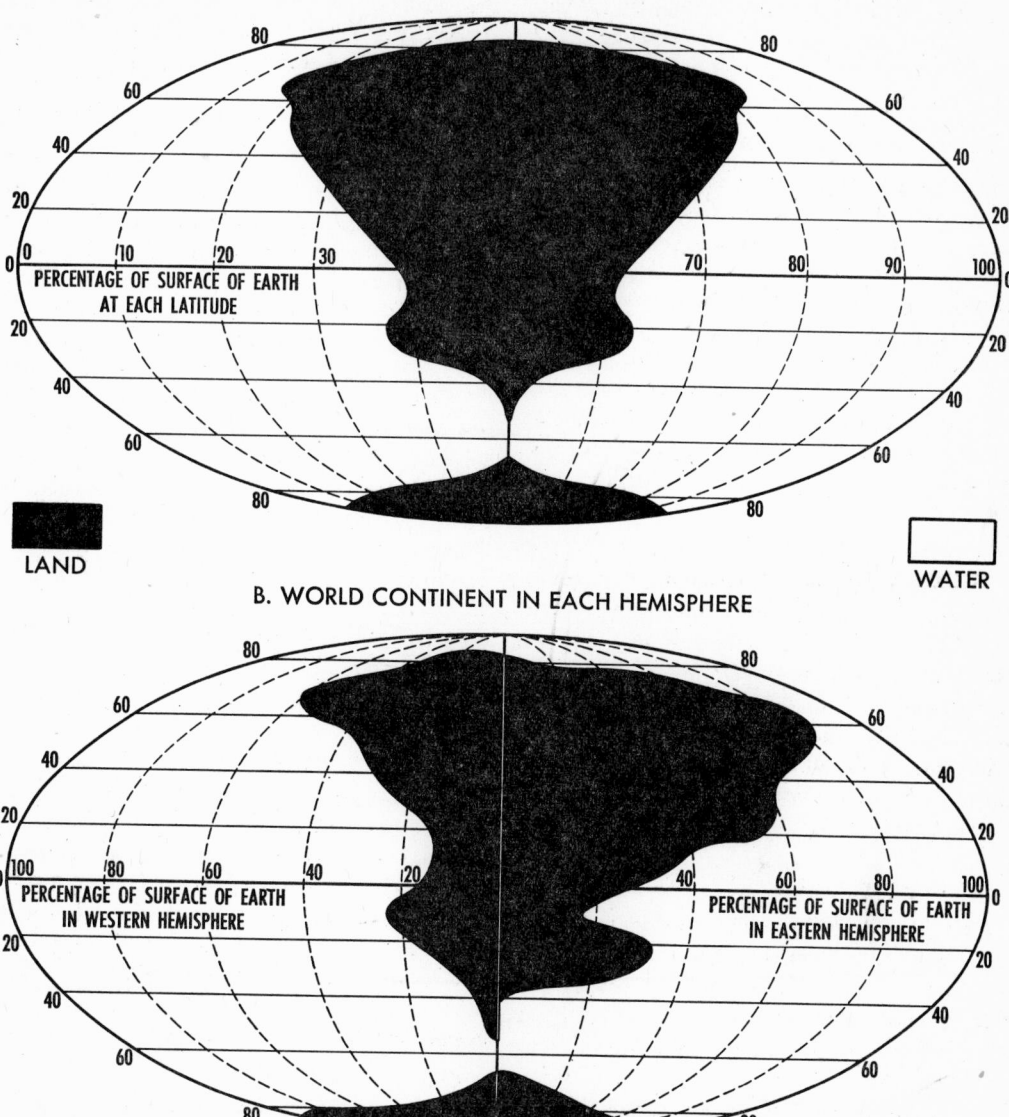

A. SCHEMATIC WORLD CONTINENT

PERCENTAGE OF SURFACE OF EARTH AT EACH LATITUDE

LAND

WATER

B. WORLD CONTINENT IN EACH HEMISPHERE

PERCENTAGE OF SURFACE OF EARTH IN WESTERN HEMISPHERE

PERCENTAGE OF SURFACE OF EARTH IN EASTERN HEMISPHERE

FIGURE 1. LAND AND WATER: PROPORTIONAL DISTRIBUTION BY LATITUDE AND HEMISPHERE

The upper panel of this figure represents the land of the world schematically as one continent surrounded by ocean. Land is concentrated in the Northern Hemisphere, between 20° and 60° N. There is a break between this mass and the land in the Antarctic region.

In the lower panel, the hypothetical world continent is divided by a vertical line between the Western and Eastern Hemispheres. The contours of North and South America appear west of the line, while east of it the land mass of Asia is clearly separated from the bulge below the equator representing Africa and Australia.

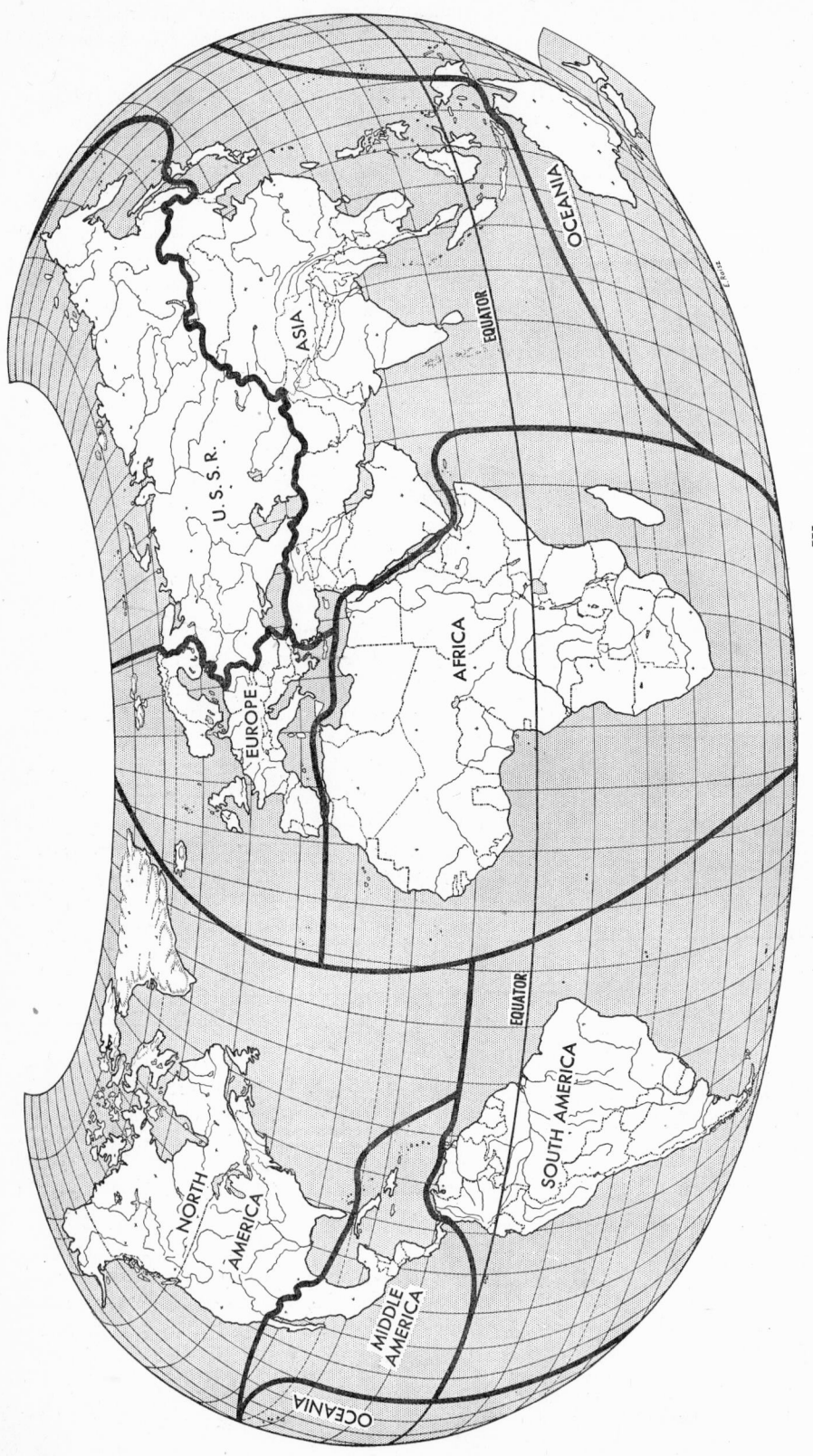

FIGURE 2. CONTINENTS AND REGIONS OF THE WORLD

The line NS crossing the Atlantic Ocean separates the two hemispheres. In the Western Hemisphere, Mexico, Central America and the Caribbean are grouped as a separate region, Middle America. In the Eastern Hemisphere, the USSR is considered as a unit apart from both Europe and Asia.

The line separating Oceania from Asia cuts New Guinea in two parts. The eastern part of the island, which is under Australian administration, is considered as part of Oceania; the western part, controlled by the Netherlands, is classified as part of Asia.

TABLE 1

CONTINENTS: AREA AND PERCENTAGE DISTRIBUTION OF LAND

Hemisphere and Continent or Region	*Thousands of Square Miles*	*Percentage of World Total*
Land surface [a]	57,400	100.0
Western Hemisphere	16,230	28.3
North America [b]	8,220	14.3
Middle America	1,150	2.0
South America	6,860	12.0
Eastern Hemisphere	35,820	62.4
Europe, excluding the USSR	1,910	3.3
Asia, excluding the USSR	10,370	18.1
USSR, in Europe and Asia [c]	8,600	15.0
Africa	11,640	20.3
Oceania	3,300	5.7
Antarctic region	5,350	9.3

Source: **1,** pp. 12–22 (adjusted to the more recent estimates of the UN).

a. Includes islands and inland waters.

b. Includes an estimated 840,000 square miles in Greenland.

c. Postwar boundaries.

published in London in 1729, Thomas Templeman estimated the surface of the "habitable world" at 30.7 million square miles, not much more than half our figure, distributed as follows (in millions of square miles): [4]

Europe	2.7
Asia	10.3
Africa	8.5
North America	3.7
South America	5.5

COAST AND HINTERLAND

Continents [5] differ strikingly from one another in shape and in coast line. Mainland represents 99 per cent of the area of South America and 98 per cent of that of Africa. The proportion is much lower in the other continents: Asia and Oceania, 80 per cent; North America, 75 per cent; and Europe, 73 per cent. In Europe and North America, the coast line is winding and deeply indented in many places. Africa and South America have the shortest coast line in

4. **22,** Plate 29. These figures do not include islands.

5. In the following discussion of physical characteristics, continents are defined as in physical geography: the USSR is divided between Europe and Asia, Middle America is included in North America.

relation to area, and a larger proportion of their areas is remote from the sea. (See Table 2 and Figure 5.)

Land along the seacoast has always been important in the economic and political life of mankind. Because of the great advantages of water transportation, almost all important industrial centers have developed within coastal regions, usually around seaports or a short distance from them. The strip of land 250 miles wide along the Atlantic, the Mediterranean, and the Pacific and the Indian Oceans (white in Figure 5) contains the most densely populated areas of the world and nearly all the cities with a million or more inhabitants.

Concentration of industry along the seacoast was particularly characteristic of the nineteenth century. More recently, progress in motor transportation and the increase of inland population in industrial countries have tended to weaken the economic supremacy of coastal regions. Since World War I, this new trend has been furthered in several countries (the USSR, Turkey and India) by the tendency of governments to transfer political and industrial centers as far inland as possible. The threat of air attacks from floating bases may cause a similar retreat throughout the world. [6]

If the trend away from the coast continues, the advantages of a long coast line are bound to decline. This will be a very slow process, however. Our present economic civilization is essentially a coastal civilization. The economic rise of the United States was favored by its unique geographic position with vast coastal regions along two oceans.

ISLANDS

The islands of the world comprise nearly 4 million square miles, somewhat more than the area of the United States including all its territories and possessions. They represent 2 per cent of the surface of the earth or 7 per cent of its land surface. (See Table 3.)

Nearly a third of this area is in the Arctic region of the Western Hemisphere and is practically uninhabitable. The political importance of these islands (Greenland, the Canadian islands and Newfoundland) is due mainly to their probable future role in intercontinental aviation. Each of the two largest islands in the tropical

6. In the United States such dispersion of strategic industries has been supported by the government.

1507

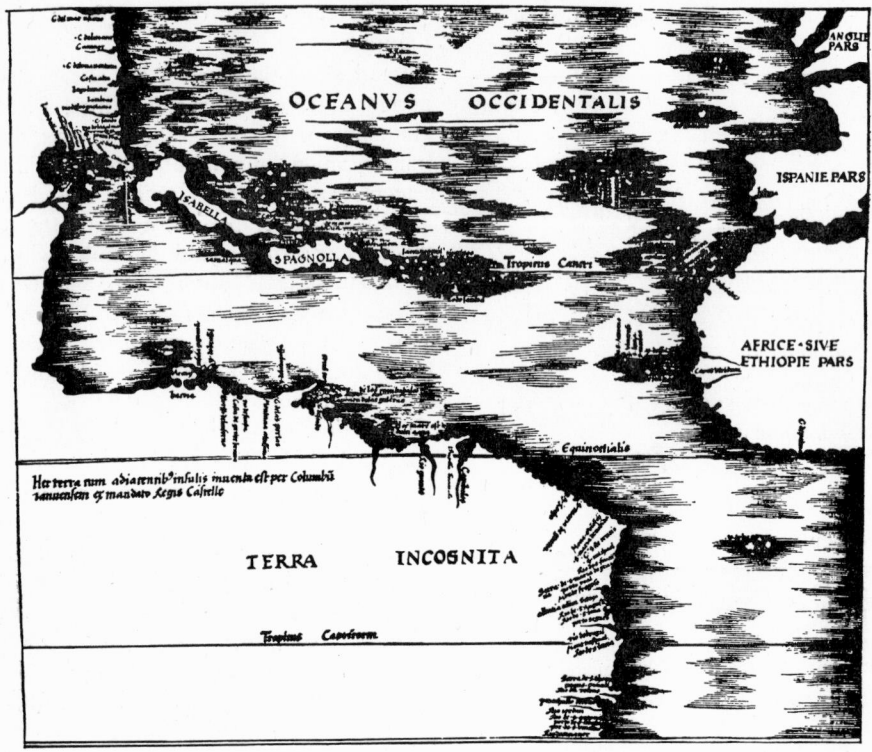

1540 - 1552

(caption opposite)

8

TABLE 2

CONTINENTS: PROPORTIONATE AREA OF MAINLAND, PENINSULAS AND ISLANDS, AND LENGTH OF COAST LINE

| | Percentage of Global Area | | | Coast Line | |
| | | | | | |
Continent [a]	*Mainland*	*Peninsulas*	*Islands*	*Length, in Thousands of Miles*	*Miles per 1,000 Square Miles of Area*
North America	75	8	17	46.7	5.0
South America	99	—	1	17.9	2.6
Europe	73	19	8	23.5	6.2
Asia	80	14	6	43.2	2.6
Africa	98	—	2	18.9	1.6
Oceania	80	5	15	12.2	3.7

Source: **19**, p. 122.

a. The USSR is here divided between Europe and Asia; North America includes Mexico and the Caribbean.

zone (New Guinea and Borneo) is slightly larger than Texas (264,000 square miles). Sumatra has roughly the same area as California (157,000 square miles), Madagascar the same as Arizona and Nevada combined (223,000 square miles). The "tiny island" of Great Britain is about twice as large as New York State or Pennsylvania or Ohio.

Some islands are outstanding because of their dense population and high level of economic and political development. Great Britain was the chief world power during the nineteenth century and is a leading center of Western civilization. The four Japanese islands (especially Honshu, which is similar to Great Britain in area and size of population) became the center of a great oriental empire. Java and the Philippines are among the most populous regions in the tropics. New Zealand's islands are outstanding in economic development and social legislation.

Islands close to the mainland have served man as stepping stones toward far horizons. Their people had at least the same chance to develop as people had on the mainland, and frequently the advantage of greater security and easier communication with other areas. On the other hand, smaller islands far from the mainland often remained long in a primitive stage of civilization, just as did regions screened from the rest of the world by forbidding mountains, jungles or marshes. Such islands were an easy prey to white men, with their superior arms, and became a part of our world as the possessions of seafaring nations. Centuries passed before they began to emerge as masters of their own destiny.

FIGURE 3. AMERICA AS SEEN BY EUROPE IN THE SIXTEENTH CENTURY (*opposite*)

These two maps are taken from Ptolemy's famous world atlas. The first was published in 1507, fifteen years after the first voyage of Columbus. In the upper right corner appear parts of England, Spain and Africa. At the left is the new continent—unknown mainland south of the Caribbean islands and a tiny coastal strip stretching northward.

The new continent begins to take shape in later editions of the Ptolemy atlas, in 1540 and 1552. It is pictured as the New World (Novus Orbis, in Latin, or Die Nüw Welt, in Dutch). At that time European scholars were aware of the general outlines of South America, the Caribbean Sea and its islands and knew of the existence of the Florida peninsula. The central part of South America had been named Brazil or America. Portugal and Spain dominated the newly discovered regions, and France had claimed the unknown lands in the north. Nobody in Europe then knew what these lands were, and geographers located them vaguely between the Caribbean Sea in the east and Japan (Zipangri), India and China (Cathay) in the west. The last three countries are shown in the upper left corner of the map.

THE ALTITUDES OF THE GLOBE

As Raymond Pearl has put it, if a giant were to roll the earth around the palm of his hand, running his fingertips over it as over a billiard ball, he would find that its surface had not been quite carefully polished. Its mountains would make it seem just a little rough in his hand — not very rough, but perceptibly short of a billiard ball's smoothness.[7]

7. **15**, p. 359.

Plate 27

North America.

	Sq. Miles	Sum Total	Length	Breadth		Leag.	dis. fr. Boston	Long.	Lat.
British Plantations to the River of S.t Lawrence	414000		1380	400	Boston	1010		70.10	42.42
					BOSTON	1010		70.10	42.42
N. England & Scotland	115000		630	400	Annapolis	995	222	66.	44.46
N. York	8100		180	90	N. York	1098	140	73.26	40.59
N. Jersey	10000		175	78	Elizabeth Town	1099	153	72.40	40.56
Pensilvania	12500		218	118	Philadelphia	1130	210	73.50	40.25
Maryland	12260		195	96	Baltimore	1190	276	72.40	39.45
Virginia	20750	236,110	225	150	James Town	1158	396	75.38	37.26
Carolina	57500		350	300	Charles Town	1240	708	78.50	32.42
Ter. di Labrador	318750		850	750					
Louisiana or Mississippi	516000		1200	645	Mobile or Fort Louis	1620		91.25	30.30
Canada and N. France	1050000	1,575,100	1450	790	Quebec	1050	distance from Mexico	74.5	47.40
Florida	118000		670	645	S.t Augustine	1300	1296	81.29	29.42
N. Mexico	300000		980	480	Sancta Fe	4380	960	109.25	35.40
California	240000		1500	360	Cape S. Lucar	4362	740	116.10	23.30
Mexico	318000		1240	665	MEXICO	4920		103.30	19.52
Guadalajara	41280		370	180	Guadalajara	5020	260	108.	20.57
Jucatan					Merida	4392	770	90.57	20.28
Guatimala	117360		750	250	Guatimala	4800	690	95.58	14.35
Honduras	48600		430	144	Valladolid	4680	852	90.47	14.
Nicaragua	23400		310	190	Leon	4710	978	90.40	11.38
Costarica	22600	1,229,240	240	165	Carthago	4662	1272	85.30	9.22
Veragua					Conception	4620	1342	83.45	9.45

SOUTH AMERICA.

	Sq. Miles	Sum Total	Length	Breadth			dis. fr. Lima	Long.	Lat.
Darien Isthmus	30000		400	120	Panama	3972	1260	81.30	9.
Terra firma	798000		1680	700	Cartagena	1502	1398	76.30	11.20
Peru	970000		1900	780	LIMA	3553		76.5	12.
Chili	206000		1800	240	S.t Jago	6540	1320	76.30	34.10
Magellanica	325000		1400	460	Mag. Str E. Mouth	2550	2410	77.	52.28
Paraguay	1150000	3,479,000	1960	1300	Assumption	5400	1500	58.	25.30
Brasil	940000		2220	900	S.t Salvador	1582	2298	40.30	12.
Land of Amazons	993600		1450	1200	Bahia de Todos los Sanctos				

Spanish Dominions — Mexico or New Spain: To Dom. To Lat.38, Fr. Dom. To Lat.46, To Lat.52, To Lat.36. To Portugal — Brasil. Little known — Land of Amazons.

‡ The Spaniards claim a right to Florida, but they are only possess'd of F.t St Augustin, and a few insignificant places on the borders of Carolina and Louisiana.

† California was always thought to be an Island till a Spanish Jesuit in 1701 discover'd that it was joyn'd to y.e Continent; of which the Royal Society receiv'd Information in 1708.

Islands of America.

	Sq. Miles	Sum Total	Length	Breadth		League to London	Long.	Lat.
Terra del Fuego	42075		315	210	Cape Horn	2612	79.30	57.35
Cuba	38400		648	126	Havana	1446	83.50	22.55
Hispaniola	36000		414	132	S.t Domingo	1300	70.5	18.28
French Hisp.	13500		300	98	Petit Guaves	1332	73.3	18.43
Spanish Hisp.	20500	36,000	410	87	S.t Domingo	1300	70.5	18.28
La Trinidad	2897		100	57	S.t Joseph	1322	61.30	10.20
Portorico	3200		115	39	Portorico	1243	65.11	18.33
Margarita	624	158,696	44	30		1323	63.20	11.10
Curisson	342		48	11		1382	68.25	12.30
Bonair	168	510	24	10		1380	67.20	12.32
Newfoundland	35500		332	194	Placentia	786	56.3	47.57
Jamaica	6000		165	50	Kingston	1424	76.30	18.
Providence	168		30	9	Fort Nassaw	1300	78.15	25.
Barbadoes	140		19	12	Bridge Town	1252	59.20	13.9
Tobago	108		29	10		1287	59.	11.5
Antegoa	100		15	11	S.t Johns Town	1212	61.	17.15
S.t Xophers	80		22	6	Basterre	1220	62.4	17.26
Bermudas	40		18	4	S.t George	910	64.6	32.28
Long Isle	800		74	20		1060	71.40	40.52
Rode Isle	36	42,972	16	5		1030	70.9	41.30
Briton	4000		112	55	Louisburg	823	61.30	45.43
Anticoste	1581		107	32	French Factory	890	63.30	50.35
Martineco	260		26	20	Fort S.t Pierre	1242	60.40	14.50
Guardalupa	180	6021	27	15	Fort Royal	1235	61.	16.10

All these Islands are subject to Spain except part of Hispaniola to France. To y.e Dutch. To Great Britain. To France.

Islands not measur'd

To G. Britain — Nevis Montserrat, Inguilla Barbuda, and Dominica.

To France { Marigalant S.t Martin Granada S.t Lucia S.t Vincent & S.t Bartholomew the Three last of the French & English have few or no Inhabitants.

S.t Eustace or Estatia and Saba (Dutch) S.t Thomas (Danes)

In some Countries where we have no knowledge of any Towns, I have supply'd y.e Vacancy by some remarkable Cape or Streight, such as Cape Horn in Terra del Fuego, Cape S.t Luca in California Streights of Magellan near Patagonia or Magellanica. And the (l) before them only Signifies that y.e distances are given from London, in Leagues by Sea.

The French have lately extended their Limits in Hispaniola, so that supposing their possessions may now be as large as those of the Spaniards, at least it is much better improv'd.

(caption opposite)

10

TABLE 3

THE LARGEST ISLANDS OF THE WORLD

Continent or Region and Island	Thousands of Square Miles	Continent or Region and Island	Thousands of Square Miles
North America		Asia	
Greenland	827	Japanese islands	
Canadian islands		Honshu	89
Baffin	198	Hokkaido	34
Victoria	80	Kyushu	16
Ellesmere	77	Shikoku	7
Banks	26	New Guinea [a]	317
Devon	22	Borneo	290
Sverdrups	21	Sumatra	168
Newfoundland	43	Philippines	116
Vancouver	12	Celebes	66
		Java	49
Caribbean		Moluccas	32
Cuba	42	Formosa	14
Hispaniola	30		
Jamaica	4	Africa	
		Madagascar	229
South America			
Tierra del Fuego	19	Oceania	
		New Zealand	
Europe		South Island	58
Great Britain	84	North Island	44
Iceland	40	Tasmania	26
Ireland	32	Solomons	16
USSR			
Novaya Zemlya	32		
Sakhalin	29		

Source: **6,** *passim.*

a. Dutch and Australian administration.

The slight surface roughness of the earth is what makes it possible for man to exist on our planet. It accounts not only for the masses of land that emerge from the ocean but also for the circulation of water on land. It is also largely responsible for the variety in climate and vegetation and in races of men.

Highlands and Lowlands

Approximately 50 per cent of all the land in the world is less than 1,000 feet above sea level;

FIGURE 4. AMERICA AS SEEN BY EUROPE AT THE BEGINNING OF THE EIGHTEENTH CENTURY *(opposite)*

These two pages from Templeman's *New Survey of the Globe,* published in London in 1729, show how North and South America appeared to English geographers half a century before the outbreak of the Revolutionary War. Templeman reports it as a new discovery that California is not an island, questions the rights of the Spaniards to Florida, and confesses that little is known about the Land of Amazons. (Cf. **22.**)

20 per cent is from 1,000 to 2,000 feet; 20 per cent, from 2,000 to 5,000 feet; 5 per cent, from 5,000 to 7,500 feet; and only 5 per cent more than 7,500 feet. (Figure 6.)

Asia is the loftiest continent in terms of mean elevation above sea level (3,000 feet), Europe the lowest (980 feet). The mean elevation of North America is 2,000 feet; of South America, 1,800 feet; Africa, 1,900 feet; and Australia, 1,000 feet. High regions (3,000 feet or more above sea level) make up a third of the land surface of Asia, more than 20 per cent of that of North America and Africa, and hardly more than one per cent of that of Australia. (See Table 4.)

Effect of Mountains on Climate

Mountains influence, at least locally, the direction of winds. Acting as barriers to passage of wind blowing landward from the ocean, they

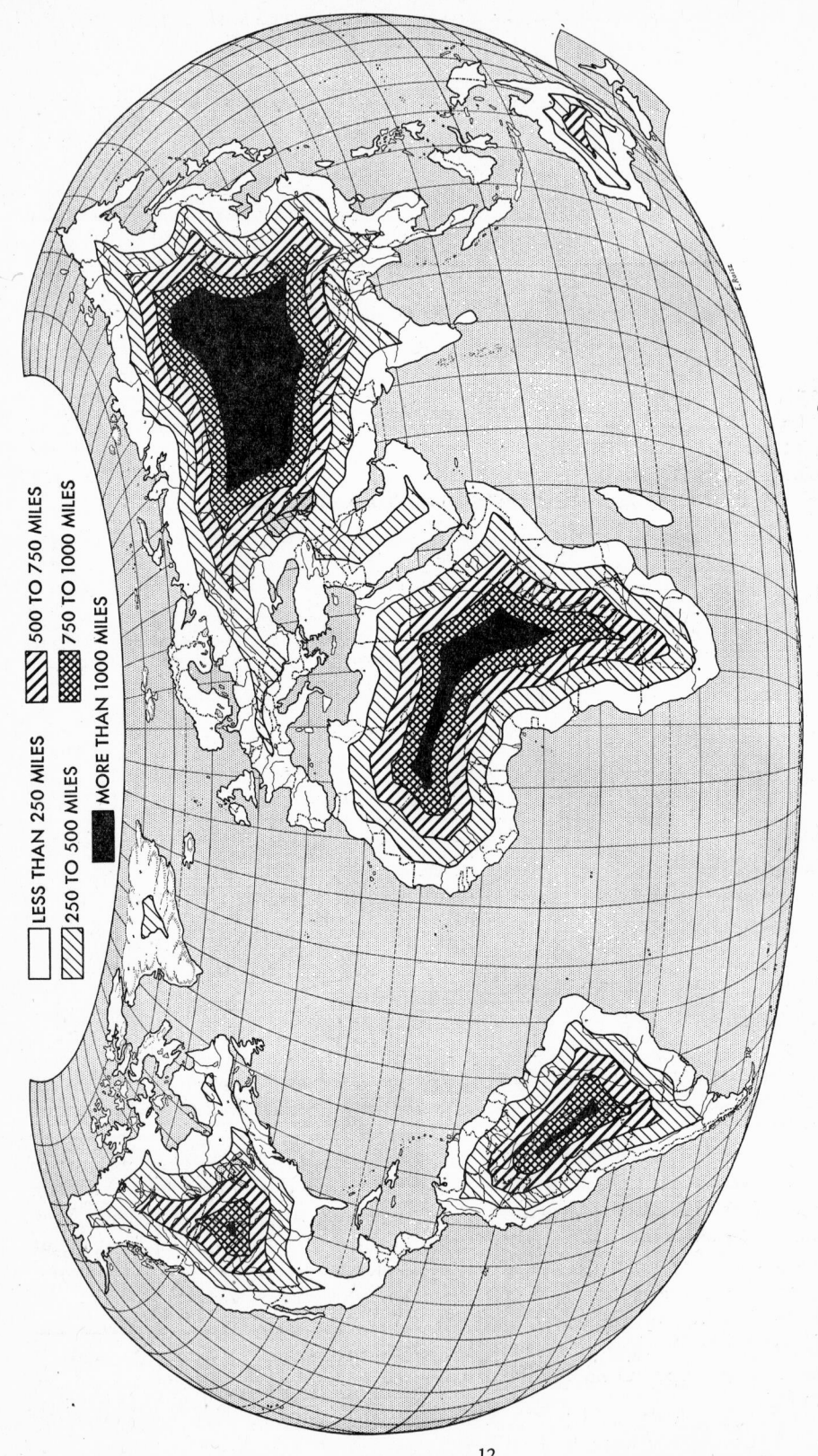

FIGURE 5. CONTINENTS: DISTRIBUTION OF AREA BY DISTANCE FROM THE SEA

This map follows the general outline of the map of Rohrback and Vidal de la Blache (25) but uses another projection and another scale to measure distances from the coast.

In Asia the area more than a thousand miles from the coast (solid black on the map) is as large as the whole United States, and in Africa, about half as large. It is smaller in South America and negligible in North America. Australia has no point more than 700 miles inland, and only a small part of western and central Europe is more than 250 miles from the coast.

LESS THAN 250 MILES

250 TO 500 MILES

500 TO 750 MILES

750 TO 1000 MILES

MORE THAN 1000 MILES

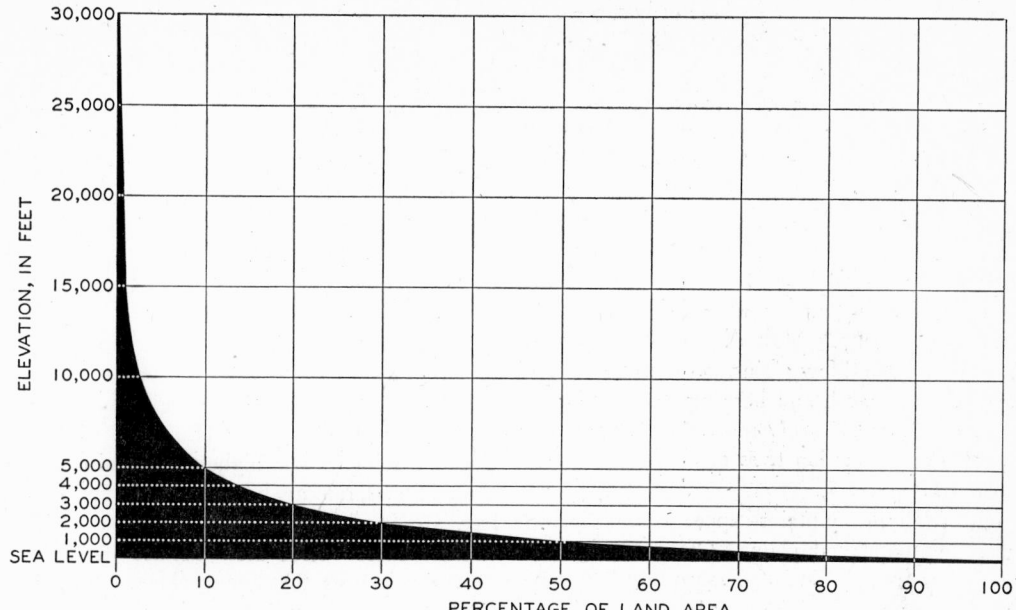

FIGURE 6. ALTITUDE: PERCENTAGE DISTRIBUTION OF LAND AREA OF THE WORLD BY ELEVATION

About half the land surface of the earth is not more than 1,000 feet above sea level; more than three fifths is below 2,000 feet, four fifths below 3,000 feet, and as much as nine tenths below 5,000 feet. Highlands and mountains cover only one tenth of the land surface. The area of high mountains does not exceed 1.5 per cent of the land surface of the earth and is less than 0.5 per cent of the total surface of the globe. (Cf. **18**, pp. 134 ff.)

TABLE 4

ALTITUDE: PERCENTAGE DISTRIBUTION OF AREA OF EACH CONTINENT [a] BY ELEVATION

Elevation above Sea Level, in Feet	North America	South America	Europe	Asia	Africa	Australia
Total	100.0	100.0	100.0	100.0	100.0	100.0
Less than 500	26.5	38.0	54.0	21.0	9.5	22.5
500-999	23.0	18.5	18.5	12.5	19.0	36.5
1,000–1,999	22.0	16.5	17.0	16.5	31.5	37.0
2,000–2,999	7.5	8.5	4.0	17.0	15.5	2.5
3,000 or more	21.0	18.5	6.5	33.0	24.5	1.5

Source: Adapted from **25**, p. 52–d. In the original, elevation is measured in meters.

a. The USSR is here divided between Europe and Asia; North America includes Mexico and the Caribbean.

affect the depth to which rains penetrate inland. Controlling the local distribution of rain, mountains frequently separate fertile valleys from deserts and determine the origin and the course of rivers. They have been a powerful factor in determining the way of life and the economic activity of men, not only in the elevated regions and valleys but also, to some extent, on the surrounding plains.

The most striking example of the influence of mountains on climate appears in the Himalayas, which control rains and winds in a vast region of southern Asia, with a population three times as large as that of North America.

Since the continental divide in North and South America is close to the Pacific coast, it influences the climate of the northern part of North America and the southern part of South

America [8] by barring the passage of winds from the Pacific, and reducing the fertile littoral plains of the Pacific coast to a narrow strip. Areas on the eastern slope of the divide, shut off from the Pacific and distant from the Atlantic, are therefore arid. In Europe the Alps play a very different role. Located between the mainland and the Apennine peninsula, they have little influence on climate but give rise to most of the rivers of western and central Europe.

Elevation is also an important determinant of population density.[9] Most of mankind has settled in valleys and low plains, not more than 600 feet above sea level, and here most of the large cities are located. Hardly more than a tenth of the world's population lives at elevations above 1,500 feet.

Historically, mountains appear as obstacles separating populated plains. Often a ridge of mountains forms a line of demarcation between two races or a natural frontier between nations, like the Andes in Chile, the Pyrenees and the Alps in Europe and the Caucasus in the USSR. A small nation surrounded by mountains has been more likely to preserve its language, religion and customs than a small nation on a plain without natural barriers.

The Roof of the World

Asia is the most mountainous continent, not only in terms of mean elevation and the proportionate area of highlands but also because it has the largest mountain masses and the highest peaks.

The Himalayas, within a region 1,500 miles long and 100 to 150 miles wide between India and Tibet, are the world's largest system of mountains. With a score of peaks towering more than 25,000 feet above sea level, they deserve to be called the roof of the world. This gigantic massif has so great an influence on the distribution of rains in some of the most densely populated parts of India that it is no exaggeration to say that some two hundred million people live in the shadow of the Himalayas. North of the Himalayas, in Hindu Kush and Pamir, other peaks of 25,000 feet and more mark the wall between India and Tibet and the Soviet Union.

Peaks of Other Continents

Europe's mountains appear small beside the Himalayas. Apart from some peaks in the Caucasus, at the border of Asia, none reaches 16,000 feet; Mont Blanc and Monte Rosa, both in the Alps, are just below this figure.

Africa's highest mountains are Kilimanjaro, in Tanganyika Territory (19,700 feet), and Kenya (17,200 feet), in the region of the same name, both of them near the eastern coast of the continent.

The loftiest peaks in North America north of the Rio Grande are in Alaska (McKinley, over 20,000 feet, Foraker, 17,000 and Bona, 16,400 feet) and western Canada (Logan, Saint Elias, Lucania, King). The highest mountains in the United States, ranging between 14,000 and 14,500 feet, are in the West; few peaks east of the Rockies exceed 6,000 feet. Mexico has several extinct volcanoes that tower above 17,000 feet (Orizaba, Popocatepetl, Iztaccihuatl), and South America has more than a score of peaks that rise from 20,000 to 23,000 feet, most of them on the Pacific coast, some on the border of Argentina and Chile and others in Peru and Bolivia. (See Table 5.)

THE WATERS

THE OCEAN

The ocean covers 71 per cent of the earth's surface, 61 per cent in the Northern Hemisphere and 81 per cent in the Southern. If the unexplored land in the Antarctic is divided evenly between the Western and Eastern Hemispheres, the same percentages hold for the share of the ocean in these two halves of the globe — 61 per cent in the Eastern Hemisphere and 81 per cent in the Western.

The ocean floor is smoother in detail but has greater differences in depth than the surface of the land. The greatest known depth of the ocean (the Philippine Drop, approximately 35,000 feet) is more than the height of Mt. Everest (29,000 feet). Likewise, the area of great depths is much larger than that of corresponding elevations of land: 77 per cent of the ocean is more than 10,000 feet deep, while 50 per cent of the land is less than 1,000 feet above sea level and only 2 per cent is 10,000 feet or more above the sea.[10]

In terms of depth, the ocean has three zones: the *continental shelf,* which borders the land and sinks gently to about 660 feet below the surface;

---

8. Pacific winds prevail in these parts of America while Atlantic winds are predominant in the middle tropical and subtropical zones.

9. See Chapter 2, pp. 36 ff.

10. **13**, pp. 43–44. Cf. **21**.

TABLE 5

ALTITUDE: THE HIGHEST PEAKS OF EACH CONTINENT

Continent and Mountain	Elevation, in Thousands of Feet	Continent and Mountain	Elevation, in Thousands of Feet
North America		Asia	
McKinley (Alaska)	20.3	Everest (Nepal-Tibet)	29.0
Logan (Canada)	19.8	Godwin Austen (K²) (India)	28.2
Orizaba (Mexico)	18.7	Kanchenjunga (Nepal-India)	28.1
Saint Elias (Canada-Alaska)	18.0	Makalu (Nepal-Tibet)	27.8
Popocatepetl (Mexico)	17.9	Dhaulagiri (Nepal)	26.8
Iztaccihuatl (Mexico)	17.3	Nanga Parbat (India)	26.7
Lucania (Canada)	17.1	Gasherbrum (India)	26.5
Foraker (Alaska)	17.0	Annapurna (Nepal)	26.5
King (Canada)	17.0	Gosainthan (Tibet)	26.3
Bona (Wrangell Mts.)	16.4	Distaghil (India)	25.9
Whitney (California)	14.5	Masherbrum (India)	25.7
		Nanda Devi (India)	25.6
South America		Rakapushi (India)	25.5
Aconcagua (Chile-Argentina)	22.8	Kamet (India)	25.4
Sajama (Bolivia)	22.3	Namcha Barwa (Tibet)	25.4
Mercedario (Chile)	22.3	Tirich Mir (India)	25.3
Huascarán (Peru)	22.2	Kungur (Pamir, Sinkiang)	25.1
		Stalin Peak [a] (Pamir, USSR)	24.6
Antarctica		Elborus (Caucasus)	18.6
Thorvald Nilsen	15.4		
Markham	15.1	Africa	
		Kilimanjaro (Tanganyika)	19.7
		Kenya (Kenya)	17.2
Europe		Peak of Tenerife (Canary Islands)	12.2
Kazbek (Caucasus, USSR)	16.5		
Mont Blanc (France-Italy)	15.8	Oceania	
Monte Rosa (Switzerland-Italy)	15.2	Carstensz (New Guinea)	16.4
Matterhorn (Switzerland-Italy)	14.8	Wilhelmina (New Guinea)	15.6
		Cook (New Zealand)	12.3

Source: **6**, *passim.*

a. Formerly Garmo Peak.

the *continental slope,* which sinks more steeply to about 8,000 feet; and the *deep ocean,* with a floor more than 8,000 feet, and in some areas 20,000 to 35,000 feet, below sea level.

The first zone, most important for sea fishery [11] and most interesting from the geological point of view,[12] covers some 6,750,000 square miles. (See Figure 7.) It is distributed by continent as follows (in thousands of square miles):[13]

North America	1,750
South America	630
Europe	810
Asia	2,440
Africa	330
Oceania	700
Antarctica	90

11. See Chapter 20.
12. See Chapter 10.
13. **13**, p. 42.

In contrast to the continents, most of which are clearly separated from one another, the world ocean is continuous. The four continental masses (the Americas, Euro-Asia, Africa and Australia) divide it into three universally distinguished oceans — the Atlantic, the Pacific and the Indian. The water around the South Pole is distributed among these three bodies of water; that around the North Pole is classified as the intercontinental Arctic Sea. Other intercontinental seas are the Mediterranean (including the Black Sea) and the Malayan and Central American Seas. (See Table 6.)

The Pacific Ocean comprises about 45.5 per cent of the marine area of the earth, the Atlantic about 22.5 per cent, and the Indian Ocean 20.5 per cent. The remaining 11.5 per cent represents the enclosed and fringing seas.

Man learned very early to cover considerable

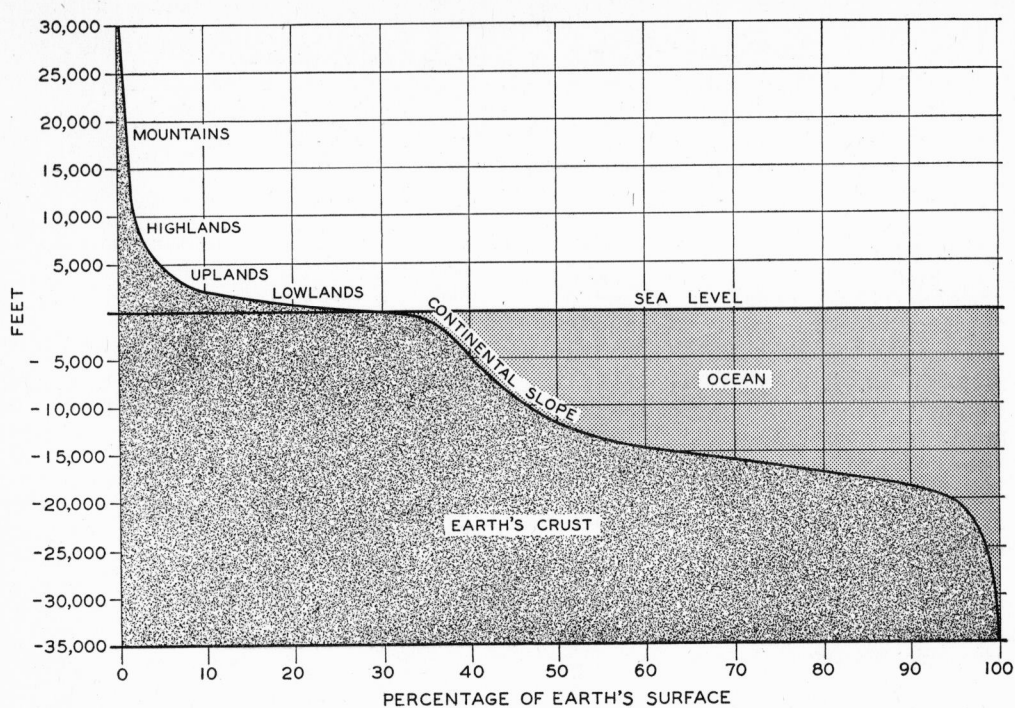

FIGURE 7. ALTITUDE: SCHEMATIC CROSS SECTION OF THE EARTH'S SURFACE
(Percentage Distribution of Earth Surface by Elevation of Land above Sea Level and Depth of the Ocean)

This figure follows the same principle as Figure 6, the only difference being that it refers not only to land area but to the whole earth's surface, land and water. The left-hand part (approximately 30 per cent of the earth's surface) shows the distribution of land area by elevation, the right-hand part, the distribution of the ocean by depth. (Cf. **18**, pp. 134–52.)

distances by sailing from island to island, and the enclosed and fringing seas became the main carriers of commerce, linking peoples to one another. A hundred miles of water was easier to travel than a hundred miles of plains, marshes, forested hills or rugged mountains.

The Atlantic

More than 6,000 miles long from Greenland to 40° S and approximately 3,000 miles wide, the Atlantic was once the great gulf between the Old World and the New. With development of marine transportation, especially since the middle of the nineteenth century, it has become the busiest water thoroughfare in the world.[14] Until the recent development of air travel, its waters carried all emigration from Europe to the Western Hemisphere, South Africa and Australia, and

it has had a major part in shaping our modern economy. The Atlantic Ocean influences the climate of the most densely populated parts of America and Europe; more specifically, its currents account for the mild climate of Great Britain.

The Pacific

The Pacific has had a very different role. Covering about a third of the earth's surface, it narrows into a strait only sixty miles wide at the Arctic Circle, widens to more than 12,000 miles at the equator, and narrows again toward the Antarctic. It strongly influences the climate in southern Asia, Oceania and America west of the Rockies, the Cordillera and the Andes. At its widest part, near the equator, it represents a formidable moat between the Western Hemisphere and the densely populated regions of Asia. Islands and trade winds enabled men to cross this expanse long before it was finally subdued by modern means of transportation, but even now

14. The central position of the Atlantic Ocean, especially the North Atlantic, in our world, is emphasized by the Raisz projection used in the maps in this book.

TABLE 6

THE WATERS: AREA AND MEAN DEPTH OF OCEANS AND SEAS [a]

Oceans and Seas	*Area, in Thousands of Square Miles*	*Mean Depth, in Feet*
Total [b]	139,600	12,750
Oceans, excluding adjacent seas	124,000	13,050
Pacific	63,800	14,050
Atlantic	31,850	12,880
Indian	28,350	13,000
Intercontinental seas	12,490	4,000
Arctic Sea	5,600	3,950
Central American Sea [c]	1,670	8,685
European Mediterranean Sea [d]	1,150	4,690
Asiatic Mediterranean (Malay) Sea	3,150	3,975
Hudson Bay	480	420
Baltic Sea	170	180
Red Sea	170	1,610
Persian Gulf	100	80
Adjacent (fringe) seas	3,110	2,870
Gulf of St. Lawrence	90	420
Gulf of California	60	2,670
English Sea and Irish Sea	70	190
North Sea	220	310
Bering Sea	870	4,715
Okhotsk Sea	590	2,751
Japan Sea	390	4,430
East China Sea	480	615
Andaman Sea	310	2,855
Bass Strait	30	230

Source: Adapted from **13**, p. 68. Cf. **20**, p. 15.

a. The purpose of this table is to show the order of magnitude and the relative depth of the main oceans and seas; the measurements are only approximate.
b. Excludes lakes and other inland waters.
c. Caribbean Sea, Gulf of Mexico and Yucatan Sea.
d. Includes the Black Sea and the Sea of Asov.

coastwise traffic on the fringing seas of the Pacific is more important than transoceanic commerce. Even the intercontinental traffic in the Pacific — for example between Tokyo and Seattle — often goes coastwise.

The Indian Ocean

The Indian Ocean is surrounded by economically underdeveloped regions with unevenly distributed populations. It brings moisture and life to the eastern coast of Africa, the littoral strip of Arabia and especially India and Indochina and, with the Pacific, influences the climate of Oceania. The topography of the adjacent continents, however, limits its direct influence to the littoral regions. As on the Pacific, coastwise traffic is more important than transoceanic commerce.

RIVERS

Apart from supplying water and influencing climate, rivers — and lakes as well — have served since early civilization as carriers of commerce, vital links between a settlement and the wider world. Although that function has diminished with progress in land transportation, inland waters are still a major factor in the economic life of nations.[15]

A river valley often attracts population in the same way as the seacoast. Many river valleys — notably those of the Indus, Ganges, Yangtze, Rhine, Danube and Nile—are among the most densely settled areas of the world. A river, however, has seldom formed a demarcation between races. In contrast to seacoasts and mountains,

15. Cf. Chapter 10.

TABLE 7

THE WATERS: DISTRIBUTION OF LAND AREA OF THE CONTINENTS BY DRAINAGE BASIN

(*Thousands of Square Miles*)

Drainage Basin	World		Continents (Area)					
	Area [a]	Per Cent	North America [b]	South America	Europe	Asia	Africa	Oceania
Total land area	52,050	100.0	9,370	6,860	3,800	17,080	11,640	3,300
Atlantic basin	27,330	52.5	7,070	6,310	3,050	5,000	5,900	—
Ocean	12,360	23.7	1,000	6,060	1,100	—	4,200	—
Arctic Sea	9,020	17.3	3,920	—	500	4,600	—	—
Mediterranean	3,550	6.8	—	—	1,450	400	1,700	—
Central American	2,400	4.6	2,150	250	—	—	—	—
Pacific basin	6,200	11.9	1,700	400	—	3,800	—	300
Indian basin	6,400	12.3	—	—	—	3,000	2,100	1,300
Continental basins [c]	12,120	23.3	600	150	750	5,280	3,640	1,700

Source: Adapted from **20**, p. 640. This table has been adjusted to the data in Table 1.

　　a. Includes inland waters and islands but excludes the Antarctic region. (Cf. Table 1.)

　　b. Includes Mexico and the Caribbean.
　　c. Without outflow to the ocean.

which tend to form natural boundaries, rivers usually mark artificial frontiers. More frequently than not, the same language is spoken on both shores of a river. When a river serves as a border between two nations, it usually divides a territory of mixed population, leaving national minorities on either side.

Drainage Basins

The outflow of rivers may be used to divide a large part of the land surface into three drainage basins — the Atlantic, the Pacific and the Indian basins. Such a classification is very rough, however, since vast regions have no distinct outflow and have to be classified as continental basins. (See Table 7.)

Because the continental divide in North and South America is near the western coast, most American rivers flow into the Atlantic Ocean or its seas. Likewise, Europe, which is geographically a peninsula in the Atlantic, belongs almost entirely to the Atlantic drainage basin. In Africa, where the highest mountains are located close to the eastern shore, the principal rivers flow to the west and north and end in the Atlantic.

All in all, the *land* area of the Atlantic drainage basin is more than four times that of the Pacific, although the *water* area of the Pacific Ocean is double that of the Atlantic. (Cf. Table 6.)

The place of the Atlantic Ocean in the river system of the world is evident also from a list-ing of principal rivers. The Atlantic Ocean, including the Arctic Sea, is the destination of the St. Lawrence River and the Mississippi in North America, the Amazon and the Paraná in South America, the Danube in Europe, the Dnieper and the great Siberian rivers in the USSR, and the Nile, Congo, Niger and Orange in Africa.

Important Rivers

The Mississippi with its tributaries and the St. Lawrence River, in combination with the Great Lakes, probably rank first among the rivers of the world in the economic importance of their basin. The Amazon, La Plata and Paraná, with their tributaries, are important in South America, as are the Rhine and the Danube in Europe, the Volga, the Don and the Dnieper in Russia, the Indus and the Ganges in India, the Yangtze in China.[16] (See Table 8.)

Some comparatively short rivers are outstanding because of their location and the cities on their shores — among them the Potomac, the Hudson and the Connecticut in the United States; the Thames in Great Britain; the Seine in France; the Po in Italy; the Ruhr in Germany; and the Neva in the USSR.

LAKES

Slightly more than one per cent of the land surface of the world (some 600,000 square miles)

16. Cf. Chapter 10.

TABLE 8

THE WATERS: LENGTH AND DRAINAGE BASIN OF PRINCIPAL RIVERS

Continent and River	Outflow	Length,[a] in Miles	Area of Basin,[a] in Thousands of Square Miles
North America			
Mackenzie	Arctic, Beaufort Sea	2,525	640
Nelson	Hudson Bay	1,650	455
Churchill	Hudson Bay	1,000	. . .
Yukon	Bering Sea	2,300	330
St. Lawrence	Atlantic Ocean, Gulf of St. Lawrence	1,900	565
Columbia	Pacific Ocean	1,200 ⎫	250
Snake	Columbia River	950 ⎭	
Mississippi [b]	Atlantic Ocean, Gulf of Mexico	2,500	
Missouri [b]	Mississippi River	2,900	
Arkansas	Mississippi River	1,500	
Red	Mississippi River	1,300	
Ohio	Mississippi River	1,300	1,300
Platte	Missouri River	1,000	
Yellowstone	Missouri River	800	
Tennessee	Ohio River	1,000	
Cumberland	Ohio River	700	
Colorado, Arizona	Pacific Ocean	2,000	250
Colorado, Texas	Gulf of Mexico	650	. . .
Rio Grande	Gulf of Mexico	1,650 ⎫	230
Pecos	Rio Grande	800 ⎭	
South America			
Orinoco	Atlantic Ocean	1,700	370
Amazon	Atlantic Ocean	3,900 ⎫	
Madeira	Amazon River	2,000 ⎪	
Japura	Amazon River	1,500 ⎬	2,800
Rio Negro	Amazon River	1,400 ⎭	
La Plata	Atlantic Ocean	2,300	. . .
Uruguay	La Plata River	1,000	. . .
Paraná	Atlantic Ocean	2,450 ⎫	
Paraguay	Paraná River	1,500 ⎪	
Pilcomayo	Paraguay River	1,000 ⎬	1,200
San Francisco	Atlantic Ocean	1,800 ⎭	
Europe, excluding the USSR			
Danube	Black Sea	1,725	320
Rhine	North Sea	700	75
Elbe	North Sea	700	55
Loire	Bay of Biscay	600	50
Oder	Baltic Sea	550	50
USSR			
Volga (Europe)	Caspian Sea	2,300	600
Dnieper (Europe)	Black Sea	1,400	200
Don (Europe)	Sea of Asov	1,100	170
Ural (Europe-Asia)	Caspian Sea	1,400	. . .
Ob (Asia)	Arctic Ocean	3,200	1,200
Lena (Asia)	Arctic Ocean	2,900	900
Yenisei (Asia)	Arctic Ocean	2,800	1,000
Amur (Asia)	Pacific Ocean	2,900	800
Amu Darya (Asia)	Aral Sea	1,500	200

(*Continued on page 20*)

TABLE 8—*continued*

Continent and River	Outflow	Length,[a] in Miles	Area of Basin,[a] in Thousands of Square Miles
Asia, excluding the USSR			
Euphrates	Persian Gulf	1,700 ⎫	300
Tigris	Euphrates River	1,150 ⎭	
Indus	Arabian Sea	1,700	370
Brahmaputra	Bay of Bengal	1,680	250
Ganges	Bay of Bengal	1,540	400
Irrawaddy	Bay of Bengal	1,250	175
Salween	Bay of Bengal	1,750	120
Yangtze	Yellow Sea	3,100	700
Hwang Ho	Yellow Sea	2,700	400
Mekong	China Sea	2,500	300
Si-Kiang	China Sea	1,650	150
Africa			
Nile	Mediterranean Sea	4,000	1,300
Congo	Atlantic Ocean	2,900	1,400
Niger	Atlantic Ocean	2,600	830
Orange	Atlantic Ocean	1,300	370
Zambezi	Indian Ocean	1,600	500
Australia			
Murray	Indian Ocean	2,300 ⎫	350
Darling	Murray River	1,150 ⎭	

Source: **6**, *passim.*

a. Length of rivers rounded in most cases to the nearest hundred miles; the area of the basin, to the nearest 10,000 square miles. Even such approximations require reservation for a margin of error in measure-ments and estimates and for changes in the length and direction of rivers.

b. Total length, Missouri-Mississippi to the Gulf of Mexico, 4,220 miles.

consists of lakes, some of them connected with oceans by rivers, others in continental basins without an outflow. Table 9 lists the largest lakes in each continent.

The Caspian Sea in the USSR, on the border of Europe and Asia, is the largest lake in the world (nearly 170,000 square miles) and has the largest drainage basin (over 3 million square miles). It has considerable influence on the climate, transportation system and economic life of the surrounding regions. The five Great Lakes on the border between the United States and Canada have, together, not much more than half the area of the Caspian Sea and a drainage basin of nearly 300,000 square miles. (See Table 10.) Their major function in the economic life of the continent is to link the agricultural Middle West with the sea, and the iron ore deposits in Minnesota with the coalfields in the Middle Atlantic states.[17] Other lakes, especially in eastern Eu-rope, Asia and Africa, are of local significance because of their influence on climate and rivers and as a source of water supply, means of water control and recreational facilities.

CLIMATE

Although man can live in exceedingly different climates,[18] development of a dense population and a thriving civilization requires a certain combination of climatic conditions. Climate acts upon man by determining the supply of food and materials for clothing and shelter, affecting health and character, and setting up barriers that limit his movements.[19]

Climate determines the supply of food and materials directly by controlling vegetation and animal life and indirectly by forming the soil. Climatic conditions — sun, rainfall and wind —

17. See Chapter 10, p. 346 and Chapter 23.

18. **17**, p. 255.
19. **10**, p. 205.

TABLE 9

THE WATERS: THE LARGEST LAKES OF THE WORLD

(*Water Area in Thousands of Square Miles*)

Continent and Lake	Area	Continent and Lake	Area
North America [a]		USSR	
Great Lakes (Canada, U. S.)		Caspian Sea (Europe, Asia)	168.9
Superior	31.8	Aral Sea (Asia)	24.6
Michigan	22.4	Baikal (Asia)	12.2
Huron	23.0	Balkhash (Asia)	8.7
Erie	9.9	Ladoga (Europe)	7.1
Ontario	7.5	Onega (Europe)	3.8
Great Bear (Canada)	12.0	Issyk Kul (Asia)	2.4
Great Slave (Canada)	11.2		
Winnipeg (Canada)	9.4	Asia	
Athabaska (Canada)	3.1	Urmia (Iran)	2.3
Reindeer (Canada)	2.4	Tsing Hai (China)	2.1
Nettilling (Canada)	2.1	Van (Turkey)	2.0
Winnipegosis (Canada)	2.1		
Nipigon (Canada)	1.9	Africa	
Manitoba (Canada)	1.8	Victoria (British East Africa)	26.6
Great Salt Lake (U. S.)	1.8	Tanganyika (Tanganyika)	12.7
Nicaragua (Nicaragua)	3.1	Nyasa (Nyasaland)	11.0
		Chad (French Equatorial Africa)	6.3
South America		Rudolf (Kenya)	3.5
Maracaibo [b]	6.3	Bangweulu (Northern Rhodesia)	2.0
Titicaca	3.2		
		Australia	
Europe		Gairdner	1.6
Vänern	2.1		

Source: **6,** *passim;* **25.**

a. Includes Middle America.　　　　　　　　　　b. An extension of the Gulf of Maracaibo.

TABLE 10

THE WATERS: THE GREAT LAKES OF THE UNITED STATES AND CANADA

(*Thousands of Square Miles*)

	Superior	Michigan	Huron	Erie	Ontario
Water area, total	31.8	22.4	23.0	9.9	7.5
United States	20.7	22.4	9.1	5.0	3.6
Canada	11.1	—	13.9	4.9	4.0
Drainage basin, total	80.9	69.0	72.4	34.7	34.6
United States	37.6	69.0	24.8	23.6	18.7
Canada	43.3	—	47.6	11.1	15.9

Source: **4,** pp. 48, 127, 291, 369 and 466.

also influence the activity of rivers, which in turn affects human life. The fundamental factor in human geography, however, is the effect of climate on the health and character of men.

The main features of climate are temperature, rainfall and wind.[20]

TEMPERATURE

Temperature is governed mainly by latitude and elevation above sea level. It rises gradually from the poles to the equator (Table 11), and declines with increase in elevation. The average monthly temperature at the equator is almost exactly the same in January and July; contrast between the summer and winter temperature increases as one moves toward the poles.

The polar circles and the tropics divide the surface of the globe into five temperature zones as follows:

	Millions of Square Miles of Land and Water	Percentage of Total Area
Total	197.0	100.0
North Polar (Arctic) Zone	8.3	4.2
North Temperate Zone	51.2	26.0
Tropical Zone	78.0	39.6
South Temperate Zone	51.2	26.0
South Polar (Antarctic) Zone	8.3	4.2

Nearly half the land in the world is in the North Temperate Zone, about a fourth is in the Tropical, and the remaining fourth is divided among the South Temperate, the Arctic and the Antarctic. (See Figure 8.) The European-American civilization is concentrated in the North Temperate Zone, and the Orient is split between this zone (China and Japan) and the tropical area.

Latitude, however, is only one of several factors that determine temperature; neither the isotherms for different months nor those for the year as a whole follow the latitudes closely. Deviations result from the planetary wind system, the monsoon type of winds, the temperature differences between the ocean and the land, ocean currents, the proportion of land and water, altitudes and mountain ridges, and local influences. There are also conspicuous differences in deviations for individual months. Two localities may fall on the same isotherm in June and be far apart in December. In Los Angeles, for example, the mean temperature in June is the same as in Huron, South Dakota (66.4° F. and 66.2° F.), but in December, mean temperatures in the two cities are 57.3° F. and 18.7° F. respectively.[21]

The isotherms for the year as a whole (see Figure 9) are closer to the latitudinal direction than those for single months. They swerve northward in the North Atlantic Ocean because of the Gulf Stream, which brings warmth and moisture to western Europe and especially to Great Britain.

Areas with an average annual temperature below the freezing point (white on the map) are practically uninhabitable. Those with an average annual temperature of more than 86° F. (solid black, in central Africa) are uninhabitable for white races because of excessive heat combined with lack of rainfall. The area between these extreme isotherms may be roughly divided into five habitable zones: the tropical zone (excluding the area of extreme heat), with an average annual temperature from 68° F. to 86° F.; the northern and southern moderately warm zones, where the annual average is from 50° F. to 68° F.; and two moderately cold zones, where the average ranges from 32° F. to 50° F.

The largest part of the United States and Japan are in the same zone as the Mediterranean region. The northeastern corner of the United States, southern Canada and the northwestern part of Europe, including Great Britain, lie close to the isotherm of 50° F. and slightly north of it. The most populous Asiatic regions (China, India and Indonesia) are in the zone with average annual temperature above 68° F.

RAINFALL

The second major aspect of climate, rainfall, is governed by the same fundamental factors as temperature — latitude, elevation, winds, ocean currents, topography. Latitude, however, is not so closely related to the distribution of moisture over the earth as to the distribution of the sun's rays; the equatorial zone includes both arid deserts and areas with almost continuous rain.

Generally, rainfall is particularly abundant in the equatorial zone, between 10° N and 10° S, where the average for all continents is about 70 inches a year. The average in the zone between 30° N and 60° N is about 20 inches a year and between 70° N and 80° N, only 12 inches.

---

20. **16,** pp. 16–17.　　　　　　　　21. **3,** 1936, p. 146.

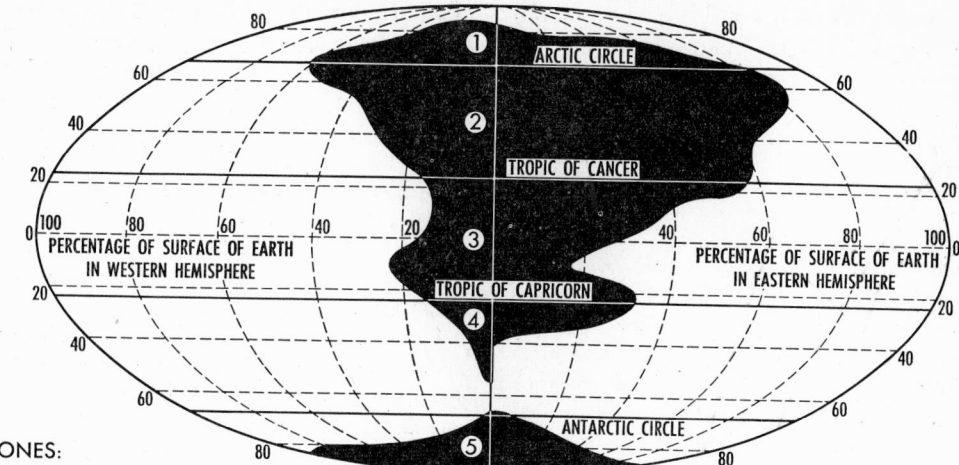

ZONES:

① NORTH POLAR; ② NORTH TEMPERATE; ③ TROPICAL; ④ SOUTH TEMPERATE; ⑤ SOUTH POLAR

FIGURE 8. CLIMATE: THE WORLD CONTINENT BY GEOGRAPHIC ZONE

This map shows the world continent schematically, as does the lower panel of Figure 1, but with the temperature zones delimited by the Polar Circles and the Tropics. The North Temperate Zone is almost evenly divided
between land and water; in the South Temperate Zone, water predominates. The Arctic forms a natural continuation of the world continent in the North Temperate Zone (as in Alaska, Canada, Scandinavia and Siberia). The
Antarctic is completely surrounded by water and separated from the world continent.

TABLE 11

CLIMATE: AVERAGE TEMPERATURE ON LAND AT SEA
LEVEL, BY LATITUDE

(*Degrees Fahrenheit*)

Latitude	Annual Average	January	July
World average	57.9	54.7	61.5
Northern Hemisphere			
North Pole	–8.9	–41.8	30.2
80°	–0.7	–28.3	35.1
70°	13.5	–15.5	44.4
60°	30.2	3.4	57.2
50°	42.6	19.2	64.4
40°	57.4	41.9	75.2
30°	68.7	58.5	81.1
20°	77.5	71.4	82.4
10°	79.3	78.4	80.4
Equator	79.3	79.7	78.1
Southern Hemisphere			
10°	77.7	79.5	75.0
20°	73.4	77.5	67.6
30°	65.1	70.9	58.1
40°	53.4	59.7	47.8
50°	41.7	47.1	37.4
60°	29.1	36.9	18.3
70°	11.3	30.6	– 8.0
80°	12.6	30.3	–24.7
South Pole	–13.0	. . .	. . .

Source: After Julius Hahn, quoted in **26**, p. 10.

Evaporation and Precipitation

The land usually obtains more moisture
through rainfall than it gives up through evaporation, receiving rain from winds blowing inland
and returning the surplus to the ocean through
rivers.

Of the estimated 112,000 cubic miles of water
evaporated during a year over land and sea
(92,000 cubic miles evaporated over the oceans
and 20,000 cubic miles over the land), the ocean
receives some 85,000 cubic miles through rainfall,
7,000 less than it loses through evaporation, and
the land receives 27,000 cubic miles, 7,000 more
than it loses. The differences in these figures
represent water that is carried inland by wind
and is returned to the ocean by the rivers. In
areas without outflow to the ocean, rainfall must
be in rough balance with evaporation; in areas
with outflow, inland winds increase the amount
of precipitation from 17,500 cubic miles, which
would be in balance with the evaporation, to
24,500 cubic miles or from 24 inches to 33.6
inches per unit of surface.[22] (See Table 12.)

Wet and Arid Regions

Each continent includes some areas with heavy
rainfall and others with an extremely arid cli-

22. Cf. the picture of the hydrological cycle in Figure
113.

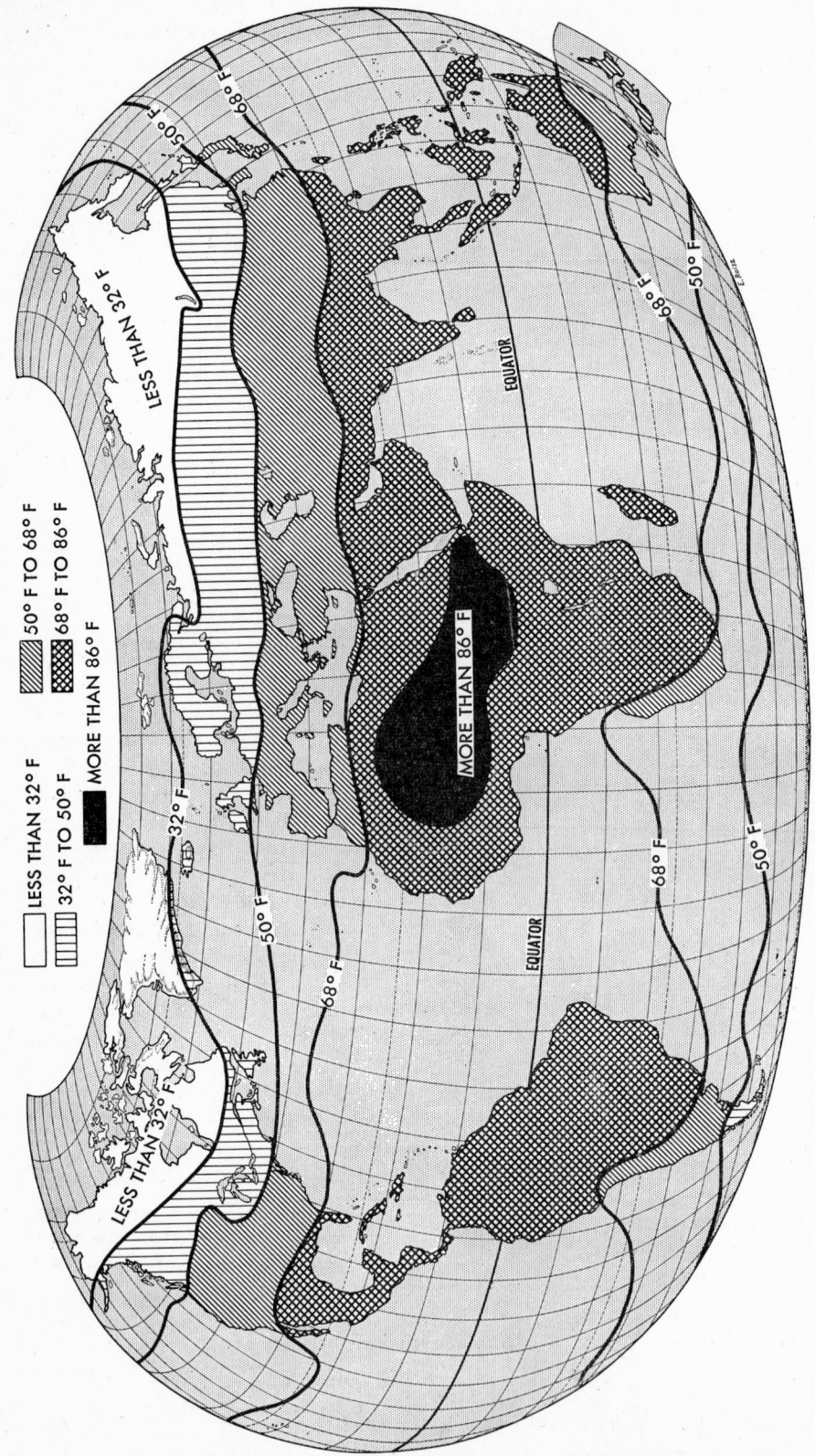

FIGURE 9. CLIMATE: SELECTED ANNUAL ISOTHERMS AND TEMPERATURE ZONES IN THE WORLD

The northern annual isotherm of 32° F. is not far from the Polar Circle in Scandinavia and sinks in the Far East to the latitude of New England. In the Eastern, it rises far above the Polar Circle in Scandinavia and sinks in the Far East to the latitude of New England.

The northern annual isotherm of 68° F. passes close to the Tropics in the Far East and swings northward in the Western Hemisphere. The largest part of the United States is between the annual isotherms of 50° F. and 68° F. The same zone includes the countries of the Mediterranean basin, Switzerland, the Balkans, the southern part of the USSR, the Near East, and most of China, Korea and Japan. The southern zone with a similar annual temperature passes through parts of Chile, Argentina, South Africa and southern Australia.

24

TABLE 12

CLIMATE: ANNUAL TURNOVER OF EVAPORATION AND PRECIPITATION OVER OCEAN
AND LAND [a]

Item	*World*	*Ocean*	*Total*	*Areas with Outflow to the Ocean* [b]	*Areas without Outflow to the Ocean* [c]
Area, in millions of square miles	197.0	139.6	57.4	40.1	17.3
Evaporation					
In inches per unit of surface	35	41	20	24	8
Total, in thousands of cubic miles	112.0	92	20	17.5	2.5
Rainfall					
In inches per unit of surface	35	38	27	33.6	8
Total, in thousands of cubic miles	112.0	85	27	24.5	2.5

Source: **26**, pp. 12–13.

a. Data are based on rough estimates and give only a general idea of the effect of oceans and winds in providing land with moisture.
b. Three ocean basins as shown in Table 7.
c. Continental basins as shown in Table 7 and Antarctica.

mate. In North America, certain regions on the Pacific coast and the Gulf of Mexico have more than 100 inches of rainfall a year, while the deserts of California, Arizona and Nevada get less than 10. In South America, rainfall is excessive in the tropical area and light in mountainous regions farther south. North Africa is arid except for a narrow strip along the Mediterranean, while rainfall in the equatorial zone exceeds 400 inches a year. In Asia, the amount of precipitation ranges from less than 10 inches a year in the desert belt to 80 inches or more in certain parts of Indonesia and 280 inches in Assam. In western Europe, the range is narrower, but in eastern Europe, especially in Russia, and in Australia and Oceania, contrasts are as striking as in the United States.

In view of these contrasts, a figure for the average annual rainfall of a continent is of little significance,[23] and precipitation should be evaluated in terms of smaller and comparatively homogeneous areas, as in Figure 10.

TYPES OF CLIMATE

Classifications of climates widely accepted in modern geography are based on various combinations of temperature and rainfall.[24]

C. Warren Thornthwaite, for example, combines five types of "precipitation effectiveness" with six types of "temperature efficiency" and four types of seasonal distribution of rainfall.[25] Since each humidity type can appear in combination with each temperature type and each type of distribution of rainfall, 120 combinations of the basic features are theoretically possible. Not all these are found, however, and some are unusual. Thirty-two may be singled out as important climatic types: 3 types of wet climate, 7 humid, 10 subhumid, 6 semiarid, 3 arid, and 3 types designated as taiga, tundra and perpetual frost.[26] On a map of the world these 32 types of climate form an extremely complicated pattern in which areas of one type are often surrounded by areas of another type.

The picture becomes simpler and clearer when classification is restricted to eight principal types of climate as shown in Table 13 and Figure 11.[27]

23. At a rough approximation, precipitation averages 25 inches a year in North America (including Mexico and the Caribbean), 55 inches in South America, 23 inches in Europe, 30 inches in Asia, 33 inches in Africa, 20 inches in Oceania and Australia, and hardly more than 10 inches in Antarctica.

24. **11**, *passim;* cf. **5**, p. 150.
25. "Precipitation effectiveness" is measured by the relationship of rainfall (in inches) to temperature. The same amount of rainfall therefore does not represent the same "precipitation effectiveness" in a temperate and a tropical zone. "Temperature efficiency" is measured by the mean temperature above 32° F. (**23**, pp. 633–55.)
26. This classification has been criticized as unnecessarily complicated (**12**, pp. C–23 and C–24).
27. **2**, p. 104.

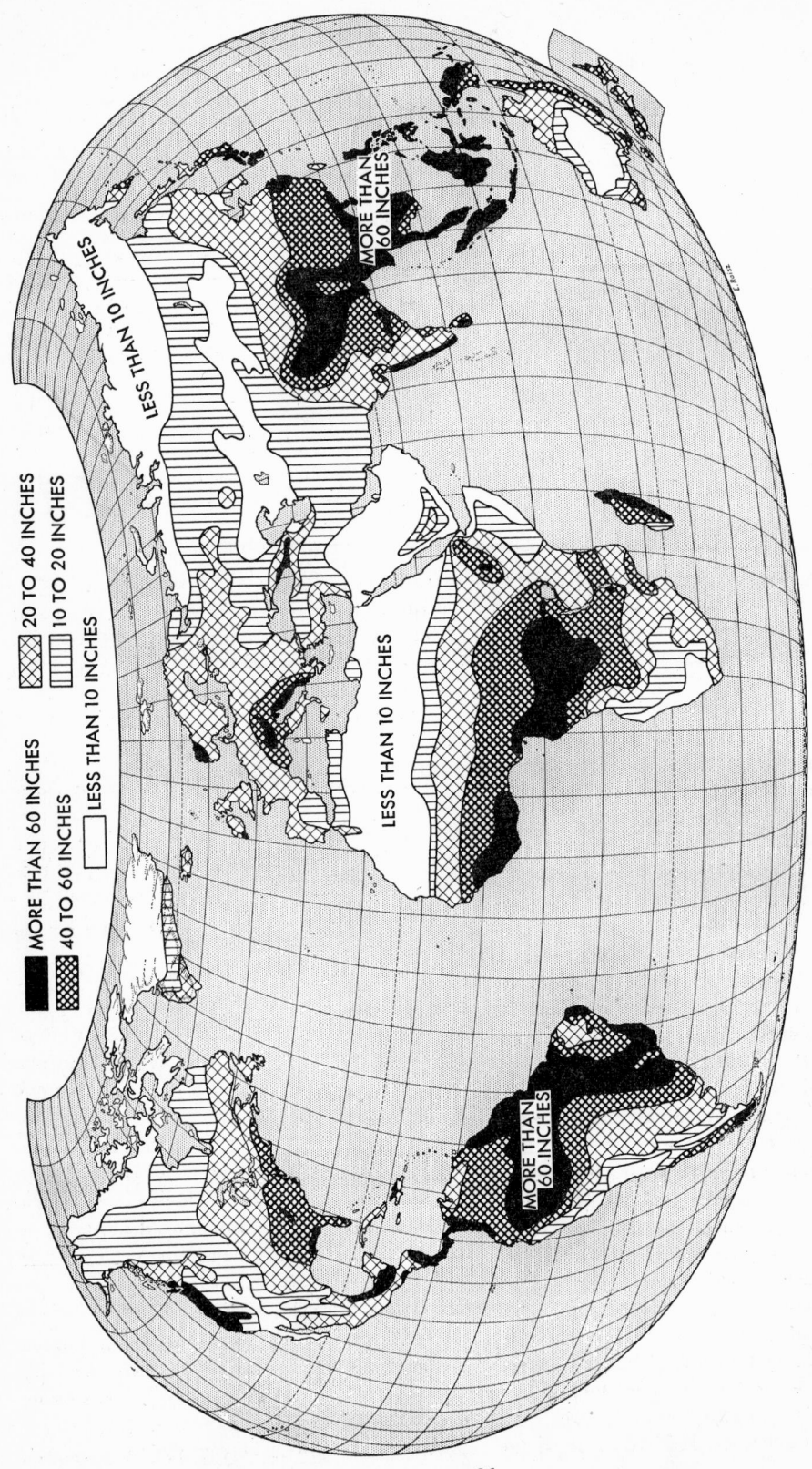

Figure 10. Climate: Distribution of Land Surface of the World by Average Annual Rainfall

A moderately humid climate with 20 to 60 inches of rainfall a year is best for agriculture. Areas of excessive rainfall (solid black in the map) are comparatively small in North America and Europe but comprise a large part of the tropical zone in South America, Africa and the Far East. Areas with insufficient rainfall form two belts. The larger crosses the Eastern Hemisphere from the Atlantic coast of North Africa to Kamchatka and the Bering Sea. The smaller cuts across North America from Canada to Mexico, following the eastern slope of the continental divide.

TABLE 13

CLIMATE: DISTRIBUTION OF LAND AREA OF THE CONTINENTS BY TYPE OF CLIMATE
(*Thousands of Square Miles*)

Type of Climate	World	North America [a]	South America	Europe [b]	Asia [b]	Africa	Oceania	Antarctic Region
All types	57,400	9,370	6,860	3,800	17,080	11,640	3,300	5,350
Wet	1,290	180	200	20	780	100	10	—
Humid	9,180	1,440	3,100	730	1,410	1,900	600	—
Subhumid	11,700	1,290	2,210	1,660	2,700	3,300	540	—
Semiarid	8,520	1,140	650	180	3,400	2,300	850	—
Arid	8,670	380	440	50	2,460	4,040	1,300	—
Taiga	7,150	2,000	220	900	4,030	—	—	—
Tundra	3,280	1,570	40	250	1,420	—	—	—
Perpetual frost	7,610	1,370	—	10	880	—	—	5,350

Source: This table follows the classification of C. Warren Thornthwaite (**24,** p. 438). Thornthwaite's classification has been condensed and all figures have been rounded to the nearest 10,000 square miles and adjusted roughly to the data for continents in Table 1.

a. Includes Mexico and the Caribbean.
b. Includes part of the USSR.

The areas with wet climate are clustered mainly along the seacoast in both hemispheres. Humid areas are widespread in the Western Hemisphere from the Amazon basin to the eastern part of the United States and the southeastern corner of Canada; this type of climate prevails also in north and central Europe, China and equatorial Africa. Subhumid climates are characteristic of the central regions of North and South America, the Mediterranean, the Balkans, a large part of the USSR and India.

The arid and semiarid areas form a wide belt in the Northern Hemisphere that passes through northern Africa and central Asia and extends over the western part of the United States; in the Southern Hemisphere, they occur in coastal and internal areas in South America flanking the Andes, southwestern Africa and the largest part of Australia. Perpetual frost, tundra and taiga climates prevail in the polar and subpolar regions, and include a large part of Canada, Scandinavia and Russia.

Regions of perpetual frost, tundra climate and arid climate — with a total area of 19.6 million square miles — are practically unfit for settlement. Semiarid climates and taiga climate represent a total area of 15.7 million square miles that supports only a thinly scattered population, hardly more than 30 million, or 1.5 per cent of all mankind. Approximately 98 per cent of the people in the world live in wet, humid and subhumid climates, which prevail over 22.2 million square miles, or 38.7 per cent of the earth's land surface. The wet-climate region includes some of the most densely populated but economically underdeveloped areas. Modern economic civilization is concentrated in areas where humid and subhumid climates prevail.

Wind

Wind is rarely used as a basic feature in classifying climate but, along with temperature and rainfall, is important in determining the opportunities that climate affords to men. "Trade winds," monsoons and cyclones have been particularly important in the development of civilization.

"Trade winds," blowing from east to west in the equatorial zone, and westerly winds prevailing above 40° N and below 40° S, were of great significance for intercontinental commerce in the era of sailing ships but have since become of less importance.

Monsoons, particularly characteristic of India, are tropical winds that blow inland from the ocean in summer and from the land toward the ocean in winter. The direction is determined by the difference between the air pressure over land and ocean. Since the temperature of water does not change with the season as sharply as that of land, air over the continent is warmer in summer and cooler in winter than that over the sea. This difference results in relatively high air pressure over the ocean in summer and over the continent in winter. Monsoons bring abundant rainfall

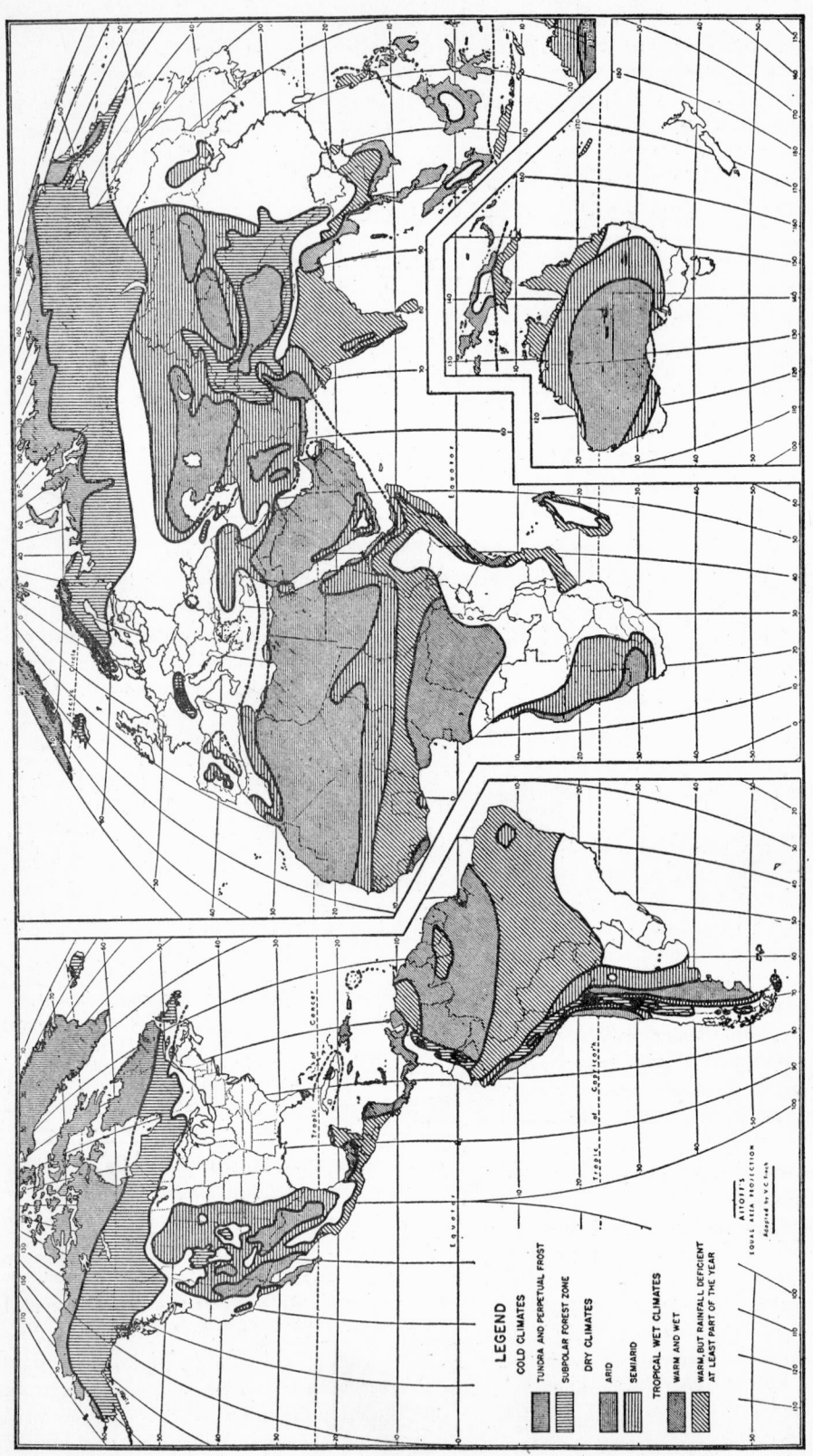

FIGURE 11. CLIMATE: DISTRIBUTION OF PRINCIPAL TYPES OF CLIMATE IN THE WORLD (C. WARREN THORNTHWAITE)

Classification of the land area of the world by type of climate is more elaborate than classification by annual temperature or rainfall. (Cf. Figures 9 and 10.) The characteristics of the types of climate designated here as subpolar forest zone ("taiga") and "tundra" are low temperature and light annual rainfall; most of the areas where such climates prevail have an average annual temperature of less than 32° F, and annual rainfall of 10–19 inches or less.

LEGEND

COLD CLIMATES
TUNDRA AND PERPETUAL FROST
SUBPOLAR FOREST ZONE
DRY CLIMATES
ARID
SEMIARID
TROPICAL WET CLIMATES
WARM AND WET
WARM, BUT RAINFALL DEFICIENT AT LEAST PART OF THE YEAR

when they blow inland and drought when they blow in the opposite direction. Favoring the culture of rice, they make it possible for an area to develop a very dense population, but they also cause periodic famines.

Cyclones are whirling winds that develop around low-pressure areas. They are characteristic of the regions of westerly winds in the temperate zones of the Northern and Southern Hemispheres. Cyclones accompanied by anticyclones are usually mild, but occasionally acquire the destructive force of hurricanes. In contrast to trade winds and monsoons, cyclones are highly irregular, and the weather changes they cause are unpredictable.

Huntington's Theory of Climatic Energy

Ellsworth Huntington has examined and classified climate in terms of its effect on human energy. More specifically, his classification relates to energy among white men in our current civilization, in which people have a rather high capacity to protect themselves from the weather by appropriate clothing, heating of houses, and the like.[28]

On the basis of studies of the efficiency of workers in different parts of the world under varying conditions of temperature and moisture, Huntington held the following conditions to be most stimulating to mind and body: mean temperature of approximately 40° F. in winter and 64° F. in summer, relative humidity of about 60 per cent at noon and high enough at night so that dew is precipitated, and variability of weather, with frequent but not extreme changes. No region on earth fully satisfies all three of these requirements, but many come fairly close to the ideal. Assigning definite weights to each factor, Huntington classified areas according to the invigorating or enervating influence of the climate [29] as shown, with minor modifications, in Figure 12.[30]

The two regions of "very high energy," where the climate is believed to be the most invigorating, are in the northeastern and north central part of the United States and the northwestern and central part of Europe (black on the map).

The area of high energy (heavily shaded) includes the remainder of the United States except the Deep South, and the remainder of Europe except southern Spain and Portugal and a sparsely populated section of Scandinavia. The high-energy area projects eastward into Russia to the border of Siberia and then gradually disappears because many cyclonic storms die out in the center of the continent and extremes of temperature and dryness prevail. It reappears in Japan at the same latitude as in Europe and North America.[31]

The Stage of History

One of the most striking aspects of the world economy is the uneven distribution of wealth among nations. Some nations have more coal, oil, water power and minerals than they can consume; others lack these riches. In some countries, a generous soil yields abundant food; in others, strenuous effort brings only a meager harvest.[32]

Still greater, however, is the inequality in the distribution of human abilities. The fertile valleys and plains of southern Asia, which gave rise to glorious systems of civilization and bred generations of warriors, artists, thinkers and statesmen, have become the abode of the deepest

---

28. **9**, p. 540.

29. **7**, pp. 228–33.

30. The Mercator projection used by Huntington has been replaced by that of Erwin Raisz (cf. **16**), and the classification of climates has been slightly simplified in that Huntington's "low" and "very low" energy are here combined.

31. **10**, p. 255. Huntington was aware, of course, that the center of civilization has moved in the last five millenniums from warm regions such as Egypt and Babylonia toward cool, stormy regions. He explains this movement as the consequence of man's technical progress. At first, man could exist only in a hot climate. After he learned to make a fire, wrap furs or skins about himself, and construct a shelter, he became able to survive adverse weather. Climate characterized by moderate temperature and changing weather then proved more stimulating and invigorating than that in which civilization was born. The controlling factor in the shift of the center of civilization "coldward and stormward" has been, according to this theory, man's increasing ability to create a comfortable, healthful artificial indoor climate when the outdoor weather is severe. (**8**, pp. 400–01. Cf. **14**.)

If this explanation is correct, the next shift of the center of civilization is unpredictable. It is possible that progress in refrigeration and air conditioning, combined with the success of modern medicine in fighting tropical diseases, will reverse the long-term northward trend and speed the rise of civilization, as we understand it, in the equatorial zone, equalizing the geographical distribution of economic power in the world.

32. See Chapter 10.

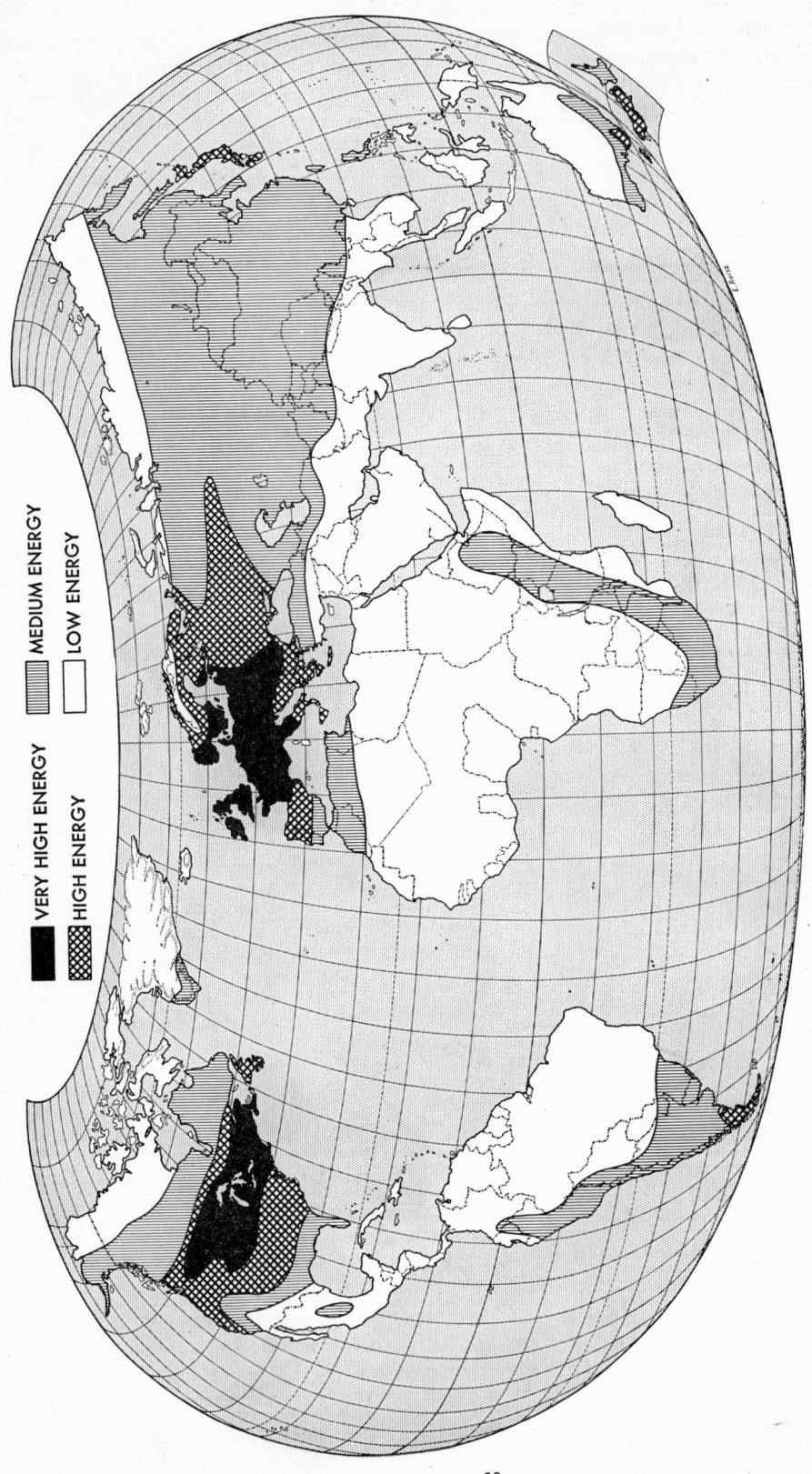

FIGURE 12. CLIMATE: DISTRIBUTION OF LAND IN THE WORLD BY "CLIMATIC ENERGY"

VERY HIGH ENERGY
HIGH ENERGY
MEDIUM ENERGY
LOW ENERGY

This map shows, in a slightly simplified form, Huntington's classification of climate according to its effect on the energy and efficiency of human beings in our present phase of civilization. The zone of "very high energy" (solid black on the map) has climatic conditions close to the optimum observed in studying the efficiency of workers under varying conditions of temperature and humidity. Climate is less stimulating in the zone of "high energy" but still favors high efficiency. In areas classified as "medium energy," continuous effort in mental or physical work is more difficult. Least favorable, according to Huntington, are climatic conditions in territory designated as "low energy" (white on the map).

poverty in the modern world.[33] Meanwhile, new generations of active men have grown up on poor soil under the cloudy northern sky. They have invented new tools and arms, have harnessed nature and conquered the oceans, and have become the masters of the world. As time goes on, deadly clashes develop among them. The new civilization is too strong to be stampeded by barbaric hordes, as was ancient Rome, but it can be blown up from within.

The setting of the drama of our time is shown on the world map by the wide dispersion of natural resources all over the globe and concentration of economic power in two comparatively small — perhaps too small — areas on both shores of the North Atlantic Ocean.[34]

33. See Chapter 12.

34. See Chapter 13.

CHAPTER 2

PEOPLES OF THE WORLD

MEN'S EFFORTS TO COUNT themselves are as old as written history. In Babylon and China, population censuses go back as far as the third millennium B. C.[1]

Ancient Censuses

Censuses have never been popular. They have often foreshadowed some unpleasant event. Conscription, confiscation or higher taxes were in the offing when a king or conqueror counted the men in a province or the sheep or the serfs. The Bible tells of violent opposition to a census in Judaea at the time of King David. Even thousands of years later, in the middle of the eighteenth century, when a census was proposed for the first time in the British House of Commons, the spokesman of the majority objected indignantly. "I did not believe," he shouted, "that there was any set of men or indeed any individual of the human species, so presumptuous and so abandoned as to make the proposal we have just heard. . . . I hold this project to be totally subversive to the last remains of English liberty." [2]

The peoples did their best to escape the census takers, and the kings, in their turn, tried to keep the results of enumerations secret — as we say today, "for administrative use only." Census data seldom became as widely known as those for the Jews after their exodus from Egypt. Apart from the census taken in the Roman Empire under Gaius Octavianus Augustus, at the beginning of the Christian era, only fragmentary information is available on the size of population in the ancient world. Practically nothing is left of the elaborate statistical surveys of old China, which were among the wonders reported by Marco Polo to his incredulous contemporaries. Only a few communities of medieval Europe — among them London, Paris and Rome — have left records that may be used to estimate population, such as the number of deaths and burials or the count, for tax purposes, of chimneys, doors and windows.

Modern Censuses

Modern censuses of population begin with those in the French and British colonies in the territory now occupied by Canada (1665) and in Iceland (1703). In 1748, periodic enumerations were introduced in Sweden; in 1769, in Denmark; and in 1790, in the United States, where the Constitution prescribed decennial censuses as a means of allocating seats in Congress among the states.[3] The first census in Great Britain was taken in 1801. During the nineteenth century, periodical enumerations became customary in almost all countries, though Russia, apart from partial enumerations for fiscal and military purposes, did not take one until 1897 and Turkey had no census until 1927. China is now the only large country that has had none in modern times.

Most modern censuses provide not only information on the number, age and sex of the inhabitants but also tell something about their work and living conditions. Some also indicate the number and composition of families, and the composition of the population by race, religious affiliation, education, language and so on. Sometimes a census of population is combined with a survey of income, housing, production (mining, manufactures, agriculture), and business.

In the last forty years — thanks largely to the efforts of the League of Nations and, more recently, the United Nations — considerable progress has been made toward uniformity of census schedules used in different parts of the world. At least threescore countries now have more or less comparable population statistics.

Most population censuses, however, have a fairly wide margin of error. Experience with American censuses teaches us not to accept such data at face value. As recently as 1940, it has

---

1. **37**, p. 761.
2. **15**, 1901, p. 4.

3. Earlier censuses were taken in Connecticut (1756) and Massachusetts (1764).

been discovered, 6.3 per cent of white native children under five years of age and 15.2 per cent of Negro children in these ages were missed by the enumerators.[4] The margin of error must be much wider in countries with poor transportation and communication and a low level of education or in totalitarian nations where the government can suppress or change the results of enumeration as it desires.

Population statistics for many countries rest on highly dubious grounds. It is not always possible to decide what is true or false in population data released by a totalitarian government. There are only rough estimates for China, which is believed to have about a fifth of the world's population.[5] Figures for such countries as Ethiopia, Liberia, Afghanistan, Iran, Turkey, Korea, Thailand, Indochina or Peru are largely informed guesses.[6]

The Statistical Office of the United Nations describes the population statistics for Africa, the Near East, and the Far East excluding Japan as "poor"; it recognizes the reports for Latin America, south-central Asia, the USSR and eastern Europe as "fair"; and accepts as "good" the data for the rest of Europe, the United States and Canada, Japan, and Oceania.[7] The Office ventures no estimate of the probable margin of error in the world totals, but suggests that an error of 3 per cent in either direction is possible.

This appraisal is, of course, open to criticism. One may question, for example, the standards according to which the nonexisting statistics of the USSR and its satellites are accepted as fair. Even the broad regions with statistical records rated as "good" have some blind spots such as Spain in southern Europe and the Pacific Islands

in Oceania. It is more likely that about a third of our statistics for world population are derived from rough estimates and doubtful sources and about two thirds from more or less reliable enumerations. The totals for the countries with dubious data may be in error by as much as 10 per cent; for the remaining countries, by 5 per cent. World population consequently may have been 160 million more or less than the estimate of 2.4 billion as of midyear 1950.

The Number of People

Large aggregations of people lived in Asia, especially in India and China at a time when most of Europe and America were still covered with virgin forests and had only scattered inhabitants. Travelers from ancient Greece were greatly impressed by the crowded communities in the valleys of the Nile and the Euphrates. The size of the cities in the Ganges valley caught the imagination of Alexander's contemporaries. Fifteen hundred years later the number of people in China amazed Marco Polo.

Beginning of the Christian Era

At the beginning of the Christian era (A. D. 30), the population of the Roman Empire, including slaves, totaled approximately 55 million,[8] distributed as follows (in millions):

Europe	23
Italy	6
Gaul	5
Spain	6
The Danube Valley	2
Greece	3
Sicily, Sardinia and Corsica	1
Africa	14.5
Egypt	8
North Africa	6
Cyrenaica	0.5
Asia	17.5
Armenia and Caucasus	2.5
Asia Minor and Syria	9
Other areas	6

How many more people may the world have had at that time? To the north of the Roman Empire lay sparsely populated regions — the British Isles, Scandinavia and heavily forested central Europe. To the east stretched borderless steppes, with only scattered settlements on rivers

---

4. **33**, p. 22.

5. The *Statistical Abstract of the Republic of China, 1947* (**13**, p. 2) shows the population as 455,592,065. This figure is the sum of data for single "localities," including Tibet and Manchukuo. Most items refer to data for July and December 1946, but those for Manchukuo were issued in 1940–1941, and the figure for Tibet reproduces an old estimate prepared in 1928. Data for 1946 rest on reports of local authorities to the Ministry of Interior. A census was taken in only nine districts of the province Szechwan, in April 1942 and December 1943; of the estimated total population of 47.1 million in this province, only 1.8 million live in the districts covered by the census. All in all, the official population figure represents an administrative estimate with a considerable margin of error.

6. **23**, p. viii.

7. **2**, 1949–50, p. 10.

---

8. Estimates of Julius Beloch (**17**), revised by Eduard Meyer (**25**, pp. 898–913).

TABLE 14

ESTIMATED POPULATION IN EACH CONTINENT, 1650–1950

(*Millions*)

Continent	1650	1700	1750	1800	1850	1900	1940	1950, Midyear
World total	545	623	728	906	1,171	1,608	2,170	2,400
North America	1	1	1	6	26	81	143	166
Middle America	6	6	5	10	13	25	42	51
South America	6	6	6	9	20	38	89	111
Europe	100	110	140	187	266	401	543	559
Asia	330	400	479	602	749	937	1,186	1,302
Africa	100	98	95	90	95	120	157	198
Oceania	2	2	2	2	2	6	11	13

Sources: For 1650 and 1750–1900, estimates of Carr-Saunders (**18**), with segregation of the data for Mexico and the Caribbean, according to the original estimate of Wilcox; for 1700, figures interpolated on basis of data for 1650 and 1750; for 1940, **1**, pp. 12–23; for 1950, **5**, July 1951, p. 1. The population of the USSR in 1940 and 1950 has been distributed between Europe and Asia, counting 30 million for the Asiatic part of the USSR and the rest for the European part.

and lakes. If we assume that the population in those regions was not much larger than that of Italy and Gaul combined, Europe may have had 11 million inhabitants outside the Roman Empire and 34 million in all.

To the south, Roman civilization had penetrated to only the northeastern fringe of Africa, but this was the most fertile part of the Dark Continent, and it probably had at least as many people as the rest of Africa. It therefore seems reasonable to assume that Africa's total population did not exceed 30 million.

In Asia, the great centers of the old and highly developed civilizations remained out of reach of Rome. A census taken in China in the second year of the Christian era showed a population of 59.5 million.[9] It is not known how many people lived at that time in India and other parts of Asia, but the aggregate population of the continent, beyond the border of the Roman Empire, was hardly less than 120 million.

Oceania and America were thinly peopled in A. D. 30, although some communities in South and Middle America may have reached a high level of civilization. All in all, the population of the earth at the beginning of the Christian era may have been between 210 and 250 million, with the most populous areas in the Far East.

Increase from A. D. 30 to 1600

Little is known about the growth of world

population from A. D. 30 to the beginning of modern times.

In Europe the early Christian era was a time of relative security. The population of the Roman Empire grew as the new order developed and began to decline when the Empire disintegrated. Depopulation of formerly prosperous cities then became a serious problem, according to the testimony of contemporary writers. By A. D. 500–600, Europe's population had dropped to a low point — perhaps close to 20 million. Time and again in the next thousand years, wars and epidemics slowed down or stopped the growth of population. By 1600 Europe had about 100 million inhabitants.[10] Thus the gain had been very slow, at an average rate of perhaps one per cent a decade or 0.1 per cent a year.

Growth of population was equally slow in America before the white man came. Probably there were never more than a million Indians in all America north of Mexico; in Mexico and Central America, where agriculture was highly developed, there may have been 3 million; in South America, with intensive farming and a carefully planned economy, possibly 4 or 5 million, concentrated chiefly about the fertile plateau of Peru and Ecuador. Thus before Columbus' voyage, the Western Hemisphere probably never held more than 10 million inhabitants.[11]

9. **32**, p. 5.

10. Estimate of Julius Beloch (**17**), confirmed by the more recent research of Walter F. Wilcox and A. M. Carr-Saunders (**18**).

11. **20**, p. 18.

Increase since the Seventeenth Century

In the past three hundred years, many attempts have been made to estimate the number of people on each continent.[12] Rough though the early estimates are, it is generally accepted that world population has been growing since the middle of the seventeenth century at a gradually increasing rate. Most spectacular has been the increase of European stock, not only in Europe itself but also in North America and Oceania. (See Table 14; cf. Figure 13, A.)

Over the three centuries 1650-1950, world population appears to have more than quadrupled. In the past century alone, from 1850 to 1950, it has more than doubled. The average decennial increase appears to have been 2.7 per cent from 1650 to 1700; 3.2 per cent in the first half and 4.5 per cent in the second half of the eighteenth century; 5.3 per cent from 1800 to 1850, 6.5 per cent from 1850 to 1900 and 8.3 per cent from 1900 to 1950.

Although these averages should not be taken too seriously, the acceleration in the growth of the world population in the last three centuries, and especially since the middle of the nineteenth century, is undeniable. This development has been due to three factors: (1) improvements in health and wealth have lowered mortality rates; (2) new means of transportation have facilitated a wider distribution of population; (3) technological progress has ensured the means of living for greater numbers of people.

"In terms of production," writes Carl O. Sauer, "what has happened is that all the major physical resources of the world have been brought into use, resource by resource and area by area, at first slowly, then with a rush. . . . The blocking out of the world as to productive capacity, and hence as to population, has been realized as never before in history." [13]

Expansion of European Stock

At least since the beginning of the seventeenth century — and possibly since ancient times — Asia has had a larger population than all other continents put together. (See Figure 13, B.) Yet that continent's relative share of the world's population has been declining steadily for the last 150 years, while the proportion in Europe and in America has been growing. (See Table 15.) Moreover, population figures for the continents fail to show all the increase in European stock in the nineteenth and twentieth centuries, since

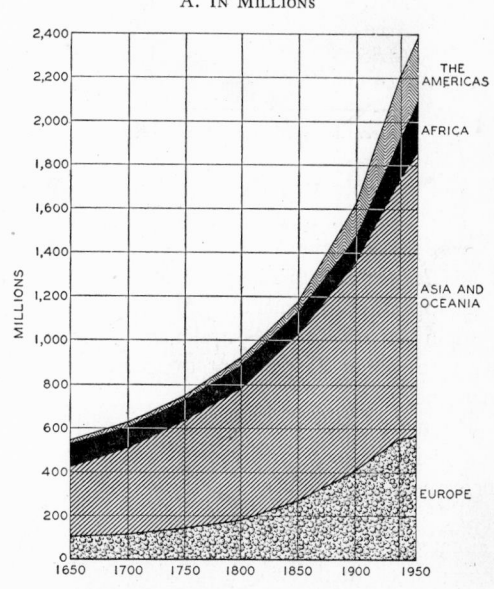

A. In Millions

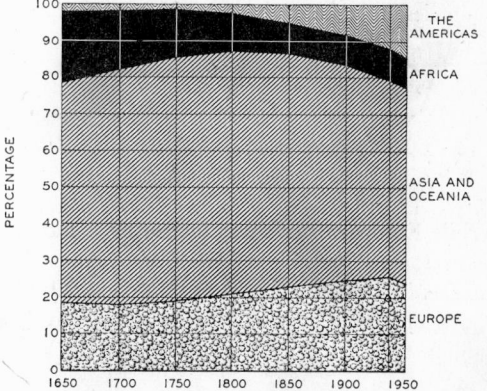

B. Percentage of Total World Population

FIGURE 13. World Population: Distribution by Continent, 1650–1950

World population has more than doubled since the beginning of the nineteenth century and has grown spectacularly since 1900. Asia and Africa accounted for 76.3 per cent of the total in 1800, but only 62.6 per cent in 1950. The proportion in Europe and other continents populated predominantly by European stock increased steadily from 1700 to 1940 but declined slightly in the last decade.

---

12. Wilcox, recording sixty-six such attempts between 1650 and 1850, has used these earlier analyses in estimating the population of the earth and of the continents from 1650 to 1929. (**36**, pp. 78 and 640.) Carr-Saunders has revised some of Wilcox's figures and has extended estimates to 1933. (**18**, p. 42.)

13. **30**, p. 9.

TABLE 15

PERCENTAGE DISTRIBUTION OF WORLD POPULATION BY CONTINENT, 1650–1950

Continent	1650	1700	1750	1800	1850	1900	1940	1950
World total	100.0	100.0	100.0	100.0	100.0	100.0	100.0	100.0
North America	0.2	0.2	0.1	0.7	2.3	5.1	6.6	6.9
Middle America	1.1	1.0	0.7	1.1	1.1	1.6	1.9	2.1
South America	1.1	1.0	0.8	1.0	1.7	2.3	4.1	4.6
Europe	18.3	17.7	19.2	20.7	22.7	24.9	25.0	23.3
Asia	60.6	64.2	65.8	66.4	63.9	58.3	54.7	54.3
Africa	18.3	15.7	13.1	9.9	8.1	7.4	7.2	8.3
Oceania	0.4	0.3	0.3	0.2	0.2	0.4	0.5	0.5

Source: Derived from Table 14.

part of it appears as the growth of the New World. Between 1850 and 1950, Europe's share of world population increased only slightly — from 22.7 per cent to 23.3 per cent — but people of European origin, including the white populations in America and Australia, grew in number from about 25 per cent to 35 per cent of mankind.

The most striking development in world population in the past three centuries has been the increase in the number of persons of European stock [14] in all parts of the world. In 1950, it is estimated, there were 800 million persons of European stock in the world, of whom some 550 million were in Europe (including the European part of the USSR) and the remainder in other countries and continents as follows (in millions):

United States and Canada	145
Latin America	48
Asia (including the Asiatic part of the USSR)	40
Africa	7
Oceania	10

While European stock was increasing eightfold, from some 100 million in 1650 to about 800 million in 1950, the non-European population in the world grew only half as rapidly, from 445 million to 1,600 million.[15] (See Figure 14.)

CONCENTRATION OF PEOPLE

Most of the earth's surface is unsuitable for dense settlement because of excessive heat or

frost, excessive or insufficient rainfall, poor soil or unfavorable topography.[16]

Regions with too cold a climate to support dense settlement comprise a large part of Canada, all Greenland, a large part of Scandinavia, the northern part of the USSR in Europe, and much of Siberia. Areas with excessive heat and rainfall stretch from the Tropic of Cancer to the Tropic of Capricorn in the Western Hemisphere — with

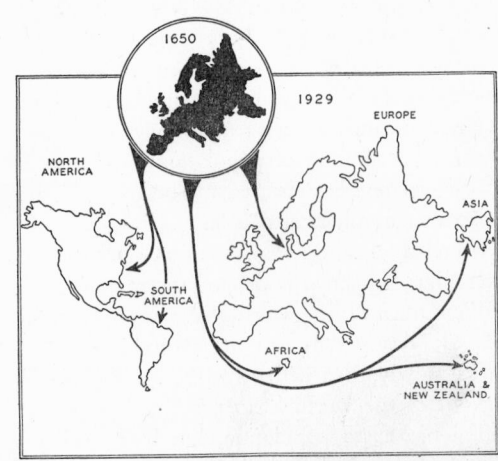

Adapted from a map in *The Problems of a Changing Population,* by the National Resources Committee

FIGURE 14. WORLD EXPANSION OF EUROPEAN STOCK, 1650–1929

The black silhouette of Europe at the top of the figure represents the population of that continent (to the Urals and the Caspian Sea) in 1650: about 100 million. The white contour map below represents, on the same scale, the population of European stock in each continent about 1929: some 500 million persons in Europe, more than 100 million in the United States and Canada, about 40 million in Latin America, and comparatively small European settlements in Asia, Africa and Oceania. (Cf. **12**, p. 19.)

---

14. The term "European stock" is somewhat vague. There is no way to count "unmixed" European population exactly in even the old European countries, and such a count is particularly difficult in Asia and South America.

15. **12**, p. 19.

16. **9**, p. 230.

interruptions in the highlands of Mexico, Central America, Colombia, Ecuador and Peru — and also include part of Brazil. In the Eastern Hemisphere such climate prevails in equatorial Africa and a large part of India, Burma, Thailand, Indochina and Indonesia. Vast arid and semiarid areas lie on both sides of the tropical wet zone, in the western part of the Americas, northern and southwestern Africa, the Middle East and Australia. (See Figure 15; see also Figure 11.)

The regions with favorable climatic conditions appear on the world map like large dots dispersed over the globe, far apart. Five are particularly important: (1) most of Europe, from the Mediterranean to 60° N, including part of the USSR and a salient eastward into southern Siberia; (2) part of North America from the Atlantic coast to the Great Plains, with a strip along the Pacific coast; (3) eastern Asia, including Japan, Korea, eastern China and the northern parts of Indochina and India; (4) the great mountainous regions of South Africa; (5) a vast region on the Atlantic coast in South America. Other areas with a climate completely suitable for dense population are located in the highlands of Mexico, Colombia and Ecuador; in southeastern Australia and on some islands, among them Madagascar, New Zealand, Tasmania, New Guinea, Borneo.[17]

Measuring Population Density

Density of population is usually measured by the average number of inhabitants per unit of area. Such an average for a large country or a whole continent is misleading, however, since part of the area may be uninhabitable and much of the population crowded into the remainder.

Comparison of population with the acreage of arable or actually cultivated soil may therefore seem preferable,[18] but this measure has other shortcomings. An area unfit for agriculture may be rich in other natural resources and thus able to support many people. Moreover, if the amount of arable land is used to measure the agricultural resources of an area, a distinction should be made between rich and poor land. Ultimately, this method leads to a comparison of population in an area with its capacity to supply food, i.e., its carrying capacity.[19]

The best way to visualize the density of population is to map the actual location of population, indicating the number of people in an area by dots, each one representing a given number of inhabitants, say 100,000 or even 1,000,000.[20] (See Figures 16 and 17.)

Populous Regions of the World

In general, settlements have grown up in easily accessible and fertile regions. Under similar climatic conditions, they seem to have been attached to seacoasts — along the North Sea in Europe, the Pacific Ocean in Asia and the United States, the Mediterranean and Indian Ocean in Africa, the Atlantic Ocean in the Americas, the southeastern coast of Australia.

In the Temperate Zone, density of population declines with increase in elevation, while in the tropics high plateaus are sometimes more densely populated than the plains. The limit of human settlements is some 7,500 feet in Europe; 8,000 feet in the United States; 12,000 in the tropical zone of Middle and South America; and 15,000 feet in Asia (Tibet).

The world has four great aggregations of population, two on the shores of the Pacific, two facing each other over the North Atlantic Ocean. The largest concentration is in eastern China, where about 400 million people are crowded into not more than a million square miles. This densely populated region extends north to Korea and Japan and reaches south to Indochina, the Philippines and Indonesia. In all, about 620 million people live in this part of the Far East on less than 1.5 million square miles — on the average, 430 persons to the square mile. The second region, including the valley of the Ganges, southern India and Ceylon, has some 410 million inhabitants in an area of approximately a million square miles — on the average, 410 persons to the square mile. The largest of the two North Atlantic agglomerations is that in Europe (including the densely populated part of the USSR). It has an aggregate population of approximately 370 million in an area of 1.2 million square miles. The fourth and smallest of the great concentrations of people is in the northeastern part of the United States, an area of

---

17. **9**, p. 230.
18. **19**, p. 4.
19. Cf. **27**.

20. In mapping populations of small and sparsely populated areas a dot may be used for each 10,000 or 1,000 inhabitants or even fewer. (Cf. population maps, **21**.)

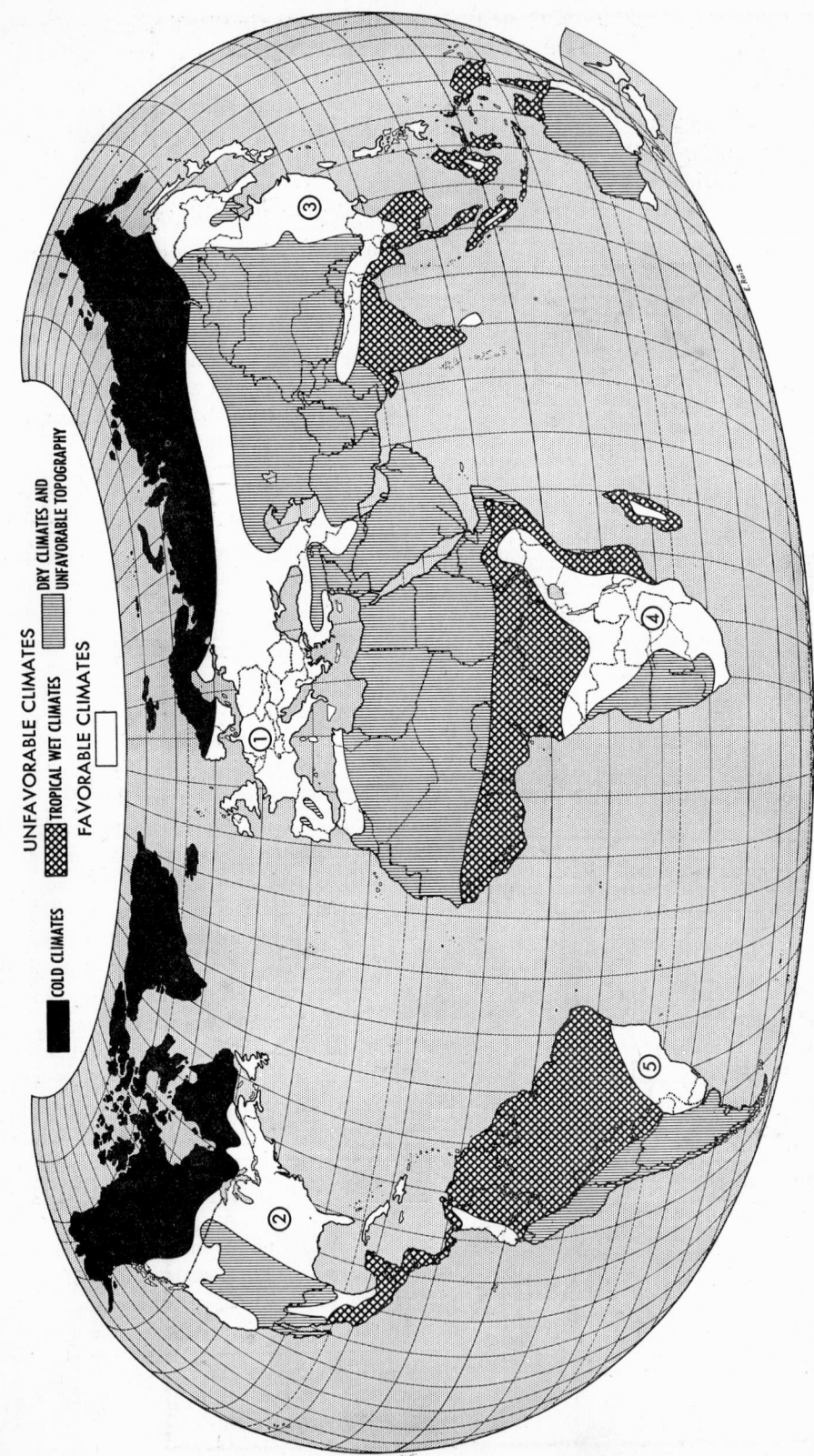

FIGURE 15. REGIONS OF THE WORLD WITH CLIMATE UNFAVORABLE OR FAVORABLE FOR DENSE SETTLEMENT

Areas of the world with climate unfavorable for dense settlement include the regions of perpetual frost and subpolar forest zone in the north, the broad belt of arid and semiarid regions in Africa and Asia and areas with similar climates in North and South America and Australia, and wet regions in tropical zones. Most of the land favorable for settlement (white on the map) is concentrated in five vast regions: 1 and 2, confronting each other across the North Atlantic Ocean; 3, in the Far East; 4, in South Africa; 5, in South America.

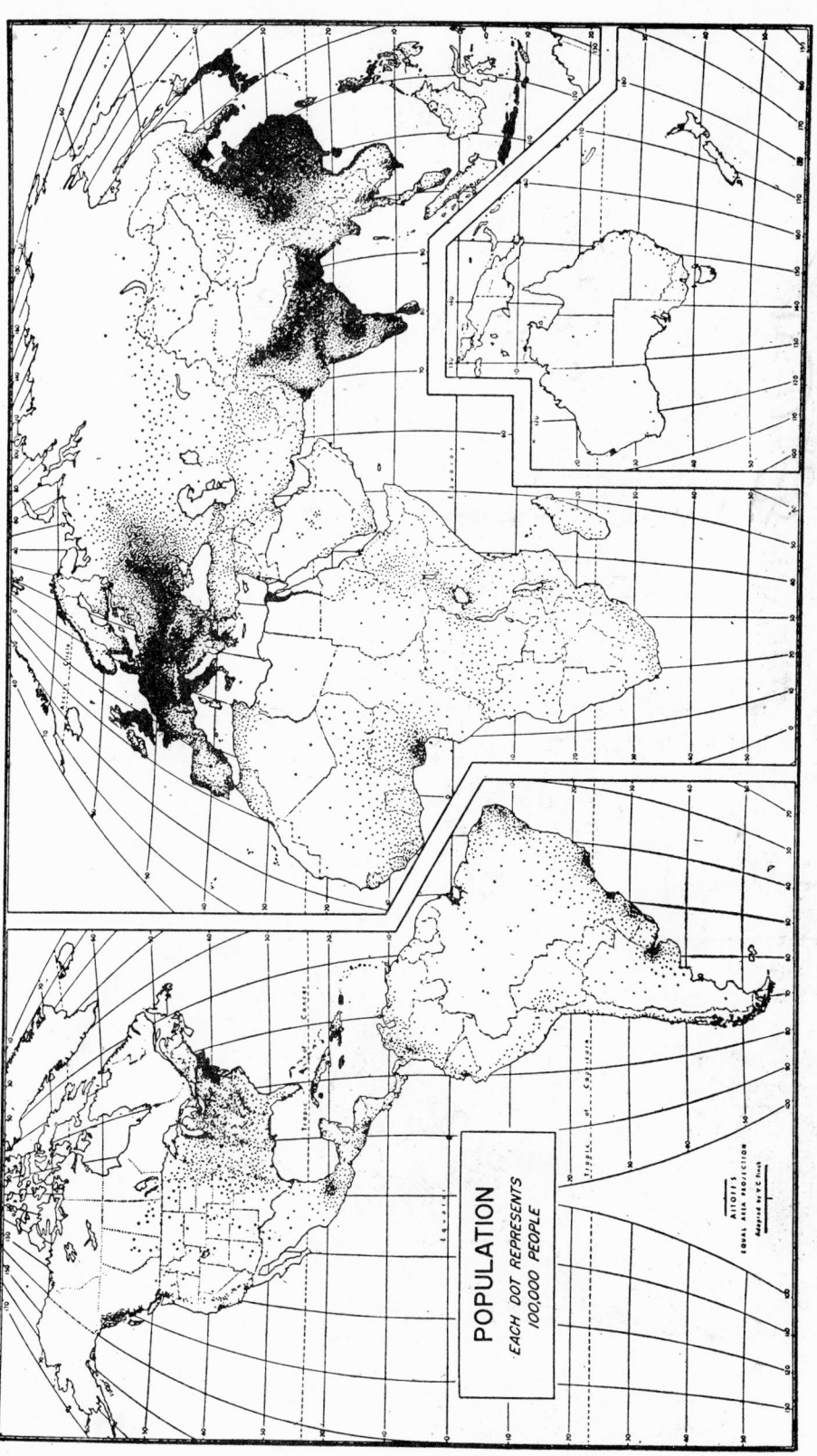

U. S. Department of Agriculture

Figure 16. Population: Geographic Distribution in the World, Around 1940. Large cities and metropolitan areas are marked by scores of dots, according to the size of their population. The dots merge into solid black in densely populated areas.

In most cases population is concentrated in the regions that appear in Figure 15 as areas with favorable climate. Striking exceptions occur in the Indian subcontinent, where population is dense in areas with unfavorable climate, and in some parts of South America and South Africa, where population is sparse despite favorable climatic conditions. (Cf. **9**, p. 229.)

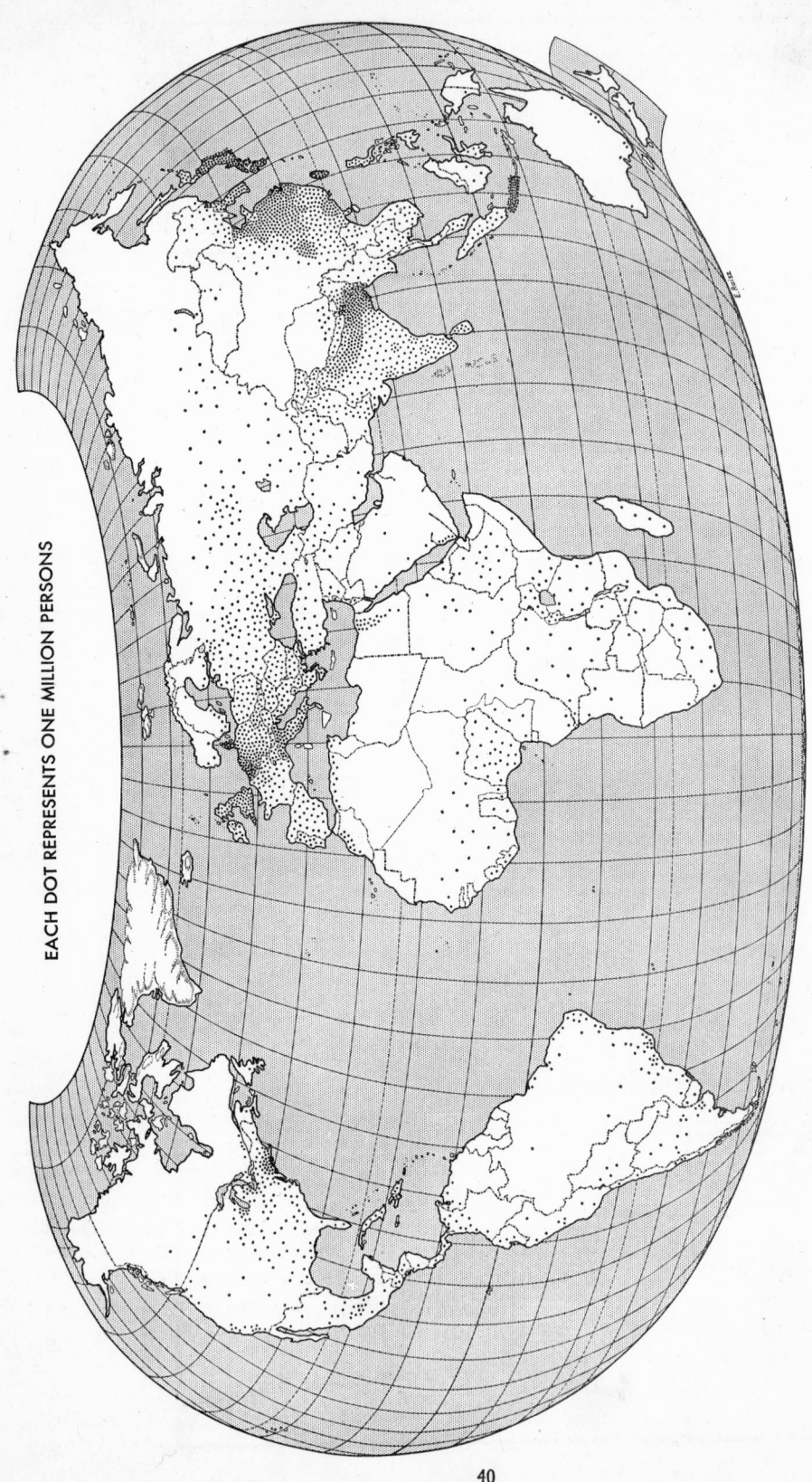

EACH DOT REPRESENTS ONE MILLION PERSONS

FIGURE 17. POPULATION: GEOGRAPHIC DISTRIBUTION IN THE WORLD, 1950

This map shows the geographic distribution of world population in 1950, based in part on estimates compiled by the United Nations. It differs from the map of continents in Figure 16 by showing the position of the continents in relation to one another and to the oceans. Using each dot to represent 1,000,000 inhabitants rather than 100,000, this map gives a clearer picture of the general pattern of distribution of people on the earth but lacks the precision of Figure 16.

TABLE 16

AREAS OF CONCENTRATION OF WORLD POPULATION, 1950

Area	Area, in Thousands of Square Miles	Population 1950, in Millions	Population Per Square Mile
World total	57,400	2,400	42
Densely populated areas	4,250	1,650	388
Far East:			
Eastern China	1,000	400	400
Korea and Japan	200	100	500
Indochina, Philippines, Indonesia	250	120	480
India and Ceylon:			
Valley of the Ganges, southern India, Ceylon	1,000	410	410
Western and central Europe:			
United Kingdom, France, Belgium, Netherlands, Denmark, Germany, Poland, Czechoslovakia, Switzerland, Austria, Spain, Portugal, Italy, Hungary, Romania, part of the USSR	1,200	370	310
America:			
Northeastern United States	500	90	180
Coastal region of North and South America, Nigeria, Egypt	100	160	160
Moderately populated areas			
Central part of the United States; South America (excluding densely populated coastal regions and tropical forests); USSR (excluding densely populated area in the west and sparsely populated tundra, taiga and arctic regions), central China, northern India, and other	17,500	710	41
Sparsely populated areas			
Semiarid, taiga, tropical forests	15,650	40	3
Uninhabitable areas			
Arctic and antarctic regions, tundra, deserts	20,000	—	—

Source: Estimated by the authors.

about 500,000 square miles with a population of 90 million.

Other densely populated areas are along the Pacific coast of North America, the Atlantic coast of South America, in the Caribbean, at the mouth of the Niger and in the Nile Valley in Africa.

In all the densely peopled regions about 1,650 million persons, more than two thirds of the world's population, are crowded into 4.25 million square miles — less than 8 per cent of the total land surface — where they average 388 persons per square mile.

Of the other 53.1 million square miles of land,

one third (17.5 million) is moderately populated, with an average of 41 inhabitants per square mile, often in concentrations scattered here and there in thinly populated regions. This area includes, among other places, the central part of the United States, a large part of South America, most of the USSR, and central China.

The remainder of the land in the world — more than 35.6 million square miles — is either uninhabitable or sparsely populated. The "uninhabitable" areas are the arctic and antarctic regions and tundra and desert regions. The sparsely populated areas include semiarid plains and subpolar forests (taiga), in all about 15.6 million

A. DISTRIBUTION OF LAND

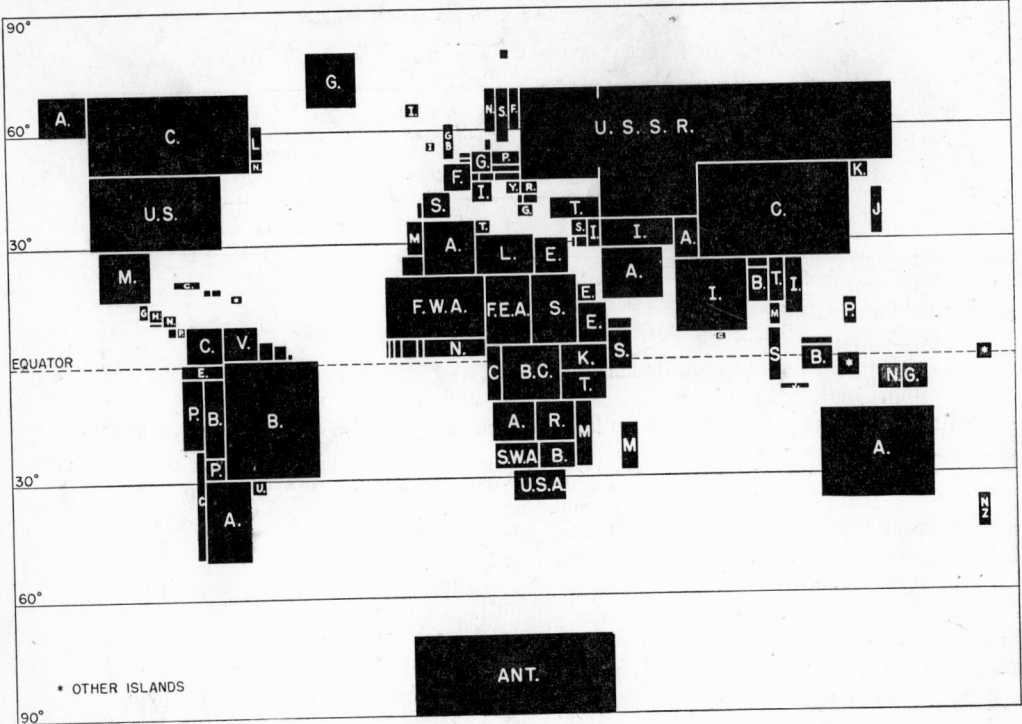

B. DISTRIBUTION OF POPULATION

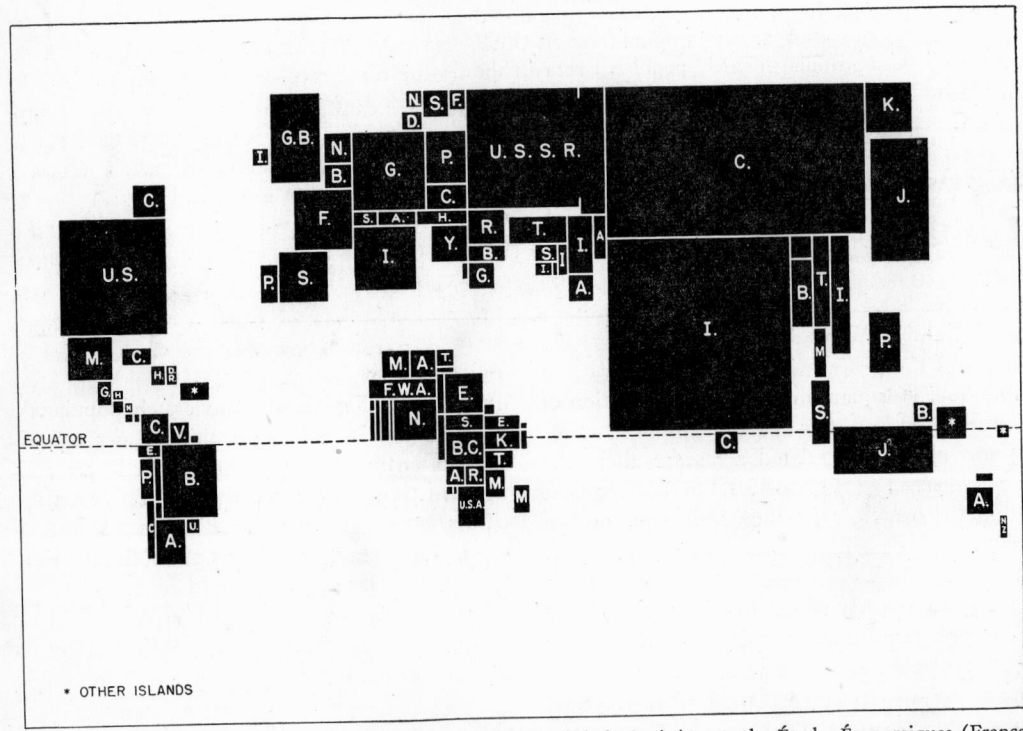

Institut National de la Statistique et des Études Économiques (France)

FIGURE 18. DISTORTED MAPS OF THE WORLD: DISTRIBUTION OF LAND AND POPULATION
BY CONTINENT AND COUNTRY

Cut prior to 9/25/68 mg7

moving to the fringes of the Empire, Africa, Asia Minor, Syria and Mesopotamia, as military potentates, administrators and officials.

The Age of Great Migrations

The first millennium of the Christian era is often called the age of great migrations. That is how the period appeared to observers within the Roman Empire, exposed to successive waves of barbaric hordes and ready to collapse under their blows. There is no evidence, however, that shifts of population in that thousand years were greater, century by century and decade by decade, than in the following millennium. They were relatively smaller than the migrations and displacements in modern times.

As Eugene M. Kulischer has pointed out, when the era of great migrations ended and Europe was entering the so-called "sedentary" era, there was not a single German at the site of Berlin, not one Russian on the shores of the Moskva River, not one Hungarian in the locality of Budapest, and only a few Turkish slaves and mercenaries lived in what was to become Istanbul.[5] The white man had not yet set foot on the soil of the New World. When the "great migrations" seemed to be at an end, the shaping of the map of the world by migration was just beginning.

The best-known migrations in the Middle Ages — the invasion of Europe by the Mongols and the drives of the European Crusaders to the Near East — were predominantly military. A process more like the colonization in the ancient world was developing at that time on the eastern European plains, where the Slavs were moving slowly but steadily eastward and northward from their original settlements on the Dnieper.

Changing Character of Migration

In the march of time, the character of migration has changed. Before men invented wheel and raft, shifts were slow and usually restricted to small groups of people who moved short distances on foot or on the backs of animals. Later, in ancient Hellas and under the Roman Empire, migrants were carried farther by sailing ships and galleys or were drawn by horses.

Many centuries later, the compass opened the oceans to migrants from Europe. By the middle of the nineteenth century, steamships made the ocean the cheapest thoroughfare for passengers and goods, and a new era in the history of migration began. Population shifts in antiquity and the Middle Ages left a deep imprint on the composition of races, languages, religions and mores of the world, but settlement of vast areas of our planet did not begin until the newer means of transportation made possible mass migrations over long distances.

MAJOR CURRENTS OF MIGRATION IN MODERN TIMES

Seven major currents are evident in migrations since the beginning of the sixteenth century, five between, and two within, nations. They are: (1) emigration from Europe to North America; (2) emigration to South America and the Caribbean; (3) emigration to South Africa, Australia and Australasia; (4) importation of slaves from Africa to the New World; (5) population shifts in the Far East, mainly from China and India to neighboring countries, such as Africa and Australasia; (6) intracontinental migration in North America, from the Atlantic coast westward; and (7) internal migration in Russia eastward. (See Figure 27.)

INTERNATIONAL SHIFTS OF POPULATION

Among the five great currents of international migration in modern times the most important have been those from Europe to the New World, beginning soon after its discovery, in the sixteenth century.

At first only fringes of the Americas were known and accessible to Europe. White men first learned to know the Caribbean — the islands of Hispaniola, Cuba and Jamaica, the peninsula of Florida, the eastern coast of South America. They had only vague ideas of what lay northward and westward and until the end of the sixteenth century, men on the other side of the Atlantic continued to regard the Americas merely as new islands located somewhere between Hispaniola and India. (See Figure 3, p. 8.)

European migration, directed first to the Caribbean and South America, gradually fanned northward. As time went on, the flow toward North America became increasingly important, but the importance of South America as a goal of European migration increased after World War I.

---

5. **33**, p. 8.

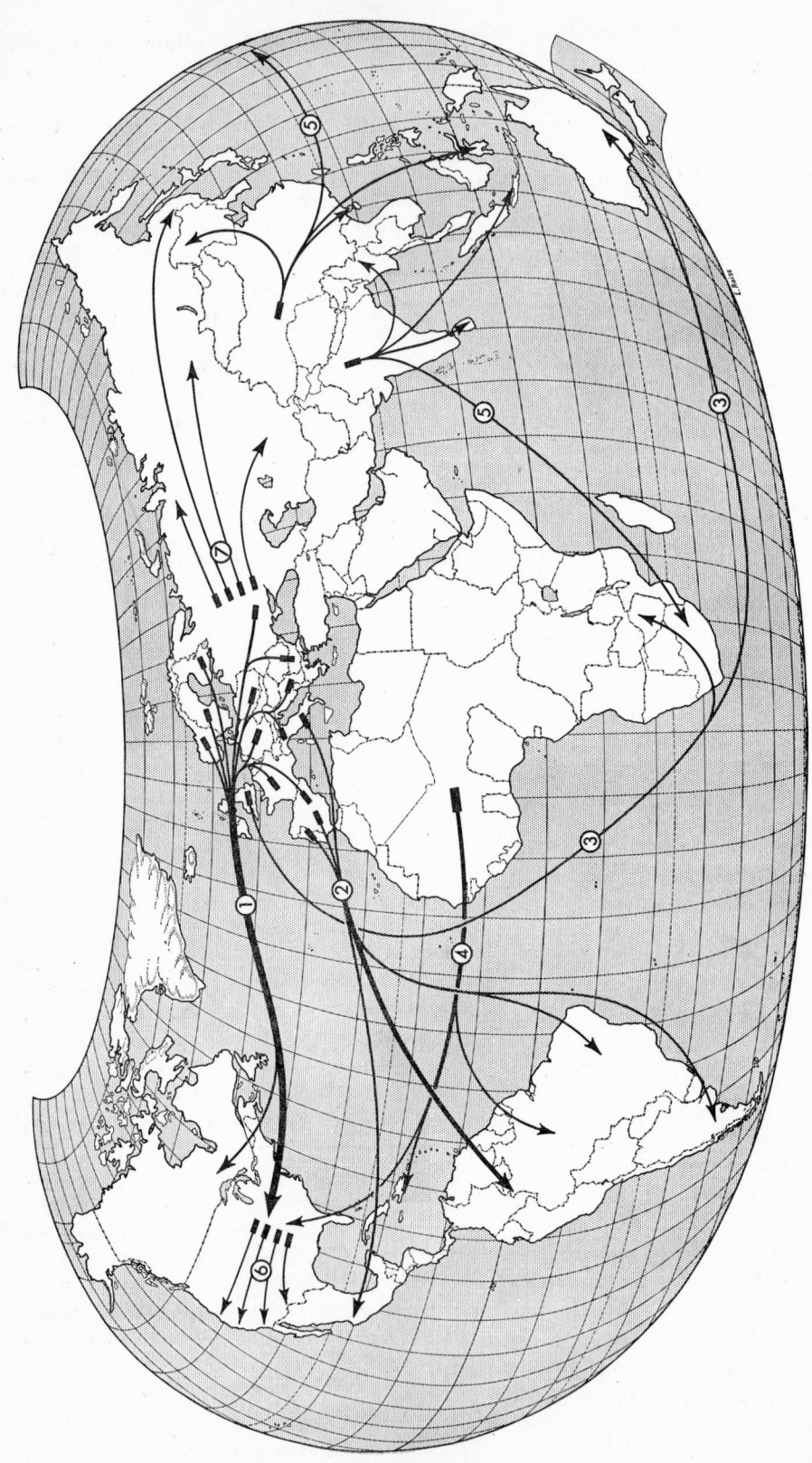

FIGURE 27. INTERCONTINENTAL MIGRATION: PRINCIPAL CURRENTS IN MODERN TIMES

The main currents of intercontinental migration since the beginning of the sixteenth century have been: (1) from all parts of Europe to North America; (2) from Latin countries of Europe to Middle and South America; (3) from Great Britain to Africa and Australia; (4) import of slaves from Africa to America. Another current (5), partly intercontinental, partly intracontinental, has flowed from China and India. The most important internal migration has been (6) westward in the United States and (7) eastward in Russia.

From Europe to North America

Nearly 45 million persons emigrated from various parts of Europe to North America between the beginning of the seventeenth century and the outbreak of World War II. Some of them returned to their old homes, but more than 25 million settled permanently in the areas now occupied by the United States and Canada. Today they account for nearly 150 million persons of European stock in these countries.

From Europe to Central and South America

Approximately 20 million Europeans, predominantly Spaniards, Portuguese and Italians, have emigrated to Middle and South America since the beginning of the sixteenth century. Some 2 million of them returned to Europe. Of those who remained, some intermingled with native Indians and imported Negroes, so that there are now close to 50 million persons in Latin America of European or partly European origin.

From Europe to Africa and Oceania

Colonization of Africa and Oceania, primarily by the British and the Dutch, has given origin to approximately 17 million persons of European stock among the 210 million who now people those continents and their islands. Together these three streams of intercontinental migration propagated European stock and European civilization over the world.

Decimation of the aboriginal population often accompanied settlement of the New World. Apart from massacres during the conquest, native populations dwindled in America, Australia and Australasia, not primarily because of oppression by the invaders, but, rather, as a result of epidemic diseases they brought with them. Ailments endemic and relatively benign in Europe became scourges among the previously unexposed natives. Death outran the white man and emptied the land for him.[6] In good measure, occupation of the New World has been replacement of its relatively sparse native population by people of European and mixed stock.

From Africa to the Americas

This flow of intercontinental migration brought persons of African stock into regions of America settled and dominated by immigrants from Europe.

The slave trade began in the sixteenth century, reached its peak at the end of the eighteenth, and continued illegally until the middle of the nineteenth. We do not know exactly how many slaves were imported into the Americas. Carr-Saunders believes that approximately 20 million Africans were taken from their homes to be sold as slaves.[7] Some died before they reached the market, and some were shipped to Asia and Europe.

The number of Negro slaves imported into the Americas is estimated at nearly 15 million: less than a million in the sixteenth century, almost 3 million in the seventeenth, 7 million in the eighteenth, and 4 million in the nineteenth.[8] The main slave markets in the Western Hemisphere were in South America and the Caribbean. Gunnar Myrdal has estimated that less than a million Negro slaves were ever imported — directly from Africa or from the West Indies — into the United States and areas that later became part of the United States.[9]

Importation of slaves had a deep impact on the early colonial economy, played a tragic role in the split between South and North in the United States, and left the country with the Negro problem of today. It has also had a deep influence on the racial composition of the population of the Western Hemisphere. (See Table 22, p. 52.)

From China and India

Migration from China had become noticeable by the beginning of the seventeenth century. In 1718, China passed a law prohibiting emigration and ordering all Chinese residing abroad to return. After 1840, emigration from China was resumed, mainly to other Asiatic countries. In 1922 the number of Chinese residing abroad was estimated at 8.2 million — 2.3 million in Formosa, 1.8 million in Java, 1.5 million in Siam, 1.1 million in the Straits Settlements, Hong Kong, Annam and Burma, 1.0 million in the East Indies, half a million in other countries.[10] In 1948 the Chinese government issued a new estimate giving the total number of Chinese abroad as 9.5 million: 9.1 million in Asia, more

---

6. **37**, p. 19.

7. **21**, p. 48.
8. **34**, p. 12.
9. **34**, p. 119.
10. **23**, p. 149; **21**, p. 57.

than 200,000 in America, 54,000 in Europe, 64,-000 in Oceania, 15,000 in Africa.[11]

Like the Chinese, most emigrants from India have settled within the confines of Asia. In 1944–45 the number of Indians abroad was estimated at more than 3.7 million: more than a million in Burma, about 750,000 in Ceylon, as many in British Malaya, some 300,000 on the island of Mauritius, 100,000 in Fiji.[12] The largest settlements of Indians outside Asia are in Trinidad and British Guiana (300,000) and in British colonies in Africa — Kenya, Tanganyika, Uganda and Zanzibar (about 100,000).

INTERNAL SHIFTS OF POPULATION

The population shifts continually within many countries, from primarily agricultural areas toward industrial centers, for example, or from densely settled to sparsely populated areas. Often these shifts have a clear geographical pattern, like the westward migration in Germany or the northward migration in Italy. Such movements are usually of only local significance, but two currents of intranational migration have played an important role in the history of mankind.

Internal Migration in the United States

In North America, migration was directed inland from the ports along the Atlantic coast. Step by step, it carried the early settlers beyond the Appalachian ridge to the Mississippi valley and beyond it, until the whole expanse between the Atlantic and Pacific was settled. Thus the colonies clustered along the seashore were transformed into a nation spanning a continent. Without intracontinental migration, the capacity of the New World to absorb immigrants would have been exhausted long ago.

Internal Migration in Russia

Internal migration in Russia, combined with the rapid growth of population and the open spaces around the original settlements, has been instrumental in developing the country from a handful of petty princedoms on the western fringe of the east European plain into one of the greatest powers in the world.

11. **4,** September 1949, p. 321.
12. **19,** pp. 921–22.

INTERCONTINENTAL MIGRATION

The composition of the successive waves of newcomers who carried European stock and ways of life to the Western Hemisphere changed as time went on. Emigration from Europe to Middle and South America was distinctly different from that to North America, and immigration to North America after the revolutionary wars was different from that in the preceding period.

IMMIGRATION INTO THE AMERICAS BEFORE 1800

The first white men who found their way to the Western Hemisphere across the Atlantic were probably fishermen and hunters from the Scandinavian countries who stayed temporarily on Newfoundland and briefly ventured onto the mainland. They had no desire to settle and left few traces of their stay in America. A wholly different situation arose when, after Columbus' discovery of the Caribbean in 1492 and especially after Cortez' conquest of Mexico in 1521 and Pizarro's seizure of Peru in 1533, swarms of adventurers and missionaries descended on the New World and took possession of it.

Adventurers and Spoilsmen: Latin America

All the unexplored regions of South America, as well as the Caribbean, Mexico and Peru, became spoils of the Spanish crown early in the sixteenth century, and the population was added to the flocks of the Catholic Church. At that time neither Spain nor Portugal was looking for new land to colonize, for they could not spare enough men to settle it. Their aim was to get gold, rare spices and other valuable products from these lands, using as few men as possible. The conquered territory was, therefore, closed to settlers. King's subjects were admitted into crown possessions, individually or in groups, only by special permission or special order. Early Spanish-Portuguese settlers in this region represented either the king's armed forces or the Catholic Church. Civil administration was divided between the two. In addition, a few craftsmen were sent overseas to make the life of the occupation forces more comfortable.

Later, Spain and Portugal adopted the custom of rewarding noblemen for services to the crown by title to land in America. This practice was in line with customs in feudal Europe, and it is natural that the tracts of land carved out in the wilderness had to be large enough to warrant the venture of sailing over the ocean to take possession of them. The new landowners came with their families and servants, often accompanied by armed guards, carpenters, bricklayers and other craftsmen. As time went on, cathedrals and cloisters were erected, old native cities were reshaped in a mixture of Indian and Spanish patterns, and in three centuries, a huge overseas empire had been built.

The number of persons who moved from Europe to the Caribbean and South America in the early colonization period is not known. It has been estimated that by 1570, when Spain's colonial administration was fairly well established, about 100,000 Spaniards and Portuguese were ruling over an Indian population of about 10 million.

Since most of the European settlers in South and Central America were adventurer-soldiers without families, marriage with native women became usual. Thus the foundation was laid for the present national and racial composition of the local population. At the beginning of the nineteenth century, the number of persons of unmixed European blood (mainly Spanish or Portuguese) was insignificant; a considerable part of the population was mixed — predominantly Indian in blood, Spanish or Portuguese in language, and Roman Catholic in religion.

Colonists and Settlers: North America

Early immigration into North America was very different. Colonization prevailed, if not from the day when the first French, British and Dutch settlers landed, then at least from the beginning of the eighteenth century.

New England was not settled originally because of agricultural attractions, nor did agriculture become the chief interest of the colonists. . . . Lack of sufficient areas of good soil and a climate marked by a brief growing season and little summer heat placed [New England] at a disadvantage with the colonies farther south. . . . It was to the middle colonies that the greatest number of people came who were by birth and training tillers of the soil. . . . From all Northwestern Europe, farmers poured into the [middle] colonies during the eighteenth century, settling from the Mohawk Valley to Pennsylvania and in the back country of Maryland.[13]

European settlements in North America were somewhat like the colonies in the ancient world. Apart from their search for religious and political freedom, colonists were lured by the vision of free land. Their goal was to develop self-supporting communities on virgin soil. This objective eventually brought them into conflict with the Indians after both groups had discovered that there was not enough land for all and that farming in the European style was incompatible with the way of life of tribes of hunters.

When each community had to rely on itself for survival, each newcomer was an asset as an additional worker and also as an additional fighter. Unlike the exploitation colonies in South America, the North American settlements needed more and still more men. Hence their policy of open gates for immigrants of all races, languages and faiths.

Benjamin Franklin estimated that North America held a million persons of British origin in 1751. Carr-Saunders believed that perhaps 250,000 persons left the British Isles for the New World in the seventeenth century and 1.5 million in the eighteenth,[14] figures that agree fairly well with Franklin's for the middle of the eighteenth century. The number of immigrants from Germany before 1800 is estimated at 200,000,[15] and the number from the Netherlands and France combined may have been about the same. Net immigration from Europe into America north of the Rio Grande may have totaled about 2 million by 1800.

INTERCONTINENTAL MIGRATION AFTER 1800

In the second half of the eighteenth century North America became the goal of overseas migration from Europe.[16] Each year from 10,000 to 15,000 colonists crossed the North Atlantic, while only an insignificant number journeyed to South America and the Caribbean. During the clash between the rebellious American colonies and Great Britain, European emigration almost ceased. It was resumed on a small scale at the beginning of the nineteenth century and skyrocketed after the end of the Napoleonic wars. In addition to the main flow toward North America, Europeans then were emigrating to South America, South Africa and Australia.

---

13. **38**, pp. 163–65.

14. **21**, p. 47.
15. **21**, p. 47.
16. Cf. **48**, pp. 113 ff.

TABLE 33

INTERCONTINENTAL MIGRATION BEFORE 1933

(*Thousands*)

Emigration (1846–1932)		Immigration (1821–1932)	
Country of Emigration	Emigrants	Country of Immigration	Immigrants
Total	53,450	Total	59,187
Europe	51,696	The Americas	53,826
British Isles [a]	18,083	United States	34,244
Sweden	1,203	Canada and Newfoundland	5,226
Norway	854	Mexico (1911–36)	226
Finland (1871–1934)	371	Cuba	857
Denmark	387	Brazil	4,431
France	519	Uruguay	713
Belgium	193	Paraguay	26
Netherlands	224	Argentina	6,405
Germany	4,889	British West Indies	1,587
Austria-Hungary [b]	5,196	Guadeloupe	42
Switzerland	332	Dutch Guiana	69
Spain	4,653	Non-American countries	5,361
Portugal	1,805	Philippines	90
Italy	10,092	South Africa	852
Russia (USSR) (1846–1924)	2,253	Mauritius	573
Poland (1920–34)	642	Seychelles	12
Non-European countries	1,756	Australia	2,913
British India	1,194	New Zealand	594
Japan	518	Hawaii	216
Cape Verde	30	Other islands	111
St. Helena	12		

Source: **21**, p. 49.

a. Includes Malta.
b. Since 1919, Austria, Hungary and Czechoslovakia.

The Great Migration from Europe

In all, at least 65 million emigrants left Europe between 1820 and 1930, and 2 million between 1930 and 1950. More specifically, 16 European countries recorded some 51.7 million emigrants from 1846 to 1932. On the receiving side, American countries listed 53.8 million immigrants between 1821 and 1932, and Australia, New Zealand, South Africa and other non-American areas recorded 5.4 million.[17] (See Table 33.) Among

17. The first statistical records on emigration date from 1815 (Great Britain); those on immigration, from 1820 (United States). More or less comprehensive international surveys of immigration begin with 1822; of emigration, with 1846. A detailed analysis of available statistics on international migration, with occasional estimates for missing items, has been prepared by the National Bureau of Economic Research, under the direction of Walter F. Wilcox, in cooperation with the International Labor Office and a score of international experts (**47**). Carr-Saunders has extended this estimate to 1932 (**21**). Cf. **47**, pp. 111 ff.

the 67 million emigrants who crossed the ocean from 1800 to 1950, approximately 60 million were Europeans and, of these, some 40 million came to the United States.[18]

Migration statistics after 1932 are not strictly comparable with those in Table 33, because of changes in classification and in routes of intercontinental migration. Moreover, they would not be very significant for countries that were predominantly emigration countries before 1932 but in recent years have had more immigrants than emigrants, such as the United Kingdom, Germany, Belgium, Italy and Sweden.

European emigration to America declined in the 1930's during the depression in the United

18. The last figure is appreciably higher than that shown in Table 33 (34.2 million, for the period 1821–1932) because, in addition to immigrants arriving directly from Europe, the United States has admitted several million immigrants of European stock from Canada and other American countries.

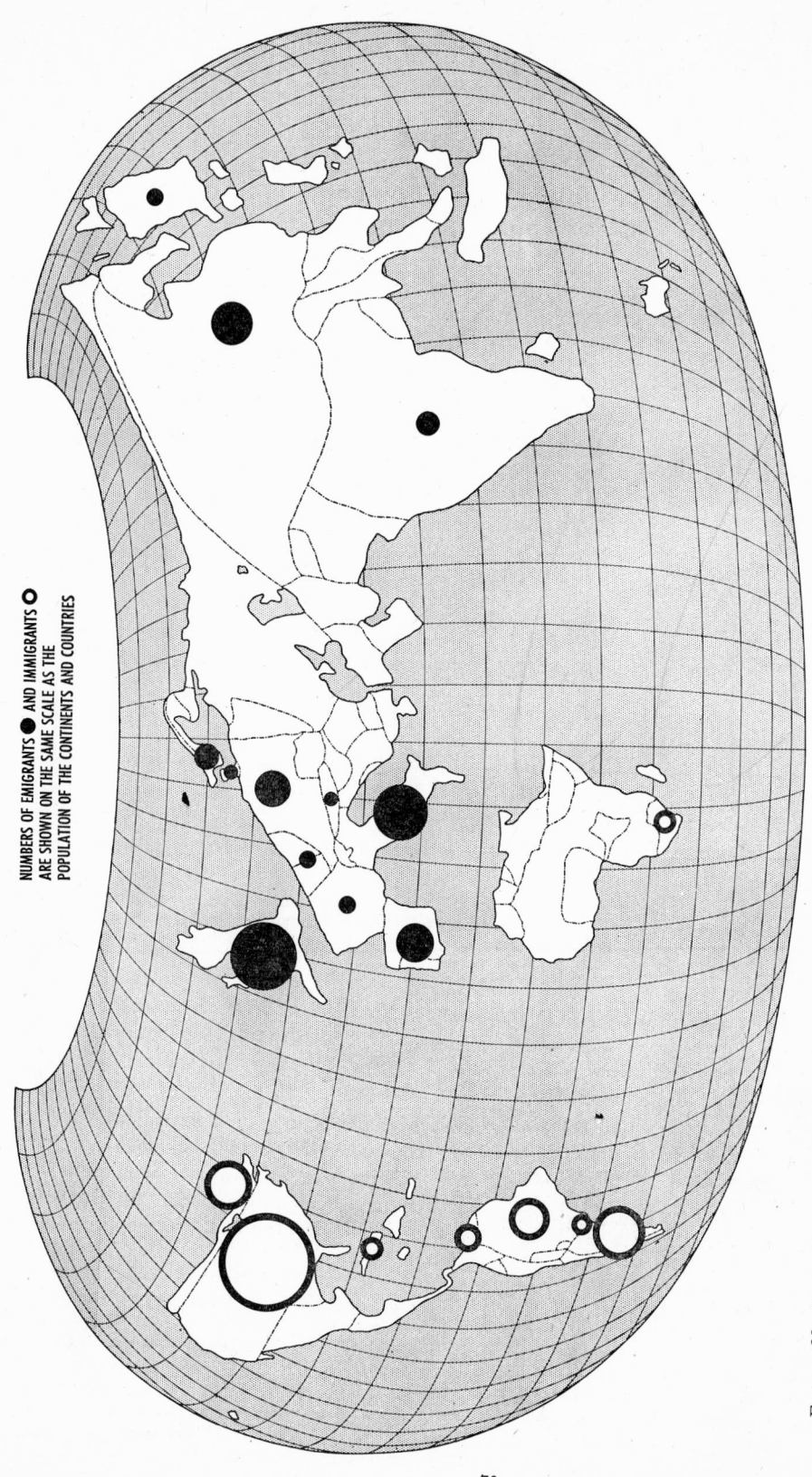

NUMBERS OF EMIGRANTS ● AND IMMIGRANTS ○
ARE SHOWN ON THE SAME SCALE AS THE
POPULATION OF THE CONTINENTS AND COUNTRIES

Figure 28. Intercontinental Migration: Total Number of Emigrants and Immigrants, 1846–1945, as Compared with Present Population of Major Emigration and Immigration Countries

Continents and countries are shown on this map on a scale proportionate to their population about 1950, so that such thinly populated regions as Canada, Siberia, Australia and central Africa appear smaller than on conventional maps, densely populated regions of the Far East and western and central Europe larger. The numbers of emigrants who have left or entered a country since the middle of the nineteenth century are shown on the same scale as the 1940 population. The circle in central Europe refers to Germany, Austria-Hungary and countries that were part of the Austro-Hungarian Empire before World War I.

The figure shows that the number of emigrants who left the British Isles from 1846 to 1945 amounted to about 40 per cent of the 1940 population of that area (including Ireland). The ratio of the total number to its population in 1940 is equally high for immigrants accepted by the United States.

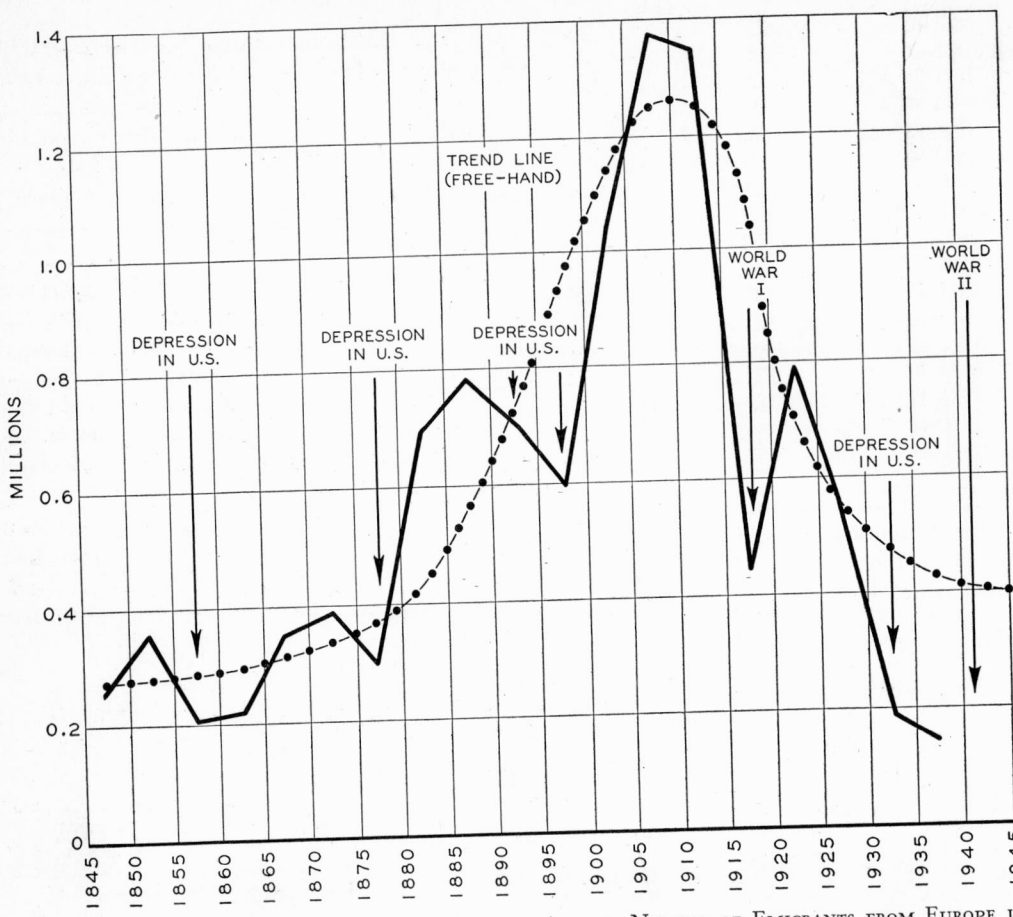

FIGURE 29. INTERCONTINENTAL MIGRATION: AVERAGE ANNUAL NUMBER OF EMIGRANTS FROM EUROPE IN EACH FIVE-YEAR PERIOD, 1846–1945

Emigration from Europe grew slowly until the middle of the 1870's, when steamships replaced sailing vessels, and then increased rapidly for forty years to a peak just before World War I. Temporary setbacks were due mainly to business slumps in the United States. The decline after World War I was caused by restrictive policies of the immigration countries. (Cf. pp. 77 ff.)

States and practically ceased during World War II. From 1933 to 1947 approximately 2 million emigrants left European ports and approximately 1.5 million persons returned to their motherland. The Netherlands ranked first in number of emigrants (nearly 600,000) but had an almost equal number of immigrants (about 580,000).[19] The era of great migration from Europe to the New World has ended, and we can now take stock of its results.

During the past 130 years, the United States, Canada, Argentina and Australia have admitted immigrants equivalent to about 40 per cent of the present population of each of these countries. The comparable figure for Brazil is about 10 per

cent, for New Zealand 35 per cent, for the Union of South Africa 5 per cent. (See Figure 28.)

Variations in the Volume of Migration

The volume of migration has varied widely, over the past century, from decade to decade and from year to year. The principal currents of intercontinental migration varied by five-year periods as follows (annual average, in thousands):[20]

	Citizens Leaving Europe	Aliens Entering the Americas
1846–50	256	299
1851–55	342	397
1856–60	201	213

19. Intercontinental and continental migrations combined.

20. For 1846–1924, **47**, Vol. I, pp. 168 and 230–31; for 1925–45, **3**, 1945–46, pp. 233–44; and **4**.

1861–65	223	207
1866–70	346	405
1871–75	372	410
1876–80	283	260
1881–85	686	650
1886–90	779	709
1891–95	729	650
1896–1900	602	528
1901–05	1,053	1,040
1906–10	1,389	1,482
1911–15	1,345	1,403
1916–20	431	375
1921–25	800	844
1926–30	552	726
1931–35	189	111
1936–40	148	116
1941–45	57	32

Migration increased after the middle of the nineteenth century, reached a peak shortly before the outbreak of World War I, and had almost ceased by the beginning of World War

II. This main movement has been overlapped by a series of shorter waves, the most significant of which were the almost complete cessation of migration in 1914–18 and the resumption immediately after World War I. (See Figure 29.)

Ups and downs in emigration in the early part of the past century resulted from economic difficulties and social turmoil in European countries. The depression in Great Britain, the potato famine in Ireland, and revolutionary upheavals in Germany were responsible for mass emigration from these countries in the 1840's. In the second half of the century, the difficult situation of farmers all over Europe, due partly to the competition of foreign grain, induced millions of farmers and farm laborers to go overseas.

The rapid increase in emigration after 1870 was due largely to progress in transportation. After the steamship replaced the sailing vessel, overseas travel became easier and less expensive.

TABLE 34

INTERCONTINENTAL MIGRATION: NUMBER OF EMIGRANTS FROM EUROPE AND ASIA, BY COUNTRY, IN EACH DECADE, 1846–1950

(*Thousands*)

Country of Emigration [a]	1846–50	1851–60	1861–70	1871–80	1881–90	1891–1900	1901–10	1911–20	1921–30	1931–40	1941–50
Total	477	2,362	2,839	3,264	7,145	6,397	11,591	7,813	6,753	1,914	…
Great Britain [b]	199	1,313	1,572	1,674	2,559	1,743	2,841	2,452	1,984	252	750
Ireland	…	…	…	175	700	406	309	135	167	10	12
Sweden	2	17	122	103	327	205	224	86	107	8	19
Norway	12	36	98	85	187	95	191	62	87	6	11
Finland	…	…	…	…	26	59	159	67	73	3	24
Denmark	…	…	8	39	82	51	73	52	64	100	133 [e]
France	11	27	36	66	119	51	53	32	4	5	…
Belgium	1	1	2	2	25	22	43	28	17	16	112
Netherlands	12	16	20	17	52	24	28	22	32	…	318 [d]
Germany	183	622	634	626	1,342	527	274	91	721	124	…
Austria-Hungary [e]	2	31	40	111	436	724	2,342	788	357	57	24
Switzerland	…	6	15	36	85	35	37	31	50	47	21 [d]
Spain	…	3	7	13	572	791	1,091	1,306	560	132	45 [e]
Portugal	…	45	79	131	185	266	324	402	995	108	40
Italy	…	5	27	168	992	1,580	3,615	2,194	1,370	235	120 [e]
Russia	…	…	…	58	288	481	911	420	80 [f]	…	…
Poland	…	…	…	…	…	90	189	183	458	160	…
India	55	242	179	189	156	170	164	56	5	138	182
Japan	…	…	…	…	…	54	132	144	122	91	…

Sources: For 1846–1924, **47**, Vol. 1, pp. 230–31; for 1925–40, **3**, various years; for 1941–50, **1**, various years.

a. Countries are arrayed by type of emigration.

b. Includes Malta and, since 1911, North Ireland.
c. Incomplete.
d. Includes continental and temporary migration.
e. Since 1919, Austria, Hungary and Czechoslovakia.
f. Estonia and Lithuania.

TABLE 35

INTERCONTINENTAL MIGRATION: DISTRIBUTION OF EMIGRANTS FROM EUROPE, BY AREA,
IN EACH DECADE, 1871–1930

(*Per Cent*)

Area	1871–80	1881–90	1891–1900	1901–10	1911–20	1921–30
Total	100.0	100.0	100.0	100.0	100.0	100.0
Northwestern Europe	65.4	51.1	37.2	30.9	35.2	35.6
Central Europe	23.4	23.4	18.0	20.9	10.9	15.8
Latin countries	9.4	21.9	36.9	39.6	46.7	41.1
Russia and Poland	1.8	3.6	8.0	8.6	7.2	7.5

Source: Derived from Table 34.

Moreover, steamship companies carried on an intensive drive to sell the golden dream of the New World to European farmers, miners and factory workers. The steep rise in immigrants coming into the United States in the last quarter of the nineteenth century was due partly to this advertising campaign and partly to the direct recruitment of European workers by agents of American industrial corporations. Shortage of labor was the main — and perhaps the only — bottleneck in the rapid economic growth of the country when it was putting the plow to the Great Plains and building railroads.

The long-range upward trend in European emigration (dotted line in Figure 29) was broken by setbacks in the late 1850's, in the 1870's and in the 1890's: world migration shrank whenever business slumped seriously in the United States. The decisive drop in the late 1920's was due largely to change in the immigration policy of the United States.

Countries of Origin and Destination

Until 1890, northwestern Europe, especially Great Britain, accounted for more than half of all intercontinental migration. After that time the flow from the Latin countries and central and eastern Europe increased steadily. (See Table 34.) In the 1870's nearly two thirds of all European emigrants came from northwestern Europe; in the 1880's about half; in 1901–30, a third. The share of the Latin countries increased from less than 10 per cent in the 1870's to more than 40 per cent in the period 1911–30. (See Table 35; cf. Figure 30.)

The change was due essentially to economic and demographic trends in emigration coun-

tries — decline in birth rates and increase in industrialization in northwestern Europe, on the one hand, and pressure of growing population and distress of farmers in southeastern Europe, on the other.

The new migrants differed from the old not only in origin and language but also in occupation and educational attainment. Skilled workers and craftsmen had predominated among emigrants from Great Britain and Germany, which were then more highly industrialized than the United States. In contrast, the Latin countries — Italy, Spain and Portugal — and the Slavic provinces of Austria-Hungary sent abroad mainly landless farmers, farm laborers and unskilled workers. In this period, however, not all farmers and farm laborers came to America to till the soil. Opportunities for settlement on free land in the New World were shrinking rapidly, but this decline was more than offset by the expansion of American industry. The open frontier for many emigrants arriving in the United States lay a few blocks from New York harbor rather than on the fringes of plowland in the West. For many Europeans, crossing the Atlantic meant a shift from farm to factory.

Emigration from Spain and Portugal was directed mainly toward Argentina and Brazil. Nineteenth-century Italian emigrants went in almost equal numbers to these two countries and the United States: from 1861 to 1900 each country received about a million. From 1901 to 1921 the main goal of Italian emigration was the United States, and then the flow again turned to Latin America.[21] The United States received about 70 per cent of all intercontinental migrants during

21. **47**, p. 271.

TABLE 36

INTERCONTINENTAL MIGRATION: NUMBER OF IMMIGRANTS ENTERING SELECTED COUNTRIES IN EACH DECADE, 1846–1940, AND 1941–48

(Thousands)

Country of Immigration	1846–50	1851–60	1861–70	1871–80	1881–90	1891–1900	1901–10	1911–20	1921–30	1931–40	1941–48
Total [a]	1,588	3,394	3,372	3,987	7,518	6,423	14,939	11,113	8,709	1,885	...
United States [b]	1,251	2,598	2,315	2,812	5,247	3,688	8,795	5,736	4,107	528	662
Canada	246	310	290	220	359	237	1,143	1,055	992	80	338
Mexico	...	...	...	...	...	...	...	107	74	96	14
British West Indies	51	73	101	98	66	61	170	459	129	...	...
Cuba	...	6	13	...	...	...	243	367	213	10	...
Brazil	5	122	98	229	531	1,144	689	792	834	283	...
Uruguay	...	...	85	112	140	90	21	57	79	53	...
Argentina	...	67	113	261	841	648	1,764	1,205	1,311	310	...
Philippines	...	...	...	...	...	...	...	55	31	...	...
Australia	...	...	116	72	213	416	1,516	902	562	103	153
New Zealand	...	33	69	145	65	35	89	91	108	18	39
Hawaii	...	...	...	...	...	...	...	85	49	...	...
Other islands	...	...	...	...	14	15	29	22	4	26	...
Union of South Africa	...	...	...	...	...	...	...	71	101	62	83
Other territories in Africa	35	185	73	38	42	89	480	109	15	376	...

Sources: For the United States, **10**, various years; other countries: for 1846–1924, **47**, Vol. 1, pp. 236–37; for 1925–40, **3**, various years; for 1941–48, **1**, various years.

a. Because of different figures for the United States, the totals in this table differ from those shown in **47**, Vol. 1, pp. 236–37.

b. Includes immigration from Canada and Mexico.

1851–90; its share declined to 60 per cent during 1891–1910, 50 per cent during 1911–30, and 20 per cent during 1931–40. In the last decade before World War II, Brazil and Argentina became the promised land. (See Tables 36 and 37; cf. Figure 31.)

IMMIGRATION INTO THE UNITED STATES

From the time of its discovery by white men, North America lay open to settlement by any who were dissatisfied with conditions in their homeland. The dream of freedom and equality, rather than the glitter of gold, lured the first throngs of pioneers to the continent. Although the new communities were poor in comparison with the emigration countries, they offered opportunities to men who were willing to work. Hundreds of thousands of immigrants were eager to seize this chance, even at the price of years of indentured labor.[22] They became the builders of the new empire.

In the nineteenth century, the United States offered newcomers incomparable economic opportunities through free homestead land, relatively high wages, and the possibility of rapid success in business and the professions. Then suddenly the traditional open-door policy came to an end.

IMMIGRATION POLICY

In colonial times, each colony regulated immigration into its territory; this responsibility was later transferred to the states. Since the 1830's, it has rested on the federal government[23] and has been a highly controversial political issue.

Selective Measures

Each economic setback in the United States brought an outburst of resentment toward aliens.

---

22. Persons deported to the American colonies by Brit-

ish courts and local authorities were another source of indentured labor.

23. **26**, p. 9; cf. **27**, *passim.*

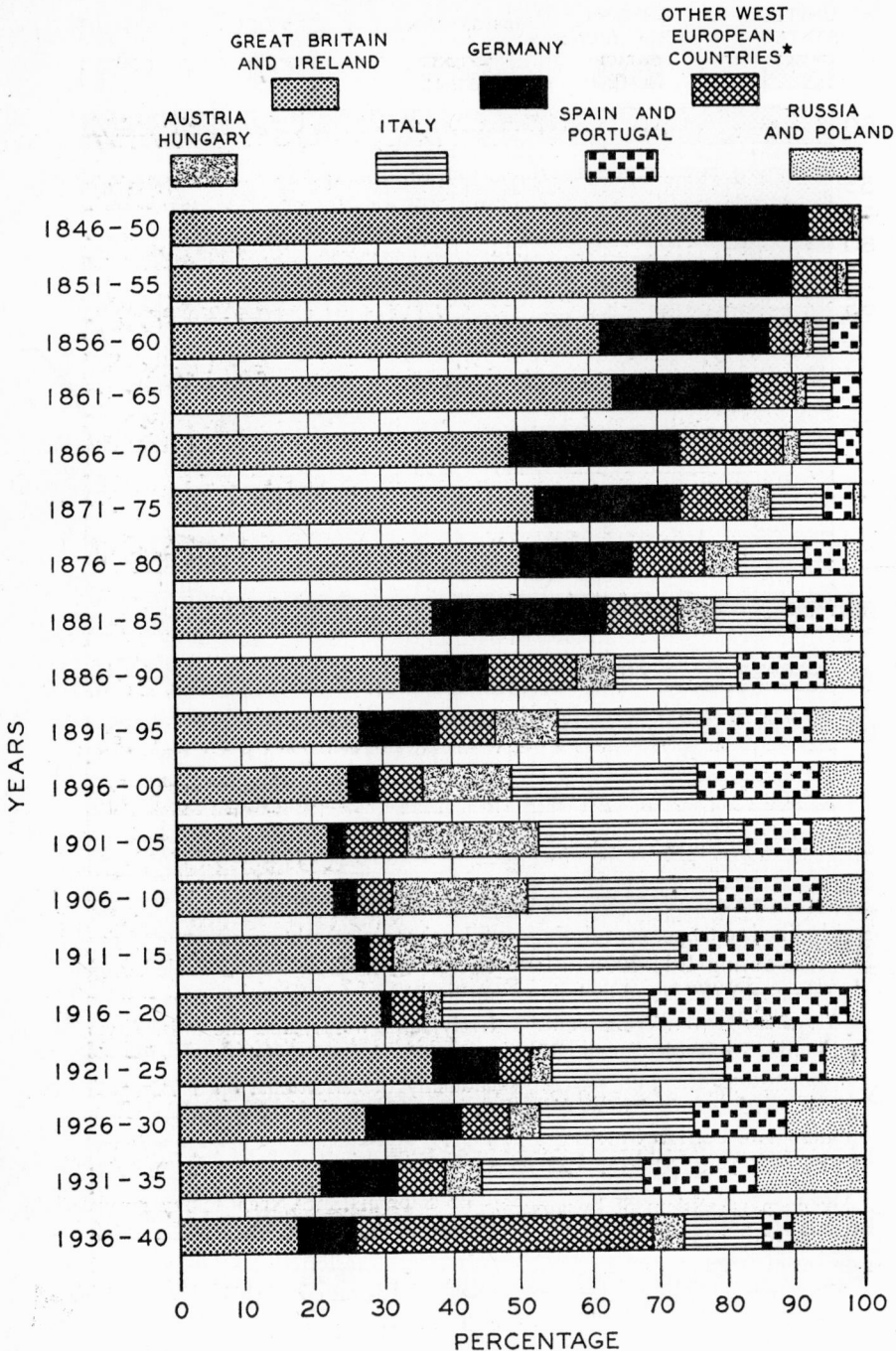

FIGURE 30. INTERCONTINENTAL MIGRATION: DISTRIBUTION OF EMIGRANTS FROM EUROPE BY COUNTRY OF ORIGIN IN EACH FIVE-YEAR PERIOD, 1846–1940

Until the middle of the 1880's, Great Britain, including Ireland, ranked first among emigration countries, and Germany held second place. By the turn of the century the number of emigrants from Latin and Slavic countries exceeded the number from Great Britain and Germany. (Cf. Table 34.)

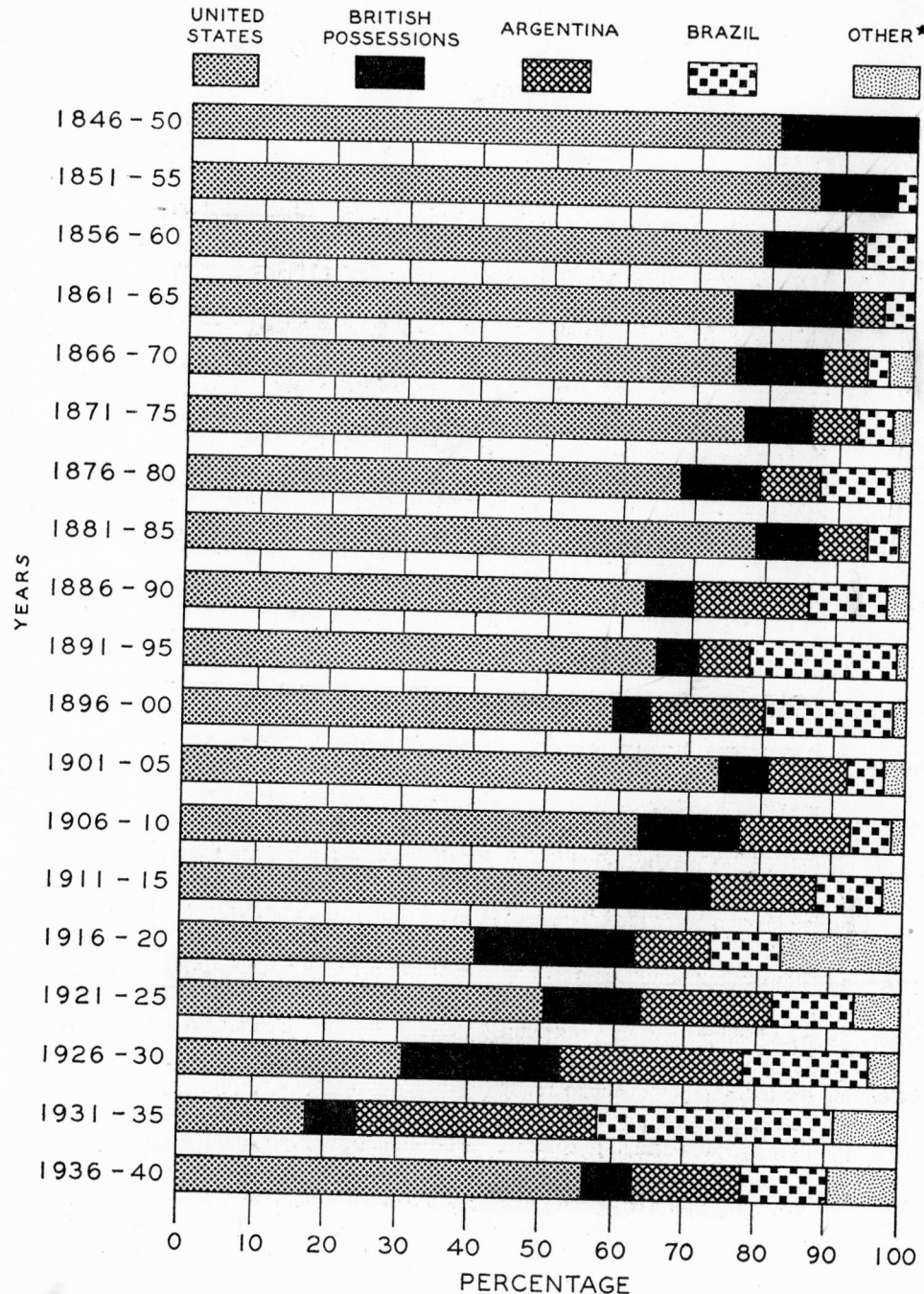

FIGURE 31. INTERCONTINENTAL MIGRATION: DISTRIBUTION OF IMMIGRANTS TO THE AMERICAS BY COUNTRY OF DESTINATION, IN EACH FIVE-YEAR PERIOD, 1846–1940

Before World War I the United States absorbed more than half of all immigration from Europe into the Americas. Since the early 1920's its share has declined as a result of restrictions on immigration. (Cf. Table 36.)

TABLE 37

IMMIGRATION INTO THE UNITED STATES: ANNUAL NUMBER OF IMMIGRANTS ADMITTED, 1821–1950 [a]

(*Thousands*)

Period or Year	Immigrants	Year	Immigrants	Year	Immigrants	Year	Immigrants
	Annual Average	1891	560	1911	879	1931	97
1821–30	15	1892	580	1912	838	1932	36
1831–40	60	1893	440	1913	1,198	1933	23
1841–50	171	1894	286	1914	1,218	1934	29
1851–55	350	1895	259	1915	327	1935	35
1856–60	170	1896	343	1916	299	1936	36
1861–65	160	1897	231	1917	295	1937	50
1866–70	290	1898	229	1918	111	1938	68
1871–75	215	1899	312	1919	141	1939	83
1876–80	347	1900	449	1920	430	1940	71
1881	669	1901	488	1921	805	1941	52
1882	789	1902	649	1922	310	1942	29
1883	603	1903	857	1923	523	1943	24
1884	519	1904	813	1924	707	1944	29
1885	395	1905	1,026	1925	294	1945	38
1886	334	1906	1,101	1926	304	1946	109
1887	490	1907	1,285	1927	335	1947	147
1888	547	1908	783	1928	307	1948	171
1889	444	1909	752	1929	280	1949	188
1890	455	1910	1,042	1930	242	1950	249

Source: **10**, 1936, p. 95, 1949, p. 93 and 1951, p. 91.

   a. 1821–1867, alien passengers arriving; 1868–1903, immigrants arriving; 1904–06, aliens admitted; beginning with 1907, immigrants admitted. Years ended June 30.

Beginning in 1836, various states petitioned Congress to take action against unwanted immigration. The demand for regulative measures became particularly insistent after 1865. The need for cheap labor, however, was too urgent to permit restriction of immigration, and Congress first adopted merely selective measures. In 1875 a law was enacted denying admission to prostitutes and alien convicts. It was followed in 1882 by acts prohibiting the immigration of the mentally ill or persons likely to become public charges. Later, in 1885, admission was denied to contract laborers. Grounds for exclusion were extended in 1891, 1903 and 1907. In 1917 the literacy test was established for immigrants over 16 years of age, and admission was denied to natives of southern and eastern Asia — the so-called Asiatic Barred Zone. The act of 1924 excluded the Japanese also.[24] Apart from these selective measures, the frontiers of the United States remained open to immigrants until World War I.

Restrictive Measures

Direct restriction of immigration was inau-

gurated by the quota act of 1921, originally passed as a temporary measure. This act limited immigration from non-American countries to 3 per cent of the number of foreign-born persons of each nationality residing in the United States in 1910; practically, the maximum for European countries and their colonies was set at 356,061 persons a year.[25] Certain groups of immigrants from Europe were, however, admitted independently of these "quotas," and no restrictions were placed on immigration from Canada and other American countries. While these provisions were in force from 1922 to 1924, the numbers of quota and nonquota immigrants admitted to the United States were as follows:

	Quota Immigrants	Nonquota Immigrants
1922	243,953	65,603
1923	335,480	187,439
1924	357,643	349,253

In 1924 a new act limited the annual number of quota immigrants to not more than 2 per cent

---

24. **26**, pp. 12–13; cf. **27**.

25. An additional 1,742 admissions were allowed for immigrants from non-European countries of the Eastern Hemisphere.

TABLE 38

IMMIGRATION INTO THE UNITED STATES: ANNUAL QUOTAS ALLOTTED AND QUOTA IMMIGRANTS ADMITTED, BY COUNTRY OR REGION, 1925–50

Country [a]	Annual Immigration Quota Allotted [b]		Quota Aliens Admitted					
	1925–29	1934–43	1925–29	1930–34	1935–39	1940–44	1945–49	1950
All countries	164,667	153,879	761,622	229,301	168,540	121,253	316,992	197,460
Europe [c]	161,422	150,501	755,387	225,725	165,471	118,301	310,094	195,671
United Kingdom	34,007	65,721	154,151	74,264	13,481	12,920	84,342	17,194
Ireland	28,567	17,853	132,715	27,528	3,633	1,777	18,738	6,444
Sweden	9,561	3,314	44,849	4,999	1,305	981	5,873	1,876
Norway	6,453	2,377	30,335	4,258	1,718	1,282	7,091	2,179
Netherlands	1,648	3,153	7,905	4,501	1,935	3,031	9,543	3,067
Belgium	512	1,304	2,661	1,926	1,166	2,364	4,354	979
Denmark	2,789	1,181	13,116	2,094	1,079	918	3,735	1,101
Finland	471	569	2,363	1,114	1,349	857	1,783	518
Germany	51,227	25,957	242,363	44,144	72,718	46,617	48,533	31,511
Austria	785	1,413	4,213	2,478	1,619		5,307	6,153
Czechoslovakia	3,073	2,874	14,668	5,210	8,464	5,019	9,989	4,058
Hungary	473	869	2,445	2,213	3,702	2,675	3,881	4,054
Switzerland	2,081	1,707	9,683	2,789	1,725	1,778	3,995	1,666
France	3,954	3,086	18,259	5,081	3,100	4,436	10,934	3,187
Spain	131	252	806	1,178	1,263	1,161	866	197
Portugal	503	440	2,453	1,309	1,543	1,519	2,075	426
Italy	3,845	5,802	18,389	14,342	15,101	4,947	17,410	5,861
Poland	5,982	6,524	29,000	12,313	15,517	13,834	39,387	50,692
Yugoslavia	671	845	3,081	1,772	2,735	1,253	3,304	5,359
Romania	603	377	3,783	1,920	1,854	1,487	2,040	2,019
Bulgaria	100	100	509	186	383	236	271	177
Greece	100	307	737	1,119	1,773	1,365	1,281	285
Turkey	100	226	679	1,104	1,070	753	829	697
USSR (Russia)	2,248	2,712	10,275	5,125	4,085	4,806	9,063	10,854
Estonia	124	116	612	251	239	233	2,073	5,387
Latvia	142	236	754	460	600	584	4,318	17,439
Lithuania	344	386	1,828	1,104	1,324	862	7,630	11,774
Other European	928	800	2,755	943	990	606	1,449	517
Asia	1,424	1,528	3,507	2,124	1,902	1,743	4,339	1,173
Africa	1,200	1,200	1,341	604	297	468	1,259	328
Pacific	621	650	1,387	848	870	741	1,300	288

Source: For immigration quotas and admissions to 1940–44, **10**, 1947, p. 111; for 1945–49 and 1950, **10**, various years.

a. Countries arrayed by type of emigration.

b. Quotas were changed several times between 1930 and 1950, but not importantly. The greatest change was effected by the act of December 17, 1943, repealing the Chinese exclusion laws and authorizing a Chinese quota of 105. In 1949 special quotas of 100 each were estab-lished for Israel, Syria and Lebanon. The quotas shown in the table were in force from 1934 to 1943. Quotas of colonies, dependencies and protectorates of European countries are included in quotas of these countries.

c. In United States immigration statistics "Europe" includes the USSR and Turkey. Quotas of colonies of European countries are included in the quotas of the respective countries, but immigrants born in colonies are counted among aliens from the continents in which these colonies are located.

TABLE 39

IMMIGRATION INTO THE UNITED STATES: AVERAGE ANNUAL NUMBER OF ALIENS ADMITTED AND DEPARTED,
1910–50

(*Thousands*)

Period Ended June 30	Admitted			Departed			Excess (+) or Deficiency (−) of Admissions over Departures
	Total	*Immigrants*	*Other*	*Total*	*Emigrants*	*Other*	
1910–14	1,215	1,035	180	552	289	263	+663
1915–19	323	235	88	236	124	113	+87
1920–24	717	555	162	323	179	145	+394
1925–29	494	304	190	247	78	169	+247
1930–34	243	85	158	254	67	187	−11
1935–39	224	54	170	206	31	175	+18
1940–44	144	41	103	94	11	83	+50
1945–49	462	131	331	300	19	281	+162
1950	676	243	427	457	28	429	+219

Sources: **10**, 1947, p. 106; **13**, 1949 and 1950.

of the number of foreign-born persons of each nationality residing in the United States in 1890. The purpose was to curtail immigration from eastern and southern Europe. The total annual quota for 1925–29 was set at 164,667 (161,422 for Europe and its colonies, and 3,245 for non-European countries). (See Table 38.) No restrictions were placed on nationals of Canada and other independent American countries. All European quotas were used to almost their full extent through 1929.

Beginning with 1930, new quotas were established: 150,000 entries a year were prorated among countries in proportion to the number of immigrants or descendants of immigrants from each among the inhabitants of continental United States in 1920. The minimum annual quota for each country was set at 100.

These provisions increased the quotas for the United Kingdom, the Netherlands, Belgium, Italy and Spain, and cut down those for Germany, Norway, Sweden, Denmark and some other countries. Then the great depression in the United States reduced immigration from Western Europe to almost nothing — especially that from the United Kingdom, the Scandinavian countries and France. For the decade 1930–39, for example, the quota of the United Kingdom and Ireland combined was 835,740, but only 110,094 immigrants from these countries entered the United States. (See Table 38.)

The annual number of quota immigrants was

very small throughout the 1930's and the 1940's: 1930–34, 45,860; 1935–39, 33,708; 1940–44, 24,-250; 1945–49, 63,398. In round numbers the total for the two decades was 836,085, only 27 per cent of the number the law permitted. The "Nordic" countries, especially the English-speaking countries, have failed to send as many persons as would have been received, while immigration from other countries has been held down by low quotas, rigorous eligibility requirements and, later, by the war.

The restrictions on immigration were relaxed after the war in favor of war refugees and alien wives, husbands and children of United States-citizen members of the armed forces. The Displaced Persons Act of 1948, amended in 1950, authorized admission into the United States of 361,000 displaced persons during the three years from July 1, 1948 to June 30, 1951. This legislation, however, was qualified by limiting provisions that make its full use unlikely. All in all, 328,851 alien displaced persons had been admitted to the United States by December 31, 1951.[26] Their visas were charged to the quotas for the respective nationalities for future years. An additional 119,693 aliens were admitted as war brides (114,691), husbands (333) and children (4,669).

In the period 1930–34 fewer aliens entered the United States than left it; during 1935–39, net immigration averaged only 18,000 a year; dur-

26. See Table 48, p. 103.

TABLE 40

IMMIGRATION INTO THE UNITED STATES: DISTRIBUTION OF IMMIGRANTS BY COUNTRY OF ORIGIN, 1851–1950

(*Thousands*)

Country of Origin [a]	1851–60	1861–70	1871–80	1881–90	1891–1900	1901–10	1911–20	1921–30	1931–40	1941–50
Total	2,598	2,315	2,812	5,247	3,688	8,795	5,736	4,107	528	1,035
Great Britain	424	607	548	807	271	526	341	330	29	132
Ireland	914	436	437	655	388	339	146	221	13	27
Canada	59	154	384	393	3	179	742	925	109	172
Germany	952	787	718	1,453	505	341	144	412	118	227
Austria-Hungary [b]	...	8	73	354	593	2,145	896	64	8	37
Netherlands	11	9	17	54	27	48	44	27	7	15
Sweden and Norway	21	110	211	569	321	441	161	166	9	21
France and Belgium	81	43	79	70	49	115	96	86	18	51
Italy	9	12	56	307	651	2,046	1,100	455	68	58
Russia (USSR) and Poland	1	5	52	265	602	1,597	926	290	18	8
Mexico	3	2	6	2	1	50	219	459	22	61
Other	123	142	231	218	277	968	921	672	109	228

Source: 10, 1947, p. 108, and 1951, p. 94.

a. Distribution of immigrants by country of origin in this table differs from the distribution in Table 38. For example, many displaced persons from Poland, the USSR and the Baltic states are counted here as arrived from Germany.

b. After World War I, Austria, Hungary and Czechoslovakia.

ing 1940–44, 50,000. The total for the past two decades, since the beginning of the great depression, has been only slightly over half a million. These figures are in striking contrast to net immigration in earlier years. (See Table 39.) *See note on page 110.*

IMMIGRANT STOCK IN THE UNITED STATES

In all, the United States has admitted more than 40 million aliens since the end of the Revolutionary War. The Irish, British and Germans predominated among immigrants in the first half of the nineteenth century. Later, the national composition of immigration changed from decade to decade. Since World War I, the proportion from Canada, Mexico and other American countries has been growing steadily. (See Table 40.) [27] Aliens from these countries represented 4 per cent of all immigrants in 1901–10, 20 per cent in 1911–20, 38 per cent in 1921–30, and 30 per cent in 1931–40.[28]

27. Totals in Table 40 are the same as those for the United States in Table 36, while trends in the distribution of migrants by country of origin are similar to those shown in Table 35.

28. 10, 1947, p. 108.

The proportion of foreign-born persons in the population of the United States fluctuated between 13 and 14.5 per cent from the Civil War to 1920 and has declined rapidly during the past thirty years. The relative number of persons born in the United States of foreign or mixed parentage increased steadily up to 1910 when it exceeded 35 per cent but has declined since then. (See Table 41.)

Language

Assimilation of new immigrants by the descendants of original settlers has been slow. As recently as 1940, English was the mother tongue of only 22 per cent of the foreign-born persons and of only 50 per cent of the persons of foreign or mixed parentage. (See Table 42.) In terms of language, complete assimilation of immigrants seems usually to take about two generations.

Concentration in Cities

Characteristically, persons of foreign stock (foreign-born or of foreign or mixed parentage) make up a much higher percentage of the population in cities than in rural areas. In 1930 they

TABLE 41

IMMIGRANT STOCK IN THE UNITED STATES, 1870–1940

(Per Cent of Total Population)

Group	1870	1880	1890	1900	1910	1920	1930	1940
Total	28.2	29.8	32.9	34.2	35.2	34.8	32.2	26.2
Foreign-born	14.4	13.3	14.7	13.6	14.7	13.2	11.6	8.7
Foreign parentage	10.8	12.7	12.8	14.0	14.0	14.8	13.8	11.5
Mixed parentage	3.0	3.8	5.4	6.6	6.5	6.8	6.8	6.0

Source: 10, 1947, p. 19, and 1950, p. 16.

TABLE 42

IMMIGRANT STOCK IN THE UNITED STATES: DISTRIBUTION OF WHITE POPULATION BY NATIVITY, PARENTAGE

AND MOTHER TONGUE, 1940

(Thousands)

Mother Tongue	Foreign-Born White	Native White — Foreign or Mixed	Native White — Native Parentage	Mother Tongue	Foreign-Born White	Native White — Foreign or Mixed	Native White — Native Parentage
Total	11,110	23,158	84,125				
Northwestern Europe				Eastern Europe			
English	2,506	12,181	78,352	Russian	357	214	14
Norwegian	233	344	81	Ukrainian	36	45	3
Swedish	423	374	34	Armenian	40	26	2
Danish	122	95	9	Lithuanian	123	141	9
Dutch	103	103	61	Finnish	97	118	15
Flemish	32	18	5	Romanian	43	20	2
French	360	534	519	Yiddish	924	774	53
Central Europe				Southern Europe			
German	1,589	2,436	925	Greek	165	102	6
Polish	802	1,429	186	Italian	1,561	2,081	125
Czech	160	279	82	Spanish	428	714	719
Slovak	172	284	29	Portuguese	84	121	12
Magyar	241	199	13				
Serbian	18	18	1	Arabic	51	53	4
Croatian	53	59	4	All other	64	35	11
Slovenian	76	97	6	Not reported	249	264	2,847

Source: 10, 1947, p. 37.

constituted 42.6 per cent of the urban population, 21.2 per cent of the nonfarm rural population, and only 14.5 per cent of the people on farms.[29] (See Table 43.)

Distribution by State

The proportion of persons who are foreign-born or of foreign parentage varies widely from

29. Censuses after 1930 do not provide comparable data.

state to state. Foreign stock is heavily concentrated along the North Atlantic coast, near the ports of entry. In 1940, for example, persons of foreign stock constituted more than 50 per cent of the population of New York State, Massachusetts, Connecticut and Rhode Island and more than 40 per cent of that of New Jersey. Another pocket of concentration lies in the north, in Wisconsin, Michigan and North Dakota. (See Figure 32.)

Foreigners entering the United States have

TABLE 43

IMMIGRANT STOCK IN THE UNITED STATES: DISTRIBUTION OF URBAN AND RURAL
POPULATION BY COLOR AND PARENTAGE, 1930

(Per Cent)

Color, Nativity and Parentage	Total Population	Urban	Rural Farm	Rural Nonfarm
All classes	100.0	100.0	100.0	100.0
White				
Native parentage	57.1	48.6	67.8	68.2
Foreign stock				
Foreign or mixed parentage	20.7	27.0	10.9	14.6
Foreign-born	10.9	15.6	3.6	6.6
Colored				
Negro	9.7	7.5	15.6	8.5
Other	1.6	1.3	2.0	2.1

Source: **7**, p. 27.

tended to join countrymen who settled in America before them. The North Central states — Illinois, Wisconsin, Minnesota and North Dakota — attracted immigrants from Sweden, Norway and Denmark. Dutch immigrants joined their countrymen in Michigan. The largest colonies of persons of German origin are in New York, Illinois, Wisconsin and Ohio. Italians are concentrated in New York, New Jersey and Pennsylvania; Czechs, in Pennsylvania, Illinois and Ohio; Poles, in New York, Pennsylvania and Illinois; Russians, in New York and Pennsylvania; Portuguese, in Massachusetts and California. The distribution of immigrants from the Irish Free State differs from that for the United Kingdom: the chief settlements of the Irish are in New York, Massachusetts and Illinois, while the English are more evenly dispersed over the country than any other national group.

Within each state, and often within a city, some areas attract people of the same origin — Irish, Dutch, Poles, Spaniards or Italians. Thus each national group preserves some of its individuality through several generations. A unique combination of geographic, economic and political conditions in the United States has resulted in a particular pattern of organization of different peoples into one community: the United States is a supernational unity rather than a multinational state of the usual type. It takes several generations for newcomers from different countries to be integrated into a homogeneous group. But long before this process is completed, they become parts of the community just as

stones in a mosaic are parts of a picture. Whatever the prevailing color in the picture, each single stone maintains its individual color and design and the variety among stones contributes to the unity of the whole.

NEGROES IN THE UNITED STATES

The United States has been less successful in handling the aftermath of its involuntary immigration. Importation of slaves into North America was never overwhelming in volume; not more than a million were brought overseas to plantations north of the Mexican Gulf and the Rio Grande.[30] The slave trade was outlawed soon after the United States became an independent nation, but the descendants of slaves have not been assimilated with other national groups in the great melting pot. Caught, bought or kidnaped from different parts of the Dark Continent, the Negroes imported into the New World had no common language, religion or cultural tradition. In the new environment they developed into a separate quasi-racial group that differs conspicuously not only from the white population in the United States but also from the black population in the land of their ancestors.

Liberation of the slaves after the Civil War did not give them equality with the white population of the states in which they were living. In the South their freedom was resented by many of their white neighbors as a symbol of defeat in the war between the states. The period of recon-

30. See **34**.

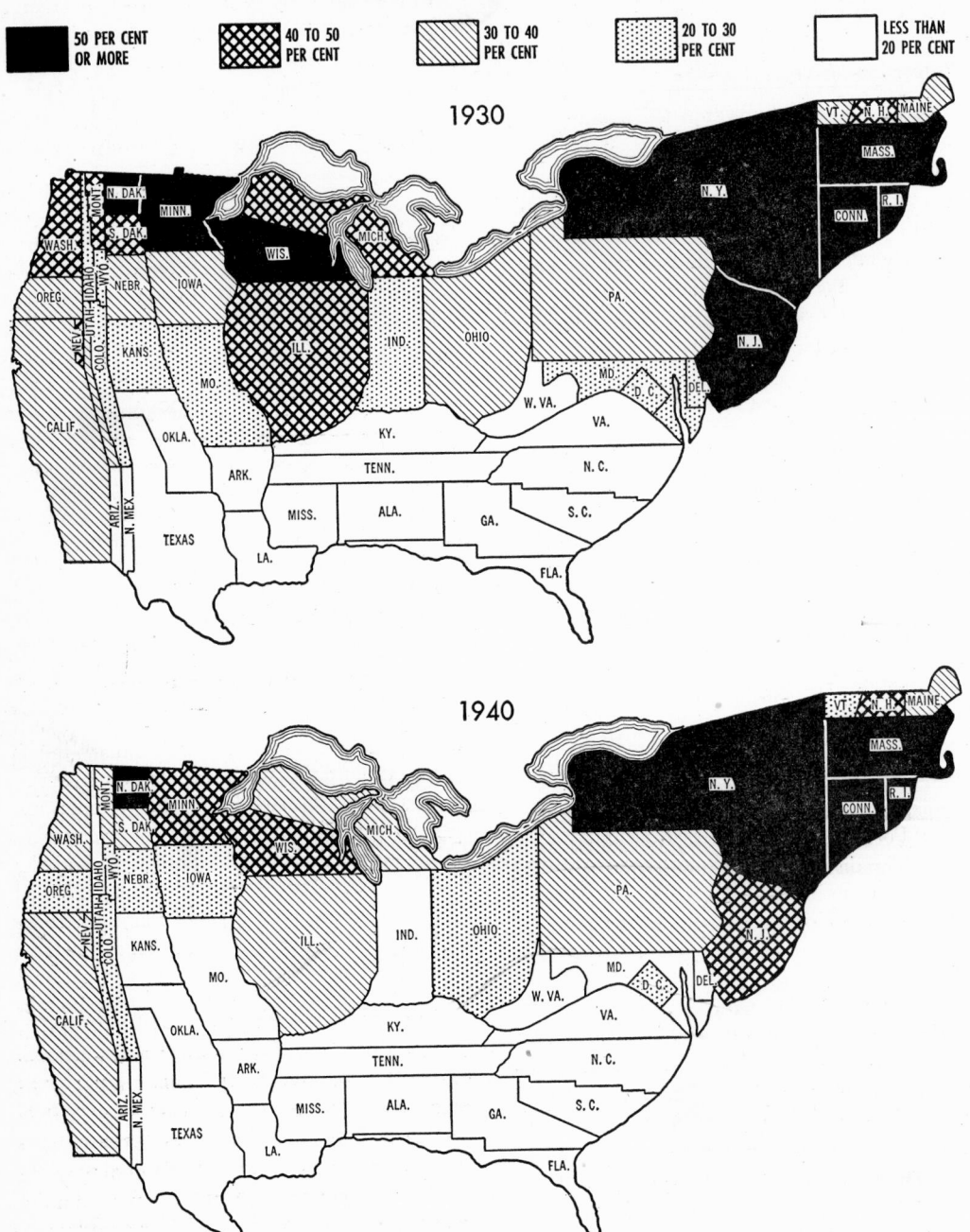

EACH STATE IS REPRESENTED
ON THE SCALE OF ITS POPULATION

50 PER CENT OR MORE | 40 TO 50 PER CENT | 30 TO 40 PER CENT | 20 TO 30 PER CENT | LESS THAN 20 PER CENT

1930

1940

FIGURE 32. IMMIGRANT STOCK IN THE UNITED STATES: PERCENTAGE IN EACH STATE, 1930 AND 1940

In 1930, eight states, all in the North, had a population composed of more than 50 per cent foreign stock (solid black on the map) and in sixteen states, all in the South, less than 20 per cent of the population was foreign-born or of foreign parentage (white on the map). Ten years later only five states were in the first group, while twenty-one were in the second. (Cf. **10**, 1947, p. 38.)

86

struction further widened the cleavage and, in many cases, left resentment to smoulder for decades to come.

Proportion of Negro Population

Because of the continuing white immigration into the United States, the proportion of Negroes declined from almost 20 per cent of the population at the beginning of the nineteenth century to 13.1 per cent in 1880 and 9.9 per cent in 1920. As the white influx has dwindled, the proportion of Negroes has become stabilized — 9.7 per cent in 1930 and 9.8 per cent in 1940. It was estimated at 9.9 per cent for 1950.

State Distribution of Negroes

Just as white immigrants concentrated near the ports of entry, so Negroes have remained in the states where their forefathers worked as slaves. Of about 13 million Negroes enumerated by the 1940 census, approximately 9 million (nearly 70 per cent) were in eleven southern states as follows:[31]

Georgia	1,085,000
Mississippi	1,075,000
Alabama	983,000
North Carolina	981,000
Texas	924,000
Louisiana	849,000
South Carolina	814,000
Virginia	661,000
Florida	514,000
Tennessee	509,000
Arkansas	483,000

Outside the South, many Negroes live in New York State (571,000 in 1940), Pennsylvania (470,000), Illinois (387,000), Ohio (339,000) and Michigan (208,000), mainly in large industrial cities. (See Figure 33.) The trend is toward a more even distribution of Negroes over the country. As Negro workers have moved steadily northward, the proportion of all Negroes who live in the southern states has declined from decade to decade. (See Table 44.) The change has been very slow, however, and up to the present, the Negro problem in the United States has been predominantly a problem of the South.

31. **10**, 1947, p. 20.

INTERNAL MIGRATION

In both the New World and the Old, internal migration has helped countries to develop their potential resources and to adjust to economic and other pressures.

INTERNAL MIGRATION IN THE UNITED STATES

The push westward dates from colonial times. The first European settlements in North America clung to the Atlantic coast or penetrated a little inland, following the bays and rivers. Before the middle of the eighteenth century, few colonists ventured more than a hundred miles inland.[32] (See Figure 34.) "West" at that time meant the other side of the Alleghenies. Later, the Mississippi Valley became the goal. Large-scale colonization of grasslands on the Great Plains, which began in the 1850's, was of epochal significance for the nation and the world.[33]

The "Center" of Population

The progress of the westward movement in the United States is best illustrated by the shifts of the "center of population." [34] (See Figure 35.) It is also shown by the rapid growth of the Pacific states as compared with the Atlantic. The population of the three Pacific states more than doubled from 1920 to 1950, rising from 5.6 million to 14.4 million, while the number of inhabitants of New England and the Middle Atlantic states (New York, New Jersey and Pennsylvania) increased by 24 and 35 per cent respectively. The growth of California has been stimulated particularly by the development of munitions industries during the war and by the postwar boom.

Mobility of Population in the United States

In addition to the westward drive, population has shifted in various directions — from New England to Florida, from Kentucky to Michigan, from Illinois to Texas. The Negro population has its own paths: northward from the Deep South, very seldom westward. A comprehensive picture of these trends can be established by

32. **40**, pp. 62, 158 and 222. Cf. **25**.

33. **44**, p. 172.

34. This term designates a point so located that to reach its longitude and latitude all persons residing west of it would have to cover the same total distance as those residing east of it and all living north of it the same distance as those living south of it.

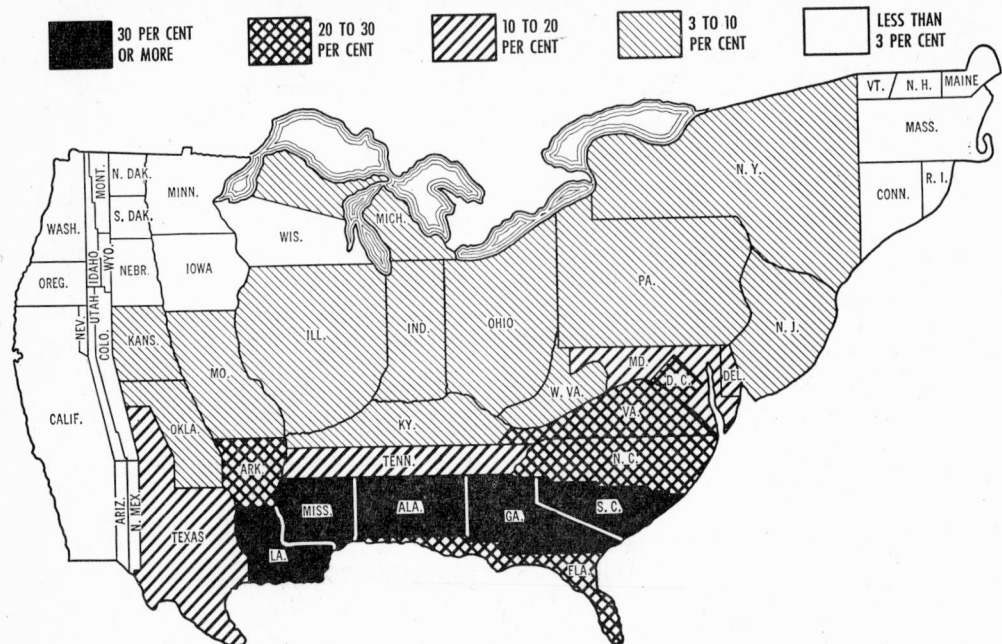

EACH STATE IS REPRESENTED
ON THE SCALE OF ITS POPULATION

FIGURE 33. NEGROES IN THE UNITED STATES: PERCENTAGE IN EACH STATE, 1940

Negroes constitute 30 per cent or more of the population in Louisiana, Mississippi, Alabama, Georgia and South Carolina and from 20 to 30 per cent in Arkansas, Florida, North Carolina, Virginia and the District of Columbia. The proportion of Negroes in a state's total population declines steadily as one moves from the Deep South northward and westward. (Cf. **8**, p. 54.)

comparing the states in which persons are living with those where they were born. Thornthwaite has used this comparison to develop maps showing the internal migration of native whites and Negroes.[35] (See Figure 36.)

In 1930 the census found that only 67.3 per cent of the persons in the United States had been born in the state in which they were living in that year, exactly the same percentage as in 1850:[36] the proportion was more than 80 per cent in the South, between 70 and 80 per cent in the Northeast, less than 40 per cent on the Pacific coast, and below 30 per cent in such states as Nevada and Arizona.[37]

The depression stopped, and in many cases reversed, the flow of migration from predominantly agricultural states toward industrial centers. The movement was resumed with recovery and was increased by the industrial mobilization during the war. During 1940-43 approximately 2 million persons moved from central agricultural states to the booming munitions centers on the Pacific coast and the iron and steel plants along the Great Lakes and in the South Atlantic states. Wartime interstate migration[38] was very similar to that in the 1920's, also a period of industrial expansion. (See Table 45.) The industrial boom that followed the war found the labor force concentrated in the regions of heavy industry where it was most urgently needed.

More recent information[39] shows the extent of interstate and intrastate migration, including changes of residence within the same county, and provides information on the personal characteristics of migrants but fails to indicate how they are distributed among states. In April 1947 approximately 70 million persons were living in a different dwelling from that in which they had lived on April 1, 1940. Some 44 million persons

35. See **42**, *passim*.
36. **7**, p. 139.
37. **7**, p. 140.

38. **50**, p. 83.
39. See **11**.

TABLE 44

NEGROES IN THE UNITED STATES: PERCENTAGE IN SELECTED STATES, 1910–50

State[a]	1910	1920	1930	1940	1950
States Where Percentage Is Increasing [b]					
Missouri	4.8	5.2	6.2	6.5	8.0
New Jersey	3.5	3.7	5.2	5.5	5.7
Kansas	3.2	3.3	3.5	3.6	4.0
Pennsylvania	2.5	3.3	4.5	4.7	6.2
Ohio	2.3	3.2	4.7	4.9	5.9
Indiana	2.2	2.8	3.5	3.6	4.5
Illinois	1.9	2.8	4.3	4.9	7.2
New York	1.5	1.9	3.3	4.2	6.3
Michigan	0.6	1.6	3.5	4.0	7.1
States Where Percentage Is Decreasing [b]					
Mississippi	56.2	52.2	50.2	49.2	45.5
South Carolina	55.2	51.4	45.6	42.9	38.9
Georgia	45.1	41.7	36.8	34.7	30.9
Louisiana	43.1	38.9	36.9	35.9	33.1
Alabama	42.5	38.4	35.7	34.7	32.1
Florida	41.0	34.0	29.4	27.1	21.8
Virginia	32.6	29.9	26.8	24.7	22.2
North Carolina	31.6	29.8	29.0	27.5	26.6
Arkansas	28.1	27.0	25.8	24.8	22.4
Tennessee	21.7	19.3	18.3	17.4	16.1

Sources: For 1910–40, **10,** various years; for 1950, *Current Population Reports,* Series PC–6 and PC–12.

a. States arrayed by decreasing percentage in 1910.
b. All nonwhite populations.

had changed residence within the same county, 13 million had changed counties within the same state, and 12 million had changed their state of residence.

The net loss to farm areas through migration from 1940 to 1947 — about 3.2 million persons — was somewhat less than at the wartime peak. The movement was in line with the long-range trend: the West remained the main immigration area and the South continued to send its surplus population to other regions. Negroes in the United States outside the South were less mobile than the white population in the period 1935–40. During 1940–47, on the contrary, they were more migratory than white persons and moved over longer distances.

INTERNAL MIGRATION IN RUSSIA

Migration developed on the eastern European plains long before the Russian nation was formed by the amalgamation of native Slavic and Fin-nish tribes. Since the twelfth century, the growing population of what is now the USSR has been expanding gradually from the southwestern corner of the area that later became European Russia toward the north and east, from the middle and upper Dnieper to the upper Volga, from Kiev to Moscow. From the new centers, migration continued northward, southward and eastward.

In the north, Russian colonists penetrated to the Arctic coast in the middle of the sixteenth century. The southward movement, which followed the great rivers of the Russian plain, the Volga and the Don, began in the sixteenth century and continued for 300 years. Eastward colonization, which followed tributaries of the Volga upstream, reached the Ural Mountains in the second half of the sixteenth century. By the beginning of the eighteenth century, under Peter the Great, the Urals had become the base of Russian munitions industries, and agricultural

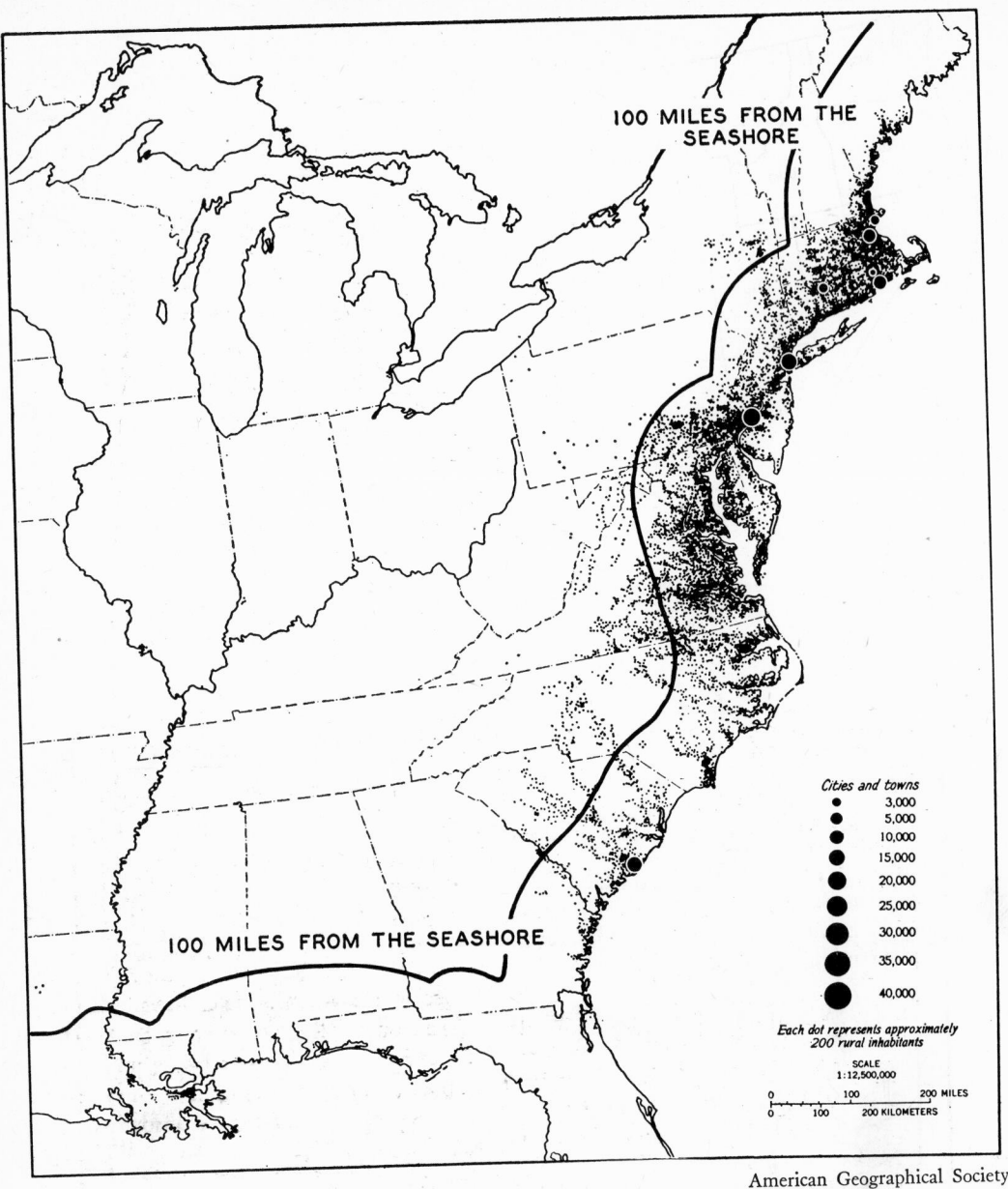

Cities and towns

•	3,000
•	5,000
•	10,000
●	15,000
●	20,000
●	25,000
●	30,000
●	35,000
⬤	40,000

Each dot represents approximately
200 rural inhabitants

SCALE
1:12,500,000

0 — 100 — 200 MILES
0 — 100 — 200 KILOMETERS

100 MILES FROM THE
SEASHORE

100 MILES FROM THE SEASHORE

American Geographical Society

FIGURE 34. DISTRIBUTION OF SETTLERS IN THE NORTH AMERICAN COLONIES, 1760

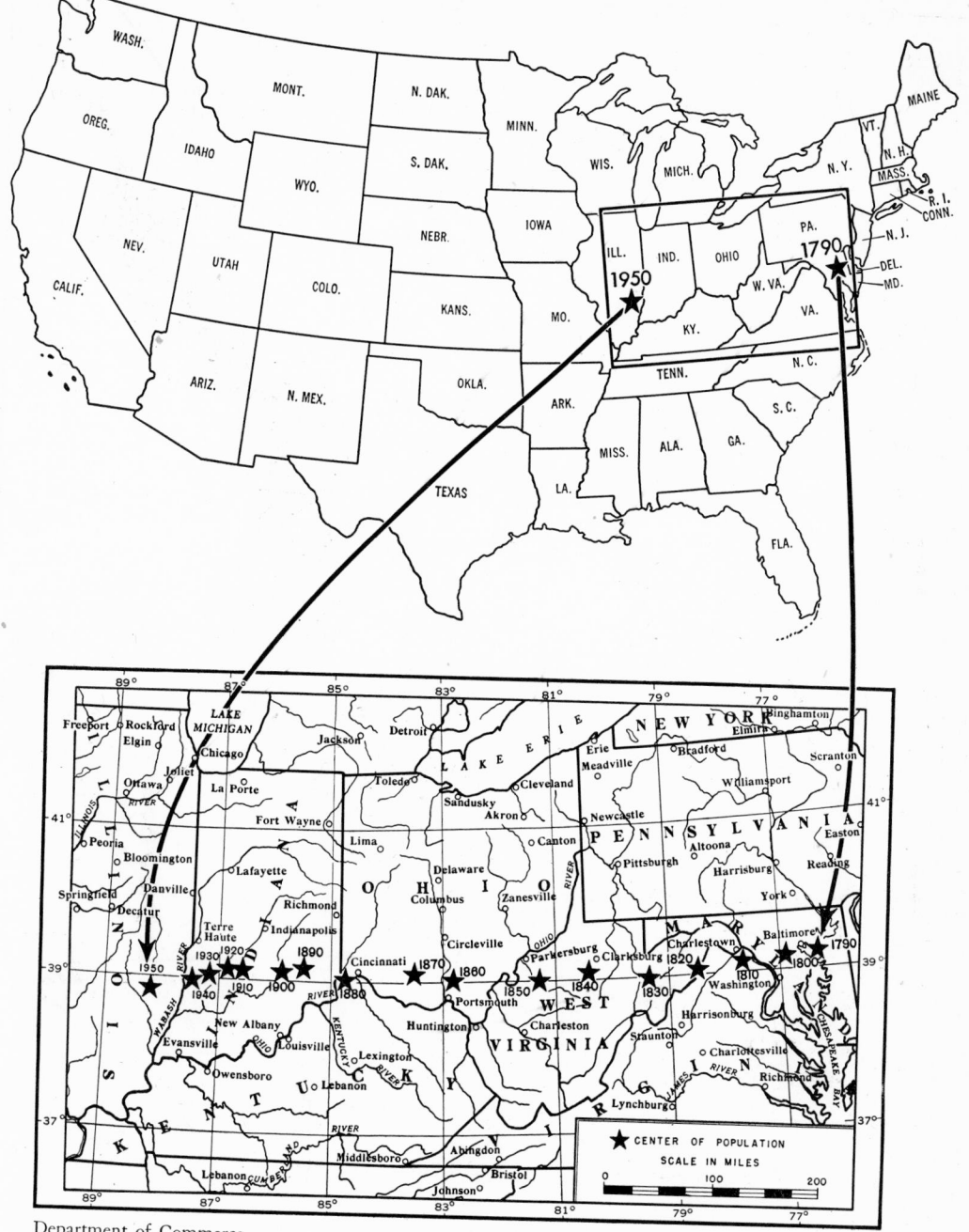

FIGURE 35. INTERNAL MIGRATION IN THE UNITED STATES: CENTER OF POPULATION, 1790–1950

Since 1790, the center of population in the United States has not deviated more than a few miles from its original latitude, close to 39° N, but it has moved steadily westward. In a century and a half the center of population has moved about 600 miles, at an average speed of four miles a year. The shift was particularly rapid (more than five miles a year) between 1830 and 1890. It then slowed down, especially after 1910, but quickened during World War II.

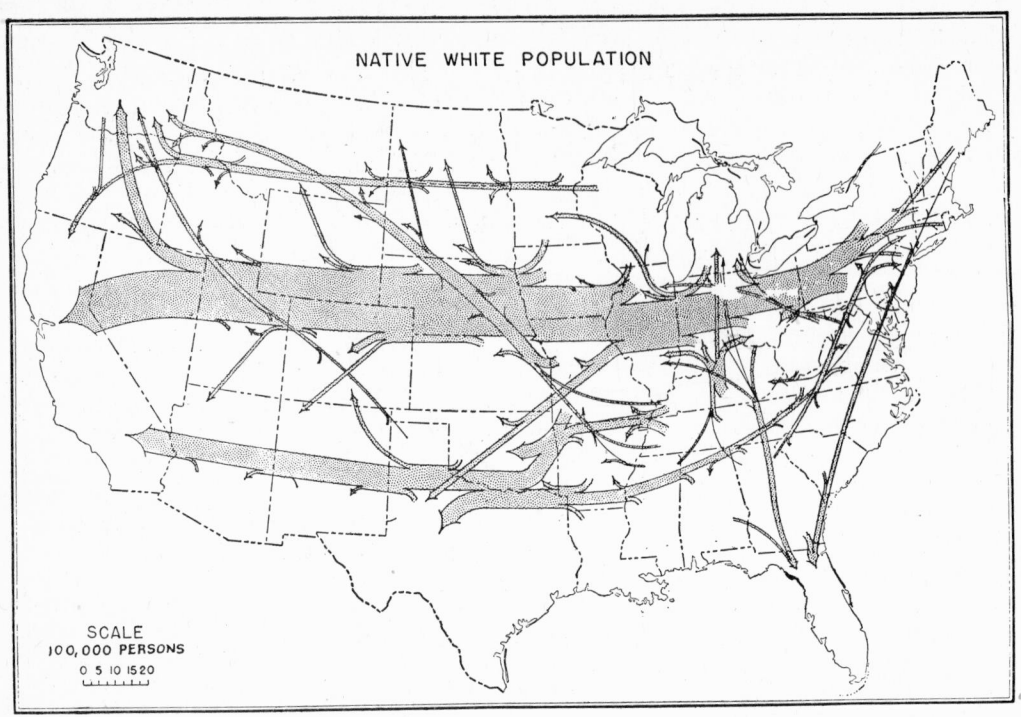

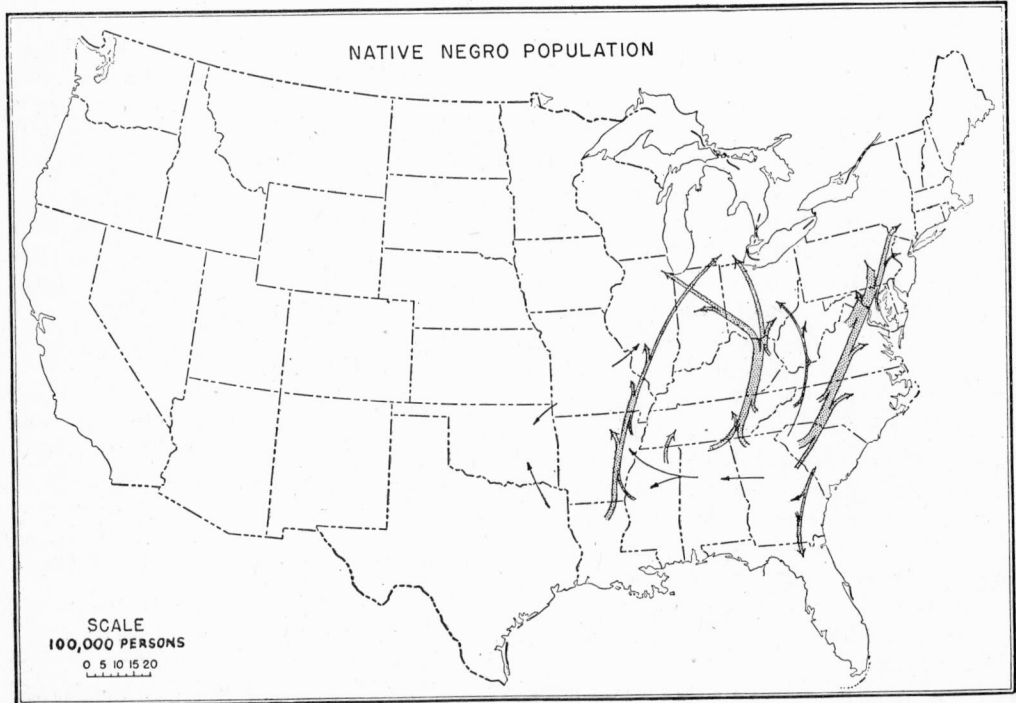

FIGURE 36. INTERNAL MIGRATION IN THE UNITED STATES: NET NUMBER OF PERSONS WHO HAD MOVED IN INDICATED DIRECTION BETWEEN TIME OF BIRTH AND 1930

The width of the bars is scaled to show the net number of persons who had migrated, since birth, in the indicated direction. Important immigration areas are the Pacific states, Texas and Oklahoma, and the Great Lakes states. Negroes are moving from the South northward. (**14**, p. 84.)

settlers were spreading farther eastward along trails blazed by outlaws and adventurous hunters. At the end of the eighteenth century, the Russians were firmly established in Alaska and had penetrated along the Pacific coast into the area now occupied by California.

The systematic agricultural colonization of western Siberia dates from the liberation of the serfs in 1861. Between that time and the outbreak of World War I, about 1.5 million peasant families settled in Siberia. Except for these, Siberia was colonized by deported criminals and political exiles. Descendants of the colonists from European Russia and the deportees formed 90 per cent of Siberia's population at the turn of the century.

During World War I and after the Soviet revolution, Russia underwent unprecedented shifts of population. Following a "scorched earth" policy, the high command of the retreating Russian armies (still under the Czar) ordered the deportation of more than 3 million persons to central and eastern Russia. During the civil war, throngs of refugees roamed the country, fleeing from the Reds and Whites; most of them pushed eastward, toward the Urals and on to Siberia and the Far East. The collapse of the anticommunist movement in southern Russia resulted in mass emigration of opponents of the new government. Including Russian war prisoners who failed to return home and foreigners who left Russia during the civil war, Kulischer estimated political emigration from Russia after World War I at 1,750,00.[40]

"Collectivization" of farms launched a new wave of population shifts during 1929–30. Some farmers were deported to the north and the east, some fled to cities, swelling the ranks of industrial workers. The famine of 1932–33, following on the heels of collectivization, resulted in the flight of people from starving villages to cities; the exact number of these migrants is unknown, but is estimated in the millions.[41]

Apart from such spontaneous shifts of population, the Soviet government has been carrying out a policy of colonization in Siberia and other Asiatic regions. Three million persons were transferred, between 1927 and 1939, to the Urals, Siberia and the Far East, and more than 2 million to central Asia, including Kazakhstan.

These figures do not include prisoners used for forced labor in the wilderness of Siberia.

During World War II, when a large part of European Russia was under German occupation, the USSR made desperate efforts to expand munitions production beyond the Urals by moving workers and machines eastward. We cannot make even a rough estimate of the number of persons involved in these shifts. No statistics are available on people who have crossed the Urals in the last twenty years, and if their number could be established, we would not know how many settled at their original destination. The main difficulty is in ascertaining the volume of involuntary shifts of population.

Labor camps are scattered all over the USSR, from its western border to the Pacific and from the borders of China, Afghanistan and Iran to the Arctic Ocean. The largest camps are located east of the Urals. They provide labor to build roads, dig canals, drain marshes and, above all, for mining. The current population of these camps is unknown, but most conservative estimates run to several millions. In view of the very high mortality among the prisoners, the labor force in the Asiatic provinces of the USSR could not be maintained at the required level without continual replacements from prisons in central Russia. From the available fragmentary information, it seems fairly certain that the number of slave laborers shipped from European Russia to Siberia in the last twenty years has been at least equal to the number of Negro slaves imported into the Western Hemisphere in the entire eighteenth century.

INTERNAL MIGRATION IN CHINA

By the end of the eighteenth century, peasants had begun to migrate to Manchuria from northern China, especially from the provinces of Shantung and Hopeh, but official prohibition of such migration was not lifted until 1878. The available statistics, which go back only to 1923, suggest that there has been a continual movement of Chinese migrants over the Manchurian border in recent decades. Some of them went to Manchuria early in the spring and returned home in the autumn; others settled on the land. Net immigration of Chinese persons into Manchuria totaled 4.4 million in the period 1923–39. This was, however, only a small part of the shift of population in China.

40. **32**, p. 56.
41. **32**, p. 98.

TABLE 45

INTERSTATE MIGRATION IN THE UNITED STATES: NET GAIN OR LOSS IN EACH STATE, BEFORE
AND DURING WORLD WAR II

(Thousands)

State [a]	Total Population			Civilians, April 1940– November 1943
	1920–30	1930–35	1935–40	
California	+1,369	+387	+665	+1,738
Michigan	+595	−81	+76	+281
Washington	+82	+26	+80	+245
Maryland	+13	+49	+61	+235
Ohio	+282	−62	−10	+231
District of Columbia	...	+122	+23	+205
Florida	+347	+188	+147	+187
New Jersey	+477	−77	+29	+185
Virginia	−231	−36	−27	+155
Oregon	+96	+19	+77	+138
Connecticut	+84	+6	+25	+127
Indiana	+35	−14	+26	+79
Arizona	+27	−12	+38	+77
Illinois	+488	−59	−19	+69
Massachusetts	+49	−74	−32	+37
Utah	−30	+51	−12	+32
Rhode Island	+18	−60	—	+30
Nevada	+5	+9	+8	+27
Delaware	−18	+49	+61	+19
Wyoming	−1	−3	+3	−9
New Hampshire	−7	+3	+6	−12
Texas	+288	+49	−22	−16
Louisiana	−22	+40	+9	−19
Colorado	−15	+12	+9	−23
Maine	−35	+7	−9	−30
Vermont	−19	−14	−6	−31
New Mexico	−20	+23	+14	−44
Idaho	−51	+7	+16	−45
Kansas	−95	−95	−111	−54
Montana	−71	−13	−11	−69
Tennessee	−117	+95	−39	−71
South Dakota	−42	−61	−61	−89
Nebraska	−81	−77	−107	−96
North Dakota	−72	−59	−67	−100
Wisconsin	−7	−13	−32	−103
Pennsylvania	−69	−252	−104	−112
Alabama	−150	−85	−73	−116
Missouri	−60	+73	−86	−117
Georgia	−416	−62	−33	−131
South Carolina	−258	−38	−16	−138
West Virginia	−53	−36	−27	−140
Minnesota	−113	+20	−18	−192
Iowa	−168	−44	−61	−193
Mississippi	−103	−73	−28	−194
New York	+1,229	+37	−57	−223
Arkansas	−214	−38	−76	−225
Kentucky	−203	−16	−55	−263
North Carolina	−8	−48	−15	−263
Oklahoma	−49	−118	−184	−304

Sources: For 1920–30, **42**; for 1930–35 and 1935–40, **49** and **50**; for 1940–43, **12**.
  a. States arrayed by net gain or loss of civilian population through interstate migration from
April 1940 to November 1943, the peak of industrial mobilization.

Torn by civil war and plagued by famines, China has been an arena of intensive migration in the past twenty years. Since the beginning of the Japanese invasion, millions of farmers, with their families, have fled before advancing armies; others have wandered from their devastated fields to cities or other farming districts where starvation seemed less imminent; some few have moved toward colonization areas; others, according to the testimony of their neighbors, disappeared to an "unknown destination." A survey of the rural exodus taken in 1935 found that almost 2 million farms had been wholly abandoned and that only elderly people remained on 3.5 million others.[42] Counting four persons for each wholly abandoned farm and two persons for each farm deserted by young family members, some 15 million persons apparently had left the areas covered by the survey.

Recent Flights and Transfers of Population

Flight of civilian population before an invading army, expulsion of a defeated tribe from its settlement, and shipment of war prisoners to slave markets are among the oldest forms of population shift. Such involuntary migration, temporarily abandoned in the nineteenth century, has been revived in our time on an unprecedented scale. During 1918–39 approximately 7 million persons were transferred or fled headlong from persecution in Russia, the Balkans and Asia Minor; during 1939–47 from 45 to 50 million in Europe alone were expelled, shipped like cattle or driven by fear. In this second period of less than a decade, more people were uprooted and forced to move to new places than had emigrated voluntarily in the whole preceding century.

Europe in the Interwar Years

The age of great flights and compulsory transfers of population began with World War I or perhaps somewhat earlier, with the Balkan wars. It started on a rather small scale and in fairly mild forms. In the shifts of European population in the interwar years, transfer of national minorities and the flight of refugees can hardly be separated from normal migration: in some cases, what started as a flight ended as an orderly migration; in others, the exchange of national minorities over a frontier appeared to be an arrangement accelerating and facilitating the usual voluntary migration.

The shifts of population in the interwar years formed an extremely complicated pattern. (See Figure 37.) In addition to massive internal migration in Russia, Europe recorded five important movements. Following the map from the Russian border westward, they involved more than 9.1 million persons, as follows:[43]

1. Emigrants from the USSR	2,500,000
2. Persons in minority groups transferred in the Balkans and Asia Minor	2,495,000
3. Germans returned to Germany	1,250,000
4. Persons reshuffled in the Balkans, Austria and Czechoslovakia	800,000
5. Immigrants into France	2,100,000

1. Emigration from Russia included political refugees (approximately 1,150,000 after subtracting the number who returned to Russia) and repatriated aliens (1,350,000), most of them Poles.

2. Transfer of minorities in the Balkans and Asia Minor was a result of the Balkan wars, which ended shortly before the outbreak of World War I. The first international agreement on a bilateral transfer of populations in that area was the convention concluded in November 1913 between Bulgaria and Turkey on the exchange of Bulgarians and Moslems and their properties within a 30-kilometer frontier zone.[44] The actual exchange, planned for about 50,000 persons on each side, was interrupted by the outbreak of World War I. Later the same principle was applied to the exchange of minorities between Greece and Bulgaria (the Convention of Neuilly of 1919) and between Greece and Turkey (the Convention of Lausanne of 1923). The Neuilly Convention resulted in the liquidation of more than 15,000 Greek peasant properties in Bulgaria and more than 30,000 Bulgarian properties in Greece.[45] The Lausanne Convention concerned not only the Turks in Greece and the Greeks in Turkey but also hundreds of thousands of Greeks who had fled from Turkey to Greece during the war.

Including voluntary migration (such as that of the Armenians), approximately 2.5 million

---

42. **15,** July 15, 1936, p. 173.

43. Estimates of Eugene M. Kulischer with minor changes (cf. **33,** pp. 248–49).

44. **39,** p. 12; cf. **16.**

45. **39,** p. 14.

FIGURE 37. RECENT FLIGHTS AND TRANSFERS OF POPULATION: POPULATION SHIFTS IN EUROPE AND THE USSR, 1918–39 (According to Eugene M. Kulischer). Shifts of population in Europe in the period 1918–39 were caused partly by World War I and the preceding Balkan wars, partly by economic factors. Exchange of Turks and Greeks, repatriation of Germans, and Russian emigration are typical of movements caused by political factors. Russian migrations; French, Polish and Italian internal migration; and migration of workers to France represent movement from agricultural regions with surplus population to industrial centers. (Cf. 33, p. 85.)

International Labor Office (ILO)

persons were moved from one country to another in the Balkans and Asia Minor to join their own people. They comprised:

Greeks returned from Turkey	1,200,000
Turks returned from the Balkan countries	600,000
Bulgarians returned from Greece	120,000
Greeks returned from Bulgaria	50,000
Hungarians returned from the Balkan countries	400,000
Armenians moving to Europe	125,000

3. Germany was an emigration country before World War I, but after its defeat hundreds of thousands of Germans living abroad returned to the Reich. The net number of Germans returning from other countries between 1918 and 1925 was as follows:

Total	1,250,000
From Baltic states and former Russian and Austrian Poland	200,000
From western Poland and Danzig	700,000
From Alsace-Lorraine	200,000
From the Balkan countries	150,000

4. The Nazi-inspired reshuffling of populations in the Balkans, Austria and Czechoslovakia and the flight of the Jews from Germany and German-dominated countries marked the beginning of Hitler's New Order, but chronologically these migrations belong to the interwar period. Hundreds of thousands of people were moved before the formal outbreak of World War II, as follows:

Total	800,000
Austrians moving to Germany	50,000
Sudeten Germans moving to Germany	250,000
Slovaks and Czechs transferred	330,000
Jews fleeing from Germany and German-occupied countries	170,000

5. Although immigration into France in the interwar years included political refugees from the USSR, Italy and Spain, it was essentially a normal economic migration. France was an emigration country before 1850 but became an immigration country in the second half of the nineteenth century. It is estimated that 4.5 million aliens settled in France between 1850 and 1950, about half of them after World War I. In the interwar years, 1918–39, France received

more than 2 million immigrants (including 200,000 political refugees from Italy and Spain):

From Poland	450,000
From Germany (Poles)	150,000
From the Balkan countries	150,000
From Italy	650,000
From Spain	450,000
From Portugal	50,000
From other European countries	100,000
From French North Africa	100,000

In 1938, on the eve of World War II, more than 3 million foreigners were living in France; in 1,700 districts the number of foreigners equaled or exceeded that of the native inhabitants.[46]

Europe during World War II

Two major movements can be distinguished in the displacements of population caused by World War II: those ordered and effected by Germany and those caused by Germany's collapse. The first movement includes compulsory redistribution of population in accordance with the Nazi ideal of national homogeneity of population in an area, transfer of workers, shipment of Jews to extermination camps, and spontaneous flight of refugees from areas directly affected or threatened by military action. The second movement includes the return of refugees and war prisoners to their homes and the expulsion of Germans from territory annexed by the USSR and Poland and areas abroad where they had lived before the war as a national minority.

The general pattern of these shifts and flights is illustrated by Kulischer's map, reproduced in Figure 38. As shown in Table 46, some 15 million Germans and 12.6 million persons of other nationalities were either transferred or compelled to flee. This enumeration, however, does not tell the whole story. Of 12 million Russians who fled or were evacuated from German-occupied areas, it lists only 1.5 million who remained, after the war, where they had settled. It does not record the 5 million Jews consigned to slaughterhouses and gas chambers, and the millions of civilians who roamed aimlessly along destroyed highways from one heap of rubble that was once a city to another.

There is hardly any way to estimate the number of this last group of displaced persons. They

---

46. **6,** p. 13.

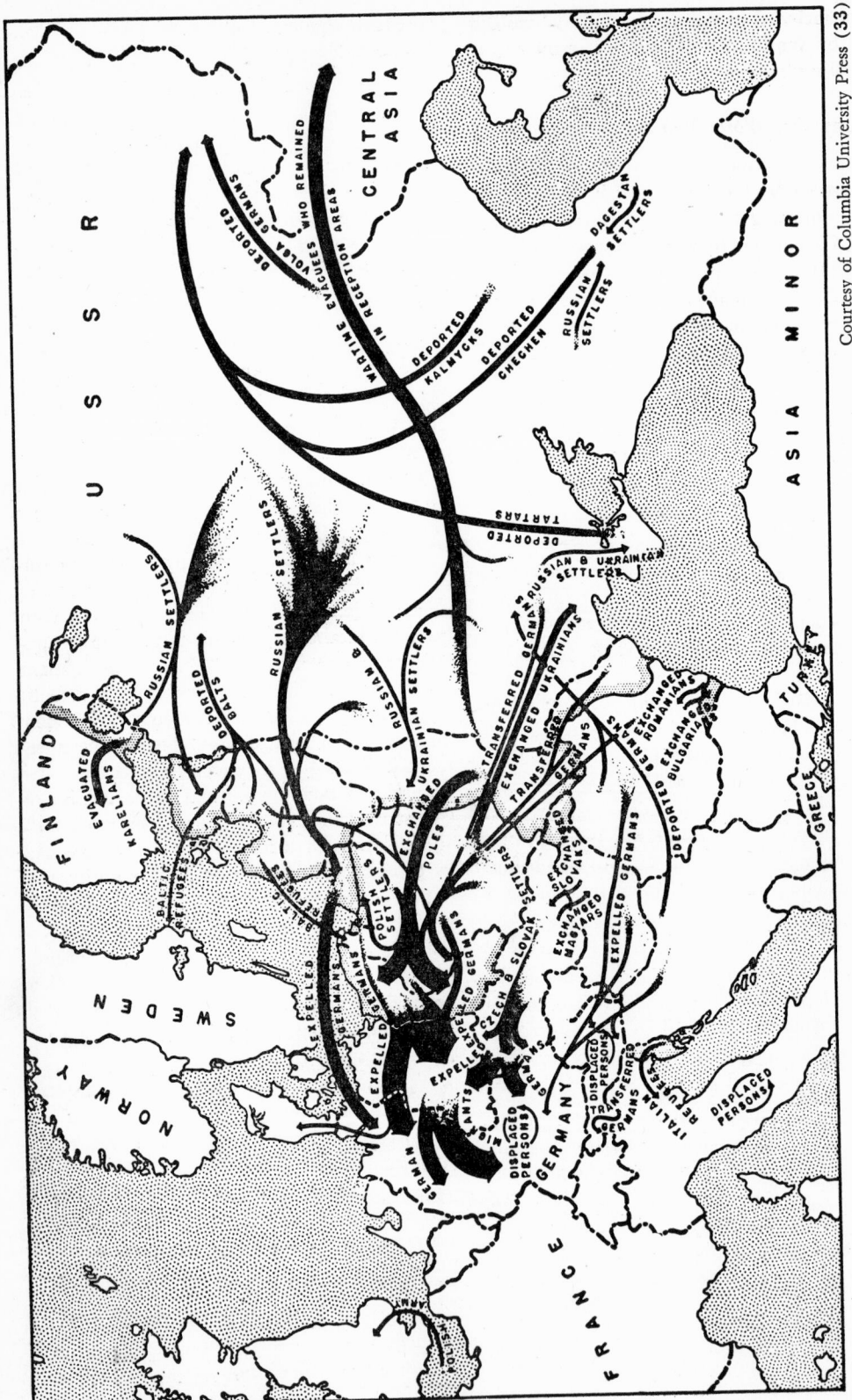

Figure 38. Flights and Transfers of Population: Shifts in Europe and the USSR Produced by World War II (According to Eugene M. Kulischer)

are not included in the number of civilians displaced by World War II, which is estimated at 45 to 50 million.

Germany after World War II

Victorious Germans were the first to use large-scale compulsory transfer of civilians for the purpose of adjusting the ethnic, or racial, distribution of a population to political boundaries. After the war, the Allies applied the same measure to the Germans. Germany lost not only all the territory it had conquered in the early part of the war — about 120,000 square miles with a population of 20 million [47] — but also one fourth of its prewar territory in the east, with a total prewar population of 9.5 million.[48]

According to the decision of the Potsdam Conference, the Germans who had lived in this area before the war, or in Czechoslovakia, Hungary, Austria and Poland, were to move back within Germany's new boundaries. It was estimated that 6,650,000 persons would be resettled: 3.5 million from Poland, 2.5 million from Czechoslovakia, 500,000 from Hungary, and 150,000 from Austria. A census taken in October 1946 showed that Germany actually had 9.7 million refugees within its postwar boundaries, 5.6 million from the eastern provinces and 4.1 million from other areas. A little less than a third of the refugees were in the Russian occupation zone, the remainder in Western Germany.[49] (See Table 47.)

In the middle of 1948 the number of German refugees in postwar Germany was estimated at 11.4 million.[50] This figure is open to criticism because of lack of information for the Russian zone, but even with allowance for possible duplication, it appears that postwar Germany has had to absorb approximately 10 to 11 million uprooted persons, roughly one refugee for each five former inhabitants of the area left to Germany.

---

47. This includes Austria, the Sudetenland in Czechoslovakia, Memel, Danzig, Eupen-et-Malmédy and a part of Poland. During the war, Germany also held as protectorates and colonies more than 80,000 square miles with a population of 27 million (Czechoslovakia, a large part of Poland, Alsace and Lorraine, Luxembourg and a part of Yugoslavia (**18**, p. 6). These figures do not include areas under military occupation, in western Europe and the USSR.

48. **17**, p. 9.

49. **22**, p. 5.

50. **22**, p. 7.

Displaced Persons

The term "displaced persons" logically would cover all the German refugees from the lost provinces and abroad, but it has been applied in a narrower sense to the persons who were displaced from the country of their birth or fled from persecution and could not return because of persecution or fear of persecution on account of race, religion or political opinions. At the end of World War II, more than a million such persons were concentrated in Western Germany and a few thousand were scattered in other areas. About 20 to 25 per cent of the displaced persons were Jews from different parts of Germany, Austria and eastern Europe who declined to return to their wrecked homes where they would be subject to humiliation if not direct persecution. The great bulk, however, consisted of refugees from the USSR and countries annexed by the Soviet Union — Poland and the Baltic states.

A special international agency, the International Refugee Organization (IRO), was created to assist these people and facilitate their resettlement. A total of 1.6 million persons were registered and assisted; 1.1 million had been either repatriated (73,000) or resettled (1,038,000) by December 1951. The main countries of destination were the United States, Australia, Israel, Canada and the United Kingdom. A few displaced persons went to France, Argentina, Brazil, Belgium, Venezuela and other countries. Less than 25 per cent of the resettled displaced persons were Jews; the overwhelming majority were refugees from the USSR and from the countries taken over by the Soviets after the war. (See Table 48.)

India and Pakistan

The partition of what was British India between two independent dominions, India and Pakistan, on August 15, 1947 was based roughly on predominance of Hindus or Moslems in different areas.[51] Because of the complicated political structure of India and the large areas with mixed population, partition was bound to leave

---

51. According to the 1941 census, Hindus formed 65.5 per cent of the total population of British India; Moslems, 24.3 per cent; members of tribal communities, 6.1 per cent; Christians, Buddhists and others, 4.1 per cent. At the time of partition, India had approximately 270 million Hindus, 100 million Moslems and 40 million members of other communities and churches.

TABLE 46

FLIGHTS AND TRANSFERS OF POPULATION IN EUROPE AND THE USSR PRODUCED BY WORLD WAR II

Years	Route	Group
	Transfer, Evacuation and Flight of Germans [a]	
1939–43	Italian Tyrol to Austria and Germany	80,000 Germans
1944	Romania to Germany and Austria	200,000 Germans
1944	Yugoslavia to Germany and Austria	250,000 Germans
1944	Romania to USSR	70,000 Germans
1944	Yugoslavia to USSR	100,000 Germans
1944–46	Hungary to Germany and Austria	200,000 Germans
1944–45	Russian East Prussia to Germany	500,000 Germans
1944–45	Old Poland to Germany	1,000,000 Germans [b]
1944–47	New Poland (former Germany) to Germany	6,000,000 Germans
1944–45	New Poland (former Germany) to Denmark	100,000 Germans
1945–46	Czechoslovakia to Germany (and partly to Austria)	2,700,000 Germans
1945–46	Soviet Zone to American and British Zones	4,000,000 Germans
	Population Movements of Non-Germans from, into and within Poland	
1939–44	Poland to Germany, Austria and Italy	275,000 Polish displaced persons
1939–47	Poland through USSR, the Balkans, and western Europe to Great Britain	160,000 members of Polish army
1944–46	USSR (former Poland) to New Poland	1,000,000 Poles
1946	USSR to Poland	50,000 Polish Jews
1944–46	Poland to USSR	518,000 Ukrainians, Byelorussians and Lithuanians
1946	Various European countries to Poland	60,000 returned Polish emigrants
1945–47	Old Poland to New Poland	3,000,000 Poles
	Population Movements of Non-Germans from, into and within Czechoslovakia	
1945–46	USSR to Czechoslovakia	63,000 Czechs and Ukrainians
1946–47	Romania to Czechoslovakia	30,000 Czechs and Slovaks
1946–47	Western and central Europe to Czechoslovakia	30,000 returned Czechoslovak emigrants
1946–47	Hungary to Czechoslovakia	100,000 Slovaks
1946–47	Czechoslovakia to Hungary	100,000 Magyars
1946–47	Inner Czechoslovakia to the border region (Sudetenland)	1,800,000 Czechs and Slovaks
1946–47	Slovakia to Bohemia and Moravia	180,000 Slovaks and Magyars
	Population Movements of Non-Germans from and into Yugoslavia	
1941–47	Yugoslavia to Germany, Austria and Italy	90,000 Yugoslavian displaced persons and refugees
1946–47	Yugoslavia (Istria, Fiume and Zara) to Italy	140,000 Italians
1946–47	Yugoslavia to Hungary	40,000 Magyars
1946–47	Hungary to Yugoslavia	40,000 Serbs, Croats and Slovenes
	Population Movements of Non-Germans from the Baltic Area	
1940–44	USSR to Finland	415,000 Karelian Finns
1941–44	USSR to Germany, Austria and Italy	165,000 Estonian, Latvian and Lithuanian displaced persons
1941–47	USSR to Belgium	35,000 Estonian, Latvian and Lithuanian displaced persons
1942–44	USSR to Sweden	30,000 Estonian, Latvian and Lithuanian refugees
1942–43	USSR (Estonia) to Sweden	6,000 Swedes
1943–44	USSR (Leningrad area) to Finland	18,000 Ingrians

(Continued on facing page)

TABLE 46—*continued*

Years	Route	Group
	Other Population Movements into and/or from Various European Countries	
1941	Bulgaria to Romania	110,000 Romanians
1941	Romania to Bulgaria	62,000 Bulgarians
1946	Greece, Bulgaria, Romania to USSR	30,000 Armenians
1941–45	USSR (former eastern Poland and old Soviet Ukraine) to Germany, Austria and Italy	150,000 Ukrainian displaced persons
1943–46	Eastern and central Europe to Germany, Austria and Italy	225,000 Jewish refugees
1940–45	Various European countries to Germany, Austria and Italy	150,000 Displaced persons and refugees
	Population Movements within the USSR	
1941	Volga region to the Asiatic part of the USSR	400,000 Volga Germans
1941–42	Axis occupied Soviet territory to inner and Asiatic parts of the USSR	1,500,000 Soviet citizens [c]
1945–46	Southern Russia to the Asiatic USSR	600,000 Crimean Tatars, Kalmyks and Chechens
1946	Russia proper and the Ukraine to the Crimea	50,000 Russians and Ukrainians
1946	Dagestan to former Chechen land	60,000 Dagestan mountaineers
1946	Various parts of the USSR to Sakhalin	50,000 Russians
1945–47	Central and western Russia proper, Byelorussia, and Lithuania to Russian East Prussia	500,000 Russians, Byelorussians and Lithuanians
1945–47	Old Soviet territory to other newly acquired western territories of the USSR	500,000 Russians, Ukrainians and others

Source: (**33**, pp. 302–04). The original table is here reproduced with some abbreviations and without original notes.

a. Transfer of 230,000 Germans from Austria to Germany is not included; it was partly a return of Reich Germans who had migrated to Austria after March 1938, and partly a transfer of Sudeten German refugees (included in the total of 2,700,000).

b. Includes also Germans from the Baltic States, Romania, Bessarabia and Bucovina.

c. Total number of evacuees (partly deportees from the new Soviet territories) estimated at 12 million, of whom the great majority returned.

considerable religious minorities on both sides of the new frontier — Moslems in Hindu-dominated India and non-Moslems in Pakistan.[52] For example, the partition of Bengal, in northeastern India, brought 11.5 million non-Moslems to Pakistan but left 5.3 million Moslems in India. Similarly, the partition of Punjab, in northwestern India, left 3.6 million non-Moslems in Pakistan, giving at the same time 5.3 million Moslems to India.[53]

Even before the partition was completed, violent clashes broke out between Moslems and Hindus. Later the friction in border provinces (see Figure 39) reached the bitterness and pro-

portions of local religious wars. Massacres of minorities and destruction of their property by mobs resulted in mass flight of Moslems from India and of non-Moslems from Pakistan. At the beginning, both governments tried to protect the minorities and discourage their exodus. Having failed in this attempt, they took measures to direct the throngs of refugees toward security and to resettle them. Spontaneous flight thus became a more or less orderly transfer of religious minorities. The operation continued from August 1947 to April 1949.

How many were transferred in all and how many perished on the way is unknown. At the beginning of 1948, the number of non-Moslems who had fled from Pakistan or awaited evacuation was estimated at 5.9 million — 4.5 million from the Punjab States, 400,000 from Sind, about a million from Bengal (Eastern Pakistan). The number of non-Moslem refugees from Eastern

52. Pakistan was formed with a population of 72 million, including 51 million Moslems. This division left almost half of all Moslems in the new Dominion of India and about 20 million non-Moslems in Pakistan.

53. **4**, August 1948, pp. 200–01.

TABLE 47

FLIGHTS AND TRANSFERS OF POPULATION: GERMAN REFUGEES IN GERMANY,
OCTOBER 1946 AND JANUARY 1948

(*Thousands*)

| | | October 1946 | | January 1948 |
Zone	Total	From Eastern Provinces Lost by Germany	From Abroad	(*in West Germany*)
Total	9,683 [a]	5,606	4,063	. . .
American Zone	2,785	750	2,021	3,163
British Zone	3,082	2,453	629	3,627
French Zone	95	37	58	157
Russian Zone	3,602	2,274	1,327	. . .
Berlin	120	92	28	. . .

Source: **22**, pp. 5–7.   a. Includes 13,000 refugees of unknown origin.

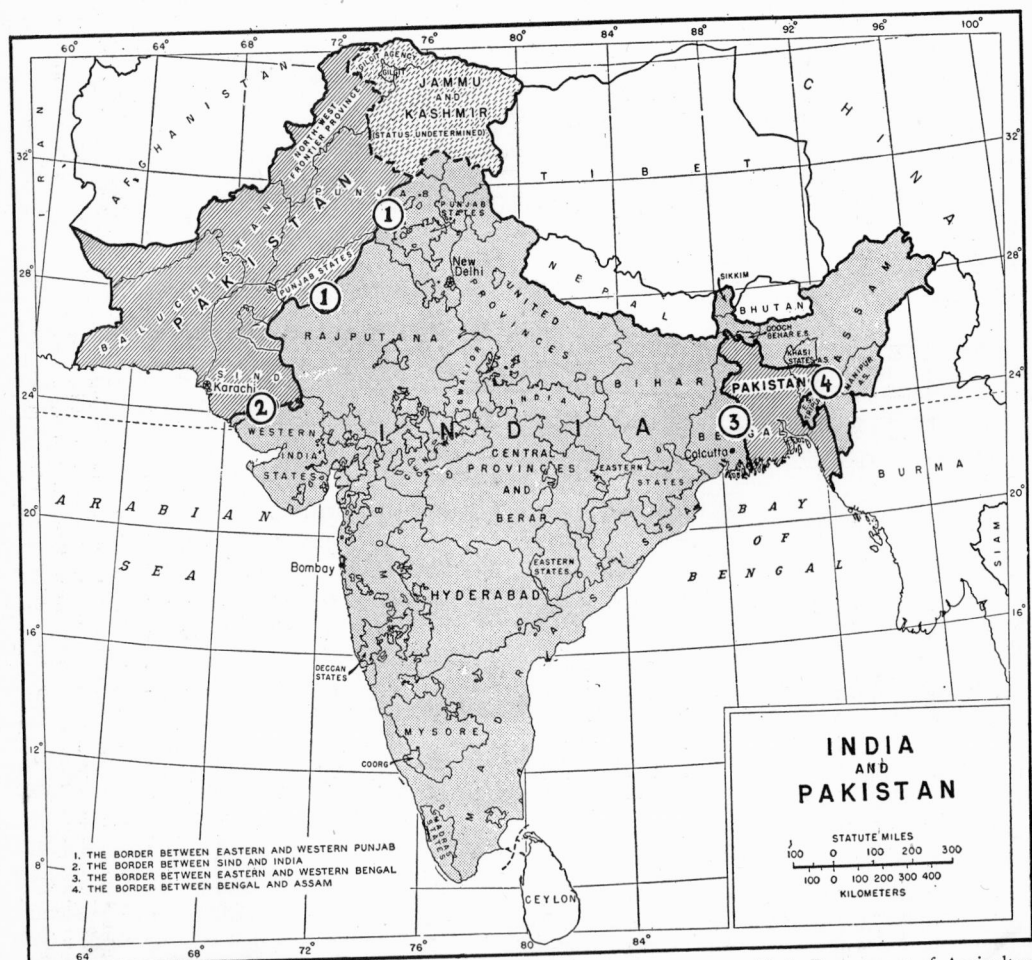

U. S. Department of Agriculture

FIGURE 39.   FLIGHTS AND TRANSFERS OF POPULATION: THE MAJOR AREAS IN INDIA AND PAKISTAN FROM
WHICH RELIGIOUS MINORITIES FLED AFTER THE PARTITION

TABLE 48

FLIGHTS AND TRANSFERS OF POPULATION: DISPLACED PERSONS RESETTLED WITH ASSISTANCE OF IRO, BY COUNTRY OF DESTINATION, FROM JULY 1947 TO DECEMBER 31, 1951

Last Residence or Citizenship, and Ethnic Group	Total	Country of Destination [a]															
		United States	Canada	Venezuela	Brazil	Paraguay	Chile	Argentina	United Kingdom	France	Belgium	Netherlands	Sweden	Israel	Australia	New Zealand	Other
Total	1,038,750	328,851	123,479	17,277	28,848	5,887	5,108	32,712	86,346	38,455	22,477	4,355	4,330	132,109	182,159	4,837	21,520
Last residence or citizenship																	
USSR, countries conquered by USSR and satellites	828,352	288,614	109,206	11,513	24,311	5,091	2,975	18,501	72,298	25,187	21,225	4,090	2,959	75,111	151,469	4,147	11,656
USSR	41,325	14,506	8,158	786	1,427	2,665	320	2,071	459	735	1,826	63	12	1,689	4,944	275	1,389
Ukraine	113,677	45,044	14,877	1,887	4,609	146	319	2,283	15,001	3,342	5,650	118	46	35	19,607	179	534
Byelorussia	2,517	1,135	152	47	336				29	56	30		2	44	670	12	4
Poland	357,635	110,566	46,961	2,814	7,770	1,443	516	6,563	35,780	11,882	10,378	2,969	563	54,904	60,308	847	3,431
Baltic states	163,476	77,454	21,296	1,749	1,350	71	216	1,444	15,271	1,538	1,872	264	1,737	1,238	35,796	976	1,205
Czechoslovakia	34,450	8,057	5,916	816	1,439	134	289	603	1,956	1,068	133	365	287	1,960	9,884	336	1,207
Hungary	62,871	16,718	7,479	1,999	3,146	166	574	3,067	3,013	3,655	450	188	155	7,191	13,320	280	1,470
Romania	23,010	4,249	2,536	257	1,365	353	245	639	501	1,558	60	19	52	7,260	2,190	918	808
Bulgaria	3,068	593	565	93	357		30	40	26	237		2	6	7	854	199	59
Stateless [b]	26,323	10,332	1,266	1,065	2,512	113	466	1,791	262	1,116	826	102	99	783	3,896	125	1,569
Other countries	126,524	35,073	12,185	5,216	4,099	214	1,935	13,510	10,342	2,581	1,092	101	1,024	5,996	26,566	652	5,938
Germany [e]	22,467	13,096	689	171	138	85	82	105	118	150	116	33	813	4,535	1,826	21	489
Austria	5,129	1,844	565	55	78	25	36	102	171	58	15	4	30	1,200	659	31	256
Spain	9,988	24	434	2,623	714	21	776	2,951	10	27				3	84	2	2,319
Yugoslavia [d]	82,090	17,213	9,828	1,997	2,581	68	867	10,105	9,817	2,085	849	57	168	83	23,350	504	2,518
Others [c]	6,850	2,896	669	370	588	15	174	247	226	261	112	7	13	175	647	94	356
Not reported [e]	83,874	5,164	2,088	548	438	582	198	701	3,706	10,687	160	164	347	51,002	4,124	38	3,927
Ethnic group																	
Jews	231,548	64,930	16,021	413	803	1,685	388	736	586	2,220	228	616	558	130,408	8,172	104	3,680
Others	807,202	263,921	107,458	16,864	28,045	4,202	4,720	31,976	85,760	36,235	22,249	3,739	3,772	1,701	173,987	4,733	27,840

Source: International Refugee Organization, *Final Statistical Report*, Geneva, 1952.

a. Countries in which more than 4,000 DP's have been resettled. The group of "other countries" includes Bolivia, British colonies, Colombia, Costa Rica, Cuba, Dominican Republic, Ecuador, Egypt, Ethiopia, Finland, French colonies, Germany, Guatemala, Hong Kong, Italy, Luxembourg, Mexico, Norway, Pakistan, Panama, Peru, the Philippines, Spain, Switzerland, Syria, Turkey, the Union of South Africa and other areas (not reported separately).

b. Includes Nansen status. This group consists mainly of refugees from the USSR.

c. Includes *Volksdeutsche*, i.e., persons of German nationality but not citizens of Germany.

d. Albania (1,104); Belgium (130); Greece (651); Turkey (362); Venezia Giulia (3,167); miscellaneous (1,436).

e. Includes "Undetermined."

103

Pakistan who reached the province of Assam was not ascertained.[54]

Of the flight and evacuation of Moslems from India, it is known that in the early, most violent phase of the movement 4.4 million Moslems from Eastern Punjab and Delhi entered Pakistan.

The refugees were temporarily kept in special camps and later distributed among the provinces of both dominions. In October 1948 a census of refugees was taken in India. On the basis of an incomplete enumeration, the non-Moslem population displaced from Western Pakistan was estimated at 5 million. Almost half the refugees were resettled near the India-Pakistan frontier, and the others were dispersed all over India.[55] Little is known about the resettlement of Moslems evacuated to Pakistan.

All in all, the number of people resettled in both dominions, not including those who perished in riots or on the way, is probably close to 10 million.

Palestine

Although not as great in volume as the migrations discussed in the preceding pages, immigration into Palestine and displacement of the Arab population of the Holy Land hold lasting political implications for the Near East.

The first Zionist settlements in Palestine were established shortly before the outbreak of World War I, when Palestine was a part of the Turkish province of Syria. In the Balfour Declaration of November 1917, the British government declared itself in favor of establishing a national home in Palestine for the Jewish people, without prejudice to the civil and religious rights of local non-Jewish communities.

From 1920 through 1924 some 47,000 Jewish immigrants were admitted into Palestine. In 1925 the number increased to more than 34,000, only to drop to a trickle in the following years when an economic crisis developed in the region. Immigration was resumed on a large scale in the 1930's, under the pressure of the rising wave of anti-Semitism in Europe. In 1935 more than 60,000 Jews were admitted. The following year the Holy Land became the scene of a bloody Arab uprising against the Jews and the British. The flow of immigrants slowed down, but acts of violence continued through 1938.

In 1939, the British government decided to limit Jewish immigration to 15,000 entrants a year. The number fell far below this limit during World War II, but when the war ended the Holy Land became the last haven of European Jews who had survived the ordeal. Jews in Palestine strongly opposed the attempt of the British administration to maintain the quota.[56]

The British mandate over Palestine was terminated in May 1948, and Palestine was divided between the Jews and the Arabs. The first step of the government of Israel was to abolish all restrictions on immigration. More than 200,000 Jewish immigrants entered Israel during its first year as an independent state. (See Table 49.)

The Jewish-Arab hostilities that marked the foundation of Israel have been followed by displacement of the native Arab population. In a report published by the United Nations Conciliation Commission for Palestine in December 1949, the number of "persons who have fled from Israel and are unable to return" was estimated at 726,000,[57] which amounts to 85 per cent of the former non-Jewish population within Israel's boundaries.

PROBLEMS OF INTERNATIONAL MIGRATION

In contrast to the terror that haunted the throngs of wartime refugees, peacetime migration is led by hope. The "pursuit of happiness" is the mainspring of free migration, international and internal alike. Even if migrants do not live to see all their dreams materialize, migration usually contributes to their welfare and that of their descendants. By bringing men closer to unused resources, intercontinental migration in the nineteenth century contributed enormously to the economic progress of the world and made it richer in material goods as well as in human freedom.

While there is far-reaching agreement on the final effect of international migration on the progress of mankind, the question of its immediate effect on the sending and receiving countries is more complicated.[58] For both sides, the impact of international migration may be considered from the standpoint of population policy, the labor market, and political and psychological implications.

54. **4**, August 1948, p. 201.
55. **4**, April 1950, pp. 449–50.
56. See **36**, *passim*.
57. **2**, p. 22.
58. **41**, pp. 378–88.

TABLE 49

JEWISH IMMIGRATION INTO PALESTINE, 1923–49

Year	Immigrants	Year	Immigrants	Year	Immigrants
1923	8,175	1932	9,553	1941	5,886
1924	13,892	1933	30,327	1942	3,733
1925	34,386	1934	42,359	1943	8,507
1926	13,855	1935	61,854	1944	14,464
1927	3,034	1936	29,727	1945	13,121
1928	2,178	1937	10,536	1946	17,760
1929	5,249	1938	12,868	1947	21,542
1930	4,944	1939	27,561	1948	119,005
1931	4,075	1940	8,398	1949	239,424
				1950	169,620 [a]

Sources: **36**, p. 46; **1**, 1951, p. 541.

a. Preliminary.

Effect of Migration on Population Growth

Population policy was of paramount importance to the New World in early colonial times and is no less important now to underpopulated countries, such as Australia and some South American republics, or countries threatened by depopulation, such as France. There is no doubt that immigration into a country tends to speed up the growth of its population.

Less clear is the effect of emigration on the growth of population in the sending country.[59] Indeed, it is questionable whether emigration has ever slowed down population growth in any country. By temporarily relieving the pressure of overpopulation as manifested in shortage of land for the growing rural population and chronic mass unemployment in urban communities, it may actually have increased the surplus of births over deaths in the homeland.

Effect on Labor Force

Through immigration, the receiving country obtains workers reared and trained at the expense of other nations. When the immigrants are skilled workers, technicians, scholars and artists, the gain is particularly great. It is enhanced by the selective process in migration. Those who decide to emigrate are seldom the most successful representatives of their profession, but they are likely to possess more than average will power, imagination, courage and flexibility — qualities particularly valuable in a new environment.

Additional labor force, however, is an advantage to the receiving country only if that country is short of labor, either because of rapid economic expansion or the slow growth (or decline) of its native population. For the same reason, emigration of workers is not necessarily an economic loss to the sending country. It is not an economic loss if the sending country thus frees itself of hands for which there is no work and of mouths for which there is not enough food.

Political and Psychological Implications

In the long run, international migration may prove to be even more advantageous to the sending country than to the receiving. Emigrants settled abroad become valuable assets to their native land: they send remittances to their relatives, promote exports from their homeland and give moral and political support abroad to their native country.

At the other end, the receiving country has to pay a price for its easy gains in labor force and population. As a rule, migration puts the newcomer in a situation requiring more difficult adjustments than those he would face in the motherland. Mass migration therefore tends to increase the proportion of unadjusted or maladjusted individuals in the receiving nation, to weaken its organic unity, and to contribute to a state of mind that may be described as "spiritual anarchy."[60] This danger can be checked by restrictive and selective immigration policies[61]

59. Cf. **46**, p. 46.

60. **41**, pp. 378–79.
61. Cf. pp. 77 ff. in this chapter.

and measures that promote the cultural assimilation of immigrants.

Cultural Assimilation of Immigrants

The cultural assimilation of immigrants is a long process.[62] It is generally controlled by the interplay of four factors: the immigrants themselves, the native inhabitants in the receiving country, and the governmental and administrative authorities in the native country on the one hand and in the receiving country on the other.

As a rule, cultural assimilation is facilitated by the dispersion of immigrants among the native population and is more difficult when they are concentrated in national self-governing communities. Obviously the process is facilitated when the native population welcomes the newcomers and is difficult when immigrants must contend with a spirit of exclusiveness and discrimination.

The policy of the motherland has often been to maintain psychological and cultural ties with emigrants by promoting national associations, holidays, conferences and so on. Sometimes this policy has gone further and has attempted political control over emigrants — for example, the principle of double citizenship of emigrants that was established by Germany before World War I and became the cornerstone of the policy of fascist and Nazi governments toward their nationals abroad.[63]

The new country's cultural structure and attitude toward foreigners is of decisive significance for the assimilation of immigrants. Maintenance of cultural and emotional ties with the old country fits assimilation as we understand it in the United States but is scorned in Australia and France. On the other hand, no receiving country can accept the principle of double citizenship and double allegiance.

In a country with rigid patterns of life, assimilation requires that immigrants become copies of the native population. This is a difficult requirement and is bound to provoke resistance on the part of those who, to be acceptable, must be remolded. In a country with a great variety of climate, types of economic life, languages, religions and customs, the newcomer need not conform exactly to any single pattern; he has practically unlimited choice, provided he accepts the fundamental political and social philosophy of the new community. Thus, relaxation of demands for external conformity increases the internal cohesion of newcomers with the native society.

Individual and Group Migration

In recent discussions of international migration, considerable attention has been given to the alternatives of individual and group emigration. Prospective emigrants who would be considered as desirable by the receiving country are often reluctant to settle abroad as individuals but would emigrate in a group of, say, a score of families if such a group were permitted to settle as a unit, at least at the beginning.[64] On the other hand, many immigration countries are opposed to group colonization as incompatible with complete assimilation of newcomers.

In the period of mass immigration into the United States, individual immigration was at the same time group resettlement; newcomers joined previous immigrants from their country and were absorbed by this local community before they became assimilated into the American nation as a whole.

OUTLOOK FOR INTERNATIONAL MIGRATION

After a quarter century with only a sluggish flow of voluntary international migration, the future outlook is not very clear. It is fairly certain that the era of uncontrolled mass migration from Europe has ended. On the receiving end, the free expanses open to colonization have shrunk; on the sending side, the reserves of people eager to settle abroad have been reduced by changes in demographic and economic conditions.

---

62. "The concept of assimilation does not mean exactly the same thing to all persons and in all countries. The conformity of immigrant behavior with that of native inhabitants does not mean total identity. An immigrant is considered as 'assimilated' if he has become part of the receiving community and resembles its inhabitants in certain essential points; if he accepts unreservedly the laws of the country in which he has settled, together with the rights and duties which that entails, and has severed all legal and political ties with his old country. Many people feel, however, that this is not enough. They would consider an immigrant as assimilated only if he speaks the language of his new country by preference and has adopted the customs and way of life of his new compatriots, so that his original outlook gives way to that of his new surroundings." (6, p. 6.)

63. 6, p. 10.

64. Many Dutch farmers would favor this type of colonization in France.

Settlement on the Land

Unused land that can be made arable now lies only on the fringes of arid regions, in tropical forests and along the border of forests in North Asia. (See Figure 40; cf. Figure 15, p. 38.) Most of this is marginal land where problems of climate, transportation, supply and outlet are still unsolved. The two important exceptions are in South America, where large areas are held back from full settlement by owners of huge estates, and in interior Asia, where land now held by pastoral peoples is capable of much more intensive agricultural settlement.[65]

Seldom, however, are large areas unexploited because no attempt has been made to settle them. More often than not, attempts have been made but have failed. With progress in means of transportation and communication, agricultural techniques and medicine, such attempts may be renewed with better chance for success. The limit of settlement and agriculture is steadily advancing, enlarging the shaded areas in Figure 40, but the advance is very slow and depends more on the action of governments and the progress of science and technology than on the individual efforts of pioneers.[66]

With a few exceptions, the establishment of emigrants as colonists on the lands of potential settlement could make little change in the distribution of the world population.[67] There are, however, limited opportunities for agricultural colonization in Canada, South America, the highlands of southeastern Africa and in Australia. There is also a possibility of partial recolonization in France. Estimates of the number of people who could be resettled in this way are highly speculative. They depend essentially on assumptions as to the capital available for investment in new colonies and the ability of prospective immigrants. In estimates announced from time to time by the countries ready to accept colonists, agricultural colonization is rarely separated from nonagricultural immigration.

Nonagricultural Immigration

Opportunities for nonagricultural settlement exist, in differing degrees, in underdeveloped areas as well as in comparatively sparsely populated and highly industrialized countries, such as the United States and Canada. Probably the most promising outlook for immigrants is in South American countries, eager to develop their natural resources by intensive industrialization. This is an opportunity for controlled and selective immigration, however, rather than free-for-all immigration like that in the nineteenth century.

Selective immigration is also a possibility for Australia, the Union of South Africa and, on a small scale, for France. Some of these countries have established long-range plans directed toward substantial increase of their population. Australia plans to double its population; some planners in Argentina envisage, or pretend to envisage, a population of 100 million; Brazil has decided to admit 2.3 million immigrants in the comparatively near future — 1.2 million from Italy, 500,000 from Portugal, 600,000 from Central Europe.[68]

All these plans, however, postulate definite selection of immigrants. Some countries have extended an invitation to persons in particular age groups on condition that they settle in prescribed areas and work in prescribed industries. Others declare themselves ready to accept single men and unmarried women, without families. Still others open their gates to persons with considerable amounts of money. In many instances, such requirements have been combined with reluctance to admit organized groups of immigrants, as, for example, twenty farmer families that would settle on land as a community.

Experience has shown that it is difficult to find enough prospective immigrants who meet all requirements of the receiving country. Those for whom the doors are open do not come, and for those who want to come, the doors are closed.

Potential Emigrants

Very little is known about the emigration potential of the overpopulated regions in Asia — Japan, China, India. Mass emigration from these areas toward the Western Hemisphere or Australia appears highly unlikely without a drastic change in the policy of immigration countries. Practically, the problem of emigration potential is a problem of Europe; more specifically, not a problem of displaced persons but one of the native populations of the Old Countries.

How many persons would emigrate from Eu-

---

65. **37**, pp. 19–20.
66. Cf. **24** and **20**.
67. **30**, p. 179.

68. **31**, p. 145.

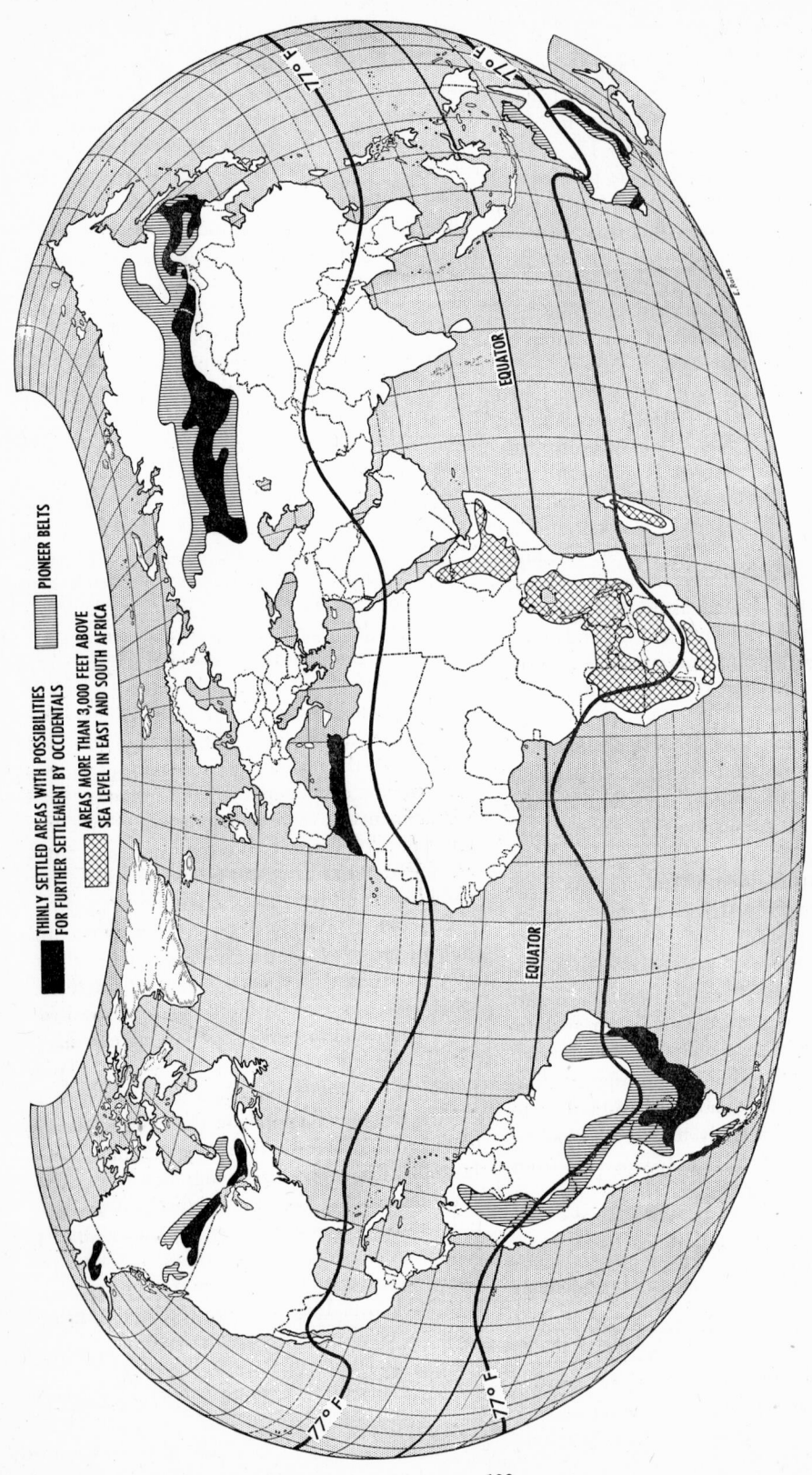

FIGURE 40. OUTLOOK FOR INTERNATIONAL MIGRATION: AREAS OF POTENTIAL SETTLEMENT

The most promising areas of possible new settlements are in Canada, South America, the highlands of East and South Africa, interior Asia and Australia. Any appreciable expansion of population in these areas, however, presumes considerable investment of capital, improvement of means of transportation, and, in some cases, changes in land ownership.

Excessive heat makes it difficult for people of the white races to establish settlements between the annual isotherms of 77° F. (Data adapted from 35.)

THINLY SETTLED AREAS WITH POSSIBILITIES FOR FURTHER SETTLEMENT BY OCCIDENTALS

PIONEER BELTS

AREAS MORE THAN 3,000 FEET ABOVE SEA LEVEL IN EAST AND SOUTH AFRICA

108

TABLE 50

Outlook for International Migration: Percentage of Various Population Groups in Europe in Favor of Emigration, According to Opinion Polls, 1948

Country and Group	Percentage	Country and Group	Percentage	Country and Group	Percentage
England		France		Italy [a]	
Total	42	Total	25	Total	29.1
Men	44	Age group		Occupational group	
Women	24	20–34 years	36	Employers	22.8
Age group		35–49	23	Farmers	23.0
21–29 years	58	50–64	19	Farm workers	38.8
30–49	47	65 years and over	13	Artisans	39.1
50–64	37	Sweden		Factory workers	34.5
65 years and over	15	Total	13	White-collar workers	29.0
Income class		Age group		Professional persons	22.0
Highest	37	20–29 years	20	Housewives	26.1
Middle	47	30–39	17	Norway	28.0
Lower	34	40–49	11	Denmark	24.0
Very poor	34	50–64	8		
Belgium	22.4	65 years and over	6		

Source: **28**, pp. 391–92.

a. Persons in favor of permanent emigration.

rope if they could find a country that would accept them?

In the spring of 1948, when Europe had just begun to win its uphill fight for reconstruction, the American Institute of Public Opinion concluded, on the basis of a number of opinion polls in eight countries of western Europe, that millions of persons in France, the Netherlands, England and other countries would want to pull up stakes and move out of their wrecked homes to find a more peaceful life in another country if restrictions against immigration were withdrawn. This conclusion seemed inescapable in the light of answers from a cross section of the population to the question: "If you were free to do so, would you like to go and settle in another country?"

It is questionable, however, whether all the persons who declared themselves in favor of emigration if they were "free to do so," thought exclusively of legal obstacles to migration. Some of them probably had in mind the various factors that usually limit an individual's freedom of choice: family obligations, property, acquired rights, social standing, possibility of economic improvement, uncertainty of the new environment, and so on. The polls reveal a deep feeling of uneasiness in Europe at the time of the canvass and show the relative strength of the desire for change among different groups of the population,

but they can hardly be accepted as indicative of the European emigration potential. (See Table 50.)

The problem of mass emigration is now vital and urgent in only two European countries on this side of the Iron Curtain, Germany and Italy. Neither nation is able to produce enough food for its growing population, and both face great difficulties in their efforts to obtain enough food from abroad in exchange for manufactured goods.

Early in 1950 the Italian government presented an estimate to the International Labor Office that 1.5 million persons were available for immediate permanent emigration in family groups. This figure included workers and their dependents and would have been considerably higher if an opportunity to emigrate had been given to persons who were underemployed.[69]

The emigration potential of Germany cannot be estimated without definite assumptions about unpredictable political factors.

In other European countries the question of mass emigration is overshadowed, perhaps only temporarily, by the shortage of labor. It seems fairly probable, however, that in the not too remote future emigration will again become a

69. **5.**

question in the United Kingdom, the Netherlands and Norway. If and when these countries face this problem, none will send its emigrants indiscriminately to any country willing to accept them. If emigration from the United Kingdom develops, it will probably be directed to the British dominions and will represent a redistribution of population within the Commonwealth.[70] Similarly, the Netherlands and Norway will try to direct their emigrants to the countries that offer them the best opportunities, preferably to areas ready to accept group immigration. The era of uncontrolled emigration, like that of unrestricted immigration, has ended.[71]

SUMMARY

The period from 1870 to 1920 can be described as the Great Resettlement. Spontaneous and individualistic in character, the international and intercontinental migration of that period brought about a new distribution of mankind — especially of European stock — over our planet. It was a major factor in molding the world of today.

The past fifteen years have been characterized by the flight of millions from their wrecked homes, the mass exodus of people haunted by fear, the mass shipment of human beings to destruction. Measured by the number of persons affected, these recent shifts of population have been of the magnitude of the economic migration of the whole preceding century.

Since the end of World War II both types of migrations have come to a standstill. The consolidation of peace will probably bring a revival of economically motivated migration, but on a smaller scale than in the nineteenth century. A new war would probably be accompanied by ever greater mass flights of people from threatened or wrecked cities. In brief, the outlook for migration depends on the outlook for peace and war.

---

70. **29**, p. 392.
71. Cf. **46**, pp. 43–46.

Note to IMMIGRATION POLICY *on pages 77–83*

Admission of immigrants to the United States is now regulated by Public Law 414, known as the McCarran Act, which was passed by Congress in June 1952 over the veto of the President. The law retained the general scale of annual immigration quotas shown in Table 38, with only minor adjustments. The total is now 154,-657. Quotas are also allocated to residents of colonial areas and Asiatic nations. The new law tightens "selective" regulations by establishing the principle of "preference" within the quota allocated to each area and by imposing restrictions based on political affiliations and activities of the applicant.

CHAPTER 4

CITIES

THE ORIGIN OF THE CITY as a cluster of dwellings with some form of communal life goes back to the Paleolithic age, before men knew anything about metals or had learned to polish the stones they used as tools. Probably the first such settlements were cave and lake dwellings and fortified villages. Some of these villages were only temporary refuges for people of the surrounding region; others included within their walls many houses, with gardens and barns for cattle.[1]

Indeed, cities are almost as old as sedentary agriculture.[2] The road is long from the cluster of huts to the modern metropolis, but our cities still bear the imprint of the past. As G. T. Renner has put it:

It took man half a million years to learn to build a hut as a protection against the elements. It took him another hundred thousand years to get his huts clustered into villages, and finally into cities. Today his cities are still located where primitive trails crossed a river, where footpaths converged upon a mountain pass, or where small fishing boats put in from the sea. The street patterns of many of our proudest cities are inherited from the cowpaths, boat landings, and stage-coach tracks of long ago.[3]

CITIES OF THE PAST

Several types of cities developed in the ancient world, different in origin, size and function.

Oriental Cities

In the Orient a city was the administrative, political and religious center of a vast agricultural territory, the capital of the strictly centralized empire, "the city of a god and of a king."[4] Palaces and temples, surrounded by the homes of dignitaries of the state and the church, formed the nucleus of such a city. Around them clustered the houses and huts of lower officials, merchants, artisans and slaves. Some of these cities were tremendous and had a million or more inhabitants.

Greek Cities

In contrast to the oriental capitals, a city in ancient Greece was essentially a community of citizens. Sometimes its power extended over the rural district around its walls and the city merged with the nearest villages; but its administrative functions were restricted to a comparatively small area and its population seldom exceeded a few thousand. Some Greek cities, such as Corinth, were predominantly commercial; others like Sparta, were agricultural; and a few, among them Athens, combined both features.

Aristotle described the "modern fashion" of a regular layout of streets in a city and conceded that such a layout was "more agreeable and generally more convenient." He pointed out, however, the advantages of the antiquated mode of city building "which made it difficult for strangers to get out of a town and for assailants to find their way in." Both plans of building should be adopted, in his opinion: "The whole town should not be laid out in straight lines, but only certain quarters and regions; thus security and beauty will be combined."[5]

After Alexander's conquests in Asia, Greece developed a new type of city, a combination of an oriental capital and a Greek urban community. These cities were closest to the modern concept of a metropolis as a center of cultural life. Some were built according to an elaborate plan, with broad, straight streets, canals and an excellent water supply. Alexandria, the most famous, had an academy of science, a public library, an art

---

1. **31**, p. 21.
2. The Bible ascribes the building of the first city to Cain, who was "a tiller of the ground," in contrast to his brother, Abel, "a keeper of sheep" (Gen. 4: 2).
3. **29**, p. 10.
4. **31**, p. 25.

5. According to Aristotle, the art of planning cities was invented by the builder of the harbor of Piraeus, Hippodamus, the son of Euryphon, from Miletus. He described this first city planner as "a strange man, whose fondness for distinction led him into a general eccentricity of life . . . for he would wear flowing hair and expensive ornaments; but these were worn on a cheap but warm garment, both in winter and summer." (**18**, Book II, Chap. 8; Book VII, Chap. 11.)

museum, a zoological garden and a highly developed municipal organization.[6]

Rome

Urban communities of the Roman Empire developed under a strong Greek influence. Before Rome became the capital of the civilized world, it was the head of the Italian league of cities. Unlike Alexandria, it grew chaotically and, in the days of its glory, became the victim of its own size. Large tracts of land around the center of the city fell into the hands of real estate speculators; the growing population was crowded into tenements; the narrow streets became intolerably congested. A municipal law, enacted under Julius Caesar, prohibited vehicular traffic within the limits of Rome. An exception was made only for carts bringing food, which could be driven in the city at night; in the daytime, only pedestrians could use the streets.

In the first century of the Christian era, Rome changed greatly. Its center was rebuilt under the Emperor Augustus, who, according to the historian Suetonius, "boasted, not without reason, that he had found Rome built of brick and left it in marble." Broad thoroughfares were cut through the maze of tenements, splendid public buildings were erected, among them huge public baths with various recreation facilities, and the city made secure against inundations and fires— "as far as human foresight could effect this," remarks the historian.[7]

Other Large Cities of Antiquity

Other large cities of the ancient world included Nineveh in Assyria; Babylon, Memphis and Thebes in Egypt; Peking, Canton and Hankow in China; Calcutta and Bombay in India. In relation to the world population at that time, these ancient cities were larger than New York or London today. Each of them may have had a million or more inhabitants in its heyday.

Medieval Cities

The cities in western Europe in the first millennium of the Christian era developed largely under the influence of Rome. Many were built around the encampments of Roman legions, others started as administrative centers or trading posts. Later, cities grew up around churches and monasteries.

Most of the urban communities of medieval Europe were relatively small. In contrast to the capitals of the ancient Orient, which dominated great agricultural regions and ruled over huge empires, they were local centers, serving and controlling a limited area. After the disintegration of the Roman Empire, they grew slowly or not at all. A place with 10,000 inhabitants was considered large in the Middle Ages. Fourteenth-century London, with a population of 35,200, was the greatest city in England and one of the greatest in Europe. York, Bristol and Frankfurt had 10,000 to 12,000 inhabitants, Nürnberg and Strasbourg, about 20,000.

The walls surrounding medieval cities may have checked the growth of some of them. An overcrowded city, however, could readily rebuild its walls to include more land.[8] Some cities — for example, Strasbourg — thus expanded, but most of them did not need additional space. The main reason for this slow growth was that they were centers of a limited territory with a stationary population.

In the late Middle Ages and in the sixteenth century, India, China and Mexico had larger cities than England, Spain, Italy and France. Rome and Venice seemed small and provincial to Marco Polo after he had seen the huge cities of China. Cortez and his Spaniards were amazed at the size of Mexico City, with its 60,000 houses, huge market places and long rows of public edifices.[9]

Despite their modest size, the cities of medieval Europe played a decisive role in preserving and developing Western civilization. By the end of the Middle Ages, some had developed into communities similar to the self-sufficient city-states of ancient Greece, as local commercial, cultural and religious centers. Later some rose in importance and became the centers of political and economic strength of larger areas.

Cities in Modern Times

Rebirth of large cities in Europe at the end of the Middle Ages was a consequence of political centralization. When large centralized kingdoms began to emerge out of the maze of medieval princedoms, the leading city of each took on

---

6. **31**, p. 40.
7. **33**, p. 70.

8. **32**, p. 68.
9. **28**, pp. 316–17.

functions similar to those of the ancient oriental capitals. The new capitals grew up around royal palaces, courts and military barracks. London, which was the king's residence and the chief port of Europe, took particular pride in being also the largest city in the Christian world, although some French writers claimed this honor for Paris. William Petty gave the following estimates of the population of the largest European cities at the end of the seventeenth century: [10]

London	696,000	Rome	125,000
Paris	488,000	Dublin	69,000
Amsterdam	187,000	Rouen	66,000
Venice	134,000	Bristol	48,000

The steady growth of London in the seventeenth century was so striking that Petty tried to express the long-range trend mathematically and to project it into the future. He assumed that the population of London would double every 40 years and that the total population of England would double in 360 years. These assumptions led him to the conclusion that by 1842 London would have 10.7 million inhabitants and England a little more than 10.9 million. Since this prospect seemed improbable, he decided that London would cease to grow by the end of the eighteenth century, at slightly more than 5 million, leaving enough people in rural areas "to perform the tillage, pasturage, and other rural work necessary to be done without the said city." [11]

Although Petty's prediction that London would reach the peak of growth in 1800 proved false, he was right in anticipating a progressive concentration of the English population in the capital. England, like the rest of Europe was entering an era of rapid urbanization. Several interrelated factors were responsible for this trend: increasing political centralization; growing sea trade; accelerated growth of population; and the Industrial Revolution, which permitted cities to absorb the surplus population of rural areas.

Urbanization in Our World

In the past century and a half, Western civilization has become increasingly a civilization of large cities, and this development has had far-reaching effects on living conditions in both cities and rural areas in industrialized nations. Cities rapidly changed in appearance and, to some extent, in function. Most of the large cities of Europe and America have been rebuilt since the middle of the nineteenth century — some, like Paris under Napoleon III and the famous Major Haussmann, according to a general plan; others piecemeal, like London, Berlin and New York. But the progress of urbanism lagged behind the growth of cities and the rising demand for better sanitary conditions, better houses, transportation facilities, free spaces for recreation, and so on. Modern cities are healthier and more comfortable places to live in than the towns and cities of the eighteenth and nineteenth centuries. But times also have changed, and standards with them.

TYPES OF CITIES

Urban communities in a modern industrially developed nation form an intricate pattern that includes places of different size with different functions and relationships to one another.

Functional Classification

Many activities performed in a city serve merely the population of the city itself. Other pursuits serve people of surrounding rural areas, other cities, the whole nation and occasionally foreign countries, and can be described as services by which the city earns its livelihood.[12] By the nature of the service which the city supplies to other communities, three functional types can be distinguished: cities as central places; cities as transport centers; and specialized-function cities. The three types are not mutually exclusive.

As *central places,* cities — large and small — serve as markets, shopping and amusement centers and provide professional, religious and other services to the surrounding ("tributary") area. This type of city is particularly widespread in nonindustrial regions. In the United States, it is best represented by farmers' towns in the Middle West, Southwest and West.

As *transport centers,* cities provide break-of-bulk and allied transportation services. Such cities usually emerge at points where the form of transportation changes, such as a transfer from water to rail, transshipment from small to large

---

10. **27**, p. 124. Petty's estimates were based mainly on the records of burials in each city, but also partly on such data as the number of houses and families. Paris, for example, enumerated 23,223 houses, 32 palaces and 38 colleges, with a total of 24,000 street doors and 81,280 households.

11. **27**, p. 35.

12. **24**, p. 7.

boats and vice versa, and so on. Typical services performed by such cities are repackaging, storing, sorting and often processing the raw materials that pass through them.

Specialized-function cities depend on local resources. They include mining centers, industrial centers, national capitals, important military centers, resorts and the like.[13]

Towns, Cities and Supercities

Classification of cities by size applies to urban centers of all three types or any combination of these types, and rests essentially on the number of inhabitants in the urban community. It stresses, however, certain characteristic features of urban agglomerations which are usually, although not always, associated with size. From this viewpoint, three types of urban places may be distinguished that, for lack of better, universally accepted terms, may be described as towns, cities and supercities.

Towns may be defined as urban agglomerations of purely local significance: farm towns serving a comparatively small rural area; factory and mining towns; and residential ("dormitory") towns. Functionally, they differ widely from each other.

Cities differ from towns in size and usually also in economic function. Whether they earn their livelihood as market and shopping centers, transportation centers or by specialized services, they are often centers of economic power, the seat of banks, industrial corporations, wholesale trade, the insurance business. As such, they exercise economic control over a large territory, including a network of towns.

A *supercity* emerges from the throng of cities as a further step in the concentration of economic power, often combined with concentration of political power. In Europe and South America most supercities are political centers. In the United States the rise of the largest urban centers has depended mainly on economic conditions, while the sites of national and state capitals have been determined by political and geographic considerations. Few state capitals, for example, have become so important in national economic affairs that they can be called supercities.

Metropolitan Areas

As a supercity grows, outlying villages and towns become its suburbs and nearby cities, its satellites. Thus a metropolitan area develops, made up of several cities, towns and villages, all attached to a central urban nucleus. Such, for example, are the areas around London, Paris, Berlin, New York, Philadelphia, Chicago and Los Angeles.

Geographical concentration of population and of industrial and commercial enterprises characterizes a metropolitan area. Such an area, however, is seldom homogeneous in density of population, the occupation of its inhabitants, or the type of buildings. It may include some rural areas completely surrounded by urban communities. It is, therefore, a matter of judgment — and sometimes of semantics — how to draw the boundary line between a metropolitan area and the surrounding independent urban or rural communities.

In the United States the development of metropolitan areas as economic units in the 1920's was related to the growth of commercial and financial enterprises and corporations rather than the growth of manufacturing.[14]

MEASURING URBANIZATION

The simplest way to measure the degree of urbanization in a country or region, or in the same country at different times, is by the relative proportion of the population in urban and in rural areas. The terms "urban" and "rural," however, mean different things in different countries and at different times.[15]

In most countries, the distinction between the two types of areas is based on the number of inhabitants in an administrative unit. Unfortunately, however, despite the recommendations of the International Statistical Institute,[16] there is no international agreement as to the minimum number of inhabitants a community must have to be called "urban." To cite the extremes, urban communities in Japan correspond roughly to cities of 30,000 or more inhabitants, while Iceland considers all places with more than 300 inhabitants as towns.[17] In France, Germany and Argentina a town is supposed to have at least 2,000 inhabitants; in the United States it must have 2,500 inhabitants and be incorporated.[18] In many coun-

---

13. **24**, pp. 8–12.

14. **23**, p. 132.
15. Cf. **8**.
16. **2**, p. 3.
17. **2**, pp. 216–17.
18. This census definition is not very satisfactory. An incorporated community may include areas with farm population; on the other hand, some suburban communi-

tries the distinction between urban and rural communities is based on the type of local government or on administrative decision.[19]

Statistics of urban and rural population become particularly confusing when a country changes its definitions of rural and urban.[20] It may be argued, however, that when that distinction is in terms of the number of inhabitants, the number used as the dividing line should change as a country grows and should not be the same for such countries as the United Kingdom and Arabia, or for the United States in 1790 and today.

Still another complication in classifying communities is that the count of inhabitants of a place is usually based on the residence of each individual, that is, the place where he sleeps, rather than the place where he works.[21] The result is to underrate cities that employ many workers who live beyond the city line. A striking example is the central business district of London (the "City"), which had a population of 14,000 by night and 420,000 by day in the early 1920's; comparable figures for the City of Westminster, another central district in London, were 42,000 and 374,000. Manhattan is supposed to have 2 million more persons during the day than at night, and the situation in Boston and the District of Columbia is similar.[22] For all these cities, census enumerators list only residents. Estimates of the daytime population are derived mainly from traffic statistics.

Serious reservations must likewise be made when urbanization in different countries or in the same nation at different times is measured in terms of the distribution of population among communities of different size — for example, those with less than 10,000 inhabitants, with 10,000 to 20,000 inhabitants, 20,000 to 50,000 inhabitants, and so on. Statistics of this type are affected by variations in administrative customs, which determine whether a densely but unevenly populated area is recorded as one large city or a dozen small towns. However, distribution of population by size of community has at least the advantage of singling out the large cities, say those with more than 100,000 or more than 500,000 inhabitants.

The development of large cities is sometimes described as *citification* as distinct from *urbanization,* which applies to the development of urban communities of any size. A similar distinction may be made between the growth of *cities* and *supercities,* two developments that do not necessarily keep pace with each other.

Proportion of Urban Population

The ratio of "urban" population to total population varies widely from country to country, ranging from less than 13 per cent in India and Korea to nearly 80 per cent in the United Kingdom. In the United States this ratio is higher than in other American countries, but lower than in some industrialized countries of Europe. (See Table 51.)

If the dividing line between urban and rural communities in all countries were like that in the United States, the proportion of the Belgian population reported as urban would probably be raised to more than 65 per cent; of the Swiss, to perhaps 40 per cent; of the Japanese, to 60 or 65 per cent. On the other hand, a lower urban proportion would be reported for Canada, the United Kingdom and most other countries that define urban communities in terms of the type of government (municipality) without reference to the number of inhabitants.

Urbanization and Industrialization

There is a clear, though not perfect, correlation between urbanization and industrialization. In general terms, the limit of possible urbanization is set by the productivity of agriculture or the ability of the country to obtain food from abroad, either through exchange of goods or by political or military force. The actual extent of urbanization, however, depends also on the political organization of the nation, often on the extent to which

---

ties around New York, Chicago, Washington and other metropolitan centers, although typically "urban" in character, have found it advantageous not to incorporate. The population in such a place is classified as "rural" by censuses, though it may run to scores of thousands. In general, the distinction between "incorporated" and "unincorporated" localities tends to overstate the relative proportion of the rural population of the United States.

19. The Statistical Office of the United Nations has tried to classify the concepts of "urban" and "rural" population used in the censuses of 51 countries. It found that most countries based the classification on the type of local government, the number of inhabitants, or a combination of both features. In nine countries the classification refers to agglomerations or clusters of population, independently of administrative divisions. (2, pp. 6–10.)

20. In the Netherlands, 93.4 per cent of population was classified as "urban" in 1930 and only 54.4 per cent in 1946. In the earlier year the census classified as "urban" all places with 2,000 or more inhabitants; in 1946, only those with a population of 20,000 or more.

21. 22, pp. 456–60.

22. 22, p. 459.

TABLE 51

URBANIZATION: PERCENTAGE OF POPULATION IN URBAN AREAS IN SELECTED COUNTRIES, AROUND 1945

Country and Year	Definition of Urban Area	Percentage of Population in Urban Areas
United States, 1940	Incorporated places of 2,500 or more inhabitants	56.5
Canada, 1941	Incorporated places of all sizes	54.3
Mexico, 1940	Populated centers of 2,500 or more inhabitants	35.1
Cuba, 1943	Populated centers of all sizes	54.6
Brazil, 1940	The principal towns of "districts" and their suburbs	31.2
Argentina, 1947	Places of 2,000 or more inhabitants	61.4
United Kingdom, 1931	Urban areas [a]	79.2
France, 1946	Communities with 2,000 or more inhabitants in the chief town	53.2
Belgium, 1930	Communities of 5,000 or more inhabitants	60.5
Netherlands, 1946	Municipalities of 20,000 or more inhabitants	54.1
Sweden, 1945	Urban areas [a]	42.3
Norway, 1946	Cities or towns	28.1
Germany, 1946	Towns and communities of 2,000 or more inhabitants	
American Zone		54.4
British Zone		78.4
French Zone		50.9
Poland, 1946	Municipalities [a]	31.4
Switzerland, 1941	Communities of more than 10,000 inhabitants	32.9
Hungary, 1941	Municipalities [a]	36.2
Portugal, 1940	Places of 2,000 or more inhabitants	31.1
Italy, 1936	Communities with less than 50 per cent of the active population engaged in agriculture	44.6
Romania, 1948	Municipalities [a]	23.4
Korea, 1944	12 incorporated cities	7.5
Japan, 1948	Municipalities of 30,000 or more inhabitants	50.9
India, 1941	Municipalities of 5,000 or more inhabitants	12.8
Egypt, 1937	Chief towns of provinces and districts	25.1
Union of South Africa, 1946	Urban communities [a]	36.4
Australia, 1947	Urban communities [a]	68.9
New Zealand, 1945	Towns of 1,000 or more inhabitants	60.5

Source: **1**, pp. 213–19.

a. No other definition given.

the rural population is exploited by the ruling classes living in towns. The old Mayan Empire, for example, was highly urbanized because a farmer could raise the amount of corn allowed for his family's consumption in 48 to 76 working days, leaving the ruling classes with sufficient corn and labor force to build and maintain large cities, palaces and temples.[23] At a given level of

23. In the tenth century of the Christian era the Mayas had at least four and perhaps six cities with a population of 200,000 or more, seventeen to nineteen cities with 50,000 to 60,000 inhabitants, and perhaps three score minor towns. All in all, 30 to 40 per cent of the population of the Mayan Empire lived in cities surrounded by suburban farms. (**25**, pp. 155, 174–75, 312–18.)

efficiency in agriculture, the higher the level of consumption among farm families, the smaller the surplus of farm products available for the cities. On the other hand, in some countries — for example, Italy, Hungary and the Netherlands — many farmers and farm laborers live in towns, while in others, artisans, small merchants and large landowners are dispersed in rural areas.

Thus industrialization and urbanization are very closely correlated in nations at the extremes of the distribution, such as India and China, at the one end, and Great Britain, Western Germany and Belgium, at the other, but are less clearly correlated in other parts of such a listing. There is no apparent correlation between ur-

TABLE 52

URBANIZATION: DISTRIBUTION OF POPULATION BY SIZE OF COMMUNITY IN SELECTED COUNTRIES, 1930–48

	Percentage of Total Population in Places with Population of:				
Country and Year	Less than 10,000	10,000 to 20,000	20,000 to 50,000	50,000 to 100,000	100,000 or More
United States, 1940	52.4	7.6	5.6	5.6	28.8
Canada, 1941	61.7	4.3	6.8	4.2	23.0
Mexico, 1940	73.7	3.9	8.8	3.4	10.2
Brazil, 1940	5.0	20.7	42.9	15.5	15.9
Chile, 1940	58.7	4.7	9.3	4.0	23.3
Argentina, 1947	48.1	4.3	4.8	3.4	39.4
England and Wales, 1931	25.6	8.4	12.1	8.7	45.2
France, 1946	62.0	6.6	9.7	5.4	16.3
Belgium, 1930	54.1	11.3	10.6	1.4	22.6
Netherlands, 1946	29.7	16.3	13.2	10.5	30.3
Denmark, 1945	58.2	6.1	9.0	2.0	32.7
Sweden, 1945	57.8	6.9	8.4	6.4	20.5
Finland, 1947	52.8	25.1	7.9	4.9	9.3
Germany, 1946					
American Zone	69.7	4.6	6.6	3.8	15.3
British Zone	42.5	9.4	10.0	7.4	30.7
French Zone	75.1	6.4	8.4	8.0	2.1
Switzerland, 1941	67.0	5.1	3.9	6.3	17.7
Hungary, 1941	54.3	11.2	12.4	6.7	15.4
Portugal, 1940	84.3	8.2	4.9	2.6	0.0
Spain, 1940	51.5	12.6	11.4	5.3	19.2
Italy, 1936	50.4	14.1	12.4	7.1	16.0
Yugoslavia, 1948	83.1	4.6	4.1	1.9	6.3
Romania, 1948	79.0	3.9	3.8	5.3	8.0
Turkey, 1945	81.8	4.2	4.6	2.1	7.3
India, 1941	89.2	2.6	2.5	1.6	4.1
Egypt, 1937	76.8	10.7	5.9	3.3	13.3
Union of South Africa, 1946	70.4	2.1	2.2	5.6	19.7
Australia, 1933	44.3	2.9	4.4	0.9	47.5

Source: **1**, 1948, pp. 220–30.

banization and average national density of population. India, for example, is more densely populated than the United States and many western European countries but has relatively few people in urban communities.

Distribution of Population by Size of Community

The proportion of population in places with less than 10,000 inhabitants ranges from less than 30 per cent in the Netherlands and England to more than 70 per cent in Mexico, Portugal, Romania and Yugoslavia, India and Turkey, Egypt and the Union of South Africa.[24] Coun-

24. Brazil, using a different definition of "place," records only 5 per cent of population in "places" with less than 10,000 inhabitants.

tries with widely differing economic structure may have about the same proportion of inhabitants in small communities. The United States, Italy, Spain, Hungary, Finland and Belgium, for example, are all in the range of 50 to 55 per cent. (See Table 52.)

Cities of 100,000 or more account for only 4.1 per cent of India's population but, at the other extreme, for 47.5 per cent of the people in Australia. The proportion is close to 30 per cent in the United States (28.8 per cent) and higher in England and Wales (45.2 per cent), Argentina (39.4 per cent), the Netherlands (30.3 per cent) and Denmark (32.7 per cent).

Using the proportion of population in large cities as a yardstick of citification, the countries of

TABLE 53

CITIES: POPULATION IN THE COUNTRIES WITH SPECIFIED PROPORTION OF POPULATION IN
LARGE CITIES, BY CONTINENT, 1950

(*Millions*)

		Population in Countries with Per Cent of Population in Large Cities		
Continent	*Total Population*	*20 Per Cent and More*	*10 to 20 Per Cent*	*Less than 10 Per Cent*
World total	2,400	467	476	1,457
America	328	205	70	53
Europe, excluding the USSR	396	158	191	47
USSR	193	. . .	193	. . .
Asia, excluding the USSR	1,272	83	. . .	1,189
Africa	198	12	20	166
Oceania	13	9	2	2

Sources: Derived from Table 52 and **1**, 1951, pp. 94–103.

TABLE 54

CITIES WITH 100,000 OR MORE INHABITANTS, BY CONTINENT, 1800 AND AROUND 1930

	1800			1930		
Continent	*Number of Cities*	*Population, in Millions*	*Percentage of Total Population*	*Number of Cities*	*Population, in Millions*	*Percentage of Total Population*
World total	36	11.5	1.3	678	243	11
America	1	0.1	0.5	162	60	22
Europe, excluding the USSR	18	4.5	3.0	248	85	29
USSR (Russia)	2	0.5	1.3	56	20	19
Asia, excluding the USSR	14	6.1	1.0	193	70	6
Africa	1	0.3	0.3	17	6	4
Oceania	—	—	—	2	2	18

Source: **4**, Vol. XXI, pp. 327–28; cf. Table 55. The data for 1940 and 1950 are incomplete.

the world can be roughly classified into three groups in which that proportion represents, respectively, 20 per cent or more of total population, 10 to 20 per cent, and less than 10 per cent. The first group includes the United States, Canada and Argentina in the Western Hemisphere; the United Kingdom, Sweden, Germany, Belgium, the Netherlands, Denmark and Austria in Europe; Japan and Australia. The Union of South Africa is very near the level of this group. The second group comprises Mexico, Cuba, Brazil and Chile; Ireland, France, Norway, Poland, Czechoslovakia, Switzerland, Hungary, Spain, Italy and Greece; Egypt, the USSR and New Zealand. The third group, with less than 10 per cent of the population in large cities, covers the rest of Middle and South America, Finland,

Portugal, Yugoslavia, Romania, Bulgaria and the largest part of Africa and Asia.

All in all, more than three fifths of mankind live in the countries where less than 10 per cent of the inhabitants are in large cities, and two fifths are almost evenly divided between the moderately and highly citified nations. (See Table 53.) The area of the first group of countries stretches continuously through the southern part of the Old World, from the Atlantic coast of Africa to the Pacific coast of Asia, including all the islands of Indonesia but not Japan. In the Western Hemisphere it includes Central America and the Caribbean. (See Figure 41.)

THE WORLD'S LARGE CITIES

In 1800 the world had thirty-six cities with more than 100,000 inhabitants. (See Table 54.)

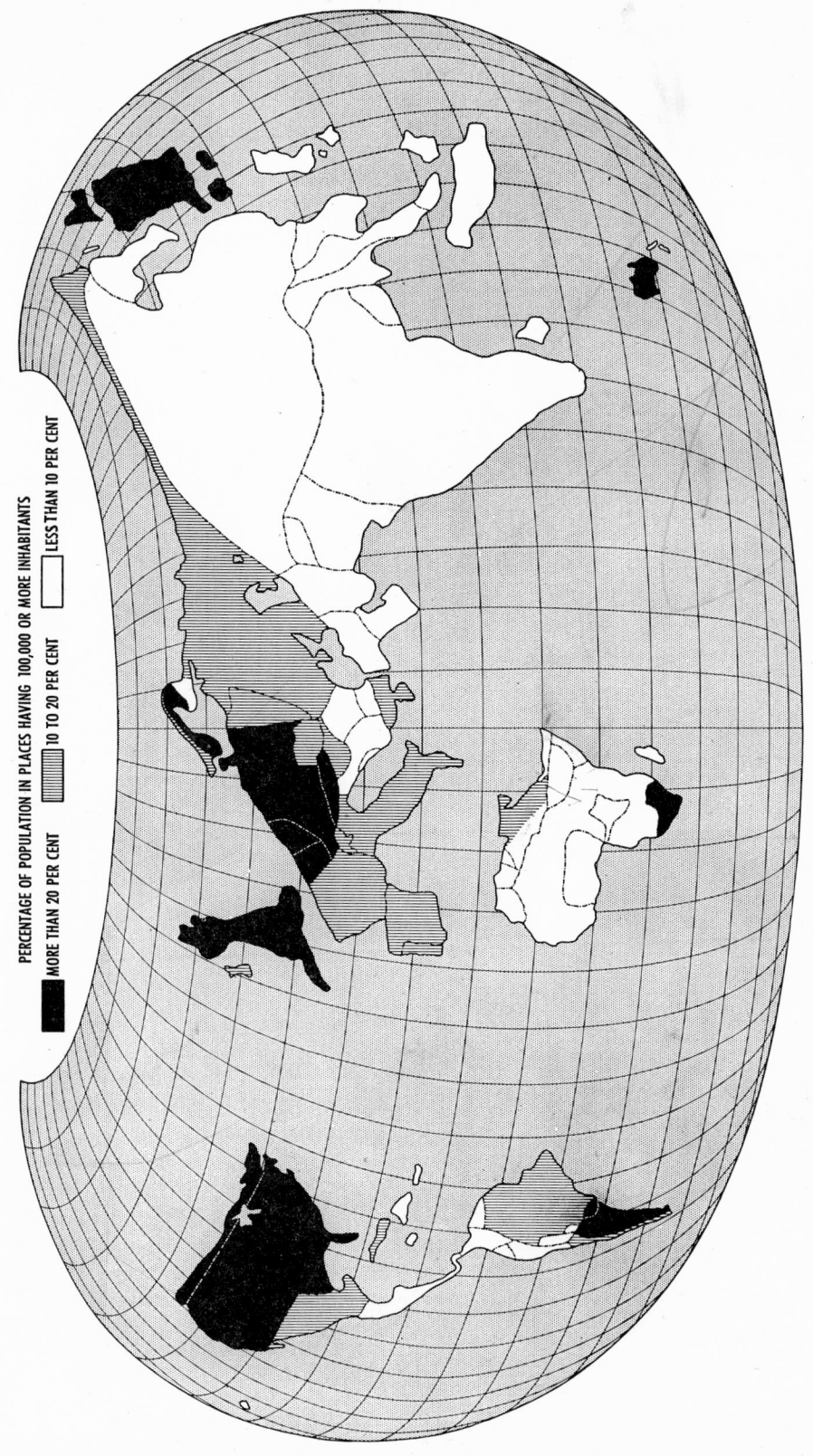

PERCENTAGE OF POPULATION IN PLACES HAVING 100,000 OR MORE INHABITANTS

MORE THAN 20 PER CENT

10 TO 20 PER CENT

LESS THAN 10 PER CENT

FIGURE 41. CITIES IN THE WORLD: COUNTRIES WITH SPECIFIED PROPORTION OF POPULATION IN LARGE CITIES, 1950

This map shows continents and countries on the scale of their 1950 population.
The highly citified regions of the world include the United States and Canada, Argentina and Uruguay, almost all western and central Europe (except Ireland, France and Switzerland), Japan and Australia. Regions with a low degree of citification comprise all continental Asia, Indonesia, almost all Africa, a part of the Balkans and the central part of the Americas, from the southern border of Mexico to Brazil. (Cf. Table 53.)

TABLE 55

THE LARGEST CITIES IN THE WORLD, 1800–1940, AND AROUND 1950

(Population, in Thousands)

Country and City [a]	1800	1850	1880	1900	1910	1920	1930	1940	Most Recent Census [b]
America									
United States									
New York	79	696	1,912	3,437	4,769	5,620	6,930	7,455	7,835
Chicago	—	30	503	1,699	2,185	2,702	3,376	3,397	3,606
Philadelphia	41	121	847	1,294	1,549	1,824	1,951	1,931	2,065
Detroit	—	21	116	286	466	994	1,569	1,623	1,839
Los Angeles	—	2	11	102	319	577	1,238	1,504	1,958
St. Louis	—	78	351	575	687	773	822	816	853
Cleveland	—	17	160	382	561	797	900	878	906
Baltimore	27	169	332	509	558	734	805	859	940
Boston	25	137	363	561	671	748	781	771	791
Pittsburgh	2	68	235	452	534	588	670	672	674
Washington, D. C.	3	40	178	279	331	438	487	663	802
San Francisco	—	35	234	343	417	507	634	635	761
Milwaukee	—	20	116	285	374	457	578	587	633
Buffalo	—	42	155	352	424	507	573	576	577
Other American countries									
Montreal (Canada)	...	...	155	268	491	619	819	1,140	...
Toronto (Canada)	...	...	96	208	382	522	631	667	...
Mexico City (Mexico)	130	...	...	345	471	615	961	1,754	...
Havana (Cuba)	...	...	...	236	297	364	550	569	...
Rio de Janeiro (Brazil)	43	266	275	811	858	1,158	1,711	1,782	1,942
São Paulo (Brazil)	—	—	31	240	400	579	1,120	1,380	1,437
Santiago (Chile)	45	...	130	292	333	507	696	1,016	...
Montevideo (Uruguay)	6	34	...	303	328	385	674	770	...
Buenos Aires (Argentina)	40	76	236	821	1,320	1,720	2,415	2,457	2,621
Rosario (Argentina)	...	...	...	120	176	265	508	522	522
Europe									
United Kingdom									
London (excluding suburbs)	959	2,363	3,830	4,537	4,522	4,485	4,397	...	...
Birmingham	71	242	437	522	842	922	1,003	...	1,096 (1948)
Glasgow	77	329	511	762	1,029	1,056	1,093	...	1,087 "
Liverpool	82	397	624	685	756	805	856	...	792 "
Manchester	77	336	462	544	719	736	766	...	693 "
Sheffield	46	135	285	381	479	512	512	...	514 "
Germany									
Berlin	172	419	1,122	1,889	3,730	3,804	4,243	4,332	3,200 (1946)
Hamburg	130	132	290	706	931	997	1,129	1,682	1,403 "
Cologne	50	97	145	373	517	643	757	450	491 "
Munich	30	110	230	500	596	646	735	828	752 "
Leipzig	40	63	149	456	590	608	713	702	608 "
Essen	4	9	57	119	295	443	654	660	525 "
Dresden	60	97	221	396	548	535	642	625	468 "
Breslau	60	114	273	423	512	532	625	615	...
Frankfurt	48	65	137	289	415	435	556	547	424 "
Dortmund	...	...	67	143	214	297	541	537	436 "

(Continued on facing page)

TABLE 55—*continued*

Country and City [a]	1800	1850	1880	1900	1910	1920	1930	1940	Most Recent Census [b]
France									
Paris	547	1,053	2,269	2,714	2,936	2,906	2,830	. . .	2,725 (1946)
Marseilles	111	195	360	491	551	586	914	. . .	636 "
Lyons	110	177	377	459	524	562	571	. . .	461 "
Italy									
Rome	153	175	300	423	520	660	931	. . .	1,600 (1947)
Milan	170	242	322	539	702	818	961	. . .	1,267 "
Naples	350	449	494	621	751	860	832	. . .	1,020 "
Turin	78	135	254	330	416	500	591	. . .	710 "
Genoa	100	120	180	378	465	542	591	. . .	656 "
Other European countries									
Brussels (Belgium)	. . .	251	421	599	720	756	869	898	916 (1946)
Amsterdam (Netherlands)	201	224	317	511	566	647	757	794	798 (1947)
Rotterdam (Netherlands)	53	90	148	319	418	516	587	612	637 "
Stockholm (Sweden)	76	93	169	301	342	419	502	530	726 (1949)
Copenhagen (Denmark)	101	129	235	401	462	561	843	. . .	762 (1948)
Barcelona (Spain)	115	175	346	533	560	710	1,006	1,301	1,133 (1947)
Madrid (Spain)	160	281	398	540	572	751	953	1,726	1,187 "
Lisbon (Portugal)	180	240	187	356	436	486	594	709	. . .
Warsaw (Poland)	100	160	252	638	864	936	1,179	477	479 (1946)
Lodz (Poland)	. . .	. . .	34	315	404	452	605	488	497 "
Vienna (Austria)	247	444	726	1,675	2,031	1,866	1,875	1,930	. . .
Prague (Czechoslovakia)	75	118	162	202	224	677	849	951	921 (1947)
Budapest (Hungary)	54	178	371	732	881	930	1,006	1,163	. . .
Bucharest (Romania)	. . .	120	. . .	276	338	348	631	984	1,042 (1948)
Istanbul (Turkey)	600	. . .	. . .	1,106	1,200	. . .	741	844	861 (1945)
USSR									
Moscow	250	365	612	989	1,506	1,028	3,642	4,137	. . .
Leningrad	220	485	877	1,133	1,911	706	2,744	3,191	. . .
Kharkov	. . .	45	. . .	175	224	284	625	833	. . .
Kiev	. . .	61	. . .	247	446	366	625	846	. . .
Gorki (Nizny)	. . .	. . .	. . .	. . .	106	106	513	604	. . .
Odessa	6	90	194	405	498	435	509	604	. . .
Baku	. . .	. . .	. . .	112	218	273	670	809	. . .
Tashkent	. . .	. . .	82	156	165	272	532	585	. . .
Asia									
China									
Shanghai	300	. . .	. . .	870	651	1,000	3,486	. . .	. . .
Peiping	700	. . .	. . .	1,000	693	805	1,556	. . .	. . .
Tientsin	600	. . .	. . .	750	800	800	1,292	. . .	. . .
Canton	600	. . .	. . .	900	900	900	1,123	. . .	. . .
Nanking	250	. . .	. . .	270	267	377	1,091	. . .	1,755 (1946)
Tsingtao	. . .	. . .	. . .	. . .	. . .	. . .	515	. . .	. . .
Hankow	550	. . .	. . .	870	826	1,320	778	. . .	. . .
Chungking	200	. . .	. . .	620	598	614	635	. . .	. . .
Wenchow (Yungkia)	. . .	. . .	. . .	. . .	100	202	631	. . .	. . .
Hangchow	400	. . .	. . .	350	350	684	537	. . .	. . .

(*Continued on following page*)

TABLE 55—*continued*

Country and City [a]	1800	1850	1880	1900	1910	1920	1930	1940	Most Recent Census [b]
Japan									
Tokyo	800	...	...	1,819	2,186	2,173	5,876	3,276	4,555 (1948)
Osaka	350	...	...	996	1,227	1,253	2,990	3,092	1,690 "
Nagoya	...	...	...	285	378	430	1,083	1,249	915 "
Kyoto	250	...	...	381	442	591	1,081	1,177	1,040 "
Kobe	...	...	...	285	378	609	912	1,006	644 "
Yokohama	...	...	...	326	394	423	704	...	855 "
India									
Calcutta	600	...	612	848	896	906	1,194	2,109	...
Bombay	200	...	773	776	979	1,176	1,161	1,490	...
Madras	300	...	406	509	519	527	647	777	...
Other Asiatic countries									
Mukden (Manchukuo)	...	...	...	...	158	160	698	864	...
Bangkok (Thailand)	...	...	...	600	629	...	493	931	...
Singapore	...	...	139	228	303	350	490	769	...
Africa									
Cairo (Egypt)	300	...	375	570	654	791	1,307	1,312	2,100 (1947)
Alexandria (Egypt)	20	...	231	320	332	445	682	686	928 "
Australia									
Sydney	...	...	225	482	636	926	1,235	1,398	1,484 "
Melbourne	...	...	283	496	589	795	992	1,077	1,227 "

Sources: For 1800–1900, **37**, pp. 132–38; for 1910–30, **11**, 1938, pp. 13*–15*; for the most recent census, statistical yearbooks of the respective countries.

a. Cities with population of approximately half a million or more in 1940. When the census gives two figures for the population of a city—one with the surrounding metropolitan area, and the other without—the lower figure has been used.

b. 1950 unless otherwise indicated.

The only large city in the Western Hemisphere was Mexico City, which had 130,000 inhabitants, perhaps a fifth of its preconquest population. In the United States, the largest cities were New York and Philadelphia.[25]

The population of all the large cities in the world totaled 11.5 million in 1800, 1.3 per cent of all the world's population. The ratio was 2.7 per cent in Europe, 1.0 per cent in Asia, and slightly less than 0.5 per cent in the Americas.

By 1930 there were nearly 700 cities with more than 100,000 inhabitants and they had, all together, 243 million inhabitants, 11 per cent of all the people in the world. The proportion was 22 per cent in the Americas, 29 per cent in Europe (excluding the USSR), 18 per cent in Oceania, 6 in Asia, and 4 in Africa. (See Table 54.)

Among the large cities of the world, 57 have from half a million to a million inhabitants and 40 have a million inhabitants or more. (See Table 55.) They are distributed by continent as follows:

	Cities with 500,000 to 1,000,000 Inhabitants	Cities with 1,000,000 or More Inhabitants
World total	57	40
North America	10	6
Middle and South America	3	5
Europe, excluding the USSR	27	12
USSR	6	2
Asia, excluding the USSR	10	12
Africa	1	1
Australia	—	2

Most of the cities with a million or more inhabitants are on the seacoast or are connected with the ocean by a navigable river. Among the few far from the sea are Chicago, Berlin, Paris, Moscow, Warsaw and Milan. (See Figure 42.)

25. **36**, p. 21.

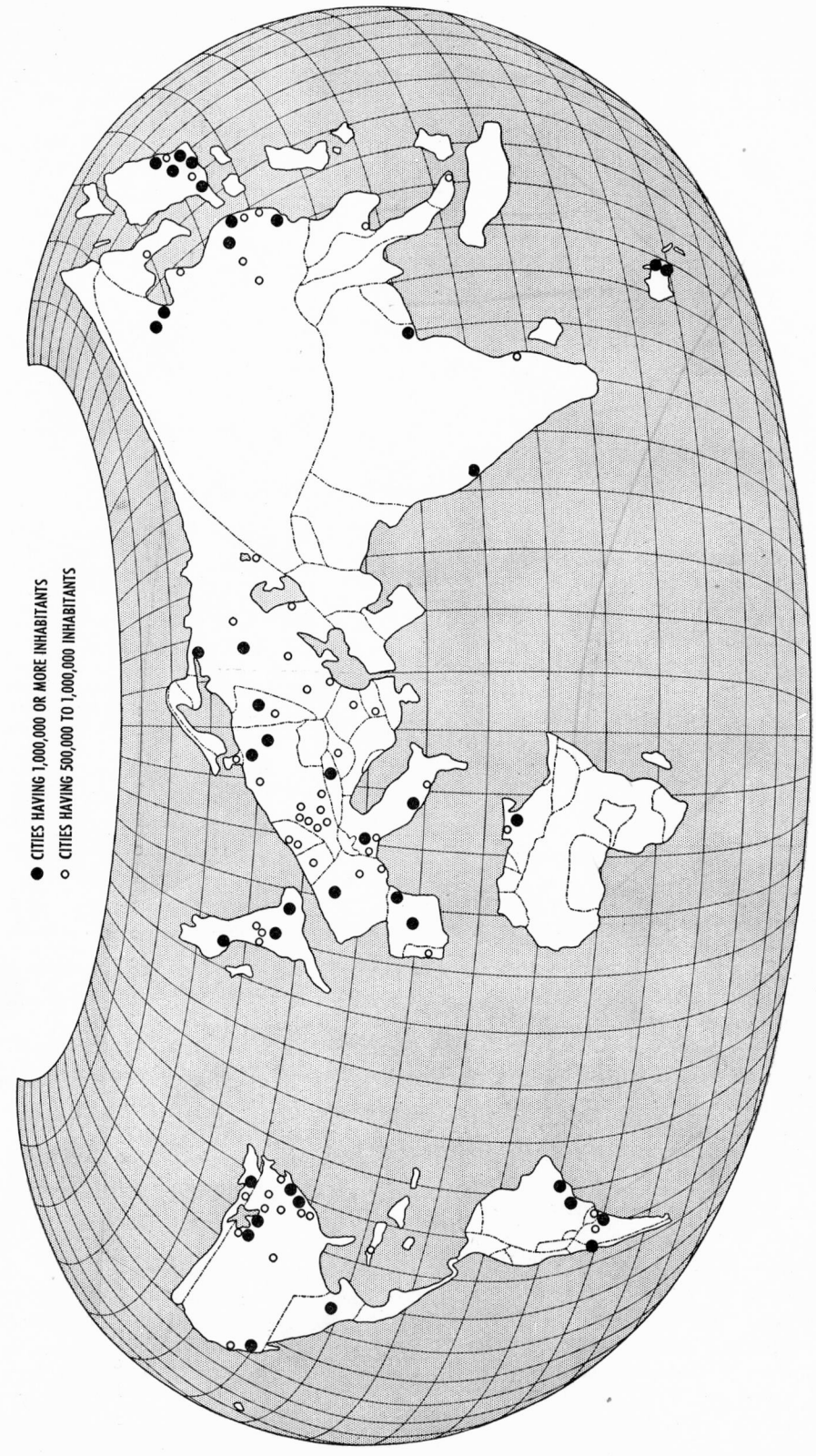

FIGURE 42. LOCATION OF THE 97 LARGEST CITIES IN THE WORLD IN RELATION TO POPULATION

This map shows continents and countries on the scale of their 1950 population.

In Europe, supercities with a million or more inhabitants are distributed fairly evenly in relation to the population, with one supercity for a population of slightly more than 30 million. The United States also has a supercity for about each 30 million persons; the rest of America, for each 40 million persons; the USSR, for 86 million; Asia, for 100 million; Australia, for 5 million.

• CITIES HAVING 1,000,000 OR MORE INHABITANTS

○ CITIES HAVING 500,000 TO 1,000,000 INHABITANTS

TABLE 56

URBANIZATION IN THE UNITED STATES: TOTAL AND URBAN POPULATION, 1790–1950

Year	Total Population, in Millions	Urban Population,[a] in Millions	Percentage of Population in Urban Areas	Year	Total Population, in Millions	Urban Population,[a] in Millions	Percentage of Population in Urban Areas
1790	3.9	0.2	5.1	1880	50.2	14.1	28.2
1800	5.3	0.3	6.1	1890	62.4	22.1	35.4
1810	7.2	0.5	7.3	1900	76.0	30.2	39.7
1820	9.6	0.7	7.2	1910	92.0	42.0	45.7
1830	12.9	1.1	8.8	1920	105.7	54.2	51.2
1840	17.1	1.8	10.8	1930	122.8	69.0	56.2
1850	23.2	3.5	15.3	1940	131.7	74.4	56.5
1860	31.4	6.2	19.8	1950	151.2	86.8	57.4
1870	38.6	9.9	25.7				

Source: **6**, p. 18; cf. **8**; for 1950, Bureau of the Census release (preliminary). The figures differ slightly from those reported by the censuses (cf. Table 57).

a. Classification in accordance with 1940 definition.

Apart from proximity to the ocean, the location of large cities has been determined by a combination of economic, geographical, political and historical factors: the need for an urban center in a vast area with abundant natural resources; interdependence of industries; transportation facilities and junction points; and considerations of security that existed when the city was founded.

URBANIZATION IN THE UNITED STATES

A century ago the United States had only four cities with more than 100,000 inhabitants. By 1900 it had become the land of the largest cities. The transformation was due to the rapid growth of population and its shift toward booming industrial centers. Since the middle of the nineteenth century most immigrants have settled in urban communities. At the same time sons and daughters of farmers moved gradually from rural areas to the nearest towns and from towns to larger cities. Until the turn of the century there was also a substantial surplus of births over deaths in urban areas. In addition, hundreds of villages became towns, while former towns developed into industrial and commercial cities. Since 1880, the farm population has increased very slowly, and nearly all the surplus of births over deaths and of immigration over emigration has been absorbed by the growing cities. (See Table 56 and Figure 43.)

The share of urban communities (places with 2,500 or more inhabitants) in the total population increased from 35.4 per cent in 1890 to 57.4 per cent in 1950. The number of cities with 100,000 or more inhabitants rose from 28 in 1890 to 93 in 1930 and 106 in 1950. The share of such cities in the total population grew from 15.4 per cent in 1890 to 29.6 per cent in 1930 and 29.3 in 1950. The 1930's represented the only decade in the history of the United States when there was no increase in the number of large cities or in the percentage of total population in such cities. The greatest increase in that decade was in cities with 25,000 to 100,000 inhabitants (10.5 per cent in 1930, 11.2 per cent in 1940). (See Table 57.) Thus, the process of *citification* had come temporarily to a standstill, while the trend toward *urbanization* continued, though more slowly. This change was due partly to the development of suburban residential settlements around the metropolitan centers and partly to the depression, which discouraged village-to-city migration. In the 1940's the middle-sized cities continued to grow, but there was also a rapid growth of population in larger cities with 100,000 to 1,000,000: their share in the population increased from 16.7 per cent in 1940 to 17.8 per cent in 1950.

State Differences in Urbanization

The proportion of population in urban communities varies in the United States from one geographic division to another and from state to state, ranging from less than 20 per cent in Mississippi to more than 90 per cent in Rhode

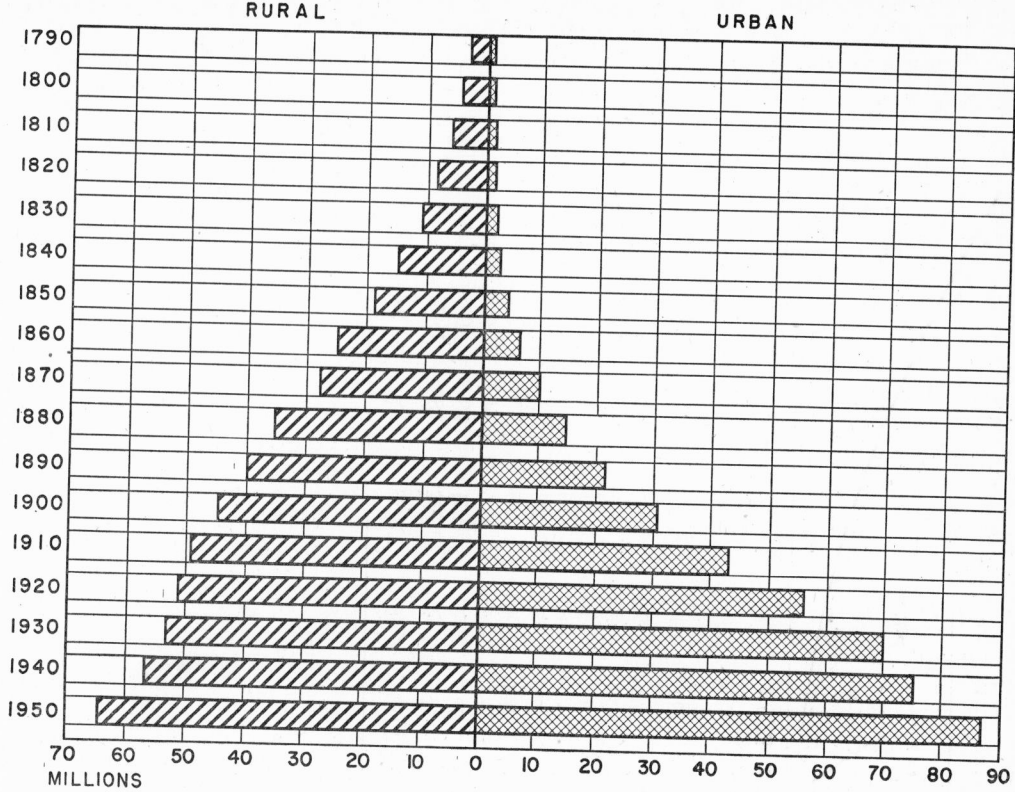

FIGURE 43. URBANIZATION IN THE UNITED STATES: POPULATION IN RURAL AND URBAN AREAS, 1790-1950

In 1870 only a fourth of the population of the United States lived in urban communities—that is, in incorporated places with 2,500 or more inhabitants. Since 1920, the urban population has exceeded the rural.

Island.[26] (See Table 58.) The degree of urbanization in Mississippi and West Virginia in 1940 was about the same as in the United States as a whole in 1860 and 1880, respectively. (See Figure 44.) Most people in the United States live in states where from 50 to 75 per cent of the inhabitants are urban. In 1940 this range included Connecticut, New Hampshire, Pennsylvania, Maryland, Delaware, Ohio, Indiana, Illinois, Wisconsin, Michigan, Missouri, Colorado, Utah, Washington, California and Florida.

The correlation between degree of urbanization and industrial development in individual states is clear only at the extremes. The highly urbanized states of Rhode Island, Massachusetts, New York, New Jersey and Illinois are, in fact, among the most industrialized in the nation, while the preponderantly rural states of Mississippi, Arkansas, the Carolinas and the Dakotas, are among the least industrialized. But it is not easy to explain why Utah and Colorado are more highly urbanized than Delaware and Missouri, why Louisiana ranks above Maine, or why Nevada, Montana, Wyoming and Arizona rank above Vermont. In these states, as all over the world, the pattern of urbanization has been determined by a combination of historical, geographical and economic conditions.

Country-to-City Migration

Country-to-city migration has been the main source of growth of cities in all countries, especially since the turn of the century, when the number of births in cities was not sufficient to offset losses through death.[27] The extent of country-to-city migration in the United States may be seen from a comparison of changes in the number of inhabitants in rural and urban communities with net balance of births and deaths in a given period.

26. Excluding the District of Columbia, which is 100 per cent urban.

27. See Chapter 5, pp. 138 ff.

TABLE 57

URBANIZATION IN THE UNITED STATES: URBAN AND RURAL PLACES AND DISTRIBUTION OF POPULATION BY TYPE AND SIZE OF PLACE, 1890–1950

Type and Size of Place	1890		1900		1910		1920		1930		1940		1950 [b]	
	Number of Places	Percentage of Population	Number of Places	Percentage of Population	Number of Places	Percentage of Population	Number of Places	Percentage of Population	Number of Places	Percentage of Population	Number of Places	Percentage of Population	Number of Places	Percentage of Population
United States, total	7,906	100.0	10,731	100.0	14,094	100.0	15,579	100.0	16,598	100.0	16,752	100.0	...	100.0
Urban places with inhabitants of 2,500 or more	1,417	35.4	1,801	40.0	2,262	45.7	2,722	51.4	3,165	56.2	3,464	56.5	4,270	57.4
1,000,000 or more	3	5.8	3	8.5	3	9.2	3	9.6	5	12.3	5	12.1	5	11.5
500,000 to 1,000,000	1	1.3	3	2.2	5	3.3	9	5.9	8	4.7	9	4.9	13	6.1
250,000 to 500,000	7	3.9	9	3.8	11	4.3	13	4.3	24	6.5	23	5.9	23	5.4
100,000 to 250,000	17	4.4	23	4.3	31	5.3	43	6.2	56	6.1	55	5.9	65	6.3
50,000 to 100,000	30	3.2	40	3.6	59	4.5	76	5.0	98	5.3	107	5.6	125	5.9
25,000 to 50,000	36	3.6	82	3.7	119	4.4	143	4.8	185	5.2	213	5.6	248	5.7
10,000 to 25,000	228	5.4	280	5.7	369	6.0	465	6.6	606	7.4	665	7.6	780	7.7
5,000 to 10,000	339	3.8	468	4.2	605	4.6	715	4.7	851	4.8	965	5.1	1,174	5.0
2,500 to 5,000	756	4.0	893	4.1	1,060	4.1	1,255	4.3	1,332	3.8	1,422	3.8	1,839	3.7
Rural places [b]	6,489	64.6	8,930	60.0	11,832	54.3	12,857	48.6	13,433	43.8	13,288	43.5	...	42.6

Sources: **5**, p. 9; **7**, 1948, p. 14; for 1950, Bureau of the Census release.

a. 1940 classification.
b. Incorporated places with fewer than 2,500 inhabitants and unincorporated areas.

TABLE 58

URBANIZATION IN THE UNITED STATES: PERCENTAGE OF POPULATION IN URBAN AREAS, BY STATE, 1940, AND IN THE UNITED STATES, 1860–1940

State	Per Cent [a]	State	Per Cent [a]	State	Per Cent [a]	State	Per Cent [a]
District of Columbia	100.0	Utah	55.5	Louisiana	41.5	New Mexico	33.2
Rhode Island	91.6	Florida	55.1	Maine	40.5	Alabama	30.2
Massachusetts	89.4	Indiana	55.1	*United States, 1900*	*40.0*	Kentucky	29.8
New York	82.8	Wisconsin	53.5	Nevada	39.3	*United States, 1880*	*28.2*
New Jersey	81.6	Washington	53.1	Nebraska	39.1	West Virginia	28.1
Illinois	73.6	Colorado	52.6	Montana	37.8	North Carolina	27.3
California	71.0	Delaware	52.3	Oklahoma	37.6	*United States, 1870*	*25.7*
Connecticut	67.8	Missouri	51.8	Wyoming	37.3	South Dakota	24.6
Ohio	66.8	*United States, 1920*	*51.4*	*United States, 1890*	*35.4*	South Carolina	24.5
Pennsylvania	66.5	Minnesota	49.8	Virginia	35.3	Arkansas	22.2
Michigan	65.7	Oregon	48.8	Tennessee	35.2	North Dakota	20.6
Maryland	59.3	*United States, 1910*	*45.7*	Arizona	34.8	Mississippi	19.8
New Hampshire	57.6	Texas	45.4	Georgia	34.4	*United States, 1860*	*19.8*
United States, 1940	*56.5*	Iowa	42.7	Vermont	34.3		
United States, 1930	*56.2*	Kansas	41.9	Idaho	33.7		

Sources: **6**, p. 18; **7**, 1948, p. 16. Cf. Table 57.

a. Incorporated communities with 2,500 or more inhabitants.

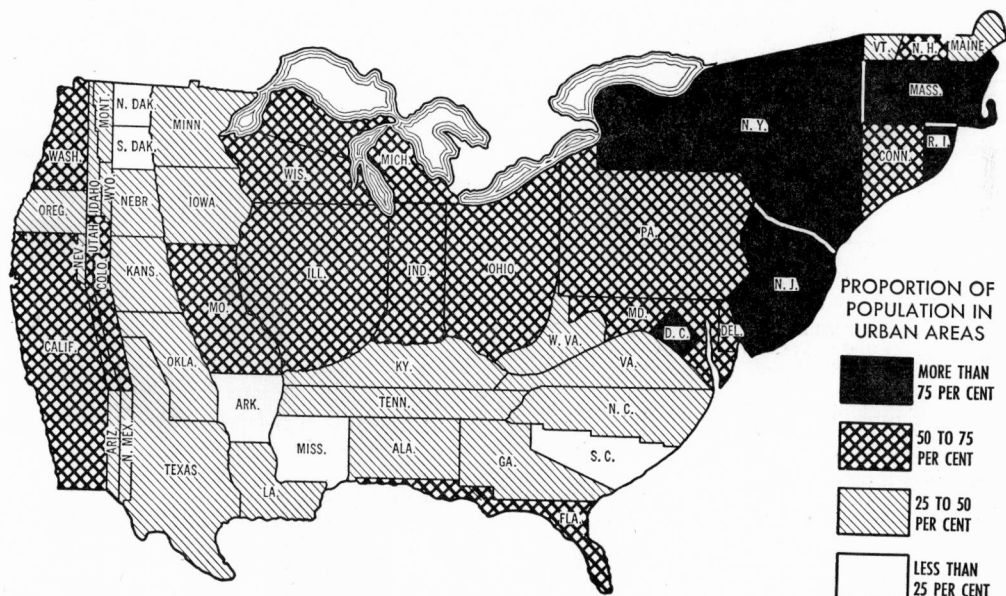

FIGURE 44. URBANIZATION IN THE UNITED STATES: PROPORTION OF POPULATION IN URBAN AREAS IN EACH STATE, 1940

Each state appears on this map on the scale of its population in 1940. The states where more people live in rural areas than in urban communities form two broad belts: in the South, from the Atlantic coast to Arizona; and in the Middle West, from the Canadian to the Mexican border. The highly urbanized states (with more than 75 per cent of total population in urban areas) are all concentrated in the East and the Northeast. (Cf. Table 58.)

In the decade 1930–1940, when net immigration into the United States was negligible, the population of either group of communities could increase because of a surplus of births over deaths or because of immigration from other communities or as a result of both factors. In 1930, 36.3 million persons lived in cities with 100,000 or more inhabitants. In 1940 these cities had about 38.0 million inhabitants, although they had recorded 4.8 million more deaths than births in the intervening years. The increase in population suggests net immigration of approximately 6.5 million persons from smaller cities or rural areas.

When such a comparison is made for communities of various sizes, it appears that almost 11 million persons moved from rural to urban areas in the decade 1930–1940 and that almost 60 per cent of this country-to-city migration was directed toward large cities. (See Table 59.)

Country-to-city migration differs in composition from international migration by sex and age. A farm family does not move to a city as a unit; rather, it is usual for rural boys and girls to look for a job in a nearby town or a more remote city after they leave school. Some later return to the country. Many a farmer's son, after having spent years in town, comes back to run the farm when his father grows old or dies.

The shift of young people from villages to cities has greatly affected the composition of population in both rural and urban areas, lowering the proportion of children in the urban population and increasing the proportion in rural areas. Similarly, it has increased the proportion of women in cities as compared with villages.

Starting with the number of children born in rural and urban areas in the preceding years, one can estimate about how many in each age group were still alive in 1940. Comparison of these estimated figures with the actual number of persons of the respective ages in urban and rural communities indicates that the urban population aged 15 or more (28.3 million males and 30.2 million females) included approximately 10.1 million men and 12 million women who were born in rural areas, most of them on the farm.[28] (See Figure 45.)

---

28. Farm girls begin to move to cities earlier than farm boys, so that the proportion of males per 1,000 females aged 15–19 years is higher on farms than in cities. By the age of 20, males leave the farm in larger numbers than females. This excess continues until about age 45, when the number of men and women in cities

URBANIZATION ABROAD

Western Europe

The number of people in Paris and Vienna, excluding their suburbs, reached its peak before World War I. London, also excluding the suburbs, was losing population after the turn of the century and Glasgow grew less than 6 per cent from 1911 to 1948. Berlin has been a dying city since World War II. In many European cities the postwar censuses (1946–49) showed a substantial loss of population since the last prewar enumeration. This is true of Glasgow, Liverpool and Manchester in Great Britain; Copenhagen in Denmark; almost all large cities in Germany; Marseilles and Lyons in France; Warsaw and Lodz in Poland; Barcelona and Madrid in Spain. On the other hand, Italian cities have continued to grow, and the number of people in Brussels, Amsterdam, Rotterdam, Stockholm and some other European cities is greater than before the war.[29] (See Table 55.)

The trend toward concentration of people in steadily growing aggregations has prevailed in England since the sixteenth century, in other countries since the middle of the eighteenth or the beginning of the nineteenth century, keeping pace with population growth and industrialization. The movement was slow at the beginning, gained momentum in the second half of the nineteenth century, and slowed down after the turn of the century. This pattern is illustrated by the experience of the Scandinavian countries, especially Norway. (See Table 60.) In England and Wales, the proportion of the city population rose from 50.2 per cent of the total in 1851 to 77.0 per cent in 1901 but has increased little since that time.[30]

Although this tendency is not universal and may be due partly to the two world wars and the intervening economic depression, it reflects far-

---

approaches an equilibrium. The increasing proportion of men on the farm in the older age classes is probably due to the return of older men from cities to villages. In the highest age classes, the proportion of women inches up because of the difference in mortality rates of the two sexes.

Our estimates make no allowance for the migration from cities to rural areas. For a discussion of economic effects of village-to-city migration, see **19**.

29. These statements refer to the size of population within the legal boundaries of the respective cities rather than metropolitan areas or the agglomeration of the city and its suburbs.

30. **12**.

TABLE 59

URBANIZATION IN THE UNITED STATES: CHANGES IN RURAL AND URBAN POPULATION, 1930–40

(Millions)

Type and Size of Community	Population (Census)		Net Change	Hypothetical Surplus of Births (+) or Deaths (−)	Hypothetical Internal Migration
	1930	1940			
United States, total	122,775	131,669	+8,894	+8,894	—
Rural places	53,820	57,246	+3,496	+14,350	−10,924
Urban places with inhabitants of					
2,500–10,000	10,615	11,708	+1,093	+160	+933
10,000–25,000	9,097	9,969	+872	−158	+1,030
25,000–100,000	12,917	14,761	+1,844	−638	+2,482
100,000 and more	36,326	37,985	+1,659	−4,820	+6,479

Sources: For population, **7**, 1948, p. 14; "hypothetical" figures are estimated on the basis of official "reproduction" rates.

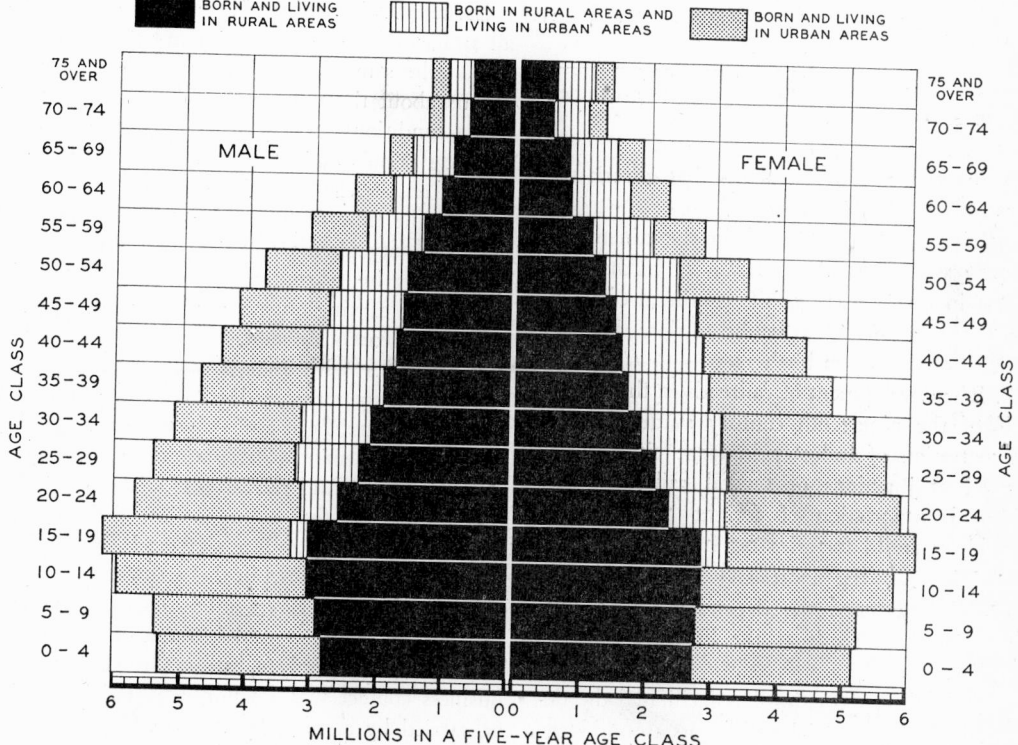

FIGURE 45. RURAL AND URBAN POPULATION IN THE UNITED STATES BY AGE AND SEX, 1940

This chart shows the pyramid of the population of the United States in 1940. Each bar represents a five-year age group. The solid black part of each bar indicates the number of persons living in rural areas; the remainder, the size of the urban population of the given age. The striped section of the pyramid shows roughly the number of persons who were born in rural areas but lived in urban communities at the time of the census.

TABLE 60

URBANIZATION ABROAD: PERCENTAGE OF URBAN
POPULATION IN SWEDEN, NORWAY AND
DENMARK, 1770–1948

Year	Sweden	Norway	Denmark
1770	...	8.9	19.9
1790	...	...	20.7
1800	9.8	8.8	20.9
1810	...	9.5	...
1820	9.8	10.4	...
1830	9.7	10.8	...
1840	9.7	11.5	20.5
1850	10.1	12.7	20.9
1860	11.3	14.5	23.4
1870	13.0	17.0	24.9
1880	15.1	20.0	28.1
1890	18.8	23.7	33.2
1900	21.5	28.0	38.2
1910	24.8	28.8	40.3
1920	29.5	29.6	44.2
1930	32.5	28.5	43.9
1940	37.4	...	47.4
1945	42.0	28.0	48.2
1948	45.0	...	...

Sources: Statistical yearbooks of the respective countries,
1949.

reaching changes in the factors that govern the
influx of people into cities.

1. Insofar as urbanization in the nineteenth
century was due to the surplus of births over
deaths in rural areas and the continual country-
to-city migration, it was bound to slow down as
a result of decline in birth rates.

2. The development of railroads in the second
half of the nineteenth century stimulated the
concentration of industry in large cities, often
located at junctions of several railroad lines.
Motor transportation of freight has made it
possible to build factories far from large cities.

3. Likewise, the increasing use of electric
power has lessened the dependence of manufacturers on railroads as the life line for coal
supplies.

4. Motor transportation has facilitated the development of residential settlements around large
cities, often beyond the limits of suburbs. As the
cities have become more and more crowded,
people have moved beyond their boundaries.

5. In many countries, the main goal of urban
planning has been to move people away from the
congested urban areas.

The Soviet Union

Urbanization developed relatively slowly in
Russia before World War I. The census of 1897
reported only 11.5 per cent of the total population as "urban." [31] In 1923 the urban proportion
was estimated at 15.5 per cent, and in 1926, 17.9
per cent. Precipitous urbanization of the country
began when the Soviet government confiscated
farm property and organized the state-operated
collective farms. From 1926 to 1939 the urban
population more than doubled and its share in
the total population rose to 32.8 per cent. (See
Table 61.)

This increase was due partly to reclassification
of localities and the surplus of births over deaths,
but mainly to large-scale country-to-city migration. Insofar as it was effected without direct
compulsion, it was essentially a flight of rural
youth from collective farms.

PROBLEMS OF LARGE CITIES

Large cities have always attracted people from
all strata of life in rural areas and small towns
and at the same time have aroused bitter complaints about the unhealthy and uncomfortable
living conditions they have offered their steadily
growing population. Complaints about the congestion and traffic difficulties in large cities go
back to the time of Rome. Equally old are the
efforts of city planners to mitigate the evils of
large cities by tearing down whole blocks of
houses and carving out new streets.

It is extremely difficult, however, to reshape
modern cities with their expensive buildings,
fixed street patterns and intricate systems of
supply of water, light and power. Despite modern improvements in transportation, housing,
medical services and recreational facilities, many
students believe that some modern cities have
outgrown their optimum size and should be
split up or redistributed in the surrounding metropolitan area. The desire of businessmen to have
their offices in the central business district was
sound when the only substitute for a personal
business contact was a letter delivered by mail
or carried by a messenger. The telegraph, and
particularly the telephone, have greatly diminished the advantage of a central location for

31. The distinction between "urban" and "rural" areas
in Russian statistics was based on administrative decision,
and many places with several thousand inhabitants were
counted as "villages."

TABLE 61

Urbanization Abroad: Country-to-City Migration in the USSR, 1926–39

	Population, in Millions		
Item	*Total*	*Rural*	*Urban*
Population			
1926	147.0	120.7	26.3
1939	170.5	114.6	55.9
Net change	+23.5	–6.1	+29.6
Sources of change			
Surplus of births over deaths	+23.5	+18.2	+5.3
Reclassification of localities	. . .	–5.8	+5.8
Country-to-city migration	. . .	–18.5	+18.5

Source: **34**, p. 30.

such offices. Nevertheless, even enterprises for which a central location represents no substantial economic advantage continue to gravitate, by inertia, to the center of the city.

Besides the long journey to work and the congestion during business hours that is an evil common to almost all large cities, each city has its special problems. The problems of large cities in the United States are distinctly different from those in western Europe and in the Orient.

The American Big City

In contrast to Europe, where almost all the largest cities are old capitals built around the royal palace and the cathedral, the center of a large city in the United States is its "downtown" area, where most of the important offices, stores, hotels, places of amusement, and public buildings are congregated.[32]

The heart of such a city is the pile of skyscrapers that accommodate the headquarters of large corporations and symbolize modern concentration of economic power. Beyond the business center lies a series of concentric belts, which the National Resources Committee in its study of the role of cities describes as follows:

The more imposing the skyscrapers at the center, the wider is the area over which they exert a blighting and depressing influence. This is reflected in actual physical deterioration, in accelerated obsolescence, vacant building sites, and in decaying commercial areas and residential slums. . . . In the center of the city are the Government administrative buildings, the offices of commercial and industrial firms and the professional and technical serv-

ices, the department stores and specialty shops, the transient hotels, the restaurants and theaters.

Beyond the city center are wholesale houses and warehouses, railroad yards, freight and passenger terminals, junk yards, and light manufacturing establishments, interspersed by dilapidated residences, rooming houses, and tenements. This area which contains the slums is the forgotten section of most American cities. . . . At its periphery, this area merges with the zone of workingmen's homes, often multiple dwellings which command relatively low rent, but are in a better state of repair than the slums. This area, in turn, shades into the middle-class apartment house area with its own local business center. . . . The last zone of the city proper is the single family residence area where more spacious individual family dwellings, with garages, yards, and larger open spaces can be bought or rented. Beyond this area is the suburban zone with scattered estates, golf courses, residential communities, and industrial areas, interspersed with truck gardens, farm lands, and embryonic residential subdivisions.[33]

This description of the typical American city is illustrated by the schematic cross section reproduced in Figure 46.[34] (Cf. Figure 47, A.) This is, however, only one of many typical patterns of the internal structure of American cities. The exact shape of each city is influenced by topography and transportation, and there are no two that have exactly the same form.[35] In some cities various sectors grew up along the main transportation routes or along the lines of least

---

33. **9**, pp. 6–7.

34. Chicago provides the most striking example of a blighted area around the nucleus of a large city; slums, tenements and underworld hangouts encircle its central business district. (**20**, pp. 109–17 ff.)

35. **21**, p. 12.

32. **35**, p. 318.

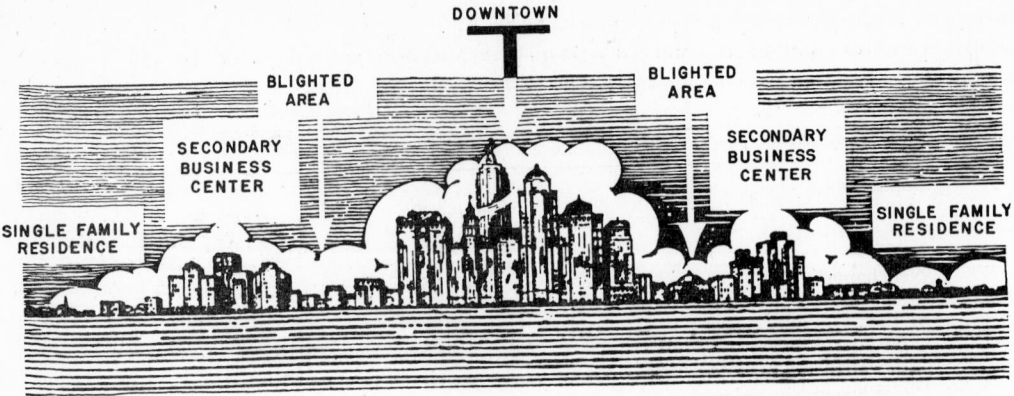

National Resources Committee

FIGURE 46. STRUCTURE OF CITIES: SCHEMATIC CROSS SECTION OF A BIG CITY IN THE UNITED STATES
(Concentric Zone Theory)

The center of this schematic cross section of a modern American city—"downtown"—is dominated by sky-scrapers, the site of corporation offices, banks, hotels, department stores and so forth. Blighted areas and slums surround this business center. Farther outside lies a middle-class residential area with secondary business centers, and next a ring of spacious single-family residences. (Cf. **9**, pp. 6–7.)

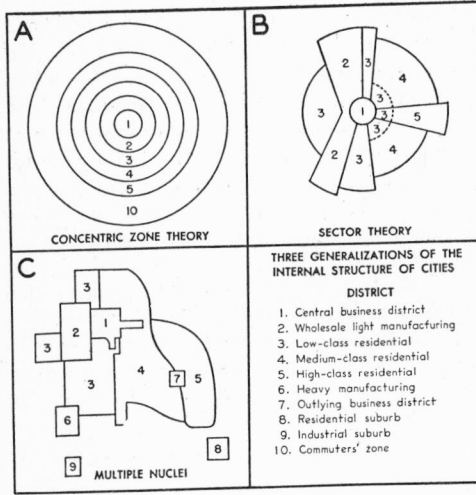

*Annals of the American Academy of
Political and Social Science* (**24**)

FIGURE 47. STRUCTURE OF CITIES: THREE THEORIES

resistance to form a star-shaped city. Thus a high-rent residential area east of the central district would tend to migrate outward, always keeping in the eastern sector of the growing city. A low-rent housing area, originally located south of the central district, would tend to extend inward to the very center of the city in that sector.[36] (See Figure 47, B.) Generally speaking, different sectors of a city present different characteristics

according to the original types of neighborhood within them.[37]

Neither the theory of concentric zones nor that of axial development is applicable to all American cities. As a result of topographic conditions, asymmetrical growth and historical factors, some cities have several nuclei, with the central business district located not in the actual center — as is implied by the concentric-zone and sector theories — but near one edge of the city.[38] (See Figure 47, C.) New York is an example of a multiple-nuclei city.

Big Cities in Europe

Products of a longer historical development, the principal cities of Western Europe have several nuclei, different in character and function. The business center is usually distinctly separate from the historical and political center, which contains public buildings. Often the amusement center is separate from the business district, hotels are clustered around railroad stations, and secondary business centers are located in various parts of the city.

Many large cities of Europe have been plagued since the middle of the nineteenth century by the same evils as the supercities of the United States: slums and blighted areas. Since the turn of the century serious attempts at slum clearance

---

36. **24**, p. 14.

37. **21**, p. 114.
38. **21**, pp. 14–16.

have been made in many European cities. The campaign has been particularly successful in the Scandinavian countries, where the principal cities have practically done away with substandard dwellings. Overcrowding, however, in terms of number of persons per room, is often still serious.

Goals of City Planning

The structural defects of large cities in the United States are largely due to the great speed with which they have grown. Its modern city, a precocious offspring of the nineteenth century, built for horse-and-buggy traffic between railroad station, residential sections and business center, is out of step with the era of electricity and the motor car. Despite all its efforts to be modern, it has not left enough space to utilize the new techniques of transportation, and it has failed to make full use of the new means of communication to eliminate congestion.

In the Old World, the defects of the large city are more deeply rooted in history, but the goals of city planning are practically the same: to move surplus population from the overcrowded central area; to separate residential sections from business districts; to broaden streets and provide more parks and open spaces; to develop shopping centers close to residential sections and to secure transportation facilities between these sections and the places where their inhabitants work. In general terms the main goal is *decentralization* of the city, with *specialization* of its various sections and their functional *integration*.

This objective cannot always be achieved within the confines of the city. In many cases, it requires dispersion of the residential settlements and industrial establishments to areas outside the city limits. Often it entails division of existing establishments.[39] Modern city planning includes the development of satellite towns that would take over certain functions of the central city — housing a part of its population, absorbing some of its industries, providing space for auxiliary services of some of its commercial establishments. Such dispersion of functions of the large city presumes a highly integrated transportation system — airfields, superhighways, subways and so on.

The London County Council projects and

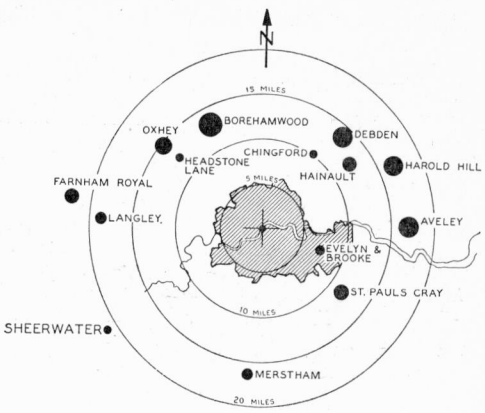

London County Council

FIGURE 48. PROBLEMS OF LARGE CITIES: RELATIVE LOCATION OF L.C.C. DEVELOPMENT AREAS OUTSIDE THE COUNTY OF LONDON

plans of the French Ministry of Reconstruction typify the new trend in city planning. While the administrative area of London lies largely within a circle with a 5-mile radius, the residential settlements designed by the London County Council are dispersed over an area that has a radius of 20 miles and includes many towns.[40] (See Figure 48.) Likewise, the plans for Paris envisage new roads, airfields, residential settlements and industrial developments in an area that stretches in all directions for scores of miles beyond the boundaries of the French capital.

In brief, aside from purely local developments that may affect only a small part of the urban area, city planning becomes more and more a part of regional planning.

EFFECTS OF WORLD WAR II ON CITY PLANNING

War Damage

Many European cities were partially or wholly destroyed during World War II. The European Economic Commission of the United Nations has estimated that in 14 European countries nearly 2.8 million dwelling units were entirely destroyed, 2.9 million partially destroyed and 8.9 million slightly damaged. In terms of total destruction, these losses are equivalent to annihilation of 5 million dwelling units.[41] (See Table 62.)

The survey did not include Germany, the USSR and Japan, the three countries that suffered the heaviest destruction. The damage inflicted on German cities was probably not less severe than

---

39. Even if the leading corporations keep their headquarters close to the business center of the city, accounting departments may be located elsewhere.

40. **13**, p. 34.
41. **3**, p. 7.

TABLE 62

EFFECTS OF WORLD WAR II: DWELLINGS DESTROYED IN EUROPEAN COUNTRIES

(*Thousands*)

Country	*Entirely Destroyed*	*Partially Destroyed*	*Slightly Damaged*	*Total*[a]	*Percentage of Prewar Dwellings Entirely Destroyed*
Total	2,756	2,923	8,942	5,034	—
United Kingdom	233	568	3,342	851	6.5
Ireland	—	3	3	2	0.3
France	600	530	1,000	1,012	7.6
Luxembourg	2	2	14	4	2.7
Belgium	68	116	300	156	6.2
Netherlands	91	51	463	163	7.8
Norway	18	1	85	27	3.6
Finland	11	2	23	19	2.1
Poland	987	1,157	630	1,500	21.5
Czechoslovakia	52	64	382	123	3.4
Austria	71	102	527	175	8.7
Hungary	59	58	58	94	3.9
Italy	355	198	700	524	4.9
Greece	208	72	1,415	386	20.7

Source: **3,** Table 19.

    a. Equivalent to entire destruction.

that of all its enemies combined, except the USSR. Assuming that the destruction in Russian cities was similar to that in Poland, it appears that some 6.5 million dwelling units in Europe have been entirely destroyed, 7 million partially destroyed and nearly 20 million slightly damaged: the total loss is equivalent to complete destruction of some 12.5 million dwelling units.

Destruction was chiefly concentrated in large cities. Except in the western provinces of the USSR and the northern tip of Norway,[42] rural dwellings and small towns were not so severely damaged as the large industrial and commercial cities. Three capitals — London, Berlin and Warsaw — are among the most severely damaged cities.

Of the European countries covered by the survey, Poland suffered the greatest destruction, while France and Great Britain rank second and third, followed by Italy and Greece. In relation to their housing resources before the war, Poland and Greece incurred the heaviest losses, with destruction of more than one house in five.

42. Cf. **15,** *passim.*

Postwar Reconstruction

Rebuilding cities naturally became a first objective of postwar reconstruction. In most countries, rebuilding began with repairing of the slightly damaged houses. In the European countries covered by the survey, 3.7 million slightly damaged and 515,000 partially destroyed dwelling units had been repaired by the end of 1947, while only 284,000 entirely destroyed units had been rebuilt. Later, partly with the aid of the European Cooperation Administration (the Marshall Plan), reconstruction gained momentum. By the middle of 1951 the program was not yet complete, but it had reached a stage at which it was possible to assess the effects of war destruction and postwar reconstruction on European cities.

In Great Britain, Belgium, the Netherlands, Norway and Italy the process of reconstruction has not been restricted to restoration. In many cases, an effort is being made to rebuild cities in accordance with a new general plan. Often the plan provides for rebuilding residences, factories and office buildings far from their prewar site. Ruined buildings have been cleared away to allow space for broader streets or parks. In London, for example, obsolete tenements around areas devastated by bombing and fire were torn down and space was thus provided to develop modern residential areas.

The rebuilding of Rotterdam is an example of this tendency in urban planning. A large part of this city was pulverized by air bombardment. After the war, the Dutch, and especially the people of Rotterdam, decided to rebuild it as a model city with broad streets, spacious parks, conveniently located business buildings and comfortable residential sections on the periphery. A completely new network of streets was laid out on the site of the old city. The work is now in full swing: a few key buildings of the planned new city are completed, others are under construction, and many are still on the drawing board. (See Figure 49.) [43]

The trend has been less spectacular in Great Britain, Italy and Norway. Reconstruction in Germany and France has been delayed by internal political factors. It is likely, however, that when the time comes, these countries will approach the task of reconstruction not merely as a restoration of damaged areas but as reconstruction of the city in accordance with modern ideas, which are essentially the same as the "modern fashion" in city planning at the time of Aristotle. It is difficult to predict how far the city planners of our time will be able to go.

Cities of the Future

The recent trend in the development of cities and in city planning has been toward decentralization.[44] Originally stimulated by the progress in transportation, communication and industrial techniques, this trend has been strengthened by the popular demand for a more healthful and comfortable environment.

The war, revealing the vulnerability of large cities, gave added impetus to decentralization of cities and dispersion of industries. Strategic considerations will probably carry considerable weight in the future in planning new factories; corporations will compare the advantages of a central location in a metropolitan area with the merits of less exposed communities. Transfer of established industrial concerns is, of course, a long process, but new industries are likely to develop at some distance from the large urban centers. This change may affect real estate values adversely in some cities, but at the same time the decline in population pressure will make it easier to replan and rezone metropolitan areas. The recent efforts of the British to integrate city planning into regional planning and to combine the regional plans in a comprehensive national plan are likely to stimulate similar efforts in other countries.[45]

The goal of city planning will be, not to introduce piecemeal improvements here and there, but, rather, to reorganize a vast area around the city so as to accomodate people and business more conveniently and efficiently, providing the facilities needed for production, trade, everyday living and recreation. Practically, such a reorganization of metropolitan areas will tend to transform them into constellations of moderate-sized communities.[46]

A metropolitan area thus organized combines features of the two types of ancient cities. The business center of the supercity plays the part of the old oriental capital in governing the economic life of a large adjacent region, while the residential areas and satellite towns are like the Greek communities of citizens, more or less self-sufficient in everyday life.

---

43. **14.**

44. Cf. **10**, *passim*. Cf. **30** and **24.**

45. As the Swedish Association for Town and Country Planning puts it: "The problems of war and reconstruction have given new life to a system of town planning and community building based on democratic cooperation within small units, organically developed from groups of dwellings via neighborhood units to whole districts, big towns, world centres—all in accordance with a sociological pattern that has been in particular described by Lewis Mumford." (**17**, pp. 3–4; cf. **16** and **26**, *passim*.)

46. **35**, p. 338.

BEFORE THE BOMBARDMENT

KEY TO THE BASIC PLAN FOR THE RECONSTRUCTED CITY OF ROTTERDAM (*on facing page*):

A — Town Hall
B — Post Office
C — Laurens Church
E — Witte Huis
F — Museum Boymans
G — Temporary Theatre
H — Gas-Works
J — s-Gravendijkwal
K — Kruiskade
L — Nieuwe Binnenweg
M — Rochussenstraat
N — Witte de Withstraat
O — Westzeedijk

Q — Zalmhaven
P — The Gardens
R — Schiekade
S — Boezem
T — Oostzeedijk
U — Kralingsche Plas
V — Oranjeboomstraat
1 — Central Station
2 — Westersingel
3 — Music centre
4 — Stationsboulevard
5 — Hofplein
6 — Coolsingel

7 — van Hogendorpplein
8 — Blaak
9 — Roundabout leading to the river
  Meuse
10 — Bridge across the River Meuse
11 — Railway bridge across the River
  Meuse
12 — Admiraal de Ruyterweg
13 — Beurs Station
14 — Maasboulevard
15 — Nieuwe Haven
16 — Haringvliet
17 — Scheepmakershaven

18 — Wijnhaven
19 — New harbour for river barges
20 — Willemsplein
21 — Maritime centre
22 — High and low Leuvehavenkade
23 — Western part Blaak
24 — van Oldenbarneveltstraat
25 — Hoogstraat
26 — Groenendaal
27 — Aert van Nesstraat
28 — Meent
29 — Jonker Fransstraat
30 — River Rotte

31 — Centre for forwarding Agents
32 — Space for special purposes
33 — Market
34 — Residential neighbourhood
  North of the Goudschesingel
35 — Goudsche Rijweg
36 — Goudschesingel
37 — Oostplein
38 — Gedempte Slaak
39 — Residential neighbourhood,
  Kralingen
40 — Oude Plantage
41 — Dwellings

Basic Plan for the Reconstructed City of Rotterdam

Ministry of Reconstruction and Housing, The Netherlands

FIGURE 49. EFFECTS OF WORLD WAR II: ROTTERDAM DESTROYED AND REBUILT

Chapter 5

BIRTHS, DEATHS, MARRIAGES AND DIVORCES

Birth and death rates reflect many and often conflicting developments in a nation and in turn greatly influence its economic and political trends. As factors controlling the size of population, the numbers of births and deaths are, indeed, the mainspring of human history. They account for the density of population in certain areas and the depopulation of others, the flow of international and internal migration, the rise and fall of empires.

Rapid increase in population usually stimulates a country's economic and political expansion but may also lead, under unfavorable conditions, to poverty and degradation. On the other hand, decline in the number of inhabitants almost always signals a country's doom, and a nation that grows less rapidly than its neighbors is likely to lose ground in international affairs.

France was supreme in Europe in the seventeenth century, lost that position in the eighteenth, failed to regain it under Napoleon, and has been losing ground since that time. Decline in its political power has paralleled the shrinkage in its share of Europe's population — from 20 per cent in 1650 and 18 per cent a century later to 15.7 per cent in 1800, 13.3 per cent in 1850, 9.7 per cent in 1900, and 7.7 per cent in 1950.[1]

BIRTHS (NATALITY)

Because of the vital importance of changes in the number of births and the complexity of the factors that can cause such changes, special methods have been developed to measure natality. None of these measures is suitable for all purposes, but they largely supplement one another.[2]

MEASURING NATALITY

Natality is measured by the *crude birth rate,* the fertility rate by age class, the *total fertility rate,* the gross and the net *reproduction rates,* and the *replacement index.*

1. **39**, p. 221.
2. **1**, pp. 50 ff. Cf. **3** and **10**.

The Crude Birth Rate

The simplest measure is the *crude birth rate,* the number of births during a year per 1,000 persons in an area or population group. The shortcoming of this measure is that it gives no regard to the age and sex distribution of the population. In appraising the number of births as a social phenomenon, in comparing natality in different countries or areas and in projecting the current population trends into the future, it is preferable to relate the number of births to that of women of child-bearing age, say 15 to 49 years.

Fertility Rates

The *fertility rate* for an age group indicates the number of children born annually per 1,000 women in the group. In computing such rates, five-year age intervals from 15 through 49 years are commonly used. The rates for the lowest and highest age groups are sometimes adjusted to allow for births before 15 and after 49 years. (See Table 71.)

The *total fertility rate* is derived from the fertility rates for each age group. It shows the hypothetical number of children who would be born to 1,000 women through the whole child-bearing period, assuming the given fertility rate for each group.[3] Among other purposes, the total

3. Since women aged 15–49 years usually represent about a fourth of the total population, a birth rate related to the number of women in this age group is about four times the crude birth rate based on total population. If there were no deaths among women aged 15–49, each woman would remain in the child-bearing age group for 35 years and the number of births per 1,000 women entering the group, through the whole reproductive period, would be 35 times the annual birth rate per 1,000 women in the group. Thus the total number of children born to 1,000 women during the reproductive period would be about 140 times the crude birth rate per 1,000 inhabitants: if, for example, the crude birth rate is 15 per 1,000, the total number of children ever born to 1,000 women (the *total fertility rate*) would approximate 2,100. This relationship, however, is affected by the deaths among women and the differences in fertility in the various age groups. Theoretically, the total

fertility rate is used to compute *reproduction rates*.

Gross and Net Reproduction Rates

The *gross reproduction rate* is the ratio of the number of girls (potential future mothers) born to a definite number, say 1,000, women passing through the child-bearing age, assuming that no woman dies before she is 50 years old.[4]

The *net reproduction rate* is computed from the gross reproduction rate with correction for mortality in the new generation of women. It is usually from 10 to 15 per cent below the gross rate and shows the anticipated ratio between births in two successive generations or the increase or decrease that would ultimately be experienced by the population in this period of time, if the current levels of fertility and mortality remained unchanged.[5] A net reproduction rate of 1.0 indicates a state of demographic equilibrium in the long run.

A net reproduction rate below one, however, does not necessarily imply that the population will decrease in the near future. As long as the population has fewer deaths than births because of its particular age composition, it continues to grow. If the net reproduction rate remains below unity, however, the decline is bound to come sooner or later. In brief, the net reproduction rate measures the vitality of the population in terms of the *long-range* trend, rather than current changes. The latter are best reflected by comparison of the crude birth and death rates.

Fertility may also be measured in terms of the number of children per family (classified by duration of marriage) or per 1,000 women (classified by age). These measurements have two advantages: first, all the information required to compute them can be derived from a census of population or a sample survey of limited scope so that they do not depend on current registration of births; second, they permit classification of births by characteristics that are not shown in birth certificates but appear in the census schedule, such as age of the father and mother, number and age of children in the family, duration of the marriage, occupation of the family head, income of the household and so on. Ratios of the number of children to those of women of child-bearing age, as recorded by a census, can be transformed into fertility rates similar to those derived from birth registration and into *replacement indices* analogous to *net reproduction rates,* which are deduced from current birth and death statistics. Although these measures are not so precise as those discussed in the preceding pages, some students prefer them for their simplicity.

BIRTH RATES

National and Regional Differences

Birth rates vary widely from country to country and often differ within the same country from one region or province to another. The contrast in natality in industrial and agricultural countries and urban and rural regions in the same nation is most conspicuous.

In 1950 the number of births per 1,000 inhabitants ranged from 48.7 in Guatemala and El Salvador, at one extreme, to 15.8 in Austria, 14.8 in Luxembourg and 10.7 in Trieste. (See Table 63 and Figure 50.) The contrast becomes particularly striking when one realizes that the registration of births in underdeveloped areas with high natality cannot be as accurate and complete as in the industrialized areas with comparatively low birth rates. Thus it appears that the number of births per 1,000 inhabitants in some underdeveloped regions may be many times the pre-World War II rates that prevailed in the nations of Western civilization.

The peoples with high birth rates are predominantly agricultural and of non-European stock. The USSR is the only European nation that reported a birth rate above 35 per 1,000 before the war but the accuracy of these statistics is questionable. Rates from 22 to 26.5 per 1,000 were usual in eastern and southern European agricultural countries before the war when in-

---

fertility rate should equal the sum of specific fertility rates for each of the hypothetical 35 age years of the child-bearing period. Practically, it is computed as five times the sum of fertility rates for the seven five-year age classes.

Occasionally the number of births is related to that of men in specified age brackets. The merits of this method, the *paternity rate,* are questionable, however.

4. If there were no difference between the numbers of boys and girls among the newborn, the number of female births would be half that of all births, and the gross reproduction rate would be half the total fertility rate. Since female births usually constitute somewhat less than half of all births (see below, pp. 158–59), the gross reproduction rate oscillates around 48.5 per cent of the total fertility rate.

5. **1**, pp. 50–51; cf. **26**.

TABLE 63

BIRTH RATES IN SELECTED COUNTRIES, AROUND 1950

(*Births Per 1,000 Inhabitants*)

Country,[a] Year	Births	Country,[a] Year	Births	Country,[a] Year	Births
Trieste, 1950	10.7	Australia, 1950	23.3	French India,[c] 1949	32.8
Angola, 1950	14.3	United States, 1950	23.4	Israel, 1950	32.9
Luxembourg, 1950	14.8	Paraguay, 1948	23.6	Panama, 1949	33.0
Austria, 1950	15.8	Bulgaria, 1947	24.0	Algeria (Moslems), 1949	34.1
United Kingdom, 1950	16.1	Finland, 1950	24.0	Colombia, 1949	35.3
Western Germany, 1950	16.2	Portugal, 1950	24.2	Dominican Republic, 1950	37.4
Sweden, 1950	16.4	New Zealand, 1950	24.6	Puerto Rico, 1950	38.5
Belgium, 1950	16.5	Argentina, 1949	24.9	Yukon (Canada), 1949	39.7
Pakistan, 1948	18.0	Union of South Africa,[b]		Belgian Congo,[b] 1950	39.8
Switzerland, 1950	18.1	1950	25.7	Ceylon, 1950	40.3
Denmark, 1950	18.6	Greece, 1949	26.1	China, 1943	40.7
Hungary, 1948	19.1	Canada, 1950	26.6	Honduras, 1949	41.3
Norway, 1950	19.3	India, 1949	26.7	Nicaragua, 1950	41.4
Italy, 1950	19.6	Thailand, 1949	27.1	Federation of Malaya,	
Romania, 1945	19.6	Indonesia,[c] 1940	28.3	1949	42.0
Spain, 1950	19.9	Japan, 1950	28.4	Venezuela, 1950	43.1
France, 1950	20.4	Bolivia, 1949	29.0	São Tomé and Principe,	
Uruguay, 1944	20.7	Yugoslavia, 1948	30.2	1949	45.2
Ireland, 1950	21.0	Peru, 1950	30.3	Mexico, 1950	45.7
Algeria,[b] 1949	21.4	Gold Coast,[c] 1949	30.7	Singapore,[b] 1950	45.7
Czechoslovakia, 1949	22.1	Korea, 1944	31.8	Costa Rica, 1950	46.5
Netherlands, 1950	22.7	Chile, 1950	32.4	El Salvador, 1950	48.7
		Burma, 1939	32.4	Guatemala, 1950	48.7

Sources: **2,** 1951, pp. 156–63; **5,** October 1951, pp. 15–18; **4,** July 1951, pp. 4–24.

a. Countries arrayed by increasing birth rate.

b. Europeans.

c. Europeans and natives.

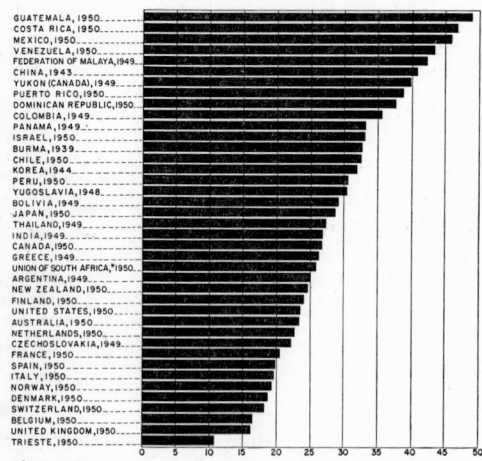

Per 1,000 inhabitants

FIGURE 50. BIRTH RATES IN SELECTED COUNTRIES, AROUND 1950

dustrial countries were reporting 10 to 12 births per 1,000 and sometimes fewer.

The correlation between the type of national economy and the birth rate remains despite the upturn of natality in industrial countries and is particularly clear when one compares the extreme ends of the distribution: for example, Guatemala or Mexico, on the one hand, and the United Kingdom or Luxembourg, on the other. It is less clear in the middle part of the distribution, among the countries in which birth rates range between 18 and 24 per 1,000. In this middle group, the United States and Australia appear very close to Portugal and Romania; Pakistan, possibly as a result of incomplete registration of births, has a place between Belgium and Switzerland. (See Table 63 and Figure 50.)

The range among the states of the United States is narrower. In 1940, the lowest birth rate — 14.1 per 1,000 — was recorded in New Jersey and the highest — 27.7 per 1,000 — in New Mexico. The comparable rates in 1948 were 20.5 and 35.9 per 1,000 inhabitants. (See Table 64.) The states with the lowest birth rates rank close to Italy, Spain and France, while the high-natality states are close to Chile and Colombia. (Cf. Table 63.)

TABLE 64

BIRTH RATES IN THE UNITED STATES, BY STATE, 1940 AND 1948

(Births Per 1,000 Inhabitants)

State [a]	1940	1948	State [a]	1940	1948
United States, total	17.9	24.2			
New Mexico	27.7	35.9	Vermont	18.6	25.8
Utah	24.6	30.9	Indiana	18.1	23.6
Mississippi	24.1	30.9	South Dakota	18.1	26.8
Arizona	23.5	27.3	Iowa	17.9	23.2
South Carolina	23.4	29.1	Maine	17.8	24.6
District of Columbia	23.1	24.1	Florida	17.8	24.5
North Carolina	22.6	28.8	Wisconsin	17.5	24.7
Idaho	22.3	27.5	New Hampshire	17.3	23.8
Kentucky	22.3	27.0	Delaware	17.2	24.2
Alabama	22.2	29.4	Nebraska	16.8	24.3
West Virginia	22.1	27.4	Pennsylvania	16.7	21.7
Louisiana	21.5	28.3	Maryland	16.6	24.8
Georgia	20.8	29.3	Ohio	16.6	23.8
North Dakota	20.8	28.5	Missouri	16.4	21.9
Virginia	20.6	26.9	Oregon	16.4	21.5
Montana	20.5	29.4	Washington	16.2	22.7
Wyoming	20.1	26.0	California	16.2	23.2
Arkansas	19.7	24.8	Kansas	15.9	22.5
Texas	19.7	26.8	Illinois	15.6	22.1
Tennessee	19.1	25.8	Massachusetts	15.3	21.0
Oklahoma	19.1	22.0	Rhode Island	15.1	22.6
Minnesota	19.0	24.8	Connecticut	14.7	21.2
Michigan	18.9	24.9	New York	14.6	21.2
Colorado	18.8	27.5	New Jersey	14.1	20.5
Nevada	18.7	22.5			

Source: **8**, 1950, p. 66.

a. Arrayed by declining birth rate in 1940.

Long-Range Trends

Records in the Scandinavian countries, some of them spanning two centuries, show that birth rates in the past fluctuated more widely from year to year than at present but, on the average, changed little for many decades. In fact, the combined average birth rate for Sweden, Norway and Finland was almost exactly the same in 1871–75 as it had been a century before, 32.7 as compared with 33.2.

In the 1870's, however, these and other European countries entered a period of declining natality. This trend continued for more than half a century until it was checked, perhaps reversed, in the late 1930's. (See Table 65 and Figure 51.)

The downward trend in birth rates in modern times started almost a century ago and spread gradually. In the first half of the nineteenth century, France was probably the only country in Europe with a steadily declining natality. In the 1870's the same trend developed in England, the Netherlands, Germany and Scandinavia. By the end of the nineteenth century it had spread over all western and central Europe. Kuczynski has computed the following combined birth rates for this area for the period from 1841–45 to 1926: [6]

1841–45	31.9	1891–95	29.7
1846–50	30.9	1896–1900	29.4
1851–55	30.8	1901–05	28.4
1856–60	31.7	1906–10	26.6
1861–65	32.1	1911–14	24.2
1866–70	32.0	1915–19	17.0
1871–75	32.7	1920–21	23.8
1876–80	32.8	1922–23	21.0
1881–85	31.4	1924–25	19.9
1886–90	30.2	1926	19.2

6. The index includes Belgium, Denmark, the United Kingdom, Ireland, Finland, France, Germany, the Netherlands, Luxembourg, Norway, Sweden and Switzerland. **37**, Vol. I, p. 9.

TABLE 65

AVERAGE ANNUAL BIRTH RATES IN SELECTED EUROPEAN COUNTRIES, 1751–1950

(*Births Per 1,000 Inhabitants*)

Period	Sweden	Norway	Finland	England and Wales	France
1751–55	37.1	34.4	45.3	...	...
1761–65	34.6	35.3	43.7	...	...
1771–75	31.3	29.4	38.8	...	...
1781–85	31.8	29.9	40.4	...	...
1791–95	33.9	33.5	41.1	...	...
1801–05	31.4	28.2	38.4	...	...
1811–15	32.9	27.1	37.0	...	...
1821–25	35.8	33.7	38.7	...	...
1831–35	32.4	31.2	34.2	...	...
1841–45	31.3	30.4	35.5	32.3	28.3
1851–55	31.8	32.5	36.3	33.9	26.2
1861–65	33.2	31.9	37.0	35.1	26.7
1871–75	30.7	30.3	37.0	35.5	25.9
1881–85	29.4	31.0	35.5	33.5	25.0
1891–95	27.4	30.1	31.8	30.5	22.6
1901–05	26.1	28.5	31.3	28.2	21.6
1911–14	23.5	25.3	28.1	23.6 [a]	18.8
1920–25	19.9	22.9	23.6	19.9 [b]	19.7
1926–30	16.0	18.0	21.2	16.7	18.2
1931–35	14.1	15.3	18.4	15.0	16.5
1936–40	14.8	15.5	19.3	18.0	14.7
1941–45	18.6	18.2	21.2	21.3	15.3
1946–50	18.2	20.7	26.6	19.0	21.0

Sources: **12**, 1938; **4**; official yearbooks for Sweden, Norway and Finland.

     a. 1911–15.   b. 1921–25.

This combined index suggests that birth rates were stable or even rose from 1841–50 to 1880 and declined rapidly thereafter. By the early 1930's, this trend would have brought the index close to 15 per 1,000, about half the rate at the end of the nineteenth century. Between 1900 and 1930, birth rates were declining in almost all European countries [7] and in the United States and Australia as well; in most countries the trend has been reversed in more recent years. (See Table 66.)

In the birth registration area of the United States the birth rate per 1,000 inhabitants has varied since 1915 as follows: [8]

1915	25.0	1918	24.7
1916	24.9	1919	22.3
1917	24.5	1920	23.7

1921	24.2	1936	16.7
1922	22.3	1937	17.1
1923	22.1	1938	17.6
1924	22.2	1939	17.3
1925	21.3	1940	17.9
1926	20.9	1941	18.9
1927	20.5	1942	20.9
1928	19.7	1943	21.5
1929	18.8	1944	20.2
1930	18.9	1945	19.6
1931	18.0	1946	23.3
1932	17.4	1947	25.7
1933	16.6	1948	24.1
1934	17.2	1949	23.9
1935	16.9	1950	23.4

In South America, Egypt, Malaya, Ceylon and Russia, rates remained very high, at the level recorded in Europe in the middle of the nineteenth century.

In almost all countries of Western civilization, the last two decades of the nineteenth century and the beginning of the twentieth were

7. With the single exception of Portugal.
8. For 1915–40, **11**, pp. 666–67. For later years, **2**, 1951; and **5**. No comparable data are available for earlier years.

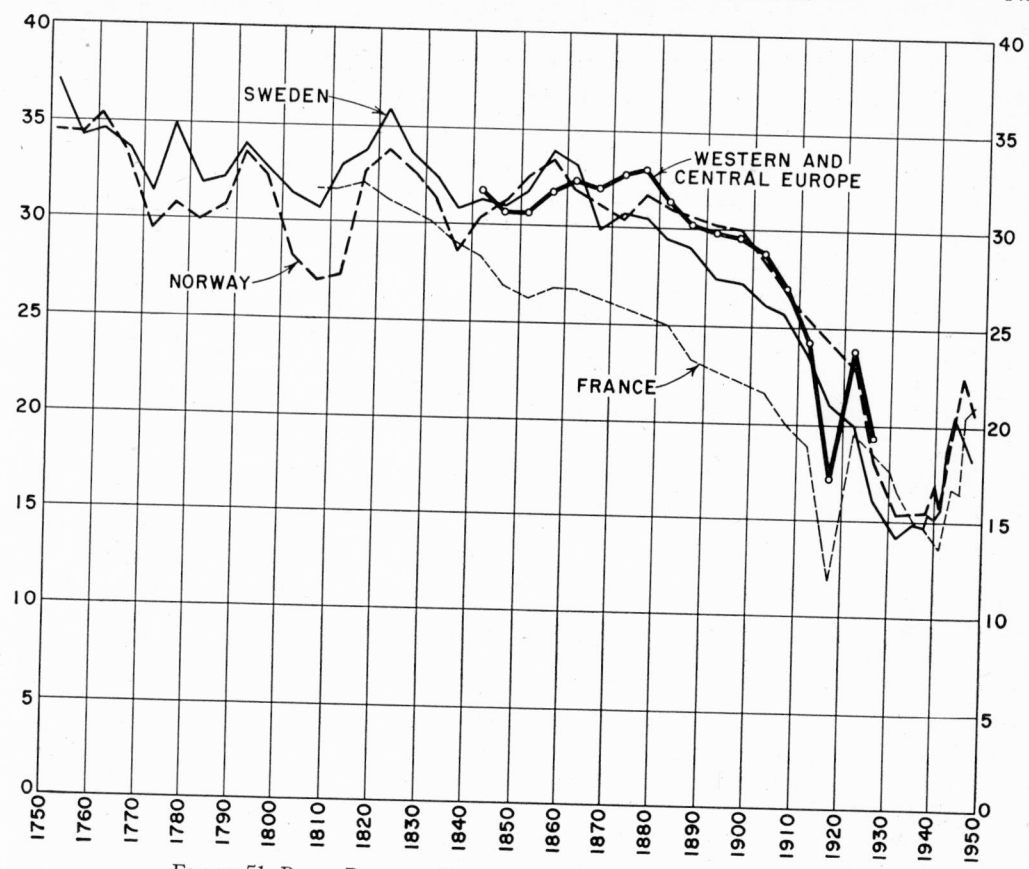

FIGURE 51. BIRTH RATES IN SELECTED EUROPEAN COUNTRIES, 1751–1950

Per 1,000 inhabitants

Birth rates have declined in France since the end of the Napoleonic Wars. In Sweden and Norway, birth rates increased at the beginning of the nineteenth century, reached a peak in the early 1820's, declined until the late 1830's, rose again, and then declined continuously from 1870 to 1930. The birth rate for western and central Europe as a whole has declined since 1880. Apart from sharp fluctuations during World War I, birth rates in Europe were at their lowest point in the mid-1930's and have since risen.

marked by unprecedented economic progress, increase in industrial production, rise in real wages, improvement in public health and education, and the growth of large cities. The simultaneous fall in birth rates may have been related to any one of these developments or a combination of them. It is easy, for example, to establish a negative correlation between the birth rate and real wages, school attendance, horsepower in industry, number of automobiles or tractors, and so on.[9] Such correlations could be supported by the differences in the birth rates in various countries — high in underdeveloped and poor countries, low in better-developed industrial nations. These would be spurious correla-

tions, however, between two simultaneous developments that may or may not have been interrelated.

The Toll of World War I

World War I and the postwar turmoil had a disastrous effect on the number of births in Europe. The deficit in births in European countries, excluding Russia, during the war years was nearly double the number of military deaths. The toll of World War I on the population of western and central Europe was 22.4 million lives: 6.6 million military deaths; 3.2 million excess deaths of civilians; and a deficit of 12.6 million births, when compared with the number that might have been expected in line with the prewar trend. (See Table 67.) The deficit would have been still larger if the decline

9. See, for example, the chart of natality and standard of living in France from 1810 to 1940 in **39**, p. 73; cf. **22**, Part II, p. 297.

TABLE 66

AVERAGE ANNUAL BIRTH RATES IN SELECTED COUNTRIES, 1871–80 TO 1948–50

(Births Per 1,000 Inhabitants)

Country	1871–80	1881–90	1891–1900	1901–10	1911–19	1920–30	1931–38	1941–47	1948–50
United States	...	...	...	...	24.3	21.3	17.2	21.5	23.8
England and Wales	35.4	32.5	29.9	27.2	22.0	18.8	15.0	17.0	16.7
Scotland	34.9	32.3	30.6	28.4	24.0	21.8	18.0	18.9	18.4
Ireland	26.5	23.4	23.0	23.3	21.0	20.8	19.5	22.0	21.4
France	25.4	23.9	22.2	20.6	15.2	19.0	15.9	16.7	20.8
Belgium	32.3	30.2	29.0	26.1	18.0	19.6	16.2	15.4	17.1
Netherlands	36.2	34.2	32.5	30.5	26.8	24.6	20.8	24.1	23.9
Denmark	31.4	32.0	30.2	28.7	25.0	21.1	17.8	21.6	19.3
Sweden	30.5	29.1	27.1	25.8	22.1	18.0	14.2	18.9	17.4
Norway	31.0	30.9	30.3	27.5	24.9	20.5	15.3	19.6	19.8
Finland	37.0	35.0	32.2	29.1	25.9	22.4	18.5 [a]	23.3	26.0
Germany	39.1	36.8	36.1	33.0	24.0	20.5	17.5	...	16.7 [b]
Switzerland	30.8	28.0	27.9	26.9	21.2	18.6	16.0	19.9	18.5
Austria	39.0	37.9	37.1	34.7	23.0	15.0	14.5	17.5	16.2
Hungary	...	44.0	40.6	37.0	28.3	27.9	21.4	19.0	...
Portugal	...	33.0	33.6	31.8	32.3	32.3	29.2	24.6	25.4
Spain	37.9	36.2	34.8	34.4	30.0	29.6	27.0 [c]	21.3	21.4
Italy	36.9	37.8	34.9	32.7	27.5	28.4	23.5	20.6	20.4
Romania	35.0	41.4	40.6	39.8	38.0	36.2	32.0	22.2	...
Russia (USSR) (European)	...	...	49.2	46.5	...	43.8	...	...	...
Japan	...	27.2	29.8	32.2	33.0	34.2	31.2 [a]	29.2	31.5
Australia	36.1	35.2	29.9	26.5	27.0	22.6	17.1	21.3	23.1

Sources: **12**, 1938; **2**, 1949–50, pp. 302–07; **5**.

a. 1931–37.

b. Western Germany.

c. 1931–35.

The Interwar Period

After a brief upswing following World War I, birth rates in western and central Europe, North America and Australia continued to fall. The decline was accelerated during the depression in the early 1930's.

On the eve of World War II, the trend in birth rates in most countries of Western civiliza-

tion was not very clear. The new population policy of the Nazis in Germany and the fascist government in Italy had been only moderately successful; it stopped the fall in the number of births but did not reverse the trend. In the United States, birth rates rose in the late 1930's, but this seemed to be a temporary phenomenon, a result of economic recovery. In most industrial countries the number of births was in precarious balance with the number of deaths.

Effects of World War II

One might have expected that World War II, with its bombing of cities, would have caused a greater decline in births than World War I. This did not occur, however. Birth rates went down in Belgium and France under German domination, but not as sharply as in 1916–17. The number of births declined slightly in England in 1941 and in Austria, Germany and Italy

in births during the war had not been partly offset by high rates in 1920–21.[10]

---

10. The totals above do not include Russia, for which statistics are lacking. During and immediately after the war and the civil war, with pestilence and famine on its heels, Russia probably lost more lives than all other belligerent countries combined. The total loss of Europe, including Russia, therefore, may have amounted to some 50 million human lives. It is likely also that the acceleration in the fall in birth rates in western Europe in the 1920's was partly due to the psychological and economic repercussions of World War I.

TABLE 67

IMPACT OF WORLD WAR I ON EUROPE'S POPULATION

(Thousands)

Country	Population, 1914	Wartime Deficit			
		Total	Military Deaths	Deficit in Births	Excess in Civilian Deaths [a]
Europe, total [b]	318,871	22,397	6,578	12,596	3,223
Allies					
United Kingdom	46,085	1,788	744	709	335
France	39,800	3,074	1,320	1,686	68
Belgium	7,662	416	40	311	65
Italy	35,859	2,735	700	1,426	609
Serbia and Montenegro	3,400	1,064	325	336	403
Romania	7,771	1,088	250	505	333
Portugal	6,155	264	4	121	139
Greece	4,732	295	25	200	70
Central Powers					
Germany	67,790	5,436	2,000	3,158	278
Austria-Hungary	53,018	5,063	1,100	3,600	363
Bulgaria	4,852	444	70	317	57
Nonbelligerent [c]	41,743	730	—	227	503

Source: **45**, p. 75.

a. Excess of deaths over age one, minus reduction in infant deaths due to the declining natality.

b. Excluding Russia. Russia's military losses are estimated at 1.5 to 2 million. Reliable population statistics for births and civilian deaths are lacking for the early postwar period, and losses caused by revolution cannot be segregated from those due to World War I.

c. Norway, Sweden, Denmark, the Netherlands, Switzerland and Spain.

in 1945; but in Norway and Denmark the number rose despite the troubled conditions of life under the German occupation; so also in Sweden and Switzerland, despite the imminent danger of invasion; and in the United States, Australia and New Zealand, birth rates increased spectacularly despite the participation of these countries in the war. All in all, the effect of World War II on natality was very different from that of World War I. (See Table 68 and Figure 52.)

After the second world war, birth rates went up in all belligerent countries and, in contrast to the experience in the 1920's, the rise proved in most cases to be more than a short-lived postwar boom. Rates declined slightly in 1948–50 but remained very high in comparison with the level in the 1930's and only slightly below that in 1913.

Recent Trend in Birth Rates

The French population expert, Alfred Sauvy, has computed combined birth rates for western

Europe, the United States, Canada, Australia and New Zealand, for the period 1913–47.[11] Continued through 1949, his series indicates that the birth rate for the group of fourteen nations, with an aggregate population of more than 300 million in 1948, averaged 24.5 per 1,000 in 1913, fell to 17.2–17.3 in 1933–37, rose to 24.0 in 1947, and was still as high as 22.1 in 1949.[12] Since the United States has nearly the same population as all other countries in this group combined, it may seem preferable to use the arithmetic mean of the rates recorded in each country, without weighting by population. The combined birth rate thus computed is 25.2 per 1,000 in 1913, ranges between 17.0 and 17.2 in 1933–37, reaches the peak of 23.7 in 1947, and falls back to 21.9 in 1949. (See Table 69; cf. Figure 53.)

The upturn of birth rates in western Europe,

11. **50**, pp. 250 ff.

12. The list includes the United Kingdom, Ireland, France, Luxembourg, Belgium, the Netherlands, Denmark, Sweden, Norway and Switzerland, in Europe; the United States, Canada, Australia and New Zealand.

TABLE 68

BIRTH RATES IN SELECTED COUNTRIES BEFORE, DURING AND AFTER WORLD WARS I AND II

(Births Per 1,000 Inhabitants)

Year	United States	United Kingdom [a]	France	Belgium	Italy	Germany [b]	Austria
			WORLD WAR I PERIOD				
1912	—	23.9	19.0	22.7	32.4	28.2	31.4
1913	—	24.1	18.8	21.6	31.7	27.5	29.6
1914	—	23.8	17.9	20.2	31.1	26.8	23.0
1915	25.1	23.0	11.6	16.5	30.2	20.4	18.5
1916	25.0	22.8	9.5	13.2	24.0	15.3	14.6
1917	24.7	19.8	10.5	11.6	19.5	13.9	13.8
1918	24.6	19.8	12.2	11.5	18.1	14.2	14.0
1919	22.3	18.8	12.6	16.9	21.2	20.0	17.9
1920	23.7	25.5	21.4	21.9	31.9	27.1	22.3
1921	24.2	22.4	20.7	21.8	30.4	26.1	23.2
1922	22.3	20.4	19.3	20.4	30.5	23.6	23.1
1923	22.2	19.7	19.1	20.4	30.6	21.0	22.4
1924	22.4	18.8	18.7	19.9	30.0	20.5	21.6
1925	21.3	18.3	19.1	19.7	27.5	20.6	—
			WORLD WAR II PERIOD				
1931–35	16.9	15.5	16.5	16.8	23.8	16.6	14.4
1936	16.7	15.3	15.3	15.4	22.4	19.0	13.1
1937	17.1	15.3	15.0	15.3	22.9	18.8	12.8
1938	17.6	15.5	14.9	16.0	23.8	19.7	13.9
1939	17.3	15.2	14.8	15.5	23.6	20.4	20.7
1940	17.9	14.6	14.0	13.6	23.5	20.0	21.8
1941	18.9	14.4	13.4	12.2	20.9	18.6	20.1
1942	20.9	15.9	14.8	13.2	20.5	15.0	17.1
1943	21.5	16.6	15.9	15.0	20.0	16.0	18.0
1944	20.2	17.9	16.4	15.3	19.4	—	18.6
1945	19.6	16.2	16.5	15.7	18.5	—	14.9
1946	23.3	19.4	20.9	18.3	22.7	15.9	15.9
1947	25.7	20.7	21.3	17.8	21.9	16.5	18.6
1948	24.1	18.1	21.2	17.6	21.6	16.4	17.7
1949	23.9	17.0	21.0	17.2	20.0	16.6	15.8
1950	23.4	16.1	20.4	16.5	19.6	16.2	15.6

Sources: **12**, 1938; **1**, p. 41; **2**, 1951, pp. 288–95; **5**.

  a. For 1912–25, England and Wales.   b. For 1946–50, Western Germany.

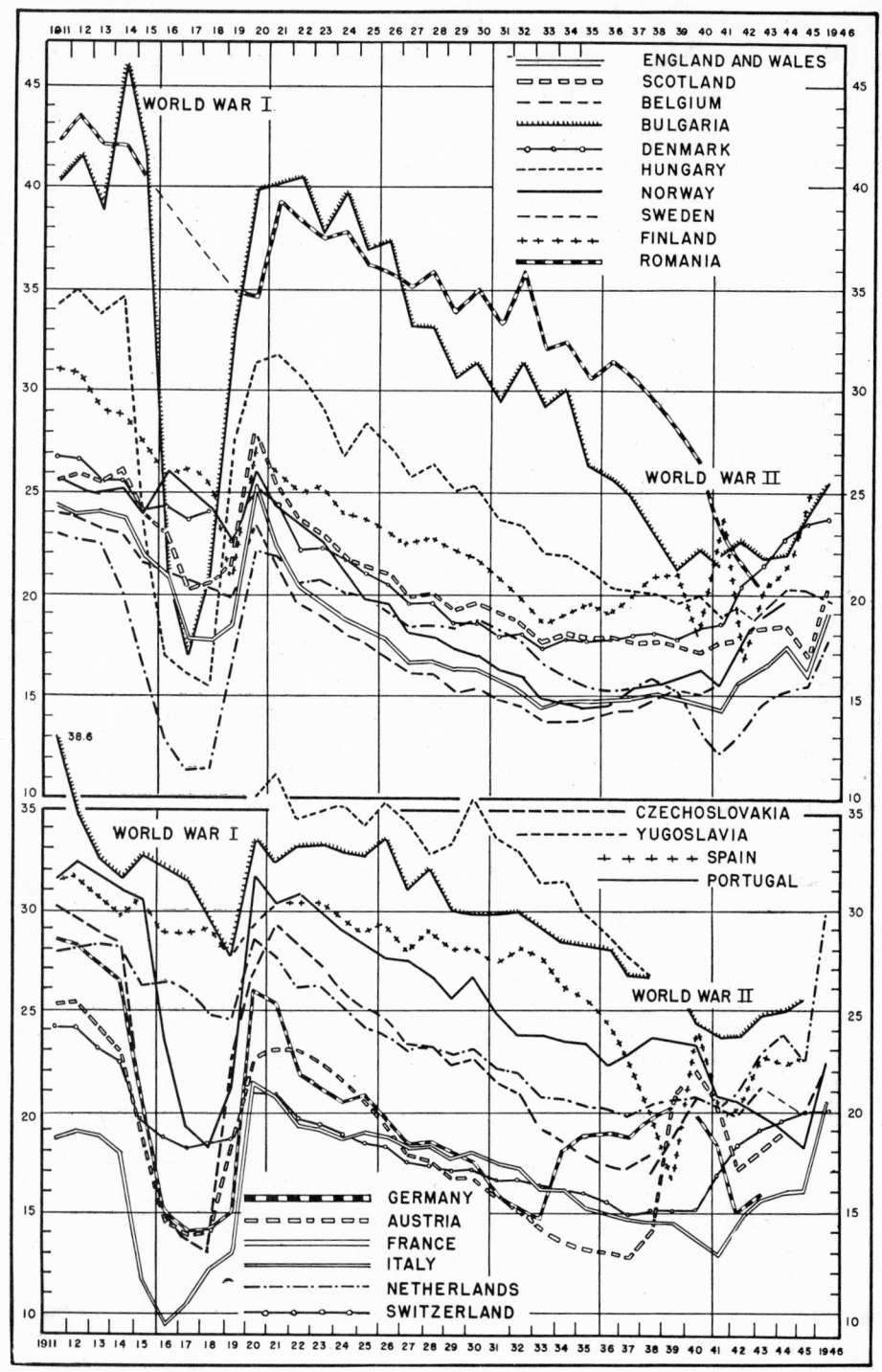

Per 1,000 inhabitants   World Health Organization

FIGURE 52. BIRTH RATES IN SELECTED EUROPEAN COUNTRIES, 1911–46

In striking contrast to the experience during World War I, birth rates in belligerent countries were only moderately affected by World War II. The range of the fluctuations in 1940–45 was surprisingly narrow in comparison with changes in the interwar years. (Cf. 6, August 1947.)

147

TABLE 69

AVERAGE BIRTH RATES FOR FOURTEEN COUNTRIES OF WESTERN CIVILIZATION, 1913–49

Year	Arithmetic Mean of 14 Birth Rates	Rate for Total Area of 14 Countries [a]	Year	Arithmetic Mean of 14 Birth Rates	Rate for Total Area of 14 Countries [a]
1913	25.2	24.5	1937	17.1	17.3
			1938	17.6	17.8
1925	21.1	21.9	1939	17.6	17.4
1926	20.7	21.4			
1927	20.0	20.6	1940	17.5	17.4
1928	19.8	20.1	1941	18.1	17.8
1929	19.2	19.4	1942	18.9	19.3
			1943	19.9	20.2
1930	19.3	19.5	1944	20.4	20.0
1931	18.6	18.8			
1932	18.0	18.3	1945	20.7	19.5
1933	17.1	17.3	1946	22.3	23.0
1934	17.2	17.6	1947	23.7	24.0
			1948	22.7	22.4
1935	17.0	17.3	1949	21.9	22.1
1936	17.1	17.2			

Sources: For 1913–46, **50**, p. 255; for 1947–49, computed on the basis of data in **5**.

a. United States and Canada; United Kingdom, Ireland, France, Belgium, Luxembourg, the Netherlands, Denmark, Sweden, Norway, Switzerland; Australia and New Zealand.

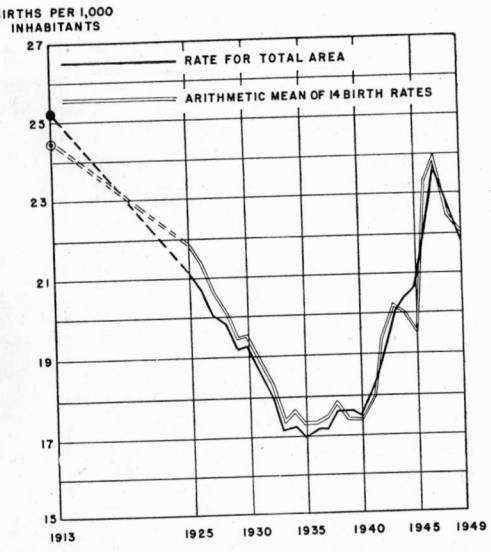

FIGURE 53. AVERAGE BIRTH RATES FOR FOURTEEN COUNTRIES OF WESTERN CIVILIZATION, 1913–49

54.) In the countries that had less than 25 births per 1,000 inhabitants in 1927, natality declined in 1927–37 and increased in 1937–50. Where the rate was more than 30 in 1927, the opposite trend prevailed. The general development has been toward equality in birth rates. The average (unweighted) for the United States, the United Kingdom, Sweden, Norway, France, Belgium, Australia and New Zealand went up from 15.9 per 1,000 in 1937 to 20.0 per 1,000 in 1950, while the average for Chile, Spain, Portugal, Bulgaria, Romania, Japan and India dropped from 28.9 to 25.0.[13]

FERTILITY RATES

Because the crude birth rate is based on a comparison of the number of births with the whole population, including children, it fails to show differences in the propensity of different nations or different groups of the population to have children. In this respect, fertility rates for women in specific age groups are preferable. Such rates are now computed in more than

the United States, Canada and Australia since the middle 1930's appears still more striking when it is compared with the long-range changes in these and other countries. Since 1937 birth rates have been rising mainly in nations where the prewar natality had been particularly low and in rapid decline. (See Table 70; cf. Figure

13. Possible reasons for these changes will be discussed below (see pp. 158 ff.), after other measurements of natality and data on natality in various population groups have been examined.

TABLE 70

BIRTH RATES IN SELECTED COUNTRIES, 1911–13, 1927, 1937 AND 1950

(Births Per 1,000 Inhabitants)

Country	1911–13	1927	1937	1950
Countries with Less than 25 Births Per 1,000 Inhabitants in 1927				
Sweden	23.1	16.1	14.4	16.3
United Kingdom	24.3	17.1	15.3	16.1
Switzerland	...	17.6	14.9	18.1
Austria	23.8	17.8	12.8	15.6
Norway	25.0	18.0	15.1	19.3
France	22.7	18.2	15.0	20.4
Belgium	28.1	18.4	15.3	16.5
Denmark	18.1	19.6	18.0	18.6
Ireland	22.7	20.3	19.2	21.0
New Zealand	26.2	20.3	17.3	24.6
United States	25.1 [a]	20.6	17.1	23.4
Australia	27.8	21.7	17.9	23.3
Finland	26.3	22.8	19.9	24.0
Netherlands	27.0	23.1	19.8	22.7
Czechoslovakia	19.6	23.3	16.2	22.1 [b]
Countries with More than 25 Births Per 1,000 Inhabitants in 1927				
Canada	...	25.3	20.0	26.5
Hungary	32.9	25.8	20.2	19.1 [c]
Union of South Africa [d]	31.9	26.0	24.9	25.7
Italy	31.7	27.5	22.9	19.6
Spain	31.2	27.9	22.4	19.9
Venezuela	29.8	29.5	33.5	43.1
Argentina	37.4	30.7	24.0	24.9 [b]
Portugal	35.3	31.6	26.7	24.2
Bulgaria	35.8	33.1	24.3	24.0
Japan	34.1	33.4	30.8	28.4 [e]
India	38.6	34.0	33.7	26.7 [b]
Romania	42.6	35.2	30.8	19.6 [f]
Philippines	32.9	35.3	33.2	...
Mexico	...	36.7	44.1	45.4
Chile	39.9	42.8	33.4	32.4

Sources: **1** and **5**.

a. 1915.
b. 1949.
c. 1948.
d. Europeans.
e. 1947.
f. 1945.

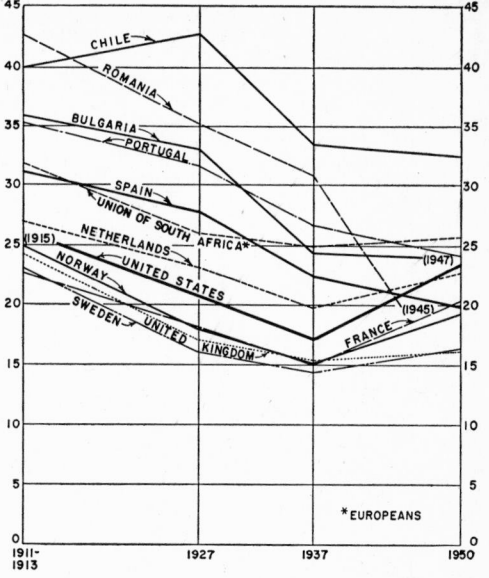

Per 1,000 inhabitants

FIGURE 54. BIRTH RATES IN SELECTED COUNTRIES, 1911–13, 1927, 1937 AND 1950

at ages 25–29, and drops abruptly after age 30. In Great Britain, France, Italy, Canada, Australia and New Zealand, the period of high fertility is in the ages 20–34 years, with the peak in the middle, at 25–29. In the Netherlands, Sweden and Norway, high fertility begins and ends somewhat later, extending from 25 years through 39 years, with the peak at ages 25–34. (See Table 71.)

These patterns are only slightly affected by changes in the general level of natality in a country. In the United States, for example, there was a striking difference between fertility rates in 1930 and 1946, but the specific rates for the various age groups changed in the same direction. There was a slight tendency toward compressing the period of births into the two decades from age 20 to 40. This tendency, however, was not as clear in all countries as in the United States.

The general impression conveyed by a comparison of age-specific fertility rates in different countries is that the distribution of births over the span of the reproductive years is determined essentially by national customs rather than biological factors.

REPRODUCTION RATES

In a population with very low mortality in the low and middle age groups, a net reproduc-

forty countries.[14] Not all are equally reliable, however, and comparison should be restricted to countries similar in economic and social structure.

In the United States, fertility is highest among women in ages 20–24 years, declines slightly

14. **2**, 1948, pp. 266–79.

TABLE 71

FERTILITY RATES BY AGE GROUPS IN SELECTED COUNTRIES

(Births Per 1,000 Women)

Country and Period	15–19 Years	20–24 Years	25–29 Years	30–34 Years	35–39 Years	40–44 Years	45 Years and Over
United States							
1920	48.5	151.8	150.5	115.5	78.4	31.1	3.8
1930	49.1	124.9	117.3	87.7	56.1	21.8	2.4
1940	48.9	125.3	114.4	77.4	41.9	13.9	1.3
1948	79.8	193.2	160.6	100.5	53.4	15.2	1.1
Canada							
1921–22	37.7	161.1	184.5	153.4	108.9	46.9	6.1
1930–32	29.6	136.7	174.4	144.9	103.2	44.8	5.4
1940	31.0	138.6	159.3	121.9	79.7	31.4	3.6
1948	42.6	178.8	197.0	140.4	89.8	32.4	3.2
Chile							
1930–33	63.5	177.0	211.3	216.6	152.3	79.7	33.1
1940	60.1	166.3	194.7	187.6	138.9	73.1	26.4
England and Wales							
1938	14.6	92.3	113.3	83.0	47.3	16.1	1.5
1946	17.2	126.0	156.6	119.1	66.3	18.9	1.4
France							
1921–22	25.3	134.7	151.7	103.7	61.6	23.4	2.2
1930–32	31.1	130.3	128.7	88.0	52.5	18.1	1.7
1940	23.3	161.0	183.6	126.1	75.4	26.0	2.3
Netherlands							
1930–31	12.5	91.8	165.7	152.9	111.5	51.5	5.2
1940	10.7	87.4	197.0	140.7	95.1	39.8	3.6
1949	12.7	97.0	187.8	172.0	120.2	49.5	4.4
Sweden							
1921–25	17.6	96.3	131.1	119.6	92.6	46.9	5.8
1930–32	18.0	79.6	97.8	85.1	60.6	28.0	3.2
1940	21.8	87.6	103.0	81.1	51.2	19.9	1.9
1947	35.3	128.7	141.3	106.4	65.1	23.4	2.0
Norway							
1910–11	10.6	105.6	186.2	188.7	165.4	93.2	17.1
1920–21	12.6	109.4	175.8	166.8	138.4	75.5	12.9
1930–31	8.1	70.5	112.2	106.5	81.0	42.8	7.1
1948	15.7	99.8	142.7	126.8	87.4	37.0	3.9
Germany							
1934	15.5	91.7	127.2	95.5	53.1	11.8	
1946 [a]	17.4	108.5	128.8	88.0	56.7	21.1	2.2
Poland							
1931–32	24.7	145.3	189.3	164.0	117.8	53.4	10.4
Switzerland							
1937	7.0	65.6	111.0	92.2	54.1	18.9	1.7
1946	11.2	100.3	163.6	138.2	78.1	26.1	2.0
Hungary							
1920–22	42.2	204.1	206.4	125.1		26.2	
1930–32	40.1	157.1	149.7	109.1	74.5	27.0	2.9
1937	14.6	103.7	143.3	110.0	61.1	21.7	2.2
Portugal							
1930	23.3	152.4	199.3	174.1	141.1	64.8	11.4
1940–41	21.3	128.3	168.7	144.4	110.4	53.3	8.5
1947	22.2	136.1	162.7	133.0	112.0	49.5	7.5
Spain							
1940	8.6	89.7	185.3	166.2	109.5	45.0	8.2
Italy							
1930–32	20.0	125.4	174.8	154.8	116.0	52.2	6.4
1936	16.6	106.6	158.8	139.4	101.9	45.8	4.6
Japan							
1925	43.2	227.8	259.3	228.3	174.0	74.8	12.4
1937	19.0	172.0	253.0	201.0	157.0	68.0	9.0
1948	17.3	180.4	256.3	211.4	147.9	58.3	4.5
Australia							
1921–22	27.1	134.3	169.6	143.5	103.7	43.7	4.2
1932–34	25.4	99.6	121.5	96.6	60.6	25.1	2.6
1947	31.8	166.2	186.4	131.1	74.1	23.4	1.8
New Zealand							
1921–22	17.5	123.8	172.7	144.3	96.6	39.9	4.7
1933–35	16.7	92.8	130.8	100.4	59.4	22.4	2.3
1948	25.3	175.9	210.1	148.6	83.1	25.8	1.9

a. American Zone.

Sources: **1**, pp. 50–57; **2**, 1948, pp. 277–79 and 1949–50, pp. 308–12; **11**, p. 669.

tion rate of 1.0 may correspond to a gross reproduction rate of 1.1 or 1.2 and to a total fertility rate of approximately 2,200 or 2,300.[15] When mortality is high, the net reproduction rate is bound to drop below one unless total fertility is at least 2,800 or 3,000 and the gross reproduction rate is 1.5 or more.

In France, the gross reproduction rate at the beginning of the nineteenth century was 2.0 while the net rate was just above one; subsequent changes in rates have been as follows: [16]

Period	Gross	Net
1806–10	1.99	1.08
1811–20	2.00	1.08
1821–30	1.94	1.06
1831–40	1.82	1.04
1841–50	1.68	1.01
1851–60	1.66	0.97
1861–70	1.71	1.02
1871–80	1.68	1.04
1881–90	1.59	1.02
1891–1900	1.43	0.97
1901–05	1.37	0.98
1906–10	1.27	0.95
1911–15	1.10	0.84
1916–20	0.80	0.59
1921–25	1.18	0.95
1926–30	1.12	0.92
1931–35	1.06	0.90
1936–39	1.04	0.80

Net reproduction rates declined in all western industrial countries after the 1920's. In the middle of the 1930's, the Netherlands and Canada were the only such nations with a net reproduction rate above one. Even in Hitlerized Germany, with its cult of rearing Nordic warriors, the rate at that time was 0.91. In recent years, the net reproduction rate has risen above one in the United States, England and Wales, Sweden, Norway, Finland, Denmark, Switzerland, Australia and New Zealand and has approached one in France. (See Table 72.)

The prevailing trends in net reproduction rates thus have been the same as in crude birth rates: a general decline to the middle of the 1930's and an upswing in more recent years, particularly in the countries that suffered the heaviest losses in births in the preceding period.

15. Cf. pp. 138–39.
16. **49**, p. 225.

DIFFERENTIAL NATALITY RATES

Communities within a nation, and social groups within a community, differ sharply in natality.

Differences by Type and Size of Community

The most striking differential in birth rates, fertility rates and the number of children per family is probably that between rural areas and cities and between urban communities of various sizes. As a general rule, the smaller the community, the higher the birth rates among women in all age classes. (See Table 73.)

Similar contrasts in the fertility of rural and urban population appear in the "standardized replacement indices" computed by Warren S. Thompson for native white and Negro population groups in the United States in 1920 and 1930 in communities of different sizes in each state.[17] The unweighted average index in six typical industrial states in 1930 was 1.36 on the farm, 1.02 in small towns, and 0.75 in large cities. The comparable figures for six predominantly agricultural states, in the South, were 1.89, 1.05 and 0.80. (See Table 74.)

The difference between natality in rural areas and cities has been observed in practically all countries in which separate birth rates are computed for areas of the two types. A comparison of crude birth rates is misleading, however. The proportion of women in child-bearing age in cities is appreciably larger than in rural areas.[18] In many countries the registration of births is incomplete, especially in rural areas. In countries with well-established public health services, women from rural communities frequently use urban maternity hospitals. All these factors tend to raise the natality rate in cities in comparison with rural areas. Therefore, one should not take seriously such birth rates as those reported by Egypt: 61.6 per 1,000 in Cairo as compared with 54.3 per 1,000 for the whole country.[19]

17. The "standardized replacement index" is similar to the net reproduction rate. It equals one when the population is reproducing itself in the long run, drops below one if natality is deficient, and is above one if it is more than sufficient to maintain the existing population.
18. See Chapter 4.
19. Similar relations between urban and rural natality rates are recorded in Chile and Peru.

TABLE 72

NET REPRODUCTION RATES IN SELECTED COUNTRIES, 1920–49

Country	Year, or Period, Closest to						
	1920	1925	1930	1935	1940	1945	1947–49
United States	1.25	...	1.08	.95	1.02	1.14	1.38 [a]
Canada	...	...	1.39	...	1.27	1.33	1.64 [b]
Chile	...	...	1.34	1.12	1.19	1.18 [c]	...
England and Wales	1.11	.98	.85	.77	.77	.91	1.10
Ireland	...	1.25	...	1.22	1.19	...	...
France	...	.95	.92	.90	.82	.94	...
Belgium	...	...	...	.83	.75	.88	1.04
Netherlands	...	...	1.30	1.14	1.18	1.43	1.76 [b]
Denmark	...	1.19	.95	.96	.99	1.30	1.20
Sweden	...	1.06	.87	.74	.80	1.15	...
Norway	1.34	...	.89	.79	.86	1.22	1.13
Finland	1.16	1.07	...	.93	.87	1.24	...
Germany	...	.97	.83	.91	...	...	...
Poland	...	1.30	1.24	1.11	...	...	...
Czechoslovakia	1.29	...	.94	.76	...	...	...
Switzerland	...	...	.85	.79	.80	1.14	1.16 [b]
Austria	...	...	.78	.74	...	...	...
Hungary	1.13	...	.99	...	.99	...	...
Portugal	...	...	1.33	...	1.09	1.17	1.15
Spain	1.34	...	1.28	1.03	1.01	1.10	...
Italy	...	1.37	1.26	1.17	...	...	...
Romania	...	...	1.45	...	...	...	...
Bulgaria	...	1.53	1.28	1.19	...	...	...
Greece	...	...	1.25	...	...	...	...
USSR	...	1.72	...	...	1.54	...	...
Japan	...	1.64	1.57	1.44	...	...	...
India	1.03	...	1.25	...	1.30	...	...
Egypt	...	...	...	1.40	...	...	...
Union of South Africa	1.54	...	1.38	1.26	1.35	...	...
Australia	1.32	...	.96	.96	1.02	1.24	...
New Zealand	1.29	1.21	1.06	.97	1.20	1.32	1.47 [b]

Source: **48**, April 1947, April 1950 and April 1951.

a. 1944–49.   b. 1946.   c. 1943.

Wherever it is possible to obtain reliable and comparable data, there is a striking difference between the high fertility on the farm and the low fertility in towns and cities. Economic reasons for this difference are obvious. Rearing children is easier and less expensive on the farm than in the city, where all food must be bought with money. Children do not interfere with the housework of the farmer's wife, while they often compel the factory worker's wife to give up work outside her home. On the farm, children become a valuable asset as workers at an age when they are still an economic liability for a city family. The decline of small family busi-

nesses in cities, the abolition of child labor, and the prolongation of education have strengthened these contrasts between the cost of rearing children on the farm and in cities. Moreover, urban families have had readier access to contraceptive information than people in rural areas.

The reasons for the difference in fertility in small towns and large cities are less obvious. To some extent it may be due to housing conditions; the housing problem of a large family is much more difficult in a city than in a small town. It is possible, however, that psychological factors and custom outweigh purely economic considerations.

TABLE 73

BIRTH RATES AMONG WOMEN IN DIFFERENT AGE GROUPS, BY TYPE AND SIZE OF COMMUNITY IN THE UNITED STATES, 1940

(Births Per 1,000 Women)

Area	All Ages[a]	15–19 Years	20–24 Years	25–29 Years	30–34 Years	35–39 Years	40–44 Years	45–49 Years
Rural communities	59.8	57.1	147.3	128.2	90.8	56.9	21.8	2.3
Urban communities								
2,500–10,000 inhabitants	56.9	55.6	137.1	121.7	79.8	42.5	13.5	1.2
10,000–25,000	49.5	43.7	117.6	111.3	73.7	35.7	10.6	0.9
25,000–100,000	47.5	43.3	112.4	107.4	70.1	33.5	9.7	0.7
100,000 or more	42.8	36.2	100.8	99.8	65.3	29.9	8.0	0.6

Source: **11**, p. 685.

a. Total female population aged 10–54 years.

TABLE 74

REPLACEMENT INDICES FOR RURAL AND URBAN COMMUNITIES IN THE UNITED STATES, IN SELECTED STATES, 1920 AND 1930[a]

State	1920 Rural Farm	1920 Rural Non-farm	1920 Urban Towns under 10,000 Inhabitants	1920 Urban Cities over 100,000 Inhabitants	1930 Rural Farm	1930 Rural Non-farm	1930 Urban Towns under 10,000 Inhabitants	1930 Urban Cities over 100,000 Inhabitants
Industrial states								
New York	1.22	1.03	.88	.70	1.37	1.12	.91	.72
Pennsylvania	1.52	1.46	1.13	.83	1.59	1.52	1.11	.81
Illinois	1.47	1.24	1.03	.72	1.42	1.21	1.01	.72
California	1.19	1.05	.86	.54	1.15	1.01	.87	.55
Michigan	1.54	1.45	1.11	.86	1.63	1.50	1.21	.90
Massachusetts	1.05	1.05	.91	.72	1.14	1.12	.99	.79
Agricultural states								
Texas	1.81	1.36	1.07	.78	1.61	1.25	.96	.73
Georgia	2.08	1.47	1.15	.83	1.90	1.35	1.12	.74
Alabama	2.08	1.64	1.26	.93	2.01	1.60	1.21	.86
Kentucky	1.91	1.67	1.04	.78	1.94	1.75	1.08	.88
Mississippi	1.91	1.43	1.07	—	1.91	1.33	.97	—
Arkansas	2.06	1.53	1.13	—	1.95	1.44	.98	—

Source: **48**, October 1938, pp. 267–76.

a. For native white population only.

Differences by Economic and Social Status

Even in ancient Rome, writers observed and deplored the low fertility of the upper classes. Equally old, however, is the observation that strong and prosperous families, especially those in rural areas, often have many children. In some agricultural countries — for example, China — the farmers who have more land usually also have more children. According to the Chinese Population Survey, the number of children who had been born per 100 farm wives varied with the size of farm as follows: [20]

	Per 100 Wives under Age 45	*Per 100 Wives Aged 45 or Over*
Small farms	263 children	503 children
Medium-large farms	274 "	528 "
Very large farms	270 "	551 "

Herbert D. Lamson found a similar diversity in Chinese cities.[21]

This pattern, however, is uncommon in the countries of Western civilization. A negative correlation between fertility and prosperity in large European cities was established more than fifty years ago by the French statistician Jacques Bertillon, who noticed that the rates of births in the poorest districts in Paris, Berlin and Vienna were twice those in the rich districts and three times those in the richest. (See Table 75.)

Bertillon's Law

Bertillon concluded that "wealth leads to sterility." This general "law" has been checked time and again since Bertillon's time. Crude comparison of urban and rural districts has been replaced by careful analysis of more or less homogeneous socioeconomic groups. Fertility rates have been computed according to the occupation of the head of the family, his and his wife's educational level, their religion and so on. Few students have challenged the Bertillon generalization, but additional information has shown that the relationship between birth rates and wealth is more complicated.[22]

TABLE 75

BIRTH RATES IN POOR AND RICH DISTRICTS IN PARIS, BERLIN AND VIENNA, ACCORDING TO BERTILLON

(Births Per 1,000 Women Aged 15–49 Years)

Type of District	Paris (1886–95)	Berlin (1886–95)	Vienna [a] (1891–94)
Total	81	102	153
Very poor	108	158	200
Poor	95	130	164
Well off	75	113	155
Very well off	66	96	153
Rich	54	62	107
Very rich	35	46	71

Source: 19, p. 103. The original table is reproduced here in abbreviated form.

a. Legitimate births only.

Experience in England

Of many studies on differential birth rates, that of J. H. C. Stevenson, based on the 1911 population census in England and Wales, has won particular attention. Stevenson showed that the number of children per 100 families in England varied widely with the socioeconomic status of the family and that the correlation with economic level depended, in turn, on the duration of the marriage. (See Table 76.) He amplified the general statement that fertility declines as one goes upward through the social scale by two reservations: (1) the difference in fertility in various economic classes is a new phenomenon; it is relatively small for marriages contracted before 1861, and increases rapidly for more recent marriages; (2) the main cause of the decline in the birth rate in the upper socioeconomic classes is voluntary restraint of parenthood, rather than lack of fertility in the biological sense.

Stevenson's conclusions sounded an alarm. The decline of fertility, he declared, "spreads throughout society from above downward. . . . The deficit in the number of children for the higher social classes is increasing with increase of duration of marriage up to 25 years. The lowest fertility rates are returned for the most purely middle-class occupations, the professions." [23]

Stevenson particularly deplored the low fertility of the "finest stock in the nation," professional people. But his observation concerning

---

20. **21**, p. 385. The Survey covered some 47,000 farm families in various parts of the country.

21. **38**, p. 320.

22. Cf. **29** and **27**. Bertillon's law refers, of course, not to biological sterility, but to the contrast in birth rates among the rich and the poor.

23. **52**, pp. 431–32.

TABLE 76

FERTILITY RATES IN VARIOUS SOCIAL CLASSES, BY DURATION OF MARRIAGE, IN ENGLAND
AND WALES, 1911

(Standardized Number of Children Born Per 100 Families)

Duration of Marriage, in Years	Social Classes							
	Upper and Middle Classes [a]				Unskilled Labor	Textile Workers	Miners	Agricultural Labor
	I	II	III	IV				
All families	277	321	353	359	392	319	433	399
0–5	80	81	86	90	100	76	105	101
5–10	171	197	211	219	242	185	263	246
10–15	242	284	314	323	362	275	399	363
15–20	303	359	405	412	463	359	517	470
20–25	357	422	482	491	541	435	610	552
25–30	413	481	544	550	596	501	671	618
30–40	497	567	615	616	652	567	717	667
40–50	607	665	696	690	715	648	777	719
50–60	662	733	746	735	763	696	797	779
Over 60	682	777	729	792	781	732	870	820

Source: **52**, pp. 414–15. Cf. **15**.

a. I, Professional occupations; II, employers and managers in business, clerical workers and generally intermediate between I and III; III, skilled workers; IV, semiskilled workers, intermediate between III and unskilled laborers.

this class has also another implication: fertility does not necessarily decline with increase in wealth. Upper capitalist groups that are better off financially than professional workers have more children per family.[24]

Experience in France and Hungary

More recent French statistics have likewise revealed holes in Bertillon's "law." Families of public officials and members of the armed forces had the fewest children, while there were more children in the families of farmers and employers and still more in households of workers, fishermen and sailors.[25]

A survey made in Hungary indicates that, after the same duration of marriage, employer families have fewer children than workers but more than public officials. (See Table 77.)

Experience in Germany

A German student of population, A. Grotjahn, found that Bavarian officials at the bottom of the bureaucratic ladder had an average of 2.5 children per family; those in the middle of the ladder, 1.7; and those at the top, 1.5.[26] Grotjahn

24. Cf. **55**.
25. **13**, pp. 26–31 and 114–15.
26. **30**, p. 79.

TABLE 77

NUMBER OF CHILDREN PER 100 FAMILIES, BY OCCUPATION OF HUSBAND, AGE OF WIFE, AND DURATION OF MARRIAGE, IN HUNGARY, 1930

Age of Wife and Duration of Marriage	Occupation of Husband		
	Employer	Public Official	Worker
Age of woman			
Under 20 years	43	33	48
20–24	112	66	116
25–29	196	102	204
30–39	284	153	306
40–49	399	225	452
50–59	475	298	537
60 and over	535	423	582
Duration of marriage			
Under 5 years	90	56	99
5–9	202	128	223
10–14	268	168	308
15–19	334	207	390
20 and over	479	312	550

Source: **49**, p. 74.

also found the characteristic contrast between birth rates in different districts of Bremen: high rates in the poorest districts, low among the rich. The difference, however, was much greater at the turn of the century than in 1925: from 1901 to 1925 the birth rate declined by more than half in the districts inhabited by workers and the middle classes but increased slightly in the wealthy areas. The number of births in those years per 1,000 inhabitants was: [27]

	1901	1925
Rich districts	12.7	14.7
Middle-class districts	28.9	14.2
Workers' districts	43.7	19.5

Experience in the Netherlands

On the other hand, a comprehensive survey made in the Netherlands shortly before the war indicated that birth rates of the upper classes were declining. This study concluded:

Both birth and death rates are higher in rural districts than in the towns, and in both areas the highest rates are in the lowest income groups.

The number of births per family declined more in the urban districts than in the rural from 1897 to 1927.

The difference between birth rates for the lower and higher income groups was larger in 1927 than in 1897.

The interval between the date of marriage and the first birth increases with rise in economic level.

Fertility is lower among married people who are well off than among poor people; it is particularly low among intellectuals.[28]

Experience in the United States

Birth and fertility statistics in the United States are in general agreement with these findings. Birth rates are high in rural areas as compared with cities, and in nonwhite families as compared with the white population. The National Health Survey (1935–36) found that among the urban white population only unemployed workers on relief had a net reproduction rate slightly above one (1.15); in all other urban white groups the rate was less than one and declined rapidly with the increase in family income. Among nonrelief families, the net reproduction rate varied with family income as follows: [29]

Under $1,000	.79
$1,000–1,499	.75
$1,500–1,999	.63
$2,000–2,999	.55
$3,000 and over	.42

The 1940 census likewise indicates a very strong inverse correlation between the number of children and the monthly rental value of the home occupied by the family. In households where the monthly rental value varied from $5 to $9, there were 4.6 children per mother; in households where the rental value was $30–$39, 3 children per mother; and in households spending $75 a month or more for rent, 2.5 children.[30]

Next to economic status, educational attainment seems to be the most important factor in differences in fertility rates in the United States. Among the families canvassed by the National Health Survey the higher the educational attainment of the head of the family, the lower was the birth rate and net reproduction rate. The fertility rate reported for families headed by college graduates would reduce their stock to half within one generation: [31]

	Births Per 10,000 Married Women	Net Reproduction Rate
Total sample	108.9	.70
College	96.9	.52
High school	102.5	.68
7th or 8th grade	117.5	.86
Under 7th grade	130.7	.97

The 1940 census recorded similar contrasts. Native white mothers aged 45–49 years with no school years completed had an average of 5.3 children; those with seven to eight years of grade school, 3.6 children; those with four years of high school, 2.6. The same average number of children — 2.6 — was recorded among mothers aged 45–49 years with one to three years of college.[32]

The same pattern appeared in the Indianapolis survey conducted in 1941 by the Committee on Social and Psychological Factors Affecting Fertility: 2.8 children per wife 15–44 years old with less than seven years of grammar school attainment; 1.8 children among those with one year of high school; 1.1 after four years of high school; and only 0.9 after four or more years of college.[33]

Recent Trends in Natality Differentials

The differences in natality among communities and among economic, social and educational

27. **30**, p. 80.
28. **43**, pp. 68–70.
29. **35**, p. 376; cf. **7**, pp. 375 ff.

30. Computed from **7**, pp. 376 ff.
31. **35**, pp. 376 and 386; cf. **7**, pp. 346 ff.
32. Computed from **7**, pp. 346 ff.
33. **57**, July 1943, pp. 245, 249 and 253.

groups suggest that average birth and fertility rates decline with economic and cultural progress. Should we not generalize Bertillon's law and say: cultural and economic progress leads to sterility?

Such a generalization would be fallacious for two reasons: (1) the observed difference between various social and economic strata may prove to be temporary differences in the behavior of people rather than in their characteristics as suggested by such concepts as fertility or sterility; (2) differentials in natality are not static but change as time goes on and there are clear indications that differences among the birth rates of the various socioeconomic classes are lessening.

Compare, for example, the birth rates of various classes in England and Wales in 1921 and 1931. In both years the lowest rates were among clerical workers and leading professional persons and employers in finance, and the highest among semiskilled and unskilled laborers. In 1921, however, the birth rates of the two labor class groups were 33 and 44 per cent higher, respectively, than among professional persons and financial employers, while in 1931 they were only 7 and 25 per cent higher.[34] In Paris, likewise, the contrast between birth rates in the poor and the wealthy districts in 1935–36 was much less sharp than at the beginning of this century.[35]

The experience in New York is striking. In 1929 the birth rate in the city's lowest economic group was 39.8 per 1,000 white persons as compared with 23.8 for the highest group. In 1942 the corresponding rates were nearly the same — 31.1 and 29.4 respectively. (See Table 78 and Figure 55.)

These facts are not wholly conclusive, but they suggest that poverty and ignorance are not necessarily the concomitants of fertility or economic and educational attainment, of sterility.

The reason why poor families have more children than the rich is not always lack of contraceptive techniques. A comprehensive survey made in Great Britain in 1946 found no substantial difference in the use of contraceptive measures by women of various socioeconomic classes married between 1920 and 1934, although there was a very pronounced difference between the families founded before 1920 and after 1934.[36] The number of live births per married

34. **33**, p. 78.
35. **49**, p. 70.
36. **17**, p. 10.

TABLE 78

BIRTH RATES IN DIFFERENT ECONOMIC GROUPS IN NEW YORK CITY, 1929–42

(Births Per 1,000 White Persons Aged 15–44 Years)

	Economic Group				
Year	I High	II	III	IV	V Low
1929	23.8	32.6	32.9	34.0	39.8
1930	24.0	32.3	32.6	33.4	36.8
1931	22.1	30.1	30.9	32.0	34.1
1932	21.1	27.5	29.4	30.8	32.9
1933	20.0	25.8	27.1	28.5	31.5
1934	20.2	25.7	27.1	27.6	28.3
1935	20.6	25.2	26.5	28.0	27.5
1936	19.9	24.3	25.8	28.0	27.2
1937	20.6	25.3	26.8	28.2	26.9
1938	20.7	25.3	26.1	27.6	27.8
1939	20.9	25.1	26.2	27.1	27.3
1940	22.5	26.3	26.9	27.6	27.5
1941	24.1	28.2	28.4	28.3	28.6
1942	29.4	33.9	32.0	30.5	31.1

Source: **34**, p. 138.

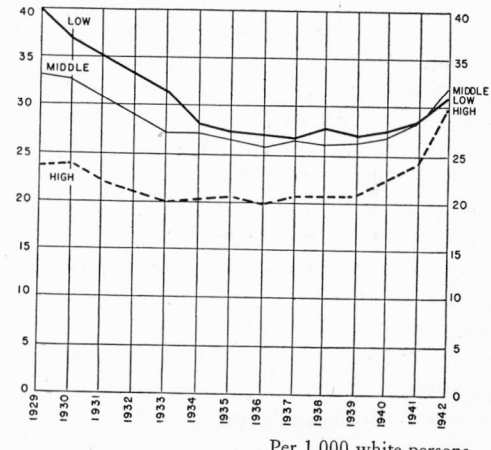

Per 1,000 white persons

FIGURE 55. BIRTH RATES IN THREE ECONOMIC GROUPS IN NEW YORK CITY, 1929–42

The striking differential in birth rates in various economic groups in New York City was reduced to less than half during the great depression. In more recent years, natality in the high and middle income groups has been increasing more rapidly than among the poor and the correlation between birth rate and family income has almost disappeared. (Cf. Table 78.)

woman in the lower social classes was somewhat higher than in the upper classes, whether or not the families used birth control. (See Table 79.)

Table 79

Average Number of Live Births Per Married Woman Who Used, or Never Used, Birth Control, in Great Britain, 1949

Date of Marriage	Birth Control Used at Some Time			Birth Control Never Used		
	Wealthy	Middle Class	Poor	Wealthy	Middle Class	Poor
1910–19	2.8	3.3	3.8	3.9	4.2	4.7
1920–24	2.7	2.8	3.0	2.7	3.4	4.9
1925–29	2.3	2.4	3.1	3.0	3.2	4.8
1930–34	1.8	2.1	2.4	2.4	2.7	3.7
1935–39	1.6	1.7	1.9	1.8	2.2	2.7
1940–47	0.8	0.8	1.0	1.2	1.4	1.5

Source: **17**, p. 66.

DISTRIBUTION OF BIRTHS

Distribution by Sex

It has long been observed that more boys than girls are born. Two hundred years ago Johann Peter Süssmilch, the German preacher and scholar whom many students consider the founder of the modern theory of population, ventured an explanation. The surplus of male births, he remarked, was established by the Creator to secure the increase of mankind in the most rational way, through monogamous marriage. Such a surplus, he explained, is indeed necessary in order that the two sexes may be approximately equal in number at marriageable age, since the death rate in the early years of life is higher for males than for females.[37]

Our knowledge of the intentions of the Creator and, more specifically, the purpose of "masculinity" of births,[38] has not made appreciable progress since the time of Süssmilch. All we know is that male births exceed female births in most countries and that the difference varies within a comparatively narrow range, usually between 104 and 106 male births to 100 female live births. The masculinity of stillbirths is never less than 120 per 1,000, sometimes rises to more than 150, and averages 130.[39] Masculinity is higher in rural areas than in cities, and higher among first births than subsequent births.[40] It has also been observed on several occasions that the proportion of male births has tended to increase during and after wars. (See Table 80.) The validity of this observation is questioned by some students, however, and the theories developed to explain it are not very convincing.[41]

Newsholme has drawn attention to an amazing parallel between changes in the proportion of male births in England from 1876 to 1918 and changes in wholesale prices.[42] (See Figure 56.)

Distribution by Birth Order

In a community where each family had two and only two children the numbers of the first and second births must be equal and there would be no third, fourth and subsequent births. A high proportion of sixth and seventh births is characteristic in a community with large families. Similarly, a change in the distribution by birth order usually indicates a change in the prevailing type of family.

In most countries the rise in natality from 1936 to 1948 was accompanied by a decline in the proportion of fourth and subsequent births. This tendency prevailed in the United States and Canada, England, Belgium, the Netherlands, Norway, Germany, Switzerland, Hungary, and Australia. The most consistent increase was in the proportion of second births. (See Table 81.)

There were a few significant exceptions, however. The proportion of seventh and subsequent births increased in Mexico, France and Italy. In Mexico there was also an increase in the proportion of fourth to sixth births, probably as a result of the war boom. In France and Italy, the proportion of fourth to sixth births has declined, but in the early 1940's more families had a seventh or subsequent child, perhaps because of the combination of low wages and comparatively high family allowances. This trend has been reversed in more recent years.

CAUSES OF THE DECLINE AND UPTURN OF NATALITY

The long-range decline of birth rates in countries of Western civilization and the upturn since the middle of the 1930's are closely connected. The forces responsible for the gradual fall have been checked, perhaps only temporarily, by other factors.

---

37. **53.**
38. **40**, p. 110.
39. **40**, pp. 121–22.
40. **40**, p. 149.

41. **46.**
42. The figures plotted are the ratios of the actual proportion of male births to female births and of the actual wholesale price index figures (of *The Economist*) to the moving ten-year averages.

TABLE 80

BIRTH DISTRIBUTION BY SEX IN SELECTED COUNTRIES, BEFORE, DURING AND AFTER WORLD WAR I

(Number of Male Births Per 1,000 Female Births)

Country	1906–14	1915–18	1919–23
Germany	1,061	1,069	1,078
France	1,056	1,063	1,073
England	1,039	1,045	1,051
Austria	1,063	1,061	1,074
Hungary	1,061	1,071	1,078

Source: **59**, p. 161.

Immediate Cause of the Decline

The immediate cause of the decline in birth rates in the nineteenth century and in the first three decades of the twentieth was the changed attitude of people toward rearing children. In all parts of the world, many married couples found it undesirable to let chance determine the number of their children and the intervals between births. "Planned parenthood" became the common practice. This was an important turning point in the history of mankind. Raymond Pearl declares:

. . . if it were not for the effect of contraceptive efforts and the practice of criminal abortion, together with correlated habits as to postponement of marriage, there would apparently be little or no significant differential fertility as between economic,

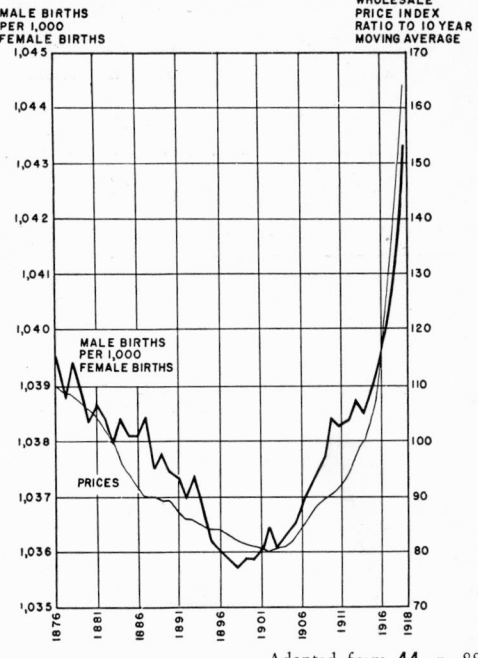

Adapted from **44**, p. 88.

FIGURE 56. DISTRIBUTION OF BIRTHS BY SEX, COMPARED WITH CHANGES IN WHOLESALE PRICES IN ENGLAND, 1876–1918

The "masculinity" of birth (ratio of male births to female births) varies from country to country and from year to year, sometimes over a fairly broad range. The causes of these variations are unknown. In England from 1876 to 1918, this ratio varied with changes in business conditions: the proportion of male births went down and up with the wholesale price index.

TABLE 81

BIRTH DISTRIBUTION BY BIRTH ORDER IN SELECTED COUNTRIES, AROUND 1936 AND 1948

(Per Cent)

Country and Year	Birth Order					
	1st	2d	3d	4th to 6th	7th and Over	Un-known
United States						
1936	34.7	22.2	13.0	18.0	8.8	3.1
1942	39.4	24.1	12.4	13.7	5.7	4.7
1948	35.6	27.6	14.3	13.4	4.6	4.6
Canada						
1936	25.3	19.2	13.4	23.8	18.2	0.1
1942	34.3	22.7	13.1	18.0	11.7	0.2
1948	31.3	25.5	15.5	18.7	9.0	0.0
Mexico						
1936	21.2	17.9	15.8	29.8	12.0	3.3
1945	21.2	18.0	14.9	32.2	12.4	1.3
Chile						
1936	29.4	18.3	13.7	34.7		3.8
1946	29.0	19.1	14.1	33.9		3.9

(Continued on page 160)

TABLE 81—*continued*

Country and Year	Birth Order					
	1st	2d	3d	4th to 6th	7th and Over	Un-known
England and Wales						
1938	41.6	25.4	13.0	14.1	5.2	0.8
1945	39.8	29.5	14.3	12.5	3.2	0.5
France						
1936	30.9	24.3	15.0	18.5	6.0	5.3
1942	29.8	22.9	14.9	19.0	7.1	6.4
1947	42.9	24.2	13.9	13.9	4.9	0.3
Belgium						
1939	38.3	25.1	14.4	16.3	6.0	0.0
1944	40.4	25.5	13.9	15.9	4.2	0.0
1949	41.5	25.3	13.7	14.9	4.6	0.0
Netherlands						
1936	28.1	21.6	14.7	23.0	12.7	0.0
1942	30.0	23.5	15.4	21.0	10.2	0.0
1949	28.9	24.3	16.0	22.2	8.5	0.0
Norway						
1936	38.4	23.2	13.7	17.6	7.0	0.1
1942	42.8	26.4	13.3	13.2	3.6	0.6
1948	37.5	28.6	16.9	14.1	2.6	0.3
Finland						
1940	35.3	21.9	14.0	19.6	8.9	0.3
1948	34.8	27.3	15.3	16.8	5.7	0.0
Germany						
1936	38.1	27.4	14.6	12.5 [a]	7.0 [b]	0.3
1948 [c]	45.2	27.9	13.2	10.8	2.6	0.3
Switzerland						
1936	37.1	24.7	14.3	17.4	6.6	0.0
1946	36.0	27.7	16.8	15.7	3.9	0.0
Hungary						
1936	32.6	21.9	14.7	20.8	9.4	0.5
1946	37.6	25.5	13.8	16.2	6.8	0.1
Italy						
1936	25.4	20.8	15.6	27.1	10.9	0.1
1942	24.7	21.6	15.8	25.4	11.3	1.0
1948	36.1	22.5	14.0	19.1	7.9	0.5
Australia						
1936	37.3	24.2	14.5	18.0	6.1	0.0
1942	40.3	26.7	14.5	14.3	4.0	0.0
1948	36.6	30.1	16.4	14.0	2.9	0.0
New Zealand						
1936	38.0	25.1	14.9	17.0	5.0	0.0
1942	32.3	27.3	19.5	17.2	3.6	0.0
1948	36.1	28.9	16.5	15.8	2.7	0.0

Source: **2**, 1948, pp. 280–91 and 1949–50, pp. 318–31.

    a. 4th and 5th births.   b. 6th and over.   c. Western Germany.

educational, or religious classes of urban American married couples. . . . The responsibility for [existing fertility differentials] appears to rest primarily, overwhelmingly, and directly upon . . . birth control. . . . Contraception is a wholly voluntary activity, free of all compulsions except the negative ones that may arise indirectly through ignorance. This single exception is at the present time being rapidly diminished in force, so far as concerns the population of America and western Europe. . . .

Classes of people have different fertility rates because of their own volition and intent, they want to have them.[43]

Increase in the use of contraception has followed the same pattern as many other customs and inventions: first, it was restricted to the wealthy and educated elite; then it found its way to the middle classes; still later it became a common practice in large cities; from the cities it penetrated into rural areas. As a consequence of this development, "planned parenthood" necessarily created a close correlation between education and prosperity, on the one hand, and childlessness, on the other.[44]

This statement requires, however, two qualifications. Two factors should be clearly distinguished in the growing practice of planned parenthood: the new birth control measures and the socioeconomic and psychological factors which determine people's decision to use these measures. The first aspect of the problem — described by Dr. Grotjahn as the technological change in birth control — should not be overrated. The second group of factors is of decisive significance: if people wished to have more children they could have them independent of the facilities for birth control at their disposal.

The second qualification is closely related to the first. While most technological developments appear as one-way movements that cannot be reversed, the direction of psychological developments changes as time goes on. The fact that the fall in birth rates was observed in all modern nations and followed the same pattern everywhere does not imply that this trend will continue indefinitely; it may be reversed under the impact of new factors. Moreover the behavior of people has changed frequently without visible and tangible cause, and such changes have been a primary cause of economic and political developments.

The importance of the recent upturn in birth rates in the region of Western civilization cannot be overrated. From 1940 to 1949, some 50 million more babies were born in the ten countries of western Europe, the United States, Canada, Australia and New Zealand than would

have been anticipated from the trend in births in 1913–29. It is difficult to interpret this phenomenon, however, because of the confusion of the times in which it occurred.

Cause of the Upturn

In 1946 the French National Institute for Population Studies canvassed population experts in eleven nations, including the United States and Canada, on their opinion on recent demographic trends. The answers revealed a wide divergence of opinion among students in the two hemispheres.

Summarizing the findings of the survey, Alfred Sauvy points out that American experts are inclined to believe there has been no fundamental change in the natality trend, while European students are open to the hypothesis that the upturn is genuine. Sauvy stresses seven factors in the recent rise of natality.

1. In the 1930's, birth rates had declined to a low level that made them very sensitive to economic and psychological changes.

2. Economic recovery stimulated the rise in the number of marriages and births.

3. A general inclination developed in favor of having more children in the family.

4. The birth rate has increased particularly in the population groups that had the lowest rates.

5. At the outbreak of World War II, this readjustment had not been completed, so that conditions favored a further rise in natality.

6. The rise was stimulated by the war economy and the wartime social policy, including deferment of fathers, special rations for children, and certain privileges for mothers.

7. After the war, the system of family allowances became an important factor in some countries.[45]

The Period of Transition

To these factors one more should, perhaps, be added. War or no war, natality, after having reached a low point, was bound to rise sooner or later. The transition from unplanned to planned parenthood necessarily starts from a situation in which many families have more children than they would have planned. Consequently, in the transition period the number of second, third and subsequent births must fall below the levels that will prevail in the same society after the

43. **47**, p. 244–47.

44. The theory that biological sterility has been one of the principal factors in declining natality, has not been completely abandoned in demographic literature (cf. **28**), but it has lost ground in the past two decades and need not be discussed here.

45. **50**, pp. 266–69.

custom of planned parenthood is firmly established. When the transition is completed, natality
will rise to the "normal" level of the given community and this level, in turn, will change as
social, economic and psychological changes bring
new scales of values, new patterns in the relationships between the individual and society, new
customs and fashions.

If this notion is correct, the lowest natality
rates in the 1930's were not current milestones
on an endless downhill road but marked, rather,
a trough that was deepened and widened by
economic conditions in the years of depression
and mass unemployment. This situation provided the conditions for an upturn. Immediately after the war, birth rates rose above the
level corresponding to the long-range plans of
prospective parents. A corrective setback was
therefore unavoidable and it came in 1948–50.
In 1950 rates probably fell below the trend line.
If this contention is correct, they will return to
a level somewhere between the low of the middle
1930's and the peak of the middle 1940's. Further
changes will be determined by the interplay of
many economic, psychological and social factors
— prosperity or depression, a sense of security
or fears for the future, rugged individualism or
stronger ties between the individual and the
community.

Deaths (Mortality)

Like natality, mortality in different groups
of population and different countries and at
different times depends on many factors that
sometimes pull in different directions.

MEASURING MORTALITY

Several methods are used to measure mortality. Like the different measures of natality,
they largely supplement one another.

The Crude Death Rate

The simplest measure of mortality, analogous
to the crude birth rate,[46] is the *crude death rate,*
the number of deaths per 1,000 persons in a
community or a particular population group.
Usually specific death rates are computed for
men and for women by 5-year or 10-year age
groups. For children under age 5, death rates
are usually computed for one-year age intervals.

The *infant mortality rate* (the number of deaths
in the first year) is usually related not to the
average number of children of this age but to
the annual number of live births. This change
in the basis of comparison is of minor significance when infant mortality is low, but becomes
important when it is high, say 100 or more per
1,000 live births.

A complete set of death rates by sex and age
measures the danger of death during the life
span of an individual.

The Life Table

A more concise picture of mortality conditions is provided by a *table of survivors* and
the *life table.*[47] A table of survivors shows the
percentage of newborn infants who may be
expected to reach the age of one year, five years,
ten years and so on up to eighty years or more,
under the existing mortality rates in each age
group. A life table derived from the survivor
table by simple mathematical manipulation,
shows, among other things, the average number
of years persons who have reached a definite
age will live, under existing death rates — that
is, the complete expectation of life at the given
age.[48]

Survivor and life tables are computed periodically in many countries. Usually separate tables
are prepared for men and women. In the United
States, life tables are based on cross classifications of population by sex and race.[49]

DEATH RATES

National and Regional Differences

The death rates reported by a country depend
on the number of deaths registered during a

---

46. Cf. p. 138.

47. For the history and theory of life tables, see **23**,
pp. 310 ff.; and **25**, pp. 3–58. Cf. **20**.

48. The first table of survivors, computed by John
Gaunt on the basis of death and burial records in London, was published in 1662. The first life expectation
table in modern times was prepared by Edmund Halley
on the basis of mortality experience in Breslau, Germany, in 1687–91. In this table, expectation of life at
birth was 33.5 years; at the age of 10, 40.0 years — very
low in comparison with our present figures. In contrast,
Halley's figure for expectation of life at the age of 60
was comparatively high: 12.1 years. **25**, p. 43.

49. Life tables for both sexes and for men and
women separately are computed for total population,
whites, Negroes and other races. Of this set of twelve
tables, the most enlightening are those for male whites,
female whites, male Negroes and female Negroes. (**9.**)

TABLE 82

DEATH RATES IN SELECTED COUNTRIES, AROUND 1950

(Deaths Per 1,000 Inhabitants)

Country,[a] Year	Deaths	Country,[a] Year	Deaths	Country,[a] Year	Deaths
Belgian Congo,[b] 1950	5.5	Western Germany, 1950	10.4	Yugoslavia, 1950	13.1
Angola,[b] 1950	6.3	Thailand, 1946	10.6	Bulgaria, 1947	13.4
Israel, 1950	6.5	Greece, 1949	10.7	Colombia, 1949	14.0
Panama, 1949	7.1	Spain, 1950	10.8	Honduras, 1949	14.7
Paraguay, 1948	7.2	Venezuela, 1950	11.0	Algeria (Moslems), 1949	14.8
Netherlands, 1950	7.5	Japan, 1950	11.0	Tunisia,[c] 1948	14.9
Iceland, 1950	7.9	Hungary, 1948	11.2	Chile, 1950	15.7
Uruguay, 1948	8.3	Bolivia, 1949	11.3	Federation of Malaya,[c]	
Union of South Africa,[b]		Algeria,[b] 1949	11.6	1950	15.8
1950	8.6	Luxembourg, 1950	11.6	India, 1949	16.0
Norway, 1950	8.9	United Kingdom, 1950	11.7	Mexico, 1950	16.4
Canada, 1950	9.0	Czechoslovakia, 1950	11.7	Madagascar,[c] 1949	16.6
Argentina, 1949	9.1	Peru, 1950	11.7	Ecuador, 1947	17.7
Denmark, 1950	9.2	Jamaica, 1950	11.8	Romania, 1945	20.0
New Zealand, 1950	9.3	Singapore,[b] 1950	12.1	Egypt, 1948	20.3
United States, 1950	9.6	Costa Rica, 1950	12.2	Indonesia,[c] 1940	20.3
Australia, 1950	9.6	Trinidad, 1950	12.2	Korea, 1944	21.2
Italy, 1950	9.8	Pakistan, 1948	12.3	Gold Coast,[c] 1949	21.3
Puerto Rico, 1950	9.9	North Borneo,[c] 1949	12.3	Guatemala, 1950	21.5
Guam, 1949	9.9	Belgium, 1950	12.4	French India,[c] 1949	21.6
Sweden, 1950	10.1	Ireland, 1950	12.6	Yukon (Canada), 1949	21.7
Switzerland, 1950	10.1	France, 1950	12.6	Burma, 1939	23.0
Finland, 1950	10.2	Ceylon,[c] 1950	12.6	São Tomé and Principe,	
Nicaragua, 1950	10.2	Austria, 1949	12.7	1949	34.0
Trieste, 1950	10.3				

Sources: **2,** 1951, pp. 198–205; **5,** October 1951, pp. 15–18; **4,** July 1951, pp. 4–24.

a. Countries arrayed by increasing death rate.
b. Europeans.
c. Europeans and natives.

definite period and the estimated population at the middle of this period. If registration of deaths is not complete or the size of the population cannot be determined with reasonable precision, the reported death rate becomes meaningless. Moreover, the gaps in registration of deaths and errors in estimates of population do not necessarily offset each other. A systematic understatement of mortality tends, rather, to result in an overstatement in population estimates.[50] This fact explains the amazingly low mortality rates reported for some colonial areas and underdeveloped areas, such as 5.4 per 1,000 inhabitants in Tangier and Lebanon; 6.2 per 1,000 in Hawaii; 7.1 in Panama; 7.9 in Spanish Morocco;

50. The recent censuses have revealed that many underdeveloped countries had fewer inhabitants than they had estimated. (See **4.**)

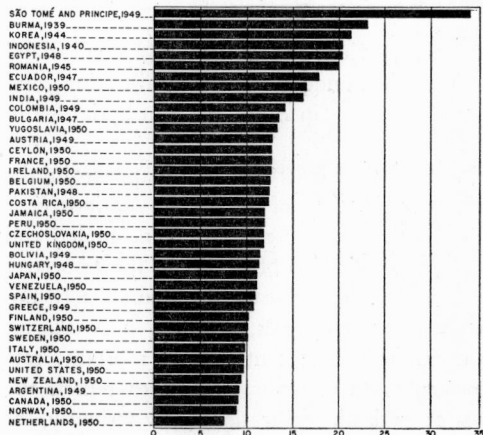

Per 1,000 inhabitants

FIGURE 57. DEATH RATES IN SELECTED COUNTRIES, AROUND 1950

TABLE 83

DEATH RATES IN THE UNITED STATES, BY STATE, 1940 AND 1948

(Deaths Per 1,000 Inhabitants)

State [a]	1940	1948	State [a]	1940	1948
United States	10.7	9.9	Louisiana	10.8	9.1
			Colorado	10.8	10.5
North Dakota	8.2	8.8	Arizona	11.0	9.4
Wyoming	8.5	8.4	Virginia	11.0	9.5
Utah	8.7	7.6	New Jersey	11.0	10.1
Arkansas	8.8	7.9			
South Dakota	8.9	9.5	Oregon	11.1	9.6
			New York	11.1	11.1
North Carolina	8.9	7.9	Florida	11.3	10.2
Oklahoma	9.0	8.3	Pennsylvania	11.3	10.4
West Virginia	9.2	9.2	Illinois	11.3	10.9
Idaho	9.3	8.4			
Minnesota	9.4	9.3	Rhode Island	11.3	11.0
			California	11.4	9.6
Nebraska	9.6	9.8	Ohio	11.4	10.3
Texas	9.7	8.7	Washington	11.5	9.0
Michigan	9.9	9.1	Missouri	11.5	11.0
Tennessee	10.0	9.1			
Wisconsin	10.0	9.9	Indiana	11.8	10.1
			District of Columbia	11.9	9.5
New Mexico	10.2	9.8	Massachusetts	11.9	11.3
Kansas	10.3	9.8	Maryland	12.0	10.4
Iowa	10.3	10.0	Delaware	12.2	11.4
Montana	10.3	11.5			
Alabama	10.5	9.2	Nevada	12.5	9.9
			Maine	12.5	11.1
Georgia	10.5	9.3	New Hampshire	12.7	11.8
Kentucky	10.5	9.8	Vermont	13.0	11.3
Connecticut	10.6	9.8			
South Carolina	10.7	9.1			
Mississippi	10.7	10.7			

Source: **8**, 1950, p. 72.   a. States arrayed by increasing death rate in 1940.

8.2 in Hong Kong; 8.3 in Tonga (a small island in the Pacific, under British administration) and Spanish Guinea (in Africa); 8.5 in Syria; 8.9 in Paraguay.[51]

Most of these mortality rates appear in the current publications of the United Nations with an explicit reservation concerning incomplete and irregular registration of deaths in the respective areas and can be discarded as completely unrealistic. In many cases, however, it is difficult to decide to what extent the low mortality rate reported in an underdeveloped area reflects the state of its death registration. How seriously, for example, should one take the official death rates of the Dominican Republic (9.3 per 1,000 inhabitants) or Thailand (10.2 per 1,000)? Or should one accept at face value statistics that

give Pakistan a lower mortality rate than Belgium and Ceylon the same rate as France?[52]

With this reservation and eliminating those data that are obviously false, mortality rates are available for three score countries and colonial areas. They range from 7.5 per 1,000 inhabitants in the Netherlands to 21.6 per 1,000 in French India. The latter rate is probably typical of many colonial areas in the tropic zone, although most of them officially report much lower rates.

Death rates in most of the countries of the Western civilization range between 9 and 13 per 1,000 inhabitants, a notably narrow range of variation when one considers the variety of economic and climatic conditions and the differences in the composition of population within this area. In less-developed countries the range

51. **4**, July 1951.   52. **4**, July 1951.

TABLE 84

DEATHS: AVERAGE ANNUAL RATES IN SELECTED COUNTRIES, 1871–80 TO 1941–50

(Deaths Per 1,000 Inhabitants)

Country	1871–80	1881–90	1891–1900	1901–10	1911–19	1920–30	1931–38	1941–50
United States	. . .	. . .	. . .	15.7	14.3	11.9	10.9	10.1
England and Wales	21.4	19.1	18.2	15.4	14.5	12.2	12.0	12.5
Scotland	21.6	19.2	18.7	16.6	15.5	13.7	13.2	13.3
Ireland	18.4	18.0	18.2	17.4	17.0	14.7	14.0	14.1
France	23.7	22.1	21.5	19.4	18.6	17.0	15.8	15.5
Belgium	22.6	20.5	19.2	16.4	15.1	13.6	12.9	13.9
Netherlands	24.3	21.0	18.4	15.2	13.2	10.2	8.9	9.4
Denmark	19.4	18.6	17.5	14.2	12.9	11.3	10.9	9.4
Sweden	18.3	16.9	16.4	14.9	13.1	12.2	11.6	10.5
Norway	17.0	17.0	16.2	14.2	13.6	11.3	10.4	9.8
Finland	22.2	21.1	19.7	18.0	17.7	14.2	12.6	15.2
Germany	27.2	25.1	22.2	18.7	15.4	12.6	11.2	13.2 [a]
Switzerland	23.5	20.8	18.8	16.8	14.5	12.5	11.8	11.0
Austria	31.5	29.5	26.6	23.3	20.7	15.4	13.5	16.5
Hungary	. . .	32.5	29.9	25.6	23.2	18.5	15.8	14.2 [b]
Portugal	. . .	22.6	21.3	20.1	22.5	20.0	17.5	15.1
Spain	30.8	31.7	29.5	25.2	23.0	19.6	16.3	13.4
Italy	29.9	27.1	24.2	21.6	20.4	16.8	14.1	12.9
Romania	31.3	27.5	29.2	25.8	29.2	22.3	20.6	19.4
Russia (USSR) (European)	. . .	. . .	34.1	29.7	. . .	22.7	. . .	. . .
Japan	. . .	19.9	20.9	20.7	20.0	21.0	17.9	16.2
Australia	15.7	15.2	13.0	11.2	10.7	9.5	9.1	10.5

Sources: **12**, 1938, p. 254; **2**, 1948, pp. 312–17 and 1949–50, pp. 380–87; and **5**, July 1951.

a. For 1941–43, all Germany; for 1946–49, Western Germany.

b. For 1941–43 and 1945–48.

of death rates is approximately 13 to 18 per 1,000 inhabitants. It is much higher in the areas with particularly poor health conditions. (See Table 82; cf. Figure 57.)

The main causes of international variations in death rates are the differences in the level of economic development, health conditions (water supply, sanitary and medical services and so on [53]) and age composition of the population. The gaps in registration of deaths in the areas with unsatisfactory public health services tend to minimize and often to conceal the contrasts.

In the interregional variations in death rates the age factor frequently prevails over other factors. In the United States, for example, the highest death rates are recorded in New England and Delaware, areas with a relatively high median age, while the states with a comparatively young population have lower death rates.

Thus the median age of population averaged 30.6 years in the five states with the highest death rates and 26.0 years in the five states with the lowest death rates, in 1940:

	Deaths Per 1,000 Inhabitants, 1940	Median Age, 1940
Vermont	13.0	29.9
New Hampshire	12.7	31.6
Maine	12.5	29.6
Nevada	12.5	31.1
Delaware	12.2	30.6
Unweighted average	12.6	30.6
South Dakota	8.9	27.4
Arkansas	8.8	24.8
Utah	8.7	24.3
Wyoming	8.5	27.6
North Dakota	8.2	25.7
Unweighted average	8.6	26.0

The correlation is less clear in the middle part of the distribution. (See Table 83.)

53. Cf. Chapter 6.

TABLE 85

DEATH RATES IN SELECTED COUNTRIES BEFORE, DURING AND AFTER WORLD WARS I AND II

(*Deaths Per 1,000 Inhabitants, Excluding Military Losses*)

Year	United States	United Kingdom	France	Belgium	Italy	Germany	Austria
WORLD WAR I PERIOD							
1912	—	13.3	17.5	14.9	18.2	16.5	20.5
1913	—	13.8	17.7	13.9	18.7	15.0	20.3
1914	—	14.0	18.8	14.2	17.9	15.5	17.7
1915	13.2	15.9	18.5	13.9	20.4	15.1	20.3
1916	13.8	14.7	17.5	13.2	19.7	14.3	19.5
1917	14.0	14.8	17.9	16.4	19.2	16.1	21.4
1918	18.1	18.3	22.0	21.0	33.0	18.9	24.9
1919	12.9	13.7	19.3	15.0	19.0	15.3	20.4
1920	13.0	12.4	17.3	13.9	18.8	15.1	19.0
1921	11.5	12.1	17.7	13.8	17.4	13.9	17.0
1922	11.7	12.8	17.5	14.1	17.7	14.4	17.4
1923	12.1	11.6	16.7	13.2	16.6	13.1	15.2
WORLD WAR II PERIOD							
1931–35	10.9	12.2	15.7	12.9	14.1	11.2	13.5
1936	11.6	12.3	15.3	12.8	13.8	11.8	13.2
1937	11.3	12.6	15.3	13.2	14.3	11.7	13.3
1938	10.6	11.8	15.8	13.2	14.1	11.6	14.0
1939	10.6	12.2	15.5	13.9	13.4	12.3	15.3
1940	10.7	14.0	19.3	16.3	13.6	12.8	14.8
1941	10.5	13.0	17.5	14.7	13.9	12.2	14.0
1942	10.4	11.6	17.1	14.8	14.3	12.3	13.3
1943	10.9	12.0	16.6	13.6	15.2	12.4	13.8
1944	10.6	11.7	20.5	16.0	15.9	—	16.0
1945	10.6	11.5	16.8	14.9	13.9	—	25.6
1946	10.0	11.7	13.5	13.6	12.0	12.0 [a]	13.4
1947	10.1	12.1	13.2	13.3	11.4	11.6 [a]	13.0
1948	9.9	10.9	12.4	12.6	10.6	10.2 [a]	12.1
1949	9.7	11.7	13.8	12.9	10.6	10.1 [a]	12.6
1950	9.6	11.7	12.6	12.4	9.8	10.4 [a]	12.7

Sources: **5** and **12**, 1938.　　　　　　　　　　　　a. Western Germany.

The Long-Range Trend

A death rate of 40 per 1,000 inhabitants was not unusual two centuries ago. A rate of 25 per 1,000 was considered exceptionally low at the end of the eighteenth century. Since that time, mortality has declined steadily from decade to decade. The Scandinavian countries have been in the lead, followed by England, France, Belgium, the Netherlands, Switzerland and Germany. Progress has been slower in Italy, Spain and the countries of southeastern Europe. Death rates in other parts of the world have also declined, although not everywhere at the same pace. (See Table 84.) In countries of Western civilization, death rates have been halved during the past two generations; in some countries, in fact, they have dropped to a level that cannot be maintained in the long run.

Some countries with complete death registration have reported nine deaths per 1,000 inhabitants (as Canada in 1950), or even fewer (as Norway and the Netherlands).[54] In a stabilized population such a death rate would imply an average duration of life of 111.1 years (1,000 ÷ 9) or less, an average we certainly have not reached. A stabilized mortality rate of 12.5 to 13 per 1,000, which would give the average newborn baby a chance to live 77 to 80 years, may be regarded as highly satisfactory under present conditions. A death rate appreciably below this level is a temporary phenomenon due

54. See Table 82.

TABLE 86

DEATHS: ANNUAL AVERAGE INFANT MORTALITY RATE IN SELECTED COUNTRIES,
1871–80 TO 1941–49

(Deaths Under One Year of Age Per 1,000 Live Births)

Country	1871–80	1881–90	1891–1900	1901–10	1911–19	1920–30	1931–38	1941–49
United States	—	—	—	—	97	72	51	37
England and Wales	149	142	153	128	102	72	52	44
Scotland	122	120	127	116	108	89	70	59
Ireland	97	95	104	96	89	75	67	68
France	172	166	164	132	126	92	65	72
Belgium	153	159	161	145	130	92	75	77
Netherlands	203	178	158	125	97	61	36	42
Denmark	138	135	135	114	95	83	59	46
Sweden	130	111	102	84	70	59	46	28
Norway	104	98	97	75	65	51	43	36
Finland	166	153	142	124	104	92	70	58
Germany	—	—	—	186	155	108	60	75 [a]
Switzerland	193	165	149	124	91	61	43	39
Austria	256	250	236	209	152	129	80	78 [b]
Hungary	—	—	234	208	214	180	134	122 [c]
Spain	—	188	203	164	154	135	120	96
Italy	200	195	175	160	146	123	104	96
Romania	198	187	214	205	213	199	183	177 [d]
Russia (USSR)	266	265	268	251	—	—	—	—
Japan	—	—	170	156	165	149	116	76 [e]
Australia	—	—	112	87	65	56	38	32

Sources: **12**, 1938, p. 256; **2**, 1949–50, pp. 411–15; **5**.

a. Western Germany, 1946–49.
b. Excludes year 1945. If this year is included, the average for 1941–48 is 87.
c. Average for the years 1941–43 and 1945–48.
d. 1941–47.
e. Average for the years 1941–43 and 1947–49.

to the high proportion of children and middle-aged persons in the population as a result of the drop in infant mortality in the past three or four decades and sometimes, as in the United States, due also to large-scale immigration of young persons.

The relatively high death rate in France is due to a high proportion of older persons as a result of the long decline in the birth rate, which began in that country earlier than anywhere else in the world.

The last century is unique in the history of mankind. It may be guilty of many sins and may deserve condemnation on more than one count, but its outstanding achievements in the struggle against death from disease are beyond question.

Recent Changes in Death Rates

Mortality statistics for the years of World War II are not inclusive. German wartime figures do not include the deaths of civilians murdered in gas chambers and prison camps. Little is known about mortality behind the Iron Curtain.

In the countries for which reliable information is available, civilian death rates show either no rise at all during these years, as in the United States, or only a temporary upswing in 1944–47, as in France, Belgium, Finland, the Netherlands, Germany, Czechoslovakia, Hungary, Italy and Japan. (Cf. Table 85.) All in all, the increase in the number of deaths of civilian population in western Europe hardly exceeded a million.

The effect of food shortages, disorganization of civilian life, and overcrowding of cities by refugees must have been offset by the progress of medical and sanitary science. Japan's toll of

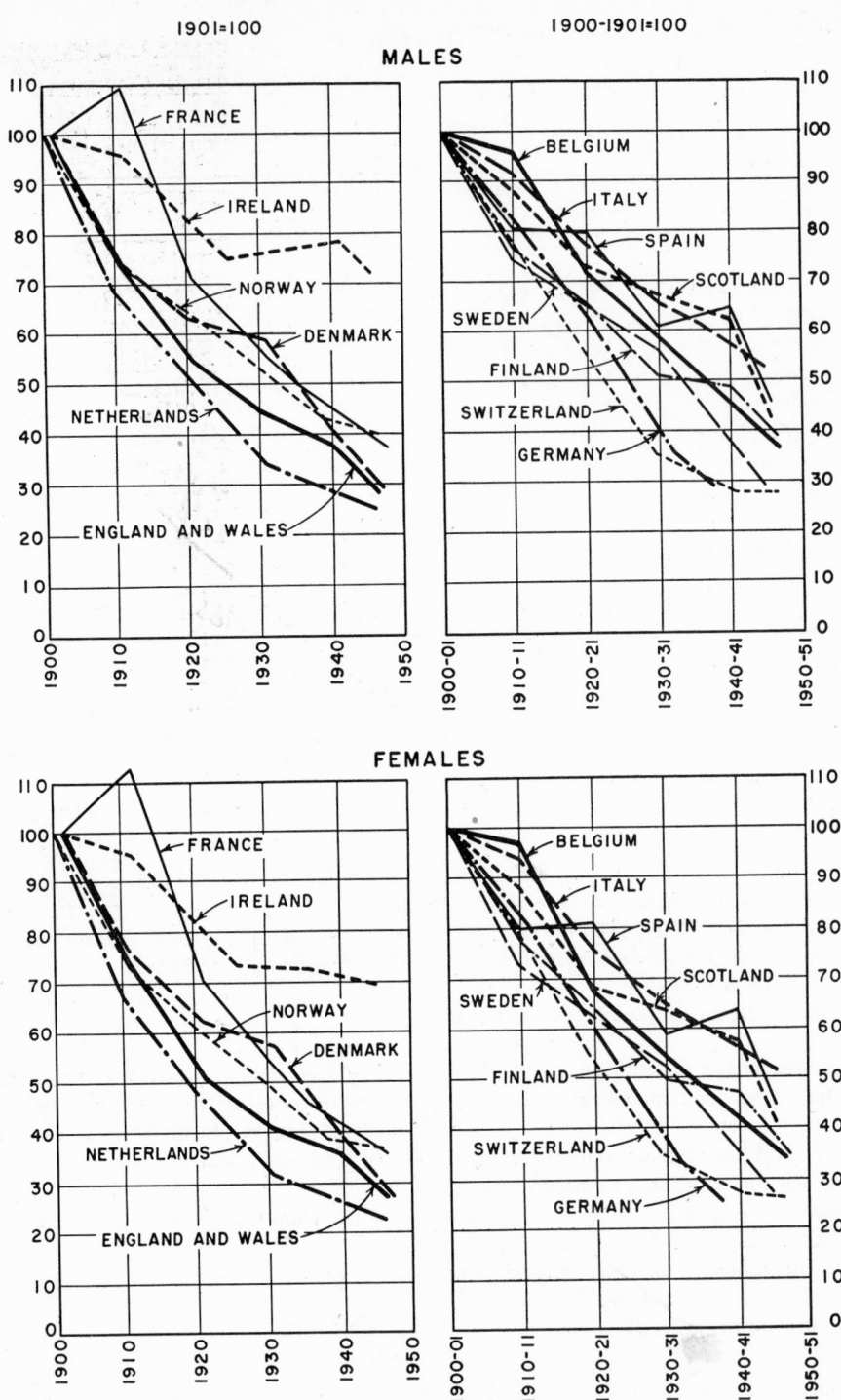

Deaths per 1,000 live births World Health Organization (**6**, February–March 1950)

FIGURE 58. INFANT MORTALITY: TRENDS IN SELECTED EUROPEAN COUNTRIES, 1900–50

excess civilian deaths about equaled the total for all European countries. The losses of the USSR in civilian population ran to several million.

Death Rates by Age Group

The decline in mortality among children has been spectacular. (See Table 86.) From 250 and 300 deaths per 1,000 live births at the beginning of the nineteenth century, the infant mortality rate has been reduced in the more advanced countries to 40 or 50 per 1,000.[55] To some extent, the struggle against infant mortality has been facilitated by the decline in the number of births. The opposite is equally true, however: the decline in infant mortality has tended to lower the birth rate.[56] From 1900 to 1950 the United States, Great Britain, Germany, the Netherlands, Norway, Denmark and Switzerland cut their infant mortality rates to about one third, and other countries of western Europe likewise recorded substantial progress. (See Figure 58.) The striking contrast between primarily agricultural regions and the industrialized nations (Figure 59) is a relatively recent development: The infant mortality rates of 200 and more per 1,000 live births recorded in 1940 in Chile and Burma are close to those that prevailed in Europe a century ago and in Italy and the Netherlands as late as 1871–80. (Cf. Table 86.)

Improvement in mortality rates among children aged 1–4 years in western Europe and the United States has been even more spectacular: In the United States the death rate in this age group in 1940 was only one sixth that in 1900; in England, Sweden and Finland, one tenth. (See Figure 60.) All in all, the proportion of newborn infants who live to reach age 5 has been increased from 60 per cent to 92–93 per cent.

Reduction in death rates in the higher age groups has been less striking, and improvement has practically stopped at the age of 75: there have been substantial declines in general mortality in the ages under 65 but only insignificant changes, mainly since 1940, in the age group 75 years and over. (See Figure 61.)

55. The stands in a village market in an underdeveloped country dramatize the high infant mortality. In Mexico, cheap children's coffins are among the staple commodities of mass consumption, along with nails and cotton shirts. Even the smallest market would not be complete without this grim display.

56. The effect of declining infant mortality on natality should not be overstated, however. Close analysis of the distribution of births shows that this is only a minor factor in the downward trend of fertility. (36.)

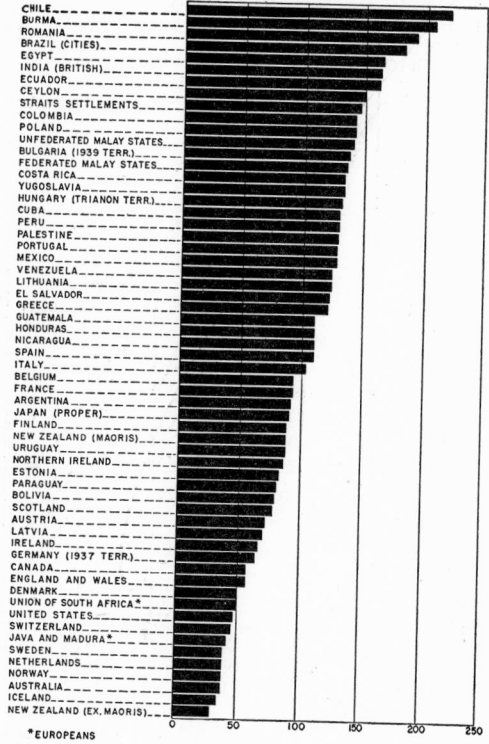

Deaths per 1,000 live births

U.S. Public Health Service, Federal Security Agency (11)

FIGURE 59. INFANT MORTALITY IN SELECTED COUNTRIES, 1940

The usual infant death rate in modern industrial countries is 40 to 50 per 1,000 live births. The rate is four or five times that figure in such countries as Chile, Burma, Romania, Brazil, Egypt and India. The unexpectedly low rates for Paraguay and Bolivia are due to incomplete registration of deaths. (Cf. 11, p. 35.)

In the United States, for example, the decrease (−) or increase (+) in death rates from 1910 to 1940 amounted, at the given ages, to the following percentages of the rates recorded at the turn of the century: [57]

	Male	Female
0–1 years	−71	−72
1–4	−85	−86
5–14	−67	−77
15–24	−61	−69
25–34	−55	−67

(*Continued on page 172*)

57. Computed from Table 87. The slight rise in mortality among older people is due to several factors: Medical science has been more successful in fighting contagious diseases and ailments of childhood than in handling ailments of the aged. (Cf. Chapter 6.) Decline in mortality among the younger age groups weakens the physical selection of those who reach older ages. The more people who live to the age of 75, the higher the proportion among them of persons with chronic ailments.

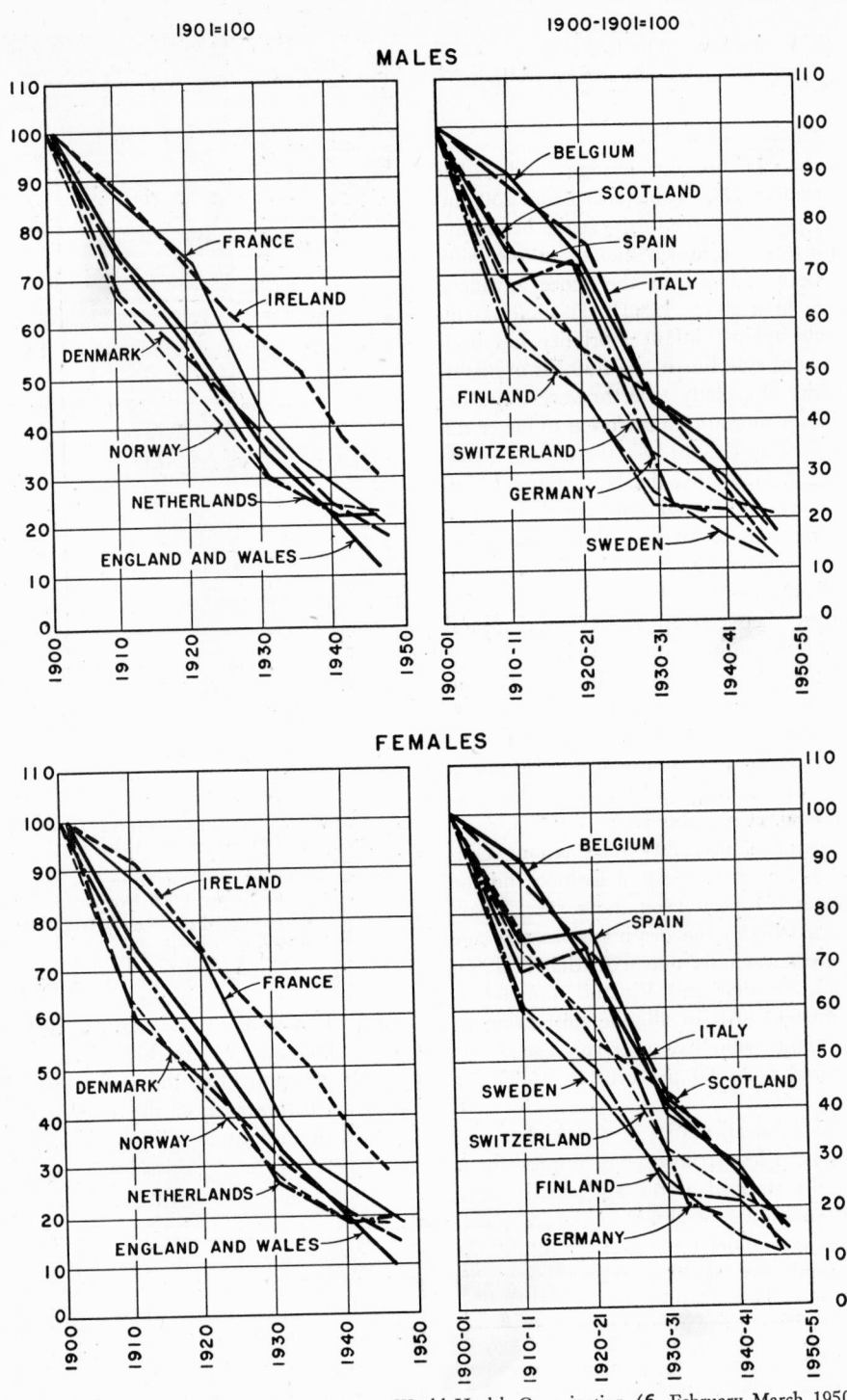

FIGURE 60. DEATH RATES AMONG CHILDREN AGED 1–4 YEARS IN SELECTED EUROPEAN COUNTRIES, 1900–50

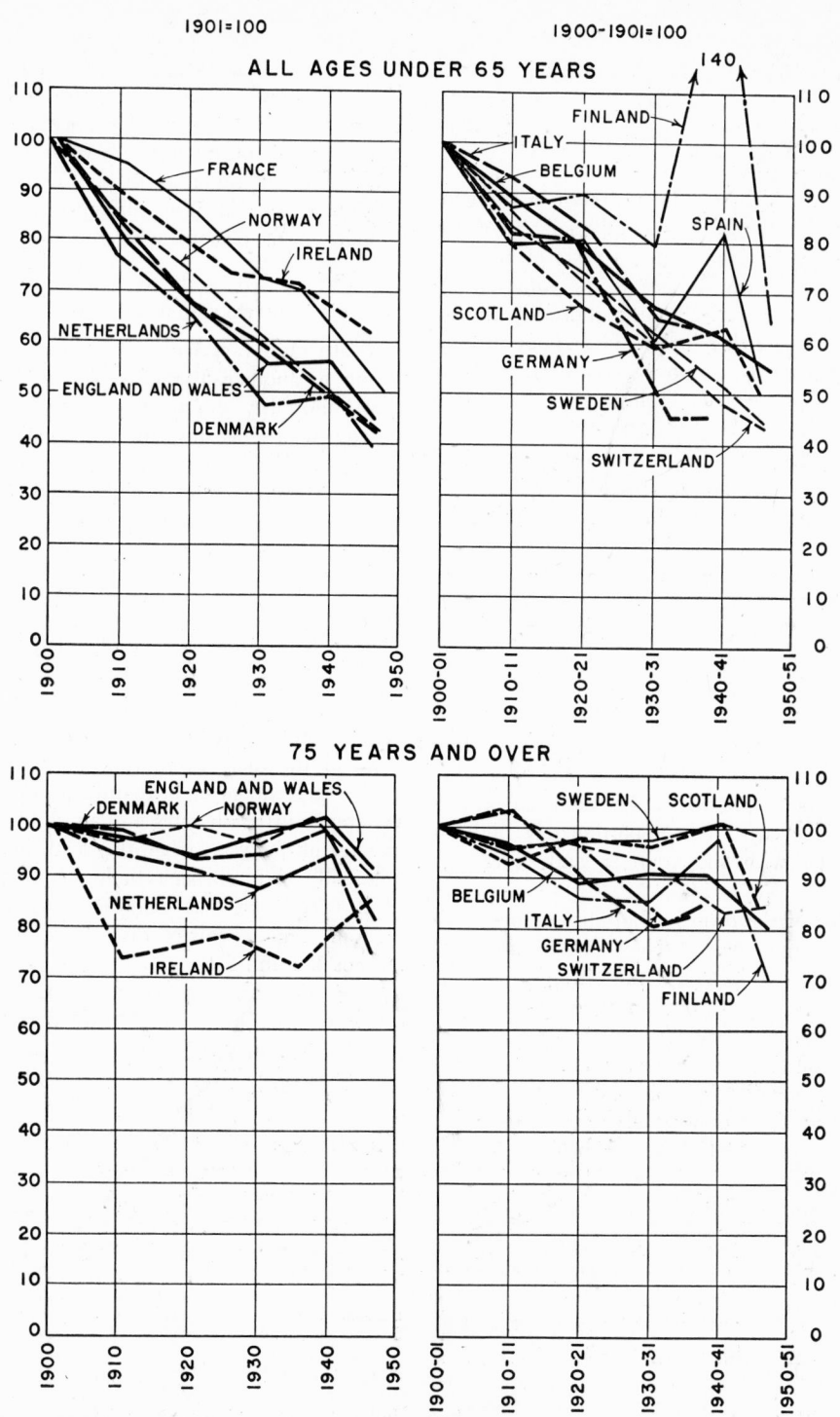

FIGURE 61. DEATH RATES AMONG MEN UNDER 65 YEARS AND OF 75 YEARS AND OVER IN SELECTED EUROPEAN COUNTRIES, 1900–50

35–44	—44	—58
45–54	—20	—39
55–64	— 8	—28
65–74	— 7	—19
75 and over	+ 3	+ 3

Apart from the striking contrasts in the general level of mortality, and especially in death rates among children under 5 years of age, the age pattern in death rates is the same in all countries: comparatively high mortality in the first year of life; the lowest death rates in ages 5–14; a gradual rise to 50–54 years, and an accelerated upswing at higher ages. (See Table 87.) The improvement in death rates in the United States since the turn of the century has not changed this pattern. (See Figure 62.)

Death rates in the highly developed industrial countries — such as Great Britain, Germany, Belgium, the Netherlands — are close to those of the white population of the United States in 1939–41; rates in backward countries are closer to the pattern for Negroes in the United States. (See Figure 63.) The only significant deviation from this pattern is Japan's surprisingly high mortality rate in the age group 20–24. More elaborate mortality tables reveal a similar phenomenon in France, where the death rate among men of 21 years is disproportionately high in comparison with the younger and older age groups.[58]

Because of the drop in mortality among children and the comparatively low death rates among young adults and middle-aged persons, deaths in modern industrialized nations are heavily concentrated in the upper age groups. In the United States, for example, only 10 per cent of a cohort of 100,000 white males will die in the first three decades of life; about 21,000 will die at ages 60–69 years, 27,000 at ages 70–79, and 19,000 at ages between 80 and 90. More than two thirds of all deaths occur after the age of 60. (See Figure 64.)

The contrast in general mortality rates between industrially developed and underdeveloped countries is due largely to the difference in mortality among children. In ages under 5 years, the death rates in Mexico, Chile and India are approximately ten times those in the United States, Sweden or Australia. At higher ages the contrast lessens. Among persons 5–24 years old, the death rates in Chile are four times as high

as in the United States; at ages 30–34 years, three times as high; at 40–44 years, twice as high. The ratio drops further to 1.6:1 for ages 50–54, to 1.3:1 for ages 60–64, while the death rate among Chileans aged 75 years and over is practically the same as in the United States, Canada or Sweden. The difference is only in the proportion of persons who reach middle and old age.

DIFFERENTIAL MORTALITY

Death rates vary widely from one population group to another. For example, in the United States mortality among Negroes is higher than among white persons; in almost all countries death rates for men are higher than for women. There is also a close correlation between mortality and occupation and, more generally, between mortality and poverty.

Death Rates by Sex

Even before birth, a male child is exposed to greater danger of death than a female child. Some experts believe that the high masculinity rate of stillbirths is due mainly to the larger head of the male child. It is possible that the higher percentage of birth injuries explains the difference in death rates among children under the age of one year, when the death rate of boys is usually 15 to 20 per cent higher than that of girls. (See Table 87.) The disparity diminishes, and in some countries disappears, in the age groups 1–4 and 5–9.

The relationship between the death rates of the two sexes in the ages 10–39 years is rather obscure; it varies from country to country, and in the same country occasionally changes from year to year. After age 40 and especially after 45, the death rate among men is higher than among women in all countries.

Very little is known about the factors controlling the changes in "masculinity" of deaths. Between 1870 and 1920, the ratio of male to female deaths leveled off in some countries and increased in others. The high index of masculinity of deaths in Australia and New Zealand contrasts strangely with the low index in European countries with similar death rates, such as Sweden and Norway. (See Table 88.)

Death Rates in Cities and Rural Areas

Comparison of death rates in cities and rural areas is sometimes misleading — first, because of

TABLE 87

DEATH RATES BY SEX AND AGE GROUP IN SELECTED COUNTRIES, 1900-49

(For Ages Over One Year, Deaths Per 1,000 Inhabitants; Under One Year, Deaths Per 1,000 Live Births)

Country, Year and Sex	Total	Age Groups, in Years																
		0-1	1-4	5-9	10-14	15-19	20-24	25-29	30-34	35-39	40-44	45-49	50-54	55-59	60-64	65-69	70-74	75 and Over
United States																		
1900 Male	17.9	179.1	20.5	3.8		5.9			8.2		10.7	15.7			28.7		59.3	128.3
1900 Female	16.4	145.4	19.1	3.9		5.8			8.2		9.8	14.2			25.8		53.6	118.8
1920 Male	13.4	103.6	10.3	2.8		4.8			6.4		8.2	12.6			29.6		54.5	122.1
1920 Female	12.0	80.7	9.5	2.5		5.0			7.1		8.0	11.7			22.4		50.5	115.9
1929-31 Male	11.4	71	6.1	2.1	1.7	3.0	4.1	4.6	5.3	6.6	8.9	11.8	16.2	23	32	48	70	139
1929-31 Female	11.2	57	5.3	1.7	1.4	2.6	3.9	4.3	4.8	5.6	7.1	9.3	12.8	18	26	39	60	129
1940 Male	10.4	52	3.1	1.2	1.1	1.9	2.7	3.1	3.7	4.9	7.0	10.1	15.1	22	31	45	68	137
1940 Female		41	2.7	0.9	0.9	1.5	2.1	2.5	3.0	3.9	5.2	7.1	10.3	15	22	33	54	122
1946 Male	10.8	11		1.0	1.0	1.7	2.5	2.5	2.9	4.1	5.9	9.1	14.0	20	29	43	61	122
1946 Female	12.0	9		0.7	0.6	1.0	1.5	1.7	2.1	3.0	4.1	6.6	8.8	12	19	30	46	108
Canada																		
1930-32 Male	10.2	91	6.6	2.2	1.6	2.5	3.3	3.4	3.5	4.4	5.4	7.2	10.6	16	23	36	57	125
1930-32 Female		73	5.8	1.7	1.5	2.4	3.3	3.8	4.1	4.8	5.5	6.8	9.2	14	20	32	50	121
1948 Male	9.9	39	3.0	0.9	0.8	1.8	2.4	2.2	3.1	3.6	5.2	8.3	13.8	21	27	42	60	85[a]
1948 Female	7.4	31	2.3	0.8	0.7	1.4	1.3	1.8	1.9	2.9	3.9	6.4	9.0	12	18	27	43	72[a]
Chile																		
1930-32 Male	23.1	241	31	4.1	3.2	6.6	9.4	9.5	10.6	11.7	14.4	18.7	23	30	41	58		121
1930-32 Female		226	31	3.9	3.7	7.3	9.5	9.5	11.1	11.1	12.6	14.0	16	23	30	47		107
1939-41 Male		221	31	3.7	3.4	6.5	9.7	9.7	10.8	11.9	14.4	17.9	23	31	38	58	78	127
1939-41 Female		206	32	3.7	3.8	7.2	9.5	10.2	10.0	11.1	11.8	13.4	17	24	29	50	61	126
England and Wales																		
1910-12 Male	13.8	121	16	3.2	1.9	2.9	3.7	4.3	5.4	7.0	9.1	12.5	17	25	36	52	81	150
1910-12 Female		98	15	3.2	2.0	2.7	3.1	3.7	4.5	5.9	7.3	9.7	13	19	27	40	66	132
1930-32 Male	11.9	72	7.5	2.3	1.5	2.5	3.3	3.3	3.6	4.8	6.4	9.3	13	19	29	46	74	150
1930-32 Female		55	6.8	2.0	1.4	2.3	2.8	3.1	3.3	3.9	4.9	6.7	9	14	21	34	55	129
1948 Male	11.5	9.7		0.9	0.6	1.2	1.5	1.8	2.0	2.5	3.8	6.6	10.3	17	27	40	61	120[a]
1948 Female	10.1	7.6		0.6	0.6	1.1	1.5	1.7	1.8	2.1	2.8	4.3	6.5	10	15	24	42	110[a]

(Continued on page 174)

TABLE 87—continued

Country, Year and Sex	Total	0–1	1–4	5–9	10–14	15–19	20–24	25–29	30–34	35–39	40–44	45–49	50–54	55–59	60–64	65–69	70–74	75 and Over
France																		
1920–22 Male	17.4	111	12.3	2.7	2.1	3.9	7.3	6.9	6.8	8.0	9.4	12.3	16	23	37	50	78	176
1920–22 Female		91	11.6	2.7	2.3	9.2	5.7	6.2	6.3	6.6	7.3	9.3	11	16	24	37	62	155
1949 Male	14.5	65	3.5	0.9	0.8	1.3	2.0	2.4	2.9	3.7	5.4	8.1	12.3	18	27	41	80[b]	
1949 Female	13.1	51	3.1	0.8	0.6	1.0	1.5	1.9	2.3	2.6	3.6	4.8	7.1	10	16	26	57[b]	
Netherlands																		
1920–21 Male	11.5	84	9.6	2.2	1.6	2.9	3.9	3.6	3.8	4.1	5.1	6.8	11	16	25	40	63	137
1920–21 Female		65	8.6	2.1	1.7	2.9	3.4	4.0	4.6	5.2	5.2	7.2	10	14	23	37	59	130
1949 Male	8.4	30	2.1	0.8	0.6	0.8	3.3	1.5	1.6	1.9	2.9	4.5	7.6	11	18	30	52	87[a]
1949 Female	7.9	23	1.7	0.5	0.4	0.5	1.6	1.0	1.2	1.7	2.5	3.8	5.9	9	15	28	50	83[a]
Sweden																		
1921–25 Male	12.1	67	6.1	2.1	1.9	3.5	5.0	4.7	4.6	4.9	5.7	7.4	10	15	22	33	58	127
1921–25 Female		52	5.3	2.0	2.0	3.4	4.3	4.3	4.5	4.9	5.7	6.9	9	12	18	29	48	123
1947 Male	10.8	28	1.7	0.9	0.6	1.4	1.9	2.1	2.3	2.5	3.4	4.8	8.5	13	19	33	53	89[a]
1947 Female	10.8	22	1.3	0.6	0.5	1.1	1.5	1.7	1.8	2.3	3.1	4.5	6.6	10	16	27	48	83[a]
Norway																		
1911–15 Male	13.4	73	8.0	3.3	2.6	5.7	8.5	7.9	7.1	7.1	7.9	9.6	12	17	23	34	52	127
1911–15 Female		60	7.3	3.0	3.0	4.9	6.1	6.3	6.0	6.9	7.6	7.8	10	13	19	28	46	116
1948 Male	9.0		8.6	1.2	0.8	1.5	2.0	2.2	2.4	2.6	3.6	5.1	7.2	11	16	23	43	71[a]
1948 Female	8.7		6.7	0.7	0.5	0.8	1.2	1.4	1.5	1.9	2.8	3.5	5.1	7	12	20	46	63[a]
Germany																		
1924–26 Male	11.9	116	7.5	1.8	1.4	2.9	4.5	4.2	4.1	4.7	66.1	8.3	12	18	29	45	73	146
1924–26 Female		94	6.9	1.6	1.3	2.5	3.6	4.0	4.3	4.8	5.7	7.3	10	15	24	39	65	137
1937 Male	12.2		21.0	2.0	1.4	2.1	3.3	3.2	3.5	4.4	5.7	7.8	11	17	27	42	102	
1937 Female	11.2		16.6	1.8	1.2	1.6	2.4	2.8	3.0	3.7	4.5	6.2	9	14	22	36	97	
Poland																		
1933–34 Male	14.7	45		3.5	2.4	3.7	5.0	4.9	5.3	6.1	7.9	11.1	16	23	35	57	76	146
1933–34 Female		38		3.5	2.6	3.6	4.6	5.1	5.8	6.5	7.2	8.5	12	16	27	40	67	135
Portugal																		
1930–32 Male	17.0	151	24	2.8	2.3	3.5	5.8	6.6	7.6	8.4	9.5	11.9	15	20	30	46	74	156
1930–32 Female		135	23	2.7	2.4	3.6	5.2	5.4	5.7	6.2	6.6	7.4	9	12	20	32	57	141
1947 Male	14.0	135	16	2.4	1.5	2.9	4.6	4.5	4.9	6.3	7.8	10.0	13	18	29	43	66	116[a]
1947 Female	12.8	121	15	2.2	1.6	2.8	4.1	3.8	3.7	4.2	4.2	5.8	7	10	18	28	49	86[a]

(Continued on facing page)

TABLE 87—continued

Country, Year and Sex		Total	Age Groups, in Years																
			0–1	1–4	5–9	10–14	15–19	20–24	25–29	30–34	35–39	40–44	45–49	50–54	55–59	60–64	65–69	70–74	75 and Over
Italy																			
1930–32	Male	14.5	116	17	2.7	2.0	3.1	4.2	4.4	4.9	5.7	6.9	8.9	12	17	26	41	67	145
	Female		103	17	2.6	2.0	3.2	4.2	4.5	4.5	5.1	5.7	6.9	9	14	21	35	60	135
1947	Male	12.0	98	8.2	1.8	1.4	2.3		3.5				9.1			22	34	94 [b]	
	Female	10.8	83	7.7	1.5	1.3	2.1		3.9				6.2			17	28	87 [b]	
Japan																			
1924–26	Male	20.2	153	25	4.4	3.0	7.6	9.5	7.9	7.4	8.4	10.9	14.6	20	31	44	66	98	169
	Female		137	25	4.7	4.2	9.5	10.6	9.6	9.5	10.1	10.5	11.1	14	21	29	46	71	138
1948	Male	12.5	73	11	2.6	1.5	3.4	7.0	7.6	7.1	7.3	8.3	10.3	15	22	57			
	Female	11.2	63	11	2.2	1.6	3.6	6.6	6.6	6.2	6.3	7.0	8.2	11	16	55			
Australia																			
1911	Male	10.7	76	6.6	2.2	1.6	2.4	3.7	4.3	5.2	6.4	8.7	10.9	15	21	32	48	71	152
	Female		61	6.2	2.0	1.6	2.2	3.5	4.2	4.8	5.9	6.3	8.1	11	15	22	36	57	132
1932–34	Male	9.0	46	4.1	1.5	1.2	1.8	2.4	2.5	3.0	3.9	5.3	7.8	12	18	26	40	62	129
	Female		37	3.6	1.2	0.9	1.4	2.1	2.6	3.0	3.7	4.4	6.1	9	12	18	29	47	111
1947	Male	10.7	32	2.0	1.0	0.7	1.4	1.7	1.7	2.0	2.6	4.2	6.6	12	17	27	42	61	97 [a]
	Female	8.6	25	1.6	0.6	0.5	0.7	1.1	1.5	1.8	2.4	3.3	4.6	8	30	16	26	43	73 [a]
New Zealand																			
1911	Male	9.4	64	5.3	2.1	1.8	2.1	2.8	3.3	4.6	5.7	7.1	8.9	14	17	26	46	63	132
	Female		49	5.3	1.7	1.2	2.3	3.2	4.4	4.3	4.7	5.3	7.3	10	15	22	32	53	121
1935–36	Male	8.5	35	2.7	1.4	0.9	1.6	2.4	2.2	2.3	3.4	4.6	6.7	10	15	23	35	56	127
	Female		29	2.3	1.1	0.7	1.0	1.9	2.1	2.7	2.9	4.1	5.5	8	12	18	29	46	111
1948	Male	10.1	26	1.9	0.7	0.7	1.2	1.8	1.5	1.7	2.0	3.1	6.0	9	14	25	37	56	122
	Female	8.1	19	1.4	0.5	0.5	0.9	1.2	1.6	1.6	2.2	2.6	3.9	6	10	15	25	40	104

a. Age 75–79. b. Age 70–79.

Sources: **1**, pp. 70–76; **2**, 1949–50, pp. 388–401; **11**.

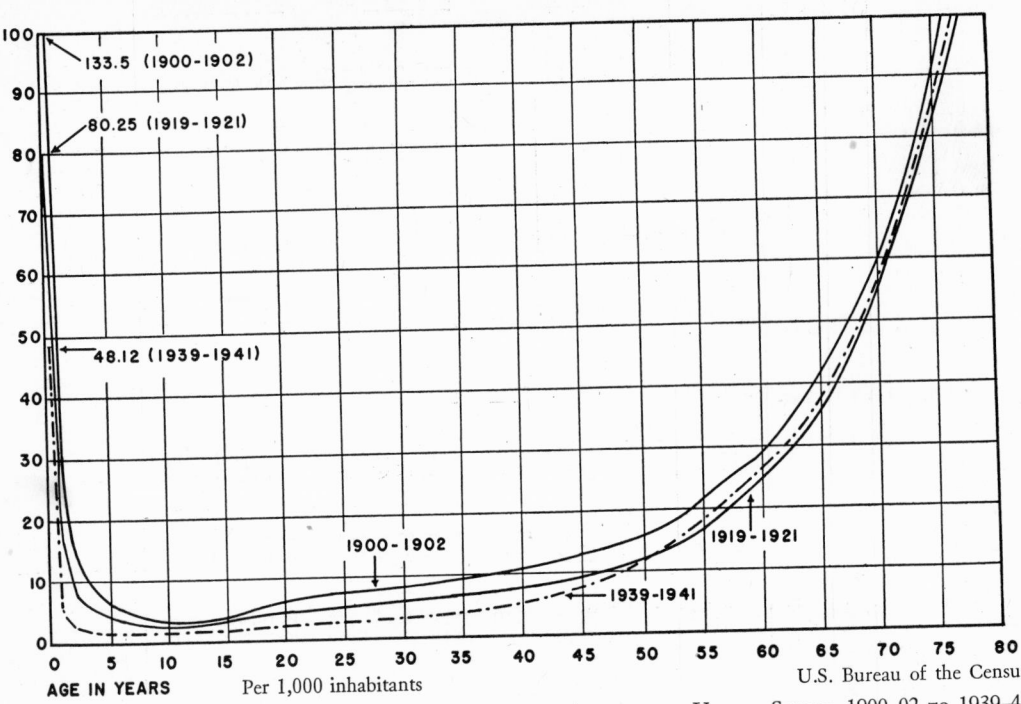

FIGURE 62. DEATH RATES AMONG WHITE MALE PERSONS BY AGE, IN THE UNITED STATES, 1900–02 TO 1939–41

Death rates in the United States have declined steadily since the turn of the century among persons of all ages. The greatest success in reducing mortality has been in the youngest age groups. Progress among elderly people has been slow. (Cf. **8**.)

TABLE 88

RATIO BETWEEN AVERAGE DEATH RATES OF MALES AND FEMALES IN SELECTED COUNTRIES, 1876–85 AND 1919–25

(Per Cent, Death Rate of Women = 100)

Country	1876–85	1919–25	Country	1876–85	1919–25
United States			Germany	113.2	109.4
Massachusetts	105.8	104.6	Switzerland	110.9	104.5
Connecticut	108.0 [a]	107.5	Austria	112.9	105.4
England and Wales	112.8	113.7	Hungary	110.7	111.9
France	108.3	112.6 [b]	Spain	109.3	110.6
Belgium	110.3	108.1	Italy	103.6	106.7 [b]
Netherlands	108.8	102.6	Japan	102.8 [a]	101.7 [b]
Sweden	108.8	101.5	Australia	121.3	126.1
Norway	109.0	104.9	New Zealand	117.6	122.2

Source: **59**, p. 208.   a. 1886–95.   b. 1906–14.

differences in the composition of the population and, second, because residents of rural areas are often brought to a city hospital for care and, if they die there, add to the urban mortality rate. Though death rates in cities are generally higher than in rural areas, the difference is neither consistent nor very large. In many countries, some cities and towns have rates below the national average while others have much higher rates.

In the United States, for example, the general death rate averaged 10.1 per 1,000 in 1947, with the rate in New York 10.7, in Baltimore 11.6, and in Detroit 8.3. In Canada the national average in that year was 9.4 per 1,000, as compared with 14.2 in 78 towns, 9.5 in Montreal,

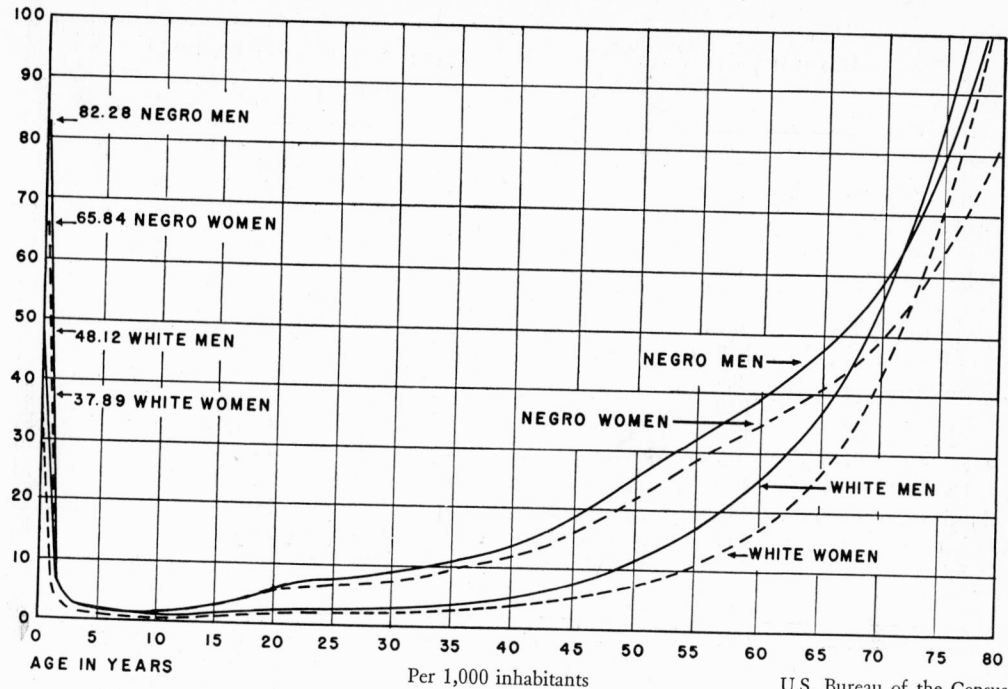

AGE IN YEARS

Per 1,000 inhabitants

U.S. Bureau of the Census

FIGURE 63. DEATH RATES BY AGE, SEX AND RACE, IN THE UNITED STATES, 1939–41

Death rates among the white population in the United States are appreciably lower than among Negroes at all ages below 73 years. Death rates among women are usually lower than among men.

Mortality for both sexes and races is high below one year, sinks to the lowest point in the ages of 5 to 10, rises gradually through middle age, then more steeply at higher ages.

Death rates for men are higher than those for women among both whites and Negroes. There is a striking difference in the death rates of the two races in the same sex and age groups. (Cf. **8**, 1950, p. 71.)

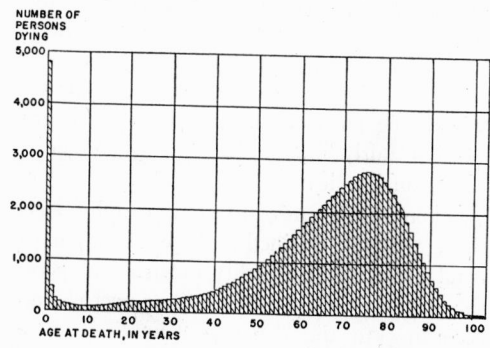

Bureau of the Census

FIGURE 64. NUMBER OF DEATHS AT EACH YEAR OF AGE IN A COHORT OF 100,000 WHITE MEN, IN THE UNITED STATES, 1939–41

According to the current death rates in the various age classes in the United States, two thirds of a cohort of 100,000 white males will live to reach some age between 60 and 79 years. The remaining third is divided almost equally between those who die before age 60 and those who live till 80 years or more.

and 15.4 in the city of Quebec. In Mexico, the rate was 16.3 for the whole nation and 18.3 for Mexico City. India reported an average death rate of 19.7 per 1,000, but 21.9 for 212

towns, 15.5 for Calcutta, 22.5 for Bombay and 35.7 for Madras. In Great Britain, Denmark, Austria, Australia and New Zealand, mortality rates in large cities are somewhat higher than in rural areas; in France, Switzerland, Spain, Hungary, the Netherlands and Sweden, the opposite relationship prevails.[59] (See Table 89.)

Death Rates by Economic Status and Occupation

The correlation between mortality and poverty seems so obvious that many people are inclined to accept it without asking for statistical evidence. However, attempts to measure the difference between the death rates for the rich and the poor have not been very successful; they have proved, indeed, that the correlation between mortality and economic conditions is often obscured or masked by other factors. In some countries, for example, large cities have a higher mortality rate than the nation as a whole despite the fact that the per capita income of their popu-

59. Cf. **18**, p. 62.

TABLE 89

DEATH RATES IN TOWNS AND LARGE CITIES IN SELECTED COUNTRIES, 1947

(Deaths Per 1,000 Inhabitants)

Country and Area	Death Rate	Country and Area	Death Rate	Country and Area	Death Rate
United States, total	10.1	England and Wales, total	12.0	Switzerland, total	11.3
New York	10.7	126 towns	13.1	10 towns	10.7
Baltimore	11.6	London	13.0	Bern	9.8
Detroit	8.3	France, total	13.0	Geneva	12.0
Canada, total	9.4	37 towns	10.5	Spain, total	11.8
78 towns	14.2	Paris	10.7	Madrid	10.7
Montreal	9.5	Lyons	10.3	Barcelona	11.5
Toronto	10.0	Bordeaux	11.3	Valencia	11.2
Quebec	15.4	Lille	13.7	Italy, total	11.3
Ottawa	9.7	Belgium, total	13.3	Rome	9.3
Mexico, total	16.3	Brussels	13.4	Milan	9.9
Mexico City (1948)	18.3	Antwerp	12.2	Naples	12.0
Chile, total	16.7	Sweden, total	10.8	Turin	11.5
Santiago	17.6	Stockholm	9.3	Genoa	11.9
Valparaiso	21.5			Florence	11.7

Source: **6,** July 1949, pp. 126–36.

lation is much higher than that of the rest of the nation. Countries and states of the United States do not always rank the same in death rate as in income and wealth.

On the other hand, in large cities mortality in poor districts is appreciably higher than in rich residential sections.[60] A clear relationship between family income and the infant mortality rate has been found in many surveys in the United States and other countries. The difference between the death rates of white persons and Negroes in the United States is largely due to the disadvantage of Negroes in income and occupational status.

To establish specific death rates for various occupational groups, the number of deaths classified by age and occupation should be compared with the number of persons in the respective pursuits. However, the occupation given on the death certificate may differ from that recorded for the same individual by the census. Some people whom the census records as skilled workers or operatives may be described as "laborers" in the death certificate. When a worker has suffered a spell of poor health and irregular employment before his death, the occupation given on his death certificate is likely to be less skilled than the one he followed in his

active years. High death rates among beggars and street peddlers,[61] unemployed workers [62] and common laborers [63] may be due partly to the fact that these occupational groups include many persons who have been squeezed out of their former jobs because of advanced age or physical handicaps. At the other extreme, the lowest death rates are found among persons in professional services (a middle-class group in income, but the uppermost group in education) and among farmers and farm laborers (a group ranking fairly low in both the economic and educational scale).

When death rates are computed by income class, without distinction between urban and rural areas, the inequality of rich and poor in the face of death does not appear overwhelming according to the experience in England and Wales, where the death rate among men in the lowest income class in 1930–32 was 11.2 per 1,000 as compared with 9.0 for the highest income group.

The range in death rates for particular occupations is much wider. When the average death rate for males aged 20–64 years is taken as 100,

60. See **31** and **32.**

61. This group has the highest death rate in England according to the much-quoted survey of "Mortality in Relation to Occupation."

62. **16,** Part 2, p. 211; cf. **14.**

63. **58.**

TABLE 90

DEATH RATES IN VARIOUS SOCIAL CLASSES, BY SEX AND AGE, IN FRANCE, 1907–08

(Deaths Per 1,000 Inhabitants)

Age, in Years	Men				Women			
	Total Population	Employers	Salaried Employees	Wage Earners	Total Population	Employers	Salaried Employees	Wage Earners
25–29	73	62	80	72	71	59	62	76
30–34	83	67	95	95	77	78	69	92
35–39	100	75	110	117	77	78	67	98
40–44	125	89	131	159	92	92	85	116
45–49	161	115	180	208	105	110	111	135
50–54	198	140	227	261	128	133	144	164
55–59	276	206	330	372	194	190	209	203
60–64	369	287	470	487	275	280	333	288

Source: **39,** p. 249.

the rates for various occupations in England in 1930–32 ranged as follows: [64]

Occupations with Low Mortality

Bank officials	62
Insurance officials	69
Clergymen	69
Farmers	73
Laundry workers	75
Farm laborers	77
Bakers	77

Occupations with High Mortality

Barmen	149
Inn, hotelkeepers, etc.	157
Glass blowers	160
Puddlers (metalworkers)	166
Stevedores	220
Cotton blow-room operatives	233
Grinders in cutlery trade	240

In France, specific death rates have been computed for employers, salaried employees and wage earners in each age class. These rates show considerable differences for men but not as wide differences for women. (See Table 90.) Furthermore, death rates in France vary more widely from industry to industry than from one social group to another in the same industry. Some of these variations may be due to differences between occupational classification in the census and in death certificates.[65]

Thompson has pointed out the role of selection in developing differences in death rates by occupation: Selection picks many of the poorer physical specimens of manhood for the worst-paid jobs, and then poor pay makes decent living impossible. It appears, however, that the contrast between the death rates of those in the more hazardous and poorly paid trades and those in the more sheltered occupations yielding larger incomes is being lessened as public health services become more widespread and more efficient. [66]

To sum up, high death rates in certain socio-economic and occupational groups are directly related to poverty, ignorance and exposure to more than average risk of illness and accident, but powerful factors tend toward equalizing all in the face of death. The germs originated in slums cannot be ordered to keep away from substantial citizens. If the community does not assure healthful conditions for all, including its poorest and least educated members, the danger of premature death increases for all, including the economic and educational elite.

LIFE TABLES

A life table indicates the mortality status of the population by showing (1) the proportion of newborn who are likely to reach the age of one year, five years, ten years and so on and (2), the average expectation of life at any given age. The proportion of the population that will survive to a given age is a measure of mortality in the preceding age groups. The expectation of life at a given age measures the mortality in the subsequent age classes. Improvement in health in a country is reflected in increase in the pro-

64. **16,** Part 2, **p. 211.**
65. **42,** pp. 525–27.
66. **54,** p. 239.

TABLE 91

LIFE TABLES: PROPORTION OF LIVE BORN SURVIVING TO A GIVEN AGE IN SELECTED COUNTRIES

(*Number of Survivors Out of 100 Live Births*)

Country and Period	Males Surviving to Age:					Females Surviving to Age:				
	1	10	30	50	70	1	10	30	50	70
United States (1939–41)										
White	95.2	93.6	90.1	80.5	46.7	96.2	94.9	92.3	85.3	58.4
Negro	91.8	89.4	81.0	60.5	27.2	93.4	91.3	83.4	64.9	32.4
Canada (1930–32)	90.0	86.9	82.3	74.2	47.7	91.6	88.2	83.5	75.1	51.4
Mexico (1930)	77.6	58.1	48.8	35.0	16.6	80.3	59.7	50.7	38.3	18.2
England (1930–32)	92.8	89.0	84.4	74.8	43.4	94.5	91.1	86.8	79.0	53.1
France (1928–33)	91.0	87.2	80.5	66.9	35.4	92.8	89.2	82.5	72.7	47.2
Belgium (1928–32)	89.9	86.1	80.7	70.5	40.7	92.1	88.7	83.3	74.7	48.9
Denmark (1931–35)	91.9	89.8	86.1	79.0	51.6	93.7	91.9	88.4	80.5	54.4
Sweden (1931–35)	94.5	92.3	87.3	79.0	53.1	95.8	93.9	88.9	81.1	57.3
Switzerland (1933–37)	94.8	92.3	87.6	77.6	43.8	95.9	93.8	89.7	82.0	54.1
Italy (1930–32)	88.5	81.7	76.3	66.9	41.2	89.8	83.0	77.5	69.3	46.5
Japan (1926–30)	86.0	76.8	66.7	54.3	24.3	87.6	78.1	66.2	54.3	31.5
British India (1921–30)	75.1	56.5	43.9	24.3	7.0	76.8	59.4	42.7	21.5	6.6
Union of South Africa (1935–37)										
White	93.4	89.9	85.0	74.2	42.5	94.7	91.4	87.5	78.6	52.3
Nonwhite	81.6	70.4	60.7	44.8	21.6	83.7	71.8	59.7	45.1	23.6
Australia (1932–34)	95.5	93.2	89.6	81.1	50.1	96.4	94.4	91.2	83.7	59.6
New Zealand (1934–38)	96.3	94.6	91.1	83.3	54.2	97.1	95.7	92.8	86.0	61.4

Source: **10**, p. 16.

portion of survivors and in the expectation of life at various ages.

On the basis of death rates classified by occupation, life tables can be computed for single social classes.[67] Such tables are of questionable value, however, because of the wide margin of error and uncertainty in the respective death rates. Moreover, a person may shift from one occupation to another. Life expectation in his current occupation may be very high but his chances of staying in this occupation until his death may be small.

Chances of Survival

The industrialized countries and the regions less developed economically differ strikingly in the proportion of the population that survives to a given age. (See Table 91; cf. Figure 65.) The number of boys who live to reach the age of 10 averaged 56.5 per cent of all born in British India in 1921–30 and amounted to 58.1 per cent in Mexico in 1930. These figures are prob-

ably close to the rates in many underdeveloped areas for which no reliable mortality data are available. On the other hand, the ratio during the 1930's was 92.3 per cent in Sweden and Switzerland, 93.2 per cent in Australia, 94.6 per cent in New Zealand. In the United States the rate in 1939–1941 was 93.6 per cent for white boys and 89.4 per cent for Negro.

In British India — under mortality conditions in 1921–30 — only 7.0 per cent of all males will live to reach the biblical age of threescore and ten. In Mexico the ratio was 16.6 per cent (1930). In contrast, 53.1 per cent of the live born will reach the age of 70 in Sweden (1931–35), 43.8 per cent in Switzerland (1933–37), 50.1 per cent in Australia (1932–34), and 54.2 per cent in New Zealand (1934–38). In the United States (1939–41) the rate was 46.7 per cent for white men and 27.2 per cent for Negroes. The former rate compares favorably with that of England, France and Belgium; the latter is near that of underdeveloped agricultural nations.

67. **56**, p. 180.

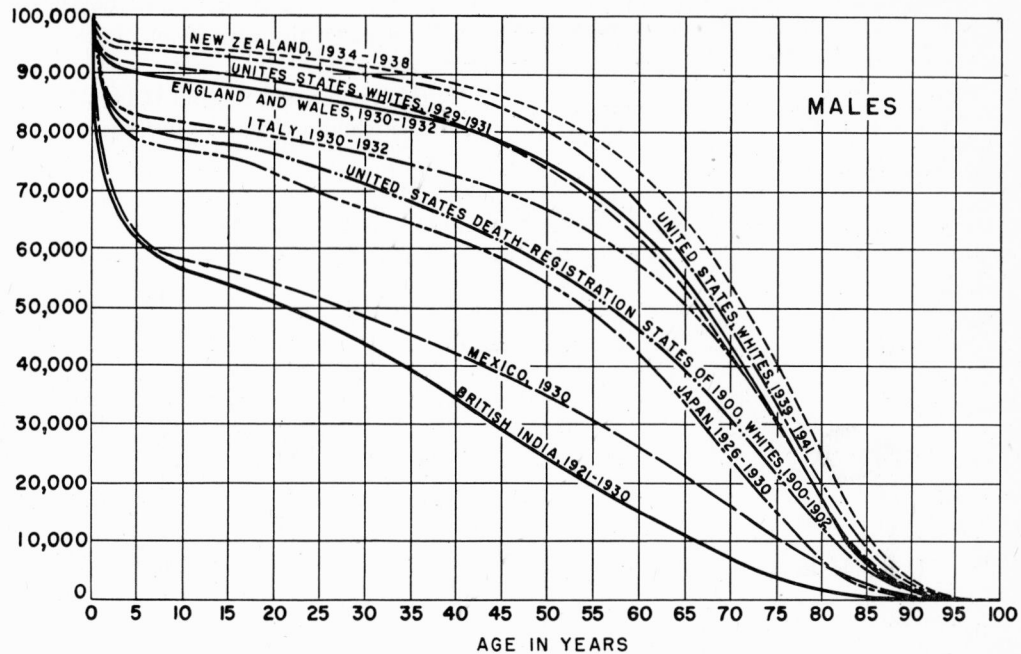

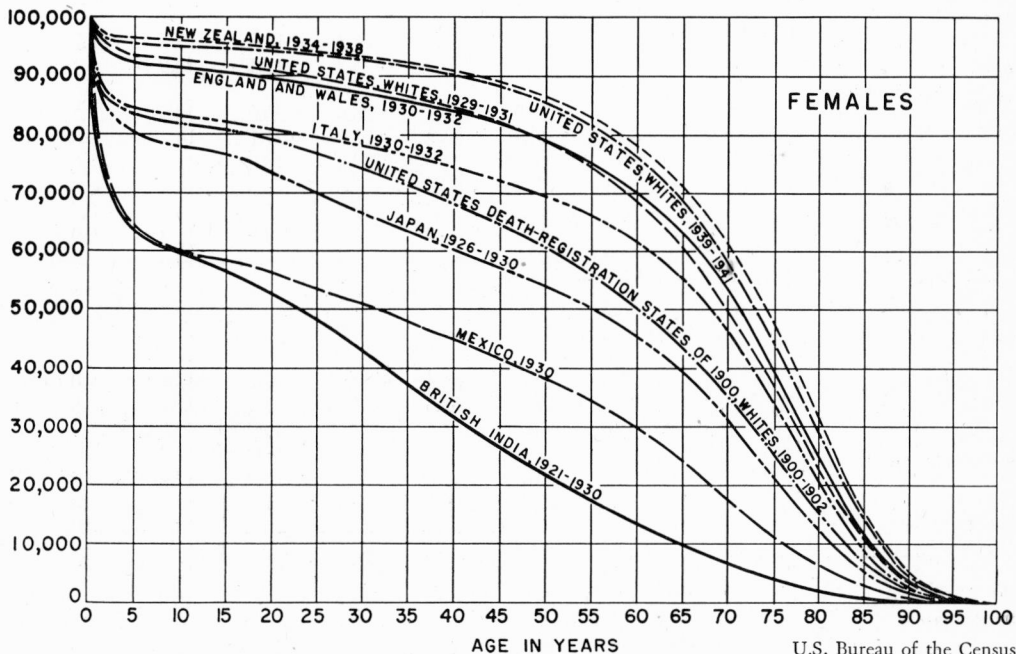

FIGURE 65. LIFE TABLES: PROPORTION OF LIVE BORN SURVIVING TO A GIVEN AGE

The proportion of live born surviving to a particular age increases with economic development and progress of public health services. In India (1921–30) less than 20 per cent lived to reach the age of 55; in the United States the proportion was over 80 per cent for women and 75 per cent for men in 1939–41; in New Zealand both rates are even higher. In India half the boys and girls born alive die before the age of 22. In the United States the corresponding medians are 68 years for male infants and 73 for female infants.

181

Trends in Life Expectancy

At the end of the eighteenth century, a new-born boy in France could be expected to live, on the average, 23.4 years. Conditions in most other European countries were less favorable. Although considerable progress had been made in the Scandinavian countries, gains in longevity came very slowly. In 1870–80, life expectation in Germany was about the same as in Mexico today. (See Table 92.)

If social progress is measured by success in assuring a child a chance to live out a full life

TABLE 92

LIFE EXPECTATION AT GIVEN AGE, IN SELECTED COUNTRIES, AT SPECIFIED PERIODS

Country, Period, and Sex		0	10	20	30	40	50	60	70	80
United States										
1929–31	White, male	59.1	55.0	46.0	37.5	29.2	21.5	14.7	9.2	5.3
	White, female	62.7	57.6	48.5	40.0	31.5	23.4	16.0	10.0	5.6
	Nonwhite, male	47.5	44.3	35.9	29.4	23.4	17.9	13.1	8.8	...
	Nonwhite, female	49.5	45.3	37.2	30.7	24.3	18.6	14.2	10.4	...
1947	White, male	65.2	58.1	48.7	...	30.6	...	15.3	...	...
	White, female	70.6	63.1	53.5	...	34.8	...	18.0	...	...
	Nonwhite, male	57.9	52.2	43.1	...	27.1	...	15.5	...	...
	Nonwhite, female	61.9	55.6	46.4	...	30.3	...	17.9	...	...
Canada										
1926–30	Male	57.7	57.2	48.4	40.0	31.5	23.4	15.9	9.7	...
	Female	59.7	97.6	48.9	40.7	32.4	24.4	16.8	10.4	...
1940–42	Male	63.0	58.7	49.5	40.7	31.9	23.5	16.1	9.9	...
	Female	66.3	61.1	51.8	42.8	34.0	25.5	17.6	10.9	...
Mexico										
1930	Male	32.4	44.6	37.2	31.0	24.8	19.0	13.5	8.7	...
	Female	34.1	45.9	38.5	32.0	25.7	19.1	12.9	8.1	...
England and Wales										
1841	Male	40.2	47.1	39.9	33.1	26.6	20.0	13.5	8.5	4.9
	Female	42.2	47.8	40.8	34.2	27.7	21.1	14.4	9.0	5.2
1881–90	Male	43.7	49.0	40.3	32.5	25.4	18.8	12.9	8.0	4.5
	Female	47.2	51.1	42.4	34.8	27.6	20.6	14.1	8.8	5.0
1920–22	Male	55.6	54.6	45.8	37.4	29.2	21.4	14.4	8.7	4.9
	Female	59.6	57.5	48.7	40.3	31.9	23.7	16.2	9.9	5.6
1937	Male	60.2	56.2	47.1	...	29.6	...	14.3	...	...
	Female	64.4	59.6	50.4	...	32.8	...	16.5	...	...
1949	Male	66.0	59.2	49.7	...	31.2	...	15.1	...	...
	Female	70.6	63.2	53.7	...	35.2	...	18.1	...	...
France										
1795	Male	23.4	44.1	36.5	30.4	24.1	18.2	13.1	9.0	5.2
	Female	27.3	46.8	39.4	33.3	27.4	21.3	15.7	10.8	6.2
1817–32	Male	38.3	47.0	40.0	34.0	27.0	19.9	13.2	8.1	4.7
	Female	40.8	47.4	40.1	33.4	26.6	19.6	13.2	8.1	4.7
1877–81	Male	40.8	48.2	40.4	33.8	26.9	20.0	13.6	8.3	4.8
	Female	43.4	49.7	42.2	35.5	28.5	21.4	14.6	8.8	5.0
1920–23	Male	52.2	51.5	42.9	35.5	27.8	20.4	13.8	8.2	4.3
	Female	55.9	54.5	46.2	38.6	30.8	23.0	15.6	9.3	5.0
1946–48	Male	62.5	58.0	48.0	...	31.0	...	16.0	...	...
	Female	68.0	62.0	53.0	...	35.0	...	18.0	...	...
Netherlands										
1816–25	Male	29.3	40.7	32.9	27.6	21.9	16.4	11.6	7.5	4.8
	Female	35.1	45.0	37.0	30.7	24.8	18.7	12.8	8.0	4.7
1870–79	Male	38.4	48.0	40.3	33.7	26.5	19.6	13.3	8.2	4.6
	Female	40.7	48.7	41.2	34.3	27.9	21.0	14.1	8.4	4.7
1931–40	Male	65.7	60.3	51.0	...	32.9	...	16.3	...	...
	Female	67.2	60.8	51.5	...	33.3	...	16.8	...	...
1947–49	Male	69.4	62.7	53.2	...	34.5	...	17.5	...	...
	Female	71.5	64.1	54.5	...	35.6	...	18.2	...	...

(Continued on facing page)

TABLE 92—*continued*

Country, Period, and Sex	Age in Years								
	0	10	20	30	40	50	60	70	80
Sweden									
1755–76 Male	33.2	43.9	36.9	30.3	23.7	17.7	12.2	7.6	4.3
Female	35.7	46.2	39.1	32.2	25.2	19.3	13.1	7.9	4.5
1816–40 Male	39.5	45.2	37.3	30.2	23.7	17.5	12.1	7.3	4.0
Female	43.6	48.6	40.7	33.4	26.4	19.6	13.2	8.0	4.5
1881–90 Male	48.5	52.2	44.2	36.9	29.3	21.9	15.1	9.1	4.8
Female	51.5	54.2	46.4	38.8	31.3	23.6	16.2	10.0	5.4
1941–45 Male	66.0	59.2	49.7	...	31.2	...	15.1	...	...
Female	70.6	63.2	53.7	...	35.2	...	18.0	...	...
Germany									
1871–80 Male	35.6	46.5	38.4	31.4	24.5	18.0	12.1	7.3	4.1
Female	38.4	48.9	40.2	33.1	26.3	19.3	12.7	7.6	4.2
1932–34 Male	59.9	57.3	48.2	39.5	30.8	22.5	15.1	9.0	4.8
Female	62.8	59.1	49.5	41.0	32.3	23.8	16.1	9.6	5.1
Poland									
1931–32 Male	48.2	52.2	43.7	36.0	27.9	20.3	13.7	8.3	...
Female	51.4	54.0	45.7	38.0	30.3	22.4	15.1	9.2	...
Italy									
1876–87 Male	35.1	47.8	40.3	33.5	26.2	19.4	13.1	8.0	4.6
Female	35.4	47.2	40.0	33.4	26.7	19.6	12.8	7.7	4.5
1930–39 Male	53.8	55.5	46.7	39.0	30.4	22.4	15.2	9.0	4.8
Female	56.0	57.1	48.5	40.4	32.1	23.9	16.1	9.6	5.2
Bulgaria									
1925–28 Male	45.9	53.7	45.8	38.4	30.7	23.2	16.4	10.9	...
Female	46.6	53.2	45.4	39.0	31.7	24.3	17.2	11.0	...
Greece									
1926–30 Male	49.1	52.4	44.3	37.1	29.8	22.6	16.0	10.6	...
Female	50.9	54.5	46.4	39.4	32.4	24.9	17.5	11.0	...
USSR (European)									
1926–27 Male	41.9	51.6	43.2	35.6	28.0	21.0	14.8	9.6	...
Female	46.8	55.7	47.4	39.7	32.1	24.4	17.1	11.0	...
Japan									
1935–36 Male	46.9	48.2	40.4	33.9	26.2	18.8	12.5	7.6	...
Female	49.6	50.5	43.2	36.9	29.6	22.1	15.1	9.0	...
1947 Male	50.1	49.5	40.9	...	26.9	...	12.6	...	...
Female	54.0	53.3	44.9	...	29.6	...	15.1	...	...
India									
1881 Male	23.6	34.0	28.5	23.8	18.9	13.9	9.2	5.4	2.9
Female	25.6	33.4	28.4	24.5	20.0	15.0	9.8	5.6	2.9
1931 Male	26.9	36.4	29.6	23.6	18.6	14.3	10.2	6.3	3.2
Female	26.6	33.6	27.1	22.3	18.2	14.6	10.8	6.7	3.2
Australia									
1881–90 Male	47.2	48.9	40.6	33.6	26.5	19.7	13.8	8.8	5.1
Female	50.8	51.9	43.4	36.1	29.1	22.1	15.4	9.7	5.3
1946–48 Male	66.1	59.0	49.6	...	31.2	...	15.4	...	...
Female	70.1	63.1	53.5	...	34.9	...	18.1	...	...
New Zealand									
1906–10 Male	59.2	56.1	47.2	38.8	30.5	22.7	15.5	9.4	...
Female	61.8	57.7	48.8	40.5	32.4	24.3	16.8	10.3	...
1934–38 Male	65.5	59.1	49.9	40.9	32.0	23.6	16.1	9.8	...
Female	68.5	61.4	52.0	43.0	34.0	25.5	17.5	10.7	...

Sources: **12**, 1938; **1**; **5**; **48**; and official statistical yearbooks of various countries.

span, some of the least developed countries appear to be half a century behind the United States, others a full century. But any nation has at least a fighting chance to catch up within two or three decades.

Life expectancy at age 10 is sometimes lower, sometimes higher, than at birth. The first relationship is typical of the countries of Western civilization with a low infant mortality rate. On the other hand, in countries with high death

TABLE 93

LIFE EXPECTATION: GAINS AT SPECIFIED AGES IN SELECTED COUNTRIES, 1920–30

| | Gain, in Years | | | | | |
| | At Birth | | At Age 10 | | At Age 50 | |
Country	Male	Female	Male	Female	Male	Female
England and Wales	7.2	7.5	2.7	3.0	1.3	1.7
France	5.8	6.6	2.2	2.9	0.6	1.3
Netherlands	10.6	10.1	4.9	4.8	1.7	1.3
Denmark	5.8	4.6	3.4	2.2	1.2	0.1
Sweden	6.7	6.1	4.0	3.2	1.0	0.3
Norway	6.2	6.1	3.4	3.3	0.4	0.6
Germany	12.5	12.1	5.2	5.1	2.8	2.4
Switzerland	8.6	9.1	3.3	4.3	0.5	1.9
Spain	8.9	9.9	2.3	4.0	0.8	1.9
Italy	7.2	8.7	3.0	4.5	1.2	2.0
New Zealand	4.5	4.9	2.6	3.1	0.9	1.3

Source: **6,** April 1949, p. 75.

rates among infants and children, life expectancy is greater for those who have survived the most dangerous age than for the newborn. Even in the countries with the lowest infant mortality, expectation of life is somewhat higher at the age of one year than at birth.

In the last two or three decades, expectation of life at birth has increased markedly in many countries; progress has been less conspicuous at the age of 10 and comparatively small at the age of 50. From 1920 to 1930 the unweighted average gain in life expectation at birth in the countries shown in Table 93 was 7.6 years for boys and 7.8 years for girls. At the age of 10, the gain averaged 3.4 years for boys and 3.7 years for girls. At age 50, gains were 1.1 years for men, 1.3 years for women. (See Figure 66.)

Patterns of progress in life expectation are strikingly similar for the same country at different dates, for different countries, and for different population groups in the same country at the same time. (See Figure 67.)

In the United States the life expectation of white men and women under 60 is appreciably higher than that of Negroes, while persons of other races rank between these two groups. At all ages, women have a greater life expectancy than men. Until the age of 25, the difference between the races is overwhelming. At higher ages the difference between the sexes becomes increasingly important. (See Figure 68.)

Longevity, as measured by the expectation of

life at birth, continues to increase. In the United States it has increased during the past 60 years at an average rate of a half year of additional life expectancy each year. That rise shows no sign of slackening according to data on life expectancy at birth computed by the Industrial Department of the Metropolitan Life Insurance Company on the basis of a comprehensive sample.[68]

	Expectation, in Years	Average Annual Gain
1879–89	34.00	—
1911–12	46.63	0.46
1919–20	51.14	0.56
1926	55.02	0.59
1936	60.31	0.53
1946	65.57	0.53

Progress has been so continuous that a figure for expectation of life computed on the basis of recent mortality rates becomes obsolete in five or six years, and international comparisons based on mortality rates for various years are biased in favor of the nation for which the most recent mortality rates are available.

An array of countries by declining expectation of life at birth shows how much certain countries lag behind others. Using the United States as a yardstick, each decade of progress should bring an additional 5 or at least 3–4 years' gain in expectation of life at birth. (See Table 94.)

68. **51,** p. 6.

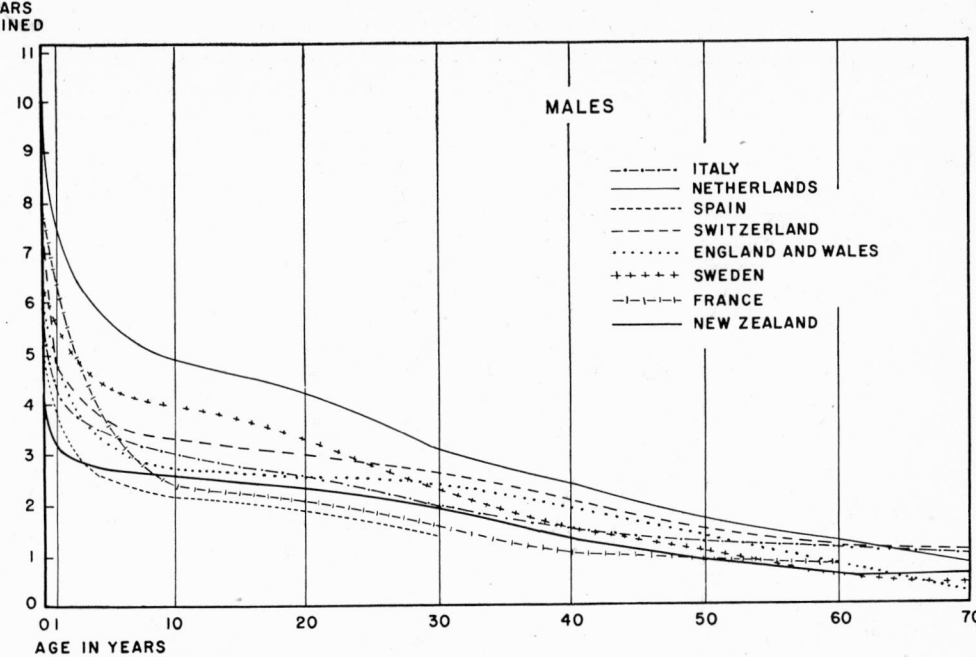

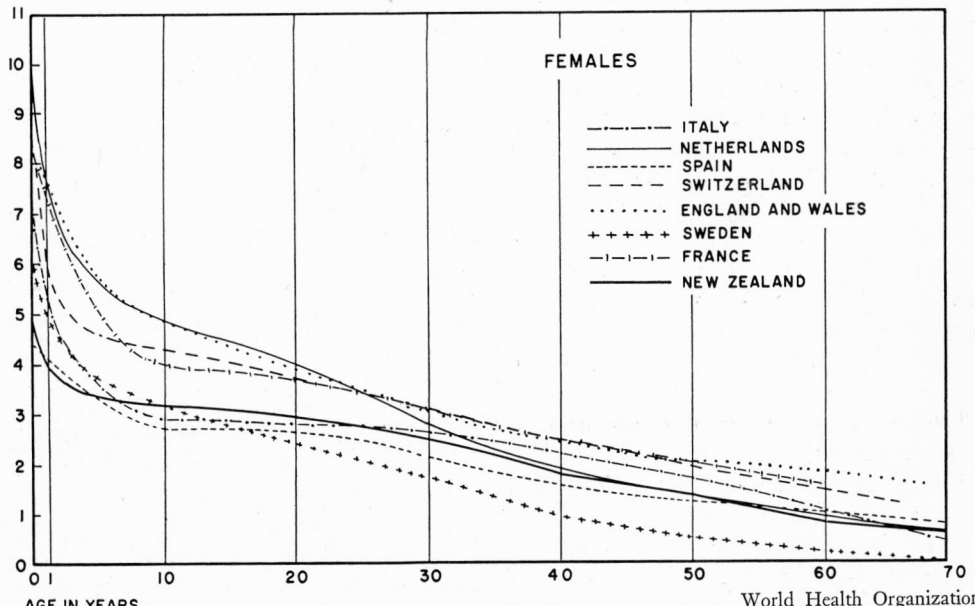

FIGURE 66. LIFE EXPECTATION: GAINS AT VARIOUS AGES IN SELECTED COUNTRIES, FROM 1910 TO 1930

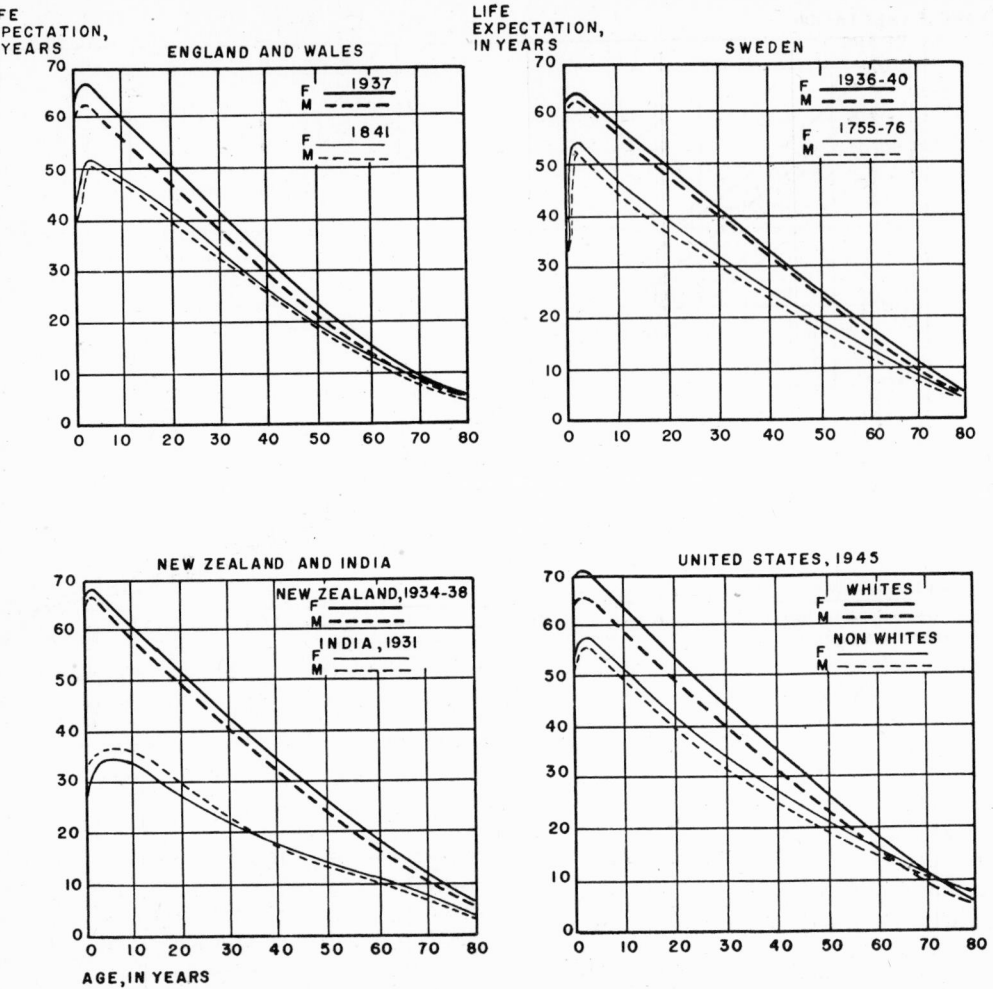

FIGURE 67. LIFE EXPECTATION AT GIVEN AGE IN SELECTED COUNTRIES, AT SPECIFIED PERIODS

A boy's expectation of life at birth has increased in England and Wales from 40.2 years in 1841 to 60.2 years in 1937. In Sweden the gain was from 33.2 years in 1755–76 to 64.3 years in 1936–40. There is a striking difference between expectation of life at birth in India and in New Zealand: 26.9 years for boys and 26.6 years for girls in India (1931); 65.5 years for boys and 68.5 years for girls in New Zealand (1934–38).

In the United States in 1929–31, life expectancy at birth was 11.4 years and 13.2 years higher for white boys and girls, respectively, than for Negro boys and girls. In 1939–41 the differences were 10.5 years and 11.7 years, and by 1947 the gap was further reduced to 7.3 years for boys and 8.7 years for girls. (Cf. Table 92.)

LIFE EXPECTATION
IN YEARS

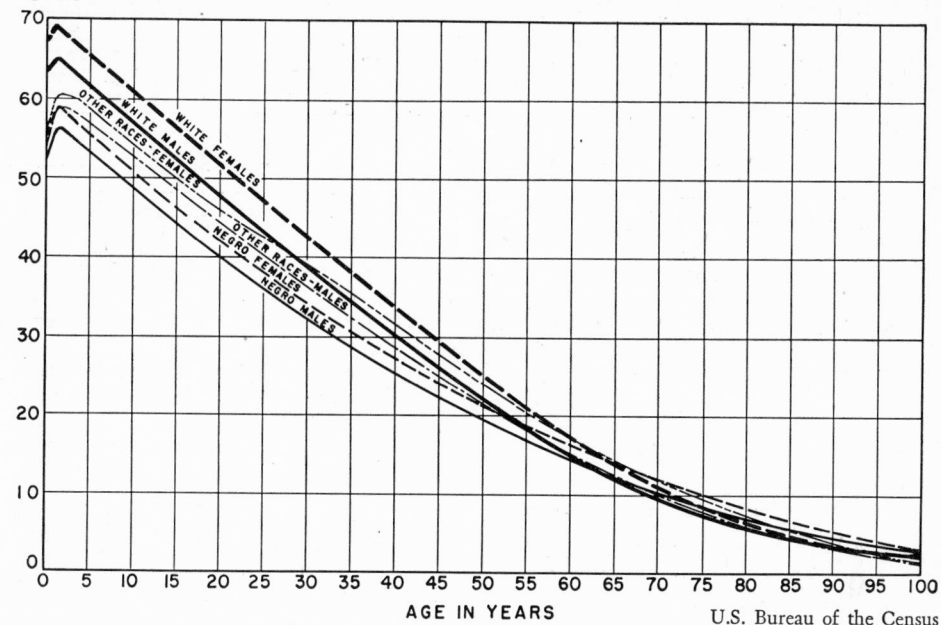

FIGURE 68. LIFE EXPECTATION AT GIVEN AGE, BY SEX AND RACE IN THE UNITED STATES, 1939–41

Increase in Average Length of Life

On the basis of fragmentary information in ancient literature and inscriptions, historians have concluded that at the time of Homer, in the Bronze Age, the average length of life was probably less than 20 years. By the time of the Roman Empire, it was somewhat longer, perhaps 22 years. The birth and death records of some cities in medieval Europe suggest an average life span of about 35 years, but how general this improvement was is not known and it is sound to assume that it was restricted to a few progressive cities. Before the outbreak of the French Revolution, life expectancy in rural communities in France was not much better than in ancient Rome, while that in Scandinavian countries was practically the same as the average attributed to medieval cities.

The upturn came toward the middle of the nineteenth century. In a hundred years, the average length of human life increased more than in the preceding eighteen centuries. (See Figure 69.) Further gains depend on a rising standard of living and progress in medical science and hygiene.[69]

69. Cf. 24.

MARRIAGES AND DIVORCES

Measuring Nuptiality

The rate of marriage — nuptiality — may be measured either by the number of marriages per 1,000 inhabitants, as in the United States, or by the number of persons married per 1,000 inhabitants. The second method obviously results in a rate twice as high as the first. The rate of divorce is measured either as the number of divorces per 1,000 inhabitants or as the ratio of divorces to the number of married couples in the nation. It can be measured also as the ratio of the number of divorces to the average annual number of marriages in the preceding decade.

Trends in Marriage

The number of marriages varies from year to year with changes in economic conditions. Since it increases with improvement in business and employment — and still more with expectation of improvement — some authors believe that the index of marriages can be used as a barometer of prosperity. Farr pointed out that marriage increased in England when there was abundance after dearth, confidence after dis-

TABLE 94

LIFE EXPECTATION AT BIRTH, AT AGE 20 AND AT AGE 60 IN SELECTED COUNTRIES,
AROUND 1940 [a]

| | Age, in Years | | | | | |
| | At Birth | | 20 | | 60 | |
Country [b]	Male	Female	Male	Female	Male	Female
Netherlands	65.7	67.2	51.0	51.5	16.3	16.8
New Zealand	65.5	68.4	49.9	52.0	16.1	17.5
Sweden	64.3	66.9	49.7	51.3	16.3	17.2
Australia	63.5	67.1	48.8	51.7	15.6	17.7
Denmark	63.5	65.8	50.3	51.1	16.0	16.6
United States, white	62.8	67.3	47.8	51.4	15.0	17.0
South Africa	61.5	66.1	47.3	51.0	12.2	13.6
Switzerland	60.6	64.6	46.5	49.6	14.3	16.0
England	60.2	64.4	47.1	50.4	14.3	16.5
Belgium *	56.0	59.8	46.0	48.4	14.5	15.9
France	55.9	61.6	43.6	48.6	13.9	16.5
Austria *	54.5	58.5	45.2	48.0	14.2	15.4
Finland	54.3	59.5	43.0	47.6	13.6	15.8
United States, Negro	52.3	55.6	39.5	42.0	14.4	16.1
Czechoslovakia *	51.9	55.2	45.3	47.4	14.3	15.3
Greece	49.1	50.9	44.3	46.4	16.0	17.5
Portugal	48.6	52.8	44.0	48.4	13.9	16.2
Hungary *	48.3	51.3	43.7	45.8	11.5	14.9
Poland *	48.2	51.4	43.7	45.7	13.7	15.1
Japan	46.9	49.6	40.4	43.2	12.6	15.1
Colombia *	46.3		43.3		14.7	
Mexico *	37.2		36.7		12.8	
Chile *	35.7	37.7	38.7	40.1	13.7	15.0
Egypt *	30.2	31.5	33.5	32.8	14.2	15.4

Source: **48,** July 1947, pp. 262–64.

   a. For countries marked with an asterisk, data around 1930.
   b. Countries arrayed in declining order of male life expectation at birth.

trust, national triumph after national disaster.[70] Apart from these short-term ups and downs, marriage rates depend on the age composition of the population, changes in the custom of early or late marriages and the frequency of divorce.

The marriage rate rises when the proportion of persons who reach marriageable age in a year increases — whether the commonly accepted age is 17, 22 or 27 years. This proportion is the higher, the larger the percentage of infants who survive to marriageable age and the shorter the life span of persons who are beyond that age. Thus the marriage rate increases as a result of a decline in death rates at premarital ages and decreases as a result of such declines in older groups.

The rate of marriage is less affected by the custom of early or late marriage than by *change* in that custom, such as general postponement or precipitation of marriage because of the outbreak of a war or a boom in business. The marriage rate also depends on the number of divorces, since a formal divorce is often followed by remarriage of one or both partners.

In most countries of western Europe, marriage rates were about the same in the 1930's as a century before. (See Table 95.) The slight rise in Germany in 1931–40 was a result of the frantic efforts of the Nazi government to encourage early marriage.

The trend in divorce rates has been sharply upward since the turn of the century in all countries for which comparable statistics are available. Apart from hectic fluctuations during and after World War I, the ratio of the annual num-

70. **44,** p. 67.

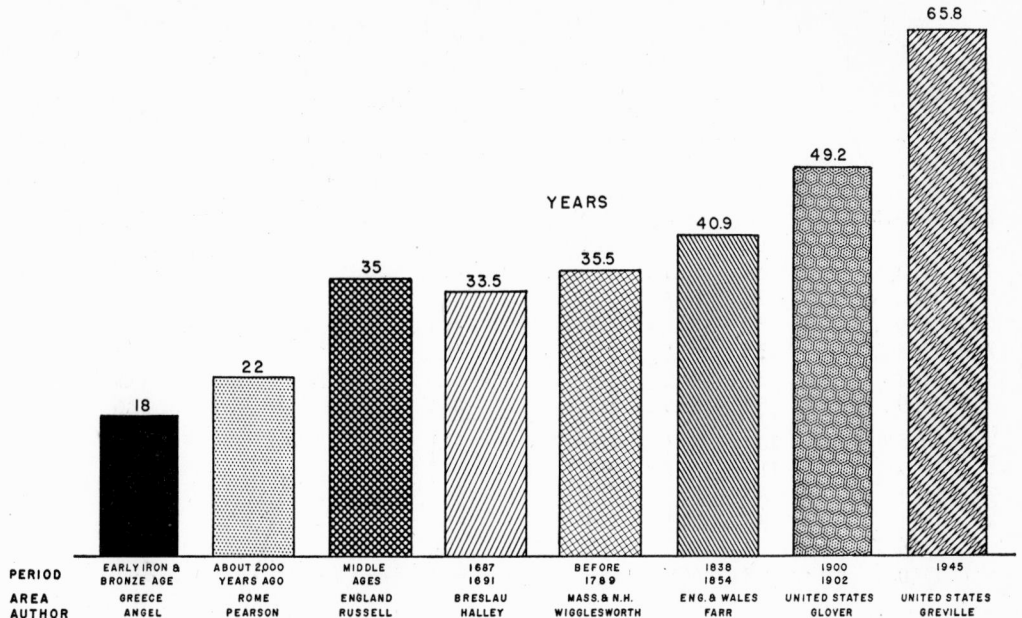

The Metropolitan Life Insurance Company

FIGURE 69. LIFE EXPECTATION AT BIRTH IN ANCIENT AND MODERN TIMES

What fragmentary information we have on the length of life in ancient times suggests that people now live three and one half times as long, on the average, as they did in the Bronze Age and Early Iron Age, and nearly twice as long as in the Middle Ages.

TABLE 95

MARRIAGE RATES IN SELECTED COUNTRIES, 1801–10 TO 1941–47 AND 1949

(*Marriages Per 1,000 Inhabitants*)

Period	Sweden	Norway	Finland	England	France	Germany
1801–1810	8.2	7.3	7.8	—	—	—
1811–1820	7.7	8.5	8.5	—	7.9	—
1821–1830	8.3	8.2	8.5	—	7.8	—
1831–1840	7.2	6.9	7.3	—	8.0	—
1841–1850	7.2	7.9	8.2	8.0	7.9	8.1
1851–1860	7.6	7.7	7.8	8.3	7.9	7.8
1861–1870	6.5	6.6	7.7	8.3	7.8	8.5
1871–1880	6.8	7.2	8.3	8.1	8.0	8.6
1881–1890	6.2	6.5	7.3	7.4	7.3	7.8
1891–1900	5.9	6.7	7.0	7.8	7.5	8.2
1901–1910	6.0	6.1	6.5	7.7	7.7	8.0
1911–1920	6.0	6.6	7.0	8.1	5.6	6.1
1921–1930	6.6	6.2	6.8	7.9	9.9	9.5
1931–1940	7.8	7.2	7.4	8.3	7.1	9.2
1941–1947	9.5	8.4	9.9	8.5	8.0	6.8
1949	7.8	8.4	9.8	8.4	8.2	10.0 [a]

Source: **12**, 1938; **2**, 1949–50, pp. 424–29.   a. Western Germany.

TABLE 96

DIVORCE RATES IN SELECTED COUNTRIES, 1910–48

(Number of Divorces in Specified Year Per 1,000 Marriages in Preceding Decade)

Year	United States	Canada	England & Wales	France	Belgium	Nether-lands	Denmark	Sweden	Norway	Switzer-land	Australia	New Zealand
1910	100.2	...	...	46.9	19.1	21.5	39.8	19.2	29.6	58.0	15.3	21.5
1911	106.9	...	2.2	50.0	18.9	23.7	38.9	18.9	29.4	61.3	16.6	21.8
1912	109.8	...	2.2	54.8	20.2	25.3	37.8	20.6	35.0	56.6	21.3	29.0
1913	103.1	...	2.2	53.2	20.8	26.4	41.4	23.9	35.7	59.8	19.3	28.1
1914	111.5	...	3.2	33.1	...	26.0	45.0	24.1	29.9	53.6	18.7	28.7
1915	111.8	...	2.5	6.6	...	26.9	44.2	25.9	38.9	54.8	18.5	26.4
1916	119.9	...	3.5	17.8	...	29.9	46.1	23.4	34.9	59.7	17.0	28.4
1917	125.4	...	2.5	34.5	...	30.8	50.4	31.4	37.4	63.9	17.5	25.4
1918	116.7	...	3.9	40.2	...	31.5	54.5	32.8	39.9	67.4	18.6	32.7
1919	140.9	...	5.8	83.5	13.2	33.7	63.1	35.4	36.9	78.9	22.6	57.5
1920	165.5	7.2	10.4	132.1	43.0	41.8	57.1	38.1	40.8	88.2	29.1	67.8
1921	150.1	8.4	11.5	105.5	65.7	40.4	64.2	40.4	36.9	75.6	36.0	74.5
1922	137.1	8.1	8.3	82.8	63.3	38.1	58.5	40.4	37.3	79.1	31.7	60.0
1923	150.1	7.4	8.5	74.1	53.4	38.4	81.7	41.6	38.6	74.6	34.7	66.4
1924	152.6	8.1	7.3	69.9	47.1	39.2	72.6	43.8	39.3	78.1	36.0	70.7
1925	154.0	8.2	8.3	66.8	37.6	39.9	67.4	46.3	39.5	80.1	43.2	65.0
1926	160.0	9.1	8.5	62.5	32.8	42.1	76.4	46.7	42.3	77.3	38.1	66.7
1927	168.2	11.0	10.4	56.7	31.0	45.0	84.2	51.3	36.2	85.6	43.6	65.5
1928	170.7	11.6	12.8	64.2	29.5	46.8	89.0	55.2	49.3	85.6	40.6	65.3
1929	172.8	11.5	10.8	63.8	25.9	46.6	85.9	56.1	49.6	90.7	43.6	68.8
1930	163.4	12.5	11.5	60.4	31.1	48.2	86.4	56.7	57.6	90.2	37.7	68.4
1931	158.7	10.1	12.4	68.3	33.1	51.1	92.2	59.7	64.7	95.6	41.7	65.2
1932	139.9	14.7	12.9	68.4	33.9	49.9	93.0	60.2	56.9	101.8	36.7	62.9
1933	142.4	13.6	13.4	69.7	36.2	50.4	101.5	63.9	56.7	99.6	42.7	65.5
1934	178.0	16.4	14.1	71.5	34.5	50.6	109.3	67.4	56.8	100.2	49.8	72.8
1935	188.3	20.7	13.1	72.5	37.3	50.8	104.8	65.2	61.2	98.2	50.6	70.2
1936	201.4	22.4	12.9	80.5	45.6	54.1	109.1	66.1	49.4	104.1	52.4	86.9
1937	209.6	25.6	15.2	81.8	47.8	57.0	110.3	70.2	55.4	108.7	56.9	91.2
1938	201.1	30.3	19.1	87.0	52.9	53.4	109.1	75.4	53.6	108.4	62.1	92.9
1939	204.4	27.6	23.9	71.5	52.5	52.8	114.9	74.3	51.8	95.5	61.6	91.6
1940	212.0	30.6	22.4	46.1	28.4	46.3	106.7	69.8	46.4	98.5	60.5	83.1
1941	226.8	29.8	17.7	57.0	43.7	51.6	113.4	68.5	50.8	97.6	59.1	75.6
1942	236.8	35.0	20.7	55.6	50.7	58.7	132.3	79.4	53.0	100.3	59.9	73.0
1943	250.2	34.4	26.6	68.7	58.6	66.9	142.7	86.0	55.7	99.4	73.0	101.6
1944	269.8	38.1	33.0	70.9	59.3	68.0	153.8	94.9	64.1	96.1	85.9	131.4
1945	323.9	49.6	42.3	101.2	57.2	68.2	166.3	109.9	79.0	113.3	105.6	136.2
1946	399.7	72.9	81.0	207.2	98.3	147.5	212.1	116.0	...	128.6	...	147.9
1947	292.9	74.0	138.5	...	...	121.4	193.3	115.2	...	124.7	...	...
1948	248.1	60.0	...	...	...	...	...	...	...	...	...	...

Source: **51**, April 1949, p. 2.

ber of divorces to the average annual number of marriages in the preceding decade increased in the United States from 100.2 per 1,000 in 1910 to 212.0 per 1,000 in 1940 and 248.1 per 1,000 in 1948. The comparable figures for England and Wales are 2.2, 22.4 and 138.5 (in 1947); for Australia, 15.3, 60.5 and 105.6 (1945);

for New Zealand, 21.5, 83.1 and 147.9 (1946); for Belgium, 19.1, 28.4 and 98.3 (1946); for the Netherlands, 21.5, 46.3 and 121.4 (1947); for Denmark, 39.8, 106.7 and 193.3 (1947); for Sweden, 19.2, 69.8 and 115.2 (1947); for Norway, 29.6, 46.4 and 79.0 (1945). In France the divorce rate per 1,000 marriages in the preceding decade was 46.9 in 1910 and 46.1 in 1940 but skyrocketed to 207.2 in 1946. (See Table 96.)

Marriage and Divorce Rates in Various Countries

The number of marriages per 1,000 inhabitants (the crude marriage rate) ranges from less than 2 in some South and Central American republics to more than 12 in the United States and among the European population of the Union of South Africa. (See Table 97 and Figure 70.) It is fairly clear that the extremely low marriage rates in such countries as Nicaragua, Bolivia, Guatemala and Haiti are due largely to incomplete registration of marriages, just as the contrast between marriages of Europeans and non-Europeans in New Zealand and the Union of South Africa is due to incomplete registra-

tion and the widespread practice of "common-law" marriage among the non-Europeans.

Apart from such reasons for differences in marriage rates, countries that are widely unlike in economic and social structure and in birth and death rates often have nearly the same marriage rate — for example, the United States and Egypt; Sweden, Denmark and Japan; Ceylon and Ireland; France and Venezuela. The proportion of the population that reaches marriageable age in a year may be low because of high birth rates and high infant and child mortality (as in Brazil, Peru, Bolivia and Guatemala) or because of low birth rates and a preponderance of older persons (as in Belgium and France). The marriage rate therefore is as high in some primitive countries as in the most industrialized nations.

TABLE 97

MARRIAGE AND DIVORCE RATES IN SELECTED COUNTRIES, 1940

(Marriages and Divorces Per 1,000 Inhabitants)

Country	Marriage Rate	Divorce Rate	Country	Marriage Rate	Divorce Rate
United States	12.1	2.0	Sweden	9.3	0.5
Canada	10.9	0.2	Norway	9.5	0.3
Mexico	8.0	0.2	Finland	7.9	0.3
Guatemala	1.5	0.1	Germany	8.7	0.7
El Salvador	3.3	0.1	Poland	8.0	—
Honduras	3.0	0.2	Czechoslovakia	9.7	0.4
Nicaragua	1.9	0.0	Switzerland	7.7	0.7
Costa Rica	5.7	—	Austria	11.7	1.0
Cuba (1939)	4.0	—	Hungary	7.7	—
Haiti	0.8	—	Portugal	6.0	0.1
Venezuela	4.6	0.1	Spain	8.3	—
Colombia	4.8	—	Italy	7.0	—
Ecuador	5.7	0.3	Yugoslavia (1939)	7.9	—
Brazil (1938)	3.4	—	Romania	8.9	0.5
Peru	3.2	—	Bulgaria	9.0	0.3
Bolivia	1.7	—			
Paraguay	5.8	—	Egypt	11.3	3.2
Chile	8.4	0.3	Union of South Africa		
Uruguay	6.7	0.2	Europeans	13.2	0.8
Argentina	6.9	—	Non-Europeans	3.5	0.0
England and Wales	11.2	0.2	Japan (proper)	9.3	0.7
Scotland	10.6	0.1	Palestine	11.8	2.1
Northern Ireland	7.6	—	Ceylon	5.6	—
Ireland	5.1	—	Australia	11.1	0.4
France	4.4	0.3	New Zealand		
Belgium	4.3	0.2	Europeans	11.3	0.7
Netherlands	7.6	0.3	Maoris	7.0	—
Denmark	9.2	0.9			

Source: **10**, pp. 228–29 and 233–34.

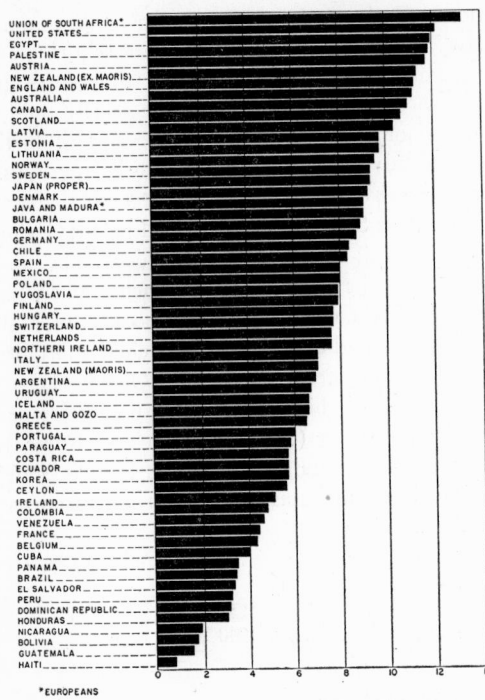

*EUROPEANS

Per 1,000 inhabitants

U.S. Public Health Service, Federal Security Agency

FIGURE 70. MARRIAGE RATES IN SELECTED COUNTRIES, 1940

The marriage rate depends on the age composition of the population, on custom and on the frequency of divorce. The low marriage rates often recorded in underdeveloped countries result from incomplete registration and from the custom of "common-law" marriage. (Cf. **11,** p. 54.)

The relative number of divorces, which also affects a country's marriage rate, likewise differs greatly from nation to nation. The contrasts are dramatically illustrated by the examples of Egypt, where one marriage out of 60 is ended each year by divorce, and England, where the ratio is one divorce to 2,000 marriages. (See Table 98 and Figure 71.)

Marriage and Divorce Rates in the United States

The marriage rate in the United States increased from 9.6 per 1,000 inhabitants in 1901 to 12.1 per 1,000 in 1945, along with the rise in the divorce rate from 0.8 per 1,000 to 3.6 per 1,000. (See Table 99.) Except for the period of the great depression, the excess of the marriage rate over the divorce rate per 1,000 inhabitants has not changed appreciably since the turn of the century.

The marriage rate varies widely from state

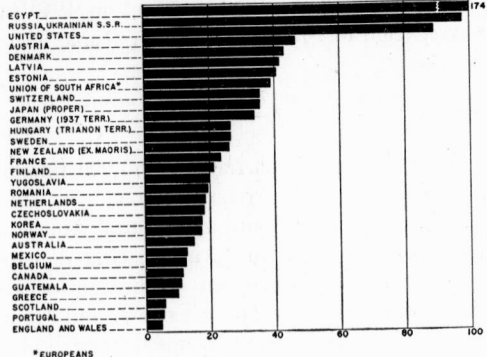

*EUROPEANS

Per 10,000 married couples

U.S. Public Health Service, Federal Security Agency

FIGURE 71. DIVORCE RATES IN SELECTED COUNTRIES, AROUND 1940

to state, mainly because of differences in state laws and the development of nationally advertised centers of the divorce and marriage industry. In Nevada, where divorces and weddings are a leading business, the marriage rate is approximately 40 times that in West Virginia or North Carolina. (See Table 100.)

Age at Marriage

The prevailing age at marriage fluctuates from year to year, probably under the impact of changing business conditions, but varies little from country to country and even from continent to continent. The median ages of bridegrooms range from a little less than 27 years in the Americas, Europe and Oceania to a little less than 29 in Japan; for brides, from 22.2 years in the Americas to 24.3 in Oceania.[71]

Contrary to widespread opinion, there is no universal tendency toward later marriages in economically developed and urbanized countries. Apart from the USSR, Bulgaria, Turkey and Mexico, where marriages are made at younger ages, most of the agricultural countries (Poland and Spain; Chile, Colombia, Guatemala, and Venezuela; Japan and Indochina) report about the same median age of bridegrooms and brides as do Germany, England, Switzerland and the Scandinavian countries. In colonial regions there seems to be no appreciable difference in the age of marriage among the native and the white populations. (See Table 101.) In countries for which comparable data for several decades are available, changes in age of marriage have been negligible.

71. **41,** p. 58.

TABLE 98

DIVORCE RATES IN SELECTED COUNTRIES, AROUND 1940

(*Divorces Per 1,000 Married Couples*)

Country [a]	Divorce Rate	Country [a]	Divorce Rate	Country [a]	Divorce Rate
Egypt	17.4	Hungary	2.7	Norway	1.7
Ukraine (USSR)	9.8	Sweden	2.7	Australia	1.5
United States	8.9	New Zealand (excluding		Mexico	1.3
Austria	4.7	Maoris)	2.6	Belgium	1.3
Denmark	4.3	France	2.4	Canada	1.1
Latvia	4.2	Finland	2.1	Guatemala	1.1
Estonia	4.1	Yugoslavia	2.0	Greece	1.0
Union of South Africa	3.9	Romania	2.0	Scotland	0.6
Switzerland	3.6	Netherlands	1.9	Portugal	0.5
Japan (proper)	3.6	Czechoslovakia	1.8	England and Wales	0.5
Germany	3.4	Korea	1.8		

Source: **10**, p. 56.   a. Countries arrayed in declining order of divorce rate.

TABLE 99

MARRIAGE AND DIVORCE RATES IN THE UNITED STATES, 1887–1949

(*Marriages and Divorces Per 1,000 Inhabitants*)

Year	Marriage Rate	Divorce Rate	Year	Marriage Rate	Divorce Rate	Year	Marriage Rate	Divorce Rate
1887	8.7	.5	1908	9.7	.9	1929	10.1	1.7
1888	8.8	.5	1909	9.9	.9	1930	9.2	1.6
1889	9.1	.5	1910	10.3	.9	1931	8.6	1.5
1890	9.0	.5	1911	10.2	1.0	1932	7.9	1.3
1891	9.2	.6	1912	10.5	1.0	1933	8.7	1.3
1892	9.1	.6	1913	10.5	.9	1934	10.3	1.6
1893	9.0	.6	1914	10.3	1.0	1935	10.4	1.7
1894	8.6	.6	1915	10.0	1.0	1936	10.7	1.8
1895	8.9	.6	1916	10.6	1.1	1937	11.3	1.9
1896	9.0	.6	1917	11.1	1.2	1938	10.3	1.9
1897	8.9	.6	1918	9.7	1.1	1939	10.7	1.9
1898	8.8	.7	1919	11.0	1.4	1940	12.1	2.0
1899	9.0	.7	1920	12.0	1.6	1941	12.7	2.2
1900	9.3	.7	1921	10.7	1.5	1942	13.2	2.4
1901	9.6	.8	1922	10.3	1.4	1943	11.8	2.5
1902	9.8	.8	1923	11.0	1.5	1944	11.0	2.9
1903	10.1	.8	1924	10.4	1.5	1945	12.1	3.6
1904	9.9	.8	1925	10.3	1.5	1946	16.3	4.3
1905	10.0	.8	1926	10.2	1.5	1947	13.9	3.4
1906	10.5	.9	1927	10.1	1.6	1948	12.4	2.8
1907	10.8	.9	1928	9.8	1.6	1949	10.7	2.6

Source: **8**, 1948, p. 89 and 1951, p. 77.

TABLE 100

MARRIAGE AND DIVORCE RATES IN THE UNITED STATES, IN SELECTED STATES, 1948

(*Marriages and Divorces Per 1,000 Inhabitants*)

States with Highest Marriage Rates	Marriage Rate	Divorce Rate	States with Middle Marriage Rates	Marriage Rate	Divorce Rate	States with Lowest Marriage Rates	Marriage Rate	Divorce Rate
Nevada	319.3	67.1	Washington	14.2	3.3	Massachusetts	9.9	1.7
Arizona	35.3	...	Montana	14.0	4.1	Wisconsin	9.9	1.5
New Mexico	28.9	4.6	Indiana	13.9	...	Pennsylvania	9.4	1.3
Maryland	26.1	2.8	District of			Oklahoma	9.0	...
Mississippi	25.4	3.2	Columbia	13.4	2.3	Delaware	8.9	1.4
South Carolina	23.6	...	Wyoming	13.1	4.4	West Virginia	8.6	...
Kentucky	22.5	...	Virginia	12.3	2.3	North Carolina	7.8	...
Arkansas	22.5	...	Illinois	12.1	...	Oregon	7.5	3.9
Georgia	21.5	...	South Dakota	12.0	1.7	Alabama	7.2	3.3
Texas	15.3	5.4	Colorado	11.7	...	Tennessee	4.8	2.6
			Nebraska	11.6	2.1			

Source: **8**, 1950, p. 82.

TABLE 101

MEDIAN AGE AT MARRIAGE IN SELECTED COUNTRIES, 1927–29, 1936 AND 1946–48

(*Years*)

Country	Around 1927–29 Bridegroom	Around 1927–29 Bride	Around 1936 Bridegroom	Around 1936 Bride	Around 1946–48 Bridegroom	Around 1946–48 Bride
Canada	26.6	23.4	27.5	23.0	26.0	23.0
Mexico	23.9	19.8	23.0	20.0	23.0	19.9
Guatemala	27.3	20.2	27.5	23.5	24.7	20.5
Venezuela	27.7	21.0	—	—	27.0	20.7
Colombia	27.4	22.4	29.5	21.5	27.5	21.5
Chile	27.5	25.5	28.0	24.5	27.0	23.0
England and Wales	26.5	24.5	26.7	24.7	26.7	24.0
France	25.9	23.2	26.7	23.7	25.7	23.0
Belgium	25.4	21.8	26.0	24.0	26.0	23.2
Netherlands	—	—	28.0	24.7	28.0	25.2
Denmark	27.9	23.9	27.5	24.0	27.5	23.7
Sweden	28.5	25.0	28.7	27.0	28.0	24.8
Norway	28.4	25.3	29.5	26.0	29.3	25.5
Germany	27.4	24.5	—	—	29.0 [a]	25.0 [a]
Poland	26.3	23.1	—	—	28.0	25.5
Switzerland	27.9	25.3	27.5	26.0	27.5	25.5
Austria	27.9	25.5	29.5	27.0	29.2	25.2
Portugal	25.3	23.2	25.7	24.5	26.0	23.5
Spain	27.4	23.9	27.5	24.0	29.0	25.2
Italy	26.7	22.9	28.0	23.7	28.5	23.5
Japan	27.7	22.4	—	—	27.0	22.5
Indochina	29.9	23.8	—	—	—	—
Egypt	—	—	27.5	20.7	28.5	21.5
Union of South Africa						
Europeans	27.7	22.7	27.5	23.5	26.0	22.0
Others	28.1	23.2	—	—	—	—
Australia	26.6	24.3	27.0	24.2	26.0	23.0
New Zealand	27.2	23.8	28.0	23.0	28.2	22.8

Sources: Data for 1927–29 from **59**, pp. 59–60; more recent data computed from **2**, 1948, pp. 468–85 and 1949–50, pp. 430–51.   a. American Zone.

TABLE 102

MEDIAN AGE AT MARRIAGE IN SELECTED COUNTRIES, 1876–85 AND 1906–15

(*Years*)

| Country | All Marriages | | | | First Marriages | | | |
| | 1876–85 | | 1906–15 | | 1876–85 | | 1906–15 | |
	Bride-groom	Bride	Bride-groom	Bride	Bride-groom	Bride	Bride-groom	Bride
Netherlands	30.5	27.9	29.2	26.7	28.3	26.5	27.6	25.8
Sweden	30.5	27.8	30.1	26.8	28.7	27.1	28.8	26.4
Finland	29.5	26.3	29.4	26.1	27.5	25.1	—	—
Italy	29.9	25.1	28.8	24.5	—	—	27.2	23.6

Source: **59**, p. 107.

In recent years a trend toward earlier marriage has been observed in France, Sweden, Norway, Austria, Australia, New Zealand, the Union of South Africa and some South American republics. Marriage of women at earlier ages was also observed in England, Denmark, Switzerland and Italy after World War II. These changes, however, may be only temporary, caused by the exceptional conditions in these years. In a few countries statistics for a longer period suggest that there has been a general tendency toward marrying at an earlier age, but the change has been very slow. (See Table 102.)

Industrialization and urbanization probably discourage early marriage. On the other hand, the breakdown of the patriarchal family tends to favor earlier marriage, and the practice of planned parenthood is likely to act in the same direction.

CHAPTER 6

HEALTH

THE STRUGGLE FOR HEALTH

THE STRUGGLE FOR HEALTH, like that for food and shelter, is one aspect of the age-old struggle between man and nature.

Beginning of Medicine

The practice of medicine began within the domain of magic and religion. The primitive physician, the shaman, was at once priest and sorcerer.[1] At a very early stage of civilization, however, rational practices began to invade the field of medicine. The broken leg and jaw, even the broken head and the battle wound, were not left to the mercy of the magician's art but were treated on the basis of experience and knowledge.[2]

Likewise, there was nothing mystical in the ancient religious customs relating to sanitary regulation. The instructions given in Leviticus[3] on testing and cleansing a leper are religious in form insofar as they rely on law established by God but rationalistic in substance. Babylonia and Assyria had the most comprehensive systems of religious medicine in which diseases were handled by spiritual and magical means, but they also recognized a purely empirical approach to disease. Herodotus tells how the Babylonians solved the problem of providing sick citizens with free medical advice:

> They have no physicians, but when a man is ill, they lay him in the public square, and the passers-by come up to him, and if they have ever had his disease themselves or have known anyone who has suffered from it, they give him advice, recommending him to do whatever they found good in their own case or in the case known to them; and no one is allowed to pass the sick man in silence without asking him what his ailment is.[4]

The Greeks developed a rational system of medicine based on empirical observation and made the two greatest discoveries in medical history: disease is not a matter of magic but a natural process; the human body has innate healing power.[5] Galen (2d century, A.D.), the great physician and thinker, is regarded as the founder of experimental physiology.

Although medicine continued to be torn between the mystical and the rationalistic approach, rationalism gradually gained ground. By the end of the seventeenth century, a considerable body of knowledge of disease had been accumulated and the foundations of scientific anatomy, physiology and pharmacology laid by scholars, among them such men of genius as Da Vinci and Harvey. At the same time, the medical profession had developed into an important learned fraternity. The effect of medicine on general health was not very satisfactory, however. It is questionable whether mortality rates were appreciably lower in seventeenth-century Europe than at the time of the Roman Empire.

Medicine in Modern Times

The turn in the history of medicine came in the eighteenth century, in the "era of enlightenment." The science and philosophy of that time advocated education as the means of ensuring a sound mind in a sound body, and the centralized state recognized the administration of health measures as one of its important functions.[6]

Chronologically, the drive to improve public health in Europe coincided with the Industrial Revolution in England and preceded the political revolution in France. In the troubled times, however, the movement lost momentum.[7] The end of the eighteenth century and the beginning of the nineteenth marked the nadir in social conditions in England and continental Europe, exhausted by war and internal conflict. Health problems and social friction became increasingly acute. At the same time, a new factor appeared on the political scene — organized labor.

---

1. **48**, p. 2.
2. **51**, p. 3.
3. Lev. 11, 13, 14.
4. **32**, Vol. I, p. 101.

5. **48**, p. 11.
6. **48**, pp. 78 ff.
7. **48**, p. 88.

Slogans asserting the citizen's right to health and the government's responsibility for the people's health became signs of the new times. The decisive campaign to improve public health began by the middle of the nineteenth century in western and central Europe. It was sustained by the remarkable progress in natural sciences. Bacteriology revealed the role of microorganisms in causing disease and made government aware of its responsibility to protect people against them. Pasteur's great discovery has probably contributed more to the health of mankind than any other single event in thousands of years.

As causes of specific diseases and the methods of their spread were revealed, an army of scientists was marshaled to seek the most effective way to prevent, control and eradicate these diseases. The widespread practice of inoculation, purification of the water supply, sterilization of food products, antisepsis and asepsis in surgery, and control of insect-borne diseases have been milestones in the progress of public health and medicine in the last six or seven decades. In the 1920's, insulin and extensive use of radiology, and in the 1930's and 1940's, the sulfa drugs, penicillin and other antibiotics were added to the weapons against disease. New horizons for medical research have been opened by progress in nuclear physics — for example, the use of radioactive isotopes.

The results of scientific progress and its application in the new public health programs became apparent in the steep decline in mortality, especially in deaths caused by the communicable diseases of childhood. In some countries, the turn came soon after the middle of the nineteenth century, in others much later. From the industrial countries of western and central Europe and North America the new methods of protecting human health and life spread slowly over other parts of the world. Medical and religious missions carried them into the wilderness of Africa, South America and Asia.

Progress in improving health and prolonging life was due to the combination of three factors: the advance in medical and sanitary science; the general improvement in economic conditions; and the growing recognition of public health protection as a primary responsibility of government. The last factor deserves particular attention. As Sigerist puts it:

If we believe that life, liberty, and the pursuit of happiness are inalienable rights of man and that

government is instituted to secure these rights, then we must conclude that man has a right to health and is entitled to having this right secured. . . . When a country establishes a constitution with the purpose of promoting the general welfare, it thereby admits that the health of the people is a direct concern of government.[8]

Moreover, a government's responsibility for its people's health does not stop at its national boundaries. No country is safe against a communicable disease if germs are close to its frontier — and our idea of "close" has changed with the increasing speed of travel and transportation. The industrialized nations have won a remarkable victory in freeing themselves from yellow fever, plague, cholera, smallpox, malaria, trachoma and typhus. But they are not safe behind their screen of quarantine so long as these diseases ravage other countries, however remote, from which an airplane may carry them in a few hours. The fight against disease has become an international task of all nations.

Where men live longer than their forefathers, it is not they who have changed by becoming healthier, stronger, more resistant to infection, but their environment, which their own efforts have so modified as to make their country a safer place in which to live.[9] The next step is to eradicate the deadly germs beyond the borders of Western civilization.

Measuring Health

Progress in health in modern times is manifested in the increase in the average length of life,[10] the complete — or almost complete — disappearance of certain diseases, the decline in mortality from other diseases, and the general increase in human stature. None of these criteria, however, shows how often, how long and how severely individuals are affected by illness during the course of their lives.

There are several methods of measuring health in a nation, but they are all inconclusive and can be misleading unless due attention is given to the particular conditions under which the measurement was effected.

Statistics of Sickness

Statistics on the incidence, severity and duration of illness are usually collected by public

8. **48,** p. 102.
9. **30,** p. 3.
10. See Chapter 5, pp. 182 ff.

health authorities and health insurance agencies and are sometimes supplemented by the findings of medical examination of recruits, school children and other groups and by special surveys. Because of differences in the organization of health services, however, these statistics cannot be used as a basis for international comparisons and historical surveys.

Often, for example, illness is classified as "nondisabling," "disabling," "not confining to bed," "confining to bed" and "hospitalized." Obviously, however, the more prosperous and health-conscious the community, the more inclined it is to handle as "bed" and "hospital" cases ailments that in another community may not be recorded at all.[11]

It is almost equally difficult to compare health conditions in various socioeconomic groups. Often it is up to the individual to call a doctor or to let his sickness take its natural course, and ailments among persons in prosperous and well-educated groups are likely to get more attention than similar ailments among the underprivileged. On the other hand, under a health insurance or assistance system a relief client may get medical care for ailments that otherwise would not be treated by a physician.

Records of Physical Examination of Recruits

Some light may be cast on health conditions in different countries by the records of physical examination of army recruits, but international comparisons of such records are misleading in view of the wide differences in standards as well as the selective factors involved. A high proportion of rejectees in a country may indicate a strict selection of men by military authorities

rather than a low standard of health among the men examined.

Statistics of Facilities for Medical Care

To some extent, the level of medical services in various countries may be measured by the number of doctors and hospital beds per 1,000 inhabitants. These data, however, are not strictly comparable and uncritical use of them may be misleading. The number of doctors and hospital beds needed to meet a definite standard of health service in an area depends on its density of population, transportation and communication facilities, the efficiency and skill of the medical personnel, and last, but not least, prevailing health conditions. An area with an unhealthy climate, poor water supply and frequently recurring epidemics needs more doctors than one where the population is less exposed to sickness.

DISEASE IN THE MODERN WORLD

Since the middle of the nineteenth century, medicine has won marked victories in the fight against communicable diseases, especially diseases of childhood. Advance in this field has kept pace with general economic progress and has been, indeed, an essential part of this progress. The struggle against such ailments as cancer, heart diseases and mental and nervous disorders, has been less successful. Thus a fairly clear chronological and geographical pattern of the distribution of diseases has developed. Particular diseases are characteristic of each stage in the economic development of nations and of each geographic region.

GEOGRAPHIC DISTRIBUTION OF DISEASE

The prevalence of different diseases forms an extremely complicated pattern on the world map. Some diseases are strictly localized, others spread over a vast area. Very roughly, for purposes of general orientation, four broad regions can be distinguished: (1) the temperate regions; (2) the region of tropical diseases; (3) the Mediterranean and middle-Asiatic region; and (4) the southern region.

The Temperate Regions

The temperate-climate regions, which comprise countries with a total population of approximately 750 million, form a broad belt encircling the globe in the Northern Hemisphere and also include Australia and New Zealand.

---

11. To take an extreme case, assume that we wish to compare the incidence of hospitalized illnesses in the United States and China. China has some 20,000 hospital beds. If each bed is occupied for 300 days during a year, the annual number of days of "hospitalized illness" in China would total 6 million. On the other hand, the United States has some 750,000 beds in general and special hospitals (excluding institutions for mental diseases) and records about 200 million days of "hospitalized illness" annually. The number of days of hospitalized illness per 1,000 inhabitants thus is 15 in China and more than 1,300 in the United States. Obviously, the difference between the two countries is not in the frequency of disabling illnesses but in the extent to which such illnesses are "hospitalized." In countries with approximately equal medical facilities the extent to which hospital beds are used depends on nearness to the hospital, custom and other factors unrelated to the state of health of the population.

About half this area (Region 1) may be described as comparatively "healthy": In this part lie a dozen countries of western and central Europe (the United Kingdom, Ireland, Sweden, Norway, Denmark, France, Belgium, the Netherlands, Germany, Austria, Luxembourg and Switzerland), the United States, Canada, Australia and New Zealand. The countries in this group — usually with an infant mortality rate below 50 per 1,000 live births — number as many as twenty if a few on the border line are added.

In these countries the prevailing major diseases are cancer, heart diseases, tuberculosis, influenza, arthritis, diabetes and mental disorders. The common cold and digestive troubles are also widespread and mortality rates from suicide and industrial and traffic accidents are comparatively high.

The same diseases prevail in the other half of the temperate region — eastern Europe, part of southern Europe, European Russia and the northern part of Asiatic Russia. General health conditions are less favorable here than in the first group of nations, infant mortality ranges from 100 to 125 per 1,000 live births, and people in some parts of this area suffer from diseases that are rare in the "healthy" area — malaria in Spain and Italy; beriberi in Japan. Essentially, however, the prevalence of diseases is like that in the rest of Region 1. (See Figure 72.)

The Region of Tropical Diseases

At the other extreme, Region 2 is ravaged by malaria, hookworm, dysentery and other parasitic diseases. This area, with a total population of approximately 1.2 billion, includes a large part of South America and the Caribbean, central Africa, India, Burma, China, Indochina and Indonesia. In some parts of it, smallpox, cholera, plague and leprosy are widespread; others are also afflicted with yellow fever, sleeping sickness, flukes and tuberculosis. Infant mortality of 200 or more per 1,000 is common.

Since a large part of this region lies between the two tropics, its diseases are often described as "tropical diseases," though it includes many areas with a distinctly nontropical climate. As Raisz has pointed out, tropical climate in itself is not unhealthy.[12] Florida has a typical wet-tropical climate in summer, while the artificial indoor climate in which people in temperate zones live in winter is very similar to outdoor conditions in dry-tropical regions.

Inhabitants of tropical and some subtropical regions fall prey to parasitic diseases because they have not yet learned how to protect themselves. Their diseases come largely from their poverty and lack of education, while their poverty is partly due to sickness and the prevailingly short span of life. Some of the dominant diseases in this region could be eradicated by controlling the water supply (typhoid fever, enteritis), others by inoculation. Hookworm is clearly a disease of poverty; not only in the tropics but in the temperate zone as well, it usually attacks those who go barefoot over infected ground.

The Mediterranean and Mid-Asiatic Region

Between the realms of the European diseases and the tropical diseases lies a wide strip that includes the Mediterranean basin, the Near East, Siberia, Manchuria, and the northwestern part of China, with a total population of approximately 370 million (Region 3). In addition to the illnesses prevailing in the adjacent areas, this region suffers from dysentery, and contagious skin and eye diseases, especially trachoma.

The Southern Region

The prevailing diseases in Region 4 in the extreme southern parts of South America and Africa are typhoid fever, influenza, tuberculosis, syphilis and flukes.[13]

The world population in mid-1950 was distributed among the four regions about as follows:

	Millions	*Per Cent*
World total	2,400	100.0
1. Temperate regions	750	31.3
2. Region of tropical diseases	1,200	50.0
3. Mediterranean and middle Asiatic region	370	15.4
4. Southern region	80	3.3

TRENDS IN DISEASE

Improvement in health conditions since the middle of the nineteenth century, and especially in the last 50 years, is clearly reflected in the decline in general and infant mortality. Some diseases have been eradicated, at least in the orbit

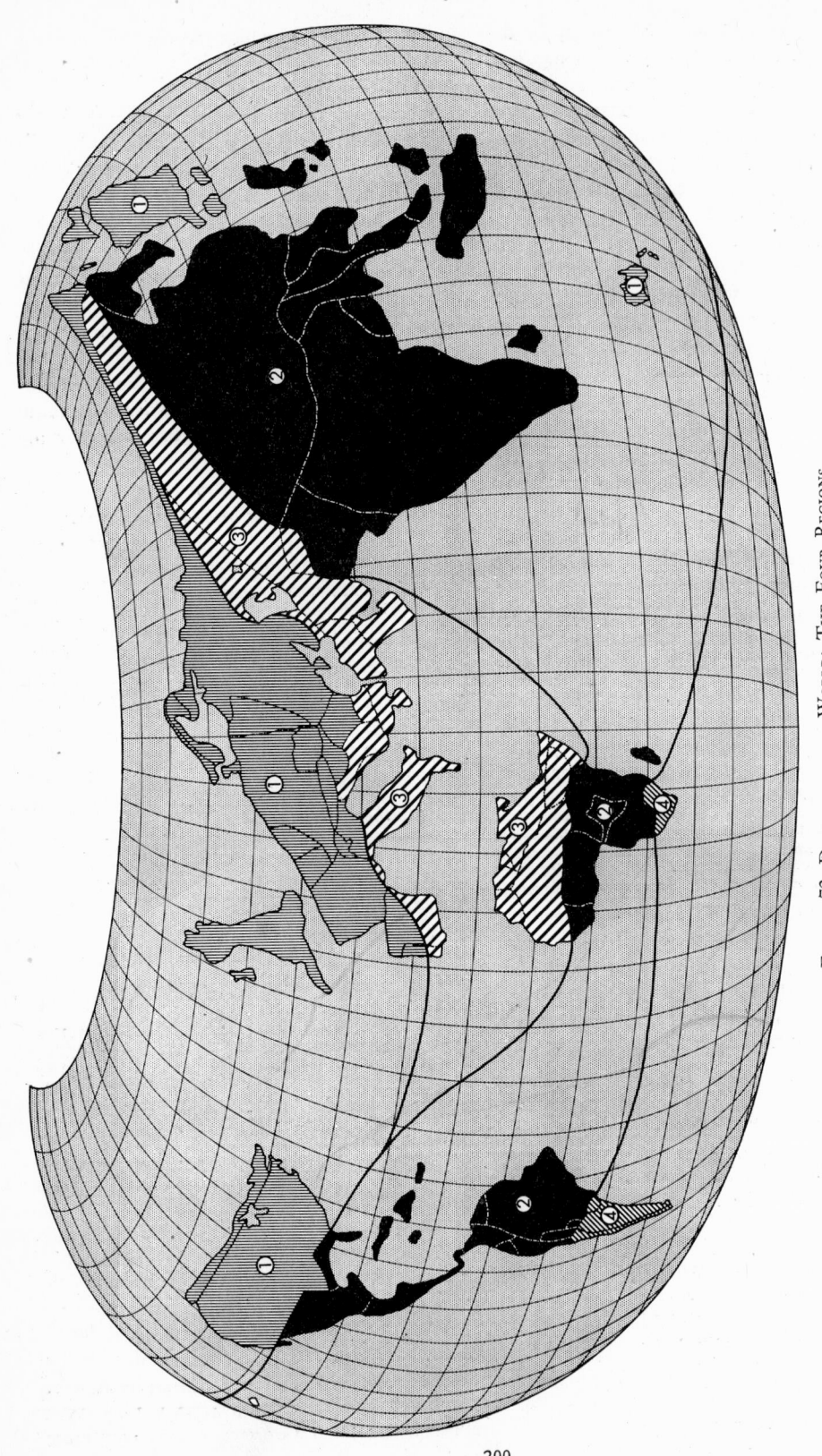

FIGURE 72. DISEASE IN THE WORLD: THE FOUR REGIONS

A distorted map showing continents and countries on the scale of their population in 1950.

The ailments prevailing in Region 1 are heart diseases, cancer, tuberculosis, pneumonia, influenza, syphilis and diabetes. Region 2, which includes about half of mankind, is ravaged by malaria, amebiasis, dysentery, hookworm, yaws and leprosy; it also suffers from tuberculosis and syphilis. Region 3, comprising southern Europe, northern Africa and a strip from Asia Minor to the Russian Far East, has the same ailments as the adjacent regions and suffers, in addition, from skin and eye diseases. The main diseases in Region 4 are typhoid fever, influenza, tuberculosis, syphilis and flukes. (Based on **39**.)

200

of Western civilization, and others have become comparatively harmless. At the same time, however, diseases that prevail in middle age and old age have become more frequent as an increasing proportion of the population lives to reach these ages. The apparent increase of some of these diseases may also reflect improvement in diagnostic techniques. Reasons for the increasing prevalence of others — for example, cancer — are not very clear.[14]

The struggle against disease continues on a broad global front. In some sectors of this front, modern medicine seems to be on the threshold of spectacular victories; in others the advance may be slow.

Recent trends in death rates from various diseases and their prevalence in economically developed countries can be summarized as follows:

1. Since the turn of the century there has been a decisive decline in mortality from communicable diseases of childhood. Some of them, such as diarrhea and diphtheria, have been practically eradicated; others like whooping cough, measles and scarlet fever have been made comparatively harmless by new therapies.

2. Equally spectacular has been the victory over typhus, typhoid and paratyphoid fevers and malaria.

3. Substantial, but less decisive, success has been achieved in the campaign against tuberculosis and pneumonia, including influenza, and senile debility.

4. Still unconquered are cancer, diseases of the heart and arteries, including hypertension and arteriosclerosis, nephritis, diseases of the nervous system (including intracranial lesions), and some other ailments, especially diseases peculiar to the first month of life and congenital malformation.

Little improvement, if any, has been recorded in the death rate from violence and from all forms of accidents combined. Death rates in the United States illustrate the trends in the prevalence and severity of various diseases. (See Table 103.)

---

14. Prevalence of mental disorders is bound to increase with the aging of the population. It is certain also that many cases of mental disorders that are being diagnosed now were not regarded and treated as diseases in the past. It is questionable, however, whether these are the only reasons for the growth of the number of patients in our hospitals for mental diseases and institutions for mental defectives and epileptics.

CONTROLLED DISEASES

Medical and sanitary sciences in modern countries have achieved their greatest progress in the field of acute infectious diseases that could be controlled or completely eradicated by improving environmental factors. (See Figure 73.)

Diarrhea

The decline in infant mortality[15] has been due partly to improvement in the care of women before and at childbirth, partly to greater concentration of births in the ages of 20 to 30 years, partly to reduction of the toll exacted by diarrhea. The largest part of the success in saving infant lives is attributable to methods of safeguarding the community's milk and water supplies.

Half a century ago, diarrhea was one of the most dangerous ailments of children under the age of 2 years. In some countries, it accounted for half of all deaths in childhood. Diarrhea still ranks first among causes of death in Egypt, where it is responsible for a third of all deaths in the total population. It also exacts a heavy toll in some predominantly agrarian countries such as Spain, Portugal, Bulgaria, Romania, Greece, Japan and Chile, where it is responsible for 10–15 per cent of all deaths and a large part of the infant mortality. In the orbit of Western civilization, however, only 1.5–2.0 per cent of all deaths are attributable to diarrhea. With effort, it could be eradicated completely.

Measles, Scarlet Fever, Diphtheria and Whooping Cough

The successful struggle against these diseases is reflected in the trend in mortality in the United States and Europe. In the United States the mortality from measles, scarlet fever, diphtheria and whooping cough, combined, amounted to 88 per 100,000 inhabitants in 1900 and has fluctuated between 3 and 4 per 100,000 in recent years. Several European countries report mortality rates from these diseases from 1901 to 1949 among the whole population and among children under one year of age. It appears that at the beginning of this century approximately one of a hundred live-born infants died from these diseases before reaching the age of one year.[16]

---

15. See Table 86.

16. In 1901, the rate was 943.5 per 100,000 live born in England and Wales; 843.3 in the Netherlands; 362.6 in Norway; 1,192.9 in Germany; 982.2 in Switzerland;

TABLE 103

TRENDS IN DISEASE: DEATH RATES FROM SELECTED CAUSES IN THE UNITED STATES,
1900–48

(*Deaths Per 100,000 Inhabitants*)

Cause of Death	1900	1910	1920	1930	1940	1948
Declining diseases						
Diarrhea, enteritis, etc.	142.7	115.4	53.7	26.0	10.3	6.0
Measles	13.3	12.4	8.8	3.2	0.5	0.6
Scarlet fever	9.6	11.4	4.6	1.9	0.5	0.0
Diphtheria	40.3	21.1	15.3	4.9	1.1	0.4
Whooping cough	12.2	11.6	12.5	4.8	2.2	0.8
Typhoid and paratyphoid fever	31.3	22.5	7.6	4.8	1.1	0.2
Dysentery	12.0	6.0	4.0	2.8	1.9	0.7
Malaria	6.2	1.1	3.4	2.9	1.1	0.1
Tuberculosis (all forms)	194.4	153.8	113.1	71.1	45.8	30.0
Pneumonia (all forms)	202.2	155.9	207.3	102.5	70.1	38.7
Influenza	26.7	14.2	70.5	19.4	15.3	3.5
Old age (senile debility)[a]	50.2	25.5	14.2	9.9	7.3	—
Unconquered diseases						
Diseases of heart (all forms)[b]	137.4	158.9	159.6	214.2	291.9	322.7
Cancer (all forms)[b]	64.0	76.2	83.4	97.4	120.0	134.9
Nephritis	88.6	94.8	88.0	91.0	81.4	53.0
Diabetes mellitus[b]	11.0	15.3	16.1	19.1	26.5	26.4
Intracranial lesions	106.9	95.8	93.0	89.0	90.8	89.7
Appendicitis	8.8	10.8	13.2	15.2	9.9	2.9
Hernia and intestinal obstruction	11.9	12.1	10.5	10.2	9.0	6.9
Cirrhosis of the liver	12.5	13.3	7.1	7.2	8.6	11.3
Congenital malformation	12.0	15.2	15.2	11.2	10.0	13.2
Diseases peculiar to the first month of life	72.3	73.2	69.4	49.6	38.9	42.1
Violent and accidental death						
Suicide	10.2	15.3	10.2	15.6	14.3	11.2
Homicide	1.2	4.6	6.8	8.8	6.2	5.8
Motor vehicle accidents	} 72.3	1.8	10.3	26.7	26.1	22.1
Other accidents		82.7	60.7	53.8	47.3	45.0

Sources: For 1900–40, **14,** pp. 210–41; for 1948, **15.**

a. The decline in the death rate from senile debility has been caused largely by changes in classification and diagnostic practices.

b. The rise in the mortality rate has been due partly to the increased proportion of aged persons in the population.

By 1949, the combined rate of infant mortality from the four diseases was cut to less than 100 per 100,000 live births in the United States, Canada, England and Wales, the Netherlands, Sweden, Norway, Switzerland, Australia and New Zealand; it remains close to 150 per 100,000 in France, Belgium, Spain and Italy and somewhat higher in Portugal. (See Table 104.)

In the struggle against diphtheria, success has

757.7 in Spain; 450.3 in Italy. There are considerable differences in reporting practices and the registration is incomplete in some countries.

been achieved by a radical reduction of the prevalence of the disease (the case rate per 100,000 inhabitants), while the case-fatality rate (the number of deaths per 100 cases) has not declined appreciably. Medicine has not succeeded in eradicating scarlet fever — there are about as many cases per 100,000 inhabitants as at the beginning of this century — but the case-fatality rate has been cut to less than a tenth. New methods of treatment likewise have made measles and whooping cough far less dangerous than they were five decades ago.

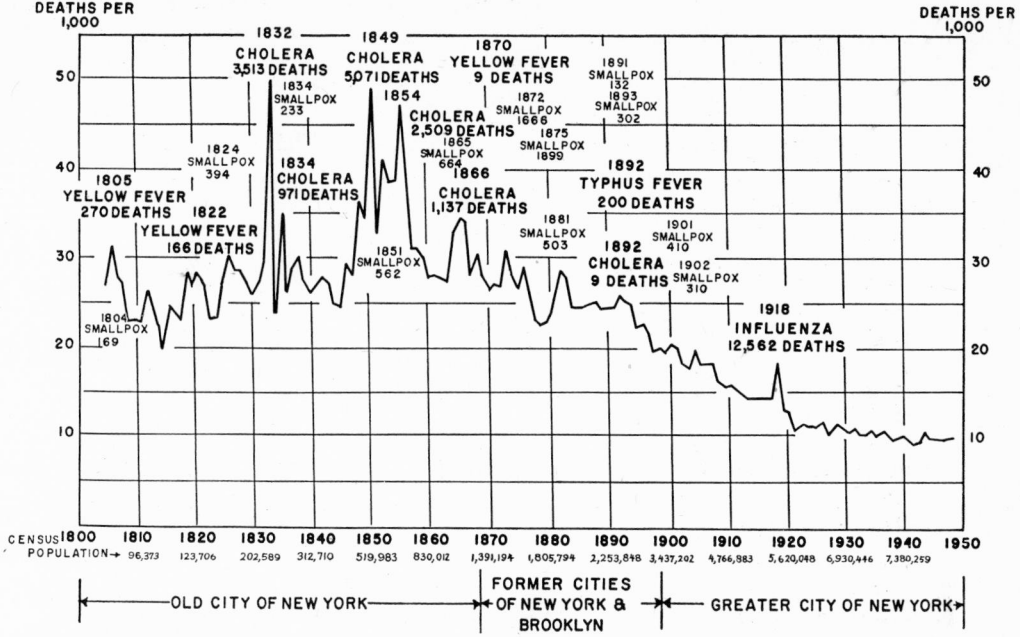

Department of Health, New York City (35)

FIGURE 73. TRENDS IN DISEASE: MORTALITY AND EPIDEMICS IN NEW YORK CITY, 1804–1948

    The trends in mortality and epidemics in New York City since the beginning of the nineteenth century illustrate changes in large cities in all modern nations.

    The first half of the nineteenth century saw no substantial improvement in the security of health and life; conditions at the mid-century were indeed disastrous. After that time epidemics became less frequent, although typhus and smallpox continued to invade the city from time to time and an effective weapon against diphtheria was not forged until near the end of the century. The progress in health is evident not only from the decline in general mortality but also from the flattening of the peaks that once marked periodic outbreaks of epidemics.

    Statistics of the least developed countries fail to report the causes of deaths of children precisely. Indochina, for example, reports 7 deaths from whooping cough, 6 deaths from measles, and none from scarlet fever in 1949 — figures that are highly improbable. International comparisons of the incidence of childhood diseases are subject to similar reservation.[17] The under-enumeration of deaths is due largely to under-enumeration of the cases. In countries with insufficiently developed public health services case-fatality rates are therefore more meaningful than the case and death rates. In Mexico and Egypt one in each 4 or 5 reported cases of measles ends in death; in France the ratio is 1 to 500, in the United States and England and Wales, 1 to 1,000. International comparison of

such rates is, however, not always possible because some countries report the number of deaths from specified causes but keep no record of the number of cases of each disease, while others report cases of communicable diseases but fail to classify deaths by cause. (See Table 105.) In countries reporting deaths from these diseases in 1949, the mortality rate per 100,000 inhabitants from whooping cough, diphtheria, measles and scarlet fever combined ranged as follows: [18]

United States (1948)	1.8
England and Wales	2.1
Canada	3.9
Switzerland	4.0
France	5.1
Netherlands	5.3
Italy	9.4
Portugal	14.2
Guatemala	17.8
Chile	23.0
Mexico	59.2

17. In 1949, for example, Indochina reported 1,108 cases of measles, 11 cases of scarlet fever and 112 cases of diphtheria. These data are in striking contrast with those for the United States: 620,905 cases of measles, 74,913 cases of scarlet fever and 8,027 cases of diphtheria. The difference is obviously in diagnosis rather than in prevalence of the respective diseases. (See Table 105.)

18. Computed from Table 105.

TABLE 104

CONTROLLED DISEASES: DEATH RATES FROM SCARLET FEVER, WHOOPING COUGH, DIPHTHERIA AND MEASLES IN SELECTED EUROPEAN COUNTRIES, 1901–49

A: Deaths per 100,000 inhabitants
B: Deaths under one year per 100,000 live births

Country, Year [a]	Scarlet Fever		Whooping Cough		Diphtheria		Measles	
	A	B	A	B	A	B	A	B
England and Wales								
1901	13.3	22.5	31.3	515.5	29.9	59.7	27.7	345.8
1911	5.2	8.2	21.7	414.2	13.6	25.4	36.3	316.1
1921	3.4	5.3	12.1	269.4	12.6	23.4	5.9	62.0
1931	1.2	3.6	5.8	178.3	6.5	16.0	7.7	113.9
1941	0.3	0.9	6.2	210.3	6.8	13.0	2.9	55.9
1949	0.0	0.3	1.2	62.4	0.2	0.8	0.7	13.8
France								
1911	2.4	18.6	7.4	210.4	7.2	65.6	10.1	162.4
1921	1.7	20.3	2.7	88.2	7.4	82.0	4.2	78.6
1931	0.6	3.3	2.3	83.0	5.5	36.2	4.0	88.4
1941	0.3	2.4	3.4	173.5	4.1	22.7	1.4	40.7
1949	0.1	0.7	2.7	105.6	0.7	6.2	1.6	39.5
Belgium								
1901	20.9	...	35.1	...	26.0	...	30.2	697.8
1911	16.6	222.2	28.0	938.7	12.9	156.5	22.3	717.6
1921	3.2	91.6	13.0	550.3	9.8	141.1	10.4	268.7
1931	1.2	40.9	8.8	356.0	5.6	64.1	4.2	147.4
1941	0.7	43.0	4.1	236.5	5.2	73.1	1.7	86.2
1949	0.1	2.7	1.5	71.1	1.3	30.3	0.8	26.6
Netherlands								
1901	1.9	0.6	23.2	387.8	17.8	43.9	52.5	411.0
1911	1.9	1.8	18.5	368.7	7.2	18.0	20.8	219.8
1921	0.8	1.0	8.3	166.7	6.2	21.6	9.5	118.7
1931	0.7	0.6	4.8	128.0	3.9	5.6	5.1	54.1
1941	0.4	...	6.1	182.5	2.4	8.2	2.0	24.2
1949	0.1	0.4	2.5	67.7	2.2	5.9	0.5	4.7
Sweden								
1901	9.4	...	17.1	...	50.8	...	7.3	...
1911	5.4	21.1	12.6	296.3	15.5	55.6	8.5	94.0
1921	1.8	5.5	7.0	231.8	11.7	32.9	3.6	58.7
1931	0.7	3.3	3.3	146.0	1.5	3.3	0.8	13.2
1941	0.3	1.0	1.5	68.2	0.3	4.4	1.1	16.0
1947	0.2	...	0.5	10.9	0.4	...	0.3	0.8
Norway								
1901	5.2	20.8	15.0	274.9	6.9	22.3	4.6	44.6
1911	3.1	21.1	13.9	317.5	19.1	47.0	8.3	76.1
1921	0.4	1.6	6.0	156.3	11.1	32.5	2.8	38.7
1931	1.4	6.5	1.9	73.9	1.8	2.2	1.9	10.9
1941	1.3	4.4	2.9	133.3	2.3	6.6	1.2	6.6
1948	0.1	3.0	0.2	10.7	1.2	10.4	0.5	3.0

(*Continued on facing page*)

TABLE 104—*continued*

Country, Year [a]	Scarlet Fever		Whooping Cough		Diphtheria		Measles	
	A	B	A	B	A	B	A	B
Germany								
1901	24.6	65.8	36.3	654.4	39.1	191.6	30.1	281.1
1911	10.6	23.8	18.6	418.3	25.1	84.2	13.0	154.8
1921	2.4	8.3	7.7	222.2	9.7	77.3	6.8	109.0
1931	1.0	2.3	3.6	162.9	6.4	19.0	2.0	41.9
1939	1.9	2.8	3.4	119.5	11.5	26.2	2.5	41.6
Switzerland								
1901	2.1	8.2	25.3	564.8	31.5	123.7	24.8	285.5
1911	3.4	11.0	10.4	249.7	13.3	35.0	9.1	107.3
1921	1.1	3.7	4.0	123.8	13.4	48.3	4.0	66.8
1931	0.8	1.5	2.2	76.2	3.1	16.1	2.1	23.4
1941	0.3	…	1.6	72.3	1.4	2.8	0.4	1.4
1949	0.2	…	2.2	89.1	1.4	2.3	0.4	3.5
Portugal								
1902	0.8	…	17.8	…	8.8	—	25.0	—
1913	0.9	3.6	15.5	251.2	9.0	59.8	12.1	99.5
1921	0.3	1.5	7.3	117.8	9.0	70.6	4.2	23.9
1931	0.6	2.4	14.9	324.3	14.5	170.0	17.4	210.2
1941	0.4	0.5	11.7	272.3	7.8	73.8	20.8	163.8
1949	0.1	0.9	5.4	140.4	2.5	23.6	6.3	65.5
Spain								
1901	6.1	17.7	20.8	368.6	33.7	88.3	98.9	283.1
1911	3.9	11.3	13.2	230.1	19.0	61.9	37.6	202.4
1921	3.9	14.3	7.4	132.7	14.2	58.6	25.4	166.7
1931	1.2	4.9	4.4	96.4	5.1	22.6	16.2	132.2
1941	0.2	2.4	2.5	70.9	6.0	51.0	2.7	83.8
1948	0.2	0.9	2.3	63.8	1.7	14.0	3.2	54.7
Italy								
1901	3.6	9.5	21.3	293.5	16.7	40.1	17.1	107.2
1911	7.3	13.5	19.7	307.3	10.6	41.6	24.7	142.4
1921	4.9	10.6	7.1	126.7	8.4	39.9	11.9	79.6
1931	4.6	9.9	7.2	155.4	7.7	30.7	8.3	70.9
1941	0.4	0.8	4.6	127.0	5.0	32.1	4.5	50.0
1949	0.2	1.0	3.4	115.7	2.2	17.9	2.3	37.5

Source: **5,** February–March 1951, pp. 56–57, 66–67, 74–75, 88–89, 94–95, 104–05, 112–13, 122–23.

a. Countries arranged geographically. Where information is not available for the specified year, data for the closest year are given.

TABLE 105

CONTROLLED DISEASES: COMMUNICABLE DISEASES OF CHILDHOOD, CASES AND DEATHS, IN SELECTED COUNTRIES, 1949

Country [a]	Scarlet Fever		Whooping Cough		Diphtheria		Measles	
	Cases	Deaths	Cases	Deaths	Cases	Deaths	Cases	Deaths
A. Number of Reported Cases and Deaths								
United States	74,913	...	68,138	...	8,027	...	620,905	...
Canada	8,518	14	7,801	202	797	79	58,126	224
Mexico	...	...	26,715 [b]	8,483 [b]	1,479 [b]	574 [b]	24,227	5,354
Guatemala	13	9	3,221	511	117	13	810	147
Colombia	57	...	21,900	369	2,143	226	24,391	288
Peru	598	...	18,993	...	542	...	5,923	...
Chile	92	6	3,860	910	913	193	2,541	199
Uruguay	442	...	591	58	372	18	159	...
England and Wales	70,649	20	102,805	528	1,897	85	385,849	308
France	12,350	53	5,799	1,134	5,237	306	36,937	676
Belgium	1,840	...	...	...	856	...	...	...
Netherlands	7,361	13	...	247	3,664	220	...	53
Denmark	9,458	...	59,899	135	84	6	24,298	...
Sweden	23,720	...	...	...	65	...	...	...
Norway	4,491	...	48,557	...	282	...	28,745	...
Finland	4,043	...	34,885	...	1,210	...	11,204	...
Germany	59,440	...	54,607	...	47,885	...	19,484	...
Poland	40,910	78	14,450	127	15,326	303	39,787	77
Czechoslovakia	...	...	13,515	...	8,561	...	5,076	...
Switzerland	6,055	9	6,097	98	1,357	62	9,467	20
Austria	19,649	38	5,702	95	10,845	272	...	...
Portugal	...	...	...	460	...	215	...	534
Spain	5,438	...	...	...	4,821	...	62,214	...
Italy	16,717	71	27,758	1,578	12,966	1,005	81,463	1,073
Yugoslavia	6,478	20	2,856	29	5,176	231	10,161	...
Bulgaria	4,559	8	8,514 [b]	89 [b]	...	...	...	...
Greece	178	...	839	23	153	11	5,823	22
Egypt	26	...	1,317	...	1,680	475	11,312	2,595
Madagascar	...	...	3,893	119	41	10	1,775	25
Japan	...	...	126,232	...	14,835	1,393	...	...
Turkey	1,586	...	3,759	46	953	112	8,857	286
Indochina	11	0	2,817	7	112	6	1,108	...
Indonesia	...	...	1,048	5	197	25	261	...
Australia	3,862	...	1,637	...	1,558	...	5,705	...
New Zealand	1,037	...	...	...	83	...	...	...

(*Continued on facing page*)

TABLE 105—*continued*

Country [a]	Scarlet Fever		Whooping Cough		Diphtheria		Measles	
	Cases	Deaths	Cases	Deaths	Cases	Deaths	Cases	Deaths
B. Reported Cases and Deaths Per 100,000 Inhabitants								
United States	50	...	46	...	5	...	416	...
Canada	63	0.1	58	1.5	6	0.6	428	1.7
Mexico [b]	...	...	109	34.8	6	2.4	99	22.0
Guatemala	...	...	85	13.5	3	0.3	21	4.0
Colombia	...	...	199	3.4	19	2.1	222	2.6
Peru	7	...	232	...	7	...	72	...
Chile	2	0.1	68	16.0	16	3.4	46	3.5
Uruguay	19	...	25	2.5	16	0.8	7	...
England and Wales	161	0.0	234	1.2	4	0.2	881	0.7
France	30	0.1	14	2.7	13	0.7	90	1.6
Belgium	21	...	...	...	10	...	...	...
Netherlands	74	0.1	...	2.5	37	2.2	...	0.5
Denmark	223	...	1,416	3.2	2	0.1	574	...
Sweden	341	...	...	...	1	...	...	...
Norway	138	...	1,500	...	9	...	880	...
Finland	100	...	869	...	30	...	280	...
Germany	86	...	79	...	69	...	28	...
Poland	167	0.3	59	0.5	62	1.2	162	0.3
Czechoslovakia	...	...	108	...	69	...	74	...
Switzerland	130	0.2	131	2.1	29	1.3	204	0.4
Austria	276	0.5	80	1.3	152	3.8	...	...
Portugal	...	...	...	5.4	...	2.5	...	6.3
Spain	19	...	...	...	17	...	222	...
Italy	36	1.5	60	3.4	28	2.2	177	2.3
Yugoslavia	40	0.1	18	0.2	32	1.4	63	...
Bulgaria	64	0.1	119	1.2	...	...	...	...
Greece	2.3	...	11	0.3	2	0.1	74	0.3
Egypt	0.1	...	6	...	8	2.4	57	13.0
Madagascar	...	...	90	3.0	1	0.2	34	0.6
Japan	...	...	153	...	18	1.7	...	...
Turkey	8	...	19	0.2	5	0.5	45	1.4
Indochina	0.4	0.0	10	0.0	0.7	0.0	4	0.0
Indonesia	...	...	1	0.0	0.2	0.0	0.3	...
Australia	49	...	21	...	20	...	72	...
New Zealand	55	...	...	...	4	...	...	...

Source: **5,** September 1950, pp. 216–38.   a. Countries arranged geographically.
b. 1946.

TABLE 106

CONTROLLED DISEASES: DEATH RATES FROM TYPHOID AND PARATYPHOID FEVERS IN THE UNITED STATES AND SELECTED EUROPEAN COUNTRIES, 1900–49

(Deaths Per 100,000 Inhabitants)

Country[a] and Year	Death Rate	Country[a] and Year	Death Rate	Country[a] and Year	Death Rate
United States		Netherlands		Switzerland	
1900	31.3	1901	9.1	1901	7.2
1910	22.5	1911	5.3	1911	4.8
1920	7.6	1921	4.0	1921	2.7
1930	4.8	1931	0.8	1931	0.9
1940	1.1	1941	0.4	1941	0.4
1949	0.2	1949	0.3	1949	0.3
England and Wales		Sweden		Portugal	
1901	15.5	1901	12.5	1902	17.4
1911	6.7	1911	4.2	1913	15.0
1921	1.6	1921	2.7	1921	32.1
1931	0.7	1931	0.7	1931	16.2
1941	0.4	1941	0.5	1941	20.5
1949	0.1	1947	0.6	1949	8.5
France		Norway		Spain	
1911	13.3	1901	7.7	1901	51.3
1921	6.6	1911	2.3	1911	26.5
1931	4.0	1921	2.3	1921	32.9
1941	3.1	1931	1.4	1931	15.2
1949	2.0	1941	0.4	1941	16.1
		1948	0.2	1948	5.4
Belgium		Germany		Italy	
1901	22.4	1901	10.6	1901	36.1
1911	10.5	1911	4.9	1911	27.5
1921	6.3	1921	4.1	1921	27.9
1931	2.3	1931	1.0	1931	14.9
1941	1.1	1939	1.0	1941	11.7
1949	0.7			1949	5.4

Sources: **5**, February–March 1951, pp. 40–41; **6**, 1950, p. 74.

a. Countries arranged geographically.

Typhus, Typhoid and Paratyphoid Fevers

Before the turn of the century, typhus and typhoid and paratyphoid fevers were common and deadly in all parts of the world. The incidence of these diseases and the mortality they cause have been largely reduced in modern industrialized countries: in the United States, from 31.3 per 100,000 inhabitants in 1900 to 0.2 in 1949; in England and Wales, from 15.5 in 1901 to 0.1 in 1949; in Belgium, from 22.4 to 0.7; in Italy, from 36.1 to 5.4, and so on. (See Table 106.) Progress in the fight against typhoid has been particularly dramatic. One city after another joined the battle against this disease by safeguarding its water supply, improving the sewage system, introducing pasteurization of milk. Each forward step in this direction was followed by a decline in the number of typhoid cases and deaths. (See Figure 74.)

In underdeveloped areas, typhus, typhoid and paratyphoid fevers still exact a high toll from the population, especially in times of national distress, such as war and famine. (See Table 107.)

For typhus, however, the available international statistics are incomplete. There are no reliable data for India, Pakistan and China, while statistics for the colonial areas of Africa record only the cases handled by European physicians. In all Asia, not more than 10,000 typhus cases and 400 deaths were reported in

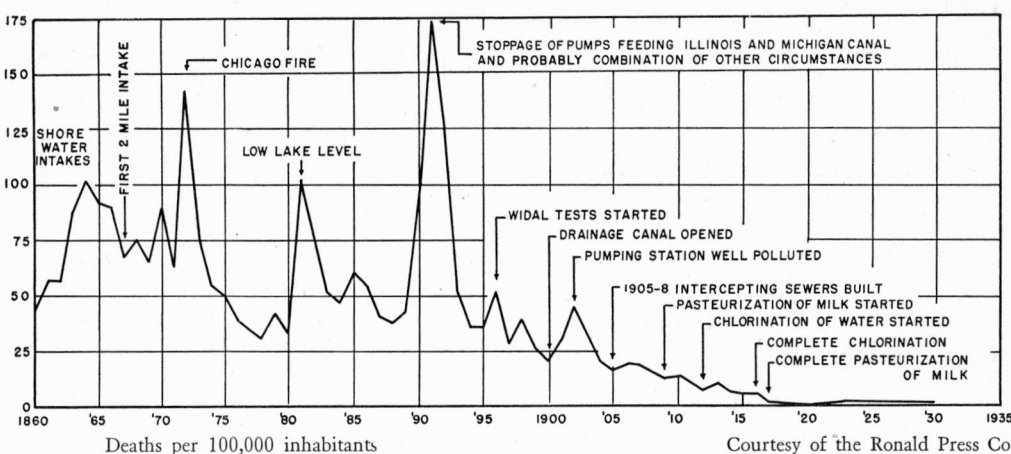

Deaths per 100,000 inhabitants   Courtesy of the Ronald Press Co.

FIGURE 74. TRENDS IN DISEASE: CONQUEST OF TYPHOID FEVER IN CHICAGO, 1860–1930

It took Chicago fifty years to conquer typhoid fever. The early attempt to improve the water supply proved insufficient. The disease seemed to be under control, only to reappear a few years later as if it had been lying in ambush. Decisive success was finally achieved by concentrated effort. "Much the same story could be told of any large city in the United States," Dublin and Lotka remark in commenting on this chart. (**29**, p. 177.)

TABLE 107

CONTROLLED DISEASES: TYPHOID AND PARATYPHOID FEVER, TYPHUS AND INFLUENZA AND
INFLUENZIAL PNEUMONIA, CASES AND DEATHS IN SELECTED COUNTRIES, 1949

Country	Typhoid and Paratyphoid Fevers		Typhus		Influenza and Influenzial Pneumonia	
	Cases	Deaths	Cases	Deaths	Cases	Deaths
A. Number of Reported Cases and Deaths						
United States	4,154	. . .	983	. . .	106,397 [a]	. . .
Canada	566 [a]	55 [a]	. . .	. . .	4,003	912 [a]
Mexico	5,349 [a]	4,260 [a]	997 [a]	851 [a]	. . .	4,144 [a]
Guatemala	879	229	58	10	7,307	503
Colombia	10,918	691	2,795	99	69,673	108
Peru	3,292	. . .	1,822	. . .	39,716	. . .
Chile	3,154 [a]	479 [a]	817 [a]	80 [a]	. . .	1,391 [a]
Uruguay	423	. . .	. . .	. . .	. . .	. . .
England and Wales	1,440	. . .	4	. . .	34,543	. . .
France	22,478	. . .	4	. . .	. . .	1,551
Belgium	1,523	. . .	. . .	. . .	. . .	. . .
Netherlands	1,977	31	0	0	. . .	2,490
Denmark	185	. . .	. . .	. . .	202,610	160
Sweden	425	. . .	. . .	. . .	. . .	. . .
Norway	81	. . .	0	0	50,910	. . .
Finland	5,876	. . .	. . .	. . .	105,500	. . .
Germany	19,966	. . .	. . .	. . .	185,221	. . .
Poland	7,975 [a]	478 [a]	345	11	71,081	. . .
Czechoslovakia	3,030	. . .	22	. . .	. . .	. . .
Switzerland	217	9	. . .	. . .	18,923	604
Austria	3,487	167	0	0	. . .	. . .
Portugal	. . .	749	4	. . .	. . .	792
Spain	21,596	. . .	0	0	359,841 [a]	912 [a]
Italy	39,208 [a]	3,160	93	7	26,064	. . .
Yugoslavia	6,803	255	267	12	. . .	. . .
Bulgaria	325	20	438	46	. . .	. . .
Greece	5,260	109	81	2	3,967	. . .

(*Continued on page 210*)

TABLE 107—*continued*

Country	Typhoid and Paratyphoid Fevers		Typhus		Influenza and Influenzial Pneumonia	
	Cases	Deaths	Cases	Deaths	Cases	Deaths
A. Number of Reported Cases and Deaths—*continued*						
Egypt	5,513 [a]	814 [a]	186	53	5,135 [a]	38 [a]
Madagascar	212	37	...	...	4,085	496
Japan	10,926	1,040	115	6	2,777	...
Turkey	214	13	230	20	...	...
Indochina	1,183	96	35	5	7,284	4
Indonesia	2,669	92	...	...	...	...
Australia	80	...	143	...	57	...
New Zealand	31	1	...	...	14	...
B. Reported Cases and Deaths Per 100,000 Inhabitants						
United States	2.8	...	0.7	...	71.3 [a]	...
Canada	4.1 [a]	0.4 [a]	...	...	29.6	6.8 [a]
Mexico	21.9 [a]	17.4 [a]	4.1 [a]	3.5 [a]	...	16.9 [a]
Guatemala	23.3	6.1	1.5	2.6	193.1	13.3
Colombia	99.3	6.3	25.4	0.9	633.3	1.0
Peru	40.1	...	22.2	...	484.3	
Chile	55.3 [a]	8.4 [a]	14.3 [a]	1.4 [a]	...	24.3
Uruguay	18.0	...	...	...	...	...
England and Wales	3.3	...	0	0	78.8	...
France	5.5	...	0	0	...	3.8
Belgium	17.7	...	...	...	...	25.0
Netherlands	19.9	0.3	0	0	478.9	3.8
Denmark	4.4	...	...	...		...
Sweden	6.1	...	...	...		
Norway	2.5	...	0	0	1,574.3	...
Finland	146.3	...	...	...	2,627.0	...
Germany	28.2	...	...	...	266.6	...
Poland	32.5 [a]	2.0 [a]	1.4	0.4	289.8	...
Czechoslovakia	24.3	...	0.2	...	...	...
Switzerland	4.9	0.2	...	...	425.8	13.6
Austria	49.2	2.3	0	0	...	...
Portugal	...	8.8	0	0	...	9.3
Spain	77.1	...	0	0	1,284.5 [a]	3.3 [a]
Italy	85.2	6.9	0.2	0	56.5	...
Yugoslavia	42.4	1.6	1.7	0.1	...	...
Bulgaria	4.5	0.3	6.1	0.6	...	...
Greece	119.6	2.5	1.8	0	90.2	...
Egypt	27.5	4.1	0.9	0.3	25.7	0.2
Madagascar	4.8	0.8	...	...	92.7	11.3
Japan	13.3	1.3	0.1	0	3.4	...
Turkey	1.1	0.1	1.2	0.1	...	...
Indochina	4.3	0.4	0.1	0	26.5	0
Indonesia	3.4	0.1	...	...	...	...
Australia	1.0	...	1.8	...	0.7	...
New Zealand	1.6	0.5	...	...	0.7	...

Sources: **5**, April 1950, pp. 82–95; July–August 1950, pp. 208–13.

   a. 1948.

1948.[19] These figures appear completely unrealistic in comparison with the data for Colombia (2,795 in 1949), Mexico (997) and Peru (1,822). (See Table 107.) In brief, international comparisons of typhus statistics should be restricted to modern industrialized countries. In such countries the incidence of typhus and of typhoid and paratyphoid fever varies widely from year to year, but the mortality rate is low even in the years of local epidemics.

Influenza

Influenza is an epidemic form of febrile respiratory catarrh. The last violent outbreak took place in 1918–19, when approximately 3 million persons died in Europe and about an equal number in India.[20] The pandemic spread in three consecutive waves of unequal virulence. The first wave appeared in western Europe in May 1918 and attained full force in central and northern Europe by midsummer. The second wave swept over the world in the autumn of the same year and exacted a much heavier toll than the first. In March 1919, a third and comparatively milder wave followed. More people died of influenza in 1918–19 than through military action in World War I.[21] Since that time outbreaks of influenza have occurred some twenty times, simultaneously or almost simultaneously in various parts of the world. Recent outbreaks have been mild in comparison with that in 1918–19 but about as large as the pandemic outbursts in the early 1890's. In the United States the cumulative number of deaths from influenza, during 1920–29, in excess

---

19. The following figures for that year were released by the World Health Organization (**5**, July–August 1950, pp. 208–13):

Country	Reported Cases	Reported Deaths
Burma	5	0
China (1947)	5,269	261
Indian Union	28	10
Pakistan	29	2
Indian States	11	4
Indochina	57	2
Iraq	225	3
Iran	150	19
Japan	488	33
Malaya	490	13
Singapore	16	2
Syria	50	. . .

20. **54**, p. 222.
21. It is unknown whether the pandemic outbreak of 1918–19 was caused by the same virus now recognized as the cause of influenza.

of the normal seasonal expectancy is estimated at more than a quarter of a million, as compared with half a million in 1918–19.

Partly because of new methods of treatment, the number of deaths in recent epidemics has been very low in comparison with the number of cases of the disease. The epidemics have therefore appeared to be mild despite the large number of cases involved.

Malaria

Malaria is not restricted to any particular continent but has important foci in many parts of the world: in Europe, in Spain, Italy and Poland; in America, in Mexico, Guatemala, Colombia, Costa Rica, Peru, Venezuela and El Salvador; in Africa, in Madagascar and practically all equatorial regions; in Asia, throughout the Far East. Statistical information on the prevalence of malaria is incomplete, however: few cases are reported in the areas where it is known to be widespread.

Malaria is endemic in many areas; often a large part of the population is infected and suffers seriously from loss of vigor and working capacity, but comparatively few deaths are reported. In the Sudan, for example, only 2 deaths from malaria were recorded in each of the years 1948 and 1949, though nearly 30,000 cases of malaria were reported each year. The reported mortality rate is low also in Indochina, Taiwan, the Cameroons, Togo, Madagascar and southern Europe but is much higher in Mexico, Guatemala and South America. (See Table 108.) The toll actually exacted by malaria is probably much greater than the deaths officially attributed to this disease. A person suffering from malaria may become an easy victim of some other disease, which will appear as the immediate cause of death in the death certificate and mortality statistics.

In recent years considerable progress toward conquering malaria has been made in the Philippines, the Pacific Islands, Italy, Greece, Iran and Latin America. In many areas the campaign was started by the military medical personnel of the United States to protect American troops and has been continued as a part of the American aid program.

Tuberculosis

Though the death rate from tuberculosis has declined substantially in all progressive countries,

TABLE 108

CONTROLLED DISEASES: MALARIA, CASES AND DEATHS IN SELECTED COUNTRIES, 1949

Country	Number		Per 100,000 Inhabitants		Country	Number		Per 100,000 Inhabitants	
	Cases	*Deaths*	*Cases*	*Deaths*		*Cases*	*Deaths*	*Cases*	*Deaths*
United States	4,239	—	2.8	—	Egypt [a]	4,515	22	22.6	0.1
Mexico [a]	93,957	23,779	384.2	97.2	Sudan	27,143	2	339.2	0
Guatemala	37,074	2,005	979.7	53.0	French West Africa	27,270	13	165.9	0.1
Colombia	97,446	596	885.8	5.4	French Equatorial				
Peru	30,179	—	368.0	—	Africa	2,704	4	67.6	0.1
					Congo	27,672	30	4,257.2	5.0
Poland [a]	9,941	9	40.6	0					
Spain [a]	56,970	62	203.4	0.2	Cameroons	67,811	65	1,695.2	1.7
Italy [a]	2,256	191	4.9	0.5	Togo	88,359	103	6,496.0	7.6
					Madagascar	434,360	2,899	10,324.0	51.9
Japan	3,732	72	4.5	0.1					
Indochina	225,333	2,402	885.0	8.7					

Source: **5**, April 1950, pp. 102–07.   a. 1948.

this disease is one of the most terrible scourges in the orbit of Western civilization. In the Orient it is overshadowed by such fearful diseases as plague and cholera.

The fight against tuberculosis proved more difficult than the campaign against some other communicable diseases, since success depends not only on early diagnosis and measures to protect others from contact with the sick person but also on long-continued care. Care is expensive, and initial success was disappointingly slow, but the number of deaths from tuberculosis was gradually declining even before Koch's discovery of the bacillus. The campaign then received new momentum and in fifty years the death rate of tuberculosis was cut in half while invalidity in the advanced phase of the disease was reduced to a third. Even this incomplete victory over tuberculosis has saved millions of human lives and the equivalent of enormous sums of money, since the disease commonly attacks people at young working ages when their responsibilities for self-support and family support are heavy.

In England and Wales, the standardized death rate from tuberculosis (all forms) declined from 347.8 per 100,000 in 1851–60 to 99.2 in 1921–30, 87.9 in 1931, 61.6 in 1938, and 51 in 1948. Thus in less than a century, mortality from tuberculosis has been cut to about a seventh.[22]

The recent report of the World Health Organization points out that many countries suffered an increase in mortality from tuberculosis during World War II or immediately after it. Despite

22. **24**, p. 231.

this temporary setback, appreciable improvement was reached from 1937 to 1949. The tuberculosis death rate varies widely from country to country, ranging from 19 per 100,000 inhabitants in Denmark and 24–30 in the United States, Canada, the Netherlands, Australia and among the white population of New Zealand to 178, and more, per 100,000 in Japan, Chile, Brazil and among the Maoris in New Zealand. (See Table 109; cf. Figure 75.)

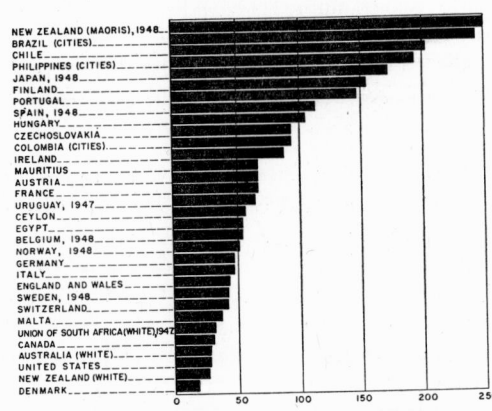

FIGURE 75. CONTROLLED DISEASES: DEATH RATES FROM TUBERCULOSIS IN SELECTED COUNTRIES, 1949

The nations with the highest death rates from tuberculosis include not only such relatively underdeveloped countries as Brazil, Chile and the Philippines but also Finland. Comparatively low death rates are found not only in the United States, the Netherlands, New Zealand, Australia and Denmark but also in Egypt, Ceylon and Uruguay. The low death rates in underdeveloped areas are largely due to the gaps in recording: the cause of death cannot be properly established in countries where the great majority of the population has no access to medical aid.

TABLE 109

CONTROLLED DISEASES: TUBERCULOSIS, DEATH RATES IN SELECTED COUNTRIES, 1937–49

(Deaths Per 100,000 Inhabitants)

Country	1937	1939	1941	1943	1944	1945	1946	1947	1948	1949
United States	54	47	45	43	41	40	36	34	30	28
Canada	60	53	53	52	48	46	47	43	37	30
Chile	253	251	252	252	243	253	236	224	226	202
Uruguay	112	101	102	114	...	103	101	100	...	...
England and Wales	68	62	73	67	63	61	55	55	50	45
Ireland	123	113	124	146	130	125	114	124	104	89
France	119	121	159	147	129	111	88	81	76	68
Belgium	71	68	98	82	82	77	66	63	55	...
Netherlands	48	41	59	70	75	86	47	37	28	24
Denmark	44	34	35	34	33	33	32	30	25	19
Sweden	86	75	75	69	67	69	55	51	42	...
Norway	98	86	80	69	74	65	64	56	52	...
Finland	200	197	196	193	193	187	178	167	156	...
Germany [a]	62	...	...	...	...	...	83	73	67	49
Switzerland	87	80	79	76	81	83	76	67	52	42
Austria	100	100	101	106	120	155	110	93	88	68
Portugal	151	143	160	152	145	152	157	153	148	149
Spain	120	122	126	113	112	112	119	124	114	...
Italy	86	76	81	100	96	91	84	77	62	49
Japan	206	218	212	232	239	280	261	186	178	...
Ceylon	62	62	61	58	59	56	60	56	57	57
Union of South Africa, White	36	33	31	31	32	30	31	31	...	...
Australia, White	40	39	38	35	33	33	32	30	28	...
New Zealand White	39	40	39	37	38	38	34	31	27	25
Maoris	357	440	440	369	383	374	386	329	250	...

Source: **5,** October 1950, pp. 242–43.   a. After World War II, Western Germany.

Tuberculosis is often considered a predominantly urban disease; in most countries, though not all, mortality is greater in large cities than in rural areas. Some large cities, however — including New York, Montreal, London, Amsterdam, Stockholm and Oslo — have been conspicuously successful in their campaign against tuberculosis in recent decades. (See Table 110.)

The comparatively low tuberculosis mortality rates recorded in some tropical and subtropical countries — for example, Mexico, Colombia and El Salvador — are due largely to gaps in medical control and diagnosis. There are also appreciable differences in the way in which deaths are classified by cause, especially when more than one disease is present. In the United States, for example, tuberculosis would be given priority when it is combined with other diseases, while in many other countries identical cases would be attributed to other causes.

Trachoma

Trachoma has been called a disease of "poverty and promiscuity." It is one of the oldest diseases known to man. Originating in ancient Egypt or China, it was brought to Europe by the Moslems early in the Middle Ages and carried on to America by immigrants. Now it is widespread in parts of South America, Spain, Italy and Greece, Siberia, northern and central Africa, the Near East, northern China and Indochina.

The fragmentary statistics on trachoma show the main foci of the disease but not the number of cases. "In the present state of our knowledge

TABLE 110

CONTROLLED DISEASES: TUBERCULOSIS, DEATH RATES IN SELECTED COUNTRIES AND CITIES, AROUND 1949

(Deaths from All Forms of Tuberculosis Per 100,000 Inhabitants)

Country and City	Death Rate	Country and City	Death Rate	Country and City	Death Rate
United States	28	Netherlands	24	Austria	68
New York	31	Amsterdam	22	Vienna	87
Canada	30	Denmark	19	Hungary [b]	106
Montreal	42	Copenhagen	23	Budapest [b]	101
England and Wales	45	Sweden [a]	42	Portugal	149
London	63	Stockholm [a]	52	Lisbon	317
Scotland	67	Norway [a]	52	Spain [a]	114
16 towns	86	Oslo [a]	45	Madrid [a]	108
Ireland	89	Finland [a]	156	Italy	49
Dublin	71	Helsinki [a]	139	Rome	77
France	68	Germany	49	Bulgaria [c]	143
Paris	62	West Berlin	115	105 towns [c]	170
Belgium [a]	55	Czechoslovakia [a]	96	Egypt	55
Brussels [a]	62	Prague [a]	90	Cairo	79
		Switzerland	42		
		10 towns	38		

Source: **5,** December 1948, p. 432, July 1949, pp. 137–39, October 1950, pp. 251–53.

a. 1948.
b. 1947.
c. 1940.

it would be hopeless to try to estimate the total number of trachoma sufferers throughout the world," the World Health Organization reports. "Some authorities speak of millions, others of tens or hundreds of millions. Perhaps the most pessimistic figures are those nearest the truth." [23] (See Figure 76.)

QUARANTINED DISEASES

Plague, cholera, yellow fever and smallpox are terrible diseases that have been barred from the western countries but keep a foothold in Asia and Africa. Medical forces in Europe and America continue to fight them actively, but immunization and quarantine are the main protection of the Western world.

23. **5,** November–December 1949, p. 270. Despite this conclusion, the present writers list trachoma among "controlled" diseases rather than among those described as "quarantined" or "unconquered." Indeed, trachoma has been overcome in many parts of the world, and efficient methods of therapy are already in use in areas where the infection is widespread. The report of the World Health Organization expresses the hope that if the national campaigns now under way are continued and meet with vigorous international support, our century may witness the disappearance of trachoma. (*Ibid.,* p. 271.)

Plague

Plague — the Black Death of the Middle Ages — has remained the most dreaded epidemic disease in the world for thousands of years. Thucydides left a pathetic decription of plague in Athens in 430 B.C. The most devastating outbreak in Europe occurred in 1348, when England lost some 2 million persons, about half the total population, and other millions perished in Spain, Italy, France and other European countries. Plague deaths in Europe in that one year have been estimated at 25 million. In 1603 and 1625 the plague returned to England, each time killing a sixth of the population of London. In the following century 91,000 plague deaths were reported in Marseilles and Toulon in 1720; 70,000 deaths in Messina in 1743; 70,000 deaths in Cyprus in 1759.[24]

There are no inclusive records of plague in Asia in past centuries, but the victims of the Black Death in its traditional domain since the middle of the past century must run to hundreds of millions. Most of Europe has been comparatively safe in this period except for sporadic outbreaks in southern countries. In 1878–79 an epi-

24. **51,** p. 152.

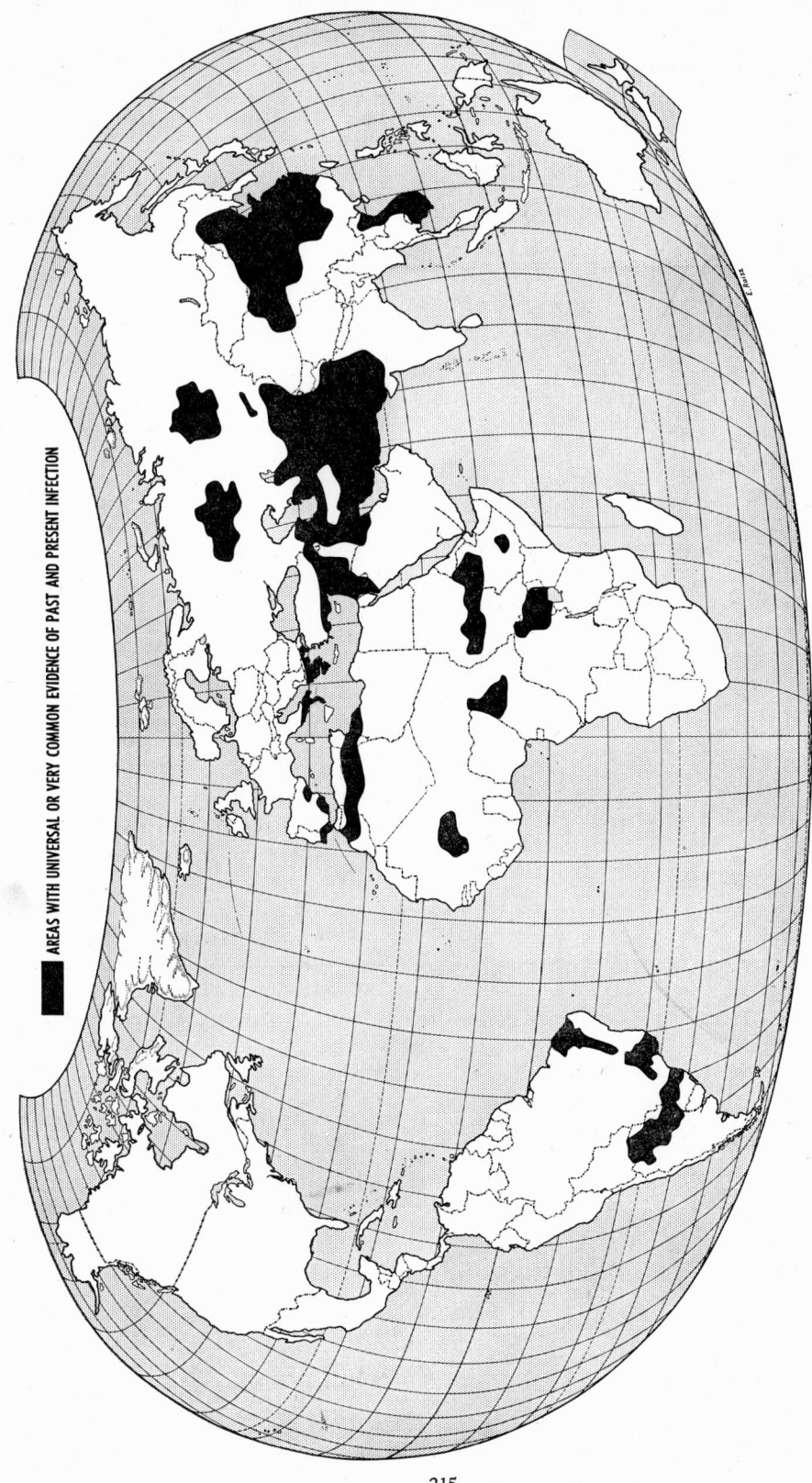

AREAS WITH UNIVERSAL OR VERY COMMON EVIDENCE OF PAST AND PRESENT INFECTION

Adapted from the map prepared by the World Health Organization

FIGURE 76. CONTROLLED DISEASES: PREVALENCE OF TRACHOMA IN THE WORLD

215

TABLE 111

QUARANTINED DISEASES: PLAGUE, CASES AND DEATHS IN THE WORLD, 1939–48

Country	1939	1940	1941	1942	1943	1944	1945	1946	1947	1948
Ecuador										
Cases	452	69	39	5	15	36	38	45	21	40
Deaths	244	50	14	2	9	11	16	19	1	3
Brazil										
Cases	81	97	179	12	67	156	192	289	77	391
Deaths	24	34	61	2	22	36	42	48	9	54
Peru										
Cases	131	180	67	98	66	83	92	126	173	73
Deaths	51	70	33	42	26	29	16	20	47	18
Argentina										
Cases	5	228	56	38	2	107	. . .	10	4	12
Deaths	4	192	28	19	1	63	3	3	0	4
China										
Cases	883	4,265	1,853	1,868	7,450	3,653	2,593	11,069	3,156	989
Deaths	. . .	2,901	1,412	1,577	5,416	2,050	1,286	5,912	1,412	419
India										
Deaths	35,367	19,892	19,114	15,010	18,962	22,145	44,398	39,917	45,038	11,696
Burma										
Cases	3,934	1,584	1,458	. . .	. . .	. . .	783	3,517	1,518	1,616
Deaths	3,398	1,314	1,266	. . .	. . .	. . .	675	2,743	1,192	1,174
Thailand										
Cases	78	104	0	36	58	57	107	72	71	122
Deaths	31	39	0	17	32	29	46	32	23	36
Indochina										
Cases	5	11	52	98	51	. . .	. . .	52	90	355
Deaths	4	11	23	85	43	. . .	. . .	24	40	105
Indonesia										
Cases	1,545	401	527	. . .	. . .	. . .	. . .	58	35	3,422
Deaths	. . .	401	524	. . .	. . .	. . .	. . .	15	19	3,365
Egypt										
Cases	169	491	14	15	163	644	218	211	15	0
Deaths	59	238	6	10	111	393	108	57	5	0
French West Africa										
Cases	0	7	0	6	292	640	58	0	0	0
Deaths	0	7	0	6	258	571	49	0	0	0
Kenya										
Cases	4	11	781	754	16	13	56	35	55	29
Deaths	4	10	196	333	13	7	21	11	16	15
Uganda										
Cases	323	277	223	356	19	7	4	12	1	0
Deaths	308	268	213	338	. . .	7	4	12	1	0
Tanganyika										
Cases	0	0	2	0	0	0	0	0	0	311
Deaths	0	0	2	0	0	0	0	0	0	173
Madagascar										
Cases	681	754	274	181	234	184	185	278	270	240
Deaths	616	689	234	163	209	161	157	248	225	184
Bechuanaland										
Cases	0	0	0	0	0	399	19	21	0	0
Deaths	0	0	0	0	0	195	17	19	0	0
Union of South Africa										
Cases	77	47	90	79	77	63	39	15	9	21
Deaths	29	20	. . .	45	39	39	24	1	3	11

Source: **5**, August 1949.

TABLE 112

QUARANTINED DISEASES: PLAGUE AND CHOLERA DEATHS IN INDIA, 1915–49

(*Thousands*)

Year	Plague	Cholera	Year	Plague	Cholera	Year	Plague	Cholera
1915	434	440	1927	44	305	1939	35	103
1916	276	288	1928	121	451	1940	20	103
1917	587	267	1929	72	295	1941	20	247
1918	621	561	1930	25	337	1942	15	235
1919	99	578	1931	46	221	1943	19	274
1920	140	130	1932	47	67	1944	22	298
1921	82	451	1933	43	68	1945	44	317
1922	102	122	1934	84	209	1946	40	80
1923	293	73	1935	29	223	1947	46	40
1924	362	293	1936	11	171	1948	12	109
1925	118	116	1937	29	107	1949	11	51
1926	196	138	1938	18	259			

Sources: **25** and **5**, various years.

demic developed in Russia, on the Volga; in 1899 there was a new and relatively mild outbreak in southern Russia and Spain.

Plague is now concentrated in Asia — in India, Burma, China, Indonesia and Indochina. In Africa the main foci are Madagascar, Morocco, Egypt, Tanganyika and Kenya; in America, Argentina, Brazil, Ecuador and Peru. In the United States, only 8 cases of plague were observed in the decade 1939–48, but there is abundant evidence of wild-rodent plague in the western part of the country. In Europe, during the same decade, a few cases of plague occurred in Italy, Corsica, Malta and Madeira.

The prevalence of plague varies widely from year to year. In Argentina, for example, 228 cases were reported in 1940 and an average of 9 cases a year in 1946–48; Ecuador reported 452 cases in 1939 and an average of about 35 cases a year in 1946–48; Egypt, 644 cases in 1944 and not a single case in 1948. (See Table 111.) India has had striking ups and downs. (See Table 112; cf. Figure 77.)

The annual number of deaths from plague in India has declined conspicuously in the past two decades but, as the World Health Organization points out, plague retains its power to spread. The violent outbreaks that followed the relaxation of national control toward the end of the war confirm this statement. Moreover, as long as plague lurks in its present foci, it remains a threat to the rest of the world.

Cholera

Like plague, cholera prevails in southeastern Asia. From this stronghold it has invaded Europe and America time and again. The outbreak in the United States in 1854 took about 2,500 lives in New York City alone.[25] Epidemics in Europe and Russia in the 1880's and 1890's were particularly devastating. Cholera reappeared in Europe during World War I, but did not spread beyond a few seaports exposed to infection from Asia.

The main foci of cholera are in India, Burma and China. The only important outbreak outside Asia in the past twenty years was in Egypt in 1947. No cases have been recorded recently in America or Europe. In Asia half the reported cases of cholera end in death. (See Table 113.)

Smallpox

Smallpox was one of the most common diseases of the eighteenth century. It has been estimated that as late as 1754 a tenth of all mankind were crippled or disfigured by smallpox and that it accounted for a tenth of all deaths.[26] The infection was still widespread all over the world half a century ago. It has since become rare in modern industrialized countries. If not precisely a disease of individual poverty, smallpox now is certainly a disease of backward

25. **51**, p. 153. Cf. Figure 73.
26. **51**, p. 153.

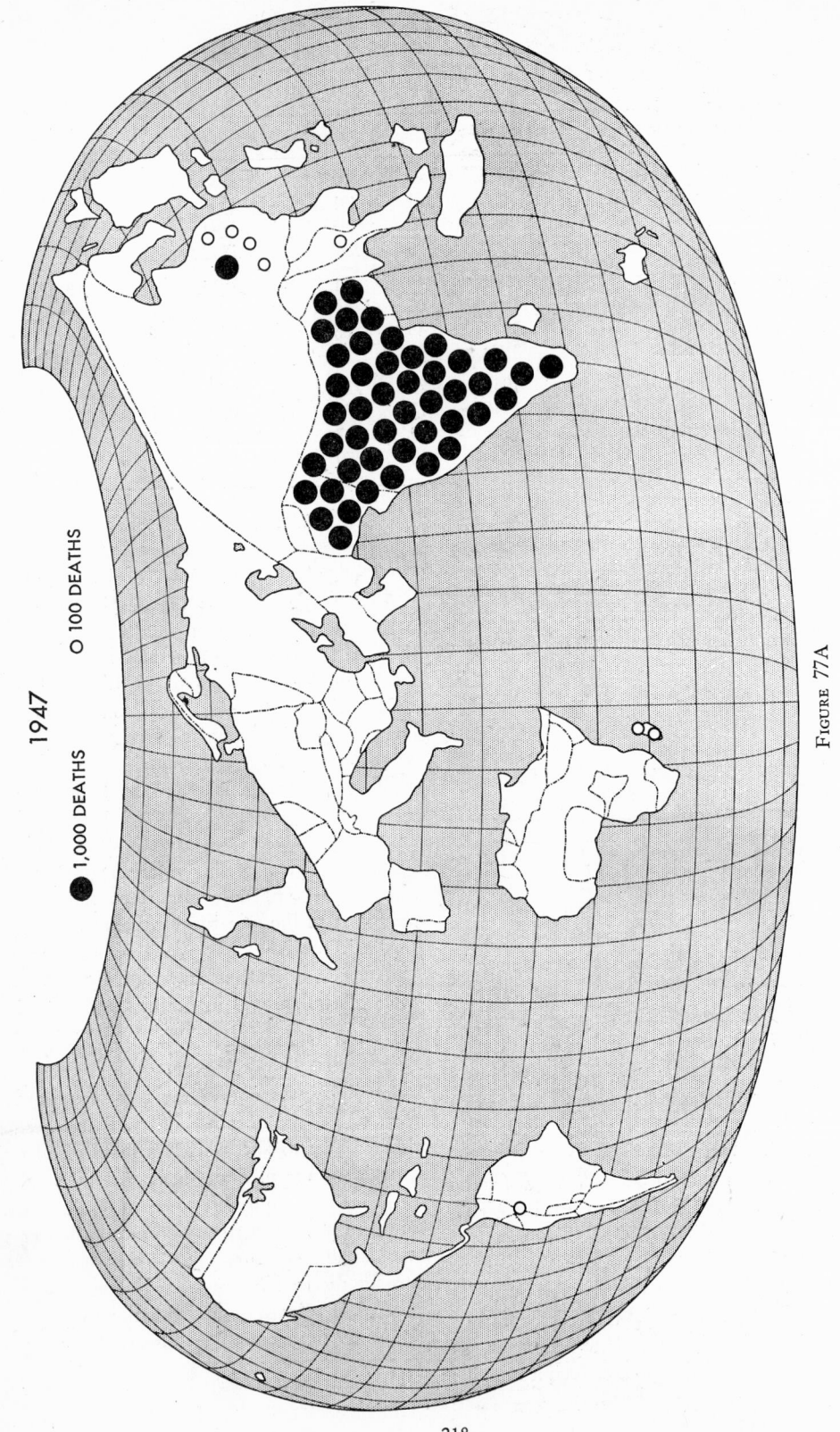

1947

● 1,000 DEATHS

○ 100 DEATHS

Figure 77A

218

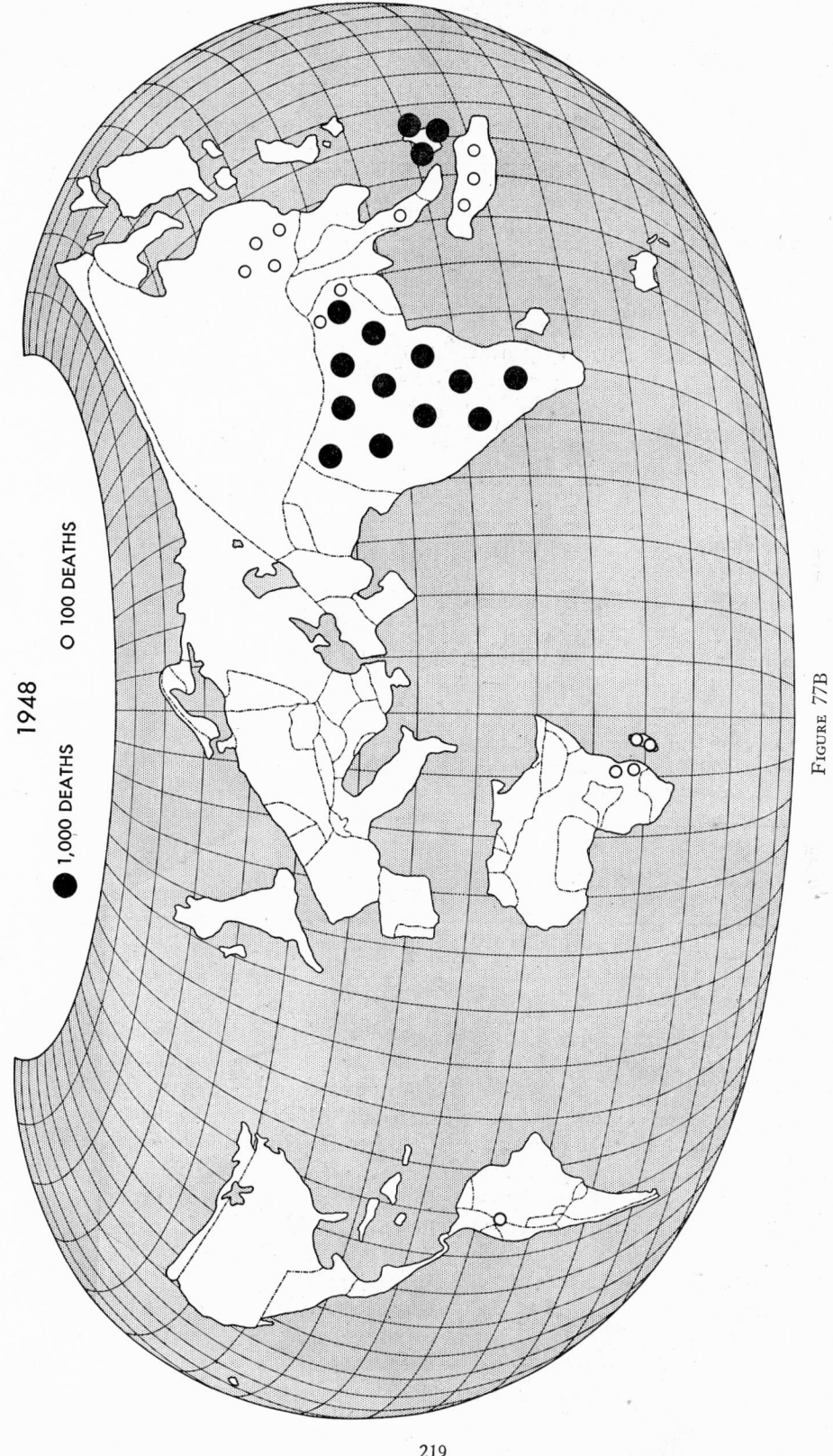

1948

● 1,000 DEATHS   ○ 100 DEATHS

FIGURE 77B

FIGURE 77. QUARANTINED DISEASES: PREVALENCE OF PLAGUE IN THE WORLD, 1947 AND 1948

Continents and countries are shown on these maps on the scale of population in 1950. The dots indicate the regions suffering from plague and the number of deaths but not the focal sites of the epidemic.

TABLE 113

QUARANTINED DISEASES: CHOLERA, CASES AND DEATHS IN SELECTED COUNTRIES, 1946–48

Country	1946		1947		1948	
	Cases	Deaths	Cases	Deaths	Cases	Deaths
Indian Union	}138,864	76,352{	89,890	45,356	214,232	108,738
Pakistan			10,572	3,979	43,527	24,006
Indian States	10,874	5,507	4,200	1,400	...	...
Burma	2,675	2,327	674	508	49	29
China	54,193	15,466	...	...	...	...
Hong Kong	514	227	6	0	0	0
South Korea	15,748	...	...	...	...	...
Indochina	1,539	1,120	1,737	1,227	1,942	1,217
Malayan Union	213	169	0	0	0	0
Thailand	6,303	4,382	3,282	2,023	33	15
Japan	1,318	...	...	...	0	0
Ceylon	73	37	...	...	0	0
Syria	...	...	45	18	0	0
Egypt	...	...	20,808	10,276	0	0

Source: **5,** December 1947, pp. 153–54, July–August 1950, pp. 202–03.

regions that fail to protect themselves against it by immunization. It occurs in Asia, Africa and South America and is kept out of Europe and North America by quarantine and compulsory vaccination.

The number of cases and deaths varies widely from year to year. There were outbreaks in many countries at the end of World War II. (See Table 114.)

UNCONQUERED DISEASES

While man has learned to protect himself against the communicable and environmental diseases, he has been less successful in his fight against the major ailments that strike people in middle age and old age.

Cancer and Diseases of the Heart

The increasing prevalence of cancer and heart diseases has been partly due to the increase in the proportion of aged persons in the population. Increase in the reported deaths from these diseases may also be due to improvement in diagnosis. The highest rates are recorded in industrially developed countries with low over-all death rates, low infant mortality and a high proportion of aged persons.

In Great Britain, Norway, Denmark, Germany and Austria the death rate from all forms of cancer approaches 200 per 100,000 inhabitants.

It is close to 150 in the Netherlands and Switzerland, and fluctuates around 135 per 100,000 in the United States. (See Table 115; cf. Table 103.) The rate is much lower in primarily agricultural countries.

All in all, cancer accounts for 12 to 15 per cent of all deaths in industrial countries and for less than 5 per cent of deaths in underdeveloped areas. Mortality from cancer is usually higher among women than among men and particularly high after the age of 50.

The pattern of mortality from diseases of the heart is similar to that from cancer, but the toll from these diseases is still higher, especially in advanced age. Diseases of the heart, including angina pectoris and arteriosclerosis, account for approximately a third of all deaths in the United States.

An international survey of mortality from cancer and diseases of the heart prepared by the United States National Office of Vital Statistics, shows the highest death rates in the United Kingdom and other industrial nations of western Europe, the United States, Australia and New Zealand, and the lowest rates in Egypt, Mexico, Venezuela, Colombia, El Salvador, Peru, Guatemala, Ceylon. (See Figure 78.) Unlike tuberculosis and acute contagious diseases, cancer and diseases of the heart are typical ailments of prosperous, industrially developed countries.

Similar is the pattern of death rates from can-

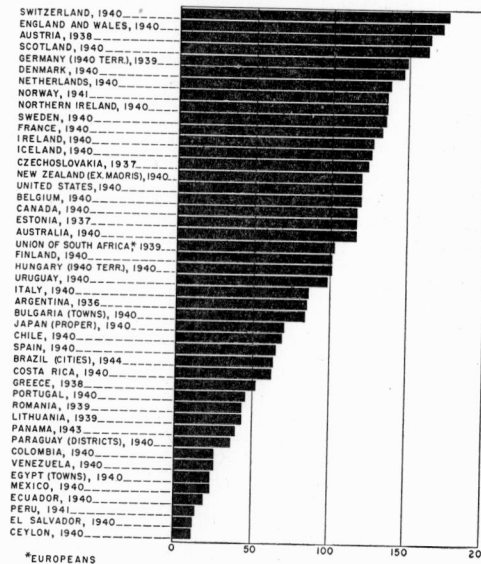

A. DEATHS FROM CANCER PER 100,000 INHABITANTS

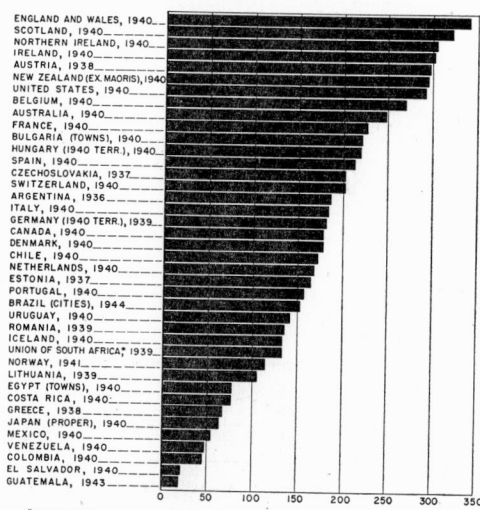

B. DEATHS FROM HEART DISEASES PER 100,000 INHABITANTS

*EUROPEANS

U.S. Public Health Service, Federal Security Agency

FIGURE 78. UNCONQUERED DISEASES: DEATH RATES FROM CANCER AND DISEASES OF THE HEART, IN SELECTED COUNTRIES, AROUND 1940

The countries with the lowest death rates from communicable diseases head the lists in death rates from cancer and heart ailments. The success of progressive countries in reducing mortality in childhood and youth and in preventing communicable diseases increases the chances of death from other causes, especially from those that prevail in middle and old age. (Cf. **13,** pp. 40 and 46.)

cer and diseases of the heart by region and individual state in the United States. Within the United States, the highest death rates from both

groups of diseases are recorded in New England and the North Atlantic states: [27]

	Cancer (Per 100,000)	Diseases of the Heart (Per 100,000)
New Hampshire	184.3	431.0
Massachusetts	183.0	440.3
New York	179.4	433.8
Connecticut	173.5	358.7
Vermont	166.1	392.3
Average	177.3	411.2

The lowest mortality is in the southeastern and southern Mountain states:

	Cancer (Per 100,000)	Diseases of the Heart (Per 100,000)
Arizona	86.6	202.3
Utah	84.3	236.7
New Mexico	77.9	161.3
South Carolina	75.5	232.7
North Carolina	75.2	211.9
Average	79.9	209.0

The regions with high death rates from cancer and diseases of the heart differ from those with low death rates in geographic location, climatic conditions, density of population, age composition of the population, the degree of urbanization and industrialization, and the general level of economic development. It is difficult, however, to appraise the impact of each single factor.

Poliomyelitis

Little is known about the world incidence of poliomyelitis (infantile paralysis) and the causes of its epidemic outbreaks. Few cases are reported outside North America and Europe.[28] The United States alone accounts for more than half of all cases recorded in the world. In recent years Iceland has had the highest number of cases per 100,000 inhabitants, followed, with a wide margin, by Sweden, the United States, Australia, Switzerland, Great Britain, Denmark and Norway — all countries with high standards of health services, comparatively favorable health conditions, low mortality and long life expectancy. (See Table 116.)

It would be natural to suspect that the difference is in diagnosis and reporting of poliomyelitis, but this hypothesis is in contradiction

27. **6,** 1950, p. 75.
28. **5,** January 1950, pp. 3–18.

TABLE 114

QUARANTINED DISEASES: SMALLPOX, CASES AND DEATHS IN SELECTED COUNTRIES, 1946–48

Country	1946		1947		1948	
	Cases	*Deaths*	*Cases*	*Deaths*	*Cases*	*Deaths*
United States	337	24	173	...	65	...
Mexico	600	561	1,123	545	...	...
Venezuela	1,819	13	5,965	110	5,280	143
Colombia	...	...	3,989	44	6,356	89
Ecuador	91	1	2,672	27	3,869	237
Peru	691	...	523	...	4,340	...
Paraguay	0	0	807	2	113	2
England and Wales	...	...	94	...	0	...
France	10	...	51	4	1	0
Portugal	...	100	...	52	...	22
Italy	772	...	44	...	9	...
China	20,562	2,593	18,393	3,462	...	...
Japan	17,800	2,823	391	38	36	1
Hong Kong	1,988	1,305	252	149	8	2
Syria	...	...	11	...	894	...
Iraq	...	...	64	16	1,740	155
Iran	114	24	849	238	1,182	195
Indian Union	} 123,033	26,849	57,773	13,695 {	62,363	17,296
Pakistan					12,453	4,094
Indian States	...	...	10,946	3,432	10,489	2,569
Burma	3,897	1,293	2,894	1,190	4,127	1,298
Indochina	...	...	5,092	1,981	4,283	1,352
Malaya	...	...	4,600	1,000	...	...
Indonesia	3	...	0	0	0	0
Algeria	565	...	533	...	422	...
Egypt	416	56	172	10	...	...
Sudan	55	2	953	173	1,464	265
French West Africa	6,721	607	2,472	254	...	...
Belgian Congo	4,122	14	2,756	13	2,969	15
Gold Coast	1,572	311	852	169	...	...
Nigeria	8,298	1,049	5,354	946	...	...
Tanganyika	12,671	1,935	...	...	1,204	206
Nyasaland	944	...	2,562	212	4,787	590

Sources: **5,** July 1947, pp. 30–33; April 1949, pp. 81–86.

to the fact that the disease is very rare in such countries as France, Belgium and the Netherlands. The rates for Iceland are far out of line with those for other countries. They appear plausible, however, when we realize that all other rates are computed for comparatively large areas that are only partly affected by the polio epidemic while Iceland has a population of only 140,000 concentrated in a small area. Since this area was a focus of the epidemic the rates computed for it are similar to those that would be obtained for a county or an even smaller area invaded by the disease. Such rates may readily

be 20 or 30 times higher than the national average in a large country.

The incidence of polio within the United States is likewise puzzling. In 1947 an epidemic broke out in Idaho and Delaware; in 1948 South Dakota and North Carolina were struck; in 1949 the main foci included Idaho, North and South Dakota, Colorado, Nebraska, Oklahoma and Maine. (See Figure 79.) On the other hand, the Deep South, New York and Pennsylvania have been comparatively safe in recent years. Thus the disease does not appear to be associated with poverty and unsatisfactory sanitary conditions or

TABLE 115

UNCONQUERED DISEASES: CANCER, DEATH RATES IN SELECTED COUNTRIES, 1861–70 TO 1949

(Deaths Per 100,000 Inhabitants)

Country	1861–70	1881–85	1901–05	1920–25	1931–35	1940	1949
England and Wales	38.6	54.8	86.7	125.1	153.4	172.3	187.1
France	...	...	75.5 [b]	81.3	95.8	133.3	169.3
Belgium	33.5	...	62.0 [b]	78.9	114.5	119.9	126.0
Netherlands	51.4 [a]	60.4	97.4	113.0	124.3	138.2	140.5
Denmark	94.7 [a]	103.9	127.6	141.7	145.0	147.4	198.1
Norway	34.8 [a]	49.2	94.8	108.6	139.7	136.2	212.7
Germany	...	59.7 [c]	77.6	103.4	139.4	149.2	186.4
Switzerland	...	102.8	128.3	139.3	153.5	176.0	163.2
Austria	39.0 [a]	44.8	74.3	134.0	170.2	164.2	202.0
Hungary	...	...	42.5	77.7	105.4	101.3	...
Spain	...	...	44.4	62.0	68.4	65.3	71.2
Italy	...	...	50.9	66.9	77.1	86.2	59.5
Japan	...	...	53.6	70.7	69.5	70.9	...
Australia	...	...	66.5	90.7	105.7	116.8	...

Sources: For 1861–70 to 1931–35, **20**, 1938, p. 263; for 1940, **13**, p. 46; for 1949, **5**.
   a. 1871–80.   b. 1906–10.   c. 1891–96.

TABLE 116

UNCONQUERED DISEASES: INCIDENCE OF POLIOMYELITIS IN THE WORLD, 1947–49

Country	Number of Reported Cases			Reported Cases Per 100,000 Inhabitants		
	1947	1948	1949	1947	1948	1949
United States	10,241	27,677	42,382	7.1	18.9	28.4
Canada	2,298	1,158	2,363	17.4	8.6	17.5
Mexico	212	65	586 [a]	0.9	0.3	...
Brazil [b]	106	97	79	0.2	0.2	...
Argentina	239	269	352 [c]	1.5	1.6	...
England and Wales	7,791	1,859	5,969	18.1	4.3	13.7
France	1,119	667	1,957	2.8	1.6	4.7
Belgium	239	144	183	3.5	1.7	2.1
Netherlands	693	81	150	7.2	0.8	1.6
Denmark	505	935	323	12.2	22.3	7.6
Sweden	1,499	826	2,584	22.0	12.0	37.1
Norway	684	509	119	21.8	16.0	3.7
Finland	228	98	341	5.9	2.5	6.0
Western Germany	4,511	5,709	2,159	9.5	11.9	4.5
Poland	282	219	112	...	...	...
Czechoslovakia	715	2,391	528	5.9	19.4	4.2
Switzerland	755	544	658	16.6	11.8	14.1
Austria	3,508	1,066	786	50.7	15.3	11.1
Spain	488	330	513	1.8	1.2	2.1
Italy	2,276	2,583	2,233 [a]	5.0	5.7	5.8
Yugoslavia	126	126	171	0.8	0.8	1.1
Bulgaria	215	190	110	3.1	2.7	1.5
Greece	17	146	261	0.2	2.1	3.3
Iceland	200	535	579 [a]	142.0	381.0	413.6 [a]
Japan	...	980	3,133	...	1.2	3.8
Union of South Africa	75	2,276	304	0.6	18.8	2.5
Australia	326	570	1,638	4.1	7.3	20.7
New Zealand	130	915	354	7.2	48.3	18.6

Source: **5**, January 1950, pp. 12 and 20–25.
   a. For ten months.   b. Twenty-two cities.   c. For nine months.

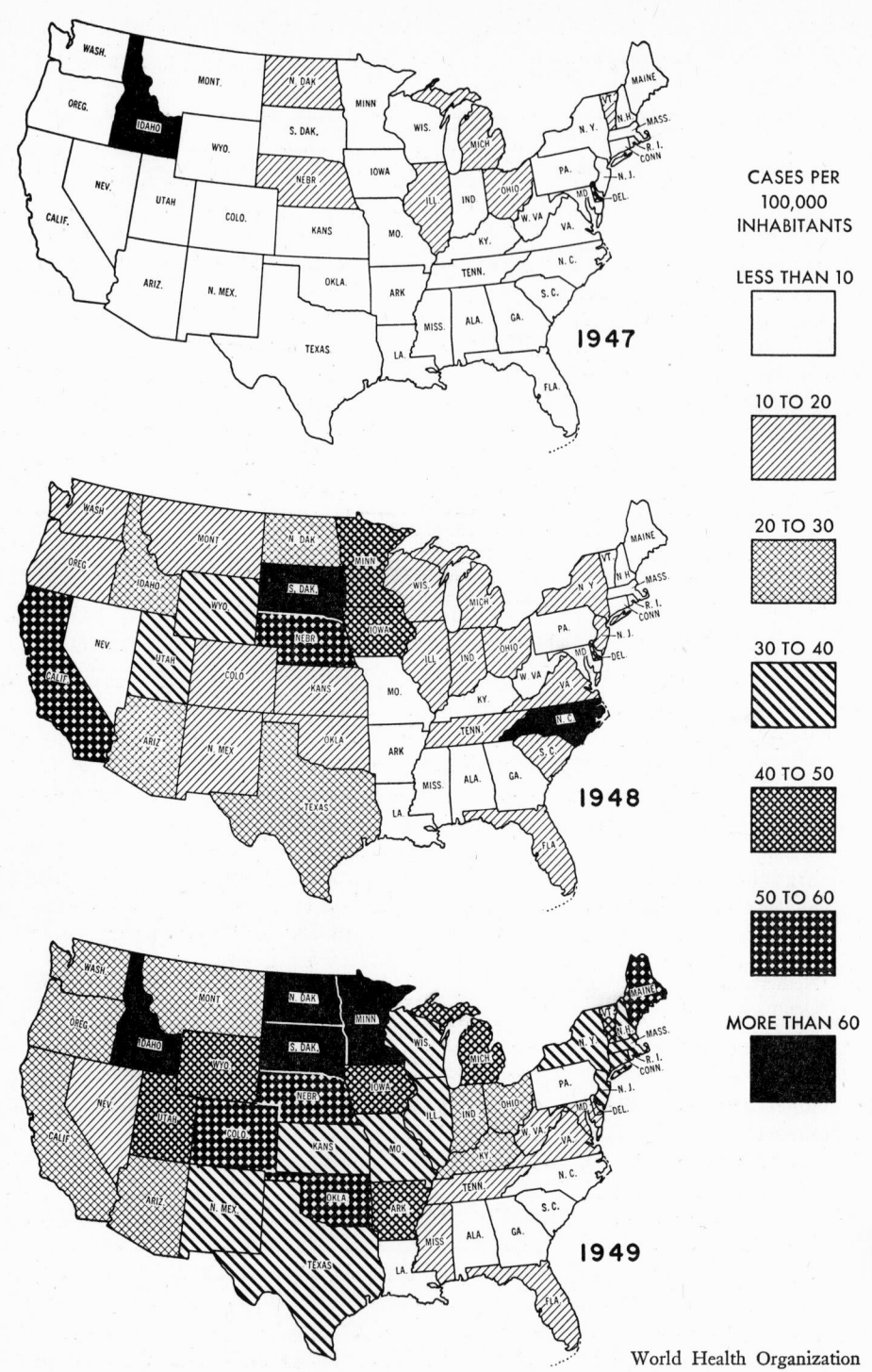

CASES PER
100,000
INHABITANTS

LESS THAN 10

10 TO 20

20 TO 30

30 TO 40

40 TO 50

50 TO 60

MORE THAN 60

1947

1948

1949

World Health Organization

FIGURE 79. UNCONQUERED DISEASES: INCIDENCE OF POLIOMYELITIS IN THE UNITED STATES, BY STATE, 1947–49

with density of population and industrialization.

The World Health Organization, in its 1950 report on the incidence of poliomyelitis in the world, emphasizes that extremely little is known about this disease compared with what is still to be learned.[29]

Mental Diseases

The number of mental and epileptic patients under medical observation is growing in the orbit of Western civilization. In the United States more than 550,000 persons are hospitalized in institutions for mental diseases, another 130,000 are in institutions for mental defectives and epileptics and nearly 100,000 on the books — on parole or in family care or otherwise absent from the institution. The total for the United States thus approaches 780,000 — or 5.2 per 1,000 inhabitants — more than for all other disabling diseases combined. Furthermore, the number of patients in mental hospitals in the United States has been increasing continuously for the past twenty or twenty-five years at a rate of 10,000 to 12,000 a year.

This trend does not necessarily reflect an increasing prevalence of mental disorder in the nation. The number of cases of mental disorders may have increased as a result of aging of the population and the strain of modern urban life, but the number of institutionalized patients has been controlled less by the number of people who needed hospitalization than by the available facilities. With increasing facilities and improved methods of diagnosis, more people suffering from mental diseases can be removed from their homes and institutionalized. The opposition of families to institutional care has weakened with the improvement of hospitals.

The United Kingdom recorded 168,669 persons of unsound mind in 1948, of whom 165,909 were in institutions. In addition, 113,000 mentally defective persons were "notified" in England and Wales and Scotland under Mental Deficiency Acts, but this registration is not complete.[30] Not counting such gaps in registration, the United Kingdom had 5.6 persons of unsound or defective mind per 1,000 inhabitants, a higher rate than in the United States.

The relatively smaller number of mental patients in some other countries does not necessarily mean less mental disease than in the United States and Great Britain.

VIOLENT AND ACCIDENTAL DEATH

The world has had little success in modern times in preventing accidental deaths, and no decline has been recorded in the rate of suicide. In England and Wales, France, Norway and the Netherlands the death rate from accidents in 1940 was double that at the beginning of this century. (See Table 117.)

The United States ranks among the countries with the highest death rates from accidents. In the 1930's, 35,000 persons died each year as a result of automobile accidents. Shortage of gasoline and curtailment of motor traffic reduced the number of accidents during the war, so that almost 50,000 fewer persons died in the five war years from this cause than would have been expected. The total rate of death due to accidents (including automobile collisions) is surprisingly constant: it was 72.3 per 100,000 in 1900, 71.0 in 1920, and 73.4 in 1940. As traffic deaths have increased, other causes of accidental death have declined.

The suicide rate varies widely from country to country. In France, Belgium and Denmark it is three times as high as in Norway, Spain and Italy. Contrary to widespread opinion, there is no close correlation between the number of suicides and industrial progress or urbanization. The number of suicides rises in some countries and declines in others, following divergent and little-known trends.

INCREASE IN STATURE

General improvement in health has resulted in progressive increases in human stature in the past century. Numerous studies in almost every country in Europe and in Japan have indicated increases in the average height of school children and college students.[31] In view of the great variety in the groups selected for measurement, an international comparison of findings of these studies is hardly possible. It appears, however, that in all countries children and college students of the same ages have become appreciably taller from generation to generation and from decade to decade.

In the United States, for example, school children aged 10 averaged 139.8 centimeters in 1927

29. **5**, January 1950, p. 3.
30. **22**, pp. 40–41.

31. **47**, pp. 264–69.

TABLE 117

ACCIDENTS AND SUICIDES: DEATH RATES IN SELECTED COUNTRIES, 1881–85 TO 1940

(Deaths Per 100,000 Inhabitants)

	Accidents				Suicides			
Country	1881–85	1901–05	1920–25	1940	1881–85	1901–05	1920–25	1940
United States [a]	...	72.3	71.0	73.4	...	10.2	10.2	14.3
England and Wales	58.7	49.0	34.9	106.6	7.5	10.1	9.9	11.3
France	...	47.7 [b]	49.3	98.4	...	21.7 [b]	18.8	18.7
Belgium	36.4	32.3	34.8	49.8	10.5	12.4	13.3	18.3
Netherlands	39.8	31.5	28.2	87.2	5.3	6.4	6.4	10.8
Denmark	...	24.1	27.5	34.2	25.9	22.7	14.0	17.7
Norway	56.8	40.6	37.1	110.2	6.8	5.5	5.6	6.9
Germany	...	40.3	43.1	50.0 [c]	...	22.2	22.1	28.4 [c]
Switzerland	62.0	64.2	55.0	53.5	23.5	23.0	23.1	23.6
Austria	31.7	32.3	38.2	31.8 [c]	16.4	17.3	26.1	44.1 [c]
Hungary	...	45.4	42.6	32.2	...	17.8	27.4	24.7
Spain	...	38.5	28.7	129.0	...	2.2	5.6	6.1
Italy	40.4 [d]	38.0	37.5	33.8	4.8	6.3	8.5	5.9
Japan	...	43.0	56.4	39.5	...	13.2	19.6	13.8
Australia	...	67.5	50.6	56.3	...	12.5	11.1	10.6

Sources: For 1940, **13**, pp. 174–89; for earlier periods, **20**, 1938, pp. 266–67.

    a. Data for 1900, 1920 and 1940 (cf. Table 103).

    b. 1906–10.   c. 1938.   d. 1886–90.

as compared with 130.7 centimeters in 1879. At age 17, the comparable figures were 175.5 centimeters and 167.2 centimeters, and at 18, 176.7 centimeters and 169.5 centimeters.[32] Students at Harvard University showed a similar increase, from an average height of 172.9 centimeters in 1856–65 to 178.0 centimeters in 1906–15 — a rise of more than a centimeter a decade.[33]

The findings for adults, especially conscripts, are equally striking. In Switzerland, for example, the average height of conscripts increased from 155.5 centimeters in 1792–99 to 165 centimeters in 1861–72.[34] In Sweden it rose from 169.2 centimeters in 1887–90 to 172 centimeters in 1911–16 [35] and gained an additional three centimeters from 1916–20 to 1946.[36] In the Netherlands the average height of 19-year-old conscripts rose from 164.1 centimeters in 1863–67 to 170.8 centimeters in 1921–25.[37] In Japan the average stature of college students increased from 159.8 centimeters in 1909 to 162.5 centimeters in

1918.[38] Similar data are available for Germany, Denmark, Norway, Italy, Spain and other countries.

While increase in height seems to have been a world-wide phenomenon in the nineteenth century and the first half of the twentieth, there are significant exceptions. French statistics, for example, reveal no consistent increase in the stature of conscripts: the average was 164.7 centimeters in 1886–90 and 165.0 centimeters in 1922.[39]

All in all, apart from racial differentials, it seems fairly probable that the average stature of adult persons in modern countries has increased by one to two inches in the past century as a result of general improvement of health. The gain for school children has been much larger. Physical development in childhood has been accelerated by better nutrition, the elimination of many childhood diseases and the virtual abolition of child labor.

FACILITIES FOR MEDICAL CARE

The quality of medical service in a community depends on the availability of a sufficient number of well-trained physicians, together with auxil-

32. **47**, p. 266.

33. **28**, p. 25. Data for 1836–45 and 1846–55 are excluded from the comparison because they refer to a small group of individuals.

34. **28**, p. 36.

35. **28**, p. 34.

36. **26**, 1947, p. 78.

37. **28**, p. 35.

38. **28**, p. 40.

39. No data for more recent years have been published. **20**, 1946, p. 25.

TABLE 118

FACILITIES FOR MEDICAL CARE: NUMBER OF PHYSICIANS IN THE UNITED STATES, 1886–1950

Year	Number	Per 10,000 Inhabitants	Year	Number	Per 10,000 Inhabitants	Year	Number	Per 10,000 Inhabitants
1886	87,521	15.1	1912	137,199	14.4	1934	161,359	12.8
1890	100,180	15.9	1914	142,332	14.6	1936	165,163	12.9
1893	103,090	15.4	1916	145,241	14.2	1938	169,628	13.1
1896	104,554	14.8	1918	146,174	14.0	1940	175,163	12.9
1898	115,524	14.7	1921	145,404	13.4	1942	180,496	13.2
1900	119,749	15.7	1923	149,966	13.4	1948	199,755	13.9
1902	123,196	15.6	1925	147,010	12.7	1949	201,277	13.5
1904	128,950	15.7	1927	149,521	12.6	1950	209,040	13.7
1906	134,688	15.8	1929	152,503	12.5			
1909	133,487	14.8	1931	156,339	12.6			

Source: **33,** August 21, 1948, May 26, 1951, and other issues.

iary personnel and such facilities as hospitals, laboratories, medical supplies. The effectiveness of medical service depends also on economic circumstances, such as nutrition and housing conditions, density of population, means of transportation and communication and the capacity of the people to pay for the medical care they need.

DOCTORS AND DENTISTS

The same number of practitioners can give good service to a larger number of persons in a populous, well-developed community than in a poor and thinly populated country. Thus a doctor can serve more people today than he could half a century ago or in the more remote past.[40] On the other hand, because of the increasing demand for specialized medical services, a community now requires more physicians than it would need if it were satisfied with the services of general practitioners.

The physician-population ratio alone does not therefore reflect the adequacy of potential medical services. The United States, for example, had 15 doctors to each 10,000 inhabitants in 1886, 16 in 1900, 14 in 1916, and somewhat less than 14 in 1950, but there is no doubt that the population is better provided with medical services now than it was sixty-five years ago. The Netherlands had 8 doctors per 10,000 inhabitants in 1850 and 7 in 1940. At the beginning of the nineteenth century, Prussia, Bavaria and Saxony had more physicians per 10,000 inhabitants than

Germany had in 1938. Many "doctors" in the first half of the nineteenth century were trained only in dressing wounds and rendering first aid.[41] Even if these so-called doctors are excluded, the training of physicians and the organization of medical services in the nineteenth century are not comparable with those of our time.

Similar differences still exist among individual countries. It is obvious that a region with one physician per 10,000 inhabitants is poorly provided with medical service, but it is not clear whether adequate service requires 7–9 doctors per 10,000 inhabitants, as in Sweden, Norway, France, the Netherlands and Switzerland; or 13–14, as in the United States. What is an adequate ratio changes with customs, with the standards of preventive medicine, the availability of hospitals and other medical facilities, the organization of medical services in schools, the prevalence of disease, and so on. "Because of the seemingly cyclic movement [in the physician-population ratio], it is difficult to conclude precisely whether at present there is a movement toward a larger number of persons per physician or in the reverse direction," remarks the Bureau of Medical Economics of the American Medical Association.[42] This contention is substantiated by variations in the number of physicians in the United States since 1886. (See Table 118.)

An upward trend in the physician-population ratio prevailed before World War II in most

---

40. **27,** p. 7.

41. **36,** pp. 539 ff.; cf. **55,** p. 329.
42. **27,** p. 9.

Table 119

Facilities for Medical Care: Trends in Practitioner-Population Ratio in Selected
Countries, 1850–1950 [a]

(*Physicians and Dentists Per 10,000 Inhabitants*)

Country	1850	1860	1870	1880	1890	1900	1910	1920	1930	Around 1940	Around 1950
France											
Physicians	...	...	4.4	3.9	3.9	3.9	5.3	5.3	6.1	6.3	7.6
Dentists	...	...	...	...	...	0.4	0.7	0.9	1.4	...	2.4
Belgium											
Physicians	4.3	4.0	4.0	3.9	4.4	5.3	5.7	5.7	6.0	7.9	11.2
Netherlands											
Physicians	8.0	7.1	6.3	4.7	4.4	4.5	5.0	5.1	...	} 8.1	6.9
Dentists	0.2	0.2	0.2	0.2	0.2	0.3	0.4	0.6	...		1.4
Sweden											
Physicians	...	1.2	1.3	1.2	1.7	2.2	2.3	2.8	3.6	4.7	6.9
Dentists	...	...	...	...	...	0.5	0.7	1.1	1.9	3.5	4.5
Norway											
Physicians	...	...	2.4	2.9	3.5	5.0	5.3	5.0	7.0	8.1	9.6
Dentists	...	...	0.1	0.2	0.5	0.9	2.0	2.2	4.5	5.3	4.9
Germany											
Physicians	...	...	...	3.2	3.4	4.6	4.8	...	} 7.4	6.2	...
Dentists	...	...	...	...	...	0.2	0.4	...		1.7	..

Sources: **55**, pp. 330–31; and official publications of the respective countries; for the most recent data, **3**, 1951, pp. 544–45.

a. Dates approximate.

European countries, but some of them had gone through long periods — in some cases several decades — with a stable or declining ratio. Increase in the relative number of dentists has been more continuous and rapid. (See Table 119.)

The number of medical practitioners in a country may be affected by the policy of the government and of the medical profession. The number may be limited by restriction of medical education and in licensing policy or, when considered necessary, it can be increased in a comparatively short time by accelerating training of medical students, as in the USSR in the 1920's and in almost all countries during the war. During World War II, India announced a plan to increase its supply of doctors from 30,000 to 300,000.[43]

Before the war, there was more than one physician per 1,000 population in the United States, Argentina, the United Kingdom, Austria, Switzerland and New Zealand. The ratio of one doctor per 10,000 inhabitants was common in underdeveloped countries such as Haiti, Guatemala, Honduras, Korea, Manchuria, India and Burma. A few Asiatic countries (China, Thailand and Indonesia) had only one doctor per 30,000 or more inhabitants. In China, according to the most recent information available, only 13,447 doctors, 371 dentists, 952 pharmacists and 5,000 midwives were available to a population of 450 million.[44] In Tibet, a country with a population of 4 million, modern medicine was represented by 4 physicians trained in medical schools in India.[45]

43. **33**, September 25, 1944. The latter number would not be excessive in a country the size of India, especially with the means of transportation and health conditions existing there. The training of an additional 270,000 physicians is a difficult and expensive proposition, however, and can hardly be completed in a decade or two unless a large part of the additional medical personnel

consists of doctors' assistants assigned to work under the general supervision of doctors.

44. These figures represent the "cumulative number" of persons in these professions registered up to December 1946. (**19**, p. 121.) The current number of practicing physicians must be appreciably lower.

45. Tibet has a Medical College in Lhasa, with a

TABLE 120

FACILITIES FOR MEDICAL CARE: NUMBER OF PHYSICIANS IN SELECTED COUNTRIES, AROUND 1940

Country	Number of Physicians	Per 10,000 Inhabitants	Country	Number of Physicians	Per 10,000 Inhabitants
North America			**Europe** (cont'd)		
United States	169,628	12.9	Czechoslovakia	11,251	7.7
Canada	7,500	6.6	Latvia	1,560	7.8
Middle America			Switzerland	7,125	17.0
Mexico	2,250	1.2	Hungary	13,274	14.2
Guatemala	365	1.1	Portugal	3,200	4.2
El Salvador	310	1.7	Spain	22,582	8.8
Honduras	130	1.2	Italy	38,983	8.9
Nicaragua	299	3.0	Yugoslavia	4,754	3.0
Costa Rica	190	3.1	Romania	8,408	6.3
Panama	144	1.3	Bulgaria	3,127	5.0
Cuba	3,100	7.2	Albania	160	1.5
Haiti	300	0.9	Greece	6,000	8.2
Dominican Republic	425	2.5	**USSR**	130,000	7.6
South America			**Asia**		
Venezuela	1,749	4.7	China	12,018	0.3
Colombia	2,997	3.3	Korea	2,906	1.2
Ecuador	793	2.6	Japan	65,000	9.0
Brazil	8,693	2.1	Manchuria	4,300	1.0
Peru	1,343	1.9	Taiwan	1,983	3.3
Bolivia	569	1.7	Turkey	1,500	0.8
Paraguay	340	3.4	Jordan	24	0.8
Chile	3,350	6.7	Saudi Arabia	50	0.1
Uruguay	1,615	7.3	India (before partition)	30,000	0.8
Argentina	16,900	11.5	Burma	1,521	1.0
Europe			Thailand	200	0.1
United Kingdom	51,539	10.6	Malaya	767	1.5
France	26,004	6.3	Philippines	4,209	2.5
Belgium	6,682	7.9	Java and Madoera	849	0.2
Netherlands	6,284	8.1	Sumatra	1,139	1.4
Denmark	3,252	8.6	**Africa**		
Sweden	3,024	4.7	Union of South Africa	4,461	4.3
Norway	2,351	8.1	**Oceania**		
Finland	1,296	3.5	Australia	6,464	9.2
Germany	49,907	7.4	New Zealand	1,804	11.3
Poland	13,600	3.9			

Sources: Data on the number of physicians in the United States from Table 118; for Germany, **21**, 1938, pp. 568–69; for other countries, from memoranda prepared during the war by the U.S. War Department. For the USSR, cf. **37**. Population data from **2**, 1948, pp. 98–105.

All in all, there were more than 800,000, perhaps as many as 850,000, doctors in the world in 1940, of whom more than 20 per cent were in the United States. (See Table 120.)

course of eight years, spent mainly in memorizing long incantations and spells. Like the medicine men of primitive tribes, Tibetan lama physicians have some knowledge of the medicinal value of certain herbs but rely more on such concoctions as the urine and excreta of the Dalai and Panchhan lamas. (**53**, pp. 229–30.)

This estimate, however, is open to criticism. Countries do not use the same methods of enumerating physicians and the concept of a physician varies widely from country to country. Only for countries on similar levels of economic development are the reported figures more or less comparable.

Another necessary reservation is that in most countries — among others, the United States —

TABLE 121

FACILITIES FOR MEDICAL CARE: NUMBER OF PHYSICIANS IN SELECTED COUNTRIES, AROUND 1950

Country	Number of Physicians	Per 10,000 Inhab- itants	Country	Number of Physicians	Per 10,000 Inhab- itants
North America			Asia (continued)		
United States	202,277	13.5	Indonesia	1,101	0.2
Canada	14,596	11.1	North Borneo	18	0.5
Greenland	16	7.1	Ryukyu Islands	212	10.0
Middle America			Africa		
Mexico	3,671	1.4	Morocco	718	0.8
Guatemala	408	1.1	Algeria	1,499	1.3
Jamaica	225	1.7	Tunisia	565	1.7
Puerto Rico	729	3.4	Egypt	4,135	2.4
			British Somaliland	9	0.1
South America			French West Africa	908	0.5
British Guiana	91	2.3	French Equatorial Africa	122	0.3
Surinam	66	3.6	Belgian Congo	441	0.4
Europe			Gold Coast	119	0.3
France [a]	25,663	6.2	Nigeria	342	0.1
Belgium	8,110	9.1	British Cameroon	15	0.2
Netherlands	7,000	7.1	French Cameroon	116	0.4
Denmark	4,120	10.0	Kenya	285	0.5
Sweden	4,354	6.2	Uganda	211	0.4
Norway [b]	2,811	9.1	Ruanda-Urundi	63	0.2
Finland	1,869	4.9	Tanganyika	266	0.4
Poland	7,869	3.3	Nyasaland	89	0.4
Switzerland	5,846	12.5	Mozambique	110	0.2
Austria	10,760	15.4	Madagascar	375	0.9
Portugal	5,675	6.7	Angola	129	0.3
Asia			Northern Rhodesia	116	0.7
Japan	65,301	8.3	Bechuanaland	14	0.5
Hong Kong	421	2.3	Union of South Africa	4,502	4.0
Turkey	2,617	1.3	Oceania		
Cyprus	355	7.7	Australia [c]	4,773	6.2
Lebanon	816	6.7	New Zealand	2,235	12.5
Indochina	390	0.1	Hawaii	492	9.1
Ceylon	537	0.8	New Guinea	20	0.2
Federation of Malaya	682	1.4	American Samoa	8	4.5
Singapore	210	2.2			

Source: Computed from **3**, 1949–50, pp. 478–85.

  a. 1943.   b. 1946.   c. 1945–46.

the reported number refers to the persons who hold official licenses to practice medicine rather than to the number actually in practice. Only 80 per cent of licensed physicians in the United States are in actual practice. On the other hand, medical services are often offered to the public by persons without an official license.

The Statistical Office of the United Nations attempted to assemble data on medical personnel and hospital beds throughout the world, especially in colonial areas. Because of differences

in definition and methods, these data are not strictly comparable with those in Table 120. For colonial areas and underdeveloped countries they include native doctors with a diploma of lower degree, many of whom work as medical assistants in public institutions, but do not include nurses and midwives.

According to these data, industrially developed countries usually have from 6 to 12.5 physicians per 10,000 inhabitants (in round numbers, a population of 800 to 1,700 per physician). A

TABLE 122

FACILITIES FOR MEDICAL CARE: NUMBER OF HOSPITALS AND BEDS IN THE UNITED STATES,
1909–50

Year	Total		Federal		State		All Other	
	Hospitals	Beds, in Thousands	Hospitals	Beds, in Thousands	Hospitals	Beds, in Thousands	Hospitals	Beds, in Thousands
1909	4,359	421	71	9	232	189	4,056	223
1918	5,323	612	110	19	303	262	4,910	331
1928	6,852	893	294	62	595	370	5,963	461
1938	6,166	1,161	330	92	523	541	5,313	528
1939	6,226	1,195	329	96	523	561	5,374	538
1940	6,291	1,226	336	109	521	572	5,434	545
1941	6,358	1,324	428	179	530	600	5,400	545
1942	6,345	1,384	474	221	530	606	5,341	556
1943	6,655	1,649	827	477	531	610	5,297	562
1944	6,611	1,730	798	551	539	609	5,274	570
1945	6,511	1,739	705	546	549	620	5,257	573
1946	6,280	1,469	464	264	557	628	5,259	576
1947	6,276	1,425	401	213	563	627	5,312	585
1948	6,335	1,424	372	185	567	648	5,396	590
1949	6,572	1,439	361	182	573	657	5,638	600
1950	6,430	1,457	355	187	552	665	5,523	605

Source: **33,** May 12, 1951, p. 110.

similar rate prevails in Greenland, Japan, the Ryukyu Islands, Hawaii and a few other colonial areas. Ratios of 1 to 2 physicians per 10,000 inhabitants prevail in Middle and South America while many less developed countries have only 1 to 2 physicians per 100,000 inhabitants. (See Table 121.)

With a reservation for the partial comparability of the available data, it seems that the world as a whole must now have more than 900,000 doctors — on the average, 4 doctors per 10,000 inhabitants. This world-wide rate is not very meaningful, however. Actually, only a fourth of mankind is amply provided with potential medical service, another fourth has only a scanty opportunity to get medical service, and one half has practically no opportunity at all.

HOSPITALS

Comparison of medical facilities in various countries is particularly difficult. The best single measurement is the number of hospital beds, but statistics of some countries segregate general hospitals from mental hospitals and special institutions, while in other countries all hospitals, mental institutions, sanatoriums, isolation wards, and convalescent and rest homes are counted together. Likewise, some countries report all med-ical institutions, others only those that meet certain standards or are under public supervision.[46]

In the United States the number of hospital beds per 1,000 inhabitants increased from 5 in 1909 to 9 in 1938, jumped to 12 during World War II, and declined slightly thereafter. The capacity of federal hospitals more than doubled during the last war, but has since declined to almost the prewar level. (See Table 122.)

Nearly half of all hospital capacity in the United States is in mental hospitals, most of them operated by state and local governments. In 1949 there were 5 beds per 1,000 population in hospitals for nervous and mental diseases, 4 beds in general hospitals, and one bed in other medical institutions. (See Table 123.) In relation to population the United States has about the same number of beds in general hospitals as other countries with well-developed medical facilities, such as Canada, Sweden, prewar Germany, France and Australia, but it has an exceptionally large number of beds for nervous and mental diseases and epilepsy.

In general hospitals, the turnover of patients and the seasonal fluctuation in illness make it

46. In the United States, for example, only bed capacity of registered hospitals which have 25 beds or more is recorded.

TABLE 123

FACILITIES FOR MEDICAL CARE: NUMBER OF HOSPITALS AND BEDS IN THE UNITED STATES BY TYPE OF
SERVICE AND AGENCY, 1949

Agency	Total		General Hospitals		Mental		Tuberculosis		Special and Institutions	
	Hos- pitals	Beds, in Thou- sands	Hos- pitals	Beds, in Thou- sands	Hos- pitals	Beds, in Thou- sands	Hos- pitals	Beds, in Thou- sands	Hos- pitals	Beds, in Thou- sands
All agencies	6,430	1,457	4,713	588	579	712	431	86	707	71
Federal	355	187	268	108	38	64	25	11	24	4
State	552	665	56	21	280	602	84	27	132	15
County and city	1,005	185	675	102	42	26	214	38	74	19
Church and nonprofit	3,169	369	2,663	320	65	11	84	9	357	29
Private	1,349	51	1,051	37	154	9	24	1	120	4

Source: **33**, May 6, 1950, pp. 26–27.

impossible to use all the hospital beds at all times. In the United States, 20 to 25 per cent of all hospital beds are vacant, on the average, although there are acute shortages of beds and urgent need for new hospitals in certain localities. The average number of patients represents about 70–75 per cent of bed capacity in general hospitals and nearly 95 per cent in mental institutions. On the other hand, the total number of patients admitted to general hospitals during a year amounts to 15 to 20 times their bed capacity or 20 to 30 times the average number of patients in a single day, while the annual number of admissions to mental hospitals is usually less than a third of the number of beds.

In 1949 more than 16 million persons were admitted to hospitals of all types in the United States, a rate of 11 admissions per 100 inhabitants. This rate is not exceptionally high in comparison with the experience of other countries.

Hospital facilities in underdeveloped countries are pathetically inadequate. In 1946, China had 2,958 hospitals, with a total capacity of 19,200 beds, an average of 6.5 beds per hospital and one bed per 23,000 inhabitants. Few of these hospitals would be registered as such in the United States.

FACILITIES IN RICH AND POOR COMMUNITIES

Medical facilities are often distributed almost as unevenly within a nation as in the world as a whole. Not infrequently, the capital and the

large cities in a country have modern hospitals and clinics while smaller cities and rural areas have only rudimentary medical facilities. This pattern is particularly characteristic of eastern Europe and South and Middle America, but medical facilities are unequally distributed nearly everywhere.

In the United States there is a direct relationship between the relative wealth of a state and the health services available to its population. New York State has 48 general-hospital beds and 20 physicians per 10,000 population, as compared with Mississippi's 19 beds and 7 physicians per 10,000. In Massachusetts, 97.2 per cent, and in Connecticut, 98.9 per cent, of all births occur in hospitals, and virtually all the rest are at least attended by a physician. In South Carolina, in contrast, only 49.7 per cent of all births are in hospitals, 20.8 per cent are attended by a doctor outside a hospital, and 29.5 per cent are attended only by a midwife or unspecified other person.[47] (See Table 124.)

Speaking in 1947 before the Annual Congress on Medical Education and Licensure of the American Medical Association, Surgeon General Thomas Parran pointed out that 40 per cent of the counties were still without a registered hospital, 81 counties had no active physician, and 141 counties had only one active physician for more than 5,000 inhabitants.[48] On the basis of

47. **12**, pp. 63–64.
48. **33**, April 12, 1947, p. 1047.

TABLE 124

FACILITIES FOR MEDICAL CARE: HEALTH SERVICES IN THE UNITED STATES, BY STATE, 1940

State [a]	Per Capita Income, 1946	General-Hospital Beds Per 1,000 Population, 1946 [b]	Days of Hospital Care Per Capita, 1946 [b]	Population Per Physician, 1940	Population Per Dentist, 1940	Percentage of Births in Hospitals, 1946	Infant Deaths Per 1,000 Live Births, 1946	Maternal Deaths Per 1,000 Live Births, 1946
Nevada	$1,703	4.8	1.27	660	2,004	96.1	39.6	1.8
New York	1,633	4.8	1.42	496	1,314	96.9	29.1	1.2
District of Columbia	1,569	5.4	1.52	296	1,337	94.9	41.2	1.7
California	1,531	3.6	1.02	580	1,268	97.1	30.7	1.2
New Jersey	1,494	3.9	1.05	716	1,547	95.4	28.5	1.3
Delaware	1,493	4.3	1.12	786	2,538	88.7	29.7	1.3
Illinois	1,486	3.9	1.13	648	1,323	93.2	30.4	1.4
Connecticut	1,465	3.9	1.13	658	1,575	98.9	27.8	.9
Montana	1,394	6.1	1.72	1,048	2,020	96.6	34.8	1.4
Massachusetts	1,356	5.1	1.38	547	1,530	97.2	31.6	1.3
Rhode Island	1,347	4.0	1.15	742	1,892	95.2	29.5	1.4
Washington	1,346	3.9	1.11	790	1,376	98.2	33.4	1.1
Ohio	1,302	3.0	.85	741	1,831	89.6	31.3	1.3
Maryland	1,293	4.2	1.18	609	2,086	80.7	34.0	1.1
Wyoming	1,264	3.4	.82	915	2,022	93.0	33.1	1.6
Idaho	1,243	3.6	.89	1,241	2,441	96.5	32.9	1.6
Pennsylvania	1,238	4.1	1.16	732	1,664	88.1	33.0	1.5
South Dakota	1,228	4.0	1.18	1,266	2,122	90.0	29.6	1.0
Michigan	1,215	4.2	1.06	826	1,978	93.4	32.7	1.2
Wisconsin	1,198	3.9	1.13	891	1,484	94.0	30.0	1.4
Colorado	1,196	4.9	1.31	572	1,687	87.8	40.0	1.9
Oregon	1,188	3.3	.93	745	1,305	98.0	27.7	1.0
Iowa	1,183	3.0	.90	823	1,564	92.2	29.9	1.1
Nebraska	1,164	3.8	1.07	805	1,430	90.9	30.2	1.0
North Dakota	1,162	4.8	1.34	1,239	2,450	90.9	34.0	1.0
Indiana	1,158	2.8	.79	830	1,890	87.3	31.5	1.3
Missouri	1,143	3.5	1.02	714	1,651	78.2	33.0	1.6
Minnesota	1,090	4.5	1.34	792	1,344	95.2	28.6	.9
Vermont	1,085	3.8	1.09	687	2,363	88.5	34.0	1.4
Utah	1,063	3.6	.87	957	1,798	96.1	27.2	1.4
Kansas	1,062	3.4	.98	870	1,776	90.3	30.6	1.5
New Hampshire	1,048	4.5	1.16	749	2,194	96.5	31.4	1.3
Maine	1,044	3.3	.91	854	2,241	86.9	41.0	1.6
Florida	1,010	2.9	.71	834	2,646	73.4	39.4	3.0
Arizona	995	3.7	.86	841	3,242	85.3	41.5	2.1
Texas	954	2.5	.64	930	3,179	72.3	41.7	1.6
Virginia	952	2.9	.79	927	3,173	65.3	38.7	1.6
West Virginia	914	3.3	.88	1,037	3,186	54.4	40.9	1.5
New Mexico	911	2.6	.64	1,211	4,665	61.6	78.2	2.0
Tennessee	843	2.3	.64	1,003	3,455	60.7	38.5	1.8
Oklahoma	825	2.4	.60	993	3,140	77.7	32.5	1.6
North Carolina	817	2.7 *	.74	1,304	4,533	61.6	37.2	2.0
Georgia	809	2.5	.62	1,106	3,786	59.6	35.9	2.6
Louisiana	784	3.5	.85	959	3,000	71.2	37.2	2.0
Kentucky	778	2.3	.61	1,031	3,575	50.7	40.0	2.0
Alabama	733	2.2	.49	1,365	4,683	49.2	37.9	2.6
South Carolina	729	2.5	.65	1,355	5,263	49.7	41.4	2.7
Arkansas	697	1.8	.46	1,066	5,077	53.6	28.3	2.1
Mississippi	555	1.9	.44	1,459	5,212	38.6	37.5	3.1

Source: **8**, p. 65.

a. States arrayed by per capita income.
b. Federal hospitals excluded.

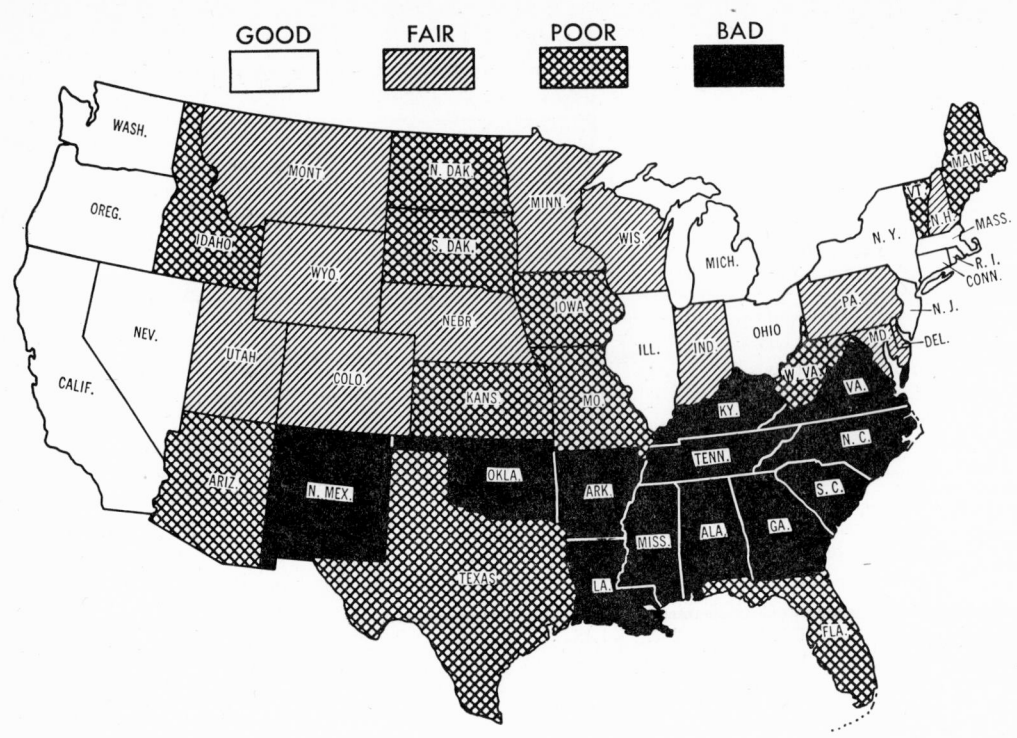

GOOD   FAIR   POOR   BAD

Research Council for Economic Security

FIGURE 80. DISTRIBUTION OF STATES IN THE UNITED STATES BY HEALTH CONDITIONS, 1946

The regional character of the health problem in the United States is illustrated by a classification of states by the combination of several factors such as education, sanitation, recreation, housing, economic conditions, public health practices.

According to the Research Council for Economic Security, health conditions are "good" in a dozen states, including Massachusetts, Connecticut, New York, Ohio, Michigan, Illinois and California, and "bad" in a dozen states in the South. In the rest of the nation they range from "poor" to "fair." (**41**; cf. Table 124.)

such factors as education, sanitation, recreation facilities, housing conditions, per capita national income, public health practice and so on, the Research Council for Economic Security has classified the states by their standing in health, as shown in Figure 80.

ECONOMIC LOSSES AND COSTS OF ILLNESS

Despite the improvement in health, even the most progressive countries still suffer severe losses through sickness, disability and death that could be avoided. The record of the United States in the fight against disease is one of the best, yet the health of the nation is still far from satisfactory.

Prevalence of Disability

In the United States, 7 million persons are disabled on an average day of the year, among

them 1,250,000 persons normally engaged in gainful pursuits and perhaps twice as many who would be in the labor force, except for physical injury, mental disorders, or disabling chronic disease.[49] These figures imply that illness and disability reduce the available labor force of the country by approximately 6 per cent.

Losses caused by illness are much higher in countries plagued by such diseases as malaria, hookworm, typhoid and paratyphoid fevers.

Incidence of Illness

The burden of illness and disability is distributed unevenly among the population. Studies made in the early 1930's in the United States indicated that, in the course of a year, illness

---

49. Estimate for 1939, based on **8**, pp. 3–8. Cf. **42** and **41**.

TABLE 125

ECONOMIC COSTS OF ILLNESS: DURATION OF DISABLING ILLNESSES BY AGE, IN 83 CITIES IN THE UNITED STATES, 1935–36 [a]

| Diagnosis Group | Days of Disabling Illness Per Year Per Person in Age Group | | | | | Average Number of Days Per Disabling Illness |
	All Ages	Under 15	15–24	25–64	65 and Over	
All causes	9.83	5.93	5.31	10.26	35.44	57
Communicable diseases	.70	2.24	.28	.19	.15	23
Respiratory diseases	1.15	1.27	.67	1.11	2.54	23
Digestive diseases	.75	.22	.53	.91	1.96	59
Puerperal state —live births only	.33	—	.65	.41	—	24
Accidents	.75	.36	.51	.88	1.97	48
Tuberculosis, all forms	.32	.09	.34	.43	.20	243
Nervous and mental diseases	1.03	.43	.81	1.28	1.99	190
Rheumatism	.69	.08	.12	.79	4.12	124
Degenerative diseases	1.76	.24	.33	1.77	12.14	122
Orthopedic impairment	.89	.28	.38	.87	5.08	306
Other causes	1.46	.72	.70	1.62	5.28	75

Source: **10,** p. 193.

a. Represents all illnesses disabling for 7 days or more and all hospital cases, confinements and fatal cases.

will strike in a group of one million persons as follows: [50]

    470,000 will suffer no serious illness
    320,000 will be sick once
    140,000 will be sick twice
     50,000 will be sick three times
     20,000 will be sick four or more times

Each age is exposed to particular ailments: communicable diseases prevail among persons under 15 years, respiratory and digestive diseases in the age groups 25–64, degenerative diseases at higher ages. All in all, disease visits the old and the poor more frequently than the young and the well-to-do, and stays with them longer. In the large cities in the United States in 1935–36, for example, persons under 25 years suffered on the average less than 6 days of disabling illness per year, those in the age groups 25–64 years had more than 10 days of illness, and those aged 65 and over, more than 35 days. (See Table 125.) The average for the whole population was 9.9 days of disabling illness per year, but the rate varied with the economic level: 16 days for the recipients of public relief; 11.6 for persons with annual income of less than $1,000;

7.9 days for the income brackets from $1,000 to $1,500; and 6.9 days for the higher income levels. (See Table 126.)

Lives That Could Be Saved

Even in countries with modern resources for protecting health, illness causes tremendous losses in life and productive work that could be avoided if full use were made of present medical knowledge. In the United States, for example, as the Federal Security Administrator stated in his report to the President, "every year, 325,000 people die whom we have the knowledge and skills to save; every year the Nation loses 4,300,000 man-years of work through bad health; every year the Nation loses $27 billion in national wealth through sickness and partial and total disability." [51] The estimated annual number of preventable deaths includes 12,000 deaths from communicable diseases, 115,000 deaths from cancer and diseases of the heart, 40,000 fatal accidents and 50,000 other cases. [52] According to this estimate, by improving health and medical services the United States could reduce its death rate by more than a fifth.

50. **31,** p. 54.

51. **8,** p. 1. The figure $27 billion refers to 1947 when national income totaled $199 billion.
52. **8,** p. 1.

TABLE 126

ECONOMIC COSTS OF ILLNESS: DURATION OF DISABLING ILLNESSES BY FAMILY INCOME
GROUP AND AGE, IN 83 CITIES IN THE UNITED STATES, 1935–36

Income Group	Average Number of Days of Disabling Illness Per Person				
	All Ages	Under 15	15–24	25–64	65 and Over
All incomes	9.9	5.7	5.4	10.5	36.1
Relief	16.0	6.8	8.6	21.8	58.8
Less than $1,000	11.6	5.0	5.9	12.4	37.6
$1,000–$1,499	7.9	5.4	4.7	8.0	30.7
$1,500–$1,999	6.9	5.3	4.2	6.8	26.7
$2,000–$2,999	6.9	5.7	3.6	6.6	27.0
$3,000–$4,999	6.6	5.8	3.4	6.4	22.8
$5,000 or more	6.9	6.3	3.1	6.0	24.6

Source: **10**, p. 194.

Wage Loss and Sickness Costs

A nation's sickness bill includes the losses in earnings and production caused by permanent and temporary disability, the decline in efficiency of workers due to partial disability and poor health, and public and private outlays for medical care and health services. For the United States the bill probably runs to 16–18 per cent of national income,[53] distributed as follows:

Total	16.0–18.0
A. Losses in earnings and production	10.0–12.0
Temporary disability of gainful workers	2.0
Permanent disability of potential workers	4.0
Diminished efficiency caused by partial disability or poor health	4.0–6.0
B. Expenditures for medical and health services	6.0
Consumer expenditures	5.0
Public expenditures	1.0

There are no strictly comparable international statistics in this field. Some countries spend less than 6 per cent of national income on health and medical services and others spend more. It is also probable that nations with only rudimentary public health service and meager resources for medical care lose a larger part of their potential income through sickness, invalidity and premature death. All in all, it seems that until a new, stronger and healthier human stock is developed, sickness will exact a toll of considerably more than a dime from every dollar's worth of potential product. It is left to nations to decide what part of this bill they will pay in cash, in money spent to prevent and care for sickness, and what part in kind, through disability, dependency and suffering.

HEALTH INSURANCE

The toll that sickness exacts from society is particularly oppressive because of the way in which the burden falls. By and large, the individual cannot predict when he will be sick or what his costs and losses will be. Since people with low incomes are sick more frequently and longer than the well-to-do, the poorer the household, the more medical services it needs. Even by spending a comparatively high percentage of its income for medical care, however, a poor family often cannot pay for adequate care. The poorer the family, the larger, on the average, is the percentage of income it spends on medical care and the smaller the amount of medical services it can buy for its money.[54] (See Table 127.)

Of course, a doctor does not charge a patient with an income under $500 the same fee he charges one with $10,000 or more, and low-income families in many places receive free medical services. Yet it is obvious that even in a rich country low-income groups cannot pay for the medical service they need, and families in comfortable circumstances may find it difficult to meet the costs of serious and prolonged illnesses.

---

53. Estimate for 1946–47, based mainly on **8**, **16** and **17**. The total does not include the losses resulting from premature (postponable) death.

54. **11**, **9**, **7**; cf. **46** and **44**.

TABLE 127

ECONOMIC COSTS OF ILLNESS: EXPENDITURES FOR MEDICAL CARE PER HOUSEHOLD, BY
INCOME CLASS, IN THE UNITED STATES, 1935–36 AND 1941–42

Income Class	Families of Two or More, 1935–36		Households, 1941–42	
	Amount	Percentage of Income	Amount	Percentage of Income
All classes	$64	4.0	. . .	. . .
Under $500	22	7.1	$26	7.9
$500–$750	29	4.7	} 39	5.1 {
$750–$1,000	28	4.3		
$1,000–$1,500	52	4.2	57	4.6
$1,500–$2,000	75	4.4	69	4.0
$2,000–$2,500	91	4.1	87	3.9
$2,500–$3,000	109	4.0	104	3.8
$3,000–$4,000	132	3.9	129	3.7
$4,000–$5,000	158	3.6	163	3.7
$5,000–$7,500	} 248	3.6 {	205	3.3
$7,500–$10,000			228	2.8
$10,000 and over	467	2.1	340	1.6

Sources: For 1935–36, **17**, pp. 5, 43; for 1941–42, **18**, pp. 20–21.

Inasmuch as society is vitally interested in the health of all its members, it is compelled to take the responsibility for providing medical services to groups that are unable to purchase them individually on a fee-for-service basis. As time goes on, free medical care for the indigent changes in form. It was provided in the past by the church, charity institutions, guilds or public authorities. In our democratic age, other ways to pay for medical care have been found in the form of health insurance.

The purpose of health insurance is to spread the costs and losses caused by sickness more equitably over the whole population. The insurance may be voluntary, like the Blue Cross and Blue Shield plans for hospitalization and medical care in the United States, or compulsory. It may be optional for certain groups of individuals but compulsory within each group in which the majority has decided to join an insurance plan, as in certain industrial medical insurance plans. Or it may be compulsory for certain income classes and occupational groups and optional for other groups. It may be voluntary but subsidized by the government and built up in such a way as to cover the large majority of the population, as in Sweden and Denmark. Or it may be compulsory for a minority of the population, as in primarily agricultural countries in which the program is restricted to factory workers. Furthermore, its scope can be nation-wide as in Great Britain and Australia, or local, as in Switzerland.

A comprehensive health insurance program covers sickness, maternity care and chronic invalidity and provides both cash benefits to offset loss of earnings and medical care to the insured persons and their dependents. In some countries, however, no medical services are accorded to dependents, and in others the program is restricted to cash sickness benefits. Coverage of the program, benefit provisions and methods of financing vary widely from country to country.[55]

Compulsory Health Insurance in the World

In one form or another, compulsory or quasi-compulsory health insurance programs are in effect in all European countries except Spain, in all South and Middle American countries, and in the USSR, Japan, Australia and New Zealand.[56]

All in all, compulsory health insurance exists in countries with a total population of more than 600 million, including all the industrially developed and prosperous countries of the Eastern Hemisphere and the comparatively poor agrarian countries of the Western Hemisphere. The list

55. **12**, pp. 62–104; **40**.
56. Cf. **40**.

of countries without compulsory health insurance (or with health insurance in a rudimentary form, as in the United States) includes the richest and poorest areas of the world. (See Figure 81.) The trend is toward widening the scope of collective responsibility in the field of health protection.

Health Insurance in the United States

The United States is the only great industrial country without a compulsory nation-wide program of health insurance or sickness benefits. Costs of sickness and medical service in the nation are met largely by consumers, except for mental disease, in which public medical care was instituted by the need for custody; tuberculosis and other communicable diseases that menace general public health; and the medical services provided for veterans.

There is ample evidence, however, of a shift of public opinion toward handling medical care as a predictable and insurable risk and collective responsibility. Four states (Rhode Island, California, New Jersey and New York) provide cash benefits during temporary sickness to workers insured under their unemployment insurance laws, and similar programs are pending before legislatures of eleven other states: Alabama, Arizona, Connecticut, Illinois, Maryland, Massachusetts, Montana, Minnesota, Nevada, New Hampshire and Pennsylvania.[57] Some 2 million additional persons are covered by provisions for cash sickness benefits under the Railroad Retirement program, and employees of the federal government are entitled to sick leave with pay under civil service regulations.

The state and federal plans are supplemented by industrial medical plans and welfare funds established by collective agreements.[58] Private insurance companies are also extending the operation of individual and group policies for hospitalization, medical care and cash indemnity. The Blue Cross and other group hospitalization plans have grown spectacularly in recent years; more than 30 million people are covered by insurance for hospital expenses. (See Table 128.)[59] The weakness of these plans, however,

57. **43**, pp. 3–4.
58. **45**.
59. Some of the items in Table 128 may be overstated and the totals may include duplication. To be insured against all the hazards of sickness an individual must have all four types of insurance shown in the table

TABLE 128

HEALTH INSURANCE: ESTIMATED NUMBER OF POLICIES PROVIDING INDEMNITY AGAINST MEDICAL COSTS AND ACCIDENTS, IN THE UNITED STATES, AS OF DECEMBER 31, 1949

(Thousands)

		Type of Policy	
Risk	*Total*	*Group Certificates*	*Individual Policies*
Hospital expense	32,426	17,697	14,729
Subscriber	17,050	8,500	8,550
Dependent	15,376	9,197	6,179
Surgical expense	24,905	15,590	9,315
Subscriber	13,755	8,396	5,359
Dependent	11,150	7,194	3,956
Medical expense	5,086	2,736	2,350
Subscriber	3,273	1,712	1,561
Dependent	1,813	1,024	789
Accidental death or dismemberment	12,769	6,669	6,100 [a]

Source: **56**, p. 207.

a. Estimated.

is that they are heavily concentrated in the rich, densely populated states. They repeat the general pattern of the distribution of medical services in the United States and in the world: insufficient facilities in the places and for the groups most urgently in need of care.

THE OUTLOOK FOR HEALTH

Man is approaching an important crossroads in his fight against death and disease. In the past century, and especially in the past fifty years, medical science has been branching out from its strongholds in western Europe and North America over all the world. Its advance has been marked by eradication of certain communicable diseases, lowering of death rates, especially infant mortality, and an increase in the average length of life. The trend has been toward better training of doctors and increase in the number of hospital beds. Further progress in this direction requires improvement of economic conditions in poor and underdeveloped countries, and must belong to the most inclusive plan of each type.

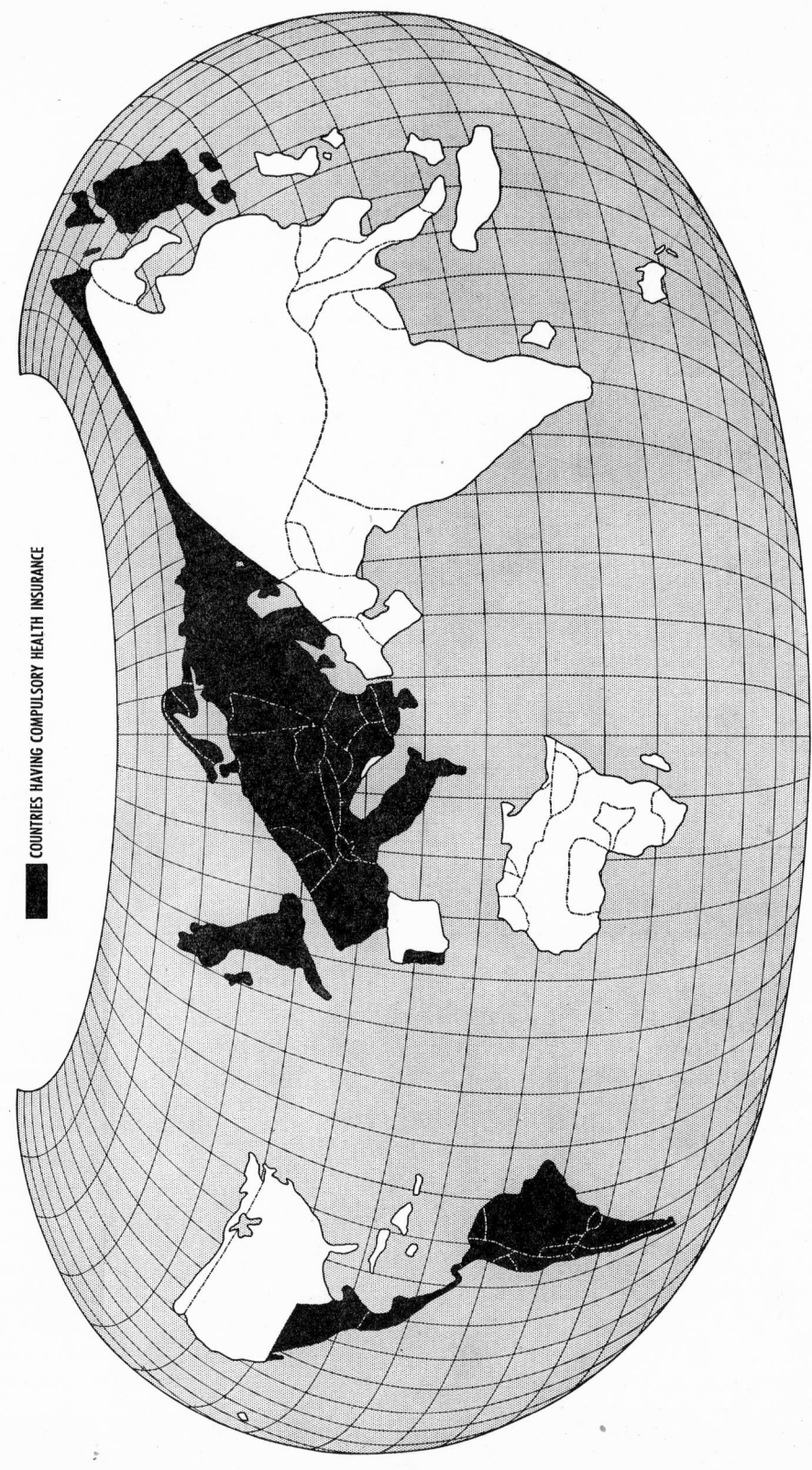

COUNTRIES HAVING COMPULSORY HEALTH INSURANCE

FIGURE 81. COMPULSORY HEALTH INSURANCE IN THE WORLD, AROUND 1948

The countries that have some form of compulsory health insurance are marked in solid black on this map. No attempt has been made to classify them by the coverage of their health insurance programs and the scope of the protection they give insured persons. There is a great difference, however, between the inclusive programs in Great Britain, the USSR and the Scandinavian countries, and programs in the Balkans and South America, which give only scant protection to comparatively small groups of workers.

which, in turn, presumes development of their latent resources and expansion of their industries. On the other hand, in the prosperous industrial countries further improvement of health conditions depends on better distribution and utilization of the available medical facilities and services. Thus health becomes increasingly an *economic* problem in underdeveloped regions and a *social* problem in industrial countries.

In still another respect, medical science has reached a crossroads. By bringing under control diseases of childhood and other communicable diseases, medicine has contributed to a substantial increase in the average length of life. But the advance in this direction meets a steady resistance: at the higher ages, formidable adversaries — cancer, diseases of the heart and mental disorders — challenge medical science. Complete practical eradication of the diseases that already have been conquered theoretically in clinics and laboratories might increase average life expectancy to 75 years, five years more than some countries have reached already. Then the progress of longevity will come to a standstill unless medical science successfully meets the challenge of the so-called degenerative diseases. Moreover, the task of reducing the suffering and waste caused by acute and chronic diseases is no less important than the further increase of the life span.

CHAPTER 7

THE FUTURE OF WORLD POPULATION

SINCE ANTIQUITY, men have been haunted by the two-edged fear of becoming too many to exist on the food and other resources available to them or too few to protect themselves and their resources against enemies. To adjust his numbers to his environment so that he could live what seemed to be the good life has always been one of man's major problems.[1] Greece was threatened by overpopulation in the time of Plato and Aristotle, and both of them considered control over the growth of population an important function of the ideal state. In the second century before the Christian era, however, Polybius wrote in his *Histories:* "All Greece suffers from the decline in births and shortage of men, so that its cities are becoming depopulated."[2] Similarly, the Roman republic was threatened by overpopulation until the third century B.C., but a few centuries later the fall in the birth rate had become a major issue of domestic policy.

In the search for means of increasing the number of workers and warriors without increasing the number of mouths to be fed, various customs have grown up, some designed to stimulate the growth of population, others to prevent overgrowth. Such considerations, which we would label population policy, probably have been responsible for many of mankind's contradictory regulations of marital and parental rights and duties.

Speculation on Future Population

Speculation on the future size of population dates from the seventeenth century. Petty, in his essays on political arithmetic, played with population projections into the future and with records of the past, back to the day when Noah with his family of seven walked down the gangplank of the Ark.[3] Realizing that the rule of geometrical progression — with a constant span of time for each redoubling of existing population — cannot be applied to long periods, he used gradually declining rates of population growth in his calculations but had no clear idea of the forces controlling long-range growth of population.

Malthus' Theory

Malthus offered a dramatic explanation of these forces. He believed that biologically a human community could double in from twenty to twenty-five years, but that actually its growth is checked by the available means of subsistence, that is, the food supply. Scarcity of food is therefore the force that limits the size of the population in any country at a given time. Practically, population growth is checked by war, famine, crime and misery.

In more modern terms, Malthus thought that the rate of population growth is controlled by economic forces. As long as the level of subsistence remains constant, population keeps pace with the production of food and other necessities. If the subsistence level rises and people demand more for themselves and their children, the increase of population must be slower than economic progress. Conversely, if because of "moral restraint," population growth is slower than economic progress — that is, if production rises more rapidly than population grows — the pressure of poverty must diminish.[4]

Few writers have left a deeper imprint on modern social science, and very few have provoked more vehement controversy. Malthus' ideas dominated the scientific study of population until the end of the nineteenth century, and it is still difficult to discuss the future of world population without thinking of his view of mankind's biological capacity for propagation and the slow and limited growth of means of subsistence.

Recent Trends

Whatever the forces were that checked population growth in the past, its increase in the orbit of Western civilization since the beginning

---

1. **32**, p. 6.
2. Quoted in **18**, pp. 45–50.
3. **25**, pp. 463–68.

4. **19**.

of the nineteenth century has been slowed down by factors other than war, famine and misery.[5] Population in the Western world has, indeed, increased with an unprecedented and growing speed but more slowly than the means of subsistence. More specifically in the last seventy or eighty years the most prosperous nations have been threatened more often by industrial and agricultural overproduction than by overpopulation.[6] The conclusion is unavoidable that the will to procreate has been tempered in modern Western nations by forces other than those described by Malthus.[7]

Nations without Youth

After World War I, the rapid decline in birth rates became a matter of serious public concern in Germany, France, Italy, Belgium and Great Britain. Although all except France still had a net surplus of births over deaths, the downward trend in the number of births in these nations threatened a decline in population in the near future. A similar prospect for all the Western world was clearly in sight. The situation seemed grave. The downward trend in the birth rate and future population was bound to reduce the military and political strength of these countries. Many people also believed that it would affect economic and social life adversely. Nations without youth would lose vitality, economic growth would slow down or stop completely, and the era of dynamism and progress would be followed by a long period of stagnation.

In the industrial countries both the public and the governments began to realize that these nations were threatened not only with a gradual decline in total population in the more or less remote future but with an almost immediate change in the composition of the population: first, a decline in the proportion of children, a decade later a decline in the proportion of young people, and so on, with a continuous increase in the relative number of the superannuated and

5. Where famine occurred — as in Ireland — it failed to check the growth of population.

6. **35**, pp. 15 ff.

7. One may stress that the main mistake of Malthus was in the underestimate of the potential growth of productive forces and the carrying capacity of land in modern times. This, however, is the central point of the whole controversy: If the growth of population tends to outrun the growth of production of food, Malthus is right; if the opposite tendency prevails, he was a false prophet.

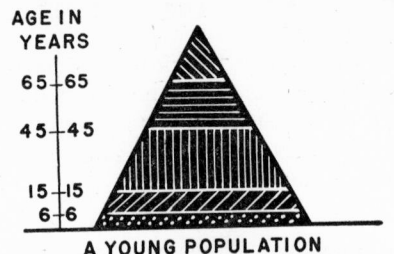

A YOUNG POPULATION

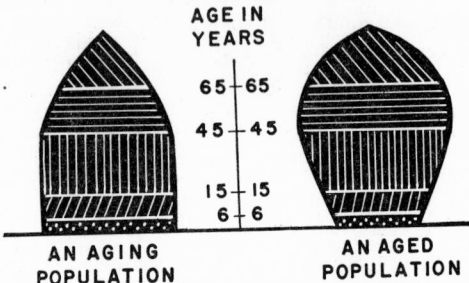

AN AGING POPULATION   **AN AGED POPULATION**

FIGURE 82. AGE STRUCTURE OF POPULATION: THREE BASIC TYPES

These three types of age pyramid characterize three phases of population growth. The regular pyramid (top) indicates a high proportion of children and a growing population. The narrow foundation and steep slopes of the pyramid (bottom, left) characterize a population that has ceased to grow. Further narrowing of the foundation, transforming the pyramid into a bulb (bottom, right), indicates the imminent danger of a decline of population. (Cf. **12**, p. 112.)

disabled. Imminent change in the type of the population pyramid ceased to be a statistical generalization and became a serious warning. (See Figure 82.)

Fiscal measures to encourage marriages and births became a cornerstone of population policy in fascist Italy and Nazi Germany. Similiar steps were taken in France and Belgium.[8]

The population trends in Asia and Africa, where Western medicine had succeeded in checking some of the most deadly diseases, added to the worries of Western nations. Mortality was rapidly falling in these areas while birth rates remained unchanged or decreased very slowly. An explosive growth in the population of Asia and Africa, similar to the nineteenth century growth of the European stock, was clearly in sight. Would the supply of food increase rapidly enough to meet the growing demand? Would overpopulation aggravate the misery in the poverty-stricken regions of the world? Would poverty add to the threat that the rapidly growing

8. **16**, pp. 72 ff. Cf. **17**.

Asiatic and African peoples present to the Western world?

These and similar questions have dominated the thinking on population problems in Europe and the United States in the last two or three decades and have generated rising interest in estimates of future population.

ESTIMATING FUTURE POPULATION

Population projections cannot be dismissed with the remark that they imply a wide margin of error and that in the final analysis no one knows what will happen in the future. Such projections are not intended as prophecies of the future; rather, they describe what is going on now and what is likely to result from these current developments provided they are not changed or blocked by new factors.

Three methods are used currently in estimating future population. They can be described in general terms as mathematical, statistical (or "component") and historical projections.

The Mathematical Approach

Projections of the mathematical type rest on the assumption that population grows in accordance with a definite mathematical formula that can be derived from past experience. The number of inhabitants might increase each year, for example, by the same number (arithmetical progression) or at the same rate (geometrical progression). The formula may allow for a decline in the rate of increase, as suggested by Petty, or treat increase as a temporary phenomenon that will be followed by a period of demographic equilibrium: gradual slowing down of population growth may be pictured by a geometrical progression in which the percentage increment drops gradually. From the mathematical point of view, however, this is a poor description; there are better formulas for expressing such a development, one of which is the "logistic" function.

Whatever the type of formula used for projection, it is agreed that it should be checked periodically and adjusted to the more recent information — for example, a new census — the general assumption being that the projection can be improved by "fitting" the curve without changing its mathematical form. The postulate that the form of the mathematical function representing past population growth will remain the same in the future is, of course, merely a working hypothesis: There is no theoretical or logical evidence in support of this assumption, just as there is no evidence that population growth can be properly described by any algebraic formula.

The Statistical Approach

Estimates of the second type, or "component projections," [9] are based on definite assumptions as to the future number of births and deaths. The example that follows explains this method.

Suppose that in 1952, soon after the release of the 1950 census data in the United States, we wish to estimate the probable population of the country in 1970. Everyone who will be 20 years old or more in 1970 had been born when the 1950 census was taken, but some persons enumerated in this census will have died by 1970. The first task is to estimate how many of the 1950 population are likely to survive the two decades. This estimate is obtained by applying, consecutively, definite mortality rates to each 5-year (or 10-year) age group of males and females recorded in the census.

The second task is to estimate the number of persons under 20 years of age in 1970, in other words, the number of survivors among those who will have been born between 1950 and 1970. This estimate requires a definite assumption about the future number of births.

This assumption can be established in different ways. For example, we may assume that the absolute annual number of births in coming years will be the same as the average in 1941–50 or 1946–50 or that the number will decline — or increase — according to some arbitrary rule.[10] Or we may start with definite assumptions as to changes in the size of families and compute the number of births accordingly, a procedure used for population projections in Great Britain. (See Figure 83.) American demographers prefer to work on the basis of assumptions for fertility in different age groups of women.[11] French demographers use assumptions for either fertility or reproduction rates.[12]

Essentially, all these procedures serve the same

---

9. **21**, pp. 200 ff.

10. Both methods were used in the alternative estimates of future population by the German Statistisches Reichsamt in the 1920's. (**12**, p. 135.)

11. Cf. **4, 5, 6, 7**; and **34**, pp. 9–20.

12. **8**; cf. **30**.

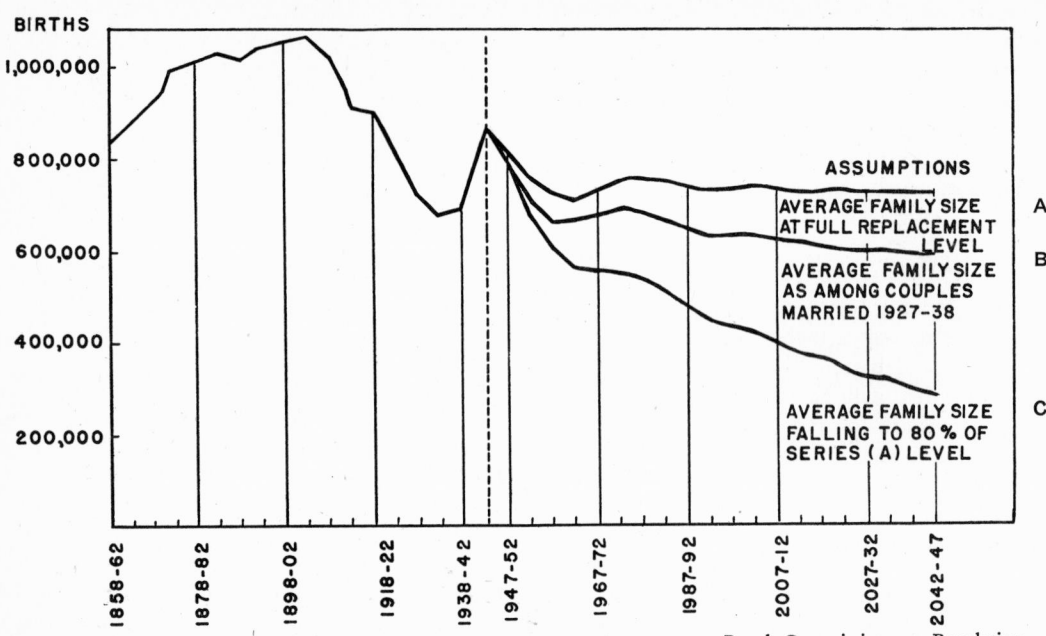

Royal Commission on Population

FIGURE 83. BIRTHS IN GREAT BRITAIN, 1858–1947, AND AS PROJECTED, 1947–2047, ON ALTERNATIVE ASSUMP-
TIONS OF SIZE OF FUTURE FAMILIES

The figure shows the three alternative assumptions about the size of family used by the British Royal Commission on Population in its estimates of annual births in Great Britain from 1947 to 2047. Each one of these hypotheses can be combined with the assumptions that the marriage rates will be the same as in 1942–47, that marriage rates will continue to decline from 1947 to 1977 at approximately the same rates as over the past fifty years,
and that there will be no net migration. (**10**, p. 81.)

purpose — to establish the anticipated or probable numbers of births in the years to come. It
then remains to estimate how many of the newborn will survive to the year 1970. This third
step in the estimate should employ definite assumptions as to mortality rates in these years
at ages under 20.

This procedure for estimating future population may be applied to the country as a whole
or to different segments — for example, to people in urban and rural areas or in different geographical regions, to white and colored people,
and so on.

Since the margin of error in such projections
depends on uncertainty as to the assumed numbers of births and deaths, alternative assumptions are often used for natality, mortality, the
number of marriages, the size of families, increase in urbanization, and other factors that
may affect population growth. These assumptions may be selected in such a way that the
range includes all conceivable patterns of development. The advantages of such a procedure
are questionable, however: If the span between

the low and high estimates of future population
is too wide, the projection becomes pointless.

The weakness of "component projections" is
that the method is necessarily restricted to countries with comprehensive statistics and cannot
be used for estimates for the world or the continents. On the other hand, it has two important
advantages: it makes clear the factors conditioning the alternative patterns of growth or decline
in a population, and it shows the age structure
associated with each pattern of population
development.

The Historical Approach

The "historical" approach considers the growth
of population as an aspect of the evolution of
mankind. Although historical events are not
subject to any rigid mathematical rule or natural
law, it is sound to assume that various countries
in the orbit of our civilization are passing
through the same population cycle and are now
in its various phases. The experience of the more
developed nations therefore casts light on what
is in store for other countries that follow them
on the road of industrialization.

The common feature of all three methods is that on the basis of experience and a definite appraisal of the current trends they offer a model of the probable future population changes. No projection pretends to be a prophecy, but each claims to portray what is likely to happen and each can be checked — *post factum* — by actual population growth or decline.

MATHEMATICAL PROJECTIONS

Among the many mathematical projections prepared in the past hundred years, probably the most interesting are one published in 1852 in New York by a retired merchant, Francis Bonynge; that developed in 1890 by a distinguished astronomer, Pritchett; and those offered in the 1920's by Raymond Pearl.

Francis Bonynge

In a pamphlet on the future wealth of America, Bonynge, who described himself as a retired merchant "for fourteen years a resident of India and West of China," ventured an estimate of the future population of the United States. Assuming definite annual rates of increase in the number of white persons, slaves and free colored persons, he concluded that the total population of the country would increase as follows (in millions): [13]

1850	23.3	1930	149.8
1860	30.9	1940	186.8
1870	39.9	1950	232.9
1880	49.7	1960	290.5
1890	61.9	1970	362.3
1900	77.3	1980	451.9
1910	96.4	1990	563.6
1920	120.2	2000	703.0

This projection (see Figure 84) almost exactly fitted the actual trend in the United States for more than eighty years but went astray after 1930. Bonynge was right in assuming a decline in the annual rate of population growth but he underestimated the progressive character of this decline.

H. S. Pritchett

In 1890, H. S. Pritchett, Professor of Mathematics and Astronomy at Washington University, offered "A Formula for Predicting the Popula-tion of the United States." Fitting a mathematical formula (a parabola of third degree) to census data from 1790 to 1890, he developed the following projection to A.D. 2900 (in millions): [14]

1890	62.6	1970	257.7
1900	77.5	1980	296.8
1910	94.7	1990	339.2
1920	114.4	2000	385.9
1930	136.9	2100	1,112.9
1940	162.3	2500	11,856.3
1950	190.7	2900	40,852.3
1960	222.1		

Pritchett was not overcome by the prospect that the population of the United States would rise to more than 40 billion in the next thousand years. He remarked:

These figures are suggestive, to say the least. With growth of population our civilization is becoming more and more complex, and the drafts upon the stored energy of the earth more enormous. As a consequence of all this, it would seem that life in the future must be subject to a constantly increasing stress, which will bring to the attention of individuals and nations economic questions which at our time seem very remote. [15]

In the light of subsequent experience, Pritchett's formula seems to fit the population trend up to 1930 more or less satisfactorily but it becomes utterly unrealistic after 2000.

Raymond Pearl

Pearl represents a school of thought that believes the growth of population follows the biological pattern: slow at the beginning, it proceeds at an accelerated pace until it reaches the maximum speed, then gradually slows down until an equilibrium is established between births and deaths. The assumption of this outcome may seem arbitrary at first sight. It appears plausible, however, if one bears in mind that the alternative is the increase of population ad infinitum, a growth that can be stopped only by some catastrophe or, as Sir William Petty put it, the world must of necessity come to an end. It can be argued, of course, that the contention that the growth of population will, sooner or later, slow down and come to a stop requires no demonstration by laboratory experiments with the growth of microorganisms.

---

13. **11**, p. viii.

14. **27**, p. 12.
15. **27**, p. 12.

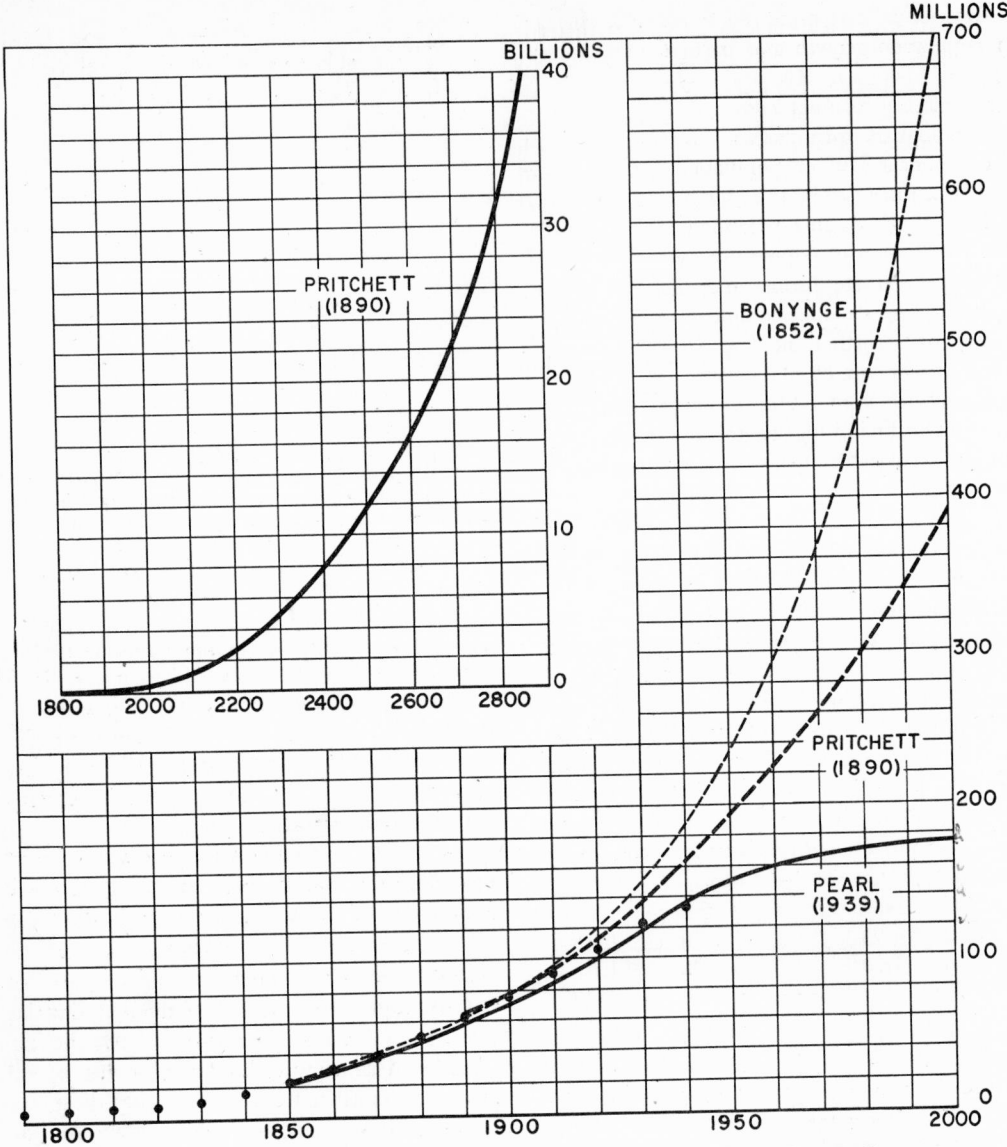

FIGURE 84. FUTURE POPULATION: MATHEMATICAL PROJECTIONS FOR THE UNITED STATES

(Francis Bonynge, H. S. Pritchett, Raymond Pearl)

This figure shows three mathematical projections of population in the United States to A.D. 2000. In the insert the Pritchett projection is carried to 2900. ·

The most recent of the projections, that made by Raymond Pearl in 1939, appears the most realistic. It fits almost exactly the actual growth of population in the United States up to 1950 and has a good chance of fitting the development in the next decade or two.

Raymond Pearl preferred to consider the law of population growth as a particular case of the general biological law and expressed it by a mathematical formula known as "logistic." [16]

The logistic formula was introduced as the mathematical law of population growth more than a century ago by the Dutch mathematician, P. F. Verhulst, as an expression of the contention that the growth of population *must* have a limit in a very remote future and that the rate of growth *must* decline as time goes on and obstacles to its further increase pile up. His arguments in support of this general law of population growth were perfectly sound, though his attempts to fit the logistic formula to the scanty population statistics at his disposal were not very successful.[17]

Moreover, the population statistics of Verhulst's time, the first half of the nineteenth century, provided no clue to aid him in expressing the anticipated leveling off of population growth in mathematical form. This could not be provided until population growth actually began to slow down. Many modern industrial countries seemed to have reached this point after World War I, and this was the time for revival of the "logistic" formula. Raymond Pearl, following a different line of thought from Verhulst's, applied this formula to the United States, selected states, several foreign countries, and the world as a whole.[18]

Pearl's latest projection for the United States so far has proved amazingly accurate: it deviated less than one per cent from the census

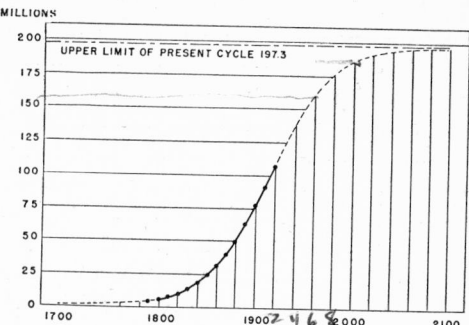

FIGURE 85. FUTURE POPULATION: PROJECTION FOR THE UNITED STATES

(Raymond Pearl's Logistic Curve)

Pearl's projection of population in the United States illustrates the use of the logistic curve. The curve starts from zero sometime before 1700, and is fitted to census data from 1790 to 1920. Projection into the future rests on the assumption that after 1914 the annual increment diminishes each year to the same extent that it rose in years preceding 1914. (**22**, p. 14.)

data for 1920 and 1930, appeared somewhat too high in 1940, and hit the bull's eye in 1950. For the future, it indicates that population in the United States will rise to 168 million in 1970 and to 185 million in 2000 and will be stabilized at approximately 197 million in the following century. (See Figure 85.)

For projections of world population, Pearl used the available estimates stretching from the middle of the seventeenth century to 1914. On this basis he concluded that the growth of the world's population would eventually stop at slightly more than 2 billion.[19] Actually, however, this figure had been exceeded by 1930. Consequently Pearl revised his formula for world population and developed a new logistic curve, reproduced in the upper panel of Figure 86. In this projection, the upper limit of world population is estimated at 2,645.5 million, 2.1 billion above the supposed number of inhabitants in the world in 1650, the year he considers the starting point of the present population cycle.[20]

For 1950 Pearl projected a world population of approximately 2,150 million, and for the year 2000, some 2,450 million. In the light of recent developments, both figures appear too low. World population had reached 2,400 million in

16. According to this formula, growth begins from zero or from a stable level. In the early phase it is slow, almost imperceptible, but it gains momentum as time goes on. Later the annual increment begins to decline. The decline is such that ten years after the turning point the annual increment is the same as it was ten years before that point; ten years later it returns to the pattern of twenty years before the turning point, and so on. Growth stops at such a level that the population at the time of the most rapid growth appears midway between the levels at which growth began and at which it stopped.

17. **33**. For criticism and further elaboration of Verhulst's formula see **15**.

18. Similarly, as there are all kinds of arithmetical and geometrical progressions and parabolas, logistic curves can be of different shapes. What they all have in common is the general form illustrated by the curve in Figure 85.

For the theory of the population logistic see **24**, 1920, pp. 275–86, and other papers presented by Raymond Pearl and Lowell J. Reed to the National Academy of Sciences (*Proceedings*, 1922, pp. 365–68, and 1925, pp. 16–22). For bibliography see **23**, pp. 384–85.

19. **22**, p. 172.

20. **23**, p. 258. Pearl estimated world population in 1650 not at 545 million (see Table 14) but at 445 million, so that in his logistic the span between population at the beginning and the end of the cycle was 2.2 billion.

1950,[21] and may reach 3,250 million by A.D. 2000.[22] Corrected so as to fit these points in 1950 and 2000, Pearl's curve would follow roughly the pattern indicated by the dotted curve in the lower panel in Figure 86 and the limit of growth of world population would be about 4 billion.[23]

The new logistic curve assumes that the growth of the population of the world will slow down after 1940, while Pearl's second projection erroneously postulated a diminishing rate of growth after the 1890's.

As Frank W. Notestein has pointed out, the rationale of logistic curves such as those plotted on Figures 85 and 86 is appropriate for many demographic situations, and they are useful as empirical descriptions of population growth although their predictive value is limited and their validity as laws of growth of population is not universally accepted.[24]

STATISTICAL PROJECTIONS

The statistical projections of population that have been made in a score of countries during the last twenty-five years have usually assumed constant birth and death rates. In the recent estimates, however, increasing attention has been paid to probable future changes in natality and mortality.[25] It has also become customary to use alternative assumptions for births and deaths. In some estimates these assumptions have been combined with alternative assumptions concerning net immigration or emigration in future years.[26]

As Notestein has pointed out, estimates of future population based on an appraisal of prevailing trends in birth and death rates have tended to flourish particularly in the countries of western and northern Europe where the decline in the birth rate has created an imminent threat of depopulation. The low estimates usually

signal the danger and tend to overemphasize the downward trend in birth rates. The high estimates stress possible improvement in natality and suggest that the danger can be overcome.

PROJECTIONS FOR SELECTED EUROPEAN COUNTRIES

Germany

One of the earliest official component projections of population was prepared by the German Statistisches Reichsamt on the basis of the 1925 census and birth and death statistics for 1927. The projection shows two possible trends: if Germany maintains the same annual number of births as in 1927, it will have about the same population in 2000 as in 1925; if its fertility continues to fall, its population is likely to decline by approximately 20 million by the turn of the century.[27] (See Figure 87.)

Great Britain

The alternative projections for population in Great Britain prepared by the Royal Commission on Population in 1949 look ahead as far as A.D. 2047. Three estimates are presented:

A. If family size increases 6 per cent the population in Great Britain will inch up very slowly during the next century.

B. If family size remains the same as among couples married between 1927–38, the population in Great Britain will be about the same in 2007 as in 1947 and will then decrease about 3 million by 2047.

C. If family size declines by 20 per cent, population will diminish nearly 20 million by 2047.[28] (See Figure 88.)

Political and Economic Planning (PEP) has published another set of projections with a much wider range between the extremes. For A.D. 2044 its estimates for England and Wales

---

21. **2**, September 1951.

22. See below, p. 259.

23. The dotted curve has been constructed in accordance with the method suggested by Lowell J. Reed and Joseph Berkson (**28**, pp. 760–79). This method is simpler than that used by Reed and Pearl (**29**).

24. **21**, p. 200.

25. **21**, pp. 200–07.

26. The last procedure unduly complicates the picture. In short-term projections, the assumed net number of immigrants can be added, or that of emigrants subtracted, after the computation is completed. In long-range projections, the effect of international migration seems unpredictable.

27. **12**, p. 135.

28. **10**, p. 34.

FIGURE 86. FUTURE POPULATION: PROJECTION FOR THE WORLD (*opposite*)

(Raymond Pearl's Logistic Curve)

As in the logistic curve for population in the United States (Figure 85), Pearl has fitted his curve of world population to a number of empirical points, from 445 million in 1650 to more than 2 billion in 1926. He assumed a decline in the speed of growth of world population after 1890.

The logistic curve in the lower panel of the figure fits the generally accepted estimates of world population for 1800, 1900 and 1950 and the authors' estimate for 2000.

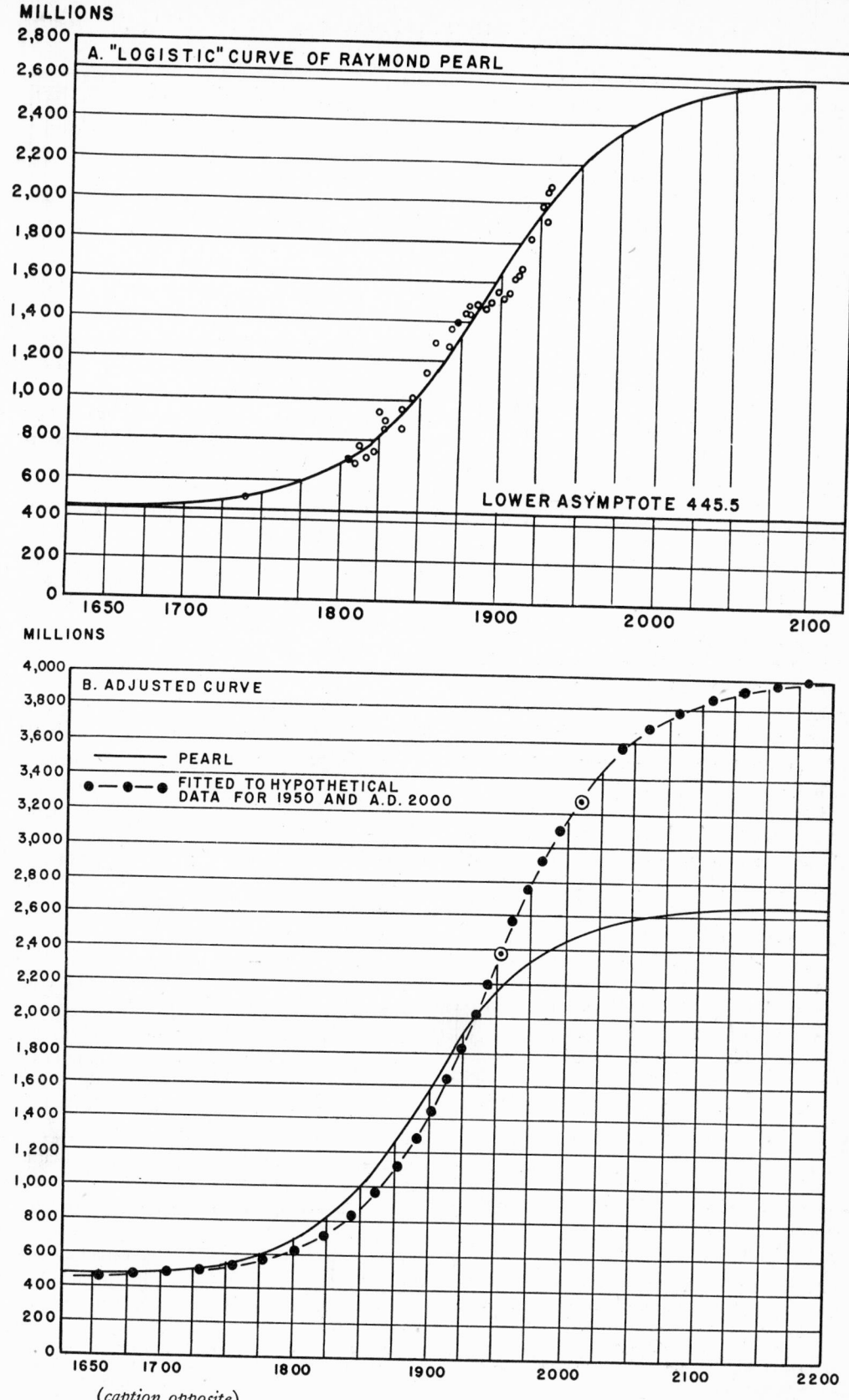

MILLIONS

A. "LOGISTIC" CURVE OF RAYMOND PEARL

LOWER ASYMPTOTE 445.5

MILLIONS

B. ADJUSTED CURVE

——————— PEARL

●—●—● FITTED TO HYPOTHETICAL DATA FOR 1950 AND A.D. 2000

(caption opposite)

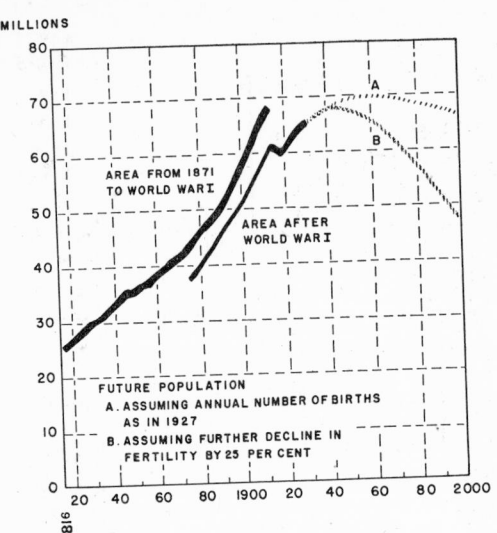

FIGURE 87. FUTURE POPULATION: PROJECTIONS FOR
GERMANY TO A.D. 2000

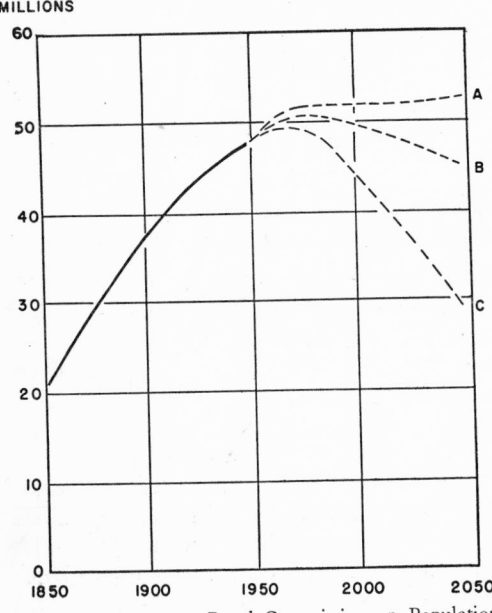

Royal Commission on Population

FIGURE 88. FUTURE POPULATION: PROJECTIONS FOR
GREAT BRITAIN TO A.D. 2050

range between 14.24 million (assuming falling mortality and a decline to 0.6 of the gross reproduction rate) and 43.43 million (assuming constant fertility at the 1944 rate and declining mortality). Three intermediate patterns fall between these two extremes.[29] (See Figure 89.)

29. **26**, p. 56.

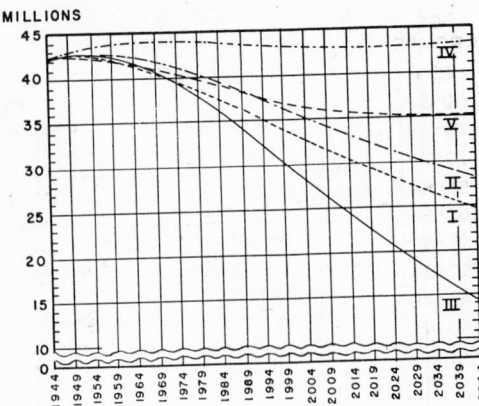

Political and Economic Planning (PEP)

FIGURE 89. FUTURE POPULATION: PROJECTIONS FOR
ENGLAND AND WALES TO A.D. 2044

The age structure of the population under the assumption of falling fertility is illustrated by a chart that looks gloomy indeed.[30] (See Figure 90.) In fact, under this assumption (gross reproduction rate = 0.6) the nation is on its way out of existence.

France

French demographers have used a still wider range of alternative assumptions. In 1946, the Institut National de la Statistique prepared ten estimates of future population, extending to 2005, based on alternative assumptions for mortality and fertility. The range of estimates for 2005 is between 48.6 million for the most favorable development (mortality as in England in 1930–32; fertility 29.4 per cent above the level in 1935–37) and 19.7 million for the most unfavorable (mortality as in France in 1933–38; fertility declining 10 per cent each five years). (See Figure 91.) [31]

In 1948, Pierre Dupoid presented a set of estimates based on alternative assumptions for the net reproduction rate, ranging from 0.7 to 1.2.[32] Dupoid's lowest figure, as well as the lowest PEP projection for England and Wales, does not appear very realistic: It seems likely that long before the reproduction rate falls to 0.7, or 0.6, the respective nation would take effective measures to meet the danger of extinction.

It can be argued, however, that the low projections of Dupoid and PEP are not intended to be

30. **26**, p. 58.
31. **8**.
32. **30**.

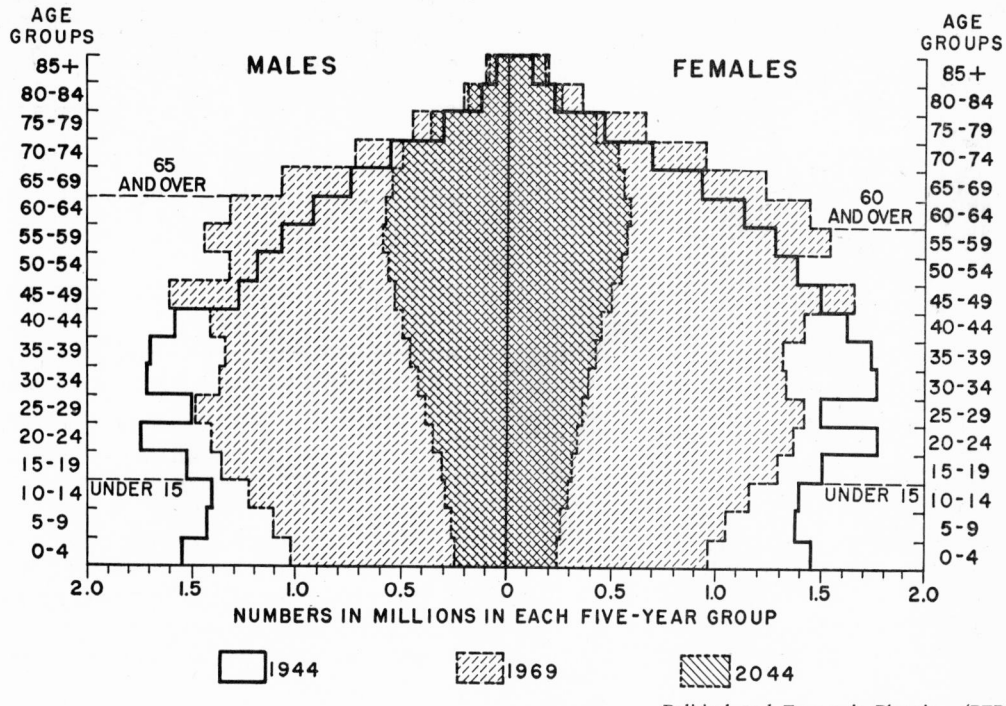

Political and Economic Planning (PEP)

FIGURE 90. FUTURE AGE STRUCTURE OF POPULATION IN ENGLAND AND WALES IN 1969 AND 2044, ON ASSUMPTION OF DECLINING BIRTH RATE

realistic but provide, rather, statistical representations of what would happen if a nation decided to commit suicide by letting its births fall far below the reproduction requirement. "Reasonably probable" assumptions can hardly include this situation.

PROJECTIONS FOR THE UNITED STATES

Five sets of "component" population projec-

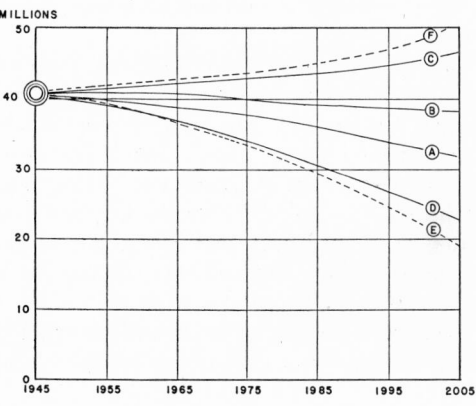

Institut National de la Statistique

FIGURE 91. FUTURE POPULATION: PROJECTIONS FOR FRANCE TO A.D. 2005

tions have been published in the United States in the last twenty-five years.[33]

The first unofficial projection, prepared by the Scripps Foundation in 1928, envisaged a leveling off of population increase, with a peak of 144.6 million in 1970 and a decline to 142.9 million in 1980.[34]

The first official projections were released in 1937 by the National Resources Committee.[35] In 1943 the National Resources Planning Board, which had replaced the Committee, released a new set of estimates, based on the 1940 census and more recent information.[36] Both projections were prepared by Warren S. Thompson and P. K. Whelpton and rest on a cross combination of three alternative assumptions for fertility (high, medium, low) with three assumptions for mortality (low, medium, high) and definite assumptions for immigration. The nine projections of each set, without allowance for net immigration, are briefly summarized in Table 129.

33. For a detailed critical appraisal of these projections see **14**, pp. 14 ff.

34. **34**, p. 16.

35. **6**.

36. **7**.

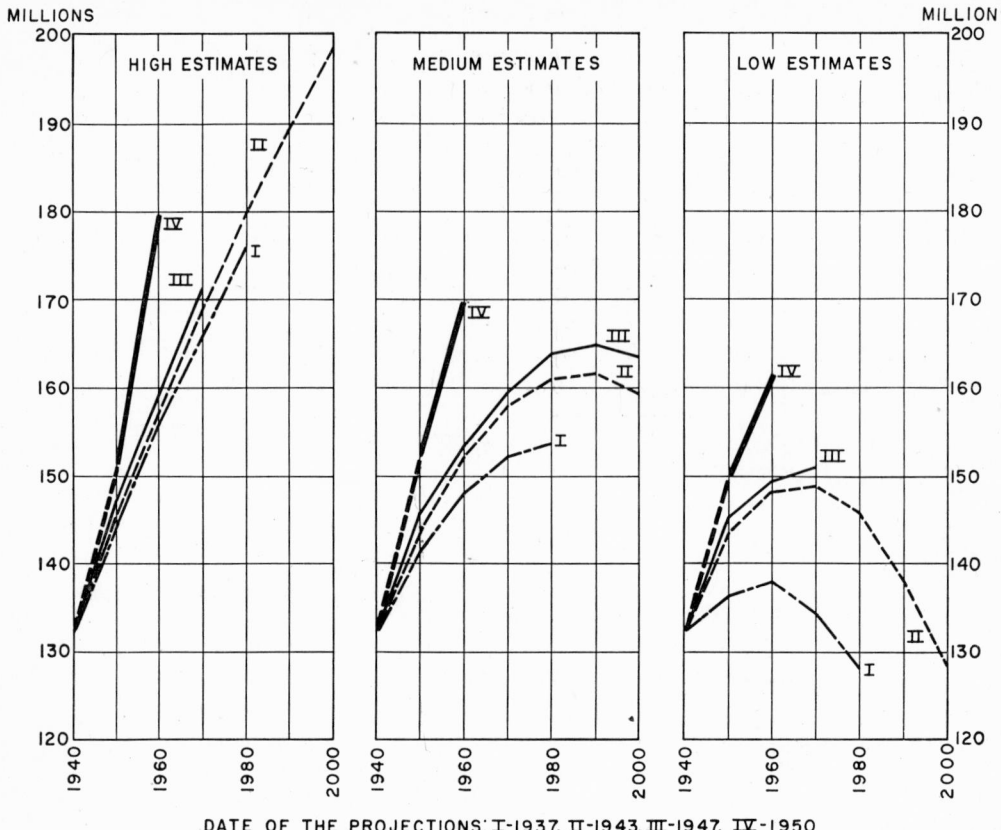

DATE OF THE PROJECTIONS: I-1937, II-1943, III-1947, IV-1950

FIGURE 92. FUTURE POPULATION: PROJECTIONS FOR THE UNITED STATES

Curves I, II and III represent the high, medium and low estimates in the three sets of projections in Table 129. Curve IV represents the projections released by the Bureau of the Census in 1950.

In both sets the assumptions have a cumulative effect: the range between the low and high estimates widens as time goes on. (See Figure 92.) For the year 1980, the range between the highest and lowest projections in the 1943 set (Table 129, middle panel) is somewhat narrower than in the 1937 set (upper panel). The gap was narrowed because of an upward revision of the low-natality projection.

In 1947, Thompson and Whelpton prepared a new set of projections for the Bureau of the Census, mostly for the period 1950–75. (See Table 129, lowest panel.) [37] In 1950 the projections for 1960 and the intermediate years 1950–59 were once more revised by the Bureau of the Census with the use of a simplified procedure. This time only three series were prepared: low, medium and high.

The striking feature in the development of

these projections is that each new set raised the figures given in earlier estimates.[38] Thus the low and high estimates for the year 1960 are as follows (in millions):

	Low	High
1937, National Resources Committee	137.6	155.3
1943, National Resources Planning Board	147.7	156.5
1947, Bureau of the Census	149.8	158.6
1950, Bureau of the Census	161.2	179.8

Although the range between the low and high estimates for 1960 is about the same in the most recent projection as in that prepared in 1937 (18.6 million as compared with 17.7 million), both of the new estimates are about 24 million higher than those made in 1937.

This upward revision of population projections in the United States has been due to the upturn

37. 4.

38. Cf. 14.

TABLE 129

FUTURE POPULATION: PROJECTIONS FOR THE UNITED STATES

(Warren S. Thompson and P. K. Whelpton, 1937, 1943 and 1947)

(*Millions*)

Fertility	Mortality	1940	1950	1960	1970	1980	1990	2000
\multicolumn{9}{c}{Projections Prepared in 1937}								
High	Low	133.3	144.6	155.3	165.6	175.2	—	—
	Medium	132.5	143.2	152.5	160.7	167.9	—	—
	High	132.3	142.2	150.0	156.0	160.7	—	—
Medium	Low	132.1	141.3	149.0	155.2	159.2	—	—
	Medium	132.6	141.2	147.6	151.8	153.6	—	—
	High	131.8	139.6	144.5	146.6	146.2	—	—
Low	Low	131.4	137.8	141.4	142.3	139.9	—	—
	Medium	131.9	137.6	139.9	138.9	134.4	—	—
	High	131.7	136.7	137.6	134.5	127.9	—	—
\multicolumn{9}{c}{Projections Prepared in 1943}								
High	Low	131.7	145.0	156.5	168.0	179.4	189.4	198.7
	Medium	131.7	144.7	155.1	164.8	174.4	182.6	190.7
	High	131.7	144.5	154.4	163.0	171.3	178.3	185.1
Medium	Low	131.7	144.2	153.1	160.5	165.9	167.7	167.0
	Medium	131.7	143.9	151.6	157.4	160.9	161.2	159.4
	High	131.7	143.7	147.8	153.5	157.2	157.9	154.5
Low	Low	131.7	143.4	149.7	153.5	153.6	149.0	140.8
	Medium	131.7	143.1	148.4	150.5	148.7	142.7	133.6
	High	131.7	143.0	147.7	148.7	145.8	138.9	129.1
\multicolumn{9}{c}{Projections Prepared in 1947}								
Highest	Low	131.7	147.0	158.6	170.8	—	—	—
High	Low	131.7	146.1	157.6	169.6	—	—	—
Medium	Medium	131.7	145.5	153.4	159.8	163.9	164.6	163.3
Low	High	131.7	144.9	149.8	151.6	—	—	—

Sources: **6**, pp. 9 ff.; **7**, pp. 20 ff.; **4**, pp. 39 ff.

in birth rates [39] and a shift in the thinking of American demographers.

In the opinion of the present writers the population of the United States in 1960 is likely to be closer to the high estimate of the Bureau of the Census than to the low. Indeed, there are indications that the decline in the birth rate leveled off in 1950 and that the rate may be rising again. The number of births per 1,000 inhabitants on an annual basis, has changed from quarter to quarter as follows: [40]

	First Quarter	Second Quarter	Third Quarter	Fourth Quarter
1949	23.5	22.6	25.6	24.3
1950	23.2	21.8	24.8	24.0
1951	24.2	23.7	25.6	24.3
1952	24.1	23.2	26.2	...

39. See Chapter 5, pp. 161 ff.

40. **3**.

If this trend continues there will be over two million more births than deaths each year during the next decade and the population of the country will exceed 170 million and be close to 175 million in midyear 1960.

PROJECTIONS FOR EUROPE AND THE USSR

Projection of the League of Nations, 1943

In 1943, at the request of the League of Nations, the Office of Population Research of Princeton University prepared estimates of the future population of Europe and the USSR, the most inclusive international population projection ever ventured.[41] These estimates, which were carried to 1970, rest essentially on the assumption of a continuous downward trend in birth and death rates as characteristic of the

41. **21**.

present demographic cycle in all nations covered by the survey. They make no allowance for international migration and war losses.

Although some of the estimates have been outdated by the effects of World War II, these projections continue to be valuable as illustrations of the underlying and orderly processes of population changes. For any use as a hypothetical model, however, these projections should be revised to take account of war casualties; the economic and psychological repercussions of the war; the upturn in birth rates and the new population policies.

The League of Nations projections (Table 130) suggest that the population of Europe, without the USSR, will rise slightly during the next few years and vary in a very narrow range in the following decade. "That Europe should reach an end to rapid population growth was a foregone conclusion," remarks the report.

No continent can continue indefinitely to increase at the rate that Europe was growing in the modern era. At the height of the Roman Empire, Europe's population has been estimated at 30 million. Had the rate of increase throughout the past 2,000 years been that of the past century, there would be 10 trillion persons alive in Europe today, a figure five thousand times that of the present population of the entire world, and predicating an average density of population throughout Europe somewhat greater than that of Central London today. Europe is already the most densely populated of the continents. Excluding European Russia, it is almost as thickly settled as India. The industrial area, including England, the Low Countries, Northern France, and Western Germany, has the greatest concentration of population in the world. Indefinite continuation of population growth would not only be disastrous; it would be impossible.

A tendency toward stabilization of population is found also in North America and Australasia, two regions peopled by European stock. The report continues:

> On the other hand, large non-European populations of Asia, Africa, and South America have reached a demographic stage comparable to that of Europe at the beginning of the period of her most rapid growth. Death rates are declining through the application of modern medicine and the control of famine, but birth rates continue high. Only a war of unheard of destruction could wipe out all the gains of modern sanitation and transportation. At the same time, birth rates in many sections of the globe are not likely to fall speedily enough to prevent a very rapid population growth for at least a generation.

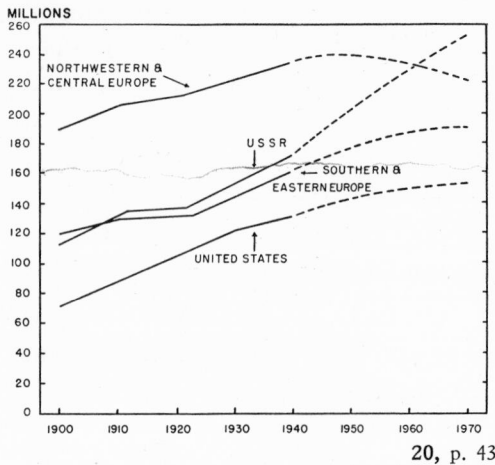

20, p. 43

Figure 93. Future Population: Projections for Europe and the USSR to 1970

(League of Nations)

Rapid population growth in the USSR contrasts with the slow advance in southern and eastern Europe and the decline in northwestern and central Europe in the projections prepared in 1943 by the League of Nations. (Cf. Table 130.) The actual developments in recent years indicate that some adjustments in these projections are necessary.

The writers conclude:

The rapid population growth of Europe is at an end. Demographically speaking, Europe has reached maturity. Such is the import of past trends and future expectations on any assumptions approximating those of the present study. For two centuries Europe and Europe overseas have had dynamic, growing populations in a comparatively slowly changing world; European populations are now approaching population stability in a rapidly expanding world. At home Europe faces economic and cultural changes made necessary by the end of population increases and the beginning of an era of stationary, if not actually declining, population. Europe has been geared to a swiftly expanding civilization, one basis of which was a growing population. This element in expansion is now disappearing.[42]

The projections of the League of Nations contrast this demographic trend in Europe with rapid growth of population in the USSR. (See Figure 93.) Combined with growth of the redoubtable colossus in the East, the decline in northern and western Europe seems to foreshadow the engulfment of Western civilization by the peoples of Russia and Asia.

---

42. **21**, pp. 57 ff.

TABLE 130

FUTURE POPULATION: PROJECTIONS FOR EUROPE AND THE USSR TO 1970

(League of Nations)

(*Thousands*)

Region and Country	1940	1945	1950	1955	1960	1965	1970
Europe and the USSR [a]	572,000	597,000	618,000	636,000	650,000	661,000	668,000
Europe (without the USSR) [a]	399,000	408,000	415,000	419,000	421,000	421,000	417,000
Northwestern and Central Europe	234,000	236,000	237,000	237,000	234,000	231,000	225,000
United Kingdom and Ireland	50,200	50,600	50,600	50,200	49,400	48,200	46,800
England and Wales	40,900	41,100	40,900	40,400	39,600	38,400	37,100
Ireland	3,020	3,080	3,140	3,190	3,230	3,240	3,240
Northern Ireland	1,300	1,330	1,360	1,370	1,380	1,390	1,380
Scotland	5,050	5,150	5,210	5,230	5,220	5,170	5,090
West-Central Europe	163,000	165,000	166,000	166,000	165,000	162,000	159,000
Austria	6,660	6,720	6,720	6,680	6,580	6,450	6,280
Belgium	8,310	8,350	8,340	8,270	8,160	7,980	7,760
Czechoslovakia	15,300	15,500	15,600	15,600	15,500	15,200	14,900
France	41,200	40,800	40,300	39,700	39,000	38,100	36,900
Germany	69,500	71,200	72,000	72,200	71,800	71,100	69,800
Hungary	9,160	9,320	9,440	9,510	9,530	9,470	9,330
Netherlands	8,840	9,230	9,550	9,780	9,950	10,000	10,000
Switzerland	4,220	4,260	4,260	4,220	4,150	4,050	3,920
Northern Europe	20,100	20,400	20,500	20,500	20,300	20,000	19,500
Denmark	3,820	3,930	4,010	4,050	4,060	4,040	3,990
Estonia	1,130	1,130	1,120	1,100	1,070	1,040	1,000
Finland	3,850	3,950	4,000	4,020	4,010	3,980	3,920
Latvia	1,990	2,010	2,010	2,000	1,980	1,950	1,910
Norway	2,930	2,980	3,010	3,020	3,000	2,950	2,870
Sweden	6,330	6,380	6,370	6,310	6,210	6,050	5,840
Southern and Eastern Europe	165,000	172,000	177,000	183,000	187,000	190,000	192,000
Southern Europe	77,500	80,100	82,300	84,100	85,500	86,300	86,500
Italy	44,200	45,700	47,000	48,100	48,900	49,400	49,500
Portugal [b]	7,620	7,980	8,290	8,550	8,780	8,960	9,090
Spain [c]	25,600	26,400	27,000	27,500	27,800	28,000	27,800
Eastern Europe	87,700	91,600	95,200	98,500	101,000	102,000	105,000
Albania	1,100	1,100	1,200	1,200	1,200	1,300	1,300
Bulgaria	6,320	6,550	6,790	7,000	7,170	7,280	7,320
Greece	7,180	7,530	7,830	8,100	8,350	8,570	8,640
Lithuania	2,460	2,530	2,580	2,630	2,660	2,670	2,660
Poland	35,200	36,700	38,100	39,400	40,400	41,000	41,400
Romania	20,300	21,300	22,200	23,100	24,000	24,800	25,300
Yugoslavia	15,200	15,800	16,400	17,100	17,700	18,200	18,500
USSR	174,000	189,000	203,000	216,000	228,000	240,000	251,000

Source: **21,** p. 56. Arrangement of countries follows original table.

a. Excluding the following areas for which projections were not made: Andorra, Channel Islands, Danzig, the Faeroes, Gibraltar, Iceland, Isle of Man, Liechtenstein, Luxembourg, Malta, Monaco, San Marino, Spitzbergen, Turkey in Europe, and Vatican City. The aggregate population of these areas in 1939 was 2.7 million.

b. Includes the Azores and Madeira.

c. Includes the Canary Islands.

League of Nations Projections Revised

It seems likely, however, that these projections have overemphasized the contrast between trends in Europe and in the USSR. As the report points out, the assumed mortality rates for the USSR were based on a life table developed as "a compromise between that for the USSR in 1926 and that of Poland in 1931–32,"[43] while the fertility rates were "assembled from a fugitive literature that prevents careful assessment of their validity."[44] These gaps in basic data necessarily suggest a wide margin of error, so that the projected increase of Russia's population from 174 million in 1940 to 251 million in 1970 is more a guess of the estimators than the result of statistical research.

Moreover, the outlook has been changed by several new factors that should be superimposed on the projected figures:

1. The most important new factor is the upturn in fertility in Great Britain, Sweden, Norway, Denmark, France, Belgium and the Netherlands. While Table 130 indicates that the population of these countries will suffer a net decline totaling 7.5 million from 1940 to 1970, the new trends in birth rates make an increase of 15–20 million more probable.

2. War losses of population, including civilian casualties, were very heavy in Germany, Poland and Greece, and especially in Russia.

According to official Russian statistics, the USSR had 193 million inhabitants in 1946 within its postwar boundaries, including 25 million in the recently conquered territories of Finland, Poland, Romania, and the Baltic states; this total is less than the 1946 population within Russia's prewar boundaries suggested by interpolation of the figures for 1945 and 1950 in Table 130. The decline has been due partly to military losses, partly to the wartime deficit in births and the excess in deaths of civilians. With the necessary adjustments, the population of the USSR in 1970 will hardly exceed 210 million within the prewar boundaries, or 240 million in the new boundaries.

3. For Germany also, a correction is required. According to the German Institute for Economic Research (Deutsches Institut für Wirtschaftsforschung), Germany had a population of 65.9 million in 1946[45] within its postwar boundaries

("Restdeutschland," or Rump-Germany) as compared with 59.8 million in the same area in 1939 and 79.4 million in all Hitler's Reich, including Austria and the provinces grabbed from Czechoslovakia. Thus Germany has lost territory with a population of 20 million, but the number of people within its postwar boundaries increased by more than 6 million from 1939 to 1946. This increase, according to the Institute, was the net result of the following changes (figures in millions):

Increase, total	12.6
Surplus of births over deaths	1.8
Displaced persons still in Germany	0.8
Germans from lost areas and from abroad	10.0
Decrease, total	6.5
War losses	4.5
German war prisoners abroad	2.0

Since this estimate was made the population within the new boundaries of Germany has continued to increase and, according to the Statistical Office of the United Nations, had reached 69 million by midyear 1950. Western Germany alone has had an annual surplus of some 300,000 births over deaths in recent years. With progressive recovery, the number of births is likely to increase. It appears, therefore, that the population of Germany within the postwar boundaries will be hardly less than 75 million by 1970, which corresponds to 85 to 90 million in the area of prewar Germany.

Because of these new factors, we would modify the general pattern of the League of Nations projection for 1970 as follows:

Add 25 million for north and central Europe and 5 million for Germany

Subtract 40 million for the USSR within the prewar borders

Transfer 30 million from southern and eastern Europe to the USSR as the probable 1970 population in the area it has annexed since World War II. The effect of these changes is shown in Table 131.

HISTORICAL LONG-RANGE PROJECTIONS

The less than satisfactory record of population projections prepared in the United States in the

---

43. **21,** p. 189.
44. **21,** p. 197.
45. **9,** pp. 18, 19. Of the total German population of 65.9 million, 45.4 million were in the regions occupied

by the Allies (22.3 million in the British Zone, 17.2 million in the American, and 5.9 million in the French); 17.3 million were in the areas held by the Russians, and 3.2 million in Berlin.

TABLE 131

FUTURE POPULATION: PROJECTIONS FOR EUROPE AND THE USSR IN 1970

(Revision of the Projection of the League of Nations)

(*Millions*)

Region	Projection of the League of Nations [b]	Revision [a]		Revised Projection
		For Trends in Population and War Losses	For Conquests of USSR in Eastern Europe	
Europe and the USSR	668	−10	—	658
Europe, excluding the USSR	417	+30	−30	417
Northern and central Europe, excluding Germany	155	+25	—	180
Germany	70	+ 5	—	75
Southern and eastern Europe	192	—	−30	162
USSR	251	−40	+30	241

a. See p. 256.   b. See Table 130.

last 25 years justifies a great amount of skepticism concerning long-range projections of world population, which must necessarily include nations and regions with very scanty statistics or no statistics at all. Despite this skepticism, however, a model of probable future world population is indispensable in a discussion of future world affairs, and the end of this century is not too remote and nebulous to be included in such a discussion. In fact, boys and girls now in college have a fair chance to be alive at that time, and babies born during World War II will not have reached old age in A.D. 2000. That year is therefore not very remote in terms of individuals. Certainly it is not too remote in terms of national and international needs and policies.

In view of considerable gaps in international vital statistics, world population at the end of this century cannot be estimated by the method of "component" projection but should be approached rather from the angle of the history of population.

NOTESTEIN'S PROJECTIONS FOR A.D. 2000

Highly enlightening projections of this type were developed in 1945 by Frank W. Notestein, who distinguishes three phases of demographic evolution: *incipient decline, transitional growth* and *high growth potential.*[46]

46. **20**, pp. 36–37.

"Incipient Decline"

The United States, nearly all the countries of northwestern and central Europe, Australia and New Zealand are now in this phase of the demographic cycle. In all these countries, Notestein finds, fertility has fallen substantially below the level required for the permanent maintenance of a stationary population at existing mortality rates, and growth continues only because of the favorable age distribution of the population, which time will alter.

"Transitional Growth"

Other countries are in an earlier stage of demographic evolution. In some of them, birth and death rates are still high and growth is rapid, but the decline of the birth rate is well established. This stage is characterized as "transitional growth." The populations of eastern Europe are nearing the end of this stage; the Soviet Union, Japan and certain Latin American countries are in the middle of this phase; Turkey, Palestine and parts of North Africa appear to be entering it.

"High Growth Potential"

Many countries have scarcely begun the demographic transition. Mortality is high and variable and is the chief determinant of growth, while fertility is high and so far has shown no downward trend. In these populations, rapid increase is to be expected as soon as medical and other developments bring about a decline in mortality. This stage of demographic development Notestein describes as "high growth potential." This is the present stage of demographic development in Egypt, central Africa, much of the Near East, virtually all Asia outside the Soviet Union and Japan, the islands of the Pacific and the Caribbean, and much of Central and South America.

World Population in A.D. 2000

Starting with these general considerations, Notestein develops the prospects for growth of population in different parts of the world to A.D. 2000. (See Figure 94.)

For North America he assumes, following Thompson and Whelpton, a rise in population to 176 million in 1980, with continuance of this figure till 2000, on the theory that increase in Canada in the intervening decades may offset losses in the United States.

For Europe west of the prewar boundaries of the USSR, his figure for A.D. 2000 is the same as his estimate for 1970, 417 million. (See Table 130.) The theory is that incipient decline in population will be forestalled by governmental population policies.

For the Soviet Union he postulates a population of 251 million in 1970 and a further rise to 298 million by the end of the century.

In Middle and South American countries, still in the stage of "high growth potential," Notestein anticipates that population will more than double from 1940 to 2000, reaching 283 million in the latter year.

For Australia and New Zealand he estimates a population of 21 million in 2000, increased by immigration rather than a surplus of births over deaths.

For Asia and Africa, for which only a very crude estimate is possible, he assumes a growth of population at an annual rate of one per cent from 1940 to 1970 and 0.5 per cent from 1970 to 2000. He thus arrives at a total of 250 million for Africa and 1.9 billion for Asia, excluding the USSR.

These figures would give a world total of 3,345 million in A.D. 2000. "On the assumption of general order and the spread of modern techniques of production the figure is probably conservative." Notestein concludes: "It implies a slightly accelerated growth between 1940 and 1970, but a sharp curtailment after that date.

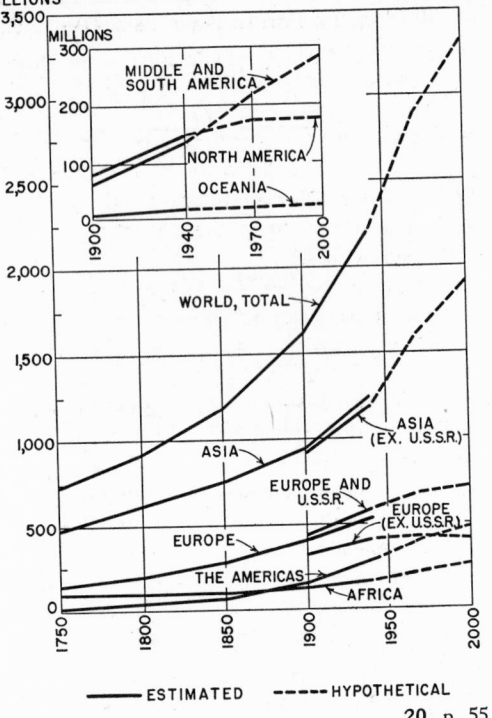

20, p. 55

FIGURE 94. FUTURE POPULATION: PROJECTIONS BY CONTINENT, TO A.D. 2000

(Frank W. Notestein)

Notestein's projections envisage a world population of 3,345 million in A.D. 2000, with nearly 57 per cent of the human race concentrated in Asia (without the USSR), and a comparatively small increase in North America and Europe. (See **20**.)

Given widespread disorder, and catastrophe, the reverse of this sequence might develop, with growth slowing in the coming generation, only to rise still higher in the next." [47] Sensible planning for the future, he believes, should be based on the assumption that the world will have at least 3 billion people by the end of this century.

In the light of recent developments, some of Notestein's projections appear too high, others too low, though all plausible adjustments fall within the unavoidable margin of error.

War losses in human lives have been less severe than might have been anticipated, and the upturn in birth rates in countries of Western civilization has been remarkable. The increased natality in the area of "incipient decline" of population has resulted in an appreciable change in

47. **20**, p. 57.

its age structure. As more people reach the age of 20–25 in the 1960's a new upsurge of births can be anticipated in the 1970's.

In the light of these developments, Notestein's estimate for North America seems too low. The population of the United States and Canada, combined, will probably reach 190 million in 1960 or a few years later, and an estimate of 220 million for the turn of the century is likely to prove conservative.

Notestein's figures for Latin America and Oceania appear realistic. The estimate for Africa should be raised if allowance is made for probable improvement in health conditions and for economic development and immigration possibilities in the eastern and southeastern part of the Dark Continent. A 40 per cent increase of Africa's population, from nearly 200 million in 1950 to 280 million by the end of the century, appears probable.

For Europe (without the USSR) Notestein assumes precisely the same population in 2000 as in 1970: 417 million. With correction for losses of territories annexed by the USSR, heavy casualties in Germany and the rise in birth rates in western Europe, the population of European countries in 1970 may total 417 million. Moderate growth from 1970 to 2000 seems probable, and an estimate of 440 million by the turn of the century will probably prove conservative. For the USSR we have assumed a population of 241 million in 1970, including the newly acquired territories. Assuming for 1970–2000 a growth of population in the USSR at the present rate in the United States, Russia may marshal a population of 260 million by the year 2000.

Notestein's projection for Asia presumes peace and order on that continent but makes no allowance for the cultural revolution now in progress in India, the Philippines and Japan, and bound to spread over China. The change in the ways of life combined with social and political turmoil, make a demographic projection for this area extremely difficult. Moreover, the current demographic trends in a large part of this area are unknown. The observation of Professor Ta Chen that China is now in the phase of declining population [48] may prove to be correct for other Asiatic countries, if not for all Asia.

It seems likely also that some of the most overpopulated Asiatic countries will develop a definite population policy long before the end

of this century and that its purpose will be to protect population equilibrium rather than to encourage population growth. On the basis of these considerations, we are inclined to assume for Asia a somewhat slower growth of population than suggested in Notestein's projection: from 1,272 million in 1950 to 1,750 million instead of 1,900 million.

Continental Trends

With these adjustments, world population would increase by 230 million from 1940 to 1950 and by 850 million from 1950 to the end of the century and reach approximately 3,250 million by the year 2000. (See Table 132.) The increment would be distributed among the continents somewhat as follows (in millions):

	1940 to 1950	1950 to 2000
World	230	850
North America	23	54
Middle and South America	32	118
Europe excluding the USSR [a]	−6	44
USSR [a]	21	67
Asia, excluding the USSR	118	478
Africa	40	82
Australia	2	7

a. Population of 25 million in areas conquered by the USSR as a result of World War II is transferred from Europe to the USSR. Without this transfer there would have been an increase in Europe and a loss in the USSR.

Of the 850 million increase from 1950 to 2000, about 300 million would be in regions with comparatively sparse population and considerable unexploited natural resources — the Americas, the USSR, Africa and Australia. A part of the additional population in Europe and Asia will probably migrate to less thickly populated regions in the same continent. The remainder, perhaps 400 million, must find places in regions that are already densely populated.

According to our projection, total world population would increase from 1950 to 2000 about 35 per cent, as compared with an estimated gain of 50 per cent from 1900 to 1950. The annual rate of growth in the second half of this century would be approximately 0.6 per cent. It would not be unduly difficult to increase the world's total food supply at an equal rate; the real difficulty is to increase it sufficiently where such an increase is needed and to improve nutrition in accordance with modern standards. To solve

---

48. **31**, p. 4.

TABLE 132

FUTURE POPULATION: PROJECTION FOR THE WORLD TO A. D. 2000

(Notestein's Projection and Its Revision)

(*Millions*)

Continent	1900	1940	Midyear 1950	2000		Increase, 1950–2000	
				Notestein	Revised	Notestein	Revised
World	1,608	2,170	2,400	3,345	3,250	945	850
North America	81	143	166	176	220	10	54
Middle and South America	63	130	162	283	280	121	118
Europe, excluding the USSR	401	402	396	417	440	21	44
USSR	—	172	193	298	260	105	67
Asia, excluding the USSR	937	1,154	1,272	1,900	1,750	628	478
Africa	120	157	198	250	280	52	82
Oceania	6	11	13	21	20	8	7

Sources: For 1900, Carr-Saunders (**13**); for 1940, **1**, 1948, pp. 28–105; for 1950, **3**, July 1951; for 2000, Notestein (**20**).

these problems, considerable progress must be achieved in agriculture and other industries.[49]

THE REMOTE FUTURE

If projections of the population in a single country for ten or twenty years ahead allow for a considerable spread between the "low" and "high" estimates, projections of world population for a century or more in advance cannot pretend even to be hypothetical models and are only illustrative of our thinking about present trends. Indeed, the searchlights of modern science are too weak to penetrate the fog of more than a few years, and visibility is bound to dwindle as distance increases. The differences in the views of students are evident from Pritchett's belief that the population of the United States alone would exceed 40 billion a thousand years hence and the conclusion Pearl drew from his first logistic, that world population would never exceed 2.1 billion. Despite the fallibility of predictions, however, many people have been impelled to visualize what the remote future has in store for mankind.

Mankind's Past Growth

Pearl presents enlightening speculations on the

49. Our projection is offered here as a description of current trends in world population and is subject to revision in the light of new facts. It does not pretend to be a prophecy.

course of the human race in his *Natural History of Population* starting from the facts established by modern anthropology and archaeology. (See Figure 95.) As a distinct and differentiated species man has been on the earth an extremely long time, probably not less than 500,000 years. For aeons he certainly increased in numbers in the normal biological way as rapidly as circumstances and environment would permit, with the result that by the middle of the seventeenth century the earth had some 445 million inhabitants.

This being so, Pearl comments, at least three possible alternatives present themselves:

The first of these is that the human population of this globe more or less steadily *grew* for 500,000 years, but at an extremely slow time rate as compared with the growth performance of any but a very few populations now existing. On this hypothesis it may be regarded as probable that growth of world population was not entirely steady and continuous along a smooth curve, logistic or other, but instead was irregular, fluctuating up and down about the ever-rising time-trend line. These fluctuations, consequent upon wars, famines, pestilences, and climatic changes, may have been relatively large at times, but absolutely well within the limit set by the 445 million asymptote finally achieved.

A second possible alternative is that for a long time — thousands of years — prior to the seventeenth century, the population of the world *stood stable* at between roughly four and five hundred million, or oscillated in waves of relatively small amplitude about some such figure. On such a view this value

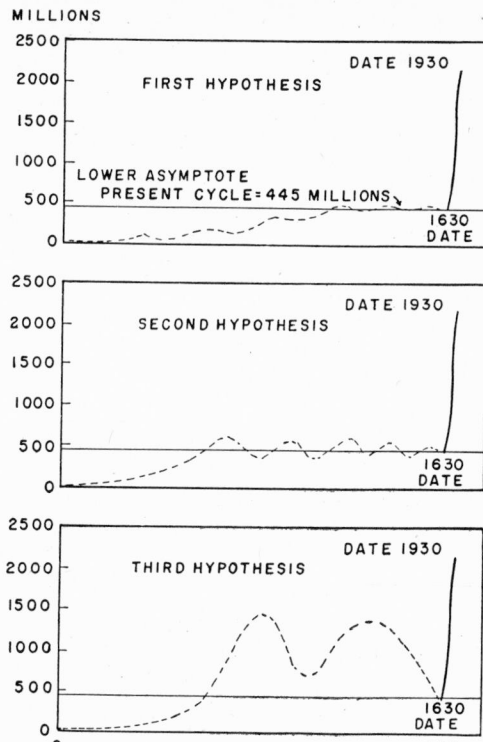

FIGURE 95. HYPOTHETICAL GROWTH OF MANKIND
FROM ITS ORIGIN TO 1930

(Raymond Pearl)

Pearl's diagram illustrates alternative hypotheses as to
the history of the human population of the earth. The
portions of the curves depicted by a continuous solid line
(1630–1930) represent the known facts about the growth
of world population. The portions of the curve drawn
in broken lines plotted to the same time scale are purely
hypothetical. (**23**, p. 262.)

would represent a relatively stable upper asymptotic
level achieved in a cycle of population growth that
was consummated long before, and at a relatively
early stage of man's evolution.

Finally, a third possible alternative is that during
some period or periods in this vast span of 500,000
odd years of man's life on the earth, the *world population was much higher* than 445 millions, and
subsequently lessened, for reasons wholly unknown,
to reach that final figure at the time when reasonably reliable population history begins.[50]

Of these three hypotheses, Pearl considers the
first the most plausible: "a very slow and irregular time rate of growth of world population over
a very long time prior to the Middle Ages, let us
say, followed by a relatively tremendous spurt
of growth not yet ended." [51]

50. **23**, pp. 261–62.
51. **23**, p. 263.

It is irrelevant whether we count the modern
history of population from the seventeenth century or some earlier date, and whether we
accept Pearl's logistic of the growth of world
population or use a different curve, not necessarily based on a mathematical formula. Pearl's
main point is the striking contrast between the
population growth in the last three centuries
and in the preceding hundreds of millenniums.
The spurt in modern times has been due to
the expansion of man's effective universe, the
breath-taking discoveries and inventions, the new
forms of society. Pearl is right when he states
bluntly that technical progress made "the gloomy
prophecies of Malthus about the future of mankind, at the end of the eighteenth century, seem
comically absurd soon after he made them."[52]

Outlook

The growth of world population in the past
three hundred years obviously does not express
the secular trend and cannot be projected indefinitely into the future. Rather, it has been a
unique, unprecedented and unrepeatable phenomenon of limited duration. It had a beginning
in the not too distant past, and it will have an
end, perhaps in the not too remote future. The
slowing down and leveling off of growth in
world population seems unavoidable. The question is only when will growth stop and at what
level.

Notestein's concept of the three phases of the
demographic cycle suggests that mankind is
gradually shifting from rapid growth to a standstill. The forces of growth still prevail and will
not have been exhausted by the turn of the
century, but the annual rate of increase is likely
to decline. Mankind may continue to grow for
a century or more, although at a gradually
diminishing rate so that stability of population
will not be reached in the twenty-first century.

From the point of view of the history of mankind, however, slow growth — say at a rate of
0.1 per cent annually — does not differ much
from stability. The important point is that the
period of rapid growth is approaching its end,
and that world population will be stabilized,
probably at a level substantially above the anticipated figure for the turn of this century (3,250
million). The limit may be 4 billion, as indicated

52. **23**, p. 265.

by our projection in Figure 86, or somewhat more.

From this point on, two types of development are possible. One is a long period of relative stability, with temporary and local changes in either direction. The other is a widening gap between mortality and natality and progressive depopulation of the earth. This process might pause at some level appreciably below 4 million and eventually be succeeded by a new cycle of growth or decline, or it might continue until the human race is extinct.

This is, however, a very remote possibility. To discuss it new hypothetical factors should be introduced. In the long range the extinction of the human race in a remote future, under the impact of unknown and hardly predictable factors, would mean that man had followed in the steps of other species that have inhabited this planet. The chance that he and his civilization will survive lies in his superior capacity to adapt himself to the environment and to adapt the environment to his needs.[53]

53. **23**, p. 288.

PART II

WORLD NEEDS AND RESOURCES

CHAPTER 8

CONSUMER NEEDS AND OUTLAYS

IN OUR WESTERN CIVILIZATION, needs, real or imaginary, have no limit. Satisfaction of one desire releases and stimulates new wants. This insatiability of demand has a twofold effect: it accounts for the dynamism of the present economic and social system and it contributes to a general feeling of dissatisfaction.

HUMAN NEEDS AND CIVILIZATION

No material progress is conceivable in a society without desires or in an environment where people can satisfy their needs without effort, such as Drummond and the first missionaries saw among the primitive tribes in Nyasaland:

Hidden away in these endless forests like birds' nests in a wood . . . are small native villages; and here in his virgin simplicity dwells Primeval Man, without clothes, without civilization, without learning, without religion — the genuine child of nature, thoughtless, careless and contented. This man is apparently quite happy; he has practically no wants . . . he does not need to work; with so bountiful a nature round him it would be gratuitous to work.[1]

When the white man first established his plantations and mines in such happy regions, he discovered that the natives, because they had no wants, were reluctant to sweat for him. Development of new needs among primitive peoples in the colonies therefore became a part of the white man's burden.

Although not completely static in early human history, needs developed quite slowly, as a result of increase in population, changes in environment, migration, war and occasional contact of one tribe with another. Material civilization began only after primitive man became aware of needs that he could not satisfy with his bare hands or the rudimentary devices handed down by his forefathers. At all stages of civilization, in all parts of the world, men have thought of life without wants and desires as the Golden Age and have attributed this era to the very remote past, never to the future.

Needs in a Primitive Community

Anthropology and archaeology have discovered traces of the existence of man as a distinct species for about 500,000 years. Traces of material civilization — characterized by use of fire and weapons — go back no further than 20,000 years. Although economic activities in a broad sense are older than the use of fire, early human history is described by some historians as pre-economic.

This is the stage of individual search for food, when, in the words of Carl Bücher,

. . . each individual has to rely entirely upon himself for his sustenance. Naked and unarmed he roams with his fellows, like certain species of wild animals, through a limited stretch of territory, and uses his feet for holding and climbing as dexterously as he uses his hands. All, male and female, devour raw what they catch with their hands or dig out of the ground with their nails: smaller animals, roots, and fruits.[2]

Work and Play

If the search for food was the everyday work of primitive man, it was work often merged with play. Purposeless imitation and experimentation has been as important for the development of the "economy" as labor. As Bücher says,

The taming of domestic animals . . . begins not with the useful animals, but with such species as man keeps merely for amusement or the worship of gods. Industrial activity seems everywhere to start with the painting of the body, and gradually to advance to the production of ornaments, masks, drawing on bark, petrograms, and similar play-products. . . . It is in play that technical skill is developed. Play is older than work, art older than production for use.[3]

Economic activities, as distinct from individual search for food and play, presume the existence of more or less stable human groups, integrated into a community. In addition to food, human needs at this stage include shelter, baked earthen

1. **16**, pp. 55–56.

2. **13**, p. 26.
3. **13**, pp. 27–29.

vessels, decorative objects, rudimentary tools, bows and arrows, and sometimes boats made from tree trunks hollowed out with fire or from pieces of bark sewn together.[4]

All these needs together, however, required much less effort than the search for food. For thousands of years, hunger remained the main motive for labor. Primitive man discovered the advantages of division of labor within the community and of exchange among tribes, established market places, tramped overland trade routes, developed rudimentary crafts and trades — and still, more often than not, was hungry. In fact, man continued to be haunted by hunger even after luxury and extravagance appeared at the top levels of the society.

Needs in Premechanized Civilization

The road was long from the life of primitive communities to the splendor of ancient Egypt, the Golden Age of Athens, the glory of the Roman Empire, the mystery of medieval cathedrals. Human civilization was growing, falling back and rising again. The social and economic fabric of society became increasingly complicated, but the methods of producing food, clothing and shelter changed little. From time to time, some methods were improved enough to meet the pressure of the growing population and to put surplus into the hands of the rulers, but never enough to raise the majority of people above bare subsistence.

The world is littered with traces of wealth in civilizations that have vanished, but this wealth was always limited to the state, personified by king, church and a thin veneer of the ruling classes. French peasants in the seventeenth century lived no better than the shepherds of Homer or the slaves who built Egypt's pyramids. In this respect, progress was disappointingly slow until the beginning of the machine age.

Dreams of Machines

There is no way of knowing when men first began to dream of using machines to perform their everyday work. Such devices appear in the folklore of all nations, from the Iliad to the Arabian Nights. Aristotle gave thought to the possibility of a mechanized civilization and discussed it in his *Politics,* but he rejected the idea

as a completely unrealistic alternative to the natural and sound institution of slavery.

If every instrument could accomplish its own work, obeying or anticipating the will of others, like the statutes of Daedalus, or the tripods of Hephaestus [he writes], . . . if the shuttle would weave and the plectrum touch the lyre without a hand to guide them, chief workmen would not want servants nor masters slaves.[5]

Karl Marx quotes a Greek poet who hailed the invention of the water wheel as the beginning of the new era giving freedom to slaves and bringing back the Golden Age:

Spare the hand that grinds the corn, oh, miller girls, and softly sleep . . . Deo has commanded your work to be done by her Nymphs, and they skip lightly over the water wheels, so that the shaken axles revolve . . . and pull round the load of the grinding stones . . . Let us rest from work and enjoy the gifts that the goddess sends us.[6]

The jubilation of the Greek poet proved to be premature. Apart from skipping lightly over the water wheels of a mill, Deo's nymphs had to be converted into steam before they learned how to replace the work of human hands.

In northern and western Europe the use of machines began in the seventeenth century, in central Europe and America in the eighteenth century, in other parts of the world in the nineteenth. Economic progress kept pace with man's growing ability to make natural forces do his work. In many parts of the world, probably for more than half of mankind, the age of machines has only started.

Needs in Modern Society

Our modern economic system makes no distinction between necessities and luxuries. Modern man claims more than what he needs, biologically, for existence. In the old days only a king could afford to say in support of his claims:

Allow not nature more than nature needs,
Man's life is cheap as beast's.

The king felt that *his* life would not be worth living if nothing but what "nature needs" were allowed to *him*. Now, the common man in modern nations feels this way. Custom, fashion, advertising, and emulative and imitative consumption unite to generate new desires and

---

4. **13**, pp. 52–53.

5. **12**, p. 57.
6. **23**, p. 446.

habits in society. We are so accustomed to living among continually changing and growing temptations that few people realize how completely this new pattern of needs has changed the manner of our life and the appearance of our cities.[7] The advertising industry is the hallmark of not only the modern supercity but also the whole modern economy.[8]

New luxuries find their way first into the households of the rich as a means of displaying wealth. Next, if advertising succeeds in inciting desire in the wider layer of well-off consumers the new article becomes a distinctive sign of social respectability. Later, it moves into the realm of mass production and mass consumption. After having invaded a sizable section of the market — perhaps a third of the population — it may become a part of the national standard of living. Soon its absence in a home is a sign of destitution, like the absence of electric light, a flush toilet or a refrigerator, all of which were out of reach of the middle classes a generation or two ago but are now regarded in the United States as necessities, even for families on the relief rolls.

How Desires Are Created

The modern technique of developing new desires and demands is illustrated by the recent triumphal march of television in the United States. The aim of the new industry was to attract commercial sponsors who would buy time on the programs to advertise their products. To attract them, manufacturers of television sets had to induce people to equip their homes with these sets. Since little could be said about the merits of television programs, the industry has made a supreme effort to win the support of the least experienced, and least critical, consumers — the children. It has succeeded in creating a psychological climate in which the absence of a television set in a home is a humiliating stigma, not only among middle-class families but also among some manual workers.[9]

Because of the instability of tastes, the high level of income, and the lack of rigid social stratification, the United States leads the world in developing new needs and demands and in expanding the realm of mass production and mass consumption. Adopting American gadgets and technics of everyday life step by step, the peoples of Europe also strive for "modernization," which is really the Americanization of the patterns of their desires.

How People Spend Their Money

Torn between numberless needs that often outrun his means, the consumer must try to spend his money in the way that provides the maximum satisfaction for himself and his family. Not always is he able to make a sensible choice either among the variety of his needs and temptations or among the articles offered him in a bewildering galaxy of brands and trademarks. Occasionally his purchases are determined in ignorance and by psychological pressure.[10] Yet there is a certain regularity in the way in which consumers divide their expenditures among broad groups of needs — food, rent, fuel and light, clothing, recreation and so on.

First Things Come First

With individual deviations, the pattern of expenditure depends on the consumer's income and occupation, the size of his family, the type of community in which he lives, and, of course, national customs and habits. The pattern changes with business conditions and with prices. Both these changes and the stability of the distribution of family expenditures at a given level of income are consistent with the principle of "marginal satisfaction," which means simply that for each consumer, first things come first.

At the lowest income level, all money is spent for the means of bare subsistence. With rising income, an increasing part is used for items that are not absolutely necessary to keep body and soul together. As a rule, each additional dollar,

---

7. See Chapter 4.

8. **19,** pp. 86 ff.

9. In describing this campaign *Life* magazine quoted arguments used by the television industry in its newspaper copy. In one advertisement the absence of a television set in the home was characterized as an act of extreme cruelty toward children. Such negligence on the part of the parents condemned their children to social ostracism, inflicted bruises deep inside and humiliated them by forcing them to beg precious television hours

from neighbors. The magazine continued with a description of spot radio announcements that tell "how little Johnnie comes home and blurts out, with sniffles, what the newspaper ads said he wouldn't tell: 'I don't know what the gang's talking about any more. They all got television sets.' A specialist in child guidance, a children's court judge and a headmaster attested in authoritative tones that the child who doesn't have television at home is a social leper." *Life,* November 27, 1950, p. 26.

10. **25,** pp. 43–69.

pound, peso or franc serves to meet needs that are less pressing than those satisfied by the preceding unit of money. Insofar as the consumer applies this principle to each part of his total expenditure his outlays for purchases which are not absolutely necessary tend to be so distributed among different items that the satisfaction he obtains from them is roughly proportionate to the price he pays for it. In other words, the consumer uses his "last dollar" for things he wishes most urgently to get and his expenditures tend to equalize the marginal satisfaction per unit of money, whatever the purpose for which it is used. Imperfect as it is, this "budgeting" by consumers governs both the distribution of the nation's purchasing power among different needs and the distribution of national resources among different branches of production.

Consumption Studies

The pattern of a nation's consumption can be indicated by showing the share of food, shelter, clothing and other needs in its total expenditures. This method is at least 250 years old. As early as the end of the seventeenth century, the great British economist Gregory King used it to compare consumption habits in England, France and Holland.[11]

As the economic system grows more complex, direct estimates of national consumption become increasingly difficult. Moreover, the distribution of a country's total expenditures among groups of needs fails to show the differences in consumption habits among different groups of its population. The latter type of information is provided by surveys of individual households, which were inaugurated in England at the end of the eighteenth century by the Reverend David Davies [12] and Sir Frederick Morton Eden.[13] Several comprehensive surveys of consumer expenditures were made in various European countries in the middle of the nineteenth century as interest in sociological problems grew. Quetelet and Ducpettiaux, Belgians; LePlay, a French-

man; and Ernest Engel, a German, were pioneers in this field.

In the United States some two hundred studies of consumer expenditures were carried out between 1869 and 1935.[14]

All these surveys were dwarfed by the Consumer Expenditures Study undertaken in 1935–36. It covered about 300,000 families and is the most ambitious and perhaps the most enlightening collection of consumption statistics in the world.[15]

In 1934–36, the Bureau of Labor Statistics also made a survey of the expenditures of about 14,500 families of wage earners and clerical workers in 42 cities. The primary purpose of the survey was to provide data necessary to compute a cost-of-living index, but its informative value is much broader.[16]

Since the end of World War I, thousands of surveys of consumer expenditures have been made by governments, local authorities, labor unions and other organizations all over the world. Because of the wide differences in scope, methods and classification, the results cannot be summarized in international statistical tables,[17] but together supplementing one another, they supply a highly enlightening picture of the structure of the needs of mankind.

Family expenditures are usually classified by family income or total outlay. Sometimes they are cross classified by income — or total outlays — and occupation of the family head, by income and size of family, by income and type of community, and so forth. From a broad economic point of view — for example, if the purpose is to ascertain the trends in the distribution of purchasing power in the nation — the classifica-

---

11. King estimated outlays for "dyet" in England at 46.2 per cent of all private expenditures (except taxes), as compared with 47.5 per cent in France and 35.7 per cent in Holland. The most conspicuous contrast he found was in drinking habits in the three countries: beer, ale, wine and liquor absorbed 36 per cent of "dyet" expenditures in England and 26 per cent in France and Holland. **20**, pp. 54–55.

12. **14.**

13. **17.**

14. Most of these studies were limited in scope. The four most important related to expenditures of 8,500 wage-earning families (in the United States and Europe) in 1890–91; of more than 25,000 families in 33 states in 1903; of 7,600 American worker families surveyed by the Board of Trade of Great Britain in 1909; and of 12,096 wage-earning and lower-salaried families in the United States in 1917–19. **21**, p. 334; cf. **2.**

15. This survey was conducted jointly by the United States Bureau of Labor Statistics, the Bureau of Home Economics of the Department of Agriculture, the National Resources Committee and the Central Statistical Board. Detailed reports for single areas were released by the Bureau of Labor Statistics and the Bureau of Home Economics. The final reports were prepared by the National Resources Committee (later known as the National Resources Planning Board). (**7**, **9** and **8.**)

16. **6**, *passim.*

17. **27**, p. 60.

tion by income level is of paramount significance. This was the chief objective of the Consumer Expenditures Study. On the other hand, sociological analysis requires classification by socio-occupational characteristics of the head of the household, type of family, and the like.

ENGEL'S LAW

The fundamental law of consumption is that *the poorer a family, the greater the proportion of its total expenditure used for food.* With some reservation, this law also holds for nations and continents: the poorer a country, a region or a continent, the larger the proportion the efforts and resources its people expend to supply themselves with food.

This correlation between the pattern of consumption and income level was established almost a century ago by the German statistician Engel and is known as Engel's law. Engel expressed this law by a hypothetical series showing the percentage of expenditures going for food at different income levels, as follows: [18]

Annual Family Income, in Francs	*Expenditure for Food as Percentage of All Expenditures*	*Annual Family Income, in Francs*	*Expenditure for Food as Percentage of All Expenditures*
200	73.0	1,000	64.0
300	71.5	1,200	62.5
400	70.1	1,400	61.3
500	68.8	1,600	60.2
600	67.7	1,800	59.4
700	66.6	2,000	58.6
800	65.7	2,500	57.4
900	64.8	3,000	56.9

These figures did not represent the findings of any particular consumer-expenditures survey but summarized, in a general way, several small-scale surveys made in various European countries in the middle of the last century. Engel described the scale of human needs as follows:

Food is of course the first need, followed by clothing and next in line by shelter and fuel and light. Satisfaction of these needs, however, is insured by public security. These five items are premises of physical and material existence; no life is possible without them, and if one of them disappears, life comes to an end. Yet, shrinkage of any of these items affects material life . . . according to a scale of the urgency of the respective needs. . . .

18. **18**, pp. 30–31. Reproduced here in abbreviated form. Cf. Figure 96.

Poverty always manifests itself as shortage of food. . . . When poverty is extreme, shelter . . . gives no protection against heat and frost. . . . Beds and linen have been sold or pawned, clothing is reduced to rags and the last shirt is given away for a piece of bread.

These seem to be universally known platitudes [Engel concludes] . . . they are, however, . . . far-reaching consequences of a natural law which is stronger than all the powers on the earth.[19]

Carle Clark Zimmerman, drawing on more comprehensive observation, stressed three types of relation between income and food:

(1) Once the starvation level is passed, additional increments of income are associated, for a period at least, with increases of the *proportion* expended for food. This occurs when the food expense is so low that the population feels underfed and intensely desires more appetizing food.

(2) Additional increases in income are associated with an increasing *amount* spent for food but at a rate which gives a decreasing *proportion* of the total income. These relations occur among populations securing food sufficient for existence and comfort. At the lower range the people have enough food

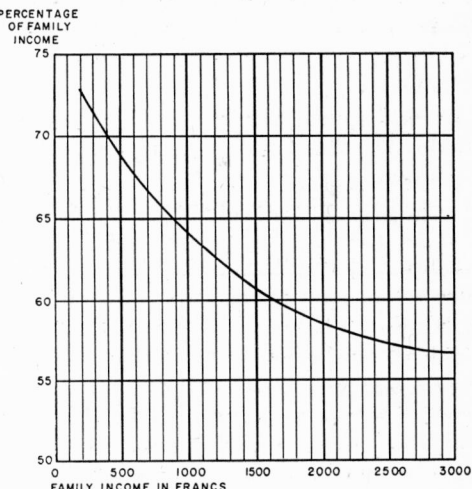

FIGURE 96. ENGEL'S LAW: PERCENTAGE OF ANNUAL INCOME USED FOR FOOD BY FAMILIES WITH DIFFERENT INCOMES

According to Engel's law, the poorer a family, the larger the share of income spent for food. Roughly, the curve in this figure postulates that with increasing income, outlays for food increase at a slightly lower and gradually declining rate, so that when a consumer's income doubles, his expenditures for food rise 90 per cent or more at a low income level; approximately 85 per cent in the middle-income bracket, and 80 per cent in households in more or less comfortable circumstances.

19. **18**, pp. 27–28.

physiologically even though it may be of an inferior economic variety. At the upper range food tends to be chosen more often on the sole basis of individual taste.

(3) Finally, as income increases further, there is some evidence that the *amount* spent for food may actually decrease. The upper sedentary and rich classes are in this category.[20]

Elasticity of Demand

Engel's law can be considered as a particular case of the general principles of declining satisfaction and elasticity of demand.

The consumer who has a strictly limited amount of money to spend for food will naturally use it for the things he needs most. This will leave many of his desires unsatisfied. If he obtains more money he will spend it on the items which were not included in his initial purchases. If he can spend still more he will add still other articles to his purchases. Since each time he buys what he wants most, the satisfaction he obtains for each additional dollar must decline. The same rule controls his outlays for clothing, furniture, recreation and so on. The principle of declining satisfaction applies to all forms of consumption: in all parts of the consumer's budget, the satisfaction he obtains declines with each additional unit of money, for the simple reason that he tries to spend each additional dollar for the things he needs or wants most.

This general principle, however, acts differently in relation to different consumption items. In some cases, the satisfaction declines rapidly and soon reaches zero: the demand is fully satisfied and further increase of consumption gives no additional satisfaction. In other cases, the satisfaction declines slowly and the demand, in changing form, remains unsatisfied. Staple foods provide an example of the first type of consumption items. All forms of luxuries in food, clothing, house accommodation, recreation, and so forth are examples of the second type. Moreover, in the realm of luxury consumption, satisfaction from the additional money spent for food declines more rapidly than that from money spent for clothing and especially for recreation.

This difference in the speed of decline in satisfaction from additional purchases is the basis of Engel's law: Since satisfaction from food expenditures declines more rapidly than that from

other outlays, the relative share of food in the total outlay must diminish as the consumer's income increases.

The elasticity of demand in relation to prices is also a consequence of the law of declining satisfaction. In general, the satisfaction an article offers per money unit increases as the price of the article declines. As a result, some persons who customarily use the article will take a larger amount than before and others who could not afford it will purchase it. Similarly, a rise in the price of an article tends to curtail the demand for it.

The response of demand to a definite change in prices depends on the character of the article and other conditions. A 10 per cent increase or decrease in the price of salt, for example, will not affect appreciably the demand for it, but a 10 per cent change in the price of apples or a particular type of house appliance may have this effect. The response of demand to a change in prices is particularly marked in the case of a competitive commodity.

As a rule, the demand for luxury goods (with slowly declining satisfaction) is more responsive to change in prices than the demand for staple commodities. A distinction can be made between the articles with an elastic and an inelastic demand: If outlets for a commodity change in more than inverse relation to its price, the total amount of its sales must increase when its price goes down and decrease when it goes up; if the demand for a commodity is inelastic, the total consumer outlay for it goes up when its price rises and goes down when it falls.

Without elaborating these general remarks, it should be mentioned here that the demand for food as a whole, tobacco and basic housing accommodation is inelastic in comparison with other items of everyday consumption. Demand is most elastic for expensive foods, luxury articles, books and recreation.

Consumer Expenditures in the United States

In the long list of studies of family expenditures carried out in the United States in the last three decades, the most important are the surveys made by the Department of Labor during 1917–19 and 1934–36 and the Consumer Expenditures Study in 1935–36. The findings of these studies are dated, of course, in the sense that they do not represent exactly the present patterns of consumption. They reflect, however,

---

20. **27**, pp. 117–18.

TABLE 133

CONSUMER EXPENDITURES: DISTRIBUTION IN EMPLOYEE FAMILIES WITH SPECIFIED
INCOME, IN THE UNITED STATES, 1917–19 AND 1934–36

	Percentage of Total Expenditure Used for:					
Annual Income	*Food*	*Rent*	*Fuel and Light*	*Furniture and Furnishings*	*Clothing*	*Other*
			1917–19			
Under $900	45.5	17.2	6.6	3.2	13.8	13.7
900–1,200	43.4	15.4	5.9	4.5	14.9	15.9
1,200–1,500	41.2	15.0	5.5	4.8	16.3	17.2
1,500–1,800	39.9	14.3	5.0	5.3	17.1	18.4
1,800–2,100	38.5	13.6	5.0	5.1	18.0	19.8
2,100–2,500	37.2	12.6	4.4	5.5	19.2	21.1
2,500 and over	37.9	10.8	3.6	4.5	21.7	21.5
			1934–36			
Under $900	40.2	18.6	8.4	3.6	8.7	20.5
900–1,200	38.2	18.3	8.3	3.7	9.2	22.3
1,200–1,500	36.4	17.5	7.8	3.9	10.0	24.4
1,500–1,800	34.8	16.8	7.2	4.5	10.6	26.1
1,800–2,100	33.7	15.9	6.5	4.2	11.2	28.5
2,100–2,500	33.8	14.6	6.3	4.1	12.2	29.0
2,500 and over	33.8	13.0	5.4	3.9	13.9	30.0

Source: **6,** p. 44.

the structure of consumer expenditures at different income levels, for families of various sizes and in various groups of the population.

Worker Families, 1917–19 and 1934–36

The surveys of the Department of Labor, designed to provide a basis for developing a cost-of-living index, were restricted to families of urban wage earners and salaried workers. They show that the share of food and rent in total expenditures declines and that of clothing increases as income rises. Within given income groups, the pattern of expenditures of worker families changed between 1917-19 and 1934-36. The percentage of the total outlay spent for food, clothing, and furniture and furnishings declined and the share of rent, fuel and light, and "other" items increased. "Other" includes expenditures for automobiles, for example, which were a luxury in the earlier period but had come into common use by the middle of the 1930's.

The rise in the share of rent in workers' budgets reflected the trend toward better and more expensive dwellings. In 1917–19, half the surveyed families had apartments without bathrooms; in 1934–36, only 10 per cent. Changes

in the share of other groups of needs were caused mainly by differences in price trends. Lower prices of food and clothing were reflected in a lower proportion of the outlay for these items, and the rise in the prices of fuel and light, in a higher proportion.[21] (See Table 133.)

Consumers, 1935–36

The Consumer Expenditures Study showed striking differences in the patterns of expenditures of the rich and the poor for food, clothing and transportation. In contrast to the surveys of workers' families, however, it suggests that the share of shelter (rent and household operation combined) in the outlays of poor and rich households varies within a comparatively narrow range and is practically the same in the income brackets $750–$1,000, $3,000–$5,000 and $15,000–$20,000.

Food accounted for nearly 45 per cent of the total outlay of the average household in the lowest income bracket, for 30 to 35 per cent among middle-class families ($1,500–$3,000 income class), and for 15 per cent among the rich.

21. **6,** pp. **34–39.**

TABLE 134

CONSUMER EXPENDITURES: DISTRIBUTION IN HOUSEHOLDS [a] WITH SPECIFIED INCOME,
IN THE UNITED STATES, 1935–36

				Percentage of Total Expenditure Used for:			
Annual Income	*Food*	*Shelter*		*Clothing*	*Auto-mobile*	*Medical Care*	*Other*
		Rent	*Household Operation*				
Under $500	44.5	22.3	9.5	7.6	2.2	3.8	10.1
500–750	42.3	20.1	9.8	9.2	3.0	3.6	12.0
750–1,000	40.3	19.2	10.0	9.5	4.2	3.7	13.1
1,000–1,250	37.8	19.0	10.4	9.6	5.7	3.9	13.6
1,250–1,500	36.3	18.4	10.2	10.0	6.5	4.1	14.5
1,500–1,750	34.5	18.4	10.1	10.1	7.6	4.5	14.8
1,750–2,000	32.9	18.5	10.3	10.2	8.6	4.5	15.0
2,000–2,500	31.2	18.3	10.1	10.8	9.7	4.6	15.3
2,500–3,000	29.9	17.9	10.9	11.2	10.2	4.7	15.2
3,000–4,000	28.1	18.3	11.0	11.7	10.3	4.9	15.7
4,000–5,000	25.9	18.2	11.4	12.6	11.3	4.9	15.7
5,000–10,000	23.2	18.5	12.2	12.6	11.5	5.7	16.3
10,000–15,000	19.7	20.7	11.5	13.6	11.1	4.2	19.2
15,000–20,000	19.2	17.7	11.9	13.6	10.4	5.0	22.2
20,000 and over	15.2	20.0	13.2	14.3	12.1	6.1	19.1

Source: **8**, p. 85 (Table 22–A).

a. Families of two or more and individuals.

The general tendency conforms with Engel's law, but in comparison with the European families observed by Engel, the American households spent relatively less for food and more for shelter.[22] (See Table 134; cf. Figure 97.)

The level of consumption among families of both city and farm workers in the United States has changed in recent years with improvement in employment conditions and earnings. A typical farm wage earner's family, for example, is much better off than before World War II. However, because of the uneven advance in prices, such a family spent about the same proportion of income on food in 1948-50 as before the war.

Families of Different Size, 1935–36

With the same income, a large family needs more food than a small family, and has therefore less money for shelter and other necessities. The Consumer Expenditures Study indicates this general relationship in that there is similarity

22. In the more recent consumer spending studies conducted by the Bureau of Labor Statistics, especially the surveys for Denver, Detroit and Houston in 1948, the pattern of expenditures for food at different income levels is less clear and does not follow Engel's law. **7**, December 1949, reprint, pp. 4, 5, 8, 12.

in the expenditure patterns of families of 2 persons with annual income of $750–$1,000, those of 3 to 6 persons in the bracket $1,500–

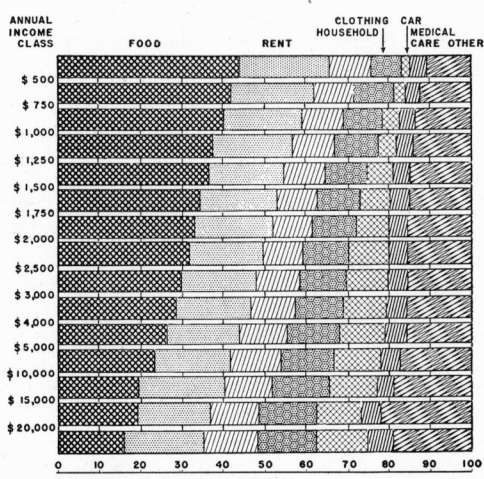

FIGURE 97. PERCENTAGE DISTRIBUTION OF EXPENDITURES OF HOUSEHOLDS IN THE UNITED STATES, 1935–36

The relative share of food in consumer expenditures declines as one moves from lower to higher income classes. The share used for rent and household operation combined is fairly stable. The relative amount spent for clothing, medical care and other items increases as income rises. (See Table 134.)

TABLE 135

CONSUMER EXPENDITURES: DISTRIBUTION IN FARM AND URBAN FAMILIES OF DIFFERENT
SIZE, WITH SPECIFIED INCOME, IN THE UNITED STATES, 1935–36

	Farm Families				Urban Families			
	Percentage of Total Annual Expenditure Used for:							
Annual Income and Size of Family	Food	Shelter	Clothing	Other	Food	Shelter	Clothing	Other
$750–1,000								
2 persons	45.1	30.2	6.4	18.3	34.6	40.3	7.0	18.1
3–6	50.9	21.3	9.5	18.3	39.1	35.3	8.2	17.4
7 or more	59.0	14.0	10.0	17.0	43.5	32.7	9.5	14.3
1,500–1,750								
2 persons	35.8	34.6	7.4	22.2	29.6	37.8	9.1	23.5
3–6	42.4	25.2	10.0	22.4	33.9	33.9	9.8	22.4
7 or more	52.3	19.0	10.5	18.2	39.6	29.0	11.7	19.7
2,500–3,000								
2 persons	30.4	37.9	6.9	24.8	26.8	36.8	10.0	26.4
3–6	37.9	26.6	10.6	24.9	29.6	33.3	11.0	26.1
7 or more	45.2	19.9	10.4	24.5	35.5	28.1	12.8	23.6
5,000–10,000								
2 persons	23.6	41.0	11.4	24.0	19.5	42.3	9.7	28.5
3–6	28.1	30.9	11.6	29.4	23.0	35.2	12.3	29.5
7 or more	39.8	23.5	13.6	23.1	26.2	28.0	13.4	32.4

Source: **10**, pp. 101–05 (recomputed).

$1,750, and those of 7 or more persons with income of $2,500–$3,000.[23] (See Table 135.) The comparison is rough, however, since other needs of a family do not increase in direct proportion to the number of its members and its needs for food.[24]

23. The same pattern of food expenditures in families of different size appears in the more recent studies of the Bureau of Labor Statistics. See **7**, April 1949 and December 1949.

24. In analyzing the actual needs of a family, not only its size but also its composition by age should be taken into account.

Engel tried to meet these requirements by using a unit of consumption related to the age of family members: 1.0 for a newborn child, 1.5 for age 5, 2.0 for age 10, 2.5 for age 15, 3.0 for age 20, 3.5 for age 25 and thereafter. He called this consumption unit "Quet," from the name of the Belgian statistician Quetelet. (**18**, pp. 4 ff.) The more recent tendency is to express family requirements in terms of those of a grown man or woman, by measuring the size of families in such units as "ammain" (adult-male-maintenance unit) suggested by Edgar Sydenstricker (**24**), or "adult-male-equivalent-units-for-food-and-other-expenditures," as used by the statistical services in Germany. A simpler method is to count the head of the family and his wife as full consumer units and each of the other members of the household as half a unit. (**26**, pp. 235–36.)

Farm and Urban Families, 1935–36

Farm families spend a larger part of their income for food than urban families with comparable income. (See Tables 135 and 136.) The difference is due to the fact that on the average farm families are larger than city families; it may also reflect the need for more food for farm workers because of the strenuous labor required of them.

Farm expenditures for food and shelter include the value of foodstuffs produced and consumed on the farm, such as grain, vegetables, fruits, milk, eggs and meat, and the imputed rental value of an owner-occupied house.[25]

CONSUMER EXPENDITURES IN OTHER COUNTRIES

International comparisons of consumer needs and expenditures must be made with great cau-

25. The distribution of the expenditures of a farm family depends largely on the way in which its receipts in kind are evaluated and added to its money income. The omission of receipts in kind in some household statistics of foreign countries result in understatement of farmers' income and particularly in understatement of their outlay for food. This understatement may be so great that it becomes inconceivable how the farm family can keep body and soul together.

TABLE 136

CONSUMER EXPENDITURES: DISTRIBUTION IN FARM AND URBAN FAMILIES WITH SPECIFIED INCOME, IN THE
UNITED STATES, 1935–36

	Farm Families					Urban Families				
	Percentage of Total Annual Expenditure Used for:									
Annual Income	Food	Shelter	Clothing	Transportation	Other	Food	Shelter	Clothing	Transportation	Other
Under $500	53.6	21.7	8.7	6.0	10.0	39.1	39.5	6.5	3.1	11.8
500–750	54.6	20.5	8.9	5.9	10.1	39.3	37.8	7.3	3.6	12.0
750–1,000	51.6	21.4	9.0	7.3	10.7	37.9	36.8	7.8	5.1	12.4
1,000–1,250	48.3	22.8	9.4	8.1	11.4	35.9	36.0	8.7	6.7	12.7
1,250–1,500	46.2	23.8	9.9	8.6	11.5	35.0	35.2	9.0	7.3	13.5
1,500–1,750	43.4	25.3	9.7	9.6	12.0	33.1	34.6	9.7	8.6	14.0
1,750–2,000	41.6	26.0	9.7	10.6	12.1	32.1	34.6	9.8	9.4	14.1
2,000–2,500	40.0	26.3	10.2	10.9	12.6	30.7	33.7	10.5	10.5	14.6
2,500–3,000	38.7	26.2	10.2	11.8	13.1	29.3	33.6	11.0	11.1	15.0
3,000–4,000	36.7	27.3	10.3	12.1	13.6	27.5	34.1	11.9	11.0	15.5
4,000–5,000	35.5	28.0	11.7	11.1	13.7	25.5	34.0	12.2	11.8	16.5
5,000–10,000	29.5	30.8	11.8	13.9	14.0	22.6	36.0	11.9	12.1	17.4

Source: **10**, pp. 51 and 61.

tion because of the wide differences in methods, selection of the sample, classification and so on.

Each of the monographic international surveys inaugurated by LePlay [26] and carried on by his school was intended to stand independently as a glimpse into the life of a particular type of family. Because of this, they did not need to be strictly comparable in statistical technique. Later the surveys were combined in groups and the main findings were tabulated as we now tabulate the more consistent data of less intensive investigations of consumer expenditures. Despite the lack of comparability, LePlay's surveys appeared to confirm Engel's law: in comparatively rich countries, such as England and Switzerland, people spend a smaller part of their means on food and a larger part on shelter and clothing than in poor and underdeveloped countries.

The correlation between the economic well-being of a family and the share of food in its total outlay is not so clear in international surveys, however, as in those of households within one country,[27] since national differences in composition of population, consumption habits and prices can be stronger than Engel's law.

26. **22**, pp. 58–91.
27. **27**, p. 109.

Families of Workers before World War II

The International Labor Office in Geneva made a comprehensive survey of the expenditures of urban employee families in 25 countries shortly before the outbreak of the last war. In Table 137, which summarizes this survey, the average annual expenditures of each group of families is expressed in United States dollars, at the current exchange rate. Because of considerable fluctuations of prices and wide differences in the patterns of consumption and the purchasing power of money in different countries, these figures give only a very rough ranking of the surveyed families in income, but they show clearly the contrast between typical patterns of expenditure in high-wage and low-wage countries.

In countries where earnings are comparatively low, outlays for food account for 50–60 per cent of all expenditures of wage-earning families; in high-wage nations, generally 35–40 per cent. In some instances, however, the working of Engel's law has been obstructed by local conditions. In Japan, for example, and perhaps also in India, the relatively low expenditure for food is due to the extreme frugality of the people, especially with respect to food. In some countries, as in Belgium and Denmark, the wide divergence in

TABLE 137

CONSUMER EXPENDITURES: DISTRIBUTION IN URBAN EMPLOYEE FAMILIES IN 25 COUNTRIES, BEFORE WORLD WAR II

Country[a] and Occupational Class[b]	Year	Percentage of Total Annual Expenditure Used for:					Average Annual Expenditure in U.S. Dollars
		Food	Rent	Household Operation	Clothing	Other	
Colombia	1936	63.9	24.1		1.3	10.6	350
Belgium	1928/29	59.6	6.4	7.9	15.8	10.3	560
(E)	1928/29	51.0	12.1	10.0	15.8	11.1	590
Estonia	1925	59.0	14.6		15.9	10.5	270
Poland	1929	57.2	4.1	8.4	17.3	13.0	387
Mexico	1934	56.4	9.7	9.5	6.6	17.8	380
China[c]	1929/30	55.8	8.5	7.9	7.4	20.4	454
Argentina	1935	54.9	18.7	4.1	10.3	12.0	—
Czechoslovakia	1931/32	54.7	6.3	9.9	13.4	15.7	517
(E)	1931/32	39.5	9.1	11.4	16.5	23.5	645
(O)	1931/32	47.9	7.1	11.2	16.7	17.1	952
Hungary	1929	52.9	10.4	7.6	10.2	18.9	820
Finland	1928	50.5	13.0	8.7	12.2	15.6	1,120
(E)	1928	41.1	15.9	8.6	13.3	21.1	1,440
(O)	1928	29.3	15.4	10.4	13.0	31.9	2,180
Austria	1934	50.3	7.7	8.3	9.8	23.9	660
Bulgaria	1927/28	50.2	13.8	9.1	12.8	14.1	301
(O)	1927/28	39.6	15.9	9.6	14.2	20.7	511
India[d]	1933/35	49.3	11.0	7.0	9.1	23.6	300
Brazil	1934	48.3	21.3	4.1	10.1	16.2	—
Norway	1927/28	47.1	12.7	8.4	13.4	18.4	1,130
(O)	1927/28	43.2	12.6	10.2	15.1	18.9	1,490
Germany	1927/28	46.6	10.6	7.9	13.5	21.4	770
(E)	1927/28	36.7	12.8	10.0	14.0	26.5	1,085
(O)	1927/28	35.5	13.2	11.1	15.4	24.8	1,740
Sweden	1933	40.2	14.7	10.1	14.0	21.0	960
(O)	1933	35.4	16.7	10.2	14.3	23.4	1,170
Netherlands	1935/36	40.1	15.8	9.4	9.0	25.7	1,040
(E,O)	1935/36	22.8	13.6	9.4	9.9	44.3	2,270
Latvia	1936/37	40.0	19.4	4.4	12.0	24.2	610
Japan	1935/36	38.5	13.6	7.7	11.3	28.9	270
(E)	1935/36	33.3	15.0	8.3	11.7	31.7	310
Denmark[e]	1931	37.5	15.1	10.0	11.3	26.1	2,040
(O)	1931	34.9	17.1	7.6	12.6	27.7	2,350
United States[f]	1934/36	36.7	21.1	7.5	11.1	23.6	—
Switzerland[g]	1936/37	35.2	23.7	8.6	9.6	22.9	1,640
(E,O)	1936/37	29.1	23.6	9.8	10.2	27.3	2,270
Union of South Africa	1936	32.8	24.3	6.5	10.3	26.1	2,830
New Zealand	1930	29.5	21.9	7.7	12.6	28.3	—

Source: 1, May 1939, p. 749.

a. Countries arrayed by declining share of food in total expenditure in households of manual workers.
b. White-collar employees: E; officials: O; all other data for manual workers.

c. Shanghai.
d. Ahmadabad.
e. Copenhagen.
f. New York.
g. Zurich.

TABLE 138

CONSUMER EXPENDITURES: DISTRIBUTION IN FAMILIES OF MANUAL WORKERS, WHITE-
COLLAR EMPLOYEES AND OFFICIALS WITH SPECIFIED INCOME, IN GERMANY, 1927–28

Occupation of Family Head and Income, in Marks	Percentage of Annual Income Used for:			
	Food	Shelter	Clothing	Other Purposes [a]
Manual workers				
Under 2,500 marks	47.9	19.3	10.4	22.4
2,500–3,000	47.3	17.8	11.6	23.3
3,000–3,600	45.6	17.5	12.7	24.2
3,600–4,300	44.5	17.0	13.4	25.1
Over 4,300	41.5	16.9	14.6	27.0
White-collar employees				
Under 3,000 marks	41.6	22.2	11.0	25.2
3,000–3,600	39.8	20.4	12.5	27.3
3,600–4,300	37.6	20.2	12.0	30.2
4,300–5,100	35.0	20.4	12.9	31.7
Over 5,100	30.5	20.9	12.9	35.7
Officials				
Under 3,000 marks	43.2	21.5	11.8	23.5
3,000–3,600	40.9	22.5	13.4	23.2
3,600–4,300	39.6	21.5	15.3	23.6
4,300–5,100	36.5	20.3	15.8	27.4
Over 5,100	29.4	22.7	13.3	34.6

Source: **11**, 1931, pp. 325–27.

a. Savings and dissavings are included in "other" outlays. Thus, in contrast to Tables 133 to 136, this table shows outlays for food, shelter and clothing as percentage of income rather than of actual expenditures.

the distribution of expenditures may reflect the selection of the surveyed families.

In general, the ILO survey warrants the following conclusions:

1. The share of food in the expenditures of workers' families ranges from about 35 per cent in the richest countries to 60 per cent in those where wages are lowest.

2. The share of rent usually varies in the inverse direction, from less than 10 per cent in the poorest countries to 21–24 per cent in the prosperous.[28]

3. The combined share of fuel, light, furnishings, household operation and clothing generally ranges between 15 and 25 per cent and is not directly correlated with the level of earnings.

4. The share of "other" expenditures increases from 10 per cent in the poor countries to more than 25 per cent in those with high earnings.

Manual and White-Collar Workers

Some of the household studies surveyed by the International Labor Office distinguish be-

tween manual workers, white-collar employees and officials. (See Table 137.) Comparable data for these occupational classes are available for Belgium, Czechoslovakia, Finland, Bulgaria, Norway, Germany, Sweden, the Netherlands, Japan, Denmark and Switzerland. In all these countries, manual workers spend more for food than white-collar employees and officials. Other differences among the three groups are less clear because of the differences in income in various occupations.

Consumer expenditures studies that provide a classification by income of households in each occupational group are more enlightening in this respect. Such double classification was used in the consumer expenditures study in Germany in 1927–28. It shows that within each occupational group the pattern of expenditure follows Engel's law: the share of food declines and that of clothing rises with rise in income, while that of shelter fluctuates within a comparatively narrow range. Within the same income group, manual workers spend more of their income for food than white-collar employees and officials. White-collar employees and officials differ chiefly

28. This item is largely affected by public housing policy and rent control in different countries.

TABLE 139

CONSUMER EXPENDITURES: DISTRIBUTION AMONG AGRICULTURAL WORKERS, IN SELECTED
COUNTRIES, BEFORE WORLD WAR II

Area and Class of Agricultural Worker [a]	Year	Food	Rent	House-hold Opera-tion	Clothing	Other	Average Annual Expendi-ture, in U.S. Dollars
Finland							
Tenants	1928	62.3	7.0	9.9	11.9	8.9	$375
Day laborers	1928	61.3	7.5	9.7	10.7	10.8	414
Foremen	1928	54.3	7.6	9.8	13.5	14.8	520
United States							
County of Laurel	1927/28	61.2	6.5	8.9	13.6	9.8	689
County of Knott	1929/30	61.0	4.1	8.2	16.9	9.8	964
County of Grayson	1928	45.3	9.7	11.5	19.0	14.5	736
Iowa	1926/27	41.2	17.1	10.6	9.9	21.2	1,558
Sweden							
Small tenants	1933	57.9	8.5	8.4	14.5	10.7	334
Tenants	1933	52.1	8.6	10.3	14.4	14.6	413
Day laborers	1933	49.8	7.6	9.8	16.7	16.1	494
Farm owners	1933/34	48.8	11.5	9.5	14.6	15.6	451
Germany							
Mainly tenants	1927	57.2	6.2	7.8	15.3	13.5	459
Netherlands							
Farm laborers	1935/36	52.1	11.1	9.8	10.9	16.1	660
Farm owners	1935/36	37.8	12.2	9.0	13.3	27.7	1,273
Japan							
Tenants	1926/27	50.7	10.2	10.7	6.9	21.5	450
Farm owners	1926/27	41.8	11.7	11.5	8.7	26.3	594

Source: **1**, April 1941, p. 530.

a. The term "tenants" as used here does not represent precisely the same type of tenure in the various countries.

in that the latter spend more for shelter and clothing. (See Table 138.)

Farmers and Farm Laborers

International household statistics for farmers and farm laborers are scanty and less conclusive. Data compiled by the ILO show characteristic differences between the budgets of farm owners, tenants and farm laborers. Farm laborers use a larger part of their earnings for food, while a larger part of the outlay of farm owners is recorded as rent, meaning usually the rental value of their own dwellings. (See Table 139.)

NATIONAL CONSUMPTION EXPENDITURES

If we know how the population of a country is distributed by income classes and how each consumer group distributes its expenditures, we

can estimate the total amount spent for food, housing, household operation, clothing and so on by various groups of the population and in the nation as a whole.

In the United States

In the United States, consumption outlays totaling somewhat more than $50.2 billion a year during 1935–36 were distributed among approximately 39.5 million consumer units. The 16.5 million households in the lowest income brackets represented, as a group, the same purchasing power — about $10 billion — as the 9 million consumer units next above them in income, the 6.5 million middle-class households, the 5 million in the next higher group, or the 2.5 million with the highest incomes. (See Tables 140 and 141.)

TABLE 140

TOTAL EXPENDITURES OF HOUSEHOLDS, WITH SPECIFIED INCOME, IN THE UNITED STATES, 1935–36

Annual Income	Number of Households,[a] in Thousands	Aggregate Annual Expenditure, in Millions, for:										
		Total	Food	Housing	Household Operation	Clothing	Automobile	Other Transportation	Personal Care	Medical Care	Education and Reading	Other
Total	39,458	$50,214	$16,865	$9,506	$6,707	$5,261	$3,781	$884	$1,032	$2,205	$1,057	$2,916
Under $500	6,711	2,817	1,254	634	306	212	63	59	60	104	40	85
500–750	5,771	3,888	1,645	781	445	356	118	81	85	140	64	173
750–1,000	5,876	5,209	2,097	999	646	495	218	99	110	197	90	258
1,000–1,500	8,734	10,294	3,819	1,924	1,352	1,002	631	176	215	414	191	570
1,500–2,000	5,186	8,072	2,720	1,487	1,092	823	654	129	168	365	152	482
2,000–3,000	4,434	9,043	2,776	1,641	1,242	991	891	134	190	418	193	567
3,000–4,000	1,354	3,631	1,020	662	524	425	375	52	71	177	85	240
4,000–5,000	464	1,494	386	271	216	187	169	21	30	74	39	101
5,000–10,000	596	2,604	602	481	399	329	299	38	51	148	68	189
10,000–15,000	153	925	182	192	137	125	103	20	17	39	38	72
15,000–20,000	68	607	116	107	89	83	63	26	10	30	37	46
20,000 and over	110	1,630	248	327	259	233	197	49	25	99	60	133

Source: Adapted from **8**, p. 89.　　　　a. Families of two or more and individuals.

TABLE 141

NATIONAL CONSUMPTION EXPENDITURES: TOTAL EXPENDITURES OF FIVE INCOME GROUPS OF HOUSEHOLDS, ACCOUNTING FOR EACH FIFTH OF NATIONAL INCOME, IN THE UNITED STATES, 1935–36

Income Group	Number of Households,[a] in Millions	Aggregate Annual Expenditure, in Billions, for:										
		Total	Food	Housing	Household Operation	Clothing	Automobile	Other Transportation	Personal Care	Medical Care	Education and Reading	Other
Total	39.5	$50.2	$16.9	$9.5	$6.7	$5.3	$3.8	$0.9	$1.0	$2.2	$1.1	$2.9
Poor	16.5	10.1	4.2	2.1	1.2	0.9	0.3	0.2	0.2	0.4	0.2	0.4
Middle-low	9.0	10.0	3.8	1.9	1.3	1.0	0.5	0.2	0.2	0.4	0.2	0.5
Middle	6.5	10.0	3.5	1.9	1.3	1.0	0.7	0.2	0.2	0.4	0.2	0.6
Middle-high	5.0	10.1	3.2	1.9	1.4	1.1	0.9	0.1	0.2	0.5	0.2	0.6
Rich	2.5	10.1	2.2	1.7	1.5	1.3	1.4	0.2	0.2	0.5	0.3	0.8

Source: Derived by free-hand interpolation from Table 140.　　　　a. Families of two or more and individuals.

278

A nation's expenditures can also be computed directly from statistics of production, imports and exports, retail trade and so on. The United States Department of Commerce has been compiling such statistics in great detail since 1929, and private estimates carry the series back for two additional decades. The percentage distribution of the total expenditures among the chief items of consumption has been more stable than might be expected on the basis of Engel's law. Changes in the distribution are slow and those after 1929 appear to be temporary fluctuations, largely due to shifts in prices, with no consistent trend in any definite direction.

Apart from changes in consumption patterns, during the war, the most conspicuous variation is in the share of food in total consumption expenditures. In accordance with Engel's law a decline in the relative expenditure might have been expected to accompany the increase in prosperity in the United States from 1909 to 1949, but such a movement has been counterbalanced by divergences in price trends. The collapse of agricultural prices during the depression of the 1930's permitted the nation to cut down its relative outlay for food, while skyrocketing food prices in the postwar boom have forced consumers to increase the proportion of their income used for food. (See Table 142.)

In the World

Germany and Great Britain also made surveys of aggregate consumer expenditures before the war. Their findings, which seem to be typical for industrially developed European countries, indicate that food, including beverages and tobacco, absorbed approximately 40 per cent of the total consumer outlay, rent and household operation, 15 per cent and clothing, 10 per cent.

It seems likely that in regions with a primitive economy, such as the Pacific Islands, Africa, some parts of South and Middle America and Asia, food accounts for as much as 80 per cent of the consumption expenditures of the population. The ratio is probably close to 70 per cent in such industrially underdeveloped countries as China, India, Iran and Iraq; 60 per cent in Mexico, Brazil, the USSR and Japan; and hardly more than 50 per cent in the agricultural countries of southern and southeastern Europe. In the industrially developed countries, the total outlay on food, beverages and tobacco probably ranges between 30 and 40 per cent of all consumer expenditures. Thus, for most nations and the majority of mankind, more than half of all expenditures goes for food, but the countries where incomes are highest spend less than half for this purpose.

We may use these tentative patterns of distribution of consumer outlays in countries at different levels of economic well-being [29] as the basis of a rough estimate of the pattern of world consumer outlays. Less than half the total consumption outlay — probably not more than 40–45 per cent — is used for food, beverages and tobacco; 10–15 per cent for clothing; and 20 per cent for housing (including rent, the rental value of owner-occupied dwellings, furniture and household operation); leaving from 20 to 25 per cent for transportation, recreation, personal and medical services, religious organizations and so on.

In addition to their outlays for personal essentials, the world's consumers, as a whole, use some of their income to pay taxes (the price of governmental services or "public security" as Engel called it), and the relatively wealthy among them acquire some savings. On the basis of available information for some two dozen countries, the rate of savings in industrial nations may be estimated at 7 to 10 per cent (probably appreciably lower in agricultural regions); and the rate of taxes (including all kinds of indirect taxes and customs duties) at 18 to 20 per cent of aggregate personal income. Thus all personal incomes in the world would be distributed, at a rough approximation, as follows:

Total personal income	100.0 per cent
Taxes	18–20
Savings	7–10
Total	25–30
Consumption expenditures	70–75
Food, beverages and tobacco	30–35
Housing	15–16
Clothing	8–12
Other needs	15–20

29. Cf. Chapter 12.

TABLE 142

NATIONAL EXPENDITURES FOR VARIOUS CONSUMPTION ITEMS, IN THE UNITED STATES, 1909–50

A. Amount, in Millions

Item	1909	1919	1929	1933	1937	1941	1945	1949	1950
Total expenditures	$28,757	$60,812	$78,761	$46,346	$67,121	$82,255	$123,079	$180,174	$193,568
I. Food, beverages and tobacco	9,881	22,304	21,374	12,777	21,629	26,476	45,924	62,870	65,347
Food produced and consumed on farms	7,427	18,814	1,585	926	1,304	1,294	2,135	2,388	2,392
Food furnished to employees and army			514	324	474	685	2,996	1,431	1,502
Food purchased			15,575	9,665	14,730	18,186	30,098	46,855	48,944
Alcoholic beverages	1,800	2,000	2,000	626	3,442	4,238	7,765	7,930	8,100
Tobacco and supply	654	1,490	1,700	1,236	1,679	2,073	2,930	4,266	4,409
II. Clothing	4,118	9,160	11,018	5,365	7,964	10,483	20,247	22,890	22,909
Footwear	767	1,913	1,839	985	1,401	1,630	2,537	3,169	3,280
Clothing, except footwear	2,784	5,951	7,514	3,664	5,427	7,295	14,818	15,943	15,769
Storage, cleaning, repair, etc.			473	230	383	513	878	1,426	1,449
Laundering, etc.	282	540	475	252	323	374	606	844	841
Miscellaneous			77	36	51	54	86	105	114
Jewelry and watches	285	756	640	198	379	617	1,322	1,403	1,456
III. Personal care	260	612	1,116	660	961	1,208	2,077	2,214	2,291
IV. Housing	5,491	7,941	11,421	7,849	8,378	9,863	12,205	18,129	19,894
Rent			4,445	3,244	3,560	4,312	4,531	5,517	6,002
Rental value of owner-occupied houses	5,491	7,941	6,727	4,452	4,607	5,313	7,333	12,108	13,370
Hotels, clubs, etc.			249	153	211	238	341	504	522
V. Household operation	4,039	7,908	10,509	6,396	9,340	11,724	14,865	23,529	26,439
Furniture, floor covering, etc.	1,125	2,709	1,652	628	1,286	1,808	2,084	3,784	4,423
Appliances, china, etc.	413	957	1,907	1,001	1,752	2,344 }	4,720	8,964	10,009
Other household supply	331	826	1,633	950	1,523	1,973 }			
Fuel and ice	985	1,492	1,608	1,152	1,417	1,707	2,225	2,892	3,163
Electricity, gas, water	362	707	1,397	1,374	1,574	1,851	2,254	3,200	3,593
Telephone, telegraph, postage and express	111	250	672	545	620	779	1,494	2,121	2,386
Domestic service	712	967	1,501	644	1,048	1,118	1,861	2,238	2,525
Miscellaneous	—	—	139	102	120	144	227	330	340
VI. Medical and death expenses	940	2,402	3,620	2,397	3,226	3,961	5,902	8,927	9,531
Drugs and appliances	201	564	735	519	723	951	1,507	1,829	1,927
Physicians and other medical personnel	434	1,152	1,777	1,065	1,424	1,700	2,342	3,688	3,889
Hospitalization	158	298	403	363	457	582	970	1,857	2,100
Miscellaneous	—	—	108	70	120	168	328	499	538
Death expenses	151	388	597	380	502	560	755	1,054	1,077
VII. Personal business	305	740	5,221	3,063	3,865	4,099	4,787	7,530	8,519
Brokerage charges, investment counsel, etc.	53	268	1,739	378	313	131	303	239	434
Expenses of handling life insurance	155	215	936	942	1,192	1,271	1,408	2,268	2,449
Legal services	97	257	402	334	402	450	620	1,003	1,066
Interest on personal debts	—	—	577	466	688	887	466	1,261	1,587
Miscellaneous	—	—	1,567	943	1,260	1,350	1,990	2,759	2,983
VIII. Transportation	1,624	5,203	7,496	3,920	6,432	8,241	6,694	19,327	22,667
User-operated car	625 [a]	3,493 [a]	5,748	2,940	5,147	6,777	3,691	16,048	19,447
Cars, tires and parts	227	1,996	3,228	1,050	2,402	3,342	1,087	9,442	12,259
Gasoline and oil	123	1,226	1,814	1,466	2,143	2,628	1,616	4,635	5,078
Repair and miscellaneous	37	189	706	424	602	807	988	1,971	2,110
Purchased transportation	999	1,710	1,748	980	1,285	1,464	3,003	3,279	3,220
Local	487	855	1,131	728	882	985	1,753	2,094	2,084
Intercity [b]	512	855	617	252	403	479	1,250	1,185	1,136
IX. Recreation	1,081	2,517	4,327	2,199	3,374	4,225	6,314	10,269	11,290
Motion pictures			720	482	676	756	1,359	1,342	1,235
Other admissions			193	91	142	181	272	460	436
Pari-mutuel and coin machines			16	15	90	147	281	385	357
Commercial participating amusements			207	121	194	210	259	394	402
Books, maps, magazines, etc.			847	571	761	870	1,537	1,934	1,970
Toys and sport equipment	1,081	2,517	551	271	472	664	931	1,736	1,879
Radio and musical instruments			1,038	209	408	672	483	2,198	3,120
Photography			73	38	77	112	254	343	358
Flowers			221	90	186	247	446	658	689
Clubs			302	208	203	203	281	460	471
Miscellaneous			159	103	165	163	211	359	373
X. Private (organized) education and research	405	734	664	481	600	692	871	1,657	1,773
XI. Religious and welfare activities	844	1,500	1,196	872	900	1,014	1,572	1,762	1,822
XII. Foreign travel and remittance (net)	124	38	799	367	452	269	1,621	1,670	1,860

TABLE 142—*continued*

NATIONAL EXPENDITURES FOR VARIOUS CONSUMPTION ITEMS, IN THE UNITED STATES, 1909–50

B. Percentage Distribution

Item	1909	1919	1929	1933	1937	1941	1945	1949	1950
Total expenditures	100.0	100.0	100.0	100.0	100.0	100.0	100.0	100.0	100.0
I. Food, beverages and tobacco	34.4	36.7	27.1	27.6	32.2	32.2	37.3	34.9	33.8
Food produced and consumed on farms	—	—	2.0	2.0	1.9	1.6	1.7	1.3	1.2
Food furnished to employees and army	25.8	30.9	0.7	0.6	0.7	0.8	2.4	0.8	0.8
Food purchased				20.8	21.9	22.1	24.5	26.0	25.3
Alcoholic beverages	6.3	3.3	22.3	1.4	5.1	5.2	6.3	4.4	4.2
Tobacco and supply	2.3	2.5	2.2	2.7	2.5	2.5	2.4	2.4	2.3
II. Clothing	14.3	15.1	14.0	11.6	11.9	12.7	16.5	12.7	11.8
Footwear	2.7	3.1	2.3	2.1	2.1	2.0	2.1	1.8	1.7
Clothing, except footwear	9.7	9.8	9.5	7.9	8.1	8.9	12.0	8.8	8.1
Storage, cleaning, repair, etc.			0.6	0.5	0.6	0.6	0.7	0.8	0.7
Laundering, etc.	0.9	0.9	0.6	0.5	0.5	0.5	0.5	0.5	0.4
Miscellaneous			0.1	0.1	0.1	0.1	0.1	0.1	0.1
Jewelry and watches	1.0	1.2	0.8	0.4	0.6	0.7	1.1	0.8	0.8
III. Personal care	0.9	1.0	1.4	1.4	1.4	1.5	1.7	1.2	1.2
IV. Housing	19.1	13.1	14.5	16.9	12.5	12.0	3.9	10.1	10.3
Rent			5.6	7.0	5.3	5.2	3.6	3.1	3.1
Rental value of owner-occupied houses	19.1	13.1	8.5	9.6	6.9	6.5	6.0	6.7	6.9
Hotels, clubs, etc.			0.3	0.3	0.3	0.3	0.3	0.3	0.3
V. Household operation	14.1	13.0	13.3	13.8	13.9	14.3	12.1	13.1	13.7
Furniture, floor covering, etc.	3.9	4.5	2.1	1.4	1.9	2.2	1.7	2.1	2.3
Appliances, china, etc.	1.4	1.6	2.4	2.2	2.6	2.8	3.8	5.0	5.2
Other household supply	0.9	1.1	2.1	2.0	2.3	2.4			
Fuel	3.4	2.4	2.0	2.5	2.1	2.1	1.8	1.6	1.6
Electricity, gas, water	1.3	1.2	1.8	3.0	2.3	2.3	1.8	1.8	1.9
Telephone, telegraph, postage and express	0.6	0.7	0.8	1.2	0.9	0.9	1.2	1.2	1.2
Domestic service	2.5	1.6	1.9	1.4	1.6	1.4	1.5	1.2	1.3
Miscellaneous	—	—	0.2	0.2	0.2	0.2	0.2	0.2	0.2
VI. Medical and death expenses	3.2	3.9	4.6	5.2	4.8	4.8	4.8	5.0	4.9
Drugs and appliances	0.7	0.9	0.9	1.1	1.1	1.2	1.2	1.0	1.0
Physicians and other medical personnel	1.5	1.9	2.3	2.3	2.1	2.1	1.9	2.0	2.0
Hospitalization	0.5	0.5	0.5	0.8	0.7	0.7	0.8	1.0	1.1
Miscellaneous	—	—	0.1	0.2	0.2	0.2	0.3	0.3	0.3
Death expenses	0.5	0.6	0.8	0.8	0.7	0.7	0.7	0.6	0.6
VII. Personal business	1.1	1.2	6.6	6.6	5.8	5.0	3.9	4.2	4.4
Brokerage charges, investment counsel, etc.	0.2	0.4	2.2	0.8	0.5	0.2	0.2	0.1	0.2
Expenses of handling life insurance	0.6	0.4	1.2	2.0	1.8	1.5	1.1	1.3	1.3
Legal services	0.3	0.4	0.5	0.7	0.6	0.5	0.5	0.6	0.6
Interest on personal debts	—	—	0.7	1.0	1.0	1.1	0.4	0.7	0.8
Miscellaneous	—	—	2.0	2.0	1.9	1.6	1.6	1.5	1.5
VIII. Transportation	5.2	8.5	9.5	8.5	9.6	10.0	5.4	10.7	11.7
User-operated car	2.2	5.7 [a]	7.3	6.3	7.7	8.2	3.0	8.9	10.0
Cars, tires and parts	0.7	3.3	4.1	2.3	3.6	4.1	0.9	5.2	6.3
Gasoline and oil	0.4	2.0	2.3	3.2	3.2	3.2	1.3	2.6	2.6
Repair and miscellaneous	0.1	0.3	0.9	0.9	0.9	1.0	0.8	1.1	1.1
Purchased transportation	3.0	2.8	2.2	2.1	1.9	1.8	2.4	1.8	1.7
Local	1.7	1.4	1.4	1.6	1.3	1.2	1.4	1.1	1.1
Intercity [b]	1.3	1.4	0.8	0.5	0.6	0.6	1.0	0.7	0.6
IX. Recreation	3.6	4.0	5.5	4.7	5.0	5.1	5.1	5.7	5.8
Motion pictures			0.9	1.0	1.0	0.9	1.1	0.7	0.6
Other admissions			0.2	0.2	0.2	0.2	0.2	0.3	0.2
Pari-mutuel and coin machines			0.0	0.0	0.1	0.2	0.2	0.2	0.2
Commercial participating amusements			0.3	0.3	0.3	0.3	0.2	0.2	0.2
Books, maps, magazines, etc.			1.1	1.2	1.1	1.1	1.2	1.1	1.0
Toys and sport equipment	3.6	4.0	0.7	0.6	0.7	0.8	0.8	1.0	1.0
Radio and musical instruments			1.3	0.5	0.6	0.8	0.4	1.2	1.6
Photography			0.1	0.1	0.1	0.1	0.2	0.2	0.2
Flowers			0.3	0.2	0.3	0.3	0.3	0.4	0.3
Clubs			0.4	0.5	0.3	0.2	0.2	0.3	0.2
Miscellaneous			0.2	0.2	0.2	0.2	0.2	0.2	0.2
X. Private (organized) education and research	0.6	0.6	0.8	1.0	0.9	0.8	0.7	0.9	0.9
XI. Religious and welfare activities	2.9	2.5	1.5	1.9	1.3	1.2	1.3	1.0	0.9
XII. Foreign travel and remittance (net)	0.4	0.1	1.0	0.8	0.7	0.3	1.3	0.9	1.0

Sources: For 1909 and 1919, **15**, pp. 700–19; for 1929–41, **4**, pp. 41–44; for 1945 and 1949, **3**, July 1950, pp. 24–25; for 1950, **5**, pp. 193 ff.

a. Includes all forms of private transportation.
b. Includes luggage.

CHAPTER 9

CONSUMPTION AND STANDARDS OF LIVING

As GOODS AND SERVICES originally designed as luxuries for the rich are incorporated into mass production and mass consumption, the community in the modern Western world raises the standard of living it considers necessary for decency and self-respect.[1]

CHANGING STANDARDS OF LIVING

In contrast to our dynamic concept of standards of living, people in earlier civilizations believed for thousands of years that frugality and restriction of wants were among man's highest virtues.

The Spartan Scale of Values

Such a "Spartan" scale of values is epitomized in a story told by Herodotus. After the sweeping victory over the Persian army at Plataea, the Spartan general Pausanias noticed the king's war tent adorned with gold and silver in the deserted Persian camp. He ordered the king's bakers and cooks to prepare a regal banquet, with all magnificence. Then he ordered his men to make ready a Spartan supper. "When the suppers were both served," continues Herodotus, "and it was apparent how vast a difference lay between the two, Pausanias called to him the Greek generals. On their coming he pointed to the two boards and said: 'I sent for you, O Greeks, to show you the folly of this [Persian] captain, who, when he enjoyed such fare as this, must needs come here to rob us of our penury.'"[2] And Herodotus leaves the impression that Pausanias would not trade his customary supper of flour and water for Persian luxury.

The social philosophy of the Catholic Church, the spokesman of medieval civilization was dominated by ascetic contempt of material goods. Charity was called upon to care for the poor, and in the idea of charity the thought that the poor had a right to a definite standard of living was eclipsed by the concept of the good deeds performed by the rich for the salvation of their souls.

The Origin of the Idea of a Standard of Living

It is difficult to determine when and where the idea of such a standard was born. There are indications that the idea dawned in England after the Industrial Revolution opened up new horizons of wealth and economic growth to the nation and, at the same time, brought degradation and misery to the working population.

So deep and widespread was the poverty among workers in eighteenth-century England that the terms "the poor" and "worker" were synonymous. The much discussed Poor Law instituted in Elizabeth's reign allowed local authorities to decide what were the necessities to which the poor were entitled. Generations later, the attempts of socially-minded students to evaluate such decisions by gathering information on living conditions among the poor led them to the problem of the standard of living.

Apology for the Poor, 1796

A page from a pamphlet published in 1796 by Rector David Davies evokes the conditions of life of English workers at the end of the eighteenth century. (See Figure 98.) The author is seeking to exonerate workers of the accusation that they eat white bread and drink tea:

Wheaten bread may be eaten alone with pleasure; but potatoes require either meat or milk to make them go down: you cannot make many hearty meals of them with salt and water only. Poor people indeed give them to their children in greasy water, in which they have boiled their greens and their morsel of bacon. . . .

Tea with bread furnishes one meal for a whole family every day, at no greater expense than about one shilling a week at an average. If anybody will point out an article that is cheaper and better, I will venture to answer for the poor in general, that they will be thankful for the discovery. . . .

---

1. The term "standard of living" is often used as synonymous with "pattern" or "level" of living. Many students believe, however, that the term "standard" has a different connotation, with emphasis on the accepted codes of what is necessary and proper; the term is used in this sense in the following pages. (Cf. **16**, pp. 9 ff.)

2. **21**, Vol. 2, Book IX, Chap. 82, pp. 311–12.

SECTION IV.

AN APOLOGY FOR THE POOR—EATING WHEATEN BREAD—NEGLECTING POTATOES—DRINKING TEA.

POOR people are often cenfured for want of frugality and œconomy in the management of their earnings. In particular, they are accufed of extravagance in eating wheaten bread; of being over-nice in neglecting as they do the ufe of potatoes; and of a luxurious excefs in drinking tea. It may be proper to fee what force there is in thefe charges.

Firft; It is afked, Why fhould our labouring people eat wheaten bread? Were they content, as the poor of this country were formerly, and as the poor of other countries are ftill, with bread of an inferior quality, they might then fpare money for other purpofes, and live with more comfort than they ufually do. It is wonderful how readily even men of fenfe give into this cenfure, neither confidering the different circumftances of different countries at the fame time, nor the different circumftances of the fame country at different rent

Facsimile from the book of Rector David Davies, *The Case of Labourers in Husbandry*

FIGURE 98. STANDARDS OF LIVING: AN APOLOGY FOR THE POOR, 1796

Still you exclaim, *Tea is a luxury.* If you mean fine hyson tea, sweetened with refined sugar, and softened with cream, I readily admit it to be so. But *this* is not the tea of the poor. Spring water, just coloured with a few leaves of the lowest-priced tea, and sweetened with the brownest sugar, is the luxury for which you reproach them. To this they have recourse from mere necessity: and were they now to be deprived of this, they would immediately be reduced to bread and water. . . .

Small indeed is the portion of worldly comforts now left them. Instead therefore of grudging them so small an enjoyment as a morsel of good bread with their miserable tea; instead of attempting to show how it may yet be possible for them to live *worse* than they do; it well becomes the wisdom and humanity of the present age to devise means how they may be better accommodated.[3]

Standards of Living in a Democratic Society

As democracy progressed in the nineteenth century, with the increasing political weight of

3. **19,** pp. 47–52.

the workers as voters and the strength of labor unions, the "morsel of good bread" and "miserable tea" in the diet of the poor ceased to be a matter of controversy. New criteria became necessary to evaluate the minimum comfort to which each member of a community is entitled.

In a democratic society, which accepts no caste barriers, the yardstick of the standard of living is determined by comparing the prevailing practices in consumption with the circumstances of persons who have not been able to adopt this way of life. When there is considerable inequality in the distribution of wealth and income, the customs of the privileged minority — say the topmost 10 per cent of the population — can hardly be recognized as the standard for the whole community. In fact, it is questionable whether most people would recognize the way of life of the median family as the national standard. On the other hand, a nation aware of the principle of a standard of living — and proud of its own standard — will probably consider that living conditions among its poorest groups are substandard.

THE MODERN CONCEPT OF A STANDARD OF LIVING

It is a matter of opinion where the line between standard and substandard should be drawn. One person feels that the lowest fifth or fourth of the community lives in substandard conditions; another will describe one third of the nation as "ill fed, ill housed and ill clad," or draw the line at different points for different categories of necessities. The essential point is that modern democratic society, which combines equality of political rights with economic inequality, feels a moral uneasiness about the conditions of life of its least fortunate members.

There is no evidence that the number or proportion of those for whom the community feels responsible diminishes as the community becomes richer. In fact, the question is not one of an absolute level of consumption but of inequality. What changes in a growing and thriving community is the target the community accepts as the standard of consumption of the underprivileged minority.

THE STANDARD FAMILY BUDGET, 1948

The United States Department of Labor's standard family budget reflects the concept of the standard of living in the nation. This budget was prepared in 1948 on the basis of extensive study of the consumption of typical urban families in different parts of the country. It was described as the point in the scale of family income and family expenditures "where the struggle for 'more and more' things gives way to the desire for 'better and better' quality."

Above this level, for example, the average family is likely to be more interested in escaping from an endless round of the cheaper cuts of meat than in increasing the number of pounds of meat that it buys. Below this level, on the other hand, people find it harder and harder to economize, being unable to shift extensively to cheaper commodities and therefore forced to "do without." [4]

Thus, the budget of the Department of Labor expressed neither a "subsistence" nor a "luxury" level of living, but a modest yet adequate standard.[5] It described this standard in terms of the following budget of goods and services that an employed worker's family of four would strive for.

Housing

The family's dwelling, which is rented, contains five rooms, including a kitchen and a bathroom, and is supplied with hot and cold running water. It has electric lighting and each room has at least one window to afford ventilation and daylight illumination. The dwelling is located within reasonable commuting distance of major centers of employment, high schools, churches and shopping, and within walking distance of food stores and elementary schools. It is equipped with the usual furnishings and the mechanical aids that are considered household necessities — a gas or electric cook stove, a mechanical refrigerator and a washing machine. Some furniture, kitchenware, appliances and household linens are purchased each year in order to maintain household inventories.

Food

The food budget provides a diet that approximates the nutritional allowances recommended by the Food and Nutrition Board of the National Research Council. Menus may be changed within these allowances to provide variety and to satisfy the tastes of individual families. A chicken or a roast may be served on Sunday and a turkey on Thanksgiving.

Clothing

The general level of the clothing budget is characterized by the following items: for the husband, one heavy wool suit every two years, one light wool suit every three years, five shirts and two pairs of shoes each year; for the wife, a heavy wool coat every four years, four dresses and three pairs of shoes each year; for the boy, one sweater or jacket, two pairs of trousers, three shirts and three pairs of shoes each year; for the girl, one snow suit or heavy coat every two years, four dresses and four pairs of shoes each year.

Other Needs

Local transportation needs in the family budget include travel to work and to high school and trips to downtown shopping areas, churches, movies, meetings of organizations, and social visits. A trip out of town every three or four years for a vacation or to visit relatives and family is also provided. The budget also includes a part of normal outlays for an automobile, on the assumption that some families have one and others have none.

The family owns a small radio, buys one daily newspaper, including a Sunday edition, and thirty-two copies of some popular-priced magazine in a year. Movies are attended by the husband, wife and daughter once in three weeks, and by the son once in two weeks. A small sum is allocated for children's toys and games, pets, camera supplies, and dues to social and recreational clubs.[6] Allowance is made for telephone calls, medical aid (4.4 calls on physicians per person annually) and dental care (one case every 2 years per person).[7]

Costs of a Family's Requirements

According to these general specifications, the Department of Labor established a detailed list of annual requirements of the hypothetical family of four and ascertained the price of each item in each of thirty-four cities. At prices as of June 1947, a household had to spend about $2,900 a year to attain this standard of living. The needs of smaller and larger families were not estimated with the same painstaking accuracy, but the available fragmentary data seem to indicate that the scale of incomes providing

---

4. **15,** February 1948, p. 131. (See also **22.**)
5. **15,** February 1948, p. 133.

6. **15,** February 1948, pp. 135–36.
7. **15,** February 1948, p. 144.

the same level of well-being to families of other sizes is very close to the simple rule of thumb: one unit for husband and wife and half of one unit for each child.[8]

The family budget developed by the Department of Labor has no particular name. In view of conflicting opinions, it is not designated officially as a "standard" budget, which it actually is. In wage negotiations it is often referred to as the "budget of the United States Department of Labor." Labor unions are endeavoring to use it as a yardstick in fixing minimum wages.

The gulf between Rector David Davies' Apology for the Poor and the standard of living implied by the budget of a working-class family in the United States epitomizes a century and a half of social and economic progress. The American budget may appear too high for France, extravagant for Italy or Spain, and out of the question for the USSR or India. In the United States likewise, the present standards would have appeared too high thirty years ago, would have impressed people as extravagant fifty years ago, and could not have been discussed seriously in the middle of the last century. On the other hand, for such countries as Australia, New Zealand, Canada, Great Britain and Switzerland, this standard budget today is a realistic target of economic and social policy.

MALTHUS REAPPRAISED

The recognition of a "living standard" in domestic social policy, and even more in discussion of international problems, marks a decisive break with Malthusian philosophy.

The Origin of the Malthus Essay

When Malthus wrote his *Essay on the Principle of Population as It Affects the Future Improvement of Society,* his purpose was to show the foolishness of the poor-law system, which, in effect, gave the poor a bonus for large families. He was not the first to explain poverty by the lack of foresight of people who rear more children than they can feed, but his brilliant style and logic gave his crusading pamphlet a much broader meaning than he intended. The practical issue of the pamphlet has long been forgotten, and the assertions of Malthus on population laws — including his idea of arithmetic and geometric progressions — have proved false. The "poor" in democratic countries have ceased to be social outcasts, as in the time of Malthus and have become a political power. For more than a century, however, the Western industrial nations have continued to consider the poverty-stricken regions of Asia and Africa as victims of over-population due to the lack of foresight of their peoples.

Nature's Mighty Feast

The first edition of Malthus' *Essay* contained a passage that became famous:

A man who is born into a world already possessed, if he cannot get subsistence from his parents on whom he has a just demand, and if the society do not want his labour, has no claim of right to the smallest portion of food, and, in fact, has no business to be where he is. . . . At nature's mighty feast there is no vacant cover for him. She tells him to be gone and will quickly execute her own orders, if he do not work upon the compassion of some of her guests. If these guests get up and make room for him, other intruders immediately appear demanding the same favour. The report of a provision for all that come, fills the hall with numerous claimants. The order and harmony of the feast is disturbed, the plenty that before reigned is changed into scarcity; and the happiness of the guests is destroyed by the spectacle of misery and dependence in every part of the hall, and by the clamorous importunity of those who are justly enraged at not finding the provision which they had been taught to expect. The guests learn too late their error, in counteracting those strict orders to all intruders, issued by the great mistress of the feast, who, wishing that all her guests should have plenty, and knowing that she could not provide for unlimited numbers, humanely refused to admit fresh comers when her table was already full.[9]

The Malthusian philosophy was based on the conviction that there is a fairly rigid limit to the possible growth of the means of subsistence. To avoid starvation man must budget these means by limiting the number of mouths to be fed.

---

8. Taking the needs of a family of four as 100, the scales are as follows:

	2 persons	3 persons	4 persons	5 persons	6 persons
According to BLS, based on adequacy of the diet	65.1	83.7	100.0	114.8	128.6
According to the rule of thumb	66.7	83.4	100.0	116.7	133.3

(Cf. **28**, pp. 237–38.)

9. **23**, p. 531. Malthus eliminated this controversial passage from the third edition of his *Essay* (1806), but there is no indication in his work that he had changed his opinion on the subject.

When Malthus spoke of the limited number of covers at nature's feast he meant his country, England, as he knew it, at the end of the eighteenth century. In contrast, most of his present-day followers are Malthusians with regard to the remote underdeveloped areas of the world. Only a few students in the United States try to apply the same yardstick to modern Europe.

Malthusianism and Peoples in Distress

A good example of neo-Malthusianism is the recent proposal of William Vogt to make American aid to European countries contingent on national programs leading toward stabilization and eventual reduction of population through voluntary action of the people:

Stabilization and eventual reduction in population in Europe would be one of the longest steps that could be made toward world peace and well-being. . . . A United States of Europe, with one-half or one-third its present population, could probably maintain a standard of living that would equal or exceed that of the United States. . . .

Where FAO [the Food and Agriculture Organization] finds overpopulation, its conservation and food production programs should include a contraception program. It should not ship food to keep alive ten million Indians or Chinese this year, so that fifty million may die five years hence. . . .

[Birth-control campaigns] should parallel, if not surpass, the other health programs of the World Health Organization.[10]

The incompatibility of these suggestions with our modern thinking in world affairs, more specifically with the foreign policy of the United States is obvious:

There is an obvious suicide-trap for any nation aspiring to world leadership in giving . . . aid with one hand and extending . . . devices for sterility with the other and saying, "both or neither." The resentment that has greeted efforts of rich foreign nations to control the political and economic life of less developed areas would be absolutely nothing compared to the permanent antagonism that would come from any statement from us that people must pay for their extra shirts, working clothes, shoes and refrigerators by giving up their sons and daughters. Not since the Minotaur of Greek legend, with his demand for a tribute of living children, has there been anything like it. Such an insult to their essential worth and their freedom offered by a foreign nation, would never be forgotten or forgiven.[11]

10. **26**, pp. 211 and 281–82.
11. **25**, pp. 36–37.

Population Problem and Conservation of Resources

The modern Malthusianism differs from the original philosophy of Malthus in that it holds man responsible for having lowered the limit of the available means of subsistence by abusing land and destroying its fertility. Vogt, for example, uses two curves to symbolize the problem of population and resources:

One of them is the curve of human population that, after centuries of relative equilibrium, suddenly began to mount, and in the past fifty years has been climbing at a vertiginous rate.

The other graph is that of our resources. It represents the area and thickness of our topsoil, the abundance of our forests, available waters, life-giving grasslands, and the biophysical web that holds them together. This curve, except for local depressions, also maintained a high degree of regularity through the centuries. But it, too, has had its direction sharply diverted especially during the past hundred and fifty years, and it is plunging downward like a rapid.

The two curves . . . have long since crossed. Ever more rapidly they are drawing apart. The farther they are separated the more difficult will it be to draw them together again.

Everywhere, or nearly everywhere, about the earth we see the results of their divergence. The crumbling ruins of two wars mark their passing. The swollen bellies of hungry babies, from San Salvador to Bengal, dot the space between them. Parching fevers and racking coughs, from Osorno to Seoul, cry about the cleavage between these curves. The angry muttering of mobs, like the champing of jungle peccaries, is a swelling echo of their passing.[12]

The current controversy between the Malthusians and the anti-Malthusians is largely in their appraisal of the ability of modern science and technology to restore and increase the carrying capacity of the earth.

Mankind's present problem has been ably stated by Fairfield Osborn:

The tide of earth's population is rising, the reservoir of earth's living resources is falling. Technologists may outdo themselves in the creation of artificial substitutes for natural subsistence, and new areas such as those in tropical or subtropical regions, may be adapted to human use, but even such resources or developments cannot be expected to offset the present terrific attack upon the natural life-giving elements of the earth. There is only one solution: Man must recognize the necessity of co-

12. **26**, p. 287.

operating with nature. He must temper his demands and use and conserve the natural living resources of this earth in a manner that alone can provide for the continuation of his civilization.[13]

This point of view does not envisage that man's cooperation with nature will ensure enough food for any number of inhabitants on our planet. The implication is, rather, that with the present density of population and present trends in birth and death rates, the essential step in attacking the problem of poverty is to create new covers at nature's table, rather than to close the doors to those guests who cannot prove that they have been invited.

The Underdeveloped Countries

If poverty in the have-not countries results from absolute overpopulation, as the Malthusian philosophy would maintain, any attempt to improve their economic situation would be foolish, and sanitary aid to them should be focused on quarantining the foci of infection. However, our modern idea of providing technical and economic aid to underdeveloped areas is based on a dynamic concept of standards of consumption and nutrition, on the realization that all modern industrial nations passed through the phase of poverty, high mortality and high natality before they reached the present phase of prosperity and relative equilibrium of population. In other words, we accept the calculated risk that there will be an upsurge of population in the underdeveloped areas, as there was in the Western world and expect that this development will be offset by the spread of modern technology and science, including modern methods of utilizing land and other natural resources.

THE WORLD'S CONSUMPTION PATTERNS

International statistics of consumption are limited, essentially, to staple foods, fibers, forest products and the principal minerals. Only fragmentary and scanty data are available on the consumption of fabricated goods and services. All we know is that most of the goods turned out by modern industry are used within a comparatively narrow circle of nations that comprise about one fourth of mankind. The more fortunate of the nations outside this circle have just enough food and protection against the elements, while the less fortunate have neither food

nor shelter in sufficient quantity or of proper quality according to modern standards.

CONSUMPTION OF AGRICULTURAL PRODUCTS

The daily diet in the economically developed nations includes a great variety of items.[14] At the top of the income ladder, selected foods replace staple foodstuffs and the per capita consumption of the staples tends to decline. At the bottom of the ladder, in many underdeveloped areas, the customary diet consists largely of a single item — bread, rice, potatoes or fish — supplemented by small quantities of such ingredients as salt, milk and sugar.[15]

Thus the choice morsels at "nature's mighty feast" are served only at the head table. Similarly the choice fibers — silk, nylon, wool — are reserved for the guests of honor in this "possessed world," while others get just enough cheap fabric to cover their nakedness.

Per Capita Consumption by Continent

Inclusive statistics of consumption of agricultural products on the various continents are available only for prewar years. They show that much the largest amount of meat per capita was consumed in the new sparsely populated continents, America and Oceania, and a smaller amount in Europe, while the diet was almost meatless in Asia and Africa, and in the USSR was midway between the European and Asiatic patterns. Per capita milk consumption in Europe lagged behind that in North America but exceeded that in any other continent, including Oceania.

North America has an extremely high per capita consumption of corn which is used as feed for cattle and serves to maintain the high per capita output of meat and milk. The USSR leads in per capita consumption of bread grains, followed by Europe and Oceania. Potatoes are consumed largely in Europe and the USSR. North America tops the list in sugar, followed by Oceania, with Europe, South America and the USSR far behind.

---

14. For example, an American worker family customarily purchases about two hundred different foods. In the family budget of the Department of Labor, 79 foods were selected for pricing. **16**, p. 18.

15. Until the nineteenth century, bread predominated in the diet of European workers. In European economic literature, the trends of real wages in the more remote past are measured by comparing money wage rates with the price of wheat or bread. **27**, pp. 175 ff.

---

13. **24**, p. 201.

TABLE 143

AGRICULTURAL PRODUCTS: PER CAPITA CONSUMPTION, BY CONTINENT,
1934–38 ANNUAL AVERAGE

(*Metric Pounds* [a])

Commodity	World	North America [b]	Middle and South America	Europe	USSR	Asia	Africa	Oceania
Bread grains	356.6	369.3	156.5	436.8	761.1	325.5	87.5	414.4
Wheat	167.6	336.9	112.0	294.1	467.4	78.3	53.8	363.8
Rye	48.1	19.8	2.0	127.0	288.8	0.7	0.2	0.0
Rice (rough)	140.9	12.6	42.5	15.7	4.9	246.5	33.5	40.6
Potatoes	240.3	192.9	56.9	841.5	787.9	9.3	7.3	106.9
Coarse grains	238.3	1,238.1	220.6	382.0	391.3	62.1	111.8	141.4
Corn	52.5	850.3	203.5	144.6	45.6	27.8	73.0	42.8
Barley	67.0	91.7	8.6	95.0	109.8	31.7	34.8	21.4
Oats	118.8	296.1	8.6	142.4	235.9	2.6	4.0	77.2
Meat	48.3	140.6	131.6	80.0	41.0	18.5	29.1	199.1
Beef	24.0	64.8	86.2	32.6	18.5	9.7	18.1	119.9
Pork	19.2	67.9	34.2	39.9	17.2	6.8	2.2	15.0
Sheep and goat meat	5.1	7.9	11.2	7.5	5.3	2.0	8.8	64.2
Milk	274.7	912.5	241.3	695.6	333.8	66.8	82.7	666.6
Sugar	26.9	99.9	41.7	47.0	25.4	10.8	12.3	87.7
Coffee	2.4	12.8	11.7	4.0	0.0	0.2	0.9	0.7
Tea [c]	13.8	14.0	1.8	20.6	3.9	14.3	7.8	88.0
Cocoa	0.7	4.2	0.7	2.0	0.0	0.0	0.2	1.8
Tobacco	3.1	7.3	2.4	3.3	2.9	2.9	0.9	2.9
Cotton	6.8	24.7	5.1	10.6	9.0	4.0	0.7	0.0
Wool	1.8	5.3	0.9	5.5	1.5	0.4	0.4	7.9
Flax	0.9	0.2	0.0	1.3	6.6	0.0	0.0	0.0
Hemp	0.7	0.0	0.0	1.1	2.6	0.2	0.0	0.4
Jute	1.5	1.1	0.7	3.3	0.2	1.5	0.0	0.4
Silk	1.0	7.1	0.0	0.7	0.4	0.7	0.0	1.4
Rubber	1.1	8.4	0.2	1.8	0.4	0.2	0.0	2.9

Source: 11, p. 56.

    a. One metric pound equals roughly 1.1 avoirdupois pounds used in English-speaking nations.
    b. Excludes Mexico and the Caribbean.
    c. In ounces.

Coffee is the favorite drink in the Americas, and tea leads in Oceania and Europe. North America has the largest per capita consumption of cotton, silk and rubber and also has a high per capita consumption of wool. Europe ranks first in consumption of jute and second in cotton and wool. Oceania is first in wool, the USSR in flax and hemp. (See Table 143.)

Per Capita Consumption in Selected Countries

Within each continent, the patterns of consumption differ greatly from country to country.

The contrast between Brazil and Argentina, Great Britain and Bulgaria, Japan and India, or Egypt and the white population in the Union of South Africa is as striking as the contrasts between continents. Moreover, the patterns of consumption vary from region to region and from community to community within each country. The differences are caused not only by relative prosperity or poverty but also by differences in climate, available supplies and habits.[16]

    16. Statistics on consumption in individual countries are not inclusive: little is known about China, prac-

Bread grains and rice. Per capita consumption of bread grains, rice and coarse grains is highest in the primarily agricultural countries of eastern and southern Europe, in Malaya, China, Japan and Egypt. The countries where consumption of bread grains, rice and coarse grains was more than 250 metric pounds (500 grams a pound) a year per inhabitant before World War II reported the following per capita rates of annual consumption (metric pounds per year): [17]

Country	1934–38 Average	1947–48 Average
Yugoslavia	457.0	351.4
Malaya	409.2	345.0
Bulgaria	404.6	341.6
Romania	404.2	359.6
Egypt	364.2	355.6
Italy	354.4	363.4
China	363.2	319.6
Hungary	328.8	349.6
Japan	325.4	279.2
Burma	298.0	338.2
Spain	292.8	226.0
Indochina	287.0	281.4
Madagascar	272.8	243.6
Ceylon	271.6	213.6
Poland	268.4	232.6
Austria	263.8	245.6
Czechoslovakia	260.4	252.8
India	259.8	232.2
Chile	258.6	264.4
Philippines	258.0	231.0
Finland	256.0	253.2
Indonesia	255.6	192.6
Ireland	255.2	267.8
France	254.6	199.8

At the other extreme, per capita consumption of grains is low in the United States, Canada, Australia, New Zealand, Great Britain, the Netherlands and Denmark. In the middle of the distribution, however, there is no visible correlation between a nation's ranking in consumption of grain and its level of economic development: the difference lies in what people eat in addition to their everyday bread or rice.[18]

Potatoes, like cereals, are not of major importance in the diet of most of the prosperous nations. On the other hand, potatoes are not necessarily associated with poverty. Per capita consumption — including potatoes used for feed and thus converted into meat — is highest in the following countries (metric pounds per year):

Country	1934–38 Average	1947–48 Average
Poland	570.0	563.2
Madagascar	518.2	309.8
Ireland	394.0	375.8
Finland	361.6	319.2
Germany	352.0	267.2
France	334.2	319.6
Czechoslovakia	319.8	296.2
Indonesia	313.4	358.6
Netherlands	261.2	310.2
Sweden	244.4	265.0
Norway	239.4	243.0
Spain	218.8	199.0
Denmark	213.0	268.2

The per capita consumption of sugar, meat and dairy products is most closely correlated with national prosperity. This correlation, however, is tempered to some extent by particular local conditions. Some tropical countries have a comparatively high per capita consumption of sugar in the form of molasses, sirups and other local preparations. Sparsely populated cattle and sheep-raising areas have an extremely high intake of meat. Milk and cheese predominate in the diet of the Scandinavian countries, which specialize in intensive husbandry.

Sugar. In 1947–48, per capita consumption of sugar (including molasses and local preparations) was highest in Colombia. The United States and Australia came next, followed by New Zealand, Cuba and Canada, Denmark, Sweden, Switzerland and Great Britain. Some comparatively poor tropical countries had a higher per capita intake than highly developed industrial nations.[19] (See Figure 99.)

Meat and fish. Argentina, New Zealand, Australia and Uruguay have the highest per capita consumption of meat. Next come Denmark, Canada, the United States and, at a considerable distance, Ireland and the Union of South Africa.

tically nothing about the USSR. Moreover, statistics for some countries may be too low because of gaps in the records of consumption on farms or in remote areas, and for others may be too high because of duplication and other statistical errors. Still more fragmentary is our information on regional variation in consumption patterns within single countries.

17. See Tables 144 and 145.

18. There is a very close correlation between the level of economic development in a country and the *relative*

share of grains and potatoes in its daily diet. Cf. pp. 304 ff.

19. The low consumption of sugar in such countries as Belgium, the Netherlands, Norway and Czechoslovakia in 1947–48 was due partly to temporary economic difficulties resulting from the war.

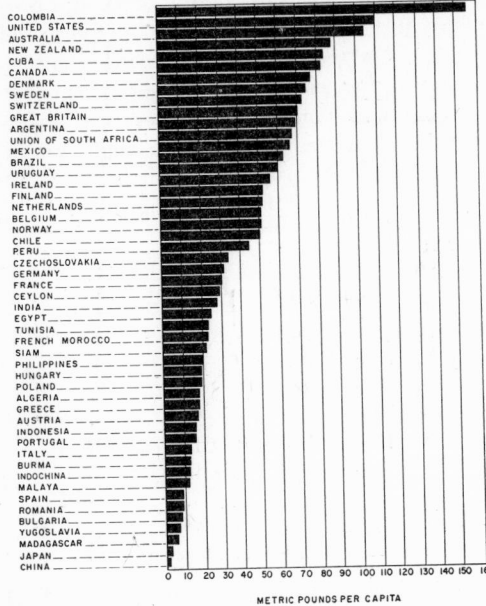

FIGURE 99. SUGAR: PER CAPITA CONSUMPTION IN
SELECTED COUNTRIES, 1947–48

Per capita consumption of sugar depends essentially
on the level of wealth in a nation and ranges from less
than 3 metric pounds a year in China to more than 80
pounds in the industrially developed countries. In addition, people in tropical areas have an abundant supply
of local sugarlike products, such as molasses, sirups,
panela, papelon and piloncillo. (Cf. Tables 144 and 145.)

Other meat-eating countries include Great Britain, France, Belgium, Sweden and Switzerland,
and, in the Western Hemisphere, Brazil, Cuba
and Chile. (See Figure 100.)

Meat consumption in Germany was very low
in 1947–48 as a result of the war; the prewar
figure was a little less than that of Great Britain
and compared favorably with the figures for the
Netherlands, Sweden and even Switzerland. (Cf.

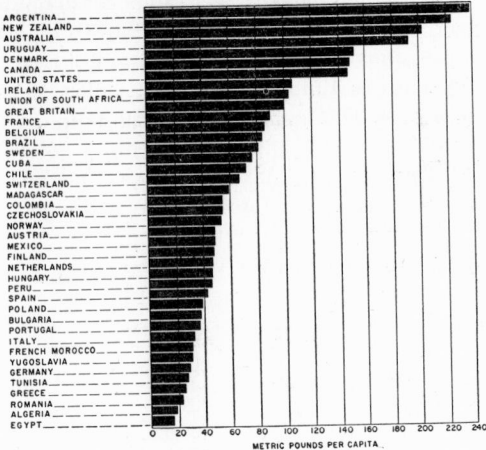

FIGURE 100. MEAT: PER CAPITA CONSUMPTION IN
SELECTED COUNTRIES, 1947–48

Tables 144 and 145.) Meat consumption is very
low in Egypt and other African countries except
the Union of South Africa and is especially low
in the Far East. For the last group of countries,
the Food and Agriculture Organization of the
United Nations (FAO) gives only total figures
covering all animal products — fats, meat, milk
and cheese, which appear very low in comparison with the respective totals for other regions.

Fish is of considerable importance in the diet
of Great Britain, Denmark, Sweden, Norway,
Portugal and Spain, Japan, Burma, Thailand,
Indochina, Malaya, the Philippines, and some
provinces of China and Indonesia.

Coffee, tea and cocoa. People in the United
States, Brazil, Sweden, Belgium and Denmark
consume a pound or more of coffee a month
per inhabitant. Great Britain, Australia and New
Zealand use half a pound of tea a month per per-

TABLE 144

PRINCIPAL FOODSTUFFS: PER CAPITA CONSUMPTION IN SELECTED COUNTRIES,
1934–38 ANNUAL AVERAGE

(Metric Pounds)

Country [a]	Bread Grains	Rice	Coarse Grains	Potatoes, Roots, Tubers	Sugar	Pulses and Nuts	Fruits and Vege-tables	Fats and Oils	Meat	Milk and Cheese	Eggs	Fish
United States [b]	179.2	—	—	128.4	98.8	14.0	366.6	44.2	127.8	322.2	33.8	10.2
Canada [b]	187.4	—	—	177.8	98.4	11.4	166.4	42.8	123.4	348.2	27.6	10.4
Mexico	103.8	—	—	9.4	46.2	28.8	142.6	9.8	52.6	159.8	4.0	7.2
Cuba	108.0	—	—	197.6	80.0	25.0	327.4	17.6	67.0	141.2	8.8	8.4

(Continued on facing page)

Table 144—continued

Country [a]	Bread Grains	Rice	Coarse Grains	Potatoes, Roots, Tubers	Sugar	Pulses and Nuts	Fruits and Vegetables	Fats and Oils	Meat	Milk and Cheese	Eggs	Fish
Colombia [b]	103.8	—	—	164.2	119.4	14.0	294.8	7.4*	55.8	138.0	11.4	1.2
Brazil [b]	160.6	—	—	91.4	49.4	45.6	176.0	10.2	105.0	150.4	5.2	2.8
Peru [b]	196.4	—	—	177.8	27.2	31.2	112.0	7.4	48.0	55.4	6.4	1.8
Chile [b]	258.6	—	—	144.8	51.2	21.6	104.2	9.0	70.0	125.6	3.4	14.4
Uruguay [b]	170.4	—	—	82.6	48.0	5.0	78.2	27.2	207.4	297.0	14.8	3.8
Argentina [b]	206.2	—	—	141.2	54.4	5.0	123.4	19.6	215.2	280.8	14.2	9.0
United Kingdom	179.0	4.0	5.4	157.2	98.2	6.8	225.8	39.6	120.8	252.4	21.8	24.2
Ireland	246.4	2.0	6.8	394.0	75.4	1.4	198.6	30.0	95.2	494.8	27.0	5.0
France	246.0	4.8	3.8	334.2	47.8	12.0	346.0	28.0	103.8	182.2	18.0	16.0
Belgium	225.2	13.2	5.2	137.4	55.6	9.4	132.0	38.4	87.2	186.6	15.0	18.0
Netherlands	172.4	10.2	14.2	261.2	67.0	5.4	211.6	44.0	79.2	293.4	11.6	15.2
Denmark	171.6	4.4	11.8	213.0	101.0	—	189.2	53.2	149.2	346.8	15.0	30.0
Sweden	170.8	3.4	27.0	244.4	88.2	3.8	160.2	34.2	94.8	511.8	16.2	46.0
Norway	113.2	3.4	21.4	239.4	60.6	4.8	104.8	51.2	75.8	349.6	13.8	42.0
Finland	224.2	7.2	24.6	361.6	56.4	6.6	133.2	26.2	64.6	525.0	6.0	12.0
Germany	215.6	5.0	2.8	352.0	48.0	4.6	171.8	45.4	101.8	239.2	14.4	24.0
Poland	264.0	2.4	2.0	570.0	17.0	18.6	138.2	14.8	52.0	328.4	7.4	4.0
Czechoslovakia	248.6	7.8	4.0	319.8	47.2	7.2	167.0	27.4	66.6	218.4	7.2	2.4
Switzerland	205.8	8.0	6.2	181.0	76.2	3.8	390.4	30.6	101.0	501.6	17.6	2.0
Austria	241.4	8.0	14.4	170.6	48.0	4.4	235.4	28.2	107.2	385.6	13.2	2.0
Hungary	296.6	5.2	27.0	179.0	20.4	12.8	189.8	20.2	68.2	223.2	12.8	1.8
Portugal	116.6	13.6	76.2	152.8	20.2	19.8	282.8	25.0	46.0	78.0	4.4	30.8
Spain	257.0	13.0	22.8	218.8	23.2	29.2	300.0	29.4	56.2	124.2	9.8	25.0
Italy	277.8	20.8	55.8	73.2	14.2	26.6	167.4	23.0	39.2	83.0	15.2	15.8
Yugoslavia	206.2	3.2	247.6	110.2	9.0	10.6	177.2	11.8	41.2	239.2	4.2	0.4
Romania	183.6	2.2	218.4	83.0	10.4	13.8	276.6	11.0	36.4	206.2	10.8	2.0
Bulgaria	354.2	4.2	46.2	17.2	5.0	22.6	245.0	16.2	44.8	155.8	8.8	2.0
Greece	224.8	5.8	11.6	26.6	20.4	15.4	167.2	36.0	36.8	96.4	9.2	10.6
China	94.6	173.8	94.8	60.2	2.4	50.6	—	12.6	28.8			5.6
Japan	20.8	267.6	37.0	134.2	25.8	17.8	—	3.8	28.2			68.8
India	23.2	158.0	78.6	15.2	29.8	44.6	—	6.6	137.8			3.2
Burma	4.8	283.6	9.6	12.2	20.4	18.2	—	8.6	62.0			74.4
Thailand	1.8	195.2	0.4	26.6	19.0	34.2	—	9.4	90.6			96.8
Indochina	1.8	279.4	5.8	36.2	13.6	9.4	—	4.4	59.2			45.6
Ceylon	8.4	253.2	10.0	25.8	26.0	220.0	—	5.2	51.8			19.0
Malaya	24.0	375.6	9.6	17.8	12.4	25.8	—	12.8	50.4			40.6
Indonesia	2.2	172.4	81.0	313.4	13.4	15.8	—	5.6	12.6			8.8
Philippines	10.6	193.2	54.2	48.0	14.6	34.4	—	6.8	48.4			96.8
French Morocco	214.2	—	—	6.6	49.6	2.2	74.4	12.6	57.0	398.2	8.6	6.0
Algeria	212.2	—	—	15.4	20.8	6.6	102.6	14.0	26.8	199.4	4.4	5.0
Tunisia	172.0	—	—	11.6	25.4	11.6	67.6	14.0	35.4	194.0	7.0	8.4
Egypt	364.2	—	—	7.8	27.0	43.0	97.6	5.8	14.6	138.0	3.4	6.0
Madagascar [b]	272.8	—	—	518.2	2.2	11.6	52.6	4.8	57.6	184.6	4.2	10.0
Union of South Africa [b]	192.6	—	—	32.6	47.2	7.8	127.4	8.2	117.6	159.0	5.8	5.0
Australia [c]	200.4	—	—	96.4	110.4	5.0	279.4	38.6	240.8	234.6	24.0	10.2
New Zealand [b]	184.2	—	—	128.0	98.2	1.0	246.8	37.2	204.0	263.4	27.2	10.8

Source: 7, pp. 48, 60, 70, 88, 102–05.

a. Countries arranged geographically.

b. 1935–39.
c. 1936–39.

TABLE 145

PRINCIPAL FOODSTUFFS: PER CAPITA CONSUMPTION IN SELECTED COUNTRIES, 1947–48

(Metric Pounds)

Country [a]	Bread Grains	Rice	Coarse Grains	Potatoes, Roots, Tubers	Sugar	Pulses and Nuts	Fruits and Vegetables	Fats and Oils	Meat	Milk and Cheese	Eggs	Fish
United States	168.4	—	—	117.2	109.8	17.0	412.0	45.0	148.4	394.0	41.4	10.0
Canada	172.8	—	—	161.8	82.8	14.0	197.8	42.4	149.2	454.4	33.6	9.6
Mexico	244.6	—	—	14.6	65.8	35.4	160.4	12.0	49.0	137.0	4.0	10.0
Cuba	214.6	—	—	183.0	83.6	28.6	277.2	27.0	76.4	151.0	6.2	11.8
Colombia [b]	127.2	—	—⎤	199.2	156.0	15.6	252.4	6.2	54.6	182.6	9.6	1.0
Brazil [e]	167.2	—	—	108.2	62.0	43.2	199.0	11.8	84.4	146.6	5.2	5.8
Peru [e]	205.2	—	—	200.4	44.8	13.8	112.4	7.2	45.2	52.2	6.6	2.5
Chile [e]	264.4	—	—	161.4	50.2	19.2	113.6	8.8	70.4	150.0	3.6	22.4
Uruguay [e]	185.0	—	—	99.0	60.0	4.0	106.8	20.6	191.2	323.2	16.6	4.6
Argentina [e]	237.4	—	—	155.6	69.8	6.8	200.6	31.4	237.8	229.2	14.6	7.6
United Kingdom	204.8	1.0	9.4	190.6	70.6	5.2	229.8	28.4	98.8	321.4	20.8	30.2
Ireland	258.4	0.6	8.8	375.8	55.8	1.4	221.4	30.4	107.4	435.0	26.8	7.4
France	187.4	0.4	12.0	319.6	30.6	6.6	327.6	20.8	89.2	144.0	15.8	10.8
Belgium	195.8	2.0	19.2	285.8	51.6	3.4	240.0	35.0	87.8	185.2	10.4	20.4
Netherlands	186.2	1.0	28.8	310.2	51.8	3.4	207.0	35.6	46.6	322.2	9.4	20.8
Denmark	140.0	—	65.8	268.2	76.2	1.0	205.2	55.2	150.8	381.4	16.2	32.6
Sweden	153.0	0.4	35.4	265.0	74.0	3.2	158.0	30.8	82.8	534.4	20.6	49.6
Norway	215.8	—	20.2	243.0	50.6	5.0	96.4	44.8	52.4	435.8	9.4	53.8
Finland	237.2	—	16.0	319.2	51.8	3.0	82.4	12.2	47.2	628.4	7.4	11.0
Germany [d]	233.6	—	25.2	267.2	31.4	6.2	150.2	10.8	29.4	181.2	2.8	12.6
Poland	213.2	—	19.4	563.2	19.2	2.2	190.0	10.5	39.0	154.6	5.2	5.8
Czechoslovakia	252.8	—	—	296.2	34.8	2.8	98.4	22.2	54.6	267.4	8.2	5.2
Switzerland	217.0	4.4	13.0	222.6	71.6	3.4	438.4	26.4	66.4	462.2	13.0	4.0
Austria	233.0	1.2	11.4	89.0	17.6	16.2	282.2	20.8	49.6	215.0	3.5	4.0
Hungary	234.2	8.2	107.2	177.4	19.4	14.0	122.8	13.6	46.0	130.0	7.4	1.0
Portugal	143.0	16.2	98.0	144.6	16.2	19.8	224.4	27.8	36.6	77.6	3.8	25.6
Spain	188.0	10.6	27.4	199.0	9.6	27.0	241.8	30.2	40.4	114.8	5.8	14.5
Italy	301.8	45.4	16.2	64.0	14.4	23.4	203.0	22.0	32.0	92.6	13.2	11.4
Yugoslavia	182.6	—	168.8	20.8	7.4	7.6	140.0	7.6	30.4	79.8	4.4	1.2
Romania	309.8	1.2	48.6	27.6	9.6	15.0	—	8.6	24.2	148.4	2.6	2.0
Bulgaria	255.6	5.2	80.8	6.2	9.2	11.2	176.0	11.8	37.0	131.6	7.0	1.4
Greece	119.4	1.8	51.6	48.0	18.6	19.4	194.2	27.4	25.6	183.6	6.0	15.4
China	83.6	149.0	87.0	69.6	1.0	48.0	—	13.0		23.0		5.4
Japan	38.8	204.8	35.6	113.4	1.4	6.8	—	1.0		7.6		75.6
India	35.6	135.4	61.2	14.4	27.2	40.4	—	7.0		119.6		2.8
Burma	2.6	324.4	11.2	15.0	13.2	21.8	—	5.6		32.8		67.2
Thailand	0.4	278.8	1.0	46.6	21.6	34.0	—	9.4		81.2		96.8
Indochina	0.6	241.0	39.8	89.4	13.0	14.1	—	3.2		10.4		24.8
Ceylon	85.8	114.2	13.6	23.0	28.6	180.3	—	11.0		39.2		14.6
Malaya	93.4	251.2	0.4	59.0	12.4	32.6	—	6.8		20.0		39.4
Indonesia	—	135.2	57.4	358.6	16.2	63.0	—	5.4		8.6		7.0
Philippines	28.4	157.4	45.2	45.8	20.0	34.8	—	10.0		37.0		92.0
French Morocco	218.4		—	2.8	23.0	3.6	61.0	9.6	30.4	230.6	6.2	8.2
Algeria	165.6		—	14.2	18.6	5.2	92.4	11.8	17.8	142.0	4.2	5.6
Tunisia	192.6		—	15.0	23.8	11.8	53.4	15.6	26.8	141.8	5.6	3.2

(Continued on facing page)

TABLE 145—*continued*

Country [a]	Bread Grains	Rice	Coarse Grains	Potatoes, Roots, Tubers	Sugar	Pulses and Nuts	Fruits and Vegetables	Fats and Oils	Meat	Milk and Cheese	Eggs	Fish
Egypt	355.6	—		13.8	26.6	32.4	93.2	6.0	16.4	138.2	3.0	6.0
Madagascar	243.6	—		309.8	5.6	5.0	51.6	3.8	58.2	175.4	3.6	9.0
Union of South Africa	340.0	—		47.2	66.8	9.4	134.8	9.4	102.4	159.8	10.4	5.2
Australia	196.6	—		120.2	104.4	8.4	295.4	32.8	200.8	26.4	283.2	7.8
New Zealand	205.8	—		117.0	86.8	8.2	234.4	28.0	223.2	27.2	392.6	12.6

Source: **7**, pp. 48, 60, 70, 88, 102–05.

a. Countries arranged geographically.
b. 1946.   c. 1947.   d. Bizone.

son. Per capita consumption of these commodities is comparatively low in southern and eastern Europe and still lower in the USSR and Asia.

Per capita consumption of cocoa before World War II was highest in the Netherlands, which was followed, at a great distance, by the United Kingdom, the United States and Switzerland. (See Table 146; cf. Figure 101.)

Tobacco. Use of tobacco is distributed more evenly throughout the world. Not all areas have abundant amounts of types that would satisfy the taste of smokers in the United States or Great Britain, but most areas in moderate and tropical zones have a sufficient supply of local nicotine plants. Per capita consumption of tobacco is about as high in Italy as in the United States and Great Britain, and people in India and China seem to smoke as much as those in France and Czechoslovakia. (See Table 146.)

Textile fibers. The consumption of textile fibers in a country depends partly on its own consumption of fabrics and partly on the extent of its production of textiles for export: mills in Great Britain and Belgium, exporters of textiles, naturally use more fibers than textile mills in countries that import fabrics. Great Britain, Japan, the United States, Belgium and Switzerland led all other countries in per capita consumption of cotton before World War II. Great Britain, Belgium and Australia led in per capita consumption of wool. The United States was first in silk and also in rubber. (See Table 146.)

Finished textile products. To estimate the actual per capita consumption of finished textile products in various countries, exports and imports of yarn and fabrics should be taken into account.

Of the three major textiles — cotton, wool

and rayon — cotton leads throughout the world. Wool obviously is needed more in temperate and cool regions than in tropical and subtropical zones. Use of rayon has increased since World War II by 20 per cent for the world as a whole and 100 per cent or more for many countries.

The United States, with some 6 per cent of the world's population, consumes more than a third of the world's textiles, 41.6 metric pounds per person. Canada comes next, with 26.4 pounds, followed by Sweden, Belgium, Switzerland, the United Kingdom, Australia, France, the Netherlands and Argentina. Germany, which was in the highest group in Europe before the war, has dropped sharply in textile consumption, from 18.0 pounds per person in 1938 to 8.1 pounds in 1948. Eastern European countries have a much lower consumption — Hungary and Bulgaria, 6.4 pounds; Yugoslavia, 5.3; Romania, 4.4. The USSR uses 5.5 pounds per inhabitant.

Most Latin American countries are on approximately the same level of textile consumption as southern and eastern Europe: Brazil resembles Poland (8.9 and 8.8 pounds per capita); Cuba and Chile resemble Greece (less than 8 pounds); Mexico is in the same class with Hungary (approximately 6.5 pounds); Colombia and Venezuela are close to Yugoslavia (less than 6 pounds); Ecuador is close to Romania (4 pounds). In Uruguay and Argentina per capita consumption of textiles is on the same level as in western Europe.

Textile consumption in Asia is exceedingly low, with Indochina and Indonesia at the bottom. Japan is the only Asiatic country that approximated the western European level before the war, with 20.0 pounds per person in 1938, but in 1948 it used as little as Iran or China.

TABLE 146

COFFEE, TEA, COCOA, TOBACCO, FIBERS AND RUBBER: PER CAPITA CONSUMPTION IN
SELECTED COUNTRIES, 1934–38 ANNUAL AVERAGE

(*Metric Pounds*)

Country [a]	Coffee	Tea	Cocoa	Tobacco	Cotton	Wool	Jute	Rubber
United States	12.3	0.6	3.9	6.3	20.0	5.5	1.1	7.7
Canada	3.1	3.1	2.1	3.7	11.6	3.1	—	5.3
Brazil	14.2	—	—	2.7	9.2	—	1.1	—
Argentina	3.6	0.3	0.8	3.5	4.8	3.5	1.5	1.1
United Kingdom	0.6	8.2	4.1	5.7	25.6	15.7	7.1	4.3
France	8.8	—	2.0	3.2	12.6	8.6	4.4	2.9
Belgium	11.4	—	2.3	6.5	17.4	12.1	12.0	2.5
Netherlands	8.4	2.9	14.5	7.5	11.6	—	2.3	1.1
Denmark	15.0	—	2.3	—	—	—	—	1.5
Sweden	15.4	—	1.8	—	10.2	—	2.5	2.1
Germany	4.9	0.1	2.4	4.3	7.4	5.1	3.2	2.3
Poland	—	—	0.4	1.1	4.0	2.2	0.8	0.3
Czechoslovakia	1.7	—	1.5	3.1	11.0	3.1	4.5	1.4
Switzerland	7.5	—	3.7	—	13.6	—	—	—
Hungary	—	—	0.9	0.9	—	—	2.2	0.6
Spain	1.2	—	0.9	—	—	—	—	—
Italy	1.7	—	0.4	7.9	7.2	2.1	2.2	1.1
USSR	0.0	0.2	0.1	2.5	8.2	1.0	0.2	0.4
China	—	1.8	—	3.0	3.0	—	—	0.0
Japan	—	0.9	—	1.8	21.0	—	0.7	1.6
Turkey	—	1.4	—	2.2	—	—	—	—
India	0.1	0.2	—	3.2	2.6	—	3.9	—
Indonesia	1.0	0.2	—	—	—	—	—	—
Egypt	0.1	0.9	—	—	3.2	—	4.2	—
Union of South Africa	3.0	1.4	—	2.1	—	2.0	—	0.7
Australia	0.5	6.1	1.9	—	—	11.0	—	3.9
New Zealand	0.4	6.0	2.0	—	—	4.2	—	—

Sources: **12**; **16**; **5**, Nos. 2–5, 1948.

a. Countries arranged geographically.

Egypt and the Union of South Africa have a slightly higher level of consumption than the USSR. (See Table 147.)

CONSUMPTION OF FOREST PRODUCTS

Timber is man's chief building material. At least two thirds of the human race uses wood for cooking food, and to that extent wood itself becomes an integral part of the world's food supply. Wood is shelter and warmth and one of the world's most versatile raw materials.[20]

At least three factors affect the consumption of wood: climate, the available supply, and the level of economic development in the country. The demand for fuelwood declines from the polar regions to the equator; consumption of round wood and lumber is high in heavily forested regions and low in sparsely wooded areas; high consumption of industrial timber, plywood and wood pulp is characteristic of industrially developed countries.

Canada, Brazil and Sweden consume more than a ton of fuelwood a year per inhabitant, as compared with 29 pounds in the Netherlands; Canada uses nearly 1.5 tons of industrial wood per capita, as compared with Guatemala's 66 pounds; per capita consumption of plywood in the United States amounted to 17.5 pounds in 1948, as compared with 5.9 pounds in Great Britain and 2.9 pounds in France. (See Table 148.)

20. **6**, pp. 6–9.

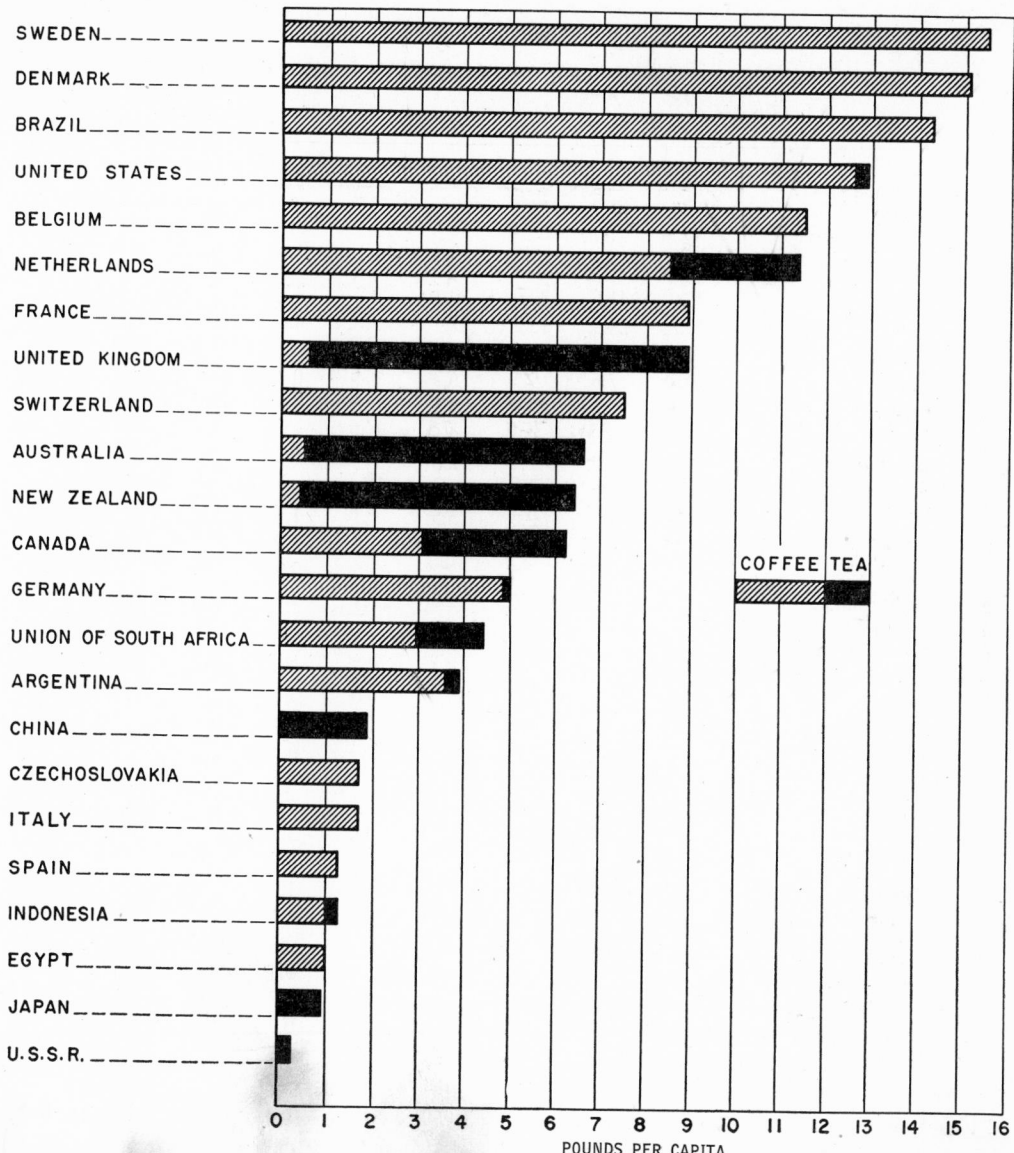

FIGURE 101. COFFEE AND TEA: PER CAPITA CONSUMPTION IN SELECTED COUNTRIES, ANNUAL AVERAGE, 1934–38

In addition to its popularity in the United Kingdom and the British Dominions (Australia, New Zealand, Canada and the Union of South Africa), tea is widely used in China and Japan, where it is the national drink, and in the Netherlands. Coffee is favored in the United States, Central and South America, continental Europe and the Near East. (Cf. Table 146.)

TABLE 147

TEXTILES: PER CAPITA CONSUMPTION IN SELECTED COUNTRIES, 1938 AND 1948

(Metric Pounds)

Country [a]	Total		Cotton Textiles		Wool Textiles		Rayon Textiles	
	1938	1948	1938	1948	1938	1948	1938	1948
World	8.6	8.1	6.6	5.9	1.1	1.1	.0.88	1.06
United States	26.6	41.6	22.0	29.3	2.2	4.8	2.35	7.50
Canada	18.7	26.4	13.2	17.4	3.7	4.6	1.61	4.42
Mexico	6.4	6.6 [b]	5.3	5.1	0.4	0.2	0.55	1.30
Cuba	10.6	7.6 [b]	9.5	6.2	0.4	0.2	0.75	2.24
Venezuela	4.2	5.3 [b]	2.6	3.3	0.2	0.1	1.23	1.91
Colombia	5.3	5.9 [b]	4.0	4.6	0.9	0.4	0.51	0.81
Ecuador	3.5	4.0 [b]	2.4	2.6	—	—	1.10	1.34
Brazil	8.4	8.9 [b]	7.7	8.1	0.4	0.4	0.31	0.57
Peru	4.2	5.0 [b]	2.6	3.5	1.3	1.3	1.20	0.13
Chile	8.4	7.5 [b]	5.5	5.1	1.8	1.5	1.01	0.84
Uruguay	5.5	11.7	3.3	7.7	1.5	2.9	0.55	0.99
Argentina	14.7	17.8	11.0	12.8	3.1	3.8	0.57	1.03
United Kingdom	27.1	24.0	18.0	14.7	6.8	5.9	2.13	3.37
Ireland	9.7	7.3	5.1	3.1	3.7	3.3	0.88	0.88
France	15.4	19.8	10.1	11.4	4.0	5.1	1.28	3.26
Belgium	20.5	24.9	13.4	16.9	5.7	5.5	1.26	2.44
Netherlands	18.0	19.1	12.9	10.1	4.4	6.2	1.28	2.77
Denmark	11.4	11.2	10.1	6.2	4.4	3.5	1.21	1.52
Sweden	19.8	25.3	14.5	13.4	3.7	6.6	1.54	4.97
Norway	13.6	13.6	8.8	7.9	4.0	3.5	0.92	2.27
Finland	15.2	11.4	10.1	5.3	2.4	2.2	2.62	3.85
Germany	18.0	8.1	7.5	3.1	3.3	1.5	7.26	3.52
Poland	6.2	8.8 [b]	4.4	6.2	1.1	1.1	0.68	1.56
Czechoslovakia	11.2	14.5	8.4	7.7	2.2	2.6	0.62	4.07
Switzerland	16.5	24.6	12.1	15.6	3.1	5.5	1.34	3.54
Austria	13.2	6.7	9.0	2.9	3.3	0.7	0.79	3.26
Hungary	8.4	6.4	5.9	5.1	1.3	0.9	0.99	0.37
Portugal	6.9	9.2	4.6	7.3	1.8	1.8	0.35	0.24
Spain	5.3	7.0	3.5	4.8	1.8	0.9	0.09	1.25
Italy	9.2	9.7 [b]	4.4	6.6	1.3	2.0	3.41	1.19
Yugoslavia	7.5	5.3	5.3	3.7	1.8	1.3	0.33	0.29
Romania	6.1	4.4	4.0	3.1	1.5	0.9	0.15	0.33
Bulgaria	9.9	6.4 [b]	7.7	4.6	2.2	1.8	...	...
Greece	10.3	7.9 [b]	8.1	5.9	2.2	1.8	0.09	0.22
USSR	8.1	5.5	7.3	4.6	0.9	0.7	...	...
China	3.7	3.1	3.5	2.9	0.1	0.1	0.02	0.02
Japan	20.0	3.3	12.8	2.4	1.5	0.2	5.65	0.75
Turkey	7.7	7.3	6.2	6.7	1.5	0.9	0.04	0.09
Lebanon and Syria	10.1	7.9	6.6	4.6	1.3	1.3	2.09	2.05
Iran	5.3	3.7	4.8	3.1	0.4	0.4	0.09	0.20
India and Pakistan	4.4	4.6	4.6	4.4	0.1	0.1	0.18	0.09
Indochina	2.2	1.1	2.2	1.1	0.02	0.02	0.13	0.07
Malaya	6.6	11.0	6.2	9.9	0.1	0.1	0.37	0.97
Indonesia	2.0	1.3	1.8	1.3	—	—	0.13	0.02

(Continued on facing page)

TABLE 147—*continued*

Country [a]	Total		Cotton Textiles		Wool Textiles		Rayon Textiles	
	1938	1948	1938	1948	1938	1948	1938	1948
Egypt	6.8	6.4	5.9	5.7	0.4	0.2	0.35	0.35
Anglo-Egyptian Sudan	3.3	2.4	3.0	2.2	—	—	0.13	0.22
Southern Rhodesia	7.5	4.8	4.4	4.6	—	—	3.08	—
Union of South Africa	7.0	6.4	5.2	4.2	1.1	1.3	0.66	0.33
Australia	18.7	21.3	9.9	11.2	5.9	6.4	2.82	3.74
New Zealand	12.1	14.7	4.4	5.1	5.5	4.2	2.11	2.09

Source: **8**, Part I, pp. 25–26.

    a. Countries arranged geographically.
    b. Raw materials (raw cotton, clean wool, rayon filament or staple fiber), semifinished (cotton yarn, tops, wool or spun rayon yarn) and manufactures.

CONSUMPTION OF MINERAL PRODUCTS

A country's per capita consumption of metal is directly related to the level of its industrial development. Per capita consumption of coal and oil depends partly on the volume of industrial activities, partly on the organization of economic life in the nation.

Steel

Annual consumption of steel ranges from a couple of pounds per inhabitant in colonial areas to 400 pounds or more in Canada, the United Kingdom, Belgium-Luxembourg and Czechoslovakia and more than 1,000 pounds in the United States.[21]

Mineral Fuels

Use of coal and oil in an area is to some extent affected by the availability of other sources of energy, especially fuelwood and hydroelectric power. In some countries, mineral fuels provide more than 90 per cent of all motive power and heat; in others, less than 30 per cent. The United Kingdom exemplifies an economy in which energy is derived mainly from coal; Finland relies chiefly on fuelwood, Norway on water power.[22] (See Table 149.)

Before World War II industrialized countries generally consumed energy from all sources equivalent to 2 tons or more of coal per inhabitant. Less than the equivalent of 1,000 pounds per capita was usual in underdeveloped areas. But the distribution of the consumed energy by source varied greatly from country to country. Thus per capita consumption of mineral fuels in some underdeveloped countries relying mainly on the energy provided by wood fuel and work animals was only a fraction of one per cent of that in the United States.

PATTERNS OF NUTRITION

The people of the world differ strikingly in the amount and type of food that represents their daily "bread."

The problem of nutrition has attracted worldwide attention in recent years. Scientific principles of nutrition have been developed through the concentrated work of international experts and it has become possible to appraise objectively nutritional habits in various parts of the world, to determine the extent of food deficiencies, and to establish nutritional targets for underdeveloped countries.

PRINCIPLES OF NUTRITION

The international discussion of principles of nutrition initiated by the League of Nations and carried on in recent years by the Food and Agriculture Organization of the United Nations (FAO) has been inspired by the recognition that it is of general concern to all nations not to let well-being drop below definite standards among any people in the world.

The Nutritional Problem

Nutrition has been recognized as an urgent problem, not because the nutritional situation has become worse during and since the last war but, rather, because of the growing conviction

---

21. For details see Chapter 29.
22. For further information on consumption of energy in the world, see Chapter 25.

TABLE 148

FOREST PRODUCTS: PER CAPITA CONSUMPTION IN SELECTED COUNTRIES, 1948

(*Metric Pounds*)

Region and Country [a]	Fuelwood	Industrial Timber	Lumber	Plywood	Wood Pulp
World	385	605	214	4.6	51
North America	660	2,740	757	20.7	257
Middle and South America	1,320	620	57	1.5	9
Europe	440	725	165	4.0	46
Near East and North Africa	155	66	20	0.7	3
Africa	385	120	15	2.0	—
South and East Asia	100	75	57	0.4	2
Oceania	1,500	1,770	525	5.0	94
United States	480	2,680	755	17.5 [b]	264
Canada	2,620	3,210	800	25.2	185
Guatemala	125 [b]	66 [b]	—	—	2
Venezuela	40	312	105	—	18
Colombia	9	97	6	—	4
Brazil	2,770	196	77	—	—
Peru	275 [b]	55 [b]	15	—	4
Chile	1,023 [b]	870 [b]	134	1.5 [b]	22
Uruguay	980	560	—	—	29
United Kingdom		682	194	5.9	59
Ireland		262	75	1.3	33
France	302	682	163	2.9	42 [b]
Belgium		750	145	7.7	66
Netherlands	29	785	227	7.9	48
Denmark	264	1,012	354	4.6	81
Sweden	2,442	2,354	447	5.1	180
Norway	484	2,618	586	—	165
Finland	7,568	3,234	469	10.1	191
Germany (Bizone)	462	726	172	3.7	13 [b]
Poland	198 [b]	550 [b]	132	1.8	—
Czechoslovakia	418 [b]	572 [b]	264 [b]	6.4 [b]	24 [b]
Switzerland	627	1,110	352	2.4	70 [b]
Austria	308	672	147	1.8	57
Hungary	198	286	53	1.3 [b]	—
Italy	407 [b]	209 [b]	53	1.8	15
Greece	682	110	33	0.7 [b]	9
South Korea	121	15	7	—	—
Japan	385	385	139	2.2	11
India	35	13	—	—	—
Burma	440	66	—	—	—
Thailand	178	64	42 [b]	—	—
Ceylon	33	35	7	1.1	2
Belgian Congo	275 [b]	33 [b]	37 [b]	—	—
Gold Coast	1,640	100	2	0.8 [b]	—
Nyasaland	4,090	66	2	—	—
Southern Rhodesia	2,145	340	46	1.3	7
Australia	1,730	1,620	470	8.8	95
New Zealand	700	2,310	763	8.6	101

Source: **10**, 1949, pp. 142–45.

a. Countries arranged geographically.　　　b. 1947.

TABLE 149

ENERGY: PER CAPITA CONSUMPTION IN SELECTED COUNTRIES, 1937

(Coal Equivalent, in Metric Pounds)

Country [a]	Total	Coal	Oil, Gas	Fuel-wood	Water Power
United States	13,310	6,150	5,125	810	1,225
Canada	10,740	4,745	1,890	1,075	3,030
United Kingdom	9,600	7,880	1,085	—	635
Belgium–Luxembourg	8,090	6,700	405	65	920
Norway	7,090	2,155	615	180	4,140
Sweden	6,550	2,895	545	1,460	1,650
Germany	6,290	4,605	585	960	140
Australia	5,440	3,000	1,210	440	790
France	4,750	3,305	625	240	580
Switzerland	3,910	1,600	370	225	1,715
Chile	3,790	695	545	2,140	410
Union of South Africa	3,570	2,530	315	20	705
USSR	2,430	1,205	465	485	275
Japan	2,340	1,200	205	435	500
Argentina	1,780	335	1,015	170	260
Italy	1,370	635	210	75	450
Portugal	1,020	445	80	420	75
Spain	1,010	660	110	70	170
Mexico	790	80	470	70	170
Brazil	680	110	80	425	60
Egypt	600	280	295	—	25
Bulgaria	600	265	35	265	35
Colombia	550	80	250	180	40
Peru	410	40	190	120	60
Iran	270	—	90	180	—
India	190	140	20	10	10
China	170	100	5	60	5

Sources: For totals: Table 400; for distribution by type of fuel: Table 396.

a. Arrayed by decreasing per capita consumption of energy.

that the peace and security of the world is endangered by the present state of affairs, wherein a small fraction of mankind enjoys all the advantages of technical progress and the majority live on the verge of starvation.

As a League of Nations report points out, the character of the food problem in the world has changed over the last half century:

Throughout many parts of the world, it practically ceased to be a problem of hunger and became rather a problem of nutrition. It is, of course, impossible to say exactly when this transition occurred; the process was gradual and imperceptible. It is, however, sufficient to compare our present preoccupations about the qualitative adequacy of diets (their animal protein, vitamin and mineral content) with the famines which decimated whole communities even as late as the first half of the nineteenth century, to realize the enormous progress that has taken place.[23]

World War II and internal turmoils interrupted this progress. Once more China and India, and much of Europe, suffered from absolute shortage of foods, but the long-range trend toward better nutrition has not been halted or reversed.

Energy-Yielding and Protective Foods

Modern standards for nutritional requirements rest on a careful analysis of the needs of the human organism and the functions of various types of food. Energy-bearing foods, valuable chiefly as a source of energy, include cereals,

23. **1**, p. 97.

potatoes and sugar. The group of protective foods, which provide minerals, vitamins and "good" protein, includes milk, eggs, meat, green and leafy vegetables, fruits and so on. Both groups of food supply calories. Lack of calories causes starvation, and lack of protective foods causes various deficiency diseases, which may develop in spite of an abundant caloric intake.[24] Rickets in the countries of Western civilization, beriberi in rice-eating communities of the East, scurvy, some defects of the teeth and eyes, pellagra and many other diseases are caused by lack of vitamins and minerals in the diet. Since protective foods are usually more expensive than energy-bearing foods, deficiency diseases are primarily the scourges of the poor.

Adequate Nutrition

A person's food requirements, in terms of calories, vary with his age and his occupation. An average adult, man or woman, in a temperate climate and not engaged in manual work, is believed to need 2,400 to 2,500 calories a day. Manual workers require more, in accordance with their muscular activity.

Adequate nutrition requires a combination of protective and nonprotective foods that supplies the requisite energy for the body's activity and contains all the necessary protective elements (vitamins and minerals) in correct balance. An unlimited number of different diets may satisfy this nutritional ideal when the intake of the different nutritive elements is properly adjusted to the age and activity of the consumer.

It is generally believed that, of the total daily requirements, about 1,400 calories should be supplied by protective foods and the rest by staple energy-bearing foodstuffs. Mankind, however, is still far from this ideal. The mixed Committee on the Relation of Nutrition to Wealth of the League of Nations declares in its final report:

Poverty and ignorance remain formidable obstacles to progress; the disparity between food prices and incomes increases the difficulty experienced by the poorer sections of the community in obtaining an adequate supply of the proper foods. . . . In countries of the most diverse economic structure and general level of consumption, appreciable sections of the population are, for one reason or another, failing to secure the food which is essential to their health and efficiency.[25]

24. **1**, p. 65.
25. **1**, p. 33.

RECENT TRENDS IN NUTRITION

During the past century the general trend in nutrition habits and nutrition standards in the countries of Western civilization has been toward a more diversified diet and increasing consumption of protective foods. In recent times, consumption of rough energy-bearing foods (cereals and potatoes) has declined in the most prosperous countries, partly because of increasing preference for better — although more expensive — food, partly because mechanization has been reducing the muscular effort required of industrial and rural workers. This trend has also been furthered by the increasing proportion of the labor force in clerical and professional jobs and by changes in tastes and fashion.

The trend in consumption of meat has not been very clear. There has been an increasing demand for tender and leaner cuts — especially in prosperous countries — but per capita consumption of all meat has risen in some countries and periods and declined in others. In general, meat consumption appears to increase with rise in wealth up to a certain point but levels off and begins to decline with greater prosperity when people shift to lighter jobs and lighter fare.

International Food Statistics

In studying changes in nutrition patterns in various countries we should keep in mind that statistics on food consumption covering only a short period of time, say a decade or less, are not conclusive. In fact, appreciable annual variations in diet in a country may be caused by changes in prices and business conditions and other temporary factors. The interpretation of dietary changes in a nation is particularly difficult when data for only a few commodities are available. An increase in consumption of bread in a poor country suggests improvement in nutrition, but in an industrial nation is likely to indicate deterioration. On the other hand, the increasing use of such foods as milk, eggs and fruit always marks an improvement. Consumption of sugar usually increases along with improvement in nutrition, although dietitians do not believe that this increase itself promotes national health.

Experience in the United States

The changes in per capita consumption of various foods in the United States in the last four decades illustrate the recent trends in food habits in modern industrial countries. (See Table 150; cf. Figure 102.)

TABLE 150

SELECTED FOODS: PER CAPITA CONSUMPTION IN THE UNITED STATES, 1909–48

(*Pounds Per Year*)

Food	1909	1919	1929	1939	1948
Cereals					
Wheat flour and cereal	210.0	198.2	174.5	154.9	138.5
Corn	140.0	132.0	155.0	121.0	133.0
Rye, rice, oats, barley	18.6	22.6	19.3	12.7	11.4
Potatoes	193.0	151.0	154.0	121.0	108.0
Sweet potatoes	26.0	29.7	22.2	19.5	14.0
Meat (carcass weight)					
Beef and veal	80.7	68.8	55.6	61.9	72.6
Lamb and mutton	6.7	5.6	5.6	6.6	5.0
Pork	66.4	63.4	69.2	64.3	68.7
Fish (edible weight equivalent)					
Fresh and frozen	4.3	6.4	6.9	5.4	6.2 [a]
Canned and cured	6.6	5.5	5.3	5.5	4.6 [a]
Poultry					
Chicken	19.4	18.8	19.7	18.7	23.0
Turkey	—	—	1.7	3.0	3.7
Eggs	36.2	37.6	41.5	38.9	48.2
Dairy products					
Fluid milk and cream	351.0	343.0	351.0	343.0	387.0
Cheese	3.9	4.2	4.6	5.9	6.8
Condensed milk	5.4	9.8	13.5	17.7	20.6
Ice cream	1.5	6.4	10.0	10.9	17.1
Fats and oils					
Butter	17.6	15.1	17.2	17.3	10.0
Lard	12.3	10.6	12.7	12.6	12.7
Margarine	1.2	3.3	2.9	2.3	6.1
Fresh fruits (retail weight)					
Apples	55.5	40.4	35.5	37.8	31.2
Citrus	15.3	22.1	37.5	47.9	51.0
Other fresh fruits	53.7	50.2	58.5	53.8	49.6
Canned fruit juices	0.5	0.3	0.3	5.9	18.1
Frozen and dried fruits	4.2	6.8	5.8	7.4	7.8
Fresh vegetables	—	193.0	221.0	243.0	251.0
Canned vegetables	15.2	21.1	25.7	31.6	36.5
Sugar (cane and beet)	73.1	85.9	96.3	100.2	95.6
Coffee	9.1	11.7	12.1	14.8	18.9
Tea	1.1	0.6	0.7	0.7	0.5
Cocoa	1.3	3.5	3.9	4.7	3.7

Source: **14**, pp. 72–86 and 114.   a. 1947.

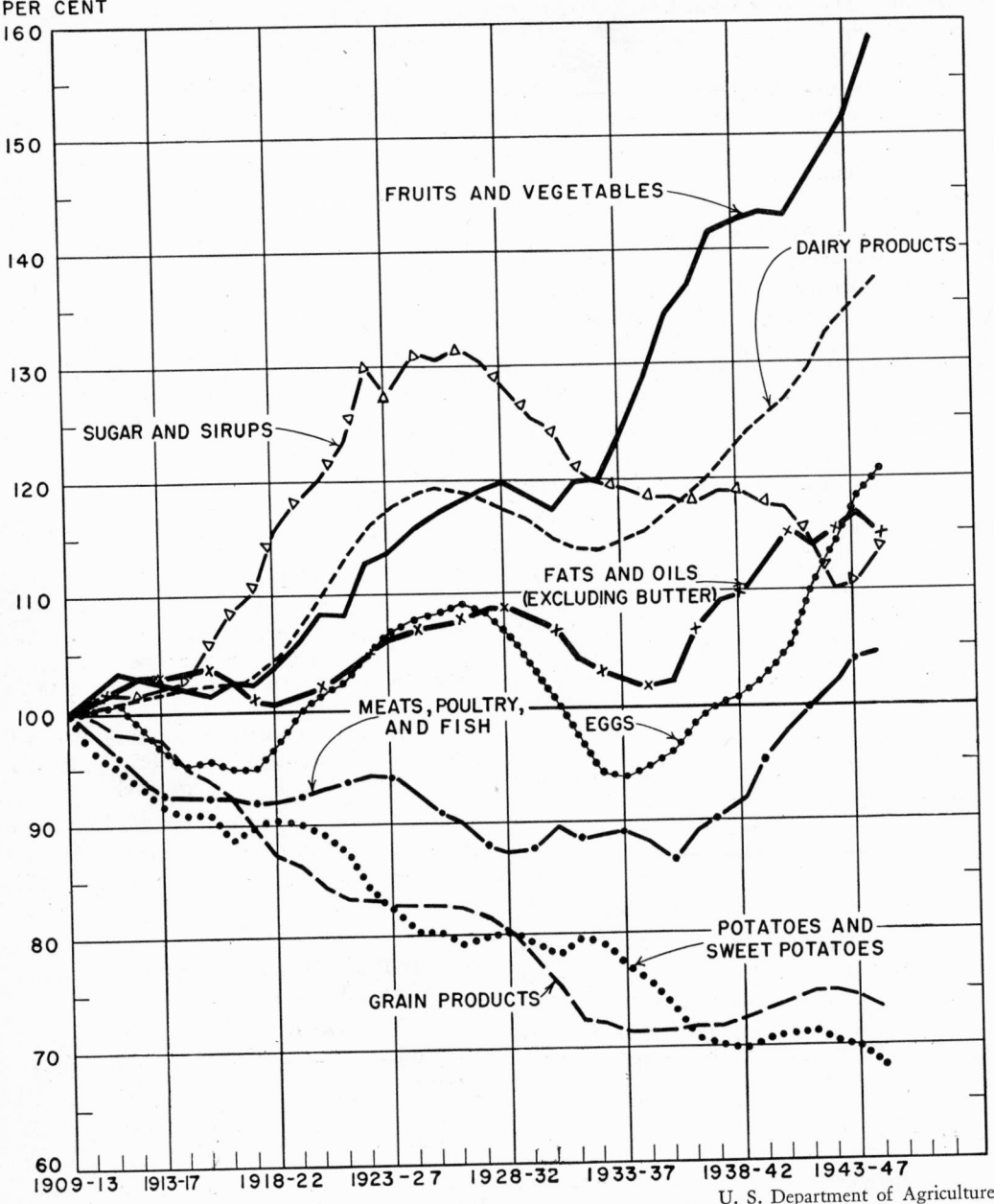

U. S. Department of Agriculture

FIGURE 102. NUTRITIONAL PATTERNS: TRENDS IN PER CAPITA CONSUMPTION OF SELECTED FOODS IN THE UNITED STATES, 1909–13—1944–48

The total per capita consumption of the foods listed in Table 150 amounted to 1,572 pounds (retail weight equivalent) in 1909, fell to 1,463 pounds in 1921, rose to 1,705 in 1946, and declined again to 1,581 pounds in 1948.[26] The changes were due to divergent trends in the price of different foods, but the extent of the change was rather small, and there has been no visible trend toward an increase or a decrease in the total intake of food, in terms of pounds per capita of population.

On the other hand, the composition of the diet of the American people changed conspicuously from 1909 to 1948. The amount of nonprotective foods, especially of cereals and potatoes, dropped from nearly 790 pounds per capita in 1909 to 405 pounds in 1948, while the amount of the protective foods was increasing. The shift was toward increasing consumption of dairy products, eggs, poultry, citrus fruits, fruit juices, fresh vegetables (other than potatoes), coffee and cocoa. Among nonprotective foods, only sugar showed an appreciable increase, and among protective foods, only meats declined. Thus improvement in diet in the United States was *qualitative* rather than *quantitative*.

Experience in Other Countries

Similar trends have been recorded in other Western countries, including Sweden, Norway, Great Britain and Belgium. (See Tables 151 and 152.)

DIETARY PATTERNS IN THE WORLD

The prevailing diet in a country or region depends on the local supply of food and on habits that have developed through centuries, mainly by dint of necessity: peoples have learned to like the kinds of food they could get. (See Figure 103.)

Scope of Deficiency

More than half the people in the world fail to get enough food, and those who have enough food in terms of total calories do not always get the proper foods in the proper proportion. The FAO summarizes the world situation as follows: [27]

In areas containing over half the world's population, food supplies at the retail level (not actual

---

26. All data in avoirdupois pounds, as used in the United States and other English-speaking nations.
27. **9,** pp. 6–7. See Figure 104.

TABLE 151

SELECTED FOODS: PER CAPITA CONSUMPTION IN THE UNITED KINGDOM, 1903–13, 1924–28 AND 1934

(Metric Pounds)

Item	1903–13 Average	1924–28 Average	1934
Wheat flour	211	198	197
Potatoes	208	194	210
Meat	135	134	143
Eggs [a]	104	120	152
Butter	16	16	25
Cheese	7	9	10
Margarine	6	12	8
Fruits	61	91	115
Vegetables (other than potatoes)	60	78	98
Sugar	79	87	94

Source: **2,** Vol. III, p. 28.

a. Number.

intake) were sufficient to furnish an average of less than 2250 calories per caput daily.

Food supplies furnishing an average of more than 2750 calories per caput daily were available in areas containing somewhat less than a third of the world's population.

The remaining areas, containing about one-sixth of the world's population, had food supplies that were between these high and low levels.

Deficiency of protective foods is even more extensive. Less than one fifth of the world's population receives adequate amounts of milk,

---

TABLE 152

SELECTED FOODS: CONSUMPTION BY THE FAMILY OF A MANUAL WORKER IN BELGIUM, 1891–1929

(Kilograms Per Year)

Item	1891	1910	1921	1929
Bread	256	242	234	200
Potatoes	232	262	258	224
Beef	22.1	18.0	25.4	22.1
Pork	2.4	10.2	8.8	8.2
Bacon	4.9	9.1	8.2	7.7
Fat	3.8	11.4	9.4	5.6
Eggs	4.4	7.8	13.1	10.1
Milk	47.4	81.9	111.4	145.1
Butter	15.2	16.6	22.4	22.9
Sugar	2.4	6.0	18.0	15.0
Coffee	5.4	7.1	8.6	6.8
Chicory	5.4	5.3	7.4	5.8

Source: **1,** p. 134.

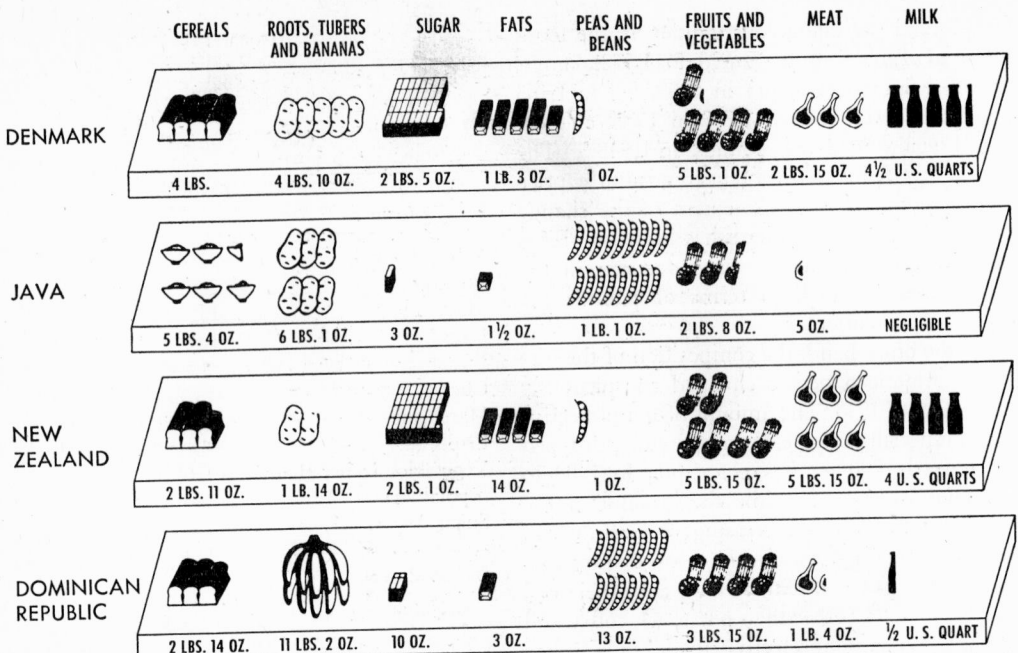

Food and Agriculture Organization

FIGURE 103. NUTRITIONAL PATTERNS: TYPICAL PREWAR DIETS IN FOUR COUNTRIES

The typical diet in a country is adjusted to its resources. Meat and milk are important in the diet of Denmark and New Zealand; rice, peas and beans in Java; bananas, peas and beans in the Dominican Republic.

eggs, meats and other protective foods. Four fifths rely mainly on cereals and potatoes.

Bread and Potato Eaters

The relative share of cereals and potatoes in the caloric intake of the population of a country

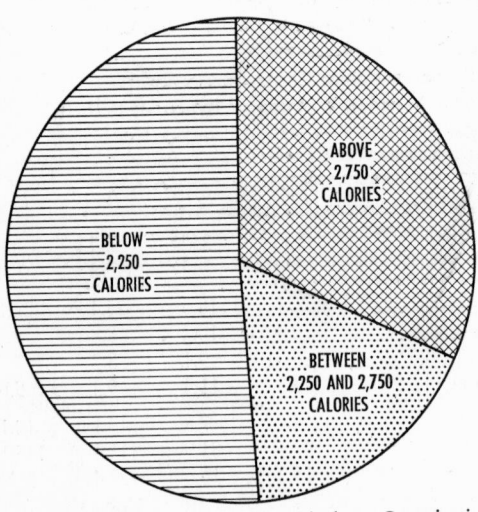

Food and Agriculture Organization

FIGURE 104. PROPORTION OF WORLD POPULATION WITH SPECIFIED DAILY CALORIC INTAKE, 1934–38

More than half the people in the world live in areas where the supply of food is not sufficient to provide 2,250 calories a day per person.

is the larger, in general, the lower the level of its economic development and well-being. The national diets computed by M. K. Bennett are in this respect most revealing.[28] Cereals and potatoes predominate in the diet of the USSR, Romania, Bulgaria, Yugoslavia and Poland; China, Manchukuo, India, Nigeria and Madagascar. Since the available figures for many countries are not very precise, no particular significance should be attached to the ranking of countries in this group. The same reservation should be made for countries where these foods represent less than half the caloric intake: the Netherlands, Austria, Norway, Denmark, Germany, Finland, Australia, the United Kingdom, New Zealand, Canada, the United States, Switzerland and Sweden. The two groups of countries are characteristic of the underdeveloped areas of the world, on the one hand, and of the economically developed regions of Western civilization, on the other. (See Figure 105.)

Meat Eaters

The practically meatless diet of Asiatic countries reflects national habits, which, in turn, are rooted in the poverty of the population and have perpetuated poverty by undermining health and

28. **18.**

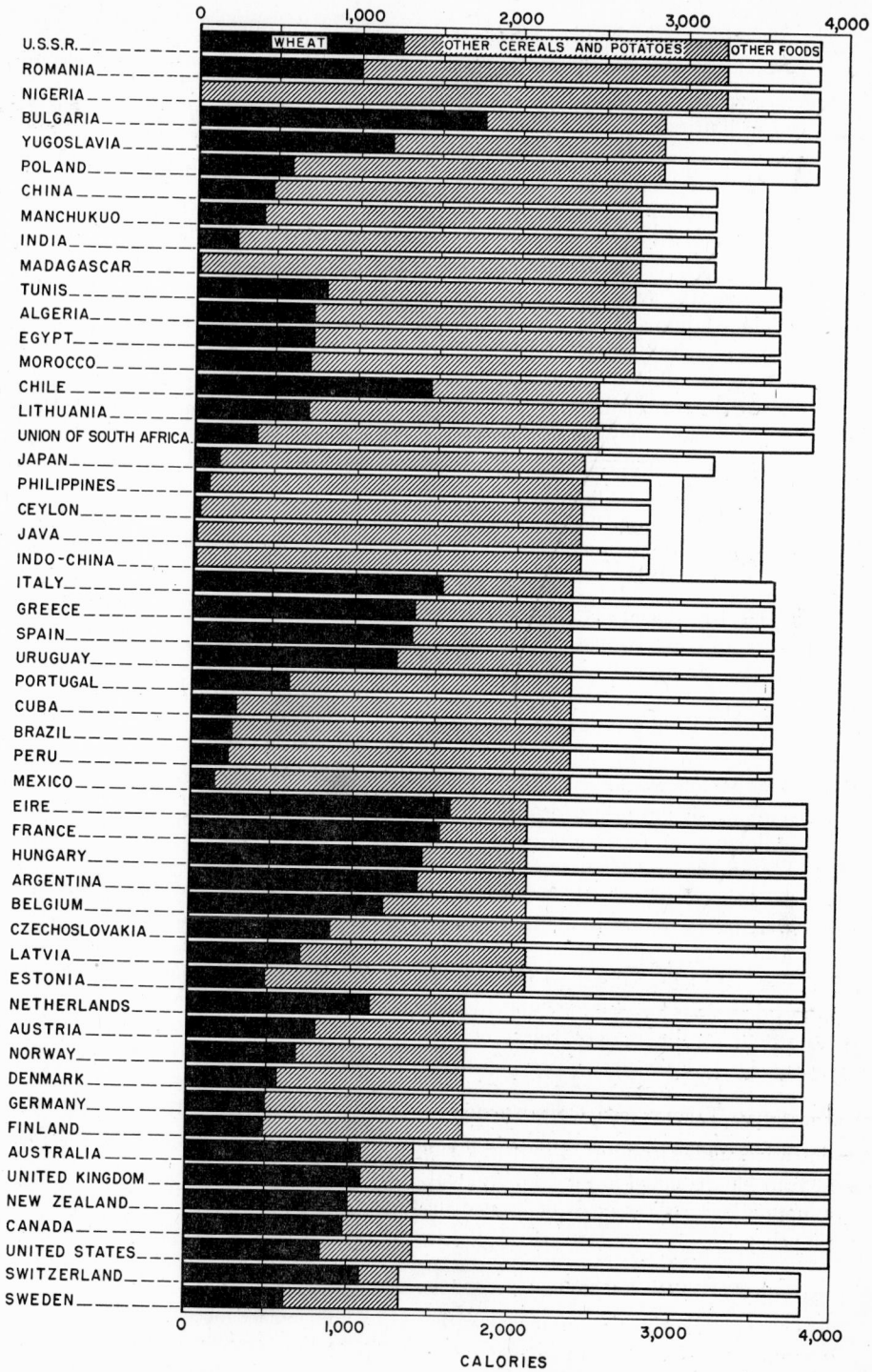

Food Research Institute, Stanford University

FIGURE 105. CALORIE DISAPPEARANCE OF CEREALS, POTATOES AND OTHER FOODS IN 52 COUNTRIES, 1933–38 AVERAGE

"Disappearance" of food includes not only its direct consumption but also the amounts wasted, lost, or diverted to industrial uses. Countries are arrayed by declining daily disappearance of cereals and potatoes per adult male. Underdeveloped, predominantly agricultural countries top the list; wealthy and industrially developed countries are at the bottom.

305

physical strength. The meatless diet of India is a striking example of the interdependence of social, economic, psychological and moral factors in the problem of nutrition.[29]

Mahatma Gandhi tells in his autobiography how the problem of meat eating precipitated the first tragedy and the first rebellion of his childhood. During a wave of "reform" then sweeping over his native province, the "reformers" secretly ate meat, committing the sin most abhorrent in the eyes of religious Hindus. A friend whom he accuses of having exercised an evil influence on him explained to Gandhi: "We are a weak people because we do not eat meat; the English are able to rule us because they are meat-eaters." Schoolboys everywhere repeated:

> Behold the mighty Englishman.
> He rules the Indian small
> Because, being a meat-eater,
> He is five cubits tall.

Gandhi let his friend convert him, and the conspirators met at a lonely spot by the river. There Gandhi saw meat for the first time in his life, a piece of goat's meat as tough as leather. He got sick and had to stop eating, but he tried again and again, tried hard, until he realized how shocked his parents would be if they learned of his sin. Without giving up his idea of eating meat and of taking up food reform, Gandhi decided that deceiving and lying to his parents would be a much worse sin than abstinence from meat.[30] Later he returned to his parents' belief that eating meat was an unpardonable sin and discovered in the ethical philosophy of his country other ways of making "the Indian small" as strong as the mighty rulers of his country.

International Targets for Consumption

The intensive studies conducted by the FAO in recent years have resulted in the establishment of consumption "targets" as goals of immediate economic policy.

NUTRITIONAL TARGETS

In 1946 the Hot Springs Conference of the FAO recommended that governments should

. . . adopt as the ultimate goal of their food and nutrition policy, dietary standards of allowances

based upon scientific assessment of the amount and quality of food, in terms of nutrients, which promote health, and distinguish clearly between these standards and the more immediate consumption goals, which necessarily must be based upon the practical possibilities of improving the food supply of their populations.[31]

In establishing the immediate nutritional targets for various countries, the experts were guided by the following principles:

(a) Per capita intake should be raised to at least 2550–2650 calories in the low-caloric countries.

(b) *Cereals.* If the daily intake in calories from cereals is between 1200 and 1800, no change should generally be recommended. If it is below 1200, and if total calorie intake is below 2600, some increase in cereal intake may be recommended unless the total calories from cereals, starchy roots and tubers and starchy fruits, sugar, fats, and pulses exceed 2000–2100.

If cereal calories exceed 1800 and total calories are high, the question of decreasing the former should be considered.

(c) *Starchy roots and tubers and starchy fruits* (for example, bananas, which in composition resemble roots and tubers). An intake of 100–200 calories from these foods may be taken as a desirable objective.

(d) *Sugar.* In general, no increase in the intake of sugar should be recommended. If calories from sugar exceed 10 to 15 per cent of total calories, some reduction may be considered.

(e) *Fats.* Total daily calories from fats (as a separate food group) should be at least 100 and preferably 150–200. Intake of fat through the medium of other food groups must be taken into consideration.

(f) *Pulses.* In countries in which meat supplies are low and pulses are an important feature of the dietary pattern, calories from this source may well reach 250–300 daily. But even when meat calories are as high as 200–250, calories from pulses may be pushed to 200–250.

(g) *Fruits and vegetables.* Total calories from these foods (excluding starchy vegetables and fruits) should be at least 100 per capita daily. Preference must be given to leafy green and yellow vegetables and fruits and to fruits and vegetables which are good sources of vitamin C.

(h) *Meat (including poultry), fish and eggs.* Not less than 100 calories daily per capita and preferably 150–200, should be derived from these sources. If intake of milk and pulses

---

29. India has nearly 20 per cent of all the cattle in the world (over 140 million head) but lets them die from starvation rather than use their meat. (Cf. Chapter 18, p. 639.)

30. **20**, pp. 53–61.

31. **9**, p. 11.

is high, that of this group can be correspondingly reduced. Fish can replace meat in countries in which the latter cannot easily be produced in quantity and where fish supplies can be readily increased.

(i) *Milk and milk products.* An intake of 300–400 calories per capita daily represents a desirable minimum level of consumption. In recommending milk-supply targets, weight must, however, be given (1) to existing dietary habits, (2) to the present level of milk intake, and (3) to the possibility of providing certain important nutrients of milk through a combination of pulses and leafy green and yellow vegetables.[32]

While accepting these general principles, the FAO realized that it was "impractical to put forward targets calling for a uniform degree of nutritional adequacy. In countries in which food supplies were insufficient in quantity as well as unsatisfactory in quality, it considered the increases in food supplies necessary to raise calorie intake to a reasonable level of sufficiency . . . For countries with sufficient calorie supplies, adjustments were made to improve the quality of the diet while the same energy value as in the prewar period was maintained."[33]

In this way "targets" were determined for eighteen areas comprising the whole world. In eight areas where present per capita intake is 2,755–3,240 calories, increase in the proportion of protective foods was recommended. In ten other areas, both increase in caloric value and change in the proportion of energy-yielding and protective foods seem necessary. (See Figure 106.)

The Cost of Adequate Nutrition

Considerable increase in the world's output of food is required to meet the established nutritional targets for the world. The problem is complicated by the fact that the need is greatest among masses of people in areas where poverty makes improvement in living standards especially difficult. The economic difficulty in meeting the requirements is increased by the emphasis of the targets on need for more animal foods. As the FAO pointed out, "When crops are fed to animals instead of being eaten directly by human beings, they lose 80 to 90 per cent of their caloric value before they reemerge in the

form of meat and milk."[34] On the average, therefore, seven "original calories" in crops are required to produce one calorie in food of animal origin.

For example, the prewar North American diet averaged about 2,200 calories per capita per day from foods of plant origin and about 870 calories from livestock products. When 870 is multiplied by seven, the value in "original calories" becomes 6,090+2,200, or 8,290. At the other end of the scale, the diet in certain islands off southeastern Asia contained about 1,940 calories from plant products and only 100 from livestock products and thus represented only 2,640 original calories (1,940+700), or about one third the value of the North American diet.[35]

The improvements suggested by the targets of the FAO require an increase of as much as 40 per cent in the "original calories" in the less developed regions, such as India and southeastern Asia. The world's output of fruits and vegetables would have to be more than doubled, that of milk increased by 60 per cent, of pulses by 44 per cent, of meats and fats by 10 per cent. On the other hand, with a better-balanced diet, the world would probably require 4 per cent less cereal food and 10 per cent less sugar.

For the world as a whole, the immediate target of better nutrition demands an increase of 20 to 25 per cent in the amount of food, in terms of original calories, and somewhat more, perhaps 30 to 35 per cent, in the value of the output.

If the value of the world output of food, at current prices on the farm, is estimated at $75 billion a year, an additional $25 billion in meat, milk, fruits and vegetables is required to supply mankind with sufficient and adequate food. This goal cannot be reached by redistributing the available agricultural surpluses by even a generous program of international aid but calls, rather, for an increase in the world's agricultural production, mainly in the economically underdeveloped areas. Thus the problem of nutritional standards becomes a problem of stimulating economic development. This objective is in conformity with our democratic concept of economic standards for all mankind but is strikingly contrary to the Malthusian philosophy that the increase in the supply of food would be followed by an upsurge of world population and result

---

32. **9**, pp. 11–12.
33. **9**, p. 14.

34. **9**, p. 19.
35. **9**.

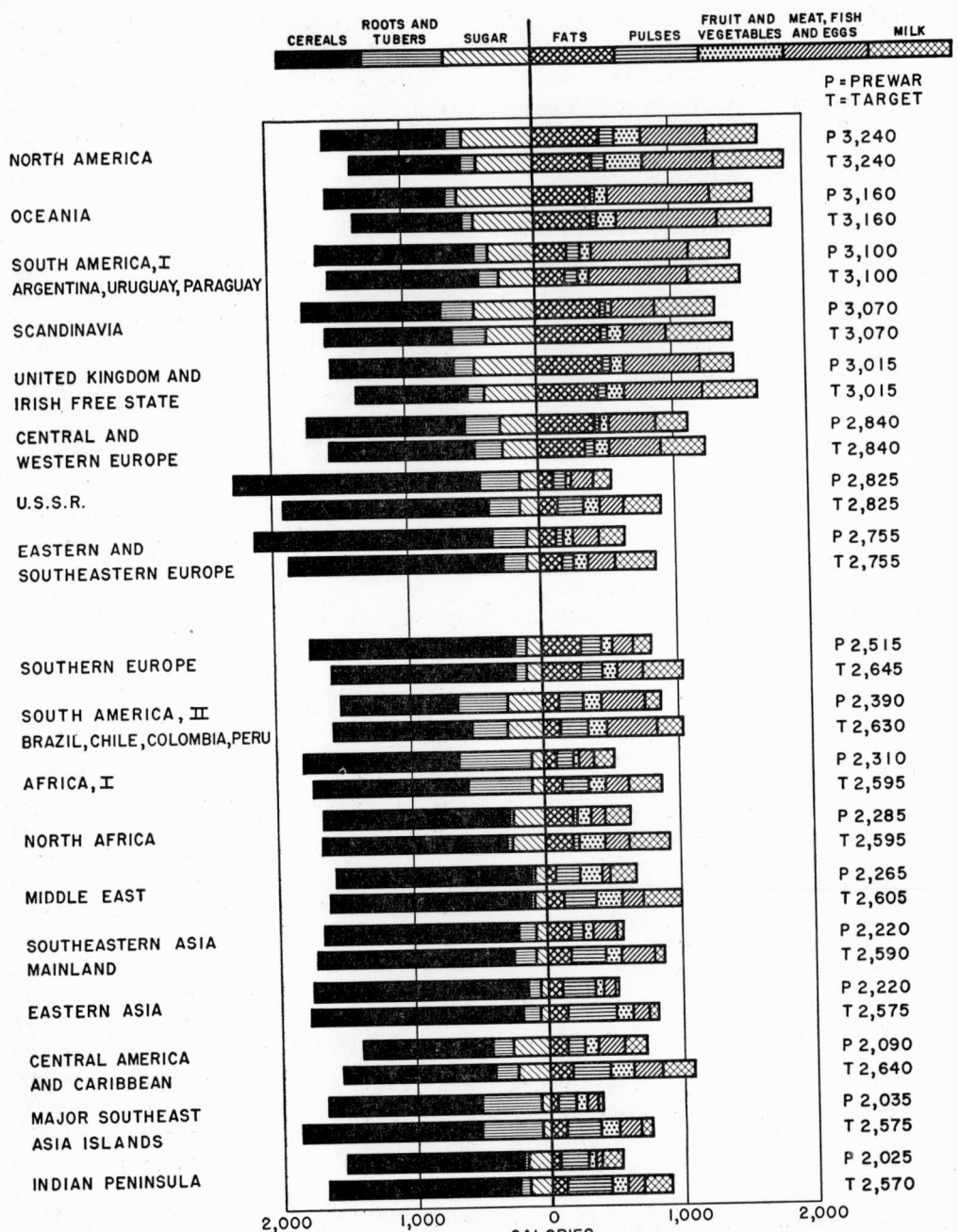

Legend (top bar): CEREALS | ROOTS AND TUBERS | SUGAR | FATS | PULSES | FRUIT AND VEGETABLES | MEAT, FISH AND EGGS | MILK

P = PREWAR
T = TARGET

Area	Prewar	Target
NORTH AMERICA	P 3,240	T 3,240
OCEANIA	P 3,160	T 3,160
SOUTH AMERICA, I — ARGENTINA, URUGUAY, PARAGUAY	P 3,100	T 3,100
SCANDINAVIA	P 3,070	T 3,070
UNITED KINGDOM AND IRISH FREE STATE	P 3,015	T 3,015
CENTRAL AND WESTERN EUROPE	P 2,840	T 2,840
U.S.S.R.	P 2,825	T 2,825
EASTERN AND SOUTHEASTERN EUROPE	P 2,755	T 2,755
SOUTHERN EUROPE	P 2,515	T 2,645
SOUTH AMERICA, II — BRAZIL, CHILE, COLOMBIA, PERU	P 2,390	T 2,630
AFRICA, I	P 2,310	T 2,595
NORTH AFRICA	P 2,285	T 2,595
MIDDLE EAST	P 2,265	T 2,605
SOUTHEASTERN ASIA MAINLAND	P 2,220	T 2,590
EASTERN ASIA	P 2,220	T 2,575
CENTRAL AMERICA AND CARIBBEAN	P 2,090	T 2,640
MAJOR SOUTHEAST ASIA ISLANDS	P 2,035	T 2,575
INDIAN PENINSULA	P 2,025	T 2,570

2,000   1,000   0   1,000   2,000
CALORIES

Adapted from a chart of the Food and Agriculture Organization

FIGURE 106. NUTRITIONAL TARGETS: PREWAR AND RECOMMENDED PER CAPITA DAILY CONSUMPTION OF FOOD IN EIGHTEEN AREAS OF THE WORLD

The first bar for each area (P) shows the composition and total number of calories in the prewar diet; the second (T), the nutritional "target." The areas are arrayed according to the prewar per capita intake in calories, from 3,240 calories a day in North America at the top of the chart to 2,025 calories in India and Burma at the bottom.

In countries in the upper part of the chart, the "target" diet has the same caloric value as the prewar supply of food, and the recommendation for improvement consists in an increase of the share of protective foods in comparison with nonprotective energy-yielding foods — cereals, roots and tubers, and sugar. In the other areas, an increase of the total energy value of the diet is needed, in most cases by means of increase in both protective and nonprotective foods.

in an increase in the number of men and women condemned to starvation.

CLOTHING REQUIREMENTS

Surveys of family expenditures indicate that the share of clothing in the total family outlay usually increases as one moves from poorer to richer households.[36] There is no evidence, however, that the same relationship exists among nations and that the richer a country, the larger the percentage of its income devoted to clothing. It can be assumed that nations all over the world spend about 10 to 15 per cent of their consumption outlay for clothing and related needs. This proportion does not meet needs in the poorer nations, but it is extremely difficult to measure their deficiency in fibers and clothing.

The FAO has made a start in tackling this problem.[37] Its economists believe that clothing materials are ample only in areas with a total population of about 300 million, less than 15 per cent of mankind. These areas include the United States, Canada, Argentina and Uruguay, most of the western European countries, Australia and New Zealand.

The per capita consumption of cotton, wool (clean) and rayon in these countries ranges between 14.5 and 29 metric pounds. Per capita consumption of textile fibers in southern and central Europe (from Italy and Portugal to Germany) and in Japan ranged between 8.6 and 14.3 pounds before the war. The areas of major dearth are South and Middle America, eastern and southeastern Europe, the USSR, China, India, southeastern Asia and Africa. In some of these areas, need for better clothing is not very urgent, thanks to the climate. Even without such areas, however, the world's output of fibers should be increased by about 25 per cent to bring per capita consumption in textile-deficient countries up to 10 pounds per year, which is less than 25 per cent of the present standard in the United States.

Since the total value of the annual output of fibers during 1934–38 averaged more than $4 billion at current prices at the site of production, the world's deficiency of fibers, according to the FAO estimate, approximated a billion dollars at that time. It may amount to $2 billion at current prices. The deficiency of finished fabrics (including the value added by transportation and processing of raw fibers and transportation and distribution of fabrics) is of course much larger. In terms of dollars and human effort, however, the world's need for fibers presents a smaller problem than the need to raise nutrition standards in underdeveloped areas.

OTHER CONSUMPTION TARGETS

The methods used here to evaluate the world's food and clothing requirements cannot be applied to other urgent needs of mankind. But all surveys of consumer budgets suggest that people in low-income brackets spend the largest part of their means for food, postponing satisfaction of other needs.[38] This fact seems to justify the conclusion that the world's need for better housing, health service and educational facilities — whether measured by the urgency of need or by the number of people affected — is comparable to the world's need for better nutrition.

Housing

Standards of housing vary as widely from country to country as standards of diet. The United States standard described in a typical budget of a worker family [39] is not much higher than the standards in Great Britain and the Scandinavian countries. In Russian cities, one room per worker family, with the right to use a common kitchen, lavatory and privy jointly with several other families, is typical. In the Far East and in tropical regions, a hut with a dirt floor, without windows or a chimney, is a standard dwelling. Almost all countries, however, are familiar with complaints of unsanitary conditions, overcrowded quarters, need for repair, and shortage of even the poorest living facilities in rapidly growing cities. Whatever a country's housing standard, there are always people who are living below it.

The extent of deficiency in housing facilities of the "ill-housed" third of the nation is illustrated by the findings of the United States Consumer Expenditures Study in 1935–36. The study showed that the third of households (families and individuals) with the lowest incomes spent approximately $1.6 billion for rent as compared with $2.6 billion spent by the middle third of the consumers.[40] Thus the

---

36. See Chapter 8.
37. **8.**

38. See Chapter 8.
39. See p. 284.
40. Computed from Table 140. The data refer to New York, 1934–36. The rate is somewhat lower in other communities. (Cf. Table 133.)

amount of deficiency in housing facilities of the first group of population was $1 billion per year, in round numbers, which amounted to more than 10 per cent of the nation's outlay for rent or 2 per cent of all current consumer expenditures. This figure probably represents the additional rental value of the new and renovated houses needed to bring the lowest third of the population up to the housing level of the middle third. The investment required for this purpose may amount to fifteen times the deficit in rental value. If this investment were stretched over fifteen years, the annual outlay would be equivalent to 2 per cent of consumer expenditures, while the current rental value of new houses would increase gradually until the cumulative increment reached 2 per cent of all consumer outlays.

There is no evidence, of course, that the urgently needed improvement of housing in other countries would absorb the same proportion of current income. The share of rent in consumer expenditures varies widely from country to country: for employee families, it ranged before the war from less than 10 per cent (in countries with rent control and in economically underdeveloped areas) to more than 20 per cent (United States, Switzerland, Union of South Africa and New Zealand).[41] But unsatisfactory housing conditions have become one of the most acute problems in European industrial countries such as Great Britain, Germany, France and Italy, and the situation is no less acute in the underdeveloped areas where improvement of housing conditions is a necessary part of the health program, especially in the struggle against tuberculosis and eye diseases. Improvement of housing facilities in poverty-stricken areas is therefore a part of their development program along with the improvement of nutrition.

There is, of course, no reason to believe that the outlay for housing must be raised in each country at the same rate as its expenditures for food. Likewise, there is no indication that the unsatisfactory housing conditions call everywhere for the 10 per cent increase in national housing expenditures suggested here for the United States. In some countries the needed expansion and improvement of housing facilities may prove greater in relation to national income, and in others, much less. Increase of world outlay for housing by 1.5 to 2.5 per cent of world income

seems to be as good a guess for the immediate target as can be ventured on the basis of the available scanty information.[42]

Medical and Educational Services

An estimate of targets for health services and education is particularly difficult. It is recognized by all students that poor health disastrously shortens length of life and diminishes physical strength and efficiency of people in underdeveloped areas.[43] However, the cost of poor health to a nation is a highly controversial issue, even in countries with abundant statistics and a well-established public health organization. It is extremely difficult to estimate the outlays required to supply all the peoples of the world with adequate sanitary and medical services. A completely satisfactory solution of this problem presumes a radical change in the level of economic well-being of the world and the ways of life of the majority of mankind. A per capita income of $100, indeed, cannot buy health conditions reached after many years of effort by nations with per capita income of $400–$500 and more.

If the immediate target is set in a more realistic way, it should be defined in terms of the most urgent requirements for healthful water supplies, sanitation, medical personnel, hospital facilities and so forth. This principle applies likewise to educational problems. A program for the underdeveloped areas cannot include all the educational facilities of the most prosperous countries, but even the most conservative program must provide for improving elementary education and developing schools of higher education.

The recent experience of countries that have tried to overcome their poverty and backwardness by adopting Western ways of life and learning Western methods of production support this contention. In all recent development programs in Middle and South American countries, schools, hospitals, sanitation projects and medical dispensaries have had priority over housing developments and dietary reforms. Similarly, the 10-year development plans for 21 British colonies envisage outlays of more than $210 million for water supplies, sanitation and health services and $125 million for education, as compared

---

41. See Table 137.

42. It is estimated that housing absorbs 15 to 16 per cent of world's income. (See Chapter 8, p. 279.)

43. See Chapter 6.

with $65 million set apart for housing projects and $5 million for nutrition.[44]

The high ranking of medical and educational needs in the development plans prepared by the peoples for which these plans are designed, reflects a definite pattern of budgeting. A program of medical and sanitary measures (for example, vaccination, elimination of malaria and improvement of the water supply) promises appreciable results in a short time and at comparatively low cost. School reform, which requires more good will than money for success, is the real foundation of future economic advance. On the other hand, improvement of nutritional patterns is expensive and often meets with strong opposition in religious precepts (as in India), firmly established habits of the population and vested interests.

It is, therefore, highly improbable that a substantial improvement of nutrition will be effected in underdeveloped areas in advance of reform of their medical and educational services. In terms of dollars, these reforms are, of course, much less expensive than the nutritional program advocated by the United Nations.

THE COST OF FREEDOM FROM POVERTY

A very considerable increase in production of consumer goods and services would be required to free the world from extreme poverty. To the

44. **17**, p. 131.

additional production of foodstuffs, estimated at some $25 billion at current prices, should be added outlays for better housing and clothing, improvement of water supplies, sanitation, medical and educational programs. The total amount will be determined by the scope of these programs. The foregoing brief discussion provides no clue for estimating this total but may cast light on the nature and order of magnitude of the requirements. In the opinion of the writers, the total may reach $40 to $50 billion annually, which means that the current world production of consumer goods and services should be increased by approximately 7 to 10 per cent to reach the described targets. The requirements will fall short of this rate for a comparatively conservative program and will exceed it if more ambitious plans are envisaged.

The difficulty of the task is that the outlay should be concentrated in areas that now account for hardly more than 10 per cent of world income. Consumption there should be nearly doubled; indeed, it should be more than doubled in the areas of extreme poverty.

Discussion of such targets may seem unrealistic. From a broad historical point of view, however, such a rise in standards of living in poverty-stricken areas is only a further step on the road that Western civilization has been traveling since the time when an apology was required for English workers who ate white bread and drank tea.

CHAPTER 10

NATURAL RESOURCES

THE NATURAL RESOURCES of a primitive community are as simple as its needs. The "unspoiled" environment — the forest, the river, the ocean — freely supplies the necessities: food, shelter, clothing, firewood, weapons and tools. Economic civilization begins with the effort of man to change his environment. A tract of land cleared of wood for planting, a flock of domesticated animals are the new economic resources. As a new environment develops around the community, its resources cease to be a free gift of nature. Most economic resources as we now know them are either man-made or have acquired value because man has developed devices that permit him to use them.

MAN-MADE ENVIRONMENT

Coal and oil have lain in the ground for aeons, but only recently have they become economically useful. Waterfalls and rapids were only obstacles to navigation until man built machines that can use their energy. Many ores were valueless rocks until man learned how to convert them into metals. Molybdenum and uranium ores would have been of little value except for recent progress in metallurgy and physics.

The attitude of men toward their environment changes as time goes on. Primitive tillers of the soil, encircled by a forest wall, fought trees as an enemy that blocked expansion of their fields. The early colonists on this continent followed the same practice. Now, a few centuries later, their descendants think sadly of the lost wealth of the vanished forests.

The inaccessibility of a place was an asset in early civilization but a handicap in a later phase. Then the location of a community at the mouth of a river, on the divide between two streams, on a strait, or at a crossing of two trails in the desert became an asset, which, in turn, often lost all value when commerce and migration abandoned old routes. Similar changes are still in progress. Development of global air routes brings to life new communities beyond the Arctic Circle. The search for oil and uranium ore creates new mining centers in the wilderness. New techniques impute new values to formerly irrelevant features of the environment, while some features cherished in the past cease to serve any purpose useful to men.

In the Ancient World

The active role of man in shaping his environment is not peculiar to modern times. Arnold Toynbee quotes a striking example of man-made resources at the dawn of Egyptian civilization. The Lower Nile Valley was colonized about 6,000 years ago by tribes from the region now known as the Libyan Desert, but which, in prehistoric times, was an earthly paradise with a fairly dense population. Then, along with other vast areas in Asia and Africa, it began to dry up. As water and vegetation disappeared, the inhabitants of this region faced a difficult choice: To change their way of life? Or to change their habitat? And if the latter, where to go?

Toynbee tells their story:

Those that changed neither their habitat nor their way of life paid the penalty of extinction for their failure to respond to the challenge of desiccation. Those that avoided changing their habitat by changing their way of life and transforming themselves from hunters into shepherds became the nomads of the Afrasian Steppe. . . . Of those that elected to change their habitat rather than change their way of life, the communities which . . . shifted northward exposed themselves, unintentionally, to a new challenge — the challenge of the northern seasonal cold . . . while the communities which avoided the drought by retreating southward . . . came under the soporific influence emanating from the climatic monotony of the Tropics. Fifthly and finally there were communities that responded to the challenge of desiccation by changing their habitat and their way of life alike, and this . . . was the dynamic act which created the Egyptiac and Sumeric civilizations.

These pioneers plunged into the jungle-swamps of the valley bottoms, never before penetrated by man, . . . into a forbidding and apparently impenetrable wilderness. As it turned out, the venture succeeded beyond the most sanguine hopes in which the pioneers can ever have indulged. The wantonness of nature was subdued by the works of man; the formless jungle-swamp made way for a pattern of ditches and embankments and fields; the lands of Egypt and Shinar were reclaimed from the wilderness and the Egyptiac and Sumeric societies started on their great adventures.[1]

Thus the forbidding swamps of the Lower Nile Valley became one of the greatest concentrations of wealth and a beacon of civilization for centuries, while the easily accessible Upper Nile Valley remained in a primitive state.

Man's destruction of natural resources is as old as his creation of new resources. In his unfinished story of Atlantis, Plato describes the "natural state" of the country around Athens as it was supposed to have been 9,000 years before his day. Woods covered the surrounding mountains and abundantly supplied fruit for men, food for cattle, and logs "long enough to cover the largest houses." In this natural state, the land "enjoyed rain from heaven year by year, . . . it received and treasured up in the close clay soil the water which drained from the heights, and let it off into the hollows, providing everywhere abundant streams, fountains and rivers." But by Plato's time the forests are gone; what is left can "only afford sustenance to bees." The denuded land is "losing the water which flows off the earth into the sea. . . . All the richer and softer parts of the soil have fallen away, and the mere skeleton of the country is left." [2] A strikingly accurate picture of a plundered and devastated land! What Plato did not know was that the natural abundance of Greece had been destroyed by man's abuse of the land, particularly by deforestation and overgrazing.

In Modern Times

The impact of man on his environment increases with growing density of population, urbanization and, most of all, development of new methods of production and transportation. In agricultural regions as well as metropolitan areas, man has reshaped the landscape. Indeed, he has acted as a new geologic force.[3] On the one hand, he has been irrigating arid plains, draining marshes and reclaiming land from the ocean; [4] on the other, he has continued to destroy forests, exhaust the soil, expose fields to erosion,

let the "richer and softer parts" of the earth be washed away by rains and floods.

Furthermore, man has also been changing the vegetable and animal life on the land. Farmers in all parts of the world raise man-made varieties of vegetable and animal species, products of thousands of years of observation, selection, crossing and breeding. Some species have lost all similarity to those from which they were developed. The economic effect of adjusting plants and animals to the climatic environment is about the same as if man had changed the climate: Since he could not give more sunshine and moisture to his wheat and corn, he developed varieties able to withstand frost and aridity.

Production of rubber since the beginning of this century provides a striking example of the substitution of man-made resources for those offered by nature. Native to South America, rubber was discovered by Europeans at the beginning of the sixteenth century and rapidly became a significant colonial product. For three hundred years, it was obtained from latex extracted from trees scattered in the tropical jungles of Brazil. Before the end of the nineteenth century plantations of *Hevea brasiliensis* had been established in Malaya, Ceylon and Indonesia. After 1910, the output of plantation latex rose from year to year while extraction of latex from free-growing jungle trees declined.[5] It would be a question of semantics to try to determine whether plantation rubber is a natural or a man-made resource.

New Horizons

As time went on, man became increasingly daring in his attempts to reshape the soil and vegetable and animal life. Modern science, not satisfied with its achievements in the breeding and culture of plants and animals, is searching for new, untapped resources of food. One of the most interesting ventures in this field lies in pending projects to utilize the stores of organic matter in the ocean.

In a report to the United Nations Conference on the Conservation and Utilization of Resources, held in New York in 1949, Dr. F. N. Woodward pointed out that the ocean, which covers about 70 per cent of the surface of the earth, contains all the minerals required for life and compares favorably with good garden soil in fertility. Acre for acre, it is more productive

1. **31**, pp. 69–70.
2. **26**, Volume 4, p. 384.
3. **24**, pp. 32 ff.
4. See Chapter 15.

5. See Chapter 17.

than the land, and there is no danger of drought or violent fluctuations in temperature and relatively little risk of disease.[6] The idea of "sea culture" converting the expanses of the ocean into plantations of algae, hotbeds of plankton [7] and fields of seaweeds may prove impractical. But even if these projects fail now, they may, like many other ventures, succeed at some later time.

The impact of modern technology and science on mineral resources is even more striking. Primitive mining was not much more than gathering the outcropping ore on the surface. Although the ancient world mined gold, silver, copper and iron ore commercially, the old mines only scratched the surface, and men could not reach the minerals hidden deep in the crust of the earth. Modern mines, like modern means of transportation, are an outgrowth of scientific progress.[8]

Man-made resources conquer space and time. Modern technology can be transferred to any corner of the world, and not infrequently the latest achievements of science are first applied in areas far remote from the place where they were conceived and developed. To some extent this may happen with the civilian use of atomic energy. In fact, an atomic pile cannot compete with the existing power plants in highly industrialized areas with abundant coal and water power; but it may prove to be of great value in remote, underdeveloped areas.[9]

Utilization of Natural Resources

In a broad sense, the objective of each study of production — whether in a nation, a geographic region or the world as a whole — is a survey of the utilization of natural resources by man. So diversified are these resources and the uses man makes of them, and so numerous and complex are the problems related to their development that when they are surveyed systematically, one at a time, little opportunity is left for appraising their interdependence and their relative position in the whole world economy. Such an over-all appraisal is attempted on the following pages.

RELATIVE VALUE

There is no point in discussing the relative significance of soil, forests, water, minerals and other natural resources for man and our civilization. An over-all comparison may be made, however, of their economic value as reflected in the value of world output of grain, meat and dairy products; fibers and other agricultural raw materials; lumber and pulp; coal, oil and hydroelectric power; metals and nonmetallic minerals. None of these products is a free gift of nature to mankind, and production of each requires a specific natural environment. No wheat can be raised in the region of eternal frost or desert; no oil can be extracted from rocks that contain no oil.

Agriculture, forestry, mining and production of hydroelectric power have many features in common: Natural environment sets limits to their expansion; man has to reckon with the danger of depletion of available resources; as time goes on, he must increasingly substitute available resources for those that become scarce.[10]

The relative economic value of the different branches of economic activity directly related to natural resources may be measured by the value of the output of agriculture, forestry and mining. The Economic Intelligence Service of the League of Nations estimated the world's output of these industries in 1938 as follows (in billions of dollars at 1930 prices): [11]

Total	$62.6
Agricultural products	49.7
Forest products	1.0
Fuels and water power	7.3
Minerals other than fuels	4.7

This estimate is not inclusive. For lack of data, the agricultural products estimate does not include poultry and eggs, skins and hides, honey, and many grains of local significance. The value of agricultural products given above should be increased at least a fourth to take account of these commodities.[12] The figure for minerals does not include the value of gold and the minerals most widely used all over the world — stone, sand and clay; allowance for these would increase the value of output of

---

6. **2,d,** p. 133.
7. See Chapter 20.
8. See Chapters 21–24.
9. See Chapter 25.

10. The related problems are discussed in Parts III and IV of this volume.
11. **1,** p. 87.
12. See Chapter 14.

minerals other than fuels from $4.7 to $8.5 billion. The value of forest products represents only a small fraction of all the products men are extracting from forests. In the light of information recently compiled by the Food and Agriculture Organization of the United Nations (FAO), world output of forest products in 1937, including fuelwood and with allowance for preliminary processing, should be estimated at $7 billion, at current prices,[13] or about $8 billion at 1930 prices.

With these corrections, the value of raw materials produced in the world in 1938 amounted to about $86 billion (at 1930 prices) distributed as follows:

	Amount, in Billions	Per Cent
Agricultural products	$62.0	72.1
Forest products	8.0	9.3
Fuels and water power	7.5	8.7
Minerals other than fuels	8.5	9.9

Since 1938, the volume of the world's output of raw materials has increased, and prices have gone up. The relative shares of the main groups of raw materials in their total value have changed little, however. As before the war the value of agricultural output overshadows that of all other raw materials combined, reminding us that tillage of the soil is still the main occupation, and food still the main concern, of most of the people in the world.

AGRICULTURAL RESOURCES [14]

The agricultural resources of the world and each of its parts are determined by physical conditions, on the one hand, and by the ability of men to use and improve these conditions, on the other.

SUITABLE LAND

Apart from man-made conditions, the two chief physical factors controlling agricultural resources are climate and soil. What one eats is "a mixture of what was once rain, rocks, air and rays of sunshine." [15] In this mixture, rain, air and rays of sunshine represent *climate,* and what was once rocks, the *soil.* Some vegetable life is possible under almost any climatic condition, from the tropics to far beyond the polar

circle and from submerged swamps to deserts. Some particular plants also have a very wide range of tolerance. The success of agriculture, however, depends on the proper amount and timing of precipitation and temperature and on the fertility of the soil, conditions very unevenly distributed in the world.

Taking 10 inches or more a year as an adequate amount of rainfall in the moderate climatic zone, with comparatively slow evaporation, and 40 inches in equatorial regions, less than half the land surface has enough rainfall and only one third has adequate rainfall at more or less the right time and in the right amounts for the production of crops. Australia has adequate rainfall in only 9 per cent of its territory, Africa in 25 per cent, and Asia in 29 per cent. Only a little more than one third of the land in North America benefits from adequate rainfall, while the percentage in South America is 70 and in Europe 79.[16] The two thirds of the world's land surface that is unfit for agriculture because of insufficient precipitation includes, among other areas, the zone of eternal frost and tundras, from which agriculture is also barred by low temperature.

A sizable part of the land surface that meets requirements as to both temperature and rainfall is unfit for agriculture because of unfavorable topography. Only a little more than one fifth of the world's land area passes all three tests — temperature, rainfall and topography — but most of this is of doubtful value for agriculture because of poor soil. All in all, only 7 per cent of the land area, or 2 per cent of the total surface of our planet, is fully suited to agricultural production. (See Table 153.) The proportion ranges from less than 3 per cent in Oceania to 37 per cent in Europe. (See Table 154; cf. Figure 107.) "Too much water, too many mountains and deserts, and too much ice on the globe," is Fernand Baudhuin's description of our planet.[17]

Natural Fertility and the Productivity of Land

When the earth does not meet their requirements, tillers of the soil must either compromise with the existing environment or try to change it. In many places, they grow food on poor soil, under unfavorable or difficult conditions. In

13. **3,** p. 67.
14. Cf. Part III, especially Chapter 15.
15. **25,** p. 20.

16. **25,** p. 27.
17. **21,** p. 22.

TABLE 153

AGRICULTURAL RESOURCES: FACTORS AFFECTING SUITABILITY OF LAND FOR
AGRICULTURE IN THE WORLD

	Area Affected	
Factor	Millions of Acres	Percentage of Total Area
Total land surface	35,700	100
Individual factors		
Adequate rainfall	15,500	43
Reliable rainfall	16,600	46
Favorable temperature	29,500	83
Favorable topography	22,700	64
Fertile soil	16,300	46
Combinations of factors		
Adequate and reliable rainfall	12,200	34
Adequate and reliable rainfall and favorable temperature	11,400	32
Adequate and reliable rainfall and favorable temperature and topography	7,400	21
The same and fertile soil	2,600	7

Source: **25,** p. 48.

TABLE 154

AGRICULTURAL RESOURCES: AREA SUITABLE FOR AGRICULTURE IN EACH CONTINENT

	Land, in Millions of Acres		Percentage of Total Suitable for Agriculture
Continent	Total	Suitable for Agriculture	
World	35,700	2,580	7.0
North and Middle America	5,500	570	10.4
South America	4,600	220	4.8
Europe	2,400	890	37.0
Asia	10,400	600	5.8
Africa	7,300	240	3.3
Oceania	2,100	60	2.9
Antarctic	3,400	0	0.0

Source: **25,** p. 50.

Finland peasants have collected soil in baskets
to cover the rocky hills. In Portugal, they have
made holes in rocks and filled them with soil
to raise grapes. In the Netherlands, men have
fought to recover thousands of salty acres from
the sea; Haarlem, the great flower garden of
the country, was originally a stretch of submerged sand and peat. In Italy, swamps and
marshes unfit for farming have been drained
and reclaimed for cultivation and terraces for
vines and olives were built on rocky hillsides.
On the other hand, the productive capacity of
the soil has been destroyed in many parts of the
world by abuse of the land, and by ignorance
or greed. Empires have crumbled and cities have

been abandoned because of the exhaustion of
formerly fertile land, often as a result of destruction of the forests.[18]

Factors in Productivity

The productivity of agriculture in different
countries and regions depends not only on the
fertility of the soil and on climatic conditions
but also on the agricultural skill of the population. The yield of cultivated land per acre is not
necessarily in direct relation to its natural fertility.[19] (See Figure 108.)

18. **32,** pp. 19 ff.

19. Following the classification used by the FAO, land
that possesses highly suitable soil and favorable climate

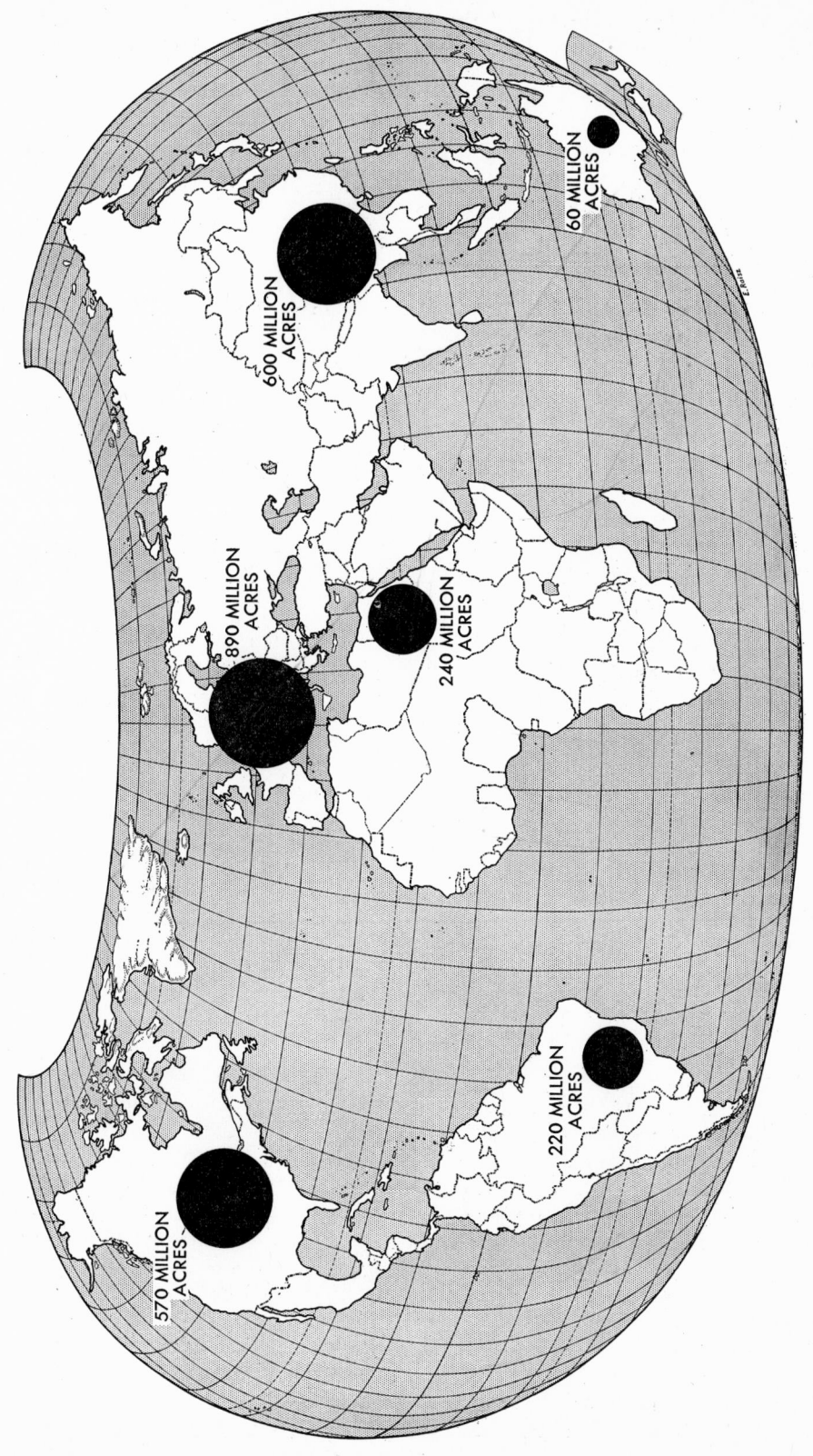

FIGURE 107. AGRICULTURAL RESOURCES: LAND SUITABLE FOR AGRICULTURE IN EACH CONTINENT

Land suitable for agriculture is scarce in the world, especially in South America, Asia and Africa. (Cf. Table 154.) The area of such land in each continent is represented on the map by black circles on the same scale as the respective continent.

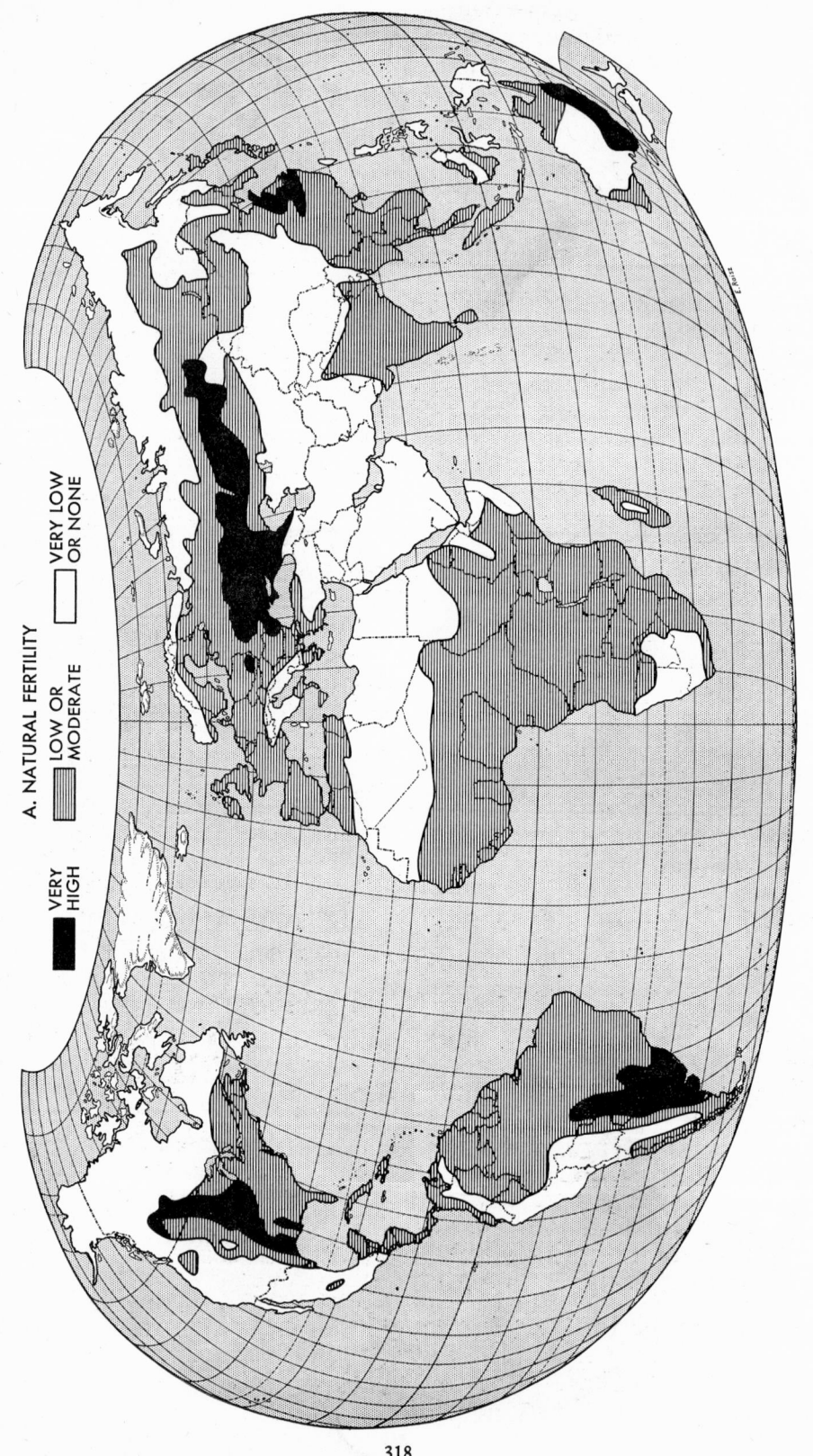

A. NATURAL FERTILITY

VERY
HIGH

LOW OR
MODERATE

VERY LOW
OR NONE

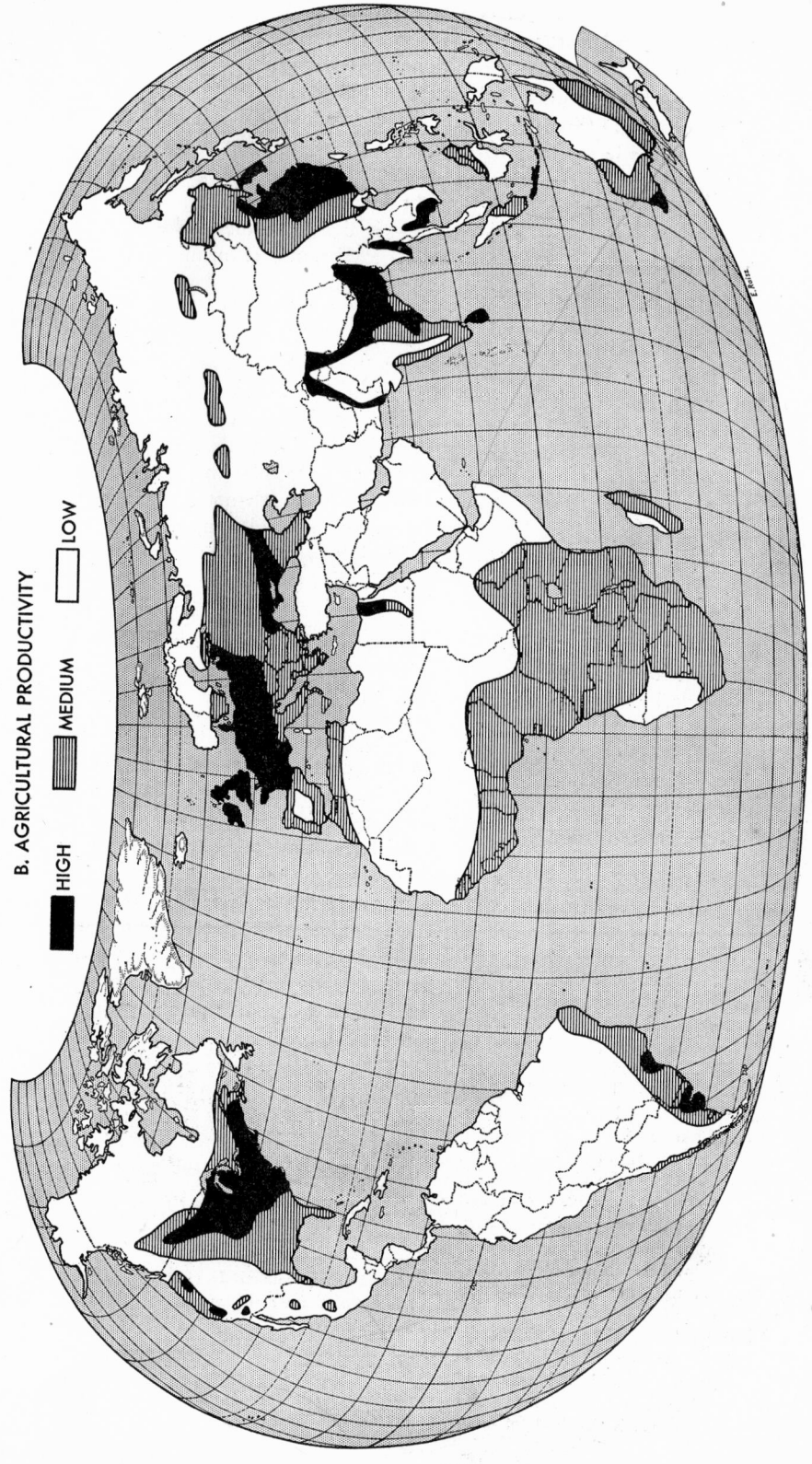

B. AGRICULTURAL PRODUCTIVITY

■ HIGH
▥ MEDIUM
☐ LOW

FIGURE 108. AGRICULTURAL RESOURCES: GEOGRAPHIC DISTRIBUTION OF LAND IN EACH CONTINENT BY NATURAL FERTILITY AND BY AGRICULTURAL PRODUCTIVITY

The land surface of the world is roughly classified here by natural fertility and actual agricultural productivity. Map A shows the FAO's appraisal of natural conditions in different areas (See 4); Map B, the actual yield per hectare of cultivated land. Productivity is high in many areas with only medium natural fertility and is medium on some land with low fertility. Inversely, large tracts of land with medium and even high fertility produce relatively little.

319

The most important areas of high productivity are northwestern and central Europe, the northeastern and north central sections of the United States, the valleys of the Indus and Ganges in India, and southeastern China. Minor areas with high yields are found in coastal provinces of Argentina and Brazil, in the southern part of the Ukraine, in the valley of the Nile, and in southern Australia. Some of these areas partly overlap areas of high natural fertility. (See Figure 108, A.) The correlation, however, is far from perfect.

The region of high productivity in the Far East stretches much farther inland than the area of high natural fertility. In Eurasia, the highly productive region includes only part of the fertile area in the east but stretches over vast spaces with medium natural fertility in the west. In North America, the highest productivity per acre is in densely populated eastern states, where the natural fertility of the soil is medium. In South America, only a small fraction of the region of high natural fertility is highly productive.

As a rule, the area of high productive capacity spills beyond the boundaries of high natural fertility under the pressure of particularly dense population. In contrast, where population is sparse, the soil is not utilized to its limit.

VALUE OF AGRICULTURAL OUTPUT [20]

The Continents

The outstanding feature of the distribution of agricultural resources among the continents is

is described as having "high natural fertility." For the most part, land of this quality is under cultivation.

Land described as having "medium fertility" meets some but not all of the requirements of agriculture. In western Europe and parts of China, Japan, and the eastern United States, such land has been raised to, and maintained at, a high fertility level by good farming methods, including diversification of crops, crop rotation, careful animal husbandry and intelligent use of fertilizers. In the tropics, much is in shifting cultivation; some of it doubtless could be brought into more permanent and productive use. Much land in this classification has been subjected to deterioration by erosion and depletion of fertility. It is chiefly within these areas, however, that soil can be improved and used to increase food production.

The third classification, "low fertility," includes the tundra of the high latitudes; mountain land unsuited to cultivation; deserts; areas of semiarid and subhumid grazing lands; and forested land in North America and Eurasia, where the growing season is too short for cultivated crops.

that Asia and Africa, which together account for more than 60 per cent of the world population, represent just over 30 per cent of world agricultural output, while countries of European stock (including the USSR), with a much smaller aggregate population, account for 70 per cent of the world's agricultural produce.

In Asia and Africa the agricultural output per capita is about half the world average. It is low in Africa because of primitive techniques, despite the abundance of land. In Asia it is low because of scarcity of land, despite the high skill of farmers in China and Japan. It is high in Europe because of intensive utilization of land and high yield per acre, and in Australia, because of the abundance of land. North and South America are in a middle position between Europe and Oceania; they are amply provided with land, although not as lavishly as Oceania in relation to population, and have a comparatively high output per acre, though not as high as in Europe. (See Table 155.)

Resources and Consumption

As a result of a long process of adjustment, the world has attained a rough balance between consumption of foodstuffs and agricultural resources, continent by continent and, with few important exceptions, country by country. The balance has been established in many cases on a level far below our modern standards, but as time has gone on, the production of food has kept pace with the increase in population. Thus large agglomerations of population have developed where there was food for them, and the available food has molded dietary habits.[21] All in all, each geographic region consumes most of the food it produces and produces most of the food it consumes. Europe is the striking exception. In 1934–38 its deficit in agricultural products (including fibers and rubber), as measured by aggregate net imports from other continents, averaged $2,450 million at current prices, or approximately 10 per cent of its own output. This deficiency was met by the other

Agricultural productivity (Figure 108, B) is measured in terms of the actual prevailing yield of staple crops in the area.

20. Agricultural output is discussed in detail in Chapters 16, 17 and 18. Here its value is examined only as an over-all measure of the distribution of world agricultural resources.

21. See Chapter 9.

TABLE 155

AGRICULTURAL RESOURCES: DISTRIBUTION OF LAND, POPULATION AND AGRICULTURAL
OUTPUT AND INDEXES OF AGRICULTURAL OUTPUT PER INHABITANT, BY
CONTINENT, 1934–38

| | | | Percentage Distribution | | | | | |
| | | | | Value of Agricultural Output | | | Index of Per Capita Output (*World* = 100) | |
Continent	Land	Popula-tion	All Products	Vege-table	Animal	All Products	Vege-table	Animal
World	100.0	100.0	100.0	100.0	100.0	100	100	100
North America	14.8	6.6	15.9	12.1	20.3	242	184	310
Middle and South America	16.0	6.0	8.8	6.7	11.3	147	112	187
Europe	4.1	18.3	29.6	24.6	35.4	160	133	191
USSR	15.9	7.9	11.9	15.4	7.9	151	196	101
Asia	20.3	53.5	27.4	36.4	17.1	51	68	32
Africa	22.5	7.2	3.6	3.8	3.3	50	53	46
Oceania	6.4	0.5	2.8	1.0	4.7	567	217	972

Source: Based on estimates of the International Institute of Agriculture (7).

continents through exports as follows: [22]

	Amount, in Millions	Percentage of Agricultural Output of Continent
Middle and South America	$710	23.4
Asia	720	7.8
Africa	420	34.2
Oceania	600	63.4

The agricultural deficit of Europe, which has been one of the main features of the world economy since the middle of the nineteenth century, is due to three factors. The chief is, of course, the density of Europe's population. The second is the high level of consumption and especially the high demand for protective foods, which implies a high intake of "original calories." [23] The third is the fact that the food deficit of Europe is aggravated by its demand for agricultural products used as industrial raw materials. Europe depends on importation of cotton, wool, silk, rubber and vegetable oils not only for its own consumption but also to produce the finished goods it must export to pay for its imported foodstuffs. Despite the efficiency of its own agriculture, Europe imports practically all kinds of agricultural products except potatoes and olive oil.

All other continents, except the USSR, which is largely self-sufficient,[24] export certain agri-

cultural products and imports others. The main export products are:

North America: wheat, tobacco and cotton

Middle and South America: wheat, rye, barley, oats, corn, sugar, cacao, tobacco, cotton, hemp, linseed, meat and wool

Asia: sugar, coffee, tea, cacao, jute, rubber, linseed, soya, ground-nuts and silk

Africa: sugar, coffee, cacao, wine, to-bacco, cotton, cottonseed, olive oil and wool

Oceania: wheat, sugar, meat, milk and wool.

Statistics for the net balance of agricultural exports and imports of the continents make various parts of the world seem more nearly self-sufficient in agricultural production than they actually are. Imports of wheat, meat and other products into the United Kingdom, Belgium, Germany, Italy, the Netherlands and Switzerland are partly offset by exports from southeastern Europe; imports of wheat and rice into Japan, Malaya and China are counter-balanced by exports from India, Indochina, Thailand, Korea and Formosa; imports of wheat into Brazil, by exports from Argentina.

In all, not more than 7 per cent of the world's

22. Based on estimates of the International Institute of Agriculture (7).

23. Cf. Chapter 9.

24. In 1934–38 the USSR had insignificant agricultural exports and negligible imports of agricultural products.

TABLE 156

AGRICULTURAL RESOURCES: PRODUCTION OF SELECTED AGRICULTURE PRODUCTS AS PERCENTAGE OF CONSUMPTION, BY CONTINENT, 1934–38 ANNUAL AVERAGE

Product	North America	Middle and South America	Europe	USSR	Asia	Africa	Oceania
Wheat	125.3	125.4	82.6	101.7	98.0	100.7	263.9
Rye	97.6	200.0	98.9	100.7	112.8	0.0	. . .
Barley	106.1	180.0	90.6	103.6	101.8	105.5	a
Oats	100.5	180.0	97.7	100.4	101.5	107.5	100.0
Corn	99.4	155.8	71.6	100.9	103.7	111.5	100.0
Rice	a	76.9	39.1	84.3	102.1	82.1	54.9
Potatoes	100.0	97.0	100.1	100.0	100.0	100.0	100.0
Sugar	25.6	286.7	72.0	105.2	119.0	128.2	421.9
Coffee	0.0	301.8	0.0	0.0	194.4	209.9	a
Tea	0.0	0.0	0.0	27.7	180.5	26.1	0.0
Cacao	0.0	555.7	0.0	0.0	133.3	3,071.0	38.6
Wine	96.8	99.2	92.7	100.0	91.0	265.7	114.1
Tobacco	135.5	137.9	49.6	100.4	104.7	116.7	21.5
Cotton	177.9	209.6	1.1	98.5	88.9	1,459.5	. . .
Flax	13.3	. . .	84.0	110.6	100.0	a	. . .
Hemp	0.0	a	98.1	100.2	102.9	. . .	0.0
Jute	0.0	0.0	0.0	0.0	193.7	. . .	0.0
Rubber	0.0	131.6	0.0	0.0	266.9	a	7.1
Linseed	33.2	934.9	14.0	100.0	218.1	. . .	0.0
Cottonseed	100.0	106.3	8.6	100.7	100.2	187.3	100.0
Soya	101.7	. . .	3.6	86.7	114.8	. . .	. . .
Groundnut	96.4	100.0	1.0	. . .	125.0	. . .	43.2
Olive oil	1.9	0.0	102.1	. . .	120.0	241.3	0.0
Beef	100.0	110.1	88.9	100.0	100.0	100.0	128.5
Mutton meat	100.0	107.6	74.1	100.0	100.0	100.0	190.2
Pork	102.4	100.5	97.8	100.0	100.0	100.0	157.8
Milk	100.5	100.0	94.8	102.0	97.5	96.0	323.5
Wool	63.9	561.3	23.7	69.3	80.4	440.5	1,560.2
Silk	0.0	0.0	40.6	100.0	252.0	. . .	0.0

Source: 7, pp. 40–46. (The faulty figures for commodities with surplus of production over consumption published by the International Institute of Agriculture have been recomputed for this table.)

a. Insignificant production, in part for export.

agricultural output — including tea, coffee, cacao, cotton, rubber and wool — is exported; the rest is consumed within the borders of the producing countries. But the discrepancy between the demand for agricultural products and domestic production at different points of the globe has been the mainspring of the international division of labor and trade. (See Table 156.)

POTENTIAL AGRICULTURAL RESOURCES

The striking contrast in the degree to which people in different parts of the world utilize their natural agricultural resources — sun, rainfall and soil — depends largely on the differences in the skill of farmers, their equipment, the availability of fertilizers, the level of agricultural technology and science, and the like. Moreover, the efforts of farmers in the most prosperous and progressive countries of the world are not necessarily directed toward obtaining the maximum yield per acre, which is the usual goal of farmers in areas where land is scarce and labor abundant.[25]

The pattern of farming depends largely on the price-cost relationship. The input of labor per

25. See Chapter 15.

TABLE 157

AGRICULTURAL RESOURCES: POTENTIALLY ARABLE LAND IN THE WORLD

(*Millions of Acres*)

Land	Total	Temperate Zones	Tropical and Subtropical Zones
A. Total land surface	36,480	21,760	14,720
B. Unsuitable for agriculture	17,280	12,160	5,120
Lack of rainfall	9,984	4,864	5,120
Cold	7,296	7,296	...
C. Land with adequate rainfall and/or adequate temperature (A–B)	19,200	9,600	9,600
D. Probably ultimately arable (⅓ C)	6,400	3,200	3,200
E. Used at present for crops or pasture	3,712	2,560	1,152
Cultivated at present	2,368	1,600	768
Arable land in pasture	1,344	960	384
F. Potentially arable, not used at present for crops or pasture (D–E)	2,688	640	2,048

Source: Rearranged after O. E. Baker, **20**, p. 25.

acre and per bushel of harvest customary in China and Japan would be wasteful in the United States. The fertilization of soil customary in northwestern Europe would be financially unsound in Argentina or Australia. The expensive farm machinery used in the United States would be of little value to farmers in some parts of Europe or China.

Agricultural experts agree that the yield per acre could be increased in almost all parts of the world if there were a real incentive to use the available technical means or if these means were available at low cost.[26]

Outlook: The Earth's Carrying Capacity

Experts differ considerably on the ultimate "carrying capacity" of the earth — that is, the number of people it can ultimately provide with food and other agricultural products. In the controversy, agricultural experts are more confident than many students of population. Among the former, O. E. Baker, for example, believes that no fewer than 6.4 billion acres in the world are "probably ultimately arable," as compared with the 2.4 billion acres now under cultivation. (See Table 157.) He reaches this conclusion on the assumption that, except for land unsuited for agriculture by reason of lack of rainfall or cold

or both, one third of the earth could be used for farming. According to this estimate, only half the potentially arable land in the temperate zone and less than one fourth in the tropical and subtropical zones is now under cultivation.[27]

Charles E. Kellogg envisages the possibility of doubling or more than doubling world output of food by utilizing a billion acres of productive but idle tropical soil.[28]

Stephen Raushenbush assumed that population in underdeveloped areas would increase from 1,644 million in 1950 to 2,721 million in 2000, and that consumption of food would rise from 2,000 calories a day per person to 2,900 calories. Even with these assumptions, he found that the required amount of food could be produced in these regions by increasing the acreage under cultivation and improving yields per acre in accordance with the standards now existing in the more progressive countries.[29]

These "optimistic" estimates do not belittle the adverse effect of scarcity of land on the well-being of such densely populated and economically underdeveloped areas as India, China or the Near East, but they stress the fact that agricultural resources in these areas can be expanded.

26. See Chapter 15.

27. **20**, p. 25.
28. Quoted in **27**, p. 13.
29. **27**, pp. 18, 34, 76.

In India, Indonesia, the Near East, Africa, such resources are actually expanding, although not so rapidly as to permit these nations to catch up with the standards of the Western world.

Agriculture in these areas is handicapped less by the scarcity or the poor quality of the soil than by the lack of good roads, storage facilities and organized markets and by disease among men, plants and animals. People of the under-developed areas can overcome these difficulties with the technical aid of industrially developed countries.

The core of the problem of the carrying capacity of the earth is not the scarcity of fertile land in comparison with the number of mouths that must be fed but the insufficient ability of men to make full use of their available resources.[30]

FORESTS

Forests originally covered about one third of all the land and more than half of all potentially habitable land, excluding the regions of permanent frost, tundra and desert. They dominated the temperate humid and subhumid zones before men cut them to clear space for fields and towns.

In prehistoric times, forests provided the people who lived in their shadow with all necessities. Later, the task of supplying food and clothing materials fell to agriculture, while the forest remained the main source of building materials and fuel. Through thousands of years, timber has successfully held its supremacy as a building material against the competition of brick, stone, glass, steel and aluminum. It has, however, lost to coal, oil, natural gas and water the leading role it once played as a source of heat and motive power. On the other hand, modern technology is increasing the importance of wood as an industrial raw material.[31]

GEOGRAPHIC DISTRIBUTION OF FORESTS

Forests are vitally important to man not only as a source of timber, fuelwood, naval stores and other products, but also as a factor protecting land against erosion and ensuring a regular turnover of water.[32] Deforestation for cultiva-

30. For further discussion of the carrying capacity of the earth and the possibility of expanding the area of arable land, see Chapter 15.

31. See Chapter 19.

32. See the picture of the "hydrological cycle" in Figure 113.

TABLE 158

FORESTS: AREA IN EACH CONTINENT, 1937

| Continent | Forest Area | | Acres of Pro-ductive Forest Per Capita |
	Millions of Acres	Percentage of Land Area	
World	9,830 [a]	27	2.7
North America	1,800	31	6.2
South America	1,870	43	15.8
Europe [a]	240	30	0.7
USSR [b]	2,340	30–40	4.0–5.3
Asia	1,280	20	0.7
Africa	2,100	28	4.0
Oceania	200	9	10.4

Source: Computed from **6**, July–August 1948, p. 166.

　a. Countries reporting to FAO.
　b. Includes the Baltic states and other European countries not reporting to FAO.

tion has been a major disaster for many regions in the United States, southern Europe, the USSR, the Near East and the Far East.

In terms of statistical totals and averages, all continents except Australia seem to be fairly well provided with forests. According to the FAO, forests still stretch over nearly 10 billion acres, 27 per cent of all the land in the world. They occupy nearly a third of North America and Europe, and more than 40 per cent of South America. The figures for Asia and Africa are 20 per cent and 28 per cent, respectively, and that for the USSR is reported to lie in the range 30–40 per cent. (See Table 158.)

If the deserts of Asia, Africa and Australia are excluded, it would appear that from 25 to 40 per cent of the land of each continent is in forest, which is about what a region needs to be protected against erosion and well provided with wood products and forest recreation areas. This picture is deceptive, however, for forests are very unevenly distributed over the world in relation to population.

In many regions in the temperate zone, the development of dense population has gone hand in hand with eradication of the woods. In the north, forests have remained because they occupy land unfavorable for agriculture and dense settlement. In the tropical zone, the wall of virgin forest has barred the advance of agricultural colonization. Thus a large part of all the world's forest is now practically inaccessible.

Such is the location of more than half the forest in the USSR, Canada, China and central and southern Asia and the overwhelming part of the tropical forest in Africa and South America.

About one third of all forest is practically useless to men, almost as useless as if it were growing on another planet. The other two thirds is being used uneconomically and destructively, not as a crop but as a quarry that will be abandoned after it has been plundered. The return obtained from forests by these methods is a small fraction of what the same area would yield under proper management. Only 15 per cent of the world forest is being used as a renewable, continuously productive resource.[33]

FOREST PRODUCTS [34]

The world's output of wood in 1948 is estimated at 1,436 million cubic meters of roundwood, or 1,000 million metric tons. The contrasts among the continents in return per acre of accessible productive forests depend less on the quality of the forests than on the ways in which they are utilized. In some underdeveloped regions there is no domestic demand for industrial timber and exploitation of forests for export is uneconomical because of lack of roads and equipment. Large forested areas are therefore used only as pasturage and for collection of fuelwood. (See Table 159.)

The United States and Europe are overcutting their forests, while Canada, South and Middle America, Asia and Africa are utilizing only a part of their timber growth. The apparent balance between annual cut and net growth in the USSR and Australia is due largely to the fact that the net growth is estimated for these areas in accordance with the recorded cut.[35]

Per capita output of timber ranges from less than 0.1 cubic meter in the Near East and North Africa and 0.3 cubic meter in South and East Asia to more than 2 cubic meters in North America. The figures for Asia and Africa would be appreciably higher if comprehensive statistics on consumption of fuelwood were available. Such a correction, however, would not change the general picture of the dearth of wood in these two continents. (See Table 159.)

TABLE 159

FORESTS: OUTPUT OF ROUNDWOOD IN EACH CONTINENT, 1948

Region	Estimated Output, in Millions of Cubic Meters	Output Per Acre of Accessible Productive Forest, in Cubic Meters
World	1,436	0.40
North America	360	0.49
Middle and South America	150	0.16
Europe	280	1.01
USSR	265	0.36
Near East and North Africa	11	0.28
South and East Asia	298	0.73
Africa	51	0.16
Oceania	21	0.36

Source: **5**, 1949, p. 1.

Resources and Consumption

A much smaller proportion of the output of wood than of agricultural products is consumed in the producing country. According to the FAO, nearly 17 per cent of the lumber produced in the world and more than 20 per cent of the woodpulp pass through the channels of foreign trade before they reach the consumer.

Lumber is exported on a large scale by Canada, Sweden, Finland, and the USSR. In all these countries, so different in economic development, lumber is a cash crop and an export crop. Pulp and pulp products are exported mainly by Norway, Sweden, Finland and Canada.

The principal importers of lumber are the densely populated industrial countries of Europe (Great Britain, Belgium, the Netherlands and Germany) and countries exceptionally poor in wood (Italy, Spain, Greece, China, India). The chief importers of pulp and pulp products are the United States and Great Britain.

POTENTIAL FOREST RESOURCES

After thousands of years of reckless burning and destructive cutting of forests, man has realized the danger of further deforestation. The principle of rotation is becoming generally recognized — although not generally followed — in economically developed countries and is penetrating underdeveloped regions. Serious efforts are being made to explore formerly inaccessible

---

33. **33**, p. 38.

34. For particulars, see Chapter 19. In the following pages forest products are discussed only in connection with the distribution of forest resources in the world.

35. See Chapter 19.

forested areas and to improve silvicultural methods by selection of species, hybridization, reproduction by sprouts, prevention of tree diseases and reduction of waste.

Experts disagree about the ultimate potential yield of the world's forests. A spokesman of the FAO presented the following estimate to the United Nations Scientific Conference: one acre of forest land in good condition can produce 1.2 cubic meters of wood a year. Thus, the world's productive forest land, with a total area of 6.5 billion acres, could yield 7.8 billion cubic meters a year, which is five times the total current consumption.[36]

In a more detailed analysis of the current and the potential yield of forests in different parts of the world, the FAO anticipates an annual yield of 1.8 billion cubic meters from coniferous forests, which represents 40 per cent of the total forest area. It ventures no estimate for broadleaved forests but states that for these "the ultimate possibilities are still greater, although their realization depends on great technological advances and even greater changes in agricultural practices in the tropics." [37] The FAO concludes that the total potential yield of the world's forests is from three to four times the current world demand.

Outlook

In terms of world totals, no shortage of wood is in sight. The world's forest can meet man's present and future requirements on a much higher level of consumption than at present. The real problems are the scarcity of forest in areas where it is urgently needed and the insufficient protection of forest in areas where its destruction endangers the water supply and soil conservation.

The situation of the world's forest resources is paradoxical. In comparison with the potential return, they have only been scratched, but in many parts of the world — in Greece, Italy and Spain, China and India, a large part of the United States, densely populated areas of South America and some regions of Africa — the advance of settlements has been marked by progressive annihilation of forests. Many nations are now facing the difficult and time-consuming task of reforestation. In other countries, some forests have been overcut and are destined to disappear

in the not too remote future, while elsewhere the growth in forests is largely wasted. The world's future supply of forest products depends on progress in silviculture and in rational management of forests.

MINERAL RESOURCES

Minerals in the earth's crust are the best example of "natural resources" — a gift of nature lavishly extended to certain areas of the world and denied to others. Actually, minerals that can be made useful to men are spread all over the world; indeed, they constitute the material of which the world is built. Their value for mankind, however, depends less on their physical properties than on the state of our economic civilization, our knowledge and technology.

The list of industrial minerals is becoming longer each year, and there is no evidence that its growth is slackening.[38] Leith, Furness and Lewis name 34 "new" minerals that gained wide use in the period between the two world wars.[39] Along with substances that are well known to laymen — for example, industrial diamonds, magnesium, molybdenum, quartz crystal and radium — the list contains rare minerals that are found only in a few places in the world and have highly specialized uses. The increasing diversity of minerals used by industry augments the interdependence of nations in mineral supplies.

VALUE OF OUTPUT OF MINERALS

Before the war, the world's annual output of minerals (including hydroelectric power) totaled about $16 billion, at 1930 prices.[40]

The Continents

North America accounted for more than 40 per cent of the total, Europe for 30 per cent and the rest of the world for the remaining 30 per cent. (See Table 160.) North America's share increased tremendously during the war, but the Marshall Plan and aid to underdeveloped countries tend to restore a relationship nearer the prewar pattern.

The relative significance of mineral resources in the economy in different parts of the world is characterized by the ratio of the value of

36. **2**, Vol. I, p. 37.
37. **6**, July–August 1948, p. 170.

38. See Chapter 22.
39. **22**, pp. 23–24.
40. See p. 315; cf. Chapter 21.

TABLE 160

MINERALS: VALUE OF OUTPUT IN EACH CONTINENT, 1938

(Millions of U. S. Dollars, at 1930 Prices)

Continent	Total		Metals		Fuels		Other Nonmetallic Minerals	
	Value	Per Cent	Value	Per Cent	Value	Per Cent	Value	Per Cent
World	$12,864	100.0	$3,808	100.0	$7,628	100.0	$1,428	100.0
North America	5,216	40.5	1,310	34.4	3,593	47.1	313	21.9
Middle and South America	803	6.3	316	8.3	389	5.1	98	6.9
Europe	3,886	30.1	922	24.2	2,281	29.9	683	47.8
USSR	1,232	9.6	468	12.3	641	8.4	123	8.6
Asia	1,164	9.0	381	10.0	626	8.2	157	11.0
Africa	410	3.2	316	8.3	53	0.7	41	2.9
Oceania	154	1.2	95	2.5	46	0.6	13	0.9

Source: Based on **1**, pp. 87, 96.

mineral output to that of the agricultural and forest products. For the world as a whole the ratio was less than 1 to 4 in 1938.[41] It was as high as 50 per cent in North America, 22 per cent in Europe, 17 per cent in Middle and South America, 14 per cent in Asia. In Oceania, a region rich in land but comparatively poor in mineral resources, the value of mineral output amounted to only 8 per cent of that of agricultural and forest products. In Africa, as a result of the exploitation of its mineral resources by European powers, the ratio was 25 per cent, i.e. higher than in Europe.[42]

The pattern seems clear: In no other part of the world are mineral resources so important in comparison with the soil and forests as in North America; Europe with its colonies in Africa ranks second; Asia trails far behind. Moreover, the ratio would be still lower in Asia were it not for the mines and petroleum wells operated by foreign capital in Malaya, Saudi Arabia and Iran.

In all continents and in individual countries, the relative value of mineral output in the total production of raw materials fluctuates widely from year to year as a result of changes in business conditions.

The United States

In the United States the ratio between the value of mineral and agricultural output is governed mainly by ... in prices. It fluctu-

ated around 45 per cent in the 1930's, jumped to 58 per cent in 1940, dropped during the war, reached a low of 32 per cent in 1946 and rose again to 46 per cent in 1948. The comparative values during the two decades are as follows: [43]

	Value in Millions		Ratio of Value of Mineral to Agricultural Products
	Agricultural Products	Mineral Products	
1930	$10,558	$4,765	45
1935	8,406	3,650	43
1940	9,618	5,614	58
1943	21,597	8,072	37
1944	22,561	8,419	37
1945	22,776	8,141	36
1946	27,488	8,896	32
1947	33,109	12,484	38
1948	33,480	15,766	46
1949	30,631	(10,580)	(34)
1950	30,423	(11,855)	(39)

RESERVES OF MINERALS

Unlike agricultural and forest resources, minerals in the earth's crust are not renewable. Each

41. See p. 315.

42. **1**, pp. 87, 93.

43. **10**, 1949, pp. 641 and 762; 1952, p. 687. The value of the agricultural output represents cash receipts of farmers for crops and livestock products, plus the value of home-consumed produce. The figure for mineral products includes, among others, the value of pig iron and other metals. Since the price of metal includes the cost of coal used for its extraction from ore, the total contains some duplications. The 1949–50 figures for mineral products are calculated on a new basis (without duplication) and are not strictly comparable with the data for previous years.

TABLE 161

MINERALS: KNOWN WORLD RESERVES AND ANNUAL OUTPUT

Metal or Mineral	Reserves	Output Around 1948	Percentage of Annual Output to Reserves
	Billions of Barrels		
Petroleum, recoverable			
Proved and indicated	75 ⎱		⎰ 4.5
Ultimate	555 ⎰	3.4	⎱ 0.6
	Millions of Metric Tons		
Coal, all types			
Coal equivalent	5,165,000	1,510	0.03
Iron ore, iron content			
Actual	19,000 ⎱		⎰ 0.48
Potential	57,000 ⎰	91	⎱ 0.16
Manganese ore (50% Mn)			
Ore equivalent	1,000	3.90	0.39
Chromite	100	2.10	2.10
Tungsten, 60 per cent WO_3	4	0.03	0.75
Copper, recoverable content	100	2.20	2.20
Lead, gross content	40	1.20	3.00
Tin, recoverable content	6	0.16	2.67
Bauxite, crude ore	1,400	6.50	0.46
Potash, gross content K_2O	5,000	3.00	0.06
Phosphate rock	26,000	14.40	0.55

Source: Adapted from **2, f,** p. 2.

intensively exploited mineral deposit is bound to be exhausted, sooner or later. How long will the world reserves of the most important metallic ores and other minerals last?

The Threat of Exhaustion

This is a very old problem. Agricola, in a classic treatise on mining and metallurgy published in A.D. 1556, tried to deny the contention that the imminent exhaustion of deposits made the mining industry highly unstable. He referred to the silver mines at Freiberg in Meissen, which had not been exhausted in 400 years; the lead mines of Goslar, which had been in operation for 600 years; and the gold and silver mines of Schemnitz and Cremnitz, which had been worked for 800 years.[44] At present rates of exploitation, hardly any mine can last for periods such as these. On the other hand, tremendous progress has been made in prospecting and in mining techniques. A race has developed between depletion of the known and easily accessible deposits and the search for new fields and new methods of exploitation.

44. **18,** p. 5.

A survey of world reserves of coal, petroleum, iron ore and ten other minerals, presented by the United States Bureau of Mines to the United Nations Scientific Conference in 1949, suggests that the world is amply provided with coal, potash, phosphate rock and iron ore (counting "potential" reserves), while from 2 to 3 per cent of all known reserves of some other minerals are being extracted each year. (See Table 161.) Of course, the statement that the world output of petroleum in 1948 amounted to 4.5 per cent of "proved and indicated" recoverable world reserves does not forecast exhaustion of those reserves in 22 years.

The Probable Length of Life

For a forecast of the probable length of life of mineral resources, two sets of assumptions must be established — one for the future rate of output, the other for the potentialities of discovery of new deposits, methods of production and conservation, and so on. The United States Bureau of Mines used three alternative assumptions for the rate of output but did not venture any assumption for future discoveries and technological progress. (See Table 162.)

TABLE 162

MINERALS: PROBABLE LENGTH OF LIFE OF KNOWN RESERVES, UNDER SPECIFIED
RATES OF CONSUMPTION

(*Years*)

Mineral	Assumed Per Capita Consumption [a]		
	In All Countries as in 1947–48	*In All Countries as in the United States in 1948*	*In the United States as in 1948; in Other Countries as in Europe (excluding the USSR) in 1948*
Petroleum			
Proved and indicated	22	2.5	20
Ultimate	160	18.0	150
Coal, all types	2,200	340.0	985
Iron ore			
Actual	200	25.0	66
Potential	625	74.0	200
Manganese ore	250	50.0	140
Chromite	47	8.0	40
Tungsten	125	34.0	b
Copper	45	5.0	20
Lead	33	4.0	11
Zinc	39	6.0	18
Tin	38	6.0	17
Bauxite	200	31.0	165

Source: **2, f**, p. 4.

   a. Without allowance for population growth.
   b. Basis for estimate not available.

The main conclusion to be drawn from the Bureau's projections is that, if the present per capita consumption in the United States existed throughout the world, the known reserves of copper, lead, zinc, tin and chromite would be exhausted in less than 10 years and the "proved and indicated" reserves of petroleum in only 2.5 years. No particular significance should be attached to these figures, but the story they tell is true: If there is to be a substantial rise in consumption of metals and other minerals in the world, in the long run "potential" reserves must be used, new deposits discovered and better methods of processing ores invented, waste in the use of fuels and other minerals reduced, the life of metal products prolonged, metals recovered from scrap, and substitute raw materials found.

Metallic Scrap

Metallic scrap materials are by-products of metallurgical industries ("residues"), metal-consuming industries ("process scrap" or "new scrap") and demolition ("old scrap"). The amount of available scrap of each metal depends on changes in technological processes, price conditions and so on. The significance of scrap in the production of iron and steel, copper, lead, zinc, aluminum, tin and nickel is increased by the fact that scrap is an automatically renewable resource. In a paper presented to the United Nations Scientific Conference, the probable recovery factor for iron and copper is estimated at 65 per cent; for lead, at 60 per cent; aluminum, 40 per cent; zinc, 25 per cent; tin and nickel, 20 per cent.[45] (See Table 163.) Scrap is an important resource in the modern economy of metals and is becoming increasingly important as technology progresses.

GEOGRAPHIC DISTRIBUTION OF MINERALS

The solid crust of the earth is made up almost

45. **2, e**, p. 29.

Metal	Total Output of Virgin Metals, 100 Years (to 1947)	Estimated Store of Scrap Metals	Current Annual Output of Scrap
Iron	—	—	—
Copper	80	51	2.2
Lead	85	51	1.5
Zinc	65	16	1.6
Aluminum	15	6	1.0
Tin	5	1	0.15
Nickel	2.5	0.5	0.13

Source: **2, e,** p. 29.

wholly of igneous rock — that is, rock that has solidified from a hot liquid condition, either as throughout crystalline "plutonic" rock, found at different depths beneath the surface, in the form of dikes or sills filling crevices, or in the form of lava flows at the surface. It is estimated that 95 per cent of the earth's crust in the topmost ten miles of its thickness consists of such rock, 4 per cent of shale and one per cent of sandstone and limestone.[46]

Composition of Igneous Rocks

Igneous rocks contain all mineral elements in varying proportions. The most common — forming nearly three fourths of the mass of the earth's crust — are oxygen and silicon. Next in volume are aluminum, iron, calcium, sodium, potassium and magnesium. Not much more than one per cent remains for more than half a hundred other elements, including nickel, copper, uranium, tungsten, zinc, lead, tin, mercury, silver, platinum and gold.

Some rare elements constitute an infinitesimal part of igneous rocks: it is estimated, for example, that the earth's crust averages one milligram of radium per 100,000 tons of rock. (See Table 164.)

In addition to the comparatively simple mixtures and chemical compounds of these elements, the earth's crust contains extremely complicated combinations of them in the form of coal, crude petroleum and natural gas.

Stone and Sand

Rocks built of the most common solid element, silicon, with the addition of some other elements in different proportions are found everywhere in the world. Such are common stones, gravel and sand. Some precious and semiprecious stones were among the first articles in international trade. On the other hand, common building stone and sand are used where they are found — or, to put it the other way, are dug wherever they are needed. In the United States, stone, gravel and sand are dug from coast to coast, and the output is distributed among the states roughly in proportion to population. (See Figure 109.)

The less common and the rare minerals occur in concentrated form only in certain areas. Except for such concentrations, it would have been difficult for man to discover the rare elements in the earth's crust and, after having discovered their presence, to use them.

Metallic Ores

The chief deposits of metallic ores occur in old, worn-down mountains with large areas of complex crystalline rock. The metal is contained in igneous rock that once was molten inside the earth and has been brought nearer the surface by the bending, breaking and erosion of the earth's crust and is concentrated at points where the rock has been broken and hot lava has forced its way into the breaks.

Mineral Fuels

Mineral fuels were formed much later than the deposits of metallic ores. They have developed from ancient vegetation and animal remains preserved in swamps and marshes and subsequently covered with sediment. Such matter could not be preserved in regions where there was intensive volcanic activity and folding of the earth's crust, or on tropical plains, where decay is too rapid.[47] Thus plains and deserts on the site of old swamps and marshes are the storehouses of mineral fuels, while stumps of washed-away mountains are the storehouses of metallic ores. Occasionally deposits of both types are found side by side in the same area. More often, however, coal and oil are found on the plains, while various minerals lie under the remains of ancient mountains.

46. **11,** p. 2,

47. **28,** pp. 136–38,

TABLE 164

MINERALS: DISTRIBUTION IN THE TOPMOST TEN MILES OF THE EARTH'S CRUST

(According to F. W. Clarke and H. S. Washington)

Common Elements	*Kilo-grams Per Ton*	*Less Common Elements*	*Grams Per Ton*	*Rare Elements*	*Milligrams Per Ton*
Oxygen	465.9	Corium, yttrium	150	Antimony	Less than 1,000
Silicon	277.2	Copper	100	Cadmium	
Aluminum	81.3	Uranium	80	Mercury	
Iron	50.1	Tungsten	50	Iodine	
Calcium	36.3	Lithium	40		
Sodium	28.5	Zinc	40	Bismuth	Less than 100
Potassium	26.0	Columbium, tantalum	30	Silver	
Magnesium	20.9	Hafnium	30	Selenium	
Titanium	6.3	Thorium	20	Platinum	Less than 10
Phosphorus	1.3	Lead	20	Tellurium	
Hydrogen	1.3	Cobalt	10	Gold	
Manganese	1.0	Borum	10		
Sulfur	.52	Glucinum	10	Iridium	Less than 1
Barium	.50			Osmium	
Chlorine	.48	Molybdenum Less than 10			
Chromium	.37	Rubidium		Indium	Less than 0.1
Carbon	.32	Arsenic		Gallium	
Fluorine	.30	Tin		Thallium	
Zirconium	.26	Bromine		Rhodium	
Nickel	.20	Caesium		Palladium	
Strontium	.19	Scandium		Ruthenium	
Vanadium	.17			Germanium	
				Radium	Less than 0.01

Source: Adapted from **11, pp. 20 and 21.**

Most rare minerals are very unevenly distributed among different parts of the world; many come from a single source or a very few sources.[48] Because of this concentration of certain minerals, no nation has all the minerals it needs within its boundaries, and few even approach self-sufficiency.

In 1943, the Brookings Institution rated eleven nations according to their potential self-sufficiency with regard to each of 26 important minerals and found that the United States was adequately supplied with 11 of the 26, Russia with 12, the British Empire with 18, Germany and Italy with 3 each, and Japan with only 2. (See Figure 110.) In several instances these figures relate to a nation and its colonies. Great Britain without its dominions and colonies, the Netherlands without Indonesia, and Belgium without the Congo are much less self-sufficient than they appear as the heads of empires.[49]

In 1951 the United States Department of the

Interior prepared a chart showing the extent to which the country is self-sufficient in 36 important industrial minerals.

The chart indicates that the United States is amply provided with 8 minerals (sulfur, molybdenum, anthracite, phosphate rock, bituminous coal, natural gas, helium and magnesium) and that its own mine output meets more than 80 per cent of the domestic demand for 4 others (nitrates, iron ore, petroleum and ilmenite). For 8 minerals (tantalum, asbestos, mica, nickel, chromite, tin, quartz crystal and industrial diamonds) the United States depends completely, or almost completely, on imports. For 4 others (cobalt, mercury, manganese and platinum metals), its own production meets less than 20 per cent of its current demand. The ratio of domestic output to primary consumption of the remaining 12 ranges from 20 per cent to 80 per cent. (See Figure 111.)

Comparing 1951 estimates with the prewar period 1935–39, the Bureau of Mines reported lowered self-sufficiency in 21 commodities, im-

48. See Chapter 21; cf. **22,** pp. 38–39.
49. **22,** p. 45.

A. CONVENTIONAL MAP OF THE UNITED STATES

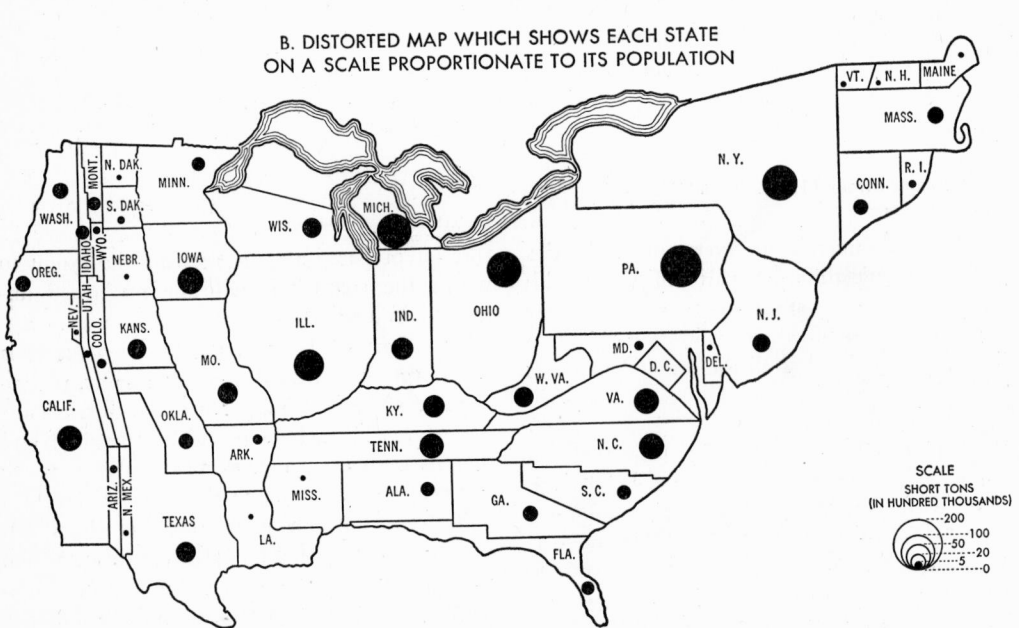

B. DISTORTED MAP WHICH SHOWS EACH STATE
ON A SCALE PROPORTIONATE TO ITS POPULATION

FIGURE 109. MINERAL RESOURCES: GEOGRAPHIC DISTRIBUTION OF THE OUTPUT OF STONE IN THE
UNITED STATES, 1939

In this figure, the value of stone sold or used by producers in each state in 1939 is plotted on the map of the United States in two ways. Map A shows a conventional map, which seems to indicate that production of stone is concentrated east of the Mississippi. Map B — a distorted map that shows each state on a scale proportionate to its population — is used as the background for the same circles measuring the output of each state. This second map shows, that in relation to the population, the output of stone is distributed rather evenly from coast to coast and from Canada to the Mexican Gulf.

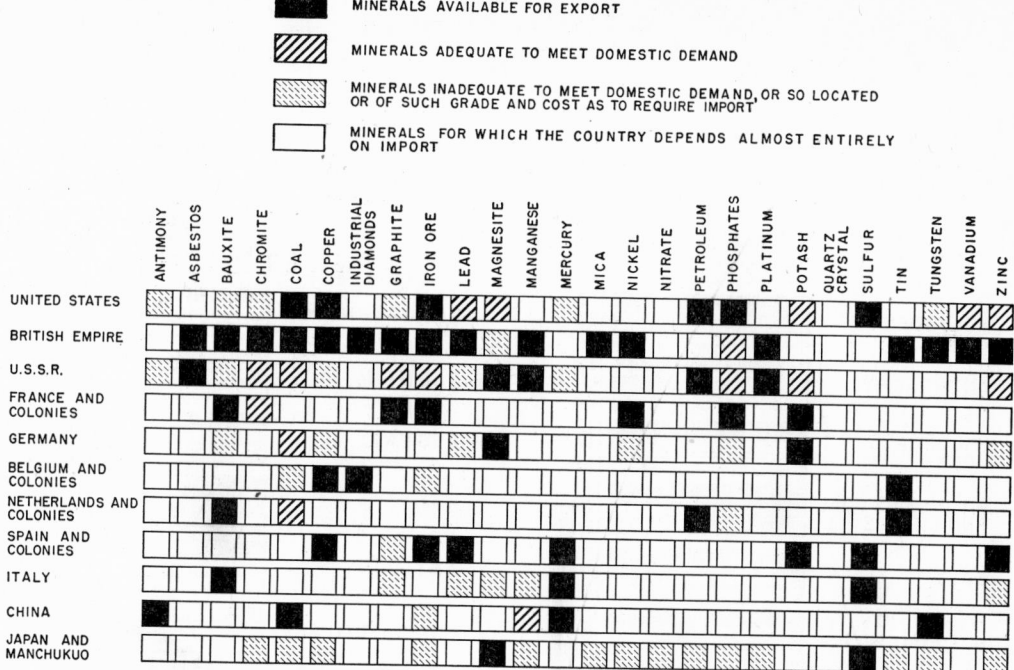

FIGURE 110. MINERAL RESOURCES: SELF-SUFFICIENCY OF SELECTED COUNTRIES IN MAJOR MINERALS

The United States has six minerals available for export and is sufficiently provided with five other minerals. The Soviet Union has surpluses of five minerals and is sufficiently provided with an additional seven. The British Empire, including all Dominions and colonies, has seventeen minerals for export but only one of these, coal, is found in the United Kingdom. (Cf. 22.)

proving self-sufficiency in 12, and an unchanged situation in 5 commodities.

SOURCES OF ENERGY

The main sources of mechanical power are coal, oil, natural gas and water power. Coal is the most widely used and has become a symbol of our mechanized civilization; the age of iron and steel is also an age of coal. The use of oil is largely concentrated in a few industrially developed countries. Natural gas is an important source of energy in the United States but of minor significance in the rest of the world. Water power is abundant in some areas and practically nonexistent in others.[50]

Coal

The main coal fields encircle the globe in the Northern Hemisphere. This coal belt stretches from the southern coast of Alaska to the Rockies and the Appalachian basin, crosses the North Atlantic and reappears in the British Isles and

in northwestern and central Europe — France, Belgium, the Netherlands, Germany, Czechoslovakia, Hungary and Poland. It extends farther through central Russia and the Ukraine, crosses the Urals and reappears again in central and eastern Siberia, in the Far East dividing into two arms, one pointing toward Kamchatka and Alaska, the other southward. (See Figure 112.) Moreover, important coal fields are dispersed here and there outside this belt, in South Africa, India and Australia.

The economic value of a coal field depends on the quality of the coal, the thickness and depth of the seams, the cost of extraction, transportation conditions and the like. Taking one foot as the minimum workable thickness of seams above a depth of 4,000 feet and two feet for the depth from 4,000 to 6,000 feet, the world's proved and probable coal reserve was estimated in 1913 at 7 trillion tons, or about 4,000 times the world's current annual demand. On the basis of more recent surveys this estimate has been scaled down to 5.2 trillion tons, or about 3,000 times the world's current annual output. (See Table 161.)

50. See Chapters 23, 24 and 25.

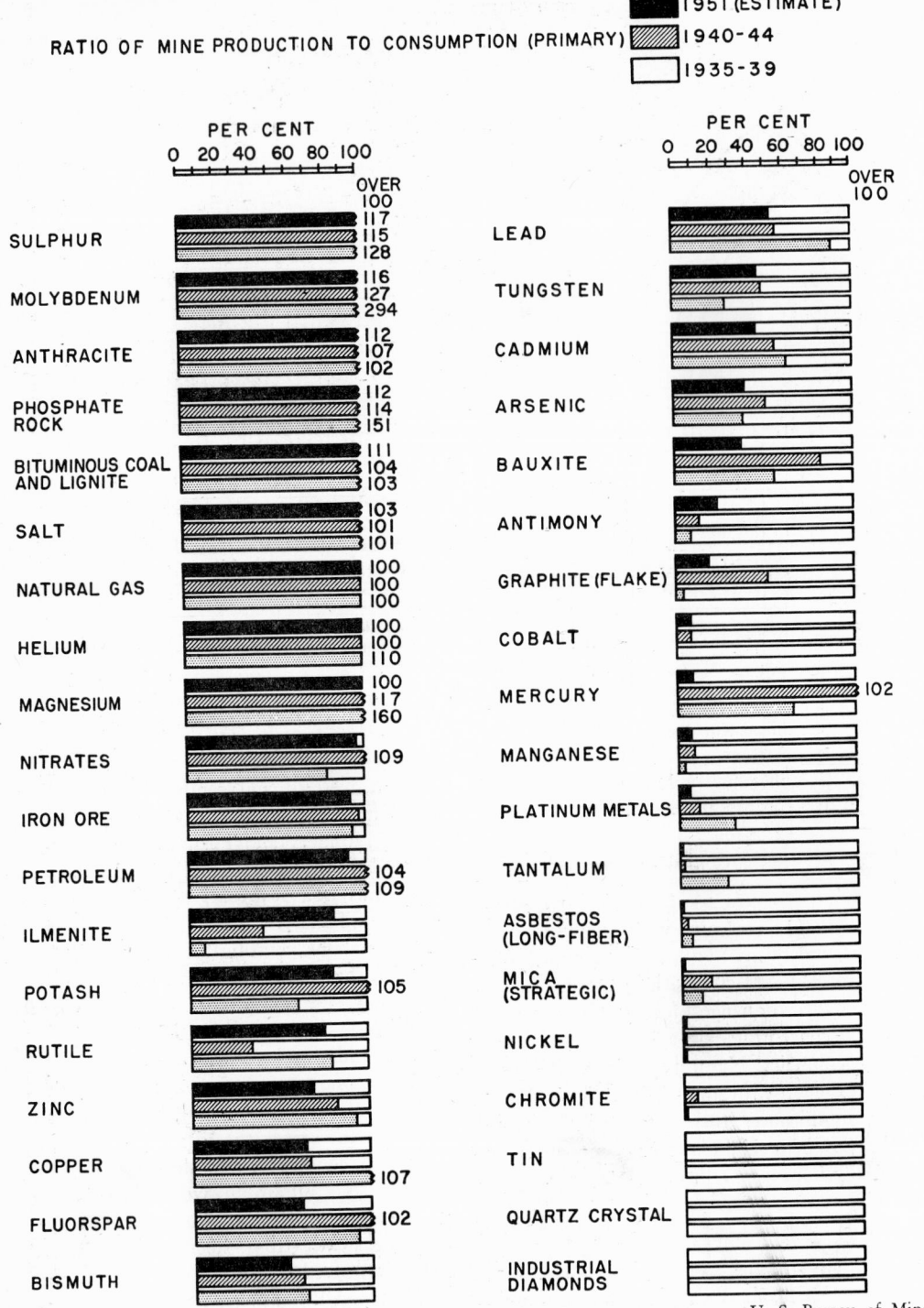

RATIO OF MINE PRODUCTION TO CONSUMPTION (PRIMARY)

■ 1951 (ESTIMATE)
▨ 1940-44
☐ 1935-39

PER CENT
0 20 40 60 80 100
OVER 100

	1951	1940-44	1935-39
SULPHUR	117	115	128
MOLYBDENUM	116	127	294
ANTHRACITE	112	107	102
PHOSPHATE ROCK	112	114	151
BITUMINOUS COAL AND LIGNITE	111	104	103
SALT	103	101	101
NATURAL GAS	100	100	100
HELIUM	100	100	110
MAGNESIUM	100	117	160
NITRATES		109	
IRON ORE			
PETROLEUM		104	109
ILMENITE			
POTASH		105	
RUTILE			
ZINC			
COPPER		107	
FLUORSPAR		102	
BISMUTH			

PER CENT
0 20 40 60 80 100
OVER 100

LEAD
TUNGSTEN
CADMIUM
ARSENIC
BAUXITE
ANTIMONY
GRAPHITE (FLAKE)
COBALT
MERCURY 102
MANGANESE
PLATINUM METALS
TANTALUM
ASBESTOS (LONG-FIBER)
MICA (STRATEGIC)
NICKEL
CHROMITE
TIN
QUARTZ CRYSTAL
INDUSTRIAL DIAMONDS

U. S. Bureau of Mines

FIGURE 111. MINERAL RESOURCES: SELF-SUFFICIENCY OF THE UNITED STATES IN IMPORTANT MINERALS, 1935–39, 1940–44 AND ESTIMATES FOR 1951

334

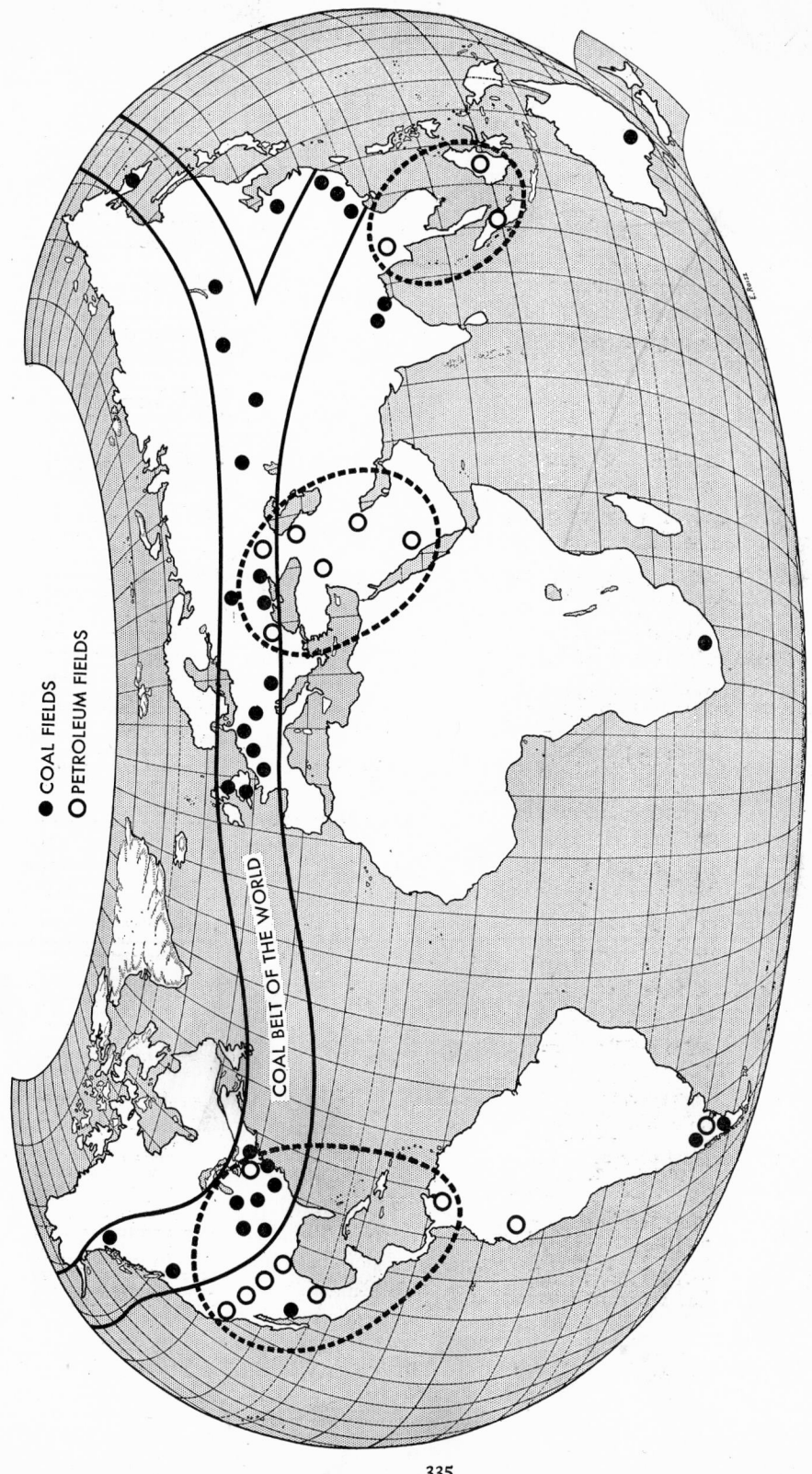

● COAL FIELDS
○ PETROLEUM FIELDS

COAL BELT OF THE WORLD

FIGURE 112. MINERAL RESOURCES: GEOGRAPHIC DISTRIBUTION OF PRINCIPAL COAL AND PETROLEUM FIELDS IN THE WORLD

The major coal fields lie in a belt encircling the world. The chief oil fields are clustered around three intercontinental breaks of land — between the Americas; between Europe, Africa and Asia; and between Asia and Australia.

In certain countries, especially those with old and highly developed coal mining, the ratio of potential reserve to annual output is less favorable. It has been estimated that, at the present annual rate of consumption, the United States faces exhaustion of coal reserves in a thousand years, Great Britain in a few centuries. These estimates are guesses, however, since nobody knows precisely how much coal is under the ground or how much will be used in the future. More real is the approaching exhaustion of some of the most profitable mines, so that production must gradually shift to poorer fields.[51]

Petroleum

The geographical location of petroleum is very different from that of coal. The world's most important oil fields lie in three groups: the western group, around and northwest of the Gulf of Mexico and the Caribbean Sea; the Black Sea or Near East group, stretching from the Balkans to Arabia and Iran; and the Far East group, including Indonesia and Indochina. Except for the fringe of the Far East region all three groups are in the Northern Hemisphere, south of the world's coal belt. In only two countries, the United States and the USSR, do oil regions and the coal belt overlap.[52] (See Figure 112.)

World reserves of petroleum are less abundant than those of coal. Although all predictions of their near exhaustion in the United States have so far proved wrong, the possibility of depletion of the known fields in a few decades should not be taken lightly. The crucial question is whether man has already discovered all the underground pools of oil or at least the most important ones.

In a paper presented at the United Nations Scientific Conference in 1949, A. I. Levorsen pointed out that "any region on the earth where an important volume of sedimentary rocks are found may be considered as potential oil and gas-producing territory . . . The apparent absence of oil and gas from a large volume of sediments may denote lack of skill or lack of persistence in the discovery effort." Levorsen believes that the plains of western Canada, the continental shelf areas, the Arctic regions, and the eastern slopes of the Andes in South America are likely to contain more petroleum than all known oil fields around the Gulf of Mexico, in

the Near East and in Indonesia. Referring to the leading experts in the field of petroleum geology, he estimates the undiscovered petroleum reserves in the world at 1,500 billion barrels, as compared with known reserves totaling 70 billion barrels.[53]

This estimate, however, is on the optimistic side, with certain reservations to be borne in mind:

1. It is largely conjectural and there is no evidence that new pools will be discovered and put in operation before the known reserves are exhausted.

2. The pools that have not yet been discovered are likely to be less accessible than those now in use, so that extraction of oil will become increasingly expensive as time goes on.

3. More specifically, two thirds of the hypothetical "undiscovered" reserves are under water in the continental shelf region, which increases the technical difficulties of exploitation.

On the other hand, "undiscovered" petroleum fields are not the only potential reserve of fluid fuel. Crude petroleum can be replaced increasingly by liquid fuel extracted from shale, bituminous coal and wastewood. Levorsen seems to be right when he points out that we are at the beginning of the era of fluid fuels rather than approaching its end.

There is a very real possibility of fundamental shifts in the global geography of petroleum, similar to the shifts of the petroleum industry's center in the United States since the turn of the century. Decline in the importance of the old oil fields and the rise of new centers of production may have a far-reaching impact on the distribution of economic power and wealth in the world.

Mineral Fuels

The distribution of coal and petroleum over the earth has been of paramount significance in molding the modern world economy. The coal belt runs through the North Atlantic areas of the highest climatic energy and includes regions held by peoples of the European stock. (Cf. Figure 112 with Figures 11 and 18.) The presence of fossil fuel deposits in soil trod by the white man is a pure coincidence, but mechanized civilization was born when the men of the North Atlantic discovered that the black rocks under their feet were loaded with energy. Soon, coal became their ally and obedient servant. The

---

51. See Chapter 23.
52. See Chapter 24.

53. **2, b,** pp. 94 ff.; cf. Chapter 24.

economic growth of the United Kingdom in the eighteenth century, and of Germany and the United States a hundred years later, was largely conditioned by their coal fields.

Petroleum arrived too late to challenge coal as the foundation of industrial empires. In the brief period of a century, between the invention of the steam engine and of the internal combustion motor, mechanized civilization came of age, and the Great Powers of the coal area could readily gain control of oil fields located in remote corners of the world. The less advanced countries, unable to develop their petroleum industry without technical and financial assistance from abroad, let their oil fields fall into the hands of the Western powers. As time goes on this arrangement is yielding to a more nationalistic policy, but so far it has helped to consolidate the predominant positions of the old coal countries.

Without challenging the supreme power of coal, petroleum has introduced three new factors into the world economy:

1. As a new source of mechanical power, in many respects superior to coal, it has accelerated technological progress, originated new industries and new means of transportation, injected new vigor into the industrial system and strengthened the leading industrial nations.

2. It has been particularly beneficial to the nations that happened to possess both coal and petroleum, the United States and Russia.

3. It has become the means of carrying mechanized economy and Western civilization southward and eastward from their original strongholds.

In the light of this experience, it seems unlikely that the discovery of new oil fields — say, in the Arctic or on the slopes of the Andes — will make these areas new world centers of economic power. It is certain, however, that the old petroleum nations, and in particular the United States, will have to rely increasingly on the importation of crude oil and that an increasing number of nations will share in the advantages of the petroleum industries.[54]

WATER RESOURCES

Introducing its report on *Water Policy for the American People* the President's Water Resources Policy Commission declared: "From the products of our land, our forests, our mines and oil fields, we have raised great cities and spanned a continent with railroads and automobile highways. But without one key resource, water, none of these miracles of human achievement would have been possible. . . . Water . . . has molded our mountains, carved our great valleys, nourished our forests, created our alluvial plains, played a major part in creating the fertility of our land and carried off our topsoil. . . . Throughout history, water has dominated human life." [55]

The Hydrological Cycle

The unique characteristic of water is that it is a dynamic substance, moving continuously from the raindrop to the land, thence to the sea or another basin, and back again to the clouds. The hydrological cycle, in combination with the physical properties of water as a particular chemical compound, determines the role of water in the world economy.[56] (See Figure 113.)

The Ocean

Man has not yet utilized the dynamics of the ocean, the power of tides and waves and the energy stored in the difference of temperature at the sea's surface and in its depths.[57] So far, the ocean has served him as a hunting ground and thoroughfare. As the source of fish and crustaceans, the ocean is important to peoples living along the seacoast in the Far East, especially in Japan, southeastern China, Burma, Thailand, the Philippines and the Pacific islands. It also plays an important role in the economic life of Great Britain, the Scandinavian countries and some regions in South America.[58] In all, probably some 200 million persons depend largely on the ocean for their everyday food, and several times as many for a supplement to their customary diet.

Much broader is the ocean's role as a carrier.[59] Most of the industrial centers of the world have developed as beachheads of sea traffic, while others have risen along waterways connecting them with the sea.[60]

---

54. Pockets of natural gas have recently been discovered in northern Italy. Some American experts believe that the presence of gas suggests that there must also be pools of petroleum. If the hypothesis proves correct, Italy will have a good chance to rise to the rank of a great economic power.

55. **17**, p. 1.
56. **8**, pp. 1–6.
57. See Chapter 25.
58. See Tables 144 and 145; cf. Chapter 20.
59. See Chapter 1.
60. See Chapter 4.

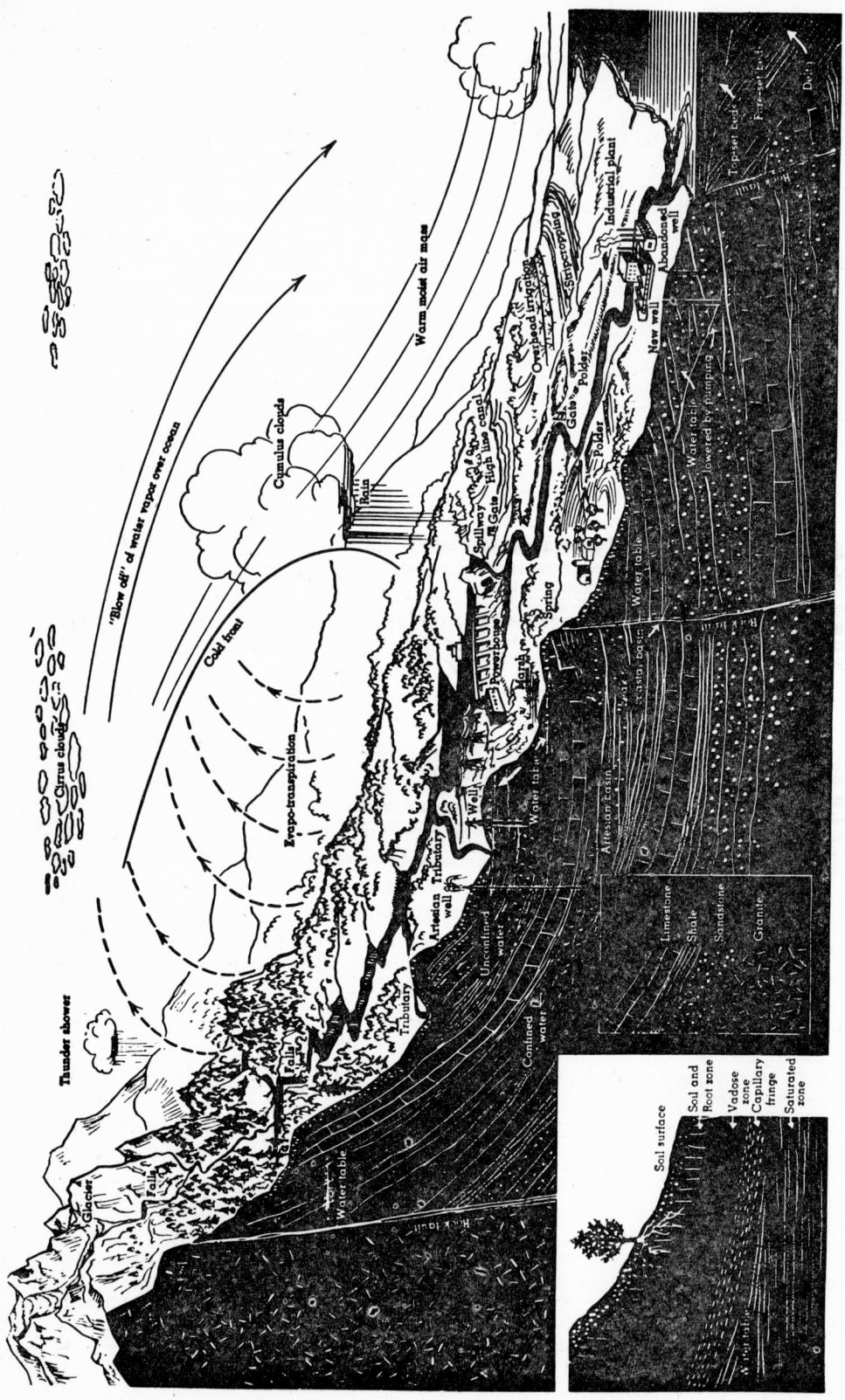

The President's Water Resources Policy Commission

FIGURE 113. WATER RESOURCES: THE HYDROLOGICAL CYCLE

The sun draws water from the sea (warm moist air masses in the figure) and the land (evapo-transpiration). Clouds form — cirrus clouds high above the earth, cumulus clouds closer to the sea level. Then rain falls. Part of the rainfall waters forests and fields, part is held by the soil, part goes into underground reservoirs (water tables, confined and unconfined waters) and part runs off, forming falls, rivers and lakes. Underground water is available by means of wells; river water can be diverted to irrigation by canals; the power of falling water can be used for generating electrical power.

Rivers

The role of a river in human life is more complicated. It acts not only as a body of water but as a stream of moving water and a phase in the hydrological cycle — by carrying traffic downstream, irrigating forests and fields (or destroying them) and providing motive power.

Rivers have been of paramount importance in determining the distribution of population on the continents and in individual countries. We have only to recall the historical role of the Nile, the Danube and the Rhine, the Dnieper and Volga, the Indus and Ganges, the Yangtze, Si-Kiang and Amur, the St. Lawrence, the Hudson and the Mississippi. Even comparatively small rivers, navigable for only part of the year, are sometimes of vital significance for the local population as the link with the world and the only practical means of sending bulky local products — especially lumber and ore — to remote markets.

Many great rivers have not yet gained a place in world economy in keeping with the expanse of their drainage basin and its natural resources. Such are the powerful rivers of the under-developed areas: the Amazon and La Plata in South America, the Niger and Congo in Africa, the Yenisei and Lena in Siberia, and many others. The eventual economic rise of the under-developed areas implies development of the corresponding drainage basins, some of which lie in more than one country. (See Figure 114.)

DEVELOPMENT OF RIVER BASINS

Full utilization of the economic assets a river represents requires careful planning for the whole drainage basin, from the headwaters of the river to its mouth. For some rivers, the main problem is navigation: maintenance of the necessary level of water, control of rapids, elimination of shoals. In others, flood control or soil and forest conservation overshadows all other problems of water policy. In some basins, every drop of water is used for irrigation and the people consider the river essentially as the carrier of fertility to their fields.[61] Still other rivers have been developed mainly as sources of hydroelectric power.

A well integrated program of river-basin de-velopment can emphasize one or another of these purposes, but the ultimate objective — complete utilization of the hydrological cycle represented by the flowing water — requires multipurpose planning, with due attention to sanitation, development of new settlements, recreation facilities and so on. (See Figure 115.) Some parts in such a program — for example, soil and forest conservation and regulation of headwaters — are closely interrelated. Other parts may eventually compete with each other. It is possible, for example, that maintaining the level of water necessary for navigation may leave too little water for irrigation and vice versa. Likewise clashes of interests may develop between different areas within the basin of a great river.[62] Such conflicts can be reconciled or compromised eventually on the basis of the tremendous gains the development of water resources brings to the whole region.

Technically, the development of a river is focused on building dams and levees that maintain a more or less even flow of water in the river, while surplus water is stored in artificial lakes in the wet season and released for navigation and irrigation in the dry season. The difference in the levels of water above and below the dam can be used as a source of electric power. The same dam can serve several purposes: flood control, navigation, irrigation and power production.

The Tennessee Valley Authority (TVA)

The idea of developing the water resources of a valley by means of the construction and operation of a multiple-purpose system of dams has been put to a test by the Tennessee Valley Authority.

For more than a century the Tennessee River had been known as a stream of great undeveloped and wasted power and "a destroyer of life and property." [63] It had several low dams to protect local navigation and ten hydroelectric stations with high dams, but these installations were inadequate to protect the valley against floods or to maintain the level of the river in drought times. The Tennessee Valley Authority Act of 1933 enumerated the goals of the new

---

61. For example, Egyptian hydrologists, direct heirs of millenniums of experience in the use of irrigation dams, show little interest in other objectives of water control. (**2**, Vol. I, pp. 390–91.)

62. The prolonged struggle around the development project of the Missouri Valley is an example of such conflicts of local interests. (See **30**, pp. 208–26 and *passim*.)

63. **2, a**, p. 369; **14**, p. 3.

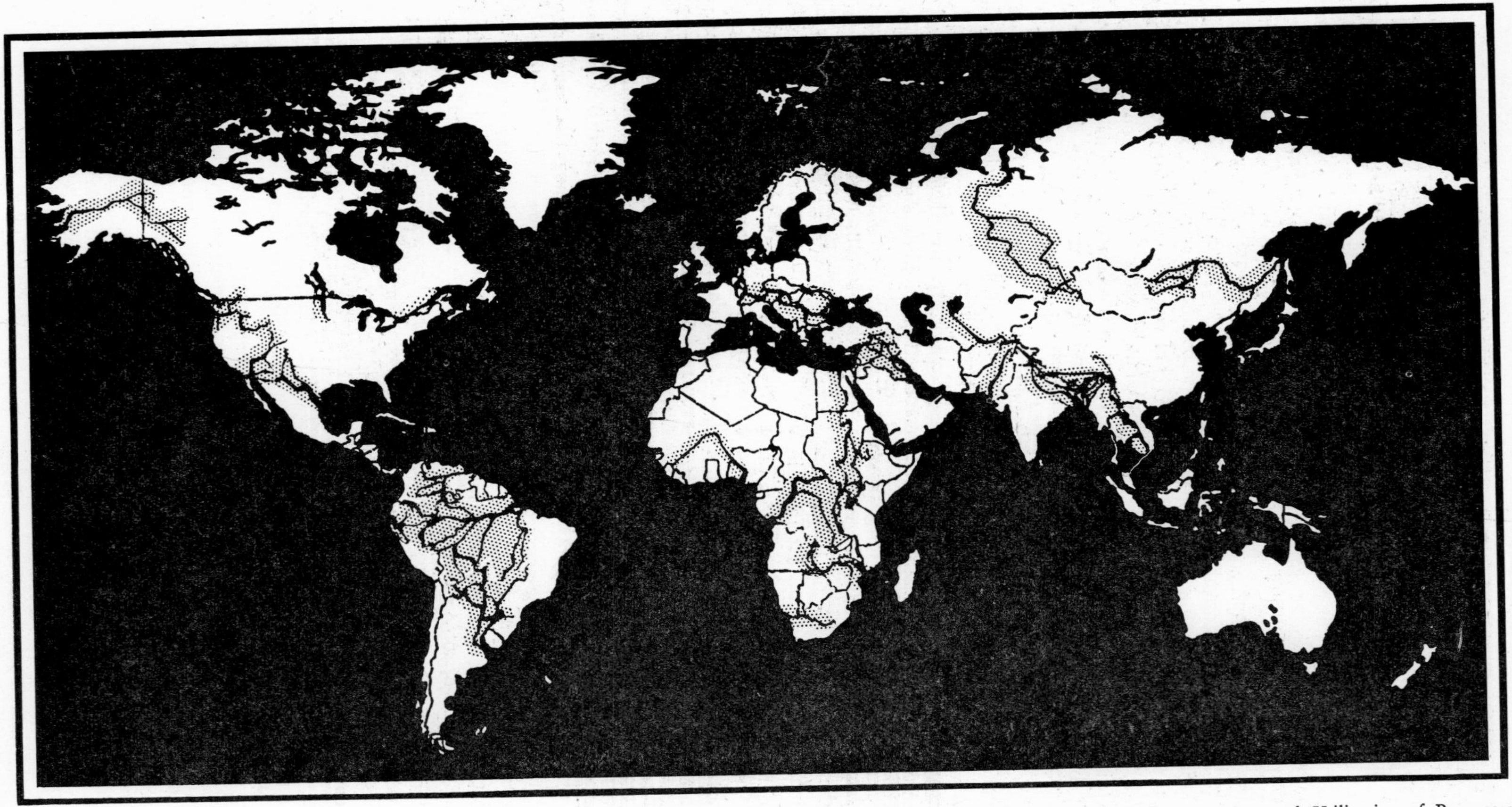

United Nations Scientific Conference on the Conservation and Utilization of Resources

Figure 114. Water Resources: Major International Drainage Basins

The President's Water Resources Policy Commission

FIGURE 115. WATER RESOURCES: A SCHEMATIC PICTURE OF A MULTIPLE-PURPOSE RIVER BASIN DEVELOPMENT

agency as follows: (1) the maximum amount of flood control; (2) the maximum development of the river for navigation; (3) the maximum generation of electric power *consistent with flood control and irrigation;* (4) the proper use of marginal lands; (5) reforestation in the drainage basin; and (6) the economic and social well-being of the people living in that basin.[64] Later, emphasis in the operations of the agency shifted increasingly to production and distribution of electric power as the most effective approach to economic development of the region.

Operations of the TVA

Up to June 30, 1949, a total of $816 million had been invested in the multiple-purpose water-control system of the Tennessee Valley. This investment was distributed as follows: [65]

	Amount, in Millions	Per Cent
Total	$816.0	100.0
Flood control	154.0	18.9
Navigation	151.5	18.6
Power	510.5	62.6

The TVA now operates a system of 27 major multipurpose dams, 17 of which were constructed by the Authority. These dams provide nearly 11.5 million acre-feet of water storage for flood control. (See Figure 116.) The power system includes 27 major hydroelectric plants, 6 steam electric generating stations, and a number of minor stations, with a total installed capacity of 2.75 million kilowatts.[66]

The system of dams on the tributaries of the Tennessee and on the river itself have made it possible to develop a navigation channel 9 feet deep and 630 miles long, from Knoxville to the mouth of the Tennessee River on the Ohio River, just above the junction of the Ohio with the Mississippi. Thus, the Tennessee Valley has been integrated in the system of waterways that connects the Southeast with industrial centers such as Pittsburgh, Chicago, Minneapolis, St. Louis and New Orleans.[67]

At the same time, the system of water controls has improved the quality of drinking water in the region, reduced the incidence of malaria, contributed to the preservation of soil, forest and wildlife, and has provided the population of the valley with unique recreation facilities.[68]

Economic Results of the TVA

Development of the Tennessee Valley has been one of the most ambitious and expensive operations of this kind in history. The investment, however, has proved to be sound. The Tennessee electric power stations are earning more than enough from power operations to repay the more than $500 million investment in power facilities with interest.[69] The investment of $154 million in flood control has eliminated flood damage estimated at $11 million a year. Electrification of the valley and improved transportation facilities have stimulated the development of farming and of new industries.[70] In brief, the control of water has greatly transformed life in the whole drainage basin, a region of 41,000 square miles [71] with a population of approximately 6 million. Indirectly, it has contributed to the economic development of the much broader area that uses electric power supplied by the TVA or sells its products in the valley.

The Impact of the TVA on Economic Planning

The TVA experience has deeply influenced the approach to water resources in the United States and abroad. Several similar projects are now under discussion in the United States, and the most ambitious of them — that of the Missouri Valley — seems to have a good chance of being realized, in one form or another, in the not too remote future. The example of the TVA has given new life to old projects for developing the Rhône Valley in France and to similar proposals in Argentina and Uruguay, the Philippines, West Africa (Niger Valley), Israel (Jordan Valley) and India (Damodar Valley).[72]

The Pacific Northwest

The Columbia River and its tributaries provide another outstanding example of the development of the natural resources of a vast

---

64. **14**, p. 6.
65. **15**, p. 10.
66. **16**, p. 3.
67. **14**, p. 17.

68. **15**, pp. 19 ff.
69. **15**, p. 11.
70. **2, c**, pp. 376 ff.
71. This is about three times the area of Denmark and nearly four times that of Belgium or the Netherlands; more than the area of Portugal, Hungary, Bulgaria or Austria; and only one fourth less than the area of England and Wales.
72. Cf. **2**, Vol. I, pp. 367 ff.

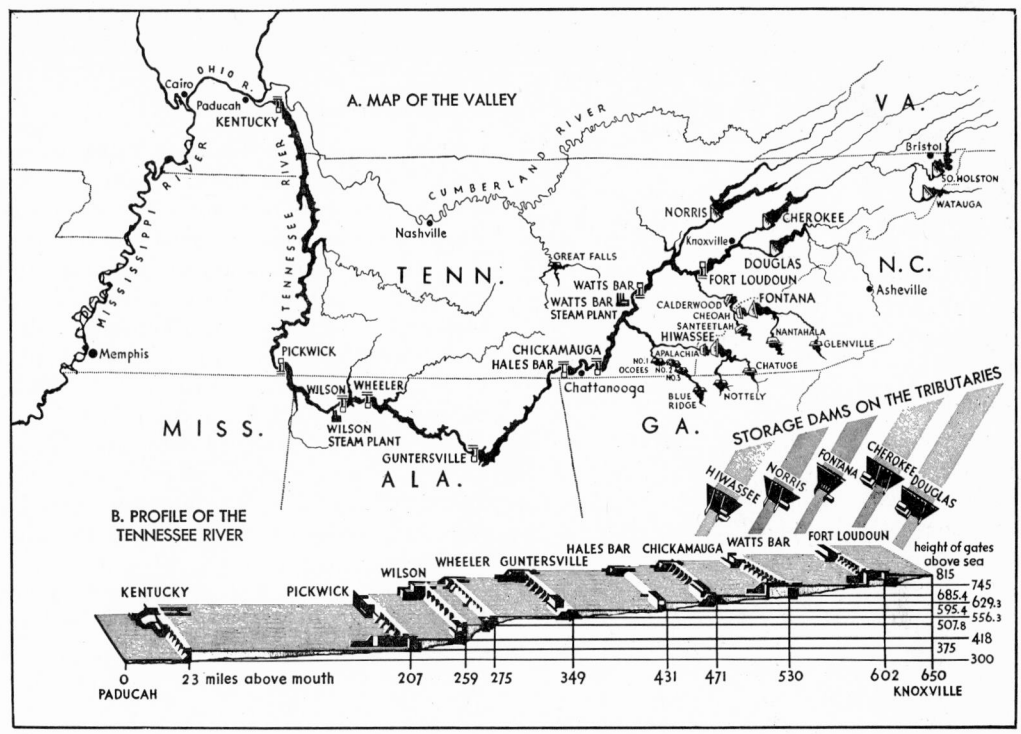

FIGURE 116. WATER RESOURCES: THE TENNESSEE VALLEY

The Tennessee Valley affords an example of the full development of a river basin. The map shows the location of multiple-purpose dams; the profile below, the water levels at their gates. The series of dams on the Tennessee River (Kentucky, Pickwick, Wilson, Wheeler, Guntersville, Hales Bar, Chickamauga, Watts Bar and Fort Loudoun, moving upstream, from the mouth on the Ohio River) is combined with a system of dams and storage reservoirs on the turbulent tributaries (Norris, Cherokee, South Holston and others).

region by controlling a river basin.[73] (See Figure 117.) The primary purpose of the management of the Columbia River basin is to produce electric power for industrial use but the dams also serve in flood control, navigation, and irrigation of arid but extremely fertile areas in the basin. When completed, the Columbia River hydroelectric plants will have a total capacity of more than 15 million kilowatts and will provide cheap energy in the states of Washington, Oregon, Idaho and Montana. The impact on mining, industry and forestry will extend over all the Northwest from the Pacific to the Great Lakes.[74]

WORLD RESERVES OF WATER POWER

Water power was used on a small scale more than 2,000 years ago. From the Middle Ages, the water wheel was a part of the standard equipment of a mine.[75] Before the invention of the steam engine, water was also the main source of motive power in industry. Even in the early part of the nineteenth century, all mills and factories in New England and the Middle Atlantic states were located on water falls and powered by water wheels. Later, water power was completely eclipsed by coal and steam engines, in both the United States and Europe. Water power did not begin its spectacular comeback until the last quarter of the nineteenth century, when men found means of transforming it into electric energy.

The capacity of installed hydroelectric plants in the world in 1947 has been estimated by the United States Geological Survey at 87 million horsepower and the potential (not harnessed) water power at ordinary minimum flow at 663.5 million horsepower — 8 times the capacity of all stations now in operation.[76]

---

73. **2, g.**

74. For more detailed discussion of use of water power in the United States, see Chapter 25.

75. See Chapter 22.

76. Cf. Chapter 25.

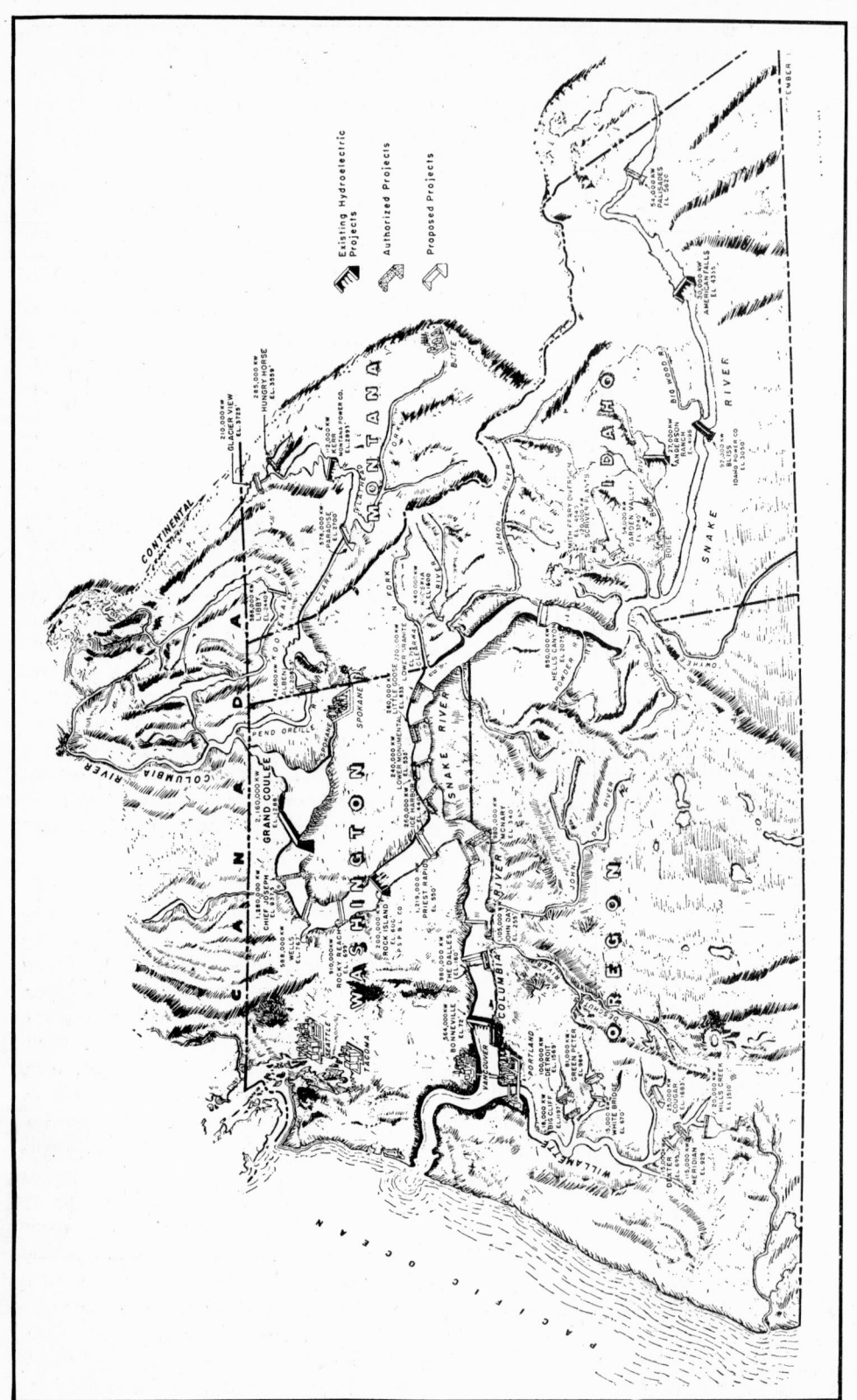

FIGURE 117. WATER RESOURCES: THE WATER CONTROL SYSTEM IN THE COLUMBIA RIVER BASIN. PRESENT AND PROPOSED DAMS

Bonneville Power Administration

This map shows schematically the location of hydroelectric installations and projects in the Columbia River basin as of December 1949. The indicated capacity is the maximum capacity of each plant after its completion. Some plants have begun operation with only a fraction of indicated capacity.

Water power is very unevenly distributed in the world and is unevenly utilized by different countries. Only a few countries — Sweden, France, Germany, Switzerland, Austria, Italy and Japan — have harnessed half or more of their supply of water power. The United States has electrified about 40 per cent of the water power available at minimum flow but still has large reserves of water power at ordinary mean flow.

In South America, the rate of utilization of available water power (installed capacity in relation to potential water power at minimum flow plus installed capacity) is approximately 3 per cent, in Middle America 5 per cent, in Europe 60 per cent, in the USSR 3 per cent, in Asia 13 per cent, in Africa slightly more than 0.1 per cent and in Oceania 6 per cent.[77]

On the whole, the unused reserves of water power are heavily concentrated in underdeveloped regions.[78] The main storehouses of water power in the world are in remote and sparsely populated regions in Central Africa and the Himalayas. From time immemorial, men have been more attracted by seashores, rolling plains, broad valleys and slowly flowing rivers than mountainous terraces, the cradle of powerful waterfalls and wild streams. Recent technological trends, however, favor development of the latent natural resources of these areas. In fact, with modern means of transportation, any machine developed on coasts of the North Atlantic Ocean can be taken to the ageless stores of water power in Central Africa and the Himalayas.[79] Moreover, just as water power facilitates the industrial development of areas that are poor in coal and petroleum and lie far from the sea, so atomic energy will probably favor industrialization of regions that possess no local energy resources and lack easy access to the ocean.

Concentration of Economic Power

The natural resources discussed on the preceding pages cannot, by themselves, assure prosperity to a region, and none is absolutely indispensable for economic progress. Great Britain has reached a very high level of prosperity although this tiny island has not enough arable land to provide a subsistence minimum for its population, is poor in forests and water power,

and has no petroleum or natural gas. At the same time, the highlands of eastern Africa are among the poorest areas in the world despite an abundance of arable land and forest, priceless deposits of all kinds of minerals and a fabulous abundance of water power.

Natural resources are worth what man has done with them. When man, as the chief actor on the historical scene, is considered in his natural environment, the relationship between the geographic distribution of economic power and the distribution of natural resources in the world becomes clearly apparent.

As shown in Chapter 9, all prosperous countries are located in the moderate climatic zone, in the areas of high climatic energy, and are inhabited by peoples of European stock. Economic power is heavily concentrated on both coasts of the North Atlantic Ocean. Characteristic of these areas are abundance of coal and high per capita consumption of energy and steel. More specifically, the two areas of concentration of economic power can be described as the strongholds of coal mining, the iron and steel industry and related branches of production.

Is the economic predominance of the two North Atlantic regions a historical coincidence or the result of a definite combination of natural conditions on both coasts of the ocean? To what extent does economic power in both regions depend on their supremacy in coal mining and the production and processing of iron and steel?

PATTERNS OF THE IRON AND STEEL INDUSTRY

In ancient times, when man was just beginning his apprenticeship in handling metals, he experimented with them wherever he found lumps of metal or ore. A siderolite could serve as an iron mine for a jungle tribe of hunters, providing them with a generous supply of arrowheads. Such finds were rare, however. Iron, which constitutes 4 per cent of the crust of the earth and is widely distributed in all parts of the world, usually occurs in the form of ore. For 4,000 years men reduced metal by heating and hammering. Ancient Rome did not improve this technique, though it used comparatively large quantities of iron for manufacturing arms and military machines. The road was long from the Catalan forge, built six hundred years ago, to the modern furnaces with a capacity of 200,000 tons and more a year.

The steel age began in the second half of the

---

77. See Table 407.
78. See Figure 275.
79. Cf. **29**, pp. 248–73.

nineteenth century, hardly more than seventy years ago. The location of steel mills, which epitomize the economic power in this age, has been governed by the availability of three factors: iron ore, coal and labor. It has been found cheaper, as a rule, to ship iron ore to coal fields than to bring coal to iron ore mines. Thus areas rich in coal became centers of the iron, and later the steel, industry in Great Britain, Germany and the United States.[80]

This pattern of development has given a decisive advantage to coal fields located close to iron ore deposits or connected with such deposits by convenient and inexpensive means of transportation. The ideal conditions were found in the areas where the world's coal belt is broken by the depression of the Atlantic.

The maze of islands, bays, fringing seas, lakes and rivers on both coasts of the North Atlantic provides an excellent network of waterways. East of the ocean, the coal and iron region stretches from the British Isles and Scandinavia to Upper Silesia; west of it, from the coast to the western corner of Lake Superior. The North and Baltic Seas and the Rhine, with its tributaries, tie coal and iron together in the East, just as the Great Lakes connect Minnesota iron ore with Appalachian coal fields in the United States. (See Figure 118.)

Apart from these two areas, the iron industry has been developed in many places that rely on the combination of local or imported iron ore or scrap with local coal or water power. In some places, wood is used for melting ore. Iron is now mined in hundreds of places all over the world. Blast furnaces and steel works, although more concentrated than iron ore mines, are operated in scores of localities, from Alabama to eastern Siberia, Manchuria and Japan; from Scandinavia to India. The exceptional combination of conditions existing in the two North Atlantic regions occurs, however, nowhere else.[81] In turn, the development of the iron and steel industry in the North Atlantic nations has had far-reaching repercussions.

To make modern steel, the producer must comb the world for such ingredients as manganese, chromium, tungsten, vanadium, molyb-denum, nickel, copper, and other alloys. The iron and steel works call into being factories that produce machinery and tools, locomotives and railroad cars, automobiles and airplanes. These factories are not necessarily attached to the site of the steel mills; they can equally well purchase finished steel from a more or less remote mill. Usually, however, industries processing steel are clustered around the place where steel is produced.

To sum up, the two North Atlantic strongholds of industrial power have risen to their present position because of the combination of the human factor — the concentration of energetic and resourceful nations — with the unique asset of coal and iron deposits linked by waterways.

The most important manufacturing region in the United States — sometimes called the "manufacturing belt" — stretches from Illinois, southern Wisconsin and Michigan, in the west, to New Jersey, Connecticut, Massachusetts and the southern part of New Hampshire and Maine, in the east, the area where the iron ores and coal meet. Contrary to other centers of manufacturing, all industry in this region has developed on the foundation of iron and steel.[82]

EXPANSION OF THE INDUSTRIAL SYSTEM

Our economic system calls for production on a continuously widening scale, steadily expanding markets and a continuously increasing variety of raw materials. In the last century and a half, it has been reaching out toward all the world through many channels — the travels of explorers, religious missions, military expeditions and conquests, the development of colonial empires, dissemination of knowledge, the global network of transportation and communication, foreign trade, international investment and so on. Coming in touch with other peoples, Western nations have been compelled to share with them their skills in techniques and organization. Europeans and Americans have taught other peoples how to build roads, bridges and harbors; how to dig coal, drill oil wells, improve soil, breed better plants and animals; and also how to operate printing presses, hold elections, and handle machine guns.

The penetration of mechanized civilization

---

80. An example to the contrary is the Magnitogorsk in the Soviet Union (Urals), where iron and steel works use local iron ore, while coal is brought more than 1,400 miles from the Kuznetsk Basin.

81. See Chapter 29.

82. **12,** p. 12.

STATES	BLAST FURNACE	STEEL FURNACE	HOT ROLLED
ALABAMA	4.44	3.76	3.63
CALIFORNIA	0.88	2.74	2.40
COLORADO	0.92	1.32	1.02
CONNECTICUT	—	0.19	0.13
DELAWARE	—	0.47	0.30
GEORGIA	—	0.19	0.15
ILLINOIS	6.95	8.52	6.55
INDIANA	8.14	11.76	10.29
KENTUCKY	0.78	1.60	1.01
MARYLAND	3.25	5.27	4.89
MASSACHUSETTS	0.20	0.25	0.24
MICHIGAN	2.04	4.77	4.55
MINNESOTA	0.58	0.92	0.25
MISSOURI	—	0.42	0.41
NEW JERSEY	—	0.21	0.22
NEW YORK	4.69	5.17	4.17
OHIO	14.69	20.77	16.48
OKLAHOMA	—	0.05	0.04
OREGON	—	0.11	0.10
PENNSYLVANIA	20.96	30.50	21.64
RHODE ISLAND	—	0.09	0.12
TENNESSEE	0.14	0.04	0.09
TEXAS	0.67	0.86	0.69
UTAH	1.70	1.44	1.60
VIRGINIA	0.05	0.01	0.04
WASHINGTON	—	0.35	0.20
WEST VIRGINIA	1.47	2.72	2.82
WISCONSIN	—	—	0.02
TOTALS	72.55	104.50	84.05

ANNUAL CAPACITIES MILLIONS OF NET TONS

ARIZONA (HAS PIPE CAPACITY)
FLORIDA (HAS WIRE CAPACITY)
IOWA (HAS WIRE AND PIPE CAPACITY)

LEGEND

BLAST FURNACE CAPACITY IN STATE
STEEL FURNACE CAPACITY IN STATE
HOT ROLLED CAPACITY IN STATE
SPECIALIZED FINISHING CAPACITY ONLY
GEOGRAPHIC CENTER OF STEEL CAPACITY
IRON ORE DEPOSITS
COKING COAL DEPOSITS
PRINCIPAL ORE DEPOSITS, ALLOYING ELEMENTS
PRINCIPAL STEEL TOWNS AND AREAS IN STATES

American Iron and Steel Institute

FIGURE 118. LOCATION OF INDUSTRIES: IRON AND STEEL INDUSTRY IN THE UNITED STATES

Iron ore is mined south and southwest of Lake Superior and is transported by water to blast furnaces in Gary, Cleveland, Youngstown, Buffalo, Bethlehem, Sparrows Point, etc. Coal moves to these centers from neighboring coal fields. The South has a minor independent iron and steel industry center, around Birmingham, near iron ore and coal deposits. (19.) Minor centers of the iron and steel industry are dispersed all over the nation from California to Tennessee but none of them approaches in importance those located close to the ore deposits of Lake Superior and the Appalachian coal fields.

into underdeveloped areas is in full swing. In his continuous search for fertile soil, petroleum, iron and other metals, the white man explores the jungles of Africa and South America and arid deserts of the Near East. Wherever he finds coveted treasures, he sends his machines to get them. Thus, the British have shipped expensive equipment to Abadan for refining petroleum and to Kenya for clearing jungles and raising peanuts; thus, Americans have established modern petroleum refineries in Saudi Arabia and Venezuela.

A recent development in this field is the discovery of fabulous iron ore deposits in Cerro Bolivar, Venezuela, deposits equal in quality and size to those at Lake Superior, which once were considered the richest in the world.[83] The plans for exploiting these deposits include building a railroad through the jungle, a bridge over the Orinoco River, port facilities in Venezuela, new ships, and blast furnaces in the United States.

Thus, new industrial centers emerge on the

83. 23.

fringe of the Western world and in the wilderness far from it. Their development is controlled by the geographic distribution of natural resources rather than by the human factor. Indeed, the human factor behind the refineries of Venezuela, Saudi Arabia and Abadan is largely the same as that behind the industrial systems of the United States and Great Britain, but the transfer of the technical know-how of these nations into a new environment, toward the new natural resources and new reserves of labor force has a deep historical meaning: the economic system that was invented east of the North Atlantic and reached full development west of the ocean is becoming universal and global.

CHAPTER 11

HUMAN RESOURCES

A SURVEY OF THE ASSETS of a nation, a geographic region or the world as a whole is not complete without an analysis of the available labor force and its utilization.[1] Indeed, of all the factors that govern the distribution of economic and political power in the world, the human factor is by far the most important. Such physical assets as fertile soil, favorable climate, sea, rivers and mineral deposits are, of course, vital for the well-being and growth of a nation. But the geographic environment is only the bare stage for the drama of history — men are the actors, and they also provide the stage with the props required by the play.

THE SIZE OF THE LABOR FORCE

A nation's labor force consists of people of various skills and abilities, some working steadily for a living, others only temporarily or occasionally engaged in gainful pursuits. The demarcation between workers and nonworkers is never rigid, and the size of the labor force, as recorded by a census of population, depends partly on the definition.

Workers and Nonworkers

Classification differs especially in the enumeration of women workers. Some countries, such as Colombia, France, Germany, Bulgaria, Romania and Yugoslavia, count farmers' wives as members of the labor force; others, like the United States, Canada, Brazil and Argentina, record most of them as nonworkers. This difference in classification materially affects the size of the female labor force reported by a census. When Colombia reports 47.6 per cent of its women as gainfully occupied and Mexico only 4.4 per cent, the difference does not mean that Colombian women are ten times more diligent or enjoy ten times the work opportunities of women in Mexico; it lies, rather, in the instructions given to the census enumerators.

1. Cf. **6**, pp. 327–65.

The Age Factor

Apart from differences in classification, the proportion of gainful workers in a country depends on the age composition of the population and prevailing customs as to working age. The high proportion of children in the population of economically underdeveloped countries tends to diminish the relative size of the labor force. On the other hand, children in such countries usually begin to work much earlier than in industrial nations. In Japan and China, as well as in Mexico and Guatemala, gainful work of children under 10 years of age is rather common, while in the United States employment of children under 14 is a rare exception. Moreover, in countries with a high proportion of children, there is a lower proportion of old people who have retired from work.

Because of these divergent factors, there is no clear correlation between the level of economic development of a country and the percentage of its population at work. In general, the proportion of gainful workers in the total male population is larger in industrially developed nations than in predominantly agricultural countries. At a certain level of economic development, however, the relative size of the male labor force in a nation begins to decline: longer school attendance keeps children out of the labor market, while social security and individual savings facilitate retirement of elderly workers.

Proportion of Workers in the Population

The proportion of workers in the male population is relatively low in such countries as Indonesia (formerly the Netherlands Indies, 48.5 per cent), Thailand (49.2 per cent), Venezuela (50.4 per cent), Peru (52.1 per cent), the Philippines (52.3 per cent), Chile (52.9 per cent). The highest rates are in Hungary (71.3 per cent), Great Britain (69.0 per cent), Switzerland (69.0 per cent), Belgium (68.8 per cent), Denmark (67.7 per cent). In countries between these extremes, the proportion of workers in the

TABLE 165

LABOR FORCE: SIZE IN RELATION TO POPULATION, IN SELECTED COUNTRIES

Country and Year [a]	Population, in Millions			Gainful Workers,[b] in Millions			Percentage of Workers	
	Total	Male	Female	Total	Male	Female	Male	Female
United States, 1940	131.7	66.1	65.6	52.7	39.9	12.8	60.7	19.6
Canada, 1941	11.5	5.9	5.6	4.7	3.8	0.9	63.6	16.4
Mexico, 1940	16.6	8.1	8.4	5.4	5.0	0.4	61.3	4.4
Guatemala, 1940	3.3	1.7	1.6	1.1	0.9	0.2	55.4	10.7
Cuba, 1943	4.8	2.5	2.3	1.5	1.4	0.2	54.6	6.9
Puerto Rico, 1940	1.9	0.9	0.9	0.6	0.5	0.1	48.8	15.5
Venezuela, 1941	3.9	1.9	1.9	1.2	1.0	0.3	50.4	14.4
Colombia, 1938	8.7	4.3	4.4	4.6	2.5	2.1	57.5	47.6
Brazil, 1940	41.2	20.6	20.6	14.0	11.8	2.2	57.1	10.9
Peru, 1940	6.2	3.1	3.1	2.5	1.6	0.9	52.1	27.9
Chile, 1940	5.0	2.5	2.5	1.7	1.3	0.4	52.9	16.8
Great Britain, 1931	44.8	21.5	23.3	21.1	14.8	6.3	69.0	26.9
Ireland, 1936	3.0	1.5	1.4	1.3	1.0	0.4	65.0	24.3
France, 1946	39.8	18.9	21.0	20.5	12.7	7.9	67.1	37.5
Belgium, 1930	8.1	4.0	4.1	3.8	2.8	0.9	68.8	24.3
Netherlands, 1947	9.6	4.8	4.8	3.9	2.9	0.9	61.0	19.5
Denmark, 1940	3.8	1.9	1.9	2.0	1.3	0.7	67.7	35.2
Sweden, 1945	6.7	3.3	3.4	3.0	2.2	0.7	67.5	22.3
Norway, 1930	2.8	1.4	1.4	1.2	0.9	0.3	62.0	23.0
Finland, 1940	3.9	1.9	2.0	2.0	1.2	0.9	60.5	43.7
Germany, 1946	63.6	28.0	35.6	28.9	17.5	11.4	62.3	32.2
Poland, 1931	31.9	15.4	16.5	15.0	9.0	6.0	58.5	36.3
Czechoslovakia, 1947	12.2	5.9	6.3	5.9	3.8	2.1	64.2	32.9
Switzerland, 1941	4.3	2.1	2.2	2.0	1.4	0.6	69.0	25.9
Austria, 1939	7.0	3.4	3.6	3.6	2.2	1.5	63.7	41.7
Hungary, 1941	9.3	4.6	4.8	4.5	3.3	1.3	71.3	26.3
Portugal, 1940	7.7	3.7	4.0	3.0	2.3	0.7	63.9	16.9
Spain, 1940	25.9	12.4	13.5	9.3	8.1	1.1	65.5	8.3
Italy, 1936	42.4	20.6	21.8	18.8	13.4	5.4	64.9	24.7
Yugoslavia, 1931	13.9	6.9	7.0	6.5	4.3	2.1	63.0	30.4
Romania, 1930	18.1	8.9	9.2	10.5	5.7	4.8	64.0	52.0
Bulgaria, 1934	6.1	3.1	3.0	3.4	1.9	1.5	62.2	50.7
USSR, 1926	147.0	71.0	76.0	84.5	45.3	39.2	63.8	51.6
Japan, 1947	78.6	38.4	40.2	34.6	21.5	13.1	55.9	32.5
Turkey, 1935	16.2	7.9	8.2	7.9	4.6	3.3	58.4	40.0
India, 1931	352.8	181.8	171.0	148.8	101.4	47.4	55.8	27.7
Thailand, 1937	14.5	7.3	7.2	6.8	3.6	3.2	49.2	45.1
Ceylon, 1946	6.7	3.5	3.1	2.6	2.0	0.6	57.8	18.3
Indonesia, 1930	60.7	30.0	30.6	20.9	14.6	6.3	48.5	20.6
Philippines, 1948	19.2	9.7	9.5	7.3	5.1	2.3	52.3	23.8
Egypt, 1937	15.9	8.0	8.0	6.1	5.2	0.9	65.2	11.3
Union of South Africa,[c] 1936	3.0	1.5	1.5	1.0	0.8	0.2	53.3	13.6
Australia, 1947	7.6	3.8	3.8	3.2	2.5	0.7	65.3	19.0
New Zealand, 1945	1.6	0.8	0.8	0.7	0.5	0.2	65.9	19.9

Source: **2,** 1948, pp. 230–31, and 1949–50, pp. 250–51; cf. **7,** 1947–48, p. 7.

a. Countries arranged geographically.
b. For the United States, persons in labor force.
c. European population.

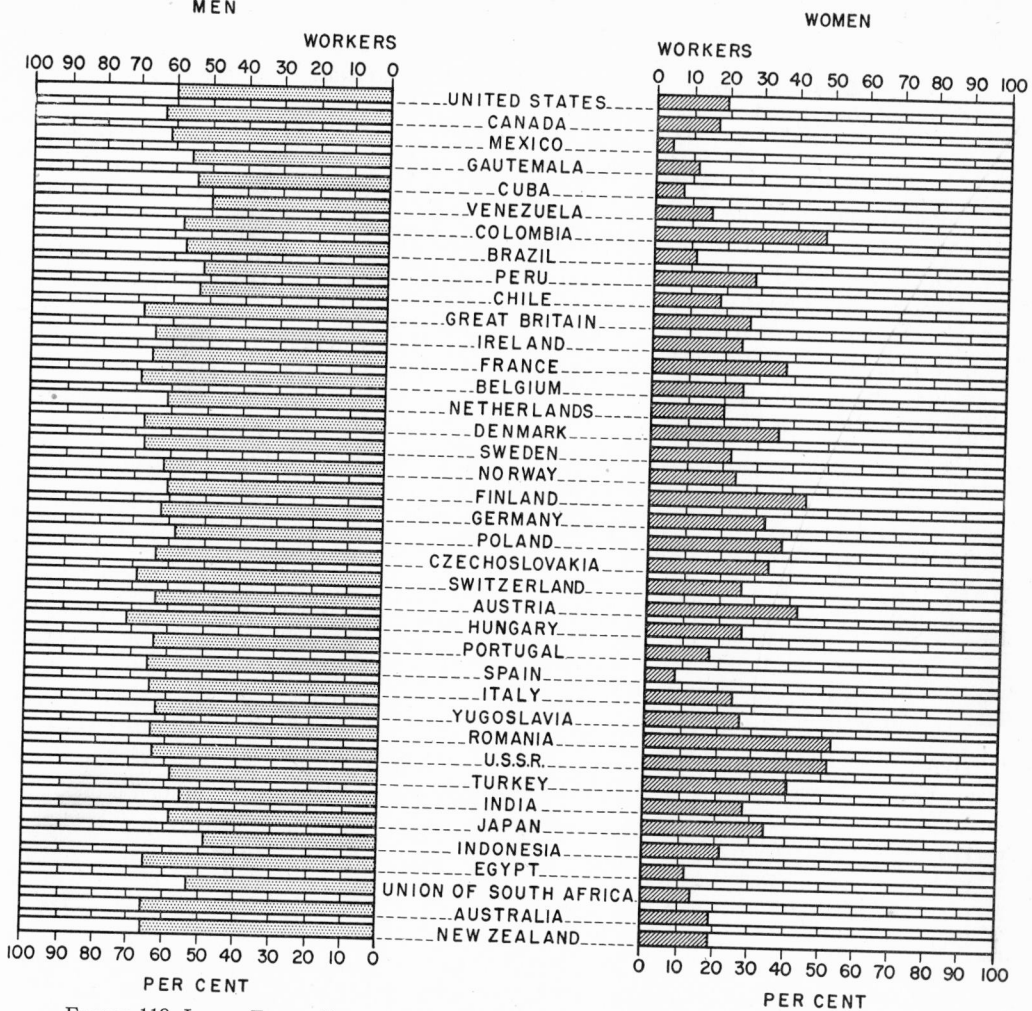

FIGURE 119. LABOR FORCE: PERCENTAGE OF WORKERS IN THE MALE AND FEMALE POPULATION,
IN SELECTED COUNTRIES

The percentage of workers in the male population varies within a comparatively narrow range. In the countries with a particularly large proportion of children (such as Cuba, Venezuela, Peru, Indonesia), it is lower than in countries with relatively few children (Great Britain, Sweden, Belgium, Denmark, Switzerland).

The percentage of workers among women depends partly on the classification of family workers in agriculture. In some countries, farmers' wives and daughters in ages over 12 and 14 years are counted as workers, while in others they are not.

male population varies without visible relationship to the level of economic development: it is about the same in Egypt, Australia, Spain and New Zealand (65.2 to 65.9 per cent); in Mexico and the Netherlands (61.3 and 61.0 per cent); in Portugal and Canada (63.9 and 63.6 per cent).

The range in the reported proportion of gainful workers in the female population is much wider — from 4.4 per cent in Mexico (1940) and 6.9 in Cuba (1943) to more than 50 per cent in Romania, Bulgaria and the USSR. (See Table 165 and Figure 119.)

The ratio of the labor force to total population in a country is usually about the mean of the rates for men and for women, and is partly affected by the way in which the country counts its female workers, especially in agriculture. It is particularly high in the countries that report a large proportion of working women (such as the USSR and Romania) but is almost as high in Denmark and Germany. It is about the same in the United States and Peru or in France and Turkey. Since these ratios depend partly on the age composition of the population, partly on the economic structure of the country and partly on statistical classification, they fail to show the differences among these countries in the actual participation of their people in the labor force.

YOUNG AND OLD WORKERS

The proportion of workers in youthful age groups depends essentially on school-attendance laws and customs which, in turn, depend on local economic conditions. It declines with progress in industrialization and improvement in standards of education. In the United States, for example, the percentage of workers among children 14 and 15 years of age has changed as follows: [2]

Year	Boys	Girls
1900	43.4	18.2
1910	41.4	19.8
1920	23.3	11.6
1930	12.6	5.8
1940	8.0	2.2

A similar trend has prevailed since 1920 in the percentage of workers in the age groups 16–17 and 18–19:

	Boys		Girls	
Year	16–17 Years	18–19 Years	16–17 Years	18–19 Years
1920	58.0	78.3	31.6	42.3
1930	41.2	70.7	22.1	40.5
1940	29.0	65.6	12.9	40.0

The relative number of old people in the labor force has also tended to decline in the United States. Among persons aged 65 years and over, the census found the following percentages of workers:

Year	Men	Women
1900	68.4	9.1
1920	60.1	8.0
1930	58.3	8.0
1940	41.5	5.9

These figures, however, are not very conclusive. The decline in the proportion of workers among persons aged 65 years or more in 1940 was due partly to a change in classification,[3] and partly to the fact that the depression in the

1930's had squeezed many elderly workers out of the labor force: after long and futile search, they began to consider themselves unemployable.

Another factor responsible for a long-range downward trend in the proportion of elderly workers is increase in industrialization. There is an important difference in the concept of "gainful work" or "economic activity" as applied to farming and nonagricultural pursuits. On the farm, the head of the family is usually the titular owner and operator of the farm. Even if he is too old to work regularly in the fields, he is likely to be recorded in the "labor force," while in cities old people who cannot work regularly usually cease to be "workers." The difference is largely in definition rather than the actual age of retirement.

These factors tend to overemphasize the downward trend in the proportion of workers among persons aged 65 years or more, in the United States, though such a trend does exist. It has been observed in many industrial countries and partly explains the contrasts in the proportion of workers among aged persons in countries representing different levels of economic development. (See Table 166.) In France, for example, the proportion of "economically active persons" among elderly people declined between 1906 and 1936 as follows: [4]

Age	1906	1926	1936
		Men	
60–64	85.1	82.4	74.0
65–69	78.0	73.8	65.4
70 and over	57.3	53.1	45.2
		Women	
60–64	44.4	39.9	36.4
65–69	37.8	33.3	29.1
70 and over	21.7	19.6	17.7

With due reservation for the limitations of the available statistics, most students agree that since the turn of the century there has been a genuine trend in most industrial countries toward later entry into gainful occupation and earlier withdrawal from work, in effect, toward limiting gainful work to the ages of about 17 or 19 through 64 years.

---

2. **11**, 1948, pp. 169–72.

3. In 1940 the census shifted from the concept of "gainful worker" to that of "labor force." In previous censuses, some persons who work irregularly from time to time could be counted as "gainful workers." In 1940,

the "labor force" of the nation was determined as consisting of persons who were at work, had a job or were seeking work during the week immediately before the day of enumeration.

4. **20**, p. 85.

TABLE 166

LABOR FORCE: PROPORTION OF WORKERS IN THE MALE AND FEMALE POPULATION IN SPECIFIED AGE GROUPS, IN SELECTED COUNTRIES

Country and Year	Male				Female			
	Total	15–19 Years	20–64 Years	65 Years and Over	Total	15–19 Years	20–64 Years	65 Years and Over
United States, 1940	60.5	40.1	91.8	41.5	19.6	22.1	29.0	5.9
Canada,ª 1941	57.1	50.8	86.8	47.2	14.9	25.8	21.6	5.5
Puerto Rico, 1940	48.8	53.0	90.9	51.1	15.5	28.4	26.0	7.9
Peru, 1940	52.1	61.2	93.5	82.6	27.9	38.0	44.9	35.8
Great Britain, 1931	69.0	88.3	96.7	47.9	26.9	75.0	31.9	8.2
Ireland, 1936	65.0	71.1	95.4	67.3	24.3	49.4	32.7	21.9
France, 1931	68.9	82.3	94.5	59.4	37.1	58.2	49.2	23.5
1946	67.1	75.6	93.2	54.4	37.5	58.7	50.0	22.3
Belgium, 1930	68.8	80.4	95.3	45.3	24.3	56.0	30.4	11.0
Netherlands, 1930	61.3	78.2	95.0	42.6	19.2	53.7	24.5	7.5
1947	61.0	66.0	95.6	35.5	19.5	48.7	25.4	6.3
Denmark, 1940	67.7	85.1	95.9	35.1	35.2	86.3	44.1	7.9
Sweden, 1930	66.1	82.3	95.6	49.8	28.7	63.4	38.5	11.0
Norway, 1930	62.0	77.2	95.1	55.4	23.0	38.9	32.8	16.5
Germany, 1933	65.5	86.1	92.7	29.7	34.2	63.7	44.1	13.1
Switzerland, 1941	69.0	78.0	95.7	54.8	25.9	59.0	32.6	12.0
Portugal,ᵇ 1940	61.2	72.3	92.7	86.4	16.2	30.4	21.8	16.5
Spain, 1940	65.5	89.1	94.7	86.7	8.3	13.7	12.0	6.3
Italy,ᶜ 1936	63.6	82.9	95.0	61.7	24.0	49.8	31.4	11.5
Japan, 1930	58.8	78.5	95.3	63.0	33.0	61.8	49.9	18.6
1949	55.4	50.4	94.5	59.5	36.7	48.3	58.0	31.1
Egypt, 1937	65.2	91.1	97.4	89.7	11.3	16.3	16.9	14.1
Union of South Africa, 1936								
Europeans	56.9	57.8	95.6	52.1	12.8	28.3	19.1	4.4
Others	50.8	78.8	98.5	64.2	15.3	42.4	26.3	8.8
Australia, 1933	65.3	80.9	96.6	34.3	19.2	52.9	23.8	5.4
New Zealand, 1936	66.8	87.9	96.3	40.0	18.9	55.6	23.5	5.0
Hawaii, 1940	61.9	47.3	94.2	43.0	20.5	23.9	35.4	7.4

Source: **2**, 1948, pp. 232–33 and 1949–50, pp. 252–53; cf. **7**, 1947–48, p. 22.

a. Excludes new workers seeking their first job, armed forces and some territories included in figures for Canada in Table 165.
b. Excludes the unemployed.
c. Excludes new workers.

WORKING WOMEN

In a primitive society, women represent the largest part of the "civilian labor force," while men divide their time between the search for food and such extra-economic activities as war, politics, administration and religious rites. Traces of such a division of work between the two sexes can still be found in some primitive countries. The situation has changed fundamentally with the development of a money economy and the broadening schism between domestic work and work for pay or gain.

In early capitalism, gainful work by women was limited to a few occupations and industries, such as domestic service and the textile and clothing industries. The ban against paid women workers was brief, however, and after the middle of the nineteenth century women appeared in numbers in the labor force of industrial countries. Their emergence has been stimulated by several factors. Industry was eager to use the available labor reserves. In some cases, hiring workers' wives and daughters proved an effective means of keeping down the wages of male workers. Technological progress and the development of the industrial system gave women new opportunities to work in factories and offices, mainly in jobs which require neither muscular effort nor long years of apprenticeship and training. At the same time, the decline in the size of the family, progress in the prefabrication of food and the dwindling scope of the home economy made it easier for married women to work outside of their homes, and it became important for many to earn money to buy goods they no longer could make economically at home.

In the United States, the proportion of women in the labor force increased from 17 per cent in 1890 to 24 per cent in 1940 and was close to 30 per cent in April 1952.[5] A similar trend has been observed in Canada, Australia, New Zealand, Germany and the USSR. In most cases, however, the change has been rather slow. In Australia the proportion of women in the economically active population increased from 18.3 per cent in 1911 to 22.2 per cent in 1933; in New Zealand, from 19.5 per cent in 1911 to 21.6 per cent in 1936; in Germany, from 33.8 per cent in 1907 to 37.0 per cent in 1939; in Denmark, from 30.9 per cent in 1911 to 34.8 per cent in 1940.

In other countries, especially in Europe, the proportion of women in the labor force has not changed appreciably. In Great Britain it was 29.6 per cent in 1911 and 29.9 per cent in 1931. In France, it amounted to 33.8 per cent in 1866 and ranged between 33.6 and 33.8 per cent in 1926–36.[6] In Belgium, it was 26.8 per cent in 1910 and 26.5 per cent in 1930; in the Netherlands, 23.9 per cent in 1909 and 24.1 per cent in 1930; in Sweden, 26.0 per cent in 1910 and 27.0 per cent in 1930; in Norway, 31.2 per cent in 1910 and 28.0 per cent in 1930.[7]

The widening scope of gainful work of women is characteristic of the young and prosperous non-European countries — the United States, Canada, Australia and New Zealand — but should not be regarded as a general historical law or the prevailing trend in all industrial nations. In many European countries women took men's jobs in factories during the war but returned to their homes when the emergency was over.

Each country has its own pattern of participation of women in gainful work. The drive toward equal work opportunity for men and women in the United States provokes little enthusiasm on the other side of the Atlantic Ocean.

THE INDUSTRIAL DISTRIBUTION OF THE LABOR FORCE

The use a country makes of its human resources is characterized by the distribution of its labor force among agriculture, manufacturing, commerce, transportation and other industries.[8]

EFFECT OF INDUSTRIALIZATION

The increase in industrialization in the last century or more has been marked by a characteristic change in the distribution of the labor force among industries. Experience in the United States and Sweden since 1870 is typical of this trend.

Trend in the United States

As recently as 1870, agriculture in the United States employed more workers than all other pursuits together. The average farm family produced just enough to provide agricultural products for itself and one nonfarm family. Including the initial processing of agricultural products and their delivery to market, agriculture probably absorbed not less than two thirds of the nation's labor force. (See Table 167.)

Then the situation changed radically. Before World War I, agriculture employed about a third of all gainful workers in the United States, while a third were employed in mining, manufacturing and building construction combined, and a third in trade, transportation and communication, public and professional service and other pursuits. At that time the average farmer grew or raised enough for his own family and two other families. After World War II, in April 1948, only a sixth of the nation's labor force was employed in agriculture. Now, a farmer provides enough agricultural products for his own family, for five or six nonfarm families and for export.

The share of mining and manufactures in the nation's labor force increased steadily in the United States before World War I, reached its

5. **24**, p. 257. For current changes see **13**.

6. **19**, p. 21.

7. Data for recent years are computed from **2**, 1948, pp. 230–31 and 1949–50, pp. 252–53; for 1910–20, see **30**, p. 71.

8. See Chapter 13.

TABLE 167

Labor Force: Distribution by Occupational Division, in the United States,
1870–1940

(Per Cent)

Occupational Division	1870	1880	1890	1900	1910	1920	1930	1940 [a]
Total	100.0	100.0	100.0	100.0	100.0	100.0	100.0	100.0
Agriculture, forestry and fishing	53.5	50.0	43.4	38.2	31.6	27.6	21.9	18.5
Mining	1.4	1.7	1.9	2.4	2.6	2.6	2.0	2.1
Manufacturing and mechanical industries	20.5	22.1	23.7	24.8	28.5	30.3	28.9	29.7
Transportation and communication	4.2	4.8	6.0	6.7	7.1	7.3	7.9	6.9
Trade, finance, etc.	6.8	7.9	8.8	10.6	9.7	10.0	12.5	22.0
Public service	0.7	0.8	0.9	1.0	1.2	1.7	1.8	3.7
Professional service	2.6	3.2	3.8	4.1	4.6	5.1	6.7	8.1
Domestic and personal service	9.7	8.8	9.6	9.7	10.1	8.0	10.1	9.1
Clerical occupations	0.6	0.9	2.0	2.5	4.6	7.3	8.2	—

Sources: For 1870–1930, **10**, p. 101; for 1940, **9**, Vol. II, p. 16.

a. In 1940, the old census classification of gainful workers by occupation was replaced by a classification of employed workers and those with work experience. The figures for 1940 are therefore not strictly comparable with those for the preceding years.

peak in the early 1920's, declined under the impact of the great depression, increased again during World War II, fell after the end of the war and skyrocketed again under the impact of the new rearmament program in the second half of 1950 and in 1951.

An increasing proportion of the human resources of the United States is being used for trade, administration and professional services of physicians, teachers and the like. The apparent stability of the share of domestic and personal services in the labor force is the product of two opposite trends. The decline in the relative number of household servants since the end of the nineteenth century has been offset by the growth of commercial enterprises that perform personal services — laundries, barber and beauty shops, eating and drinking places, hotels and so on.

Trend in Sweden

The change in the distribution of Sweden's labor force reveals a similar trend. During the 75 years between 1870 and 1945, the proportion of the labor force engaged in agriculture declined from 72.4 to 29.7 per cent, while industry's share rose from 14.6 to 39.7 per cent

and that of commerce and communication, from 5.2 to 20.9 per cent. (See Table 168.)

NATIONAL AND REGIONAL VARIATIONS

Apart from a few extreme cases, the range of variation in the industrial distribution of the labor force in various parts of the world and in individual countries is only slightly greater than the differences between 1870 and the present time in the United States or Sweden. (See Table 169; cf. Figure 120.)

The Share of Agriculture in the Labor Force

The proportion of workers engaged in agriculture ranges from 6 per cent in Great Britain to more than 70 per cent in Nicaragua, Colombia, Yugoslavia, Romania, Egypt and the Philippines and exceeds 80 per cent in Bulgaria, Turkey, Thailand and many colonial areas that are not listed in Table 169. When countries included in this table are arrayed by increasing share of agriculture in the labor force, the United States, the Netherlands, Belgium, Australia and New Zealand, along with Great Britain, are in the group in which agriculture absorbs less than 20 per cent of the labor force. Most of the countries of Latin America, Asia, Africa and southern

TABLE 168

LABOR FORCE: DISTRIBUTION OF POPULATION BY INDUSTRY DIVISION, IN SWEDEN, 1870–1945

(*Per Cent*)

Industry Division [a]	1870	1880	1890	1900	1910	1920	1930	1940	1945
Total	100.0	100.0	100.0	100.0	100.0	100.0	100.0	100.0	100.0
Agriculture, forestry and fishing	72.4	67.9	62.1	55.1	48.8	44.0	39.4	34.1	29.7
Industry	14.6	17.4	21.7	27.8	32.0	35.0	35.7	38.2	39.7
Commerce and communication	5.2	7.3	8.7	10.4	13.4	15.2	18.2	19.5	20.9
Public service, etc.	7.8	7.4	7.5	6.7	5.8	5.8	6.7	8.2	9.7

Source: **16**, p. 33.

a. The figures include gainful workers and members of their households.

TABLE 169

LABOR FORCE: DISTRIBUTION BY INDUSTRY, IN SELECTED COUNTRIES

(*Per Cent*)

Country and Year [a]	Agriculture, Forestry, Fishing	Mining	Manufacturing and Construction	Trade	Transportation, Communication	Government, Armed Forces	Professions	Personal and Domestic Service	Other and Unknown
United States, 1940	18.5	2.1	29.7	22.0	6.9	3.7	8.1	9.1	—
Canada, 1941	29.2	2.2	28.9	13.2	6.4	3.3	6.3	8.6	1.8
Mexico, 1940	65.4	1.8	10.9	10.4	2.5	3.3	0.7	3.1	1.9
Nicaragua, 1940	72.9	1.4	11.2		0.7	0.4		2.3	11.1
Panama, 1940	52.6	0.2	11.0	5.0	15.6[b]	5.0		9.7	1.0
Cuba, 1943	41.4	0.4	14.2	9.8	2.2	6.1		5.2	20.7
Puerto Rico, 1940	38.2	0.2	23.9	8.4	3.6	25.7 [c]			
Venezuela, 1941	51.3	1.9	16.7	8.1	3.5	18.6			
Colombia, 1938	72.7	1.7	11.7	3.5	1.4	1.7	1.6	3.5	2.9
Brazil, 1940	67.4	2.8	10.0	5.7	3.4	3.4	7.3		
Peru, 1940	62.6	1.8	17.3	4.5	2.1	3.5	8.4		
Chile, 1940	35.6	5.5	20.4	9.3	4.3	12.7		11.9	0.2
Great Britain, 1931	6.0	6.1	40.0	15.8	6.9	7.7	4.1	12.6	0.9
Ireland, 1936	48.4	0.4	14.8	7.8	5.1	2.2	5.0	9.8	6.6
France, 1946	36.5	1.8	28.0	8.6	6.3	18.8			
Luxembourg, 1947	24.9	0.0	39.7	19.2		16.2			
Belgium, 1930	17.0	5.9	41.9	14.5	6.8	13.9			
Netherlands, 1947	19.3	1.3	32.0	14.1	6.2	27.1			
Denmark, 1940	28.5	30.7		12.4	5.8	7.0		14.8	0.7
Sweden,[d] 1945	24.4	1.1	36.7	14.5	7.2	10.3		4.1	1.5
Norway, 1930	35.3	1.7	24.8	12.5	9.3	1.5	4.1	10.2	0.4
Finland, 1940	57.4	0.1	18.4	5.5	3.5	15.1			
Germany, 1939	26.1	2.0	40.1	10.0	5.5	9.4		7.0	—
Western Germany, 1946	29.1	38.5		15.4		13.0		3.9	

(*Continued on facing page*)

Europe use more than a half, and often more than two thirds, of their labor force in agriculture. Indeed, in countries representing more than half of mankind (an aggregate population of 1.3 billion) production of daily bread occupies more persons than all other pursuits combined.

Thus, at one extreme, a farmer produces enough food for his own household and four or five other families, while at the other, the surplus output of three or four farmers is required to support one family off the farm.

The Share of Mining and Manufacturing

The highest proportion of the labor force engaged in mining and manufacturing (including handicrafts, building construction, electricity, water and gas) is recorded in Belgium (47.8 per cent), Great Britain (46.1 per cent), Switzerland (43.5 per cent), Germany (42.1 per cent in 1939) and Luxembourg (39.7 per cent). Next come Sweden, Czechoslovakia and Australia. The United States is in the group with Canada, the Netherlands, Denmark and Austria; in all these countries from 30 to 35 per cent of the labor force is engaged in mining and manufacturing, including handicrafts and building construction.

Apart from production for export, the industrial plant in most modern countries absorbs approximately a third of the labor force, so that

TABLE 169—*continued*

Country and Year [a]	Agriculture, Forestry, Fishing	Mining	Manufacturing and Construction	Trade	Transportation, Communication	Government, Armed Forces	Professions	Personal and Domestic Service	Other and Unknown
Poland, 1931	65.0	1.2	15.7	5.4	2.3	2.0	2.0	2.8	3.6
Czechoslovakia, 1947	37.8	2.4	35.0	6.4	4.9	10.5		2.7	0.3
Switzerland, 1941	20.8	0.4	43.1	10.0	3.8	7.4		10.3	4.1
Austria, 1939	39.0	0.7	31.4	7.7	5.2	8.8		7.2	—
Hungary, 1941	47.8	1.2	23.5	5.8	3.1	8.0		3.5	7.1
Portugal, 1940	48.9	0.7	20.0	6.2	2.9	5.6		10.3	5.5
Spain, 1940	51.7	1.1	22.6	6.2	3.3	14.9			
Italy, 1936	47.1	0.7	26.8	8.6	3.7	4.7	1.4	3.5	3.4
Yugoslavia, 1931	78.7	11.1		2.6	1.6	4.7		1.3	
Romania, 1930	78.7	0.5	6.7	3.4	1.7	4.6			4.3
Bulgaria, 1934	80.0	0.2	7.7	2.4	1.3	2.2	1.2	2.5	2.5
Greece, 1928	53.7	0.2	15.7	7.6	3.9	1.7	3.1	2.1	12.0
Japan, 1947	52.5	2.0	21.3	7.2	4.4	3.7	3.3	2.5	3.1
Turkey, 1935	81.8	0.2	8.0	2.8	1.5	5.0		0.6	—
India, 1931	67.1	0.2	10.3	5.5	1.5	1.2	1.6	7.3	5.2
Thailand, 1937	88.4	0.3	2.0	4.4	0.8	1.6	—	2.1	0.3
Philippines, 1939	72.9	0.7	9.8	5.2	3.3	0.8	1.7	5.4	—
Egypt, 1937	70.7	0.2	9.8	7.5	2.3	2.8	2.5	4.2	—
Union of South Africa (Europeans) 1946	18.9	6.0	21.4	15.8	13.8		19.7		4.4
Australia, 1947	15.6	1.7	33.3	15.0	9.2		25.2		
New Zealand, 1946	19.9	26.3		14.3	10.2	24.1		4.7	0.5
Hawaii, 1940	30.7	0.1	14.6	10.3	3.5		40.8		

Sources: **3**, 1948, pp. 62–79 and 1949–50, pp. 64–85. For the United States **9**, Vol. II, p. 16 (cf. Table 167); these data do not include unemployed workers without work experience and differ substantially from those reported in **3**, 1949–50, pp. 67–68.

a. Most recent data available.
b. Including persons employed in the Canal Zone.
c. Including unemployed.
d. Because of differences in classification these data for Sweden, 1945 differ from those in Table 168.

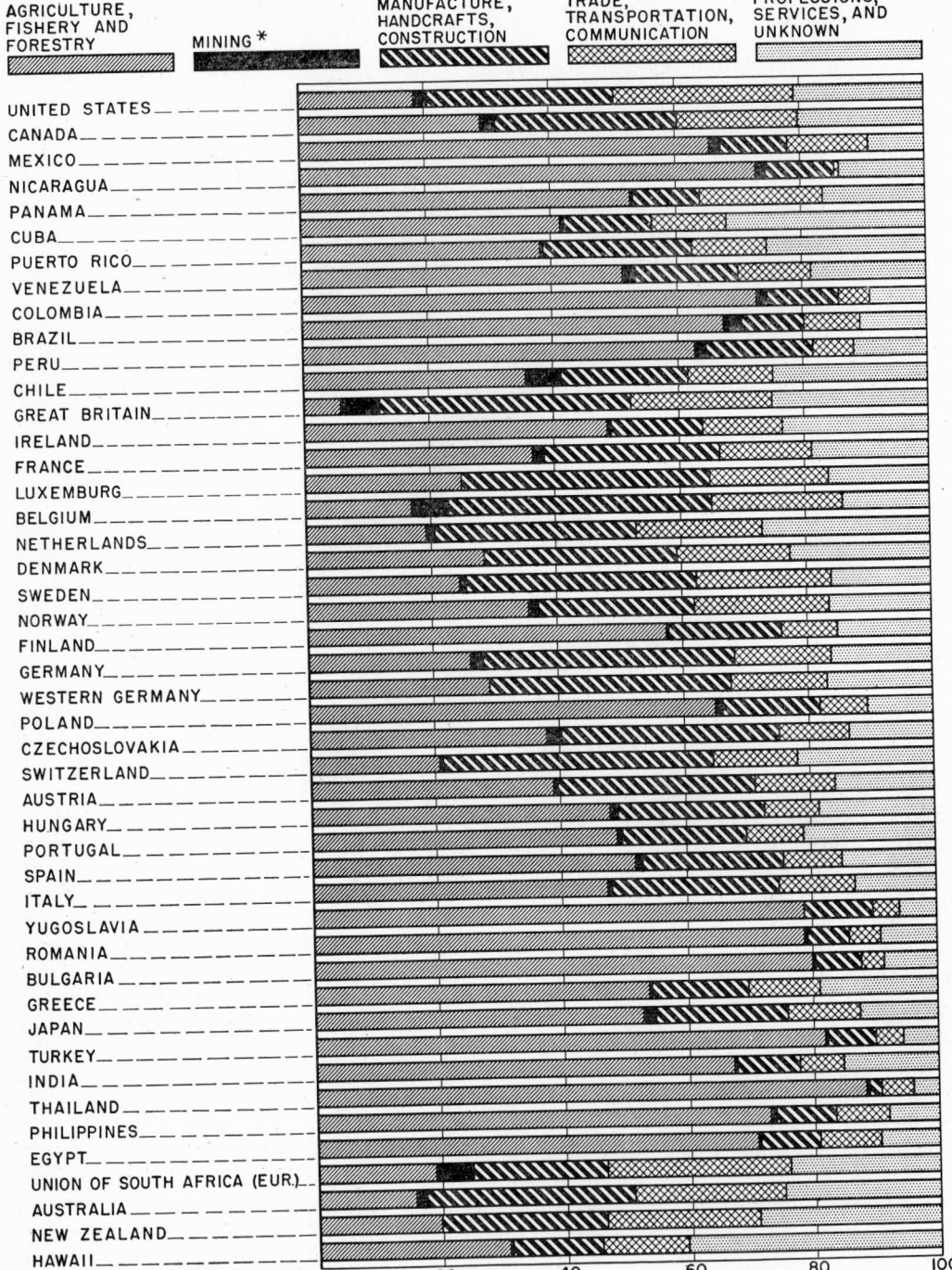

FIGURE 120. LABOR FORCE: DISTRIBUTION BY INDUSTRY, IN SELECTED COUNTRIES
(Most Recent Data Available)

an industrial worker turns out enough goods to satisfy the demand of three families (including his own), to maintain tools and machinery and assure the maintenance and growth of national capital.

In many primarily agricultural countries, such as Mexico, Cuba, Panama, Colombia, Brazil, Egypt and Hawaii, from 10 to 15 per cent of the labor force is engaged in industries and handicrafts. In some countries, however, such as Romania, Bulgaria and Turkey mining and manufacturing, in a broad sense, use less than 10 per cent of the labor force. Occasionally the census reports even fewer workers in these pursuits, as in Thailand, where the rate is 2.3 per cent. In such areas its seems likely that handicrafts and building trades are not differentiated from farming, hunting and fishing and therefore are not counted as separate pursuits.

The Share of Commerce, Transportation and Communication

The proportion of the labor force engaged in commerce, transportation and communication ranges from 5 per cent or less in Colombia, Romania, Bulgaria, Yugoslavia and Turkey to more than 20 per cent in the Netherlands (20.3 per cent), Belgium (21.3 per cent), Sweden (21.7), Norway (21.8), Great Britain (22.7), Australia (24.2), New Zealand (24.5) and the United States (28.9).

In many primarily agricultural countries a large part of the agricultural produce is either consumed directly on the farm or is taken by the farmer to a market in the nearest town. In both cases, the produce remains in the hands of the farmer until it reaches the ultimate consumer. In industrialized countries, on the contrary, farm products travel far before they are consumed and their transportation and distribution absorb more labor than does production.

The share of commerce, transportation and communication in the nonagricultural labor force varies from country to country in a narrower range, usually between 20 and 30 per cent, as illustrated by the following examples: [9]

Industrial Countries	Per Cent
Great Britain, 1931	24.1
France, 1946	23.5
Belgium, 1930	25.8
Netherlands, 1947	25.0
Australia, 1947	28.7

9. Computed from Table 169.

Agricultural Countries	Per Cent
Colombia, 1938	18.0
Peru, 1940	17.1
Poland, 1931	22.0
Bulgaria, 1934	18.5
Turkey, 1935	23.6

The ratio is exceptionally high in the United States: 35.1 per cent.

The Share of Government and the Professions

The proportion of a country's labor force engaged in government depends partly on the political organization of the country and partly on statistical classification. In modern democratic nations, the ratio varies within a comparatively narrow range, from 2 to 5 per cent, not including the armed forces, the size of which is determined essentially by the state of international affairs.

Professional services (in education, in medicine, recreation, the press, science, art, and so on) tend to absorb an increasing share of the labor force as one moves from primitive to industrially developed countries. Such services, for example, employ less than 2 per cent of the labor force in Colombia, Romania, Bulgaria and India, 4 to 5 per cent in Great Britain, Norway and France and 8.1 per cent in the United States (1940).

In view of inconsistencies in separating the "professions" as special industrial and occupational groups from "government" or "public administration," it may be advisable to count both groups together. Their combined share averages about 10 per cent of the labor force in industrially developed countries (United States, Canada, Great Britain, Sweden, Western Germany), and is closer to 5 or 6 per cent in predominantly agricultural nations.

The Share of Domestic and Personal Services

Domestic and personal services represent about the same proportion of the labor force in Great Britain and Chile, Switzerland and Portugal, Austria and Brazil, Germany and India. (See Table 169.) This phenomenon is similar to the trend observed in the United States (see Table 167) and probably is to be explained similarly: the proportion of persons in household domestic service declines while that of the service industries, such as hotels, restaurants, beauty shops, laundries, increases as one moves from predomi-

TABLE 170

LABOR FORCE: DISTRIBUTION BY INDUSTRY OF EMPLOYED MALE AND FEMALE WORKERS IN THE UNITED STATES, BY STATE, 1940

(*Per Cent*)

State	Agriculture, Forestry, Fishing	Mining	Manufacturing	Construction	Transportation, Communication	Trade, Finance, Insurance	Business Services	Personal Services	Professional Services and Recreation	Government	Unknown
					A. Male						
United States	23.5	2.7	24.2	5.9	8.1	19.2	2.3	3.3	5.2	4.2	1.3
New England											
Maine	19.0	0.3	33.4	5.8	7.4	17.2	2.5	3.2	4.7	4.6	2.0
New Hampshire	12.5	0.2	40.2	7.2	6.1	16.9	2.6	3.6	5.2	3.6	1.9
Vermont	31.5	1.5	23.7	5.8	7.1	14.5	2.5	2.7	4.4	4.5	1.8
Massachusetts	3.8	0.1	38.1	6.4	8.1	23.7	2.5	4.1	6.6	5.1	1.5
Rhode Island	3.0	0.1	44.1	7.2	6.1	21.2	2.2	4.0	5.3	5.7	1.1
Connecticut	5.5	0.1	44.8	6.8	5.9	20.1	2.2	3.9	5.5	3.6	1.5
Middle Atlantic											
New York	5.9	0.2	27.5	6.7	10.3	27.1	2.9	4.9	7.3	5.2	1.9
New Jersey	4.2	0.3	36.9	6.9	10.0	23.3	2.6	3.9	5.7	4.1	2.1
Pennsylvania	7.8	9.2	34.2	5.8	9.3	18.4	2.2	3.1	5.1	3.3	1.4
East North Central											
Ohio	14.1	1.8	36.4	5.5	8.8	18.6	2.3	2.8	5.3	3.2	1.2
Indiana	22.3	1.5	31.5	5.5	8.1	17.1	2.2	2.4	5.1	2.9	1.4
Illinois	13.1	2.3	30.0	5.4	10.5	22.1	2.7	3.4	5.5	4.0	1.1
Michigan	14.7	1.1	43.0	5.0	6.1	16.8	2.1	2.5	4.5	3.1	1.0
Wisconsin	31.8	0.3	27.1	4.7	6.4	16.7	2.2	2.1	4.7	2.9	1.1
West North Central											
Minnesota	38.2	1.1	13.2	5.1	8.0	19.5	2.5	2.4	5.4	3.6	1.0
Iowa	43.8	0.9	11.9	5.1	7.3	17.6	2.4	2.0	4.7	2.7	1.5
Missouri	30.2	1.2	18.2	5.6	8.9	20.5	2.5	3.2	5.1	3.3	1.3
North Dakota	63.0	0.6	2.6	2.4	5.5	14.0	2.2	1.5	4.3	3.0	1.1
South Dakota	57.5	1.7	4.8	3.7	4.6	14.6	2.3	1.6	5.0	3.2	1.1
Nebraska	46.2	0.2	7.2	4.8	8.6	18.6	2.6	2.3	4.9	3.7	0.9
Kansas	38.5	3.2	9.6	5.3	9.5	18.4	2.6	2.4	5.3	4.0	1.3
South Atlantic											
Delaware	18.1	0.1	29.9	9.0	9.7	16.5	2.1	3.7	4.4	4.2	2.3
Maryland	13.8	0.8	27.8	7.6	10.3	19.3	2.3	3.5	5.4	7.3	1.8
District of Columbia	1.3	0.1	10.1	10.9	9.6	22.9	2.4	5.4	8.2	27.6	1.4
Virginia	30.4	3.3	20.2	6.6	8.2	13.9	1.6	3.0	3.8	7.8	1.2
West Virginia	18.2	26.6	18.3	4.8	8.6	12.1	1.5	2.0	4.4	2.3	1.2
North Carolina	41.7	0.3	25.1	5.2	4.2	12.4	1.4	2.7	3.3	2.4	1.2
South Carolina	44.8	0.3	23.7	4.7	3.8	11.8	1.2	2.6	3.1	3.1	0.8
Georgia	43.2	0.5	18.4	5.1	5.8	13.9	1.5	3.2	3.3	4.1	1.0
Florida	23.1	0.5	13.7	8.9	8.6	23.8	2.4	6.7	5.8	4.9	1.5
East South Central											
Kentucky	43.4	8.6	11.0	5.0	7.0	12.7	1.8	2.3	3.7	3.1	1.1
Tennessee	41.1	2.0	17.7	5.8	6.4	14.8	1.7	3.1	3.8	2.5	1.1
Alabama	45.7	4.4	19.0	4.2	5.2	11.4	1.2	2.5	3.0	2.5	1.0
Mississippi	64.4	0.3	9.9	4.3	3.6	9.0	1.1	2.2	2.7	1.7	0.9
West South Central											
Arkansas	58.4	1.2	11.0	3.5	4.7	11.1	1.4	2.1	3.1	2.0	1.2
Louisiana	39.5	2.5	14.9	5.9	7.9	16.1	1.8	3.3	4.2	3.1	1.0
Oklahoma	40.1	6.2	8.6	5.0	5.4	18.2	2.5	3.0	5.6	3.8	1.5
Texas	35.9	3.6	11.0	6.5	7.5	19.5	2.4	3.8	4.6	4.1	1.1
Mountain											
Montana	38.0	8.7	8.4	5.7	8.9	15.6	2.4	2.2	4.4	4.5	1.0
Idaho	43.5	5.0	8.8	5.4	7.1	16.1	2.4	2.2	5.0	3.2	1.4
Wyoming	34.4	8.6	5.9	5.7	11.7	13.8	2.3	2.5	4.7	9.3	1.0
Colorado	26.6	5.8	11.4	6.5	9.5	20.7	3.1	3.3	6.4	5.4	1.4
New Mexico	39.0	7.8	5.3	7.4	7.7	16.0	2.5	3.0	5.6	4.1	1.6
Arizona	26.2	10.8	8.1	7.4	8.9	19.4	2.6	4.0	6.3	4.9	1.3
Utah	23.7	8.3	11.6	6.6	11.6	20.3	2.6	2.7	6.5	4.7	1.4
Nevada	17.9	18.0	5.1	8.8	14.2	16.3	2.4	3.9	6.5	5.2	1.7
Pacific											
Washington	17.7	1.1	25.1	7.7	9.6	19.9	2.6	3.0	5.5	6.6	1.2
Oregon	23.2	1.0	24.4	6.7	9.1	19.3	2.8	2.9	5.4	3.8	1.4
California	13.7	2.4	18.5	7.9	9.2	24.9	3.2	4.7	7.8	6.6	1.1

TABLE 170—*continued*

LABOR FORCE: DISTRIBUTION BY INDUSTRY OF EMPLOYED MALE AND FEMALE WORKERS IN THE UNITED STATES, BY STATE, 1940

(*Per Cent*)

State	Agriculture, Forestry, Fishing	Mining	Manufacturing	Construction	Transportation, Communication	Trade, Finance, Insurance	Business Services	Personal Services	Professional Services and Recreation	Government	Unknown
					B. Female						
United States	4.4	0.1	20.8	0.3	3.1	22.3	0.7	25.8	17.3	3.0	2.1
New England											
Maine	1.3	—	31.4	0.2	2.8	16.0	0.4	26.5	16.7	2.7	1.9
New Hampshire	1.0	—	37.8	0.2	2.6	14.4	0.4	22.4	16.6	2.5	1.9
Vermont	2.0	0.1	16.3	0.2	3.6	17.0	0.5	33.6	21.2	3.1	2.5
Massachusetts	0.3	—	33.8	0.3	3.2	20.9	0.6	17.9	18.1	2.4	2.3
Rhode Island	0.2	—	49.4	0.3	2.2	16.4	0.4	14.4	13.3	2.0	1.5
Connecticut	0.6	—	40.4	0.3	2.4	18.0	0.4	17.8	15.9	2.1	2.2
Middle Atlantic											
New York	0.5	—	26.8	0.4	3.4	22.5	1.1	22.1	17.6	2.4	3.3
New Jersey	0.5	—	35.3	0.3	3.4	20.5	0.6	19.2	15.0	2.0	3.1
Pennsylvania	0.6	0.2	30.1	0.3	2.9	21.9	0.5	21.5	16.9	2.6	2.4
East North Central											
Ohio	1.0	0.1	23.7	0.4	3.0	25.6	0.7	23.0	17.6	2.7	2.2
Indiana	1.6	0.1	24.6	0.3	3.0	25.0	0.6	22.8	17.0	2.7	2.2
Illinois	0.7	0.1	24.7	0.4	4.6	27.8	1.1	20.5	16.3	2.1	1.9
Michigan	1.4	—	21.7	0.3	3.2	26.1	0.9	23.0	18.4	2.9	2.1
Wisconsin	5.0	—	19.5	0.3	3.3	23.1	0.6	22.4	20.6	2.8	2.3
West North Central											
Minnesota	3.4	—	10.0	0.3	3.4	28.8	0.8	24.8	23.3	3.3	1.9
Iowa	3.2	—	9.7	0.4	3.6	26.3	0.7	25.9	24.6	2.8	2.8
Missouri	2.3	—	21.0	0.3	3.6	25.6	0.7	25.3	17.0	2.5	1.7
North Dakota	5.9	—	2.2	0.1	3.1	21.6	0.4	28.9	29.2	6.2	2.5
South Dakota	5.6	0.1	3.5	0.2	3.2	24.6	0.5	24.1	29.9	5.8	2.5
Nebraska	3.0	—	5.4	0.3	4.6	27.5	0.7	26.3	25.9	4.4	1.8
Kansas	3.3	0.2	7.1	0.3	4.4	26.4	0.5	27.0	24.5	4.1	2.2
South Atlantic											
Delaware	1.7	—	25.9	0.5	2.0	19.1	0.5	29.4	15.1	2.4	3.2
Maryland	1.3	—	21.4	0.3	3.2	21.8	0.5	28.4	15.5	4.8	2.8
District of Columbia	0.1	—	2.7	0.3	3.1	17.7	0.6	28.9	14.3	31.0	1.4
Virginia	4.6	0.1	19.9	0.3	2.5	16.2	0.3	34.5	15.7	4.5	1.6
West Virginia	2.5	0.6	14.9	0.3	2.9	21.3	0.4	30.2	20.7	3.8	2.3
North Carolina	11.1	—	32.2	0.2	1.2	9.9	0.2	29.3	12.7	1.7	1.5
South Carolina	27.2	—	20.7	0.1	0.8	7.7	0.1	30.3	10.6	1.5	1.0
Georgia	13.5	—	18.9	0.2	1.9	12.3	0.3	38.8	11.2	1.7	1.2
Florida	8.6	—	6.9	0.3	1.9	22.5	0.4	42.3	13.3	2.2	1.5
East South Central											
Kentucky	4.1	0.2	15.9	0.3	2.9	21.6	0.5	32.1	17.4	3.0	2.0
Tennessee	6.3	—	20.3	0.2	2.2	17.1	0.4	35.3	14.5	2.3	1.4
Alabama	21.3	0.1	12.1	0.2	1.5	11.9	0.2	36.8	12.4	2.1	1.4
Mississippi	37.9	—	6.8	0.1	1.1	9.4	0.1	31.2	10.4	1.8	1.2
West South Central											
Arkansas	18.1	0.1	4.5	0.2	2.1	17.6	0.3	36.4	15.8	3.2	1.9
Louisiana	13.1	0.2	6.4	0.2	2.3	18.1	0.3	40.4	15.1	2.6	1.1
Oklahoma	4.4	1.6	3.8	0.3	3.5	26.6	0.6	31.3	21.6	4.0	2.4
Texas	8.1	0.3	5.8	0.3	3.0	23.9	0.5	37.4	16.9	2.4	1.4
Mountain											
Montana	4.9	0.4	2.5	0.2	3.6	27.4	0.6	24.1	27.5	6.2	2.4
Idaho	4.2	0.2	3.4	0.2	4.1	28.6	0.6	25.6	25.2	5.3	2.6
Wyoming	4.2	0.4	2.0	0.2	3.6	25.7	0.7	27.2	28.1	6.2	1.6
Colorado	2.5	0.2	6.0	0.3	4.0	29.0	1.0	25.7	24.5	4.3	2.4
New Mexico	4.6	0.2	11.0	0.2	2.4	19.9	0.5	29.2	23.8	6.0	2.1
Arizona	5.6	0.3	9.4	0.3	2.4	23.5	0.5	29.5	22.3	4.4	1.8
Utah	1.4	0.3	8.3	0.2	5.8	30.8	0.7	20.1	24.4	5.7	2.2
Nevada	2.9	0.7	1.6	0.3	3.7	27.1	0.8	28.7	24.0	7.0	3.1
Pacific											
Washington	3.1	0.1	8.5	0.3	4.2	33.0	1.0	23.3	20.8	3.7	2.0
Oregon	3.5	0.1	8.6	0.3	3.6	31.1	1.0	24.2	21.4	4.1	2.3
California	2.2	0.2	10.6	0.4	4.2	31.4	1.1	23.8	20.4	3.9	1.8

Source: **9**, Vol. II, pp. 107–11.

nantly agricultural to highly developed industrial countries.

Regional Differences in the United States

Regional contrasts in the distribution of the labor force are as wide as national differences. In the United States, for example, the proportion of male workers in agriculture in 1940 ranged from 3.0 per cent in Rhode Island to 64.4 per cent in Mississippi; the share of mines in employment of male workers varied from 0.1 per cent in Massachusetts to 26.6 per cent in West Virginia. For manufacturing, the range was from 2.6 per cent in North Dakota to more than 40.0 per cent in New Hampshire, Michigan, Rhode Island and Connecticut; for transportation and communication, from 3.6 per cent to 14.2 per cent; for commerce, from 9.0 per cent to 27.1 per cent. (See Table 170, A.) The pattern of distribution of female workers among industries is different, but state differences are equally wide. (See Table 170, B.)

A comparison of the distribution of the labor force in particular states of the United States and in foreign countries (see Table 169) shows some similarity between the Middle Atlantic States and Great Britain, while the pattern in some of the southern and central states, such as Mississippi, Arkansas, North and South Dakota, resembles that in Mexico, Brazil and Peru, or southeastern Europe.

Such a comparison is only partly correct, however. That about 40 per cent of the labor force in Iowa is engaged in agriculture does not mean that a farmer in this state produces just enough food to support himself, his dependents and an urban family and a half. Interstate commerce is carried on much more readily and intensively than the exchange of products among nations. A predominantly agricultural region which supplies other areas of the same nation with agricultural products may divert a large part of its labor force to agriculture even though the yield of an average farm is enough to support ten urban families.

Independent Workers and Hired Labor

The labor force of a nation contains several "classes" of workers: employers, self-employed persons, salaried employees and officials, wage earners, unpaid family workers.

The distinction between these groups is not always very clear. A person may be an employer,

an employee and self-employed in the course of a year or even simultaneously. A farmer, for example, may employ hired labor in the harvest season and work for wages in winter. If he runs a grocery store and serves as local postmaster he may be classified as self-employed on his farm, as an employer in the store and as an employee, a public official, when postal operations are carried on in the corner of the store. A salesman or insurance agent working on commission may be classified either as an independent worker or an employee, according to the terms of his contract with the firm. The status of farm tenants is most confusing: some are independent operators, while others work for the landowners and differ little from hired laborers who are paid in accordance with the harvest. At the other extreme, in partnerships and corporations, the owner of the enterprise often appears in statistics as a salaried officer of the firm.

The classes of workers do not necessarily represent layers of an economic pyramid, with employees at the bottom, employers at the top, and self-employed persons in the middle. Salaried employees and officials may be found close to the top of the pyramid, while some "independent" farmers and dealers are close to the bottom.

With reservation for inconsistencies in classification, the proportion of independent workers and of hired workers is an important characteristic of the economic system. A high proportion of self-employed persons indicates the predominance of small enterprises, while a high proportion of wage workers is characteristic of large-scale industry.

National Variations

International statistics of classes of workers are not strictly comparable because of the inconsistency in counting "unpaid family workers" and the considerable number of persons whose occupational status is not recorded by the census. In some countries the last group includes unemployed workers, in others, the armed forces.

Excluding unpaid family workers and persons of "undefined status," we may compare two groups — employers and self-employed, on the one hand, and employees, on the other. (See Table 171.) In most countries hired workers outnumber independent workers. The ratio ranges between 11 to 10 and 12 to 10 in Colombia (1938) and Poland (1931); between 13 to 10

TABLE 171

LABOR FORCE: NUMBER OF INDEPENDENT WORKERS AND EMPLOYEES IN SELECTED COUNTRIES

(*Thousands*)

Country and Year [a]	Total			Agriculture			Other Pursuits		
	Total	Inde-pendent	Depend-ent	Total	Inde-pendent	Depend-ent	Total	Inde-pendent	Depend-ent
United States, 1940	48,027	9,981	38,046	7,855	5,237	2,618	40,172	4,744	35,428
Canada, 1941	3,853	1,036	2,817	966	694	272	2,887	342	2,545
Mexico, 1940	4,326	1,263	3,063	3,131	1,218	1,913	1,195	45	1,150
Cuba,[b] 1943	1,136	656	480	474	403	71	662	253	409
Colombia, 1938	3,012	1,409	1,603	1,912	937	975	1,100	472	628
Peru, 1940	2,117	1,086	1,031	1,240	733	507	877	353	524
Chile,[e] 1940	1,742	443	1,299	620	160	460	1,122	283	839
Great Britain, 1931	18,455	2,453	16,002	1,089	382	707	17,366	2,071	15,295
Ireland, 1936	1,074	360	714	403	263	140	671	97	574
France,[e] 1946	20,520	7,480	13,040	7,130	3,975	3,155	13,390	3,505	9,885
Belgium, 1930	2,855	753	2,102	398	267	131	2,457	486	1,971
Netherlands,[e] 1947	3,365	720	2,645	492	251	241	2,873	469	2,404
Denmark, 1940	1,858	396	1,462	476	206	270	1,382	190	1,192
Sweden, 1945	2,833	588	2,245	607	368	239	2,226	220	2,006
Norway, 1930	1,086	323	763	332	213	119	754	110	644
Finland, 1940	1,361	525	836	537	309	228	824	216	608
Western Germany, 1946	16,309	3,342	12,967	2,982	1,440	1,542	13,327	1,902	11,425
Poland, 1931	9,821	4,532	5,289	4,816	3,332	1,484	5,005	1,200	3,805
Czechoslovakia, 1947	4,678	1,126	3,552	1,091	722	369	3,587	404	3,183
Switzerland, 1941	1,814	421	1,393	298	190	108	1,516	231	1,285
Austria, 1939	2,838	615	2,223	673	340	333	2,165	275	1,890
Hungary, 1941	3,892	1,191	2,700	1,562	790	772	2,330	401	1,928
Portugal, 1940	2,193	627	1,566	1,086	454	632	1,107	173	934
Italy, 1936	14,355	4,895	9,460	5,330	2,875	2,455	9,025	2,020	7,005
Yugoslavia, 1931	3,615	2,130	1,485	2,259	1,770	489	1,356	360	996
Romania, 1930	4,833	3,348	1,485	3,121	2,915	206	1,712	433	1,279
Bulgaria, 1934	1,554	975	578	895	754	141	658	221	437
Japan, 1947	20,355	8,498	11,857	6,250	5,343	907	14,105	3,155	10,950
Egypt,[e] 1937	5,352	1,972	3,480	4,243	1,389	2,854	1,209	583	626
Australia, 1947	3,054	608	2,447	459	286	173	2,595	321	2,274
New Zealand, 1945	578	114	464	129	66	63	449	48	401

Source: **7**, 1947–48, pp. 8–21.

a. Most recent data available.

b. Family workers are counted as independent.

c. Family workers are counted as dependent.

and 19 to 10 in Japan, Finland, Egypt, Italy and France; between 20 to 10 and 29 to 10 in Hungary, Norway, Mexico, Portugal, Belgium, Canada and Chile; and between 30 to 10 and 40 to 10 in Czechoslovakia, Switzerland, New Zealand, Denmark, Austria, the Netherlands, Sweden, the United States and Western Germany. It is 40 to 10 in Australia and 65 to 10 in Great Britain.

With a few exceptions, due partly to inconsistencies in enumeration, the ratio increases as one moves from agricultural areas to the strongholds of the modern industrial economy.

In agriculture, the proportion of wage workers in the labor force varies from 6.6 per cent in Romania and 15.7 per cent in Bulgaria to more than 60 per cent in countries as different as Great Britain, Egypt, Mexico and Chile. (See Table 172.) There is no clear correlation between economic development and the ratio of hired farm workers to independent farmers. The United States ranks high in the proportion of employees in urban pursuits, while on the farms the proportion of hired workers is lower than in Cuba.

TABLE 172

LABOR FORCE: PROPORTION OF EMPLOYEES AMONG WORKERS IN AGRICULTURE AND OTHER PURSUITS, IN SELECTED COUNTRIES

(*Per Cent*)

Country and Year	Agricul-ture	Other Pursuits	Country and Year	Agricul-ture	Other Pursuits
United States, 1940	33.3	88.2	Western Germany, 1946	51.7	85.7
Canada, 1941	28.1	88.2	Poland, 1931	30.5	76.0
Mexico, 1940	61.0	96.2	Czechoslovakia, 1930	33.8	88.7
Cuba,[a] 1943	14.9	61.7	Switzerland, 1941	36.2	84.7
Colombia, 1938	50.9	57.0	Austria, 1939	49.5	87.3
Peru, 1940	40.9	59.7	Hungary, 1941	49.4	82.8
Chile,[b] 1940	74.2	74.8	Portugal, 1931	58.1	84.4
			Italy, 1936	46.1	77.6
Great Britain, 1931	64.9	88.1	Yugoslavia, 1931	21.6	73.4
Ireland, 1936	32.5	85.5	Romania, 1930	6.6	74.7
France,[b] 1946	44.2	73.8	Bulgaria, 1934	15.7	66.4
Belgium, 1930	32.9	80.2			
Netherlands,[b] 1930	48.9	83.7	Japan, 1947	14.5	77.6
Denmark, 1940	56.7	86.2	Egypt,[b] 1937	67.2	51.7
Sweden, 1940	39.3	90.1			
Norway, 1930	35.8	85.4	Australia, 1947	37.6	87.6
Finland, 1940	42.4	73.7	New Zealand, 1945	45.8	89.3

Source: Computed from Table 171.

a. The ratios are underrated because family workers are counted as independent.

b. The ratios are overrated because family workers, especially in agriculture, are counted as dependent.

THE WORLD'S LABOR FORCE

Because of lack of statistics for China, insufficient information on other Asiatic countries and the statistical blackout over the USSR,[10] a precise estimate of the size and distribution of the world's labor force is impossible. The following figures are merely illustrative.

World Total

The ratio of gainful workers to total population averages, for the world as a whole, 40 to 45 per cent. It is closer to 40 per cent — and in some cases less than 40 per cent — in an area comprising more than half of the world's population, in Asia and Africa. It is a sound guess, therefore, that of the total world population of 2.4 billion, as of midyear 1950, the number of gainful workers was close to a billion, in round numbers, including unpaid family workers insofar as they were enumerated by censuses. Of the total some 300 million were women and 700 million, men.

In Agriculture and Other Pursuits

More than half of the world's labor force, probably not less than 530 million persons, were engaged in agriculture and the rest, about 470 million persons, in nonagricultural pursuits.[11] (See Figure 121.) The two groups, however, are not mutually exclusive. Many rural workers, men and women, are engaged not only in agriculture but also in various kinds of handcrafts, such as spinning and weaving, making bricks and adobe, preparing pottery and tools for personal use or for the market.

With this reservation, the distribution of the

10. With a population of 193 million in 1946, the USSR probably now has a labor force of approximately 100 million. Its exact size and distribution by industry are, however, strictly guarded secrets. Only the number of "workers and employees" was given, as confidential information, to the Congress of Soviets. The number was set at 32 million in 1942 and later raised to 32.7 million. This figure does not include the members of 19 million families in "collective" and "soviet" farms, inmates of labor camps, and the armed forces. The last available official statistics on the labor force in the USSR are those for 1926. (See Table 165.)

11. This estimate is based on extrapolation of available information (3, 1949–50, pp. 64–85; and 7, 1947–48, pp. 8–21). The distribution of the labor force of India and Indonesia is applied to Burma, Indochina and China; the structure of the labor force in Turkey is considered as typical for the whole Near and Middle East; the labor force in the USSR is estimated on the basis of the size and probable age structure of its population.

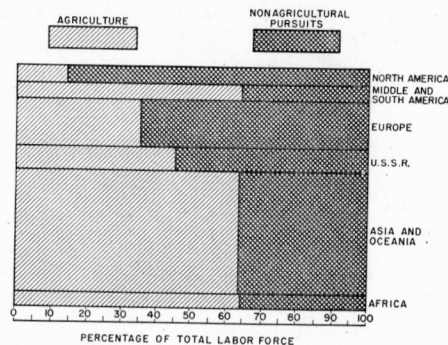

FIGURE 121. LABOR FORCE: DISTRIBUTION OF THE WORLD'S AGRICULTURAL AND NONAGRICULTURAL LABOR FORCE, BY CONTINENT, MIDYEAR 1950

agricultural and nonagricultural labor force among the continents may be estimated as follows (in millions):

	Total	In Agriculture	In Nonagricultural Pursuits
World	1,000	530	470
North America	70	10	60
Middle and South America	70	45	25
Europe	200	70	130
USSR	100	50	50
Asia and Oceania	490	310	180
Africa	70	45	25

About 60 per cent of the agricultural labor force as compared with less than 40 per cent of the nonagricultural labor force is in Asia and Oceania. On the other hand, North America and Europe account for some 15 per cent of the world's agricultural labor force and 40 per cent of the nonagricultural workers.

Independent and Wage Workers

Of the estimated 530 million persons engaged in agriculture, perhaps 390 million are farmers and members of their families and 140 million are hired farm laborers.

Among the 470 million nonagricultural workers in the world as a whole, employees outnumber employers and self-employed persons 3.7 to 1. In all nonagricultural pursuits, the world may have as many as 370 million employees (including public officials and domestic servants) and some 100 million independent producers, dealers and professional workers distributed among the

great industrial divisions, at a rough approximation, as follows (in millions):

	Total	Employers and Self-employed	Employees
All nonagricultural pursuits	470	100	370
Manufactures, mines, handicrafts and building	190	30	160
Trade and transportation	180	50	130
Professional and personal services, public administration and the armed forces	100	20	80

In the World and the United States

The structure of the world's labor force is in striking contrast to that in the United States. Agriculture absorbs only 18.5 per cent of the country's labor force, as compared with 53 per cent in the world as a whole. The United States has relatively more workers in manufacturing, trade and services, and a much higher proportion of wage and salary workers. (See Figure 122.)

HOURS OF WORK

The input of labor in an economic system can be measured either in terms of the number of workers, or in terms of the number of hours worked. The great advantage of the first method, used in the preceding pages, is its simplicity and the availability of international statistics which either give the number of gainful workers in the nation or make it possible to estimate the number with a reasonable margin of error. The second method, however, is preferable for many purposes, as for example, for measuring the productivity of labor.

THE LONG-RANGE TREND

The social issue of working hours does not arise in a society based on independent labor or in one based on slavery; in both, the length of the working day is a technical or personal question.[12] It acquires social significance only in a stratified society.

The Middle Ages

The oldest method of limiting working time is by alternating days of work with days of rest

---

12. **31**, p. 479.

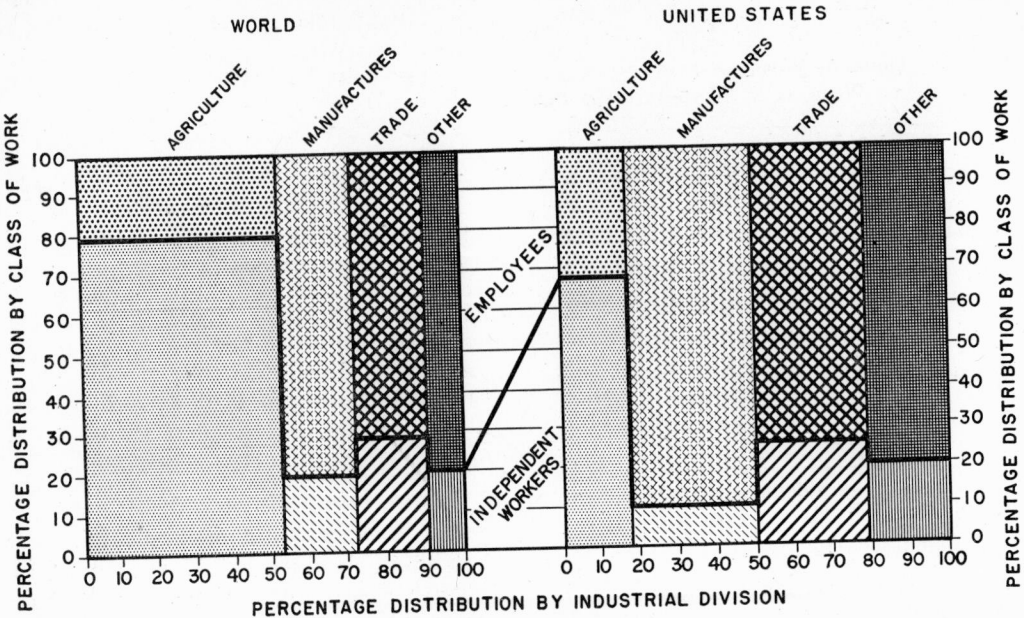

FIGURE 122. LABOR FORCE: DISTRIBUTION BY INDUSTRIAL DIVISION AND CLASS OF WORK, FOR THE WORLD, 1950 AND THE UNITED STATES, 1940

and suspending work on the Sabbath or Sunday and holidays. During the Middle Ages and until the Industrial Revolution in England, work from sunrise to sunset was customary in workshops as well as in the fields. Longer hours of work were unusual at that time because of primitive methods of illumination and the danger of fire inherent in work after dusk. In fact, many cities forbade such work by law. The work week was further shortened by frequent holidays and church celebrations. All in all, a 48-hour week was not unusual in medieval Europe, but the actual duration of the work day varied widely with the season.[13]

Early Capitalism

The rise of capitalism brought longer hours of work. At the close of the seventeenth century, the 10-hour day prevailed in England and continental Europe. The Industrial Revolution and the introduction of expensive machines further stretched the working day. Fourteen hours was regarded as normal in factories and mines at the end of the eighteenth century, and only a "day" of 17 or 18 hours attracted attention as excessive.

13. Legend attributes to King Alfred the Great the saying: "Eight hours' work, eight hours' sleep, eight hours' play, make a just and healthy day."

By the beginning of the nineteenth century, the hours of labor had been extended to the limit of human endurance. It is characteristic of that time that the great social reformer, Robert Owen, defended an 8-hour day in his writings but maintained a work week of 63 hours in his factories. In the 1840's, a work week of 72 hours was customary in England and the United States, while 80 hours and more was usual in continental Europe. Since the middle of the nineteenth century, hours of work have been reduced from decade to decade, partly under the pressure of demands by labor, partly because of changes in techniques of production.

Recent Changes

Although the trend has been toward shorter hours of work, the 48-hour week or the 8-hour day remained a remote ideal of labor until recent years. This goal was proclaimed by British unions in the 1870's and accepted by unions in other countries in the late 1880's — as a long-range goal, rather than a target of immediate action. Not until the turn of the century did the 8-hour work day begin to make its way into industries in the United States, Great Britain, Australia and New Zealand. The movement gained momentum in Europe after World War I and in the United States during the great

TABLE 173

HOURS OF WORK: AVERAGE NUMBER OF HOURS WORKED PER WEEK BY PRODUCTION
WORKERS IN MANUFACTURING INDUSTRIES IN THE UNITED STATES, 1923–51

Year	Hours of Work	Year	Hours of Work	Year	Hours of Work
1923	45.6	1933	38.1	1943	44.9
1924	43.7	1934	34.6	1944	45.2
1925	44.5	1935	36.6	1945	43.4
1926	45.0	1936	39.2	1946	40.4
1927	45.0	1937	38.6	1947	40.3
1928	44.4	1938	35.6	1948	40.1
1929	44.2	1939	37.7	1949	39.7
1930	42.1	1940	38.1	1950	40.5
1931	40.5	1941	40.6	1951	40.7
1932	38.3	1942	42.9		

Sources: **11**, 1951, p. 201; **14**, March 1952, p. S. 12.

depression, when it became part of the social reforms of the New Deal.

At a rough approximation, the trend in weekly hours of work in the United States and Europe during the last century has been as follows:

Year	United States	Europe
1850	72 hours	84 hours
1870	66	78
1890	60	69
1910	54	60
1930	48	56
1950	40	48

These figures, of course, are only approximate averages. At any time and in every country, there has been a considerable range in the work week in different industries and occupations. The trend, however, has been the same in most countries of the world. In terms of hours of work, the exertion required from a worker has been reduced in the last century by a third or more.

The grim emergency of World War II brought this progress to a standstill. Some industrial countries devastated and ruined by the war have been compelled to work overtime. There is little doubt, however, that the trend toward shorter hours of work will be resumed as soon as the pressure of reconstruction is over. It is also fairly certain that the industrialization of underdeveloped countries will be accompanied by reduction in hours of work.

In the long run, the trend toward shorter working hours means simply that people are splitting the advantages afforded by technologi-

cal progress between two goals — increasing material comfort and extending leisure. The ratio of the split is determined by the interplay of numerous factors, such as technological requirements, the balance of social forces and the propensities of a people facing the choice between more goods or more leisure.

SHORT-TERM VARIATIONS

The long-range trend toward a shorter work day and work week is overlaid by hectic ups and downs caused by changes in business conditions — overtime work in prosperity, part-time work in depression. In the United States, for example, production workers in manufacturing industries averaged 44.2 hours per week in 1929, 34.6 hours in 1934, 45.2 hours in 1944, 39.7 hours in 1949 and 40.7 hours in 1951. (See Table 173.) Because of these fluctuations, precise international comparisons of hours of work require analysis of business conditions in the respective countries.

PREVAILING HOURS OF WORK

The 48-hour week now prevails in industrial establishments in most industrial countries. Only two countries — the United States and New Zealand — have firmly established a 40-hour week. In New Zealand, it is accepted in all industries; in the United States, it prevails in most industries, while a work week of 35–36 hours is customary in coal mining and printing and the movement in favor of a similar reduction of hours of work is gaining momentum in many other industries.

TABLE 174

EMPLOYMENT: INTERNATIONAL INDEXES, 1929–47

(1937 = 100)

| | World | | Europe |
Year	Mining, Manufacturing, Transportation and Communication (14 Countries [a])	Manufacturing (20 Countries [b])	Manufacturing (7 Countries [c])
1929	96	94	103
1930	93	84	95
1931	86	75	86
1932	79	68	82
1933	80	72	85
1934	86	81	88
1935	89	85	89
1936	94	91	93
1937	100	100	100
1938	99	99	98
1939	103	106	103
1940	101	106	101
1941	108	115	106
1942	113	123	111
1943	116	133	110
1944	114	133	106
1945	111	122	102
1946	116	119	103
1947	124	129	...

Source: **7,** 1947–48, p. 35.

a. United States, Canada; Great Britain, Ireland, France, the Netherlands, Germany, Poland, Czechoslovakia, Austria, Hungary, Yugoslavia; Japan; Union of South Africa (Europeans only).

b. United States, Canada, Chile; Great Britain, Ireland, France, the Netherlands, Denmark, Sweden, Norway, Finland, Germany, Poland, Austria, Hungary, Switzerland, Italy; Union of South Africa (Europeans); Australia, New Zealand.

c. Great Britain, France, Denmark, Sweden, Norway, Finland, Switzerland.

A 44-hour week is universally accepted in Australia and is stipulated in some collective bargaining agreements in Canada, Great Britain and the Union of South Africa.

A 46- or 47-hour week is usual in most industries in Great Britain; a 48-hour week prevails in Ireland, France, Belgium, the Netherlands, Sweden and Norway, Switzerland and many other countries as well as in manufacturing in such countries as Mexico, Peru, Venezuela and Colombia.

The prevailing work day in Japan is 9 hours and in China (Shanghai), 11 hours.[14]

UTILIZATION OF HUMAN RESOURCES

Perfect utilization of human resources would

require that each individual have an opportunity for the full development of his abilities, as defined on the basis of some objective criterion. It also requires that the available labor force be distributed by industry and occupation in accordance with the abilities of each individual and the requirements of each job, and that continuous employment be assured to each man and woman able and willing to work. No known economic system has attained all these objectives. Our industrial system leaves a considerable margin of freedom to individuals to develop their abilities, choose their occupations, change jobs, shift from one place of work to another. In these respects the United States is probably ahead of the older countries, with their more rigid social structure. Even in the United States, however, access to higher education is

14. **7,** 1947–48, pp. 85–111.

TABLE 175

EMPLOYMENT: INDEXES FOR SELECTED COUNTRIES, 1929–50

$(1937 = 100)$

Year	United States	Canada	Argentina (Buenos Aires)	Great Britain	Germany	France	Nether- lands	Czecho- slovakia
1929	102	104	79	89	96	. . .	109	111
1930	95	99	80	85	90	127	112	108
1931	85	90	78	82	78	118	105	102
1932	75	77	75	81	68	103	93	92
1933	75	73	78	84	71	101	93	84
1934	83	84	83	88	82	98	95	83
1935	87	87	90	90	87	94	92	85
1936	94	91	95	95	93	94	93	91
1937	100	100	100	100	100	100	100	100
1938	94	98	103	98	106	103	104	89
1939	99	100	105	102	112	104	109	57
1940	105	109	102	99	102	. . .	107	59
1941	118	133	107	100	103	92	118	59
1942	130	152	111	101	101	93	115	63
1943	137	161	117	99	104	97	110	67
1944	135	160	123	97	102	92	. . .	67
1945	130	153	123	93	. . .	94	. . .	. . .
1946	135	152	. . .	97	100	100	118	104
1947	141	158	. . .	106	103	105	133	105
1948	144	165	. . .	100 [a]	100 [b]	108	147	. . .
1949	140	165	. . .	100 [a]	103 [b]	109	. . .	. . .
1950	144	168	. . .	102 [a]	107 [b]	110	. . .	. . .

Sources: For the United States, Bureau of Labor Statistics; for other countries, **7**, 1947–48, pp. 33–34 and **8**, July 1951.

a. New series, 1948 = 100.   b. Western Germany, 1948 = 100.

often restricted by financial requirements, and the leading positions in industrial concerns are not always distributed according to the abilities of the candidates. Moreover, even on the lower occupational levels the actual distribution of labor is often determined by chance. What people are actually doing for a living is a sort of compromise between what they would like to do, what they are able to do and what somebody is willing to pay them to do. Our industrial system also has not yet solved the problem of instability and insecurity in employment.

Major Causes of Labor Waste

The main causes of wastage of labor are temporary disability of workers, seasonal variation in the demand for labor, depressions and excessive labor turnover.

Illness and industrial accidents account for about a week of disability per year of work in the countries with favorable health conditions and for much larger losses in other regions. Seasonal variations in the demand for labor are partly offset by fluctuations in the size of the labor force, as in the United States, but in some industries as much as 10 per cent of the potential labor is lost through seasonal slumps.

Unemployment

Major depressions cause much larger losses. (See Tables 174 and 175.) In examining employment indexes of different countries and international indexes computed by the International Labor Office (ILO), one should keep in mind that the basis of comparison is usually the average number of workers employed a particular year (1937 in Tables 174 and 175) rather than full employment of the steadily growing labor force.

It is reasonable to assume that the industrial

labor force in the 14 countries covered by the world employment index of the ILO increased at least one per cent each year, and was 8 to 10 per cent larger in 1937 than in 1929. Since the ILO index had risen only 4 points between these years, employment in the 14 countries had lagged behind the increase in the labor force by 4 to 6 per cent since 1929. Moreover, average annual employment in 1929 — including the last quarter, which was affected by the beginning of the depression — cannot be regarded as representing perfect utilization of human resources. If 95 per cent of the labor force was utilized in that year, hardly more than 90 per cent was employed in 1937. Similar correction should be made for the intermediate years.

The wide range of annual fluctuation in employment in industrial countries shows that, except at the peak of a boom or in a national emergency, the economy fails to use all the available labor force.

The Total Cost of Labor Waste

It is hardly possible to estimate with a reasonable margin of error the wastage of labor through avoidable illness, excessive labor turnover and seasonal and cyclical slumps. Experts disagree in the estimates of work time lost through "avoidable" disability. The concept of excessive labor turnover depends on the definition of the extent of labor turnover necessary for adjustment of the labor force to changing industrial conditions. It can be argued also that in the event of change of job the laid-off worker needs some time to find and choose a new position: a reasonably short interruption between two jobs may be preferable for him to an immediate transfer from one job to another. Obviously, only a part of the work time lost through illness, labor turnover and unemployment can be considered as "waste."

"Waste" thus defined might average — in the past two decades — some 10 to 15 per cent of potentially available work time in industrially developed countries; it is likely to be appreciably larger, possibly twice as large, in underdeveloped regions with poor health conditions and a continuously shifting labor force.

To these forms of waste must be added the waste that occurs when several men are doing work that could be performed in the same time by one man with adequate tools. This waste of human resources deserves close attention.

According to the League of Nations estimate, North America (practically, the United States and Canada) accounted for 19.5 per cent of the world agricultural output in 1934–38, while Asia's share, excluding the USSR, averaged 18.7 per cent.[15] At uniform 1930 world prices, the agricultural output of the two continents amounted to $9.4 and $9 billion, respectively. The first figure represents the return from the labor of approximately 10 million farmers and farm laborers; the second, from more than 300 million agricultural workers. The per capita value of the output of workers engaged in agriculture was slightly more than $900 in the United States and Canada and approximately $30 in Asia. On the average, the produce of a year's work of an American farmer or farm laborer was more than 30 times that of a tiller of the soil in China, Korea, India, Burma and other Asiatic countries. Even with allowance for an underestimate of the output in Asiatic countries, the contrast between them and North America is overwhelming.

It is true that the output of North American farmers depends not only on their own efforts but also on production of fertilizer, gasoline, tractors and machinery and so on. It is also true that the efficiency of the American farmer depends on abundance of land and an intricate system of marketing, transportation, credit, and technical assistance from the government — conditions that are not duplicated in Asia. But it is no less true that the most precious asset of a nation, its labor force, is wasted when ten farm families work on a patch of land that could be cultivated successfully by one family with comparatively inexpensive tools.

In this sense agricultural overpopulation represents a waste of human resources similar to that caused by mass unemployment in industrial countries during a severe depression. The difference is only that in underdeveloped agricultural countries this waste is widespread year after year. Waste of labor force in agriculture is one of the most striking manifestations of the inefficiency of an economic system and, at the same time, one of the most difficult problems for such a system to solve.

To eliminate this evil, fundamental changes in the economic system are required: larger holdings, regional redistribution of crops, im-

---

15. 1, p. 93. This estimate differs from that of the International Institute of Agriculture (cf. Table 206).

provement of means of transportation, development of a market economy, education, improvement in public health and so on. Moreover, elimination of waste of human resources in agriculture serves no useful purpose unless workers freed from the farms can be employed more efficiently in other sectors of the national economy and the increased aggregate output is used to raise the level of living of the people.

VALUE OF HUMAN RESOURCES

What is the value of human resources in comparison with other wealth of a nation? What is the contribution of the human factor to the income of a country, as compared with the contribution of land or capital?

Some students will question the soundness of such comparisons, holding that the economic value of the human factor (the labor force, in a broad sense, including self-employed persons and employers) cannot be segregated from that of other factors of production. Labor, land and capital, they declare, are not additive factors. The economic value of each depends, in fact, on its integration in an industrial system based on specialization and division of labor: the most fertile soil is of no economic value without labor and capital; the most skilled labor force cannot produce much without technical means. The conclusion is that the contributions of the human and technical factors or their relative economic value cannot be measured precisely and objectively.

Yet, in a rough and not wholly objective way, the different factors in production — and among them, the human factor — are continuously weighed, measured and appraised in modern society. They are appraised in the process of distributing the social product and allocating the respective shares to personal effort and to ownership of land and capital.

Petty's Formula

In his treatise, *Political arithmetik,*[16] published in 1691, after his death, Petty approached the question of the value of human individuals from the point of view of a king who owns the land with all that is on it, including its inhabitants. According to this point of view, what a king's subject earns is the king's return, just as

rent is a return of the landowner or interest a return of the capitalist.

Starting from this concept, Petty tried to determine the share of labor in the national income of England. He set that income at £42 million, including £8 million as the rent of the land and £8 million as the yearly return on all personal property. The remaining £26 million appeared to be the result of personal effort or the remuneration of people for their work, whatever their type of activity. Capitalizing the yearly return of the national labor force at an interest rate of 5 per cent, Petty arrived at the money value of the population of England: $20 \times £26$ million $= £520$ million. Dividing this amount by the estimated number of inhabitants — 6 million — his calculation gives a value of more than £80 for each "Head of Man, Woman, and Child," and twice as much for each adult person. "From whence," Petty concludes, "we may learn to compute the loss we have sustained by the plague, by the slaughter of men in war, and by sending them abroad into services of Princes."

American Criticism of Petty

Louis I. Dublin and Alfred J. Lotka have criticized Petty's reasoning, pointing out two defects. The first is the one already mentioned: Petty treats human effort, land and capital as additive items, as if "the contribution of the individual alone could be deduced by the naïve expedient of deducting rent on land and profit of personal estates from the total national income."[17] This, however, is an objection to any evaluation of the labor force, rather than to the particular method used by Petty. The second defect of Petty's estimate is that it rests on capitalization of gross earnings of individuals, with no allowance for the cost of maintaining the individual.

Avoiding these pitfalls, Dublin and Lotka computed the money value of a man measured by the *present* value of his future net earnings, that is, of his gross future earnings less what he will expend on himself. Thus the money value of a man is defined as the actuarial value of that part of his future earnings which will be available for the use of his dependents or will be left to them in the form of his lifetime savings.[18] This approach is of course defensible for certain purposes but there is no reason why this point

---

16. **27.**

17. **22,** p. 9.
18. **22,** p. 169.

of view should exclude the appraising of a man's earning capacity from his own point of view or, in a broader sense, from that of the whole community.[19]

Moreover, whether one capitalizes the net or gross future earnings of a worker, his "money value" will necessarily include the effect of the existing technology and economic organization. If the effects of these factors are included in the money value of the man, there is nothing wrong in Petty's method of appraising the contribution of human effort to national income by deducting from this income rents and profits as income based on property rights, rather than individual effort. If the value of the labor, diligence and skill in a nation is to be compared with the value of its other resources, the best yardstick is the relationship between earnings based on individual effort and those obtained from property. Practically, the application of this yardstick is limited by the almost insurmountable difficulties of disentangling income accrued as a result of personal effort from various forms of capital gains. Therefore, only a very rough appraisal of the contribution of the human factor to national income is possible.

LABOR'S SHARE IN NATIONAL INCOME

The share of the human factor in national income includes not only wages and salaries but

also the earnings of independent producers such as farmers, craftsmen and professional persons and, in general, all entrepreneurial withdrawals insofar as they can be separated from what businessmen get as return on their investment in their own business. Income based on property rights, as distinguished from the remuneration of individual effort, appears in the national income in the form of rent, interest, dividends and undistributed corporate profits.

Distributive Shares of National Income

Statistics which clearly distinguish the "distributive shares" of national income are scarce. In many countries all earnings other than wages and salaries are classified as proprietary income; in others, entrepreneurial withdrawals are merged with wages and salaries and contrasted with income based on ownership of land and capital. When entrepreneurial income is listed separately from employees' compensation and return on capital and landownership, it is difficult to determine what part of it results from individual effort (the human factor) and what part is derived from property. There is therefore a wide margin of uncertainty in statistics showing the share of the human factor in national income, and the following data are offered only as an approximation.

Trend in the United States

In the United States, labor's share in national income has increased in depression years and declined in prosperity,[20] while the share of farmers has been controlled essentially by variations in agricultural prices. (See Table 176.) Apart from these short-term ups and downs, a definite long-range trend since the beginning of this century can be discerned — an increase of the share of salaries and wages and a contraction of all other shares, especially net rents, royalties and interest. (See Figure 123.) This general trend has continued in the last two decades.

During 1947–49, the share of civilian employees (wages and salaries and supplementary payments to labor) averaged 65.1 per cent of national income; pay and allowances of the armed forces accounted for 2 per cent; and rent and net interest together for 5.6 per cent; corporate profits amounted to 9.2 per cent; and income of proprietors (including farmers, self-employed

---

19. Whether the money value of a man is determined by capitalizing his future "net" or "gross" earnings, this value is roughly offset in the balance sheet of the nation by the liabilities he represents: "net" earnings by his future expenses for maintenance of his family, "gross" earnings by his anticipated outlays for the family and himself. By taking too seriously the "netness" of the money value of a man, the dean of Italian statisticians, Corrado Gini, arrived at a striking discovery of the origin of prosperity in the United States. He calculated that the money value of 27.5 million immigrants who were admitted to the country during the 110 years from 1821 to 1930, and did not return to their old homes, was close to $830 billion, in 1930 dollars. This capital, Gini concludes, invested at annual interest of 4 per cent, would have amounted now to $6 trillion! By a series of adjustments he cuts this amount to $1,000 billion (**25**, pp. 8–16). He stresses that this "net" contribution of immigration to the wealth of the United States was several times larger than the total wealth of the United States as estimated by the National Industrial Conference Board (**28**, Vol. I, p. 231). Actually, the whole money value of immigrants has been invested in the running concern of the whole economy of the United States. Their contribution to national income and the increment of wealth in the country have been roughly proportionate to their and their descendants' share in the national labor force.

20. Cf. **32**, Chapter 8.

TABLE 176

DISTRIBUTIVE SHARES IN NATIONAL INCOME, IN THE UNITED STATES, 1929–50 [a]

(Per Cent)

Year	Compensation of Employees	Pay and Allowances of Armed Forces	Proprietors' Income (Unincorporated)		Rental Income of Persons	Net Interest	Corporate Profits [b]
			Farm	Business and Professional			
1929	59.1	0.3	6.6	9.7	6.8	7.6	9.9
1930	65.2	0.4	5.5	9.9	6.8	8.7	3.5
1931	70.0	0.5	5.2	9.5	6.5	10.6	−2.3
1932	75.8	0.7	4.3	7.9	6.2	13.5	−8.5
1933	70.5	0.7	5.5	7.1	4.9	12.2	−0.9
1934	69.7	0.5	4.8	8.8	4.3	9.8	2.0
1935	65.7	0.5	8.7	8.9	4.1	8.1	4.0
1936	66.1	0.5	6.0	9.5	4.2	6.7	7.0
1937	65.6	0.5	7.8	9.2	4.4	6.1	6.5
1938	67.9	0.6	6.8	9.7	5.0	6.6	3.5
1939	66.1	0.5	6.3	9.4	4.8	5.9	7.0
1940	65.3	0.6	6.3	9.8	4.6	5.2	8.2
1941	63.2	2.0	7.0	9.7	4.4	4.2	9.5
1942	62.0	5.0	8.3	9.9	4.3	3.1	7.4
1943	60.7	9.3	7.5	9.6	3.9	2.1	6.8
1944	58.9	12.1	6.9	10.1	3.8	1.8	6.3
1945	58.4	13.1	7.3	10.9	3.6	1.7	4.9
1946	62.0	4.5	8.4	11.7	3.8	1.6	7.9
1947	64.4	2.1	8.1	10.3	3.7	1.8	9.6
1948	64.1	1.9	8.3	10.4	3.5	1.9	9.8
1949	66.8	2.1	6.6	10.3	3.7	2.3	8.3
1950	65.8	2.3	6.1	9.9	3.6	2.4	10.1

Source: Computed from **14**, July 1950, p. 9 and 1951, *National Income* (Supplement), p. 150.

a. National income excluding corporate profits tax and inventory valuation adjustment.
b. Only dividends and undistributed profits (corporate profits after taxes).

businessmen, professional people and so forth) made up the remaining 18.0 per cent.[21] The percentage distribution of national income in 1929 and during 1947–49 by broad groups of payments is as follows:

	1929	1947–49 Average
Total	100.0	100.0
Labor income (allocated to the human factor including the armed forces)	59.4	67.1
Capital income (based on property rights)	24.3	14.9
Mixed income (entrepreneurial withdrawals)	16.3	18.0

21. These rates refer to national income without corporate profit taxes and corporate inventory valuation adjustment and differ therefore from the rates given in **4**, p. 220.

"Mixed income," especially the income of farmers, small retail dealers and independent professional persons (physicians, lawyers, artists and the like), depends much more on individual skill and effort than on the capital these individuals have invested in their business or profession. The capital gain in the gross earnings of a farmer is usually completely offset by the interest he has to pay on his mortgage debt and does not appear in his net earnings as recorded in national income. In many small businesses entrepreneurial withdrawals are little more than the usual remuneration of a salaried manager or professional employee. If the mixed income is divided between the personal factor and the property factor at the rate of 3 to 1, it appears that the total proportion allocable to the human factor during 1947–49 averaged 80.7 per cent of private national income and that based on prop-

TABLE 177

DISTRIBUTIVE SHARES IN NATIONAL INCOME, IN GREAT BRITAIN, 1911–35

(*Per Cent*)

Type of Income	1911	1924–25 Average	1926–30 Average	1931–35 Average
Total	100.0	100.0	100.0	100.0
Labor income				
Wages	35.0	38.0	38.0	40.0
Salaries	14.0	23.0	24.0	26.0
Entrepreneurial and capital				
Government	—	—	1.0	1.0
Rent	10.0	7.0	8.0	9.0
Other	41.0	32.0	29.0	24.0

Source: **17**, pp. 82 and 94.

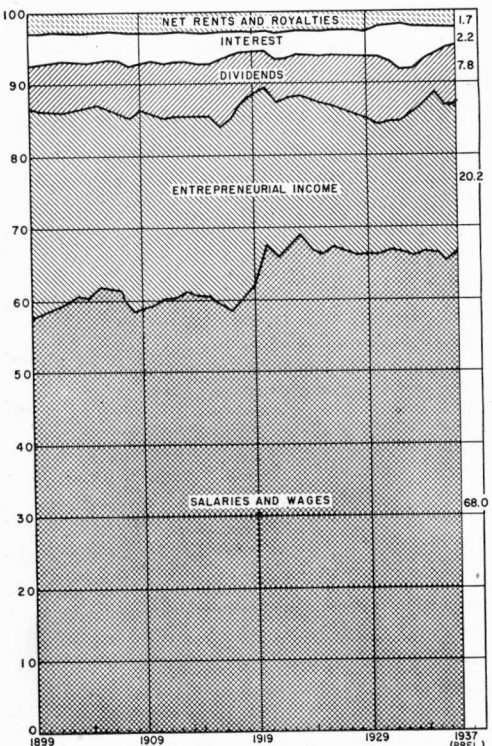

National Industrial Conference Board

FIGURE 123. DISTRIBUTIVE SHARES OF PRIVATE PRODUCTION INCOME IN THE UNITED STATES, 1899–1937

"Private production income," as used here, includes wages and salaries, entrepreneurial income, dividends, interest and net rents and royalties received from private industries and occupations (**26**, p. 18). Wages and salaries amounted to approximately 60 per cent of this aggregate from 1899 to 1917 and to 68 per cent from 1920 to 1937 (*ibid.*, p. 26). The rise during World War I was due mainly to the change in price level and the decline in the farmers' share in national income.

erty rights amounted to 19.3 per cent.[22] Comparable rates for 1929 were 71.6 per cent for the human factor and 28.4 per cent for property.

In this respect the trend from 1929 to 1947–49 was very similar to that from 1899 to 1929.[23] (See Figure 123.) According to Robert F. Martin, the share of wages and salaries (excluding remuneration of the personal effort of independent producers) has represented the following percentages of national income:

1899	1904	1909	1914	1919	1924	1929
57.6	60.4	58.9	60.7	62.2	67.4	66.7

Trend in Great Britain

A similar trend has been observed in the United Kingdom, where entrepreneurial and capital income together accounted for 51 per cent of national income in 1911 and 34 per cent, on the average, in 1931–35. (See Table 177.) Since the income of farmers in the United Kingdom is a comparatively small part of the total, probably the human factor in entrepreneurial withdrawals is not as large as in the United States. Yet some of the income listed by British statisticians in "entrepreneurial and capital income" must be attributable to personal effort. If a fourth of entrepreneurial and capital income

22. It is assumed that all farmers' income and half of business and professional (unincorporated) income are the result of personal effort. These rates are only illustrative. Changing them, however, does not affect our conclusions.

23. **26**, p. 11. Because of differences in classification these data are not strictly comparable to those shown in Table 176.

other than rent is assigned to the human factor, the share of labor in the national income in the United Kingdom amounted to 59 per cent in 1911 and 72 per cent in 1931–35.

According to another estimate, the share of wages and salaries in home-produced income in the United Kingdom increased from 55 per cent in 1911 to 67 per cent in 1930, while that of capital and entrepreneurial income (including rent) declined from 45 to 33 per cent.[24]

More recent trends in the distribution of national income in Great Britain are not very clear in view of changes in the system of taxation and in business practices. Private personal income in the United Kingdom was distributed as follows: [25]

| | *Millions of Pounds* | |
	1938	1948
Total	£4,886	£9,592
Wages and salaries	2,923	6,071
Rent, dividends, interest	1,109	1,479
Mixed income	584	1,379
Transfer income	270	663

| | *Per Cent* | |
	1938	1948
Total	100.0	100.0
Wages and salaries	59.8	63.3
Rent, dividends, interest	22.7	15.4
Mixed income	12.0	14.4
Transfer income	5.5	6.9

Trends in France and Germany

Similar trends were observed before the war in Germany and France. In Germany, wages and salaries, together with social security and relief payments and war pensions, increased from 48.3 per cent of national income in 1913 to 63.1 per cent in 1938; the comparable rates for France were 44.7 per cent and 55.9 per cent. In the same period, the share of proprietary income (interest, dividends and rent) declined in Germany from 19.5 per cent to 11.3 per cent, and in France from 19.6 to 16.5 per cent. Although the figures for the two countries are not strictly comparable, the similarity in trends is striking.

(See Table 178.) The change in labor's share in Belgium and Switzerland has followed a similar pattern.

Agricultural Countries

In predominantly agricultural European countries, exemplified by Hungary and Poland, the prewar share of wages and salaries in national income was comparatively small (less than 50 per cent), but a large part of the social dividend went to farmers. Since farmers' income in this area represents essentially the remuneration for their work rather than a profit from capital investment, labor's share in the national income of these countries appears higher than in industrial nations.

Even higher is labor's share in Chile, a country with a premechanized agricultural and pastoral economy. (See Table 179.) The part of native capital in the national income of that country (excluding the profits of foreign companies) fluctuated between 1.5 per cent in 1931–32 and 9 per cent in 1933–34 and averaged 4.7 per cent in 1929–34. All the rest of the Chilean national income consisted of wages, salaries, earnings of farmers, craftsmen, and professional persons and other forms of entrepreneurial withdrawals.[26]

According to more recent estimates, wages and salaries in Chile (including pay and allowances of the armed forces) averaged 74.8 per cent of national income in 1940–43, while income of all enterprises, incorporated and unincorporated and private and public, amounted to 16.8 per cent, and rent represented 8.5 per cent.[27] This distribution suggests that appreciably more than 80 per cent of Chile's national income was allocated to the personal factor.

Industrial Countries

In most industrial countries of Western civilization, approximately three fourths of the national income serves to remunerate personal effort. The remaining fourth goes to owners of land and capital and includes the imputed value of owner-occupied houses, interest on the national debt and pensions and other items which are not income from capital in the proper sense of this term. The share of the national dividend

---

24. **17**, pp. 82 and 94. The decline was partly due to the loss of British foreign investments, which tend to increase the part of capital gains in the prewar national income of Great Britain.

25. **4**, p. 170.

26. **29**, p. 90.

27. **4**, p. 217.

TABLE 178

DISTRIBUTIVE SHARES IN NATIONAL INCOME, IN GERMANY AND FRANCE, 1913–38

(*Per Cent*)

Type of Income	1913	1923	1928	1933	1938
Germany					
Total	100.0	100.0	100.0	100.0	100.0
Wages and salaries	45.3	—	56.5	55.8	53.6
Social security and relief payments, etc.	3.0	—	11.2	18.3	9.5
Entrepreneurial income					
Farms	12.5	—	7.7	8.3	7.3
Business and professions	20.1	—	16.2	13.8	18.6
Rent, dividends and interest	14.5	—	4.8	6.7	5.1
Undistributed profits and net income of publicly owned enterprises	5.0	—	5.0	2.4	6.2
Other items and adjustments for duplications	—0.4	—	—1.4	—5.3	—0.2
France					
Total	100.0	100.0	100.0	100.0	100.0
Wages and salaries	43.3	47.0	45.4	50.7	50.0
Pensions and relief payments	1.4	2.6	4.1	7.3	5.9
Mixed income (capital and labor)					
Farms	23.2	15.6	19.0	13.0	15.7
Business	11.0	14.6	13.0	8.9	10.1
Professions	1.6	1.8	1.8	2.0	1.8
Income of capital	19.6	18.3	16.7	18.0	16.5

Sources: **15,** 1939, p. 607; **23,** 1937, p. 549, and 1939, p. 560.

TABLE 179

DISTRIBUTIVE SHARES IN NATIONAL INCOME, IN CHILE, 1929–34

(*Per Cent*)

Type of Income	1929	1930	1931	1932	1933	1934
Total	100.0	100.0	100.0	100.0	100.0	100.0
Labor and entrepreneurial income						
Agriculture	26.5	23.1	24.4	31.9	27.1	25.5
Mining, manufacturing and construction	25.4	25.0	22.2	22.2	20.5	21.4
Other private pursuits	29.2	29.9	33.1	29.3	29.4	29.9
Government	13.2	14.5	17.1	13.6	12.4	13.3
Employers' social security contributions	1.7	4.0	1.7	1.5	1.3	1.4
Capital income	4.0	3.5	1.5	1.5	9.3	8.5

Source: **29,** p. 90.

received by owners of the means of production seldom exceeds 20 per cent. This leaves 80 per cent or somewhat more for the remuneration of personal effort, either directly as current earnings or in the form of pensions, interest from savings or the imputed rental value of owned homes.

Changes in Labor's Share in National Income

In a given year, the share of wages and salaries in national income may be affected by changes in prices, harvest, depression, taxes and political factors.

In general, the share of the human factor in national income appears to change with economic progress. It is futile to speculate on its amount in a slave economy or a feudal society. It is probably larger in an economy dominated by independent farms and handcrafts than in the modern system of huge enterprises. It is likely to decline in the period of transition, when independent firms are being crushed by the rising monopolistic concerns, men are blindly displaced by machines, and poverty grows at one pole of the society while wealth piles up at the other.[28] Then a stage is reached at which labor, including the labor of technicians and salaried organizers of production, becomes increasingly important in the life of the community. The available, somewhat fragmentary, information suggests that at this stage the trend in the distribution of national income is reversed: a larger part goes to remunerate the human factor, and a smaller part for income based on property rights.

---

28. This was the pattern of the economic system in Great Britain and part of western Europe at the beginning of the nineteenth century. Karl Marx, in his *Capital*, gave a striking picture of this phase in our industrial system.

CHAPTER 12

ABUNDANCE AND SCARCITY

IN A COMMUNITY CLOSE to the subsistence level, poverty is the common lot. Economic inequality, wherein some people enjoy relative abundance while others struggle for necessities, presumes a higher level of economic development. Economic progress, however, is not necessarily accompanied by accumulation of wealth at one pole of the society and growing misery at the other pole. Patterns in the distribution of wealth and income within a community are not the same in all countries or at all times, and they do not always change in the same direction as mankind advances from poverty to abundance.

On the other hand, the contrast between the poorest and richest countries tends to increase with economic progress: The standard of living of modern prosperous nations is rising steadily, while the lowest limit of poverty does not change appreciably and in the least developed areas most people are living as close to the level of bare subsistence as in prehistoric times.

NATIONAL INCOME

Study of abundance and scarcity requires a yardstick to measure the economic welfare of nations. This task is approached in the same way as measuring the economic condition of a family. To appraise the latter, we must know how much the breadwinner and other family members earn, what their money can buy, and how many mouths it must feed. Similarly, to measure the economic welfare of a nation, we try to ascertain its means of existence per person in the population, in other words, its per capita income.[1]

---

1. Some students believe that income per worker is a better measure of the efficiency of an economic system. As Colin Clark pointed out, "average real income produced per head of the working population is higher in Germany than in France. But income per head of the population is higher in France than in Germany, the simple reason being that the average age of the French population is much higher than the German, and the proportion of dependent children is smaller." (24,a, p. 32.) This argument is not convincing. The ratio of workers to population depends largely on classification of marginal workers, such as unpaid family workers on the farm, children who earn some money after school

MEASURING NATIONAL INCOME

Computation of national income is a highly complicated operation. Success depends on the availability of statistical information on various economic activities in the nation and involves a variety of methodological and theoretical problems. The method of using a single over-all measure of the economic level in a country is rather tricky and requires certain reservations.

Money Units

The first reservation is that national income relates to money and prices and the application of this concept to economic activities which do not produce marketable goods and services presents serious difficulties. Even in the United States it is difficult to measure the farmer's income in terms strictly comparable with those that measure urban incomes. The problem is particularly difficult in the areas where most of the products of farming are consumed on the farm and a subsistence economy has predominance over a money and market economy.

As far as the market economy is concerned, money amounts are added in computing national income in the same way as they are handled in the accounts of a tax collector: each dollar, each pound, each franc of income is counted as a unit, regardless of the economic situation of the man who earned it or the ways in which he spends it. In the budget of a poor family, however, a dollar does not represent the same goods and services or the same amount of "satisfaction" as in the hands of a rich man. The two dollars are equivalent only as money units and only as such are interchangeable.

Similarly, a million dollars in national income in a primitive country does not represent the same amount of goods and services or the same "satisfaction" as a million dollars in a prosperous

---

and so on. This ratio also depends on the extent to which a country permits work by children. Income per capita of population in different countries is therefore more comparable than income per worker.

nation. The two identical sums are comparable only as equal amounts of money.

Because of this fact, national income provides an over-all measurement of the productive activity in a nation but not of the average well-being of people, in the sense of satisfaction of their needs and desires. Indeed, people's needs vary from country to country and depend on such factors as custom and climate. To use the example given by Corrado Gini, a Swede or a Canadian requires heavy and expensive clothing and a well-built and well-heated house, while an Indian or an Egyptian can obtain the same level of well-being with light clothing and makeshift shelter.[2] This difference does not invalidate the concept of national income but shows only that because of the severe environment, a Swede or a Canadian needs a larger income to keep body and soul together than an Indian or an Egyptian. Similarly, under equal climatic conditions, the income the community must produce to meet its needs increases as the needs grow in number and extent. A rise in income reflects the growing productive activities in the community, but there is no evidence that the feeling of well-being (satisfaction) in the community has increased in the same proportion.

Differences in Concept

Another reservation is that the aggregate loosely termed "national income" does not mean the same thing in different countries.[3] The difference is in the scope of goods and services included in national income and in the "netness" of the evaluation, that is, the way of handling intermediate consumption. There are at least four definitions of "national income," each of which is defensible for certain purposes. The national income, broadly defined (with certain duplications resulting from counting intermediate consumption), may be 20–25 per cent more than the net national income included in the narrow definition.[4] The narrowest concept of national income — national income at factor cost — is used mainly in the following pages.

Differences in Scope

In evaluating national income, various countries handle certain items differently. Some countries, for example, list the home housework of married women as a part of national income, but more often this item is omitted. Not all countries include the imputed rental value of owner-occupied houses in their income, but some add not only this amount but also allowance for the service of other durable goods such as furniture and cars. Similarly, there is no universally accepted practice for handling interest on the national debt, transfer payments of the government, social security contributions and benefits, and so on.[5]

The Changing Yardstick

These are minor factors, however, in disparities in estimates of national income. The main difficulty in historical, international and interregional comparisons of national income data is that the money unit is not a stable yardstick for measuring the level of a people's wealth. As a measure of real things — either in production or in consumption — the money unit changes as time goes on. It changes likewise in real value when it crosses the border between two countries. As a measure of satisfaction, it changes even when it passes from one individual to another.

NATIONAL INCOME AT CURRENT AND CONSTANT PRICES

The instability of the money unit as a yardstick for measuring economic activities is partly

---

2. **28**, p. 5.

3. See **3**, pp. 21 ff.; **5**, pp. 5–7; **27**.

4. In the broadest sense, the volume of economic activity in a nation is measured by the value of all goods and services the nation produces at market prices — the *Gross National Product* (GNP). After allowance for depreciation of houses and maintenance of industrial plants, public buildings, roads and the like, has been excluded, the remaining amount represents the *Net National Product,* which may be some 10 per cent less than the GNP. After further exclusion of indirect taxes which appear in the market prices of goods and services,

a new aggregate is found defined as *National Income at Factor Cost.* This is the narrowest concept of net national income. It does not include gifts between persons or transfer payments of public authorities, such as subsidies, pensions, public assistance, and social insurance benefits. Adding these items and making other minor adjustments gives a somewhat wider aggregate *Private Income before Taxes.* For some purposes it appears desirable to distinguish *Personal Income before Taxes* from other private income. Sometimes taxes are excluded from the aggregate and in this way either *Disposable Personal Income* or *Disposable Private Income* (including incomes of private organizations) is determined. In using national income statistics, attention should be given to the exact meaning of the terms. (**5**, pp. 6–7. See **12**, July 1947; cf. *National Income*, Supplement, for more detail.)

5. **5**, pp. 8–22.

offset by the distinction between national income at current (changing) and at constant prices.

In aggregate national income as well as in per capita income, the real goods and services that people produce and consume are represented by prices. When prices (and wages as the price of labor) go up, national income seems to increase; when prices go down, it seems to diminish. The effect of the price factor on national income expressed in money units often overshadows all other factors. Figures showing the money income of a nation therefore become meaningless in periods when prices are rising or falling rapidly. Such figures are equally meaningless in historical comparisons stretching over a considerable period of time. The crucial problem in such comparisons is, therefore, how to eliminate the influence of the price factor on the *nominal* income of individuals and nations and to measure their *real* income.

Adjusting National Income to Prices

In historical series — comparisons between one period of time and another — several approaches are possible. The first is to adjust ("deflate") different types of expenditures or income by appropriate price indexes; the second, to use an index of the volume of production in different industries. Both methods are very cumbersome and have been applied, with varying degrees of success, in only a few countries.[6]

Usually a short-cut method is used. The influence of prices on national income is checked by adjusting ("deflating") the nominal national income by a price index which is assumed to express the over-all change in purchasing power of the national money unit. This assumption is correct when all prices in the country vary in the same direction and at the same rate, but is not valid when prices for different commodities are moving in divergent directions or at different rates.

Suppose, for example, that the "cost of living" index is used as the adjustment factor. This index is supposed to reflect changes in the purchasing power of money spent by a household with definite characteristics — usually a middle-sized urban family with a moderate income. It is likely to be too high or too low for other types of households — for example, farm families or people in high income brackets or families of a different size or composition. Moreover, the available cost-of-living index often relates to a single city and there is no evidence that it correctly reflects the movement of prices in the whole country.[7] In addition, the range of consumer expenditures on which the cost-of-living index is based differs widely from country to country. Some indexes cover a great variety of commodities and services, while others are restricted to a few food items.

The index of wholesale prices is an even less satisfactory correction factor. Apart from the limitations it suffers in common with the cost-of-living index, wholesale prices are often oversensitive to changes in business conditions, and the wholesale price index tends to overstate the effect of the rise or fall of prices on consumers' incomes.[8]

In brief, although the cost of living is a very imperfect measure of the average purchasing power of the national currency unit, in practice historical comparisons of national income must rely on it.[9]

---

6. The Statistical Office of the United Nations (UN) has released a comparison of "real" national incomes in ten countries for 1938 to 1947. For three countries (Austria, Italy and the Philippines), the governments have given no explanation of the method used by their statistical agencies for adjustment. For four others (Argentina, Bulgaria, Greece and Hungary), the agencies that computed real income had to rely on highly doubtful statistics of production. In one (France), the original national income estimates are so rough that deflation cannot add much to their reliability. In only two — Denmark and Norway — are the "real income" figures actually what they claim to be. (**5**, pp. 133–35; cf. **1**, 1950, p. 410.)

7. The Statistical Office of the UN currently publishes cost-of-living indexes of more than 50 countries, but four fifths of them refer to a single city: Argentina is represented by Buenos Aires, Austria by Vienna, Brazil by São Paulo, China by Shanghai, Czechoslovakia by Prague, Egypt by Cairo, France by Paris, India by Bombay, Poland by Warsaw, Portugal by Lisbon, Turkey by Istanbul and so on.

8. It can also be argued that since the ultimate consumer spends most — or all — of his money on the retail market, changes in wholesale prices do not directly affect the purchasing power of the currency unit in his hands.

9. There is no completely satisfactory and workable substitute for this method. Some statisticians have tried to solve the problem in its most general form, developing a procedure for comparison of the purchasing power of the currency unit in two or more "situations" (at different dates in the same place, in different places at the same time, or at different dates and places). These methods, however, require a number of more or less arbitrary assumptions and are not very convincing (see for example **41**, pp. 230 ff.). In the opinion of the

"Real Income"

The nominal national income divided by the cost-of-living index gives of course only a very rough approximation of "real income." When the result of such computation is described as income "at 1929 prices" or "in 1938 dollars," these conventional terms mean simply that the recorded changes in national income at current prices are being compared with the changes in prices for definite groups of commodities or costs of living for definite types of households.[10]

CHANGES IN ECONOMIC PATTERNS

In comparing per capita income in different periods or in different areas, it is extremely important to consider the general pattern of the economy at each time or in each place. Suppose, for example, we wish to measure general economic progress in the United States over the last century. For 1949, we take the official estimate of national income prepared by the United States Department of Commerce. For the middle of the nineteenth century, no official statistics of national income are available, but on the basis of decennial censuses of population and manufactures and with the aid of other more or less fragmentary information, estimates of national income have been computed for the years preceding the decennial censuses of 1800–1900.[11] With reservation for a considerable margin of error, the estimated national income of 1849 can be used for comparison with the official data for 1949. Thus per capita income in the United

States at the two dates can be computed as follows: [12]

	1849	1949
National income, in millions	$2,420	$216,716
Population, in millions	22.4	149.2
Per capita income	$107	$1,455

Immediately the question arises, what is the relationship between a dollar in 1849 and one in 1949? Since there is no price index to bridge the two dates, the time lapse between them must be divided into several periods that can be bridged. In this particular case, two price indexes can be used, one linking the years 1849 and 1926, the other bridging 1926 with 1949. Thus it is found that an 1849 dollar was worth about $2.20 at prices as in 1926 and that a consumer's dollar in 1949 had, in relation to 1926, a purchasing power of only 75 cents. Since the dollar of a century ago represented a purchasing power roughly equivalent to $3 at 1949 prices, $107 in 1849 was equivalent to about $321 in 1949. The conclusion is that the real per capita income has increased more than fourfold but not quite fivefold over the century.

This conclusion is open to criticism, however. Many of the things a dollar could buy in 1849 have long since disappeared from the market and have been replaced by other products. Many goods and services we now buy were unknown in 1849. The displacement of old commodities by new ones usually indicates the preference of consumers; each shift to new articles represents more satisfaction for their money.[13] The method of linking price indexes to one another tends to underestimate this effect of changing patterns of production and consumption on the real value of money. But whatever the purchasing power of a dollar in 1849 as compared with that in 1949, the United States in the middle of the nineteenth century was a predominantly agricultural country with large families and small neighborhood shops. Its people were less dependent on the money economy than they are now and needed relatively less money to satisfy their wants.

There is no completely satisfactory way to reconcile the conflicting factors, and it is anybody's guess whether the real purchasing power of $107 in 1849 was more, or less, than $321 in 1949.

present writers, in intertemporal comparisons (for the same country), the cost-of-living method has at least two merits: it is simple and does not pretend to give more than a roughly approximate measurement of changes in national income. Moreover, the results it provides do not differ much from those obtained through much more elaborate procedures. The United States Department of Commerce has computed the Gross National Product of the country for 1929–49 in constant prices, using more than 400 deflation factors for various items. The series shows an increase of 26.0 per cent from 1941 to 1949 and 59.1 per cent from 1929 to 1949. When the conventional rough method is used and the nominal Gross National Product is deflated by the consumers' price index, the comparable rates of gain are 23.2 per cent and 65.6 per cent, respectively. (**12**, January 1951.)

10. Even with this reservation, this method does not work in periods of excessive price fluctuation as, for example, runaway inflation. At such times, however, all statistics of national income break down.

11. **35.** These estimates are of questionable accuracy and are used here only as an illustration of the method of adjusting national income to changing prices.

12. Table 180.

13. **45,** pp. 182–84.

The longer the period of time covered by historical comparison of national incomes and the greater the changes in economic patterns in this period, the wider is the margin of error in trying to measure real income by adjusting money income to prices.

INTERREGIONAL AND INTERNATIONAL DIFFERENCES

Interregional and international variations in economic patterns are similar to the variations over a period of time. Differences between Alabama and Pennsylvania, for example, are analogous to those that occur over a few decades; contrasts between Belgium and Tibet are like those between two periods in time separated by centuries. Therefore, interregional differences in economic levels may be measured roughly in terms of per capita income, even without correction for difference in prices, but such a comparison becomes meaningless when it is applied without qualification to two countries widely different in economic structure.

The difference between Tibet and a modern industrial nation is, indeed, qualitative rather than quantitative. There, each family produces its own food, clothing, work tools, furniture, shelter, and lives almost wholly outside the market and money economy. Here, each step of each individual is recorded in the flow of national income; he has to pay for each bit of food, each hour of recreation, almost each breath of fresh air; his necessities include even the fare from his home to his place of work and back again. The difference is not in prices but in the patterns of daily life in two different civilizations and different eras.

When China records an annual per capita income equivalent to $17, this figure does not imply that an average Chinese family of five persons lives in the same way as it would live in the United States for $85 a year. Low as the subsistence level in China is, it certainly cannot be equivalent to a nickel a day per capita at our prices. The recorded per capita income of China shows only the amount originated in economic activities measured and rewarded in money-units that are superimposed on the home economy still prevailing in that country.[14]

Since it is practically impossible to estimate with any degree of precision the money value of goods and services produced outside the market and money economy, there are only two

ways of handling the situation. One is to recognize that national income estimates for China and other countries of similar economic structure are incomparable with statistics for modern industrial countries, and for this reason to maintain that estimates of world income and its distribution among continents and countries or groups of countries are meaningless and that comparison should be restricted to nations on more or less similar levels of economic development. The other approach is to try to adjust the national income figures for such countries as China upward so as to make them more nearly comparable with those for industrially developed countries preserving, at the same time, the proper ranking of individual countries of this group and keeping their national income estimates low enough in comparison with more prosperous industrially developed nations.[15] It is a matter of judgment whether the first or the second approach is used. The present writers prefer the second method as one which provides some useful insight into the relationships in the world economy.

TRENDS IN NATIONAL INCOME

Isolated attempts to estimate national income as the general basis of evaluating the fiscal and military capacity of a nation can be traced back to the seventeenth century — for example, in the writings of Sir William Petty. In the nineteenth century, estimates of national income were developed in the United Kingdom (beginning in 1870), France (1860), Germany (1891), Sweden (1851), Belgium (1846) and Italy (1860). Since the turn of the century, and especially since World War I, research in national income has gained momentum, and official or unofficial estimates are now available for more than seventy countries.[16] Annual estimates covering most or all the period from 1919 to 1949 have been made for more than thirty countries.

No nation has entered the stage of history as a land of plenty. The present contrasts between scarcity and abundance have resulted from unequal speed in economic progress, largely in the last century.

EXPERIENCE IN THE UNITED STATES

For the United States several series are available. The official series of the Department of

---

14. Cf. Chapter 13.

15. Cf. **32**, pp. 237–38.
16. **5, 6,** and **1,** 1951, pp. 430–38. Cf. **46**, pp. 153 ff.; **24,b,** pp. 38–162.

TABLE 180

NATIONAL INCOME: TOTAL AND PER CAPITA IN THE UNITED STATES, 1799–1950

Year [a]	National Income, in Millions	Per Capita Income		Year [a]	National Income, in Millions	Per Capita Income	
		Current Prices	1929 Prices [b]			Current Prices	1929 Prices [b]
1799	($677)	($131)	($221)	1932	$ 41,690	$ 334	$ 419
1809	(915)	(130)	(212)	1933	39,584	315	418
1819	(876)	(93)	(180)	1934	48,613	385	493
1829	(975)	(78)	(171)	1935	56,789	453	567
1839	(1,631)	(98)	(206)	1936	64,719	505	623
1849	(2,420)	(107)	(244)	1937	73,627	572	682
1859	(4,311)	(140)	(308)	1938	67,375	519	631
1869	6,827	180	246	1939	72,532	554	683
1879	7,227	147	321	1940	81,347	616	753
1889	10,701	173	398	1941	103,834	780	908
1899	15,364	205	501	1942	137,119	1,018	1,071
1909	26,456	292	580	1943	169,686	1,243	1,231
1914	31,213	319	587	1944	183,838	1,404	1,370
1919	62,945	599	645	1945	182,691	1,309	1,439
1924	67,003	592	634	1946	180,286	1,277	1,124
1929	87,355	717	717	1947	198,688	1,380	1,062
1930	75,003	609	625	1948	223,469	1,523	1,092
1931	58,873	475	535	1949	216,716	1,455	1,068
				1950	238,963	1,593	1,140

Sources: For 1799–1924, computed from **35**, pp. 6–7; from 1929 on, based on official estimates of the United States Department of Commerce (**12**).

     a. Until 1859, rough estimates.   b. Adjusted by cost-of-living index.

Commerce starts with 1929; the preceding decade is covered by the series of the National Bureau of Economic Research (Simon Kuznets); the series of the National Industrial Conference Board (Robert F. Martin) goes back to the first census taken in 1799.[17]

Per capita income in the United States, with adjustment for changes in the cost of living, rose little, if any, in the first half of the nineteenth century. (See Table 180.) With reservation for the doubtful character of the estimates related to so distant a period, it appears that people in the United States were not much better off in 1849 than in 1799. The country was growing rapidly in that half century: its area increased fourfold and its population, eightfold. The group of rebellious colonies on the fringe of the world was becoming the nucleus of a new world power, but the expansion was too rapid to permit the new settlers to improve their level of living appreciably in terms of per capita income. Then came the Civil War, followed by inflation and depression. As a result of all these factors,

per capita income in 1869, adjusted to prices, was only slightly above that in 1799.[18] (See Figure 124.)

In the 1870's, the United States entered an era of rapid economic progress. Per capita income, adjusted to the cost of living, more than doubled between 1869 and 1899 and, after violent fluctuations and a temporary setback in the early 1930's, nearly doubled again between 1909 and 1942. The little group of colonies had become the richest nation in the world.

EXPERIENCE IN OTHER COUNTRIES

Canada

Changes in national income in Canada in the last three decades have paralleled those in the United States. (See Tables 180 and 181 and Figure 125.) Apart from temporary deviations during the depression in the early 1930's and

17. **35**; cf. **10**, p. 14.

18. According to Martin, per capita income increased from $216 in 1799 to $237 in 1869 at prices as in 1926. A change of this magnitude falls within the margin of error of the computation.

TABLE 181

NATIONAL INCOME: TOTAL AND PER CAPITA IN CANADA, 1919–50

| Year | National Income, in Millions | Per Capita Income | | Year | National Income, in Millions | Per Capita Income | |
		Current Prices	1929 Prices			Current Prices	1929 Prices
1919	$3,816	$459	$428	1942	$ 8,373	$ 727	$756
1924	3,867	423	431	1943	9,102	772	801
1929	4,274	526	526	1944	9,741	811	835
1934	3,149	294	373	1945	9,788	809	826
1938	3,986	360	429	1946	9,819	798	788
1939	4,289	382	460	1947	10,916	867	780
1940	5,255	466	542	1948	12,474	975	768
1941	6,594	579	636	1949	13,169	970	735
				1950	14,308	1,044	733

Sources: For 1919–37, **42**; for 1938–50, **15** and **16**, supplemented and corrected on the basis of **1**, 1951. Data for 1903 and 1911 used by Colin Clark (**24,b**, p. 54) seem unreliable to the authors.

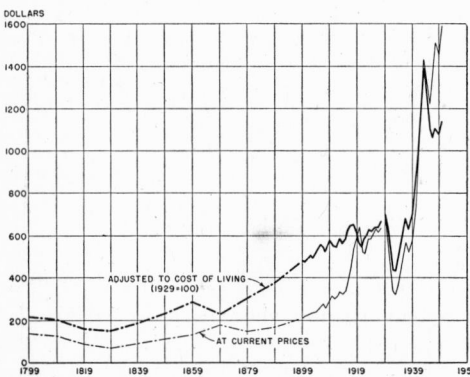

FIGURE 124. PER CAPITA INCOME IN THE UNITED STATES, 1799–1950

In 1869, per capita income in the United States, after adjustment to the cost of living, was only slightly higher than in 1799. The amount doubled between 1869 and 1899 and almost doubled again between 1899 and 1942. (Cf. Table 180.)

during World War II, the correlation between the two countries in per capita income has been very close. The similarity is evident in the ratio (per cent) of per capita income in Canada to that in the United States:

| 1919 | 66 | 1933 | 79 | 1943 | 65 |
| 1929 | 73 | 1938 | 69 | 1948 | 70 |

The United Kingdom

Per capita income in the United Kingdom, expressed in terms of constant purchasing power, lagged conspicuously behind the gain in real per capita income in the United States. In 1870, it

amounted to £24 6s. or $120 at 1900 prices ($164 at 1929 prices), about two thirds of the amount in the United States in 1869. From 1870 to 1920, it increased 93 per cent, while the comparable gain in the United States was 162 per cent. From 1920 to 1946 it rose less than 45 per cent as compared with the 74 per cent gain in the United States. Thus, real per capita income in the United Kingdom is now approximately half that in the United States. (See Table 182.)

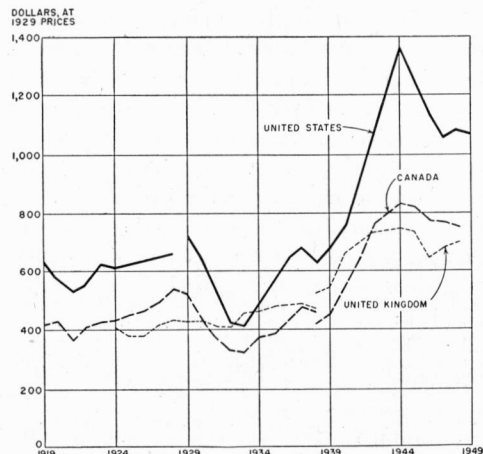

FIGURE 125. PER CAPITA INCOME ADJUSTED TO PRICES IN THE UNITED STATES, THE UNITED KINGDOM AND CANADA, 1919–49

Changes in per capita income in Canada, after adjustment to the cost of living, are very similar to those in the United States. Per capita income in the United Kingdom has fluctuated in a narrower range and has lagged, in the long run, behind that in the United States and Canada. (Cf. Table 181.)

TABLE 182

NATIONAL INCOME: TOTAL AND PER CAPITA IN THE UNITED KINGDOM, 1870–1950

| Year | National Income, in Millions | | Per Capita Income, 1900 Prices |
	Current Prices	1900 Prices	
1870	£ 929	£ 768.4	£24.63
1875	1,085	889.3	27.15
1880	1,073	929.8	26.97
1885	1,118	1,118.0	31.05
1890	1,399	1,430.5	38.16
1895	1,442	1,581.1	40.42
1900	1,756	1,756.0	42.67
1905	1,818	1,798.2	41.84
1910	2,063	1,955.4	43.54
1915	(2,591)	(1,916.4)	(41.66)
1920	5,664	2,078.5	47.56
1925	3,980	2,069.7	45.89
1930	3,957	2,293.9	49.98
1935	4,109	2,615.5	55.77
1936	4,388	2,717.0	57.68
1937	4,616	2,728.1	57.68
1938	4,716	(2,745)	(58.78)
1939	5,012	(2,665)	(61.78)
1940	5,952	(2,951)	. . .
1941	6,839	(3,128)	(64.86)
1942	7,540	(3,422)	(71.97)
1943	8,000	(3,631)	(75.02)
1944	8,224	(3,732)	(76.49)
1945	8,302	(3,710)	(75.71)
1946	8,411	(3,759)	(76.43)
1947	9,226	(4,060)	(82.49)
1948	10,057	(4,164)	(84.00)
1949	10,466	(4,050)	(81.00)
1950	11,196	(4,389)	(87.15)

Sources: For 1870–1937, **39**; for 1938–50, **7**. Figures in parentheses estimated by the authors on the basis of **20, 19,** and **1,** 1951.

Germany

The growth of national income in Germany has been interrupted three times in the last forty years — by World War I, the depression in the early 1930's, and World War II. (See Table 183.) These setbacks wiped out all the gains Germany had achieved through decades of hard work: adjusted to prices, per capita income in 1925 was approximately the same as in 1891. The amount sank below this level in the early 1930's, recovered before the outbreak of the last war, and dropped again after the military collapse of the Reich.

According to the German Institut für Wirtschaftsforschung, the national income of Ger-

many within its postwar borders (west of the Oder-Neisse Line) amounted to $25 billion (62.3 billion marks) in 1947 and $26 billion (64.5 billion marks) in 1949, at 1938 prices. These sums indicate a per capita income of approximately $320 (900 marks) in 1947 and $350 (990 marks) in 1949 at current prices or $250 and $270 (708 and 762 marks) respectively, at 1929 prices. This is approximately two-thirds the per capita income at the turn of the century and probably not much more than what the tiny German princedoms produced per capita of population before Bismarck hammered them together into the formidable empire.

According to an estimate of the United Na-

TABLE 183

NATIONAL INCOME: TOTAL AND PER CAPITA IN GERMANY AND FRANCE, 1891–1950

	Germany [a]			France [b]		
	National Income, in Billions	Per Capita Income		National Income, in Billions	Per Capita Income	
Year		Current Prices	1929 Prices		Current Prices	1929 Prices
1891	M 24.8	M 498	M 1,034	Fr. ...	Fr. ...	Fr. ...
1901	31.3	550	1,074	...	...	...
1911	45.6	698	1,136	...	...	...
1913	45.7	766	1,183	36	900	5,030
1920	...	...	...	110	2,820	4,590
1925	60.0	961	1,043	172	4,240	5,880
1929	75.9	1,188	1,188	245	5,940	5,940
1930	70.2	1,092	1,134	243	5,840	5,550
1931	57.5	889	1,005	229	5,470	5,370
1932	45.2	696	889	206	4,920	5,160
1933	46.5	713	931	199	4,750	5,060
1934	52.7	804	1,023	184	4,390	4,720
1935	58.6	876	1,095	176	4,250	4,980
1936	65.8	978	1,210	195	4,704	5,270
1937	73.8	1,080	1,338	275	6,520	5,880
1938	82.1	1,200	1,481	377	8,480	6,730
1939	89.8	1,305	...	...	...	...
1940	92.5	1,322	...	...	...	...
1941	97.8	1,405	...	...	...	...
1942	98.0	1,400	...	...	...	...
1943	99.0	1,606	...	...	...	...
1944	90.0	1,271	...	...	...	...
1945	...	...	...	...	...	...
1946	48.0	700	543	2,618	61,900	7,440
1947	62.3	900	708	3,303	79,000	5,910
1948	52.0	750	590	5,430	141,000	6,670
1949	64.5	990	762	6,530	160,000	7,000
1950	73.4	(1,080)	(880)	7,395	(163,000)	(7,000)

Sources: **42**; **18** and **17**; **5, 6, 1**, 1951; **4** and **12**. Figures in parentheses estimated by the authors.

a. Until 1938, adjusted to wholesale prices; beginning with 1946, adjusted to cost-of-living index. Earlier estimates are omitted as unreliable.

b. Beginning with 1938, new series; since 1946, national income at 1938 prices. Earlier estimates are omitted as unreliable and incomparable with the more recent data. (Cf. **24,b**, p. 80.)

tions in 1949, the per capita income in Western Germany amounted to $320 as compared with $482 in France, $773 in the United Kingdom and $1,455 in the United States.[19]

France

France's record proves that continuous growth is not a general law in the modern economy, even in a nation on a very high level of economic civilization.

Per capita income in France, adjusted to prices,

showed no visible gain from 1913 to 1936. At 1929 prices, it amounted to $197 (5,030 francs) in 1913 and $207 (5,270 francs) in 1936. (See Table 183.) Apparent gains during 1936–38 are not significant in view of a change in methods of calculation; the old series shows a decline of the adjusted per capita income in these years. In 1947, per capita income in France was roughly equivalent to $200 at 1929 prices, or about the amount before the outbreak of World War I. In 1913 per capita income in the United States was nearly $600 and by 1947 it had increased to more than $1,000, at 1929 prices, while the

19. **4**, p. 15.

TABLE 184

NATIONAL INCOME: TOTAL AND PER CAPITA IN SWEDEN, 1861–1950 [a]

Year	National Income, in Millions	Per Capita Income		Year	National Income, in Millions	Per Capita Income	
		Current Prices	1929 Prices			Current Prices	1929 Prices
1861	Kr 780	Kr 201	Kr 395	1938	Kr 12,240	Kr 1,946	Kr 1,863
1870	950	228	470	1943	18,300	2,817	2,012
1880	1,363	298	564	1944	19,000	2,892	2,080
1890	1,498	313	641	1945	19,000	2,866	2,060
1900	2,238	437	843	1946	22,110	3,296	2,370
1910	3,330	597	1,055	1947	24,060	3,536	2,430
1920	12,837	2,185	1,361	1948	26,730	3,881	2,605
1930	9,324	1,521	1,568	1949	28,030	4,039	2,680
				1950	29,720	4,080	2,686

Sources: For 1861–1930, **42**; for 1938–49, computed from **5, 6,** and **1,** 1949–50, pp. 405–07; corrected on the basis of **7**.

a. For 1861–1930, includes domestic work of women; for 1938–49, gross national product at factor cost.

people in France had very little more than they had had a third of a century earlier.

Sweden

The economy of this tiny country is as dynamic as that of the United States. Per capita income, adjusted to prices, doubled from 1861 to 1900, more than doubled from 1900 to 1938, and has continued to increase since World War II. (See Table 184.) It was equivalent to somewhat more than $100 in 1861, to $225 in 1900, and approached $580 in 1947 (all figures at 1929 prices).[20] Although the amount is less than that in the United States, Sweden has had a higher rate of economic growth during the last 70 years in terms of per capita income and has suffered less from cyclical setbacks.

Other European Countries

Similar data on changes in national income since the turn of the century, with more or less rough estimates for the preceding period, are available for Denmark, Norway, Belgium, the Netherlands, Switzerland, Hungary, Spain, Italy and several other European countries. In all of them a general upward trend in per capita income at constant prices is overlapped by marked fluctuations due to changes in business conditions and to war and its repercussions. Apart

20. Roughly comparable figures for the United States are $308 in 1859, $501 in 1899 and $1,062 in 1947. (See Table 180.)

from these short-term deviations, the pace of long-range growth of real per capita income differs from decade to decade: a long period of economic expansion may be succeeded by a spell of stagnation, followed by a new period of economic progress, as happened in the United States.[21] Continuous progress at a steady rate for several decades as in Sweden, for example, is a rare exception rather than a general rule.

The fragmentary data available for other parts of the world suggest that economic progress in these regions has been as uneven and jerky as in Europe and America.[22]

The Union of South Africa

The white population of South Africa is highly prosperous, while the natives live in a primitive pastoral economy. When the aggregate national product, derived mainly from mining and trade, is prorated among the whole population, per capita income appears rather low in comparison with industrial countries of Europe and America and fails to reflect the level of either major group in the population.

Per capita income in the Union has fluctuated widely in the last 40 years, but increased little

21. Cf. **24,b,** pp. 83–118.

22. In some cases sudden and erratic changes in the real national income in a country may be accounted for by the method of its measurement. In fact, it is measured as the ratio between two values — the nominal national income and the price index — which cannot be established with perfect precision.

from 1911–12 to 1932–33. Since that time it has risen rapidly.[23] The amount, in dollars, at 1929–30 prices, has been as follows:

1911–12	$137	1932–33	$141
1917–18	129	1935–36	188
1920–21	127	1938–39	201
1923–24	143	1941–42	227
1926–27	152	1944–45	213
1929–30	148	1946–47	224
		1947–48	232

Australia

Australia's per capita income is approximately three times South Africa's. The difference lies less in the level of prosperity of the white population in the two countries than in the fact that the whites are a minority in South Africa but constitute nearly all Australia's population.[24] The figures for Australia, in dollars at 1929–30 prices, are as follows:

1901–03	$408	1932–33	$525
1914–15	452	1938–39	539
1917–18	389	1941–42	612
1920–21	423	1944–45	651
1922–23	525	1946–47	690
1926–27	593	1947–48	700
1929–30	569	1949	729

International Comparisons

Despite the pitfalls in international comparisons of national income, such comparisons cannot be avoided if one wishes to visualize the structure and distribution of wealth in the world. Indeed, the concept of *world income* assumes that incomes of individual nations can be expressed in identical units and added together just as incomes of individual persons are added in national income.

National income statistics for 1938 show the structure of world income before the war. The changes caused by the war appear in the data for 1948. To compare the data for the two years, the figures expressed in national currencies should be converted into a single stable currency, for example, United States dollars. For countries in which the free exchange of currency was suspended, the "unofficial" exchange rate or the lowest of the several official exchange rates should be used, so that United States dollars in 1938 will be considered as equivalent to 36 francs in France, 3.3 rupees in India and so on.

A given money amount expressed in dollars or any other common unit, of course, does not represent precisely the same purchasing power in the various countries. But neither does a dollar in the hands of a Mississippi sharecropper possess the same purchasing power as a dollar earned by a business executive in New York. If two such dollars are added in computing national income in the United States; if a franc earned in Paris is handled in the same way as one originating in a fishing village in Normandy; if, in a computation for Brazil a reis earned in Rio de Janeiro is added to one earned in the upper Amazon river — the same technique should be used in estimating the amount and distribution of world income.[25]

PER CAPITA INCOME IN VARIOUS COUNTRIES, 1938

According to the current official and unofficial estimates, per capita income in various countries in 1938 ranged from the equivalent of less than $20 to more than $500 a year, without upward adjustment of recorded figures in the countries in which a considerable part of goods and services are produced outside the market and money economy. (See Table 185.)

The Have and Have-not Nations

Annual per capita income of more than $500 was recorded in the United States, Australia and New Zealand.[26] From $250 to $500 per capita

---

25. Colin Clark has attempted to express national incomes of various countries in "International Units" defined as "the amount of goods and services which one dollar would purchase in the United States over the average of the period 1925–34." (**24,a**, pp. 39–41.) Advantages of this method are questionable. These "amounts of goods and services" are neither produced nor purchased in the poor predominantly agricultural countries for which the International Unit is designated, and it is not very clear what their equivalent is in such countries.

The "ideal" index used for conversion of various currency units into "International Units" is likewise confusing. This index for each country is defined as the square root of the ratio of American prices weighted according to the distribution of consumption in the respective country to the prices prevailing in the United States weighted in accordance with the American consumption pattern. (**24,b**, p. 17.) Because of lack of adequate statistical data, most of the index numbers computed in this way are meaningless.

26. In 1938 the United States had not yet recovered from the depression and its per capita income lagged approximately 12 per cent behind the 1929 peak ($631 as compared with $717 at 1929 prices). This explains the ranking of the United States behind Australia and New Zealand in per capita income in this year.

---

23. **42, 5,** and **6.**

24. For 1901–03 to 1932–33, **42.** For more recent years, **14** and **1.**

TABLE 185

NATIONAL INCOME: TOTAL AND PER CAPITA IN SELECTED COUNTRIES, 1938

Country	Population, in Millions	National Income, in Millions of Dollars	Per Capita Income, in Dollars
United States	129.8	$67,375	$519
Canada	11.2	3,986	357
Mexico	19.1	1,100	58
El Salvador (1940)	1.8	45	25
Honduras (1941–42)	1.1	37	34
Panama	0.6	79	127
Cuba	4.2	400	95
Jamaica	1.1	94	85
Dominican Republic	1.6	64	40
Puerto Rico	1.8	207	115
Venezuela	3.5	440	125
Colombia	8.7	625	72
Ecuador	3.0	250	83
Brazil	39.5	1,990	50
Peru	6.0	370	62
Bolivia	3.3	147	44
Paraguay	1.0	100	100
Chile	4.6	840	183
Argentina	14.3	2,657	186
United Kingdom	47.5	22,100	465
Ireland	2.9	724	250
France	41.1	10,800	260
Luxembourg	0.3	95	285
Belgium	8.4	2,200	262
Netherlands	8.7	2,730	314
Denmark	3.8	1,170	308
Sweden	6.3	2,830	449
Norway	2.9	1,000	345
Finland	3.7	625	169
Germany	68.6	23,000	335
Poland	34.9	3,350	96
Czechoslovakia	10.8	2,000	185
Switzerland	4.2	1,850	440
Austria	6.8	1,051	154
Hungary	9.2	1,500	167
Spain (1939)	16.6	2,875	173
Italy	43.7	5,830	133
Yugoslavia	15.4	2,640	171
Bulgaria	6.2	682	110
Greece	7.1	550	77
USSR	170.0	17,850	105
China	450.0	7,700	17
Japan	70.6	6,070	86
Turkey	17.8	1,060	60
Palestine	1.4	142	100
India	375.4	12,670	34
Ceylon	5.8	260	45
Netherlands Indies	68.0	1,490	22
Philippines	15.8	640	40

(*Continued on page 390*)

TABLE 185—*continued*

Country	Population, in Millions	National Income, in Millions of Dollars	Per Capita Income, in Dollars
Egypt	16.3	$1,034	$ 63
Belgian Congo	11.0	600	55
Nyasaland	1.6	19	12
Northern Rhodesia	1.5	40	27
Southern Rhodesia	1.4	24	17
Union of South Africa	10.0	1,860	186
Australia	6.9	3,825	556
New Zealand	1.6	907	567

Sources: Computed mainly on the basis of national income, price and exchange rate data published by the Statistical Office of the United Nations (**5** and **6**). Data for El Salvador, Honduras, Panama and Ecuador from **24,b**, pp. 158–61.

was characteristic of such nations as the United Kingdom, Sweden, Switzerland, Canada, Norway, Germany, the Netherlands, Denmark, Luxembourg and France.

The group of countries with annual per capita income ranging from $150 to $200 includes Argentina and Chile in the Western Hemisphere and Czechoslovakia, Yugoslavia, Finland, Austria and Spain in the Eastern. The Union of South Africa appears also in this group, although actually its European community is among the most prosperous in the world, while its native population is close to the bottom of the scale.

Next comes a group of countries with annual per capita income between $50 or $60 and $125: Cuba, Puerto Rico, Jamaica, Ecuador, Paraguay, Colombia and Peru; Poland, Bulgaria and Greece; Japan and Egypt. Portugal, though not included in Table 185, also belongs in this group; Panama is on the borderline between this and the more prosperous group, while Brazil and Turkey are probably on the borderline of this group and that of the poorest nations.

The realm of extreme poverty embraces countries with a recorded annual per capita income of less than $50 in 1938 — some countries of Middle America, India, China, the Netherlands Indies, the Philippines, all the Near East except Palestine and Turkey, and the largest part of Africa.

National income reported for some of these countries is obviously understated. Because of inequality in the distribution of incomes, most people get less than the national per capita income. This implies that most people in Nyasaland are supposed to live on less than one dollar per month; most people in China and Southern Rhodesia, on less than $1.50; and most people in El Salvador, on less than $2.00. Even with allowance for the difference in prices and purchasing power of the dollar, this would mean an existence far below the subsistence minimum. The conclusion is inescapable that either there must be some error in the estimates of national income in underdeveloped countries or our concept of national income does not apply to them. Without attempting a correction for the probable understatement of national income in each country, one can group all countries in which national income has been estimated at less than $50 per capita as countries of extreme poverty.

The USSR

The position of the USSR in this classification is not very clear. According to the official statistics, the national income of the Soviet Union in 1938 amounted to 105 billion "rubles at 1926–27 prices." It is not known, however, what this unit was worth in American cents in 1938. If the ruble is valued at more than 20 cents, the Soviet Union was in the group with Czechoslovakia and Finland; if it was worth 15 cents, in the group with Poland and Bulgaria. The available fragmentary information suggests that the standard of living in the prewar USSR was lower than in the neighboring countries, including not only Finland but also Poland, Latvia and Estonia. It is possible, however, that its per capita consumption was low in comparison with its per capita income because of huge outlays for armament and capital formation. This consideration justifies an assumption that the USSR ranked between Bulgaria and Poland in per capita income in 1938.

The Ranking of Countries in Per Capita Income

If countries listed in Table 185 are arrayed by 1938 per capita income and countries for which no such statistics are available are placed close to those on a similar level of wealth or poverty, the nations of the world may be classified by per capita income in 1938 as follows: [27]

More than $500
New Zealand, Australia, United States

$400 to $500
United Kingdom, Sweden, Switzerland

$300 to $400
Canada, Norway, Germany, the Netherlands, Denmark

$200 to $300
Luxembourg, Belgium, France, Ireland

$150 to $200
Union of South Africa, Argentina, Czechoslovakia, Chile, Spain, Yugoslavia, Finland, Hungary, Austria

$100 to $150
Italy, Panama, Venezuela, Puerto Rico, Newfoundland, Bulgaria, Albania, Iceland, Algeria, Morocco, Tunisia, the USSR, Uruguay

$75 to $100
Paraguay, Palestine, Poland, Romania, Cuba, Japan, Jamaica, Ecuador, Portugal, Greece

$50 to $75
Colombia, Egypt, Peru, Turkey, Mexico, Belgian Congo, Brazil

Less than $50
Ceylon, Bolivia, Philippines, Dominican Republic, Guatemala, Honduras, El Salvador, Haiti; India, Netherlands Indies, Indochina, Korea, China; other areas in Asia, Africa, South America and the Pacific Islands not listed above.[28]

This ranking differs in several points from that offered by Clark for 1925–34, the source of the discrepancy being in the methods used in the two computations and the dates to which

they refer,[29] but the general pattern of contrast between the have and have-not nations is the same in both classifications. Moreover, this ranking has not changed much since the outbreak of World War II.

PER CAPITA INCOME IN VARIOUS COUNTRIES, 1948

Statistics of national income have been greatly improved and expanded in the last ten years. Much attention has been given to the conceptual comparability of international income statistics.[30] On the other hand, the statistical blackout in countries behind the Iron Curtain, unsettled political conditions in the East, disorganization of international exchange rates and lack of free circulation of goods in the world make it extremely difficult to evaluate current national income in different parts of the world in a uniform currency. The difficulties were greatly increased in 1949 by the devaluation of currency

---

29. Clark classified countries of the world by real income per capita of the working population, in International Units, as follows:

1200–1400 Units:	United States, Canada, New Zealand
1000–1200	Great Britain, Switzerland, Argentina
800–1000	The Netherlands, Australia
600– 800	Ireland, France, Denmark, Sweden, Germany, Belgium, Uruguay
400– 600	Norway, Austria, Spain, Chile, Czechoslovakia, Yugoslavia, Iceland, Brazil
300– 400	Greece, Finland, Hungary, Poland, Latvia, Italy, Estonia, the USSR, Portugal, rest of America, Japan, Palestine, Philippines, Algeria, Egypt, Hawaii
200– 300	Bulgaria, Romania, Lithuania, Albania, Turkey, Syria, Cyprus, South Africa, Morocco, Tunis
Under 200	China, India, Dutch Indies, rest of Asia, Africa and Oceania

(24,a, p. 54)

In this classification Greece is assigned a higher per capita income than Italy (397 International Units as against 343) on the theory that the purchasing power of a drachma in relation to a lira is nearly double their relative values at international exchange rates. Similarly per capita income for Spain and Chile is corrected upward and that for Norway downward. Figures in International Units used by Clark seem to the authors less plausible than those in dollars in international exchange rates.

30. See **26, 27**; cf. **3, 5, 6**.

---

27. In each group countries are arrayed by declining per capita income as shown in Table 185.

28. Cf. Chapter 13.

TABLE 186

NATIONAL INCOME: TOTAL AND PER CAPITA IN SELECTED COUNTRIES, 1948

Country	Population, in Millions	National Income, in Millions of U. S. Dollars	Per Capita Income, in U. S. Dollars
United States	146.6	$223,500	$1,525
Canada	12.9	11,538	895
Mexico	23.9	2,541	106
Guatemala (1949)	3.7	380	103
El Salvador (1944)	1.9	217	114
Panama	0.7	125	179
Cuba	5.2	1,550	296
Jamaica	1.3	262	201
Dominican Republic	2.2	165	75
Puerto Rico	2.2	600	275
Venezuela	4.6	1,478	322
Colombia	11.0	1,456	132
Ecuador	3.4	134	40
Brazil	49.0	5,530	112
Peru	8.1	662	82
Bolivia	4.0	221	55
Paraguay	1.3	109	84
Chile	5.6	1,013	180
Uruguay	2.3	779	331
Argentina	16.1	5,068	315
United Kingdom	50.0	39,000	777
Ireland	3.0	1,455	485
France	41.5	17,336	418
Belgium-Luxembourg	8.8	5,690	646
Netherlands	9.8	4,756	487
Denmark	4.2	3,280	781
Sweden	6.9	5,600	805
Norway	3.2	1,760	550
Finland	4.0	2,276	569

(Continued on facing page)

in the sterling area. In 1948, nearly all countries had a considerably higher per capita income expressed in United States dollars, than in 1938. (See Table 186.) The gains, however, were largely offset by the rise in world prices: in 1948 a United States dollar in the hands of the consumer represented hardly more purchasing power than 60 cents in 1938. Thus per capita income in 1948 in the United States and Canada ($1,525 and $895) was roughly equivalent to $900 and $530, respectively, at 1938 prices.

With corresponding correction for change in the price level, real per capita income in most European countries in 1948 was below the 1938 level. Real income increased appreciably during 1949–51 under the impact of the recovery, in part accelerated and supported by American aid under the Marshall Plan.

DISTRIBUTION OF WORLD INCOME

The relative economic power of various continents, geographical areas and nations can be characterized in terms of their respective shares in the aggregate world income. The limitations of this method should be kept in sight. "World income" is not a tangible, exactly defined and measurable value but an artificial statistical aggregate, a sum of single items that are not strictly comparable. With all these reservations, however, many experts and laymen feel that this aggregate helps them to visualize some important features of the structure of world economy.

TABLE 186—*continued*

Country	Population, in Millions	National Income, in Millions of U. S. Dollars	Per Capita Income, in U. S. Dollars
Germany			
Western	41.7	$15,000	$360
Eastern	26.0	7,800	300
Poland	23.9	4,504	190
Czechoslovakia	12.3	4,240	345
Switzerland	4.6	4,365	950
Austria	7.0	2,560	368
Hungary	9.2	1,490	163
Spain	27.8	5,063	182
Italy	45.7	10,900	225
Bulgaria	7.0	800	113
Greece	7.8	737	95
USSR	193.0	35,000	181
Japan	80.2	11,523	143
Turkey	19.5	2,796	143
Pakistan (1949)	74.4	5,000	67
India (1946)	346.0	26,000	75
Burma (1946)	17.7	705	40
Thailand	18.0	1,460	81
Ceylon	7.1	561	79
Philippines	19.4	799	41
Egypt (1945)	18.4	2,060	112
Belgian Congo	10.9	380	35
Kenya	5.4	250	47
Northern Rhodesia	1.6	87	54
Southern Rhodesia	2.0	210	105
Union of South Africa	11.8	4,096	347
Australia	7.7	6,256	812
New Zealand	1.9	1,755	933

Sources: Computed from official statistics of the respective countries and data collected by the Statistical Office of the United Nations (**4** and **7**; cf. **8**, Part 2, p. 495).

Before World War II (1938)

In 1938, the aggregate national income of the world probably totaled $260 billion [31] including estimates for countries for which no statistics on national income are available and making allowances for underenumeration of income in China, India, the Netherlands Indies, African colonies and so on.[32] This total agrees fairly well with the estimate prepared by Clark for 1925–34.[33]

For all mankind, per capita income in 1938

31. Of this total $221 billion is for countries listed in Table 185; approximately $20 billion is the estimated total for countries for which no national income statistics are available; and $19 billion is added as a correction for underestimate of income in countries in which the home economy prevails over money transactions.

32. No allowance for underenumeration is made in Tables 185 and 186, which present the widely accepted official and private estimates of national income for the respective countries.

33. Clark estimated the average world total of national income in 1925–34 at 254.4 billion "International Units," that is, United States dollars with correction for assumed difference in prices (**24,a**, p. 56). Since for most countries (except Australia, Norway, South Africa, Sweden and Denmark) the national income figures in dollars were adjusted upward, the total in straight dollars, at international exchange rates, would probably be close to $235 billion at 1925–34 prices or $220 billion at 1938 prices. The discrepancy between this total and our estimate is due largely to the growth of population and income in the world from 1925–34 to 1938.

averaged $120. Puerto Rico, Panama, Venezuela and Bulgaria were closest to this average.

Close to 40 per cent of all world income in 1938 originated in Europe, nearly 30 per cent in North America and as much in the rest of the world. (See Table 187.)

Three countries representing somewhat less than 7 per cent of the world's population (the United States, Australia and New Zealand) enjoyed more than 28 per cent of the world's income in 1938. The next highest income group of twelve countries in the array in Table 186, representing approximately 10 per cent of mankind had 24 per cent. Thus, 16–17 per cent of the world's population had 52 per cent of the world's income.

At the other extreme, more than 60 per cent of the world's population shared less than a fourth of the world's income.[34] (See Figure 126.)

After World War II (1948)

World income in 1948 is estimated at $548 billion, distributed by continent as follows:[35]

	Billions of U. S. Dollars	Per Cent
World, total	$548	100.0
North America	235	42.9
Middle America	7	1.3
South America	16	2.9
Europe	145	26.4
USSR	35	6.4
Asia	86	15.7
Africa	16	2.9
Oceania	8	1.5

From 26 per cent in 1938, the share of the United States in world income increased to 40.7 per cent in 1948 while Canada's share grew from 1.8 per cent to 2.2 per cent. The relative shares of most of the Old World countries went

34. For further discussion of the distribution of income by type of economic system and level of development, see Chapter 13.

35. This estimate rests essentially on the data collected by the Statistical Office of the UN, but the total suggested here differs slightly from that given by the UN in a press release in July 1949 ($531 billion). The discrepancy is due partly to recent revisions made by various countries in their preliminary estimates of national income; in addition, the authors have assumed somewhat higher per capita income for several underdeveloped countries for which dependable national income statistics are not available.

down, with the conspicuous exceptions of Great Britain, Denmark, Sweden and Switzerland.

When continents and individual countries are plotted on a world map on the scale of their income in the same way as they are plotted on the scale of population on distorted population maps, the United States appears to be twice as large as Asia and one and one half times the size of Europe, while the USSR is smaller than the United Kingdom. (See Figure 127.)

The distribution of world income among peoples in different continents is illustrated by the distorted map of world population on which each $5 billion of national income is represented by a dot. (See Figure 128.) The dots are crowded heavily in North America, less heavily in northwestern Europe and are thinly dispersed over South America, eastern Europe, Asia and Africa.

CHARACTERISTICS OF RICH AND POOR NATIONS

The ranking of nations in per capita income reveals definite features characteristic of the have and have-not nations. In examining these features, limitations of national income statistics should be kept in mind.

It should be remembered that figures for per capita income in countries with widely different climatic conditions, customs and economic structure are not strictly comparable. Moreover the amounts are affected by the methods of computation and various short-term factors such as fluctuations in business conditions, prices and exchange rates. Minor disparities in per capita income between individual countries are therefore meaningless. No significance can be attached, for example, to the ranking in Table 188 of Australia ($812), Sweden ($805), Denmark ($781) and the United Kingdom ($777), or of Austria ($368), the Union of South Africa ($347), Germany ($336), Uruguay ($331), Venezuela ($322) and Argentina ($315).

If the methods of computation are modified and a year other than 1948 is used, the ranking of individual countries within these groups may readily change. The same reservation applies to Poland, Spain, the USSR, Chile and Hungary; to Bulgaria, Brazil, Mexico, Southern Rhodesia and Guatemala; to Peru, Ceylon and the Dominican Republic; and so forth.

The second limitation in comparisons of per capita income is that such data are not inclusive. Most of the nations of Asia and Africa are either on the level of the poorest countries listed in

TABLE 187

WORLD INCOME: DISTRIBUTION BY CONTINENT AND AMONG COUNTRIES WITH SPECIFIED
PER CAPITA INCOME, 1938

Continent and Per Capita Income	Population		Income	
	Millions	*Per Cent*	*Billions of U. S. Dollars*	*Per Cent*
Total	2,140	100.0	$260	100.0
Continent				
North America	142	6.6	72	27.7
Middle America	41	1.9	3	1.1
South America	87	4.1	8	3.1
Europe	396	18.5	100	38.5
USSR	170	7.9	21	8.1
Asia	1,138	53.2	45	17.3
Africa	156	7.3	6	2.3
Oceania	10	0.5	5	1.9
Per capita income				
More than $500	138	6.4	73	28.1
$250 to $500	206	9.6	70	26.9
$125 to $250	114	5.3	18	6.9
$ 60 to $125	350	16.4	35	13.5
Less than $60	1,332	62.2	64	24.6

Source: Table 185.

Table 188 or below that level. Data should be extrapolated to include these nations if one wishes to visualize the contrasts between abundance and scarcity in the world.

With these reservations, the ranking of nations by per capita income in 1948 reveals a fairly clear pattern of the contrast between abundance and scarcity, from the United States, Switzerland, New Zealand, Canada and Australia at the top of the list to the Dominican Republic, Bolivia, the Philippines and Ecuador at the bottom, with China, India and the African colonies beyond the lower limit of the tabulation.[36]

General Characteristics

All rich countries enjoy moderate climate; all are located in Huntington's zones of "high" and "very high" energy.[37] All are inhabited by people of European stock, with a strong predominance of northwestern and central Europeans.

Apart from these common features, countries on a similar level differ from one another in size, geographic location, density of population and so on. Both large and small countries appear

at the top of the list (the United States and New Zealand), at the bottom (China, India and Nyasaland[38]), and in the middle (the USSR and Puerto Rico). Similarly, throughout the distribution comparatively young nations are found along with the old. No visible correlation exists between prosperity or poverty, on the one hand, and density of population, on the other. Switzerland, with nearly 300 inhabitants per square mile, has about the same per capita income as Canada with 3.5 inhabitants per square mile. Ceylon, as densely populated as Switzerland, has about the same income level as such thinly populated countries as Peru or Paraguay. (See Table 188.)

Urbanization

As a rule, the degree of urbanization increases as one moves from poor to rich countries, but this correlation is not very close. The highest proportions of population in cities with 100,000 inhabitants or more are found in Australia (47.5 per cent), the United Kingdom (45.2), Argentina (39.4), New Zealand (34.5) and Denmark (32.7). The United States is eighth while Switzerland ranks after Spain.

36. Cf. Table 185, for the year 1938.
37. See Chapter 1, pp. 29 ff.

38. See Table 185.

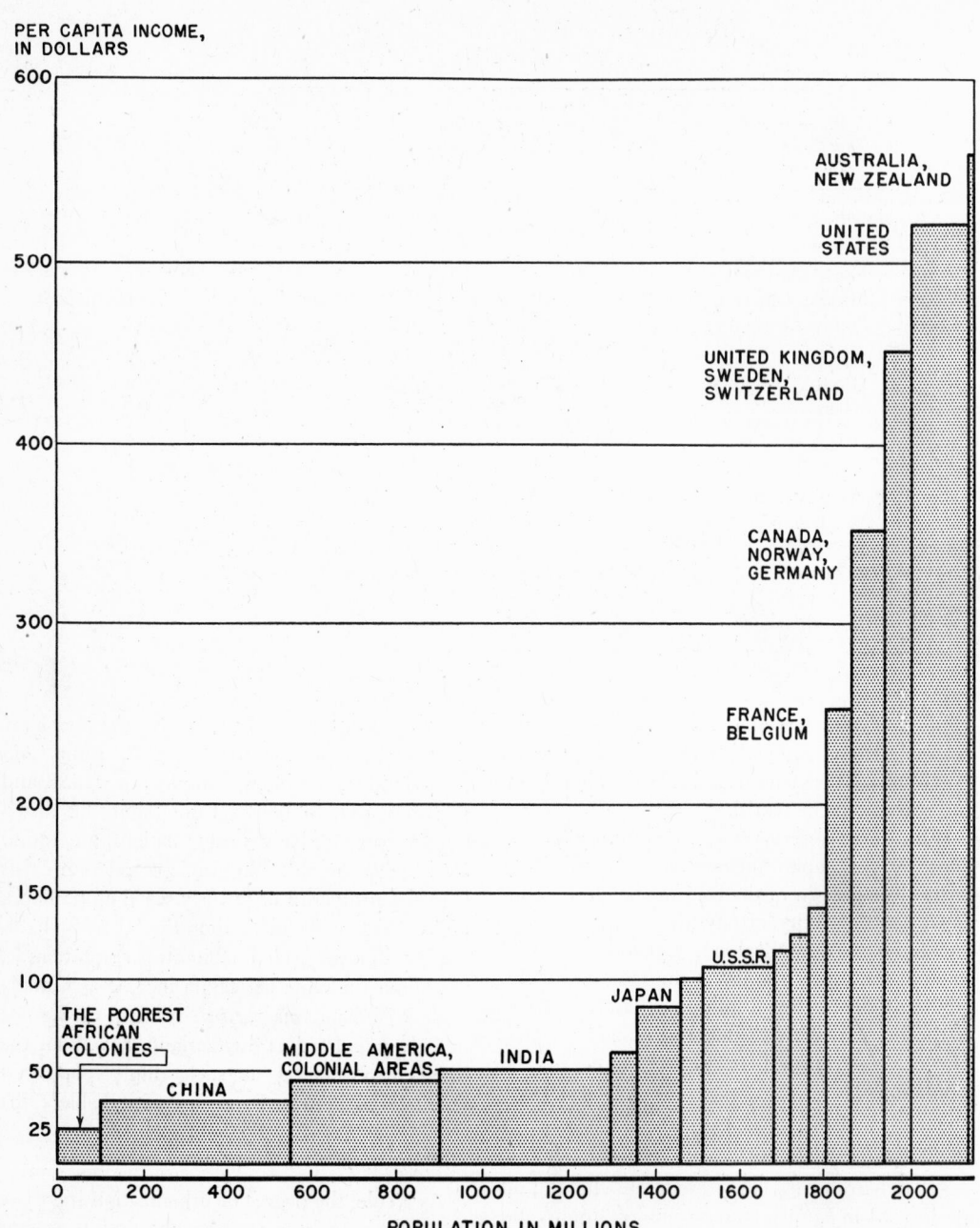

FIGURE 126. WORLD INCOME: DISTRIBUTION AMONG COUNTRIES, 1938

The peoples of the world are arrayed on this chart in accordance with their annual per capita income. The number of persons is shown in millions on the horizontal scale, the per capita income in 1938 on the vertical scale, in dollars. Thus, the income of a nation or a group of nations is proportionate to the surface of the respective rectangle or column. First, at the left, come primitive colonial peoples (100 million persons, with per capita income of $20), then China (450 million, per capita income $35, which is approximately double the official estimate, but still suggests extreme poverty), other underdeveloped countries (estimated 350 million, per capita income $40), India and a few other countries on a similar economic level (400 million, average per capita income $50). Japan ($86) follows some underdeveloped South American countries and Greece. The USSR, with its 170 million inhabitants, is shown with per capita income of about $100. Over each column are the names of countries that are typical of the group.

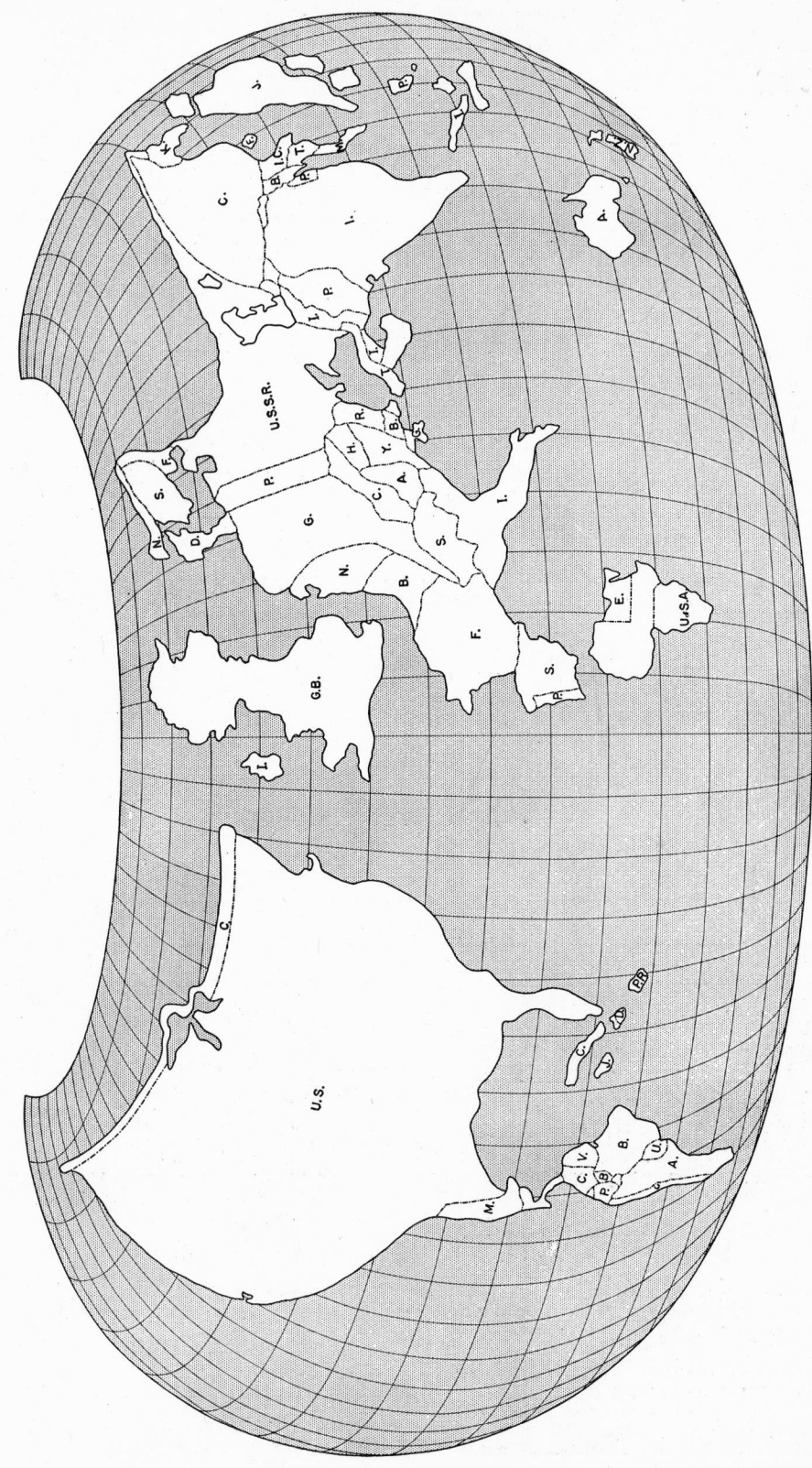

FIGURE 127. GEOGRAPHIC DISTRIBUTION OF WORLD INCOME: DISTORTED MAP OF THE WORLD SHOWING EACH REGION AND COUNTRY ON THE SCALE OF INCOME, 1948

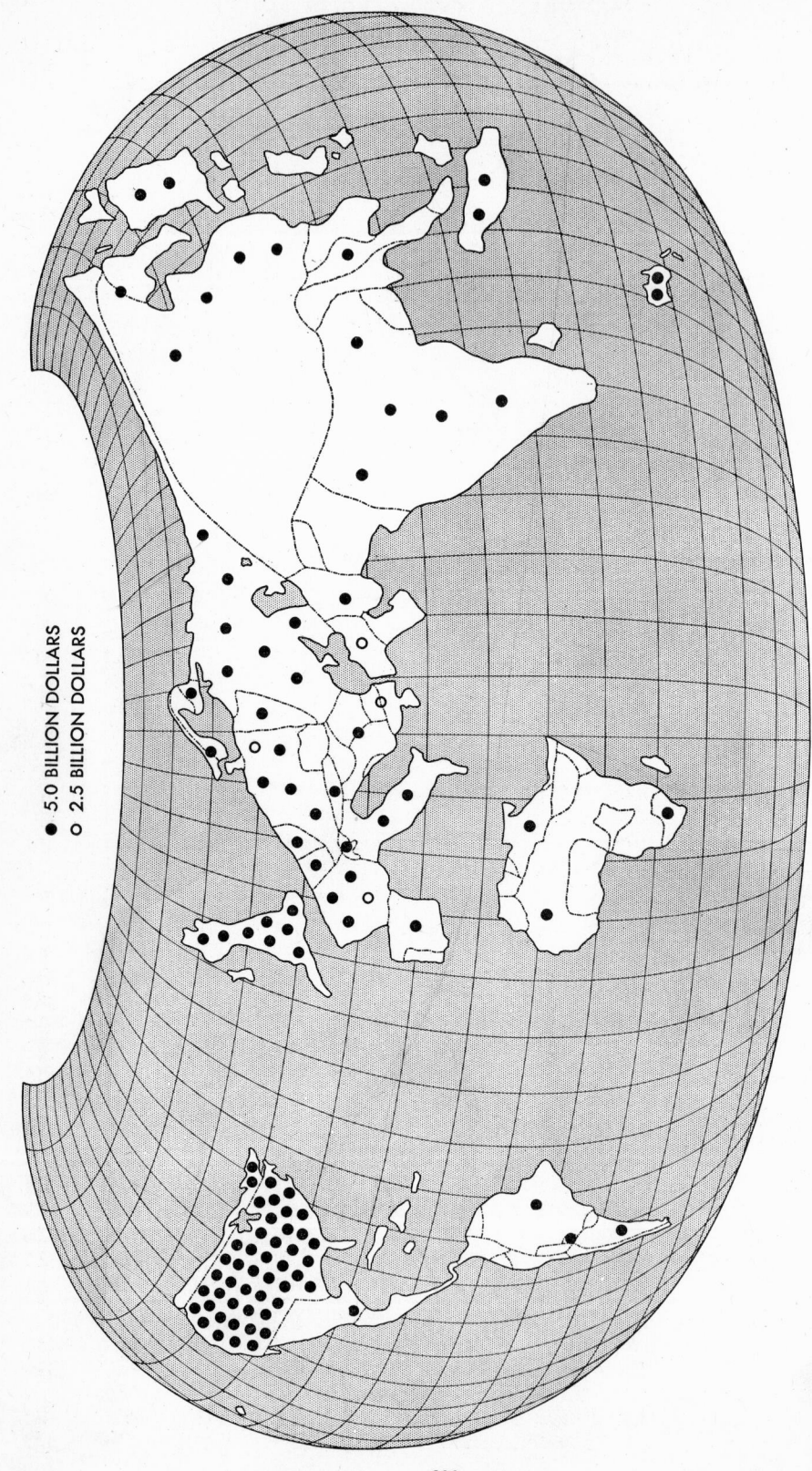

● 5.0 BILLION DOLLARS
○ 2.5 BILLION DOLLARS

Figure 128. Geographic Distribution of World Income: Map of World Population Showing National Income of Each Region or Country, 1948

On this map continents and selected countries are plotted on the scale of their population in 1950. Each dot represents $5 billion, at a rough approximation, and is located in the area where aggregate income of this amount was received in 1948. The density of dots in different parts of the world illustrates the contrasts between rich and poor areas.

398

TABLE 188

PER CAPITA INCOME AND POPULATION CHARACTERISTICS, VARIOUS COUNTRIES, AROUND 1948

Country	Per Capita Income, in U.S. Dollars	Population, in Millions	Inhabitants Per Square Mile	Per cent of Population in Places with:		Births Per 1,000 Inhabitants	Deaths Per 1,000 Inhabitants	Deaths of Infants Per 1,000 Births	Percentage of Children under 15 Years
				Less than 10,000 Inhabitants	100,000 or more Inhabitants				
United States	$1,525	146.6	48.4	52.4	28.8	24.1	9.7	31.1	24.6
Switzerland	950	4.6	287.5	67.0	17.7	18.4	10.7	34.3	22.1
New Zealand	933	1.9	18.3	...	34.5	24.9	9.1	23.8	25.7
Canada	895	12.9	3.5	61.7	23.0	27.0	9.2	42.8	27.9
Australia	812	7.7	2.6	44.3	47.5	22.9	9.5	25.3	25.1
Sweden	805	6.9	40.0	57.8	20.5	17.4	10.0	23.2	21.6
Denmark	781	4.2	247.0	58.2	32.7	18.9	8.9	35.3	24.6
United Kingdom	777	50.0	526.3	25.6 [a]	45.2 [a]	17.0	11.7	34.1	21.4 [a]
Belgium-Luxembourg	646	8.8	677.0	54.1 [b]	22.6 [b]	17.2 [b]	12.9 [b]	57.2 [b]	22.9 [b]
Finland	569	4.0	30.5	52.8	9.3	25.8	11.3	48.3	26.9
Norway	550	3.2	24.0	...	...	19.6	8.8	29.6	23.1 [f]
Netherlands	487	9.8	750.0	29.7	30.3	23.7	8.1	26.8	30.6
Ireland	485	3.0	111.1	...	16.9	21.4	12.7	51.5	27.8
France	418	41.5	198.0	62.0	16.3	21.0	13.8	56.0	21.8
Austria	368	7.0	210.0	...	31.8	15.8	12.6	75.6	21.1
Union of South Africa	347	11.8	25.0	70.4	19.7	27.0 [c]	9.1 [c]	40.1 [c]	31.5 [c]
Czechoslovakia	345	12.3	246.0	73.7	13.7	23.3	11.5	83.2	24.3
Germany	336	67.7	490.6	...	...	16.6 [d]	10.0 [d]	58.2 [d]	24.7
Uruguay	331	2.3	33.0	...	...	20.7	8.9	65.7	...
Venezuela	322	4.6	13.0	...	...	43.3	12.5	99.6	40.9
Argentina	315	16.1	14.9	48.1	39.4	24.4	9.4	79.0	38.4 [e]
Cuba	296	5.2	118.1	...	...	...	...	...	36.4
Puerto Rico	275	9.2	733.3	...	9.0	40.2	12.0	67.6	40.6
Italy	225	45.7	390.6	50.4	16.0	20.0	10.4	74.1	30.9
Poland	190	23.9	196.7	...	...	...	...	...	28.3 [f]
Spain	182	27.8	142.0	51.5	19.2	21.4	11.4	74.1	30.0
USSR	181	193.0	22.4	...	...	...	...	...	36.1
Chile	180	5.6	19.5	...	22.4	33.2	18.1	169.1	37.1
Hungary	163	9.2	255.5	54.3	15.4	19.1	11.2	99.6	26.0
Turkey	143	19.5	65.7	81.8	7.3	...	...	...	41.3
Japan	143	80.2	554.0	...	...	33.2	11.6	62.0	36.1
Colombia	132	11.0	24.9	34.4	8.6	35.1	14.3	136.6	41.9
Bulgaria	113	7.0	166.0	...	...	24.0	13.4	129.5	35.6
Brazil	112	49.0	15.9	5.0	15.9	...	...	...	42.5
Mexico	106	23.9	31.3	73.7	10.2	44.6	16.8	102.3	41.1
Southern Rhodesia	105	2.0	13.2	...	...	27.7 [c]	7.0 [c]	32.2 [c]	...
Guatemala	103	3.7	89.0	31.7	5.6	...	...	109.9	43.6
Greece	95	7.8	157.0	68.2	12.5	27.0	12.4	...	33.0
Paraguay	84	1.3	8.2	...	...	31.7	8.9	52.0	...
Peru	82	8.1	16.7	...	...	25.9	10.8	106.8	42.0
Ceylon	79	7.1	284.0	...	...	39.9	12.6	87.0	37.2

(*Continued on page 400*)

TABLE 188—*continued*

Country	Per Capita Income, in U.S. Dollars	Population, in Millions	Inhabitants Per Square Mile	Per cent of Population in Places with:		Births Per 1,000 Inhabitants	Deaths Per 1,000 Inhabitants	Deaths of Infants Per 1,000 Births	Percentage of Children under 15 Years
				Less than 10,000 Inhabitants	100,000 or more Inhabitants				
Dominican Republic	75	2.2	115.8	88.8	0.0	36.2	9.3	77.3	46.5
Bolivia	55	4.0	9.6	83.6	0.0	30.7	12.7	113.1	...
Philippines	41	19.6	167.2	...	...	...	...	96.0	43.0
Ecuador	40	3.4	31.7	...	...	...	...	122.0	...

Sources: For per capita income and population, Table 187; for density of population, Table 19 (adjusted to 1948); for urbanization, Table 52 and **2**, 1948, pp. 220–30; for birth and death rates, **2**, 1949–50, pp. 288–95, 380–87 and 410–15.

a. England and Wales.
b. Belgium.
c. White population.
d. Western Germany.
e. 1914.
f. Estimate.

Similarly, the percentage of population living in communities with less than 10,000 inhabitants tends to decline with the rise in the level of per capita income, but there are exceptions. The ratio is approximately the same in the United States, Spain and Hungary; in Switzerland and Greece; in the Netherlands and Guatemala. (See Table 188.)

Geographic Location

The ranking of nations by per capita income is headed by countries with easy access to the ocean: the United States, Canada, Australia, New Zealand, Sweden, Denmark, the United Kingdom. But one country — Switzerland — in this top-ranking group is completely barred from the sea. At the other extreme, such maritime countries as Haiti and the Philippines are close to the lower end of the distribution.

In brief, it is difficult to point to any objective and statistically measurable feature related to the distribution of population and its physical environment that can be considered a controlling factor in the level of national economic well-being.[39]

Birth and Death Rates

A more significant correlation exists between per capita income, on the one hand, and birth and death rates, on the other. As one moves from prosperous to poor countries, both birth and death rates tend to increase. In recent years, for example, birth rates have been close to 24–25

per 1,000 inhabitants in the United States and New Zealand and 23 per 1,000 in Australia, as compared with 40 or more per 1,000 in Ceylon, Puerto Rico, Venezuela and Mexico. Death rates have been below 10 per 1,000 inhabitants at the top of the list and 12 to 18 per 1,000 in many poor countries.

The correlation, however, is not perfect. Birth rates in old European countries — Austria, Germany, the United Kingdom, Belgium, Sweden, Switzerland, Hungary, Norway, France — are lower than in the prosperous nations of the New World. In many countries with very low per capita income the recorded death rates are low because of faulty registration. When Paraguay reports 8.9 deaths per 1,000 inhabitants (as compared with 9.7 in the United States, 10.7 in Switzerland and 11.7 in the United Kingdom) the rate reflects the inadequacy of local statistics rather than the enviable health of the population. This is the situation in such countries as the Dominican Republic, Ceylon and Peru. (See Table 188.)

Gaps in registration also affect the infant mortality records in underdeveloped countries. The contrasts, however, are too great to be masked by statistical inadequacies; the death rate among children under one year increases sharply as one moves from rich to poor countries. The infant mortality rate ranges between 25 and 35 per 1,000 live births in the modern industrial countries and rises to 100 and more per 1,000 in the poverty-stricken areas. Whenever a country with per capita income of less than $100 reports infant mortality of less than 100 per 1,000 live

39. Cf. Chapter 10.

births (as in Paraguay, Ceylon, the Dominican Republic or the Philippines) there can be strong doubt as to the completeness of death registration.

The proportion of children in the population is also closely correlated with a country's per capita income. The usual rates are 20 to 25 per cent in prosperous nations and 35 to 45 per cent in underdeveloped areas. The contrast is due to the differences in birth and death rates.

The impact of differences in the level of economic well-being on the health of people is revealed also by comparison of per capita income and life expectation at birth: 60 to 65 years and over in rich nations,[40] 30 to 40 years in areas dominated by poverty. This contrast, however, is tending to decline with progress in medical science and the introduction of modern sanitation in the underdeveloped countries.

Nutritional Patterns

The have and have-not nations differ strikingly in the patterns of consumption of various foodstuffs, industrial raw materials and energy.

Only rich peoples have an adequate and properly balanced diet,[41] while the populations of poor countries often suffer from caloric insufficiency and especially from lack of protective foods in the diet. The comparatively poor countries usually consume more bread grains per capita of population than the prosperous nations: 244.6 metric pounds per capita in Mexico and 255.6 pounds in Bulgaria, as compared with 168.4 pounds in the United States and 153.0 pounds in Sweden. (See Table 189.) In rice-eating Asiatic countries, however, the consumption of bread grains is very low (85.8 pounds per capita in Ceylon, 38.8 pounds in Japan).

Consumption of meat and sugar on the other hand, declines as one moves from prosperous to poor countries, though with some exceptions. Per capita consumption of meat is particularly high in cattle-raising areas (Argentina, Uruguay, Australia, New Zealand), while sugar is a staple food in some tropical countries with sugar cane plantations (Ceylon, Colombia, Cuba, Costa Rica).

Consumption of Raw Materials and Energy

The real contrast between the have and have-

not countries is in the consumption of manufactured goods, industrial raw materials, especially steel, and fuels.

Statistics on consumption of textiles tend to minimize the contrast between abundance and scarcity, since they record only the weight of the fabrics consumed but fail to show the difference in quality. The contrast between the two groups of countries is much clearer in data on consumption of industrial timber, steel and other metals, coal, petroleum, energy and electric power.

The economic structure of modern nations is too complex and they differ too widely from one another to permit a one-dimensional measurement, as, for example, by consumption of energy. Fuel consumption (as a source of energy) is exceptionally high, in relation to national income, in the United Kingdom, Belgium and Germany because of the predominance of heavy industries in these countries. It is high in Norway and Canada because of the abundance of cheap water power; in Chile, because of the relative preponderance of mining; and in the USSR, because of the primarily military character of the economy. It is high in relation to per capita income in Japan because the deficiency of arable land and other natural resources keeps that country's national income low in relation to its industrial development. On the other hand, per capita consumption of energy is relatively low in Switzerland, Denmark, Uruguay, Venezuela, Argentina and Puerto Rico, to mention only countries listed in Table 189. Apart from such anomalies, however, per capita income in various countries is roughly related to the amount of energy the country consumes.

Contrasts in the use of electric power are particularly striking. The United States consumes approximately 100 times as much electricity per capita as the Philippines and more than 1,000 times as much as China, while its per capita income is only about 40 to 50 times the amounts in these countries.

Insofar as consumption of energy is the best single measure of the industrial development in a nation, it appears that per capita income is closely related to the level of industrialization. This general formula is, however, subject to serious reservations.[42]

INTERREGIONAL COMPARISONS

Our modern economic civilization is an ag-

40. Cf. Table 92.
41. See Chapter 9.

42. See Chapter 13.

TABLE 189

PER CAPITA INCOME AND CONSUMPTION, VARIOUS COUNTRIES, AROUND 1948

| Country | Per Capita Income, in U.S. Dollars | Per Capita Consumption, in Metric Pounds Per Year [a] | | | | | | | |
		Bread Grains	Sugar	Meat	Tex-tiles	Indus-trial Timber	Steel	Energy, Coal Equiva-lent	Electric Power in Kilo-watt Hours
United States	$1,525	168.4	109.8	148.4	41.6	2,680	1,300	13,310	2,560
Switzerland	950	217.0	82.8	66.4	24.6	1,110	...	3,910	2,230
New Zealand	933	205.8	71.6	223.2	14.7	2,310	...	4,510	1,600
Canada	895	172.8	86.8	149.2	26.4	3,210	506	10,740	4,120
Australia	812	196.6	104.4	200.8	21.3	1,620	330	5,440	1,160
Sweden	805	153.0	74.0	82.8	25.3	2,354	640	6,550	2,580
Denmark	781	140.0	76.2	150.8	11.2	1,012	...	3,940	500
United Kingdom	777	204.8	70.6	98.8	24.0	682 [b]	595	9,600	1,115
Belgium-Luxem-bourg	646	195.8 [e]	51.6 [e]	87.8 [e]	24.9 [e]	750 [e, b]	548	8,090	986 [e]
Finland	569	237.2	51.8	47.2	11.4	3,234	...	4,280	1,000
Norway	550	215.8	50.6	52.4	13.6	2,618	...	7,090	5,310
Netherlands	487	186.2	51.8	46.6	19.1	785	383	4,930	725
Ireland	485	258.4	55.8	107.4	7.3	262 [b]	...	3,780	300
France	418	187.4	30.6	89.2	19.8	682	404	4,750	790
Austria	368	233.0	17.6	49.6	6.7	672	198	2,310	900
Union of South Africa	347	340.0	9.4	102.4	6.4	...	...	3,570	890
Czechoslovakia	345	252.8	34.8	54.6	14.5	572	429	3,890	730
Germany	336	233.6 [d]	31.4 [d]	29.4 [d]	8.1 [d]	726 [d]	207	6,290	925 [d]
Uruguay	331	185.0	60.0	191.2	11.7	560	...	1,120	165
Venezuela	322	...	...	...	5.3	312	...	1,820	105
Argentina	315	237.4	69.8	237.8	17.8	...	...	1,780	255
Cuba	296	214.6	83.6	76.4	7.6	...	...	...	142
Puerto Rico	275	...	...	...	...	...	...	670	260
Italy	225	301.8	14.4	32.0	9.7	210	116	1,370	535
Poland	190	213.2	19.2	39.0	8.8	550	157	2,000	375

(Continued on facing page)

glomeration of heterogeneous economic patterns. Old and new methods of production, old and new forms of enterprise elbow one another in today's world. Modern airfields, highways, radio stations and power plants are scattered over all parts of the globe. On the other hand, remains of primitive economies persist in the most progressive nations. This diversity of economic patterns, combined with diversity in geographic conditions and natural resources, accounts for contrasts in per capita income within a nation.

In the present study, interregional comparisons serve a double purpose: on the one hand, they cast light on the structure of national income in individual countries; on the other, they help to visualize the origin and nature of international contrasts in per capita income.

The United States

In 1948 the per capita income payment in the United States as a whole was $1,383,[43] greater than the per capita income in any other country in the world. However, Mississippi, with per capita income of less than $750, trailed such countries as Canada, the United Kingdom, Denmark, Sweden, Switzerland, Australia and New Zealand. Such states as Louisiana, Virginia and New Mexico had a per capita income slightly above that of the richest countries, Switzerland and New Zealand. Ten states — New York,

43. "Per capita income payment" as estimated by the Department of Commerce is approximately 10 per cent less than national per capita income computed by dividing total national income by number of inhabitants. (Cf. Tables 186 and 189.)

TABLE 189—*continued*

Country	Per Capita Income, in U.S. Dollars	Per Capita Consumption, in Metric Pounds Per Year [a]							
		Bread Grains	Sugar	Meat	Tex-tiles	Indus-trial Timber	Steel	Energy, Coal Equiva-lent	Electric Power in Kilo-watt Hours
Spain	182	188.0	9.6	40.4	7.0	...	40	1,010	225
USSR	181	...	...	...	5.5	...	176	2,430	456
Chile	180	264.4	50.2	70.4	7.5	870	...	3,790	260
Hungary	163	234.2	19.4	46.0	6.4	286	144	1,290	483
Turkey	143	...	...	...	7.3	...	11	410	38
Japan	143	38.8	1.4	7.6 [e]	3.3	385	44	2,340	540
Colombia	132	127.2	156.0	54.6	5.9	97	...	550	62
Bulgaria	113	255.6	9.2	37.0	6.4	...	...	600	66
Brazil	112	167.2	62.0	84.4	8.9	196	22	680	55
Mexico	106	244.6	65.8	49.0	6.6	...	25	790	175
Southern Rhodesia	105	...	...	...	4.8	340	...	...	...
Guatemala	103	...	...	...	...	66	...	200	20
Greece	95	119.4	18.6	25.6	7.9	110	...	490	73
Paraguay	84	...	...	...	...	...	...	210	20
Peru	82	205.2	44.8	45.2	5.0	55	...	410	28
Ceylon	79	85.8	180.3	39.2 [e]	...	35	...	490	11
Bolivia	55	...	...	...	...	...	...	...	43
Philippines	41	28.4	34.8	37.0 [e]	...	...	...	...	43
Ecuador	40	...	...	...	4.0	...	...	220	23
								360	38

Sources: For per capita income, Table 188; for consumption of bread grains, sugar and meat, Table 144; for textiles, Table 147; for industrial timber, Table 148; for steel, cf. Chapter 29; for energy and electric power, Tables 400 and 415.

a. One metric pound equals approximately 1.1 avoirdupois pounds used in English-speaking countries.
b. Including fuelwood.
c. Belgium.
d. Western Germany.
e. Including dairy products and eggs.

Illinois, Nevada, Connecticut, Montana, California, New Jersey, Delaware, the District of Columbia and South Dakota — had per capita payments of more than $1,550, or more than twice the per capita income of the United Kingdom and Denmark. (For 1929–50 data, at 3-year intervals, see Table 190; cf. Table 186.)

In the United States the contrasts in state per capita income have lessened in the past two decades. In 1929, the average for the three richest states was four times the average for the three poorest states. The ratio increased to 6.5 at the depth of the depression, returned to 3.9 in the late 1930's, declined to 2.3–2.5 in more recent years and amounted to 2.4 in 1950.[44] In brief, depression widened the gap between the rich

and poor areas in the nation and prosperity has narrowed it.[45]

Canada

In the early 1920's, Alberta and British Columbia were the richest provinces of Canada, with per capita income almost double that in Nova Scotia and New Brunswick. The contrast has since been reduced. In 1938 the average for Alberta and British Columbia was less than half again as much as the average for Nova Scotia and New Brunswick.

Germany

Although the contrasts between economic levels in different parts of prewar Germany

44. In 1950 per capita income in the three richest states (District of Columbia, Delaware and Nevada) averaged $1,920 and that in the three poorest states (Mississippi, Arkansas and South Carolina), $790.

45. This phenomenon was due largely to changes in agricultural prices — collapse during the depression and rise during the war.

TABLE 190

PER CAPITA INCOME PAYMENTS IN EACH STATE IN THE UNITED STATES, 1929–50

(*At Current Prices*)

State	1929	1932	1935	1938	1941	1944	1947	1950
New England								
Connecticut	$918	$558	$659	$710	$1,055	$1,513	$1,610	$1,766
Maine	566	367	428	450	569	1,040	1,137	1,161
Massachusetts	897	594	634	677	879	1,296	1,402	1,600
New Hampshire	652	422	502	531	665	1,055	1,229	1,282
Rhode Island	851	562	626	639	909	1,320	1,412	1,561
Vermont	601	369	439	454	622	959	1,138	1,184
Middle East								
Delaware	919	522	634	682	1,018	1,424	1,513	1,909
District of Columbia	1,191	926	955	1,044	1,096	1,328	1,473	1,986
Maryland	703	460	524	594	834	1,284	1,314	1,547
New Jersey	947	586	630	699	914	1,444	1,557	1,689
New York	1,125	671	743	791	984	1,535	1,713	1,864
Pennsylvania	767	429	510	553	748	1,213	1,368	1,523
West Virginia	464	261	342	369	477	807	995	1,049
Southeast								
Alabama	305	155	213	233	364	702	775	836
Arkansas	305	153	204	236	345	655	756	825
Florida	484	287	360	418	516	1,013	1,043	1,210
Georgia	329	189	264	280	387	761	855	969
Kentucky	371	198	260	283	374	704	821	911
Louisiana	415	230	286	341	433	827	861	1,045
Mississippi	273	125	177	185	281	583	662	698
North Carolina	309	176	270	289	396	713	860	951
South Carolina	252	147	222	241	361	673	769	831
Tennessee	349	185	260	280	411	808	862	962
Virginia	422	276	347	380	559	924	993	1,158

(*Continued on facing page*)

were not as sharp as in the United States, per capita income in predominantly agricultural areas (East Prussia) was less than half that in Hamburg and Berlin.[46] The general trend has been toward less inequality between regions. East Prussia, Pomerania, Silesia, Bavaria and Württemberg, all of which had per capita income far below the national average in 1913, were catching up with the more prosperous areas, such as Hesse-Nassau, Rhine Province, Saxony and Hamburg. The average for the first group of areas was 574 marks in 1913, 799 marks in 1926 and 768 marks in 1936, at current prices (unweighted); comparable averages for the second group were 986 marks, 1,184 marks and 1,094 marks, respectively. In 1913 per capita income in the rich areas was 72 per cent higher than in the poor areas; by 1936 the gap had narrowed to 43 per cent.

46. **18**, p. 76; **29**, 12–35.

One of the factors contributing to the gradual ironing out of interregional inequalities in per capita income has been the fight of labor unions for equalization of wage rates in all parts of a country. Another factor, at least in the United States, has been the increasing geographic mobility of labor: workers are moving from areas with comparatively low wages to high-wage areas. Thus the pressure of a surplus supply of labor increases in the cities with high wages and diminishes in communities with particularly low wages.

INEQUALITY IN INCOME

The strongest accusation against the capitalist system of production has been that it leads to luxury and extravagance at one pole of society and to poverty and destitution at the other. Since the concept of poverty is relative the crucial question is whether our civilization is mov-

TABLE 190—*continued*

State	1929	1932	1935	1938	1941	1944	1947	1950
Southwest								
Arizona	573	271	355	436	525	959	1,057	1,240
New Mexico	383	192	272	322	418	799	972	1,109
Oklahoma	455	212	281	327	467	940	990	1,070
Texas	465	248	319	387	498	972	1,105	1,278
Central								
Illinois	932	456	543	616	870	1,337	1,606	1,752
Indiana	583	296	392	449	705	1,156	1,283	1,451
Iowa	546	248	357	423	619	1,036	1,191	1,417
Michigan	745	382	524	535	795	1,331	1,410	1,583
Minnesota	566	320	403	474	593	975	1,227	1,332
Missouri	612	349	413	455	620	1,039	1,205	1,401
Ohio	748	388	507	554	814	1,311	1,387	1,582
Wisconsin	634	325	413	466	651	1,124	1,316	1,431
Northwest								
Colorado	616	342	412	475	611	1,023	1,354	1,392
Idaho	518	241	338	406	540	1,029	1,288	1,287
Kansas	532	267	337	382	558	1,164	1,372	1,338
Montana	602	290	455	488	684	1,208	1,548	1,605
Nebraska	557	251	353	384	518	1,122	1,257	1,467
North Dakota	389	181	269	302	537	1,075	1,582	1,298
South Dakota	417	171	273	318	492	1,048	1,347	1,308
Utah	537	276	362	434	585	1,061	1,162	1,271
Wyoming	687	371	477	537	672	1,092	1,450	1,509
Far West								
California	946	533	617	714	951	1,535	1,574	1,751
Nevada	817	479	614	645	907	1,383	1,667	1,875
Oregon	640	342	447	507	729	1,302	1,357	1,523
Washington	713	374	470	558	838	1,495	1,451	1,642

Source: **12**, August 1951, p. 18.

ing toward greater equality in the distribution of the social product or greater inequality.

Unfortunately, precise measurement of economic inequality in different countries and at different times is very difficult. Various definitions of "inequality" [47] and different ways of measuring frequently give contradictory results.

MEASURING INEQUALITY

The most convincing way to measure inequalities of income in a community is to array its people — from the poorest to the richest — and to ascertain what part of the aggregate social product goes to the 10 per cent of households at the lowest end of the distribution, how much goes to the lowest 20 per cent and so forth.[48]

47. **45**, pp. 1–16, 197 ff. and 251–55.
48. A simpler but less conclusive method is to compare income in the lowest and highest quartiles or deciles. (See **22**, *passim*, and **45**, pp. 2 ff.)

Under conditions of perfect equality, each tenth of the households would receive 10 per cent of the aggregate income. Under conditions of inequality, the lowest tenth of the households will get less than 10 per cent of the aggregate, the first 20 per cent get less than 20 per cent and so on. Then the inequality in the distribution of income will be measured by the lag between the share of the respective groups of population in total income and their equality rates. The advantage of this method is that it permits a very simple graphic presentation of inequality. (See Figure 129.)

The Lorenz Curve

If all incomes are equal, the cumulative income of 10, 20, 30 per cent of the households will represent an evenly rising series (the line of equal distribution on the plot). If the low-income households get less than their propor-

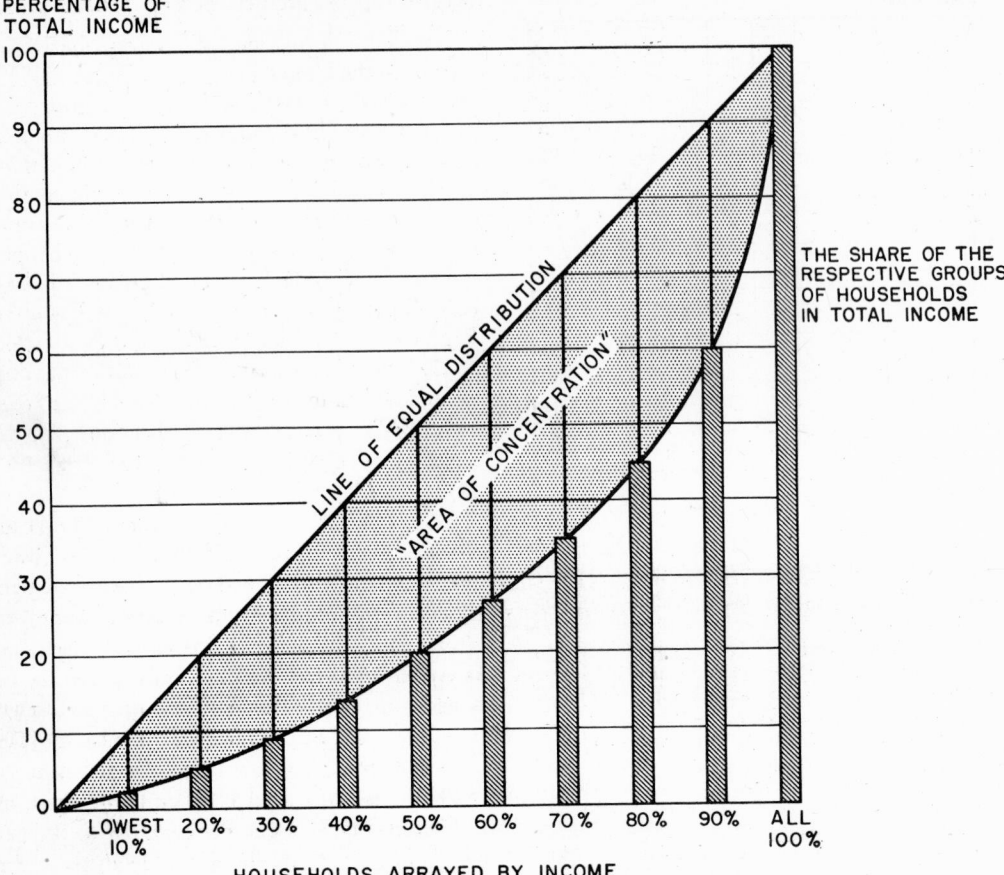

FIGURE 129. INCOME DISTRIBUTION: CONSTRUCTION OF A LORENZ CURVE

tionate rate, the cumulative incomes form a series rising slowly at the beginning and sky-rocketing at the end. In other words, the cumulative decile income will form a concave curve (the Lorenz curve), and its concavity (or distance from the line of equal distribution) can be used as the measure of inequality.[49] Practically, inequality in distribution of income, or income concentration in the hands of the rich, is measured by the "area of concentration" between the curve measuring the cumulative share of households in total income and the straight line of equal distribution. This, in brief, is the justification for describing inequality in distribution of incomes in terms of the percentage share of each tenth (or each fifth) of recipients of the national income.[50] In fact, such percentages can be readily plotted, as in Figure 130, and in this

way the distributions at different dates or in different areas can be compared with one another.

Interpreting the Lorenz Curve

The wider the distribution of income in a community, the narrower is the gap between the rich and the poor, and likewise the concentration area. Under conditions of extreme inequality, assuming that most members of the community have practically no income and almost all aggregate income is concentrated in the hands of a small minority, the concentration area will expand over almost the whole surface ABC in Figure 130.

Sometimes, however, two distribution curves cross each other (Curves 3 and 4 on Figure 130). This crossing usually indicates that in one case (Curve 3) there is less inequality in the low income groups and more among the rich, and

49. **34**, pp. 209–19.
50. **45**, pp. 1–16.

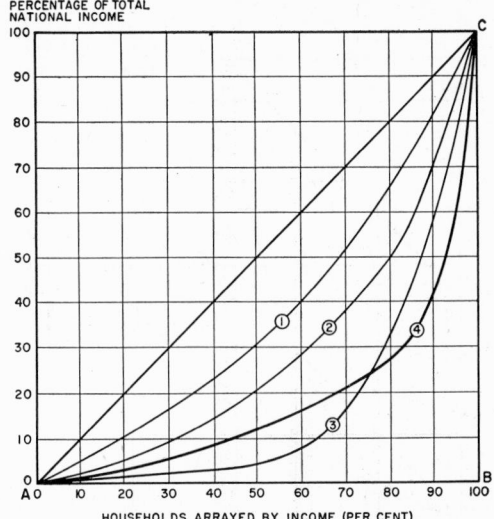

PERCENTAGE OF TOTAL
NATIONAL INCOME

HOUSEHOLDS ARRAYED BY INCOME (PER CENT)

FIGURE 130. INCOME DISTRIBUTION: EXAMPLES OF
LORENZ CURVES

The four curves on this plot represent different patterns
of income distribution. Curve 1 indicates that the poorest fifth of the households get 10 per cent of national income; the poorer half, somewhat more than 30 per cent,
and 90 per cent of the households account for more
than 80 per cent. This is a case of a fairly even distribution of income. Curve 2 shows a distribution that allocates only 20 per cent of aggregate income to the poorer
half of the households. Curve 3 leaves them only 4 per
cent — an extreme case, hardly possible in modern society. Curve 4 gives to the poorer half of households
12 per cent of national income and allocates nearly 60
per cent to the upper 10 per cent of population — also
an example of extreme inequality.

in the other case (Curve 4) a considerable number of persons have comparatively low income
but the distribution of higher income is more
nearly equal.

When comparing inequalities of income distributions in different communities and different
times, the influence of purely statistical factors
on visible inequality should be borne in mind.
A very large and heterogeneous community is
likely to have a more unequal distribution of
incomes than its more or less homogeneous component parts. The visible inequality of incomes
in a community depends also on the way in
which its units are defined. In a community
where large families prevail and all family members pool their earnings, the proportion of households with very small earnings must be lower
than in a community which includes many one-
person households.

INEQUALITY OF INCOME IN THE UNITED STATES

Detailed information on the distribution of
income in the United States is available for 1935–
36, a period of severe depression and mass unemployment.[51] For more recent dates only estimates based on comparatively small samples are
at our disposal. With reservation for the margin
of error, these estimates show that the distribution of income in the United States has changed
since 1935–36 in the direction of greater equality.
(See Table 191; cf. Figure 131.) *The Economic
Report of the President,* 1949, records a reduction of the relative share of the rich in national
income and an increase of the share of the lower
and middle groups.[52] A further shift in the
same direction was indicated in the President's
Report in 1950.[53]

There are also clear indications of a significant
change in the distribution of incomes of wage
and salary earners. According to an estimate published in the *Journal of the American Statistical
Association* the share of income of wage and
salary earners (families and individuals) in the
lowest third of the income distribution amounted
to 11 per cent of all earnings of such families
and individuals in 1939, and 15 per cent in
1949. In the same period of time, the share of
the middle third went up from 27 to 33 per
cent, and that of families and individuals in the
highest third of the income distribution declined

TABLE 191

DISTRIBUTION OF MONEY INCOME AMONG FIVE EQUAL
GROUPS OF FAMILIES IN THE UNITED STATES,
1935–36, 1941, 1947 AND 1948

Family Units, Ranked by Income	1935–36	1941	1947	1948
Total	100.0	100.0	100.0	100.0
Lowest fifth	4.0	3.5	4.0	4.2
Second fifth	8.7	9.1	9.8	10.5
Third fifth	13.6	15.3	15.4	16.1
Fourth fifth	20.5	22.5	22.6	22.3
Highest fifth	53.2	49.6	48.2	46.9

Source: **9**, 1949, pp. 91–92 and 1950, p. 97.

51. **13**, p. 95.
52. **9**, 1949, pp. 91–92.
53. **9**, 1950, p. 97.

A. UNITED STATES

PERCENTAGE OF TOTAL.
NATIONAL INCOME

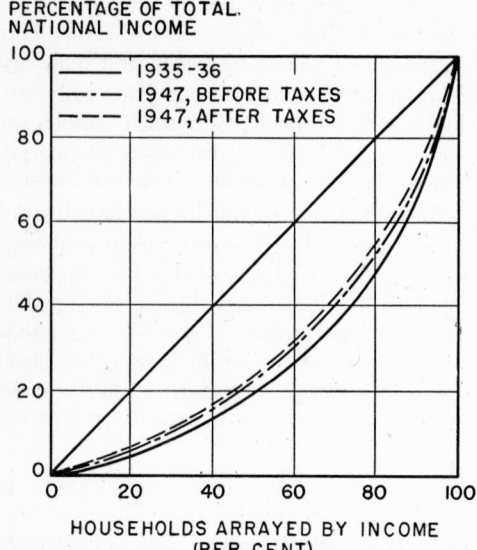

HOUSEHOLDS ARRAYED BY INCOME
(PER CENT)

B. GERMANY

PERCENTAGE OF TOTAL
NATIONAL INCOME

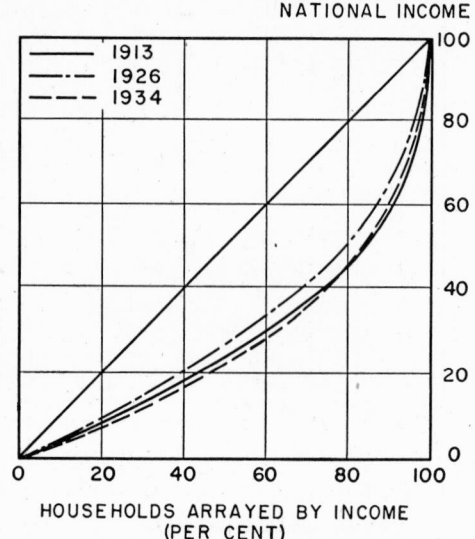

HOUSEHOLDS ARRAYED BY INCOME
(PER CENT)

FIGURE 131. INCOME DISTRIBUTION: CHANGES IN THE UNITED STATES AND GERMANY

These graphs show the changes in the degree of inequality of income. The curve of distribution in the United States in 1947 was closer to the line of equal distribution than in 1935–36, indicating a trend toward more nearly equal distribution. A similar trend prevailed in Germany from 1913 to 1926. Under the impact of the depression and the Nazi regime, inequality again increased in Germany, and the relative share of the poor in national income in 1934 was much lower than in 1926 and even lower than in 1913.

from 62 to 54 per cent.[54] In other words, the relative share of the low-income and the middle groups increased by approximately 15 per cent, while that of the high-income group was cut by approximately 12 per cent.

The change in the pattern of distribution of money income after taxes was particularly significant. In 1935–36, the average money income of the highest fifth of the consumer units was 3.9 times that of the middle fifth. In 1947, the ratio was 3.1 before taxes and 2.9 after taxes.[55]

INEQUALITY OF INCOME IN OTHER COUNTRIES

Economic inequality in the foreign countries for which comparable statistics are available resembles that in the United States in 1935–36: the highest fifth of the households usually receive more than 50 per cent of the aggregate

income, while the lowest fifth have shares ranging from 3 per cent (New Zealand, 1938–39) to 7 per cent (the United Kingdom, 1929). (See Table 192.)

Germany illustrates the impact of political and economic factors on the distribution of income in a nation. (See Figure 131.) Before World War I, the top fifth of the consumers in Germany received 55 per cent of the national income but the remaining national income was distributed rather evenly, so that the lowest fifth of the consumers had 8.0 per cent of the total, the second fifth, 10.0 per cent, the third, 12.3 per cent, and the fourth, 14.7 per cent.[56] After World War I, the share of the rich declined and that of the poor increased, but this trend was reversed by the depression.[57]

New Zealand has comparatively low income at

---

54. The computation refers only to families and individuals with no other income than wages or salaries. (**37**, pp. 438–41.)

55. The incidence of taxes by income level cannot be established with absolute certainty. An estimate published by Rufus S. Tucker suggests that the share of lower incomes in total national income was larger and their share in taxation smaller than indicated in the President's *Report*. (See **43**.)

56. Cf. data for the United States (Tables 189 and 190).

57. As a rule an economic depression accompanied by mass unemployment tends to increase inequality in the distribution of national income, at least if the inequality is measured on the basis of a Lorenz plot (cf. **36**). The contrast between employment and unemployment in lean years appears to outweigh the increase in profits made in fat years.

TABLE 192

NATIONAL INCOME: DISTRIBUTION AMONG TEN EQUAL GROUPS OF HOUSEHOLDS IN
SELECTED COUNTRIES, BEFORE WORLD WAR II

Family Unit, Ranked by Income	United Kingdom 1929	Germany					Poland 1929	New Zealand 1938–39
		1913	1926	1928	1932	1934		
Total	100.0	100.0	100.0	100.0	100.0	100.0	100.0	100.0
Lowest tenth	3.0	3.5	3.8	3.7	3.5	3.0	1.7	1.0
Second tenth	4.0	4.5	4.9	4.8	4.5	4.0	2.8	2.0
Third tenth	5.0	4.8	5.4	5.2	4.8	4.5	4.7	4.0
Fourth tenth	6.0	5.2	5.6	5.4	5.2	5.0	5.3	4.8
Fifth tenth	6.5	6.0	6.4	6.2	6.0	5.5	6.0	5.7
Sixth tenth	7.0	6.3	6.9	6.8	6.3	6.0	7.2	7.5
Seventh tenth	8.5	6.7	7.0	7.0	6.7	7.0	8.5	11.0
Eighth tenth	9.0	8.0	10.0	10.0	8.0	10.0	10.4	14.0
Ninth tenth	10.0	14.0	14.0	14.1	15.0	15.0	14.4	16.0
Highest tenth	41.0	41.0	36.0	36.8	40.0	40.0	39.0	34.0

Sources: Computed from the Lorenz curves plotted for the respective distributions by freehand method on the basis of official statistics on the percentage distribution of families and their aggregate income by income level. **25**, p. 109; **17**, p. 660; **44**, p. 74; **21**, 1941, p. 694.

the low end of the distribution. Poland's income distribution in 1929 was not much different from that recorded in the United States during 1935–36.

Distribution of income in France in 1938 followed a similar pattern. (Compare the dotted curve in Figure 132 with the heavy black curve in Figure 131, A.) After World War II, however, the visible inequality in income distribution in France declined by nearly half. (See the heavy black line in Figure 132.) [58] The origin of this shift is not very clear, however. It may be due partly to a decline in the share of interest and rent in national income.[59] Another plausible explanation is that since official income statistics in France, as in other countries, are necessarily restricted to legitimate income, they fail to register black-market profits that mushroomed in the early years of the postwar economy. This gap would result in an understatement of incomes in the upper brackets and make the postwar income distribution appear more nearly equal than it actually was.

58. **23**, pp. 29, 30 and 46.
59. The two items totaled 17 per cent of national income in France in 1938 and only 2 per cent in 1946. (**23**, p. 32.)

EFFECTS OF CHANGES IN FISCAL LAWS

Changes in the distribution of taxed incomes do not always reflect the changes in the distribution of income of the whole population. A fiscal reform that lowers the tax exemption and increases the number of taxpayers often results in an increase of the visible inequality of taxed in-

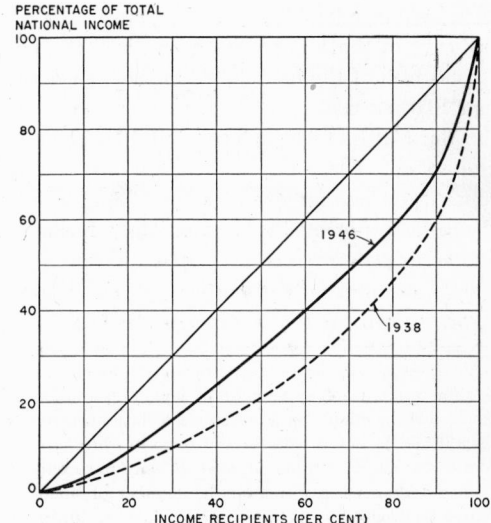

FIGURE 132. INCOME DISTRIBUTION: CHANGES
IN FRANCE

comes — whether the inequality is measured by the Lorenz curve or by any other yardstick.[60] Similarly, a general rise in prices and money wages that brings small incomes into the bracket above the exemption limit results in an increase in the visible inequality among taxpayers.

LONG-RANGE TRENDS IN DISTRIBUTION OF NATIONAL INCOME

The contrasts in scarcity and abundance examined on the preceding pages permit some generalizations on the trends in inequality of incomes, and in interregional and international differences in per capita income.

PARETO'S THEORY

Using a very rough method of measurement, Vilfredo Pareto, the Swiss economist, claimed to have found that inequality in income is about the same in all countries and at all times.[61] Experience has proved that he was wrong. Distribution of income can change appreciably in a comparatively short time, as it changed in the United States from 1935–36 to 1947 and in Germany from 1913 to 1926 and from 1926 to 1934. It varies also from country to country.

What is true in Pareto's observation is that the poor and the rich sometimes have similar relative shares in national income in communities of widely different economic and social structure. For example, the lowest fifth of the households received 4.5 per cent of the national income in Poland in 1929, as compared with 4.0 per cent in the United States in 1935–36. The second fifth of the households in these countries had 10.0 per cent and 8.7 per cent respectively; the third fifth, 13.2 per cent and 13.6 per cent and so on. There are also indications that in some countries, for example, in Great Britain, the pattern of inequality in wages did not change appreciably over several decades in the nineteenth century.[62] Without repeating Pareto's error, we can say that the range of variation in

the distribution of income is not very wide, at least, within the scope of our observation.[63]

THE THEORY OF VARIABLE TRENDS

A plausible theory of changes in distribution of income was offered by the German economist, Gustav Schmoller, in an article which appeared in 1895, almost simultaneously with the theory of Pareto.

With economic progress, an increasing differentiation in individual income is as unavoidable as increasing social differentiation. However, in certain periods contrasts in individual income become much more pronounced than differences in individual abilities, partly because of personal success or inheritance of one generation from another, partly as the result of ruthlessness, shrewdness, violence and exploitation. Since none of these factors favors the same groups constantly, continuous growth in inequality in income is out of the question. The very fact that the highest and lowest layers of society often degenerate and decline more rapidly than the middle classes can result in the increasing importance of the last group. It may be expected that with moral progress and a growing sense of equity, violence will be checked and the progress of general education will diminish inequality of opportunities and favor a more even distribution of income. In all probability, periods of growing inequality in income will be followed by periods in which contrasts will be partly ironed out. . . . The prevailing historic trend is neither a steadily growing inequality of income nor a steadily growing equality, but a temporarily progressing differentiation, followed by opposite movements which tend to reduce inequality.[64]

According to this theory, the early phase of industrial expansion — as in the eighteenth century in England or in the middle of the nineteenth century in the United States — is characterized by increasing inequality in income: the rich become richer and the poor, poorer. The opposite tendency is more likely to prevail

---

60. Income statistics of the United Kingdom recorded 3 million taxed incomes in 1938 and 10.4 million in 1947. The inequality in 1947 seems to be much greater than in 1938, but a shift in the opposite direction becomes obvious if 7 million lowest incomes are excluded from the 1947 records or a similar number of small incomes is added to the taxpayers of 1938. (Cf. **20**, p. 13; **39**.)

61. **38**, pp. 320 ff.

62. **22**.

---

63. The economic system of the Soviet Union seems to favor a greater equality of income than the capitalist economy. However, by piecework payment and unrestricted use of incentive wages, this system tremendously increases differences between the earnings of common labor and of the elite of the labor force. It also increases the contrast in the living conditions of rank-and-file workers and supervisory and administrative staff. A precise comparison of inequality of incomes under the Soviet system and in the capitalist economy is impossible in view of the statistical blackout in the Soviet Union.

64. **40**, pp. 1076–77 and 1094.

in the more advanced phase of a free-enterprise economy. In recent years, democratic countries have supported this tendency by wage policies, progressive income taxes based on ability to pay, price controls, subsidies to producers of staple foodstuffs, social security plans and similar measures.

TRENDS IN INTERREGIONAL DIFFERENCES

Interregional differences in per capita income are determined by numerous factors, such as climate, soil, natural resources, transportation facilities, the level of industrialization and urbanization. The average size of farms or the density of agricultural population is an important factor in per capita income in rural areas. The distribution of industrial plants and large cities within the country is often of decisive significance.[65] In the United States, the high per capita income in such states as Nevada and Montana is a reminder of the advantages of young areas over older regions.

Modern techniques of transportation and communication tend to level interregional contrasts. It becomes easier for workers to move to places where they can obtain better wages and easier for employers to shift their plants to areas where they can find cheap labor. Organized labor strives for equality in regional wage rates. Governments often support this drive and take various measures to stimulate well-being in underdeveloped regions. All these factors tend to narrow the range of interregional differences in per capita income. It seems, therefore, that the trends observed in the United States, Canada and prewar Germany reflects a fairly common tendency of modern times.

TRENDS IN INTERNATIONAL CONTRASTS

Recent trends in international differences in per capita income are less clear. In modern technology, the more developed nations are blazing the trail for other countries and are giving them an opportunity to achieve considerable progress in a short time, at comparatively low cost and without risk of losses in a period of experimentation. In the last half century, British, Belgian,

American and German engineers have built railroads, highways, factories and power stations all over the world. The United States has launched a far-reaching, world-wide campaign to strengthen the productive forces of the world by means of loans and technical assistance to underdeveloped countries as well as other nations willing to cooperate in this plan.

Yet inequality in per capita income in the world is probably greater now than half a century ago. Incomes of a large majority of the population in China, Tibet, Iran and Egypt are about the same as at the beginning of this century; in the modern progressive countries per capita income has doubled since then. The increase in inequality in the distribution of world income, however, appears to have been a result of exceptional conditions in recent years rather than a manifestation of a historical trend.

Never before have the less prosperous countries had a better opportunity to develop their natural resources by using the experience and machinery of the more advanced nations. Never before has financial and technical assistance been offered to them on more generous terms or with fewer political strings.

Foreign investments have ceased to be a device of industrial powers to exploit backward areas. The purpose, of course, is profit, just as in the days of colonial conquests. But underdeveloped countries have learned how to defend themselves. A concession for exploitation of natural resources in such a country is a poor risk unless it is integrated with the local economy and promises to contribute to the prosperity of the native population.

Ambitious plans for economic revival have been developed in recent years in different parts of South America, the Near East and Far East. Large-scale experiments are in progress in Africa.

The conspicuous shift in the relations among the industrial nations is even more important. Economic cooperation inaugurated by the Marshall Plan and through international productivity councils has replaced the traditional policy of cut-throat competition. The United States leads in this drive. It has opened its secrets of efficiency and technical and managerial know-how to its potential competitors, urging them to send their experts to its factories and mines to learn American methods of production and industrial organization.

---

65. The Consumer Expenditure Study of 1935–36 revealed a clear correlation between the level of income and the size of community: in all geographic regions, the average family income in villages and small cities was appreciably lower than in large cities. (**30**, pp. 206–31.)

This policy is without precedent, just as the present concentration of economic power in the hands of a single nation is without precedent. But peace, political stability in the world, economic revival of underdevedoped areas, and prosperity in free nations are vital to the United States. It has no chance to survive as an isolated island of abundance in an ocean of poverty. Its economic supremacy will become highly vulnerable if the economic trend proves to be toward accumulation of wealth in one part of the world and desolation in others.

CHAPTER 13

ECONOMIC PATTERNS

TIME AND SPACE are largely interchangeable factors in shaping economic patterns. A backward area on the fringe of the civilized world often has economic characteristics similar to those which archaeology and history attribute to communities that existed thousands of years ago. Moreover, old and new economic patterns often are intermingled within the same nation.

CLASSIFICATION OF ECONOMIC PATTERNS

The purpose of any classification is to reduce the apparently chaotic variety of phenomena to a logical system. A classification of economic patterns, to be meaningful, should be applicable to historical as well as international and interregional variations.

CLASSIFICATION BY HISTORICAL STAGE

The oldest known classification of economic systems was based on the idea of stages in historic development. This is, indeed, the simplest approach to the problem, directly suggested by everyday observation of differences between new and old ways of life, progress and backwardness, developed and underdeveloped areas.

From "Primitivity" to Trade

From the time of Ancient Rome to the nineteenth century, most scholars believed that all countries are predestined to pass through the same economic sequence. This concept can be traced back to Varro, a Roman scholar of the first century B.C., who offered the following classification of the economic system:

1. Primitive life supported by free gifts of nature (hunting, fishing, gathering)
2. Pastoral life (herding, domestication of animals)
3. Agriculture

For Varro, the agricultural economy was the highest conceivable form of economic civilization and urban crafts appeared as a superstructure of agriculture. This concept was in harmony with the economic patterns known at that time. Not until the end of the eighteenth century did the urban crafts and trades reach such importance that it became necessary to extend Varro's classification by adding industry and trade as an economic stage succeeding agriculture.

In the first half of the nineteenth century the German economist Friedrich List carried this sequence further. Each nation, he taught, is predestined to pass through five phases of economic growth: [1]

1. Savagery
2. Pastoral life
3. Agriculture
4. Agriculture and manufactures
5. Agriculture, manufactures and trade

History and anthropology have proved the fallacy of this idea. Human society does not always follow the same path of development. More specifically, List's classification is an oversimplified description of the experience of Great Britain, but it does not fit the history of other countries. [2]

An agricultural economy has not always been a transitory phase which follows a pastoral economy and precedes manufactures. [3]

From Home Use to Market

Largely because of doubts as to the soundness of the theory that economic systems follow

---

1. **27**, pp. 49 ff.
2. **25**, pp. 326–27.
3. Eduard Hahn has elaborated the concept of "agriculture" as a succession of different types of economic systems, some preceding the pastoral economy, others paralleling or following it. According to his theory, hoe-or-hack agriculture develops at a very early stage of civilization, along with the primitive hunting and fishing. Herding and domestication of animals (the pastoral economy) comes later, while plow agriculture is characteristic of a still higher level of economic civilization (**24** and **23**). In his world map of economic patterns — the first map of this type in modern times — Hahn distinguished the hunting and fishing economy and five forms of agriculture: primitive hoe agriculture, the plantation economy (in colonial areas), plow agriculture, animal husbandry, and gardening.

a definite sequence from primitive agriculture to modern trade, some students have classified economic patterns according to the type of disposal of the product or the area of interrelated economic activities. Hildebrand distinguished between barter economy, money economy and credit economy.[4] Bücher described three stages in the expansion of areas of economic operation:

1. Independent domestic economy (production for one's own use, absence of exchange)

2. Town economy (custom production, direct exchange of products by producers)

3. National economy (wholesale production, wide circulation of goods) [5]

This type of classification, however, is not very useful for analysis of economic patterns in various parts of the modern world. The fact that the native farmers of Java produce rubber for the world market while truck gardens and dairy farms in New York State deliver their products to the "local" market does not imply that upstate New York lags behind Indonesia in economic development. On the other hand, Bücher's sharp distinction between the domestic economy and the market economy — town or national — is enlightening. Although the domestic economy seldom occurs in a pure form, even now most people in the world satisfy most of their needs by their own produce and themselves consume most of what they raise or make. Domestic production or the subsistence economy continues to prevail in a large part of the world, while the market-and-money economy is the way of life of only a minority of mankind.

These two basic economic types are not mutually exclusive. Subsistence farming exists in areas where the money economy is dominant and vice versa.[6] Indeed economic history shows that the two patterns have coexisted since very remote times. What has changed is their relative importance.

From Vacuum to Maturity

Many analysts have surveyed the diversity of economic patterns of the past and, in our time, of different parts of the world, from the vantage

4. **25**, p. 330.

5. **19**, p. 89.

6. The word "subsistence" is often used in the sense of a subsistence minimum, almost as a synonym of poverty and destitution. Here the term has no such connotation but is applied to economic systems based on production for consumption within the producer's household.

point of the economic system that has been developed recently in the most progressive Western countries and is characterized by mechanized mass production and an intricate network of financial and industrial institutions. They have considered this system (mature capitalism) as the final goal of historical development and have arrayed all other economic patterns as rungs of a ladder leading from the economic vacuum of prehistoric times to the pinnacle of our civilization.

A typical example of this pattern of thinking is the classification developed in 1930 by Ernest Wagemann, who divided all countries into four groups: (1) the noncapitalist (Asiatic Russia, the Belgian Congo, French West Africa, Sudan, Tripolitania); (2) the neocapitalist (Central and South America, Australia, South Africa); (3) the semicapitalist (European Russia and all Asia except Russia and Japan); and (4) the mature capitalist (all Europe — except Russia — the United States, Turkey and Japan).

Wagemann describes the first group as an economic vacuum. Its peoples live in a state of nature insofar as economics are concerned. They presumably have no relations with other economic units and represent portions of the earth's surface that have not yet been brought within the economic orbit of "historical" nations. The characteristic feature of the area of mature capitalism is the large quantity of capital and labor power per unit of territory. In the neocapitalist area, the quantity of each of these is small, while in a semicapitalist area, there is little capital but a great deal of labor power per unit of territory.[7]

Practically, individual countries are arrayed in this classification according to density of population, consumption of machinery, per capita foreign trade, and the part of finished goods in imports and exports. This results in a rather strange ranking of individual countries: Bulgaria, Yugoslavia and Albania appear as mature capitalist; Australia, the Union of South Africa and Argentina, as neocapitalist, behind China, India and even Saudi Arabia. Asiatic Russia gets a place among the African colonies.

The fallacy is in overrating the significance of density of population as a characteristic of the type of economy, an error that is often committed in the discussion of types of economy. Wherever population is unevenly distributed within the boundaries of a nation — as in the

7. **37**, pp. 257 ff.

United States, Canada, Argentina, the USSR, Sweden, Norway, Australia — the average ratio of inhabitants per square mile is meaningless. On the other hand, the density of population in India, southern China or Indonesia does not contribute to the maturity of the economy in these regions.

Similarly, per capita imports and exports are a poor yardstick of the level of economic development. Other conditions being equal, a small country needs larger per capita imports and exports than a great nation that possesses a wider variety of resources and industries. In fact, Iceland ranks above Great Britain in foreign trade per capita, Chile above the United States. Moreover, many colonial territories have very high per capita exports and imports in relation to their per capita national income.

Stages in Industrialization

Other economists who have surveyed the world economy by comparing its patterns with the modern industrial system have tried to classify countries by the extent of industrialization or the relative significance of heavy industries (production of capital goods).

An example of the first type is the classification prepared by Folke Hilgerdt for the League of Nations.[8] It distinguishes between "typical industrial countries," "other industrial countries," "less industrialized countries," and "countries lagging in industrial development." The first group includes the United Kingdom, Belgium, the Netherlands, Switzerland, the United States, Czechoslovakia, Germany, Austria, Sweden, France, Italy and Japan. The second comprises Canada, Argentina, Norway, Denmark, the Union of South Africa, Australia and New Zealand — all countries in which agriculture employs more labor than manufacturing. The list of "less industrialized countries," arrayed by declining stage of industrialization, includes Chile, Uruguay, Ireland, Cuba, Portugal, Palestine, Hungary, Greece, Spain, British Malaya, Finland, Poland, Estonia, Latvia and the USSR. "Countries lagging in industrial development" include Egypt, Mexico, Indochina, India, Thailand, Colombia, Venezuela, China, the Netherlands Indies, Peru, Brazil, the Philippines, Iran, Romania, Yugoslavia, Lithuania, Bulgaria and Turkey.[9]

In this classification countries with widely different economic structures (for example, the United Kingdom and Japan) appear in the same group while some countries of similar structure are in different groups. There is, indeed, no substantial difference between the economic patterns prevailing in the United States, and in Canada, Australia and New Zealand or between those in Sweden and Norway, or the Netherlands and Denmark, or Yugoslavia and Poland, or Poland and Hungary. Italy and Japan are hardly "typical industrial countries," and China is certainly not more developed industrially than Romania and Yugoslavia.

Consumer Goods and Capital Goods

A classification offered by Walther Hoffmann is based on measuring the extent of industrialization by the ratio between the net value of the output of consumer goods and of capital goods. At an early stage of industrial development, the value of the first is usually 4 to 5 times that of the second; in highly developed industrial countries the two are approximately equal and in some cases the output of capital goods may even exceed that of consumer goods. The ratio of the net value of the output of consumer goods to that of capital goods in various countries in different stages of economic development varies as follows: [10]

	Ratio (Per Cent)
Brazil, 1919	620
Chile, 1912	520
1925	490
Argentina, 1908	470
British India, 1908	420
New Zealand, 1906	550
1916	480
1924	340
Belgium, 1846	520
Great Britain, 1851	470
1871	390
France, 1861–65	450
Switzerland, 1882	400
Japan, 1900	480
1913	270
1925	240
Netherlands, 1920	180
Denmark, 1897	260
1925	180

(*Continued on page 416*)

---

8. **1.**

9. **1**, pp. 26–27.

10. **26**, pp. 178–81.

	Ratio (Per Cent)
Canada, 1901	200
1924	170
1927	130
Hungary, 1926	180
South Africa, 1915–16	200
1926–27	180
Australia, 1914	190
1924–25	170
1926–27	160
Great Britain, 1901	170
Switzerland, 1895	210
United States, 1850	240
1870	170
1880	180
Germany, 1895	230
France, 1896	230
Belgium, 1896	170
Great Britain, 1907	180
1924	150
Switzerland, 1911	150
1923	130
1929	100
United States, 1890	150
1900	120
1914	90
1920	80
France, 1921	150
Germany, 1907	150
1925	110
Sweden, 1926	110
Belgium, 1926	110

This list shows that the share of capital goods in industrial output has been steadily increasing in all modern countries. There is, however, a serious objection to using this yardstick as a basis for international comparison. The character of industrial production in a country depends largely on the available raw materials. In this respect, conditions in New Zealand, Australia or Denmark, for example, differ substantially from those in Sweden or Belgium. Ranking of countries by the prevailing type of output tends to understate the level of industrial development in areas with ample agricultural resources and to overstate that in countries which are less favored by nature or are overpopulated in relation to their carrying capacity.

CLASSIFICATION BY TYPE AND LEVEL OF
DEVELOPMENT

All the classifications of economic systems described on the preceding pages are based on the idea of one-way economic evolution. We can gain better insight into the economic patterns in the world by stressing various types of economy which do not necessarily succeed, or evolve from, one another, and distinguishing the various levels of development within each type.

Type of Economy

Two general types of economic organization of society can be distinguished:

1. The domestic or subsistence economy, in which different economic activities are not clearly differentiated and each household meets most of its needs by its own production.

2. Economic systems in which specialized economic units perform different functions, such as production of clothes, tools and weapons, construction, building of houses, exchange and transportation of goods and so on. To meet its needs under such a system, each household must exchange or sell its products. In other words, a differentiated economy is necessarily a market or money economy.

In a subsistence economy, agriculture usually prevails over all other activities. In a market economy, the available resources are divided between agricultural and nonagricultural pursuits and the relationship in which they are divided largely determines the economic structure of the community. It appears plausible, therefore, to distinguish three types of economic systems dominated by market or money relations: primarily agricultural, agricultural-industrial and primarily industrial.

The fact that several modern countries have passed from a primarily agricultural economy to a primarily industrial type does not imply that such is the historically predetermined road of economic growth of all nations and that the three types of market and money economy correspond to three successive stages of historical development. The present economic structure of the most industrialized countries — Great Britain, Belgium, Switzerland and Western Germany — does not necessarily foreshadow the future of other industrial nations. Some features in their economy are neither a result of their free choice nor an advanced station on the road of economic progress, but rather a consequence of the pressure of overpopulation and scarcity of arable land. Without these unfavorable conditions, these countries would probably have maintained their agricultural production on a much higher level. A more balanced type of economy would have made them appear less industrialized than they are now.[11]

Level of Development

Since the economic development of a nation cannot be reduced to its shift from agriculture to industry and the level of development cannot be measured by the expansion of its industrial sector in comparison with the agricultural, some other yardstick must be found for ranking different economic systems. Such a ranking must be based on a criterion that meets three requirements: it must be strictly quantitative and continuous and applicable to various types of economic communities. Per capita income meets these requirements for an over-all measurement of the efficiency of the economic system.

The use of the concept "efficiency" in this connection should not be misunderstood. It does not imply that an economic organization is good or bad but accepts the values that prevail in the community and measures them as the community itself appraises them. Since this is the meaning of per capita income as a yardstick of economic progress, it must not be taken as a measure of "satisfaction" or psychological well-being of the community.[12]

Theoretically, there are two reasons for using per capita income as a yardstick of economic development: it provides the best measurement of the over-all technical efficiency of an economic system,[13] and technical efficiency is the only continuous characteristic of economic progress.[14]

Economic Patterns

Classification of stages of economic develop-

---

11. The most prosperous countries are of the agricultural-industrial type rather than the primarily industrial. (Cf. pp. 436 ff.)

12. As far as economic growth creates new needs and desires, it tends to originate dissatisfaction of people with their present economic status. It is an open question, indeed, whether most people in an economically prosperous nation are more "satisfied" than in a comparatively poor country. In each community the feeling of poverty and destitution of people at the bottom of the economic pyramid stems from comparison of their living conditions with the standards prevailing in the community. This feeling cannot be measured by dividing the aggregate income of a community by the number of its members (cf. Chapters 9 and 12). It is fairly probable that poverty is felt more keenly in the countries with a prevailing money economy than in the areas where a subsistence economy prevails.

13. **30**, pp. 117 ff.

14. Cf. **17**, *passim.*

ment by per capita income stresses the contrast between countries that are underdeveloped and developed, poor and rich, nonmechanized and mechanized. In view of the range of contrast, the dual classification "rich" and "poor," "developed" and "underdeveloped," "progressive" and "backward" appears insufficient and a third intermediate type, "mixed" or "transitional," is required. Thus, all countries with a differentiated market economy have been classified here by the relative significance of agricultural and industrial pursuits and then ranked by per capita income. Each economic system is identified in this way by its *type* and *level* — but not necessarily its stage — of development. In this classification, nine economic patterns are distinguished. (See the circles in Figure 133.)

THE SUBSISTENCE ECONOMY

An economic system in which farming for home use predominates over all other forms of economic activities can be described as a subsistence (or domestic) economy. Subsistence farming, however, is usual in many areas with developed market and money relations, such as the countries of southeastern Europe, France, Italy, Spain, and even the United States, where it exists side by side with commercial farming. On the other hand, commercial enterprises such as plantations, mines, local factories exist in regions where subsistence agriculture predominates. Indeed, even in regions with a primitive subsistence economy, money relations prevail in urban communities.

The difference is in the relative significance of work for home consumption and production for market.

TYPES OF SUBSISTENCE AGRICULTURE

In addition to crop growing and livestock raising, subsistence agriculture, in a broad sense, includes primitive hunting and fishing. Often it is combined with handcrafts. Sometimes, after having paid taxes and satisfied the landowner, the farmer retains a meager surplus that can be exchanged or sold on the local market.

Although compatible with a high development of individual skills and arts, subsistence farming excludes far-reaching division of labor and substantial capital investment and seldom provides farmers with much more than an existence minimum. Most of the regions with this type of farming are therefore among the poor-

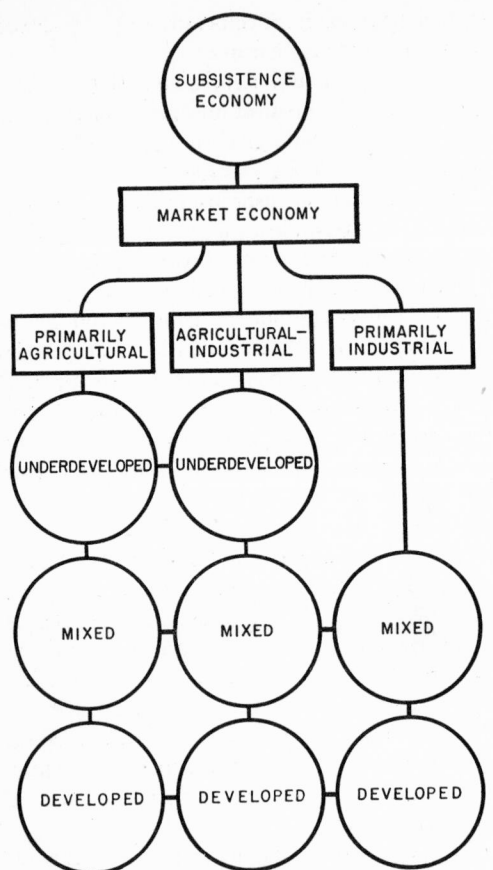

FIGURE 133. ECONOMIC PATTERNS: CLASSIFICATION OF
ECONOMIC SYSTEMS

Classification of economic systems here begins with the segregation of areas with a prevailing subsistence economy — that is, production for one's own household — from the areas where a market economy predominates. The main occupations of people in the areas of subsistence economy are agriculture, fishing and hunting. Countries with a predominant market economy are further classified by the relative significance of agriculture and other industries: primarily agricultural, agricultural-industrial and primarily industrial. In each group, countries are classified by level of development as reflected in per capita income. An underdeveloped, primarily industrial, economy is omitted since this pattern does not occur among existing economic systems.

est areas in the world. Under favorable climatic conditions, however, some subsistence farmers are able to satisfy their moderate needs.

Moreover, large urban communities often develop in areas of subsistence farming. Cities of India and China with millions of inhabitants exemplify islets of market economy surrounded by an ocean of subsistence farming. Even the people directly engaged in subsistence hunting, fishing or tillage of the soil are seldom completely independent of markets and money.

Whittlesey [15] distinguishes five types of subsistence economy: (1) primitive hunting and fishing; (2) nomadic herding; (3) shifting cultivation and rudimentary sedentary tillage; (4) intensive subsistence tillage; and (5) subsistence crop and stock farming in areas where money-market relations prevail.

In view of the scarcity of statistical data, these five types cannot be characterized by objective statistical criteria. The distinction between them is qualitative rather than quantitative and can be ascertained only by direct observation. In this, the economist must rely on the findings of economic geography, which must also be used to distinguish the regions of prevailing subsistence economy from the regions of commercial agriculture.

Primitive Hunting and Fishing

This form of economy is found among the natives of the arctic region (in Alaska, northern Canada and Siberia), in South America, Indonesia, central Africa and the Pacific Islands.

Hunting and fishing are often combined with primitive tillage of the soil. A subsistence economy of this type is an example of ancient obsolete ways of life surviving through the ages — a "fossil civilization," as Toynbee describes it. At a very rough approximation, it prevails in areas embracing about 10 million people, including as many as 200,000 natives in the Arctic and perhaps 2.5 million on Borneo, Papua and other Indonesian and Pacific Islands; most of the remainder are in Africa.

Nomadic Herding

Nomadic herding, described by Whittlesey as the aboriginal form of husbandry, evolved in the arid Eurasian-African steppes and is still typical of the sparsely populated regions of the Sahara, Saudi Arabia, Turkey, Iraq, Iran, Afghanistan, northern India, Tibet, Mongolia and Manchuria — in all, an area with a population of approximately 100 million, including the cities.

Shifting Cultivation and Sedentary Tillage

These are the agricultural types of the economy in humid low latitudes. Shifting cultivation is widespread in the rain forest and on its bor-

---

15. **38.**

ders in Africa, Indonesia, India, Indochina, Taiwan and Hainan.

Rudimentary sedentary tillage (usually hoe agriculture) is widespread in Central and South America, in southern Mexico, Guatemala, Colombia, Peru, Brazil. In Africa (except the coast of the Mediterranean, Egypt and Madagascar), it represents the highest type of native agriculture. In many places, it is losing ground to commercial plantation tillage.

The areas in which shifting cultivation and rudimentary sedentary tillage prevail, have a population of approximately 200 million, 100 million in Africa and about as many in Central and South America.

Intensive Subsistence Tillage

Intensive subsistence tillage is the prevailing type of agriculture in humid regions of southern and eastern Asia and the adjacent islands. Where the season is long enough for paddy rice to mature, this crop, yielding more grain per acre than any other crop in the world, predominates. Where the season is shorter, the farmers grow other grains, oilseeds and cotton and, on slopes too steep to till, tea, mulberry, pepper and other trees. The region of intensive subsistence tillage includes some of the most densely populated areas of the world and supports a population of around a billion persons.

Subsistence Crop and Stock Farming

This type of farming differs from small-scale commercial farming in that its main objective is to produce food for the farmer's household rather than for market.

SCOPE OF THE SUBSISTENCE ECONOMY

According to Whittlesey, these types of subsistence agriculture — excluding subsistence crop and stock farming in industrially developed areas, but including commercial plantations and livestock ranching in areas of prevailing domestic economy — cover a large part of the earth's tilled and grazed land and support nearly 70 per cent of the world's population.[16] This total, however, includes regions of commercial livestock ranching and plantations. Without these, subsistence farming, hunting and fishing sup-

port a population of approximately 1.5 billion or 60 per cent of mankind.[17]

The area of a *prevailing subsistence economy* is narrower. Production for home consumption may prevail in the agricultural sector of an economic system while money and market relations are firmly established in the nonagricultural sector. The preponderance of one pattern or the other in such an economic system depends on the relative importance of the agricultural and nonagricultural sectors, and the degree to which the agricultural sector is dominated by the production for domestic consumption. If, for example, 75 per cent of the national income originates in the agricultural sector and 80 per cent of the agricultural produce is consumed within the farmers' households, production for home use represents 60 per cent of all economic activity in the nation and money relations dominate the remaining 40 per cent. If the agricultural sector represents 60 per cent of the system and 75 per cent of the agricultural produce is consumed directly by the farmers, only 45 per cent of the country's economic activity lies outside the market pattern. In the first case, the economic system as a whole is characterized by the predominance of domestic production; in the latter, by predominance of money relations.

Moreover, per capita income in the agricultural sector of a national economy may be lower than in the nonagricultural sector. Agriculture may, for example, absorb 80 per cent of the national labor force but account for only 50 per cent of the national product. If 80 per cent of the agricultural output in such an economic system is consumed directly by the producers and 20 per cent is sold, market relations control 60 per cent of the nation's economic activity and prevail in the country as a whole.

It is not always possible to establish the exact demarcation between a subsistence and a market economy. These hypothetical examples suggest, however, that only those countries can be classified as subsistence-economy areas in which agriculture predominates overwhelmingly over other activities and subsistence farming outweighs other forms of tillage and husbandry.

As thus defined, a subsistence economy prevails in practically all Asia except Japan, in all Africa except the Mediterranean coast, Egypt, and the Union of South Africa; and in the

---

16. 38, p. 226.

17. See Chapter 14.

Pacific Islands. Vast regions in various countries of Middle and South America are also in this group. The 1948 population of these countries and regions is estimated at 1,300 to 1,350 million or approximately 55 per cent of mankind. (See Figure 134.)

On the whole, these are the areas of underdeveloped natural resources and primitive techniques, but it would be a mistake to think of them as economic and cultural vacuums. Countries in these areas differ from each other in the level of economic development, in religion and political organization. Their annual per capita income — with an allowance for underestimation of agricultural production — ranges from $50 or less to more than $100.

The borderline between the comparatively prosperous countries in the subsistence-economy area and underdeveloped countries with a primarily agricultural money economy is not very clear.[18] As is shown subsequently in Figure 138, the income of the subsistence-economy area represented about $83 billion or about 15 per cent of the world income of $549 billion in 1948.[19]

THE MONEY ECONOMY

The realm of the money economy comprises North America, the larger part of Middle and South America, all Europe, the USSR, Japan, the Mediterranean strip of Africa, Egypt, the Union of South Africa, Australia and New Zealand. (See Figure 134.) They comprise all the economically developed countries of the world. These countries have a total population of slightly more than one billion or from 40 to 45 per cent of the world total in 1948, and they control about 85 per cent of the world income.

The market-and-money economy is, essentially, the economic system of nations of European and mixed stock, although it has made inroads into regions of other nations.

TYPES OF MONEY ECONOMY

The area where the money economy prevails includes countries on different levels of

economic development with widely different climatic conditions, different historical traditions and political institutions. It would be futile to try to reduce to a few simple and measurable features the great variety of patterns of agriculture, mining, manufacturing and trade in this area.

The main features that distinguish the various economic systems based on market relations from one another are the relative importance of the agricultural and nonagricultural sectors in each and the level of the technical efficiency of the economy. The first determines the type of the economy, the second the level of its development.

Economic activities in a community dominated by market-and-money relations include, in addition to agricultural and industrial production, trade, transportation and services, including governmental services — activities that are equally important for agriculture and manufactures. In classifying economic systems, a tripartite grouping of these pursuits is often used:

Primary activities. Farming, including forestry, hunting and fishing

Secondary activities. Mining, manufacturing, production of electric power and gas, building construction

Tertiary activities. Commerce, transportation and communication, finance, professional and personal services, public administration and the armed forces

The three headings — primary, secondary, tertiary — used in this classification are somewhat misleading. Perhaps it would be better to distinguish between the agricultural and nonagricultural sectors of the economic system, including in the agricultural sector forestry, hunting and fishing. The next step would then be to distinguish between two types of nonagricultural pursuits: production of goods and production of services. Another approach would be to start with the distinction between production of goods and services, and then subdivide the goods-producing sector between agricultural and nonagricultural activities. Some activities could then be classified in different ways (for example, supplying electricity, gas and water), but these borderline cases do not affect the results of the analysis appreciably. (See Figure 135.)

The relative significance of agricultural and industrial production in an economy is best characterized by a comparison between its primary

---

18. This statement refers particularly to the demarcation between Asiatic and European Turkey; or between Syria, Lebanon and Jordan, on the one hand, and Egypt on the other.

19. Including allowance for understatement in the available official and private estimates of income in underdeveloped countries.

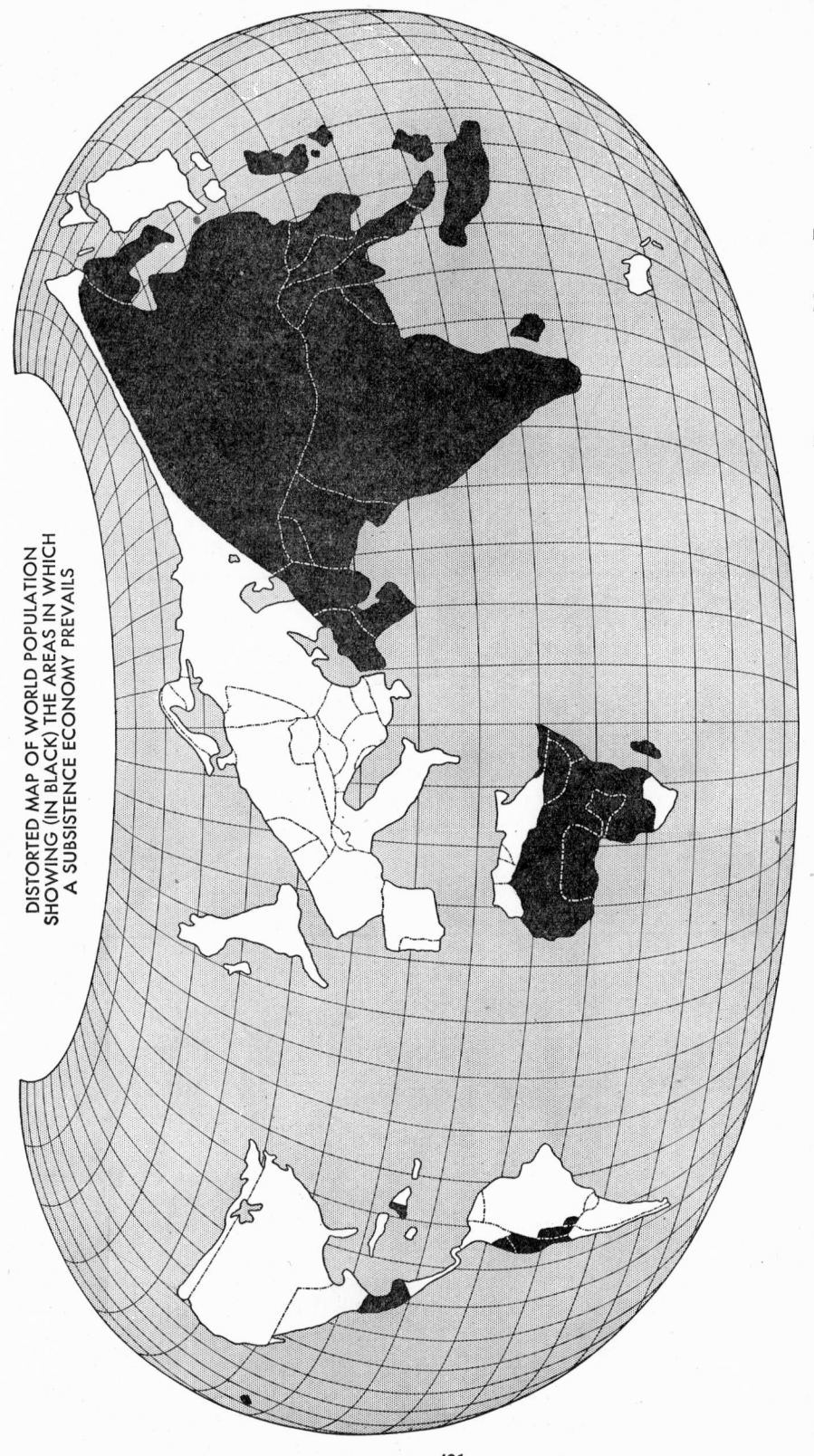

DISTORTED MAP OF WORLD POPULATION
SHOWING (IN BLACK) THE AREAS IN WHICH
A SUBSISTENCE ECONOMY PREVAILS

FIGURE 134. ECONOMIC PATTERNS: GEOGRAPHIC DISTRIBUTION OF THE PREVAILING SUBSISTENCE ECONOMY AND MONEY ECONOMY.

Because of the scarcity of statistical information for many underdeveloped regions, the borderline between the prevailing subsistence economy and money economy cannot be established with precision. The purpose of this map is to suggest the approximate distribution of the world between the two economic patterns. (Cf. **31**.) Continents and countries are shown here on the scale of their population in 1950.

421

A

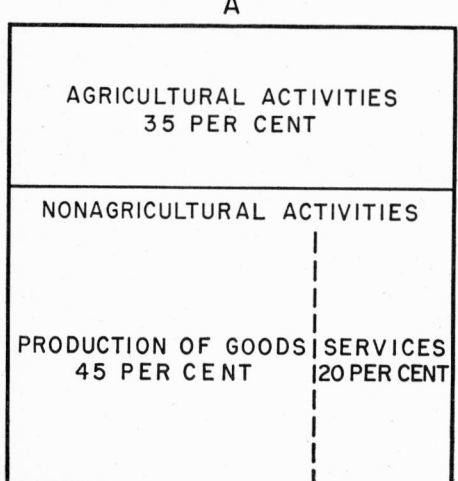

B

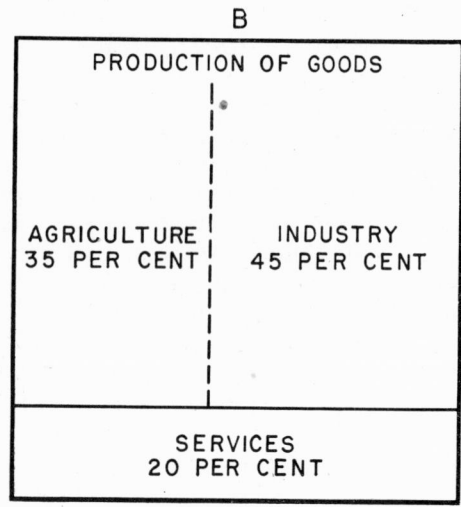

C

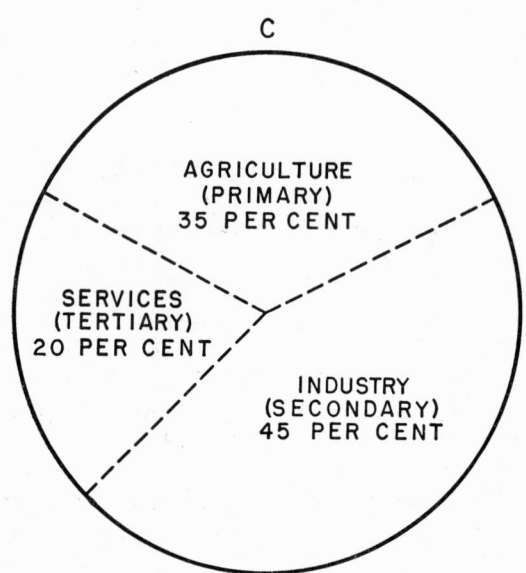

FIGURE 135. CLASSIFICATION OF ECONOMIC ACTIVITIES AS PRIMARY, SECONDARY AND TERTIARY

The purpose of this classification is to illustrate the distribution of the labor force among broad groups of activities. It can be interpreted in several ways. The upper left plot, A, shows a split between agricultural (35 per cent) and nonagricultural (65 per cent) activities and a further split of the latter between the production of goods and of services. On the upper right plot, B, all activities are divided between the production of goods (80 per cent) and of services (20 per cent); production of goods is divided between agricultural and nonagricultural products. The three sections correspond to the "primary," "secondary" and "tertiary" activities in the widely used classification, as in the circle C.

422

and secondary sector,[20] as on the upper right plot in Figure 135.

The Relative Significance of Agriculture and Industry

The primary and secondary sectors of an economic system may be compared with each other in terms of either the input of labor or the value of output. Several considerations favor use of the former. Statistical data on the distribution of the labor force by industrial division are available for a larger number of countries, are more reliable and, with some reservation, more nearly comparable than data on distribution of national income by industrial origin. Moreover, the relative shares of agricultural and industrial production in national income are largely affected by temporary variations in the price structure and business conditions. In addition, statistics of national income in various countries differ widely in handling the value of farm produce consumed on the farm, which is a very important item in primarily agricultural areas.

INPUT OF LABOR

Distribution of the Labor Force

The distribution of the labor force among broad groups of activities varies widely from country to country. (See Table 193.) [21] Contrasts in the percentage of the labor force engaged in agriculture and related pursuits are especially enlightening, though the percentages derived from national censuses are not strictly comparable because of differences in classification.[22] This shortcoming is not very important in view of the very wide range in the recorded figures: from 6.0 per cent to 88.4 per cent for labor force in agriculture; from 2.3 per cent to 47.8 per cent for industrial production; and from 9.3 per cent to more than 50 per cent for commerce, services and government. Whether we consider the proportion of the labor force in agricultural or in industrial production, or the ratio between the two, the range is so broad that classification of countries is only slightly

affected by the differences in the methods of enumeration.

The ratio between the numbers of workers in agricultural and industrial production seems to be the best index of the relative significance of the two broad divisions of the economic system. After countries are arrayed according to this characteristic (see Table 194), it remains to select the demarcation points between countries designated as primarily agricultural, agricultural-industrial and primarily industrial. The selection necessarily rests on judgment, and any choice will leave some doubtful cases and will be open to criticism.

Tentatively, countries in which agriculture employs at least twice as many workers as secondary industries may be classified as *primarily agricultural,* and those in which secondary occupations absorb at least twice as much labor as agriculture may be listed as *primarily industrial.* Then, the classification can be corrected for the marginal cases, on the basis of other information on the economic structure of the respective countries. This classification leaves in the *agricultural-industrial* group the countries where the ratio of primary to secondary employment ranges between 50 and 200 per cent.[23]

Primarily Industrial Countries

In four of the countries listed in Table 194 — Great Britain, Belgium, Australia and Switzerland — industrial production absorbs more than twice as many workers as agriculture. This classification, however, requires two corrections.

Australia employs few people in agriculture, but because of the particular character of its agriculture, with a tremendous expanse of land and considerable investment of capital per worker, it has substantial surpluses of agricultural products for export. Australia's agriculture is too important to justify classification in the same group with Belgium, the United Kingdom and Switzerland, and it seems more realistic to describe the country as an agricultural-industrial nation, in the same group with New Zealand, Canada and the United States.

On the other hand, Germany's population censuses tend to overstate the proportion of agricultural workers in the labor force by the very liberal enumeration of unpaid family workers.

---

20. The question whether the relative development of the tertiary sector is characteristic of economic growth is more controversial. (Cf. pp. 426 ff. in this chapter.)

21. Cf. Chapter 11.

22. In some countries all farmers' wives are counted as engaged in agriculture; in others they are included in the labor force only if they work in the field, or are not counted at all.

---

23. These demarcation points are of course arbitrary, but a shift in either direction would imply a reclassification of only a few countries.

TABLE 193

LABOR FORCE: DISTRIBUTION IN SELECTED COUNTRIES BY BROAD INDUSTRIAL DIVISION

(*Per Cent*)

Country [a] and Year	Agriculture, Forestry, etc.	Industrial Production	Commerce, Services, etc.
Great Britain, 1931	6.0	46.1	47.9
Australia, 1947	15.6	35.0	49.4
Belgium, 1930	17.0	47.8	35.2
United States, 1940	18.5	31.8	49.7
Union of South Africa, Europeans, 1946	18.9	27.4	53.7
Netherlands, 1947	19.3	33.3	47.4
New Zealand, 1946	19.9	26.3	53.8
Switzerland, 1941	20.8	43.5	35.7
Sweden, 1945	24.4	37.8	37.8
Luxembourg, 1947	24.9	39.7	35.4
Denmark, 1940	28.5	30.7	40.8
Western Germany, 1946	29.1	38.5	32.4
Canada, 1941	29.2	31.1	39.7
Norway, 1930	35.3	26.5	38.2
Chile, 1940	35.6	25.9	38.5
France, 1946	36.5	29.8	33.7
Czechoslovakia, 1947	37.8	27.4	24.8
Puerto Rico, 1940	38.2	24.1	37.7
Austria, 1939	39.0	32.1	28.9
Cuba, 1943	41.4	14.6	44.0
Italy, 1936	47.1	27.5	25.4
Hungary, 1941	47.8	24.7	27.5
Ireland, 1936	48.4	15.2	36.4
Portugal, 1940	48.9	20.7	30.4
Venezuela, 1941	51.3	18.6	30.1
Spain, 1940	51.7	23.7	24.6
Japan, 1947	52.5	23.3	24.2
Panama, 1940	52.6	11.2	36.2
Greece, 1928	53.7	15.9	30.4
Finland, 1940	57.4	18.5	24.1
Peru, 1940	62.6	19.1	18.3
Poland, 1931	65.0	16.9	18.1
Mexico, 1940	65.4	12.7	21.9
India, 1931	67.1	10.5	22.4
Brazil, 1940	67.4	12.8	19.8
Egypt, 1937	70.7	10.0	19.3
Colombia, 1938	72.7	13.4	13.9
Philippines, 1939	72.9	10.5	16.6
Nicaragua, 1940	72.9	12.6	14.5
Romania, 1930	78.7	7.2	14.1
Yugoslavia, 1931	78.7	11.1	10.2
Bulgaria, 1934	80.0	7.9	12.1
Turkey, 1935	81.8	8.2	10.0
Thailand, 1937	88.4	2.3	9.3

Source: Computed from Table 169 (cf. **9**, 1945–46, and **2**, 1949–50, pp. 250–75).

a. Arrayed by increasing percentage of labor force in agricultural production.

TABLE 194

LABOR FORCE: RELATION BETWEEN THE NUMBERS OF WORKERS IN AGRICULTURAL AND INDUSTRIAL
PRODUCTION AND SERVICES IN SELECTED COUNTRIES

(*Per Cent*)

Country [a] and Year	Agricultural to Industrial Production	Services to All Nonagricultural Activities	Country [a] and Year	Agricultural to Industrial Production	Services to All Nonagricultural Activities
Great Britain, 1931	13.0	50.9	Japan, 1947	225.3	51.0
Belgium, 1930	35.5	42.4	Portugal, 1940	236.1	59.5
Australia, 1947	44.6	58.5	Venezuela, 1941	275.8	51.5
Switzerland, 1941	47.8	45.1	Cuba, 1943	284.2	75.0
Netherlands, 1947	58.0	58.7	Finland, 1940	311.1	56.6
United States, 1940	58.1	61.0	Ireland, 1936	320.5	70.7
Luxembourg, 1947	62.7	47.1	Peru, 1940	327.7	48.9
Sweden, 1945	64.5	50.0	Greece, 1928	337.7	65.7
Union of South Africa,[b] 1946	69.0	66.3	Poland, 1931	384.6	51.7
Western Germany, 1946	75.6	45.7	Panama, 1940	469.6	76.3
New Zealand, 1946	75.7 [c]	67.2	Mexico, 1940	514.9	63.3
Denmark, 1940	92.8	57.1	Brazil, 1940	526.6	60.7
Canada, 1941	93.9	56.1	Colombia, 1938	542.6	59.9
Czechoslovakia, 1947	100.1	40.0	Nicaragua, 1940	580.1	53.1
Austria, 1939	121.4	47.4	India, 1931	638.1	68.1
France, 1946	122.4	53.1	Philippines, 1937	694.3	61.2
Norway, 1930	133.2	59.2	Egypt, 1937	707.0	65.9
Chile, 1940	137.4	59.8	Yugoslavia, 1931	709.0	47.9
Puerto Rico, 1940	158.5	61.0	Turkey, 1935	997.6	54.9
Italy, 1936	171.3	48.0	Bulgaria, 1934	1,012.6	60.5
Hungary, 1941	193.5	52.7	Romania, 1930	1,094.0	66.2
Spain, 1940	216.0	50.5	Thailand, 1937	3,834.0	80.2

Source: Computed from Table 193.

  a. Arrayed by increasing ratio between labor force in agricultural and industrial production.

b. Europeans.

c. Mining is included in agricultural production.

Downward adjustment to make German statistics of labor force comparable with those of other modern countries shows that German industry employs more than twice as many workers as agriculture.[24] Germany belongs, therefore, in the group of primarily industrial nations.

24. The 1939 census reported 9.0 million workers in agriculture of whom 4.8 million were unpaid family workers. Without unpaid family workers, the ratio between labor force in primary and secondary industries in Germany would amount to 29 per cent. If the number of unpaid family workers on the farm were estimated at half of the total number of farmers, hired farm laborers and salaried employees, the ratio would be 43.7 per cent.

In 1946 German agriculture accounted for a greater than usual number of workers, but industrial employment and production had not yet recovered from the paralyzing blow of military collapse.

Agricultural-Industrial Countries

The group of agricultural-industrial countries, according to Table 194, includes the United States, Canada, Chile and Puerto Rico in the Western Hemisphere; a large part of western and central Europe (France, Luxembourg, the Netherlands, Denmark, Sweden, Norway, Czechoslovakia, Austria, Italy and Hungary); New Zealand and the Union of South Africa.

There can be some doubt about the classification of Puerto Rico among agricultural-industrial countries. In that country the predominant industrial establishments are sugar mills, closely connected with the growing of sugar cane. Most workers shift between seasonal work in the fields and in the mills. The whole economic life of the country depends ultimately on its agriculture, and the area should be classified as primarily agricultural.

Primarily Agricultural Countries

In all other countries included in Table 194, agriculture, including forestry, fishing and hunting, employs more than twice the number of workers engaged in industrial production. This group includes most of Latin America; Ireland and Finland, Portugal and Spain, Poland, Bulgaria, Romania, Yugoslavia and Greece; Asia and most of Africa. Indeed, it covers not only primarily agricultural nations with a prevailing money economy but likewise all the subsistence-economy areas represented in the table by such countries as Thailand, Turkey, the Philippines, India and Nicaragua.

This classification raises serious objections concerning Japan. The census of 1947 recorded 17.8 million workers in agriculture, forestry and fishing as compared with 7.1 million in mining, manufacturing and building construction. The first number, however, does not seem strictly comparable with statistics of the agricultural labor force in most other countries. It includes 5.3 million farmers, 0.9 million hired laborers and 11.6 million unpaid family workers (3.7 million male and 7.9 million female). Even with allowance for the particular significance of family work in Japan, it appears that the number of agricultural workers in the country is largely inflated and that the reported relationship between labor input in farming and industrial production is too high. A downward adjustment brings Japan into the group of agricultural-industrial nations.

The USSR

There is no information on the current distribution of the labor force of the USSR. The Five Year Plan for 1938–42, submitted to the Eighteenth Congress of the Russian Communist Party in 1939, contained a distribution of 32 million workers and employees by industrial division: 11.9 million in mining and manufacturing, 1.8 million in building construction, 2.7 million in agriculture and forestry. These figures, however, do not include members of the kolkhozy, estimated at 19 million families. Assuming two workers per family, total employment in agriculture and forestry in the USSR may be estimated at 40.7 million as compared with 13.7

million workers and employees in industrial production.

Both figures are too low, however. A kolkhoz family must have more than two workers to earn the subsistence minimum. On the other hand, the official figure of workers and employees does not include the inmates of labor camps that supply a large part of the labor force for mining, road building, lumbering and many other industries. It is fairly possible also that some members of kolkhoz families are engaged mainly in administrative work such as policing other kolkhoz members. Thus, the number of workers in agriculture and forestry would be close to 50 million and the number in industrial production is likely to approach 20 million.

The USSR probably employs more than twice as large a labor force in agricultural pursuits as in industrial production. According to our definition, it should therefore be described as a primarily agricultural country, though close to the borderline of the agricultural-industrial type. Such a classification, however, would be in contradiction with the general character of the Soviet economy: the ruthless exploitation of agricultural labor by the state, the frantic drive toward industrialization, the high rate of investment in heavy industries, the rapid progress in urbanization, and so on. The yardstick we use in classification of countries in which free enterprise prevails simply does not fit the peculiar conditions in the Soviet Union. Either the USSR should be excluded from the classification, or it must be described as an agricultural-industrial country in which agriculture is the main pursuit of the population, but the urban, industrial sector prevails in the distribution of the social product and determines the economic policy of the government.

Employment in Commerce and Services

The percentage of the labor force employed by service industries — including commerce, transportation and communication, government and the armed forces — ranges from 9.3 per cent in Thailand and 10 per cent in Turkey to 49.7 per cent in the United States and 53.8 per cent in New Zealand. (See Table 193.) The ratio is necessarily low in primarily agricultural areas and increases as one moves to urbanized and industrialized nations and regions.

The correlation between the proportion of workers in agriculture and the relative significance of production of goods and services in the nonagricultural sector of the economy is not very clear. According to the old theory of Petty, recently revived by Colin Clark, economic progress is marked by movement of the labor force from agriculture to manufacturing and from manufacturing to commerce.[25]

This observation is supported by the changes in distribution of the labor force in several industrialized countries,[26] but is not corroborated by international and interregional comparisons. Areas with widely different economic patterns often have about the same relationship between employment in nonagricultural production of goods and in services. In Great Britain and France, the two divisions employ approximately equal percentages of workers. The same is true for Sweden, Hungary, Poland, Japan, Nicaragua and Peru. In the United States, on the other hand, services, including commerce and transportation absorb one and a half times as many workers as nonagricultural production of goods. (See Table 193.) Brazil, Bulgaria, Greece, Romania, Egypt and India record a similar or higher ratio.

All in all, it appears that the ratio between employment in services and in nonagricultural production of goods is somewhat higher in predominantly agricultural nations than in primarily industrial or agricultural-industrial areas. In most cases the role of a city in a primarily agricultural area is to provide services for the surrounding rural population, while many cities in industrialized regions are primarily centers of manufacturing production.[27]

---

25. Clark quotes Petty's observation "There is much more to be gained by *Manufacture* than *Husbandry;* and by *Merchandise* than *Manufacture,*" and adds the comment: "the vast majority of the world still remains quite unaware of the significance of Petty's brilliant and entirely correct generalization [and] the great majority of economists and those concerned with economic policy still act as if they too were entirely unaware of what might be called, in all fairness, Petty's Law." (**20,a**, pp. 176–77; **20,b**, p. 395.) Petty was a spokesman of mercantilism, an economic philosophy that was eclipsed in the eighteenth century by the physiocrats and Adam Smith but reappeared in the form of economic nationalism in the nineteenth century (List) and gained considerable influence among "those concerned with economic policy" in the twentieth century. In the last fifty years much greater effort has been directed to support industry and trade than to develop agriculture and conserve soil and forests.

26. **20,a**, pp. 185–203.

27. In this respect a typical city and a supercity in an

Labor Force Distribution in the United States

The method of ranking different areas by the ratio between the numbers of workers in agriculture and those engaged in nonagricultural production of goods, can be applied to the individual states in the United States. Since most farmers' wives are not counted as gainful workers (or members of the labor force) by the censuses, it seems preferable to rate individual states according to the industrial distribution of male workers only. (See Table 195.) On this basis, 24 states are agricultural-industrial, 9 are primarily agricultural and 16, including the District of Columbia, are primarily industrial. In most agricultural-industrial states, manufacturing and other branches of nonagricultural production of goods employ more workers than agriculture.

On a map of the conventional type, the primarily industrial states seem to represent a rather small part of the nation. They are more densely populated, however. The 16 states described as primarily industrial averaged 131.6 inhabitants per square mile in 1940, while the 9 primarily agricultural states averaged 22.5 persons and the 24 agricultural-industrial, 26.7. On a "distorted" map showing each state on the scale of its population, the expanse of the primarily industrial states therefore appears much larger than on a conventional map, while the primarily agricultural region is reduced to a narrow strip running across the country from Canada to the Gulf. (See Figure 136.)

There is no visible correlation between the level of industrial development of different regions in the United States and the ratio of the labor force in services to all workers in nonagricultural pursuits. (See Table 195.) The highest ratio is recorded in such primarily agricultural states as North Dakota, South Dakota, Nebraska, Kansas, Wyoming and Iowa. Indeed the share of commerce and services in nonagricultural employment in these states is higher than in New York, Massachusetts, Connecticut and Illinois.

DISTRIBUTION OF NATIONAL INCOME

Along with the distribution of the labor force,

---

industrial country differ sharply. The main functions of a supercity are often management of finance, insurance, distribution and so on — that is, activities classified as services. (Cf. Chapter 4.)

TABLE 195

LABOR FORCE: DISTRIBUTION OF EMPLOYED MALE WORKERS, BY BROAD INDUSTRIAL
DIVISION, IN EACH STATE IN THE UNITED STATES, 1940

State [a]	Agriculture, Forestry, etc. A	Industrial Production B	Commerce, Services, etc. C	Ratio (Percentage) A : B	C : (B + C)
	Percentage of Total				
District of Columbia	1.3	21.1	77.6	6.2	78.6
Rhode Island	3.0	51.4	45.6	5.8	47.0
Massachusetts	3.8	44.6	51.6	8.5	53.6
New Jersey	4.2	44.1	51.7	9.5	54.0
Connecticut	5.5	51.7	42.8	10.6	45.3
New York	5.9	34.4	59.7	17.1	63.4
Pennsylvania	7.8	49.2	43.0	15.8	46.6
New Hampshire	12.5	47.6	39.9	26.3	45.6
Illinois	13.1	37.7	49.2	34.7	56.6
California	13.7	28.8	57.5	47.6	66.6
Maryland	13.8	36.2	50.0	38.1	58.0
Ohio	14.1	43.7	42.2	32.3	49.1
Michigan	14.7	46.1	39.2	31.9	46.0
Washington	17.7	33.9	48.4	52.2	58.8
Nevada	17.9	31.9	50.2	56.1	61.1
Delaware	18.1	39.0	42.9	46.4	52.4
West Virginia	18.2	49.7	32.1	36.6	39.3
Maine	19.0	39.5	41.5	48.1	51.2
Indiana	22.3	37.5	40.2	59.5	51.7
Florida	23.1	23.1	53.8	100.0	70.0
Oregon	23.2	33.9	42.9	68.4	55.9
Utah	23.7	26.5	49.8	89.4	65.3
Arizona	26.2	26.3	47.5	100.0	64.4
Colorado	26.6	23.7	49.7	112.2	67.7
Missouri	30.2	25.0	44.8	120.8	64.2
Virginia	30.4	30.1	39.5	101.0	56.8
Vermont	31.5	31.0	37.5	101.5	54.8
Wisconsin	31.8	32.1	36.2	99.1	52.9
Wyoming	34.4	20.2	45.4	170.3	69.2
Texas	35.9	21.1	43.0	170.1	66.6
Montana	38.0	22.8	39.2	166.6	63.3
Minnesota	38.2	19.4	42.4	196.9	68.6
Kansas	38.5	18.1	43.4	212.7	70.6
New Mexico	39.0	20.5	40.5	190.2	66.4
Louisiana	39.5	23.3	37.2	169.5	61.5
Oklahoma	40.1	19.8	40.1	202.5	66.9
Tennessee	41.1	25.5	33.4	161.2	56.7
North Carolina	41.7	30.6	27.7	136.2	47.5
Georgia	43.2	24.0	32.8	180.0	57.7
Kentucky	43.4	24.6	32.0	176.4	56.5
Idaho	43.5	19.2	37.3	226.6	64.0
Iowa	43.8	17.9	38.3	244.7	68.2
South Carolina	44.8	28.7	26.5	156.1	48.0
Alabama	45.7	27.6	26.7	165.6	37.7
Nebraska	46.2	13.2	40.6	350.0	75.5

(*Continued on facing page*)

TABLE 195—*continued*

State[a]	Agriculture, Forestry, etc. A	Industrial Production B	Commerce, Services, etc. C	Ratio (Percentage) A : B	Ratio (Percentage) C : (B + C)
	Percentage of Total				
South Dakota	57.5	10.2	32.3	563.7	76.0
Arkansas	58.4	15.7	25.9	372.0	62.3
North Dakota	63.0	5.6	31.4	1,125.0	84.9
Mississippi	64.4	14.5	21.1	444.1	59.3

Source: Computed from Table 170 (cf. **12**, Vol. II, pp. 107–11).

a. States arrayed by increasing percentage of labor force in agricultural production.

the distribution of national income between agricultural and industrial sectors is one of the most important characteristics of our economic system. (See Table 196.)

Agricultural and Nonagricultural Income Disparities

In most countries in which the share of agriculture in national income is recorded, it is considerably lower than its share in employment. The disparity in primarily agricultural countries is particularly striking. In Peru, for example, nearly two thirds of the gainful workers in 1940 (62.6 per cent) were engaged in agriculture, but their share in national income was only one third (35 per cent in 1949). These figures suggest that per capita income in nonagricultural pursuits is about three times as high as in agriculture. In Bulgaria, the ratio is 5 to 1, in Colombia 6 to 1. In modern industrially developed countries the contrast is less striking, but the ratio is close to 2 to 1 in the United

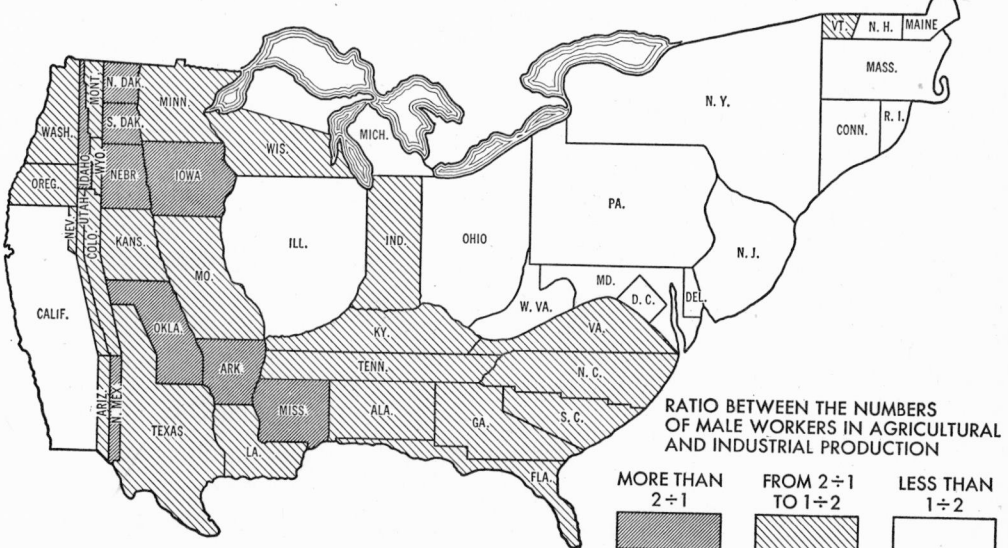

EACH STATE IS REPRESENTED ON A SCALE PROPORTIONATE TO ITS POPULATION

RATIO BETWEEN THE NUMBERS OF MALE WORKERS IN AGRICULTURAL AND INDUSTRIAL PRODUCTION

MORE THAN 2÷1   FROM 2÷1 TO 1÷2   LESS THAN 1÷2

FIGURE 136. DISTRIBUTION OF LABOR FORCE: A DISTORTED MAP OF THE UNITED STATES SHOWING THE PERCENTAGE OF MALE WORKERS IN AGRICULTURE, BY STATE, 1940

A "distorted" map of the United States, on which each state is represented by an area proportionate to its population in 1940, indicates the importance of the industrial states in relation to population. The 16 states in which nonagricultural production of goods employs more than twice as many men as agriculture occupy only 16 per cent of the area of the United States but account for 55 per cent of its population.

TABLE 196

NATIONAL INCOME: DISTRIBUTION, BY INDUSTRIAL ORIGIN, IN SELECTED COUNTRIES, AROUND 1948

(Per Cent)

Country and Year	Agriculture	Manufacturing and Construction	Trade	Transportation and Communication	Government	Other
United States, 1950	7	38	18	9	10	18
Canada, 1950	14	39	15	10	8	15
Dominican Republic, 1946	41	20	21	3	8	7
Colombia, 1949	39	22	9	7	7	16
Peru, 1949	35	28	18	6	7	7
Chile, 1948	18	33	16	7	7	20
Argentina, 1945	24	27	22	9	9	9
Great Britain, 1950	5	46	13	10	10	15
Ireland, 1950	31	25	21		7	16
France, 1949	16	40	12	9	11	12
Netherlands, 1949	13	40	14	11	10	12
Denmark, 1950	22	36	15	9	7	11
Norway, 1950	15	46	12	17	11	3
Finland, 1950	29	39	13	6	9	8
Western Germany, 1950	12	55	8	8	9	1
Poland, 1948	24	47	18	10	—	18
Hungary, 1946	26	46	10	—	10	8
Italy, 1950	30	34	10	8	10	9
Bulgaria, 1946	43	24	12	4	8	9
Greece, 1949	38	25	11	6	10	9
India, 1948	48	17	19		5	11
Philippines, 1948	62	7	13	2	5	11
Union of South Africa, 1949	14	36	14	9	14	14

Sources: **3,** 1951, pp. 435–38; **8,** pp. 23–28.

States, Canada, France, the Netherlands and Norway.[28]

Although there are a few exceptions to this general rule — for example, Australia and India — this distribution of national income between agriculture and other economic activities seems to confirm the first half of Petty's law — that much more is to be gained in urban industries than by tillage and husbandry. To some extent, however, the contrast in agriculture's share of labor and in national income is due to statistical factors, such as understating the income of farmers and overstating the amount of labor absorbed by agriculture.

Even with this reservation average per capita earnings on the farm are probably lower than in urban industries. This disparity is rooted partly in conditions of the agricultural and industrial economy, partly in disparity between the growth of population in rural and in urban areas.[29]

Long-Range Trend in the United States

Economic progress in all modern countries has been marked by the increasing importance of industrial production as compared with farming. This trend is shown in the distribution of national income as well as labor force among the respective industrial divisions.

In the United States, according to estimates

28. **5,** pp. 211–15; **36,** *passim.* For further analysis, cf. Chapter 14.

29. Cf. Chapter 14.

TABLE 197

NATIONAL INCOME: DISTRIBUTION, BY INDUSTRIAL DIVISION, IN THE UNITED STATES, 1929–50 [a]

(*Per Cent*)

Year	Agri-culture	Mining	Manufac-turing	Contract Construc-tion	Trade	Finance	Trans-porta-tion, Communi-cation	Services [b]	Govern-ment	Income from Abroad
1929	9.2	2.4	25.2	4.2	15.0	15.0	10.8	11.7	5.9	0.7
1930	8.0	2.2	24.3	4.1	16.0	14.3	11.1	12.0	7.1	0.8
1931	7.9	1.7	21.1	3.6	16.3	14.5	11.7	13.1	9.3	0.8
1932	7.4	1.6	17.3	2.5	15.1	15.5	13.0	14.4	12.4	0.9
1933	8.9	1.7	19.1	1.9	13.6	14.3	12.6	13.8	13.5	0.7
1934	7.3	2.4	22.4	2.1	16.2	12.1	11.3	12.6	13.0	0.5
1935	11.0	2.2	23.5	2.2	15.8	11.1	10.5	11.5	11.9	0.4
1936	8.2	2.4	25.0	3.0	15.9	11.1	10.3	11.3	12.6	0.3
1937	9.8	2.6	26.2	2.7	16.2	10.8	9.8	10.9	10.6	0.2
1938	8.9	2.2	22.3	2.9	17.3	11.9	10.0	11.5	12.7	0.5
1939	8.4	2.2	24.7	3.1	16.7	11.3	10.2	11.1	11.8	0.3
1940	8.1	2.3	27.5	3.2	16.9	10.4	9.8	10.6	10.8	0.3
1941	8.6	2.3	31.7	4.2	15.3	9.2	9.2	9.4	10.1	0.2
1942	9.5	1.9	33.1	5.1	13.3	8.0	8.9	8.0	12.0	0.2
1943	8.6	1.6	34.2	3.3	12.7	7.2	8.6	7.3	16.2	0.2
1944	8.4	1.6	32.8	2.3	13.1	7.2	8.3	7.4	18.9	0.1
1945	9.0	1.6	28.3	2.3	14.5	7.5	8.3	7.9	20.4	0.1
1946	10.4	1.8	26.7	3.4	18.4	8.3	8.4	9.5	13.0	0.1
1947	9.5	2.0	30.5	4.3	18.5	8.1	8.3	9.3	9.2	0.2
1948	9.8	2.4	30.1	4.7	19.2	7.7	8.4	8.9	8.8	0.2
1949	8.0	2.0	29.0	4.8	19.7	8.2	8.6	9.4	10.1	0.2
1950	7.4	2.1	31.1	5.1	18.1	8.4	8.6	9.2	9.8	0.2

Sources: **15**, July 1950; **14**, pp. 158–59.

a. Figures are not strictly comparable with those in Table 198. They include income derived from public service and publicly owned enterprises, which are not listed in private production income. Moreover, there are considerable differences in industrial classifications in the two tables.

b. Includes the professions.

of Martin based on decennial censuses, agriculture's share in private production income declined from 39.5 per cent in 1799 to 12.7 per cent in 1929, while the share of industrial production increased from 12.8 per cent to 36.2 per cent.[30]

Thus, production of agricultural and nonagricultural goods together accounted for 52.3 per cent of private national income in 1799 and 48.9 per cent in 1929. The ratio of income derived from agriculture to that derived from nonagricultural industrial production was about 3 to 1 in 1799 and 1 to 3 in 1929. The share of services in total income remained amazingly constant, while its ratio to all nonagricultural income declined from 78.6 per cent in 1799 to 58.5 per cent in 1929.[31]

Our official statistics from 1929 on, not strictly comparable with these data, show no consistent trend toward decline in the share of agriculture in national income but reveal appreciable short-term variations in income distribution caused by changes in business activities and prices. (See Table 197.) During the depression in the early 1930's, the joint share of agriculture, mining, manufacturing and construction in national income declined (from 41 per cent in 1929 to 28.8 per cent in 1932), while the share of services increased. The war in its early phase brought a sudden increase in the share of manufactures and building construction, and of government.

30. The data for 1799 are very rough and largely conjectural, but the trend revealed by this comparison seems plausible enough.

31. **29**, pp. 60–61; **13**, p. 14.

TABLE 198

NATIONAL INCOME: DISTRIBUTION, BY INDUSTRIAL DIVISION, IN CANADA, 1919–48

(*Per Cent*)

Year	Agri-culture	Mining	Manu-fac-turing	Con-struc-tion	Trade	Finance	Trans-porta-tion, Com-munica-tion	Profes-sions	Domestic and Other Services	Govern-ment
1919	29	2	20	4	12	7	10	5	5	6
1924	23	3	15	4	12	12	10	5	6	10
1929	21	3	19	4	12	13	10	5	5	10
1934	15	5	20	1	12	11	9	7	7	13
1938	17	7	20	2	12	9	8	5	6	14
1947	14		39		16	6	10		9	8
1948	16		39		14	...	10		...	8

Sources: **36**; **4**, 1938–48, p. 49; **3**, 1951, p. 435.

These short-term fluctuations have over-shadowed any long-range trends that may have existed in the last two decades. The main changes in the distribution of national income by indus-trial origin, from 1929 to 1949–50, occurred in the increase in the share of manufacturing (from 25.2 per cent to 30.0 per cent); in trade (from 15.0 to 18.9 per cent); in government (from 5.9 to 10.0 per cent); and in the decline in the share of finance (from 15.0 to 8.3 per cent).

Trends in Other Countries

In Canada, agriculture's share in national in-come declined from 29 per cent in 1919 to 16 per cent in 1948, while that of mining, manu-factures and construction grew from 26 per cent to 39 per cent. The share of trade, finance, trans-portation, communication, the professions and domestic and other services including govern-ment, continued at about 45 per cent. (See Table 198.)

In Sweden, agriculture, forestry, fisheries and hunting accounted for 38 per cent of national income (without duplications) in 1861 and 12 per cent in 1930. The share of mining, manu-facturing, construction and handcrafts increased from 10 per cent to 31 per cent and that of transportation, communication, trade and fi-nance, from 15 per cent to 26 per cent. (See Table 199.) The fragmentary information avail-able for other countries (see Table 200) reveals similar shifts.

TABLE 199

NATIONAL INCOME: DISTRIBUTION BY INDUSTRIAL DIVISION, IN SWEDEN, 1861–1930

(*Per Cent*)

Year	Agri-culture	Mining, Manufac-turing, etc.	Transpor-tation, Communi-cation	Trade and Finance	Dwellings and Durable Goods	Domestic Services	House-wives	Govern-ment	Correc-tion for Duplica-tion
1861	38	10	1	14	14	4	18	3	–2
1870	36	14	3	15	11	3	17	4	–3
1880	37	11	4	16	11	3	17	4	–3
1890	32	14	5	17	12	2	17	4	–3
1900	28	25	5	17	11	2	16	4	–4
1910	23	25	6	18	11	2	15	4	–4
1920	20	26	6	21	7	2	18	5	–5
1930	12	31	7	19	11	2	17	6	–5

Source: **36**.

TABLE 200

NATIONAL INCOME: DISTRIBUTION, BY INDUSTRIAL DIVISION, IN SELECTED COUNTRIES AND SPECIFIED YEARS

(*Per Cent*)

Country and Year	Agriculture and Forestry	Mining, Manufacturing, Construction	Trade and Finance	Transportation and Communication	Other
Chile					
1929	26.5	25.4	14.5	5.3	28.3
1934	25.3	21.4	14.3	6.2	32.8
1948	18.0	33.0	15.0	7.0	26.0
Ireland					
1926	35.4	18.7	13.6	4.1	28.2
1932	30.4	22.3	13.6	4.0	29.7
1944	36.0	19.0	21.0		24.0
Finland					
1926	34.9	19.8	18.2		27.1
1938	33.2	22.0	19.8		25.0
1948	34.3	39.2	12.7	6.1	7.7
Hungary					
1924–25	41.0	26.6	4.4	1.1	26.9
1936–37	33.6	32.6	7.4	3.4	23.0
1946	25.7	46.1	10.2	18.0	
Bulgaria					
1925	52.3	22.3	10.4	1.6	13.4
1935	43.5	20.8	10.5	2.9	22.3
1946	43.0	24.0	12.0	4.0	17.0
USSR					
1913	43.3	37.6	8.6	5.7	4.8
1928	37.6	40.8	12.0	6.4	3.2
1937	15.4	66.0	12.2	5.4	1.0
Japan (Empire)					
1930	23.5	33.6	42.9		
1939	20.7	42.0	37.3		
1949 [a]	28.4	32.2	14.0	8.3	17.1
Israel, 1950 [a]	9.6	36.6	14.9	6.3	32.6
Union of South Africa					
1911–12	16.1	34.3	13.7	8.8	27.1
1924–25	20.0	29.4	17.8	6.5	26.3
1934–35	12.8	36.4	17.0	6.6	27.2
1943–44	13.6	33.9	15.1	8.3	29.1
1948	14.0	33.0	14.0	10.0	29.0
Australia					
1928–29	24.7	27.5	21.9		25.9
1935–36	24.9	28.0	21.5		24.6

Sources: **4**, 1938–48, pp. 211–15; **3**, 1949–50, pp. 411–13; **5**, p. 23.

a. Net geographical product.

PREVAILING SUBSISTENCE ECONOMY

PER CAPITA INCOME, IN U.S. DOLLARS	COUNTRIES AND REGIONS	POPULATION, IN MILLIONS	NATIONAL INCOME, IN MILLIONS OF U.S. DOLLARS
LESS THAN 60	PACIFIC ISLANDS, MOST OF AFRICA, SOME COLONIAL AREAS IN ASIA	160.0	7,640
	CHINA, MONGOLIA, KOREA, BHUTAN, NEPAL, BAHREIN, BURMA, INDOCHINA, INDONESIA, PHILIPPINES	641.5	34,800
	SAUDI ARABIA, YEMEN, AFGHANISTAN	25.0	1,370
	HAITI, ECUADOR AND FOREIGN POSSESSIONS IN AMERICA	9.6	560
OVER 60 TO 80	INDIA, PAKISTAN, CEYLON, THAILAND	445.5	33,021
	BOLIVIA	4.0	221
OVER 80 TO 100	IRAN, IRAQ	22.0	1,870
	PARAGUAY, PERU	8.4	770
OVER 100	GUATEMALA, SYRIA, LEBANON, JORDAN, TURKEY (IN ASIA)	23.3	2,750

PREVAILING MONEY ECONOMY

AGRICULTURAL-INDUSTRIAL ECONOMY

PER CAPITA INCOME, IN U.S. DOLLARS	COUNTRIES AND REGIONS	POPULATION, IN MILLIONS	NATIONAL INCOME, IN MILLIONS OF U.S. DOLLARS
LESS THAN 300	JAPAN	80.2	11,523
	U.S.S.R.	193.0	35,000
	CHILE	5.6	1,013
	HUNGARY, ITALY	54.9	12,390
OVER 300 TO 500	AUSTRIA, CZECHOSLOVAKIA	19.3	6,800
	UNION OF SOUTH AFRICA	11.8	4,096
	FRANCE	41.5	17,336
OVER 500 TO 750	NETHERLANDS, NORWAY	13.0	6,516
OVER 750 TO 1000	DENMARK, SWEDEN	11.1	8,880
	CANADA (INCL. NEWFOUNDLAND), NEW ZEALAND, AUSTRALIA	22.5	19,550
OVER 1000	UNITED STATES	146.6	223,500

PRIMARILY AGRICULTURAL ECONOMY

PER CAPITA INCOME, IN U.S. DOLLARS	COUNTRIES AND REGIONS	POPULATION, IN MILLIONS	NATIONAL INCOME, IN MILLIONS OF U.S. DOLLARS
LESS THAN 150	EGYPT, ALGERIA, TUNISIA, MOROCCO, ISRAEL	41.2	4,700
	MEXICO, EL SALVADOR, HONDURAS, NICARAGUA, COSTA RICA, DOMINICAN REPUBLIC	31.0	3,310
	COLOMBIA, BRAZIL	60.0	6,986
	EUROPEAN TURKEY, GREECE, ALBANIA	10.6	1,300
OVER 150 TO 200	YUGOSLAVIA, BULGARIA	22.9	3,430
	PANAMA	0.7	125
	SPAIN, PORTUGAL, ROMANIA, POLAND	76.1	14,000
OVER 200 TO 300	CUBA, JAMAICA, PUERTO RICO	8.8	2,412
OVER 300	ARGENTINA, URUGUAY, VENEZUELA	23.1	7,325
	IRELAND, FINLAND	7.0	3,731

PRIMARILY INDUSTRIAL ECONOMY

PER CAPITA INCOME, IN U.S. DOLLARS	COUNTRIES AND REGIONS	POPULATION, IN MILLIONS	NATIONAL INCOME, IN MILLIONS OF U.S. DOLLARS
LESS THAN 300			
OVER 300 TO 500	GERMANY	67.7	22,800
OVER 500 TO 750	BELGIUM AND LUXEMBOURG	8.8	5,690
OVER 750 TO 1000	UNITED KINGDOM, SWITZERLAND	54.6	43,365
OVER 1000			

FIGURE 137. COUNTRIES AND REGIONS OF THE WORLD CLASSIFIED BY TYPE OF ECONOMY AND PER CAPITA INCOME, 1948

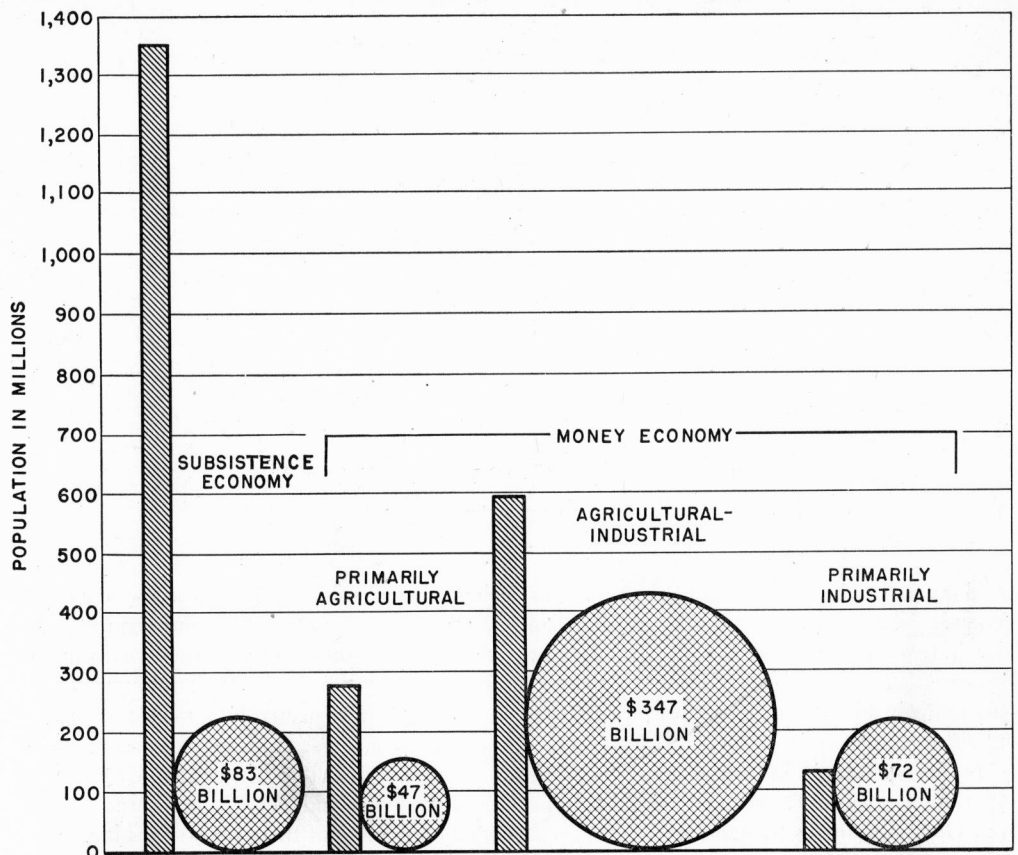

FIGURE 138. ECONOMIC PATTERNS: DISTRIBUTION OF WORLD POPULATION AND INCOME BY TYPE OF ECONOMY, 1948

The prevailing trend thus has been toward an increase in the share of manufacturing in national income at the expense of agriculture. There has been no universal increase in the share of services compared to the production of goods. The relative income of the professions and government has risen but not in all countries as rapidly as that of industry. Domestic services have lost ground to service industries.

ECONOMIC PATTERNS IN THE WORLD

Classification of the countries of the world by type of economy results in a rough distribution of the world's population and income among four vast areas. (See Figure 137.)

The area of prevailing subsistence economy embraces more than 100 countries, including colonial possessions and mandates, which had, in 1948, a population of more than 1.3 billion and aggregate income of $83 billion. Primarily agricultural countries with a prevailing money economy accounted for a total population of 281 million and an aggregate income of $47 billion. Industrial-agricultural countries, with a total population of 600 million, controlled an aggregate income of $347 billion. Primarily industrial countries, with 131 million people, had an income of $72 billion, in round numbers.

Annual per capita income was, in round numbers, $60 in the area of prevailing subsistence economy, $170 in primarily agricultural countries with a money economy, $580 in agricultural-industrial countries, and $550 in primarily industrial nations. (See Figure 138.)

DISTRIBUTION OF WORLD POPULATION AND INCOME BY TYPE OF ECONOMY

A subsistence economy prevails in the largest part of Asia and Africa, on the Pacific Islands and in some parts of Latin America.

Primarily agricultural countries with a prevailing money economy form two blocks on the

*TABLE 201

ECONOMIC PATTERNS: DISTRIBUTION OF WORLD POPULATION, BY TYPE OF ECONOMY, 1948

(*Millions*)

Continent	Total	Prevailing Subsistence Economy	Money Economy		
			Primarily Agricultural	Agricultural-Industrial	Primarily Industrial
World	2,351	1,339	281	600	131
America	316	27	123	166	—
Europe	389	—	118	140	131
USSR	193	—	—	193	—
Asia	1,248	1,168	—	80	—
Africa	193	141	40	12	—
Oceania	12	3	—	9	—

Source: Figure 137.

world map. In the Western Hemisphere, this economic pattern prevails south of the Rio Grande (except for the areas with a subsistence economy); in the Eastern Hemisphere it dominates in Spain and Portugal, southeastern Europe and the Mediterranean strip of Africa.

The four primarily industrial countries form a continuous strip in western and central Europe from Great Britain to Switzerland.

Countries classified as agricultural-industrial are dispersed over all parts of the world: the United States, Canada and Chile; France, Italy, the Netherlands, Denmark, Sweden, Norway, Austria, Hungary and Czechoslovakia; the Union of South Africa; the USSR; Australia and New Zealand. (See Table 201 and Figure 139.)

A reclassification of single countries close to the demarcation lines between the four types of economy, does not change this general geographic pattern appreciably.

PER CAPITA INCOME

Per capita income is lower in most of the primarily agricultural countries than in industrial nations and is particularly low in the areas with a subsistence economy.[32] It seems, however,

that the available national income data[33] for these areas are understated and require an upward adjustment to be comparable with national income estimates for industrial countries.[34]

The group of primarily agricultural countries comprises a great variety of countries, from Egypt and Brazil to Argentina, Uruguay, Ireland and Finland. Per capita income in the more developed of these countries is higher than in the agricultural-industrial USSR or Japan.

On the other hand, the richest countries of the world are agricultural-industrial rather than primarily industrial.

THREE LEVELS OF DEVELOPMENT

In the classification of countries of each type by level of economic development in 1948, as in Figure 140, the economic level of primarily agricultural nations is designated as low if they have per capita income of less than $150, as medium if their per capita income ranges between $150 and $300, and as high if it exceeds $300; in other areas, the level of countries with per capita incomes under $300 are described as low, those with income from $300 to $750 as

---

32. The measurement of national income in countries in which most products are consumed in the household of the producer, without reaching the market, is difficult, of course, and cannot be very accurate. However, without such an estimate, no comparison of the over-all level of living in these areas and the rest of the world is possible. Such estimates have been made repeatedly in China, India, Southern Rhodesia, Nyasaland and other underdeveloped

countries. These studies usually start with the sectors of the economy in the area in which money and market relations prevail. These observations are subsequently extrapolated and applied to other economic sectors. Some of the studies on national income in the areas of subsistence economy have been made with considerable skill and reasonable accuracy. (See, for example, **21** and **28**.)

33. See **4** and **6**; cf. **10**.

34. Cf. **18**.

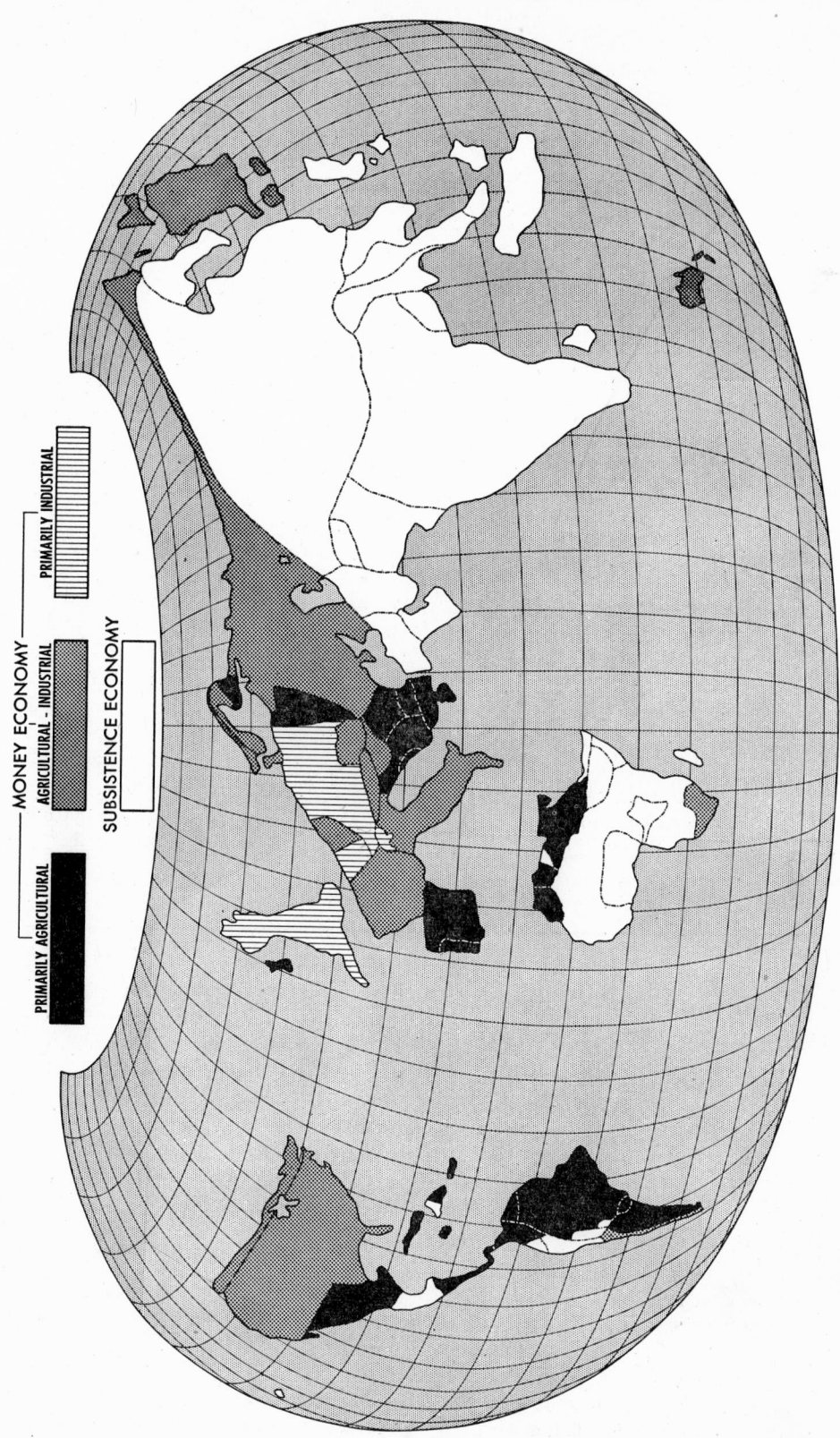

FIGURE 139. ECONOMIC PATTERNS: A DISTORTED MAP OF THE WORLD SHOWING THE AREAS OF PREVALENCE OF SPECIFIED TYPES OF MONEY ECONOMY

Continents and countries are shown here on the scale of their population in 1950. The map indicates the distribution of world population among the realms of subsistence and money economies, and among the different types of money economy.

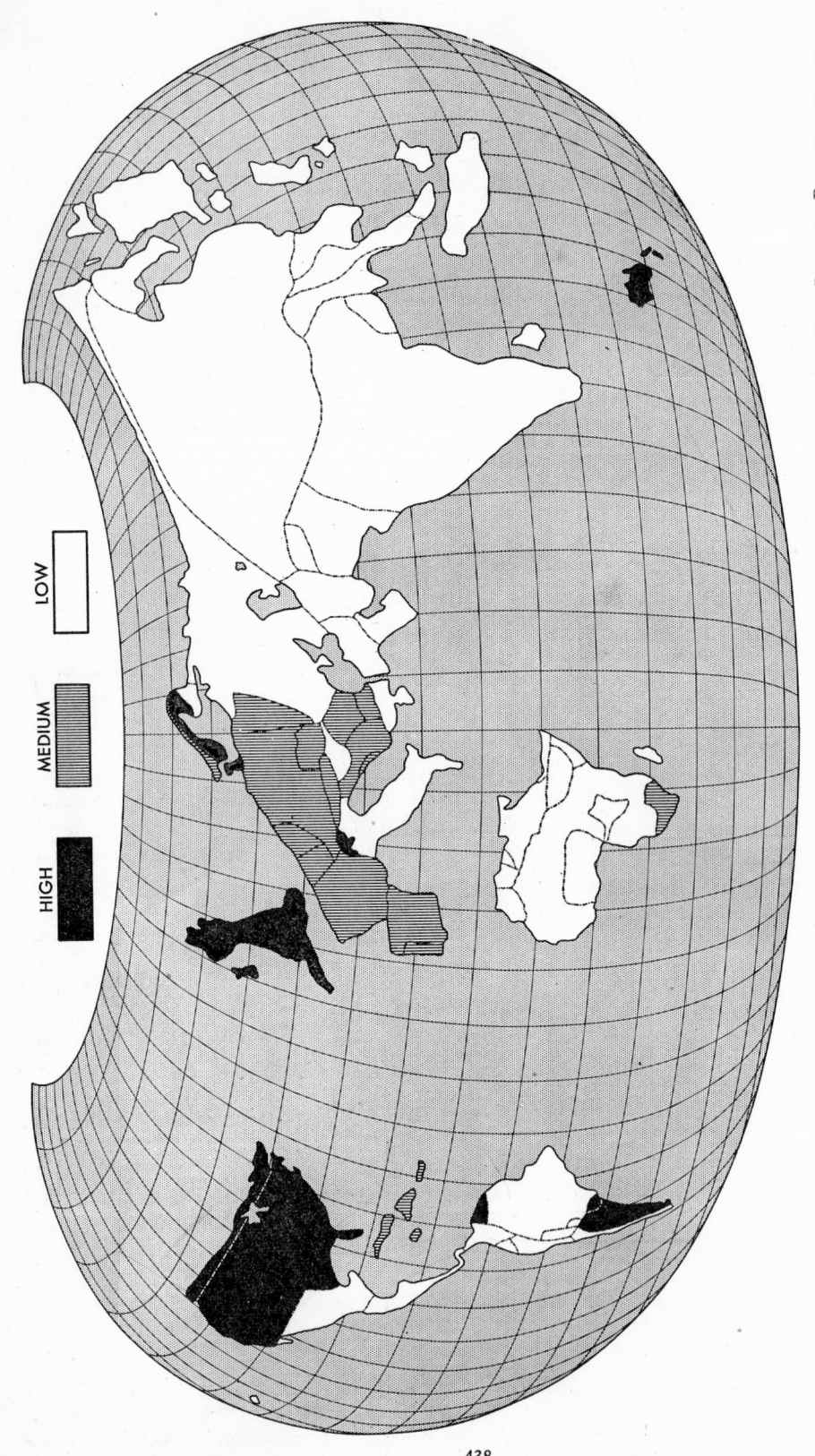

FIGURE 140. ECONOMIC PATTERNS: A DISTORTED MAP OF THE WORLD SHOWING THE AREAS WITH DIFFERENT LEVELS OF WELL-BEING IN RELATION TO THE PREVAILING TYPE OF ECONOMY

Countries are classified on this distorted map by per capita income in relation to the type of economy prevailing in the respective country. Italy, Hungary, the USSR, Chile and Japan, for example, had per capita income in 1948 that compared favorably with that in most of the primarily agricultural nations. (Cf. Table 187 and Figure 138.) In the area of agricultural-industrial economy, however, they are the poorest countries.

TABLE 202

ECONOMIC PATTERNS: DISTRIBUTION OF WORLD POPULATION AND INCOME BY TYPE OF
ECONOMY AND ECONOMIC LEVEL, 1948

Level of Well-Being	*Total*	*Prevailing Subsistence Economy*	Prevailing Money Economy		
			Primarily Agricultural	*Agricultural-Industrial*	*Primarily Industrial*
Population, in Millions					
Total	2,351	1,339	281	600	131
Low	1,816	1,339	143	334	—
Medium	271	—	108	86	77
High	264	—	30	180	54
Income, in Billions					
Total	$549	$83	$47	$347	$72
Low	159	83	16	60	—
Medium	84	—	20	35	29
High	306	—	11	252	43

Source: Figure 137.

medium, and those with more than $750 as high.[35]

Nations classified, according to these standards, as being of "low" level of development represent some 77 per cent of the world's population and account for less than 30 per cent of the world's income.[36] The other 70 per cent of income is distributed among the medium and high groups of countries, which are about equal in aggregate population. The medium group controls 15 per cent of the world's income and the group of highly developed nations accounts for the remaining 55 per cent. (See Table 202 and Figure 137.)

35. This grouping is tentative and open to criticism. The use of a double yardstick for primarily agricultural and industrialized areas is justified by two considerations. First, it is recognized that national income figures for primarily agricultural countries, especially those in which subsistence economy prevails, are not completely comparable with those for industrial nations. The latter use an appreciable part of their income on needs which are unknown or insignificant in agricultural areas. Second, the concepts of wealth and poverty are relative and describe the state of a group of population or an area in comparison to other groups or other areas. Venezuela, Uruguay and Argentina are poor in comparison with the United States, Canada and the United Kingdom, but they are rich in comparison with other nations in Latin America and in comparison with agricultural countries in other parts of the world. Such comparisons within the group of nations of more or less similar type seem more meaningful than the use of a uniform yardstick for all countries.

36. Data for population from **3**, 1949–50, and **7**.

ECONOMIC PATTERNS IN THE UNITED STATES

When the states are arrayed by declining ratio between the number of workers in agriculture and industrial production, from the Dakotas and Mississippi, to New Jersey, Massachusetts and Rhode Island, some of the poorest states are found in the primarily agricultural regions and some of the richest in the highly industrialized areas. This correlation is not very close, however. Such primarily agricultural states as Idaho and Iowa have higher per capita income than primarily industrial West Virginia. The agricultural-industrial group includes states on widely different economic levels. Wyoming and Montana, for example, have about the same distribution of labor force between agricultural and industrial production as Alabama and Georgia but have nearly double the per capita income of the latter. (See Table 203.)

In 1938, per capita income in primarily agricultural states ranged from $185 to $423; in industrial-agricultural states, from $233 to $645; and in primarily industrial states, from $369 to $791. The contrasts were less pronounced in 1950: from $698 to $1,467 for primarily agricultural states; $831 to $1,872 for agricultural-industrial states; $1,049 to $1,909 for primarily industrial states.

In 1938, the poorest primarily agricultural states in the United States, Mississippi and Arkansas, had about the same per capita income as Hungary, Yugoslavia and Finland and double

TABLE 203

ECONOMIC PATTERNS: PER CAPITA INCOME IN STATES CLASSIFIED BY RELATIVE IMPORTANCE OF
AGRICULTURE, IN THE UNITED STATES, 1938 AND 1950 [a]

Primarily Agricultural States	1938	1950	*Agricultural- Industrial States*	1938	1950	*Primarily Industrial States*	1938	1950
Mississippi	$185	$ 698	Alabama	$233	$ 836	West Virginia	$369	$1,049
Arkansas	236	825	South Carolina	241	831	Maine	450	1,161
North Dakota	302	1,298	Georgia	280	969	New Hampshire	531	1,282
South Dakota	318	1,308	Tennessee	280	962	Michigan	535	1,583
Oklahoma	327	1,070	Kentucky	283	911	Pennsylvania	553	1,523
Kansas	382	1,338	North Carolina	289	951	Ohio	555	1,582
Nebraska	384	1,467	New Mexico	322	1,109	Maryland	594	1,547
Idaho	406	1,287	Louisiana	341	1,045	Illinois	616	1,752
Iowa	423	1,417	Virginia	380	1,158	Rhode Island	639	1,561
			Texas	387	1,278	Massachusetts	677	1,600
			Florida	418	1,210	Delaware	682	1,909
			Utah	434	1,271	New Jersey	699	1,689
			Arizona	436	1,240	Connecticut	710	1,766
			Indiana	449	1,451	California	714	1,751
			Vermont	454	1,184	New York	791	1,864
			Missouri	455	1,401			
			Wisconsin	466	1,431			
			Minnesota	474	1,332			
			Colorado	475	1,392			
			Montana	488	1,605			
			Oregon	507	1,523			
			Wyoming	537	1,509			
			Washington	558	1,642			
			Nevada	645	1,872			

Source: Computed from **15**, August 1951.

a. States are classified by the ratio of the number of male workers engaged in agriculture to that in industrial production in 1940. (Cf. Table 195.) Within each group, states are arrayed by increasing per capita income in 1938.

the amount in Poland, Romania and the USSR. The richest primarily agricultural states were on the same economic level as the United Kingdom and Switzerland, and considerably above Belgium and Luxembourg.

Per capita income in agricultural-industrial states ranged from the pattern characteristic of France and Ireland ($233 in Alabama, $280 in Tennessee and Georgia) to that found abroad only in Australia and New Zealand ($537 in Wyoming, $558 in Washington, $645 in Nevada). Per capita income was highest in New York, New Jersey, Connecticut, Massachusetts and California. In other primarily industrial states per capita income was not appreciably higher than in wealthy agricultural-industrial states of the West and Midwest.

PRODUCTIVITY OF LABOR

Per capita income in a nation is closely correlated with output per worker. Essentially, these are two ways of measuring the same characteristic of the economic system: its efficiency in utilization of human resources for production of goods and services.

Direct measurement of the over-all productivity of labor (or the over-all efficiency of the economic system) is very difficult, however. It is not enough to compare the output of an industry, in physical units, with the input of labor in terms of man-years or man-hours worked in this industry. To the input of labor in the industry should be added the labor input in mechanical energy consumed by the industry, the labor represented by the amortization of capital equipment and other items.

A comparison of productivity of labor in a single industry in different years likewise presents serious difficulties. If comparison is restricted to a short period — say, less than a decade — differences may be due to temporary factors such as cyclical variations in business

TABLE 204

PRODUCTIVITY: TREND IN COAL MINING IN THE UNITED STATES, 1890–1948

	1890	1900	1910	1920	1930	1940	1942	1944	1946	1948
Production, in millions of tons	111	212	417	569	468	461	583	620	534	600
Workers, in thousands	192	304	556	640	493	439	462	393	396	442
Tons, per man										
Per year	579	697	751	881	948	1,049	1,261	1,575	1,347	1,357
Per day	2.50	2.98	3.46	4.00	5.06	5.19	5.12	5.67	6.30	6.26
Mechanization:										
Cutting (per cent)	(5.3)	24.9	41.7	60.7	81.0	88.4	35.4	90.5	90.8	90.7
Loading (per cent)	—	—	—	—	10.5	89.7	45.2	52.9	58.4	64.3
Cleaning (per cent)	—	—	3.8	3.3	8.3	22.2	24.4	25.6	26.0	30.2
Strip mines (per cent)	—	—	—	1.5	4.3	9.4	11.5	16.3	21.1	23.3

Source: **16**.

conditions. If it covers a long period, changes in product, methods of production, and hours of work must be taken into consideration.

Coal mining in the United States is one of the few industries for which strictly comparable data are available for more than 50 years. (See Table 204.) The output of coal per man-year increased from 579 tons in 1890 to 1,357 tons in 1948, though the miners' work week was cut almost half. During that period the trend in other industries was very uneven. Progress was occasionally interrupted by periods of stagnation and setbacks, as in the 1930's.

PRODUCTIVITY IN VARIOUS COUNTRIES

In recent years, extensive studies have been made to compare the productivity of manufacturing industries in Great Britain, the United States and other industrially developed countries.

Comparison of output and employment in 32 manufacturing industries in 1935–39 indicated that the average productivity per worker in the United States was about 2.2 times that in Great Britain. If the difference in hours of work is taken into consideration, it appears that the output per man-hour in the United States was perhaps 2.8 times that in the United Kingdom.[37] These conclusions remain unchanged when the data for single industries are combined in a composite weighted or unweighted index. Indexes of physical output per worker in selected industries in different countries show that before the war the productivity of labor in Germany and Sweden was about the same as in

Great Britain, in the Netherlands somewhat higher, and in the United States more than twice as high as in any one of the surveyed European countries. Only in the cement industry was the output per worker lower in the United States than in Great Britain and the Netherlands. (See Table 205.)

The gap between the productivity of American and British factories has developed gradually through decades. From 1907 to 1937, output per wage earner increased, on the average, 1.4 per cent a year in Great Britain and 1.8 per cent a year in the United States, while the output per man-hour rose 1.7 per cent in Great Britain and 2.1 per cent in the United States.[38]

From 1924 to 1939, output per man-hour in manufacturing industries in the United States increased 65 per cent, so that the output per worker rose 36 per cent despite the reduction of the normal work week by one sixth. During the same period (more precisely, from 1924 to 1938), Great Britain gained 25 per cent in output per worker, without appreciable change in the hours of work. (See Figure 141.)

FACTORS IN PRODUCTIVITY OF LABOR

In comparison with the present level of per capita income in the industrially developed countries, all nations started from the same fairly low level not very long ago; indeed, contrasts in well-being in different parts of the world were not overwhelming in the middle of the nineteenth century. Inequality has developed as a result of the unequal rate of growth

37. **32**, p. 35.

38. **32**, p. 53.

TABLE 205

PRODUCTIVITY: RELATION OF OUTPUT PER WORKER IN SELECTED INDUSTRIES IN THE
UNITED STATES, GERMANY, SWEDEN AND THE NETHERLANDS TO OUTPUT PER
WORKER IN GREAT BRITAIN (According to L. Rostas)

(Output Per Worker in Great Britain, 1935–37 = 100)

Industry	United States 1935–37	Germany 1936	Sweden 1937	Netherlands 1937–38
Pig iron	364	} 141	...	...
Steel works and rolling mills	166		...	...
Foundries	167	120	...	...
Machinery	...	110	...	...
Cement	94	92	90	170
Brick	121	...	...	...
Coke	236	152	...	...
Motor cars	306	98	...	...
Radio sets	...	70	...	...
Cotton spinning	150	120	...	...
Cotton weaving	200	68	84	...
Rayon and silk	146	132	...	81
Jute	...	106	...	...
Hosiery	161	92	...	...
Boots and shoes	153	110	68	...
Rubber tires	276	117	...	...
Soap	276	117	...	228
Breweries	202	67	...	90
Tobacco	...	30	153	...
Margarine	136	81	100	62
Beet sugar	106	34	43	...
Grain milling	170	93	95	...
Paper	...	...	140	...

Source: **32**, pp. 46–50.

of productivity of labor in agriculture as well as in manufacturing.

The conditions that control progress in agriculture differ from those in industry. A country with abundant agricultural resources usually tends to organize its farming in such a way as to obtain a maximum yield per worker without necessarily maximizing the yield per acre. On the contrary, in a densely populated country, the high cost of land, high rents and the smallness of holdings compel farmers to increase the yield per acre from even marginal land. The rising input of labor per unit of agricultural product in such a country is not always favorable for increase of output per farm worker. Thus, in terms of agricultural output per worker (rather than per acre), young and sparsely populated countries such as the United States, Canada, Australia and New Zealand have a considerable advantage over the older nations. (See Chapter 15.)

In forestry, fishing and mining, the output per worker depends largely on natural condi-

tions, but also on man's ingenuity in using what nature puts at his disposal.

In manufacturing, the first major factor in productivity of labor is, of course, the use of machinery. A worker in a modern factory produces more than a craftsman of former times, not because his skill is superior but because he has better tools and machines run by mechanical power.

Factories in the United States used 2.18 horsepower per operative in 1899, 2.88 in 1909, 4.91 in 1929 and 6.42 in 1939. In the United Kingdom, the factory operative was supported by 1.10 horsepower in 1899 and 3.54 in 1939. For other industrially developed countries, Rostas gives the following figures (horsepower per worker): [39]

Germany (1933)	3.76
Switzerland (1937)	2.70
Netherlands (1937)	3.80

39. **32**, p. 72.

1924=100

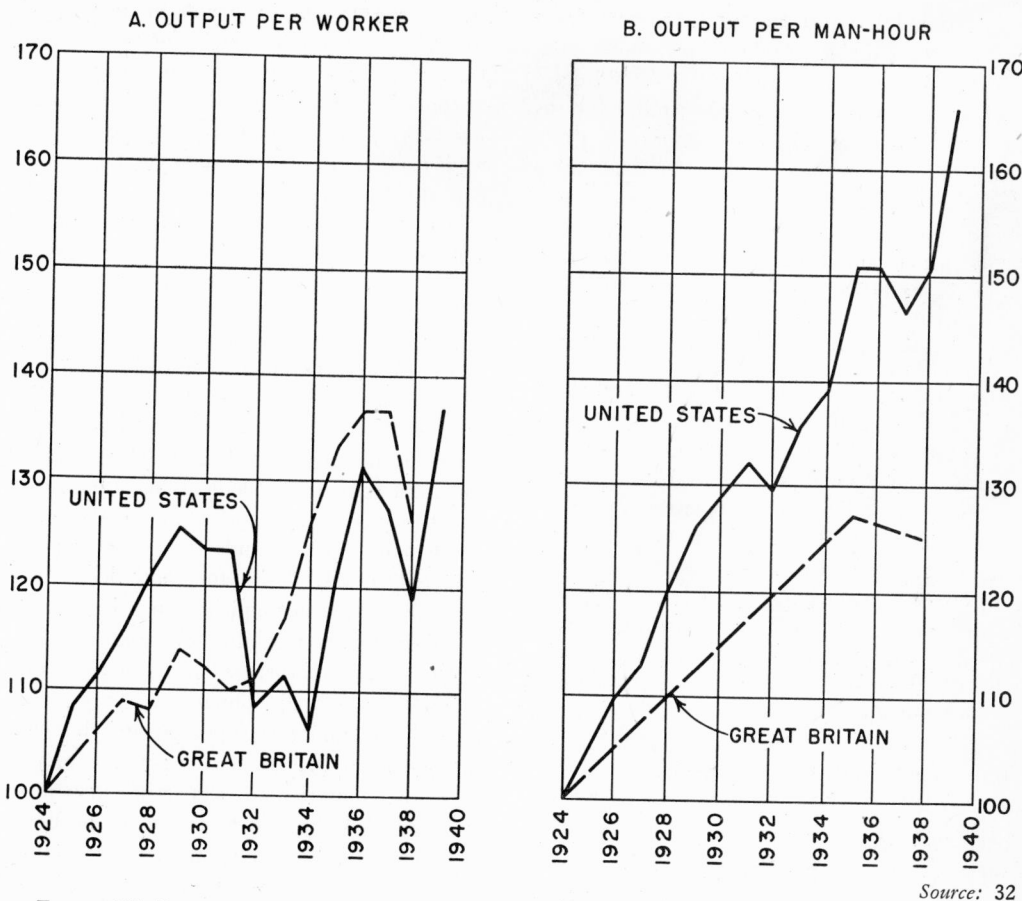

Source: 32

FIGURE 141. PRODUCTIVITY IN MANUFACTURING: THE UNITED STATES AND GREAT BRITAIN, 1924–39

The ratio between the output per worker in the United States and Great Britain is about the same as the ratio of energy consumed in manufacturing per factory worker in the two countries. It would be erroneous, however, to generalize this relationship. In some countries, the output per worker lags far behind the input of mechanical horsepower. There is also a considerable difference in the demand for horsepower by individual industries and in the efficiency of utilization of horsepower in different countries.[40] A closer comparison of conditions in 27 industries in the United States and Great Britain does not suggest a close correlation between the relative amount of horsepower per worker and relative productivity.[41] The general trend of manufacturing technique in recent

years has been neither entirely in the direction of using better and more expensive machinery nor of increasing horsepower.[42] The way in which machines and horsepower are used in production is of decisive significance.

The high output per man-hour in the United States is due to the concentrated efforts of industry to reduce labor cost by such devices and methods as the assembly line, scientific organization of work operations, automatic hand tools, standardization and interchangeability of parts, simplification of design, reduction of variety of patterns. Other means which serve the same general purpose have been the reduction of hours of work and improvement of lighting, heating and ventilation and other working conditions, such as periods for meals and for relaxation between work operations.

40. **32**, Chapter 25.
41. **32**, p. 74.

42. **32**, p. 76.

The Road of Economic Progress

The world has just started the ascent from scarcity to abundance. Only 11 per cent of the world's population live in countries on a "high" level of economic development and about as many live in areas with an economy of "medium" type, according to modern standards. The predominant economy in the world is still the traditional tillage of soil, handwork and small-scale local trade. As Gini puts it, the natural state of the economy is "primitivity." [43]

Industrialization vs. Colonization

The modern economic system has been built up by a dozen nations of European stock on the two coasts of the North Atlantic Ocean and has been spreading out from these two centers over a steadily expanding area, progressing at an uneven pace in various directions. Other peoples hated this development as long as it proceeded in the form of *colonization* but now are eager to promote it in the form of *industrialization*.[44] The diversity of economic patterns in different parts of the world and the contrasts between scarcity and abundance reflect the stages reached by the different nations that are traveling the road from primitivity to mechanization.

The Cause of Contrasts

The cause of the striking contrasts in the use of mechanical power and other technical devices and in the organization of production in different parts of the globe can be reduced to two factors: differences in the speed of economic growth and in the time when this growth, in the sense of the modern mechanized economy, began.

Economic progress is not a single process such as biological growth but, rather, a system of interrelated, more or less independent developments in the different fields of economic activities.[45]

The controlling factor in economic advance of a nation has been less the availability of local natural resources than what people have been able to do with these resources and their own hands and brains.

Premises of Economic Growth

In his study of the origin of modern capitalism, Werner Sombart has shown that the new forms of economy were born in Europe at the dawn of modern times, when people first learned to consider money not merely as treasure and a means of living in luxury, but as capital, a means of acquiring more money and power.[46] He describes as "feverish, greedy money madness" the capitalist spirit that shook the immovable society of the Dark Ages to its foundation.[47]

The economic system of our time is very different from that of the sixteenth or seventeenth century. No less than early capitalism, however, it depends on a definite pattern of human behavior. An exhaustive analysis of this pattern is not within the scope of the present study, but some of its elements have been mentioned in preceding chapters: the steadily growing demand for all kinds of economic goods, tempered by the desire for more leisure; the drive toward greater equality on a higher level of consumption; flexibility of production and occupational patterns; a spirit of individual initiative and self discipline.

People of underdeveloped areas who claim their share in the fruits of economic progress are neither hungrier nor less secure than in the past, but they have seen the ways of life of wealthier nations and want these ways for themselves. The first manifestations of the wakening of the underdeveloped areas seem to threaten the foundations of our civilization; actually, it broadens them. The civilization of men expert in building and using machines ceases to be the privilege and weapon of the white race and becomes the universal, global civilization.

Factors in Growth

Economic progress has different aspects in the different parts of the world. In developed countries, the forward drive is stimulated by economic inequality. The lowest third of the population feels ill-clad, ill-fed and ill-housed even when its living conditions are far above the average standards in poorer nations. Moreover, not only the poor in the wealthy countries but the countries as a whole are haunted by fear of economic setbacks, exhaustion or depletion of their

---

43. **22**, pp. 6 ff.

44. The question of colonies is discussed by the authors in their study of world trade and government, now in preparation for the Twentieth Century Fund.

45. **33**, p. 490.

46. **34**, pp. 378 ff.

47. **35**, p. 2 and *passim*.

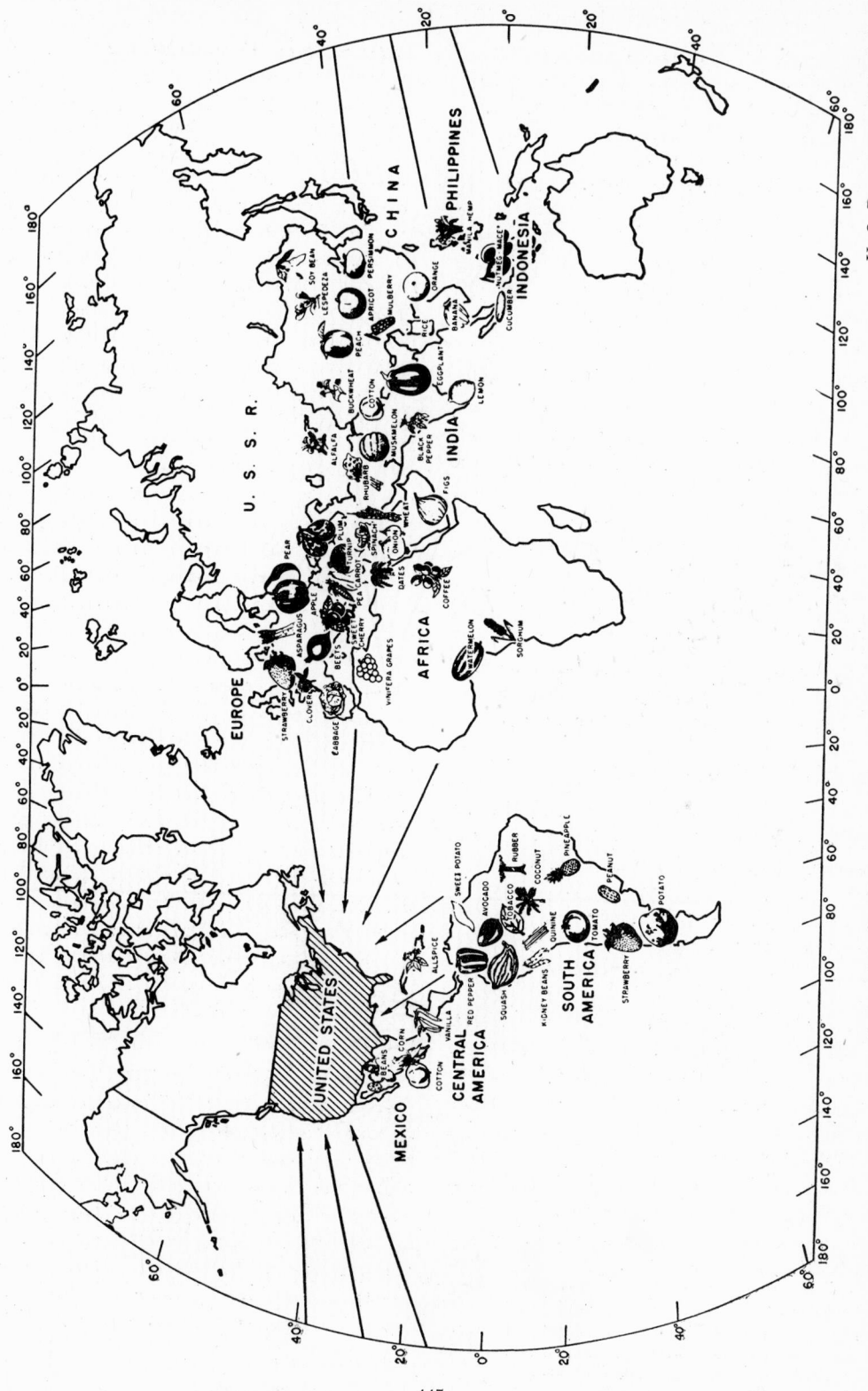

FIGURE 142. THE WORLD'S CONTRIBUTION TO AGRICULTURE IN THE UNITED STATES

U. S. Department of Agriculture

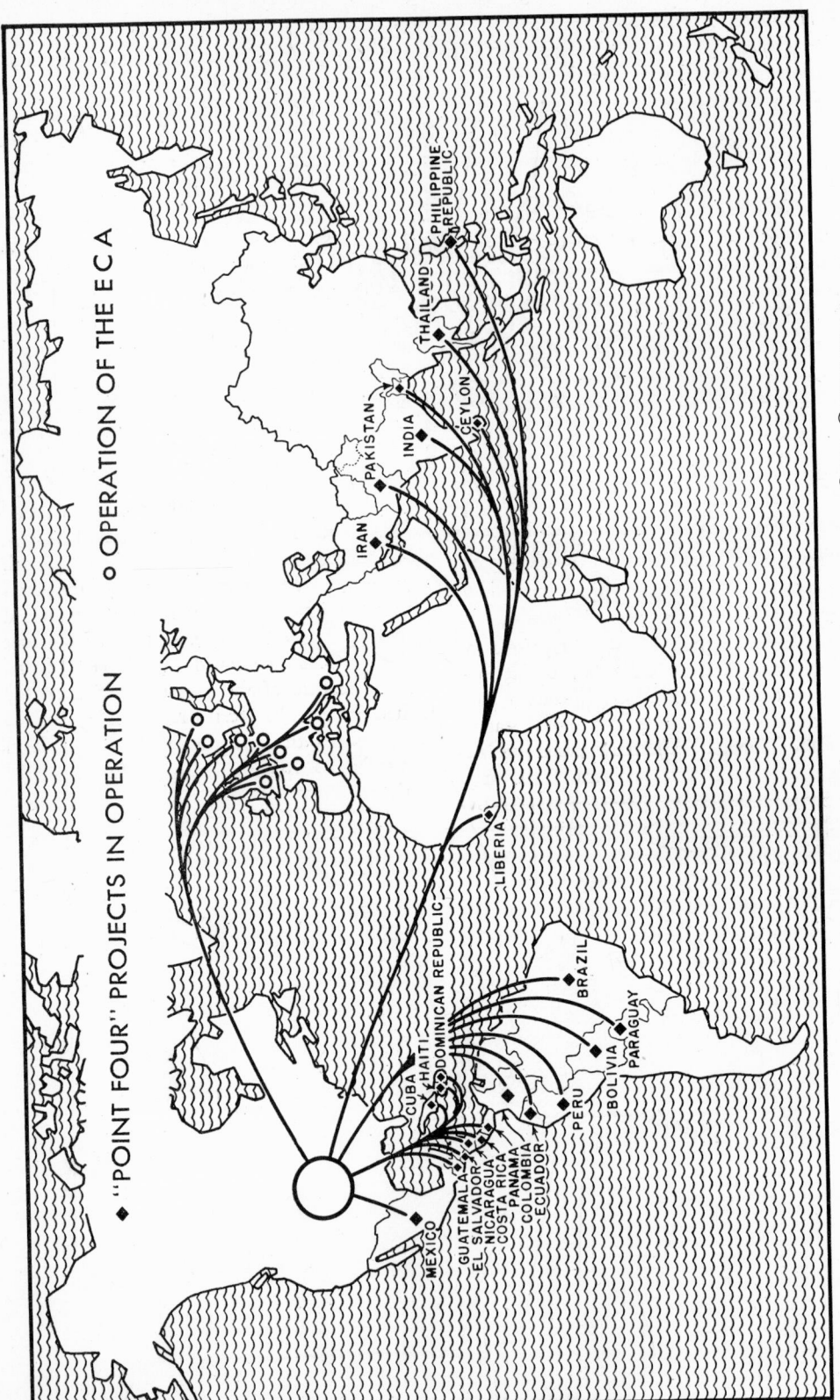

FIGURE 143. THE UNITED STATES' CONTRIBUTION TO AGRICULTURE IN OTHER COUNTRIES

Agricultural cooperation under "Point Four" program and operation of the Economic Cooperation Administration (Marshall Plan).

natural resources, international insecurity. For them the problems of economic progress include conservation of natural resources, prevention of depressions, a better distribution of income.

For nations on a lower economic level, the goal is to catch up with the more prosperous countries.

On a still lower level of economic development, the goals of economic progress become increasingly imitative. Sometimes imitation is manifested more or less superficially, as in the style of buildings and uniforms of the army, but more often the underdeveloped country calls for foreign capital to develop local resources, hires foreign technical advisers, sends its youth to foreign colleges. Imitation and adaptation of experience of other nations has always been a vehicle of economic progress, and the United States passed through a long period of imitating the old countries before it became a model that older nations are eager to copy.

The United States and the Old World

The pattern of agricultural development in the United States illustrates the relationship between that country and the world. None of the important crops grown in the United States, none of the animals commonly raised on its farms is native to North America. Corn and tobacco were brought to North America by Indians migrating from the south in precolonial days; wheat, horses and cattle were brought from Europe; oats trace their ancestry to South America and Australia; alfalfa came from Turkistan, tomatoes from Peru. In brief, the agriculture of the United States has been built on the heritage of many countries and many civilizations.[48] (See Figure 142.)

But on this foundation the nation has developed new agricultural techniques, new methods of selection and breeding, new machines. Now it repays its debts by participating in joint agricultural programs with the governments of fifteen Latin American republics; by sending agricultural missions to Japan, the Philippines, Syria, Lebanon, Iraq, Saudi Arabia, Egypt, Greece and other countries; by supplying tractors and combines to the old countries of Europe. (See Figure 143.)

Since the beginning of civilization, wealthier nations have been the bearers of economic progress to other peoples. Often they played this role unwillingly; they were unable to hide their superior technique from the rest of the world even when they did their best to keep it for themselves. As mentioned in Chapter 12, the peculiar feature of the present position of the United States is its acceptance as the goal of its foreign policy the reduction of the gap between its standard of living and that of the rest of the world.

---

48. **11,** April 1949, pp. 75 ff.

PART III

AGRICULTURE

CHAPTER 14

AGRICULTURE IN THE WORLD ECONOMY

AGRICULTURE HAS BEEN the chief occupation of mankind since time immemorial. Even now it directly engages more than half the world's labor force. Including persons who divide their time between farming and other pursuits, nearly three fifths of the world's people get their living from tilling the soil, raising livestock or carrying on forestry or fishing.

Many other people are engaged in processing foodstuffs, plant and animal fibers and forest products. The exchange of agricultural and forest products in raw or finished form accounts for more than half of all international trade. In all, farming, and the processing, transportation and distribution of agricultural products occupy about three fourths of the world's labor force.

Agriculture differs from all other economic activities in that its basic processes are not mechanical or chemical, as in other industries, but biological. The possibility of speed-up is limited: "a wheat grain will not mature, an apple ripen, a calf become a cow before the right time." [1] This statement, written thirty years ago, may require some qualification today, in view of the progress in agricultural technology. Nevertheless, it is true that acceleration such as that in shipbuilding during the war, when the construction time for certain types of ships was cut from three or four years to a few weeks, is unthinkable in agriculture.

Nor can the farmer fully control the quantity or the quality of his product. A steelmaker can calculate in advance the tonnage and type of product he will obtain from the amounts of iron ore, coal and flux material he puts into a furnace. Not so the farmer who is dependent on the structure and the condition of the soil and the topography of his land, on rainfall and sunshine and the inherent requirements of each plant. After he has prepared the ground and planted the seed, he may see all his labor put at naught by too much or too little rain, late frost or a sudden hailstorm, insects or blight.

The technical revolution in the eighteenth century that marked the beginning of our mechanical civilization reached agriculture a century or more later and it has not been as complete in agriculture as in mining, manufacturing, transportation and communication. There is little room on the farm for division of labor comparable to that in industry. Work cannot be separated into a number of single operations performed by different workers. Moreover, unlike most industrial processes, many types of farm work cannot be carried on uninterruptedly throughout the year. In winter, the work load is low and farmers, farm animals and machinery are idle; in the busy season, labor is in short supply. On the other hand, agriculture is carried on throughout the entire world, while industrial production is localized.

All these characteristics determine the exceptional position of agriculture in the world economy as well as in the economy of individual nations.

PATTERNS IN AGRICULTURE

World agriculture has developed many different patterns as the result of the extreme variety in physical conditions (soil, climate, topography) and in the requirements of different plants and animals, the size and form of agricultural holdings, methods of farming, marketing and transportation systems and so on. Among the many patterns, however, two broad types can be distinguished — subsistence farming and commercial farming.

The difference between these types is in the main objective: production for home use or production for the market. Although the demarcation is not always wholly clear, and many farmers grow crops and raise animals partly for home consumption and partly for sale, the prevailing purpose determines the general pattern. [2]

Subsistence Farming

Subsistence or self-sufficing farming dates from the beginning of agriculture. In earlier days, it

---

1. **17**, pp. 11–12.

2. See Chapter 13.

451

provided the farmer and his family with nearly all their basic needs — food, shelter, clothing and so on. Its pure form is now rare, for today's subsistence farmers have adjusted themselves to a money economy to some extent. Their basic objective, however, is still to produce mainly to meet their own needs by means of their own labor and produce.

Subsistence and commercial farming illustrate stages in the development of agriculture. Tribes of hunters and fishermen, the Eskimos of North America, the Tungus and the Yakuts in the extreme north of the USSR, and the Lapps in the north of Scandinavia and the USSR, tribes of nomadic herders in Africa and Asia today represent agricultural patterns of the past although they occasionally sell some surplus products at trading posts. Shifting cultivation, the once prevalent practice of obtaining land for crops by burning forests and moving on to new forest land when the fertility of the soil declined, is still widespread in Africa, southeastern Asia and some parts of South America

These forms of agriculture, however, are now only fringes on the predominant patterns — permanent tillage, largely on a self-sufficing basis, which supports some 60 per cent of mankind, and commercial farming, geared to the money economy. According to D. S. Whittlesey,[3] the general geographic domain of these two basic types may be mapped by drawing a line roughly along the Tropic of Cancer. In the Western Hemisphere, the realm of subsistence farming is south of this line, with some exceptions such as the commercial ranches, grain farms and tropical plantations in Latin America. In the Eastern Hemisphere, subsistence farming stretches northward in Asia beyond this line and includes nomadic herding over vast areas in China. South of the line, subsistence farming prevails on almost the entire continents of Africa and Asia, except for plantations. Australia and New Zealand, however, are largely engaged in commercial farming.

Commercial Farming

The other general pattern of world agriculture, commercial farming, also stems from early times, when royal families, religious bodies and the nobility owned huge tracts of land and raised quantities of agricultural produce for use by armies and servants and also for exchange. Only in recent centuries, however, has commercial farming begun to take the form we know today — independent private farms producing largely for the open market. The domain of commercial farming is north of the Tropic of Cancer, with exceptions such as nomadic herding in the extreme north and in China, plantations and ranches in southeastern Asia, Latin America and Oceania.

In the world as a whole, not more than one farmer in five is engaged in commercial farming. Commercial farmers are concentrated in western and central Europe, North America, Australia and New Zealand and constitute only a small minority of the farmers in other regions.

In the USSR, where all land is state owned, farming is organized in enterprises, "kolkhozy," operated by the state. A large part of the produce of these collective farms is taken over by the state for sale outside the producing areas, and the rest is paid to the producers on the basis of their working time and efficiency. This system is more like the plantation system in underdeveloped regions than like the independent commercial farming elsewhere. The Russian peasants actually are wage workers, although they lack the mobility of farm laborers in other countries.[4]

Subsistence and commercial farming sometimes exist side by side, as, for example, plantations, ranches and huge estates in the midst of native farms in underdeveloped regions, or the many tiny farms in industrial countries that produce chiefly for home use. For example, the 1945 census reported 1.3 million subsistence farms in the United States.[5]

Patterns in the United States

Almost every conceivable type of agriculture is represented in the United States. Except for certain tropical products such as rubber, tea, coffee, cacao, bananas and spices, nearly all crops are grown: grain, tobacco, cotton, sugar cane, oil-bearing products, vegetables, fruits and nuts are included in a list of more than 200 types.

---

3. **23,** pp. 199 ff. Cf. Chapter 13.

4. See Chapter 15 for a more detailed description of this system.

5. The 1945 census, however, used a definition of subsistence farms that does not fully describe subsistence farms in other parts of the world: a farm was thus classified if the value of produce used by the farm household exceeded the total value of produce marketed (**11,** 1950, p. 586).

Livestock production is no less diversified. It includes cattle for meat and milk; sheep for mutton and wool; poultry and eggs; and dairy products.

Along with diversification goes considerable regional specialization. Eight major types of farming can be distinguished in the United States. In the heart of the country lies the Corn Belt, which is also the Hog Belt. Northeast of it, the dairy region extends to the Canadian border; southeast lies the area of general farming.

Cotton is king in ten states in the South, although general farming has made some inroads. The subtropical coastal edge along the Gulf of Mexico specializes in sugar cane and citrus fruit; the subtropical southern fringe of the Pacific, in fruit, truck gardening and special crops. Deciduous fruit is raised in other parts of the country wherever climate and soil permit.

The bread basket (wheat and small grains) of the United States lies in the Great Plains, the Columbia Plateau and the winter wheat region, southwest of the Corn Belt. Millions of cattle and sheep graze on vast expanses of treeless, nontillable pasturage, which represents dozens of acres per head. Tobacco raising and general farming are found in many eastern and central eastern states — Virginia, Maryland, Connecticut, Kentucky and others. (See Figure 144.)

AGRICULTURAL PRODUCTION

Types of Products

Agricultural products can be grouped under three broad headings:

Grains and other food and feed crops, including fruits and vegetables, edible oils (Chapter 16)

Fibers, rubber, tobacco, industrial oils and similar technical crops for industry (Chapter 17)

Livestock and animal products, including dairying and poultry (Chapter 18)

In analyzing agricultural production, a distinction is usually drawn between plant and animal products. Only highly specialized commercial farms and plantations, however, fully separate these two branches of production. In subsistence farming and on commercial family farms, the farmer usually divides his time and effort between crops and animal husbandry. He produces feed crops for his livestock, and he keeps livestock to have draft power, to fertilize

his soil and to obtain milk and meat for himself and his family.

The advantage of rotating crops and the seasonal character of agricultural work favor this combination. On such a farm, wooded land or poor land unfit for food crops and gardening may be left for grazing, and fields that are pastures today may be plowed up for crops next year, or vice versa. On a mixed farm, "any one crop, such as wheat, is inextricably linked with the others; it utilizes fertilizer residues left in the soil from previous crops, it leaves certain residues for the crop which follows it, it shares with other crops the available labour of men and horses, the use of machinery, carts and barns. . . ." [6] Diversity of production not only supports the proper utilization of the farmer's time and land but also helps to safeguard him against losses through adverse weather or drops in prices for one product or another.

In Denmark, a model of intensive and diversified farming, nearly all farmers grow three or four cereals, three or four kinds of roots, often two or more grass mixtures, plus, in a great many cases, some fodder and very often one or more seed crops. Almost all of them also keep horses, cattle, pigs and poultry and market a variety of dairy products. [7]

The farmer's dollar of the United States reflects the diversity of the output of American farms. Although meat production as a whole represents almost a third of farmers' income, no single product accounts for as much as 15 per cent of their total receipts in the United States. (See Figure 145.)

Agricultural Production and Consumption

In the world as a whole the greatest part of farm output is consumed on farms, and patterns of national production and consumption are generally more or less adjusted to each other.[8] Meat and dairy products, for example, usually constitute a larger part of the national diet in cattle-raising countries than in countries where grains predominate in agricultural output. When city people begin to consume more meat and dairy products, farmers shift to animal husbandry. When the demand for fruits and vegetables increases, truck gardening is expanded. Climate and soil, however, limit the possibilities of ad-

---

6. **25**, p. 23. See also **18**, pp. 19–21.
7. **15**, pp. 36–37.
8. See Chapters 8 and 10.

A. TYPES OF FARMING

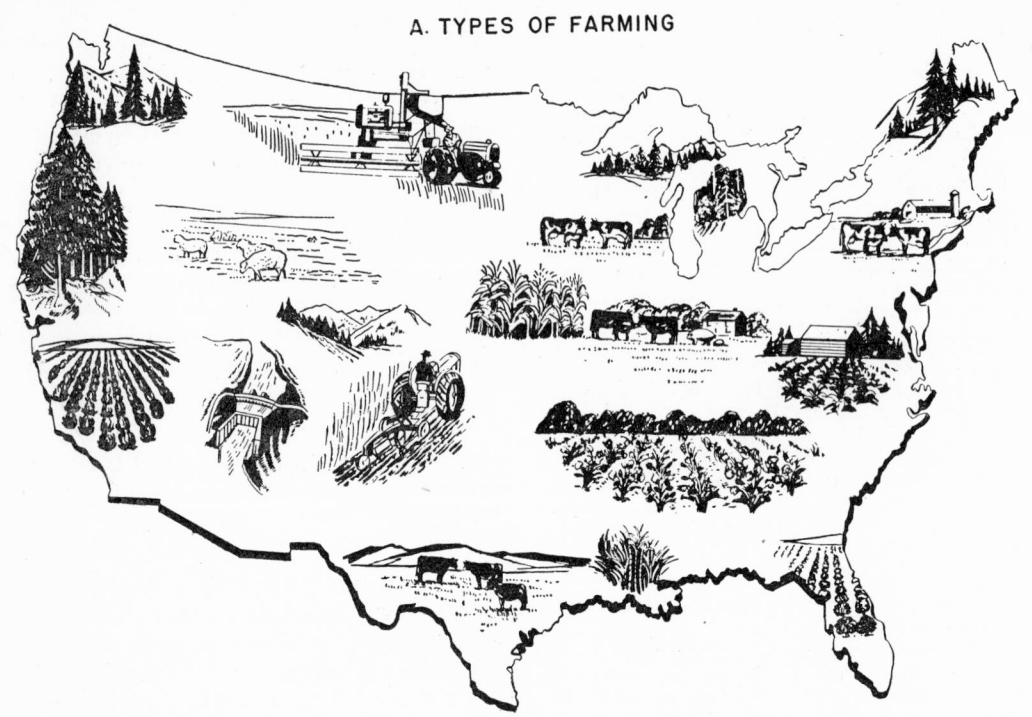

B. GEOGRAPHIC LOCATION OF PREVAILING TYPES OF FARMING

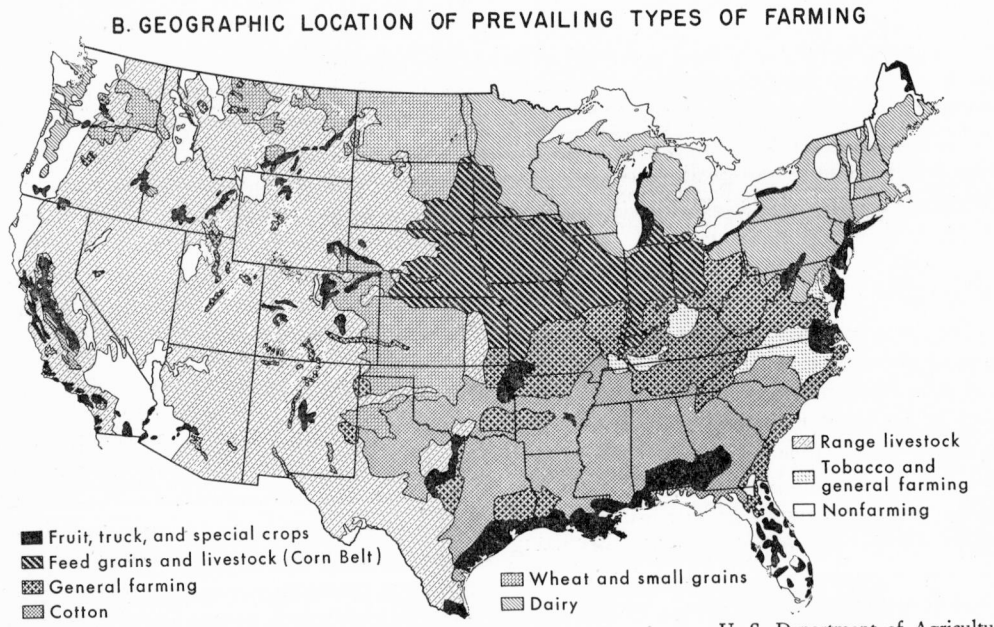

Range livestock

Tobacco and general farming

Nonfarming

Fruit, truck, and special crops

Feed grains and livestock (Corn Belt)

General farming

Cotton

Wheat and small grains

Dairy

U. S. Department of Agriculture

FIGURE 144. PATTERNS IN FARMING IN THE UNITED STATES

In the northern part of the United States, dairying extends from the Atlantic seaboard toward the center of the country. South of this belt lies a region of general farming and tobacco growing. Further south, the land belongs to cotton, then to citrus fruits in Florida and sugar cane in Louisiana. A region stretching from north to south in the central part of the country is largely in grain: spring wheat in the north; corn in the center and winter wheat farther south. Cattle and sheep roam over hundreds of millions of acres in the West and Southwest, though irrigation has opened areas in the latter to cotton and other special crops. Truck gardening and fruit growing are important along the southern part of the Pacific coast.

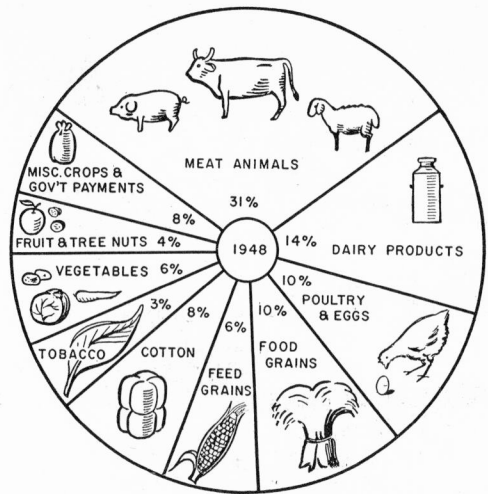

Courtesy of Viking Press (19)

FIGURE 145. SOURCES OF THE FARMERS' DOLLAR IN
THE UNITED STATES, 1948

In the United States as a whole, the farmers' dollar in
1948 included 75 cents from the sale of food products, of
which food grains supplied 10 cents; meat animals, 31
cents; dairy products, poultry and eggs, 24 cents; fruits,
nuts and vegetables, 10 cents. Cotton, tobacco, feed grains,
miscellaneous crops and government payments accounted
for the remainder.

justing agricultural production to consumer demands. Hence, the specialization of certain
world regions in particular types of farming,
which, along with surpluses of agricultural products in other regions and the scarcity of land in
densely populated areas, accounts for international trade in agricultural products.

VALUE OF WORLD AGRICULTURAL OUTPUT

The interdependence of the many different
lines of production on the farm makes it difficult to ascertain the cost of producing any single
item in terms of manpower or capital investment. It is also difficult to establish the total
value of the output of a farm by commodity,
since a part is consumed by the farmer and his
family, another part by the livestock. Estimating
the total agricultural output of the whole country is even more complicated.

Limitations of Statistics

Precise evaluation of world agricultural output is next to impossible. Some countries have
no statistics of even arable land or harvested
crops or livestock, and others report only on the
chief agricultural commodities. Some countries

carefully record or estimate consumption on the
farm as a part of national income, and others
disregard it. In some instances export statistics
are the only available substitute for data on output. Furthermore, prices vary from month to
month, and the relationship between prices at
the farm and on local markets differs among
countries. Under such conditions, the purpose
of an estimate of the world agricultural output
is not to give precise amounts but to show the
approximate value of agricultural output compared with other branches of primary production
in the world and the continents; to ascertain the
relative significance of different products in the
total value; and to provide a background for
appraising agricultural production in individual
countries.

The average agricultural output of the world
in 1937–38 has been roughly estimated at $62
billion at 1930 prices, compared with an aggregate value of $24 billion for world output of
other raw materials — mineral fuels, metallic
ores and other minerals, water power and forest
products.[9] Before World War II, agriculture
provided more than 70 per cent of the total
value of primary products (foodstuffs and industrial raw materials). Since that time, prices and
the output of many commodities have changed
radically. The total value of annual primary production in the world rose from $86 billion (at
1930 prices) to more than $150 billion in 1949–
50 (at current prices), but the relative share of
the broad groups of commodities did not change
much.[10] As before the war, the value of agricultural output exceeds that of all other raw
materials combined.

Conflicting Estimates

For a closer analysis of the distribution of the
value of agricultural production among continents and commodities, less comprehensive estimates have to be used. The two best known
estimates of the world's agricultural output in
prewar years are those of the League of Nations
and of the International Institute of Agriculture.

Using 1930 prices, the League of Nations estimated world agricultural output in 1938 (in-

9. See Chapter 10.
10. For 1938, see Chapter 10. The value for 1949–
50 has been computed on the basis of changes in
world production and prevailing prices, as reported by
the Statistical Office of the United Nations.

cluding fisheries but excluding production of wood) as follows (in millions): [11]

Total	$49,694
Cereals and sugar	12,043
Fruits and vegetables	3,423
Meat	11,991
Sea fish	693
Milk	13,395
Wine and hops	842
Coffee, tea, cocoa	726
Tobacco	888
Oil materials and oils	1,891
Textile fibers	3,580
Rubber	222

In sharp contrast, the International Institute of Agriculture, using gold dollars, estimated the world's annual average production during 1934–38 at a much smaller amount. The figures were (in millions): [12]

Total	$20,417
Wheat	3,120
Rye	714
Rice (raw)	1,569
Potatoes	1,118
Sugar	252
Coffee	225
Tea	243
Cacao	42
Wine	578
Tobacco	800
Cotton	994
Flax	136
Hemp	76
Jute	58
Manila hemp	9
Sisal and other	16
Rubber	174
Linseed	93
Cottonseed	155
Soya	184
Groundnut	183

11. Adapted from **2**, p. 87. Crops fed to livestock are not included since their value appears in that of meat and milk.

12. **8**, p. 17. The Institute assumes that barley, oats, corn and half of all potatoes are used to feed livestock and therefore appear in the value of meat and milk. It estimates the average cost of processing sugar beet and cane, plus accessory expenses, at 50 per cent of the value of sugar, and of converting silk cocoons into silk, at 25 per cent of the value of the silk. Accordingly, the total for the commodities listed excludes the value of barley, oats and corn, half the value of potatoes and sugar and 25 per cent of that of silk.

Copra	$ 46
Palm kernels	15
Olive oil	135
Palm oil	16
Beef	1,788
Mutton and goatmeat	553
Pork	2,503
Milk	4,082
Wool	454
Silk	86

The discrepancy in these two sets of estimates is due mainly to differences in method: recalculated in current dollars, rather than gold dollars, the estimate of the International Institute totals $34.6 billion. Correction for the difference in prices between 1930 and 1934–38 raises the figure further to $39.8 billion. Adding the value of products included in the estimate of the League of Nations but omitted by the Institute (such as fruit, vegetables, rapeseed, hops, sea fish and crude whale oil) brings it still higher, to $45.4 billion. With these adjustments, the two estimated totals are not far apart — $49.7 and $45.4 billion, respectively.

The remaining discrepancy is chiefly due to the difference in the period covered by the estimates, and the methods of pricing. The year chosen by the League of Nations (1938) was marked by a higher agricultural output in the world as a whole than the average during 1934–38. Moreover, the League of Nations used the prevailing national prices for each country; the International Institute, the average price for each commodity in main exporting countries — generally countries not directly influenced by governmental protective measures. The second method has the advantage, for purposes of international comparisons, of eliminating the excessive disparity of prices in different markets. The estimate of the International Institute is therefore used in the following discussion but all values are expressed in current dollars, rather than gold dollars.

The estimate of the International Institute of Agriculture omits such important products as poultry, eggs, vegetables, fruits, lard, tallow, hides and skins, sorghum, millet and many kinds of oilseeds and oils, such as sesame, sunflower, castor and tung. Fully aware of these gaps, the Institute rightly stresses, however, that the commodities included represent the bulk of the world's agricultural products.

TABLE 206

WORLD AGRICULTURAL OUTPUT: VALUE, BY CONTINENT, 1934–38 ANNUAL AVERAGE

Continent	Value, in Millions			Percentage Distribution, by Continent			Percentage Distribution, by Type		
	Total	Vegetable	Animal	Total	Vegetable	Animal	Total	Vegetable	Animal
World	$34,570	$18,542	$16,028	100.0	100.0	100.0	100.0	53.7	46.3
North America	5,503	2,245	3,258	15.9	12.1	20.3	100.0	40.8	59.2
Middle and South America	3,056	1,253	1,803	8.8	6.7	11.3	100.0	40.9	59.1
Europe	10,244	4,565	5,679	29.6	24.6	35.4	100.0	44.6	55.4
USSR [a]	4,116	2,851	1,265	11.9	15.4	7.9	100.0	69.2	30.8
Asia [b]	9,475	6,739	2,736	27.4	36.4	17.1	100.0	71.2	28.8
Africa	1,227	694	533	3.6	3.8	3.3	100.0	56.7	43.3
Oceania	948	195	754	2.8	1.0	4.7	100.0	20.5	79.5

Source: Adapted from **8**, pp. 19–20.

a. The USSR undoubtedly has a smaller share in agricultural output than is shown above. The International Institute of Agriculture has used the official Russian harvest statistics, which report the so-called "biological" harvest or crop forecast, not the barn harvest. In view of the wide discrepancy between crop forecasts and crops harvested in the USSR, the Russian data must be reduced by not less than 15 to 20 per cent to make them roughly comparable with those for the rest of the world.

b. Experts believe that China's recorded output is about 40 per cent lower than the actual output. The value of agricultural output in Asia would thus be 10–15 per cent greater than these figures indicate.

Distribution by Continent

Europe, the smallest continent, accounted for almost 30 per cent of the world's agricultural output before the war, while the Western Hemisphere produced a little less than 25 per cent. Asia contributed 27 per cent, and Africa and Oceania, about 4 and 3 per cent, respectively.

Products of plant origin accounted for $18.5 billion, or 53.7 per cent of the value of the total agricultural output. The actual proportion was larger, since grain fed to livestock (barley, oats, corn) and half the potatoes were included in the value of animal products. Including the value of these ($6.8 billion), vegetable output represented $25.3 billion, or 73.1 per cent of the total. (See Table 206 and Figure 146.)

Distribution by Type of Product

The relative importance of the output of vegetable and animal products varies from continent to continent. When income and the standard of living rise, people generally shift more and more from starchy food of plant origin to a diet containing more animal proteins. In North America and western and central Europe production of meat, butter and milk has increased steadily. Food of animal origin is more expensive, however, in terms of land and labor. It has been estimated that one hectare (2.5 acres)

in grain, potatoes or sugar beets provides enough calories for from 7 to 20 people, while a hectare used to raise livestock feeds only one person.[13] Animal husbandry also requires work throughout the year and in many ways is more specialized than crop farming.

Poverty in the USSR and Africa and the pressure of the extremely dense population in Asia make it impossible for millions of people to have a balanced diet with an adequate supply of animal proteins, and forces them to raise cereals, the cheapest of foodstuffs. In Europe, vegetable products represent less than 45 per cent of the value of the total agricultural output, and in North and South America, just over 40 per cent. The ratio in North America is low because of dietary habits of the population and in Middle and South America, because of the production of meat for export. Specialization in wool and animal foodstuffs for export accounts also for a low ratio in Oceania.

In terms of use, agricultural products can be divided into foodstuffs and industrial raw materials. In crowded Europe, foodstuffs account for nearly the total value of agricultural output (97.7 per cent); in Oceania, where the population is small and wool is a major product, the ratio is less than 3 to 1. For the world as a whole, it is about 8 to 1.

13. **16**, p. 120.

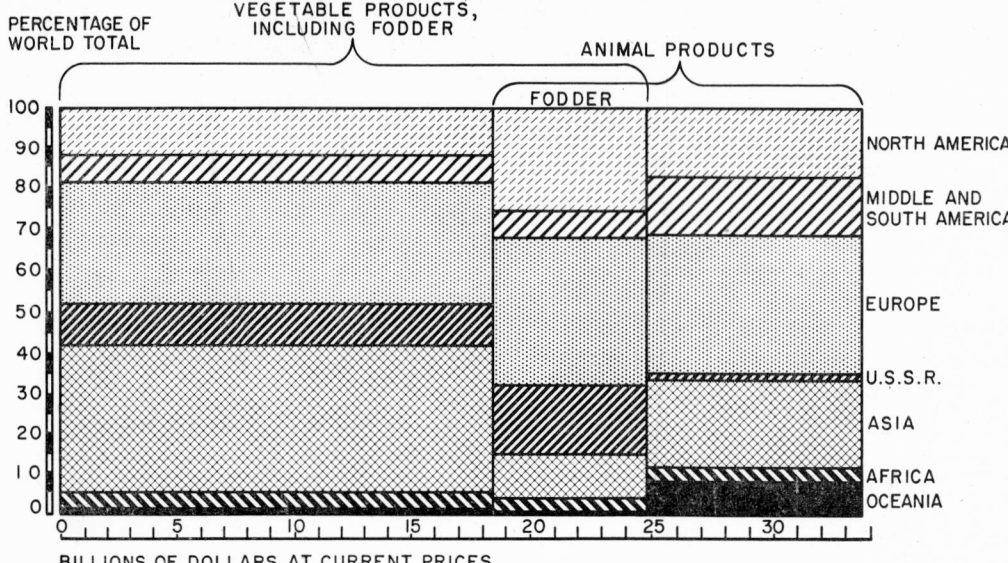

PERCENTAGE OF
WORLD TOTAL

VEGETABLE PRODUCTS,
INCLUDING FODDER

ANIMAL PRODUCTS

FODDER

NORTH AMERICA

MIDDLE AND
SOUTH AMERICA

EUROPE

U.S.S.R.

ASIA

AFRICA
OCEANIA

BILLIONS OF DOLLARS AT CURRENT PRICES

FIGURE 146. WORLD AGRICULTURAL OUTPUT: VALUE IN EACH CONTINENT, 1934–38, ANNUAL AVERAGE

North America accounts for one eighth of the value of world output of vegetable products and one fifth of that of animal products; Europe, for one fourth and more than one third respectively; Asia produces more than one third of the vegetable output, in terms of value, but only one sixth of that of animal products.

Value of Output Per Capita

For the world as a whole the annual value of agricultural output before the war averaged $16.27 per capita. In Oceania, where wool and animal foodstuffs are produced for export, the average value was more than five times higher ($92.19); it was also high in North America ($39.45). The figure appears practically the same in Middle and South America ($23.84), Europe ($25.96) and the USSR ($24.70), but this similarity does not mean that the three areas have equal amounts of agricultural products for domestic consumption. (See Table 207.) South America exports an appreciable part of its agricultural output, especially meat, coffee, wheat, corn, flaxseed and wool. Europe, in addition to its own produce, has sizable agricultural imports from other continents. In the USSR, figures for agricultural output are disproportionately high because of the method of computing the harvest (see Table 206, footnote a). With allowance for this factor, the per capita amount in the USSR is not more than that which South America uses domestically.

AGRICULTURAL POPULATION

Out of every ten persons in the world, six live on farms and depend on agriculture for a livelihood, as workers or other members of a farm household. The ratio varies considerably from continent to continent. In North America, only two persons out of ten depend on agriculture, in Latin America more than six and in Asia and Africa seven or more.

Nearly two thirds of the world's agricultural population are in Asia. Some 9 per cent are in Europe, and a little more than 2 per cent are in North America. Latin America and the USSR each account for 7 per cent; Oceania, for about one third of one per cent. (See Table 208.)

Recent Trends

In the last two decades, the total agricultural population has increased by 76 million but trends have differed substantially among the continents. In Asia, the agricultural population increased by 69 million; in Africa, by 36 million, and in Latin America, by 21 million. The rise in North America and in Oceania was about one million. Europe's agricultural population declined by 11 million, largely because of the loss of territory to the USSR. A decline from 140 million to 99 million in the USSR was due to collectivization and mechanization, which forced peasants to migrate to urban areas.

Variations by Country

Agriculture's share in total population is smallest in the United Kingdom — only 6 per cent.

TABLE 207

WORLD AGRICULTURAL OUTPUT: PER CAPITA VALUE, BY CONTINENT, 1934–38 ANNUAL
AVERAGE

Continent	Total	Product		Purpose	
		Vegetable	Animal	Food	Other
World	$16.27	$8.74	$7.53	$14.41	$ 1.86
North America	39.45	16.10	23.35	33.00	6.45
Middle and South America	23.84	9.75	14.09	21.05	2.79
Europe	25.96	11.58	14.39	25.36	0.61
USSR [a]	24.70	17.11	7.60	21.98	2.72
Asia	8.37	5.96	2.41	7.08	1.29
Africa	8.09	4.59	3.50	6.09	2.00
Oceania	92.19	18.93	73.26	66.20	25.99

Percentage Distribution

World	100.0	53.7	46.3	88.6	11.4
North America	100.0	40.8	59.2	83.6	16.3
Middle and South America	100.0	40.9	59.1	88.3	11.7
Europe	100.0	44.6	55.4	97.7	2.3
USSR [a]	100.0	69.3	30.7	89.0	11.0
Asia	100.0	71.2	28.8	84.6	15.4
Africa	100.0	56.7	43.3	75.3	24.7
Oceania	100.0	20.5	79.5	71.8	28.2

Source: Adapted from **8**, pp. 57–59.

a. See Table 206, footnote a.

TABLE 208

AGRICULTURAL POPULATION, IN THE WORLD AND CONTINENTS, 1930 AND 1948

Continent	Total Population, in Millions		Agricultural Population [a]					
			Number of Persons, in Millions		Percentage of Total Population		Percentage of Total Agricultural Population	
	1930	1948	1930	1948	1930	1948	1930	1948
World	2,022	2,352	1,301	1,377	64.3	58.5	100.0	100.0
North America	134	160	31	32	23.1	20.0	2.4	2.3
Middle and South America	117	155	76	97	65.0	62.6	5.8	7.0
Europe	379	387	139	128	36.7	33.0	10.7	9.2
USSR	161	197	140	99	87.0	58.0	10.8	7.2
Asia	1,079	1,248	805	874	74.6	70.0	61.9	63.5
Africa	142	193	107	143	75.4	74.0	8.2	10.4
Oceania	10	12	3	4	30.0	33.0	0.2	0.3

Sources: **22**, pp. 2–3, and **6**, January 1950, p. 4.

a. Since there are no inclusive international statistics of farm and nonfarm population as defined in the United States censuses, these estimates of the Royal Institute of International Affairs (1930) and the Food and Agriculture Organization of the United Nations (1948) are rough approximations. They rest essentially on census data for occupational distribution of gainful workers between agricultural and nonagricultural pursuits around 1930 and 1940, with allowance for differences in age composition and family size in rural and urban areas in various countries. In the estimate for 1948, population increase and occupational shifts since preceding censuses have been taken into account.

TABLE 209

AGRICULTURAL POPULATION IN SELECTED COUNTRIES

Country [a] and Year	Agricultural Population		Country [a] and Year	Agricultural Population	
	Number of Persons, in Millions	Percentage of Total Population		Number of Persons, in Millions	Percentage of Total Population
United States, 1948	27.5 [b]	19	Spain, 1930	11.9	50
Canada, 1941	3.2 [b]	27	Italy, 1936	18.9	45
			Yugoslavia, 1948	11.1	71
United Kingdom, 1931	2.5	6	Romania, 1941	9.7 [c]	72
France, 1946	10.2	25	Bulgaria, 1934	4.4 [c]	73
Belgium, 1930	1.2	15	Albania, 1930	0.8	80
Netherlands, 1930	1.5	18	Greece, 1940	3.8	52
Denmark, 1940	1.0	26			
Sweden, 1945	2.0	30	USSR, 1939	97.1	57
Norway, 1946	0.8	25			
Finland, 1940	1.9	50	China, 1946	331.8	73
Western Germany, 1946	8.1 [c]	18	Japan, 1946	34.5	47
Poland, 1931	19.3	60	Iran, 1930	—	76 [e]
Czechoslovakia, 1947	3.4 [c]	28	India,[f] 1931	234.8 [c]	67
Switzerland, 1941	0.9	20	Thailand, 1930	—	72 [e]
Austria, 1947	1.9	27	Indochina, 1930	—	71 [e]
Hungary,[d] 1941	4.5 [c]	49	British Malaya, 1930	—	56 [e]
Portugal, 1940	3.1	40	Belgian Congo, 1947	9.1	84

Sources: **5**, 1950, p. 15; **1**, pp. 26–27; **21**, p. 26.

   a. Countries are arranged geographically.
   b. Total population of communities in which the majority of residents depend on agriculture.

c. Includes forestry and fishing.
d. Present boundaries.
e. Share of total population dependent on agriculture.
f. Includes Burma.

In continental Europe, the proportion ranges between 15 and 20 per cent in the Low Countries, Switzerland and Western Germany and between 25 and 30 per cent in the Scandinavian countries (except Finland), Austria and Czechoslovakia, and rises to about 50 per cent in Hungary, Spain, Greece and Finland. The highest group before World War II included Bulgaria (73 per cent), Romania (72 per cent) and Yugoslavia (71 per cent). The United States figure was 19 per cent. (See Table 209.)

In the countries of Asia and Africa, from two thirds to more than four fifths of the population make their living in agriculture. The exceptions are Japan, the most industrialized country in Asia, and possibly the Union of South Africa. In most Latin American countries, it is estimated, from two thirds to three fourths of the population make their living through agriculture; for Brazil, the estimate is about four fifths.[14]

Variations by Region

A single country may have nearly as great differences in this respect as exist even among continents. In the United States, in 1940, for example, the farm population (all persons living on farms without regard to occupation) constituted 2.4 per cent of the total population in Rhode Island, 3.4 per cent in New Jersey and Massachusetts, 9.7 in California, 16.6 in Michigan, 36.8 in Virginia, 47.4 in Alabama, 51.1 in North Dakota and 64.3 in Mississippi.[15]

AGRICULTURAL LABOR

Because of differences in age composition of rural and urban population and in the average size of families, world agriculture represents a somewhat smaller share in total labor input than in total population. Nevertheless, agriculture employs more people than all other pursuits together.

---

14. **14**, p. 9.

15. **11**, 1950, p. 42.

In the World

It has been estimated that of the billion persons in the world's labor force, 530 million are engaged in agriculture, including forestry, fishing and hunting. Subsistence farming probably accounts for nine tenths of the agricultural labor in Africa, three fourths in Asia, two thirds in Middle and South America, one fifth in North America and one tenth in Europe, and for more than three fifths in the agricultural labor force in the world as a whole. The agricultural labor force is distributed between subsistence and commercial farming, as follows (in millions): [16]

	All Agriculture	Subsistence Farming	Commercial Farming
World	530	325	205
North America	10	2	8
Middle and South America	45	30	15
Europe	70	7	63
USSR	50	—	50
Asia	310	246	64
Africa	45	41	4
Oceania	1	...	1

In contrast to the amount of labor it absorbs, subsistence agriculture accounts for only a small fraction of the world's agricultural output. It provides food and a scanty supply of fibers for about 56 per cent of mankind, along with some products used in the rest of the world. Commercial farming, on the other hand, uses less than 40 per cent of the world's agricultural labor force but produces much more abundant food for 44 per cent of mankind and supplies them with a great quantity and variety of raw materials for industrial processing.

In Selected Countries

Agriculture's share in the labor force varies widely among countries. Indeed, the relative number of persons engaged in agricultural and nonagricultural production is the most significant criterion of the economy of an area.[17]

On a world map, countries in which more than 60 per cent of the working population is employed in agriculture form two blocks: the huge eastern block including the whole of Asia (except Japan), Africa (except the European population of the Union of South Africa) and eastern Europe; the smaller western block covering Mexico, the Caribbean and a part of South America. The United States and Great Britain are the only great powers in which less than 20 per cent of the labor force is engaged in agriculture.

Census data for various countries are not strictly comparable, however. The greatest discrepancy among countries is in the enumeration of unpaid family workers on the farm. In the United States, Canada, Great Britain, Australia, New Zealand and some other countries, farmers' wives and daughters are not counted as members of agricultural labor while elsewhere they are ordinarily included.[18] In France women constitute 42 per cent of the labor force on farms; in Czechoslovakia, Romania, Bulgaria and Turkey, about 50 per cent. Germany and Austria in 1939, and Japan in 1940, had more women than men in agriculture, in contrast to previous censuses. When men shifted to munition plants, women were called upon to take their place in the fields.

While the work of farm women in the United States or Canada is likely to be chiefly care of poultry, help in the dairy and other tasks that are much less heavy than the work of women in the fields of China or even Italy, they do constitute an important part of agricultural labor that is not recorded by the census.

In general, agriculture absorbs from 20 to 30 per cent of the national labor force in highly industrialized countries and from 60 to 70 per cent or more in agricultural countries.

Agriculture's share in the labor force of Switzerland and Sweden is 21–24 per cent, while it approaches 80 per cent in the Balkan countries. The proportion in Latin American countries fluctuates around 60 to 70 per cent. In some Asiatic areas, such as Thailand, it is nearly 90 per cent. In Australia only 16 per cent of the labor force is engaged in agriculture; in New Zealand 20 per cent. (See Table 210.)

The relative size of the agricultural labor force in some countries is affected by an international division of labor. A country that relies on imported foodstuffs may reduce its agricultural output below the limit set by conditions of soil and climate and use only a small fraction

---

16. Estimated as of midyear 1950, assuming total world population of 2.4 billion (cf. Chapter 2).

17. See Chapter 13, *passim*.

18. In the United States, the census counts only Negro farm women as members of the agricultural labor force.

TABLE 210
AGRICULTURAL LABOR FORCE IN SELECTED COUNTRIES [a]

Country and Year	Total Labor (Gainful Workers), in Thousands	Agricultural Labor,[b] in Thousands			Agricultural Labor as Percentage of Total Labor
		Total	Men	Women	
United States, 1940	52,712	9,317	8,799	518	18
1949	60,835	7,820	6,749	1,071	13
Canada, 1941	4,670	1,227	1,207	20	26
Mexico, 1940	5,858	3,831	3,791	40	65
Guatemala, 1940	1,093	778	771	7	71
Nicaragua, 1940	353	258	248	10	73
Panama, 1940	208	109	103	6	53
Cuba, 1943	1,521	631	619	11	41
Venezuela, 1941	1,241	636	595	41	51
Colombia, 1938	4,566	3,320	1,758	1,563	73
Brazil, 1940	14,020	9,454	8,183	1,270	67
Peru, 1940	2,475	1,546	1,060	486	63
Chile, 1940	1,742	620	580	40	36
Argentina, 1947	5,680	2,045	...	...	36
Great Britain, 1949	23,188	1,273	...	...	5
Ireland, 1936	1,339	648	542	107	48
France, 1946	20,520	7,480	4,218	3,263	36
Belgium, 1930	3,750	638	497	141	17
Netherlands, 1947	3,866	745	577	169	19
Denmark, 1940	1,971	562	435	127	29
Sweden, 1945	2,992	730	683	46	24
Norway, 1930	1,182	412	372	41	35
Finland, 1940	2,017	1,157	629	529	57
Germany,[c] 1939	34,617	8,985	4,065	4,920	26
Western Germany, 1946	19,154	5,587	2,735	2,852	29
Poland, 1931	15,006	9,752	5,429	4,323	65
Czechoslovakia, 1947	5,852	2,207	1,123	1,084	38
Switzerland, 1941	1,992	415	385	30	21
Austria, 1939	3,649	1,423	655	767	39
Hungary, 1941	4,503	2,153	1,604	550	48
Portugal, 1940	3,050	1,488	1,263	225	49
Spain, 1940	9,254	4,781	4,519	262	52
Italy, 1936	18,755	8,843	6,412	2,431	47
Yugoslavia, 1948	9,785	7,363	3,290	4,073	72
Romania, 1930	10,458	8,231	4,055	4,177	79
Bulgaria, 1934	3,433	2,745	1,348	1,397	80
Greece, 1946	2,466	1,436	1,183	253	58
Korea, 1938	22,237	16,994	...	...	76
Japan, 1947	33,881	17,812	9,044	8,768	53
Turkey, 1935	7,921	6,480	3,383	3,097	82
India, 1931	148,817	100,037	72,021	28,016	67
Burma, 1931	6,199	4,321	—	—	70
Thailand, 1937	6,824	6,044	3,031	3,014	89
British Malaya, 1931	1,987	1,212	...	...	61
Indonesia, 1940	20,871	14,364	...	...	69
Philippines, 1939	6,108	4,451	3,182	1,268	73

(*Continued on page 463*)

TABLE 210—*continued*

| Country and Year | Total Labor (Gainful Workers), in Thousands | Agricultural Labor,[b] in Thousands | | | Agricultural Labor as Percentage of Total Labor |
		Total	Men	Women	
French Morocco, 1946	2,282	1,529	1,398	131	67
Egypt, 1937	6,095	4,308	3,605	703	71
Nigeria, 1931	8,497	6,260	...	...	74
Union of South Africa, White population, 1946	888	168	160	8	19
Nonwhite population, 1936	4,607	3,212	1,549	1,663	70
Australia, 1947	3,196	498	474	24	16
New Zealand,[d] 1945	679	135	124	11	20

Sources: **7**, 1947–48, pp. 8–21; **3**, 1949–50, pp. 64–85; **5**, 1950, pp. 17–19; official statistical yearbooks.

a. In contrast to Table 171, includes unpaid family workers and persons of undefined status, if reported separately by the censuses.

b. Includes forestry, fishing and hunting in the United States, Canada, France, the Netherlands, Norway, Denmark, Peru, Venezuela and Australia; includes forestry and fishing in Mexico, Colombia, Brazil, Belgium, Germany, Sweden, Poland, Czechoslovakia, Portugal, Switzerland, Austria, Romania, Spain, Italy, Yugoslavia, Japan, the Philippines and the Union of South Africa; includes fishing in Chile, Great Britain and Ireland; includes forestry in Finland and Hungary.

c. 1937 boundaries.

d. Primary production.

of its labor in farming. On the other hand, countries that export large quantities of agricultural produce divert a larger share of their labor force to agriculture than the level of their industrial development would suggest.

Recent Trends

The relative number of persons engaged in agriculture has been steadily declining with the increase in industrialization and in the productivity in agriculture per worker and per unit of land.

In the United States, agriculture accounted for more than 90 per cent of the working population until 1820; 77.5 per cent in 1840, and 38.2 per cent in 1900. By 1940 the proportion had dropped to 18.5 per cent.[19] The same trend is evident in many other countries. Between 1900 and 1940, the share of agricultural labor in Canada's total labor force fell from 42.6 per cent

19. **9**, 1940, p. 350; **12**, p. 101. The 1949 figure (13 per cent) in Table 210, based on monthly sample reports, is not strictly comparable with the census figure for 1940. The share of agricultural labor in the total labor force has declined, however, due to the rapid increase in employment in the industrial sector of the economy.

to 26.3; in Sweden's, from 55.1 to 34.1. In Switzerland, farm labor represented 37.5 per cent of all gainfully occupied in 1890 and only 20.8 per cent in 1940. (See Table 211.)

With the increasing use of mechanical power and machinery in agriculture, this trend is likely to continue. The closer the alliance between agriculture and modern technology, the fewer workers will be needed to obtain an even larger amount of agricultural produce than farms supply today. In early days the average American farm provided food for 4 persons; in 1950, for 25–30 persons.

Farmers and Hired Labor

Agriculture is essentially the realm of small producers working on their own account. Of the 530 million persons engaged in agriculture, 390 million, or nearly four fifths, are farmers and working members of their families.[20] The other 140 million are landless farm laborers. The latter figure includes more than 30 million in India, possibly 20 million in China and 10 million in other Asiatic countries, 3 million in Egypt and

20. See Chapter 11.

TABLE 211

AGRICULTURAL LABOR FORCE: SHARE IN TOTAL LABOR FORCE IN SELECTED COUNTRIES,
1890–1940

(*Per Cent*)

Country	1890	1900	1910	1920	1930	1940
United States	43.4	38.2	31.6	27.6	21.9	18.5
Canada [a]	—	42.6	37.1	35.1	31.2	26.3
Great Britain	—	—	8.1	7.1	6.0	—
France [b]	—	—	42.8	41.5	35.7	36.5
Sweden	62.1	55.1	48.8	44.0	39.4	34.1
Germany [c]	42.2	36.4	34.0	30.5	28.8	26.1
Switzerland	37.5	31.0	26.8	25.8	21.3	20.8
Italy	—	59.3	55.7	55.7	46.7	—
Australia	—	—	28.2	22.2 [d]	18.6 [e]	15.6 [f]

Sources: Official statistical yearbooks, or censuses, for various years. For the United States,
   12, p. 101; for Sweden, agricultural population in relation to total population (cf. Table 168).

a. Farming, fishing, trapping and logging.
b. 1906, 1921, 1931, 1946.
c. 1882, 1895, 1907, 1925, 1933, 1939.
d. 1921.
e. 1933.
f. 1947.

about 15 million in Europe. The 50 million workers of the "collective farms" in the USSR are also counted here with hired workers. The proportion of hired farm laborers in the total agricultural labor force ranges in Europe from 2.5 per cent in Romania to 48.0 per cent in Denmark where male family workers receive wages and are reported with hired laborers; in America, from 22.2 per cent in Canada to 74.2 per cent in Chile.

Where small holdings and mixed farming prevail, the farmer needs hired help only occasionally, in the rush season. In specialized agricultural enterprises — whether large estates, as in Great Britain, prewar Hungary, and Chile, or comparatively small farms engaged in intensive animal husbandry, as in the Netherlands and Denmark — hired labor performs a considerable part of the work. (See Table 212.)

In the United States, independent and family labor predominate. Out of 5.3 million reporting farms, only 900,000 had hired help in the last week of March 1940; 500,000 among them had hired help by the month and others employed only week- and day-workers. Of the total 9,694,000 persons working on farms at that time,

1,753,000 were wage workers, and the rest belonged to the family labor force.[21]

AGRICULTURE'S SHARE IN NATIONAL INCOME

The total income derived from agriculture in the world as a whole is estimated for 1948 at approximately $120 billion, or 21 per cent of all income. In areas where subsistence farming prevails, agriculture may account for half or more of all income; in industrial countries, for as little as 10 per cent or even less.

In Ceylon, for example, agriculture provides 72 per cent of the national income, and in the Philippines, 62 per cent. On the other hand, it furnishes only 7 to 13 per cent of all income in the United States and the Netherlands, and from 14 to 16 per cent in the Union of South Africa, Canada, Norway and France. The weak position of agriculture in Great Britain is evidenced by its tiny share in that nation's income — 3.8 per cent in 1934, though the wartime and postwar emphasis on expansion of

21. **11**, 1946, p. 609. Agricultural employment in the United States varies widely from season to season. The annual average is usually higher than the labor force on farms in the last week of March.

TABLE 212

AGRICULTURAL LABOR FORCE: HIRED WORKERS IN SELECTED COUNTRIES

Country and Year	Hired Workers		Country and Year	Hired Workers	
	Number, in Thousands	Percent-age of Agricul-tural Labor		Number, in Thousands	Percent-age of Agricul-tural Labor
United States, 1940	2,805	24.0	Western Germany, 1946	1,542	27.6
1949 [a]	2,430	22.6	Poland, 1931	1,494	15.3
Canada, 1941	272	22.2	Czechoslovakia, 1947	369	16.7
Venezuela, 1941	336	52.8	Switzerland, 1941	108	26.0
Colombia, 1938	975	29.4	Austria, 1939	333	23.4
Brazil, 1940	3,164	33.5	Hungary, 1941	772	35.9
Peru, 1940	507	32.8	Portugal, 1940	632	42.5
Chile, 1940	460	74.2	Italy, 1936	2,455	27.8
			Yugoslavia, 1931	489	9.6
Great Britain, 1931	707	56.2	Romania, 1930	206	2.5
Ireland, 1936	140	21.6	Bulgaria, 1934	141	5.1
Belgium, 1930	131	20.5			
Netherlands, 1947	241	32.3	Japan, 1947	907	5.1
Denmark, 1940	270	48.0	India, 1931	31,480	31.5
Sweden, 1945	239	32.7	Egypt, 1937	2,854	66.2
Norway, 1930	119	28.9	Australia, 1947	173	34.7
Finland, 1940	228	19.7	New Zealand,[b] 1945	63	46.7

Sources: **7**, 1947–48, pp. 8–21; **3**, 1949–50, pp. 64–85; **11**, 1950, p. 180; **24**, p. 53. As in Table 210, labor force includes unpaid family workers and persons of undefined status, not counted in Tables 171 and 172.

a. Annual average includes all persons working for pay one or more hours during the last week of the month surveyed.

b. Primary production.

agricultural production increased the percentage to 5.1. (See Table 213.)

Agricultural Income and Labor Input

An international comparison of the shares of agriculture in national income and labor input (or labor force) is very difficult, because of differences in the methods of classification of the working population and of distribution of national income by industrial origin. Moreover, in many cases the available data on labor force (or employment) and national income do not refer to the same years. This discrepancy in dates affects the comparability of figures even more, since the shares of agriculture in employment and national income often fluctuate in opposite directions: during the depression of the 1930's, for example, the share of agriculture in total employment increased while its share in national income declined; the opposite fluctuations characterized the war economy.

In all countries for which more or less comparable data are available, agriculture's share in national income lags behind its share in the labor force. (See Figure 147.) This discrepancy has several sources, some of which are purely statistical:

1. The farmer's actual income may well be somewhat higher than it appears in statistics of national income. Foodstuffs produced and consumed on farms are usually listed in income statistics at "farm-gate" prices, much lower than prices in retail trade. Figures on agricultural income do not include fuelwood, and in many countries do not consider imputed rent on owner-occupied farm dwellings, while urban rents are likely to take 20 per cent or more of the earnings of low-income groups.

2. The income of the urban population must often be used for business expenditures such as carfare or other costs of transportation between the home and the place of work, clothing to wear to work, meals outside the home. Costs of such items are lower for rural families.

TABLE 213

AGRICULTURE'S SHARE IN NATIONAL INCOME, BEFORE AND AFTER WORLD WAR II

Country [a] *and Year*	Agricultural Income as Percentage of National Income	*Country* [a] *and Year*	Agricultural Income as Percentage of National Income
United Kingdom [b]		Finland [b]	
1934	3.8	1938	35.4
1950	5.1	1950	28.7
United States [b]		Italy [b]	
1938	8.9	1938	29.1
1950	7.4	1950	29.5
Western Germany [b]		Ireland [b]	
1936	13.4	1944	36.9
1950	12.1	1950	30.5
Netherlands [b]		Peru [b]	
1938	7.6	1942	32.0
1949	12.6	1949	34.9
Union of South Africa [b]		Greece [b]	
1938	12.7	1938	37.5
1949	13.9	1949	38.4
Canada [b]		Colombia [b]	
1944	15.6	1949	39.0
1950	14.2	Dominican Republic	
Norway [b]		1940	39.0
1938	15.5	1946	40.9
1950	14.5	Kenya [b]	
France [b]		1949	42.6
1938	21.8	Bulgaria	
1949	15.8	1939	42.0
Chile		1946	43.0
1940	19.0	Turkey	
1948 [b]	17.7	1943	47.6
Denmark [b]		1948	43.0
1938	22.3	Egypt [b]	
1950	21.9	1938	49.1
Argentina		1945	44.4
1938	27.0	Guatemala	
1945	24.0	1949	45.5
Puerto Rico [b]		India [b]	
1939	30.4	1948	47.5
1948	24.1	Philippines	
Hungary		1938	51.0
1938	33.6	1948	62.0
1946	25.7	Ceylon	
Japan [b]		1938	64.7
1946	33.9	1947	72.2
1949	28.4		

Sources: **4,** 1938–1947, pp. 43–46; 1938–1948, pp. 211–15 and Supplement 1938–1950, pp. 20–25; Series H, No. 1, pp. 23–28; **3,** 1949–50, pp. 411–13.

a. Countries are arrayed by the increasing share of agriculture in national income in recent years.

b. The share of agriculture in net geographic income, which differs from the national income concept by excluding income received from, and including income paid to, the rest of the world. Estimates are not fully uniform from country to country in the items of income covered and the industrial classification used.

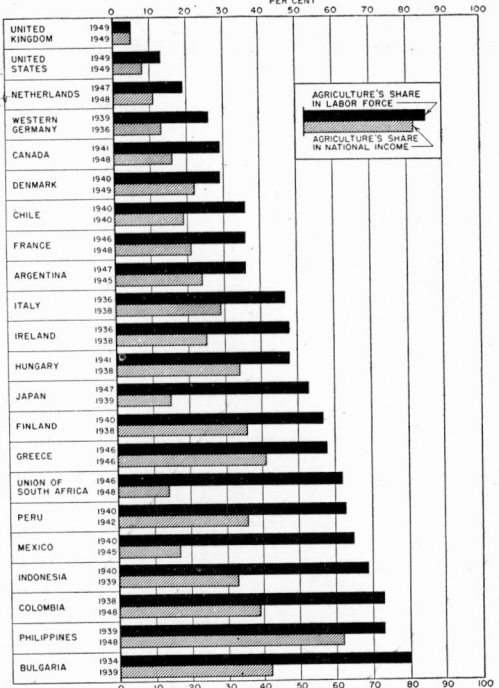

FIGURE 147. AGRICULTURE'S SHARE IN LABOR AND
NATIONAL INCOME IN SELECTED COUNTRIES

The black columns in this figure measure agriculture's
share in the labor force of the respective countries; the
striped columns, its share in the national income. The
general pattern of relationship between the two columns
is striking. In all these countries, agriculture has a
much smaller share in the national product than in the
nation's labor force.

3. In these figures, as in other surveys of
this type, income derived from agriculture is
compared with the number of workers attached
to agriculture. Many of these workers, however,
earn additional income from nonagricultural
pursuits.[22] Some people counted as farmers earn
more from work off the farm than from farming. For a valid comparison of the share in national income and in the labor force, either
earnings of farmers off the farm should be added
to their earnings from farming or the number
of persons engaged in agriculture should be
expressed as the number of full man-years
worked in agricultural pursuits.

Even with such adjustments, however, agri-

22. In Japan, for example, 85 per cent of the farmers
carry on some outside occupation (**22**, p. 163). In the
United States, 27 per cent of all farm operators reported
part-time work off the farm in 1944, and almost 70 per
cent of these worked 100 days or more off the farm
(**11**, 1950, p. 581).

culture's share in national income is low in comparison with its share in the national labor force.
There may be various explanations:

1. Agriculture is less adaptable to changes in
demand than industry. A manufacturer can reduce or stop production if prices for his commodity seem too low to him. A farmer, on the
contrary, cannot change his plans once the fields
are sown, or stop milking the cows or feeding
his horse. When the financial prospect is dark,
he continues to work even harder in the hope
of getting a greater crop.

2. At the same time, the demand for foodstuffs is less elastic than that for industrial products. As soon as normal demand is satisfied,
prices for foodstuffs fall more rapidly than those
for industrial goods, and the fall usually fails
to open up new outlets. Thus periodically recurring overproduction inflicts heavy losses on
agriculture. As the French king, Charles X, explained in 1826: "His Majesty has no power to
protect his subjects against the consequences of
a good harvest."[23]

3. The investment per worker in agriculture
is usually lower than in industry, and the value
of the output per worker is accordingly smaller.

4. Agriculture often employs more people
than it actually needs, including many marginal
workers.

Farm Income in the United States

Agriculture's share in total income varies
greatly in the different parts of the United
States, reflecting the wide differences in its importance in the local economy. The proportion
in 1950 was less than 2 per cent in such highly
industrialized states as Rhode Island (0.5 per
cent), Massachusetts (1.0) and New York (1.3);
it ranged between 2 and 5 per cent in New
Hampshire, Maryland, West Virginia, Pennsylvania, Delaware, Michigan and Ohio. At the
other extreme, agriculture accounted for 20–30
per cent of all income in some predominantly
agricultural states such as Arkansas and Mississippi, Idaho and Montana, and for 38.6 and
38.3 per cent, respectively, in North and South
Dakota.

Comparison of agricultural income with manufacturing payrolls reveals similar contrasts.
While the ratio of manufacturing payrolls to
farmers' income is higher than 10 to 1 in many

23. **20**, p. 11.

TABLE 214

Agriculture's Share in Labor Force and National Income in Selected Countries and States of the United States

Agriculture's Share (Per Cent)	Countries	States of the United States [a,b]
A. Share in Labor Force		
Up to 10	Great Britain	Rhode Island, Massachusetts, Connecticut, New York, New Jersey, Pennsylvania, District of Columbia
10.1–20	United States, Belgium, Australia, New Zealand	Maine, New Hampshire, Ohio, Illinois, Michigan, Delaware, Maryland, West Virginia, Nevada, Washington, California
20.1–30	Canada, Denmark, Norway, Sweden, Netherlands, Germany, Switzerland, Union of South Africa [c]	Indiana, Arizona, Utah, Oregon, Florida, Colorado
30.1–40	Chile, Argentina, France, Austria, Czechoslovakia	Wisconsin, Missouri, Minnesota, Virginia, Louisiana, Montana, Wyoming, New Mexico, Kansas, Texas, Vermont
40.1–50	Cuba, Ireland, Portugal, Italy, Hungary	Iowa, Nebraska, North Carolina, South Carolina, Georgia, Kentucky, Tennessee, Alabama, Oklahoma, Idaho
50.1–60	Venezuela, Spain, Portugal, Japan, Greece, Panama, Finland	South Dakota, Arkansas
60.1–70	Mexico, Brazil, Peru, Poland, India, Indonesia, Burma, British Malaya, Union of South Africa [d]	North Dakota, Mississippi
70.1–80	Guatemala, Nicaragua, Colombia, Yugoslavia, Romania, Korea, French Morocco, Egypt, Nigeria, Philippines	None
80 and over	Bulgaria, Turkey, Thailand	None
B. Share in National Income		
Up to 10	United States, Great Britain	Rhode Island, Delaware, Connecticut, Massachusetts, Maine, New Hampshire, Maryland, New Jersey, New York, Pennsylvania, West Virginia, Florida, Virginia, Louisiana, Tennessee, Illinois, Indiana, Michigan, Wisconsin, Ohio, Utah, California, Washington, Oregon
10.1–20	Canada, Norway, Netherlands, Chile, Union of South Africa, Western Germany	Vermont, Alabama, Georgia, Kentucky, North Carolina, South Carolina, Arizona, Texas, Oklahoma, Minnesota, Kansas, Missouri, Colorado, New Mexico, Wyoming, Nevada
20.1–30	Argentina, Puerto Rico, Denmark, Hungary, Japan, Finland, Italy	Mississippi, Arkansas, Idaho, Montana
30.1–40	Ireland, Peru, Greece, Colombia	Iowa, Nebraska, North Dakota, South Dakota
40.1–50	Dominican Republic, Bulgaria, Turkey, Egypt, Kenya, India	None
50.1–60	None	None
60.1–70	Philippines	None
70.1–80	Ceylon	None
80 and over	None	None

Sources: Tables 211 and 213.

a. Data for 1940 (**10**. pp. 107–12). Male agricultural labor.
b. Data for 1950 (**13**, August 1951, p. 16).
c. White population.
d. Native population.

468

states, in 1950 there were 17 states in which agricultural income exceeded manufacturing payrolls.[24]

The United States has about the same percentage of the labor force in agriculture as Belgium has, but its income from manufacturing and service industries is so much larger than in Belgium that the share of American agriculture in national income is one third smaller than that of Belgian farming.

In agriculture's relation to total income and labor force, Rhode Island and New York have about the same pattern as Great Britain. Mississippi devotes approximately the same part of its labor force to agriculture as Mexico or Brazil and derives the same percentage of its total income from these pursuits as Argentina or Hungary. In North Dakota, agricultural income accounts for about the same share in total income as in Ireland or Greece, and its farm labor force for approximately the same share in total labor force as in Poland or India. (See Table 214.)

There are no states, however, where agriculture absorbs as large a percentage of the total labor force as in Guatemala or the Philippines, and no states where agriculture has as important a part in income as in Turkey or the Dominican Republic.

Protection of Farm Income

In recent years many countries have tried to solve the problem before which the king of France stood helpless — to lessen the risks incurred by farmers through their dependence on prices and to assure them a fair income. In some countries support of farmers has been defended as a matter of population policy to encourage

population increase and prevent decline in birth rates. Other countries have used the argument of national defense, closely related to the population argument, and self-sufficiency. Support of farmers has sometimes been advocated as a means of widening the domestic market and providing jobs for industrial workers. Often the argument of fair play in the distribution of national income has dominated the discussion. In a more general way, it appears that farmers, who represent a large part of the voters in small towns, have learned to use their political power to influence government policy.

Thus, the United States has introduced the policy of parity prices to compensate the farmer if crop prices drop considerably below prices of the industrial products he purchases. The English Agricultural Act of 1947 empowered the government to fix prices for agricultural products and provided that prices for crops should be announced one year, and those for livestock and products two to four years, in advance. Many countries have tried such measures as restricting imports to uphold prices for domestic agricultural products, paying subsidies to raise the output of specific commodities, controlling production of some crops or buying up and distributing quantities of surplus products. The recent trend in prices has strengthened the position of farmers. During and since World War II, agricultural prices in most countries have risen in comparison with those of manufactured products.

Thus, agriculture's share in national income has been rising in most industrial countries, while its share in the labor force has declined. The gap between the remuneration of agricultural and industrial work is narrower than it was 20 years ago but it has not disappeared. Despite the political successes of farmers and the efforts of governments to increase their income, farming remains the most common but not the most lucrative human activity.

---

24. Arkansas, Florida, Mississippi, Arizona, New Mexico, Oklahoma, Texas, Iowa, Colorado, Idaho, Kansas, Montana, Nebraska, the Dakotas, Wyoming and Nevada (**13**, August 1951, p. 17).

Chapter 15

LAND, FARMS AND FARMING

IN EACH COUNTRY, and often in each region of a large country, farmers face problems of their own, but the fundamental factors on which they must depend are the same the world over. Whether the farmer grows food crops, raises livestock or produces so-called technical crops for industry, four basic factors control the results of his work — the climate, his land, the type of his farm, and farming practices, including his skills.

The effect of climate and other natural conditions on agriculture is discussed in Chapter 10. Consideration here is focused on the distribution and use, or abuse, of arable land. The type of farm is determined by such characteristics as its ownership and changes in ownership in the course of agrarian reforms, the form of land tenure, and the farmer's major objective — whether to produce chiefly for his family's subsistence or for the market.

Farming practices include, in addition to practices in land use, the selection of seed, techniques of livestock breeding, use of tools and machinery, electrification of farm operations, fertilization of the soil, and so on.

LAND

In all parts of the world, the sight of fields stretching to the horizon is likely to conceal the basic fact of world agriculture: land fully suitable for cultivation is scarce.

ARABLE LAND

Only 9 per cent of all the land in the world is cultivated, according to the Food and Agriculture Organization (FAO) of the United Nations, and some of this is mediocre or marginal. The United States Department of Agriculture figure is even lower — 7.5 per cent — because it estimates Africa's cultivated land at 138 million acres instead of 462 million and that of the USSR at 414 million instead of 556 million.[1] While using different terms — arable land and orchards (FAO), and cultivated land (USDA)

— both estimates are based on a similar definition: cropland, forage, gardens, tree and bush crops, temporary meadows and fallow land.[2]

Differences among Continents and Countries

Arable land is very unevenly distributed among continents and countries. Asia, with more than half the world's population, has less than a third of the world's cultivated area; North America, with 7.5 per cent of the population, has about a fifth. Within the continents, arable land constitutes some 12 per cent of the total area in North America, 3.6 per cent in South America, nearly 30 per cent in Europe and only 2.2 per cent in Oceania. (See Table 215 and Figure 148.)

In some regions, as in South-West Africa or the Sudan, only a fraction of one per cent of the land is arable; in Peru the figure is a little more than one per cent; in Brazil, Colombia and Australia about 2 per cent; in Canada and Ecuador, 3 to 4 per cent; in China and the USSR about 10 per cent. In contrast, in most of Europe except the Scandinavian countries and mountainous Switzerland, the proportion of land that is arable ranges from about 21 per cent in Ireland to about 62–63 per cent in Denmark and Hungary. (See Table 216; cf. Figure 149.) Favorable climate and soil account for part of this high rate of cultivation, but incessant human effort, stimulated by the great pressure of population, and technical knowledge have been important contributing factors.

The 89 countries and territories included in Table 216 cover 29.5 billion acres, or nearly nine tenths of the land on our globe. Some 40 per cent of this territory is in the group of countries where less than 5 per cent of the land is arable, and less than 0.5 per cent lies in countries where as much as 50 per cent of the land is arable. (See Table 217.)

The proportion of arable land used annually for crops varies from region to region. In Europe and Asia, almost all cultivated land is in crops;

---

1. **102**, pp. 1–2. See also Chapter 10.

2. **19**, 1950, p. 257 and **102**, p. 2.

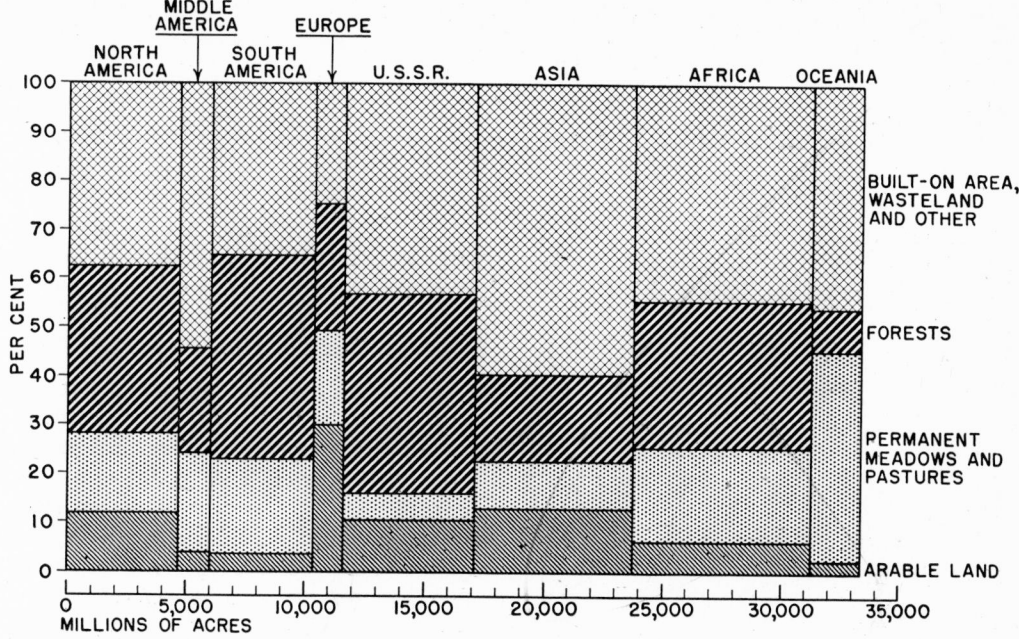

FIGURE 148. LAND USE, BY CONTINENT, 1947-49

TABLE 215

LAND USE, BY CONTINENT, 1947–49

| | Millions of Acres | | | | | Percentage Distribution | | | | |
| | Agricultural Area | | | | | | Agricultural Area | | | |
Continent	*Total Area*	*Arable Land*	*Permanent Meadows and Pastures*	*Forests and Woodlands*	*Built-on Area, Wasteland and Other* [a]	*Total Area*	*Arable Land*	*Permanent Meadows and Pastures*	*Forests and Woodlands*	*Built-on Area, Wasteland and Other* [a]
World	33,381	3,039	5,405	9,943	14,994	100.0	9.1	16.2	29.8	44.9
North America	4,671	545	771	1,604	1,752	100.0	11.7	16.5	34.3	37.5
Middle America	1,328	51	269	284	724	100.0	3.8	20.3	21.4	54.5
South America	4,396	158	848	1,843	1,547	100.0	3.6	19.3	41.9	35.2
Europe	1,218	363	237	316	301	100.0	29.8	19.5	25.9	24.7
USSR	5,503	556	306	2,273	2,367	100.0	10.1	5.6	41.2	43.1
Asia	6,632	855	635	1,166	3,976	100.0	12.9	9.6	17.6	59.9
Africa	7,517	462	1,431	2,268	3,356	100.0	6.1	19.0	30.2	44.6
Oceania	2,115	47	909	188	971	100.0	2.2	43.0	8.9	45.9

Source: Adapted from **19**, 1950, pp. 3–7. Continental and world totals include estimates of the FAO for various countries for which no official information was available. For some countries, particularly in Asia and Africa, no estimates have been made for "permanent meadows and pastures" and "forests and woodlands" because of complete lack of any bases for such estimates. The totals for these two groups somewhat understate the actual area. (*Ibid.*, p. 258.)

a. Includes unused but potentially productive land.

TABLE 216

LAND USE, IN SELECTED COUNTRIES, 1947–49

(*Millions of Acres*)

| Country [a] | Total Area,[b] Including Inland Waters | Agricultural Area | | Forests and Woodlands | Unused But Potentially Productive Land | Built-on Area, Wasteland and Other |
		Arable Land	Permanent Meadows and Pastures			
United States	1,934.3	454.9	662.0	623.9	15.0 [e]	178.4
Canada [d]	2,389.7	91.2	78.6	837.2	208.6	1,174.2
Mexico	486.5	24.7	247.1	158.1	24.7	31.9
Guatemala	26.9	7.4	1.5	17.8	...	0.2
El Salvador	8.4	1.1	0.4	4.9	...	2.0
Honduras	37.8	1.4	0.5	24.0	...	12.1
Nicaragua	36.6	1.7	0.7	16.1	7.9	10.4
Costa Rica	12.6	2.0	0.5	9.9	...	0.3
Panama	•18.3	0.3	...	16.1	...	2.0
Cuba	28.3	4.9	9.6	7.4	0.1	6.3
Dominican Republic	12.2	1.7	1.5	8.4	...	0.6
Puerto Rico	2.2	1.0	0.6	0.2	...	0.4
Venezuela	225.4	3.7	74.1	90.2	45.7	11.6
Colombia	281.4	5.2	65.0	177.9	...	33.4
Ecuador [e]	68.0	2.8	4.9	35.3	13.1	11.9
Brazil [f]	2,104.3	46.5 [f]	327.7	978.3	72.4 [f]	679.5
Peru	308.6	4.0	33.4	173.0	32.1	66.2
Bolivia [g]	264.1	0.8	...	116.1	...	147.3
Paraguay	100.6	3.8		20.8 [e]	...	76.1
Chile	183.3	14.3	16.8	40.3	...	111.7
Uruguay	46.2	3.5	31.8	1.2	...	9.9
Argentina	694.1	74.1	284.7	120.1	...	215.2
United Kingdom	60.3	18.3	29.9	3.7	...	8.3
Ireland	17.3	3.7	7.9	0.2	...	5.4
France [h]	136.2	52.2	30.2	27.5	...	26.2
Belgium	7.6	2.5	1.8	1.3	...	2.0
Netherlands	8.6	2.7	3.2	0.6	5.9 [i]	2.1
Denmark	10.6	6.7	1.2	0.9	...	1.9
Sweden	110.9	9.1	2.3	58.1	7.4	41.3
Norway	80.1	2.0	0.6	18.5	...	59.1
Finland	83.3	6.2	1.0	53.4	...	22.7
Germany:						
Western	60.3	21.4	13.6	17.3	...	8.0
Soviet Zone	26.4	12.6	3.2	7.3	...	3.5
Poland [j]	77.1	41.5	10.0	17.0	...	8.4
Czechoslovakia	31.1	13.6	5.0	10.0	...	2.5
Switzerland	10.1	1.2	2.5	2.5	...	4.0
Austria	20.6	4.4	5.7	7.7	...	2.7
Hungary	23.0	14.3	3.9	2.7	...	2.0
Portugal [g]	22.0	8.4		6.1	6.6	1.0
Spain	124.3	47.4	58.1	12.6	...	6.4
Italy	74.4	38.1	12.8	14.8	3.0	5.7
Yugoslavia	63.5	19.5	14.6	21.5	...	7.9
Romania	58.6	23.0	8.4	16.3	...	10.9
Bulgaria	27.4	10.6	0.6	9.1	...	7.2
Greece	32.4	8.2	6.0	4.7	0.2	13.2
USSR	5,502.9	556.0	306.4	1,551.8	29.7	3,059.0

(*Continued on facing page*)

TABLE 216—*continued*

Country [a]	Total Area,[b] Including Inland Waters	Agricultural Area		Forests and Woodlands	Unused But Potentially Productive Land	Built-on Area, Wasteland and Other
		Arable Land	Permanent Meadows and Pastures			
China	2,405.8	224.9	479.6	207.6	...	1,493.7
Korea	50.7	10.9	...	39.0	...	0.9
Japan	90.9	14.8	1.2	61.6	...	13.3
Turkey [h]	192.0	36.6	106.0	29.7	...	19.8
Syria	42.3	6.2 [g]	9.6	1.0	8.4	17.2
Jordan	22.5	1.2	1.5	0.1	...	19.8
Iraq	107.5	6.7	9.9	3.7	...	87.3
Iran	407.2	41.5	24.7	46.9	81.5	212.5
Afghanistan	148.3	3.0 [g]	...	2.5 [g]	...	143.0
Pakistan	241.0	51.1	...	7.9	22.2	159.9
India	664.9	305.9	86.5 (⌣ combined)		91.7	180.6
Burma	167.5	21.6	...	96.6	13.8	35.3
Thailand	127.0	11.7	...	80.6	...	34.6
Indochina	181.9	11.6	...	76.6	...	93.7
Ceylon	16.2	3.6	...	8.6	1.5	2.4
Malaya	32.4	5.2	...	24.5	1.9	0.9
Indonesia	470.5	27.2	...	299.0	...	144.3
Philippines	73.9	20.3	2.4	39.3	6.7	5.4
Morocco (French)	97.9	18.8	19.0	9.8	...	50.2
Algeria	544.9	14.1	102.1	7.5	...	421.3
Tunisia	38.5	9.4	10.4	2.5	...	16.3
Egypt	247.1	6.0	...	...	...	241.1
Anglo-Egyptian Sudan	619.2	1.7	59.3	232.5	1.5	325.4
Ethiopia	261.9	27.2	49.4	2.5	158.1	24.7
Somaliland	172.7	19.7	81.5	66.7	...	4.9
French West Africa	1,155.4	24.7	61.8 (⌣ combined)	420.0	...	648.9
French Equatorial Africa	620.2	165.6 (⌣ combined)		376.6	...	78.1
Belgian Congo [h]	584.4	121.1	21.2	247.1	...	...
Liberia	27.4	4.4	0.6	9.6	6.7	6.2
Gold Coast	50.4	3.0	14.8	27.4	...	5.4
Nigeria	216.7	16.1	...	94.6	...	106.0
French Cameroons	109.0	19.8	12.4	71.2	...	5.7
Kenya	144.1	4.0	29.7	3.7	...	106.7
Uganda	60.0	5.4	...	4.9	...	49.6
Ruanda-Urundi	13.3	3.2	6.8	0.8	...	2.7
Tanganyika	232.0	7.3	32.8	96.4	2.0	93.7
Nyasaland	30.6	0.5	...	4.4	...	25.7
Madagascar	145.8	12.4	91.4	17.3	0.6	24.1
Northern Rhodesia	185.8	80.1 (⌣ combined)		96.1	...	9.6
Southern Rhodesia	96.1	3.0	...	56.8	...	36.3
South-West Africa	203.4	0.1	126.3	12.4	24.7	39.8
Union of South Africa	296.5	15.1	200.2	9.1	...	72.2
Australia	1,903.7	32.1	876.0	76.4	20.0	899.4
New Zealand	66.4	2.4	30.4	16.8	0.3	16.3

Source: **19**, 1950, pp. 3–7.

a. Countries arranged geographically.

b. Since mixed growth such as grassland or forests is counted twice in some countries, the totals for such countries are smaller than the sum of the components.

c. Excludes grazing and forest areas suitable for cropland if cleared or otherwise improved.

d. Includes Newfoundland. A part of potentially productive land also included under forest and woodland.

e. Incomplete.

f. Data of 1940 farm census.

g. Prewar data.

h. Inland waters included in the various land use categories.

i. Being reclaimed from the sea; not included in total area.

j. Prewar data for present boundaries.

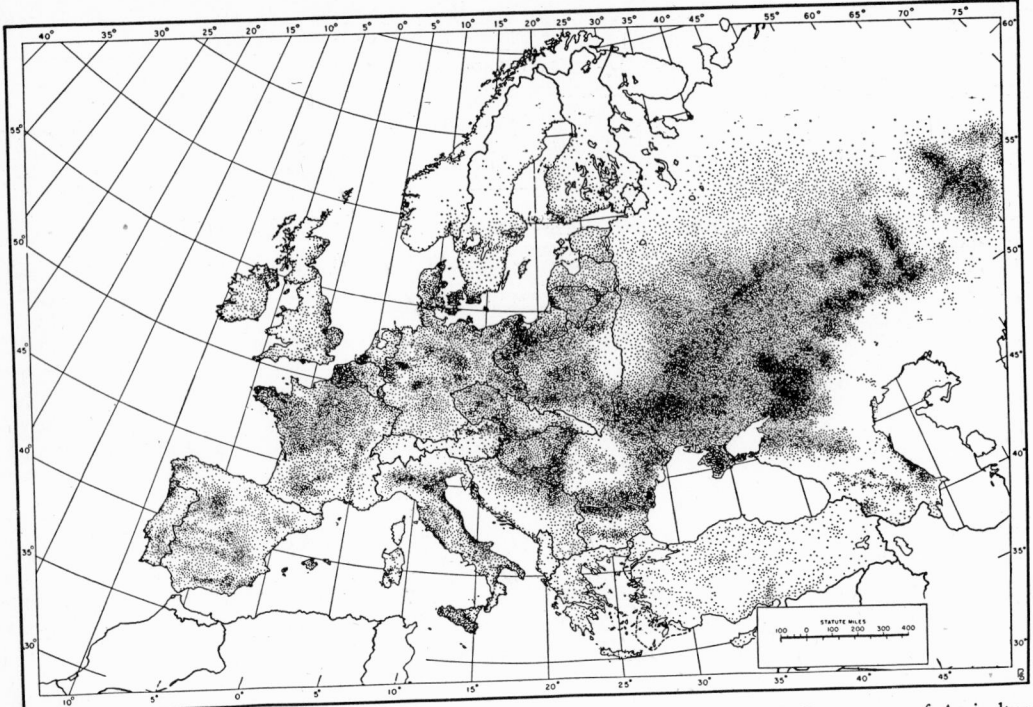

U. S. Department of Agriculture

FIGURE 149. ARABLE LAND IN EUROPE, THE NEAR EAST AND THE WESTERN PART OF THE USSR, 1932–38

in Latin America, 60 to 70 per cent; in the USSR, about 60 per cent (1938).[3]

Differences within Countries

A single country may have as great contrasts within its own borders as those between Nicaragua or Iraq and Denmark or Hungary. In the United States, less than 5 per cent of Wyoming or Arizona, for example, is arable while more than 60 per cent of Iowa is under cultivation. (See Table 218.)

In the USSR, land is most intensively utilized in the black earth area (chernozem), where 60 to 80 per cent is plowed. The percentage declines as one goes northward to the Baltic Sea and eastward to the Urals. In the European part of the USSR, the proportion of arable land amounts to nearly 30 per cent of the total area.[4]

Since the turn of the century, the amount of arable land in some countries has declined because some poor soil has been withdrawn from cultivation, as in France, or turned into pasture, as in Belgium. In some areas, this shift has been largely offset by higher yields per acre of the remaining cultivated area.

DENSITY OF FARM POPULATION

A much larger part of the total territory is cultivated in Europe than in the United States or Canada, and the farming area is much more densely settled. International data on the arable acreage per capita of population, total or agricultural, are not fully comparable because of differences in land classification or absence of statistics for the agricultural population. The available data often relate to a postwar year for arable land and a prewar year for agricultural population. Nevertheless, the figures in Table 219, while not strictly comparable, show that Oceania has more acres of arable land (3.71) per capita of population than any other continent. North America and the USSR have about the same acreage per capita of total population (3.40 in 1948 and 3.26 in 1939, respectively), while North America has three times as many acres per capita of farm population as the USSR (18.0 and 5.73). Figures for Canada are even higher than for the United States. Land hunger in China and Japan is illustrated by the pitifully small arable acreage

3. **10**, p. 11 and **139**, p. 102.
4. **139**, p. 102.

TABLE 217

LAND USE: PERCENTAGE DISTRIBUTION

Less than 5	5.0–9.9	10.0–19.9	20.0–29.9	30.0–39.9	40.0–49.9	50.0 or More
			America			
Canada	Mexico	Cuba	United States		Puerto Rico	
Nicaragua	Chile	Dominican	Guatemala			
Honduras	Uruguay	Republic				
Panama		Argentina				
Venezuela		El Salvador				
Colombia		Costa Rica				
Ecuador						
Brazil						
Peru						
Bolivia						
			Europe and the USSR			
Norway	Sweden	Switzerland	Ireland	United Kingdom	Germany	Poland
	Finland	USSR	Austria	France	(Soviet Zone)	Italy
			Greece	Belgium	Czechoslovakia	Denmark
				Netherlands		Hungary
				Western		
				Germany		
				Spain		
				Yugoslavia		
				Romania		
				Bulgaria		
			Asia			
Afghanistan	China	Japan	Korea		India	
	Jordan	Turkey	Pakistan			
	Thailand	Syria	Ceylon			
	Indochina	Iran	Philippines			
	Indonesia	Burma				
	Iraq	Malaya				
			Africa			
Algeria	Nigeria	Morocco	Congo			
Egypt	Uganda	Ethiopia	Ruanda-			
Sudan	Madagascar	Somaliland	Urundi			
French West	Union of	Liberia	Tunisia			
Africa	South Africa	French				
Kenya	Gold Coast	Cameroons				
Tanganyika						
South-West						
Africa						
Southern						
Rhodesia						
Nyasaland						
			Oceania			
Australia						
New Zealand						
			Total Land Area, in Millions of Acres			
11,187	4,995	7,869	3,049	546	724	186
			Arable Land, in Millions of Acres			
257	393	856	697	197	333	101

Source: Computed from Table 216.

TABLE 218

LAND USE IN THE UNITED STATES: DISTRIBUTION OF STATES BY PROPORTION OF AREA USED AS ARABLE LAND,[a] 1945

(Per Cent)

Less than 5	5.0–9.9	10.0–19.9	20.0–29.9	30.0–39.9	40.0–49.9	50.0 or More
Wyoming	Maine	Massachusetts	New York	Wisconsin	Ohio	Indiana
New Mexico	New Hampshire	Connecticut	New Jersey	Minnesota	Nebraska	Illinois
Arizona	Vermont	Virginia	Pennsylvania	Missouri		North Dakota
Utah	Rhode Island	West Virginia	Michigan	South Dakota		Kansas
Nevada	Florida	Louisiana	Maryland	Delaware		Iowa
	Oregon	Texas	South Carolina	North Carolina		
	California	Montana	Georgia	Oklahoma		
		Idaho	Kentucky			
		Colorado	Tennessee			
		Washington	Alabama			
			Mississippi			
			Arkansas			

Source: Adapted from **45**, 1949, pp. 3 and 616.   a. Cropland harvested, crop failure and cropland idle or fallow.

TABLE 219

ARABLE LAND: PER CAPITA OF TOTAL AND AGRICULTURAL POPULATION

(Acres)

Continent and Country [a]	Per Capita of Population		Country [a]	Per Capita of Population	
	Total	Agricultural		Total	Agricultural
World	1.28	2.20	Poland	1.5	2.7
North America	3.40	18.0	Czechoslovakia	1.1*	3.8
Middle America	1.02	} 2.47	Switzerland	0.3*	5.9
South America	1.47		Austria	0.6*	5.3
Europe	0.96	2.87	Hungary	1.5*	4.0
USSR	3.26	5.73	Portugal	. . .	3.1
Asia	0.64	0.94	Spain	1.7	4.6
Africa	2.22	2.99	Italy	0.8	2.7
Oceania	3.71	11.12	Yugoslavia	1.2*	3.2
			Romania	1.7*	3.3
United States	3.1*	16.5*	Bulgaria	. . .	2.5
Canada	5.3*	28.5*	Greece	1.1	2.9
United Kingdom	0.4	12.0	China	0.29	0.7*
France	1.2	5.5	Japan	0.20	0.8
Belgium	0.3	3.5	Iran	2.47	. . .
Netherlands	0.3	3.4	Pakistan	0.69*	. . .
Denmark	1.7	6.5	India	0.89*	. . .
Sweden	1.4*	5.4	Australia	4.06*	. . .
Norway	0.7*	4.1			
Germany	0.7	5.1			

Sources: For continents: **10**, p. 12; for data on area per capita of total population, **102**, p. 2; on agricultural population, **127**, p. 22; cf. also **19**, 1950, pp. 13–15.

a. Continents: data for 1947–49; single countries: data for prewar years except for those marked with asterisks.

per capita of both total and agricultural population. (See Table 219.)

Such contrasts in arable acreage per capita are of paramount significance, since the relative amount of farm land determines whether the controlling factor in a country's agriculture is land or manpower. Where farm land is relatively scarce, all efforts must be directed toward obtaining the maximum yield per acre. If cultivation is diversified and intensive and agricultural techniques are well developed, a comparatively high standard of living may be achieved on even a few acres, as in the Low Countries or Scandinavia. Where land is abundant, but relatively few people are available to work it, as in the New World, farmers resort to mechanization to obtain as great an output per man as possible.

This difference between Europe and the United States was recognized as early as the time of Thomas Jefferson, who said: "In Europe the objective is to make the most of their land, labor being abundant; here it is to make the most of our labor, land being abundant." Wherever labor is abundant, men, indeed, become "accessories to teams and machines," in contrast to the United States where "tractor, truck and team are accessories to the farmer." [5]

SOIL DEPLETION

When man began to till the soil, he also began to destroy it.

Soil is not inert and static, but a living and dynamic substance, the product of nature's ageless work, a mixture of organic and inorganic materials formed by the interaction of climate, vegetation and animal organisms. Highly intricate chemical changes and biological processes are in operation within it, activated by innumerable microorganisms, many millions of them per gram of rich surface soil.[6] This microbial population decomposes fallen leaves, decaying roots, insects and dead animal matter into highly complex organic matter without which plants cannot grow. The nitrogen-fixing bacteria are among the most important of these microorganisms. They live on the roots of leguminous plants and produce nitrogen, essential to plant nutrition. The ancient Greeks and Romans recognized that legumes were useful in maintaining the fertility of the soil, and practiced legume rotation and green manuring centuries ago.[7]

Proper operation of the soil factory is endangered when the same crop is grown year after year, extracting the same nutrients, which are then carried away, or when row crops requiring clean tillage, such as corn, tobacco and cotton, are planted continuously on the same land. If the soil does not receive the equivalent of the nutrients it yields to growing vegetation, it loses fertility. Such losses do not appear in the budget of the nation or individual farmer or in trade balances. Nor are they calculated in the domestic or export prices of foodstuffs. Considering that gradual soil depletion is universal, Sir Josiah Stamp has declared that the world at large has been fed below cost for the last hundred years.[8]

EROSION

Even more serious is the danger of erosion. Normal or geological erosion is the ageless work of water and wind on rock surfaces of the earth. Man-made erosion begins when the plant cover that keeps the soil in place is removed, when underbrush is cleared and forests [9] are burned to provide plow land or when land is overgrazed. Then the soil, unprotected by vegetation, lies open to wind and rain, and the precious topsoil is washed or blown away much faster than it can be renewed.

The vast difference between the slow process of geological erosion and the exceedingly rapid process of man-made erosion is shown clearly by measurements taken by the U. S. Department of Agriculture at many experimental stations. For example, at the station in Statesville, North Carolina, the accelerated erosion on land planted to cotton year after year removed an average of 31.2 tons of soil per acre annually and resulted in a loss of 12.4 per cent of the annual rainfall. In contrast, geological erosion removed only 0.002 of a ton of soil per acre during a year from the same kind of soil and only 0.06 per cent of the rainfall was lost as run-off.[10]

Erosion may be of various degrees and of various types — gully erosion, sheet erosion, wind erosion. Soil that has not been too seriously eroded may be restored. On the other hand,

5. **26**, p. 23.

6. Soil tests in the famous Rothamsted experimental station, in England, have shown that one gram may contain as many as 45 million bacteria plus millions of fungi and other living organisms (**97**, pp. 339–41).

7. **101**, pp. 32–34.

8. **129**, p. 260.

9. See Chapter 19.

10. **36**, 1948, p. 72.

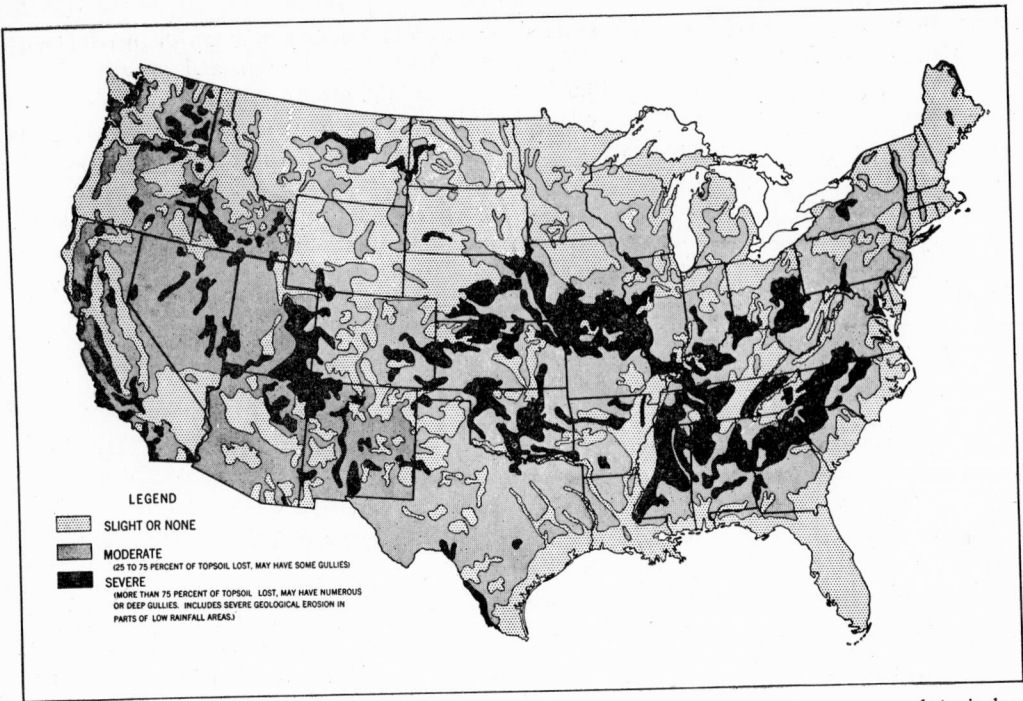

U. S. Department of Agriculture

FIGURE 150. SOIL EROSION IN THE UNITED STATES, 1934

erosion may destroy soil completely in that all the organic matter and lighter particles are removed, leaving only gravel, coarse sand or stubborn clay. If not checked, erosion may increase in both extent and destructiveness. It takes only fifty years to wash down seven inches of topsoil that it has taken thousands of years to build up.

The United States

The alarming situation in the United States was suddenly dramatized for the unsuspecting country in the 1930's, when dark clouds from the Dust Bowl blackened the sky over many states, even in the East. The survey of 1934 showed that of the 400 million acres of cropland, about 50 million had been ruined, 50 million were approaching that condition, 100 million were severely damaged by the loss of from half to all topsoil, and another 100 million were suffering from active erosion.[11] Three billion tons of solid earth were being washed out of the fields and pastures every year; one fourth was carried into

the Gulf of Mexico. The annual costs of erosion were estimated at almost $4 billion, and about a million acres were being ruined each year for further cultivation.[12] (See Figure 150.)

These conditions resulted from a combination of factors: ruthless clearing of forests; the frequent use of land susceptible to both gully and sheet erosion for crops requiring a clean cultivation, such as cotton, corn,[13] or tobacco; the vast expansion of wheat fields in the Great Plains, with the resulting destruction of the grass cover.

Latin America

In Latin America, much of the land in densely populated areas is extremely susceptible to erosion. In western and northern Venezuela a large part of cultivated steep hills has been severely eroded. Clearing land for coffee has depleted large areas in central Brazil. On the great plains of Argentina, Uruguay and southern Brazil, some areas show the destructive work of wind

11. **85**, p. 7.

12. **86**, p. 4, and **36**, 1948, p. 77.
13. Continuous growing of corn, for example, keeps soil uncovered during 207 days and exposes it to erosion (**81**, p. 286).

erosion. In El Salvador and Haiti erosion has affected a large acreage.[14]

Oceania and Asia

In Australia erosion is spreading rapidly and many millions of acres have been denuded of topsoil. In New Zealand more than two fifths of the total area and more than two thirds of the occupied area are subject to rapid erosion.[15]

Efficient cultivation has checked erosion in many areas of China, but in others man-made erosion has reached appalling proportions.[16] Erosion has played havoc in large areas where forests have been destroyed for fuel or cut to make room for farming. In the northwestern part of that country, where farming was extended to semi-arid grazing grounds, the wind has blown away the topsoil during the dry years. This vast region is now barren and ruined even for grazing livestock, its original best use.[17] Rivers wash away the loose soil on denuded hillsides and banks. The Yellow River alone carries off as much soil from its watersheds every year as all the rivers of the United States together. In South China, nearly all the cleared hillsides are stripped of soil cover, and run-off water carries sand, gravel, even boulders to the fields in the valleys and on the plains. In many places the sterile clay subsoil has been exposed.[18]

In India, uncontrolled grazing by millions of cattle and faulty practices of cultivation have caused widespread erosion. Sheet and gully erosion has seriously damaged cultivated and uncultivated lands on many plains close to rivers and streams. In the United Provinces, for example, 5 million acres are barren ravines and salt-impregnated wasteland; 8.7 million acres represent the so-called "cultivable waste" that could be restored to cultivation through soil conservation measures. But very little is done to protect the land, and some 40 million head of scrub cattle continue to ravage it. In Bengal, gully erosion has exposed the subsoil; in Orissa, it causes immense damage.[19] Punjab has 2 million acres of ravine lands that are not only unpro-

ductive but a menace through the flood damage they cause on lands at great distance.[20]

In the Middle East, soil erosion is visible everywhere. In extreme cases, whole hillsides are but barren rocks. Harmful cultivation practices, destruction of forests and overgrazing have turned this land, once fertile, to a desert. Traces of the past, which can be discerned in the ruins of ancient waterworks, explain eloquently why the land around them is dry and sterile.

Africa

The African continent is a monument to the destructive work of erosion, due largely to "shifting agriculture." This type of farming in which one wooded area after another is burned and its fertile soil used for crops until it becomes depleted, may not have been dangerous in itself, for in time, new forest growth revegetated the abandoned plots. The increase in population, however, forced the natives to return to old plots before they had regained fertility. As a result, only a poor forest growth or even savanna had been established and new cropping was practically impossible. Animal grazing then replaced cropping, and the coarse unpalatable grass was often burned in a futile attempt to obtain better forage.[21] In such areas, moreover, the effect of the scanty rainfall is largely lost because of intense evaporation and the run-off caused by the lack of soil cover. Thus, the desert is virtually advancing throughout all Africa, but particularly in areas bordering the Sahara.[22]

Europe

There is no large-scale erosion in western and central Europe except in Spain, where large forests have been ruthlessly destroyed. Yet even in France the 1949 investigation by the Ministry of Agriculture found erosion in scattered areas totaling some 11 million acres, mostly in mountainous departments.[23] Sicily and Sardinia, once the granaries of Europe, and Latium (Campagna di Roma), "the cradle of the Latin race," now have barren land. In Western Germany large tracts of arable land are endangered by unchecked wind erosion.[24] In eastern Europe ero-

---

14. **16**, pp. 47–49 and **10**, p. 10.

15. **96**, p. 111.

16. On rice fields ("paddies") erosion is controlled in southwestern and central China, but where rice is grown on steep slopes erosion is so severe that only two or three years of cultivation are possible (**85**, pp. 912–13).

17. **3**, p. 78.

18. **16**, pp. 42–43.

19. **70**, pp. 74–75.

20. **100**, p. 142.

21. **113**, pp. 50–51; **16**, pp. 110–14.

22. **32**, March 1950, pp. 62–63.

23. **64**, p. 11.

24. **49**, p. 18.

sion affects great expanses. The wooded hilltops and grass-covered mountain slopes of Greece have been ruined by the destruction of forests and by grazing; probably not more than 2 per cent of the entire country has its original topsoil today, and crops are grown on subsoil.[25] In Yugoslavia, the southern mountain regions suffer from erosion directly attributable to the destruction of forests and the grass cover. As a consequence, streams become choked with silt and arable valleys are flooded.[26]

The USSR

Erosion and moving dunes plague the USSR in the Ukraine, central Russia, Turkestan and the Caucasus. It has been estimated that all the topsoil in the Transcaucasus may be gone within a decade or two.[27]

Soil Reclamation and Conservation

Scarcity of arable land, heightened by the growth of population has long compelled many peoples to turn their attention to areas that are idle but potentially productive. Reclamation of such land through drainage or irrigation has often called for vast engineering projects, extending over many years, even decades, and usually carried out by public authorities. Measures to conserve soil on individual farms and to maintain or improve its fertility are ordinarily the responsibility of the farmers themselves. These less dramatic measures benefit the individual farmer initially and require his continuous, patient effort year in and year out. Pragmatic measures to conserve the soil have been practiced for centuries. They are part and parcel of Chinese and Japanese agriculture, for example, in which the accumulated experience of innumerable generations turns tiny patches of land into veritable gardens. Only in our time, however, has a comprehensive scientific system of soil conservation been launched on a nationwide scale with the active support and on the initiative of government — that is, in the United States in the 1930's.[28]

Soil Reclamation in Europe

Perhaps the most daring and dogged example of soil reclamation the world has ever recorded is that which Holland has been carrying on for centuries.

The Netherlands

The Dutch began to drain lakes and pools and reclaim coastal areas for cultivation in the Middle Ages. Large lakes were transformed into fertile regions, and the sea was pushed further and further back. More ambitious projects were undertaken as experience in drainage increased and more effective pumping became possible, by means of windmills from the fourteenth century on and much later by steam-drawn and electrical machinery. In the middle of the nineteenth century, drainage of the eighteen-mile long Haarlem Lake added nearly 50,000 acres of valuable agricultural land.

After World War I, Holland started the gigantic Zuider Zee project to reclaim part of the ocean floor for farming. The first step was to build a dam about 19 miles long, in the turbulent sea from northern Holland to the Frisian coast. Four polders (areas enclosed by dykes) were then to be created by drainage and desalting, to provide, in all, some 544,000 additional acres — about 10 per cent of Holland's arable land. Work began in 1919, and the first polder, Wieringermeer, was put into cultivation between 1930 and 1941 while the second, the North East Polder, was dry in 1942. (See Figure 151.) In 1945 the retreating Germans opened the dykes and flooded the Wieringermeer polder. Drainage was resumed immediately after liberation,[29] and the polder is again under cultivation.

France

Late in the eighteenth century France began to reclaim more than 250,000 acres in the department of Landes from the invading sands. Carried by wind from the sea, the sand had buried villages and forests, fields and pastures and, hindering the normal flow of water toward the sea, had created marshes in the interior. The

25. **122**, p. 104.

26. **32**, September 1950, p. 191.

27. **85**, p. 911.

28. **38**, December 1945, p. 124. The Soil Conservation Service states in its annual report of 1949: "We have, thus far, been unable to find anywhere in the annals of ancient agriculture — and we have looked carefully through the literature of the world — that our modern methods of soil conservation (treating the land according to the adaptability and need) have ever been used anywhere in any extensive way prior to the establishment of the Soil Erosion Service on the 19th of September, 1933. . . ." **36**, 1949, p. 80.

29. **73**, pp. 20–24.

A. AREAS RECLAIMED SINCE A. D. 1500   B. RECLAMATION OF THE ZUIDER ZEE

 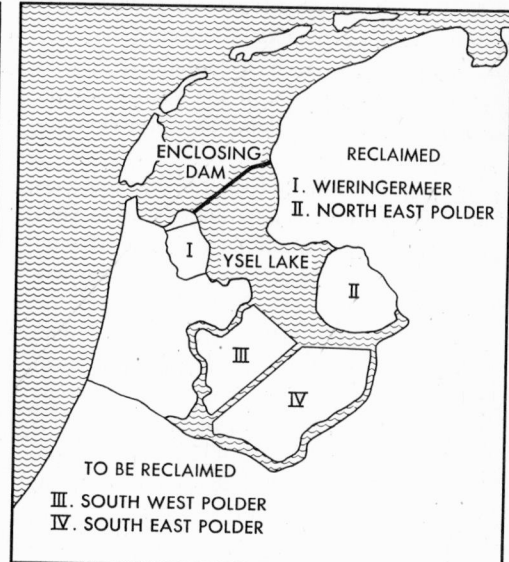

FIGURE 151. SOIL RECLAMATION IN THE NETHERLANDS SINCE A.D. 1500

The black areas on the left (A) have been wrested from the ocean by the Dutch since A.D. 1500. They include the Wieringermeer (49,500 acres), formerly the northwestern corner of the Zuider Zee, and the North East Polder (118,500 acres), once the northeastern part of that sea. The right side of the figure (B) shows the progress of reclamation of the Zuider Zee. The two northern polders have been reclaimed, and work has started on the reclamation of the South East Polder (272,000 acres) and the South West Polder (141,000 acres). In order to maintain the present level of ground water in the mainland, these polders will be built up as artificial islands. Stretches of water will be left between them and the mainland, and a wide channel will separate the two polders from each other.

entire area was deserted. A vast engineering project — which took many decades to accomplish — included the building of a high sand dune parallel to the coast and stabilizing it by means of a special hardy, coarse plant that creates a thick maze of roots. Behind this dune, seeds of selected trees were sown and immediately covered with twigs and branches topped with sand. Small crooked trees could grow under the protective mulch and its decomposition provided the necessary nutrients. Behind these two defense lines pine forests were planted, and the area gradually became a flourishing region.[30]

Great Britain

Centuries of effort have restored the fenlands on England's eastern coast to fertility. Drainage work begun in the second half of the seventeenth century reclaimed about half a million acres without the help of modern machinery. Then a new difficulty arose, which still harasses the fen farmers. The drained soil, of spongy peat, began to sink, and the general level of the fenlands,

originally about five feet above the coastal silt belt, is now as much as ten feet below it. When heavy winter rains swell the rivers, as in 1937 and 1939, the flat fenland is flooded. A project has been approved to build a new channel that will reduce flood levels to below the safety line.[31] During World War II, Great Britain cleared and drained a considerable acreage of swamp and scrubland to increase the output of essential food crops.[32]

Italy

An important program of land reclamation, whose beginnings go as far back as 1870, was under way in Italy before World War II. By July 1938, 7 million acres had been reclaimed, and an additional 8 million were in process of reclamation. The Pontine Marshes, where formerly only a few hundred people could barely exist during the summer, had a population of 60,000 after the reclamation. The northern and central parts of Italy have been the chief bene-

---

30. **64,** pp. 47–48. See also Chapter 19.

31. **38,** December 1945, pp. 136–38 and 142.
32. **100,** p. 142.

ficiaries of reclamation projects. Nearly a million acres were reclaimed in the north between 1882 and 1924, but the south added only 10,000 acres, and some of its provinces in greatest need of land improvement, such as Calabria, gained only about 30 acres. Nor in the years that followed was a single reclamation project completed in the south.[33]

With the help of the Marshall Plan, numerous reclamation projects are now under way in various parts of Italy. It is estimated by the Mission to Italy (Economic Cooperation Administration) that the result will be to irrigate about a million acres, reclaim some 800,000 acres, protect some 400,000 acres from flood, supply 330,000 farm people with electric power and 410,000 people with drinking water, and bring about various other benefits. (See Figure 152.) In addition, ECA funds are being used to expand or complete old projects. The entire program involves about 8 million acres.[34]

Germany

Western Germany has a 10-year plan in operation to bring some 400,000 acres of moors and wasteland in the Emsland into cultivation. It is planned to fill in some 1,000 square kilometers, regulate the rivers and construct several dykes, thereby increasing agricultural and forest land by 40 per cent.

Other Countries

Denmark has brought more than half its wasteland into cultivation since the second half of the nineteenth century. After World War I, Greece and Bulgaria reclaimed vast marshland areas to settle repatriated nationals.

Yugoslavia recently began to drain marshes in Croatia, Macedonia and some other areas and started work on irrigation in semiarid subtropical regions. It is reported that more than 13,000 acres have been reclaimed in Macedonia, largely by youth brigades without the help of heavy equipment. However, many projects included in that country's Five Year Plan are either in the initial stage or merely on paper.[35]

In Austria, several drainage and irrigation projects supported by the ECA are under way

and are expected to add 1.6 million acres to the country's arable land.[36]

Greece started reclamation projects before the war, the largest of them in central and eastern Macedonia and various smaller works in Thessaly, Peloponnesus, central Greece and elsewhere. Interrupted during the war, the work was resumed after liberation. By the end of 1949, some 800,000 acres had been reclaimed — some drained or irrigated, others protected from floods.

In 1950 work was in progress on 48 reclamation and flood control projects, and various measures had been taken to fight the upland soil erosion. Extensive well-drilling for irrigation purposes was under way.[37] Marshall Aid funds have been assigned to various projects.

The USSR

Drainage and irrigation projects are being carried out in the USSR to increase the area suitable for crop production. Before World War II, the USSR had about 15 million acres of irrigated land and more than 7.5 million acres of land reclaimed by drainage.[38] The first postwar Five Year Plan (1946–50) envisaged drainage of 667,000 acres of agricultural land in White Russia and 100,000 acres in the Ukraine, and irrigation of more than 1.6 million acres of new land. Reportedly, 943,000 acres of this land had irrigation in 1949.[39] New extensive multiple-purpose projects were announced in 1950 to irrigate the acid and semiacid land in the south and southeast and use the water to generate power and improve the climate. Cotton will be one of the principal crops to be planted in the Crimea and southern Ukraine when the irrigation project is completed. The old irrigation system on more than 25 million acres is also to be improved.[40]

SOIL RECLAMATION AND CONSERVATION IN THE UNITED STATES

Soil Reclamation

Irrigation, controlled by a system of dams and reservoirs, has made it possible to farm and raise livestock on more than 21 million acres in the western part of the United States [41] where the

33. **93**, p. 264.

34. Information received from the ECA Mission to Italy.

35. **32**, September 1950, pp. 192–96.

36. **32**, December 1949, p. 277.

37. **59**, April 1951, p. 22.

38. **83**, p. 368.

39. **76**, January 1, 1950.

40. **139**, pp. 105–06.

41. "Had it not been for the big and little reclamation projects, the West as we know it today would not exist,

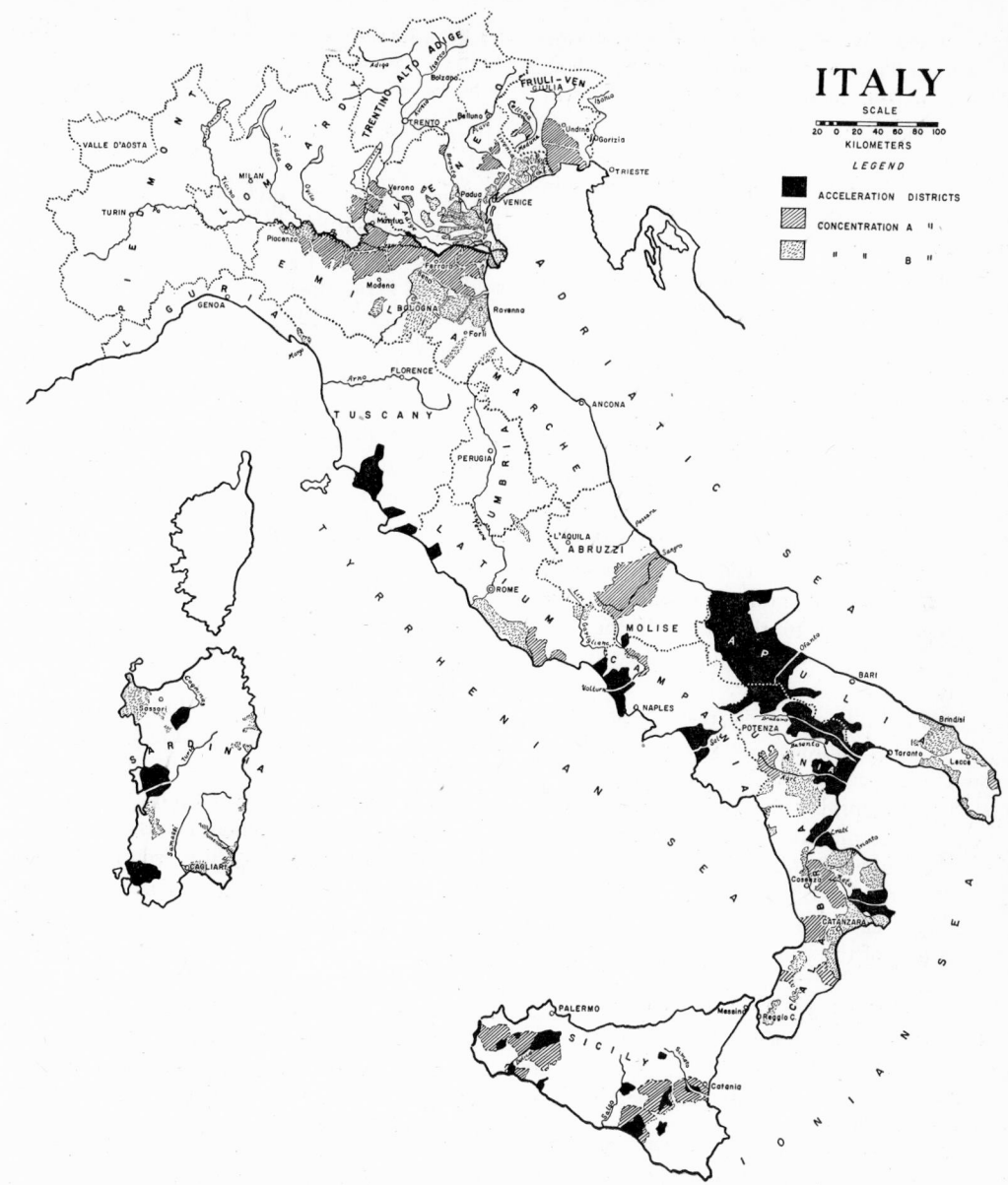

FIGURE 152. SOIL RECLAMATION PROJECTS IN ITALY, 1949

Soil reclamation projects are in progress in all parts of Italy: in the north, in the Po River Valley, along the coasts of the Adriatic and Tyrrhenian Seas; in the south, where the need for arable land is particularly urgent, in Sardinia and Sicily.

Acceleration districts, which are concentrated in southern Italy, Sicily and Sardinia, have first call on the extraordinary public funds. They are to be completed by 1953–55.

Concentration A districts are scattered throughout Italy over an area of 2 million acres but particularly in the Po River Valley and Sicily. They require four years of work for completion.

Concentration B districts, located in various parts of the country, are well advanced or completed.

annual precipitation is very low, and in some other areas, including Texas and Louisiana. About four fifths of this area is irrigated by private companies; the remainder by the federal government.[42] In 1940 the system included 34,544 diversion dams and 4,607 storage dams (as compared with 23,894 and 3,931 respectively, in 1920) and reservoirs with an aggregate capacity of 33.8 million acre feet (as compared with 21.2 million in 1920). Water was carried to the fields by 127,534 miles of canals [43] and 28,585 miles of pipes. More than a billion dollars had been invested in this irrigation system.[44]

A large part of the best agricultural land in the country depends on drainage.[45] From the time of the early settlers, farm land has been drained by means of open ditches, but systematic reclamation by drainage did not begin until the middle of the nineteenth century. The so-called Swamp Act of 1850 granted public lands too wet for cultivation to the states if the states would assume the task of drainage. Few projects were carried out, however, largely because of lack of funds. It also took many years before engineering techniques were developed and more efficient equipment, such as deep dredgers and large pumps, became available. Most of the work was accomplished after 1890, but even in 1922 the United States had nearly 100 million acres of unreclaimed swamps and tidal marshes.

Drainage enterprises are concentrated in the eastern part of the United States, but some have been carried on in the western states in connection with irrigation.[46] In 1940, drainage enterprises in 38 states involved 87 million acres, of which 75 million were drained and made suitable for raising normal crops and nearly 5 million were partly drained.[47]

Soil Conservation

A program of soil conservation unlike any previously undertaken anywhere began in the United States in 1935, when the Soil Conservation Service was established.[48]

About a hundred different methods are now used to halt erosion, conserve rainfall and improve the land — terracing, contouring, strip and cover cropping, crop rotation, stubble mulching, woodland improvement, gully planting and so on. Each technique is designed to meet a particular problem on a given piece of land and to support other measures. The program is carried out in cooperation with the farmer on his fields, pastures, woodlots and idle land after a plan has been worked out with him in accordance with his means and the particular problem of his land.[49]

Soil conservation districts — public organizations composed of local farmers and ranchers — have been organized in every state to carry out the necessary measures with the assistance of the Soil Conservation Service. By July 1, 1950, 2,285 such districts had been established in the continental United States, Puerto Rico, the Virgin Islands, Hawaii and Alaska. The work had to do with about 4.8 million farms and ranches containing about 850 million acres of land.[50] The acreage surveyed, planned and treated for soil conservation purposes, expands each year: 10.9 million acres in 1943, 19.0 million in 1946 and 29.2 million in 1950. (See Figure 153.) One of the most striking examples of conservation is the Dust Bowl, where, in 1935–36, more than 6 million acres were subject to severe erosion and, in 1939, less than a million, mostly on the outlying fringes of the area. The Dust Bowl now produces more grain than it did before its plight was realized.[51]

All in all, detailed conservation plans had been carried out on 218 million acres by June 30, 1950; on about 121 million of these, a combination of conservation techniques had been used. The Soil Conservation Service believes that the United States could control and overcome erosion within

for impounded water alone makes possible not only agriculture, but the very life of the people in this vast semiarid region." (**57**, Vol. I, p. 152.)

42. **41**, 1943–47, p. 602. The participation of the federal government in irrigation was initiated by the Reclamation Act of 1902.

43. Most of this mileage, however, consists of unlined, untreated earth channels, permitting seepage losses of as much as 70 per cent or even more. Treating channel surfaces with light oil, sand traps and other measures is still necessary. (**41**, 1943–47, pp. 603–04.)

44. **43**, pp. xxxiii–xxxiv.

45. **81**, p. 28.

46. Wherever irrigation is practiced, drainage is likely to become a problem: as the higher lands in a valley are irrigated, the lower lands become waterlogged (**41**, 1943–47, p. 606).

47. **45**, 1950, p. 553. The New England states, New

York, New Jersey and Pennsylvania were not included in the canvass.

48. This agency replaced the Soil Erosion Service, created in 1933 within the Department of the Interior.

49. **3**, p. 75; **36**, 1949, p. 13.

50. **36**, 1950, pp. 12–13.

51. **3**, p. 32.

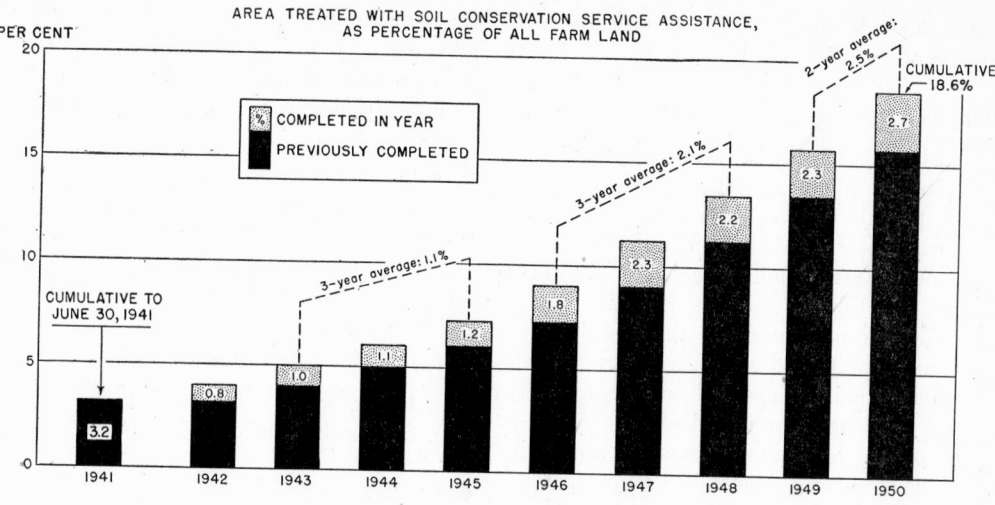

AREA TREATED WITH SOIL CONSERVATION SERVICE ASSISTANCE, AS PERCENTAGE OF ALL FARM LAND

U. S. Department of Agriculture

FIGURE 153. SOIL CONSERVATION IN THE UNITED STATES, 1941–50

twenty years by strengthening its present conservation work.[52]

SOIL RECLAMATION AND CONSERVATION IN ASIA AND AFRICA

The Far East has used irrigation for thousands of years. More than a third of the land in major crops — some 200 million acres — is under irrigation in the area as a whole.[53] If only land in food crops, cotton and sugar cane is considered, the proportion of irrigated area amounts to almost 46 per cent.[54]

China

China is at once a classic illustration of the damage of unchecked erosion and an example of the value of drainage and irrigation carried on by endless generations. Large irrigation canals were built about 2,000 years ago. That built in the Szechwan Province, for example, brings water to nearly 750,000 acres and, according to modern engineers, still complies with every principle of hydraulics. The Chinese have dug ponds, drilled wells and dyked land to prevent floods; they have terraced slopes, constructed diversion channels and so on, all with only human and animal labor and primitive tools, such as shov-

els.[55] The prevailing practice in old times was to direct water by gravity to the fields in the valley and store run-off water in tanks or artificial ponds above the fields from which it was drawn as needed by gravity. In this century China, like other Asiatic countries, has been building weirs and barrages across rivers, with gates to control the flow into canals from which water is carried to the fields through small distributive channels.

About half of China's farm land (more than 100 million acres) is irrigated, chiefly for rice. The network of irrigation canals is about 70,000 miles long. In the rice areas, irrigation involves not only supplying water to the fields but leveling the land to be kept flooded. About a fourth of the total cultivation area of China has been terraced.[56]

Various other parts of Asia present similar contrasts between primitive, but exceptionally effective, efforts to protect land and failure to save it from erosion.

The Philippines

In the Philippines, the impressive stone-walled rice terraces built some 2,000 years ago by the Ifugao tribe on the inaccessible mountains of Luzon are the highest and best in the world. They cover an area of 250 square miles and rep-

52. **36**, 1950, pp. 7 and 11.
53. **6**, 1949, pp. 368–69.
54. **6**, 1950, p. 23.

55. **3**, pp. 226–28.
56. **92**, pp. 6–7.

resent an exceptional feat even in terms of modern engineering.[57]

India and Pakistan

British India has carried through great irrigation projects. About 20 million acres had been irrigated by the turn of the century, and many more have been added since. The total irrigated area now covers 45 million acres. While these projects established a modern irrigation system of canals, primitive methods such as those of small tanks, wells, and water carried by animals and even human beings, still supply some 40 per cent of all irrigation in India.[58]

The present long-term reclamation project in independent India is designed to restore part of the 10 million acres of formerly cultivated land that have fallen into disuse through neglect and the difficulty in coping with deep-rooted grass that defies primitive implements. Some 2 million acres, including jungle areas, are scheduled for clearing.[59] West Bengal and the United Provinces are engaged in irrigation projects covering more than 3 million acres, and all projects in India, when completed, are expected to provide irrigation for almost 13 million additional acres.[60] In some of these projects, the emphasis is on multiple-purpose reservoir schemes.

After China and India, the largest area in the Far East under irrigation is in Pakistan with more than 22 million irrigated acres, nearly four fifths of which are served by canals. The largest project under construction, the barrage in the lower Sind, is designed to irrigate some 2.3 million acres.[61]

Japan

Japan has carried on an intensive battle against erosion since the beginning of the twentieth century, and has salvaged a large area and checked accelerated erosion of farm land everywhere. In 1945, a 15-year reclamation plan was put in operation to increase the cultivated area by 4.1 million acres, or more than 25 per cent. The government has acquired about 3 million acres of uncultivated land for reclamation. Of these, one million acres have been reclaimed and allocated to more than 195,000 new settlers. Some 700,000 farmers have been provided with additional land for reclamation.[62]

Israel

The state of Israel completed farm conservation planning on thirty-one settlements (27,000 acres) during 1950 and started work on eight other settlements (15,000 acres).[63]

Egypt

In Egypt, whose very life depends on irrigation, farmers have used various primitive methods since ancient times to supply their fields with water. Large-scale irrigation did not begin until the second half of the nineteenth century, when foreign engineers were called in. Since that time, a perennial irrigation system of canals, dams, barrages and reservoirs has been established to serve more than 4 million acres.

SOIL CONSERVATION IN LATIN AMERICA

Peru, Ecuador, Venezuela, Chile, Brazil, Costa Rica and some other American countries also have programs to conserve soil and control erosion. Peru has undertaken to maintain and restore to cultivation the old Inca terraces, which hold the topsoil. Brazil is trying to protect its valuable coffee land from erosion.

Between 1926 and 1946, Mexico placed 2.5 million acres under irrigation; in the last six years of that period, the government allocated 10 per cent of the national budget for this purpose.[64] In 1947–52 it planned to reclaim and irrigate nearly 3 million acres. The two most important works under construction are the Papalcapan and Tepalcatepec projects. The Papalcapan valley suffers from soil erosion and lack of water and also from disastrous floods. The project is similar to the reclamation of the Tennessee Valley in many respects and actually was inspired by this example. Development of an integrated economy will be sought by improvement of the soil and methods of farming, building of high-

---

57. **32**, August 1949, p. 182.

58. **6**, 1949, pp. 370–71 and **69**, 1939–40, p. 551.

59. **13**, p. 74. A $10 million loan for this purpose was granted by the World Bank in 1949 to purchase tractors and other equipment.

60. **59**, October 1948, p. 9 and **6**, 1950, p. 26.

61. **3**, p. 370 and **6**, 1950, p. 26.

62. **59**, July 1951, p. 32.

63. **36**, 1950, p. 73.

64. More than nine tenths of the country's cropland needs irrigation but only one eighth is irrigated. Four fifths of all the cropland is considered "temporal," producing crops only during the rainy season (**142**, pp. 9–10).

ways and establishment of hydroelectric plants, canning factories for regional products and a tourist center. One of the dams will have a reservoir capacity of 6.3 billion cubic meters, making it the largest in Latin America.[65]

Venezuela, Colombia and Ecuador have completed irrigation projects for 80,000 acres; works covering nearly 300,000 additional acres are in various stages of completion. Peru has under construction two large projects to provide water to almost 200,000 acres of new or insufficiently irrigated land and is considering two other projects involving about 2 million acres.

Argentina's five-year irrigation program includes 46 projects for an area of more than 3.5 million acres but no information is available either on the location or the present status of these projects. Uruguay is carrying on integrated land improvement and irrigation to benefit some 40,000 acres.

Brazil has completed various small irrigation works and is considering some large projects. The largest project of integrated development — not only in Brazil, but in South America — is the irrigation of a drought area ("Poligono das Secas") covering more than 200 million acres in which use of the São Francisco River is contemplated. Work has already begun. In other Latin American countries various irrigation projects are being studied or are under construction.[66]

WORLD NEEDS

On a world-wide basis, the problem of soil conservation involves changing the use of hundreds of millions of acres scattered over practically every farm on the globe. Some of these acres should be shifted from intertilled crops to grass, grain or trees; others from forest, grass, swamp or idle land to cultivation and so on. In addition, all worthwhile arable land should have the appropriate combination of measures needed to maintain its productivity indefinitely, whether it is used for crops or grazing or for timber or wild life.[67]

The United States Soil Conservation Service is actively aiding many countries in both hemispheres. The Union of South Africa, Mexico and Australia have adopted its method of working through farmers' groups that establish the targets

for the local conservation program for two or three years in advance. In 1949, 47 countries were carrying on work patterned on that of the Soil Conservation Service. The programs range from national projects in Mexico and the Union of South Africa to smaller programs in parts of India.[68]

FARMS

Small and medium-sized farms predominate in most countries but the meaning of these terms differs from country to country. A farm of less than 25 acres is considered small in the United States, but "very, very large" in China. In New Queensland, Australia, from 25,000 to 35,000 acres is considered the right size for a cattle ranch; in the United States, this would be a huge holding.

SIZE OF FARMS

Various criteria may be used to define the size of farm holdings — the acreage, number of workers, value of investment, number of draft animals, amount of mechanized equipment and so on.

The measure common to all farms is land.[69] The number of acres, however, does not in itself determine the farmer's living, though it is a very important factor. A few acres well equipped and used in intensive animal husbandry may provide a satisfactory living for the farmer and his family and yield a substantial amount of produce for the market. The same acreage, with poorer soil, used for grain and cultivated with primitive implements, would yield very little. In Belgium 73 per cent, and in Spain 77 per cent, of all farmers have less than 2.5 acres of land, but Belgian farmers have an incomparably higher standard of living than Spanish peasants and play a more important role in the national economy.

Another often used criterion relates to employment of hired labor. A small farm may be defined as one operated by the farmer and his family, without hired help or with only occasional help. Often the farmer himself works off-farm in the dull season. On a medium-sized farm the farmer and members of his family perform a substantial part of the work, but hired labor is often needed, particularly at harvest time. On a large farm the owner supervises the

65. **10**, p. 22.
66. **10**, pp. 21–25.
67. **36**, 1948, pp. 47–48.

68. **36**, 1949, p. 72.
69. **135**, p. 170.

TABLE 220

FARMS: AVERAGE ACREAGE IN SELECTED COUNTRIES, AROUND 1930

(*Acres*)

Country	Average Area Per Farm		Country	Average Area Per Farm	
	Total Farm Land	Arable Land		Total Farm Land	Arable Land
United States	156.8 [a]	139.6	Czechoslovakia	20.3	13.6
Canada	223.8	...	Switzerland	15.1	14.8
Mexico	378.7	325.8	Austria	43.5	23.0
			Hungary	12.6	...
Chile	461.5	312.6	Italy	15.6	12.4
Uruguay	135.6	...	Bulgaria	12.1	...
England and Wales	76.3	50.9	Greece	1.7	1.7
Scotland	168.2	61.0			
Ireland	38.0	29.9	Japan	13.6	3.2
France	28.7	20.5	Philippines	61.5	36.6
Belgium	4.4	4.2	Egypt (Nile region)	6.4	4.7
Netherlands	14.3	...	Union of South Africa [c]	2,109.9	127.7
Denmark	...	39.0			
Sweden	75.8	17.8	Australia	717.8	208.2
Norway	13.1	8.2	New Zealand	509.1	...
Finland	132.1	27.4			
Germany [b]	33.3	21.5			

Source: **132**, pp. 22-23.

a. In 1945, according to the census, the average size of a farm was 195 acres (**136**, p. 92); in 1950, 215 acres.

b. Farms with over one acre.

c. Farms of Europeans.

work of hired laborers and is chiefly a manager. Each of the groups of farms defined above includes, of course, agricultural units of distinctly different character and efficiency.

Small versus Large Farms

From the standpoint of agricultural efficiency, both large and small farms have their advantages. The first can be mechanized more readily, not only because their owners ordinarily are better able to afford expensive machinery but also because such machinery will be used more continuously than on small farms. On the other hand, the difficulties of supervising operations on very large farms may decrease the efficiency of work which is generally less routine than in a factory and requires constant attention to detail. While small farms [70] cannot attain the

technical and marketing economies available to large holdings, their operating costs may be no higher per unit if they are managed efficiently and with the care that only personal interest can command.[71] Moreover, small farms can benefit from cooperatives, as they do in Denmark and Sweden, both in selling their products and in buying equipment and fertilizers.

Small farms predominate in Asia and parts of Europe. Medium-sized farms are characteristic of North and South America, while large agricultural holdings are typical of Australia and New Zealand.

Average Acreage of Farms

There are usually differences in the size of farms raising specific crops. In the United States, for example, the 1945 census found that the

70. By "small farms" we mean here farms without hired labor but with enough land to provide work and a living for all members of the family. The tiny farms numerous in many parts of the world have too little

ground to use the available family labor and on them hidden unemployment and poverty go hand in hand.

71. **94**, pp. 49–56.

average for various types of farms was as follows (in acres): [72]

Livestock	610
Forest products	208
General	179
Dairy	143
Vegetable	83
Fruit and nut	81
Poultry	70
Self-sufficing	61
Horticultural-specialty	49

The average size of farms also differs from
country to country. In Europe, the average
ranges from 1.7 acres in Greece to 76.3 acres in
England and Wales. Although there are many
small farms in the New World, the average size
of the farms is considerably larger than in Europe — 150 to 200 acres. Farms in Asia and
Africa are generally very small except for the
holdings of Europeans in the Union of South
Africa, where they average more than 2,100
acres.[73] (See Table 220.)

Distribution of Farms by Acreage

Since farms in many countries range from tiny
holdings that cannot provide enough food for
the farmer and his family to huge enterprises
that extend over thousands of acres, information
on average acreage must be supplemented by
data on the distribution of agricultural holdings
by size.

In the world as a whole, from 65 to 75 per cent
of the farmers work on tiny plots; together, they
may till about one third of all arable land. The
remaining two thirds of the land is distributed
unequally among middle-sized farms, large holdings and huge enterprises, owned and operated
by the government, as in the USSR.

Europe. In most European countries, from 75
to 85 per cent of all farms have between 2.5 and
25 acres. Within this range countries vary
greatly. Farms under 5 acres represent 17.0 per
cent of all farms in England and Wales, 23.5
per cent in Switzerland, 28.5 per cent in Sweden;
in Spain 76.8 per cent of all farms have less than
2.5 acres. On the other hand, Europe has rela-

tively few farms with 125 acres or more, but
they represent a considerable part of all farm
acreage. The most striking examples are Italy,
where 1.1 per cent of the holdings account for
41.6 per cent of all farm land, and Spain, where
nearly 60 per cent of the land is held by 2.3 per
cent of the landowners. In prewar Hungary
1.7 per cent of the holdings accounted for more
than 51 per cent of agricultural land. (See
Table 221.)

The Americas and Oceania. In contrast to
Europe, more than two fifths of the farms in
the United States, and about two thirds in
Canada and Oceania, have more than 100 acres.
Large farms count their acres in thousands, and
from 75 to more than 90 per cent of all farm
land in these regions is in holdings of 200 acres
and more. (See Table 222.)

In South America, farms are larger on the
whole than in Europe and most of the land is
concentrated in the hands of a few landowners.
Some of the private owners and land companies
in Brazil, for example, hold individual tracts as
large as 7 million acres.[74] Less than 7 per cent
of the holdings in Chile (1930), those with
500 acres or more, accounted for nearly 90 per
cent of all the farm land; in Brazil (1940) about
8 per cent of the holdings accounted for more
than 73 per cent:[75]

	Chile	Brazil
Acreage	*Percentage of Farms*	
Under 12.5	39.2	21.8
12.5–50		29.2
50–125	} 43.1	23.9
125–500	11.0	17.2
500 and more	6.7	7.8
	Percentage of Farm Land	
Under 12.5	0.3	0.5
12.5–50		3.2
50–125	} 4.2	7.2
125–500	6.0	15.9
500 and more	89.5	73.3

In Chile, the typical holding is the large estate,
almost exactly the grant by the Crown to an
early Spanish conquistador. In 1935–36, more
than half the agricultural land was in estates of
12,350 acres or more each; 626 holdings averaged
57,160 acres each.[76] In some parts of Venezuela,

72. **44**, p. 28.

73. Comprehensive data on the average acreage of
farms in different countries were provided by the first
world agricultural census of 1930.

74. **59**, July 1951, p. 19.

75. **24**, No. 3, p. 9, and **148**, p. 56.

76. **52**, p. 8.

TABLE 221

FARMS: ACREAGE AND SIZE IN EUROPE, AROUND 1945–48

Country	Number of Farms and Total Farm Acreage	Acreage[a]						
		Under 2.5	2.5 to 5	5 to 12.5	12.5 to 25	25 to 50	50 to 125	125 and More
	Farms, in Thousands	*Percentage of Farms*						
England and Wales[b]	361.7	17.0		19.1	13.5	11.9	25.8	12.8
France	...	35.0			60.0		5.0	
Belgium[c]	1,131	74.2	17.2		5.0	2.5	0.9	0.2
Netherlands	369.6	33.6	28.8		16.5	13.3	7.2	0.6
Denmark	208.1	11.4		10.7	26.8	15.1	23.4	12.7
Sweden	414.4	14.3	14.2	26.0	22.9	14.1	6.7	1.8
Norway[d]	328.2	41.6	13.4	23.8	13.7	5.7	1.7	0.1
Finland	283.3	14.0	12.8	25.3	22.6	20.0	4.3	1.1
Germany:								
Western[e]	1,978.1	17.8	15.1	27.5	20.2	12.9	5.7	0.8
Soviet Zone[e]	...	29.2		16.2	33.4	15.1	5.5	0.6
Poland[f]	3,143	11.4	15.0	31.6	26.6	12.6	2.2	0.6
Czechoslovakia[e]	1,649	28.1	42.7		15.7	8.9	3.6	1.0
Switzerland[g]	210.3	9.4	14.1	28.5	28.0	11.3	7.4	1.3
Hungary	1,827.2	67.7			17.3	13.3		1.7
Spain	...	76.8	1.9		8.6	10.6		2.3
Italy[e]	4,196.3	35.6	43.0		11.7	6.1	2.6	1.1
Yugoslavia[e]	...	34.0		33.8	20.5	8.7	2.7	0.3
Romania[e]	3,067	76.1			17.8	4.9	1.0	0.2
Bulgaria[e]	...	27.0		30.4	30.3	11.3	0.9	0.1
Greece[e]	...	79.3			14.3	5.9		0.5

(Continued on facing page)

the 1932 census reported that from 80 to 85 per cent of the land was held in a few large estates.

Of the 1.2 million privately owned holdings in Mexico in 1940, 40.8 per cent comprised less than 2.5 acres and an additional 35.4 per cent from 2.5 to 12.5 acres;[77] in contrast, nearly 10,000 holdings had 2,500 to 12,500 acres each.

Asia and Africa. Information for Asia is scanty. In Japan in 1930, about 2 million farm families (34 per cent) had holdings of less than 1.25 acres; another 2 million had from 1.25 to 2.5 acres; 250,000 had from 2.5 to 5 acres, and about 600,000 families had 5 acres or more; this last group included some owners of estates of 4,000 acres or more.[78] Similar conditions exist in India where millions of peasants have an acre or less of cultivated land.[79] In China, a survey in 1929-33, covering about 17,000 farms in 22 provinces, found that more than 60 per cent of the farms averaged less than 5 acres in size and an additional 20 per cent averaged 7.17 acres. The largest average acreage, 23.38 acres, represented only one per cent of the total.[80] This survey classified farms with 4.92 to 7.17 acres as medium-size, and those with more than 20 acres as "very, very large."

Holdings in French Indochina are even smaller. In Tonkin province, for example, 62 per cent of all farm families have less than 0.9 acre in rice fields, and 30 per cent have less than 0.4 acre.[81] In Annam province 69 per cent of the peasants have less than 1.2 acres of rice land and 25 per cent have from 1.2 to 6.2 acres.[82]

In Egypt, holdings with less than an acre

77. **110**, p. 10.

78. **72**, pp. 2–3.

79. **129**, pp. 56–58, and **126**, p. 33.

80. **92**, pp. 271–72.

81. About 85 per cent of cultivated land is used for rice production in Indochina. (See Chapter 16.)

82. **31**, pp. 9–11.

TABLE 221—*continued*

Country	Number of Farms and Total Farm Acreage — Acres, in Millions	Under 2.5	2.5 to 5	5 to 12.5	12.5 to 25	25 to 50	50 to 125	125 and More
		(Percentage of Total Acreage)						
England and Wales [b]	23,020	0.8		2.7	4.2	7.0	35.3	49.9
France	...	5.5		65.0			29.5	
Belgium [c]	936	6.6	26.0		20.7	19.9	15.9	10.9
Netherlands	5,939	1.9	11.2		18.3	28.7	31.8	8.1
Denmark	7,850	1.3		2.6	12.1	11.7	31.3	41.0
Sweden	9,179	1.3	2.7	10.7	19.4	22.9	22.8	20.2
Norway [d]	2,790	3.1	6.3	23.3	28.5	22.9	13.6	2.5
Finland	5,634	1.0	2.2	10.2	19.7	36.8	17.7	12.6
Germany:								
Western [e]	33,255	1.7	3.0	13.4	21.1	26.2	24.1	10.4
Soviet Zone [e]	...	3.5		7.2	32.3	27.3	21.5	8.2
Czechoslovakia [e]	33,256	1.6	13.8		13.6	15.3	12.3	43.4
Switzerland [g]	2,770	19.4			31.5	21.0	20.9	7.2
Hungary [e]	22,799	14.6			12.0	22.1		51.3
Spain	...	13.2	5.6		7.1	15.0		59.1
Italy [e]	64,870	2.5	17.1		13.3	13.5	12.1	41.6
Yugoslavia [e]	...	7.0		21.0	27.0	23.0	12.3	9.7
Romania [e]	...	28.1			20.0	19.7		32.2
Bulgaria [e]	...	5.0		24.1	37.3	25.6	6.4	1.6
Greece [e]	...	16.9			11.7	21.6		49.8

Sources: Adapted from statistical yearbooks of the respective countries; **23**, *passim* and **132**, pp. 22–23 and 34–43; for Germany: Western Germany: **66**, April 1, 1950, pp. 2–5; Soviet Zone, **20**, December 1950, p. 25; for France: **9**, E/ECE/SR. 5/16, June 30, 1950, pp. 24–25; for Poland: **78**, 1948, p. 38; for Romania: **59**, October 1949, p. 46; for Spain, Yugoslavia, Bulgaria, Hungary, Greece: **120**, pp. 82–83 and **32**, October 1951, pp. 216–21.

a. In a few countries the size of farms is reported in categories somewhat different from those used here. The deviations are (in acres):
  England and Wales: under 5 acres; 5 to 15; 15 to 30; 30 to 50; 50 to 150; over 150.

Denmark: under 7.5; 7.5 to 12.5; 12.5 to 25; 25 to 37.5; 37.5 to 75; over 75.
Switzerland (three last groups): 25 to 37.5; 37.5 to 75; over 75.
Italy (three last groups): 25 to 52.5; 52.5 to 125; over 125.
Finland (three last groups): 25 to 62.5; 62.5 to 125; over 125.
b. 1941.
c. 1930.
d. 1939.
e. 1949. Land under cultivation; preliminary data.
f. Old territory of Poland in 1947.
g. 1939. Excludes some 28,000 holdings with less than 1.25 acres; cultivated acreage only.

constitute 70.7 per cent of all farms, and those with 1 to 5 acres, 22.9 per cent. Only 0.5 per cent of the farms have more than 50 acres, but this small group accounts for 37.1 per cent of all the farm land.[83]

FRAGMENTATION OF LAND

Many farms, especially in Europe and Asia, consist of several small patches of land scattered over a considerable area among lots and strips belonging to other farmers. A Belgian farm of 30 acres may be divided into 20 or 30 scattered strips, some of them a mile or two apart and so narrow as not to permit cross-plowing.[84] (See Figure 154.) Often a farmer must cross other people's property to reach his land. In Switzerland the census of 1939 reported that about 63,000 holdings were divided into more than ten strips, and of these nearly 5,000 were scattered into fifty or more patches. Some of these holdings

83. **140**, p. 10; cf. **2**, p. 9.

84. **84**, p. 87.

TABLE 222

FARMS: ACREAGE AND SIZE IN NORTH AMERICA AND OCEANIA, AROUND 1941-46

Country	Number of Farms and Total Farm Acreage	Acreage				
		Under 50	50 to 100	100 to 200	200 to 1,000	1,000 and More
	Farms, in Thousands			*Percentage of Farms*		
United States [a]	5,859	38.4	19.8	20.5	19.5	1.9
Canada [b]	729	17.0	20.4	31.4	24.1 [c]	6.5 [d]
Australia [b]	201	23.9	10.3	48.7		17.1
New Zealand	86	29.3	14.8	19.5	28.4	8.0
	Acres, in Millions			*Percentage of Farm Land*		
United States [a]	1,141	4.1	7.3	14.2	34.1	40.3
Canada [b]	163	1.8	7.9	22.2	37.8 [c]	30.3 [d]
Australia [b]	145	0.6	1.1	28.0		70.3
New Zealand	43	0.9	2.2	5.5	24.5	67.0

Sources: Official statistical yearbooks; for Australia, **132**, pp. 40–43.

a. The classification of farms by acreage is: 50–99; 100–179; 180–999; 1,000 and more.

b. 1930.
c. 200–639 acres.
d. 640 acres and more.

represented *in toto* less than 2.5 acres.[85] Many French farms include strips as small as 0.1 of an acre.[86] In Bulgaria the average farm had 17 strips, according to the 1934 census.[87]

It is estimated that from a fourth to a third of the arable land in western Europe, and an even higher proportion in eastern Europe, is in ribbon-like strips.[88]

In Romania, for example, most of the peasant holdings consist of scattered strips, and many patches are a mile or more apart, in opposite directions from the village. The land reform of 1945 did nothing to eliminate such fragmentation of land.[89] In Czechoslovakia, in 1947, some 1.4 million farms comprised 33 million plots, averaging about five-eighths acre each.[90]

Conditions in Asia are even worse. A Chinese farm of less than an acre may consist of six or seven plots. In addition, the traditional custom of sharing land with the spirits of the ancestors subtracts space for graves from even so tiny a lot; not infrequently the graves are placed in the center of the largest parcel.[91] In Indochina

(Tonkin and Annam) the custom of dividing property equally among all children has led to tiny holdings, split into many strip parcels.[92] In India, the farm is rarely a single unit. A five-acre farm may consist of five plots scattered over a couple of square miles.[93]

This fragmentation of land, largely rooted in custom — especially practices in inheritance — is a serious economic handicap. It has been calculated that the value of the yield per acre doubled when farm strips in certain Swiss areas were combined to make larger blocks.[94] In France, the cost of growing wheat on a plot of two fifths of an acre was 70–80 per cent higher than on one of two and a half acres.[95] In addition, disputes are frequent, and much time is wasted.

Many countries are trying to consolidate farm land into larger units. In 1865 the French government began to consolidate holdings by paying most of the costs and relieving the farmers of formalities, but few availed themselves of this opportunity. The Act of 1919 authorized the

85. **149**, p. 362 and **74**, 1945, p. 158.
86. **79**, p. 57.
87. **59**, April 1949, p. 46.
88. **150**, p. 41.
89. **32**, October 1951, p. 221.
90. **32**, July 1950, p. 158.
91. J. L. Buck estimates that in the 22 provinces

surveyed, removal of graves would release 2.5 million acres for cultivation and could support 400,000 additional families (**92**, p. 179).
92. **31**, p. 9.
93. **32**, May 1950, p. 98.
94. **84**, p. 89.
95. **150**, p. 42.

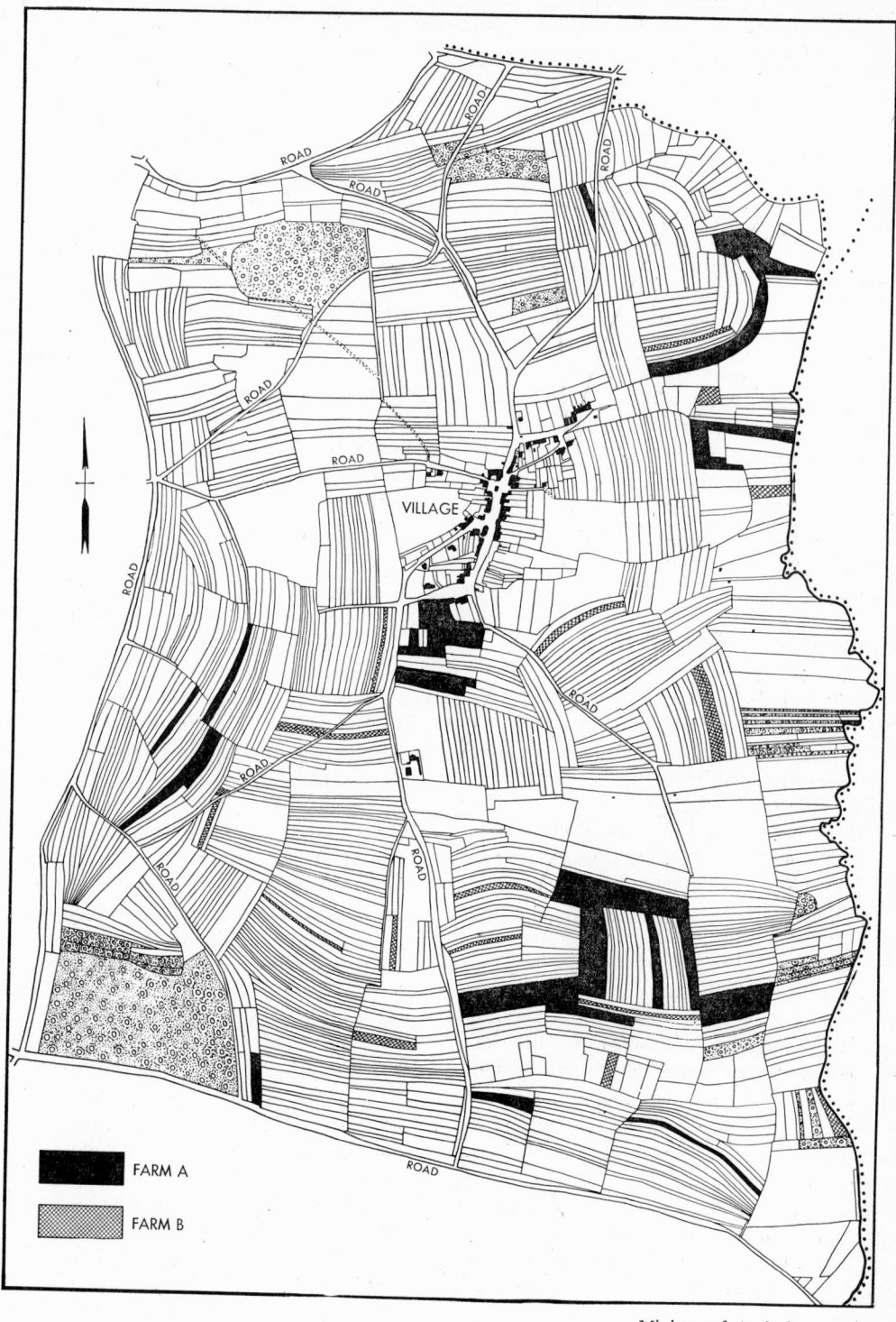

VILLAGE

FARM A

FARM B

Ministry of Agriculture, Belgium

FIGURE 154. LAND DISTRIBUTION ON TWO TYPICAL FARMS IN A BELGIAN COMMUNITY, 1949

state to carry out regrouping of holdings in the war-devastated regions, and between 1919 and 1927 more than 0.5 million acres were consolidated. Further legislation was enacted in 1935 and 1939, but the end of World War II still found an excessive fragmentation in a large part of agricultural land, and many communes once regrouped had reverted to old practices.[96] France expects to reassemble about 25 million acres under the Monnet Plan. Some 1.3 million acres in small strips have been consolidated since 1946, and operations now under way involve nearly 4 million acres. By 1952 more than 10 million acres were in process of reassemblage.[97]

In Belgium, a law for voluntary reassemblage of scattered farm strips, with some aid from the government, was passed soon after the war. The results were disappointing, since only about a dozen applications were received. Obligatory consolidation of strip farm land is under consideration.

In some countries of eastern Europe, likewise, agrarian reforms since World War II are tending to reduce such uneconomic subdivision of lands.[98]

Some provinces in India have passed legislation for reassemblage of farm strips. The province of Bombay has fixed 5 acres as the minimum size of a farm. A farmer who wishes to dispose of less than 5 acres must sell the land to a neighbor in the same group. By 1949 about 1.6 million acres had been consolidated, and the number of plots reduced from 4.3 million to 0.6 million.[99]

LAND TENURE

Most of the world's farmers own all or part of the land they occupy and till, but various forms of tenancy are widespread in many countries. In some areas tenancy is a survival of the feudal system of land ownership; in others, it represents a traditional stage in shifting from one owner to another. Poverty is often the cause of tenancy and helps to perpetuate it. Millions of people working the land have no means of purchasing even a small lot of their own and the necessary equipment. Many landless peasants throughout the world work as sharecroppers,

using the equipment, seed and fertilizers provided by the landowners. Living from crop to crop, they often go into debt to the landlord for the barest necessities of life, repaying him at harvesttime.

Tenancy of feudal origin prevails in Great Britain, particularly in Scotland, where more than three out of four farmers work rented land. In the Netherlands, every second farmer is a tenant; in the United States and China, every third. In contrast, only 5 per cent of all farmers rent land in Denmark and Western Germany, and only 8 per cent in Norway. (See Table 223.)

Between outright ownership and tenancy are various forms of part ownership established through inheritance or for the purpose of later acquisition of the land. Not infrequently a small landowner rents additional land to extend his farm operations.

Trends in Tenancy

In some countries farm property is held rigidly, generation after generation, as in France, where the number of farm owners has changed only a fraction of one per cent in the last sixty years. In others, the ratio between farm owners and tenants has been changing in one direction or the other. In England and Wales, farm ownership is gradually increasing — from 12.2 per cent of all operated farms and 10.7 per cent of all cultivated land (crops and pastures) in 1908 to 35.0 and 33 per cent, respectively, in 1941.[100]

In the United States tenancy was on the increase until the 1930's; in 1880, 25 per cent of all farmers were tenants; in 1930, 42.6 per cent. Then tenancy declined to 38.9 per cent in 1940 and 31.7 per cent in 1945;[101] a sample survey of the Bureau of Agricultural Economics, covering 15,000 farms, showed a further drop in January 1947 to 26.9 per cent.[102] The greatest decline is in the South, where much land formerly operated by tenants is now cultivated by the owners themselves, while the tenants have been "tractored off." The extent of tenancy varies from one type of farming region to another. (See Table 224.)

Tenancy in China is largely concentrated in the south. Tenant farmers predominate in

---

96. **79**, pp. 58–61.
97. **65**, p. 136. Marshall Plan funds have aided in financing this work.
98. See pp. 503 ff.
99. **32**, May 1950, p. 98; **2**, p. 13.

100. **67**, p. 20.
101. **45**, 1949, p. 623.
102. **28**, May 1948, p. 13. According to the preliminary report of the 1950 census, the tenancy percentage was 26.8.

TABLE 223

FARM TENANCY IN SELECTED COUNTRIES

Country and Year	Tenants, as Percentage of All Farmers [a]	Rented Land, as Percentage of All Farm Land	Country and Year	Tenants, as Percentage of All Farmers [a]	Rented Land, as Percentage of All Farm Land
United States, 1945	31.7	22.0	Western Germany, 1949	5.4	4.0
Canada, 1941	12.9	15.6	Czechoslovakia, 1930	7.8	9.4
Chile, 1929–30	5.3	. . .	Switzerland, 1939	17.7	22.1
Argentina, 1937	62.1	. . .	Austria, 1930	9.4	4.6
			Italy, 1930	23.8	28.6
England and Wales, 1941–43	65.0	67.0	Greece, 1929	19.3	. . .
Scotland, 1934	77.6	68.5			
Ireland, 1932	. . .	2.5	China, 1946	35.0	. . .
France, 1946	26.0	40.0	Japan, 1938	20.0 [c]	. . .
Belgium, 1942	. . .	67.0	Taiwan, 1948	40.0	. . .
Netherlands, 1930	46.7	49.1	India, 1931	53.0	. . .
Denmark, 1946	5.0	. . .	Philippines, 1939	35.0	32.4
Sweden,[b] 1944	18.9	26.7			
Norway, 1939	8.0	. . .	New Zealand, 1941	25.9	29.7
Finland, 1929	11.1	. . .			

Sources: For the United States, **45**, 1949, p. 623; for Canada, **60**, 1945, p. 242; for Argentina, **99**, p. 254; for England and Wales, **67**, p. 93; for China, **61**, p. 19; for the Philippines, **103**, pp. 66–67; for Taiwan and Japan, **6**, 1950, pp. 183–88; for other countries, either statistical yearbooks, or **23**, Vols. II–V.

a. An additional 11.3 per cent (in 1945; 26.7 per cent in 1950) of farmers in the United States, 11.6 per cent in Canada, 3.8 per cent in Germany, 14.8 per cent in

Italy, 25 per cent in China, 51 per cent in Japan, 15.6 per cent in the Philippines, 27 per cent in Taiwan and 11.8 per cent in New Zealand, are owners as well as tenants. In Switzerland about 30 per cent of farm owners use some rented land.

b. Farms with more than 5 acres.

c. Large estates are often divided among tenants. An estate of 4,000 acres, for example, was recorded as having 2,486 tenants (**125**, p. 118).

Kwantung and Szechwan, while only 10 per cent of farmers in the northern provinces occupy rented land.[103] The Philippines show even greater contrasts. In some areas, such as Mountain Province on Luzon, tenants work less than 2 per cent of all farms, while in Central Luzon, two thirds of the farmers are tenants.[104] In India, tenancy predominates, and rentals average 50 or even 60 per cent of the gross produce. Two types of tenants are distinguished; the occupancy-tenants, with an inheritable right to occupy the rented land, and the tenants-at-will, with little security of tenancy.[105]

Forms of Tenancy

The legal and economic aspects of tenancy vary from country to country. In Great Britain, tenants generally have the security that elsewhere is conveyed only by ownership and not infrequently the same tenant family occupies a parcel

of land generation after generation. In the United States, in contrast, a third of the farm land operated by tenants changes hands every year. In Belgium, farm leases for 9 years are common and leases for 15 and 18 years are not rare. In China, a tenant may live on a piece of rented land all his life, and his son may continue to rent it.

The laws of most countries protect tenants who have made capital investments on rented land and entitle them to some compensation if they leave. In Great Britain, the landlord and the tenant often worked out a plan for improvements and shared the costs. If the tenant left before some of these improvements had been fully exploited, he was recompensed for the difference.[106] The Agricultural Act of 1947 put legal foundations under the customary relationships between landlord and tenant and established further provisions to improve holdings and safeguard the rights of tenants. Long-range improvements are subject to the consent of the

103. **62**, p. 7.
104. **103**, p. 65.
105. **6**, 1950, p. 186.

106. **98**, pp. 209–10; **135**, pp. 402–04.

TABLE 224

FARM TENANCY IN THE UNITED STATES, BY
TYPE-OF-FARM REGION, 1935

| Type-of-Farm Region | Total Number of Farmers, in Thousands | Tenant Farmers | |
		Number, in Thousands	Percentage of All Farmers
All types	6,812	2,865	42.1
Cotton	1,824	1,187	65.1
Corn	928	417	44.9
Tobacco	535	255	47.6
General farming	746	220	29.5
Dairy	799	149	18.7
Wheat	350	147	42.1
Rice	34	20	58.7
Sugar cane	12	5	45.5
Other	1,584	465	29.3

Source: **56**, p. 38.

landlord or, if that is not available, to that of the
Ministry of Agriculture. When the tenancy ex-
pires the tenant is entitled to a payment equal
to the increase in the value of the holding due to
those improvements. On the other hand, the
landlord may claim indemnity from the tenant
for damage to his property. Unless the tenant has
neglected his duties as a farmer or has failed to
make the payments due, he is entitled to an indemnity ranging from one to two years' tenure
payment if his contract is broken by the landlord. Moreover, the Ministry of Agriculture may
refuse its consent to such a break. It has been
observed in England that tenants are usually the
better farmers. They have capital available for
investment, while the farmer owning the land
is often impoverished.[107]

A French law passed in 1946 assures the tenant of renewal of the lease even against the will
of the landowner and grants him, if he leaves,
indemnity for the increase in the capital value
of the holding.

The problem of indemnifying tenants is more
complex in tropical regions, where such commercial plantings as orange, coffee and cacao
trees have a comparatively long life span, and
the planters' outlay cannot be recovered in two
or three years. To encourage tenants to plant
such trees, the Brazilian Civil Code has provided
that the term of the lease must cover the harvesting of the first crop.[108]

In Japan the law of October 1946 introduced
overdue protection from exploitation by landlords — among other measures, a cash-rent ceiling not exceeding 25 per cent of the value of
the rice crop and 15 per cent of that of other
crops. As a result of the land reform carried out
in 1946–48, tenant-operated land has been reduced from 46 to 12 per cent of all cultivated
land.[109]

In some states of India (Bombay, Hyderabad,
Saurashtra, West Bengal), legislation has been
passed in recent years to protect tenants. For
example, the Bombay Tenancy Act of 1948 stipulated that the lease must be secure for at least
10 years and conferred permanent tenancy on a
large number of the so-called "protected tenants." They were also given the right to purchase land at fair prices, as established by a
tribunal. Various acts have been passed in Punjab and Sind (Pakistan) to protect tenants from
overcharging, ejection and other mistreatment.[110]

THE STRUGGLE FOR LAND

The farmer's struggle for land is almost as old
as farming itself. Pressure for more land existed
in ancient Palestine, where periodic redivision
was customary. The size of individual land holdings in ancient Greece was limited by law. The
Roman Empire enacted various legislative measures to control land ownership.[111] It is in the
nature of farming that every farmer believes he
could do better if he had more land. Equally
ancient is the belief that control over farm land
assures domination of the population.

Landholding in most countries today is the
result of a long historical process not yet consummated. Revolutions have been fought in
some countries to effect changes in land ownership, while others have achieved the distribution
of land among small farmers more or less peace-
fully. On the whole, Europe has followed a one-
way road since the time of the French Revolution, from the concentration of land in the hands
of the few — crown, church, nobility — to its
distribution among the many who till the soil.
Until World War I, however, the system of large
landed estates persisted over all the continent
except in France, the Low Countries and Scandinavia.

Then a wave of agrarian reforms swept across

107. **3**, p. 69.
108. **82**, pp. 6–14.

109. **59**, April 1948, pp. 78–79 and **6**, 1950, p. 189.
110. **6**, 1950, pp. 187 and 190.
111. **151**, pp. 165–66.

TABLE 225

AREA AND BENEFICIARIES OF LAND REDISTRIBUTION IN EUROPE AFTER WORLD WAR I

Country	Area Redistributed		Area, in Millions of Acres, Allocated to			Plots, in Thousands, Allocated to		
	Millions of Acres	Percentage of All Agricultural Land	State[a]	Former Owners	Other Farmers	New Farmers	Small Farmers	Former Tenants
Total	60.3	...	16.5	7.9	35.8	...	...	...
Finland	3.7	2.1	—	2.2	1.5	22	10	97
East Germany	1.0	...	—	—	1.0	16	28	...
Poland[b]	3.7	6.1	—	—	3.7	109	200	...
Czechoslovakia	9.9	14.1	4.9	0.2	4.7	1.7	303	...
Hungary	1.7	9.7	—	—	1.7	549	113	...
Yugoslavia	4.9	4.6	1.2	2.5	1.2	...	256	...
Romania	14.8	29.7	2.2	—	12.6	...	1,369	...
Bulgaria	0.5	2.0	—	—	0.5	...	17	...
Greece	3.2	—	—	1.2	2.0	...	229	...
Latvia	9.1	42.4	5.2	0.5	3.5	64	13	7
Lithuania	2.0	17.5	0.2	—	1.7	36	19	...
Estonia	5.7	25.0	2.7	1.2	1.7	33	...	27

Source: **133**, pp. 28–34.

a. Often includes woodlands or wasteland.

b. By 1937 about 6.5 million additional acres had been redistributed among some 700,000 purchasers (**130**, p. 53).

central and eastern Europe. Some countries, among them Latvia and Lithuania, confiscated large estates outright; others granted compensation of some kind to former landowners, together with part of the acreage. In most countries expropriated woodland became state property. The USSR undertook an agrarian revolution of a completely different character; all farm land was confiscated and became the property of the all-powerful government, while former farmers were practically forced to become landless farm laborers employed by the state.

AFTER WORLD WAR I

Agrarian Reforms in Europe

In twelve European countries that carried out agrarian reforms after World War I, some 60 million acres or 11 per cent of the total territory was redistributed. More than half this acreage was allocated to former tenants, landless workers and owners of tiny plots whose farm land was increased. About a fourth was taken over by the state, and some 8 million acres were left to former landlords. In Czechoslovakia the 10 million acres redistributed under the reform were about equally divided among the state and new owners; in Romania, about five sixths of the 15 million acres were allocated to new owners,

and the rest went to the state. (See Table 225.)

To satisfy the largest possible number of claimants, expropriated land was divided into small lots except in the Baltic countries, where the program envisaged strong medium-size farms. Preference among claimants usually was given to veterans, subsistence farmers, former tenants, repatriated nationals. On the other hand, expropriation more often than not began with alien landlords. In Romania, land was taken preferably from Hungarian, Russian, Bulgarian and Turkish owners; in Yugoslavia, from Hungarian and Macedonian settlers; in Czechoslovakia, from Germans and Hungarians; in Poland, from Russians and Germans.[112]

The immediate economic results of the reforms were not wholly encouraging. The distributed land was not always of adequate quality, lots were small and the new farmers had little equipment or capital. In some countries, as in Czechoslovakia, cooperative banks supplied credits on easy terms and helped the new farmers to establish themselves, but such resources were not available in most of the countries. The national agricultural output declined since the new small holdings could not produce marketable surpluses on a scale approaching that of the former larger estates.

112. **106**, pp. 114–16; see also **90**, pp. 39–41.

In Romania, where large estates were confiscated, the cultivated area decreased from 15.6 to 11.6 million acres by 1920, and the output of wheat dropped 40 per cent; of rye, 36 per cent; and of corn, 16 per cent.[113] In Yugoslavia, the output of wheat dropped 25 per cent, and of oats, 47 per cent, between 1920 and 1926.[114] The new peasant farms, however, raised more barley and other feed for their livestock than the big commercial estates had produced. In general, farmers themselves had more to eat than they had had before the reform, but in the first years after the change the small farms had little surplus to market in the cities or ship abroad.

This outcome, however, does not mean that the agrarian reforms failed. The primary purpose was not to increase the country's output, but to achieve a more equitable distribution of land and thus improve the position of landless agricultural workers or poor farmers. Because the purpose of these reforms was social and political, rather than economic, few nations introduced changes in landholding that might increase output — for example, by prohibiting the parceling of farms through inheritance.[115] In many cases, the holdings established under agrarian reforms have proved inadequate to meet even subsistence standards.[116]

Turkey, where most of the land belonged to the ruling class and the church, undertook land reform after the revolution of 1924. A long-range plan of gradual land redistribution was initiated with the result that today almost two thirds of the farmers are owners.[117]

Agrarian Revolution in the USSR

While the agrarian reforms in Europe were intended to strengthen small farmers, the USSR abolished individual farming as a form of agricultural enterprise. In its final phase, this revolution amounted to a straight expropriation of all independent farms in the country.

Redistribution of Land. This process was preceded by agrarian reform similar to that in European countries. Immediately after World War I the estates, which belonged largely to the imperial family, the church and the aristocracy, were expropriated. This change did not substantially increase the land available to peasants. Before the revolution they had owned two thirds of all farm land in European Russia (exclusive of Poland and Finland) and had leased, at a high price, a substantial part of the rest from large proprietors; in Siberia almost all farm land was in the hands of peasants.[118] The 1916 census reported 89 per cent of the cropped plowland in the hands of peasants. The grain production by landlords was estimated at 12 per cent of the total.[119]

As the amount of land confiscated under the soviets was not large enough to satisfy the land hunger of the peasants, it could not be divided systematically and so fell into the hands of those who grabbed it, taking advantage of the chaotic conditions of the civil war. For a few years, land was redistributed almost every year and small tracts were divided and redivided among new claimants, many of whom came from the starving cities. The number of farms increased from 18 million in 1916 to 25.6 million in 1928.[120] These subsistence plots had little surplus produce for the urban population and nothing for export. Many of them had no draft animals and equipment and consisted of scattered strips.

Collectivization. The Soviet government then reversed its policy of individual land ownership and, against the violent opposition of the peasants, carried out a compulsory alienation of land from the peasants. Collective farms, "kolkhozy," were established throughout the country. Farm livestock, implements, stables, barns, even seed and forage supplies were also collectivized. By 1938 the completed program covered 19 million peasant households and 99.3 per cent of all cultivated land. At the beginning of 1940, Russia had more than 236,000 kolkhozy with 371 million acres and about 4,000 huge state farms, "sovkhozy," with 4.7 million acres. Both kolkhozy and sovkhozy are served by state-owned machine-tractor stations.[121] Before the members of the kolkhozy are remunerated for their work, the government quota for grain and other agricultural products [122] must be delivered,

113. **107**, p. 51.

114. **108**, p. 40.

115. A detailed description of European agrarian reforms after World War I is given in **147**, pp. 33–35. For the evaluation of economic results of agrarian reforms see **120**, pp. 99–106 and **2**, pp. 68–74.

116. **22**, p. 54.

117. **59**, July 1947, p. 72.

118. **138**, p. 244 and **139**, p. 11. Public domain, situated mostly in the north, had little agricultural importance.

119. **114**, pp. 145–46.

120. **139**, p. 13.

121. **77**, pp. 5 and 24; **139**, p. 22.

122. Delivery provisions aim at obtaining the total

taxes paid, the motor stations paid for their services, seed loans returned, the full annual requirements for livestock for the kolkhozy and the next year's seed set aside, and funds for repairs, building materials and improvements replenished. Produce must be turned over to the state as it is harvested, directly from the combine or thresher. Free-market prices are, as a rule, 15 to more than 40 times as high as government procurement prices.[123]

Members of the kolkhozy are paid in proportion to the number of days they work. The work day (*trudoden*) is the unit of payment, but a day's work at different jobs is evaluated at various amounts, on the basis of piece work.

Since the pay has been very low, the Soviet government has had to concede members of collective farms the right to work a tiny plot, the produce of which is their own. If land is available, from 0.6 to 1.2 acres (in some sections up to 2.5 acres) may be allotted to a kolkhoz family for homestead and cultivation. The eagerness of the members to possess a strip of land of their own and the effort they put into its cultivation are demonstrated by the fact that in 1937 these small individual plots, which comprised together about 4 per cent of the total crop area in the USSR, accounted for more than 20 per cent of the total agricultural output.[124] Yet, according to the Soviet statistics, the labor time available to men on collective farms for private purposes was only 12.4 days out of 288 potential workdays during the year.[125] Obviously, the individual plots must have been cultivated before and after the official working time.

The comparatively large output from the individual plots so concerned the government that in September 1946 it ordered a special check-up of the amount of land thus used, which showed that the excess above the permitted amount averaged less than 0.1 of an acre per kolkhoz household.[126]

All in all, agrarian reform in Russia has culminated in a form of organization of agricul-

tural production that has no parallel in the modern capitalist economy but resembles the plantation system in underdeveloped countries and is vaguely reminiscent of the precapitalist pattern in medieval Europe and the system in South America before its conquest by Europeans.

AFTER WORLD WAR II

Agrarian Reforms in Western Europe

Germany. No significant changes in land ownership were made in Germany when the first wave of agrarian reforms rolled through central and eastern Europe after World War I. (See Table 225.) According to the agricultural census of 1939, large estates with 250 acres and more, representing 1.1 per cent of all agricultural holdings, had more than a third of all the farm land in the country and a sixth of all the cultivated land. In contrast, 53.5 per cent of all the farms, with less than 12.5 acres each, together accounted for only 8.3 per cent of all the farm land and 13.4 per cent of the cultivated land. Many of these small farmers were tenants. It was therefore to be expected that land reform would be the order of the day when World War II ended. The expulsion of millions of German farmers and farm laborers from neighboring countries made land reform even more urgent.

Germany's four zones included 21,000 holdings of more than 250 acres each and about 7 million acres of cultivated land in all, distributed in 1939 as follows: [127]

Region	Thousands of Acres	Per Cent
Rump Germany	6,993	100.0
Soviet zone	4,695	67.1
American zone	692	9.9
British zone	1,384	19.8
French zone	222	3.2

Thus, two thirds of cultivated land in large holdings was in the Soviet zone, about a fifth in the British, and a tenth in the American.

A radical redistribution of land was carried out in the Soviet zone immediately after the end of the war. All land, livestock, buildings and machinery of farms with more than 250 acres, all estates of war criminals and leading Nazis and all state land were expropriated. Churches, schools and experimental institutions were exempted. Of the 4.7 million acres thus obtained,

---

output of cotton, sugar beets and some other technical crops and of hides, skins and, to a large extent, wool (**114**, p. 369). During 1935–37 (the latest available data) compulsory deliveries to the state averaged 68 per cent of meat and animal fats and 45 per cent of the milk (**139**, p. 37).

123. **114**, pp. 364–69; **139**, p. 38; **117**, pp. 542–43.
124. **138**, pp. 249–50.
125. **114**, p. 394.
126. **114**, p. 58.

127. **116**, p. 157.

3.9 million have been redistributed among half a million farm laborers, former tenants, small landowners, small artisans who had lived on these estates before the reform, and new settlers. Some land was allotted to breeding stations, public institutions and mutual aid committees, and some was left undivided.

This reform has effected very considerable changes in the distribution of land among large and smaller holdings: [128]

Size of Holding	Percentage of Holdings	Percentage of Cultivated Land
1.25–12.5 acres		
1939	56.0	9.0
1950	45.4	10.7
12.5 to 50 acres		
1939	33.0	31.8
1950	48.5	59.6
50 to 125 acres		
1939	8.5	22.4
1950	5.5	21.5
125 to 250 acres		
1939	1.4	8.4
1950	0.5	4.6
More than 250 acres		
1939	1.1	28.2
1950	0.1	3.6

Thus after the reform, nearly 11 per cent of the holdings were still of less than 12.5 acres (and many within this group, of less than 5 acres), but the large estates accounted for only 3.6 per cent of cultivated land, rather than 28.2 per cent.

The new landowners must compensate the state for the allotted land at the rate of the value of a year's crop of bread grain — about 880 to 1,320 pounds per acre, depending on the quality of the soil — in installments over 10–20 years, according to the financial conditions of the new settlers. While the beneficiaries of the land reform did not receive credits for the purchase of livestock and implements, they were assigned lower ratios for obligatory delivery of produce to the state. The new settlers in Saxony and Thuringia, for example, deliver 10 per cent less grain and potatoes, and 15 per cent less oilseed than the older farmers.[129]

Machine-tractor stations were established and received all expropriated tractors (6,004), trucks (450), threshing machines (5,546) and other machinery. The state authorities deny that they have any plans for collectivization.

A different course was taken in Western Germany. There the large holdings represented only 4.8 per cent of all cultivated land, in comparison with 28.2 per cent in the Soviet zone. Moreover, a good many landowners hastily distributed their land among relatives to cut down the size of their holdings. No party but the Communist advocated land reform energetically; some held it a violation of property rights, and others expected it would have an adverse effect upon the production of foodstuffs. This latter argument also concerned the occupation powers who wished to avoid the need to provision Germany. All these factors resulted in delays, protracted negotiations and half measures.

The land reform ordinance was promulgated in the American zone in September 1946, in the British and French zones a year later. The American ordinance provided for a progressive land levy ranging from 10 per cent for holdings of 250 acres to 90 per cent for those of more than 3,750 acres. Church land was not exempted from expropriation. The British ordinance decreed that no one should own more than 375 acres of land, and permitted the German provincial governments to scale down this limit.[130] Similarly, the ordinance in the French zone affected holdings of more than 375 acres. It is estimated that about 1.6 million acres might be made available for resettlement under these ordinances: American zone, 300,000; British zone, 1,250,000; French zone, 30,000.[131] Opposition of landowners and their efforts to obtain exemptions, for whatever reason, may reduce this acreage considerably.

The implementation of the reform is in the hands of the German state and federal authorities. The governments of the three states in the American zone issued decrees for such implementation in 1946. In the British zone, the most active state in carrying out the land reform is Schleswig-Holstein, more crowded with refugees than most other states. It enacted the necessary

---

128. **118**, p. 14.

129. **146**, October 1949, p. 34. The amount of obligatory deliveries, at lower than market prices, varies from region to region and for farms of different size. For example, deliveries per acre ordered in Saxony for 1950

for old farmers with less than 12.5 acres were: 529 pounds of grain, nearly 2 short tons of potatoes, 49 pounds of meat, 269 pounds of milk, 660 pounds of pulse, 17 eggs and so on. (**118**, pp. 38 and 67.)

130. The limit was later reduced to 250 acres.

131. **116**, pp. 138–42.

legislation in 1949, but even so planned to settle only 4,250 households during the next five years. North Rhine-Westphalia, in the British zone, passed the land reform law in June 1949. It is reported, however, that at least 300,000 acres have been distributed by landowners among their kinsfolk and thus made unavailable for the land reform. Because of disagreement among German parties the land reform in Lower Saxony was ordered by the Military Government in June 1949. Here too, as in North Rhine-Westphalia, prospects for successful implementation of the program are slight.

The French zone has few large holdings and the influx of refugees has been small, so that the demand for land so far has not been very vigorous.

By the end of 1948, some 325,000 acres in the American zone had been accumulated for redistribution, partly from private landowners and partly from confiscated land of the Reichswehr, of which 95,000 had been allotted to local farmers and refugees. In the British zone (Schleswig-Holstein) about 110,000 acres were to be taken from landlords who possessed several holdings.[132]

Italy. Land ownership continues to be a major problem in Italy. This country, like Spain and Portugal, has been a classical example of large landed estates operated by hired workers and tenants. Various forms of labor dues and obligatory services for the landlord persisted until the early 1930's. They were abolished only to establish land enclosures, sometimes for monetary compensation or allocation of a part of land to the communes.[133] Estates in the south, in Sicily and in Sardinia — some ranging from 2,500 to 10,000 acres — total more than 2 million acres.[134] The owners are often nonresidents. In Italy as a whole, large holdings constituted one per cent of all the farms and about 42 per cent of all farm land in 1930. (See Table 221.) Backward practices have been common on some of the largest holdings and much of the land has lain idle for centuries. Tenants and laborers have lived under intolerable conditions, and the productivity of land and labor has been very low.

The difficulty in changing these inequitable conditions through agrarian reform lies to some extent in the fact that, by the process of inheritance, many of the large estates are now owned by more than one person and often by many people. Each owner's share may be within the size permitted under the planned reform.

Consolidation of holdings is also a problem. For centuries land has been divided and subdivided among the local families, and a peasant may own a dozen strips, totaling an acre, in different localities and may have a great attachment to particular strips that have been made into veritable gardens by the patient work of his family for generations.

In view of these and other difficulties, and most of all, in view of the opposition of the large landowners and the political groups that support them, progress in drafting laws for land reform has been very slow. The only part of Italy where land redistribution is near realization is Calabria. There the demand for land is so great that widespread seizure, mostly of untilled estates, was staged by land-hungry peasants late in 1949. This forced the government to initiate measures to expropriate and redistribute land in this area. A reform law was passed in May 1950 providing for settlement on the Sila plateau, and for expropriation, against payment, of land in private holdings exceeding 750 acres or forming parts of properties which together hold more than this acreage. A central agency, "Opera-Sila," was created to carry out this action and allocate the land thus obtained to landless laborers and peasants who had less than 2.5 acres. Nearly 200,000 acres have been expropriated, and redistribution has begun. During September-October 1951, for example, 64,000 acres were allotted to 4,900 Calabrian peasant families in nine villages and in November, 15,000 additional acres. In this area, allocations are limited to 15 acres per household, but large families may obtain up to 35 acres; in some other areas, with better soil, allocations range from 7.5 to 11.5 acres.

The new landowners have to pay for the land in installments over 30 years, with interest at the rate of 3.5 per cent. They receive credits for the purchase of equipment, fertilizer and seed, and a tractor pool has been established. Any reclamation work carried out by the new owners will be partly compensated by Opera-Sila and partly by other state funds, so that their own share will be a little more than 40 per cent.

Changes brought about by the Sila law can be summarized as follows: holdings of 750 acres and more, which previously represented 83 per

---

cent of the land in this area, have disappeared. Farms of less than 25 acres now comprise 68 per cent of all the land; those of 25 to 125 acres, 4 per cent; the remainder is in holdings of from 125 to 750 acres.

In September 1950 the so-called "extract" law was passed by the legislature as an emergency preliminary measure of the reform law for all Italy. It covers the Po delta, southern Tuscany, the Fucino Basin, the lower Volturno and Garigliano rivers, Sardinia, Sicily and the latifundia in the southeast. The "extract" law is the first reform affecting possession of private land in Italy. The estimate of the government, though considered by some too optimistic, is that 1.5 million acres may become available through this reform for redistribution among some 200,000 peasant families. The law declares null and void all gratuitous transactions or alienations of land made after January 1, 1948, in anticipation of expropriation. When two thirds of a property is expropriated, the last third, not to exceed in any case 750 acres, may not be sold. The basis for the expropriation is the taxable land income of the entire property on January 1, 1943 and average taxable land income per hectare, except for forest land and uncultivated productive land. Indemnity to the landlords is to be paid in bonds, redeemable in 25 years; the interest rate is set at 5 per cent.

Bills still to be approved by the parliament seek land expropriation in limited areas, immediate improvement of this land for settlement purposes and resale to peasants at low prices on easy terms over 30 years. These bills would involve 1.25 million acres, or roughly a third of the whole target of land reform.[135]

Agrarian Reforms in Satellite Countries

Land redistribution was carried out throughout eastern Europe immediately after the end of World War II. In some countries where large holdings were few, as in Bulgaria, the redistribution as such has not resulted in substantial changes. In others, as in Hungary, which had more agricultural land in large estates than any other Danubian country, the reform was more important.

In all satellite countries, however, another aspect of change in land ownership has become more significant than land redistribution. As in the USSR, this has been only the first step toward eliminating individual holdings. According to the Soviet pattern, these must be replaced by collective farms. Following this pattern, two types of farms are being established: "collective farms" in which the peasants pool their land to work under government supervision, and "state farms" owned and run by the central power.

Poland. Under the reform carried out between September 1944 and January 1948, the Polish government expropriated some 8 million acres in nearly 9,500 estates within its former territory and took title to about 2.5 million acres of German land in the new areas. About 4 million acres were parceled out to farm workers and small farmers and about as much land was retained in nearly 5,000 state farms. The maximum size of the new holdings was set at 12.5 acres, and additional plots allocated to small farmers ranged from 2.5 to 10 acres.[136]

The FAO Mission to Poland found this distribution "uneconomic and socially undesirable," since neither the little new farms nor even the small old ones with a little additional land could provide a living for a family. The mission also reported that the buildings and machinery of the former estates had fallen into a progressively worse state of disrepair. In the new territory acquired by Poland after World War II, 466,000 families had been settled on what had been 364,000 farms. Thus, on more than 100,000 farms, two families had been placed where there was formerly one.[137]

Collectivization of agriculture made slow progress at first; by the beginning of 1949 about 40 collective farms had been established. The drive was stepped up, and by October 1950, more than 1,800 such farms were in operation. A large proportion of these farms are in the western part of Poland — Pomerania, East Prussia and Silesia, where the new Polish settlers have been more dependent on government aid than in other parts of the country.[138]

Czechoslovakia. Confiscation, without compensation, of land belonging to the Germans, Hungarians and collaborators preceded the revision of the Land Reform Act of July 1947. Some 4.4 million acres of farm land and 3.2 million acres of forest land were expropriated, by confiscation, between 1945 and 1947.

135. **59**, April 1950, p. 23.

136. **78**, 1948, pp. 38–39.
137. **14**, pp. 39 and 43.
138. **59**, October 1950, p. 44 and April 1951, p. 64.

The Reform Act also expropriated, with a small indemnity, some additional 1.5 million farm acres from Czech landowners. Of the 5.9 million acres of confiscated farm land, 3.3 million were distributed among small and medium farms. Allotments to farmers ranged from 12.4 to 37 acres, depending on the quality of the soil. About 150,000 farm households were the beneficiaries of such allotments, and 35,000 additional families obtained small plots for home sites and gardens. Land so acquired was to be regarded as private and inheritable property. Payment for it amounted to one or two years' harvest value and, for the buildings, from one to three years' rent.[139]

At the same time, a law was passed to limit the splitting up of fields [140] and prevent further land fragmentation by sale or inheritance.

The Communists, in power since February 1948, enacted a new land reform law in March of that year, limiting the size of holdings to 125 acres, including woodland, and expropriating inventory and livestock in the same proportion as the land. In itself, this act has not resulted in any substantial change since only 670 holdings had more than 125 acres each, and together, these had at most 215,000 acres of agricultural land.[141]

The Communist government immediately began to create state farms that totaled 235,000 acres in September 1948 and 1.5 million acres at the end of 1949. The goal for the first half of 1950 was set at 1.6 million acres, or more than 8 per cent of all agricultural land in Czechoslovakia. It was estimated that 0.8 million additional acres were retained in state ownership for the expansion of this program. Collectivization of farms has proceeded much more slowly: only some 2,500 collective farms with a total area of about 250,000 acres had been established by early 1951.[142]

Hungary. Land reform was overdue in Hungary, where redistribution of land was carried out on only a small scale between the two wars and feudal land holding controlled most of the country's agricultural resources. The demand for land was so great that even before the reform law was promulgated in 1945, the land-hungry peasants and landless agricultural workers took matters into their own hands and redistributed the large estates during the chaos following the military and political collapse.

The land reform law of March 1945 sanctioned the *fait accompli* and provided for expropriation of all land in holdings with more than 142 acres while permitting a farmer working his own land to hold twice, and a distinguished soldier three times, as much.

The changes in land ownership were sweeping. The proportion of land in holdings of more than 72 acres fell from 55 per cent to 29 per cent of the total, and of this 29 per cent, two thirds was in communally owned pastures or state estates that could not be divided. Private holdings of more than 280 acres, which represented nearly a fourth of all agricultural land in 1935, have disappeared. Some 600,000 families, mostly of landless laborers and small farmers, have been the beneficiaries. About a million families still are landless, however, and about 7 holdings out of 10 are of less than 7 acres.[143]

The collectivization drive was somewhat delayed in starting. The entering wedge was the cooperatives, largely of the market and credit type, which had existed in Hungary for many years. In December 1948 "Production Group Cooperatives" were introduced by government decree. They are subdivided into three groups, according to the extent of collective work and distribution of the resulting income. All must make deliveries of farm products to the state, on the basis of total acreage, amount of tillable land, and land taxation. To encourage membership, such collective farms are not asked to make as large deliveries of produce to the state as the individual peasants, and even greater reductions are made for the third group, which in its constitution and practices is almost a replica of the Soviet kolkhoz.

So far, government efforts have found little support among the farm households despite the enthusiastic reports of peasant delegations to the USSR about the achievements of collective farms there. Only 4 per cent of the country's farm households, with 7 per cent of the agricultural land, joined the government "cooperatives." An equal percentage of the farm acreage was turned over by the government to the state farms.[144] (See Table 226.)

---

139. **32**, July 1950, pp. 156–58.
140. See p. 492.
141. **32**, July 1950, pp. 158–59 and **59**, January 1949, p. 48.
142. **59**, April 1951, p. 64.

143. **59**, April 1949, pp. 48–49.
144. **32**, October 1951, pp. 218–21.

TABLE 226

COLLECTIVE AND STATE FARMS IN SATELLITE COUNTRIES, DECEMBER 1950

| | Collective Farms | | | | State Farms | |
| | Number of Households | | Cultivated Land | | Cultivated Land | |
Country	In Thousands	Percentage of Total	In Thousands of Acres	Percentage of Total	In Thousands of Acres	Percentage of Total
Hungary	90	4.1	1,153	7.1	1,170	7.2
Yugoslavia	415	18.1	5,475	21.9	1,147	5.8
Romania	66	2.1	662	2.3	2,105	7.4
Bulgaria	564	51.3	5,535	50.3	210	1.9

Source: **32**, October 1951, pp. 220–21.

Romania. Under a law of March 22, 1945, Romania expropriated without compensation the land and inventory of holdings with more than 124 acres (in some cases, 148 acres). This action affected only 0.5 of the holdings but about 20 per cent of the arable land, more than 7 million acres. This land was distributed in 12-acre allotments to landless laborers, and in proportionate allotments to peasants with less than 12 acres, to bring their property up to that limit. Draft animals were also apportioned, but the government kept the farm machinery from large estates for the state machine-tractor stations.

As in other satellite countries, the government is trying to introduce collectivization. In July 1949 the campaign against the "kulaks," that is, farmers who had more than 48 acres of land or employed hired labor, was intensified. Extra delivery quotas, discriminatory taxation and restriction of credit are some of the weapons employed against them. A farm with 7 acres has to deliver 27 per cent of its total output to the state; one with about 48 acres must turn over 58 per cent, at about a fifth the free market price.[145]

The first five full-fledged collective farms, copied from the Soviet kolkhozy, were established in July 1949. Each family was allowed to retain its dwelling, from 0.6 to 1.2 acres, a cow, a few sheep and poultry, shelter for the animals and the necessary farm tools; all the land and livestock in excess was taken over by the collective farm. This system seems to find little favor with Romanian peasants; by the end of 1950, only 2.1 per cent of farm households were in collective farms. At that time the state-controlled sector of the country's farming operated about

10 per cent of all arable land: 2.3 per cent in collective farms and 7.4 per cent in state farms. (See Table 226.)

Bulgaria. Large estates were uncommon in old Bulgaria where 68 per cent of arable land was in holdings of less than 25 acres. (See Table 221.) Southern Dobruja, incorporated into Bulgaria after World War II, had fairly large estates. The law of March 1946 limited holdings to 49 acres in Bulgaria proper and to 74 acres in Dobruja.

Even before the land reform law was enacted, the collectivization drive had started. The government introduced various measures to force farmers into the new organization and to break the resistance of the more prosperous among them. Use of labor on leased land and sale of land are prohibited, service from machine stations is more expensive for private farms than for collective farms, and taxes and compulsory grain deliveries are heavier.[146] To some extent, the Bulgarian government had easier going than some of the other satellite nations, because of the traditional system of cooperatives in the country's agriculture. The campaign for collective farming has been steadily gaining in intensity, with numerous incentives to joiners and increasing hardships for individual peasants, such as higher taxes and stiffer crop collections. By the end of 1950 more than half the farm households were combined in 2,568 collective farms. State farms are less important in Bulgaria than in other Danubian countries — by the end of 1950 they were operating about 2 per cent of the country's agricultural land, as against 50.3 per cent in collective farms.

Yugoslavia. Only 3 per cent of the land hold-

145. **59**, October 1949, pp. 46–47.

146. **59**, January 1950, p. 13.

ings in Yugoslavia exceeded 49 acres each at the end of World War II, but they represented more than a fifth of the arable land. (See Table 221.)

The land reform law of August 1945 expropriated all land in holdings with more than 49 acres (86 acres in exceptional cases) and land belonging to peasants of German origin. Some of the expropriated land was immediately organized in state farms; some was distributed to land-needy peasants on the condition that it would be operated on a collective basis. The first thirty-one collective, or "cooperative," farms were in operation by December 1945.

In May 1949 a new law concerning agricultural cooperatives went into effect, providing for four types, with gradations in compensation to be made for land turned over to the collective farm. Members of all four types may retain up to 2.5 acres for gardening near their homesteads, some livestock and poultry and, in some regions, a small pasture. In turn, they must transfer to the collective all farm buildings, implements, and, in excess of permitted limits, all draft and breeding animals, fodder and seed. Part of the year's output was to be used for deliveries to the state and payment of farm administration, use of machinery, depreciation costs and contributions to various funds. Feed and seed for the collectives were to be put aside from the remainder; a fixed ration per member and per head of his livestock was then to be calculated, and the members paid in accordance with their workdays — some more, and some less, than the stipulated ration (law of June 1951). Any remainder is to go into a special fund. The entire industrial crop, except for seed, must be delivered to the state at a fixed price.

The attitude of the peasants [147] and the poor harvest of 1951 forced the government to make at least a temporary halt in collectivization and to grant various privileges to already established collective farms, which composed 18 per cent of farm households at the end of 1950. It can be expected, however, that the government will make further efforts to promote collectivization.[148]

Agrarian Reforms in Asia

Efforts to strengthen the position of small farmers are in progress in various parts of Asia.

Japan. The reform law of 1946 provided for government purchase of about 5 million acres, or 80 per cent of the land under tenancy, for resale to tillers of the soil. Absentee landowners were asked to give up all their land; noncultivating resident owners, all but 2.5 acres; in Hokkaido, because of the prevailingly larger farms, all but 10 acres was asked. Owners who worked their land were restricted to 7.5 acres (in Hokkaido, to 30 acres). Both the landlords and the tenant purchasers had to deal with the government. Prices were fixed officially, and the tenant obtained the land at the price the government paid the landlord, in long-term annuity bonds. The buyer pays in annual installments over 30 years at 3.2 per cent interest.

By April 1949 about 4.5 million acres of cultivated land (almost a third of the total) had been acquired by the government, and 3 million farmers, about half of all farm households, had obtained land under this arrangement. This reform was completed by the end of 1949 "without the shedding of blood, pillage, or a yen's worth of damage" and has greatly benefited the Japanese farmers, 70 per cent of whom are now owners of the land. Only 5 per cent own less than 10 per cent of the land which they till.[149]

Korea. In 1945, the Military Government took title to all public or private Japanese-owned land in South Korea. Some 600,000 acres were sold in 1948 to more than 500,000 tenant operators, against payment of triple average values of the annual crop. The payment was to be effected in yearly installments at the rate of 20 per cent of the annual crop, in all in 15 years. The title to the land was to pass to the farmer after payment was completed. Though the addition for each family was small, it was of great importance in a country where about half the farming population did not own any land, and another third owned only tiny plots. Moreover, the land the Japanese held was the best paddy land in the country.

The second step was the promulgation of the land reform law in June 1949, providing for purchase of land from landlords to be distributed among tenants and part-tenants, against a payment of 30 per cent of the value of the average annual output during five years. More than a

---

147. Many peasants who joined the collective farms are trying to withdraw, and many others have kept away despite all incentives.

148. **32**, October 1951, pp. 217–18.

149. **6**, 1950, pp. 188–89 and **32**, September 1951, pp. 187–89.

million acres have been distributed among 1.2 million tenants.[150]

In North Korea, after occupation by the Russians, all privately owned land above a certain minimum acreage was seized by the government and parceled out in small plots, but title was not transferred to the individual farmer. He received only the right to cultivate it in return for payment of a yearly tax amounting to 27 per cent of the rice crop.[151]

China. The National government of China made weak attempts, first by the Land Law of 1930 and again after World War II, to reduce the usual land rent from 50 per cent of the main crop to 37.5 per cent. But the laws were not enforced, and the failure of the government to protect tenants and redistribute land largely accounted for its downfall.

The Communist government had carried out large-scale land reform in areas under its administration and extended this program over the entire territory of China when it obtained control of the country. By the end of June 1950, redistribution of land had been completed in Manchuria and most of the north — an area with a rural population of more than 140 million people. In the winter of 1950–51 land reform was carried out in other parts of China with a farm population exceeding 130 million. Some 80 million peasants in these areas obtained about 25 million acres of land — a little more than one third acre per capita, on the average. It is expected that land distribution in the remaining areas, where there are some 130–140 million people on farms, will be completed by the end of 1952 except for areas with minority nationalities (about 20 million persons) for which the date of implementing the reform is still undetermined.[152]

Taiwan. In mid-1951 the Chinese National government enacted legislation providing for the sale of public and some formerly Japanese-owned land to tenant farmers on a 10-year installment basis. The annual payment is to be fixed at 37.5 per cent of the value of the main crop.

The rent for land was limited in 1949 to 37.5 per cent of the annual value of the main crop. The 1951 law continues this rate and provides additional protection to tenants, such as a lease

contract of not less than six years; exemption of rent payments in poor-crop years; priority in purchasing the rented land if it is offered for sale.[153]

India. Land hunger is great in India, and redistribution of land is an urgent problem. More than two thirds of the rural population are either tenants or landless laborers.

Land reform is in the hands of provincial governments that have either recently enacted legislation outlawing the existing ownership system or are considering such legislation. In a number of provinces, landowners (zamindars, who subrent the land and are responsible for the payment of the land revenue) and intermediaries [154] (tenure holders between the landlord and the cultivator) have been eliminated by payment of compensation to the landowners, usually on the basis of the existing high rents. To replace them, the traditional system of individual ownership, the so-called ryotwar, has been introduced. Some provincial laws prescribe that a landowner must cultivate his land; others have restricted landholding to from 50 to 250 acres. In Bihar it will take twenty years to pay the full compensation, in Madras only three years. It is estimated that the present program of land reform, if fully implemented, will affect half the cultivated area of India.

There have been legal difficulties, and the landowners have taken the disputes to court and challenged the constitutionality of the reform laws. In June 1951 the Indian Parliament amended the constitution to enable the states to alter the agrarian system in favor of the underprivileged inhabitants. The legality of the amendment was upheld by the High Court a few months later, thus clearing the way to implementation of the legislation. In 1951–52 some real progress was achieved. Five million acres were taken over by the state in Madras for redistribution, and transfer of proprietorship was also under way in Kashmir.[155] In Uttar Pradesh the state obtained from four hundred absentee landlords some 60 million acres against payment

---

150. **6**, 1950, pp. 189–90.

151. **32**, October 1950, pp. 234–35 and **6**, 1950, p. 189.

152. **6**, 1950, pp. 183–86.

153. **6**, 1950, pp. 183–84.

154. In some provinces it is not rare for five or six such middlemen to hold financial interest in a single plot. Each collects rent from the one immediately below him to pay to the one above him, while the cultivator must pay enough to satisfy all of them. (**32**, September 1951, p. 202.)

155. **6**, 1950, pp. 186–88; **2**, p. 53.

and began to distribute them among thirteen million peasants. The land is to be paid off in ten-year installments, equal to annual rent.

Burma. Soon after having gained its independence, Burma passed the Land Nationalization Act (October 1948) by which the state took title to all land in the possession of nonagriculturists (absentee landlords). In Lower Burma, this meant about half the cultivated land; in Upper Burma, a little over 10 per cent. Limits concerning the amount of land held by cultivators are set so high, by Burmese standards,[156] that only about one or 2 per cent of this group of landowners will be affected. The compensation for nationalized land is relatively low and in most cases may be paid out over a 12-year period.

The act was expected to provide the state with 8 million acres for distribution among landless peasants and allotments to those with tiny land patches. During the adjustment period the present tenants were to continue the cultivation of the land as tenants of the state. The rapid spread of civil unrest, however, has so far prevented the carrying out of the program. In the absence of any public authority, tenants seized, in a disorderly manner, the land which the government had expected to take title to.[157] In the province of Syriam the state had redistributed some 60,000 acres by May 1950.[158]

Turkey. A new bill passed in May 1945 granted small holdings to peasants who had not obtained land through Turkey's earlier agrarian reform. About 20 million acres including state and church holdings, reclaimed and uncultivated land, and private holdings in excess of 1,120 acres in a single estate are to be redistributed through allotment of 20 acres to each qualifying family. The dispossessed landowners are to receive compensation over a period of 20 years in 4 per cent "soil" bonds.[159] By the end of 1950, about 1.3–1.4 million acres had been distributed to peasants under this law, and the allocation of an additional 650,000 acres was under way.[160]

THE LAND PROBLEM IN THE NEW COUNTRIES

In the Western Hemisphere, new countries were more concerned at first with the settlement of vast unoccupied expanses than with redistribution of land. In the United States, a series of laws beginning with the Ordinance of 1787 and ending with the Homestead Act of 1862 were designed chiefly to transfer pieces of the public domain to individual settlers who were willing to cultivate them.[161] By 1923, 265 million acres had been distributed, and by 1934 the public domain was virtually closed.

Australia has followed the opposite policy and the major part of the area is in the public domain, within which individual farmers lease land under various provisions. In 1943, more than 90 per cent of the public domain was operated under Crown lease; only 7.4 per cent of public domain had been alienated, and 2.2 per cent was in the process of alienation.[162]

Redistribution of Land in Mexico

After the Spanish conquest, all land in Mexico was declared the property of the Spanish Crown. Later, the Crown granted large holdings to various dignitaries in return for their services. By the end of the nineteenth century, ownership was more highly concentrated in Mexico than in any other Latin American country. In 1900, some 70 per cent of the territory was held by only 2 per cent of the people; by 1910 almost all village land was incorporated in big estates or "haciendas."

Land hunger, high rents and the miserable living conditions of millions of peasants have led to many upheavals in Mexico during the present century. Redistribution of land began officially in 1917, but the census of 1930 reported that about a third of the country's territory, more than 170 million acres, was still in the hands of less than 2,000 owners.

In spite of many setbacks, however, agrarian reform, intensified since 1934, has transferred a substantial part of the agricultural land to *ejidos,* village communities. *Ejidal,* or communal land, cannot be sold, rented, mortgaged or left idle. A member of the community, *ejidatario,* may use communal pastures, woods and water, and receives a permanent lease to a plot of land. The succeeding head of the family inherits his rights. Between 1917 and 1934 more than 20 million acres were distributed, and during 1935–37, some

---

156. 50 acres for rice land, 25 for dry land and 10 for alluvial land. **2,** p. 58.
157. **30,** p. 11.
158. **6,** 1950, pp. 182–83.
159. **59,** July 1947, pp. 73–74.
160. **4,** p. 35; **2,** pp. 58–59.

161. Various subsequent laws amending the Homestead Act were aimed chiefly at effecting adjustments necessitated by land conditions in particular states.
162. **58,** 1944–45, p. 105.

29 million additional. In 1940, 48 per cent of all the arable land and 60 per cent of the cultivated land was held by more than 14,500 communities, with an average of 1,200 acres of arable land per *ejido* or 9.4 acres per *ejidatario*.[163]

By the end of 1946, more than 76 million acres had been placed in the hands of 1.7 million beneficiaries. (See Figure 155.) Thus Mexico distributed more land in the period 1917–46 than all the European countries together through their land reforms between the two wars. Nevertheless, hundreds of thousands of landless peasants still clamor for an *ejido* share, and many members of *ejidos* complain that their plots are inadequate. Since there is not enough land to satisfy all the claimants, the government is seeking a solution by bringing idle land into cultivation through irrigation and by developing new centers of population to which villagers can move to work in urban pursuits. During 1946–48, about 4 million additional acres were cleared for farming.[164]

The land ownership system as it now stands consists, on the one hand, of *ejidal* farming by small farmers and, on the other, of thousands of medium-size land holdings, from 375 to 750 acres each. Some *ejidos* have taken the form of collective enterprises. Although technical development has been more rapid in such enterprises and in medium-size holdings, the economic condition of all farmers has been improved. Other important consequences are a certain degree of diversification in farm production, development of irrigation and establishment of state and private credit systems to provide the new landowners with the necessary capital.[165]

Argentina

The government of Argentina purchased some large holdings in 1949 and expropriated others with the object of dividing the land into small farms and selling it to new owners. Land rentals have been reduced by 36 per cent since 1940. While the government promises to help small farmers obtain more land, it has set rather high limits below which a farm may not be divided or expropriated: 250 acres for grain farms and from 3,750 to 5,000 acres for livestock farms.[166]

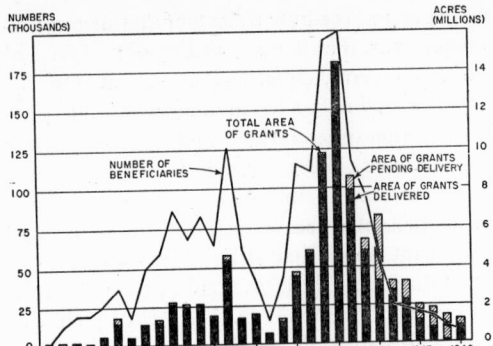

U. S. Department of Agriculture

FIGURE 155. AGRARIAN REFORM IN MEXICO, 1917–46

FARMING

Scientific farming is a product of recent times. For thousands of years, agriculture developed by the imperceptibly slow adjustment of tradition to experience. Beginnings were often accidental, as probably were the discoveries by prehistoric man of such plants as wheat, maize, the sweet potato, rice and tobacco. Yet in the subsequent thousands of years, man has not discovered a single species of equal importance to him and has not domesticated any additional animal.[167]

Farming in the Ancient World

In farming practices, the ancients did not know "why" but they gradually learned "how." Plowing scenes on Egyptian papyri date from the fifteenth century B.C.[168] Plowing and cultivating and the practice of letting land lie fallow are mentioned in the Bible.

The Chinese, "farmers of forty centuries," apparently started even earlier. They even recognized various types of soil at a very early date, as witnessed by the first known classification of soil, made for taxation purposes by Emperor Yao in 2361–57 B.C.[169] In many places they have succeeded in maintaining the fertility of their soil through countless generations by manuring, terracing and irrigating their land, and they frequently have three crops at different stages of maturity growing simultaneously in the same field. In Japan, where, as in China, labor is the only surplus resource, soil has been cultivated so untiringly that the land longest in use, often

163. **53**, pp. 18–21.
164. **32**, October 1948, pp. 221–24 and **59**, January 1950, p. 24.
165. **10**, p. 7.
166. **59**, April 1950, pp. 2–3.

167. Of the 3,500 species of mammals, only 19 have been domesticated (**112**, Chapter 13).
168. **141**, p. 7.
169. **143**, p. 4.

by countless generations of the same family, is valued more highly than virgin soil.

As archaeological research has shown, terracing was practiced in the Mediterranean and in Britain some twenty centuries B.C. Irrigation was widely used in many parts of the world long before our era, whether water was carried through hollow trunks such as the Fijians laid, or extensive aqueducts, as in Ceylon, Mexico, Peru. Ancient irrigation ditches have been traced in Arizona, and it is believed that prehistoric people had 100,000 acres under irrigation in the Salt River valley.[170]

But the progress based on accumulation of occasional experience came to a halt many centuries ago. Ancient Rome added little to the agricultural methods developed in Greece, although it suffered from shortage of grain. The role of the Romans in agriculture, like their general role in our civilization, was to systematize the heritage of Greece, to spread it over the nations in the orbit of their Empire and to preserve it for coming generations. Cato the Elder (234–149 B.C.) taught intensive cultivation, crop rotation, use of leguminous plants to improve the soil. Varro (116–27 B.C.) stressed the adaptability of crops to different soils and the importance of green manure. Columella (about A.D. 45) recommended growing clover and lucerne (or alfalfa), advocated green manure, dung and ashes for soil conditioning, and preached the high value of turnips.[171]

The downfall of Rome in the fifth century brought a relapse in agriculture in Europe, where an era of unrest began. Many centuries passed before agricultural progress was resumed.

The Scientific Foundation of Farming

A new page in the history of agricultural technology was begun in the second half of the nineteenth century with systematic attempts to implement farming with new technical devices, new metals, new motor power and, most important of all, new knowledge of chemistry and biology. In 1840 Justus von Liebig laid the scientific foundation for agriculture, which for millenniums had been purely empirical. Since that time, and particularly since the 1890's, discoveries in every field of agriculture have succeeded one another at such a rate that agricultural tech-

niques have been improved vastly more in the last fifty years than in the preceding two thousand.[172]

MODERN AGRICULTURAL TECHNOLOGY

In 1940 the United States Department of Agriculture described agricultural technology in the following terms:

[It is] science, art and invention. It is tractors, combines, cornpickers. It is the testing and breeding of animals and the conquest of diseases. It is hybrid corn, new kinds of wheat, soybeans, and lespedeza. It is the way to feed cows, plants and men. It is road building and rural electrification. It is contour plowing, conservation of soil, management of forests, protection of wild life. It is marketing and distribution. It is a race between insect pests and ways to kill them. Technology is the workshop, barn, grove, field and home.[173]

To this description should be added many other methods developed since then. Such, for example, are grassland farming; weed spraying; the feeding of antibiotics to livestock to check or destroy various disease-producing microorganisms (bacteria, fungi and others) and, in some animals, to stimulate growth and faster gain in weight.

Each of these methods and practices holds promise, but the proper combination of improved techniques multiplies the advantages and assures success. Because of the interaction among factors in plant growth, a multifactor approach has given striking results, for example, with corn, small grains, soybeans and other crops in the United States. Corn yields that had never averaged more than 20 bushels per acre in the southeastern states have risen to 60 bushels when fertilization, hybrid seed, shallow cultivation and closer spacing of plants were combined. Some fields returned a yield five or more times greater than before.[174]

The fascinating story of the invasion of agriculture by modern science and technology is beyond the scope of this volume. It is impossible, however, to survey the world economy and especially world agriculture, to discuss the interrelation between continents, or to appraise the earth's capacity to support mankind, without mentioning recent trends in farming. The following pages briefly outline recent improvements

---

170. **141**, pp. 5–6.
171. **141**, pp. 9–10.

172. **41**, 1938, p. 125.
173. **40**, p. 3.
174. **3**, p. 86.

in plants and livestock, mechanization of agricultural processes, electrification and the use of fertilizers.

Improvement of Plants

Among the achievements of agricultural technology in the last century, "none has brought about such progress as the improvement of plants through selection and crossbreeding." [175] The explanation is that while many other improvements require considerable financial outlay, the use of better varieties of seed is within the reach of even a poor farmer. Thus the introduction of better seed strains into Japan and Korea two or three decades ago has already produced tangible results in increasing the yield.

Moreover, many new techniques may not be transferred as conveniently as new seed varieties can be exchanged. Topography, the prevailing size of farms, conditions of land ownership and patterns of farming may be so fundamentally different as to make techniques suitable in one area practically impossible in another. But better seed varieties adapted to similar soil and climate will thrive in any part of the world. Furthermore, improved seed varieties may be used to breed those specifically adapted to the area where they will be used.[176]

The experience in Indonesia is particularly indicative. When peasants living in extreme poverty were supplied with fertilizers and produced more food, the extra food inevitably was eaten and they had nothing with which to buy the next year's fertilizer. But even the poorest peasant will not eat his seed for the next crop. More productive seed therefore had a greater influence on farming in Indonesia than fertilizer.[177]

Plant Breeding

This branch of agricultural technology rests on the pioneering work of Gregor Johann Mendel on the basic principle of plant genetics (the laws of inheritance) which went unnoticed for more than thirty years and was discovered and republished in 1900. The science of genetics has permitted plant breeding to improve and intensify the characteristics of commercially desirable plant species. Many new varieties have been developed. Strains have been created that are more tolerant of extremes of cold and heat, drought and moisture, or more resistant to diseases and insects; existing varieties have been acclimatized to new environments and hybrid strains of greater efficiency have been produced.

One of the most spectacular achievements in this field has been the development of hybrid corn that yields 15 to 20 per cent more than open-pollinated varieties. More than fifty improved varieties of wheat have been developed and distributed to American farmers in the past decade. They resist leaf or stem rust, or both, loose and stinking smut; some mature a week or more earlier and thus escape damage from drought. The crossing of an almost sugarless wild cane with a superior variety has resulted in the disease-resistant and prolific Java cane, registered under the name P. O. J.[178] 2878, which in barely a century has raised the sugar yield from less than one ton to ten tons per acre. In the United States, breeding stations have developed disease-resistant sugar cane varieties adapted to various regions where cane is grown, by crossing strains from the temperate zone with tropical varieties, some of them from Java.

Development of earlier-maturing varieties of plants increase the yield in existing areas and extend production to new areas. Thus wheat varieties maturing a week earlier than usual — in advance of the hottest weather — are used on the Great Plains to raise the yield. Similarly, commercial corn production has been extended hundreds of miles northward with the introduction of early-maturing varieties.[179]

The search for improved varieties of wheat, corn, barley, rice, beans, oilseed, sugar cane and other crops has been intensified in the last decade even in countries previously not aware of this factor. Experimental stations are now at work on this problem in almost every Latin American country, for example. Much of this research is conducted in cooperation with the United States Department of Agriculture.[180] To some extent, crops are being fitted to mechanized culture by the production of strains adaptable to mechanical operations, which cannot exert the same degree of selectivity as manual labor.[181] In some

---

175. **22**, p. 291. The U. S. Department of Agriculture also believes that "The use of improved varieties, 'tailor-made' for the areas in which they are grown, is probably the easiest and surest way to get more food out of every acre in any one crop." (**33**, p. 11.)

176. **3**, p. 87.

177. **3**, pp. 89–90.

---

178. Proefstation Oost Java.

179. **3**, p. 85.

180. **10**, pp. 36 ff.

181. **13**, p. 22.

countries, the use of better seed is compulsory. For example, the Netherlands prohibits the sale of seed not approved by a special testing service.[182] In turn, improved seed, more sensitive in many respects and requiring better care, has been a factor in improving methods of cultivation in many regions.

Since Pasteur's epochal discoveries, science has turned its attention increasingly to the permanent worries of all farmers — insects and other pests and plant diseases that threaten the harvest. Treatment of seeds before planting, more powerful dusts and sprays, more efficient equipment for spraying and dusting and introduction of disease-resistant strains have done much toward alleviating these dangers in areas where farmers make use of the new technology.

Weed Control

Weeds appear so commonly in cultivated fields and pastures that many farmers have tended to take them for granted. They occupy space needed by the crop for fuller growth, retard this growth by consuming a large part of the plant nutrients and moisture in the soil, and, by shading, hinder crops in maturing. Various disease-spreading insects, such as white grubs, some bugs, and potato beetles feed on weeds. They are the cause of great losses. In the United States, for example, the farm loss from weeds is estimated at about $5 billion a year. This is many times the loss from all animal diseases and more than that from destruction caused by insects and plant diseases.[183] In Great Britain, the loss of crop is often 40 to 50 per cent, and sometimes a crop may be a total failure because of weed infestation.[184]

Certain mechanical and cultivation practices in weed control have long been applied by farmers, but chemical control has been developed only recently. In 1938 France released a weed-killing chemical (Sinox), and during World War II research in the United States produced the chemical 2,4-D which is not toxic to livestock. The first test on a large scale with this weed-killer was made in a corn field in Kentucky in 1946. The test was so successful that the usefulness of 2,4-D was rapidly recognized throughout the country and abroad. Many new chemicals for specific weeds and crops have since been developed, and many more are being tested and worked on.[185] Some sprays cause the weed to burn up the food reserves in its leaves, stems and roots, so that it actually starves to death.

Methods and equipment for spraying, dusting and fumigating have been improved. Seed and soil treatment before planting is effectively controlling seed- and soil-borne fungus diseases. Flame is used successfully in weed control in cotton and promises to be effective in other crops.[186]

New and more efficient insecticides have also been discovered and new techniques for their application developed. Great care is necessary in applying them in some cases, however, to prevent injury to neighboring plants. Precise timing of chemical control is essential.

Grassland Farming

Grassland agriculture is an important part of farming in most European countries and is coming into wider use in other parts of the world. In some areas this implies extensive farming, but elsewhere, as in the northwestern countries of Europe, it is very intensive — as much so as vegetable farming. It may be used in combination or rotation with other crops.

The importance of grassland farming is gaining more and more recognition in the United States, where the grasslands, including hay and forested range lands, cover more than a billion acres — nearly 60 per cent of the total land area. These lands furnish about half of the feed for all livestock, and more than half of the farms and ranches depend largely on grassland feed.[187] Grassland farming for improving the soil and controlling erosion now constitutes one of the measures applied to soil-conservation districts throughout the nation. Improved plant species are used in many areas, alone or in seeding mixtures; useful varieties from foreign countries, such as lespedeza, have been introduced; new grazing, harvesting and storage techniques have been adopted.

Improvement of Livestock

Empirical crossbreeding by selection of animals was practiced long before our era. (See

---

182. **73**, p. 14.
183. **80**, p. 9.
184. **119**, p. 1.

185. **119**, pp. 4–6.
186. **3**, p. 85.
187. **41**, 1948, p. 25.

Figure 156.) Varro, for example, gives farmers pointed instructions on the selection of animals in his *Rerum Rusticarum.*

Empirical breeding, however, long ago reached a point beyond which little progress was possible. After Mendel's discoveries on the manner in which characteristics are passed on from generation to generation, livestock breeding entered a new phase, shifting from empirical selection to scientific crossbreeding. The object was to obtain progeny with predetermined characteristics — greater efficiency in converting feed into meat and milk, greater and more regular reproductive capacity, earlier maturity, and the like. Crossbreds generally gain more rapidly during the feeding period, have fewer digestive disturbances and show higher dressing percentages.

Many breeds of livestock have been developed. Since the genetic value rather than the quality of a given animal has become the chief purpose of breeding, the breeding value of an animal is appraised by progeny tests. Special registers of such tests, mostly applied to male animals, have been established in agriculturally advanced countries. Only animals with exceptional progeny, in comparison with their ancestry, are listed in these registers. Productivity tests are carried out in many countries: milk tests for dairy cows, fattening and reproductive capacity tests for pigs, wool-production tests for sheep, egg-laying tests for hens, and so on.

Genealogical herdbooks of the best livestock breeds are kept and coordinated in various Latin American countries, where the improvement of livestock production is of great concern. Costa Rica, for example, is trying to improve cattle by introducing specialized breeds (beef cattle and dual-purpose cattle) and to develop breeds that will mature in three instead of five years. Venezuela is conducting similar work. Peru is importing pedigreed bulls and heifers, mostly from Holland, to improve its dairy herds.[188]

To improve cattle breeds, crossbreeding with sires of outstanding characteristics has been widely practiced. Bull clubs for this purpose were first founded in Denmark around 1880. Artificial insemination, one of the latest methods for improving genetic strains, is being used increasingly.[189]

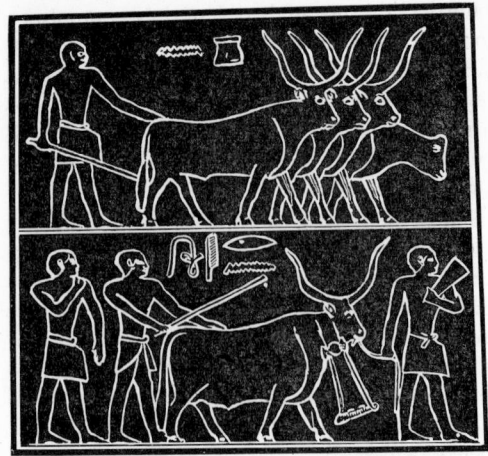

Courtesy of *The Field*

FIGURE 156. BREEDING OF CATTLE IN ANCIENT EGYPT
(After a Stone Carving, 4000 B.C.)

These stone carvings, which were found in Egypt in the tomb of Mehenwetre, show that people in the Nile Valley more than 4,000 years ago were aware of the difference between ordinary and improved cattle.

The United States has many centers, each with dozens of bulls of different breeds whose semen is used in many parts of the country. About one million cows were artificially inseminated in 1946; in 1947, a million and a half.[190] Semen is also sent to other countries, such as Argentina, by air. In Denmark, about 35 per cent of all dairy cows are artificially inseminated, and in Italy sterility and genital diseases of cows have been fought successfully by artificial insemination. In some countries, for example in Chile, where livestock raising is almost always on a large scale, methods of artificial insemination as applied in the United States and Europe, meet with difficulties. The great size of Chilean holdings is an obstacle to cooperation and use of the semen material. Efforts are being made, however, to overcome these difficulties.[191]

The feeding of animals has become an important adjunct to breeding. In the light of better knowledge of nutritional requirements and values, the composition of feed and methods of feeding have undergone substantial changes. The Scandinavian countries have worked out a special system for measuring the energy and protein value and the optimum amount of different

188. **10**, pp. 46 ff.

189. The first experiments in artificial insemination were made in Russia in 1907, but application of this method on a vast scale in the United States, Denmark, the United Kingdom, the USSR and some other countries dates from the late 1930's. (**91**, p. 126.)

190. **88**, pp. 16–20. See also **145**, p. 292.

191. **10**, p. 47.

feeds. These standards have been put into general practice throughout Scandinavia.[192] World War II activated research on the best diets and feeding methods for animals in the United States, when it became of utmost importance to obtain the maximum in foodstuffs in return for the least feed. Needs of livestock for energy materials, proteins, mineral elements and vitamins were carefully studied, and new feed standards developed for each category of livestock.[193]

These and other efforts have resulted in substantial progress in animal breeding, such as improvement in the frame and productivity of cattle, the flavor of meat, the yield of milk and butterfat per cow, the quantity and quality of wool per sheep. Animal strains have been obtained that gain weight on less feed than others: in the Corn Belt, for example, the amount of feed per 100 pounds of pork has been cut by 10–15 per cent.[194]

The use of various parasiticides in the destruction of worms, ticks and grubs that infest the larger animals, has become an effective weapon of livestock producers. Painstaking experiments have been carried out with hogs, cattle and sheep, for example, to develop specific drugs for each type of parasite and to find the best methods of using them as preventives or cures.[195] The animal kingdom is beginning to benefit from the science of antibiotics in the control of many diseases for which no cure was known a decade ago. Some antibiotics are mixed with the feed to cure sick animals or prevent a threatening disease. Vitamins are added to the feed to compensate for deficiencies.

More efficient control has checked some diseases and reduced losses from others. In Denmark, for example, a twenty-year campaign against bovine tuberculosis has eliminated this disease.[196] In the United States, the first survey of bovine tuberculosis, completed in 1922, indicated an infection of 4 per cent of all cattle in the country, and of 15 per cent in the eastern dairy region. A considerable percentage of hogs

and poultry were also infected.[197] An intensive campaign for eradication of tuberculosis was started, and today no state has an incidence of more than 0.5 per cent although some traces of infection show up in almost every state. Whenever postmortem examination in slaughterhouses discloses tuberculosis in animals, the origin of the infected animals is traced; the herd is then tested and the disease eradicated by slaughter. This method, coupled with general cattle testing, is gradually reducing bovine tuberculosis to the vanishing point.[198]

Like the better varieties of seed, the improved breeds of animals generally require better care. Their sensitivity to weather and type of feed has given an impetus to provide better and more hygienic accommodations. The work involved in the care of a high-grade animal and in conditioning it to a desired breeding type, such as the Danish hog (increased body length, thinner back, thicker belly) is illustrated in Figure 157.

FARM MECHANIZATION

The use of farm machinery and mechanical power in agriculture is comparatively recent. Even in Europe and North America, crude agricultural implements, such as wooden plows, scythes, hand-made flails, hoes and hand rakes were in universal use as late as the middle of the nineteenth century. Farming operations were carried out chiefly by hand. It was inevitable, however, that technical progress in industry and transportation should extend to agriculture. Rapid growth of the population and the rise in the standards of living progressively increased the demand for foodstuffs. This increase in turn stimulated greater efficiency in production, which has been achieved largely through the introduction of farm machinery. New implements — cast iron plows, steel plows, threshers, mowers, reapers, binders — appeared on the market. Gradually, industry began to supply increasing numbers of better-quality implements.

In the New World, particularly in the United States, land was abundant but labor was in short supply. At harvesttime when the need for labor was especially urgent, it was difficult, or impossible, to get enough help and wages were high. At the same time, both domestic and foreign markets for food crops were growing.

192. **63**, pp. 30–31.
193. **41**, 1943–47, pp. 95 ff.
194. **41**, 1943–47, p. 925.
195. **41**, 1943–47, pp. 71–79.
196. In Great Britain, tuberculosis among livestock is still a serious concern. In Poland the incidence of tuberculosis ranges from 30 to 80 per cent in dairy herds, with the higher percentages in the larger herds. It is believed that much of the tuberculosis prevalent among Polish children was contracted by drinking milk. (**14**, p. 96.)

197. **109**, p. 96.
198. **41**, 1943–47, p. 85.

Courtesy of Longmans Green and Company (149)

FIGURE 157. BREEDING OF HOGS IN DENMARK

The Danish farmer shows how he achieves the remarkable flavor and delicacy in his custom-tailored bacon, so popular in the United Kingdom. Sixty years of systematic selective breeding were needed to develop the hogs that yield this bacon.

TABLE 227

FARM MECHANIZATION: TRACTORS AND DRAFT ANIMALS IN THE WORLD, 1930 TO 1948–49

(Millions of Power Units ^{a} *)*

	1930			1938–39			1948–49		
Region ^{b}	Total	Draft Animals	Tractors	Total	Draft Animals	Tractors	Total	Draft Animals	Tractors
World	221.9	214.2	7.7	225.2	210.3	14.9	230.6	199.2	31.4
North America	23.5	17.4	6.1	22.0	12.4	9.6	29.4	7.2	22.2
Latin America	37.7	37.6	0.1	42.3	42.1	0.2	45.6	45.2	0.4
Europe, excluding the United Kingdom	22.0	21.3	0.7	22.4	21.2	1.2	20.9	17.9	3.0
United Kingdom	0.9	0.8	0.1	1.2	0.8	0.4	2.2	0.5	1.7
USSR	25.2	24.8	0.4	16.0	12.9	3.1	14.1	11.1	3.0
Near East	7.8	7.8	—	8.6	8.6	—	9.3	9.2	0.1
Far East	89.6	89.6	—	98.1	98.1	—	90.1	90.0	0.1
Africa	13.5	13.4	0.1	12.9	12.8	0.1	17.4	17.1	0.3
Oceania	1.7	1.5	0.2	1.7	1.4	0.3	1.6	1.0	0.6

Source: **13**, p. 3.

a. Conversion factors for draft power units: horse or mule, 1; buffalo, 0.9; draft cattle, 0.5; tractor, 6.

b. Regions are defined as follows: North America: United States, including Alaska and Hawaii, Canada; Latin America: Middle and South America, and the Caribbean; Europe, excluding the United Kingdom; Near East: Turkey, Iraq, Iran, Afghanistan, Syria, Lebanon, Israel, Saudi Arabia and neighboring territories, Egypt, Anglo-Egyptian Sudan, Ethiopia, Eritrea; Far East: southeastern Asia; Africa: all areas not comprised in Near East; Oceania: Australia, New Zealand, and islands in the southwestern and central Pacific.

These factors created the demand for labor-saving devices; the soil and topography of the United States lent themselves to the use of large machinery.

At first most of the new implements were horse-drawn and later some were steam-powered. The former were too slow, the latter were too heavy and cumbersome. In the twentieth century, the internal combustion engine finally opened the way to construction of powerful and fast-operating equipment — tractors and combine-harvesters.

TRACTORS IN THE WORLD

The world's farmers had 1.3 million tractors in 1930, 2.5 million in 1939 and 6.1 million in 1951. The distribution by region in 1951 was as follows (in thousands): [199]

World total	6,130
North America	4,168
Latin America	122
Europe	971
USSR	564
Near East	16
Far East	23
Africa	100
Oceania	166

As of January 1951 North America had 68 per cent of the world's tractors; Europe, 15.8 per cent; the USSR, 9.2 per cent; and the rest of the world, 7.0 per cent. The Far East, with half the world's farmers and about a fourth of the world's arable land, had only 0.4 per cent of the tractors.

Despite the increasing use of tractors which nearly quintupled between 1930 and 1951, draft animals supply over 85 per cent of the power used on the world's farms. While animals provide only about a fourth of all farm draft power in North America and the United Kingdom, farmers in Latin America, the Near and Far East and Africa depend almost exclusively on them for work in their fields. The ratio between the use of animal power and tractors varied in 1948–49 from 1 to 3 in North America to about 1,000 to 1 in the Far East. (See Table 227.)

The spread of tractorization in the world's agriculture, slow until 1939, except for the

199. **7**, pp. 5–6.

TABLE 228

FARM MECHANIZATION: TRACTORS IN SELECTED COUNTRIES, 1939, 1949 AND 1951

| Country | Number of Tractors,[a] in Thousands | | | Acres of Arable Land Per Tractor, 1951 |
	1939	1949	1951	
World	2,498.0	4,626.0	6,130.0	494
United States	1,447.0	2,950.0	3,825.0	119
Canada	...	324.0	368.0	247
Mexico	...	22.0	32.0	772
Guatemala	...	0.6	...	24,710
El Salvador	...	0.3	...	3,541 [b]
Honduras	...	0.3	...	4,529 [b]
Nicaragua	...	0.3	...	5,592 [b]
Costa Rica	...	0.4	...	4,695 [b]
Panama	...	0.3	...	1,154 [b]
Cuba	...	5.0	8.0	608
Venezuela	...	5.4	7.7	482
Colombia	...	3.2	6.5	806
Ecuador	...	0.6	...	4,732 [b]
Brazil	...	6.2	15.7	2,965
Peru	...	2.5	3.6	1,127
Bolivia	...	0.6	...	1,408 [b]
Chile	...	5.0	6.0	2,394
Uruguay	...	7.0	10.5	331
Argentina	...	23.9	25.0	4,732
United Kingdom	55.0	280.0	325.0	57
Ireland	3.8	13.0	17.0	217
France	30.0	89.0	135.0	385
Belgium	1.4	5.0	7.0	351
Netherlands	5.0	12.0	19.0	143
Denmark	4.0	11.0	22.0	316
Sweden	20.0	52.0	60.0	153
Norway	2.8	7.0	10.0	198
Finland	4.0	8.0	12.0	514
Germany				
Western	} 60.0	70.0	126.0	168
Soviet Zone		5.0	12.0	1,028
Poland	1.5	14.0	22.0	1,888
Czechoslovakia	6.0	22.0	29.0	469

(Continued on facing page)

United States and the USSR, gained momentum in the postwar years. Between 1939 and 1949, the United States and Switzerland doubled the number of tractors; the United Kingdom quintupled the number; France, Denmark, Yugoslavia and New Zealand about tripled it. The Union of South Africa had only 1,600 tractors in 1939 and 30,000 in 1949.

In the past few years tractorization continued at an accelerated rate. From 1949 to 1951 Australia, Western Germany, Colombia, the Union of South Africa and some other countries about doubled the number of tractors on their farms. Spain is the only European country that showed little progress in comparison with its prewar position. (See Table 228 and Figure 158.)

The density of tractors in agriculture (the number of tractors per 1,000 acres of arable land or the number of acres per one tractor) depends on the extent of mechanization and the size of farms. As a general rule, when farms are equally mechanized, in terms of the distribution of power between draft animals and tractors, there must be more arable land per tractor in coun-

TABLE 228—*continued*

Country	Number of Tractors,[a] in Thousands			Acres of Arable Land Per Tractor, 1951
	1939	1949	1951	
Switzerland	8.2	17.0	20.0	62
Austria	2.2	10.0	16.0	279
Hungary	7.0	13.0	18.0	796
Portugal	1.0	3.0	5.0	2,866
Spain	10.0	8.0	15.0	3,160
Italy	39.0	52.0	66.0	198
Yugoslavia	2.3	7.0	7.0	2,792
Romania	2.0	11.0	15.0	1,532
Bulgaria	3.0	3.0	5.0	2,125
Greece	1.5	3.0	5.0	1,631
USSR	483.5	400.0	564.0	988
China	. . .	1.4	2.0	112,431
Japan	0.1	1.8	. . .	50,265 [b]
Turkey	1.0	4.0	8.0	4,571
Israel	0.1	0.8	3.0	1,648
Syria	—	0.3	. . .	20,591 [b]
Saudi Arabia	—	0.1	. . .	494 [b]
Iraq	—	0.5	. . .	13,096
Iran	—	0.6	1.2	3,435
Pakistan	—	2.1	2.6	19,691
India	0.1	7.0	15.0	20,398
Indonesia	—	0.1	. . .	271,810
Philippines	0.1	1.3	2.1	9,625
French Morocco	0.2	5.1	5.6	3,353
Algeria	0.3	8.2	12.5	1,122
Tunisia	0.3	3.0	4.2	2,216
Egypt	0.2	5.4	9.2	657
Northern Rhodesia	—	0.4	1.5	5,337
Southern Rhodesia	—	2.1	5.6	882
Union of South Africa	1.6	30.0	58.0	259
Australia	. . .	76.3	132.0	247
New Zealand	9.6	25.9	34.0	72

Sources: **13,** *passim;* **10,** p. 29; **9,** 1950, p. 184; **8,** p. 42; **7,** *passim.* Data for the beginning of each year.

a. Excludes garden tractors.
b. 1949.

tries with large holdings than in those where smaller farms prevail.

In January 1951 the world as a whole had one tractor per 494 acres of arable land; North America, one per 131 acres; Europe, one per 423 acres; and the USSR, one per 988 acres. Farmers in Latin America had at their disposal one tractor per 1,722 acres; in the Near East, one per 6,333 acres; and in the Far East, one per 31,908 acres. Africa counted one tractor per 4,275 acres while the level of mechanization in Oceania (Australia and New Zealand) was half-

way between that in North America and Europe — one tractor per 208 acres.

The United Kingdom, Switzerland and New Zealand have the largest number of tractors in relation to the area of arable land — about 14 to 18 tractors per 1,000 acres.[200] The United States, the Netherlands, Sweden, Western Germany,

200. In New Zealand, tractors are also used extensively on pasture land covering nearly 30 million acres, and for forestry. Therefore the density of tractors in relation to arable land does not show that New Zealand is reaching the saturation point in tractors. **7,** p. 144.

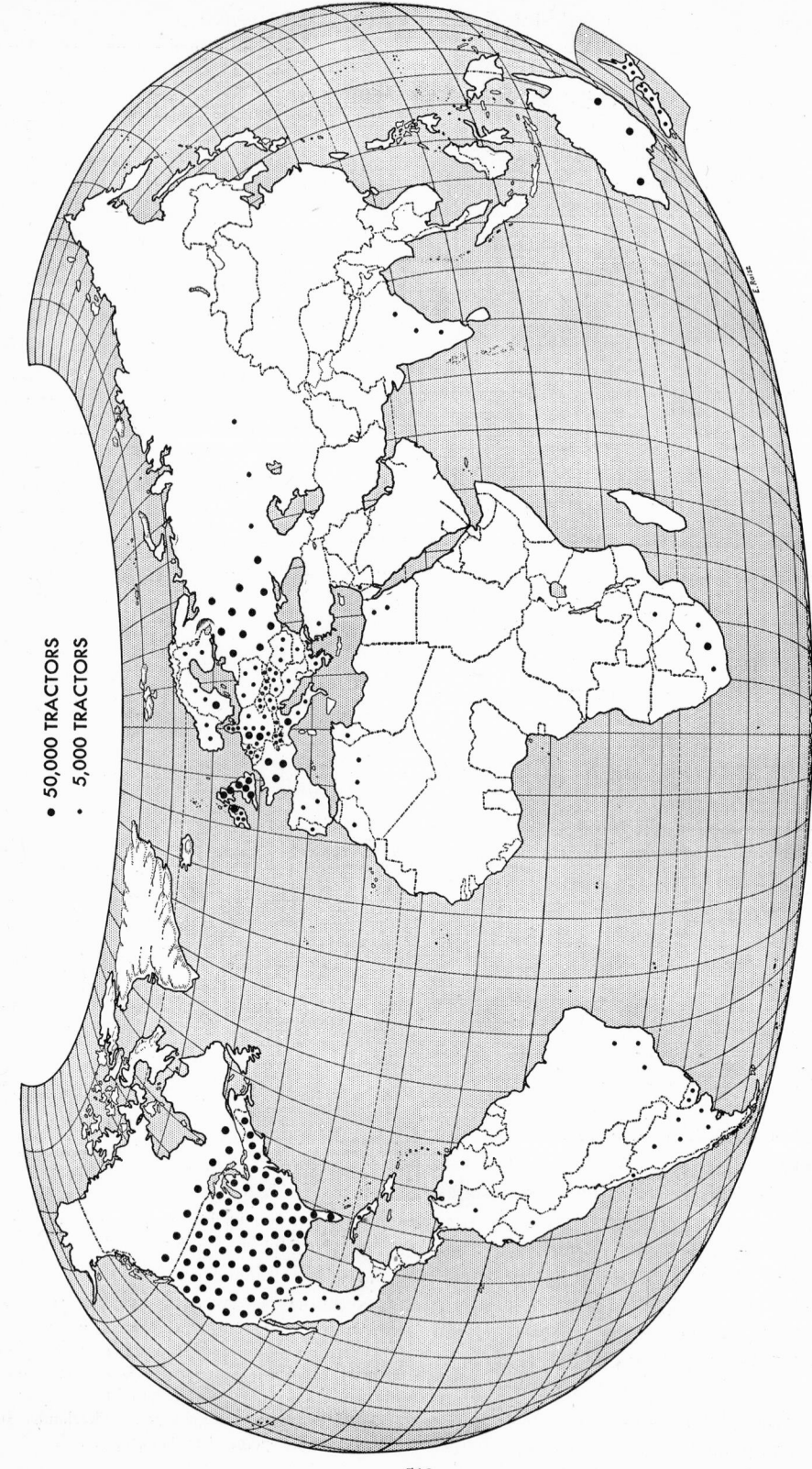

● 50,000 TRACTORS

· 5,000 TRACTORS

FIGURE 158. FARM MECHANIZATION: WORLD DISTRIBUTION OF TRACTORS IN RELATION TO ARABLE LAND, 1951

Italy and Norway are next in line with 5 to 9 tractors per 1,000 acres; they are followed by Ireland, Canada, Australia, the Union of South Africa, Austria, Denmark, Uruguay, Belgium and France (3 to 5 tractors per 1,000 acres). Less than one tractor per 10,000 acres is used in Iraq, Pakistan, India, Syria, Japan, China and Indonesia — an area with more than a billion inhabitants. (See Figure 159.)

FARM MECHANIZATION IN SELECTED COUNTRIES

The United States

The number of tractors on American farms has risen rapidly in the past three decades: [201]

Year	Thousands of Tractors
1910	1
1915	25
1920	246
1925	549
1930	920
1935	1,048
1940	1,545
1945	2,422
1950	3,825

Tractors first displaced horses and mules on the large, level grain farms of the Middle West, excellently suited to their use; later, on medium-sized farms in various parts of the United States. Some states use tractors much more extensively than others. In January 1948 there were 133 tractors per 100 farms in North Dakota, 114 in South Dakota, 109 in Iowa, 102 in Illinois and 98 in Kansas, but only 17 tractors per 100 farms in Georgia, 14 in Kentucky and 12 in Mississippi.[202]

The use of tractors in planting and cultivating corn and cotton came much later than for small grains but usage is developing. In 1938, for example, tractors were used to plant 13 per cent of the corn and 21 per cent of the cotton; in 1946 the corresponding figures were 41 and 43 per cent.[203]

The most significant developments in the tractorization of American farming have been the introduction of rubber tires instead of steel wheels and the appearance of small tractors and small power attachments for farms of 40 acres

or less. The latest important improvement is the adoption of hydraulically operated mounted implements.[204]

The combine-harvester, which also had to wait for the combustion engine to reveal all its advantages,[205] has made great headway on American farms. Until the 1920's, combines were very large and expensive and could be used effectively only on large acreages. Since the middle of the 1930's, midget combines that derive their power from tractors have had the largest use. Recently, self-propelled combines have been introduced and are now increasingly used in larger areas of small grains. In 1920, the United States harvested only 5 per cent of its wheat with combines; in 1938, 50 per cent. In 1945 the American farms counted 440,000 combines; in 1950, 714,450.[206]

Tractors and combines spread from the United States to other countries, especially Canada, Argentina, Australia and the USSR, where the types of farms and the topography invite the use of such machinery. The United States, the largest manufacturer of agricultural machinery, has exported tractors and combines to all parts of the world and has established tractor plants in Canada, Australia, Sweden, France and Great Britain.[207]

Western Europe

In western Europe generally, farm technology is advanced and factory-built equipment of all kinds is widely used. Tractors, however, did not make much headway before World War II, because of the high investment and operating costs they entail, the small size of European farms and the often unsuitable topography. Only some of the larger farms and estates used tractors.

According to the FAO, Europe lost during the war more than 15 per cent of its draft animals, which had normally accounted for about 85 per cent of all farm power.[208] This loss,

201. **27**, 1951, p. 8; **29**, 1950, p. 574.
202. **29**, 1949, pp. 567 and 653.
203. **28**, October 1948, p. 10.

204. **54**, p. 17; **8**, p. 17.
205. The first combine-harvester, drawn by thirty to forty horses, was tried out in California as early as 1880. Later a steam-powered model appeared but also proved disappointing.
206. **41**, 1940, p. 515 and **29**, 1945, p. 460. Economic as well as climatic conditions account for the fact that in 1938 California harvested as much as 95 per cent of its grain with combines; Kansas, 82 per cent, and North Dakota, 23 per cent. **114**, pp. 476–77.
207. For details, see **50**, *passim*. Cf. Chapter 30.
208. **13**, pp. 36–37.

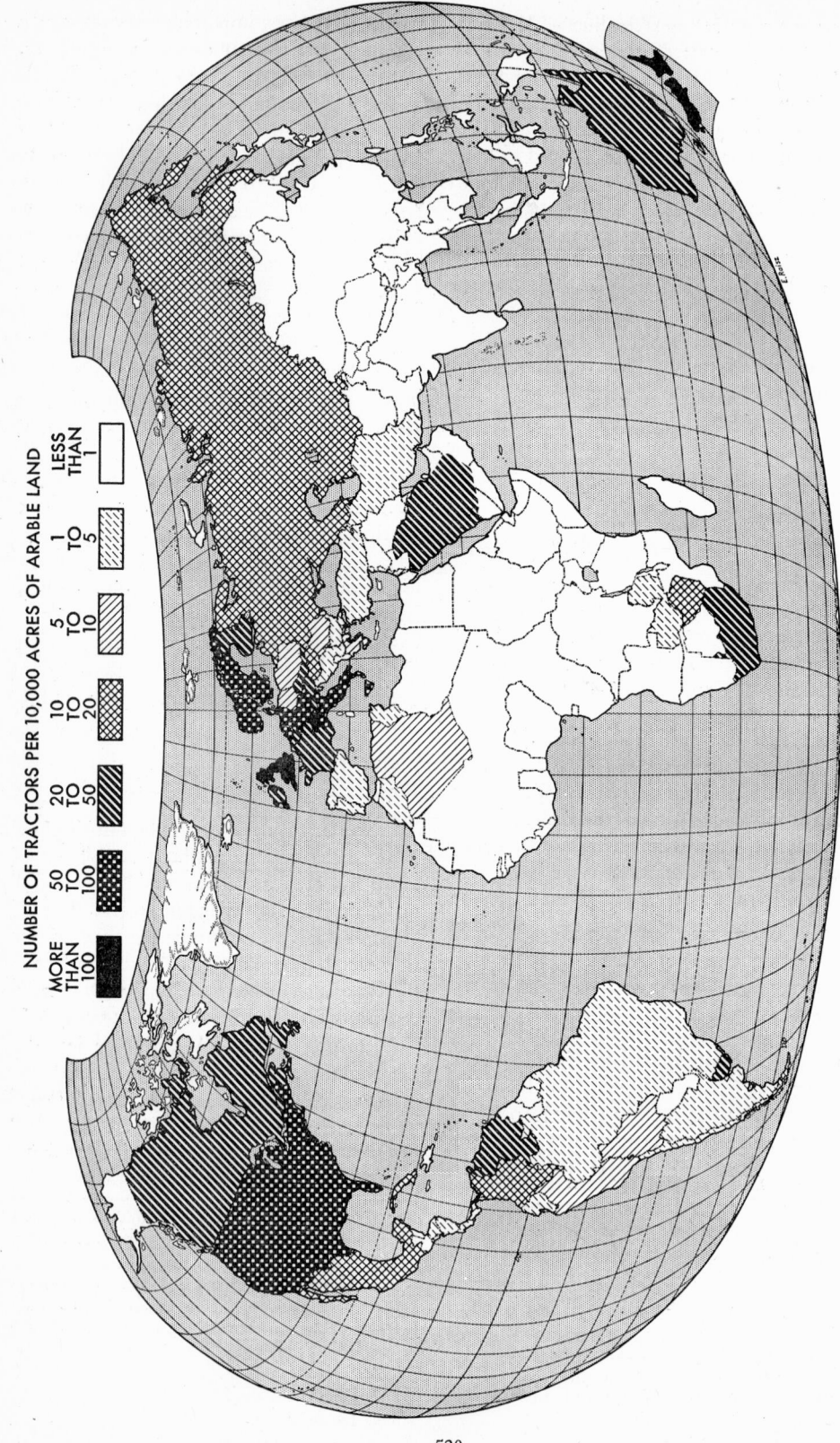

NUMBER OF TRACTORS PER 10,000 ACRES OF ARABLE LAND

| LESS THAN 1 | 1 TO 5 | 5 TO 10 | 10 TO 20 | 20 TO 50 | 50 TO 100 | MORE THAN 100 |

FIGURE 159. FARM MECHANIZATION: DENSITY OF TRACTORS IN THE WORLD, 1951

coupled with the shortage of farm labor and the urgent need to raise more food, focused attention on mechanical power.

Britain's answer to the wartime emergency was to triple the number of tractors, and American industry supplied much of the needed machinery. After the war, the number of tractors in the United Kingdom continued to increase. The generally heavy soil, particularly in land recently put in cultivation, and the short time between rains make it desirable to have greater draft power than animals can provide.[209] Moreover, the shortage of labor in manufacturing and mining made it likely that agricultural workers would continue to shift to jobs in towns and cities. Farmers were encouraged to buy tractors and other farm machinery on credit and a special income tax depreciation allowance of 40 per cent on the initial cost of agricultural equipment was introduced.[210]

By January 1951, Great Britain, with 325,000 tractors, had almost half of all in the Marshall Plan countries — one on nearly every farm — and some people began to wonder whether British agriculture was overmechanized.

France increased the number of tractors from 30,000 in use in 1939 to 135,000 in 1951, and the Monnet Plan envisages bringing the total to about 250,000. This number should release for food crops some 2.5 million acres now needed for the upkeep of draft animals.[211] The use of tractors rose also in Western Germany, the Low Countries, Italy, Scandinavia, Austria, Switzerland, and other countries, doubling in some and increasing even more in others. (See Table 228 and Figure 159.)

In northwestern Europe, the service of tractors, combines and some other expensive farm machinery has long been available under contract. Another practice, particularly in the Scandinavian countries, is to purchase expensive equipment on a cooperative basis. Since the war, many countries have encouraged these practices through governmental loans and subsidies. The United Kingdom, for example, has established an Agricultural Machinery Service, publicly financed and supervised. In 1949 this service had 10,000

tractors and tractor plows, 375 combine-harvesters and many other machines. It operates in sixty-one counties and either works directly for the farmers under contract or rents its machinery to farmers or small contractors. As British farmers obtain additional equipment of their own, this service is being reduced or withdrawn.[212] In many countries of Western Europe, farmers are provided with special credits for the purchase of tractors and taxation on tractor fuel has been reduced; training schools have also been established.[213]

Southeastern Europe

In eastern and southern Europe, farming is generally on a much lower technical level. In Greece, not every farmer had a plow in 1929, only one in six had a harrow, and wooden plows and harrows were more common than those of iron or steel.[214] In Hungary, even big estates sometimes used oxen and wooden plows before World War II. The owners asserted that tractor-plowing was more expensive and actually let tractors lie idle for that reason. In recent years, however, use of mechanical power has increased in southeastern Europe, although in considerable areas the wooden plow persists along with the flail and the winnowing fork, essentially like the implements of primitive areas in Asia and North Africa.[215] The collective and state farms in satellite countries are served by government machine-tractor stations, though a few individual farms may own such equipment. In Greece, the number of tractors in 1949 was considerably larger than before the war, and imports have continued in recent years. However, the level of mechanization in eastern Europe, with a third of all arable land and about a tenth of the tractors in Europe, is still much lower than in the western part of the continent, except for Portugal and Spain.[216] Czechoslovakia, with the most mechanized agriculture among the satellite countries, has one tractor per 469 acres of arable

---

209. **48**, Vol. II, p. 152.
210. **7**, p. 86.
211. **59**, October 1948, p. 34. The Economic Commission for Europe considers that the Monnet Plan underestimated the requirement of French agriculture for tractors. **7**, p. 94.

212. While machinery cooperatives are little developed in North America, the contract use of machinery is widespread. For example, private companies contract to harvest the wheat crop on many farms. Their combines move northward from the southern states as the grain ripens, and then to Canada. (**13**, pp. 34–35 and 45–46.)
213. **7**, p. 29.
214. **68**, 1936, p. 123.
215. **13**, p. 36.
216. **13**, pp. 37–38.

land; Hungary, one per 796 acres and Romania, one per 1,532 acres.[217]

The USSR

Although the USSR built its first tractor plant in 1923, most of the tractors used in Russian agriculture until 1932 were imported from the United States. Then Russia established, with American technical assistance, three new tractor plants — in Stalingrad, Kharkov and Cheliâbinsk — and imports ceased. From 1940 to 1947 about 13,000 tractors were shipped to the USSR by the United States — first for military purposes, and after the end of the war under the auspices of UNRRA.

In 1930 the USSR had 66,332 tractors; in 1939, 483,500. On the eve of the war, the USSR used mechanical power for more than 70 per cent of the plowing, 45–50 per cent of the sowing and harvesting of grain, and 95 per cent of the threshing. The southern and eastern steppe regions (the Ukraine, North Caucasus and Lower Volga) used more mechanical power than the north and west: 90 to 100 per cent of the spring plowing, for example, was done by mechanical power in 1937 in the first group, compared to 40 or less per cent, in the second.[218]

During the war, much mechanized equipment was destroyed. Some tractor plants were also destroyed, others shifted to the production of tanks. In 1946, the USSR had only about 300,000 tractors; most of them were obsolete, others unusable. It has been estimated that all would be obsolete by 1950.[219] During 1946–50, some 264,000 were produced, and as of January 1951, the total supply was estimated at 564,000 units. The Economic Commission for Europe estimates that even if the planned production of tractors during the next five years is fulfilled, the USSR will be short about one million tractors. Inadequate supplies of fuel is a serious problem and until recently the lack of rubber prevented the introduction of pneumatic tires. Track-laying tractors are therefore preferred to wheeled, and this hampers the use of tractors for many purposes.[220]

The number of combines in the USSR (185,-400 units in 1940) has increased since the end of the war. Use is largely dictated by the advantage of controlling the harvest and preventing concealment or theft of grain, rather than for economic reasons. Since harvesting by combines ordinarily leaves no time for the grain to dry between cutting and threshing, and the green weeds cut with the grain often transfer moisture to the kernels, the grain must be dried after it is harvested.[221] Both the number and the quality of dryers in the USSR are inadequate, even on the state farms, and many kolkhozy dry their grain in very primitive ways.[222]

The Soviet government owns practically all the tractors, combines and other agricultural machinery. A small part of this equipment is on state farms, but most of it is in government machine-tractor stations that serve the kolkhozy. The concentration of mechanical farm equipment in its hands provides the government with powerful control of all farm operations.[223]

The Underdeveloped Regions

Manual labor and animal draft power predominate in a large part of the world's farming. In Africa, hand tools are used, and men frequently pull the plow. Only in some areas are animals used for plowing.[224] A major obstacle to replacing the hoe and manual labor is the inability of draft animals to survive in large areas because of disease transmitted by the tsetse fly.[225]

In Chile, wheat is often cut with a sickle and bound by hand.[226] The mattock and spade are the chief agricultural implements of the Indians in Guatemala. Man's first agricultural implement, the digging stick, is still used by the

217. **7**, pp. 5–6.
218. **139**, pp. 55–65; **114**, p. 452.
219. **114**, pp. 454–55.
220. **7**, pp. 107 and 109.

221. **17**, p. 1 and **117**, p. 168.
222. **114**, pp. 179–80. Some kolkhozy have recently found a novel, and apparently workable method, since the official organ of the Ministry of Agriculture of the USSR reports it with commendation. Grain is spread, for drying, on one side of the asphalt-covered highways: "The broad and even highway between Moscow and Riazan stretches for many kilometers. . . . For tens of kilometers the asphalt is covered with a thin layer of grain. . . . It is recommended . . . that the grain be spread so as not to impede traffic." (**76**, August 24, 1950, p. 2.)
223. In Soviet publications, machine-tractor stations are acknowledged to be "one of the most important levers in the hands of the state for the reorganization of the structure of agricultural economy." See, for example, **117**, p. 140.
224. **137**, pp. 25–26.
225. **13**, p. 77.
226. **52**, p. 9.

Maoris in Australia and Bushmen in Africa.[227]

In China, wooden spades and hoes are in common use, and corn is often threshed upon a stone. The Chinese rely today, as they did thousands of years ago, on the sickle for harvesting wheat and on the water buffalo for draft power. If a farmer has no work animal, he or some member of his family pulls the plow.[228]

Yet even in areas where the digging stick and the wooden plow of biblical times are the principal farm implements, tractors and combines are operating successfully in increasing numbers.[229] In Egypt, for example, a tractor or combine or disk plow may be seen alongside a hoe, hand sickle or wooden plow. In Turkey, the barren soil of the Malaye Desert, which had never been plowed, is now cultivated with the use of the most modern machinery, practically all American-made.[230]

"Tractor mindedness" has never been as intense as at present, and despite all the difficulties the tendency to greater use of mechanical power is bound to prevail in world farming.

ECONOMIC AND SOCIAL EFFECTS OF FARM MECHANIZATION

The use of machinery and mechanical power on farms depends on so many factors that it may offer great advantages under some conditions and be much less important under others. Topography and the size of the farm may be conducive to mechanization or may make it difficult. Fragmentation of land militates against mechanization or at least lessens its effectiveness. Cost of machinery and its maintenance, the availability and price of fuel and spare parts, lack of skill in proper handling and, in particular, repair of the machine when it breaks down are serious problems in many countries. Agricultural overpopulation in areas where there are few other work opportunities discourages the use of mechanical power. Moreover, in areas of subsistence farming draft animals are kept not only for power but also for transport and food.

While the use of tractors, combines and other machinery has been spreading at a much faster rate since World War II than before, the time is still distant when mechanical power will displace animal and human labor on farms in the world at large to the extent it has displaced them in the United States, the USSR and the United Kingdom. More use of machines can be expected wherever particularly heavy work is required as, for example, clearing jungles in India and Brazil, or breaking dry soil with tough roots in Africa and the Middle East.[231]

In general, a mechanized farm becomes more and more a commercial unit, less dependent on hazards of weather but increasingly dependent on market hazards and the business cycle. At the same time, it is knit more closely into the industrial system.

Farmers once did the whole job with their hands, perhaps aided by animals they raised and fed. In our day, industry participates indirectly in producing agricultural raw materials by supplying the farmer with machinery, chemical fertilizers and the like.[232] In a country with highly mechanized agriculture, the production of food actually begins in the coal and iron ore mines, in oil wells, refineries and steel-rolling mills. It is carried forward in factories where trucks, tractors and agricultural machines are built, and fertilizers, dusts and sprays manufactured. The farmer is only a link in the chain that stretches through food-processing plants, wholesalers and retailers to the consumer.

In the United States the ever-growing use of mechanical power on the farms has had many and far-reaching consequences. Fewer and fewer workers have been needed to produce the same amount of crops: between 1800 and 1940, the number of man-hours required to produce 100 bushels of wheat dropped from 373 to 47; of corn, from 344 to 83; of a bale of cotton, from 601 to 191.[233] Savings in human labor have released many millions of farm workers for factory jobs. The number of persons at home and abroad whom one American farm worker could supply with agricultural products rose from 4.5 in 1820 to 14.5 in 1940.[234]

At the same time the number of draft horses and mules on farms decreased from 26.7 million in 1918 to 14.8 million in 1939, and 7.5 million in 1950. (See Figure 160.) Further decrease is certain.[235]

227. **32**, September 1949, p. 203.
228. **121**, p. 754.
229. **5**, Part II, p. 4.
230. **32**, December 1948, pp. 268–70.

231. **13**, pp. 16–22.
232. **124**, p. 43.
233. **41**, 1943–47, p. 921 and **115**, p. 256.
234. **95**, p. 5.
235. The number of colts is far short of that needed to replace the normal death rate, let alone to offset the

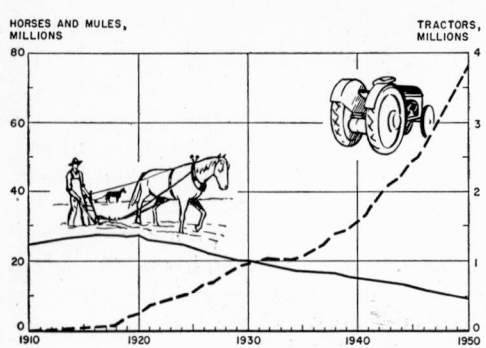

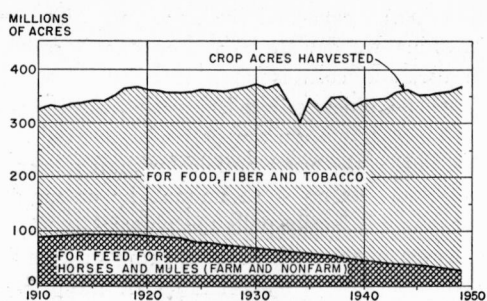

U. S. Department of Agriculture

FIGURE 161. FARM MECHANIZATION: CHANGES IN THE
DISTRIBUTION OF ACREAGE IN THE UNITED
STATES, 1910-50

U. S. Department of Agriculture

FIGURE 160. FARM MECHANIZATION: DRAFT ANIMALS
AND TRACTORS IN THE UNITED STATES, 1910-50

This decline has released for food crops and fibers more than 65 million acres previously used to produce feed. (See Figure 161.) The continuing decrease in draft animals releases about 2 million additional acres of cropland each year.[236]

Mechanization of agriculture is changing the social structure of the farm population and the relationship between farming and industry. The large investment required in modern farming makes it difficult for a farm laborer or tenant to climb the agricultural ladder, despite the fact that wages of farm workers in countries with mechanized agriculture are much higher than in areas where hand methods predominate.

RURAL ELECTRIFICATION

While the New World has led in the introduction of mechanical power on farms, it has lagged in a related modern development in farm operation — rural electrification.

The United States

In 1925, only 3.2 per cent of the farms of the United States were electrified; in 1935, only 10.9 per cent. Since the private utility companies, controlling more than 90 per cent of the electric power industry in the country, had not found it advantageous to extend their lines into rural areas, the government began an intensive program of rural electrification in 1935. By 1940, the number of electrified farms had risen from

744,000 to 1.7 million; by 1945, to 2.7 million. In 1950, 5.1 million farms out of a total 5.9 million were electrified.[237]

Densely populated industrial states in the East and on the Pacific coast, where hydroelectric power has been greatly developed in recent decades, are more completely served than some states in the South and on the Great Plains. The range is between 99.9 per cent in Connecticut and Rhode Island and 55.6 per cent in North Dakota. In the country as a whole, 86.3 per cent of all farms received central station service in June 1950 and only nine states had less than 75 per cent of farms with this service. (See Figure 162.) Farms in the West use, on the average, nearly two and a half times as much electric current as those east of the 100th meridian because of the high consumption of energy for irrigation pumping.

European Countries

In rural electrification, the United States has only recently been catching up with the countries of western Europe. Even before World War II, electricity had been carried to more than 55 per cent of the farms in Norway, 65 per cent in Sweden, 85 per cent in Denmark, 90 per cent in Germany, 90-95 per cent in Italy and to practically every farm in the Netherlands and Switzerland.[238]

Progress in rural electrification in both Europe and North America has generally gone hand in hand with density of population. Where rural communities are close to industrial areas or large towns and cities, they have had no special difficulties in being connected with power lines;

---

record slaughter of horses in 1947 and 1948. (**28**, March 1949, p. 3.)

236. **27**, 1951, p. 9. In the United States and western Europe, about 3 acres are needed to support a draft animal. (**13**, p. 19.)

237. **35**, 1950, p. 14.
238. **51**, p. 98 and **41**, 1940, p. 791.

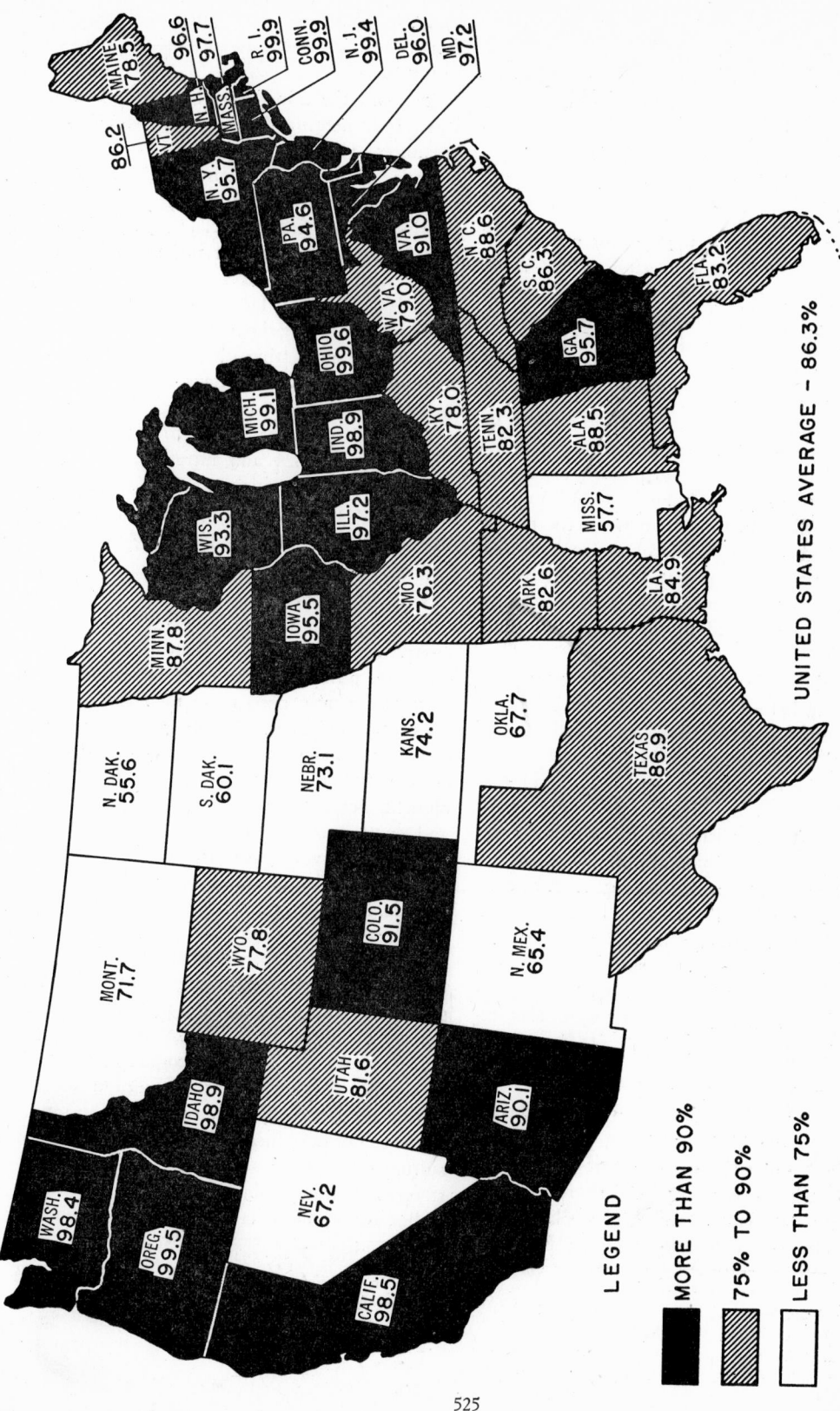

MAINE 78.5
96.6
97.7
R. I. 99.9
CONN. 99.9
N. J. 99.4
DEL. 96.0
MD. 97.2
86.2
N. H.
MASS.
N. Y. 95.7
PA. 94.6
VA. 91.0
N. C. 88.6
S. C. 86.3
FLA. 83.2
W. VA. 79.0
OHIO 99.6
GA. 95.7
MICH. 99.1
IND. 98.9
KY. 78.0
TENN. 82.3
ALA. 88.5
WIS. 93.3
ILL. 97.2
IOWA 95.5
MO. 76.3
ARK. 82.6
MISS. 57.7
LA. 84.9
MINN. 87.8
N. DAK. 55.6
S. DAK. 60.1
NEBR. 73.1
KANS. 74.2
OKLA. 67.7
TEXAS 86.9
COLO. 91.5
N. MEX. 65.4
MONT. 71.7
WYO. 77.8
UTAH 81.6
ARIZ. 90.1
IDAHO 98.9
WASH. 98.4
OREG. 99.5
NEV. 67.2
CALIF. 98.5

LEGEND

MORE THAN 90%

75% TO 90%

LESS THAN 75%

UNITED STATES AVERAGE – 86.3%

U. S. Department of Agriculture

FIGURE 162. PROPORTION OF FARMS ELECTRIFIED IN THE UNITED STATES, MIDYEAR, 1950

In the northeastern part of the United States (except for Maine and Vermont), in the Middle Atlantic and Great Lakes areas and along the Pacific Coast, all states have electricity on more than 90 per cent of all farms. The states where rural electrification is least prevalent—from 56 to 75 per cent of all farms—extend from North Dakota southward through Oklahoma and also include Montana, Nevada and New Mexico

villages in sparsely inhabited areas cannot afford the high costs of extending the lines and the high rates of commercial service. In this respect, conditions in Europe have been much more favorable for rural electrification than in the United States.

The USSR

Rural electrification has made little progress in the USSR, where the capacity of all rural electric stations was only 66,000 kilowatts in 1940.[239] In 1937, 8,500 kolkhozy with 600,000 households had electric service. The third Four-Year Plan envisaged building 6,000 small stations with a capacity of 800,000 kilowatts,[240] but the war interrupted the work and resulted in the destruction of many existing power stations. The postwar Four-Year Plan projects expansion of the electric supply on farms to 2.3 million kilowatts. All or most of the new electric power is to be produced in small local stations operated by water power, with peat or even by wind, since supplies of oil and of coal, except possibly lignite, are too limited to permit use for rural electrification.[241]

A number of small rural plants were constructed in 1946–49 but only 30,000 collective farms, out of more than 250,000, had electric power at the beginning of 1950. Most of the kolkhozy in the Moscow and Leningrad districts and all in the Sverdlovsk district were provided with electricity; in many other areas electrification still remained in the offing.

It was planned to raise the proportion of electrified kolkhozy to 15 per cent by the end of 1950 and to increase the use of electric power for various farm operations, such as milking of cows and clipping of sheep. Successful experiments with 30 electric tractors were also reported.[242]

FERTILIZERS

The era of artificial fertilizers actually began in 1840, when Justus von Liebig published the results of his experiments on plant growth. He showed that there is a chemical relationship between the soil and plants and that plants need certain elements which they extract from the soil, such as potash, phosphorus and soda, and from the air, such as carbon dioxide and nitrogen.

At about the same time, Sir John B. Lawes was experimenting in England with various "manures" (including bone dust, guano, nitrate of soda, potassium and ammonium salts) for potted plants. In 1842 he patented superphosphate, the first artificial fertilizer in the world, having produced it by treating ground bones with sulfuric acid. The next year he erected a fertilizer factory at Rothamsted in England. The experiments carried out in the laboratories and testing grounds of Rothamsted for more than a century have made this center world famous.

The United States began to import guano from Peru in 1824 and nitrate of soda from Chile in 1830. Domestic production of phosphate fertilizers started about 1850, with the application of Lawes's process to phosphate rock.[243]

Major Fertilizers

The three indispensable soil fertilizing elements are nitrogen, phosphate and potash.[244] Of these, nitrogen is the most important, since plants frequently need more than the soil supplies. Its function is to promote the growth of stems and leaves. Phosphates give the plant a good start and greatly promote its root development. Potash strengthens resistance to disease and encourages the growth of plant cells, the formation of various essential plant substances and the capacity of leaves to assimilate carbon dioxide. Nitrogen, phosphates and potassium are complementary, rather than competitive. Soil, climate and the properties of the crop determine the proper proportion of one to another at a given time and place and the practical limits to the use of any of them.[245]

Nevertheless, it is now recognized, from innumerable tests at various agricultural stations during the last twenty-five years that the return to the soil of only the three major fertilizers plus sulfur and sometimes calcium does not fully restore its nutrient balance. Many carefully controlled experiments have shown that when any

239. **114**, p. 475.
240. **75**, pp. 5–9.
241. **114**, p. 475.
242. **139**, p. 69.

243. **41**, 1943–47, p. 554.
244. In addition, many "trace" elements are important for plant life, among them iron, manganese, copper or boron.
245. **8**, p. 5.

necessary nutrient element is lacking, be it only a trace element, the plant responds by accumulating increased quantities of some other elements. Inversely, an increased supply of one element leads to a smaller accumulation of some other by the plant. Thus, if a maximum return from cropland is to be achieved, a proper balance must be maintained not only among the major nutrients but between them and trace elements in the soil. This requires integration and application of all available knowledge, still not fully adequate, of the requirements of each crop, the supply of nutrients in the soil and the effects of the rate of added supply of each element on the accumulation and function of all other elements in the plant.[246]

The main minerals from which the three major fertilizers are made are: for nitrogen, nitrate salts from Chile; for phosphates, phosphatic rock from the United States, North Africa, Oceania; and for potash, potassium deposits, of which the largest are in Germany.

During World War I, Germany was cut off from the nitrogen supplies of Chile and began synthetic production of nitrogen compounds through the fixation of atmospheric nitrogen. After the war, synthetic production spread to other countries, and new methods were discovered to obtain nitrogen from the air. This was a crucial development for world agriculture, since it opened up an inexhaustible source of this irreplaceable plant food: the supply in the air is practically limitless — about 35,000 tons per acre of the earth's surface.[247] Raw materials to produce phosphates and potash are also plentiful in the world.[248]

It is difficult to measure the exact effect of fertilizers on the yield per acre since countries using more fertilizer are often also advanced in other fields of agricultural technology. It is estimated roughly that a ton of nitrogen increases the cereal yield per acre by 12 to 15 tons. It may increase the output by as much as 20 tons if the appropriate balance of soluble phosphate and potash is used.[249]

The science of soil fertilization has made great progress since Liebig's discoveries. Although he considered the amount of certain mineral elements most important, he overlooked the biological and dynamic processes operating in the soil and in plants. Modern science aims to use fertilizers to modify the microbiological content of the soil as well as to enrich it.

Artificial versus Natural Fertilizers

Whether commercial fertilizers are more effective than farmyard manure is an open question. Apparently soil will not accept indiscriminate amounts of commercial fertilizers, but neither will it take farmyard manure indiscriminately. As far as can be ascertained from prolonged observation, the effect of farmyard manure is more even and lasting, while the reaction of the soil to commercial fertilizers is very strong at first but gradually falls off. Moreover, manure improves the texture of the soil and restores humus.[250] In the United States, and elsewhere to a lesser extent, the amount of available manure on farms has considerably decreased since the introduction of tractors, making the application of commercial plant food more necessary than before.

Consumption of Fertilizers

Before World War II, the world's farmers outside of the USSR consumed, on the average, about 8.1 million tons of commercial fertilizers a year (in terms of nitrogen, phosphate and potash content). Close to two thirds of the total was fed to the soil of Europe, followed by North and Middle America, together taking about 19 per cent and Asia, with 11 per cent. Much smaller quantities were used in other parts of the world.

Europe. In recent years, the need for fertilizers has become particularly acute in Europe and other areas where the soil suffered during the war from both lack of nutrients and more intensive cropping. Moreover, the decline in livestock has resulted in a substantial decrease in farmyard manure, in some countries by as much as 50 per cent. The available manure is also less effective because the animals get less feed.

All continents have increased consumption of commercial fertilizers since 1946. The total used in the world rose from an average of 8.1 million

246. **41**, 1943–47, pp. 592–601.
247. **40**, pp. 169–70.
248. See Chapters 22 and 31.
249. **47**, p. 43 and **8**, p. 3.

250. The opinion of the late Sir Alfred D. Hall of Rothamsted is that, given equal amounts of nutrients, manure is less effective in increasing crop yield despite its other beneficial effects on the soil. (**104**, p. 190.)

TABLE 229

FERTILIZERS: CONSUMPTION OF COMMERCIAL PLANT FOOD BY CONTINENT, 1936–38 AND 1950–51

| | Consumption, in Thousands of Metric Tons [a] | | | | | | | | Percentage Distribution | |
| | 1936–38 Average | | | | 1950–51 | | | | | |
Continent	Total	Nitro-gen	Phos-phate	Potash	Total	Nitro-gen	Phos-phate	Potash	Prewar	1950–51
World [b]	8,131	2,283	3,507	2,341	13,446	3,887	5,648	3,911	100.0	100.0
North and Middle America	1,511	380	714	417	3,962	1,026	1,912	1,023	18.6	29.5
South America	64	32	22	10	184	65	93	26	0.8	1.4
Europe	5,110	1,297	2,043	1,770	7,124	1,872	2,600	2,652	62.8	53.0
Asia	890	470	302	118	1,287	767	360	160	10.9	9.5
Africa	173	87	75	11	309	131	144	34	2.1	2.3
Oceania	383	17	351	15	581	25	539	17	4.7	4.3

Sources: **12**, p. 14 and **11**, pp. 16–17 and 20–23.   b. Excludes the USSR.

   a. Conversion factor: one metric ton = 1.1023 short tons.

tons a year during 1936–38 to 13.4 million during 1950–51. The increase in North and Middle America was 160 per cent; in Europe and Oceania, about 40 and 50 per cent, respectively, and in Asia, 45 per cent. North and Middle America [251] now account for 30 per cent of the world's consumption, as against 19 per cent before the war; Europe, for 53 per cent, as compared with its prewar 63 per cent. (See Table 229.)

The Netherlands has been and still is the world's largest consumer of commercial plant food per acre of arable land. Land there is so scarce, yet so responsive to intensive feeding and is devoted so preponderantly to horticulture that the Dutch farmers use fertilizers abundantly, coaxing from their soil the highest yields in the world. (See Table 230.)

Asia. Japan has led all other Asiatic countries in the use of commercial fertilizers, chiefly because of pressure on land. With only 15 million acres of arable land and 8 million acres suited only for grazing, Japan has 83 million people. Land rents have been seven times as much as in England, and tenants have had to supply seed, fertilizers and implements and to pay all assessments and dues and erect their own houses. Clearly, they needed to wrest everything possible from the soil.[252] Moreover, a large part of the

land in Japan carries two crops a year and thus requires more fertilization than land used for only one crop.

The United States. Before the war the United States consumed less commercial plant food per acre of arable land than any country in western Europe. Its demand for fertilizers was concentrated chiefly in the cotton and tobacco states of the South, where soil suffers from the one-crop system and is subject to leaching, and in the fruit-growing states of Florida and California. American agricultural experts consider that, on the whole, not enough plant food was supplied to the soil each year to restore the organic matter lost. The annual soil loss in nitrogen was estimated at 4.3 million tons, in potassium at 31.4 million, in calcium 39.8 million and in organic matter at 222 million tons. (See Table 231.)

During the war the United States used commercial fertilizers increasingly and many farmers employed them for the first time. The consumption of mixed commercial fertilizers rose from an annual average of 7.3 million tons during 1935–39 to more than 11.7 million in 1943. The rise continued after the war and in 1948 the country used nearly two and a half times as much mixed fertilizers as a decade before. (See Table 232.)

Though consumption increased everywhere, the rate of increase varied greatly among the states. The increase in the yearly consumption of

---

251. Middle America consumes only small quantities of fertilizers, and some countries there use almost none.
252. **125**, p. 119.

mixed commercial fertilizers has been especially great in the Middle West: [253]

State	Thousands of Short Tons 1935–39 Annual Average	1948
United States	7,310	17,596
Illinois	44	973
Wisconsin	39	398
Minnesota	12	252
Iowa	9	368
North Dakota	0.5	22
South Dakota	0.2	10
Nebraska	1	38
Kansas	12	113

TABLE 230

FERTILIZERS: CONSUMPTION OF COMMERCIAL PLANT FOOD IN SELECTED COUNTRIES, BEFORE WORLD WAR II

Country [a]	Plant Food, in Pounds Per Acre of Arable Land			
	Total	Nitro-gen	Phos-phate	Potash
Netherlands	300.3	56.5	91.7	152.2
Belgium	158.7	41.8	65.0	51.8
New Zealand	124.9	4.7	112.8	7.5
Germany	96.0	26.3	26.0	43.7
Japan	86.8	37.4	34.4	15.1
Switzerland	64.1	69.6	42.8	14.4
United Kingdom	53.0	8.7	31.1	13.0
Denmark	46.8	13.6	22.5	10.8
Norway	39.0	7.6	15.3	16.1
Egypt	33.5	29.8	3.7	0.1
France	33.2	6.7	15.3	11.3
Sweden	30.2	6.6	12.1	11.4
Peru	28.3	12.0	10.2	6.1
Ireland	28.0	4.6	18.3	5.1
Portugal	26.7	8.6	17.6	0.5
Italy	24.1	1.5	9.5	3.2
Australia	19.4	0.9	17.8	0.6
Finland	18.1	2.7	9.9	5.4
Spain	16.9	5.9	9.4	1.6
Czechoslovakia	15.4	3.6	7.4	4.3
Austria	12.2	2.3	5.8	4.1
United States	8.8	2.1	4.4	2.3
Union of South Africa	8.4	1.4	6.4	0.4
Poland	6.8	1.2	1.6	3.9
Canada	2.7	0.5	1.2	0.9
USSR	2.7	0.5	1.5	0.6
Mexico	0.5	0.5	—	—
Brazil	0.2	0.2	—	—

Source: **34**, p. 56.

a. Arrayed according to total consumption of plant food.

PRODUCTIVITY IN AGRICULTURE

The farmer in Belgium or the Netherlands worries chiefly about the scarcity and high cost of land; the farmer in the New World, about the scarcity and high cost of labor. The European farmer has achieved and maintained the highest yield per acre on his small patches of

TABLE 231

FERTILIZERS: ANNUAL BALANCE SHEET OF THE SOIL IN THE UNITED STATES, BEFORE WORLD WAR II

(Millions of Short Tons)

Plant Nutrients	Gross Loss [a]	Plant Nutrients Added [b]	Net Loss
Nitrogen	16.1	11.8	4.3
Phosphorus	2.5	1.1	1.4
Potassium	36.2	4.8	31.4
Calcium	53.6	13.8	39.8
Magnesium	16.8	4.6	12.2
Sulfur	11.3	8.7	2.6
Organic matter	322.0	100.0	222.0

Source: **98**, p. 209.

a. Through crop harvests, grazing, pastures, leaching and erosion.

b. Through artificial fertilizers, crop residues, manure, rainfall and irrigation waters and nitrogen fixation.

TABLE 232

FERTILIZERS: CONSUMPTION OF COMMERCIAL FERTILIZERS IN THE UNITED STATES,[a] 1929–49

(Thousands of Short Tons)

Year	All Ferti-lizers	Plant Food [b]			
		Total	Nitro-gen	Phos-phoric Acid	Potash
1929	8,208	1,464	352	774	338
1932	4,545	817	212	413	192
1934	5,794	1,067	275	530	262
1936	7,222	1,373	350	673	350
1938	7,758	1,521	384	744	393
1940	8,656	1,771	420	915	436
1942	10,131	2,076	398	1,131	547
1944	13,330	2,692	635	1,408	649
1946	16,087	3,279	756	1,671	852
1948	17,596	3,640	841	1,842	957
1949	18,000	3,816	882	1,890	1,044

Source: **29**, 1950, p. 652.

a. Includes Hawaii and Puerto Rico.
b. Average plant food content.

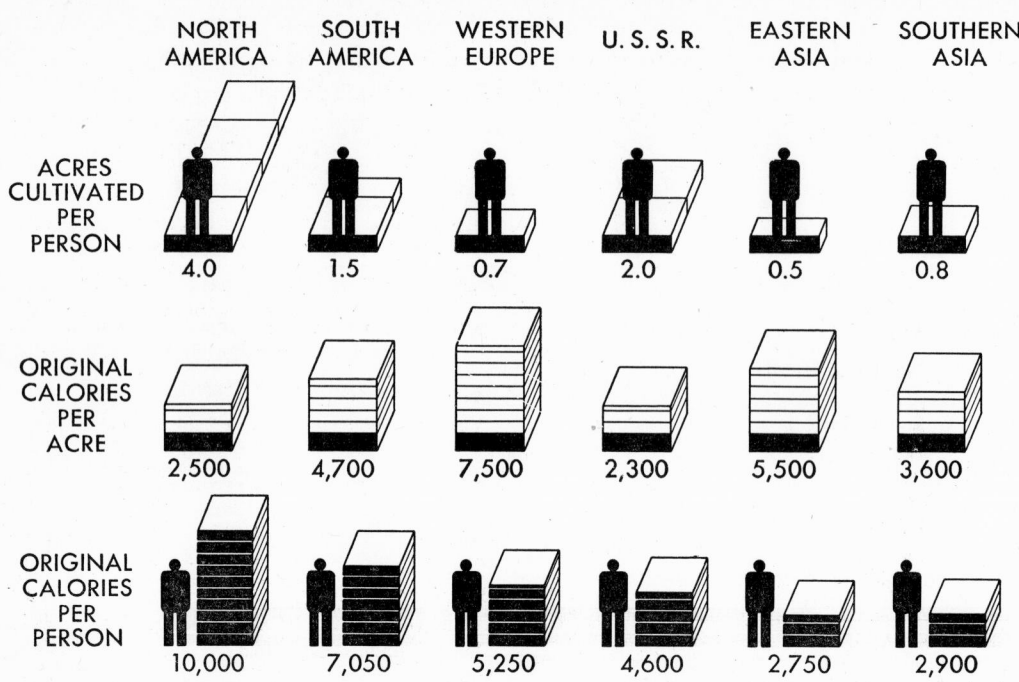

	NORTH AMERICA	SOUTH AMERICA	WESTERN EUROPE	U. S. S. R.	EASTERN ASIA	SOUTHERN ASIA
ACRES CULTIVATED PER PERSON	4.0	1.5	0.7	2.0	0.5	0.8
ORIGINAL CALORIES PER ACRE	2,500	4,700	7,500	2,300	5,500	3,600
ORIGINAL CALORIES PER PERSON	10,000	7,050	5,250	4,600	2,750	2,900

Food and Agriculture Organization

FIGURE 163. AGRICULTURAL PRODUCTIVITY: FOOD OUTPUT PER CAPITA OF POPULATION AND PER ACRE IN SELECTED AREAS, BEFORE WORLD WAR II

North America, with technical resources and land, follows an extensive type of farming. It has four acres of cultivated land per capita of population and obtains 2,500 original calories, on the average, from each acre, so that its total output per capita amounts to 10,000 original calories. South America, with only 1.5 acres of cultivated land per capita, produces 4,700 original calories per acre and 7,050 original calories per capita. Western Europe, with only 0.7 acre of cultivated land per capita, farms more intensively and produces 7,500 original calories per acre and 5,250 per person. In eastern Asia, which has few technical resources and even less farm land than Europe (0.5 acre of cultivated land per capita), cultivation is also fairly intensive, and yields 5,500 original calories per acre, but the output of food furnishes only 2,750 original calories per capita.

land,[254] while the United States, Canada, Argentina and Australia have the largest output per worker in agriculture and per capita of total population. Figure 163 illustrates this difference in terms of so-called original calories.[255]

RANKING OF THE CONTINENTS

The FAO has estimated that Europe led the continents in 1936 in the yield of the eight major crops per acre, expressed in terms of the wheat equivalent.[256] South America and Asia ranked second and third, while North and Middle America and Oceania tied for the next place. Africa was far behind them. In 1947–48, North and Middle America held the first place, followed by South America and Europe. Asia and Oceania were on an equal footing. The change was due largely to the exceptionally poor harvest in Europe in 1947, but also to the spectacular improvement in agricultural practices in the United States and Canada, the two major producers of crops in North (and Middle) America.

In output per capita of the agricultural population, Oceania is first in livestock and South America ranks second; North and Middle America considered together, are first in crop production, outdistancing Oceania and even more, Europe. Asia and Africa have an extremely low output per capita, particularly in crops. (See Table 233.)

254. The situation is similar in Egypt where the pressure of the population on land is very heavy: the yield per acre is extremely high, that per man extremely low. (**55**, September 1949, p. 203.)

255. When crops are fed to animals instead of being consumed directly by human beings, they lose 80 to 90 per cent of their caloric value before they emerge in the form of meat and milk. About seven *original* calories (calories yielded by crops) are required to produce one calorie in the animal products. (**18**, p. 19.)

256. The conversion factor based on calories was: wheat, 100; rye, 95.8; barley, 64.8; oats, 58.4; corn, 106.3; rice, 82.9; raw sugar, 105.4; potatoes, 21.0. (**20**, September 1949, p. 4.)

TABLE 233

AGRICULTURAL PRODUCTIVITY: OUTPUT PER ACRE AND PER CAPITA OF AGRICULTURAL POPULATION, BY CONTINENT, 1936 AND 1947–48

| Continent | Crop [a] Output Per Acre, in Metric Quintals of Wheat Equivalent | | Output Per Capita of Agricultural Population | | | |
| | | | Crops, in Quintals of Wheat Equivalent | | Livestock, in Units [b] | |
	1936	1947–48	1936	1947–48	1936	1947–48
World [c]	5.0	5.3	4.2	4.2	0.51	0.48
North and Middle America	4.3	6.1	18.0	25.7	1.58	1.63
South America	5.2	5.6	5.8	4.8	1.94	1.87
Europe	6.1	5.4	10.4	8.8	0.82	0.70
Asia	5.1	4.9	2.4	2.2	0.25	0.23
Africa	3.1	3.0	1.2	1.2	0.51	0.54
Oceania	4.3	4.9	19.4	23.8	8.04	7.92

Source: **20**, September 1949, p. 4.

a. Eight crops supplying more than 85 per cent of the world's food intake. Conversion factors (calorie basis): wheat, 100; rye, 95.8; barley, 64.8; oats, 58.4; corn, 106.3; rice, 82.9; raw sugar, 105.4; potatoes, 21.0. One metric quintal of wheat = 3.67 bushels.

b. Conversion factors: cattle, 0.8; pigs, 0.2; sheep, 0.1.

c. Excludes the USSR.

AGRICULTURAL PRODUCTIVITY IN THE UNITED STATES

Until recent years, improvement in yield per acre in the United States was slow and uncertain; for most crops, productivity in 1926–35 was only slightly above that in 1866–75. Progress did not accelerate until World War II, when American farmers were called upon to produce food not only for their own country but also for much of the world, and agricultural technology was used intensively. More has been achieved in a few recent years than in the preceding threescore.

The yield per acre of every important crop was considerably larger in 1948 than in 1926–35; corn yielded 42.8 bushels per acre as against 23.9; wheat, 18.0 and 13.8 bushels, respectively; oats, 37.1 and 27.7 bushels, respectively. The potato yield per acre nearly doubled, and that of cotton rose by nearly 80 per cent. (See Table 234.)

Gains in the over-all output per agricultural worker in the United States have been more continuous. For agricultural production as a whole, farm output per man-hour in 1949 was twice that of 40 years earlier as is shown by the following index (1935–39 annual average = 100):[257]

1910	74
1915	80
1920	81
1925	82
1930	87
1935	96
1940	112
1945	134
1949	151

(See Figure 164.)

Before World War I, it took about 35 manhours to grow and harvest an acre of corn; 15.2 hours an acre of wheat and 15.7 hours for an acre of oats. In 1945–48 the labor requirements were 23.7, 6.1 and 8.1 hours, respectively. The drop would have been greater if the yield had not increased. The combined effect of fewer hours and more bushels per acre has resulted in more than halving labor requirements per unit of production. The number of man-hours required in 1910-14 per 100 bushels of corn was 135, of wheat, 106 and of oats, 53; in 1945–48, the corresponding figures were 67, 34 and 23 hours, respectively.[258] It is estimated that productivity per man on farms in the United States is about four and a half times that in the USSR.[259]

THE AGRICULTURAL OUTLOOK

Although no exact and strictly comparable data are available for the world's agricultural out-

257. **27**, 1951, p. 5.

258. **105**, pp. 9 and 11. See also **46**, pp. 2–5.
259. **114**, p. 17.

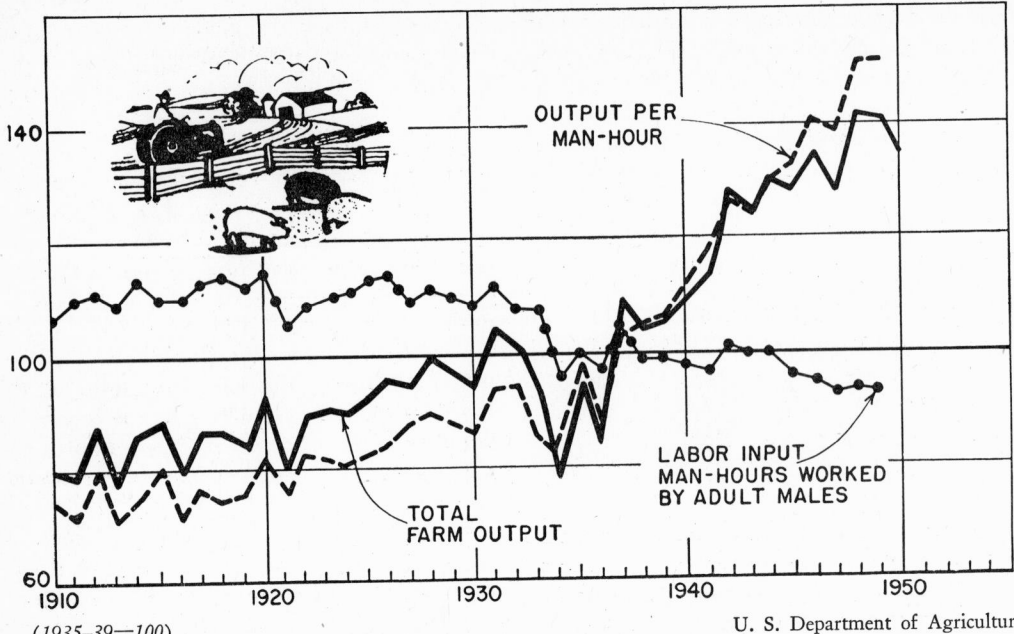

(1935–39=100)   U. S. Department of Agriculture

FIGURE 164. AGRICULTURAL PRODUCTIVITY: INDEXES OF FARM OUTPUT AND LABOR INPUT IN THE
UNITED STATES, 1910–50

put from 1850 to 1950, it is fairly certain that
the increase in output has been more rapid than
the growth of world population. The diet of the
population in a steadily growing number of

TABLE 234

AGRICULTURAL PRODUCTIVITY: ANNUAL YIELD OF
SELECTED CROPS IN THE UNITED STATES,
1866–75 TO 1950

(*Bushels per Acre*)

Period or Year	Corn	Wheat	Oats	Potatoes	Cotton[a]
1866–75	25.6	12.3	26.5	86.9	162.6
1876–85	26.2	13.0	27.5	83.5	172.2
1886–95	25.4	13.7	26.8	81.2	181.5
1896–1905	27.1	13.8	29.7	88.1	190.6
1906–15	27.0	14.8	29.2	99.7	191.5
1916–25	26.5	13.5	30.6	101.9	160.5
1926–35	23.9	13.8	27.7	111.1	179.3
1940	28.4	15.3	35.2	133.1	252.5
1946	36.7	17.2	34.7	186.3	234.5
1948	42.8	18.0	37.1	215.5	311.2
1950	37.4	16.1	36.1	240.7	269.0

Source: **45**, 1952, pp. 615–17.

a. Pounds.

countries has improved appreciably.[260] While
malnutrition is still common in large areas of
the world, famines are no longer common or
customary. The crucial question of mankind is
whether the future yield of world agriculture
will keep pace with the steadily growing population and rising demand for cereals, and vegetable
and animal products.

Future Demand for Food

The world's population may be close to 3,250
million by A.D. 2000. The rate of increase is
expected to be greatest in Asia, where most of
mankind lives, but considerable increase is also
expected in South America, Africa and the
USSR.[261]

An increase from 2.4 to 3.3 billion in the next
fifty years obviously requires a proportionate increase in food, if the present level of nutrition
is to be maintained. A billion additional guests
will press their way to nature's table. Their
number alone makes it necessary to increase the
number of seats at this table and the amount of
food by 46 per cent. However, neither the new
guests nor the old will be satisfied if they are
served just as people are now served. In many

260. See Chapter 8.
261. See Chapter 7.

areas the average diet today is inadequate both in the number of calories and in the composition of the caloric intake. (See Chapter 9.)

The target set by the FAO for a better and more balanced nutrition pattern throughout the world would require the following increases by 1960:[262]

Food	*Percentage Increase*
Cereals	21
Roots and tubers	27
Sugar	12
Fats	24
Pulses	80
Fruits and vegetables	163
Meat	46
Milk	100

This goal means that the world must produce, in excess of the prewar output, 60 million tons of cereals, 30 million tons of meat, 250 million tons of fruits and vegetables, and about 35 billion gallons of milk. The projected food requirements by the year 2000 call for more staggering increases. Can agriculture meet this challenge? To answer this question we must consider whether more land can be farmed and whether more food can be produced per farm acre.

Factors in Increasing the Supply

Extending Cultivation. Doubtless all continents, even Europe, can extend the area of cultivation. It has been estimated, for example, that Western Germany has at least 1.2 million acres and probably 2.5 million or more of wasteland, moors, brushland, heath land and tideland that could be reclaimed.[263]

The United States could reclaim many millions of acres of marshland or land subject to flooding. Drainage has already improved almost 45 million acres,[264] and it is estimated that about 12.5 million additional acres could be reclaimed by drainage, irrigation and clearing within the next decade, and additional land in later years.[265] The U. S. Department of Agriculture estimated early

in 1949 that some 80 million acres or more of undeveloped land are suitable for farming; about 60 million acres need drainage or clearing and 20 million western acres can be irrigated.[266]

Canada has 25–27 million acres of unused, reasonably accessible land suitable for agriculture.[267] It is estimated that if 10 per cent of the potential farm land in the north of Canada and the USSR were used for dairying and cold-weather vegetables, on the pattern of Scandinavia, world agriculture would gain many million acres.[268]

Tropical Areas. The really great areas of undeveloped soil, however, are in the tropics — Latin America, Africa and Asia. Mexico has some uncultivated fertile areas, chiefly along the Gulf Coast and the Pacific Ocean.[269] In South America, vast areas now unused could be brought into cultivation.[270] Southeastern Africa also has large unused areas of potentially arable land. In Australia and Africa, irrigation and an intensive campaign against erosion could increase land suitable for food production by many millions of acres. Even Asia still has significant potentialities for increasing land under cultivation. It is estimated that irrigation could increase Iraq's arable land from 6 million acres to 20 million and Syria's from 4 to 10 million acres. Turkey could enlarge its crop area from 25 to 40 million acres; Egypt, from 6 to 7 million acres.[271]

The example of India, where vast irrigation projects have added millions of arable acres in the last five or six decades has demonstrated what engineering skill and large capital investment can achieve. India still has about 90 million acres of "cultivable wasteland," and the India Food Grains Policy Committee estimates that a substantial part of it could be used for rice and wheat if funds for land reclamation and equipment were available.[272] In Bengal

262. **18**, p. 18. The target was calculated on the basis of a minimum energy value per person and certain minimum quantities of protective foods, and adjusted to regional differences in consumption habits and production possibilities. Cf. Chapter 9.
263. **49**, p. 18.
264. **42**, p. 46.
265. **25**, p. 9.
266. **28**, January 1949, p. 6.
267. **87**, p. 401.
268. **3**, p. 32. In fact, the USSR has several experimental stations at the edge of the Arctic that are trying to develop plant varieties which will grow under Arctic conditions. Some results have been achieved. The stations raise hardier vegetables, such as cabbage and some fodder crops, and maintain some dairy livestock. (**59**, July 1947, pp. 39–40.)
269. **21**, p. 78.
270. Particularly in Patagonia, on the plateau of Mato Grosso in Brazil, Bolivia and the eastern slopes of the Andes. (See **89**, p. 51.)
271. **32**, May 1948, p. 102.
272. **15**, p. 9.

alone, 4 million acres could be reclaimed in the province.[273] Proper drainage could restore millions of acres of waterlogged land and land heavily impregnated with salt, now uncultivable, in the valley of the Indus.[274] The wasteland in Burma that can be converted to farm land is estimated at 19 million acres, slightly less than the cultivated area. Much of this land is potentially as valuable as the surrounding rice land.[275]

Increasing the Yield. Modern agricultural technology probably holds the greater promise for expanding food production in the world. Where farmers have taken advantage of the opportunities it has created, the results have been striking. In 1948, for example, farmers harvested the largest total crops ever produced on farms of the United States, largely because of improvement in agricultural techniques rather than important expansion of acreage or the accident of good weather. During the war, farmers in many countries accomplished the seemingly impossible task of increasing the output of food from the same or only slightly increased acreage with less labor but more fertilizer and equipment. This increase was substantial enough to outweigh, for the world as a whole, the severe slump in food production in Europe.[276]

Potential Capacity of Agriculture

The United States. According to the Department of Agriculture[277] the United States could increase its agricultural output sufficiently in a decade to provide food, at American per capita standards, for 380 million people or appreciably more than the estimated population of the country in A.D. 2000. (See Figure 165.)[278] The results attainable in an emergency could not be duplicated in normal times but they indicate that a much larger future output is possible.

Other Countries. Even now, it is believed, China could raise agricultural yields by 20 to 30 per cent[279] through the use of better seed.

The increase in yield per acre attainable in that country through various improved practices could amount to 20 per cent in the output of wheat, some 30 per cent in that of rice, and 40 and 55 per cent, respectively, for corn and barley.[280] India is believed to be able to double rice yields by improved seed and better tillage.[281] If the peasants of India would put animal dung into the soil instead of using it for fuel and letting the "fertility of their soil go up in smoke,"[282] they could provide their fields with large quantities of badly needed humus and other nutrients and thus substantially increase the harvests. India's agricultural scientists believe that India can feed itself if modern practices and the nation's agricultural resources are fully utilized. Where these two potentials have been combined, farm productivity has increased by from 60 to 400 per cent. Yet it is estimated that India, as a whole, needs only a 10 per cent increase in its food production to become self-sufficient,[283] though at its present level rather than at the level set by the FAO.

Yields in eastern Europe and the USSR, now 30 to 40 per cent below the European average and half or two thirds below that in the most advanced European countries, may also improve. It has been estimated that by 1960 the USSR could attain, through a combination of better agricultural techniques, the following increases in the yield per acre over 1935–39 averages: 20 per cent for wheat; 20–25 per cent for corn, barley and oats; more than 30 per cent for sugar; and nearly 50 per cent for potatoes.[284]

In yields per unit of land it was believed, a decade ago, that the intensity of cultivation in western Europe had very nearly reached the limits set by today's technology.[285] Yet important increases in yields of various crops per acre have been achieved in the last few years in many countries with the most intensively cultivated land.

Latin American countries have considerably expanded food production in recent years, but

273. **134**, p. 50.
274. **128**, p. 47.
275. **30**, p. 15.
276. See Chapter 16.
277. **33**, p. 24.
278. A. E. Parkins and J. R. Whitaker quote an estimate by the U.S. Department of Agriculture of potential *ultimate* acreage of cropland of the United States, exploited to its *extreme physical possibility,* as amounting to 973 million acres, or about three times the present area. (**123**, p. 621.)
279. **136**, p. 69. J. L. Buck considers that a 25 per cent

increase of China's agricultural production is a conservatively estimated possibility and that China could feed itself with the adoption of modern transportation, economic organization and technical improvements in agriculture. (**92**, pp. 165 and 203.)
280. **131**, p. 534.
281. **144**, pp. 262–64.
282. **111**, pp. 573–77.
283. **32**, May 1950, p. 95.
284. **131**, p. 534.
285. **22**, p. 242.

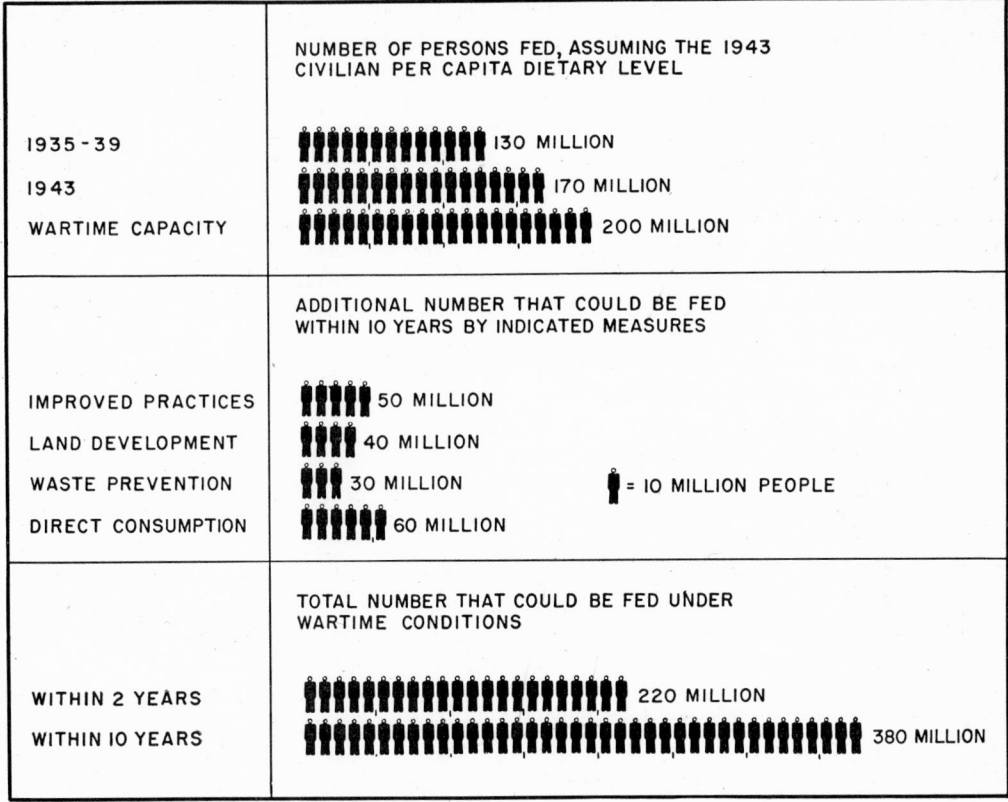

U. S. Department of Agriculture

FIGURE 165. AGRICULTURAL OUTLOOK: POTENTIAL CAPACITY OF AGRICULTURE IN THE UNITED STATES

This estimate of the potential capacity of agriculture in the United States was prepared by the Department of Agriculture in 1944. "Wartime capacity"—food for 200 million persons—shows the agricultural capacity in 1945, allowing for only normal rates of technological improvement.

To this number, the lower panel of the figure adds food for 20 million persons as reserve wartime capacity that can be tapped if necessary without a vigorous emergency program. Food for an additional 180 million persons above the 1945 potential capacity could be obtained by carrying through the measures listed in the middle panel, including diversion to human consumption of produce now fed to livestock and converted to animal products.

still are far from their potential limits. Some practical results have been achieved by their technical cooperation with agricultural services of the United States. In El Salvador, farmers now use seed corn yielding 30 to 40 per cent more than before; those in Guatemala plant wheat with double the previous yield. Middle America is raising legumes particularly suited to the tropics. The cooperative station in Guatemala has developed a formula for a balanced poultry feed from tropical products. Aid in pest control has relieved many Latin American farmers of constant plagues. The coffee development program has found a way to treble yields. Some improvements have been accepted immediately by the farmers; others come about more slowly,

but the wheels of agricultural progress are moving in the Western Hemisphere.[286]

The World at Large. A combination of increased acreage and better use of land, it is estimated, would more than double the world's output of cereals and milk, more than triple the harvest of potatoes, tubers, fruits and vegetables and result in vastly greater quantities of other foodstuffs. (See Table 235.) This estimate of R. M. Salter is based on the following assumptions:

1. More intensive use of present world cropland would result in a substantially higher output of various foodstuffs.

286. **39**, p. 20.

TABLE 235

AGRICULTURAL OUTLOOK: ATTAINABLE AGRICULTURAL OUTPUT IN THE WORLD [a]

(*Millions of Metric Tons*)

Output	Cereals	Roots and Tubers	Sugar	Fats and Oils	Pulses and Nuts	Fruit and Vege- tables [b]	Meat [c]	Milk
Prewar output	300	153	30	15	36	156	66	150
Attainable increase in output:								
From present cropland by more intensive use	60	77	5	3	7	55	13	30
From additional 1 billion acres of tropical soil [d]	358	240	143	52	12	259	10	9
From additional 300 million acres out- side tropics [e]	36	66	0	1	1	0	7	135
Total attainable output	753	536	178	71	56	470	97	323

Sources: **131**, p. 534 and **115**, p. 25.

  a. Estimate for 70 countries with 90 per cent of world population.
  b. Includes bananas.
  c. Includes fish and eggs.
  d. Obtained by applying the approximate average production per crop acre in the Philippines to one billion acres.
  e. Obtained by applying the approximate average pro-
duction per crop acre in Finland to 300 million acres of soils of the Northern Hemisphere. Fats, oils, fruits and vegetables are underestimated because of lack of data on these items in Finland.

2. Some 300 million additional acres could be developed in the northern part of the North Temperate Zone, where only about one per cent of the land is now cultivated. To judge by the experience of Scandinavian countries, soils of this zone are responsive to management and can be made to support dairying and gardening. Finland has been chosen as a yardstick for the calculation of the possible output from these 300 million acres, its average yields being representative for the soils of this group.

3. One billion acres could be added to world agriculture if a part of the unused red tropical soils (say 20 per cent) in South America, Africa and on islands such as Madagascar, Sumatra, Borneo and New Guinea were made available or reclaimed for cultivation. The average yield in the Philippines was taken as the basis for calculating the resulting increase in world food production because this is one of the tropical countries fully representative of the tropical soil region and has nearly complete food production records.[287]

A more intensive fight against insects, weeds and plant diseases could also become a factor in increasing world food supplies. China suffers

great losses from insects and plant diseases; in extreme cases, the whole crop is destroyed.[288] In the United States, it is estimated, annual losses from insect infestation and rats exceed 13 million tons of food grain; losses from weed infestation are also very considerable. For the world as a whole, losses from destructive pests may amount to 10 per cent of all field crops.[289]

Reducing losses in crops between their maturity and consumption by means of better storage and conditioning may also increase the proportion available for human needs. At present, such nutritional losses, visible and invisible, are very great.

Moreover, further mechanization of agricultural production may release some land now in feed crops for food crops. Similarly, some additional acreage for food production will probably be gained with the increasing use of synthetic fibers rather than natural fibers.

The difficulties in reclaiming the hitherto unused land in the tropics or in the north should not be minimized, however. Much of it is in "difficult acres" that must be surveyed and studied before any settlement programs can be con-

287. **131**, p. 534.

288. **37**, p. 6.
289. **1**, p. 201.

sidered. Most of it requires clearing, drainage or irrigation and road building. New settlements would have to be established with the necessary utilities and educational and medical facilities. The cost would be tremendous. Financial investments alone, no matter how great, cannot carry through this gigantic job. The concentrated effort of millions of people, kindled by the prospect of better living and supported by all the weapons of modern engineering, will be required if jungles, marshes, deserts and frozen wastes are to be turned into new granaries.[290]

The agricultural frontier is still open and holds much promise to the growing world population but the climb to the targets set by the FAO will be hard and slow. The transfer of technological knowledge to less developed regions and its application there can be achieved only gradually, as the implements of technology — better seed, fertilizer, insecticides, mechanical power, drugs, schools and roads — penetrate into these areas. Many techniques that have been successful in some places will prove ineffective in others. Lack of funds and of trained agriculturists, on the one hand, and the traditional conservatism of farmers, on the other, are additional obstacles.

The greatest difficulty in feeding the additional throngs of mankind will be in achieving a more even distribution of food supplies over the globe. The core of the problem is whether enough food can be supplied where it is most ur-

gently needed: that is, in Asia, where the largest and poorest part of the world's population now lives and where the greatest increase in population is anticipated.

In the past, famine has limited population in some countries and migration has helped other nations to maintain those who remained. Now we no longer tolerate starvation and the prospects for migration are limited, at least in the near future.

Modernization of farm production is needed to increase the supply of food in overpopulated countries as well as in underdeveloped areas. But countries cannot modernize agriculture without modernizing the whole economy — industry, transportation, marketing. For success these processes must go hand in hand. Such a development can assure better utilization of the world's human and natural resources. It would also enable the underdeveloped areas in Asia and other continents to buy additional foodstuffs with exports of some of their products, not in the form of raw materials, as at present, but in semifinished or finished goods.

The modernization of agriculture and the industrialization of underdeveloped countries can be achieved only if the advanced countries help them to attain higher economic standards through full utilization of their own resources by means of modern techniques. Here economic problems merge with political considerations.

290. Cf. Chapter 10.

Chapter 16

FOOD CROPS

Food is the major objective of world agriculture. In the world as a whole, food crops represent more than half the value of the total agricultural output, and they account for a much larger proportion, perhaps as much as three fourths, of all effort of farmers and farm laborers. Some 85 per cent of the world's population obtain the majority of the calories in their daily diet from cereals. Raising these cereals and other food crops, such as sugar and oilseeds, is the prime task of farmers the world over, and there are few who raise no food crops at all.

The Value of the World's Vegetable Output

Plant products, including crops fed to livestock, represent nearly three fourths of the total value of the world's agricultural output; excluding feed crops, they account for more than half.[1] Of all vegetable production, in turn, food and feed crops together account for more than four fifths. The rest is divided among tobacco, nonedible oils,[2] fibers and other technical crops. The value of the grain output (bread grain and coarse grain) alone represents more than half of that of the world's total vegetable output.

The estimate of the International Institute of Agriculture from which these figures on vegetable production are taken relates to prewar years and includes grain, potatoes, sugar plants, coffee, tea and cocoa, certain oilseeds and vegetable oils, wine, tobacco and other technical crops (fibers, rubber and others). It omits, for lack of data, the value of some important agricultural products, including fruit and vegetables and some food crops, such as millet and sorghum.[3] Although there are no strictly comparable estimates of current output, it is fairly certain that

there has been no change in the two outstanding features: the preponderance of vegetable products in the total agricultural output, and among these products, the predominance of grain.

In prewar years, Asia accounted for the largest part of the world's vegetable output (29.6 per cent), Europe ranked second (27.9 per cent), while the USSR and North America competed neck-and-neck for the third and fourth places. (See Table 236 and Figure 166.) [4]

Grain

The overwhelming majority of mankind depends chiefly on grain for food. "The development of cereal grains, probably more than any other factor, permitted the earliest tribes to change from nomadic life to more settled existence. They learned that cultivation of cereal grains provided more food with less effort than did any other crop. No other crop offered such security in existence. In addition, grain could be easily stored to provide food between harvests." [5]

Of the world's population in 1935 (2,095 million), 1.8 billion were distributed by the percentage of total calories derived from grain and potatoes [6] as follows (see also Figure 167):

Per Cent	Millions of Persons
30–39	205
40–49	93
50–59	93
60–69	169
70–79	156
80–89	1,125

1. See Table 206 and p. 457.

2. The value of oil-bearing products is divided in this survey equally between edible and nonedible oils, according to the estimate of the League of Nations. 2, p. 87.

3. The method and limitations of this estimate are discussed in Chapter 14.

4. The International Institute of Agriculture, like all government bodies, used official data for the USSR. These are 15 to 20 per cent too high, because Russian statistics relate to the harvest as estimated on the field during the period of growth (the so-called biological crop) and not the harvested or barn crop.

5. 25, 1950-51, p. 331.

6. 33, p. 57. Potatoes, also a carbohydrate food, are important only in Europe and the USSR.

TABLE 236

VEGETABLE OUTPUT: VALUE IN EACH CONTINENT, 1934–38 ANNUAL AVERAGE

(*Millions* [a])

Continent	Total	Grains [b]	Potatoes [c]	Sugar Beets and Cane	Coffee, Tea, Cocoa	Wine	Oil-Bearing Products and Vegetable Oils	Tobacco	Other Technical Crops
World	$25,305	$14,018	$3,786	$427	$864	$979	$1,400	$1,355	$2,477
North America	3,965	2,545	200	27	—	29	164	281	720
Middle and									
South America	1,678	711	52	113	359	58	112	91	181
Europe	7,081	3,308	2,465	100	—	753	208	130	115
USSR	4,011	2,426	974	32	2	25	63	103	386
Asia	7,479	4,531	78	108	427	5	704	716	911
Africa	874	334	8	17	75	105	139	30	166
Oceania	217	163	8	29	2	3	10	2	—

Source: Adapted from **10**, p. 21.

a. The value is given in current dollars, instead of gold dollars as used by the International Institute of Agriculture.

b. Including grains fed to livestock (barley, oats, corn).

c. Including potatoes fed to livestock.

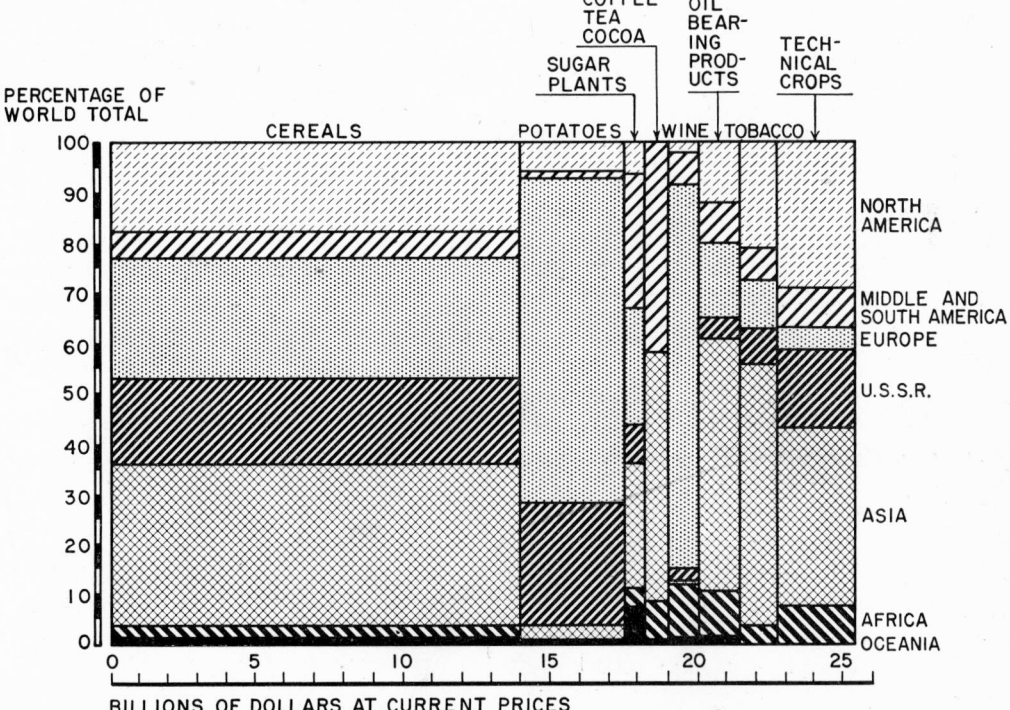

FIGURE 166. VEGETABLE OUTPUT: VALUE IN EACH CONTINENT, 1934–38 ANNUAL AVERAGE

Grain represents about 55 per cent of the total value of the world's prewar vegetable output (excluding fruit and vegetables); potatoes account for about 15 per cent; a further 15 per cent was in technical crops and tobacco. Asia, which includes more than half the world's population and lives almost wholly on a vegetarian diet, is responsible for the largest share in the output of grain and oil-bearing products; it also leads in production of tea, tobacco and technical crops, largely for export. Europe leads in production of potatoes, Latin America in sugar. North America ranks second in technical crops and third in grain and oil-bearing products. The estimate on which these figures is based includes the value of grain and potatoes fed to livestock. (Cf. Table 236.)

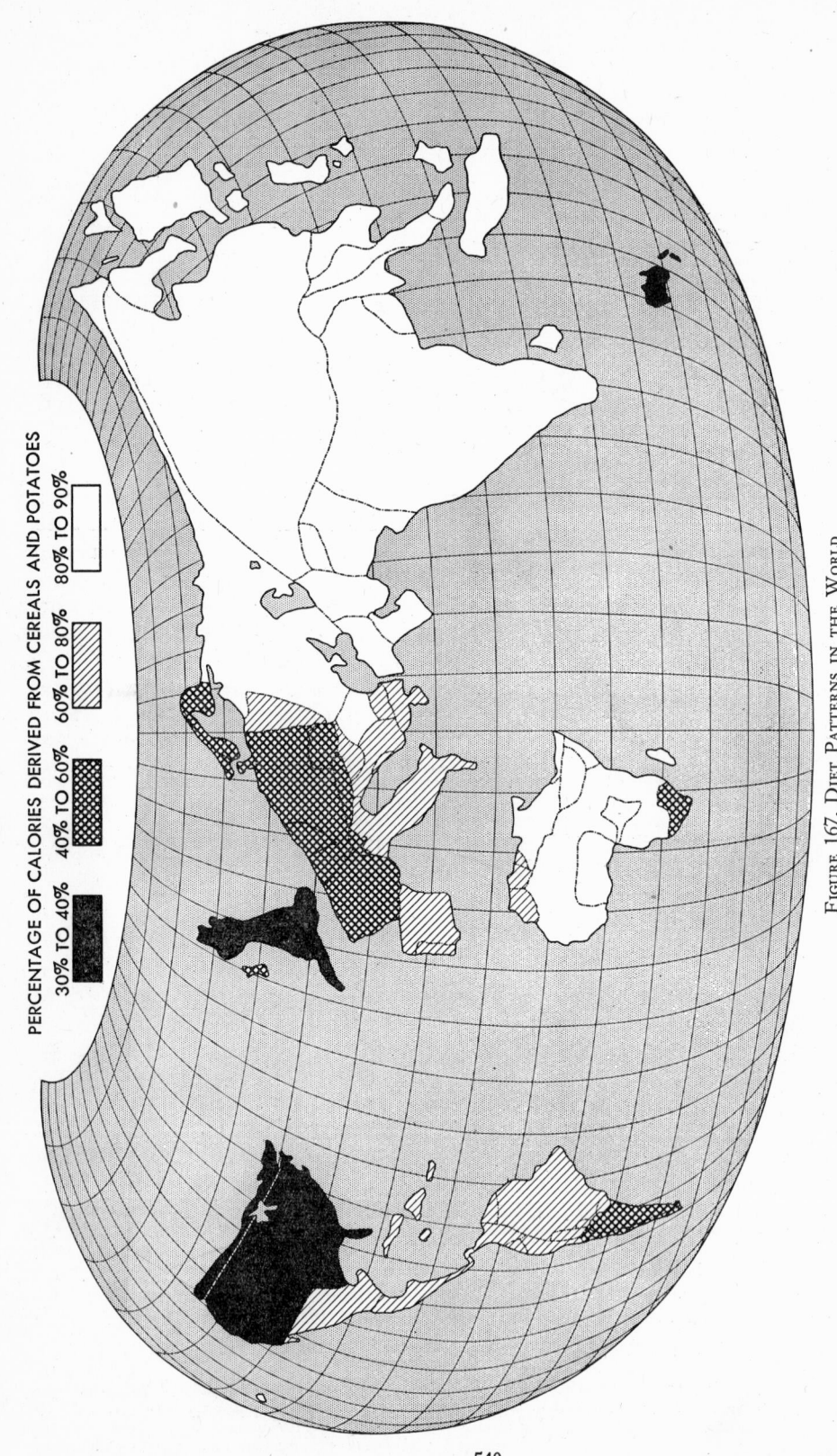

PERCENTAGE OF CALORIES DERIVED FROM CEREALS AND POTATOES

30% TO 40%   40% TO 60%   60% TO 80%   80% TO 90%

FIGURE 167. DIET PATTERNS IN THE WORLD

On this map continents and countries are shown on the scale of their population. It indicates, therefore, the number of people with different diet patterns, rather than the area in which such patterns prevail.

About two thirds of the people in the world—in Asia, the USSR and Africa—derive from 80–90 per cent of the calories in their diet from carbohydrates, chiefly grain. At the other extreme, this type of food represents less than 40 per cent of the calories consumed by people in the United States, Canada, Great Britain and Oceania. Grain accounts for 50–60 per cent of the calories in the diet of many Latin American countries. Potatoes are an important food in Europe and the USSR.

540

TABLE 237

GRAIN: VALUE OF OUTPUT IN EACH CONTINENT, 1934–38 ANNUAL AVERAGE

(*Millions*)

Continent	Total	Wheat	Rye	Rice (rough)	Corn	Barley	Oats
World	$14,018	$5,283	$1,209	$2,657	$2,242	$1,151	$1,476
North America	2,545	872	32	20	1,048	142	430
Middle and South America	711	268	7	37	361	19	20
Europe	3,308	1,417	586	22	362	352	569
USSR	2,426	1,173	574	5	68	196	410
Asia	4,531	1,287	10	2,533	290	379	32
Africa	334	122	—	37	110	58	7
Oceania	163	144	—	2	3	5	8

Source: Adapted from **10**, p. 17. See Table 236, footnote a.

Rice was the dominant cereal for the largest number of people in 1934–38; wheat came next: [7]

Grain	Millions of Persons
Rice	946
Wheat	368
Wheat-Rye	283
Wheat-Corn	38
Wheat-Barley	16
Corn	54
Rye	35
Uncertain	100

In prewar years, Asia accounted for almost a third of the value of the world's grain output; Europe for nearly one fourth and North America for less than a fifth. (See Table 237.) If millet and sorghum had been included in the estimate, Asia's share would have been even larger.

Wheat is the leading grain in Europe, the USSR and Oceania.[8] In North America, wheat is the chief bread grain but represents a smaller part of the total grain output than corn, used chiefly for feeding livestock. Rice is the leading grain in Asia.

Acreage in Grain

Grain occupies nearly half the world's arable land and from 75 to 90 per cent of all arable land in Canada, Mexico, Egypt, Japan, Indochina, the Balkan countries and some others.

Cereal grains are interchangeable to some ex-

tent in various food uses, and are almost completely interchangeable as feed. As raw materials in processing industries, they are less competitive one with another, since only a particular type fully meets a specific combination of chemical and physical properties required for a particular purpose.[9]

Within a crop-producing area, various types of grain compete for land among themselves and with other crops. Competition is governed by the physical requirements and yielding capacity of the crop, on one hand, and by the relationship between the cost of production and the price, on the other. For example, on land suitable for either, it is more profitable to produce corn, a heavier yielder, than wheat. Wheat is therefore relegated to dryer regions where corn would not grow well. On the other hand, corn has to give way to cotton, which has even more exacting requirements and brings higher prices.[10]

In recent years, government policy has frequently influenced the acreage in grain. In countries such as India, where the pressure of population is great and grain constitutes the largest part of the diet, the government has adopted various measures to encourage planting of grain rather than crops less vitally needed. The United States government, on the other hand, limited the wheat acreage to which price support provisions could be applied in 1950, thus causing a considerable contraction of the wheat area.

---

7. **33**, p. 62.

8. While Table 237 indicates that wheat is also the chief grain in Africa, millet and sorghum, not included in these comparisons for lack of data, are actually more important.

9. **25**, 1950-51, p. 336.

10. **53**, pp. 60–61. N. Jasny (**42**, p. 197) considers that yield is the principal, if not the only, factor in the choice of grains grown for the larger part of world production of all grains.

TABLE 238
GRAIN: WORLD ACREAGE AND OUTPUT, 1934–38 ANNUAL AVERAGE AND 1950

Grain	Area, in Millions of Acres		Output, in Millions of Metric Tons [a]	
	1934–38	1950	1934–38	1950
All varieties	1,367.0	1,414.3	637.9	664.6
Wheat	416.9	431.9	161.6	176.2
Rye	103.5	110.5	46.5	42.8
Barley	114.7	117.6	51.3	52.9
Corn	220.1	212.6	114.8	132.2
Oats	142.8	129.9	65.0	60.2
Rice	209.0	233.3 [b]	149.6	153.0 [b]
Millet and sorghum [c]	159.9	178.5 [d]	49.1	47.3 [d]

Sources: Tables 239 to 246.

a. Conversion factors: one metric ton = 1.1023 short tons = 2,204.6 pounds.
b. Includes the insignificant prewar acreage and output of the USSR, for lack of later data.
c. Excludes the USSR, where in 1939 more than 13 million acres were in millet.
d. 1949.

During the past forty years, the world's combined acreage in wheat, rice, rye, corn, barley and oats has increased on the whole, despite occasional setbacks — from an annual average of about 608 million acres during 1910–14 to 990 million during 1925–29, 1,207 million in 1934–38 and 1,236 million in 1950. About 180 million additional acres are planted to millet and sorghum, and probably further millions to various local grains. In all, as many as 1.5 billion acres may be devoted to grain. (See Table 238.)

The World's Grain Crop

The world's output of the six major crops has also increased notably, from an annual average of 451 million tons in 1910–14 [11] to 589 million during 1934–38 and 617 million in 1950. This increase has been due chiefly to greater acreage rather than higher yields per acre. Only corn has had a considerably higher yield per acre, benefiting, in the last decade, from hybrid seed. The total output of wheat, rice and corn (in millions of metric tons) is considerably greater than the annual average during 1910–14, while that of rye and oats has decreased slightly: [12]

Grain	1910–14, Annual Average	1950
Total	451.2	617.3
Wheat	106.6	176.2
Corn	99.6	132.2
Rice	100.5	153.0
Rye	44.3	42.8
Barley	35.9	52.9
Oats	64.3	60.2

11. **58**, p. 112.
12. **58**, p. 112, and Table 238.

WHEAT

Wheat occupies a larger acreage than any other crop and about double that used for either corn or rice. It used to occupy 17 per cent of all cultivated land in the world and 11 per cent of all land where conditions of temperature, moisture, topography and soil permit its cultivation.[13] In recent decades, its share in the world's cultivated land has declined to about 13–14 per cent. It is harvested in some part of the globe in each month of the year.[14]

Climatic and Soil Requirements

Wheat is grown almost everywhere — on the plains, in the highlands and even on mountains; close to the equator and within the Arctic Circle; in areas with as little as four inches of annual precipitation (as in Egypt, under irrigation) and in areas where annual rainfall amounts to 60 inches and more (as in some parts of Japan or southeastern China). The distribution of the world's wheat acreage among regions with various amounts of precipitation is as follows: [15]

Inches a Year	Percentage of Acreage
Under 14.9	10
15 to 24.9	53
25 to 34.9	22
35 to 39.9	8
Over 40	7

The best yields are in regions where a cool, moderately moist germinating season changes to

13. **31**, p. 31, and **30**, p. 25.
14. **36**, p. 13.
15. **34**, p. 272.

a warm, sunny, preferably dry period during growth and harvest. In the Northern Hemisphere, such conditions prevail in coastal regions with the Mediterranean climate (rainy winters and dry summers), and in the interior of the continents. (Cf. Figure 170.) Wheat grows on a wide range of soils, but the best wheat soils are fertile, well drained, free of weeds, not too acid and with a large humus content.

Varieties of Wheat

About 300 million acres, or 75 per cent of the world's total wheat acreage, are in winter wheat, planted in the fall and harvested in summer.[16] Among 30 countries where wheat acreage exceeds a million acres, only the United States, Canada, the USSR and Manchuria use less than 90 per cent for winter wheat.[17] The proportionate acreage in winter and spring wheat in the United States is close to the world average: 53.2 and 18.3 million acres respectively in 1950.[18]

The first hard winter wheat seeds were brought to the United States by Mennonites emigrating from Russia, and this variety, called Turkey, proved so successful that for more than half a century it was the most widely grown type in the country. Tenmarq, which matures a few days earlier and has excellent milling and baking qualities, was introduced in 1932 and by 1944 was grown more widely in the United States than any other variety of wheat.[19] A cross with Tenmarq produced three new varieties of hard red winter wheat (Pawnee, Comanche and Wichita) which, together with Westar, another new strain, have gained great popularity in the Middle West since 1946.

Another variety, Red Fife, originating in Poland, reached Canada via Scotland. The seeds of this hard spring wheat were first sown in winter, however, and only a single plant survived. Successful wheat growing in Canada is credited to the seed of this plant. Later, Red Fife, crossed with a wheat strain from India, produced the famous Marquis wheat which ripens as much as ten days earlier than Red Fife and is outstanding in yield and excellently qualified for milling and bread making. It remained the king of wheats for twenty years in Canada, and its introduction, extending the Canadian wheat belt several hundred miles to the north, was of great importance to the world grain market.[20] Marquis, however, is susceptible to both stem and leaf rust and was gradually displaced by Thatcher, a stem-rust-resistant variety of hard red spring wheat released to the farmers in 1934. Its acreage increased rapidly (14.5 million acres in the United States in 1939) until its weak resistance to leaf rust was established. It has lost ground in the United States although Canada still had 17 million acres in Thatcher in 1944. Since then several new varieties have been developed, more resistant to stem rust than Marquis and to leaf rust than Thatcher, and these are grown extensively in both the United States and Canada. New high-yielding varieties have also been developed, and the bumper crops of postwar years are partly due to their adoption by farmers in the United States. For example, Kansas, which accounted for a fifth of the 1947 wheat crop, used nearly half its wheat acreage for three varieties developed within the past five years.[21] Many other varieties of winter and spring wheat are grown in the United States.

In other important wheat-producing areas, such as Australia and the USSR, intensive wheat breeding has also resulted in the introduction of new and better varieties adapted to local conditions. About 180 winter wheat varieties and 140 spring wheats are recorded in the USSR, and some of them, such as Kubanka, Kharkov and Arnautka, have been introduced in the United States.[22]

Where winters are dry and cold, with little or no snow, and the ground freezes, as in Canada, most wheat is planted in the early spring and harvested in autumn. Spring wheat occupies nearly 95 per cent of the acreage in Canada and practically all the wheat area in eastern Montana, North Dakota and Minnesota. In the USSR, it dominates the wheat acreage everywhere north and east of the Ukraine, in the Caucasus, much of the Volga region, the Urals, Siberia, Kazakhstan and Central Asia and accounts for about two thirds of the total wheat acreage.[23]

---

16. **44**, p. 345.
17. **34**, p. 269.
18. **14**, 1951, p. 62. In the USSR before the war, winter wheat occupied 35 per cent of the total area sown in wheat but acreage was increasing rapidly. (**32**, p. 377, and **55**, p. 114.)
19. **25**, 1943–47, p. 381.

---

20. **42**, p. 278.
21. **4**, 1948, p. 148.
22. **55**, pp. 117–18.
23. **32**, p. 374, and **55**, p. 112.

Wheat Regions

During 1934–38 about 410 million acres, and in 1950 some 430 million acres, were planted to wheat in countries for which data, though not always complete, are available. Additional millions of acres were planted in countries that have no crop statistics. The major wheat regions of the world are (cf. Figures 168–170):

In the Western Hemisphere
> The Great Plains of the United States and Canada
> Eastern and central Argentina

In the Eastern Hemisphere
> The Mediterranean (France, Spain, Italy, French North Africa)
> Southeastern Europe (the Danube basin)
> The USSR
> Northwestern and central India (largely in the valleys of the Ganges and Indus rivers)
> Northeastern China (mostly between the valleys of the Yangtze and Yellow rivers)
> Southeastern Australia

Together, these eight regions account for more than 80 per cent of the world's wheat acreage. The United States belt is about 1,000 miles long and 200 miles wide [24] and that of Canada, 750 miles long. The Danube basin and the Russian belt along the Black Sea and across Siberia up to Lake Baikal together make a strip more than 3,600 miles long and 200 miles wide.

The USSR has the largest wheat acreage, further increased by its territorial acquisitions since the war. Next in rank are the United States, China, India, Canada, Argentina and Australia.

The United States has four wheat-producing areas of unequal importance: (1) the hard winter wheat region in the southern part of the Great Plains, centering in Kansas, Nebraska and the Panhandles of Oklahoma and Texas; (2) the eastern winter wheat region stretching from Kansas over Missouri, Illinois, Indiana and Ohio to Pennsylvania, and merging with the hard winter wheat region; (3) the western or Columbia Plateau region, including the eastern part of Washington and parts of Oregon and Idaho; (4) the spring wheat region, in the northern part of the Great Plains, including the two Dakotas, western Minnesota and northeastern and north central Montana and merging with the spring wheat belt of Canada in the largest

continuous area of spring wheat in the world. (See Figure 168.) Hard red winter wheat, the most important commercial class of wheat in the United States, supplies about 45 per cent of the country's total output.

In Europe, the four most highly concentrated areas of wheat production are in the Danube Valley, where rich soil and moderate moisture particularly favor the growing of this crop; the Po Valley, where the Romans built the necessary drainage system centuries ago; central Germany, with its intensive cultivation of the rich soil coupled with heavy fertilization and much legume-grass growing; and the northeastern part of France, where modern cultivation practices are employed.[25] (See Figure 170.)

Acreage and Output

The world's wheat crop averaged 160 million tons a year during 1934-38 and totaled some 176 million tons in 1950. In prewar years, Europe accounted for more than one fourth, 44 million tons, and France and Italy were the largest European producers. Asia produced 42.9 million tons, of which China accounted for 21.7 million; the USSR, 30.9 million; and the United States, 19.5 million.

During World War II, the world's output of wheat was at about the prewar level, chiefly because of much greater yields in the United States and Canada; the output of continental Europe fell sharply from the average of 42.3 million tons during 1934–38 to 33 million in 1942.

Postwar recovery, although interrupted by a severe setback in Europe in 1947, brought the 1948 output above the prewar average and the 1950 world crop, 176 million tons, was the largest on record. The output in Europe and Middle and South America nearly regained the prewar level, while that in the USSR, within the present boundaries, was considerably below it. In the United States, Canada and Australia, the crop exceeded the prewar average by 43, 75 and 19 per cent, respectively. (See Table 239 and Figures 169 and 170.)

Yield per Acre

With a much higher yield per acre, prewar Europe produced considerably more wheat from its somewhat smaller acreage than either North America or the USSR. Every European country,

---

24. The Pacific Northwest area in the United States is also an important wheat producing area.

25. **13**, p. 34.

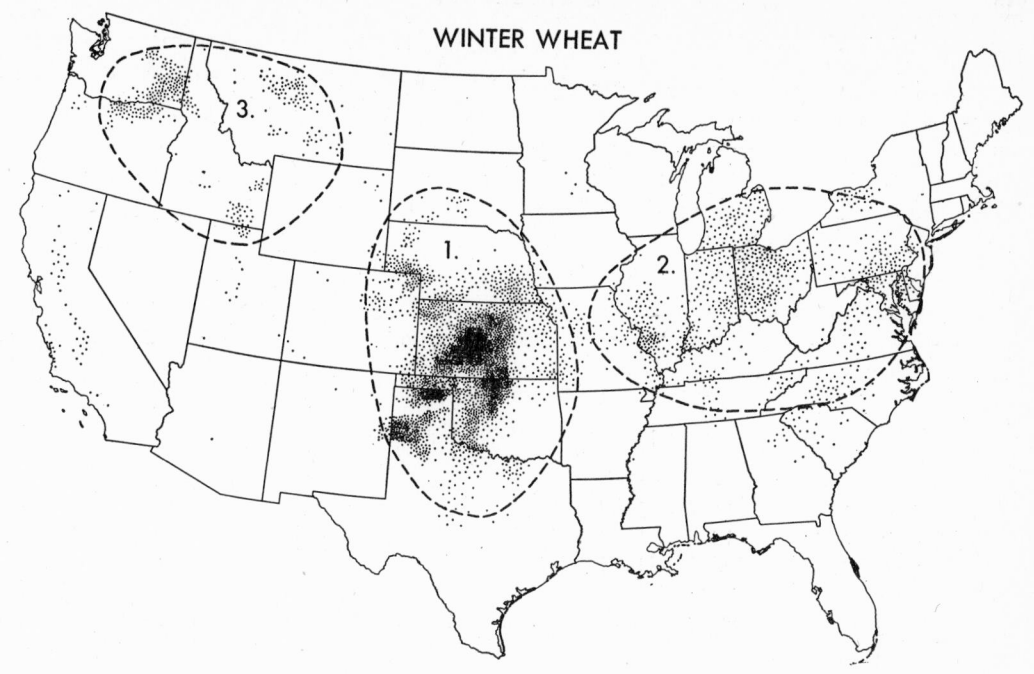

WINTER WHEAT

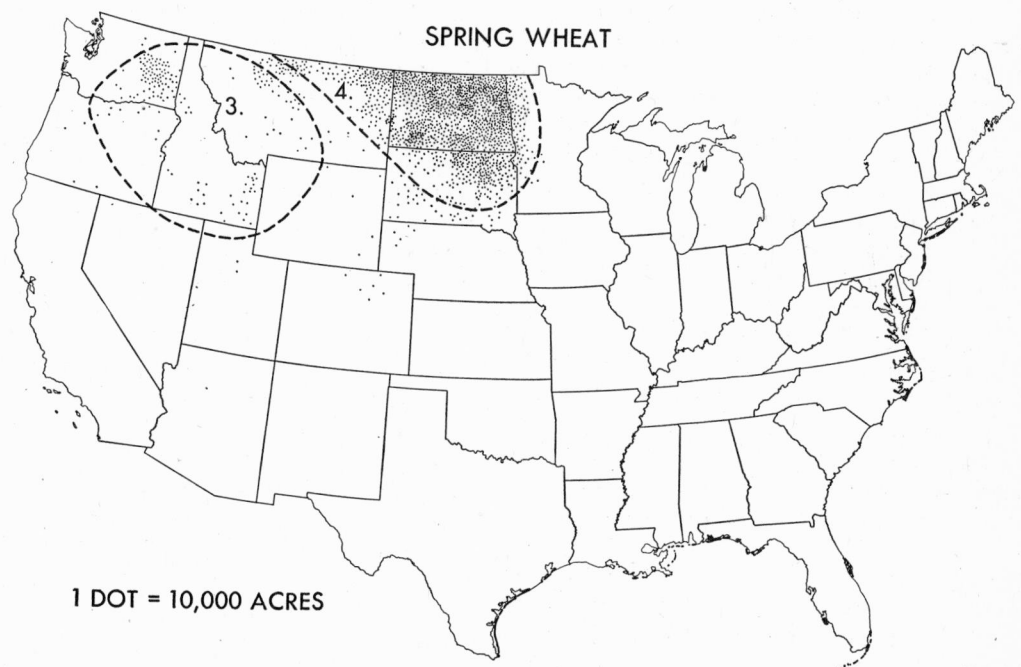

SPRING WHEAT

1 DOT = 10,000 ACRES

FIGURE 168. WHEAT: PRINCIPAL PRODUCING AREAS IN THE UNITED STATES

The main center (1) of wheat production in the United States is the central hard winter wheat region. Other important centers of winter wheat are in the northeastern part of the country (2) and in the Columbia Plateau region (3). In this last, spring wheat is also raised. The Dakotas and Montana (4) lead in production of spring wheat.

TABLE 239

WHEAT: ACREAGE AND YIELD IN EACH CONTINENT AND SELECTED COUNTRIES, 1934–38 ANNUAL AVERAGE, 1949 AND 1950

Country and Continent [a]	Area, in Thousands of Acres			Output, in Thousands of Metric Tons			Yield Per Acre, in Metric Quintals		
	1934–38	1949	1950	1934–38	1949	1950	1934–38	1949	1950
World (with the USSR)	416,920	434,115	431,935	160,000	169,300	176,245	3.8	3.9	4.1
World (without the USSR)	315,800	331,115	324,935	129,000	139,300	146,000	4.0	4.2	4.5
North America	80,468	104,290	88,760	26,646	41,200	40,510	3.3	4.0	4.6
United States	55,427	76,750	61,738	19,476	31,202	27,944	3.5	4.1	4.5
Canada	25,041	27,540	27,020	7,170	10,000	12,566	2.9	3.6	4.7
Middle and South America	22,459	18,040	21,200	8,575	7,700	8,244	3.8	4.3	3.9
Mexico	1,208	1,322	1,507	374	503	544	3.1	3.8	3.6
Brazil	395	1,050	1,211	144	438	519	3.6	4.2	4.3
Chile	1,977	2,059	2,034	851	831	973	4.3	4.0	4.8
Uruguay	1,196	1,238	1,191	365	452	435	3.0	3.7	3.7
Argentina	16,761	11,204	13,677	6,634	5,144	5,500	4.0	4.6	4.0
Europe									
Prewar boundaries	*78,801*	—	—	*43,940*	—	—	*5.6*	—	—
Present boundaries	73,636	67,460	70,670	42,300	40,100	41,500	5.7	5.9	5.9
United Kingdom	1,863	1,962	2,475	1,743	2,239	2,648	9.4	11.4	10.7
France	12,909	10,435	10,672	8,143	8,082	7,701	6.3	7.7	7.2
Belgium	408	378	430	450	596	547	11.0	15.8	12.7
Netherlands	351	245	225	430	425	295	12.2	17.3	13.1
Denmark	311	205	210	383	299	298	12.3	14.6	14.2
Sweden	717	759	838	696	698	739	9.7	9.2	8.8
Germany									
Prewar boundaries	*5,330*	—	—	*4,855*	—	—	*9.1*	—	—
Western Germany	2,807	2,291	2,503	2,505	2,471	2,614	8.9	10.8	10.4
Soviet Zone	1,562	1,159	1,260	1,553	926	815	9.9	8.0	6.5
Poland									
Prewar boundaries	*4,295*	—	—	*2,064*	—	—	*4.8*	—	—
Present boundaries	3,319	3,571	3,941	1,965	1,781	1,854	5.9	5.0	4.7
Czechoslovakia									
Prewar boundaries	*2,256*	—	—	*1,550*	—	—	*6.9*	—	—
Present boundaries	2,179	1,967	1,977	1,513	1,573	1,540	6.9	8.0	7.8
Austria	618	511	539	417	350	384	6.7	6.8	7.1
Hungary	3,926	3,506	3,620	2,220	1,830	2,040	5.7	5.2	5.6
Portugal	1,240	1,626	1,641	477	415	576	3.8	2.6	3.5
Spain	11,260 [b]	9,810	9,884	4,364 [b]	3,305	3,380	3.9 [b]	3.4	3.4
Italy									
Prewar boundaries	*12,508*	—	—	*7,280*	—	—	*5.8*	—	—
Present boundaries	12,454	11,671	11,661	7,254	7,020	7,625	5.8	6.0	6.5
Yugoslavia									
Prewar boundaries	*5,261*	—	—	*2,430*	—	—	*4.6*	—	—
Present boundaries	5,313	4,411	4,403	2,455	2,516	1,827	4.6	5.7	4.1
Romania									
Prewar boundaries	*8,560*	—	—	*3,359*	—	—	*3.9*	—	—
Present boundaries	6,269	…	…	2,600	…	…	4.1	…	…
Bulgaria									
Prewar boundaries	*3,096*	—	—	*1,588*	—	—	*5.1*	—	—
Present boundaries	3,343	…	…	1,690	…	…	5.1	…	…
Greece									
Prewar boundaries	*2,071*	—	—	*754*	—	—	*3.6*	—	—
Present boundaries	2,078	1,883	2,142	756	839	850	3.6	4.5	4.0

(*Continued on facing page*)

TABLE 239—*continued*

Country and Continent [a]	Area, in Thousands of Acres			Output, in Thousands of Metric Tons			Yield Per Acre, in Metric Quintals		
	1934–38	1949	1950	1934–38	1949	1950	1934–38	1949	1950
USSR									
Prewar boundaries	*95,956*	—	—	*30,920*	—	—	*3.2*	—	—
Present boundaries	101,121	103,000 [e]	107,000 [e]	32,560	30,000 [e]	30,245 [e]	3.2	2.9 [e]	2.8 [e]
Asia	112,185	114,900	117,867	42,900	40,200	46,100	3.8	3.5	3.9
China [d]	49,800	52,632	...	21,743	20,600	...	4.4	3.9	...
Japan	1,688	1,866	1,883	1,287	1,297	1,338	7.6	7.0	7.1
Turkey	8,525	9,904	11,063	3,412	2,517	3,872	4.0	2.5	3.5
Iraq	1,633	1,236	1,236	478	500	544	2.9	4.0	4.4
Iran	3,835	4,942	6,153	1,869	2,000	2,263	4.9	4.0	3.7
Pakistan	9,306	10,823	10,714	3,183	4,162	4,022	3.4	3.8	3.8
India	25,481	22,338	24,026	7,140	5,741	6,320	2.8	2.6	2.6
Africa	13,838	13,590	14,579	3,800	4,000	4,400	2.7	2.9	3.0
French Morocco	3,170	2,587	3,111	631	638	755	2.0	2.5	2.4
Algeria	4,174	3,630	3,823	952	947	1,061	2.3	2.6	2.8
Tunisia	1,853	2,053	1,717	385	540	460	2.1	2.6	2.7
Egypt	1,453	1,470	1,423	1,184	1,167	1,018	8.1	7.9	7.2
Union of South Africa	2,044	2,800 [e]	3,109	427 [e]	372	680	2.1	1.3	2.3
Oceania	13,215	12,355	11,861	4,400	6,100	5,100	3.3	4.3	4.3
Australia	12,980	12,230	11,700	4,200	5,939	4,991	3.2	4.3	4.3
New Zealand	215	126	146	183	133	161	8.5	10.6	8.8

Sources: **12**, 1941–42 to 1945–46, Vol. I, pp. 4–13; **9**, December 1951, p. 3.

a. For the USSR and European countries whose boundaries have undergone changes since World War II, data for 1934–38 in prewar boundaries are given in italics, for comparison. World or continent totals include the FAO estimate for gaps in reporting of acreage and output. Conversion factors: one metric ton of wheat = 10 metric quintals = 36.7 bushels.

b. 1931–35.

c. Estimate of the U. S. Department of Agriculture (**55**, p. 114, and **22**, March 17, 1952, p. 213).

d. Data for 22 provinces, with nearly 90 per cent of the total population.

e. European farms and estates.

even such underdeveloped countries as Bulgaria or Romania, had a higher yield per acre than the United States, Canada or the USSR; Denmark, the Netherlands and Belgium outdistanced the United States by more than 3 to 1.

While most European countries increased their already high yields per acre during the past half century, the average yield in the United States and Canada was either stationary or on the downgrade before World War II.[26] Since the war, yield per acre has risen considerably in both countries because of greater use of fertilizers and more intensive cultivation, better seed and favorable weather. (See Table 240.) Yields in many European countries are also higher than in 1934–38.

RICE

In many Oriental languages, the word rice is synonymous with food. While wheat is at home in many parts of the world, rice has only one major habitat.[27] Rice is the staple food of about half of mankind for whom it constitutes from 70–90 per cent of the diet. Of the 233 million acres devoted to rice in the world, Asia accounts for about 217 million. Failure of the rice crop may spell actual famine for millions in the "rice bowl" of southeastern Asia. Its importance in agriculture in the Orient is shown by the proportion of all cropland used for it:

Region	Per Cent	Region	Per Cent
Thailand	90	Japan	53
Indochina	85	India	65
Burma	57	Pakistan	40
Indonesia	57	Korea	36

In these regions, "rice is the peasant farmer's means of subsistence, his first need and principal

26. **6**, p. 67.

27. **56**, p. 264.

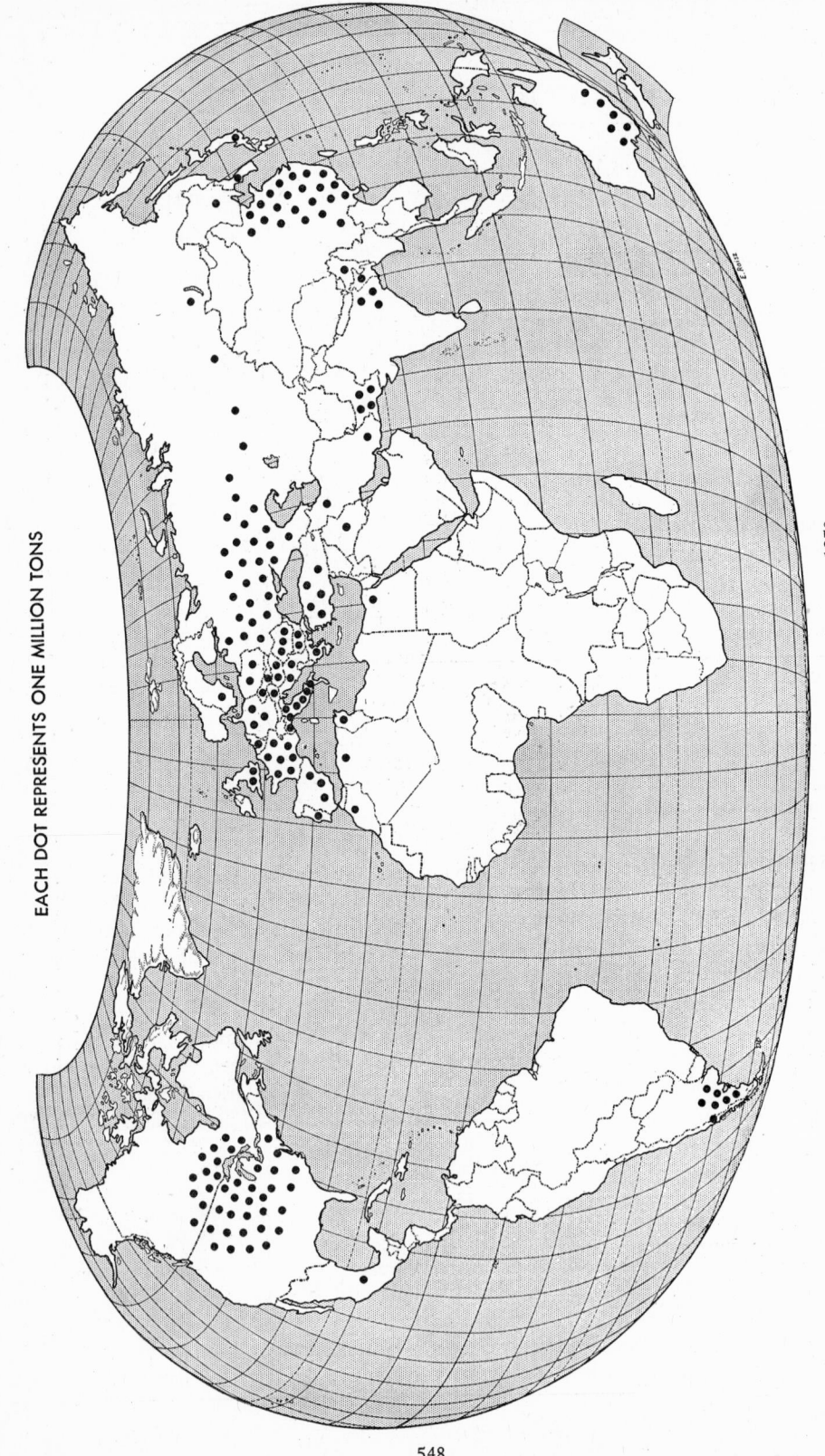

EACH DOT REPRESENTS ONE MILLION TONS

FIGURE 169. WHEAT: WORLD OUTPUT, 1950

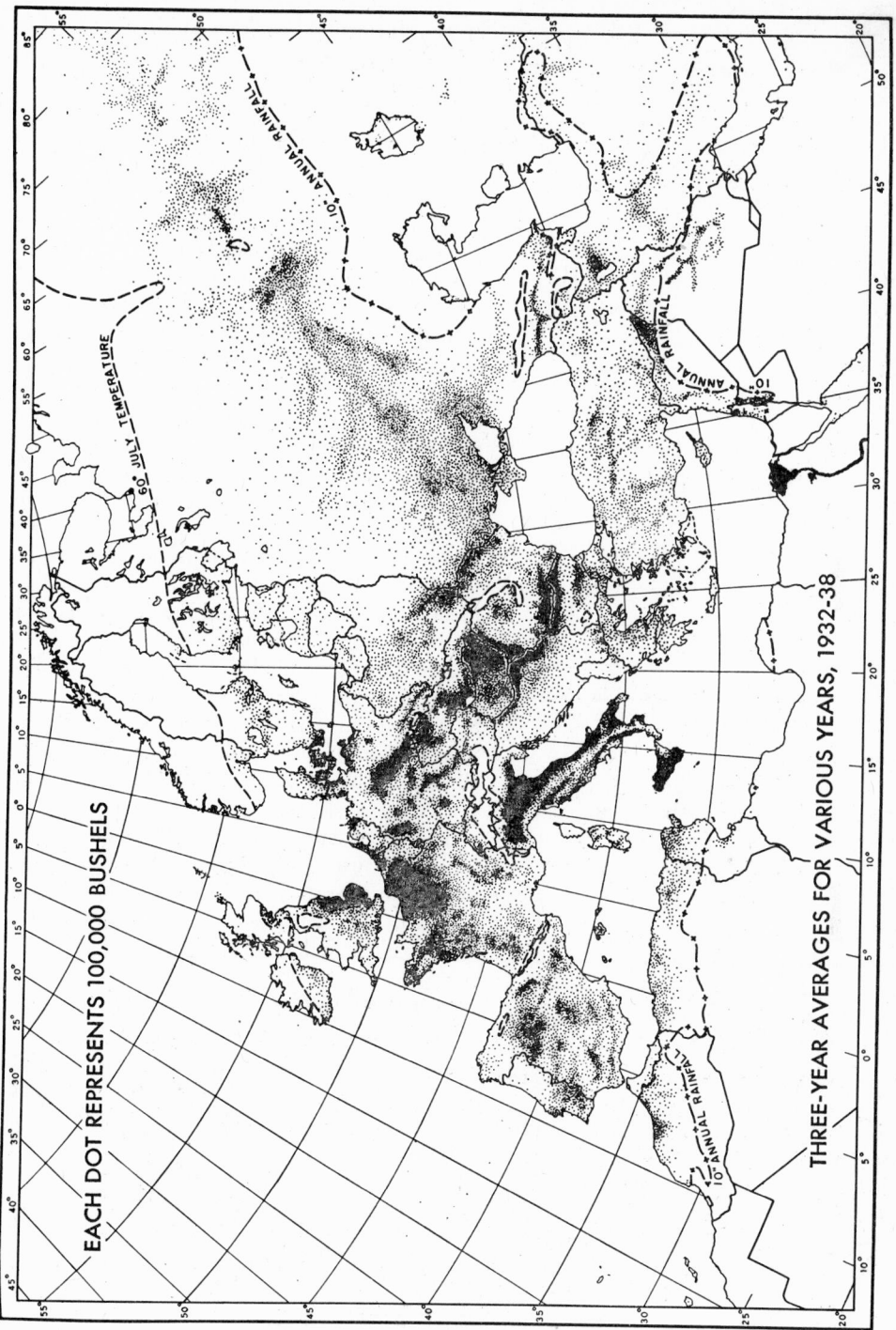

EACH DOT REPRESENTS 100,000 BUSHELS

THREE-YEAR AVERAGES FOR VARIOUS YEARS, 1932-38

Figure 170. Wheat: Output in Europe and the Near East

U. S. Department of Agriculture

Four areas in Europe and the Near East are outstanding in production of wheat: the Valley of the Danube, where richness of the soil and moderate moisture particularly favor wheat growing; the Apennine Peninsula and Sicily; central Germany; and the northeastern part of France.

Country[a]	Annual Average Yield Per Acre, in Metric Quintals[b]		
	1885–89	*1934–38*	*1949–50*
Denmark	10.3	12.3	14.4
United Kingdom	8.2	9.4	11.1
Netherlands	7.6	12.2	15.2
Belgium	7.6	11.0	14.3
Germany	5.7	9.1	10.6[e]
Hungary	4.9	5.7	5.4
France	4.9	6.3	7.5
Romania	4.4	3.9	—
Canada	4.1	2.9	4.3
Bulgaria	3.8	5.1	—
United States	3.5	3.5	4.3
Italy	3.5	5.8	6.3
Argentina	2.7	4.0	4.3
Yugoslavia	2.7	4.6	4.9
Australia	2.2	3.2	4.3
Russia (USSR)	2.2	3.2	2.9

Sources: **61**, p. 31; Table 239.
   a. Countries are arrayed by yield per acre in 1885–89.
   b. Conversion factor: one metric quintal of wheat =
3.67 bushels.
   c. Western Germany.

possession, his medium of exchange and standard of value." [28] Outside Asia, rice is of only
minor importance.

Rice Culture

Rice grows in standing water and requires
high temperatures during the entire growing
season. Since the chief soil requirement is water-
holding capacity, the best rice soils are silts or
loams, stretched over a layer of clay. Alluvial
plains and deltas are ideal for this crop.

As much as 80 per cent of the crop is raised
on swampy, muddy fields — paddies. The paddies must hold the water at a uniform depth,
and no amount of work is spared to level the
rice beds. Seedlings are raised in highly fertilized
seedbeds and transplanted in small bundles by
hand. The rice fields are flooded several times
during the period of growth. When water cannot be brought to a field by irrigation canals, it
is carried, even in buckets. As the harvest approaches, the fields are drained to permit the

kernels to ripen. Apart from paddy rice, there is
upland rice, grown on terraced hillsides, under
irrigation.

Rice is a heavy yielder and supplies more food
per unit of land than any other grain. Double
cropping is common in Asia. An enormous
amount of work is involved in rice production
in the monsoon countries, where almost all operations are done by hand. Only the abundance
of cheap labor makes it possible to grow rice by
such methods.

In the United States, which has a comparatively small output of rice (though one of the
largest outside of Asia), the crop is raised with
about as much use of machinery as for any other
and, except for irrigation, there is little difference
between growing rice and other grains.[29] Rice
planting from airplanes has become general practice in California. In Rio Grande do Sul, the rice
exporting state of Brazil, and in the Sonora Valley of Mexico, rice is also raised with the aid of
modern machinery. Italy and Egypt use machine
methods along with hand labor.[30]

Rice is an economical crop, requiring only 3–5
per cent of the yield for seed, as against from
8 to 15 per cent for wheat. It may be grown year
after year on the same paddy and in a moist, hot
climate can be stored much better than wheat or
corn.[31]

The importance of rice to Asia is enhanced by
its various uses other than for food. In China
and Japan, rice straw serves for thatching roofs,
for fuel, feed, fertilizer, and for making footwear, baskets and so on.

Acreage and Output

The world acreage in rice was about 10–12 per
cent greater in 1949 and 1950 than in 1934–38.
Much of this expansion took place in India,
Pakistan and Thailand, on marginal or even
submarginal land. Despite the increase, the
world output was only slightly larger than the
prewar.

Asia produces 93–95 per cent of the world's
rice. Most of the remainder is raised in the
Western Hemisphere and Africa, while small

28. **57**, pp. 31 and 312; **21**, June 1948, p. 115. The
percentage for Indochina increases to 91 when the
temporary dry rice fields in the upland are included.

29. For over 200 years, from 1685 to 1888, rice was
grown only in the Carolinas and Georgia. After the
Civil War, shortage of labor affected rice production in
those states. The crop moved westward, first to Louisiana
and then to Texas, California and Arkansas. **25**, 1938,
p. 419.

30. **21**, June 1948, p. 117.

31. **56**, p. 270.

quantities are grown in Europe and the USSR.

The major producing countries are China, India, Pakistan, Japan, Indonesia, Indochina, Thailand and Burma. While China ranks first, millions of the northern Chinese have never tasted rice and for tens of millions it is a luxury eaten only once or twice a year.[32] Burma, Indochina and Thailand, the "Big Three" exporters, are the world's rice granary; today, as before World War II, they account for about two thirds of the world's rice trade. Of these three countries — the "rice bowl" of southeast Asia — only Thailand has considerably increased its rice acreage and output in recent years. In contrast, Burma, normally the largest rice-surplus country in the world, produces 1.5–1.7 million tons less than before the war. Military operations and unsettled political conditions in Indochina have resulted in a substantial slump in rice production in that country. Japan, the Philippines, India and Taiwan have increased their output, but not in proportion to the growth of the population. The United States, Brazil and Egypt have doubled their output and tripled their combined exports, while the Far East has less home-grown rice to feed 110 million more people than it had before the war.[33]

Almost all countries in the Far East have initiated projects to expand rice acreage by reclaiming wasteland, extending irrigation and improving soil fertility. If and when such plans are implemented, rice production in the Far East may rise to levels that would supply this area adequately and provide a surplus for export.

Italy, with a small rice crop, has the world's highest yield per acre (18.4 quintals in 1950). Egypt's and Japan's yields are also very high. (See Table 241 and Figure 171.)

Recently rice has been grown in Greece, where the Economic Cooperation Administration has introduced this crop on salt flats barren since ancient times, which now yield 1.5 quintals or more per acre — a very small yield on good soil but unusual on this sterile land. It was expected that by 1952 the salt would have been washed out by constant flushing of the land with fresh water, so that other crops, such as wheat, could be grown.[34]

RYE

Rye is the only grain except wheat commonly used to make bread. Once the principal grain for large masses of the population in Europe, it has been losing ground to wheat for use in bread throughout this century. Since rye bread is generally considered less palatable than wheat bread and not as easily digestible, it has largely become the poor man's bread even in rye-producing countries. Rye bread, moreover, is often made with some wheat flour. Rye is used increasingly for feed, though livestock do not relish it and suffer from digestive troubles when it forms more than half the grain ration.

In spite of the distinct preference of human consumers for wheat bread and of livestock for corn, oats or barley, rye remains an important crop largely because it is cheap and has less exacting requirements than other grains as to soil and moisture. In the large rye-producing and rye-consuming areas no other cereal will consistently yield as much human food per acre as rye at such a low cost.[35] Moreover, rye is also raised as a cover crop and for pasturage, soil conditioning and green manuring.

Acreage and Output

Rye, a winter hardy crop, is grown mostly in temperate and cool regions; it ripens earliest of all the small grains. Rye holds its own on about 110 million acres in the world, largely because no other grain will tolerate such poor and acid soil. A small increase in rye acreage since the turn of this century is due largely to the fact that rye-producing countries have brought additional inferior land under cultivation.[36] Not infrequently, however, fairly good soil is given over to rye for rotation purposes.

Rye is eminently a European crop: 96 per cent of the world output is harvested in Europe and the USSR. The European prewar acreage was about half that in the USSR and is still smaller now: France, the Low Countries, Sweden, Czechoslovakia, Austria and some other countries have reduced their acreage in rye while almost 8 million acres under this crop were taken by the USSR (the Baltic states and parts of Poland, Romania, Germany, Czechoslovakia and Finland). The yield per acre in Europe is much higher than in Russia — in many countries,

TABLE 241

RICE (PADDY): ACREAGE AND YIELD IN EACH CONTINENT AND SELECTED COUNTRIES,
1934–38 ANNUAL AVERAGE, 1949 AND 1950

Continent and Country	Area, in Thousands of Acres			Output, in Thousands of Metric Tons [a]			Yield Per Acre, in Metric Quintals [a]		
	1934–38	1949	1950	1934–38	1949	1950	1934–38	1949	1950
World (with the USSR)	209,020	...	...	149,618	...	...	7.2	...	...
World (without the USSR)	208,700	229,062	233,015	149,300	151,000	152,700	7.2	6.6	6.7
North and South America	4,275	8,401	8,278	3,000	6,200	6,200	7.0	7.3	7.5
United States	956	1,841	1,609	956	1,736	1,722	10.0	9.4	10.7
Brazil	2,362	4,571	4,497	1,365	2,980	2,995	5.8	6.5	6.7
Europe	544	642	741	1,140	1,080	1,200	21.0	16.8	16.2
Spain	116 [b]	141	143	293 [b]	275	240	25.4 [b]	19.5	16.8
Italy	351	319	376	753	610	690	21.5	19.1	18.4
USSR	366	...	...	318	...	...	8.7	...	...
Asia	199,311	213,000	216,707	142,900	140,300	141,700	7.2	6.6	6.5
China [c]	48,854	45,714	45,714	50,065	44,500	47,000	10.2	9.7	10.3
South Korea	3,005	2,580	...	2,726	3,197	2,935	9.1	12.4	...
Japan	7,831	7,784	7,398	11,501	11,660	12,005	14.7	15.0	16.2
Pakistan	18,686	21,772	22,400	11,169	12,403	12,490	6.0	5.7	5.6
India	58,877	71,660	75,272	29,645	34,709	30,981	5.0	4.8	4.1
Burma [d]	12,185	9,318	9,264	6,971	5,170	5,200	5.7	5.5	5.6
Thailand	8,327	12,264	13,084	4,357	6,782	6,018	5.2	5.5	5.2
Indochina	13,813	11,196	...	6,498	4,600	...	4.7	4.1	...
Indonesia	9,496	9,197	...	6,081	6,075	...	6.4	6.6	...
Philippines	4,917	5,387	5,580	2,179	2,596	2,795	4.4	4.8	5.0
Africa	4,547	6,919	7,166	2,170	3,400	3,500	4.8	4.9	4.9
Egypt	430	729	726	609	1,168	1,241	14.2	16.0	17.1
French West Africa	1,433	1,962	2,051	405	505	531	2.8	2.6	2.6
Madagascar	1,236	1,389	1,539	613	750	802	5.0	5.4	5.2
Oceania	25	74	74	50	80	80	20.0	12.2	10.8

Sources: **12**, 1941–42 to 1945–46, Vol. I, pp. 36–41; **9**, December 1951, p. 5.

a. Conversion factors: one metric ton of rice = 10 metric quintals = 49 bushels.

b. 1931–35.
c. 22 provinces.
d. Incomplete data.

at least double. Germany and Poland together account for two thirds of the European crop.

Production of rye declined in Europe very considerably during the war and has never regained the prewar level. The output in the USSR is also smaller despite the 15 per cent increase in acreage, because of a slump in the yield per acre.

In the United States, most of the rye harvest is fed to livestock or used in the distilling industry. Three states, the Dakotas and Minnesota, raised about half the crop during 1934–38. Acreage decreased after 1942 and in 1948, despite the high price, rye had only about half its 1938 acreage. The output, however, was only a third less than

that before the war.[37] In 1950 both acreage and output increased somewhat, while remaining well below the prewar average. (See Table 242 and Figure 172.)

CORN

Most corn leaves the farm on the hoof and reaches the ultimate consumer as pork or beef, or in the form of butter, cheese, eggs and the like. Corn is the leading cereal for only some 50–60 million people, but hundreds of millions consume it in the form of animal products.

The processing of corn by animals is costly.

37. **26**, 1949, p. 669.

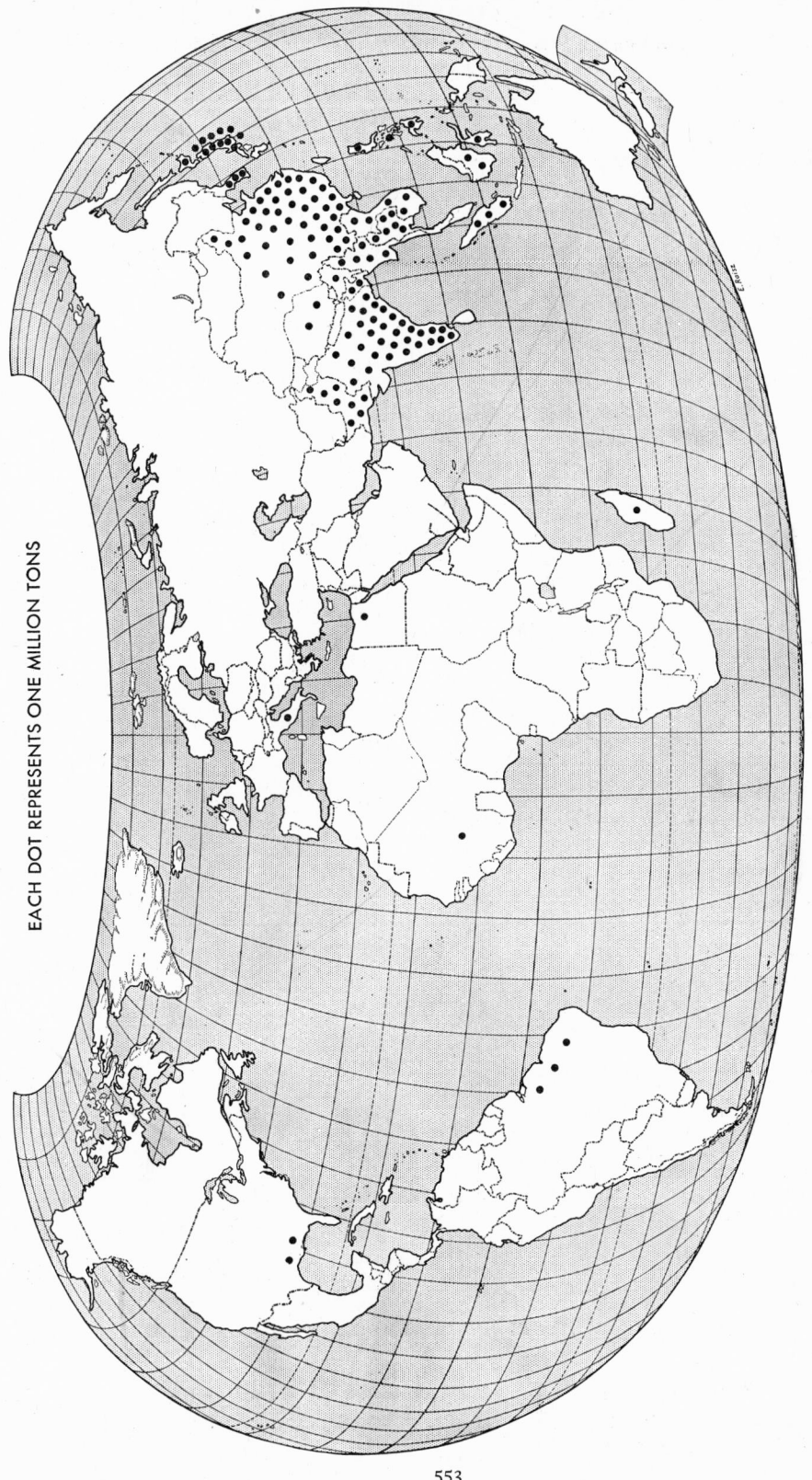

EACH DOT REPRESENTS ONE MILLION TONS

FIGURE 171. RICE: WORLD OUTPUT, 1950

Rice is primarily an Asiatic grain. Both production and consumption are heavily concentrated in the Far East, where 93–95 per cent of the world's rice is grown. The rest of the rice crop is so widely scattered over the continents that it is hardly noticeable on the map. (Cf. Table 241.)

TABLE 242

RYE: ACREAGE AND YIELD IN EACH CONTINENT AND SELECTED COUNTRIES, 1934–38 ANNUAL AVERAGE, 1949 AND 1950

Continent and Country [a]	Area, in Thousands of Acres			Output, in Thousands of Metric Tons [b]			Yield Per Acre, in Metric Quintals [b]		
	1934–38	*1949*	*1950*	*1934–38*	*1949*	*1950*	*1934–38*	*1949*	*1950*
World (with the USSR)	103,535	111,936	110,454	46,500	43,960	42,800	4.5	3.9	3.8
North and South America	5,214	4,003	4,843	1,490	1,030	1,360	2.9	2.6	2.8
United States	3,319	1,559	1,821	1,028	476	584	3.1	3.1	3.2
Canada	734	1,181	1,169	180	254	339	2.5	2.2	2.9
Argentina	1,072	1,154	1,752	254	277	413	2.4	2.4	2.4
Europe									
Prewar boundaries	*40,942*	—	—	*22,650*	—	—	*5.5*	—	—
Present boundaries	33,359	30,888	29,900	19,100	18,400	17,800	5.7	6.0	6.0
France	1,638	1,290	1,245	769	650	606	4.7	5.0	4.9
Belgium	440	235	220	424	258	238	9.7	11.0	10.8
Netherlands	539	467	432	496	517	421	9.2	11.1	9.7
Denmark	363	482	381	262	469	330	7.2	9.7	8.7
Sweden	526	334	314	409	277	244	7.8	8.3	7.8
Finland									
Prewar boundaries	*593*	—	—	*371*	—	—	*6.3*	—	—
Present boundaries	524	358	351	340	218	234	6.5	6.1	6.7
Germany									
Prewar boundaries	*10,870*	—	—	*7,611*	—	—	*7.0*	—	—
Western Germany	4,117	3,496	3,368	7,081	3,021	3,178	7.5	9.5	9.0
Soviet Zone	2,987	3,205	3,398	2,070	2,130	2,130	6.9	6.3	6.3
Poland									
Prewar boundaries	*14,268*	—	—	*2,558*	—	—	*4.8*	—	—
Present boundaries	13,225	12,765	12,108	6,854	6,759	6,503	5.2	5.3	5.4
Czechoslovakia									
Prewar boundaries	*2,441*	—	—	*1,598*	—	—	*6.5*	—	—
Present boundaries	2,417	1,749	1,779	1,568	1,339	1,170	6.5	7.7	6.6
Austria	907	596	615	539	365	388	5.9	6.1	6.3
Hungary	1,559	1,680	...	697	...	...	4.5	...	...
Spain	1,465 [c]	1,606	1,581	551 [c]	460	560	3.8 [c]	2.9	3.5
Romania									
Prewar boundaries	*1,038*	—	—	*391*	—	—	*3.8*	—	—
Present boundaries	442	...	...	165	...	...	3.7	...	...
USSR									
Prewar boundaries	*56,166*	—	—	*21,970*	—	—	*3.5*	—	—
Present boundaries	63,925	75,500	74,000	25,500	24,100	23,100	4.0	3.2	3.1
Asia	939	1,236	1,359	360	330	490	3.7	2.7	3.6
Turkey	865	1,045	1,206	336	274	443	3.9	2.6	3.7

Sources: **12**, 1941–42 to 1945–46, Vol. 1, pp. 20–21, and **9**, December 1951, p. 4.

a. For the USSR and European countries whose boundaries have undergone changes since World War II, data for 1934–38 in prewar boundaries are given in italics, for comparison. World totals include the FAO estimate for gaps in reporting of acreage and output.

b. Conversion factors: one metric ton of rye = 10 metric quintals = 39.37 bushels.

c. 1931–35.

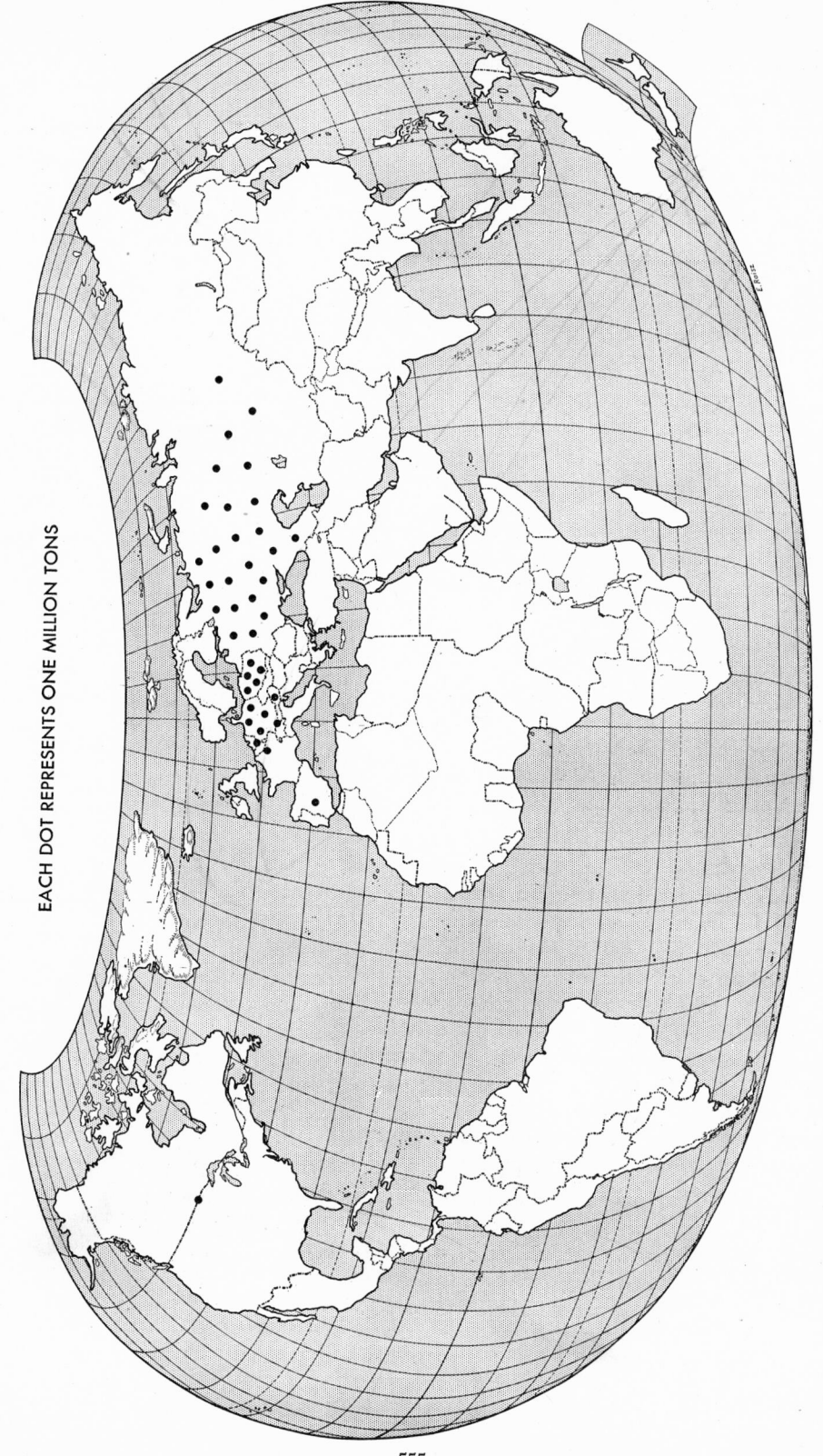

EACH DOT REPRESENTS ONE MILLION TONS

FIGURE 172. RYE: WORLD OUTPUT, 1949–50

It takes from 5 to 6 pounds of corn to produce a pound of pork, and 10 to 12 for a pound of beef. A bushel of corn consumed as whole corn meal supplies the daily requirements of twenty-three persons for food energy and protein, but the same amount of corn consumed in the form of eggs provides only two persons with their requirements for food energy and eight persons with those for protein. Somewhat larger amounts are supplied by corn fed to cows and hogs. (See Figure 173.)

Climatic and Soil Requirements

Corn, a native American crop, requires an abundance of moisture and sunshine, an average growing season of at least 140 days [38] and soil that is well drained and aerated, rich in humus, dark and fertile. Only a few regions combine these climatic and soil conditions in large continuous areas. The Corn Belt of the United States, 900 miles long and 150 to 300 miles wide, with ideal conditions for this crop, is unique in the world.

No other cereal is distributed so widely over the globe as corn, and only wheat occupies a larger acreage in the world. Corn, however, is not grown to any significant extent in the Northern Hemisphere north of the fiftieth parallel, except for green fodder, or in the Southern Hemisphere south of the fortieth parallel.[39]

Acreage and Output

The world's corn crop rose from an annual average of 115 million tons during 1934–38 to 132 million in 1950. The United States leads, with nearly 60 per cent of the total. Before the war, Argentina ranked second as a producer but led all other countries, including the United States, as an exporter. In normal years it had considerable surpluses for export because of the exceptionally high output per capita of population and the comparatively low domestic demand: its hog industry is less extensive than that of the United States, and cattle are fattened with alfalfa instead of corn. Argentina had several years of bad crops during the war, and its corn output continued to decline in postwar years. In 1949 the lowest point in corn production was

reached, the output amounting to little more than 10 per cent of the 1934–38 average. At the close of 1949, the government requested the farmers to sow about 12.5 million acres to corn (10.8 million in 1934–38) and fixed prices 30 per cent above those in 1949. The farmers about doubled the acreage in 1950 and obtained a triple crop, but both acreage and total yield remain far below the prewar averages.

Brazil, Mexico and some other Latin American countries raise corn largely for human consumption. The yield per unit of land in Mexico is one of the lowest in the world, less than half the world average, but the crop itself is of extreme importance to the population and occupies a considerable percentage of all cultivated land. Efforts are now being made to obtain higher yields by better farming methods and abandonment of marginal land.[40]

About 10 per cent of the world's corn crop is raised in Europe, chiefly in the Balkans, Hungary and Italy. Corn acreage in the USSR is nearly triple Italy's but the harvest in 1950 was only twice as high. In the USSR corn occupies less acreage (some 8.5–9.0 million acres) than any of the major grains, except rice. It is grown in the southern Ukraine, some parts of the Caucasus, particularly Georgia, and in the territory acquired after the war from Romania.

In Asia, China ranks first, followed by India and Indonesia. (See Table 243 and Figure 174.)

Output of Corn in the United States

Corn has been the most important grain crop in the United States for more than a century. The farm value of harvested corn has consistently exceeded, with a few exceptions, that of all other grains combined (wheat, barley, oats, rye, rice, sorghum and buckwheat).[41] The yield per acre before the war was just above the world average, and has risen since the war by about two thirds. Apart from the Corn Belt, which accounts for about 70 per cent of the country's total yield, this crop is of considerable importance in the South. (See Figure 175.)

More than 85 per cent of the corn produced in the United States is fed to livestock — about 40 per cent to hogs, 20 per cent to horses and mules, 15 per cent to cattle and 12 per cent to poultry, sheep and other stock. Some is used by the starch, sirup and distilling industries. Only about

38. There are strains, however, that require only 60 to 70 days to mature, and others that need from 300 to 340 days. **21**, July 1948, p. 140.

39. **21**, July 1948, p. 141.

40. **3**, p. 54.

41. **26**, 1952, pp. 615–18.

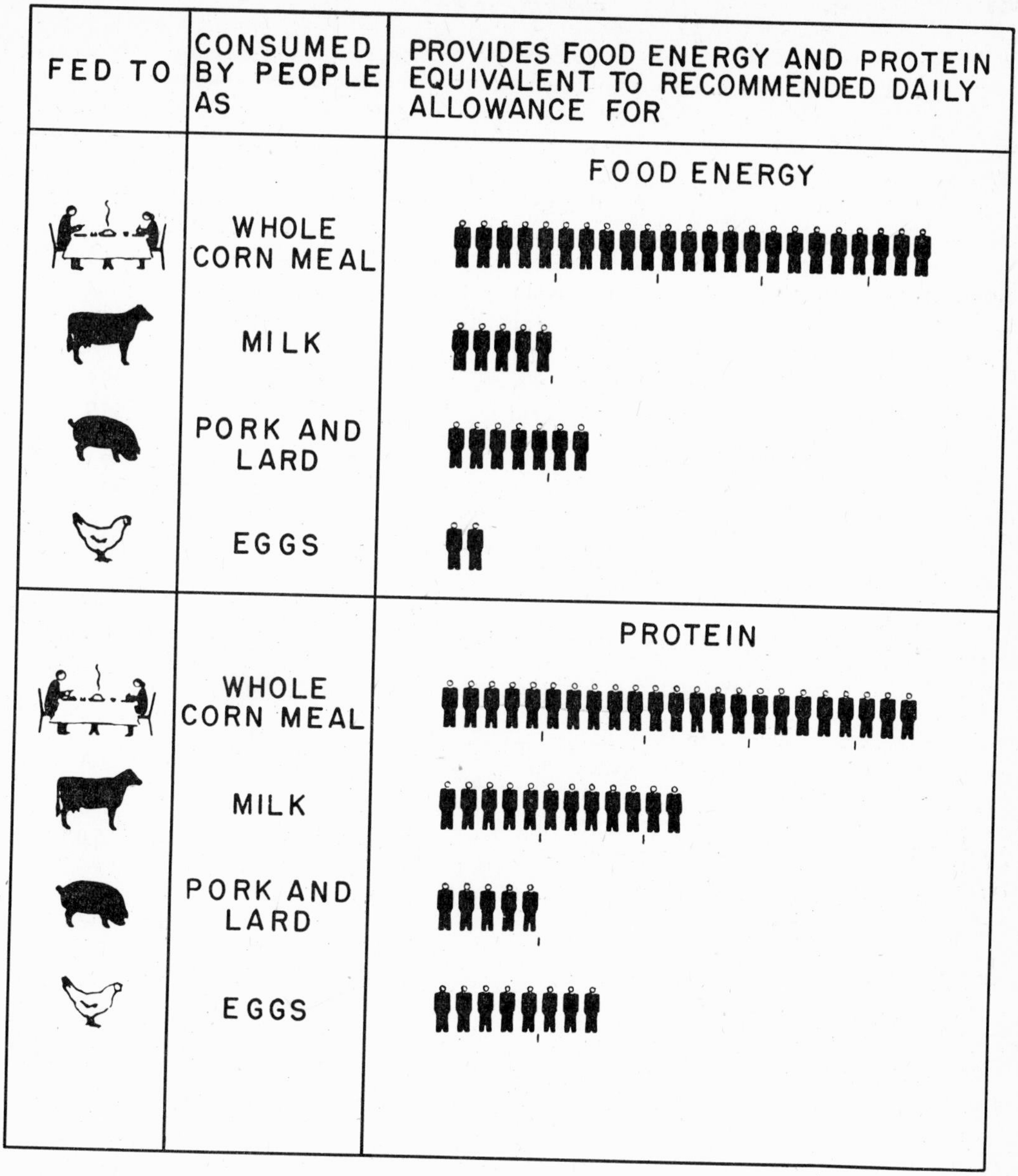

FED TO	CONSUMED BY PEOPLE AS	PROVIDES FOOD ENERGY AND PROTEIN EQUIVALENT TO RECOMMENDED DAILY ALLOWANCE FOR
		FOOD ENERGY
	WHOLE CORN MEAL	👤👤👤👤👤👤👤👤👤👤👤👤👤👤👤👤👤👤👤👤👤👤👤
	MILK	👤👤👤👤👤
	PORK AND LARD	👤👤👤👤👤👤👤
	EGGS	👤👤
		PROTEIN
	WHOLE CORN MEAL	👤👤👤👤👤👤👤👤👤👤👤👤👤👤👤👤👤👤👤👤👤👤👤
	MILK	👤👤👤👤👤👤👤👤👤👤👤👤
	PORK AND LARD	👤👤👤👤👤
	EGGS	👤👤👤👤👤👤👤👤

U. S. Department of Agriculture

FIGURE 173. CORN: FOOD ENERGY AND PROTEIN PROVIDED BY ONE BUSHEL

Consumed as cereal (whole corn meal) a bushel of corn provides 23 persons with food energy and protein sufficient to meet a day's needs.

Converted into milk, it contains the food energy equivalent to the daily requirements of 5 persons, and the protein equivalent required by 12 persons.

In the form of pork and lard, the same amount of corn supplies a day's food energy for 7 persons and protein for 5 persons.

In the form of eggs, it supplies sufficient food energy for only 2 persons and the protein required by 8 persons.

TABLE 243

CORN: ACREAGE AND YIELD IN EACH CONTINENT AND SELECTED COUNTRIES, 1934–38 ANNUAL AVERAGE, 1949 AND 1950

Continent and Country [a]	Area, in Thousands of Acres			Output, in Thousands of Metric Tons [b]			Yield Per Acre, in Metric Quintals [b]		
	1934–38	1949	1950	1934–38	1949	1950	1934–38	1949	1950
World (with the USSR)	220,112	216,730	212,610	114,848	141,605	132,210	5.2	6.5	6.2
World (without the USSR)	209,368	205,530	203,610	110,200	138,050	128,400	5.3	6.7	6.3
North America	93,650	87,300	82,123	53,240	86,183	78,123	5.7	9.9	9.5
United States [c]	93,480	87,029	81,817	53,066	85,836	77,671	5.7	9.9	9.5
Canada	168	272	306	172	347	352	10.2	12.8	11.5
Middle and South America	34,595	32,290	34,110	17,960	15,907	16,260	5.2	4.9	4.8
Mexico	7,354	9,880	9,880	1,665	2,300	2,499	2.2	2.3	2.6
Guatemala	593	1,334	. . .	237	378	. . .	4.0	2.8	. . .
Colombia	1,369	1,747	1,705	496	738	585	3.6	4.2	3.4
Brazil	10,111	11,560	. . .	5,677	6,162	5,790	5.6	5.3	. . .
Argentina	10,779	2,330	4,940	7,892	838	2,600	7.4	3.6	5.3
Europe									
Prewar boundaries	*32,023*	—	—	*18,580*	—	—	*5.8*	—	—
Present boundaries	28,911	26,193	25,946	17,400	15,400	13,100	6.0	5.9	5.0
Hungary	2,856	3,284 [d]	. . .	2,306	2,862 [d]	. . .	8.1	8.7 [d]	. . .
Italy	3,603	3,062	3,067	3,000	2,211	1,924	8.3	7.2	6.3
Yugoslavia									
Prewar boundaries	*6,561*	—	—	*4,691*	—	—	*7.1*	—	—
Present boundaries	6,603	5,453	5,760	4,708	3,718	2,085	7.1	6.8	3.6
Romania									
Prewar boundaries	*12,647*	—	—	*5,141*	—	—	*4.1*	—	—
Present boundaries	9,585	10,645 [e]	. . .	4,032	5,279 [e]	. . .	4.2	5.0 [e]	. . .
Bulgaria									
Prewar boundaries	*1,707*	—	—	*812*	—	—	*4.8*	—	—
Present boundaries	2,004	1,878 [e]	. . .	913	890 [e]	. . .	4.6	4.7 [e]	. . .
USSR									
Prewar boundaries	*7,630*	—	—	*3,100*	—	—	*4.1*	—	—
Present boundaries	10,744	8,500 [f]	9,000 [f]	4,648	3,556 [f]	3,810 [f]	4.3	4.2 [f]	4.2 [f]
Asia	33,606	39,610	38,510	15,200	16,256	15,494	4.6	4.1	4.0
China (22 provinces)	11,643	12,300	. . .	6,497	6,483	. . .	5.5	5.3	. . .
Turkey	1,092	1,474	1,466	557	725	628	5.1	4.9	4.3
Pakistan	813	1,004	941	364	430	374	4.5	4.3	4.0
India	5,518	8,046	7,561	1,647	2,041	1,708	3.0	2.4	1.7
Indonesia (Java and Madoera)	5,061	5,560	. . .	1,978	1,850	. . .	3.9	3.3	. . .
Africa	18,285	21,250	21,250	6,200	7,500	7,000	3.2	3.5	3.3
French Morocco	1,065	1,243	1,290	213	400	127	2.0	3.2	1.0
Egypt	1,604	1,552	1,507	1,616	1,250	1,306	10.1	8.1	8.7
French West Africa	1,621	1,184	1,063	532	310	262	3.3	2.6	2.5
Union of South Africa [g]	5,824	8,154	7,907	1,995	2,633	2,470	3.4	3.2	3.1
Oceania	321	198	173	200	160	130	6.2	8.1	7.5
Australia	311	193	170	186	152	120	6.0	7.9	7.1

Sources: **12**, 1941–42 to 1945–46, Vol. I, pp. 28–35; **8**, 1950, pp. 36–38; **19**, FG, 5–51, pp. 2–3; **9**, February 1952, p. 5.

a. For the USSR and European countries whose boundaries have undergone changes since World War II, data for 1934–38 in prewar boundaries are given in italics, for comparison.

b. Conversion factors: one metric ton of corn = 10 metric quintals = 39.37 bushels.

c. Corn used for all purposes, including "hogged" and silo corn.

d. 1948.

e. 1947.

f. Estimate of the U. S. Department of Agriculture (**55**, p. 126).

g. European farms and estates.

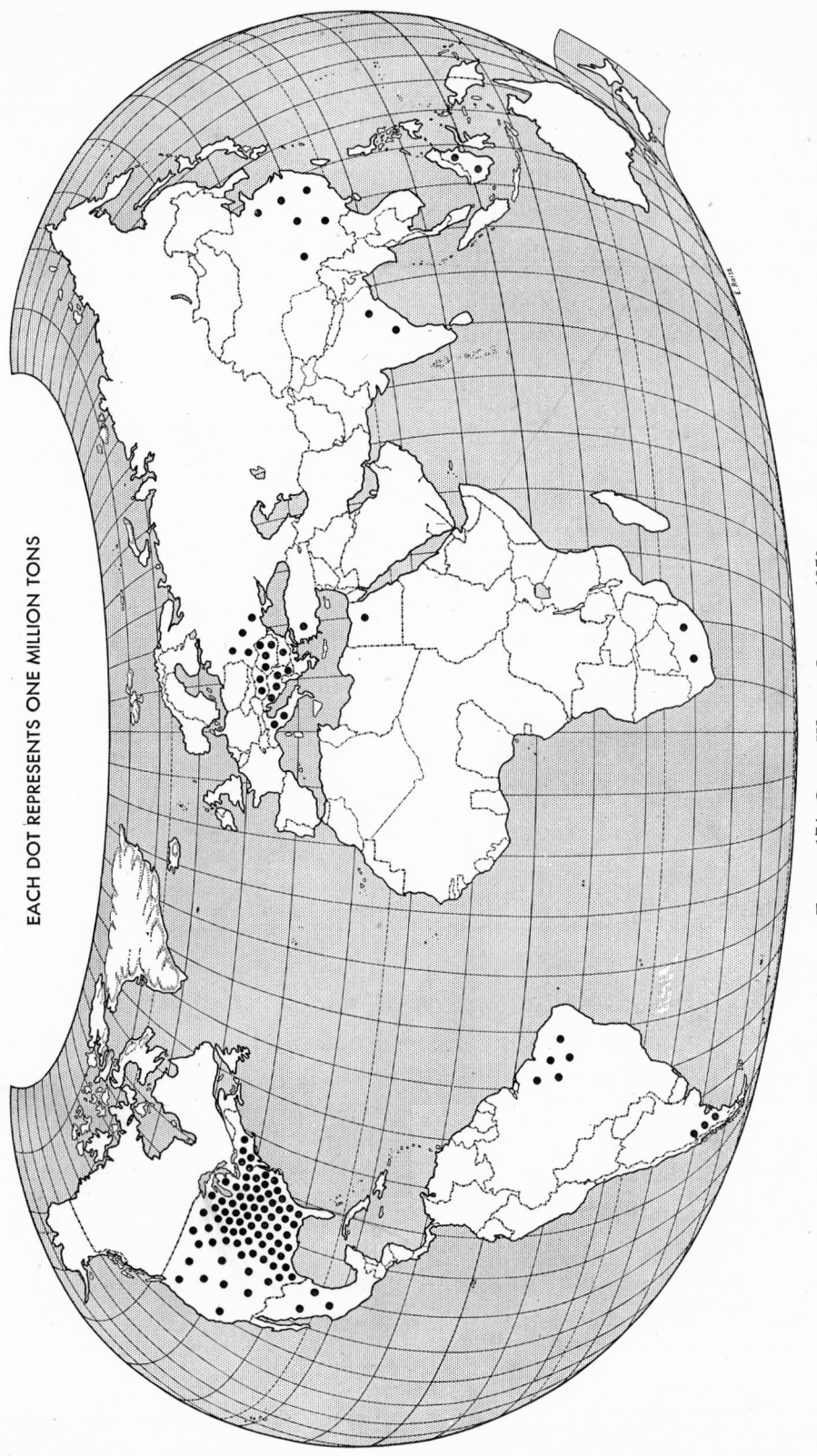

EACH DOT REPRESENTS ONE MILLION TONS

FIGURE 174. CORN: WORLD OUTPUT, 1950

The United States leads in production of corn and accounts for about 60 per cent of the world's output. Southeastern Europe—Italy, the Balkans and Hungary—is another important producing area. Other corn regions are in Brazil and Argentina, China and Indonesia, the USSR, Egypt and South Africa. (See Table 243.)

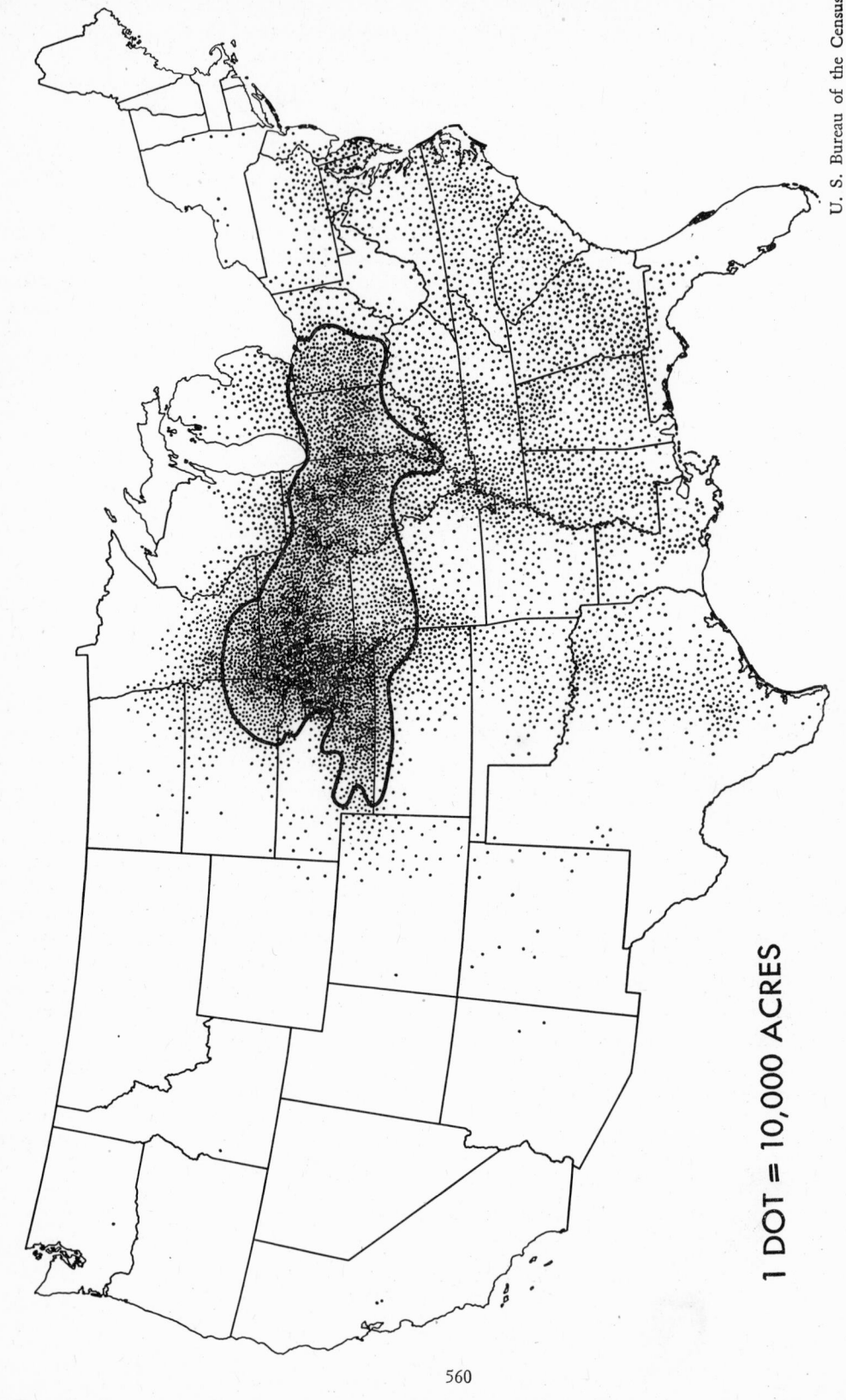

1 DOT = 10,000 ACRES

Figure 175. Corn: Major Producing Areas in the United States

The Corn Belt raises about 70 per cent of the corn crop of the United States. Most of the rest comes from southern and southeastern states.

3 per cent goes directly into human food — corn meal, grits, flour, corn on the cob, breakfast cereals and the like.[42]

High-yielding hybrid corn is rapidly displacing the open-pollinated strains: less than ten years ago it grew on only 7.9 per cent of the total corn area, and now it covers 77.7 per cent. In 1933, only a little more than one acre in a thousand was in hybrids; now hybrids are planted on more than three acres out of four.[43] More than 94 per cent of the corn acreage in the north central states was in hybrids in 1949. In Indiana, 99.0 per cent of the corn sown is hybrid, and Iowa and Illinois use it entirely.[44] It is estimated that the use of hybrid seed in the United States added about 14 million tons to the 1944 crop and that 16 million additional acres would have been needed to get the same harvest from ordinary seed. The principal type grown in the Corn Belt is Dent, which accounts for more than 90 per cent of the United States output. Flint is another popular variety.[45] In the South, hybrid seed was adopted later, but the trend shows a rapid upward movement.[46]

BARLEY

Barley is primarily a feed grain, although it is used for human consumption in some countries in Asia and North Africa.[47] A relatively small amount of a special variety, malting barley, is used in the beer industry.

Barley, a short season crop, is grown under a wide range of climatic conditions — near and even within the Arctic Circle and on the Sahara, the plains of India and the high plateau of Tibet, even the slopes of Mount Everest. While barley can stand drought and frost, it grows best in moderate temperatures. It needs well-drained soil and is sensitive to acidity. Malting barley has more exacting requirements than feed barley.

The USSR, China and the United States are the three big producers of barley. In the USSR, barley grows mostly near the Black Sea, but also in the far north (the Archangel Oblast and the Yakutsk Republic). In the latter area, spring barley ripens better than other grain crops and is used for food.[48] The USSR's yield per acre is a third below the world average.

In the United States, more than 11 million acres were sown to barley in 1950, principally in California, the Dakotas and Minnesota. Colorado and Montana are next in line, and the six states together produced about two thirds of the total output.[49] Nearly 60 per cent of the crop is fed to livestock, 28 per cent is used for making beverages and other purposes, and the remainder is exported or stocked.[50]

China leads in Asia and consumes nearly its whole crop. India and Turkey are next in importance. Japan, with a smaller output, ranks first in Asia in yield per acre. In Africa, barley is grown chiefly along the Mediterranean coast — in French Morocco, Algeria, Tunisia and Egypt. (See Table 244.)

OATS

The world's crop of oats has maintained its position despite the displacement of horses by automobiles and tractors. Oats are a well-balanced feed and the straw has a higher feed value than that of any other grain.

In the Corn Belt of the United States, oats are grown in rotation with other crops, mostly corn and clover.[51] No other crop fits this purpose so well or so well utilizes land and labor which might otherwise be unproductive.[52]

Oats thrive in a moist, cool climate and are less demanding in soil requirements than any other small grain except rye. Three fourths of the acreage in oats in the USSR, almost all in Poland, and more than half in Germany is in poor acid soil unfit for either wheat or barley.[53]

Oats exceed barley and rye in world output. In the United States, oats hold third place, immediately after corn and wheat, but in many countries they either rank second to wheat, as in Canada and France, or about equal the largest crop (rye), as in Germany. In the USSR only two crops — wheat and rye — occupy more acreage.

North America, Europe and the USSR together account for about 95 per cent of the oats

42. **16**, 1946, p. 46.
43. **15**, August 1950, p. 4.
44. **16**, 1950, p. 47.
45. **25**, 1943–47, p. 923, and 1950–51, p. 333.
46. Hybrid corn is also gaining ground in other countries — in Brazil, Mexico, Ecuador, Japan and many countries of Europe.
47. Barley was used for feed by the time of the Roman Empire. (**54**, p. 137.) In continental Europe, it was one of the chief bread grains until the sixteenth century but was gradually replaced by rye and wheat.

48. **32**, p. 384.
49. **17**, p. 21.
50. **23**, p. 12.
51. **25**, 1950–51, p. 333.
52. **35**, p. 9.
53. **42**, p. 538.

TABLE 244

BARLEY: ACREAGE AND YIELD IN EACH CONTINENT AND SELECTED COUNTRIES, 1934–38
ANNUAL AVERAGE, 1949 AND 1950

Continent and Country [a]	Area, in Thousands of Acres			Output, in Thousands of Metric Tons [b]			Yield Per Acre, in Metric Quintals [b]		
	1934–38	1949	1950	1934–38	1949	1950	1934–38	1949	1950
World (with the USSR)	114,730	113,420	117,620	51,270	49,800	52,900	4.5	4.4	4.5
World (without the USSR)	88,315	91,920	96,120	41,020	43,000	45,900	4.6	4.7	4.8
North America	13,729	15,874	17,777	6,259	7,776	10,340	4.6	4.9	5.8
United States	9,585	9,857	11,152	4,495	5,154	6,608	4.7	5.2	5.8
Canada	4,144	6,017	6,625	1,764	2,622	3,732	4.2	4.4	5.6
Middle and South America	2,577	2,656	3,039	921	1,030	1,362	3.6	3.9	4.5
Argentina	1,324	971	1,448	503	395	708	3.8	4.1	4.9
Europe									
Prewar boundaries	*27,528*	—	—	*16,020*	—	—	*5.8*	—	—
Present boundaries	23,227	21,251	21,991	14,400	14,300	14,300	6.2	6.7	6.5
United Kingdom	924	2,061	1,779	782	2,163	1,738	7.9	10.5	9.8
France	1,833	2,214	2,377	1,074	1,431	1,572	5.9	6.5	6.6
Denmark	914	1,122	1,221	1,103	1,571	1,615	12.1	14.0	13.3
Germany									
Prewar boundaries	*4,082*	—	—	*3,577*	—	—	*8.7*	—	—
Western Germany	1,999	1,223	1,515	1,699	1,213	1,473	8.5	9.9	9.7
Soviet Zone	1,085	625	704	1,029	458	515	9.5	7.3	7.3
Poland									
Prewar boundaries	*2,963*	—	—	...	—	—	...		⌐
Present boundaries	2,570	2,078	2,088	1,632	1,028	1,076	6.4	4.9	5.2
Czechoslovakia									
Prewar boundaries	*1,616*	—	—	*1,112*	—	—	*6.9*	—	—
Present boundaries	1,614	1,408	1,544	1,109	1,116	1,225	6.9	7.9	7.9
Hungary	1,134	1,886	...	608	...	...	5.4	...	...
Spain	4,683 [c]	...	...	2,394 [c]	1,460	1,500	5.1 [c]	...	...
Romania									
Prewar boundaries	*3,857*	—	—	*1,031*	—	—	*2.7*	—	—
Present boundaries	2,073	...	...	596	...	...	2.9	...	...
USSR									
Prewar boundaries	*22,113*	—	—	*8,628*	—	—	*3.9*	—	—
Present boundaries	26,415	21,500 [d]	21,500 [d]	10,250	6,800 [d]	7,000 [d]	3.9	3.2 [d]	3.3 [d]
Asia	37,806	38,548	39,536	16,700	15,500	16,400	4.1	4.0	4.1
China [e]	16,652	15,320	...	7,871	6,600	...	4.7	4.3	...
South Korea	2,142	1,722	...	819	723	...	3.8	4.2	...
Japan	1,888	2,476	2,513	1,556	2,074	1,958	8.3	8.4	7.8
Turkey	4,379	4,346	4,699	1,954	1,247	2,047	4.5	2.9	4.4
Iraq	1,836	1,853	2,471	575	800	900	3.1	4.3	3.6
Iran	1,576	1,730	2,286	793	850	875	5.0	4.3	3.8
Pakistan	487	610	561	153	182	157	3.1	3.0	2.8
India	5,792	7,712	7,650	1,968	2,241	2,187	3.4	2.9	2.9
Africa	10,378	12,602	12,602	2,500	3,900	3,000	2.4	3.1	2.4
French Morocco	4,240	4,527	4,848	1,148	1,368	1,075	2.7	3.0	2.2
Algeria	3,071	2,748	2,953	704	890	784	2.3	3.2	2.7
Tunisia	1,114	1,542	939	167	400	200	1.5	2.6	2.1
Oceania	593	1,087	1,137	240	500	540	4.0	4.6	4.7
Australia	573	1,040	1,080	219	443	497	3.8	4.3	4.6

Sources: **12,** 1941–42 to 1945–46, Vol. I, pp. 14–19; **9,** February 1952, p. 3.

a. For the USSR and European countries whose boundaries have undergone changes since World War II, data for 1934–38 in prewar boundaries are given in italics, for comparison.

b. Conversion factors: one metric ton of barley = 10 metric quintals = 45.9 bushels.

c. 1931–35.

d. Estimate of the U. S. Department of Agriculture (**55,** p. 125, and **22,** October 8, 1951, p. 359).

e. 22 provinces.

produced in the world. The yield per acre was about the same in the United States and in the USSR in 1934–38; since the war, yield has considerably increased in the United States and has declined in the USSR.

In prewar Europe, France, Germany, Poland and the United Kingdom were important producers of oats. After the war, output declined in the first three countries but increased in the United Kingdom by about 35 per cent. In the world as a whole, exclusive of the USSR, the output of oats since 1948 has been above the prewar level. (See Table 245.)

MILLET AND SORGHUM

Millet and sorghum are grown in Europe and North America chiefly for livestock and poultry feed, but are used largely for human food in Asia, Africa and the USSR.[54] In the world as a whole, these two crops share almost equally in acreage and output. Many reporting countries combine the data on acreage and production for both crops.

Millet

Millet has been used for food in Asia and Africa since prehistoric times. It was a major food of the poorer people in Europe in the Middle Ages but in the nineteenth century was replaced by wheat and rye and, in some areas, by corn or potatoes.

Millet grows on soil that will not support other grain and needs little cultivation. It requires only a short growing season and survives drought by reverting to a dormant state. Of the many kinds of millet produced in the world, five varieties are of dietary importance. Finger millet is so hardy that it grows in the Himalayas at an altitude of 6,000–7,000 feet. Cattail or pearl millet is an important food in India and is also grown in China and the USSR. Bread millet (proso) grows farther north than any other millet, for example, in central Russia. Proso, a staple food throughout the USSR, is eaten mostly in the form of thick porridge (*kasha*).[55]

Millet occupies some 75–80 million acres, possibly more, in the world, not including the USSR. The annual output in reporting countries averaged about 24 million tons in 1934–38 and was 20 million tons in 1949. The U. S. Department of Agriculture estimates the prewar world output, including that in nonreporting countries, at 26 million tons. The leading producers of millet are China and India, but Egypt has the highest yields per acre, three or four times the world average. India and Pakistan have very low yields per acre. (See Table 246.)

Sorghum

Sorghum, also an ancient crop in Asia and Africa, was brought to the Western Hemisphere in slave ships from Africa, its native home. While millions of people in Asia and Africa eat sorghum in the form of bread, porridge or confectionery or make a beverage from it, it is grown in the United States almost exclusively for feed. Sweet sorghum (sorgo) is grown for forage and sirup, and another variety (broomcorn) for making brooms.[56]

This prolific crop is well adapted to very hot climates and needs only a short growing season. It is widely grown in the monsoon regions of Asia and south and north of the tropics in Africa. In the United States, the only important producer outside Asia and Africa, sorghum is largely grown in the dry, hot southwestern states where its ability to remain dormant during a long drought and resume growth in a moist period has earned it the name of "crop camel." Texas and Oklahoma lead in sorghum production.

The numerous varieties of sorghum (kafir, milo, durra, sorgo, and so on) vary widely in such characteristics as height, yield, the time needed for maturity, size and shape of seeds. Together they occupy about 70 million acres in the world as a whole. World output ranges between 20 and 21 million tons a year. China, India, the United States and French West Africa account for more than 80 per cent of the total. More than 32 million acres are reported in millet and sorghum combined; how these are distributed between the two crops has not been estimated. (See Table 246.)

POTATOES

World production of potatoes centers in Europe and the USSR. While potatoes originated in the Andes, there are few places in the world where they are as much at home as in the cool,

---

54. **8,** 1949, p. 230.
55. **21,** November 1948, pp. 236–38.

56. Broomcorn was introduced into the United States by Benjamin Franklin, who found the seed in a broom imported from Europe. **25,** 1936, p. 527.

TABLE 245

OATS: ACREAGE AND YIELD IN EACH CONTINENT AND SELECTED COUNTRIES, 1934–38
ANNUAL AVERAGE, 1949 AND 1950

Continent and Country [a]	Area, in Thousands of Acres			Output, in Thousands of Metric Tons [b]			Yield Per Acre, in Metric Quintals [b]		
	1934–38	1949	1950	1934–38	1949	1950	1934–38	1949	1950
World (with the USSR)	142,800	129,660	129,910	65,030	58,800	60,200	4.6	4.5	4.6
World (without the USSR)	93,455	92,660	92,910	45,000	47,500	49,300	4.8	5.1	5.3
North America	48,395	51,827	52,306	19,000	24,200	26,955	3.9	4.7	5.1
United States	34,960	40,438	40,732	13,973	19,297	20,473	4.0	4.8	5.0
Canada	13,435	11,389	11,574	5,018	4,903	6,482	3.7	4.3	5.6
Middle and South America	2,498	2,000	2,224	910	739	889	3.6	3.7	4.0
Europe									
Prewar boundaries	*40,944*	—	—	*25,147*	—	—	*6.1*	—	—
Present boundaries	36,071	32,123	31,876	23,000	20,400	19,300	6.4	6.4	6.1
United Kingdom	2,444	3,252	3,106	2,019	3,043	2,735	8.3	9.4	8.9
France	8,100	6,019	5,814	4,572	3,225	3,305	5.6	5.4	5.6
Denmark	944	761	687	1,024	982	834	10.8	12.9	12.4
Sweden	1,641	1,240	1,240	1,257	840	807	7.6	6.8	6.9
Finland									
Prewar boundaries	*1,144*	—	—	*726*	—	—	*6.4*	—	—
Present boundaries	1,030	1,048	1,119	654	723	722	6.3	6.9	6.2
Germany									
Prewar boundaries	*7,055*	—	—	*5,755*	—	—	*8.2*	—	—
Western Germany	3,472	2,805	2,861	2,843	2,600	2,545	8.2	9.3	8.9
Soviet Zone	1,826	1,626	1,754	1,587	1,087	1,140	8.7	6.7	6.5
Poland									
Prewar boundaries	*5,560*	—	—	*2,558*	—	—	*4.6*	—	—
Present boundaries	4,823	4,384	4,248	2,830	2,333	2,126	5.9	5.3	5.0
Czechoslovakia									
Prewar boundaries	*1,905*	—	—	*1,238*	—	—	*6.5*	—	—
Present boundaries	1,848	1,554	1,515	1,212	1,107	818	6.6	7.1	5.4
Spain	1,917 [c]	1,606	1,606	670 [c]	500	500	3.5 [c]	3.1	3.3
Italy	1,050	1,159	1,169	539	415	553	5.1	3.6	4.6
Romania									
Prewar boundaries	*1,910*	—	—	*596*	—	—	*3.1*	—	—
Present boundaries	1,668	...	...	528	...	...	3.0	...	...
USSR									
Prewar boundaries	*44,429*	—	—	*17,884*	—	—	*4.0*	—	—
Present boundaries	49,346	37,000 [d]	37,000 [d]	20,030	11,300 [d]	10,900 [d]	4.1	3.1 [d]	2.9 [d]
Asia	3,947	3,707	3,706	1,400	1,200	1,300	3.5	3.0	3.5
China [e]	2,560	2,323	...	881	730	...	3.4	3.1	...
Africa	889	914	939	310	330	330	3.5	3.2	2.6
Algeria	457	427	460	150	142	142	3.3	3.3	3.2
Oceania	1,631	1,804	1,804	360	550	500	2.2	3.0	2.8
Australia	1,569	1,747	1,757	308	498	460	2.0	3.1	2.6

Sources: **12,** 1941–42 to 1945–46, Vol. I, pp. 20–25; **9,** February 1952, p. 4.

a. For the USSR and European countries whose boundaries have undergone changes since World War II, data for 1934–38 in prewar boundaries are given in italics, for comparison.

b. Conversion factors: one metric ton of oats = 10 metric quintals = 68.9 bushels.

c. 1931–35.

d. Estimate of the U. S. Department of Agriculture (**55,** p. 123, and **22,** October 8, 1951, p. 361).

e. 22 provinces.

TABLE 246

MILLET AND SORGHUM: ACREAGE AND YIELD IN EACH CONTINENT AND SELECTED COUNTRIES, 1934–38 ANNUAL AVERAGE, 1948 AND 1949

Country	Area, in Thousands of Acres			Output, in Thousands of Metric Tons [a]			Yield Per Acre, in Metric Quintals [a]		
	1934–38	1948	1949	1934–38	1948	1949	1934–38	1948	1949
				MILLET					
World (excluding the USSR)	85,250	73,636	76,354	23,800	20,900	20,000	2.8	2.8	2.6
America	100 [b]	272 [b]	...	60 [b]	170 [b]	...	6.1 [b]	5.9 [b]	...
Europe	568	420	395	200	150	140	3.5	3.6	3.6
Poland	...	170	151	103	69	63	...	4.0	4.1
Romania	138	64	...	38	18	...	2.7	2.8	...
USSR	...	...	...	2,752	...	...	...	...	...
Asia	59,057	62,022	64,740	18,530	18,000	17,000	3.2	2.9	2.6
China [c]	17,257	15,931	16,232	8,229	8,316	7,058	4.8	5.2	4.3
South Korea	...	415	...	...	114	...	...	2.8	...
Pakistan	1,982	2,298	2,439	301	379	...	1.5	1.7	...
India	20,329 [b]	33,811	35,639	6,159 [b]	5,321	5,745	...	1.6	1.6
Africa	25,451	10,526	10,625	5,000	2,400	2,500	2.0	2.3	2.3
Egypt	348	546	516	426	559	567	12.3	10.2	11.0
Ethiopia	...	7,413	7,413	...	1,400	1,400	...	1.9	1.9
French West Africa	10,845	12,281 [d]	...	2,315	2,029 [d]	...	2.1	1.7 [d]	...
French Equatorial Africa	4,492	1,853 [d]	...	395	550 [d]	...	0.9	3.0 [d]	...
Nigeria	...	11,369	11,369	...	2,581	2,581	...	2.3	2.3
French Cameroons	1,137	1,581 [d]	...	290	386 [d]	...	2.5	2.4 [d]	...
Tanganyika [d]	...	2,948	2,842	...	880	850	...	3.0	2.0
				SORGHUM					
World (excluding the USSR)	58,563	68,200	69,979	21,700	19,800	20,800	3.7	2.9	3.0
America	4,077	7,487	6,845	1,310	3,410	3,950	3.2	4.6	5.8
United States	3,879	7,297	6,612	1,241	3,343	3,877	3.2	4.6	5.9
Europe	99	124	124	50	60	60	5.1	4.9	4.9
USSR	...	...	...	145	...	...	...	...	...
Asia	48,926	55,845	57,821	18,800	15,000	15,300	3.8	2.7	2.6
China [c]	12,681	10,578	10,788	7,016	6,386	5,448	5.5	6.0	5.1
Pakistan	1,921	2,298	2,439	203	216	...	2.0	2.0	...
India	25,091 [b]	36,541	37,453	7,325 [b]	5,097	5,856	...	1.4	1.6
Africa	5,436	4,645	5,189	1,500	1,300	1,500	2.8	2.8	2.9
Oceania	5	52	...	1	27	...	2.0	5.1	...
				MILLET AND SORGHUM [e]					
World	16,062	32,370	32,123	3,600	6,870	6,500	2.2	2.1	2.0

Source: **8**, 1950, pp. 39–41.

a. Conversion factors: One metric ton of millet or sorghum = 10 metric quintals = about 44 bushels.
b. Incomplete data.

c. 22 provinces.
d. Includes sorghum.
e. Figures for both grains combined; exclusive of world totals indicated above.

moist regions of northern Europe or the USSR.

Potatoes need soil of loose texture, friable, acid and naturally cool. In the sandy soils of Germany, they require large quantities of fertilizer. In the United States, the soil of Maine (notably in Aroostock County), of shale formation, is considered ideal.

Acreage and Output

In Europe, the prewar potato crop represented more than a third of the value of all vegetable produce and more than that of wheat and rye combined. In the USSR, potatoes ranked second to wheat, the chief crop. (See Tables 236 and 237.) Together, Europe and the USSR account for 85–90 per cent or more of the world's potato output (56 and 32 per cent in 1950, respectively). Germany, Poland, France and the United Kingdom together produce 70–75 per cent of the European crop. Germany, with about 5 million acres in potatoes, is the leading producer,[57] far exceeding Poland, despite the latter's larger acreage (6.5 million acres).

The potato acreage of the USSR is nearly five times that of Germany, but the output is less than double, the yield per acre being one of the lowest in Europe. In the USSR, the average yield per acre in 1949 (3.3 tons) was only slightly higher than Germany's in 1879–83 (3.1 tons).[58] (See Table 247 and Figure 176.) The highest yields in Europe were in the Low Countries, particularly in the Netherlands (more than 9 tons per acre during 1949–50, on the average).

Output in the United States

The United States is the only important producer of potatoes outside Europe and the USSR. Although the acreage is 40 per cent less than the average during 1934–38, output is about 20 per cent greater than in those years because the yield per acre has more than doubled. Maine and Idaho are the two chief producers of late potatoes; California leads in spring potatoes. Potatoes are used chiefly for table purposes. Since the crop is bulky to ship and perishable, most of the producing centers are near large metropolitan areas. Idaho and Maine potatoes have a national reputation, however, and are marketed throughout the country.

SUGAR

Sugar beets and sugar cane provide an identical product (in processed form) though they grow under entirely different climatic and soil conditions, and one is a root crop, the other a stalk crop.

Since both sugar beets and sugar cane consist largely of water and are bulky to transport, sugar mills are usually located within the growing area.[59] The mill produces sugar from sugar beets in one continuous process, while cane sugar is the product of two distinctly different operations: raw sugar is made in a mill near the plantation and then shipped to a refinery, often situated in another continent.

Cane sugar was first brought to Europe by the Moors in the eighth century.[60] From Spain it spread to Sicily, the Canary Islands and Madeira. The Spaniards introduced sugar cane into the New World, but output was limited, and sugar was among the greatest luxuries. The price in England in the fifteenth century was so high that it was "considered too extravagant for prudent purchase, and too much to expect from any host." [61]

Until 1800, sugar was made from cane only.[62] Europe depended on the West Indies and Brazil for its sugar supplies. The war between England and France interrupted this trade, which moved largely through channels controlled by England. Napoleon, to meet the challenge, called a sugar beet industry into being in 1811 by encouraging cultivation of sugar beets and subsidizing sugar mills. The first results were disappointing because of the low sucrose content of the beets. Somewhat later, Germany succeeded in raising the sugar content of the root and improving the

---

57. Before the war, Germany used 28 per cent of the potato crop for table food, 40 per cent for feeding livestock, 12 per cent for seed. Half the rest was taken by the alcohol and starch industries, the other half wasted through decay, shrinkage and so on. (**52**, p. 359.)

58. **38**, p. 14.

59. Though production of sugar from sugar beet and sugar cane is a food-processing industry, it is so closely tied to the raising of the crops that it is usually discussed in this connection in publications of the International Institute of Agriculture and its successor, the FAO. This chapter will follow the same course.

60. Sugar cane is mentioned in Indian scripts of 5000 B.C. Among the first Europeans to see it were Alexander the Great and his soldiers, when they reached India in 327 B.C. The Saracens introduced sugar cane into Egypt in the seventh century A.D. Sugar cane reached the West Indies with Columbus. From there it came to the French colony of Louisiana and later to Florida. (**41**, pp. 9–10, and **25**, 1950–51, p. 293.)

61. **49**, pp. 656–57.

62. Except for small pioneering attempts in Germany to use sugar beets for this purpose.

TABLE 247

POTATOES: ACREAGE AND YIELD IN EACH CONTINENT AND SELECTED COUNTRIES, 1934–38 ANNUAL AVERAGE, 1949 AND 1950

Continent and Country [a]	Area, in Thousands of Acres			Output, in Thousands of Metric Tons [b]			Yield Per Acre, in Metric Quintals [b]		
	1934–38	1949	1950	1934–38	1949	1950	1934–38	1949	1950
World (with the USSR)	54,865	55,030	55,525	233,800	222,100	248,925	42.4	40.3	44.8
World (without the USSR)	33,606	31,630	32,125	159,400	145,900	170,000	47.4	46.1	52.9
North and South America	5,387	4,571	4,497	14,880	18,340	19,780	27.6	40.1	44.0
United States	3,190	1,913	1,846	10,024	11,201	11,961	31.4	58.6	64.8
Canada	526	511	504	1,859	2,428	2,651	35.3	47.5	51.9
Brazil	161	383	366	380	748	740	23.6	19.5	20.2
Peru	400	492	563	820	1,115	1,364	21.0	22.7	24.2
Argentina	284	492	494	663	1,167	1,500	23.3	23.7	30.4
Europe									
Prewar boundaries	*28,557*	—	—	*154,660*	—	—	*54.2*	—	—
Present boundaries	24,858	22,980	23,475	135,300	116,400	138,900	54.4	50.7	59.2
United Kingdom	731	1,307	1,236	5,011	9,180	9,660	68.5	70.2	78.2
Ireland	334	351	336	2,583	2,735	2,920	77.3	77.9	86.9
France	3,511	2,777	2,768	17,158	10,976	14,431	48.9	39.5	52.1
Belgium	390	220	247	3,169	2,047	2,309	81.3	93.0	93.5
Netherlands	334	457	410	2,720	4,605	4,052	81.4	100.8	98.8
Denmark	195	262	257	1,349	1,794	1,850	69.2	68.5	72.0
Sweden	326	334	321	1,847	1,720	1,734	56.7	51.5	54.0
Norway	126	143	146	892	1,099	1,116	70.8	76.6	76.4
Finland									
Prewar boundaries	*213*	—	—	*1,288*	—	—	*60.5*	—	—
Present boundaries	183	215	210	1,105	1,157	1,210	60.4	53.8	57.6
Germany									
Prewar boundaries	*7,052*	—	—	*48,199*	—	—	*68.4*	—	—
Western Germany	2,921	2,777	2,819	19,603	20,875	27,959	67.1	75.2	99.2
Soviet Zone	1,955	2,006	2,002	13,649	8,499	13,060	69.8	42.4	65.2
Poland									
Prewar boundaries	*7,163*	—	—	*35,007*	—	—	*48.9*	—	—
Present boundaries	6,810	6,178	6,528	38,014	30,900	36,835	55.8	50.0	56.4
Czechoslovakia									
Prewar boundaries	*1,873*	—	—	*10,029*	—	—	*53.6*	—	—
Present boundaries	1,767	1,394	1,507	9,635	6,263	7,500	54.5	44.9	49.8
Austria	511	440	455	2,845	2,008	2,548	55.7	45.6	56.0
Hungary	719	722	692	2,133	1,920	1,200	29.7	26.6	17.3
Spain	1,087 [e]	890	890	4,954	2,560	3,000	45.6 [e]	28.8	33.7
Italy	988	964	946	2,626	2,606	2,374	25.5	27.0	25.1
Yugoslavia	665	576	591	1,498	2,060	1,019	22.5	35.8	17.2
Romania									
Prewar boundaries	*738*	—	—	*2,023*	—	—	*27.4*	—	—
Present boundaries	556	445	450	2,007	1,225	812	36.1	27.5	18.0
USSR									
Prewar boundaries	*17,453*	—	—	*53,973*	—	—	*32.1*	—	—
Present boundaries	21,258	23,400 [d]	23,400 [d]	73,933	76,200 [d]	78,925 [d]	34.8	32.6 [d]	33.7 [d]
Asia	2,842	3,558	3,534	8,120	9,500	9,740	28.6	26.7	27.6
Africa	272	395	395	590	950	1,020	21.7	24.1	25.8
Oceania	148	148	148	470	560	520	31.8	37.8	35.1

Sources: **12,** 1941–42 to 1945–46, Vol. I, pp. 42–47; **9,** January 1952, p. 4.

a. For the USSR and European countries whose boundaries have undergone changes since World War II, data for 1934–38 in prewar boundaries are given in italics, for comparison. World and continental totals include the FAO estimates of gaps in reporting of acreage and output.

b. Conversion factors: one metric ton of potatoes = 10 metric quintals = 36.7 bushels.

c. 1931–35.

d. Estimate of the U. S. Department of Agriculture (**22,** November 5, 1951, p. 468).

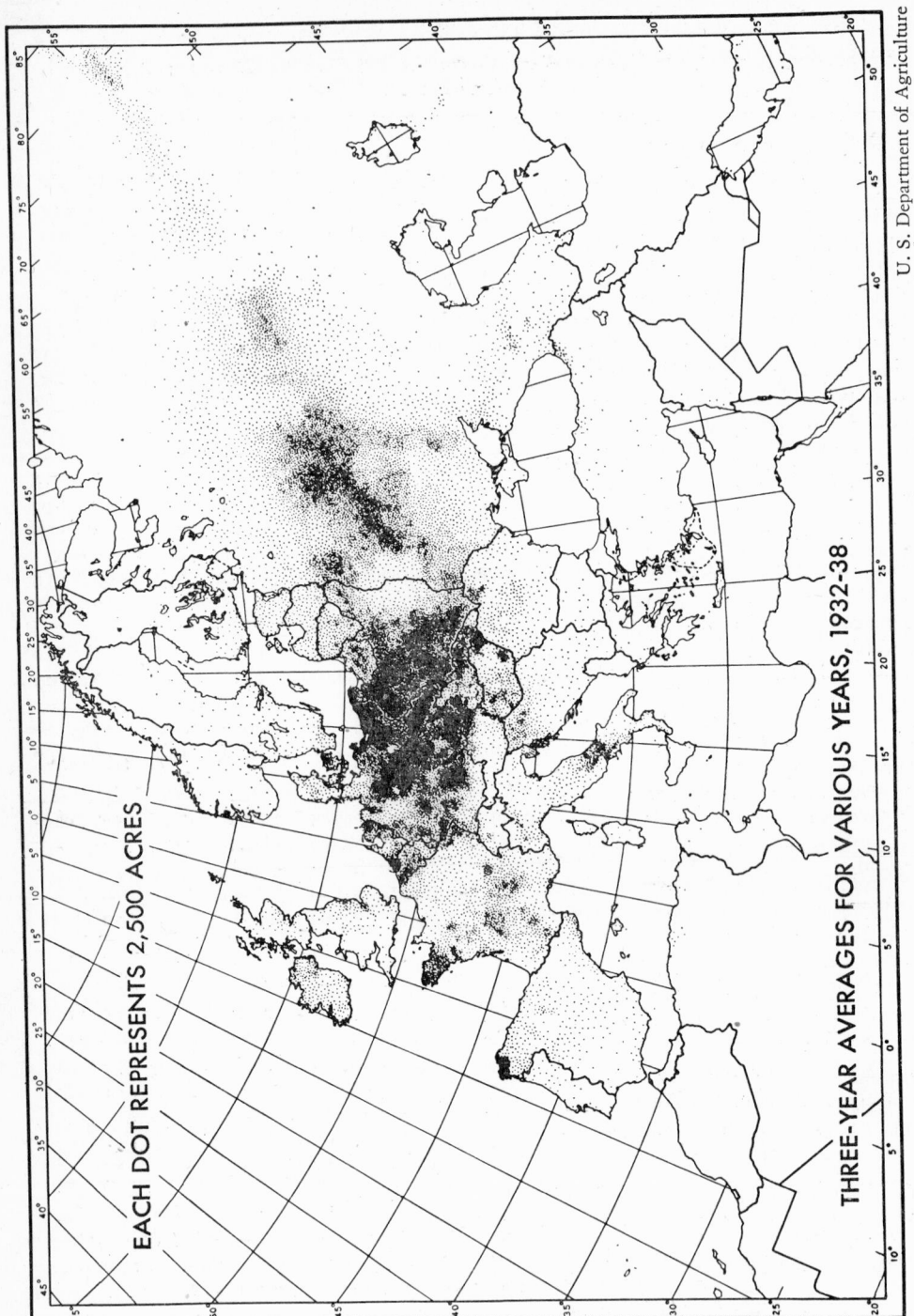

EACH DOT REPRESENTS 2,500 ACRES

THREE-YEAR AVERAGES FOR VARIOUS YEARS, 1932-38

U. S. Department of Agriculture

FIGURE 176. POTATOES: ACREAGE IN EUROPE AND THE EUROPEAN PART OF THE USSR, 1932-38

technique of extraction, opening the way for the intercontinental competition between sugar beets and sugar cane.

SUGAR BEETS

Sugar beets, one of the few plants developed in modern times, need a cool growing season and a moderate, well-distributed rainfall. Extremes in weather — drought, night frost, overabundance of moisture — affect the sugar content of the beets. Desirable soils are friable, fertile loams, rich in lime and with good drainage and aeration. The culture of sugar beets involves a good deal of labor. While machinery is customarily used for planting, cultivating and harvesting, the weeding and thinning is done by hand, often by entire families including men, women and children.

The sugar beets introduced into Germany in the nineteenth century contained 7–8 per cent of sucrose. Persistent work by German scientists to improve seed varieties has resulted in a sucrose content of 18–20 per cent or even more. At the same time, the yield has risen from 4 quintals per acre to 12 and more. The tops and the pulp left after the extraction of sucrose are excellent feed for cattle. The harvested tops from an acre of beets, plus the pulp after the extraction, equal the stock-feeding value of the entire product from an average acre of corn.[63]

The introduction of sugar beets gave a strong impetus to other branches of agriculture in many European countries. Although sugar beets require intensive and expensive cultivation and much nutriment, production proved advantageous since it could be included in a rotation system and assured higher yields of succeeding crops. Moreover, by supplying excellent feed, sugar beets enabled the farmers to keep more livestock and to improve the soil with farmyard manure.

Europe accounts for about 65 per cent of world output of sugar beets, the USSR for 17–18 per cent, and the United States for about 12 per cent. In Europe, Belgium, the Netherlands and Western Germany had the highest yields, 17.5, 17.6 and 15.5 tons of beets per acre, respectively, in 1950, while yields in the USSR and Asia are among the lowest in the world. The yield in the United States is about 13 tons per acre. (See Table 248.)

In the United States, mechanical harvesting is rapidly replacing the hand methods used since the industry was introduced about eighty years ago. Only fifteen or twenty machines were in commercial use before 1943; in 1949, some 9,100 were used and an additional 1,900 were bought by farmers. In that year, 54 per cent of the acreage in sugar beets in the country as a whole was machine-harvested; about 73 per cent in California, and more than 60 per cent in Idaho, Washington, Oregon and Utah. Average labor requirements for harvesting an acre by hand have been 30 to 35 hours, as against 6 to 7 hours for machine harvesting.[64]

SUGAR CANE

Sugar cane is a tropical plant, and its main habitat is in Asia, the Pacific Islands and the Caribbean. This crop needs a high temperature, much sunshine and rather abundant rainfall.

Cultivation

Usually small pieces of stalks with one or more joints are planted in furrows, and the canes take 12 to 24 months to mature. Under favorable conditions, several crops can be obtained from one planting. The ripe stalk is cut to the ground, and a new growth starts from the stubble (ratoon). In Java and India, only one crop can be obtained from one set of canes, while in Cuba, where climate and soil are ideal for sugar cane, four to eight crops a year from the same planting are usual. The culture of sugar cane is a laborious process, and in the tropics almost all labor is done by hand, but in Hawaii, the United States and Australia, the crop is handled mechanically.

The mechanization of harvesting in the United States was speeded up during World War II when the demand for sugar was great and manpower in short supply. Within five years, Louisiana mechanized as much as 90 per cent of the harvesting. Cutting and loading equipment has been improved, and better methods of handling the cane throughout the entire operation have been worked out.[65]

Java and Hawaii are outstanding in intensive cultivation of sugar cane. Sugar plantations there have employed every practicable method to achieve the highest possible yield — irrigation, heavy fertilization, improved varieties of cane

---

63. **25**, 1950–51, p. 307.

64. **25**, 1950–51, pp. 300–01.
65. **25**, 1950–51, pp. 295–96.

TABLE 248

SUGAR BEETS: ACREAGE AND YIELD IN EACH CONTINENT AND SELECTED COUNTRIES, 1934–38
ANNUAL AVERAGE, 1949 AND 1950

Continent and Country	Area, in Thousands of Acres			Output, in Thousands of Metric Tons [a]			Yield Per Acre, in Metric Tons [a]		
	1934–38	1949	1950	1934–38	1949	1950	1934–38	1949	1950
World (with the USSR)	8,400	9,077	9,896	74,700	76,767	92,415	8.9	8.5	9.3
World (without the USSR)	5,288	6,227	7,042	57,050	61,200	76,900	10.8	9.8	10.9
North and South America	848	781	1,038	8,600	10,057	13,319	10.1	12.9	12.8
United States	798	687	927	8,138	9,251	12,244	10.2	13.5	13.2
Canada	47	84	101	426	779	1,023	9.1	9.3	10.0
Uruguay	3	7	10	13	27	52	4.3	3.9	5.2
Europe	4,250 [b]	5,164	5,634	47,500	49,600	61,800	11.2	9.6	11.0
United Kingdom	356	421	429	3,195	4,026	5,300	9.0	9.6	12.4
France	786	773	749	8,785	8,599	10,000	11.2	11.1	13.4
Belgium	124	148	153	1,459	2,348	2,670	11.8	15.9	17.5
Netherlands	106	161	166	1,637	2,943	2,913	15.4	18.3	17.6
Denmark	101	153	180	1,483	2,130	2,624	14.7	13.9	14.6
Sweden	128	121	133	1,888	1,770	1,978	14.8	17.5	14.9
Germany									
Western	287	368	459	4,118	4,240	7,016	14.3	11.5	15.5
Soviet Zone	460	499	519	5,467	3,545	5,400	11.9	7.1	10.4
Poland	556 [b]	618	709	5,962	5,085	6,377	10.7	8.2	9.0
Czechoslovakia	403 [b]	531	544	4,664	4,446	...	11.6	8.4	...
Austria	106	64	72	1,130	480	821	10.7	7.5	11.4
Hungary	114 [b]	279	284	960	1,801	1,723	8.4	6.5	6.1
Spain	220 [c]	230	222	2,150 [c]	1,330	1,379	9.8 [c]	5.8	6.2
Italy	284	324	430	2,879	3,619	4,470	10.1	11.2	10.4
Yugoslavia	67 [b]	220	242	509	1,095	851	7.6	5.0	3.5
USSR	3,106 [b]	2,850 [d]	2,854 [d]	17,537	15,567 [d]	15,515 [d]	5.6 [b]	5.5 [d]	5.4 [d]
Asia	198	297	346	1,000	1,500	1,800	5.1	5.1	5.2

Sources: **8**, 1950, p. 48; **22**, October 22, 1951, p. 412; **9**, January 1952, p. 5.

a. Conversion factor: one metric ton = 1.1023 short tons.

b. Postwar boundaries.
c. 1931–35.
d. Estimate of the U. S. Department of Agriculture.

and intensive tillage. In contrast, Cuba, the chief world producer, has made little effort to raise the yield per acre. While Java produces, on the average, up to 57 tons of cane per acre and Hawaii 67–68 tons, the Cuban yield is 15–17 tons.

Raw cane sugar varies greatly. India's sugar (gur) is good only for domestic consumption; that grown in Cuba, Hawaii, Puerto Rico, the Philippines and Peru needs refining; the white sugar of Java and Mauritius may go directly into consumption.[66]

Sugar cane is also raised in some subtropical regions — Louisiana and Florida, for example — but only fast ripening varieties can be grown

66. **37**, p. 5.

there because of the danger of frost. The plant has only about eight months to mature, and the sugar content is lower than in the tropics.

Acreage

Sugar cane occupies a larger acreage in India than in any other country, despite the competition of other food crops. The output, however, does not meet domestic requirements and additional quantities are imported from other Asiatic countries. Sugar cane production in Indonesia has not yet recovered from the devastation of war and civilian strife.

In the Western Hemisphere, Brazil is second to Cuba in output of sugar cane. Brazil led in

TABLE 249

SUGAR CANE: ACREAGE AND YIELD IN SELECTED COUNTRIES, PREWAR, 1948 AND 1949

Country	Area, in Thousands of Acres			Output, in Millions of Metric Tons [a]			Yield Per Acre, in Metric Tons [a]		
	Prewar	*1948*	*1949*	*Prewar*	*1948*	*1949*	*Prewar*	*1948*	*1949*
United States [b]	284	309	314	5.1	5.7	5.7	18.0	18.4	18.2
Mexico	200	427 [e]	...	3.8	7.2	...	19.0	16.9 [e]	...
Cuba [b]	1,507	2,693	...	26.2	41.7	...	17.4	15.5	...
Trinidad and Tobago [b]	77	...	...	1.3	1.2	...	16.9	...	...
Jamaica	42	89	...	1.1	2.7	...	26.2	...	...
Puerto Rico [b]	299	326	341	7.3	10.0	9.6	24.4	30.7	28.2
Colombia	672	...	...	...	6.4 [d]	...	...	...	...
Brazil	1,144	2,024	1,930	17.4	29.0	30.0	15.2	15.3	15.5
Peru	...	124	148	3.2	...	...	...	...	...
Argentina [b]	457	563	600	5.9	7.0	...	12.9	12.4	...
China,[b] 22 provinces	...	961 [e]	...	3.6	5.2 [e]	...	...	5.4	...
Japan	15	7	5	0.2	...	...	...	...	...
Taiwan [b]	287	301	...	7.4	6.2	...	25.8	20.6	...
Pakistan [b]	521	714	751	...	...	...	...	...	...
India [b]	3,277	3,791	3,640	67.5	50.0	...	20.6	13.2	...
Thailand [b]	25	69	...	0.7	0.6	...	28.0	8.7	...
Indochina	99	20	...	0.9	0.2	...	9.1	10.0	...
Indonesia [e]	200	...	...	10.3	...	...	51.5	...	...
Philippines	581	...	919	8.2	6.5	...	14.1	...	...
Egypt [b]	67	82	89	2.2	1.9	1.9	32.8	23.2	22.5
Mauritius	143	156	163	2.4	3.2	3.4	16.8	20.5	20.9
Madagascar	42	54	...	0.2	0.3	...	4.8	5.6	...
Union of South Africa [f]	361	385	...	3.8	4.7	4.5	...	...	...
Australia [b]	247	267	289	5.2 [g]	6.8 [g]	...	...	...	...
Hawaii [b]	131	100	109	8.0	6.8	7.3	61.1	68.0	67.0

Source: **8**, 1950, pp. 45–47.

  a. Conversion factor: one metric ton = 1.1023 short tons.

  b. Harvested area.

c. 1937.
d. 1946.
e. Java and Madoera.
f. Area refers to farms and estates.
g. Factory-crushed sugar cane.

production in the seventeenth and early eighteenth centuries, when sugar was the country's most important commodity in international trade, and hundreds of thousands of slaves were brought from Africa to work on the plantations.[67] After the price collapsed because of overproduction in the world, Brazil turned its efforts to gold and diamond mining. Nevertheless, sugar cane still occupies a large acreage in Brazil and is grown in every state. High-yielding and disease-resistant varieties have been introduced from Java, and the nation's output meets its own requirements. Yield per acre, however, is lower than in Puerto Rico. (See Table 249.)

67. **40**, pp. 37 and 131; **60**, p. 78.

In Peru, the acreage in sugar is not large but the yield is the highest in the Western Hemisphere. Conditions in Peru are exceptionally favorable for raising sugar cane, which can be cut at any time during the year.

Statistics on acreage and output of sugar cane are scattered and few, and even the available data are frequently unreliable and only approximate. For some countries, as the Dominican Republic, for example, where sugar production plays an important role, statistics are lacking. In tropical countries almost every village family has a patch of land in sugar cane, from which it extracts, in the most primitive way, the sucrose to make molasses, sirup and other sweets. It is practically impossible to estimate this acreage and output

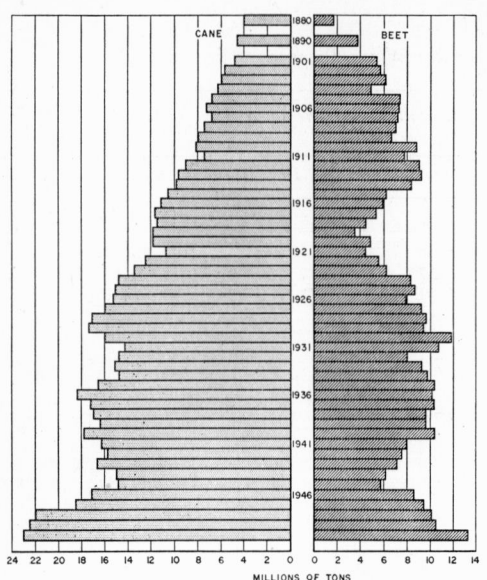

FIGURE 177. SUGAR: WORLD OUTPUT OF BEET AND
CANE SUGAR, 1880–1950

even in such small countries as El Salvador or
Guatemala.

PRODUCTION OF SUGAR

By the beginning of the twentieth century,
more sugar was produced from beets than from
cane. Since that time, cane sugar has made much
greater headway than beet sugar. While the output of cane sugar increased from 4.8 million tons
in 1900 to 23.1 million in 1950, that of beet sugar
rose only from 5.4 to 13.4 million tons. At the
turn of the century, less than half of all sugar
came from cane; in 1950, about two thirds. (See
Table 250 and Figure 177.)

The Western Hemisphere and Asia account
for about 85 per cent of the world's output of
cane sugar, while Europe and the USSR produce
about the same percentage of all beet sugar.
Cuba is the largest producer of cane sugar, and
also the greatest single supplier of sugar to the
United States. India accounts for as much as half
of Asia's output of cane sugar, but the chief exporter in prewar years was Java, with a little less
than a third the output of India but only a tenth
of India's population.

Except for an insignificant amount in Canada,
the United States is the only producer of beet
sugar in the Western Hemisphere. It ranks next
to the USSR and has a larger output than either
Germany or France, the leading European
producers.

TABLE 250

SUGAR: WORLD OUTPUT OF BEET AND CANE SUGAR,
1900–50

Annual Average, or Year	*Output, in Millions of Metric Tons* [a]			*Cane Sugar as Percentage of Total Sugar Output*
	Total [b]	*Beet Sugar*	*Cane Sugar*	
1900–01	10.2	5.4	4.8	46.7
1910–11	15.2	7.8	7.4	48.5
1920–21	15.1	4.4	10.7	70.8
1930–31	25.0	10.7	14.3	57.2
1938–39	26.0	9.6	16.4	63.1
1940	28.2	10.4	17.8	63.1
1941	24.3	8.0	16.3	67.1
1942	23.3	7.6	15.7	67.4
1943	23.8	7.2	16.6	69.7
1944	21.2	6.2	15.0	70.8
1945	20.7	5.8	14.9	72.0
1946	25.8	8.6	17.2	66.7
1947	28.0	9.5	18.5	66.1
1948	32.1	10.1	22.0	68.5
1949	33.0	10.5	22.5	68.2
1950	36.5	13.4	23.1	63.3

Sources: **45**, p. 9; **4**, 1947, pp. 54–56; **9**, July–August
1951, p. 3.

a. Conversion factor: one metric ton = 1.1023 short
tons.

b. Includes the USSR: 1940–46 as estimated by the
FAO (**8**, 1947, p. 56) and 1947–50 as estimated by the
U. S. Department of Agriculture (**22**, June 11, 1951,
p. 671).

Sugar production was seriously affected by
war and postwar dislocations — fighting and
political turmoil in many parts of Asia, shortage
of fertilizer and manpower in western and central Europe and so on. Nevertheless, production
in the world as a whole and on every continent
except Asia and the USSR has recovered more
fully than most other branches of agriculture.
The output of sugar from both cane and beets
exceeds the prewar volume on even a per capita
basis despite the considerable increase in the
world's population. The greatest expansion has
been in Cuba, which doubled its prewar output.
Brazil, Puerto Rico, Mexico and Argentina have
also substantially increased production. (See Table 251 and Figure 178.)

Further increase in the output is probable,
since many countries are stressing it, partly to
become self-sufficient, partly for military reasons.
Moreover, high prices for sugar and foreign exchange difficulties have stimulated domestic pro-

TABLE 251

SUGAR: OUTPUT OF CANE AND BEET SUGAR IN EACH CONTINENT AND SELECTED COUNTRIES, 1934-38 ANNUAL AVERAGE AND 1948-50

(Thousands of Metric Tons [a])

Continent and Country	Cane Sugar			
	1934–38	1948	1949	1950[b]
World[c]	18,400	22,000	22,510	23,100
America	8,110	12,830	13,300	13,460
United States	430[d]	430	463	510
Mexico	319	645	628	726
Cuba	2,838	5,228	5,558	5,770
Dominican Republic	436	476	475	507
Puerto Rico	888[d]	1,158	1,167	1,161
Brazil	1,031	1,751	1,732	1,730
Peru	382	472	470	420
Argentina	410	565	549	613
British West Indies	436	626	673	708
Asia	7,250	5,700	5,790	6,010
Taiwan	1,200	631	554	400
Pakistan	417	663	678	570
India	2,902	3,175	3,200	3,328
Java and Madoera	1,153	...	...	...
Philippines	960	662	621	890
Africa	1,180	1,480	1,470	1,620
Egypt	146	191	170	180
Mauritius	310	410	416	456
Union of South Africa	453	570	509	622
Oceania	1,840	1,960	1,950	1,970
Australia	756	958	959	920
Hawaii	889[d]	867	872	953

Continent and Country	Beet Sugar			
	1934–38	1948	1949	1950[b]
World	10,345	10,060	10,500	13,400
America	1,445	1,338	1,534	1,965
United States	1,377[d]	1,243	1,425	1,820
Canada	69	94	109	145
Europe	6,450	6,730	6,770	9,010
United Kingdom	435	632	523	740
France	971	960	881	1,434
Belgium	237	261	343	445
Netherlands	235	281	398	409
Denmark	191	264	322	360
Sweden	301	291	291	330
Germany	1,663[e]			—
Western	565	618	614	1,017
Soviet Zone	900	680	555	800
Poland	954	694	828	1,056
Czechoslovakia	633	635	627	880
Hungary	124	243	265	255
Spain	308	261	184	177
Italy	335	448	475	610
USSR	2,300	1,800[f]	2,000[f]	2,200[f]
Asia	150	190	200	230

Source: **9**, July–August 1951, p. 3.

a. Conversion factor: one metric ton = 1.1023 short tons.
b. Preliminary.
c. Includes Spain (20,000 tons).
d. 1935–39.
e. Territory of 1937.
f. Estimate of the U. S. Department of Agriculture (**22**, June 11, 1951, p. 671).

573

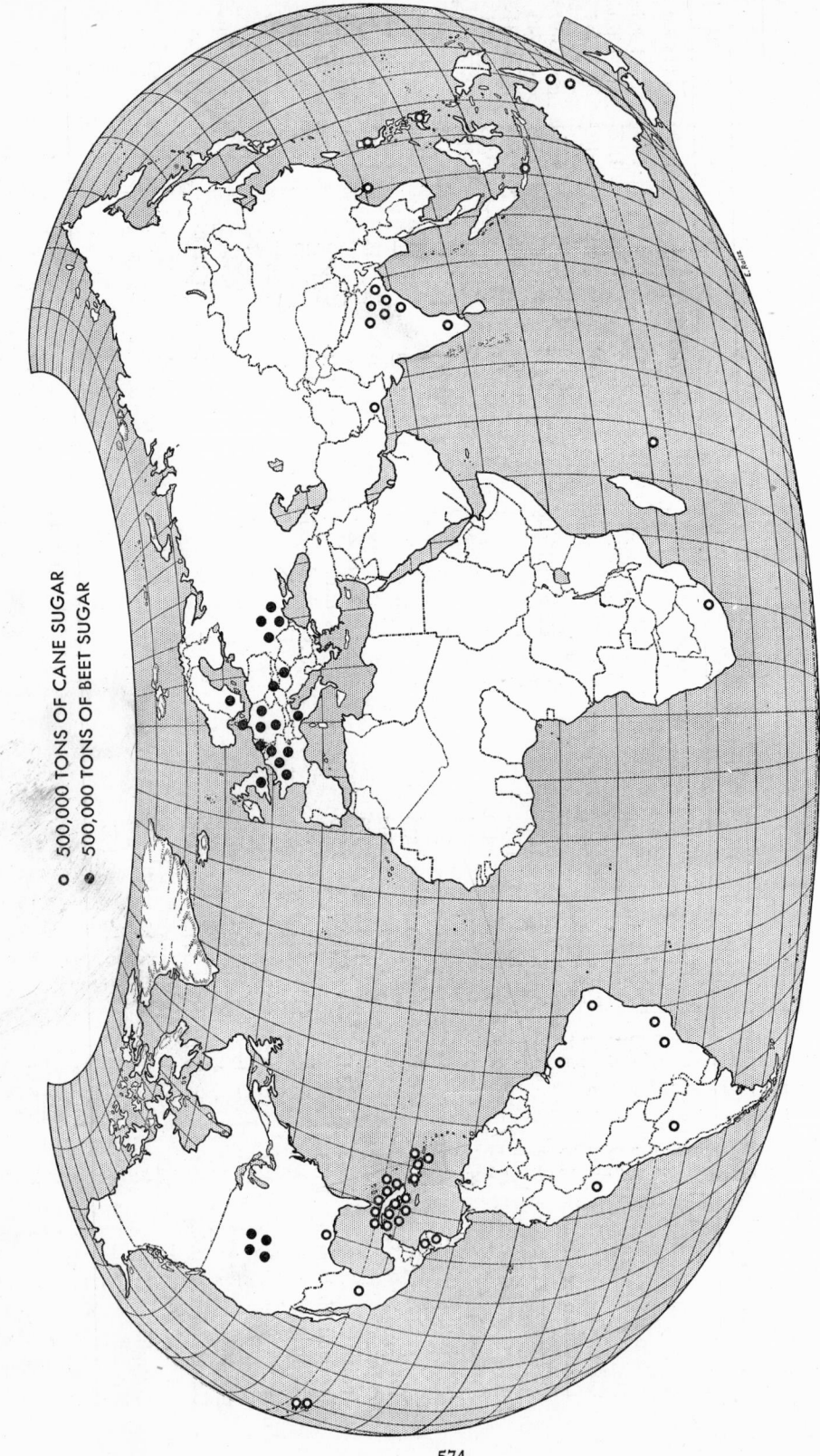

○ 500,000 TONS OF CANE SUGAR

● 500,000 TONS OF BEET SUGAR

Figure 178. Sugar: Geographic Distribution of World Output, 1950

duction. Many areas where sugar previously could be produced only with governmental support and subsidies now find themselves in a position to compete with imported sugar.[68]

Increase in sugar production is further stimulated by the many uses, some old and others recently discovered, for the by-products from processing both cane and beets. Sugar cane yields fiber (bagasse), an industrially used acid, molasses and a valuable wax. The fiber is often used for fuel, especially in primitive mills; in the United States, it has been used since the first world war to manufacture insulating wallboard, and as a mulch and poultry litter. Shortly before World War II the manufacture of a molding plastic from bagasse was introduced, and much research is being done on the use of the fiber in paper production. Sugar itself is also used for many nonfood purposes — in tanning leather and silvering mirrors, in photographic materials, pharmaceuticals, explosives and so on.[69]

COFFEE, TEA, CACAO

Coffee is produced mainly in Middle and South America, tea in Asia, cacao in Africa. Of the three crops, coffee is the most important in international trade.

COFFEE

The coffee tree grows from seed and requires high temperatures and abundant rainfall during the growing season. A drought, strong winds or too heavy rainfall may affect the yield substantially. The trees cannot stand great heat and must be shaded by higher trees. The first crop of any consequence is obtained in the fourth year, but the maximum yield is usually not expected until after the seventh and then is maintained for about five years. Thereafter the coffee tree continues to bear in commercial quantities for some years, depending on soil and climatic conditions. In some districts of Brazil, for example, the tree may produce for sixty years; in others, twenty to thirty years; and in the state of Espíritu Santo, only eight years.[70] Brazil, with

about half the world's output, is by far the largest producer. Coffee was introduced into that country from Ethiopia early in the eighteenth century, and cultivation spread widely since climate and soil (terra rossa, or red earth) are very favorable.[71] Coffee now holds as dominant a position in the Brazilian economy as sugar in the Cuban. It accounts for about 6 to 7 million acres, about 15 per cent of the country's arable land. In 1942, 1.3 million workers were employed in growing and picking coffee berries.[72]

Colombia is the second largest producer of coffee. Although its output is much smaller than Brazil's the quality is higher. In Brazil, the berries are stripped from the trees by hand and allowed to fall to the ground, then swept into containers, together with leaves and other trash, to be hauled to the farm headquarters.[73] In Colombia, the berries are picked carefully, one at a time, and the imperfect or unripe are rejected. This selection requires repeated pickings, but a better product is obtained.

Transportation facilities from the coffee plantations to markets or ports are inadequate in both countries. In Brazil, the coffee is hauled by oxen or mule carts to local markets or export houses, then by rail to ports. Motor trucks have recently come into some use. In Colombia, coffee is carried on pack mules and must be reloaded many times during the haul. In both countries, the government aids coffee planters through subsidies and other measures.

While Asia produces less coffee than the Western Hemisphere, the Asiatic product is highly valued for its fine flavor. Java holds first place in Asia and has a considerable number of plantations, both European and native-owned. The former are greatly superior in technology and mechanization.

The world's prewar coffee crop averaged 2.4 million tons. The output dropped substantially during the war and is still below the prewar level. The demand for coffee is inelastic; a relatively small change in the supply causes considerable fluctuations in price. Coffee growers, while responsive to price changes, cannot adjust production to prices as readily as can producers of annual crops. Although high prices induce intensive plantings, there is a lag of 5-7 years before the growers can cash in. (See Table 252.)

68. **5,c**, pp. 12–13. Probably no other agricultural product has been controlled by national governments to such an extent as sugar. It has enjoyed the protection of tariffs, subsidies and special bounties and has been subjected to price controls, import quotas and other restrictions. International agreements on production and export quotas have been tried more than once.

69. **25**, 1950–51, pp. 293–99.

70. **60**, p. 68.

71. **40**, p. 66.

72. **27**, p. 26.

73. **59**, p. 8.

TABLE 252

COFFEE: OUTPUT IN EACH CONTINENT AND SELECTED COUNTRIES, 1934–38 ANNUAL AVERAGE AND 1948–50

(*Thousands of Metric Tons* [a])

Continent and Country	1934–38	1948	1949	1950
World	2,420	2,170	2,200	2,100
Middle and South America	2,117	1,830	1,874	1,743
Mexico	56	53	59	64
Guatemala	69	71	65	55
El Salvador	64	76	75	68
Honduras	11	18	16	17
Nicaragua	15 [b]	14	20	15
Costa Rica	23 [b]	18	23	18
Cuba	32	31	35	30
Haiti	27	35	40	36
Dominican Republic	21	22	28	22
Puerto Rico	8	10	10	9
Venezuela	58	42	52	...
Colombia	251	368	345	320
Ecuador	14 [b]	19	21	...
Brazil	1,446	1,038	1,068	1,000
Asia	160	68	78	90
India	16	15	23	21
Indonesia	124	...	31	45
Africa	140	265	240	280
Ethiopia	...	...	...	24
French West Africa	8 [b]	42	36	47
Belgian Congo	17	19	20	21
Uganda	11 [b]	38	38	36
Tanganyika	15 [b]	14	13	19
Madagascar	24	25	29	31
Angola	17	53 [b]	37	58
Oceania	6	4	4	3
Hawaii	4	3	3	2

Source: **9,** November 19, 1951, p. 4.

    a. Conversion factors: one metric ton = 1.1023 short tons = 2,204.6 pounds.
    b. Exports.

In the past, overproduction has repeatedly caused breaks in prices. In the late 1930's, for example, there was no outlet for Brazil's bumper crop despite extremely low prices, and millions of bags were burned or dumped.[74] The Brazilian government has often intervened during such catastrophes with various schemes of coffee valorization, with intermittent success. Many superannuated trees have been uprooted to clear the land for competitive crops.[75] For a time, the government prohibited the planting of additional trees, but this order was rescinded in 1943.

TEA

Asia accounts for more than 95 per cent of the world's output of tea; the rest is grown in Africa and the USSR. (See Table 253.) China produces more tea than any other country — about half of all in the world — but consumes most of its crop, exporting only some finer varieties. Data on production are lacking. The estimate for prewar years was from 300,000 to 500,000 tons.[76] India, Formosa, Ceylon and Java grow tea on large European and small native plantations for their own population and the rest of the world. In contrast to China's inefficient

74. On the other hand, high prices fail to lessen the consumer demand to any marked degree.
75. **40,** p. 79.

76. **10,** p. 101.

TABLE 253

TEA: OUTPUT IN EACH CONTINENT AND SELECTED
COUNTRIES, 1934–38 ANNUAL AVERAGE
AND 1948–50

(*Thousands of Metric Tons* [a])

Continent and Country	1934–38	1948	1949	1950
World [b]	500.0	490.0	510.0	550.0
Asia	486.0	470.0	490.0	530.0
China [c]	41.0	12.7	. . .	. . .
Japan	49.3	26.0	31.0	. . .
Pakistan	25.6	19.3	17.6	23.8
India	167.6	254.3	254.0	274.6
Indochina	10.9 [d]	1.0	. . .	. . .
Ceylon	103.9	135.6	135.4	138.9
Indonesia [e]	75.2	12.9	27.2	35.3
USSR	5.1	. . .	. . .	. . .
Africa	8.9	16.0	19.0	19.0

Sources: **8**, 1950, p. 97; **9**, November 1951, p. 6.

a. Conversion factors: one metric ton = 1.1023 short tons = 2,204.6 pounds.
b. Excludes the USSR in 1948–50, and domestically consumed part of output in China and other countries, for which data on exports only are available.
c. 22 provinces, exports only.
d. 1938.
e. Estates only, in postwar years.

and often careless tea growing and harvesting, tea culture in most other parts of Asia, particularly Japan, is elaborate and scientifically managed, both in the small native tea gardens and on the large plantations.

Tea grows on bushes, kept small to facilitate plucking the leaves. It needs a hot and moist climate and a soil with good drainage and an abundant supply of humus. After the first harvest, successive crops, "flushes," occur at intervals of a week or two during the season. In China, the tea leaves are plucked three to four times a year; in India (Assam), up to sixteen times, and in Ceylon, even more frequently. Tea leaves must be picked as soon as they are ripe, since flushes from the same bush may differ in quality and the leaves are sorted by grades.

CACAO

The cacao tree, native to the New World, thrives only within twenty degrees of the equator and needs well-aerated, deep, rich soil and considerable, evenly distributed rainfall. It suffers from strong winds and needs the protection of taller trees. It bears its first fruit in the fourth or fifth year. The maximum yield is reached when the tree is about ten to fifteen years old and is maintained for about twenty years. The crop from a single tree is small, some twenty pods yielding about two pounds of dry beans. Recently higher-yielding strains have been developed, which promise to produce up to six pounds per tree.

Brazil and Ecuador dominated the world's production of cacao beans in the nineteenth century, but the output was comparatively small. Mass production of cacao did not begin until this century: from 82,000 tons at the turn of the century, the world crop rose to an annual average of 730,000 tons during 1934–38, and 770,000 tons in 1950.

The increase in production came largely through the incidental introduction of cacao beans on the Gold Coast of Africa late in the nineteenth century. The cultivation of the cacao tree spread rapidly, and in the course of a few decades made the Gold Coast the world's largest producer and exporter of cacao beans. The output of cacao in this region increased from 34 tons in 1896 to 9,000 in 1906, 73,000 in 1916, 230,000 in 1926 and an average of 265,000 tons during 1934–38. The beans of this region are inferior in quality to those of Ecuador, Venezuela and the West Indies, but the output of the Gold Coast is so much larger that manufacturers of chocolate and cocoa found ways to use it for fine products.

The sudden appearance of immense quantities of beans from the Gold Coast resulted in the collapse of prices. But consumption of cacao and chocolate is much more elastic than that of many other foodstuffs. Lower prices increased the demand and the output rose in the old producing countries of Latin America as well as in Africa.

Africa now supplies nearly 67 per cent of the world's cacao, Latin America, 32 per cent; and Asia and Oceania together, about 1 per cent. The four main producing areas of Africa have more than a billion bearing trees, of which some 400 million are on the Gold Coast. A disease of cacao trees, swollen shoot, which reduces the yield and ultimately kills the tree, is widespread in Africa. The only effective method to protect the healthy trees is to destroy the infected ones, but this remedy is violently opposed by native owners of groves.

Brazil ranks next to the Gold Coast in production. (See Table 254.) About a third of its output is consumed at home, and the rest is

TABLE 254

CACAO BEANS: OUTPUT IN EACH CONTINENT AND SELECTED COUNTRIES, 1934–38
ANNUAL AVERAGE AND 1948–50

(*Thousands of Metric Tons* [a])

Continent and Country	1934–38	1948	1949	1950
World	730.0	770.0	780.0	770.0
Middle and South America	238.0	253.0	282.0	242.0
Costa Rica	6.8	6.3	4.3	5.0
Panama	4.7 [b]	3.0	2.9	2.4
Dominican Republic	23.4	30.0	33.4	27.0
British West Indies [c]	21.7	13.6	12.3	12.7
Venezuela	16.5 [b]	23.8	15.0	17.4
Colombia	10.5	11.2	13.5	8.3
Ecuador	20.0 [b]	20.2	22.5	23.0
Brazil	124.0	128.5	161.5	128.6
Asia	6.0	4.0	4.0	4.0
Africa	484.0	506.0	487.0	523.0
French West Africa	47.1 [b]	50.6	55.4	55.0
Gold Coast	265.1	255.7	250.4 [d]	274.3 [d]
Nigeria	90.8 [b]	101.6	96.0	106.7
French Cameroons	24.8 [b]	35.9	43.1	45.7
Oceania	3.0	4.0	3.0	3.0

Sources: **11**, p. 163; **8**, 1950, pp. 95–96; **3**, p. 123; **9**, November 1951, p. 5.

  a. Conversion factors: one metric ton = 1.1023 short tons = 2,204.6 pounds.
  b. Exports.
  c. Data for 1949 and 1950 incomplete.
  d. Includes British Togoland.

exported. Brazilian cacao is of about the same quality as that of the Gold Coast, but the yield per acre is somewhat lower. Many old trees have been replaced with newly developed varieties, and increase in the Brazilian crop may be expected.[77] The 1950 crop, however, was much smaller than that in 1949, partly because of unfavorable weather and partly because of a normal tendency of cacao trees to "rest" after an unusually heavy yield.[78]

EDIBLE VEGETABLE OILS

The world produces a wide variety of oil-bearing crops — some from annual plants, others from trees; some raised for this purpose, others obtained as a by-product from a plant grown for other purposes. Oils extracted from oil-bearing seeds, nuts or fruit can be roughly distinguished as edible or industrial, as in the following classi-

fication of the U. S. Department of Agriculture: [79]

Edible Oils	*Industrial Oils*
Cottonseed	Linseed
Olive	Castor bean
Peanut	Rapeseed
Sesame seed	Tung
Soybean	
Sunflower seed	
Coconut	
Palm kernel	
Palm	

Edible and industrial oils are frequently interchangeable. An oil used in the manufacture of soap, for example, may also be used to make shortening or margarine, and an oil considered industrial in one country may be eaten commonly in another or may enter into human consumption in an emergency.

77. **5,b**, pp. 4–6.
78. **22**, December 18, 1950, p. 619.

79. **18**, p. 125. Some less common oils have been omitted here. Discussion in this chapter is limited to edible oils. Industrial oils are described in Chapter 17.

Oil meal, the residue after extraction of the oil, is excellent feed for livestock because of its high protein content. Oil crops thus not only supply oils for direct human consumption but also contribute to the production of animal fats, their competitors in the field. Until the invention of the hydraulic press in Europe just before the end of the eighteenth century, oil was extracted from seeds with equipment known to antiquity and still used in the Orient — the wedge press, edge runner and screw press. The new press, further improved, raised the rate of oil extraction markedly and has been used in much of the world for processing various oilseeds. In the United States, the processing methods have been revolutionized through an American invention of a continuous screw press. This press is used today throughout the world for processing every known type of oilseed. In the United States, it is used mainly for processing soybeans, flaxseed and copra and to a lesser extent for a variety of other oil-bearing products.

The difference between the American press and its prototype in Europe is that the first is designed to remove almost all the oil by the use of much higher pressure while the second removes only a part of the oil and leaves a greater amount of meal for re-extraction by other methods.[80]

Along with improvements in the continuous screw press, which reduced the residual oil content in soybeans, for example, to 3.5–4.5 per cent, efforts were made to obtain even this residue by nonmechanical methods. Extraction of oil by organic solvents had been practiced in Europe on a fairly large scale since 1870, and fifty years later especially efficient equipment was developed in Germany. Further perfected in Europe and then in the United States, such equipment, of three different types, is now in use in all but a few plants in the United States and in most European plants.

In the last twenty-five years the efficiency of oil recovery has risen so that nearly all in the seed is extracted. It is considered that little more can be done to increase the recovery of oil from the meal containing only 0.6–0.8 per cent of oil.[81] Underdeveloped countries, however, still use primitive equipment and methods and could raise the extraction rate substantially.

---

80. **25,** 1950–51, pp. 497–98 and 504–12.
81. **25,** 1950–51, pp. 498–99.

Output of Oil-Bearing Products

The principal products used for extraction of edible oils are, in the order of their importance, peanuts, soybeans, rapeseed, coconuts and cottonseed. Next in order are sunflower seed, palm nuts and sesame seed. Olives also rank high in "good years."

Somewhat less than half of the world's crop of cottonseed and soybeans comes from the United States. China, India, the USSR and Egypt are other important producers of cottonseed. China's output of soybeans trails that of the United States. India and China together account for more than half the world's peanut crop and seven tenths of that of sesame seed. The USSR leads in output of sunflower seed. (See Table 255.)

OUTPUT OF EDIBLE OILS

World production of major edible oils, in terms of oil equivalent,[82] rose from an annual average of 6 million tons in 1909–13 to 10.2 million in 1950 and 11.7 million in 1951. (See Table 256.)

Europe and North America are deficit areas, while Asia, Africa and South America have large surpluses for export. Asia, in particular, is an outstanding producer, accounting for 85 per cent of the world's output of sesame oil, 63 per cent of the coconut oil, 50–55 per cent of the peanut oil, and 30–35 per cent of the cottonseed oil. Asia's position in this field is further strengthened by its large share in the output of

---

82. Statistics on the production of both oil-bearing products and oils are scattered and usually incomplete. For seeds, only data on the production are often available, and for oils, usually only export figures. Sometimes production figures for seeds, too, are missing. Consequently, the output of oil is usually estimated on the basis of data on the output of oil-bearing crops minus amounts put aside for next year's seeding, in terms of the oil equivalent of the crop. When only data for exports of oils are available, local consumption is estimated and added to exports to arrive at total production. The only exception is olive oil, for which most producing countries have more or less adequate statistics for both production and exports. We use the estimate of world production of vegetable oils prepared by the Office of Foreign Agricultural Relations, U. S. Department of Agriculture. This makes allowance for oil-bearing products used for seed and also for use for feed and human consumption, as well as for losses. For example, coefficients used for cottonseed are 75 per cent; soybeans, 65 per cent; peanuts, 60 per cent; olive oil, 100 per cent; coconut and palm oil, 125 per cent (i.e., 25 per cent added to export data). **22,** March 6, 1950, p. 189.

TABLE 255

OIL-BEARING CROPS: OUTPUT IN SELECTED COUNTRIES, 1934–38 ANNUAL AVERAGE, 1949 AND 1950

(Thousands of Metric Tons[a])

Crop and Country	1934–38	1949	1950[b]
Cottonseed			
World (with the USSR)	12,830	13,090	11,952
World (without the USSR)	11,540	11,915	
United States	4,927	5,950	3,670
Mexico	127	408	488
Brazil	778	566	653
Peru	139	180	181
Argentina	146	298	213
Greece	36	34	54
USSR	1,290	1,175[c]	...
China[d]	1,520	864	1,184
South Korea	...	60	42
Turkey	104	206	260
Iran	69	46	63
Pakistan	} 2,290	463	572
India		1,194	1,346
Egypt	771	870	850
Anglo-Egyptian Sudan	101	148	211
Belgian Congo	66[i]	102	91
Uganda	117	131	131
Sunflower seed			
World (with the USSR)	2,465	3,550	...
World (without the USSR)	515	1,850	1,940
Chile	—	55	67
Uruguay	3	58	42
Argentina	154	712	920
Hungary	26	212[i]	...
Yugoslavia	12	130	121
Romania	173	...	...
Bulgaria	130	108[h]	...
USSR	1,949	1,692[c]	...
Turkey	—	93	66

Crop and Country	1934–38	1949	1950[b]
Soybean			
World (without the USSR)	12,260	14,118	17,187
United States	1,164	6,284	7,811
Brazil	...	23	35
China[d]	6,093	4,880	...
Manchuria	3,851	1,800	...
South Korea	280	181	...
Japan	321	243	333
Indonesia[e]	236	265	...
Peanut			
World (without the USSR)	8,800	10,070	10,125
United States	540	851	924
Mexico	10	37	40
Brazil	13[f]	135	115
Argentina	80	139	100
China[d]	2,739	2,925	...
India	3,196	3,454	3,384
Indonesia[e]	251	312	...
French West Africa	713	675	565
Belgian Congo	128	145	164
Nigeria[g]	356	454	363
Uganda	71	159[h]	...
Union of South Africa	14	63	52
Sesame			
World (without the USSR)	1,600	1,690	1,820
Mexico	22	110	90
China[d]	851	830	...
Turkey	27	35	30
Pakistan	43	25	34
India	397	385	428
Anglo-Egyptian Sudan	30	72	168
Ethiopia	...	30	...

Sources: **8**, 1950, *passim;* **3**, pp. 117–19; **22**, 1951: April 30, p. 494; May 21, pp. 569–70; November 5, p. 471; November 19, pp. 509–10; cf. **9**, October 1951, pp. 4–8.

a. Conversion factors: one metric ton = 1.1023 short tons = 2,204.6 pounds.
b. Preliminary.
c. Estimate of the U. S. Department of Agriculture (for cottonseed, 1949: **22**, November 5, 1951, p. 471; for sunflower seed, 1948: **55**, p. 133).

d. 22 provinces; 1931–37 in column for 1934–38.
e. Java and Madoera.
f. 1939.
g. Includes British Cameroons.
h. 1948.
i. 1947.

TABLE 256

EDIBLE OILS: WORLD OUTPUT, 1909–13 TO 1951

(Thousands of Metric Tons in Terms of Oil Equivalent[a])

Oil	Annual Average				1948	1949	1950	1951[b]
	1909–13	1924–28	1929–33	1935–39				
Total	5,959	8,615	9,979	9,648	8,643	10,442	10,241	11,694
Cottonseed	1,466	1,729	1,712	1,560	1,361	1,471	1,361	1,651
Soybean	1,575	1,702	1,941	1,229	1,494	1,374	1,769	1,733
Peanut	1,000	1,746	2,418	1,506	1,701	1,751	1,760	1,783
Sesame	330	664	768	653	653	703	703	694
Sunflower seed	165	503	592	562	835	875	758	925
Olive	590	753	845	871	481	1,064	549	1,338
Coconut	386	802	914	1,932	1,297	1,742	1,805	2,073
Palm	300	475	539	372	472	404	435	395
Palm kernel	147	241	250	962	349	1,057	1,102	1,102

Sources: **39**, *passim;* **22**, February 18, 1952, p. 119.   b. Preliminary.

a. Conversion factors: one metric ton = 1.1023 short tons = 2,204.6 pounds.

the fruit of coconut, copra and palm trees, from which edible oils are extracted.

Cottonseed Oil

Before World War II the average annual output of cottonseed oil in the world amounted to 1.6 million tons, or about 16 per cent of the total tonnage of edible oils. It declined during the war and did not regain the 1934–38 level until 1951.

The United States by far outranks every other producing country and accounts for about half the world's total. Its output shrank during the war but now exceeds the average in 1934–38. (See Table 257.)

While the chief cotton-growing countries are also the chief producers of cottonseed (the United States, India, China, the USSR and Brazil), some cottonseed oil is also produced by the United Kingdom, which imports the seed for processing and has a well-established crushing industry. Before World War II it was the world's largest consignee of cottonseed and the largest exporter of cottonseed oil.

Olive Oil

Olive oil, the finest of all vegetable oils, is marketed without refining. Almost the entire output comes from the Mediterranean region. Spain, Italy and Greece account for about 70 per cent of the world production, though in

1950 their share was about 65 per cent. (See Table 257.)

Olive oil largely replaces animal fats in the Mediterranean countries and only 15–20 per cent of the output enters into world trade; some countries export the finest grades of oil and import inferior grades for domestic consumption.

The olive tree is unusually long-lived; some still productive trees are five to six hundred years old. The tree is sensitive to weather conditions, however, during the pollination and early growth of the fruit. During the war, world production of olive oil slumped, largely because of adverse weather, though the fluctuation was less, on the whole, than in earlier crop years, as shown in the following figures (in thousands of tons): [83]

1926–27	570	1939–40	909
1927–28	1,057	1940–41	812
1928–29	675	1941–42	938
1929–30	1,258	1942–43	753
1930–31	454	1943–44	944

The first large output of olive oil after the war was in 1947, when Greece had the largest crop in a decade and Italy, the largest in twenty-five years, while the world total approached 1.2 million tons. Spain also had an exceptionally good crop. Catastrophe followed in 1948, when world output was less than half a million tons. The yield was high in 1949 and low once more

83. **29**, p. 164; **18**, p. 37.

TABLE 257

EDIBLE OILS: OUTPUT IN SELECTED COUNTRIES, 1934–38 ANNUAL AVERAGE AND 1948–50

(*Thousands of Metric Tons in Terms of Oil Equivalent*[a])

Oil, and Country	1934–38	1948	1949	1950	Oil, and Country	1934–38	1948	1949	1950
Cottonseed					Olive				
World	1,475	1,361	1,471	1,361	World	870	480	1,064	549
United States	645	635	700	...	Spain	353	142	318	159
Brazil	125	88	110	...	Italy	213	120	200	159
United Kingdom	94	...	...	...	Greece	115	47	225	38
USSR	189	...	...	...	Portugal	46	29	99	40
China	155	170	165	...	Turkey	37	30	50	45
India	339	...	...	...	Algeria	12	23	23	18
Egypt	115	85	110	...	Tunisia	45	42	105	40

Sources: **8**, 1950, p. 80; **19**, FFO 7–51, April 27, 1951, p. 2, and FFO 3–51, March 16, 1951, p. 2; **22**, February 1952, p. 119.

a. Conversion factor: one metric ton = 2,204.6 pounds.

in the "off year" 1950, when severe insect attacks and unfavorable weather further restricted the crop.[84] In 1951 the output rose to an all-time high, with more than 1.3 million tons.

It is expected that a large share of the expropriated and redistributed land in Italy, under the land reform programs, will be planted to olive trees.[85]

Peanut Oil

Peanuts supply about a sixth of the world's output of edible vegetable oils. An increase of about 15 per cent above the prewar level has been uniformly maintained in the world output during recent years. (See Table 256).

Asia raises about three fourths of the world's peanuts and produces a somewhat smaller proportion of the peanut oil.[86] About half the output is consumed in the producing area, where it is an essential part of the diet. India alone accounts for nearly a third of the world's production and has more than doubled its crushing capacity since the war. China ranks second.

Europe has a negligible output of peanuts but an important processing industry. In prewar years, France, Germany, the United Kingdom and the Netherlands together produced more than a fourth of the world's peanut oil from imported nuts. Both peanut oil and oil cake, the other products of processing, were in great demand, and peanut oil was second only to olive oil in use for cooking and salads.

In the United States, peanuts are consumed mostly in the form of peanut butter or salted and roasted nuts and in candy. About a million acres are planted for hogs, which are allowed to root out and eat the peanuts.[87] The output of peanut oil is comparatively small. Since mills for crushing cottonseed can also be used for processing peanuts, the potential crushing capacity for the production of peanut oil far exceeds the requirements.[88]

Of the 1947 crop, about 18 per cent was kept on the farm for seed and household use, 45 per cent entered trade as peanut butter, candy and salted peanuts and 37 per cent was crushed for oil and exported.[89]

Sesame Oil

Of the annual world output of 1.6 million tons of sesame seed during 1934–38, Asia supplied about 95 per cent (China about 50 per cent, India more than 20 per cent). Less than 10 per cent was exported.

China and India also accounted for about 80 per cent of the world output of sesame oil, which averaged 653,000 tons a year during 1935–39. Sesame oil, obtained by primitive meth-

84. **22**, December 25, 1950, p. 649; **19**, FFO 7–51, *passim*.

85. **22**, April 9, 1951, p. 412.

86. Shelled peanuts yield 35–45 per cent of oil. Peanuts yield more per acre than most other oilseeds. A leguminous plant, the peanut supplies nitrogen to the soil and is valued for rotation purposes, and the cake, high in protein, is a valuable feed.

87. **28**, Part 5, p. 50.

88. **18**, p. 15.

89. **25**, 1950–51, p. 611.

ods of crushing, is consumed domestically in both countries, and only small surpluses are exported. The output of sesame seed and oil declined during the war, rose somewhat in 1949 and exceeded the prewar average in 1950. The proportion of oil entering international trade dropped after the war to 5 per cent or less.

In the Western Hemisphere Mexico is the largest producer. It has multiplied its output four- or fivefold during the last decade, and further expansion is expected.[90]

Sunflower Oil

Sunflower seed is the most important oil-bearing crop in the USSR and in the territory the USSR acquired from Romania after World War II. The oil is the basic vegetable food oil in the USSR; the oil cake is used for feed, the husk of the flower for fuel and the ashes of the stalk for fertilizer.[91] The average rate of oil extraction is about 25 per cent.

The USSR formerly accounted for about 80 per cent of the world's output of both the seed and the oil; the Danubian countries, for about 15 per cent. Russia consumed almost all of its sunflower oil domestically, while Romania and Bulgaria exported a part of the output.

During World War II, when a large part of the USSR's producing area was occupied by the Germans, production dropped considerably. It has been recovering in the last years but is still below the prewar level in the present boundaries.

In the mid–1930's, Argentina began to devote a large acreage to this crop, expanding it from an average of less than a million acres in 1934–38 to more than 4.5 million in 1949. The output was estimated at 920,000 metric tons in 1950; the goal for 1952–53 was even higher. An efficient crushing industry has been established, and Argentina has become the world's only substantial exporter of sunflower oil.[92] Domestic requirements absorb nearly two thirds of the output; the rest is exported, principally to the United Kingdom. Consumption in 1950 is estimated at 175,000 short tons, and shipments of oil abroad, at more than 113,000 short tons.[93]

In Chile, sunflower seed represents one of the main sources of edible oil. The seed output of 67,000 tons in 1950 was double that of a few years earlier. Uruguay, likewise, has expanded its acreage to many times the prewar, but the yield per acre is so much lower than in Chile that the crop from the considerably larger area was less than Chile's in 1950.[94]

Soybean Oil

Soybeans, one of the oldest crops grown by man, have been an important item in the diet of Asia for many centuries. The beans yield 15–17 per cent of oil, depending on the variety and the extraction technique. Asia formerly raised as much as 90 per cent of the world's soybean crop, and China and Manchuria together raised more than 75 per cent. While China needed the crop for domestic consumption,[95] Manchuria dominated the world markets in soybeans and oil, and in 1935–39 annual exports averaged about 2 million tons of soybeans and 70,000 tons of oil.

Many countries have recognized the value of soybeans and soybean oil in recent decades. The United States has expanded the acreage in this crop spectacularly — from 50,000 acres harvested for beans in 1907 to 0.7 million in 1929, 11.2 million in 1947 and 13.3 million acres in 1950.[96] With a crop of 7.8 million tons, the United States now holds first place in world soybean production. China ranks next.

Before the war, the world produced on the average about 1.2 million metric tons of soybean oil in a year, of which China accounted for about half. Now the United States, with more than 800,000 tons, accounts for some 48 per cent, China, for 35–37 per cent, and Manchuria, for 6–7 per cent.

Within the United States, the Corn Belt dominates soybean production, with about 80 per cent or more of the total crop.[97] The United States uses soybeans primarily for oil but also for feed, flour and other purposes. Output of soybean oil now exceeds that of cottonseed oil, previously the chief vegetable oil produced in the country.[98]

90. **3**, p. 63.
91. **55**, pp. 132–33.
92. **3**, pp. 61 and 117; **18**, pp. 29–31.
93. **19**, FFO 10–51, p. 4.

94. **3**, p. 117.
95. According to surveys made in the 1930's, Chinese farmers used 55 per cent of the crop as food, 27 per cent for oil, 10 per cent for feed and 8 per cent for seed.
96. **23**, p. 53, and **16**, 1950, p. 148.
97. **15**, November 1950, p. 13.
98. **28**, Part 5, p. 93.

Coconut Oil

Coconut oil is produced from copra, the dried meat of coconuts. This oil is used chiefly by the soap industry, but also in the manufacture of margarine and for other food purposes. The coconut trees grow in equatorial regions and supply the natives with food, drink, textile fibers and building material. They begin to bear fruit eight years or more after planting and continue to bear for about fifty years. Small native groves supply no less than 85 per cent of the world crop; large plantations, the rest. The world's output of copra and coconut oil amounted to 2.1 million tons in 1951, about 7 per cent more than the average in 1935–39.

Indonesia is the leading grower of coconuts. In prewar years its annual output of copra was estimated at about 1.2 million tons and came almost exclusively from the native groves. More than half a million tons of oil were extracted in 1939, three fifths by natives on farms, the rest in the mills. Only about 15,000 tons of coconut oil, from the mills, were exported. Much more important were shipments of copra, which totaled about half a million tons. No coconut oil was exported after the war, and exports of copra in 1949 and 1950 had dropped by 40–50 per cent.[99]

The Philippines follow Indonesia in production and ranked first in exports in prewar years. In 1939, the Islands had about 140 million coconut trees, of which 85 million were bearing. During 1934–38, the annual production of copra averaged about 655,000 tons, and of coconut oil, 225,000 tons. About 90 per cent of the crop was exported, approximately 45 per cent as copra, 36 per cent as coconut oil, and 9 per cent as dried coconut. Most of the oil and the dried coconut and more than two thirds of the copra was shipped to the United States.[100]

During the war, the output of copra and oil in the Philippines declined, and the liberation found this industry paralyzed. The copra areas had no bags, trucks, work animals, storehouses or ships, and tenants and laborers had abandoned the groves. The industry has recovered gradually and the profitable prices have stimulated the increase in production. The 1950 output rose to about 900,000 long tons of coconut products — copra, coconut oil and dried coconut

(in terms of copra equivalent), and a still larger output was forecast for 1951.[101]

The Philippines now export considerably less coconut oil than in 1935–39 but more than double the prewar tonnage of copra.

In Ceylon, which was the chief wartime source of copra and coconut oil for the Allies, exports of copra declined from an annual average of 60,000 long tons during 1935–39 to somewhat more than 21,000 in 1949 and 1950; those of coconut oil, on the other hand, rose from an average of 59,000 tons in the prewar years to 89,200 in 1949 and nearly 110,000 tons in 1951.[102]

Malaya, also an important producer, had more than 600,000 acres in coconut trees in 1940 — one fifth of them in plantations. The commercial copra output averaged 225,000 tons a year before the war, and native production was also considerable. A crushing industry was gradually establishing itself, and coconut oil exports were increasing. Exports of copra declined, however, despite considerable imports of copra for processing from Indonesia and other neighboring areas.[103]

Palm Oil

Palm oil, obtained from the pulp of the palm fruit, is used chiefly for industrial purposes; most palm-kernel oil is consumed as food. Africa and two regions in Asia (Indonesia and Malaya) account for nearly all the world's output of these oils.

Asia's palm oil industry is comparatively young. Before World War I, only a few thousand acres were planted to these trees in Indonesia and Malaya. Since the mid–1920's plantings have expanded rapidly and in 1940 comprised 250,000 acres in Sumatra and more than 100,000 acres in Malaya, all on European plantations. Production was highly mechanized, and the yields were high in both areas.

The quality of the Malayan palm oil is uniformly high, and the 1950 output amounted to about 55,000 metric tons. Since domestic consumption is limited, nearly all was exported to the United Kingdom.

Indonesia also exports practically all its palm oil and kernels because the natives consume coconut oil instead. Production has suffered from unsettled political conditions throughout the post-

---

99. **19,** FFO 17–51, p. 6.
100. **46,** pp. 28 and 60.

101. **18,** pp. 45–47; **22,** July 30, 1951, p. 115.
102. **19,** FFO 17–51, p. 1; **22,** April 14, 1952, p. 320.
103. **18,** pp. 48–49; **22,** April 7, 1952, p. 293.

war years, and the exports are about half the prewar: 212,685 short tons in 1935–39, on the average, and 109,058 in 1950.

In Africa, millions of wild palms are grown, but the natives utilize only a small percentage of them. Oil is extracted chiefly by hand, with pestles and mortars, and the quality is low as compared with that from the mechanically equipped refineries in Indonesia and Malaya. Use of mechanical equipment is spreading, however, along with other improvements in processing, cultivation, transportation and marketing.

Nigeria and the Belgian Congo are the largest producers of palm oil. Nigeria accounts for about a third of the world's exports and about one half of the shipments from Africa. About 90 per cent of the palm oil is produced by boiling the fruit and skimming off the oil. These crude methods recover only about 55 per cent of the oil, as against 93 per cent in a factory mill, and the oil has a high fatty acid content.[104] The British government is encouraging the use of the so-called pioneer mills, which usually extract 85 per cent of oil and result in a better quality product. Several of these mills are in operation and more are expected to be put in use.

The Belgian Congo, next in importance as a producer and exporter, is steadily increasing its output. It is establishing modern plantations, with wider use of high-yielding varieties of trees. The 1950 output of 182,000 short tons marked a continuous increase, the result of more intensified exploitation of wild trees by the natives rather than of a rise in production on European plantations. Steadily rising prices and increases in obligatory minimum prices ordered by the colonial government to be paid to native producers have been the incentives. Native output accounts for about 55 per cent of the total, and the European plantations, for 45 per cent. About a fifth of the output is consumed in crude form by the native population.[105]

By 1952–53, the total output of palm oil is expected to approximate 275,000 short tons per year; by 1958, some 385,000 tons.[106]

Production of palm oil is also expanding in French West Africa, where it is one of the main vegetable oils. The 1950 output was about 90,000 metric tons but only a small part was exported.

The greater part is produced with native hand presses, and the extraction is only 70–73 per cent, as compared with 90–93 per cent obtained in the three new plants built by the French government corporation, which also produce a higher quality. Five more plants are to be completed by 1954. With the recent completion of a palm oil factory and five others under construction, it is expected that oil from French West Africa will be as high in quality as that from any other part of the world.[107]

Some palm oil is also produced in Middle and South America.

Data on production of palm oil and palm kernel, as for many other tropical products, are often not available. Exports of the principal producing countries together averaged 487,000 metric tons of palm oil during 1935–39 and were again at about the same level in 1949 and a little larger in 1950 after a decline during the war years. During the same periods, exports of palm kernel were 725,000, 772,000 and 762,000 metric tons, respectively.

FRUIT AND VEGETABLES

The League of Nations estimated the value of the world's annual output of fruit and vegetables during 1934–38 at $3 billion. Fruit and vegetables ranked third in value among the world's food crops, after wheat and potatoes. The value was distributed among the continents as follows (per cent): [108]

	1925–29 Average	1937–38 Average
North America	16.2	15.3
Middle and South America	6.9	7.2
Europe	55.9	54.0
USSR	14.4	16.7
Asia	3.4	3.8
Africa	2.4	2.2
Oceania	0.8	0.9

Between 1925 and 1938 the world output of fruit and vegetables increased in volume by about 30 per cent. The greatest increase was in the production of citrus fruit, particularly grapefruit.

---

104. **20**, p. 30.

105. **22**, April 9, 1951, pp. 416–17, and April 16, 1951, pp. 436–39.

106. **20**, p. 34.

107. **22**, April 16, 1951, p. 437, and June 25, 1951, p. 756.

108. **2**, pp. 87 and 94. This item is not included in the estimate of the value of the world's vegetable production by the International Institute of Agriculture, summarized in Table 236.

Three factors account for this rise: new nutritional concepts of the importance of vitamins supplied by fruit and vegetables; increase in yield through greater use of commercial fertilizers; progress in canning, refrigeration, storage and, last but not least, in speedy transportation by truck and air. While these perishable products once were consumed only within the growing area or in nearby cities, and largely only during the season, they now can be transported over great distances and marketed throughout the year.

To compensate for shortage of other foodstuffs during the war, the acreage and output of vegetables expanded throughout Europe as well as in the United States and many other countries. Production of fruit followed a different trend. In Europe (except France) output declined, largely because of the severe winters in 1939–40 and 1941–42 and the lack of fertilizer and insecticides. In the United States, the prewar volume was maintained.

Noncommercial production of vegetables in home gardens has risen considerably in most countries. France, for example, now has about 750,000 acres in commercial production of vegetables, and about the same acreage in noncommercial production; the latter increased during the war by some 70 per cent. There is no information for countries in eastern Europe, but it is believed that production and consumption of vegetables has increased in only a few areas and that of fruit has declined.[109]

In the United States, more than 3 million acres were devoted to the commercial production of vegetables before the war and more than 5 million to fruit and nuts. Commercial acreage expanded by about 45 per cent during the war years,[110] and there also was a large increase in noncommercial production. In India, where vegetable food makes up most of the diet, more than 50 million acres are used for vegetables.[111] In the USSR, vegetables occupied about 3.4 million acres in 1938, and 4.1 million in 1946.[112]

In many countries, statistics on the commercial production of fruit and vegetables are inadequate, and for noncommercial production there is none, despite its importance in many countries. The available data for some fruits are summarized below.

109. **7**, pp. 5–6.
110. **26**, 1949, p. 667.
111. **12**, 1941–42 to 1945–46, Vol. I, p. 150.
112. **32**, p. 409, and **55**, p. 150.

APPLES AND PEARS

Apples and pears are the most important fruits in the Temperate Zone. The world's annual crop of table, cooking and cider apples during 1935–39 averaged 10.9 million tons a year (exclusive of the USSR). The United States produced about 25 per cent, and Europe, 60 per cent, with France (mostly cider apples) in the first place. The output in France before the war averaged 3.6 million tons.

The year 1950 witnessed a record apple crop of 14.7 million tons in the world as a whole, excluding the USSR, for which data are not available. The crop in the United States was somewhat smaller than in average prewar years and much smaller than in 1949. France raised over a million tons more than in 1935–39, and Western Germany, the United Kingdom, the Low Countries, Italy and many other countries also harvested considerably larger crops than before the war.

The world's pear crop averaged about 3 million tons during the years 1935–39 and exceeded 3.5 million in 1950. The United States and France (producing mostly cider pears) are the leading countries. (See Table 258.)

PEACHES, CHERRIES, PLUMS AND PRUNES

The peach crop of the world averaged about 1.9 million tons in prewar years and was somewhat greater in 1950. The United States is the largest producer, with about two thirds of the total; western states account for nearly 60 per cent of the country's crop. Europe as a whole produces only about a third as much as the United States.

Europe grows about 80 per cent of the world's cherry crop. Romania and Germany were the leading producers during 1935–39 but the Romanian output had fallen catastrophically by 1950 (from 194,000 to 9,000 tons). Germany and Italy now lead in Europe, while the United States has become the largest producer, with about a fifth of the total.

The United States grows close to a fifth of the world's crop of plums and prunes, which totals 2.4 million tons a year. In Europe, which accounts for more than two thirds of the total, the leading producers are Yugoslavia, Germany, Romania, Czechoslovakia and France. Yugoslavia now produces considerably less than its average prewar crop while France has almost tripled its output.

TABLE 258

FRUIT: OUTPUT IN SELECTED COUNTRIES, 1935–39 ANNUAL AVERAGE AND 1950

(*Thousands of Metric Tons* [a])

Country	Apples [b]		Pears [b]		Peaches		Plums and Prunes		Cherries	
	1935–39 Average	1950	1935–39 Average	1950	1935–39 Average	1950	1935–39 Average	1950	1935–39 Average	1950
World, total	10,850	14,700	2,955	3,540	1,905	1,975	2,570	2,443	925	980
United States	2,771	2,681	651	712	1,230	1,164	725	454	140	211
Canada	317	352	13	20	22	27	6	13	5	8
Mexico	26	48	7	15	30	49	3	5	...	...
Chile	22	20	2	2	15	5	3	12	d	d
Argentina	30	229	55	113	63	100	13	30	3	2
United Kingdom	305	566	23	24	...	...	86	66	12	15
France	3,581	5,117	533	923	65	113	49	134	51	76
Belgium [c]	124	317	48	138	...	...	13	34	14	26
Netherlands	78	274	36	132	1	1	8	24	5	17
Denmark	61	280	11	23	...	...	...	...	d	d
Sweden	104	211	24	41	...	...	10	13	9	8
Norway	24	59	4	10	...	...	9	14	5	4
Germany										
Western	786	1,082	270	406	17	13	250	270	87	101
Soviet Zone	235	242	90	70	4	2	125	95	60	62
Poland	179	163	50	57	...	...	81	45	54	64
Czechoslovakia	151	198	92	72	2	3	168	163	52	82
Switzerland	358	660	160	400	...	...	11	35	23	60
Austria	292	210	144	210	3	5	56	35	16	18
Hungary	47	57	17	17	...	...	33	23	9	14
Spain	118	85	69	43	58	25	36	30	29	30
Italy	281	512	201	292	239	283	50	88	71	104
Yugoslavia	155	111	63	82	15	36	543	385	38	59
Romania	71	83	25	10	...	...	80	163	194	9
Bulgaria	24	37	14	36	...	...	72	118	...	...
Greece	9	27	20	19	9	8	5	10	11	7
Korea	70	22	2	1	5	3	...	...	...	...
Japan	165	438	167	78	47	33	43	40	5	3
Turkey	112	119	79	105	9	6	55	55	33	38
Union of South Africa	25	33	19	15	13	17	10	7	...	...
Australia	227	214	56	69	48	54	19	18	4	5
New Zealand	63	71	7	12	5	7	2	3	d	d

Sources: **22**, 1951: September 10, pp. 235–37, and September 24, pp. 310–11.

a. Conversion factors: one metric ton = 1.1023 short tons = 2,204.6 pounds = 45.9 bushels of apples or peaches and 44.08 bushels of pears. Estimates for countries with boundary changes after World War II adjusted to postwar.

b. Cooking, dessert and cider apples and pears.

c. Includes Luxembourg for apples and pears.

d. Less than 1,000 tons.

GRAPES

Grapes are predominantly a European crop, though they are grown in other parts of the world. Grapes are used chiefly as fresh fruit and for wine and raisins. The main European producers — France, Italy, Spain, Portugal and Romania — and Chile and Argentina use most of the crop for wine, and Greece, for raisins. Turkey produces grapes chiefly for table use.

The United States uses grapes for all three purposes. "Table use" includes grapes consumed on farms and fresh and canned grapes. Dried grapes (raisins) are produced only in California. Wine grapes include, in addition to those crushed for this purpose and for brandy and juice, the quantities processed for jam and jelly and those processed by freezing.[113]

The world's acreage in vineyards before the war exceeded 20 million acres, of which more than three fourths were in Europe. Grapevines were grown along with other crops on millions of acres. Italy, for example, had about 2.5 million acres in vines alone, and some 7.5 million acres on which vines shared the land with other crops.

About 36 million tons of grapes were produced annually, on the average, during 1935-39. Europe accounted for two thirds of the total. Over 30 million tons were processed for wine, about 3 million tons were consumed as fresh fruit, and the rest were dried to make raisins.

The world's grape crop in 1950 was about 6 per cent below the prewar average. Europe grew 63 per cent of the world's crop; Africa, 16 per cent; the Western Hemisphere, 14 per cent; Asia, 6 per cent; and Oceania, a little more than one per cent. (See Table 259.)

CITRUS FRUIT

World production of citrus fruit increased from 4 million tons in 1919 to an average of nearly 9 million during 1935-39 and more than 12 million in 1950. Oranges and tangerines made up 77 per cent of the 1950 total; grapefruit, 15 per cent; and lemons, limes and kumquats, the remainder. About 40 per cent of the oranges and 90 per cent of the grapefruit are produced in the United States.

In Europe, Spain is the leading producer of oranges; in Asia, Japan; in Latin America, Brazil. In Africa, Egypt, Algeria and the Union of South Africa are the largest producers. (See Table 260.)

BANANAS

Bananas, the most traded fruit, are produced chiefly in Brazil, Costa Rica, Guatemala, Honduras, Colombia, Mexico and other Latin American countries and, outside this area, in the Canary Islands, Nigeria, the Cameroons, Tanganyika, Ruanda-Urundi, and some other territories of Africa. The Philippines and Taiwan are the only substantial producers in Asia.

Commercial production requires large financial outlays. It is estimated that a few big com-

panies have invested $300 million in this business. The largest is the United Fruit Company, which controls more than 2 million acres and employs more than 70,000 workers in Middle and South America, the Canary Islands and the West Indies.

The reported world output of bananas in 1950 amounted to 9.5 million tons. It probably was larger but information is wholly lacking for some producing areas and for others, only exports are known.[114]

The figures for the chief producers in 1948 and 1950 were (in thousands of metric tons): [115]

	1948	1950
Brazil	2,726	3,169
Tanganyika	2,012	. . .
Honduras	850	. . .
Philippines	346	575
Ruanda-Urundi	480	. . .
Mexico	300	257
Ecuador	174	. . .
Guatemala	282	. . .
Colombia	229	373
Dominican Republic	250	. . .
Costa Rica	190	222
Panama	130	115
Taiwan	110	. . .
Puerto Rico	112	. . .

Brazil consumes the greatest part of its output; Honduras was the largest exporter until recently and now ranks second to Costa Rica. The United States takes nearly two thirds of the world's exports.

FOOD PRODUCTION DURING WORLD WAR II

The world's output of foodstuffs during 1943-44, in terms of calories, was 5-7 per cent above the prewar level and thus had about kept pace with the increase in the world's population.[116]

114. Bananas are counted by stems or bunches, which vary greatly in weight depending on the producing country and the year.

115. **8**, 1951, pp. 70-71. Data for Costa Rica and Panama refer to exports; those for Honduras and Guatemala to 1947.

116. This estimate of the U. S. Department of Agriculture is based on data for total food production in 30 countries, with about 60 per cent of the world's population, and for production in all countries of five leading food crops, which provide about half the world's supply in calories. It has been assumed that these countries and crops together present a reasonably accurate picture of the over-all output of food on farms since the beginning of the war.

113. **19**, FDAP 8-49, p. 1.

TABLE 259

GRAPES: OUTPUT IN SELECTED COUNTRIES, 1935-39 ANNUAL AVERAGE, 1949 AND 1950

(*Thousands of Metric Tons*[a])

Country	Total			For Table Use			For Drying			For Wine		
	1935–39	1949	1950	1935–39	1949	1950	1935–39	1949	1950	1935–39	1949	1950
World (without the USSR)	35,748	33,015	33,736	3,041	4,413	3,736	2,315	2,189	1,797	30,392	26,413	28,202
United States	2,200	2,396	2,285	598	544	540	846	944	540	755	907	1,205
Brazil	206	200	225	81	76	81	—	—	—	125	123	144
Chile	455	614	624	27	75	80	6	4	4	422	535	540
Uruguay	98	134	135	5	4	4	—	—	—	93	130	131
Argentina	1,354	1,726	1,395	230	219	180	16	20	18	1,107	1,488	1,197
France	8,035	5,706	7,762	148	126	175	—	—	—	7,887	5,580	7,587
Germany [b]	385	172	351	—	—	—	—	—	—	385	172	351
Hungary	634	763	630	38	71	54	—	—	—	596	692	576
Portugal	1,082	1,135	1,131	—	—	—	—	—	—	1,082	1,135	1,131
Spain	3,004	2,268	2,788	142	109	140	57	34	38	2,805	2,125	2,610
Italy	6,395	5,868	5,060	331	445	437	1	11	9	6,062	5,412	4,614
Yugoslavia	785	832	540	78	67	40	—	—	—	706	765	500
Romania	1,216	990	792	172	148	90	—	—	—	1,044	841	702
Bulgaria	512	585	450	133	135	90	—	—	—	379	450	360
Greece	1,203	987	1,255	80	109	136	607	480	442	517	397	677
Turkey	975	2,168	1,470	560	1,840	1,172	265	297	257	149	31	40
Syria [c]	198	80	90	142	57	65	30	12	13	26	11	12
Iran	130	80	178	—	—	—	130	80	178	—	—	—
Algeria	5,296	4,492	4,657	13	22	22	—	—	—	5,285	4,470	4,635
Tunisia	265	140	168	34	18	22	—	—	—	230	121	147
Union of South Africa	250	486	504	13	43	50	40	35	36	197	408	418
Australia	435	435	405	14	13	13	316	259	247	104	162	144

Source: 22, December 18, 1950, pp. 622–25.

a. Conversion factor: one metric ton = 1.1023 short tons.

b. Western Germany; output in the Soviet Zone of Germany is negligible.

c. Includes Lebanon.

TABLE 260

CITRUS FRUIT: OUTPUT IN THE WORLD, CONTINENTS AND SELECTED COUNTRIES, 1935–39 ANNUAL AVERAGE AND 1950

(Thousands of Metric Tons [a]*)*

Continent and Country	Oranges and Tangerines		Grapefruit		Lemons	
	1935–39	1950 [b]	1935–39	1950 [b]	1935–39	1950 [b]
World, total	6,775	9,450	1,280	1,825	798	971
North America	2,128	3,736	1,153	1,665	329	448
United States	2,128	3,736	1,153	1,665	329	448
Middle and South America	1,980	2,280	46	76	21	93
Mexico	151	349	...	...	...	...
Cuba	33	48	14	7	...	...
Jamaica	14	32	8	18	...	...
Dominican Republic	13	48	...	...	...	...
Puerto Rico	26	32	16	19	...	...
Brazil	1,094	1,003	...	...	...	...
Bolivia	95	117	...	7	75	...
Paraguay	159	130	...	...	...	52
Argentina	292	381	2	...	...	
Europe	1,188	1,642	—	—	398	363
Spain	768	970	—	—	50	43
Italy	371	578	—	—	332	290
Greece	47	89	—	—	16	30
Asia	911	753	60	52	23	22
Japan	505	432	...	...	—	—
Turkey	32	32	...	...	3	2
Palestine	284	146 [c]	52	38 [c]	3	3 [c]
Iran	16	45	...	...	...	...
Africa	480	927	19	29	14	25
French Morocco	30	155	[d]	2	[d]	3
Algeria	101	257	[d]	[d]	3	3
Tunisia	6	32	—	—	2	7
Egypt	203	278	—	—	3	5
Union of South Africa	127	184	18	26	5	7
Oceania	89	111	[d]	3	13	20

Source: **22**, June 25, 1951, pp. 728–31.

a. Conversion factors: one metric ton = 31.5 boxes of oranges = 27.6 boxes of grapefruit = 29 boxes of lemons.

b. Preliminary.

c. Production in Israel only: about 90 per cent of total Palestine acreage.

d. Less than 1,000 tons.

This over-all balance, however, concealed considerable shifts, both regional and structural.

While North America increased its output of food by 32 per cent and South America by 16 per cent, western Europe and North Africa produced 9 per cent less, and Oceania and South Africa, 14 per cent less, than in prewar years. In the latter areas, the decline in the total output of food was due to the adverse weather, on the one hand, and, on the other, to use of a larger part of the acreage for feeds. While the index for cereal output in these continents during 1943–44 was 70 (1934–38 = 100), that for animal products had risen to 109. (See Table 261.)

Wartime Output in Europe and Asia

The urgent need to raise more food at home when foreign sources of supplies were cut off forced many areas to change the composition of food production considerably. Western Europe,

TABLE 261

WARTIME OUTPUT OF FOOD: INDEXES FOR SELECTED REGIONS, 1943–44 ANNUAL AVERAGE

(*1934–38 Average=100*)

Region	All Food [a]	Vegetable Products					Animal Products		
		Total	Cereals	Fruit and Vege-tables	Edible Oils	Sugar	Total	Meat, Poultry, Eggs	Dairy Products
World [b]	105	106	105	108	125	99	105	107	102
North America [c]	132	127	128	121	154	95	142	159	119
South America	116	115	94	130	375	128	122	121	122
Western Europe and North Africa	91	97	98	104	102	82	74	61	90
Middle East	99	100	106	86	69	115	86	91	78
Oceania and South Africa	86	78	70	117	d	99	109	119	96
South and East Asia	103	104	103	101	114	105	91	e	98

Sources: **48**, p. 247; **47**, p. 3.

a. Total output of food crops and livestock products at the farm.

b. The countries included are:

North America: United States, Canada, Mexico
South America: Brazil, Uruguay, Argentina, Chile
Western Europe and North Africa: United Kingdom, Ireland, Sweden, Norway, Denmark, France, Germany, Italy, Spain, Bulgaria, Algeria, Tunisia, French Morocco

Middle East: Egypt, Palestine, Turkey, Greece
Oceania and South Africa: Australia, New Zealand, Union of South Africa
South and East Asia: India, Unoccupied China, Japan

c. The high index is partly the consequence of low agricultural output in the base period because of droughts in 1934 and 1936 in the United States.

d. Production insignificant.

e. Estimate made for Japan only: 64 (includes fish).

normally a deficit area in grains, shifted from feed crops and livestock production to food crops. During the war years it had only 70 per cent of its peacetime output of meat, and only 61 per cent of that of poultry and eggs. In contrast, its cereal crop, although affected by shortage of seed, fertilizer and manpower, remained at nearly the prewar level. Inevitably, the diet deteriorated and rationing was necessary to spread the supplies among the growing population and to feed the army. A slight increase in oil crops, stepped up to meet the shortage of fats, helped somewhat, as did the raising of vegetables in millions of "victory gardens."

Within Europe, output of foodstuffs increased rather substantially in some countries and slumped badly in others. In the United Kingdom, the area in grain grew to an unprecedented size and the per acre yield of every food crop was above the prewar average. British farming became the most highly mechanized in Europe.[117] The output of cereals nearly tripled and that of fruit and vegetables rose by 45 per cent.

On the other hand, the United Kingdom produced only a little more than half its peacetime output of meat, poultry and eggs and, as always, depended on foreign food supplies. Norway went all-out for production of cereals and more than quintupled its output but produced a smaller amount of animal foodstuffs. France, Italy and Spain were the worst off, with sharp declines in almost every food item.[118]

India, Japan and other countries in Asia shifted from technical crops to food crops. While the output of foodstuffs in southern and eastern Asia was 3 per cent above the prewar level, it did not meet the requirements of the rapidly expanding population, even at the peacetime malnutrition standard.

Output in the Western Hemisphere

The Western Hemisphere, in contrast, showed a rising curve for all groups of agricultural commodities during the war years.

In the United States, the increase was beyond

117. **1**, p. 101.

118. **47**, p. 35.

the most hopeful expectations. With a farm labor force smaller by nearly 15 per cent but working longer hours and more days per year, farm output, in 1944, was 24 per cent above the level of 1935–39; the marketable output per worker increased by 40 per cent.[119] Weather was favorable, but it is estimated that not more than one fourth of the increase was due to this factor. The vast resources of agricultural technology — better seed, greater use of cover crops, fertilizer and lime, full use of mechanical power, pest and disease control and other measures — helped to realize the great potential capacity of agriculture in the United States. More of everything was produced — crops, animal foodstuffs, fruit and vegetables, oil crops. The population and the armed forces were abundantly provided with food, and enough remained to supply the Allies and build up stocks to aid in supplying the world's postwar needs.

Expansion in Canada and other American countries was also very substantial. Canada increased the output of both vegetable and animal foodstuffs and shipped great quantities of both to the United Kingdom. In Mexico, the production of edible oils had tripled by 1943–44, and that of sugar had increased by 50 per cent. Argentina tripled its output of pork, doubled that of cheese, increased the production of mutton and lamb by 80 per cent and of butter, by 50 per cent. The output of oilseeds in Argentina rose to four or five times the prewar amount, and the increase in Uruguay was even greater. Brazil greatly expanded production of oilseeds and rice.

PRODUCTION IN RECENT YEARS

After the war ended, world agriculture was beset with many difficulties. Obsolescence of equipment, lack of new machinery and parts and shortage of fertilizer, quality seed, labor and draft animals were combined with unsettled political conditions in many regions. Livestock had been decimated in belligerent countries for lack of feed. Soil needed reconditioning after years of inadequate fertilization. Lack of goods to offer farmers in exchange for foodstuffs was another obstacle. In addition, weather struck a heavy blow in western Europe just as agriculture was starting to recover.[120]

Between 1946 and 1950, the only substantial progress for the world as a whole was in the production of sugar. While the output of bread and coarse grain in 1950 exceeded the average during 1934–38 by 5 and 7 per cent, respectively, the increase was not enough to keep pace with the increase in population. The world's output of rice, the staple food for almost half of mankind, has barely exceeded the prewar level. (See Table 262.) All in all, the world is still producing less food per capita of population, in terms of calories, than it produced before the war, sugar being the only exception.[121]

Crop production is abundant in some areas and deficient in others. North America's increase has so far exceeded the growth of population that this continent has become the world's chief supplier of grain. The picture of Oceania is also bright because of the great increase in output of its two most important food crops, wheat in Australia and sugar in Hawaii.

In Latin America, adverse weather and government policies regulating grain prices and allocating acreage in various countries are the chief reasons for the stagnation in production of bread and coarse grains. The high indexes for rice and potatoes (see Table 262) mean little, since the total output is small. The output of sugar has risen spectacularly, because of the rapid expansion in Cuba.

Europe, the USSR and Asia continue to struggle to regain the prewar level of food production but have not yet reached it for all major crops. Sugar production in Europe is an exception effected through active governmental initiative. The only gain in the USSR is in potatoes.

For Africa, the important increases are in grain and, to a lesser extent, in sugar. In that continent, rice and potatoes play a minor role in the diet.

In summary, the problem of food continues to be acute in the world at large because of the growth of population and, even more, the uneven distribution of the existing food. As a result, per capita consumption of food in regions where most of humanity is concentrated is even lower than before the war, while per capita consumption in other regions has increased by 15 per cent or more.

---

119. **43**, pp. 264 and 268.

120. A severe winter in 1946–47 hit a large proportion of fall-sown crops; then the most severe drought in many years seriously affected spring-sown food, feed and root crops. Pastures dried up. As a result, Europe raised 35.6 million tons of the all-important bread grains, wheat and rye, in 1947, as against the average of 61.4 million in 1934–38. (**6**, pp. 2 and 58–60.)

121. **24**, 1951, p. 1.

TABLE 262

POSTWAR OUTPUT OF FOOD: INDEXES FOR THE WORLD AND EACH CONTINENT, 1946–50 ANNUAL AVERAGE

(1934–38 Average=100)

Crop and Year	World	North America	Middle and South America	Europe [a]	USSR [a]	Asia	Africa	Oceania
Bread grain								
1946	90	153	92	75	71	98	103	75
1947	92	171	109	58	81	95	87	139
1948	102	169	92	86	89	103	100	120
1949	102	152	90	95	93	94	105	139
1950	105	149	100	96	92	108	108	116
Coarse grain [b]								
1946	103	152	97	69	44	95	102	100
1947	98	117	102	78	65	99	113	188
1948	118	159	97	89	62	105	119	150
1949	108	150	75	91	62	98	126	150
1950	107	150	88	86	62	101	109	155
Rice								
1946	94	157	196	61	c	91	140	200
1947	97	167	191	88	c	94	154	200
1948	97	178	181	96	c	94	173	200
1949	101	182	217	95	c	98	157	180
1950	103	180	219	105	c	100	157	160
Potatoes								
1946	81	129	127	76	81	112	149	149
1947	82	106	140	81	75	112	134	153
1948	104	123	127	100	105	128	149	143
1949	95	115	163	87	103	114	163	132
1950	103	123	173	98	105	117	166	130
Sugar								
1946	102	100	162	78	d	d	100	73
1947	111	117	168	69	65	d	119	84
1948	112	94	161	104	78	80	125	107
1949	115	106	167	105	87	81	125	106
1950	127	132	171	140	96	84	137	107

Source: Adapted from Tables 239 to 251.

a. Present boundaries.

b. Corn, barley, oats.

c. Negligible quantity of rice is produced.

d. Data not available.

OUTLOOK

Food production has been encouraged increasingly in many areas during recent years, and substantial progress has been achieved. It is expected that the spreading use of improved agricultural techniques developed during the past decade will result in still larger output of foodstuffs. On the other hand, the defense program in many countries has created a greater demand on production factors which are also important in agriculture, such as labor, chemicals and raw materials for machinery. It would appear therefore, that, given the present international situation, substantial progress in food production in countries of intensive cultivation can hardly be expected unless labor input is used more effectively. Conditions are different in areas of agricultural overpopulation and where defense effort is inconsequential.[122] In such areas, expansion of acreage and, even more, better utilization of available land and use of better techniques could

122. **24**, 1951, p. 4.

result in considerably larger output of food crops.

To some extent, efforts in this direction have been aided by the defense program in industrial countries, because of higher prices which the underdeveloped areas (with the possible exception of India) now obtain for many of their agricultural materials and foodstuffs. Exports of rubber, jute, copra, coffee, tea and some other products have established new income records for these areas. Various plans for agricultural development in southern and southeastern Asia, Latin America and Africa, which call for considerable financial outlays, have become more feasible since they can be financed largely by the increased income.

In the long run, all countries of the world, including those with the most developed agricultural techniques, can achieve a greater output of food crops, as technology progresses, better use is made of manpower, idle land is brought under cultivation, pest and weed control is intensified, and waste of harvested crops is reduced. When primitive processing of oil-bearing crops is replaced by effective extraction, the world supply of vegetable oils will be increased considerably. When more fertilizer is used and is more effectively applied, yields will be raised to provide more food from the same land.

No one can know when the limit of the "carrying capacity" of the earth will be reached. All we do know is that for centuries, if not millenniums, man did not have the scientific tools for the production of food that are now at his disposal to open vistas he heretofore could not imagine.

CHAPTER 17

TECHNICAL CROPS

IN ADDITION TO FOOD, the world's farmers produce many essential raw materials for industry, some of plant origin, others of animal origin. The products of plant origin, the so-called technical crops, include textile fibers, rubber, tobacco and seeds from which industrial oils are extracted. Wool and silk, though of animal origin, are so closely associated with the processing of other fibers that it seems more logical to consider them in this connection — as is done in this chapter — than as part of animal production.

VALUE OF THE WORLD'S TECHNICAL CROPS

Before the war, the value of the world's technical crops (including wool and silk) averaged $5.4 billion a year, about a fourth as much as that of food and feed crops combined ($21.5 billion). Fibers accounted for nearly three fifths of the total value of technical crops; tobacco, for about a fourth and oil-bearing products and rubber for nearly a fifth.[1] Among the textile fibers, cotton represented more than half the value of the average annual output during 1934–38:

	Millions of Dollars	Per Cent
All textile fibers	3,097	100.0
Cotton	1,683	54.3
Wool	769	24.8
Flax	231	7.4
Silk	146	4.7
Hemp	129	4.2
Jute	98	3.2
Manila hemp, sisal, etc.	42	1.4

Share of the Continents

Before the war Asia accounted for 40 per cent of the value of the world's technical crops. It produces nearly all the rubber, accounts for more than half the value of oil-bearing products and tobacco, and competes closely with North Amer-

ica for first place in textile fibers. North America ranks second in the value of total output, followed by Europe and Latin America.

Textile fibers rank first in value among the technical crops in all the continents, representing 38 per cent of the total in Asia, nearly 50 per cent in Europe, almost 70 per cent in North America, 76 per cent in the USSR, and more than 97 per cent in Oceania. (See Table 263 and Figure 179.)

Technical Crops in World Trade

In contrast to foodstuffs, which are consumed largely within the producing areas, the technical crops raised in predominantly agricultural countries are mostly shipped to industrial countries for processing. One of the few exceptions is the cotton crop of the United States. This country is the world's largest producer of textiles as well as of cotton and processes most of its cotton domestically.

On the whole, the production of technical crops is more specialized and localized than that of staple foodstuffs. A few areas supply the rest of the world with cotton and silk; a few others, with rubber. Such specialization is due largely to the exacting physical requirements of the plants or to economic factors. While underdeveloped countries have an abundant supply of cheap labor for the tedious and intensive work involved in producing technical crops,[2] the technological knowledge and skill required for processing these crops are largely confined to industrialized areas.

Technical crops consequently play an important role in international trade. While they represent only about 16 per cent of the value of the total agricultural output, they are among the

---

1. **13,** p. 17; in accordance with the method used by the League of Nations (**3,** p. 83), the value of oil-bearing products is divided equally between products for human consumption and products for industry.

2. In terms of labor per unit of land planted, the cultivation of technical crops is more intensive than that of most others. In the United States the cotton acreage in 1949 was less than 8 per cent of the total harvested acreage in 52 crops but absorbed 26 per cent of all man-hours in crop production. In contrast, wheat, with an acreage about three times as large, absorbed only 4 per cent of all man-hours (**16,** 1950, pp. 592 and 649). In Egypt, cotton growing absorbs five or six times as much labor per unit of land as any other crop (**10,** 1947, pp. 47–48).

TABLE 263

TECHNICAL CROPS: VALUE OF OUTPUT IN EACH CONTINENT, 1934–38 ANNUAL AVERAGE

Continent	Total	Textile Fibers	Tobacco	Rubber	Oil-Bearing Products
		Millions of Dollars			
World	$5,446	$3,097	$1,355	$295	$700
North America	1,180	818	281	—	81
Middle and South America	452	298	91	7	56
Europe	463	228	130	—	105
USSR [a]	560	426	103	—	31
Asia	2,185	831	716	286	352
Africa	338	237	30	2	69
Oceania	268	261	2	—	5
		Percentage Distribution, by Continent			
World	100.0	100.0	100.0	100.0	100.0
North America	21.7	26.4	20.8	—	11.6
Middle and South America	8.3	9.6	6.7	2.4	8.0
Europe	8.5	7.4	9.6	—	15.0
USSR [a]	10.3	13.8	7.6	—	4.4
Asia	40.1	26.9	52.9	97.0	50.4
Africa	6.2	7.7	2.2	0.6	9.9
Oceania	4.9	8.4	0.1	—	0.7
		Percentage Distribution, by Product			
World	100.0	56.9	24.9	5.4	12.9
North America	100.0	69.3	23.8	—	6.9
Middle and South America	100.0	65.9	20.1	1.5	12.4
Europe	100.0	49.2	28.1	—	22.7
USSR [a]	100.0	76.1	18.4	—	5.5
Asia	100.0	38.0	32.8	13.1	16.1
Africa	100.0	70.1	8.9	0.5	20.4
Oceania	100.0	97.4	0.7	—	1.9

Source: Adapted from **13**, p. 17.

a. Figures for the USSR are relatively too high because of the official method of reporting, which relates to the biological crop in the fields, not the actually harvested or "barn" crop.

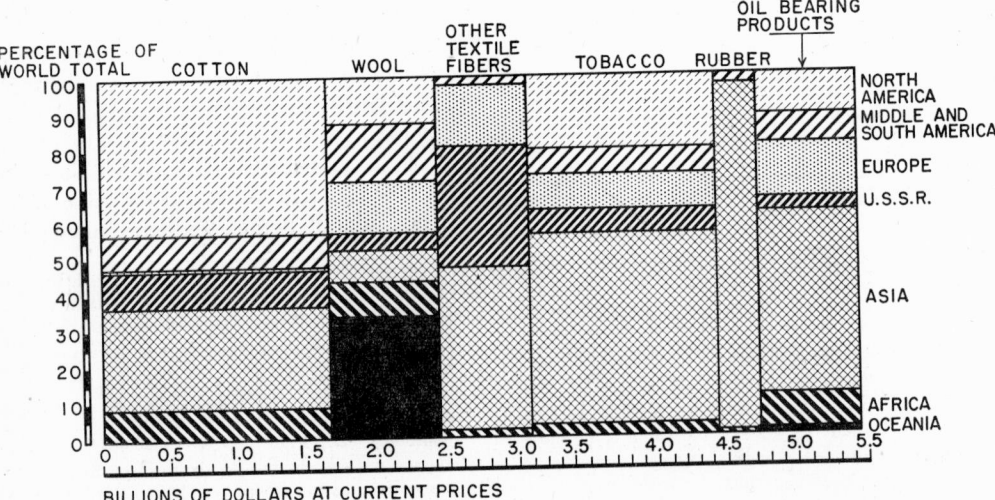

FIGURE 179. TECHNICAL CROPS: VALUE OF OUTPUT IN EACH CONTINENT, 1934–38 ANNUAL AVERAGE

leading items in world trade, as evidenced by their place in a ranking of the value of leading exports in 1938 (in millions of dollars): [3]

Cotton	*$600*	
Wheat ($442) and		
wheat flour ($127)	569	
Coal	530	
Crude petroleum	448	
Meat	438	
Wool	*435*	
Gasoline	394	
Tobacco	*359*	
Sugar	340	
Copper	325	
Butter	304	
Gas and fuel oil	298	
Rubber	*287*	
Coffee	263	
Corn	220	
Tea	202	
Rice	197	
Iron ore	149	
Silk	*124*	
Tin (metal)	123	
Citrus fruit	103	

In many countries that produce textile fibers these products accounted for a considerable percentage of the value of all exports, both before and after World War II: [4]

	1936–38 Annual Average	1946
Peru (cotton)	23	23
Brazil (cotton)	19	19
Uruguay (wool)	46	46
Argentina (wool)	9	9
India (cotton and jute [a])	42	39
Philippines (abacá)	14 [b]	11
Egypt (cotton)	74	73
Sudan (cotton)	63	51
Tanganyika (cotton and sisal)	52	48
Union of South Africa (wool)	29	33
Australia (wool)	35	32
New Zealand (wool)	24	27

a. Including jute manufactures.
b. 1936–37.

Europe remains the chief consignee for fibers, taking some 60 per cent or more of world imports, as shown by the following figures: [5]

Cotton	1938–39 average	62
	1948	69
Wool	1934–38 average	80
	1948	63
Jute	1938	80
	1948	67
Sisal	1938	63
	1948	55

TEXTILE FIBERS

Textile fibers have been used for cloth and cordage for thousands of years. Linen mummy cloths dating back to 5500 B.C., and some even to 12000 B.C., have been found in Egypt. Flax remained the most important textile fiber in Europe until the end of the eighteenth century. Hemp was used by the Thracians for making garments,[6] but was not introduced to other parts of Europe until the Christian era.

India used cotton for fabric and ropes as early as 3000 B.C., and held the lead in the world's cotton weaving until the fifteenth century.[7] In North America, cotton cloth was known long before the arrival of the white man; remains of it have been found in prehistoric pueblo ruins of Arizona. The Indians of Peru used cotton for making yarn and cloth in pre-Inca times, some 800–900 years ago.[8]

China produced silk several millenniums before our era. Marco Polo relates that the Chinese "have vast quantities of raw silk, and manufacture it, not only for their own consumption, all of them being clothed in dresses of silk, but also for other markets." [9] In the first centuries of the Christian era cultivation of silk worms began to spread, first through Korea to Japan, where it became an important industry, then to India, Byzantium, and finally to Europe. Spain was the first country in western Europe to raise silkworms; later, in the eleventh and twelfth centuries, Portuguese silk became famous throughout Europe.

Wool is mentioned in some of the oldest records of human history. Rome produced the finest wool in the world in the time of its glory. Its sheep received extraordinary care. Their bodies were covered with skins to produce a lustrous and wavy gloss; the fleece was combed and moistened with the rarest oils and frequently with wine. Sheep houses were washed frequently and fumigated regularly.[10]

In our time, the chief plant fibers are cotton,

---

3. **2**, p. 30. The listing includes only commodities with an export value exceeding $100 million in 1938, representing in the aggregate about a third of the value of world trade in that year.
4. **10**, 1948, p. 8.
5. **10**, 1949, p. 14.

6. **46**, Vol. I, p. 316.
7. **34**, pp. 3–5.
8. **22**, 1950–51, p. 418.
9. **53**, p. 227.
10. **37**, p. 1.

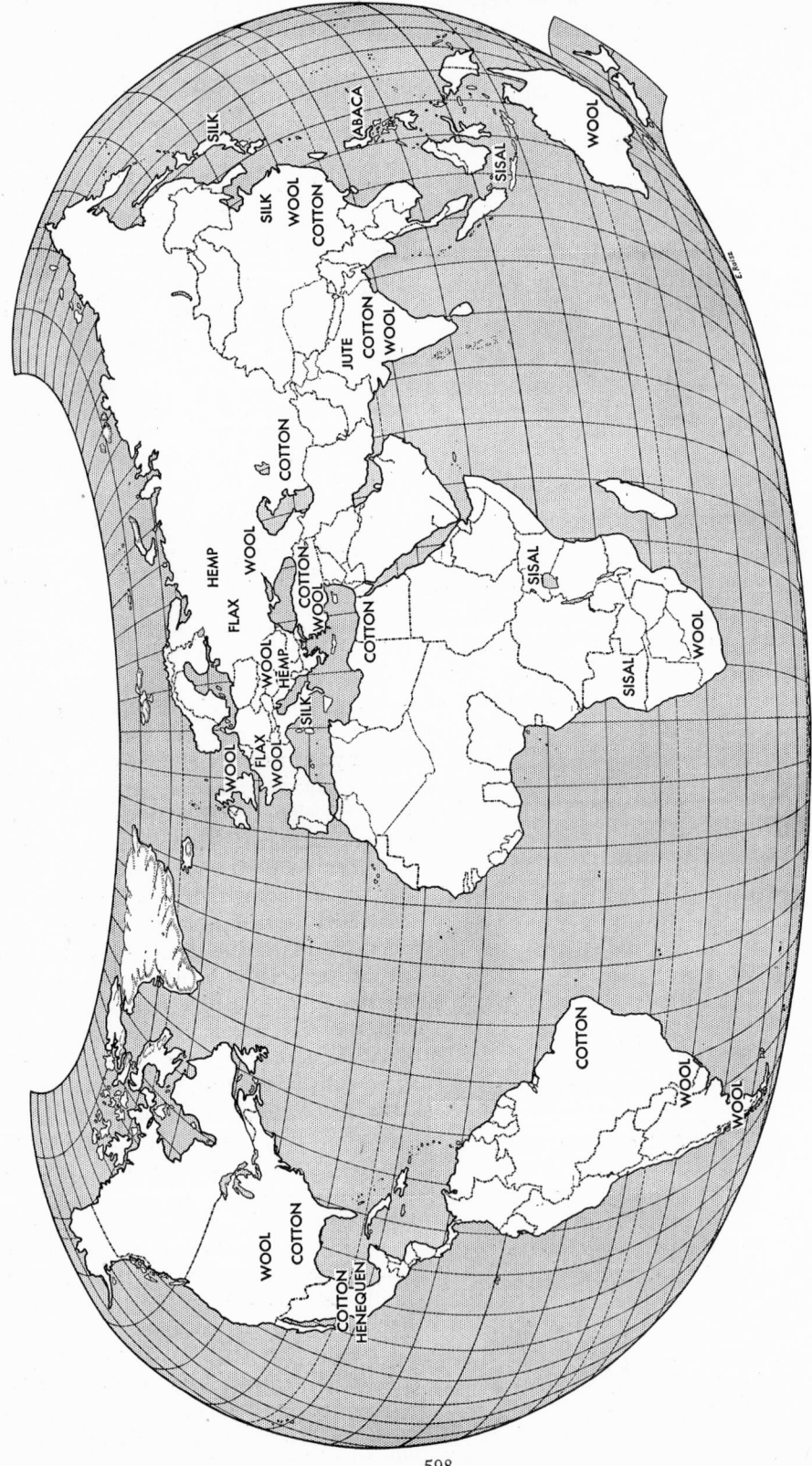

FIGURE 180. TEXTILE FIBERS: CHIEF PRODUCING AREAS IN THE WORLD

598

flax, hemp, jute, manila hemp (abacá), sisal and henequen; the chief animal fibers, wool and silk.[11]

Chief Producing Areas

Textile fibers are produced in all parts of the world. North America (the United States) leads in cotton, which is also grown in considerable quantities in Middle and South America (Brazil and Mexico), in the USSR, Asia (India and China) and Africa (Egypt). Flax and hemp grow mostly in Europe and the USSR. Jute, abacá and silk are produced in Asia (some silk is also grown in Italy and a few other countries), sisal in Asia and Africa. Oceania leads in the output of wool, which is also produced on all other continents. (See Figure 180.)

Major Groups of Fibers

Though fibers are interchangeable to some extent, they may be roughly divided into two groups: those used mainly for apparel and household purposes (cotton, wool, silk and some flax), and those used mainly by industry (hemp, abacá, jute, henequen, sisal). The dividing line is not sharp, since some are used for both purposes.[12] With this qualification, it is estimated that apparel and household fibers account for about 70–75 per cent and industrial fibers for 25–30 per cent of the world's fiber output.

Trends in Output

Between 1909–13 and 1939 trends in world production of apparel fibers and industrial fibers differed sharply.

The output of apparel fibers rose by about 33 per cent, with setbacks due to depressions, thus more or less keeping pace with the increase of the world's population.[13] Cotton held first place, although twice the output dropped sharply — in the early 1920's and again from 1927 to 1935. Peak production was reached in 1937. The

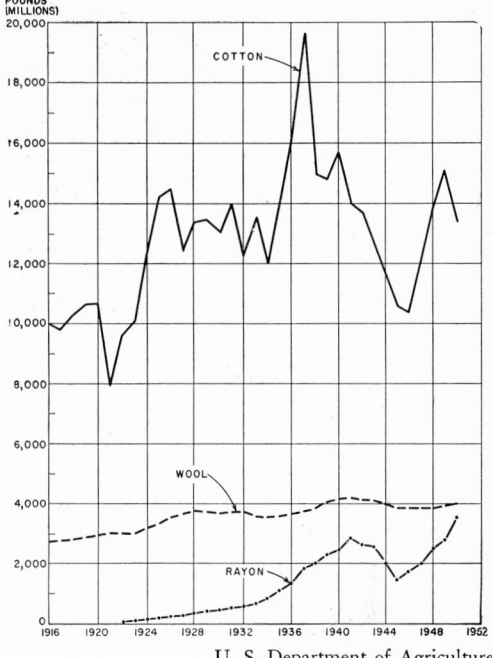

U. S. Department of Agriculture

FIGURE 181. TEXTILE FIBERS: WORLD OUTPUT OF MAJOR APPAREL FIBERS, 1916–50

upward trend in wool output was less spectacular but steadier. (See Figure 181.) Silk had its record year in 1939.

In contrast, the output of industrial fibers increased slowly, by some 10 per cent from the average during 1909–13 to the volume in 1939. Only abacá recorded a rise, about 220 per cent, though the actual quantity was too small to influence the general trend of the group.

Production of fibers declined considerably during World War II. With the disruption of international trade and the greater need for food, there was less incentive to raise cotton, normally a cash crop, and the cotton acreage decreased in many countries. Wool, however, assured of buyers by contracts with the United Kingdom and the United States, was less affected, but the output fell in the last war years. Production of silk nearly collapsed. All industrial fibers experienced a severe setback.

In postwar years, pent-up demand and high prices stimulated an increase in fiber production, but the recovery was rather slow. Cotton is the only fiber for which output was above the prewar level in 1949 and again in 1951. Production of wool in 1950 was smaller than in 1939 by some 3 per cent, of jute by 17, and of abacá by about 10 per cent. (See Table 264.)

---

11. Lack of space precludes discussion of minor fibers of plant origin (such as ramie, kapok, sunn and coir) and of animal origin (mohair and alpaca).

12. In the United States in 1939, for example, 63 per cent of the raw cotton was consumed in the manufacture of apparel and household goods and 37 per cent in making industrial goods (automobile-tire fabric, cotton bags, tents, awnings, belting and so on). **25**, p. 25.

13. Moreover, supplies of apparel fibers were substantially increased by the appearance of synthetic fibers, the output of which rose in this period from 9,000 tons to more than a million. See Chapter 28.

TABLE 264

TEXTILE FIBERS: WORLD OUTPUT OF MAJOR TYPES, 1909–13 ANNUAL AVERAGE AND 1929–50

(*Thousands of Metric Tons*[a])

Year	Apparel Fibers				Industrial Fibers				
	Total	Cotton	Wool[b]	Silk	Total	Flax[c]	Hemp[d]	Jute	Abacá
1909–13	6,191	4,662	1,500	29	2,962	786	569	1,547	60
1929	7,668	5,823	1,784	61	3,009	619	497	1,880	213
1934	7,053	5,342	1,654	57	2,744	689	322	1,553	180
1939	8,211	6,280	1,870	61	3,278	920	415	1,750	193
1944	7,026	5,236	1,777	13	. . .	. . .	. . .	1,140	. . .
1946	6,423	4,692	1,720	11	1,681	350	232	1,050	49
1948	8,041	6,318	1,710	13	2,275	535	250	1,395	94
1949	8,588	6,815	1,758	15	1,769	200	260	1,210	99
1950	7,873	6,041	1,817	15	2,015	190	200	1,450	175

Sources: **10**, 1949, p. 81; **12**, June 1951, pp. 4–9; **20**, May 14, 1951, p. 547, and January 28, 1952, pp. 59–60: data for cotton since 1948.

a. Conversion factor: one metric ton = 2,204.6 pounds.
b. Greasy basis. Wool is marketed "in the grease," but the value is based on the estimated clean yield, which may represent from 55 to 45 per cent or less of the total weight.
c. Excludes, in 1949 and 1950, the USSR (1948 output: 345,000 tons, as estimated by the U. S. Department of Agriculture, **57**, p. 146).
d. Excludes the USSR since 1946.

All in all, a larger world population has a smaller amount of natural fibers per capita than before World War II. The total output is only beginning to approach the prewar level. The current value of the world's output of natural fibers is not known, but the relationship among the various types may have remained about the same. Before the war, cotton surpassed all other fibers taken together in both volume and value. It outranked wool four to one in volume and more than two to one in value. (See Table 265.)

Share of the Continents

While each continent produces some fibers, Asia and North America together supply more than 60 per cent of the volume of world output. In ranking, these two continents have changed places. Before the war, Asia accounted for 38 per cent of the average yearly volume of the world's total output and North America for 25 per cent; in 1948–49, North America, with 33 per cent, exceeded Asia's 28 per cent.[14]

	Per Cent	
	1934–38	*1948–49*
World	100	100
North America	25	33
Latin America	9	11
Europe	4	5
USSR	14	10
Asia	38	28
Africa	7	9
Oceania	3	4

14. **10**, 1949, p. 5.

COTTON

At the beginning of the nineteenth century only 4 per cent of all the fabric produced in a year was of cotton, as compared with 74 per cent of wool and 18 per cent of flax. A hundred years later, the figures were 78 per cent for cotton, 20 per cent for wool and 6 per cent for flax.[15] During World War II, cotton supplied about 83 per cent of the military textile requirements in the United States, in comparison with 11 per cent for wool and 6 per cent for rayon.[16]

Physical Requirements

The cotton plant requires a frost-free season of about 200 days or more, a minimum rainfall of 20 inches well distributed throughout the growing season, a mean annual temperature above 60°F., and much sunshine. In addition to these exacting climatic requirements, it needs, for the best results, well-drained and aerated soil that can retain moisture, such as loam with clay subsoil. Only a few areas in the world satisfy these requirements, although cotton is grown on all continents.

The narrow physical limits of cotton culture and the universal demand for this fiber make it a powerful competitor for land. (See Chapter 15.) This valuable cash crop normally displaces corn and wheat in areas capable of producing either cotton or these food crops. But where

15. **40**, p. 25.
16. **22**, 1950–51, p. 386.

TABLE 265

MAJOR FIBERS: VOLUME AND VALUE OF OUTPUT IN EACH CONTINENT,
BY TYPE, 1934–38 ANNUAL AVERAGE

	Thousands of Tons						Millions of Dollars					
Continent	Cotton	Flax and Hemp	Jute	Manila, Hemp, Sisal, Etc.	Wool	Silk	Cotton	Flax and Hemp	Jute	Manila, Hemp, Sisal, Etc.	Wool	Silk
World	6,441	1,342	1,506	551	1,683	58.2	$1,683	$359	$98	$42	$769	$146
North America	2,754	1	—	—	214	—	720	0	—	—	98	—
Middle and South America	629	5	—	112	270	—	164	2	—	8	124	—
Europe	22	422	—	—	232	3.2	5	110	—	—	107	7
USSR	673	756	—	—	79	1.6	176	210	—	—	36	3
Asia	1,776	156	1,506	286	156	53.4	466	37	98	22	71	135
Africa	586	2	—	153	158	—	152	0	—	12	73	—
Oceania	—	—	—	—	574	—	—	—	—	—	261	—

Source: **13**, pp. 14–17.

there is pressure for produce more essential to human life, cotton has to retreat, as it retreats before rice in India. The total cotton acreage in a given year is determined largely by the level of prices. When the price is sufficiently high, cotton is grown even on marginal land; a drastic drop in price usually cuts down the acreage.

Output

The major cotton-producing countries are the United States, the USSR, India, China, Egypt, Brazil, Pakistan and Mexico. Together, they grow about nine tenths of the world's output. The world's postwar output exceeded the 1934–38 average in 1949; the 1950 crop was considerably smaller, mostly because of the slump in the United States due to acreage control, heavy boll weevil damage and adverse weather. (See Table 266 and Figure 182.)

Major cotton countries (exclusive of the USSR) have maintained about the same ranking in output during the last forty years. (See Figure 183.)

The United States. The share of the United States shrank from more than 60 per cent of the total before World War I to 41 per cent during 1934–38 because of the decline in its crop and increases elsewhere, chiefly in Brazil and the USSR. Since the end of the war, except for 1950, it has again raised the lion's share of the world's cotton crop (51 per cent in 1948; 52 in 1949; and 36 per cent in 1950).

Cotton acreage in the United States, reduced during and immediately after the war, chiefly because of labor shortage, began to expand under the stimulus of high prices and approached the prewar extent in 1949. Acreage control in 1950 reduced the cotton land by some 10 million acres, but control measures were removed in 1951, and the goal for output was set at about 3.5 million tons (16 million bales), as much as had been produced in 1949.

Cultivation is concentrated in the South's Cotton Belt, one of the most specialized agricultural regions in the world. Within the Cotton Belt, there has been a shift from the eastern states (South Carolina, Georgia, Alabama) toward the west (Oklahoma and Texas). In recent years the westward movement has extended beyond the borders of the old Cotton Belt to the hot, irrigated valleys of California, New Mexico and Arizona. (See Figure 184.) The supremacy of the Cotton Belt remains unchallenged, however, in that it produces about 80 per cent of the country's crop. For geographic distribution of cotton output in 1949 see Figure 185.

India and Pakistan. Before World War II, India ranked second in cotton output. The cotton acreage of the subcontinent as a whole was only about 13 per cent smaller than that of the United States, but its yield was 60 per cent less. The need to stress food production has reduced the acreage in both India and Pakistan, and their combined output in 1949–50 was more than 30 per cent below the average of 1934–38. Their

TABLE 266

COTTON: ACREAGE AND OUTPUT IN THE WORLD AND SELECTED COUNTRIES, 1934–38 ANNUAL AVERAGE
AND 1948–50

Country	Area, in Millions of Acres				Output, in Thousands of Metric Tons [a]			
	1934–38	1948	1949	1950	1934–38	1948	1949	1950
World	82.0	63.0	69.6	66.8	6,480	6,318	6,815	6,041
United States	28.4	22.9	27.4	17.8	2,756 [b]	3,226	3,514	2,181
Mexico	0.7	1.1	1.4	1.8	66	124	204	244
Brazil	5.2	4.1	4.5	4.7	389	325	283	327
Peru	0.4	0.4	0.4	0.4	82	64	76	81
Argentina	0.8	1.2	1.1	1.1	60	98	140	100
USSR	5.0	4.1	4.6	5.6	645	564	588	. . .
China	7.4	6.3	5.3	7.7	630	459	370	545
Korea [c]	0.5	0.3	0.3	0.3	40	16	28	20
Turkey	0.6	0.7	0.8	1.1	55	67	97	122
Pakistan	}24.7{	2.8	2.9	2.8	}1,150{	193	217	267
India		11.1	12.2	13.9		547	512	577
Egypt	1.9	1.5	1.8	2.1	400	398	391	382
Belgian Congo	0.8	0.7	0.8	0.8	31	48	48	43
Uganda	1.5	1.6	1.6	1.6	59	70	62	65
Other countries	4.0	4.2	4.5	5.0	117	120	75	. . .

Sources: **11**, 1950, pp. 102–03; **20**, January 28, 1952, pp. 59–60.

a. Conversion factors: one metric ton = 2,204.6 pounds = 46 bales.

b. Not including the output of linters, amounting to about 293,000 tons.

c. In 1948–50, South Korea.

share in the world's cotton crop fell from 18 per cent before the war to 12 per cent in 1949–50.

Increased cotton production is planned in India, to be achieved through more extensive sowing of higher-yielding varieties, greater use of fertilizer and intercropping of cotton with peanuts. It is believed that the target increase in output by a third is possible in this way, without affecting adversely the production of food crops.[17]

China. The combination of unsettled political conditions, high prices for food crops and unfavorable weather cut down acreage and output in 1948 and 1949. The 1949 crop was about 40 per cent below the prewar average. While the acreage in 1950 slightly exceeded the prewar, the output was about 14 per cent smaller because of lower yields. (See Table 266.)

The USSR. The USSR, now the second largest producer of cotton, raises it in the old irrigated areas of Central Asia and Transcaucasia and in new nonirrigated regions farther north.[18]

Climatic conditions are favorable, although less so than in the irrigated parts of the United States. In Central Asia cotton is cultivated farther north than any place else in the world.[19]

In 1928, the Soviet government began to extend the cultivation of cotton into the southern Ukraine, the Crimea, the delta of the Volga and some areas of North Caucasus, where cotton is "rain-grown" on nonirrigated soil. In 1938, these areas had 1.3 million acres in cotton, or nearly a fourth of the total cotton acreage. The growing season is short, 130–150 days, and frost is a serious problem. Very low yields of inferior quality, or even complete failure of the crop, occurred before World War II.[20]

During the war, almost all the nonirrigated cotton area lay in the path of the German invasion, and production was insignificant. In the first postwar years, the acreage in this region was less than a third that before the war, but in 1950 it

in irrigated regions in 1915, and the output amounted to about 320,000 tons.

17. **9**, p. 70.

18. Cotton was raised on more than 2 million acres

19. **48**, p. 506.

20. **57**, pp. 133–40, and **18**, November 1947, p. 7.

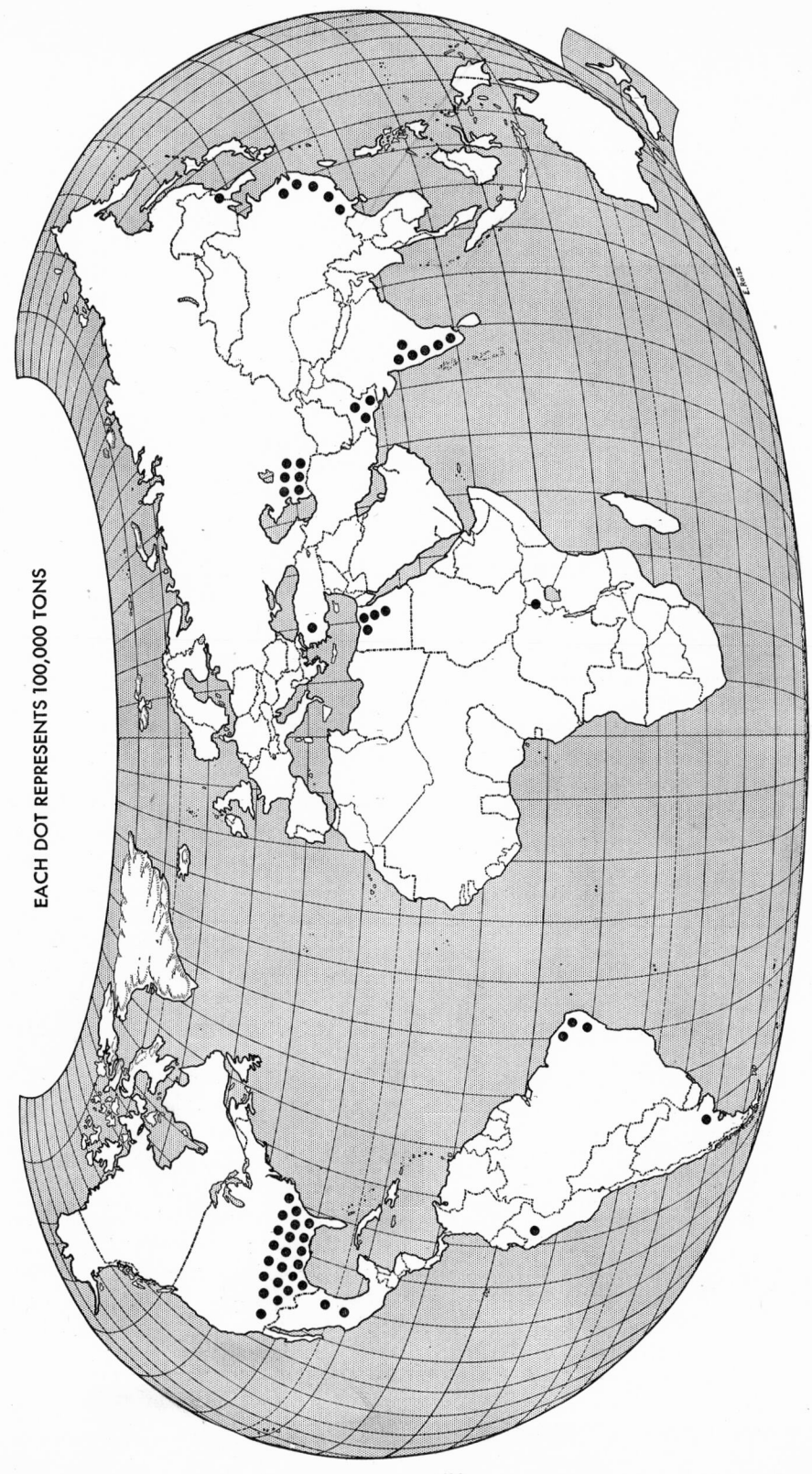

EACH DOT REPRESENTS 100,000 TONS

FIGURE 182. COTTON: GEOGRAPHIC DISTRIBUTION OF WORLD OUTPUT, 1950

The United States is the world's largest producer of cotton. The USSR ranks second. Other important cotton-raising countries are China (southeastern provinces), Pakistan, Egypt, Brazil and Mexico.

MILLION METRIC TONS

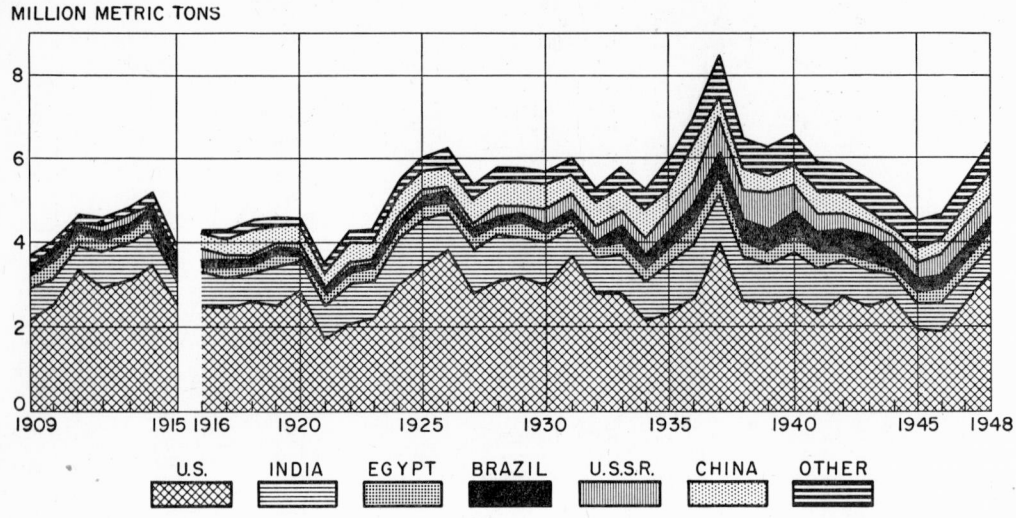

Food and Agriculture Organization

FIGURE 183. COTTON: OUTPUT IN THE WORLD AND SELECTED COUNTRIES, 1909-48

The world's output of cotton was at a peak in 1937, declined during World War II and turned upward after its end. Data shown in this figure do not include China for the period of 1909–15. The years charted relate to the season beginning August 1.

exceeded the prewar figure. The total cotton acreage was larger than in 1934–38 (5.6 and 5.0 million acres, respectively). (See Table 266.)

The government has complete control over cotton cultivation; it distributes seed and fertilizer, allocates the use of water for irrigation and decides upon practices to be used. The entire crop must be delivered to government warehouses.[21]

Egypt, Brazil and Mexico. Egypt, Brazil and Mexico are next in importance in cotton raising.

Egypt's whole economy is dependent upon its "white gold" and cotton generally is planted on 30–40 per cent of the country's arable land. The cotton acreage declined during World War II because of governmental measures to increase food production, but by 1949 it had regained about the prewar area and in 1950 exceeded it. Until recently, Egypt has exported almost all its cotton. During 1930–31, Egyptian textile factories consumed only one tenth of one per cent of the crop, but in 1947–48, they were using 17 per cent.[22]

In Brazil, expansion of the acreage in cotton was stimulated by the collapse of coffee prices and also by the crop restriction program in the United States; development of better seed and

improvement of ginning have also contributed to the increase in output.[23] As farmers shifted from coffee to cotton, Brazil nearly quintupled its output from 1930–31 to 1944. The center of cotton production is in the south, particularly in the state of São Paulo. In recent years, when coffee and foodstuffs commanded higher prices, some land was diverted from cotton to other crops. Plant diseases, scarcity of labor and less favorable weather have further reduced the output.

Mexico has considerably increased its cotton acreage in recent years — from less than an average 700,000 in 1934–38 to 1.4 million acres in 1949, 1.8 million in 1950 and more than 2.2 million in 1951. Better insect control and increased mechanization have contributed to a rise of 40–50 per cent in yield per acre.

Yield Per Acre

The average yield of cotton per acre differs from country to country and from year to year. India's yield (about half a metric quintal per acre) is only half the world average because of frequent drought, inferior seed and soil depletion. The yield in the United States before World War II was just above the world average, but in recent years it has been raised by greater use

21. **57**, p. 142.

22. Egypt prohibits the use of foreign cotton by its textile factories. **40**, pp. 136–37.

23. **58**, p. 70.

EACH DOT REPRESENTS 10,000 ACRES (HARVESTED) ON COUNTY BASIS

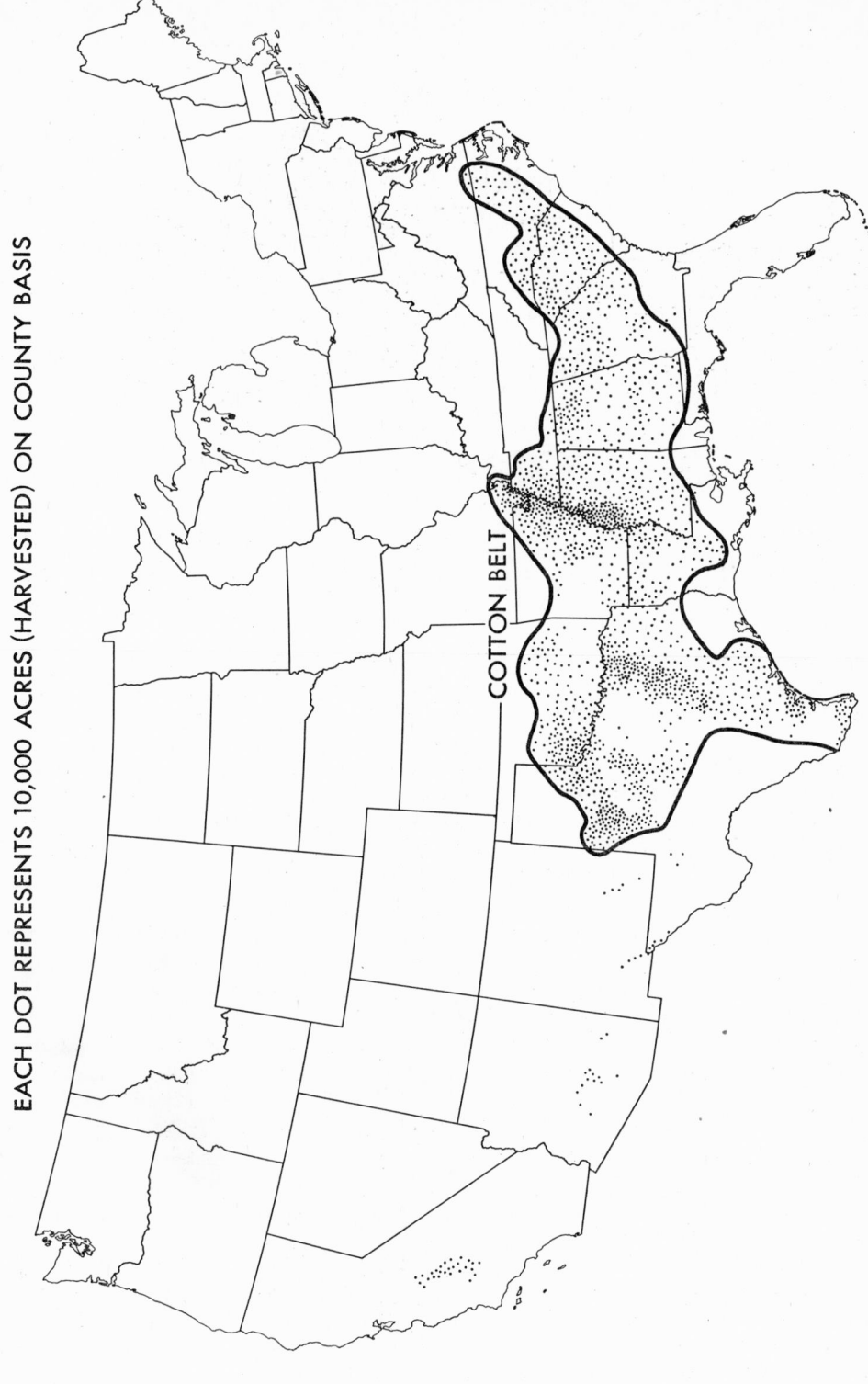

COTTON BELT

U. S. Bureau of the Census

FIGURE 184. COTTON: GEOGRAPHIC DISTRIBUTION OF ACREAGE IN THE UNITED STATES, 1944

The Cotton Belt extends eastward from the lower Mississippi nearly to the Atlantic coast and westward to the border of New Mexico. It includes parts of the Carolinas, Georgia, Alabama, Tennessee, Arkansas, Mississippi, Louisiana, Oklahoma and Texas. Except for Florida, it covers the largest part of the "Deep South." Cotton is also grown in irrigated valleys of California, Arizona and New Mexico.

EACH DOT REPRESENTS 200,000 BALES (500 POUNDS GROSS)

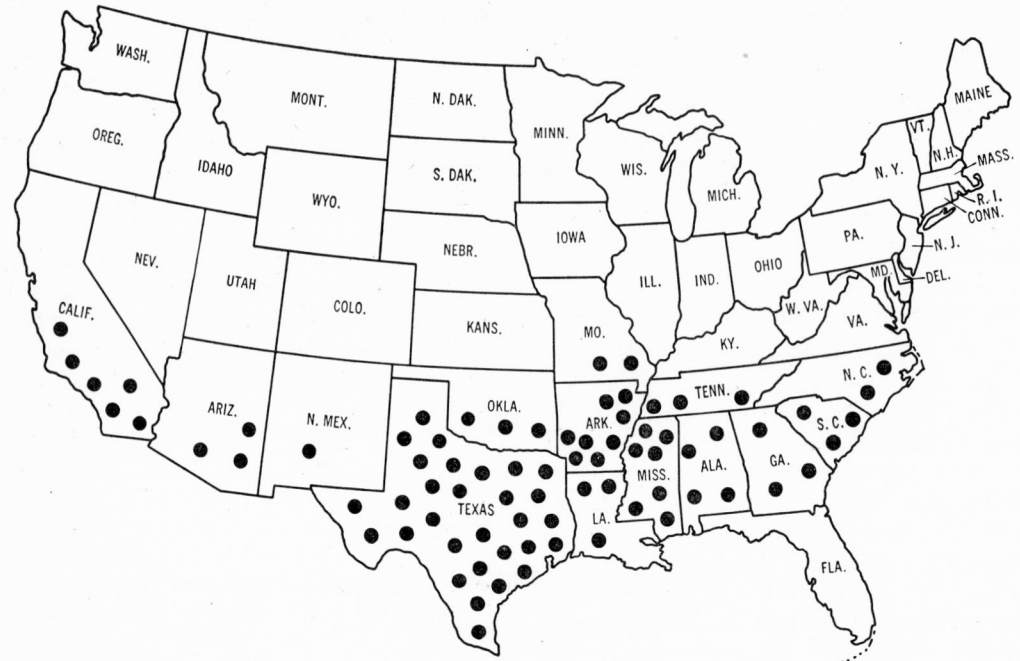

FIGURE 185. COTTON: GEOGRAPHIC DISTRIBUTION OF OUTPUT IN THE UNITED STATES, 1949

Texas is the leading cotton state, with more than 20 per cent of the total crop of the United States. Arkansas and Mississippi are next in line. California's share is growing rapidly.

of fertilizers and high-quality seeds, crop rotation and better cultural practices. The country's highest yields are not in the old realm of cotton but in the irrigated valleys of California, New Mexico and some parts of Texas. Egypt, which has climate and soil exceptionally favorable to cotton and uses much fertilizer and great care in cultivation, has the world's highest yield per acre. In 1950 Egypt grew 6.3 per cent of the world's cotton on only 3.1 per cent of the world's cotton acreage.

Types of Cotton

The finest cotton in the world, the "aristocrat of cotton fibers" is Sea Island cotton, produced in the British West Indies and Puerto Rico in only very small quantities. Sea Island cotton grew for more than a century in the humid areas of Florida, Georgia and South Carolina, but the boll weevil practically wiped it out by 1922. Recently attempts have been made to plant more resistant strains in the Gulf Coast areas of some states.

Egyptian cotton is similar in quality to the Sea Island variety, although it does not have as long and fine a fiber. Small quantities of this type of cotton are also produced in the United States, Peru, the USSR, India and North Africa. In normal years, half the world's long-staple cotton and three fourths of the extra-long staple have come from Egypt.[24]

Next in quality are American upland long-staple and short-staple varieties. The first has a somewhat shorter staple than Egyptian cotton; the second is considerably shorter.[25] The short-staple type constitutes about 90 per cent of the cotton crop in the United States and about 70 per cent of the world's output. Outside the United States, Uganda is practically the only source of fine-fibered, long-staple upland cotton. In spinning quality, the silky Uganda cotton is just under the shorter Egyptian cotton.[26]

The Asiatic type of cotton, grown in India and China, has a very short and coarse but strong fiber. Nearly half the Chinese cotton crop is grown from American seed. In the indigenous

---

24. **10**, 1947, p. 52.

25. Shorter-staple and earlier maturing varieties have been generally adopted to reduce the damage from the boll weevil.

26. **42**, pp. 8–9.

plant of China and India, very short ($\frac{7}{8}$ inch) staple cotton predominates.[27]

In addition to annual cotton plants, there is a perennial wilt-resistant variety ("Tanguis"), grown in Peru, where it accounts for more than 80 per cent of the country's annual crop. The British West Indies and Haiti also have indigenous perennial cotton plants. A large part of Brazil's crop comes from long-staple tree cottons ("Moco").[28]

Mechanization of Production

Cotton culture in the United States has lagged behind other branches of agriculture in mechanization. The explanation lies partly in its geographic location, partly in technical difficulties. With its sharecroppers and tenants, the Cotton Belt has a relatively larger supply of low-cost labor than the Middle West or West. Many cotton farms are small, and the rolling topography of the South also fails to provide the incentive to develop machines to harvest cotton that was offered by the vast level wheat fields of the Great Plains.

Moreover, no completely satisfactory machinery has yet been produced. The mechanical cotton picker gathers less lint than the human picker, and mechanically picked cotton is lower in grade than that carefully picked by hand. Machine-picked cotton contains extra moisture from the spindles and a considerably larger percentage of trash, especially of leaf material, than the hand-picked cotton. This complicates the ginning and calls for additional cleaning at the mill. Machine picking has recently been improved by the application of chemicals to the spindles to reduce the amount of moisture transferred from the spindles to the fiber. In addition, the plant is often defoliated before the machine picking. Although less leaf is then tangled in the fiber, full removal is almost impossible without excessive loss of lint. About 16 per cent of the cotton crop was machine-picked in the United States in 1950.[29]

The mechanical stripper removes all the bolls from the plants, whether or not they are ripe. In dry cotton-growing areas, picking may be postponed until the crop is completely mature, but in humid regions, postponement is difficult. The price discount for the loss in grade often counterbalances the saving in labor through mechanization.[30]

The need for labor in cotton growing — bedding and planting, cultivating and hoeing, and finally picking — has discouraged many farmers from introducing expensive machinery for one or two of these processes.

Use of mechanical equipment, however, saves a substantial amount of labor. While 1,500 man-hours are spent in Egypt to produce 500 pounds of cotton and 208 hours are used by a man with one-row mule-drawn equipment in the coastal plains of the southeastern United States, only 15 hours are required on the high plains of Texas with complete mechanization.[31] West of the Mississippi River, increasing numbers of tractors are used for bedding, planting and cultivating, while labor is imported for picking. When mechanical equipment is perfected, integrated mechanization doubtless will be applied to cotton as to other crops in the United States.

WOOL

A considerable share of the world's sheep do not count at all in production of wool. Of more than 700 million head, from a third to a half (probably nearer a half) produce no wool used as fiber or only a small amount of low-quality wool. These include the majority of the sheep in Asia and a large part of the flocks in the USSR, Africa (except the Union of South Africa) and many parts of Central America.[32]

Raising sheep primarily for wool is practicable only in countries with extensive land for grazing. Sheep are also raised on farms in more densely populated areas, as in some midwestern states of the United States, where lambs can be fattened and marketed readily and wool represents only part of the income from the flock.

Development of Wool Growing

Until the second half of the nineteenth century, England, Spain and, later, Germany were the most important wool-producing countries. Spain produced the finest wool, unchallenged in quality for centuries. It had a world monopoly of merino wool and, until the beginning of the nineteenth century, forbade export of live merinos from the country under penalty of death.

27. **30**, p. 20, and **38**, May 3, 1948, p. 146.
28. **22**, 1941, p. 360.
29. **22**, 1950–51, pp. 441–43.

30. **28, b**, pp. 168–69, and **10**, 1949, p. 32.
31. **41**, p. 5.
32. **30**, p. 38.

Some sheep, nevertheless, did cross Spain's borders, chiefly as royal presents to rulers of other lands. In 1786 France imported a few hundred merinos, which, placed in Rambouillet, near Paris, established the Rambouillet merino breed.[33] Germany and Austria similarly produced the Saxony and Silesian merino breeds. In Saxony, in particular, a merino breed was developed with an exquisite fineness of wool, never attained in Spain. Except for England, European countries began to raise merinos as soon as they could avail themselves of the original stock.[34]

England had its own breeds of sheep, with both short and long wool. Only the former suffered from the competition of merino wool, finer and more delicate in fiber. The long wool of England was known throughout Europe, and much was exported. The domestic demand for this fiber, in a country of cold climate, was also great. In those days "wool was the chief source of wealth of traders and of the revenues of the Crown. It controlled the foreign policy of England, supplied the sinews of our wars, built and adorned our churches and private houses."[35]

A few merinos were smuggled into the New England colonies in North America, but they could not adjust themselves to the severe winters and also suffered from predatory animals and lack of care. Their wool was lusterless and, in general, not to be compared with that of the original strain. Even for ordinary unimproved breeds of sheep, able to forage for themselves and withstand many hardships, the conditions in colonial New England were too hard at first.[36] During the Napoleonic wars, it became possible to import large numbers of merinos into the United States, and a "mania for [merinos] swept the country in 1810–16." [37] Interest in the breed slackened about the middle of the nineteenth century and was not revived until its last decade.

The most important event, however, was the shipment of a number of merinos to Australia in the beginning of the nineteenth century. The natural conditions suited them perfectly, and they multiplied rapidly. As a result, the center of wool production shifted from Europe to Australia, which now holds first place in this field.

Yield Per Sheep

The output of wool depends not only upon the size of the flock but also on the weight of the fleece. Progressive countries have long been trying to increase the yield per sheep. In Great Britain, the average weight of the fleece rose from 4.5 pounds during 1876–81 to about 9 pounds during 1935–39. In 1936, Australian fleece averaged 7.7 pounds; New Zealand, 8.4 pounds. Argentina has about 10 million sheep, which yield an average of 12.1 pounds of fine fleece, and more than 3 million criollo sheep averaging not more than 3.3 pounds of coarse or carpet-type wool.[38] In the United States, the fleece of shorn wool averaged only 2–3 pounds in colonial times; in 1949, the average was 8.0 pounds for the country and ranged from 3.3–3.6 pounds in Florida, Mississippi and Louisiana to nearly 10 pounds in Idaho and Wyoming.[39]

Types of Wool

The three chief types of wool are (1) merino, the finest; (2) crossbred; and (3) carpet wool.[40] The first two are used mostly for clothing; carpet wool, for upholstery and carpeting. Each of the principal types includes many varieties differing in the length, fineness, purity, strength and smoothness of the fiber.[41] The official classification of wool in Australia includes 1,500 types; in New Zealand, 950; in South Africa, 350.[42]

Raw wool is sold before cleansing, but the price is based on the estimated clean yield or weight in scoured wool. The difference varies from country to country: some coarse wools of New Zealand lose only 20 per cent in weight through scouring, while some range-grown wools of the United States may lose 70 per cent or more if the sheep have been kept in particularly dusty areas.

About 80 per cent of the world's average wool

---

33. The pure Rambouillet stock, raised without crossbreeding since the nineteenth century, now comprises only 150 head. **49**, p. 15.

34. **45**, p. 18, and **37**, p. 1.

35. **45**, p. 2.

36. **43**, p. 61.

37. **43**, p. 223. Thomas Jefferson was very much interested in the introduction of merinos into the country.

38. **44**, p. 49.

39. **16**, 1950, pp. 391–97, and **54**, p. 682.

40. Crossbred wool means wool of medium fineness, coarser than merino wool, but does not imply that the sheep from which it is shorn are crossbred (**45**, p. 11).

41. The properties of wool may vary not only among different flocks or among sheep in the same flock, but even within a single fleece. **51**, p. 403.

42. **10**, 1947, p. 82.

clip is of the merino and crossbred types; the remainder is carpet wool. More than 90 per cent of the output in the southern wool belt — Australia, New Zealand, Uruguay, Argentina and the Union of South Africa — is merino and crossbred wool. The Union of South Africa produces merino wool almost exclusively. In Australia this type of wool represents three fourths of the total output. New Zealand's wool is chiefly of the medium crossbred type. Uruguay produces predominantly fine crossbred wool.[43]

In the Northern Hemisphere, the United States is the largest producer of merino wool, which represents about half its total output. In Europe as a whole, about 70 per cent of the wool is of apparel types (merino and crossbred); the USSR produces chiefly coarse (carpet) wool. In Spain, the homeland of merino, less than a fifth of the clip is of that type. Merino wool constituted the following percentages of the total output in various countries in 1947–48: [44]

Union of South Africa	98
Hungary	90
Australia	74
United States	50
Germany	23
Spain	18
USSR	17
France	15
Argentina	14
Uruguay	13
New Zealand	2

Production of carpet wool extends from the Balkans and Asia Minor (Turkey, Iran) to Asiatic Russia and southeastern China. This is the only type of wool grown in these countries or in any part of Africa except the Union of South Africa. No carpet wool is grown in the United States.[45]

Output

The world's clip of wool averaged 1.7 million tons a year (on a greasy basis) during 1934–38. This amount was exceeded in 1949 by 2 per cent and in 1950 by 5 per cent.

Five countries in the Southern Hemisphere — Australia, Argentina, New Zealand, the Union of South Africa and Uruguay — and the United States together account for two thirds of the

world's output. The southern wool belt has a substantial surplus to export, while the United States imports large quantities.

The share of various producing areas in world output of wool has changed markedly since World War II. In the United States, wool production fell by more than 10 per cent, largely because of the better return from the sale of fat lambs for slaughter and competition from other farm produce, such as cattle and market grain.[46] The decline has been halted and an upturn was expected by the spring of 1952.[47] The output of South America — particularly in Uruguay, but also in Chile, Argentina and Brazil — exceeded the prewar level by about 20 per cent in 1950 and was estimated at a still higher figure for 1951.[48] The clip in Oceania has also risen in recent years. Australia, in particular, recovered from the heavy losses of sheep from drought in 1944–45, and increased its output of wool considerably in the following seasons. The 1951 clip was expected to reach an all-time record of about 550,000 tons.[49] Output in the Union of South Africa and in China and India has declined. That of the USSR rose, partly because of acquisition of new areas. (See Table 267 and Figure 186.)

In the United States, wool growing extends from the Canadian to the Mexican border and from the Atlantic to the Pacific, but the principal centers are in Texas, the Rockies and California. Texas accounted for almost 25 per cent of the nation's clip in 1949. In the West, which produced more than 47 per cent of the total in 1949 and 1950, the leading states are Wyoming, Montana, California, New Mexico and Utah.[50] (See Figure 187.)

Reclaimed Wool

Wool reclaimed from rags constitutes an important supplement to the supply of virgin wool. In the United Kingdom and Germany, the output of recovered wool in prewar years amounted to about 25 per cent of that of virgin wool;[51] in the United States, to about 15 per cent. It has

---

43. **20,** June 18, 1951, p. 700.
44. **10,** 1949, p. 88.
45. **26,** p. 1, and **8,** p. 18.

46. **20,** June 19, 1950, p. 604.
47. **20,** June 18, 1951, p. 697.
48. **12,** June 1951, p. 9, and **20,** June 18, 1951, pp. 698–99.
49. **29,** January 1951, p. 1.
50. **16,** 1950, pp. 396–97.
51. **32,** Tables 6 and 11. According to the League of Nations, the production of recovered wool exceeded that of virgin wool in Germany and nearly equaled it in the United Kingdom. **1,** 1938–39, p. 124.

TABLE 267

WOOL: OUTPUT IN THE WORLD AND SELECTED COUNTRIES, 1934–38 ANNUAL AVERAGE AND 1948–50

Country	Output, in Thousands of Metric Tons [a]				Percentage of Total			
	1934–38	1948	1949	1950	1934–38	1948	1949	1950
World	1,728	1,710	1,758	1,817	100.0	100.0	100.0	100.0
North America	212	139	125	125	12.3	8.1	7.1	6.9
United States	204	134	120	120	11.8	7.8	6.8	6.6
Canada	8	5	5	5	0.5	0.3	0.3	0.3
Latin America	278	316	321	330	16.1	18.5	18.3	18.2
Brazil	18	20	20	20	1.0	1.2	1.1	1.1
Peru	9	8	9	9	0.5	0.5	0.5	0.5
Chile	15	16	17	17	0.9	0.9	1.0	0.9
Uruguay	51	65	74	78	3.0	3.8	4.2	4.3
Argentina	170	193	188	195	8.4	11.3	10.7	10.7
Europe	228	206	209	208	13.2	12.0	11.9	11.4
United Kingdom	50	36	40	41	2.9	2.1	2.3	2.3
France	24	16	16	16	1.4	0.9	0.9	0.9
Germany	18	12	13	12	1.0	0.7	0.7	0.7
Hungary	6	2	2	3	0.3	0.1	0.1	0.2
Spain	27	47	41	39	1.6	2.7	2.3	2.1
Italy	14	15	16	16	0.8	0.9	0.9	0.9
Yugoslavia	15	15	16	16	0.9	0.9	0.7	0.9
Romania	20	13	14	14	1.2	0.8	0.8	0.8
Bulgaria	10	13	13	12	0.6	0.8	0.7	0.7
Greece	8	8	8	8	0.5	0.5	0.5	0.4
USSR [b]	100	127	132	145	5.8	7.4	7.5	8.0
Asia	167	158	165	168	9.7	9.2	9.4	9.2
China [c]	50	35	35	35	2.9	2.0	2.0	1.9
Turkey	24	34	32	33	1.4	2.0	1.8	1.8
Iraq	7	11	12	13	0.4	0.6	0.7	0.7
Iran	17	14	15	16	1.0	0.8	0.9	0.9
Afghanistan	7	7	8	8	0.4	0.4	0.5	0.4
Pakistan	}43{	11	11	25	}2.5{	0.6	0.6	0.6
India		25	25	11		1.5	1.4	1.4
Africa	155	129	127	138	9.0	7.5	7.2	7.6
French Morocco	19	12	10	12	1.1	0.7	0.6	0.7
Algeria	8	5	5	7	0.5	0.3	0.3	0.4
Tunisia	5	4	4	5	0.2	0.2	0.2	0.3
Egypt	2	3	3	4	0.1	0.2	0.2	0.2
Union of South Africa [d]	118	103	102	108	6.8	6.0	5.8	5.9
Oceania	588	634	680	703	34.0	37.1	38.7	38.7
Australia	452	468	503	534	26.2	27.4	28.6	29.4
New Zealand	136	166	177	169	7.9	9.7	10.1	9.3

Source: **12**, June 1951, p. 9.

a. Conversion factor: one metric ton = 2,204.6 pounds. Weight on a greasy basis. (See Table 264, footnote b.)

b. In prewar boundaries, but including the Baltic states. The U. S. Department of Agriculture's estimates for the USSR's present boundaries are as follows (in thousands of metric tons): 1936–40 annual average, 141; 1948, 132; 1949, 143; 1950, 147 (**20**, June 18, 1951, p. 698).

c. China proper (22 provinces).

d. Includes Basutoland and South-West Africa.

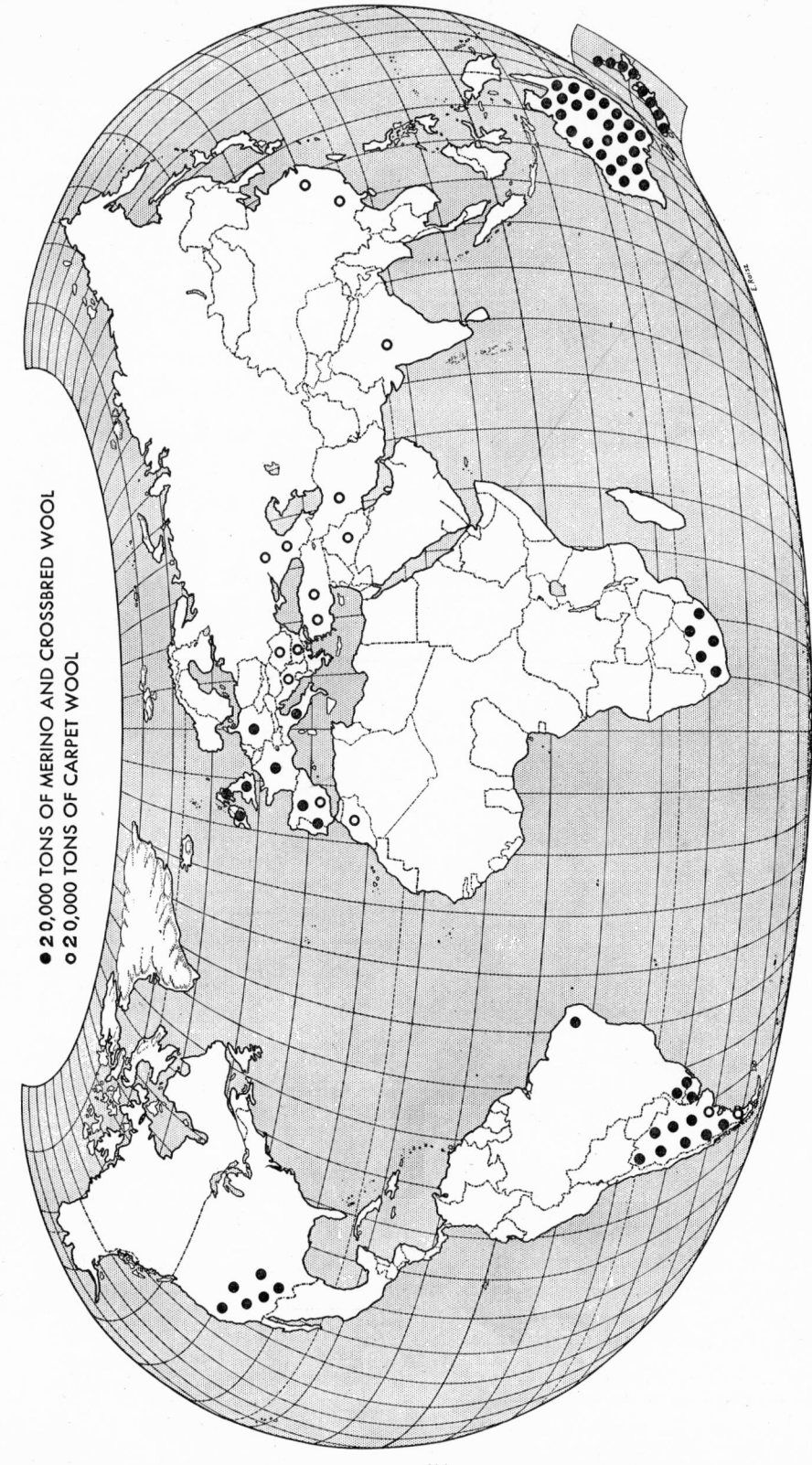

FIGURE 186. WOOL: GEOGRAPHIC DISTRIBUTION OF WORLD OUTPUT, 1950

● 20,000 TONS OF MERINO AND CROSSBRED WOOL
○ 20,000 TONS OF CARPET WOOL

EACH DOT REPRESENTS 1,000 SHORT TONS OF SHORN WOOL

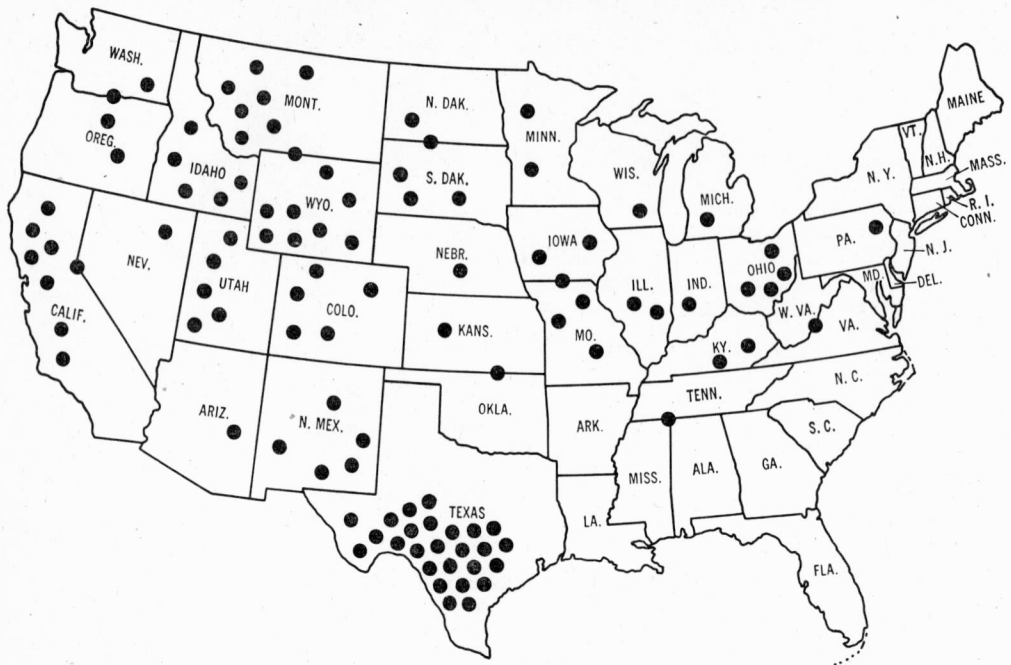

FIGURE 187. WOOL: GEOGRAPHIC DISTRIBUTION OF OUTPUT IN THE UNITED STATES, 1949

been estimated that the world's annual output of reclaimed wool is nearly 160,000 tons, about a fifth of the amount of virgin wool on a clean basis.[52]

SILK

While all raw silk shares certain characteristics — light weight, long wear, resilience and absorbency — there are differences in texture, luster and fineness. Japanese silk is generally finer than Chinese, particularly the "wild" silks of northern China — tussah and pongee — from worms fed on oak leaves; on the other hand, China's tsatlee silk, from the lower Yangtze Valley, is the finest white silk in the world.

Because of its supreme qualities as a textile fiber, coupled with the comparatively small supply, silk commands higher prices than any other fiber. Used chiefly for apparel, it also has great importance for munitions, since silk protects shells from salt air more effectively than any other material. It is also used for parachute canopies, for insulation of military wireless sets, linings of flying apparel and so on.

52. **44**, p. 43.

Cultural Requirements

Silk culture is time consuming and requires a great deal of attention during every phase, since the slightest negligence may make the cocoons valueless. The mulberry leaves fed to silkworms must be freshly picked for each meal and finely chopped. The voracity of the worms is extraordinary.[53] They must be fed several times during the day and twice at night. Worms hatched on the same day must be kept together so that their four sleeping periods, when nourishment is not necessary, coincide; otherwise, some may not get food in time, while leaves will be wasted on others.

Trays on which silkworms are kept must be cleaned every day, yet the worms must not be disturbed. They are so sensitive to noise that workers walk barefoot in the operating quarters. Care must be taken not to crowd the worms at spinning time; otherwise two worms may spin a

53. The worms hatched from each pound of silkworm eggs consume about ten tons of leaves. It takes thirty to forty mulberry trees to supply one ton of leaves, and enormous quantities of leaves are plucked each spring in Japan to feed the silkworms. **55**, p. 601.

TABLE 268

SILK: OUTPUT IN THE WORLD AND SELECTED COUNTRIES, 1924–28 AND 1934–38 ANNUAL AVERAGE, AND 1947–50

(*Tons*)

Country	1924–28	1934–38	1947	1948	1949	1950
World	50,900	53,900	12,500	12,500	14,500	15,000
Japan	34,000	42,300	6,700 [a]	8,100 [a]	9,900	10,000
China	9,000 [b]	4,700 [b]	500 [b]	400 [b]	400 [b]	500 [b]
Other Asiatic countries	900	1,800	...	500	500	500
France	270	60	...	...	...	...
Italy	4,600	2,600	2,300	1,000	...	...
Greece	110	260	...	...	...	...
Turkey	90	220	...	...	...	...
USSR	800	1,460	1,500	1,500	...	...
Other countries	1,130	500	1,500 [c]	1,500 [c]	...	...

Sources: **1**, 1931–32, p. 125; 1942–44, p. 140; **10**, 1949, p. 61; **4**, 1950, p. 222.

   a. Commercial production only.
   b. Exports.
   c. Includes estimates by the FAO for countries for which data are not available.

single cocoon which cannot be reeled into fine silk.

These are only a few of the exacting requirements. It is no wonder that so many attempts to introduce sericulture in various countries have broken down, usually for lack of efficient but cheap labor.

Output

The world's center of sericulture is Japan, where skills in this field have become traditional, and about a third of all farms, comprising some million households, were engaged before the war in raising silkworms. Actually, the silkworm has been the chief domestic animal in Japan, receiving a great deal more care than any other. Japan's prewar production of raw silk amounted to about 80 per cent of the world's total.

China, the cradle of sericulture, is now second to Japan. It also has an abundance of traditionally skilled and undemanding labor and a seemingly inexhaustible supply of mulberry trees, producing two or more leafings during the season. It lacks, however, Japan's dynamic scientific techniques and modern reeling methods, which have achieved a 15 per cent increase in the yield per cocoon. Consequently Chinese production of raw silk is far below that of Japan.[54] The most

important silk-growing areas in China, in the central and southern provinces, account for three fourths of the country's output of raw silk.[55]

In Europe, Italy ranks first in sericulture; the USSR is second to Italy.

A slight increase in the world's output of silk from the level during 1924–28 to that during 1934–38 was due chiefly to the expansion of sericulture in Japan, which more than outweighed severe setbacks in China and Italy. (See Table 268.)

During World War II, production of silk declined severely. The drop in Japan was nothing less than catastrophic. With the loss of its chief customer, the United States, and the need for greater food production, the acreage in mulberry trees was cut down by government order. By the end of the war, only 40 per cent of the former acreage was in mulberry trees, and the output of silk had fallen even more drastically because reeling equipment had been scrapped for military purposes. Since the end of the war, Japan has been making great efforts to restore sericulture, for silk is still one of its most important exports to the United States, totaling 40 per cent of all dollar receipts in 1948. Silk exports, however, cannot be expected even to approach the prewar level, since nylon has replaced silk in hosiery manufacture in the United States.[56]

54. It is larger, however, than Table 268 indicates, since the figures show only the exports, while domestic consumption is considerable.

55. **15**, p. 113.
56. See Chapter 28.

FLAX

Flax fiber is almost exclusively European. Of the average 790,000 tons produced in the world in 1934–38, Europe and the USSR raised all but 2.5 per cent.

Cultural Requirements

Flax is grown commercially for seed and for fiber. While the seed from fiber flax is as valuable for oil and meal as that from seed flax, the fiber from the seed varieties is coarse and not well suited for textiles.[57]

Within Europe, flax is grown mostly in areas with heavy soil and moist subsoil. It requires cool weather and rainfall during the growing season, and warm and relatively dry weather in the maturing period.

Flax growing involves many tedious processes, each requiring the greatest of care. All the processes of weeding, pulling the matured plant, combing, retting (partial rotting to loosen the fiber from the rest of the plant), drying, rolling, breaking the woody core of the stalks, and scutching must be carried through without damage to the fiber. Since much of this work still is done by hand, cheap labor is essential.

The best flax fiber is produced in Courtrai, Belgium, along the river Lys, where flax is retted in crates sunk in the river. Since the natural conditions — climate, soil and the physical characteristics of the water — are particularly favorable, growing flax has become the major occupation in this region. The highest skills in handling flax are traditional, and a considerable part of the French flax straw is moved across the border to be retted by Belgian workers.

Output

Before World War II, the USSR produced 70 per cent of the world's flax fiber. Lithuania, Latvia and Estonia together accounted for about 7 per cent and Poland for about 5 per cent. Belgium and the Netherlands, which together produced only about 5 per cent, had, as for other crops, the highest yield per acre. Yugoslavia also had high yields.

Under the impact of the war, the output of flax in the USSR shrank from an average of some 560,000 tons a year to less than half that amount in 1944. The flax-growing areas of the

Baltic states and Poland fell to Russia after the end of the war, but even including their territory, the acreage in flax in 1948 was a third less than before the war (3.7 million acres in contrast to 4.7 million). With the lowest yield per acre in the world, the USSR produced only 345,000 tons of flax in 1948. Nevertheless, it still raised more than 60 per cent of the world crop.

Other flax-producing countries maintained or even increased their output during the war, to compensate for lack of other fibers. This incentive disappeared after the war, and with it, the governments' wartime support. For example, the British Dominions, which grew only about 6,000 metric tons of flax fiber in a prewar year, raised their output to 165,000 tons in 1944 and cut it back to 62,000 tons in 1946 and about 15,000 tons in 1949. The United Kingdom alone increased its output of flax fiber from an average of 5,000 tons in 1935–39 to 132,000 tons in 1944 and then reduced it to 11,000 tons in 1949 and 10,000 in 1950.[58] (See Table 269.)

In the United States, fiber flax was one of the first crops grown by the Pilgrims at Plymouth and by the early settlers at Jamestown. Flax growing increased until the cotton gin was invented in 1793 and declined rapidly thereafter because cotton could be produced more cheaply.[59] Before World War II, the country's annual production of flax fiber averaged only some 400 tons. In 1942 the output of flax straw soared to 36,900 short tons only to drop back to the prewar level in 1948 and 1949.[60]

The combined output of flax fiber outside the USSR in 1950 was about 27 per cent larger than the average during 1934–38.

HEMP

Hemp, a coarse-textured bast fiber, is grown almost entirely in Europe and the USSR. The methods of separating the fibers from the woody stalks resemble those used for flax. Since much manual work is required, hemp is not grown in high-wage areas.

Hemp is stronger and more durable than any other soft fiber except flax. It has been used for many centuries for rope and twine, canvas, sails and the like. It is subject to competition from

---

57. **22,** 1950–51, p. 484. For flaxseed see pp. 623–24.

58. **10,** 1947, p. 121; **11,** 1950, pp. 104–05; **12,** May 1952, p. 23.
59. **22,** 1950–51, p. 484.
60. **16,** 1950, p. 90.

TABLE 269

FLAX AND HEMP: OUTPUT IN THE WORLD AND SELECTED COUNTRIES,
1934–38 ANNUAL AVERAGE AND 1948–50

(*Thousands of Tons* [a])

Country	Flax [b]				Hemp [b]			
	1934–38	*1948*	*1949*	*1950*	*1934–38*	*1948*	*1949*	*1950*
World (with the USSR)	790	535	...	...	454	...	...	...
World (without the USSR)	150	190	200	190	250	250	250	200
United Kingdom	5 [c]	10	11	10	—	—	—	—
Ireland	1	4	2	1	—	—	—	—
France	21	22	26	29	4	6	5	4
Belgium	22	19	22	20	[d]	[d]	[d]	...
Netherlands	12	18	21	16	—	—	—	—
Finland	1	4	3	1	—	—	—	—
Western Germany	9	5	5	4	4	1	1	1
Poland	24 [e]	32	42	46	5 [e]	4	6	9
Czechoslovakia	8	7	10	...	4	4	...	...
Italy	3	6	6	4	90	77	71	66
Yugoslavia	11	4	5	3	47	60	70	30
Romania	7 [e]	4	...	...	27 [e]	27	...	...
USSR [f]	640 [e]	345	...	...	203 [e]	...	...	...
Japan	5	4	3	3	8	2	2	2
Turkey	3	5	3	2	8	10	11	8
Egypt	2	6	6	2	—	—	—	—

Sources: **14**, Vol. I, pp. 142–43; **11**, 1950, pp. 104–06; **12**, May 1952, pp. 23–24.

a. Conversion factors: one metric ton = 1.1023 short tons = 2,204.6 pounds.
b. Scutched fiber including tow.
c. 1939.

d. Less than 500 tons.
e. In present boundaries.
f. The USSR acquired, after World War II, territories which produced an average of about 78,000 tons of flax fiber a year, while its output averaged about 560,000 tons. Output in 1948 as estimated by the U. S. Department of Agriculture (**57**, p. 146).

manila fiber, abacá, which is stronger, and jute, which is less durable but cheaper.

Output

The USSR, Italy, Yugoslavia and Romania, in the order given, were the chief producers of hemp before World War II. The USSR alone accounted for almost 45 per cent of the world crop. Italy had the highest yield per acre, about two and a half times the world average; the USSR had the lowest.

Because of increased military requirements for rope and twine and the disappearance of peacetime sources of supply, production of hemp expanded during the war in most countries. In German-occupied territories, various incentives to enlarge the acreage were offered. In the United States, where only a few hundred tons a year were grown before the war, the government in-

stituted an intensive program that increased the output to 64,000 tons in 1943. World production of hemp (except for the USSR) rose 40 per cent in the early phase of the war, then slowed down somewhat, though remaining above prewar levels.

In the USSR, the chief hemp producer, both acreage and output shrank during the war by about 60 per cent. As a result of the war, Russia acquired hemp-growing areas of Poland and Romania. Nevertheless, the hemp acreage planned in postwar years was one third smaller than the comparable prewar acreage.[61]

In Italy, a decline in hemp production started in 1943 and continued through 1945. Then a slow recovery began, but the 1948–50 output was below the prewar. (See Table 269.)

---

61. **10**, 1949, p. 66.

JUTE

Jute, another coarse-fiber plant, is exclusively Asiatic and pre-eminently Indian.

It is used to make burlap, coarse yarns, rope and similar products. It deteriorates rapidly when moist and, being woodier in texture, is inferior to both flax and hemp. It is more easily spun than either of these fibers, however, and is generally much cheaper and therefore in greater demand as packaging material. Coffee, raw sugar, grain, cotton, wool, fertilizer and many other commodities are shipped all over the world in jute sacks. Jute is consumed in larger quantities than any other textile raw material except cotton.

India and Pakistan

East Bengal, now a part of Pakistan, is the center of jute production. The partition of the subcontinent has created two separate jute economies — one in Pakistan, with great centers of jute culture but no processing industry, and another in India, with a small part of the output of raw jute but the greatest concentration of jute processing in the world and vast facilities for marketing and exporting jute manufactures.[62] While Bengal used to export almost the entire crop in a raw state, except for some 10 per cent consumed by the villagers, more than 100 jute mills with modern processing facilities were established in or close to Calcutta.[63] With abundant cheap labor and raw material close at hand, these mills produced the largest part of the world's burlap and jute bags and absorbed about 60 per cent of Bengal's raw jute output.

This well-functioning system has been seriously affected by the division of the subcontinent of India into two independent states. Pakistan, in whose economy jute plays a key role, was faced with a critical surplus problem when trade relations with the Indian Union were disrupted in 1949. The Union, in turn, found itself cut off from the normal source of raw material for a vital industry. The rest of the world suffered, too, from a shortage of jute, raw and processed: Pakistan does not have shipping facilities to export this bulky raw commodity, and large jute-processing factories in the United Kingdom (with Dundee, Scotland, as its center) and other European countries felt the pinch.[64]

Although the crisis was resolved by a trade agreement between Pakistan and India in 1950, the latter country has strengthened its drive for self-sufficiency in jute and has been steadily increasing the acreage in this crop — from 835,000 acres in 1948 to more than 1.4 million in 1950. Pakistan, in its turn, has made plans to process at least part of its jute crop in domestic mills and to build three mills, each equipped with 1,000 looms.[65]

Output

The world's output of jute during 1934–38 averaged about 1.9 million tons a year, of which all but a few thousand came from the subcontinent of India.[66] There it grows primarily on small peasant holdings, where it is the principal cash crop. Much of the land suitable for jute is adaptable to rice growing. Before World War II, changes in the price relationship between these two crops often caused shifts in this acreage. During the war and the postwar food crisis, a substantial part of the acreage in both India and Pakistan was diverted from jute to rice, and their combined output in 1948, 1949 and 1950 was a quarter or more below the 1934–38 average. (See Table 270.)

Plantings in Pakistan in 1951 were about 40 per cent larger than in 1950; India's chief aim in that year was to raise the average yield per acre which had declined by more than 14 per cent in 1950.[67]

Substitutes for Jute

The wartime scarcity of jute stimulated the output of substitute fibers in many countries. Kenaf, a fiber plant native to India, is now being developed in the Caribbean countries and Florida. Kenaf fiber, of soft texture, is taken from the bark and is so outstanding in quality, yield and ease of cultivation that it may become an effective competitor of jute for use in twines, bagging, burlap, fishing nets, floor matting, rug backing and so on.[68] Rapid commercialization of kenaf

62. **10,** 1948, p. 45.

63. **24,** pp. 39–42.

64. The United States has a large jute-bag manu-

facturing industry, second only to that of India, but it imports jute cloth, rather than raw jute, from India.

65. **4,** 1950, p. 250.

66. The actual output may have been larger than that reported, since recorded exports and domestic consumption together consistently exceeded the estimates of the crop. **10,** 1947, p. 133.

67. **20,** July 1951, pp. 20 and 22; **12,** May 1952, p. 24.

68. **39,** pp. 345–46. Kenaf seed yields oil up to 20 per cent of its weight; the oil has about the same uses as cottonseed oil.

TABLE 270

JUTE: ACREAGE AND OUTPUT IN THE WORLD AND SELECTED COUNTRIES, 1934–38 ANNUAL AVERAGE AND 1948–50

Country	Area, in Thousands of Acres				Output, in Thousands of Metric Tons [a]			
	1934–38	1948	1949	1950	1934–38	1948	1949	1950
World	3,534	2,716	2,716	2,716	1,875	1,395	1,210	1,450
Pakistan	} 3,509 {	1,875	1,561	1,260	} 1,860 {	994	605 [b]	808 [b]
India		835	1,163	1,447		373	560	597
Other Asiatic countries	25	87	71	. . .	15	19	5	. . .
Brazil	—	20	22	. . .	—	9	13	20

Sources: **7**, p. 14; **4**, 1950, p. 221; **20**, July 2, 1951, pp. 20 and 22; **12**, May 1952, p. 24.

a. Conversion factor: one metric ton = 2,204.6 pounds.

b. Trade estimate is considerably larger: 907,000 tons for 1949 and 1,089,000 tons for 1950. (**20**, July 2, 1951, pp. 20–22.)

production in the Western Hemisphere is expected. Yields per acre in Florida compare favorably with jute yields in India.[69]

The Union of South Africa, formerly a large importer of jute bags and cloth, is using homegrown fibers to make bags, and Australia and the Philippines are experimenting with indigenous fibers. Cultivation of so-called Congo jute is expanding in the Belgian Congo. Brazil has a jute strain developed by Japanese living in the Amazon Valley. During the war, Brazil took the land from the Japanese but encouraged continued cultivation of the fiber. The main difficulties are shortage of labor and lack of transportation facilities: it costs twice as much to bring jute from the Amazon Valley to consuming areas in southern Brazil as it does to ship jute from India to the factories in São Paulo.[70]

In many countries, moreover, use of other packaging materials, especially paper, has made heavy inroads into the use of jute for bagging.

HARD FIBERS

The three most important hard fibers are abacá (manila hemp), sisal and henequen. They are used in making cordage and twine and also for upholstery padding, carpet yarns and in paper making. The largest single use of these fibers is for binder twine. They are interchangeable to some extent in the manufacture of various kinds of rope, twine and cord.

Abacá

Abacá is the strongest of the hard fibers and is used for rope that has to withstand great strains, such as that used in well drilling or for hoisting. It is particularly valued for marine cables since it does not swell or disintegrate in salt water. Fiber waste and worn-out ropes are ground and made into manila paper.

Before World War II, abacá was grown almost exclusively in the Philippines, which produced, on the average during 1934–38, 170,000 tons out of the world's total of 171,000 tons a year.[71] The plant is grown throughout the Islands, but the main centers of production are in southern Luzon and southward. The most common method of extracting the fiber is by hand stripping, though large plantations have introduced stripping machinery. Small producers account for a substantial share of the output.

During the war, abacá stands suffered severely, particularly on the large plantations in Mindanao, through neglect and overcutting by invaders and guerillas. As a result, the Philippine output dropped to 50,000 tons, less than one third the prewar average. In 1948, it amounted to 74,000 tons, in 1949 to 99,000 tons. (See Table 271.) A project to develop abacá stands on some 20,000 acres of virgin land in Davao was initiated early in 1950. Plantings were to be completed late in 1952.[72]

In the meantime, old experimental abacá plantings in Panama were expanded with the aid of the United States government, and new plantings were made in Costa Rica, Guatemala and Honduras. These stands have begun to produce and should continue to bear for at least fifteen years.

69. **22**, 1950–51, p. 476.
70. **58**, pp. 81–82, and **7**, p. 13.

71. **10**, 1949, p. 96.
72. **6**, p. 4.

TABLE 271

HARD FIBERS: OUTPUT OF ABACÁ, SISAL AND HENE-
QUEN IN THE WORLD AND SELECTED COUNTRIES,
1934–38 ANNUAL AVERAGE AND 1948–50

(*Thousands of Metric Tons*[a])

Fiber and Country	1934–38	1948	1949	1950
Abacá				
World	171	94	99	175
Guatemala	—	5	4	4
Honduras	—	4	2	1
Costa Rica	—	6	4	2
Panama	—	4	3	3
British North Borneo	1	1	1[b]	1
Philippines	170	74	99	175
Sisal				
World	245	265	283	314
Haiti	6[b]	30	31	33
Brazil	—	26	32	53
Indonesia[c]	84	6	2	7
Uganda and Kenya	30	37	38	42
Tanganyika	90	123	128	124
Mozambique	21	17	18	19
Madagascar	3[b]	4	6	5
Angola[b]	6	17	20	21
Henequen				
World	108	136	120	114
Mexico	96	123	104	98
Cuba	12	13	16	16

Sources: **11**, 1950, pp. 107–08; **12**, May 1952, p. 25.

a. Conversion factor: one metric ton = 2,204.6 pounds.
b. Exports.
c. Exports including small amounts of other hard fibers.

Plantings in Panama supplied 5,000 tons of abacá in 1947, all of which was shipped to the United States under a contract with the growers. In 1948, Central American countries together produced 19,000 tons of abacá. In 1949, stands suffered from plant disease, and the output dropped to 13,000 tons,[73] and in 1950, to 10,000 tons.

Sisal

Sisal is grown chiefly in British East Africa, Indonesia and Portuguese Africa, but small quantities are produced in Haiti, Madagascar and

73. **20**, July 19, 1948, p. 49; **6**, p. 4.

some other areas. Brazil recently entered the field. During 1934–38, the world's annual output of sisal averaged 245,000 tons, half of which came from British East Africa. The wartime demand for hard fibers stimulated production in that region, and expansion has continued. Despite a serious drought, British East Africa increased slightly its share in world output in 1950: 166,000 tons out of 314,000. In contrast, output in Indonesia, plagued by civil unrest, dropped from an average of 84,000 tons a year during 1934–38 to a few thousand tons in recent years. Portuguese Africa, Brazil and Haiti together produced 126,000 tons in 1950 (40,000, 53,000 and 33,000 tons, respectively). (See Table 271.)

Henequen

Until the 1920's, henequen was an exclusively Mexican fiber. Cultivation centered in Yucatan. Cuba subsequently developed a small output. Of the average world crop of 108,000 tons a year during 1934–38, 96,000 tons came from Mexico and the rest from Cuba. The Mexican output has increased since the war and in 1948 exceeded the prewar average by about 30 per cent. In 1949, influenced by overcutting in preceding years, unfavorable weather and a decline in demand, Mexico's output dropped to 104,000 tons but was still above the prewar level. In 1950, the output declined further. (See Table 271.)

RUBBER

Rubber is indigenous to the Amazon Basin of Brazil, Peru, Ecuador and Colombia. Columbus, on his second voyage to South America, and other early European explorers, watched the Indians play with balls made from the milky juice of an unknown tree. Yet two centuries passed before Europe saw its first samples of rubber brought by the French. Rubber attracted little attention until two inventions opened up important possibilities for its use: vulcanization of rubber, by Goodyear, in 1839, and the pneumatic tire, by Dunlop, in 1888.

DEVELOPMENT OF RUBBER GROWING

During the nineteenth century, rubber was produced only in the Amazon Valley of Brazil, by tapping the wild rubber trees (*Hevea brasiliensis*). By the end of the century, it became one of the chief exports of that country. Though prices were high and millions of rubber trees dotted the Amazon Valley, it was hard for Brazil to increase its output of rubber as world demand grew.

Wild Rubber

The trees in Brazil are scattered over 2 million square miles. The best stands are in inaccessible jungles. Not infrequently the tapper has to live and make his rounds in a canoe. A worker can tap only a few trees a day because of adverse weather and other conditions during the season — from May to September. It was impossible to find enough workers who were willing to work in dense, humid forests, threatened by frequent floods and wild animals and plagued by insects, and provided, at best, with poor living quarters. It was often necessary to hire inexperienced tappers who actually killed many trees. Yet, despite these conditions, the rubber "barons" made enormous fortunes.[74]

Plantation Rubber

In 1876, the British succeeded in bringing some 70,000 seeds of *H. brasiliensis* from Brazil to London. Young plants raised from them in hothouses were shipped to Ceylon and Malaya. Somewhat later, the Dutch established rubber plantations in the East Indies. In all these areas climate, soil and other conditions were most favorable for rubber growing. Trees were planted close to one another and could be tapped the year around. Native labor was abundant. In addition, the plantations were located near the coast, on trade routes between the Orient and the chief rubber-consuming countries, which facilitated the marketing of the product.

Scientific research and improved techniques of tapping and planting raised the yield of latex per acre in that part of the world. It was found, for example, that latex flows more freely when tapping is done early in the morning. Bud grafting from better trees contributed to the development of more productive stands.[75] The use of seedlings from high-yielding varieties has raised the average yield to 1,000–1,200 pounds per acre and in some individual cases to 2,000 pounds

per acre, in Malaya and Indonesia.[76] However, almost all these developments chiefly benefited the estate plantations, supported by official aid and their own large financial means. Little, if any, technical assistance was given to small native holdings, where the chief advantage was family labor. Nevertheless, the native planters have learned to produce cleaner, less adulterated rubber than that from wild trees in Brazil. They have a lower yield per tree than the estate owners, but a higher yield per acre on their densely planted holdings.[77]

The land planted to rubber trees in British Malaya and Ceylon increased from 5,000 acres in 1900 to 150,000 in 1905, a million in 1910 and 1.5 million in 1911.[78] With the rise of the automobile and the apparently unlimited demand for rubber, the area of plantations in southeastern Asia (British Malaya, Ceylon, the Dutch East Indies) increased from 1.25 million acres in 1910 to 4.25 million in 1920 and 8.5 million by 1937.[79] In the past decade the area in plantation rubber totaled 9.4 million acres, of which Asia had 8.8 million and Africa nearly 0.5 million while the rest was scattered in Central and South America and Oceania.[80]

European and Native Holdings in Asia

Production of rubber in southeastern Asia is divided between estates owned almost exclusively by Europeans (about 55 per cent) and small holdings operated by native producers (45 per cent). In some regions, such as Thailand, the natives produce all the rubber; in Sarawak, nearly all. In Indonesia, the estates had nearly two thirds of the acreage in rubber in 1929, but by 1933 the acreage of the native holdings exceeded that of the estates.[81] The trend in all southeastern Asia is toward increase in the share of native producers. (See Table 272.)

Rubber Growing in Other Areas

Numerous attempts have been made to establish rubber plantations in other regions: in Liberia (Firestone); in Nigeria and the Belgian Congo (United Africa Company); in Costa Rica and Panama (Goodyear); and in Brazil

---

74. **47**, pp. 114–20.

75. Five-year-old seedling trees produce 60 pounds of rubber per acre, and budded trees of the same age, 400 pounds. Three years later, yields are 500 and 1,200 pounds, respectively. **50**, p. 67.

76. **35**, p. 264.
77. **35**, p. 363.
78. **50**, p. 9.
79. **31**, p. 100.
80. **33**, September 1951, p. 38.
81. **35**, p. 29.

| | Area, in Thousands of Acres | | Output, in Thousands of Long Tons [a] | |
Year	Estates	Small Holdings	Estates	Small Holdings
1909	425	75	5.5	. . .
1920	2,545	1,650	250	65
1930	4,020	3,930	465	335
1940	4,538	4,275	765	610
1950	. . .	. . .	765	1,095

Sources: **50**, p. 11, and **33**, September 1951, p. 3.

a. Conversion factors: one long ton = 1.12 short tons = 2,240 pounds.

(Ford). The USSR has been trying to grow rubber on collective farms. In 1925 when plantings of tropical seeds proved unsuccessful, the USSR began searching for indigenous plants that would produce rubber. An expedition to Kazakhstan in 1930–31 reported that latex was a component of the roots of three wild dandelion plants — kok-saghyz, krym-saghyz and tau-saghyz.[82] Commercial growing of rubber plants, mainly of kok-saghyz, was started in the Ukraine and White Russia in 1937. By 1940, 165,000 acres were in rubber-bearing plants.

During World War II the United States, confronted with the critical shortage of natural rubber, intensified both the production of synthetic rubber[83] and the search for possible domestic sources of natural rubber. The Department of Agriculture was charged by Congress with the task of planting a large acreage of guayule, a rubber-yielding shrub, and carrying out research in domestic opportunities for growing rubber. Most of the plantings and the mills for extracting rubber are in California. Of various plants that have been studied, the most practical and promising is the guayule, and the second-best is the kok-saghyz.

Guayule rubber is chemically identical with *Hevea* rubber but is less pure and deteriorates rather rapidly during storage. Research has shown that these drawbacks can be eliminated

through various processes and that guayule rubber, when purified, is uniformly high in quality, essentially equivalent to *Hevea* in most physical characteristics. Because of its immediate promise of high yields and low-cost production, guayule is receiving major attention in current research, but the possibilities of obtaining natural rubber from kok-saghyz are also being explored. During the war, two sacks of seed were flown from Russia to the United States, and more than 600 acres were planted to kok-saghyz, largely in Michigan and Minnesota. The seed was not uniform, and it is believed that selection and breeding may lead to a higher and more uniform rubber content than that obtained from the original seed.

The results of road tests of tires made of kok-saghyz rubber showed that it approaches plantation rubber in physical characteristics. Kok-saghyz has the advantage of yielding a rubber crop in a shorter time than guayule.[84]

OUTPUT

As the use of rubber increased, the plantations of the Far East captured the insatiable world market from Brazil with the greatest of ease.

Brazil

As late as 1906, Brazil supplied 98 per cent of the world's rubber but the actual volume of its exports was very small and lost significance when the demand began to grow rapidly. Unable to satisfy this demand, Brazil lost its rubber trade to the continuously expanding plantations in southeastern Asia. The exorbitant price which Brazil obtained as late as 1911 and 1912 — a dollar a pound — began to tumble when cheap plantation rubber appeared on world markets. It fell, some years later, to a few cents a pound. Faced with increasing competition and falling prices, Brazilian producers reduced their output from 37,500 tons in 1912 to some 6,000 in 1932.[85]

Under the stimulus of high prices during World War II, when rubber supplies from Asia were cut off, production in Brazil was revitalized to some extent, but the boom was short-lived. Brazil's share in the world's output of rubber is now less than 2 per cent, some 20,000 tons out

82. **36**, pp. 8–9 and 18–19.
83. For production of synthetic rubber, see Chapter 31.

84. **22**, 1950–51, pp. 367–74.
85. **58**, p. 93.

TABLE 273

NATURAL RUBBER: WORLD OUTPUT, BY TYPE, 1900–50

(*Thousands of Long Tons* [a])

Year	Wild Rubber	Planta-tion Rubber	Year	Wild Rubber	Planta-tion Rubber	Year	Wild Rubber	Planta-tion Rubber
1900	52	—	1917	53	214	1934	9	1,025
1901	55	—	1918	37	184	1935	13	875
1902	52	—	1919	48	350	1936	16	856
1903	58	—	1920	37	317	1937	21	1,138
1904	62	—	1921	23	277	1938	22	890
1905	65	—	1922	26	373	1939	22	978
1906	68	—	1923	28	379	1940	26	1,385
1907	77	1	1924	31	398	1941	44	1,556
1908	71	2	1925	39	480	1942	40	600
1909	76	4	1926	36	586	1943	53	412
1910	83	11	1927	40	567	1944	62	298
1911	76	17	1928	28	789	1945	59	191
1912	80	32	1929	26	995	1946	44	794
1913	65	53	1930	20	960	1947	46	1,214
1914	46	76	1931	15	820	1948	45	1,480
1915	51	116	1932	7	713	1949	40	1,448
1916	50	160	1933	10	857	1950	40	1,810

Sources: **52**, p. 41; **33**, July 1950, p. 3, and September 1951, p. 3.

a. Conversion factor: one long ton = 1.12 short tons. Includes rubber in the form of latex.

of more than 1.8 million. (See Table 273 and Figure 188.)

Asia

In 1939, Asia produced 97 per cent of the world's rubber. British Malaya accounted for about 36 per cent of the output, Indonesia for 38 per cent, Ceylon and Indochina together for some 13 per cent, and the rest of Asia for 10 per cent. During the war, production dwindled in both Malaya and Indonesia, occupied by the Japanese, more for lack of outlets than because of destruction, which was not very serious. In Malaya, the Japanese felled only 5-7 per cent of the rubber trees.[86]

After 1945 recovery was very rapid initially, partly because of the flush production from the rested trees, but mostly because of high prices and freedom from international regulations and restrictions.

The world output in 1949 was about 50 per cent larger than in 1939, and that of 1950 was the highest on record, about double the prewar. In Malaya, Ceylon, Thailand, Indonesia and other areas the small holder's production is run-

86. **35**, p. 340.

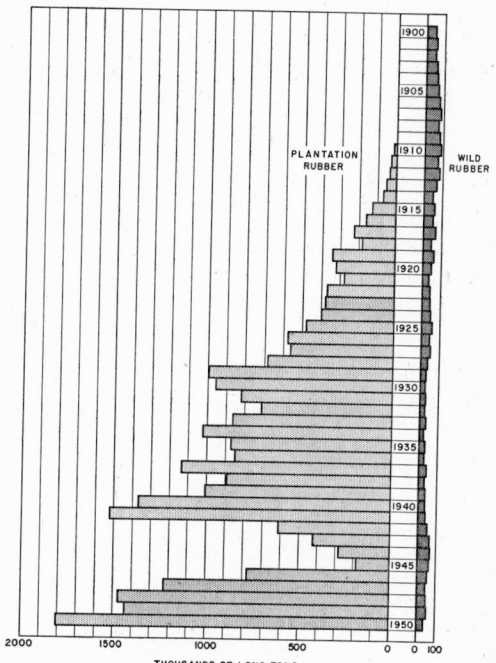

FIGURE 188. NATURAL RUBBER: WORLD OUTPUT, 1900–50

ning high. Estates in Malaya are turning out more rubber than at any time in the past, but

TABLE 274

NATURAL RUBBER: OUTPUT IN THE WORLD AND SELECTED AREAS, 1939–50

(*Thousands of Long Tons*[a])

Area	1939	1941	1942	1943	1944	1945	1946	1947	1948	1949	1950
World	1,000	1,600	640	465	360	250	838	1,260	1,525	1,490	1,860
Malaya[b]											
Estates	244	370	55	35	25	—	174	361	404	401	377
Small holdings	116	230	100	40	—	9	230	286	295	271	317
Indonesia											
Estates	195	300	100	50	25	5	—	13	102	168	175
Small holdings	183	350	100	50	25	5	175	265	331	264	521
Ceylon	60	100	102	106	99	98	94	89	95	90	114
Indochina	68	75	76	70	60	12	20	38	44	43	48
India	13	17	16	17	17	16	16	16	15	16	16
Sarawak	24	35	10	5	—	—	9	37	40	39	56
Other Asiatic areas	60	78	15	5	3	2	32	80	128	125	152
Africa	15	17	30	45	55	54	47	39	42	45	55
Brazil	17	17	22	23	29	24	24	26	20	21	19
Other Latin American areas	3	9	14	19	21	23	16	9	9	6	8
Oceania	2	1	1	1	2	2	1	1	1	1	2

Source: **33**, September 1951, p. 3.

a. Conversion factor: one long ton = 1.12 short tons. Includes dry-rubber content of latex.
b. Includes Singapore.

their output in Indonesia is considerably below the prewar level. Indochina is the only rubber-producing area in Asia, however, where the total output remains below capacity. (See Table 274.)

Although the output of rubber from regions outside southeastern Asia will increase when all the planted trees begin to bear, Asia will continue to hold its overwhelming lead. If its supremacy is endangered, the threat will come not from plantations elsewhere but from synthetic rubber.[87]

RECLAIMING RUBBER

Since the 1920's the United States has supplemented supplies of natural rubber with rubber recovered from scrap.[88] Until World War II, this process was used almost exclusively in the United States, which reclaimed 23,000 tons in 1920, 87,000 tons in 1930 and 115,000 tons in 1940.[89] The United Kingdom, Canada and some other countries also made efforts in this direction during the war. The USSR had a small output

of reclaimed rubber — about 10,000 tons — in 1935.

In postwar years, about 80–85 per cent of all reclaimed rubber was recovered in the United States, which is also the largest consumer of this product. The United Kingdom accounted for 7–8 per cent. Germany re-entered the field in 1949 and now reclaims nearly as much rubber as the United Kingdom. (See Table 275.)

INDUSTRIAL OILS

Industrial and edible oils cannot always be clearly distinguished, since some edible oils[90] — for example, peanut and soybean — are also used in making soap, paints, pharmaceuticals and the like. On the other hand, linseed oil, though valued chiefly in the manufacture of paint and varnish, linoleum and oilcloth for its excellent drying capacity, is also used as an edible oil in the USSR and the Balkans. Shifts from one use to another may be occasioned by changes in price and relative abundance or scarcity. The oils predominantly used as industrial raw materials are, according to the classification of the

---

87. For synthetic rubber, see Chapter 31.
88. Reclaimed rubber is used in combination with natural rubber, plus carbon black and various chemicals.
89. On the average, 1.8 tons of scrap rubber yields one ton of reclaimed rubber.

90. See Chapter 16.

TABLE 275

RECLAIMED RUBBER: [a] OUTPUT IN THE WORLD AND SELECTED COUNTRIES, 1944–50

(*Thousands of Long Tons* [b])

Country	1944	1945	1946	1947	1948	1949	1950
Total	300	275	334	324	301	278	380
United States	261	243	296	291	267	224	313
Canada	3	3	4	4	4	3	5
United Kingdom	29	22	28	22	25	21	30
Germany	...	...	...	...	...	24	25
Australia	7	6	6	6	5	6	8

Source: **33,** September 1951, p. 30.

a. Natural and synthetic.
b. Conversion factor: one long ton = 1.12 short tons.

U. S. Department of Agriculture, linseed, rapeseed, castor and tung.

Linseed Oil

Linseed oil is obtained from a variety of flaxseed grown especially for this purpose. The oil content of the seed averages 33–34 per cent.

Argentina accounted for almost half the prewar production of flaxseed and was the chief exporter. The USSR, India and the United States together produced an additional 40 per cent.

The leading prewar producers of linseed oil, largely from imported seed (except for the USSR), were the United States, the USSR, the Netherlands, the United Kingdom, France and Germany. Together, they accounted for three fourths of the world's output. Argentina and India marketed their seed abroad and produced relatively small quantities of oil. Lacking sufficient crushing facilities, they found it easier, and occasionally more profitable, to export flaxseed than to export both oil and oilcake.

This pattern of world output and trade in flaxseed and linseed oil changed drastically during World War II. When most supplies of oil-bearing products and oils from Asia were cut off, the United States government tried to extend production of domestic oilseeds, including flaxseed, by farm subsidies and other measures. The output in 1943 was nearly six times the average during 1934–38, but even so did not meet the greatly increased requirements of the industry. Even during the short slump following the end of the war, the output was consistently higher than before the war, and since 1948 it has been five or more times the 1934–38 average. This quantity not only meets the country's own needs but also provides an exportable surplus.

Like the United States, Canada expanded its acreage during the war and has become an exporter rather than an importer. Although the 1950 flaxseed crop was far less than the record harvest in 1948 — 115,000 metric tons, as compared with 450,000 tons — it was still nearly four times the prewar average.

In contrast, Argentina's acreage in flaxseed has decreased very considerably, from 6 million acres in 1935–39 to 2.7 million in 1950. Moreover, the acreage harvested in 1950 was only a little more than 2 million, the smallest area harvested since the country became a major producer. Losses were attributed to late frosts, excessive rains and hot drying wind during the flowering period. Argentina has established a large crushing industry, which is trying to maintain its ground and is bidding for the available supplies of domestic flaxseed. In 1950 Argentina exported about 227,000 tons of linseed oil, while some 33,000 tons were consumed domestically.[91]

The United States now leads in world output of both flaxseed and linseed oil, outranking Argentina two to one and accounting for about 30 per cent of the total. (See Table 276.) In the USSR, flaxseed production suffered heavily during the war, both in German-occupied and uninvaded regions. Although some recovery has been achieved, the output has not yet reached the prewar level in the country's postwar boundaries.

91. **19,** FFO 18–51, pp. 6–7, and FFO 15–51, p. 6.

TABLE 276

OILSEED AND OILS: OUTPUT OF FLAXSEED AND RAPESEED IN THE WORLD AND SELECTED COUNTRIES, 1934–38 ANNUAL AVERAGE AND 1948–50

(Thousands of Metric Tons [a]*)*

Country	Flaxseed 1934–38	1948	1949	1950	Country	Rapeseed 1934–38	1948	1949	1950
World (with the USSR)	3,555	3,735	3,610	...	World	3,968	4,640[d]	4,930[d]	5,200[d]
World (without the USSR)	2,710	3,390	2,860	2,650	France	13	110	143	127
United States	209	1,385	1,116	1,022	Germany				
Canada	32	450	58	115	Western	40	54	140	81
Mexico	2	49	50	36	Soviet Zone	30	38	140	...
Uruguay	89	117	75	89	Poland	48	36[e]	117	116
Argentina	1,702	490	676	532	USSR	88	...	...	...
USSR	845[b]	345[c]	...	...	China [f]	2,473	3,080	3,060	3,090
China	54	...	...	...	Japan	120	27	39	118
Turkey	7	46	52	28	Pakistan	232	269	240	282
India	433	430	418	391	India	753	747	806	839

Sources: **11**, 1951, pp. 78–79 and 81; **19**, FFO 15–51, *passim.*

a. Conversion factor: one metric ton = 2,204.6 pounds.
b. In present boundaries.

c. Estimate of the U. S. Department of Agriculture (**57**, p. 147).
d. Excludes the USSR.
e. 1947.
f. 22 provinces.

Rapeseed Oil

Rapeseed oil is used chiefly for lubrication but in China, India and some European countries it is a popular edible oil. The oil content of rapeseed is about 35 per cent.

Asia accounts for about 90 per cent of the total output of rapeseed and China is the chief producer, followed by India and Pakistan. In contrast to the processing of flaxseed, the producing countries largely extract rapeseed oil. Less than 5 per cent of the crop enters into international trade.

During the war, Europe made strenuous efforts to increase its normally small output, and by 1943 the total yield was four times the prewar average. Germany, in particular, urged extension of acreage within its borders and in occupied territories. China and India maintained their prewar output with some fluctuations, and later China even increased its crop by about 20 per cent.

The world output of rapeseed has dropped considerably from its wartime peak but it is still about 25 per cent larger than in an average prewar year. Europe as a whole raises much more rapeseed than before the war. Germany has tripled its output, and France now harvests a crop ten times larger than in 1934–38. In 1948–49 the output in Japan was only about one third of the prewar average, but nearly reached that level in 1950. (See Table 276.)

In the United States, the small domestic production of rapeseed and still smaller imports are ordinarily used for bird feed.

Castor Oil

The castor-oil plant grows throughout the tropics, mostly along roads, at the edges of fields, around native houses, and around refuse dumps and other wasteland. In India the plant is grown mixed with other field crops. In Brazil it grows wild on almost every farm but cultivated plantings have recently accounted for an increasing proportion of the total output.[92]

Brazil has led in production of castor beans since it outdistanced India in the mid-1930's. The USSR is also an important producer, though current information on output is not available.

Because the castor bean grows wild, often in the interior of tropical underdeveloped countries, more or less accurate statistics are difficult to

92. **23**, Part 5, p. 78.

obtain, and the crop is usually estimated for various areas.

A record was set in 1948, with a world output of 490,000 metric tons. Each following year the crop has been smaller, but even the lowest estimate for 1951 was somewhat higher than the average for 1935–39. Brazil and India together account for about 60 per cent of the world output. Prewar production in the USSR averaged 110,000 metric tons.

The United States, the largest importer and consumer of castor beans and oil, produced large quantities of castor beans in the nineteenth century, mostly in Illinois, Kansas, Oklahoma and Missouri. Production has since declined, but in 1918–19 the southern states produced a few thousand tons to meet the demand for aircraft lubricants. Output in the decades that followed was negligible until research developed seed better suited to domestic conditions. To assure a supply of castor oil for national defense, contracts were negotiated for some 84,000 acres, partly on irrigated land and partly on dry land, in western and southwestern states. About 9,500 metric tons were harvested in 1951. About 120,000 acres were planted in 1952, mostly in Texas,[93] but the domestic crop would supply only a small fraction of the total civilian and military consumption at the recent rate.[94] Imports from Brazil in 1952 were therefore likely to be as large as possible because of the increased requirements of the defense program and for stockpiling.[95]

Like linseed oil, castor oil is used in paint and varnishes, oilcloth and linoleum; it is also used for coating food containers and lubricating airplane motors and as a plasticizer. The bean residue (pomace) is used as a fertilizer. Its medicinal use is well known but accounts for only a small amount in comparison with industrial uses. The oil content of the bean is about 45 per cent of its weight, and the oil surpasses linseed oil in fast-drying qualities.

Brazil used to export most of the crop, but domestic use has increased substantially with industrialization. Extraction facilities have been enlarged, and Brazil's export of castor oil, rather than beans, is steadily increasing — an average

of 322 short tons in 1935–39; 11,700 tons in 1949; and 27,100 tons in 1950.[96]

India and the USSR keep two thirds or more of their output for domestic use. The United States and the industrial countries of Europe process imported castor beans.

Tung Oil

Tung oil, one of the most valuable drying oils, is produced from the nuts of a tree indigenous to China. The Chinese have used the oil for centuries, but not until the twentieth century did Europe and America know how to utilize its unique properties for water- and chemical-resistant coatings.

China, which had a monopoly in tung oil until 1930, extracts the oil by the crudest possible method: hand-picked nuts are heaped to ferment, and the seeds husked by hand and ground to meal in stone mortars. The steamed meal is shaped into cakes, wrapped in straw and placed in a hollow log; a wood block is then placed against the cakes, and the oil is pressed by driving wedges between the log and the block. By such methods an average of 120,000 metric tons were produced annually in 1934–38, a third of which was used in domestic consumption for waterproofing wood, paper, cloth and other material.

During prewar years, exports of tung oil represented about 10 per cent of the total value of Chinese exports.[97] Nevertheless, this product has never been a major source of income for individual farmers, since each has only a few trees. In the Province of Szechwan, some 1.7 million growers raise tung trees, planting them on hillsides, along roads, and on wasteland and gathering the nuts without regard to quality.[98] During World War II, China's tung trees suffered severely. Many were cut for fuel, and others were destroyed by disease.

The first commercial plantings of tung trees in the United States were made in 1925 on an experimental basis, and the first processing mill was established in 1928. While tung trees are used as a forest crop in China, they are considered a horticultural crop in the United States, and are planted in orchards and cultivated intensively. By 1930, 351,000 tung trees had been planted, and by 1940, almost 13 million, chiefly in Mississippi but also in Florida and Louisiana

93. **20,** October 29, 1951, pp. 452–55; **5,** October 1952, p. 33.

94. **5,** October 1951, p. 23.

95. **18,** November 1951, p. 239.

96. **19,** FFO 22–51, p. 5.

97. **21,** pp. 129–31.

98. **21,** pp. 31 and 132–34.

and, to a small extent, in Georgia and Alabama.

When commercial cultivation of tung trees was started in the United States, the recovery of tung oil by modern processes and equipment was nonexistent. It took years of research and experimentation to work out the best methods for storing, drying and processing the tung nuts and designing the most practical equipment. Now the partly dried nuts are processed by decorticating and hulling, then preheating and grinding the kernels and recovering the oil in a continuous press which discharges the residue at one end of its cylinder while the oil flows out between the bars of the cylinder, to be filtered and pumped into storage tanks.[99]

In the United States more than 80 per cent of the tung oil is used by the coating industry; the rest, by the oilcloth and electrical industries and for many other purposes.

The world output of tung oil in 1949 was estimated at 120,000 short tons; in 1950 at 135,000 tons — still 10 per cent below the prewar level.[100]

In 1944 the United States harvested 26,680 short tons of tung nuts; in 1946, 57,400; in 1949, 88,000 tons.[101] More than 10,000 tons of tung oil were produced in 1949, and a record volume of 13,000 tons in 1950.[102] The tung oil produced in the United States is of better quality than the Chinese and commands higher prices, but the domestic supply is too small to meet the demand. In 1948, net imports exceeded the domestic output by more than 7 to 1; in 1949, by 3 to 1; in 1950, by nearly 4 to 1. Imports of Chinese tung oil virtually ceased after the embargo on trade with China was declared.

Because of high prices and the uncertainty of Chinese supplies, groves of tung trees have been established in many other areas. Argentina had a record crop in 1950 and produced some 14,000 tons of oil. In Brazil, the average output of tung oil in recent years has amounted to about 2,000 tons; in Paraguay, to 1,500 tons. Many trees are still to come into bearing in these areas as well as in the United States. Tung plantations are being rapidly expanded in Nyasaland and an oil output of 11,000–12,000 tons is expected in a few years.[103]

TOBACCO

The white man discovered tobacco when he discovered America. Tobacco was in general use by the Indians on the Caribbean islands visited by Columbus, by the people in Mexico conquered by Cortez, by a Brazilian tribe visited by French monks.[104]

In contrast to rubber, tobacco at once became popular in Europe. A few decades after its discovery, it was grown in France, Spain, Portugal and England, and by 1600 it had been introduced into almost all European countries, Asia and the west coast of Africa.

In the North American colonies the first tobacco plantings were made in Jamestown in 1612. Tobacco culture spread so rapidly that 200,000 pounds of the product were exported to England seven years later. By 1639, exports from Virginia and Maryland had risen to 1.5 million pounds, and by the outbreak of the Revolutionary War, to 100 million pounds.[105] Since tobacco was at first one of the very few exportable commodities, more and more was raised. It was also highly valued as a cash crop in Virginia itself, where ministers were paid in tobacco.[106] It became so popular that it was often grown at the expense of essential food crops and even the streets and the market place in Jamestown were planted in this crop. In 1616 the Governor of Virginia forbade farmers to plant tobacco before each had sown two acres of corn for himself and each male servant, but this prohibition could not keep tobacco growers from devoting every acre they possibly could to the highly profitable commodity.[107]

Climatic and Soil Requirements

Although tobacco is tropical in origin, it is cultivated as far north as central Sweden. More than 90 per cent of the world's crop grows north of the equator and south of 40° N.[108]

Despite the wide range of conditions under which tobacco can grow, few plants are more sensitive to changes in weather and to the com-

104. This tribe was even known as the "tobacco nation" because it produced tobacco not only for its own use but also for trading purposes. **47**, p. 22.

105. **22**, 1936, p. 810.

106. In contrast, "men of God were paid in tar, pitch, and pork" in North Carolina. **56**, p. 3.

107. **43**, pp. 65–66.

108. **22**, 1941, p. 365.

99. **22**, 1950–51, pp. 584–85.

100. **19**, FFO 3–51, p. 13.

101. **17**, 1950, p. 30.

102. **16**, 1950, p. 155; **19**, FFO 3–51, p. 13.

103. **5**, October 1951, p. 25.

position of soils. Plentiful, well-distributed precipitation, 100–120 frost-free days and well-drained soil with a large content of humus are essential. Moreover, the interrelation of soil and climate is important in determining the type of tobacco leaf produced. The elasticity, texture, color, size, weight and, particularly, the flavor and aroma of the leaf depend entirely on this interrelationship, and a great variety of grades result. The influence of environmental conditions is so great that there are often very substantial differences in tobacco grown on fields near one another. For example, in some sections of Cuba, known for the world's finest cigar filler, one farmer may produce a top-notch product while his neighbor, using the same seed and cultural methods on an apparently similar soil, obtains a low-grade leaf.[109] Being a "heavy feeder," tobacco requires more fertilizer than many other crops.

In Sumatra, whose cigar wrapper is the world's standard of excellence, only one crop of tobacco is grown on the same land in each eight or ten years. The next crop is usually rice, and then the land is permitted to revert to jungle. Thus, tobacco is always planted on virgin soil. The concessions of four large companies cover more than 600,000 acres, practically all the land suitable for tobacco, of which usually less than 10 per cent is planted to tobacco in any one year.

In contrast, Greek and Turkish farmers grow tobacco on the same land year after year. Soil is manured by sheep and goats herded on the fields in late winter. If the soil is sandy, green manure is used. In Turkey, tobacco is raised chiefly on small farms, and only a few large estates engage in tobacco culture.

Labor Requirements

Tobacco culture requires a vast amount of manual labor. It has been estimated that from 300 to 400 man-hours are required to prepare, grow and harvest an acre. Harvesting requires extreme care. Leaves at the bottom of the plant mature earliest, then the leaves in the middle and finally those at the top. The picking is usually done separately for each series of leaves, since the degree of maturity affects the color, aroma and other properties of the leaf. In Sumatra, for example, only two leaves from each plant, beginning at the bottom, are harvested at a time, at two-day intervals. After the harvest comes the additional work of curing the leaves. Because of the labor required, the usual one-family farm has only four or five acres in tobacco.[110]

In spite of the numerous hazards involved in tobacco growing, the crop, under favorable conditions, is attractive to an average farmer because it promises him substantial returns if it is of high quality.[111]

Types and Grades of Tobacco

Commercial requirements for tobacco leaf are exacting. For one type of product, a leaf may be valued for its extreme length and narrowness, while for another a small broad leaf is needed. In some instances a light, in others a dark color is preferred, or a strong or weak aroma and so on. Since each area produces certain types and grades of leaf, tobacco culture is highly localized and specialized. Sumatra, the Connecticut Valley and the vicinity of Quincy, Florida, produce the finest grades of cigar wrappers; some sections of Greece and Turkey grow excellent grades of cigarette tobacco; western Cuba raises the best cigar filler. A single tobacco-producing country may raise various types of tobacco. In the United States, southern Maryland produces tobacco used in the manufacture of most cigarettes,[112] Pennsylvania and Ohio lead in production of cigar filler, and some other areas specialize in pipe and chewing tobaccos. In addition to such specialized areas, there are some regions in China and India where a nondescript type of tobacco is grown.

Output

The world's output of tobacco has risen about 10 per cent above the prewar average. Every continent, with the exception of Asia, now has a larger crop, though the rate of increase varies greatly. In 1950 North America and Africa harvested from 55 to 57 per cent more than the 1934–38 average; Middle and South America, about 40 per cent more; Europe, 22 per cent more.

Before World War II Asia (exclusive of the USSR) accounted for more than half the world's output of tobacco; North America, for more than a fifth; and Europe, for a tenth. Since the war

---

109. **22**, 1936, p. 786.

110. **51**, p. 360.
111. **22**, 1936, p. 805.
112. The quantity produced is small, but Maryland tobacco has a capacity for holding fire and is therefore added to other kinds to improve their "burn."

TABLE 277

TOBACCO: OUTPUT IN THE WORLD AND EACH CONTINENT, 1934–38 ANNUAL AVERAGE AND 1948–50

Continent	Output, in Thousands of Metric Tons [a]				Percentage Distribution			
	1934–38	1948	1949	1950 [b]	1934–38	1948	1949	1950 [b]
World (without the USSR)	2,710	3,150	3,020	3,000	100.0	100.0	100.0	100.0
North America	619	956	958	975	22.8	30.3	31.7	32.5
Middle and South America	201	294	322	284	7.4	9.3	10.7	9.5
Europe	280 [c]	330	330	340	10.3 [c]	10.5	10.9	11.3
USSR	235 [c]	174 [d]	...	...	...	...	...	...
Asia	1,540	1,460	1,290	1,290	57.0	46.3	42.7	43.0
Africa	70	110	120	110	2.6	3.5	4.0	3.7
Oceania	3	4	4	4	0.1	0.1	0.1	0.1

Sources: **11**, 1950, pp. 99–101; **20**, June 4, 1951, pp. 645–46.

a. Conversion factor: one metric ton = 2,204.6 pounds.

b. Preliminary.

c. Present boundaries. In prewar boundaries the output of Europe is estimated at 294,000 tons and that of the USSR at 221,000 tons (**11**, 1947, pp. 90–91).

d. Estimate of the U. S. Department of Agriculture (**57**, p. 149).

North America's share has risen to more than 32 per cent and Asia's has declined considerably. (See Table 277.)

The United States, China and India are the three major producers, in 1949 together accounting for almost 60 per cent of the world crop. Italy, Greece and France are the main European producers. The yield per acre in various countries varies widely, as is the case for all crops. Germany leads with a yield of nearly 11 quintals per acre, followed by Japan and France. The United States, which once had a yield below that of Canada, Argentina, Italy, the USSR, China, India and New Zealand, exceeded all of them in this respect in 1950. By heavier fertilization and better cultivation practices, it has raised its average yield per acre by about 50 per cent. (See Table 278.) In tobacco culture, however, the quantity of the crop is less important than its quality; a small amount of a type in great demand may bring a higher profit than a much greater amount of an indiscriminate or low-grade variety.

In the United States, the chief tobacco states are North Carolina (nearly 40 per cent of the country's total crop in 1948 and 1949), Kentucky (about 22–24 per cent), Virginia, South Carolina and Tennessee (each with about 7 per cent), and Georgia (about 6 per cent). Between 1936–40 and 1949, the country's annual output increased by about a third, though the acreage remained about the same.[113]

113. **16**, 1950, pp. 118–19.

In China and India tobacco is produced almost everywhere, under all kinds of climatic and soil conditions. While it is grown throughout the Philippines, high-grade tobacco (cigar filler and wrapper) is limited to some parts of Luzon. Small tobacco farms predominate although there are several large plantations. About the same situation exists in Java. In Sumatra almost all tobacco is grown on large plantations averaging 7,000 acres each.

The best cigarette-tobacco regions in the USSR are in the Crimea and along the Black Sea coast of the Caucasus. A large part of the makhorka (a low-grade tobacco with a high nicotine content) is grown in the northern part of the Ukraine.

OUTLOOK FOR TECHNICAL CROPS

During and since World War II, the world has been short of almost all technical crops. Some alleviation has come from the expanding production of synthetic fibers and rubber, which have become serious competitors of natural products. (See Chapter 31.)

In the long run, we can reasonably expect a surplus rather than a shortage of most technical crops, particularly of textile fibers. The average yield of cotton per acre has increased nearly 50 per cent in recent years in the United States, the world's greatest producer. Brazil continues to expand its cotton output. Experts believe that

TABLE 278

TOBACCO: ACREAGE AND OUTPUT IN SELECTED COUNTRIES, 1934–38 ANNUAL AVERAGE AND 1948–50

Country [a]	Area, in Thousands of Acres				Output, in Thousands of Metric Tons [a]				Yield Per Acre, in Metric Quintals [a]		
	1934–38	1948	1949	1950 [b]	1934–38	1948	1949	1950 [b]	1934–38	1949	1950 [b]
United States	1,502	1,555	1,631	1,604	590	899	895	922	3.9	5.5	5.7
Canada	59	111	110	105	29	57	63	53	4.8	5.7	5.0
Mexico	44	89	96	64	15	36	39	27	3.4	4.1	4.2
Cuba	111	106	146	117	22	20	42	33	1.9	2.9	2.8
Puerto Rico	47	32	30	...	14	12	12	12	3.0	4.0	...
Brazil	255	356	368	297	93	118	97	99	3.6	2.6	3.3
Argentina	30	52	62	82	13	25	25	33	4.3	4.0	4.0
France	44	64	75	71	36	46	44	51	7.9	5.9	7.2
Germany [c]	32	22	23	27	31	14	24	29	10.6	10.4	10.7
Hungary	37	49	54	...	21	27	...	...	5.7	5.5	...
Italy	82	144	135	144	44	74	74	67	5.3	5.5	4.7
Yugoslavia	37	86	86	...	14	29	31	17	3.8	3.6	...
Bulgaria	86	200	...	...	31	20	...	...	3.6	...	...
Greece	220	177	199	253	57	37	58	56	2.6	2.9	2.2
USSR [d]	492	509	...	...	224	174	...	...	4.4	3.4	...
China [e]	1,411	1,530	1,211	...	650	720	540	...	4.7	4.5	...
Japan	86	125	124	134	64	99	85	99	7.4	6.9	7.4
Turkey	178	262	469	317	55	74	91	84	3.0	1.9	2.6
Pakistan	351	200	...	...	151	91	79	...	4.3	...	...
India	899	783	803	790	344	236	236	...	4.6	2.9	...
Indonesia [f]	435	...	...	...	98	...	...	...	2.3	...	...
Philippines	166	84	119	141	35	17	26	32	2.1	2.2	2.3
Algeria	57	64	78	53	19	21	20	19	3.3	2.6	3.6
Nyasaland	52	...	163	160	8	12	10	14	1.5	0.6	0.9
Madagascar	17	7	15	...	6	2	3	3	3.5	2.0	...
Southern Rhodesia	47	128	158	174	11	38	49	38	2.3	3.1	2.2
Union of South Africa	35	...	...	...	9	19	21	21	2.6	...	...
Australia	10	4	5	5	2	2	2	2	2.0	4.0	4.0
New Zealand	2	4	4	4	1	2	2	2	5.0	5.0	5.0

Sources: **11**, 1950, pp. 99–101; **20**, June 4, 1951, pp. 645–66.

a. Conversion factors: one metric ton = 10 metric quintals = 2,204.6 pounds. Figures for different countries are not always strictly comparable: while the crop is generally estimated on the basis of the weight of tobacco sold after curing, the weight of stalks is included in some countries and the moisture content varies from country to country. Some countries report planted acreage, others the harvested. Data for 1950: harvested acreage.

b. Preliminary.

c. For postwar years, data for Western Germany only.

d. Data for prewar from **11**, 1947, pp. 90–91; for 1948 from **57**, p. 149.

e. 22 provinces.

f. Java and Madoera.

selective breeding and wide adoption of progeny testing of rams can ensure a much higher yield of wool per sheep.[114] On plantations in the Far East, vast numbers of rubber trees are coming into bearing. Selection of seed and improvement of farm practices may be expected to increase the output of various industrial oilseeds.

114. **10**, 1947, p. 92.

While an increase in the output of synthetic products is likely, there should be room for both these and natural products in an expanding world economy. In the event of a prolonged setback in economic conditions, on the other hand, intensified competition between synthetic products and products of the soil would probably develop and might lead to a fall in prices.

Chapter 18

LIVESTOCK AND ANIMAL PRODUCTS

Though more than four fifths of the people in the world live largely on plant food, animal husbandry is very important in world agriculture. Since animal foodstuffs are the preferred fare of wealthy people and nations and thus command relatively high prices, the cash value of the world's output is only a little less than that of vegetable products. For each calorie obtained for human nutrition, it costs much more to produce animal foodstuffs than cereals.

In addition to foodstuffs, livestock supplies farmers with draft power and transportation. In 1948–49, more than 85 per cent of the world's farms used animals for draft power. Oxen and buffaloes work in the fields in South America, Asia, Africa and eastern Europe. In central Europe, where the thin topsoil does not permit deep plowing, milk cows are used in cultivating the soil.[1] Even in France, about a million oxen and two million cows worked in the fields in 1948.[2] In many countries farmers rely on horses for transportation as well as for work in the fields. Manure, although not represented in farmers' cash receipts, has been important for centuries, if not millenniums, in maintaining soil fertility and assuring the success of crops.

On the whole, a farmer usually gets a larger and more dependable income when he combines crops and stock, feeding part of his crops to livestock and marketing animal products, than he does when he raises crops alone.[3] The combination makes it easier for him to use his labor and equipment throughout the year. Grazing livestock during the summer releases labor for work in the fields. The soil is fertilized by manure, especially when high-protein concentrates are added to the livestock feed. Rotation of food and feed crops improves the soil and increases yields. Furthermore, stockraising permits the farmer to utilize grass and roughage, and to store them and surplus grain "in the hide," so to speak, in the form of livestock to be used or sold when prices are advantageous.

While livestock farming thus complements the raising of food crops, it, in turn, depends largely on crop farming, particularly in countries where natural pasturage is insufficient to maintain the herds. As modern agriculture becomes more complex, its two principal branches become more and more interdependent. Yet in many countries crop growing and livestock raising still vie with each other for supremacy, as in the biblical story did Cain, the tiller of the soil, and Abel, the shepherd. In our day, the conflict finds expression in the competition between cropland and pasturage.

Patterns in Animal Husbandry

Climate, soil and topography have influenced the patterns of animal husbandry as they have influenced crop farming. In general, level, fertile land, adequate rainfall and a mild climate encourage cattle raising. Regions with semiarid or arid climate and rugged topography are suitable only for sheep and goats, which can live on scattered bits of grass and need little water. Least demanding are hogs, which, being scavengers, can live in almost any climate under almost any conditions of soil and topography and have followed man throughout the world. On the whole, livestock farming is concentrated in the Temperate Zone, and is unimportant in tropical areas.

The specialization of certain areas within a continent or a country in the output of a particular type of livestock is determined also by the kinds of crops that can be raised most profitably. The abundance of corn and other feed crops in the Corn Belt of the United States has favored hog and cattle raising and "finishing" in that region. Where soil or limited rainfall or topography make it less profitable to grow grain than to keep the land in pasture, dairying often develops, particularly when markets for dairy products are within reach.[4]

DEVELOPMENT OF ANIMAL HUSBANDRY

The very different patterns in livestock production today in various parts of the world reflect

1. **14**, p. 48.
2. **32**, January 1949, p. 40.
3. **42**, p. 5.

4. **47**, p. 11.

to some extent successive stages in the development of animal husbandry.

Men first obtained meat by hunting wild animals and game. Archaeological explorations have shown that people had animal food in the Paleolithic and Neolithic eras. Primitive stone weapons have been found in the remains of the carcasses of early animals, and evidences of bones crushed for the extraction of marrow have been discovered.

The domestication of cattle must have started about 6000 B.C. Cattle existed in Europe before the final retreat of the glaciers, but none were native to America.[5] Sheep were among the first animals to be domesticated. Domestication of hogs started about 4900 B.C. The Babylonians rode horses in 2000 B.C.[6]

With the domestication of animals, man began to shift from a primitive hunting economy to animal husbandry. Cattle began to roam on flat grasslands, and sheep and goats multiplied in drier regions, on hills and mountains.

As the population increased, grain fields began to encroach upon pastures, gradually displacing the animals. Tillage for food crops, however, exhausted the productive capacity of the land when crops were carried away and the fertility of the soil was not renewed by manure.[7] When cropping thus became less productive, the fields again were given over to livestock. That return signaled the beginning of general farming, which is now the most widely distributed form of stock farming in the world.

With further increase in the density of population in industrialized countries and the rise in the level of consumption, demand for animal foodstuffs became more urgent. Yet less land was available to maintain large herds of livestock. This situation encouraged stock breeding on relatively small farms.

All these stages in the development of animal husbandry still exist in the world. Hunting tribes, although crowded out almost everywhere by pastoral or soil-tilling farmers, can still be found in unsettled regions in Asia, the USSR, Africa, Australia and America. The nomadic herds of some African or Asiatic tribes in our times have essentially the same characteristics that herds once had in Europe. Sheep raising in South Africa

today is not much different from what it was in England in the time of Queen Elizabeth.[8]

The extensive type of animal husbandry, with animals roaming freely over great expanses and feeding almost entirely on natural vegetation, still exists, as it did centuries ago, in sparsely populated regions. Commercial livestock production of the extensive type prevails in range areas of the United States, Argentina, Uruguay, Australia and New Zealand. Intensive livestock production is best developed in northwestern Europe but is also found in some parts of central Europe and North America. The Corn Belt of the United States is one of the best examples of animal husbandry as a form of general farming.

Within the three main patterns of animal husbandry — extensive, intensive and as part of general farming — there are many variations, sometimes overlapping one another. Moreover, this classification does not include the livestock held on almost every farm for home use — a cow or a draft animal, a few sheep or goats, a couple of pigs or a few chickens. In the world as a whole, such livestock outnumbers that on commercial farms.

EXTENSIVE STOCKRAISING

Stockraising of the extensive type is important in the United States, Argentina, New Zealand and some other countries.

The United States

Extensive stockraising characterizes the range areas of the Great Plains, the Rocky Mountain, Intermountain and Pacific Coast Regions. Originally immense herds of cattle grazed freely in these areas, but overstocking and overgrazing gradually destroyed the protective vegetation.[9] Homesteading and conflicts among cattle herders for more and better ground, close to water sources, led to fencing.[10] Gradually, commer-

---

5. **67**, p. 94.
6. **42**, pp. 325, 468 and 627.
7. See Chapter 15.

8. **56**, p. 189.
9. Of the 728 million acres of the western range, more than 630 million produce considerably less forage than previously, and almost all are in a state of erosion. On about 80 million acres of this damaged land, the better forage plants have practically disappeared. **24**, 1943-47, p. 897.
10. The story of fencing the cattle holdings within the range is filled with conflict and adventure. Big landholders who could afford to buy barbed wire and have armed men protect their property fenced enormous areas. One fenced ranch in Texas covered 210,000 acres. **56**, p. 920.

cial grazing evolved. Although the overused land has lost more than half its capacity to maintain livestock, the range still supports about 40 per cent of all the cattle in the United States. Since this system of husbandry usually requires several acres to support one animal, ranches must have hundreds, and often thousands, of acres. Moreover, to supplement grass feeding, many ranchers grow feed crops, particularly for the winter season.

The range, however, does not produce enough feed for its great numbers of livestock, and a division of labor has developed between the herders on the range and the "finishers" in the Corn Belt. Since it is usually more economical to move cattle to feed than to ship feed to cattle,[11] millions of animals are moved each year to the Corn Belt, where they are fattened on corn and other feed crops before they are marketed for slaughter.[12] However, great numbers of cattle — chiefly calves and yearlings — are shipped directly to market. It is estimated that about two thirds of the cattle shipped from the western grazing areas each year are sold for immediate slaughter, and a third go to the Corn Belt and other feeding grounds for fattening.[13] There are feeding centers in the western states also, such as the cottonseed cake area in Texas and the area in northeastern Colorado where cattle are fattened on the pulp left after extraction of beet sugar.

Argentina

The extensive animal husbandry of Argentina has more favorable natural conditions than the range in the United States affords in its present state. Vast natural grasslands with ample rainfall and sunshine provide excellent grazing grounds during the entire year, and shelter from weather is not needed. Here cattle are fed and fattened exclusively on pasture — first on natural grassland, then, after about two years of grazing, on alfalfa pasture for from six months to a year before they are shipped to market. Only in times of extreme drought do the breeders resort to corn for cattle finishing. Because of this complete dependence on pasture, the quality of pasture

grasses largely determines the kind, quality and number of livestock.[14]

Alfalfa is the chief fattening feed in Argentina, where it occupies over 15 million acres. While seven acres of grass are needed to support a steer, two acres of alfalfa suffice. Moreover, one planting of alfalfa lasts up to eight years.

The alfalfa zone, watered by the La Plata and its tributaries, is spreading, and even invading the territory in food crops.[15] Since pasturage is pivotal in Argentine cattle raising, there is constant competition for the use of land, not only between animal husbandry and grain farming but also within the livestock industry itself. As a result, the sheep industry is gradually being forced from the central grasslands to semiarid barren lands, such as those in the south.[16]

Most of the Argentine livestock farms (*estancias*) are holdings of 6,000–12,000 acres. The agricultural census of 1937 reported 480 *estancias* of more than 12,500 acres each in the Province of Buenos Aires alone. There were fifty *estancias* with 70,000 acres each. In rugged Patagonia, where sheep fear no competition from cattle because of the cold and stormy winds, extreme temperature variations and sparse natural forage, virtually all holdings exceed 1,600 acres and many, half a million acres.[17]

New Zealand

In New Zealand, permanent meadows and pastures comprised more than 30 million acres in 1947–49. To increase productivity, over a million tons of fertilizer are used annually for top-dressing.[18] The renewal of pastures also requires the sowing of very considerable quantities of grass seed each year, which is grown almost entirely in New Zealand.

Government agencies in that country are working to improve grass strains, and some superior varieties have been developed. The quality and

11. **42**, p. 26.

12. In Great Britain, cattle are moved for feeding from Wales to the Midlands, and cattle imported from Ireland are taken to fattening centers in England. **65**, p. 80.

13. **47**, p. 18.

14. **58**, p. 56.

15. **29**, pp. 64-66.

16. A similar movement may be observed in the United States. Each census has reported a further westward shift of the center of the sheep population. At present, it is located in southwestern Nebraska. The chief cause is the same: competition for land and feed. **42**, p. 472.

17. **29**, pp. 65 and 74.

18. **36**, pp. 26-27.

"pedigree" of seeds are certified by the government; distribution is channeled through commercial outlets. Although grass is the main crop in New Zealand and livestock can graze at all seasons, hay or ensilage, green fodder and root crops are also used as feed, chiefly to protect the pastures from overgrazing and to maintain livestock in uniformly good condition throughout the year.[19] Landholdings in New Zealand's cattle-raising area are large, stretching over many thousands of acres. About a fourth of all farm land is in holdings of 20,000 acres or more.

INTENSIVE ANIMAL HUSBANDRY

Denmark is probably the world's outstanding example of intensive animal husbandry. In this small country, livestock production has achieved almost the perfection of an art. Highly skilled labor, close association with science, use of modern installations and machinery, and versatility in farm management and marketing have assured, in intimate combination, the uniformly high standard of Danish animal husbandry. An excellent cooperative system, including as much as 90 per cent of all the farms, rigorously controls the quality of every product of its members.[20]

Special trade marks, such as the "Lur" brand for butter and, since 1947, for cheese, or the mark *Danish* for eggs, have been introduced by voluntary cooperation through farmers' organizations. Not until they were firmly established were such marks for quality control made obligatory by law. Only first-grade butter may bear the Lur brand, and only this butter may be exported.[21]

Yet natural conditions in Denmark are not very favorable. Though the climate is mild and humid, livestock must be kept in solidly built, well-insulated buildings during six or seven months of the year. The soil is fertile and pasturage is lush in some parts of the country, but there are large areas of sand and bogs.

Much of the land in Denmark is in pasture, natural or sown, and by far the greatest part of the arable land is in feed and root crops.

Cultivation is so intensive and fertilizers are applied so lavishly that whatever the crop, it has a higher yield per acre than in any other country. Nevertheless, the country depends largely on foreign concentrates and other feedstuffs for its animal husbandry. In other words, Denmark depends not only on its own soil but also on the fertility of faraway countries for the feed that it transforms into dairy products. In this way, corn production in the Western Hemisphere and animal husbandry in Denmark complement each other.

Although Danish farms are somewhat larger than the Dutch and, particularly, the Belgian, they are small by American standards. All branches of farm work are closely integrated, each supporting the other without waste. This intensive and highly organized system of production, combined with proximity to great centers of population and large markets, pre-eminently in the United Kingdom, has determined the success of the Danish livestock industry.

ANIMAL HUSBANDRY WITHIN GENERAL FARMING

The Corn Belt of the United States is a perfect example of animal husbandry carried on within the framework of general farming. With less than 10 per cent of the total area of the country, this region produces about half the corn and oats and a considerable part of the other feed and food crops raised in the United States. At the same time, it accounts for about half of the hogs and a fifth of the cattle raised in the country.

Ample rainfall, good soil and level land, adapted to extensive use of machinery, have encouraged the development of crop farming on a large scale. All land suitable for cultivation is under the plow. Corn is the main crop, and the second in importance is oats. Planted before corn can be sown and harvested after the corn fields have been cultivated, oats are essential to the rotation system customary in the northern part of the Corn Belt.

Pastures, originally abundant, have yielded somewhat to crops. Putting land to crops makes it possible not only to raise livestock on local farms but also to fatten cattle brought from the range and hogs brought from western and southwestern states.[22] The fattening of hogs from

---

19. **39**, 1947-49, pp. 909-10.

20. Every package of butter must be of standard quality and show the date it was produced. Each egg is marked and can be traced back to the producer. A dissatisfied customer in the United Kingdom or Germany can get a refund, and the Danish producer must return his money and also pay a fine to the cooperative.

21. **34**, pp. 37-38. The care given livestock in Denmark is well illustrated by Figure 157.

22. The fattening grounds are already spreading beyond the Corn Belt; they stretch out into Nebraska, Minnesota and South Dakota. The herders of the United States have even begun to search for open spaces in

other areas is the less important operation, since hogs are sold to farmers in the Corn Belt only when the fodder is poor in the breeding areas.

The animal husbandry of the Corn Belt is highly diversified and includes the breeding and finishing of cattle, dairying, and hog and poultry raising. The central location of this area between the range and the great consumption centers in the east is of commanding importance. Farms are generally large, usually from 100 to 200 acres, but many holdings are of 1,000 acres or more. Most of the work is performed by family labor with occasional hired help, and mechanical power is used extensively.

FEED VERSUS FOOD

Feedstuffs[23] are a link between crop farming and stockraising. Having domesticated animals, man had to assume the responsibility of feeding them and has had to devote a large part of all farm land to this purpose.

In some countries, permanent pastures and rotation meadows take up from 50 to 75 per cent of all agricultural land. In cattle-raising countries, pastures often compete for land with crop fields. Thus, in Great Britain between 1871 and 1938, cultivated land shrank from 18 to 12 million acres, largely to the advantage of pastures.[24] In Belgium, grasslands were extended a million acres between 1880 and 1939 at the expense of cereal raising. Even in the open stretches of Argentina, cattle raising and grain farming compete keenly for land.

Sharing Crops and Land

In many parts of the world, herds have greatly outgrown the available pastures and grazing alone no longer suffices to maintain them. Thus, mankind has been compelled not only to shift a part of the fields from food crops to feedstuffs but also to share the food crops with domestic animals. While farmers once raised livestock to help them produce crops, they now grow crops to produce and maintain livestock. The share of

human beings and animals in the consumption of various crops produced in the United States is estimated as follows (per cent):[25]

	Human Food	Feed	Seed, Storage, Export
Wheat	65	15	20
Buckwheat	65	20	15
Rice	50	5	45
Barley	30	60	10
Rye	25	50	25
Corn	3	85	12
Oats	3	95	2
Sorghum	—	100	—
Hay	—	100	—

Less than 20 per cent of the combined output of wheat, rye, corn, barley, oats and rice in the United States is consumed directly as human food.[26] About 65 per cent goes to feed animals, and the remainder is used for seed, storage or export. In prewar Europe, the annual consumption of grains was about equally divided between human population and livestock: 53 and 47 per cent, respectively.[27] While countries differ widely, in the world as a whole a considerable proportion of all crops is fed to livestock. Some experts believe that a larger part of the world's productive land, including crop areas and pastures, is used to feed animals than to grow food crops for mankind. In the United States, about six tenths of all land is used for hay and pasture and two thirds of all cropland for producing feed and forage crops.[28]

Converting Feed into Food

Animal feeds are largely produced from such crops as bread grain, coarse grain, potatoes and fodder roots, on the one hand, and pasture grasses, on the other. The animals that convert these feeds into human food can be broadly classified into two groups: refiners and condensers. Cattle and sheep are equipped with digestive systems that permit them to consume roughage that human beings cannot eat, and they refine coarse crops into meat and dairy products. Hogs and poultry have digestive systems more like

---

Mexico and other Latin American countries. **57**, pp. 75-77.

23. Following the International Institute of Agriculture, the terms forage, fodder and feedstuffs are used here interchangeably without differentiating between fodder or forage (grass, hay, straw, roots and tubers); cereals and their by-products (bran, husk and so on); and industrial residues.

24. Since 1943, the relationship has been almost exactly reversed. **35**, 1938-48, p. 171.

25. **60**, p. 72.

26. **23**, p. 15.

27. In addition to 56 million tons of grain, Europe's livestock consumed annually about 14 million tons of mill by-products, such as wheat bran, rye bran, flour offals, rice meal dust and sweepings. **2**, pp. 14 and 19.

28. **24**, 1948, p. 26, and **27**, p. 3.

man's and condense crops largely fit for human consumption into more nutritious products — pork, poultry and eggs.[29]

FEED SUPPLIES AND LIVESTOCK PRODUCTION

The problem of fodder is the problem of land use. Livestock products are expensive in terms of land. An average acre in food crops in the United States yields six times as many calories for human consumption as one in feed crops yields in terms of the eventual animal products. More specifically, an acre of wheat supplies nineteen times as many calories for direct human consumption as are provided when the same wheat is fed to fatten cattle from the range.[30]

Consequently, only countries with vast pasturage and plenty of cropland can feed great numbers of livestock the free gifts of nature as well as crops raised for them. In overpopulated parts of the world where food crops occupy all the land that farmers know how to use, and yet fail to supply enough for the people, it would be sheer waste to use large tracts for grazing. In such countries, food crops must come first and man takes for himself not only the customary food crops but also the coarse grains used elsewhere almost exclusively for feed.

Corn, for example, is an important food in many parts of Asia, Africa, South America, eastern and southeastern Europe; barley, in Asia and Africa. In India all grains are considered to be food, and in China about 90 per cent of all grain is consumed directly by human beings. Less than 6 per cent of the farms in China have any pasture, and in Japan and the Philippines pastures occupy less than 10 per cent of all agricultural land.[31] Although India, with more than 350 million people, has nearly 135 million cattle, man uses the land almost exclusively for himself, letting the animals feed themselves as best they can. Where people live in poverty, livestock must be poor, too.

Intercontinental Division of Labor

The densely populated countries of western and, particularly, northwestern Europe have found a way of getting around the dilemma of food versus feed crops, fields versus pastures. With rising standards of nutrition, they faced a demand for animal products beyond the capacity of the nation's agriculture. The alternatives were to import additional supplies of meat, butter, cheese, as does the United Kingdom, or to import feedstuffs and transform livestock raising into a processing industry. Denmark, the Netherlands, Belgium and some other countries chose the second method. By importing large quantities of feed crops and concentrates from the Western Hemisphere,[32] they have been able to develop an intensive animal husbandry.

As long as the demand for animal products and the ratio between prices for them and imported feedstuffs were favorable, and as long as an uninterrupted flow of feed from abroad was assured, this intercontinental division of labor functioned well.[33] But a poor harvest in countries exporting feed, or wartime paralysis of foreign trade, inevitably inflicted heavy losses and difficulties on all nations involved. Because of such experiences during World War I and difficulties in foreign exchange during the depression, Germany, Sweden, Denmark, the Low Countries, Italy and Austria made great efforts in the 1930's to produce more and better fodder within their borders. In southern Europe, where cereals are of prime importance to human beings,[34] little can be spared for livestock, and a poor harvest or a drought results in the slaughter of many animals so that the rest can be maintained.

Pasturage

In the USSR, pastures supply about half the fodder. The main pasture lands are in Kazakhstan, central Asia and eastern Siberia. Together these three regions account for nearly 83 per cent of the total pasture area. Root crops are concentrated in the Ukraine and extend somewhat north of it. Clover is sown in the nonchernozem and central chernozem regions, the Urals, the Ukraine and Siberia; alfalfa predominates in the Caucasus, the southern part of the Ukraine and central Asia. Clover occupies twice as large an area as alfalfa.[35]

The United States assures its supply of fodder by its great output of corn, oats, barley and other crops, on the one hand, and by hundreds of

---

29. **60**, pp. 72-73.
30. **59**, pp. 3 and 6. Cf. Figure 173, p. 557.
31. Table 216, p. 473; cf. **46**, p. 173.

32. Some feed has also been imported from the Danubian countries.
33. The final link in the international chain was the export of animal products from Denmark and the Netherlands, chiefly to the United Kingdom and also to Germany, France and other European countries.
34. See Chapter 16.
35. **43**, pp. 428-29; **54**, p. 453.

millions of acres of pastures, improved and unimproved, on the other. In an average year pasture supplies more than 35 per cent of the forage; hay, almost 16 per cent; corn, 24 per cent; and other grain, more than 10 per cent. (See Figure 189.) Through the nineteenth century, the United States relied primarily on pasturage, while increasing quantities of corn were exported to Europe. The peak year of such exports was 1897, when more than 5 million tons were shipped abroad. Increase in the population and in the demand for animal food resulted in an increase in the number of livestock and the need for more feed. At the same time the pasturage began to deteriorate because of overgrazing. Feed crops, once predominantly exported, had to be used for domestic livestock. Thus, corn from the United States almost disappeared from the European markets and was replaced first by Russian barley, then by corn from Argentina.[36]

While the supply of feed in the United States normally is adequate, a poor harvest may disrupt the balance. In the drought years 1934 and 1936, feed was in such short supply that, in spite of imports of corn, chiefly from Argentina, heavy slaughtering of livestock became inevitable.

On the whole, large and sudden fluctuations in the supply of feed are particularly dangerous for countries with well-developed animal husbandry, since high-grade livestock is less able to survive want than primitive, slow-developing breeds.

The World's Livestock

Domesticated livestock is roughly divided into two groups: workstock, or animals used chiefly to provide draft power (horses, buffaloes, oxen, mules and asses), and productive animals that supply foodstuffs (cattle, hogs, sheep and goats). Animals serving both purposes are classified according to their main function in farming. Thus horses are counted as workstock though horse meat and milk are used in some countries,[37] and

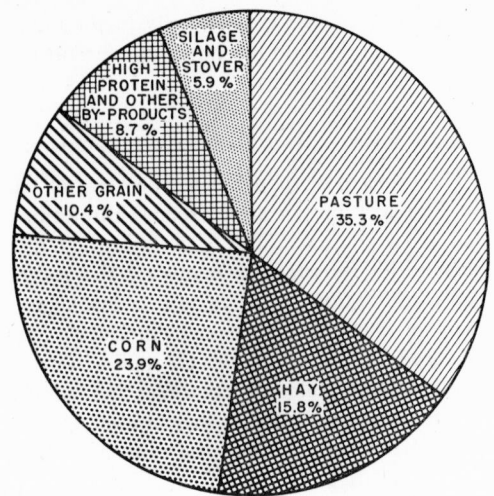

U. S. Department of Agriculture

FIGURE 189. FEEDS: RELATIVE IMPORTANCE IN LIVESTOCK PRODUCTION IN THE UNITED STATES

oxen are counted with other cattle even when they serve as draft animals. Buffaloes are counted as workstock although buffalo meat and milk are used for human consumption in Asia.[38]

Though the number of cattle in a country is changing continually, it is less subject to annual fluctuations than crop yields. The numbers of hogs and sheep are subject to wider fluctuations and are affected by the season. They are highest in the late spring and summer and lowest in the winter. Consequently, international statistics referring to different times of the year are not wholly comparable. Many countries do not enumerate livestock and for them only rough estimates are available; for some others, statistics cover only those animals registered for taxation.

Workstock

Horses are the principal draft animals in the Temperate Zone — in Europe, the Americas and the USSR. Buffaloes predominate in Asia, particularly in the monsoon regions. Mules and asses are used chiefly in the tropical parts of Latin America and Asia, but also in the Mediterranean region and in the southern part of the United States. Oxen work in the fields of Asia, Africa, South America and some European countries.

Greece, which uses all types of workstock, has kept statistical records of their labor. In 1938,

36. Since World War II, the United States has become an important exporter of corn, while Argentina's exports have declined considerably. In 1950, the United States exported 2.4 million tons of corn, as compared with Argentina's 0.8 million. **8,** February 1952, p. 17.

37. Horse meat was the poor man's meat in continental Europe, but in the postwar shortage of meat, consumption has become more general. Horses unfit for work are slaughtered for meat, and others are imported for slaughter from Ireland. On the whole, "a dead horse is in many parts of Europe today more valuable than a live one." **32,** January 1949, p. 31.

38. In India, for example, buffaloes produce 45 per cent of all the milk consumed. **38,** p. 179.

TABLE 279

WORKSTOCK: USE OF DRAFT ANIMALS ON FARMS IN GREECE, 1938

	All Workstock	Buffaloes	Horses	Oxen	Cows	Mules	Asses
Number	1,247,003	17,967	268,346	341,665	124,185	150,170	344,670
Average number of work days per animal	...	147	162	129	105	161	153
Average daily wage per animal, in U. S. cents [a]	...	44.6	51.5	39.8	36.4	47.1	24.1

Source: **37**, 1938, Appendix I, p. 221.

a. In Greek statistics the term "average daily wage" signifies the cost of keeping the animal.

TABLE 280

WORKSTOCK IN EACH CONTINENT, 1928, 1938 AND 1950

(*Millions*)

Continent	Horses			Mules and Asses			Buffaloes		
	1928	1938	1950	1928	1938	1950	1928	1938	1950
World	114.1	90.5	76.0	45.7	54.5	...	69.4	75.2	...
North America [a]	17.6	13.4	7.0	5.5	4.2	2.4	...	...	...
Middle and South America	22.7	21.6	21.6	9.1	16.0	...	b	b	b
Europe	23.6	20.0	16.4	5.5	5.1	...	0.7	0.7	1.0
USSR	33.5	17.5	13.7 [c]	0.6	0.7	...	0.5	0.6	...
Asia	12.4	13.0	12.2	19.4	19.7	...	67.4	72.9	72.0
Africa	2.0	3.0	3.8	5.6	8.8	...	0.8	1.0	1.0
Oceania	2.3	2.0	1.3	b	b	b	b	b	b

Sources: **11**, pp. 461, 466, 470 and 474; **19**, FLM 5–51, pp. 6–7.

a. Includes Mexico and Cuba in 1928.

b. Insignificant number.

c. Official estimate of the USSR for 1951. Planned for 1948, 12.9 million (**40**, pp. 935–36).

for example, about a million and a quarter animals provided 180 million work days. The largest average number of work days per animal was supplied by horses and mules (162 and 161, respectively), the smallest by cows (105). The cost of keeping work animals, or their "average daily wage" (a term used in Greek statistics), was highest for horses and mules, lowest for asses. (See Table 279.)

HORSES

The number of horses in the world has been declining continuously, from 114 million in 1928 to 90.5 million in 1938 and 76 million in 1950, chiefly because of the introduction of motor power in agriculture and transportation, as well

as in the armed forces. The decline in North America has been particularly steep, from about 18 million head in 1928 to 7 million in 1950. The number in the USSR also has dropped sharply, first during the enforced collectivization and then during the war; mechanization of agriculture was an important contributing factor. The number of horses in Europe has also decreased, but Latin America maintained the previous level throughout the war. (See Table 280.)

While the continuing spread of mechanization is tending to reduce the world's stock of horses, this decline may be offset by increases in the USSR, eastern Europe, Asia and some parts of Africa. It is believed that the USSR and many European countries will continue to make some

TABLE 281
WORKSTOCK: HORSES IN SELECTED COUNTRIES, 1928, 1938 AND 1950
(*Thousands*)

Country [a]	1928	1938	1950 [b]	Country [a]	1928	1938	1950 [b]
United States	14,203	10,995	5,274	Austria	. . .	231	282
Canada	3,376	2,821	1,683	Hungary	918	814	569 [c]
				Spain	598	555	600 [c]
Mexico	1,887	2,200	2,722 [c]	Italy	943	793	791
Colombia	929	930	1,180	Yugoslavia	1,109	1,264	1,097
Brazil	6,045	6,713	6,928	Romania	1,945	2,158	939 [d]
Peru	432	. . .	518	Bulgaria	482	584	549 [g]
Chile	441	528	460	Greece	290	363	232
Uruguay	623	644	575 [d]				
Argentina	9,858	8,262	7,238 [e]	USSR	33,537	17,500	13,700 [h]
United Kingdom	1,309	1,100	549	China [i]	3,500	4,080	2,023 [d]
Ireland	433	442	391	Japan	1,494	1,432	1,120
France [f]	2,936	2,692	2,414	Turkey	424	964	1,134
Denmark	519	564	503	Pakistan	}2,282{	1,461	470
Sweden	628	633	440	India		762	1,401
Finland	. . .	342	427	Ethiopia	. . .	. . .	1,100
Germany	3,729	3,037	. . .	Union of South			
Western	. . .	1,566	1,629	Africa	836	778	684 [d]
Soviet Zone	. . .	811	695				
Poland	4,047	3,148	2,677	Australia	1,943	1,724	1,057
Czechoslovakia	. . .	662	640	New Zealand	307	262	195

Sources: **1**, 1931–32, pp. 74–76; **12**, 1941–42 to 1945–46, Vol. I, pp. 177–81; **7**, 1950, pp. 114–17; **19**, FLM 5–51, pp. 6–7; **8**, February 1952, pp. 8–9.

a. December–January estimates for 1950 (and often for prewar years) are given for the United States, Mexico, Colombia, Brazil, Germany, Czechoslovakia, Austria, Italy, Yugoslavia, Romania, Bulgaria, Greece, Japan, Turkey, India and New Zealand; March–April, for Spain and Australia; May–August, for Canada, Chile, Argentina, the United Kingdom, Ireland, Denmark, Sweden, Finland, Poland, Hungary, the USSR, China and the Union of South Africa; similar information not available for other countries. Estimates for October–December of 1949 reported under 1950.
b. Preliminary.
c. 1949.
d. 1948.
e. 1946–47.
f. Excludes army horses.
g. 1947.
h. Official estimate of the USSR for 1951.
i. 22 provinces.

use of horses in agriculture so as to economize on fuel.[39]

In various countries, the trends have been in opposite directions. In the United States the number of horses on farms declined, because of mechanization, from 14.2 million in 1928 to 5.9 million in 1949, and 5.3 million in 1950.[40] The number also decreased in Canada in this period for the same reason, from 3.4 to 1.7 million; in the United Kingdom, from 1.3 million to 549,-000; in Australia, from 1.9 to 1.1 million. The considerable decline during the war and postwar years in Greece, Romania and Hungary resulted from feed shortage and requisitioning by the Germans and the Russians; the number dropped further in 1950 when severe drought reduced the supplies of forage and feed. In contrast, the number of horses has increased in Mexico, Colombia and Brazil. (See Table 281.) In Argentina, horsepower is still used considerably but is declining as the use of tractors increases. In Uruguay, saddle horses maintain their numbers, but draft horses are gradually being replaced by mechanical power.[41]

MULES, ASSES AND BUFFALOES

Mules and asses are widely used in farming in Asia and Latin America; Brazil and Mexico have more than 4 million each. They are also used considerably in the United States, though the number dropped from 5.4 million in 1930 to

39. **19**, FLM 5-51, p. 3.
40. **16**, 1950, p. 412.

41. **19**, FLM 5-51, p. 3.

2.1 million in 1950. The change in countries for which data are available has been as follows (figures in thousands): [42]

	Prewar	*1950*
United States	4,621	2,149
Spain	2,190	1,900 [a]
Turkey	1,499	1,790
Italy	1,370	1,139
Iran	1,186	1,245
India	1,165	1,175
French Morocco	845	759
Colombia	760	800
Greece	567	517
Algeria	527	557
Peru	407	582
Iraq	380	393
France	331	196
Tunisia	229	170
Syria	149	321

a. 1949.

Asia has nearly all the world's buffaloes. (See Table 280.) India and China together account for about three fourths (61 and 17 per cent, respectively). These animals are well adapted to the muddy, marshy land used for rice and they withstand conditions under which no other animal would work. India has slightly increased the number of its buffaloes, but the herds in Pakistan, the Philippines and Thailand are smaller than before the war (figures in thousands): [43]

	Prewar	*1950*
China [a]	11,574	9,460 [b]
Pakistan	6,200	5,600 [b]
India	41,000	41,500
Burma	1,035	721 [b]
Thailand	5,300	4,000
Indochina	1,912	1,270
Indonesia	3,219	2,665
Philippines	2,919	2,035

a. 22 provinces.   b. 1948.

A few buffaloes have been introduced into southeastern Europe and Italy from Asia. In Italy, buffaloes practically disappeared after the reclamation of the Pontine Marshes.[44] Bulgaria used more than 300,000 buffaloes in 1947, Greece had about 60,000 in 1948–50, and Yugoslavia, 65,000.[45]

PRODUCTIVE LIVESTOCK

Cattle, sheep and hogs, taken together, are almost as numerous as men. Asia has the largest number of cattle and hogs. Oceania has more sheep than any other continent but relatively few cattle and only 2 million hogs. Hogs outnumber sheep in North America, while Africa has more sheep than cattle and hogs together. Cattle and sheep are the chief productive animals in Middle and South America.

In the world at large, cattle herds increased by about 10 per cent between 1928 and 1938 and in 1950 exceeded the prewar number. In contrast, the number of hogs has been almost stationary.

The Western Hemisphere has considerably more cattle than before World War II, but Europe, despite great efforts, has not yet rehabilitated its herds. The USSR has more sheep but fewer cattle and hogs than before the war. (See Table 282 and Figure 190.)

Quality of Livestock

Numbers alone, however, give only a partial picture of animal husbandry in the various continents and countries. The usefulness and relative value of livestock depend greatly on the quality of the animals — weight, breed, efficiency, reproductive capacity, age, general physical condition and so on.

The Dominion of India has nearly 20 per cent of all the cattle in the world and about 60 per cent of the cattle of Asia, but its herds include millions of old, worn-out, often sick animals, destined to die from starvation since religious traditions forbid slaughtering. Hence, the tremendous cattle population of India (about 135 million) is probably the least productive in the world — growth is slow, the milk yield very low and the interval between calvings nearly three years.[46] Indeed, India would fare much better with smaller numbers of better cattle.

The situation in Africa is not much better. There wealth and social standing are measured by the number of cattle a man owns and little attention is paid to quality.[47] Here, as in vast

---

42. **19**, FLM 5-51, pp. 8-9. (Countries are arrayed by the declining number of mules and asses in prewar years.)

43. **19**, FLM 5-51, pp. 819. **8**, September 1951, gives somewhat different figures.

44. **45**, p. 251.

45. **7**, 1951, p. 130.

46. **48**, pp. 200-01.

47. In many parts of Africa cattle are used as local currency (**63**, p. 171). The British Agricultural Commission for Kenya came to the conclusion that the custom of

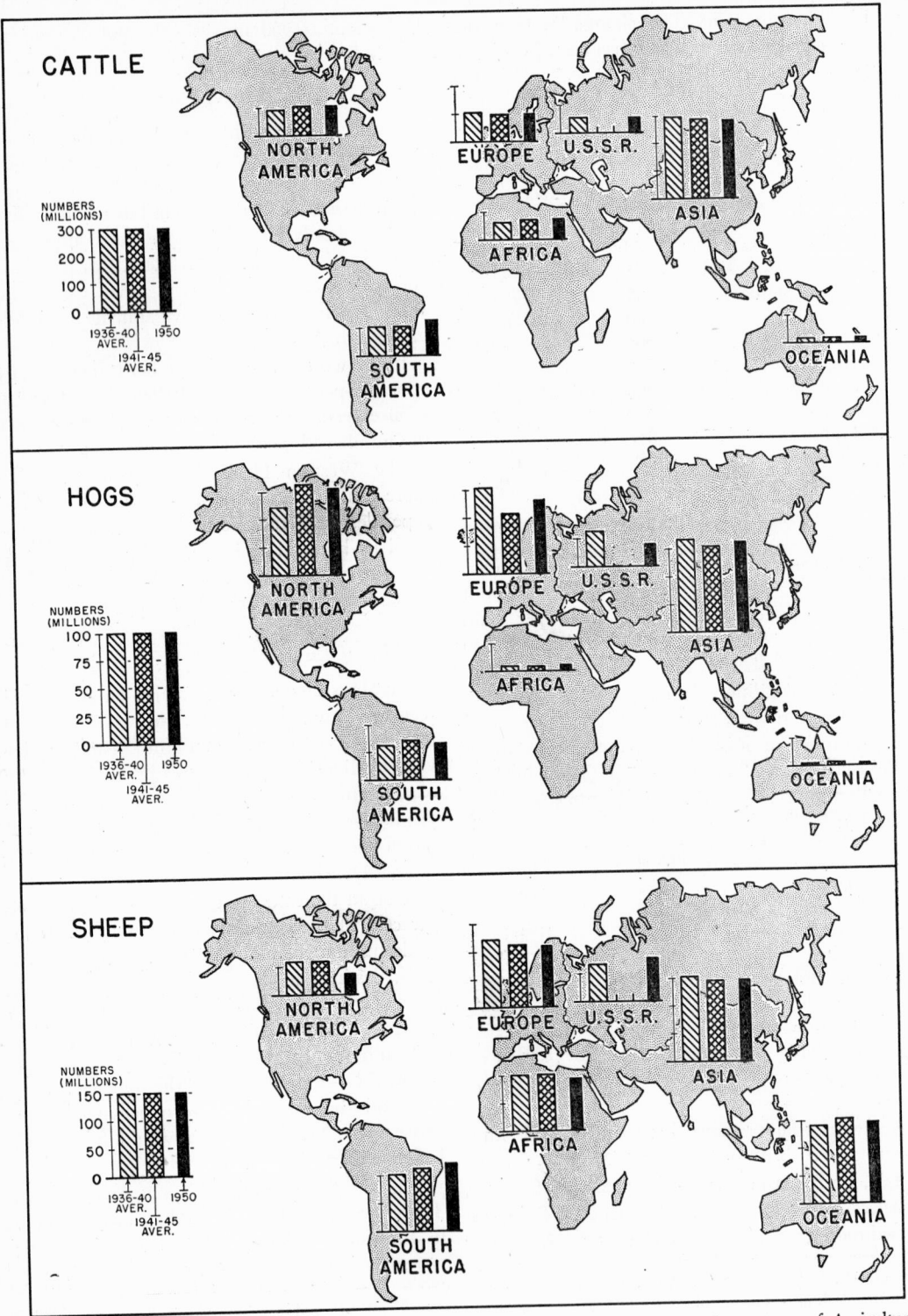

FIGURE 190. PRODUCTIVE LIVESTOCK IN EACH CONTINENT, 1936–40, 1941–45, AND 1950

TABLE 282

PRODUCTIVE LIVESTOCK IN EACH CONTINENT, 1928, 1938 AND 1950

(*Millions*)

Continent	Cattle			Sheep			Hogs		
	1928	1938	1950	1928	1938	1950	1928	1938	1950
World	635	694	725	733	707	718	290	290	288
North America [a]	67	74	88	52	54	32	63	55	66
Middle and South America	115	134	158	105	104	129	37	37	45
Europe	104	102	97	125	119	101	71	78	69
USSR [b]	71	63	56	133	57	78	26	31	19
Asia	204	227	220	98	127	121	89	85	83
Africa	60	76	86	90	103	110	3	3	4
Oceania	15	18	20	131	143	147	2	2	2

Sources: **11**, pp. 433, 441 and 449; **8**, August 1951, pp. 7–8, and January 1952, pp. 10–11.

a. Includes Mexico and Cuba in 1928.

b. Data for 1950 estimated by the U.S. Department of Agriculture (**19**, FLM 1–51, p. 1; 2–51, p. 1; and 3–51, p. 1).

areas of Asia, cattle live in a semiwild state, and many of them provide only skins or, sometimes, labor.

In some other underdeveloped areas where there is extensive cattle raising or nomadic herding, animals serve chiefly for labor or milk and are slaughtered only when they are entirely worn out. Consequently, the meat is tough and is consumed only locally, without entering even the internal trade of the country. Statistical information on the quality of cattle, sheep and hogs is lacking for most countries.

CATTLE

Cattle are raised chiefly for either meat or dairy products. In Argentina and in some places in the United States, steers are bred and slaughtered for beef only and cows are used principally for calving,[48] but in the world at large, animals bred for both purposes outnumber single-function animals.

Great Britain first populated its colonies, then the world, with some of the finest pedigreed breeds of cattle. English breeds came to the United States with the first settlers. In South American countries, such as Argentina and

Brazil, they were introduced much later. Even now, America, continental Europe and Oceania import pure-bred animals from the United Kingdom to maintain the quality of their stock. Argentina, where four fifths of the cattle are of the best English breeds,[49] is still the United Kingdom's best customer for breeding stock and has much better cattle than any other Latin American country and among the best in the world.

Selected Countries

With more than 80 million head of cattle, the United States is second only to India. Brazil and Argentina together account for about 60 per cent of all the cattle in South America. Brazil has the larger number, but the value of its output of meat, hides and by-products is considerably smaller than Argentina's. Very few of the cattle are grain-fed, and many of the ranges have poor grass. Generally, the cattle suffer from insects and the debilitating climate.[50]

In Africa, Ethiopia ranks first in number of

raising cattle and goats without regard to utilization is a form of social competition.

48. It has been estimated that half the supply of beef and veal in the United States comes from beef cattle, about a third from dairy cattle, and the remainder from cattle raised for both purposes. **15**, August 1941.

49. Of the more than 33 million cattle in Argentina before the war, only about 7 million were of poor stock. These were raised in remote areas, partly because of their greater resistance to epidemics. **13**, p. 255; **29**, p. 64. No price was too high for a pure-bred bull to Argentine cattle breeders, who again and again outbid the British and United States breeders at the European auctions up to World War II. **49**, p. 31.

50. **69**, pp. 108–09.

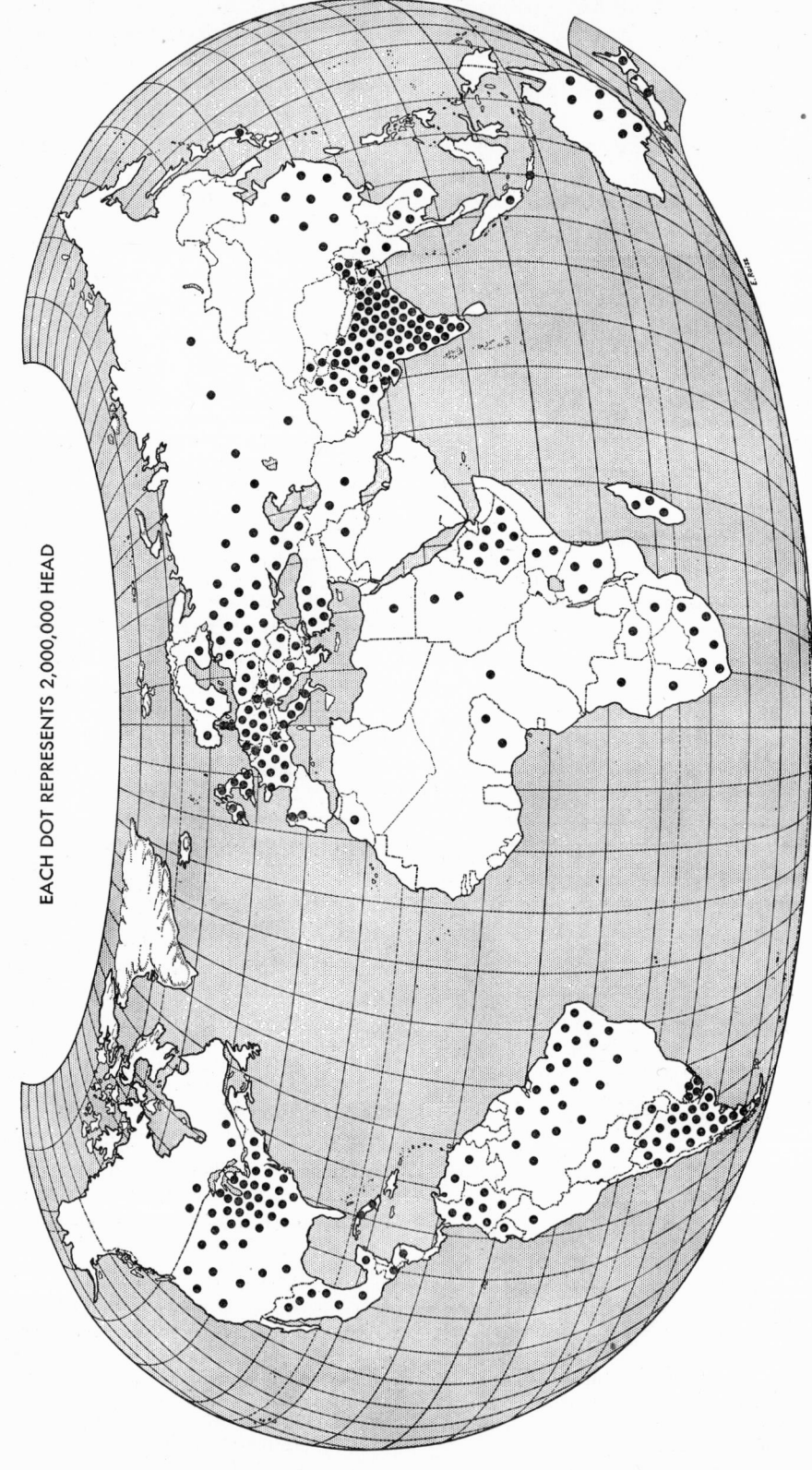

EACH DOT REPRESENTS 2,000,000 HEAD

FIGURE 191. CATTLE: GEOGRAPHIC DISTRIBUTION IN THE WORLD, 1950

cattle and the Union of South Africa second (18 million and 12 million, respectively). Australia is also an important cattle-raising country, with about 14 million in 1949–50. (See Table 283 and Figure 191.)

Europe's cattle are concentrated chiefly in France, the United Kingdom, Ireland, the Low Countries and Denmark and along the northwestern coast of Spain and in the Po Valley of Italy. (See Figure 192.) Ireland, with its green pastures, has more than twice as many cattle per square mile as Iowa.[51] Germany had the largest herd in prewar Europe but, like almost all European nations, has suffered severe losses. In eastern Europe (Hungary, Romania, Poland, Greece) as many as half the cattle were requisitioned by the Germans and the Russians or slaughtered for lack of feed. Although the shortage of feed has continued, cattle-raising countries have made great efforts to restore the size of their herds. The United Kingdom, Ireland, Belgium, Italy and Yugoslavia reported more cattle in 1949-50 than before the war. France has almost regained its prewar level, while herds continue to be smaller in Czechoslovakia, Poland, Greece and some other countries.[52]

The USSR ranked second in number of cattle in 1928 but lost more than 7 million between 1928 and 1938 as a result of enforced collectivization, and about 17 million between 1938 and 1945, according to an official estimate, as a result of the war. It is estimated that 6.4 million cattle have been transferred from occupied countries to the USSR through requisition or as reparations.[53] For 1950 the target of the Five-Year Plan was to raise the number about 3.3 per cent above the 1938 level. In 1950, however, the country had only 56 million, or some 11 per cent less than before the war. In 1938 the Ukraine, Siberia and the Caucasus accounted for 57 per cent of all cattle in the USSR.[54]

The United States

The number of beef cattle on farms and ranches in the United States fluctuates periodically over a cycle that usually lasts from fifteen to twenty years. The trough and the peak of each

succeeding cycle are usually higher than those of the cycle immediately preceding. The number of dairy cows has been increasing steadily. (See Figure 193.)

Between 1938 and 1945, the total number of cattle in the United States increased by about 21 million, from 65 million to 86 million. This large increase is partly explained by the fact that 1938 was a low point in the cattle cycle, while the outbreak of World War II coincided with the beginning of an upward movement. This upward phase of the present cycle, the fourth since 1890, has been rather like that of preceding cycles although it started from a higher level. In 1949, the number of cattle on farms was 78.3 million; in 1950, 80.3 million; in 1951, 84.2 million. Barring drought or severe economic disturbances, the present increase is likely to continue and may set a new record during the next few years.[55]

The greatest concentration of cattle is in the corn and dairy regions. (See Figure 194.) Texas has the largest herd, 9.3 million. Next in line are Iowa, with more than 5 million, and Nebraska and Wisconsin, each with nearly 4 million.[56] Eighty per cent of the farms reporting in 1945 had cattle, with an average of 17.6 head, as compared with 12.5 in 1940 and 11.3 in 1930.[57]

SHEEP

Sheep are naturally grazing animals. They feed mostly on grasses and weeds and browse on woody plants. In the United States, they are sometimes used to clear pastures of weeds.[58] While sheep are found everywhere in the world, there are few in equatorial or subarctic regions.

Two distinct types of sheep are bred: wool breeds and mutton breeds, with many variations within each group. Meat obtained from wool breeds is inferior in quantity and quality to that from mutton breeds.

Wool and mutton prices affect the number of sheep on farms by putting a premium on either wool growing or the raising of lambs. A high price for wool encourages the producers to expand their flocks by keeping the breeding ewes and slaughtering fewer sheep and lambs. A higher return for meat reverses these practices and increases the number of slaughterings. A

51. **14**, p. 51.
52. The change in boundaries partially accounts for the considerable decrease in the number reported for Poland and Romania.
53. **32**, April 1946, p. 11.
54. **41**, *passim*, and **43**, p. 420.

55. **15**, March 1950, p. 8.
56. **26**, 1951, p. 632.
57. **26**, 1949, p. 709.
58. **24**, 1948, p. 95.

TABLE 283

CATTLE IN SELECTED COUNTRIES, 1928–29, 1938–39 AND 1950

(*Thousands*)

Country [a]	1928–29	1938–39	1950 [b]	Country [a]	1928–29	1938–39	1950 [b]
United States	57,878	65,249	80,277	Belgium	1,751	1,600	1,902
Canada	8,772	8,224	8,243	Netherlands	2,366	2,817	2,517
				Denmark	3,016	3,226	3,053
Mexico	10,083	17,588	14,500	Sweden	2,898	2,975	2,648
Guatemala	298	605	800	Norway	1,221	1,455	1,237
El Salvador	284	451	765 [c]	Finland	1,917	1,954	1,844
Honduras	517	⋯	950	Germany	18,481	19,911	10,883 [e]
Nicaragua	800	⋯	1,275	Poland	9,057	10,553	6,837
Costa Rica	399	⋯	527	Czechoslovakia	4,458	4,938	4,140
Cuba	4,421	4,900	4,550	Switzerland	1,587	1,711	1,530
Dominican Republic	900	818	887	Austria	2,313	2,620	2,203
Venezuela	2,750	4,300	⋯	Hungary	1,812	2,372	2,050
Colombia	7,343	9,018	14,500	Portugal	⋯	905 [f]	1,000 [c]
Ecuador	1,280	1,420	1,600 [d]	Spain	3,660	3,738	3,300 [c]
Brazil	37,392	40,744	46,400	Italy	7,089	7,590	8,331
Peru	1,843	⋯	2,883	Yugoslavia	3,654	4,332	5,236
Bolivia	1,855	1,849	3,849	Romania	4,436	3,494	3,048 [g]
Paraguay	2,973	3,219	3,865	Bulgaria	1,498	1,512	1,711 [g]
Chile	2,388	2,356	2,331	Greece	910	974	675
Uruguay	7,128	8,297	8,600	USSR	70,543	63,200	56,000
Argentina	32,212	33,207	42,000				
United Kingdom	7,978	8,902	10,036	China (22 provinces)	20,000	23,081	18,200 [c]
Ireland	4,125	4,057	4,322	South Korea	⋯	922	685 [d]
France	15,005	15,622	15,432	Japan	1,484	1,967	2,461

(*Continued on facing page*)

Table 283—continued

Country [a]	1928–29	1938–39	1950 [b]
Turkey	4,366	9,311	10,204
Iraq	...	250	1,245
Iran	...	2,920	3,500
Pakistan	} 154,547	24,444	24,296 [e]
India	}	137,929	133,841
Burma	4,256	5,194	4,488 [c]
Thailand	...	5,858	5,000
Indochina	...	2,050	1,486
Indonesia	4,407	4,577	3,618
Philippines	1,096	1,349	735
French Morocco [h]	...	1,871	1,951
Algeria [h]	887	886	766
Egypt	792	1,217	...
Anglo-Egyptian Sudan	...	2,700	3,500
Ethiopia	...	18,000	18,000
French Equatorial Africa	...	1,000	2,992
Belgian Congo	...	384	637
Nigeria [h]	...	2,847	5,274
Kenya	3,482	5,273	4,785 [c]
Tanganyika	4,813	5,125	6,380 [d]
Madagascar [h]	6,901	5,266	5,742
Angola	1,074	977	1,116
Northern Rhodesia	...	634	878
Southern Rhodesia	2,326	2,326	3,004
South-West Africa	655	1,053	1,500
Bechuanaland	625	671	983 [d]
Union of South Africa	10,473	11,852	12,242 [d]
Australia	11,301	12,862	14,640
New Zealand	3,274	4,528	4,949

Sources: **11**, p. 433; **1**, 1931–32, pp. 74–76; **8**, October 1951, pp. 10–11, and March 1952, pp. 11–12; **19**, FLM 2–51, pp. 12–13.

a. December–January estimates for 1950 (and often for prewar years) are given for the United States, Canada, Mexico, Cuba, Colombia, Brazil, Bolivia, Paraguay, France, Belgium, Denmark, Germany, Czechoslovakia, Austria, Portugal, Italy, Yugoslavia, Romania, Bulgaria, Greece, the USSR, South Korea, Japan, Turkey, Pakistan, India, Burma, Thailand, Indochina, Indonesia, the Philippines, French Morocco, French Equatorial Africa, Kenya, Tanganyika, Madagascar, Northern and Southern Rhodesia, and New Zealand; March–April, for Switzerland, Hungary and Australia; May–August, for Guatemala, El Salvador, Honduras, Dominican Republic, Chile, Uruguay, Argentina, the United Kingdom, Ireland, the Netherlands, Sweden, Norway, Poland, China, the Union of South Africa. Estimates for October–December 1949 are reported under 1950.

b. Preliminary.

c. 1948.

d. 1949.

e. Western Germany; eastern Germany: 3.3 million.

f. 1934.

g. 1946–47.

h. Animals registered for taxation.

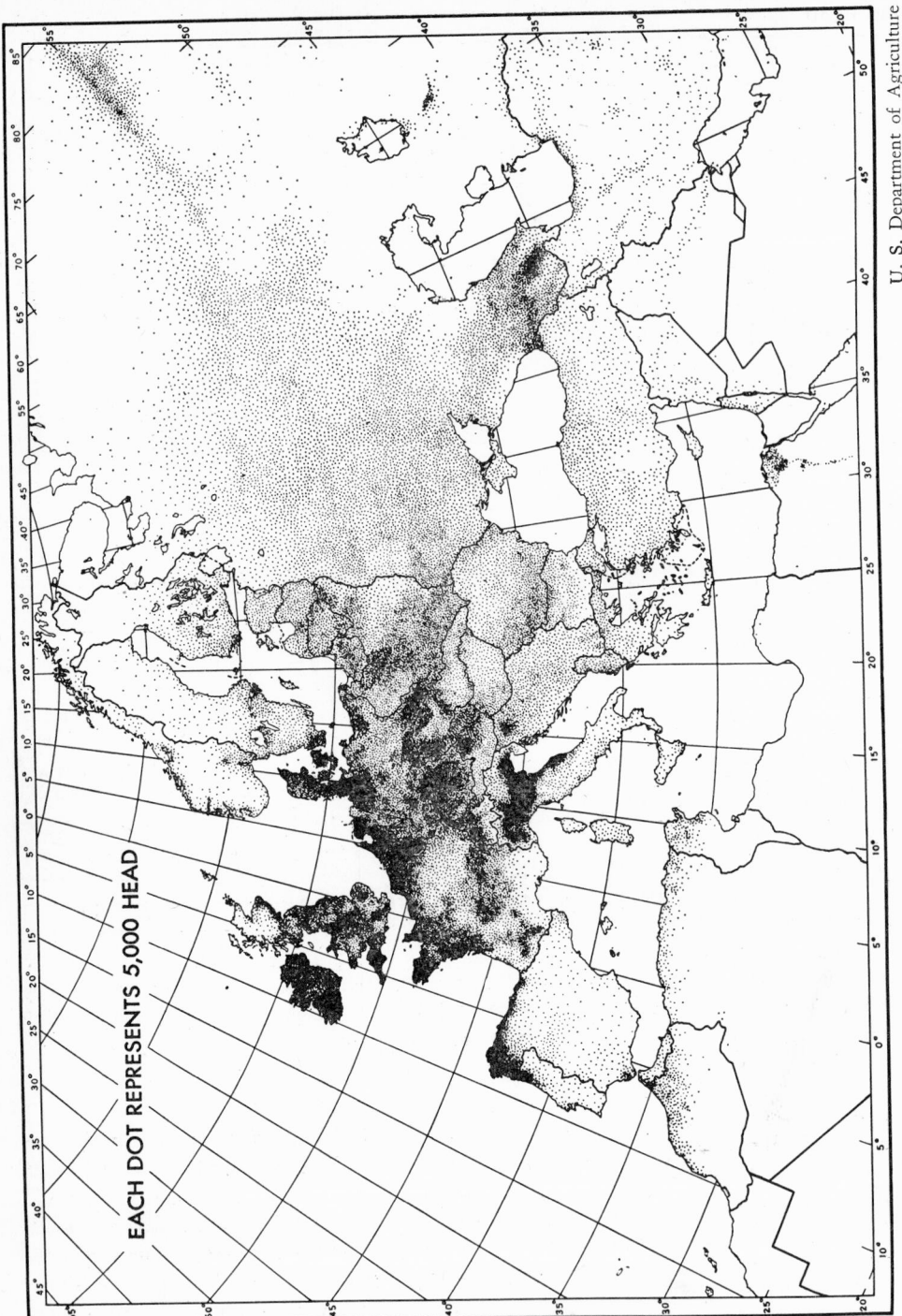

EACH DOT REPRESENTS 5,000 HEAD

U. S. Department of Agriculture

Figure 192. Cattle: Geographic Distribution in Europe and the Near East, Before World War II

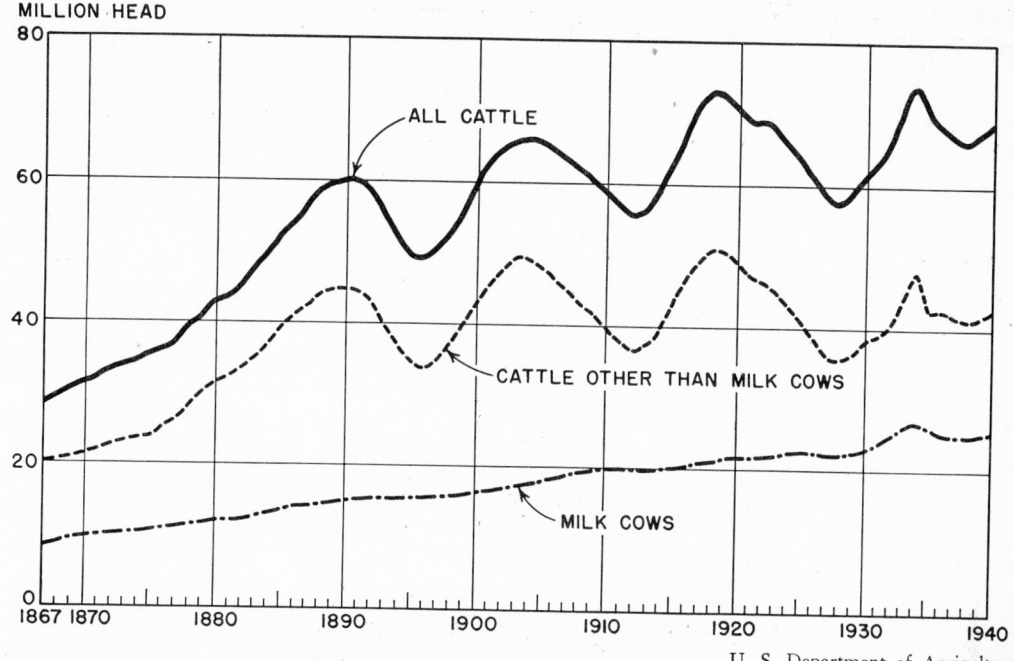

FIGURE 193. CATTLE CYCLE IN THE UNITED STATES, 1867–1940

severe drought affects the number of both types of sheep.

Australia, which raises sheep chiefly for wool, outranks all other countries in sheep husbandry. (See Table 284 and Figure 195.) Australian flocks increased spectacularly after the first imports of merino sheep from Spain, from 238,000 head in 1825 to 20 million in 1860 and more than 115 million in 1951.[59] About half of Australia's sheep are concentrated in New South Wales, with Queensland and Victoria in second and third place, respectively. In contrast to Australia, New Zealand concentrates on mutton sheep.

In the Western Hemisphere, Argentina and the United States are the principal sheep breeders. Argentina had slightly fewer sheep than the United States before the war, but now has a much larger number.

The United States

The flocks of the United States declined consistently after the peak year 1942 (56.2 million head) and totaled only 30.7 million head in 1950. More than half of the sheep in the United States are in western and southwestern states, with Texas in the lead. (See Figure 196.)

During the latter part of the nineteenth century, the United States raised sheep in arid areas primarily for wool, in humid areas for meat, and in semiarid places for both purposes. Today meat is the chief purpose of sheep breeding, and this fact has reduced the age at which sheep are sent to market. While three fourths of the marketed sheep previously were from four to eight years old, in the 1920's about 80 per cent were sold before reaching the age of one year. The proportion of lambs rose to nearly 94 per cent during 1939–41, declined during the war and was 89.7 per cent in 1949.[60]

Selected Countries

The USSR led all other countries in number of sheep in 1928, but its flocks decreased by 76 million, or about 57 per cent, between 1928 and 1938, and by 27 million during World War II, according to official estimates.[61] The target for 1950 set by the Five-Year Plan was 121 million head in the postwar territory,[62] but the number in 1950 was estimated at 78 million, little more than half that in 1928. Sheep breeding is particularly important in central Asia, Kazakhstan and

59. **44**, p. 8; **8**, December 1951, p. 10.

60. **47**, p. 30; **16**, 1950, p. 393.
61. **32**, April 1946, p. 13.
62. **41**, *passim*.

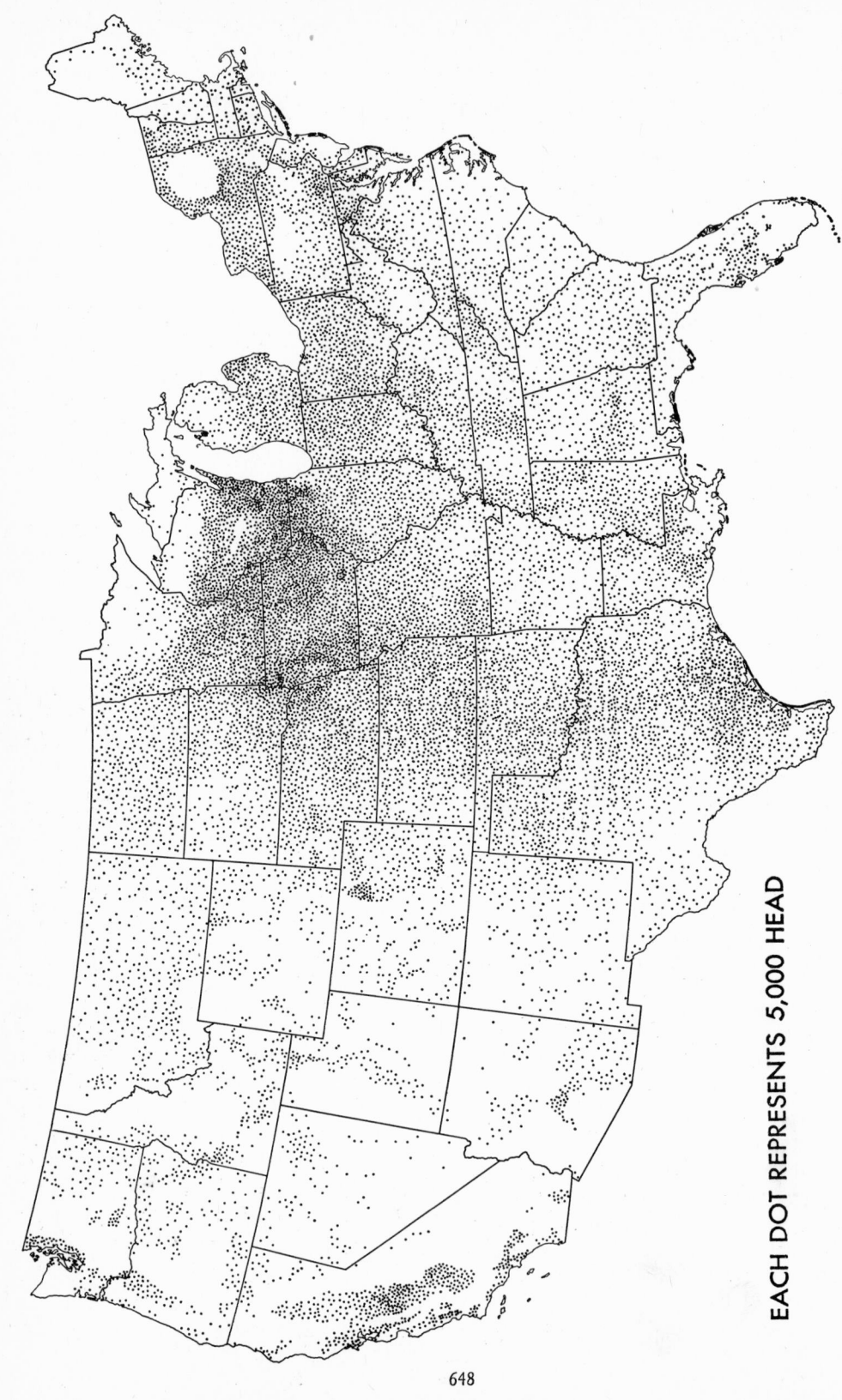

EACH DOT REPRESENTS 5,000 HEAD

U. S. Bureau of the Census

FIGURE 194. CATTLE: GEOGRAPHIC DISTRIBUTION IN THE UNITED STATES, JANUARY 1, 1945

TABLE 284

SHEEP IN SELECTED COUNTRIES, 1928, 1938 AND 1950

(Thousands)

Country [a]	1928	1938	1950 [b]	Country [a]	1928	1938	1950 [b]
United States	40,689	51,595	30,743	Bulgaria	8,740	9,413	8,800 [d]
Canada	3,416	3,415	1,259	Albania	...	1,576	1,700 [g]
Mexico	3,674	6,203	5,100	Greece	6,920	8,139	6,656
Guatemala	241	378	610	USSR	133,265	57,300	78,000
Colombia	810	883	1,200	China	15,000	12,411 [h]	10,450 [h,d]
Ecuador	700	735	1,800 [c]	Japan	19	114	364
Brazil	10,709	14,167	13,390 [e]	Turkey	11,176	17,752	23,073
Peru	11,209	14,900	19,000	Syria	2,149	3,100	2,750
Bolivia	5,552	2,608	4,195 [d]	Iraq	...	5,525 [i]	7,489
Paraguay	195	146	202	Iran	14,000	14,011	13,572
Chile	6,263	5,749	6,000	Afghanistan	...	...	14,000 [d]
Uruguay	20,558	17,931	22,646	Pakistan	35,506 {	5,941	6,145 [d]
Argentina	44,413	45,917	47,000	India		41,505	35,846
United Kingdom	24,602	20,805	14,832	Indonesia	1,408	1,338 [i]	2,334
Ireland	3,263	3,197	2,385	French Morocco [i]	8,035	10,162	10,375
France	10,445	9,872	7,480	Algeria [i]	5,614	6,406	4,541
Netherlands	485	690	390	Tunisia [i]	2,173	2,687	2,390
Sweden	806	406	279	Egypt	1,180	1,897 [i]	1,875 [d]
Norway	1,654	1,744	1,812	Anglo-Egyptian Sudan	2,201	2,500	5,600
Finland	1,319	923	1,330	French West Africa	...	11,950	11,700
Germany	3,637	3,766	2,020 [e]	French Equatorial Africa [i]	...	788	890
Poland	2,492	1,940	1,617 [d]	Belgian Congo	348	333	300
Czechoslovakia	836	519	480	Nigeria	1,785	1,836	2,236
Austria	272	318	375	Kenya	2,297	...	3,290
Hungary	1,566	1,868	650 [c]	Southern Rhodesia	359	302	315
Portugal	3,721	3,224 [f]	4,000 [d]	South-West Africa	1,524	3,452	2,717
Spain	19,370	19,093 [f]	23,000	Union of South Africa	42,500	39,118	31,908 [e]
Italy	10,288	9,736	10,295	Australia	103,431	113,372	112,891
Yugoslavia	7,722	10,292	10,042	New Zealand	27,134	32,379	33,857
Romania	12,801	12,767	7,300 [d]				

Sources: **11**, p. 499; **1**, 1931–32, pp. 74–76; **8**, December 1951, pp. 9–10; **19**, FLM 3–51, pp. 8–9

a. December–January estimates for 1950 (and often for prewar years) are given for the United States, Canada, Mexico, Colombia, Brazil, Bolivia, Paraguay, the United Kingdom, Germany, Greece, the USSR, Turkey, Syria, Iraq, Pakistan, India, Indonesia, French Morocco, Tunisia, French Equatorial Africa and Southern Rhodesia; March–April, for Finland, Iran, Australia and New Zealand; May–August, for Guatemala, Chile, Uruguay, Argentina, the Netherlands, Hungary and China. Estimates for October–

December 1949 are reported under 1950.

b. Preliminary.
c. 1949.
d. 1948.
e. Western Germany; Soviet Zone: 0.9 million.
f. 1934.
g. 1946.
h. 22 provinces.
i. Animals registered for taxation.

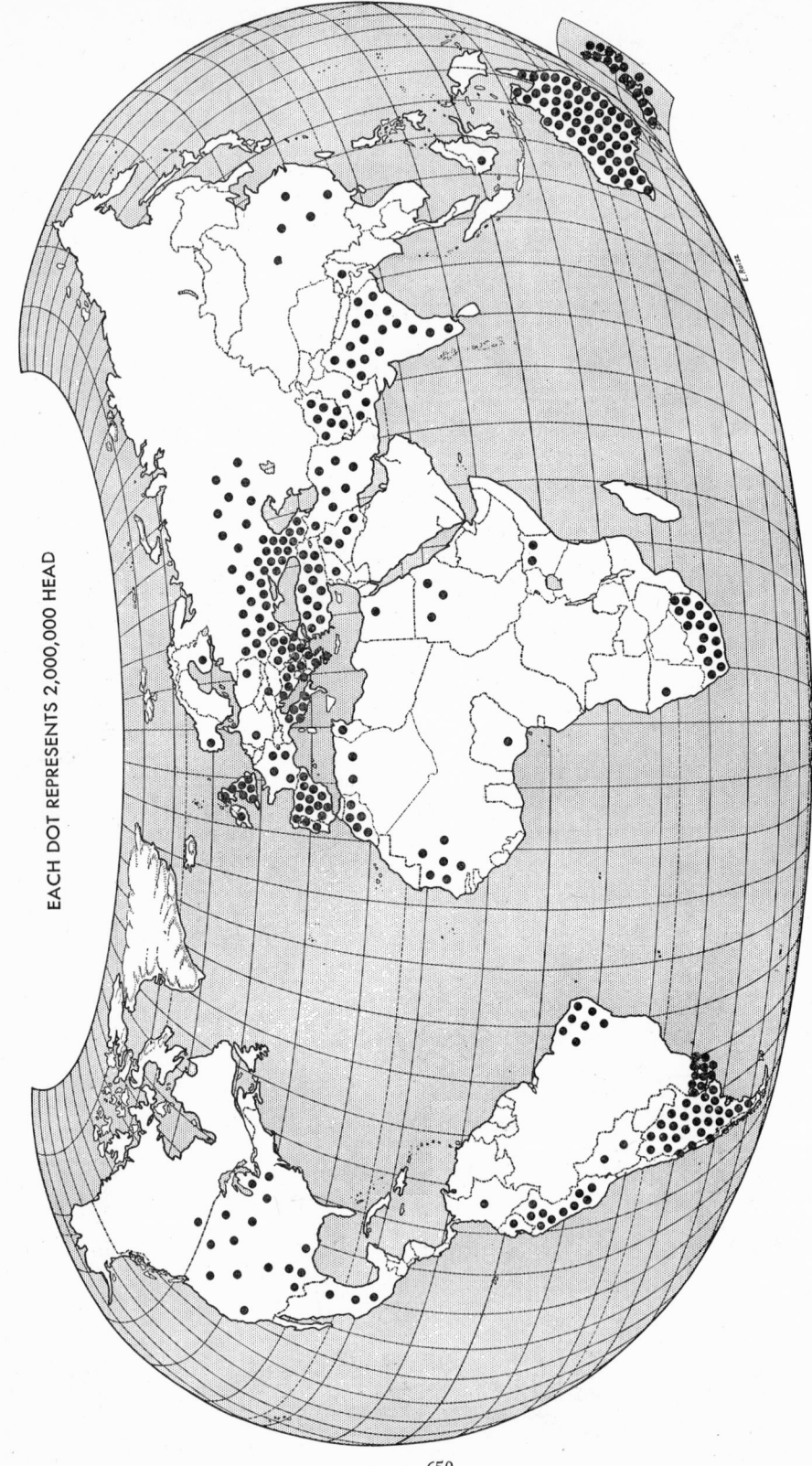

EACH DOT REPRESENTS 2,000,000 HEAD

FIGURE 195. SHEEP: GEOGRAPHIC DISTRIBUTION IN THE WORLD, 1950

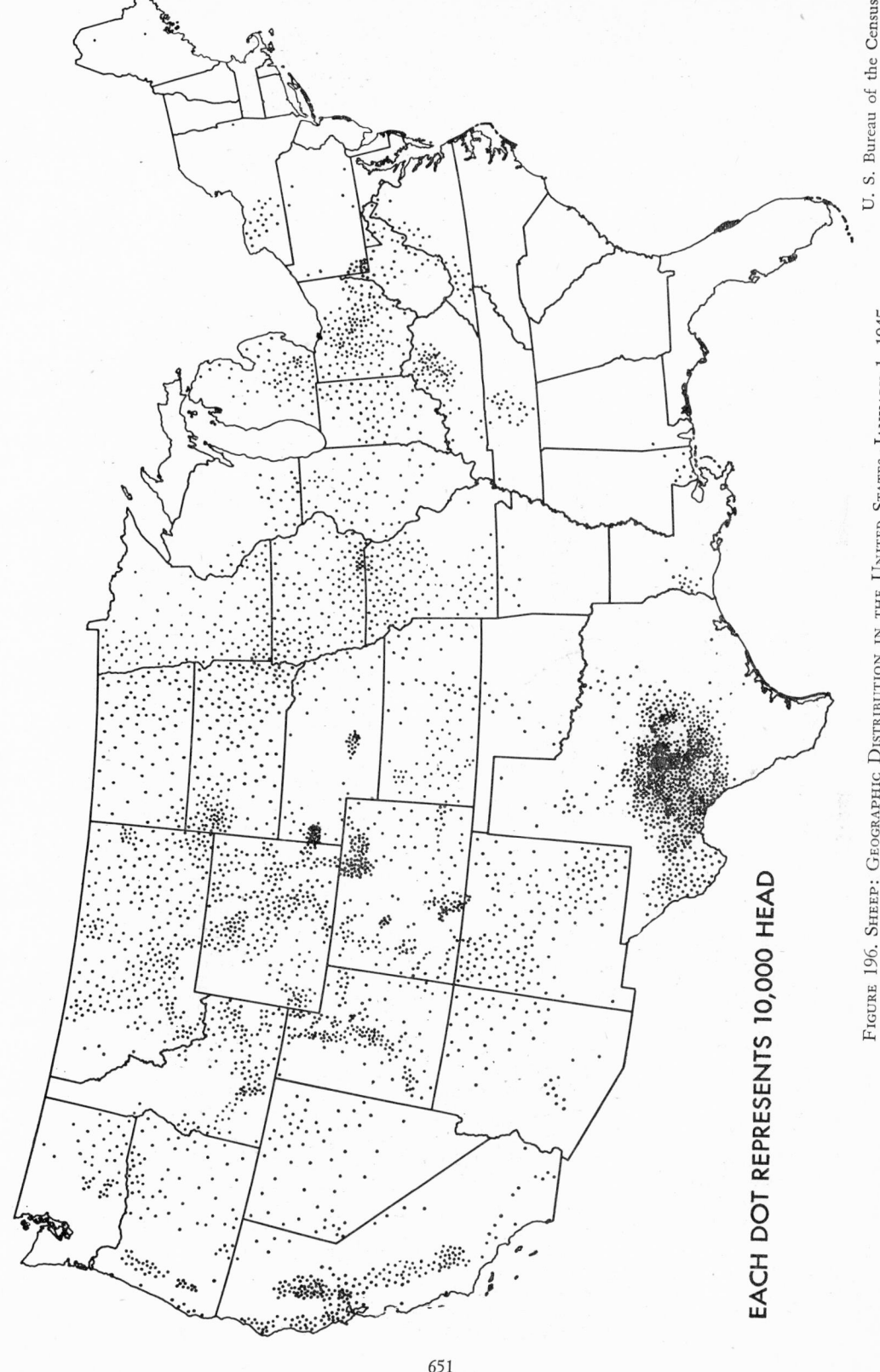

EACH DOT REPRESENTS 10,000 HEAD

FIGURE 196. SHEEP: GEOGRAPHIC DISTRIBUTION IN THE UNITED STATES, JANUARY 1, 1945

U. S. Bureau of the Census

the Caucasus. In central Asia and the Transcaucasus, sheep graze on mountain pastures; in Kazakhstan, they live on the scant vegetation of the arid steppes.

For a long time Great Britain was the greatest sheep-producing country in Europe, and some of the most famous sheep pastures of the world are in the low ranges of England's chalk hills.[63] With the growth of population and its concentration in urban areas, England began to develop breeds of mutton sheep, the first specialized breeds of this type in the world. These breeds are believed still to retain their pre-eminence.[64] Except in Scotland, where sheep can be kept on rough grazings, the number, however, has been generally declining (figures in millions):

1871–75 average		28.8
1881–85	"	25.3
1891–95	"	27.3
1901–05	"	25.6
1911–15	"	24.9
1921–25	"	21.2
1938, December		20.8
1950, December		14.8

Although the policy is to encourage production, the competition of dairy cattle keeps the flocks from regaining prewar size. A small increase was noted in 1950, as compared with 1948–49 (13.7 million).

France also reports a general downward trend: 29.5 million head in 1862, 20.6 million in 1902, 11 million in 1922, 9.9 million in 1938 and 7.5 million in 1950.[65]

Since the war Spain has had the largest flock in Europe — 23 million in 1950. The United Kingdom, Italy, Yugoslavia, Bulgaria and France are next in line. (See Table 284.)

The concentration of sheep in Mediterranean lands is due to their ability to subsist on scanty summer forage in the mountains. (See Figure 197.) Throughout this region, sheep and goats outnumber cattle, in some places by as much as 10 to 1.[66]

HOGS

Two distinct types of hogs are bred, the lard type and the bacon type. The former predominates in the United States, the latter in northwestern Europe.

The most important hog-raising countries are the United States, Brazil, China, the USSR and Germany. (See Table 285 and Figure 198.) Together, these countries account for more than 60 per cent of the world total.

The United States

Hog raising in the United States is largely concentrated in the Corn Belt, which is also the Hog Belt. Iowa alone accounts for about a fifth of all the hogs raised in the country. Illinois is second, with about a tenth. (See Figure 199.) The other important area is the Cotton Belt.

Annual fluctuations in the number of hogs on farms in the United States are controlled by the relation between market prices for hogs and corn. The farmer usually faces the alternatives of selling his corn as such or feeding it to his hogs. When corn prices rise, he markets the crop; when they slump, he raises more hogs. The price of one product affects the price of the other. When more corn, and less pork, is on the market hog prices go up and corn prices down. Then the farmers produce more hogs, and the relationship is reversed.[67] In January 1951 the number of hogs was 4.5 million above the preceding year. The increase was attributed chiefly to a favorable relationship between hog and corn prices and the strong demand for pork and pork products during 1950. Spring farrowings in 1951 were also up.[68]

Selected Countries

In China, where pork is a favorite item in the diet, hogs are raised throughout the country, even where there is little suitable feed and they must subsist on vegetation. Usually the better-off farmers keep sows, the poor or disabled farmers, boars, which provide income in the form of mating fees.[69]

In the USSR, the Ukraine accounts for nearly a third of the hogs. There, as in the Volga region and the North Caucasus, hogs are raised on grains and offal or, near large cities, on garbage. Hogs are also raised extensively in the nonchernozem area, and the central chernozem

---

63. **14,** p. 54.
64. **50,** p. 3.
65. **55,** p. 10.
66. **14,** p. 54.

67. **66,** p. 93.
68. In other corn-growing countries, the corn-hog price ratio plays a similar though lesser role. An increase in hogs in 1951 in Brazil was also largely due to the advantage in marketing hogs. (**19,** FLM 1-51, p. 2.)
69. **61,** pp. 123 and 133.

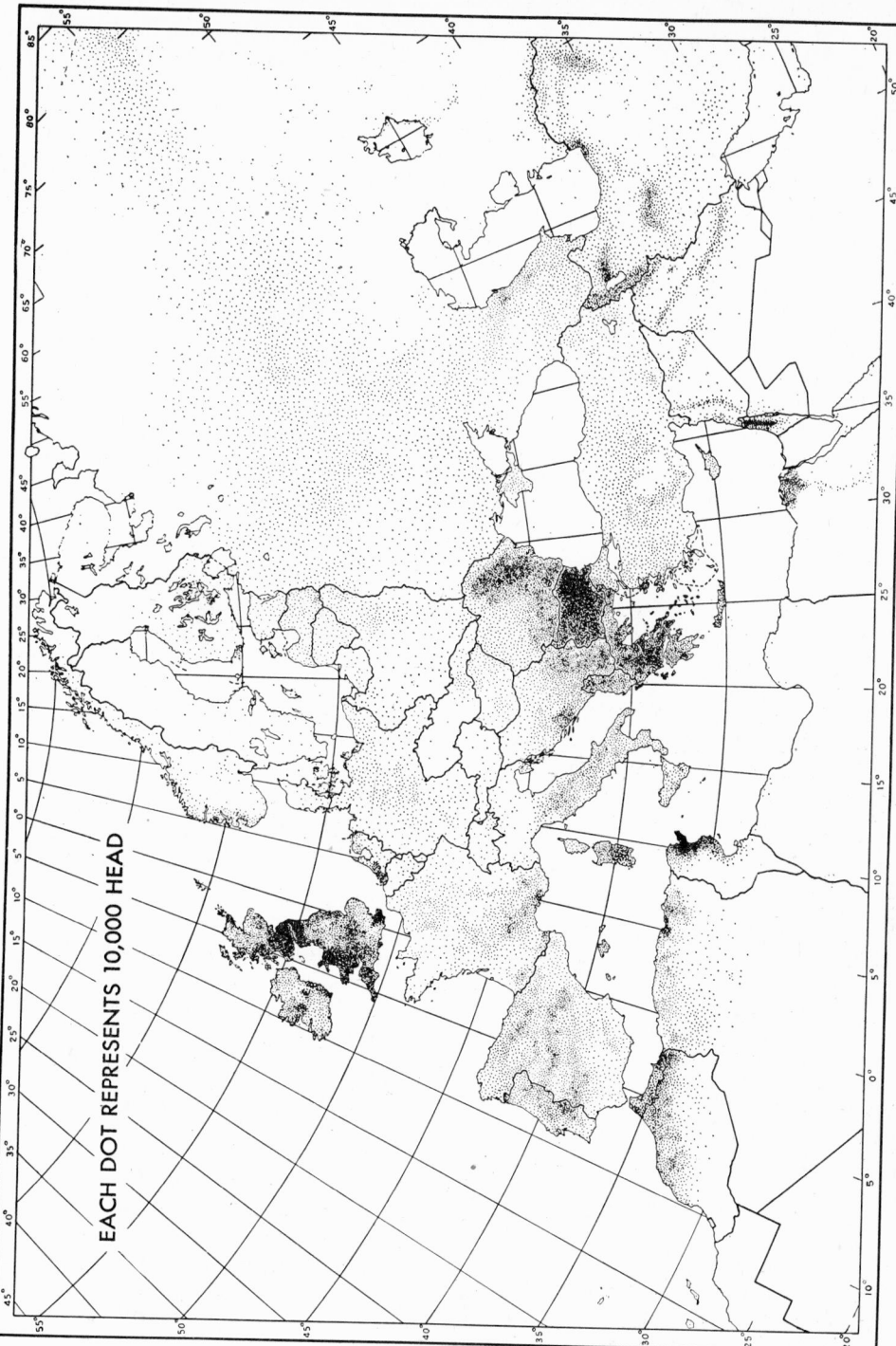

EACH DOT REPRESENTS 10,000 HEAD

U. S. Department of Agriculture

FIGURE 197. SHEEP: GEOGRAPHIC DISTRIBUTION IN EUROPE AND THE NEAR EAST, BEFORE WORLD WAR II

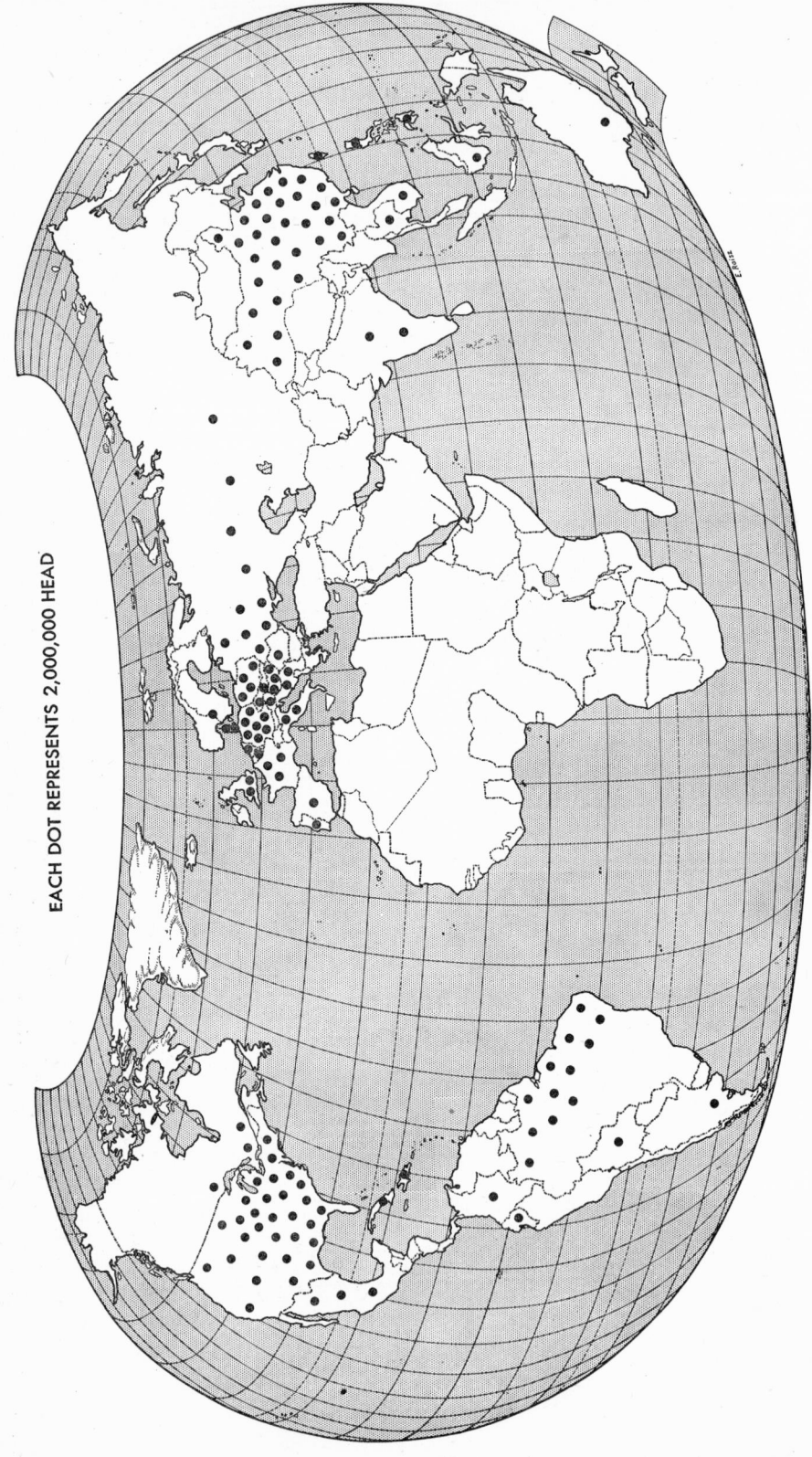

EACH DOT REPRESENTS 2,000,000 HEAD

Figure 198. Hogs: Geographic Distribution in the World, 1950

Table 285

Table 285

Hogs in Selected Countries, 1928, 1938 and 1950

(Thousands)

Country [a]	1928	1938	1950 [b]
United States	61,873	50,012	60,502
Canada	4,497	3,569	5,413
Mexico	3,698	4,965	5,600
Guatemala	70	155	415
El Salvador	355	248	348 [c]
Honduras	298	...	407
Nicaragua	400	...	664 [c]
Cuba	591	904	1,800
Haiti	200	335	...
Dominican Republic	1,100	783	1,140
Colombia	1,434	1,622 [d]	2,200
Ecuador	150	350	1,140 [e]
Brazil	22,147	23,543	24,500
Peru	689	...	960
Bolivia	336	523	1,200 [e]
Chile	331	572	600
Argentina	3,769	3,381	2,600
United Kingdom	3,396	4,383	3,140
Ireland	1,183	959	645
France	6,017	7,127	6,760
Belgium	1,139	993	1,329
Netherlands	2,018	1,538	1,795
Denmark	3,363	2,706	3,235
Sweden	1,369	1,371	1,268
Norway	283	362	422
Finland	435	531	470
Germany	20,194	18,003	
Western		12,280	9,698
Soviet Zone		5,707	4,310
Poland	4,829	7,525	7,659
Czechoslovakia	2,776	3,612	3,242 [e]
Switzerland	926	923	908
Austria	1,965	2,830	1,927
Hungary	2,662	3,110	6,500
Portugal	1,157	1,206	1,200 [e]
Spain	4,773	6,942	2,688 [e]
Italy	3,318	2,940	4,375 [e]
Yugoslavia	2,663	3,542	4,287
Romania	2,832	3,165	1,459 [e]
Bulgaria	1,002	902	825 [e]
Greece	419	430	530
USSR	25,989	30,600	19,000
China [f]	69,000	62,639	59,510 [e]
South Korea	...	828	545 [e]
Japan	764	1,140	800
Taiwan	1,718	1,849	1,500
India	...	2,704	3,653
Burma	...	530	402 [e]
Thailand	...	1,366	2,000
Indochina	...	4,535	1,900
Malaya	...	764	311
Indonesia	930	1,131	1,234
Philippines	2,381	3,348	4,673
Algeria	89	60	140
Belgian Congo	17	143	159
Madagascar	328	507	391
Angola	278	360	228 [e]
Southern Rhodesia	68	132	107
Union of South Africa	835	1,037	761
Australia	910	1,156	1,123
New Zealand	587	757	560

Sources: 1, 1931–32, pp. 74–76; 8, January 1952, pp. 10–11; 19, FLM 1–51, pp. 8–9.

a. December–January estimates for 1950 (and often for prewar years) are given for the United States, Canada, Mexico, Cuba, Colombia, Brazil, Belgium, the Netherlands, Denmark, Germany, Portugal, Yugoslavia, Bulgaria, Greece, the USSR, South Korea, Japan, India, Burma, Indochina, Indonesia, the Philippines, the Belgian Congo, Madagascar and Southern Rhodesia; March–April, for Finland, Switzerland, Romania and Australia; May–August, Guatemala, El Salvador, Honduras, Chile, Argentina, the United Kingdom, Ireland, Sweden, Poland, Italy, Burma, and the Union of South Africa. Estimates for October–December 1949 are reported under 1950.

b. Preliminary.
c. 1948.
d. 1934.
e. 1949.
f. 22 provinces.

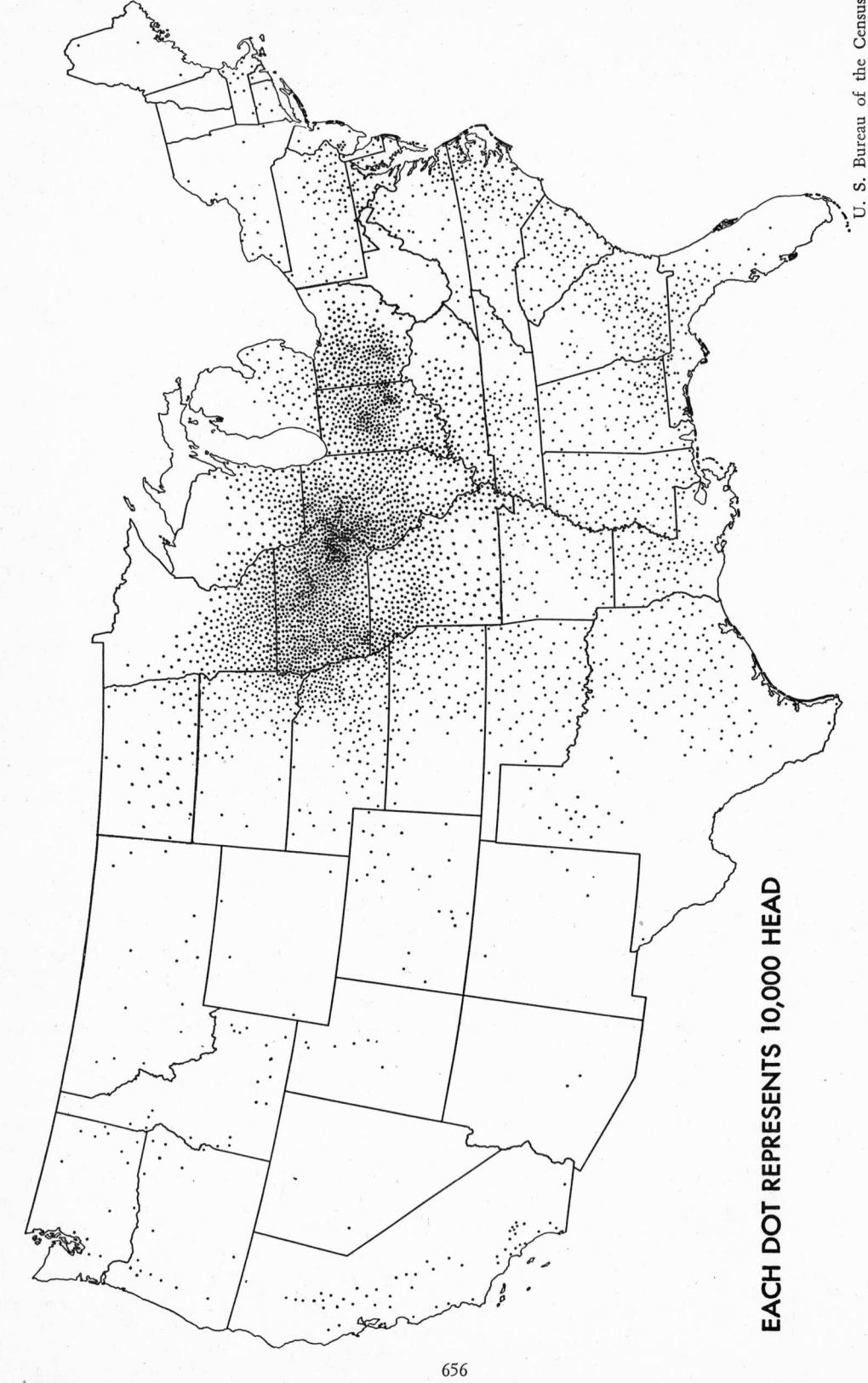

EACH DOT REPRESENTS 10,000 HEAD

FIGURE 199. HOGS: GEOGRAPHIC DISTRIBUTION IN THE UNITED STATES, JANUARY 1, 1945

region where potatoes are the prevailing feed.[70] The number of hogs in the USSR decreased by 20 million, or more than 60 per cent, during World War II, and the loss could not be made good by transfer from occupied territories, since hogs cannot be driven on the hoof over long distances. Although the Five-Year Plan aimed at restoring the herds to the 1938 number (31 million) by 1950, the estimate for that year was only 19 million.

Brazil has more hogs than any other country in Latin America but the number increased slowly between 1928 and 1950. The industry is not commercial, as in Argentina, and is mostly in the hands of small farmers, each with a few animals.[71] As in the United States, hogs are raised chiefly in the Corn Belt — Rio Grande do Sul and neighboring states.

Turkey reports no hogs, and few are raised in other Moslem regions, such as North Africa, Asia Minor and Pakistan.

The potato-growing area, particularly Germany, is the center of hog raising in Europe, but many hogs are also raised in northwestern countries, where skimmed milk, potatoes and barley are available for feed. (See Figure 200.) During World War II, the number slumped considerably, because of the diversion of potatoes to human consumption. Official statistics, reporting postwar numbers far below the 1938 level, are believed to have underestimated the actual hog count. Ample feed and forage, especially the large potato crop, and good prices for pork stimulated hog-raising production in 1950, and the estimate for 1951 was at nearly the prewar level.[72]

The Low Countries and, particularly, Denmark, which had lost from one to two thirds of their hogs during the war, have stepped up production in recent years, taking full advantage of good supplies of fodder. The numbers of hogs in 1950 and 1951 were well above the prewar level. Rising prices of imported and domestic feed may, however, dim the prospects of further increases.

The Danubian countries suffered great losses in hogs during the war, more because of requisitioning than because of shortage of feed. Production is up in Yugoslavia, but Bulgaria and Romania have not yet reached the prewar level.

Greece has effected a gradual postwar increase, through the importation of foreign breeds and voluntary limitations on the slaughter of breeding sows.

India, Indonesia, Thailand and the Philippines have more hogs than before the war, but most other Asiatic countries have fewer. The number in Australia continues to decline from the high wartime level, but has remained stationary in New Zealand during the postwar period.

DENSITY OF LIVESTOCK

Domesticated animals, like human beings, are unevenly distributed over the surface of the earth, and the relation between the human and animal population differs greatly in different parts of the world. Where land is abundant and people are few, many animals can be raised but the density of the animal population is low since many acres, on the average, are devoted to each animal. Where land is scarce and people are crowded, animals are crowded too.

Generally, the more inhabitants in a given area, the more livestock per 1,000 acres but the fewer per 1,000 inhabitants. With a very low density of population, Australia and New Zealand have a larger number of cattle and sheep per 1,000 inhabitants than any other country in the world; in fact, together they have twice as many cattle and about fifteen times as many sheep as people.

In Middle and South America, cattle and sheep are almost as numerous as human beings, while densely populated Europe and Asia have fewer livestock per 1,000 inhabitants than the world average. (See Table 286.)

Hogs, less attached to the soil than either cattle or sheep, are distributed more evenly among the human race except in those regions of Asia and Africa from which they are barred by custom and religion.

The Food and Agriculture Organization (FAO) of the United Nations has calculated the density of the world's livestock in terms of uniform units. According to this estimate, the number of livestock units in the world as a whole dropped from 794 million in the prewar years to 778 million in 1949. Europe and Asia suffered the largest losses, 20 and 17 million units, respectively, while South America increased its livestock units by 16 million, Africa by 5 million, and Oceania by 1 million. (See Table 287.)

There are now fewer animals per person than

---

70. **43**, p. 431.
71. **30**, p. 56.
72. **19**, FLM 1-51, pp. 2 and 5.

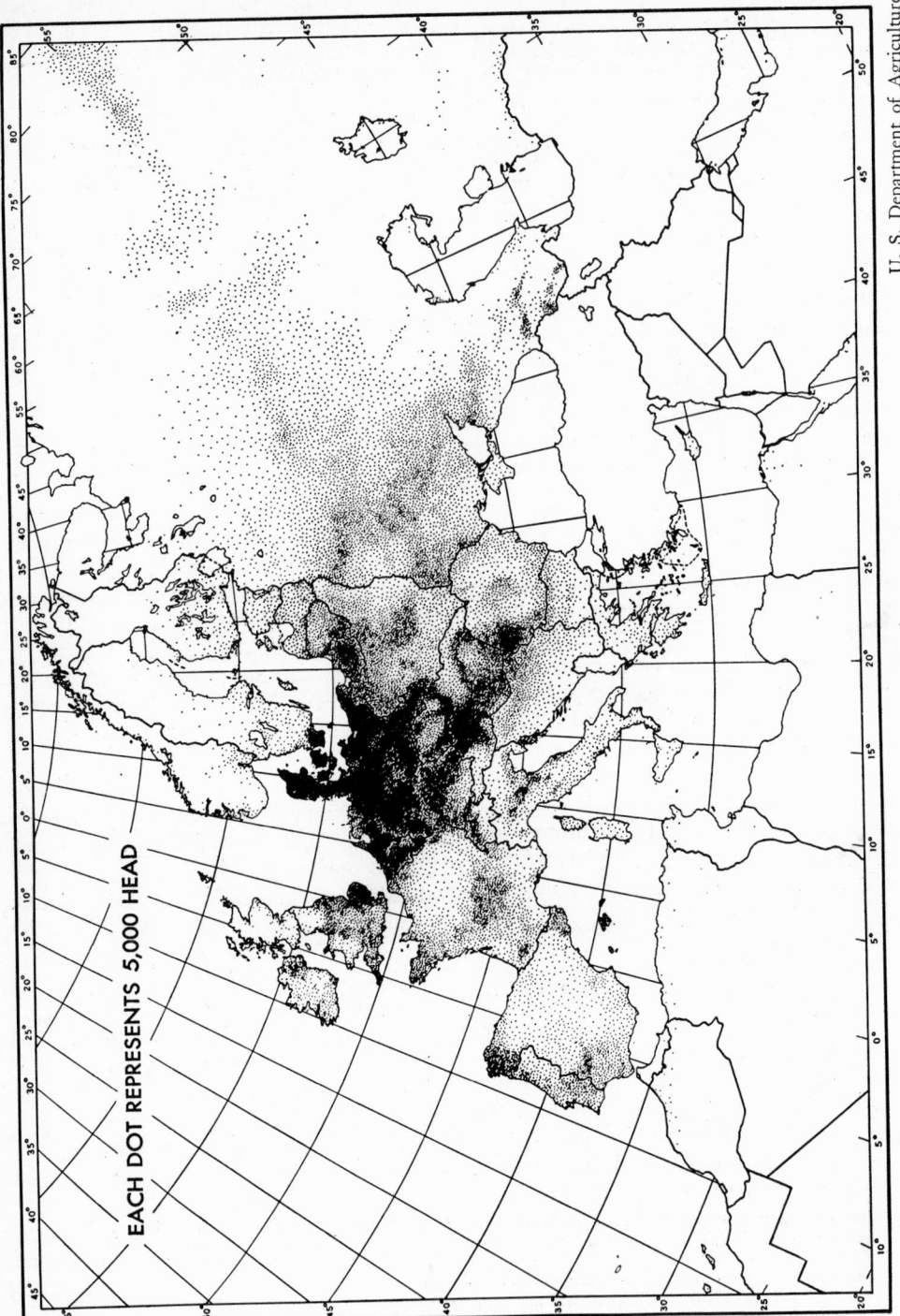

EACH DOT REPRESENTS 5,000 HEAD

U. S. Department of Agriculture

FIGURE 200. HOGS: GEOGRAPHIC DISTRIBUTION IN EUROPE AND THE NEAR EAST, BEFORE WORLD WAR II

TABLE 286

LIVESTOCK DENSITY IN EACH CONTINENT, 1938

Continent	Human Population Per Square Kilometer [a]	Animals Per 1,000 Acres of Land Surface				Animals Per 1,000 Inhabitants			
		Work-stock	Cattle	Sheep	Hogs	Work-stock	Cattle	Sheep	Hogs
World	16.3	6.5	21	23	8.9	102	316	342	137
North America [b]	8.1	4.0	17	13	12	127	530	403	375
Middle and South America	5.6	6.1	23	18	7	271	993	813	309
Europe	73.8	22	83	100	62	72	277	337	208
USSR	8.1	3.6	12	18	5.7	110	371	543	180
Asia	42.6	16	33	16	13	96	191	96	74
Africa	5.3	2	8.5	13	0.4	59	407	608	20
Oceania	1.2	0.8	8.5	69	0.8	197	1,969	13,741	191

Source: **11**, *passim.*   b. Includes Mexico and Cuba.

a. Conversion factors: one square kilometer = 100 hectares = 247.1 acres.

TABLE 287

LIVESTOCK DENSITY IN EACH CONTINENT, PREWAR AVERAGE AND 1948–49

(*Livestock Units* [a])

Continent	Total Units, in Millions		Units Per 1,000 Acres of Agricultural Land, 1948 [b]	Units Per 1,000 Inhabitants	
	Prewar	1949		Prewar	1949
World [c]	794	778	105	410	360
North and Middle America	123	122	77	690	570
South America	125	141	134	1,490	1,320
Europe	133	113	178	360	290
Asia	306	289	194	270	230
Africa	77	82	49	460	420
Oceania	30	31	32	2,790	2,490

Source: **8**, June 1950, p. 4.

a. The conversion factor used to express livestock in uniform units is: horses, mules and buffaloes, 1; cattle, 0.8; hogs, 0.2; and sheep, 0.1. The conversion factor assumes constant world-wide weight relationships among the several species.

b. Arable land and permanent meadows and pastures.

c. Excludes the USSR, for which data are not available.

TABLE 288

LIVESTOCK DENSITY IN SELECTED COUNTRIES, 1938

Country	Human Population Per Square Kilometer [a]	Livestock Per 1,000 Inhabitants			Country	Human Population Per Square Kilometer [a]	Livestock Per 1,000 Inhabitants		
		Cattle	Sheep	Hogs			Cattle	Sheep	Hogs
United States	16.6	513	413	377	Switzerland	101.6	408	41	220
Canada	1.2	722	305	318	Hungary	97.5	239	179	343
Mexico	9.9	831	294	260	Spain	50.4	147	854	272
Colombia	7.7	937	98	182	Italy	141.8	174	215	67
Brazil	5.2	949	321	534	Romania	67.3	210	643	159
Paraguay	2.1	3,371	152	36	Greece	54.7	136	1,145	60
Uruguay	11.4	3,908	8,446	163	USSR	7.9	371	543	180
Argentina	4.6	2,563	3,387	306	China	43.0	53	49	148
United Kingdom	195.1	187	562	92	Japan	188.8	26	2	16
Ireland	42.6	1,381	1,089	327	Turkey	22.5	417	1,033	—
France	76.2	372	235	170	India	89.9	439	112	—
Belgium	274.9	202	24	115	Indonesia (Java and Madoera)	355.6	106	20	16
Netherlands	249.1	317	75	176	Kenya	5.8	1,485	1,039	4
Denmark	88.0	834	50	716	Rhodesia	3.6	1,058	121	59
Sweden	14.1	481	52	217	Union of South Africa	8.2	1,160	3,920	95
Finland	9.9	510	258	139	Australia	0.9	1,856	16,360	159
Germany	146.2	290	70	342	New Zealand	6.0	2,785	20,112	422
Poland	89.0	305	99	218					
Czechoslovakia	108.6	324	13	237					

a. Conversion factors: one square kilometer = 100 hectares = 247.1 acres.

Source: 11, passim. For some countries the year closest to 1938 has been used.

660

TABLE 289

ANIMAL PRODUCTS: VALUE OF OUTPUT IN EACH CONTINENT, 1934–38 ANNUAL AVERAGE

Continent	*Value, in Millions of Dollars* [a]				*Percentage Distribution*			
	Total	*Meat*	*Milk*	*Other Products* [b]	*Total*	*Meat*	*Milk*	*Other Products* [b]
World	$16,028	$8,201	$6,912	$914	100.0	100.0	100.0	100.0
North America [c]	3,258	1,644	1,515	98	20.3	20.0	21.9	10.7
Middle and South America	1,803	1,314	366	123	11.3	16.0	5.3	13.5
Europe	5,679	2,482	3,083	113	35.4	30.3	44.6	12.4
USSR	1,265	559	667	39	7.9	6.8	9.6	4.3
Asia	2,736	1,654	875	207	17.1	20.2	12.7	22.6
Africa	533	317	144	73	3.3	3.9	2.1	8.0
Oceania	754	232	261	261	4.7	2.8	3.8	28.5

Source: Adapted from **9**, p. 22.

a. The value is given in current dollars, instead of gold dollars used by the International Institute of Agriculture.

b. Includes wool and silk.
c. Includes Mexico and Cuba.

before World War II, largely because the world's animal husbandry has not kept pace with the increase in population. The number of cattle increased only 4 per cent, from 694 million in prewar years to 725 million in 1950, while the number of draft animals declined 13 per cent.[73]

Density of livestock per 1,000 inhabitants varies from country to country. Uruguay, Paraguay and New Zealand have the largest number of cattle in relation to human population; New Zealand, Australia and Uruguay, the largest number of sheep. Among European countries, pastoral Ireland has the largest number of cattle per 1,000 inhabitants. Denmark is next in line. (See Table 288.)

ANIMAL PRODUCTS

In addition to meat, fats, dairy products, poultry and eggs, animal husbandry supplies raw materials for industry — hides and skins, wool, hair, feathers, bristles, and so on. Beekeeping for honey (apiculture) was an important branch of agriculture in some countries in ancient times, but is insignificant in the modern economy.

VALUE OF ANIMAL PRODUCTS

The International Institute of Agriculture has estimated that animal products before World War II accounted for nearly half the total value

73. **8**, June 1950, p. 4.

of the world's agricultural output. On the basis of the available data, the Institute valued animal products at $16.0 billion a year and total agricultural output at $34.6 billion, on the average, during 1934–38.[74] This estimate rests largely, however, on extrapolations of fragmentary statistics and includes items for which only conjectural guesses could be made. It is subject to serious reservations therefore, but is, nevertheless, worth attention.

Europe ranked first before World War II in value of output of meat and milk, Oceania in that of wool. North America was second in output of milk; Asia, in industrial raw materials of animal origin. The value of the meat output of these two continents was approximately the same. (See Table 289 and Figure 201.)

The relative importance of the three groups of animal products during 1934–38 varied from continent to continent. In North America, as in the world as a whole, meat constituted about half the total value of livestock production; in Middle and South America, almost three fourths; in Asia and Africa, about 60 per cent;

74. The figure for animal products includes meat (beef and veal, mutton and goat meat, and pork), milk, wool and silk. It excludes, for lack of data, poultry and poultry products, hides, skins and other animal products. The figure for total agricultural output excludes also, for the same reason, vegetables, fruits, millet, sorghum and other locally raised grains. (See Chapters 14 and 16.)

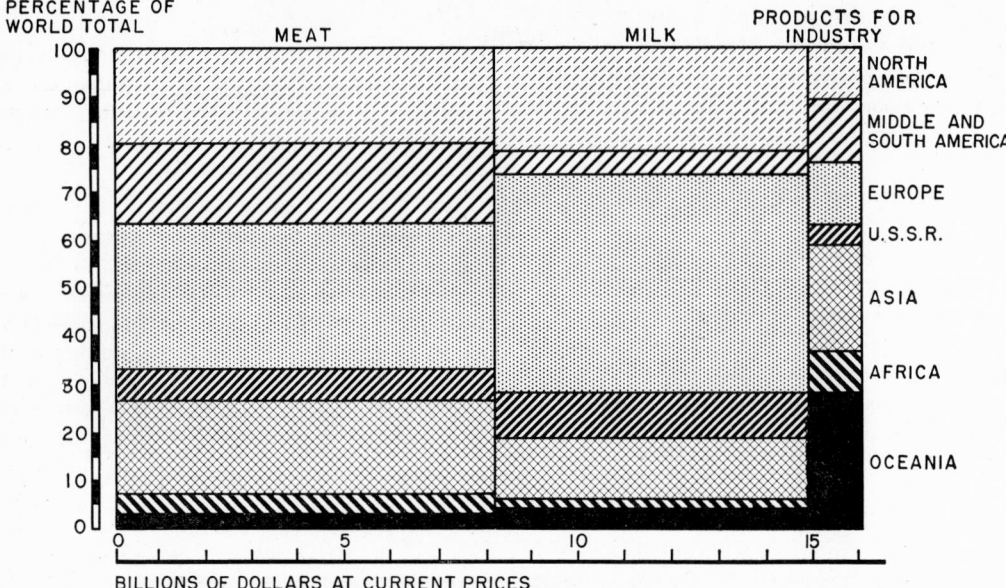

FIGURE 201. ANIMAL PRODUCTS: VALUE OF OUTPUT IN EACH CONTINENT, 1934–38 ANNUAL AVERAGE

in Europe and the USSR, less than 45 per cent; in Oceania, less than a third. The following figures show the percentage distribution of the value of animal products in 1934–38:

	Meat	Milk	Other Products
World	51.2	43.1	5.7
North America [a]	50.5	46.5	3.0
Middle and South America	72.9	20.3	6.8
Europe	43.7	54.3	2.0
USSR	44.2	52.7	3.1
Asia	60.5	32.0	7.5
Africa	59.4	27.0	13.6
Oceania	30.8	34.6	34.6

a. Includes Mexico and Cuba.

While the prewar value of animal products in the world as a whole was less than that of crops, in some areas it was much higher. Thus, in 1928 and also in 1938, 70 per cent of the value of the total agricultural output in the United Kingdom was attributable to animal husbandry. The percentages in 1928 for Ireland, the Union of South Africa, Australia and New Zealand were 80, 60, 65–70, and 85–90, respectively.[75] In the British Empire (the United Kingdom and the Dominions), about two thirds of the value of the total farm output came from animal hus-

bandry,[76] and in Denmark as much as 90 per cent of gross agricultural income was derived from animal products.[77] In the United States cash receipts from livestock and animal products in 1949 accounted for about 55 per cent of all cash receipts of farmers, including government payments — $15.4 billion out of $28.3 billion.[78] In addition, the value of the produce that the farm families themselves consumed amounted to $1.7 billion for livestock products, as against $0.8 billion for crops.

MEAT

Half the meat produced in the world is beef and veal; four tenths is pork; somewhat less than a tenth is mutton; goat and horse meat together account for one hundredth. Between 1934–38 and 1950, there was a slight shift to beef and veal at the expense of the two other major varieties of meat (figures in per cent): [79]

	1934–38 Average	1950
Beef and veal	48.6	50.7
Pork	41.3	39.9
Mutton and lamb	9.1	8.3
Goat and horse meat	1.0	1.1

75. **48**, p. 218.

76. **52**, p. vii.
77. **33**, p. 186.
78. **16**, 1950, pp. 637-39.
79. **19**, FLM 4-51, p. 11.

Pork ranks first in output in Europe, but in Africa and Oceania is exceeded by both beef and mutton. In North America, production of beef and of pork are equal, while in South America beef output far exceeds that of other kinds of meat.

In countries that breed fine stock the quality of meat has risen in recent decades. Complying with the tastes of consumers, who began to demand smaller cuts and joints and leaner meat, and in line with the faster finishing of the animals, cattle raisers produce "baby beef" from animals aged 12–18 months, "ultra baby beef" from those aged 8–10 months, and "hothouse lamb." These luxuries are produced in only a few countries where modern farms can avail themselves of first-class stock, highly skilled labor and the best feed, and where consumers can afford to pay fancy prices. In countries with a developed dairy industry, cows discarded as too old or unproductive are an important source of meat. In the United States a third of the combined beef and veal supply, and in the United Kingdom four tenths of the beef supply, comes from dairy animals.[80] Most countries, however, derive meat largely as a residual product from cattle of nondescript breed.

A steer raised on a modern farm is much more effective as a source of meat than one raised in a country with primitive husbandry. It matures more rapidly and thus is fed for a shorter time. Since the capacity of an animal to convert feed into meat declines with age, a young animal gains weight more rapidly than an older one and has less inedible fat and waste.[81] While about four years were once required for a bullock to mature, it now takes only about two and a half years.[82]

Within a country, the live weight of slaughtered animals may vary greatly from area to area, depending on the composition and quality of feed, feeding practices and other conditions. For example, the average live weight of slaughtered cattle in the United States in 1949 ranged from 632 pounds in Mississippi to 1,040 pounds in Nevada; that of calves, from 97 pounds in New England to 417 in Texas.[83]

Output

The output of meat increased steadily during the nineteenth century, in line with urbanization and the rise in the standard of living, but the increase has been uneven in the past two decades, modified by depression and war.

International statistics on output of meat are neither complete nor strictly comparable.[84] The computation of continental and world totals requires so many conjectures that the FAO has not attempted such estimates at all, and the United States Department of Agriculture has limited its estimate to a few broad regions comprising 41 countries for which comparatively reliable statistics are available. On the other hand, the International Institute of Agriculture, the forerunner of the FAO, ventured an estimate of world meat output in 1934–38.

According to the Institute's estimate, Europe accounted for a considerably larger proportion of the world's prewar output of meat than any other continent. (See Table 290 and Figure 202.) While its output of beef was not much greater than Asia's it produced twice as much pork. Pork production is an adjunct to the dairy industry in northwestern Europe, since the skimmed milk left after butter is churned is fed to hogs. In central Europe, pork production is associated with potato growing. Nearly all farms keep hogs in southeastern Europe, feeding them waste and unmarketable crops. Europe accounted for more than 28 per cent of the world's meat, while North America and Asia each produced about a fifth, the USSR less than 7 per cent, and Africa and Oceania about 4 and 3 per cent respectively.

In view of the state of international statistics on meat production, these ratios do not pretend to be exact, but they convey a generally correct idea of the distribution of the world's meat output by continent and kind of meat in prewar years.

The United States Department of Agriculture's estimate of meat output in regions that together accounted for nearly 95 per cent of the 1938 output in 67 countries, excluding China, shows how World War II has affected meat production in different parts of the world. At the end of the

---

80. **47**, p. 21, and **65**, p. 79.
81. A two-year-old prime British steer equals, in weight of carcass, three five-year-old steers of low breed. **56**, p. 81.
82. **52**, p. 121.
83. **16**, 1950, p. 365.

84. Most countries report only slaughterings in publicly controlled slaughterhouses, or only commercial production; some make allowances for slaughterings on farms. (See **13**, pp. 202 and 215; **8**, January 1952, p. 9.) Some countries include edible offal, or fat; others do not.

TABLE 290

MEAT: OUTPUT IN EACH CONTINENT, 1934–38 ANNUAL AVERAGE

Continent	Thousands of Short Tons				Per Cent			
	Total	Beef	Mutton and Goat	Pork	Total	Beef	Mutton and Goat	Pork
World	51,147	25,540	5,259	20,349	100.0	100.0	100.0	100.0
North America [a]	9,921	4,520	551	4,850	19.4	17.7	10.5	23.8
Middle and South America	9,039	6,063	772	2,205	17.7	23.7	14.7	10.8
Europe	14,551	5,732	1,103	7,716	28.4	22.4	21.0	37.9
USSR	3,417	1,543	441	1,433	6.7	6.1	8.3	7.1
Asia	10,472	5,512	1,103	3,858	20.5	21.6	21.0	19.0
Africa	2,205	1,378	662	166	4.3	5.4	12.6	0.8
Oceania	1,544	794	629	122	3.2	3.1	11.9	0.6

Source: Adapted from **9**, p. 171. a. Includes Mexico and Cuba.

war the world found itself with much less meat than before, although the Western Hemisphere, with abundant feed supplies, increased its output considerably. In Europe and the USSR — where forced wartime slaughterings caused by shortage of feed sharply reduced the herds — the slump in output was severe. But high prices for meat and greater feed supplies have gradually begun to stimulate an increase in the herds and the number of animals marketed. Meat output rose everywhere in Europe in 1950, but was still 17.3 per cent below the prewar level.[85] In contrast, North America produced 36.5 per cent more meat than in prewar years; the seven Latin American countries enumerated in Table 291, 22.6 per cent more; the Union of South Africa, 41.1 per cent more; and Oceania, 8.3 per cent more. (See Table 291.) The increase was largest in pork and moderate in beef; these increases more than offset the decline in production of mutton and lamb, which was partly due to the attractive prices for wool.[86]

Figures on output in individual countries likewise show the effects of war and uneven rates of postwar recovery. In 1950 Western Germany produced 20 per cent less meat than before the war; Austria 14 per cent less, and the United Kingdom 8 per cent less. Most other western Eu-

ropean countries either had a somewhat smaller output than in 1934–38 or just barely exceeded that level. Information for eastern Europe is lacking or unreliable, but it is known, for example, that Czechoslovakia's output in 1949 was almost 30 per cent less than in prewar years. Severe drought conditions in southern Europe during 1950 forced slaughterings despite the poor finish of most livestock and raised the meat output, which remains, nevertheless, below the prewar level. A different situation prevails in countries that could increase their herds and flocks in wartime and are not dependent on imported feed. Mexico has raised its meat output about 47 per cent above the prewar level; Canada and the United States, about 45 and 37 per cent, respectively; Brazil, 32 per cent; and New Zealand, about 22 per cent. (See Table 292.)

Output per Capita

Oceania, particularly New Zealand, leads in per capita production of meat. In South America, Argentina and Uruguay are outstanding, but their output per capita is still somewhat below the prewar level. The United States and Canada, on the other hand, have increased per capita output, despite the growth of the population, by 17 and 9 per cent, respectively. In Europe, Denmark ranks first in per capita output, but more of its meat goes into exports than into domestic consumption. No European country except France and Belgium has yet regained its prewar per

85. Western Europe produced 7 per cent and eastern Europe 20 per cent less meat in 1950 than before. (**5**, p. 1.)

86. **19**, FLM 4-51, p. 1.

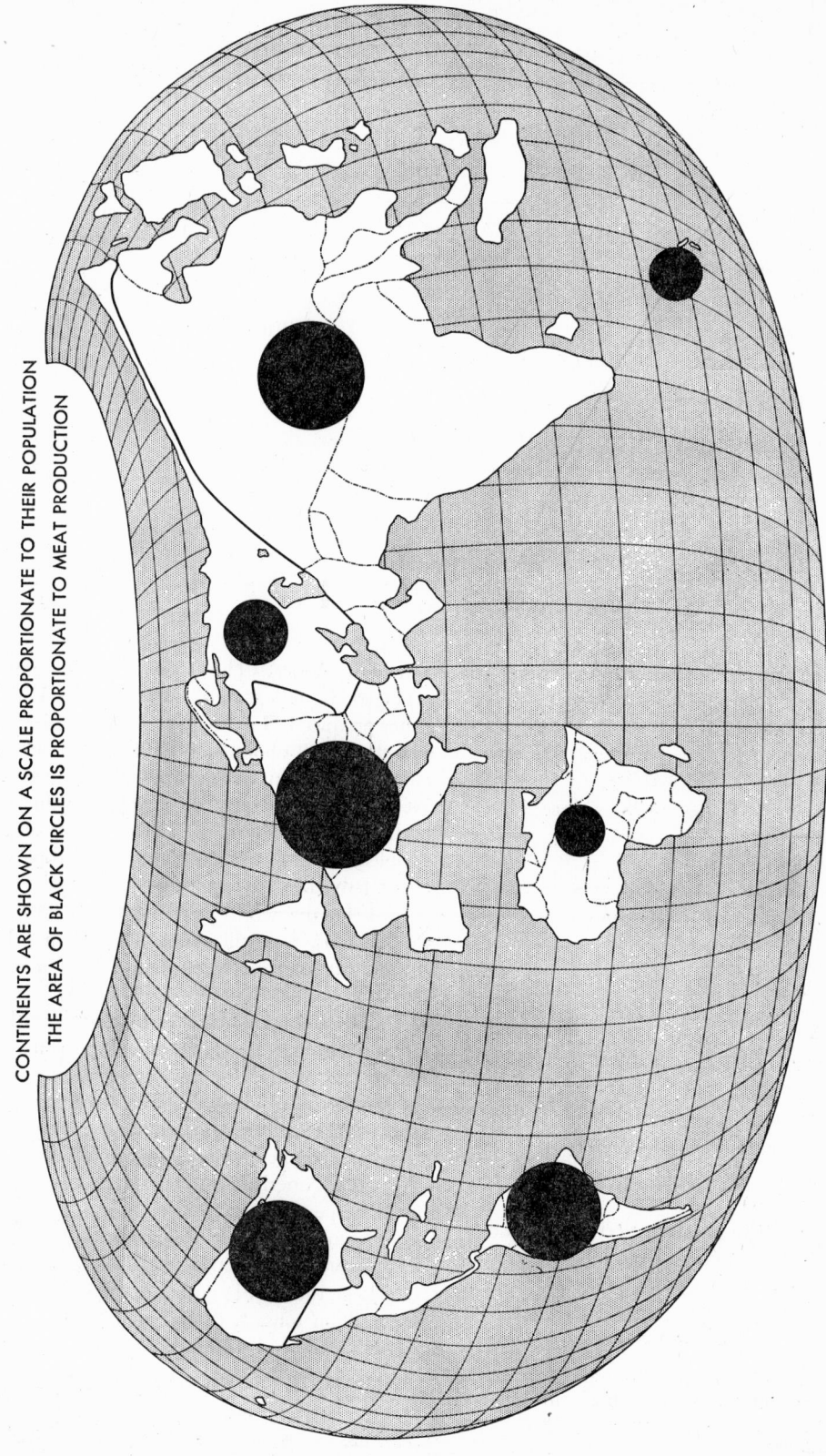

CONTINENTS ARE SHOWN ON A SCALE PROPORTIONATE TO THEIR POPULATION

THE AREA OF BLACK CIRCLES IS PROPORTIONATE TO MEAT PRODUCTION

FIGURE 202. MEAT: OUTPUT IN EACH CONTINENT IN RELATION TO POPULATION, 1934–38 ANNUAL AVERAGE

T<small>ABLE</small> 291

M<small>EAT</small>: O<small>UTPUT IN</small> S<small>ELECTED</small> R<small>EGIONS</small>, 1934–38 A<small>NNUAL</small> A<small>VERAGE</small>, 1949 <small>AND</small> 1950 [a]

	Thousands of Metric Tons [b]			*Percentage Increase (+) or Decrease (—) from 1934–38 to 1950*
Region	*1934–38*	*1949*	*1950*	
North America	7,983 [c]	10,730	10,898	+36.5
Middle and South America [d]	4,015	4,999	4,931	+22.6
Europe	12,167	9,752	10,063	–17.3
USSR	3,308	...	...	...
Middle East [e]	635	...	...	...
Union of South Africa	304	433	430	+41.1
Oceania	1,463	1,613	1,584	+8.3

Source: **19**, FLM 4–51, p. 1, and 9–51, p. 1.

    a. Excludes offal, lard, rabbit and poultry meat.
    b. Conversion factor: one metric ton = 2,204.6 pounds.
    c. 1935–39.
    d. Mexico, Cuba, Argentina, Brazil, Chile, Paraguay and Uruguay.
    e. Egypt, Turkey, Iraq and Iran.

capita output, as the following figures show (in pounds):[87]

	Prewar [a]	*1950* [a]
United States	125	146
Canada	127	138
Mexico	38	40
Uruguay [b]	383	355
Argentina [b]	325	297
United Kingdom	61	52
Ireland	114	107
France	96	103
Belgium	83	83
Netherlands	104	88
Denmark	295	262
Sweden	103	95
Switzerland	101	86
Australia	321	274
New Zealand	640	649

    a. Carcass meat, excluding offal, lard, rabbit and poultry meat.
    b. Commercial establishments only.

Asia and Africa produce very little meat in relation to population, and the USSR does only slightly better.

LARD AND TALLOW

Lard and unrendered pork fat are produced everywhere except in some countries in Asia and Northern Africa. The prewar world output averaged 3 million tons, of which the United States produced 27 per cent, Germany 13 per cent and the USSR about 11 per cent. Other important producers in Europe are Italy, France and Poland. In Asia, China is the largest producer of lard. During the war, the United States almost doubled its output of lard; that in Europe was about halved.

In 1949, the world's production of lard, 2.7 million tons, was still about 10 per cent below the prewar average. More than half of it came from the United States.[88]

Tallow is obtained chiefly from rendered beef fat and also from the fat of sheep, goats and horses. The world's prewar output averaged 1.5 million tons annually. The United States — where tallow and greases, derived mainly from hogs, are counted together — produced 38 per cent; other American countries some 20 per cent; and Europe about 27 per cent. Asia, the USSR and Oceania shared about equally in the remainder; Africa's output was negligible.[89]

In 1949, the world's output of tallow amounted to 2 million tons. A decline in Europe's output was offset by gains in Latin American countries, and the total produced outside the United States

---

87. **20**, p. 66.

88. **22**, March 6, 1950, pp. 189 and 192.
89. **62**, pp. 98 and 111.

TABLE 292

MEAT: OUTPUT IN SELECTED COUNTRIES, 1928, 1934–38 ANNUAL AVERAGE, AND 1949–50

(*Thousands of Metric Tons*[a])

Country	Beef and Veal				Mutton and Lamb [b]				Pork			
	1928	1934–38 Average [c]	1949	1950	1928	1934–38 Average [c]	1949	1950	1928	1934–38 Average [c]	1949	1950
United States	2,963	3,617	4,885	4,884	300	395	275	273	4,100	3,328	4,687	4,929
Canada	354	333	450	415	28	28	20	16	380	236	413	437
Mexico	...	223	339	322	...	6	11	9	...	76	102	117
Cuba	...	122	170	170	...	1	1	1	...	17	17	16
Colombia	...	205	268	280	...	2	2	2	...	21	29	30
Brazil [d]	542	826	1,032	1,066	14	7	17	18	122	167	234	240
Chile	108	107	107	115	19	33	37	38	13	18	24	25
Uruguay	253	279	288	290	34	64	81	75	5	14	14	14
Argentina	1,628	1,653	2,037	1,950	119	168	209	150	...	154	102	136
United Kingdom	663	632	537	644	277	203	142	151	360	459	272	398
Ireland	...	47	58	62	...	17	15	15	...	88	59	72
France	968	998	990	980	129	101	110	110	569	678	770	800
Belgium	121	138	122	129	4	3	2	2	142	166	136	169
Netherlands	165	140	86	139	12	9	7	9	314	249	164	247
Denmark [e]	140	164	121	157	...	4	2	2	377	329	266	340
Sweden	103	132	114	114	7	4	3	3	41	148	174	176
Norway	38	43	39	41	14	15	15	16	31	40	34	49
Finland	48	52	36	40	6	5	5	7	38	55	65	64
Germany [f]	942	1,313	454	596	39	49	24	20	2,130	2,306	667	980

(*Continued on page 668*)

TABLE 292—continued

Country	Beef and Veal				Mutton and Lamb [b]				Pork			
	1928	1934–38 Average [c]	1949	1950	1928	1934–38 Average [c]	1949	1950	1928	1934–38 Average [c]	1949	1950
Poland	220	342	…	…	10	14	…	…	348	751	…	…
Czechoslovakia	189	186	104	…	52	3	2	…	127	272	185	…
Switzerland	37	98	82	88	…	2	2	2	29	86	79	91
Austria	90	105	61	79	…	8	5	5	…	163	113	152
Italy	509	320	290	304	248	49	49	50	66	295	295	290
Romania	…	111	…	…	…	50	…	…	…	170	…	…
Greece	…	15	10	10	…	62	38	34	…	18	17	18
USSR [g]	1,841	1,295	…	…	779	444	…	…	1,318	1,569	…	…
Japan	51	70	44	79	…	—	—	—	41	61	36	57
Turkey	…	20	34	36	…	39	46	53	—	—	—	—
Union of South Africa	182	…	306	307	…	89	84	79	74	29	47	49
Australia	460	578	594	630	264	325	374	311	17	96	87	78
New Zealand	131	166	181	188	207	251	323	337	27	48	40	41

Sources: 13, pp. 317–19; 7, 1950, p. 153; 19, FLM 4–51, pp. 8–9.

a. Carcass meat basis; except in 1928, excludes offal and lard. Conversion factor: one metric ton = 2,204.6 pounds.
b. Includes goat meat for Austria, France, Sweden, Italy, Greece, Romania, Yugoslavia and the Union of South Africa.
c. 1935–39 for the United States, Canada, Denmark, Sweden and Finland; 1936–40 for Cuba; 1933–37 for Australia; 1936 for Czechoslovakia; 1936–38 for the United Kingdom, Greece and Australia; 1938 for Poland and the USSR.
d. Excludes farm production.
e. Includes carcass meat equivalent of live animal exports.
f. Western Germany in postwar years.
g. Prewar territory.

remained practically unchanged. The increase in world output is thus mainly attributable to the rise in tallow production in the United States from 0.5 to 1 million tons, which resulted from the larger number of cattle and the greater recovery of fat per animal slaughtered. Argentina, too, has doubled its output of tallow and has become the largest producer after the United States. Tallow production in the USSR, according to the estimated number of livestock, may approximate the prewar output of some 100,000 tons.[90]

DAIRY PRODUCTS

The production of butter and cheese, as well as of milk, may be as old as recorded history. Milk and milk products are mentioned many times in the Bible, and the earliest Greek authors speak of dairying. Cheese was probably made before butter. Plutarch called cheese one of the most nourishing foodstuffs. It was believed to strengthen the body and was given to Greek and Roman soldiers before battle.

MILK

Milk and milk products are among the most important items in the world's agricultural output. Most farms have some milk-producing animals — a cow, a goat or a sheep or, in Asia, a buffalo. In the Temperate Zone, many farmers count on milk and its products as a chief source of cash income. Dairying plays a lesser role in tropical areas, largely because of the great perishability of milk products in hot climates and the generally poor and unproductive livestock breeds.

Commercial dairying has developed only in recent times, chiefly during the twentieth century. It requires substantial capital investment in livestock and equipment, high skill in the handling of animals, painstaking care in all operations, and the greatest attention to sanitation. Tenant farming is therefore less common in dairying than in any other type of agriculture. Formerly, proximity to urban markets was essential; today, refrigerated trucks and special milk trains carry milk and other dairy products over comparatively great distances.

The dairy farms of northwestern Europe, particularly those of Denmark and the Netherlands, are outstanding. Great Britain, Germany, Switzerland and the other Scandinavian countries

have also achieved a high level of quality and efficiency in dairying. New Zealand has one of the finest dairy industries in the world.

In North America, dairy farming is concentrated chiefly in the northeastern part of the continent, on both sides of the border between the United States and Canada. More than half of all the cows in both countries are in this densely populated region, near metropolitan areas. Another important dairy region in the United States is on the Pacific Coast, oriented toward the cities.

Milk Cows and Yield per Cow

The output of milk depends on the quality as well as the number of milk cows. Before World War II, it is estimated, there were about 180 million milk cows among the world's 694 million cattle, but this estimate is only an approximation, since not all countries have statistics on the sex of cattle and even the term "cow" is used differently in various countries.[91] The United States far outranks all other countries in number of cows — nearly 23 million in 1950. In the 1920's the USSR held first place, but it lost about 30 per cent during the introduction of collectivization and suffered further losses during the war.[92] In prewar Europe, Germany and France had the largest numbers.

Rather opposite trends can be observed in the number of milk cows in many countries. The United States, Canada, Denmark, Sweden, Norway, Switzerland, Austria, Australia and some other countries had fewer milk cows in 1950 than in an average prewar year. Among the European countries, the most noticeable increase has been in the United Kingdom; a lesser increase took place in the Netherlands. New Zealand, too, now has more milk cows than before. (See Table 293.)

In countries with a developed dairy industry, the milk yield per cow has increased steadily in recent decades. A Dutch cow now produces 8,385 pounds a year, while the average cow in India gives only 1,400 pounds.[93] In Venezuela and Greece, annual production per cow is also some 1,400 pounds; in Northern Rhodesia, about 1,035 pounds; and in Ethiopia, only 660.[94]

The upward trend was interrupted by World

---

90. **22**, May 2, 1949, pp. 417-20, and March 6, 1950, p. 189.

91. **13**, pp. 247 and 252.

92. Moreover, the USSR data refer to all cows, not solely milk cows.

93. **3**, p. 9, and **53**, p. 51.

94. **7**, 1950, pp. 160-61.

TABLE 293

MILK: MILK COWS AND OUTPUT PER COW IN SELECTED COUNTRIES, 1934–38 ANNUAL
AVERAGE AND 1950

Country	Milk Cows, in Thousands [a]		Milk Output Per Cow, in Pounds	
	1934–38	1950	1934–38	1950
United States	23,933	22,779	4,291	5,292
Canada	3,816	3,609	4,138	4,554
United Kingdom	3,300	3,765	5,583	6,136
France	8,400	8,400	3,929	4,057
Belgium	967	950	7,022	7,309
Netherlands	1,460	1,521	7,658	8,385
Denmark	1,658	1,577	7,047	7,566
Sweden	1,922	1,664	5,327	6,482
Norway	807	766	3,660	4,678
Finland	1,309	...	4,268	4,564 [b]
Germany	10,076	...	5,270	4,740 [c]
Switzerland	902	858	6,297	6,349
Austria	1,210 [d]	1,170	4,630	3,674
Italy	3,466	...	3,968	3,417 [b]
Australia	2,545	2,354	4,629	5,508
New Zealand	1,787	1,850	5,694	5,623

Source: **22,** May 21, 1951, pp. 573–74.

  a. For the United States and Canada, cows kept mainly for milk; for other countries, cows producing above the requirements of the calf.
  b. 1949.
  c. Western Germany, 1949.
  d. 1934.

War II but regained its course in most countries as soon as the supply of feed became more plentiful. Between 1934–38 and 1950, milk yield per cow in Canada increased from 4,138 to 4,554 pounds; in the United Kingdom, from 5,583 to 6,136 pounds; in Denmark, from 7,047 to 7,566 pounds, and so on.

Because of selective culling and better feed, the yield per cow in the United States has risen and averaged 5,292 pounds in 1950. California leads the states, with 7,310 pounds per cow (1949), followed by New Jersey (7,210) and Rhode Island (7,000). The yield is lowest in Louisiana and Mississippi.[95]

The average milk yield per cow in the USSR is low — 2,300 pounds in 1935 and 2,083 pounds in 1945. Cows are not specialized for milk production in that country, and are widely used for draft power, especially since the war.[96]

Output

World output of milk from cows, ewes, goats

and buffaloes averaged more than a quarter billion metric tons in prewar years. Europe and North America together accounted for about two thirds of the total:[97]

	Millions of Tons	Per Cent
World	264.5	100.0
North America	58.0	21.9
Middle and South America	14.0	5.3
Europe	118.0	44.6
USSR	25.5	9.6
Asia	33.5	12.7
Africa	5.5	2.1
Oceania	10.0	3.8

Trends in milk production during the war were like those in output of meat. With dwindling numbers of cows and less feed per animal, the total yield of milk declined in most European countries and particularly in France, Belgium, the Netherlands and Denmark. In the United States, output rose considerably despite the de-

95. **16,** 1950, p. 427.
96. **68,** pp. 162-63.

97. Adapted from **9,** p. 177. North America includes Mexico and Cuba. Data for Asia and Africa may be too low. One metric ton = 2,204.6 pounds.

TABLE 294

MILK: OUTPUT IN SELECTED COUNTRIES, PREWAR AND 1948–50

(*Millions of Metric Tons* [a])

Country	Prewar	1948	1949	1950	Country	Prewar	1948	1949	1950
United States	47.8	52.4	55.4	56.0	Poland	10.3	3.4 [b]	...	...
Canada	6.8	7.6	7.6	7.5	Czechoslovakia	4.4	2.3	2.6	...
Chile	0.3	0.6	0.8	0.6	Switzerland	2.7	2.3	2.4	2.7
Argentina	2.6	4.2 [b]	...	...	Austria	2.0	1.6	1.7	1.9
United Kingdom	8.2	9.1	9.8	10.5	Hungary	1.5	0.9	1.1	...
Ireland	2.3	2.2	2.3	2.4	Italy [e]	6.5	4.9	5.6	...
France	14.2	11.2	13.0	15.0	Greece [e]	0.4	0.3	0.2	...
Belgium	2.8	2.6	3.1	3.2	USSR	28.9 [d]	...	...	...
Netherlands	4.9	4.4	5.5	5.8					
Denmark	5.3	4.1	4.9	5.4	Turkey [e]	2.3	3.2	2.0	3.2
Sweden	4.6	4.4	4.6	4.9	India [e]	16.8	18.2 [e]	...	...
Norway	1.3	1.4	1.6	1.6	Egypt	1.6	1.9 [b]	1.3	...
Finland	2.6	1.9	2.2	2.5	Union of South				
Germany:	20.0	—	—	—	Africa	0.9 [f]	1.7	1.7	1.8
Western	15.0	8.6	11.9	14.0	Australia	5.4	5.5	5.7	5.9
Soviet Zone	4.9	2.0	2.4	...	New Zealand	4.5	4.2	4.7	5.0

Sources: **7**, 1951, pp. 149–50; **22**, October 29, 1951, p. 451; **8**, January 1952, p. 8, and April 1952, p. 12.

a. Conversion factor: one metric ton = 2,204.6 pounds.
b. 1947.

c. Includes sheep, goat and buffalo milk.
d. 1938.
e. 1945.
f. Farms and estates.

cline in the number of cows, and this increase is continuing.

The United States is the world's largest single producer of milk; its output in 1950 was 56 million tons. It produces more than the combined output of the United Kingdom, France, Western Germany, the Low Countries and Denmark. In 1944, 77 per cent of all farms in the United States produced some milk, and more than half of them sold milk or dairy products. Less than half of all farms, those with more than two milk cows per farm, produced 90 per cent of all the milk.[98]

The USSR was the next important milk producer before World War II, with 28.9 million tons in 1938. More recent data are not available. France, Germany and the United Kingdom are the chief milk-producing countries in Europe, but little Denmark produces more than half as much as the United Kingdom. (See Table 294.)

Utilization

The allocation of milk to various uses depends largely on price relationships among dairy products. Other determining factors are its perishabil-

ity, the availability of transportation and manufacturing and marketing facilities, and sometimes also government policy.

Before the war, 35–40 per cent of all the milk produced in the world was consumed in liquid form, about 40 per cent went into butter, nearly 10 per cent was used to make cheese, and the remainder was fed to livestock or utilized for other products — such as condensed milk, dried milk, ice cream.[99]

These ratios varied from country to country. In the United Kingdom, more than 60 per cent of all milk produced was consumed in liquid form; in the Low Countries, only 21 per cent; in Denmark, some 12 per cent; in the United States, 41 per cent. On the other hand, the proportion of milk used for butter ranged from 15 per cent in the United Kingdom to 80 per cent in Denmark and Australia.

The relative use of milk has changed substantially since the war. Between the period 1934–38 and 1948, the largest shift was the rise from 32 to 41 per cent in the proportion consumed as fluid milk in western and central Europe.[100] In the

98. **18**, p. 1.

99. **3**, p. 12.
100. **4**, p. 7.

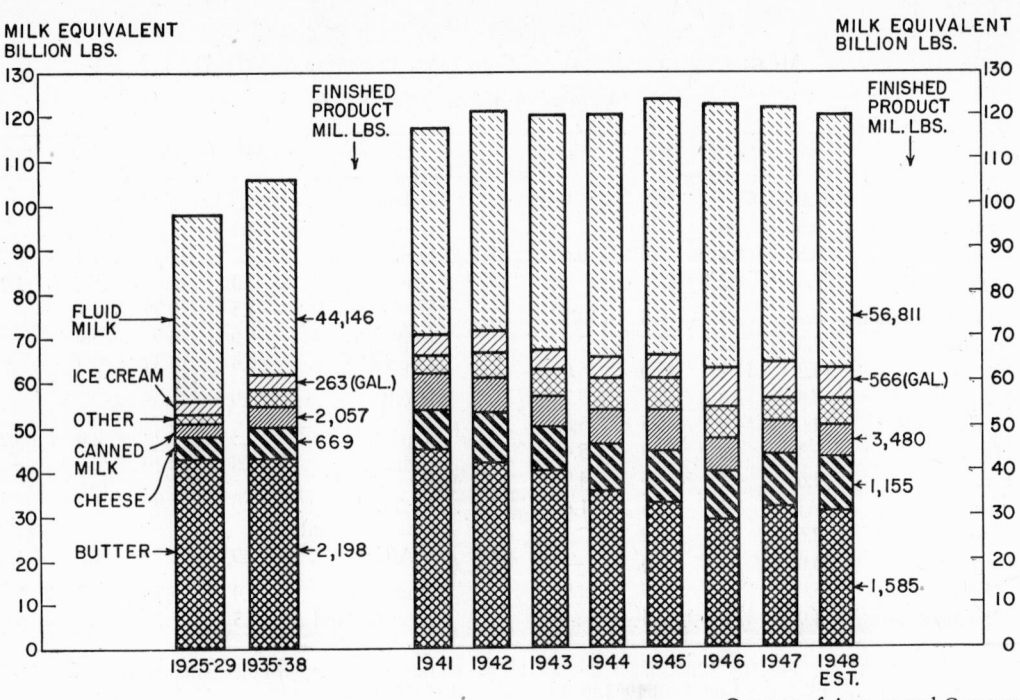

Courtesy of Armour and Company

FIGURE 203. MILK: USE, BY TYPE, IN THE UNITED STATES, 1925–48

United States, too, more milk is now consumed in fluid form and less is used for butter. (See Figure 203.)

The United States and New Zealand use 2.8 to 2.7 per cent of their milk to feed livestock, while the proportion in Italy is 15.0 per cent and in France, about 21 per cent. (See Table 295.)

Skim milk is the by-product of processing cream and butter. In major butter-producing countries, the output of skim milk represents more than half of the whole milk produced. It is estimated that most countries normally consume less than 50 per cent of their skim milk for human use. Much is used for feeding animals, some is used for cheese, and some is wasted.[101]

BUTTER

Butter is churned on most farms, but in countries with advanced agriculture the greater part of it is produced in factories — about 80 per cent in the United States and Canada; nearly 100 per cent in the Netherlands.

Before World War II, the annual output of butter in the world exceeded 4.3 million metric

tons. Europe, North America, British India[102] and Oceania accounted for the largest part — about 29, 26, 17 and 9 per cent, respectively. The USSR produced about 4 per cent.

The world's output of butter, including ghee, is estimated at 3.5 million metric tons for 1949, and at 3.6 million for 1950.[103] Despite the increase in milk production, the output of butter is smaller in many countries than before the war, because proportionately more milk is consumed in liquid form. In 1950, for example, the United States, with about 14 per cent more milk, produced only about 64 per cent as much butter as before the war. The United Kingdom had nearly 20 per cent more milk in 1950 and produced only 57 per cent as much butter as in prewar years. In Canada, the output of butter in 1950 was about 25 per cent less than in 1934–38, although milk output increased 10 per cent. Although Europe has achieved a considerable recovery in butter production in recent years, only a few countries have a larger output than before the war. (See Table 296.)

102. India, like Turkey, Egypt and other Middle Eastern and Far Eastern countries, produces a semifluid butter, the so-called ghee.

101. **4,** p. 8.

103. **22,** June 4, 1951, p. 640.

TABLE 295

MILK: USE, BY TYPE, IN SELECTED COUNTRIES, 1934–38 ANNUAL AVERAGE AND 1950

(Per Cent)

Country	1934–38						1950					
	Fluid Milk[a]	Butter	Cheese	Canned Milk	Other Uses[b]	Feed	Fluid Milk[a]	Butter	Cheese	Canned Milk	Other Uses[b]	Feed
United States	41.3	41.5	6.1	4.4	4.1	2.6	47.4	27.0	9.5	5.6	7.8	2.8
Canada	29.4	51.9	8.9	1.7	3.0	5.0	35.6	44.0	7.0	3.6	3.4	6.4
United Kingdom	60.3	15.2	5.5	3.5	3.7	11.9	76.1	6.0	5.6	3.3	2.3	6.7
Ireland[e]	18.0	68.0	1.0	[d]	1.0	12.0	21.0	61.0	1.0	5.0[d]	—	12.0
France	25.0	51.0	—	—	—	24.0	25.7	34.9	16.7	[d]	1.3	21.3
Belgium	21.1	63.6	2.4	0.2	0.6	12.0	28.1	57.2	1.9	0.2	0.1	12.5
Netherlands	20.8	49.5	20.5	[d]	4.6	4.6	26.9	40.2	19.4	6.5	1.8	5.2
Denmark	12.3	79.7	2.8	[d]	0.5	4.7	13.3	71.9	7.6	2.4	0.4	4.3
Sweden	32.0	50.5	7.6	[d]	0.4	9.4	34.8	49.5	9.4	[d]	1.2	5.1
Norway	38.0	37.6	16.6	[d]	1.8	6.0	46.2	30.2	15.4	[d]	2.1	6.1
Finland[e]	45.8	48.9	3.6	—	—	1.6	48.0	45.0	—	—	—	7.0
Germany	30.3	52.9	4.5	—	0.9	11.3	37.0	51.0	—	—	—	12.0
Poland[e]	52.0	40.0	—	—	—	8.0	55.0	37.0	—	—	—	8.0
Czechoslovakia[c]	56.0	37.0	—	—	—	7.0	54.0	34.0	—	[d]	—	12.0
Switzerland[e]	35.2	24.8	21.7	[d]	0.8	17.7	42.6	14.3	25.7	[d]	1.8	15.5
Austria	54.8	21.6	11.8	—	—	11.8	44.1	35.8	4.7	—	—	15.3
Hungary[c]	56.0	27.0	—	—	—	17.0	64.0	17.0	—	—	—	19.0
Italy[e]	26.9	19.6	26.2	0.2	4.5	22.5	29.0	56.0	—	—	—	15.0
Australia	13.7	80.4	3.8	2.2	—	—	20.2	65.2	8.0	2.4	4.2	—
New Zealand	5.6	73.2	18.6	[d]	0.6	2.0	9.0	65.0	20.3	[d]	3.0	2.7

Sources: **4**, pp. 9 and 48; **22**, May 21, 1951, pp. 573–74.

a. Includes milk used for cream.
b. Ice cream and dried milk, whole milk, other products, waste.
c. Postwar data shown are for 1948.
d. Included under other uses.
e. Includes goat milk.

TABLE 296

BUTTER AND CHEESE: OUTPUT IN SELECTED COUNTRIES, 1928–50

(*Thousands of Metric Tons* [a])

Country	Butter					Cheese				
	1928	1934–38	1948	1949	1950	1928	1934–38	1948	1949	1950
United States	931	988	686	769	630	199	292	498	545	532
Canada	117	158	159	152	119	66	52	43	55	46
Brazil [b]	13	21	20 [c]	22 [c]	25 [c]	7	40	19	21	. . .
Argentina [d]	31	30	42	39	45	17	35 [e]	83	99	103
United Kingdom	49	47	16	20	27	50	50	27 [f]	34 [f]	56 [f]
Ireland [g]	82	63	50	55	59	. . .	2	3	3	3
France	220	202	160	183	225	229	270	180	240	299 [h]
Belgium [g]	63	64	23	66	32	. . .	7	3	6	6
Netherlands	85	98	71	84	93	132	121	96	128	127
Denmark	166	182	120	156	179	27	33	56	64	61
Sweden	. . .	92	95	104	109	26	34	52	66	52
Norway [g]	. . .	23	17	18	20	14	23	14	21	26
Finland [d]	. . .	28	19	29	36	5	10	7	12	14
Western Germany	. . .	. . .	173	246	270	. . .	. . .	92	150	136
Czechoslovakia [b]	. . .	13 [i]	23	30	. . .	. . .	11 [i]	13	14	. . .
Switzerland	. . .	26	14	15	19	71	50	50	54	56
Austria	. . .	24	22	25	23	. . .	31 [j]	5	8	13
Italy [k]	42	51	54	55	54	217	237	237	240	261
Greece [h]	. . .	6	4	3	3	. . .	55	39	38	43
USSR	408	168 [l]	248	. . .	. . .	12	35 [l]	. . .	. . .	. . .
Union of South Africa [b]	12	18	27	26	27	3	5	9	8	9
Australia	132	207 [l]	166	168	177	14	30	42	44	46
New Zealand	104	170 [m]	157	169	175	91	90	88	101	107

Sources: **1**, 1937–38, pp. 74–76; **8**, September 1951, p. 9, and January 1952, p. 8; **7**, 1950, pp. 162–65; **22**, June 4, 1951, pp. 641–42, and March 24, 1952, p. 239.

a. Conversion factor: one metric ton = 2,204.6 pounds.
b. Butter: factory production only.
c. Government-inspected only.
d. Butter and cheese: factory production only.
e. 1938.
f. Excludes processed cheese.

g. Cheese: factory production only.
h. Cheese made of milk from cattle, sheep and goats. For Greece, also made of milk from buffaloes.
i. Prewar boundaries.
j. Includes cottage cheese.
k. Includes sheep cheese.
l. 1938–39.
m. 1936–39.

CHEESE

Cheese is made in some five hundred varieties, and from the milk of many animals. The Lapps and Eskimos make cheese from reindeer milk, the Arabs from camels' milk; llama cheese is popular in the Cordilleras in South America, and zebu cheese in Ceylon and India.[104] Some varieties have been made for centuries; in places in Switzerland, cheese is prepared exactly as it was first made by monks in the tenth century. Some countries produce large quantities of skim milk cheese or cheese made partly of skim milk. Most European countries now produce **more** cheese

from skim milk than before the war, with a consequent decrease in average butterfat content.[105] With this qualification, the output of cheese shows a tendency to gain at the expense of milk and butter. Many countries report a growing interest in the manufacture of cheese as a market for milk, whole or skim.

The United States has nearly doubled its cheese output during recent years, and the output of Argentina has tripled. Denmark and Sweden have raised output considerably above the prewar level, while Italy, Switzerland, the United Kingdom and many other countries have barely ex-

104. **51**, p. xv.

105. **4**, p. 12.

ceeded it. Output has decreased in Canada, Greece and Austria. (See Table 296.)

POULTRY AND EGGS

Chickens require little room, little feed and not much care; they reproduce rapidly and, except on commercial poultry farms, often live as scavengers on scraps and waste. Poultry raising is therefore particularly adapted to small farming. Moreover, in many countries, chickens are raised in towns and cities, in backyards, on roofs, even in kitchens.[106] Entrance into chicken raising and egg production on a commercial scale is made attractive by the fact that investment can be smaller and returns are both quicker and more certain than from other livestock enterprises. Chicken meat and eggs are readily marketable and do not require processing. Moreover, chickens use feed economically, producing in almost direct proportion to the feed they obtain, and, more readily than for other livestock, the number on the farm can be adjusted to feed supplies.

COMMERCIAL POULTRY FARMING

Commercial raising of poultry has developed primarily in countries with abundant grain production, such as the United States, Canada and Australia, and also in countries with relatively high standards of living and large grain imports, as in western Europe. In contrast, in regions with barely sufficient or inadequate amounts of grain and low levels of consumption, poultry farming is largely a "backyard" industry. In the United States about 15 per cent of all animal protein consumed per capita in recent years has been derived from poultry meat and eggs; in Canada and France, 14 per cent; in all western and central Europe, about 8–10 per cent.[107]

Poultry and poultry products represent a considerable share of cash farm income. In the United States, for example, they accounted for $3 billion, or 11 per cent of all farm cash receipts, in 1949, more than receipts from the sale of food grains ($2.3 billion) or of all vegetables and fruit together ($2.9 billion). The proportion in other leading poultry-producing countries is similar.[108]

In recent decades, poultry farming has been expanding in many countries as a result of the increase in population and in demand for lighter protein fare — chicken meat and, especially,

eggs. The growth of the industry has been marked by vast improvement in breeding and feeding, as well as in storage, transportation and marketing.

The commercial production of poultry is influenced by the relationship between the cost of feed, the price of eggs and the price of chickens. When feed prices go up more than the price of eggs, the output of poultry ordinarily declines, and vice versa. Similarly, it may be more advantageous for the farmer to sell eggs at one time and to raise chickens for meat at another.

Poultry Meat versus Eggs

Poultry meat is a comparatively expensive food for areas short on grain, such as Asia and some European countries. In such areas, chickens are kept chiefly for egg production, while countries with adequate or surplus grain supplies raise proportionately more poultry for meat. Thus in 1949, Belgium, the Netherlands, Norway, Sweden, Switzerland and Greece produced about 2.2 pounds of poultry meat for every laying hen, while the United States had about 11.0 pounds per laying hen.[109]

The United States is the world's largest producer of poultry (chickens, turkeys, ducks); China is next in line. In Europe, the United Kingdom and France lead in output. (See Table 297.)

CHICKENS

Chickens predominate among farm poultry almost everywhere. In the world as a whole, some 2.5 billion chickens account for about 90 per cent of all poultry. In the United States, Canada and Great Britain, chickens represent over 98 per cent of the total; in western Germany, about 94 per cent; and in France, 76 per cent.

In the United States, all farms covered by the 1945 agricultural census were raising chickens. In size of the flocks, the farms were distributed as follows:[110]

	Percentage of Reporting Farms	Percentage of Chickens
Total	100.0	100.0
Under 20 chickens	16.0	2.3
20–49	33.6	11.6
50–99	22.0	15.8
100–199	17.8	25.8
200–399	8.4	23.8
400 and more	2.2	20.7

---

106. **10**, Vol. III, pp. 117 and 227.
107. **6**, p. 3.
108. **16**, 1950, p. 637; **21**, May 1949, p. 108.

109. **6**, p. 6.
110. **25**, p. 26.

Table 297

POULTRY: OUTPUT IN SELECTED COUNTRIES, PREWAR AND 1949–50

Country and Month or Season	Number of Poultry, in Millions			Number of Chickens, in Millions			Poultry Meat, in Thousands of Tons [a]		
	Prewar	1949	1950	Prewar	1949	1950	Prewar	1949	1950
United States, January [b]	414.2	454.2	487.3	408.2	448.7	480.8	1,197.0	2,066.0	2,135.0
Canada, June	62.4	70.0	. . .	58.5	69.0	61.5	96.0	139.0	. . .
United Kingdom, June	94.6	114.2	118.0	90.0	109.7	111.4	79.0	102.0	105.0
Ireland, June	19.5	22.2	23.0	16.0	18.5	18.9	25.0	29.0	30.0
France, Fall	188.0	192.0	192.0	145.0	146.0	146.0	250.0	250.0	250.0
Belgium, Winter	20.0	18.4	20.0	19.0	18.0	19.0	13.0	12.5	14.0
Netherlands, May	30.8	23.0	26.0	29.6	20.3	25.0	8.0	4.2	5.5
Denmark, July	29.0	31.1	33.3	27.6	28.0	30.0	27.0	25.0	27.0
Sweden, September	11.2	17.5	17.7	10.9	17.1	17.4	8.0	13.0	14.0
Norway, June	5.8	5.8	5.9	3.7	3.7	3.9	2.9	2.7	2.7
Finland, March	3.1	2.9	3.5	2.9	2.7	3.0	1.2	1.3	1.5
Germany (Western), December	57.0	47.0	53.0	54.6	44.2	50.0	45.0	32.4	37.0
Poland, June	56.0	48.4	. . .	50.0	42.9	. . .	. . .	. . .	. . .
Czechoslovakia, January	38.5	16.4	17.2	31.9	15.0	15.7	46.0	. . .	. . .
Switzerland, April	5.6	6.2	6.2	5.5	6.1	6.1	4.0	3.5	3.5
Austria, December	9.3	5.5	6.5	8.9	4.9	6.2	4.0	2.7	3.0
Italy, Fall	80.5	67.8	72.0	76.0	64.0	68.0	64.0	51.0	54.0
Greece, December	12.3	10.2	11.6	11.7	9.7	11.0	11.0	9.0	10.0
China [c]	341.0	248.0 [d]	. . .	266.0	200.0 [d]	. . .	320.0	250.0 [d]	. . .
Japan, February [e]	51.6	16.6	23.3	51.1	16.4	22.8	29.0	9.0	14.0
Turkey, December	19.1	22.0	22.7	17.7	20.3	21.0	30.0	27.0	25.0
Philippines, December	26.4	21.2	28.5	25.4	20.4	27.4	29.0	10.4	11.0

Source: **6**, pp. 16–17.

a. Dressed weight.
b. Chickens on farms, excluding commercial broilers. Chickens not on farms may amount to 10 per cent of the number on farms.
c. Month or season not reported.
d. 1947–48.
e. Prewar data refer to month of July.

Iowa has more chickens than any other state — 34 million in 1950. Minnesota had 28 million in that year; Texas and Pennsylvania had 27 million each; and Missouri, Illinois and California, 23–24 million. About 25 per cent of all the chickens raised on farms are consumed by the farm household.[111]

The hatchery industry in the United States has grown since 1918, when it became possible to ship chicks by parcel post. In 1930 commercial hatcheries produced 672 million chicks; in 1947, 1.3 billion; in 1949, 1.5 billion.[112] Indiana, Illinois, Iowa and Missouri each hatch about 100 million chicks a year.

PRODUCTION OF EGGS

The relative number of laying hens and their laying capacity differ from country to country.

111. **16**, 1950, pp. 456-57.
112. **16**, 1950, p. 468, and **17**, 1950, p. 69.

In the United States and Belgium, at least 9 out of every 10 chickens are laying hens; in Canada, less than 4 out of 10; in the United Kingdom, about 5 out of 10.

The United States is the world's largest producer of eggs, with an output exceeding that of all Europe. Characteristically, its output of eggs in 1950 was about 70 per cent above that in prewar years, while the number of laying hens had risen less than 20 per cent. (See Table 298 and Figure 204.) The greater productivity of the laying stock is attributable to better breeding and feeding, more careful selection of laying strains, better "living quarters," use of light in hen houses to lengthen "working time," improved sanitation, and similar measures. Some other countries report the same trend. Belgium, with the same number of laying hens in 1950 as before the war, produced almost 25 per cent more eggs. (See Table 298.)

TABLE 298

EGGS: OUTPUT IN SELECTED COUNTRIES, PREWAR AND 1949–50

Country	Number of Laying Hens, in Millions			Number of Eggs, in Billions [a]			Annual Number of Eggs Per Hen		
	Prewar	*1949*	*1950*	*Prewar*	*1949*	*1950*	*Prewar*	*1949*	*1950*
United States [b]	366.2	413.2	439.1	35.5	56.6	60.0	97	137	137
Canada	24.0	24.2	...	2.6	3.8	3.7	108	157	...
United Kingdom	46.4	51.0	54.0	5.1	5.0	5.8	110	98	107
Ireland	8.9	9.1	9.8	1.1	1.0	1.0	124	110	102
France	71.0	75.0	75.0	6.2	6.8	7.1	87	91	95
Belgium	17.0	16.0	17.0	1.7	1.9	2.1	100	119	124
Netherlands	14.7	9.3	10.4	2.0	1.5	1.9	136	161	183
Denmark	12.2	13.0	14.5	2.0	1.9	2.1	164	146	145
Sweden	7.3	12.4	12.7	0.9	1.3	1.5	123	105	118
Norway	3.4	3.5	3.7	0.4	0.3	0.5	118	86	135
Finland	2.7	2.5	2.8	0.3	0.3	0.3	111	120	107
Germany (Western)	45.0	36.6	42.0	3.7	2.8	4.1	82	77	98
Poland	26.0	20.1	...	3.5	...	...	135	...	...
Czechoslovakia	15.5	12.6	14.4	2.0	1.4 [c]	...	129	111	...
Switzerland	4.2	4.3	4.3	0.4	0.6	0.5	95	140	116
Austria	8.3	4.1	5.1	0.7	0.4	0.5	84	98	98
Italy	61.0	51.0	54.0	5.5	4.6	5.0	90	90	93
Greece	7.9	6.6	7.5	0.6	0.4	0.5	76	61	67
China	210.0	160.0	...	...	...	...	...	...	...
Japan	27.1	12.1	13.7	3.6	1.2	1.6	133	99	117
Turkey	15.6	17.5	18.0	1.0	0.9	0.9	64	51	50
Philippines	10.1	8.1	10.9	...	0.7	0.7	...	86	64
Australia	...	...	...	0.7	1.4	1.4	...	...	...
New Zealand	...	...	...	0.4	0.5	...	...	...	...

Sources: **6**, pp. 16–17; **22**, March 17, 1952, pp. 207–08.

a. Production on farms in the United States and Canada; total output in the United Kingdom. Data for other countries not explicit on this point.

b. Number of laying hens on hand on January 1. The average number of laying hens on hand during the year was as follows (in millions): 1938, 276; 1949, 341. The average number of eggs per layer on hand during the year was as follows: 1938, 135; 1949, 165 (**16**, 1950, p. 486).

c. Possibly underreported.

The average rate of lay in the United States in 1949 and 1950 was 137 eggs per hen on farms on January 1, and 165 per layer during the year. Vermont and Massachusetts led in 1949, with 204 and 200 eggs per hen, respectively.[113] There is also much less seasonal variation than formerly in egg production in the United States, with a considerable increase in the proportion of the annual output produced in the fall and winter.[114]

The average annual output in Canada (1949) is 157 eggs per hen; in the Netherlands, 183. In Turkey and the Philippines, on the other hand, hens average only 50 and 64 eggs per year, respectively.

113. **16**, 1950, pp. 484–85.
114. **15**, September 1950, p. 8.

Before the war, China was the most important producer of processed eggs. Since the war, Australia has engaged in a large processing production, and liquid and dried eggs now represent nearly 30 per cent of its total output. To save shipping space, the United States processed as much as 25 per cent of its eggs during the war; in 1949, about 15 per cent were processed.

In 1950, the output of the major egg-producing countries (exclusive of China and the USSR) was about 30 per cent above the prewar average, largely because of the rise in output in the United States. In 1951 the world's egg output failed to show a significant increase for the first time since the end of World War II. The reversal of the trend was particularly marked in Western Eu-

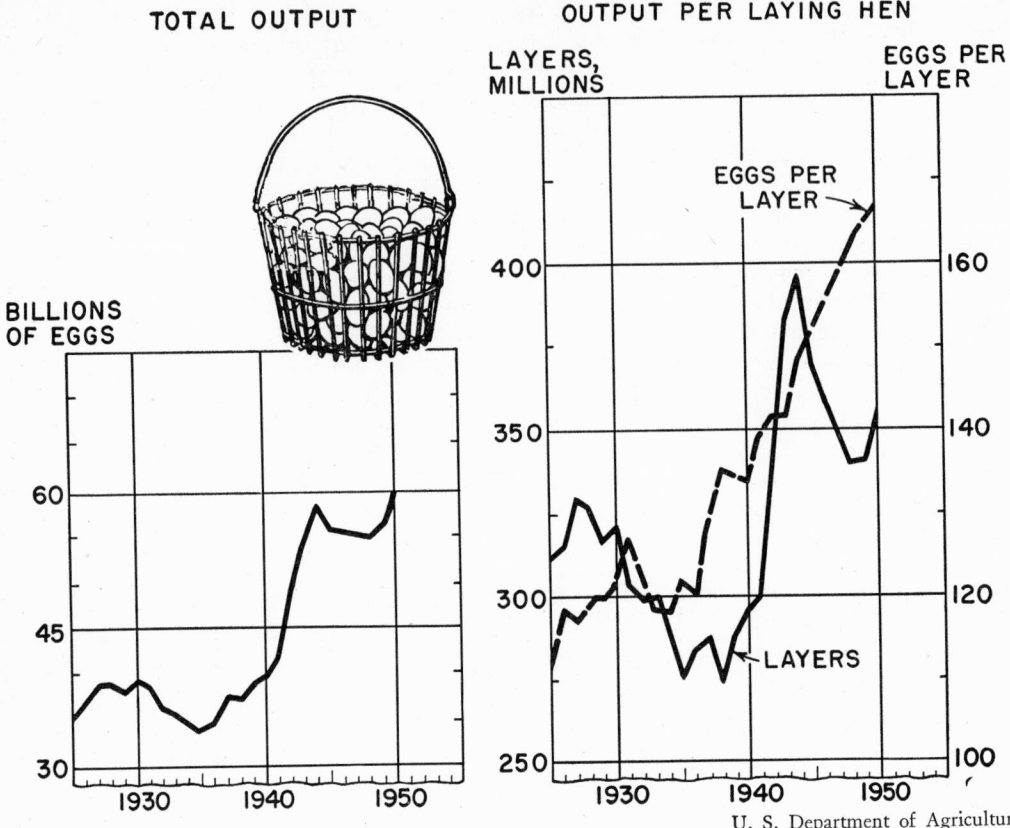

FIGURE 204. EGGS: OUTPUT IN THE UNITED STATES, 1930–50

rope, except Germany, Austria and Italy. Countries exporting eggs, such as Belgium, Ireland and the Scandinavian countries, were affected by unsatisfactory export prices in relation to feed prices and other costs. High prices for poultry meat in relation to eggs encouraged liquidation of flocks in the United Kingdom and some other countries.[115]

HIDES AND SKINS

Since hides and skins are by-products of animal husbandry, the output depends primarily on the slaughter of livestock for meat and does not respond to changes in the demand for leather. When meat requirements and meat prices go up, more animals are slaughtered, more hides and skins appear on the market, and prices for hides and skins tend to decline.[116] On the other

hand, high demand and rising prices for hides and skins result primarily in the marketing of inferior grades, ordinarily rejected, and only occasionally in some small influx of supplies from marginal or more remote sources. In other words, supplies of hides and skins are inelastic to changes in prices.

Goat and kid skins are generally more sensitive to prices than other hides and skins. Goat meat is cheaper and less in demand than other meat and the skins of goats and kids therefore represent a larger part of the value of the animal than the skins of calves or sheep. Even so, higher prices for goat and kid skins ordinarily result not in increased flocks but in increased slaughtering and in the marketing of skins from sources generally not available.

Quality

Hides and skins are sold either wet or dry. Most wet hides and skins come from meat-packing houses and are of high quality because they have been removed expertly. Dry hides and skins

115. **22**, March 17, 1952, p. 206.

116. In the United States, the price of the hide amounts to about 9 per cent of the total value of high-quality steers, to 15 per cent of the value of low-grade cows, and to 20 per cent of the value of calves. **42**, p. 145.

usually come from areas with inferior stock and few facilities for wet preservation. In Latin American countries, important world sources of these products, the custom of branding cattle to identify ownership, often on the butt, the most valuable part of the hide, lowers the quality and price of the product. Moreover, the skinning is often inferior, and the hides may be ticky and grubby and hence less desirable to the leather industry than those from healthier animals. Cattle hides from Argentina, however, and particularly those from packing houses (the so-called *frigorificos*), as well as hides from Uruguayan packing houses, are of good, and often excellent, grade.

Differences in quality in other parts of the world are about equally great. In a country like Sweden, hides are uniformly good, while in India they are generally defective and little is done to improve the quality. In India, the percentage of "fallen" hides (taken off fallen animals by special flayers) is three times larger than that of hides from slaughterhouses.[117] Competition on international markets for available supplies is so intense, however, that efforts of government and private interests to raise the quality of the national production of hides and skins — for example, in Brazil — have often had little result.[118]

Chief Types and Uses

The four main kinds of hides and skins are cattle hides, calf and kip[119] skins, sheep and lamb skins, and goat and kid skins. These four types represent about 95 per cent of all the hides and skins used in the world and in the United States. The remainder is made up of hides and skins of horses, buffaloes, pigs, reptiles, fish, kangaroos, deer, elk and so on.

Cattle hides are used as they come to produce heavy sole leather, belting and harness leather, or are split into various thicknesses for lighter and more flexible leather (shoe uppers, upholstery and other products). No other kind of leather is as suitable for soles.[120]

Calf and kip skins are used mostly for shoe uppers but also for handbags, garments, uphol-

stery, luggage and the like. While only the predominantly agricultural countries have large surpluses of cattle hides, some industrial countries where the dairy industry is well developed, as in northwestern Europe, have surplus calf and kip skins, since practically all male calves of dairy cows are slaughtered young; the quality of these skins surpasses even the uniformly good quality in the United States.

Leather from sheep and lamb skins is less durable and stretches more than other leather and is the least expensive. It is used for gloves and garments, shoe linings and fancy leather goods. Sheep and lamb skins are produced in much greater quantities than any other hides and skins. Demand for mutton and lamb increases the output of skins, while demand for wool encourages the farmer to hold the animals for additional shearings.

About 95 per cent of all goat and kid skins are used for uppers and for lining footwear, the rest for gloves, bookbinding and other leather products. Goats, the poor man's animal, are usually raised on small farms, and skins are collected from farm to farm by local dealers, who ship them to larger companies for marketing. Goat and kid skins from Brazil, especially from the southern state of Rio Grande do Sul, are of excellent quality and command premium prices on the world markets.

Output

In the average prewar year, about half a billion hides and skins were produced in the world, as follows: [121]

	Millions of Pieces	Per Cent
Total	494	100.0
Hides	100	20.2
Calf and kip skins	70	14.2
Sheep and lamb skins	180	36.4
Goat and kid skins	120	24.3
All other hides and skins	24	4.8

World totals for postwar years are not available, but they must be considerably higher since almost all countries outside Europe report increases in output. The United States raised its output of cattle hides and calf skins from 24.5 million pieces a year during 1934–38 to 35.3 million in 1949; India from 6.7 to 20.9 million;

---

117. **28**, October 1947, p. 1.

118. **64**, p. 3.

119. Immature or undersized cattle and buffaloes.

120. In the United States, the manufacture of footwear consumes 85 per cent of all cattle hides, 90 per cent of all calf and kip skins, 95 per cent of all goat and kid skins, and about 30 per cent of all sheep and lamb skins. **31**, p. 15.

121. **31**, pp. 18–19.

Table 299

Hides and Skins: Output in Selected Countries, 1934–38 Annual Average and 1949

(*Thousands of Pieces*)

Country	Cattle Hides [a]		Calf Skins [b]	Sheep and Lamb Skins		Goat and Kid Skins	
	1934–38	*1949*	*1934–38*	*1934–38*	*1949*	*1934–38*	*1949*
United States	15,050	35,255	9,451	21,988	15,170	...	210
Canada	1,208	1,906	1,130	1,535	700	...	...
Mexico	1,900	2,420	...	435	1,080	...	1,510
Colombia	1,020	2,800	...	101	420	21	200
Brazil	3,750	7,080	...	2,600	3,640	...	2,755
Peru	445	525	...	1,618	3,420	709	600
Chile	413	465	...	2,850	2,680	57	109
Argentina	7,460	9,850	725	12,815	12,000	4,800	2,400
United Kingdom	2,500	3,600	1,200	12,250	6,660	...	...
France	2,342	5,400	4,853	6,550	2,440	1,323	...
Belgium	445	900	503	132	60	11	380
Netherlands	406	1,200	860	258	160	...	85
Denmark	556	1,000	543	79 [c]	25	...	...
Sweden	466 [d]	1,300	1,265 [d]	178 [d]	110	140 [d]	...
Germany	3,744	4,300	4,841	1,640	1,400	607	500
Poland	1,318	1,660	2,395	534	400	...	260
Czechoslovakia	694	730	901	203	190	401	300
Switzerland	...	400	431	90	60	...	66
Hungary	151	570	394	216	210	2	20
Spain	...	630	...	7,000	7,450	2,157	3,930
Italy	1,300	2,000	1,700	3,000	3,650	...	890
Yugoslavia	357	615	328	1,075	3,000	195	490
Romania	1,032	990	...	1,495	2,500	...	75
Bulgaria	98	130	48	1,630	3,000	1,800	390
Greece	167	170	...	1,750	2,740	2,325	1,510
USSR	7,017	14,800	6,370	22,600	25,100	5,000	6,100
China	1,500	7,000	...	8,850	4,100	11,500	5,040
Japan	322	475	34	2	...	50	...
Turkey	...	900	70	6,200	8,000	4,980	6,060
India	6,103	20,890	550	15,225	16,980	34,500	21,100
Indonesia	579	1,500	...	111	600	830	2,550
Philippines	...	420	...	162	120	588	710
Egypt	...	...	...	600	450	...	520
French West Africa	860	...	...	2,615	3,100	...	6,600
British West Africa	...	...	...	5,500	4,900	...	...
British East Africa	1,265	...	...	1,111	1,200	2,500	3,700
Union of South Africa	693	1,920	...	13,383 [c]	10,600	...	1,850
Australia	2,480	3,400	1,550	18,759	20,760	...	...
New Zealand	557	1,900	1,302	13,422	16,000	...	...

Source: Textile and Leather Division of the U. S. Department of Commerce.

a. Data for 1949 include cattle and buffalo hides, calf and kip skins.

b. 1949 data included in figure for cattle hides.
c. Includes goat and kid skins.
d. 1939.

Argentina from 8.2 to 9.9 million; Brazil from 3.8 to 7.1 million; the USSR from 13.4 to 14.8 million. Production of sheep and lamb skins showed greater fluctuations. It fell in the United States, Canada, Chile, Argentina, most European countries, China, the Union of South Africa, but increased in the Balkans, the USSR, India, Australia, New Zealand, and some other countries. (See Table 299.)

The United States has been for many years the chief world producer of cattle hides. Argentina, next in importance in the Western Hemisphere, produced about half as many hides as the United States before the war, but had less than a third of the output of the United States in 1949. Because of much lower consumption at home, Argentina ordinarily exports about 70 per cent of its products. The USSR produces considerable quantities of all four kinds of hides and skins.

In the production of sheep and lamb skins, the leading countries are the USSR, Australia, India, New Zealand and the United States. India was the chief world producer of goat and kid skins before the war, and China ranked next.

OUTLOOK

People have become keenly aware of the nutritive value of animal foodstuffs.[122] Meat and dairy

---

122. Cf. Chapter 9.

products are no longer considered the proper fare of only the privileged classes and nations. We realize today that they should form a sufficient portion of the human diet to make it nutritionally adequate. The value of "protective" foods has been stressed in innumerable publications, public speeches, national and international conferences on food problems; it reappears in every comparison of living standards among countries. The new attitude toward, and active interest in, animal foodstuffs encourages the development of the livestock industry in many parts of the world.

The problem is that the production of animal foodstuffs cuts into grain supplies and requires more labor than the production of an equivalent number of calories in cereals. The intrinsically high prices of animal foodstuffs are further increased by the growing demand.

At present, the supply of meat and dairy products per capita of world population is smaller than before World War II, despite a considerable recovery in the livestock industry in most countries: the human population has increased faster than the livestock herds. Nevertheless, it can be confidently expected that the stimulus of high prices, on the one hand, and rising income, on the other, will increase livestock production. Furthermore, the spread of better techniques in breeding and feeding holds promise of raising the quality of livestock and increasing their effectiveness as producers of food.

CHAPTER 19

FORESTS AND FOREST PRODUCTS

FORESTS ARE one of the world's most valuable natural resources. They serve mankind in many intangible ways, and their economic value increases as science and technology find new ways to utilize wood. In contrast to other natural resources, such as coal, petroleum and minerals, the wealth of the forests can be inexhaustible. All that is needed to make them last forever is a clear understanding of the nature of forests and the care necessary to enable them to renew and perpetuate themselves — that is, to treat forests as a crop, not as a mine.

THE LIFE OF A FOREST

A forest is a world in itself, full of action and conflict. The trees, ruling the biological functions within the forest, are engaged in a continuous life-and-death battle. They struggle with one another for sun, water and food, stretching upward to reach the light and extending their roots underground to wrest food and moisture from the soil. No quarter is given to the weak — they must perish so that the stronger trees can live and grow.

On a larger scale, there is also a perpetual conflict between the two basic types of trees — softwoods or conifers (Gymnospermae), and hardwoods or broadleaved species (Angiospermae).[1]

The first — pines, cedars, spruces, firs, hemlocks — are the older inhabitants of the earth. Their cells are of a relatively primitive kind; they have only one simple and rather mechanical process to heal their wounds, the manufacture of oleoresin. The second group — oaks, elms, birches, maples and other hardwoods — have strong specialized cells, some for food storage, others linked in one system to speed the flow of sap from the roots to the crowns and back to the roots. Their seedlings are more tolerant of physical conditions than those of softwoods.[2] Because of their strength and adaptability, the hardwoods, although latecomers in the world, have been able to take the best land from the softwoods. The latter have maintained themselves mostly on the drier, or colder, and generally less favorable sites.

Like all living things, forest trees become toughened in the struggle for existence. Through natural pruning, they drop their lower branches, useless in the battle yet demanding food. They grow tall and straight, sometimes stretching without limbs for a hundred feet above the ground. Wood from trees that are hardened by adversity is much more valuable to man than the knotty wood of the more decorative trees growing freely in the open and branching in every direction.

To the victors in the battle within a forest go the spoils: with assurance of food, moisture, light and air, they can grow to maturity. If left undisturbed, they gradually attain an ideal balance with natural conditions and form the so-called climax forests. When the old trees reach their maximum height, they begin to spread their crowns in all directions. Finally growth becomes almost imperceptible. Then they occupy soil for which they "pay no rent."[3]

With old age, infirmities beset the trees: their annual shoots become less vigorous, the annual rings narrower, and the leaves smaller; dead branches multiply, and their wounds do not heal as easily as in their youth; their moisture content decreases, and it is increasingly difficult for them to provide water for their vital functions.[4]

Other living organisms in the forests — animals, insects, birds, bacteria, innumerable plants — also know no peace. Every member of a forest community is food for some other member. The plants, even the trees, provide food for animals and insects. Insects are the food of birds. The weaker animals fall prey to the stronger, the vegetarian animals to the carnivorous.

Yet, even in the midst of this ceaseless struggle, there is cooperation within the forest community. The trees protect one another from the wind, and the bigger and stronger trees break the

---

1. The hardwoods may be subdivided into tropical (mahogany, ebony, teak, rosewood, balsa and others), and temperate (oak, maple, poplar, birch and so on).
2. **14**, p. 3.

3. **23**, p. 52.
4. **12**, 1948, p. 9.

heavy snow that would crush the younger and weaker. Trees build up the soil for their neighbors, as well as themselves. Even the defeated trees that die enrich the soil for others. Birds and squirrels scatter seeds, which start new trees. Bacteria and infusoria work on dead animal and plant matter and convert it into substances that fertilize the soil.

TYPES OF FORESTS

The forests of the world can be classified in two ways: according to the predominant type of tree — coniferous or broadleaved — and according to characteristics of the forest as a whole in relation to man — productive and accessible or the opposite.

Coniferous and Broadleaved Forests

Coniferous and broadleaved temperate forests often intermingle to form mixed forests. Man makes much more use of conifers than of the broadleaved types or hardwoods. Since the conifers are usually less tolerant of shade, hardwoods often gradually displace them in mixed areas.

Coniferous forests stretch from Alaska to Kamchatka in a broad belt just below the tundras of northern Canada, Scandinavia and Siberia. This belt covers the larger part of Canada, stretches over a considerable area in the northwestern United States and runs uninterruptedly across the entire northern part of Europe and the USSR. In addition, there is an important coniferous area in the western and southern regions of the United States and also in Brazil and in central Europe. (See Figure 205.)

The geographic distribution of the hardwoods is very different. In the Western Hemisphere the temperate hardwoods are concentrated in the eastern part of the United States, from its northern border to the conifer area in the south, and in the extreme south of Chile and Argentina. They cover a substantial area in central Europe and the USSR, extending in a narrow line between the Black and Caspian Seas, and, in Asia, run from Tibet to the Pacific coast. There are isolated areas in Asia and Africa, but on the whole, these temperate hardwood forests, having been cleared from land suitable for agriculture, are rather scattered, covering a considerably smaller area than the conifers, and are often surrounded by almost treeless expanses.

The tropical hardwoods form a broken belt, interrupted by deserts, savannas and swamps.

The greatest concentrations are in South America and along the equator in western and central Africa and southeastern Asia. Tropical hardwoods occupy roughly half the world's forest area, the other half being divided among the coniferous, temperate broadleaved and mixed forests.[5]

About 95 per cent of the conifers and 90 per cent of the temperate hardwoods are in the North Temperate Zone, where nearly three fourths of the world's people live.

Productive and Accessible Forests

Forests that are capable of producing crops of industrial wood, such as saw logs, pulpwood, poles, posts and crossties, are generally classified as productive. About 60 per cent of the world's forest area falls within this definition, but only about half of this is now accessible. The other half has not been penetrated because of topographic and climatic obstacles or other factors that so far have made commercial exploitation too great a risk. Some of these productive but inaccessible forests constitute a potential reserve of timber and may be opened up eventually.

The tropical hardwood forests, in particular, will become economic assets and yield large quantities of timber if and when they can be made accessible. They contain numerous species of trees — 2,700 kinds of palm alone — whose properties for the most part have not yet been established. The wood of some trees in these forests is so heavy that it will not float, while that of others is lighter than cork. Unfamiliarity with the tree species, absence of transportation facilities and difficulties in finding and keeping labor have combined to make these forests too great a risk to attract capital investment in logging and marketing. What little use is now made of them consists of slow and highly selective felling. Some trees, for example, are spotted in the jungles, girdled and left to dry for two years or more so that they will lose weight and their removal will be made easier.

The nonproductive forests consist of the slow-growing trees, often stunted or dwarfed, usually found in unfavorable sites — on the fringes of

---

5. Since there is some intermingling, all forests in which 75 per cent or more of the stand is of coniferous or needle-leaved species are classified as coniferous. The same principle is applied to broadleaved forests. The remainder are mixed forests. For statistical data on forest areas see below, pp. 692 ff.

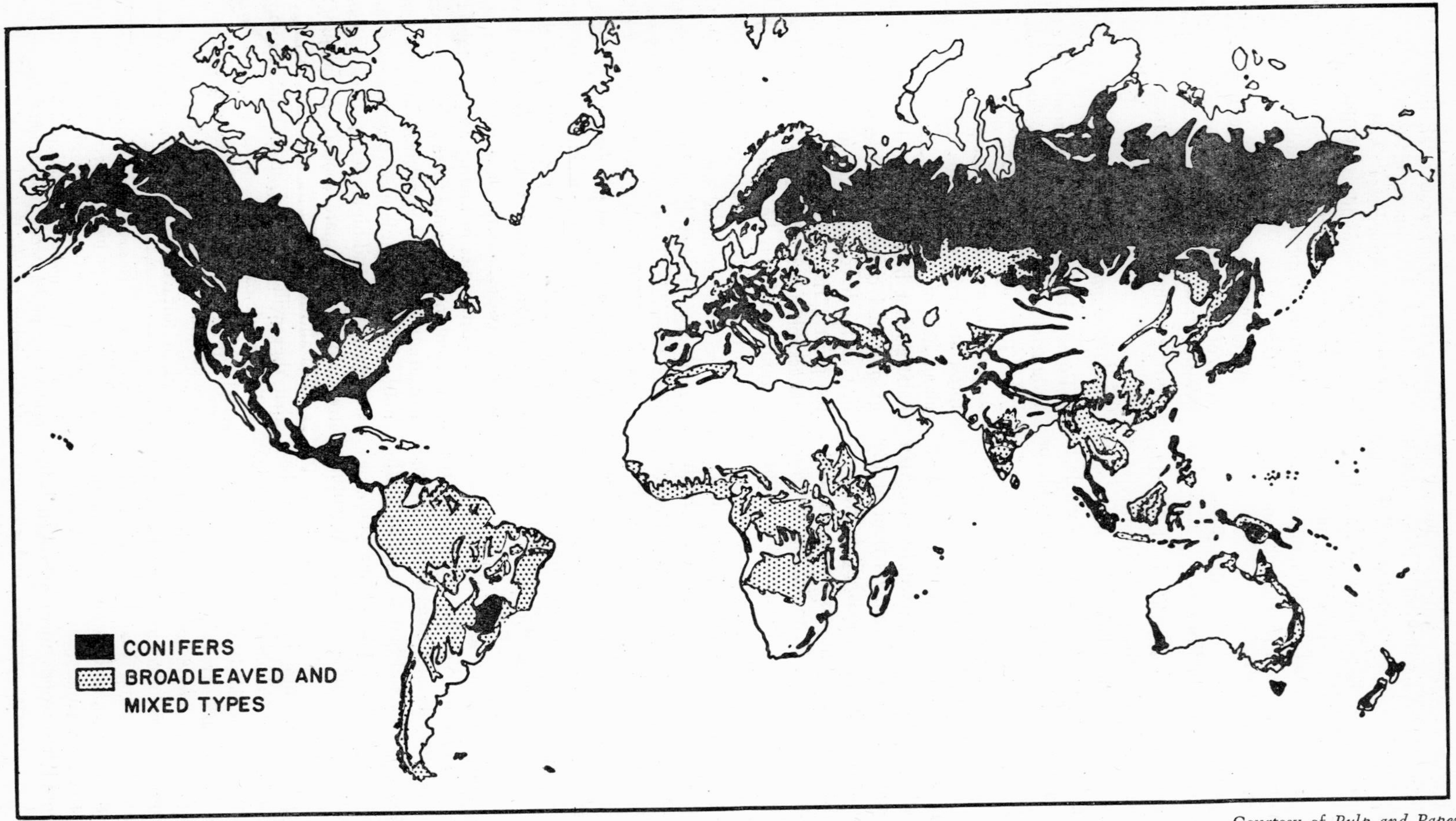

Courtesy of *Pulp and Paper*

FIGURE 205. TIMBER AREAS IN THE WORLD, BY TYPE

CONIFERS

BROADLEAVED AND
MIXED TYPES

tundras, in arid savannas bordering the deserts of Africa and at high altitudes near the limits of tree growth. While such forest land may be made productive, it is highly improbable that it it will ever provide more than small and occasional supplies of fuel.[6]

WHAT FORESTS MEAN TO MANKIND

Forests serve mankind in a thousand and one ways, both directly, through their products, and indirectly, by safeguarding man's environment.

PRODUCTS

Wood is one of the world's most versatile raw materials. Lumber is still the chief building material, and at least two thirds of mankind use wood as fuel for heating and cooking. As much as 90 per cent of all paper is made of wood. More than two thirds of the world's railways have wooden crossties.[7] Coal mines depend on wooden pit props, and millions of miles of electric wires are carried on wooden poles. Rayon fiber, explosives, alcohol, and in some countries even cattle feed, are made of wood pulp, and many experts think that new uses of pulp for plastics and fabricated building materials may soon double the demand for it. In addition to wood, forests supply man with rubber, tanning materials, naval stores, cork, oils, camphor, cinchona bark and other products.

SERVICES

Conserving Soil and Water

Apart from providing so many and such diversified products, forests guard the soil and regulate distribution of water. The heavy underground network of tree roots safeguards the topsoil.[8] This is particularly important on sloping land where rainfall and streams would otherwise carry away the soil, after the surface has been denuded and the way opened to erosion. "Except for a layer of concrete, there is nothing known that will hold the soil so firmly on sloping land

as a cover of trees." [9] Where the hillsides are bare and sun-scorched, like too many in the United States and many other countries, the run-off water carves deep channels and eventually causes devastating erosion. By preventing or weakening the run-off from hillsides, the forests also keep streams, reservoirs and irrigation ditches from filling with silt. In the southern Appalachians, fifty times more silt is carried down from treeless than from forested hills.[10]

In the United States, where more than 75 per cent of the land is sloping and potentially subject to erosion if used for clean-tilled crops or grazing, forest protection of watersheds is vitally important. The wooded slopes of mountains in the West receive several times as much rain and snow as the valleys and supply virtually all the ground water to feed perennial streams. "Without them the valleys, and indeed most of the West, would be an arid waste." [11]

Breaking the Winds

Forests also act as windbreaks and help to keep the hot summer winds from drying out the soil and destroying the crops. They catch the blown soil and hold it, thus keeping it from being deposited on fields or other places. This is why deforestation leads to the development of dust bowls, dunes and deserts. Reforestation helps to stop the loss of soil and is the important step toward reclaiming land that has lost fertility.

The most striking example of this effect of forest destruction and of reforestation is Landes, in southwestern France.[12] After the pine forests of Landes were burned by the Vandals in the fifth century A.D., west winds began to blow sand over the devastated area. In time, sand dunes covered about half a million acres and choked the streams, thus forming marshes. More than 2 million acres became swampland, and malaria soon depopulated a once productive region. Napoleon began the battle against sand dunes in this area by reforesting it with pines and building littoral dams. It took a century to drain the marshes, restore the soil, and reforest the land, but today Landes, with two thirds of its territory in forest (1.5 out of 2.3 million acres), is the most heavily forested of all the depart-

6. **2**, p. 6.

7. More than a billion wooden crossties are in use in the United States. Cheapness, strength, resistance to shock, relative ease of replacement and long life (sometimes thirty to forty years) have helped them to withstand the competition of other materials. **30**, pp. 16–17.

8. The total length of all the roots of a big spreading oak tree amounts to many hundreds of miles. **12**, 1948, p. 3.

9. **22**, p. 3.

10. **23**, p. 112.

11. **13**, p. 15, and **11**, p. 122.

12. **33**, pp. 50–51. See also Chapter 15, pp. 480–81.

ments of France and has thriving timber and resin industries.

China presents another extreme. Forest lands that once extended far to the arid northwestern mountains are now a desert because of the removal of trees, which had acted as natural windbreaks and soil-holding agents. Northwest winds, meeting with no resistance, bring the desert farther down into the Chinese valleys. Intensive pressure of population and the need for crop cultivation have resulted in a virtual elimination of forests throughout many of the more densely populated parts of the country.[13]

Controlling Floods

Forests cannot prevent floods, but they help to control them. The tree trunks and undergrowth divide the rushing water into weaker separate streams; dead and living roots and dead trees on the forest floor spread the water over the surface and help it infiltrate the soil and rock mantle. Moreover, the forest floor is covered with mosses, ferns and lichens, all of which absorb water,[14] as does the spongy, loose forest soil. If the flow of water is heavy, the forest soil may not absorb it all, but it will lessen the speed and destructiveness of the flow.

Other Services

Forests increase the amount of moisture in the wind and thus provide additional precipitation in the areas beyond their limits. Wind absorbs at least as much moisture in passing over a square mile of forest as over a square mile of water.[15] Wooded areas above the headwaters of streams that supply the cities with drinking water help to safeguard the purity of the supply.

The protection the forests afford in retarding the water run-off, in distributing rainfall, preventing erosion, reducing wind damage and safeguarding water supplies is often valued more than their output of wood. In many countries, the so-called protective forests have been taken under public control and are in turn protected from destruction.

In addition, forests supply forage by serving as grazing grounds for millions of domestic animals. In the United States, about 350 million

acres, more than half of all forest land, are used for range; in the West, the proportion is nearly 70 per cent. If properly managed, forests can be grazed without impairing the forage or other values.[16]

Because forest air is pure and healthful, recreation centers, resorts and sanatoriums for convalescents have long been established in wooded areas. To millions of people, the forests are not only playgrounds, but also a link with nature. Throughout the ages, man has sought spiritual relaxation in the solitude of forests. Recognition of such intangible values was expressed in the ancient custom of consecrating certain forests to gods.

What Man Has Done to and for Forests

In the course of human history, the relationship between man and the forest has changed frequently, though many of the ancient relationships still persist in one part of the world or another. "Barely one thousand years ago . . . , forests occupied the largest part of the earth's surface, with the possible exception of Asia and the Mediterranean seaboard." Today the manmade change in the face of the earth is so great as "to be comparable with the variations brought about by the preceding geological ages." [17]

USE OF FORESTS IN THE PAST

To primitive man, forests offered hunting grounds and a retreat from enemy attacks. Most of all, the forest was a larder containing such foods as nuts, seeds, berries, fruits, acorns and roots, in addition to the meat of animals and birds. When men began to domesticate animals, forests served as pastures.

Often the forest was a barrier to the migration of tribes in search of new sources of food. Later, when the Romans were extending their power into Asia and Africa, they hesitated to engage their legions in the thick woods of central Europe. Thus, forests often became boundaries between tribes and nations.

Primitive Agriculture

Generally speaking, men must have begun to consider the trees as obstacles when they shifted from the nomadic to the agricultural way of life. Primitive agriculture has always treated forests

---

13. **3**, p. 39, and **7**, November–December 1948, p. 306.

14. Mosses, for example, can absorb as much as 900 times their weight in water.

15. **35**, p. 124.

16. **14**, p. 15.

17. **1**, p. 34.

as enemies. Almost everywhere, the common way to get land for crops has been to set fire to the woods and thus clear the virgin soil, especially fertile when enriched with ashes. People soon learned that forest soil was rich at the beginning but became unproductive after a few years. Then they abandoned the old site, moved to another place and repeated the performance.

The destruction of forests for cropfields was not disastrous on more or less level land if the land was let alone and if soil and climate were suited to forest growth. The trees recaptured the lost ground as soon as people vacated the area. Bushes and other thickets reappeared, then small trees displaced them. In time, the soil recovered, weak trees capitulated, and the original character of the forest was more or less restored. On hillsides, however, the destruction was often final, since forest trees found it difficult to recolonize soil that had been exposed to the ravages of water and wind. Scrub would invade the naked hills, and if goats or sheep were brought to browse on the poor forage, erosion was likely to overwhelm the land.[18]

Use for Lumber and Fuel

As population increased, people needed not only more land for crops but also more lumber for shelter and more fuel for cooking and heating. More and more trees were felled, more and more forests were burned, in all parts of the world — by the Incas in Peru, the Mayas in Mexico, the Teutons in Germany, the Normans in Great Britain, the Romans and the Greeks, the Slavs on the Russian plains, the native tribes in Africa and, later, the early settlers in North America. To some extent destruction of forests was inevitable, since land had to be cleared in the new communities and wood had to be cut to build houses and barns and meet the many other needs for which it was used almost universally. The destruction, however, often greatly exceeded the actual requirements. Moreover, while wood was plentiful, nobody worried much about forest fires or about having wood rot on the ground.

As time went on the demand for wood, the customary material for houses, boats, plows, carts, coaches, furniture, continued to grow; more charcoal was needed for expanding industries. Such demands increased the rate of wood cutting in many parts of the world.

Choice Timber for Shipbuilding

In the time of the Roman Empire as well as in the following centuries, construction of warships and merchant vessels consumed large amounts of choice timber, and the sea power of a country depended largely on its timber resources. To some extent, timber conditioned shipbuilding: vessels could not exceed 230 feet in length because it was difficult to find trees exceeding this size. Some parts of ships, particularly of warships, had to be made of single pieces from trunks with definite curves. England has been reminded several times of the close relationship between sea power and timber resources. In 1588, the Spanish Armada carried orders to set fire to the royal oak forests along the British coast as soon as invasion was effected. Though the Armada was defeated, the threat was not forgotten. About a century later, during their fight against Dutch sea power, the British anticipated the destruction of their coastal forests and started inland oak plantings. Although this project was abandoned after the British victory, it was revived a century later during the war against Napoleon. These plantings had just begun when iron replaced wood in shipbuilding.

USE OF FORESTS IN MODERN TIMES

The primitive practice of shifting cultivation still prevails in many wooded areas of the world where forests retreat before the fires set to obtain forest soil and sunshine for crops. In tropical Africa, the dry season, which lasts more than seven months, prevents regrowth of burnt-over forests. Instead, the savanna type of grass or bush takes over the deforested land. Flames and smoke columns are a part of the panorama every year during the dry season in Africa's immense savanna belt.[19]

Shifting cultivation, with the concomitant burning of forests, is still widespread in Asia as well — in Indochina, for example. In Brazil, some of the best forests have been burned to make room for coffee trees and corn or are cut for firewood.[20] Wasteful and primitive manufacturing of charcoal takes a heavy toll of valuable species in Argentina. Railroads in El Salvador, Peru, Brazil, Mexico and many other Latin American countries use wood for fuel. In

18. **28**, p. 39.

19. **1**, p. 56.
20. **9**, Vol. II, p. 66.

Brazil, where the major use of wood is for fuel, cordwood for locomotives is transported as much as ninety miles by truck or cart. Most of the railroads burn coal only when wood is not available.[21]

Cutting Practices

Even in advanced countries, cutting practices are often wasteful and destructive. Either the best trees are cut haphazardly, leaving only poor stands, or young stock is felled prematurely and the vigorous growth of the forest is checked. In one way or another, many countries are rapidly destroying their forest stands.

Cutting practices in the United States in 1945 were classed as poor or destructive on 64 per cent of all private forest land (which constitutes about three fourths of all forest land), fair on 28 per cent, good on 7 per cent, and of high order on only one per cent.[22] (See Figure 206.) On public land, cutting is notably better, but the practices on private timberland, supplying 90 per cent or more of all timber, make the national showing poor. Small farm woodlands get particularly bad treatment; only 4 per cent of the cutting in 1945 was rated good or better.[23] It is estimated that such practices and the present rate of cutting, if continued, would reduce the timber resources of the country by some 27 per cent in the next twenty years.

Pasturage

Much forest land has been ruined by indiscriminate use for pasture. While light grazing does not affect forests seriously, overgrazing has the same ultimate effect as fire or excessive cutting, though the destruction is slower. It is practiced, however, not only in remote areas like Java, where buffaloes know no other pastures,[24] but even in the United States, where overgrazing on farm woodlands is common. The number of livestock grazing in farm woods of the central states, for example, is five times the carrying capacity of the woods. More than 5 million animals were permitted to graze in national forests in 1945.[25]

Forest Fires

Ineffective fire protection, and often the complete lack of protection, has probably done more to devastate forests in many regions than uneconomic cutting practices.

In the United States, about 100 million acres of forest had no organized fire protection whatsoever in 1948. The country had 194,611 forest fires in 1949, and even this figure is moderate as compared with the 234,000 forest fires in 1938. The area burned over in 1949 was 15.3 million acres, as against 33.7 million acres in 1938.[26] The majority of the fires are in unprotected forest areas, but almost 79,000 fires in 1949 were in protected forests and more than 10,000, within national forests. Some 60 million acres have been completely devastated by fire. Each year adds about a million acres to this total.[27]

In Canada, more than 2 million acres on the average have been burned over each year during the last decade. These fires have destroyed about half as much marketable timber each year as is used by the Canadian pulp and paper industry.[28]

In some forest areas of Argentina, not less than 30 per cent of the stand has been destroyed by fire. In some regions of Chile, the loss by fire is nearly four times the amount of the annual cut.[29] The slopes above many hill towns of South America are bare, and no forests are left around the large cities.

Both in the United States and other countries, most forest fires can be traced to neglect and irresponsibility, though some start from natural causes, such as lightning. Once started, the fire is too often fed by litter and branches left after cutting. As long as forests were well stocked and free from man's interference, they resisted occasional natural fires in their own way and managed to survive. Today, they need protection but too seldom get it.

DEFORESTATION

Half the original forests of the world have been eliminated from the face of the earth.[30] The extent of deforestation varies from region to region. In western Europe, about two thirds of the original forest area has been cleared; in the Mediterranean the percentage is even higher,

21. "Occasionally one sees . . . in Brazil an anomaly of a wood-burning engine pulling a train load of coal." **31**, p. 237; see also **48**, p. 106.

22. **46**, p. 40. A field survey of commercial forests only.

23. **13**, p. 48.

24. **25**, p. 40.

25. **12**, 1938, p. 744, and **16**, p. 123.

26. **10**, 1950, p. 740.

27. **12**, 1938, p. 741.

28. **5**, p. 34.

29. **3**, pp. 33–35.

30. **37**, p. 38.

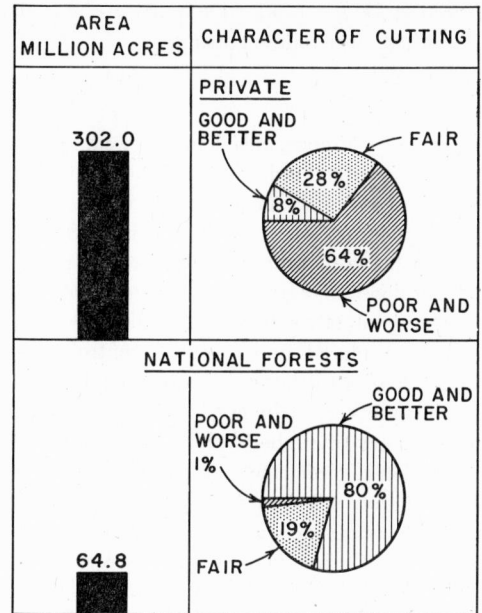
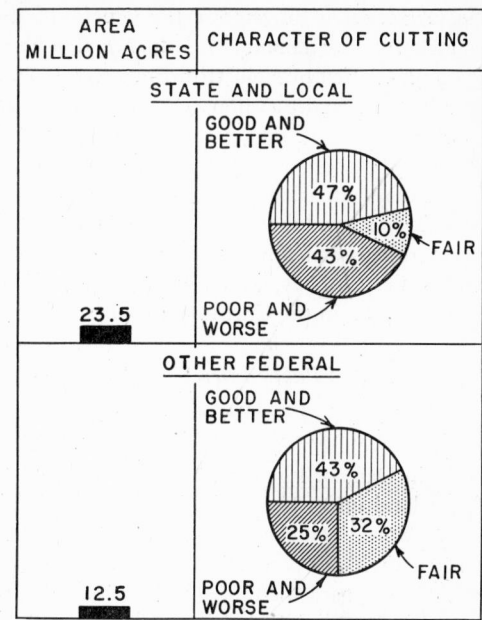

U. S. Department of Agriculture

FIGURE 206. CUTTING PRACTICES IN THE UNITED STATES, 1945

while in central Europe it is lower. In Great Britain, only 5 per cent of the original forest area has been preserved; in France, about 19 per cent of the forests, which originally covered some three fourths of the land. In Italy no virgin forests survive; many areas of the Middle East, which once gloried in abundance of wood, are now denuded.[31] Forests have been almost completely destroyed in many parts of China, so that firewood is weighed on scales and costs so much that few families can afford to buy more than a handful of sticks at a time.[32] In the United States, the original forest area has been reduced by about a third, largely by land clearing and fire. What is now classed as forest land, covering about 624 million acres, is mostly cutover land on part of which there is second growth, although the West still has much virgin timber. Some of the cutover land is so depleted by logging and fires that it should be classed as wasteland.[33]

The Caribbean has only remnants of its old forests. In Brazil, the area around Rio de Janeiro has been so deforested that domestic wood for fuel costs more than coal imported from Europe.[34]

FOREST POLICY

Only about a fifth or less of the world's productive and accessible forest area is managed properly, while about half is being exploited without regard for continued productivity. The rest has been neglected, often to such an extent as to become worse than valueless.

The disastrous consequences of forest destruction were recognized by some rulers more than two thousand years ago. Asoka, a legendary sovereign of the Indian Kingdom, which exceeded the borders of former British India, initiated the planting of trees and ordered the use of stone for building instead of wood, of which even the city walls and palaces had been constructed. Forest conservation measures in many respects comparable to modern practice existed in China during the Chow Dynasty, which began in 1100 B.C. and lasted almost a thousand years.[35] The Romans introduced provisions to protect forests in their penal code, the *Lex XII Tabularum* (Twelve Tables), in 450 B.C.[36]

Medieval Europe, however, did little to preserve forests. Royal ordinances against wanton destruction, which were issued in various countries, were more concerned with the preservation of game for hunting by the nobility than with

31. **26**, p. 10.
32. **7**, November–December 1948, p. 299.
33. **12**, 1941, p. 485.
34. **49**, Vol. II, p. 709.

35. **1**, p. 14.
36. **7**, November–December 1947, p. 3.

the protection of forests for the benefit of the population. The famous Ordonnance des Eaux et Forêts drafted by Colbert in France in 1669, a model of forest legislation for other European countries for more than a century, was inspired primarily by concern for timber to build warships. One provision specifically protected the coastal forests and the objective of another was to force tree growth upward to provide the masts for the French navy, which prided itself as having the tallest in the Christian world.[37]

The Concept of Public Interest

The concept of public interest in forests appeared forcefully for the first time in a law enacted in Denmark in 1805.[38] This law placed all forest land under reservation and provided that no purchaser could cut timber during the first ten years without permission of the state forester, who was to mark the timber to be removed. The law stated explicitly that "where there is now high forest there must always be high forest." Grazing was forbidden and various measures were specified to maintain forest growth.

As a result Danish forests, which occupied only 5 per cent of the country and were in danger of virtual extinction at the beginning of the nineteenth century, are now in excellent condition and extend over 8 per cent of the land. The forest law was modernized in 1935 to compel all woodland owners to replant when trees are felled and to give adequate attention to drainage, weeding out of inferior species, road maintenance and so on. The area in hardwood may not be diminished.

The French Forestry Code of 1827 prohibited the clearing of protective forests, such as those on mountain slopes and summits. The code was expanded in 1859, 1922 and again in the 1930's. The forest law enacted by Austria in 1852 provided for a sustained-yield operation of forests and reforestation, regulated grazing and removal of forest litter and branchwood, and laid down special rules for the treatment of protective forests, such as prohibition of large clear-fellings at high elevations and on steep slopes. This law had a great influence on the development of better forest practices in most European countries, many of which ruled that forest land might be

cleared only for productive purposes and that replanting must follow cutting.

Continental Europe

Germany, France, Sweden, Norway, Czechoslovakia, Switzerland, Finland and some other countries have established an efficient and rational management on a sustained-yield basis, with distinction between protective forests that serve to prevent floods and erosion and protect water supplies and all other forests. Usually the former have been placed under special control of the state. Even for the latter, however, regulations on clearing are very stringent in many countries.

An owner of timberland in France must ask permission to clear land four months in advance. Reforestation is encouraged by various governmental means, such as grants and direct technical aid.[39] Germany also requires a state permit for clearing. In both countries cutting without permit is subject to fine. Italy has a similar law. Sweden enacted "diameter limit laws" in 1874 and 1882, requiring special permission for cutting trees less than 7 inches in diameter at 16 feet from the ground.[40] The Swedish law of 1903 made replanting after cutting compulsory in all forests, and the law of 1923 introduced a further restriction by prohibiting cutting in "younger forests" except thinning to improve the remaining trees. Since the owners could not decide easily whether a particular stand was considered younger forest in terms of the law, they began to ask the Forest Conservation Board to mark the trees to be cut. Today, most of the trees cut for sale, and even some cut for home use, are marked by the Board's foresters. Forestry in Sweden, which considers its woods as its "green gold," is of a high order, and there is little distinction between public and private forests.[41]

Norway also has comprehensive forest legislation. The Forest Act of 1863 covers all forests and forbids use of them for grazing and any other damage to the woods. The even more important law of 1932 established rules for timber cutting, compulsory cultivation and the like. No felling that can jeopardize the natural regeneration or unduly reduce the timber supplies is permitted. The Forest Fire Act provides a foundation for protection against fires; since 1911

---

37. **25**, p. 130.

38. Various acts for the protection of forests had been passed previously in that country, beginning with 1680. (**21**, p. 17.)

39. **21**, pp. 42–49.

40. **49**, Vol. I, pp. 129, 147 and 338.

41. **42**, pp. 37–44.

Norway has had a mutual forest fire insurance organization. In 1938, a national long-range afforestation scheme was adopted.[42]

In the Netherlands, where there was little interference before World War II with the freedom of private owners to use their forests as they saw fit, no tree can now be felled without the sanction of the forest administration, and replanting is compulsory.[43]

Great Britain

Great Britain, well provided with coal and able to import necessary supplies of timber, has done little to protect its forest stands. Some concern about the dwindling supplies of timber has been shown since the sixteenth century.[44] This interest has been revived during each new emergency, but measures to preserve the remaining woodland or plant new forests have never been followed up consistently. More than four fifths of the productive forest area is privately owned and there is no control except over entailed property.[45] The owner may clear woods, leaving devastation, or sell them to the same end. As a result, most of Britain's forests present a sad picture. Many private owners are interested only in the protection of game for hunting.

The two world wars inflicted great damage on the small remaining reserves of standing timber in Great Britain. During World War I, when Great Britain was cut off from foreign supplies of timber, the greater part of its mature forest and large areas of immature woodland were cut.[46] The Forestry Act of 1919 provided for afforestation of 1.8 million acres on an eighty-year basis, and nearly half a million were planted between 1919 and 1939. During World War II large numbers of young trees were sacrificed to obtain urgently needed pit props, poles and the like, and older stands were felled for timber. At least half the 1939 stand has gone. The postwar plan calls for afforestation of 3 million acres of bare land and 2 million of existing woodland during the next fifty years.[47] Planting will consist mostly of conifers, since 94 per cent of Britain's consumption is of coniferous timber, almost wholly from foreign sources.[48] Whether some measure of control over the forest policy of private owners will also be established remains to be seen.

The United States

In comparison with many European countries, the United States has made little headway in forest legislation. Until the middle of the past century no thought was given to the need to protect the forests. The "Timber Culture Act" of 1873 provided for grants of free public land for planting certain areas to timber in treeless western states. Later, some states also passed legislation penalizing the setting of forest fires. None of these laws was seriously enforced. More and more forest land passed out of public control as the federal government distributed public land to settlers and purchasers, and, in the form of grants, to railroad companies — nearly 40 million acres to the Northern Pacific Railroad, for example. The states followed the same practice, disposing of their timberland either by grants or by selling it at ridiculously low prices. North Carolina sold some of its finest hardwood forests for 10 cents an acre. The legitimate price for the best timberland was held to be $2.50 an acre.[49] To control subsurface rights, mining companies acquired considerable forest areas either by outright grants or at bargain prices.

In 1891, a beginning was made in reserving some forest lands for the nation for the purpose, among others, of protecting watersheds. At that time, however, the only large remaining areas of public land were in the West. To return some eastern woodland to public ownership, federal legislation was passed in 1911 for the purchase of forested land on the watersheds of navigable streams; the act also provided for cooperation with the states in forest fire protection. This law was extended by a 1924 act to include the purchase of forest lands for timber production. Most of the national forests east of the Great Plains have been established under these acts.[50]

42. **9**, Vol. I, pp. 12–13, and **21**, p. 77.

43. **21**, p. 54.

44. The preamble to the Statute of Woods (1543), which provided for the enclosure of all forests, begins as follows: "The King and Sovereign Lord perceiving and right well knowing the great decay of timber and wood universally within his realm . . ." **44**, p. 9.

45. A forest owner must not cut trees on such property without replanting, except with the sanction of the heir-in-law. **45**, p. 29.

46. **40**, pp. 31–33.

47. **7**, September–October 1947, p. 29.

48. Much domestic timber — estate-grown hardwood, knotty and overripe — is not adaptable to modern commercial uses. **44**, p. 1.

49. **38**, pp. 22–23.

50. **49**, Vol. II, pp. 543–44, and **12**, 1949, pp. 299–300.

The 1924 act expanded the principle of federal aid for the protection of state and private forests, such aid to be given only to states that have a legally established system of fire protection. By 1948 the cooperative federal-state program had been extended to 43 states and Hawaii and covered nearly 340 million acres of forest land, but about 100 million acres of potentially valuable forest land still lacked any organized fire protection.[51] There is no general regulation of cutting practices in private forests, which account for three fourths of the nation's forest land, although twelve states have enacted legislation providing for such control.

The picture is not completely dark, however. Protection of forests is being steadily strengthened. The United States has the world's greatest system of public (national) forests, effectively managed. The state forests are for the most part under sound control. Forest research has made great progress, particularly in recent years. The Forest Service gives direct technical advice and assistance to many thousands of individual forest owners, and extension work in farm forestry is expanding. Many private owners, particularly pulp companies and the larger wood-using plants, are steadily improving their cutting practices and encouraging other owners to do likewise. The Sustained Yield Unit Act of 1944, which provides for cooperation between public and private owners in pooling forest holdings into sustained-yield units, promises better management of limited areas of interrelated public and other forest lands.[52]

Canada

Organized fire protection in Canada covers an area of nearly 900,000 square miles, about 70 per cent of the total forested area. Both government and industry are giving increased attention to improvement of logging methods and more effective use of timber and to research in both forestry and wood utilization.[53] Forest management is at about the same level as in the United States.

Latin America

Forest policy in most Latin American countries is in an initial stage. Brazil does not control the cutting practices of private operators who obtain concessions to cut public timber. Although a forestry code was recently adopted to prevent the destruction of forests and provide for reforestation, enforcement is hampered by lack of trained foresters. Bolivia has no forest service whatsoever. Peru is considering the introduction of legislation. In Argentina, both public and private forest stands lack good management. Mexico has laws regulating cutting practices, but enforcement is not always effective.

Asia

Japan's private forests produce only a third the timber they could produce under good management. Although from 200,000 to 300,000 acres were reforested each year before World War II, some 7 to 8 million acres of cutover land are in need of reforestation. Burma, India and Pakistan have a well-developed forest service, and India's forest research center at Dehra Dun is famous throughout the world. Other Asiatic countries exercise little supervision over the use of forests.

THE WORLD'S FORESTS

Measuring Forest Areas

"Forest" means different things in different countries.[54] Originally, the word was understood to mean a large tract of land, consisting of woody grounds, pastures and whole villages, where the king had the right of chase.[55] Later, with the decline of the feudal system, "forest" began to mean natural woodland. Today, in countries with advanced forestry, it includes not only natural growth but also planted trees. In some countries, any wooded area may be reported as forest, even thin stands of short, scrubby trees that may possibly supply fuel for local needs but can hardly be of value for the production of sawed lumber, poles, crossties and the like. Some such areas are so classified in the United States.[56]

An estimate of the forest area of many countries can be only a rough approximation, particularly in the vast forested expanses in the extreme

51. **15**, 1949, p. 40.

52. **15**, 1949, pp. 38–40. In return for committing his forests to a coordinated management, the private owner can purchase national-forest timber without competition at the appraised value.

53. **5**, p. 35.

54. Nine different interpretations of "forest" are cited in **32**, p. 26.

55. In England "forest" once meant land belonging to the king and used for hunting, whether it had trees or not. This use of the word is still applied to Scottish deer "forests," mainly mountainous country without trees and sometimes above the tree line. **28**, p. 26.

56. **12**, 1949, p. 743.

north and in the tropics. Man has never set foot on large parts of these areas. Estimates have relied not infrequently on reports of dubious accuracy, and aerial surveys over some areas mapped as forest have shown that many parts are actually treeless. Because of incomplete and inexact surveys and conceptual difficulties, international comparisons of forest statistics may be misleading, and figures for some countries have a wide margin of error. Estimates of the forest area of Peru, for example, range from 174 to 224 million acres; of Guatemala, from 11 to 20 million; of the USSR, from 1,235 to 2,347 million acres. Even the United States, with a well-organized forest survey of some twenty years standing, has sizable regions in which the forest area, volume, growth and loss are estimated only roughly.[57]

During 1947–48, the Food and Agriculture Organization of the United Nations undertook a systematic survey of the world's forest resources and gathered information from countries with about two thirds of the world's forest area and three fourths of its population.[58] Although some countries are not included and some others could answer the questions only in part, the survey provides more complete and more consistent information than any previously available.[59]

According to the FAO survey, the world's forests cover about 10 million acres, an area approximately equal to that of the Western Hemisphere. Of the total forest acreage, 66 per cent is classified as productive, and about half that proportion as both productive and accessible.

About 36 per cent of the world's productive forests are coniferous. The remaining 64 per cent are in broadleaved species, 14 per cent in temperate hardwoods and 50 per cent in tropical hardwoods.[60]

While not much more than a third of the productive forests are coniferous, the conifers supply 70 per cent of all wood used for construction and for industrial purposes. In the United States, for which the census of 1810 was the first record of lumber output, softwoods have consistently supplied more than 75 per cent, and in many years more than 85 per cent, of all lumber produced.[61] (See Figure 207.)

DISTRIBUTION OF FORESTS AMONG CONTINENTS

Over 90 per cent of Europe's forest area is both productive and accessible. In North America, about 70 per cent is productive but only two thirds of the productive forest and less than half the total area are accessible.[62] Coniferous forests predominate in North America, Europe and the USSR; broadleaved forests, in South America, Asia, Africa and Oceania. (See Table 300.)

Because of differences in the density of population, the continents rank differently in forest area per inhabitant than in total forest area. Oceania, with the smallest forest area in the world, has more productive forest area per capita of population than any other continent except South America. Asia and Europe have only 0.7 acre of productive forest per capita. The per capita area of total and of accessible productive forests in different continents is as follows (in acres):

	Total	Accessible
World	2.7	1.5
North America	7.2	4.7
Middle America	2.7	2.0
South America	15.8	7.4
Europe	0.7	0.7
USSR	5.2	2.7
Asia	0.7	0.4
Africa	4.0	2.0
Oceania	10.4	5.2

FORESTS IN SELECTED COUNTRIES

Forests grow on less than 5 per cent of all land in Uruguay, Ireland, Algeria, Ethiopia, the Union of South Africa and Australia and, by contrast, on more than 60 per cent in Guatemala, Colombia, Peru, Finland, Indonesia, Malaya, Thailand and some African territories. The area of productive forest per capita of population is 0.03 hectare in the United Kingdom, Ireland, the Netherlands; more than 8 hectares in Brazil, 11 hectares in the Belgian Congo, and 17 hectares

---

57. **12**, 1949, p. 742.

58. Information was not received from the USSR, Iran, Arabia, Spain, Romania, Yugoslavia, Mexico, Bolivia and a few other Latin American countries, or from some territories in Africa. The FAO made estimates for nonreporting countries.

59. During 1948 and 1949 the FAO received information from countries that had not reported earlier, and in its latest yearbook (1950) it introduced some changes in the figures published in previous yearbooks. Since the latest yearbook gives no breakdown by type of forest, however, this chapter uses the data for the distribution of forests by type in 1947.

60. **12**, 1949, p. 749.

61. **41**, p. 10.

62. In the United States alone, 52 million acres of productive forest are inaccessible. **12**, 1949, p. 744.

BILLION FEET B.M.

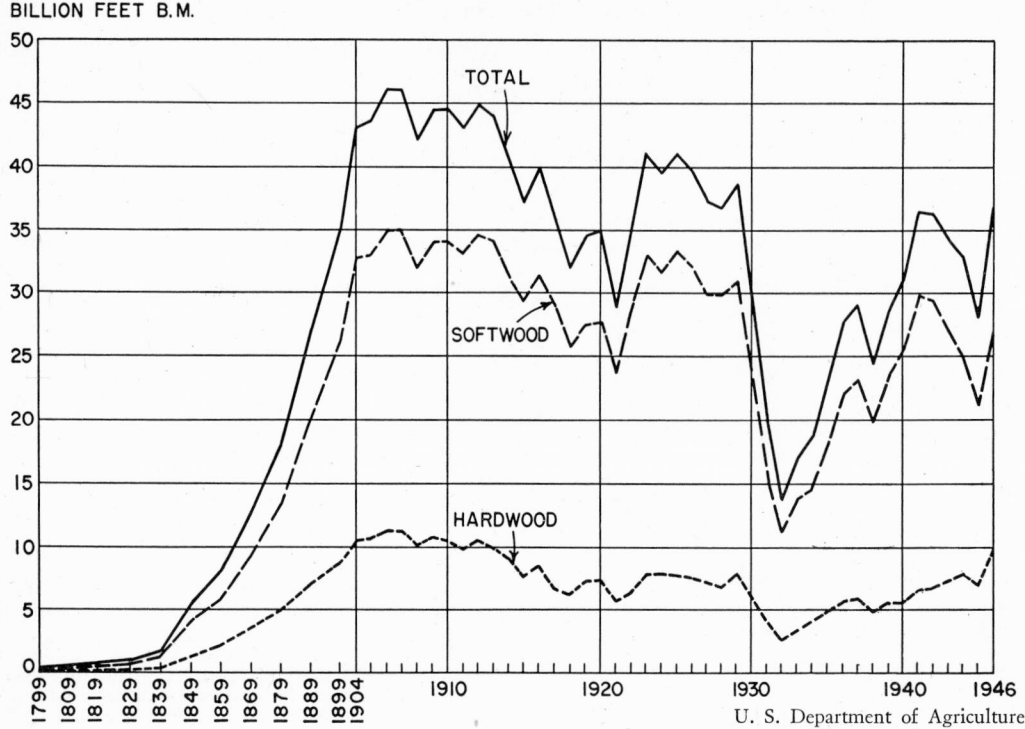

U. S. Department of Agriculture

FIGURE 207. OUTPUT OF HARDWOOD AND SOFTWOOD IN THE UNITED STATES, 1799–1946

in Canada. Alaska, with tiny settlements lost in a wilderness of virgin forests, has nearly 600 hectares of productive forests per inhabitant.

With a few exceptions, large areas of inaccessible forest are located in countries that extend above the polar circle (Canada, Alaska, the USSR) and in the tropical countries. The softwood forests are more unevenly distributed than are all forests. The only substantial softwood areas are confined to the United States, Canada and the USSR. Latin American countries either have no softwoods or, as in Brazil and Colombia, only an insignificant part of their total productive forest area is in softwoods.

The United States and the USSR have the largest area of accessible productive forests in the world; next come Brazil and Canada. Most of the accessible forest in the USSR and Canada is, however, in trees of pulpwood size, rather than saw-log size. Trees in inaccessible productive forests of these countries tend to be even smaller, on the average. In Brazil, which has more than half of all forest land in Middle and South America,[63] almost all forest area is rated as productive,

but much of it is inaccessible. Until unit air surveys became possible, this wilderness could not even be mapped; only scientific explorers and workers gathering rubber had penetrated some parts of the jungle. In spite of this abundance, Brazil's long-settled areas suffer from shortage of wood for both construction and fuel, and afforestation has begun in some places.

In Europe, the most densely forested countries are Finland, Sweden and Norway, where the area of productive forest per inhabitant is 5.31 hectares, 3.42 hectares, and 1.97 hectares, respectively.

Indonesia accounts for about 23 per cent of all forest land in Asia, but it is so densely populated that productive forest represents only 0.93 hectare per capita. West Africa, French Equatorial Africa and the Belgian Congo together have about half of all African forests. All forest land in the Belgian Congo is rated productive, but in West Africa and French Equatorial Africa about 30 and 18 per cent, respectively, are classified as such. (See Table 301.)

---

63. The very name of Brazil came from a tree, brazilwood, famous for its rich purple dye. The exportation

of woods having been a monopoly of the Portuguese crown, brazilwood became the first important item of export after the discovery of that country. **31,** p. 227.

TABLE 300

FOREST AREA IN EACH CONTINENT, BY TYPE, 1947

(*Millions of Hectares* [a])

| Continent | All Forests | Productive Forests | | | | | Nonproductive Forests |
| | | Total | Accessible | | Inaccessible | | |
			Coniferous	Broadleaved	Coniferous	Broadleaved	
World	3,978	2,612	543	870	399	800	1,366
North America	653	454	173	125	130	26	199
Middle America	75	53	7	29	5	12	22
South America	755	664	10	297	5	352	91
Europe [b]	104	98	61	34	2	—	7
USSR [c]	942	629	255	74	210	91	312
Asia	520	358	31	143	43	141	162
Africa	849	306	2	148	—	156	543
Oceania	80	50	4	20	4	22	30

Sources: Adapted from **7**, July–August 1948, pp. 166–67 and 172–75, and April–June 1950, p. 58; FAO data have been adjusted to the classification of continents used in this volume; the combined data for Europe and the USSR have been segregated. See also **12**, 1949, p. 744.

a. Conversion factor: one hectare = 2.471 acres.
b. Excludes nonreporting Albania, Romania, Yugoslavia and Spain.

c. Includes Albania, Romania, Yugoslavia and Spain. Estimates for the USSR appear to be too high. In 1941, the area of productive forests in the USSR was estimated at nearly 500 million hectares. Postwar acquisition of territory from Finland, Poland, Romania, Czechoslovakia, Japan (southern Sakhalin), and the annexation of the Baltic states, have increased the total area by 16 million hectares (**7**, May–June 1949, p. 127).

FORESTS IN THE UNITED STATES

The forest area in the United States, 624 million acres, is usually divided into two broad categories: commercial forests, suitable for growing marketable timber, with 461 million acres, and noncommercial forests, with 163 million acres. (See Table 302.)

Commercial Forests

About three fourths of the commercial forests are east of the Great Plains. (See Figure 208.) Not all the western commercial forests can yet be used economically.[64]

In terms of quality, however, the picture is reversed. The commercial forests of the East are badly depleted and poorly stocked and are largely second growth. Almost half of the area and in many parts more than half, bears only seedlings or saplings and is denuded. Another large part is in timber too small for saw logs. The urgent demand for pulpwood and various products that can be made from small trees encourages premature cutting and thus perpetuates the shortage of large timber. In the West, in contrast, about 40 per cent of the commercial forest area and almost 80 per cent of the sawtimber are in virgin stands.

In the United States as a whole, virgin stands represent only a small part of commercial forests, 44.6 million acres out of 461 million acres; of these, more than 41 million acres are in the West. The quality of even the western stands is not uniformly high, and frequently is downright poor, as is evident from the following percentage distribution of virgin forest in the nation and the West:[65]

	Good	Medium	Poor
United States	25	38	37
Pacific Northwest	39	40	21
Other western areas	12	36	52

Figure 209 shows how each state would look if its area corresponded to its amount of standing timber. The best remaining timber is far from the great centers of consumption. Little timber remains in Pennsylvania, New York and Michigan, each of which once led the nation in timber production.

64. **13**, p. 14.

65. **13**, p. 23.

TABLE 301

FOREST AREA IN SELECTED COUNTRIES, BY TYPE, 1947

(Millions of Hectares [a])

| | All Forest Land | | Productive Forests | | | | | |
| | | | All Types | | Accessible [b] | | Inaccessible [b] | |
Country	Area	Percentage of Total Territory	Total Area	Hectares Per Inhabitant	Coniferous	Broad-leaved	Coniferous	Broad-leaved
United States	252.5	33	191.8	1.36	88.4	82.4	19.4	1.6
Alaska	61.9	42	47.8	596.94	8.1	3.2	27.1	9.3
Canada	334.4	37	210.6	17.12	72.8	39.8	83.0	15.0
Mexico	25.9	13	25.9	1.13	...	...	...	...
Guatemala	7.2	66	5.0	1.39	...	...	...	...
Colombia	72.0	68	72.0	6.99	1.5	58.5	0.4	11.7
Brazil	395.9	47	377.2	8.08	5.3	147.4	3.5	221.1
Peru	70.0	62	50.0	6.41	—	15.0	—	35.0
Chile	16.2	22	6.7	1.24	0.4	4.6	1.7	
Uruguay	0.5	2	0.5	0.20	—	0.4	—	0.1
Argentina	48.6	17	22.9	1.45	—	17.1	0.1	5.7
United Kingdom	1.3	6	1.3	0.03	0.6	0.7	—	—
Ireland	0.1	1	0.1	0.03	0.05	0.05	—	—
France	11.0	20	11.0	0.27	3.0	8.0	—	—
Belgium	0.5	18	0.5	0.06	0.2	0.3	—	—
Netherlands	0.3	8	0.3	0.03	0.2	0.1	—	—
Denmark	0.3	8	0.3	0.08	0.2	0.1	—	—
Sweden	23.5	57	22.9	3.42	17.2	5.0	0.7	
Norway	7.5	24	6.1	1.97	4.5	0.7	0.8	0.1
Finland	21.7	71	20.7	5.31	15.9	4.8	—	—
Germany	7.5	21	7.5	0.11	5.3	2.3	—	—
Poland	6.9	22	6.5	0.27	5.7	0.8	—	—
Czechoslovakia	4.0	32	4.0	0.30	2.6	1.4	—	—
Switzerland	0.9	22	0.8	0.18	0.5	0.2	0.1	—
Austria	3.1	38	2.8	0.40	1.9	0.6	0.2	0.1
Hungary	1.1	12	1.1	0.12	0.1	1.0	—	—
Portugal	2.5	28	2.5	0.30	1.2	1.3	—	—
Italy	6.0	20	5.6	0.12	1.1	4.5	—	—
Bulgaria	3.7	35	3.1	0.44	0.3	2.7	—	0.1
Greece	2.0	16	0.6	0.08	0.3	0.2	0.1	
China	82.8	9	56.3	0.12	13.5	3.4	34.9	4.5
Japan	22.3	59	22.3	0.30	7.7	12.0	1.0	1.6
Turkey	10.0	13	10.0	0.51	1.9	1.1	4.6	2.4
India and Pakistan [e]	44.5	20	33.3	0.11	3.3	30.0	—	—
Burma	39.1	58	25.4	1.49	—	25.4	—	—
Thailand	32.4	63	32.4	1.79	—	10.7	0.2	21.5
Malaya	10.1	77	7.3	1.24	—	2.0	—	5.3
Indonesia	120.0	63	70.0	0.93	—	11.0	—	59.0
Philippines	17.5	59	13.2	0.69	...	...	...	...
Algeria	3.0	2	1.9	0.22	0.6	1.0	0.2	0.1
Anglo-Egyptian Sudan	93.2	37	3.5	0.53	—	1.3	—	2.2
Ethiopia	1.2	1	1.2	0.08	0.1	0.1	0.5	0.5
French West Africa	170.0	36	50.0	3.09	—	25.0	—	25.0
French Equatorial Africa	152.4	61	27.0	6.76	—	12.0	—	15.0

(Continued on facing page)

TABLE 301—continued

| Country | All Forest Land | | Productive Forests | | | | | |
| | | | All Types | | Accessible [b] | | Inaccessible [b] | |
	Area	Percentage of Total Territory	Total Area	Hectares Per Inhabitant	Conifer- ous	Broad- leaved	Conifer- ous	Broad- leaved
Belgian Congo	120.3	53	119.5	11.27	—	69.0	—	50.5
Gold Coast	16.1	67	9.1	2.52	—	4.1	—	4.9
Nigeria	40.7	42	7.0	0.32	—	0.9	—	6.1
Tanganyika	39.1	44	34.1	6.20	0.2	5.2	—	28.7
Northern Rhodesia	38.9	52	5.4	3.40	—	0.3	—	5.2
Southern Rhodesia	23.0	59	7.1	4.18	—	5.5	—	1.6
South-West Africa	5.2	6	5.2	12.94	—	0.1	—	5.0
Bechuanaland	69.8	97	0.2	0.65	—	0.2	—	—
Union of South Africa	3.7	3	0.8	0.72	0.1	0.7	—	—
Australia	30.9	4	20.3	2.70	1.6	12.1	0.1	6.4
New Zealand	6.8	26	2.0	1.10	0.6	0.1	0.3	1.0

Sources: **2**, pp. 26–35; **7**, May–June 1948, p. 111, July–August 1948, pp. 172–75, and April–June 1950, p. 58.

a. Conversion factor: one hectare = 2.471 acres.

b. Area of mixed wood is divided equally between coniferous and broadleaved forests.

c. 1938 estimates.

Farm Woodlands

Some 139 million acres of commercial forest, about 30 per cent of the total, are divided, usually in comparatively small tracts, among some 3.5 million farms. Of these, 130 million acres are east of the Great Plains. (See Figure 210.) In the West, farm woodland is overshadowed by pub-

TABLE 302

FOREST AREA IN THE UNITED STATES, BY REGION, 1945

(Millions of Acres)

Region	All Forest	Commer- cial	Noncom- mercial
United States	623.8	461.0	162.8
New England	31.1	30.9	0.2
Middle Atlantic	44.2	41.6	2.6
Lake	55.7	50.3	5.4
Central	44.9	44.2	0.7
Plains	35.8	3.3	32.5
South Atlantic	43.8	42.9	0.9
Southeast	91.9	89.4	2.5
West Gulf	51.1	50.9	0.2
Pacific Northwest	53.9	46.2	7.7
California	45.5	16.4	29.1
North Rocky Mountains	53.2	29.1	24.1
South Rocky Mountains	72.7	15.8	56.9

Source: **13**, p. 15.

licly owned forests (69 million acres) and forests belonging to industrial companies and other large owners (29 million acres).

Theoretically, farm woodland could represent a part of the nation's permanently productive forest area. Under a stable ownership and at only small managerial cost, it could give the farmer a continuing source of income and enable him to use his time productively in the slack season. Practically, most farmers know little of forestry, and farm woodland, on the whole, has probably been more abused than any other major farm crop with the possible exception of natural pasturage.[66] About a third of the total area has no fire protection and about half is so deteriorated that it cannot yield a reasonable return. For the most part, woodlots are still the backyard of the farm, used indiscriminately for cutting and pasturage. In recent years, however, some progress has been made in improving these stands.[67]

DISTRIBUTION OF FORESTS BY OWNERSHIP

The world's productive forest area is almost evenly divided between public and private ownership, but with wide differences from country to country. Much of the private woodland is so scattered that it defies systematic management

66. **12**, 1940, p. 468.
67. **12**, 1949, p. 708.

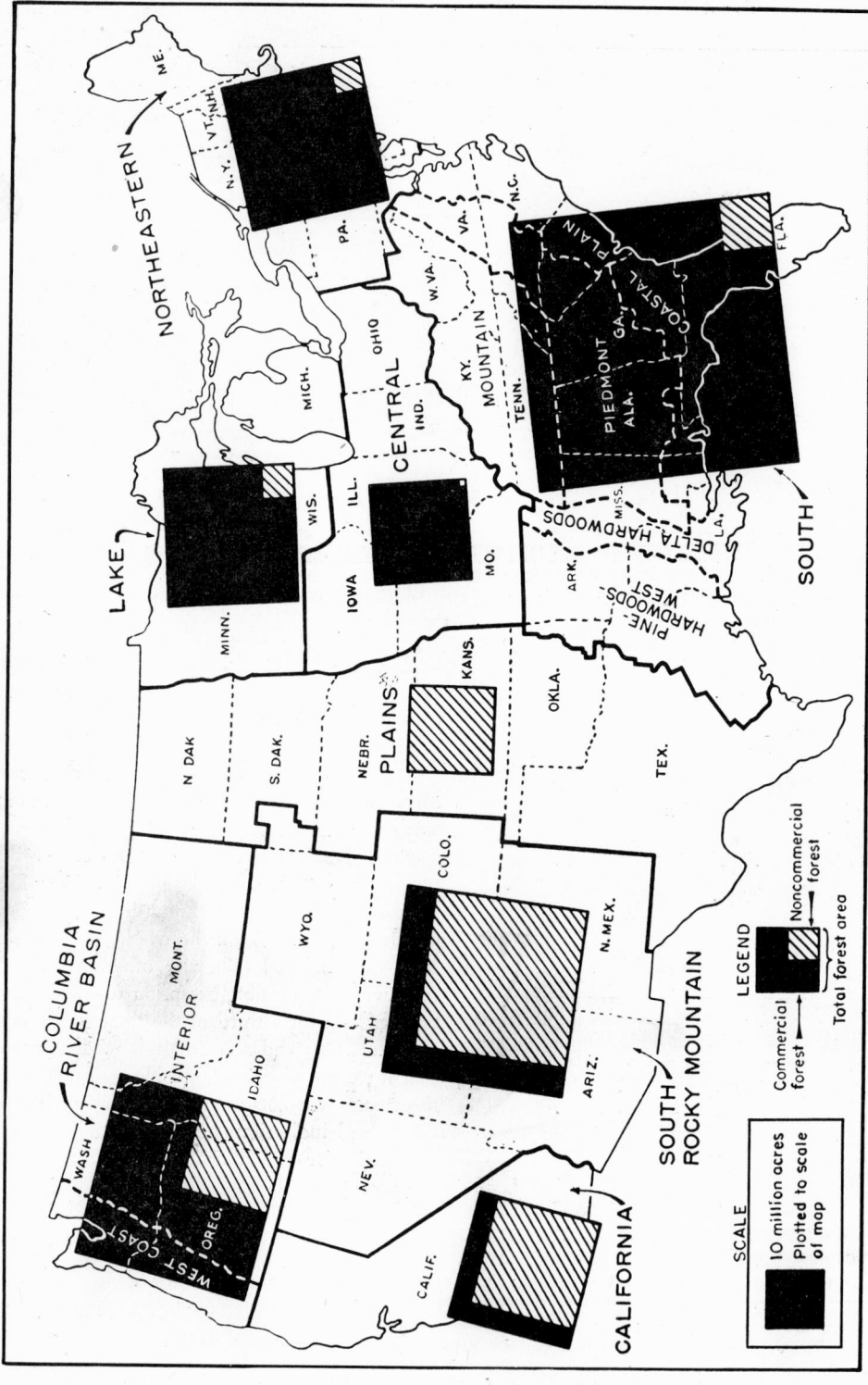

FIGURE 208. FOREST AREA IN THE UNITED STATES, BY REGION, 1938

U. S. Department of Agriculture

698

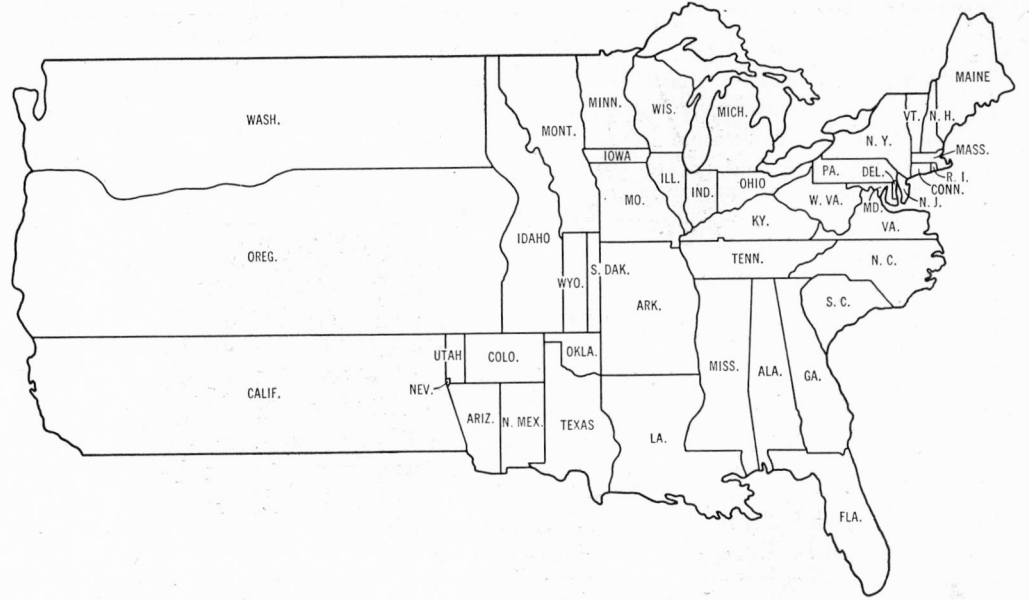

FIGURE 209. DISTORTED MAP SHOWING EACH STATE IN THE UNITED STATES IN RELATION TO AMOUNT OF TIMBER IN THAT STATE

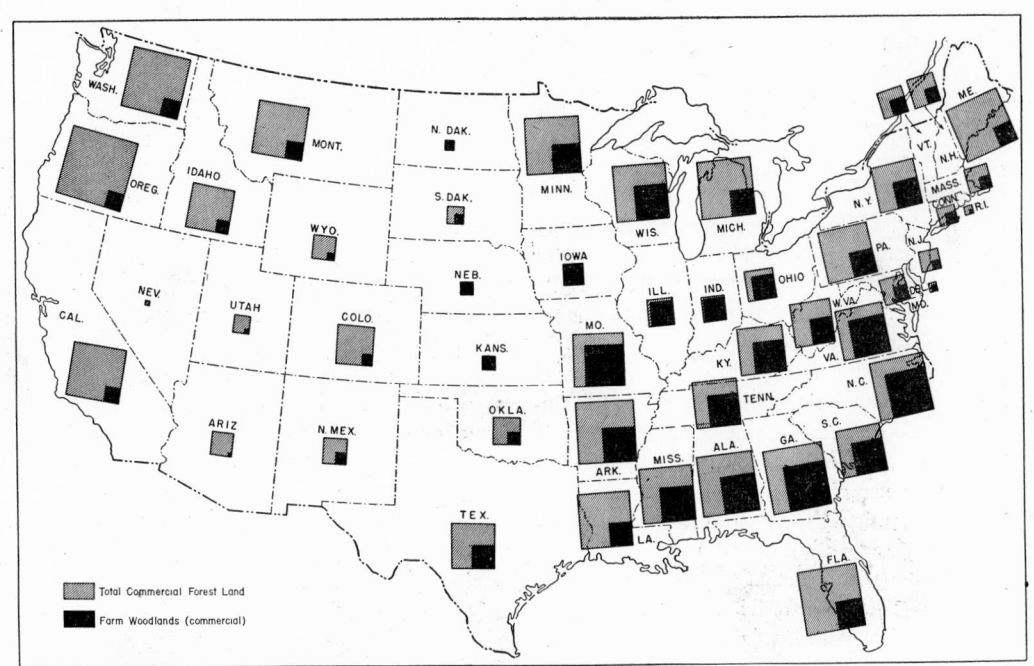

FIGURE 210. ALL FOREST LAND AND FARM WOODLAND IN THE UNITED STATES, BY STATE

Forested areas are shown on the same scale as the whole surface of the country.

and is used mostly for the immediate farm needs of the owner.

Public ownership predominates in a few European countries, as in eastern Germany, Czechoslovakia, Poland and Switzerland. In the USSR, all forests, like all other land, are state owned.

Since 1891, when the United States inaugurated the policy of public ownership of some forest areas, about 215 million acres have been placed under public ownership or management. The federal government owns or manages some 177 million acres,[68] of which 123 million acres are in the so-called national forests; the remainder includes Indian reservations, national parks, wildlife refuges and areas for recreation and farm resettlement. The slow but unmistakable trend is toward increase in publicly owned forests through purchase, lease, grants and the like. About half of all publicly owned or managed lands are noncommercial.

In some other countries of the Western Hemisphere, as in Canada and Colombia, public ownership predominates. The contrast between Canada and Brazil is particularly striking: in the former, nearly nine tenths of the productive forest is publicly owned; in the latter, practically none. In Argentina, most of the forests are owned in large tracts by private corporations.

In colonies, throughout the world, almost all forests are owned by the mother country. (See Table 303.)

The type of ownership has greatly influenced the way in which forests are exploited. Both public and private ownership have advantages and limitations, and forests may be well or badly managed under either, but the emphasis is usually on different objectives.

Public ownership ordinarily results in greater concern for permanent economic and social values than for immediate financial return. It tends to maintain the forests on a sustained-yield basis, to assure the necessary protection of watersheds, promote recreational use of the forests and preserve wild life.

. Private ownership aims first and foremost at profit but is not necessarily incompatible with far-sighted forest policy. In the long run, profits can be derived only on the basis of the sustained yield, and a greater or smaller part of the private forests in various countries is thus operated. Generally speaking, however, not many private owners have been willing to exchange the immediate profits to be obtained from indiscriminate cutting for a rotation system extending over several generations.

In most countries, including the United States, sustained-yield forestry is practiced in only a small part of the privately owned forest land. Small farm woodlands present the greatest difficulties in introducing sustained-yield management in the United States. To the individual farmer, his woods are only a minor resource. Hard pressed for cash and lacking knowledge of forestry, he often accepts a lump-sum price for his wood, which then is cut without restriction. Nonfarm absentee ownership is another obstacle to good forest management.[69] The situation is different when practices in private forests are regulated by law as in the Scandinavian countries, France and Germany.

FOREST GROWTH AND DRAIN

Wood can be grown and harvested like other crops, with the major difference that harvesting methods affect the amount and quality of the future yield. Another difference is that trees mature slowly, some species requiring fifty or sixty years or more.

Principles of Rational Management

The objective of rational exploitation of a forest is to assure perpetual yield while increasing productivity or, at the least, not destroying it. Some cutting benefits the forest as a whole — for example, the elimination of "wolf trees" that take too much food and light from other trees. On the whole, regular thinning enhances both the quantity and the quality of the forest crop. If trees are allowed to grow beyond the age at which the rate of growth is at its peak, the current increment begins to decrease.

The two basic principles of rational harvesting of tree crops are that the cut, in the long run, must equal the growth, while harvesting should be such as to assure the renewal of the crop. To maintain an annual crop of marketable timber, a forest should contain trees of various ages, from seedlings up to fullgrown timber, so younger trees will take the place of mature trees that are felled.[70] When these basic requirements are fulfilled, the crop taken will be replaced as time goes on, without damage to the stands.

68. **12**, 1940, pp. 471–72.

69. **13**, p. 96.
70. **12**, 1949, p. 717.

TABLE 303

PRODUCTIVE FORESTS: AREA PUBLICLY AND PRIVATELY OWNED IN SELECTED COUNTRIES, 1947

Country	Area, in Millions of Hectares [a] — Ownership		Percentage of Forest Area Publicly Owned	Country	Area, in Millions of Hectares [a] — Ownership		Percentage of Forest Area Publicly Owned
	Public	Private			Public	Private	
United States	52.2	139.6 [b]	27	China	31.9	24.4	57
Alaska	47.8	—	100	South Korea	1.4	5.0	22
Canada	184.7	25.9	88	Japan	10.6	11.7 [b]	44
Colombia	44.6	27.4	62	Burma	25.4	—	100
Brazil	0.4	376.8	—	Indonesia	70.0	—	100
Chile	2.9	3.8 [b]	43	Philippines	12.9	0.3	98
United Kingdom	0.2	1.1	16	Algeria	1.6	0.3	85
France	4.0	6.9	37	Anglo-Egyptian			
Sweden	5.2	17.7 [b]	23	Sudan	3.5	—	100
Norway	0.8	5.3 [b]	14	French West			
Finland	7.4	13.3	36	Africa	49.7	0.3	99
Germany	5.4	2.1	72	French Equatorial			
Poland	5.7	0.7	89	Africa	27.0	—	100
Czechoslovakia	2.3	1.6 [b]	59	Belgian Congo	119.4	—	100
Switzerland	0.6	0.2	73	Gold Coast	9.1	—	100
Austria	0.7	2.1 [b]	25	Tanganyika	33.9	0.2	99
Italy	1.7	3.9	31	South-West Africa	5.0	0.1	97
USSR	625	—	100	Australia	14.2	6.0	70
				New Zealand	1.6	0.4	80

Source: **7**, July–August 1948, pp. 176–77, and April–June 1950, p. 58.

a. Conversion factor: one hectare = 2.471 acres.
b. Includes forests owned by institutions.

Simple as these principles may sound, they involve a high degree of technical knowledge, large investments, and willingness on the part of the forest owners to distribute their profits over a series of years. Only a fraction of the world forests is treated as a crop. The extractive method of exploiting forests — mining them, so to speak — too often prevails.

Measuring Growth and Drain

The balance sheet of a well-managed forest shows net annual growth (total growth minus losses from natural causes) on one side, annual cut on the other. The difference, described as "over-cut" or "under-cut," indicates whether the forest has been felled too heavily or has not been fully utilized. Measurement of growth and drain is a very complex undertaking and requires not only highly skilled personnel but also an efficient system of supervision and records of all timber cut. There must also be some method for measuring the losses due to windstorms, pests, tree diseases, lightning and the like. No one method of

measuring forest drain has been universally accepted. The current estimates of forest growth and cut in the various countries and continents are only approximations and for many countries show only the theoretical quantities which the forests might produce under reasonable management.

Only the western and central European countries take regular inventories of timber stands and growth. In the United States, where vast forest expanses make the cost of such inventories almost prohibitive, sampling methods, based on measurement of trees on selected representative plots, have been developed. As these methods have been improved, estimates of forest growth have been raised from 1.9 cubic feet per acre in 1931 to 2.9 cubic feet in 1945.[71] There is no evi-

71. **7**, July–August 1947, pp. 28–29. The first complete survey of the forest resources of the United States was authorized by Congress in 1928. Field work began in 1930 and about 300 million acres were surveyed during the 1930's. Interrupted by World War II, the survey was resumed at an accelerated rate — to cover the unexplored forest areas and make a reinventory of originally sur-

dence, however, that the improvement of techniques of measurement in some other countries would not result in downward revision of their estimates. The reports of economically underdeveloped countries are likely to be incomplete and inaccurate, since valid estimates can be prepared only after forests have been placed under systematic management.

TIMBER CUT

Since fluctuations in weather and business conditions make short-term averages of growth and drain unreliable, a ten-year average has been computed by the FAO for accessible productive forests of selected countries.

Timber cuts in the decade 1937–47 were somewhat affected by the war, which necessitated overcutting in many countries that normally husband their timber carefully. The Scandinavian countries managed to maintain a positive forest balance despite considerable exports of timber and pulp before and after the war and the unavoidable substitution of wood for coal during the war, but with few other exceptions, overcutting was general. The average cut in the United Kingdom was more than three times the net growth of the stands and was due in part to the urgent wartime need for pit props.

In the United States, there was overcutting in the coniferous forests and nearly as great undercutting in broadleaved stands. The excess of drain over growth is particularly noticeable in trees of saw-timber size, amounting to about 50 per cent. Comparable figures are not available for European countries but in general the saw-timber supply there seems to have kept well in balance with the allowed cut. Some countries are considering a reduced rate of cutting for such trees, to offset the severe drain during the war.[72] In Chile, losses in timber from natural causes, particularly fire, exceed the annual growth, and the cut, not too heavy under normal conditions, becomes a serious factor in the destruction of forest stands. (See Table 304.)

Statistics for China are believed to be highly unreliable. In the Belgian Congo, the enormous total growth, almost equal to that in all North America, seems not to have been utilized at all. In French West Africa, the ratio of 5–1 between

total and net growth emphasizes the disproportionately great forest losses from natural causes and shifts in cultivation of land for crops. The annual cut in the USSR was estimated for 1940 at 233 million cubic meters of roundwood; annual fellings in 1940 in areas acquired by the Soviet after the war are estimated at about 35 million. The USSR's output of wood in 1950 is estimated at 280 million cubic meters.[73]

FOREST PRODUCTS

The chief forest product is wood. Most of it is used for industrial purposes and as fuel. Other forest products are naval stores, tanning materials, rubber, cork, nuts, berries, and so on.

WOOD

The world's output of wood totaled nearly 1.4 billion cubic meters of roundwood in 1937 as well as in 1949, according to the estimate of the FAO.[74] Europe and North America together produced about 45 per cent of the total in 1949, although they had only 23 per cent of the world's productive forests. In contrast, Latin America and Africa, with 37 per cent of the productive forest in the world, accounted for only 13 per cent of the total output.[75] The share of North America in the world's total was greater than that of any other continent:

	Millions of Cubic Meters [a]	*Per Cent*
World	1,397	100
North America	361	26
Latin America	132	9
Europe	265	19
USSR	269	19
Asia	300	22
Africa	51	4
Oceania	19	1

a. 1 cubic meter equals 35.31 cubic feet.

The United States is the world's largest producer of wood. Next in line in the Western Hemisphere are Brazil and Canada; in Europe, Sweden, Finland and Germany; and, in Asia,

---

veyed ones. By 1950, nearly 100 million acres of forested land had been covered for the first time, and 89 million acres had been resurveyed (**15**, 1949, p. 21).

72. **12**, 1949, p. 750.

73. **19**, No. 2–3, 1946, p. 10; **1**, p. 35.

74. Most wood is removed from the felling site for use as fuel or for conversion into lumber, veneer and other products. Some products, however, including hewn railway crossties and posts, are often processed prior to removal. The estimate above gives the solid volume of roundwood. **6**, 1949, p. 153.

75. **6**, 1950, p. 1.

TABLE 304

PRODUCTIVE ACCESSIBLE FORESTS: NET GROWTH AND CUT IN SELECTED COUNTRIES, 1937-47 ANNUAL AVERAGE

(Millions of Cubic Meters of Roundwood [a])

Country	All Forests			Coniferous			Broadleaved		
	Net Growth	Cut	Balance [b]	Net Growth	Cut	Balance [b]	Net Growth	Cut	Balance [b]
United States	336.8	345.0	+8.2	168.6	208.1	+39.5	168.2	136.9	-31.3
Canada	62.6	69.3	+6.7	⋮	⋮	⋮	⋮	⋮	⋮
Chile	-11.7	4.9	+16.6	-0.1	0.5	+0.6	-11.6	4.3	+16.0
Uruguay	2.2	1.4	-0.8	—	—	—	2.2	1.4	-0.8
United Kingdom	1.3	4.6	+3.3	0.9	2.6	+1.8	0.5	2.0	+1.5
France	28.6	31.0	+2.4	7.7	9.2	+1.4	20.9	21.9	+1.0
Belgium	1.2	1.2	0	0.7	0.7	0	0.1	0.07	-0.03
Netherlands	0.6	0.3	-0.4	0.5	0.2	-0.4	0.9	1.5	+0.6
Denmark	2.3	2.4	+0.1	1.4	0.9	-0.5	7.5	6.0	-1.5
Sweden	45.6	41.2	-4.4	38.1	35.2	-2.9	1.6	1.5	-0.1
Norway	10.6	10.0	-0.6	9.0	8.5	-0.5	⋮	⋮	⋮
Finland	39.1	34.5	-4.6	⋮	⋮	⋮	⋮	⋮	⋮
Germany	27.0	63.7 [c]	+36.7	⋮	⋮	⋮	0.7	0.7	0
Poland	9.0	10.0	+1.0	8.3	9.3	+1.0	2.4	3.2	+0.8
Czechoslovakia	10.4	13.5	+3.1	8.0	10.3	+2.3	0.8	1.2	+0.4
Switzerland	2.7	4.1	+1.4	1.9	2.9	+1.0	1.2	1.1	-0.1
Austria	8.2	7.0	-1.2	7.0	6.0	-1.1	⋮	⋮	⋮
Hungary	1.9	3.0	+1.1	⋮	⋮	⋮	4.3	4.0	-0.3
Bulgaria	5.4	4.9	-0.5	1.1	0.9	-0.2	0.3	0.4	+0.1
Greece	0.9	1.1	+0.2	0.6	0.7	+0.1	10.0	3.0	-7.1
China	44.1	9.9	-34.2	34.0	6.9	-27.1	42.5	⋮	⋮
Japan	39.9	66.5	+26.6	⋮	⋮	⋮	⋮	⋮	⋮
India [d]	44.6	⋮	-7.5	2.1	⋮	⋮	⋮	⋮	⋮
Indonesia	11.0	3.5	-3.0	⋮	⋮	⋮	5.0	2.0	-3.0
French West Africa	5.0	2.0	⋮	⋮	⋮	⋮	⋮	0.4	⋮
Belgian Congo	⋮	0.4	⋮	⋮	0.4	-0.7	0.7	2.0	+1.3
Union of South Africa	1.8	2.3	+0.5	1.1	0.9	-0.7	7.1	7.3	+0.3
Australia [e]	8.6	8.2	-0.4	1.5	⋮	⋮	⋮	⋮	⋮
New Zealand	1.4	2.4	+0.9	⋮	⋮	⋮	⋮	⋮	⋮

SOURCE: 7, July–August 1948, pp. 179–81.

a. Conversion factor: one cubic meter = 35.31 cubic feet. Solid volume of roundwood.

b. Plus (+) = overcut; minus (−) = undercut. For Chile, minus (−) net growth indicates excess of losses from natural causes over the annual growth.

c. 1947.

d. British India, 1938. Commercial species only.

Japan. Many countries in Latin America, Asia and Africa do not record wood produced and consumed on farms and must have a substantially greater output than is reported. The USSR produces somewhat more wood than all Europe.

Types and Uses of Wood

Of the world's output of roundwood in 1949, 23 per cent was used for lumber, 8 per cent for wood pulp, 12 per cent for other industrial purposes and 57 per cent for fuel. Thus, slightly less than half the cut was consumed for construction and industrial purposes, and slightly more than half for fuel. About 80 per cent of coniferous wood was used for building and industry, and the rest for fuel. For the broadleaved species, the relationship was almost exactly the opposite.[76]

In the United States, about 56 per cent of the 1949 output was used for saw logs and veneer logs, about 20 per cent for fuel, somewhat less for pulp, and the remainder mostly for various industrial purposes. Of Canada's 1949 cut, nearly 36 per cent went for saw logs, more than 32 per cent for pulp, about 25 per cent for fuel, and the rest to satisfy other needs. The largest single item in Sweden's use of wood was pulp, while Finland consumed almost half of its wood output for heating. (See Table 305.)

Generally speaking, the industrial countries produce more saw timber and industrial wood than fuelwood, while the agricultural or underdeveloped countries use more wood for fuel. Obviously, a country which has coal, oil or natural gas prefers them for fuel. Brazil, Southern Rhodesia and Nyasaland use 90 per cent of their output of wood for fuel; the United States, ordinarily only about a sixth, more than half of which consists of tops and limbs of trees, dead and dying trees, mill waste, and the like.[77]

In Europe as a whole, except for a few Danubian countries, fuelwood represents about 42–46 per cent of the total cut, but differences among the countries range from about 17–24 per cent in Austria to 35 per cent in the Netherlands and 90 per cent in Greece.

Out of the 280 million cubic meters produced in 1950 in the USSR, only about 13 per cent was saw timber.[78] Most of the cut is fuelwood, of which many industrial plants consume enormous quantities. Moreover, most of the wood is poorly seasoned and may contain as much as 55 per cent moisture. It has been estimated that one and a half times more wood is consumed each year than would be used if it were dry, to say nothing of the extra burden in transportation. During the war, small round timber and firewood were floated on rafts to large cities. A great deal of firewood is shipped to Moscow on the Moscow-Volga Canal, from forests along the tributaries of the upper Volga 300–500 miles away. The Soviet government is said to be trying to expand transportation of firewood by water in order to relieve the railroads.[79]

In the more than one hundred countries and territories reporting to the FAO, fuelwood accounted for 45 per cent of the total cut in 1948 and 1949. In view of underreporting of the cut of fuelwood everywhere (in Asia by two thirds, in Africa by more than nine tenths and in Latin America by half), the FAO estimates 57 per cent for the world cut.[80]

Sawed lumber follows fuelwood in the world's output of wood. In 1948 and 1949, the United States and Canada together produced two thirds of all saw logs and veneer logs in the reporting countries. In 1949 the former supplied 151 million cubic meters of roundwood and the latter, about 32 million. Europe accounted for 55–57 million cubic meters; while Latin America, with its enormous forest reserves, produced only 10–11 million and Africa, 2.8–2.9 million cubic meters.[81]

Europe led in pulpwood production before the war, but in postwar years the output of the United States alone has greatly exceeded that of all Europe. Canada nearly matches the European output and uses about a third of its cut to make pulp. The increasing output of pulpwood in

76. **6**, 1950, p. 2.

77. Consumption of fuelwood in the United States began to decline around 1880 when saw lumber dislodged fuelwood from the lead in forest drain. In three hundred years of American history (1630-1930) fuelwood accounted for about half the total cut and more than twice the volume cut for lumber. (**39**, p. 8.) Up to World War II, 2.4 trillion board feet of timber had been cut in the forests of the United States — enough to build 52 million urban houses, 12 million farmhouses, 2 million schools and libraries, 650,000 churches and 450,000 factories. (**36**, p. 3.)

78. **1**, p. 35.

79. **7**, May–June 1949, p. 127.

80. R. Zon and W. H. Sparhawk, who also emphasize the underreporting of the fuelwood cut in their classic study of forest resources, consider that the actual cut for fuel may be 50 per cent greater than is reported. **49**, Vol. I, p. 37.

81. **6**, 1950, pp. 14–19.

TABLE 305

WOOD: OUTPUT, BY TYPE, IN SELECTED COUNTRIES, 1948 AND 1949

(Millions of Cubic Meters [a])

Columns headed "Saw Logs and Veneer Logs", "Pulpwood", and "Other [c]" together form the "Industrial Wood" group. Values shown spanning two sub-columns (braces in the original) are placed in a single cell. "..." denotes no data.

Country	1948 Total Cut[b]	Saw Logs and Veneer Logs	Pulpwood	Other[c]	Wood for Charcoal[d]	Fuelwood	1949 Total Cut[b]	Saw Logs and Veneer Logs	Pulpwood	Other[c]	Wood for Charcoal[d]	Fuelwood
United States[e]	280.0	162.0	45.8	16.5	0.5	46.4	271.1	150.9	40.2	15.5	0.4	55.5
Canada	90.6	35.4	30.1	2.2	0.1	21.6	89.5	31.9	28.9	2.1	0.1	22.7
Mexico	3.5	2.0	f	0.3	0.5	0.5	...	...	...	...	...	...
Brazil[g]	94.0	6.5	0.2	0.3	3.5	83.5	101.4	6.8	0.2	0.4	4.0	90.0
Uruguay	1.5	f	f	f	0.6	0.9	...	...	...	...	...	...
United Kingdom	0.3[h]	...	...	0.3	...	...	0.3	...	...	0.3	...	...
France[i]	21.8	9.5	0.9	2.6	0.8	7.5	17.4	7.8	0.7	2.2	0.6	5.5
Belgium	1.9	0.9	1.0		...	...	1.6	0.7	0.9		...	...
Netherlands[j]	0.5	0.1	—	f	0.1	0.2	0.5	0.1	—	0.1	0.2	0.2
Denmark	1.7	0.8	0.1		f	0.7	1.8	0.9	0.1		...	0.7
Sweden	35.4	9.2	12.4	1.3	0.9	10.0	37.1	11.1	13.8	0.9	0.7	9.0
Norway[k]	7.4	2.8	3.1	0.2	—	1.0	9.0	3.4	4.2	0.2	—	0.8
Finland[j]	39.7	8.0[l]	6.2	1.5	...	19.5	28.3	8.5[l]	8.3		...	11.5
Germany: Bizone	30.8[l]	12.4	2.3	3.1	0.1	12.3	...	...	...	...	...	...
Czechoslovakia	9.9	4.0	1.3	1.1	—	3.3	...	...	...	...	...	...
Switzerland	4.0	1.7	0.3	0.1	f	1.8	3.7	1.5	0.4	0.1	f	1.7
Austria	5.8	2.9[l]	1.1	0.4	...	1.4	6.3	3.7[l]	1.1	0.4	...	1.7
Italy	15.4	2.6	0.2	0.9	3.8	7.3	15.0	2.7	0.2	1.0	3.7	6.7
Greece	3.5	0.1	—	f	0.3	3.2	4.3	0.1	—	f	0.2	4.0
South Korea	2.5	0.2	f	0.1	0.2	2.0	...	...	...	...	...	...
Japan[m]	40.1	14.2	0.8	2.5	13.3	6.9	34.1	13.0	1.2	1.8	12.4	...
Turkey[n]	6.6	0.6	f	0.1	f	5.8	5.2	0.6	f	0.1	0.1	4.2
India[o]	10.2	2.2	...	...	...	7.9	...	...	...	...	0.1	4.3
Burma	5.9	0.8			0.1	4.9	3.6	0.2			0.1	3.3
Thailand[p]	2.4	0.8	...	...	0.8	0.8	2.8	1.3	...	...	0.7	0.8

(Continued on page 706)

TABLE 305—*continued*

Country	1948 Total Cut[b]	1948 Industrial Wood: Saw Logs and Veneer Logs	1948 Industrial Wood: Pulpwood	1948 Industrial Wood: Other[c]	1948 Wood for Charcoal[d]	1948 Fuelwood	1949 Total Cut[b]	1949 Industrial Wood: Saw Logs and Veneer Logs	1949 Industrial Wood: Pulpwood	1949 Industrial Wood: Other[c]	1949 Wood for Charcoal[d]	1949 Fuelwood
Indochina	1.0	0.3	—	[f]	0.1	0.6	. . .	. . .	. . .	. . .	. . .	. . .
Malaya	1.3	0.7	—	0.1	0.1	0.4	1.4	0.8	—	0.1	0.1	0.4
Indonesia	1.9		0.8		0.2	0.9	. . .	. . .	. . .	. . .	. . .	. . .
Gold Coast	4.4	0.3	—	[f]	0.1	4.0	4.7	0.3	—	0.2	0.3	3.9
French Cameroons	3.4	0.2	—	—	—	3.3	. . .	. . .	. . .	. . .	. . .	. . .
Nyasaland	5.8	[f]	—	0.1	[f]	5.7	5.8	[f]	—	0.1	[f]	5.7
Southern Rhodesia	3.1	[f]	—	0.3	—	2.8	3.1	0.1	—	0.1	—	2.9
Australia	15.1	5.5	0.4	0.7	—	8.5	15.3	5.7	0.4	0.7	—	8.5
New Zealand	3.3	2.3	[f]	0.1	—	0.8	. . .	2.3	[f]	. . .	. . .	. . .

Source: **6,** 1950, pp. 14–19.

a. Conversion factor: one cubic meter = 35.31 cubic feet. Solid volume of roundwood.
b. Includes, for some countries, all other wood output.
c. Pit props, hewn crossties, poles, piling and posts.
d. Includes wood for distillation.
e. Excludes wood waste and wood from dead trees.
f. Insignificant quantities.
g. Incomplete data for 1948; figures for charcoal and fuelwood refer to 1946.
h. Incomplete data.
i. Excludes farm fuelwood, almost as large as reported fuelwood figure.
j. 1947–48 and 1948–49.
k. Excludes consumption on farms.
l. Volume with bark.
m. Only quantities reported by control agencies.
n. Excludes unauthorized fellings, estimated to be as large as reported figures.
o. Only data of the Department of Forestry.
p. Excludes "unreserved" wood removed for use in villages.

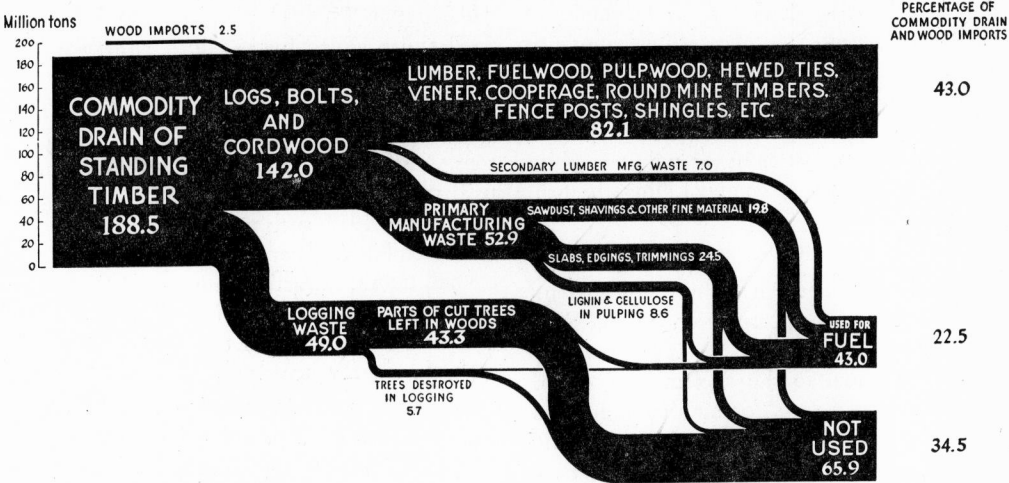

U. S. Department of Agriculture

FIGURE 211. USE AND WASTE OF WOOD IN LOGGING AND MANUFACTURING IN THE UNITED STATES, 1944

Figures show number of tons, in millions, in accordance with scale at left.

North America reflects the steadily rising demand for paper for packing, wrapping, printing, paperboard, building board, rayon and other purposes.[82]

Wastage of Wood

Only a small part of the cut wood is utilized. Waste begins in the forest, where limbs and tops, broken trunks and cull logs are discarded. The most wasteful cutting is done by the veneer logger, who takes only the butt end of the stem and abandons more than two thirds of the tree. A saw logger cuts about half the tree, while the pulp logger wastes only 30 per cent, since pulp mills can use smaller logs.

Wood processing in the mills is no less wasteful. The sawmills make little use of slabs, trimmings and shavings, and finished lumber represents about 25 per cent of the original tree. Veneer and pulp mills waste about half the wood they receive, and their end products amount to about 15 and 35 per cent, respectively, of the original material.[83] Not counting fuelwood, only 20 per cent of the total cut reaches the ultimate consumer. Even in the Scandinavian countries, where wood cutting and manufacturing are much more efficient and economical than elsewhere, only about half the annual cut reaches the consumer.

In the United States, 34.5 per cent of all wood cut (and imported) was wasted in 1944; 22.5 per cent was used for fuel; only 43 per cent appeared in products such as lumber, pulpwood, hewed ties, veneer, shingles and so on. Of the 108.9 million tons (oven-dry) wasted, logging accounted for 45 per cent, primary manufacture for 49 per cent, and secondary manufacture for the rest. (See Figure 211.) Part of the waste was used for fuel: 7 per cent of the logging waste, 62 per cent of the waste in primary manufacture, and 6 per cent in secondary manufacture of lumber.[84]

Even when wood is used as fuel it is not fully utilized, since much of the heat value is lost by inefficient equipment. Open fires and fireplaces yield only 5 per cent of the heat produced by burning the wood, and wood stoves, about 25 per cent. Research has shown that combustion of fuelwood could yield 80 per cent of the heat generated and that modern equipment could give as much heat as the stoves habitually used, with less than a third of the wood now consumed.[85]

In pulping processes, more than half the original wood is separated in solution and largely wasted. About half the waste consists of lignin, representing 20–30 per cent of the weight of the original wood. Although lignin has been studied for a hundred years, it is still a riddle. It is not

---

82. The per capita consumption of tissue paper in the United States about equals in tonnage the per capita consumption of all kinds of paper in the USSR. **3**, p. 55.

83. **27**, pp. 120–21.

84. **13**, p. 64.

85. Germany was one of the first countries to modernize its wood-burning practices and reduced the share of fuelwood in the total cut by 70 per cent between 1930 and 1940. **3**, pp. 63 and 67.

even known whether it is a single substance or a mixture of several substances. This ignorance makes it extremely difficult to utilize lignin waste, which, in pulping liquors alone, amounts to millions of tons a year. The greatest part is still discharged into streams as pulping sulfite liquor, polluting the water and killing the fish.

TANNING MATERIALS

Tanning materials are used by the leather industry to coagulate the protein in hides and skins and thus produce resistant leather. This procedure was known to the ancients, who used the bark of certain trees for tanning hides and skins. The Chinese tanned hides three thousand years ago. Well-tanned leather products have been recovered from the tombs of Egypt.

Tannins of forest origin are used in making heavy leather for soles, belting, harness, luggage and the like. While lighter hides and skins for uppers may be chrome-tanned or processed by a blend of forest and mineral tannins, vegetable tannins dominate in the production of leather. The most widely used tanning materials are chestnut and quebracho wood; oak, hemlock, mangrove and wattle bark; nuts, acorns, or pods of the myrobalan, Turkish oak and divi-divi trees; and sumac leaves. Usually two or more tannins are blended.

Chestnut wood, one of the oldest and most widely used tannins because of its fast penetration of hides, has been produced chiefly in the United States, France, Italy and Yugoslavia. Although blight has killed most of the chestnut trees in the United States, dead chestnut trees still supply most of the tannin produced in the country.[86]

Argentina and Paraguay produce one of the most valuable tannins in the world, quebracho wood.[87] This is one of the hardest and heaviest woods known; it will not float in water. Until recently, quebracho logs were shipped to all parts of the world for extraction of tannin, but the excessive cost of transporting the logs encouraged the development of a domestic industry producing a much less bulky extract for export. As a result, exports of logs shrank from nearly

440,000 tons in 1911 to about 75,000 tons in 1939 and declined further during the war (436 tons in 1943) because of the shipping shortage. In contrast, exports of the extract nearly tripled from 1911 to 1937 (about 68,000 and 198,000 tons, respectively). Until recently Argentina used much of the cut of the quebracho tree for fuel, but in 1950, such use of this precious wood was prohibited.[88] Paraguay has also developed a small tannin-extracting industry based on four plants.[89] Venezuela and Colombia supply small quantities of the pods of divi-divi trees and the bark of mangrove trees.

In Asia, the mangrove jungles of Indonesia contain an inexhaustible supply of tannin. Modern extracting plants in Borneo operate almost exclusively for export purposes. Mangrove tannin is used extensively because of its low price and the much higher avidity of hides for it than for any other tanning extract. India supplies the nuts of the myrobalan tree. Africa provides mangrove and wattle bark; Australia, wattle bark.

France, Italy and Yugoslavia have large chestnut forests; Italy also possesses an abundance of sumac groves, assuring it a world monopoly in the production of tannin from sumac leaves; Turkey and Greece produce a very valuable tannin (valonia) from the acorns of the valonia oak.

Only scattered data are available on the production of tanning materials (in thousands of tons): [90]

Brazil, quebracho, 1949	9.5
black wattle, 1949	4.0
France, oak and chestnut extract, 1948	20.0
Italy, sumac, 1949	1.5–2.0
Turkey, valonia oak, 1949	56.0
India, myrobalan, 1947–48	85.0–100.0
Union of South Africa, wattle bark extract, 1949	103.5

The FAO also has published statistics on the output of tanning bark. (See Table 306.)

NAVAL STORES

"Naval stores" is a trade term for turpentine and rosin which dates from the days when the ropes of wooden sailing vessels were lubricated

---

86. It has been discovered recently that a small annual plant, canaigre, native to the Southwest, has a high tannin content. **1**, p. 134.

87. Ninety-five per cent of the quebracho stands are in Argentina, where the wood is used also for crossties, pilings, posts and paving blocks. **18**, p. 9.

88. **18**, pp. 84–85; **17**, No. 17, August 1950, pp. 3–4.
89. **20**, p. 84.
90. **17**, 1949–50, *passim.*

TABLE 306

TANNING MATERIALS: OUTPUT OF BARK IN SELECTED COUNTRIES, 1946–48

Country	Thousands of Tons			Country	Thousands of Tons		
	1946	1947	1948		1946	1947	1948
United States	71.0	. . .	. . .	Poland	2.1	0.6	. . .
Mexico	6.2	3.3	. . .	Czechoslovakia	13.0	7.4	90.0
Jamaica	1.0	. . .	. . .	Switzerland	3.3	2.3	1.6
Venezuela	. . .	. . .	2.2	Austria	16.0	17.6	16.5
Colombia	0.9	. . .	150.0	Hungary	3.7	. . .	. . .
				Italy	1.3	1.4	1.8
United Kingdom	0.9	1.0	1.0				
France	9.2	6.0	. . .	Japan	1.6	1.1	0.5
Luxembourg	6.9	7.8	4.1	French Morocco	7.6	5.7	. . .
Belgium	1.5	1.3	. . .	Zanzibar	11.9	. . .	. . .
Denmark	1.0	0.8	0.8	Madagascar	5.0	0.3	. . .
Sweden	8.5	8.0	3.8	Union of South Africa	2.2	. . .	59.4[b]
Western Germany	. . .	62.7	46.6[a]	Australia	10.2	10.0	10.0

Source: **6,** 1948, pp. 116–17, and 1949, pp. 108–09.   a. Bizone.   b. Exports of wattle bark.

and the seams calked with pitch and tar.[91] Although the term persists, these products are little used today on ships, but are consumed in hundreds of other ways. Turpentine is used chiefly for thinning paints and varnishes and also in many polishes, waxes and pharmaceutical preparations, such as synthetic camphor. Rosin is one of the most versatile industrial materials in the world and is used in packing plants and in innumerable products, such as paper, varnishes, soap, linoleum, oils and greases, roofing, adhesive tape, rubber products and printing ink.

The main world supplies of both products come from the United States, which accounts for 70 to 78 per cent of all turpentine and rosin. France is the most important producer outside the United States, its share ranging from 8 to 9 per cent for turpentine, and from 9 to 10 per cent for rosin. Portugal, Spain, Mexico and Greece produce almost all the rest of the known output. (See Table 307.)

The United States

Production of naval stores developed first in New England. With the encouragement of England, which needed these products for its navy and merchant marine, it had become an important industry in North Carolina by 1700. In 1728

England forbade the American colonies to export naval stores directly to foreign countries. Trees near navigable streams were tapped, and the crude gum was shipped to England for processing. Later, distillation centers were established in North Carolina.[92]

To assure the safety of United States ships on the high seas the states, after gaining their independence, continued for many years to pay tribute in naval stores to pirates.[93] Production continued to expand, and in 1850 the Carolinas accounted for 95 per cent of the total output in the United States. Cutting in these states failed, however, to leave enough seed trees for reproduction, and the output in the Carolinas has dwindled almost to zero; in 1947, it amounted to less than half of one per cent of the nation's total.[94]

The industry began to move, first to Georgia, then to Florida, and more recently to Alabama, Louisiana and Texas. Today the naval stores belt extends across the coastal plain, from the Savannah River to the Mississippi. Forests occupy almost three fourths of the area, in which field crops are of only minor importance. The

91. Rosin from trees was used by the Greeks and Romans for their warships. In the Middle Ages, tar and pitch were produced chiefly in the region of the Baltic Sea, and Sweden was the main exporter. (**36,** p. 417.)

92. **36,** p. 417.

93. In 1815, the United States defeated the pirates in Tripoli, Tunisia and Algiers and ceased to pay tribute. (**12,** 1949, pp. 286–87.)

94. Nevertheless, an abundant second growth of the longleaf and slash pines, the most prolific sources of gum, has somewhat reactivated the industry in South Carolina in recent years. (**12,** 1949, p. 287.)

TABLE 307

ROSIN AND TURPENTINE: OUTPUT IN SELECTED COUNTRIES, 1939 AND 1948–49

Country	Rosin, in Thousands of Tons			Turpentine, in Millions of Gallons		
	1939	1948	1949	1939	1948	1949
World [a]	594.1	642.8	636.4	43.4	45.3	46.4
United States	433.2	490.5	471.7	30.2	33.0	33.2
Mexico	22.4	20.0	20.0	1.7	1.5	1.3
France	61.8	51.6	55.0	5.4	4.3	4.6
Portugal	28.6	39.3	42.7	2.0	3.0	3.2
Spain	26.0	34.7	34.7	2.4	3.1	3.1
Greece	22.1	6.7	8.2	1.6	0.5	0.7
Other	—	—	4.1	—	—	0.3

Source: **34,** 1948, p. 33, and 1950, p. 23.

    a. Excludes the USSR.

TABLE 308

ROSIN AND TURPENTINE: OUTPUT IN THE UNITED STATES, 1897–1950

Year [a]	Rosin, in Thousands of 520-Pound Drums			Turpentine, in Thousands of 50-Gallon Barrels		
	Total	Gum	Wood	Total	Gum	Wood
1897–98	1,332	1,332	—	500	500	—
1907–08	1,558	1,558	—	585	585	—
1917–18	1,513	1,385	128	548	520	28
1927–28	2,060	1,732	328	727	650	77
1937–38	2,050	1,388	661	700	518	182
1938–39	2,090	1,466	624	709	534	175
1939–40	1,835	1,054	782	605	383	222
1940–41	1,717	939	779	566	344	222
1941–42	1,708	792	917	549	285	264
1942–43	1,656	869	787	560	322	238
1943–44	1,463	784	679	508	288	220
1944–45	1,318	692	626	471	245	226
1945–46	1,452	694	758	488	244	244
1946–47	1,720	753	968	570	270	300
1947–48	1,991	828	1,163	641	294	347
1948–49	2,076	921	1,155	659	324	335
1949–50	2,024	925	1,099	673	323	350

Source: **34,** 1948, pp. 35–37, and 1950, pp. 25–26.

    a. The annual period for which output is recorded extends from April 1 through the following March 31.

pine forests, especially the longleaf and slash pine stands, are used chiefly for the extraction of resin or gum, from which both turpentine and rosin are obtained through distillation.

Once distillation of pine gum was the only, and then the chief, process used in this industry. In the last two decades, however, distillation of pine stumps has been initiated and has gradu-

ally become more important than the distillation of resin. (See Table 308.) More recently, large amounts of naval stores have been recovered at some pulp mills in the South. Production methods have been greatly improved. Formerly, individual turpentine producers distilled their gum in primitive fire stills. Today more than 400,000 "turpentine farmers" bring their product to thirty-two central distilling plants, where the gum is cleaned and converted to products of high quality. In 1948, these plants processed more than 80 per cent of all the gum produced in the United States.

In 1947–48, Georgia accounted for 69.7 per cent of the country's output of naval stores; Florida, for 22.4 per cent; Alabama, for 6.9 per cent and other states for the rest.[95]

In the United States, the percentage distribution of industrial consumption of turpentine and rosin in 1949 was as follows: [96]

	Turpentine	Rosin
Chemicals and pharmaceuticals	67.2	28.3
Ester gum and synthetic resins	14.0	17.1
Paints, varnish, lacquer	10.8	8.0
Paper and paper size	—	31.3
Railroads, shipyards	3.9	0.7
Soap	—	6.3
Shoe polish, shoe materials	2.7	0.4
Linoleum and floor covering	—	2.7
Rubber	0.1	0.8
Other	1.2	4.4

Other Countries

In France, the industry is concentrated in the heavily forested department of Landes, where its commercial success dates from the 1860's. When the United States ceased to export turpentine during the Civil War, Landes captured the foreign markets and has kept most of them.[97] The trees, maintained on a rotation system, are first tapped when they are thirty years old. After thirty or forty years of tapping, they are cut for timber.

The USSR has extensive pine forests covering about 225 million acres. Although they largely consist of Scotch pine, a poor producer of oleoresin, they must yield considerable quantities of rosin and turpentine. Until 1935, the USSR exported a part of its output, but exports ceased in the last prewar years. Apparently, the country's growing industry consumed all domestic supplies of these products.[98]

Production in Greece dropped catastrophically during the country's occupation by the Germans and Italians, who felled 4 million fully grown pine trees for military purposes. In addition, lack of fuel during the war years caused de-

forestation near the cities, and the gathering of cones for fuel prevented the development of seedlings.[99]

OTHER PRODUCTS

Cork

Cork was well known in antiquity. According to Pliny, the Romans used it in swimming and in fish nets, ship anchors, jug stoppers and winter shoes for women. The early monasteries in Europe had walls and ceilings lined with cork for protection from heat. With the invention of the glass bottle in the fifteenth century, the use of cork became more general, but the real beginnings of the cork industry date from the seventeenth century. By 1760 cork production was firmly established in Spain, and later it was extended to France, Portugal, Italy and North Africa.[100]

Cork is obtained from the bark of the evergreen cork oak, grown in the Mediterranean region. The cork oak may live as long as a hundred and fifty years, and its soil requirements are modest. The bark is first stripped when the tree is fifteen or twenty years old and thereafter every eight or ten years. With each stripping the cork becomes lighter, softer and more compressible.

Cork is used for bottle stoppers, life buoys and other similar articles and in the production of linoleum, shoe linings and soles, and the like. As new uses were found for cork, and later for cork shavings and waste, production increased from 68,000 tons in 1888 to 167,000 in 1935 and about 310,000 tons on the eve of World War II.

The chief producers of cork are Portugal, Spain and North Africa; smaller quantities are produced in France, Italy, the Balkans, Turkey and the USSR. (See Table 309.)

In 1947, the annual rate of output of Algeria amounted to 35,000 tons; of French Morocco, to about 18,000 tons; and Tunisia, 3,500 tons.[101] Production in these regions is largely controlled by the government, and most cork is exported in a crude state. Most of Portugal's exports are likewise raw; a high percentage of Spain's consists of cork products.[102]

Various attempts have been made to acclimatize cork oak trees in California, which

95. **34**, 1948, pp. 35–37.
96. **10**, 1950, p. 749.
97. **25**, pp. 121–22.
98. **36**, p. 451.

99. **34**, 1948, p. 76.
100. **24**, p. 5.
101. **6**, 1949, p. 12.
102. **24**, pp. 26–27.

TABLE 309

CORK: STANDS AND OUTPUT IN SELECTED COUNTRIES
BEFORE WORLD WAR II

Country	Cork Oak Stands, in Thousands of Acres	Annual Output, in Thousands of Metric Tons[a]	Annual Yield Per Acre, in Pounds
World	5,312	308.5	127.5
France	346	12.0	76.9
Portugal	1,705	150.0	193.4
Spain	840[b]	70.0	183.7
Italy	198	11.0	123.0
Spanish Morocco	99	2.0	44.5
French Morocco	766	18.0	51.8
Algeria	1,087	40.0	81.3
Tunisia	272	5.5	44.5

Source: **8**, p. 84.

a. Conversion factor: one metric ton = 2,204.6 pounds.
b. Other estimates of the area of the Spanish stands are considerably lower, ranging from 336,000 to 534,000 acres.

now has some 2,000 trees. Experimental stripping of the bark in 1940 yielded about 11 tons, of a quality equal to that of imported cork of the same grade. New plantings have been made in California, Arizona and some other southwestern states.[103]

Pharmaceutical Products

Camphor and quinine are the two chief drugs produced from trees.

Camphor is obtained from the wood of the camphor laurel, which grows wild in Formosa, China and Japan.[104] The total world output is estimated at 6,000 to 7,000 tons a year, of which Formosa supplies about half. In Formosa and Japan, camphor forests are publicly owned, and the industry is under government control.

The wood of camphor trees sixty or more years old is chopped into small pieces, which, after distillation, yield camphor amounting to about 3 per cent of the weight of the wood. Recently methods have been found in Japan to obtain camphor from the leaves and twigs of young trees.

Quinine, used in fighting malaria, is produced

from cinchona bark.[105] The cinchona tree requires a mean temperature of 70–80 degrees and a well-distributed rainfall of about 100 inches. It is difficult to cultivate, grows very slowly, and the bark is taken fifteen to eighteen years after planting, when the quinine content is at its peak. The tree, with its roots, is taken from the soil and cut into short logs. The bark is then stripped with wooden mallets. The bark contains about 70 per cent water but, after having been exposed to the sun for a few days, retains only about 13 per cent moisture. The excess water is removed in special drying furnaces, and the dry bark is either pulverized or broken into small chips before the extraction of quinine begins.[106]

Like rubber, cinchona bark was originally obtained from a wild tree, which is native to Ecuador, Colombia, Bolivia and Peru. Since 1850, cinchona cultivation has been attempted in practically every tropical country and many subtropical regions. The most successful plantations are in Java, where the Dutch government used a small lot of seeds obtained from Charles Ledger in 1865. This seed proved to be so prolific that the strain has been called *C. ledgeriana.* Around 1890 overproduction of quinine resulted in a severe drop of prices. Most private planters in India, Ceylon, Burma, Malaya, the Sudan, the West Indies, Australia and elsewhere destroyed the trees and turned to tea and other crops as more promising enterprises. The high yields of *C. ledgeriana,* however, enabled the Dutch plantings to survive.[107] Combining patient work with the use of soil science, genetics, climatology and forest ecology, the Dutch put their plantations on such a solid foundation that Java was able to establish a world monopoly in quinine production.

Recently cinchona plantations have been established in Guatemala, with good prospects of success. Except for the plantings at Toro Negro National Forest, various attempts to grow cinchona trees in Puerto Rico have failed so far.[108] Some other Latin American countries still produce relatively small amounts of cinchona bark but none can compete with the Javanese plantations.

103. **36**, pp. 502–03.
104. Camphor is also produced synthetically. It is used in the pharmaceutical industry and in the manufacture of nitrocellulose products, such as cellulose, smokeless powder, photographic film.

105. Synthetic drugs, such as atabrine, are also used for this purpose.
106. **43**, pp. 71–73. Some other alkaloids are extracted from the roots.
107. **47**, p. 2.
108. **47**, p. 2.

OUTLOOK

World War II made people increasingly forest and wood conscious. Great Britain was again sharply reminded of the vital link between its lifeline, the coal industry, and its supply of pit props. In the United States, wood was one of the bottlenecks in war production. At the same time, timber-exporting Sweden, having lost its usual outlets, began to look for new ways to utilize its great forest resources for various other products in short supply, such as textiles, cattle feed and yeast. It also used wood to alleviate the shortage of coal for heating and of petroleum for transportation. The critical postwar shortage of timber for building construction in most European countries focused attention even more sharply on the value of forests.

New Products and Uses

New types of wood, "wood alloys," combining the features of wood with certain qualities of steel, stone and rubber, have been developed by permeating the wood structure with special synthetic resins.

Durable weather-resistant plywood has appeared on the market as a construction material. The new field of plastics has evolved, and new processes have been invented that promise both increased yields of pulp and new industries based on wood. Structural paper has been created — impregnated with synthetic resin, laminated and pressed under heat, it becomes hard and strong and can be bonded to metals. Sawdust, once a waste material, can now be converted to cattle feed, ethyl alcohol and other products.

Many experts believe we are on the threshold of new inventions enabling us to make liquid hydrocarbons from lignin and other wood waste material. The significance of the manufacture of hydrocarbons from wood is summarized by the FAO as follows: "By duplicating in minutes what nature took millions of years to perform, science could enable forests to augment the world's nonrenewable oil resources." [109] It is believed that this new source of power for the internal combustion engine may accelerate industrialization in countries poor in coal but rich in forests, such as some in South America and Africa.[110] Experiments have been made in feed-

ing wood molasses and wood yeast to livestock, and some scientists believe that commercial production of these commodities is now possible; intensive tests at various agricultural colleges in the United States have shown that they are satisfactory feed. The possibility of making wood sugar for human consumption has come closer in recent years.[111]

These and other new uses for wood, combined with its customary utilization for fuel, building, paper and other purposes, may increase the world demand for it very substantially, particularly if the growth of world population is accompanied by rising standards of living.

Adequacy of Supplies

Are the world's forest resources adequate to meet the growing demand? The foresters say yes, on two conditions: forests must be managed as a renewable crop and forest destruction must be stopped.

The present growth rate of coniferous forests in the United States is 33 cubic feet per acre, and it is believed that improved management could raise it to 57 cubic feet. The reported present growth rates for coniferous forests in Europe range from 104 cubic feet per acre in Denmark to 23 in Poland and 21 in Great Britain. In the two latter countries forests suffered greatly during World War II, but an increase to 43 cubic feet per acre is considered possible. An estimate of growth in the coniferous forests of the USSR is 28 cubic feet per acre; because of the northerly location of many of the forests, it is unwise to estimate a higher average rate for the future.[112] In Canada, the current rate of growth in the coniferous forests is about 14 cubic feet per acre, and a rate of 28 is considered attainable with better management.

The world's accessible coniferous forests could produce, assuming reasonably good management, a total of more than 40 billion cubic feet. It is estimated that inaccessible coniferous forests could yield, under the same assumption, some 22 billion cubic feet per year. Thus, with good management and over a period of years, the world's coniferous forests could be expected to provide 62 billion cubic feet annually, as compared with the present normal use of about 26 billion cubic feet. The future productivity of

109. **4**, p. 228.
110. **29**, p. 26.

111. **1**, pp. 141–43.
112. **12**, 1949, p. 749.

broadleaved forests in Europe and North America can also be increased substantially. In tropical regions, such an increase will depend on finding uses for many species not utilized at present and on curbing destructive practices, now so widespread.[113]

Moreover, better utilization of the cut would substantially improve the world's tight supply of timber. If the world could attain the Swedish efficiency in utilizing the forest cut — so that 50–55 per cent reaches the ultimate consumer — timber requirements could be met much more easily.

Technological progress in silviculture opens new horizons for the future. It is anticipated that in the not too distant future hybrid forest trees will grow to harvest size in half or even a third the time required by a good nonhybrid tree. There is already a hybrid pine which, at three years, is more than twice as high and three times as heavy as the better type of the parent stock. It is confidently predicted that hybrid tree strains will be as common in twenty years or so as hybrid corn is today. When that time comes, commercial plantations could produce two or three times as much timber as is produced by natural growth or by planting standard stock.[114]

---

113. **12,** 1949, p. 749. See also Chapter 10.

114. **12,** 1943–47, p. 465.

CHAPTER 20

FISHERIES

MORE THAN TWO THIRDS of our globe is covered by water. Like the land area, this part of the planet teems with life, though the forms of life are different.

Despite the progress of biology and hydrography, the ocean is still a frontier and a challenge to man. We know very little about its life, make relatively little use of its resources and have not yet begun to till the waters of the earth as we have tilled the land. Awareness of the tremendous potential resources beneath their surface is growing, however. Under the pressure of threatening shortages of other resources, scientists are exploring water life increasingly, seeking out paths across the frontier that separates water from land. Some experts believe that the "time will come when we shall cast our bread upon the waters and see it multiplied manyfold." [1]

LIFE IN THE WATER

The Population of the Water

The waters of the world are the habitat of an extremely numerous and diversified population — crustaceans, mollusks and other aquatic animals, including seals and whales. Science has identified 40,000 different kinds of fish, nearly twice as many as the varieties of all other vertebrates — birds, mammals and others — put together.[2] There may be, in all, a thousand or more commercial species in the water. Though some fish are not used, none seem to be useless.[3]

The habits and living conditions of these creatures vary greatly. Some species are accustomed to the temperature of hot springs, others live in icy waters. Some are vegetarians, others carnivorous, still others are practically omnivorous. Some can only swim, others can fly or jump; some few can even walk on land. There are fish that "burrow like moles, hibernate like bears, and fight like tigers."[4] Some migrate in search of food or to reproduce their kind, others are sedentary.

Aquatic animals range in length from a fraction of an inch to 85 feet or more; in weight from 2–5 grams to 75 tons. Most of them see in the water, some can see in the air, and others are almost blind. All fish "hear" and recognize sounds in water; some of them like to hum, as does, for example, the toad fish guarding its eggs cemented to rock or crevices. Some fish are able to give off electric impulses, the electric eel so powerfully that it can fell or even kill a horse. Demersal or ground fish, such as the cod, haddock and pollack live at the bottom; the pelagic species, such as herring, menhaden, mackerel, pilchard, tuna, salmon and shad, keep close to the surface; still others live at various depths below the surface.[5] Some fish travel in schools, some move singly. Some are powerful swimmers, mackerel, for example, and are widely distributed; others, among them sea bass and white perch, have a narrow geographic range.[6]

The breeding habits of fish also differ greatly. Some spawn in water as they swim, others migrate to special spawning grounds. Anadromous species, such as salmon or trout, return generation after generation from the ocean to the fresh river waters, their birthplace, to spawn and die. Catadromous fish, such as eels, migrate from fresh water to the sea for spawning. The European eel swims three thousand miles to spawn in waters near Bermuda. The young eels soon begin their journey back from the sea to fresh water. The young American eel has to travel only about one thousand miles, which takes him about a year; the European eel may be under way for nearly three years.[7] Some species bury their eggs in mud, others build nests at the bottom, and still others carry eggs and young in their mouths, as the catfish and the cardinal do.

---

1. **1**, Vol. I, p. 33.
2. **44**, p. viii. Other estimates range from about 24,000 to some 100,000. **47**, p. 315, and **51**, p. 7. This chapter deals only with commercial fish species, seals and whales.
3. **47**, p. 315.

4. **44**, p. viii.
5. **44**, pp. viii, 156–58 and 167–68.
6. **51**, pp. 172–73.
7. **51**, p. 171.

The pipefish and the sea horse transfer their eggs to the abdominal brood pouches of the males. There the eggs are incubated, and later the males "give birth" to the young.[8] Sometimes, as with the ocean perch, the young are perfectly formed and sizable at birth.[9]

Most species have a tremendous reproductive capacity. The female often produces several hundred thousand eggs in a spawning season, but the cod may spawn more than 9 million eggs in one breeding period. If all the eggs hatched and all the young survived, the waters of the earth would have been overcrowded long ago. Nature prevents this by exposing the larvae to so many perils that only one or a very few out of many thousands reach maturity.

The food of aquatic animals consists chiefly of countless microscopic plant and animal organisms (collectively called "plankton"), so translucent that they are not perceptible to the naked eye. Fish eggs discharged in water drift with the plankton, which covers vast areas and serves as the first link in the food chain of all aquatic creatures. Various species of even the largest of all marine animals, the whale, live on plankton almost exclusively, although they also swallow small fish.[10] Many fish eat fish, in addition to plankton, small ones serving as food for the larger and stronger, which, in turn, fall prey to fish that exceed them in strength and adroitness. Fish "eat each other's eggs, they eat each other's young, they eat their own young, they eat one another."[11] Thus actually all live on plankton, directly or indirectly. In apparently calm waters, a free-for-all fight for food goes on relentlessly.

The Marine Environment

The distribution of fish in the world, like that of plants, depends on climatic conditions and physical environment, with water instead of soil as the habitat. The ocean offers a wide range of environmental conditions, some static and others dynamic. The most significant factors are temperature, salinity and currents. Some authorities believe that the change of temperature may be the most important single factor controlling the distribution of marine animals.[12]

The temperature of the water, which depends on the amount of solar radiation, decreases with depth and with distance from the equator. Very deep waters close to the equator may be about as cold as surface waters close to the poles.[13] The minimum temperature is about 28° F., the maximum 108° F., but the temperature in the open ocean seldom exceeds 86° F.

The temperature of the water has a direct bearing on the physical processes of the fish population, such as breeding, incubation and the larval period, rate of growth and seasonal migration, and it affects them indirectly by influencing the amount and distribution of plankton.[14] All inhabitants of the sea have an optimum range of temperature, below and above which are the lethal limits. They require different temperatures in different biological phases; the lobster, for example, grows to a large size in cold waters, though the larvae can survive only in warm waters.[15]

The salinity of sea water varies with latitude and with the rate of evaporation and precipitation. It is lowest near the equator, an area of torrential rains, and highest in latitudes about 20° N and 20° S, decreasing again at higher latitudes. For all oceans, the average salinity is 35 parts per thousand. In the Red Sea, where evaporation is extreme, the salinity is about 40; in the Gulf of Bothnia in the Baltic Sea, with low evaporation and a large influx of fresh water, it is almost zero.[16]

Salinity decreases with depth to about 800–1,000 fathoms, then increases again. The ice-cold surface waters around the poles, diluted by rain, snow and melting ice, are lowest in salt content, while the deeper layers are saltier.[17] The effect of changes in salinity on the various marine species is very considerable, although some can tolerate changes within certain limits. An inflow of warmer and saltier water imperils a species not adjusted to it, a disaster the herring in the North Sea suffered in 1921.[18]

---

8. **51**, p. 174.

9. **44**, p. 28.

10. The sperm whale, however, depends for food mainly on squids moving at great depths, and the killer whale eats marine mammals and birds as well as fish.

11. **47**, p. 313.

12. **27**, p. 21.

13. **33**, p. 11.

14. Because of the high conductivity of water, all changes in its temperature cause changes in the body temperature of fish. **46**, p. 844.

15. **24**, p. 154.

16. **24**, p. 124. The salts of the ocean contain various minerals, such as calcium, magnesium, bromine and potassium, in different proportions. **47**, p. 36.

17. **27**, p. 21. See the conclusions of the famous scientific expedition of the *Challenger,* which explored ocean and marine life in 1872–76. **50**, pp. 12–13.

18. **29**, p. 66.

The currents and, in general, the constant circulation of oceanic waters affect the life of fish in many ways, mainly by dispersing plankton throughout the various layers of water. Fish eggs and larvae are carried along with the plankton, many succumbing while others survive.

The currents largely account for the distribution of both temperature and salinity in sea water. They move vast masses of warm equatorial waters toward the poles, and the cool waters of the Arctic and Antarctic toward the tropics. In addition, water masses in high latitudes sink vertically. These large water masses plow through the oceans without merging completely with other water except along their fringes; they roll over and thereby cause involuntary migrations of fish to regions often fatal to them. The Gulf Stream, for example, forces various tropical pelagic fishes into cold waters in high latitudes. "Currents, in fact, play the same role in marine economy as do railroads, or any other transportation system on land." [19] When two currents of contrasting temperature and salinity collide, they sweep large masses of water up or down and with them multitudes of fish and quantities of plankton.

Another important function of the currents is to aerate the depths and renew the supply of oxygen. Otherwise, the depths would be filled with toxic waste because of the respiration of innumerable animal organisms and the oxidization of decaying animals and plants. Indeed, except for the circulation of water, all but the uppermost layer of the sea would become an emptier waste than the Sahara. [20]

A most intimate interdependence exists between sea water and marine life, the former influencing the life cycles of animals and plants, the latter altering by its functions the very character of the water environment.

Migration of Fish

In the ever moving oceans, fish, too, are almost always on the go. Whole schools move to some bank at certain seasons and depart when the season ends. Herring visit the northern part of the Temperate Zone in the early spring and then migrate to its more southern part, while mackerel move in the opposite direction during the same seasons.

In the main, fish migrate in search of food as well as for breeding. Thus, schools of fish retreat in masses before the advance of a warm current that carries less plankton. Migrations of cod, herring and mackerel are examples in point, while the migrations of salmon in the North Pacific, of both American and European eels, and of fur seals in the Arctic are motivated by breeding purposes.

The migration of fish has important bearings on the operations of fisheries. When a run toward a bank begins, more often than not, fishermen are already lying in wait. When the exodus gets under way, the fishing season in that area is at an end. The catch is unpredictable — sometimes overabundant, sometimes meager. It may remain at a high level for several years, then suddenly decline. Such a hegira occurred in the past decade in the world's three great sardine-fishing grounds, off the coasts of the United States, Japan and the Iberian Peninsula. The predominant species of sardines in each of these is different, but each area ordinarily accounted for a substantial proportion of the country's total annual fish catch before the war — in the United States, a fourth; in Japan, a third or more; in Portugal, more than half. After years of plenty, these fishing grounds have met with a marked loss of sardines — for Japan, since 1941; for the United States, since 1944; and for Spain and Portugal, since 1947. [21] The sardine (pilchard) catch in the United States ranged from 300 million pounds in 1931 to 1,241 million pounds in 1939, 531 million in 1946 and 272 million in 1947. Thereafter the fish began to appear in gradually increasing numbers, and the catch amounted to 373 million pounds in 1948, 634 million in 1949 and 712 million in 1950. [22] In Portugal, the sardine reappeared in 1950, and landings rose 80 per cent. [23]

Considerable research in these areas has so far not resulted in any satisfactory explanation. A special investigation of the life history and dynamics of the sardine population has been under way in California since 1949.

In general, mystery still surrounds the routes that fish follow and the mechanisms that enable them to navigate thousands of miles. Nor are these the only secrets hidden in the ocean depths. Although much has been learned about marine

19. **24**, pp. 129 and 260.
20. **24**, p. 261.

21. **5**, May–June 1950, pp. 56–57; **4**, 1947 and 1948–49, *passim*.
22. **11**, 1952, p. 680.
23. **5**, July–August 1951, p. 13.

life in recent years, little is yet known about even such common species as the menhaden, the catch of which, in some years, approximates half a million tons in the United States alone.[24] Least is known about the largest marine animal, the whale. It can be studied only when dead, and then it decomposes rapidly.[25]

The unpredictable migrations of fish, and consequently the alternating gluts and scarcities in the catch, involve great risks for the fisheries. In times of overabundance, the industry suffers from shortage of manpower and from the great perishability of the product. When fish suddenly disappear, equipment, machinery, storage houses and labor are idle and underutilized. This raises the overhead expenses of the industry, and fish — the free gift of nature and therefore among the least expensive foods at the point of production — goes up in price.

MAJOR FISHING AREAS

Like other living organisms, fish naturally gravitate toward sources of food. Plankton, the chief pasturage of the sea, is more abundant in cold waters than in warm; in shallow layers, exposed to sunlight, than in the depths; in coastal waters than in the open sea.[26]

Continental Shelves

The subsurface plateaus along the coasts of the continents combine these favorable conditions. The continental shelves differ in width, being very broad in the North Atlantic and very narrow in the Caribbean. The seaward edge of the shelf drops rapidly to the bottom of the sea, but the greatest depth of the most important shelf for world fisheries, that of the North Atlantic, does not exceed 100 fathoms and averages 50 fathoms. The most abundant and variegated plankton is found on elevated parts of the shelves, the so-called banks, where both marine life and fisheries are concentrated.

The richest and most productive banks are in the Northern Hemisphere. The world's fisheries are concentrated in the North Temperate Zone, north of the isotherm of 54° F. In both temperate zones, only small fishing centers exist between the isotherms of 54° F. and 68° F. The tropical region, between the isotherms of 68° F. north

and south of the Equator, has many species of fish, but none is as numerous as any of the major species in the Temperate Zone. South of the isotherm of 54° F. in the South Temperate Zone there is only one area where fish are concentrated on the continental shelf — around the tip of South America. (See Figure 212.)

Fishery Centers

The Northern Hemisphere accounts for 98 per cent of the world's fish catch. Its major sea fisheries in the North Atlantic extend from the White Sea (USSR) along the entire length of the European coast to the Bay of Biscay, and from Labrador to the southern edge of New England. The most important banks in this area are the Grand Bank near Newfoundland and the Georges Bank close to the New England shore; the Dogger Bank in the center of the North Sea, close to Great Britain; the banks of Lofoten (Norway), the Faroes and Iceland. In the North Pacific, the important fishery areas are the Bering Sea and the stretch from the Gulf of Alaska to Lower California and waters off the coast of Siberia down to southern China.

Japan's fishing areas are along the coast and offshore — in cold waters surrounding the island of Hokkaido; in temperate waters off the coasts of Honshu, Kyushu and Shikoku; and in subtropical waters south of Japan and in the deepsea waters of the Pacific Ocean east of that country.[27]

The most important fresh-water fisheries in the Northern Hemisphere are in the Great Lakes and on the Mississippi and its tributaries; on rivers flowing into the North Pacific (salmon fisheries); and in the inland waters of southeastern Europe, the USSR (particularly the Caspian Sea), China and Japan.

In the Southern Hemisphere, marine resources are little utilized, although the makings of a fishing industry exist in many areas. Argentina faces wide continental shelves; off the coast of Chile and Peru, the cold Peruvian current provides an excellent environment for a wealth of marine life. The waters of the desert coast of northern Chile and Peru are among the world's richest in sardines and anchovies, available throughout almost all the year. The Galapagos fishing grounds, where United States fishermen catch tuna, are among the richest of the American Pacific Coast. The entire coast line of Brazil

24. **7**, p. 71.
25. **48**, p. 312.
26. **32**, p. 22.

27. **17**, p. 27.

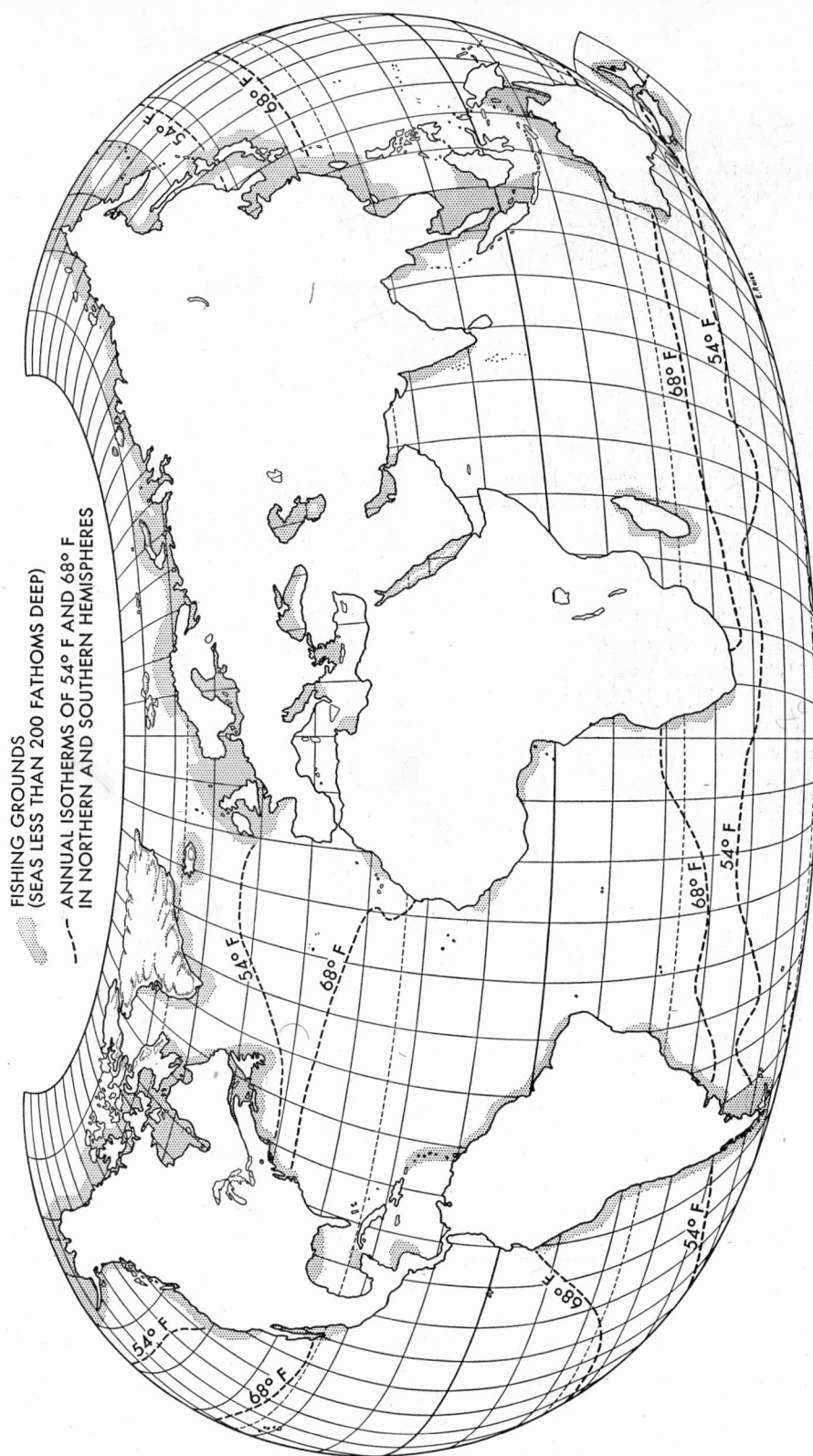

FISHING GROUNDS
(SEAS LESS THAN 200 FATHOMS DEEP)

- - - ANNUAL ISOTHERMS OF 54° F AND 68° F
IN NORTHERN AND SOUTHERN HEMISPHERES

FIGURE 212. FISHERIES: LOCATION OF PRINCIPAL FISHING GROUNDS IN THE WORLD

is one large potential fishing area. Fresh waters in Brazil, Argentina and Venezuela, with their extensive river network, also could be exploited more effectively than they now are.[28]

The main fishing areas of the Union of South Africa are on the west coast between Capetown and Walvis Bay, with trawling grounds between the depths of 13 and 300 fathoms. These cold waters are rich in pilchard, stockfish and other species.

Products of the Sea

Mankind's foremost use of aquatic resources has always been for food. For coastal regions, especially countries with such limited agricultural resources as Japan, Norway and Iceland, the proteins supplied by fish are vitally important. The cheapness of fish, as compared to meat, has also been a factor in expanding its consumption in poorer countries and among poorer people. Before World War II fish accounted for 2 per cent of the total food consumption in France and for at least 15 per cent in Japan.[29] Whale flesh is eaten in some countries (Norway, Japan, China),[30] and whale oil is used extensively in Great Britain and Germany in the manufacture of margarine.

Marine life is also and increasingly an important source of feed, fertilizers and industrial raw materials. At one time small fry and little-known species were unmarketable and were thrown overboard. The United States Fish and Wildlife Service estimates that even now the otter and shrimp trawls operating off the New England coast and in the Gulf of Mexico discard about 50,000 tons a year. By and large, however, the fishing industry is utilizing the inedible part of the catch for fish meal and scrap, constituents of animal feeds, and for fertilizers. In the United States, for example, 200,000 tons or more of fish meal were produced annually before World War II.

Oils constitute another valuable by-product of fisheries. Fish oils are obtained from all parts of the body; fish-liver oils, rich in vitamins, from the liver only.[31] Fish oils, derived principally from pilchard, menhaden and herring but also from many other species, are used in making soap, insecticides, paints and varnishes and other products. Many species of fish-liver oils are used in the pharmaceutical industry, and lower grades, in processing leather. Cod-liver oil, of which the United Kingdom, Iceland and Norway are the chief producers, is particularly valued for medicinal purposes.

The sperm oil of whales goes into the making of liquid waxes and lubricants; whale oil proper is used, after refining, as a constituent of margarine and other shortenings and, to a lesser degree, for making soap. Shells of oysters, mussels and other shellfish are used in poultry feed, for making lime and stucco and for other purposes. The skin of fish, particularly that of sharks, is used for leather.

New ways of using every part of the catch continue to develop. Complete utilization of some species would seem to have been achieved. In France, reportedly, nothing is left after the processing of a shark — skin, flesh, fins, liver oil, stomach, blood, teeth, glands are fully utilized. Fishermen of many countries, however, still discard the shark after skinning it and removing the liver. Such examples of diverse practices could be multiplied.

Seaweed (Irish moss, kelp, algae) is a valuable and unique material. Agar-agar, from red seaweed, is used in making bacteriological media and is essential in hospitals. In some countries, for example Japan, seaweed is eaten. In France (Brittany), seaweed is used for soil improvement. Sponges are another widely used product of marine life.

Fishery in the Past

Fishing, together with hunting, is one of the oldest industries, if not the oldest. No one knows when or where it originated, but it is certainly older than any recorded history.

Fishery in Ancient Times

Rudimentary harpoons found in Europe and Peru have been traced back to about 10,000 B.C. The many fish hooks uncovered in some lacustral villages originated either in the same mesolithic

---

28. **5**, May–June 1951, pp. 4–5 and 11.

29. **48**, p. 611.

30. In the Middle Ages, whale meat, particularly the head and tail, was royal food in England. Whale, as well as sturgeon and porpoises, belonged to the crown unless subject to a special grant. **43**, pp. 264–66. The German army was fed whale meat in nutrition tests on the eve of World War II. **51**, p. 709.

31. In salmon, herring, menhaden, mackerel, shad and many other species, most of the oil is in the body; in shark, cod, tuna, halibut and several other species, in the liver. **47**, p. 357. The oil content varies greatly in different species, and in the same species according to size, fishing season and area. **1**, Vol. VII, p. 84.

period as harpoons (which may have been used for either fishing or hunting) or in the later neolithic era. Fishing techniques reached a comparatively high level at a very early period. Remnants of fish nets, with square or round bark floats, have been preserved from neolithic times. Improvements in implements continued throughout the Stone and Bronze Ages; the old bronze hooks and nets with bronze shuttles resemble those used today in some European countries.

Elaborate Egyptian paintings of fishing with lines or nets and of fishing from boats, and paintings showing the cooking of fish, date from about 2000 B.C. While the Egyptians as well as the Hebrews fished in rivers, the Phoenicians preferred sea food, which their nets drew from the Mediterranean. Before 2000 B.C. the Assyrians had artificial pools in every town and close to every temple to provide fresh fish for cooking.[32] Wealthy Romans later adopted the same custom. In the Far East, fishing has been practiced since early times all along the sea coast — in China, Japan, Indochina. Paintings made in 1500 B.C. on wood and bone show that the Chinese then knew the use of both fishlines and nets.

Large accumulations of fish bones and shells, together with broken parts of primitive kitchen utensils, on the coasts of England, France, Portugal, Russia, the Baltic countries and in the Western Hemisphere testify that fish has been a very important part of the diet since prehistoric times. Some of these kitchen middens, such as those along the Baltic Sea, are from one to three yards high and stretch over an area one hundred to three hundred yards long and fifty to one hundred and fifty yards wide.[33]

Very early, man discovered that to utilize his catch properly he had to keep the fish from rotting. Salting of fish, one of the oldest methods of food preservation, was practiced in prehistoric times. The Egyptians knew about drying and salting fish. When they established trade relations with India, they exchanged salted fish for spices. The Romans salted fish and also maintained a supply of fresh fish that arrived in barrels filled with salt water. In winter, salmon packed in snow or ice were sent to Rome from the Rhine or Loire. In spite of primitive transportation facilities, Rome, with more than a million inhabitants in the first century A.D., never lacked fish.

Fishery in the History of Europe

Fishery has played a very important role in Europe. It has supplied the population with protein food at seasons when meat supplies were meager, and has been the Lenten and Friday fare of Catholic Europe and part of the regular diet of soldiers as well as of sailors on long voyages.

Whale and sperm oils once were essential for lighting streets and houses. As recently as the early nineteenth century it was predicted that cities and homes would be dark when mass slaughtering had exterminated the whales.[34]

Fishing served as a training school for future sailors in the British, Dutch, French and Spanish navies, which reshaped the map of the world.

Trade in herring is generally considered to have been one of the main sources of the power of the Hanseatic League in the thirteenth century. Migration of the herring in the fifteenth century to the North Sea, from which they failed to return in schools, undermined the wealth and power of the Hanse and became an important factor in the economic and political power of the Dutch.[35] A seventeenth-century author, Cardinal Bentivoglio, said of the herring's contribution to human liberty: "Without forests and wood, Holland has built more ships than all the rest of Europe. It owes this success to the herring fishery. With the arms of those engaged in this trade it checked the plans of Spanish tyranny and emerged from surrounding waters free of oppression." [36] Voltaire remarked, "Although fishing and the art of salting herring do not appear to be an important item in world history, they have been the basis of Amsterdam's grandeur, and further, they have made out of a country once despised and sterile, a rich and respected power."

Fishery had a most crucial role in the rise of England's sea power. It stimulated the naval arts and gave impetus to shipbuilding and foreign trade. Fishing craft off the Yarmouth coast, the center of the herring industry, formed the nucleus of the British navy and called into being the confederation of the Cinque Ports.[37] England's reliance on its fishermen was so great that Sir William Monson, Admiral of the Narrow Seas, reported to James I: "He that hath the trade of fishing becomes mightier than all the world."

---

32. **48**, p. 48.
33. **42**, p. 15.
34. **50**, p. 28.
35. **50**, p. 27.
36. Translated from **48**, p. 238.
37. **43**, p. 260.

Sir Walter Raleigh pointed out that fishermen were necessary to England:

1. For taking Gods blessing out of the Sea to enrich the Realm, which otherwise we lose.

2. For setting the people on work.

3. For making plenty and cheapness in the Realm.

4. For encreasing of Shipping, to make the Land powerful.

5. For a continual Nursery for breeding and encreasing our manners.[38]

In perhaps no other country, however, has fishery played so important a role as in Norway. "The entire Norwegian economic structure could not have developed without its fishing." [39] Fishing has been practiced all along the Norwegian coast for thousands of years, and the great abundance and variety of fish encouraged settlements on even the northern tip of the country. The configuration of the coast, protected by thousands of islands, islets and rocks, and cut by long and narrow fjords, offers great opportunities for what is still the chief source of livelihood for the majority of the coastal population. (See Figure 213.) Fishing is often combined with farming. Many farms along the coast are so small that fishing has had to provide a subsidiary cash crop for centuries.[40] Fish and fish products constituted two fifths of Norwegian exports up to the end of the nineteenth century and, even before World War II, were second only to wood pulp and wood.

France had a fishing fleet of 40,000 boats in the fifteenth century, and more than 300,000 persons were occupied in the herring fishery alone.[41]

Fishery in the History of the New World

Fisheries were instrumental in expanding European civilization. The spirit of adventure sent some fishermen of western and northern Europe farther and farther from their native shores — sometimes to hunt whales, a trade known since the ninth century, or to follow the moving schools of cod. The Norwegians (Northmen) thus reached Iceland, where they established a colony in the ninth century. Cod fishing became

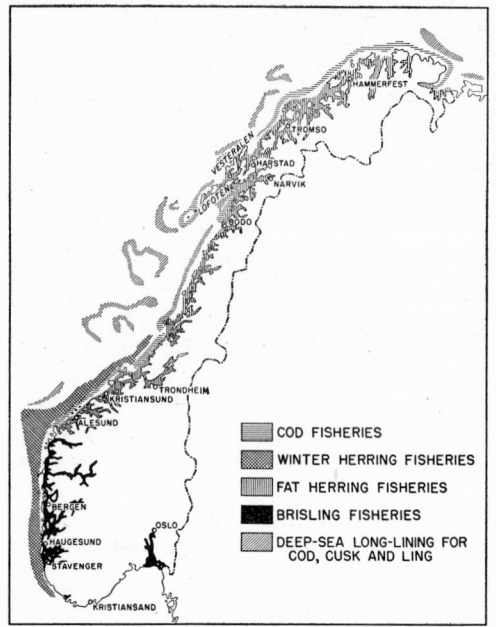

Courtesy of Norwegian Export Council

FIGURE 213. FISHERIES: NORWAY'S COASTAL FISHING GROUNDS

its chief occupation, and the fish served as currency in the payment of rents and other dues.

Sixteenth-century fishermen of France, Spain, Portugal and England extended the economic frontiers of Europe to the New World, especially North America. The attraction of North America was not gold, as in Peru, but cod and whales. Newfoundland, where fishermen used to summer, was the bridgehead. Gradually, they began to leave a part of the crew there over the winter and also moved westward, to and beyond the Gaspé Peninsula. In time, the settlements expanded, and the colonization of Canada began. White men were active on the coast of Quebec before Jacques Cartier officially discovered Canada.[42] By the end of the sixteenth century, fisheries operated not only on the Great Banks but also in the Gulf of St. Lawrence.

With the defeat of Spain, England obtained a firm hold on Newfoundland, which later became one of the channels for migration from England to the New World. Many English colonists came in the fishing ships and remained in New England when the ships returned home with their cargoes.[43] The settlers in New England learned from the Indians to use fish re-

---

38. **40**, pp. 197–98. In 1722 William Wood wrote in *A Survey of Trade* (London), "It is a certain maxim that all states are powerful at sea as they flourish in the fishing trade."

39. **52**, 1948, p. 43.

40. **36**, p. 12.

41. **29**, pp. 12–13.

42. **35**, p. 76, and **21**, p. 3.

43. **30**, pp. vii–viii.

mains to fertilize the soil. The Pilgrims might not have survived without the abundant supplies of cod, herring and mackerel. Whaling was also important, since it provided illuminating oil, candles and whalebone.

Fishery Today

Technical progress has reshaped fishery, as it has other industries, though to a much lesser extent. Schooners have been replaced by trawlers; steam and diesel power have replaced sail; the fathometer and the sonic depth finder aid in the locating of fish; the general use of radio-telephone speeds up the arrival of a larger number of fishing units in areas where a fish concentration has been discovered; experiments are under way to use underwater electric currents for directing fish to the desired point; nylon nets have been introduced.[44] Big commercial companies have modern fishing fleets, extensive shore installations for processing fish and a large labor force.

The Atlantic menhaden fleet uses airplanes to spot fish, and California tuna clippers locate bait and tuna with the aid of planes and helicopters.[45] Utilization of the catch has been intensified. Salting and drying in the sun have given way to refrigeration and, recently, to quick freezing.

A new invention, so far only in the experimental stage, may revolutionize commercial fishing and, at the same time, "be one of the most conservative fishing methods as yet practiced." Its purpose is to suck the fish directly from the open sea into the boat, without the use of a net. The fish are to be directed toward a large suction pump and drawn into the hold of the vessel by electric devices. The range of voltage to be used is such that small fish should not be affected. It is estimated that the cost of the electrical equipment and its installation amounts to only 3–5 per cent of the value of a medium-sized vessel.[46]

Though fishing, which was once a trade, is becoming an industry, more and more mechanized and commercialized, it still maintains its traditionally diffuse character, not only in the world at large but even in most industrialized countries. Composed of numerous small enterprises and family fisheries along the coast and beset with uncertainty in supply, it cannot keep pace with the development of other industries.

The unique feature of the industry is the international character of the exploitable resource: Fish have no nationality until caught. Fishermen of all countries can congregate at a fishing ground and take their share of nature's bounty. For example, a considerable part of the catch of the United States comes from waters off foreign coasts, and nationals of other countries fish off the coasts of the United States.

Because fishing is not a very profitable business, and large fortunes cannot be made as fast as in some other industries, such as oil, it has never attracted large venture capital. It also cannot give a producer the protection of exclusive ownership that he holds for a farm or a mine. The farmer can till his acres as he sees fit and is free to introduce new machinery, but the fisherman is often restricted by law, even in inshore operations, from using more efficient gear for the catch, a measure necessary to prevent the depletion of resources in particular areas. For example, the kind, size and location of nets, traps, purse seines and the use of the catch and so on are subject to many restrictions in every fishing state of the United States. California limits the percentage of the sardine catch that may be used to manufacture meal and oil.[47] International restrictions of sorts are also in force, though often only on paper. Whether such restrictions aim at the protection of fisheries in the interest of all and serve to protect certain fish species in danger of exhaustion,[48] is no matter: to commercial fisheries and to small fishermen, they are limits on their freedom in exploiting the waters and diminish the attractiveness of the occupation.

Hazards of the Industry

The hazards of fishing are great. First, the wide fluctuations in the catch caused by weather or other conditions result in erratic price movements. Peril to life, particularly on small craft, is considerably greater than in other occupations.

The product itself is one of the most perishable. Some of the fishing grounds are far from consuming centers, and preservation of the product is difficult. Salting is the least expensive process, but the salted product is less and less popular. The latest method of preservation, freezing,

44. **47**, p. 310; **1**, Vol. VII, p. 99. On the use of electric currents by the USSR, see p. 730.

45. **5**, May–June 1951, pp. 26–27.

46. **51**, p. 274.

47. **47**, p. 308.

48. See below, pp. 739 ff.

TABLE 310

FISHERIES: FISHERMEN AND FISHING CRAFT IN SELECTED COUNTRIES BEFORE AND AFTER
WORLD WAR II

Country [a]	Number of Fishermen		Number of Fishing Craft	
	Prewar	Postwar	Prewar	Postwar
United States [b]	124,795	153,056	71,810	88,823
Canada	68,817	60,419	34,606	30,599
Newfoundland [c]	25,220	28,000	492	251
Mexico	...	15,000	2,195	5,698
Cuba	...	19,500	...	2,509
Venezuela	...	20,000	...	4,250
Brazil	80,002	67,911	31,300	11,000
Peru	6,588	7,669	2,404	3,234
Chile	5,617	7,655	2,410	4,272
Argentina	...	7,500	...	4,000
United Kingdom	58,000	...	11,503	12,977
Ireland	7,237	10,232	4,278	4,370
Iceland	5,003	...	1,100	...
France	130,710	...	21,812	19,649
Belgium	1,784	...	510	484
Netherlands	17,570	...	3,201	2,838
Denmark	18,486	19,665	15,436	15,828
Sweden	23,114	23,333	20,376	21,051
Norway	83,029	79,176	23,443	...
Germany	30,000	...	20,000	...
Poland	1,822	...	953	2,669
Portugal	33,126	40,846 [d]	13,181	15,738
Spain	195,000	277,229 [e]	40,000	37,832
Italy	108,000	120,000	42,051	32,804
Yugoslavia	18,294	29,523	6,293	6,800
Greece	...	26,000	...	7,668

(Continued on facing page)

assures the best results but requires a large investment.

Adequate fishing equipment is expensive. Since the ocean is open to all, fishermen from more distant and advanced countries may arrive with larger trawlers and capture the season's harvest, leaving only a scanty remainder for those who, though near the great fishing grounds, are poor and not so well equipped.

Small fishermen are often hard pressed for capital to improve or replace gear and boats. Unlike farmers, they have no land or farm buildings to mortgage; their boats are often uninsured because of very high insurance costs and thus cannot be used as collateral. Fishing as an occupation also fails to provide the small fisherman with at least the minimum essentials of living derived from subsistence farming.[49]

Often small fishermen combine into groups and work for a specific share of a catch; commercial shore plants own the equipment and hire the ships' crews for a season. For the most part, piece wages are paid — per barrel or pound or otherwise. This practice tends to make wages more dependent on luck than on individual efficiency.

Fishing as an Occupation

The number of fishermen in the world at large has been estimated at 2 million for 1800; 3 million for 1900; 4 million for 1936.[50] In that prewar year Asia accounted for 2.8 million, or 70 per cent of the total; America, for 270,000; and Europe, for 626,000. Today, some 5 million persons or more are directly engaged in fishing as a source of livelihood.

49. See the description of fisheries in **47**, pp. 304–28.

50. **31**, pp. 16 and 23.

TABLE 310—*continued*

Country [a]	Number of Fishermen		Number of Fishing Craft	
	Prewar	*Postwar*	*Prewar*	*Postwar*
USSR	250,000	...	...	...
Japan	1,102,502	...	366,267	294,989
Taiwan (Formosa)	100,000	...	10,000	...
Hong Kong	...	50,000	...	5,036
Iran	...	8,000	...	200
Ceylon	...	112,600	...	...
Malaya	27,069	44,379	11,167	16,215
Indonesia	25,000	...	4,050	...
Philippines	...	60,000	...	480
Kwantung	305,000	...	...	...
French Morocco	2,323	...	511	1,440
Algeria	3,609	...	1,081	...
Tunisia	10,820	3,130	10,076	2,064
Egypt	52,800	60,000	10,022	12,018
French West Africa [f]	...	20,000	...	200
Gold Coast	...	50,000	...	800
Union of South Africa	...	7,000	...	2,566
Australia	9,081	18,429	5,462	8,594
New Zealand	2,218	1,550	1,279	891

Sources: **3**, pp. 212–15; **4**, 1948–49, pp. 14–25; **5**, May–June 1951, p. 6; **52**, *passim*.

　　a. Prewar data for different countries range from 1936 to 1940; postwar data, from 1945 to 1948.
　　b. Includes Alaska. In 1950: about 170,000 fishermen and 92,500 fishing craft (**5**, March–April 1952, p. 69).
　　c. Cod fisheries.
　　d. Includes 4,280 fisherboys.
　　e. Includes 52,134 fisherboys and 6,916 fisherwomen.
　　f. Senegalese fisheries only.

Before the war Japan reported the largest number — 1.1 million. It is estimated that the total must run high for other countries in the Far East such as China, India and Indochina, where hundreds of thousands of persons fish to feed themselves and their families and for the market.[51] In the United States, about 170,000 persons are engaged in fishing. Canada, including Newfoundland, counts about 90,000, and the number in the USSR and the Middle and Near East must be considerable. Incomplete data for Europe indicate that large numbers of people derive their livelihood from fishing in Spain, Italy, France, Norway and other countries with long coast lines. (See Table 310.)

Data on total fishing craft in various countries are not wholly comparable because of diversity in the tonnage and efficiency of the vessels. Trawlers, steam and motor vessels, small rowboats and diesel-powered vessels are counted each as a unit

though they are entirely different in amount of investment and as means of production. About 60 per cent of the craft of United States fisheries are motor-powered, for example, while 77 per cent of Japanese craft are without power.[52]

The world's prewar fishing fleet is estimated at about a million units, of which nearly a fifth were motor-powered. The United States and Japan together had more than half the world's motor boats; Norway, Canada and France, nearly three tenths.[53] The United Kingdom had fewer vessels but the proportion motor driven was the highest in the world (figures in per cent):[54]

United Kingdom	76
United States	47
Norway	32
Japan	16–17
USSR	8–10
China	0.2

51. **2**, 1949, p. 7.

52. **4**, 1948–49, pp. 16 and 21.
53. **31**, pp. 22 and 33.
54. **41**, p. 57.

TABLE 311

FISHERIES: LANDINGS, BY CONTINENT, BEFORE AND AFTER WORLD WAR II

(*Thousands of Metric Tons* [a])

Continent	Annual Average for the Prewar Decade	Average in Recent Years	
		Accounted For	Estimated
World	16,683	23,192	25,000
North and Middle America	2,691	3,693	3,750
South America	213	426	500
Europe	4,750	5,909	6,000
USSR	1,557	1,560	2,000
Asia	7,238	10,976	12,000
Africa	179	533	600
Oceania	56	96	150

Source: **4,** 1948–49, p. 3.

a. Conversion factor: one metric ton = 2,204.6 pounds.

SEA FISHERIES

All the great sea fisheries are concentrated in the Northern Hemisphere, from which come nearly all recorded landings of fish. The marine resources of the Southern Hemisphere, with the exception of whales, have so far remained almost untapped.

The Fish Catch, by Continent

International statistics on fishing have great gaps. For some of the world's waters there are no figures at all, for others only scattered data. A chaotic medley of weights, measures and names of species is used in reports of landings. The world's catch of fish in 1800 is estimated roughly at about 4 million tons; in 1900, at 12 million; and in an average prewar year, at about 17 million tons,[55] of which the Pacific Ocean accounted for about 10 million and the Atlantic, some 7 million.[56]

The FAO has been trying since 1946 to develop statistics of fisheries on a world-wide scale and has made considerable progress in this pioneer work. Although complete coverage has not been achieved in view of the many statistical gaps and semantic difficulties, it considers its

estimates, based largely on official reports, fairly realistic.

According to these estimates, the world's fishing catch is now about 50 per cent greater than in prewar years: 25 million tons as against 16.7 million.[57] Asia accounts for the largest share, ranging from more than 43 per cent before the war to 48 per cent in recent years. Europe and North and Middle America follow, accounting for 24 and 15 per cent, respectively, of the world's postwar catch. (See Table 311.) While Asia's percentage share has increased, those of Europe and North and Middle America have declined in postwar years:

	Prewar	Postwar
World	100.0	100.0
North and Middle America	16.1	15.0
South America	1.3	2.0
Europe	28.5	24.0
USSR	9.3	8.0
Asia	43.4	48.0
Africa	1.1	2.4
Oceania	0.3	0.6

The importance of fishing to the various continents can be measured by the relative output of fish and of meat. In the world as a whole, the weight of the fish catch was a third that of the

55. **31,** pp. 16 and 23.
56. **41,** pp. 58–59. **1,** Vol. VII, gives 17.7 million tons for the world's prewar catch, with a somewhat different distribution by ocean.

57. Subsistence fishing, angling and unrecorded commercial catch may have provided an additional million tons before the war. **3,** p. 183. No estimate of the amount from these sources in postwar years is available.

output of meat in prewar years but the percentage varied among the continents: [58]

	Tonnage of Fish Catch as Percentage of Meat Output
World	33
Western Hemisphere	16
Europe	33
USSR	47
Asia	69
Africa	8
Oceania	4

Comparable data for the postwar years are available only for America as a whole, Europe and Oceania: The weight of the fish catch rose, in comparison with the output of meat, from 16 to 27 per cent in America, from 33 to 59 per cent in Europe and from 4 to 9 per cent in Oceania.

The Fish Catch, by Country

Japanese fishermen took more than a fifth of the world's commercial catch of fish in an average prewar year. Other leading nations in the industry were China, the United States, Korea, the USSR, the United Kingdom and Norway. Their combined landings in 1938 were in the neighborhood of 11 million tons, or two thirds of the total. In recent years, the catch in Korea has dropped considerably, but precise data are not available. The Chinese catch has also declined, while that of the United States and the USSR has risen.

The fishing industry of many countries has been developing rapidly since the war. The landings of Brazil, Denmark, Sweden, Spain and other countries exceed the prewar level. (See Table 312.)

Japan

Japan leads all other countries in fishery in terms of number of persons employed, size of fishing fleet and volume of catch. The fishing industry is the principal source of protein in the diet of the people and also provides much of the country's fertilizer, animal oils, skins and so on. Coastal fishing is carried on in a multitude of tiny villages, while deep-sea fishing is concentrated in a few ports with good harbor facilities. Before World War II Japanese fishing was almost world-wide. Japan operated salmon fisheries in northern waters of the Okhotsk and Bering seas, trawled in the Yellow and East China seas, whaled in Antarctic waters, and had small fisheries off the coasts of Canada, the United States, Mexico and other Latin American countries and in Indian and Australian waters.[59]

Immediately after the war, Japan experienced great difficulties in rebuilding its fishing fleet, though the occupation forces imported great quantities of nets, twine and other materials after 1948. Hundreds of refrigerator cars have been built, and others are under construction. The number of vessels in 1950 exceeded the prewar total. For fear of stock depletion, the Japanese Diet ordered the reduction of the East China Sea fleet from 1,000 to 700 vessels.[60] A strict inspection has been established at all landing ports, and no distribution of fuel oil is made in exchange for fish of substandard quality.[61] Until Japan was permitted in May 1950 to extend its fishing area 900 miles east of the islands, landings were below the prewar level: 2.5 million tons in 1948 and 3.0 million in 1949. (See Table 312.) In 1950, total landings increased to 3.8 million tons, or 27 per cent above 1949.[62]

The United States

The United States is the second largest producer of fish.[63] With its two coasts, each thousands of miles long, it has a greater variety of marine life than any other nation. The North Atlantic and the North Pacific, with their warm and cold currents in close proximity to the coast, provide a natural feeding ground for nearly all important commercial varieties of fish.[64] The capitalized value of United States fishery resources was estimated by the Fish and Wildlife Service of the Department of the Interior at $5.9 billion for 1943.[65]

---

58. Cf. Tables 311 and 290, p. 664.

59. **17**, p. 29; see also **16**, *passim*.
60. **2**, 1950, pp. 227–28.
61. **52**, 1950, pp. 66–67.
62. **5**, July–August 1951, p. 4.
63. China may have a larger catch but only rough estimates of its landings are available. The USSR claims to have a larger catch than the United States (**23**, p. 330), but supporting evidence is not available.
64. **45**, p. 412. See the description of species caught in **7**, *passim,* and of fisheries by regions and states in **13**, *passim*.
65. **7**, p. 127.

TABLE 312

FISHERIES: LANDINGS, IN SELECTED COUNTRIES, 1938 AND 1948–50

(*Thousands of Metric Tons* [a])

Country	1938 [b]	1948	1949	1950	Country	1938 [b]	1948	1949	1950
United States [c]	2,291	2,075	2,175	2,652	Romania	30	30	30	...
Canada [d]	874	1,033	870	927	Greece	25	34	35	...
Mexico	19	49	55	...	USSR	1,716	1,445	1,791	...
Cuba	18	14	14	...	China	2,700	2,500	...	...
Venezuela	22	92	75	...	North Korea	1,300	...	...	...
Brazil	103	145	153	...	South Korea	629	285	295	219
Peru	5	36	45	...	Japan	3,059	2,454 [e]	2,980 [e]	3,794 [e]
Chile	31	65	76	...	Hong Kong	29	21	...	...
Argentina	55	71	64	...	Turkey	23 [f]	...	...	...
United Kingdom	1,194	1,196	1,159	988	Pakistan	...	23	...	...
Ireland	13	26	18	15	India	...	...	503	...
Iceland	274	465	384	368	Thailand	...	196	...	...
France	444	435	435	432	Indochina	266 [f]	...	...	...
Belgium	43	71	68	60	Malaya	...	54	72	...
Netherlands	236	269	249	244	Indonesia	472 [g]	350	...	...
Denmark	106	226	255	251	Philippines	270 [g]	195	238	220
Sweden	144	208	202	203	French Morocco	30	56	96	123
Norway	1,139	1,387	1,297	1,468	Algeria	19	...	...	...
Finland	22	46	66	66	Tunisia	10	10 [h]	...	...
Western Germany	669	380	513	555	Egypt	41 [i]	42	...	...
Poland	13	48	58	...	Angola	26	123	131	130
Portugal	241	274	281	307	Union of South Africa	30	...	125	250
Spain	299	527	551	576					
Italy	171	138	180	190	Australia	36	47	39	...
Yugoslavia	13	18	20	...	New Zealand	19	34	34	32

Sources: **4,** 1948–49, pp. 4–9; **5,** May–June 1951, p. 5, and supplement to March–April 1952, pp. 3–5; **52,** 1950, p. 74 (data for the USSR). For earlier data, see **53,** pp. 256–61; for the United States, **12,** 1949, front page.

a. Conversion factor: one metric ton = 2,204.6 pounds. The FAO gives somewhat higher figures, resulting from the use of round fresh weight for mollusks and related species instead of edible weight published by the U.S. Department of the Interior. The difference is not so great as to affect the comparability of the data.

b. 1938 or 1939.

c. Includes Alaska.

d. Includes Newfoundland.

e. Includes estimated unreported landings (in thousands): 368 in 1948, 447 in 1949 and 569 in 1950.

f. Prewar.

g. 1940.

h. 1947.

i. 1935.

The menhaden fishery, extending from the North Atlantic through the Gulf, has become the most important in volume in recent years, overshadowing the pilchard (sardine) fishery on the southern Pacific coast. On the Atlantic coast, the cod, haddock, herring and mackerel fisheries are very productive, and the largest shrimp fishery in the world is in the South Atlantic and Gulf states. Although pilchard landings have declined recently,[66] this branch, on the southern Pacific coast, still accounts for landings both large in volume and high in value. The northern Pacific coast provides abundant supplies of salmon, halibut and some other species. Tuna fishing is pursued on the high seas bordering the Western Hemisphere, 2,500 miles from home ports. (See Figure 214.) Tuna and tunalike fish (bonito, bluefin, yellowfin, albacore and others) are captured in increasing quantities. Landings of these species along the Pacific coast in 1949 (332 million pounds) were the highest on record.[67]

The potential yield from United States fish-

66. See p. 717.

67. **12,** 1949, p. 7.

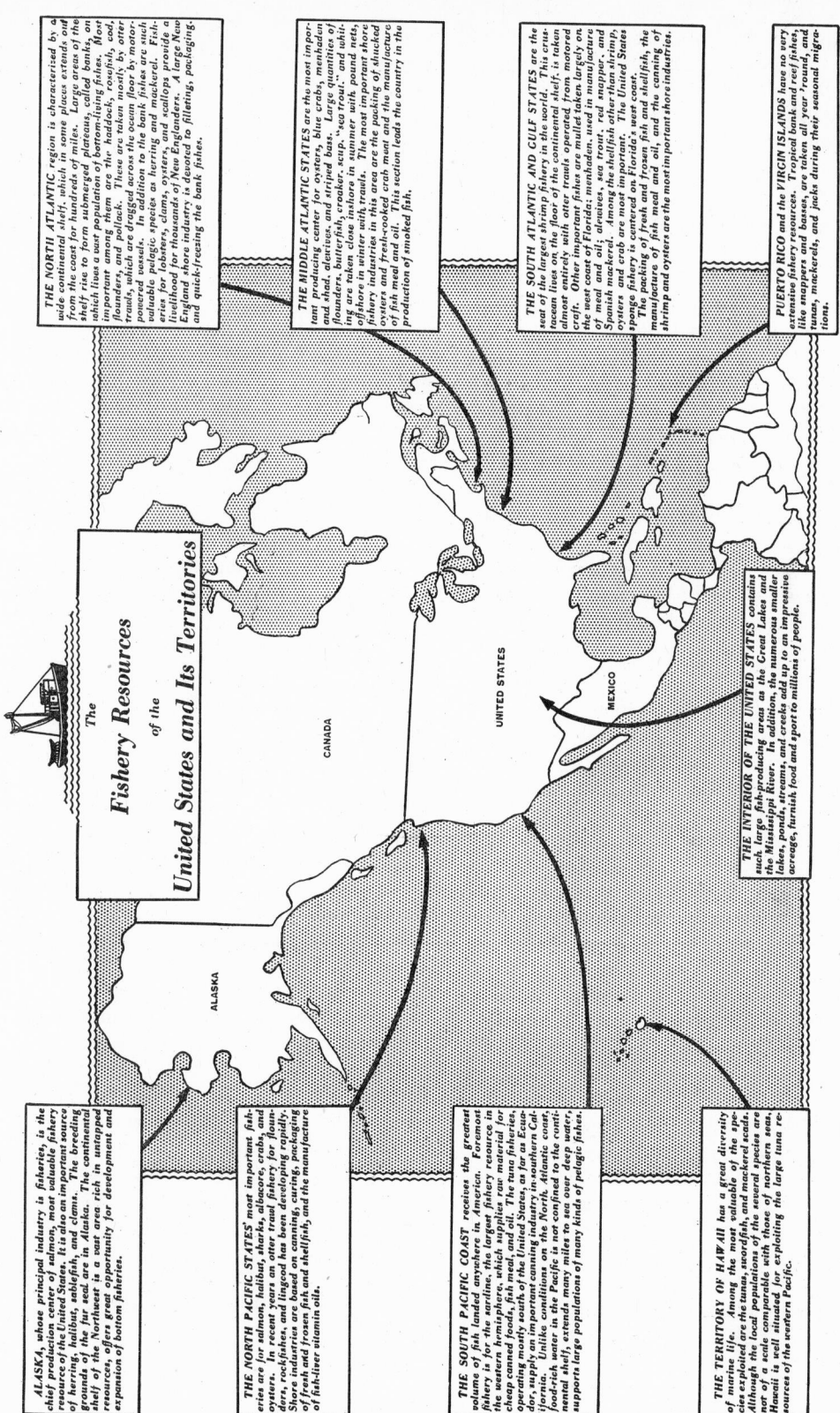

U. S. Department of the Interior

FIGURE 214. FISHERIES: RESOURCES OF THE UNITED STATES AND ITS TERRITORIES, 1944

eries has been estimated at 7 billion pounds (about 3.2 million metric tons).[68] The value of the 1950 catch totaled some $365 million, or almost quadruple the 1939 value ($96.5 million), although the difference in volume was rather insignificant (4.4 billion pounds in 1939; 4.9 billion in 1950). The average price per pound was 2.17 cents in 1939 and 7.45 cents in 1950.[69]

The United Kingdom and Norway

Both the United Kingdom and Norway have excellent fishing grounds off their coasts, and efficient fleets with large numbers of experienced fishermen; in both countries fishing is a traditional trade. Their fishing fleets suffered severely during the war, but many new vessels have been built in recent years. In 1949 the United Kingdom launched forty new long-distance trawlers. The Norwegian fleet has been fully restored and, except for incomplete replacement of old motors, is in better condition than before the war.[70] The 1951 catch of the United Kingdom was about 1.1 million metric tons; of Norway, 1.8 million.

The USSR

The center of fishing operations in the USSR has shifted from the Caspian Sea, which used to account for about two thirds of the total catch, to the Far East and the Barents Sea. The Caspian Sea now provides only some 23 per cent of the national catch; the Far East, 25 per cent; and the Barents Sea, nearly 21 per cent.

Several types of sturgeon, pike perch, pike, catfish and other species are caught in the Caspian Sea. The Barents Sea is rich in cod, haddock and herring, which are caught with trawlers. In the Pacific Ocean, fishing is carried on along the shores of Kamchatka and the Maritime Territory. The rivers in the western part of Kamchatka are spawning grounds for the salmon coming from the cold Okhotsk Sea. Fishing in the Black Sea is negligible.

The Soviet fisheries have many thousands of motor vessels and about a hundred trawlers; airplanes are used to survey the shoals of fish.[71] The Far Eastern fishing fleet is reported to use underwater electric current for taking in the shoals of herring, and it was believed that by 1950 the entire Soviet fishing fleet would be equipped with underwater reflectors. Fifty motor-driven vessels were obtained from Sweden under the postwar trade contract, and twenty-five more were ordered.[72]

Other Countries

The fishing fleets of other countries are also being restored and modernized. Iceland increased the number of its trawlers in 1949, and France launched 27 new steel vessels.

The badly depleted Greek fleet now exceeds its prewar size. Much of the Dutch fishing fleet has been restored and modernized. Germany, which lost about half its fishing fleet, has been permitted to build a hundred new trawlers.[73] India purchased two trawlers from the Netherlands for deep-sea fishing off Bombay. Interest in the development of marine resources is increasing in Latin America. The development of fisheries in the Union of South Africa, long overdue, is now in full swing and the supply of fish, barely touched until recently, is increasingly being utilized.[74]

On the whole, the catch exceeds the prewar tonnage, but Germany is an exception: there the catch was about 17 per cent smaller in 1950 than in 1938. (See Table 312.)

Output of Fish Per Capita and Per Fisherman

The importance of fish in a nation's economy can be measured — though only approximately because of the inadequacy of the basic data — by the number of pounds caught per capita of population. Iceland, whose economy is keyed to fishery and exports of fish, tops the list with a catch of 7,152 pounds per capita in 1949. Data for Newfoundland, now a part of Canada, are calculated separately, to stress the importance of fishery in that area — 2,813 pounds per capita in prewar years and 1,820 pounds since the war. Norway, with a small population and an intensive fish industry, leads the remaining countries and assigns a large part of its output to exports. In contrast, a number of countries produce only a few pounds of fish per capita — among them Peru, Argentina, Yugoslavia, Italy, Greece and Egypt. Japan, though it has the largest fish catch in the world, caught fewer pounds of fish per capita than Canada in 1949 and 1950.

The fish catch per fisherman is highest in Ice-

68. **51**, p. 216.
69. **12**, 1948, front page; **11**, 1951, p. 665.
70. **5**, January–February 1950, pp. 4–5; **36**, p. 41.
71. **23**, pp. 330–31.

72. **52**, 1950, p. 74.
73. **8**, p. 195.
74. **15**, pp. 6–10.

TABLE 313

FISHERIES: OUTPUT PER CAPITA AND PER FISHERMAN IN SELECTED COUNTRIES, 1938 AND 1949 [a]

(*Metric Pounds*)

Country	Per Capita		Per Fisherman	
	1938	1949	1938	1949
United States [b]	35	29	36,716	28,590
Canada	97	116	15,984	22,079
Newfoundland	2,813	1,820	...	1,766 [c]
Mexico	22	48	3,818	8,157
Cuba	92	63	1,000	3,748
Venezuela	14	43	2,400	9,860
Brazil	59	82	2,838	4,945
Peru	2	9	1,434	13,007
Chile	14	33	12,164	21,895
Argentina	9	9	...	19,180
United Kingdom	56	54	...	...
Iceland	5,162	7,152	91,500	...
France	24	24	7,490	...
Belgium	11	18	...	...
Netherlands	60	54	...	...
Denmark	63	139	12,658	28,578
Sweden	50	66	13,715	18,986
Norway	866	814	30,242	29,445
Finland	13	39	...	...
Western Germany	...	23	...	...
Portugal	72	81	14,705	15,412
Spain	26	47	3,067	5,040
Italy	9	8	3,167	2,533
Yugoslavia	2	3	1,645	1,490
Greece	8	10	...	2,960
USSR	21	21	14,120	...
Japan	113	82	6,115	...
Philippines	39	23	...	2,500
Egypt	6	5	1,366	1,550
Union of South Africa	7	25	...	3,943
Australia	12	11	8,681	4,667
New Zealand	26	44	18,935	47,741

Sources: Tables 310 and 312.

a. Whenever data for 1938 and 1949 were not available, the years closest to them were used.
b. Includes Alaska.
c. Cod fisheries.

land, New Zealand, Norway, the United States and Denmark, followed by Canada, Chile, Argentina and Sweden. (See Table 313.)

Consumption of Fish Per Capita

Fish is of greater importance in the diet in many Asiatic countries, where traditionally little meat is used, than elsewhere. Thailand and the Philippines consume more than 100 pounds of fish a year per capita; Japan, 83.3; Burma, 74.0. On the other hand, fish is only a minor item in the diet in China, Turkey, India and Pakistan. In Europe, Iceland, Norway, Sweden and Denmark, all countries with well-developed fisheries, top the list of fish consumers, while the Danubian countries use fish hardly at all. The per

TABLE 314

FISHERIES: CONSUMPTION PER CAPITA IN SELECTED COUNTRIES, 1947–48

Country [a]	Metric Pounds Per Year	Country [a]	Metric Pounds Per Year
Thailand	106.7	New Zealand	13.9
Philippines	101.4	Italy	12.1
Japan	83.3	France	11.9
Burma	74.0	United States	11.5
Iceland	67.9	French Morocco	9.0
Norway	59.3	Austria	8.6
Sweden	54.7	Egypt	6.6
Malaya	43.4	Algeria	6.2
Korea	39.7	China	6.0
Denmark	39.4	Czechoslovakia	5.7
United Kingdom	33.3	Union of South Africa	5.7
Portugal	28.2	Turkey	4.9
Indochina	27.3	India	3.1
Netherlands	22.9	Pakistan	3.1
Belgium	22.5	Germany, Soviet Zone	2.2
Greece	17.0	Bulgaria	1.5
Spain	16.1	Yugoslavia	1.3
Ceylon	16.1	Hungary	1.1
Finland	15.7	Romania	1.1
Germany, Bizone	13.9		

Source: **51,** pp. 214–15; **5,** January–February 1952, p. 7, reports higher figures for most European countries in 1949.

a. Countries arrayed by diminishing order of consumption of fish products.

capita consumption of fish in the United States is only 11.5 pounds a year, about as much as in Italy or France. (See Table 314.)

The Fish Catch, by Species

Conclusive data on the world's catch of various species of fish are not available, but the largest part consists of cod and herring and related species. The eighteen countries that reported their landings in 1949 by species had a total yield of nearly 11 million tons, distributed as follows:[75]

	Thousands of Tons	Per Cent
Total	10,975	100.0
Herring and related species	3,312	30.2
Cod and related species	2,538	23.1
Crustaceans and mollusks	1,308	11.9
Tuna, true mackerel and related species	544	5.0
Flatfish	370	3.4
Perch, bass and other	324	3.0
Salmon and related species	318	2.9
Freshwater fish (carp, pike, minnow and other)	181	1.6
Other	2,080	19.0

75. **4,** 1948–49, pp. 38–44.

In the United States the chief species are menhaden, pilchard (sardine), salmon, herring, tuna, rosefish (ocean perch) and haddock, but the catch varies widely from year to year, especially for some species, as is shown by the following figures (in millions of pounds):[76]

	1931	1939	1949
Menhaden	230	575	1,076
Pilchard (sardine)	300	1,241	634
Mackerel	62	114	92
Salmon	601	527	484
Tuna	60	182	336
Ocean perch	[a]	78	237
Haddock	195	179	135
Cod	112	124	71
Herring, sea	170	263	205

a. 237,000 pounds.

In the catch of the United Kingdom, cod accounts for two thirds of the total (760,000 tons out of 1,152,000 tons in 1949); herring, for about

76. **11,** 1951, p. 668; **12,** 1949, pp. 5–7. Data in the last column include 1945 figures for the South Atlantic states and, in the last two columns, 1931 figures for the Mississippi River and its tributaries, for which more recent data are not available.

TABLE 315

FISHERIES: LANDINGS, BY SPECIES, IN SELECTED COUNTRIES, 1938 AND 1949

(*Thousands of Metric Tons* [a])

Country	Herring and Related Species	Cod and Related Species	Salmon and Related Species	Tuna, True Mackerel and Related Species	All Other
		1938			
United States [b]	995	137	239	83	837
Canada [c]	181	123	82	13	100
United Kingdom	283	734	—	10	167
Iceland	156	112	1	—	5
France	116	159	[d]	34	135
Netherlands	124	19	1	7	85
Denmark	15	36	2	7	46
Sweden	77	32	1	5	28
Norway	662	409	1	8	59
Portugal	120	48	—	4	69
Spain [e]	. . .	. . .	. . .	. . .	. . .
Japan	1,128	194	221	311	1,205
		1949			
United States [b]	921	175	220	152	707
Canada [c]	265	384	73	18	130
United Kingdom	212	760	2	7	171
Iceland	71	282	[d]	—	41
France	85	89	—	43	218
Netherlands	117	15	—	7	97
Denmark	38	66	3	17	131
Sweden	104	52	2	10	33
Norway	733	355	1	16	61
Portugal	63	125	—	10	85
Spain [e]	127	93	—	29	278
Japan	659	159	23	219	1,920

Sources: **4**, 1948–49, pp. 38–44; for the United States: **12**, 1949, pp. 5–8.

a. Conversion factor: one metric ton = 2,204.6 pounds.
b. Includes Alaska; prewar figures for 1939.
c. Includes Newfoundland in 1949.
d. Insignificant quantity.
e. Landings by Spanish craft in 1948.

TABLE 316

UTILIZATION OF FISH IN SELECTED COUNTRIES, 1949

(Thousands of Metric Tons [a]*)*

Country	Total Landings	Marketed Fresh [b]	Frozen	Dried, Smoked, Salted	Canned	Reduced to Oil and Meal	Other Uses	Offal for Reduction [c]
United States [d]	2,175	730	...	42	738	625	39	418
Canada	605	132	88	141	78	137	30	...
Newfoundland	266	7	35	214	1	8	—	11
United Kingdom	1,152	804	46	215	19	68	e	203
Iceland	394	177	102	69	e	46	—	35
France	435	273	...	124	39	—	—	...
Netherlands	236	114	3	96	14	4	5	5
Denmark	255	145	31	16	18	27	18	91
Norway	1,166	246	52	280	54	468	65	86
Finland	66	53	1	9	e	3	—	—
Italy	152	129	1	15	7	—	—	—
Japan [f]	2,533	718	89	1,129	23	261	313	—
Philippines	75	67	e	5	2	—	1	—

Sources: **4**, 1948–49, pp. 12–13; for the United States: **11**, 1951, p. 668.

a. Conversion factor: one metric ton = 2,204.6 pounds.

b. Includes marketed frozen fish.

c. Offal from quantities shown in six preceding columns.

d. Includes Alaska.

e. Small quantities.

f. Reported landings only.

18 per cent, and in some years for more. In successful years, herring represents 50 per cent or more of the Scottish landings.[77]

The predominant species in Norway's inshore fishery are also herring and cod, the former constituting up to two thirds of the average annual catch, the latter some 30–35 per cent. During the run of herring, gear and craft are crowded to such an extent that strict regulations are necessary to prevent collisions. From 60 to 80 per cent of the annual catch is effected in a short time, between January and April, and during this period some 3,000 vessels with 12,000 fishermen are concentrated around a few Norwegian villages whose permanent population numbers only a few hundred persons.[78]

In Japan, herring is the all-important species, and the catch in prewar years exceeded a million tons. Herring and cod constitute practically the entire catch of Iceland, their importance alternating from year to year. (See Table 315.)

Utilization of the Catch

About two thirds of the world's catch is used for human food in various forms — fresh, frozen, canned or otherwise preserved. The rest is reduced to oil and meal.[79]

National preferences and the final destination of the catch — whether for domestic consumption or for export — largely determine the form in which fish is marketed. In the United States, almost equal amounts of fresh and canned fish are sold. Frozen fish is capturing more and more of the market, and about a fourth of the catch is reduced to oil and meal. In contrast, the United Kingdom, with an annual catch half that in the United States, markets more fresh and frozen fish (850,000 tons as against 730,000 tons for the United States) but uses only small quantities for canning. In no country does the share of canned fish in the total catch even approach that in the United States. (See Table 316.)

Fish Meal

Certain species of nonedible fish and the waste from processing the edible kinds are reduced to meal and oil. Fish meal is used increasingly for feed, as the value of its high-quality concentrated protein has been recognized. The waste of fish

77. **22**, pp. 177 and 179.
78. **38**, p. 57.

79. **51**, p. 202.

TABLE 317

Utilization of Fish: Output of Oils and Meal in Selected Countries, 1948 and 1949

(Thousands of Metric Tons [a] *)*

Country	Cod-Liver Oil 1948	Cod-Liver Oil 1949	Herring Oil [b] 1948	Herring Oil [b] 1949	Herring Meal [b] 1948	Herring Meal [b] 1949	Other Fish Meal 1948	Other Fish Meal 1949
United States [c]	0.7	0.7	51.1	49.6	111.0	137.4	47.0	66.4
Canada	1.4	1.3	12.0	11.9	30.8	27.4	10.0	12.7
Newfoundland	2.0	3.7	0.5	1.2	1.0	1.0	1.4	2.1
Great Britain	10.0	10.0	0.5	1.8	d	d	43.1	51.7
Iceland	9.0	8.5	17.5	7.6	22.9	7.7	5.0	7.0
France [e]	0.9	1.3	—	—	—	—	—	—
Belgium	0.1	0.1	...	...	0.1	0.1	0.6	0.6
Netherlands	...	...	...	...	d	d	5.8	1.5
Denmark	...	...	0.1	0.1	0.4	0.5	11.2	11.5
Norway	7.2	7.8	42.2	26.6	111.0	72.0	13.5	12.7
Japan	0.3	0.6	0.8	1.5	8.2	14.6	22.4	35.0

Sources: **5,** May–June 1950, p. 48; **4,** 1948–49, pp. 120–33.

a. Conversion factor: one metric ton = 2,204.6 pounds. Product weight.

b. Includes related species.
c. Includes Alaska.
d. Herring meal included with other fish meal.
e. Includes Corsica.

species that contain little oil in their bodies, such as cod, haddock and redfish, is converted into so-called liquid fish, a kind of liquid protein. When fish is reduced to oil, the water remaining after the separation of the oil still contains some portions of fish and various minerals. The solids are screened and added to the meal. The water, known as stickwater, was formerly discarded in ignorance of its value for feed. Years of research and experimentation have resulted in the development of a process for concentrating stickwater into a product with high vitamin B content, greatly valued for inclusion in mixed feed and considered to be a special factor in animal growth.[80] The United States and Norway are the chief producers of fish meal, followed by Great Britain, Japan and Canada. (See Table 317.)

Fish Oils

Fish oils are interchangeable to some extent with vegetable oils. Fish-liver oils have been used for medicinal purposes for centuries; they were prescribed for rickets in the Middle Ages. The discovery of their vitamin content has led to their use in vitamin oils and concentrates.[81]

The world's output of fish oils averaged 284,000 tons a year during 1934–38. The United States led, and Japan was second. During World War II the annual output of the United States declined by about 25 per cent, and that of Japan and Norway fell catastrophically. In the United Kingdom, the fishing fleet was requisitioned for military purposes, and production of fish oil ceased altogether. Only Iceland produced more fish oil than before the war. In 1948, the world's output of fish oils amounted to 213,000 metric tons; in 1949, to 263,000 tons.

In the United States, by far the greater part of the fish-liver oils is provided by the Pacific Ocean, from sharks, tuna, swordfish and halibut. The industry, however, has been affected increasingly by the competition of manufactured vitamins. The last vitamin in which the fisheries held a monopoly was vitamin A, but even this is being synthesized chemically in a pilot plant in the United States.[82]

Great Britain, Iceland and Norway account for the largest share of the cod-liver oil produced in the world, while the United States leads in the production of herring oil. (See Table 317.) Norway benefits from the fact that its fishing industry is carried on close to the coast, at low temperatures that make it possible to process

80. **51,** pp. 469–87; **1,** Vol. VII, p. 87.
81. **51,** p. 493.

82. **47,** pp. 327–58.

millions of fish livers in the shortest possible time.[83]

FRESH-WATER FISHERIES

In many countries fresh-water fisheries supply a substantial part of the nation's protein food. The Great Lakes provide the United States and Canada with about 50,000 tons of fish a year. In northern Europe and Asia likewise, fresh-water fisheries are of considerable importance.

The United States

Fishing in lakes and streams is usually carried on by individuals, each of whom gets only a small daily catch. Even on the Great Lakes, one of the largest fresh-water areas in the world, the commercial companies are comparatively small. The boats, usually 25–60 feet long, have a limited cruising range and return to shore daily to distribute the catch among the many small ports scattered along the shore. Normally, more than 5,000 fishermen and 2,000 boats are engaged in fishing on the United States side of the Great Lakes.[84]

Noncommercial fishing, however, usually accounts for a larger total haul than commercial fishery in the United States. In a normal year, it is estimated, anglers land about 120,000 tons of fish, or nearly two and a half times as much as is landed on the Great Lakes by the commercial fishery of the United States and Canada combined. In 1943, at least 12 million anglers took advantage of recreational fishing resources in the United States.[85] In 1948, 14.6 million persons obtained fishing permits. Besides, many people fish on their own properties or in small streams, where no permit is required. In all, the Department of the Interior estimates that more than 20 million persons, or about one out of seven inhabitants of the United States, engage in fishing as a sport. From $800 million to $1 billion is spent every year for equipment and other necessities connected with this sport.[86]

Latin America

Inland fisheries are important as a food resource in Argentina, Brazil and Venezuela. The Amazon River contains many fresh water species,

among them the pirarucú. This gigantic fish which weighs up to 200 pounds and is found only in the Amazon, is dried and shipped all over Brazil as a substitute for cod. The river also teems with turtles, the meat, fat and eggs of which are consumed throughout the region.[87] In most of Latin America, fresh-water fisheries are operated by fishermen owning no more than a small canoe and a few hooks and lines. Lack of capital blocks the introduction of modern equipment.[88]

Pond Fishery

Fish are reared in ponds in many countries. The practice originated about 500 B.C. in China, where it is especially used on paddy fields. On many Pacific islands, ponds near the sea or connected with it contain both fresh-water and salt-water species. Pond culture was introduced into central Europe during the fourteenth century, and later into the Balkans. In the European fish ponds, the principal species is the common carp; in southeastern Asia and Japan many species are reared.

The United States has about 1.1 million ponds occupying 530,000 acres, but they are valued not so much for food supply as for watering livestock, water storage and the control of soil erosion, and for recreation. Construction of ponds in the United States is a development of the last fifteen years, during which about a hundred times as many have been created as in the two preceding centuries. While some artificially fertilized ponds have yielded as much as 400 pounds of fish to the acre, the yield in many regions is low, chiefly because fishermen want the ponds stocked with game fish that are relatively free of bones and thus discourage the use of many prolific species. Little attention has been paid to raising fish in ponds on a commercial basis, except for minnows for bait.[89]

In the Far East pond fish are raised in relatively small bodies of water; boglands, swamps and ravines are utilized, as well as the waters of irrigation canals and reservoirs. In many areas (China, Japan, Java and others), fish are raised on flooded rice paddies. Annual yields of one or more tons to the acre are not infrequent.[90]

83. **37**, p. 156.
84. **7**, p. 111.
85. **7**, p. 103.
86. **34**, p. 3; cf. **1**, Vol. VII, pp. 138-39.

87. **14**, p. 26, and **19**, p. 70.
88. **5**, May–June 1951, p. 11.
89. **3**, pp. 186–187; **5**, March–April 1950, p. 32, and July–August 1950, pp. 84–85.
90. **5**, January–April 1951, p. 31.

Israel started fish farming before World War II and introduced the carp from Yugoslavia into its fish ponds. In 1948, 2,300 tons of carp were produced, and the objective is an annual yield of 10,000 tons.[91]

Whaling and Sealing

Whaling in the Past

The whaling industry dates from the eighth century, when French and Spanish Basques first began to hunt whales in coastal waters. Later the Basques extended their activities to waters off Iceland, Greenland and even Newfoundland. In the ninth century the Finns hunted whales. At the end of the eleventh century, an association of whalers, Societas Walmanorum, existed in France, at Fécamp.[92] In the seventeenth century, the English and Dutch joined, and soon they dominated the industry. The main implements were harpoons and lances, and the annual catch totaled about 1,500–2,000 Greenland (right) whales. With the extermination of right whales in the second half of the nineteenth century, Arctic whaling came to an end.

Throughout the eighteenth century and during a large part of the nineteenth, Americans hunted whales, especially sperm whales, in all parts of the globe. The number of their whaling ships was several times that of all foreign vessels combined.[93] Sperm oil became the basis of important candle manufactures in the United States, for both domestic needs and export. In the middle of the nineteenth century, the United States whaling industry employed 735 boats and 40,000 persons. It represented an investment of $40 million, and the annual catch was worth about $8 million.[94]

Soon thereafter the American industry began to wane. The most serious blow was the discovery of petroleum in Pennsylvania in 1859.[95] Moreover, the annual catch began to reflect the mismanagement of whaling resources.

Modern Whaling

The second period of world whaling was coming to an end when modern whaling came upon the stage, with effective equipment for hunting and processing whales. (See Table 318.) Operations shifted to the Antarctic, which now accounts for some 95 per cent of the catch — about 90 per cent in the Antarctic itself and the remainder from shore stations used as centers for hunting herds that move to and from the Antarctic.

Norway leads in this international industry. Whaling is an old trade for the Norwegians. They hunted first along the coasts and from small sailing vessels at sea. Whalers launched their attacks from small boats using hand harpoons or lances. This type of whaling, mostly for local use, was profitable as long as right (Greenland) whales frequented waters not too distant from Norway. Since the second half of the nineteenth century when right whales were exterminated, Norwegian whaling has concentrated on the blue whale, the finback and the humpback.

Only large-scale operations could make the pursuit of these less valuable species profitable, since it took from 5 to 15 finner whales to equal the value of one right whale. Permanent land stations were established along the Norwegian coast, from which small, fast sailing vessels pursued the animals. Harpoon guns and explosive harpoons replaced the old weapons. Yet, in the forty years between 1864, the beginning of Norway's commercial whaling, and 1904, only 32,176 whales were captured, less than were caught in 1949–50 in the Antarctic.[96]

In modern whaling, the prey is processed on a specially equipped "factory" ship. Norway sent the first floating factory to the Antarctic in 1905 and in the following years built the world's largest and most modern whaling fleet. Its floating factories have equipment to process 20–25 whales a day and can dispose of a 100-ton blue whale in less than an hour and a half.[97] The tonnage of such ships has been increased continually, from 1,500 to 30,000 gross registered tons. A factory ship can provide living quarters and twenty-four-hour working space for 450 men and requires many accessory boats — six, eight or more catcher boats to supply the whales; tankers to remove whale oil and bring fuel; and transport ships to take whale meat, bone meal and so on.[98]

The number of floating factories increased

91. **5,** March–April 1950, pp. 32–33; **1,** Vol. VII, pp. 147–48.
92. **29,** pp. 8–9.
93. **51,** p. 680.
94. **7,** p. 45. Many of the boats, however, were of small size and are not included among sailing vessels in the international survey in Table 318.
95. Chapter 24.

96. **37,** pp. 135–36.
97. **9,** January 1949, p. 21.
98. **51,** p. 711.

TABLE 318

WHALING: CHARACTERISTICS OF THE TRADE IN THREE MAJOR PERIODS

Item	Old Whaling (Arctic)	Intermediate Whaling	Modern Whaling
Peak period	1650–1750	1820–50	Since 1925
Chief participating countries	England, Holland, Germany	United States	Norway
Chief grounds	Arctic	All oceans	Antarctic
Season	Summer	All year	December–April
Chief species caught	Greenland (right) whale	Sperm whale	Blue and fin whale
Implements	Hand harpoons	Hand harpoons, bomb lances	Harpoon cannons, grenades
Number of ships at peak period	250–300 sailing vessels	500–700 sailing vessels	About 30 "floating factories," [a] 200–250 catcher or killer boats
Average annual number of whales at peak period	1,500–2,000	7,000–10,000	25,000–30,000

Source: **39**, p. 7.

a. Since publication (1938) of the source, the peak number of floating factories has reached 41.

from 6 in 1919–20 to 34 in 1938–39; the number of catcher boats even more, from 44 to 281. The results of the whale hunt — the numbers caught and the volume of oil extracted — seemed to have justified the investment in this expensive equipment. (See Table 319.)

Although Norway practically monopolized whaling in northern seas during 1864–1904, other countries began to participate in the Antarctic catch. These newcomers at first had their ships fitted in Norwegian ports and engaged Norwegian crews and managers.[99]

The United Kingdom is second in importance to Norway. Japan, Germany, Argentina, the USSR and Portugal also are active in this field. For the world as a whole, the record catch of nearly 55,000 whales was made in the season 1937–38. Norway sent eleven floating factories, as many as the entire British Empire; Japan sent four, Germany five, the United States two, Panama and the USSR one each.[100]

Whaling in Postwar Years

Many whaling vessels were destroyed during

the war, including 25 floating factories. Japan lost all its factory ships and Norway and Great Britain lost most of theirs. Whaling all but ceased. The catch in 1943–44 numbered less than 2,000 whales; only one factory ship was in operation.

In the years since, however, Norway has regained leadership. Its fleet in the 1949–50 season — 10 floating factories and 126 killer boats — exceeded the fleets of all other nations combined.[101] Argentina is building the world's largest floating factory, to hold about 30,000 tons of whale oil and related by-products, and, according to the United States Department of Agriculture, has ordered 10 catcher boats from Japan.[102]

On the other hand, the whaling industry of the United States has almost disappeared, chiefly because of the competition of other products.[103] In 1943 only three American boats, with crews totaling 59 persons, were engaged in whaling; the investment was less than a million dollars, and the season's catch was valued at only $44,000. In 1947, 6 boats, totaling 1,000 gross tons, brought back 335 tons of whale products.[104]

99. **37**, pp. 138–40.
100. **4**, 1947, p. 297. The catch in the Antarctic was 46,039 whales; the rest were caught in operations from shore stations.

101. **10**, March 27, 1950, p. 292.
102. **10**, May 8, 1950, p. 461.
103. **7**, p. 45.
104. **11**, 1949, pp. 576 and 752.

TABLE 319

WHALING: OPERATIONS IN THE ANTARCTIC, 1919–20 TO 1949–50

Item	1919–20	1928–29	1938–39	1943–44	1948–49	1949–50
Shore stations	6	6	2	1	3	3
Floating factories	6	26	34	1	18	18
Catcher boats	44	111	281	15	212	237
Total number of whales	5,441	20,341	38,356	1,799	31,435	32,396
Number of whales per boat	124	183	136	120	148	137
Oil production (thousands of barrels)	272.8	1,631.3	2,820.8	132.0	2,219.6	2,166.5

Source: **28**, 1951, p. 13.

The total catch in the Antarctic during the whaling season in 1948–49 was 31,435 whales; in 1949–50, 32,396. Norway accounted for the preponderant share; the United Kingdom had the next largest catch. (See Table 320.)

It is not expected that the output in coming years will exceed the prewar maximum, since whaling reached its zenith long ago and the catch is now subject to international control.[105] According to Johan Hjort, the well-known ichthyologist, there are probably not more than 300,000 whales in Antarctic waters.[106]

Whale Oil

Whale products are not very palatable and are generally considered inedible, though the Japanese eat them. In Europe whale oil has been used in margarine since methods of refining were devised to remove its objectionable odor. Since 1930, when the use for margarine began on a commercial scale, whale oil has been in particular demand in Germany, the United Kingdom, the Netherlands, Norway and Denmark. These five countries consumed about 90 per cent of the world's prewar output. In the United States, whale oil goes primarily into soap, but is also used for lubrication, leather, paints and printing ink.

Whale oil comes largely from the Antarctic, where 96 per cent of the total output in the 1938–39 season was extracted.[107] Great Britain and Norway dominated the industry until 1933, together accounting for 97 per cent of the world output. Later their combined share fell to about two thirds of the world total. Japan, Germany, and, to a lesser extent, the Union of South Africa,

the United States and Panama, together accounted for almost all the remainder.

The output of whale oil fell very considerably during the war but has begun to recover slowly in recent years. During each of the seasons 1948–49 and 1949–50, about two thirds of the prewar amount of whale oil was produced. (See Table 321.)

Sealing

Seals provide industrial and edible oils and fats, and their pelts are utilized for fur and leather. Seal fisheries are important in the economies of coastal populations in the Arctic areas of the United States, Canada and the USSR.

Since 1911, when an international agreement forbade pelagic (open-sea) sealing, fur seals have been killed on breeding grounds. Formerly, indiscriminate pelagic sealing took a heavy toll of both the immature females and the bulls needed to reproduce the species and threatened extinction of the breed. Now enough males of every age class are left for breeding purposes.

The main breeding areas are on the Pribilof Islands (the largest seal rookery in the world) and the Commander, Robben and Kuril Islands in the Arctic. (See Figure 215.) Before World War II, the annual catch of fur seals on these grounds averaged 55,000, of which the Pribilof herd, the largest, accounted for 80 per cent.[108]

CONSERVATION OF MARINE RESOURCES

Marine resources are like forest resources in that they are renewable and represent a crop that can be harvested year after year. Like forests, they are not inexhaustible. Overfishing has depleted many areas, as evidenced by the decrease

---

105. **3**, p. 188. See below, pp. 742–46.
106. **45**, p. 432.
107. **25**, p. 5.

108. **49**, pp. 107 and 109. See below, p. 745.

TABLE 320

WHALING: CATCH IN THE ANTARCTIC, 1929–30 TO 1949–50

Country	Number of Whales Caught in Season				
	1929–30	*1937–38*	*1938–39*	*1948–49*	*1949–50*
World	37,674 [a]	46,039	38,356	31,435	32,396
United States	655	1,560	1,106	—	—
Panama	—	1,527	907	—	—
Argentina	1,386	1,062	1,024	919	946
United Kingdom	12,204 [b]	13,286	10,022	7,596	7,786
Netherlands	—	—	—	1,366	1,295
Norway	21,609	14,960 [c]	11,521 [c]	16,196	16,799
Germany	—	5,237	5,066	—	—
USSR	—	—	—	1,107	1,574
Japan	1,312	5,582	7,540	1,643	2,114
Union of South Africa	[d]	2,825	1,170	2,608	1,882

Source: **28**, 1931, p. 61 and 1951, pp. 30–31.

     a. Includes 258 whales caught by Denmark and 250 by Chile.
     b. British Empire.
     c. Includes the catch of two Norwegian expeditions hired by Germany (1937–38: 2,158 whales; 1938–39: 1,658 whales).
     d. Included in the figure for the United Kingdom.

in the total catch at certain fishing grounds and in the yield per vessel and by the prevailingly younger age of the fish taken.[109] Much harm has also been caused by sewage from cities and mill waste of all kinds dumped into streams and bays, and by oil from ships in harbor.

The commercial sturgeon fishery of the United States, once of major importance, is now virtually extinct. The Delaware River alone yielded 5 million pounds in 1890, but since 1929 the total annual catch in the country has not exceeded half a million pounds and has been incidental to other fishing.[110] Cod was taken for centuries,

---

109. Experts differ on the causes of stock depletion. Some attribute the decline in supplies of particular species to overfishing and the destruction of immature fish; others, Hjort for one, consider it the result of a low reproduction rate in certain years when conditions for hatching and for the survival of the fry have been unfavorable. In the seasonal herring fisheries on the Norwegian coast, the 6–7-year-old herring (age is counted by year rings on scales and bones) predominate, as compared to 9–10-year-old cod. The Norwegian Directorate of Fisheries holds it possible to estimate in advance the size of the year classes at the spawning grounds and to forecast the size of the catch for some years ahead (**36**, p. 29). H. B. Bigelow, on the other hand, thinks that modern science knows practically nothing about the causes underlying good and poor years. See **1**, Vol. VII, pp. 2ff., for discussion of fluctuations in fish population.

110. **20**, Part 2, pp. 19 and 149.

seemingly without exhaustion of the stock, but today the catch is much smaller than before, despite the much more efficient equipment. Certain species once abundant in the waters of

TABLE 321

WHALING: OUTPUT OF WHALE OIL, BY COUNTRY, 1937–38 TO 1949–50

(*Thousands of Barrels* [a])

Country	1937–38	1948–49	1949–50
World	3,340	2,220	2,167
United States	114	—	—
Panama	118	—	—
Argentina	52	53	41
United Kingdom	960	596	518
Netherlands	—	110	83
Norway	1,158 [b]	1,108	1,106
Germany	357	—	—
USSR	—	73	103
Japan	389	119	169
Union of South Africa	194	161	145

Source: **28**, 1951, Vol. 26, pp. 30–31.

     a. Conversion factors: one barrel = 170 kilograms = 374.8 pounds.
     b. Includes the output of Norwegian expeditions hired by Germany: 0.2 million barrels.

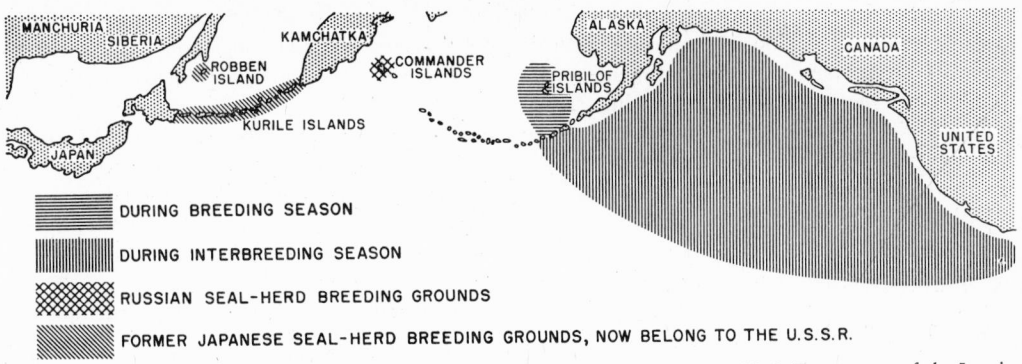

DURING BREEDING SEASON

DURING INTERBREEDING SEASON

RUSSIAN SEAL-HERD BREEDING GROUNDS

FORMER JAPANESE SEAL-HERD BREEDING GROUNDS, NOW BELONG TO THE U.S.S.R.

U. S. Department of the Interior

FIGURE 215. SEALING: CHIEF BREEDING GROUNDS

the Great Lakes (bluefin, sturgeon and the Lake Erie herring, called cisco) are gradually disappearing from the market. The cisco catch, for example, which supplied some 8 to 39 million pounds a year up to 1925, provided only 600,000 pounds in 1928 and less than a million a year ever since.[111] Herds of marine animals were subjected to what was virtually organized massacre, with the result that some species of whales are almost extinct and the fur seals of the Pribilof Islands were reduced from 3 million in 1867, when Alaska was purchased by the United States, to 216,000 in 1912.

While overfishing and the use of destructive gear have caused stock depletion in particular areas, migration, sometimes for reasons not yet understood, is also important. It has been observed that a certain species disappears from an area for a long time, and then is again taken in large quantities. For example, the sea trout, which has appeared in New England waters in commercial quantity and disappeared several times over the centuries, is now absent from New England, but assures a relatively stable and high yield in the Middle Atlantic states. The bluefish was totally absent from New England between 1764 and 1830.[112] The chub mackerel shows great variations in its availability at customary fishing grounds.[113] Some experts therefore stress the difference between abundance of fish and their availability to fishermen at times and places where they are expected to appear.[114]

H. F. Taylor believes that the total fish supply and its composition are subject to wide fluctua-

tions—with great variation locally from day to day, less in larger areas from month to month and still less in very large areas from year to year. In his opinion, the yield of "the sea fisheries as a whole or of any considerable region has not only been sustained but has generally increased with increasing human population, and there is as yet no sign that they will not continue to do so. No single species so far as we know has ever become extinct, and no regional fishery in the world has ever been exhausted."[115] Scarcities have always applied to particular species, not to the total stock of fish in world waters.

While this may be true, fishermen are concerned not with the total supply of fish but with particular species at specific fishing grounds. Disappearance of fish or a reduction in the catch for a season or more has serious consequences for them. The fishing industries have made up some of their losses in particular kinds of fish by turning to species previously neglected and by shifting to other fishing grounds. The problem of conservation, however, remains as great as ever.

Principles of Conservation

If marine resources are considered a crop, harvesting must be done so as to permit the stock to reproduce itself. Enough adult fish of a species must be left to assure a reproduction rate that will cover the losses from natural causes and through fishing, and fish should be caught at the period in their life cycle when they offer most for human use.[116] For example, the Fish and Wildlife Service of the United States Depart-

---

111. **45**, p. 415, and **7**, p. 113.
112. **47**, p. 314.
113. **7**, p. 64.
114. **45**, p. 72.

115. **47**, p. 314.
116. **49**, p. 45.

ment of the Interior has concluded that the spawning stock of haddock should be nearly double its present size to provide for adequate reproduction. Maintaining the spawning stock at the required level and leaving fish smaller than two pounds in the ocean to grow would raise the haddock catch from the New England banks by 50 million pounds or more a year.[117]

The principles of harvesting marine resources have much in common with those of harvesting forest resources, but the continual migration of fish and marine animals makes marine conservation much more complicated than the conservation of forests. To be effective, the protection of marine life must be based on international collaboration, since overfishing of a species in one area may reduce the yield in another. The main obstacle is that knowledge of many of the basic facts concerning fishing on the high seas is still inadequate. Much disagreement exists among experts about the soundness and effectiveness of such proposals as the establishment of a closed season, closure of nursery grounds or a minimum size for the mesh of nets.[118]

A more or less universally accepted principle of conservation is the setting of a quota for the annual catch. This principle, however, raises a number of difficult problems, the chief one being how to divide the total quota among the many interested nations. When only two countries are involved, an agreement can be worked out. Thus, the United States and Canada have agreed on equal quotas in the yield of sockeye salmon on the Fraser River, while they have decided to leave the sharing of the total halibut catch in the Pacific to the play of economic forces.[119] It has been much more difficult to reach an agreement for the distribution of a quota among many nations.

The Pacific Halibut Convention

The case of the Pacific halibut shows how international agreement can restore a species that has been nearly exterminated. Halibut fishery, which extends 2,200 miles from California to the Bering Sea and now yields more than 25,000 tons a year, began to suffer from an alarming decrease in stock as early as 1916. In 1924, the United States and Canada adopted the Pacific Halibut Convention to conserve breeding stocks and increase available supplies. This convention was broadened in 1930 and again in 1937.

The entire Pacific coast was divided into four areas. Two areas with predominantly small fish were closed to fishing, and for the other two a limit was placed on the total number of pounds of halibut that the two countries could take during the season. When the quota was reached, the season was closed. Stocks of halibut have increased markedly since 1930, and the annual yield has been considerably greater than under unrestricted fishing before the convention. Canada's share in the catch rose from 15 per cent during 1925–30 to 25 per cent in the war years.[120]

Regulation of Whaling

Among the various attempts to achieve broad international cooperation in the conservation of marine resources, only the two concerning whales and fur seals have so far shown real results.

A Convention for the Regulation of Whaling — prepared in 1931, ratified by seventeen nations and acceded to by eight others — became effective in 1935. It applied to all the waters of the world, including the high seas and territorial and national waters. It forbade the killing of all right whales and of all calves, sucklings and accompanying female whales. In 1937 the International Conference for the Regulation of Whaling established a minimum legal size for killing certain species and prescribed the fullest possible use of the carcass. Certain zones were closed to factory ships or to all operations. (See Figure 216.) In addition, Norway and Great Britain, the two most active participants in whaling, formed a production cartel to keep the industry within reasonable limits.[121]

While this convention has been the most effective to date, it did not limit the number of whales to be caught. Moreover, not all whaling nations became signatories. After two further conferences on whaling in London in 1944 and

---

117. **7**, p. 52.
118. Some of these measures are centuries old. In the thirteenth century, a minimum mesh size was introduced in England, and destruction of nets with smaller meshes was ordered. Salmon weirs stretching across the river were not permitted in some parts of England; a free passage had to be left in midstream. The opening, as specified by law in 1278 and again in 1293, was to be wide enough for a sow with five little pigs to pass through. **43**, p. 270.
119. **49**, pp. 52–54.

120. **7**, pp. 21–22, and **20**, Part 2, p. 8.
121. **25**, pp. 92–94.

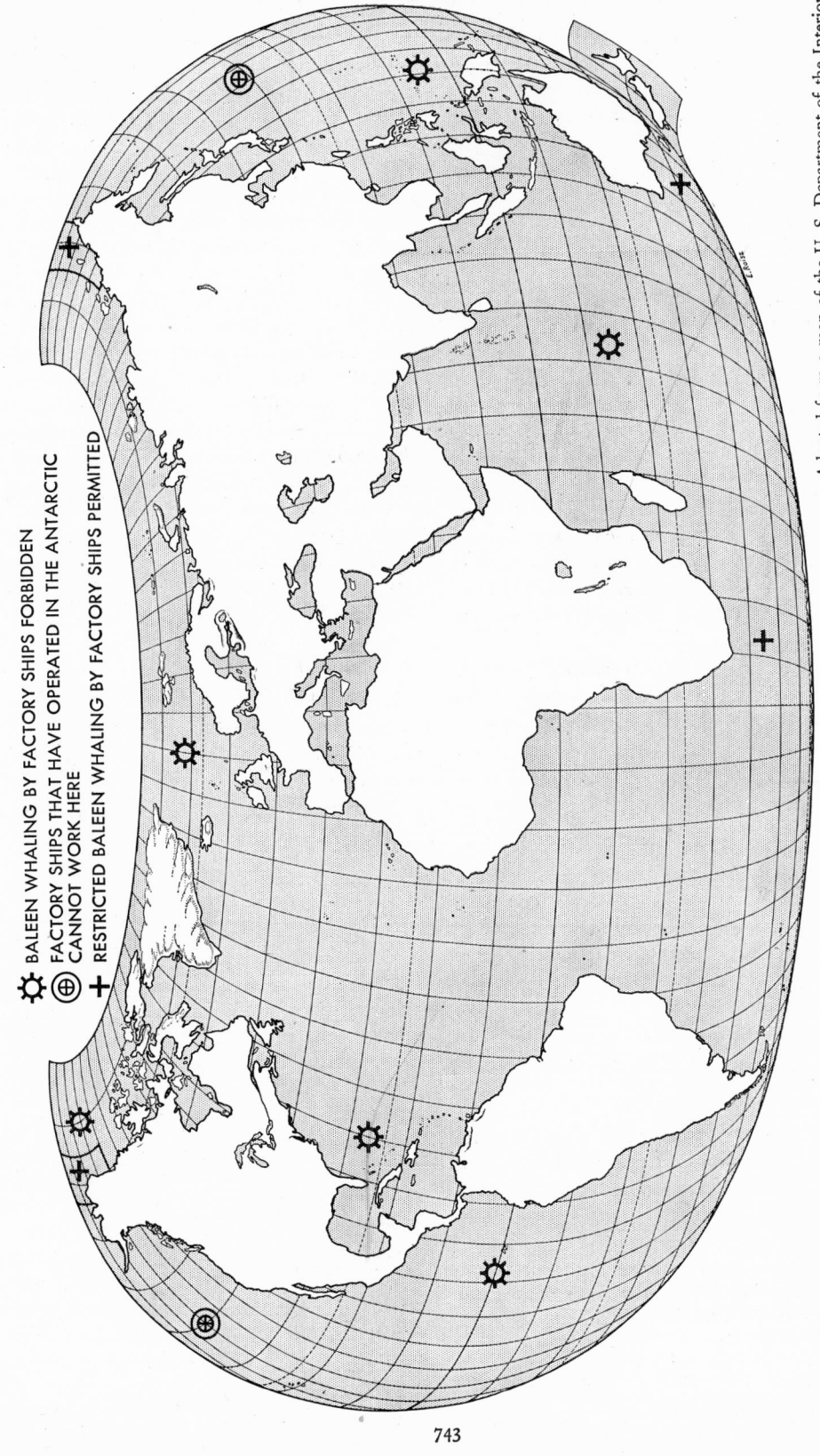

☼ BALEEN WHALING BY FACTORY SHIPS FORBIDDEN

⊕ FACTORY SHIPS THAT HAVE OPERATED IN THE ANTARCTIC CANNOT WORK HERE

✛ RESTRICTED BALEEN WHALING BY FACTORY SHIPS PERMITTED

FIGURE 216. WHALING: AREAS REGULATED BY INTERNATIONAL AGREEMENTS

A 100-TON BLUE WHALE

WEIGHS AS MUCH AS

25 ELEPHANTS

OR 150 OXEN

FIGURE 217. WHALING: A BLUE WHALE

1945, a meeting was held in Washington in 1946, at which an International Whaling Commission was established with fourteen member nations. At this meeting an International Convention for the Regulation of Whaling was signed, and by late summer of 1948 it was ratified by the requisite number of governments. The schedule annexed to the convention limits the taking of baleen whales during the Antarctic season to 16,000 blue-whale units.[122]

The blue whale was selected by the International Bureau of Whaling Statistics and introduced into the schedule of the 1946 convention as the basis for measurement because it is the largest whale ("in fact, the most gigantic sea or land animal of all time") and supplies the largest quantity of oil — from 100 to 120 barrels.[123]

(See Figure 217.) By the International Whaling Commission's regulations, the blue-whale unit equals 2 fin whales, 2.5 humpbacks or 6 sei whales.[124] Within the quota of 16,000 blue-whale units, a catch of not more than 1,250 humpbacks was permitted during each of the seasons 1949–50 and 1950–51. The minimum length of whales captured in pelagic operations has been set for blue whales at 70 feet, fin whales at 55, sei whales at 40, and humpbacks and sperm whales at 35 feet.[125] The International Commission sets the length of the whaling season in advance but is entitled to close it earlier when the total catch has reached the permitted limits; the whaling seasons of 1949–50 and 1950–51 were closed before schedule for this reason.

Only the future will show whether these meas-

122. **26,** p. 22; **6,** p. 3.
123. **51,** p. 687.

124. **10,** January 22, 1951, p. 79.
125. **28,** 1951, pp. 7–8; **6,** p. 16.

ures will restore and perpetuate the world's whale herds. It is encouraging that the legal protection given a few species, such as the humpback since 1938, has restored their previous abundance in the Antarctic. The right whale, which had almost disappeared, has begun to be seen again now that it is fully protected by international law.[126]

Regulation of Sealing

A highly effective international agreement on fur seals on the Pribilof Islands has been in force since 1911.[127] It was signed by the United States, Canada, Russia and Japan; Russia participated only in the interest of herds on its side of the Pacific. Pelagic sealing was forbidden. The United States took over the herd on the Pribilof Islands and, to compensate Great Britain and Japan for refraining from pelagic sealing, obligated itself to turn over to each of them 15 per cent of the fur seals taken each year. Similar provisions were made for skins taken by the Rusians in the Commander Islands, by Japan on Robben Island, and by Canada, if seals should choose her territory for breeding. The herd of seals increased from 250,000 in 1911, when the treaty was signed, to nearly 3 million in 1944, although the number of seal skins taken has increased many-fold during this period.

Regulation of Coastal Fishing

Freedom of the high seas is a firmly established principle, and each nation has access to the sea's riches. It is also generally accepted that a country has exclusive right to exploit its coastal waters. Since the end of the eighteenth century, the United States and Great Britain have defined coastal waters as a three-mile belt along the shore. Great Britain, France, Belgium, the Netherlands, Denmark and Germany agreed on the same principle in 1882.

Many countries, however, have insisted that a three-mile belt is not satisfactory. The Scandinavian countries claim that the configuration of their coast line necessitates a four-mile limit; Chile, Uruguay and Turkey want five miles; and France, Portugal and Spain, six miles. The USSR has established a twelve-mile limit for its shores.

The controversy has a long history, and the League of Nations failed to induce its members to accept a six-mile limit as the common principle. There have been individual agreements between interested nations — for example, between Russia and Japan with respect to fishing in Siberian waters.

The question of conserving resources in and under water has been equally controversial. The League of Nations was forced to recognize the impossibility of general international action to conserve fish in the high seas, such as herring and cod. The problem varies from area to area and from species to species. It was left to the countries directly concerned with the fishing industries in a particular area to follow up the changing conditions and husband their resources collectively on a regional basis. So far, however, no agreement for the effective conservation of fish has been concluded, although some protective measures, such as the requirement of a minimum size for fish to be marketed and for the mesh of nets, were accepted by a number of countries at the London Conference of 1937 and by a conference in London in 1946.

The United States, Canada, Denmark, Iceland, Norway, Italy, Portugal, Spain, France and the United Kingdom signed the International Convention for the Northwest Atlantic Fisheries in Washington in 1949.[128] Its purpose is the protection and conservation of the fisheries of the Northwest Atlantic Ocean in order to maintain a maximum sustained catch. The convention covers all except territorial waters. The International Commission for the Northwest Atlantic Fisheries is to make scientific investigations and to propose to the member governments measures to keep the stocks of fish species supporting international fisheries in the convention area at a level permitting the maximum sustained yield: the establishment of closed and open seasons; the closing to fishing of spawning grounds and of portions of the subarea populated by small or immature fish; prescription of size limits for any species, of fishing gear and appliances and of an over-all limit on the catch of any species.[129] Any such proposals shall become effective four months after receipt of notification of acceptance from the governments concerned

---

126. **51,** pp. 687–88.
127. The convention expired in 1941 with the withdrawal of Japan, and a provisional agreement was signed by the United States and Canada until a new treaty can be negotiated.

128. France and Spain signed the convention with reservations on some points. Newfoundland, which also signed the convention, is now a part of Canada.
129. **18,** *passim.* The convention area is divided into five subareas.

with a particular subarea. Withdrawal from the convention is permitted after it has been in force ten years.

In 1945, the President of the United States issued a proclamation asserting the jurisdiction of the country over the fishing resources of the continental shelf under the high seas contiguous to the coasts of the United States and its territories. The purpose of this proclamation is to protect the coastal fishery resources from destructive exploitation and to establish conservation zones in those areas of the high seas contiguous to the coasts of the United States where fishery has been or may be developed on a substantial scale. That such protection is in order can be seen from the example of the Alaskan salmon fishery, which constitutes one of the most valuable fisheries of the country. Great efforts have been made to maintain the salmon, but with the fish spending a large part of its life in the open sea, uncontrolled fishing by the nationals of either the United States or other countries represents a real menace to salmon fishery. The right of free and unimpeded navigation over such conservation zones is not affected by this proclamation.

Outlook

Despite the improvement in fishing craft and equipment and a considerable increase in the world's catch, fish has not yet taken an important place in the diet of many countries. The world's waters supply only 3 per cent of the foodstuffs and 2 per cent of the proteins consumed by mankind. Yet the great advantage of the ocean's food resources is that they replenish themselves, without the effort required to produce food on land. Fisheries, moreover, supply animal proteins and fats, the most expensive and most needed kinds of food. Marine resources, although not inexhaustible, are very great. While there is not enough information to compare the costs of food values in protein and fat per unit of weight obtained from meat and fish, it is believed that fish supply proteins and fats at a much lower cost at the point of production than livestock.[130]

The increase in world population makes it imperative to produce more food, and especially more animal proteins, of which there is a deficiency. The main obstacles to a more effective exploitation of marine resources have been insufficient knowledge of marine life, insufficient recognition of the food value of fish, conservatism in eating habits, and lack of international cooperation in the management of marine resources. International good will is needed not only to exploit the world's marine wealth more effectively but even to learn how to manage aquatic life in accordance with its laws of reproduction. Better utilization of marine resources will depend, therefore, on closer cooperation among the nations most directly concerned.

---

130. **47**, pp. 301–03.

PART IV

ENERGY AND MINING

CHAPTER 21

MINING IN THE WORLD ECONOMY

THE ART OF MINING, by which minerals are obtained," wrote Aristotle, "has many branches, for various kinds of things are dug out of the earth." [1]

MINING THROUGH THE CENTURIES

Mining is as old as man's use of stone, clay and metals. The ruins of pyramids, temples, palaces and walled cities testify to its existence in the most remote times. In the sixth millennium B.C. some 8,000 workers were employed in copper and turquoise mines on the Sinai peninsula of Egypt.[2] Tribes that were not familiar with extractive trades have left few traces on the face of the earth.

The Ancient World

In his introduction to Agricola's *De Re Metallica,* Herbert Clark Hoover has tried to indicate the periods when particular operations in mining and metallurgy appeared on the historical horizon. In prehistoric times, he points out, gold was washed from alluvial soil, copper was reduced from ore by smelting, and bitumen was mined and used. Before 2000 B.C., tin, iron, silver and lead were reduced from ore by smelting, bronze was made, soda was mined, gold was reduced from ore by concentration, and silver was separated from lead by cupellation. Before 1500 B.C. bellows were used in furnaces; before 1000 B.C. steel was produced; and before 500 B.C. base metals were separated from ores by water concentration, gold was refined by cupellation, and sulphide ores were smelted for lead. Before the beginning of the Christian era, men learned to use the touchstone, reduce quicksilver from ore, make brass, obtain zinc oxides, extract antimony and make vitriol and alum.[3]

The Beginning of Modern Times

By the middle of the sixteenth century, the art of mining had developed into a science and mining had become one of the most advanced industries in Europe. Complicated machinery was already in use for airing subterranean tunnels, pumping water, and bringing ore to the surface.[4] Despite this conspicuous technical progress, many people questioned the usefulness of mining. Agricola's treatise of 1556 began with an eloquent defense of minerals and metals against their detractors:

They contend that, inasmuch as Nature has concealed metals far within the depths of the earth, and because they are not necessary to human life, they are therefore despised and repudiated by the nobles, and should not be mined, and seeing that when brought to light they have always proved the cause of very great evils, it follows that mining is not useful to mankind but on the contrary harmful and destructive.[5]

Agricola's strongest defense of metals was theological:

Those who speak ill of the metals and refuse to make use of them, do not see that they accuse and condemn as wicked the Creator Himself, when they assert that He fashioned some things vainly and without good cause, and thus they regard Him as the Author of evils, which opinion is certainly not worthy of pious and sensible men.[6]

Measured by today's standards, mining progressed rather slowly from the middle of the sixteenth century to the beginning of the nineteenth. The Industrial Revolution in England started in the cotton mills rather than in heavy industries and did not spread to mining until the end of the eighteenth century.

After the Industrial Revolution

In the first two decades of the nineteenth century, the value of the world yield of mines averaged $67 million a year, of which the United States accounted for less than a million; in 1821–40, the world total rose to $80 million a

---

1. **15,** Book I, Chapter 11.
2. **18,** pp. 185–86.
3. **14,** p. 354.

4. See Chapter 22.
5. **14,** pp. 11–12.
6. **14,** p. 12.

year, and the United States share to $2 million.[7] Progress was faster after the middle of the century as a result of railroad building and the increased demand for coal, iron and, later, steel.

By the turn of the twentieth century, the value of the world's mineral output was approaching $3 billion.[8] By that time, petroleum had taken an important place in world affairs, iron was losing ground to steel, electricity was opening new outlets for copper.

Up to the 1890's, Great Britain led in world mining,[9] but by the turn of the century it had fallen behind the United States. Of the aggregate value of world output of minerals in 1912, approximately $4 billion, the United States accounted for 40 per cent, Great Britain for 12.5 per cent, and Germany for 10.5 per cent. Russia came fourth with 8.5 per cent, followed by France, Chile, Australia, Austria, Hungary and Belgium.[10]

Recent Trends

Since the beginning of World War I, the volume of the world's mineral output has more than tripled, many previously unknown or unused minerals have appeared on the market, petroleum has made further gains, and the relative positions of the principal mineral producers have changed more than once. The general pattern of world mining, however, has remained about the same as in 1912–14: coal, petroleum and iron dominate the picture; the United States leads in all three fields while, on the other side of the Atlantic, about an equal total mineral output is divided among a half dozen nations.

Mining and quarrying are carried on today in all parts of the world, at least on a small scale and in rudimentary form; but extraction of minerals is unevenly distributed among the continents and nations, according to the accessibility of natural resources, demand for the product, availability

of labor, transportation facilities and cost-price relationships. Where these conditions are favorable, modern mining is developed far from the industrial centers where the equipment is built, the technical personnel trained and the product used. Mines and oil wells become spearheads of industrial civilization as it advances into areas of primitive economy.

Geographical Concentration

The geographical concentration of mineral resources [11] increases the economic interdependence of continents and nations. The more industrialized a country, the more urgent is its demand for various minerals not found within its borders. Even the United States, with all its abundance and variety of mineral resources, depends on imports for tin, nickel, zinc, bauxite, manganese, titanium, industrial diamonds, quartz crystals, mercury, asbestos, mica, antimony, arsenic and many other minerals. Assuring free access of all nations to world resources is largely a problem of mineral products. Similarly, stockpiling strategic materials for a national emergency is essentially a problem of minerals.

MINERAL OUTPUT

According to the Economic Intelligence Service of the League of Nations, the value of the world's annual output of minerals (including water power but excluding gold and most products of quarrying) amounted in 1937–38 to $12–$13 billion, at 1930 prices. The total was close to $16 billion if gold, stone and sand are included.[12] The output of the minerals covered by the League's survey was distributed among the continents as follows (per cent):[13]

	Fuels and Power	Metals	Nonmetallic Minerals
World	100.0	100.0	100.0
North America	45.4	30.0	23.0
Middle and South America [a]	5.1	8.8	6.9
Europe	30.5	26.2	46.9
USSR	8.9	13.5	8.5
Africa	0.8	8.6	2.9
Asia	8.6	10.2	11.0
Oceania	0.7	2.7	0.8

a. No data available for Middle and South America separately.

---

7. **20**, p. 97. All values, here and below, at current prices.

8. **17**, pp. 6–7. Contrary to the practice of the U. S. Bureau of Mines, these figures do not include value added to the metallic ores by processing in smelters, refineries and blast furnaces.

The long-range trend in wholesale prices was downward in the nineteenth century, so that a pound or a dollar had a somewhat larger purchasing power in 1900 than in 1920–40. **19**, pp. 55 and 156–57.

9. It controlled approximately three fourths of the world output of minerals in the period of the Napoleonic wars, two thirds in the 1840's, and half after the 1860's. **20**, p. 97.

10. **17**, p. 4.

11. See pp. 757 ff.; cf. Chapters 10 and 22.

12. **2**, p. 87. Cf. Chapter 10.

13. **2**, p. 96. Averages for 1937 and 1938.

TABLE 322

VALUE OF OUTPUT OF METALS AND MINERAL FUELS IN THE WORLD AND THE
UNITED STATES, 1880–1940

(Millions, at Average 1923–25 Prices)

	World			United States		
Year	*Total*	*Metals* [a]	*Fuels* [b]	*Total*	*Metals* [a]	*Fuels* [b]
1880	$1,355	$376	$979	$362	$70	$292
1890	2,163	581	1,582	749	155	594
1900	3,244	862	2,382	1,187	269	918
1910	5,106	1,344	3,762	2,250	466	1,784
1920	6,030	1,280	4,750	3,121	583	2,538
1921	5,287	907	4,380	2,519	301	2,218
1922	5,870	1,219	4,651	2,632	456	2,176
1923	6,925	1,556	5,369	3,647	649	2,998
1924	6,993	1,636	5,357	3,403	637	2,766
1925	7,185	1,785	5,400	3,473	683	2,790
1926	7,354	1,849	5,505	3,777	720	3,057
1927	8,009	1,972	6,037	3,801	690	3,111
1928	8,195	2,097	6,098	3,773	716	3,057
1929	8,903	2,293	6,610	4,110	790	3,320
1930	8,190	2,074	6,116	3,601	621	2,980
1931	7,222	1,618	5,604	3,042	407	2,635
1932	6,288	1,163	5,125	2,522	218	2,304
1933	6,720	1,270	5,450	2,774	237	2,537
1934	7,471	1,581	5,890	2,943	281	2,662
1935	8,008	1,820	6,188	3,178	367	2,811
1936	8,884	2,151	6,733	3,703	548	3,155
1937	10,015	2,655	7,361	4,164	719	3,445
1938	9,393	2,397	6,996	3,553	471	3,082
1939	10,035	2,653	7,382	3,924	616	3,308
1940	. . .	. . .	. . .	4,375	781	3,594

Source: **16,** pp. 214 and 221.

 a. Includes iron ore, aluminum, copper, lead, tin, zinc, nickel and silver.
 b. Includes coal and crude petroleum.

This distribution was affected to some extent by the state of world affairs on the eve of World War II: the United States had not fully recovered from the great depression, while Germany and the USSR were expanding their heavy industries, bracing themselves for the approaching clash of arms.

LONG-RANGE TRENDS

Large-scale modern mining is a child of the age of steel, petroleum and electricity. Its history and statistical records begin with the last quarter of the nineteenth century.

World Output, 1880–1939

According to the Brookings Institution, the value of the annual world output of metals and fuels, at average 1923–25 prices, rose from $1,355 million in 1880 to $3,244 million in 1900, $6,030 million in 1920 and $10,035 million in 1939,[14] nearly doubling every twenty years. The largest element in this increase was the growth of mining in the United States. This was interrupted in the 1930's by the great depression but, after a decade of stagnation, was resumed at a speed reminiscent of the 1920's. (See Table 322.)

Progress has not been steady in all countries and all parts of the world. The general long-

14. **16,** p. 214. These figures are not strictly comparable with the totals reported by the League of Nations for 1937–38, since they do not include nonmetallic minerals other than coal and petroleum.

range trend — a doubling every twenty years — is the product of divergent developments in various countries and various branches of mining and quarrying.

Mineral Output in the United States

In the United States, the physical volume of the mineral output doubled from 1899 to 1914, almost doubled from 1914 to 1929, remained constant from 1929 to 1939, and increased by more than 50 per cent from 1939 to 1951. In all, it rose almost sixfold in fifty-two years. (See Table 323.)

The long-range trends in mineral production in the United States and in the rest of the world have differed appreciably. From 1890 to 1939 the value of the output increased as follows (in millions, at average 1923–25 prices, as shown in Table 322):

	1890	1939	Percentage Increase
United States			
Metals	$155	$616	+297
Fuels	594	3,308	+457
All other countries			
Metals	426	2,037	+378
Fuels	988	4,074	+312

In the United States, production of mineral fuels (especially petroleum and natural gas) surpassed the output of metals, while in the rest of the world the two branches of mining kept pace with each other.

CURRENT VALUE OF MINERAL OUTPUT

The simplest way to estimate the current value of the world's mineral output is to start with the value in the United States, the largest producer, and to appraise the yields of other parts of the world at prevailing United States prices.

Output in the United States

The U.S. Bureau of Mines has estimated the value of mineral production in the United States at $4,363 million in 1938, $12,484 million in 1947, and $15,670 million in 1948. The increase was partly due to the rise of prices. At 1938 prices the value was close to $9,250 million in 1947 and $9,600 million in 1948. These totals, however, include the value added to ore through processing in blast furnaces, smelters and re-

TABLE 323

INDEXES OF VOLUME OF MINERAL OUTPUT IN THE UNITED STATES, 1899–1951

Year	Total [a]	Metallic	Nonmetallic	
			Fuels	Other
Indexes of Physical Output (National Bureau of Economic Research) *(1899 = 100)*				
1899	100	100	100	100
1904	138	125	142	149
1909	184	170	187	255
1914	202	172	218	258
1919	234	184	259	235
1924	310	207	346	389
1929	389	252	434	507
Indexes of Mineral Production (Federal Reserve Board) *(1929 = 100)*				
1929	100	100	100	...
1930	87	76	88	...
1931	75	51	80	...
1932	63	27	70	...
1933	71	38	78	...
1934	75	43	81	...
1935	80	54	86	...
1936	93	76	96	...
1937	105	95	106	...
1938	91	84	96	...
1939	99	100	102	...
1940	109	111	111	...
1941	117	110	118	...
1942	121	94	121	...
1943	123	84	128	...
1944	131	84	140	...
1945	128	66	139	...
1946	126	74	138	...
1947	139	69	150	...
1948	145	69	155	...
1949	126	66	135	...
1950	138	78	147	...
1951	153	83	164	...

Sources: For 1899–1944, **8**, p. 141; for more recent years, **10**, 1949, February 1950, 1951, 1952 and Statistical Supplements.

a. For the index of the Federal Reserve Board (1929–50), metals and mineral fuels only.

fineries. Thus, the value of coal used in processing ore is counted twice — in the value of the output of coal mines and as part of the price of pig iron and other metals. The duplication is most significant for iron, since pig iron is worth more than five times as much as the iron ore used in making it.

TABLE 324

VALUE OF MINERAL OUTPUT IN THE UNITED STATES AND ITS PERCENTAGE RELATION TO
WORLD OUTPUT, 1947–49

Mineral	1947		1948		1949	
	Value, in Millions	Percentage of World Output	Value, in Millions	Percentage of World Output	Value, in Millions	Percentage of World Output
Total	$9,612.0	...	$12,273.0	...	$10,555.0	...
Metallic minerals	1,084.0	...	1,219.0	...	1,101.0	...
Antimony ore and concentrates	3.3	13	4.3	13	1.1	3
Bauxite	6.9	19	8.7	18	6.8	14
Copper	356.0	35	362.3	32	296.6	31
Gold	64.0	7	61.8	7	61.7	6
Iron ore, usable	317.6	51	391.2	48	377.6	40
Lead	110.6	31	139.7	26	129.5	26
Manganese ore (35% or more Mn)	4.2	} 3	4.4	3	5.2	} 3
Manganiferous ore (5–35% Mn)	3.4		ᵃ	...	4.0	
Mercury	1.9	14	1.1	14	0.8	9
Molybdenum ore and concentrates	15.2	86	20.4	86	19.3	...
Silver	32.4	23	34.4	23	31.3	21
Titanium concentrates	5.6	31	6.4	32	6.7	53
Tungsten concentrates	4.3	...	6.4	...	4.4	...
Vanadium ore and concentrates	1.3	55	ᵃ	...	ᵃ	...
Zinc	153.1	46	168.0	42	148.9	41
Other metals	4.2	...	9.9	...	7.1	...
Mineral fuels	7,181.0	...	9,495.0	...	7,887.0	...
Coal						
Bituminous	2,614.6	} 37	2,983.5	} 34	2,126.2	} 26
Lignite	5.5		7.0		7.3	
Pennsylvania anthracite	413.0	44	467.1	40	358.0	31
Natural gas (valued at mills)	274.7	86	333.2	88	355.5	...
Natural-gas liquids	295.0	} 61	459.0	} 59	372.1	} 54
Petroleum	3,577.9		5,245.1		4,667.5	

(*Continued on page 754*)

Excluding the value added to iron ore through processing, the value of the mineral output of the United States amounted to $4,081 million in 1938, $11,097 million in 1947 and $13,832 million in 1948 at current prices (approximately $8,220 million in 1947 and $8,540 million in 1948 at 1938 prices).

These figures, however, still contain some duplications and costs of processing and transportation. In order to evaluate the net mineral production in the United States and to make the national totals comparable with the data for the individual states, the U.S. Bureau of Mines has prepared another set of estimates for 1947, 1948 and 1949.[15] The total value of mineral produc-

tion in the United States as estimated on the new basis was $9,612 million in 1947, $12,273 million in 1948 and $10,555 million in 1949 at current prices. (See Table 324.) For 1947 the new series is 23 per cent below the old series; for 1948 the difference is 22 per cent.

World Output

For most of the minerals mined in appreciable quantity in the United States, the Bureau of Mines also reports the relationship between the output in the country and the world as a whole. (See Table 324.) For other products, rough es-

15. The following changes were made: natural gas is valued at wells rather than at points of consumption; the series for aluminum, pig iron, magnesium, nickel and

refined platinum-group metals are replaced, respectively, by bauxite, iron ore, magnesium chloride, nickel ore and crude platinum-group metals; smelter and refinery by-products are omitted; and the clay series is modified. (**11**, 1949, p. 30.)

TABLE 324—*continued*

Mineral	1947		1948		1949	
	Value, in Millions	Percentage of World Output	Value, in Millions	Percentage of World Output	Value, in Millions	Percentage of World Output
Other nonmetallic minerals	1,345.0	...	1,559.0	...	1,567.0	...
Abrasive stone	0.7	...	0.6	...	0.4	...
Asbestos	0.9	3	1.8	3	2.6	1
Asphalt and related bitumens	5.5	...	5.0	...	5.6	...
Barite (crude)	6.2	56	6.7	53	5.6	53
Boron minerals	11.8	...	11.1	...	11.5	...
Bromine	14.8	...	14.8	...	16.3	...
Cement	356.6	38	446.5	36	475.1	33
Clays (including fuller's earth)	71.3	25 [c]	81.0	25 [c]	74.6	25 [c]
Feldspar	2.4	61	2.6	61	2.3	56
Fluorspar	11.0	45	11.2	38	8.3	33
Gypsum (crude)	16.5	42	19.1	40	18.3	36
Lime	63.4	...	74.7	...	68.9	...
Magnesium compounds [b]	5.8	21	6.9	...	5.0	13
Phosphate rock	46.6	55	50.5	48	51.4	47
Potassium salts	34.7	31	36.0	30	35.1	28
Salt (common)	52.1	38	54.2	35	54.0	...
Sand and gravel	212.6	25 [c]	252.2	25 [c]	245.7	25 [c]
Sand and sandstone (ground)	5.2	...	5.8	...	5.3	...
Slate	11.7	...	12.9	...	12.2	...
Sodium carbonate (natural)	5.9	...	6.6	...	4.2	...
Sodium sulfate	3.3	...	4.2	...	2.7	...
Stone	286.8	25 [c]	326.7	25 [c]	339.4	25 [c]
Sulfur	85.3	92	89.6	92	86.3	91
Talc	7.7	45	8.3	43	7.5	37
Other nonmetallic minerals	26.2	...	30.0	...	28.7	...

Sources: **11**, 1949, pp. 26, 32–34 and *passim.*

a. Included in the value of other metals.

b. From sea water and brines.

c. Estimated roughly by the authors.

timates of world output may be ventured. Thus the world output of minerals may be estimated at $23.8 billion in 1947, $30.7 billion in 1948, and $30.2 billion in 1949, at U.S. prices.[16] (See Table 325.) These totals do not include the value added to iron ore through processing into pig iron, but do include the value of smelting and refining for nonferrous metals. Unlike Table 324 they include aluminum (rather than bauxite).

The increase from 1947 to 1948 is due partly to the rise in production in the United States and Europe and partly to the rise in prices, especially of petroleum. The physical volume of mineral production in the world did not increase more than 5 or 6 per cent, so that the 1948 output, evaluated at 1947 prices, hardly exceeded $25 billion and postwar inflation raised this amount to $30.7 billion.

VALUE OF LEADING MINERALS

Of the total value of world mineral produc-

16. This estimate is not strictly comparable with the prewar estimates of the League of Nations. First, most products are estimated at U. S. prices. Second, the value of nonferrous metals in Table 325 relates to the output of smelters or refineries, while for iron only the value of iron ore is counted. Table 325 also includes the value of the world output of stone, sand and clay products, although the lack of statistical data makes a precise estimate of these items impossible. The present estimate rests on the following considerations: the output of stone, gravel and sand in the United States represents approximately 5 per cent of the value of the total mineral output. The ratio is likely to be somewhat higher for the rest of the world, since quarrying is the prevailing branch of the extractive industries in underdeveloped areas. On the other hand, per capita production of building materials declines as one moves from rich to poor areas. These considerations suggest that the share of the United States in the world output of stone, sand and gravel is hardly more than 25 per cent.

TABLE 325

VALUE OF WORLD MINERAL OUTPUT, 1947–49

(*Millions*)

Mineral	1947	1948	1949	Mineral	1947	1948	1949
Total	$23,835	$30,715	$30,170	Other nonmetallic minerals	$4,490	$5,360	$5,720
Metallic minerals	4,655	5,350	5,355	Abrasive stone [b]	40	45	45
Antimony ore and concentrates	25	33	37	Asbestos	30	60	260
Aluminum	340	400	415	Asphalt	10	10	10
Copper	1,030	1,140	975	Barite	11	13	11
Gold	1,010	1,040	1,070	Cement	940	1,240	1,440
Iron ore	625	815	945	Clays	280 [c]	320 [c]	300 [c]
Lead	350	535	500	Feldspar	4	4	4
Manganese	250	250	300	Fluorspar	14	30	25
Mercury	14	8	9	Gypsum	40	48	50
Molybdenum	18	24	22	Lime	250	300	275
Nickel	110	125	130	Magnesium compounds	30	34	38
Platinum	50	50	42	Phosphate rock	85	105	110
Silver	140	150	150	Potassium salts	110	120	125
Tin	300	300	320	Salt (common)	140	155	155
Titanium	17	20	13	Sand and gravel	850 [c]	1,010 [c]	980 [c]
Tungsten	30	40	50	Stone	1,150 [c]	1,305 [c]	1,360 [c]
Vanadium	2	[a]	[a]	Sulfur	90	100	95
Zinc	335	400	360	Talc	15	20	20
Other metallic minerals	9	20	17	Other nonmetallic minerals [d]	400	440	417
Fuels	14,690	20,005	19,095				
Coal							
Bituminous and lignite	7,080	8,795	8,205				
Anthracite	940	1,165	1,155				
Natural gas	320	380	400				
Petroleum and natural gasoline	6,350	9,665	9,335				

Sources: Table 324 and **11**, 1949, *passim.*

a. Included in the value of other metallic minerals.
b. Includes industrial diamonds.
c. Estimated roughly by the authors.
d. Includes diamonds and other precious stones (rough estimate).

tion (including the smelting and refining of non-ferrous metals but not the processing of iron ore) the United States accounted for about 40 per cent in 1947 and 1948 and 35 per cent in 1949. (See Table 326 and Figure 218.) The country's share in world output of various individual minerals ranged from zero for diamonds to more than 85 per cent for natural gas. The United States accounted for nearly half of the world's mineral fuels and for nearly 30 per cent of the aggregate of all other minerals, including the roughly estimated output of sand, gravel and stone.

Mineral Fuels

Fuels constitute the main item in world mineral production. They represent more than 60 per cent of the value of the total mineral output in the world as a whole, nearly 75 per cent in the United States, about half in other countries.

World output of the three mineral fuels in 1947, 1948 and 1949 was valued at the following amounts (in millions):

	1947	1948	1949
Coal (bituminous and anthracite)	$8,020	$9,960	$9,360
Petroleum and natural gasoline	6,350	9,665	9,335
Natural gas	320	380	400

In 1948 and 1949 the world output of petroleum and natural gasoline represented almost exactly the same value as that of coal (at current U.S.

TABLE 326

VALUE OF MINERAL OUTPUT IN THE WORLD AND THE UNITED STATES,
BY CLASS OF PRODUCT, 1947–49

Product	World		United States		Other Countries		U. S. Output as Percentage of World Output
	Value, in Millions	*Per Cent*	*Value, in Millions*	*Per Cent*	*Value, in Millions*	*Per Cent*	
				1947			
Total	$23,835	100.0	$9,765	100.0	$14,070	100.0	41.0
Metallic minerals	4,655	19.5	1,239	12.7	3,416	24.3	26.6
Fuels	14,690	61.6	7,181	73.5	7,509	53.4	48.9
Other nonmetallic minerals	4,490	18.8	1,345	13.8	3,145	22.4	29.9
				1948			
Total	$30,715	100.0	$12,445	100.0	$18,270	100.0	40.5
Metallic minerals	5,350	17.4	1,391	11.2	3,959	21.7	26.0
Fuels	20,005	65.1	9,495	76.3	10,510	57.5	47.5
Other nonmetallic minerals	5,360	17.5	1,559	12.5	3,801	20.8	29.1
				1949			
Total	$30,170	100.0	$10,739	100.0	$19,431	100.0	35.6
Metallic minerals	5,355	17.7	1,285	12.0	4,070	20.9	24.0
Fuels	19,095	63.3	7,887	73.4	11,208	57.7	41.3
Other nonmetallic minerals	5,720	19.0	1,567	14.6	4,153	21.4	27.4

Sources: Tables 324 and 325. The figures for the United States (for metallic minerals and total output) differ slightly from those of the U.S. Bureau of Mines (**11**, 1949, pp. 32–34) reproduced in Table 324, because they include the value of output of aluminum.

prices), and each roughly equaled the value of all minerals other than fuel (including, for nonferrous metals, the value added by smelting and refining).

Metals

In comparing the values of different metals, the cost of processing the crude ore should be taken into account. Extraction of ore from the soil is only the initial phase in the processing, which goes on to cleaning, sorting, grinding, floating, smelting, refining and so on.[17] The chain of operations is shorter for some ores, longer for others and longest of all for iron, the most commonly used metal in our age. A comparison of the value of iron ore at the mouth of the mine (as in Table 324) with that of smelted copper and zinc or refined lead and aluminum is, therefore, misleading. To be valid, the comparison should be made in terms of finished

metals. Thus compared, pig iron far outranks all other metals. In fact, the value of the annual output of pig iron exceeds that of gold, silver, platinum, copper, lead, tin and zinc combined.

The world output of pig iron (including ferroalloys) represented a value of $4,465 million in 1948 and $5,117 million in 1949. The world output of steel (154 million metric tons in 1948 and 157 million tons in 1949) had a value of $11.6 billion in 1948 and $12.8 billion in 1949, at average U.S. prices.[18] (See Figure 219.) These figures include, of course, the cost of the coal, lime, alloys and scrap used in processing the ore to make pig iron and the pig iron to make finished steel. Similar processing costs are included in the value of copper, lead, zinc and other nonferrous metals in statistics of mineral output. (See Tables 322, 324 and 325.) There is a difference, however, in the magnitude of these costs: they amount to hundreds of millions of dollars for

17. Cf. Chapter 22.

18. Computed from **11**, 1949, pp. 634, 647.

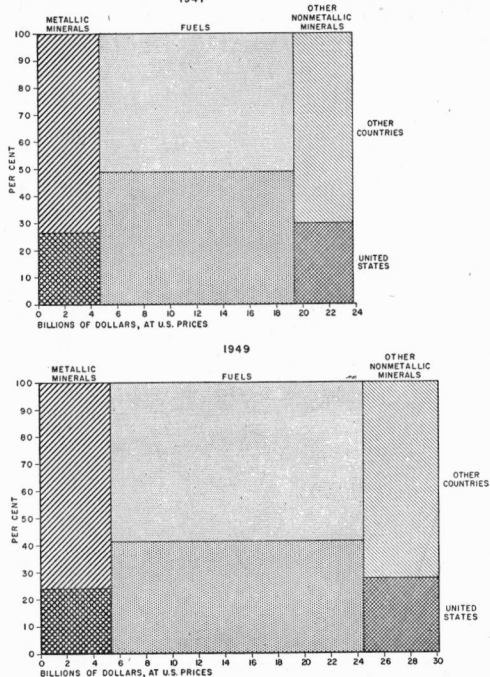

Source: Table 326.

FIGURE 218. VALUE OF MINERAL OUTPUT IN THE
WORLD AND THE UNITED STATES, BY CLASS
OF PRODUCT, 1947 AND 1949

The world's output of minerals amounted to $23.8 billion in 1947 and $30.2 billion in 1949, at U.S. prices. More than 60 per cent of this total represented mineral fuels—coal, petroleum and natural gas. Metallic ores (estimating the value of copper, zinc, lead and aluminum after smelting and refining) accounted for 19.5 per cent in 1947 and 17.7 per cent in 1949. Nonmetallic minerals other than fuels had about the same value as metals. The share of the United States in fuels was 40–50 per cent; in other minerals and metals, less than 30 per cent.

processing nonferrous metals, to many billions for making steel.[19]

Nonmetallic Minerals

The estimate of the value of the world output of nonmetallic minerals other than fuels — $4,490 million in 1947, $5,360 million in 1948, $5,720 million in 1949 — is very rough. The main products in this group are various building materials (clay, cement, gypsum, stone, gravel and sand); fertilizers; mineral pigments; and so on. The group also includes diamonds and gem stones. In the world as a whole, building materials for local

19. This quantitative difference is the only reason for the difference in the handling of the value of iron, steel and other metals in the estimates of the world mineral output.

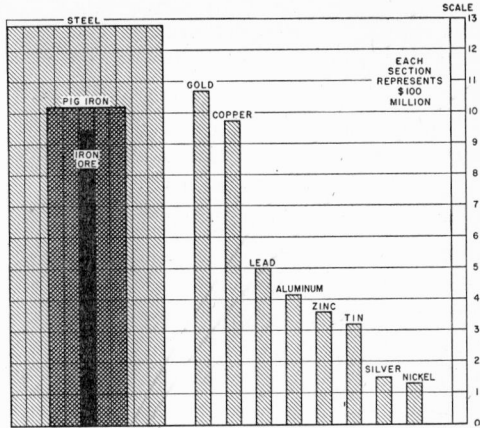

Source: Table 325.

FIGURE 219. VALUE OF WORLD OUTPUT OF PRINCIPAL
METALS, 1949

The world's output of steel in 1949 was valued at $12.8 billion at U.S. prices, far more than the value of all other metals combined. The figure for steel includes the value of the raw materials used to make it: pig iron, manganese and ferroalloys, scrap, coal, lime and so on. The value of pig iron, manganese and ferroalloys is shown in the figure as a part of the value of steel. The value of pig iron ($5.1 billion) includes, in turn, that of iron ore and coal as well as the costs of transportation and processing. The value of the iron ore ($945 million) is shown separately as a component of the value of pig iron and steel.

use predominate in this sector of mineral production.

GEOGRAPHIC DISTRIBUTION OF MINING

The geographic distribution of mining operations in the world is controlled by four factors or groups of factors: the heavy concentration of industrial activities in the United States and western and central Europe;[20] the predominance of coal in northwestern Europe; the concentration of petroleum around the Gulf of Mexico and in the Near East; and the deposits in Africa and Asia of minerals that are rare in Europe and North America.

The production of individual minerals is highly concentrated geographically. The largest single producing country accounts for more than

20. The most important concentration of heavy industry outside these two areas is in the USSR. The Statistical Office of the United Nations has estimated the share of the USSR in the world's mineral output as follows: coal, 10–11 per cent (1935–38); petroleum, 11–12 (1935–38); pig iron, 18 (1936–38); steel, 16 (1936–38); copper, 4–5 (1936–38); zinc, 20 (1933–34); cement, 8 (1935–36). **4,** 1948, pp. 131, 135, 145, 231, 237, 239, 241.

TABLE 327

SHARE OF LARGEST PRODUCERS IN WORLD OUTPUT OF SELECTED
MINERALS, AROUND 1949

Mineral [a]	*Largest Producer*	*Percentage of World Total*	*Second Producer*	*Percentage of World Total*
Quartz crystal	Brazil	100	—	—
Columbite	Nigeria	99	—	—
Sulfur (native)	United States	91	Italy	3
Molybdenum	United States	89	Chile	5
Nickel	Canada	80	USSR	17
Cadmium	United States	76	Mexico	16
Cobalt	Belgian Congo	75	Northern Rhodesia	17
Diamonds	Belgian Congo	68	Union of South Africa	10
Asbestos	Canada	67	Southern Rhodesia	8
Platinum metals	Canada	62	USSR	16
Tantalite	Belgian Congo	60	Brazil	22
Graphite	Korea	60	Mexico	15
Vanadium (1947)	United States	55	Peru	26
Corundum	Union of South Africa	55	Canada	31
Petroleum	United States	54	Venezuela	14
Barite	United States	53	Germany	30
Titanium concentrates	United States	52	Norway	13
Phosphate rock	United States	47	French Morocco	18
Manganese (ore) (1947)	USSR	46	Gold Coast	15
Aluminum	United States	42	Canada	25
Iron ore	United States	40	France	14
Mercury	Italy	39	Spain	29
Fluorspar (1948)	United States	38	Mexico	9
Talc	United States	37	Japan	23
Gypsum	United States	36	Canada	17
Gold	Union of South Africa	36	USSR	27
Tungsten	China	36	United States	6
Salt	United States	35	USSR	...
Potash	Germany	34	United States	25
Tin	Malaya	34	Bolivia	21
Zinc	United States	32	Canada	15
Copper	United States	32	Chile	15
Silver	Mexico	30	United States	20
Antimony (ore)	Bolivia	30	Mexico	17

Source: **11**, 1949, *passim.* Cf. **6**, p. 44.

a. Minerals are arrayed by the degree of geographic concentration of their production as measured by the share of the largest producer in world output. Only minerals for which the share of the largest producer is 30 per cent or more are listed. Because of differences in dates some of the ratios in this table deviate slightly from those given in surveys of output of respective minerals in Chapters 23–25.

half of the world's output of seventeen of the minerals listed in Table 327, and the two largest producers together, for more than half the output of ten others. The United States alone produces more than half of the output of seven minerals and 40–47 per cent of three others. Canada leads in the production of asbestos, nickel and platinum metals; the Belgian Congo in cobalt, tantalite and diamonds; the Union of South Africa in gold and corundum; the USSR in manganese; Brazil in quartz crystal; Nigeria in columbite; Korea in graphite.[21] Thus, many countries play an important role in world mining

21. The share of individual countries in the world output of different minerals varies widely from year to year. In recent years such variations have been particularly sharp. The ratios shown in Table 327 refer to 1949 or the last year for which information is available.

as producers of a coveted mineral. (See Figure 220.)

Mineral Fuels

Europe — excluding the USSR but including its European satellites — leads in coal production, accounting for approximately 44–45 per cent of world output; the United States mines approximately 33–35 per cent, and the remainder (20–23 per cent) is evenly divided between the USSR and the rest of the world. Including production in satellite countries,[22] the Soviet government holds directly or indirectly, 18–20 per cent of the world output of coal.[23]

The distribution of petroleum and natural gas presents a different picture. The United States accounted for 61 per cent of the world's output of petroleum in 1947, for 59 per cent in 1948 and 54 per cent in 1949. It accounts also for 86–88 per cent of the world's output of natural gas. Other important producers in the Western Hemisphere are Venezuela and Mexico; in the Eastern Hemisphere, the USSR, Romania, Kuwait, Iraq and Saudi Arabia. Capital from the United States predominates in the petroleum industry in Central and South America and Arabia; Great Britain established oil production in Iran. All in all, about three fourths of the world output of petroleum is handled, directly or indirectly, by the United States, and a fourth is evenly divided between western European interests and the USSR with its satellites. (See Table 328; cf. Tables 324 and 325.)

In terms of potential heat and power, the world output of coal represents two and a half times as much energy as petroleum and natural gas together.[24] The latter sources, however, can be utilized more efficiently than coal, and command higher prices per potential unit of heat or power.

All in all, the United States accounts for nearly half the world output of mineral fuels; Europe (excluding satellites of the USSR), for approximately 17 per cent, and the Soviet bloc for 13–15 per cent. More than 70 per cent of the petroleum produced in other areas is actually controlled by the United States or the United Kingdom. If this is allocated to the respective countries, the United States accounts for 60 per cent of the world supply of mineral fuels and Europe for more than 20 per cent.

Metals

Metallic ores are widely but unevenly distributed among the nations. Production of silver is currently reported in 66 countries. In recent years, 86 countries have dug gold. Even molybdenum, one of the rarest metals, was produced before World War II in 16 countries, and nickel in 17.[25] The production of most metals, however, is dominated by a single country or a small group of nations. The United States leads in molybdenum, iron, aluminum, zinc and copper; the USSR in manganese; Canada in nickel and platinum metals; the Union of South Africa in corundum and gold; Bolivia in antimony; Malaya in tin; Italy and Spain in mercury; Mexico in silver; China in tungsten. (See Table 327).

In the world economy all other metals are overshadowed by iron and its finished form, steel. Concentration of iron and steel production on both coasts of the North Atlantic Ocean has been the salient feature of the world economy since the middle of the nineteenth century.

The United States had an overwhelming lead in this field after the turn of the century but fell back in the 1930's. In 1938, it accounted for 26.5 per cent of the world output of steel, while the second largest producer, Germany, delivered 21.4 per cent. Ten years later, however, the United States alone produced more steel than all the rest of the world combined. In 1947–49 the percentage distribution of the world output of steel was as follows:[26]

Area	*1947*	*1948*	*1949*
World	100	100	100
United States	57	52	45
Western Europe (excluding satellites)	25	27	30
USSR and satellites	14	15	18
Other areas	4	6	7

For other metals, the relative shares of the United States and western Europe are much smaller and those of South America, Asia and Africa, larger. In 1947–49, despite its leading position in production of copper and aluminum,

---

22. Czechoslovakia, Hungary, Poland and Romania.

23. The distribution of the world output of coal among continents and individual countries varies from year to year. The rates given here refer to 1948–50. (See **4**, 1949–50, pp. 141–43.)

24. See Chapter 25. Cf. **13**.

---

25. **16**, p. 33.

26. **11**, 1949, p. 648.

A. METALLIC MINERALS

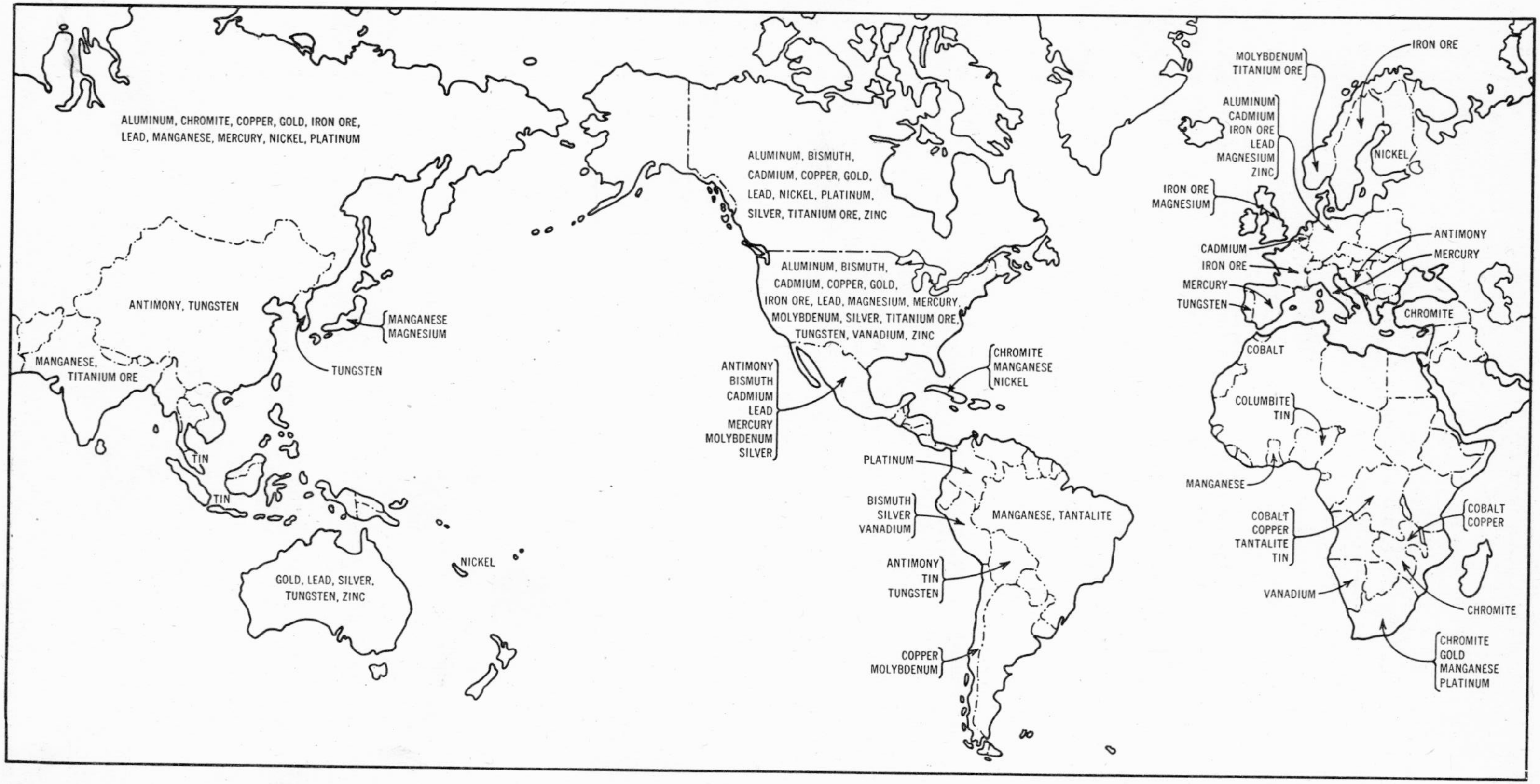

IRON ORE

NICKEL

ANTIMONY
MERCURY
CHROMITE

CHROMITE

COBALT
COPPER

CHROMITE
GOLD
MANGANESE
PLATINUM

MOLYBDENUM
TITANIUM ORE

ALUMINUM
CADMIUM
IRON ORE
LEAD
MAGNESIUM
ZINC

CADMIUM
IRON ORE
MERCURY
TUNGSTEN

COBALT

COLUMBITE
TIN

COBALT
COPPER
TANTALITE
TIN

VANADIUM

IRON ORE
MAGNESIUM

MANGANESE

ALUMINUM, BISMUTH,
CADMIUM, COPPER, GOLD,
LEAD, NICKEL, PLATINUM,
SILVER, TITANIUM ORE, ZINC

ALUMINUM, BISMUTH,
CADMIUM, COPPER, GOLD,
IRON ORE, LEAD, MAGNESIUM, MERCURY,
MOLYBDENUM, SILVER, TITANIUM ORE
TUNGSTEN, VANADIUM, ZINC

CHROMITE
MANGANESE
NICKEL

MANGANESE, TANTALITE

ANTIMONY
BISMUTH
CADMIUM
LEAD
MERCURY
MOLYBDENUM
SILVER

PLATINUM

BISMUTH
SILVER
VANADIUM

ANTIMONY
TIN
TUNGSTEN

COPPER
MOLYBDENUM

ALUMINUM, CHROMITE, COPPER, GOLD, IRON ORE,
LEAD, MANGANESE, MERCURY, NICKEL, PLATINUM

NICKEL

MANGANESE
MAGNESIUM

TUNGSTEN

ANTIMONY, TUNGSTEN

TIN

TIN

GOLD, LEAD, SILVER,
TUNGSTEN, ZINC

MANGANESE,
TITANIUM ORE

760

B. NONMETALLIC MINERALS

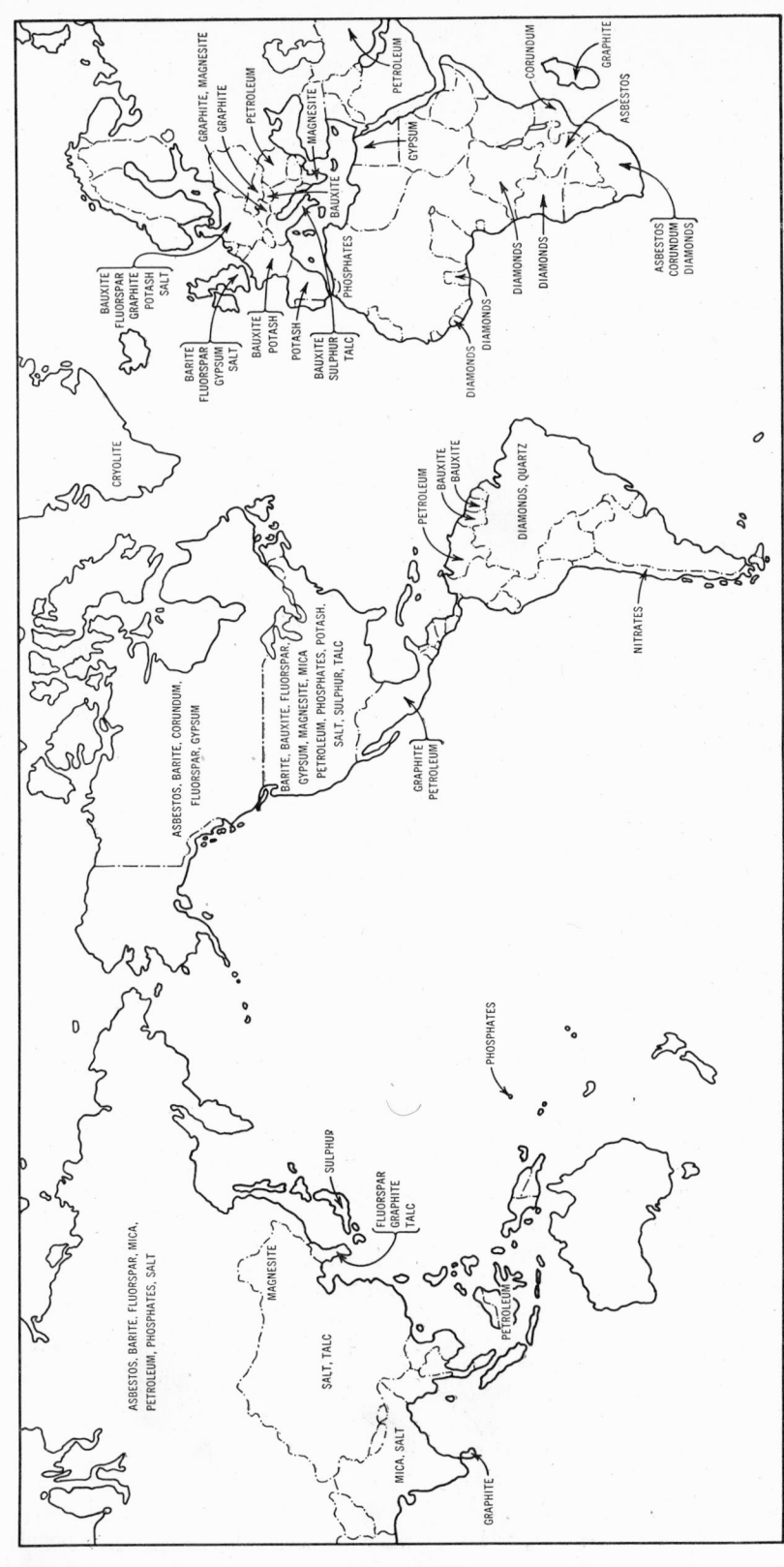

United Nations Scientific Conference on the Conservation and Utilization of Resources

FIGURE 220. PRINCIPAL PRODUCERS OF METALLIC AND NONMETALLIC MINERALS IN THE WORLD

These maps indicate only the countries that normally account for 10 per cent or more of the world's output of selected metals and minerals. They are intended, not to show all the known sources but rather, to indicate the location of the most active mineral areas.

761

TABLE 328

VALUE OF OUTPUT OF MINERAL FUELS IN BROAD AREAS, 1947–49

(Millions)

Year and Area	All Fuels	Coal	Petroleum [a]	Natural Gas [b]
		1947		
World total	$14,690	$8,020	$6,350	$320
United States	7,181	3,033	3,873	275
Europe (excluding satellites)	2,810	2,775	32	3
USSR and satellites	1,892	1,413	476	3
Other areas	2,806	799	1,969	39
		1948		
World total	$20,005	$9,960	$9,665	$380
United States	9,495	3,458	5,704	333
Europe (excluding satellites)	3,555	3,503	48	4
USSR and satellites	2,684	1,936	744	4
Other areas	4,271	1,063	3,169	39
		1949		
World total	$19,095	$9,360	$9,335	$400
United States	7,887	2,492	5,040	355
Europe (excluding satellites)	3,257	3,200	52	5
USSR and satellites	2,838	2,068	765	5
Other areas	5,113	1,600	3,478	35

Sources: Tables 324 and 325; **11**, 1949, pp. 340–42, 388, 818, 991; **4**, 1949–50, pp. 141–47.

    a. Includes natural gas liquids (rough estimate).

    b. Rough estimate for Europe and USSR with its satellites: one per cent of world output for each area.

the United States accounted for less than a fourth of the total output of all nonferrous metals combined, including gold, silver, platinum and nickel. (Cf. Tables 324 and 325.)

Nonmetallic Minerals

Man knew nonmetallic minerals long before he learned to use metals. Salt, stone, clay, sand and gravel were widely used in primitive communities and are now produced practically everywhere in the world. However, the output of most of the nonmetallic minerals is concentrated geographically. Thus, quartz crystal comes mainly from Brazil; sulfur from the United States; diamonds from the Belgian Congo; potash from Germany, the United States and France; asbestos from Canada; and mica from India.

In many countries, nonmetallic minerals absorb more human labor and represent a greater market value than metallic ores, though in highly industrialized areas they are overshad-owed by metals and mineral fuels. The quarrying of stone, clay, sand and gravel, or the extraction of salt, is frequently taken for granted as a local trade in underdeveloped areas, while the mining of minerals for export is considered an important branch of the national economy. In areas embracing the great majority of mankind, however, local quarrying is vitally important.

EMPLOYMENT IN MINING

The place of mining in the economy of a country or an area is reflected by its share in national income and employment. Income statistics are available for only a few countries, but nearly two score nations provide census data on employment in mines and quarries.

In the World

Statistics on employment in mining are available for an area with an aggregate population of

TABLE 329

LABOR FORCE IN MINING AND QUARRYING IN SELECTED COUNTRIES, AROUND 1940

	Labor Force, in Thousands		Labor Force in Mining, as Percentage of	
Country and Year	Total	In Mining and Quarrying	Total Labor Force	Nonagricultural Labor Force
United States, 1940	52,712.3	1,100.5	2.1	2.5
Canada, 1941	4,670.1	93.0	2.0	2.7
Mexico, 1940	5,858.1	106.7	1.8	5.2
Panama, 1940	207.7	0.4	0.2	0.4
Cuba, 1943	1,520.9	5.5	0.3	0.8
Venezuela, 1941	1,240.7	23.5	2.0	3.9
Colombia, 1938	4,566.2	75.4	1.5	6.0
Brazil, 1940	14,020.1	390.6	2.8	8.5
Peru, 1940	2,475.3	44.7	1.8	4.9
Chile, 1940	1,741.5	96.1	6.5	9.6
United Kingdom, 1931	21,074.8	1,281.1	6.1	6.5
Ireland, 1936	1,339.1	3.0	0.3	0.5
France, 1946	20,520.0	360.0	1.8	2.8
Belgium, 1930	3,750.3	221.7	5.9	7.1
Netherlands, 1947	3,866.4	52.0	1.4	1.7
Sweden, 1940	2,992.2	33.8	1.1	1.6
Norway, 1930	1,181.8	13.2	1.1	1.7
Finland, 1940	2,017.2	2.7	1.3	3.1
Germany, 1939	34,616.6	733.6	2.1	2.9
Poland, 1931	15,006.1	175.1	1.1	3.3
Czechoslovakia, 1947	5,852.4	142.6	2.4	3.9
Switzerland, 1941	1,992.5	7.5	0.4	0.5
Austria, 1939	3,648.9	26.9	0.7	1.2
Hungary, 1941	4,503.1	55.3	1.2	2.3
Portugal, 1940	3,049.9	21.7	0.7	1.4
Italy, 1936	18,754.7	128.4	0.7	1.4
Romania, 1930	10,457.6	52.7	0.5	2.4
Bulgaria, 1934	3,433.1	8.4	0.4	1.2
Japan, 1947	33,881.0	667.5	2.0	4.1
Turkey, 1935	7,921.2	18.7	0.2	1.3
India, 1931	148,816.9	346.0	0.2	0.7
Philippines, 1939	6,107.7	42.0	0.7	2.6
Egypt, 1937	6,095.0	10.8	0.2	0.6
Union of South Africa, 1946 [a]	888.2	53.6	6.0	7.5
Australia, 1947	3,196.4	54.4	1.7	2.0

Sources: Computed from **3**, 1948, pp. 234–51; **4**, 1949–50, pp. 64–84.

a. Whites only.

nearly a billion, approximately 40 per cent of mankind, and a total labor force of 450 million. In these countries, 6.2 million workers were employed in the extractive industries around 1940. (See Table 329.) Though a large part of the world's mining is concentrated in this area, the countries for which no occupational statistics are available include several with extensive mining, among them the Soviet Union, the Belgian Congo and Manchuria. In all, countries not included in Table 329 may have 2.5 to 3 million mine workers.[27] Mining and quarrying thus

27. Including native mine workers in the Union of South Africa.

may have employed approximately 9 million workers before World War II.

In Various Countries

The development of mining in a country depends on both the incidence of local mineral resources and the extent to which the available resources are being exploited. Frequently, rich mineral deposits call into being large-scale modern mining in the midst of a primitive subsistence economy, as exemplified by Bolivia, Chile, Saudi Arabia, Iran, Kuwait, Malaya, the Belgian Congo and Rhodesia. On the other hand, Switzerland has reached a high level of economic development with practically no mining industry. In most regions, however, development in mining has kept pace with industrial progress.

The geographical distribution of the labor force employed in mining shows the concentration of the extractive industries in the Northern Hemisphere, especially in the region where coal and iron ore meet,[28] the "power belt" that encircles the earth, starting with the United States, crossing northwestern Europe and the USSR and extending to Manchuria and Japan. (See Table 329; cf. Figure 221.)

The proportion of the nonagricultural labor force engaged in mining in the countries listed in Table 329 ranges from 9.6 per cent in Chile and 8.5 per cent in Brazil to 0.5 per cent in Switzerland and 0.4 in Panama. Belgium, with 7.1 per cent, and the United Kingdom, with 6.5 per cent, are near the head of the list; the United States is in a class with Canada, Germany and France, with 2.5–3.0 per cent.[29]

Coal mining probably employs as many workers as all the other branches of mining and quarrying combined. In the United Kingdom, France, Belgium, Germany and Poland, it accounts for more than 80 per cent of all mine and quarry workers.

In the United States

Nearly 60 per cent of the workers engaged in extractive industries in the United States are in coal mining, 20 per cent are in the production of crude petroleum and natural gas, and 20 per cent mine or quarry other nonmetallic minerals and metallic ores. Coal mining is concentrated in Pennsylvania, Virginia, West Virginia, Ohio, Illinois, Kentucky and Alabama. Texas, Oklahoma and California lead in petroleum. Other mines and quarries are dispersed in various parts of the country, especially in California, Arizona, Montana, Michigan and Pennsylvania. (See Table 330 and Figure 222.)

In many states — among them New York, New Jersey, Massachusetts and Connecticut — not more than 0.2 per cent of all workers were employed in mining and quarrying in 1940. In contrast, the proportion was 7 per cent or more in Pennsylvania, Kentucky, Montana, Wyoming, Arizona and Utah, 15.4 per cent in Nevada, and 21.8 in West Virginia. In the Mountain states (New Mexico, Arizona, Utah, Nevada and Wyoming), and in West Virginia, more workers are employed in mining than in manufacturing.

The Share of Mining in National Income

In statistics of national income, the direct contribution of mining appears in the form of wages, salaries and profits yielded by enterprises classified in the economic division "Mining" or "Extractive Industries." In the United States, this division comprises only mines and quarries, but in some other countries it also includes smelters, blast furnaces and refineries. The actual contribution of mining to national income and wealth is far greater than its share in wages and profits, however. The process that starts with extraction of ore from the earth and continues in smelters and blast furnaces is carried further by rolling mills, machinery factories and other industries until the finished product is delivered to the ultimate buyer, either for direct consumption or as productive equipment.

This process may be continuous, as when a firm not only operates coal and iron ore mines, blast furnaces and rolling mills but also makes bridges, ships and other finished products. But the long chain of operations may start in a country rich in mineral deposits and be completed elsewhere, in an area rich in technical knowledge. In the first case, mining serves as the foundation for a great variety of industrial activities in the country; in the second, its contribution to the national income of the country ends with delivery of the ore at the harbor.

---

28. Cf. Chapter 10.

29. These percentages are not strictly comparable. Some countries include quarrying in "extractive industries," others do not; in some countries blast furnaces and smelters are included with mining, in others they are classified as manufacturing establishments. These inconsistencies, however, are of minor significance in comparison with the range in the percentages.

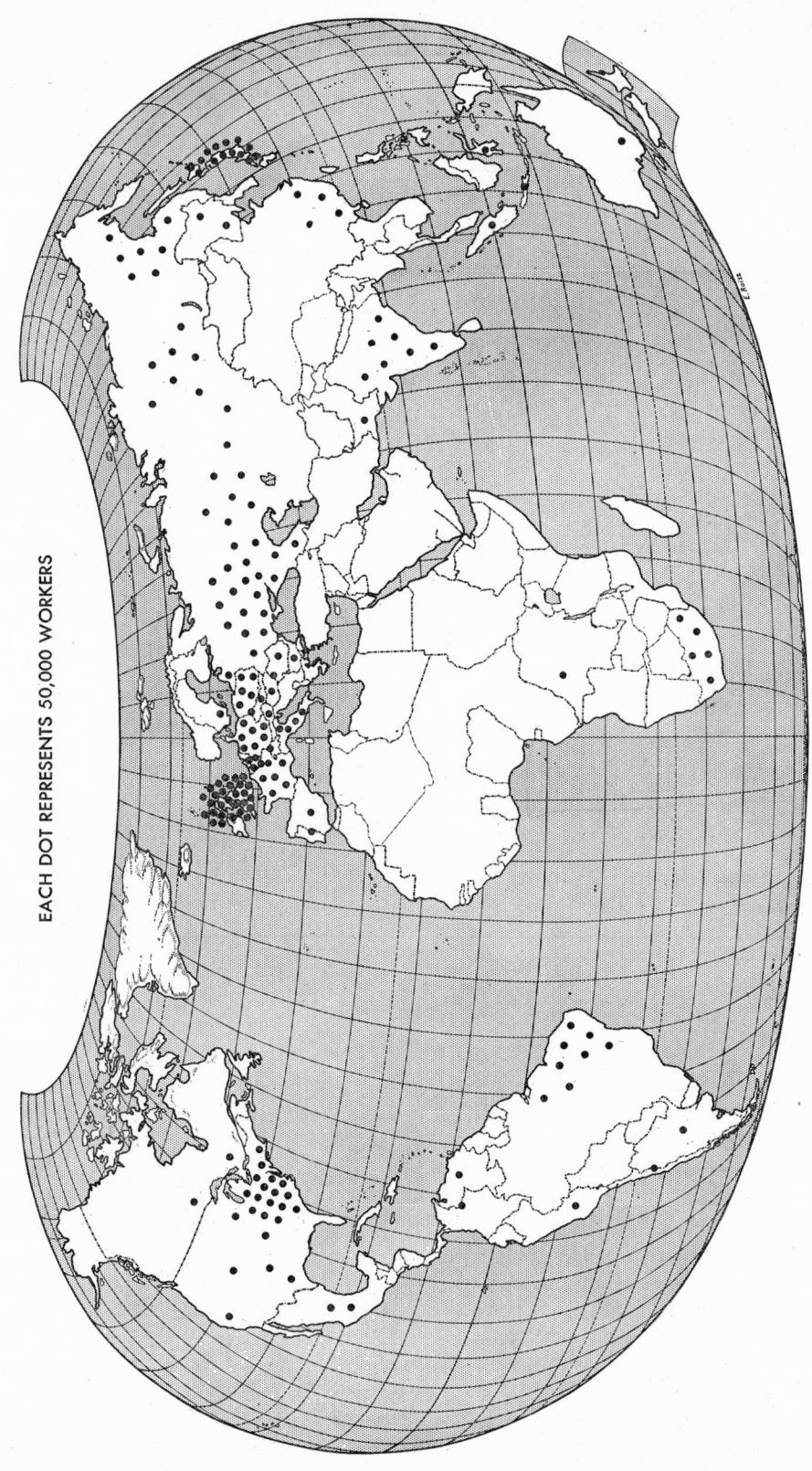

EACH DOT REPRESENTS 50,000 WORKERS

FIGURE 221. LABOR FORCE IN MINING IN THE WORLD, AROUND 1940

Work in mines is heavily concentrated in the Northern Hemisphere, in a wide belt that embraces the United States and northwestern Europe and stretches across the USSR to Japan. For the Union of South Africa the map shows not only European workers enumerated by the census (cf. Table 329), but also native workers.

TABLE 330

EMPLOYMENT IN MINING IN THE UNITED STATES, BY STATE, 1940

Geographic Division and State	Employed Workers, in Thousands		Workers in Mining, as Percentage of all Employed Workers
	Total	In Mining	
United States	45,166	913.0	2.0
New England			
Maine	279	0.6	0.2
New Hampshire	176	0.3	0.2
Vermont	126	1.5	0.2
Massachusetts	1,535	1.5	0.1
Rhode Island	265	0.2	0.8
Connecticut	680	0.6	0.1
Middle Atlantic			
New York	4,975	8.9	0.2
New Jersey	1,569	3.6	0.2
Pennsylvania	3,230	224.9	7.0
East North Central			
Ohio	2,345	32.4	1.4
Indiana	1,151	13.5	1.1
Illinois	2,874	49.2	1.7
Michigan	1,825	15.9	0.8
Wisconsin	1,061	2.5	0.2
West North Central			
Minnesota	931	7.9	0.8
Iowa	863	6.3	0.7
Missouri	1,297	12.5	1.0
North Dakota	200	1.0	0.5
South Dakota	205	2.9	1.4
Nebraska	423	0.6	0.1
Kansas	574	15.2	2.6
South Atlantic			
Delaware	103	0.1	0.1
Maryland	691	4.0	0.6
District of Columbia	309	0.1	0.0
Virginia	933	24.2	2.6
West Virginia	519	113.4	21.8
North Carolina	1,309	2.9	0.2
South Carolina	661	1.3	0.2
Georgia	1,607	4.1	0.3
Florida	683	2.6	0.4

(*Continued on facing page*)

In the United States

The United States not only has its own un-rivaled array of mines, quarries and oil wells but also imports ores, minerals and metals from other parts of the world to manufacture machinery, automobiles, airplanes, chemicals and so on. In all, more than half the national income originated in the United States by manufacturing is attributable to industries processing metals and minerals. (See Table 331.) Domestic mines provide most of the raw material and mineral fuel required for manufacturing and building activities in the United States.

In 1948 a million workers, in round numbers, were engaged in the United States in extracting metallic ores, crude petroleum and other minerals, and 7.6 million worked in the processing of these products, which added $37.7 billion to the national income. If income from the transportation and distribution of minerals and fabricated products (included in nonmanufacturing industries in Table 331) is taken into account, more

TABLE 330—*continued*

Geographic Division and State	Employed Workers, in Thousands		Workers in Mining, as Percentage of all Employed Workers
	Total	In Mining	
East South Central			
Kentucky	848	60.5	7.1
Tennessee	942	14.4	1.5
Alabama	894	30.2	3.3
Mississippi	727	1.9	0.3
West South Central			
Arkansas	584	5.9	1.0
Louisiana	771	14.8	1.9
Oklahoma	659	35.0	6.3
Texas	2,138	61.1	0.3
Mountain			
Montana	186	13.5	7.3
Idaho	159	6.7	4.2
Wyoming	87	6.3	7.2
Colorado	250	15.9	6.4
New Mexico	140	8.8	6.3
Arizona	150	12.8	8.5
Utah	149	10.1	7.0
Nevada	41	6.3	15.4
Pacific			
Washington	608	5.4	0.9
Oregon	390	3.0	0.7
California	2,525	45.7	1.8

Source: **7**, pp. 99–106. Only employed workers.

than $60 billion worth of goods and services was produced in the United States on the foundation of the $5,445 million yield of its mines and quarries.[30]

In Other Countries

The direct share of mining in national income ranges among countries from slightly more than 1 per cent (India, China, Greece) to 10 per cent or more (Peru, the Union of South Africa, Chile); in most of the modern industrialized countries for which information is available (the United States, Canada, France, the Netherlands) the percentage falls between these two extremes:[31]

Peru, 1942	14.0
Union of South Africa, 1946	12.8
Chile, 1943	10.0
Mexico, 1946 [a]	7.3
Canada, 1938	7.0
Japanese dependencies, 1939	6.0
Burma, 1931–32	5.7
France, 1947 [b]	5.6
Luxembourg, 1946	3.3
Japan, 1939	3.0
United States, 1947	2.0
Hungary, 1936–37	1.9
Netherlands, 1942	1.8
Argentina, 1945	1.8
Yugoslavia, 1923–25	1.3
Greece, 1929	1.2
India, 1925–29	1.2
China, 1936	1.1

a. Mining and metallurgy.
b. Includes blast furnaces and building materials.

30. The concept of "income originated" in an industry is narrower than that of "value added" by the industry and represents only a fraction of the gross value of the product. The value of the mineral products produced in the United States in 1948, $12.3 billion, includes the income originated in mining proper ($5,445 million), in processing of petroleum products ($3,632 million), in refining nonferrous metals (a part of $2,079 million) and a part of that from making and processing iron. It also includes allowances for depreciation of equipment and payments of mines to railroads, utilities, insurance companies and banks.

31. Computed from **5,** and publications of the respective countries.

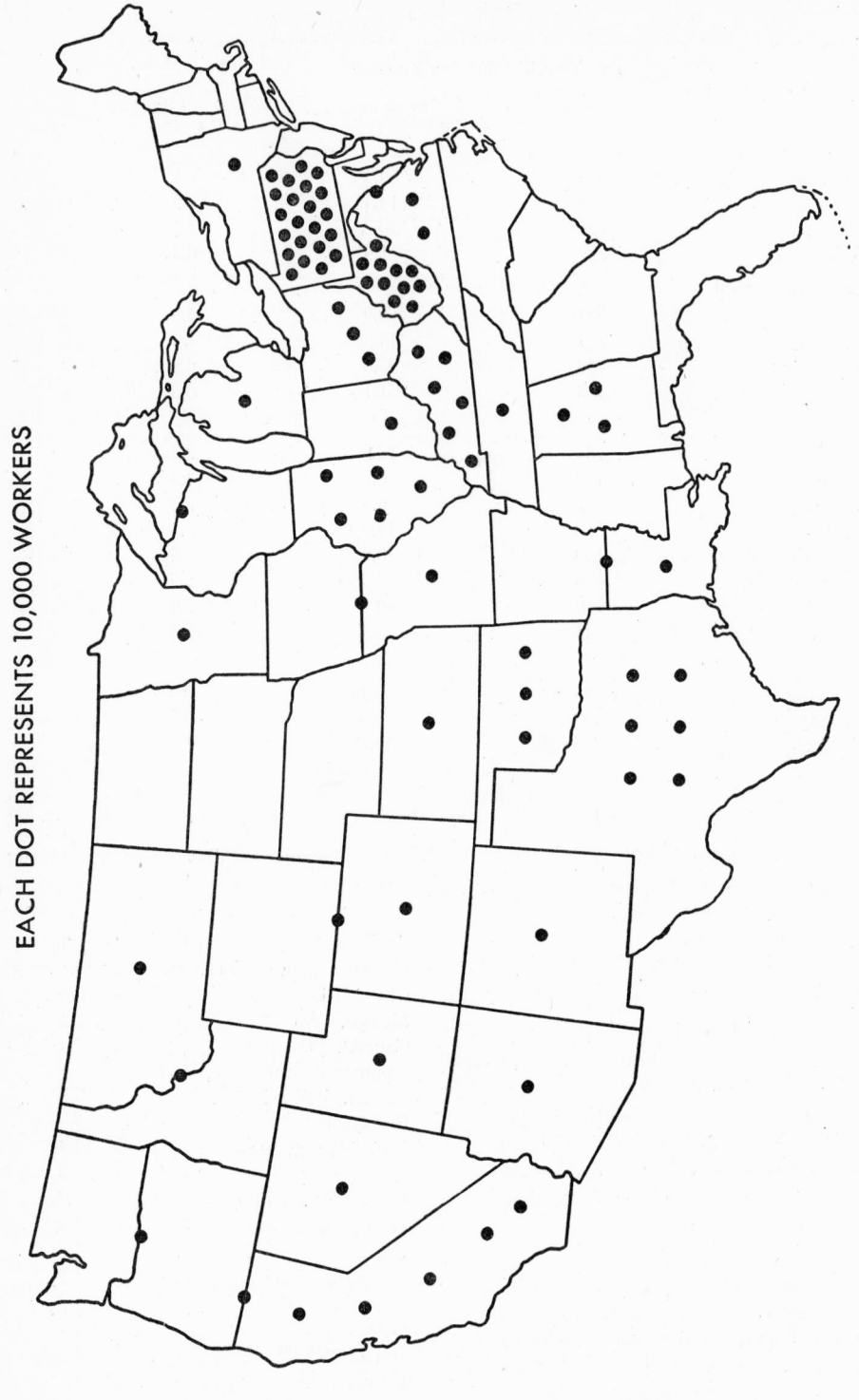

EACH DOT REPRESENTS 10,000 WORKERS

Source: Table 330.

FIGURE 222. EMPLOYMENT IN MINING: GEOGRAPHIC DISTRIBUTION IN THE UNITED STATES, BY STATE, 1940

In the United States, mining is concentrated in the Appalachian coal fields in West Virginia, Pennsylvania and neighboring states, and in the Rockies. In relation to population and labor force, mining is the leading industry in West Virginia and the Mountain states.

TABLE 331

EMPLOYMENT AND INCOME ORIGINATED IN MINING AND MANUFACTURES PROCESSING
MINERALS AND METALS IN THE UNITED STATES, 1948

Industry	National Income, in Millions	Persons Engaged in Production, in Thousands [a]
All industries	$223,469	58,646
Mining	5,445	1,032
Coal	2,455	542
Crude petroleum and gas	1,870	276
Metal ores and minerals	1,120	187
Manufactures processing metals and minerals	37,743	7,562
Products of petroleum and coal	3,632	235
Chemicals and allied products	4,383	727
Iron and steel and their products	8,713	1,878
Nonferrous metals and their products	2,079	482
Machinery (excluding electrical)	7,115	1,580
Electrical machinery	3,661	890
Transportation equipment, except automobiles	1,874	472
Automobiles	4,132	767
Stone, clay and glass products	2,154	531
Other manufactures	29,472	7,895
Nonmanufacturing industries	150,809	42,157

Source: **9,** pp. 159, 181, 187.   a. Equivalent of full-time man-years.

Apart from the Union of South Africa, where the national economy is built around gold, mining yields the highest percentage of national income in underdeveloped countries (such as Chile, Peru, Bolivia, Saudi Arabia, Kuwait) that do not process their minerals but ship them abroad. In highly industrialized countries, the share of national income originated in the fabrication of metals and other raw materials overshadows that originated in mining.

MINERAL PRODUCTS IN WORLD TRADE

Most of the output of minerals is processed in the country of origin, but some ores and other minerals are dug primarily for export.

Natural gas is practically nonexistent in international trade. Of the world output of coal, more than 90 per cent is consumed by producing countries or used by them for bunkers, and less than 10 per cent is exported, partly as coke or briquettes. Petroleum is used for domestic needs in the United States but is mainly exported by Mexico, Venezuela, Peru, Colombia, Iraq and Iran, Kuwait, Saudi Arabia and Indonesia. In all, however, more than 80 per cent of the world output of petroleum is consumed in the producing countries.

Of iron ore likewise, approximately 80 per cent of the world output is processed to iron and steel and used for further fabrication in the producing countries, the remainder exported. The proportionate domestic consumption of copper and lead is even higher. On the other hand, nickel, tin, chromite, antimony, uranium, gold and gem stones are mined mainly for export.

In all, approximately 20 per cent of the world output of minerals (in terms of value) moved through the channels of international trade before the war, representing about 15 per cent of the total value of world trade.[32]

Exports of the minerals figuring most impor-

32. 1. According to the estimate of the German Central Statistical Office, the value of mineral products in world exports totaled $2,850 million, and that of finished metals amounted to $1,750 million, in 1937. The total represents more than 18 per cent of all world exports but includes the cost of processing iron ore into pig iron, steel and finished-steel products.

tantly in world trade represented the following values in 1938 (in millions of dollars): [33]

Coal	$540
Crude petroleum	448
Petroleum	394
Copper (unworked)	325
Gas and fuel oil	298
Iron ore	149
Tin (unworked)	123
Iron and steel scrap	74
Lead (unworked)	74
Tin ore	72
Pig iron	50
Zinc (unworked)	34
Manganese ore	21
Bauxite	10

The movement of minerals in international trade forms an intricate design on the world map, each mineral following its own well-established pattern. Some merely cross a frontier, as in the shipment of coal and nickel between the United States and Canada or the shipment of coal and iron ore betwen Germany and France. Others travel thousands of miles from producing to consuming country.[34]

Progress in Mining

Since the time of Aristotle, the number of things men dig out of the earth has multiplied many times, and the list continues to grow. C. K. Leith names thirty-four "new" minerals that became well established in commercial and technical use in the period between the two world wars. Two or three decades ago, some of these were produced in only negligible quantities and others were known only as laboratory specimens or were not known at all.[35]

Modern mining has been affected not only by technological progress in extracting minerals and drilling oil wells but also by changes in the processing and use of minerals and metals. Progress in geology, chemistry, electrochemistry and related sciences makes it possible to utilize comparatively poor deposits. The use of scrap iron

and the recovery of secondary metals reduce the demand for ore per ton of metal. The increasing demand for steel of superior qualities stimulates the search for alloys.

The most far-reaching changes have taken place in the technology of coal and petroleum. The trend has been toward mechanizing coal mining and improving methods of coal burning so that more coal is mined per worker, more heat is produced per ton of coal, more power is obtained per heat unit, and more useful work is performed per unit of power. The progress of technology promises new outlets for coal by converting it into gaseous or liquid form.

The petroleum industry has succeeded in improving the quality of gasoline to satisfy the exacting requirements of aviation. Aware of the threat of exhaustion of oil fields in some more or less remote future, and as a precautionary measure against interruption of imports, the industry is getting ready to utilize synthetic fuels obtained from coal.

The various branches of mining are becoming increasingly interdependent. The oil industry depends on iron for pipe; coal mines depend on petroleum for fuel for their motors and trucks; steel makers depend on coal and petroleum and some two score minerals and metals. Africa and Asia are the only sources of many "rare" minerals coveted by industrial countries; on the other hand, industrial countries are the only buyers interested in minerals dug in Africa and Asia.

In the following chapters, problems of world mining are discussed under four headings. Chapter 22 deals with metallic and nonmetallic minerals other than fuels. In that chapter, nonferrous metals are followed through smelters and refineries but consideration of iron ore goes only as far as the blast furnace.[36] Chapters 23 and 24 deal with coal, petroleum and natural gas from their origin to the fuel product ready for consumption. The concluding chapter of this section gives an over-all picture of world economics of energy, including not only coal, petroleum and natural gas but also water power, fuel wood and work animals.[37]

---

33. **2**, p. 32.

34. This question is discussed by the authors in a study of world trade and government now in preparation for the Twentieth Century Fund. Cf. the map of the free world lifelines in the report of the President's Materials Policy Commission, *Resources for Freedom*, 1952, Vol. I, p. 157.

35. **16**, pp. 23 ff.

36. For further discussion of the economics of iron and steel, see Chapter 29.

37. The use of metals and minerals in industrial production is discussed further in Chapters 30 and 31. The flow of mineral products and metals in international trade is considered by the authors in another study (see footnote 34).

CHAPTER 22

METALLIC AND NONMETALLIC MINERALS

OUR YOUNG MECHANIZED CIVILIZATION is an off-spring of the mineral kingdom. It uses minerals in a thousand and one ways to provide comfort in peacetime and to cause destruction in war. The early American colonists met their need for metals with small supplies of iron for tools and weapons, lead for ammunition, copper for household utensils, gold and silver for ornaments. In contrast, their descendants, two centuries later, require great quantities of more than a hundred minerals.

Consumption of metals and minerals has grown with the development and spread of western civilization. The amount of mineral products consumed in the last fifty years exceeds by far the amount consumed during man's entire preceding existence on earth,[1] and there is no evidence of any slackening in our demand for an ever-increasing quantity and variety. Men are combing the globe in search of new sources of supply, while the ground under them is being emptied of minerals at an increasing rate.

Minerals can be conveniently divided into two major classes: (1) mineral fuels (coal, petroleum and natural gas) and (2) all other minerals, metallic and nonmetallic. This chapter deals with the more important members of the second group. These, in turn, may be classified in five groups of metallic ores (or metals) and six groups of nonmetallic minerals, apart from mineral fuels, as follows:

Metallic Ores and Metals
    Iron ore
    Ferroalloying ores
    Nonferrous metals
    Precious metals
    Minor metals
Nonmetallic Minerals
    Building materials
    Abrasives
    Industrial and manufacturing
        materials
    Metallurgical materials
    Chemical minerals
    Fertilizers

The estimated value of the world's output of these minerals in 1949, at U.S. prices, was $11.1 billion, of which the United States, with $2.7 billion, accounted for 24 per cent.[2]

TECHNIQUES OF MINERAL PRODUCTION

The production of minerals begins with prospecting, the search for, and appraisal of, deposits of useful minerals.

MINERAL DEPOSITS

The importance of a mineral deposit depends both on physical factors such as the size of the deposit, the richness and chemical properties of the ore, the degree of concentration, and the characteristics of the gangue (that is, the non-metallic minerals associated with it in the deposit and usually discarded as waste); and on economic factors such as the cost of extracting, processing and transporting the minerals, the distance from consuming centers, and industrial demand. An iron ore deposit near Lake Superior, for example, is far more valuable than a deposit of the same grade and size in the Arctic or the Brazilian jungles. Only deposits that can be profitably exploited with present techniques are considered "ore deposits."

A new milling technique or a new use for a mineral may convert a worthless deposit into a valuable one. Thus, the vast disseminated porphyry copper deposits, which now account for two thirds of the copper produced in the United States, were of little importance until methods were developed to mine and concentrate low-grade ores economically. The value of beryllium deposits increased overnight because of the combination of a new technique in production (directly from ore by electrolysis) and new uses for beryllium in copper alloys.

If the price of the product is high and other conditions are favorable, it may be profitable to work a mine yielding as little as a fraction of an ounce of metal to a ton of ore, as, for example,

---

1. **3, a**, p. 39.

2. See Tables 324 and 325. This estimate includes the cost of processing copper, lead, zinc, tin and nickel.

the gold mines of the Union of South Africa. On the other hand, the United States has billions of tons of rocks containing 500 pounds of iron to the ton for which there is no market since American ferrous metallurgy operates only with ore containing twice as much iron.

EXTRACTION OF MINERALS

Once a deposit has been discovered and its exploitation planned, the next important task is to mine it.

Primitive Methods

For millenniums the simplest hand tools were used to dig out mineral ores buried in the ground. Underground water, foul air, fumes emanating from sulfurous and other ores, and slides of loose rock constantly menaced the lives of the diggers. Miners drained the tunnels by carrying the water up in buckets and tried to improve the ventilation underground by swinging cloth or their jackets to and fro over the mouth of the mine. Gradually techniques were developed to reach minerals as deep as 100 to 200 feet, with relative safety.

By the end of the Middle Ages, mining was making use of various techniques and installations that were the early forerunners of modern equipment. Agricola has left an impressive description of mines in Saxony in the middle of the sixteenth century, and the woodcuts in his famous *De Re Metallica* testify to the ingenuity of the mining technicians of his time.[3]

Shafts were sunk into mines, windlasses were set up, usually with sheds for protection against the weather, and timbers were used as supports. (See Figure 223, A.) Water was drawn up by a chain of dippers, or water bags made of two or more ox hides were lowered and hoisted by windlass. Various types of pumps were used to control flooding, and ventilating machines were built to blow fresh air into the shaft or draw out foul air. (See Figure 223, C.) Goats or horses were used at some mines to operate the pumping or ventilating machines. Miners, however, still descended into the mines by ladder or by steps cut in the rock, or were lowered by rope, sitting on a stick or sliding on the dirt. (See Figure 223, B.) If the rock was too hard to be cut, it was shattered by setting a fire in the mine and then, usually, quenching it with water. (See Figure 223, D.)

In brief, men engaged in mining in the sixteenth century faced essentially the same problems they face today and sought solutions in the proper direction, even though the machinery they developed was inefficient and cumbersome. The men whom we would now call mining engineers were handicapped by lack of cheap iron to make heavy installations and by lack of mechanical power to turn the wheels of their wooden machinery.

Modern Techniques

The steam engine and the availability of iron and, later, of steel and electricity revolutionized the extraction of minerals. Today, underground mines are entered by shafts, vertical or inclined, or by tunnels. Ore is broken by drilling and blasting and is loaded onto cars for delivery at the surface or to the shaft, where the ore is hoisted and automatically dumped into ore bins. Mines have attained depths of more than 9,000 feet. Mechanical drainage and ventilation, electric lights and telephone systems are common. Work underground is largely mechanized, as are the descent into the mines and underground transportation.

Surface mining of deposits that lend themselves to such operations is almost completely mechanized. Before the end of the nineteenth century, small steam shovels and dump cars drawn by teams of animals or "dinky" automobiles over narrow-gauge tracks came into use in open-pit operations. Now the mines use fully revolving electric shovels with enormous dippers and caterpillar traction, electric locomotives and motorized pit haulage, and conveyor belt systems for transporting the ore from the pits. The efficiency of the new methods and equipment is such that in the Bingham copper mine in Utah, for example, 125,000 tons of ore and 200,000 tons of waste can be removed daily.[4] In placer deposits, huge dredges lift the subaqueous gravel from 100 feet beneath the surface, screen out and stack the barren debris, sluice the sands to washing tables and reject the washed tailings.

ORE DRESSING

Few metallic ores are marketable in the form in which they are extracted from the earth. They contain too many impurities and must be freed of the gangue before they are shipped for fur-

---

3. **36**, *passim*.

4. **41**, pp. 399–400.

A. Shafts and Tunnels

B. Descending the Shafts

THREE VERTICAL SHAFTS, OF WHICH THE FIRST, A, DOES NOT REACH THE TUNNEL; THE
SECOND, B, REACHES THE TUNNEL; TO THE THIRD, C, THE TUNNEL HAS NOT YET BEEN
DRIVEN. D—TUNNEL.

A—DESCENDING INTO THE SHAFT BY LADDERS.   B—BY SITTING ON A STICK.   C—BY
SITTING ON THE DIRT   D—DESCENDING BY STEPS CUT IN THE ROCK.

C. Ventilation of the Shafts

D. Breaking Rock by Fire

A—TUNNEL. B—PIPE. C—NOZZLE OF DOUBLE BELLOWS.

A—KINDLED LOGS. B—STICKS SHAVED DOWN FAN-SHAPED. C—TUNNEL.

FIGURE 223. MINING IN THE SIXTEENTH CENTURY: EXTRACTION OF MINERALS

(GEORGIUS AGRICOLA)

ther processing. Thus mining is to some extent a processing, as well as an extractive, industry.[5]

Primitive Methods

We do not know when ore dressing was first introduced. Herbert Hoover points out in his comments on Agricola's work that smelting of ore antedates human records and was practiced before ore concentration. He believes that ore milling and concentration must have been in use before the third century B.C.[6]

As long as small supplies of minerals satisfied the market, it was sufficient to pick coarse metallic fragments out of the ore by hand, relying on color, luster or general appearance to identify the mineral. In the time of Agricola, ore was sifted and sorted on large tables. The metallic parts were put into trays, which were emptied into tubs or buckets. Then the sorted fragments were broken by hammer, or otherwise crushed, and roasted. Or, if the ore was rich in metal, it was sifted and then washed in tubs, or in ditches on a slope over which a stream of water would be diverted, or in open boxes over troughs hollowed out from trees. The bottoms of such boxes had holes of the desired size, and rushing water would force the pieces of metal down into the troughs. (See Figure 224, A, B, C.)

Modern Techniques

Modern large-scale mineral production calls for speedier and more efficient techniques of ore concentration.

Now practically all ore is crushed, ground to fine powder and sorted mechanically by the size of the grain. Almost all mines, except the very small ones that ship crude ore for treatment elsewhere, have concentrating mills for this preliminary processing and for flotation or leaching and, if needed, magnetic concentration. If flotation is used, oil and chemicals are added to the powder, which flows to different cells. A froth of oil-coated air bubbles is then formed, which attaches itself selectively to certain minerals and carries them to special troughs, while the gangue material sinks. Some nonmetallic minerals, pre-

treated for flotation, are also concentrated in this way. Magnetic concentration is used to separate minerals with magnetic properties from waste. Other minerals can be concentrated only through leaching by some solvent or water.

The ratio of concentration varies from ore to ore. The higher the ratio, the lower the freight and smelting charges. High-grade ores are moved to smelters without preliminary milling, but supplies of such ores are rare, and few mines can ship run-of-the-mine ore.

The new concentration techniques have made it feasible to work many deposits of vitally needed materials that formerly were left unmined because of their low-grade or too complex ores, such as some ores in the western states of the United States left unmined for many years despite their high content of lead and zinc. Selective flotation has made it possible to obtain a high-grade lead concentrate with very little zinc, and vice versa.[7] Such techniques are being constantly improved, and it is anticipated that many marginal or submarginal deposits will become valuable ore deposits.

SMELTING AND REFINING

Primitive Methods

Copper was reduced from ore by smelting before recorded history, and tin before 3500 B.C.[8] Charcoal was used in smelting from the beginning through Agricola's time and down to the eighteenth century. Agricola gives a comprehensive description of the furnaces and the smelting procedures in furnaces, pots or trenches, and of the fluxes used. Bellows were used before 1500 B.C. After smelting, the metal flowed into the forehearth, while the slag was skimmed and resmelted. (See Figure 224, D.)

Separation of silver from lead by cupellation has been practiced for more than 2,000 years and that of silver from copper was known long before Agricola's time. Four complicated processes were used in the Middle Ages to separate gold from silver.[9] Thus, with few tools and no mechanical power, the ancients found ways to reduce metallic ores and refine metals, although the quantities produced were necessarily small and the prices accordingly high.

5. This chapter follows the processing of nonferrous ores through smelting and refining, but considers iron ore only until it is shipped to blast furnaces. Because of the exceptional importance of iron and steel for the world's economy and the complexity of their production, they are discussed separately, in Chapter 29.

6. **36,** pp. 279 and 281.

7. **15,** pp. 385–86.
8. **36,** p. 354.
9. **36,** pp. 458, 465, 494.

A. Sifting Ore

A—Sieve. B—Its handles. C—Tub. D—Bottom of sieve made of iron wires. E—Hoop. F—Rods. G—Hoops. H—Woman shaking the sieve. I—Boy supplying it with material which requires washing. K—Man with shovel removing from the tub the material which has passed through the sieve.

B. Sorting Ore

A—Long table. B—Tray. C—Tub.

C. Washing Ore

A—Box. B—Perforated plate. C—Trough. D—Cross-boards. E—Pool. F—Launder. G—Shovel. H—Rake.

D. Smelting Ore

A, B, C—Three furnaces. At the first stands the smelter, who with a ladle pours the alloy out of the forehearth into the moulds. D—Forehearth. E—Ladle. F—Moulds. G—Round wooden rammer. H—Tapping-bar. At the second furnace stands the smelter, who opens the tap-hole with his tapping-bar. The assistant, standing on steps placed against the third furnace which has been broken open, chips off the accretions. I—Steps. K—Spatula. L—The other hooked bar. M—Mine captain carrying a cake, in which he has stuck the pick, to the scales to be weighed. N—Another mine captain opens a chest in which his things are kept.

FIGURE 224. MINING IN THE SIXTEENTH CENTURY: PROCESSING OF ORES

(GEORGIUS AGRICOLA)

Modern Techniques

In our time, both run-of-the-mine and concentrated ore are melted in blast or reverberatory furnaces. Molten metal settles at the bottom, and the slag, containing most of the impurities, is removed. Some ores undergo further processing. Thus "matte," an intermediate product in copper smelting with about 15–60 per cent metal, is put through converters to eliminate most of the remaining impurities and obtain "blister" copper, 96 or more per cent pure. Lead ore is roasted and smelted to bullion, which is tapped off and cast into pigs. Zinc is volatilized in retorts, condensed to liquid metal, drawn off, and cast into slabs.

Since smelter products still contain some extraneous materials, most of them are further refined, either by fire or electrolysis, to recover precious metals and remove the baser metals, lead and zinc. The cost of refining is usually less than the value of the precious metals recovered. Refining of blister copper yields gold, silver or lead and results in 99.9 per cent pure copper, used for electrical transmission. In the United States more than 95 per cent of the copper in raw materials other than scrap is refined. Lead bullion is refined to separate silver, and the purest grades of zinc, used mainly in die casting, are obtained through electrolysis.[10]

METALLIC MINERALS

The value of the world output of metallic minerals about equals that of nonmetallic minerals other than fuels: $5,355 million and $5,720 million, respectively, in 1949, at U.S. prices.[11] Metallic minerals represent a smaller share of the total if the costs of processing copper, lead, zinc, tin, aluminum and so on are excluded. However, the importance of metals in the economic life of industrialized countries exceeds the monetary value of the output.[12] They are, in fact, the basic raw materials for the industries that represent the foundation of our modern mechanized civilization and are vital for the munitions industries. Many important metallic minerals are highly concentrated geographically and play a prominent role in foreign trade and world politics.[13]

IRON ORE

The economic significance of iron ore mining stems less from the value of the ore itself than from the fact that this ore is a starting point for a long manufacturing process. The world's output of iron ore in 1949 was valued at $945 million, at U.S. prices, but the value of pig iron was $5.1 billion and that of steel, produced from pig iron with the addition of ferroalloys and scrap, was $12.8 billion.

Iron ores are found under different geological conditions, commonly along with silica, phosphorous, manganese, sulfur and other impurities. Iron is usually found in oxides, sulfides or other chemical compounds. Of the four most important iron ore minerals, three (magnetite, hematite, limonite) are oxides, and the fourth (siderite) is a carbonate. The maximum iron content of these four ores, in their pure form, varies from 48 per cent for siderite to 72 per cent for magnetite; because of impurities and water in the ores, however, the iron content seldom reaches these upper limits and may be as low as 27–28 per cent.

MAJOR DEPOSITS

While at least fifty countries mine iron ore, the world has only a few important deposits. (See Figure 225.)

The United States

The "ranges" of the Lake Superior region in Minnesota, Michigan and Wisconsin constitute the main source of iron ore (hematite) in the United States. The iron content of the ore averages 50 per cent. The largest deposits are in the Mesabi Range, which accounts for about eight tenths of the ore mined in the Lake Superior region during a year. Most of the ore in the ranges is mined from open cuts or shallow workings.

Next in importance is the Birmingham district in Alabama. Its ore is of lower grade (about 35 per cent iron content) but is self-fluxing.[14] Mining operations are underground throughout almost the entire district. Magnetite ore has been produced for many years in the Northeast (New

---

10. For a description of progress in smelting and refining as well as other processes of metal recovery, see **39**, pp. 126 ff.

11. See Table 325.

12. See Table 331.

13. See Table 327. The role of minerals in world trade

is discussed in detail by the authors in a study of world trade and government, now in preparation for the Twentieth Century Fund.

14. Self-fluxing ore does not require the addition of any substance, such as lime or fluorspar, to remove impurities and cause the metal to settle at the bottom of the furnace, from which it can then be drawn.

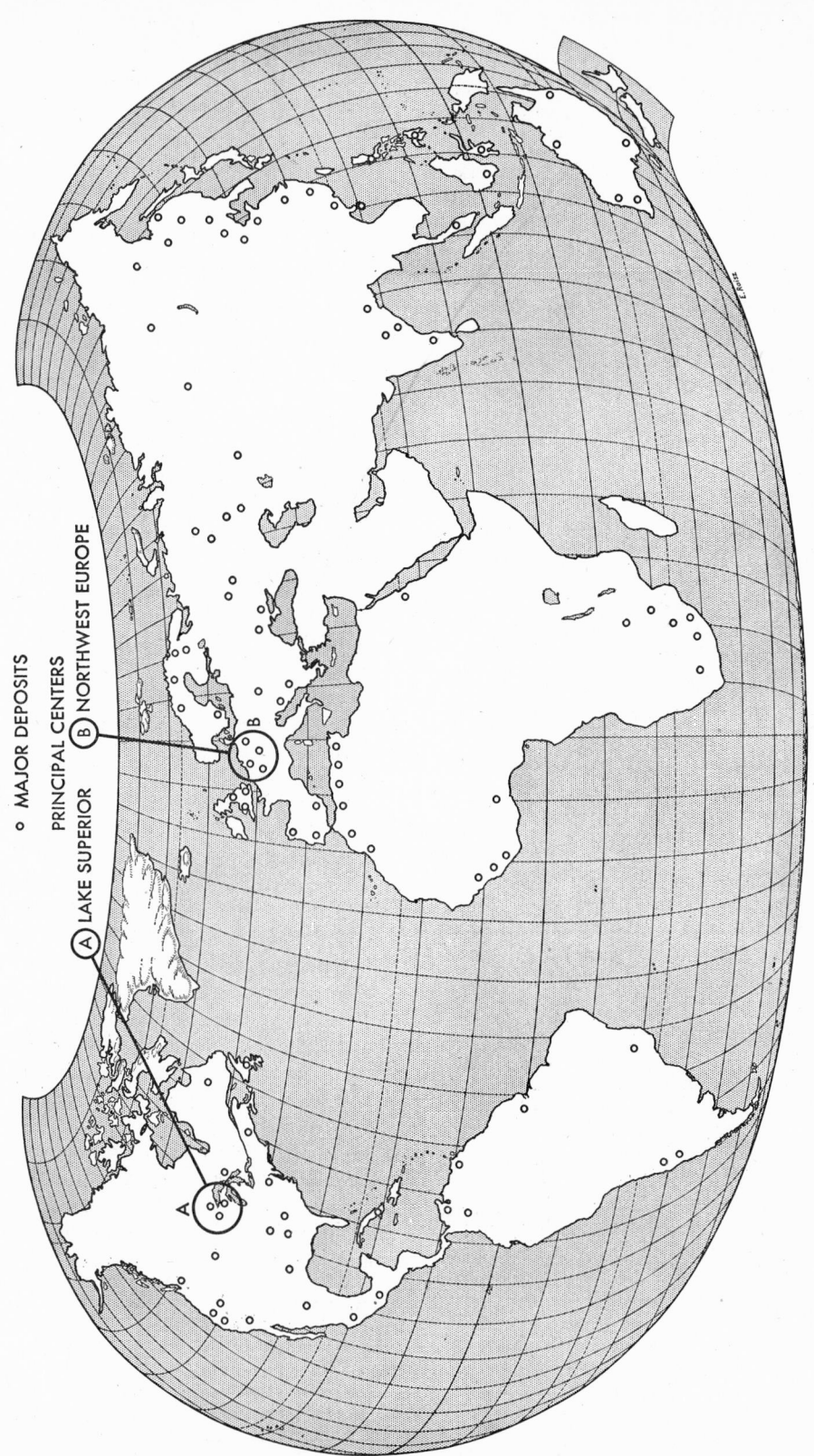

FIGURE 225. IRON ORE: GEOGRAPHIC DISTRIBUTION OF MAJOR DEPOSITS IN THE WORLD

Deposits of iron ore are scattered all over the globe, but the world's output of iron and steel comes mainly from a few large deposits, chiefly in North America and western Europe.

York, New Jersey and eastern Pennsylvania), and small deposits are worked in many other states.

Other American Countries

Canada developed deposits of high-grade hematite ore at Steep Rock, Ontario, during World War II. Recently, intensive drilling has disclosed large deposits (of 68 per cent iron content, on the average) at Sawyer Lake, Labrador. The Wabana district in Newfoundland has ore with 44 per cent iron content, but this ore is also high in phosphorus. The beds are uniform in thickness and quality and advantageously located close to a harbor that permits entrance of ocean-going ships. The deposits extend under the sea. In one mine that extends more than two miles under Conception Bay, the ore deposit is covered by 600 feet of water and 1,500 feet of rock.

Cuba possesses very large deposits of iron ore in the northeast. Some ores have as much as 50 per cent iron and a high alumina content; others, of somewhat lower grade, contain chromium, nickel or cobalt.

Venezuela possesses large deposits of hematite ore near Pao, on the Orinoco River. Commercial exploitation, just beginning, is controlled by the Bethlehem Steel Corporation. A new deposit of high-grade ore, Cerro Bolivar, was discovered in Venezuela in 1950 by the U.S. Steel Corporation, which obtained a 99-year concession for its exploitation. Estimates of the amount of iron ore contained in this deposit range from more than half a billion tons to more than a billion.[15]

In Chile, deposits of almost pure hematite ore, mined by open-quarry methods, are near the port of Coquimbo.

Brazil has very extensive deposits of high-grade iron ore (iron content 65 per cent) in its central province, Minas Gerais. There are no facilities for shipping, however, and the region lacks coking coal. As a result, these large reserves remain almost untouched and are of little present economic importance to the world or Brazil itself. C. K. Leith considers them the largest world reserve of high-grade hematite ore discovered to date.[16]

Rich deposits of ore with 67 per cent iron content have been discovered in the Dominican Republic. In Argentina, exploration has begun of deposits near Sierra Grande (Territory of Río Negro), which are reported to be extensive and rich.[17]

Europe

Only Ireland, Switzerland and Denmark lack domestic sources of iron. Deposits stretch from the United Kingdom to Greece, with the most important in the United Kingdom, France and Sweden. (See Figure 226.)

France has very large deposits of low-grade iron ore, the so-called "minette," in Lorraine. The ore contains only 30–35 per cent iron and is high in phosphorus but self-fluxing. Minette is suitable for the basic Bessemer steel.[18] These deposits extend into Luxembourg and Germany. French iron ore deposits in Normandy, Brittany and Anjou in the west and in the Pyrenees in the south are much smaller, but the ore is richer, some beds yielding ore with iron content of 60 per cent.

Great Britain has large deposits — in Europe second only to those of France — but the iron content of the ore is even lower, under 30 per cent. The deposits located in the southwest extend to the English Channel. The famous deposits of high-grade ores in Cumberland and Lancaster have been depleted and supply only about 5 per cent of the national output.

Sweden has extensive deposits of iron ore in the north. The metal content averages 62 per cent, but higher grades are often obtained. The most important deposit is at Kiruna; those at Gällivare and Tuolluvarra are next in line. Two types of ore are mined, the one containing titanium and vanadium and low in phosphorus, the other highly phosphoric.

Germany's two largest deposits are in Siegenland and Peine-Salzgitter, both in Western Germany. The ore of the first contains 35 per cent iron and when roasted yields 48 per cent iron and 8 per cent manganese. The Salzgitter ore is highly phosphoric, with about 30 per cent iron. The Lahn-Dill district, with deposits of slightly higher-grade ores, is also important.

Spain has high-grade ores in the Bilbao deposit.

The USSR

The Krivoi Rog deposits of high-grade ores (up to 68 per cent iron content) resemble those

---

15. **32,** p. 22; **60,** p. 190; **18,** 1949, p. 629.
16. **57,** p. 97.

17. **18,** 1949, pp. 626–27.
18. See Chapter 29.

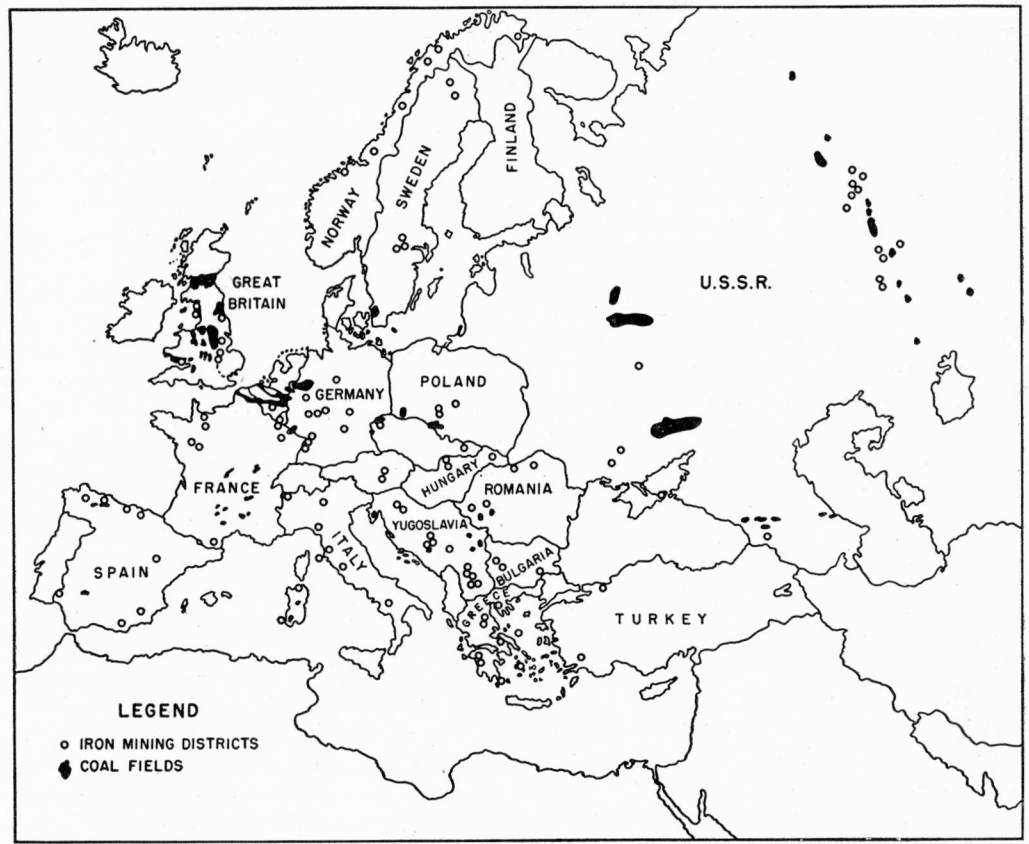

FIGURE 226. IRON ORE: GEOGRAPHIC DISTRIBUTION OF MAJOR MINING DISTRICTS AND COAL FIELDS IN EUROPE AND THE EUROPEAN USSR

This map, originally prepared by C. W. Wright for the U.S. Bureau of Mines in 1939, has been somewhat simplified here and modified to show the postwar boundaries.

of the Lake Superior region in importance but lack their uniformity in grade and extent. Mining operations are underground. In the Urals, the USSR has large deposits of magnetite, the chief range being the Magnitnaya mountain. Discovery of new deposits in Siberia and the Caucasus has been reported. It is claimed that the mineral zone in the Nizhne-Angarski district, extending over more than 2,000 square miles along the lower reaches of the Angara River, contains large veins of high-grade hematite ore.

Asia

India possesses very extensive deposits of ore with 60 per cent metal content, on the average, and only insignificant percentages of sulfur and phosphorus. The reserves, located in the iron ranges of the Central Provinces, may be as great as those of the Lake Superior region. Other de-

posits, to the southwest of Calcutta — in Orissa, Mysore and Madras — are also important.

China's most extensive deposits are in Chihli and Manchuria. The best Chinese ores, containing 56 per cent iron, are found along the lower Yangtze Valley.[19]

The Philippines and Indonesia also have considerable deposits of iron ore. (See Figure 227.)

Africa

The deposits of the Union of South Africa, concentrated in the province of Transvaal, have an iron content of 49–54 per cent. Recently discovered iron ore deposits in Southern Rhodesia are considered the largest in Africa. Liberia's deposits are considerable and contain mostly ore of open-hearth grade. Open-pit operations are

19. **5**, 1949, p. 345.

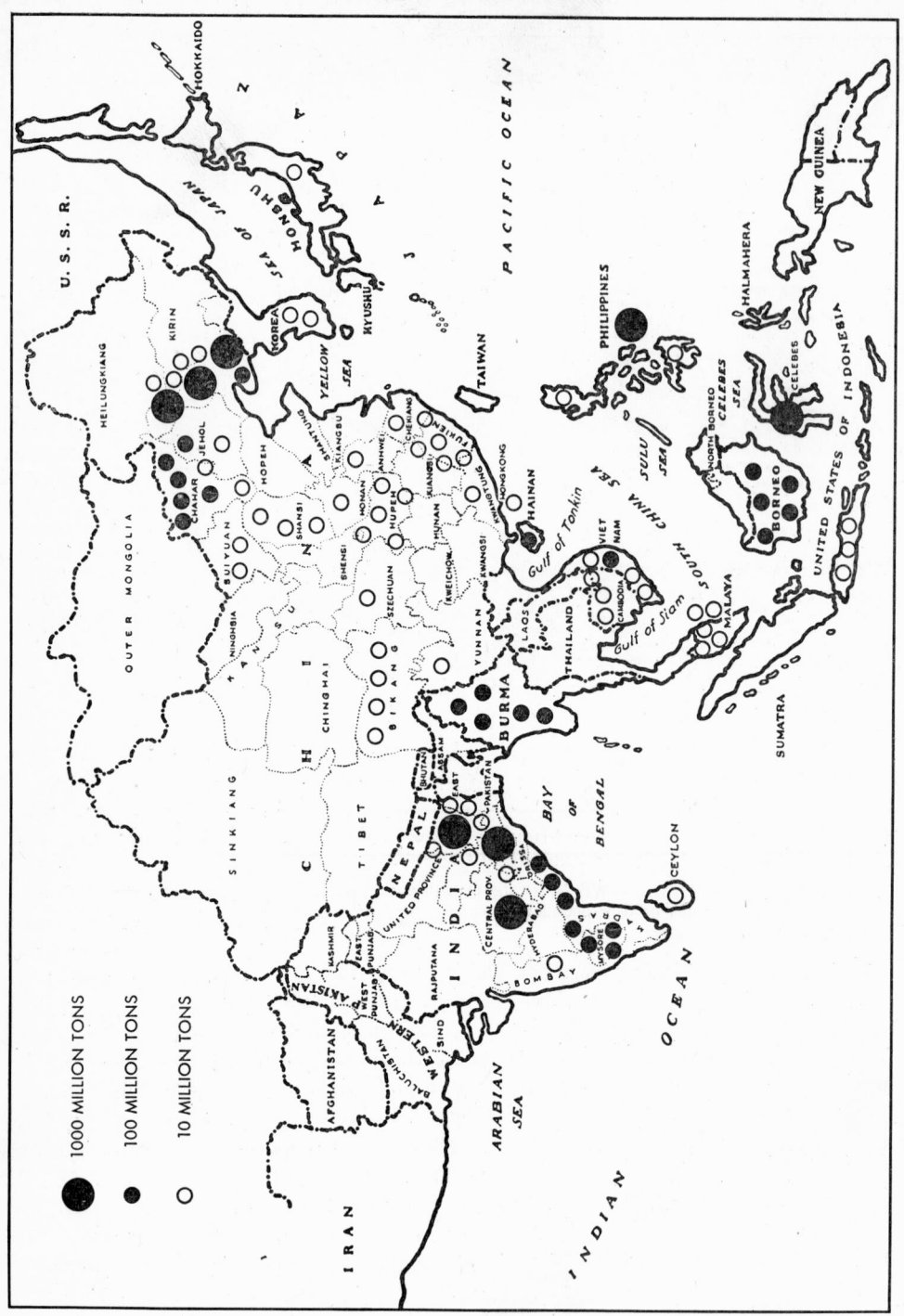

United Nations, Economic Commission for Asia and the Far East

Figure 227. Iron Ore: Geographic Distribution of Known Reserves in Asia and the Far East

(Redrawn and simplified from the original map)

TABLE 332

IRON ORE: RESERVES IN THE WORLD AND EACH CONTINENT

(*Billions of Metric Tons* [a])

Continent	H. M. Mikami, 1944			United Nations, 1950 [c]		
	Total	*Actual* [b]	*Other*	*Total (Potential)*	*Probable*	*Other*
World	200.0	35.2	164.9	293.4	53.9	239.5
North America	84.2	5.2	79.0	75.2	5.7	69.5
Middle and South America	31.5	7.4	24.1	36.3	10.1	26.2
Europe	30.6	11.6	19.0	25.1	13.7	11.4
USSR	21.9	4.5	17.4	10.9	4.5	6.4
Asia	18.2	4.9	13.3	26.1	12.4	13.7
Africa	13.2	1.2	12.0	119.4	7.3	112.1
Australia	0.5	0.4	0.1	0.4	0.2	0.2

Sources: **4**, pp. 66–68, and **64**, pp. 22–23.

a. Conversion factor: one metric ton = 1.1023 short tons.

b. "Actual" reserves are those which because of size, content, composition and location constitute an economically available source of iron ore. Other (potential) reserves, as classified in this estimate, are those which cannot be exploited economically at present.

c. Total (potential) reserves include: (1) "probable" reserves, for which a reliable calculation of the extent of the deposits, based on actual investigation, has been carried out, and (2) other deposits, for which only an approximation could be carried out.

carried out on an ore face outcropping a hundred and fifty feet high and half a mile long.[20]

RESERVES

In the World and Each Continent

Until recently H. M. Mikami's estimate of the world's reserves of iron ore, issued in 1944, was the most widely accepted. According to Mikami, the reserves total 200 billion tons, of which only 35 billion represent "actual" reserves, that is, an economically available source.[21] The rest is in "potential" deposits that cannot be exploited profitably at present. The potential deposits of North America are the largest in the world, but the actual deposits of Europe and Latin America are considerably more important.

In 1950 the United Nations published its estimate of 293 billion tons for total (or potential) world reserves. This includes 54 billion tons in "probable" reserves, "for which a reliable calculation of the extent of the deposits, based on actual investigation has been carried out," and

239 billion tons in "other deposits for which an approximate estimate could be carried out." [22]

According to this latest estimate, Africa has the largest total (potential) reserves of iron ore (119 billion tons). The next largest reserves (75 billion tons) are in North America. Except for Oceania, which is almost completely without iron ore, the USSR, with about 11 billion tons, has smaller potential reserves than any of the continents. (See Table 332 and Figure 228.) Europe and Asia have about the same total reserves — 25 and 26 billion tons, respectively; Latin America has more, about 36 billion tons.

The amount of ore in the deposits must be evaluated in terms of the iron (Fe) content. Ore with a low iron content may not be economical to extract and thus may remain useless in the earth while high-grade ore is hauled for processing from another country or even another continent. In fact, the United Kingdom imports high-grade iron ore from Chile and Newfoundland, and the United States obtains small quantities from Sweden and is preparing to transport ore from Venezuela and Liberia. On the other hand, some grades of ore that are utilized in the

---

20. **18**, 1949, p. 628. The Republic Steel Corporation bought an interest in the Liberian Mining Company, and additional financial aid has been provided to Liberia by the Export-Import Bank of Washington.

21. **64**, pp. 22–23.

22. **4**, p. 67.

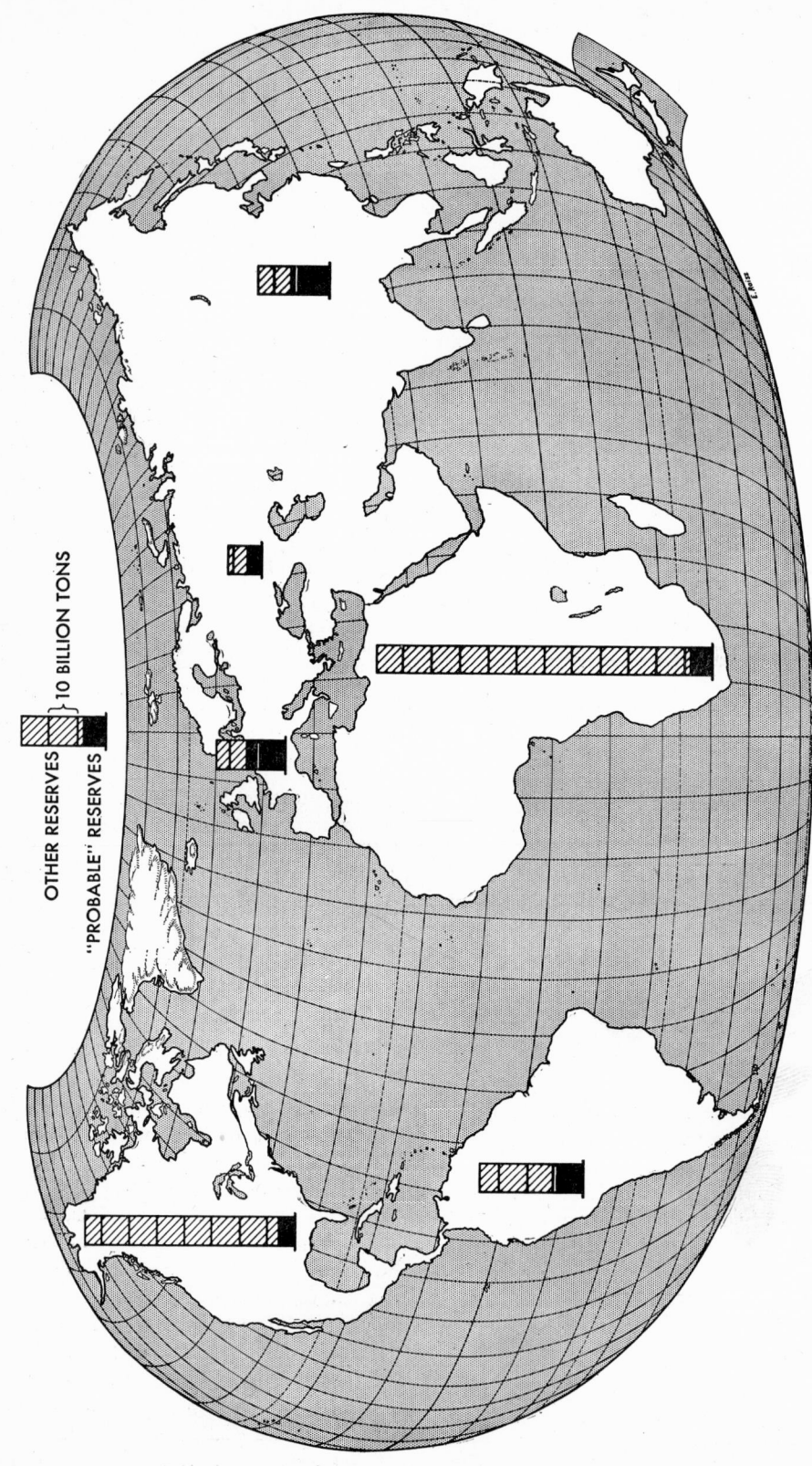

OTHER RESERVES
"PROBABLE" RESERVES } 10 BILLION TONS

FIGURE 228. IRON ORE: RESERVES IN EACH CONTINENT
(As estimated by the United Nations, 1950)

Source: Table 332

TABLE 333

IRON ORE: RESERVES IN SELECTED COUNTRIES

(As Estimated by the United Nations, 1950)

Country	Iron Ore Reserves, in Millions of Metric Tons [a]		Average Iron Content of Ore (Per Cent)		Approximate Iron Content of Reserves, in Millions of Metric Tons [a]	
	Total [b]	Probable	Total [b]	Probable	Total [b]	Probable
United States [c]	70,800	3,800	36	45	25,488	1,710
Canada [d]	4,355	1,937	51	48	2,221	930
Cuba	15,000	3,000	36	40	5,400	1,200
Venezuela [d]	960	360	51	60	490	216
Brazil	19,650	6,300	55	65	10,807	4,095
United Kingdom	3,400	2,400	27	28	918	672
France	10,500	6,700	37	38	3,876	2,546
Sweden	2,500	2,200	64	64	1,600	1,408
Norway [e]	2,170	170	34	48	738	82
Germany	2,800	800	30	32	840	256
Spain	1,800	800	35	45	630	360
USSR [f]	10,862	4,504	40	45	4,345	2,027
China [g]	2,700	1,800	45	45	1,215	810
India [e]	20,320	9,347	51	60	10,272	5,608
Indonesia	1,500	100	48	49	720	49
Philippines	1,016	1,016	47	47	478	478
French West Africa	2,030	2,000	50	50	1,015	1,000
Southern Rhodesia	105,564	2,240	48	51	50,671	1,142
Union of South Africa	10,828	2,712	47	47	5,089	1,275
Other countries	4,636	1,732	...	...	2,030	855

Source: **4**, pp. 66–68.

a. Conversion factor: one metric ton = 1.1023 short tons.
b. See the definitions of total (potential) and probable reserves as used by the UN, p. 781.
c. The combined estimate of the U.S. Bureau of Mines and the U.S. Geological Survey (**42**, p. 118) is close to those given here: total reserves, 68,396 million tons; potential, 62,915 million; measured and indicated, 3,726 million; inferred, 1,755 million. The latest estimate of the U.S. Geological Survey, for January 1951, evaluates United States total reserves at 67,350 million

tons, of which 6,436 million are of a "commercial" nature (usable under present economic and technological conditions) and the rest of a "submarginal" character, which may become usable under future conditions. (**18**, 1949, p. 605.)
d. Recent discoveries of iron ore deposits are not fully represented.
e. Official estimate, conservative in comparison with estimates by other sources.
f. Ferruginous quartzites, of 25 to 35 per cent iron content, at Kursk and Krivoi Rog not included.
g. Estimates of China's iron ore reserves differ widely.

United Kingdom are not even counted in the estimates of United States reserves.[23]

The metallic content of the world's total reserves, according to the United Nations, is estimated at 128.8 billion tons, of which Africa has 57.2 billion and North America, 27.7 billion. Europe has twice as much iron in its deposits as the USSR. (See Table 333.)

In Selected Countries

Eight countries — the United States, Cuba, Brazil, France, the USSR, India, Southern

Rhodesia and the Union of South Africa — hold about 90 per cent of the world's total reserves of iron ore. The United States and Southern Rhodesia together account for 60 per cent (24 and 36 per cent, respectively). The probable reserves of these two countries are, however, comparatively small — 3.8 billion tons in the United States and 2.2 billion tons in Southern Rhodesia.

In terms of probable reserves, as defined by the United Nations, India ranks first, followed by France, Brazil, the USSR, the United States, Cuba, the Union of South Africa and the United Kingdom. These eight countries together account for about 72 per cent of the world's total.

23. **4**, p. 12.

The metallic content of the probable reserves in the United States amounts to 1.7 billion tons, in Brazil to 4.1 billion tons, in India to 5.6 billion, in France to 2.5 billion and in the USSR to 2 billion.

Southern Rhodesia is believed to have twice as much iron in its total reserves as the United States, five times as much as India, and nearly twelve times as much as the USSR. (See Table 333.)

Reserves per Capita

The iron content of reserves per capita of population is, obviously, largest in sparsely populated areas with vast ore reserves. Thus an inhabitant of Southern Rhodesia has much more iron in his country's deposits than people in any other country on earth, though he has hardly ever had a piece of iron in his hands. For Africa as a whole, the per capita iron content in probable reserves is estimated at 18.6 tons, in potential reserves at 295.2 tons; for North America, at 16.5 tons and 173.3 tons, respectively. Asia has the smallest amount — 5.6 tons and 10.3 tons, respectively.

In terms of iron content, the highly industrialized and densely populated United Kingdom has 13.4 tons per capita in probable reserves, and Germany only 3.8 tons. The USSR has 10.5 tons per capita, the United States 11.7 tons, as against 193.1 tons per capita in Luxembourg and 232.6 tons in Cuba. These and other countries rank as follows in number of metric tons per capita:[24]

	Probable Reserves	Total (Potential) Reserves
Southern Rhodesia	576.8	25,591.0
Cuba	232.6	1,046.5
Sweden	204.6	232.6
Luxembourg	193.1	269.0
Union of South Africa	107.2	428.0
Brazil	84.5	223.0
Canada	70.4	168.1
French West Africa	63.0	63.0
France	61.3	93.4
Venezuela	48.1	109.1
Sierra Leone	29.0	29.0
Norway	25.8	232.1
Philippines	24.0	24.0
Australia	16.3	25.7
India	16.1	30.0
Spanish Morocco	14.0	14.0
United Kingdom	13.4	18.3
Spain	13.0	22.7
United States	11.7	173.9
USSR	10.5	22.5
Germany	3.8	12.3
China	1.7	2.6
Italy	0.7	0.7

Depletion of Reserves

While Southern Rhodesia has not yet begun to exploit its iron ore reserves, and Brazil and India have barely touched theirs, the United States and the United Kingdom are extracting a sizable slice of their higher-grade deposits each year. Some of the best deposits in the United Kingdom have already been exhausted.

The United States, facing the same danger,[25] has recently begun to stretch the supply of the best ores through beneficiation of lower grades, that is, preparation for smelting by concentration or other methods. Plants for this purpose have been erected at many deposits, including the Mesabi Range. Efforts are being made to utilize, by concentration, the large reserves of taconite, a mixture of magnetite and hematite ores with a high proportion of impurities. The complex technical problems have not yet been fully solved, however. The large steel companies are making intensive efforts to secure rights to the exploitation of iron ore deposits in foreign countries, as in the concessions obtained by the U.S. Steel Corporation and the Bethlehem Steel Corporation affecting vast deposits in Venezuela.[26]

OUTPUT

Since iron and steel are used mainly in construction and in the production of machinery, transportation equipment and munitions, demand for iron ore varies sharply with the business cycle and the state of world affairs. Apart from the long-range upward trend, output rises during prosperity and wars and drops during economic slumps and in peacetime.

From 30 million tons in the early 1870's, the world's annual output of iron ore rose to 90 million tons by the end of the century. It averaged 150 million tons a year during World War I, dropped to less than half that figure in

24. **4**, pp. 66–67.

25. For example, an important mine in the Lake Superior area (in the Menominee Range) was exhausted and closed in 1945, after having produced continuously since 1887. **18**, 1945, p. 560.
26. **4**, p. 29, and **60**, p. 190. See p. 778.

TABLE 334

IRON ORE: OUTPUT IN SELECTED COUNTRIES, 1880–1950

(*Millions of Metric Tons* [a])

Country	1880	1890	1900	1913	1918	1929	1934	1939	1944	1949	1950
World	44.0	58.0	92.0	178.0	127.0	203.0	121.0	204.0	203.0	218.0	245.0
United States	7.2	16.3	28.0	63.0	70.8	75.5	25.0	52.6	94.6	86.3	99.7
Canada	—	0.1	0.1	0.3	0.2	b	b	0.1	0.5	}3.4	3.3
Newfoundland	—	b	0.3	1.5	0.8	1.5	0.5	1.7	0.5		
Brazil	—	—	—	—	—	b	b	0.4	0.7	1.6	1.9
Chile	—	—	—	—	—	1.8	1.0	1.6	0.7	2.6	3.3
United Kingdom	18.3	14.0	14.3	16.3	14.8	13.4	10.8	14.7	15.7	13.6	13.2
France	2.9	3.5	5.4	21.9	1.7	50.7	32.0	36.1	9.4	31.0	30.0
Luxembourg [e]	—	—	—	—	3.1	7.6	3.8	5.1	2.9	4.1	3.8
Sweden	0.8	0.9	2.6	7.5	6.6	11.5	5.3	15.2	7.3	14.0	13.9
Norway	b	b	b	0.5	0.1	0.7	0.5	1.5	0.3	0.4	0.4
Germany [d]	7.2	11.4	19.0	35.9	18.4	6.4	4.3	12.1	10.3	9.1	10.9
Czechoslovakia	—	—	—	—	e	1.8	0.5	1.4	0.5	1.4	1.4
Austria [f]	1.1	2.2	3.7	5.3	1.2 [g]	1.9	0.5	2.9	3.0	1.5	1.9
Spain	3.6	6.1	8.7	9.9	4.7	6.6	2.1	3.5	1.5	1.8	2.1
Russia (USSR)	1.0	1.8	6.1	9.5	—	7.2	21.8	30.9	16.0	22.5 [h]	...
Korea	—	—	—	0.1	0.2	0.6	0.6	1.0	3.4	e	e
India	—	—	0.1	0.4	0.5	2.5	1.9	3.2	2.4	2.3 [h]	3.0
Spanish Morocco	—	—	—	—	—	1.1	0.8	1.0	0.7	0.9	0.9
Algeria	0.6	0.5	0.6	1.3	0.9	2.4	1.3	2.9	0.8	2.5	2.6
Union of South Africa	—	—	—	—	—	b	0.2	0.5	0.8	1.2	1.2
Australia	—	—	b	0.2	0.4	0.9	1.3	2.7	2.2	0.8	...

Sources: **49**, p. 249; **25**, 1920, Part I, p. 382, and 1926, Part I, p. 108; **18**, various years; **17**, August 1950, p. 18, and April 1951, *passim*.

a. Conversion factor: one metric ton = 1.1023 short tons.
b. Output negligible.
c. Included in output of Germany until 1918. Output (in millions of tons) in 1880, 2.2; 1890, 3.4; 1900, 6.2; 1913, 6.6.

d. Includes eastern Upper Silesia in 1944; for 1949 and 1950, Western Germany.
e. Data not available; estimate of the U.S. Bureau of Mines included in the total.
f. Until 1918, Austria-Hungary.
g. Boundaries after World War I.
h. 1948.

1921, rose again to more than 200 million tons in 1929, and dropped back, under the impact of the depression, to a low of 76 million tons in 1932. Subsequent changes have been brought about primarily by political factors — the approach, course and aftermath of World War II. The world's output of iron ore was slightly higher in 1939 than in 1929, rose 20 per cent by 1942, had fallen considerably by the end of the war, and declined further in 1946. Since then the trend has been upward, and output in 1950 was about 20 per cent above the prewar level. (See Table 334 and Figure 229.)

Fluctuations in the output of iron ore in the United States have been most spectacular. From 77 million tons during World War I, the volume dropped to 30 million tons in 1921, rose to 75.5 million in 1929 and shrank in 1932 to 10 million tons, the lowest point since 1886. During the recession in 1938, output fell from the 1937 level of 73 million tons to 28 million tons. In 1942–43, the annual output skyrocketed to more than 100 million tons. It declined again before the end of the war but has risen subsequently. Output of iron ore in the United States has varied as follows in comparison with

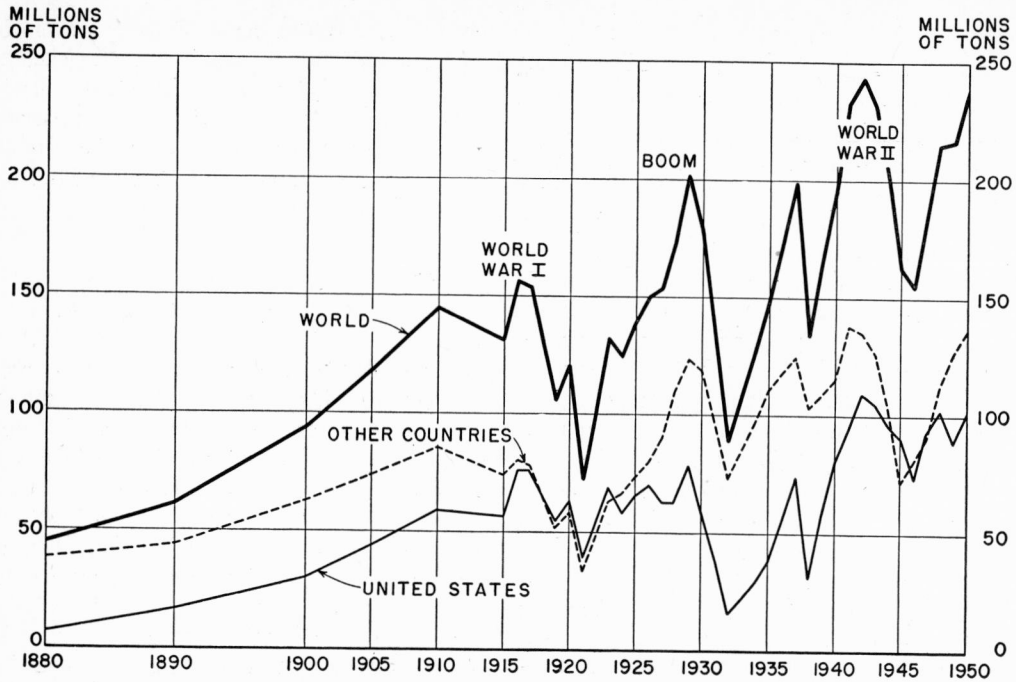

FIGURE 229. IRON ORE: OUTPUT IN THE WORLD AND THE UNITED STATES, 1880–1950

Production of iron ore fluctuates sharply with changes in business conditions. Output increased during World War I, dropped after the Armistice, reached a new peak during the boom in 1929, declined by more than half during the depression, skyrocketed with economic recovery, suffered a new setback in the recession of 1938, broke all previous records in the early years of World War II, went down in the later war years after the basic armament of the Allied armed forces had been completed, and has been increasing since 1946.

world output (figures in millions of metric tons):[27]

	World	United States	
		Total	Per Cent
1871	30.7	3.4	11.1
1900	91.8	28.0	30.5
1917	(148.0)	76.8	(51.9)
1921	68.0	29.8	43.8
1929	202.6	75.5	37.3
1932	76.2	10.0	13.1
1936	170.0	48.8	28.7
1938	167.0	28.4	17.0
1942	245.0	107.2	43.8
1944	203.0	94.6	46.6
1948	216.0	102.6	47.0
1949	218.0	86.3	39.6
1950	245.0	99.7	40.7

Until World War I, the United States, the United Kingdom, Germany, France, Sweden and Russia together controlled, with occasional variations, more than eight tenths of the world's output of iron ore.

27. **75,** pp. 167–68; **18,** various years.

Since 1890 the United States has led except during the years 1931–35 and 1938. The United Kingdom, second to the United States until the turn of the century, now ranks after France and the USSR and competes with Sweden for fourth place. Germany, when in possesssion of Lorraine and Luxembourg, had a growing production, in 1913 almost equaling the combined output of the United Kingdom and France. With the loss of these sources after World War I, Germany's output declined considerably and was about a third that of France on the eve of World War II. France came into prominence after World War I, with the return of Lorraine. Sweden began to expand its output after the turn of the century and increased its exports to Germany, the United Kingdom and France. Russia's production fell after World War I and remained low until the 1930's. Just before World War II, the USSR held third place. Spain, an important producer of high-grade ore at the beginning of the century, now mines relatively little. (See Table 334.)

FERROALLOYS

Ferroalloying ores are used to make special metals, ferroalloys, which are added to carbon steel in order to improve its properties — malleability, hardness, toughness, resistance to corrosion and abrasion — for special uses. Each alloying metal has distinct properties and imparts specific properties to the steel. The chief alloying elements are manganese, chromium, nickel, tungsten, molybdenum, cobalt and vanadium; silicon and phosphorus are also used for certain steels. Some "additive" alloys, such as boron, zirconium, titanium and tantalum, are used in minute quantities to lower the requirements for a major alloying element.

Manganese occupies a unique position among the alloys in that it is indispensable in the production of any steel, regardless of type, and there is no adequate substitute for it. Its main task is to remove oxygen and sulfur. From 13 to 14 pounds of manganese per short ton of steel, on the average, is considered standard. Addition of large quantities of manganese increases the resistance of steel to abrasion.

Chromium, when added to steel in small quantities, contributes strength, resistance to wear, and "hardenability";[28] in large quantities, it gives resistance to corrosion and oxidation. Nickel increases tensile strength and, if used in large amounts, resistance to corrosion. Tungsten makes steel hard, even at red heat, and is a strong carbide-forming agent. Molybdenum improves the strength of steel. Cobalt is unique in cementing tungsten carbide. Vanadium makes steel tough and resistant to repeated shocks, controls the grain size, and, as a carbide-forming agent, increases hardness and toughness. It is also an intensive deoxidizer and an excellent catalyst.

Nearly every alloying metal has uses aside from steel-making. Manganese of high purity is essential for dry-cell batteries; tungsten, for the manufacture of filaments for electric bulbs, radio and X-ray tubes, and for cross hairs in telescopes; cobalt, for magnets and as a catalyst; chromium, as a refractory for furnace linings and in the chemical industry.

MAJOR DEPOSITS

Ferroalloying ores are very unevenly distributed in the world. Some of them are practically limited to a single area, as nickel to Canada or molybdenum to the United States. Some others are found mainly in industrially underdeveloped regions far from the world's steel-making centers and are mined exclusively for export. (See Figure 230.)

Manganese

The USSR and India have large reserves of manganese ore. The reserves of the USSR are estimated at 650 million tons, of which those in Nikopol (Ukraine) represent 390 million tons and those at Chiatura (Georgia) 160 million.[29] The Nikopol ore has about 30 per cent manganese content and after concentration 40–50 per cent; the Chiatura ore, with 40 per cent manganese content, is enriched through concentration to 44–52 per cent. Manganese deposits in India have, on the average, 50 per cent manganese content. The reserves are estimated at 100 million tons of ferro-grade ore and 200 million tons of ore of lower quality.[30]

The vast reserves of manganese ore northwest of Kimberley in the Union of South Africa are roughly estimated at a billion tons. The Nsuta mine on the Gold Coast is considered the largest single manganese deposit in the world. The ore, of high grade, crops out on a ridge for two and a half miles and is mined by open-cut methods. Other manganiferous rocks are spread through an area of six hundred miles but are of uncertain grade and not exploited.[31]

In the Western Hemisphere, Brazil is outstanding for its manganese deposits of high-grade ore, of which the chief are in the states of Minas Gerais, Baía and Mato Grosso and the Territory of Amapá. The Urucum deposit in Mato Grosso is estimated to contain more than 33 million tons of manganese ore averaging 45.6 per cent manganese and is exploited by the United States Steel Corporation. The reserves in the Amapá deposit have been estimated at 7.4 million tons, but latest indications are that they may be much greater. The manganese content averages 48.4 per cent, and the deposit

---

28. "Hardenability" is the ability of steel to harden deeply, when heat treated, by quenching and tempering.

29. **47**, 1948, p. 445. According to Russian sources, the Nikopol reserves, including inferred reserves, amount to 522 million tons; those of Chiatura, to 175 million. **40**, p. 252.

30. **27**, Vol. I, p. 99.

31. **41**, p. 581, and **18**, 1949, p. 757.

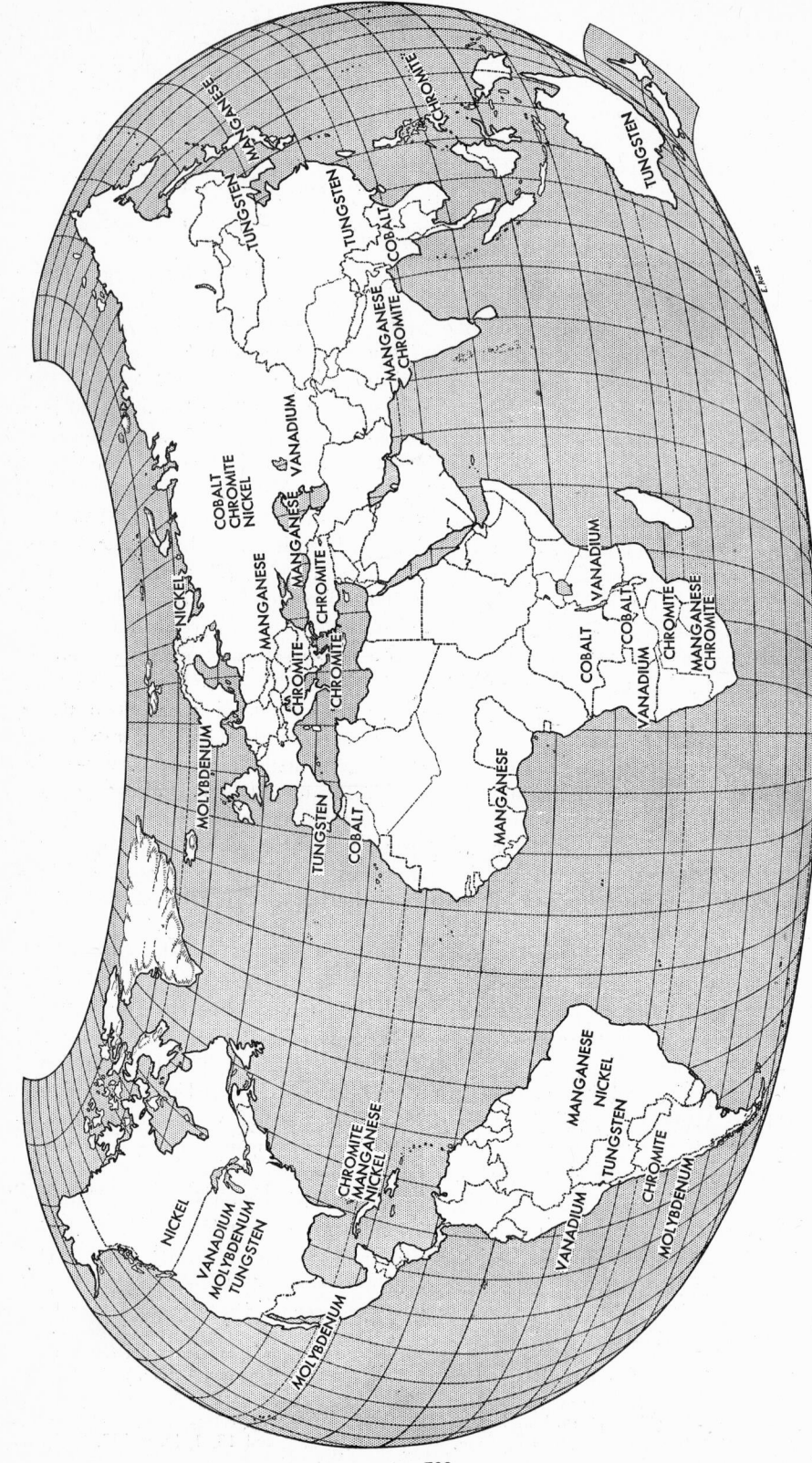

FIGURE 230. FERROALLOYING ORES: GEOGRAPHIC DISTRIBUTION OF MAJOR DEPOSITS IN THE WORLD

is under development by the Bethlehem Steel Corporation.[32] Cuba has many small deposits, and in 1951 Peru and Venezuela reported the discovery of manganese. The United States has almost exhausted its small deposits of high-grade manganese. The large deposits of low-grade ores were mined during both world wars, but peacetime exploitation, with present technology, is not economical, since the ore cannot compete with foreign ore in price.

Chromite

The chief deposits of chromite are in Turkey, the USSR, New Caledonia (with exceptionally high-grade ores), Southern Rhodesia and the Union of South Africa. Next in importance are the deposits in India, Chile, the Philippines, Yugoslavia and Greece. The United States has no reserves of refractory-grade chromite and has only negligible deposits of metallurgical grade, in the West. Large deposits of low-grade ores in the United States have been worked, like domestic manganese deposits, mostly under emergency conditions; their exploitation is unprofitable in peacetime. The USSR has deposits in the Urals (Saranovskaya and Donskoye); the grade is low, 32–35 per cent metal content.

Nickel

Sudbury, Canada, is the world's chief source of nickel. Reserves are estimated at more than 200 million tons of ore, containing 2–3 per cent metal. New Caledonia has high-grade nickel deposits (3.8 per cent metal content) throughout the island. In the 1930's, the USSR discovered rather extensive low-grade deposits in the Urals, and it also has nickel reserves in the vicinity of apatite deposits on the Kola Peninsula. Finland's deposits at Petsamo were ceded to the USSR in 1944. Brazil has large deposits of high-grade ores (12–13 per cent metal content) in the state of Goiaz, about 1,600 km. from the coast, and smaller but better located deposits in Minas Gerais. Cuba, the Philippines and Celebes also possess some nickel deposits. The nickel deposits in the United States are of such low grade that they were not utilized even during World War II.

Tungsten

Tungsten deposits are concentrated in China,

Burma, Korea and the Malay States. The United States, Bolivia, Argentina, Spain, Portugal and Australia also have deposits. All the tungsten deposits recently discovered in the USSR are in Siberia. During World War II, an important tungsten deposit was found in northeastern Brazil, and France has reported the discovery of a promising deposit.

Molybdenum

The world's greatest known deposit of molybdenum is at Climax, Colorado, at an altitude of more than 11,000 feet. Molybdenum is also recovered from copper ore in Utah and New Mexico; Nevada has a small deposit. Canada, Mexico, Chile, Norway and Australia have minor deposits. In 1944 the USSR reported the discovery of a deposit in the Caucasus, near Nalchik, and Yugoslavia was to begin operation of a molybdenum mine in 1951. Molybdenum deposits have also been found in Sweden.

Cobalt

The world's most extensive deposit of cobalt is in the Belgian Congo (Katanga); that in Northern Rhodesia is next in importance. Burma and French Morocco also have cobalt-bearing deposits. The Canadian deposits are nearly depleted. The USSR reports pure cobalt deposits in the Urals, Kazakhstan and the Transcaucasus.

Vanadium

The chief vanadium deposits are in Peru (at the Minas Ragra mine, owned by the American Vanadium Corporation), southwestern Africa and Northern Rhodesia. The USSR recently reported the discovery of vanadium-bearing ores in Kazakhstan. In the United States, the phosphate beds of Idaho and Wyoming contain vanadium, and low-grade vanadium is recovered from sandstone in Colorado, Utah, Arizona and New Mexico. Vanadium is also obtained in Venezuela from the smokestacks of tankers on Lake Maracaibo, and from the boilers of power plants using fuel oil.

OUTPUT OF FERROALLOYING ORES

In 1929, 70 per cent of the world's manganese was produced by the USSR, India and the Gold Coast. The League of Nations estimated the

---

32. **18**, 1949, p. 756.

USSR's output in 1938 at 1.2 million tons.[33] While data for later years are lacking, it is certain that the USSR is by far the most important producer and the only large steel-producing country that is self-sufficient in manganese. There is no way of telling, however, how the vast output is used. Exports are comparatively small, and the iron and steel industry of the USSR, with an output of 25–30 million tons a year, cannot possibly consume half the world's manganese, even if losses during concentration of the ore are high.[34] According to the U.S. Bureau of Mines, Russia uses manganese for alloying purposes to a far greater extent than does the United States and may also stockpile it at steel centers east of the Urals. The offering of Russian ferromanganese on the European market has been reported.[35]

India was the largest exporter of manganese in prewar years, but its output has declined, from 505,000 tons in 1929 to 429,000 in 1939 and 386,000 tons in 1950. In contrast, the Gold Coast, now the ranking exporter, and the Union of South Africa have increased output considerably. (See Table 335.)

The world's supply of tungsten came chiefly from China, Burma and the United States in prewar years. China supplied 237,252 metric tons of tungsten, or 28 per cent of the world's total output (almost 847,000 tons), during the forty-four years 1905–48, despite the fact that it started producing only in 1914. The United States and Burma each accounted for about 13 per cent, and Bolivia, Portugal and Korea together for 22 per cent. The remainder came from small workings in many countries.[36]

In the United States, California, Nevada and North Carolina are the most important producers.

The Union of South Africa, **Turkey** and Southern Rhodesia together accounted for 70 or more per cent of the world's output of chromium. The Union of South Africa, with a steadily increasing output, is the only producer of chromium of acceptable chemical grade.

In molybdenum, the United States, and in nickel, Canada, have continued to maintain their overwhelming pre-eminence. Of the world's vanadium, about a third comes from the United States; Peru and Northern Rhodesia together produced an equal amount before World War II, but in 1949 their output was only 70 per cent of the prewar amount. Cobalt comes chiefly from the Belgian Congo, which produced only 20 per cent of the world total in 1939 (1,000 tons out of 5,000) but 5,100 tons out of the total 7,100 in 1950. (See Table 335.)

NONFERROUS METALS

The term "nonferrous metals" is often applied by laymen to all metals except iron, but mineralogists generally use it to include only copper, lead, zinc, tin and aluminum.[37]

Most nonferrous metals were known thousands of years before the Christian era and all but the newcomer to industry, aluminum, were in use before iron. Copper tools and other articles were made in the Near East and Egypt about 3500 B.C. A thousand years later, with the probably accidental discovery that the addition of tin strengthens copper, bronze came into use, ushering in the Bronze Age. By 2200 B.C., bronze products were made in China and India as well as in the Mediterranean countries. About this time the Chinese used lead for money and for lining tea chests. By about 1500 B.C., the Phoenicians were trading in tin from Britain. Lead deposits were worked in Greece in 1200 B.C. Lead was then used chiefly for coins, ornaments and solder; later the Romans used it also for plumbing, in the water pipes at Pompeii, for example. Zinc as a metal was not discovered until 1520, but the Romans made brass, an alloy of copper and zinc, before the beginning of the Christian era. [38] Yet commercial large-scale production of zinc, as of many other metals, did not begin until 1900, when mining techniques and milling practices had been developed.

Copper ranks first among the nonferrous metals in value of output. World output of copper in 1949 was valued, at U.S. prices, at $975

---

33. **1**, 1938–39, p. 144.

34. F. Friedensburg comments on the Russian manganese riddle: "Domestic consumption must then be extraordinarily high if compared with steel output, about twelve times as high (per ton of steel) as in the United States." **47**, 1938, p. 402.

35. **18**, 1949, p. 757.

36. **18**, 1949, p. 1241.

37. This classification is followed in the present study and is also used by Alan M. Bateman. **41**, p. 481. Some mineralogists include magnesium in this group, others add some minor metals.

38. **36**, pp. 409–10; **41**, pp. 527–28 and 546; **51**, pp. 389–91.

TABLE 335

FERROALLOYING ORES: OUTPUT IN CHIEF PRODUCING COUNTRIES, 1929–50

(Thousands of Metric Tons [a]*)*

Country	1929	1939	1949	1950	Country	1929	1939	1949	1950
Manganese (Metal Content)					**Chromium (C_2O_3 Content)** [g]				
World	1,952	1,155 [b]	1,420 [b]	...	World	299	560	730 [b]	800 [b]
United States [c]	27	13	64	70	Cuba [d]	23	22	29	48
Cuba [d]	2	53	25	23	Yugoslavia	14	15	30	31
Brazil	137	124	111	...	Greece	10	22	1	5
Chile	2	5	14	17					
Italy	3	12	7	5	USSR	20	90 [h]	...	...
Romania	15	15	21	...	Japan	3	26	10	12
USSR	650	...	...	...	Turkey	8	92	221	206
Japan	10	27	36	49	India	28	25	9	6
India	505	429	255	386	Philippines	—	60	91	95
Malay States	8	10	—	—	Southern Rhodesia	130	68	122	146
Philippines	—	14	12	12	Union of South Africa	27	73	182	223
French Morocco	6	26	98	115	New Caledonia	26	28	45	43
Egypt	61	35	40	60	**Tungsten (WO_3)** [i]				
Gold Coast [e]	217	178	385	376	World [b]	9.3	25	27	30
Union of South Africa	4	175	262	316	United States	0.5	2.3	1.7	2.3
Nickel (Metal Content)					Bolivia	1.0	2.0	1.5	1.5
World [b]	57	119	121	119	Argentina	0.1	0.8	...	...
Canada	50	103	117	112	Portugal	0.2	2.1	2.7	2.2
Norway	0.4	1	—	—	Spain	0.2	0.1	0.5	0.5
Greece	0.3	1	—	—	China	5.8	7.1	8.0	11.0
Burma	0.8	1	—	—	Korea	...	2.6	0.9 [j]	...
New Caledonia	5	12	3	6	Burma	0.9	4.7	0.7	...
Molybdenum (Metal Content)					Malay States	0.3	0.4	f	f
World [b]	2	16	11	14	Union of South Africa	—	0.1	0.3	0.1
United States	2	14	10	13	Australia	0.1	0.6	0.8	1.2
Mexico	—	0.5	—	—	**Cobalt (Metal Content)**				
Peru	—	0.2	—	—	World	...	5.0	5.9	7.1
Chile	—	f	0.6	1	Canada	0.4	0.3	0.3	0.3
Norway	0.1	0.4	0.1	0.1	Burma	...	0.8	...	—
Vanadium (Metal Content)					French Morocco	...	0.7	0.2	0.4
World [b]	0.9	2.5	1.8	...	Belgian Congo	2	1	4.4	5.1
United States	...	0.9	k	k	Northern Rhodesia	2	2	0.4	0.7
Peru	0.9	0.6	0.5	0.4					
Northern Rhodesia	0.2	0.4	0.2	...					
South-West Africa	0.3	0.5	0.2	0.3					

Sources: **1**, 1938–39 and 1942–44, *passim;* **2**, 1951, pp. 142–43 and 154–57; **17**, January 1951, p. 25; **18**, various years.

a. Conversion factors: one metric ton = 1.1023 short tons = 2,204.6 pounds.
b. Excludes the USSR.
c. Excludes ores containing 10–35 per cent manganese.
d. Exports to the United States.
e. Beginning with 1939, exports.
f. Negligible output.
g. Estimated chromic oxide content.
h. 1937.
i. Concentrates containing 60–65 per cent WO_3.
j. South Korea.
k. Data not disclosed by U.S. Bureau of Mines.

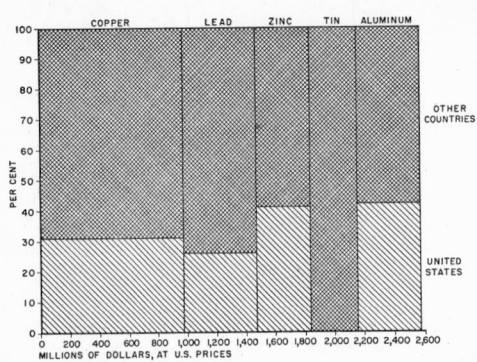

FIGURE 231. NONFERROUS METALS: VALUE OF OUT-
PUT IN THE WORLD AND THE UNITED STATES, 1949

copper, readily recovered from scrap, old and new.[40]

The difference between mine, smelter and refinery statistics is illustrated by the following data on copper output in the United States in 1949 (in thousands of short tons): [41]

Mined (copper content)	753
Smelter, from domestic ore	758
Refined:	
Total	1,140
From domestic ore	695
From foreign ore	233
From old and new scrap	212

million; that of aluminum, at $415 million, and of zinc and lead at $360 and $500 million, respectively. Tin ranks fifth in this group, with $320 million. (See Figure 231 and Table 325.)

MEASURING OUTPUT

The output of nonferrous metals may be measured in terms of output at the mine, the smelter or the refinery. The data on mine production reflect only approximately the recoverable metal content of ore or concentrates. From the international point of view, mine yield is the most important measure, since it indicates the geographical source of the ore. The recorded output of smelters shows the actual recovery of metal in a given country from domestic or foreign ore or both. Refinery statistics are best for showing recovery of metal but indicate only in a general way the source of the crude material treated. There are usually small differences in the three sets of figures on output of metals from domestic ore, due mainly to overlap or time lag between mining, smelting and refining; about ninety days, for example, are required to produce refined copper from newly mined ore.[39]

Statistics on the world output of metals usually indicate only the recoverable metal content of mined ore and the smelter output; data on refinery production are available for only a few countries, and consequently the exact amount of the world's metal output is not known. This lack is the greater in that, in addition to regular refining, there is recovery from scrap. This omission is particularly important for metals like

The 1949 copper output of refineries was about 50 per cent greater than the smelter output from domestic ores; scrap and foreign raw materials made up the difference.

In most countries smelters are located near the mines or near the ports where foreign ores arrive, to avoid hauling worthless gangue for long distances. In contrast, refineries are more usually near metal-consuming centers, irrespective of the distance from the mines.

COPPER

Properties and Uses

Copper possesses excellent resistance to certain kinds of corrosion, has high electrical conductivity, exceeded only by silver, and good thermal conductivity. It is also indestructible in many uses, and therefore a high proportion returns for reuse as scrap; in combination with other metals, it forms many useful alloys.

Because of its superior electrical conductivity, copper is almost irreplaceable in electric motors and much other electrical equipment. Alloyed with zinc, it is used in ammunition, valves, fittings and pipes, where resistance to corrosion is essential. Bronze is much used for bearings, bushings and the like. These and other uses accounted for the following percentages of all

40. Typical examples of old copper scrap are used pipe, cartridge cases, lithographers' plates, trolley wire; of new scrap, defective castings, refuse from the manufacture of copper products, such as punchings, clippings and borings. **18**, 1949, p. 473.

41. **18**, 1949, pp. 463 and 472. Excludes small quantities of copper compounds refined from scrap by both primary and secondary plants.

39. **33**, p. 17.

copper consumed in the United States in 1935–40:[42]

Total	100
Light and power lines, telephone, telegraph, other electrical wire	26
Generators, motors, electric loco-motives, etc.	25
Automobiles, excluding genera-tors, starters, ignition	13
Buildings, excluding electrical work	11
Castings	5
Radio sets	3
Ammunition	2
Other uses	15

Deposits

The world's major deposits of copper are in the United States, Canada, Chile, Peru, the Belgian Congo and Northern Rhodesia. (See Figure 232.)

The United States. The main deposits are at Butte, Montana, and (porphyry ores) in Utah, Arizona, Nevada and New Mexico. Together, these sources account for more than nine tenths of the total domestic mine output.

The Butte district has been called the richest hill on earth and ranks next to the Rand gold deposits in South Africa in metallic wealth extracted.[43] Copper occurs at Butte in fissure veins. An extraordinary geological feature is the splitting of some veins into brush-like aggregations of smaller veins, "the horsetails." [44] The ore contains, on the average, 3–4 per cent copper and some silver.

The disseminated copper ore deposits at Bingham, Utah, gave rise to the greatest copper-producing mine in the world. The ore, averaging less than one per cent copper content, is open cut by highly mechanized mining methods.

While Utah's copper comes predominantly from one mine, the state of Arizona, the largest producer in the United States, has a number of important copper districts, among them Globe-Miami, Jerome, Bisbee, Copper Mountain. Some of them began producing in the early 1870's and have extensive underground workings. In the Globe-Miami district, for example, workings under the surface extend for several hundred miles.

Copper deposits in the Lake Superior district lie in a belt a hundred miles long and two to four miles wide. The mines are very deep, some vertical shafts being the deepest in the world; the Tamarack mine is 5,800 feet deep, and its inclined shafts are about a mile and a half long.[45] This deposit is the only place in the world, except for a small deposit in Bolivia, where native copper (metal content 100 per cent) is the chief source of this metal. The deposit is, however, nearly exhausted.[46]

Canada. The chief copper deposits are at Sudbury, Ontario, though the main product of these mines is nickel. Actually more copper than nickel is produced, but the ratio in value per pound is about 1 to 4. Other important deposits are in western Quebec and Manitoba.

Latin America. Chile, second only to the United States in copper production, has three substantial deposits of porphyry copper — at Chuquicamata, Potrerillos and Braden. The first, located in the desert more than 9,000 feet above sea level, close to the Pacific, is considered the largest porphyry copper deposit in the world. The copper ores of Chile are richer than those of similar formations in Utah, and Chuquicamata is believed to contain more proven copper ore than any other single deposit in the world. The deposits of Peru, chief of them Cerro de Pasco, are at an altitude exceeding 14,000 feet. The ore contains a variety of other metals — gold, silver, lead, zinc, bismuth.

Africa. The very extensive copper districts of the Belgian Congo (Katanga) and of Northern Rhodesia form a belt about two hundred miles long. The copper content is high, ranging from 3.4 to 4.4 per cent in Northern Rhodesia and from 1 to 8 per cent in Katanga. The beds are unusually uniform in metallization, and some of the ore is fit for direct smelting. The importance of the African deposits is increasing.

Europe and the USSR. Europe's main deposits are Bor in Yugoslavia; Mansfield (mined since the Middle Ages) in Saxony, Germany; Minas de Riotinto, known to have produced copper from the days of the Phoenicians,[47] in Spain-Portugal (pyrite deposits, also yielding copper); and Outokumpu, beneath a swamp in Finland. Finland has large reserves in its deposit, which is consid-

42. **33**, p. 16.
43. **41**, p. 491.
44. **53**, Vol. I, p. 48.

45. **74**, pp. 170–73.
46. **41**, pp. 483 and 496. The smelter product of this district is known as "furnace-refined." **48**, p. 6.
47. **69**, p. 31.

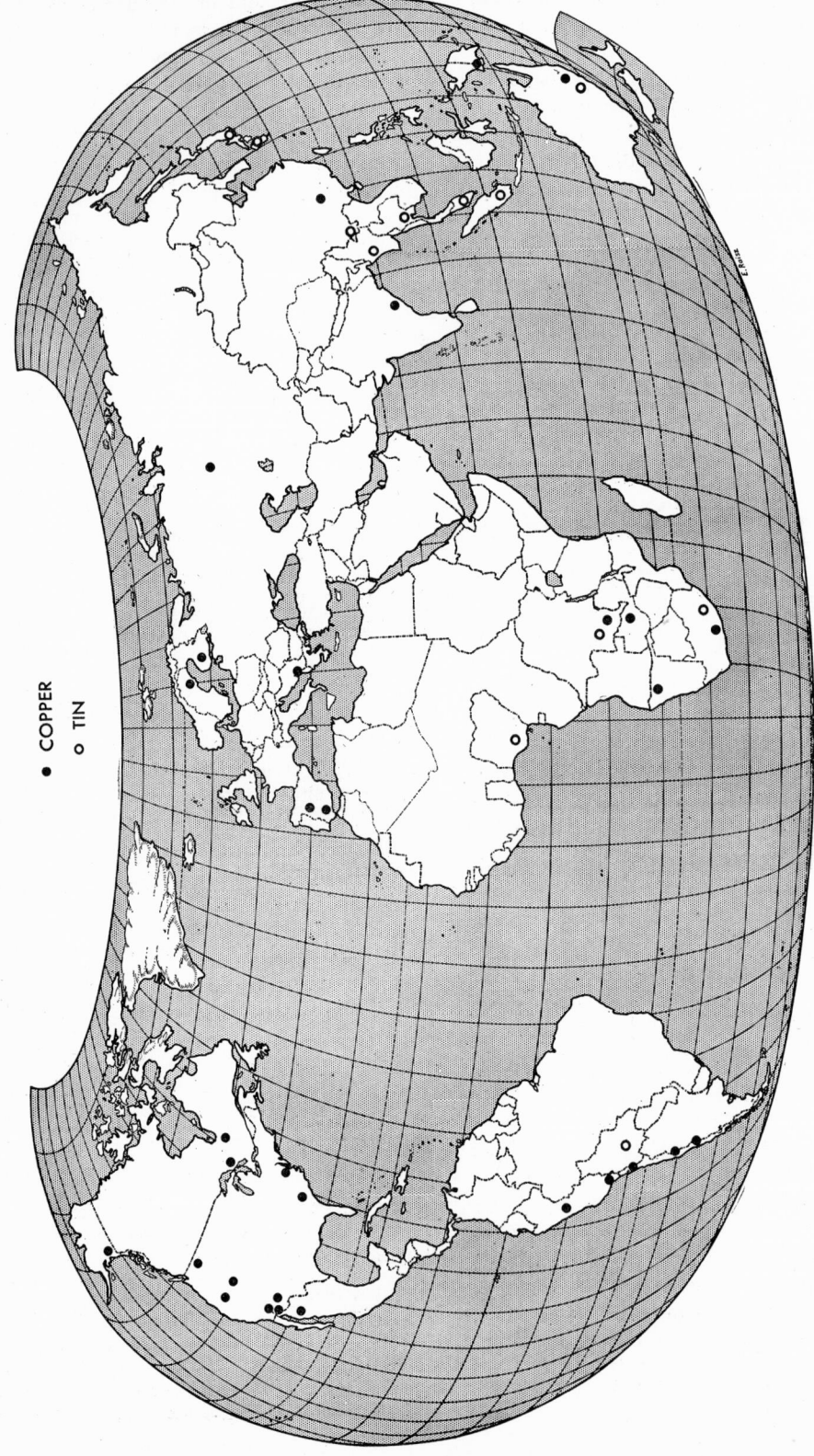

COPPER

TIN

Figure 232. Copper and Tin: Geographic Distribution of Major Deposits in the World

ered one of the largest single deposits in Europe.

The chief deposits of the USSR are in Kazakhstan, the Urals and the Transcaucasus. The ores are of low grade, with an average copper content of 1.76 per cent; the ores of Kazakhstan have a 2.2 per cent copper content. The Kounrad mine on the shores of Lake Balkhash provides ores containing one per cent copper, molybdenum, tungsten and silver.[48]

Reserves

The sixteenth International Geological Congress, held in 1933, estimated the world's actual reserves of copper ore and metallic copper as follows (in millions of metric tons): [49]

	Copper Ore	*Copper Content*
World	3,536	74
United States	1,568	18
Canada	267	5
Chile	1,052	22
Belgian Congo	86	6
Northern Rhodesia	549	23
Other countries	14	1

E. W. Pehrson, of the U.S. Bureau of Mines, estimates the recoverable copper content of the world's present reserves, inclusive of the USSR and some new deposits, at 100 million tons.[50] According to Pehrson, the present reserves would provide the world with copper, at today's rate of consumption per capita and without adjustment for population increase, for forty-five years; at the present rate of consumption per capita in the United States, for five years; and if the rate of consumption in the United States were to remain the same and the rate in the rest of the world were to equal the present rate in Europe, excluding the USSR, for twenty years.

According to the latest estimate of the U.S. Geological Survey and the Bureau of Mines, the copper deposits of the United States contained (as of January 1944) 15 million tons of measured and indicated reserves and 5 million tons of inferred reserves. The lowest grades of ores in inferred reserves are those from some vein deposits with 0.8 per cent metal content and porphyry copper with 0.4 per cent, as well as ores with 0.2 per cent from some reserves that yield copper as a by-product. New discoveries of deposits and new developments in technology may provide additional reserves.[51]

Output

The world's output of smelter copper began to grow in the last decade of the nineteenth century, largely because of the expansion of electrical systems in all industrialized countries. In 1889, the world's smelters turned out 266,000 tons; in 1899, 478,000; in 1909, 858,000. World War I raised the annual output to more than 1.4 million tons in 1917 and 1918. During the postwar depression production fell to less than half that figure. The next peak was in 1929, with more than 1.9 million tons.[52] During World War II, output reached an all-time high of 2.8 million tons a year in 1942 and 1943.

The United States. This country has been the leading producer of copper since 1880, when it overtook Chile and Great Britain.[53] Smelter production in the United States from domestic ores represented an increasing share of the world's smelter output until the end of World War I, with 60.4 per cent in 1918, and then declined. Even in 1944, it was less than 40 per cent of the world's total and it has since decreased. (See Table 336.)

The total production of copper in the United States, however, is much greater than these figures indicate, because of the substantial recovery from scrap. Exports of refined copper have normally been considerably larger than imports, but since World War II that situation has been reversed.

Four companies integrate and control all stages of copper production in the United States, from the mining of the ore through the fabrication of copper products. These companies produce more than 80 per cent of all the copper mined, have about 83 per cent of all the primary smelting capacity, about 70 per cent of the primary refining capacity, and more than 60 per cent of the copper and brass fabricating facilities.[54]

Other Countries. Chile, Northern Rhodesia, Canada and the Belgian Congo are the next important producers. Chile smelted 42,000 tons

48. **41**, p. 525; **66**, March 1951, p. 36.
49. **69**, pp. 32–33.
50. **3,b**, p. 2.

51. **42**, pp. 96–97; **10**, pp. 240–42.
52. **38**, 1947, p. 105.
53. As early as the 1870's Great Britain had almost exhausted its deposits and practically ceased to produce virgin copper. Instead, it began to import copper ore and smelter copper for refining. **48**, p. 2.
54. **33**, p. 17.

TABLE 336

OUTPUT OF SMELTER COPPER IN THE WORLD AND THE
UNITED STATES, 1889–1950

| Year | Output, in Thousands of Metric Tons [a] | | U. S. Output as Percentage of World Total |
	World	United States	
1889	266	103	38.7
1899	478	264	55.2
1904	654	366	56.0
1909	858	496	57.8
1914	924	517	56.0
1918	1,433	866	60.4
1919	986	579	59.7
1924	1,392	735	52.1
1929	1,922	908	47.2
1934	1,303	220	16.9
1939	2,175	698	32.1
1944	2,584	1,022	39.6
1948	2,394	840	35.1
1949	2,403	780	32.5
1950	2,480	915	36.9

Sources: **20**, p. 15; **38**, 1947, p. 105; **18**, 1949, p. 484; **67**, May 1951, p. 13.

a. Conversion factors: one metric ton = 1.1023 short tons = 2,204.6 pounds.

of copper in 1913, and more than eight times that amount in 1950. Canada increased its output between those years from 35,000 to 218,000 tons. An even more spectacular increase occurred in Northern Rhodesia, from 6,000 tons in 1929 to 264,000 in 1949, and 280,000 in 1950. (See Table 337.)

Belgium has a large smelting capacity for its colonial ores, and in 1939 produced 66,000 tons of smelter copper, as much as Germany, from imported ores. Prewar Germany also had a considerable refining capacity for recovery from domestic and imported scrap and alloys. Both Belgium and the Belgian Congo have raised their output of smelter copper considerably above the 1939 level.

The output in the USSR in 1949 is estimated by the U.S. Bureau of Mines at 200,000 tons; by the Economic Commission for Europe (UN), on the basis of Russian official statistics, at 235,000 tons for 1949 and 255,000 for 1950.[55]

International Control

Most of the foreign copper deposits outside the USSR are owned or controlled by companies in the United States, Great Britain and Belgium. American companies own the principal deposits in Chile and some deposits in Peru, Bolivia and Mexico, and have interests in Canadian, Rhodesian and South African copper reserves; in all, they control about three fourths of the world's copper output, but their interests are primarily in the lower-grade mines.[56] Rhodesian properties are largely controlled by British capital, and Belgian capital predominantly owns and controls the deposits in the Belgian Congo.[57] Virtually all copper entering into world competition is controlled by fewer than a dozen companies or financial groups.[58]

LEAD AND ZINC

Properties and Uses

Lead and zinc are very commonly associated in mineral deposits. The most important lead mineral is galena; and sphalerite (zinc blende) is the most common source of zinc mineral. In pure form, galena is 86.6 per cent lead, but such ore occurs in only a few deposits. Usually galena also contains silver, zinc and titanium. The percentage of zinc in pure zinc blende is 67.

Lead is outstanding in malleability and weldability, resistance to corrosion and in its excellent antifriction properties; zinc, as a corrosion inhibitor, especially as a protective coating on steel in galvanized products.

Lead is used in storage batteries, and for cable covering; in ammunition, bearings, type metal, brass, bronze and terneplate; for packing foil, for solder and for ballast. The chief uses of zinc are in galvanizing iron and steel and in the manufacture of brass; the major use of zinc-base alloys is for die castings. The roasting of zinc blende produces sulfur dioxide gases from which sulfuric acid is made. In 1949, nearly 477,000 short tons of sulfuric acid were obtained in zinc blende roasting plants in the United States. Zinc oxide is used in rubber, paint and ceramic industries.

In the United States, consumption of slab zinc in 1949 was distributed as follows: galvanizing, 49.3 per cent; die castings, 28.4 per cent; brass products, 12.0 per cent; rolled zinc, 7.8 per cent;

55. **6**, 1950, p. 39. Another source estimates the output in 1944 at 170,000 tons and in 1949 at 225,000 tons (**62**, January 3, 1950, p. 7).

56. **51**, pp. 369–70.
57. **33**, p. 19.
58. **26**, p. 175.

TABLE 337

COPPER: OUTPUT IN SELECTED COUNTRIES, 1913–50

(*Thousands of Metric Tons* [a])

Country	1913	1918	1929	1939	1944	1949	1950
			Ore (Metal Content)				
World	1,006	1,417	1,951	2,200	2,527	2,235	2,250 [b]
United States	561	859	998	661	882	683	825
Canada	35	54	124	276	248	239	238
Mexico	53	70	95	44	41	57	62
Peru	28	44	63	36	32	24	30
Chile	42	114	353	339	499	371	363
Belgium	—	—	—	—	—	—	—
Sweden	5	3	1	10	16	16	16
Norway	3	3	19	20	14	15	16
Finland	—	—	5	12	16	21	17
Germany [c]	26	35	29	24	25	1	1
Spain	50	63	64	—	11	7	. . .
Yugoslavia (Serbia)	6	1	21	64	23	38	43
Russia (USSR)	34	5	26	. . .	. . .	. . .	. . .
Japan	66	90	83	52	87	33	39
Turkey	—	—	—	—	—	11	12
Belgian Congo	8	20	130	—	—	—	—
Northern Rhodesia	—	—	—	—	—	—	—
Union of South Africa	8	5	13	11	23	30	33
Australia	48	43	14	22	29	14	15
			Smelter Output				
World	989	1,433	1,922	2,175	2,584	2,403 [d]	2,480 [d]
United States	555	866	908	698	1,022	780	915
Canada	35	54	80	229	224	204	218
Mexico	53	70	73	39	33	49	49
Peru	28	44	54	34	27	21	23
Chile	42	115	303	326	490	351	346
Belgium	1	. . .	9	66	4	133 [e]	137 [e]
Sweden	4	3	5	11 [f]	15 [f]	14 [f]	17 [f]
Norway	3	3	2	10	1	9	9
Finland	—	. . .	. . .	14	8	21	18
Germany [e]	50	40	54	67	30	103 [g]	134 [g]
Spain	31	45	28	10	11	9	9
Yugoslavia (Serbia)	—	—	21	42	23	49	40 [e]
Russia (USSR)	34	5	25	131	135 [h]	200 [h]	. . .
Japan	—	—	76	96	66	36	37
Turkey	1	—	—	7	11	11	12
Belgian Congo	—	—	—	123	166	141	176
Northern Rhodesia	—	3	6	215	224	264	280
Union of South Africa	8	5	9	14	23	30	33
Australia	46	39	11	18 [f]	20 [f]	10 [f]	14 [f]

Sources: **75,** p. 176; **25,** various years; **18,** various years; **2,** 1951, pp. 146–47 and 255–56.

  a. Conversion factors: one metric ton = 1.1023 short tons = 2,204.6 pounds.

  b. Excludes the USSR, Spain and a few minor producing countries.

  c. For 1939 and 1944, includes occupied territories; for 1949 and 1950, Western Germany.

  d. Without the USSR.

  e. Refined copper including secondary copper.

  f. Refined copper.

  g. Electrolytic copper (1936, 121,700 metric tons).

  h. Estimate of the U.S. Bureau of Mines.

various other purposes, 2.5 per cent.[59] In 1949, 31 per cent of all lead went into storage batteries, 15 per cent for cable covering, 11 per cent for pigments, 6.5 per cent for solder, 10 per cent for chemicals, and the rest for various other uses.[60]

Deposits

The United States. The world's greatest deposits of lead and zinc are in the United States: the "lead belt" in southeastern Missouri and the zinc deposits in the Tri-State region (Kansas, Oklahoma and southwestern Missouri). The Tri-State region also produces large quantities of lead, and other important deposits of lead and zinc are at Coeur d'Alene, Idaho, and Bingham, Utah, along with copper. Franklin, New Jersey, has unique zinc deposits.[61] The zinc belt of eastern Tennessee and southwestern Virginia is an important mineral area. (See Figure 233.)

Other Countries. Canada's chief deposit, accounting for nearly all the country's lead output and three fourths of its zinc, is at Kimberley, British Columbia. The chief lead deposits in north central Mexico are in Chihuahua and Coahuila; Chihuahua and San Luis Potosi have the largest zinc mines.[62]

The principal European lead-zinc district is in Upper Silesia (Poland). Italy, Spain and Yugoslavia have lesser deposits. Burma has lead-zinc ores (Bawdwin mine), some of them of the highest grade in the world.

In the USSR, lead and zinc deposits at Altai, Kazakhstan, account for 62 per cent of all the lead and 42 per cent of all the zinc reserves of the country.

The deposits in Australia, in New South Wales and Queensland, are extensive and contain rich ores, particularly the New South Wales deposit. (See Figure 233.)

Reserves

The world reserves of lead content in the ground were estimated in 1950 at 45 million tons: 12.7 million in Australia; 8.3 million in the United States; 4.6 million in Canada; 3.6 million in Mexico, Peru and Argentina; 3 million in the

USSR; 2 million in Germany; and the remainder scattered in a score of countries. The measured and indicated reserves of zinc content in the ground were estimated for the world at 70 million short tons in 1950, of which the United States is credited with 8.5 million, the rest of the Western Hemisphere with 20 million, Europe with 13.5 million, the USSR with 6 million, Asia and Africa each with 4 million and Australia with 14 million.

The inferred zinc reserves of the United States are estimated at 12.7 million short tons as of January 1950; of these, about 9.8 million are recoverable. The measured and indicated reserves of lead in the United States were estimated at 2.6 million short tons, as of January 1944; the inferred reserves, at 5.2 million tons. (See Table 338.) A later estimate of lead reserves in the United States indicated 8.3 million tons in 1951.[63]

Output of Lead

The output of the world's lead smelters amounted to 1.2 million tons of primary lead in 1913 and 1.7 million in 1939. Between these years, production in some countries increased greatly — in Canada, for example, from 17,000 to 173,000 tons and in Mexico, from 62,000 to 214,000. In some others the output declined — in Spain, from 199,000 to 26,000 tons.

The United States, with 401,000 tons in 1913, reached the peak in 1929 (703,000 tons) but smelted only 404,000 tons in 1939, little more than in 1913. Germany treated lead ore and bullion from foreign sources for the most part and had about the same output on the eve of World War II as at its entry into World War I.

The USSR increased its output very considerably but still ranked eighth in 1939. Altai, the chief center of ore production, also accounts for a fourth of the lead smelting in the USSR but has no zinc smelting capacity. Thus, most of the concentrates of both metals are transported for smelting over long distances to other regions — the Ukraine, North Caucasus and so on.[64]

Belgium has a large smelting capacity and is an important European producer of lead from imported ores.

Together, the United States, Canada, Mexico, Germany and Australia accounted for about

---

59. **18**, 1949, p. 1280.
60. **18**, 1949, p. 681.
61. Franklin is generally renowned for its mineralogical wealth. More than a hundred minerals occur there, some of which have not been discovered anywhere else. **41**, pp. 536–37.
62. **19**, pp. 111–19.

63. **19**, pp. S–15 and III–10; **27**, Vol. II, p. 150.
64. **40**, p. 262.

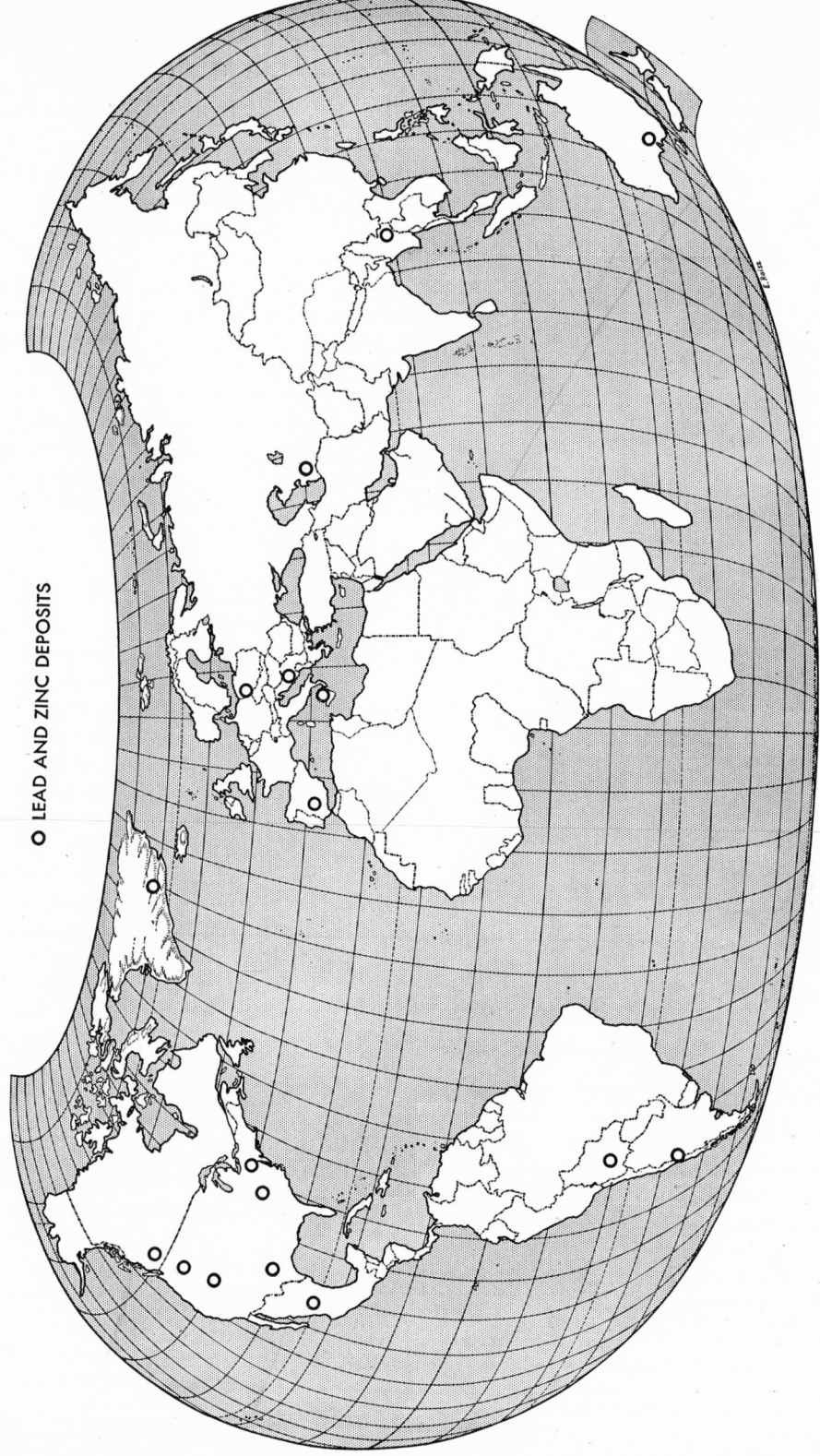

○ LEAD AND ZINC DEPOSITS

FIGURE 233. LEAD AND ZINC: GEOGRAPHIC DISTRIBUTION OF MAJOR DEPOSITS IN THE WORLD

TABLE 338

LEAD AND ZINC: ESTIMATED RESERVES IN THE UNITED STATES

(Thousands of Short Tons of Metal Content)

	Lead, January 1944		Zinc, January 1950	
	Gross Content in Ground	Recoverable Content	Gross Content in Ground	Recoverable Content
Total	7,750	6,580	21,200 [a]	16,300 [a]
Measured and indicated reserves	2,600	2,200	8,480	6,530
Inferred reserves	5,150	4,380	12,700	9,800
Additional metal in deposits workable under new technological or industrial conditions	Nil	—	3,840 [b]	...

Sources: **42**, p. 126; **19**, p. III–10.

a. Rounded figures.

b. Includes 3.4 million tons of measured and indicated reserves and 0.4 million tons of inferred reserves.

seven tenths of the world's lead output in 1939.

During World War II, trends differed among countries. The United States increased its smelter output by about 25 per cent from 1939 to 1941–42 but by 1945 was back at the 1939 level. Labor shortages restricted production in Australia, and Burma's output dropped 75–80 per cent as a result of the destruction by the Japanese of many installations at the famous Bawdwin smelter. Belgian smelters could not operate for lack of ore.

In postwar years, the world's output of smelter lead has fluctuated and has been lower than in 1939; in 1949 and 1950 it amounted to about 1.6 million tons. The share of the United States increased from 23 to 28 per cent while that of Australia declined somewhat. (See Table 339.)

The United States meets a large part of its requirements for lead with secondary lead obtained from domestic lead waste in manufacturing and old lead alloys. During the past decade, such sources actually supplied more lead than was obtained from mine production. Secondary lead is important in other industrial countries also, but adequate statistics are not available.

Output of Zinc

The world's output of smelter zinc approximates that of lead — 1.1 million tons in 1913, 1.7 million tons in 1939. The chief producers before World War II were the United States, Germany, Belgium, Canada and Poland. The United States increased its output very considerably during the war, and in the peak year, 1943,

produced 85 per cent more zinc than in 1939. Production subsequently declined but is still about 65 per cent above the prewar level. In 1950, the United States accounted for more than 40 per cent of the world's total. Western Germany's output in 1950 (122,800 tons) exceeded that in 1936 (96,000 tons). The 1950 output of smelter zinc in almost all other producing countries was larger than in 1939. (See Table 340.)

TIN

Properties and Uses

Tin is outstanding in its high antifriction property, extreme malleability, high resistance to corrosion, low melting point (a quality it imparts to alloys) and ability to adhere closely to metals, a quality useful in soldering. The chief single use of tin is for making tinplate, which accounts for a third of the world's tin consumption. Other important uses are for soldering, in alloys (babbit, bronze and brass), terneplate and type metal. Tin alloys are used in the manufacture of bearings and many other products.

The United States consumes more than 40 per cent of all the tin annually produced in the world; the United Kingdom, the next largest user, takes some 17–18 per cent, and its per capita consumption is larger than that in the United States. Export of tin products, however, accounts for about a fourth of the tin used in the United Kingdom. In the United States, about 40 per cent of the tin consumed in 1949 went into tinplate, 21 per cent was used for solder and 26 per cent for alloys. The United Kingdom used the bulk of its tin in 1948 for

TABLE 339

LEAD: OUTPUT IN SELECTED COUNTRIES, 1913–50

(*Thousands of Metric Tons* [a])

Country	1913	1929	1939	1949	1950
			Ore (Metal Content)		
World	1,228	1,684	1,650	1,400 [b]	1,500 [b]
United States [c]	454	590	376	372	391
Canada	17	148	176	}145	154
Newfoundland	—	11	28		
Mexico	62	248	220	221	242
Peru [d]	—	21	46	57	62
Bolivia [e]	—	15	14	26	31
Argentina	—	3	28	16	20
United Kingdom	18	19	17	2	3
France	10	11	5	10	12
Germany [f]	79	61	96	41	45
Poland	—	12	—	…	…
Spain	182	127	29	31	36
Italy	25	31	47	36	40
Yugoslavia	—	9	73	71	84
Russia (USSR)	—	8	56 [h]	…	…
Japan [d]	4	5	15	9	11
Burma	6	104	90	…	…
Tunisia [d]	…	17	18	15	18
Australia [d]	246	197	285	217	223
			Smelter Output		
World	1,219	1,819	1,735	1,563	1,610 [b]
United States [c]	401	703	404	433	461
Canada [d]	17	138	173	133	155
Mexico	62	230	214	212	231
Peru [d]	—	19	24	36	35
Argentina	—	9	14	18	18
United Kingdom	31	11	13	2	3
France	29	20	42	55	62
Belgium [g]	104	60	96	79	62
Germany [d, f]	191	98	186	98	118
Poland	43	37	20 [i]	17	…
Spain	199	143	26	27	35
Italy	22	23	39	26	38
Yugoslavia	—	10	11	57	57
Russia (USSR)	2	6	75	90	…
Japan [d]	…	3	13 [i]	8	10
Burma	6	82	78	8	…
Tunisia [d]	…	19	22	20	24
Northern Rhodesia	—	2	…	14	14
Australia [d]	118	180	247	187	203

Sources: **75**, p. 180; **22**, Table 33; **1**, various years; **25**, various years; **18**, various years; **2**, 1951, pp. 148–49 and 258–59.

a. Conversion factors: one metric ton = 1.1023 short tons = 2,204.6 pounds.

b. Without the USSR.

c. For smelter output, lead refined from domestic and foreign ores; excludes lead from foreign base bullion.

d. Smelter output: refined lead.

e. Exports.

f. For 1939, includes Austria, Bohemia and Moravia; for 1949 and 1950, Western Germany.

g. Smelter output includes scrap in 1949 and 1950.

h. 1937.

i. 1938.

TABLE 340

ZINC: OUTPUT IN SELECTED COUNTRIES, 1913–50

(*Thousands of Metric Tons* [a])

Country	1913	1929	1939	1949	1950
	Ore (Recoverable Zinc)				
World	1,139	1,713	1,870	1,675 [b]	1,850 [b]
United States	375	657	530	538	566
Canada	3	90	179	262	282
Mexico	7	174	134	178	224
Peru	...	...	21	68	89
Bolivia	—	—	8	18	20
United Kingdom	6	1	9	—	—
France	26	10	1	11	12
Belgium	—	5	—	—	—
Norway	—	1	6	7	6
Germany [c]	244	143	190	58	69
Poland	—	105	70 [d]	...	...
Spain	38	53	46	47	...
Italy	64	87	106	74	86
Yugoslavia	—	5	33	44	45
Russia (USSR)	31	3	90	...	...
Japan [c]	16	18	58	44	52
Burma	...	56	55	...	...
Northern Rhodesia	...	20	15	23	23
Australia	191	157	221	185	206
	Smelter Output				
World	1,053	1,450	1,650	1,840	1,870 [b]
United States	315	567	460	739	765
Canada [e]	3	78	159 [f]	188 [f]	186 [f]
Mexico	—	15	36	54	49
Peru	...	...	...	1	1
United Kingdom	66	59	52	65	71
France	68	87	63	61	72
Belgium	204	198	177	177 [e]	177 [e]
Netherlands	24	26	21	16	20
Norway [e]	9	6	46	41	43
Germany [e]	279	102	231	87	123
Poland	8	169	108 [d]	87 [g]	...
Spain	6	12	13	20	21
Italy [e]	—	16	35	27	38
Yugoslavia	—	6	5	9	11
Russia (USSR)	11	3	85 [d]	110	...
Japan [e]	1	22	57 [f]	32 [f]	49 [f]
Northern Rhodesia	—	12	13 [f]	23 [f]	23 [f]
Australia	4	53	72	83	85

Sources: **75,** pp. 182–84; **24,** Table 15; **1,** various years; **25,** various years; **2,** 1951, pp. 150–51 and 257.

a. Conversion factors: one metric ton = 1.1023 short tons = 2,204.6 pounds.
b. Without the USSR.
c. For 1939, includes occupied territories; for 1949 and 1950, Western Germany.
d. 1938.
e. Includes secondary zinc.
f. Refined zinc.
g. 1948.

TABLE 341

TIN: CONSUMPTION IN THE UNITED STATES, 1949, AND THE UNITED KINGDOM, 1948

(Thousands of Long Tons)

| Product | United States, 1949 | | | United Kingdom, 1948 [a] |
	Total	Primary	Secondary	
Total	72.4	47.2	25.2	32.0
Tinplate	29.6	29.6	—	} 10.7
Terneplate	0.6	0.3	0.3	
Solder	15.4	8.2	7.2	5.3
Babbit, bronze, brass	19.0	4.4	14.6	12.0
Collapsible tubes and foil	0.9	0.9	0.1	2.0
Tinning	2.1	1.9	0.2	1.0
Type metal	1.8	0.1	1.7	} 1.0
Other uses	3.0	1.8	1.1	

Source: **18,** 1949, p. 1201; **7,** May 1949, pp. 28–29.

a. Separate data on use of primary and secondary metal not available.

alloys (37.5 per cent), tinplate and terneplate (33.3 per cent) and solder (16.7 per cent). (See Table 341.)

Tinplate consumption per capita in 1948 was 43.4 pounds in the United States, 32.9 pounds in Canada, 30.1 in Australia, 18.3 in the United Kingdom, 9.2 in the Union of South Africa, 8.9 in the Netherlands, 4.6 in France and 0.4–0.5 pounds in Japan and India. The world's average consumption per capita (exclusive of the USSR) was 4.2 pounds.[65]

Deposits

The world's chief tin deposits are in the Malay States, Indonesia and Bolivia. The Malayan reserves are the largest and most productive; the ore is of alluvial origin, and large-scale dredging operations are employed. Deposits in Indonesia are similar in character. In contrast, Bolivia has lode deposits, with tin ore in narrow veins. The ore contains as much as 8 per cent tin and also silver and some other minerals, but extraction of tin from lodes is more complex than from the placer deposits in southeastern Asia. The Bolivian tin mines are at elevations of from 12,000 to 17,000 feet. One of the principal mines, in the department of Potosí, is believed to be the largest tin lode deposit in the world and has more than a hundred miles of underground workings.[66] Indonesia's deposits are on the islands of Bangka, Billiton and Sing-

kep. The first is the largest producer of tin ore.

Deposits in other areas (Nigeria, the Belgian Congo, Thailand, Burma, China, Australia, Germany, Portugal, Spain and a few others) are of lesser importance. (See Figure 232.)

Great Britain's famous Cornwall deposit, worked hundreds of years before the Christian era and still the leading world source of tin seventy-five years ago, is now almost entirely exhausted. Spain and Portugal have tin deposits; they were intensively worked during World War II but the peacetime output is small. Investigations during the past sixty years have shown that known deposits of the United States are too small or of too low grade to permit profitable operations or to represent a significant resource.[67]

Output

The Malay States, Indonesia and Bolivia are the leading producers of tin ore. Together they once accounted for 75–80 per cent of the world total, but their combined share declined to about 60 per cent in 1939, when production began to rise in some lesser areas, such as the Belgian Congo, Nigeria and Thailand. In 1949, they again accounted for 73 per cent of the total output of tin ore. (See Table 342.)

Before World War II, tin smelting was concentrated in British Malaya, which had the largest smelter plant in the world, at Penang, and also in Singapore, the United Kingdom, the

65. **8,** p. 49.
66. **30,** p. 15.

67. **42,** p. 194.

TABLE 342

TIN: OUTPUT IN SELECTED COUNTRIES, 1913–50

(*Thousands of Metric Tons* [a])

Country	1913	1918	1929	1939	1944	1949	1950
Ore (Metal Content)							
World	136	125	199	168	101	164	164
Bolivia [b]	26	30	47	28	39	34	32
United Kingdom [c]	5	4	3	2	1	1	1
China	8	8	7	13	2	4	4
Burma	—	—	3	6	1	2	2
Thailand	6	8	10	16	3	8	11
Malay States	50	37	73	48	9	56	58
Indonesia	20	19	36	28	7	29	33
Belgian Congo	—	—	1	8	17	14	15
Nigeria	4	6	11	10	13	9	9
Australia	—	—	—	4	3	2	3
Smelter Output							
World	136	128	196	176	95	170	175
United States	—	—	[d]	[d]	31	37	33
United Kingdom [c]	23	22	58	38	29	29	28
Belgium	—	—	1	4	—	9	10
Netherlands	—	—	1	15	—	20	21
China	8	9	7	13	2	4	4
Thailand	7	9	. . .	. . .	4	. . .	. . .
Malay States	53	42	107	82	5	64	70
Indonesia	—	—	14	14	6	—	—
Belgian Congo	—	—	—	3	10	3	4
Australia	8	5	2	3	2	2	2

Sources: **23**, Table 24; **18**, various years; **7**, May 1949, pp. 6–9; **2**, 1951, pp. 152 and 260.

    a. Conversion factors: one metric ton = 1.1023 short tons = 2,204.6 pounds.
    b. Exports.
    c. Data on smelter output include production from imported scrap.
    d. Negligible.

Netherlands and Belgium. In 1942–43, when Malaya was cut off, the United States government built a huge tin smelter (Longhorn) at Texas City, which accounts for all tin production in the country. The Longhorn, the smelters in Malaya and Singapore, and those in the United Kingdom, Belgium (Hoboken) and the Netherlands (Arnhem) together delivered 93 per cent of the world's tin in 1950. After World War II, the world output of smelter tin began to expand, reaching 175,000 tons in 1950. The world's smelting capacity is estimated at 300,000–350,000 tons, or about double the present output.

Consumption of tin declined to 119,000 tons in 1949, largely because of the development of the electrolytic process in tin-plating. The new process requires only half as much tin as hot-dipping and is less expensive. Both the United States and the United Kingdom now produce more than half their tinplate electrolytically.[68] Another long-term trend may be the loss of ground to substitutes, such as lead and aluminum.[69] In 1950, the world consumption of tin, 152,000 tons, was smaller than the output.[70]

The USSR's output is not known; the main

68. **18**, 1949, p. 1200, and **67**, May 26, 1950, p. 550.
69. **8**, p. 34.
70. **63**, 1951, p. 441.

producing countries exported no tin concentrates or metal to the USSR in 1949. Only 510 tons are known to have been shipped to it in the first half of 1950, though exports from China were reported. The USSR purchased 560 tons of tin-containing white metal from the Netherlands in 1948, and 640 tons in 1949.[71]

Properties and Uses

Aluminum's most important features are lightness, malleability,[72] resistance to corrosion, high electrical and thermal conductivity, high power to reflect light and radiate heat, and great tensile strength. Because of these properties, it is used for innumerable purposes in many industries— including aircraft and automobiles; building and ship construction; refrigeration equipment; diesel engines; chemical equipment and endless products for household use. In the United States, the building trade has become the best customer of the aluminum industry in recent years. It uses aluminum for roofing and siding, window frames, shingles, gutters and downspouts, prefabricated housing panels, heating and ventilating ducts, electric conduits and accessories, and many other purposes. In the United Kingdom, many thousands of prefabricated aluminum bungalows have been built since the war (75,000 for the domestic market alone), and school buildings, warehouses, bridges and other structures are made increasingly of aluminum.[73]

Aluminum alloys (with copper, tin, zinc, nickel and other metals) are the basic structural material in aircraft, and use of them in motor vehicles, ships and rolling stock is growing. More and more aluminum is used in high-voltage lines — for example, more than 1.5 million miles of aluminum conductor cable are now in use in the United States in high-voltage and rural distribution lines.[74]

Aluminum, one of the metals most abundant in the earth's crust,[75] is found in most common rocks except limestone and sandstone. Nevertheless, it has never been found in nature in metallic form and was not isolated until 1827. Then almost sixty years passed before the electrolytic method for its extraction was discovered, simultaneously and independently, by H. M. Hall in the United States and P. L. T. Héroult in France.

Aluminum is produced commercially from only one ore, bauxite, which is also used in the manufacture of chemicals, abrasives, refractories and cement, in oil refining; and as a flux in steel and ferroalloy industries.

Deposits of Bauxite

The world's chief deposits of bauxite are in British Guiana, Surinam, Brazil, France and Hungary. Brazil's deposits are handicapped by their land-locked location and the lack of transportation facilities. Most of Hungary's bauxite is low grade.

The chief deposits in the United States are in Arkansas, which supplied 97 per cent of all the bauxite mined in the country in 1943. Bauxite from deposits in the East Gulf Plain, with high silica and iron content, is used chiefly in chemical and refractory industries.

The USSR has low-grade deposits in the Urals, the Leningrad area and Siberia. The Gold Coast's deposits contain many thick beds of high-grade ore. Indonesia has, on Bintan Island, the largest known deposits of bauxite in the Far East. Italy's deposits on the Istrian Peninsula, which supplied 70 per cent of the national output before World War II, were ceded by the peace treaty to Yugoslavia; its remaining bauxite deposits are in the Foggia and Bari areas. (See Figure 234.)

Reserves of Bauxite

In 1944, the world's total reserves of bauxite were roughly estimated at between 700 million and 1.2 billion tons; those of high-grade ore, at 374 million tons. Later estimates raised total reserves to 2 billion tons (in round numbers). Estimates for the various countries are as follows: [76]

	Millions of Metric Tons	Per Cent of Alumina Content
World	2,000	. . .
United States	50	50
Jamaica	315	50
Haiti Dominican Republic	}30	}47

(*Continued on page 807*)

---

71. **8**, p. 40.

72. Aluminum can be drawn into wires as thin as one ten-thousandth of an inch and rolled into extremely thin sheets.

73. **3,c**, p. 248.

74. **18**, 1948, pp. 120–21.

75. Cf. Chapter 10.

76. **46**, p. 20; **27**, Vol. II, p. 138.

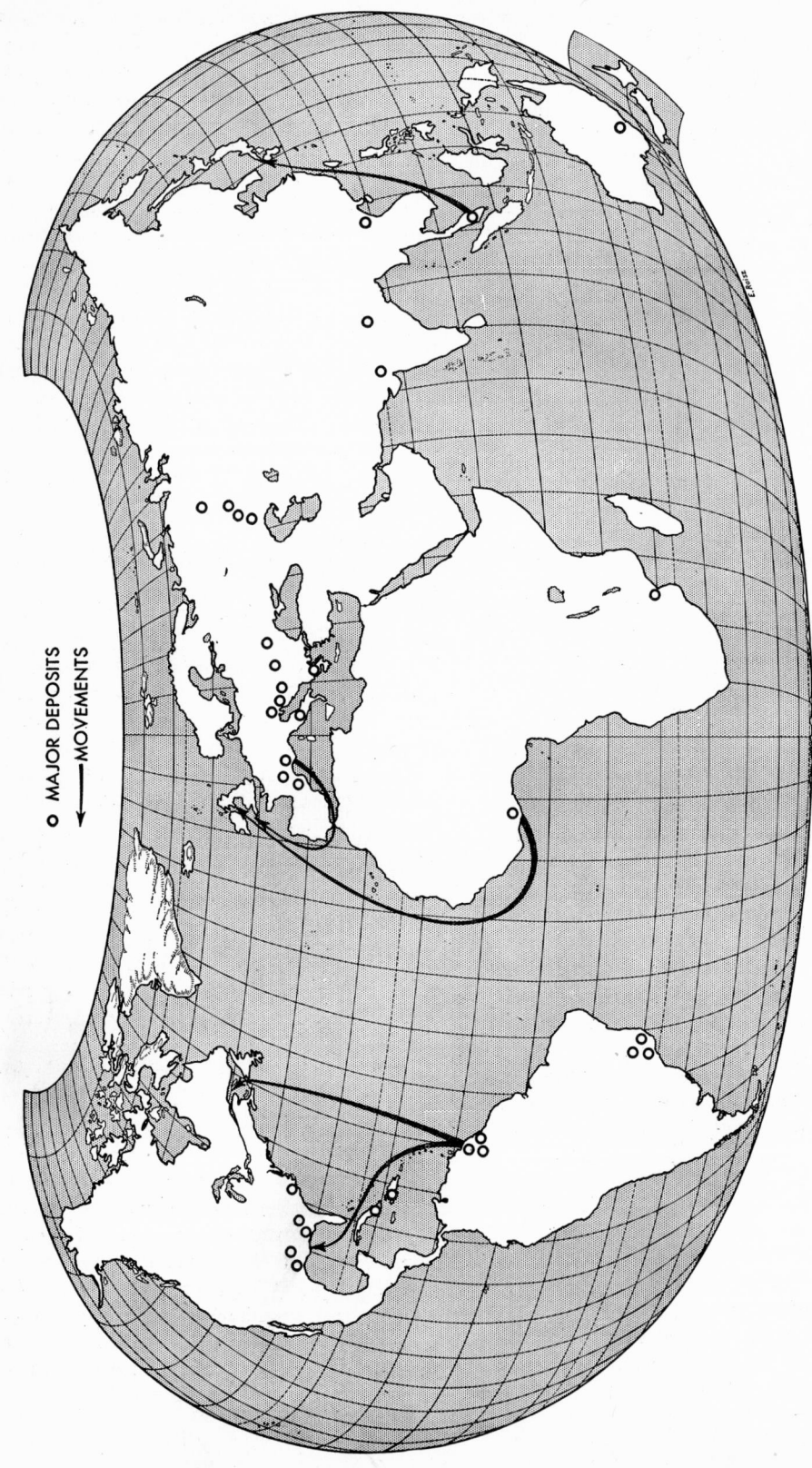

MAJOR DEPOSITS

MOVEMENTS

FIGURE 234. BAUXITE: LOCATION OF MAIN FIELDS AND PRINCIPAL MOVEMENTS OF BAUXITE, BEFORE WORLD WAR II

Adapted from a map of the U.S. Tariff Commission

	Millions of Metric Tons	Per Cent of Alumina Content
Surinam	50	59
British Guiana	65	61
Brazil	150	61
France	60	61
Hungary	250	46–65
Italy	5–10	. . .
Yugoslavia	100	60
Romania	20	57
Greece	60	57
USSR	50	58
China	200	56–65
India	250	60
Malaya	10	56
Indonesia	25	54
French West Africa	50	60
Gold Coast	230	53
Nyasaland	20	42
Australia	20	39

The United States has very small reserves of high-grade bauxite and not much more of second grade. It has vast deposits of low-grade bauxite and clay, but it is less economical to use these than to import foreign high-grade ore. In an emergency, when cost is disregarded, the low-grade deposits could assure the necessary raw materials.[77]

Output of Bauxite

In 1939, France, Surinam, Hungary, British Guiana, Italy, the United States and Yugoslavia together produced about 80 per cent of the world's 4.4 million tons of bauxite. In 1943, world output reached the all-time high of about 14 million tons, of which the United States, with 6.3 million tons, accounted for 45 per cent. The total dropped to 7.0 million tons in 1944 and 3.5 million in 1945. The trend has since been upward, and the 1950 output (exclusive of the USSR) was 7.5 million tons. (See Table 343.)

Output of Aluminum

Bauxite is so stable chemically that separation of the aluminum is very difficult. A large amount of electric power is used in this process, and bauxite is shipped from the mines to sources of cheap power. The separation of aluminum is achieved by two processes. First alumina (cal-

cined aluminum oxide) is recovered from bauxite, then aluminum is produced from alumina. Two tons of high-grade bauxite combined with flux material (soda ash and chemical lime) yield one ton of alumina. One ton of coal is usually required to generate the heat for this operation. Two tons of alumina and about 18,000 to 22,000 kilowatt-hours (the equivalent of about 8 tons of coal) are needed to produce one ton of aluminum. In addition, about 1,200 pounds of electrodes and almost 200 pounds of cryolite are required. In this process, powdered alumina mixed with cryolite is charged into a cell where an electric current both fuses the mixture and separates the metal, which sinks to the bottom of the cell. The metal is then drawn off and cast into pigs or ingots containing roughly 99.7 per cent aluminum. These are remelted for either refining or alloying.[78]

The unit price of electrodes is about the same as that of pure alumina and is therefore an important cost factor. The greatest consideration is the availability of cheap and abundant power. Since most of the world's bauxite mines are at a great distance from the aluminum smelting plants, transportation costs also play a role. It sometimes costs about as much to transport alumina to the aluminum plant as to produce it.

The world produced 11 tons of aluminum in 1884, 66,700 tons in 1913,[79] 273,000 tons in 1929 and 1.9 million in 1943. In 1939, Germany, which has only small domestic supplies of bauxite, led in aluminum production. (See Table 343.)

The United States accounted for 35 or more per cent of the world's total aluminum output until the 1930's, when its share fell to 20–22 per cent. During the war, the country greatly expanded its output and in 1943, the peak year, produced more than five times as much as in 1939 and more than two fifths of the world total. The movement of bauxite ore to alumina plants and of alumina to aluminum plants during the war is shown in Figure 235.

Until 1941, the Aluminum Company of America (Alcoa) was the sole producer of alumina in the United States and the largest producer of aluminum. No other domestic company produced both alumina and aluminum before World War II. More than two thirds of the wartime expansion of productive capacity was financed by the government, which also supported an increase

---

77. **10**, pp. 220–22.

78. **28**, p. 38 and pp. 64–65.
79. **72**, p. 225.

TABLE 343

BAUXITE AND ALUMINUM: OUTPUT IN SELECTED COUNTRIES, 1924–50

(Thousands of Metric Tons [a]*)*

Country	1924	1929	1939	1943	1949	1950
			Bauxite			
World	...	2,149	4,370	13,970	7,700 [b]	7,500 [b]
United States [c]	353	· 372	396	6,333	1,167	1,369
British Guiana [d]	188	220	484	1,919	1,786	1,609
Surinam [d]	60	216	512	1,655	2,162	2,045
United Kingdom	5	2	...	108	—	—
France	389	666	800	916	766	805
Germany [e]	3	7	93	12	...	...
Hungary	...	389	500	1,001	300 [f]	...
Italy	141	193	484	292	105	153
Yugoslavia	19	103	314	...	368	201
Romania	—	1	11	13	...	...
Greece	1	6	187	25	45	...
USSR	...	...	270	313	500 [g]	...
Japan	...	...	23	...	...	...
India	24	9	9	25	41	52
Malay States	—	—	94	168 [h]	—	—
Indonesia	—	—	231	650	678	531
Gold Coast	—	7	24	163	148 [d]	117 [d]
			Aluminum			
World	168	273	670	1,946	1,308 [b]	1,300 [b]
United States	68	102	149	835	548	652
Canada	12	29	75	450	335	358
United Kingdom	8	8	25	57	31	30
France	16	29	50	46	54	61
Norway	20	29	31	24	36	47
Germany [e]	20	33	200	250	29	28
Switzerland	19	21	28	19	21	19
Hungary	—	—	2	9	14	...
Italy	2	7	34	46	26	37
Yugoslavia	—	—	2	2	2	2
USSR	—	—	50	62	140 [g]	...
Japan	...	...	22	108	21	25
India	—	—	—	1	4	4

Sources: **1,** various years; **18,** various years; **2,** 1951, pp. 153 and 261.

  a. Conversion factors: one metric ton = 1.1023 short tons = 2,204.6 pounds.
  b. Without the USSR.
  c. Beginning with 1939, dried equivalent of crude ore.
  d. Exports.
  e. For 1939, includes Austria; for 1949 and 1950, Western Germany.
  f. 1948.
  g. Estimate (**17,** September 1950, p. 4).
  h. Imports into Japan, Taiwan and Korea.

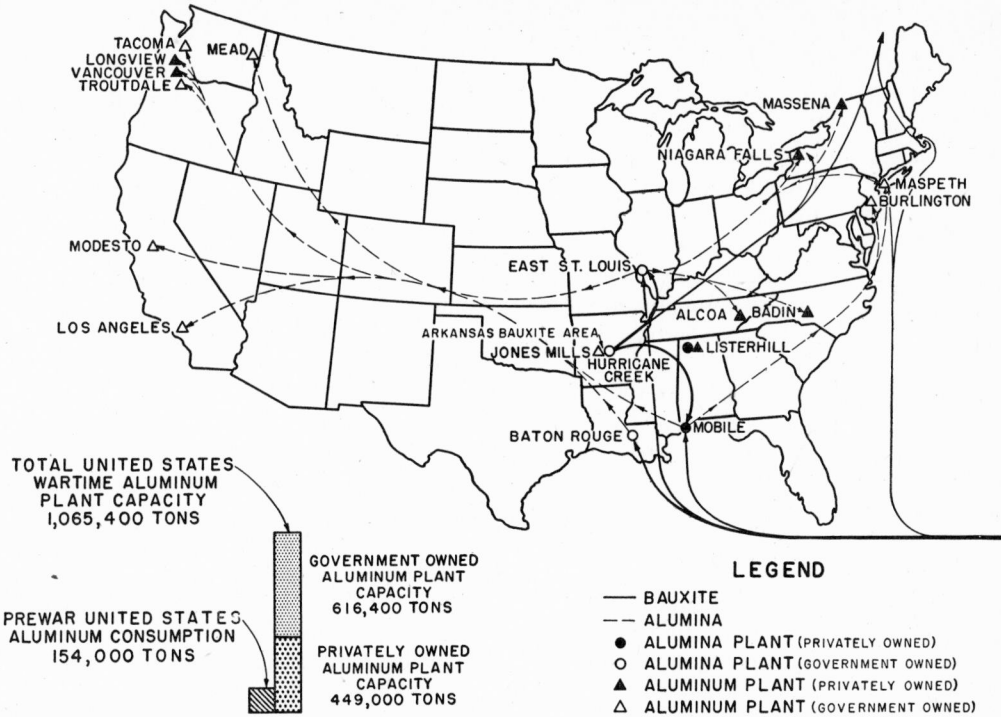

TOTAL UNITED STATES
WARTIME ALUMINUM
PLANT CAPACITY
1,065,400 TONS

PREWAR UNITED STATES
ALUMINUM CONSUMPTION
154,000 TONS

GOVERNMENT OWNED
ALUMINUM PLANT
CAPACITY
616,400 TONS

PRIVATELY OWNED
ALUMINUM PLANT
CAPACITY
449,000 TONS

LEGEND
—— BAUXITE
— — ALUMINA
● ALUMINA PLANT (PRIVATELY OWNED)
○ ALUMINA PLANT (GOVERNMENT OWNED)
▲ ALUMINUM PLANT (PRIVATELY OWNED)
△ ALUMINUM PLANT (GOVERNMENT OWNED)

U. S. Tariff Commission

FIGURE 235. ALUMINUM: LOCATION OF THE INDUSTRY AND MOVEMENTS OF BAUXITE AND ALUMINA IN THE UNITED STATES DURING WORLD WAR II

The United States obtains bauxite partly from domestic deposits in Arkansas, partly from British Guiana and Surinam. Most of its alumina plants are located in the Southeast — in Louisiana, Arkansas and Alabama — but there is one plant in Illinois. Aluminum plants are concentrated near sources of cheap hydroelectric power — in the Columbia River Basin, at Niagara Falls, in the Tennessee Valley; and others are scattered on the Pacific Coast. Thus, bauxite travels from Surinam to Baton Rouge and Mobile, and alumina is shipped from these cities to Tacoma and Mead in the state of Washington to be transformed into aluminum. The metal is then shipped back to eastern factories in Michigan, Illinois and Pennsylvania.

in Canadian capacity through contracts for a large part of the production and partial prepayment for purchases.

In 1944, Alcoa owned 44 per cent of the total alumina-producing capacity in the United States and 35 per cent of the aluminum capacity. It also operated two alumina plants representing an additional capacity of 52 per cent of the total, and eight aluminum plants with an additional 56 per cent — all of them owned by the government. With its Canadian affiliates, Alcoa controlled more than a third of the world's aluminum production in 1944.[80] In 1946, however, the government-owned facilities built in the war years were sold to other companies, considerably reducing Alcoa's share in aluminum production at all stages, though its lead remained great.[81]

When the war ended, production of aluminum in the United States shrank to less than half the 1943 peak volume, though it was still about three times as much as in 1939. Peacetime demand and the cold war, however, stimulated the industry to increase the output, which amounted to 548,000 tons in 1949 and 652,000 in 1950.

Canada ranks next to the United States, its chief asset being abundant and cheap hydroelectric power. Raw materials are imported: bauxite from Guiana, coal and coke from the United States, cryolite from Greenland.[82] In 1950, Canada produced almost as much aluminum as all Europe and the USSR together, and about a fourth of the world's total. Its reduction plant at Arvida, in the Saguenay Valley, is the largest

80. **28**, pp. 5–6 and 75.
81. **9**, pp. 105–09.

82. **34**, p. 1. Fluorspar used to be imported from Newfoundland, now a part of Canada.

in the world. In contrast, Guiana and Surinam, with a very large output of bauxite, produce no aluminum.

The USSR. With small reserves of domestic bauxite, the USSR has tried to utilize various other sources such as nephelin, a by-product of the apatite in the Kola Peninsula, and alunite in the Baku area.[83] Economic considerations have been of less importance, particularly during the war, than the drive to self-sufficiency and military objectives. Since the war, supplies of bauxite from Hungary have been supporting aluminum production in the USSR. The current output is estimated at 200,000–250,000 tons a year. A dismantled German aluminum plant has been re-erected in Kamensk Uralski, where the equipment from two Russian plants has also been transferred. The largest plant in Siberia is in Stalinsk.[84]

Japan started with an output of 19 tons of aluminum in 1933, which grew by 1943 to 150,000 tons, of which about 108,000 tons were produced in the home islands, the rest in Korea, Taiwan and Manchuria. In the last year of the war, however, production was cut down to about 16,000 tons by the success of American submarines in blocking bauxite imports from the Indies and Malaya. The capacity of the Japanese plants is still large, but during the occupation production of aluminum was held within the limits permitted by the occupation forces (25,000 metric tons in 1950).[85]

MAGNESIUM

Properties and Uses

Magnesium, the lightest of engineering metals, readily alloys with various other metals and gives the alloys tensile strength equal to that of structural steel. Its machinability is superior to that of other metals,[86] but its drawback is low resistance to corrosion in sea water. Lately, however, corrosion-resistant magnesium alloys have been developed that are comparable with high-grade aluminum alloys. The fear of igniting magnesium prevalent before World War II has been greatly reduced by improved handling techniques.

Magnesium is used in its pure form for fire-

works, flashlights, signal flares and incendiary bombs; as a deoxidizer; and for high-grade refractories and in metallurgy; but its chief use is in the form of alloys, mainly with aluminum. Magnesium castings are the strongest commercial castings for their weight and permit easier and faster machining than any other commercial machining material.[87] Magnesium alloys are used in portable and pneumatic tools, bearings, parts for rapidly moving machinery, field glasses, cameras, microscopes and various types of surveying and industrial equipment. The magnesium industry is intensively experimenting with new processes for the use of the metal. Among the outstanding developments are new processes for electroplating magnesium and for arc welding heavy magnesium plates, as well as the alloying of magnesium with various other metals, such as cerium, zirconium and lithium.[88]

Transportation equipment, chiefly aircraft, remains the chief consumer of magnesium products in the United States. For example, more than five tons of magnesium sheet are used in the production of a B-36 airplane. Research in the use of magnesium powder as a jet-engine fuel is under way.[89]

Sources

Magnesium is produced from sea water or underground brine and from ores (magnesite, brucite and dolomite). Large deposits of magnesite are found in many parts of the world. The United States has magnesite deposits in California, Washington and Nevada; Canada, in Quebec; Austria, in Styria; Greece, in Euboea. Czechoslovakia has a 75-mile belt with many deposits. The USSR's magnesite deposits are in the Urals. The world's largest deposits are in Manchuria, within a 9-mile belt.

Magnesite has been the chief source of magnesium, but during World War II it was displaced by sea water. The reserves of magnesium in sea water and underground brine are practically inexhaustible. One cubic mile of sea water may contain as much as 5.4 million tons of magnesium, vastly more than has been produced from all other sources since magnesium was discovered more than a hundred and forty years ago.[90]

The production of magnesium from sea water

83. **47,** 1948, p. 448.
84. **66,** March 1951, pp. 35–36.
85. **58,** April 1949, p. 10.
86. **46,** p. 163.

87. **3,c,** p. 250.
88. **18,** 1948, pp. 752–58.
89. **18,** 1949, pp. 729–31.
90. **3,d,** p. 258.

TABLE 344

MAGNESIUM: OUTPUT IN SELECTED COUNTRIES, 1938–50

(*Thousands of Metric Tons* [a])

Country	1938	1940	1942	1944	1946	1948	1949	1950
World	23.7	37.8	104.9	209.6	24.0	32.0	35.0	40.0
United States	2.2	5.7	44.4	142.5	4.8	9.1	10.5	14.3
Canada [b]	—	—	0.4	4.8	0.1	...	...	1.6
United Kingdom [c]	2.2	6.0	14.9	13.1	0.6	3.9	5.2	4.8
France [d]	1.8	2.6	1.3	0.7	0.7	1.5	0.7	0.3
Norway	—	—	2.0	2.0	...	...	...	...
Germany	14.0	17.7	30.0	33.6	—	—	—	—
Switzerland	0.7	0.7	1.5	1.0	0.3	—	...	...
Italy	0.1	0.4	2.4	1.4	1.0	0.6	...	...
USSR [e]	0.5	1.5	5.0	5.0	...	...	...	...
Korea	—	—	0.2	1.6	—	—	...	...
Japan	1.5	2.7	2.0	2.9	—	—	—	—
Australia	—	—	0.5	0.1	—	—	—	—

Sources: **29**, p. 19; **18**, various years, and 1950 preprint; **2**, 1951, p. 259.

a. Conversion factors: one metric ton = 1.1023 short tons = 2,204.6 pounds.
b. Refined magnesium.

c. For 1948–50, secondary magnesium (metal and alloys).
d. Includes secondary magnesium.
e. The USSR's present output is estimated at 40,000 tons a year. (**66**, March 1951, p. 36.)

is fairly simple but requires large amounts of lime or calcined dolomite and about as much electric power per ton as the production of aluminum. Plants are located as close as possible to the sea, preferably near sea level, to reduce pumping expenses. In general, the output of magnesium depends not so much on the availability of the raw material as on cheap electric power, the market price of the product and other economic considerations.

Output

Germany, the first country to produce magnesium commercially, dominated the world market until World War II. In other countries, production did not begin until the early 1930's, except for a negligible output in the United States, and was entered upon at first on a small scale.

The world's output of magnesium in 1925 was only 1,800 metric tons; in 1938, 23,700 tons. In 1944, nine times as much, 209,600 tons, was produced. Output in the United States increased even more spectacularly — from 2,200 tons in 1938 to 142,500 tons in 1944. The production

built up for war purposes was discontinued at the war's end. The world output of magnesium in 1946 was only 24,000 tons; that of the United States, less than 5,000.

There has been only a very slow postwar revival in magnesium production. In 1949 the total output was 35,000 tons, of which the United States produced some 10,500 tons. The USSR, the United Kingdom and France produced almost all the rest. A substantial part of the output of the two latter countries was in secondary metal. (See Table 344.)

The entire output of primary magnesium in the United States comes from a plant at Freeport, Texas, which produces it from sea water.[91] Seven government-owned magnesium plants remaining from World War II have been reconditioned to stand-by readiness.

One deterrent to a larger output of primary magnesium has been the availability of scrap; the output of secondary magnesium in 1949 totaled more than 5,000 metric tons in the United States.

Of the five magnesium plants operating in

91. **18**, 1949, p. 727.

Germany during World War II, the Russians dismantled three and kept one, the Bitterfeld plant, for the production of calcium metal. The only plant in Western Germany has also been dismantled.

PRECIOUS METALS

Gold by far outranks the other two precious metals, silver and platinum, in value of annual output. In 1949, the world's output of gold represented more than a billion dollars, as compared to $150 million for silver and $42 million for platinum.[92]

GOLD AND SILVER

Properties and Uses

Gold and, next to it, silver are the most malleable of all metals. A gram of pure silver can be drawn into a wire more than a mile long, a gram of gold into one a mile and a half long. An ounce of gold, hammered to a leaf 1/200,000 inch thick, can cover 100 square feet of surface.[93] Silver is the best conductor of heat and electricity. Gold has a high resistance to corrosion and is practically indestructible; its stability and the ease with which it can be separated from other metals have permitted its recovery in an extremely pure state since very early days. Commercial gold is 99.95 to 99.99 per cent pure.[94]

Both silver and gold are used primarily for monetary purposes — silver predominantly in Asia, gold in the rest of the world. Considerable quantities are used for jewelry and other ornamental purposes. High marriage rates and increased earnings during and since World War II have stimulated a large consumption of gold in the form of wedding rings, watches and jewelry. Gold is also used in dentistry, precision instruments, X-ray equipment and various chemicals; silver, in photography, soldering and sterilizing compounds and other chemicals.

During World War II, silver was used in the United States in many types of weapons and equipment, engine bearings and electrical appliances, and, in considerable quantities, for military insignia. The ratio between monetary and other uses of silver varies in the United States from year to year. It was about 1 to 2 in 1940, 1 to 1.2 in 1943, 1 to 4 in 1947.[95]

Deposits

Gold is obtained chiefly from ore deposits (placers, veins or lodes), but often is also extracted as a by-product of the mining of base-metal ores. Silver is ordinarily separated from the ores of base metals, although there are a few mines where silver is found alone, as in Coeur d'Alene, Idaho. Gold and silver commonly occur together. The close association of silver with copper, lead and zinc, on the one hand, and with gold, on the other, is illustrated by the fact that since the beginning of the world's known production of gold and silver, the "silver-bearing ores which produced 91 per cent of the world's silver also produced 85 per cent of the world's gold, 69 per cent of the world's lead, 66 per cent of the world's copper and 46 per cent of the world's zinc." [96] On the other hand, the wartime increase in production of base metals in the United States resulted in the extraction of large quantities of gold as a by-product, while many gold mines were closed.[97] Both gold and silver are found in minute quantities in sea water, but no technique has yet been developed to extract them profitably.

The chief world deposits of gold are in the United States, the Union of South Africa, the USSR, Canada, Mexico and Australia; of silver, in the United States, Mexico, Canada, Peru and Australia.

The most important gold deposits of the United States are in South Dakota, California, Colorado and Alaska; of silver, in Idaho, Montana, Nevada, Utah. The main Canadian deposits of gold are in Ontario; of silver, in British Columbia, Quebec and Saskatchewan.

The most famous gold deposit in the world is the Witwatersrand, or simply the Rand, of South Africa (Transvaal), where gold has been mined to a depth of about 10,000 feet. The world's greatest silver mines, some of which have been producing since the early 1500's, are in Mexico. Bolivia and Peru also have important silver deposits.

The USSR has gold lodes in Transbaikalia and on the Lena; placer deposits in the Urals, on the Yenisei River in the Yakutsk region, on the Kolyma and the Amur, and in Altai. Silver is extracted from polymetallic ores in Altai, Chimkent, North Ossetia and other regions.

In Australia, West Australia is the chief gold

---

92. See Table 325.
93. Both metals are beaten to leaves by the same method as was used 5,000 years ago. (**74**, p. 288.)
94. **68**, p. 142.
95. **38**, 1947, p. 89.

96. **13**, p. 3.
97. The Bingham, Utah, copper district became the leading producer of gold during the war.

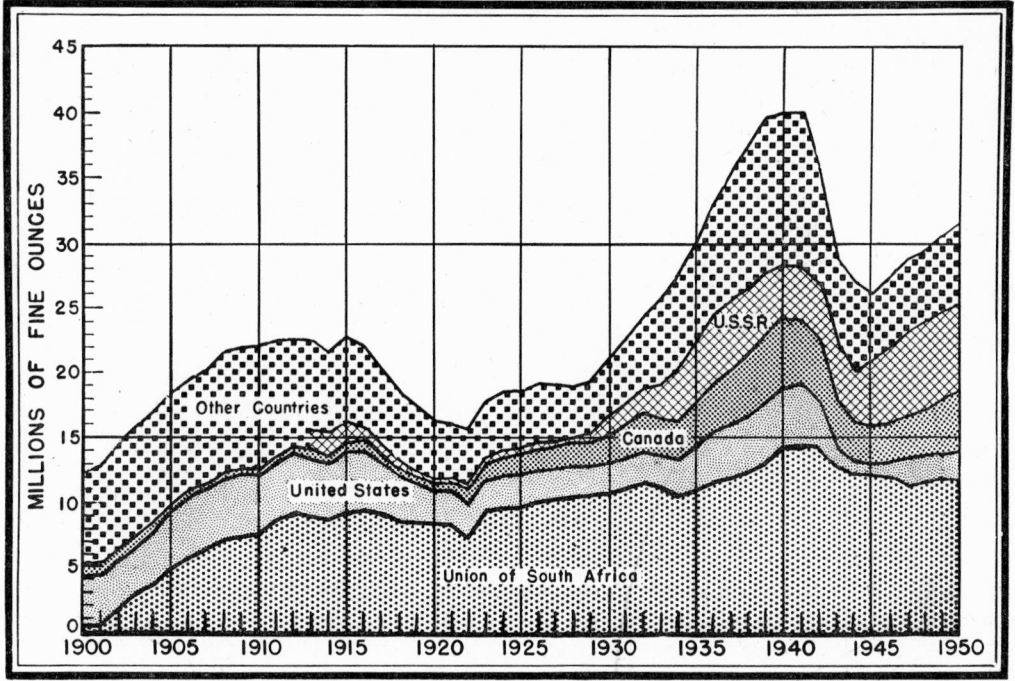

U. S. Bureau of Mines

FIGURE 236. GOLD: OUTPUT IN THE WORLD AND SELECTED COUNTRIES, 1900–1950

producer; New South Wales and Queensland have the largest silver deposits. India has one of the world's great gold deposits, in the Kolar district.

Development of World Output

Statistics of the output of gold and silver traditionally begin with 1493, the year after Columbus had discovered the New World. After that time, gold and silver from Mexico, Peru, Chile and Bolivia began to flow to Europe, chiefly to Spain and Portugal. Gold was not discovered in the United States until 1801, silver not until the 1860's.

The chief producers of gold are the Union of South Africa, the USSR, Canada and the United States (see Figure 236); of silver, Mexico, the United States, Canada and Peru (see Figure 237).

The following figures show the development of the world's output of precious metals over the centuries (in millions of fine ounces, cumulative within each period): [98]

	Gold	Silver
1493–1600	23.0	746.9
1601–1700	28.8	1,271.9
1701–1800	61.2	1,832.8
1801–1900	374.3	5,098.6
1901–25	477.5	4,901.3
1926–50	653.3	5,442.4

At one time gold money circulated freely, and all other types of money could be converted into it. Since World War I, the gold stock has been held largely by central banks and government treasuries as a legal reserve or for the stabilization of exchange rates. Some quantities of both gold and silver, particularly of gold, are hoarded by private individuals, a tendency that has been greatly stimulated by the depreciation of currencies in many countries. Since little gold is lost through war or otherwise, the world has, at any given time, almost all the gold produced since 1493. In fact, part of the gold treasure that the Spaniards brought from Mexico and Peru in the sixteenth century can still be traced and identified. Some of the gold now at Fort Knox, Kentucky, may have been a part of the treasures of the Pharaohs.[99]

The Federal Reserve System has estimated the world's reserves of gold in monetary funds, private hoards and other sources at one billion

---

98. **21**, p. 6; **13**, p. 3; **63**, 1951, pp. 649 and 660.

99. **61**, p. 22.

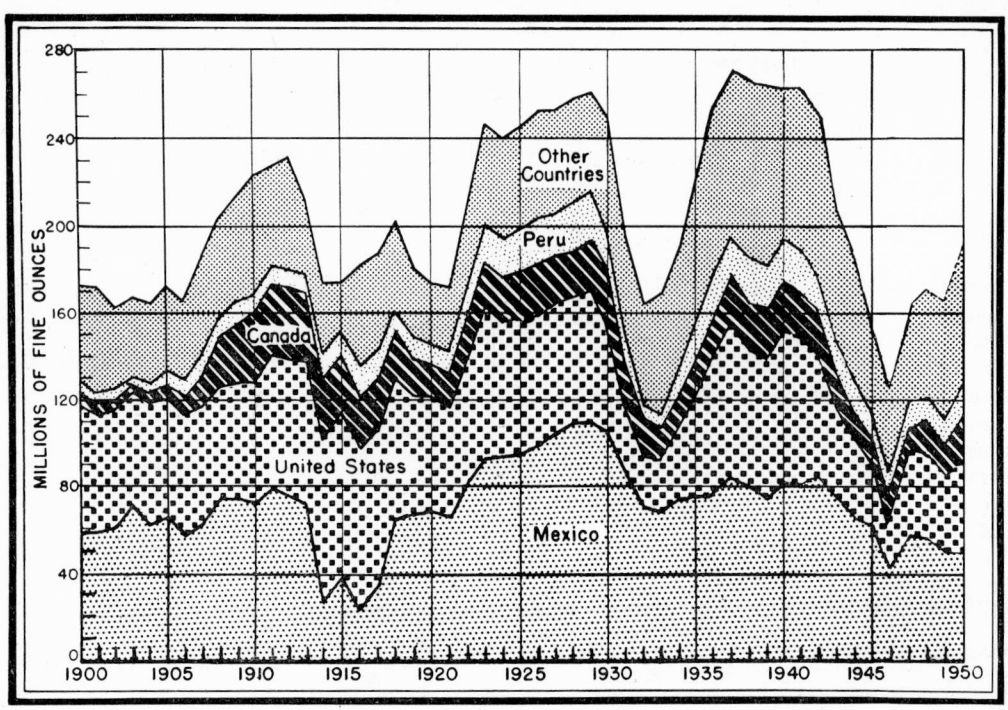

U. S. Bureau of Mines

FIGURE 237. SILVER: OUTPUT IN THE WORLD AND SELECTED COUNTRIES, 1900–1950

ounces in 1945. This figure is fairly close to the cumulative production of gold in the preceding four and a half centuries. After having traveled all over the world, more than half this stockpile (about 62 per cent) has landed in Kentucky.[100]

Current Production of Gold

The Union of South Africa, the USSR, Canada and the United States together accounted for 70 per cent of the world's gold output in 1939 and 80 per cent in 1950. (See Table 345 and Figure 236.)

The Union of South Africa. From 1884, when production statistics were introduced in the Union of South Africa, until 1929, the Rand produced 220 million fine ounces of gold out of the country's total of 229 million,[101] and it produced an equal amount between 1929 and 1950. This one deposit alone has accounted for nearly 30 per cent of the world's total output between 1493 and 1950. A new "Rand" district in the Free Orange State has been discovered, and work in the mines has begun.

The United States. California accounted for almost 38 per cent of all gold produced in the United States between 1898 and 1945; Colorado, for nearly 15 per cent; Alaska and Nevada, for 9–10 per cent each.[102]

The production of gold has not yet returned to the prewar all-time peak, which was reached in 1940 (4.9 million ounces). The industry resumed work after the war on a smaller scale, because of the unchanged price of gold and the difficulties of recruiting labor, on the one hand, and, on the other, the higher prices for equipment and higher wages and the need, in many instances, to make large outlays to rehabilitate gold mines that were closed during the war. Slightly more than 2 million ounces were produced in 1950, over 70 per cent in California, South Dakota, Alaska and Utah.[103]

The USSR. Production of gold in the USSR has been kept highly secret since the middle of the 1930's. Even the geological formation of the newly discovered deposits and the metal content of their ores have not been reported. It is believed that, except in the war years, produc-

100. **18**, 1945, p. 107.
101. **52**, pp. 337–38.

102. **18**, 1945, p. 96.
103. **18**, 1950, preprint.

TABLE 345

GOLD AND SILVER: OUTPUT IN SELECTED COUNTRIES, 1493–1950

Country	Cumulative 1493–1900	Cumulative 1901–25	1929	1939	1949	1950
	Gold, in Thousands of Fine Ounces					
World	487,291	477,527	19,500	40,040	30,800	31,600
United States	115,392	93,916	2,060	4,620	1,922	2,289
Canada	6,969	21,180	1,930	5,094	4,124	4,481
Mexico	11,783	18,926	650	842	406	408
Nicaragua	...	...	27	110	219 [a]	229
Venezuela	2,596	550	46	147	61	34
Colombia	42,796	4,703	136	570	359	379
Ecuador	40	596	39	89	99	92
Brazil	34,680	3,076	110	253	184	180
Peru	5,533	1,393	120	267	138	129
Bolivia	9,670	34	2	9 [b]	34	2 [a]
Chile	9,337	1,087	33	369	179	207
French Guiana	1,820	2,151	49	39	15 [a]	12
British Guiana	1,166	1,140	6	36	14	12
Sweden	51	22	35	216	80	c
Germany [h]	1,071	100	6	5	c	c
Czechoslovakia	—	54	9	10	c	c
Hungary [d]	16,586	1,560	...	5	c	c
Yugoslavia	—	36	33	72	c	c
Romania	—	261	71	154	113	c
Russia (USSR)	62,533	24,625	1,100	5,200 [e]	7,000 [e]	7,000 [e]
China	5,683	5,249	78	302	60 [e]	160 [e]
Korea	843	3,565	178	844	c	c
Japan	500	4,939	490	836 [e]	84	132
India	3,024	12,642	360	315	164	197
Philippines	—	918	152	1,040	288	334
Belgian Congo	—	1,283	158	522	334	339 [e]
Gold Coast	...	...	208	793	677	680 [e]
Southern Rhodesia	241	14,359	560	796	528	511
Union of South Africa	20,520	178,437	10,410	12,822	11,705	11,664
Australia [f]	91,388	54,495	430	1,646	982	995
New Zealand	13,471	8,163	118	179	85	77
Fiji	—	—	...	108	104	103

(*Continued on page 816*)

tion of gold and the search for new gold reserves have been intensified. Forced labor is largely used to work the deposits in remote regions, some of them near the Arctic Circle. Apparently the placer deposits of the Lena region have been exhausted, but important gold veins have been discovered in Transbaikalia, on the Kolyma, and particularly in Kazakhstan, hailed in the Russian press as the "Soviet Transvaal."

Without issuing information to substantiate the statement, the USSR claims to be second only to the Union of South Africa in gold production, surpassing Canada and the United States.[104] A substantial part of its gold output must come from polymetallic ores of the Urals. Since only small amounts of Russian gold appear on international markets, it is supposed that the USSR is hoarding gold, possibly outside as well as within its borders, for unknown purposes.[105]

104. **40**, p. 267.
105. **47**, 1948, p. 433.

Table 345—*continued*

Country	Cumulative 1493–1900	1901–25	1929	1939	1949	1950
	Silver, in Millions of Fine Ounces					
World	8,950	4,901.3	261	267	174	192
United States	1,338	1,530	61	64	35	42
Canada	30	465	23	23	18	22
Mexico	3,306	1,615	109	76	49	49
Peru	1,072	240	22	19	11	13
Bolivia [a]	1,447	...	5	7	7	7
Chile	242	...	2	1	1	1
Germany [h]	363	124 [i]	6	6	2	c
Hungary [d]	294	...	...	g	g	g
Spain	100	88 [i]	3	g	1	1
Russia (USSR)	87	5 [i]	...	7	c	c
Japan	132	99 [j]	6	10	3	4
Belgian Congo	...	...	...	3	5	4
Australia [f]	156	253	9	15	10	11

Sources: **21**, pp. 12–13 and Appendix; **13**, pp. 8–11; **18**, various years; **17**, December 1950, p. 9; **75**, pp. 196–97; **67**, May 1951, pp. 7–9.

a. Exports.
b. Purchases by the State Central Bank.
c. Data not available. Estimate (U. S. Bureau of Mines) included in the total.

d. Austria-Hungary; Hungary from 1919 only.
e. Estimate. (U. S. Bureau of Mines.)
f. Includes New Guinea.
g. Less than half a million ounces.
h. Western Germany in 1949 and 1950.
i. Data incomplete.
j. Includes Taiwan and Korea.

Current Silver Production

Mexico, the United States, Canada and Peru together accounted for 68 per cent of the world's output of silver in 1939 and 66 per cent in 1950. Australia, Japan and the USSR together produced an additional 12 per cent in 1939; Australia, Bolivia and Japan together, about 11 per cent in 1950. (See Table 345 and Figure 237.)

Montana, Colorado and Utah each accounted for about 19 per cent of all silver produced in the United States from 1858–62 to 1945; Nevada, for about 15 per cent.

With the increase in output of polymetallic ores in the USSR, production of silver has probably been rising in that country. Exact information is not available, however, and trade statistics of other countries show no imports of silver from the USSR since 1936.[106]

PLATINUM

Platinum usually occurs in combination with other rare metals — osmium, palladium, iridium, rhodium and ruthenium — which therefore are called the platinum-group metals. Their outstanding common properties are a high melting point and great catalytic capacity.

Uses

Platinum has been used primarily for jewelry, although Russia used it in the middle of the nineteenth century for coinage as well. It is now employed chiefly for industrial purposes — in the chemical and electrical industries, dentistry, medical equipment, measuring and recording devices. During World War II, platinum and related metals were used extensively for radar, the bombsight in superfortresses, and in the manufacture of explosives. The use of platinum and its alloys for jewelry was prohibited in the United States. Indeed, platinum, it was said, "has taken off its white collar and put on overalls." [107] In 1949, 53 per cent of the platinum used in the United States went into jewelry; 40 per cent into chemical and electrical industries; 6 per cent into dentistry; and the rest for miscellaneous purposes.[108]

106. **47**, 1948, p. 436.

107. **70**, p. 127.
108. **63**, 1951, pp. 668–69.

TABLE 346

PLATINUM-GROUP METALS: OUTPUT IN SELECTED COUNTRIES, 1929–50

(*Thousands of Troy Ounces* [a])

Country	1929	1934	1939	1942	1945	1948	1949	1950
World [b]	213.0	281.7	543.0	773.0	964.0	529.0	576.0	585.0
United States [c]								
Placer platinum	0.8	3.7	32.5	23.2	26.6	13.7	17.2	
From refineries:								
Platinum	}5.2	1.1{	5.3	4.3	1.1	1.3	1.8	}37.9
Related metals			3.4	5.5	3.4	4.3	5.8	
Canada								
From refineries:								
Platinum	}12.5	116.2{	148.9	285.2	208.2 [d]	121.4	153.8	121.1
Related metals			135.4	222.6	458.7 [d]	148.3	182.2	148.3
Colombia [e]	45.6	54.8	39.1	49.2	30.9	40.0	20.8	26.4
USSR [f]	115.8	70.7	100.0	100.0	150.0	125.0	100.0	100.0
Ethiopia [e]	7.7	5.6	6.0	1.0	...	0.5	0.4	...
Belgian Congo [g]	1.3	1.3	4.2	...	...	0.2	0.1	...
Union of South Africa:								
Platinum	25.4	27.5	59.2 [h]	73.3 [h]	74.9 [h]	68.9 [h]	87.3 [h]	144.2 [h]
Osmiridium from gold ores	...	...	7.0	...	6.3	5.5	6.0	6.4
Australia [i]	0.1	0.2	0.3	0.1	0.1	0.1	[j]	[j]

Sources: **65**, p. 436; **18**, various years; **17**, October 1950, p. 25.

a. Conversion factor: one pound = 14.6 troy ounces.
b. Total includes small output in Italy, Japan, Indonesia, Sierra Leone, Papua and New Zealand.
c. Placer platinum includes small quantities of platinum in ores. Data on refineries cover new metals recovered from domestic gold and copper materials.

d. Includes some metal produced in 1938–44 but not reported previously in the statistics.
e. Placer platinum.
f. Estimated placer platinum and platinum recovered from nickel-copper ores.
g. Data include palladium and platinum.
h. Platinum and concentrates of platinum-group metals.
i. Largely osmiridium.
j. Less than 50 troy ounces.

Output

The world's main centers of platinum production are Sudbury, Canada; the Urals, in the USSR; and the Bushveld, in the Union of South Africa. Alaska and the Choco district of Colombia have smaller centers. Sources of platinum metals in other countries are of minor significance.

In the United States, platinum is obtained chiefly from placers, but some metal is recovered in refining gold and copper. Almost all of Canada's output comes from the refining of nickel-copper ores. The Union of South Africa is the only place in the world where straight platinum ore is mined.

The world's annual output of platinum fluctuated between 625,000 and 750,000 troy ounces during the latter part of the nineteenth century, with Russia almost the exclusive producer. After World War I, the output declined to an average of about 50,000 troy ounces and Russia dropped from first place. First Colombia, and later Canada, advanced to the lead.

World War II brought a temporary increase in production, especially in Canada. World output reached its peak in 1945. After the war, production declined rapidly, but it began to recover in 1949, when the output was greater than in 1939, and increased again in 1950. Canada remains the ranking producer. (See Table 346.)

OTHER METALS

In the group of other metals, which are used mainly in alloys or as auxiliary raw materials in various industries, uranium holds a unique position because of its strategic importance.

URANIUM AND RADIUM

Properties and Uses

Although uranium metal was first isolated about a hundred years ago, it was so little known before 1940 that even its exact melting point had not been established. Substantial amounts of high-purity uranium were needed for the atomic bomb project of the United States, but until the end of 1941 only a few grams were available. Pure uranium was not obtained until 1942.[109] Uranium salts have been used chiefly as a ceramic colorant, a mordant in dyeing, a component of photographic chemicals, and a catalyst for radium and luminous paints, and in medicine. Since World War II, the relationship between radium and uranium has been reversed. Most of the uranium now produced is used for atomic energy, and radioactive elements useful in medicine are by-products of the production of uranium.[110]

Sources

Uranium is a ubiquitous mineral, occurring in all rocks and also in natural waters, but generally in such low concentration that its presence can be detected only by special, sensitive instruments. Mines capable of producing uranium in significant quantity exist in a few localities only, and their production from about 1898 until recent times was dictated entirely by the demand for radium, while uranium was merely a by-product.[111]

The chief ores of uranium and radium are pitchblende and uraninite and carnotite. The world's two largest and richest pitchblende deposits are in Canada and the Belgian Congo. The ore in Canada (at Great Bear Lake, Northwest Territories) is of such high grade that it has paid to transport it by air in winter to a plant in Ontario for the recovery of radium.[112] The Shinkolobwe mine at Haut Katanga in the Belgian Congo is the world's largest producer of pitchblende and one of the main sources of uranium metal produced in the United States. Both these deposits are very extensive.

The Joachimsthal deposit in Czechoslovakia, from the pitchblende of which the Curies extracted radium in 1898, is now controlled by the USSR. A pitchblende deposit in Erz Gebirge, eastern Germany, is also under Russian control. The USSR may obtain uranium from ores in Bulgaria and the uraniferous black marine shales

in Estonia, extending into the Leningrad area.[113] The USSR is known to have uranium ore deposits in the Caucasus, central Asia, the Altai Mountains of Asia and the Urals. Small deposits are scattered in many other areas — Norway, France, Portugal, Spain, Argentina and Madagascar.

The carnotite deposits in the United States (Colorado Plateau) contain uranium and also vanadium, the content of which increases in lower-grade ores. These deposits have experienced several periods of development. First they were exploited primarily for radium, then for vanadium. The mines were closed for a time and reopened for extraction of vanadium in 1934, when Peru introduced a new export tax on its vanadium ore. By the outbreak of World War II, the Colorado Plateau mines were the major source of vanadium. Tailings from these operations were used for the Manhattan Project, and today production is largely concentrated on uranium.[114]

Uranium ore has been discovered in an abandoned copper-silver mine in Australia (New South Wales) and in eastern China (Kwangsi Province). It is believed that the gold mines of the Rand (Union of South Africa), oil shales in Sweden and marine phosphate deposits in the United States may eventually produce uranium as a by-product.[115]

Output

There is only scattered information on the production of radium and almost none on uranium. An intensive global hunt for uranium is being carried on, mainly because of its military importance, but all nations keep secret the quantities they mine, export or refine.

Until about 1940, uranium ores were mined primarily for the production of radium, an extremely rare element. About three tons of uranium ores had to be processed to obtain one gram of radium.[116]

France was the first country to produce radium, using ore imported from Portugal, the United States and other countries, but its output slumped

109. **18**, 1945, pp. 825–30.
110. **18**, 1946, p. 1217.
111. **44**, pp. 1–2.
112. **74**, p. 343.

113. **18**, 1949, p. 1257. According to recent reports, the Joachimsthal deposit now provides decreasing amounts of uranium. (**66**, March 1951, p. 35.)
114. **66**, March 1949, pp. 37–38; and **67**, December 29, 1950, p. 637.
115. **67**, December 29, 1950, p. 637.
116. **72**, p. 95.

during World War I. The carnotite deposits of Colorado and Utah, with 1–1.5 per cent uranium content, were discovered in 1903. The United States soon gained the lead in radium production; its output rose from 10 grams in 1913 to 22 grams in 1914 and 35 in 1921; by 1923 the cumulative total was 215 grams, valued at $120,000 a gram. In addition, 1.6 millions pounds of uranium oxide, at $1.75 a pound, were produced, and more than 300,000 tons of carnotite ore were dumped or blocked out in mines.

In 1922, the Colorado radium industry was ruined overnight when radium from the Belgian Congo suddenly appeared on world markets. Actually, pitchblende ore had been discovered in the Belgian Congo around 1913, but use of it to produce radium was kept in the greatest secrecy until Belgium announced its possession of large quantities of finished radium. By 1930, the Belgian Congo was producing 60 grams a year.[117] In that year, the Great Bear Lake deposit in Canada was discovered, and a radium plant was installed at Port Hope, Ontario. Before World War II, Canada produced 70–90 grams a year; the Belgian Congo, more than 100; the United States, 8; Germany (from Czech pitchblende) from 1 to 3 grams, and Czechoslovakia, from 3 to 4.[118]

The world's cumulative output of radium from the time of its discovery until World War II amounted to about 1,180 grams, of which 600 came from the Belgian Congo, 300 from the United States, 140 from Canada, 55 from Czechoslovakia, 51 from France, and the remainder from five other countries. The price of radium declined by 1935 to about $70,000 a gram, and after World War II, to about $25,000.[119]

Since 1941, the United States has produced the following amounts of radium (in grams): [120]

	From Domestic Ore	From Canadian Ore
1941–43 average	2.0	—
1944	0.2	21.8
1945	0.2	31.4
1946	0.2	17.4
1947	16.4	—
1948	4.2	3.5

117. **66,** March 1949, pp. 37–38; and **45,** pp. 36–40.
118. **41,** p. 619. Figure for the Belgian Congo estimated; official statistics not published after 1933.
119. **45,** p. 59; and **72,** p. 97.
120. **18,** 1948, p. 1266. Data for 1941–43 and 1944 exclude confidential figures representing certain shipments from October 1943 to May 1944.

The estimated value ranged from $18,000 to $26,000 per gram.

ANTIMONY

Properties and Uses

The outstanding property of antimony is expansion on solidifying, in contrast with the prevailing tendency of other molten metals to shrink in cooling. By adding a proper amount of antimony to other metals, an alloy is obtained which, when cast, solidifies so as to fill a mold with perfect precision. This property of antimony is valued in making type metal. Although only small quantities are thus consumed, the metal is of great importance for this use alone.

The largest single use of antimony is in an alloy with lead, making the lead so hard that it can be used in ways otherwise not feasible.[121] In the United States, for example, about half the consumption of antimony is in lead-alloy form. Antimony is used for storage batteries, the sheathing of cables, pipes in chemical industries, ammunition and antifriction bearings. The nonalloy uses are in paints, enamel and safety matches, and for vulcanizing, soldering and so on. The industrial consumption of primary antimony in the United States has been distributed as follows (in short tons): [122]

	1944	1949
Metal products	12,247	6,899
Antimonial lead	5,287	}4,737
Battery metal	2,341	
Bearing metal and bearings	2,637	873
Cable covering	422	172
Castings	115	49
Collapsible tubes and foil	114	14
Sheet and pipe	326	306
Type metal	841	587
Solder	71	155
Ammunition	93	6
Nonmetal products	11,509	4,631
Flameproofed textiles	7,063	422
Paints and lacquers	2,490	874
Frits and ceramic enamels	501	1,155
Other	1,455	2,180

Deposits

The world's chief deposits of antimony are in China (Hunan Province), which has the largest field, containing 1.5 million tons of metallic

121. **71,** pp. 939–40.
122. **18,** 1949, p. 128.

antimony, and about 0.5 million tons in other fields; in Bolivia, which has large reserves of high-grade ore (about 500 million tons); and in Mexico, which has many large and small fields (also about 500 million tons).[123] Yugoslavia, Czechoslovakia, Algeria, the Union of South Africa and Australia also have antimony deposits.

The principal source of antimony in the United States is the Yellow Pine mine in Idaho, where antimony is obtained as a by-product in mining tungsten and gold. Various other western states have small deposits.

Output

The world's output of antimony in 1939 exceeded 37,000 tons; in 1943, 53,000 tons. After the decline in postwar years, the world's output in 1950 amounted to 38,000 tons. China, the largest producer before the war, now ranks fifth. In contrast, the Union of South Africa, which produced only 7 tons in 1939, now vies with Bolivia for first place. Of the 1950 total output, Bolivia accounted for 23 per cent; the Union of South Africa for 21 per cent; and Mexico for some 15 per cent. The output of the United States in 1950 was only about half the wartime peak, but about seven times as large as in 1939. (See Table 347.)

In addition, a considerable amount of antimony is recovered from lead alloys. In the United States, secondary recovery has yielded more in recent years than primary metals, domestic and foreign. Plates, grids and sludge from discarded storage batteries are the main source of these supplies.

MERCURY

Properties and Uses

Mercury is the only common metal that remains liquid even at the lowest natural temperature in moderate climates. Before the development of cyanidation, mercury was used largely in the recovery of gold and silver because of its ability to amalgamate.[124] Now mercury has many and diversified uses: in thermometrical and electrical instruments, in boiler plants for the generation of power, in amalgamation for recovering gold and silver from ores, in dentistry and in chemicals, for detonating high explosives, in tracer

bullets, and in antifouling paints for ship bottoms, red pigments, mirrors and so on. During World War II mercuric oxide was used in dry-cell batteries.[125]

The 49,215 flasks of mercury consumed in the United States in 1950 were used for the following purposes: electrical, industrial and control instruments, 35 per cent; in agriculture, about 9 per cent; pharmaceuticals and dental preparations, about 15 per cent; redistillation, 15 per cent; as a catalyst, about 5.5 per cent; and the remaining 20.5 per cent for many other purposes.[126]

Deposits

The world's principal deposits of cinnabar, the principal commercial mercury mineral, are along the northern part of the Mediterranean and on the Pacific coast of the United States. The Almadén mine in Spain is the richest in the world. Worked for more than 2,000 years, it still holds the largest known reserves, sufficient to meet the world's needs for the next century. By 1944, the cumulative output of Almadén, recorded since 1500, amounted to 6.5 million flasks, more than had been produced by all other mercury mines together.[127] Next in importance is the cinnabar deposit in Tuscany, Italy, though its ore averages only one per cent mercury as against 8 per cent and, in some parts, 14 per cent in the Almadén body. There is also a cinnabar deposit in Trieste.

In the United States, the two chief mines are in California: New Idria, with workings 1,200 feet deep; and New Almaden, the world's deepest mercury mine (nearly 2,500 feet). For many years before World War II, New Almaden's output was negligible, but operations were expanded in 1941. Almost all the western states, as well as Arkansas and Texas, work cinnabar deposits, but the Cordero mine in Nevada and the Bonanza mine in Oregon, both important producers, have been closed. The closing of the Bonanza mine is said to be permanent.[128]

Minor deposits are worked in the USSR, Czechoslovakia, Germany, China, Japan, Canada, Mexico, Peru, Algeria and some other countries.

123. **41**, p. 608, and **27**, Vol II, p. 140.

124. The gold rush in California gave impetus to the development of mercuric mining in the United States. **59**, pp. 533–49.

125. This new use called for large quantities of mercury. Efforts are now being made to adapt this battery to large-scale peacetime use. Mercuric batteries for hearing aids are already on the market.

126. **18**, 1949, p. 765.

127. **18**, 1945, p. 722.

128. **18**, 1949, p. 758.

TABLE 347

ANTIMONY: OUTPUT IN SELECTED COUNTRIES, 1929–50

(*Metric Tons, Metal Content*)

Country	1929	1933	1939	1943	1947	1949	1950
World [a]	30,267	20,531	37,400	53,200	34,000	35,000	38,000
United States	78 [b]	532	328	4,638	4,823	1,484	2,265
Canada	—	—	550	465	522	72	295
Mexico	3,582	1,950	7,391	12,585	6,926	5,753	5,868
Peru	111	11	753	2,472	1,292	1,790	971
Bolivia [c]	3,779	1,896	9,225	16,536	10,857	10,275	8,781
France	1,950	385	. . .	153	201	295	355
Czechoslovakia	695	1,363	1,012	2,294	1,434	1,600	. . .
Italy	384	364	674	522	497	503	517
Yugoslavia	159	—	3,337	. . .	1,361	2,789	3,205
Greece	68	168	1	. . .	—	. . .	. . .
China [c]	18,753	13,310	12,017	505	1,780	2,400 [d]	. . .
French Morocco	15 [b]	33 [e]	420	409	403	700	706
Algeria	180	97	224	902	110	1,338	1,250
Union of South Africa	—	—	7	1,560	3,280	4,500	8,310
Australia	27	48	477	532	202	199	. . .

Sources: **1**, 1938–39, pp. 158–59; **18**, 1945, p. 781, and 1949, p. 132; **2**, 1951, p. 158; **17**, October 1950, p. 5.

a. Excludes the USSR.
b. 1928.
c. Exports.
d. 1948.
e. 1934.

Output

The world's mercury output totaled 145,000 flasks in 1939, soared to almost twice that volume in 1941 and declined subsequently. In 1949 and 1950, it was considerably below the prewar level.

Italy and Spain accounted for about 70–80 per cent of the world's peacetime output of mercury. Most of the remainder came from the United States, Mexico, the USSR and Canada. The United States nearly tripled its mercury output between 1939 and 1943, but production in 1948–50 was below the 1939 level. (See Table 348.)

The 1950 output in the United States was at the lowest level in the hundred years covered by production records. Because of the ample supply of mercury on the world's markets and the nearly complete strategic stockpile of this product, producers were not disposed to reopen inactive mines, which would require considerable expenditures, recruitment of personnel and installation of new equipment. Stocks of mercury in consumers' hands were very large.

BERYLLIUM

Beryllium, one of the "new" metals, is second only to magnesium in lightness of weight. The process of extracting it from beryl ore through electrolysis was not worked out until the 1930's. The extraction of beryllium is considered one of the most difficult processes in metallurgy.[129] Great advances have been made very recently in producing high-purity beryllium metal and in fabricating items of a size and intricacy previously unattainable.[130]

Uses

Beryllium acquired great importance when it was found that the addition of small quantities of it to copper, followed by heat treatment, gives that metal great tensile strength and resistance to corrosion and fatigue superior to that of spring steel, without impairing its high electrical and

129. **55**, p. 104.
130. **18**, 1949, p. 1298.

TABLE 348

MERCURY: OUTPUT IN SELECTED COUNTRIES, 1929–50

(*Thousands of Flasks, of 76 Pounds*)

Country	1929	1933	1939	1941	1943	1948	1949	1950
World	162.7	59.8	145.0	275.0	236.0	104.0	115.0	136.0
United States	23.7	9.7	18.6	44.9	51.9	14.4	9.9	4.5
Canada	—	—	a	7.1	22.2	—	—	—
Mexico	2.4	4.5	7.4	23.1	28.3	4.8	5.3	3.7
Chile	—	—	—	1.3	2.6	0.5	a	a
Germany	...	...	1.2	0.9	—	a	a	a
Czechoslovakia	1.9	—	2.7	a	a	0.8	a	a
Spain	71.8	19.6	35.9	86.5	47.8	22.7	32.3	50.0
Italy	58.0	17.6	67.2	94.2	58.0	38.2	44.5	53.3
USSR	3.8	—	8.7 b	a	a	a	a	a
China	0.6	—	4.9	2.8	3.1	0.3	a	a
Japan	—	—	0.6	4.3	6.7	1.7	2.5	1.3
Turkey	0.2	—	0.4	0.4	0.2	c	...	a
Union of South Africa	—	—	—	0.2	1.2	—	—	—

Sources: **1**, 1938–39, p. 159; **18**, various years; **17**, June 1951, p. 23.

  a. Data not available; an estimate by the U.S. Bureau of Mines is included in the total.
  b. 1938.
  c. Negligible amount.

thermal conductivity. Recently another important application has been its use in an aluminum alloy remarkably resistant to corrosion at high temperature. The use of beryllium in industrial radiography is also growing. Very small amounts of beryllium added to magnesium-rich alloys minimize their inflammability. Beryllium alloys are used for springs and in electrical equipment and instruments. Pure beryllium is used in X-ray instruments and for many purposes in the field of atomic energy.

Sources

The world's chief sources of beryllium are in Brazil and various parts of Africa: the Union of South Africa, Madagascar, Southern Rhodesia and South-West Africa. Rich deposits were discovered in Manchuria during the Japanese occupation. The United States has deposits in Colorado, South Dakota (the Black Hills), Maine, New Hampshire (where clusters of very large beryl crystals were discovered in 1948) and New Mexico. In the USSR, beryl occurrences are numerous and widespread. Of these, the emerald mines in the vicinity of Sverdlovsk (Urals), deposits east of Lake Baikal (Sherlova Gora) and in eastern Kazakhstan are the most important.

Australia has commercial deposits in every state except Victoria. India's chief deposit is in the United States of Rajasthan.

Output

The world's output of beryllium ore (beryl concentrates) amounted to only 676 tons in 1939. In 1943, 5,374 tons were produced, of which Brazil accounted for nearly 40 per cent and India for about 30 per cent. Output in the United States rose from 23 tons in 1938 to 323 in 1943; in India, from 18 tons in 1938 to 1,486 in 1943.

In 1945, the world's output dropped to 929 tons; but it soon began to rise again under the stimulus of high prices, reaching 4,450 tons in 1949 and 6,640 in 1950. Brazil held the lead, with 3,078 tons in 1949 and 2,625 in 1950; the United States produced 314 and 530 tons in those years; the Union of South Africa, 223 and 844; South-West Africa, 239 and 659. The year 1950 saw the appearance of Madagascar and Southern Rhodesia as important producers, with 486 and 823 tons, respectively. (See Table 349.)

In 1949 the United States imported 3,457 tons of beryl concentrates; 4,248 tons in 1950 and 3,916 in 1951. The bulk of the 1951 imports came from the Union of South Africa, Brazil, South-

TABLE 349

BERYLLIUM: OUTPUT IN SELECTED COUNTRIES, 1938–50

(*Metric Tons* [a])

Country	1938	1939	1943	1945	1948	1949	1950
World	1,026	676	5,374	929	2,470	4,450	6,640
United States [b]	23	86	323	35	90	314	530
Brazil [c]	203	276	2,027	510	1,783	3,078	2,625
Argentina	753	299	881	190	50	. . .	. . .
India	18	9	1,486	108	. . .	. . .	. . .
French Morocco	—	—	—	—	51	211	56
Mozambique	. . .	. . .	6	2	81	. . .	260
Madagascar	. . .	. . .	67	10	. . .	. . .	486
Southern Rhodesia	. . .	. . .	. . .	. . .	. . .	. . .	823
South-West Africa	. . .	. . .	36	5	90	239	659
Union of South Africa	. . .	. . .	. . .	. . .	. . .	223	844
Australia	—	6	534	47	56	21	23

Source: **18**, 1945, p. 816; 1949, p. 1300, and 1950, preprint.

   a. Conversion factor: one metric ton = 1.1023 short tons.
   b. Mine shipments.
   c. Exports.

ern Rhodesia and India. Consumption of beryllium increased from 200 short tons in 1936 to 3,058 tons in 1943 and amounted to 3,175 short tons in 1950.[131]

NONMETALLIC MINERALS

Nonmetallic minerals include some products that are valued by the carat (0.2 gram), like diamonds, and others, like stone, clay or gravel, for which the unit of measurement is the ton or the cubic yard. Some are extremely rare, others widely distributed over the globe. Nonmetallic minerals other than fuels are commonly divided into six groups: building materials, abrasives, industrial minerals, chemical minerals, fertilizers and precious stones.[132]

BUILDING MATERIALS

Building materials account for more than two thirds of the total annual value of output of nonmetallic minerals, other than fuel, in the world as well as in the United States. The value of the output of this group of products in 1949

131. **18**, 1950, preprint; **27**, Vol. II, p. 59.
132. Discussion of nonmetallic minerals in this chapter excludes mineral fuels; for these see Chapter 23 and Chapter 24. Metallurgical and refractory materials, which are sometimes treated as a separate group, are included with industrial minerals.

was distributed as follows (in millions of dollars, at U.S. prices): [133]

	World	*United States*
Nonmetallic minerals (except fuels)	$5,720	$1,567
Building materials	4,130	1,153
Stone	1,360	339
Sand and gravel	980	246
Cement	1,440	475
Gypsum	50	18
Clays	300	75

With reservation for a broad margin of error in the estimate of the world output, production of building materials is, except for fuels, the main objective of nonmetallic mining and quarrying in the world.

CEMENT

Properties and Uses

The term "cement," in its broad sense, covers a wide variety of building materials from clay and other binders used five thousand years or more before the Christian era to modern rapidly hardening materials varying in type and composition. Portland cement, the type most commonly used today, was first made in England in 1824, but its superiority over natural cement, a burned

133. Table 324 and Table 325.

and pulverized cement rock, was not recognized in Europe until the 1850's. In the United States, production of Portland cement began twenty or twenty-five years later, and the real development of the cement industry came after the turn of this century.[134]

Cement materials are found almost everywhere, but some areas have no outcrops of limestone or cement rocks. New England, for example, with crystalline rock, obtains the bulk of its cement materials from other parts of the country.[135] In some other areas, as in the Lehigh Valley, large deposits of "natural cement" rock have been discovered and worked. They contain the minerals used in the manufacture of Portland cement in about the proportions required, except that some limestone must be added.

While a great variety of cement products are made by different methods, cement is, in general, a mixture of calcareous and argillaceous materials applied in suitable proportions for specific purposes. Portland cement, which constitutes 99 per cent of all the hydraulic cement made in the United States, is made by burning a mixture of clay or shale, limestone, gypsum and other materials to clinkers. It is manufactured in thirty-six states and in Puerto Rico.

Output

The United States ranks first as a producer of cement: of the 93 million tons produced in the world in 1939, it accounted for more than 21 million; of 122 million tons in 1950, for 38.5 million. Heavy motor traffic, requiring better highways, has largely contributed to the rapid growth of cement production in this country; concrete highways are more expensive to build but require much less maintenance than other roads.

Germany was next in cement output before the war, with 14.5 million tons; the United Kingdom, France, Italy, Japan and the USSR also produced considerable amounts.

Production of cement varies widely with changes in business conditions. In the decade before World War II, output in the United States fluctuated as follows: 29.5 million tons in 1929, 10.9 million tons in 1933 and 21.3 million tons in 1939. United States output rose to 31.6 million tons in 1942 and dropped to 15.7 million tons in 1944. With the end of hostilities, however,

it began to rise again, partly because of a shortage of lumber.

In 1950 the United States produced nearly a third of the world's total cement output. In Europe, repair of war damage and the backlog of construction work created a great demand for cement. Shortages of coal, manpower and suitable equipment still hamper production, particularly in Germany, but recovery is noticeable in many areas. Output in the United Kingdom, France and some other countries exceeds the prewar level. In Latin America, output, stimulated by the war-deferred demand for construction, is increasing in most countries. Japan's output in 1950 was about two thirds the 1939 level. (See Table 350.)

GYPSUM

Properties and Uses

Gypsum, known and used for many thousands of years, has become one of the most important nonmetallic minerals during this century. Three varieties — massive or rock gypsum, alabaster and gypsite, an impure, earthy substance — are used commercially. Most gypsum is calcined before use and then hardens rapidly. Calcined gypsum is used chiefly for plastering of one type or another and for making molds and casts. Uncalcined gypsum is used as a retarder in making Portland cement, a filler in brewer's fixe, an agricultural agent in soil dressing, and for various other purposes.

Deposits

The chief deposits of gypsum in the United States are in New York, Michigan, Ohio, Oklahoma, Texas, Nevada and California. In Canada the chief centers are in Nova Scotia and New Brunswick. The United Kingdom has workings in various parts of the country. The gypsum beds north of Paris, some sixty feet thick, have been worked since ancient times and gave rise to the term "plaster of Paris." Germany's deposits are centered in the Harz Mountains, Thuringia and Saxony. Poland reports enormous deposits (200 million tons) of very high-grade gypsum at the River Nida. Spain has extensive deposits.

India has large deposits of gypsum in the state of Bikaner, and a new deposit containing some 40 million tons was discovered recently. Pakistan has a gypsum deposit in the Salt Range, in West Punjab. Iraq owns large deposits of gypsum not yet exploited.

---

134. **37**, pp. 174–75.
135. **59**, p. 174.

TABLE 350

CEMENT: OUTPUT IN SELECTED COUNTRIES, 1929–50

(*Thousands of Metric Tons* [a])

Country	1929	1939	1949	1950	Country	1929	1939	1949	1950
World	73,600	93,000	107,900 [b]	121,900 [b]	Austria	582	429 [f]	1,098	1,289
					Hungary	403	343 [d]	640	...
United States	29,481	21,267	35,939	38,546	Spain	1,820	1,194	1,864	2,103
Canada	1,945	910	2,527	2,658	Italy	3,497	5,112	4,037	5,004
Mexico	225	410	1,228	1,479	Yugoslavia	874	663	1,300	1,219
Colombia	...	167	476	579	Romania	317	531	560	657
Brazil	196	698	1,281	1,308	Bulgaria	151	180	...	...
Peru	49	120	288 [c]	341	Greece	155	343	326	...
Chile	145	341	495	513					
Uruguay	...	174	278	305	USSR	2,367	5,700	...	...
Argentina	350	1,128	1,457	1,569	China	185	540	...	...
United Kingdom	4,766	8,344	9,364	9,908	Japan	3,277	6,199	3,275	4,462
France	5,787	4,121 [d]	6,674	7,421	Turkey	65	284	376	396
Belgium	3,248	2,552	2,925	3,557	Pakistan			431	...
Netherlands	210	541	565	593	India	} 570	1,748 {	2,136	2,655
Denmark	799	696	834	873	Indochina	184	306	153	144
Sweden	570	1,182	1,698	1,936	Indonesia	149	170	...	...
Norway	319	390	593	583	Egypt	180	372	889	952
Finland	278	563	656	743	Union of South				
Germany	7,206	14,540	8,460 [e]	10,877 [e]	Africa	376	949	1,364	1,845
Poland	1,008	1,719 [d]	2,344	2,512	Australia	720	883	1,076	1,177
Czechoslovakia	1,250	1,128 [f]	1,738	...	New Zealand	80	235	254	252
Switzerland	...	...	977	1,085					

Sources: **1**, 1938–39, p. 131; **18**, various years; **2**, 1948, pp. 229–31, and 1951, pp. 244–46.

a. Conversion factor: one metric ton = 1.1023 short tons.

b. Excludes the USSR and China.
c. 1948.
d. 1938.
e. Western Germany.
f. 1937.

Output

Before the war, the world's annual output of gypsum was about 10–11 million tons, of which the United States accounted for about a fourth. The United Kingdom, France, Germany, Canada and Spain were also important producers. Increased construction activities have accounted for a considerable increase in the world's postwar output: 18.3 million tons in 1948, 17.7 million in 1949, and 20.7 million in 1950. The United States produced less in 1949 than in 1948 but, even so, more than in the prewar peak years 1925–26 (5 million tons).[136] Its share in the world's total in 1948–50 was about 35 per cent; Canada's, about 16 per cent. (See Table 351.)

While production and consumption of gypsum are largely local in most countries, the United States is unique in that, in addition to its domestic supplies, it imports considerable quantities of crude gypsum from Canada and Mexico,[137] and recently also from the Dominican Republic. In 1949 the United States imported about 2.6 million tons of gypsum, of which more than 2.4 million came from Canada.[138]

ABRASIVES

Metal and engineering industries use abrasives in cutting, boring, grinding and polishing; the lumber industry, in grinding wood for paper pulp; the soap industry, for scouring; the optical industry, for polishing lenses. Some abrasives are hard, others soft, and some are used in the form of powder. There are also artificial abrasives, and some mineral compounds, various oxides for example, are also employed as polishing agents. Certain carbides, such as boron and tungsten carbides, are used for their abrasive properties or

136. **11**, p. 147.

137. **14**, p. 39.
138. **18**, 1949, p. 595.

TABLE 351

GYPSUM: OUTPUT IN SELECTED COUNTRIES, 1929–50

(Thousands of Metric Tons [a])

Country	1929 [b]	1939	1942	*1948*	*1949*	*1950*
World	. . .	. . .	9,350	18,300	17,700	20,700
United States	4,551	2,927	4,262	6,581	5,995	7,432
Canada	1,112	1,390	723	3,164	2,855	3,256
Argentina	34	97	89	c	c	c
United Kingdom	983	1,043	1,232	1,175	c	c
France	2,558	1,320 [d]	840	2,541	569	2,100
Germany [e]	800	1,700 [d]	. . .	316	515	344
Switzerland	. . .	38	38	165	80	80
Spain	. . .	. . .	862	1,422	1,292	2,252
Italy	530	433	344	298 [f]	c	c
USSR	493	. . .	. . .	c	c	c
China	51	70	38	55	c	c
Japan	. . .	. . .	187	114	117	115
India	54	70	64	107	142	c
Algeria	91	33 [d]	24	33	32	46
Egypt	130	. . .	119	95	c	c
Union of South Africa	7	41	51	79 [g]	88 [g]	104 [g]
Australia	55	181	90	281	292	205 [h]

Sources: **35**, passim; **14**, p. 42; **18**, 1948, pp. 620–21, and 1950, preprint, p. 11.

a. Conversion factor: one metric ton = 1.1023 short tons.
b. 1928 for Argentina, Italy, the USSR, Algeria, Union of South Africa and Australia.
c. Data not available; estimate by the U.S. Bureau of Mines included in the total.
d. 1937.
e. For 1948–50, Western Germany.
f. 1947.
g. Sales.
h. Excludes New South Wales.

because of their great hardness.[139] Alan M. Bateman points out that fluctuations in the demand for abrasives reflect the ups and downs of some industries — for example, automobile production.[140]

INDUSTRIAL DIAMONDS

Properties and Uses

The hardest of all abrasives is the industrial diamond, which has unique properties. It is the most imperishable and hardest substance known. It consists of a single element and comes from the deepest rocks in the earth's crust.[141] The origin of diamonds remains something of a mystery. The major puzzle is the great difference in physical properties between the diamond and ordinary carbon, with which it is chemically identical.

For industrial purposes, the chief types are the black diamond of Brazil, "carbonado," the toughest and hardest of all diamonds, and "bort." Carbonadoes, once considered almost worthless and shipped in kegs to Amsterdam as ballast, now fetch a higher average price than any except some South African stones (from Namaqualand).[142] Bort, the flawed, broken or impure diamond, is a by-product of all diamond mining and accounts for about half the output of abrasive diamonds.

The most important uses of industrial diamonds are in dies for wire drawing — no other material is so durable and produces so uniform

139. **18**, 1948, p. 114.
140. **41**, p. 821.
141. Diamonds used in jewelry are unexcelled in brilliance and "fire" (display of spectral colors) when skillfully cut.

142. **41**, p. 845.

TABLE 352

DIAMONDS: OUTPUT IN SELECTED COUNTRIES, 1928–50

(*Thousands of Carats*)

Country	1928	1933	1939	1943	1945	1947	1949	1950
World	7,630	3,774	11,330	8,694	14,384	9,750	14,175	15,300
Venezuela	...	...	8	...	...	62	56	60
Brazil [a]	50	34 [b]	350	302	275	275	250	200
British Guiana	132 [a]	62 [b]	32	275	15	25	35	37
French Equatorial Africa	—	—	16 [a]	56	83	107	123	148
French West Africa	—	—	56	36	80	54	95	126
Belgian Congo	1,648	1,931	7,201 [a]	4,882	10,386	5,474	9,650	10,147
Gold Coast [c]	661	864	1,088	1,318	812	852	973	950 [a]
Angola	238	374	682 [a]	795	804	799	770	539
Sierra Leone	—	32	600 [a]	834	504	606	494	655
Tanganyika [c]	25	1	3	53	116	92	192	195
South-West Africa	503	18 [b]	35	94	153	180	280	488
Union of South Africa	4,373	507	1,247 [a]	302	1,141	1,205	1,254	1,748
Other countries [a]	2	2	19	30	15	4	3	3

Sources: **18,** various years and preprint 1950, p. 7; **67,** January 5, 1951, p. 7. Data for 1947 and 1950 are rounded figures (U.S. Bureau of Mines).

　a. Estimated.
　b. 1932.
　c. Exports.

a wire; in rock drilling — carbonado was used formerly but is now largely replaced by bort (bits are set with many small borts), at half the cost; in watches, electric meters and other precision instruments; for cutting the diamond itself and other gems; for cutting carbides, particularly hard metals, and for fast-cutting wheels. The use of diamond drills increased greatly during the war and has continued to expand, particularly for exploring and breaking (blast-hole drilling) and in drilling oil wells. The use of diamond-impregnated wheels for shaping carbide tools is also increasing.

Output

Africa (mainly the Belgian Congo and the Union of South Africa) has become the world's diamond continent. Until 1721, when diamond placers were discovered in Brazil, India was the home of diamonds, though Indian diamonds have since vanished from the world's markets. To overcome the prejudice of buyers against non-Indian diamonds, Brazilian producers had to ship their diamonds to India and sell them there.

More than one hundred and fifty years later, diamonds were shipped from South Africa to Brazil for the same reason and re-exported.

The output of diamonds rose during World War II, when industrial types were in great demand and jewelry was much sought after largely as a safeguard against inflation and for smuggling capital out of a country. A subsequent temporary setback in production was followed by rapid recovery, and the diamond output in 1949 was 25 per cent greater than in 1939; in 1950, 8 per cent greater than in 1949.

Industrial diamonds represent about 80 per cent of the world's output of all types in terms of weight but only 20 per cent in terms of value. Separate statistics for industrial and jewelry diamonds by country are not available. Africa accounts for 96–98 per cent of the world's entire output; the Belgian Congo alone, for about 65–70 per cent. Smaller quantities come from Brazil, Venezuela and British Guiana. (See Table 352.)

The United States imported 10.4 million carats of industrial diamonds in 1948, partly for current consumption and partly for stockpiling. Later data are not available.

CORUNDUM AND EMERY

Corundum is another natural abrasive, second only to diamonds in hardness. Emery, a mixture of corundum and iron oxides, has been used as an abrasive for centuries. The amount of corundum present in emery determines its hardness and cutting properties. Both are used for abrasive wheels and in cutting metal and polishing hardwood.

The chief deposits of corundum are in the Union of South Africa, which has supplied most of that consumed in the United States. Canada, India, Madagascar and the USSR have small commercial deposits. Efforts during World War II to discover sources within the United States were unsuccessful and have been discontinued.[143]

Statistics on the production of corundum are incomplete. The world's output, exclusive of the USSR, amounted to 3,910 metric tons in 1940; 7,029 in 1942 and 2,750 in 1949. The Union of South Africa produced 3,820, 6,274 and 2,464 tons in those years. Canada obtained 1,195 tons of corundum from tailing dumps in 1945 and 673 tons the next year. Later data are not available, and information on output in the United States is withheld by the U.S. Bureau of Mines.[144]

Emery comes largely from Greece and, in small amounts, from the United States and Turkey. The main deposit in the United States is in New York State, and the entire domestic output in recent years has come from this source.

INDUSTRIAL AND MANUFACTURING MATERIALS

Various nonmetallic minerals are used for making products which consist entirely of them or in which they constitute an important part. This group includes mica, asbestos, talc, mineral fillers and filters, optical minerals, meerschaum and others. The first two are discussed below.

MICA

Properties and Uses

Mica has an unusual combination of properties: transparency, flexibility, heat resistance, high dielectric strength, nonabsorption, luster and perfect cleavage. This last makes it possible to split natural crystals of mica into thin sheets or film, the regular practice calling for a thickness of not more than one one-thousandth of an inch.

As recently as 1920, Sir Thomas Holland, the famous English mineralogist, declared that there would never be synthetic mica,[145] but work on mica synthesis, which began at the Colorado School of Mines in 1946 and at Norris, Tennessee, in 1947, now holds promise of success.[146] A pilot plant for making "integrated mica" is nearing completion after ten years of research. Thus, the United States, the world's largest importer of mica from India, may become self-sufficient with respect to some grades when production at prices competitive with natural mica becomes feasible.[147] The Germans reported the synthesis of mica before the war, but the process had not reached the commercial stage.[148]

Of the many varieties of mica minerals, only two — muscovite and phlogopite — are important commercially. Both are comparatively abundant, but deposits large and high-grade enough for economic exploitation are rare.

Mica is indispensable for many purposes. Nearly 90 per cent of the world's output of sheet mica is used for insulation.[149] Mica splittings are used for facing tapes, cloth and paper, and for insulating. Ground mica is used in dusting tires, in asphalt shingles and rolled roofing, as a filler in rubber goods, in heat insulation, paints, ceramics and many other fields. The strategic uses of mica are in radar equipment, airplane spark plugs, radio tubes, magneto-condensers and the like.

Output

India is the leading producer of mica, accounting for about 80 per cent of the world's total. The most important mines are in Bihar and the Nellore district, but many deposits are found in a belt covering some 1,500 square miles. Because of the absence of good all-weather roads, many of them are inaccessible. Under present-day mining methods, depths of

---

143. **18**, 1946, p. 104.
144. **18**, 1949, p. 104.

145. **50**, p. 18.
146. In the United States, ceramic sheet for condensers, promising to stand higher temperatures than mica types, has been produced by the National Bureau of Standards and the Massachusetts Institute of Technology.
147. **67**, November 24, 1950, p. 504; cf. **27**, Vol. II, p. 95.
148. **18**, 1945, p. 1508.
149. **73**, p. 414.

500–600 feet are common and efforts are being made to bring electricity to mica mines to attain greater depths. In the Bihar mine, 100,000 women are employed in splitting mica, and in all mines child labor is much used for this delicate work.[150]

The United States produces chiefly scrap and ground mica from its eastern deposits of muscovite, but also some sheet and punch mica. The Southeast accounts for most of this production, with North Carolina in the lead. Mica production is believed to be the oldest mining industry in North America. Most operations — sorting, cleaning, grading, trimming and cutting — are still done primarily by hand, since no adequate machinery has been developed.[151] Because of the very rigid specifications and the hand processing characteristic of mica production, the domestic industry faces stiff competition from the Indian product, more carefully graded and trimmed, yet available at lower prices. The waste in processing in the United States is very great; 90 per cent or more of the original block is cut away and used only as scrap for grinding.

Canada produces sizable quantities of mica from its phlogopite deposits in Quebec and Ontario, which contain an especially desirable type. Brazil, Argentina, the Union of South Africa, Norway, Madagascar, the USSR and some other countries also contribute to the world's supply. In the past, much Brazilian mica (phlogopite type) was processed in India, but now Brazil plans to cut and split mica at home.[152] Some other countries, even Madagascar, ship all or part of their mica to India for splitting.[153]

Data on world production of mica convey little real information because of the lack of specifications. All countries except the United States simply report mica output.[154] Moreover, the largest producer, India, issues statistics only on exports, rather than production.[155] Exports in

1938 and during World War II fluctuated around 10,000 tons. In 1949, they amounted to 20,000 tons; in 1950, to about 21,000, of which two thirds were splittings.[156]

ASBESTOS

Properties and Uses

The two outstanding features of asbestos are fibrous structure and infusibility.[157] The first quality permits asbestos to be spun and woven into textiles, much as animal and vegetable fibers are used; the other makes such textiles fire-resistant. Some asbestos can withstand temperatures of more than 3,000° F. While asbestos can be worked like fiber, it has the resistance of granite.[158] At the same time, the fibers of some asbestos are so fine that they can be separated almost indefinitely, depending on the precision of the tools used and the skill in manipulation.[159]

The chief commercial variety of asbestos is chrysotile, which has silky fibers, extremely fine yet strong; a thread of such fibers 32,000 feet long weighs about one pound. The other variety in great demand is the "blue asbestos" (crocidolite) of South Africa, which has lower fusibility but high resistance to acids. The amosite variety is also used extensively. The length of the fiber determines whether asbestos is of spinning or nonspinning grade, and the price of asbestos otherwise of the same quality depends on the fiber length.

The chief uses of spinning chrysotile are for brake linings, for which there is no substitute, and for clutch facings, gaskets for steam fittings essential in power plants, and firemen's clothing. The nonspinning fibers are utilized for fireproofing and heat insulation materials. Blue asbestos has many important uses in the chemical industry and in building materials, asbestos-

---

150. **17**, April 1951, pp. 41–44.

151. **16**, pp. 8 and 16. The National Bureau of Standards has made available plans for a mechanical splitter with which an untrained worker could produce 60 films a minute, as against the average rate of 15 to 20 films by hand splitting. (**18**, 1948, p. 812.)

152. **65**, p. 380.

153. **73**, p. 465.

154. **18**, 1947, p. 792.

155. Since India produces mainly for export and re-exports are small, the export statistics are actually

more reliable, especially in view of extensive thieving in different phases of production. Thus, the reported output during 1915–35 was 40,300 tons as against nearly 77,000 tons exported. **71**, p. 352; and **73**, p. 467.

156. **18**, various years; and **17**, April 1951, p. 44.

157. Both qualities of asbestos were known to the ancients. Strabo, who lived in the first century of the Christian era, describes this mineral thus: "At Carystus there is found in the earth a stone, which is combed like wool, and woven, so that napkins are made of this substance, which, when soiled, are thrown into the fire and cleaned, as in the washing of linen." (Quoted in **36**, p. 440.)

158. **67**, September 20, 1947, p. 597.

159. **12**, p. 3.

TABLE 353

ASBESTOS: OUTPUT IN SELECTED COUNTRIES, 1929–50

(Thousands of Metric Tons [a]*)*

Country	1929	1939	1942	1945	1948	1949	1950
World [b]	370	440	540	555	855	775	1,065
United States [c]	2.9	14.0	14.0	11.1	33.6	39.4	38.5
Canada	277.7	330.7	398.7	423.6	650.3	521.6	796.2
Italy	2.6	5.2	6.5	. . .	13.0	15.9	21.4
USSR	29.5	86.0 [d]	. . .	. . .	. . .	. . .	. . .
Cyprus	14.3	8.9	1.6	3.2	8.1	12.6	15.0
Southern Rhodesia	38.7	52.9	50.6	51.1	62.6	72.2	64.9
Swaziland	. . .	4.2	23.2	21.2	29.4	30.8	29.6
Union of South Africa	29.2	19.9	31.4	25.6	41.5	64.3	79.3

Source: **2**, 1948, p. 159, and 1951, p. 165.

   a. Conversion factor: one metric ton = 1.1023 short tons.
   b. Excludes the USSR.
   c. Sold or used by producers.
   d. 1938.

cement covering of pipes, furnaces, floors, walls and the like. Amosite is used extensively in making high-temperature molded insulation that resists corrosion to insulate underground steam pipes [160] and for various fireproof materials for ships and so on.

Deposits

The main deposits of chrysotile asbestos, of exceptionally high quality, are in the Quebec area of Canada. Rhodesia, Swaziland and the USSR also have chrysotile. The principal deposit of the USSR, with large reserves, is in the Urals (Bayanovka); Siberia and the Caucasus have minor beds. The Union of South Africa has unique deposits of blue asbestos, and also large beds of amosite and high-grade chrysotile. Although the United States has a few minor asbestos deposits in Vermont, Arizona and some other states, it depends almost completely on foreign supplies.

Output

Canada accounts for about 75 per cent of the world's output of asbestos. Next in importance are Southern Rhodesia and the Union of South Africa. Italy, once "the cradle of the asbestos industry," and the world's chief source of this mineral until the discovery of Canadian deposits in 1878, now produces little.[161]

The world's output of asbestos, stimulated by increasing demand, rose nearly 55 per cent from 1945 to 1948. The decline in 1949 was largely caused by a strike in the Canadian mines, and the loss in the output of that country was only partly offset by increased production in Africa. In 1950, world output reached an all-time high, with 1,065,000 tons. (See Table 353.)

The United States is the largest consumer of asbestos and manufacturer of asbestos products, followed by the United Kingdom. The United States consumes about 60 per cent of the world's supply. In 1949 it imported 515,000 short tons, of which more than nine tenths came from Canada.[162]

No effective substitute for asbestos has been found, although the shortage of this mineral has stimulated research in various directions. On the other hand, new uses for asbestos have been developed, which tax the available supply.[163] Much work is under way to find methods for asbestos synthesis at the Norris, Tennessee, station of the U.S. Bureau of Mines.

160. Preshrunk paper made of asbestos does not absorb moisture and when used as a pipe covering does not shrink under heat, thus preventing gaps through which heat could escape. **12**, p. 9.

161. **12**, p. 42.
162. **18**, 1949, p. 143.
163. **55**, p. 55.

TABLE 354

FLUORSPAR: OUTPUT IN SELECTED COUNTRIES, 1929–50

(*Thousands of Metric Tons* [a])

Country	1929	1939	1943	1945	1948	1949	1950
World	...	560	1,037	674	791	673	730
United States	133	166	368	294	301	215	258
Canada	16	...	10	7	10	} 56	59
Newfoundland	—	11	56	25	48		
Mexico [b]	—	—	22	50	75	56	59
United Kingdom	42	39	55	44	71	68	54
France	53	[c]	24	15	32	40	40
Germany [d]	107	162	199	...	38	34	35
Spain	13	8	36	10	43	60	33
Italy	6	13	34	3	40	18	32
Korea	1	22	50	19	...	1 [e]	...
Union of South Africa	...	...	5	4	4	5	7

Sources: **18**, various years; **27**, Vol. II, p. 90.

  a. Conversion factor: one metric ton = 1.1023 short tons.
  b. Exports.
  c. In 1938: 52,000 tons. Estimate for 1939 included in the total.
  d. 1948–50, Western Germany.
  e. South Korea.

Although synthetic asbestos may differ from the natural in chemical composition, it is expected to have similar physical properties.[164]

METALLURGICAL MATERIALS

Various nonmetallic minerals, such as fluorspar, graphite and cryolite, are used for metallurgical purposes. Of these, fluorspar, needed in the production of steel, is of critical importance.[165]

FLUORSPAR

Properties and Uses

Fluorspar (fluorite) is used chiefly as flux in the basic open-hearth process of the steel industry to move sulfur and phosphorus into the slag and give it fluidity. The discovery of this process in the late 1890's stimulated the production of fluorspar, which is also in demand in the manufacture of hydrofluoric acid needed in the production of synthetic cryolite and for other purposes, including the atomic bomb.[166]

Output

The outstanding world producers of fluorspar are the United States (where the largest deposits are in Illinois, Kentucky, Colorado, Utah and New Mexico), Mexico, Canada and the United Kingdom. Germany ranked second before World War II, but the current German output is small. Recently a large deposit of fluorspar was discovered in southwestern Africa.

Of the 560,000 tons of fluorspar produced in 1939, the United States and Germany each accounted for about 29 per cent. During the war, output increased greatly in the United States and slightly in Germany but fell in France.

The growing production of the steel industry during and after the war stimulated the demand for fluorspar, about half of which is used in the United States in open-hearth steel making. United States output broke all records in 1943, with 368,000 tons, but was considerably smaller in 1950 (258,000 tons). (See Table 354.) United States consumption and imports of fluorspar were at an all-time high in 1950, and Mexico was, for the tenth consecutive year, the largest supplier of imported fluorspar.[167]

164. **18**, 1949, p. 144.
165. **41**, p. 734.
166. **18**, 1945, p. 1422.

167. **18**, 1950 preprint, p. 1.

CHEMICAL MINERALS

SALT

Salt, the only mineral directly consumed in food, has played an important role in human history. It became a necessary seasoning at a very early date, and was considered essential in sacrificial offerings.[168] Its ability to keep food from spoiling has made it a symbol of durability.[169]

Wars have been fought for the acquisition of salt supplies, and ancient routes of commerce were often the salt roads. Thus the great trade routes between the Phoenician ports and the Persian Gulf converged at the salt-trading city of Palmyra. The ancient trade between the Aegean and southern Russia was developed to obtain salt from the salt pans at the mouth of the Dnieper. The salt mines of India were the focus of trade in Alexander's time. According to Marco Polo, salt was used as money in the western provinces of China and in Tibet: small cakes of salt impregnated with the stamp of the Great Khan circulated in commerce.

Since very early times, salt has been subject to taxation. Salt obtained from the works on the banks of the Tiber was the first mineral to provide Rome with revenue.[170] Cash paid to Roman officers and soldiers to purchase salt (*salarium,* whence our "salary") was a substitute for an allowance in kind.

Properties and Uses

It is estimated that the average person today consumes 12 pounds of salt a year.[171] Mankind may use 15–20 million tons of salt, about half the total output, in food and for livestock. The rest is used for industrial purposes.

A basic raw material in the chemical industry, salt is used in the manufacture of chlorine, bleaches, soda ash, soap, dyes, acids, emulsions, drugs and other chemical products; in processing hides, skins, textiles; in packing meat, curing fish, canning and processing dairy products and other foods; in refrigeration, metallurgy and ceramics; for road surfacing, oil refining; in treating water, making synthetic rubber and DDT, and for many other purposes. In the United States, 70 per cent of the annual output of salt is used by the chemical industry, the remainder in food processing and other manufacturing industries and in households.[172]

Sources

Salt occurs as rock salt in various kinds of deposits (sedimentary beds, surface deposits, salt domes) and is also obtained from sea water or brines by solar or artificial evaporation. Practically every country in the world has either rock salt or brine.

To obtain salt from salt beds, water is poured into them and left for saturation, then pumped up and heated. Various methods of separating salt from brine were known and used in antiquity. Most of the coastal African countries obtain salt by solar evaporation. Sea water is the sole source of salt in Japan; in Peru, Italy, Ceylon, the West Indies and many other areas, more than half the salt comes from sea water. In Australia, salt is obtained from lake deposits and sea water.

In the United States, wells supply by far the greatest part of the output. Some wells supplying artificial brine are 7,000 feet deep. Mines are next in importance. The remainder is obtained from sea water, the brine of the Great Salt Lake and various desert sources, where simple methods of separation are used. The chief producing states are Michigan, New York, Louisiana, Ohio and Texas; together they account for more than eight tenths of the national output.

Output

The United States is the leading producer of salt, accounting in 1950 for 15.1 million tons, or a third of the world's total output of 48.9 million tons. Brazil and Canada are the next largest producers in the Western Hemisphere. The United Kingdom and Germany were the most important producers in Europe before the war, but France now ranks second to the United Kingdom. The USSR has a large output, but whether the trend is up or down is not known. China's output is believed to have declined considerably, while India produces much more than in 1939. (See Table 355.)

---

168. "With all thine offerings thou shalt offer salt." Lev. 2: 13.

169. The permanent hope in God's blessings was, to the Hebrews, "a covenant of salt for ever before the Lord." Num. 18: 19.

170. **54**, pp. 10–11.

171. **41**, p. 776.

---

172. **42**, p. 179.

TABLE 355

SALT: OUTPUT IN SELECTED COUNTRIES, 1929–50

(*Thousands of Metric Tons* [a])

Country	1929	1939	1944	1949	1950
World	...	31,972	33,603	43,600	48,900
United States	7,751	8,317	14,258	14,127	15,086
Canada [b]	300	386	633	679	719
Mexico	80	108 [e]	126	157 [d]	...
Colombia	70	105	134	126	141
Brazil	326	509	547	806	792
Peru	31	42	54	56	...
Argentina	198	304	451	...	...
United Kingdom	2,006	3,254	3,439	3,796	4,266
France	2,190	2,135	957	2,506	...
Netherlands	45	200	124	330	413
Germany	3,835	3,629	4,020	1,800 [e]	2,469 [e]
Poland	570	650	—	836	...
Czechoslovakia	166	174 [e]	...	...	...
Switzerland	88	96	85	99	104
Austria	178	263	251	198 [d]	237
Spain	1,079	819	692	836	1,210
Italy	910	1,365	483	580	...
Yugoslavia	56	75	...	109	131
Romania	322	375	154	314 [f]	...
Bulgaria	29	77 [e]	...	120 [d]	...
Greece	82	76	17	52 [d]	...
USSR	2,670	4,350 [g]	...	...	...
China	3,300	3,300	3,600	2,000	...
Korea	...	384	268	188 [h]	...
Japan [i]	644	636	353	395	330
Turkey	143	240	257	319	305
Israel (Palestine)	8	9	20	...	...
Syria	...	10	22	22	30
India	1,736	1,523	2,100	2,022 [j]	2,613 [j]
Burma	24	59	...	30	32
Thailand	177	134	113	...	...
Indochina	255	214	148	114	71
Ceylon	26	36	29	29	68
Indonesia	514	91 [e]	431	177	214
Algeria	15	68	51	117	...
Tunisia	120	106	52	90	99
Egypt [k]	149	443	199	466	539
Sudan	15	41	36	44	41
French Somaliland	39	78	43	68	80
Angola	—	23	38	41	41
Union of South Africa	89	106	124	163	106
Australia	137 [l]	85 [l]	171	246	298

Sources: **1**, 1938–39, pp. 142–43; **18**, various years; **2**, 1951, pp. 167–69.

a. Conversion factor: one metric ton = 1.1023 short tons.

b. Manufactured salt.

c. 1938.

d. 1948.

e. Western Germany.

f. 1947.

g. 1935.

h. South Korea.

i. Production in government-licensed plants only.

j. Excludes Pakistan.

k. Exports.

l. Incomplete data.

Countries differ enormously in per capita output, which is about 200–220 pounds in the United States, less than 100 pounds in prewar Germany and about 114 pounds in Western Germany (1950), about 188 pounds in the United Kingdom, some 15–16 pounds in India, and less than 10 pounds in China.

SULFUR

Uses

Sulfur, the basic material for production of sulfuric acid, is one of the most important raw materials in the chemical industry. In the United States, the leading producer of sulfur, about half is used for heavy chemicals, 20 per cent in fertilizers, 10 per cent in pulp and paper, and the rest in explosives, dyes, paints, varnish, rubber and miscellaneous products.

Sources

Sulfur is obtained from deposits of native sulfur (brimstone) and from pyrites. Brimstone is mined in its natural state and marketed as crude sulfur. Pyrites — metallic sulfides in which sulfur is combined with iron and other metals — are treated for sulfur recovery and constitute the largest source of sulfur in the world.[173]

Sulfur is also obtained from the smelting of copper, zinc and lead ores and from coke-oven gas and natural and other industrial gases.

The United States, like the rest of the world, depended on Italy's brimstone deposits (in Sicily) for sulfur until the Frasch process was discovered and used for the recovery of sulfur from the deposits in Louisiana.[174] Although brimstone deposits are found in many other countries, they are small and contain low-grade mineral, and some are inaccessible. The Eastern Hemisphere derives its sulfur largely from deposits of pyrites, which usually contain about 53 per cent sulfur. The chief workable deposits are in Spain, Portugal, Norway, Italy, Germany, the USSR and Canada. The United States has substantial pyrite deposits in Arizona and California, but native sulfur dominates the production.

Germany, which consumed some 700,000 tons of sulfur in 1935 but produced only one third of this amount, was experimenting before the war with extraction of this mineral from its

coal, which contains 1.3–1.6 per cent sulfur. The coal consumed in that country in a single year contained some 4 million tons of sulfur, which evaporated when the coal was burned. A new process was developed in 1935 that provided Germany with 70,000 tons of sulfur from the cokeries, gas plants and the like. An output of 250,000 tons a year was expected by 1940.[175]

Output

In prewar years, the world's output of native sulfur was 2.8–3.0 million tons; of sulfur from pyrites, around 4 million tons. The United States accounted for about 80 per cent, and Italy for 14 per cent, of all the native sulfur produced in 1939.

During World War II, the great increase in production in the United States raised the world's output of native sulfur to 4 million tons. In contrast, production of sulfur from pyrites fell in Spain and elsewhere in Europe, lowering the world output of that type to a little more than 2 million tons a year.

In recent years the output of sulfur from both sources has increased considerably. In 1950, production of native sulfur was more than twice as large as in 1939, while that of pyritic sulfur was in the neighborhood of the prewar volume. (See Table 356.)

FERTILIZERS

The chief fertilizers are phosphates, potash and nitrates. Phosphates are obtained chiefly from phosphate rock, apatite and marine phosphate beds, though also from slag produced in the manufacture of basic Bessemer pig iron from high-phosphorus iron ore,[176] such as French minette ore and certain grades of Swedish iron ore. Potash is obtained mostly from underground mines. Nitrates in mineral form are found only in Chile, and today the vastly more important source of nitrates is the air, from which nitrogen is obtained by fixation.[177]

PHOSPHATE ROCK

Uses

Phosphate rock is used chiefly in fertilizers, either directly, in powdered form, or after treat-

---

173. **27,** Vol. II, pp. 85–86.
174. See Chapter 31.

175. **72,** p. 405.
176. See Chapter 29.
177. See Chapters 15 and 31.

TABLE 356

SULFUR: OUTPUT IN SELECTED COUNTRIES, 1929–50

(*Thousands of Metric Tons* [a])

Country	1929	1939	1945	1948	1949	1950
			Native Sulfur			
World	2,846	2,700	4,100	5,250 [b]	5,150 [b]	5,670 [b]
United States (crude)	2,400	2,091	3,753	4,947	4,821	5,276
Chile	16	27	21	13	8	22
Spain	. . .	4	5	10	9	8
Italy	345	376	74	189	208	229
Japan (refined)	. . .	. . .	70	41	62	92
			Sulfur Content of Pyrites			
World	3,260	4,215	2,100	4,000 [b]	4,400 [b]	4,000 [b]
United States	122	223	301	395	385	399
Canada	35	104	100	79	107	137
France	92	81	68	75	87	104
Sweden	32	87	131	182	205	202
Norway	324	457	110	322	325	330
Finland	30	101	102	130	135	117
Germany	150	208	526 [c]	153 [d]	173 [d]	212 [d]
Poland	4	36 [e]	. . .	25	36	. . .
Portugal	192	309	77	253	280	. . .
Spain	1,425	620	378	589	601	673
Italy	306	455	47	372	393	407
Yugoslavia	25	54	13	38	32	13
Greece	64	99	3	9	10	. . .
Japan	280	855	178	490	648	787
Cyprus	148	409	17	283	325	296
Algeria	8	21	12	15	13	10
Union of South Africa	2	13	17	16	16	. . .

Sources: **1**, 1938–39, p. 165, and 1942–44, p. 155; **18**, various years; **2**, 1951, pp. 170–71 and 174.

    a. Conversion factor: one metric ton $= 1.1023$ short tons.
    b. Excludes the USSR and a few minor producers.
    c. 1943. Includes Poland.
    d. Western Germany. Practically all of the prewar output came from this area.
    e. 1937.

ment by sulfuric acid, in the form of "super-phosphate."[178] About nine tenths of the phosphate produced in the United States is utilized as fertilizer. The rest is used for phosphorus compounds, safety matches, ammunition, fireworks, drugs, photography, ceramics and many other purposes.

Deposits

The largest deposits of phosphate rock are in the United States — blanket deposits in Florida and Tennessee, and immense, practically inexhaustible beds of phosphatic shales and phosphate rock in Utah, Wyoming, Idaho and Montana, which are as much as 230 feet thick in some places.

Other deposits of phosphate rock are in northern Africa (Egypt, Algeria, Tunisia and French Morocco) and on islands in the Pacific: Nauru, Ocean, Angaur and Makatea. All the Pacific deposits originate from guano, the manure of birds, which has filled the underlying coral rock and blanketed the entire surface.

The USSR has vast deposits of apatite, in the

178. See Chapter 31.

Table 357

Phosphate Rock: Output in Selected Countries, 1929–50

(*Thousands of Metric Tons* [a])

Country	1929	1939	1945	1948	1949	1950
World	10,680	11,583	11,420	18,493	19,412	21,250
United States	3,883	3,817	5,463	8,808	9,131	10,418
Curaçao [b]	103	65	9	59	64	91
France	180	25	75	85	68	74
Belgium	40	34	18	69	45	42
Spain	8	10	20	23	23	10
USSR	211	1,618 [c]	1,626 [c]	2,032 [c]	...	...
Japan	28	234	53 [d]	4	1	...
Christmas Island, Straits [b]	122	214	119	108	255	...
French Morocco	1,650	1,703	1,654	3,226	3,626	4,022
Algeria	747	500	401	671	648	685
Tunisia	2,511	1,628	706	1,864	1,442	1,448
Egypt	215	548	349	300	350	397
Pacific Islands: [b]						
Makatéa (French)	263	175	259	183	240	255
Nauru and Ocean Island	558	1,280	—	472	780	1,200

Sources: **1**, 1938–39, p. 167; **18**, various years; **2**, 1949–50, p. 178, and 1951, p. 172; **67**, January 19, 1951, p. 58.

a. Conversion factor: one metric ton = 1.1023 short tons.
b. Exports.
c. Apatite.
d. 1944.

Kola Peninsula, which when concentrated forms a high-grade phosphate product.

Output

Before World War II, the United States accounted for about a third of the world's output of phosphate rock, the combined output of the three French territories in North Africa for about the same percentage, and the USSR for about 14 per cent. During the war, the United States increased its output of phosphate rock by more than 50 per cent, while production in some other areas dropped substantially.

The world's output of phosphate rock in 1949–50 was nearly double the prewar volume. The United States and French North Africa (French Morocco in particular) accounted for most of the increase. In other producing areas, output is now fluctuating at about the 1939 level. (See Table 357.)

POTASH

Uses

Potash, like phosphates, is used primarily for fertilizers. Not more than 10 per cent of the output is taken by the chemical industries for drugs, matches, explosives, photography and other purposes. Potash is marketed in compounds, the potash content of which is calculated in K_2O.

Sources

Potash is abundant in nature. The oceans contain an inexhaustible supply, little of which, however, is drawn on. Potash deposits formed by the evaporation of sea water are mined by underground methods; in Germany, the workings are as deep as 2,000 feet. The extracted crude salts range in potash content from 9 to 26 per cent and are concentrated to higher grades.

The world's largest potash deposits are at Stassfurt, Germany, which supplied the world's needs until 1925, when deposits were discovered in many other areas — the United States, France, Poland, Spain, the USSR, Palestine. Exploration had been stimulated during World War I, when German supplies were cut off.

In the United States, the deposits in New

TABLE 358

POTASH: OUTPUT IN SELECTED COUNTRIES, 1929–50

(Thousands of Metric Tons of K₂O)

Country	1929	1939	1945	1948	1949	1950
World [a]	2,470	2,700	2,370	3,500	4,000	4,400
United States	56 [b]	283	793	1,034	1,015	1,167
France	484	519	144	691	896	1,018
Germany	1,788	1,750	850	1,020	1,447	1,835
Poland	64	108 [c]	[d]	[d]	[d]	[d]
Spain	24	26	270	165	166	165
USSR	...	122	...	...	...	...
Israel-Jordan	—	32	47	50	—	—

Sources: **1,** 1938–39, p. 169; **18,** various years and 1950, preprint, p. 15; **2,** 1951, p. 173.

    a. Conversion factor: one metric ton = 1.1023 short tons.
    b. Industrial production.
    c. 1938.
    d. There are now no potash mines in Poland.

Mexico, where production began in 1931, contain large reserves and account for four fifths of the national output. In California and Utah, potash is also obtained from saline lake brine. Potash salts have been found in deep borings in other western localities but have not been fully explored. It is believed that potential reserves of potash salts in the United States are extensive.

The United Kingdom recently announced the discovery of large, rich and workable deposits in Yorkshire. The beds are about 5,000 feet deep and contain potash in a comparatively pure form.[179]

France has deposits in Alsace of a character similar to those in Germany, at depths of 1,600–2,800 feet. In 1925 the USSR discovered considerable deposits at Solikamsk, north of Molotov; although worked since 1931, they have not yet been completely explored. Potash deposits have also been found in the Emba and Fergana areas of the USSR.

Output

The world's output before World War II was in the neighborhood of 3 million tons, in terms of pure potash (K₂O). Germany supplied about 60–65 per cent, France almost 20 per cent and the United States 10 per cent. In the years 1942–44 the United States more than doubled its output, while production in Germany increased slightly and in France remained, with some ups and downs, more or less at the prewar level.

In 1950, about 63 per cent more potash was produced in the world than in 1939, the United States accounting for 27 per cent of the total, Germany for 42 per cent and France for about 23 per cent. (See Table 358.)

NITRATES

Nitrogen, essential for plant life, is now obtained chiefly from nitrate deposits and from fixation of nitrogen in the air. Some is also obtained from coal distillation as well as from guano and other organic refuse.[180]

Virtually the only commercial deposits of mineral nitrogen in the world are the caliche deposits of Chile, on the eastern slopes of the Andes, at elevations of 4,000–7,500 feet. The deposits form an irregular belt, some 400 miles long and 5–40 miles wide. These beds contain a mixture of minerals (sodium and potassium nitrate, sulphates of sodium and calcium, common salt and many others), from which an ideal fertilizer is produced. The reserves are very large. The title to all nitrate properties has been vested since 1933 in the government, which closely supervises the industry.[181]

179. **17,** February 15, 1951, pp. 34–35.

180. Only natural nitrates are discussed here. For synthetic nitrogen see Chapter 31.
181. **31,** pp. 19–20.

Chilean nitrates were almost the only source of nitrogen for fertilizer until the fixation process was developed in Germany during World War I. This development, later adopted in other countries, seriously affected not only Chile's nitrate industry but also its entire economy, since for many years about three fourths of the total value of the country's exports had been derived from nitrates. In 1913, Chile produced more than 3 million tons of nitrate (about 382,000 tons in terms of contained nitrogen); in 1933, less than half a million tons.[182] Improvements in mining and processing methods and government assistance in the 1930's helped the Chilean nitrate industry survive the competition of synthetic nitrogen, although its output today, of which 98 per cent is exported, is only about half that in 1913.

A new process of nitrate recovery, the "butterfly" process, was introduced in February 1950. This process employs a solar evaporation technique as does the other (Guggenheim) process in use, but does not utilize ponds. The nitrate solution is sprayed on the ground and after evaporation leaves a thin coating of the salts. The mineral is gathered when it has reached a thickness of about two and a half inches. The yield is a concentrated mixture of nitrate salts, which must be processed further.[183]

OUTLOOK

Only a few years ago it seemed certain that there was "hardly room left on the earth's surface for the discovery" of great mineral deposits such as have been found during the last fifty or more years.[184] The exhaustion of many of the world's commercial mineral deposits through the steady rise in consumption began to appear ominously close at hand.

Yet, within the past few years, large commercial deposits of various essential minerals have been discovered that may change the mineral geography of the future. The Cerro Bolivar, a vast deposit of high-grade iron ore, was found in Venezuela as recently as 1950. An important deposit of iron ore has been discovered at Steep Rock, Canada, and productive oil fields have been found in Alberta. Southern Rhodesia has suddenly appeared on the scene as one of the world's major possessors of iron ore. In the Union of South Africa, exploitation of a new gold deposit, comparable only to the Rand, the world's richest gold-bearing source, has just begun. The United Kingdom has discovered vast beds of potash, and the USSR has reported newly found sources of many important minerals. Uranium deposits have been found in many countries. The search for minerals proceeds feverishly in every part of the globe, and remote regions whose very names were unfamiliar a few years ago have been brought onto the mineral map of the world.

Prospectors today have many tools that did not exist a few decades ago. Their new equipment enables them to reach almost to the entrails of the earth and the bottom of the oceans. In their exploration, they are supported by advanced technology. The very threat of exhaustion of existing deposits has stimulated the search for new mineral supplies. The great industrial enterprises of the world send technical missions to regions where there are even slight prospects of success. At the same time, the underdeveloped countries, awakening to their opportunities, invite technicians from the West to explore their dormant resources.

No less important, "the curve of technologic advance is rapidly rising."[185] The techniques for utilizing low-grade ores are becoming more and more effective, and the use of processed minerals has become more efficient.

All in all, it begins to look as if the mineral frontier of the world has not been closed, as was believed not long ago, and as if mineral wealth still hidden in the earth may become available to future generations. Nevertheless, it must be remembered that mineral resources are not renewable like forests, and that mineral output is a one-time crop. Moreover, advanced technology has not yet found ways of working various low-grade ores at costs that permit large-scale commercial operation. As the President's Materials Policy Commission puts it:

The realm of difficulty for technology lies elsewhere —in costs. . . . The all-embracing problem for technology is to do the things that must be done to ensure a steady, concentrated flow of materials, rich in diversity, at costs that will make possible their wider and wider utilization. The wonders of science are

182. **31**, p. 19; and **43**, February 1939, p. 112.
183. **18**, 1949, p. 855.
184. **57**, p. 88.

185. **56**, p. 29. Cf. **27**, Vol. IV, on the promise of technology.

not at issue here; what is at issue is the hard facts of economics.[186]

The demand for minerals has been increasing uninterruptedly and can be expected to rise even more rapidly as mechanization spreads over the globe and new customers are brought into the world's markets. The hope for the future therefore lies not only in new discoveries but also in the conservation of existing resources; in more effective protection from corrosion of metals in use; in cutting down waste in mining and processing of minerals, and in their more efficient utilization; in creating, in many cases, substitutes from more abundant sources; and in the active cooperation of highly industrialized nations in the development of potential mineral resources in areas lacking in technical know-how and domestic capital.

---

186. **27,** Vol. IV, p. 2.

CHAPTER 23

COAL

OUR INDUSTRIAL CIVILIZATION has been geared to the use of coal from the beginning. As long as wood, wind and water were the only sources of energy, and metals were smelted by means of charcoal and shaped by hand, large-scale industry, requiring abundant mechanical power, could not develop. Moreover, the decline in the forest reserves in Great Britain, the cradle of the world's manufacturing, increasingly limited even artisan production of iron and other metals. While the great inventions of the eighteenth century had to await a new source of power, coal, on the other hand, awaited these inventions. Through most of that century only small quantities of coal were mined, largely from outcroppings, since underground water and gases caused great difficulties in deeper mines. The Newcomen steam engine, perfected by Watt and patented in 1769, solved the problem of pumping water out of mines and opened the way to greater coal production.

The coal-fed steam engine invigorated the entire economic life of Great Britain and other European countries. The new and abundant source of power first made possible rapid growth of the iron and steel industry. Next, coal began to turn factory wheels, move locomotives and transport cargoes. Some decades later, coal replaced wind in propelling ships across the ocean. Increase in manufacturing and expansion of international trade further stimulated the demand for coal. Coal became the basis of technical progress, and the coal industry, in turn, benefited greatly from that progress: new techniques made it possible to mine coal at greater depths with greater safety and efficiency and paved the way to mechanization of coal mining.

COAL IN THE MODERN ECONOMY

Coal ranks second among mineral products (after petroleum and natural gasoline and natural gas) in value of annual output and first in number of workers employed. In 1949 it accounted for nearly a third of the value of the world's mineral production, $9.4 billion out of $30.2 billion, at prices in the United States. In the world as a whole, coal mining engaged about 4.5 million workers before World War II, probably as many as all other branches of mining together. In the United States, 60 per cent of all miners were in coal mines.[1]

While coal no longer holds the almost exclusive position it had in the nineteenth century as a source of heat and power and now must meet three strong competitors — oil, gas and hydroelectric power — it remains the most important source of energy in the world.[2] Until 1920, coal provided more than three fourths of the energy used in the United States. With increasing use of petroleum and natural gas, its share had fallen to about 47 per cent by 1948. (See Figure 238.) In countries with less abundant supplies of other mineral fuels, coal plays a much greater role as a source of energy. In the world as a whole, except for the United States, coal provides more than twice as much energy as all its rivals together, including wood. Europe derives some 80 per cent of its energy from coal; the United Kingdom and Germany, even more.

In one field, moreover, there is no substitute for coal: in smelting iron, coke is indispensable as a fuel and a reducing agent. Coal is also used in many industrial-chemical processes requiring heat — calcination, burning clay, tempering and the like.

Apart from its role as a source of heat and power, coal is one of the most important raw materials of the ever-expanding chemical industry. Coal's components — gas, oils and tar — are converted into fertilizers, explosives, drugs and dyes. The black mineral that was only a fuel to our grandfathers is today

. . . a storehouse of raw materials essential in the making of countless things. From coal today we derive all of the colors of the rainbow, the scents of flowers, healing drugs, plastics, brush bristles, fine hosiery, fabrics, explosives, and an endless list of products. Once we saw coal in that light, and industrial techniques were developed for its more efficient utilization as a chemical raw material, coal's

1. **5**, Vol. II, pp. 2–3; see also Chapter 21.
2. Chapter 25, pp. 930 ff.

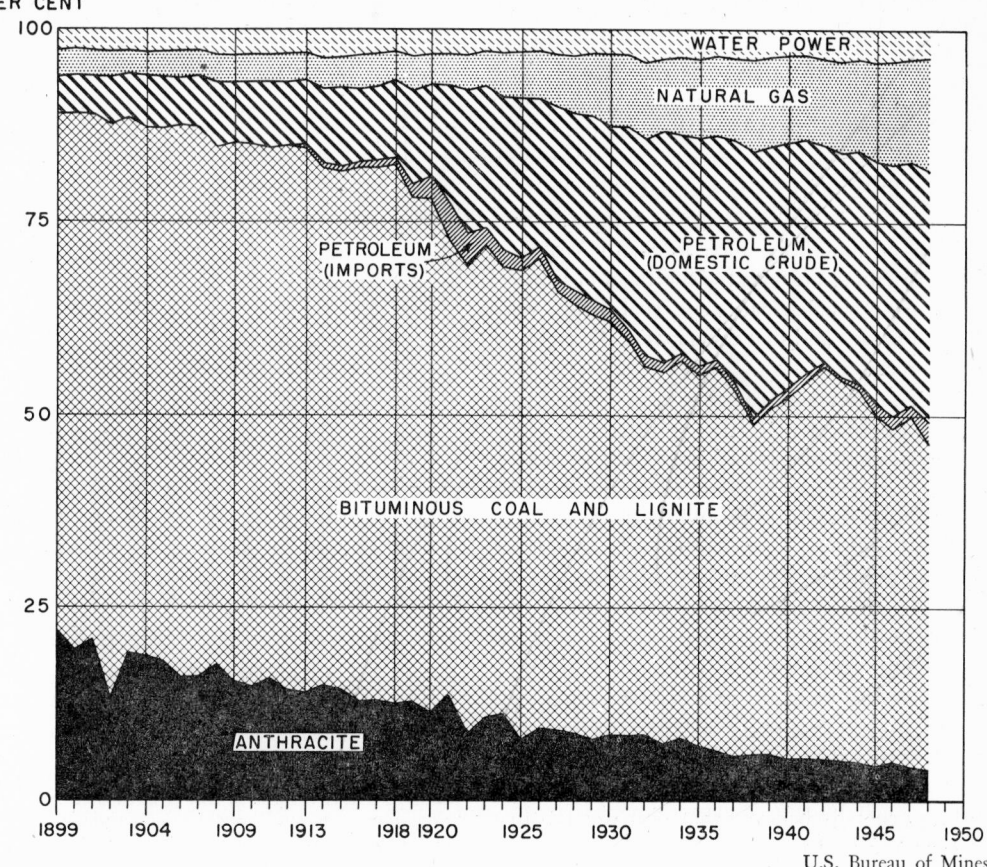

PER CENT

U.S. Bureau of Mines

FIGURE 238. COAL: PERCENTAGE SHARE IN THE SUPPLY OF ENERGY IN THE UNITED STATES, 1899–1948

Coal supplied more than 85 per cent of the energy derived from mineral fuels and water power in the United States in 1899, close to 50 per cent in 1945, and about 47 per cent in 1948. Percentages are computed in terms of the BTU equivalent of the annual supply of each form of potential energy, without regard to the purpose for which each product was used. The coal equivalent of water power is calculated on the basis of the performance of all coal-bearing central electric stations for each year. Exclusion of oil used as an industrial raw material — for example, for making lubricants — would raise the share of coal in the annual supply of heat and power by several percentage points.

influence was felt in such diverse fields as the growing of indigo in India, of roses in Persia, of hogs in Mongolia, of silkworms in Japan, and of rubber in Malaya.[3]

ORIGIN, TYPES AND USES OF COAL

Chemically, coal consists of carbon, hydrogen, oxygen, nitrogen and impurities (sulfur and ash).

Origin

Coal is the product of a long chain of processes: the slow decay of luxuriant swamp vegetation of early geological periods under fresh and brackish water; the mixing of the decomposed

plant matter with mud and sand; the loss of much of its moisture and gases under heat and the pressure of overlying strata; and, as a result, the accumulation of a growing proportion of carbon in the product of this transformation. This process, metamorphism, was hastened and often distorted by volcanic disturbances, intrusions of igneous rocks, crushing stresses within the earth's crust, and inundations. At the same time the vegetable matter was subjected to chemical alterations through the work of innumerable microscopic bacteria and fungi.

There are two main theories of coal formation. One holds that the plant remains accumulated *in situ,* that is, at the place where the vegetation was growing, and that these accumulations, un-

3. **62**, pp. 824–25.

dergoing the processes described above, gradually turned into coal. The other, the drift theory, is that great masses of vegetable matter were transported by water and deposited at the bottom of the sea or lakes, where they built up layer after layer, which, under pressure, became gradually solidified to rock.[4] Evidence to support each of these theories is found in the composition of coal in certain areas, such as South Wales in Great Britain or areas on the continent of Europe. It seems probable that some coal fields were formed *in situ* and that others were the result of drift processes.

Since areas where coal has been formed supported a different vegetation at different geological periods and metamorphism varied in degree, length and character, there are many varieties of coal, differing in rank and grade, amount of ash and sulfur, proportion of volatile matter, capacity to coke, resistance to weathering and the like. The rank of coal designates its maturity, the degree to which the original vegetable matter has undergone changes in composition. Coal of high rank has less moisture and volatile ingredients and a higher percentage of fixed carbon than younger coal. The grade of coal can be improved by purification but not the rank.[5]

It is generally believed that peat was the first step in the transformation of vegetable matter into coal and that the following stages were, in turn, lignite, subbituminous coal, bituminous coal and anthracite.[6] This transformation began millions of years ago and is still going on. Although coal is not as old as gold or nickel, the high-rank coals date from the Carboniferous period, some 200–240 million years ago. The lower-rank coals were formed much later, during the second great coal cycle in the Cretaceous and early Eocene periods, some 80–90 million years ago. Subbituminous coal and lignite date from the late Tertiary period, separated from us by only a few million years.[7]

Types

The standard classification of coal by rank used in the United States was established in 1939 by the American Society for Testing Materials.

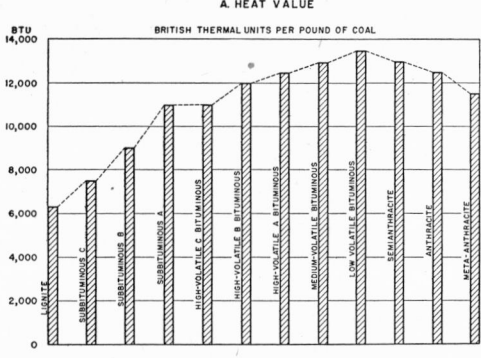

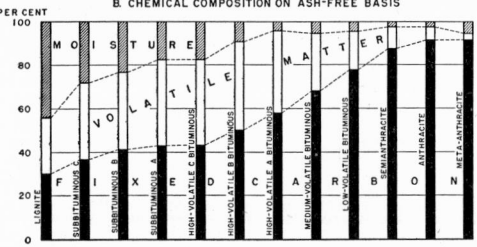

U.S. Geological Survey

FIGURE 239. COAL: HEAT VALUE AND COMPOSITION, BY TYPE

Anthracite has the highest proportion of fixed carbon but less heat value per unit of weight than high-rank bituminous and semibituminous coals. Lignite is of lesser value as a fuel because of low heat capacity and a high proportion of moisture per unit of weight. The bituminous coals, with high heat capacity and abundant volatile matter, are the most valuable in a nation's economy.

It considers four main groups: (1) anthracite; (2) bituminous; (3) subbituminous; and (4) lignite, including the brown coal of Europe. The four groups vary widely in heat value and in amount of moisture (2 to more than 40 per cent), volatile matter (2 to 40 per cent) and fixed carbon (30 to 94 per cent). Some of the groups are subdivided. (See Table 359 and Figure 239.)

Bituminous and semibituminous coals [8] are the most important types of coal for modern industry, since they are the source of coke and gas. These two types, indispensable in the steel and chemical industries, are much less abundant than other varieties and are highly valued. A country may produce enough coal to meet its needs for heating, but if it does not have coking coal, it has to turn to foreign sources for coke to make iron and steel.

Anthracite and semianthracite, the oldest

4. **50**, p. 214.

5. Coal containing little ash is, for example, a "high-grade" coal while an impure coal is "low-grade." **16**, p. 9.

6. **63**, p. 5.

7. **64**, pp. 42–43.

8. M. R. Campbell and some other experts suggest that a more exact name for semibituminous would be superbituminous coal. **37**, pp. 5–6.

TABLE 359

COAL: HEAT VALUE AND COMPOSITION [a]

| Type of Coal | Total | Percentage Distribution | | | Heat Value, in British Thermal Units [b] |
		Moisture	Volatile Matter	Fixed Carbon	
Anthracite					
Meta-anthracite	100	4	2	94	11,500
Anthracite	100	2	5	93	12,500
Semianthracite	100	2	10	88	13,000
Bituminous					
Low-volatile	100	3	19	78	13,500
Medium-volatile	100	4	28	68	13,000
High-volatile					
A	100	3	39	58	12,500
B	100	10	40	50	12,000
C	100	18	40	42	11,000
Subbituminous					
A	100	18	40	42	11,000
B	100	23	36	41	9,000
C	100	28	35	37	7,500
Lignite	100	43	27	30	6,250

Source: Adapted from **31**, pp. 6–7.

a. On an ash-free basis.

b. The British thermal unit is the amount of heat required to raise the temperature of one pound of water one degree Fahrenheit.

forms of coal, have a high percentage of fixed carbon and little volatile matter. Since the heat value of coal is greatest when fixed carbon and volatile matter are most effectively balanced, rather than when the percentage of fixed carbon is highest, anthracite gives less heat per unit of weight than semibituminous or high-rank bituminous coal.[9]

Subbituminous coal is on the borderline between bituminous and lignite. Some varieties approach bituminous in grade, while others are almost as low in quality as lignite. Subbituminous coal is entirely noncoking.

Lignite is the lowest coal in both rank and grade. It disintegrates on exposure to air and is subject to spontaneous combustion if not properly stored. In view of these characteristics and the costliness of transportation in terms of heat value, it cannot be used economically at great distances from the mine.

Uses

Certain kinds of coal are preferred for certain purposes. Price differentials are often the de-

cisive factor in the selection; a lower-grade, and therefore cheaper, coal may be more practical for certain purposes than a more expensive better variety. The possibilities of substitution are limited, however, and certain types of coal are eminently adapted for special purposes. Thus, while any type of coal can be used for raising steam, semibituminous is considered best for steamship and naval use since it has the greatest heat value and thus requires less bunker space per unit of heat and, in addition, is nearly smokeless.

The ideal domestic coal is one low in ash content and comparatively clean and smokeless. Anthracite best satisfies these qualifications.[10] On the other hand, anthracite is not the best fuel for industry because of its comparatively low heat value. (See Table 359.)

9. **20**, p. 5.

10. All kinds of coal are used for heating, however. Germany originated briquettes — lumps of various sizes and shapes made of small pieces of coal or coal dust, usually waste, mixed with binding material and compressed. The manufacture of briquettes has been taken up in most coal-producing countries. In 1938 the world output of briquettes exceeded 65 million tons, of which Germany produced 51 million.

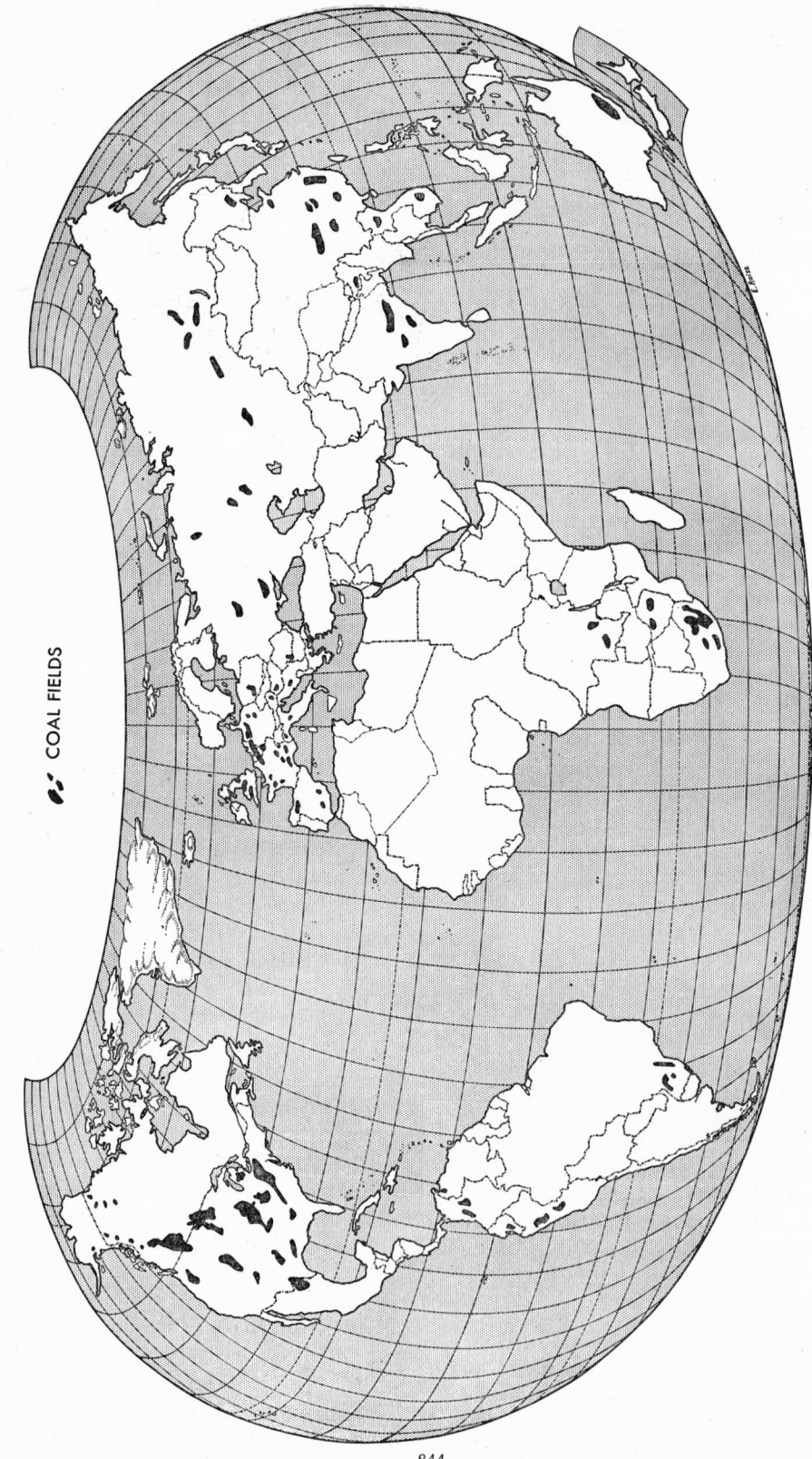

COAL FIELDS

Figure 240. Coal Fields: Geographic Distribution in the World

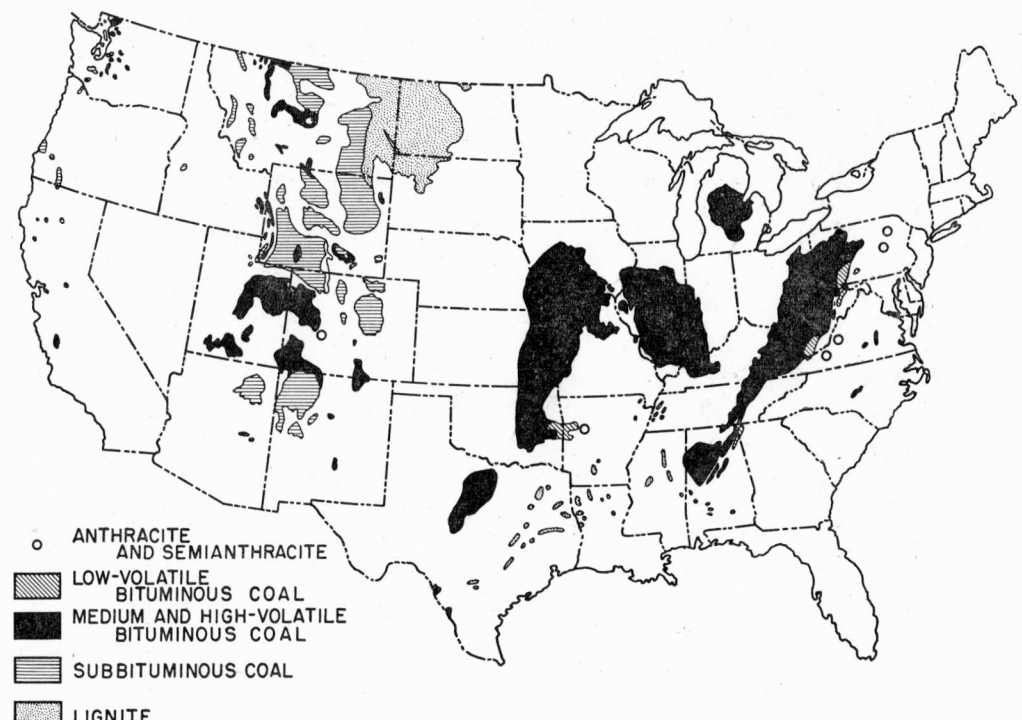

   ○   ANTHRACITE
          AND SEMIANTHRACITE

     LOW-VOLATILE
          BITUMINOUS COAL

     MEDIUM AND HIGH-VOLATILE
          BITUMINOUS COAL

     SUBBITUMINOUS COAL

     LIGNITE

FIGURE 241. COAL FIELDS: GEOGRAPHIC DISTRIBUTION IN THE UNITED STATES

Bituminous coal includes gas and coking varieties and is also used for raising steam and as a domestic fuel. Its noncoking varieties are preferred in making cement and burning tile. Subbituminous coals are generally used for generating power. In Germany and the USSR, lignite (or brown coal) is used in electric power plants located at open mines.

MAJOR COAL FIELDS

The coal fields most important to the economic life of the world form a large belt on both sides of the Atlantic — in North America at one side and in Europe (mainly Great Britain and Germany) at the other. (See Figures 240 and 112.) Before World War II these fields accounted for more than 70 per cent of the world's output of bituminous coal and anthracite and for 91 per cent of its lignite.

The United States

The major coal area of the United States is the Appalachian field of about 70,000 square miles. (See Figure 241.) It consists of two chief coal fields — the anthracite bed in eastern Pennsylvania, covering 480 square miles, and the bi-

tuminous and semibituminous coal beds stretching over the rest of this vast area.

The anthracite bed has comparatively small reserves, but the coal is of high rank and excellent grade and at almost no other place in the world is there a major field of such uniformity. The seams are folded, however, and have steep dips, and the beds are thin at many places. These characteristics, coupled with the hardness of anthracite, make it more expensive to mine than other coal.

The bituminous beds stretch from western Pennsylvania and eastern Ohio into western Maryland, West Virginia, eastern Kentucky, Tennessee, Georgia and Alabama. They contain the largest store of high-volatile and coking coal in the world and are the center of the greatest coal-mining activity in the United States. In the northern part of this area, many coal seams, regular and gently dipping, are seven feet thick over an extent of more than 2,500 square miles. In the South, the seams are folded and often dip steeply, though the deepest point is no more than 2,000 feet below the surface.[11]

In the middle of the country, the most im-

11. **37**, p. 11.

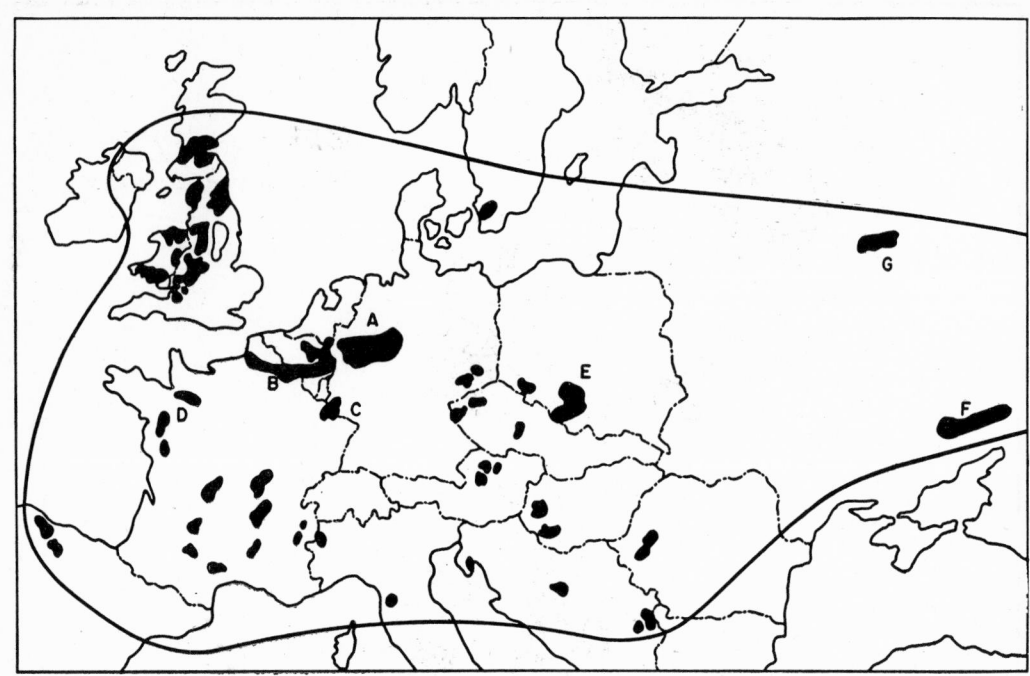

FIGURE 242. COAL FIELDS: GEOGRAPHIC DISTRIBUTION IN EUROPE

Among Europe's coal fields, here shown in greater detail than in Figure 240, the most important is the famous Ruhr field in the western part of the Westphalian coal region (A). West of that area stretches the Somme-Meuse region (B), which supplies coal to France and other parts of the continent. South of it are the Saar fields (C). Farther west are the coal fields of Normandy (D). On the border between central and eastern Europe lies the coal region of Upper Silesia (E), which belonged to Germany before the war and is now part of Poland.

The main coal regions in the European part of Russia shown on the map are the Donets Basin (F) in the Ukraine and the Tula-Moscow region (G).

The coal fields of Great Britain are pictured in greater detail in Figure 243.

portant coal basin lies in Illinois, Indiana and western Kentucky and extends into Michigan, Iowa, Missouri, Oklahoma, Kansas, Arkansas and Texas.

Extensive fields of subbituminous coal in the Rocky Mountain area and the northern plains and deposits of lignite and subbituminous coal in Wyoming, Montana, the Dakotas, New Mexico and Colorado have not yet been fully developed, and the mines serve only local markets. The Alabama coal basin contains coal of similar rank. Thirteen states have no known coal deposits of any kind.

The thickest coal seam in the country is the 84-foot Adaville bed at Elkol, Wyoming. The Mammoth anthracite bed in Pennsylvania is from 50 to 60 feet thick. The greatest part of all coal mined, however, is in seams from 3 to 7 feet thick, rarely as much as 20 feet. The Pittsburgh bed averages 7 feet in thickness.[12]

Canada

The comparatively small beds of Nova Scotia and New Brunswick contain high-rank coal. About two thirds of Canada's largest deposits, in Alberta, are of various types of bituminous coal and about a third of subbituminous. Seams in British Columbia are mostly bituminous, while the Saskatchewan coal fields contain lignite. The western Canadian coal beds are a continuation of seams in the northern Great Plains of the United States.

Europe

Coal fields are widely dispersed in Europe, from the Bay of Biscay to the Black Sea and from the British Isles to the Balkans. The most important deposits are in the United Kingdom, Germany, northeastern France and the Low Countries. (See Figure 242.)

The United Kingdom. In relation to its area, Great Britain possesses the most extensive coal fields in the world. (See Figure 243.) The coal

---

12. **33**, p. 643. Other writers credit the Adaville coal seams with 90-foot thickness. **34**, 1951, p. 49.

FIGURE 243. COAL FIELDS: GEOGRAPHIC DISTRIBUTION IN THE UNITED KINGDOM

Great Britain is rich in coal deposits, most of them situated at great depths, a few under the sea. The most important fields are in South Wales; in Somersetshire and Gloucestershire (Bristol), York, Derby and Nottingham; in Staffordshire, Durham and Lancashire; and in Scotland: Fife, Clackmannan, Clyde, Lanark, Ayr and Midlothian.

847

is of excellent quality, and its value is increased by closeness to consumption centers and ports. The world-famous South Wales field, which covers about 1,000 square miles, has anthracite seams in the west and northwest, first-class steam coal [13] in the center, coking coal in the southeast. Some of the coals mined in the Midlands and in the north are of unsurpassed quality, notably Durham coal. The most important field in Scotland, in number and total thickness of seams, is the Edinburgh.

Most seams of coal in the United Kingdom are continuous and horizontal and are seldom interbedded with other minerals, but their depth is considerable. In North Staffordshire, for example, coal shafts reach a depth of 3,000 feet and near Manchester, 3,500 feet.[14] In some parts of the country, coal seams lie as deep as 10,000 feet, too deep for present mining methods. The average thickness of the beds is 4 feet.[15]

Germany. The most important coal field of Germany — indeed, of Europe — is the Ruhr, in Westphalia. (See Figure 244.) Of Carboniferous origin, this field stretches eastward from the Dutch border for about 60 miles and is as much as 30 miles wide. The seams are more than 6,000 feet deep and contain all varieties of high-rank coal. Excellent coking coal is abundant.

The Aachen coal field, to the west, is similar in rank and grade. It was probably the earliest in Europe to be mined. The Silesian fields, which produced 60–70 million tons a year, were lost to Poland by Germany after World War II.

Apart from other bituminous coal fields of lesser size and importance, Germany has very extensive fields of lignite despite the loss of a great part of its lignite reserves to Poland.

France and the Low Countries. France has two main coal basins, dating mostly from the Carboniferous period: in the north, the Somme-Meuse region (B in Figure 242), a continuation of the seam from Aachen across the Netherlands and Belgium; in the east, the coal fields of Lorraine and the Saar (C). The first contains much coking coal; the second, mostly coals with a high percentage of volatile matter. Scattered fields are worked in central France (Loire Basin).

Since 1920 Belgium has developed the Cam-

pine basin in the north, its most promising coal field, which has various kinds of bituminous coals and more regular seams than the old southern basin. In the latter, with larger reserves, the veins are deep. Belgian coal mines have been worked to a depth unknown in any other country, sometimes 4,000 feet below the surface. The seams are thin, often interbedded, highly distorted and difficult to develop.

In the Netherlands, two comparatively extensive seams, at Limburg and Horst (west and northwest from Aachen), have been actively developed during this century. They are of about the same type and age as the Aachen seam of Germany.

Poland. As a result of its acquisition of the German coal fields in Upper and Lower Silesia (E in Figure 242), postwar Poland has become one of Europe's greatest coal-producing countries. Mining conditions are less difficult than in the Ruhr. While most coal from these beds will not coke, it is suitable for raising steam or manufacturing gas.

The principal old Polish coal fields, in East Upper Silesia, Dombrau and Krakow, are extensions of the former German fields in Silesia. The Dombrau Basin has lignite, while the coal of the other beds is very hard and some of it is of coking quality. There are also lignite beds in southern and southeastern Poland.

The USSR

The chief coal field in the European part of the USSR is the Donets Basin, dating from the Carboniferous period. It contains anthracite in its eastern part and coking coal in the western. The ash content is rather high, however, and the seams are thin (about two feet) and faulted. This basin, favored by the proximity of large deposits of high-grade iron ore in Krivoi Rog and manganese in Nikopol, was the foundation of the metallurgical industries in old Russia and still accounts for at least half the coal output.

The Tula-Moscow coal field consists of subbituminous coal and lignite, of low heat value and high ash and sulfur content. The thickest seams are in the central part and appear, in contrast to the Donets Basin, in the form of pockets. (See Figure 245.)

The Asiatic coal beds of the USSR are very extensive. The most important is the Kuznetsk Basin, with large reserves of good coking coal. Another important bed of coking coal is in Kara-

13. In Great Britain "steam coal" designates the grade suitable for use by the navy and by fast steamships and locomotives.

14. **56**, pp. 9–13.

15. **34**, 1949, p. 46.

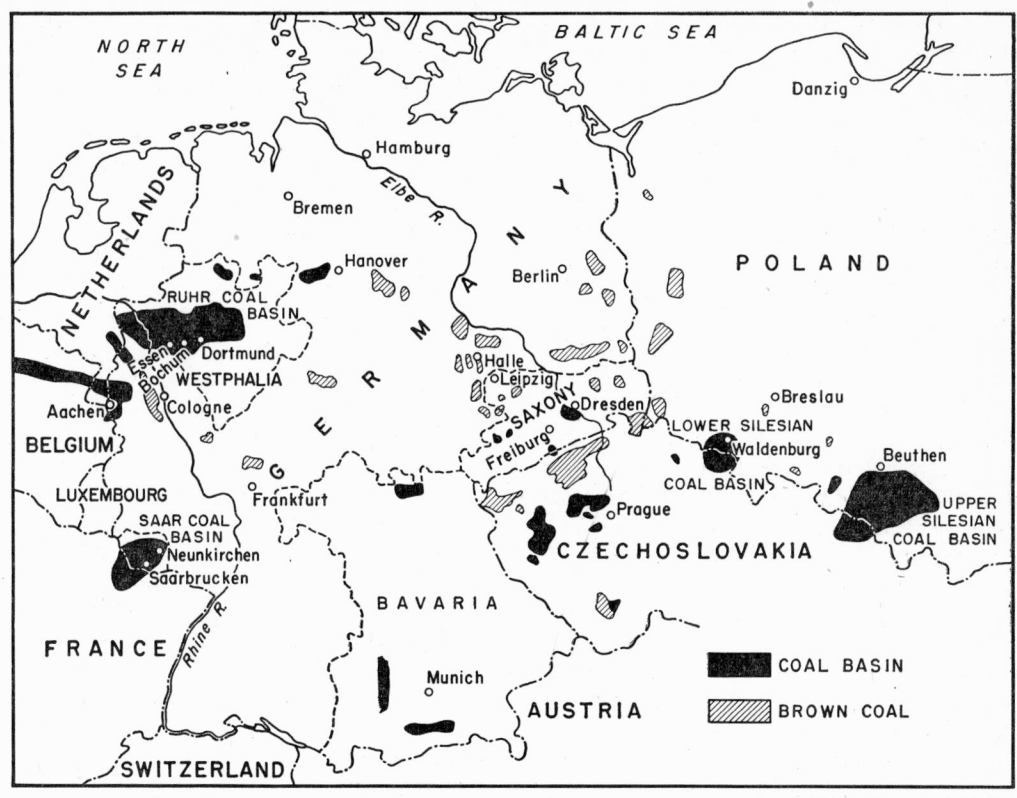

U. S. Bureau of Mines

FIGURE 244. COAL FIELDS: GEOGRAPHIC DISTRIBUTION IN GERMANY

ganda, Kazakhstan. The Cheremkhovo Basin in eastern Siberia has substantial reserves. Large but little explored lignite fields lie in the Lena and Yenisei Basins, and in the Tungus Basin; many small beds are mined in the Far East and other areas.[16]

Asia

Asia has only a few important fields of high-grade coal and coking coal. Lignite deposits are scattered in many areas, as in Burma, Indonesia, Pakistan, Thailand and the Federation of Malaya. Ceylon has only peat deposits.

China's largest deposit of anthracite and bituminous coal is in the east, in Shansi province. Other important coal beds are in Shensi, Szechwan and Honan. The much smaller fields in Hopei and Shantung are of greater economic importance, however, because of their proximity to the coast and better transportation facilities. Small deposits of coal are found in almost all the Chinese provinces.

India's main coal fields, which have broken seams of medium thickness lying deep, are in the Damodar Valley, Hyderabad. The Central Provinces have extensive beds of lignite and subbituminous coal. (See Figure 246.)

Australia

Australia has the largest coal reserves in the Southern Hemisphere. The field along the coast in New South Wales contains about nine tenths of the country's reserves. Much of the mining is under water. Victoria has the thickest beds of lignite in the world. This coal is mined by open-pit methods and is used for generating electric power and making briquettes.

COAL RESERVES

The exceptional importance of coal for the world economy has stimulated interest in appraising mankind's reserves of this fuel. Difficulties in making such an appraisal are many: in many coal-producing countries, inadequate knowledge of the extent and geological structure of the fields

---

16. **32**, pp. 211–13.

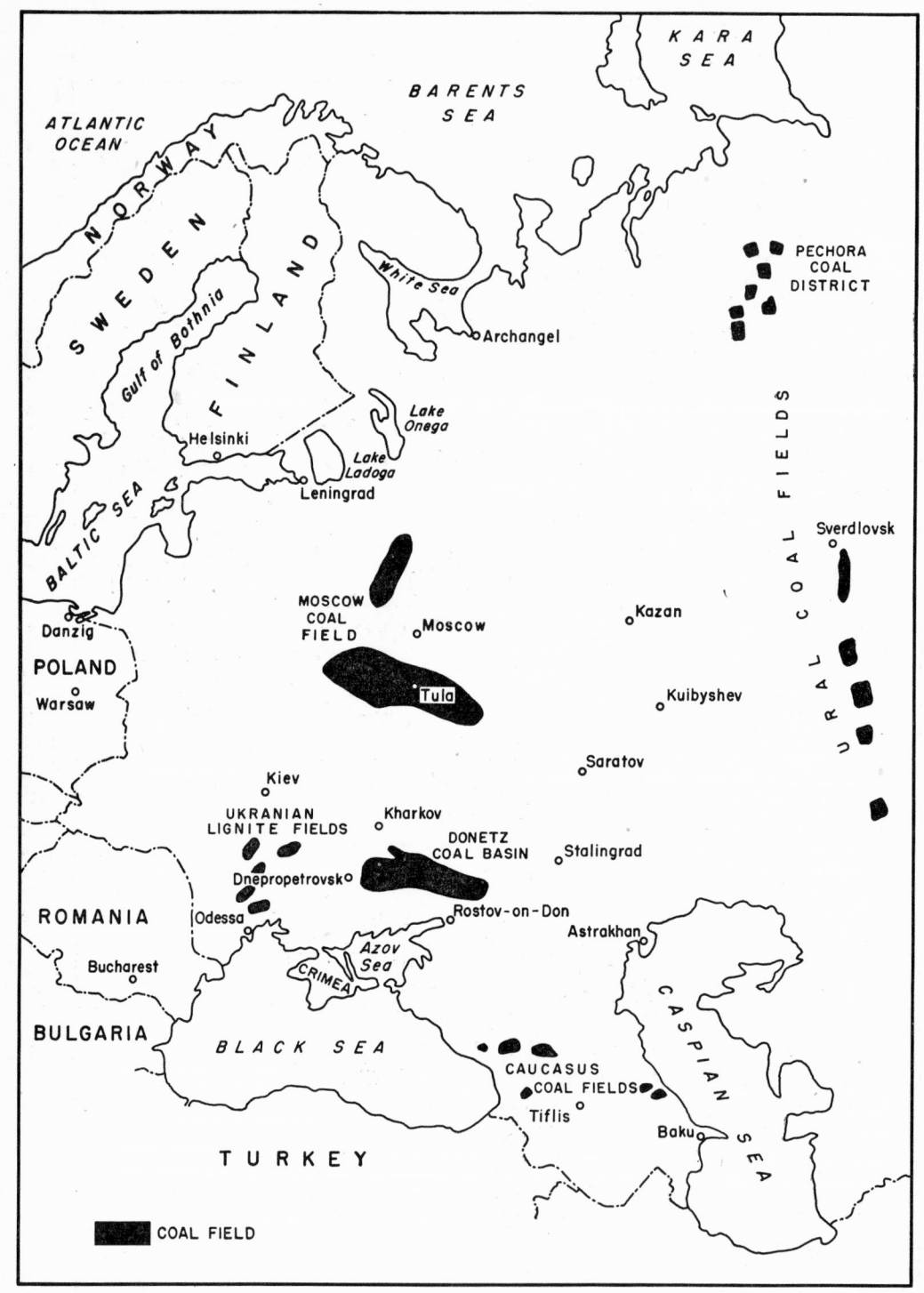

FIGURE 245. COAL FIELDS: GEOGRAPHIC DISTRIBUTION IN EUROPEAN USSR

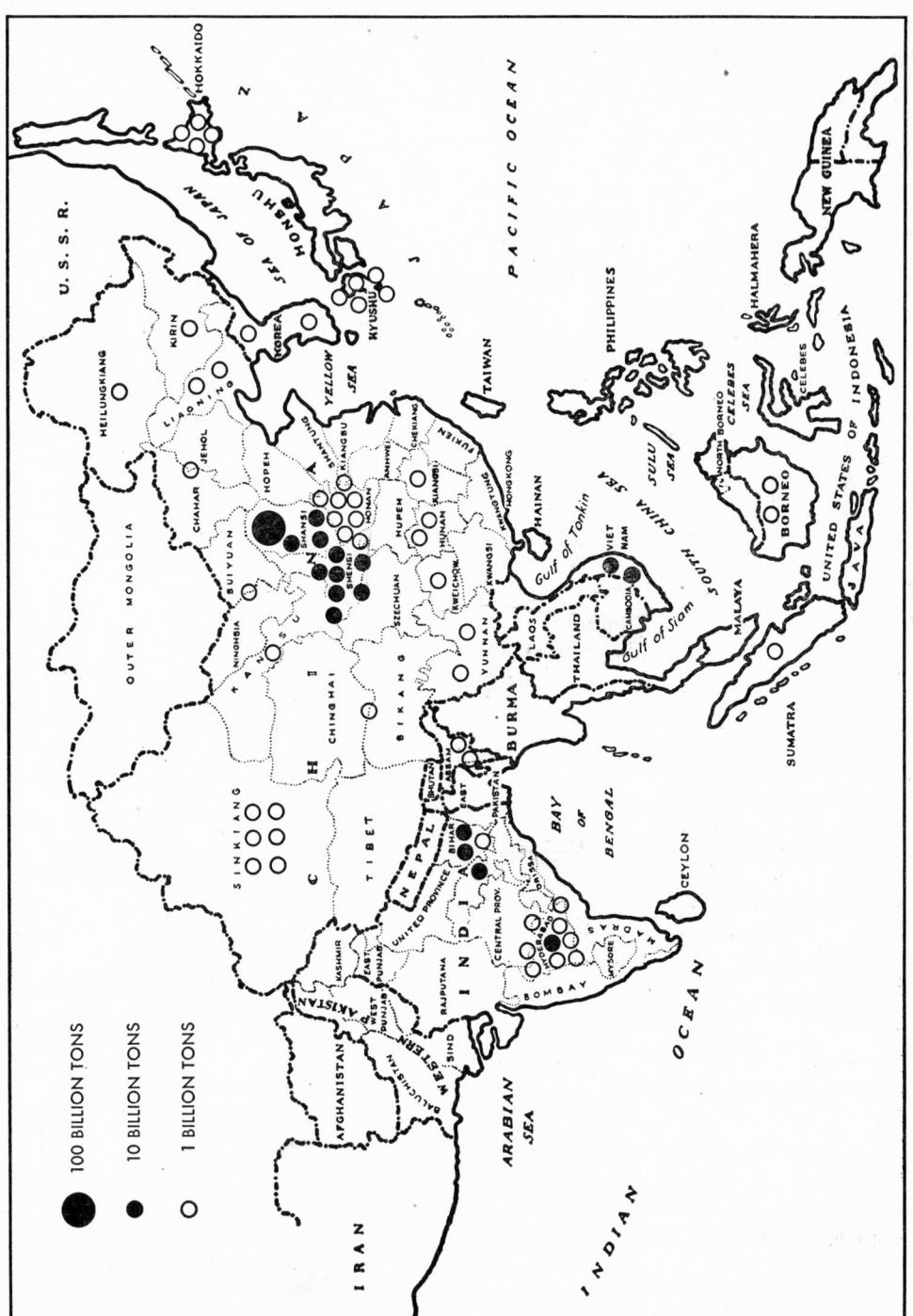

FIGURE 246. COAL RESERVES: GEOGRAPHIC DISTRIBUTION IN ASIA AND THE FAR EAST

Adaptation of map from United Nations, Economic Commission for Asia and the Far East

and the workable thickness of the seams; insufficient exploration of remote or isolated fields; differences in the rate of extraction in different mining areas; the possibility that coal beds will be discovered in regions so far unexplored, and so on.

ESTIMATES OF THE WORLD'S COAL RESERVES

The first authoritative estimate of the world's coal reserves was prepared by the twelfth International Geological Congress in 1913, on the basis of reports submitted to it by individual countries. This estimate was universally accepted and remained the sole official appraisal of the world's coal reserves until another authoritative international organization, the World Power Conference, published its estimate in 1933–34 and revised it in 1948.[17]

International Geological Congress, 1913

The reliability of an estimate of coal reserves depends on both the quality of the available information and the yardstick applied. The reserves reported by individual countries were divided, by the Geological Congress, into two groups: (1) actual reserves, based on knowledge of the actual thickness and extent of seams; (2) probable and possible reserves ("probable" when only an approximate estimate could be made, "possible" when no estimate in figures could be presented). The uniform yardstick set for the appraisal was one foot as the minimum workable thickness of seams down to a depth of 4,000 feet, and two feet at depths of 4,000–6,000 feet.[18]

On this basis, the world's coal reserves were estimated at 7.4 trillion tons, of which about 10 per cent were described as "actual reserves" and the rest as "probable and possible." According to this estimate, the Northern Hemisphere accounted for about 96 per cent of the total reserves, and the United States, for more than half. Canada ranked second, with total reserves exceeding those of Asia and Africa together. Europe and

Russia together were also believed to have smaller coal reserves than Canada. (See Table 360 and Figure 247.)

World Power Conference Estimate, 1948

The World Power Conference considered that the main shortcoming of the 1913 estimate was that it had made little real distinction between reserves actually surveyed and those evaluated on the basis of insufficient information.[19] The new estimate classified the world's coal reserves under two headings: (1) proven reserves of economic value for which reliable data on the actual thickness and extent of seams were available; (2) probable reserves, or proven reserves *plus* such further reserves of economic value as may, from incompleted investigations or from the relation to proven reserves, be reasonably assumed to exist but with respect to which only approximate estimates can be given. The standard for thickness of seams was about the same as in 1913, but that for depth was cut considerably: for bituminous, subbituminous and anthracite, to not more than 3,940 feet below the surface, including workable submarine seams; for lignite and brown coal, 1,640 feet below the surface.[20]

According to the 1948 estimate, the world's total reserves amount to 6.3 trillion tons (instead of 7.4 trillion), of which 690 billion tons (plus an unknown quantity in the United States) are proven reserves. While revisions were made for various countries, the difference in the world total is due chiefly to changes affecting three — the United States, Canada and the USSR. For the United States, the estimate gave reserves of 2.9 trillion tons instead of the 3.8 trillion accepted in 1913; for Canada, 89 billion tons instead of 1.2 trillion; and for the USSR, 1.2 trillion instead of 234 billion. (See Table 361.)

The 1948 estimate of the World Power Conference reflects the increase in information on coal reserves in individual countries and growing experience in exploration and mining. For example, the 1913 estimate of Russian coal reserves had shown practically no actual coal reserves in Russia, which, in the face of growing coal production, defied the realities. Although the 1948 figures for the USSR may not be more than an over-all appraisal of possible deposits at considerable depths in insufficiently explored fields and

---

17. The 1936 estimate was more than double that of the International Geological Congress in 1913. The difference was due largely to the increase in the figure for China from 996 billion tons to 10,113 billion tons. (**9**, 1933–34, pp. 16 and 21.) This fantastic figure remained uncorrected for twelve years until, in its latest publication in 1948, the World Power Conference stated that the figure for probable reserves of coal in China had been "magnified ten times by the accidental insertion of an extra 0." (**9**, 1948, p. 21.)

18. **7**, Vol. I, p. x.

19. **10**, p. 23.
20. **9**, 1948, p. 16.

Table 360

Coal Reserves in the World

(International Geological Congress, 1913)

(Billions of Metric Tons[a])

Continent	Total (Actual, Probable and Possible)	Actual				Probable and Possible			
		Total	Anthracite	Bituminous	Brown Coal and Lignite	Total	Anthracite	Bituminous	Brown Coal and Lignite
World	7,398	716	23	282	411	6,681	474	3,621	2,586
North America	5,073	415	0.7	29	385	4,659	21	2,211	2,427
United States	3,839	b	b	b	b	3,839	20	1,956	1,863
Canada	1,234	415	0.7	29	385	820	1.5	255	563
South and Middle America	32	2.1	—	2.1	—	30	0.7	29	—
Europe	724	274	13	237	24	450	3.7	436	11
Great Britain	190	142	11	130	—	48	—	48	—
Germany	423	104	—	95	9.3	319	—	315	4.1
Russia [c]	234	0.1	—	0.1	0.01	234	38	87	110
Asia	1,106	20	8.9	11	0.3	1,085	399	683	3.7
China	996	19	8.9	10	—	977	379	598	0.6
India	79	0.4	—	0.2	0.2	79	—	76	2.4
Africa	58	0.5	—	0.3	0.2	57	12	45	0.9
Oceania	170	4.1	0.1	2.4	1.6	166	0.6	131	35

Source: Adapted from **7**, Vol. I, pp. xxviii–xxxix.

a. Conversion factor: one metric ton = 1.1023 short tons.

b. No distinction made between "actual" and "probable and possible" in estimate submitted to the International Congress. All reserves included under the latter.

c. In Europe and Asia.

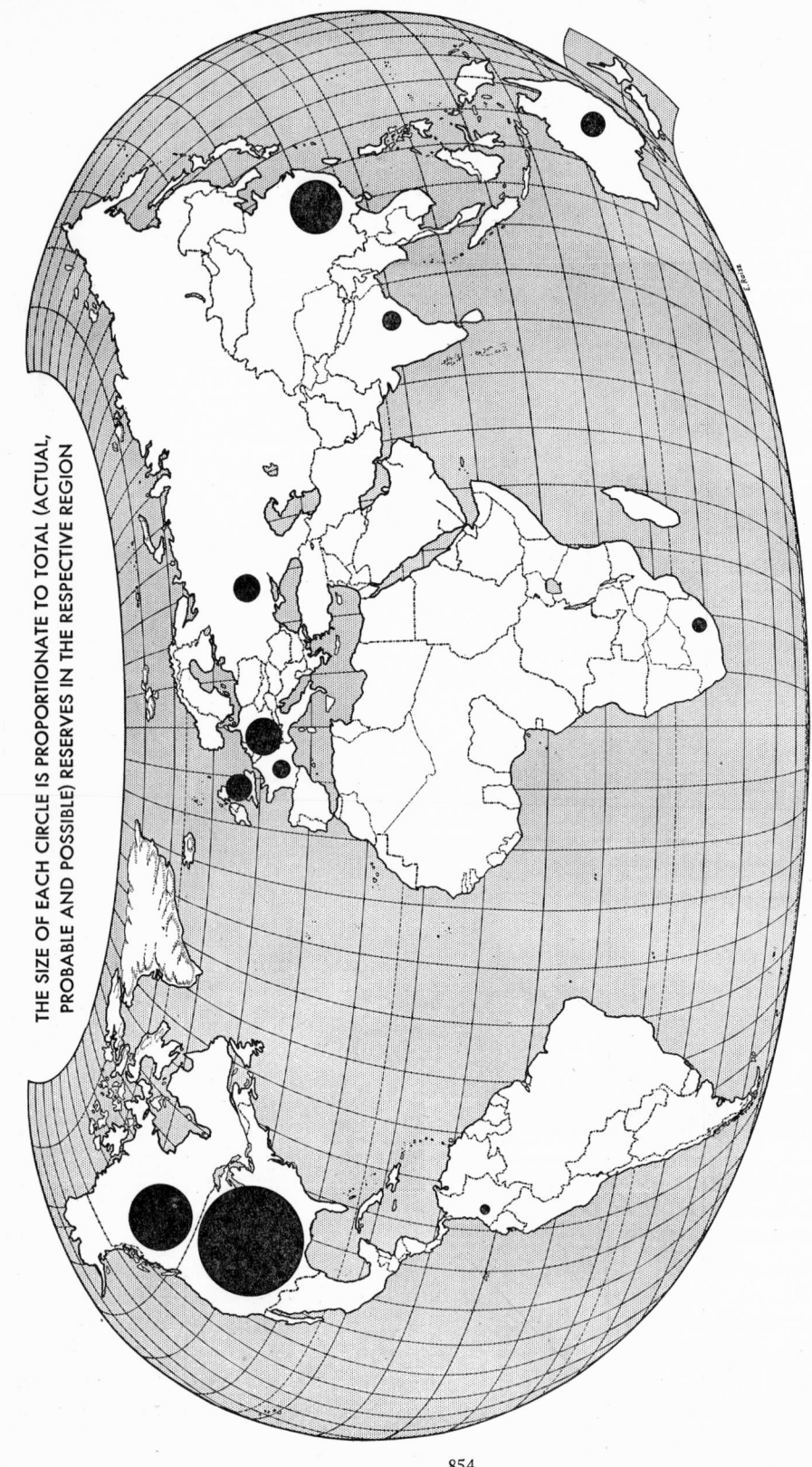

THE SIZE OF EACH CIRCLE IS PROPORTIONATE TO TOTAL (ACTUAL, PROBABLE AND POSSIBLE) RESERVES IN THE RESPECTIVE REGION

FIGURE 247. COAL RESERVES: GEOGRAPHIC DISTRIBUTION, AS ESTIMATED BY THE INTERNATIONAL GEOLOGICAL CONGRESS, 1913

Since the International Geological Congress made the 1913 estimate of the world's coal reserves pictured on this map, major countries have revised the figures they submitted to the Congress at that time, some raising, others lowering their own estimates of the coal within their boundaries. All estimates here relate to total coal reserves, including both actual and probable and possible.

854

TABLE 361

COAL RESERVES IN THE WORLD

(World Power Conference, 1948)

(*Billions of Metric Tons* [a])

Continent	Total	Anthracite, Bituminous and Subbituminous		Brown Coal and Lignite	
		Probable [b]	Proven	Probable [b]	Proven
World	6,266	4,984	616 [c]	1,282	75 [c]
North and Middle America	3,066	2,115	42	951	20
United States	2,880	2,028 [d]		852 [d]	
Canada	89	57	38	33	18
South America	3	3	2	—	—
Europe	638	553	252	85	37
United Kingdom	172	172	130	—	—
Germany	337	280	80	57	29
Poland	98	80	15	18	—
USSR	1,200	998	296	202	13
Asia	1,101	1,097	11	4	—
China	1,012	1,011	—	0.6	—
India	65	62	5	3	—
Africa	206	206	9	—	—
Oceania	54	14	4	40	5

Source: **9**, 1948, pp. 21 and 24–25. Data for the United States and Canada are for 1946; the United Kingdom, 1947; India, 1945; USSR, 1933; Germany, 1937; Poland, 1935 (bituminous coal) and 1945 (lignite); China, 1913.

a. Conversion factor: one metric ton = 1.1023 short tons.
b. Includes proven reserves.
c. Excludes the United States.
d. Data on "proven" reserves not available; includes Alaska.

may have an upward bias, they are more plausible than the incredibly small and overcautious figures of 1913.

The World Power Conference made the reservation that the totals for continents and the world are not inclusive and that the figures reported by different countries refer to different dates. The main significance of the available information was seen in the fact that the reserves "are at the very least as great as the quantity" shown in the published total. Nevertheless, this estimate is bound to be revised again, more probably downward than upward. The coal reserves of the United States, for example, were reappraised shortly after the publication of this last world estimate to a considerably lower figure.[21]

Moreover, in summarizing the estimates sub-mitted by individual countries, the World Power Conference did not and perhaps could not touch on the most important economic factor in appraising coal reserves, namely, the proportion of the reserve that is recoverable. Canada was the only country to include this factor in its estimate.[22] Recently the U.S. Geological Survey introduced the factor of recoverability in coal mining and revised the estimate of United States coal reserves from this point of view.

It can reasonably be assumed that when the world's coal reserves are reappraised from this point of view, the estimate will be much smaller than that in Table 361. In fact, some experts believe with C. A. Carlow "that if not from geological and scientific, then from practical and economic viewpoint, a sweeping reduction in the

21. See pp. 856–60.

22. See p. 860.

estimate of world coal reserves is necessary and that the reserves, instead of being stupendously large, will be found to be perilously small." [23]

ESTIMATES FOR SELECTED COUNTRIES

The United States

The estimate of United States coal reserves generally used until recently rested largely on data issued by the U.S. Geological Survey in 1907 and submitted to the International Geological Congress in 1913.[24] (See Table 360.) These data were based on geological information and made allowance for reserves in coal areas for which precise information was not available.[25]

Although M. R. Campbell, of the Geological Survey, who had prepared this estimate for the International Congress, made various reservations in his report, such as statements that some of the reserves were of low-rank coal, that others were not minable and the minable beds might not be accessible, and that the estimate rested "on entirely insufficient data," his over-all figure of more than 3 trillion tons of coal reserves became a byword in technical, economic and political discussions in the United States. This report, reprinted by the Survey in 1917 and again in 1929, contains Campbell's warning that the great bulk of the reserves is in low-rank coal, as shown by their composition at the end of 1918. (See Table 362.) As against the conclusion drawn from the total reserves that they were sufficient for more than 3,000 years, Campbell pointed out that with an increasing rate of consumption, the exhaustion is more probably within some 100 years than 4,000 years. This statement went unnoticed, however, since the estimate of the reserves, made "on entirely insufficient data," remained for a long time "nearly as it was originally made." [26]

In the early 1920's, the United States Coal Commission made a survey of the country's *recoverable* coal reserves, basing its estimate on the data of the Geological Survey and various state surveys, which it had "revised and reduced to allow for losses in mining and for thin and unavailable coal included in these estimates but

not considered as of special value." [27] Because of the limitation to "recoverable coal," the Commission's figure, as of 1923, indicated less than half the tonnage previously accepted — only 1,640 billion tons for total reserves. (See Table 362.)

Nevertheless, Campbell's estimate continued to be used widely. In 1936, T. A. Hendricks, of the Geological Survey, in his report to the National Resources Committee, appraised the coal reserves of the United States at 3.2 trillion tons.[28] In May 1947 the U.S. Bureau of Mines and the Geological Survey presented a joint estimate at hearings before the Senate Committee on Public Lands, indicating national coal reserves of 3.1 trillion tons as of January 1944. The estimate was described as "reasonably accurate," except for small reserves of some 30 billion tons in Texas.[29] (See Table 362.)

In August 1948, A. B. Crichton presented a paper on United States coal reserves to the Coal Division of the American Institute of Mining and Metallurgical Engineers, in which he sharply criticized the official estimate for overevaluation of coal seams. He pointed out that many seams are less deep than believed and that many mines were abandoned because they were either unproductive or unprofitable. The percentage of waste was, he said, higher than the accepted figure. He ventured to estimate total United States reserves at only 223 billion tons. Although many technicians participating in the discussion considered Crichton's estimate much too low, the consensus was that a radical reappraisal of national coal reserves was in order.[30]

In March 1949, Arno C. Fieldner, of the U.S. Bureau of Mines, published, in a symposium on the nation's fuel reserves, the following estimate of *recoverable* reserves of coal in the United States as of January 1, 1948 (in billions of short tons): [31]

Total	1,562
Bituminous	675
Subbituminous	409
Lignite	470
Anthracite	8

This estimate is rather close to that of the U.S. Coal Commission as of 1923.

23. **29**, pp. 681–82.

24. The yardstick was a minimum seam thickness of 14 inches for anthracite and bituminous, two feet for subbituminous and three feet for lignite, with a maximum cover of 3,000 feet.

25. **34**, 1949, p. 24.

26. **37**, pp. 25–26.

27. **12**, p. 1032.

28. **18**, p. 282.

29. **13**, p. 234.

30. **38**, pp. 26–32.

31. **44**, p. 139.

TABLE 362

COAL RESERVES: ESTIMATES FOR THE UNITED STATES, 1918–50

(Billions of Short Tons)

| Item | U.S. Geological Survey, 1918 [a] | U.S. Coal Commission, as of 1923 | U. S. Geological Survey, as of | | |
			1936	1944	1950
Original reserves	3,553	1,640	3,216	3,144	2,485
Bituminous [b]	1,491	690	1,435	1,362	1,281
Subbituminous	1,002	390	819	819	469
Lignite	1,038	544	940	940	712
Anthracite	22	16	22	24	24
Mined and wasted	13	...	34	41	59
Available:					
Bituminous	...	...	1,408	1,330	1,233
Subbituminous	...	...	818	818	468
Lignite	...	...	939	939	711
Anthracite	...	...	15	16	14

Sources: **37**, pp. 24–25; **12**, p. 1033; **18**, p. 285; **31**, p. 4.

   a. Excludes 667 billion tons of coal below surface at depths of 3,000–6,000 feet.
   b. Includes 50 billion tons of semibituminous coal.

Meanwhile, in 1948, the U.S. Geological Survey began a ten-year program of reappraising the nation's coal reserves. This program is intended to make a detailed, state-by-state inventory of each state's reserves by field surveys and test drilling, placing emphasis on the amounts of coal in terms of the various types, the thickness of seams and the thickness of overburden.

The Geological Survey issued its first progress report toward the end of 1950. It covered only portions of ten states and about 15 per cent of all coal reserves. On the basis of this partial resurvey, total reserves of the United States, as of January 1, 1950, are estimated at 2.5 trillion tons, instead of the 3.1 trillion reported as of 1944. The Bituminous Coal Institute assumes that as the resurvey continues, further downward revisions of the old estimates in other states will be made.[32]

Indeed, mining activities in the past decades have shown that some coal deposits previously considered continuous have been broken up by ancient erosion channels or by glacial scouring, while some other beds that are generally continuous are very thin in spots.[33] Moreover, with the introduction of mechanized mining in advanced countries, the potential importance of their beds has decreased. Actually, only accessible reserves in the thicker beds with less than 1,000 feet or, at most, 2,000 feet of overburden can be profitably mined today in the United States.[34]

The total reserves of bituminous coal in the ground as of January 1, 1950 are estimated at 1.3 trillion tons; approximately half of it is in four states — Colorado, Illinois, Kentucky and West Virginia. Of the nearly half a trillion tons of subbituminous coal, Colorado, Montana and Wyoming have about three fourths. North Dakota has six sevenths of the nation's lignite, and Pennsylvania nearly all the anthracite. (See Table 363.)

In its latest estimate the Geological Survey also attacked the problem of the recoverability of coal from the mines. Losses in mining vary from mine to mine, amounting to 20 per cent in some and more than 50 in others. According to H. N. Eavenson, 50–70 per cent of the coal in seams that have been mined has not been recovered, and this proportion tends to increase.[35] The Geological Survey has decided to use 50 per cent as a yardstick for the recoverability of coal and has halved the estimate of reserves in the ground to give a realistic appraisal of the coal potentially available to the nation.[36] The total recoverable reserves are estimated at 1.2 trillion tons, of

32. **34**, 1951, p. 42.
33. **34**, 1949, pp. 24–25.

34. **11**,a, p. 3.
35. **42**, p. 198.
36. **31**, p. 3.

TABLE 363

COAL RESERVES IN THE UNITED STATES, BY STATE, JANUARY 1, 1950
(Geological Survey)
(Millions of Short Tons)

State	Estimated Original Reserves					Mined and Wasted by January 1, 1950 [a]	Remaining Reserves, January 1, 1950	Recoverable Reserves [b]
	Total	Bituminous	Subbituminous	Lignite	Anthracite			
United States	2,484,637	1,280,736	468,544	711,693	23,664	59,071	2,425,566	1,212,783
Alabama	67,570	67,570	—		—	1,643	65,927	32,963
Arkansas	1,716	1,396	—	90	230	184	1,532	766
Colorado	317,346	213,071	104,175	—	100	942	316,404	158,202
Georgia	933	933			—	23	910	455
Illinois	171,905	171,195	—		—	6,264	165,641	82,821
Indiana	53,051	53,051	—		—	1,968	51,083	25,542
Iowa	29,160	29,160	—		—	686	28,474	14,237
Kansas	17,574 [c]	17,574 [c]	—		—	20 [d]	17,554	8,777
Kentucky	123,327	123,327	—		—	3,904	119,423	59,712
Maryland	8,043	8,043	—		—	520	7,523	3,762
Michigan	297	297	—		—	77	220	110
Missouri	79,362	79,362	—		—	516	78,846	39,423
Montana	222,047	2,363	132,151	87,533	—	314	221,732	110,866

(Continued on facing page)

TABLE 363—continued

| State | Estimated Original Reserves | | | | | Mined and Wasted by January 1, 1950 [a] | Remaining Reserves, January 1, 1950 | Recoverable Reserves [b] |
	Total	Bituminous	Subbituminous	Lignite	Anthracite			
New Mexico	61,755	10,948	50,801	—	6	243	61,512	30,756
North Carolina	110	110	—	—	—	2	108	54
North Dakota	600,000	—	—	600,000	—	136	599,864	299,932
Ohio	86,497	86,497	—	—	—	3,389	83,108	41,554
Oklahoma	54,951	54,951	—	—	—	318	54,633	27,317
Pennsylvania	97,898	75,093	—	—	22,805	24,666	73,233	36,616
South Dakota	1,020	—	—	1,020	—	2	1,018	509
Tennessee	25,665	25,665	—	—	—	649	25,016	12,508
Texas	31,000	8,000	—	23,000	—	124	30,876	15,438
Utah	93,340	88,184	5,156	—	—	397	92,943	46,471
Virginia	21,649	21,149	—	—	500	1,097	20,552	10,276
Washington	63,878	11,413	52,442	—	23	286	63,592	31,796
West Virginia	116,618	116,618	—	—	—	9,959	106,660	53,330
Wyoming	121,554	13,235	108,319 [e]	—	—	725	120,829	60,415
Other states [f]	16,370	820	15,500	50	—	18	16,352	8,176

Source: 31, p. 5.

a. It is assumed that losses equal production.
b. Assuming 50 per cent recovery.
c. Reserves on January 1, 1946.

d. Production from January 1, 1946 to January 1, 1950.
e. Includes small reserves of lignite.
f. Includes reserves of bituminous coal in Arizona, California, Idaho and Oregon; of subbituminous in Arizona, California and Oregon; of lignite in California and Louisiana.

859

which a large part is lignite (more than 300 billion tons) and subbituminous coal (about 240 billion tons).

While United States coal reserves are abundant, "exhaustion is a matter of hundreds rather than thousands of years." [37] Whatever the yardstick used, it must be remembered that the best coal is being mined while the less valuable remains in the ground. Reserves of the best coking types are rather limited, and some day the steel industry may have to adapt itself to inferior coal or alter its methods of ore reduction.[38]

Canada

The Canadian Royal Commission on Coal of 1946 concluded that the 1913 estimate of 1,234 billion tons submitted to the International Geological Congress can in no circumstances be considered "as an approximation of reserves of coal which, assuming present mining techniques, are physically available without exceptional engineering problems and prohibitive mining costs. . . . No coal one foot thick has been mined in Canada below a depth of five hundred feet, and it is extremely unlikely that it will be" in the near future.[39] Applying different yardsticks to particular Canadian fields,[40] the Commission found that the total reserves of the country (probable and possible) amounted to only 99 billion tons instead of 1,234 billion,[41] or to less than 10 per cent of the amount estimated in 1913.

The Commission has also distinguished between minable and recoverable coal resources since, in its opinion, it is unusual to recover anywhere near all the coal in a mine. The degree of extraction varies from mine to mine, but for Canada as a whole, 50 per cent recovery of the minable coal was considered likely.[42] Moreover, the Commission believes that precise determination of minable and recoverable coal can be made only with respect to relatively small areas

that have been extensively drilled and at least partially exploited. For an area as large as the Canadian coal fields, these requirements cannot be adequately met at the present time.

All in all, the Commission estimates that only half the Canadian coal resources — that is, 49 billion tons — is recoverable. Of these 49 billion tons, 31 billion represent probable reserves, "which by direct mining experience and by drilling, contiguity to existing workings and areas drilled, or extensive geological data, can be reasonably expected to exist." The remaining 18 billion tons are possible reserves, including coal "the reasonable existence of which is based on limited geological data and prospecting, and coal, the recovery of which is problematical due to its inferior quality and its relative inaccessibility." [43]

In its report to the Fourth World Power Conference, held at London in 1950, the Canadian government estimated the reserves of minable coal in Canada at 89.6 billion tons — 56.4 billion tons in probable reserves and 33.3 billion tons in possible reserves.[44]

Great Britain

The earliest official estimate of British coal reserves was made by the First Royal Commission in 1871. Without speculating on the probable existence of coal beds in the south of England, but allowing for losses of mining, it estimated the country's coal resources at 146.5 billion tons in seams a foot or more in thickness and not more than 4,000 feet below the surface. Each following evaluation, except that made in 1905, has shown higher figures (in billions of tons): [45]

1871.	First Royal Commission	146.5
1905.	Second Royal Commission	140.4
1912.	Strahan, Director of the British Geological Survey	178.7
1913.	International Geological Congress	189.5
1915.	Professor H. S. Jevons	197.0
1938.	Reichskohlenrat	209.2

In 1944–45, the estimate of the Ministry of Fuel and Power introduced a more realistic yardstick — seams 18 inches in thickness at depths not exceeding 3,940 feet. Without taking account of unexplored coal fields or undersea extensions of the northern and Scottish fields, the Ministry

---

37. **44**, p. 138.
38. **34**, 1949, p. 27.
39. **20**, p. 9.
40. For Nova Scotia, coal of a minimum thickness of 3 feet with not more than 4,000 feet of cover; for New Brunswick, average thickness of 18 or more inches, at a depth not exceeding 500 feet; for lignite of Saskatchewan, Ontario and Manitoba, a minimum thickness of 3 feet to a maximum depth of 500 feet, and so on.
41. **20**, pp. 8 and 11.
42. In the United States the recovery in bituminous mines was considered to be about 65 per cent in 1943. **46**, p. 64. The Geological Survey estimates it at 50 per cent. **31**, p. 8.

43. **20**, p. 10.
44. **11,c**, p. 4.
45. **27**, p. 17; **22**, 1938, p. 5.

computed total reserves at only 44.7 billion tons. In 1946 the Department of Scientific and Industrial Research made the first analysis of national coal reserves in terms of type and quality, and this assessment of reserves was later revised by the National Coal Board. According to the Board there is sufficient coal for another century (1942–2042) at the present annual rate of consumption, and ample evidence that it will be possible to maintain output for a considerable period beyond the year 2042. It is expected that about 22 billion tons will be consumed between 1942 and 2042, of which more than half will be mined in Yorkshire, South Wales, Fife and Clackmannan, Nottinghamshire and North Derbyshire.[46]

The USSR

The 1913 estimate of Russia's coal reserves presented to the International Geological Congress was revised upward by Soviet experts from 234 billion tons to 1,654 billion tons (91 billion tons of anthracite, 1,352 billion of bituminous and 211 billion of lignite) in the report presented to the seventeenth International Geological Congress, held in Moscow in 1937.[47]

The well-known coal fields in the European part of the USSR constitute, according to the 1937 estimate, less than 10 per cent of the total (150.4 billion tons). The rest is in the Asiatic USSR, where, with the exception of the Kuznetsk Basin (450 billion tons), there has been comparatively little exploration. The Donets Basin is evaluated at 89 billion tons; the Tungus field, at 440 billion; Bureya, at 203 billion; and the reserves in the north central section of the Soviet Arctic, at 103 billion.

China

Chinese coal resources, estimated in 1913 by the International Geological Congress at 996 billion tons, were whittled down in the evaluation of the Chinese Geological Survey in 1934 to only 235 billion tons, including 4 billion tons for Manchuria.[48] The 1913 and 1934 estimates of the various types of coal are as follows (in billions of tons):

	1913	1934
Anthracite	387	46
Bituminous	608	182
Lignite	0.6	5

46. **11,b**, pp. 1–3.
47. **8**, pp. 196–97.
48. **29**, pp. 656–57. 1934: includes reserves not classified by type.

The 1934 estimate was accepted by the United Nations Economic Commission for Asia and the Far East in a survey of mineral resources.[49] (See Figure 246.)

THE LIFETIME OF COAL RESERVES

Attempts have been made time and again to estimate the lifetime of coal reserves of the world and of particular countries. The problem involves two unknown factors: the quantity of coal that can eventually be extracted from the earth, and the rate at which it will be extracted in coming years and centuries. An attempt to solve the problem by dividing a hypothetical and highly controversial total by an arbitrarily assumed annual demand for coal only confuses the issue.

For example, one may take as "probable" the coal reserves of the world as estimated in 1948 by the World Power Conference — 6,266 billion tons — and assume that 1,000 billion tons represent "proven" reserves.[50] One may then assume that coal will continue to be mined at the present rate, about 1.7 billion tons a year. On these premises "proven" coal reserves will last approximately 600 years and "probable" reserves an additional 3,000 years.

Such an estimate would be misleading, however. Even if the estimate of reserves is taken at face value, the assumption that coal will be dug through centuries and millenniums at the present rate is utterly unrealistic. If allowance is made for a gradual increase in coal output at the rate of one per cent a year, approximately 290 billion tons would be extracted from the earth in the next century, 780 billion tons in the century following and 2,110 billion tons and 5,700 billion tons, respectively, in the third and fourth centuries. Thus the "proven" reserves would approach exhaustion in less than 200 years, and all "probable" reserves would be gone in less than 350 years.

Allowance for a 2 per cent annual increase in coal consumption during the next hundred years would mean that about 830 billion tons would be mined during the next century and 7,600 billion tons in the century following, between A.D. 2150 and 2250. Thus the world would ex-

49. **3**, 1949, p. 335. In addition, 8 billion tons of unclassified coal reserves are considered possible.

50. Inclusive of the proven reserves in the United States, roughly estimated for this purpose at 320 billion tons.

TABLE 364

COAL RESERVES: PROBABLE LIFETIME IN THE WORLD AND SELECTED COUNTRIES

(Institut für Konjunkturforschung, 1937)

Country	Reserves, Proven and Probable [a]	Average Annual Output, 1925–35	Probable Lifetime, in Years, under Assumption of Production		
			At the Rate of 1925–35	With Yearly Increase of:	
				0.5 Per Cent	2 Per Cent
	(In Millions of Metric Tons)				
World	4,600,000	1,234	3,730	595	217
United States	1,975,000	536	3,686	593	217
Canada	286,000	11	25,310	969	314
Great Britain	200,000	230	868	329	147
Germany	289,000	148	1,951	470	186
Poland	138,000	38	3,651	590	216
USSR	1,075,000	30	35,478	1,037	330
China	220,000	17	13,330	892	282

Source: **54**, p. 47.

    a. Only bituminous and anthracite to a depth of 2,000 meters.

haust its "proven" reserves before A.D. 2070 and its "probable" reserves some 70 years later.[51]

The Institut für Konjunkturforschung (Institute for the Study of Business Conditions) followed a similar line of reasoning in its alternative estimates. (See Table 364.) Using lower figures for the world's reserves than those established by the International Congress in 1913 and a lower annual output than that assumed above, it concluded that the world's coal reserves are bound to be exhausted in the not too remote future. This danger would seem more imminent now that it has become increasingly questionable whether all known reserves can ever be recovered.

Although the Institute's opinion appears more realistic than the theory that the known world coal reserves will last many millenniums "at the present rate of production," its projections require two corrections. First, geometrical progression as the law of growth in demand for coal should not be taken too seriously. The declining rate of growth of world population and the probability of its stabilization in the future [52] may imply a decline in the rate of the growth of world demand for coal, even when allowance is made for the progressive industrialization of un-

derdeveloped countries and the increasing use of coal for chemicals. Second, demand for coal may be cut down further by the factors that checked growth in output after World War I: greater efficiency in coal consumption and greater use of other sources of energy. While a new demand for coal may arise from its conversion to liquid fuels, new sources of fuel and power yet untapped may, in turn, lessen the rate of coal consumption.

To sum up, it seems probable that, in the long run, demand for coal will increase at a declining annual rate rather than a constant rate, and that the exhaustion of existing reserves is a question of the comparatively remote future. Moreover, it is possible that new coal fields will be discovered, and it is reasonable to expect that technological progress will result in recovery of a higher percentage of the coal from the mines.[53]

COAL MINING

Primitive Techniques

In early days coal was extracted by hand, generally only from outcrop deposits close to the surface. "Bells" (shallow, bell-shaped pits) were lined with wooden boards and, when water appeared, undressed sheep skins to prevent cave-ins. The coal was lifted out in baskets until the pit was exhausted. Then a new hole would be dug a few yards away. Before the sixteenth century, pits 25 feet below ground were considered deep.

---

51. The assumption of a 2 per cent annual increase in coal output implies that the demand would rise from 1.7 billion tons in 1950 to 12.3 billion tons in 2050 and would be close to 52.5 billion tons by 2150. (Compare the estimate of the U.S. Bureau of Mines of the lifetime of the world's coal reserves in Table 162, p. 329.

52. Cf. Chapter 7, pp. 261–62.

53. Cf. Chapter 25.

In the seventeenth century the depth increased to 180 feet, and galleries were usually dug from the bottom of the shaft along the face of the coal to reach and follow the underground seams. Gunpowder was not used to blast coal in English mines until the end of the seventeenth century, and borers came into use at about the same time.

The miners worked underground in near darkness. To avoid the danger of candles or open lamps underground, flint and steel were put to work. The shower of sparks resulting from this friction gave a light just sufficient to work by.[54]

Provisions for ventilation were primitive in England and in the United States, where there was virtually none as late as 1840. Rooms about 50 feet long were cut out in all directions, with scarcely any pillars to hold up the overburden. Not until 1850 was the double entry for air circulation introduced in the coal mines of the United States; by 1870 it had become general.

The coal was carried to the surface, mostly by women groping along dark galleries and up ladders, with lighted candles in their teeth. The ordinary load for a woman was 170–175 pounds, carried in a basket supported by a leather strap across her forehead. The father of a family usually worked as a hewer, and his wife and daughters, of 7 or 8 years, and sometimes even younger, as "bearers." These were rarely paid anything at all, as for example in Scottish mines, their work being considered merely a contribution to the earnings of the family head.[55] About 1650, wooden-wheeled wagons were introduced in England (somewhat earlier in Germany), and two women were employed at a wagon, one pulling it by a chain at her belt, the other pushing it from behind. Some mines later introduced wagon ways with wooden rails, fastened to ties by wooden pins, and used horses for hauling. Wagons with cast-iron wheels appeared around the middle of the eighteenth century. In the second half of that century, man-operated windlasses for hoisting coal were introduced.

Water, the ever present danger in early mines, was once pumped by hand in an endless chain of buckets, operated by a windlass at the mine head.[56] The Watt steam engine solved the drainage problem late in the eighteenth century, and Humphrey Davy gave the mines the safety lamp

in 1816. By the middle of the nineteenth century, power-driven machinery for pumping, ventilating and hauling was in common use, and somewhat later coal-cutting machinery appeared.[57]

Women and children meanwhile continued to work underground, putting in 12 to 14 hours a day. Not until 1842, after the report of the Royal Commission on work conditions underground aroused the country, was the work of women and boys under 10 years of age forbidden in England's coal mines. In most other countries female labor and the "bearing system" were also discontinued during the nineteenth century.

In the United States all bituminous coal was still undercut and drilled for shooting, or shot from the solid seam and loaded by hand as late as 1871. The coal cars were pushed by hand to haulage ways or pulled by mules; in some Illinois mines, dogs were used for this purpose as late as 1903.[58] The first coal-cutting machine was introduced in Indiana in 1873.

Modern Techniques

Modern coal-mining techniques are geared to the use of electricity. Coal can be cut by electric machines at any level, vertically or horizontally. Power drills make the holes in the face of the coal, and the charge of explosives can be fired electrically. The coal is then loaded mechanically and transported either to a gathering place in the mine or directly to the tipple at the surface. Drop-bottom cars unload coal automatically at any designated point. Recently, some mines have introduced shuttle cars — self-unloading electric trucks shuttling between the working face and the haulage center.[59]

In general, coal mining has become a highly mechanized industry, particularly in the United States. All important coal-producing countries have been mining an increasing percentage of their coal mechanically, especially in the last twenty-five years. In 1949, 91.4 per cent of the underground bituminous and lignite output of the United States was cut by machine and 67 per cent was loaded mechanically.[60] In the United Kingdom, 76 per cent was cut mechanically in 1948. Mechanical pneumatic picks (rather than cutting machines) were used before World War II for the entire output of Germany and Belgium

54. **40**, p. 41.

55. **51**, Vol. II, p. 189.

56. **48**, p. 126; **30**, pp. 15–34; **57**, p. 31; **61**, pp. 42–57.

57. **48**, pp. 70–71.

58. **29**, p. 225.

59. **20**, pp. 80–81.

60. **34**, 1951, p. 72.

and for about 90 per cent of that of France. Coal is commonly conveyed by machinery in these European countries, but it is generally shoveled to the conveyor by hand. Thus, in the United Kingdom, 75 per cent of the coal output was conveyed mechanically in 1948 but power loading was used for only 2.5 per cent. Apparently, a suitable power loader has not yet been developed for the British mines, where underground gradients are steeper than in the United States.[61] The USSR claimed in 1938 that 99 per cent of its coal was mechanically mined.[62]

Recent Technological Developments

One of the latest developments in mining techniques is a new machine, a kind of combine for simultaneous cutting and loading of coal into the conveyor or shuttle car. This machine, the nearest approach to "automatic" mining, can, it is claimed, cut and load up to 2 tons of coal a minute with a crew of 4–7 men. Drilling and blasting are eliminated. In 1950, at least a hundred robots of this type, though of different construction, were used in United States mines. In the United Kingdom a similar British-built machine is used in a number of advanced mines, while the American combine and the German "coal plow" of similar type are being used experimentally.[63]

Continuous mining machines raise new problems, however. Haulage to the surface must keep pace with them; roof-propping must also be adjusted to their speed, to assure operational safety.[64] In the United Kingdom it has been found that the machine can be used only if the seam is at least three feet thick and not too faulted, the gradient is not too steep, the roof is strong and the floor solid.[65] On the whole, it is to be expected that such universal machines will be modified in design and that ways will be found to assure their full effectiveness through the coordination of all the operations involved.[66]

Mechanical Cleaning

Mechanization of mining made it necessary to clean coal mechanically. The usual practice had been to pick out impurities, such as "bone," by

hand, mostly from large-size coal. Small-size coal went into the cars without further preparation. With mechanical loading, hand picking was largely abandoned, and the proportion of dirt and "fine" coal increased. In some cases, the amount of refuse nearly trebled. The percentage of large-size coal, on the other hand, dropped considerably with the replacement of traditional techniques by continuous mining.[67]

To check these conditions, surface processing of coal has been greatly developed. The cleaning plant at the tipple, receiving the run-of-the-mine coal, removes the impurities, by wet or dry mechanical methods, and screens the coal to "tailor-size" lumps for various groups of consumers. In the United States more than half of the bituminous mines have cleaning plants; practically all anthracite is cleaned.[68] In 1949, 69 per cent of the bituminous coal mechanically loaded underground was cleaned in special plants, as compared with 19 per cent of the hand-loaded coal. In that year 17 tons of refuse were discarded in cleaning every 100 tons of run-of-the-mine coal, while only 9 tons of refuse had been rejected in 1936.[69] Another important trend in coal preparation is the growing distinction between the preparation of coal for fuel use and for special purposes, such as metallurgy, when coal is cleaned to ash and sulfur specifications.[70]

Although half the coal output in the United Kingdom is treated in cleaning plants (not counting the hand-picked large coal), much of the coal is dirtier than it used to be, chiefly because mechanical processing lags behind the mechanization of mining. New cleaning plants of increased capacity are being installed, and some coal is transported for cleaning to neighboring collieries with spare processing capacity.[71]

Types of Mines

An underground mine can be opened (1) by driving a more or less level tunnel, called a drift, into the coal seam; (2) by driving an inclined entry, called a slope, down to the seam; or (3) by sinking a vertical shaft to the coal level. In the United States the first two methods are commonly used in hilly or mountainous country and the third in flat country. (See Figure 248.)

---

61. **11,b**, p. 16; **26**, 1949, p. 15; and **34**, 1949, p. 150.
62. **59**, p. 215.
63. **34**, 1951, pp. 75–76; and **25**, pp. 51–52.
64. **34**, 1949, p. 148.
65. **26**, 1949, p. 16.
66. **11,d**, pp. 11–13.

67. **11,d**, p. 15.
68. **42**, p. 194.
69. **15**, 1950, preprint, p. 40; **34**, 1950, p. 149.
70. **11,a**, p. 6.
71. **26**, 1949, p. 18.

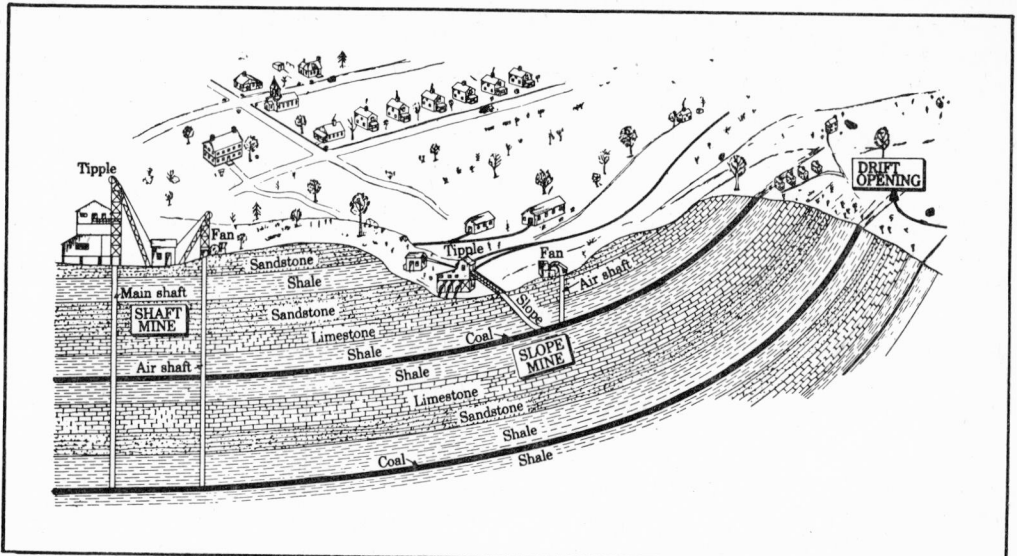

U.S. Bureau of Mines

FIGURE 248. COAL MINING: TYPES OF UNDERGROUND MINES

Drift, slope and shaft mines differ chiefly in the way men, materials and coal are moved between the underground workings and the surface. Trains of mine cars, called trips, are hauled into and out of drift mines by specially designed electric locomotives. Trips may be taken into and out of slope mines in the same way, if the grade is gentle. At many slope mines, however, trips are moved by a cable operated by a hoist or windlass, which pulls them to the surface and keeps them from going downgrade too fast. Sometimes endless-belt conveyors are used instead of mine cars. Men, materials and coal are taken into and out of shaft mines in cages or skips.

In addition to underground mining, several countries have strip or open-cut coal mining. The overburden is first shoveled off, and extraction consists largely in scooping up the coal. Open-cut mining has been facilitated by improvements in earth-moving machinery. In the United States, 23.3 per cent of the coal mined in 1950 was extracted by stripping, as compared with 3.0 per cent in 1927 and 7.1 per cent in 1937.[72] In Great Britain, 1.3 per cent of the coal was open-cut in 1942, 8.7 per cent in 1944, and 11.8 per cent in 1948.[73] Before World War II, Germany extracted more than 80 per cent of its lignite from open pits, Czechoslovakia about 20 per cent.[74]

In the USSR, only 3.8 per cent of all coal was open-cut in 1940; by 1945, the percentage had risen to 11.8. Since the war, surface mining has been increasing more rapidly than underground production.[75]

Surface mining obviously results in higher productivity per man-day than work underground. In some Canadian mines, where 15 per cent of the coal was mined by stripping in 1945, output per man was as much as 14 tons a day. In the United States, strip mining averaged 15.3 tons per man-day in 1949, as much as 25 or 30 tons a day in some mines, and 79.3 tons a day in one Montana mine, as against an average of 5.4 tons a day in underground mining for the country as a whole and an average of 10.2 tons for the highest state.[76]

Systems of Mining

Most of the world's coal mining is carried on underground, by one of two main systems: room-and-pillar or longwall mining.

With the first system, part of the coal is left in the room in the form of pillars to keep the roof from caving in. If the pillars are not mined, less than half the coal in the room may be extracted. Gradual withdrawal of the pillars, as in some mines in Pennsylvania, may raise the rate of extraction to 90 per cent.

72. **15**, 1950, preprint, p. 2; and **34**, 1950, pp. 64–65.
73. **24**, p. 122.
74. **4**, Vol. I, p. 25.

75. **59**, p. 216.
76. **20**, p. 76; **15**, 1950, preprint, pp. 21 and 28–34.

In longwall mining, the coal is removed from a continuous working face. The workers may begin at the part of the coal face nearest the entrance and move inward, or they may start at the end limit of the working face and mine all the coal out to the entrance. The overburden is either permitted to cave in and fill the space, or is supported by rock waste that comes down with the coal.

Geological, physical, economic and engineering factors — the thickness of the seam, its inclination and faulting, the formation of the roof, the cost of production per unit, and so on — which vary from district to district and mine to mine, govern the choice between room-and-pillar and longwall mining. In general, room-and-pillar mining pays only if the pillars can be recovered. The extent to which they are removed is largely determined by the cost of operation, the price of coal, legal regulations and the extent of the coal deposits. In the United States several states have regulations prohibiting full extraction of coal because of surface conditions. In some areas it has been found cheaper to leave the coal in the pillars, while in others coal is mined entirely and the pillars are removed because of the scarcity of the type of coal.

The room-and-pillar system has many advantages, such as greater productivity per man-shift, support of all roadways by solid coal, and free use of cutting and loading machines. In longwall mining, on the other hand, a larger percentage of the coal is extracted from a seam without waste. This method also permits better control of cave-ins and is safer for the miners.

The United States mines 90 or more per cent of its coal by the room-and-pillar method; in Canada, more than half of the mines in the west and about half of those in Nova Scotia use this method.[77] In contrast, longwall mining predominates in Europe, where the seams are thin and so deep that pillars might break under the heavy overburden.[78] Backfilling is strictly enforced in Europe to avoid sinkage of the surface.

In the United Kingdom, about three fourths of all coal is produced by the longwall method, and the rest is about equally divided between the room-and-pillar method and open-pit mining. In some of the British coal beds conditions are ideal for longwall mining — a hard bottom, enough waste rock for backfilling, a uniform and flat bed, a roof strong enough to span a sufficient space between the coal face and the pack-wall with the aid of props.[79]

Coal Mining in the United States and Europe

On the basis of a special study of coal mining in Europe before World War II, the U.S. Bureau of Mines made the following comparison:

Our coal resources are much greater than those of European countries; the natural conditions of the coal deposits now being used are more favorable, in that our coal seams on the average are thicker, are more easily opened . . . and in many places can be attacked through the outcrop. Moreover, the daily output per coal mine worker is much greater in this country, because of the more widespread application of mechanization. However, . . . in spite of our natural advantages and our technical advancement, the coal extraction in our fields remains less complete and our accident rate is worse than in Europe.[80]

Loss of coal in European mines may be as little as 2 or 3 per cent if the seam is not too thick and the roof is good, somewhat greater under adverse conditions. In the United States, losses in the 1920's in mining (coal left in room entry and panel pillars, on the roof and the bottom) and in handling and preparation amounted to 35 per cent of the available bituminous and 39 per cent of the available anthracite. With mechanization, the proportion of waste has increased, since extra pillars are left behind to protect the machines and many small pillars are abandoned to permit continuous use of machinery. Today, losses in mining coal equal output. (See Table 363.)

COAL PRODUCTION

The Chinese used coal long before the Europeans. The first mention of it goes back to the reign of Han in the second century before Christ. The use of coal in China was first described in

77. **60,** p. 17.

78. In Belgium seams are from 8 to 12 inches thick, in other countries up to 18 inches. The average thickness of seams mined in the United States is 30 to 36 inches. (**56,** p. 42.) East of the Mississippi, where 92 per cent of today's coal is mined, the seams are generally from 36 to 72 inches thick, averaging 66 inches. The geologically younger beds are even thicker — nearly 156 inches, on the average, in Wyoming and more than 200 inches in Montana. **34,** 1951, p. 49.

79. **56,** p. 78.
80. **56,** p. 62.

European literature by Marco Polo in the thirteenth century:

> Throughout this province there is found a sort of black stone, which they dig out of the mountains, where it runs in veins. When lighted, it burns like charcoal, and retains the fire much better than wood; insomuch that it may be preserved during the night, and in the morning be found still burning.[81]

Coal may also have been known to the ancient Greeks and Romans. Theophrastus, the pupil of Aristotle, thus describes "stones" that must have been coal:

> Some of the more brittle stones there also are which become as it were burning coals when put into a fire, and continue so a long time: of this kind are those about Bena, found in mines and washed down by the torrents, for they will take fire on burning coals being thrown on them, and will continue burning as long as anyone blows them; afterward they will deaden, and may after that be made to burn again. They are therefore of long continuance, but their smell is troublesome and disagreeable.[82]

Cinders found near the Roman walls in Northumberland and in the ruins of Roman forts testify that coal must have been used in England as early as the Roman occupation. The first written record of its use in Anglo-Saxon chronicles dates from A.D. 852.

Use of Coal in Medieval Europe

England was probably the first European country to mine coal. Coal could not have been considered of any importance, however, since the Domesday Book (A.D. 1086), the first stocktaking of England's resources, does not even mention it. References to commercial coal mining begin to appear in the thirteenth century in British chronicles, contracts, records of monasteries, pacts, donations and testaments. Coal seams in Fife and Northumberland fields were outcropping and often covered by sea water. Women and children collected "sea coal," lumps left behind when the water receded.[83] After the middle

of the thirteenth century, coal began to be shipped to London, and in the fourteenth century small mines were worked in England, France and Germany. In Belgium, coal was mined as early as the twelfth century.

In England, sea coal was welcomed particularly by the smiths after Parliament prohibited the cutting of timber in various parts of the country to smelt iron.[84] There was strong opposition to the new fuel, however. With the common medieval practice of building the household fire in the middle of the room and letting the fumes escape through a flue in the roof, coal filled the dwelling with choking, ill-smelling smoke, and black soot covered the furnishings. The people, alarmed for their health, petitioned for the prohibition of coal burning. Even the use of coal by smiths was objected to, because the smoke was believed to pollute the air.[85] King Edward I commanded all subjects except the smiths to make fires of wood. Later, when the use of coal continued, a Royal Commission was named to punish all violators and destroy all coal-burning furnaces. At about the same time, even the smiths in some provinces of France were fined for using coal.[86] Similar measures were taken in Germany. As late as the sixteenth century, coal was the fuel of the poor in England, and persons of high rank would not enter houses heated with coal or eat food cooked over a coal fire.

Development of Production, 1600–1850

Neither orders nor fines nor social discrimination, however, could stop the advance of this cheap and abundant fuel in England or continental Europe. By 1600, England was producing a million tons of coal a year, exporting some of it to France, where coal was considered "that thing that France can no more lyve without than the fyshe without water." [87] In England, coal became "the general fewell . . . , used in the houses of the nobilitie, cleargy and gentrie in London and in all other cityes and shires of the Kingdom as well as for dressing of meate, washing, brewing, dyeing as otherwise." [88]

The real impetus to coal production, however, did not come until the end of the eighteenth century, after the invention of coke-making

81. **53**, p. 167.
82. **28**, p. 34. "Coals," as used here, means charcoal.
83. **48**, p. 3. The term "sea coal" persisted for centuries. In London, there was a "Secole Lane" in 1228. This term, in use in England until about 1780, was taken over in the United States. The first map showing coal locations in Pennsylvania, Ohio and Kentucky bears the inscription: "sea-coal here." (**41**, p. 9.)

84. **48**, p. 255.
85. **51**, Vol. I, p. 13.
86. **57**, pp. 26–27; **58**, p. 29.
87. **4**, Vol. I, p. 1.
88. **48**, p. 7.

TABLE 365

COAL OUTPUT IN THE WORLD AND SELECTED COUNTRIES, 1868–1949 ANNUAL AVERAGE [a]

(*Millions of Metric Tons* [b])

Annual Average	World	United States	Canada	Great Britain	France	Belgium	Germany
1868–69	209	33	1	107	14	13	34
1870–74	251	44	1	123	15	15	42
1875–79	290	54	1	136	17	15	50
1880–84	374	85	2	159	20	17	66
1885–89	442	117	2	168	22	18	78
1890–94	533	156	3	183	26	20	94
1895–99	643	192	4	205	31	22	121
1900–04	827	286	6	230	33	23	157
1905–09	1,048	393	9	260	36	24	203
1910–14	1,232	474	13	274	40	23	247
1915–19	1,269	545	13	247	24	15	244
1920–24	1,280	521	15	240	34	23	249
1925–29	1,448	548	15	227	52	26	316
1930–34	1,251	388	12	223	50	25	265
1935–39	1,488	408	14	233	47	29	351
1940–44	1,821	555	16	209	40	23	444
1945–49	1,560	553	15	201	46	24	233

Annual Average	Poland	Czechoslovakia	Russia (USSR)	China	Japan	India	Union of South Africa
1868–69	—	—	1	—	—	—	—
1870–74	—	—	1	—	—	—	—
1875–79	—	—	2	—	—	—	—
1880–84	—	—	4	—	1	—	—
1885–89	—	—	5	—	2	—	—
1890–94	—	—	7	—	4	3	—
1895–99	—	—	11	—	5	5	—
1900–04	—	—	17	—	9	7	—
1905–09	—	—	23	9	14	11	—
1910–14	—	—	27	13	19	15	—
1915–19	—	—	28	21	26	20	9
1920–24	22	32	11	21	30	20	12
1925–29	38	34	31	24	35	22	15
1930–34	33	28	73	28	34	22	12
1935–39	40	32	133	27	46	26	17
1940–44	83	46	135	59	56	28	20
1945–49	58	37	181	14	31	30	24

Source: **34**, 1950, p. 74.

a. Includes anthracite and bituminous coal, and lignite.

b. Conversion factor: one metric ton = 1.1023 short tons.

(1735), the steam engine (1769), the puddling process (1789) and illuminating gas,[89] all of which originated in England. By about 1820, England was producing some 10 million tons of coal a year, Germany and France a million each, and the United States 3,000 tons.[90]

The growth of iron production increased the

89. Use of coal gas for public lighting was an innovation of London's celebration of the battle of Waterloo in 1815.

90. **67**, p. 119. The first authentic record of the discovery of coal in the United States (at the Illinois River) dates from 1679. Early in the eighteenth century, coal was discovered in Virginia, where mining operations

demand for coal. The coal industry was enabled to meet the increasing demand by the opening of new beds and the use of deeper seams, in England and on the continent. Around 1850, England produced 35 million tons a year, Germany more than 4 million, France more than 2 million, and the United States about 6 million.

Many difficulties had to be overcome and many technical and engineering problems solved before coal production could gain real momentum. The deeper men dug for the hidden treasure, the greater became the hazards of explosions and the difficulties of haulage. Even after the coal had been brought to the surface, the problem of transporting this bulky and heavy product was formidable. England's leadership in production was due partly to the fact that its coal fields lie close to seaports. Once canals were built to link the coal fields to the harbors, exports of coal to the continent began to grow. The advent of railways, raising the demand for coal, stepped up the pace of production in England and other countries.

From 1850 to World War I

Between 1850 and 1860 the world's output of coal rose from about 50 million metric tons to 136 million. In 1860, England produced 85 million tons, the United States more than 15 million, and Germany and France more than 12 and 8 million tons, respectively.[91] The revolutionary invention of steel-making processes by Bessemer in 1856 and Siemens-Martin in 1861 [92] and the increase in output of steel gave a powerful impetus to coal production. From 1860 to the beginning of World War I, the world's coal output (in millions of metric tons) grew as follows: [93]

Year	Total	Bituminous	Lignite
1860	136	—	—
1870	218	—	—
1880	339	—	—
1890	513	474	38
1900	766	700	66
1910	1,143	1,039	105
1913	1,340	1,215	125

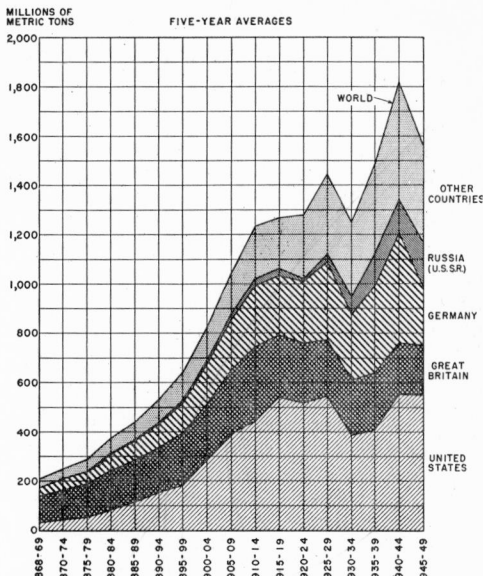

FIGURE 249. COAL: OUTPUT IN THE WORLD AND SELECTED COUNTRIES, 1868–69 TO 1945–49

By 1880 the United States was producing more coal than Germany, and at the turn of the century it overtook Great Britain. Except in 1938, it continued to hold the lead. (See Table 365 and Figure 249.) In 1913, these three countries together accounted for 81 per cent of the world's output — the United States for 38.6 per cent, Great Britain for 21.8 per cent and Germany for 20.7 per cent.

From World War I to World War II

After World War I, the upward trend in coal production was interrupted. In each decade preceding that war, the world's output increased by 50 per cent or more, but in 1924 only 6 per cent more coal was mined than in 1913. Even in the peak year 1929, the world's coal industry produced only slightly more coal than in 1913. The lowest point was reached during the depression in 1932. Thereafter output began to rise slowly, but in 1938 it barely exceeded the 1913 level, despite intensified production, in preparation for war, in Germany, Japan and the USSR. (See Table 366.)

Many reasons accounted for this slowdown in the world's coal production. First, oil was being used increasingly in factories and on ships and railroads, and water power also cut down the demand for coal. At the same time, coal lost a part of its market as the steel industry began to

started around 1750. Coal was first used in the vicinity but by 1789 was shipped to Philadelphia, New York and Boston. The Pittsburgh bed has been worked since 1760. (**61**, pp. 4–5.)

  91. **65**, p. 378.
  92. See Chapter 29.
  93. **7**, Vol. I, p. xix; **21**, 1924, pp. 262–63.

TABLE 366

COAL OUTPUT IN THE WORLD AND SELECTED COUNTRIES, 1929–50 [a]

(*Millions of Metric Tons* [b])

Country	1929	1930	1931	1932	1933	1934	1935	1936	1937	1938	1939
World, excluding USSR and China	1,623	1,341	1,172	1,035	1,069	1,157	1,186	1,295	1,385	1,302	1,402
United States [c]	552	487	400	326	348	378	384	448	451	358	405
Canada	17	14	11	11	13	13	14	14	14	13	14
United Kingdom	262	248	223	212	210	224	226	232	244	231	235
France [d]	55	55	51	47	48	49	47	46	45	48	50
Belgium	27	27	27	21	25	26	27	28	30	30	30
Netherlands	12	12	13	13	13	12	12	13	14	14	15
Saar	14	13	11	10	11	11	11	12	13	14	13
Germany [e]	338	293	252	227	226	262	279	308	355	364	385
Poland	46	38	38	29	27	29	29	30	36	38	23 [f]
Czechoslovakia	53	34	31	27	26	26	26	28	35	32	38
Spain	8	7	7	7	6	6	7	3	2	6	7
USSR	42	49	57	65	76	94	109	124	128	133	145
China [g]	25	27	38	26	...	32	...	...	...	...	...
Japan	34	32	28	28	33	36	38	42	45	47	52
India [h]	24	24	22	20	20	22	23	23	25	29	28
Union of South Africa	13	12	11	10	11	12	14	15	15	16	17
Australia	13	12	11	11	12	13	13	15	16	16	18

Country	1940	1941	1942	1943	1944	1945	1946	1947	1948	1949	1950
World, excluding USSR and China	1,471	1,431	1,610	1,625	1,535	1,180	1,291	1,440	1,486	1,394	1,493
United States [e]	465	517	584	590	620	574	539	624	596	436	505
Canada	13	15	17	17	16	15	15	16	17	17	17
United Kingdom	228	210	208	202	196	186	193	201	213	219	220
France [d]	41	44	44	42	27	35	49	48	45	51	52
Belgium	26	27	25	27	14	16	23	24	27	28	27
Netherlands	12	14	13	13	10	5	9	11	11	12	12
Saar	11	14	15	16	12	3	9	11	13	14	15
Germany [e]	396	406	416	425	376	60	106	130	153	176	187
Poland	...	...	...	...	...	...	49	64	75	79	82
Czechoslovakia	43	44	47	52	50	27	34	39	41	44	46
Spain	9	10	10	11	12	12	12	12	12	12	12
USSR	166	...	...	...	...	149	161	175	209	236	264
China [g]	6	6	6	7	6	5	18	19	9	16	37
Japan	58	56	56	58	52	24	23	30	36	40	40
India [h]	30	30	30	26	27	30	30	31	31	32	33
Union of South Africa	17	19	20	21	23	24	24	24	24	25	26
Australia	16	19	20	20	19	18	20	21	22	22	24

Sources: **1**, 1942–44, pp. 152–53; **2**, 1948, pp. 130–32, and 1951, pp. 135–38; **15**, 1950, preprint, pp. 81–83. For the United States: **14**, p. 142; and **15**, 1950, preprint, p. 81.

a. Includes bituminous coal, anthracite and lignite.
b. Conversion factor: one metric ton = 1.1023 short tons.

c. Output of anthracite in 1929 equaled 67 million metric tons; in 1939, 47 million; in 1949, 40 million.
d. 1940–44 without Lorraine, which produced 6.7 million tons in 1938 and 8.2 million in 1948.
e. Beginning with 1945, Western Germany.
f. First six months.
g. Includes Manchuria in 1929–34.
h. Beginning with August 1947, excludes Pakistan.

shift more and more to open-hearth methods and the use of scrap. Open-hearth furnaces smelt a ton of scrap with about a fifth of the coal needed to smelt a ton of pig iron in blast furnaces.[94]

Increasing efficiency in the use of coal helped curtail the demand. The iron and steel plants of the United States produced 1,478 pounds of pig iron per ton of coal used in 1948, in comparison with 1,310 pounds in 1920. The electric power plants needed 6.4 pounds of coal for each kilo-watt-hour produced in 1902, 3 pounds in 1920, and only 1.19 pounds in 1950. The railroads used one ton of coal for every 17,505 gross-ton-miles of freight and for every 125 passenger-car-miles in 1947, while a ton of coal in 1920 accounted for only 11,628 ton-miles and 106 car-miles.[95] Coal consumption per unit of manufactured gas dropped a third between 1909 and 1939.[96]

In 1920, the Canadian Pacific Railway used 148 pounds of coal for freight trains and 262 pounds for passenger trains per 1,000 gross-ton-miles, but on the eve of World War II, only 97 and 181 pounds, respectively.[97] In the United Kingdom, the coke and coal consumed per million kilowatt-hours in electric power stations fell from 1.49 long tons to 0.69 between 1920–21 and 1934–35. Coke consumption per ton of pig iron dropped from 2.06 tons in 1913 to 1.66 in 1936.[98] In Japan, steam power plants used 2.1 tons of coal in 1915 to produce 1,000 kilowatts and only 0.7 ton in 1932.[99]

In the United States, where nearly 24 billion tons of coal were mined from 1800 through 1938, the first peak in coal output (more than 616 million metric tons) came in 1918, at the end of World War I. From that year until the entrance of the United States into World War II, output was generally on the downgrade. In 1938 it was about 58 per cent of the 1918 level.

In the United Kingdom, coal output declined from 292 million tons in 1913 to 226 million in 1935. Domestic consumption decreased only slightly, but foreign demand dropped considerably because of competition from oil and cheaper German coal and because of a decrease in requirements for bunkering.

In contrast, Germany's coal output increased

after the depression of the 1930's, and on the eve of World War II exceeded that of Great Britain even in thermal value, although more than half the German output was lignite, which is low in heat value. The Ruhr-Aachen area accounted for 70–75 per cent, and Upper and Lower Silesia for about 19 per cent, of the total bituminous output. Germany's production of lignite, about three fourths of the world's total, was stimulated by new methods of utilizing this type of coal for power plants, briquetting and, later, hydrogenation. In 1938, the output of lignite (192 million tons) exceeded that of bituminous coal (172 million tons).

The USSR and Japan made great efforts during the 1930's to produce more coal, the USSR tripling its output and Japan increasing its by about 62–63 per cent from 1930 to 1939. In many coal-producing countries — France, Belgium, the Netherlands, Czechoslovakia, Poland and India — production remained more or less stationary in that decade, except for a slump during the depression years. In contrast, the Union of South Africa and Australia increased output by 50 per cent. (See Table 366.)

During World War II

The United States. The output of bituminous coal in the United States rose more than 70 per cent between 1938 and 1944 and that of anthracite about 38 per cent. The increase was achieved with about 11 per cent fewer workers, but in 1944 the average number of working days per man — 278 — was the highest in the history of coal mining in the country; even in 1918, a peak year in coal production, the average had been only 249. A higher percentage of coal was mechanically loaded and stripped in 1944 than in 1938, and open-pit mining was greatly developed. The mines operated around the clock — twenty-four hours a day, seven days a week. Average output per worker rose by about 12 per cent, from 4.85 to 5.67 tons a day.[100]

Great Britain. In Great Britain, on the other hand, production declined in each successive war year and in 1945 was some 19 per cent below 1938. The main reasons were shortage of labor and the drop in productivity. Some 70,000 experienced miners were lost to other industries at the outbreak of the war, and the replacements, at first voluntary, later compulsory (the so-called

94. **36**, pp. 20–21. See Chapter 29.
95. **18**, p. 108; **34**, 1951, p. 76; **15**, 1950, preprint, p. 65.
96. **19**, p. 157.
97. **20**, p. 469.
98. **52**, p. 111.
99. **5**, Vol. I, p. 28.

100. **15**, 1945, pp. 853–54.

Bevin boys), had no mining experience and only brief training.[101] Moreover, although the miners received a larger food ration than most other workers, they felt the shortage and produced less than before the war.

Continental Europe. In France, Belgium and the Netherlands, coal production went down between 1938 and 1944 as a result of the unwillingness of miners to work under German control, sabotage, shipment of miners to German mines,[102] food shortage, lack of maintenance and parts, and so on.

In Germany, production of bituminous coal remained at about the prewar level until 1944, when it dropped 4 per cent. The output of lignite was increasing steadily, however, and in 1943 reached the peak volume of 255 million tons.

The USSR and China. Only rough and contradictory estimates are available for the USSR. Apparently coal production continued to rise until 1942, when the Donets Basin fell into German hands. This loss reduced the country's total output of bituminous coal to 90 million tons (as against 166 million in 1940). Then strenuous efforts were made in the Kuznetsk and Moscow Basins, and the national output began to rise, reaching 149 million tons in 1945.[103]

In China, coal production slumped considerably, but it is believed that the official figures presented in Table 366 greatly understate the actual output. Under pressure of the Japanese occupying forces, Manchuria's output increased by two thirds between 1938 and 1942.[104]

After World War II

World War II brought marked changes in the distribution of Europe's coal resources and in mining methods, as well as in the coal trade and the supply of labor, the consequences of which will probably be felt for a long time to come.

An adequate supply of coal has been a vital problem in the reconstruction of the shattered economies of Europe. The first goal has been to bring output to at least the prewar level, but obsolescence of equipment, shortage of manpower and low productivity of labor have made this a difficult problem. Many miners who were mobilized for war service or dispersed among other industries have not been eager to return to the mines, and mining work underground has had less appeal to young people than work in factories. The traditional importation of cheap labor from Poland, Italy and the Balkans stopped almost altogether. Temporary relief was sought through the use of German war prisoners, but their efficiency was too low. Coal-producing countries have therefore tried various measures to attract labor to the coal mines — better rations, higher pay, pensions and so on. In France, for example, a decree of 1946 exempted young miners from military service. The increasing mechanization of mining is also expected to attract young workers to the industry.

Throughout 1946–48, shortage of coal was one of the chief bottlenecks in the European recovery program, particularly because the two chief coal-exporting countries, the United Kingdom and Germany, had little coal to share. The shortage created difficulties for Italy, Sweden and Switzerland, whose industries customarily worked on imported coal, and also for France, which had imported large amounts to supplement domestic supplies.

In the United States, coal output reached an all-time high in 1947, with 631 million short tons of bituminous coal and 57 million tons of anthracite.[105] Since that time, the total has declined, partly because of strikes and partly because of competition from other fuels and a decrease in exports to Europe. Nearly 38 million short tons were shipped to Europe in 1947, 16 million in 1948, less than 9 million in 1949, and less than a million in 1950.

In Japan, coal production declined after the war, while Canada, India, the Union of South Africa, Australia and Turkey raised their output slightly. The target of the USSR for 1950 was 250 million tons; in 1949, output reached 236 million tons, and it is estimated that the 1950 output exceeded the target. (See Table 366.)

PRODUCTIVITY OF LABOR IN COAL MINING

The output of coal per man-shift depends to a considerable extent on natural conditions, such as

101. **6**, p. 25.

102. According to the estimate of the International Labor Organization, some 60–70 per cent of all miners in Germany in the war years were foreigners.

103. **59**, p. 214.

104. **2**, 1949–50, p. 141; and **15**, 1945, p. 914.

105. Includes coal used at mines for power and heat, coal used by mine employees, and so on.

Table 367

PRODUCTIVITY OF LABOR IN COAL MINING: OUTPUT PER MAN-SHIFT
IN SELECTED COUNTRIES, 1913–49 [a]

(*Metric Tons* [b])

Country	1913	1925	1930	1935	1938	1944	1948	1949
United States [c]	3.8	4.6	5.1	4.6	4.9	5.8	5.9	6.0
Canada [d]	...	2.2	2.2	2.3	2.4	...	3.0	...
United Kingdom	1.1	1.2	1.4	1.5	1.5	1.4	1.5	1.6
France	...	0.8	1.0	1.3	1.2	0.9	1.0	1.1
Belgium	0.7	0.7	0.8	1.1	1.1	0.8	0.9	0.9
Netherlands	1.1	1.2	1.7	2.6	2.4	1.6	1.7	1.7
Germany (Ruhr)	1.2	1.2	1.7	2.2	2.0	...	1.3	1.4
Saar	...	...	...	1.3	1.6	1.6 [e]	1.2	1.3
Poland	1.7	1.5	1.9	2.7	...	...	1.8	1.8
Czechoslovakia	...	1.1	1.3	1.7	1.5	1.1	1.5	...

Source: **34,** 1951, p. 160.

a. Excludes workers above ground at underground mines and workers at surface mines, except 1913.

b. Conversion factor: one metric ton = 1.1023 short tons.

c. Output per man-day in bituminous mines.

d. Includes surface mines.

e. 1943.

the thickness, depth and structure of seams, as well as on the underground transport system for men and coal, the degree of mechanization, and mining methods. In highly mechanized collieries with favorable natural conditions, as in the United States, output per man-shift is several times larger than it is where seams are often faulted and very deep, as in Belgium.

Throughout the modern history of coal mining, the average output per man-day in the United States has been the highest in the world. It rose in bituminous mines from 2.6 metric tons in 1890 to 3.8 in 1913, 4.9 in 1938, 5.8 in 1944 and 6.0 in 1949. Canada comes next, with 3 tons per man-shift in 1948. In both countries, the impressive average is due largely to a high degree of mechanization and the structure of the seams.

Output per man-shift in British mines is about a third or a fourth that in the United States; in Belgian mines, it is lower, substantially below the British. Poland, Germany (the Ruhr) and the Netherlands reached their peak in productivity in 1935 and the present output per man-shift is only about two thirds as much. (See Table 367.)

The Technical Advisory Committee appointed by the British government during World War II to explore the decline in productivity of labor in coal mines found that the low output per man-day was due to many causes: poor haulage [106] and lack of facilities for transporting workers underground; lack of uniformity in the quality and size of coal seams; insufficient training of young miners; and many other shortcomings. The committee traced these inadequacies to the basic weaknesses of the British coal industry: the dispersion of ownership, the traditionalism of the mine owners, the ineffective layout of many mines. Many small mines dating from the early years of the industry had not been able to adapt themselves to technical progress and had continued to use outdated methods. Where mechanization had been introduced, it was often used unsystematically, so that not all its advantages were realized.

Since the publication of the committee's report, the British coal mines have been nationalized (1946). Many changes and improvements have been introduced, and much greater stress has been laid on mechanization. While the output of coal has risen considerably, productivity per man-shift remains low. Some progress was made in 1949–50, when output was increased with simultaneous reduction of manpower.

106. One fourth of all the workers underground are engaged in transporting coal. One worker is needed for every 5 tons of coal produced, as against one for every 20–25 tons in the Netherlands and one for every 50 tons in the United States. **25,** p. 33; and **17,** p. 25.

CONSUMPTION OF COAL

Chief Consumers and Uses

Four fifths of the world's output of coal is used to provide heat and generate power. The remainder is consumed as raw material in metallurgical and chemical industries and gas works. Five countries — the United States, Great Britain, Germany, France and the USSR — consumed more than three fourths of the world's output before World War II. Seven other countries — Canada, Belgium, Poland, Czechoslovakia, India, China and Japan — accounted for an additional 15 per cent.

The purposes for which coal is used differ from country to country, according to the requirements of industries (particularly metallurgical and chemical industries, railroads and steamships), climatic conditions, and the availability of other sources of power and heat. General manufacturing and heavy metallurgy took 40–50 per cent of the coal consumed in the United States, Great Britain, France and Germany before the war; in the USSR, heavy metallurgy was the largest consumer.

Fuel for locomotives accounts for about 20–25 per cent of the coal used in most countries with a well-developed railway system but plays a minor role in countries relying largely on water transportation, such as the Netherlands. Italy and Spain use little coal for domestic heating because of their mild climate, while in northern Europe and the United States domestic heating consumes about as much coal as railways. China uses half its output for domestic heating. (See Table 368.)

Factors Affecting Demand

The current demand for coal by various groups of consumers depends partly on short-run factors, such as changes in economic conditions, prices and weather, and partly on long-run factors, such as growth of population and industrial production, efficiency in coal utilization and competition between coal and other sources of power and heat.

About 24 per cent of the world's coal consumption, mainly that of the metallurgical industries, is highly sensitive to fluctuations in business conditions, and the 44 per cent used for manufactures, railroads and steamships is moderately sensitive to business changes. Weather conditions strongly affect only the supply used for heating homes and public buildings; other forms of consumption react sluggishly to changes in weather.

Increase in the efficiency with which coal is used for fuel affects, to a varying extent, more than 75 per cent of the total demand. About half the consumption is sensitive to the competition of other fuels and water power. In contrast, the reaction to price changes is relatively weak among all groups of consumers. (See Table 369.)

Per Capita Consumption

In 1937 the United Kingdom, Belgium–Luxembourg and the United States had the highest consumption of coal per capita of population, six or seven times the world average. Per capita consumption for these countries was as follows (figures in pounds):

United Kingdom	7,880
Belgium–Luxembourg	6,700
United States	6,150

Canada, prewar Germany, France and Australia came next, with a per capita consumption three to four times the world average (figures in pounds):

Canada	4,745
Germany	4,605
France	3,305
Australia	3,000

Sweden (2,895 pounds), the Union of South Africa (2,530 pounds) and Norway (2,155 pounds) were next in line. The rate was as low as 140 pounds per capita in India, 110 in Brazil, 100 in China, 80 in Mexico and Colombia, and 40 in Peru.[107]

COAL PRODUCTS

Coal yields a great variety of products when its volatile ingredients are separated from the carbon. This process usually starts with carbonization of coal in a coke oven.

COKE

Coking coal, that is, coal that can be released by heat from its volatile ingredients to almost a graphite or fixed-carbon state, constitutes a relatively small part of the world's coal resources. Coke is indispensable in the iron and steel indus-

---

107. See Table 149, p. 299. This study was in an advanced stage of printing when more recent data on coal consumption in various countries became available. (See **34**, 1952, pp. 142–43.)

TABLE 368

COAL CONSUMPTION: PERCENTAGE DISTRIBUTION, BY PURPOSE, IN SELECTED COUNTRIES, 1936

Country	Consumption, in Millions of Metric Tons	Percentage Distribution								
		Total	Collieries	Railways	Steamships	General Manufacturing	Metallurgical Industries	Gas Works	Central Electric Stations	Domestic Heating[a]
Total	1,116	100.0	4.3	16.3	1.6	26.6	19.6	3.5	7.1	21.0
United States[b]	430	100.0	0.9	19.4	0.4	29.3	14.8	1.2	10.1	24.0
Great Britain	182	100.0	6.7	7.2	0.8[e]	35.6	12.0	10.1	7.7	19.9
France	67	100.0	8.1	14.4	1.5	25.4	14.8	5.9	5.6	24.3
Netherlands	11	100.0	[d]	4.0	6.0	56.0	[d]		11.0	23.0
Germany	164	100.0	12.4	8.1	2.2	18.6	22.7	3.8	6.8	25.3
Poland	21	100.0	[d]	19.2	0.1	42.5	20.1	1.6	3.8	12.7
Hungary	3	100.0	8.3	20.3	[d]	36.3	[d]	3.9	12.2	18.9
Spain	8	100.0	2.1[e]	23.7	...	52.7	12.9	3.2	3.2	2.2
Italy	8	100.0	—	24.0[f]	[g]	35.0	19.0	15.0	[g]	7.0[h]
USSR[i]	118	100.0	...	28.5	1.6	6.2	51.6	...	...	12.1
China	20	100.0	7.6	8.4	5.4	21.5	[d]	[d]	7.1	50.0
Manchuria	8	100.0	3.0[e]	21.8	15.1	13.9	13.9	0.8	4.7	26.8
Japan[j]	39	100.0	[k]	10.1	9.3	40.1	17.1	5.4	8.3	9.7
India	23	100.0	5.3	31.9	7.6	30.8	24.4	[d]	[d]	[d]
Union of South Africa	13	100.0	26.1[e]	31.8	6.6	22.6	[d]	[d]	[d]	12.9

Source: **4,** Vol. I, p. 48.

a. Frequently includes heating of public buildings, hospitals, theaters and so on, as well as coal used for agricultural undertakings, retail and commercial buildings and miscellaneous small workshops.

b. Bituminous coal only; as much as 75 per cent of anthracite coal, which constitutes about one tenth of total coal consumption, is used as domestic fuel. In 1948, about 90 per cent of the anthracite consumed was used for heating purposes.

c. Coastwise trade only.

d. Included in manufacturing.
e. All mines.
f. Includes street trolleys.
g. Included in domestic consumption.
h. Also includes steamship bunkers.
i. Deliveries of coal by seven principal coal basins, accounting for about 90 per cent of total output.
j. Bituminous coal only.
k. Included in metallurgical industries.

875

TABLE 369

COAL CONSUMPTION IN THE WORLD: PERCENTAGE DISTRIBUTION BY INDUSTRY AND FACTORS AFFECTING DEMAND, 1936

Use	Percentage of World Consumption	Sensitivity to Short-Run Factors			Sensitivity to Long-Run Factors		
		Business Conditions	Prices[a]	Weather[b]	Progress in Fuel Combustion	Changes in Use of Fuel[c]	Population Growth
Heavy metallurgy	19.6	V.H.	V.L.	V.L.	V.H.	V.L.	M.L.
Collieries	4.3	V.H.	V.L.	V.L.	M.H.	V.L.	M.L.
Manufactures	26.6	M.H.	V.L.	V.L.	M.H.	M.H.	M.L.
Railways	16.3	M.H.	M.L.	V.L.	V.H.	V.H.	M.L.
Steamships	1.6	M.H.	M.L.	V.L.	V.H.	M.L.	M.L.
Electric stations	7.1	M.L.	M.L.	V.L.	M.L.	M.L.	M.L.
Gas works	3.5	M.L.	V.L.	V.L.	V.L.	M.L.	M.L.
Domestic heating	21.0	V.L.	M.L.	V.H.	V.L.	M.L.	M.L.

Percentage Distribution by Degree of Sensitivity

Total		100.0	100.0	100.0	100.0	100.0	100.0
Very high		23.9	0.0	21.0	44.6	1.6	0.0
Moderately high		44.5	0.0	0.0	30.9	42.9	0.0
Moderately low		10.6	46.0	0.0	3.5	31.6	100.0
Very low		21.0	54.0	79.0	21.0	23.9	0.0

Source: 4, Vol. I, pp. 102–03.
V.H. = Very High; M.H. = Moderately High; M.L. = Moderately Low; V.L. = Very Low.

a. Changes in the price of coal, other fuels, water power.
b. Changes in length and coldness of the winter season.
c. Trends toward use of other fuels and water power.

try, and the liquid products released through carbonization (tar, light oils and ammoniacal liquor) are important raw materials for the chemical industry. Coke is also used as a domestic fuel and for the manufacture of gas.

The amount of volatile matter contained in coking coal affects the character of the coke. Low-volatile coal, when carbonized, produces a hard coke, which is strong enough to carry the load of iron ore in a blast furnace, while high-volatile coal gives a light, porous coke. The yield of coke is interrelated with the amount of liquids and gases produced. The more coke obtained from carbonization, the less liquids and gases obtained and vice versa.

Output

Manufacture of coke is concentrated in a few industrial countries. The two largest producers before World War II were the United States and Germany; the former led in 1929, accounting for 38 per cent of the world's total, the latter in 1938, with 31 per cent (including the Saar). The coke output of the USSR increased rapidly between these years and by 1938 was about half as large as that of Germany.

The United States greatly increased its output during the war, from 29.5 million tons in 1938 to 67.2 million in 1944. Germany more or less maintained its prewar level, while output in France, Belgium, the Netherlands and the USSR slumped seriously. In the world as a whole, the output of coke in 1944 was about a fifth greater than in 1938.

After a slump in the immediate postwar years, coke production began to recover in most countries. Although an upward movement has been noticeable in Western Germany, where output reached bottom in 1945 and rose to 23.4 million tons in 1949, war damage to coke plants and territorial changes have affected that country's position considerably. Germany now produces about as much coke as the USSR, while the lead of the United States, re-established in 1940, is unchallenged. (See Table 370.)

Production Methods

The old method of producing coke in beehives resulted in coke only; oils and gases went up in smoke. The modern method of coking in high-temperature (by-product) ovens preserves not only the volatile ingredients, highly valued by the

TABLE 370

COKE: OUTPUT IN SELECTED COUNTRIES, 1913–50 [a]

(Millions of Metric Tons [b]*)*

Country	1913	1925	1929	1935	1938	1944	1948	1949	1950
World	...	...	144.0	118.0	139.5	169.5	160.6	164.0	...
United States	42.0	46.2	54.3	31.9	29.5	67.2	67.9	57.7	66.0
Canada	1.4	1.0	2.2	1.8	1.8	3.1	3.1	3.3	3.4
United Kingdom	13.0	11.2	13.6	12.1	13.0	14.3	15.6	15.7	15.7
France	4.0	6.0	9.1	7.1	7.6	2.9	6.1	6.8	6.9
Belgium	3.5	4.1	6.0	4.4	4.4	1.5	3.7	3.5	...
Netherlands	...	1.1	2.5	2.9	3.2	1.6	2.3	1.5	...
Germany	34.6	28.4	39.4	29.8	43.5 [e]	41.6 [d]	19.0 [e]	23.4 [e]	25.2 [e]
Poland	—	1.0	1.9	1.4	2.3	4.5	5.2	5.8	5.9
Czechoslovakia	—	2.0	3.2	1.6	2.8	4.5	5.2	6.6	...
USSR [f]	4.4	1.4	5.0	16.7	20.7	11.0	20.0	24.0	...
Japan	...	0.8	1.5	1.9	3.7	4.9	1.9	2.6	2.7
India	...	0.5	2.5	2.7	1.7	1.7	1.7	2.0	2.1
Australia	0.3	0.7	0.6	0.7	1.2	1.4	1.4	1.2	1.3

Sources: **67**, p. 129; **1**, 1934–35, pp. 130–31; **23**, 1928, p. 46*, and 1938, p. 61*; **15**, 1949, p. 444; **2**, 1951, pp. 240–42.

  a. Coke produced in coke ovens.

  b. Conversion factor: one metric ton = 1.1023 short tons.

  c. Includes the Saar (3.1 million tons).

  d. Includes Silesian production.

  e. Western Germany.

  f. Estimate of the U.S. Bureau of Mines from 1944 on.

chemical industry, but also produces more coke. Out of a short ton of coal, a beehive usually yields 1,300 pounds of coke, while a high-temperature oven yields about 1,500 pounds of coke plus 9,500–11,500 cubic feet of gas, 8 gallons of tar, 2.5–3.5 gallons of light oil, and 20 pounds of sulfate of ammonia.[108] The amazing variety of products obtained from these raw materials is illustrated by Figure 250. Oils and gases yielded by high-temperature ovens in the United States represent about 25 per cent of the total value of the output. (See Table 371.)

The United States was much slower than Europe in shifting to ovens; at the turn of the century it produced 95 per cent of its coke in beehives. The delay was due partly to lack of demand by the young chemical industry for the by-products and partly to the country's abundance of natural gas and its tremendous coal reserves, which did not suggest any need for economy in coal consumption. By 1930, however, the ratio between the output of beehives and high-temperature ovens had been reversed. Because beehives can be put into and taken out of

operation easily, some idle beehives were activated during the war to meet the peak demand.

HYDROGENATION OF COAL

In the past few decades, two synthetic processes have been invented in Germany to convert coal into oil — the Bergius and the Fischer-Tropsch methods. The essence of this transformation is to increase the amount of hydrogen (from 6 to about 14 per cent) in coal, remove oxygen, nitrogen and sulfur and break down the large molecules of which coal is composed.

Processes

Coal hydrogenation was first attempted in France by P. E. M. Berthelot, but Friedrich Bergius was responsible for the first practical advance in this field.[109] The Bergius process of direct hydrogenation first liquefies coal, which yields a distillable middle oil; then it purifies this oil of nitrogen, which would otherwise poison the catalyst used in the following stage of the process; finally it converts the purified oil into gasoline. At all three stages, a stream of hydrogen flows

---

108. **60**, p. 13; and **34**, 1950, p. 115.

109. **39**, Vol. III, p. 2154.

TABLE 371

COKE: OUTPUT IN THE UNITED STATES, 1900-1950

Year	Number of Beehives	Number of High-Temperature Ovens	Ouput of Coke, in Millions of Short Tons Total	Ouput of Coke, in Millions of Short Tons Beehives	Ouput of Coke, in Millions of Short Tons High-Temperature Ovens	Value at Plant, in Millions of Dollars Beehive Coke	Value at Plant High-Temperature Ovens Total	Value High-Temperature Ovens Coke	Value High-Temperature Ovens By-Products
1900	57,399	1,085	20.5	19.4	1.1	47	. . .	. . .	. . .
1905	84,405	3,103	32.2	28.8	3.4	72	. . .	. . .	. . .
1910	100,362	4,078	41.7	34.6	7.1	75	33	25	8
1915	93,110	6,268	41.6	27.5	14.1	57	79	49	30
1920	75,298	10,881	51.3	20.5	30.8	163	418	313	105
1925	57,587	11,290	51.3	11.4	39.9	52	354	211	143
1930	23,907	12,831	48.0	2.8	45.2	10	368	200	168
1935	13,674	12,860	35.1	0.9	34.2	4	286	173	113
1940	15,150	12,734	57.1	3.1	54.0	14	428	260	168
1945	12,179	14,510	67.3	5.2	62.1	38	661	470	191
1948	14,078	15,139	74.9	6.6	68.3	79	1,151	849	302
1949	13,662	15,104	63.6	3.4	60.2	44	1,067	799	268
1950	17,708	14,982	72.7	5.8	66.9	77	1,202	900	302

Source: **15**, 1949, p. 408, and 1950, preprint.

through the reaction zone at a pressure of several thousand pounds per square inch. The Fischer-Tropsch process begins with production of water gas, removes sulfur, adjusts the ratio of hydrogen to carbon monoxide, and obtains a so-called synthesis gas; the contact of synthesis gas with a catalyst converts the former into hydrocarbons of a wide molecular size, from which gasoline, diesel oil, lubricants and other products can be processed.[110]

Synthesis gas can be made from all ranks of coal, including lignite, and this process can be more widely applied than the direct hydrogenation process, which is best adapted to lower-rank coals. Roughly, one barrel of gasoline can be produced by the Bergius method from 0.6 ton of bituminous coal, or from 1.8 tons of lignite with 50 per cent moisture; the Fischer-Tropsch method requires 1.1 tons of bituminous coal, but tar and gas are also obtained.[111]

The gasoline produced from coal is so similar to that from petroleum that it was very difficult to determine the origin of the fuel in captured German equipment. This gasoline met the same aviation specifications as that from petroleum.

Production

Large-scale application of these processes is de-termined by cost considerations. As long as the price of oil from coal is higher than the price of oil from wells, countries abundantly provided with petroleum will make little use of coal hydro-genation, but this process is extremely important to a country that is cut off from supplies of nat-ural oil. Germany, having felt the pinch during World War I, developed hydrogenation methods in order to have a supply of oil in another emer-gency. The first Bergius plant was built in 1927, and Fischer-Tropsch plants were erected between 1933 and 1939. It was expected that the total quantity of motor fuel produced by the new processes would amount to 1.2 million tons, or about two thirds of Germany's total 1935 con-sumption.[112] During World War II, production expanded greatly, and Germany's plant capacity has been estimated at 5 million tons.[113]

Before World War II, Great Britain installed one direct hydrogenation plant at Billingham, with an annual capacity of 150,000 tons. France, Belgium and Japan built small plants, based on German designs, more for experiment than for protection. The USSR built its first hydrogena-tion plant in 1939.

In the United States, little research was carried out in this field before 1935. More recently, the study of both German processes has been ex-

110. **20**, pp. 493–505.
111. **20**, pp. 497 and 502.

112. **56**, p. 34.
113. **1**, 1942–44, p. 148.

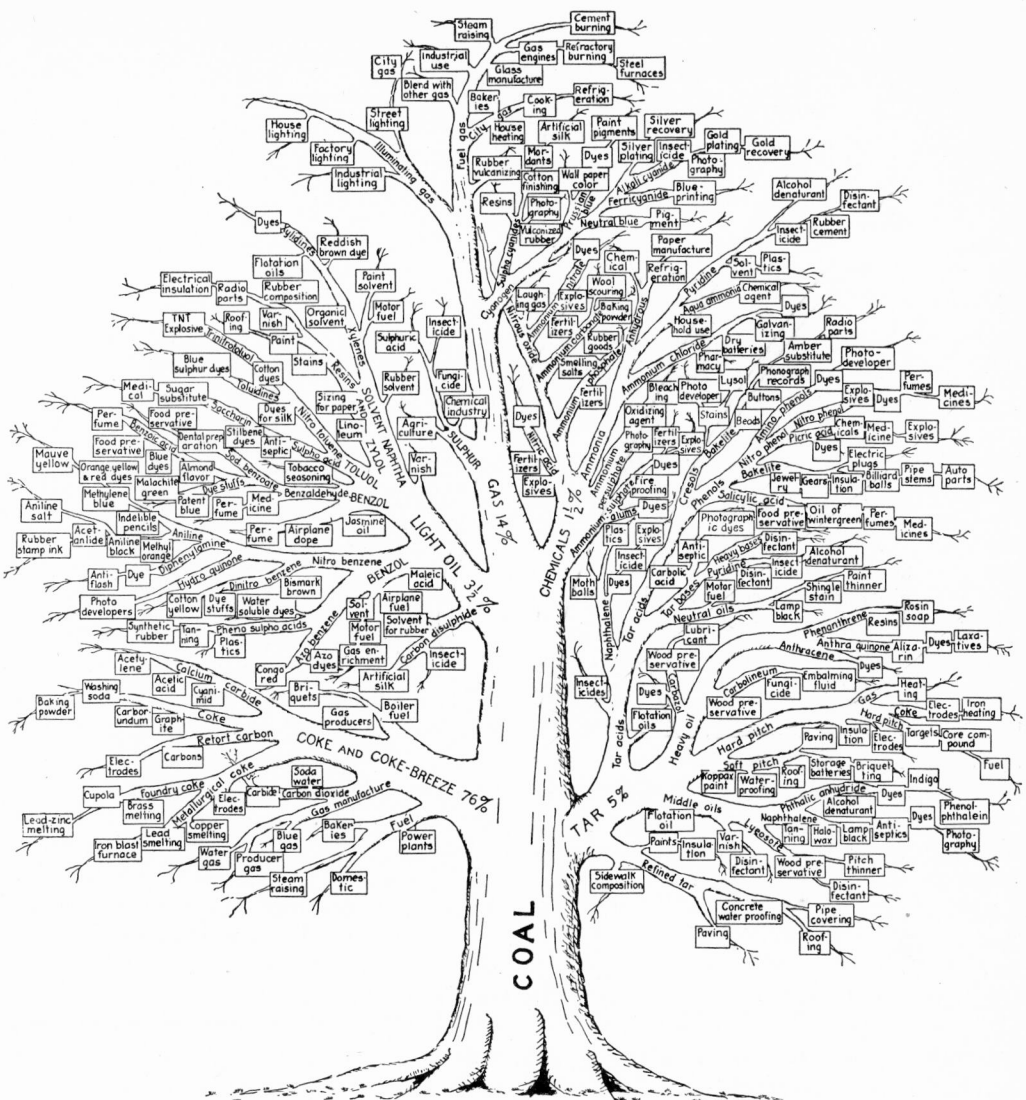

U.S. Bureau of Mines

FIGURE 250. COAL PRODUCTS: SUBSTANCES OBTAINABLE THROUGH CARBONIZATION IN A HIGH-TEMPERATURE OVEN

A short ton of bituminous coal yielded in 1949, on the average, 1,515 pounds of coke, 7.8 gallons of tar, 20.1 pounds of sulfate of ammonia, 10,250 cubic feet of fuel gas, and 2.8 gallons of crude light oil. The coal-products tree illustrates the further ramifications of processing and indicates the products obtainable.

panded, and pilot plants have been built by the U.S. Bureau of Mines. Interest is centered chiefly on improving the Fischer-Tropsch process through production of cheap oxygen for use in the mixture of hydrogen and carbon monoxide and stricter control of the vast amount of heat liberated in the process.

The American process consists in reducing coal to a fine powder, which, together with a finely powdered catalyst, forms gas in a fluidiz-

ing reaction generator; this gas is then converted to synthetic oil, both gasoline and diesel.[114] There are already many variations of this process, differing mainly in the way in which the gas is converted into oil. Since a large quantity of chemical by-products is released in hydrogena-

114. Germany used a cobalt catalyst, which the American experts have found unsatisfactory. Instead of the 128 reaction vessels used in Germany, only two are needed in the United States. **66,** August 1948, pp. 87–90.

tion, it is believed that this process may become a substantial source of basic organic chemicals, particularly those used in manufacturing plastics and acetate rayon.[115]

The U.S. Bureau of Mines is working on both processes of synthesizing liquid fuels from coal. It is thought that these processes can best be applied to the lignite, subbituminous and low-rank bituminous coal fields in the West. The vast reserves of poorly coking coals of Ohio, Indiana and western Kentucky are also suitable for both processes, while the limited supplies of coal of metallurgical grades are to be kept for the steel industry.[116]

GASIFICATION OF COAL

Some countries are now conducting experiments in gasifying the coal seams in mines, without digging out the coal.

In the United States, a coal seam 3 feet thick, 100 feet wide and 300 feet long at Gorgas, Alabama, was the object of such an experiment, conducted by the U.S. Bureau of Mines and a private power company. Coal burned out clean and without wastage. Trapped gases were analyzed and found to have a low heating value because of an excess of carbon dioxide. For the second experiment, a 300-acre tract in Alabama was chosen, with a 40-inch coal seam and a 100-foot cover.[117]

Another method, under trial in Missouri, is to apply high-voltage current through an unmined coal seam. The heated coal is gasified, and when it is hot enough to begin to burn, the current is cut off and air or oxygen is pumped into the seam to maintain combustion.

If the experiments are successful, underground gasification of coal will revolutionize coal mining, providing cheaper fuel for electric power at the mine and easier transportation of fuel energy as electric power rather than bulky coal.[118] Moreover, this method would eliminate the tedious and dangerous work of underground mining. Gasification of coal would make it possible to exploit seams now considered too thin or too deep to work, and to make use of worked-out mines that still contain some coal.

The USSR experimented with coal gasification before the war. It built a few pilot plants, of which those in Gorlovka (Donets Basin) and in the Kuznetsk Basin were particularly active. The method was to start a fire in a blocked mine, blow air in through two openings, and capture the gas escaping through another.[119]

The Donets station was to produce 14 million cubic feet of gas an hour, equivalent to 0.5 million tons of coal a year. The target set for 1950 was an annual production of 920 million cubic meters of fuel gas. It is claimed that underground gasification in the Tula coal bed results in recovery of from 80 to 90 per cent of the coal, instead of the previous 60 per cent, and in great reduction of manpower underground.[120]

OUTLOOK

Coal is likely to retain its position as a main source of energy for a long time to come. The industrialization to which many underdeveloped countries aspire implies an increase in the demand for coal. New chemical industries — plastics, synthetic rubber and the like — will also create a need for more coal.

Since the world has much larger reserves of coal than of other sources of energy, coal is unlikely to yield much ground to its competitors. It may even be called upon to supplement some of these sources, such as oil, or replace them, should they become exhausted.

The world has already exceeded its 1938 output of coal. While some further increase in output can reasonably be expected, competition of other sources of energy and greater efficiency in thermal methods of combustion may slow down the demand. A time may even come when coal will be produced chiefly to obtain synthetic oil and to supply ingredients for the chemical industry. Whereas a few generations ago the most efficient "utilization of coal might have been considered to be achieved by the invention of a better coal-burning furnace, it is now not beyond possibility that, a few generations hence, the use of coal as fuel alone may be prohibited by law as criminally wasteful." [121]

---

115. **47**, 1948, p. 105.
116. **44**, p. 138–40.
117. **66**, August 1948, pp. 87–90.
118. **43**, p. 125–27.

119. **45**, October 10, 1936, pp. 1035–37.
120. It is reported that the Russian technicians found that gasification is limited to certain seams and types of coal and by the availability of cheap oxygen. **49**, January 1, 1949, p. 8; and **55**, p. 273.
121. **62**, pp. 824–25.

The shares of particular countries in the world's output of coal will differ in the near future from their shares in prewar years. The United States may account for 40 per cent of the total, or perhaps even more, as compared with 25 per cent in the 1930's. The United Kingdom may exceed its 1938 coal output. Germany will have a smaller share of the world's total, while the USSR and Poland will produce more coal than before the war.

With the further spread of mechanization in coal mining, output per man-day is likely to rise despite the inevitable shift to more difficult and less productive seams.

CHAPTER 24

PETROLEUM AND NATURAL GAS

PETROLEUM AND NATURAL GAS, with their allied products, rank first among all mineral products in the value of the world's output. In 1949, they accounted for $9.7 billion of the $30.2 billion worth of mineral products in the world, as compared with $5.4 billion for all metallic ores, $5.7 billion for all nonmetallic ores and $9.4 billion for coal. (See Table 325.) They are even more important in the mineral output of the United States, where they account for 51 per cent of the total value.

PETROLEUM IN THE MODERN ECONOMY

Petroleum entered our economy less than a hundred years ago. Its present leading role in world politics dates back only a few decades. Yet in the twentieth century the exploitation of oil has brought about a revolution comparable in its consequences with the rise of coal in the nineteenth century. [1]

In the middle of the nineteenth century, tallow candles and whale oil were the only means of lighting houses the world over, and wood was the chief means of heating. Horse-drawn stage coaches were the common means of travel. Coal-fed steamships were just beginning to appear on the seas, but sailing vessels predominated. There were only a few railroads. "A factory smelled of the rancid animal and vegetable oils used to lubricate engines and machines whose shrieks and groans were deafening. Cumbersome steam engines stopped because their bearings became overheated or acid-eaten." [2] Oil changed this picture.

The first commercial oil drilling started in Romania in 1857 and in the United States (Pennsylvania) in 1859. The first product that the petroleum industry distilled from crude oil was kerosene, but it took years to free it of inflammable constituents, smoke and odor.

Development of lubricating oils also came about slowly, through endless, truly international laboratory work in refining and processing. Experimentation was carried on in the United

States, Great Britain, France and Russia until lubricants were made that met any specification of heat, speed or friction. Since oil lubricants assured smoother functioning of machinery than animal or vegetable fats, oxidized less, lasted longer and were less sticky, they gradually displaced greases for use in factories and on railroads and steamships. [3] In fact, for modern machinery there is no substitute for lubricating oils made from petroleum, and some experts think that our technical civilization is hardly imaginable without them. [4] Petroleum lubricants have also been an important factor in the development of machinery, making it possible to design machines that can operate at greater speeds and higher temperatures.

Combined with the internal combustion engine, petroleum has revolutionized farming, the transportation of goods, travel — actually, everyday life. As the chemical industry has developed, oil has invaded the production of dyestuffs, plastics, paint and varnishes, solvents, synthetic rubber, rayons, drugs, detergents, explosives, insecticides, anesthetics, acids and numerous other commodities.

As a source of energy and as an industrial raw material, petroleum has not displaced coal, which still remains the foundation of modern industrial civilization. But it has become a potent competitor of coal as a source of heat and power, and its products are used for many purposes for which coal is not fitted. It has also become a potent factor in world affairs and the economic life of the leading industrial countries and especially in the worldwide system of transportation. [5]

ORIGIN AND COMPOSITION OF PETROLEUM

In spite of intensive research in all fields con-

3. Today mineral oil supplies practically all the lubricants. Lubricants from vegetable oils are high in quality but negligible in amount. **25**, Vol. I, p. xii.
4. **30**, p. 445.
5. See Chapter 25. The subject is further discussed by the authors in a study of world trade and government, now in preparation for the Twentieth Century Fund.

1. **25**, Vol. I, p. ix.
2. **26**, p. xii.

nected with petroleum, its origin still remains somewhat of a mystery.

Origin

Whether petroleum originated from inorganic or organic matter was a subject of scientific controversy for many decades. The organic theory is now universally accepted.

The inorganic theory traced the origin of oil to extensive chemical reactions within the earth's crust — reactions between descending waters and metallic carbides underground (D. I. Mendelejeff), or from the contact of water charged with carbon dioxide with metallic sodium (P. E. M. Berthelot). The theory that oil is of volcanic origin is a modification of the inorganic hypotheses.[6] As oil and the sediment that surrounds it have been subjected to intensive analysis, however, the inorganic theory has gradually lost ground. The remains of marine fossils, both plant and animal, that abound in shale and limestone in oil fields point to an organic origin.

According to the organic theory, vegetable and animal matter, partly land-derived but mostly consisting of plankton,[7] was deposited in geologic times with mud and sand on the sea bottom, where such deposits were free from scavenger action and oxidation. During the great invasions of land by ocean waters, marine sediment was deposited on the surface of the earth around the margins of the continents. In repeated inundations, sea water often reached far inland, where it carried vast accumulations of marine sediment with decomposed organic matter and thus formed the basic pattern of the oil deposits known today. Under the impact of heat and pressure of overlaying strata, the organic matter in such sediment began to yield liquid or gaseous hydrocarbons. While the amount of organic matter in marine sediment is appreciable, it is believed that only a small part of the original source material survived to reach the final form of petroleum. The further evolution of oil in the earth's crust consisted in the decrease of the size of the molecules and increase in the content of hydrogen in relation to carbon. Oils in older rocks have smaller molecules and, often, a paraffin base. Younger oils have large and heavy molecules and usually an asphalt base.[8]

Oil is usually found in porous sandstone, in proximity to shale and limestone, which are rich in organic matter and relatively compact and impervious. Some oil fields, however, have been discovered in limestone. Sandstone does not contain organic remains, and its chief role has been to serve as a reservoir for the accumulation of oil.

Oil is a vagrant fluid and has moved to sandstone from the beds in which it originated. The factors responsible for this migration are numerous: presence of gas, gravity, capillary action, pressure of water, bacterial action and so on.[9] Once oil moves out of its source bed along joints and crevices, it seeps through the porous sandstone until it reaches impervious rock. If the rock is so arched or domed as to form a trap, oil is imprisoned and accumulates in a pool. Such traps vary greatly in their structure, but most of the world's major oil pools have been found on anticlines, upward arches of the bed of the earth's surface, or domes.

Composition

Petroleum is an extremely complex and diversified substance. It consists of carbon and hydrogen combined in various proportions with each other and other elements.[10] Some of these compounds are solid, others liquid or gaseous. About a hundred hydrocarbons constituting oil have been isolated, and it is believed that the number still unexplored may be very great. Some oils contain few compounds, others a great many.

Petroleum is usually classified by its base — paraffin, with a high hydrogen content; asphalt or naphthene and mixtures. Gasoline, kerosene, diesel fuel, heavy fuel oils, lubricating oils, various gases and some solids are derived from paraffinic petroleum. With a few exceptions, all petroleum gases so far identified belong to the paraffinic series.[11] The asphalt series is more complex than the paraffinic, and a typical asphalt-base oil contains a wide range of gases, liquids and solids. Since the heavier compounds are

---

6. **25**, Vol. I, p. 33.

7. Plankton is the collective name for animal and plant substances, chiefly minute, that drift in all sea waters and provide food for fish. See Chapter 20, p. 716.

8. **41**, p. 16.

9. V. C. Illing distinguishes between primary migration, when oil and gas moved from more compact "source rocks" to porous and coarse reservoir rocks, and secondary migration, when oil, gas and water became separated and, in accordance with their density, moved to different layers in the reservoir — water at the bottom, gas at the top, oil between them. **25**, Vol. I, p. 209.

10. The carbon content ranges from 82.2 to 87.1 per cent; hydrogen from 11.7 to 14.7; sulfur, 0.1 to 5.5; nitrogen, 0.1 to 2.4; oxygen, 0.1 to 1.2; and various minerals, between 0.1 and 1.2 per cent. **32**, p. 30.

11. **19**, pp. 197–98.

soluble in the lighter, asphalt may be found in oil in a liquid form.

Oil Reservoirs

We have only recently begun to understand the nature of oil reservoirs and the behavior of the fluids and gases they contain. The practices used twenty years or so ago in withdrawing oil from a reservoir are now considered wasteful and inefficient.

An oil reservoir contains not only oil but also gas in solution and sometimes free gas in the cap, as well as water. When a well is drilled, the equilibrium among oil, gas and water is disrupted, and the forces of gravity and gas and water pressure are released. Oil itself has no lifting energy, but release of the energy of other forces propels it to the surface. Oil is expelled from the reservoir by the drive of water, of the gas in the cap or of gas in solution.

When water is the propulsive agent, it advances as the oil begins to flow and takes the place previously filled with oil. In advancing, the water flushes the oil from the oil-bearing sands and exercises pressure on it, forcing it toward the well. Such a water drive is considered the most effective agent for removing oil. Under favorable conditions, it may assure complete withdrawal of recoverable oil.[12]

In a reservoir with a cap-gas drive, the expansion of gas is the expulsive force driving the oil to the well bore. This force also prevents the gas in solution from leaving the oil. Again, conditions being favorable, almost all recoverable oil can be extracted from the reservoir.

When gas in solution is the only agent for oil removal, the pressure of gas, which leaves the oil as it begins to flow, voids some space in the reservoir. Usually only from 20 to 40 per cent of the oil in the pool is recovered.

The interplay of natural forces in the reservoir is often more complicated because of various physical conditions, and it is greatly affected by operating practices. For example, if the cap gas is permitted to escape, as was done in the past,[13]

the force that could drive oil to the well bore is lost. The tendency now is to keep and use the natural forces within the reservoir and recover as much oil as possible through their operation. Efforts are made to hold all the gas in the cap, to preserve the water pressure and to maintain a low gas-oil ratio by slow withdrawal of the oil from the reservoir. The modern science of reservoir engineering has also stimulated the development of secondary projects to recover additional oil from fields partially emptied by earlier and less efficient methods.[14]

MAJOR OIL FIELDS

One of the two main areas of oil concentration in the world is in the Western Hemisphere — the Gulf Coast, Caribbean [15] and Mid-Continent; the other, in the Eastern Hemisphere, along the Black and Caspian Sea and the Persian Gulf. These two regions encompassing landlocked seas have afforded an ideal environment for the development of petroleum and contain the greatest known reserves.

Large petroleum reservoirs have also been found in California, Canada, southeastern Asia, the Volga-Ural area and Siberia, but they do not compare in importance with the two first mentioned.[16] (See Figure 251.)

The United States

The most imporant oil fields in the United States lie in the Mid-Continent, stretching from Kansas City through Oklahoma and southern Arkansas, into Texas and northern Louisiana and also including oil fields in Mississippi and Missouri. (See Figure 252.) Within this vast territory, there are many single fields, some discovered in the 1890's, others only in recent years. They vary from shallow fields in the "shoestring sands" of Kansas and underwater fields on Caddo Lake in Louisiana to salt dome and sand bar fields in Texas. The biggest single field is the East Texas, which is 30 miles long and has about 25,000 wells. Between 1930, when it was discovered, and 1938, it produced more oil than Europe, Africa, Japan and Sakhalin together

---

12. Because some oil saturates the sand in the reservoir and cannot be removed, and because of the presence of water in the sand pores, 60 to 80 per cent of the oil is the maximum recoverable. **27**, 1945, p. 89.

13. The function of gas in the reservoir was not known until recently, and cap gas was considered a nuisance and was blown into the air. The presence of gas in oil was also discovered only about two decades ago, when it was established that oil contains less gas when it leaves the well than when it is in the reservoir.

14. **6, b**, p. 10.

15. The Caribbean area as discussed in this chapter includes the West Indies, Trinidad, Venezuela, Colombia, the eastern part of Mexico, and, in the United States, Louisiana, Florida and the southern parts of Georgia, Alabama, Mississippi and Arkansas.

16. **42**, pp. 325–26.

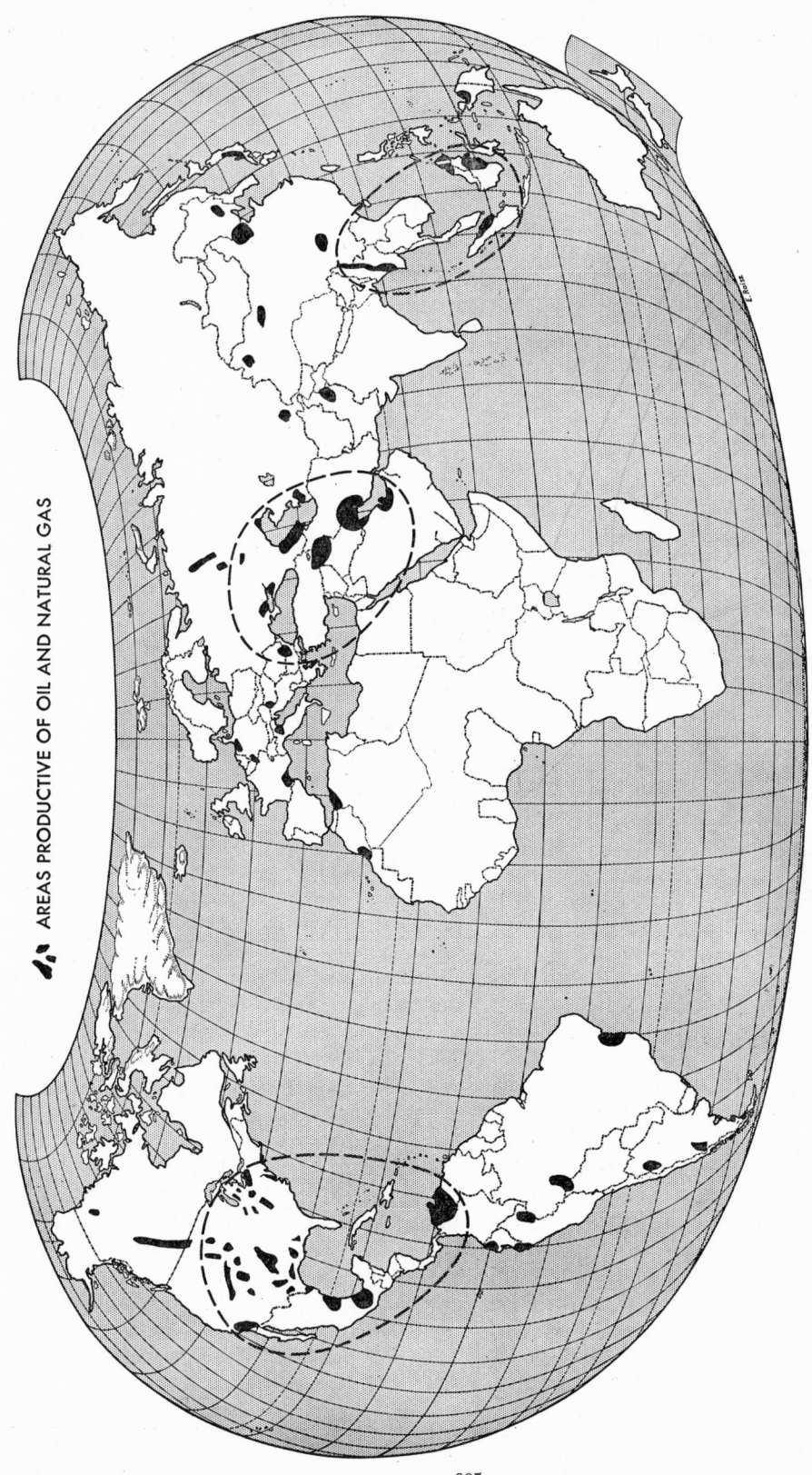

AREAS PRODUCTIVE OF OIL AND NATURAL GAS

FIGURE 251. MAJOR OIL FIELDS: GEOGRAPHIC DISTRIBUTION IN THE WORLD

The most important petroleum fields are clustered in two intercontinental depressions: in the Western Hemisphere, areas around the Mexican Gulf and the Caribbean; in the Eastern Hemisphere, around the Black Sea, the Caspian Sea and the Persian Gulf. The richest petroleum fields in the United States (including the Mid-Continent district), Mexico and Venezuela belong to the first system. The petroleum fields of the Middle East, the southern part of the USSR and Romania are all in the second area.

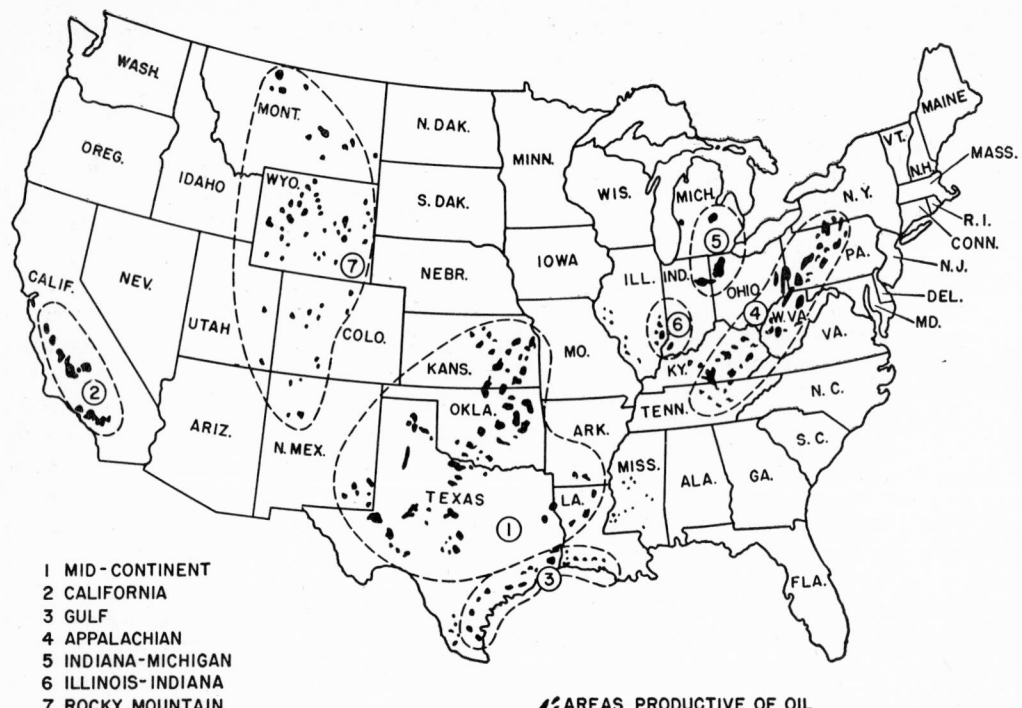

1 MID-CONTINENT
2 CALIFORNIA
3 GULF
4 APPALACHIAN
5 INDIANA-MICHIGAN
6 ILLINOIS-INDIANA
7 ROCKY MOUNTAIN

*: AREAS PRODUCTIVE OF OIL

FIGURE 252. MAJOR OIL FIELDS: GEOGRAPHIC DISTRIBUTION IN THE UNITED STATES

have produced in their entire history.[17] Another area of growing importance is the Permian basin, which covers an area of some 50,000 square miles in West Texas and southeastern New Mexico. Although some fields in this area were discovered in the 1920's, its potentialities were not fully recognized until two decades later. Extensive exploration and use of geologic data and the latest geophysical methods resulted in discovery of substantial reserves. In 1950, this basin accounted for a fifth of the United States output.[18]

The California field ranks next. Its oil-producing sands are unusually thick — some 1,500 feet, as compared to less than a couple of hundred feet in the rest of the United States. Two geologic areas — the San Joaquin Valley between the Sierra Nevada and the Coast Range, and the Los Angeles Basin — are the main centers of production.

Oil production is also concentrated along the Gulf Coast — in Texas, where oil is mostly found in salt domes, and in Louisiana, where wells are largely drilled from barges in swamps and bayous. A new important field, West Catahoula Lake, was discovered in Louisiana in 1949: twenty-five oil wells have been completed without defining its limits.

The Appalachian field, where the first well in the United States was drilled, extends from New York, through Pennsylvania, West Virginia and southeastern Ohio and reaches into Kentucky. For several decades it steadily produced oil free of sulfur and easily refined. Then the output began to decline, and today the field is more important for the high quality of its motor oil than for the volume of its production.

Three other oil-producing centers, Indiana-Michigan, Illinois-Indiana, and Rocky Mountain — together supply a small percentage of the national output.

Venezuela

The Lake Maracaibo basin in the northwestern part of Venezuela contains some of the world's largest oil fields. They are found under water and on lake shores, and shallow wells have been drilled at many places. The largest single field is the Bolivar coastal field, on the northeast border of the lake. The limits of its productive area have not yet been fully outlined after a quarter of a century of development.[19]

17. **19**, p. 357.
18. **49**, September 1951, pp. 108–11.

19. **42**, p. 60.

The Orinoco basin is second to the Maracaibo region and has a large daily production and great reserves. The most productive field is the Quiriquire field; its crude oil is relatively heavy, and the gasoline obtained in cracking is of high-octane rating. Explorations in the Apure area began as recently as 1947 and prospects are considered promising.[20]

Colombia

Two major oil-producing areas are the Magdalena basin and the portion of the Maracaibo basin within Colombia. Ten American companies operate in Colombia.[21]

Canada

Two large fields have recently been discovered in Alberta, near Edmonton — Leduc in 1947 and Redwater in 1948. The fields are relatively shallow (6,000 feet deep), and the potential area is vast. Every important American and Canadian oil company is participating in an intensive search for oil in Canada's western provinces.[22]

Conditions in the Leduc field resemble those producing oil accumulations in the older fields of the West Texas basin in the United States. The whole sedimentary area in the Prairie Provinces, stretching to the Arctic Ocean, covers about 475,000 square miles and ranks as prospective oil territory.[23]

In 1950, two new oil fields were discovered: Heart's Hill in Saskatchewan, and Acheson-Stony Plains, 8 miles west of Edmonton. The first major field in British Columbia was discovered in November 1951, after thirty years of unsuccessful explorations, along the Alaska highway.

Mexico

The chief old oil fields in the Tampico embayment — the northern fields and the Golden Lane — are located between the Gulf Coast and Sierra Madre Oriental and on the Isthmus of Tehuantepec, south of Vera Cruz. A new field, Poza Rica, south of the Golden Lane, has become the most important oil producer in Mexico. Another field, the Moralillo, was discovered in 1948; it had produced more than a billion barrels by January 1, 1950.[24]

The USSR

Some of the greatest oil fields yet discovered are in the USSR, on Apsheron Peninsula (Baku) and nearby islands. Oil springs in this area were known long before the Christian era. Two other fields, under development since the late 1890's, are the Grozny and Maikop districts, the former along the north side of the Caucasus, the latter north of the Black Sea.

In the heart of the Volga basin, north of the Caspian Sea, a very extensive oil field was discovered in the late 1930's. Because of the abundance of oil and the great promise it holds, it has been named "Second Baku." South of this field, at about the same distance from Baku, is another oil area, Emba-Uralsk. Although oil began to flow here in 1911, the area is still little developed. The Emba reserves are estimated to be very considerable.

A new oil field, Buzonow, was discovered recently northeast of Baku, on the Apsheron Peninsula. In the Far East, the USSR has oil fields on Sakhalin Island, which it has possessed completely since World War II; formerly part of the island belonged to Japan.

The Middle East

The sun-scorched Middle East, with vast desert areas, has emerged as the world's richest and most productive oil region. It is unique in the concentration of giant fields and the productivity of single wells. Immense oil fields, still little explored, stretch throughout Iran, Iraq, Saudi Arabia and Kuwait, on the Persian Gulf, and on the Bahrein Islands off the coast of Arabia. The Burgan oil field in Kuwait now ranks as the world's largest single oil reservoir.

The Far East

Only relatively small fields have been discovered and exploited in the Far East: in Indonesia (Sumatra and Java), British Borneo (Brunei and Sarawak) and central Burma. The northwestern part of China is believed to contain important oil-bearing areas.[25]

20. **42,** pp. 64 ff.
21. **42,** p. 114.
22. **42,** 150.
23. **39,** pp. 4–5.

24. **49,** January 1951, p. 216.
25. **4,** 1949, pp. 339–40.

OIL RESERVES

In contrast to coal, for which recoverable reserves seem to have been overestimated, the estimates of the world's proven oil reserves (oil recoverable by present methods, at a profit, in such parts of oil reservoirs as have been drilled) have had to be increased consistently as exploration has been extended and drilling has revealed the full extent of known reservoirs. The estimates will probably continue to rise, particularly with the exploration of areas potentially productive of oil.

PROVEN RESERVES

As late as 1939, the proven oil reserves of the world were estimated at 34.2 billion barrels. On January 1, 1951, after twelve years in which some 25 billion barrels were extracted, the remaining reserves were assessed at 95.2 billion barrels. Discovery of new fields had raised the estimate of Asia's reserves from about 7 billion barrels to 49.4 billion, that for Venezuela, from 2.5 billion to 9.5 billion, and for the United States, from 17.3 billion to 26.2 billion. (See Table 372.)

In October 1951, the estimate of the world's reserves rose to 110–115 billion barrels, chiefly because of the higher evaluation of reserves in the Middle East. The estimate for the United States at that time was some 27 billion barrels.[26]

Different estimates of the proven USSR oil reserves are cited in American sources, ranging from 4.3 to 7.6 billion barrels. Although the estimates are attributed to different dates — 7.6 billion at the end of 1947 and 5.6 billion on January 1, 1951 — the difference indicates variance in the judgment of estimators rather than an actual decrease in reserves.[27] However, E. L. DeGolyer, who believes that his estimate of 4.3 billion barrels of proven reserves of the USSR is too high, rather than too low, agrees that the potential oil reserves of the USSR are very large.[28]

POTENTIAL RESERVES

Geologic considerations lead to the belief that the world's potential oil reserves are many times

the estimated 115 billion barrels in proven reserves. All petroleum accumulations are intimately associated with sedimentary rock in marine basins or along shore lines where streams and rivers, flowing to the ocean, deposit debris from the land. From this fact, geologists conclude that any region on the earth with a vast volume of sedimentary rock may be considered a potential oil- and gas-producing area.

Since sedimentary rock is usually found in basins and lowlands, large petroleum reservoirs must have been formed in areas where the sea floor has subsided, mostly in depressions of the earth's crust occupied by landlocked seas, between the main continental land masses, where marine organic matter was buried in sediment from the shores.

There are four such great areas in the world: (1) the Middle East, land along the Black, Caspian and Red Seas, and the Persian Gulf, between Europe, Africa and Asia; (2) the area in the Gulf of Mexico and Caribbean Sea, between North and South America; (3) the Far East, with the islands of Java, Sumatra, Borneo and New Guinea, between Asia and Australia; and (4) land fringing the Arctic Sea in North America, Europe and Asia. All these areas have vast sedimentary formations, normally containing petroleum reservoirs, and show seepages of oil and gas at the surface.[29] Although only a small part of this total area has been drilled or even explored, it is believed that it must contain considerable accumulations of oil and gas. The three most recent estimates of undiscovered oil reserves in the world's land areas, offered by Joseph E. Pogue, L. G. Weeks and W. E. Pratt, are as follows (in billions of barrels):[30]

	Pogue (1946)	*Weeks* (1948)	*Pratt* (1950)
World	490	487	600
Western Hemisphere	145	154	210
United States	50	54	100
Eastern Hemisphere	345	333	390
USSR	100	139	150

In addition, the continental shelf is believed to house vast stores of oil. All the debris carried by rivers from the continents to the sea comes to rest on the shelf or its edges, and waters over the shelf abound in marine life, the original source material of oil. Drilling on the shelf in

---

26. **31,** October 1951, p. 11.

27. According to Russian sources, the proven oil reserves of the USSR are close to 58 billion barrels, thus approximating the combined oil reserves of North America and the Middle East, as estimated for January 1, 1949. **21,** p. 20.

28. **36,** December 30, 1948, p. 146.

29. **27,** 1945, pp. 117–19.

30. **34,** p. 96, and **27,** 1950, p. 149.

TABLE 372

OIL RESERVES IN THE WORLD AND INDIVIDUAL COUNTRIES, 1939–51

Continent and Country	Proven Reserves, in Millions of Barrels				Percentage of Total		Ratio of Reserves to 1950 Output (Years of Supply)
	January 1, 1939	End of 1947	January 1, 1949	January 1, 1951	1949	1951	
World	34,248 [a]	61,683 [b]	77,647	95,208	100.0	100.0	25.2
North America	—	21,688	27,826	27,418	35.8	28.8	13.7
United States	17,348	21,488	27,326 [c]	26,218	35.2	27.5	13.3
Canada	...	...	500	1,200 [d]	0.7	1.3	41.5
Middle and South America	...	10,712	10,883	11,884	14.0	12.6	16.8
Mexico	600	1,058	850	1,300	1.1	1.4	18.0
Trinidad	150	300	250	250	0.3	0.3	12.4
Venezuela	2,500	8,350	9,000	9,500	11.6	10.0	17.4
Colombia	400	500	300	375	0.4	0.4	11.0
Ecuador	...	...	30	26	[e]	[e]	0.7
Peru	200	150	160	150	0.2	0.2	16.6
Argentina	200	275	250	270	0.3	0.3	10.0
Europe	...	789	604	707	0.8	0.7	12.0
Netherlands	...	...	50	53	[e]	[e]	10.9
Germany	...	80	45	160 [g]	[e]	0.2 [g]	20.4
Poland	...	20	20	12	} 0.1	} 0.1 {	12.9
Austria	...	70	75	60			9.5
Hungary	...	72	40	35			10.1
Romania	700	475	350	340	0.5	0.4	10.8
USSR	5,000	7,590	4,275	5,570	5.5	5.9	21.2
Asia	...	20,763	33,888	49,446	43.6	51.9	67.6
Japan	—	—	15	22	[e]	[e]	10.7
Saudi Arabia	—	3,600	9,000	10,000	11.6	10.5	50.1
Bahrein Islands	—	—	170	300	0.2	0.3	75.5
Kuwait	—	4,500	10,950	15,000	14.1	15.8	119.3
Qatar [f]	...	...	500	1,000	0.6	1.1	87.3
Iraq	1,500	5,000	5,000	8,700	6.4	9.1	186.1
Iran	3,500	5,625	7,000	13,000	9.0	13.7	53.8
Pakistan	—	—	32	20	[e]	[e]	16.0
India	...	...	...	15	[e]	[e]	4.9
Burma	—	—	50	48	[e]	[e]	8.4
Indonesia	1,600	850	1,000	1,000	1.3	1.1	19.9
British Borneo	—	—	150	250	0.2	0.3	15.2
Africa	—	142	122	183	0.2	0.2	11.1
Egypt	—	141	120	180	0.2	0.2	11.1
Oceania	—	0.05	50	0.5	[e]	[e]	62.5

Sources: For 1939: **18**, 1939, p. 60; for 1947: **49**, July 1948, p. 31; for 1949: **42**, pp. 22–23; **49**, July 15, 1951, p. 66.

a. Includes 500 million barrels for countries for which separate figures are not available.
b. Includes some undistributed reserves.
c. Includes 4,046 million barrels for reserves of natural gasoline and liquefied petroleum gases.
d. This estimate became obsolete before it was released. The oil reserves of Alberta alone were estimated at 2 billion barrels by the end of 1950.
e. Less than one tenth of one per cent.
f. Sheikdom on the isthmus in the Persian Gulf.
g. Western Germany.

the Gulf of Mexico off the coasts of Texas and Louisiana seems to confirm this belief.[31] Seven out of ten exploratory wells drilled off the Gulf Coast have been successful.

Using the drilling experience in the United States as a yardstick, the majority of the experts believe that the world's oil resources may ultimately prove to be many times as great as the known reserves. Some estimate the possible oil reserves on the continental shelf at 600 billion barrels, and others at as much as a trillion barrels.[32] However, difficulties of operating under water and the location of a great part of the continental shelf in the Arctic limit the prospects of exploring these potential resources in the near future.

RESERVES IN THE UNITED STATES

The first estimate of the proven oil reserves of the United States in 1914 was 6 billion barrels. Since that time, estimates have risen consistently with the discovery of additional oil fields. The latest estimate, for January 1, 1952, is 27.5 billion barrels. In the meantime, about 40 billion barrels have been produced, and the cumulative total since the beginning of commercial oil production in 1859 is about 43 billion barrels. (See Table 373 and Figure 253.) The largest reserves are in Texas (13.5 billion barrels), Oklahoma (11.3 billion), California (3.8 billion) and Louisiana (1.9 billion).[33]

There are still vast unexplored areas where geology points to structural features favorable to accumulation of oil. (See Figure 254.) Greater depth of drilling also holds promise of possible new discoveries. The United States, however, has less to expect from discoveries than some other areas, such as the Middle East or Venezuela. Its most promising areas have been intensively explored, and enormous quantities of oil have been extracted. Yet the intensified search, reflected also in the steep rise of wild-cat drilling, has more than offset the amounts of oil extracted from existing fields: from 1941 to 1952, 19.4 billion barrels were extracted and 27.8 billion discovered. Thus reserves on January 1, 1952 were 8.4 billion greater than in 1941.[34]

31. **27**, 1950, pp. 141–43.
32. **34**, pp. 98 and 110. Pratt (**41**, p. 127), J. Crowther (**23**, p. 12) and J. E. Grantley (**36**, September 1948, p. 82) are also of the opinion that the world's oil reserves are vastly larger than the drilling has yet shown.
33. **18**, 1950, p. 183. Data for January 1, 1950.
34. **18**, various years.

TABLE 373

PETROLEUM: ESTIMATED RESERVES AND CUMULATIVE OUTPUT IN THE UNITED STATES, 1914–52

(*Millions of Barrels*)

Estimating Authority and Year	Estimated Reserves at Beginning of Year [a]	Cumulative Output Prior to Estimate
Ralph Arnold		
1914	6,000	3,070
U.S. Geological Survey		
1915	7,500	3,335
1921	9,000	5,430
American Petroleum Institute		
1925	7,500	7,906
U.S. Geological Survey		
1934	13,300	15,690
American Petroleum Institute		
1935	12,177	16,598
1937	13,063	18,695
1938	15,507	19,972
1939	17,348	21,186
1940	18,483	22,450
1941	19,025	23,802
1942	19,589	25,206
1943	20,083	26,591
1944	20,064	28,095
1945	20,453	29,773
1946	. . .	31,510
1947	20,874	33,236
1948	21,488	35,087
1949	23,280	37,089
1950	24,649	38,908
1951	25,268	40,919
1952	27,468	43,164

Sources: **18**, 1939, p. 60, and 1950, p. 182; **12**, various years.

a. Beginning with 1946, reserves of crude oil only. Earlier figures include some condensate.

This increase does not, however, remove the danger of imminent exhaustion of the oil reserves of the United States. With an annual output of nearly 2 billion barrels, as in 1950, the ratio of estimated reserves to output showed a supply of oil for 13.3 years. (See Table 372.)

OIL SHALES AND TAR SANDS

Two hitherto almost untapped sources of crude oil — oil shale and tar sand — may become important in the future.

Reserves of Oil Shales

Oil shales consist of mud or clay consolidated

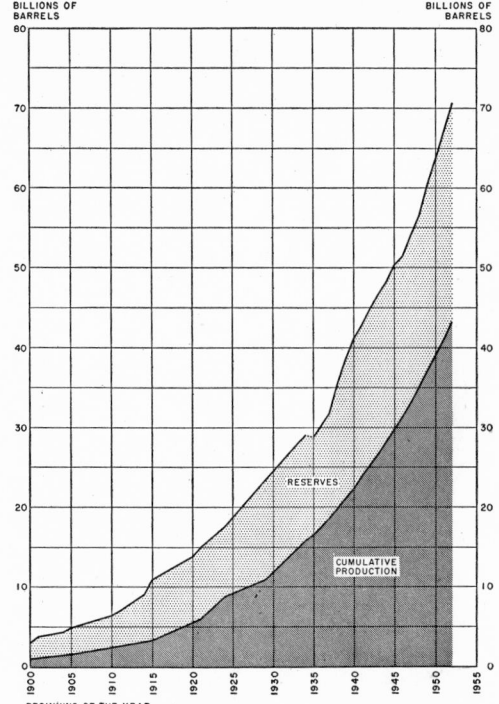

FIGURE 253. PETROLEUM: ESTIMATED RESERVES AND
CUMULATIVE OUTPUT IN THE UNITED STATES, 1900–50

into rock from which oil and gas can be produced
by destructive distillation. Although they do not
carry oil or gas, and oil seeps are unknown, they
contain organic materials that can be broken up
into oil and gas.[35]

Oil shales are widely scattered over the earth,
with vast concentrations in a few areas. The
organic origin of oil in this sediment of very fine
texture and laminated structure has apparently
been definitely established.[36] The organic matter
in the shale, the so-called kerogen, decomposes at
high temperature and is converted to oil, gas
and fixed carbon. The yield of oil from a ton of
oil shale ranges from less than one gallon to
ninety gallons or more.

The greatest single deposit in the world is the
Green River formation in Colorado, Utah and
Wyoming, stretching over 16,500 square miles.
The richest bed, about 500 feet thick, is north-
west of Rifle, Colorado, where the outcrop forms
an almost vertical cliff.

According to Dean E. Winchester, whose estimate of oil reserves in shale deposits of the
United States was prepared in 1928 after long
exploration, these potential reserves contain more

than three times the oil in proven reserves. He
estimates that 92 billion barrels could be recovered from oil shale in the country, of which
Colorado and Utah would account for almost 80
per cent, as follows (in billions of barrels): [37]

	Total	*Recoverable*
Total	144.2	92.1
Colorado	79.6	47.6
Utah	42.8	25.7
Kentucky	11.0	9.9
Indiana	7.7	6.9
Wyoming	3.0	1.8

Even more optimistic estimates have been
made recently. The preliminary evaluation of the
U.S. Bureau of Mines of recoverable shale oil is
as follows (in billions of barrels): [38]

Total	250,319
Colorado	200,000
Utah	25,680
Wyoming	1,826
Nevada	4
Indiana	6,912
Kentucky	9,881
Pennsylvania	16
California	6,000

In Sweden, deposits of oil shale are estimated
at 5 billion tons, of which 630 million tons can
be mined by open-cut methods. The Estonian
deposits, now in the USSR, of 1.5 billion tons,
have an average yield of 60 U.S. gallons of oil
per long ton. Manchuria has large deposits in
Fushun (540 million tons), but the yield of oil is
low, averaging 15–17.5 U.S. gallons per ton.
Australian deposits, in New South Wales, Tasmania and Queensland, are considerable and
those in New South Wales are outstanding because of their exceptionally high yield — up to
120 U.S. gallons of oil per long ton.[39]

Reserves of Tar Sands

The vast deposits of tar sands in the Athabaska
Valley of Canada are another potential source of
oil. These sands hold not only a kerogen-like
compound convertible into oil but also oil itself.
The Dominion Bureau of Mines has estimated

35. **29**, p. 480.
36. **25**, Vol. II, p. 99.

37. **48**, pp. 13–14. Only oil shale that might be mined
by open-cut steam-shovel methods was considered in this
estimate. Most estimators agree that these figures are
conservative. (**27**, 1945, pp. 188–89.)
38. Quoted from **35**, December 1948, p. 91.
39. **22**, pp. 4–7.

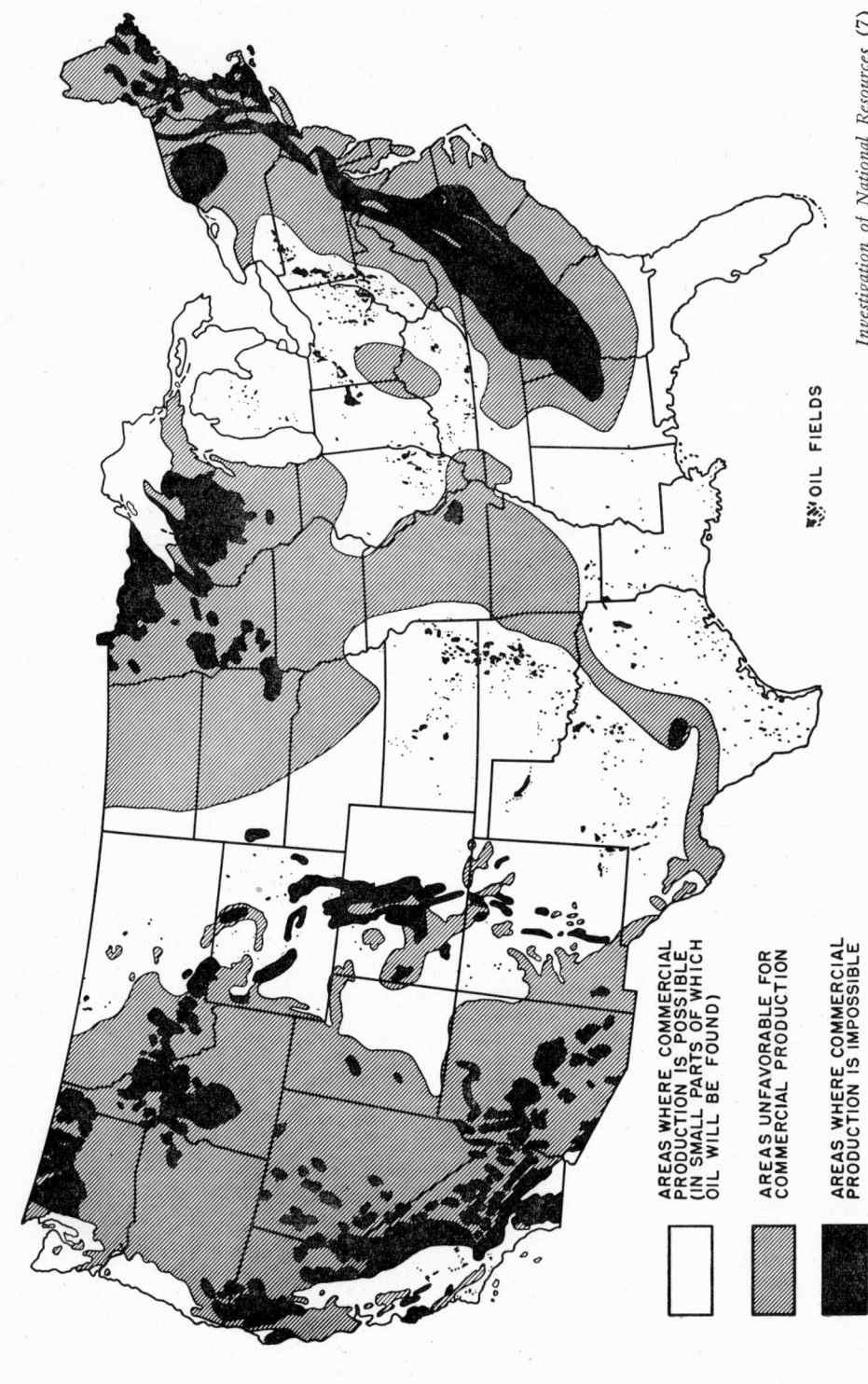

OIL FIELDS

AREAS WHERE COMMERCIAL
PRODUCTION IS POSSIBLE
(IN SMALL PARTS OF WHICH
OIL WILL BE FOUND)

AREAS UNFAVORABLE FOR
COMMERCIAL PRODUCTION

AREAS WHERE COMMERCIAL
PRODUCTION IS IMPOSSIBLE

FIGURE 254. OIL RESERVES: AREAS IN WHICH OIL CAN EXIST IN THE UNITED STATES

Approximately half the surface of the United States either is known to contain oil fields or, because of its geological structure, may have such fields. Another half consists of areas which are considered either "impossible" or "unfavorable" for commercial production of oil.

Investigation of National Resources (7)

that at least 100 billion barrels of oil could be recovered from these sands. The United States Bureau of Mines estimates that this reserve may contain 250 billion barrels.[40] Other estimates are much more modest, indicating that 27.5 billion barrels of oil can be recovered from all tar sands in the Western Hemisphere, principally those in Canada.[41] For the British Commonwealth, which has only small oil fields, these tar sands constituted the only large potential reserve until large oil fields were discovered in Canada in 1947–48.

Exploitation of Reserves

While the estimates of the oil contained in shales and tar sands are impressive, recovery of crude oil from these sources hinges on the solution of many technical and economic problems. With present methods of mining and processing, the product is too expensive to compete with the natural crude oil. Small-scale exploitation of oil shales so far has taken place only in countries that have no domestic sources of petroleum, and the exploitation of tar sands in Canada is only in a preparatory stage.

France began to exploit its oil shale deposits in Saône-et-Loire and Allier more than a century ago, but production fell when cheap American petroleum reached Europe in the 1870's. France still produces some shale oil, with governmental support — about 80,000 barrels a year.

Canada began commercial oil-shale retorting in New Brunswick in 1815, and between 1850 and 1860 the United States had more than fifty plants on the eastern seaboard for the distillation of oil from Canadian shale. This industry was abandoned after the discovery of oil in Pennsylvania.

In Scotland, oil shale has been mined since 1850 and has provided a complete range of petroleum-like products and excellent grades of paraffin wax. The output rose to 3 million tons during World War I and declined thereafter because of the competition of natural petroleum. Moreover, the yield of oil began to decline with depth — from a barrel per long ton of shale to little more than half a barrel.[42]

Estonia produced about a million barrels of oil from oil shale in 1938. A large plant built in Manchuria in 1929 had about the same annual output before World War II.

In the United States, exploitation of shale deposits is still in an experimental stage. Government demonstration plants in Colorado produce, after the crushing and retorting processes, around 50 barrels of oil per day. This product requires some further processing to equal crude petroleum.[43] Special difficulties stand in the way of large-scale commercial production. Such production would require a considerable amount of water, yet the chief beds of oil shale are in the arid western states. Disposal of the ash resulting from conversion of shale to oil (more than a ton of ash, a sterile material, for every barrel of oil), prevention of pollution of streams and ground waters from chemical solutions and the protection of surface land are also expected to present great difficulties.[44]

Canada is moving toward a solution of the problem of extracting heavy oil from tar sands; in 1949 the pilot plant at Bitumount processed some 500 tons a day and recovered about 90 per cent of the oil content. Present production methods are complicated, however, and various changes are contemplated. One drawback is that the impregnation of the beds with tar is very erratic. In some areas the sand is completely impregnated, in others, only at the top or bottom or in the middle of the bed.[45]

OIL PRODUCTION

The production of petroleum begins with the search for oil pools and continues with drilling wells and withdrawing and processing crude oil. In addition, the operations of the petroleum industry normally include storage and transportation of oil. The large oil companies commonly integrate the entire process, from prospecting for oil fields to delivering the finished products.

THE SEARCH FOR OIL

Although drilling at random, without technical knowledge, has resulted in the discovery of many oil fields, among others the great East Texas field, petroleum companies now draw heavily on the help of science in their search for oil.

Geology guides exploration of the surface and subsurface structure of the prospective area. Paleontology supplies supplementary information on the age of fossils and helps to establish a correla-

---

40. **19**, p. 373, and **41**, pp. 44–45.
41. **46**, p. 587.
42. **25**, Vol. IV, p. 3081, and **22**, p. 4.

43. **31**, August 1948, pp. 49–50.
44. **27**, 1950, p. 230.
45. **49**, February 1951, p. 205.

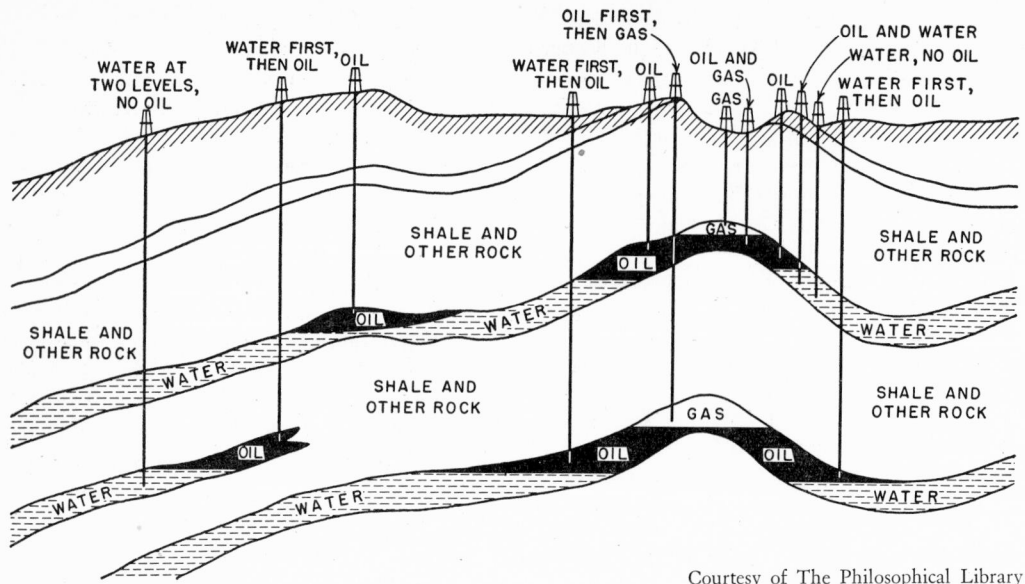

WATER AT TWO LEVELS, NO OIL

WATER FIRST, THEN OIL OIL

OIL FIRST, THEN GAS

WATER FIRST, THEN OIL OIL

OIL AND GAS GAS

OIL AND WATER WATER, NO OIL WATER FIRST, THEN OIL

OIL

SHALE AND OTHER ROCK

GAS

SHALE AND OTHER ROCK

OIL

SHALE AND OTHER ROCK

OIL

WATER

WATER

SHALE AND OTHER ROCK

WATER

WATER

SHALE AND OTHER ROCK

OIL

GAS

SHALE AND OTHER ROCK

OIL

OIL

WATER

WATER

WATER

Courtesy of The Philosophical Library

FIGURE 255. HOW OIL IS FOUND AND MISSED IN TYPICAL FIELDS

tion of geological strata among widely separated wells. Mineralogy is used to examine the constituents of the rocks. Subterranean structures four miles or more underground can now be located more accurately by geophysical methods than rocks just below the surface were plotted some twenty-five years ago. Analysis of actual samples of oil-bearing rocks and reservoir liquids has been developed to assess the oil content quantitatively and to estimate the native energy of the reservoir for propelling the oil.[46] Scientific prospecting has been much more successful than "wild-catting." Since the beginning of oil production in the United States, 225 oil fields have been discovered with the aid of science, and only 65 by random drilling.[47]

The wealth of information supplied by preliminary explorations still points only to the probable presence of oil. The final test is provided by drilling. (See Figure 255.) The drilled well may be productive or a "dry hole" or a "teaser"; on the average, three out of ten wells drilled in the United States are found to be without oil.[48] When two productive wells are drilled, the area is considered an oil field. Then additional wells are drilled, until the field is delimited by dry holes on all sides.

---

46. **6, b,** p. 9.
47. **15,** p. 236.
48. **18,** 1950, p. 130.

OIL WELLS

Number

Of the 471,000 oil-producing wells in the world in 1949, the United States had almost 450,000, or about 96 per cent; in 1950, it counted nearly 468,000 wells. More than a million wells, productive and dry, have been drilled in the country. Other oil-producing countries have only a tiny fraction of that number. Venezuela, for example, with about a fourth of the oil output of the United States, has little more than one per cent of the world's producing wells. Iran, Iraq, Kuwait and Saudi Arabia together had 220 wells in 1949, and 261 at the end of 1950.

Overdrilling in the United States has been caused both by the tremendous demand for oil and the intense search for it and by the "law of capture," which ruled supreme throughout the first sixty or seventy years of oil production in the country and is still officially on its books. Under this law, as upheld by a court in Pennsylvania in 1889, oil is *ferae naturae* (of a wild nature) and therefore subject to the same legal regulations as wild game: it belongs to the person who captures it in his tank, not to the owner of the land under which it exists. An underground reservoir, however, is a unit in which the natural forces of pressure and gravity act like a single mechanism, no matter how many persons own the surface land. The reservoir can be

TABLE 374

OIL WELLS IN SELECTED COUNTRIES, END OF 1950

Country	Number of Wells			Average Output, per Day	
	Total [a]	Flowing	Artificial Lift	Total, in Thousands of Barrels	Per Well, in Barrels
World [b]	...	...	...	10,953	...
United States	467,776	53,587	414,189	5,681	12.1
Canada	3,469	...	...	84	24.3
Mexico	1,215	...	...	211	173.8
Trinidad	2,053	635	1,418	57	27.7
Venezuela	6,915	2,810	4,105	1,650	238.6
Colombia	1,312	145	1,167	103	78.7
Argentina [e]	1,332	7	1,325	63	47.4
Romania	...	...	...	75	...
USSR	...	...	...	721	...
Saudi Arabia	95	95	—	618	6,503.9
Bahrein Islands	69	...	...	30	437.4
Kuwait	78	78	—	403	5,171.4
Qatar	10	10	—	44	4,375.0
Iraq	11	11	—	159	14,446.3
Iran	77	73	—	718	9,324.7
Indonesia	1,629	742	887	134	82.2
British Borneo	268	...	...	81	303.6
Egypt [c]	109	32	77	44	406.8

Source: **49,** July 15, 1950, p. 54, and July 15, 1951, p. 80.

a. World total available only for 1949: 470,883.
b. Excludes the USSR, for lack of data.
c. 1949.

tapped at different points, and an enterprising driller can capture the oil from adjoining lands. As a result, a great number of offset wells were drilled to keep the oil from flowing to neighbors' wells, with complete disregard of both market demand and efficient recovery of oil from the common pool.[49]

In most wells in the United States (414,189 out of 467,776 in 1950) oil is extracted by artificial lift. In the Middle East, all wells flow through the operation of natural forces. (See Table 374.)

Daily Yield

In 1950 the average well in the United States yielded 12.1 barrels of oil a day; in Venezuela, 238.6 barrels; and in the Middle East, many thousands.[50] The yield depends not only on the capacity of the well but also, to a considerable degree, on operating practices. A well in a field like the East Texas could yield hundreds, perhaps thousands, of barrels daily, but the oil flow is controlled for reasons of rational production, the proration system and so on.

The depth of oil wells has been increasing steadily. (See Figure 256.) The first well drilled in the United States, in 1859, was 69.5 feet deep; in 1947 the deepest wells reached more than three miles below the surface and in 1949, nearly four miles.[51] Wells a few thousand feet deep are now regarded as shallow, the average depth in southern Louisiana, for example, being 9,000 feet.

Deeper drilling became possible with the shift from the cable-tool system to the rotary method,[52]

Virginia). On the other hand, wells in Louisiana, East Texas and California yield 40–50 barrels daily and in Mississippi, almost 100 barrels.

49. **38,** pp. 17–18.
50. About a third of the wells in the United States, some 140,000–150,000 average as little as half a barrel a day (in Pennsylvania, New York, Ohio and West

51. 17,823 feet in Oklahoma; 18,734 feet in California; and 20,521 feet in Wyoming. All three wells are dry **18,** 1950, p. 138.
52. In the cable-tool, or percussion, method, the drill-

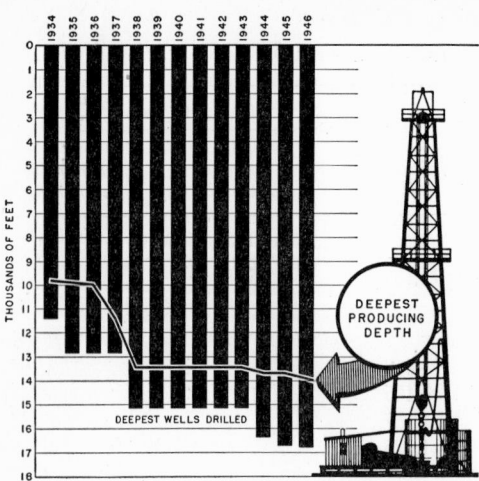

American Petroleum Institute

FIGURE 256. THE DEEPEST WELLS DRILLED AND PRODUCING IN THE UNITED STATES

progress in making alloy steel and improvement in drilling equipment. The record in cable-tool drilling was established in 1949, with 10,312 feet. Experimentation with the jet-bit rock type continues, and several wells have been drilled with this new equipment.[53] Special drilling methods are used in swampy or offshore areas: underwater barges in some parts of Louisiana; in Venezuela, wooden pilings on deep foundations; in California, wharves extending in water 40–50 feet deep.

PRODUCTION METHODS

Modern methods of oil production tend to utilize the forces of pressure and gravity within the oil reservoir. When these natural forces are not sufficient to drive oil toward the mouth of the well, they are augmented by various means. If, for example, an oil reservoir has an insufficient gas-cap drive or none at all, gas can be injected to increase the volume or create a cap. Water is sometimes injected around the walls of the reservoir to maintain water pressure within it. Recently acids have been injected into the oil to facilitate its flow.

Since maintenance of the original pressure within a reservoir is the essence of the new technology, efforts are being made to determine the maximum efficient rate of production for a given field and to restrict oil withdrawals to this rate, as against the uncontrolled, wide-open flow formerly permitted. It is believed that adjusting the rate of production to the play of natural forces in the reservoir results in a greater ultimate recovery of oil.

The new technology is also used to rejuvenate depleted or abandoned oil pools that still contain reserves of oil but lack energy to expel it. Compressed gas or air is injected or reservoir sands are flooded with water to stimulate the flow of oil. In northeastern Oklahoma, for example, 40 to 60 per cent of the oil remaining in the ground is extracted by flooding methods.[54] The world's largest operation of this type has been under way in Burbank, Oklahoma, since 1951. This secondary oil recovery project is expected to add 140 million barrels from a reservoir which, through wasteful production practices, has supplied only 25 per cent of the oil initially in place, despite supplementary gas repressuring.[55]

Some experts believe that from one to five billion barrels of oil may ultimately be obtained by secondary recovery methods in the United States.[56]

Unitization of production is practiced in the Middle East and other countries, where oil concessions affecting a vast area have been granted to a single company.

THE OUTPUT OF CRUDE OIL

Although petroleum was known in Asia and the Caucasus long before the Christian era and is often mentioned under various names in writings of Greek and Roman authors,[57] commercial

---

ing bit is suspended at the end of the rope, and lifted and dropped intermittently to crush the rock and force the passage downward. In the rotary method, the bit is fastened to the bottom of the drill pipe and cuts the passage by rotation. Both methods require heavy equipment driven by powerful engines at the surface. The rotary method is much faster but it did not become fully efficient until metallurgy developed alloy steels, so that the bit could cut through the hardest rock. (**42**, pp. 27–28.) The Chinese used a kind of a cable-tool system in 2000 B.C. for drilling brine wells.

53. **49**, February 15, 1950, pp. 87–88.

54. **44**, p. 357.
55. **49**, October 1951, pp. 60–61.
56. **27**, 1945, p. 96.
57. Bitumen had been used by Sumerians (in Mesopotamia) to bind the mud bricks in 4000 B.C. Nebuchadnezzar's hanging gardens had stone terraces waterproofed with bitumen. This material was also used for caulking boats and, in dried form, for fuel. Liquid petroleum, obtained from seepage, served as an illuminant and as medicine (internal and external) in China and along the Persian Gulf. The famous "Greek fire," a powerful weapon until the invention of gun powder, was a self-igniting mixture of petroleum and quicklime. Flames of

TABLE 375

OUTPUT OF CRUDE OIL IN EACH CONTINENT, 1913–50

(*Millions of Barrels*)

Continent	1913	1918	1923	1928	1933	1938	1943	1948	1949	1950	Cumulative Total as of January 1, 1951
World	385	504	1,016	1,325	1,442	1,978	2,231	3,398	3,399	3,783	65,539
North America	249	356	733	902	907	1,220	1,515	2,028	1,863	2,000	41,108
Middle and South America	26	70	166	206	204	297	293	629	635	713	9,864
Europe	23	16	18	38	61	58	66	50	58	59	1,819
USSR	63	27	39	85	153	205	206	212	240	270	6,569
Asia	24	33	59	92	113	195	143	466	587	723	6,027
Africa	0.1	2	1	2	2	2	9	13	16	17	154
Oceania [a]	…	…	…	…	…	…	…	…	…	…	…

Sources: **12,** various years; **36,** December 30, 1948, p. 149; **49,** July 15, 1951, p. 54.

a. Less than 100,000 barrels.

production did not begin until the 1850's — in Romania in 1857 and in the United States in 1859. Since that time, more than a score of countries have entered the field.

OUTPUT OF THE WORLD AND THE CONTINENTS

In 1913, the world produced 385 million barrels of oil; in 1928, about three and a half times as much (1,325 million barrels), and in 1950 nearly three times as much as in 1928 (3,783 million barrels). The Western Hemisphere dominates the world's oil output, supplying more than seven tenths of the total. Asia's share has been increasing rapidly with the exploitation of the oil fields in the Middle East, particularly in Saudi Arabia, Iraq and other areas. The USSR accounts for about 7 per cent of the world's present output, while Europe and Africa together provide only about 2–3 per cent. Oceania's output is negligible. (See Table 375 and Figure 257.)

The world's cumulative output of crude oil natural gas escaping from oil fields on the Apsheron Peninsula were worshiped by the Zoroastrians, and Hindus made pilgrimages there from Burma and India as early as 2500 B.C. In ancient Mexico bitumen was an article of commerce. Production of oil from hand-dug pits on the peninsulas of Kerch and Taman is described by ancient Greek historians. Indians in North America used crude oil for its purgative effects, for painting their bodies and for making fires during their religious ceremonies. The early settlers of New York, Pennsylvania, Ohio and other states used "rock oil" and "Seneca oil" for treating various ailments. (**43,** Vol. I, pp. 1 ff.; **23,** p. 8.)

from 1857 through 1950 totaled 65.5 billion barrels, of which North America produced 41 billion barrels, or nearly two thirds. Latin America accounted for about 15 per cent of the total; Asia, for 9 per cent and Russia (USSR), for 10 per cent. (See Figure 258.)

OUTPUT IN SELECTED COUNTRIES

Ranking of Countries

The United States, which has been the major producer of petroleum except in 1898–1902, ac-

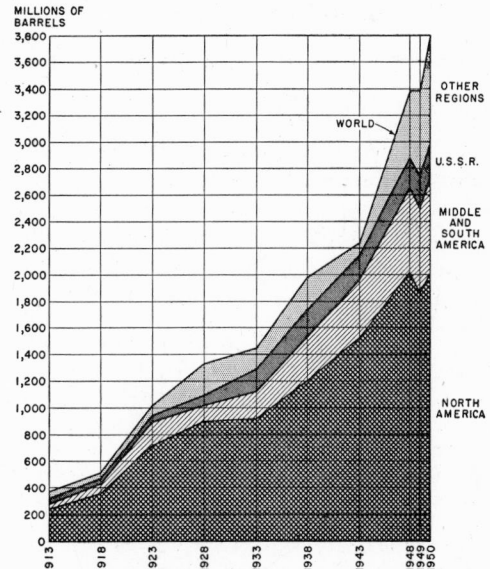

FIGURE 257. OUTPUT OF CRUDE OIL IN THE WORLD AND SELECTED REGIONS, 1913–50

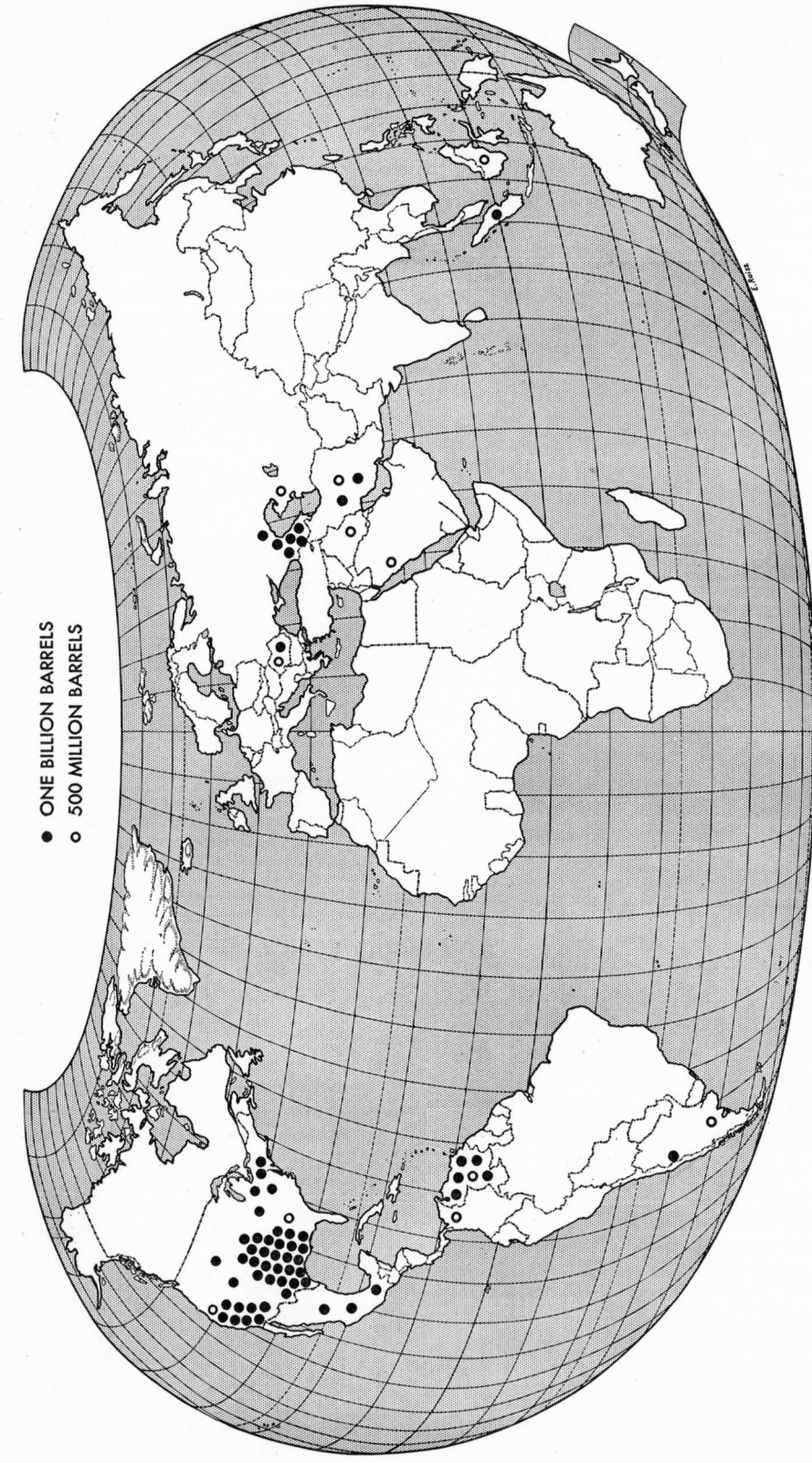

FIGURE 258. OUTPUT OF CRUDE OIL: CUMULATIVE OUTPUT IN THE WORLD TO JANUARY 1, 1951

● ONE BILLION BARRELS
○ 500 MILLION BARRELS

TABLE 376
OUTPUT OF CRUDE OIL IN SELECTED COUNTRIES, 1913–50

Country	Output, in Millions of Barrels									Percentage of World Total	
	1913	1918	1923	1928	1933	1938	1948	1949	1950	1938	1950
World	385	504	1,016	1,325	1,442	1,978	3,398	3,399	3,783	100.0	100.0
United States	248	356	732	901	906	1,214	2,017	1,842	1,972	61.4	52.1
Canada	0.2	0.3	0.2	0.6	1	7	12	21	29	0.4	0.8
Mexico	26	64	150	50	34	39	59	61	72	2.0	1.9
Trinidad	0.5	2	3	8	10	18	20	21	20	0.9	0.5
Venezuela	—	0.3	4	106	118	188	490	482	545	9.5	14.4
Colombia	—	—	0.4	20	13	22	24	30	34	1.1	0.9
Peru	2	3	6	12	13	16	14	15	15	0.8	0.4
Argentina	0.1	1	3	9	14	17	24	23	23	0.9	0.6
Romania	14	9	11	31	54	48	31	34	32	2.4	0.8
USSR	63	27	39	85	153	205	212	240	270	10.4	7.2
Saudi Arabia	—	—	—	—	—	0.5	143	174	200	—	5.3
Bahrein Islands	—	—	—	—	—	8	11	11	11	0.4	0.3
Kuwait	—	—	—	—	—	—	47	90	126	—	3.3
Iran	2	9	25	43	54	78	190	205	241	3.9	6.4
Iraq	—	—	—	0.7	0.9	33	26	31	47	1.7	1.2
India [a]	8	8	8	9	9	9	2	2	3	0.5	0.1
Indonesia	11	13	20	32	43	57	32	45	50	2.9	1.3
British Borneo (Sarawak and Brunei)	[b]	[b]	4	5	4	7	19	25	30	0.4	0.8
Egypt	0.1	2	1	2	2	2	13	16	16	0.1	0.4
Other	9	12	10	10	12	10	15	31	47	0.5	1.3

Sources: **12,** various years; **49,** February 15, 1950, p. 195, and July 15, 1951, p. 54.

a. Includes Burma through 1933. Burma's output in 1938: 7.5 million barrels. (**18,** 1950, p. 448.)
b. Negligible output.

counted for 52 per cent of the world's total in 1950. It supplied more than 90 per cent until 1875, when Russia began to produce increasing quantities from its Baku fields. Between 1898 and 1902, Russia's output slightly exceeded that of the United States. Since 1902 no country has challenged the lead of the United States.

Russia held second place until 1918, then Mexico, through 1926. Meanwhile an important new producer — Venezuela — began to contend for second place. In recent years, Venezuela has been exceeded only by the United States. (See Table 376.) In oil exports Venezuela ranks first, sending about a third of its oil to the United States. About 60 per cent of its output consists of heavy crude oil, serving largely as a source of residual fuel oil. It supplies much of the world's bunker requirements and is also used in industrial plants.[58]

Canada has recently become an important oil producer in the Western Hemisphere, and its territory holds great promise of new oil discoveries as the search is intensified. During 1949–51 new fields were discovered in Alberta and British Columbia. Canada's output is rising by leaps and bounds.

The USSR now occupies third place in oil production, which was stepped up during the war in spite of the officially reported destruction of more than 3,000 wells with an average annual production of some 36 million barrels. In the first postwar years, the output was considerably smaller than in 1944, but in 1949, the war peak level was reached. The increase was due mainly to the growing production in Second Baku; the output of the southern oil fields rose only slightly. This fact points not only to slow recovery from war damage but also to progressive depletion of the older fields in this area.

58. **40,** p. 7.

In 1950, the output was more than 10 per cent above that in the preceding year. All the war-damaged installations in Maikop, Grozny and the Western Ukraine have been fully restored. Oil fields in Sakhalin Island are receiving much attention, and oil resources in the Kazakhstan, Uzbek and Turkmen Republics are being developed.[59]

From the point of view of the world oil economy, nothing has been more important in the postwar years than the spectacular increase in output in the Middle East. Iran tripled its pre-war output and in 1950 was just behind the USSR. Production in Saudi Arabia, only recently initiated, is making rapid strides — from 7.8 million barrels in 1944 to 21.3 million in 1945 and 200 million in 1950. Kuwait is also rapidly increasing its output. The tremendous potentialities of the Middle East are more important than the present production. Until recently, exploration has been meager, few wells have been drilled, and equipment has been insufficient. Nevertheless, these three underdeveloped countries produced about twice as much oil in 1950 as their neighbor, the USSR.

Iran's cancellation, in 1951, of the Anglo-Iranian Oil Company's concession is of world-wide significance, the more so because it raises the problem of similar action toward foreign concessions in other areas. The drop in oil output, however, is of more immediate concern, particularly for western Europe, which had begun to orient its purchases toward this source; Iranian oil, flowing through new pipe lines directly to ports from which it could be taken by tankers, is closer at hand and cheaper for western European countries than Venezuelan oil. Entirely apart from any potential political dangers in the Iranian situation, the affair has been of great concern to the United States, which has felt it necessary to replace the Iranian oil in western Europe.

Despite the drastic decline in Iran's production during 1951 (from 241 million barrels to 128 million), the world's output rose almost 13 per cent above the 1950 level, from 3.8 billion barrels to 4.3 billion. More than half of this increase came from the United States, but the Middle East, exclusive of Iran, also contributed a good deal and more than offset the loss in Iranian output.

The USSR was estimated to have raised its output inconsiderably, by only 18–20 million barrels. Romania's output remained on the 1950 level, and a small increase was achieved in Austria and Hungary.

The world's output in 1952 was expected to reach 4.6 billion barrels, with the United States accounting for somewhat more than half. A substantial increase in production was expected in the USSR and the countries within its orbit.[60]

Cumulative Output

Romania, the world's pioneer in crude oil, had produced only about 2 per cent of the world's cumulative output by January 1, 1951; the United States, which started two years later, had produced 62.4 per cent, and Russia (the USSR) beginning in 1863, 10.1 per cent. Venezuela, which has been a producer since 1909, accounted for 8.5 per cent of the cumulative total, and Mexico, starting in 1901, for 3.8 per cent. Canada, which began commercial production in 1862, had chalked up only 0.3 per cent. The Middle East produced only 6 per cent of the cumulative total up to 1951, but its share will grow each year. (See Table 377 and Figure 258.)

The United States

The country's production of petroleum has risen continuously, though the quantities produced until the turn of this century were relatively small. The output, in millions of barrels, has increased as follows:[61]

1880	26.3
1890	45.8
1900	63.6
1910	209.6
1920	442.9
1930	898.0
1940	1,353.2
1950	1,971.8

This rise has been due not only to the discovery of many large oil fields and use of modern technology but also to more efficient operating practices. The majority of the oil fields prorate the allowable output among individual producers and some fields are operated as a unit.

This development has not come overnight. Competition among oil producers, fostered by the law of capture, resulted in overdrilling, an

---

59. **49,** July 15, 1951, pp. 218–20.

60. **36,** January 28, 1952, p. 232.
61. **9,** p. 146; cf. Table 376.

TABLE 377

OUTPUT OF CRUDE OIL: CUMULATIVE AMOUNT TO
JANUARY 1, 1951, IN SELECTED COUNTRIES

Country and First Year of Commercial Production	Amount, in Millions of Barrels	Percentage of World Total
World	65,539	100.0
United States, 1859	40,917	62.4
Canada, 1862	191	0.3
Mexico, 1901	2,482	3.8
Trinidad, 1897	413	0.6
Venezuela, 1909	5,549	8.5
Colombia, 1921	505	0.8
Ecuador, 1917	49	0.1
Peru, 1896	402	0.6
Argentina, 1908	458	0.7
Netherlands, 1944	14	a
Germany, 1880	107	0.2
Poland, 1874	279	0.4
Austria, 1935	64	0.1
Hungary, 1937	50	0.1
Romania, 1857	1,257	1.9
Russia (USSR), 1863	6,649	10.1
Japan, 1875	98	0.2
Saudi Arabia, 1936	719	1.1
Bahrein Islands, 1933	121	0.2
Kuwait, 1946	284	0.4
Qatar, 1940	12	a
Iraq, 1927	489	0.8
Iran, 1913	2,385	3.6
Burma, India, Pakistan, 1890	345	0.5
Indonesia, 1893	1,270	1.9
British Borneo, 1913	214	0.3
Egypt, 1911	153	0.2
Other	63	0.9

Source: **49**, July 15, 1951, p. 54.

a. Less than 0.1 per cent.

excessive rate of withdrawal, high costs of production and wastage of great quantities of oil and natural gas. Thousands of wells were abandoned as exhausted when as little as 20 per cent, and sometimes not more than 10 per cent, of the potentially obtainable oil had been recovered.

The first legal restrictions on production were introduced in Oklahoma in 1915, when an oversupply of oil on the market caused the prices to drop to very low levels. The Conservation Act of Oklahoma aimed at limiting the output to the market demand and restricting waste in production. Almost all the leading oil-producing states now have legislation requiring proration; California practices proration on a voluntary basis.[62] Proration has been supported by the federal government, and the Connally Act forbids interstate oil shipments in excess of state proration quotas.[63] In 1935, the Interstate Oil Compact Commission was created. The Commission apportions each state's share of the total output, and the state, in turn, distributes its quota among fields or pools.

The effect of the proration system, established to stabilize and protect individual rights of co-owners of a common pool, has been beneficial for some fields, negligible or even harmful for others. The consensus among oil experts is that proration alone is not sufficiently effective and that only the exploitation of a reservoir as a unit, regardless of surface boundaries, assures a high rate of oil recovery and longevity of the wells.[64] The major features of unit operation are scientific exploration of fields, pooling of interests, use of natural energy in the reservoir and control of the withdrawal of oil.

Texas ranks first with about 45 per cent of the country's total petroleum output, followed by California and Louisiana. Of the cumulative total 43 billion barrels produced in the United States, Texas accounts for 14.8 billion barrels, or one third; California, for more than one fifth and Oklahoma, for about one sixth. Louisiana, which did not enter the field until 1902, is behind Oklahoma in cumulative output but ahead of it in current output. (See Table 378 and Figure 259.)

The physical properties of oil produced in the United States vary greatly. The Mid-Continent's crude oil yields a good grade of gasoline and fair grades of lubricating oils; Pennsylvania supplies lubricating oils of the finest quality; several California fields yield crude oils, of which some have a high, others a low, gasoline content.[65]

62. Various criteria are used in allocating production quotas for states and oil fields: the number and depth of wells, acreage, potential productivity of wells, size of reserves, market demand and the like. Because of variations in physical conditions of oil pools and often the irreconcilable interests of individual producers, none of these methods has proved completely satisfactory.

63. **15**, p. 240; **44**, p. 212.

64. It has been estimated that the competitive system of production frequently yields only 30–35 per cent of the obtainable oil, while exploitation of the same reservoir as a single mechanism could raise the rate to 50–75 per cent. **33**, p. 478; see also **39**; **38**, p. 19.

65. **33**, p. 46.

TABLE 378

OUTPUT OF CRUDE OIL IN THE UNITED STATES, BY STATE, 1946–51 AND CUMULATIVE, THROUGH 1951

(*Output, in Millions of Barrels*)

State[a] and First Year of Commercial Production	Annual Output						Cumulative through 1951	
	1946	1947	1948	1949	1950	1951	Output	Per Cent
Total, 1859	1,734	1,857	2,016	1,840	1,972	2,243	43,232	100.0
Texas, 1889	760	820	903	744	832	1,006	14,783	34.2
California, 1876	315	333	340	333	328	355	9,012	20.9
Oklahoma, 1891	135	141	154	151	164	187	6,385	14.6
Louisiana, 1902	144	160	181	191	210	232	2,834	6.6
Kansas, 1889	97	105	111	100	107	114	2,200	5.1
Illinois, 1889	75	66	65	65	62	60	1,554	3.6
Pennsylvania, 1859	13	13	13	11	12	11	1,148	2.7
Wyoming, 1919	39	45	54	47	61	69	984	2.3
Arkansas, 1920	28	30	32	30	31	30	846	2.0
New Mexico, 1894	37	41	48	48	47	53	735	1.7
Ohio, 1876	3	3	3	3	3	3	621	1.4
West Virginia, 1876	3	3	3	3	3	3	446	1.0
Michigan, 1900	17	16	17	16	16	14	336	0.8
Mississippi, 1939	24	35	46	38	39	37	321	0.7
Kentucky, 1883	11	9	9	9	10	12	264	0.6
Indiana, 1889	7	6	7	10	11	11	211	0.5
New York, 1860	5	5	5	4	4	4	180	0.4
Montana, 1916	9	9	9	9	8	9	177	0.4
Colorado, 1887	12	16	17	24	23	28	175	0.4
Other	1	1	1	3	1	5	—	—

Sources: **12,** 1949, p. 875; **36,** January 28, 1952, p. 217.

a. States are arrayed by the cumulative output through 1951.

Canada

In the last few years, the development of Canada's oil industry has been reminiscent of the gold-rush days in California. The prairie province of Alberta suddenly became the center of extraordinary activity. More than a hundred geologic groups are exploring its vast area in all directions, hundreds of wells are being drilled, and the Interprovincial, the first major Canadian pipeline, has been built from this territory. The estimate of Alberta's oil reserves is constantly rising. The two biggest fields, Leduc-Woodbend and Redwater, have grown as follows since their discovery in 1947 and 1948, respectively: [66]

	1948	1949	1950
Number of producing wells:			
Leduc-Woodbend	151	351	519
Redwater	1	278	733
Output, in millions of barrels:			
Leduc-Woodbend	4.7	9.7	10.6
Redwater	0.04	4.8	10.7

66. **49,** July 15, 1951, p. 150.

The output could have been greater but has been kept down for lack of market and storage facilities. Both fields operate on a proration system, and the allowable quotas have been lowered several times. The Interprovincial pipeline, recently completed, will alleviate the situation. The fields have a storage capacity of 800,000 barrels, but the terminus of this line at Superior, Wisconsin, on the western boundary of the Great Lakes, can store 1.8 million barrels, as much as the entire line holds. From there, the two largest fresh-water tankers, newly built, are to transport the crude oil to Ontario for refining. Consumption of petroleum in Canada itself, though steadily rising, does not offer adequate outlets for the new potentialities. The Pacific Northwest is considered one of the potential new markets.

The USSR

The Baku fields provided about 71 per cent of the total oil output of the USSR in 1939 and were expected to supply 66 per cent of the out-

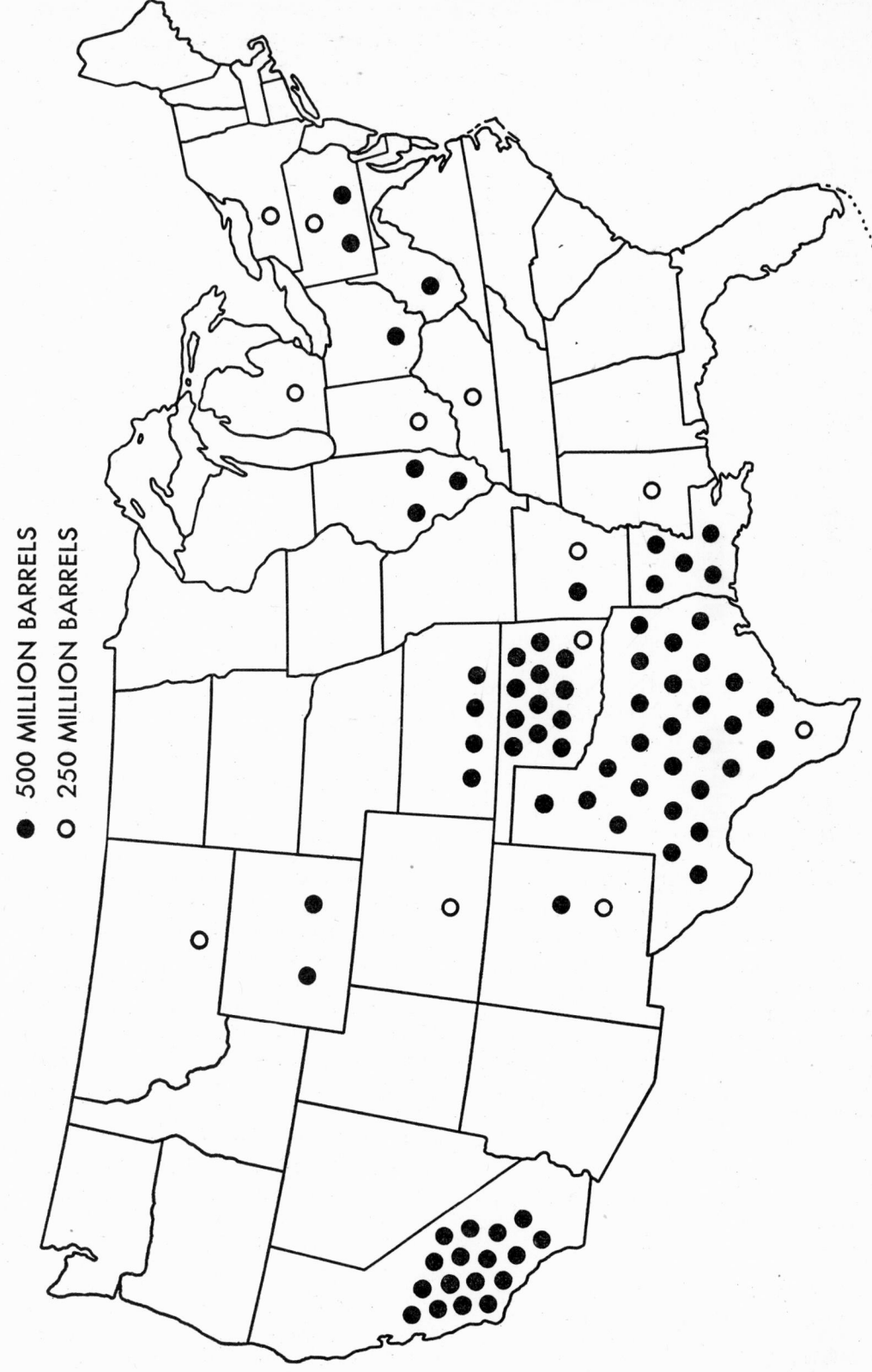

● 500 MILLION BARRELS
○ 250 MILLION BARRELS

FIGURE 259. OUTPUT OF CRUDE OIL: GEOGRAPHIC DISTRIBUTION OF CUMULATIVE OUTPUT IN THE UNITED STATES, BY STATE, TO JANUARY 1, 1951

put in 1941. Efforts have been made to develop new fields, particularly the Second Baku between the Volga River and the Urals. (See Figure 260.) The output of the chief fields, except for a small amount in the part of Sakhalin which belonged to Japan before the war, was as follows (in millions of barrels): [67]

Area	1939	1944, Estimated
Total	218.8	240.6
European USSR	210.4	216.8
Asiatic USSR	8.4	23.8
Baku	154.3	143.8
Grozny	15.8	12.0
Maikop	18.0	6.4
Ural-Volga (Second Baku)	12.9	25.2
Bukhara-Fergana	1.5	9.1
Turkmen	3.5	6.8
Emba-Uralsk	5.1	10.2
Dagestan	1.4	6.8
Kura River	1.1	4.9
Sakhalin	3.5	6.0

The target for 1950 was 260 million barrels (35.4 million tons), of which the Ural-Volga fields were expected to supply 36 per cent. Although this goal was not achieved, it was slightly exceeded in 1951.

After World War II the USSR gained the oil area in the eastern part of Poland, with about four fifths of Poland's former capacity. Moreover, the oil fields in Austria, Hungary and Romania, with an approximate annual production of some 40 million barrels, are likewise controlled by the USSR.

REFINING CRUDE OIL

In a complete plant, refining of crude petroleum is an integrated process. Under accurately controlled temperature, pressure and other conditions, oil is separated into gasoline, kerosene, fuel oils, lubricating and gas oils, paraffin oils and residue.[68] (See Figure 261.) Incomplete, or skimming plants, usually produce only gasoline and kerosene and sell the residue to complete refineries for further processing.[69]

Methods

When kerosene was the chief product obtained from crude oil, all refining was done by primitive distillation methods and gasoline and light gases

were wasted; gasoline was often poured into rivers, polluting the water. With the advent of the automobile, the demand for gasoline began to grow rapidly. It had been discovered accidentally, in 1861, that crude oil decomposed under high temperatures into lighter materials, chiefly gasoline and gas. This discovery was not commercialized during the next half century because there was no demand for such products.[70]

By 1914, however, the "cracking" method had been introduced. In this process, crude oil is subjected to great heat and pressure in special stills to break down the large molecules into those of gasoline range.[71] In the United States, "cracking" increased the gasoline yield of a barrel of crude oil from 11 per cent in 1909 to 45 per cent in 1939. (See Table 379.) It is estimated that if straight-run distillation had been used, the United States would have needed 26.8 billion barrels of crude oil to make the 6.1 billion barrels of gasoline produced between 1920 and 1938: actually, only 15.6 billion barrels of crude oil were used.[72]

The latest development in refining crude oil is catalytic cracking, with the use of clay or a synthetic silica alumina as the catalyst in oil fractionation. This process yields a high-octane gasoline, used during World War II mostly for aviation. Installation of catalytic cracking equipment has increased greatly since the war, and the present daily capacity exceeds 1.7 million barrels.[73] It was estimated in 1945 that, with the maximum use of catalytic and other cracking facilities in the United States, the average yield of gasoline from crude oil could be raised to 57 per cent.[74]

Another new process is polymerization, the opposite of cracking, which liquefies fixed or dry gases formed in the cracking process or found in nature and, by subjecting them to heat and pressure, combines their small molecules into larger ones, which are then condensed to gasoline. As a result, gases that had been wasted or burned as fuel are converted to high-quality gasoline. During the war various other refining methods were developed to produce special aviation gasolines with octane ratings of 100 and more.

67. **49,** July 1948, pp. 251–55, and **49,** July 15, 1950, pp. 45–46.
68. **25,** Vol. I, p. ix.
69. **15,** p. 242.

70. **6, a,** p. 5.
71. A somewhat similar "cracking" followed by "hydrogenation" marks the evolution of heavier to lighter oils in nature's laboratory. **41,** p. 16.
72. **18,** 1939, p. 87.
73. **18,** 1950, p. 263.
74. **26,** p. 60.

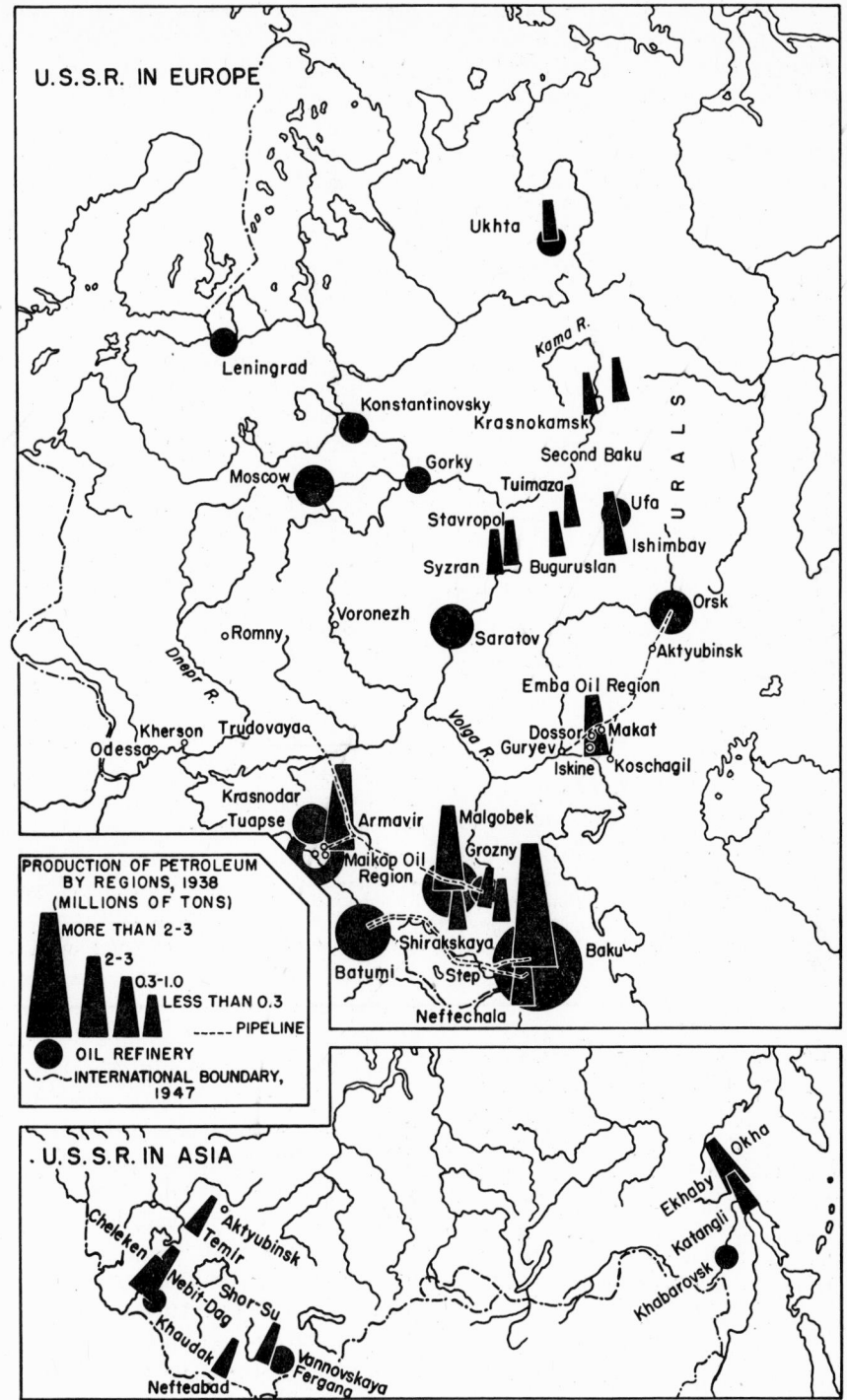

U.S.S.R. IN EUROPE

Ukhta

Kama R.

Leningrad

Konstantinovsky
Krasnokamsk

Second Baku

U R A L S

Moscow

Gorky

Tuimaza

Ufa

Stavropol

Ishimbay

Syzran

Buguruslan

Orsk

Voronezh

Saratov

Aktyubinsk

o Romny

Emba Oil Region

Dnepr R.

Kherson Trudovaya o
Odessa

Volga R.

Dossor
Guryev

Makat

Iskine Koschagil

Krasnodar
Tuapse

Armavir

Malgobek

PRODUCTION OF PETROLEUM
BY REGIONS, 1938
(MILLIONS OF TONS)

Maikop Oil
Region

Grozny

MORE THAN 2-3

2-3

0.3-1.0
LESS THAN 0.3

Shirakskaya

Baku

Batumi

Step

----- PIPELINE

OIL REFINERY

Neftechala

INTERNATIONAL BOUNDARY,
1947

U.S.S.R. IN ASIA

Okha

Ekhaby

Aktyubinsk

Cheleken Temir

Katangli

Nebit-Dag

Shor-Su

Khabarovsk

Khaudak

Vannovskaya

Nefteabad

Fergana

Adapted from **20**, p. 216.

FIGURE 260. OUTPUT OF CRUDE OIL: GEOGRAPHIC DISTRIBUTION IN THE USSR, 1938

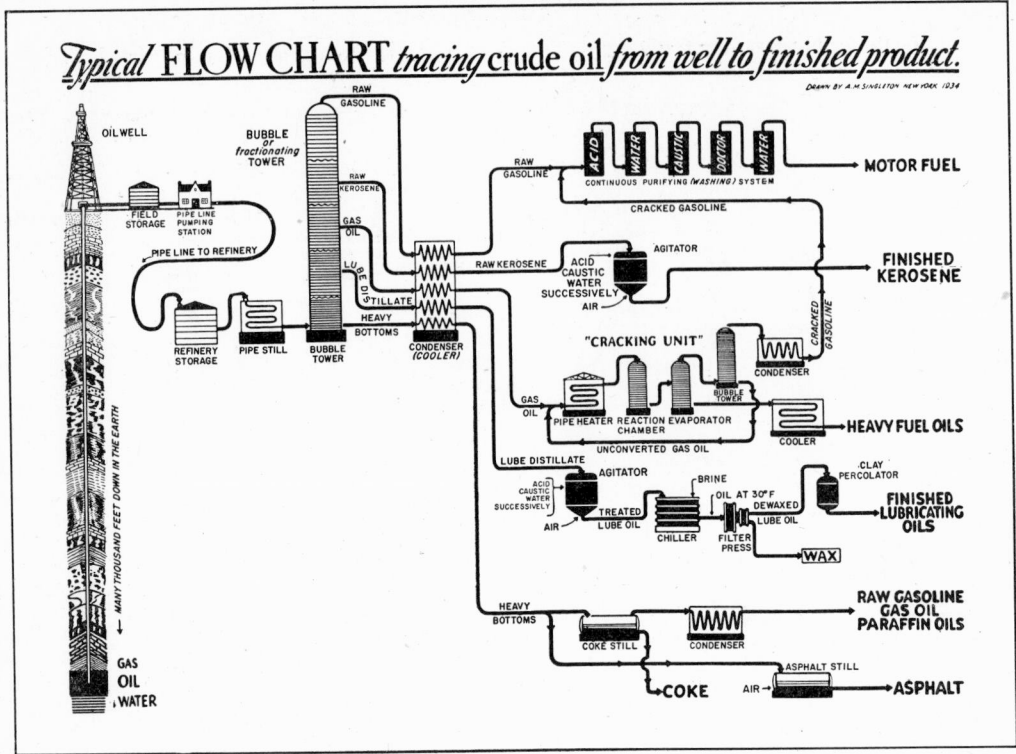

FIGURE 261. OIL REFINING: FLOW FROM WELL TO FINISHED PRODUCT

　　　Crude oil is transferred, by a system of pipes, from the oil well to the refinery. Refining is carried out in a bubble, or fractionating, tower. Various products — raw gasoline, raw kerosene, gas oil, lube distillate and others — are moved from the tower to the cooler. Here begins a separate processing of each product. Raw gasoline, combined with cracked gasoline obtained from gas oil, is processed to motor fuel. Raw kerosene is purified into finished kerosene. Gas oil is cracked and used partly for the production of motor fuel, and partly for heavy fuel oils. Lube distillate yields lubricating oils and wax. "Heavy bottoms" serve to produce coke, asphalt, raw gasoline, gas oil and paraffin oils.

TABLE 379

OIL REFINING: AVERAGE YIELD OF PRINCIPAL PRODUCTS FROM CRUDE OIL IN THE
UNITED STATES, 1880–1950

(*Per Cent*)

Year	Gasoline	Kerosene	Gas Oil and Distillates [a]	Residual Fuel Oil [b]	Lubricating Oils	Other
1880	10.3	75.2	. . .	. . .	2.1	12.4
1889	12.8	65.9	. . .	. . .	7.7	13.6
1899	12.9	57.6	14.0	. . .	9.1	6.4
1909	10.7	33.0	33.6	. . .	10.7	12.0
1919	25.2	15.4	50.2	. . .	5.6	3.6
1929	39.3	5.7	45.5	. . .	3.5	6.0
1939	45.0	5.5	13.1	24.7	2.8	8.9
1948	40.1	6.0	18.5	23.5	2.5	9.4
1949	43.7	5.2	17.5	21.7	2.3	9.6
1950	43.0	5.6	19.0	20.2	2.5	9.7

Source: **18**, 1952, p. 144.

　　a. Includes residual fuel oil through 1929.
　　b. Prior to 1930, included in the preceding column.

TABLE 380

OIL REFINING: NUMBER AND CAPACITY OF PLANTS IN SELECTED COUNTRIES, AS OF JANUARY 1, 1950

| Country | Number of Plants | Capacity, in Thousands of Barrels per Day | | Country | Number of Plants | Capacity, in Thousands of Barrels per Day | |
		Crude Oil	Cracking			Crude Oil	Cracking
World	685	11,375	3,483.1	Hungary	8	19.7	0.4
				Portugal	1	7.5	—
United States	367	6,696.3	1,820.7	Spain	2	5.7	5.4
Canada	33	328.8	166.8	Italy	16	107.2	21.6
Mexico	7	160.4	25.9	Yugoslavia	5	8.3	—
Cuba	6	7.3	1.1	Romania	16	181.5	50.0
Dutch West Indies	3	617.0	511.0				
				USSR	25	650.0	250.0
Trinidad	5	104.3	45.0				
Venezuela	15	253.7	32.0	China	2	17.9	—
Colombia	2	23.7	—	Japan	12	34.3	1.0
Ecuador	2	4.7	—	Turkey	1	1.4	—
Brazil	4	12.0	2.5	Palestine (Israel)	1	83.0	33.0
Peru	3	35.0	6.6	Saudi Arabia	1	140.0	20.0
Bolivia	3	7.2	—	Bahrein Islands	1	150.0	30.0
Uruguay	1	15.7	2.0	Kuwait	1	25.0	—
Argentina	18	152.3	89.5	Iraq	2	9.0	—
				Iran	2	502.1	155.0
United Kingdom	21	196.8	19.2	Lebanon	1	6.0	—
Ireland	1	0.6	—				
France [a]	16	305.7	73.4	Pakistan	1	4.8	2.0
Belgium	7	15.8	3.5	India	1	5.8	1.5
Netherlands	2	77.0	24.4	Burma	2	4.0	—
Denmark	3	0.6	—	Indonesia	8	203.1	58.0
Sweden	4	25.8	2.9				
Norway	1	1.0	—	Egypt	2	39.0	7.0
				Union of South Africa	1	—	2.0
Germany	26	71.1	9.5	Canary Islands	1	10.0	5.0
Poland	6	7.1	—				
Austria	9	26.1	3.7	Australia	5	14.0	1.6

Source: **18,** 1950, pp. 454–55.

a. The Monnet Five Year Plan envisaged the expansion of daily capacity to 348,000 barrels by July 1, 1952.

Capacity

The world's capacity for refining petroleum increased from 7.1 million barrels per day before World War II to 9.3 million in 1948 and 11.4 million at the beginning of 1950. By the end of that year, the number of refineries in the world rose to 689, and their daily charging capacity of crude oil to 12.8 million barrels. Of these, the United States had 347 plants with a daily capacity of 6.9 million barrels of crude oil; Canada, 39 and 303,800, respectively; and the USSR, 27 and 970,000, respectively.[75] The United States had, in 1950, more than half the world's cracking

capacity: 1.8 million barrels per day out of a total of 3.5 million. (See Table 380.)

Texas and California account for about 40–45 per cent of the refining capacity of the United States. Next come Pennsylvania, Louisiana, Illinois, New Jersey and Indiana. The largest refinery (235,000 barrels per day) is in Louisiana, and the three next largest (190,000–230,000 barrels per day) are in Texas.[76]

The two largest refineries of the world, however, are outside the United States: the plant at Abadan, Iran (crude charging capacity, 500,000 barrels a day) and the Standard Oil plant on the

75. **49,** July 15, 1951, p. 84.

76. **42,** p. 37.

TABLE 381

PETROLEUM PRODUCTS: OUTPUT IN SELECTED COUNTRIES, 1938–49

(*Millions of Barrels*)

Country	Gasoline			Kerosene			Fuel, Gas, Diesel Oil			Lubricating Oils		
	1938	1948	1949	1938	1948	1949	1938	1948	1949	1938	1948	1949
United States	556.0	921.9	954.0	60.0 [a]	121.9	102.1	475.8 [a]	846.8	764.8	38.3 [a]	51.4	45.1
Canada	18.7	35.4	41.7	0.6	3.3	4.0	13.8	33.1	34.8	0.6	1.8	1.6
Mexico	16.1	9.9	10.6	0.3	2.4	2.6	21.7	30.6	33.7	0.4	0.3	0.2
Dutch West Indies	29.6	40.2 [b]	...	4.8	9.4 [b]	...	111.1	164.9 [b]	...	2.2	1.4 [b]	...
Venezuela	1.1	4.1	6.6	0.1	0.7	2.2	8.0	38.0	43.3	—	—	—
Peru	2.3	3.9	4.0	1.0	0.9	1.1	2.7	6.8	7.0	0.03	0.07	0.07
Argentina	7.6	8.5 [b]	...	1.7	3.3 [b]	...	10.8	12.2 [b]	...	0.4	...	...
United Kingdom	5.4	7.7 [b]	...	0.8	...	...	8.0	3.7 [b]	...	0.5	2.3 [b]	...
France	20.3	15.1	22.0	2.1	2.1	2.2	18.8	33.3	49.3	1.6	1.5	1.4
Germany	13.2	1.4 [b]	...	0.6	0.3 [b]	...	4.0	2.4 [b]	...	1.1	0.4 [b]	...
Poland	0.8	0.3 [b]	...	1.0	0.1 [b]	...	1.2	...	...	...	0.1 [b]	...
Italy	3.6	3.6	4.8	1.2	1.5	1.0	4.7	9.9	13.4	0.5	0.2	0.3
Romania	12.9	9.4 [b]	...	6.5	4.1 [b]	...	20.4	13.6 [b]	...	0.5	0.7 [b]	...
USSR	36.3 [c]	23.9 [b]	...	46.8 [c]	37.4 [b]	...	83.1 [c]	59.8 [b]	...	9.4 [c]	7.7 [b]	...
Japan	5.1	0.2 [b]	...	1.0	0.2 [b]	...	4.7	0.6 [b]	...	2.2	0.3 [b]	...
Saudi Arabia	...	7.7 [b]	...	...	3.9 [b]	...	...	17.8 [b]	...	—	—	—
Bahrein Islands	2.6	8.9 [b]	...	1.1	4.5 [b]	...	3.3	20.6 [b]	...	—	—	—
Iran	21.0	29.4 [b]	...	5.5	9.2 [b]	...	48.2	78.4 [b]	...	—	—	—
Indonesia	19.3	0.1 [b]	...	7.2	0.2 [b]	...	19.3	0.7 [b]	...	0.2	...	...
Egypt	0.8	1.5 [b]	...	0.1	0.5 [b]	...	1.1	5.0 [b]	...	—	—	—

Source: **11,** various years.   b. 1946. (**18,** 1950, pp. 457–58.)

    a. 1939.   c. 1940. (**14,** p. 16.)

island of Aruba (400,000 barrels). The Aruba plant and the Dutch Shell plant on the island of Curaçao (217,000 barrels), both in the West Indies, process crude oil from Venezuela almost exclusively.[77] During the war both plants built new units for producing 100-octane gasoline. The Abadan plant is among the largest and most modern for production of such gasoline.

The two oil-producing areas in the Middle East — Saudi Arabia and the Bahrein Islands — also have modern refineries. Iraq's newest refinery, south of Basra, with a daily capacity of 700,000 barrels was scheduled for completion late in 1952. In comparison with the Middle East, Europe and the USSR have a rather modest refining capacity.

An important postwar development is the considerable increase in the refining capacity of western Europe, partly through its own efforts and partly with the aid of the Economic Cooperation Administration. Further expansion can be expected, which, coupled with the growing crude oil output in the Middle East, makes the Eastern Hemisphere more and more independent of the Western, previously the chief source of finished petroleum products. If this tendency continues and the flow of crude oil from the Middle East is assured, the two hemispheres may become independent producing and consuming areas although some marginal amounts of petroleum and petroleum products will be traded between them.[78]

The USSR, without a single petroleum-cracking refinery unit in 1928, had, by 1937, obtained about six tenths of its gasoline by the cracking

77. The sand bars off the petroleum-producing shores of Venezuela do not permit tankers to enter. Specially built shallow ships carry the oil from Venezuela to Aruba and Curaçao for processing. Foreign tankers use the deep harbors of these islands to load the refined products for delivery to various parts of the world. **13,** p. 132.

78. **31,** October 1951, p. 11.

TABLE 382

PETROLEUM PRODUCTS: OUTPUT IN THE UNITED STATES, 1920–50

(Millions of Barrels [a]*)*

Product	1920	1925	1930	1935	1940	1945	1948	1949	1950 [b]
Total	437	760	971	997	1,333	1,790	2,107	2,030	2,190
Gasoline	116	260	432	458	597	774	896	939	998
Kerosene	55	60	49	56	74	81	122	102	119
Fuel oil:									
Distillate	}211	365{	82	100	183	249	379	341	399
Residual			291	260	316	469	486	425	425
Lubricating oil	25	31	34	28	37	42	51	45	52
Wax	1.9	2.1	2.0	1.6	1.8	2.9	3.5	3.2	4.5
Coke	0.1	5.3	9.9	7.3	7.6	10	14	17	17
Asphalt	0.02	15	18	17	20	39	52	49	58
Still gas	. . .	. . .	5.4	51	76	103	81	83	84
Other	30	21	48	18	20	20	39	26	43

Sources: **10**, p. 15; **12**, 1945, p. 1096; 1946, p. 924; 1948, p. 959; **18**, 1950, p. 217; **8**, 1951, p. 697.

a. Conversion factors: 280 pounds of wax to the bar-rel; 5 short tons of coke and 5.5 short tons of asphalt to the barrel; 3,600 cubic feet of still gas to the barrel.

b. Preliminary.

process.[79] By January 1, 1950 it had, in its 25 refineries, a daily capacity of 650,000 barrels, of which 250,000 barrels were in cracking units.

PETROLEUM PRODUCTS

Motor and fuel oils, kerosene, still gases and lubricants are the chief products obtained from petroleum. In the United States, these products together account for about 95 per cent of the refined yield of all crude petroleum.[80] (See Table 382.) The remainder goes into waxes, road oil, asphalt and many other products. Some petroleum-derived products that consume only a small percentage of the crude oil output are nevertheless of great importance. Among these are

79. **45**, pp. 220–21.

80. For about half a century after the beginning of petroleum production in the United States, kerosene and lubricating oils were the principal products. After the turn of the century, fuel oils also became important, and after 1910 the demand for gasoline began to grow until it finally became the chief product of refining. **24**, p. 331.

The first known use of oil as fuel was in Russia in 1861, and in 1882 nearly a hundred and fifty locomotives on one Russian railroad were converted to oil. In the United States, oil was used experimentally as fuel for marine boilers in California in 1865, and in the late 1880's experiments were made in the use of oil as a fuel for locomotives. The British Admiralty pioneered in the naval use of oil, and in 1909–10 the American navy introduced auxiliary oil burners on some battleships. (**17**, pp. 276–77.)

butadiene, the most important raw material in the production of synthetic rubber; and various petroleum oils, gases and residues used in plastics, drugs and anesthetics, insecticides and fumigating compounds.

The output of refineries in the United States quintupled between 1920 and 1950, increasing from 0.4 billion barrels to 2.2 billion. The greatest increases were in the output of gasoline from 116 to 998 million barrels and in that of fuel oil, from 211 to 824 million barrels. (See Table 382.)

TRANSPORTATION OF PETROLEUM

Modern methods of transporting oil, used more or less in all oil-producing countries, include pipelines,[81] tankers, tank cars and trucks.

Pipelines are used chiefly to bring crude oil from the oil fields to refineries, although they also transport some refined products. Previously of modest length and diameter, they are now laid over great distances and may be thirty inches or even more in diameter.

Tankers, the "water pipelines," distribute enormous quantities of petroleum and its products all over the world. Some tankers have a carrying capacity of 165,000 barrels yet can dock

81. The earliest known pipeline system existed 2,000 years ago in China where natural gas for heating the palaces was carried through bamboo pipes. **28**, p. 304.

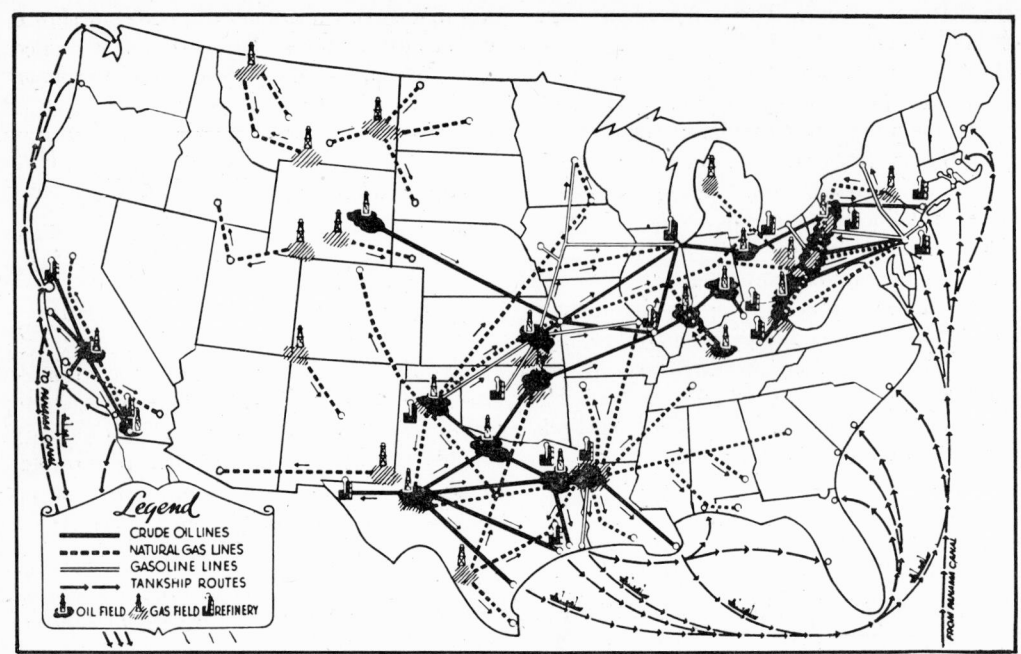

American Petroleum Institute

FIGURE 262. TRANSPORTATION OF PETROLEUM IN THE UNITED STATES, 1948

This map shows only the important pipeline systems and the more heavily traveled tank-ship routes that make petroleum and its refined products available to every section of the United States. The arrows indicate the direction of the flow from important oil fields to refineries and from refineries to the major consuming centers.

and unload within 24 hours.[82] Oil stations have largely replaced the old coaling stations in international trade.

Tank cars and, more recently, tank trucks transport both crude oil and refined products.

THE UNITED STATES

The United States has the largest and most efficient system of oil and gas transportation in the world. (See Figure 262.)

Pipelines

In 1949, the country had about 160,000 miles of oil pipelines, laid across mountains and rivers, under swamps and bayous, railways, highways, canals and city streets. They operate day and night throughout the year and deliver their products on schedule, like trains on a railroad. Like railroads, the pipelines have stations, switch systems, depots and terminals. Pipelines are made today of seamless, high-alloy steel, are electrically welded, and require no maintenance for many years.

It has taken many decades to develop this system. When production started in the United States, oil was carried from the fields in every imaginable container — barrels, buckets and even bottles. Soon teamsters started moving oil in wooden barrels to rivers on which boats carried it downstream to railroad stations. Railroads, too, first carried oil in barrels, later in tank cars.

Attempts in the 1860's to move oil through pipelines met with violent opposition from teamsters who, trying to protect their jobs, often cut the lines. In 1874, when the first trunk line was laid from oil fields to refineries, the railroads also began to fight this new means of transportation. They destroyed the pipes, refused right of way across their land and used their influence in legislatures to forbid the lines.[83] But the economic and technical advantages were on the side of the pipelines. Their rates were cheaper and they moved oil faster and more conveniently. These advantages, however, were not realized immediately. The early pipelines leaked, corroded, moved the oil slowly and in jerks, and needed frequent repairs. Only gradually were

---

82. **33**, p. 507.

83. **26**, pp. 104–06.

these defects overcome. The first seamless pipe was laid in 1928.

Pipelines are common carriers and are subject to regulation by the Interstate Commerce Commission if they cross state lines. About 84 per cent of the pipeline mileage in the United States is interstate, the rest intrastate. Except for a few independent lines representing about a tenth of the total mileage, the lines belong, in one way or another, to the big oil companies.

About three fourths of all crude oil supplied to the refineries comes directly through pipelines, and practically all crude oil produced in the United States is believed to be piped at least part of the way to the refineries.[84] In 1949, pipelines transported 2.5 billion barrels of oil.

During World War II, the system of pipelines was expanded and rebuilt. In particular, it was essential to increase the movement of oil to the eastern ports. Two new lines, longer and larger than any previously built, were laid from the Southwest to Philadelphia and New York with government financing — the Big Inch (24-inch pipe) over 1,254 miles and the Little Big Inch (20-inch pipe) over 1,475 miles. Their combined daily capacity is about half a million barrels. The flow in some existing lines was changed; for example, the flow from east Texas to the Gulf Coast was reversed to pour oil into the Big Inch at Longview, Texas. The pipelines also began to carry a larger volume of gasoline than before, in 1944 more than a third of the national output.

In 1947 a new and still bigger pipeline, 26 to 30 inches in diameter, began to stretch from Texas to the Los Angeles district.

Tankers

In contrast to the pipelines, most tankers are largely owned and operated by shipping companies rather than oil companies. Before World War II, tankers supplied the refineries with about 22 per cent of the crude oil produced, but their main task has been to transport petroleum products from refineries to markets. About two hundred and fifty tankers were in regular service between the Gulf and Atlantic ports; tankers carried some 97 per cent of the petroleum products consumed in the Atlantic area. Other ships served the Pacific Coast.

Early in the war, many tankers were lost through submarine attack, yet it was necessary to ship tremendous quantities of petroleum abroad for the armed forces. The government carried out a vast shipbuilding program with the following results: [85]

	September 1, 1939	September 30, 1945
Number of tankers	389	949
Gross tonnage, in thousands	2,837	8,659
Dead-weight tonnage, in thousands	4,451	13,820

After the war, the government disposed of almost all its tankers. Many hundreds were sold to private owners at home and abroad. On January 1, 1949, of the 793 tankers it had constructed, the government held only seventeen in the reserve fleet and four under repair for sale. [86]

Tank Cars and Trucks

Most of the tank cars hauled by the railroads belong to the oil companies. Of the 152,183 railroad tank cars in service on January 1, 1950, only 9,219, or about 6 per cent, were railroad-owned.[87] During the war, this service became of great importance. Railroad tank cars were called upon to replace the tankers moving in convoys to the overseas fronts and to carry petroleum overland from the producing centers to the ports. While the railroads (and trucks) supplied only 0.3 per cent of all petroleum to the Atlantic Coast area in 1940, in 1942 they delivered 51 per cent and in 1943, 60 per cent.[88]

Substantial quantities of petroleum products are transported by truck from terminal centers to distribution stations. The number of tank trucks in the United States has been estimated at 40,000, most of them controlled by the large oil companies.[89]

OTHER COUNTRIES

The world's demand for oil has become so great that pipelines are pushing out through remote areas and tankers traverse the seven seas.

Pipelines

Pipelines outside the United States exceed 85,000 miles in length. Every oil-producing coun-

---

84. Except perhaps a small amount delivered from the wells directly to tank cars and trucks. **18**, 1947, p. 137.

85. **18**, 1947, p. 146.
86. **36**, December 30, 1948, p. 154.
87. **18**, 1950, p. 292.
88. **13**, p. 72.
89. **33**, p. 532.

try in the Western Hemisphere has built some lines to refineries or shipping ports. Canada has built its first major line, the Interprovincial (1,127 miles long), from Alberta to the Great Lakes.[90] The first two sections — a 20-inch pipeline (439 miles) from Edmonton to Regina, and the 16-inch line (336 miles) to Gretna, Manitoba — were completed in 1950 and by the spring of 1951 were in full operation, with a daily capacity of 95,000 barrels. Crude oil is moved in this line from Alberta across the prairies to Lake Superior and transshipped by tankers to the refineries at Sarnia, Ontario.[91]

No sooner was the Interprovincial line completed than the need for its expansion became evident. Many pumping stations are being added, and some 100 miles of the central section are being looped. One major pipeline is under construction, and another is planned, to transport petroleum products from expanding Canadian refineries to eastern markets.[92]

Venezuela recently laid a 144-mile line of 24–26-inch pipe.

The USSR has several thousand miles of pipelines. Russia's first pipeline, 9 miles long, was laid in 1879 from Baku to a refinery. In 1905 the important line from Baku on the Caspian Sea to Batum on the Black Sea, 550 miles long, was completed. A few years later, the line from Grozny to Makhachkala was laid to transport oil to the Caspian Sea and thence by sea to the Volga. Under the Soviets, additional lines have been built, of 8–12-inch pipe and, for the most part, less than 100 miles long.[93] All the lines together pipe only 11.4 per cent of the oil in the USSR; 45.9 per cent is transported by water and 42.7 per cent by rail.[94]

Romania has pipelines from the oil fields to the port of Constantsa on the Black Sea.

Iran has eleven pipelines, all laid by the Anglo-Iranian Company, and a huge 34–36-inch line was planned. In Iraq, two pipelines from the main Kirkuk field were in operation, one to Haifa and the other to Tripoli; an additional line to Haifa was under construction. Saudi Arabia has a few lines built in recent years, with a total carrying capacity of almost 900,000 barrels daily. The world's largest pipeline (Tapline, built by

the Trans-Arabian Pipe Line Company), 30–31 inches in diameter and 1,068 miles long, was completed in September 1950. Stretching from the Persian Gulf to the Mediterranean, it will move crude oil from Saudi Arabia's oil fields across the desert to Sidon, Lebanon, and is expected to obviate 3,500 miles of tanker runs around the Arabian peninsula and to change the entire pattern of oil distribution from the Middle East to Europe.[95]

During World War II the United States government built a 2,000-mile pipeline from Calcutta to China.[96]

Africa's first pipeline has been laid to transport refined products to Tanganyika.

Tankers

On the eve of World War II, the tanker fleet of countries outside the United States comprised 1,047 vessels, with a total gross tonnage of 7.3 million. The United Kingdom, with 406 units and 2.9 million gross tons, had a larger fleet than any other country, including the United States. Norway was also very active in oil transportation, with 263 tankers totaling 2.1 million gross tons.

Both these countries and the Netherlands, France and some other European countries lost many tankers during the war, and there was no replacement by new units, as in the United States. By September 30, 1945, the world fleet of tankers, (except for the United States) had shrunk to 857 units totaling 5.9 million gross tons. (See Table 383.) While the United States increased its tanker fleet far beyond its peacetime needs, the fleets of European countries were substantially smaller at the close of the war; in fact, the United States had a much greater capacity than all other nations combined.

Since that time, the world's tanker fleet has gradually shifted toward its prewar distribution. Great Britain and Norway launched large construction programs, placing orders in Great Britain, the United States and Sweden. In 1949-50 the world's tanker fleet consisted of 2,089 vessels totaling 15.8 million gross tons. The share of the United States in the gross tonnage of the world's tanker fleet was about 28 per cent in 1939, rose to almost 60 per cent in 1945 but fell to about 30 per cent in 1949–50. The United Kingdom and Norway now have larger tonnages

90. Cf. p. 902.
91. **49,** November 1950, p. 304.
92. **49,** December 1951, pp. 233 ff.
93. **49,** July 1948, p. 263.
94. **21,** p. 221.

95. **49,** November 1950, p. 285.
96. **30,** p. 435.

TABLE 383

TRANSPORTATION OF PETROLEUM: TANKER FLEETS OF THE WORLD, BY COUNTRIES, 1939–50

	September 1, 1939		September 30, 1945		1949–50	
Country	*Number*	*Gross Tonnage, in Thousands*	*Number*	*Gross Tonnage, in Thousands*	*Number*	*Gross Tonnage, in Thousands*
World	1,436	10,147	1,806	14,594	2,089	15,824
United States [a]	389	2,837	949	8,659	544	4,736
Canada	11	94	30	164	59	237
Panama	53	468	66	479	186	1,525
Venezuela	23	63	23	65	36	108
Argentina	25	140	24	146	32	188
United Kingdom	406	2,862	347	2,451	493	3,690
France	49	321	24	164	65	545
Belgium	10	70	4	29	4	33
Netherlands	105	526	77	388	95	485
Denmark	13	105	10	87	17	142
Sweden	20	169	36	316	42	374
Norway	263	2,073	168	1,393	241	2,131
Spain	...	...	...	...	24	137
Italy	...	...	...	...	72	513
Greece	7	31	4	18	—	—
USSR	22	122	16	83	32	140
Japan	—	—	—	—	31	194
Other	40	266	28	152	166	644

Sources: **18,** 1947, p. 143; **36,** December 30, 1948, p. 153; **37,** January 26, 1951, p. 61.

a. Includes vessels owned by the Army and Navy.

than before the war but their share in the total is somewhat smaller.

CONSUMPTION OF PETROLEUM

Consumption of petroleum is increasing rapidly in many parts of the world under the impact of progress in mechanization in agriculture and motorization of transport. Relative gains are most spectacular in countries that only recently shifted to the use of petroleum for these purposes.

Detailed data on petroleum consumption are available for prewar years only. Some of them have become obsolete, but nevertheless they stress the general pattern in the distribution of petroleum consumption in the world at large and in individual countries.

In 1938, the world consumed 1.9 billion barrels of petroleum: 771 million of motor fuel, 749 of fuel oil, 147 million of kerosene, and 54 and 198 million barrels, respectively, of lubricants and of all other products. Lubricating oils, though all-important in our modern economy, represented less than 3 per cent of the total.

North America accounted for about two thirds of the total consumption; Europe used less than a sixth; and the USSR less than a tenth. In North America, Europe and Oceania, motor fuel was the major item of consumption; in Latin America, the USSR, Asia and Africa, fuel oil was most important. (See Table 384.)

Among petroleum-consuming countries, the United States is in a class by itself. With about 6.5 per cent of the world's population, it uses more petroleum than all the rest of the world. Motor fuel ranks first in its consumption and fuel oil comes next.

In the USSR, the second important consumer, agriculture consumed before the war 60 per cent of all petroleum, and fuel oil was the major product consumed, followed by kerosene. It is reported that 80 per cent of all fuel oil and nearly 70 per cent of all kerosene were used in agriculture as a source of power. Gasoline constituted about 15–17 per cent of all refined products.[97]

In the United Kingdom, France, Canada and Germany, motor fuel accounted for half or

97. **47,** p. 85; **14,** p. 16.

TABLE 384

CONSUMPTION OF PETROLEUM IN EACH CONTINENT, BY TYPE OF PRODUCT, 1938

Continent	Millions of Barrels						Per Cent					
	Total	Motor Fuel	Kero-sene	Lubri-cants	Fuel Oil	Other Products	Total	Motor Fuel	Kero-sene	Lubri-cants	Fuel Oil	Other Products
World [a]	1,918	771	147	54	749	198	100.0	40.2	7.7	2.8	39.1	10.3
North America	1,189	551	57	22	426	133	100.0	46.3	4.8	1.9	35.7	11.2
Middle and South America	117	21	5	2	83	6	100.0	17.9	4.3	1.7	70.9	5.1
Europe	295	130	20	14	108	23	100.0	44.1	6.8	4.7	36.6	7.8
USSR	165	27	42	10	65	21	100.0	16.4	25.5	6.1	39.4	12.7
Asia	96	18	16	4	44	14	100.0	18.7	16.7	4.2	45.8	14.6
Africa	28	10	4	1	11	1	100.0	35.7	14.3	3.6	39.3	7.1
Oceania	26	15	2	1	7	1	100.0	57.7	7.7	3.8	26.9	3.8

Sources: **18**, 1947, pp. 212–13 and 218–21.

a. World totals include small undistributed amounts.

Military consumption not included, except in the United States.

nearly half of the total consumption. In contrast, Italy, Romania and Japan used more fuel oil than motor fuel. (See Table 385.)

In postwar years, consumption of petroleum increased throughout the world, and in 1948 was nearly 80 per cent greater than in 1938: the daily demand for petroleum was 9.3 and 5.3 million barrels, respectively. In the United States, the daily consumption rose from 3.2 million barrels in 1938 to 5.8 million in 1948. In some other areas, the rate of increase was even higher: in Africa, for example, nearly three times as much petroleum was consumed in 1948 as in 1938.

Current consumption of petroleum continues to rise at an accelerated rate throughout the world — more in other countries than in the United States. Domestic demand in the United States rose by about 12 per cent between 1948 and 1950; in the rest of the Western Hemisphere, by 17 per cent; in Europe, by 36 per cent; in the USSR, by some 25 per cent, and in the Middle East, by about 40 per cent.

As this trend gains momentum, the share of the United States in the world's consumption of petroleum, although still predominant, declines: in 1948, it amounted to 61.8 per cent; in 1950 to 59.1 per cent. The rest of the Western Hemisphere now consumes more than 11 per cent and Africa 2.5 per cent of the world's total, as compared with 8.6 and 1.5 per cent, respectively, in 1938. The shares of Europe and the USSR in the total consumption are also rising, but are still below the prewar level. (See Table 386.)

Per Capita Consumption

Per capita consumption of petroleum products in various countries is controlled by three factors: industrial development; the transportation system; and the national output of oil. The United States, with its high degree of industrialization and large use of motorized transportation, as well as its leading position in oil output, ranks first. Its per capita consumption of 8.8 barrels in 1938 was more than four times the rate in the United Kingdom or Argentina, and about nine times that in the USSR. In 1945, per capita consumption in the United States was 12.7 barrels, and in 1950, 15.7 barrels.

Canada comes next, with 4.6 barrels per capita in 1938, and 9.1 barrels in 1949. The USSR raised its per capita consumption from 1 to 4 barrels between 1938 and 1950, and Sweden, from 1.4 to nearly 4 barrels. An increase in per capita consumption, of varying magnitude, is characteristic of all countries for which information is available: consumption rose in the United Kingdom from 1.9 to 2.9 barrels; in France, from 1.3 to 1.9 barrels; in Norway, from 1.4 to 3.4 barrels. (See Table 387.)

Consumption in the United States

The United States, with its more than fifty million motor vehicles and thousands of aircraft, uses more motor fuel than it does any other petroleum product. While it consumed almost twice as much fuel oil as motor fuel in 1918, demand for the latter has outstripped that for fuel

TABLE 385

CONSUMPTION OF PETROLEUM IN SELECTED COUNTRIES, BY TYPE OF PRODUCT, 1939 [a]

(*Millions of Barrels*)

Country	Total	Motor Fuel	Kerosene	Lubricants	Fuel Oil	Other Products [b]
United States	1,236.1 [c]	560.5	60.5	23.7	458.5	132.9
Canada	49.2	24.3	1.0	1.3	18.4	4.2
Mexico	18.6	3.5	0.8	0.2	12.7	1.4
Panama [d]	3.1	0.1	0.03	0.03	2.9	0.04
Puerto Rico	1.9	0.6	0.09	0.04	1.2	0.05
Trinidad	5.1	0.1	0.08	0.04	4.4	0.5
Dutch West Indies	19.9	0.3	0.05	0.05	15.5	4.0
Venezuela	9.5	1.2	0.04	0.04	8.0	0.2
Colombia	3.4	0.9	0.1	0.03	2.2	0.1
Brazil	9.3	3.3	0.8	0.3	4.8	0.1
Peru	2.4	0.5	0.2	0.03	1.5	0.2
Chile	5.3	0.8	0.07	0.08	4.3	0.06
Uruguay	3.3	0.8	0.3	0.04	2.1	0.05
Argentina	31.0	8.0	1.9	0.6	18.6	1.9
United Kingdom	88.2	44.0	7.0	2.9	29.9	4.4
France	44.2	22.0	1.4	1.8	15.0	4.0
Belgium	6.8	4.0	0.2	0.5	1.6	0.5
Netherlands	11.8	4.1	2.0	0.6	4.3	0.8
Denmark	6.9	2.9	0.9	0.2	2.7	0.2
Sweden	11.0	5.1	1.0	0.5	3.7	0.7
Norway	5.3	2.0	0.4	0.1	2.6	0.2
Finland	2.4	1.5	0.6	0.1	0.1	0.1
Germany [e]	56.7	25.9	0.8	4.0	18.7	7.3
Poland [e]	3.1	0.8	1.0	0.3	0.6	0.4
Czechoslovakia [e]	2.2	1.2	0.4	0.2	0.4	—
Switzerland	3.3	1.6	0.2	0.2	1.2	0.1
Hungary	2.4	0.8	0.6	0.1	0.7	0.2
Portugal	1.6	0.6	0.4	0.08	0.5	—
Spain	5.3	3.0	0.2	0.2	1.8	0.1
Italy	21.8	5.7	1.0	1.0	12.2	1.9
Yugoslavia	1.1	0.4	0.2	0.07	0.3	0.1
Romania	14.4	1.3	1.5	0.2	10.0	1.4
Bulgaria	0.8	0.2	0.3	0.05	0.2	0.07
Greece	2.9	0.6	0.2	0.08	1.9	0.1
USSR	170.6	28.0	44.0	9.6	67.0	22.0
China	4.4	0.8	1.7	0.2	1.4	0.3
Japan	25.4	8.0	1.5	1.8	12.0	2.1
Turkey	1.3	0.45	0.35	0.06	0.4	0.02
Palestine	1.8	0.4	0.5	0.03	0.7	0.2
Iraq	4.2	0.4	0.3	0.06	2.7	0.8
Iran	11.1	0.7	1.3	0.5	6.0	2.6
India	15.7	3.1	6.1	1.0	4.6	0.9
Burma	1.6	0.2	0.05	0.05	1.0	0.3
Thailand	0.6	0.1	0.2	0.03	0.2	0.06
Indochina	0.9	0.3	0.3	0.04	0.2	0.1
Ceylon	3.2	0.4	0.2	0.02	2.5	0.1
British Malaya	4.9	1.1	0.3	0.1	3.2	0.2
Indonesia	11.5	1.5	2.0	0.3	6.2	1.5
Philippines	4.3	1.1	0.4	0.1	2.5	0.2

(*Continued on page 916*)

TABLE 385—*continued*

Country	Total	Motor Fuel	Kerosene	Lubricants	Fuel Oil	Other Products [b]
French Morocco	1.5	0.9	0.1	0.05	0.3	0.2
Algeria	2.0	1.0	0.3	0.09	0.5	0.1
Egypt	6.3	0.9	2.6	0.3	2.2	0.3
French West Africa	5.8	0.4	0.1	0.05	5.2	0.02
Union of South Africa	10.3	5.8	0.7	0.4	3.0	0.4
Australia	16.3	10.5	1.2	0.5	3.1	1.0
New Zealand	5.2	3.3	0.2	0.1	1.3	0.3
Hawaii	4.1	1.2	0.2	0.1	2.5	0.1

Source: **18,** 1947, pp. 212–13 and 218–21.

    a. Excludes military consumption except in the United States.
    b. Includes related fuels: natural gasoline, benzol, power alcohol, and synthetic mineral oils from coal and shale.
    c. Includes small amounts of butane-propane.
    d. Panama Canal Zone.
    e. 1938.

TABLE 386

CONSUMPTION OF PETROLEUM IN MAJOR REGIONS, PER DAY, 1938–50

Region	Thousands of Barrels Per Day				Percentage Distribution			
	1938	1948	1949	1950	1938	1948	1949	1950
World	5,250	9,340	9,747	10,978	100.0	100.0	100.0	100.0
United States	3,125	5,775	5,792	6,491	59.5	61.8	59.4	59.1
Rest of the Western Hemisphere	452	1,045	1,089	1,221	8.6	11.2	11.2	11.1
Europe	808	1,070	1,227	1,451	15.4	11.5	12.5	13.2
USSR	452	618	707	770 [a]	8.6	6.6	7.3	7.0
Africa	77	213	237	276	1.5	2.3	2.4	2.5
Middle East	} 334 {	182	212	256	} 6.4 {	2.0	2.2	2.3
Far East and Oceania		438	484	512		4.6	5.0	4.7

Source: **49,** July 15, 1951, p. 51.

    a. The estimate for 1951 is about 10 per cent higher. **31,** October 1951, p. 10.

oil since the mid-1930's. In 1950, the United States consumed more motor fuel per day than some European countries in a whole year.

Consumption of fuel oil in the United States rose from 501 million barrels in 1940 to 823 million in 1949. Distillate fuel oil accounted for about 40 per cent of the consumption in 1949, and residual fuel oil for 60 per cent. The chief use of distillate oil is for heating, while smelters, mines and manufacturing industries, as well as ships' bunkers and railroads, are the chief consumers of residual oil.

The United States consumed nearly 70 million barrels of kerosene in 1940 and 103 million in 1949, for illumination, cooking and, to a small extent, for tractor fuel. The increase was due largely to the growing demand for range oil.

The three most important markets for kerosene, accounting for some 60 per cent of the nation's consumption, are the New England, Middle and South Atlantic states.[98]

Consumption of lubricating oils increased from 24.7 million barrels in 1940 to 33 million in 1949. (See Table 388.)

INTERNATIONAL CAPITAL IN THE OIL INDUSTRY

American, British and Dutch capital play a very important role in many oil-producing countries in all phases of the oil industry — production, refining, transportation and marketing. This capital is provided by a few big companies, which may operate independently or combine their interests.

98. **18,** 1950, p. 37.

Six American companies, one British (Anglo-Iranian) and one Dutch (the Dutch-Shell Group, with Dutch and British capital) accounted before World War II for half the world's output of oil outside the United States or for about 80 per cent of that output excluding production in the USSR and Mexico, where it is government controlled. In 1939, the world output of 2,085 million barrels was distributed as follows (in millions): [99]

United States	1,265
USSR	217
Mexico	43
All other countries	560
American companies	203
British companies	85
Dutch companies	150
Local and other	122

The share of American capital in the oil industries in other countries is illustrated by the percentage of output and reserves that were American-owned in various years: [100]

	Annual Output	Estimated Reserves
Canada	29	14
Venezuela, 1944	71	74
Colombia, 1943	100	90
Peru, 1943	80	81
Bolivia	100	. . .
Argentina	5	. . .
Hungary, 1937	99	. . .
Italy	63	. . .
Saudi Arabia	100	100
Bahrein Islands	100	100
Kuwait	50	50
Indonesia, 1939	27	35
Ethiopia	100	. . .

In 1944, American interests controlled 72 per cent of the proven oil reserves in the Caribbean area; 24 per cent in other Latin American countries; 27 per cent in Europe; 30 per cent in the Near and Middle East; and 29 per cent in the rest of the Eastern Hemisphere except the USSR. In 1939, the American share in the total run of foreign refineries (except in the USSR) was 31 per cent.

Concessions in the Middle East are distributed by nationality of holders of concessions as follows: [101]

	Term of Concession, in Years	Nationality of Concessionaire
Saudi Arabia		
360,000 square miles (1933)	66	American
80,000 square miles (1939)	66	American
Jordan, all (1947)	75	British
Bahrein Islands and territorial waters, all (1940)	55	American
Kuwait, all (1934)	75	Anglo-American
Oman and Dhofar, all (1937) [a]	75	British
Iraq, all (1925–38)	60–75	International [b]
Qatar, all (1935)	75	International [b]
Syria, 41,700 square miles (1940)	75	International [b]

a. Exploration permit only.
b. Anglo-Dutch-French-American.

The Anglo-Iranian Oil Company had a 60-year concession in Iran which was terminated in 1951 by the Iranian government; all installations for the output of crude oil were nationalized.

NATURAL GAS

Natural gas consists essentially of hydrocarbons in numerous combinations, and some varieties also contain nitrogen, helium or carbon dioxide. It occurs wherever oil is found and has also been discovered in other areas. In the oil reservoirs, gas exists in solution and also often on top of the oil, as the cap gas.

Most natural gas is obtained from fields that produce gas only, but some "wet" (casing-head) gas is produced with petroleum and distributed from many oil fields. Gas is also produced from condensate wells in which the liquids obtained at the surface occur in the reservoir as gas and are formed by the drop in pressure and temperature after the gas has left the reservoir. In the United Sates, most condensate wells are in Texas and Louisiana.[102]

Some gas fields are very extensive. That in

---

99. **13**, p. 96.
100. Cf. **42**, p. 340.

101. **42**, pp. 177–78.
102. **7**, p. 270. The "wet" gas is rich in gasoline fractions, the "dry" gas has none or insignificant amounts of such fractions.

Gasoline recovered from gas is called "natural gasoline" and is used largely for blending.

TABLE 387

CONSUMPTION OF PETROLEUM: PER CAPITA IN SELECTED COUNTRIES, 1938 AND 1950

(*Barrels*)

Country	1938	1950	Country	1938	1950
United States	8.83	15.72	Czechoslovakia	0.19	0.23
Canada	4.63	9.10 [a]	Switzerland	0.85	. . .
Mexico	1.09	. . .	Hungary	0.20	. . .
Venezuela	2.38	. . .	Italy	0.41	0.74
Brazil	0.18	. . .	Romania	0.75	. . .
Peru	0.42	. . .	USSR	0.99	. . .
Chile	1.09	. . .	Japan	0.25	. . .
Uruguay	1.20	. . .	Palestine	1.27	. .
Argentina	2.19	. . .	Iraq	1.34	. . .
United Kingdom	1.91	2.89	Iran	0.71	. . .
France	1.29	1.91	India	0.05	. . .
Belgium	0.69	1.86	Indonesia	0.19	. . .
Netherlands	1.27	2.35	Egypt	0.38	. . .
Denmark	1.65	3.25	Union of South		
Sweden	1.44	3.98	Africa	0.74	. . .
Norway	1.43	3.43			
Finland	0.54	. . .	Australia	2.13	. . .
Germany	0.67	0.55 [b]	New Zealand	2.76	. . .
Poland	0.10	. . .			

Sources: Computed on the basis of **5,** 1950, p. 172; and **18,** 1950, p. 464.

a. 1949.
b. Western Germany. Includes consumption of synthetic oil.

TABLE 388

CONSUMPTION OF PETROLEUM IN THE UNITED STATES BY TYPE OF PRODUCT, 1918–50

(*Thousands of Barrels*)

Year	Total	Motor Fuel	Kerosene	Distillate Fuel Oil	Residual Fuel Oil	Lubricating Oil	Other Products and Losses
1918	359.4	74.5	34.4	[a]	142.8 [b]	13.8	94.0
1920	455.8	101.2	33.1	[a]	186.0 [b]	14.7	120.8
1925	727.0	223.9	40.0	[a]	307.0 [b]	20.6	135.5
1930	926.5	394.8	34.7	[a]	368.5 [b]	21.6	107.0
1935	983.7	434.8	47.6	86.0	280.7	19.7	115.0
1940	1,326.6	589.5	68.8	160.9	340.2	24.7	142.5
1945	1,772.7	696.3	75.6	226.1	523.4	35.3	216.0
1946	1,792.8	735.4	89.1	242.9	480.0	34.9	210.5
1947	1,989.8	795.0	102.5	298.3	518.5	36.5	239.0
1948	2,113.7	871.3	112.2	340.6	500.5	36.0	273.0
1949	2,118.2	913.7	102.7	329.3	496.0	33.1	243.5
1950	2,375.1	994.3	117.8	394.9	553.8	38.9	279.4

Source: **18,** 1952, p. 3.

a. Included with residual fuel oil.
b. Includes distillate fuel oil.

TABLE 389

NATURAL GAS: PROVEN RECOVERABLE RESERVES AND CUMULATIVE OUTPUT IN THE UNITED STATES, 1925–51

(Billions of Cubic Feet)

Year, as of December 31	Reserves	Cumulative Output
1925	23,000	17,363 [a]
1930	46,000	24,238
1934	62,000	30,806
1938	70,000	37,300
1940	85,000	42,440
1945	147,800	59,400
1948	173,870	73,160
1949	180,381	79,405
1950	186,160	85,685
1951	193,800	93,682

Sources: **16,** 1948, p. 20, and 1949, p. 18; **12,** various years; **49,** February 15, 1951, p. 149; **36,** March 17, 1952, p. 172.

a. Marketed production from 1906, when records of natural gas were first established in the United States. The U.S. Bureau of Mines estimates the country's cumulative consumption before 1906 at 2.4 trillion cubic feet.

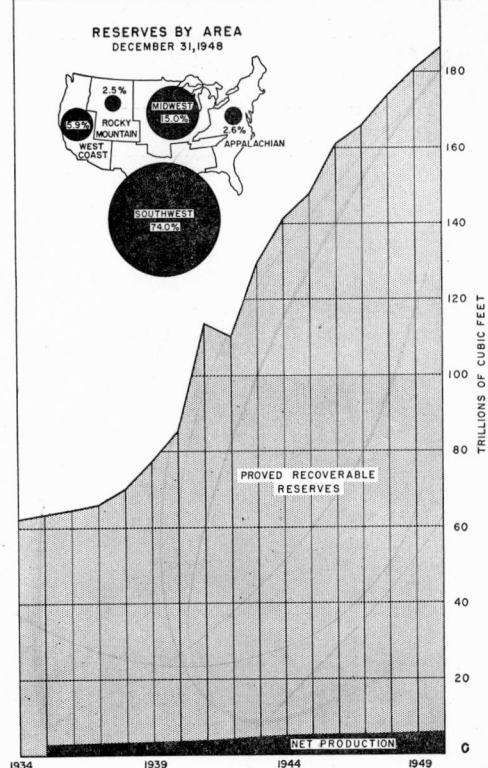

Adapted from a chart of the American Gas Association

FIGURE 263. NATURAL GAS: RECOVERABLE RESERVES AND ANNUAL NET OUTPUT IN THE UNITED STATES, 1934–50

southwestern Kansas is the largest single sulfur-free gas reservoir in the world; it covers nearly 4 million acres and has a reserve of more than 30 trillion cubic feet. Another, in the Panhandle of Texas, extends over 1.5 million acres.[103]

Reserves

Reserves of natural gas in the United States are considered to be more abundant than those of petroleum. Estimates for the world as a whole are not available.

The gas reserves of the United States were estimated as of the end of 1925 at 23 trillion cubic feet. As with oil reserves, the estimates of gas reserves have been raised frequently in more recent years as new gas fields have been discovered and old fields extended. The proven gas reserves were estimated in 1938 at 70 trillion cubic feet; by the end of 1949 at 180 trillion, and by the end of 1951, at almost 194 trillion cubic feet. (See Table 389 and Figure 263.) Yet, about 76 trillion cubic feet of natural gas were produced and marketed between 1925 and 1951, and many trillions were wasted in production and transport or blown into the air. This situation led G. E. McLaughlin of the National Resources Committee to state in 1939 that natural gas is being discovered faster

than it is consumed.[104] Texas, with about 100 trillion cubic feet, accounts for the lion's share in the national gas reserves, and Louisiana, with 27 trillion, is next.

The reserves of natural gas in the USSR are estimated at 34.8 trillion cubic feet. In 1946, Poland discovered an important gas reserve in the Debowiec field.[105] Mexico has gas fields in the northern part of the country that promise the largest reserves yet found. It is considered possible that these fields will replace the gas now piped from Texas to the Monterrey area.[106]

In 1951 two natural gas fields were discovered in Canada at Wizard Lake. Their reserves have not yet been defined, but are estimated to be considerable.

Output

The recent rapid rise in the world's output

103. **29,** p. 466.

104. **44,** p. 130.
105. **49,** July 1948, p. 239.
106. **12,** 1949, p. 818.

TABLE 390

NATURAL GAS: OUTPUT IN SELECTED COUNTRIES, 1929–50

(*Billions of Cubic Feet*)

Country	1929	1939	1944	1949	1950
World	. . .	2,998.0	4,167.0 [a]	6,215.0 [a]	. . .
United States	1,917.7	2,476.8	3,711.0	5,487.0	6,281.1
Canada	28.4	35.2	44.7	75.0	71.2
Mexico	10.7 [b]	37.8	25.5	48.1	59.2
Venezuela	—	130.7	178.1	499.0	557.2
Argentina	2.7 [b]	18.2	23.1	. . .	. . .
France	—	—	3.0	8.1	8.7
Poland	16.5	27.0	. . .	. . .	. . .
Austria	—	—	5.3	2.1	1.8
Hungary	—	0.5	2.8	35.6 [c]	. . .
Italy	0.2	0.7	1.7	8.3	17.8
Romania	28.5	60.1	32.6	41.5 [c]	. . .
USSR	13.0	102.4	. . .	. . .	. . .
Japan	1.0	1.9	1.5	2.1	2.4
Indonesia	24.0	34.6	. . .	20.9	21.9
Brunei	. . .	4.0	. . .	20.5	26.6

Sources: **25**, Vol. I, p. 28; **1**, 1931–32, p. 138, and 1942–44, p. 152; **2**, 1951, p. 139; **3**, February 1952, p. 26.

a. Excludes the USSR.
b. 1930.
c. 1947.

TABLE 391

NATURAL GAS AND NATURAL GASOLINE: OUTPUT IN THE UNITED STATES, 1906–49

Year	Natural Gas, in Billions of Cubic Feet [a]	Natural Gasoline, in Millions of Gallons	Year	Natural Gas, in Billions of Cubic Feet [a]	Natural Gasoline, in Millions of Gallons
1906	383	—	1942	3,146	2,071
1911	513	7	1943	3,516	2,115
1916	753	103	1944	3,815	2,188
1921	662	450	1945	4,042	2,499
1926	1,313	1,363	1946	4,153	2,691
1931	1,722	1,832	1947	4,582	2,744
1936	2,225	1,796	1948	5,148	2,979
1941	2,894	2,208	1949	5,487	3,008

Sources: **12**, 1949, pp. 798 and 820; **9**, p. 146; **16**, p. 45.

a. Marketed production; from 1931, calculated on a new basis to include net volume stored and lost in transmission. Comparable figures, on old basis, for 1931 and 1941 are: 1,686 and 2,813 billion cubic feet, respectively. The gross output of natural gas is considerably larger; it includes quantities of gas used in repressuring and wasted. In Table 390 and in text tabulation by state: only data for 1948–50 on a new basis.

of natural gas has been due to the increase in the United States output, which is estimated at about nine tenths of the total. Its output of natural gas has been steadily increasing, from 798 billion cubic feet in 1920 to 1,918 billion in 1929, 3,711 billion in 1944 and 6,281 billion cubic feet in 1950.

In the past decade and particularly since World War II, output in Venezuela has been increasing rapidly. Its output in 1950 was more than four times that of the prewar period.

In 1939, the USSR produced about 3 per cent of the world's output of natural gas. The last prewar Five Year Plan envisaged raising output from 105 to 245 billion cubic feet a year.[107] The country is reported to have completed several transmission lines.

The United Kingdom, France, Germany, Yugoslavia and satellite countries also produce natural gas. Germany and the United Kingdom use their small output for industrial purposes.

Italy has a small production of natural gas, which is, nevertheless, of great national importance since the country has little coal. Relatively large fields were discovered during the war in the western part of the Po Valley. Two of these produce dry gas; in the third, light oil is also present.[108] In 1949, 4.6 billion cubic feet were collected from Lodi, the one western field so far exploited, and nearly 4 billion cubic feet from the fields in the eastern part of the Po Valley. The output rose to 17.8 billion cubic feet in 1950. (See Table 390.)

In the United States, Texas accounts for almost half the total output, and Louisiana, California and Oklahoma, next in line, together produce about a third. The output in the country and these four states has been as follows (in billions of cubic feet): [109]

	1944	1948
United States	3,711	5,148
Texas	1,526	2,290
Louisiana	535	686
California	502	571
Oklahoma	311	481
Kansas	158	245
New Mexico	88	195

107. The slow development of the gas industry in the USSR is attributed, in Russian economic literature, to the work of "saboteurs," who "have tried in every possible way to prevent the extraction and utilization of natural gas." **20**, p. 222.

108. **42**, p. 265.

109. **12**, 1949, p. 799. Data for 1948 include gas stored and lost in transmission.

The output of natural gasoline in the country also shows an upward trend, from 7 million gallons in 1911 to 450 million in 1921; 1,832 million in 1931, 2,208 million in 1941 and 3,008 million in 1949. (See Table 391.)

The United States has more than 65,000 producing gas wells. Pennsylvania and West Virginia account for more than half the number of wells but for a relatively small part of the output.

Transportation

By the end of 1950, the natural gas industry of the United States operated 292,334 miles of pipeline and more than 32,000 additional miles of pipeline were projected or under construction.[110] In mileage, the gas pipeline greatly exceeds both the oil lines and the railroads.

A new pipeline, the largest and longest ever installed as a single undertaking, has been laid between the Lower Rio Grande Valley and New York City. It extends 2,250 miles (1,840 miles of main trunk and 410 miles of gas feeder and sales distribution lines), most of it with a 30-inch diameter. The line, which has a daily capacity of 505 million cubic feet, brought natural gas from Texas directly to New York City, for the first time in history.[111] The main line cuts across seventy-six rivers, chiefly under water. The most difficult crossing was that at the Hudson River, a mile wide and forty feet deep, where the pipe was laid from 25 to 30 feet under the river bottom.

The largest gas pipe yet laid, 30 inches in diameter in one portion and 34 inches in another, is now being installed to provide the Pacific Coast with Mid-Continent natural gas. The first section of 506 miles, from Arizona to the San Francisco area, has been completed.[112]

The longest gas line in the USSR is between Saratov and Moscow, about 500 miles, and is 12¾ inches in diameter.[113] In 1949 Argentina completed a 10-inch pipeline, 1,100 miles long, from the Comodoro Rivadavia field to Buenos Aires; and Mexico, a 20-inch pipeline, from Poza Rica to Mexico City.[114] In the same year France completed a 114-mile pipeline from Toulouse to Bordeaux to move 12 million cubic feet of gas per day from the St. Marcet field.

110. **49**, February 15, 1951, p. 206.

111. **12**, 1948, p. 850; **49**, February 15, 1951, p. 128.

112. **42**, p. 33; **36**, February 25, 1951, p. 219.

113. **49**, July 1948, p. 255.

114. **12**, 1949, pp. 817–18.

TABLE 392

NATURAL GAS: CONSUMPTION, BY USE, IN THE UNITED STATES, 1906–48

(*Billions of Cubic Feet*)

Type of Use	1906	1911	1916	1921	1926	1931	1936	1941	1948
Total	389	513	753	662	1,313	1,684	2,161	2,805	4,945
Domestic and commercial	110	175	235	248	289	381	455	587	1,219
Industrial	278	338	518	414	1,024	1,303	1,706	2,218	3,726
Gas fields	—	—	—	182	478	571	618	686	1,022
Carbon black	—	—	—	51	131	196	283	365	481
Oil refineries	—	—	—	a	121	76	93	148	441
Electric power plants [b]	—	—	—	24	53	138	156	205	478
Portland cement plants	—	—	—	a	a	31	37	54	72
Other industrial	—	—	—	157	240	291	517	759	1,232

Source: **12,** various years.   b. Includes some manufactured gas.

a. Included under other industrial.

Consumption

The United States consumes 88 per cent of all natural gas in the world. Venezuela accounts for about 8–9 per cent, and the small remainder is consumed in a dozen or more countries, with Canada and Mexico taking the largest part.

About three fourths of the natural gas produced in the United States is used by industry, and the remainder for domestic and commercial purposes. (See Table 392.)

The industrial use of natural gas begins with consumption on the gas fields themselves, for drilling, pumping, repressuring, operation of natural gasoline plants and the like. Industry also uses gas in the manufacture of carbon black,[115] in operations in petroleum refineries and in plants producing electric power, Portland cement and other products.

OUTLOOK

Recent decades have witnessed an unprecedented demand for petroleum. The use of petroleum products is extending simultaneously in many directions: agriculture is becoming increasingly mechanized in many countries; motor

---

115. About 60 per cent of the carbon black supply is used in the manufacture of rubber tires; it toughens the rubber and gives the tires a stronger road-gripping surface. It has been estimated that tires made with carbon black last two and a half to three times as long as tires made with the next most suitable substitute. (**44,** p. 182.) Carbon black is also employed in making printer's ink, for which purpose there is no substitute, and in paints, typewriter ribbons, phonograph records and many other products.

transportation of persons and of freight is growing rapidly; the railroads and the bunkers of the world's merchant fleet require ever greater quantities of fuel and diesel oil; civil and military aviation is increasing its consumption of petroleum; heating of homes with fuel oil is expanding in many countries. This trend is likely to continue, though business setbacks may cause temporary slumps in demand.

It is unlikely that per capita consumption of petroleum and its products in the rest of the world will catch up with that in the United States, but it is certain to rise from decade to decade, and even from year to year. This increase makes the problem of exhaustion of existing oil reserves very serious not only for the United States, but for the world as a whole. Although this is not a problem of the near future, neither is it centuries away. The world's proven reserves of oil as of January 1951 would last only 25 years at the 1950 rate of output (see Table 372), and fewer years at an increasing rate of extraction. True, less than a year later the estimated reserves were greater by 10–15 per cent and the estimates will doubtless continue to rise. Nevertheless, a shortage on a world-wide scale may develop before the end of this century.

The crucial point is where the new reserves will be found and whether they will be available to the countries that need them most. The immense reserves in remote areas difficult to develop or in countries where growing nationalism may impede their utilization are not an immediately available asset. The industrialized countries will be the first to feel the shortage, but if such reserves are left untapped in the ground, the world as a whole will be the loser.

The menace of exhaustion, or at least of shortage, of this vital source of energy calls for the greatest possible efforts both in intensive exploration and in the most effective utilization of available supplies. The time has passed for affording loss of oil through evaporation or seepage from storage tanks; drilling unnecessary wells and spacing them inappropriately; and inefficient use of reservoir energy.[116] In the opinion of all petroleum experts, the time has come for recovery of all the oil and natural gas that coordinated effort

and the most effective methods of exploration can provide.

The main hope for industrialized countries lies therefore in technology, the "great multiplier" of natural resources. Technology promises not only further discoveries of new oil fields and better utilization of known sources but also the creation of new sources of supply, from coal, oil shales and tar sands.

The era of liquid fuels inaugurated less than a century ago will not end with the exhaustion of reserves of natural oil. It will continue as technical know-how calls to life new products to meet human needs developed when oil was abundant.

---

116. Cf. **46**, pp. 563–64.

Chapter 25

THE ECONOMICS OF ENERGY AND POWER

A MECHANIZED CIVILIZATION is a high-energy civilization.[1] Without control over a supply of energy far superior to their own muscular force, men would have little use for machines and, in fact, could not build them.

Coal, oil, natural gas and hydroelectric power are the Big Four in the modern economy of energy. Man, however, still uses other sources of motive power and heat: the muscular energy of human beings and pack and work animals, fuel wood, wind harnessed by sails and windmills, streams carrying ships and turning water wheels.[2]

In the world as a whole, about 75 per cent of all energy is provided by mineral fuels, and supplying these fuels is the main task of modern mining: combustibles represent approximately 60 per cent of the value of the world's mineral output. (See Figure 264; cf. Chapter 21.)

MEASURING ENERGY AND POWER

In view of the great variety of the sources of energy and power used in the modern economy, it is necessary to have universal units for measuring them.

Units of Energy

"Energy" is the capacity to do work, that is, to overcome resistance through a definite distance. The simplest example of energy is the capacity of a bent spring to raise a weight to a certain height, overcoming the earth's attraction. Energy is measured by the work it can perform; as, for example, in such units as a *foot pound,* the work of raising one pound one foot. Since mechanical work can be transformed into heat and vice versa, mechanical and thermal energy can be measured with the same yardstick. A *calorie* (or *small calorie;* symbol, *cal.*), a widely used unit of thermal energy, is the amount of heat required at a pressure of one atmosphere to raise the temperature of one gram of water one degree

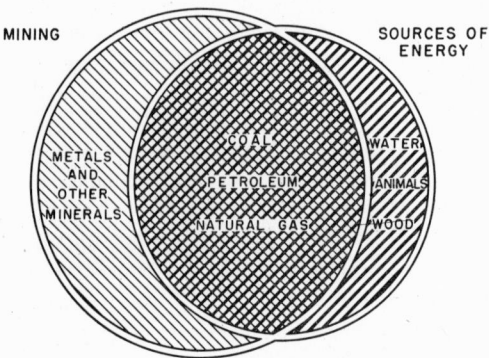

MINING — SOURCES OF ENERGY

FIGURE 264. ENERGY: MINERAL FUELS IN THE WORLD'S ENERGY SUPPLY AND MINE OUTPUT

The circle at the left represents the value of the world's mine output — coal, petroleum and natural gas, metals and other minerals. The right-hand circle indicates the world's energy supply obtained from all sources — mineral fuels, water, work animals and fuel wood. The inequality in the size of the two circles reflects the fact that the relative share of mineral fuels in the world's energy supply is even greater than their share in the value of mine output. They represent about 75 per cent of the total energy supply and approximately 60 per cent of the total value of mine output.

Centigrade. One thousand such units (*great calorie;* symbol, *Cal.*) are required to raise the temperature of one kilogram of water one degree Centigrade. Another popular unit of heat is the *British thermal unit* (BTU), the amount of heat required to raise the temperature of one pound of water one degree Fahrenheit, which equals about one fourth of a great calorie.[3]

Since heat and mechanical energy are interchangeable, calories and BTU can be converted into foot pounds and vice versa.[4]

If we know the quantity of heat that is released by burning a ton of coal of definite quality, or a barrel of oil or cubic meter of fuel wood or gas of a particular type, we can express the equivalent of the potential energy in each fuel in such units as foot pounds, calories or BTU.[5] The po-

---

1. **39**, p. 1.
2. Explosives, a special source of energy widely used in construction and mining, are not included in the following discussion.

3. More exactly, BTU = 0.252 Cal.
4. A great calorie is the equivalent of 3,087 foot pounds; one BTU amounts to 778 foot pounds.
5. It is estimated, for example, that a metric ton of ordinary bituminous (or burning) coal is equivalent to 7.2 million great calories or approximately 28.8 million

tential energy of each fuel can also be expressed as the equivalent of a definite quantity of coal.[6]

In using these measures one must keep in mind their meaning: practically, a large part of the potential energy is lost in the course of conversion and utilization. The theoretical amount of energy in the fuel depends on its physical properties, but the amount man obtains for his purposes depends on the efficiency of the devices he uses in processing the fuel, burning it, transforming heat into mechanical or electric power and transferring it to a working machine.[7]

Units of Power

"Power" is the capacity to perform a definite amount of work or release a definite amount of energy in a unit of time, as, for example, per second. Therefore, when energy is measured in, say, foot pounds, power is measured in *foot pounds per second*. The commonly used units of power are *horsepower* and *kilowatt*. One horsepower amounts to 550 foot pounds per second.[8]

The kilowatt, another popular unit of power, was introduced originally for measuring electric power but, like horsepower, can be used for measurement of any power. One kilowatt is about one third larger than one horsepower.[9]

BTU, which corresponds, roughly, to 13,100 BTU per pound of coal. The energy value of anthracite is somewhat lower, 12,700 BTU per pound, that of peat, 4,600 BTU per pound. Petroleum is estimated, on the average, at 5.9 million BTU per barrel, natural gas at 1,075 BTU per cubic foot, fuel wood at 1.8 million great calories or 7.2 million BTU per cubic meter and so on.

6. The following conversion coefficients are used in this chapter: 1 metric ton of oil = 1,400 kilograms of coal; 1 ton of peat = 350 kilograms of coal; 1,000 cubic feet of natural gas = 40 kilograms of coal.

These are only conventional averages, however. Actually, different sorts of coal, oil, peat and natural gas represent different amounts of energy.

7. See pp. 946 ff.

8. There is no agreement among experts on the relationship between this unit of power and the power of a real horse. Agricultural economists in the United States consider the strength of a horse on the farm as roughly equivalent to one horsepower, with the reservation that the horse works only 500-600 hours during a year, on the average. In Europe, horsepower is often set as the equivalent of the strength of 2.2 horses. Sometimes the work of a horse during a year is set at 800 horsepower-hours. **29**, p. 124.

9. More exactly: one horsepower = 0.746 kilowatt; one kilowatt = 1.34 horsepower = 737 foot pounds per second.

Horsepower and kilowatts can be expressed also in terms of BTU per second. In round numbers: one kilowatt = 0.95 BTU per second; one horsepower = 0.71 BTU per second.

Units of Work

The work performed by a power depends on this power and the duration of its action. Thus, a *kilowatt-hour* (the work of a kilowatt during an hour) amounts to approximately 3,412 BTU, and one *horsepower-hour* to 2,544.5 BTU.

Since the work performed is measured in the same units as energy, it can be converted also into foot pounds or the coal equivalent. Likewise, the energy of a fuel can be expressed in kilowatt-hours or horsepower-hours.[10]

HOW MUCH ENERGY AND WORK WE USE

In 1948 the United States produced 596 million metric tons of coal, more than 2 billion barrels of crude petroleum and 146 billion cubic meters of natural gas. These fuels represent, theoretically, nearly 35 quadrillion BTU. Assuming their utilization to be 20 per cent of capacity, they would perform work equivalent to 7 quadrillion BTU. The additional work performed by water power, fuel wood and work animals brings the total to approximately 8 quadrillion BTU or 3 trillion horsepower-hours. This amount of work is equivalent to the performance of 1.5 billion horsepower delivered in 2,000 hours during the year or 10 horsepower per capita of the population. Since one horsepower is roughly equivalent to the muscular strength of 10–15 men,[11] the equivalent of 10 horsepower in work performance is the work of some 120 manual laborers for 2,000 hours.

This comparison is inexact, however. The total includes not only the work of motors of all kinds

---

10. Two procedures can be used. First, the theoretical energy value of a fuel (for example, 13,100 BTU per pound of ordinary burning coal) can be expressed as the equivalent work output, in kilowatt-hours or horsepower-hours (13,100 ÷ 3,412 = 3.84 kilowatt-hours, or 13,100 ÷ 2,544 = 5.15 horsepower-hours). (See **37**, p. 142.) Second, the work performed by each fuel can be estimated with the aid of a conventional efficiency factor, assuming, for example, 20 per cent efficiency in the ultimate utilization of energy. (See **29**, p. 123.) Both methods are defensible, but they give widely different results. In using statistics of energy, attention should be given to the method of computation, which may relate to the *theoretical* energy value of the fuel or to the work it *actually* performs. For measuring energy efficiency see pp. 946 ff.

11. The conversion factor is very rough and controversial. According to Rudolf Laemmel (**44**) a man is capable of continuing effort representing approximately 22 foot pounds (3 kilogram-meters) per second, as compared with 550 foot pounds per second of one horsepower. Other experts estimate the muscular work of a man at 1/12 horsepower (**29**).

but also the equivalent of work consumed as heat in our homes and public buildings and as a source of chemical reactions.

The United States is the world's largest consumer of coal, petroleum, natural gas and water power. It accounts, roughly, for 30 per cent of the world's coal output; more than 50 per cent of its petroleum; 85 per cent of its natural gas; and nearly 50 per cent of its electric power; but other countries exceed it in use of fuel wood and animate energy. All in all, if the potential energy of fuels and electricity consumed in the United States is close to 1.5 billion horsepower delivered in 2,000 hours a year, the total for the world is likely to exceed 3.5 billion. At a very rough approximation, the world outside the United States consumes fuels and electricity with potential energy approximately equivalent to 2,000 hours of work of one horsepower per capita per annum, one tenth the amount in the United States.

The Sun as the Source of Energy

The main source of the energy used by man is the solar radiation originated by nuclear transformations on the sun. This energy travels a long road before it reaches our planet and undergoes a series of transformations before we can use it. Only morsels of it finally serve man as a source of heat, motive power and chemical reactions.

Solar Radiation Reaching the Earth

The earth obtains through solar radiation approximately one two-billionths of the energy emitted by the sun into interstellar space. About 50 per cent of the solar energy that reaches the earth is reflected back into space by its atmosphere, 15 per cent is reflected by the earth's surface and 35 per cent is absorbed by land, water and air. The largest part of the last amount remains on the earth for only a few hours: almost all the solar energy absorbed by the earth during the day is lost at night into interstellar space by the earth's radiation. In fact, while the part of our globe turned to the sun absorbs solar energy, the other hemisphere radiates it back into space. Thus, the earth is a transmission station rather than a storehouse of solar energy.

Solar Energy Retained by the Earth

Only the difference between the energy absorbed by land, water and air during the day and that radiated back into interstellar space at night remains on the earth. The land surface retains the energy used in formation of wood and other combustible materials from the carbon dioxide of the air. The water surface uses a considerable part — 40 per cent — of the absorbed solar energy in evaporating water and raising vapor above the earth's surface. In the latter operation, however, the earth functions likewise as a transmission station rather than a storehouse of energy. The condensation of vapor into water in the form of clouds, rain and snow consumes all the solar energy absorbed by the water surface for evaporation. Thus, only the solar energy used in raising water vapors against the force of gravity remains in the clouds.[12] Subsequently it can be transformed into the energy of falling water in rivers.

In terms of a power station designed to meet mankind's demands for energy, this system is not very efficient.

Recoverable Solar Energy

According to Eugene Ayres, about one per cent of the solar energy used for raising vapor above the earth — a little more than two thirds of our current energy requirement — could be recovered ultimately. Water-power experts estimate, however, that less than 10 per cent of the potential power of rivers is practically recoverable under present conditions.[13] All in all, only 0.001 per cent of solar energy absorbed in the evaporation of water can be used eventually as water power.

Other forms of solar energy received by the earth are stored in part in its crust. Vegetation can be burned to produce about as much energy as the amount of solar energy absorbed during its growth or can be converted into alcohol with a considerable loss of energy. Petroleum, natural gas and coal, which are often called "stored sunlight," can be used similarly.

Wind

Wind is, essentially, a consequence of solar radiation. It is estimated that 2.5 per cent of the solar energy absorbed by the earth is transformed into wind power.[14] This figure, however,

12. This form of energy is comparable to that of a bent spring or a weight raised high above the surface of the earth and able to perform work in its fall.
13. Cf. pp. 949 ff.
14. **51**, p. 5.

is as controversial as the question of the extent to which wind power can be utilized by men.[15] Ayres believes that only winds of moderate velocity blowing close to the land surface can be harnessed — velocities under 20 miles per hour are useless and those much above 30 miles per hour are dangerous and unmanageable.[16] Other experts think that the cut-off points on winds of low or high velocities are a matter of design of the wind turbine. Percy H. Thomas stresses that such a turbine should not necessarily rely on winds blowing close to the land surface but could harness high-level winds of greater velocity. The aerogenerator he has designed is supported by a steel tower several hundred feet above the ground and is able to utilize winds of a wide range of velocities.[17]

Direct Utilization of Solar Energy

Several methods of direct utilization of solar energy have attracted the attention of scholars and technicians in recent years, and some are now the subject of extensive research and experimentation. Various types of "solar collectors" have been developed, some with parabolic mirrors [18] and others with flat glass, as in hothouses. The question is no longer whether it is possible to catch solar energy by such devices but whether this can be done on a large scale and at a cost comparable with that of conventional sources of energy. Two types of projects are under consideration: solar collectors installed in arid regions for delivering energy to remote populations and industrial centers; and direct heating of houses by sunrays, with storage of heat for periods when the direct supply of sunrays is insufficient.[19] Many experts believe that the most promising projects are those based on the idea of artificial photosynthesis, that is, artificial absorption of solar energy in the same way as it is absorbed by plants in the process of their growth. Other projects likewise related to the employment of solar energy deal with the possibilities of heating and cooling houses by utilizing the differences between the temperature of the earth and the atmosphere or the surface and depths of the ocean ("heat pumps"), or of making use of the high temperature of tropical waters.

OTHER CONTINUOUS SOURCES OF ENERGY

Apart from solar energy, other continuous sources of energy are the heat of the earth, the tides and the atmospheric electricity.

Theoretically the internal heat of the earth can become an inexhaustible source of energy but practically it is beyond our reach. According to Laemmel, the problem would be solved if we could dig a shaft approximately 60 miles deep and penetrating into the zone with a temperature of 3,000°C.[20] This, however, is an utterly unrealistic project.

Experiments in utilizing the tides and the volcanic heat of the earth are in progress in various countries, but on a comparatively small scale and under local conditions that do not occur in other places.[21]

Ayres points out that mankind now draws the potential equivalent of 1.7 trillion horsepower-hours per year from continuous sources of energy, mainly vegetation and water power. He thinks that this amount is less than 0.001 per cent of the total continuous energy available on the earth, and he ventures a forecast that within a century we shall use more than 40 trillion horsepower-hours per year from these sources. This would be 60 per cent more than the world's present total demand and would probably cover a substantial part of the demand to be anticipated by the middle of the twenty-first century. (See Table 393.)

PRODUCTION AND CONSUMPTION OF ENERGY

Modern economy requires the concentration of large quantities of energy in limited space. As long as energy was supplied by the muscular strength of men and animals, it was an engineering feat to concentrate the power of a hundred horses or a thousand manual laborers at one point. (See Figure 265.) Now 100 horsepower is brought inconspicuously under the hood of a car; 100,000 horsepower operates under the roof of a medium power plant; a million horsepower may be engaged in turning the wheels of factories in an industrial city.

The main difficulty in utilizing the inexhaustible supply of solar energy and wind power is that this energy is extremely diffused. The modern economy rests on the utilization of energy available in concentrated form — coal, petro-

---

15. **37**, p. 117.
16. **37**.
17. **49**, p. 18. Cf. pp. 980 ff.
18. **51**, p. 12.
19. **37**, pp. 114 ff.

20. **44**, p. 48.
21. **17**.

TABLE 393

ENERGY: CONTINUOUS SOURCES

(According to Eugene Ayres)

(*Trillions of Horsepower-hours Per Year*)

Source	Maximum Available	Now Used	Possible within a Century
Total	17,676	1.7	41.9
Vegetation	60	1.0	10.0
Solar collectors for power	17,000	Trace	20.0
Solar collectors for space heating	9 [a]	Trace	4.5
Waterfalls	360	0.7	6.0
Wind	2	Trace	Trace
Heat pumps	2	Trace	0.2
Tropical waters	20	—	0.7
Earth heat	200	Trace	0.5
Tides	13	—	0.05
Atmospheric electricity	10	—	—

Source: **37**, p. 119.   **a.** Current demand for space heating.

leum, natural gas, fuel wood, water power. All these; however, are only particular forms of solar energy retained on the surface or in the crust of the earth. Since the sun is the source of all life and energy on our planet, the flow of human economic activities can be represented as a cycle in the transformation of solar radiation. (See Figure 266.)

THE WORLD'S SUPPLY OF ENERGY

For the world as a whole, it can be assumed that the annual supply of energy available for consumption equals the annual output. For continents and single countries, imports and exports of fuel and electric power must also be considered. Disregarding changes in stocks, the annual supply of energy in a country can be measured

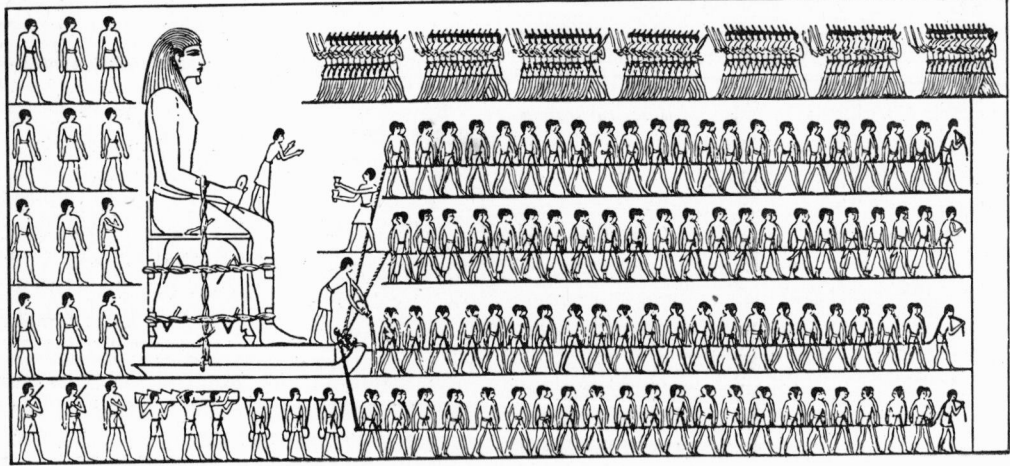

FIGURE 265. ENERGY: MOTIVE POWER IN ANTIQUITY

The building of pyramids, temples and palaces in ancient Egypt depended on the command of slave labor. This picture shows some two hundred men arranged in pairs dragging the sledge of a huge statue by four ropes. Upon the pedestal stands a man who pours water — or perhaps oil — on the planks under the sledge. Another man stands upright on the knees of the statue and marks time with his hands. At the side of the statue walk men carrying instruments and water, overseers and relays of workers to take the places of those who may drop out of the ranks from fatigue. For thousands of years, this was the prevailing type of motive power.

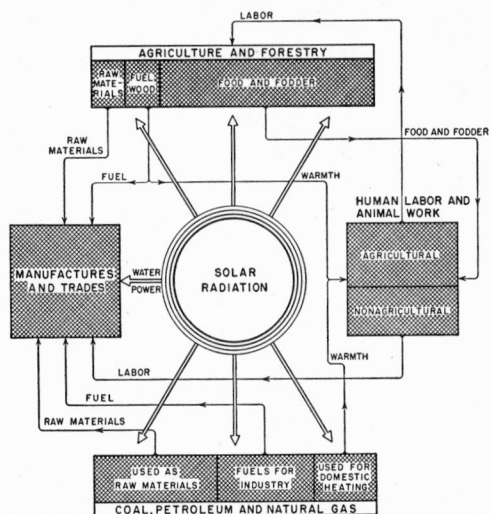

FIGURE 266. ENERGY: FLOW IN THE ECONOMIC SYSTEM

This chart traces the flow of energy in the modern economic system. Solar radiation activates agriculture and forestry (the bar at the top of the plot), whose energy has been preserved in the earth in the form of coal, petroleum and natural gas (the bar at the bottom). It also gives rise to water power.

By producing food and fodder, agriculture converts solar energy into the energy of work animals and human beings, while forestry provides fuel for industries and homes. Other products of agriculture and forestry flow to industry as raw materials. On the other hand, most of the mineral fuel flows directly to industry, either as raw material or as a means of generating heat and motive power, while the rest serves to provide mankind with warmth.

Human labor and animal work (the square at the right) depend on the current of food and fodder and of warmth originated partly by fuel wood and partly by mineral fuels. A large part of the energy of men and work animals is used in agriculture, the rest in manufactures and trades.

This flow chart reproduces in a simplified and modified form Sir Alfred Egerton's diagram of human activities. (**41**, p. 393.)

as the sum of current production and imports minus exports.

Trends since 1820

The world's consumption of coal increased tenfold from 1820 to the early 1860's and more than tenfold from the 1860's to our times. The rate of increase has slowed down in the twentieth century, partly as a result of the increasing role of petroleum, natural gas and water power, partly because of the improved efficiency in converting fuels into energy.[22] Under the impact of the depression the total consumption of fuel declined in the 1930's, but increased use was re-

sumed during World War II and has continued. (See Table 394.) While the oldest sources of energy — domestic animals and wood — were outdistanced by mineral fuels in the last century, they have not disappeared from the scene.

At a rough approximation, the world's working livestock includes 100 million horses and mules and as many other work animals — oxen, buffaloes, camels and so on. In round numbers, they supply draft power equivalent to 100 million horsepower operated 2,000 to 2,500 hours a year or to 100 million tons of ordinary burning coal utilized to one fifth of its theoretical potential energy.[23] The estimates of the energy supplied by fuel wood (including waste, manure and so on) vary widely — from an equivalent of 100 million tons of coal [24] to 400 million tons.[25] The latter is probably the more realistic, since it takes account of consumption of wood on farms in industrialized countries and, especially, of fuel wood consumption in countries that have no regular statistics of wood cut. The primitive means of using wind and water power — sail, windmills, water mills and the like — are less important and probably fall within the margin of error in the estimate for wood.

All in all, energy provided by animals, fuel wood and primitive utilization of wind and water, may be roughly equivalent to 500 million tons of coal per year. This quantity of energy, widely diffused over the world, has changed little in the last fifty years. The decline in the number of pack and work animals and in consumption of fuel wood in European industrial countries during this period has been much less spectacular than in the United States. Probably it has been offset by the increase in the number of work animals and the consumption of wood in primarily agricultural areas. At a rough approximation, it can be assumed that farm animals and the forest provided energy equivalent to 400 million tons of coal a year in the second half of the nineteenth century and to 500 million tons since the turn of the century. If this supply of energy, sometimes

---

23. This conversion is based on the estimate of the potential energy of a ton of coal at 28.8 million BTU. Utilized to a fifth of its potential capacity, one ton of coal delivers 5.76 million BTU. On the other hand, one horsepower is equivalent to 0.71 BTU per second or 2,556 BTU per hour. Energy equivalent to one ton of coal utilized to one fifth of its capacity therefore is equivalent to 2,250 horsepower-hours, in round numbers, or one horsepower delivered 8 hours a day for 281 days.

24. **44**, p. 80.

25. **43**, p. 27.

22. See Chapter 23, pp. 869 ff.

TABLE 394

THE WORLD'S SUPPLY OF ENERGY: MINERAL FUELS AND WATER POWER, 1820–1948

(*Coal Equivalent, in Millions of Metric Tons* [a])

Year	Total	Coal	Oil	Natural Gas	Water Power
1820	15	15	—	—	—
1840	60	60	—	—	—
1860	136	136	—	—	—
1880	319	310	6	3	—
1900	778	735	28	10	5
1920	1,431	1,250	140	20	21
1929	1,859	1,445	290	80	44
1938	1,865	1,318	395	100	52
1948	2,395	1,440	658	217	80

Sources: For 1820–1920, **50**, pp. 73, 119–23, 143–44; for 1929, **1**, 1934–35, pp. 128–36; for 1938 and 1948, **2**, 1949–50, pp. 141–47.

a. Conversion factors: one ton of lignite = 0.5 ton of coal; one ton of oil = 1.4 tons of coal; one hp. of hydroelectric installation = 0.94 ton of coal.

called "green coal," is added to mineral fuels and water power, the increase in the total supply since the turn of the century is less steep than it appears in Table 394: from the coal equivalent of 1,278 (778+500) million tons in 1900, the world's demand rose to 1,931 (1,431+500) million tons in 1920 and 2,895 million in 1948.[26] (See Figure 267.)

It should be remembered that these figures refer to the potential energy of fuels and work animals rather than actual output of motive power and heat. Because of the increasing efficiency in the use of energy, the motive power and heat available for human use have increased more rapidly than the coal equivalent of the fuels consumed.

Distribution of Energy by Source, 1948

Of the world's total supply of energy in 1948 (in terms of the coal equivalent), 49.7 per cent was provided by coal, 22.7 per cent by oil, 7.5

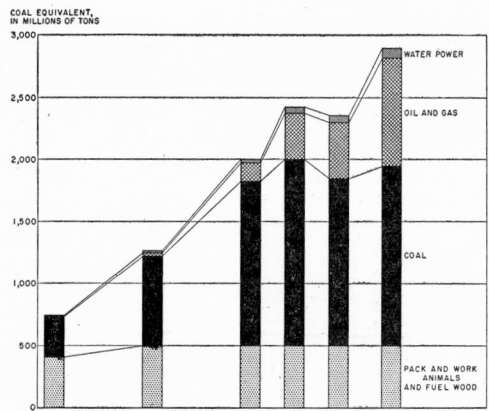

FIGURE 267. THE WORLD'S SUPPLY OF ENERGY, BY SOURCE, 1880–1948

The amount of energy (in the form of motive power or heat) the world derived from coal and oil doubled from 1880 to 1900 and has doubled again since the turn of the century. The amount supplied by pack and work animals and fuel wood increased slowly during the nineteenth century and the first decade of the twentieth. After World War I, the number of pack and work animals declined in industrial countries, but rose in primarily agricultural areas, where it probably kept pace with the growth of the population. The trends in consumption of fuel wood were likewise divergent. There is no precise information on changes in the total supply of energy from animals and fuel wood, but it can hardly have changed much in the last fifty years. In this chart, it is assumed to have remained constant.

per cent by natural gas, 17.3 per cent by wood and domestic animals, and 2.8 per cent by hydroelectric power.[27] (See Table 395.)

---

26. Sir Harold Hartley estimates the current world consumption of every kind of energy, food for men and beasts, heat, light and power, at the equivalent of 4 billion tons of coal. (**42**, p. 113.) This is the sum of the equivalent of 840 million tons of coal provided by food from agriculture; 1,640 million tons provided by coal and lignite; 240 million by wood; 980 million by oil; 260 million by natural gas; and 40 million by hydroelectricity. In our estimate, the energy provided by agriculture is counted only in the form of work of animals and the contribution of fuel wood has been increased in view of the probability of underestimate in underdeveloped areas; other deviations of Table 395 from Hartley's estimate are due mainly to the difference in conversion factors.

27. The considerable margin of error in the available statistics, and especially in estimates necessary for filling

TABLE 395

THE WORLD'S SUPPLY OF ENERGY, BY CONTINENT AND SOURCE, 1948

Region	Total	Work Animals	Fuel Wood, Manure, etc.	Coal	Oil and Natural Gas	Water Power
			Coal Equivalent, in Millions of Tons			
World	2,895	100	400	1,440	875	80
North America	1,254	10	55	577	580	32
Middle and South America	233	25	55	6	144	3
Europe	694	15	70	568	13	28
USSR	347	10	90	199	43	5
Asia	271	30	100	42	88	11
Africa	72	9	30	29	3	1
Oceania	25	1	—	19	5	—
			Percentage Distribution by Source			
World	100	3.5	13.8	49.7	30.2	2.8
North America	100	0.8	4.4	45.9	46.4	2.5
Middle and South America	100	10.7	23.6	2.6	61.8	1.3
Europe	100	2.3	10.1	81.8	1.9	4.0
USSR	100	2.9	25.9	57.4	12.4	1.4
Asia	100	11.1	36.9	15.5	32.5	4.1
Africa	100	12.5	41.6	40.2	4.2	1.4
Oceania	100	4.0	—	76.0	20.0	—
			Percentage Distribution by Continent			
World	100.0	100.0	100.0	100.0	100.0	100.0
North America	43.5	10.0	13.8	40.1	66.3	40.0
Middle and South America	4.6	25.0	13.8	0.4	16.5	3.8
Europe	27.4	15.0	17.5	39.4	1.5	35.0
USSR	12.3	10.0	22.5	13.8	4.9	6.2
Asia	8.7	30.0	25.0	2.9	10.0	13.7
Africa	2.6	9.0	7.5	2.0	0.3	1.4
Oceania	0.9	1.0	—	1.3	0.6	—

Source: Estimated by the authors as explained in text. The table shows potential energy of fuels and other sources without allowance for differences in degree of utilization.

This computation does not include human muscular energy. Its supply can be roughly estimated on the assumption that approximately half the working men and women in the world,

the gaps in statistical data, should be borne in mind. The estimate of the energy supplied by animals is very rough.

The estimate of the energy of fuel wood includes waste and manure. The power of water and wind used in primitive forms such as water and windmills, sailing vessels and so on, is not listed separately.

Figures for coal include anthracite, bituminous coal, lignite and peat, converted into burning coal.

Oil and gas have been converted into the coal equivalent at the average conversion rates mentioned above.

Hydroelectric power is converted into the equivalent of coal on the basis of production in kilowatt-hours.

i.e., some 500 million persons, are regularly engaged in heavy manual work and that the muscular exertion of each is equivalent to one tenth the performance of a horsepower for 2,000–2,500 hours. Under these assumptions, the annual supply of human muscular energy is roughly equivalent to the performance of 50 million horsepower, which corresponds, theoretically, to the potential energy of approximately 10 million tons of average burning coal and practically, to the amount of motive power derived from burning 50 million tons of coal.[28]

28. Assuming that the potential energy of coal is utilized to one fifth in conversion into motive power.

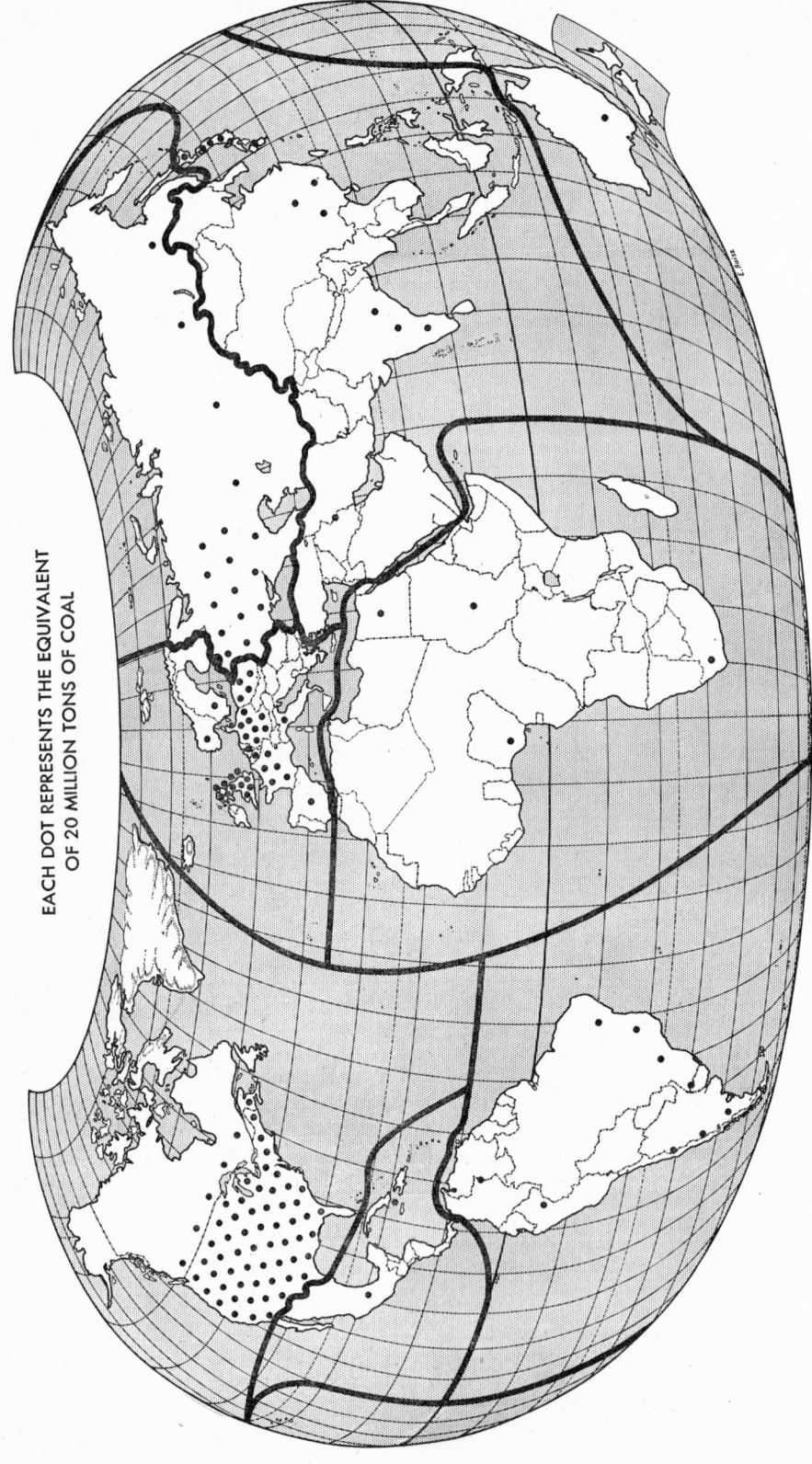

EACH DOT REPRESENTS THE EQUIVALENT
OF 20 MILLION TONS OF COAL

FIGURE 268. THE WORLD'S SUPPLY OF ENERGY: GEOGRAPHIC DISTRIBUTION
Energy is heavily concentrated along both sides of the North Atlantic Ocean. (Cf. Table 395.)

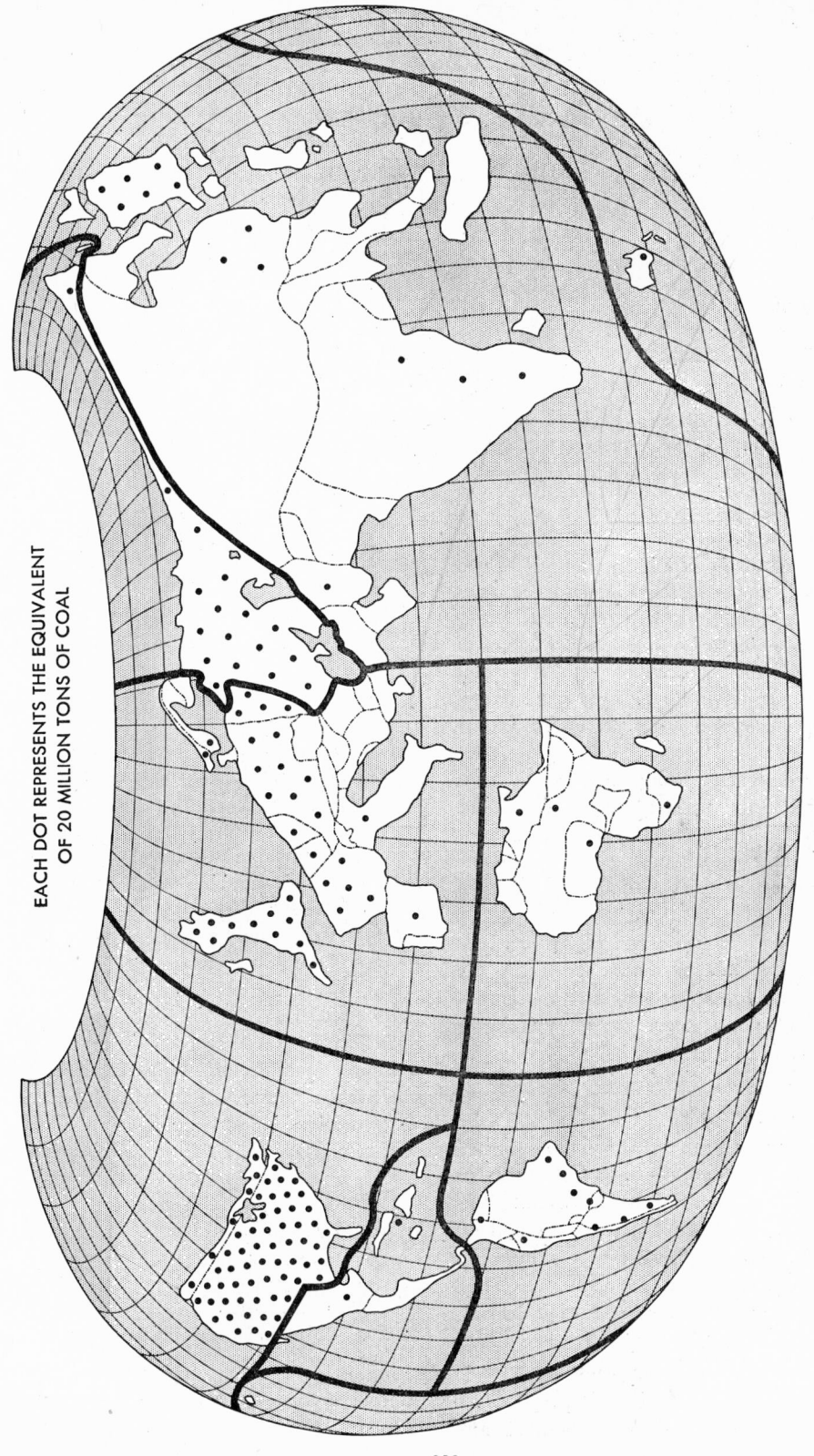

EACH DOT REPRESENTS THE EQUIVALENT
OF 20 MILLION TONS OF COAL

FIGURE 269. THE WORLD'S SUPPLY OF ENERGY: GEOGRAPHIC DISTRIBUTION IN RELATION TO POPULATION, 1948

A distorted map of the world shows the distribution of sources of energy in relation to population. The peoples of North America are best supplied with fuel. Oceania and Europe come next, followed by the USSR. Africa and Asia are at the bottom of the list.

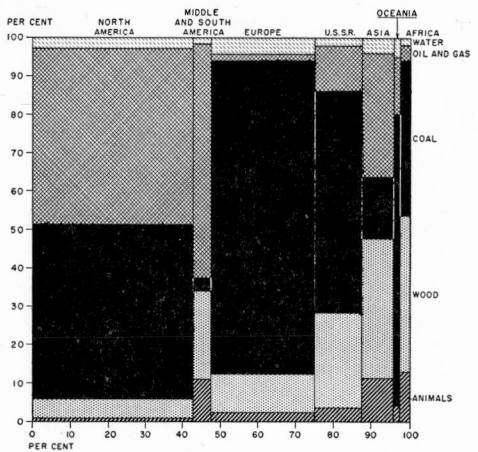

FIGURE 270. THE WORLD'S SUPPLY OF ENERGY: DISTRIBUTION BY SOURCE AND BY CONTINENT, 1948

Coal is the main source of energy in Europe, the USSR and Oceania. Fuel wood predominates in Asia and Africa, and oil and natural gas in the Americas.

If animate sources of energy and fuel wood are excluded, the world's output and consumption of energy was equivalent to approximately 2.4 billion tons of coal — one ton per capita of world population. Coal accounted for 60 per cent of this total, petroleum for 27.5 per cent, natural gas for 9 per cent and water power for 3.5 per cent.

The low percentage assigned to hydroelectric power is due to the method of computation: the figures refer to the potential energy of various sources of heat and power rather than the amounts of heat or work actually derived from them. Because of the difference in the efficiency of utilization, the actual share of hydroelectric power in the supply of motive power in the world is several times that suggested by the distribution of the potential energy supply as shown in Table 394 and Figure 267.

Distribution of Energy by Continent, 1948

North America (north of the Rio Grande) had 43.5 per cent of the world's output of energy in 1948. It controlled two thirds of the energy derived from petroleum and natural gas and 40 per cent of the coal and water power, but only 13.8 per cent of the fuel wood and 10 per cent of the animate sources of energy. Europe had almost the same output of coal and water power as North America but little petroleum and natural gas. (See the bottom section of Table 395.)

The greatest concentrations of energy at the

disposal of man are along both coasts of the North Atlantic. (See Figure 268.) A distorted map which shows continents on the scale of their population, dramatizes the concentration in North America — more than 40 per cent of the world's energy developed and used by slightly more than 6 per cent of the world's population. (See Figure 269.)

The relative importance of the various sources of energy varies widely from continent to continent. Domestic animals and fuel wood provide a third of the output of energy in Middle and South America, about half in Asia and Africa and nearly 30 per cent in the USSR, but only 12.4 per cent in Europe and 5.2 per cent in North America. (See Figure 270.)

THE SUPPLY OF ENERGY IN INDIVIDUAL COUNTRIES

Current statistics on the supply and use of energy in individual countries are less comprehensive than those for the years just before World War II, and prewar data remain in many respects the source of information on the patterns of the economy of energy in different parts of the world.

Prewar Patterns

A survey prepared by the United States Department of State during the war and published in 1949 contains detailed statistics on energy resources and their utilization in 1937 in more than 160 countries and colonial territories. (See Table 396.) Although not all these data are equally reliable [29] they reveal the important role of fuel wood not only in tropical regions but also in some European countries (Albania, Estonia, Latvia, Lithuania, Yugoslavia); the predominance of oil in the Caribbean region and the Near East; the significance of hydroelectric power in mountainous regions poor in coal — not only Sweden, Norway, Finland and Switzerland but also Italy, Japan, Spanish Morocco and the Belgian Congo. (Cf. Figure 271, showing the patterns of energy supply around 1950.)

Recent Trends

The consumption of energy has increased appreciably since 1937 in the United States and

---

29. The statement, for example, that Basutoland, Bechuanaland, Italian Somaliland and Kuwait obtained all their mechanical energy from oil, while Spanish Guinea (Africa) and Yemen met their total needs with fuel wood, are bound to provoke doubt.

TABLE 396

SUPPLY OF ENERGY IN EACH CONTINENT AND SELECTED COUNTRIES,
BY SOURCE, 1937

Continent and Country	Consumption, Electricity Equivalent in Billions of Kilowatt-hours [a]	Percentage Distribution			
		Wood and Peat	Coal	Oil and Gas	Hydro-electric Power
World	3,530.1	10.5	54.7	23.3	11.5
North America	1,427.7	6.4	46.0	37.1	10.5
United States	1,332.9	6.1	46.2	38.5	9.2
Canada	91.9	10.0	44.2	17.6	28.2
Middle and South America	95.4	10.5	9.1	68.8	11.6
Mexico	11.6	9.0	9.8	59.6	21.6
Guatemala	0.5	51.1	0.3	36.6	12.0
Panama	1.9	2.4	10.3	81.4	5.9
Cuba	2.9	15.8	21.8	52.5	9.9
Jamaica	0.9	15.1	21.4	61.3	2.2
Puerto Rico	0.9	21.6	4.1	62.1	12.2
Venezuela	4.8	8.8	0.6	89.1	1.5
Colombia	3.6	32.3	15.2	45.3	7.2
Brazil	22.8	62.7	16.4	12.0	8.9
Peru	2.0	28.7	9.3	47.3	14.7
Bolivia	0.3	24.8	18.2	45.1	11.9
Paraguay	0.1	79.2	—	11.8	9.0
Chile	13.4	56.5	18.3	14.4	10.8
Uruguay	1.8	11.6	27.7	48.5	12.2
Argentina	17.5	9.7	18.7	57.0	14.6
Europe	1,234.2	5.3	70.9	10.8	13.0
United Kingdom	347.2	—	82.1	11.3	6.6
France	153.0	5.1	69.6	13.1	12.2
Belgium–Luxembourg	53.9	0.8	82.8	5.0	11.4
Netherlands	32.8	2.4	72.6	14.9	10.1
Denmark	11.4	6.1	68.6	15.5	9.8
Sweden	31.7	22.3	44.2	8.3	25.2
Norway	15.8	2.5	30.4	8.7	58.4
Finland	12.5	50.4	23.1	4.3	22.2
Germany	326.8	2.2	73.2	9.3	15.3
Poland	53.0	14.3	73.3	6.0	6.4
Czechoslovakia	45.7	4.8	81.3	5.0	8.9
Switzerland	12.6	5.8	40.9	9.5	43.8
Austria	12.0	13.0	58.3	9.8	18.9
Hungary	8.9	12.7	65.3	7.7	14.3
Portugal	5.6	41.2	43.5	8.0	7.3
Spain	19.9	6.8	65.6	11.0	16.6
Italy	46.1	5.3	46.3	15.5	32.9
Yugoslavia	9.0	44.3	42.5	3.0	10.2
Romania	13.0	30.2	11.1	50.4	8.3
Bulgaria	2.9	43.8	43.9	6.2	6.1
USSR	319.3	19.9	49.5	19.2	11.4
Asia	318.2	21.4	56.3	10.9	11.4
China	57.4	35.1	57.3	3.3	4.3
Korea	11.1	38.0	49.8	7.6	4.6
Japan (1936)	128.1	18.6	51.4	8.7	21.3

(*Continued on page 936*)

TABLE 396—*continued*

Continent and Country	Consumption, Electricity Equivalent in Billions of Kilowatt-hours [a]	Percentage Distribution			
		Wood and Peat	Coal	Oil and Gas	Hydro-electric Power
Asia (continued)					
Turkey	5.1	24.7	65.9	6.8	2.6
Saudi Arabia	0.1	88.5	3.0	8.5	—
Iraq	0.6	26.4	0.8	70.2	2.6
Iran	2.4	66.9	—	32.5	0.6
India	50.5	6.4	78.0	11.5	4.1
Burma	2.2	33.2	32.9	29.3	4.6
Africa	100.3	49.9	30.1	13.5	6.5
French Morocco	1.1	28.5	28.6	30.7	12.2
Spanish Morocco	0.1	—	23.6	27.3	49.1
Egypt	7.3	—	46.6	49.5	3.9
Ethiopia	0.4	96.2	—	3.0	0.8
Belgian Congo	1.4	50.7	22.9	6.1	20.3
Nigeria	28.0	97.5	2.1	0.3	0.1
Union of South Africa	26.9	0.6	70.8	8.8	19.8
Oceania	35.0	7.5	52.3	24.2	16.0
Australia	27.7	8.1	55.2	22.2	14.5
New Zealand	5.4	5.4	49.3	22.1	23.2

Source: **29**, pp. 92–93.

a. One million kilowatt-hours is approximately equivalent to potential energy of 625 tons of average burning coal. The world total shown in this table is equivalent to 2.3 billion tons of coal. This table gives a lower estimate of consumption of wood and peat than Table 395, but a much higher estimate for hydroelectric power. The difference is accounted for by allowance for the degree of utilization of energy from different sources in its conversion into heat.

other countries in the Western Hemisphere and in some parts of western Europe, especially the United Kingdom, France, the Netherlands, Sweden, Norway, Czechoslovakia and Spain. For the Eastern Hemisphere as a whole, these gains were partly offset by the setback in Japan and Germany. Production and consumption of energy in the USSR in 1948–49 were somewhat above the prewar level, but these gains were due partly to the annexation of new territory after World War II.

The United Nations Economic Commission for Europe points out that the consumption of electric power and petroleum in Europe increased from the coal equivalent of 165 million metric tons in 1938 to 241 million tons in 1949 while the consumption of coal and lignite declined from the coal equivalent of 559 million tons to 483 million. (See Table 397.) These divergent changes resulted in an appreciable shift in the percentage distribution of energy consumption in Europe by type of energy: [30]

	1938	1949
Coal, coke and brown coal [a]	86.3	80.7
Petroleum products	7.9	11.4
Water power	5.8	7.9
Total	100.0	100.0

a. Includes consumption of thermoelectric plants.

The search for new sources of energy is characteristic of recent trends in Europe's economy of energy.[31] After many years of unsuccessful search for petroleum, natural gas has been found in France and Italy.[32] Production of natural gas in the Po Valley in Italy has substantially improved the economic outlook for this region. Many European countries are making serious efforts to develop their water-power resources. Norway, for example, one of the most highly electrified countries in the world, is considering installation of additional capacity of 150,000 kilowatts each year for the next decade, with the ultimate goal of producing enough hydroelectric power to meet 80 per cent of the demand for space heating and 50 per cent of the industrial demand for motive power.[33]

Production of electric power in Europe (ex-

30. **7**, 1949, p. 12.

31. **13**.
32. **15** and **23**.
33. **12**.

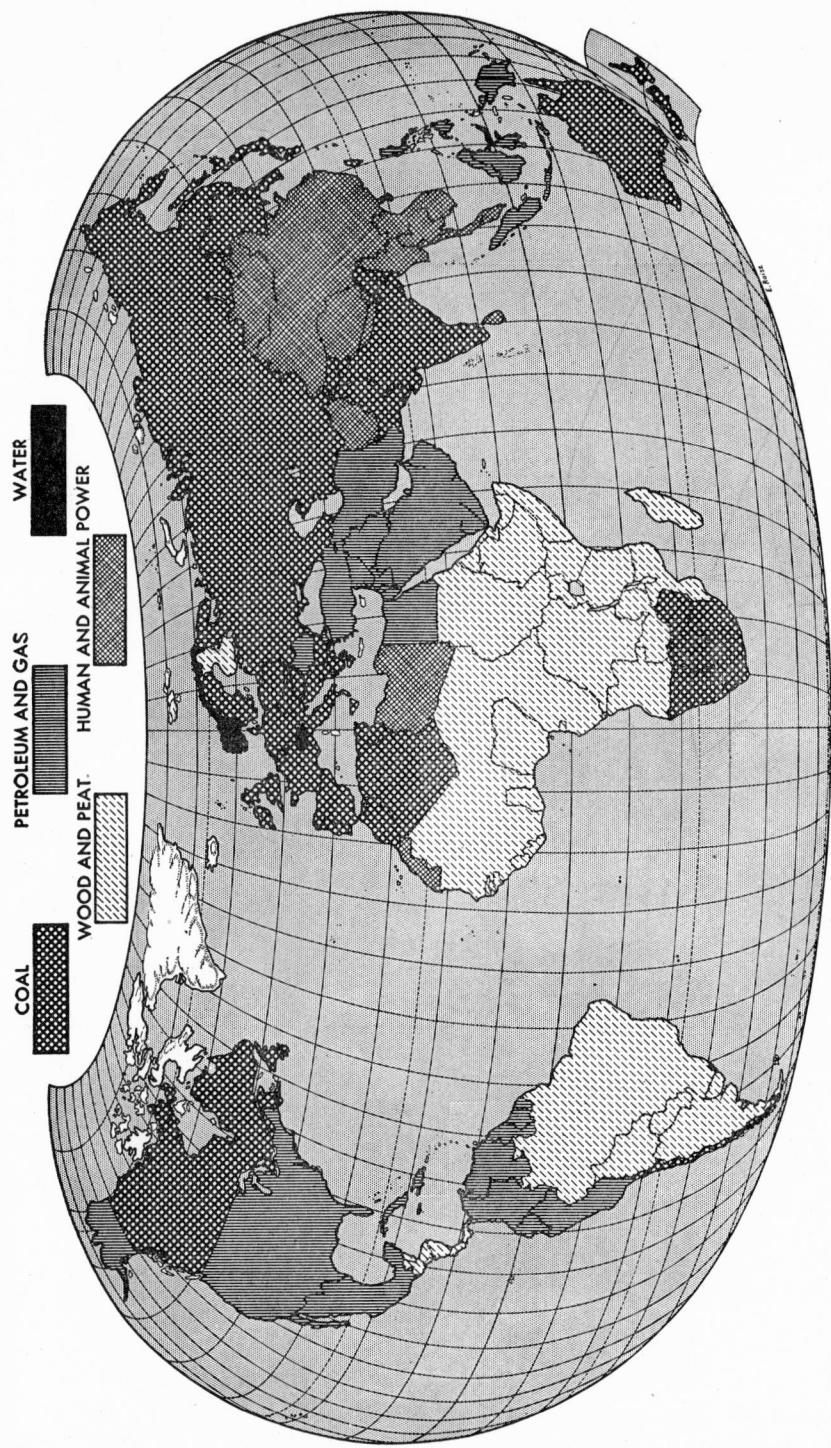

FIGURE 271. SUPPLY OF ENERGY: GEOGRAPHIC DISTRIBUTION OF CHIEF SOURCES IN THE WORLD, 1949

Coal is the main source of energy in Canada, the greater part of Europe (excluding Norway, Finland, Switzerland and Romania), the USSR, Japan, India, the Union of South Africa and Australia. Oil and natural gas predominate in the United States, Mexico, the Caribbean, the northern part of South America, Argentina, Uruguay, Romania, the Near East, Egypt and Indonesia. Hydroelectric power is the major source in Norway and Switzerland. There is no clear dividing line between the area where fuel wood and peat predominate and the area where energy is supplied mainly by the muscular force of men and animals; often a country appears in this or that class because of gaps in statistical information. China and other countries of the Far East are sometimes classified in the area where coal prevails, and all North Africa in the area relying chiefly on human and animal force. (Cf. **46**, p. 371.)

The classification used in this map is based on energy statistics for 1937 and the available information on more recent trends, and does not agree in all cases with Table 396. The map offers a simplified schematic picture of patterns of the energy economy in broad areas rather than a precise description of the situation in each country.

937

TABLE 397

SUPPLY OF ENERGY IN EUROPEAN COUNTRIES, BY SOURCE, 1938 AND 1949

(Coal Equivalent, in Millions of Tons)

Country	Total		Coal and Lignite		Petroleum		Hydroelectric Power	
	1938	*1949*	*1938*	*1949*	*1938*	*1949*	*1938*	*1949*
Europe	724	724	559	483	57	83	108	158
United Kingdom	210.6	231.0	178.3	172.4	17.0	27.7	15.3	30.9
France	85.7	100.3	62.4	67.6	11.6	14.9	11.7	17.8
Belgium–Luxembourg	31.0	32.4	26.5	24.6	1.2	2.6	3.3	5.2
Netherlands	15.1	19.4	10.6	11.3	2.3	4.3	2.2	3.8
Denmark	6.7	7.8	4.7	4.6	1.3	2.1	0.7	1.1
Sweden	14.7	20.7	7.5	5.7	2.0	4.9	5.2	10.1
Norway	9.8	12.9	2.7	1.1	0.9	2.2	6.2	9.6
Finland	3.8	3.4	1.5	0.7	0.4	0.5	1.9	2.2
Germany	221.0	123.6 [a]	177.8	83.6 [a]	8.1	5.3 [a]	35.1	34.8 [a]
Poland	27.6	13.6	24.3	38.6	0.8	—	2.5	5.0
Czechoslovakia	22.9	33.2	19.7	28.0	0.6	—	2.6	5.2
Switzerland	8.6	9.4	3.5	1.9	0.7	1.5	4.4	6.0
Austria	6.3	12.1	3.8	7.7	0.6	1.4	1.9	3.0
Spain	8.5	16.0	6.3	11.0	0.5	1.9	1.7	3.1
Italy	27.0	26.1	13.6	8.4	3.7	4.6	9.7	13.0
Other European Countries	24.8	32.1	15.4	16.3	5.6	8.9	3.8	6.9

Source: **7**, 1949, p. 12.   a. Western Germany.

TABLE 398

SUPPLY OF ENERGY IN THE UNITED STATES, BY SOURCE, 1889–1948

Year	Consumption, in Quadrillions of BTU [a]	Percentage Distribution			
		Coal	Oil	Natural Gas	Hydroelectric Power
1889	7.5	89.1	4.5	3.2	3.2
1900	8.0	88.9	4.8	3.2	3.1
1905	11.9	86.9	6.8	3.1	3.2
1910	15.6	84.9	8.1	3.5	3.5
1915	17.1	81.8	10.4	4.0	3.8
1920	22.2	78.0	14.9	3.8	3.3
1925	22.2	68.9	22.3	5.8	3.0
1930	22.7	62.2	25.3	9.2	3.3
1935	20.2	55.3	30.5	10.2	4.0
1940	25.6	52.7	32.7	11.2	3.4
1941	27.7	54.2	31.5	10.9	3.4
1942	29.7	56.9	28.2	11.1	3.8
1943	31.2	54.8	29.2	11.8	4.2
1944	33.6	53.4	30.7	11.9	4.0
1945	33.1	50.4	32.6	12.8	4.4
1946	32.3	48.4	33.9	13.4	4.3
1947	36.0	50.2	32.5	13.3	4.0
1948	36.7	46.6	35.1	14.3	4.0

Source: **28**, 1948, pp. 284–86.

a. A metric ton of ordinary burning coal is equivalent to 28.8 million BTU. One billion BTU is therefore equivalent to 34.7 tons of coal. For 1948, for example, 36.7 quadrillion BTU is roughly equivalent to 1.25 billion tons of coal.

cluding the USSR and Germany) increased from 115 billion kilowatt-hours (equivalent to 70 million tons of coal, in round numbers) in 1938 to 194 billion in 1949 and approached 250 billion (equivalent to 140 million tons of coal) in 1951.[34]

Coal's share in generating energy in the United States declined from 89 per cent in 1900 to 46.6 per cent in 1948, while that of petroleum and natural gas combined increased from 8.0 per cent to 49.4 per cent. The increase in the use of water power has been comparatively slow: from 3.1 per cent in 1900 to 4.0 per cent in 1935, with no consistent change in either direction since the latter year.[35] (See Table 398 and Figure 238.)

THE PER CAPITA SUPPLY OF ENERGY

With allowance for loss of energy which occurs in converting fuels into heat and mechanical power, the peoples of the world had at their disposal in 1948, in heat and mechanical work performed, the equivalent of 1.6 horsepower per capita working 2,000 hours during the year.[36]

Continents, 1948

The per capita consumption of energy in 1948 was as follows in each continent:

the USSR: 3,300–4,000 pounds coal equivalent or 2,000 hours of the work of 2.0–2.4 horsepower. North America has 4.5 times that rate while Africa has only a fifth the average European rate and Asia, only about half the African.

The contrasts between individual countries are even wider.

Selected Countries, 1929–50

International statistics on per capita supply and consumption of energy are neither exhaustive nor completely reliable.

In releasing its new estimates for a large number of countries for the years 1929, 1937, 1949 and 1950 the United Nations warns that they are of an approximate and somewhat provisional character. "In certain cases, some of the minor component items have been partly or wholly estimated; in others, calendar-year data for production have had to be combined with fiscal year for trade." [37] The UN figures refer to the gross domestic consumption of mineral fuels and water power, expressed in terms of coal equivalent. The production data employed cover coal and lignite; petroleum, shale oil, natural gasoline and, when available, motor alcohol; natural gas; and hydro-

	Potential Energy Produced, Coal Equivalent, in Pounds	Heat Generated and Motive Power Delivered; Horsepower Per Capita Working 2,000 Hours a Year
World	2,706	1.6
North America	17,240	9.8
Middle and South America	3,307	2.0
Europe	3,924	2.4
USSR	3,955	2.2
Asia	478	0.3
Africa	816	0.5
Oceania	4,508	2.4

Per capita consumption of energy is about the same in Middle and South America, Europe and

34. **7**, 1949, p. 282; **4**, April 1952, pp. 57–59.

35. The figures refer to potential energy of the respective sources, rather than amount of heat and work actually derived from them.

36. Potential energy from Table 395. Per capita horsepower computed on assumption of 20 per cent utilization for fuels, and 100 per cent for water power and animals. Conversion factor: one ton of coal equivalent, fully utilized = 11,250 horsepower-hours.

This estimate requires an important reservation: only part of the heat generated by fuel is actually used in space heating or chemical reaction. Similarly, only part of the motive power delivered to machines performs useful work. The rest is wasted. (See pp. 946 ff.)

electric power. The trade data include the foregoing and their derivatives. Fuel wood and other vegetal fuels and peat have been omitted for want of adequate data.

According to these estimates, in 1929 per capita consumption of mineral fuels and water power ranged from the equivalent of some 20 pounds coal equivalent in such areas as Haiti and Tanganyika to 9,045 pounds in the United Kingdom, 9,970 pounds in Belgium, 11,465 pounds in Can-

37. **2**, 1951, p. 294. This volume was in an advanced stage of printing when the Statistical Office of the UN released the report *World Energy Supplies in Selected Years, 1929–1950* (Statistical Paper), 1952.

ada and 14,455 pounds in the United States. Under the impact of the depression, per capita consumption of energy declined in most of the industrial countries. In 1937, it was below the 1929 level in the United States, Canada, Norway, Belgium, Czechoslovakia, New Zealand, France, Switzerland, Poland, the Netherlands, Austria and many other countries. It increased, however, in the United Kingdom, Sweden, Australia, Germany, Denmark, Finland, Japan and especially in some underdeveloped countries such as Northern Rhodesia, Colombia, Turkey.

The trends between 1937 and 1950 were likewise divergent but, all in all, gains prevailed over losses. During this period per capita consumption of mineral fuels and water power increased about 40 per cent in the United States and the Union of South Africa; 35 per cent in Canada and Australia; 30 per cent in Sweden; and 25 per cent in Norway. Appreciable progress was also recorded in other European countries as well as in the Belgian Congo and Morocco; in Mexico, Cuba, Bolivia, Colombia, Brazil and Peru; in Turkey and Iraq; and in Spain and Yugoslavia. On the other hand, per capita consumption declined in Germany and Japan. (See Table 399.) The USSR does not appear in the list. Its per capita consumption of energy from all sources was estimated at 2,430 pounds coal equivalent in 1937 and was probably about the same in 1950 — lower than in modern industrialized countries, but much higher than in primarily agricultural regions in Asia and Africa.

These data understate the supply of energy in areas that use substantial quantities of fuel wood, waste and manure for heating. If these sources of energy were taken into account, total per capita supply of energy would be increased appreciably for such countries as Sweden and Finland, Portugal and Spain, Poland and Bulgaria, Brazil and Puerto Rico, Burma and Ceylon.

Estimates of per capita consumption of energy from *all* fuel sources and water power in 1937 and 1949 are given in Table 400. In contrast with Table 399, which covers only mineral fuels and water power, these estimates also include wood fuel, waste and manure. In addition, the 1949 data in Table 400 make allowance for consumption in rural areas (fuels derived from "noncommercial sources"); which are roughly estimated although not recorded in current statistics for the respective countries.

With the reservation for a considerable margin of error in the 1937 data, the following types of per capita consumption of energy can be distinguished:

1. Negligible consumption of energy (100 pounds, or less, coal equivalent per capita), in primitive countries with a prevailing subsistence economy and warm climate.

2. Low consumption of energy (100 to 1,000 pounds per capita), in primarily agricultural nations on varying levels of economic development.

3. Medium consumption of energy (1,000 to 3,000 pounds per capita), in agricultural countries on a higher level of economic development than in the preceding group, and in agricultural-industrial countries.

4. High consumption of energy (3,000 to 5,000 pounds per capita), in a heterogeneous group of countries that include prosperous agricultural areas and areas with a predominance of mining.

5. The highest consumption of energy (more than 5,000 pounds coal equivalent per capita), in the most prosperous and highly industrialized countries. (See Table 400.)

The figures (in Table 400) for 1949 in underdeveloped areas include allowance for "noncommercial" sources of energy and do not drop below the coal equivalent of 500 pounds per capita, which is supposed to be the minimum requirement, whether reported by statistics of production of sources of energy or not.

The exceptionally high consumption of energy in the United States is due chiefly to three factors:

1. Because of its large area, the country needs more draft power per capita for transportation than densely populated countries in northwestern Europe.

2. Agriculture, mining and manufacturing in the United States are more highly mechanized, in terms of horsepower per worker, than in the Old World.

3. Automotive transport is much more developed and consumes more gasoline per passenger-mile than in other countries.

Uses of Energy

About 42 per cent of all potential energy — mineral fuels, water power, wood and work animals — produced in 1937 was used in industrial establishments for generating heat, providing motive power and as raw material for chemical processes; 32 per cent was used for heating dwellings and commercial and public buildings, for lighting, and for agricultural and other

TABLE 399

PER CAPITA CONSUMPTION OF MINERAL FUELS AND WATER POWER, SELECTED COUNTRIES, 1929–50

(*Coal Equivalent, in Pounds*)

Country [a]	1929	1937	1949	1950	Country [a]	1929	1937	1949	1950
United States	14,455	12,720	15,975	17,515	Northern Rhodesia	242	814	924	900
Canada	11,465	10,275	13,840	13,865	Yugoslavia	395	395	790	880
United Kingdom	9,045	9,420	9,460	9,680	Colombia	155	420	660	680
Norway	8,165	7,570	8,650	9,460	Bulgaria	285	310	615	660
Belgium	9,970	8,845	7,590	7,700	Panama	...	...	680	660
Sweden	4,005	5,500	6,205	7,175	Malaya	790	725	595	615
Australia	4,135	5,195	6,405	7,000	Cyprus	155	265	530	595
Iceland	3,895	4,095	6,580	...	Portugal	505	530	550	570
New Caledonia	6,470	6,645	6,515	...	Turkey	200	310	595	570
Czechoslovakia	4,335	3,915	6,160	6,515	Costa Rica	350	375	485	530
Germany	6,470	6,645	5,325 [b]	5,785 [b]	Greece	310	420	460	485
New Zealand	4,775	4,310	5,195	5,195	Brazil	220	265	440	485
France	5,325	4,665	4,885	4,755	Peru	310	285	460	440
Switzerland	4,050	3,980	4,160	4,685	Ecuador	45	130	330	440
Denmark	3,565	3,785	3,740	4,600	Iraq	45	90	350	420
Poland	2,330	1,650	4,270	4,600	Jamaica	130	175	350	...
Netherlands	4,095	3,940	4,025	4,315	Tunisia	375	350	330	350
Union of South Africa	2,310	2,905	4,115	4,115	Guatemala	130	90	310	350
Austria	3,300	2,290	3,235	3,390	Algeria	395	310	310	350
Finland	1,275	2,265	2,135	2,575	Honduras	570	420	330	330
Ireland	2,110	2,420	2,110	2,330	Morocco	135	175	285	330
Hungary	1,740	1,585	2,070	2,155	Egypt	310	285	310	330
Israel	...	...	1,385	1,760	India	155	175	220	240
Argentina	1,495	1,585	1,560	1,695	Belgian Congo	155	90	175	200
Chile	1,630	1,540	1,740	1,670	Ceylon	200	175	175	175
Japan	1,630	2,045	1,670	1,670	Bolivia	65	90	155	175
Southern Rhodesia	1,100	...	1,410	1,540	Nicaragua	90	110	155	...
Italy	1,340	1,450	1,275	1,385	El Salvador	90	90	130	...
Uruguay	990	925	1,300	1,365	Indonesia	130	110	90	130
Mexico	640	770	1,340	1,340	Pakistan	...	...	90	65
Spain	1,120	880	1,210	1,255	Tanganyika	20	20	65	65
Cuba	1,300	790	1,055	1,210	Indochina	90	90	45	45
Puerto Rico	...	420	925	1,055	Burma	...	110	45	45
Romania	530	815	925	...	Haiti	20	20	45	...
Surinam	...	265	790	925	Thailand	45	20	20	45

Source: Computed on the basis of **2**, 1951, pp. 294–96.

a. Countries are arrayed by declining per capita consumption in 1950. Countries for which the 1950 data are not available are ranked according to the data for 1949.

b. Western Germany.

TABLE 400

PER CAPITA CONSUMPTION OF ENERGY FROM ALL FUEL AND WATER POWER
SOURCES, SELECTED COUNTRIES, 1937 AND 1949

(Coal Equivalent, in Pounds)

Country [a]	1937	1949 [b]	Country [a]	1937	1949 [b]
Over 5,000 Pounds			Brazil	680	1,540
			Puerto Rico	670	2,310
United States	13,310	16,100	Korea	640	750
Canada	10,740	15,600	Egypt	600	700
United Kingdom	9,600	9,500	Bulgaria	600	1,030
Australia	5,440	7,330	Colombia	550	1,120
			Greece	490	880
Over 3,000 to 5,000 Pounds			Ceylon	490	700
Netherlands	4,930	4,160	Peru	410	1,030
France	4,750	4,970	Turkey	410	1,120
Finland	4,280	5,170	Ecuador	360	730
Denmark	3,940	4,290	Iran	270	970
Chile	3,790	2,160	Philippines	220	770
Ireland	3,780	3,670	Iraq	220	810
Union of South Africa	3,570	4,220	Paraguay	210	590
			Guatemala	200	880
Over 1,000 to 3,000 Pounds			Burma	190	570
			India	190	770
USSR	2,430	...	Belgian Congo	180	880
Japan	2,340	1,960	China	170	...
Austria	2,310	3,670	Haiti	130	550
Poland	2,000	4,400			
Venezuela	1,820	1,830	**100 Pounds or Less**		
Argentina	1,780	2,110			
Uruguay	1,120	1,690	Liberia	100	570
Portugal	1,020	1,080	Ethiopia	80	550
Spain	1,010	1,580	Thailand	70	640
			Afghanistan	70	550
Over 100 to 1,000 Pounds			Saudi Arabia	20	920
			Basutoland	16	...
Romania	860	1,320			
Yugoslavia	760	1,230			

Sources: For 1937: **29**, pp. 90–91; for 1949: United Nations, *World Energy Supplies in Selected
Years, 1929–1950*, pp. 94–96. For 1937, electricity in kilowatt-hours has been converted into
the coal equivalent at the rate of 1 kilowatt-hour = 1.3 pounds of coal.

a. Countries are arrayed by decreasing per capita consumption of energy in 1937.
b. Data for 1949 include allowance for consumption of fuels from "noncommercial" sources,
particularly important in underdeveloped areas, and are therefore not comparable with 1937
figures.

purposes; as much as 22 per cent was consumed
in transportation by tankers, railways and automotive vehicles and so on; the rest was wasted.[38]

Distribution of Energy by Use, 1937

International comparisons of the use of energy
are subject to serious reservations: classification
varies from country to country; reliable statistics
are available for only a few countries; particular
types of use must often be estimated on the basis

of indirect evidence. The differences in the use of
energy in various countries are so wide, however,
that clear patterns can be derived from the available data despite reservations for the margin of
error. (See Table 401.)

In underdeveloped countries, the main use of
energy is for space heating. Heating and lighting (including public services and agriculture)
also absorb a large part of the energy consumed
in the northern European countries—Finland,
Denmark, Norway and Sweden.

In some underdeveloped countries located at

38. **29**, pp. 86 ff.

TABLE 401

USES OF ENERGY, IN EACH CONTINENT AND SELECTED COUNTRIES, 1937

(Per Cent)

Continent and Country	Transportation [a]	Industry	Heating, Lighting [b]	Military Use; Lost, Stored and Unknown
World	22.4	42.4	31.9	3.3
North America	26.2	40.8	29.0	4.0
United States	26.4	40.9	28.6	4.1
Canada	23.4	37.6	35.9	3.1
Middle and South America				
Mexico	21.7	57.9	17.1	3.3
Guatemala	34.6	63.5		1.9
Panama	23.4	—	5.5	71.0
Cuba	27.6	40.4	29.2	2.8
Jamaica	78.5	3.2	17.9	0.4
Puerto Rico	59.1	10.0	29.2	1.7
Venezuela	17.4	6.8	12.2	63.6
Colombia	18.1	34.4	33.8	13.7
Brazil	34.2	14.7	49.1	2.0
Peru	27.4	37.6	32.8	2.2
Bolivia	43.0	18.2	37.1	1.7
Paraguay	29.8	2.1	66.7	1.4
Chile	12.8	20.8	62.7	3.7
Uruguay	46.3	27.6	24.3	1.8
Argentina	42.7	36.0	17.5	3.8
Europe	16.6	50.3	30.5	2.6
United Kingdom	18.0	50.9	29.1	2.0
France	18.8	50.8	27.5	2.9
Belgium	9.4	67.7	21.1	1.8
Netherlands	29.7	42.5	25.5	2.3
Denmark	15.4	30.4	52.4	1.8
Sweden	11.8	43.8	40.7	3.7
Norway	9.0	42.8	44.2	4.0
Finland	9.1	30.8	57.7	2.4
Germany	14.0	54.8	29.2	2.0
Poland	17.2	36.7	44.0	2.1
Czechoslovakia	11.8	62.7	24.2	1.3
Switzerland	10.7	49.2	34.7	5.4
Austria	20.2	43.7	32.2	3.9
Hungary	21.6	32.3	41.5	4.6
Portugal	17.8	27.8	51.9	2.5
Spain	28.2	46.2	21.6	4.0
Italy	19.5	54.2	17.7	8.6
Yugoslavia	18.7	26.8	53.4	1.1
Romania	24.4	37.7	37.1	0.7
Bulgaria	16.2	19.3	63.4	1.1
USSR	24.5	47.0	33.7	1.1
Asia				
China	10.2	18.3	70.6	0.9
Korea	7.1	52.7	39.6	0.6
Japan	13.4	46.8	32.9	6.9
Turkey	41.2	4.0	50.2	4.6

(Continued on page 944)

TABLE 401—*continued*

Continent and Country	Transporta-tion [a]	Industry	Heating, Lighting [b]	Military Use; Lost, Stored and Unknown
Asia (continued)				
Saudi Arabia	8.5	—	91.5	—
Iraq	57.0	0.1	41.4	1.5
Iran	24.0	3.2	72.7	0.1
India	34.6	38.2	26.3	0.9
Burma	25.7	35.1	38.5	0.7
Africa	29.3	13.0	56.2	1.5
French Morocco	32.2	27.1	38.9	1.8
Spanish Morocco	43.4	2.2	47.1	7.3
Egypt	67.0	5.0	27.4	0.6
Ethiopia	2.3	—	97.7	—
Belgian Congo	59.8	25.1	13.1	2.0
Nigeria	1.2	1.2	97.6	—
Union of South Africa	43.4	37.8	15.8	3.0
Oceania	36.4	31.3	28.2	4.1
Australia	36.7	31.9	28.3	3.1
New Zealand	22.1	29.7	33.1	5.1

Source: **29,** pp. 88–89.

    a. Includes overseas and local bunkers, railways and automotive vehicles.
    b. Includes all types of use for domestic, commercial, public and agricultural purposes.

crossroads of world trade or dominated by foreign capital, energy is used mainly for transportation, primarily for overseas bunkers, as in Jamaica, Egypt, the Belgian Congo.

Industry's share in the consumption of energy is appreciably higher in industrialized European countries than in the United States — 50.9 per cent in the United Kingdom; 54.8 per cent in Germany; 67.7 per cent in Belgium; 62.7 per cent in Czechoslovakia; compared with 40.9 per cent in the United States.

There is also a conspicuous variation in the distribution of energy consumed in transportation among overseas and local bunkers, railways and automotive vehicles. In the United States, automotive vehicles use about as much fuel as railways. In Europe, the ratio between these two types of consumption is 1 to 3; in Africa, 1 to 5; in Asia and the USSR, nearly 1 to 10. Before World War II, the United States used 3.1 per cent of its energy for bunkers; Europe, 4.7 per cent; Asia, 0.6 per cent; the USSR, 2.7 per cent; Africa, 13.7 per cent; and Oceania, 9.8 per cent.[39]

Use of Energy in Industry

The United States and Canada rank first in consumption of energy per worker in mining

and manufacturing. They are closely followed by Norway, the country of waterfalls and hydroelectric stations, and Belgium, the country with the greatest concentration of heavy industry. There is a surprising similarity in input of energy per worker in mining and manufacturing in such widely different countries as Sweden and the Union of South Africa, the USSR and Germany, Japan and France. (See Table 402.)

Comparable data for the United States are available for 1939 and 1946. In both years the chemical and iron and steel industries were the largest consumers of energy, followed by paper and allied products, food industries, textile mills and nonferrous metals industries. The paper industries consume about as much energy as the production of automobiles, machinery and electrical equipment combined. Coal mining consumes less than the food industries. (See Table 403.)

Chemical industries rank first not only in the total amount of energy they require but also in consumption per worker — in 1946, more than 30,000 kilowatt-hours or the equivalent of some 23 tons of coal per worker. Processing of petroleum and coal comes next in energy consumption per worker, and the nonferrous metals industries are third, far ahead of the iron and steel and machinery industries. (See Table 404.)

39. **29,** pp. 88–89.

TABLE 402

USE OF ENERGY PER WORKER IN MINING AND MANUFACTURING,
SELECTED COUNTRIES, 1937

(*Coal Equivalent, in Tons*)

Country	Tons	Country	Tons
United States	20.7	Japan	6.0
Canada	15.9	Australia	5.7
Norway	13.1	Ireland	4.6
Belgium–Luxembourg	12.2	Chile	4.5
United Kingdom	10.9	Romania	3.6
Finland	9.2	Denmark	3.3
Sweden	7.8	Hungary	1.9
Union of South Africa	7.2	Greece	1.4
USSR	6.8	Colombia	1.2
Netherlands	6.8	Turkey	1.1
Germany	6.5	Latvia	0.9
France	6.4	Estonia	0.9
New Zealand	6.1	Lithuania	0.8

Source: **29**, p. 8.

TABLE 403

USE OF ENERGY IN MINING AND MANUFACTURING IN THE UNITED STATES, 1939 AND 1946

(*Millions of Kilowatt-hours* [a])

Industry	1939	1946	Industry	1939	1946
Total	79,004	133,682	Manufactures (continued)		
			Electrical machinery	1,432	2,955
Manufactures, total	70,518	120,280	Machinery	1,985	4,796
Food and kindred products	6,386	9,603	Automobiles	2,467	4,245
Tobacco	115	176	Transportation equipment	482	2,782
Textiles	6,800	8,895	Miscellaneous	466	830
Apparel	357	658			
Lumber and timber	1,245	1,601	Government-owned industries, total	441	1,701
Furniture	605	977	Shipbuilding	180	957
Paper and allied products	9,097	12,154	Arsenals	90	267
Printing and publishing	859	1,213	Miscellaneous	171	477
Chemicals	9,747	21,565			
Products of petroleum and coal	3,438	6,385	Mining, total	8,085	11,701
Rubber products	1,584	3,015	Metal mining	2,895	3,503
Leather	402	587	Coal mining	3,525	5,546
Stone, clay and glass	4,851	6,627	Nonmetallic mining and		
Iron and steel	12,246	19,406	quarrying	828	1,646
Nonferrous metals	5,954	11,811	Crude petroleum and natural gas	837	1,006

Source: **26**, 1950, p. 758.

a. One thousand kilowatt-hours of useful energy is the equivalent of about 1,300 pounds of coal or coal equivalent consumed at 20 per cent efficiency.

TABLE 404

Use of Energy Per Worker in Manufacturing in the United States, 1939 and 1946

(Thousands of Kilowatt-hours [a])

Industry	1939	1946	Industry	1939	1946
Food and kindred products	5,357	6,207	Rubber products	10,560	11,334
Tobacco	1,095	1,778	Leather	1,050	1,439
Textiles	5,506	6,795	Stone, clay and glass	13,890	13,981
Apparel	392	584	Iron and steel	10,458	11,620
Lumber and timber	2,677	2,529	Nonferrous metals	21,308	26,541
Furniture	1,571	2,018	Electrical machinery	4,034	4,358
Paper and allied products	2,842	2,719	Machinery	2,877	3,495
Printing and publishing	1,531	1,841	Automobiles	5,294	5,326
Chemicals	23,152	30,373	Transportation equipment	2,497	4,429
Products of petroleum and coal	23,387	29,288	Miscellaneous	1,498	1,517

Sources: **26**, 1950, p. 758; **17**, pp. 15–16. In view of discrepancies in industrial classification, the figures for the two years are not strictly comparable.

a. One thousand kilowatt-hours is the equivalent of about 1,300 pounds of coal or coal equivalent consumed at 20 per cent efficiency.

Use of Energy in Agriculture

World agriculture absorbs almost all the energy of work animals and a large part of human muscular energy. Both sources of energy together are the equivalent of about 1.3 trillion horsepower-hours per year. In only a few countries is agriculture a major consumer of fuels. The United States and the USSR lead in such consumption, but in the world as a whole, energy consumed by tractors remains a small fraction of the total input of farm work.[40]

There are few statistics on the consumption of energy in agriculture. Apart from figures on the use of draft animals and tractors on farms, collected by the Food and Agriculture Organization of the United Nations,[41] the most inclusive report is the survey prepared by the United States Department of State for 1937.[42] (See Table 405.)

According to this survey, the wealthy young countries — Australia, the United States, Canada and New Zealand — outrank Europe in energy consumption per agricultural worker. The ranking is reversed, however, in the input of energy per acre of agricultural land. The contrast between the United States and Japan is most striking. In 1937, the United States used the equivalent of 2,270 kilowatt-hours per agricultural worker but only 26 kilowatt-hours per acre of agricultural land, while Japan used the equiva-

lent of 191 kilowatt-hours per person in agriculture and 354 kilowatt-hours per acre.[43] The difference is due to the fact that the United States had more than 100 acres of agricultural land per agricultural worker and Japan had only 0.6 acre.

ENERGY-USE EFFICIENCY

When a hunter makes a campfire to warm himself and boil a quart of water, he uses only a small fraction of the energy released by the burning wood; the rest is dispersed into space. Similarly, when logs or coal are burned in an open fireplace only a small part — not more than 10 per cent — of the energy contained in the fuel is utilized. Although the efficiency of modern domestic furnaces can be raised to 75 per cent it seldom reaches 50 per cent. On the whole, much more potential energy is wasted in domestic furnaces and fireplaces than is actually used for raising the temperature of the air in the rooms.

Waste of Energy

Ayres quotes examples of losses in utilization of energy. Theoretically, if there are no losses, one pound of coal is equivalent to approximately 4 kilowatt-hours, but actually generators installed in the United States consume, on the average, 1.3 pounds of coal per kilowatt-hour, which represents an efficiency of 20 per cent.[44] The work-

40. Cf. Chapter 15, p. 515.
41. See Table 227, p. 515.
42. **29.**

43. For further details on use of energy in agriculture see Chapter 15.
44. **37**, p. 133.

TABLE 405

USE OF ENERGY IN AGRICULTURE, SELECTED COUNTRIES, 1937

	Total Consumption of Energy in Agriculture, in Millions of Kilowatt-hours				Consumption in Kilowatt-hours Equivalent:	
					Per Person Engaged in Agriculture	Per Acre of Agricultural Land
Country [a]	Total	Human Energy	Draft Animals	Fuels		
United States	20,748	1,371	8,667	10,700	2,270	26
Japan	5,100	4,000	860	240	191	354
Germany	4,172	1,407	2,065	700	444	61
Poland	3,844	1,452	2,334	58	394	63
France	3,181	1,157	1,724	300	442	35
Romania	2,647	1,236	1,353	58	—	—
Canada	2,516	184	1,732	600	2,051	19
Italy	2,495	1,326	794	375	—	—
Yugoslavia	1,574	764	798	12	—	—
Australia	1,476	88	1,052	336	2,506	47
United Kingdom	1,173	210	663	300	835	37
Czechoslovakia	898	400	423	75	—	—
Hungary	889	305	484	100	—	—
Sweden	688	156	372	160	661	60
Greece	649	222	409	18	—	—
Lithuania	506	162	331	13	—	—
Denmark	503	84	331	88	—	—
Finland	452	166	228	58	408	73
Latvia	365	115	235	15	—	—
Netherlands	326	96	180	50	—	—
Belgium–Luxembourg	312	98	169	45	—	—
New Zealand	257	26	167	64	1,477	13
Estonia	208	67	126	15	466	31
Switzerland	158	62	86	10	—	—

Source: **29,** pp. 7 and 96.

a. Countries are arrayed by total amount of energy consumed in agriculture.

ing efficiency of railway locomotives averages 6–8 per cent.

This is what happens to coal used in the production of electric power:

We start with 100 horsepower-hours of coal in a mine. By the time this is collected and transported to a power plant, we have 90 horsepower-hours. By the time we have burned the coal to make steam to drive a generator, we come out with 18 horsepower-hours. By the time this power reaches our motor or stove, we have 14.4 horsepower, and this is the energy delivered.[45]

Still lower is the energy efficiency in motor transport. A hundred horsepower-hours worth of crude petroleum being refined

. . . becomes 90 horsepower-hours. When this has

been delivered to the tank of a motor car, it becomes 81 horsepower-hours. When it is burned in the motor, the energy produced is about 29 per cent of 81, or 23.5 horsepower-hours. Engine (and auxiliary) losses bring it down to 16.7 horsepower-hours. Then, by the time the energy reaches the road, it is 5 horsepower-hours.[46]

Thus, Ayres finds that

. . . the joint efforts of the automotive and chemical engineers have now reached the point where 95 per cent or more of the energy in a ton of [crude petroleum] would be used not to move the car along the road, but: 1, to evaporate huge quantities of water in the conversion plant; 2, to carry the gasoline to the filling station; 3, to heat water in the radiator and the gas in the exhaust; 4, to

45. **37,** p. 134.

46. **37,** p. 135.

TABLE 406

ENERGY-SYSTEM EFFICIENCY IN THE UNITED STATES

(According to Eugene Ayres)

Use of Energy	Energy, in Billions of Horsepower-hours per Year			*Loss as Percentage of Total Consumption*
	Consumed	*Utilized*	*Lost*	
Total	10,400	3,620	6,780	65.2
Space heating	3,450	1,700	1,750	50.7
Mining and manufacturing	3,120	1,390	1,730	55.4
Transportation	3,360	410	2,950	87.8
Miscellaneous	470	120	350	74.5

Source: Adapted from **37**, p. 136.

operate motor car auxiliaries; and 5, to overcome friction in gears and tires.

Apart from this waste of energy in its utilization, the United States uses for space heating, mining and manufacturing, transportation and other purposes, 3,620 billion horsepower-hours per year, but requires an additional 6,780 billion horsepower-hours to cover losses in burning, conversion, transmission and so on. (See Table 406.) The ultimate efficiency of energy utilization is much lower than 20 per cent — the rate used in the preceding discussion. When this rate is used for converting the potential energy of fuels into units comparable with those for water and work animals, it expresses the hypothesis that, on the average, the ultimate efficiency rate of the latter kinds of energy is five times that of fuels.

Long-Range Trends

As time goes on, the efficiency of the energy system increases. If changes in the uses of energy and the efficiency of its utilization are taken into account, it appears that since the middle of the nineteenth century, the work performed by fuels and water power in the United States has increased more than twice as rapidly as the amount of potential energy consumed.[47]

The considerable losses in energy in the course of its utilization widen the contrasts in the per capita supply of energy in various countries. The potential energy of coal can be better utilized

47. **39**, pp. 3–4. The figures on which this conclusion is based are being revised and the corrected figures will appear in the forthcoming revised edition of *America's Needs and Resources*, Twentieth Century Fund, New York.

than that of wood or manure. Oil and gas suffer less loss in conversion than coal. Losses in hydroelectric power are less than in mineral fuels. Modern machinery has less friction and therefore higher efficiency than older machinery. Thus, underdeveloped countries obtain less service than modern countries in terms of the actual heat or work they receive from each unit of potential energy they consume. Even their pack and work animals are less efficient than those developed through careful breeding in industrialized countries.

The Flow of Energy in the World

To visualize the extent of waste of energy in the world one may begin with the various forms of fuel and water power and the animate energy of men and work animals or one may go back further to the potential energy of the food and feed used to maintain human workers and animals. If the second method is used, the list of primary sources of energy includes the "original calories" of food and feed crops as well as hydroelectric energy, fuel wood and the array of mineral fuels.

The next step is to estimate the useful motive power and utilized heat derived from all these sources. More than 90 per cent of the original calories in food and feed crops are lost in the conversion of vegetable products into animals or animal products and in the further conversion of the caloric value of feed and food into "animate energy," that is, the actual efforts of work animals and men. Similar, though smaller, losses occur in utilizing the potential energy of fuels. Of this, nearly 10 per cent is lost in the conversion of fuels (refining of petroleum, fabrication

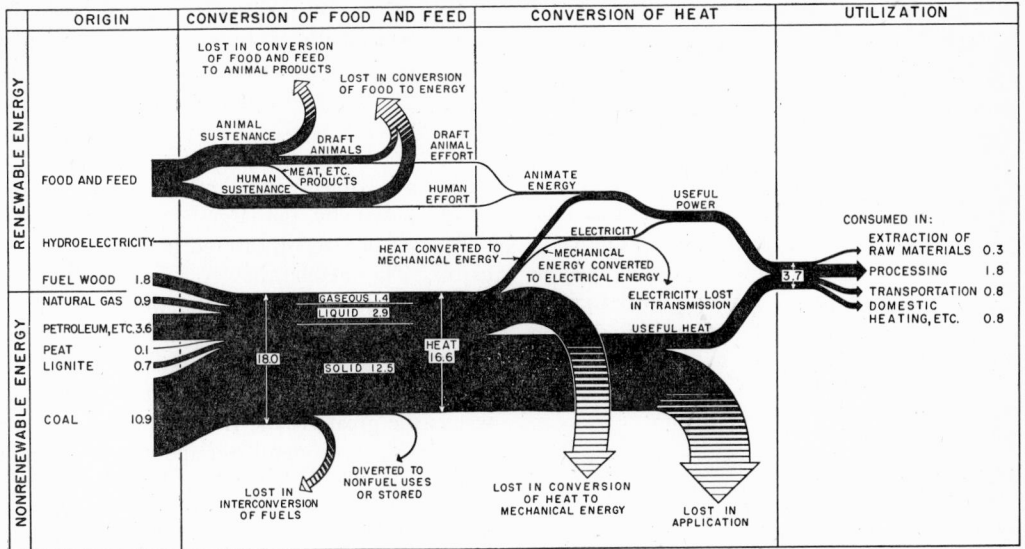

FIGURE 272. ENERGY-SYSTEM EFFICIENCY: ORIGIN AND UTILIZATION OF THE WORLD'S SUPPLY OF ENERGY, 1937

of coke and so on) or is diverted to nonfuel uses; more than 25 per cent is lost in converting heat into mechanical energy; less than half the heat generated by burning fuels is actually utilized by men. Thus, all in all, the motive power and heat used by men represent less than a sixth of the potential energy they have at their disposal in the form of food, feed, water power and mineral fuels.

The flow of energy in the world in 1937, illustrated by Figure 272, shows the following changes in the amount of energy, in kilowatt-hours and coal equivalent, as it goes through the conversion process from origin to utilization: [48]

Energy	Trillions of Kilowatt-Hours	Coal Equivalent, in Billions of Tons [a]
Origin		
Total potential energy	23.2	13.92
Food and feed	5.0	3.00
Hydroelectricity	0.2	0.12
Fuels	18.0	10.80
Wood	1.8	1.08
Coal, lignite, peat	11.7	7.02
Petroleum	3.6	2.16
Natural gas	0.9	0.54
Loss in conversion		
Total	6.1	3.66
Food and feed	4.7	2.82
Fuel	1.4	0.84

48. Adapted from **29**, Figure 1.

Converted into animate energy, electricity and heat		
Total	17.1	10.26
Animate energy	0.3	0.18
Electricity	0.2	0.12
Heat	16.6	9.96
Loss in conversion of heat and in transmission		
Total	13.4	8.04
Burning	8.6	5.16
Transformation of heat into mechanical energy	4.7	2.82
Transmission of electricity	0.1	0.06
Remainder for consumption	3.7	2.22
Consumed in		
Extractive industries	0.3	0.18
Processing (manufactures)	1.8	1.08
Transportation	0.8	0.48
Domestic heating	0.8	0.48

a. Conversion factor: 1,000 kilowatt-hours = 0.6 ton of coal equivalent.

WATER POWER

Water, in its modern form of hydroelectric power, has been a junior partner among the sources of energy. In 1945 it provided less than 3 per cent of the world's supply of potential energy, including animate energy and fuels. Indeed, in the list of sources of potential energy water was below natural gas, fuel wood and even work animals. (See Table 395.) Its importance in the world economy, however, is much greater than this comparison suggests. First, water power can be transformed into motive power or heat with comparatively small losses while potential energy of fuels is seldom utilized at a rate above 25 per cent. Second, water power is continuously renewable. Third, in some areas that are short of other sources of energy, water is the mainspring of the whole economy. It is believed also that the role of water in the world's economy will increase with the depletion of the most profitable deposits of coal, oil and natural gas.

WATER-POWER RESOURCES

While the sail and the water wheel are among the oldest mechanical devices known to man, water power could not be used on a large scale until turbines and dynamos were invented.

The use of water power has certain limitations. Power plants cannot utilize all the energy of a river, measured by the total amount of water it carries and the total fall during its course. The fall must be sufficiently great and the flow sufficiently uniform during a large part of the year. On the other hand, when the fall is very great, even a comparatively small stream can generate a considerable amount of electric power.

The conditions that make a site on a river suitable for a hydroelectric plant change with progress in the technique of building dams and turbines and the methods of transmitting high-tension electric current. They change also with the demand for power (the "load"). Some sites that are now regarded as potential reserves of water power could not have been utilized two or three decades ago. When better cement, stronger pipes and cheaper dynamos become available, sites that are now of no economic value will become potential sources of water power. The trend in estimates of potential water power, therefore, has been upward. Another factor that has contributed to utilization of certain sites for development of hydroelectric power is the new practice of using water power for a part of the year, in conjunction with steam.

The Potential Power of Rivers

A paper presented to the World Power Conference in London, 1950, suggested estimating the hydroelectric power of the world by multiplying the arithmetic mean flow of each river by the elevation above sea level of the point where this flow begins.[49] By this short-cut procedure, the total capacity of the world's rivers is estimated at 5.6 billion kilowatts, which is the equivalent of an energy supply of more than 49 trillion kilowatt-hours per year.

This total was erroneously described in the paper as "Usable Water Power Resources of the World." Actually, the largest part of the potential power of rivers measured in this way is not usable. The method, however, has the merit of describing the network of the world's rivers as an energy system, quite independent of the ability of men to use it. This approach shows four main concentrations of powerful streams of water: the great Asiatic rivers flowing from the Himalayas; the Congo River and its tributaries in Africa; the Columbia River Basin in North America; and the rivers of the Pacific coast in South America. (See Figure 273.) The streams on the southern and eastern slopes of the Himalayas are probably the most powerful. A single site on the upper Brahmaputra at Lusa (Tibet) is capable of generating 15 million kilowatts,[50] almost as much as all the existing hydroelectric stations in the United States.

Most of the sites of river power shown in Figure 273, however, have never been explored, and not all of those explored have been found "usable."

Usable Water Power

In estimating usable water power in an area, account is taken only of sections of rivers where water can be harnessed to hydroturbines at reasonable cost. Less than 10 per cent of the total potential power of rivers meets this requirement. According to the United States Geological Survey, potential water power, at ordinary minimum flow at the sites where hydroelectric installations can be built, totals 650–700 million horsepower, or about 500 million kilowatts. Some 40 per cent of this water power is found in Africa, 23 per cent is in the Americas, and only 13 per cent in Asia. (See Table 407.)

Many sites that are technically suitable for hydroelectric development are located, however, in areas where there is little demand for electric power. Mountainous regions with vast plateaus towering one above another are highly favorable for the large-scale accumulation of water power

49. 22.
50. 6, 1949, p. 372.

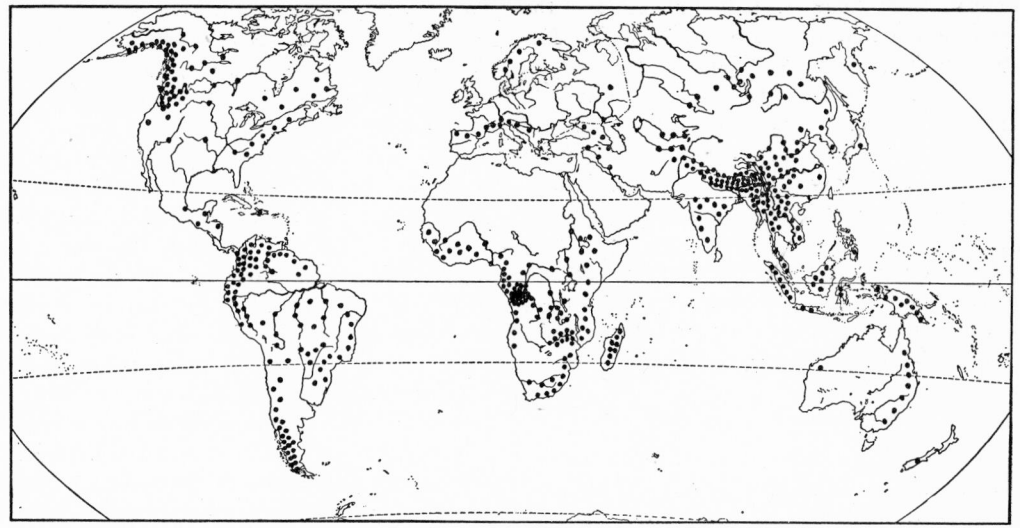

World Power Conference, London, 1950

FIGURE 273. WATER POWER: POTENTIAL RESERVES IN THE WORLD

Each dot represents 10 million kilowatts

The map is reproduced here as it was presented to the World Power Conference. Its accuracy seems questionable at some points, especially the basin of the Yellow River in China.

but not for the development of dense population. On the other hand, fertile plains and coastal lowlands, which are the most densely populated areas, rarely include waterfalls and rapids — Niagara Falls being one of the rare exceptions. Thus, the world's largest reserves of water power are far from its industrial centers.

HYDROELECTRIC PLANTS

Capacity

The total capacity of the world's hydroelectric plants doubled between 1920 and 1930 and almost doubled again between 1930 and 1947, according to estimates of the United States Geological Survey:

Year	Millions of Horsepower	Index (1920 = 100)
1920	23.0	100
1923	29.0	126
1926	33.0	143
1930	46.0	200
1934	55.0	239
1936	60.0	261
1938	63.9	278
1940	69.4	302
1941	71.6	311
1945	77.8	338
1947	86.9	378

In 1947, plant capacity totaled 86.9 million horsepower as compared with potential power totaling 663.5 million horsepower (Table 407). These figures seem to indicate that the capacity of existing water-power plants represents less than a seventh of the potentially usable water power in the world. If, however, all the potential water power estimated by the Geological Survey were harnessed, the capacity of the new plants would be from 15 to 20 times that of the existing hydroelectric installations.[51] In other words, the

51. The potential water power of a definite section of a stream is measured on the basis of the ordinary minimum flow available 50 per cent, 90 per cent or 95 per cent of the time, assuming a definite percentage of efficiency in utilization, sometimes 70 per cent, sometimes 100 per cent. The flow available 50 per cent of the time is naturally larger than that available for 90 per cent of the time; in the United States, the difference is close to 40 per cent. In general, an estimate based on the flow during half the time and 70 per cent efficiency is not far from an estimate based on the flow during 90–95 per cent of the time and 100 per cent efficiency.

The developed water power in an area is measured by the capacity of installed water wheels, which is usually two to four times the potential power at low flow at the same sites. The United States Geological Survey therefore assumes that the ultimate installed capacity of water wheels in a site about equals the power available at this site at mean flow, assuming 100 per cent efficiency, which is much higher than the standard estimate of potential

TABLE 407

WATER POWER: CAPACITY OF PLANTS AND UNDEVELOPED POWER, BY COUNTRY, 1947

(Thousands of Horsepower)

Continent and Country	Capacity of Existing Plants	Undeveloped Power — Ordinary Minimum Flow	Undeveloped Power — Mean Flow
World	86,890	663,500	...
North America	34,993	68,700	...
United States	24,206	34,700	113,000
Alaska	35	1,400	...
Canada	10,491	32,000	72,000
Newfoundland	261	600	...
Middle America	856	15,700	...
Mexico	646	8,500	...
Guatemala	35	2,100	...
El Salvador	5	300	...
Honduras	7	1,400	...
Nicaragua	1	1,100	...
Costa Rica	31	1,400	...
West Indies	91	200	...
Panama	40	700	...
South America	2,392	66,600	...
Venezuela	15	4,300	...
Colombia	30	5,400	...
Guiana	0	5,400	...
Ecuador	21	1,300	...
Brazil	1,520	28,000	...
Peru	275	6,400	...
Bolivia	44	3,600	...
Paraguay	0.5	2,800	...
Chile	322	3,600	...
Uruguay	90	400	...
Argentina	75	5,400	27,000
Europe	32,917	53,615	...
United Kingdom	485	700	...
Ireland	168	300	...
Iceland	22	700	...
France	6,100	6,000	12,000
Belgium	32	Small	...
Netherlands	1	25	...
Denmark	16	30	...
Sweden	3,820	4,000	21,000
Norway	3,800	10,000	27,000
Finland	820	2,500	...
Germany	2,600	2,500	5,000
Poland	128	1,350	3,600
Czechoslovakia	370	700	1,700
Switzerland	3,700	3,600	...
Austria	2,000	1,550	4,000
Hungary	5	160	300
Portugal	146	450	...
Spain	1,980	5,700	...
Italy	6,250	6,000	...
Yugoslavia	250	4,000	...
Romania	127	3,000	8,000
Bulgaria	70	300	1,000
Albania	1	200	...
Greece	10	350	...
Turkey	16	Small	...
USSR	2,362	78,250	375,000
In Europe	2,020	14,250	50,000
In Asia	342	64,000	325,000
Asia	11,717	86,600	...
China	3.5	22,000	...
Manchukuo	208	1,000	...
Korea	1,800	3,000	...
Japan	8,600	7,200	...
Taiwan	237	1,000	...
Asia Minor	48	22,000	41,000
Iran	1	300	...
Afghanistan	2	700	...
India and Ceylon	767	39,000	...
Thailand	50	5,700	...
Indochina	0.2	6,000	...
Africa	368	273,890	...
Morocco	81	350	...
Algeria	105	300	...
Egypt	10	850	...
Ethiopia	1	5,700	...
Rio de Oro	—	350	...
French Guinea	—	3,000	...
Sierra Leone	—	2,500	...
French Equatorial Africa	—	50,000	...
Belgian Congo	70	130,000	...
Liberia	7.5	5,700	...
Ivory Coast	—	4,000	...
Gold Coast	—	2,000	...
French Sudan	—	1,400	...
Nigeria	11	13,000	...
French Cameroons	—	18,500	...
Tanganyika	18	4,000	...
Nyasaland	—	1,700	...
British East Africa	10	6,700	...
Mozambique	—	5,000	...
Madagascar	4.5	7,000	...
Angola	4	5,700	...
Rhodesia	41	3,500	...
Union of South Africa	4	2,500	...
Other areas	1	140	...
Oceania	1,284	20,150	...
Australia and Tasmania	352	1,000	...
New Zealand	670	2,000	3,600
Philippines	65	2,000	...
Borneo and New Guinea	5	10,500	...
Celebes	0.5	1,400	...
Java	140	1,100	...
Hawaii	32	150	...

Source: Adapted from mimeographed releases of the U.S. Geological Survey.

potential continuously renewable water power in the world could theoretically satisfy about half of mankind's current demand for energy. The potential water power of Asia, including the Asiatic part of the USSR, at ordinary minimum flow is 6 times and at mean flow perhaps 20 times the capacity of all the hydroelectric plants in the United States. Africa has water power sufficient to generate 10 times as much electricity as all the present hydroelectric plants in North America or Europe.

The United States ranks first in capacity of hydroelectric plants, with more than 24 million installed horsepower at the end of 1947; Canada is second (10.5 million); Japan third (8.6 million); Italy and France come next (over 6 million each), followed by Sweden, Norway (3.8 million each) and Switzerland (3.7 million). These eight countries together control more than two thirds of the capacity of the hydroelectric plants in the world. Hydroelectric plants in the USSR and Germany have a capacity of 2 to 2.6 million horsepower in each country; Austria, Spain and Korea have from 1.8 to 2 million each; Brazil has 1.5 million; Mexico, Finland, India and New Zealand, from 640,000 to 820,000 each. At the end of 1947, no other country had as much installed capacity as 500,000 horsepower. (See Table 407; cf. Figures 274 and 275.)

A large part of the capacity of existing hydroelectric plants is concentrated in three areas — North America, western Europe and Japan. (See Figure 274.) Potential water power, in contrast, is scattered all over the world. (See Figure 275.) The greatest storehouse is the Belgian Congo in Central Africa. The Asiatic part of the USSR — mainly Siberia, with its tremendous rivers — ranks second, followed by French Equatorial Africa, India, Brazil and China, all of which are areas with a comparatively low level of industrial development.[52]

Undeveloped Power in the United States

The Federal Power Commission publishes periodic estimates of undeveloped water power, by state, comparable with its reports on the capacity of existing installations.[53] Undeveloped power is rated as the probable capacity of generators which would normally be installed at hy-

droelectric developments, assuming reasonable regulation of flow by storage and taking into account factors pertinent to the best over-all development of the river for power and other purposes.

As of January 1949, the capacity of existing hydroelectric power plants in the United States totaled 25 million horsepower and that of undeveloped water power, 117 million horsepower.[54] The ratio of actual to total potential capacity (actual and undeveloped) varies widely from state to state. More than half the total potential water power has been harnessed in Rhode Island, Delaware, Michigan, Wisconsin, Tennessee and Nevada. Less than 10 per cent is being utilized in New Jersey, Ohio, Illinois, Missouri, North Dakota, South Dakota, Kansas, West Virginia, Mississippi, Arkansas, Oklahoma, Montana, Idaho, Wyoming, Colorado and Utah. The largest unharnessed reserves of water power are in the West, in the Mountain and Pacific states. (See Table 408 and Figure 276.)

Large Plants in the World

Hydroelectric plants range in size from small barrages for the owner's private use to huge installations which affect the life of a whole region.

According to the information assembled by the Federal Power Commission, some 185 hydroelectric plants dispersed all over the world had a capacity of 75,000 kilowatts or over, in January 1951. Of the total, 170 plants could be exactly located while the whereabouts of large hydroelectric installations in the USSR remained unknown and their number was estimated as "probably about a dozen."

Most of the large hydroelectric plants—97, excluding those in the USSR — have a capacity of 100,000 to 250,000 kilowatts, the usual size of large plants of regional and national significance in Great Britain, France, Germany, the Scandinavian countries, Italy, India, Japan and Manchuria. Only a few plants have a capacity of more than 250,000 kilowatts. In January 1951 there were 27 such stations in the world, including the USSR: 18 in the United States, 6 in Canada, and one each in France, Sweden and the USSR (Dneprostroi). All plants with a capacity of more than 500,000 kilowatts are in the

---

(undeveloped) water power based on ordinary minimum flow for 95 per cent of the time.

52. Cf. **35**, pp. 12, 13 and 20.

53. **14**.

54. The first figure is close to that given for the United States in Table 408; the second is somewhat higher than the undeveloped power at mean flow as estimated in 1947.

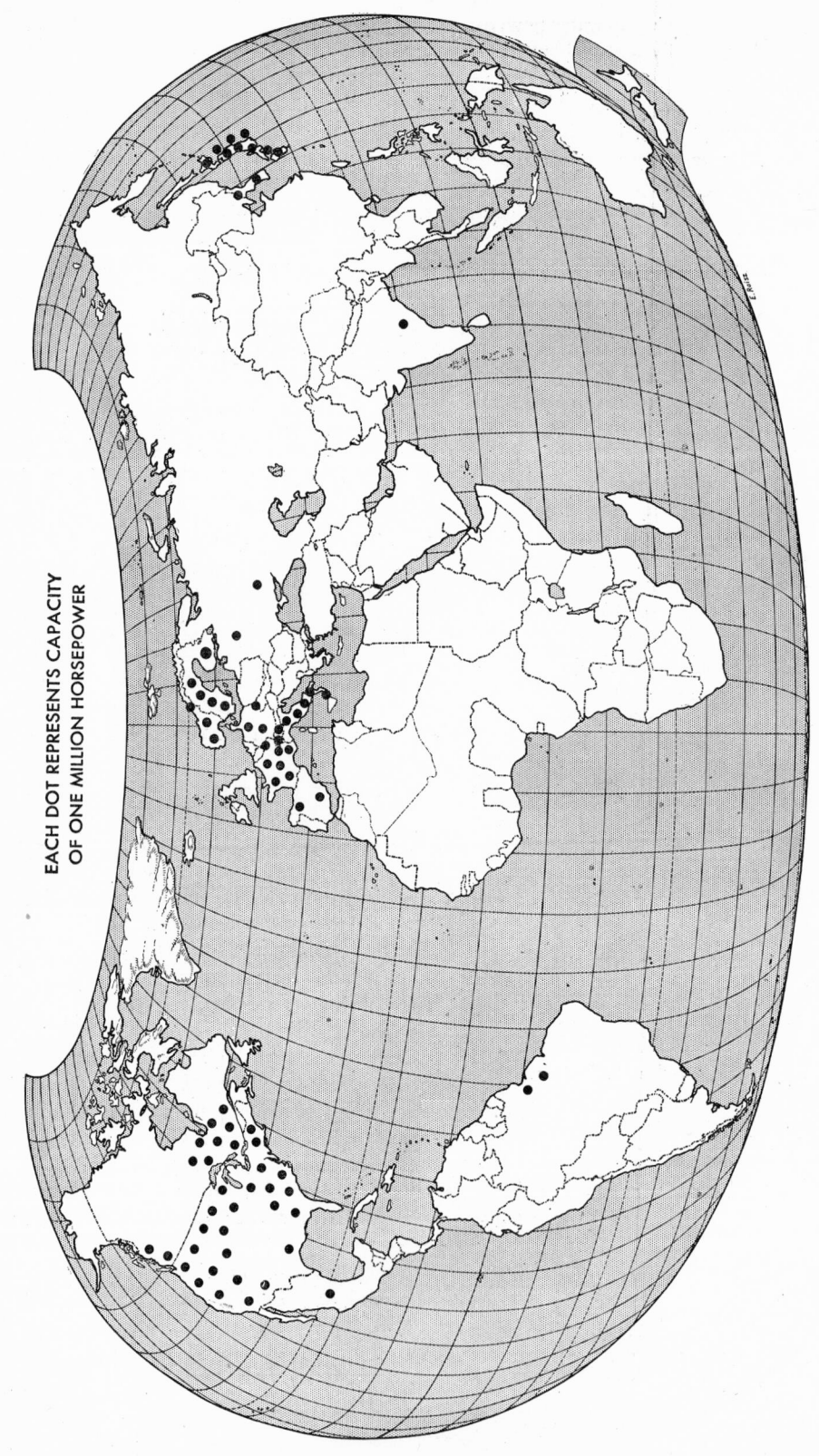

EACH DOT REPRESENTS CAPACITY
OF ONE MILLION HORSEPOWER

FIGURE 274. WATER POWER: GEOGRAPHIC DISTRIBUTION OF PLANT CAPACITY IN THE WORLD, 1947

Most of the world's hydroelectric plants are located in North America, western Europe and Japan. These three areas together had an installed capacity of 76.5 million horsepower in 1947, as compared with 10.4 million in the rest of the world.

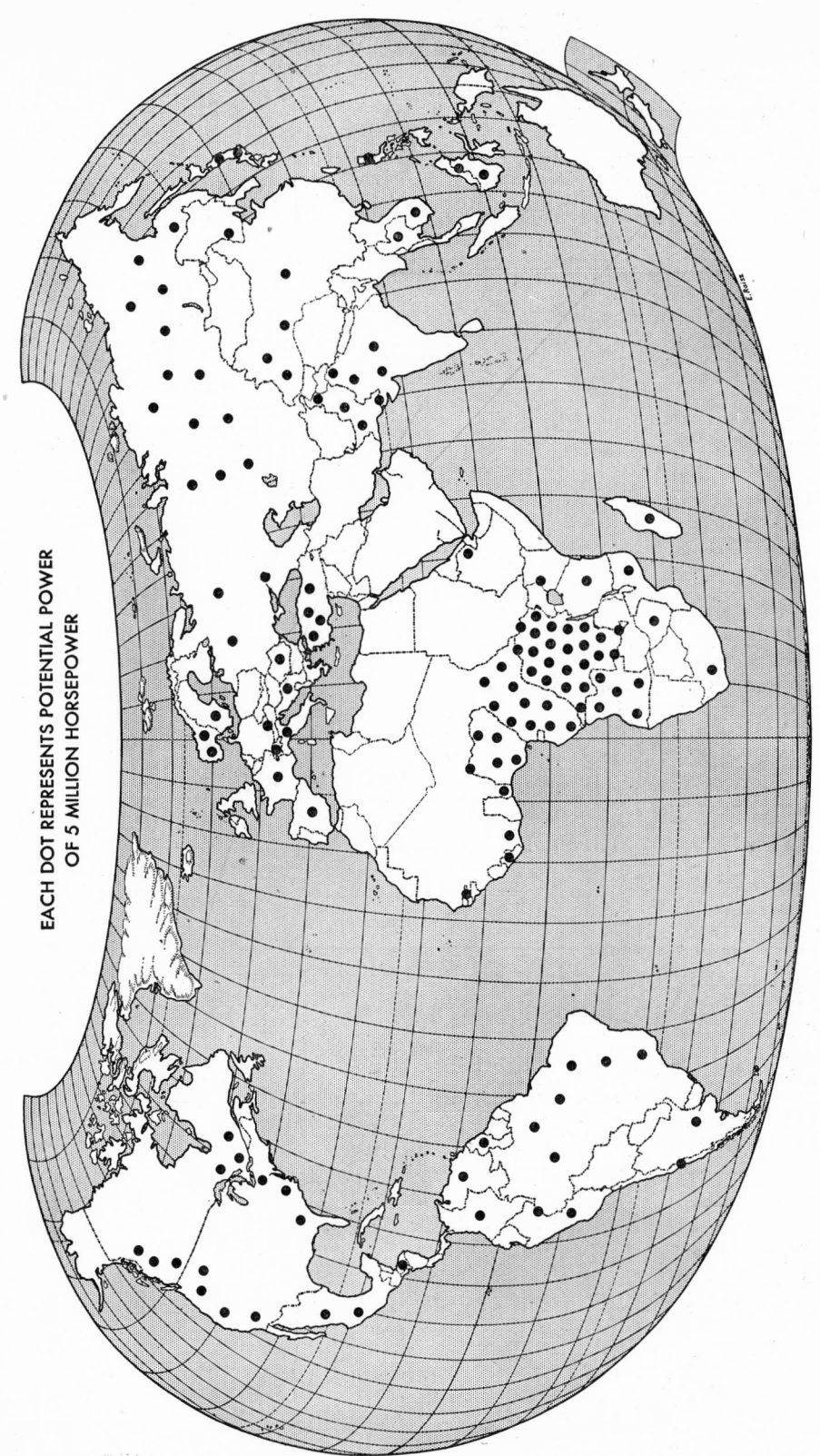

EACH DOT REPRESENTS POTENTIAL POWER
OF 5 MILLION HORSEPOWER

Figure 275. Water Power: Geographic Distribution of Potential Reserves in the World, 1947

According to the U. S. Geological Survey, Africa is the main storehouse of potential water power. Considerable reserves also exist in the United States, Canada, Brazil, Siberia, and especially in the Far East. The United Nations Economic Commission for Asia and the Far East gives much higher estimates for the potential power of the rivers of China, but this correction does not change the ranking of continents suggested by this map.

TABLE 408

WATER POWER: CAPACITY OF PLANTS AND UNDEVELOPED POWER IN THE UNITED STATES, BY STATE, END OF 1948

(Thousands of Horsepower)

Division and State	Existing Plants	Estimated Undeveloped Power	Percentage of Total Capacity Developed	Division and State	Existing Plants	Estimated Undeveloped Power	Percentage of Total Capacity Developed
United States	25,024	117,389	18	South Atlantic (continued)			
				District of			
New England	1,656	4,255	28	Columbia	4	80	5
Maine	524	2,159	20	Virginia	276	1,837	13
New Hampshire	418	803	34	West Virginia	278	2,810	9
Vermont	257	837	24	North Carolina	1,288	1,566	45
Massachusetts	299	301	43	South Carolina	909	1,260	42
Rhode Island	15	—	100	Georgia	569	2,736	17
Connecticut	144	153	49	Florida	17	121	12
				East South Central	3,656	6,346	37
Middle Atlantic	2,249	8,806	20	Kentucky	363	2,112	15
New York	1,641	4,088	29	Tennessee	1,659	1,300	56
New Jersey	12	302	4	Alabama	1,635	2,385	41
Pennsylvania	595	4,417	12	Mississippi	—	549	0
East North Central	1,268	3,141	28	West South Central	625	4,781	12
Ohio	20	284	7	Arkansas	198	2,273	8
Indiana	49	433	10	Louisiana	—	67	0
Illinois	72	1,489	5	Oklahoma	99	1,290	7
Michigan	535	478	53	Texas	328	1,151	22
Wisconsin	531	457	54	Mountain	3,063	31,410	9
				Montana	571	9,159	6
West North Central	843	7,739	10	Idaho	591	11,894	5
Minnesota	242	304	44	Wyoming	106	1,068	9
Iowa	183	555	25	Colorado	124	2,184	5
Missouri	201	3,312	6	New Mexico	33	240	12
North Dakota	—	874	0	Arizona	724	4,959	13
South Dakota	16	1,714	9	Utah	126	1,757	7
Nebraska	191	591	24	Nevada	787	149	84
Kansas	9	389	2	Pacific	8,013	39,889	17
South Atlantic	3,707	10,922	25	Washington	3,473	21,319	14
Delaware	1	—	100	Oregon	1,049	8,509	11
Maryland	365	512	42	California	3,491	10,061	26

Source: Federal Power Commission.

BY GEOGRAPHIC DIVISIONS

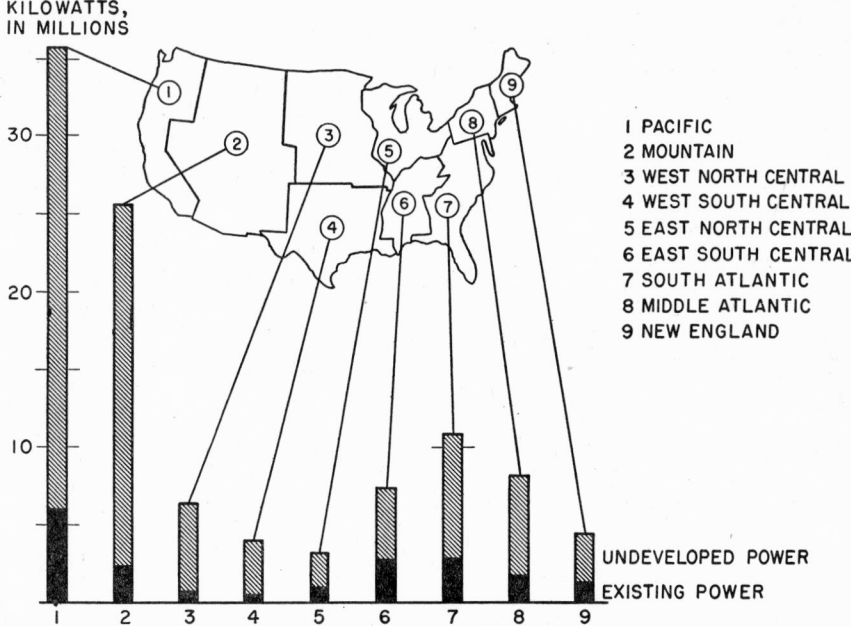

1 PACIFIC
2 MOUNTAIN
3 WEST NORTH CENTRAL
4 WEST SOUTH CENTRAL
5 EAST NORTH CENTRAL
6 EAST SOUTH CENTRAL
7 SOUTH ATLANTIC
8 MIDDLE ATLANTIC
9 NEW ENGLAND

BY MAJOR DRAINAGE BASINS

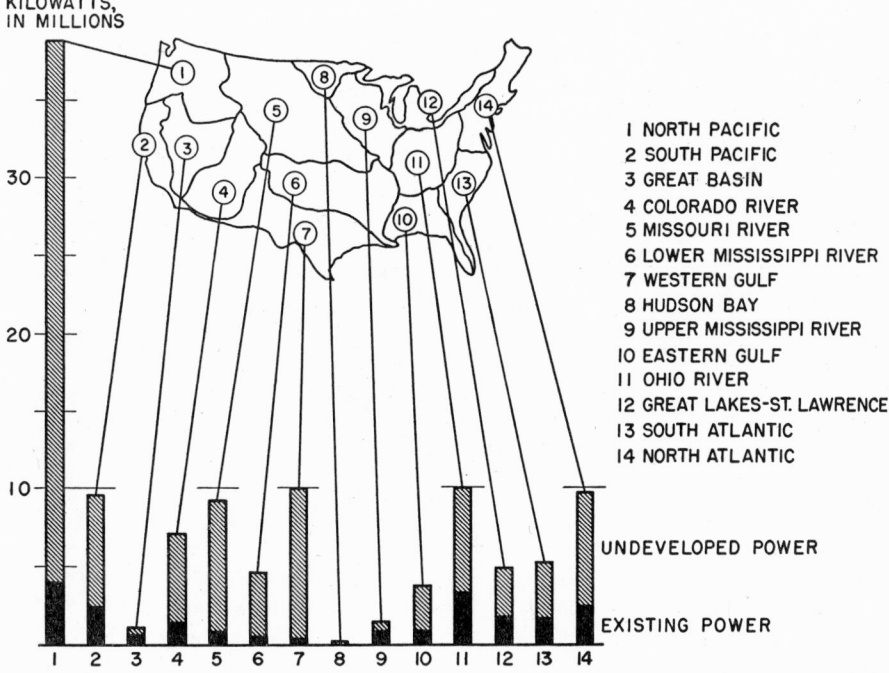

1 NORTH PACIFIC
2 SOUTH PACIFIC
3 GREAT BASIN
4 COLORADO RIVER
5 MISSOURI RIVER
6 LOWER MISSISSIPPI RIVER
7 WESTERN GULF
8 HUDSON BAY
9 UPPER MISSISSIPPI RIVER
10 EASTERN GULF
11 OHIO RIVER
12 GREAT LAKES-ST. LAWRENCE
13 SOUTH ATLANTIC
14 NORTH ATLANTIC

U. S. Federal Power Commission

FIGURE 276. WATER POWER: GEOGRAPHIC DISTRIBUTION OF EXISTING AND UNDEVELOPED POWER
IN THE UNITED STATES, JANUARY 1, 1951

Nearly 60 per cent of the potential water power of the United States is in the West. The East has
about one third of the potential water power and 60 per cent of the installed capacity. The central
states are sparsely provided with water power.

TABLE 409

LARGE HYDROELECTRIC PLANTS IN THE WORLD: NUMBER IN EACH COUNTRY,
BY SIZE, JANUARY 1, 1951

		Capacity, in Thousands of Kilowatts [a]				
Country	Total	75–100	101–250	251–500	501–1,000	Over 1,000
World, total [b]	170	47	97	19	4	3
United States	65	14	33	13	2	3
Canada	31	7	18	4	2	—
United Kingdom	1	—	1	—	—	—
France	9	2	6	1	—	—
Sweden	7	2	4	1	—	—
Norway	10	2	8	—	—	—
Finland	2	—	2	—	—	—
Western Germany	7	2	5	—	—	—
Switzerland	7	4	3	—	—	—
Austria	4	2	2	—	—	—
Spain	3	1	2	—	—	—
Italy	8	3	5	—	—	—
Japan	5	2	3	—	—	—
Taiwan	1	1	—	—	—	—
Manchuria	2	—	2	—	—	—
India	3	1	2	—	—	—
Australia	1	1	—	—	—	—
New Zealand	4	3	1	—	—	—

Source: Federal Power Commission.

a. As far as possible plants are classified by capacity as of January 1, 1951. Some plants in the United States, however, are classified by ultimate planned capacity, which may not have been reached at that date.

b. Excludes the USSR.

United States and Canada. (See Tables 409 and 410.)

The twenty-five largest hydroelectric installations in the world are:

	Installed Capacity in Kilowatts
Grand Coulee (United States)	1,974,000
Chief Joseph (United States)	1,280,000 [a]
Hoover (United States)	1,030,000
McNary (United States)	980,000 [a]
Shipshaw No. 2 (Canada)	900,000
Beauharnois (Canada)	635,000
Bonneville (United States)	518,400
Dneprostroi (USSR)	500,000 [b]
Oahe (United States)	490,000 [a]
Wilson (United States)	436,000
Garrison (United States)	400,000 [a]
Isle Maligne (Canada)	400,000
Shasta (United States)	375,000
Queenston–Chippawa (Niagara: Canada)	373,000
Shawinigan Falls (Canada)	365,000
Ross (United States)	360,000 [a]
Des Joachims (Canada)	358,000
Schoellkopf (United States)	334,800
Bull Shoals (United States)	320,000 [a]
Fort Randall (United States)	320,000 [a]
Hungry Horse (United States)	300,000 [a]
Harsprånget (Sweden)	290,000
Clark Hill (United States)	280,000
Wolf Creek (United States)	270,000
Genissiat (France)	260,000

a. Ultimate capacity as envisaged in 1949.
b. Approximate.

The large plants (with a capacity of 75,000 kilowatts and over) represent some 60 per cent of the total installed capacity of hydroelectric stations in Canada; 30 per cent in the United States, Germany, Finland; approximately 25 per cent in Sweden, Norway, Austria, the USSR, Manchukuo; and 15 per cent in France and Italy. Several large stations are under construction in India and other countries.

TABLE 410

LARGE HYDROELECTRIC PLANTS IN THE WORLD: NAME AND LOCATION IN EACH COUNTRY, JANUARY 1, 1951

Country and State or Province	Name of Plant	River	Capacity, in Thousands of Kilowatts
United States			
Washington	Grand Coulee	Columbia	1,974,000
Washington	Chief Joseph	Columbia	1,280,000 [a]
Arizona–Nevada	Hoover	Colorado	1,030,000
Washington–Oregon	McNary	Columbia	980,000 [a]
Oregon	Bonneville	Columbia	518,400
Missouri	Oahe	South Dakota	490,000 [a]
Alabama	Wilson	Tennessee	436,000
Missouri	Garrison	North Dakota	400,000 [a]
California	Shasta	Sacramento	375,000
Washington	Ross	Skagit	360,000 [a]
New York	Schoellkopf	Niagara	334,800
Arkansas	Bull Shoals	White	320,000 [a]
South Dakota	Fort Randall	Missouri	320,000 [a]
Montana	Hungry Horse	Flathead	300,000 [a]
Georgia–South Carolina	Clark Hill	Savannah	280,000 [a]
Kentucky	Wolf Creek	Cumberland	270,000 [b]
Alabama	Wheeler	Tennessee	259,000
Maryland	Conowingo	Susquehanna	252,000
Pennsylvania	Safe Harbor	Susquehanna	230,000
Arizona	Davis	Colorado	225,000 [b]
West Virginia–Virginia	Bluestone	Kanawha	180,000 [b]
Washington	Rock Island	Columbia	180,000 [b]
Texas–Oklahoma	Red	Denison	175,000 [b]
South Carolina	Pinopolis	Santee	163,000 [b]
Kentucky	Kentucky	Tennessee	160,000
Tennessee	Watts Bar	Tennessee	150,000
Washington	Gorge	Skagit	144,000
New Hampshire	Comerford	Connecticut	140,000 [b]
Arkansas	Norfolk	White	140,000 [b]
South Carolina	Santee Cooper	Santee	132,600
South Carolina	Saluda	Saluda	130,000
Missouri	Osage	Osage	129,000
California	Pit No. 5	Pit	128,000
Tennessee	Fort Loudoun	Tennessee	128,000
Tennessee	Calderwood	Little Tennessee	121,500
Washington	Diablo	Skagit	120,000
Arizona–California	Parker	Colorado	120,000
Washington	Chelan	Chelan	120,000 [b]
Tennessee	Cherokee	Holston	120,000 [b]
Iowa	Keokuk	Mississippi	117,600
North Carolina	Hiwassee	Hiwassee	115,000 [b]
California	Rock Creek	Feather	113,000 [b]
Montana	Kerr	Flathead	112,000
Pennsylvania	Holtwood	Susquehanna	111,000 [b]
California	Electra	Mokelumne	109,000 [b]
North Carolina	Walters	Pigeon	108,000
Georgia	Allatoona	Etowah	108,000 [b]
California	Big Creek No. 3	San Joaquin	106,500

(*Continued on page 960*)

TABLE 410—*continued*

Country and State or Province	Name of Plant	River	Capacity, in Thousands of Kilowatts
United States (continued)			
Tennessee	Norris	Clinch	100,800
Alabama	Jordan	Coosa	100,000
Oregon	Detroit	Willamette	100,000 [b]
Alabama	Martin	Tallapoosa	99,000
Washington	Merwin	Lewis	91,000
Tennessee	Center Hill	Caney Fork	90,000
California	New Electra	N. F. Mokelumme	89,100
Tennessee	Douglas	French Broad	86,000
Alabama	Lay	Coosa	81,000
Tennessee	Chickamauga	Tennessee	81,000
Kentucky	Ohio Falls	Ohio	80,320
California	Big Creek	San Joaquin	80,000
New York	Adams	Niagara	80,000
Idaho	Bliss	Snake	75,000
Virginia	Claytor	New	75,000
California	Keswick	Sacramento	75,000
Tennessee	Apalachia	Hiwassee	75,000
Canada			
Quebec	Shipshaw No. 2	Saguenay	900,000
Quebec	Beauharnois	St. Lawrence	635,000
Quebec	Isle Maligne	Saguenay	400,000
Ontario	Queenston–Chippawa	Niagara	373,000
Quebec	Shawinigan Falls	St. Maurice	365,000
Ontario	Des Joachims	Ottawa	358,000
Quebec	Shipshaw No. 1	Saguenay	224,000
Ontario	Abitibi Canyon	Abitibi	179,000
Quebec	Paugan	Gatineau	178,000
Quebec	Chat Falls	Ottawa	167,000
Quebec	La Tuque	St. Maurice	165,000
Quebec	Cedar Rapids	St. Lawrence	154,000
Ontario	De Cew Falls	Welland Canal	153,000
Quebec	Grand 'Mere	St. Maurice	150,000
Quebec	Rapids Blanc	St. Maurice	150,000
British Columbia	Bridge River	Bridge	138,000
Ontario	Ontario	Niagara	134,000
Manitoba	Seven Sisters	Winnnipeg	130,000
Quebec	La Gabelle	St. Maurice	128,000
Quebec	Chelsea	Gatineau	127,000
Manitoba	Great Falls	Winnipeg	125,000
Ontario	Chenaux	Ottawa	119,000
Ontario	Toronto	Niagara	108,000
British Columbia	Ruskin		105,000
Quebec	Trenche	St. Maurice	95,000
Quebec	High Falls	Lièvre	90,000
Quebec	Farmers	Gatineau	90,000
Manitoba	Pine Falls	Winnipeg	85,000
Ontario	Chat Falls	Ottawa	80,500
Quebec	Chaudière Falls	Ottawa	80,000
Manitoba	Pointe du Bois	Winnipeg	77,500

(*Continued on facing page*)

TABLE 410—*continued*

Country and State or Province	Name of Plant	River	Capacity, in Thousands of Kilowatts
United Kingdom			
Scotland	Loch Sloy		130,000
France	Genissiat	Rhone	260,000
	Brommat	Truyere	167,000
	Kemos	Rhine	150,000
	Mareges	Dordogne	140,000
	Sarrans	Truyere	102,000
	L'Aigle	Dordogne	100,000
	Lac Noir	Cere	100,000
	St. Étienne–Cantales	Cere	75,000
	Le Sautet	Drac	75,000
Sweden	Harsprånget	Lule	290,000 [b]
	Krangede	Indal	210,000
	Porjus	Lule	135,000
	Trollhättan	Gota	130,000
	Hjalta	Flaxälven	125,000
	Stadsforsen	Indal	91,000
	Midskogsforsen	Indal	90,000
Norway	Tyin	Ardal	150,000
	Nore	Numedalslågen	145,000
	Vemork	Mana	145,000
	Saheim	Mana	117,000
	Mar	Mana	114,000
	Sauda		105,000
	Tysse I	Sorfjord	104,000
	Haugvik		100,000
	Holingsdal		84,000
	Vama	Glomma	81,000
Finland	Imatra		127,000
	Pyhakoski		108,000
Western Germany	Witznau		176,000
	Herdecke	Rhine	132,000
	Altjoch		125,000
	Waldeck	Eder	115,000
	Nausern Eicholz	Schwarza	110,000
	Toging	Inn	84,000
	Ering	Inn	75,000
Switzerland	Innertkirchen	Aar	170,000
	Dixence	La Dixence	130,000
	Ryburg-Schworstadt	Rhine	108,000
	Etzel	Sihl	92,000
	Handeck	Aar	88,000
	Vernayaz	Trient-Triege	85,000
	Albruck-Dogern	Rhine	75,000
Austria	Rodund	Ill	170,000
	Vermunt	Ill	119,000
	Kaprun	Tauern	80,000
	Achensee		77,000

(*Continued on page 962*)

TABLE 410—*continued*

Country and State or Province	Name of Plant	River	Capacity, in Thousands of Kilowatts
Spain	Los Peares	Mino	120,000
	Esla	Esla	118,000
	Villal Campo		77,000
Italy	Galleto	Terni	160,000
	S. Francesco	Liri	140,000
	San Giacomo	Teramo	132,000
	Bressanone	Isarco	120,000
	Piave	Piave	100,000
	Fadalto	Piave	86,000
	Ampollino	Fiorre	86,000
	Ponte	Val Toggia	75,000
USSR	Dneprostroi	Dnieper	500,000
Japan	Shinanogawa	Shinano	165,000
	Senju	Shinano	150,000
	Yamabe	Shinano	106,000
	Kurobe No. 4	In Honshu	93,000
	Kurobe No. 3	In Honshu	90,000
Taiwan	Jitsugetsuntan (Sun Moon)	Dokusui-Kei	100,000
Manchuria	Ta-feng-man	Sungari	140,000
	Supung Dong	Yalu	120,000
India	Bhira	Near Bombay	141,000
	Jog	In Mysore	120,000
	Bhivpuri	Near Bombay	78,000
Australia and Tasmania	Derwent, Tasmania		78,000
New Zealand	Arapuni	Waikato	152,000
	Waikaremoana	Waikaretaheki	92,000
	Karapiro	Waikato	80,000
	Waitaki	Waitaki	75,000

Source: Federal Power Commission.

a. Ultimate capacity as envisaged in 1949.
b. May not yet be completed to this ultimate capacity.

With progress in methods of construction and transmission of power and integration of hydroelectric power with that originated by steam, the share of large stations in total installed hydroelectric capacity is steadily increasing.

Large Plants in the United States

The federal government owns the largest hydroelectric power plants: Grand Coulee Dam, Hoover, Bonneville, Wilson, Shasta and so on. By the end of 1949 there were 20 federal stations with an ultimate capacity of 100,000 kilowatts or more in operation and 15 others were under construction. The initial capacity of plants (planned or existing) with an ultimate capacity of 100,000 kilowatts or more was 7.6 million kilowatts, but ultimate total capacity was estimated at 12.4 million. In addition, there were 22 privately owned and 4 public nonfederal power plants with an existing or ultimate capacity of 100,000 kilowatts or more each that would have a total ultimate capacity of 4.6 million kilowatts.[55] The largest privately owned plants are Conowingo and Safe Harbor, both on the Susquehanna River. (See Table 411.)

Development Projects

The development of water power has become the backbone of the program of industrialization in many countries.[56] The plan for hydroelectric

55. Federal Power Commission; cf. 21.
56. See, for example, 25 and 20.

TABLE 411

LARGE HYDROELECTRIC PLANTS IN THE UNITED STATES: BY OWNERSHIP,[a] JULY 1, 1949

	Existing Plants			Plants under Construction		
		Capacity in Thousands of Kilowatts			Capacity in Thousands of Kilowatts	
Ownership	Number	Initial	Ultimate	Number	Initial	Ultimate
Total	45	7,493	11,335	16	3,162	5,683
Federal	20	4,568	6,853	15	3,060	5,552
Nonfederal, public	4	327	907	—	—	—
Privately owned, public utilities	21	2,598	3,575	—	—	—
Industrial plant	—	—	—	1	102	131

Source: **21,** pp. 3–4.

  a. Plants with ultimate capacity of 100,000 kilowatts or more.

power development presented by the Indian government to the World Power Conference in London is typical.[57]

This plan envisages the addition of 27 new stations, with a total capacity of more than 6.6 million kilowatts to India's present 18 electric power plants, which together have a capacity of 1.3 million kilowatts. Seven of the proposed stations are thermal plants and 20 are hydroelectric, with a total capacity of 5.7 million kilowatts. The projected network includes huge installations at the foot of the Himalayas, such as Kosi Dam (1,800,000 kilowatts), Bhakra (400,000), Yamuna (200,000). (See Figure 277.) Two important projects — Damodar and Mahanadi — are under way as part of unified, multipurpose plans for river-basin developments. Both are located in the densely populated eastern provinces of India south of the Ganges River. Apart from flood control, irrigation of four million acres and improvement of the navigability of the rivers, these projects promise to add more than a million kilowatts to the country's supply of hydroelectric power. Further expansion of the Mahanadi river project is in sight, with a possible installation of much more powerful generators.[58]

Another interesting plan is under consideration in Egypt, a country almost completely deprived of natural sources of energy. In view of the limited possibility of harnessing the Nile, the Egyptian government has taken up the old idea of Dr. John Ball of utilizing the Qattara Depression in the northern part of the Libian Desert for generating power by directing into it water from the Mediterranean Sea. This depression, which became known all over the world at the time of the battles for Alexandria in World War II, is a great natural hollow, 186 miles long and 90 miles wide, with an average depth of 200 feet and its lowest point 440 feet below sea level. (See Figure 278.)

In the proposal now under study, water would be led from the Mediterranean over a distance of forty miles, first in an open channel, then in a tunnel leading to the edge of the depression and hence to the turbines. A salt lake would eventually be formed with a surface about 150 feet below the level of the Mediterranean; because of evaporation, however, it would take 200 years to reach this point. The projected hydroelectric station, with a capacity of 300,000 kilowatts, would be only 120 miles from the center of the densely populated area of the Delta.[59]

In the USSR, work is in progress to utilize the water power of the Volga and its tributaries.

These various projects are in different phases of development and most of them are not new. Technological progress, however, and especially the development of heavy equipment for excavating, have brought latent water resources all

___

59. **17.** In view of the role assigned to the evaporation of water from the artificial lake formed in the Qattara Depression, Sir Harold Hartley links this plan with projects to utilize solar radiation. **42,** p. 116.

57. **18.**
58. **6,** 1949, p. 374.

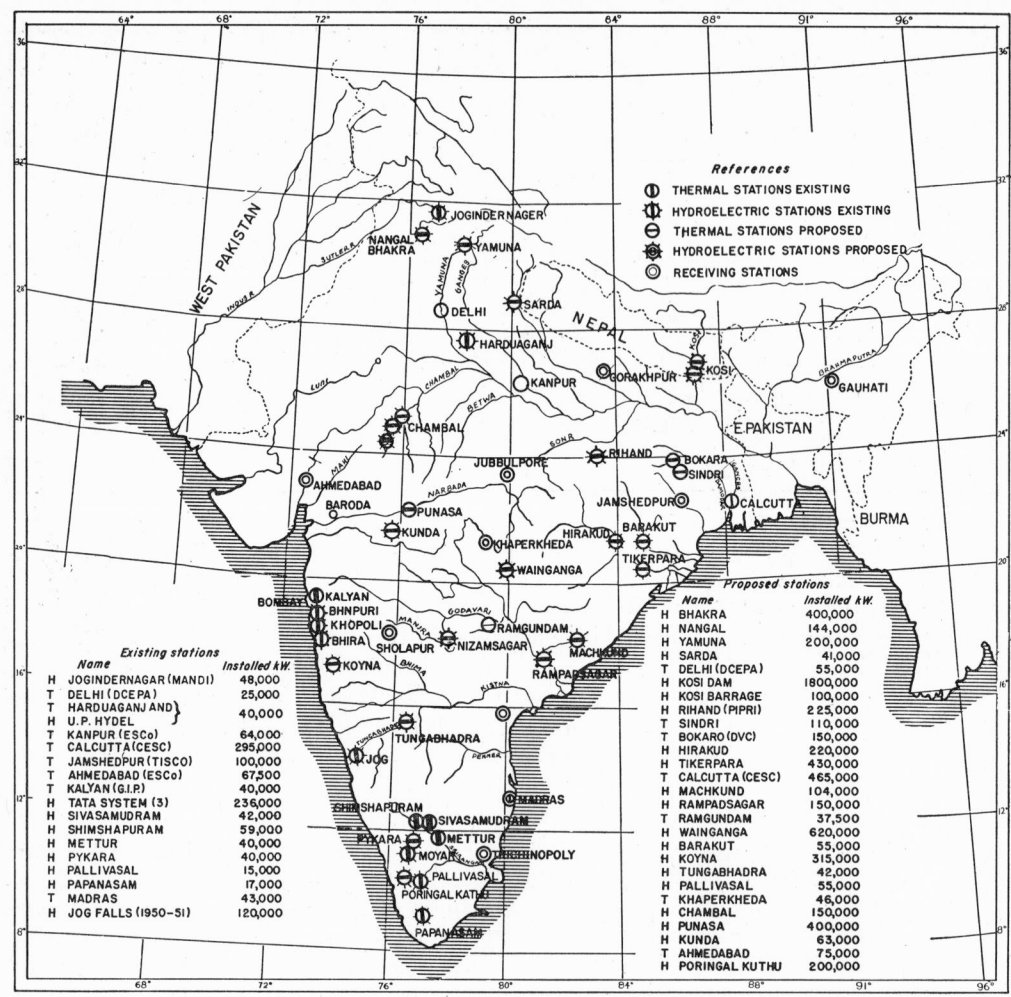

World Power Conference, London, 1950

FIGURE 277. DEVELOPMENT OF WATER POWER: EXISTING AND PROPOSED PLANTS IN INDIA

over the world within the reach of men, and utilization is only a question of time.

ELECTRICITY

The energy originated by mineral fuels and water power travels a long way before it reaches the ultimate consumer. Part of it goes through hydroturbines or steam engines in electric power plants, is transformed into electric current, transferred by wire to electromotors at the site of its use, and then reconverted to motive power.

PRODUCTION OF ELECTRIC POWER

Unlike coal, oil, natural gas and falling water, electricity is a *form,* not a *source,* of energy. It occurs in nature only in the form of static electricity in the clouds, which is practically unman-

ageable and useless to man, but it can be generated artificially from any source of energy — mechanical power, heat or chemical reaction. In most cases it has only a transitory existence and is almost immediately reconverted to mechanical power, heat, light or chemical energy. The objective, and economic advantage, of this dual conversion stems from the unique qualities of electric power — ease of transfer, distribution and control.[60] Indeed, electric power can be transmitted over comparatively long distances with little loss. It can therefore be produced for the market and sold to consumers as a commodity deliverable to their factories and homes.[61] At

60. **38**, p. 409.

61. Heat can also be distributed to consumers in the form of heated air, steam or water, but this practice is not

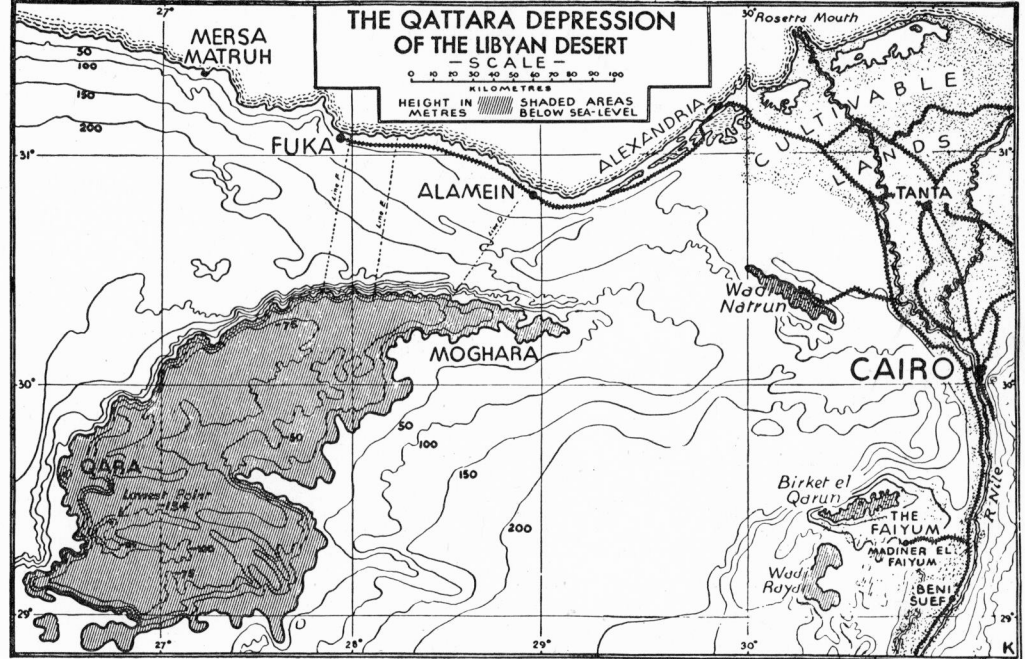

World Power Conference, London, 1950

FIGURE 278. DEVELOPMENT OF WATER POWER: THE QATTARA DEPRESSION PROJECT IN EGYPT

Lines D, E and F show the possible routes of channels and tunnels leading water from the Mediterranean (at top of map) to the Qattara Depression.

present, transmission is limited to a distance of 300–400 miles, but experts are confident that much larger distances could be covered, if necessary.

The Beginning of the Age of Electricity

The modern economy of electric power is the result of a long development. The electrogenerator and motor trace their ancestors to the beginning of the nineteenth century. The most revolutionary invention in this field, however, did not come until the early 1880's, when Thomas Edison realized that electric current could be generated by special plants and delivered to buyers like water, a loaf of bread or the morning newspaper.

The first hydroelectric plant was established in Appleton, Wisconsin, in 1882. Then the first commercial utility plant, with a steam generating capacity of 1,200 horsepower, began operating in New York, supplying light to a dozen city blocks. A few months later, another electric plant was opened in London. A decade later,

electric utilities — some of them public, others privately owned — were in operation in all parts of the United States and in England and continental Europe.

The original objective of all electric utilities of that time was distribution of light. They were called electric lighting companies and the early acts regulating their operation in Great Britain were characteristically called electric lighting acts.[62]

The first public power supply system was inaugurated in England in 1901. Application of Edison's idea to distribution of motive power has drastically changed the system of power supply in modern economy. A factory no longer must itself produce all the energy it needs for operation. Some factories generate part of the energy they need and purchase the rest from utilities; others use only purchased energy. Moreover, modern establishments which operate their own power plants have replaced the old transmission and shaft by a system of electrogenerators and motors: whether they generate their power or purchase it, the energy is usually brought to the site of the work by wire.

very common yet. Electricity is the only form of energy thus sold in large quantity.

62. **38**, p. 410.

TABLE 412

ELECTRIC POWER: OUTPUT, SELECTED COUNTRIES, 1930–51

(Billions of Kilowatt-hours)

Year	World [a]	United States	Canada [b]	Great Britain	France	Sweden	Norway	Germany	Italy	Japan
1930	271	114.6	18.1	12.3	16.9	5.1	7.6	29.1	10.7	13.6
1931	270	109.4	16.3	12.8	15.7	5.1	...	25.8	10.5	16.1
1932	259	99.4	16.1	13.7	15.0	4.9	7.2	23.5	10.6	17.6
1933	274	102.7	17.3	15.0	16.4	5.3	7.2	25.7	11.7	19.7
1934	302	110.4	21.2	16.9	16.7	6.0	7.1	30.7	12.6	21.9
1935	333	118.9	23.3	18.9	17.5	6.9	7.8	36.7	13.8	24.9
1936	371	136.0	25.4	21.5	18.5	7.4	8.0	42.5	13.6	27.3
1937	408	146.5	27.7	24.2	20.1	8.0	9.0	49.0	15.4	30.4
1938	423	142.0	26.2	25.7	20.8	8.2	9.6	55.3	15.5	32.7
1939	464	161.3	28.3	27.7	22.1	9.1	10.2	61.4	18.4	34.1
1940	482	179.9	30.1	30.0	18.8	8.7	8.7	63.0	19.4	34.7
1941	536	208.3	33.3	33.6	20.4	9.1	9.0	70.0	20.8	37.7
1942	575	233.1	37.4	36.9	20.2	9.8	9.6	71.5	20.2	37.5
1943	625	267.5	40.5	38.2	21.2	11.0	11.0	73.9	18.2	38.6
1944	626	279.5	40.6	39.6	16.1	12.4	11.1	...	13.5	37.1
1945	572	271.3	40.1	38.6	18.5	13.5	9.8	...	12.6	23.2
1946	603	269.4	41.7	42.7	23.0	14.2	11.3	...	17.5	29.1
1947	664	307.3	43.4	44.0	25.9	13.5	11.3	...	20.6	32.6
1948	727	336.8	42.4	48.0	29.0	14.1	12.4	30.8 [c]	22.7	35.6
1949	766	345.1	46.7	50.6	30.0	16.1	15.2	35.7 [c]	20.8	41.0
1950	855	388.7	50.9	56.3	33.1	18.1	17.3	44.0 [c]	24.7	44.9
1951	954	432.3	57.4	60.0	36.0	19.6	17.3	51.4 [c]	29.3	41.1

Source: **2**, 1949–50, pp. 280–85, and 1951, pp. 277–84; **4**, January 1953.

a. Excludes the USSR and some minor producers.
b. Only hydroelectric stations.
c. Western Germany.

Producers of Electric Power

Large-scale production of electric energy began at the turn of the present century. The capacity of all the generating plants in the world was close to 2.5 million kilowatts in 1900, more than 10 million kilowatts in 1910, 40 million kilowatts in 1920, 100 million in 1928, 150 million in 1938, and over 250 million in 1948.[63] The United States has led the way, and through a large part of the period has accounted for 40–45 per cent of world output.

About 18 per cent of the electric energy produced in the United States is generated by industrial plants for their own consumption; the remaining 82 per cent is produced by electric utilities for sale to consumers. Public utilities — commercial and government-owned — account for 90 per cent of the electricity generated in Japan;

85 per cent in Australia; 75 per cent in Mexico, the Netherlands, Sweden and Switzerland; 55 per cent in Norway; 50 per cent in Turkey.[64] In many countries statistics of production of electric energy are limited to public utilities.

World Output, 1930–51

The world's output of electric energy in 1930 totaled 271 billion kilowatt-hours, according to the estimate of the Statistical Office of the United Nations.[65] This total does not include the USSR, China, Newfoundland, Cuba, Egypt and some small producers. Correction for these gaps would bring the world's output close to 300 billion kilowatt-hours, in round numbers. Output declined in the early 1930's during the depression but after 1935 advanced rapidly. Excluding the USSR, it

---

63. These figures are based in part on rough estimates.

64. **2**, 1949–50, pp. 277–85.
65. **2**, 1949–50, p. 280.

TABLE 413

ELECTRIC POWER: PLANT CAPACITY AND OUTPUT, SELECTED COUNTRIES, 1950

(According to P. B. Seymour, Federal Power Commission)

Continent and Country	Installed Capacity, in Thousands of Kilowatts	Production, in Millions of Kilowatt-hours	Continent and Country	Installed Capacity, in Thousands of Kilowatts	Production, in Millions of Kilowatt-hours
World, total	231,691	915,028	Europe	84,709	280,610
North America	92,987	438,859	United Kingdom [a]	15,730	55,015
United States	82,487	388,064	Ireland [b]	350	903
Canada	10,500	50,795	France	13,680	31,447
			Luxembourg	169	700
Middle America	2,115	7,334	Belgium	3,182	8,365
Mexico	1,150	4,410	Netherlands	2,241	5,500
Caribbean	965	2,924	Denmark	882	1,814
South America	5,779	15,922	Sweden	4,130	18,464
Venezuela	275	522	Norway	3,070	17,200
Colombia	360	710	Finland	1,400	4,119
Ecuador	44	130	Germany		
Guiana	10	25	West	8,500	43,700
Brazil	2,000	5,500	East	5,000	18,000
Peru	400	1,200	Poland	2,970	9,065
Bolivia	60	240	Czechoslovakia	3,240	9,720
Paraguay	25	60	Switzerland	2,930	9,058
Chile	780	1,535	Austria	1,800	5,000
Uruguay	225	600	Hungary	1,540	4,500
Argentina	1,600	5,400	Portugal	393	937
			Spain	2,440	6,316
Asia	16,157	56,064	Italy	7,870	21,300
China	700	2,250	Yugoslavia	1,730	5,000
Manchuria	500	1,250	Romania	801	2,500
Korea	1,500	4,500	Bulgaria	203	800
Japan	10,500	38,840	Greece	343	850
Taiwan	230	920	Islands	115	342
Turkey	412	732	USSR	22,400	88,000
India and Pakistan	1,425	5,063			
Indonesia	245	600	Oceania	3,794	14,182
Philippines	115	456	Australia	2,750	10,300
Other areas	530	1,453	New Zealand	750	3,020
			Hawaii	175	550
Africa	3,750	14,057	Other islands	119	312
Union of South Africa	2,500	10,770			
Other areas	1,250	3,287			

Source: Courtesy of Mr. P. B. Seymour. There are minor discrepancies in the totals for the same countries and the same years in this table and Table 414.

a. Excludes Northern Ireland.
b. Includes Northern Ireland.

reached 954 billion kilowatt-hours in 1951. (See Table 412.)

The world's output of electricity has increased since the end of World War II, at an annual rate of 8–10 per cent — from 700 billion kilowatt-hours in 1947 to 915 billion in 1950, including the USSR and other areas that are not covered by the current statistics of the United Nations. (See Table 413; cf. Figure 279.) According to

this estimate, the United States controls more than 42 per cent of the world's output of electric power; the USSR claims nearly 10 per cent;[66] Germany accounts for nearly 7 per cent; the United Kingdom for 6 per cent; Canada for 5.5; Japan for 4.3; France for 3.5; Italy for 2.3; Aus-

66. Data for the USSR in Table 413 and Figure 279 are based on official publications of the Soviet government. They may be on the optimistic side.

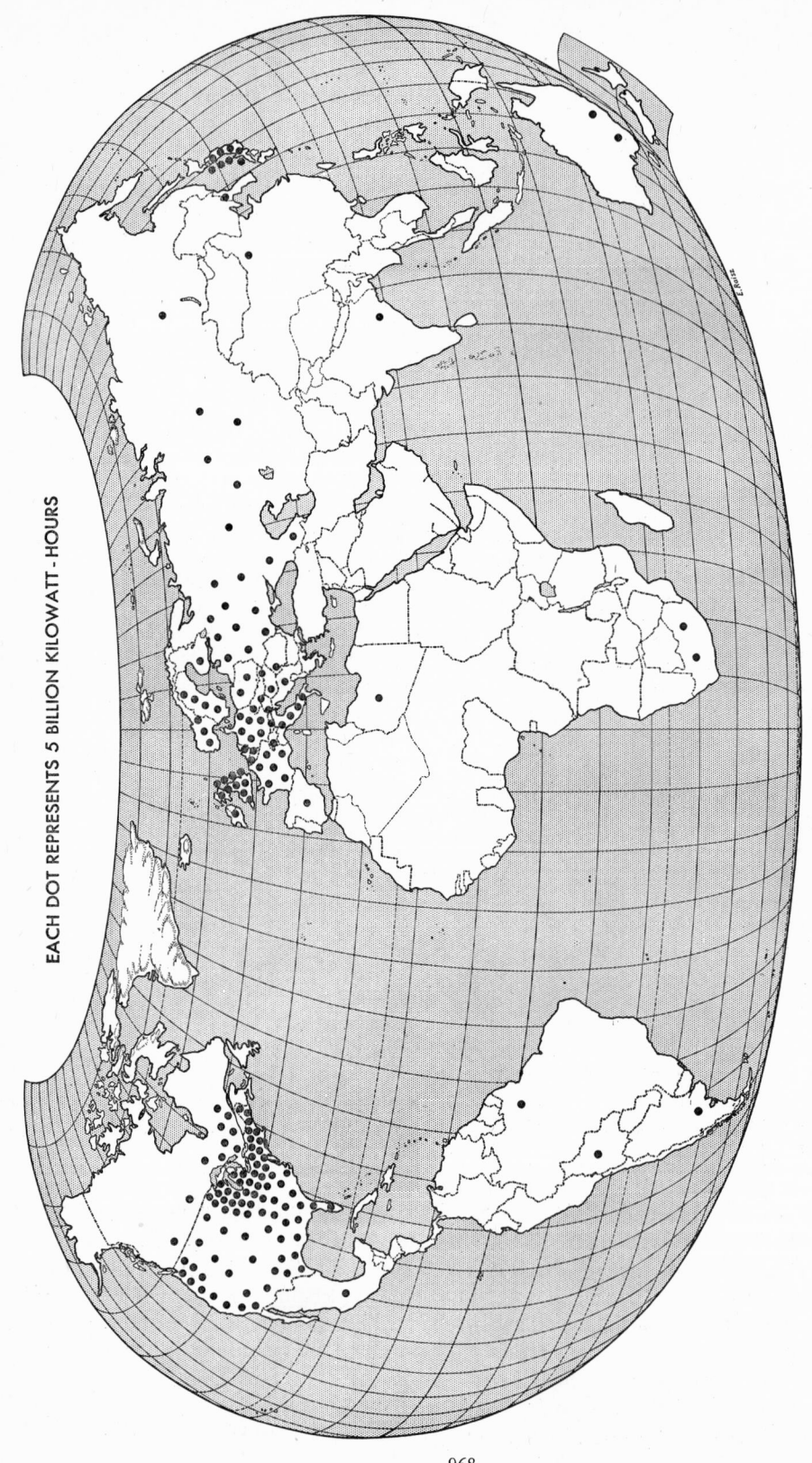

EACH DOT REPRESENTS 5 BILLION KILOWATT-HOURS

FIGURE 279. ELECTRIC POWER: GEOGRAPHIC DISTRIBUTION OF OUTPUT IN THE WORLD, 1950

Production of electric power is heavily concentrated on both coasts of the North Atlantic Ocean. The United States and Canada account for 48 per cent of the world's output, western and central Europe for 30 per cent. Other important producers of electric power are the USSR, Japan, Italy, Australia and the Union of South Africa.

TABLE 414

ELECTRIC UTILITIES: CAPACITY AND OUTPUT, SELECTED COUNTRIES

Country and Year	Installed Capacity, in Thousands of Kilowatts			Output, in Millions of Kilowatt-hours
	Total	Thermo	Hydro	
United States, 1950	81,851	64,176	17,675	. 388,674
Canada, 1946	8,290	381	7,909	41,737
Mexico, 1947	893	484	409	3,598
Jamaica, 1947	15	10	5	46
Colombia, 1946	175	50	125	463
Brazil, 1947	1,486	238	1,248	2,204
Chile, 1947	—	—	—	2,204 [a]
Uruguay, 1947	159	95	64	465
Argentina, 1946	—	—	—	3,052
United Kingdom, 1950	15,502	14,960	542	56,337
Ireland, 1947	214	95	110	618
France, 1950	14,460	8,360	6,100	33,070
Belgium, 1949	2,860	2,836	24	8,163 [b]
Netherlands, 1949	2,260	2,260	—	6,250 [b]
Denmark, 1946	580	566	14	1,141
Sweden, 1949	4,410	1,022	3,388	16,043
Norway, 1949	2,897	113	2,784	15,183
Finland, 1950	1,144	486	658	4,166
Western Germany, 1950	6,901	5,021	1,880	44,017
Poland, 1947	1,196	1,056	140	6,613
Austria, 1947	1,243	230	1,013	3,902
Portugal, 1950	339	192	147	937
Spain, 1950	2,136	607	1,529	6,005
Italy, 1950	7,944	1,200	6,744	20,574
Japan, 1950	10,543	3,984	6,559	44,890
India, 1950	2,296	1,734	562	5,103 [a]
Ceylon, 1950	17	16	1	56
Australia, 1949	2,286	2,013	273	9,053 [b]
New Zealand, 1950	727	87	640	3,070

Sources: **9,** pp. 100–07 and **2,** 1951, pp. 273–82.

a. Hydro.
b. Thermo.

tralia and Czechoslovakia, Poland and Switzerland for about one per cent each.

Sources of Electric Power

The share of water power in the output of electricity ranges from more than 99 per cent in Switzerland and Norway, and almost 90 per cent in Austria, Italy and Japan, to less than 3 per cent in the United Kingdom, Denmark, Belgium and the Netherlands. Coal accounts for most of the remainder.

Since hydroelectric plants are generally better utilized in relation to their capacity than fuel-operated plants, the share of water power in the output of electricity is usually greater than its share in the installed capacity of generators. (See Table 414.) In 1945–47, the share of hydropower in the capacity of installed generators and in the output of electricity by electric utilities in selected countries was as follows: [67]

	Percentage of Capacity	Percentage of Output
Switzerland	—	99.9
Norway	95.5	99.8
Sweden	—	98.8
Canada	95.4	97.7

(*Continued on page 970*)

67. **9,** 1948, pp. 160–75, and 1950, pp. 100–07.

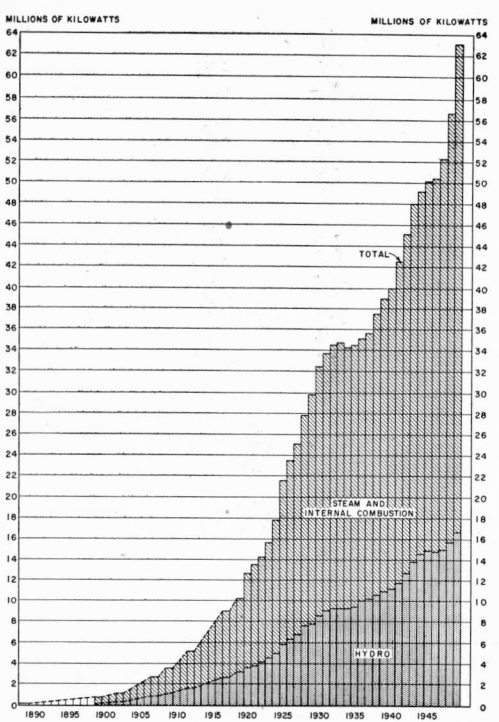

U. S. Federal Power Commission

Figure 280. Electric Utilities: Capacity in the
United States, 1889–1949

Electric utilities have grown rapidly since the beginning of this century. The installed capacity of generating
plants in the United States totaled 2 million kilowatts in
1905, 8 million in 1915 and nearly 22 million in 1925.
Growth slowed down during the depression of the 1930's
but was resumed with economic recovery and accelerated
under the impetus of the defense program and war.

	Percentage of Capacity	Percentage of Output
New Zealand	83.6	95.5
Brazil	83.1	—
Austria	80.0	88.7
Japan	—	87.6
Finland	47.3	84.3
Spain	77.5	76.3
Colombia	71.4	—
Ireland	52.0	64.7
Turkey	65.4	59.0
France	46.4	58.3
Portugal	45.0	51.4
Bulgaria	38.5	46.0
United States	29.5	35.1
Uruguay	20.6	31.1
Czechoslovakia	—	25.8
Romania	8.5	11.9
United Kingdom	—	2.9
Denmark	2.3	2.8
Belgium	2.1	1.8
Netherlands	0.0	0.0

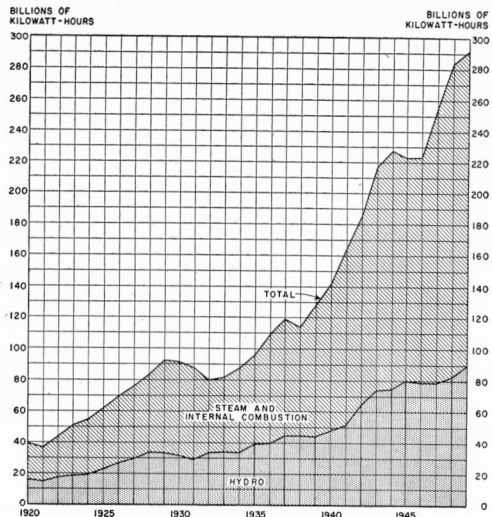

U. S. Federal Power Commission

Figure 281. Electric Utilities: Energy Output in
the United States, by Type of Station, 1920–49

Hydroelectric plants supply approximately 30 per cent
of all power; gas and oil 12–15 per cent; the rest is
supplied by coal.

In the United States, hydroturbines account
for some 30 per cent of the electric power generated by utilities and only 10 per cent of that generated by other industrial establishments.[68]

The share of water power in the total output
of electricity by utility companies has varied
within a narrow range (30–35 per cent) since
1920. (See Figures 280 and 281.) At the end
of 1949, utility plants in the United States had a
total capacity of 63.1 million kilowatts distributed among sources as follows (in millions of
kilowatts):[69]

	Total	Private Utilities	Public Utilities
All sources of energy	63.1	50.5	12.6
Water power	16.6	9.3	7.3
Coal and oil	46.5	41.2	5.3

Water power is the chief source of energy generated in publicly owned electric plants, especially
those of the federal government. Many such
plants are parts of multipurpose projects that
include regulation of the flow of the rivers, soil
conservation, irrigation, flood control and so on.

There is a clear geographic pattern in the relative share of various movers in generating elec-

68. **31,** pp. ii and 30; cf. **30.**
69. **31,** p. xi.

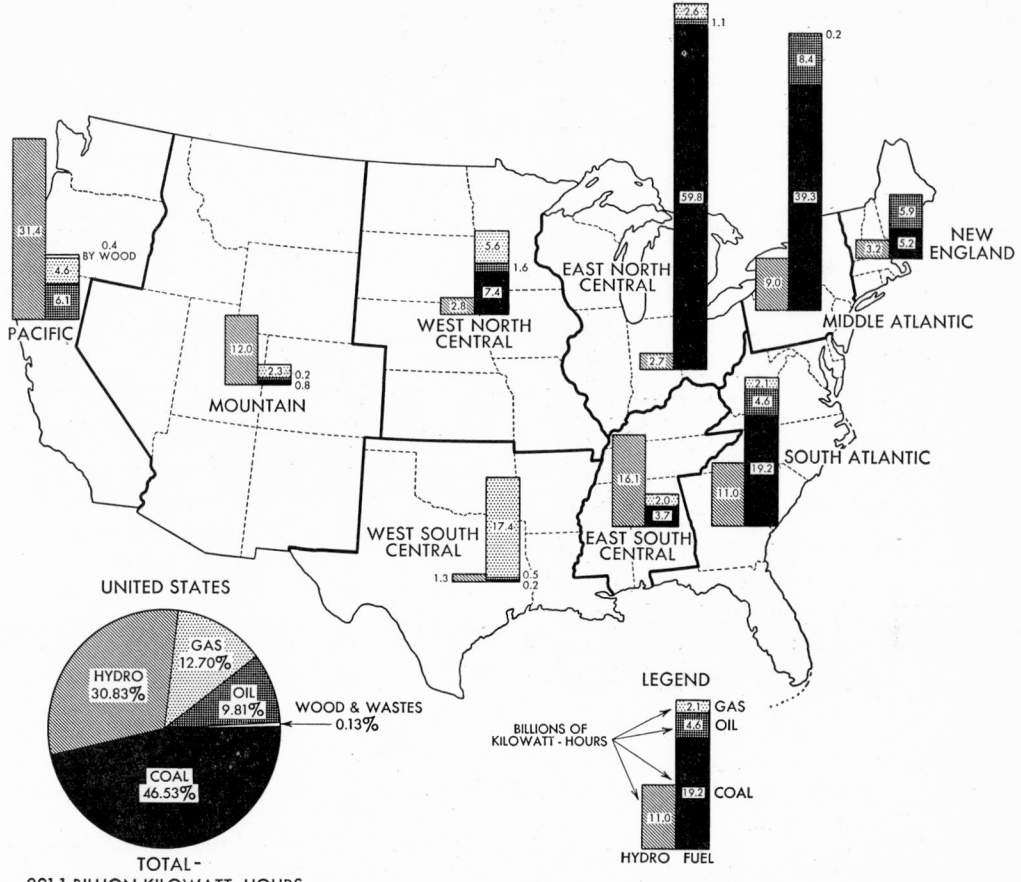

U. S. Federal Power Commission

FIGURE 282. ELECTRIC UTILITIES: SOURCES OF ENERGY IN THE UNITED STATES, BY GEOGRAPHIC DIVISION, 1949

Water power predominates in the production of electricity by utility companies in the Mountain and Pacific and in the East South Central States. Coal predominates in the East.

tricity: coal prevails in eastern states and the North Central Region; gas in the West South Central Region; water power in the Pacific and Mountain states and in the East South Central Region — Tennessee, Kentucky, Mississippi and Alabama. (See Figure 282.)

CONSUMPTION OF ELECTRICITY

Per Capita Consumption

The pattern of per capita consumption of electric energy in the world changes with progress in electrification. Apart from the close correlation between the level of industrial development and the use of electricity, countries rich in water power consume more electricity than those in which electricity is generated by coal. Sparsely populated areas need more electricity per capita

than regions with a similar economy but a dense population. Such strongholds of heavy industry as Luxembourg and Belgium use more electricity per capita than nations with more diversified industries, such as France, the Netherlands and Denmark.

Despite its leading position in the production of electric power, and especially in construction of huge dams and hydroelectric plants, the United States lags behind Norway, Canada and Sweden in per capita consumption. (See Table 415; cf. Figure 283.)

Uses

Electricity is used for lighting, heating, refrigerating, operating motors and for electrolytic and other processes. In 1949, electric utilities in

TABLE 415

CONSUMPTION OF ELECTRICITY PER CAPITA, SELECTED COUNTRIES, 1950

(*Kilowatt-hours*)

Country	Consumption	Country	Consumption
Norway	5,310	Cuba	142
Canada [a]	4,120	Romania [a]	130
Sweden	2,580	Malaya	115
United States	2,560	Portugal	110
Luxembourg	2,320	Venezuela [a]	105
Switzerland	2,230	Panama	100
New Zealand	1,600	Greece	73
Iceland	1,350	Algeria	68
Australia	1,160	Bulgaria	66
United Kingdom	1,115	Jamaica	63
Finland	1,000	Colombia [b]	62
Belgium [a]	986	Brazil [b]	55
Western Germany	925	Belgian Congo	50
Austria	900	Bolivia	43
Union of South Africa	890	Tunisia	40
France	790	Turkey	38
Czechoslovakia	730	Dominican Republic	37
Netherlands	725	Peru [b]	28
Japan	540	Syria	25
Italy	535	Philippines	23
Denmark [a]	500	Paraguay	20
Poland	375	Guatemala	20
Israel	365	India	14
Ireland	300	Korea	12
Chile [b]	260	Ceylon	11
Puerto Rico	260	Liberia	11
Argentina	255	Iraq	7
Spain	225	Angola	6
Mexico	175	Nigeria	5
Uruguay	165	Thailand	3
Yugoslavia	150	Pakistan [a]	2

Source: Computed from **2**, 1951, pp. 21–31 and 277–82.   a. Thermo.
                                                          b. Hydro.

the United States counted nearly 43 million ultimate customers distributed as follows: [70]

	Customers, in Thousands	Sales in Millions of Kilowatt-hours
Total	42,851	248,473
Residential or domestic	35,375	58,136
Rural	1,804	7,384
Commercial and industrial	5,523	166,964
Other	149	15,989

Industrial establishments are the largest customers of electric utilities. In addition industry

70. **26**, 1950, p. 474.

produces electricity on a large scale for its own use. (See Figure 284.)

In most countries — Great Britain, France, Belgium, Luxembourg, the Netherlands, Denmark, Sweden, Norway, Austria, Portugal, Spain — as in the United States, industry consumes from 50 to 70 per cent of the energy sold by utilities. In Canada and Finland, industry's share is more than 80 per cent; and in Switzerland, only 35 per cent. (See Table 416.)

Industry uses the electric power, purchased or generated by its own plants, mainly for installed motors and traction, but also for lighting, electrolytic processes, furnaces and other purposes. In

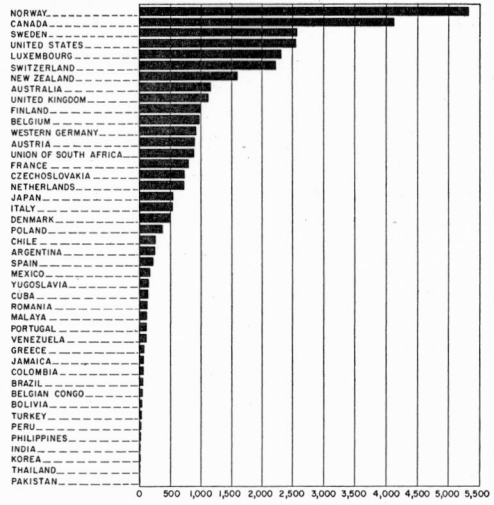

FIGURE 283. CONSUMPTION OF ELECTRICITY PER
CAPITA, SELECTED COUNTRIES, 1950

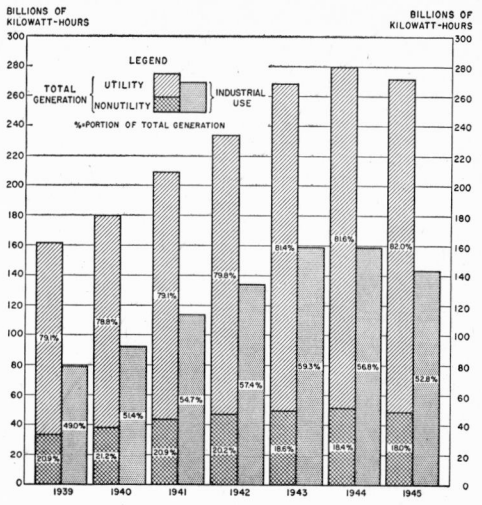

U. S. Federal Power Commission

FIGURE 284. CONSUMPTION OF ELECTRICITY: SHARE OF
INDUSTRIAL USERS IN THE UNITED STATES, 1939–45

The age of electricity has not yet dawned in China, Indonesia, Pakistan, Thailand, the Near East and most of Africa, an area with an aggregate population of approximately 900 million. Countries representing some 500 million people — India, Korea, the Philippines and other Asiatic countries and some South American countries — are just entering the electric era and consume from 10 to 100 kilowatt-hours per capita. These two groups combined, with nearly 60 per cent of the world's population, use hardly more than 20 billion kilowatt-hours a year, approximately 2 per cent of the world's total.

At the other extreme, ten countries with a total population of some 250 million and a per capita consumption of 1,000 kilowatt-hours or more per capita per year, account for two thirds of the world's output of electric power.

Between these two extremes are nations at different levels of economic development — ranging from Venezuela and Portugal to Western Germany and Belgium, with per capita consumption of 100–1,000 kilowatt-hours. Their peoples total some 750 million, and their combined share in the world's supply of electricity in 1950 amounted, in round numbers, to 250 billion kilowatt-hours.

the United States, the share used for motors ranges from 20.2 per cent in the manufacture of nonferrous metals to 93.7 in the mining and petroleum industries; lighting absorbs from 2.5 per cent in nonferrous metals industries to 34.3 per cent in the apparel industries; electrolytic cells and electric furnaces account for 49.8 per cent of the consumption of electricity in chemical industries and for 75.9 per cent in nonferrous metals industries. (See Table 417.[71])

Of the electric energy left for use after all kinds of loss and waste in the course of conver-

71. This table refers to power purchased by industries — a little more than half of all power sold by utilities.

The left-hand column for each year shows the annual output of electricity in billions of kilowatt-hours and the part (percentage) of the output attributable to each of the two groups of producers: utilities and other industrial establishments that operate power plants for their own use. The second column for each year shows the amount of electricity used by industry and its proportion (percentage) of the total output.

sion, transformation and transfer, about 60 per cent is ultimately consumed for lighting and heating dwellings, melting ore and metal and other industrial processes, and about 40 per cent is used as motive power — for transportation and for turning the wheels of machines.

STEAM ENGINES AND MOTORS

The steam engine and the motor have radically changed the pattern of life and the structure of modern society. From time immemorial, the muscular effort of slaves and animals had been the main motive power at the disposal of the community. The engine and the motor made large-scale production possible without slave labor.

PRIME MOVERS AND ELECTROMOTORS

From the point of view of the master, machines contrast favorably with slaves and work animals in that they demand no food when they do not work. It is economical therefore to build machines for special purposes, even if they are not used to capacity most of the time. In fact, many machines and mechanical means of transportation are operated for only a small part of a

TABLE 416

CONSUMPTION OF ELECTRICITY: DISTRIBUTION OF UTILITY OUTPUT
BY TYPE OF CONSUMER, SELECTED COUNTRIES

Country and Year	Total Sales, in Millions of Kilowatt-hours	Percentage Distribution				
		Traction	Industry	Public Lighting	Homes and Shops	Agriculture
United States, 1947	217,581	3.3	52.2	1.1	40.9	2.5
Canada, 1945	33,998	1.9	82.9	0.7	14.1	0.5
Mexico, 1947	1,078	7.3	56.2	11.3	25.1	—
Uruguay, 1947	379	12.8	49.7	3.7	33.8	—
United Kingdom, 1946	35,049	3.9	51.1	0.7	44.3	—
Ireland, 1947	492	1.4	36.6	2.4	59.6	—
France, 1947	17,059	4.9	67.7	1.2	26.2	—
Luxembourg, 1947	72	5.3	50.6	2.4	26.2	15.4
Belgium, 1947	3,731	8.1	62.6	1.0	28.3	—
Netherlands, 1946	2,330	5.1	53.6	1.4	40.0	—
Denmark, 1946	1,068	7.4	57.2	1.8	33.6	—
Sweden, 1947	9,110	13.4	56.8	29.8		—
Norway, 1946	9,975	1.5	60.4	38.1		—
Finland, 1947	2,544	0.7	82.1	0.5	16.7	—
Germany (Bizone), 1947	12,230	4.5	44.6	14.4	36.5	—
Poland, 1946	2,705	78.0		0.5	19.9	1.6
Switzerland, 1947	6,283	7.7	35.0	46.4		10.9
Austria, 1948	2,603	4.7	60.0	1.2	31.3	2.8
Portugal, 1947	527	12.5	61.1	3.9	21.9	0.6
Spain, 1947	4,175	8.9	69.3	1.9	17.2	2.7
Bulgaria, 1947	385	4.4	55.3	1.0	32.7	6.4
Japan, 1947	26,772	...	...	...	...	...
Turkey, 1947	267	6.4	55.4	4.9	33.3	—
India, 1948	3,722	7.9	70.1	1.4	17.3	3.3
Ceylon, 1948	65	3.5	—	96.5		—
French Morocco, 1947	288	18.0	19.6	55.4		6.9
Algeria, 1947	348	13.2	47.6	24.7		14.5
New Zealand, 1946	1,998	3.4	24.0	67.7		4.9

Source: Computed from **9**, 1950, pp. 108–13.

day and motors have a considerable reserve capacity for emergencies. The aggregate capacity of motors installed in factories, locomotives, motor vehicles, airplanes and steamships is therefore much larger than they use, all together, at any time during a year.

When a factory uses purchased electric power, prime movers, i.e., machines generating power, are installed in power plants operated by public utilities, while electromotors in the factory serve to transform electricity to motive power.

The United States

In 1939, electric utilities were equipped with steam, hydro and other prime movers with a total capacity of approximately 52 million horse-power. Factories had prime movers with a total capacity of 21.2 million horsepower and used, for producing electricity for their own use, generators with an aggregate rating of 10 million horsepower. Their electric motors had a total capacity of 45.3 million horsepower, 29.2 million driven by purchased power and 16.1 million by energy generated in their own power plants. (See Table 418.) The mining industries (including extraction of crude petroleum and natural gas) had motors with an aggregate rating of 14.3 million horsepower, including 8 million for prime movers and 6.3 million for electromotors driven by purchased power.

Thus mines and manufacturing establishments together had electromotors with an aggregate

TABLE 417

CONSUMPTION OF ELECTRICITY: DISTRIBUTION BY INDUSTRY
AND USE IN THE UNITED STATES, 1946

Industry	Total, in Millions of Kilowatt-hours	Percentage Distribution				
		Lighting	Motors	Electrolytic Cells	Electric Furnaces	Other
Total	133,682	7.7	63.2	13.1	13.7	2.2
Manufactures	120,280	7.8	62.1	14.0	13.9	2.2
Food	9,603	10.6	87.3	1.6	—	1.5
Tobacco	176	14.8	84.3	0.3	—	0.6
Textiles	8,895	9.8	89.4	—	0.2	0.6
Apparel	658	34.3	64.6	—	—	1.1
Lumber	1,601	12.3	85.4	—	—	2.2
Furniture	977	12.2	85.8	—	0.3	1.8
Paper	12,154	3.9	93.1	2.2	0.2	0.6
Printing, etc.	1,213	20.1	75.0	0.5	2.1	2.3
Chemicals	21,565	4.5	44.7	21.9	27.9	1.0
Petroleum and coal	6,385	5.6	93.7	—	—	0.7
Rubber	3,015	12.1	87.5	—	0.2	0.2
Leather	587	15.2	84.1	—	0.1	0.6
Stone, clay, glass	6,627	6.2	88.0	0.1	4.4	1.3
Iron and steel	19,406	7.2	72.0	0.4	18.7	1.7
Nonferrous metals	11,811	2.5	20.2	61.3	14.6	1.3
Electrical machinery	2,955	19.0	42.6	1.9	30.1	6.4
Machinery	4,796	19.8	59.2	0.5	14.3	6.2
Automobiles	4,245	19.4	68.0	0.2	7.3	5.1
Transport equipment	2,782	27.0	46.6	0.2	9.4	16.7
Miscellaneous	830	18.4	73.0	0.2	5.1	3.3
Mining	11,701	4.0	93.7	0.1	—	2.1
Government [a]	1,701	14.6	40.5	3.9	37.7	3.3

Source: **32**, pp. vii–xi.   a. Shipbuilding, arsenals, ordnance, etc.

TABLE 418

MOTIVE POWER: EQUIPMENT IN MANUFACTURING IN THE UNITED STATES,
BY TYPE, 1899–1939

Item	1899	1909	1919	1929	1939
Number of establishments reporting power equipment	131,309	181,994	219,398	190,091	179,674
Total capacity of prime movers, in thousands of horsepower	9,586	16,365	19,432	19,329	21,239
Steam engines	7,999	13,806	13,346	9,158	6,533
Steam turbines	—	—	3,099	7,410	11,296
Internal combustion	133	740	1,223	1,203	1,806
Hydro	1,454	1,819	1,764	1,558	1,604
Total capacity of electric motors, in thousands of horsepower	475	4,582	15,612	33,844	45,291
Purchased energy	178	1,669	8,965	21,794	29,213
Own energy	297	2,913	6,647	12,050	16,078

Source: **26**, 1950, p. 757.

capacity of 59.6 million horsepower, 35.5 million in motors driven by purchased power, and 24.1 million in those driven by power generated in their own power plants.

Electric utilities, factories, and mines together had installed prime movers with an aggregate capacity of more than 80 million horsepower, about two thirds of which was owned by public utilities.

Much larger, however, was the aggregate capacity of motors installed in cars, trucks and railroad locomotives, which is estimated as follows: [72]

	Number, in Thousands	Average Capacity, in Horse-power	Total Capacity, in Millions of Horse-power
Total	30,661	—	2,106
Passenger cars, buses and taxis	26,140	60	1,568
Motor trucks	4,476	100	448
Locomotives	45	2,000	90

Including the motors of electric railways, motor-cycles, merchant and naval vessels, and civil and military aircraft, the aggregate capacity of motors in transportation equipment in the United States in 1939 was close to 2.3 billion horsepower, more than 20 times the capacity of all prime movers in public utilities, factories and mines combined.

Other Countries

International statistics on prime movers and motors are fragmentary and fail to provide a clear and internally consistent world picture.

In 1930 the United Kingdom had prime movers with an aggregate capacity of 9.2 million horsepower in electric utilities and 21.3 million in all other trades.

In 1938 Germany reported an aggregate capacity of generators of electric power of 10 million horsepower in electric utilities and 7.7 million in other industrial establishments.[73] The capacity of prime movers was probably one third larger, close to 24 million horsepower. In addition, German industry used 9 million horsepower for mechanical application of power to machines. Thus, the capacity of installed prime movers in German utilities and industry was about 33 million horse-

power, somewhat more than Great Britain had eight years earlier.

In France, the industrial census taken in 1931 recorded 161,243 establishments with prime movers (including electric utilities) with an aggregate capacity of 15 million horsepower.

The aggregate capacity of industrial prime movers in these three European industrial countries together was nearly 80 million horsepower before the war, about the same as in the United States.

For the world as a whole, the prewar capacity of all *installed* steam engines, hydroturbines and other prime movers may be roughly estimated at 220 million horsepower.

The aggregate capacity of motor-vehicle motors in foreign countries was less than half that in the United States. On the other hand, the aggregate capacity of locomotives used by foreign countries on their railroads was at least double that of the United States railroads; the aggregate capacity of motors in their ships and other installations was at least equal to that in similar installations in the United States.

Manufacturing

Motive power in an industry or single industrial establishment can be measured either as the sum of the capacities of installed prime movers and electric motors driven by purchased power, or as the sum of the capacities of all electric movers and prime movers directly driving machinery. The two methods often give appreciably different results, but for all manufacturing industries as a whole the differences partly offset each other. The international data for different manufacturing industries are not strictly comparable because of the differences in industrial classification, measurement of capacity of movers, the date of enumeration, and so on.

Despite these limitations, the available statistics of the use of motive power in manufacturing industries reveal characteristic contrasts between different branches of production and between different countries.

The paper industry ranks first in installed horsepower per worker in the United States, Sweden, Norway, Finland, Czechoslovakia and Austria. Manufacturing of metals ranks first in the United Kingdom, France and Italy; chemical industries head the list in Belgium, Germany and Poland. These three industries and the production of building materials can be described as

---

72. Authors' estimate.
73. **36**, 1939–40.

those having the most powerful engines. At the other extreme are such industries as clothing, printing and leather, which require much less horsepower per worker.

Because of the predominance of the pulp and paper industry in Sweden and Norway, these two countries use more horsepower per person employed in manufacturing industries than any other nation, including the United States. In most industries, the United States ranks first in horsepower per worker, but there are important exceptions to this rule and the country's lead over the next nation in horsepower per worker in single industries is not overwhelming. (See Table 419.)

The countries ranking first and second in horsepower per worker in given industries are as follows:

Metals: United States (9.5); Italy (8.9)
Engineering: United States (3.7); Switzerland (3.1)
Building materials: United States (8.5); Denmark (6.9)
Timber: Norway (6.8); Sweden (6.1)
Leather: Denmark (3.2); Norway (3.0)
Rubber: Switzerland (9.5); United States (6.2)
Textiles: Switzerland (4.2); United States and Sweden (3.0)
Clothing: Chile (2.2); Romania (0.8)
Paper: Finland (23.2); Norway (19.6)
Food, drink and tobacco: Peru (5.6); Romania (5.1)
Chemicals: United States (10.7); Norway (10.6)
Printing: Czechoslovakia (2.1); Switzerland (1.5)

A closer analysis discloses the reasons for the apparent anomalies in these rankings. Norway, Sweden, Finland and Switzerland hold their high ranking largely because of the abundance of cheap hydroelectric power. Peru and Romania appear prominently in the food, drink and tobacco industries because this industrial group is represented here mainly by flour mills, which in all countries use considerable horsepower per worker.

As a general rule, horsepower per worker increases as one moves from poorer and less developed to more prosperous and highly industrialized countries, but this tendency is overlapped and partly overshadowed by numerous other factors: the prevailing character of industry, the supply of energy, organization of production and so on. The pulp industry uses more horsepower per worker than production of airplanes, precision instruments or watches, but the latter require more skill and a higher industrial organization.

The World

The aggregate capacity of prime movers in the world in 1938 was probably between 3.6 and 3.9 billion horsepower, distributed as follows: industry (including electric utilities), 200–250 million horsepower; motor vehicles, 2,800–2,900 million; steam railroads, 250–300 million; ships and miscellaneous installations, 350–450 million.

These hypothetical totals include steam engines and motors of all types but not the power of pack and work animals. With allowance of 100 million horsepower for this item, the total for the world's animals and prime movers represented from 3.7 billion to 4.0 billion horsepower in 1938.

Since that year, the capacity of prime movers in the United States has increased by about 60 per cent for electric utilities and at least 30 per cent for motor vehicles, and has more than tripled for aircraft, merchant vessels and ships. The aggregate capacity of all prime movers in the United States probably exceeds 3 billion horsepower. Trends in other countries have been diverse. Gains in Canada, South America, Great Britain, the Scandinavian countries, Switzerland and Australia have been partly offset by losses in Germany. On the whole, it may be assumed that the aggregate capacity of prime movers in foreign countries has increased, although not in the same proportion as in the United States. From 1.5–1.8 billion horsepower in 1938, it may have risen to 1.7–2.0 billion, which would bring the world total, including the power of work animals, close to 5 billion horsepower, in round numbers.

The share of the United States in the total capacity of prime movers in the world increased from 57 per cent before the war to perhaps 62 per cent, and is disproportionately high in relation to its share in the world's supply of energy. The disproportion is due to the fact that car motors, which prevail over all other power equipment in the country, are operated least regularly during the year. An average United States family keeps 40–100 horsepower in its garage, but does not use this power more than a couple of hours a day.

OUTLOOK

Three general factors control the outlook of the world economy of energy and power: (1) the increasing demand for energy; (2) the progressive depletion of petroleum, natural gas, fuel

TABLE 419

MOTIVE POWER PER WORKER IN MANUFACTURING, SELECTED COUNTRIES

(*Horsepower*)

Country and Year	Total	Metals	Engineering	Building Materials	Timber	Leather	Rubber	Textiles	Clothing	Paper	Food, Drink, Tobacco	Chemicals	Printing	Miscellaneous
United States, 1939	4.8	9.5	3.7	8.5	4.6	2.5	6.2	3.0	0.3	12.3	4.0	10.7	1.4	1.4
Peru, 1936 [a]	2.4		0.8	0.6	0.7	...	...	1.1	...	0.7 [b]	5.6	1.9	...	0.3
Chile, 1939 [a]	3.2		1.6	1.6	1.7	...	1.1	2.2	2.2	6.4 [b]	4.0	0.8	...	—
United Kingdom, 1939	2.4	6.2	1.8	2.5	1.7	1.7	3.3	2.5	0.2	3.9	1.5	4.4	0.9	0.8
Ireland, 1936	1.7	1.1	0.9	1.3	2.3	1.2	...	1.2	0.3	1.5	3.0	2.1	1.0	2.5
France, 1931	2.2	6.5	1.3	1.9	1.6	0.7	2.1	1.9	0.2	4.2	2.5	3.2	0.6	0.5
Belgium, 1937	2.3	3.7	2.0	2.4	1.8	1.7	2.3	1.8	0.5	3.5	2.8	3.9	0.8	—
Netherlands, 1930	2.0	3.2	1.7	2.0	1.8	2.0	3.1	2.9	0.2	7.3	2.0	4.5	0.8	0.5
Denmark, 1949	3.2	3.7	2.5	6.9	4.3	3.2	3.8	2.1	0.5	5.9	3.9	5.8	1.3	3.0
Sweden, 1948	5.0	7.7	2.9	5.6	6.1	2.0	4.7	3.0	0.5	19.3	4.5	5.7	1.1	1.5
Norway, 1947	4.9	3.2	2.3	4.9	6.8	3.0	3.5	2.4	0.5	19.6	3.8	10.6	1.4	1.4
Finland, 1947	4.4	5.9	2.2	4.5	3.7	2.5	3.2	2.7	0.4	23.2	2.9	3.2	0.8	1.0
Germany, 1933	2.4	5.4	2.5	3.4	2.2	1.5	2.8	1.8	0.1	5.9	1.9	6.3	0.9	0.8
Poland, 1936	2.8	4.1	2.2	2.3	2.2	1.7	1.8	1.4	...	6.3	4.3	6.3	0.6	0.3
Czechoslovakia, 1930	1.4		1.9	1.0	1.3	1.2	1.5	1.3	0.1	3.1	2.1	2.0	2.1	0.4
Switzerland, 1944	3.3	3.9	3.1	6.8	3.4	2.5	9.5	4.2	0.5	6.9	4.3	6.9	1.5	0.7
Austria, 1930	1.4	2.1	2.1	1.4	1.4	0.9	1.3	1.2	...	4.7	1.6	2.4	0.5	0.7
Hungary, 1938 [c]	2.5	3.7	2.1	2.5	1.6	1.5	2.6	1.3	0.2	4.1	4.4	2.8	0.8	0.5
Italy, 1937–40	1.6	8.9	1.4	1.9	0.7	1.5	2.9	1.4	0.1	3.9	1.5	4.3	0.6	0.9
Romania, 1947	2.3		2.4	2.3	0.8	1.5	...	1.8	0.8	3.6	5.1	3.9	...	0.9
Bulgaria, 1934	1.1	0.4	0.5	2.9	0.6	1.0	2.5	0.9	...	2.0	3.1	1.5	0.3	0.9

Sources: For all countries except Chile and Peru, **3**, First Quarter 1951, p. 27; for Chile and Peru, computed from **18**, pp. 258–59 and 269.

a. Prime movers and electric movers.

b. Includes printing.

c. Large establishments only.

wood reserves and the most profitable coal fields; and (3) progress in the production and utilization of energy, including the discovery of ways to utilize new sources.

Future Demand for Energy

The demand for energy in the next few years can be estimated with reasonable precision, but an estimate looking as far ahead as a decade or two requires a system of more or less arbitrary assumptions of the growth of population, the speed of economic progress, technological improvements in utilization of energy and so on. An attempt to visualize the situation at the end of this century — almost five decades ahead — necessarily implies a considerable margin of error and is only illustrative of the current trends as the writers see and appraise them.

The following estimate rests on the assumption of a continuous growth of world population, continuous increase in per capita consumption of motive power and heat, and steady progress in the efficiency of the whole energy system.

World population by the end of the century is set at 3,250 million.[74] The average rate of increase in world per capita demand for motive power and heat is set conservatively at 2.5 per cent per year, and it is assumed that the efficiency of utilization of potential energy of fuels will be doubled in the next fifty years, so that twice as much useful work and heat will be produced from each ton of coal or unit of potential energy expressed as coal equivalent.

According to these assumptions, the world's annual demand for sources of energy will more than double, increasing from the equivalent of 2.9 billion tons of coal in 1948 to 6.0 billion, in round numbers.[75]

The questions to be answered are whether a demand of such magnitude can be met by the available sources, and what the future role of different sources of energy will be in meeting this demand.

74. Cf. Chapter 7, pp. 257–62.

75. This estimate is probably on the conservative side. It conforms to the projection of the Bureau of Mines for the United States. The Bureau has estimated that the demand for energy supply, measured in BTU, in the United States will increase slightly more than 30 per cent between 1947 and 1965, or an annual increase of approximately 1.5 per cent. (**27**, p. 25.) Our projection suggests the same rate of growth in demand for the world as a whole.

Exhaustion of Sources of Energy

Depletion of the known reserves of coal, petroleum and natural gas is discussed in Chapters 23 and 24. Known reserves of coal are neither unlimited as many people have believed, nor are they approaching exhaustion. The "proven" and "probable" reserves, together, would last for thousands of years if they were all recoverable and if the future demand for coal were stabilized at the present rate. Both these assumptions, however, are utterly unrealistic. Not all the coal can be extracted, and it is fairly certain that the world demand for coal will increase with the progress of industrialization, especially in the areas where consumption of coal is now almost nil. On the other hand, the life of the coal reserves may be prolonged by improvements in extraction and utilization techniques and by the discovery of new deposits.

On the basis of the available information, the best guess is that exhaustion of coal reserves is a matter of two or three centuries. Long before this, man will have had to shift from the currently used seams to less profitable and more difficult fields, though the increasing difficulties of extraction will be offset by steadily improving techniques.

The known reserves of petroleum and natural gas could be depleted in a few decades at the present rate of extraction. It is believed, however, that new reserves will be found, and that predictions of approaching exhaustion of known fields will prove as unwarranted as in the past.

Like coal production, but at an earlier date, the production of petroleum and natural gas is bound to shift to new fields, which means that the United States will have to rely increasingly on imported or synthetic liquid fuels. Production of liquid fuel from coal will probably become a common practice sooner or later.

The supply of water power in the world is likewise limited. If hydroelectric plants were to be established at all sites of falling water — including the powerful waterfalls in central Africa, the Amazon River, the rivers of Siberia and the Himalayas — and if the energy produced were delivered without heavy loss to places where it is needed, it could satisfy about half the current demand of the world. Its great advantage in comparison with coal, oil and natural gas is that it is renewable, that is, within certain limits, inexhaustible.[76]

76. Because of deterioration of dams and silting of

To sum up, exhaustion of the energy resources of our planet is a very serious question in terms of individual sources — natural oil, natural gas, wood or particular coal fields — but appears less grave when we take account of all sources of energy and their convertibility and interchangeability. The world is full of energy in amounts that exceed not only the needs of men but even their imagination.

The Future Supply of Energy

Man's supply of energy in the future depends on his growing ability to harness the forces of nature. It is fairly certain that there will be increasing pressure on all available sources, especially in the industrialized areas. It is also fairly probable that this pressure will be met effectively.

A few trends are clearly discernible:

1. Long before the end of the century, the demand for liquid and gaseous fuels will probably be met increasingly by synthetic oil and gas, derived from coal, shale or other raw materials.

2. The increasing demand for coal will stimulate technological progress in mining.

3. The use of fuel wood and domestic animals as sources of energy will probably decline, although not in all parts of the world as rapidly as in the United States.

4. Water power will be used on a much larger scale than now, in most places to the limit of potential capacity.

New Sources of Energy

Less certain are developments in the utilization of new sources of energy, such as wind, solar radiation, the heat of the earth and, most of all, atomic energy.

Experiments with these and other sources of energy are going on in the United States and other countries. Although the results are unpredictable, none of the new sources can be discarded as unrealistic. In fact, in everyday life we are using scores of mechanical devices that seemed fantastic a few decades ago when they were taking shape in the imagination of scholars or dreamers. Moreover, the current search for new sources of energy has long since outgrown the stage of dreaming.

In the United States the interest of the Federal Power Commission in harnessing wind as an auxiliary source for generating electricity illustrates this point. Wind is an inexhaustible source of energy but all attempts to harness it for production of power on a large scale have failed. The only exception has been the Grandpa's Knob wind turbine on a mountain ridge a few miles west of Rutland, Vermont. It is mounted on a steel tower 110 feet high and is able to deliver more than 1,000 kilowatts. This modest installation, operated commercially by the Central Vermont Public Service Corporation, proved so successful that on the basis of this experience a turbine designed to use much more powerful aerogenerators has been developed by Percy H. Thomas, an expert of the Federal Power Commission. This project envisages a wind turbine with twin wheels 200 feet in diameter, capable of using wind velocities of 10 to 50 miles per hour, mounted on a tower 475 feet above the ground. (See Figure 285.) Such a unit would have a capacity of 6,500 to 7,500 kilowatts and could be erected at an initial maximum cost of $68–$75 per rated kilowatt (at 1946 prices) if mass produced. By combining several such units at appropriate sites, "batteries" with a capacity of 20,000 kilowatts and more could be developed.[77]

A bill to authorize the building of an aerogenerator as designed by Thomas is pending in Congress. If the experiment succeeds, it will open a new page in the history of the use of energy. Wind power will be given a chance to join the big four sources of energy — coal, petroleum, natural gas and water.

Another potential competitor to the old sources of energy, and possibly their successor in the world economy, is the atom. However, the question of the immediate impact of the discovery of atomic energy on the existing economic system is highly controversial. From the point of view of the economy of energy and power, the use of atomic energy means that a definite amount of energy can be condensed in an extremely small space for future use and preserved in this form or delivered to the site where needed. The possibilities of such transformation of energy may have far-reaching economic repercussions. Most experts are inclined, however, to minimize the economic role of the atom in the immediate future.

In 1946 the Canadian Royal Commission on Coal considered the future of atomic energy as

---

storage reservoirs, hydroelectric installations have a limited life span. This span is rather long, however, and can be prolonged by proper maintenance.

77. See **48** and **49**. Cf. **19**.

U. S. Federal Power Commission (Ink sketch by Percy H. Thomas)

FIGURE 285. NEW SOURCES OF ENERGY: A TWIN-WHEEL WIND TURBINE, 6,500 KILOWATTS

a possible competitor of coal. The Commission's report quotes the predictions of Dr. C. J. Mac-kenzie, President of the Canadian National Research Council: [78]

Within five years. No industrial use of atomic

78. **34,** pp. 415–16.

power, except on a pilot-plant scale for purely experimental purposes.

Within ten years. Limited use under special circumstances, where cost is not a consideration. Examples are military use; rockets to the moon; very long-range aircraft; naval use to give effectively unlimited cruising range; supply of power in remote areas such as the Far North.

Within fifteen years. Industrial uses beginning to develop. Considerable decrease in cost, but price probably still high enough so that effect on coal is negligible.

Within twenty years. Costs possibly beginning to approximate coal or hydroelectric power. New uses may very well lead to increased power consumption.

More than five years have elapsed since the predictions were made. We are now in the second five-year phase, described by Mackenzie as the period of "limited use under special circumstances." In contrast to the revolutionary effect of the atom on armament, military policy and scientific research, progress in economic utilization of atomic energy has been very slow.

At the Fourth World Power Conference in London in 1950, the general attitude toward the prospects for industrial use of nuclear energy was characterized by great caution. Sir John Cockraft, Director of the British Atomic Energy Research Establishment, expressed the opinion that we are unlikely to embark on any large-scale development of nuclear power for at least another decade.[79] The United States spokesman, Ward F. Davidson, was doubtful whether the cost of electricity generated by nuclear energy could be much lower than that for coal-burning and hydroelectric plants.[80] The general report on atomic energy presented to the Conference pointed out that all pending projects for industrial utilization of nuclear energy were much more conservative than earlier plans.[81]

Similarly, the United Nations Scientific Conference on the Conservation and Utilization of Resources, held in New York in 1949, did not reveal much enthusiasm for industrial use of atomic energy in the near future.[82]

This cautious approach to the problem of nuclear energy seems to be a sound reaction to the exaggerated expectations that followed the explosion of the first atom bombs. In the near future — a decade or two from now — the atom will hardly play a role in the world economy even remotely similar to that of coal, oil, natural gas and water power. It may, however, be of great significance for regions without easy access to coal and other sources of energy.[83]

All in all, it is extremely difficult to define the place of atomic energy in the world picture by the end of this century. Large-scale production of atomic piles would require an additional demand on energy derived from conventional sources now in use. For a certain period of time, perhaps for several decades, more energy would be consumed in this process than would be released by the piles in operation. Another element of uncertainty is that we do not know which raw materials will be used for production of atomic energy and the extent of their reserves in the world. Indeed, we do not know surely whether the atom will ultimately be used as a source of energy or reserved for other purposes.

For all these reasons atomic energy seems to be a blind spot in speculations on the future sources of energy.

Another blind spot is the direct utilization of solar radiation, a problem that has been given increasing attention by experts in recent years. Eugene Ayres' estimate of the possible energy supply from this source within a century — 24.5 trillion horsepower-hours, the equivalent of more than 10 billion tons of coal, or about four times the total current consumption of energy — may be on the optimistic side. However, the significance of this source of energy should not be minimized. Tentatively, we would assume that by the end of this century, man will have harnessed solar radiation equivalent to one trillion horsepower-hours or the coal equivalent of about 400 million tons per year.

Aeroelectric power, the atom and solar radiation are the newcomers in the world economics of energy and power. Some experts believe that by A.D. 2000 they will provide most of the energy required by man. According to a more conservative view they will become increasingly important sources of energy in the next five decades, but their predominance over fuels and waterpower will come — if ever — much later. Our projection is based on the latter point of view.

The Hypothetical Supply of Energy, A.D. 2000

World demand for energy by the end of the century, estimated at the equivalent of 6.0 billion tons of coal, will be met mainly from old,

79. **11.**
80. **16.**
81. **10.**
82. **5.**

83. See **45** and **47.**

conventional sources. The share of the new sources in total supply is estimated tentatively at 20 per cent, or the equivalent of 1.2 billion tons of coal, evenly distributed among aeroelectric power, solar radiation and atomic energy.[84]

This would leave a demand for the coal equivalent of 4.8 billion tons to be met from the old sources — work animals, fuel wood, coal, petroleum, natural gas and hydroelectric power.

The recent trend in the production of hydroelectric power, the capacity of plants under construction and plans for new and more powerful plants justify the assumption that the supply will increase in the next fifty years at an average annual rate of at least 5 per cent. At this rate of growth the world's supply of hydroelectric power would increase from the coal equivalent of from 80 billion tons in 1948 to 800 billion tons in A.D. 2000.

The supply of petroleum and natural gas will be appreciably reduced by the year 2000; some writers think that it will have been exhausted long before the end of the century.[85] Without accepting this extreme point of view, it is sound to assume that the supply of energy from this source will drop to less than half the current supply — say, from the coal equivalent of 875 million tons to 400 million tons.

The role of work animals will probably decline in industrial countries and increase in underdeveloped countries that are now in the stage of hoe agriculture: in these areas human muscular energy is likely to be replaced by pack and work animals before the latter yield to the steam engine and electricity. It seems reasonable, therefore, to assume that the demand for energy derived from work and pack animals in the world as a whole will be larger in the year 2000 than it is now. Tentatively, it is estimated at the coal equivalent of 200 million tons by the end of the century as compared with 100 million tons in 1948.

The anticipated decline in the use of fuel wood will be more than offset by the increasing demand for wood as a raw material for produc-

84. The relative importance of the three new sources of energy fifty years from now is, of course, unpredictable. The important points in our reasoning are (1) that these sources will play an important role and (2) that the predominant position will still belong to the old sources of energy.

85. **44**, p. 83.

TABLE 420

THE WORLD'S HYPOTHETICAL SUPPLY OF ENERGY IN A.D. 2000 AS COMPARED WITH 1948

(Coal Equivalent, in Millions of Tons)

Source of Supply	1948	2000
Total energy supply	2,895	6,000
Old sources		
Work animals	100	200
Wood	400	800
Coal	1,440	2,600
Petroleum and natural gas	875	400
Hydroelectric power	80	800
New sources		
Aeroelectric power	—	400
Solar radiation	—	400
Atomic energy and other new sources	—	400

Sources: For 1948, Table 395; for 2000, estimated by the authors, as explained in text.

tion of liquid and gaseous fuels. The total supply of energy from work animals and vegetation — the coal equivalent of 500 million tons in 1948 — may double by the end of the century.

The remaining demand for energy would be met by 2.6 billion tons of coal. (See Table 420.)

These hypothetical figures do not pretend to be a forecast; single items and the total rest on arbitrary assumptions and by changing these assumptions we would arrive at different sets of figures. The projections given in Table 420 are purely illustrative: they show how the situation *may* look half a century from now.

The use of fuels extracted in liquid and gaseous form from the earth's crust will probably prove to be a short-lived episode in the history of world energy economy: it began less than seventy-five years ago and will probably approach its completion by the end of this century. The era of coal, which began a hundred and fifty years earlier, is likely to continue longer and leave a deeper impact on mankind. In the long run, however, if our mechanized civilization survives, man will probably move from utilizing the crumbs of energy he collects here and there in the soil to deliberate control over the energy in his environment. Like many other resources, the supply of energy in the world economy will be controlled by the creative genius of mankind.

PART V

MANUFACTURES

CHAPTER 26

MANUFACTURES IN THE WORLD ECONOMY

MANUFACTURING, IN A BROAD SENSE, includes all the activities involved in transforming raw materials into commodities for direct consumption or further processing. There is no sharp borderline between the production of raw materials — by agriculture, fishing, hunting, logging, mining, quarrying and so on — and the processing of them. The initial processing — sorting, cleaning and the like — is usually considered to be part of the production of a raw material. Manufacturing begins when the product has reached a state in which it can be moved to another establishment for futher handling.

The product need not actually change hands at this point: frequently the same enterprise combines manufacturing and primary production. A commercial farm, for example, may operate a cannery; a steel-making concern may own iron and coal mines. In a highly developed industrial society, as in a primitive economy, the same economic unit may carry on all the phases from the production of raw materials to the delivery of the finished product to the consumer, thus engaging in both primary production and manufacturing. The borderline between the two processes is not the point at which the product actually changes hands but the point at which it customarily can pass from an economic unit specializing in primary production to one that specializes in transforming raw materials.[1]

Moreover, it is not always possible to draw a precise line between manufacturing and repair services. In a handicraft economy, repair services are ordinarily combined with the processing of raw materials. In a developed industrial system, repairs are made either in factories or in service establishments that specialize in these operations or combine them with retail trade.

In brief, the concept of manufacturing varies from country to country.

_____

1. In coffee-producing countries, for example, the processing of berries is often considered as a special industry although the large plantations usually process their "cherries" and some small plantations process the crops of other small producers as well as their own.

THE ORIGIN AND DEVELOPMENT OF MANUFACTURING

In its rudimentary form of handicrafts, manufacturing can be traced back to the primitive economy of hunters, fishermen and tillers of the soil. Even now, in areas where subsistence farming prevails, many people are engaged in making pottery, carving, spinning, weaving, making simple tools and ornaments, and so on. For some of these people, these are auxiliary occupations; for others, their main or sole means of livelihood. Counting persons who work for local or broader markets, selling their products directly to consumers or to middlemen, this primitive manufacturing employs at least as many people as modern factories in the world as a whole. Factory-made clothing, footwear, household articles and tools are used by a minority of mankind and have not yet reached the throngs in Asia, Africa and South America.

The main difference between primitive handicrafts and modern factories is that, despite all the skill and diligence of primitive craftsmen, their work is pathetically inefficient in comparison with that of the modern factory equipped with power tools and all the other means of mass production. Moreover, in the areas where raw materials are processed by hand, the customers are usually so poor, and the price they can pay for purchased articles is so low, that local craftsmen earn little more than a bare subsistence. The total market value of their output is very small indeed in comparison with the input of labor and the number of potential customers. In relation to other nonagricultural activities, however, manufacturing is nearly as important in the area where this pattern of production prevails as it is in industrialized countries.

Development of the Modern Factory

The modern factory is a product of long development; the term "manufacture" (Latin: to make by hand) reflects its origin in the handicraft shop. The foundations for the development of manufacturing in the nineteenth century were laid by the growth of handicrafts, which had achieved a high level of commercialization, especially in England and northwestern Europe, by the end of the sixteenth century. The rise of manufacturing was facilitated as national and international trade became well established and as production was specialized regionally. Further expansion of production was stimulated and accelerated by the marvelous succession of technical inventions in the eighteenth century. Some of these inventions were not completely new but, rather, made use of centuries-old technical ideas that had had no practical application before the Industrial Revolution.[2]

In retrospect, the transformation of the old handicraft economy into the factory system appears to have been almost a sudden, revolutionary change. Actually, however, the process was a long one. At almost every stage progress seemed to have come to the end of the road. People considered the new production technique to leave little room for the ingenuity and inventiveness of future generations. Because the transformation of the system of production that started in the eighteenth century was gradual, few thinkers realized its historical meaning and its promise for the future.[3]

Since the middle of the eighteenth century, factory production has been expanding in western Europe and North America. Originally it contributed little to the economic well-being of people in these areas. Output rose slowly, craftsmen displaced by the machine could not find work in factories, and social tensions increased with rising unemployment. At the dawn of the modern industrial system, the end of the eighteenth century and the beginning of the nineteenth, workers' living conditions were at their lowest point in modern times.[4] The turning point, in the latter part of the nineteenth century, was heralded by the appearance of new factors on the economic scene: steel, electricity, oil and the internal combustion motor. The output of manufactures has since grown at an increasing rate, and the proportion of people sharing in the fruits of technological progress has been expanding continually.

Mass Production and Mass Consumption

In the modern economic system mass production and mass consumption are two sides of the same coin. Rise in standards of consumption depends on the availability of consumer goods — that is, on increasing output — while, on the other hand, progress in mass production depends on a large, fairly uniform and steadily expanding market for a growing variety of goods. In fact, modern mass production requires a political climate that favors rising standards of living for the majority of the population and at the same time permits luxury at the top of the social ladder.

The salient features of manufacturing in modern industrial countries are dynamism, acceleration of technological progress by the concentration of production in large plants, frequent change in fashion and pattern, and continual increase in output per man-hour.

These features make the factory system strikingly different from the handicraft economy with its traditional technique, rigid pattern for the product and wide field for application of individual skill, inherited from past generations and raised to perfection by many years of apprenticeship. The factory system recognizes no traditional methods of production. Its only incentive is profit. But profit is bound to shrink unless management finds ways to beat competition, improve the product, market new models, and reduce the cost of production. This last goal can be reached by better organization, better machinery, elimination of waste, development of by-products, use of new materials, and so on. Thus the principle of competition demands flexibility in techniques.

In order to combine fluidity of the production program with continuity of operation, the factory system tends to concentrate changes in certain parts of the finished product or certain stages of production, leaving other parts of the product and other phases of production intact. This problem is solved by the principles of standardization and interchangeability of parts.[5] The same standardized parts can be used in innumerable different products, and each product can be improved

---

2. For further information on technical progress in that time see Chapters 27–31.

3. One of the few was Adam Smith, but his disciples overlooked or forgot his understanding of the dynamism of the new economic system represented by the factory.

4. David Ricardo and, later, Karl Marx described this stage of economic development as fully developed capitalism.

---

5. For a discussion of these principles and their application in modern production see Chapter 30.

without changing its general design by replacing a few parts. This principle — completely foreign to the handicraft system — stimulates further progress in specialization.

The assembly line is a logical application of the same principle: when parts are interchangeable and fit one another perfectly, production of them can be separated from the final phase in the manufacturing process. The latter can be reduced to "assembling" the parts, and the same assembly line can serve intermittently for the production of several models, which differ from one another in particular features added in the respective phases of the continuous production process. The same principle is applied in the increasing prefabrication of parts in building construction and shipbuilding.

The craftsman of old depended on his hand tools, and his skill included his ability to sharpen, fix and repair them. By divorcing tool making from the further phases of production, the modern factory system has made it possible to specialize hand tools and develop portable powered tools for almost all forms of manual work. Thus manual labor becomes increasingly the manipulation of powered hand tools; skilled labor, the supervision of more elaborate machines. The process of production spreads from the workshop to the laboratory, test station, drafting department, management office.

Within this intricate system, new tendencies develop: a new traditionalism, as in Great Britain and France after the end of the nineteenth century, and monopolistic practices, as in the United States.

International competition tends to correct these evils. The country that indulges in the use of traditional methods of production rapidly loses the world market. After a period of spectacular profit, monopolistic practices lead to stagnation.

The modern factory system, the system of mass production and mass consumption, is not streamlined. It is full of internal strains and contradictions. But it is a living thing, a phase of historical progress characterized by a dynamism that was absent from the old systems of production, and this inherent feature of the factory system permits it to overcome its weaknesses and evils.

In contrast to the economists of the nineteenth century, many scholars of our time have learned to consider the existing production system as a dynamic, continually changing process, an aspect of man's never-ending struggle with nature and the progressive adjustment of environment to the needs of mankind.

In no other country are these features of the factory system so conspicuous as in the United States. The dynamism of consumption and production has made the country the spearhead of modern industry. While manufacturing in a broad sense absorbs a considerable part of the labor force all over the world, in terms of the volume or value of output it is heavily concentrated in a score of countries that have developed the factory system. Large parts of the world have just entered an apprenticeship in the art of building and running factories.

EMPLOYMENT IN MANUFACTURING

The share of manufacturing in the labor force and in employment may be measured in several ways, starting either from censuses of population and industries or from current reports of unemployment insurance agencies and other administrative bodies. Each method has certain merits, but population censuses have the advantage of providing more inclusive information for a larger number of countries.

National Patterns

According to censuses of population, the proportion of the labor force engaged in manufacturing and handicrafts ranges from 10 per cent or less in such primarily agricultural countries as Brazil, Colombia, Panama, Bulgaria, Romania, Turkey, the Philippines, Egypt and Hawaii to 35 per cent or more in highly industrialized countries, such as the United Kingdom, Belgium, Luxembourg, Western Germany and Switzerland. (See Table 421.)

There is a clear correlation between the share of manufactures and handicrafts in the *nonagricultural* labor force and the degree of industrial development in a country. That share is less than 25 per cent in Hawaii, Thailand, Panama, Cuba and Ireland; 40 per cent or more in highly industrialized nations that export manufactured goods in exchange for raw materials and foodstuffs — the United Kingdom, Belgium, Germany, Switzerland, Czechoslovakia. In many primarily agricultural countries, however, among them Italy, Peru and Turkey, manufactures and handicrafts absorb about the same proportion of the nonagricultural labor force as in Belgium and Germany. This phenomenon is illustrated

TABLE 421

LABOR FORCE IN MANUFACTURING: SELECTED COUNTRIES, MOST RECENT CENSUS [a]

Country and Year [b]	Labor Force, in Thousands		Labor Force in Manufacturing as Percentage of:	
	Total	In Manufacturing	Total Labor Force	Nonagricultural Labor Force
United States, 1940	52,789.5	12,314.7	23.3	28.3
Canada, 1941	4,670.1	966.0	20.7	28.1
Mexico, 1940	5,858.1	533.7	9.1	27.6
Nicaragua, 1940	352.7	36.1 [c]	10.3	38.0
Panama, 1940	207.7	14.7	7.1	14.9
Cuba, 1943	1,520.9	190.1	12.5	21.8
Puerto Rico, 1940	602.0	104.2	17.3	28.1
Venezuela, 1941	1,240.7	164.8	13.2	27.2
Colombia, 1938	4,560.2	441.0	9.7	35.3
Brazil, 1940	14,020.1	1,400.1 [d]	10.0	30.6
Peru, 1940	2,475.3	380.3	15.4	40.9
Chile, 1940	1,741.5	298.0	17.1	26.5
United Kingdom, 1931	21,074.8	8,435.8 [e]	40.0	42.6
Ireland, 1936	1,339.1	136.5	10.2	23.1
France, 1946	20,520.0	4,654.0	22.6	35.7
Luxembourg, 1947	134.3	53.3	39.6	53.7
Belgium, 1930	3,750.3	1,340.0	35.7	42.9
Netherlands, 1947	3,866.4	925.4	23.9	29.7
Denmark, 1940	1,971.4	474.1	24.1	33.6
Sweden, 1945	2,992.2	887.2	29.6	39.2
Norway, 1930	1,181.8	227.8	19.3	29.6
Finland, 1940	2,017.2	327.5	16.2	38.1
Western Germany, 1946	19,153.8	7,385.6	38.5	54.4
Poland, 1931	15,006.1	2,362.6	15.7	45.0
Czechoslovakia, 1947	5,852.4	2,042.3 [d]	34.8	56.0
Switzerland, 1941	1,992.5	722.9	36.2	46.0
Austria, 1939	3,648.9	894.3 [f]	24.5	40.2
Hungary, 1941	4,503.1	1,057.2	23.3	45.0
Portugal, 1940	3,049.9	468.3	15.3	28.3
Spain, 1940	9,254.1	1,703.8	19.4	31.1
Italy, 1936	18,754.7	3,980.0	21.2	40.1
Yugoslavia, 1931	6,477.8	717.0	11.1	57.9
Romania, 1930	10,457.6	632.1	6.3	28.4
Bulgaria, 1934	3,433.1	266.4 [c]	7.7	38.7
Japan, 1947	33,881.0	5,721.9	16.9	35.6
Turkey, 1935	7,921.2	637.7	8.0	44.2
India, 1931	148,816.9	15,352.0 [c]	10.3	31.5
Thailand, 1937	6,823.6	110.4	1.6	14.2
Philippines, 1939	6,107.7	601.3	9.8	36.3
Egypt, 1937	6,095.0	478.2	7.7	26.7
Union of South Africa, 1946 [g]	888.2	134.3	15.1	18.6
Australia, 1947	3,196.4	799.2	25.0	27.6
New Zealand, 1945	679.5	178.8 [c]	26.3	32.9
Hawaii, 1940	188.2	14.9	7.9	11.4

(See opposite page for footnotes)

by the following array of the countries listed in Table 421 by the percentage of the total non-agricultural labor force engaged in manufacturing (including handicrafts):

Hawaii	11.4
Thailand	14.2
Panama	14.9
Union of South Africa [a]	18.6
Cuba	21.8
Ireland	23.1
Chile	26.5
Egypt	26.7
Venezuela	27.2
Mexico	27.6
Australia	27.6
Canada	28.1
Puerto Rico	28.1
United States	28.3
Portugal	28.3
Romania	28.4
Norway	29.6
Netherlands	29.7
Brazil	30.6
Spain	31.1
India	31.5
New Zealand	32.9
Denmark	33.6
Colombia	35.3
Japan	35.6
France	35.7
Philippines	36.3
Nicaragua	38.0
Finland	38.1
Bulgaria	38.7
Sweden	39.2
Italy	40.1
Austria	40.2
Peru	40.9
United Kingdom	42.6
Belgium	42.9
Turkey	44.2
Poland	45.0
Hungary	45.0
Switzerland	46.0
Luxembourg	53.7
Western Germany	54.4
Czechoslovakia	56.0
Yugoslavia	57.9

a. White population.

Sources: **9**, pp. 8–21; **3**, 1949–50, pp. 254–75; **8**, 1947–48, pp. 8–21; cf. **28**, Vol. IV, p. 4.

a. The figures in this table are not strictly comparable with those in Table 169 (p. 356), in which building construction and electricity, gas, water and sanitary services are counted together with manufacturing. Here handicrafts are included in manufacturing but repair services

The World

We do not know exactly how many persons are engaged in manufacturing and handicrafts in the world as a whole, but the number can be estimated within a reasonable margin of error on the basis of the statistics available for areas representative of different economic types.

On the assumption that the share of manufactures and handicrafts in the total labor force of Mexico and Cuba (see Table 421) is more or less representative of all the countries of Middle America, the number of workers attached to manufacturing in the area from the Rio Grande to the Panama Canal, including the Caribbean, can be estimated at about 1.4 million around 1940 and 1.6 million in 1950.

The number of workers in manufactures and handicrafts in Brazil was about 1.4 million in 1940 and the number in Bolivia, Ecuador, Uruguay and Paraguay combined was probably not far from 500,000. All South America may have had 4.2–4.3 million industrial workers in 1940 and in 1950, allowing for increase in population and progress in industrialization, 4.7 million.

In Africa, in an area with a population of 170 million (excluding Egypt and the white population of the Union of South Africa but including the Mediterranean region), probably more than 6 million workers were employed in manufacturing and handicrafts around 1950. Including Egypt and the white population of the Union of South Africa, the total for the continent is likely to have been close to 7 million.

The distribution of Turkey's labor force is likely to be representative of that in Afghanistan, Iran, Iraq and the whole Middle East, while the data recorded in India and the Philippines may be used for a rough estimate for China, Korea, Burma, Indonesia and other areas of the Far East. Allowing for the growth of population since the censuses cited in Table 421, and with reservation for a considerable margin of error, it appears that in 1950 Asia had approximately 58.5 million workers in manufactures and handi-

(so far as censuses permit such classification) are excluded. This classification could not be applied to countries where censuses do not separate building construction from manufacturing.

b. Most recent data available.
c. Industry and commerce.
d. Industry and construction.
e. Industry.
f. Manufacturing and quarrying.
g. European population only.

crafts (3 million in the Middle East, 6 million in Japan, 18.5 million in India, and 31 million in China, Korea, Indochina, Indonesia and other Asiatic countries).

A figure for the USSR is the weakest point in the estimate. Judging from the size of the population, as many as 20 million workers may be employed in Soviet manufacturing industries, but this is a guess rather than a scientific estimate.[6]

For the European countries, Australia and New Zealand, the census data in Table 421, adjusted for population growth, suggest a total of 55 million in 1950. The estimated world total thus would be 165 million, distributed as follows (in millions):

World	165.0
North America	18.2
Middle America	1.6
South America	4.7
Europe	54.0
USSR	20.0
Asia	58.5
Africa	7.0
Oceania	1.0

Europe, North America and Oceania account for 44.4 per cent of the world's industrial labor force; Asia, Africa and South and Middle America, for 43.5 per cent; and the USSR, for 12 per cent.

In relation to total population, more people, of course, are engaged in manufacturing and handicrafts in industrialized countries than in the areas where an agricultural subsistence economy prevails. (See Figure 286.)

---

6. A tentative estimate in the third Five-Year Plan, submitted to the eighteenth conference of the Communist party in March 1939, anticipated that in 1942 manufactures would employ 11.9 million workers out of a total of 32 million, including wage earners, white-collar employees, technical personnel, service workers and apprentices. (*23, passim.*) These figures, however, account for less than half the probable labor force of the USSR, which, apart from workers on collective farms and inmates of labor camps, includes supervisory and administrative personnel and the armed forces. The present estimate of the number of workers in manufacturing industries makes allowance for the labor force in the areas conquered by the Soviet Union in World War II, partial demobilization of the armed forces, and growth of population. The greatest margin of error is in the estimate of forced labor employed in manufacturing. The assumption made here is that not more than 10 per cent of the slave workers are employed in manufacturing and that the rest are used in mining, logging, road building and so on.

The United States

Within the United States, the proportion of employed workers who had jobs in manufacturing industries in 1940 ranged from more than 40 per cent in New England to less than 10 per cent in Nebraska, Kansas, Mississippi, Arkansas, Oklahoma, Texas, the Dakotas and the Mountain states. (See Table 422.) On a regional basis, a larger proportion of the labor force is employed in manufacturing in the Northeast than in the South and the West. (See Figure 287.)

The relative share of manufacturing in nonagricultural employment varies more widely from state to state in the United States than it does from country to country. (Cf. Tables 422 and 421.) The highest ratios of employment in manufacturing to total nonagricultural employment (46.7 per cent in Rhode Island, 45.3 in Connecticut, 43.7 in New Hampshire, 43.5 in Michigan) are close to the percentages reported by censuses of population in the United Kingdom (42.6), Belgium (42.9) and Switzerland (46.0). In 23 states, at the other extreme, manufacturing accounted for less than 20 per cent of nonagricultural employment and in 6 states for less than 10 per cent, ratios very unusual in international statistics.

This contrast is due to the fundamental difference between the patterns of national and regional economic specialization. Because of the free exchange of goods among different areas of a nation, a state or province depends less than a nation on products manufactured within its borders.

MANUFACTURING ESTABLISHMENTS

Large factories with hundreds and thousands of workers predominate in industrialized countries, while small shops where a craftsman often works without hired help are characteristic of a premechanized civilization. The two patterns in manufacturing are not mutually exclusive, however. The difference between the industrially developed and underdeveloped areas is essentially in the proportion of establishments of one type or the other.

Number of Establishments and Workers

In the United States, 4,800 manufacturing concerns, with 500 or more workers each, employed a total of more than 10 million workers in the

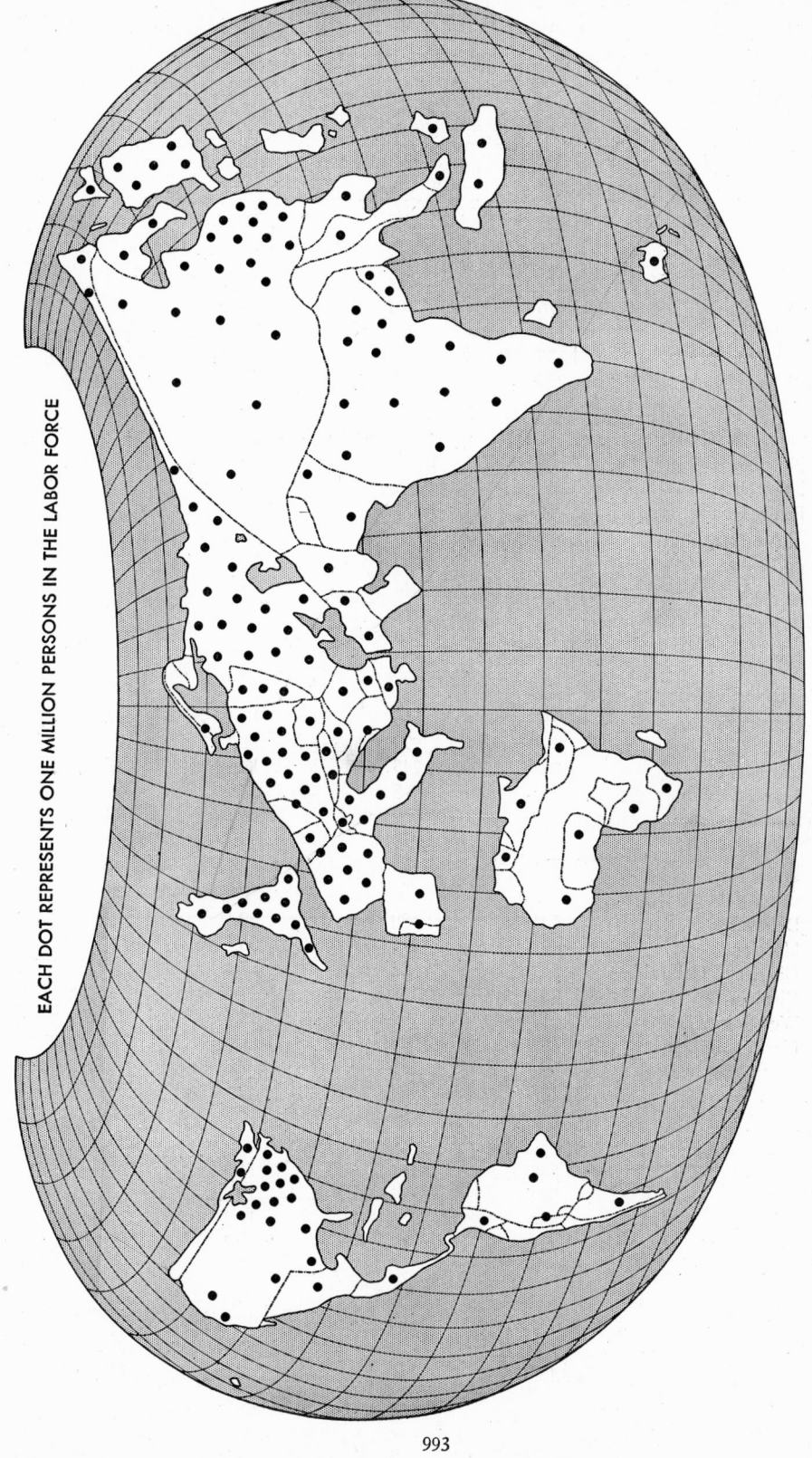

EACH DOT REPRESENTS ONE MILLION PERSONS IN THE LABOR FORCE

Figure 286. Labor Force in Manufacturing: Geographic Distribution in the World in Relation to Population, 1950
Continents and countries are shown here on the scale of their population in 1950.

TABLE 422

LABOR FORCE IN MANUFACTURING: THE UNITED STATES, 1940

Division and State	Labor Force,[a] in Thousands		Labor Force in Manufacturing as Percentage of:	
	Total	In Manufac-turing	Total Labor Force	Nonagricul-tural Labor Force
United States	45,166	10,573	23.4	28.8
New England				
Maine	279	92	32.9	38.4
New Hampshire	176	70	39.7	43.7
Vermont	125	27	21.6	28.7
Massachusetts	1,535	564	36.7	37.7
Rhode Island	265	121	45.6	46.7
Connecticut	680	296	43.5	45.3
Middle Atlantic				
New York	4,975	1,357	27.2	28.4
New Jersey	1,569	572	36.4	37.6
Pennsylvania	3,230	1,073	33.2	35.3
East North Central				
Ohio	2,345	783	33.4	37.5
Indiana	1,152	346	30.0	36.5
Illinois	2,874	821	28.6	31.7
Michigan	1,825	700	38.3	43.5
Wisconsin	1,061	270	25.4	34.2
West North Central				
Minnesota	931	116	12.4	17.9
Iowa	863	99	11.5	17.8
Missouri	1,297	245	18.8	24.7
North Dakota	200	5	2.5	5.3
South Dakota	205	9	4.5	8.8
Nebraska	433	30	6.9	11.0
Kansas	584	53	9.1	13.2
South Atlantic				
Delaware	103	30	29.1	33.7
Maryland	691	181	26.1	29.2
District of Columbia	309	22	7.1	7.1
Virginia	933	188	20.2	26.7
West Virginia	519	92	17.7	20.9
North Carolina	1,209	326	26.9	40.1
South Carolina	661	151	22.8	37.8
Georgia	1,107	105	9.5	14.6
Florida	683	80	11.7	14.4
East South Central				
Kentucky	848	101	11.9	18.7
Tennessee	942	172	18.2	27.3
Alabama	894	155	17.3	29.4
Mississippi	727	67	9.2	19.9
West South Central				
Arkansas	584	58	9.9	20.4
Louisiana	771	99	12.8	19.2
Oklahoma	659	51	7.7	11.5
Texas	2,138	212	9.9	14.2

(*Continued on facing page*)

TABLE 422—*continued*

| Division and State | Labor Force,[a] in Thousands | | Labor Force in Manufacturing as Percentage of: | |
	Total	In Manufacturing	Total Labor Force	Nonagricultural Labor Force
Mountain				
Montana	186	14	7.5	11.1
Idaho	159	13	8.2	13.0
Wyoming	87	5	5.7	8.2
Colorado	350	36	10.3	13.0
New Mexico	140	9	6.4	9.5
Arizona	150	13	8.7	11.1
Utah	149	16	10.7	13.3
Nevada	41	2	5.0	6.0
Pacific				
Washington	608	131	21.5	25.1
Oregon	390	82	21.0	25.8
California	2,525	417	16.5	18.5

Source: Computed from **13**, pp. 93–106.   a. Excludes 2,530,000 persons in public emergency work.

EACH DOT REPRESENTS 100,000 PERSONS IN EXPERIENCED LABOR FORCE

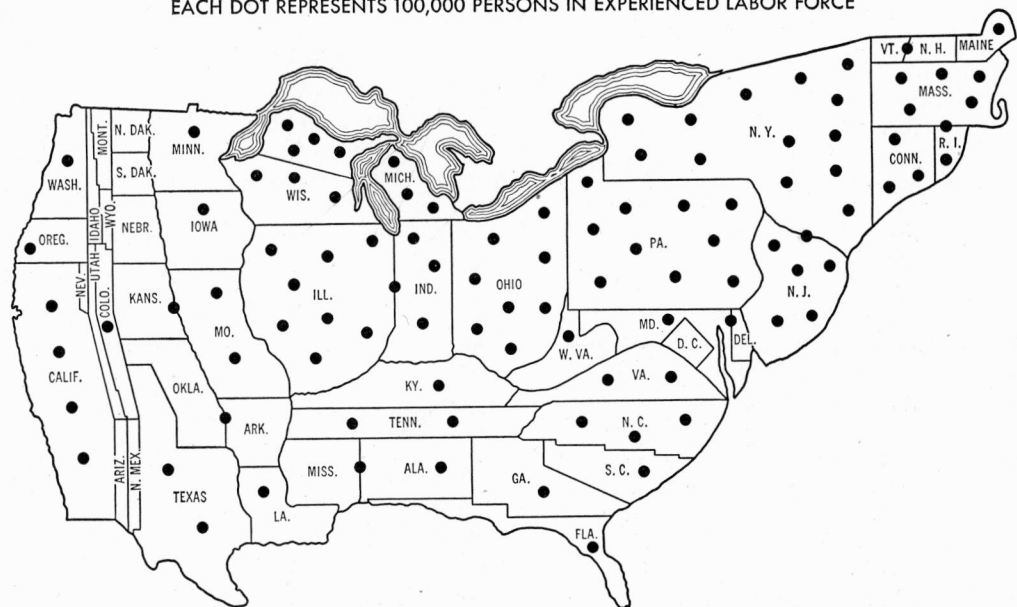

FIGURE 287. LABOR FORCE IN MANUFACTURING: GEOGRAPHIC DISTRIBUTION IN THE UNITED STATES IN RELATION TO POPULATION, 1940

States are shown here on the scale of their population in 1940.

first quarter of 1947 and accounted for about three fourths of all manufacturing output. At the same time, 66,000 small establishments, with not more than 3 workers each, had a total work force of 100,000 and accounted for hardly more than 0.5 per cent of the manufacturing output.[7]

At the other extreme, in India, the census of

7. These figures, based on the 1947 Census of Manufactures, are not strictly comparable with the 1940 data provided by the Sixteenth Census of Population.

population enumerated 15.3 million persons in manufacturing and handicrafts in 1931; the number probably reached 17 million in 1938, but only 1.7 million workers were then employed in 9,743 factories subject to the Indian Factories Act.[8] In China, 7,851 factories were registered by March 1947, most of which were engaged in the preparation of food and drink (1,888 establishments) and the manufacture of textiles (1,679) and of chemical and allied products (1,840).[9] These were small but more or less modern factories, with machinery and prime movers averaging 30 horsepower per establishment. On the basis of a partial registration, the number of their workers may be estimated at 400,000–500,000, hardly more than 2 or 2.5 per cent of the number of persons in China who make their living by handicrafts.

International statistics on the number of establishments fail to show all the contrasts in the structure of manufacturing. For many countries the statistics cover only those establishments that have an output above a certain limit ($5,000 in the United States) or employ at least three, four or five workers, or use motive power, and so on. The number of manufacturing establishments reported therefore depends largely on the method of classification. Where small shops are included, the number of establishments is high in relation to population and the average number of workers per establishment is low; where all or most small shops are excluded, the number of establishments is small and the number of workers per establishment is large.[10] (See Table 423.)

Of the estimated 165 million workers in the world's manufacturing and handicrafts in 1950, hardly more than 75 million were employed in industrial establishments that can be identified as factories. Among the countries for which statistics of such establishments are available, the United States ranks first in number of factory workers, number of large establishments and value of manufacturing output. Data are not available for the Soviet Union, but it probably has about as many factory workers as the United States and its government-owned "trusts," embracing whole branches of industry in large regions, employ more workers than the largest concerns in the United States. Next in order are Germany and the United Kingdom, followed by France, Japan and Italy. (See Table 423.) In these seven countries together, manufacturing employs approximately 60 million workers, or 80 per cent of the estimated 75 million factory workers in the world.

Measuring the Value of Output

The geographic concentration of manufactures is even greater in terms of value of output than in terms of labor force. (See Table 423.) Statistics on industrial output, however, are somewhat confusing because of the lack of a clear distinction between the concepts of "gross" and "net" value of production.

The gross value of manufacturing output in a country is the sum of all sales effected by manufacturing establishments, including sales of semifinished products, parts and containers, contract work performed by one establishment for another, and so on. It therefore not only includes the value of agricultural and mineral raw materials and fuels used in manufacturing, costs of transportation, trade and insurance, profits, excise taxes and duties, and costs of maintaining plants and amortizing capital, but also incorporates many duplications of these items. When, for example, a factory making car motors buys parts from specialized establishments and sells the finished motors to an automobile factory, the value of each motor appears twice in the gross value of total manufacturing output, and the value of the parts of the motor three times. Some semifinished products used in making the parts, such as screws or wire, may be counted four times.

The net value of a factory's production is the "value added" by manufacturing, the amount that remains after the costs of raw materials, fuel, purchased energy and contract work have been deducted from the gross value. It includes, essentially, the remuneration of workers, the maintenance cost of the industrial establishment, rent, interest on capital, and profits. Often it also includes taxes, such as corporate profit and excise levies.

The net value of output is a better measure of manufacturing production in a nation than the gross value. For a manufacturer, however, it is easier to report the gross value — that is, the amount of his sales — than to compute the net value. Some countries, therefore, record only the gross value of manufacturing.

The relationship between the two aggregates varies widely from nation to nation and from industry to industry in the same country. Gen-

---

8. **22**, 1944, pp. 590–607.

9. **18**, p. 31.

10. See statistics on manufacturing establishments in Chapters 27–30.

TABLE 423

MANUFACTURING ESTABLISHMENTS IN SELECTED COUNTRIES

Country and Year [a]	Establish-ments	Persons Em-ployed, in Thousands	Value, in Millions			Horsepower, in Thousands
			Gross Value of Products	Cost of Materials	Net Value of Products	
United States						
1939	184,230	8,936	$56,843	$32,160	$24,683	50,450
1947	240,801	14,292	. . .	. . .	74,426	. . .
Canada, 1948	33,447	1,156	11,877	6,937	4,940	7,867
Mexico, 1944	50,894	559	1,017	. . .	. . .	. . .
Cuba, 1938	2,200	27	60	25	35	. . .
Dominican Republic, 1949	3,185	45	108	. . .	. . .	. . .
Venezuela, 1936	8,025	48	69	28	41	. . .
Colombia, 1944–45	7,853	135	365	282	83	. . .
Brazil, 1948	11,180	540	2,861	. . .	. . .	. . .
Peru, 1945	325	26	51	. . .	. . .	47
Bolivia, 1943	1,221	13	24	. . .	. . .	. . .
Chile, 1946	3,224	150	53	29	24	208
Uruguay, 1945	. . .	85	255	. . .	. . .	. . .
Argentina, 1943	19,315	816	2,046	1,426	620	1,396
United Kingdom, 1935	48,944	5,158	13,910	8,116	5,794	. . .
Ireland, 1948	3,227	120	688	463	225	. . .
France, 1936	493,917	3,926	. . .	. . .	. . .	9,400
Belgium, 1937	153,300	942	. . .	. . .	. . .	. . .
Netherlands, 1949	9,200	744	4,180	. . .	. . .	. . .
Denmark, 1948	7,406	267	1,504	807	697	755
Sweden, 1948	16,509	775	5,456	. . .	. . .	3,848
Norway, 1948	5,926	225	1,350	686	664	. . .
Finland, 1948	5,794	290	1,711	. . .	. . .	1,290
Germany, 1936 [b]	110,400	6,001	20,030	9,645	10,385	. . .
Poland, 1947	28,996	1,443	. . .	. . .	. . .	. . .
Switzerland, 1939	98,572	661	. . .	. . .	. . .	972
Hungary, 1947	4,342	350	948	474	474	1,076
Italy, 1937–39	903,668	3,539	5,020	3,457	1,563	1,418
Romania, 1947	3,834	338	. . .	. . .	. . .	761
Bulgaria, 1934	85,928	212	. . .	. . .	. . .	224
Japan, 1948	100,116	3,632	. . .	. . .	. . .	. . .
India, 1947	4,880	1,633	2,247	1,515	732	. . .
Egypt, 1945	129,231	458	. . .	. . .	. . .	1,009
Union of South Africa, 1945–46	9,988	443	1,487	806	681	906
Australia, 1946–47	34,294	794	3,171	1,891	1,280	2,638
New Zealand, 1946–47	7,498	128	658	421	237	397

Sources: **2,** 1949–50, pp. 181–85, and official publications of respective countries.

a. Most recent data available.

b. In 1939 in Germany (1937 boundaries) 8,242,000 persons were employed by 94,531 manufacturing establishments with 11 workers or more (**20,** pp. 238–43).

erally, the net value of manufacturing production is equal to 40–50 per cent of the gross value, but there are conspicuous deviations from this range. In Italy, Ireland and Argentina, for example, the net value of manufactured products is about 30 per cent of the gross value, while in Colombia the ratio is less than 25 per cent. (See Table 423.) In the United States the ratio in 1939 averaged 43.4 per cent for all manufactures but ranged among industry groups from 22.8 per cent in products of petroleum and coal and 26.4 per cent in tobacco manufactures to 63.2 per cent

TABLE 424

MANUFACTURING ESTABLISHMENTS IN THE UNITED STATES, BY INDUSTRY GROUP, 1939 [a]

Industry Group	Establishments	Wage Earners, in Thousands	Value, in Millions			Net Value as Percentage of Gross Value
			Gross Value of Products	Cost of Materials	Net Value of Products	
All industries	184,230	7,887	$56,843	$32,160	$24,683	43.4
Food and kindred products	51,448	824	10,618	7,062	3,556	33.4
Tobacco manufactures	765	88	1,322	972	350	26.4
Textile mill products	6,444	1,083	3,931	2,109	1,822	46.3
Apparel	20,206	751	3,325	1,944	1,381	41.5
Lumber and timber	11,520	361	1,122	504	618	55.1
Furniture	8,457	294	1,268	641	627	49.4
Paper and allied products	3,279	265	2,020	1,150	870	43.1
Printing and publishing	24,878	325	2,578	812	1,766	68.5
Chemicals and allied products	9,203	287	3,734	1,880	1,854	49.6
Products of petroleum and coal	989	105	2,954	2,278	675	22.8
Rubber products	595	121	902	496	406	45.0
Leather	3,508	328	1,390	806	584	42.0
Stone, clay and glass	7,024	288	1,440	529	911	63.2
Iron and steel	8,994	966	6,592	3,636	2,956	44.8
Nonferrous metals	5,600	229	2,573	1,749	824	32.0
Electrical machinery	727	95	625	251	374	59.8
Machinery, excluding electrical	9,506	523	3,254	1,285	1,969	60.5
Automobiles and equipment	1,133	399	4,048	2,725	1,322	32.6
Transportation equipment	968	157	883	411	472	53.4
Miscellaneous	7,699	239	1,163	469	694	59.6

Source: 11, pp. 22–23.

a. Data on gross value of products by industry group were not computed by the 1947 Census of Manufactures.

in stone, clay and glass products and 68.5 per cent in printing and publishing.[11] (See Table 424.)

THE WORLD'S INDUSTRIAL OUTPUT

The industrial output of the world includes countless commodities produced under widely differing conditions. It is impossible to evaluate them precisely in uniform currency units, but a rough estimate may be ventured to show the order of magnitude of industrial activities in different parts of the world.

MEASURING THE VALUE OF OUTPUT

Industrial output comprises the output of min-

ing and quarrying, including the processing of ores, and the net value (that is, value added) of manufacturing. Production indexes serve to measure annual, quarterly and monthly changes in this volume. Data on value of output are found mainly in industrial censuses and current reports of industrial establishments.

National Indexes of Production

Indexes of production for broad industrial groups are derived by applying a system of weights to the indexes of single industries. The current index of mineral production in the United States, for example, covers mineral fuels, ores, precious metals, nonmetallic minerals and so on. The changes in the volume of output of each item are ascertained either from current reports of producers or by special surveys. Then

11. The 1947 Census of Manufactures reports only net value of products of industry (value added by manufacturing). (See 12, Vol. II, pp. 22 ff.)

the indexes for single products are weighted in accordance with their value in the period selected as the basis of comparison and in this way the recorded changes are combined to form a general index of mineral production.

A similar procedure is followed in all countries that compute national indexes of manufacturing production. The bench mark is usually a census of manufactures that shows the net value of the output of each industry. Indexes showing the current changes in the volume of production of individual industries are established on the basis of periodic reports of producers, sample surveys, data on the consumption of basic raw materials, employment and hours of work, and so on. These indexes are then weighted in accordance with the net value of output of the respective industries in the base period and are combined in a general index of the volume of manufacturing production.

When indexes for mining and manufacturing are merged in an over-all national index of industrial production, the production indexes of the two economic divisions are likewise weighted by the net value of output in the base period. The same procedure — weighting by value in the base period — is repeated for the fourth time when production indexes of individual countries are combined to arrive at an index of the world's industrial production.

Thus, although values and prices do not appear in production indexes, a production index shows, essentially, the changes in the aggregate value of industrial production at *constant* prices. By reversing the procedure used in computing it, a production index can be expressed in absolute figures, in currency units at prices that existed in the base period or at any other time for which the necessary information is available.

The World Index of the United Nations

The new world production index of the United Nations, published in April 1951, summarizes current production statistics of some thirty countries representing approximately 93 per cent of the world's industrial output. The key to this index is the system of "weights" that shows the probable distribution of the total dollar value of output in the covered areas in 1937.[12]

(See Table 425.) These weights have been applied to the indexes prepared by the governments of individual countries (Table 426) in computing a world index of mineral and manufacturing production (Table 427).[13] The world index of the United Nations for recent years would be lower if countries for which no current production statistics are available were included.[14] This, however, is a minor source of error in comparison with that inherent in the data for the USSR. The Soviet government claims that its industrial output has more than doubled since 1937. There is no way to check this assertion, but it does not appear very trustworthy in the light of the scanty information that comes from behind the Iron Curtain. On the other hand, as a result of the industrial predominance of the United

---

1937 but in a proximate year, the census figures were extrapolated to 1937 by means of the national index of production and indexes of prices or wages. The data for manufacturing industries were adjusted, wherever possible, to cover establishments with 5 or more employees. In a number of cases in which no census had been taken in a year reasonably close to 1937, data on net national product by industrial origin were utilized as the basis of estimation. In a few cases where neither census figures nor national income statistics were available, the weights were derived from statistics of the labor force employed and from estimates of the value of net output per worker in countries broadly similar in economic structure and degree of industrial development, or from statistics of energy consumed in industry.

"The estimates of the net value of mining and manufacturing output in national currencies thus derived were then converted to U.S. dollars. . . . To check the estimates thus derived, comparisons were made with labor employed and with energy consumed. In addition, the mineral output of all countries in which mining was important was valued directly in U.S. prices, at mine, quarry or well. In most cases the results corresponded reasonably well with the figures of gross value of output in national currency converted to U.S. dollars at the official rate of exchange. In the case of the United Kingdom, however, the discrepancy was significant. The outputs of mineral products in the United Kingdom and the United States were therefore compared, using the prices in each country in turn as weights, and the results were averaged to give the final estimate of the value of U. K. mining output in U.S. dollars." **6**, April 1951, pp. 1-2.

13. The UN index begins with 1937. The period 1925–37 was covered by a similar index of the League of Nations. (**1**, 1937–38, p. 175.) The German Institute for the Study of Business Conditions (Institut für Konjunkturforschung) computed an index of world industrial production for 1913–31. (**19**, p. 67.)

14. The world index does not include the following: Asia, except India and Japan and oil and tin production in other Asiatic countries; Africa, except the Union of South Africa and mining in other African countries; a large part of South America and the Caribbean; Spain, Portugal, Hungary, Romania, Yugoslavia and Albania.

---

12. The UN *Monthly Bulletin of Statistics* describes the procedure as follows: "[The] estimates are based, wherever possible, on data obtained from industrial censuses. For countries in which a census was taken not in

TABLE 425

INDUSTRIAL OUTPUT: PERCENTAGE DISTRIBUTION OF
WORLD OUTPUT AMONG SELECTED
COUNTRIES, 1937

Area	Percentage of Output Covered by UN Indexes	Percentage of Estimated World Output
World, total	—	100.00
Covered by the UN indexes	100.00	93.00
America		
United States	37.00	34.41
Canada	2.40	2.23
Mexico ᵃ	0.30	0.28
Chile ᵃ	0.10	0.09
Argentina ᵃ	0.50	0.47
Other countries ᵃ	0.70	0.65
Europe		
United Kingdom	11.20	10.42
Ireland	0.20	0.19
France	5.40	5.02
Luxembourg	0.10	0.09
Belgium	1.60	1.49
Netherlands	1.00	0.93
Denmark	0.40	0.37
Sweden	1.20	1.12
Norway	0.30	0.28
Finland	0.20	0.19
Germany ᵇ	11.10	10.32
Western	8.00	7.44
Eastern	3.10	2.88
Saar	0.20	0.19
Poland ᶜ	1.90	1.77
Czechoslovakia	1.70	1.58
Austria	0.50	0.46
Italy	2.70	2.51
Bulgaria	0.10	0.09
Greece	0.20	0.19
USSR	10.70	9.95
Asia		
Japan	4.30	4.00
India	1.20	1.12
Other countries ᵈ	0.40	0.37
Africa		
Union of South Africa	0.80	0.74
Other countries ᵃ	0.30	0.28
Oceania		
Australia	1.10	1.02
New Zealand	0.20	0.19

Source: **6,** April 1951, p. 2.

a. Mining only.
b. Postwar territory, excluding Berlin.
c. Postwar territory.
d. Only crude petroleum and tin production.

States, the world index of industrial production depends largely on fluctuations of business conditions in the United States. In fact, the ups and downs in that production outweigh the combined effects of changes in other countries.

The UN has met these difficulties by computing separate series of production indexes for the world as a whole; for the world excluding the USSR; for the world excluding the United States; and for the world excluding both the United States and the USSR. All four index series have the same base year, 1937, and in methodology are strictly comparable with one another. In combination with the indexes for individual countries, they cast light on changes in the volume of the world's industrial output and its distribution. (See Table 427.)

TRENDS IN INDUSTRIAL OUTPUT, 1913–51

In the past forty years the world has undergone two major wars, a succession of revolutionary upheavals of unprecedented violence, and an economic depression of exceptional duration and severity. Indexes of industrial production, of course, reflect these and other political and economic developments.

The World and the United States

There are no comprehensive international statistics on industrial production during World War I. By the end of the war, Germany and Russia were knocked out, economic life in France and Italy was deeply disorganized, and the southeastern European countries were readjusting themselves to new political boundaries. In 1921 the United States and Great Britain suffered a brief but severe economic setback, during which world industrial production (excluding the USSR) dropped some 16 per cent below the 1913 level.

The following eight years were marked by continual growth of production in the world. The recovery proceeded at about the same speed in Europe and the United States. A peak — nearly 48 per cent above the 1913 level for the world without the USSR — was reached in 1929. In the next three years the depression in the United States and Germany wiped out all the gains and in 1932 the world's output was again below the 1913 level. Recovery was not yet complete by the end of the 1930's. Except in 1936–38, neither the United States nor the world as a whole (excluding doubtful data for the USSR)

TABLE 426

INDUSTRIAL OUTPUT: INDEXES FOR SELECTED COUNTRIES, 1938–51
(United Nations)

(1937 = 100)

Country	1938	1939	1940	1941	1942	1943	1944	1945	1946	1947	1948	1949	1950	1951
United States	79	96	111	143	176	212	208	180	150	165	170	156	176	195
Canada	95	101	121	146	172	184	184	163	147	163	168	171	184	195
Mexico	100	97	97	101	106	111	114	122	126	131	131	141	155	163
Guatemala	...	...	...	...	...	...	...	...	100	106	110	114	116	115
Chile	...	105	119	129	126	130	129	141	159	158	163	169	169	194
Argentina	...	109	...	114	...	122	137	137	153	175	178	173	178	183
United Kingdom	94	...	...	...	...	...	...	...	90	98	109	117	126	130
Ireland	97	102	102	94	77	79	83	96	109	117	128	139	155	169
France	92	...	...	...	51	47	30	39	73	87	102	112	113	128
Luxembourg	69	...	...	...	...	...	...	...	59	75	100	96	101	121
Belgium	81	86	...	...	...	...	...	31	72	86	92	94	98	108
Netherlands	101	112	104	89	72	65	43	31	75	95	114	127	140	146
Denmark	100	107	86	82	86	88	87	74	101	116	129	138	152	156
Sweden	101	110	101	98	104	109	115	113	137	141	150	156	163	168
Norway	100	106	94	94	83	81	76	69	100	115	125	132	141	149
Finland	103	101	75	77	80	92	86	90	108	121	137	146	149	177
Western Germany	...	...	...	...	...	...	...	...	...	63	90	114	136
Poland	...	...	...	...	...	...	...	...	106	146	177	230	...
Czechoslovakia	...	...	...	...	...	...	...	...	87	103	111	...	...
Austria	...	...	...	...	...	...	...	...	58	93	123	146	166
Italy	100	...	...	...	...	...	...	...	95	99	109	126	143
Greece	...	100	...	...	...	...	...	33	53	67	73	87	110	125
Japan	107	112	114	119	115	133	146	61	34	40	52	67	79	104
India	105	103	110	118	111	117	117	120	100	98	109	107	106	118
Morocco [a]	122	117	75	41	46	27	65	97	136	138	150	172	185	234
Algeria [a]	100	113	58	36	43	50	84	93	152	170	192	232	236	255
Tunisia [a]	109	90	60	45	37	14	25	33	61	82	96	81	88	103

Source: **6**, July 1951, pp. 30–34, and August 1952, pp. 18–21.

a. Mining.

regained the 1929 peak during that decade.[15] (See Table 427.)

The war emergency brought a phenomenal increase in industrial production in the United States, Canada, Australia, Japan and some other countries. In the United States, the index of output more than doubled from 1939 to 1943.[16] More specifically, the index of output of durable manufactured goods more than trebled. The course of world production during World War II is not very clear, since statistics of civilian production were among the first casualties of the war in many countries.

There are, moreover, serious doubts as to the comparability of "industrial output" in wartime and peacetime. During an all-out war, a large part of the industrial capacity of a nation is diverted to the production of articles that are produced in insignificant amounts in peacetime. The problem of weighing "guns" against "butter" cannot be solved in a production index. The unavoidable waste in a war economy, combined with the inflated prices of military goods, pushes the index up. Whether industrial output in the United States more than doubled from 1939 to 1943 or whether it increased only 50–60 per cent, there is no doubt that the industrial plant of the country was operating at full capacity during the war, and after a brief setback during the reconversion, regained the acquired momentum.

15. **19**, p. 67; **1**, 1937–38, p. 175.
16. **14**, 1950, p. 755.

TABLE 427

INDUSTRIAL OUTPUT: INDEXES FOR THE WORLD, 1913–51

(*1937 = 100*)

Period	World	World, Excluding the USSR	World, Excluding the United States	World, Excluding the United States and the USSR
1913	55	67	52	53
1921	47	56	43	47
1922	67	68	49	57
1923	62	73	47	55
1924	63	76	53	61
1925	68	82	57	60
1926	69	84	55	54
1927	72	89	62	60
1928	75	93	64	64
1929	80	99	69	68
1930	70	88	62	55
1931	61	81	56	76
1932	55	61	...	...
1933	62	69	...	...
1934	68	75	...	...
1935	77	84	...	...
1936	88	94	...	...
1937	100	100	100	100
1938	93	91	102	100
1946	105	105	79	73
1947	119	117	92	83
1948	132	127	109	96
1949	136	128	124	108
1950	157	145	144	121
1951	176	161	162	135

Sources: The series for the world and the world excluding the USSR, 1913–31, are based on **19**, p. 67. The same series for the world, 1932–36, are based on **1**, 1937–38, p. 175. The other two series, 1913–31, are computed by the authors. All data for 1937–51 are taken from **6**, July 1951, p. 1, and July 1952, p. xv.

For the world without the United States and the USSR, industrial production at the end of World War II was far below the prewar level: the United Nations index stood at 73 in 1946 (1937=100), then rose to 135 in 1951. (See Table 427.)

Assuming that production in 1948–50 in the United States corresponded to the current state of productive capacity under reasonably favorable business conditions and that production in other countries, including the USSR, was gradually rising and, by 1951, had completely recovered from the setback caused by the war, the general trend of growth can be estimated for the United States and for the world, including the USSR, as in Figure 288. The trend lines in the chart are fitted to the respective production in-dexes by the freehand method. Apart from the erratic ups and downs and the uncertainty as to the real meaning of wartime production, these lines indicate for the world (including the USSR) an average growth of 2 per cent a year and for the United States an average growth of 3 per cent a year; for the world without the USSR and the United States the rate of growth was 1.3 per cent a year.

Various Countries

The supremacy of the United States in manu-facturing production was firmly established in the second half of the nineteenth century and has not been challenged. The value of manu-facturing output in the twelve leading industrial

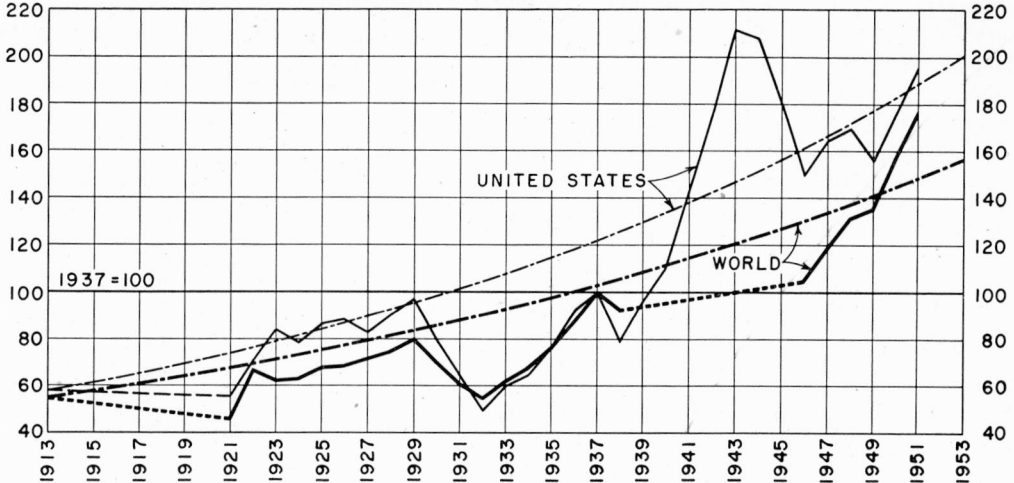

FIGURE 288. INDUSTRIAL PRODUCTION: INDEXES FOR THE WORLD AND THE UNITED STATES, 1913–51
The "world" index includes the United States and the USSR.

countries in 1888 has been estimated as follows (in millions): [17]

World	$22,370
United States	7,215
Great Britain and Ireland	4,100
Germany	2,915
France	2,425
Russia	1,815
Austria	1,265
Italy	605
Belgium	510
Spain	425
Sweden	250
Netherlands	175
Switzerland	160
Other countries	510

Twenty-five years later, before World War I, Germany outranked Great Britain; and Japan, Canada and British India, industrial newcomers, outranked Spain, Sweden, the Netherlands and Switzerland.[18] The struggle between Great Britain and Germany for first place among European industrial powers precipitated World War I.

Russia remained in fourth place in Europe until the revolution in 1917. Its industrial capacity, practically annihilated during the civil strife in 1918–22, was restored in the late 1920's, increased appreciably before World War II, suf-

fered terrible destruction during the German offensive and occupation, and has been rebuilt and increased in recent years. With due caution in assessing the exaggerated claims of the Kremlin, it is certain that the USSR is now one of the greatest industrial countries of the world, probably outranked only by the United States, Great Britain and Germany.

THE VALUE OF WORLD INDUSTRIAL OUTPUT

Before World War II

According to the "weights" established by the Statistical Office of the United Nations, the United States accounted for 34.4 per cent of the world's industrial output in 1937 (including mining and manufacturing). (See Table 425.)

The net value of United States manufacturing output in that year was $25.2 billion;[19] the value of mineral output (including the processing of ores), $5.4 billion.[20] Industrial production therefore totaled $30.6 billion in the United States; the figure for the world, at current U.S. prices, was close to $89 billion.[21]

In terms of type of economy,[22] this total rep-

---

17. **24**, p. 365; cf. **28**, Vol. IV, p. 16. The estimate refers to manufacturing in the narrow sense.

18. Computed from **19**, pp. 38 and 64.

19. **14**, 1950, p. 753.

20. **14**, 1950, p. 689.

21. The German Institute for the Study of Business Conditions estimated the net value of world industrial production in 1928 at 350 billion Reichsmarks ($83 billion). (**19**, p. 38.) The two estimates agree fairly well; both the volume of world industrial output and prices in 1937 were slightly above the 1928 level.

22. For the classification of nations and geographic regions by type of economy, see Figure 140, p. 438.

resents all the primarily industrial and agricultural-industrial areas except Switzerland and Hungary, most of the comparatively prosperous primarily agricultural countries (Ireland, Finland and Argentina), and a few less prosperous agricultural nations (Poland, Bulgaria, Greece and Mexico). The areas where a subsistence economy prevails are represented by a single country, India.

All in all, apart from partial coverage of "other countries" in Middle and South America, Asia and Africa, the United Nations index of world industrial production relates to an area with a total population of approximately 800 million and an aggregate income of $430 billion in 1948. In other words, it includes about a third of the world's population and four fifths of its income.[23]

The claim that the areas covered by the index controlled more than 90 per cent of the world's industrial output [24] seems realistic if "industry" is defined in the narrower sense as excluding handicrafts. Inclusion of handicrafts would raise the net value of world industrial output in 1937 to approximately $96 billion and increase the relative share of underdeveloped areas in this aggregate.

According to the UN index, the net value of industrial production in individual countries in 1937 was as follows (in millions):

World, total	$89,000
United States	30,600
Germany [a]	9,345
United Kingdom	9,260
USSR	8,849
France [b]	4,466
Japan	3,556
Italy	2,233
Canada	1,985
Poland	1,571
Czechoslovakia	1,406
Belgium	1,323
Sweden	992
India	992
Australia	910
Netherlands	827
Union of South Africa	662
Argentina	414
Austria	414

Denmark	$331
Norway	248
Mexico	248
Ireland	165
Greece	165
Finland	165
New Zealand	165
Chile	83
Luxembourg	83
Bulgaria	83

a. Territory as after World War II, excluding Berlin.
b. Includes the Saar.

The industrial output of all other countries totaled $7,450 million.

In 1947

By a similar method of analysis, the UN index of world industrial production indicates that world output in 1947 had a value of $182.2 billion, at current U.S. prices,[25] of which mining output represented $29.4 billion [26] while manufactures (including handicrafts) accounted for $152.8 billion. Since mining is not separated from manufacturing in the production indexes of many countries, the following discussion relates to industrial production as a whole.[27]

We can estimate the value of industrial output in individual countries in dollars, at U.S. prices, by distributing the estimated world total ($182.2 billion) in accordance with the share of each country in the world's industrial output in 1937 (Table 425) and the relative change in its output (Table 426) in comparison with that of

25. Industrial production in the United States was 65 per cent greater in 1947 than in 1937, while the world index advanced only 19 per cent. The relative share of the United States in the world's industrial output therefore increased from 34.41 per cent to 47.71 per cent. The value of industrial output in the United States totaled $86,910 million at current prices — $12,484 million for mineral products and $74,426 million for the value added by manufacturing, as shown by the Census of Manufactures. (**14**, 1950, pp. 689 and 753; cf. Chapter 21.) These amounts indicate that the value of the world's industrial output was approximately $182.2 billion.

26. The world output of mining, as such, is estimated at $26,370 million, at current U.S. prices. This total differs from that shown in Table 326, p. 756. The latter does not include the value of pig iron, which appears in the total value of mineral production in the United States. When the value of pig iron replaces that of iron ore in the world total, the resulting amount is as shown above. (Cf. Chapter 21.)

27. In most countries the value of mineral output (including the costs of processing the ores, smelting and refining) is between 15 and 25 per cent of the net value of total industrial output.

23. In 1948, world population totaled 2,351 million and world income $549 billion. (See Table 202, p. 439; cf. Table 187, p. 395.)

24. More exactly, 91.7 per cent, if "other countries" listed in Table 425 are not counted.

TABLE 428

INDUSTRIAL OUTPUT: TOTAL AND PER CAPITA IN SELECTED COUNTRIES,
1947 AND 1950

(*At U.S. 1947 Prices*)

Country	Total, in Millions		Per Capita	
	1947	*1950*	*1947*	*1950*
United States	$86,910	$93,170	$606	$620
Canada	5,560	6,275	430	458
Mexico	565	640	23	26
Chile	215	240	39	41
Argentina	1,255	—	78	—
United Kingdom	15,630	20,255	325	405
Ireland	335	440	113	147
France	6,760	8,775	168	209
Luxembourg	110	150	380	503
Belgium	1,960	2,235	232	258
Netherlands	1,350	1,990	140	197
Denmark	660	865	159	202
Sweden	2,420	2,800	356	499
Norway	490	600	155	184
Finland	350	430	86	105
Western Germany	—	10,560	—	218
Poland	2,880	4,725	120	189
Czechoslovakia	2,100	—	173	—
Austria	415	1,030	60	146
Italy	3,640	4,560	80	99
Greece	200	325	26	41
USSR [a]	[18,000]	[38,000]	[93]	[191]
Japan	2,450	4,780	31	56
India	1,680	1,775	7	7

Source: Computed as explained in text.

a. Data shown are of doubtful accuracy, although they conform to the UN production indexes. They should be deflated, probably by one third in 1947 and one half in 1950, to be comparable to those for other countries. There are indications of a considerable increase in industrial output in the USSR — especially in heavy industries — since 1950.

the world as a whole (Table 427). (See also first column in Table 428.)

The United States and Canada accounted for approximately half the world's industrial output in 1947; northwestern Europe, for 20 per cent. The USSR claimed the equivalent of 10 per cent of the world's total (about $18 billion, at current U.S. prices). The remaining 20 per cent was widely dispersed. (See Table 428; cf. Figure 289.)

The geographical distribution of industrial output at that time shows the repercussions of World War II. Production was below the prewar level in Germany, Japan and most European countries (cf. Table 426), but above the prewar level in the Americas, the Union of South Africa and Australia. The whole industrial economy of the world was badly out of balance. Restoration of equilibrium depended primarily on the rapid restoration of industrial capacity in the old European countries, which was one of the main objectives of the Marshall Plan.

In 1950

The comparatively short period 1947–50 brought about considerable changes in the volume and geographic distribution of the world's industrial output. All in all, the trend was toward the prewar pattern but on a higher level.

According to the UN index, the volume of the world's industrial output increased by 32 per

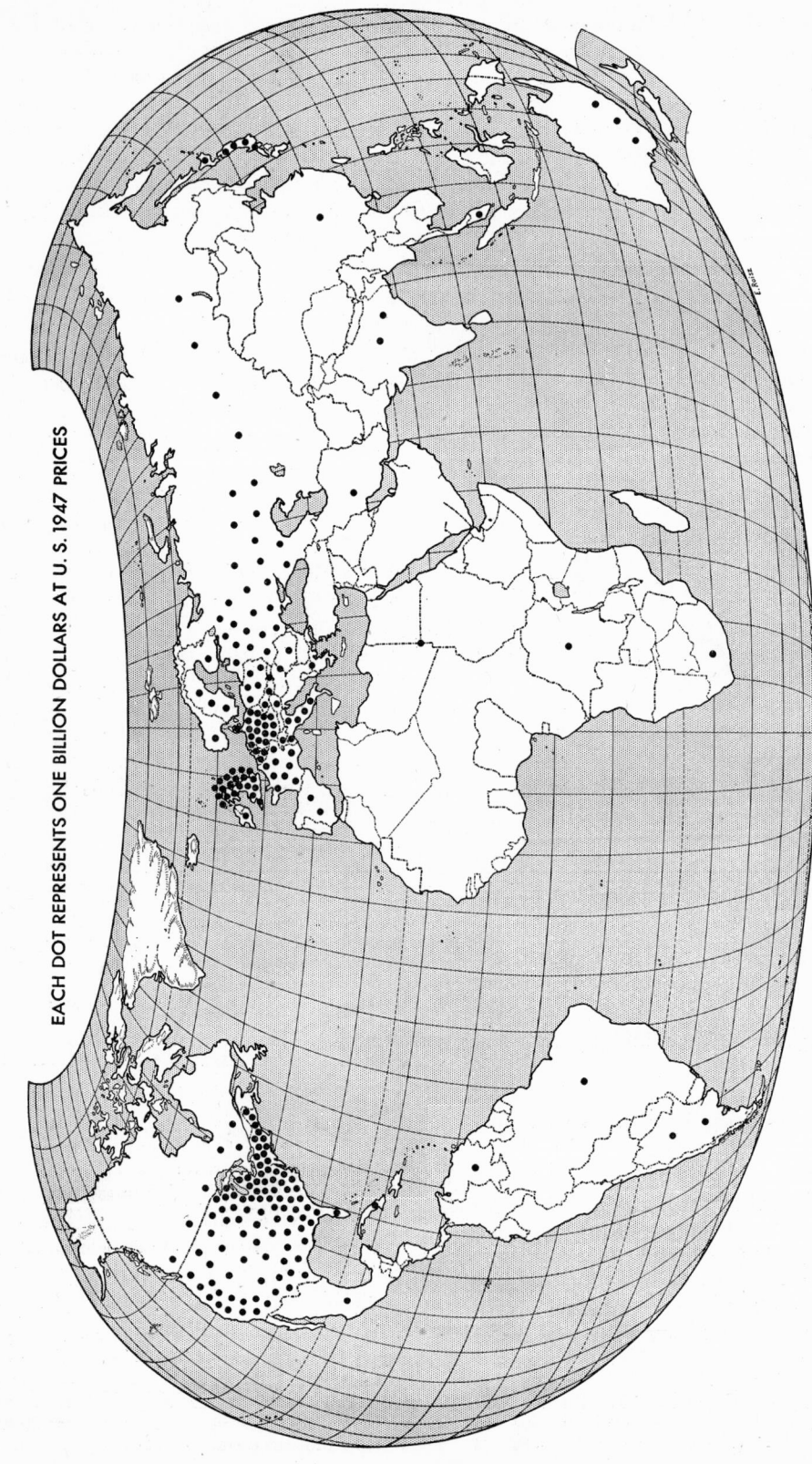

EACH DOT REPRESENTS ONE BILLION DOLLARS AT U. S. 1947 PRICES

FIGURE 289. INDUSTRIAL PRODUCTION: GEOGRAPHIC DISTRIBUTION IN THE WORLD, 1950

For purposes of comparability the data for the USSR have been deflated by 25 per cent. No correction has been made for the satellite countries.

cent from 1947 to 1950.[28] Assuming prices as in 1947, this gain would bring the value of the world's industrial output to $239 billion. With allowance for a general price rise of 7 per cent, the total would be close to $255 billion. If the exaggerated claims of the USSR and satellite countries are deflated, the amount is reduced to about $235–$240 billion at current prices or $220–$225 billion at 1947 prices.

The world's industrial production is now even more heavily concentrated on both coasts of the North Atlantic than before the war. Its geographic concentration is particularly striking in relation to population. This may be pictured by drawing a line along the Rio Grande in the Western Hemisphere and through the Eastern Hemisphere across Italy, the Balkan Peninsula, the Black and Caspian Seas and along the border between the USSR and China. In 1947, less than 30 per cent of mankind lived north of this line, but these peoples accounted for more than 90 per cent of the world's industrial output, while the remaining three fourths south of the line accounted for only 10 per cent. (See Figure 290.)

Industrial production is distributed more evenly in relation to national income. The areas of intensive industrial activity are in most cases also the areas of concentration of wealth. (See Figure 291.)

INDUSTRIAL OUTPUT PER CAPITA

The per capita value of industrial output in 1950 ranged from $7 in India (and probably even less in China) to $620 in the United States. Typical of prosperous, highly industrialized countries that export fabricated products were the following per capita values (at U.S. 1947 prices):

Luxembourg	$503
Sweden	499
Canada	458
United Kingdom	405

In such countries as Belgium, Western Germany, France and Denmark, industrial output ranged between $260 and $200 per capita; in the Netherlands and Norway it was just below

$200 and in Ireland and Austria below $150. (See Figure 292.) Under these conditions it is difficult or impossible to accept the USSR's claim to have attained an industrial output equivalent to approximately $190 per capita, at U.S. 1947 prices. For similar reasons, the spectacular increase of industrial output reported for Poland after the Kremlin took over can hardly be regarded seriously.

THE SHARE OF MANUFACTURING IN NATIONAL INCOME

The part of a nation's income that originates in manufacturing is usually smaller than the value added by manufacturing (the net value of manufacturing output). This discrepancy arises mainly from outlays by manufacturers for maintenance of plant and amortization of capital. As a part of production costs, this item appears in the value of the finished product and the net output. On the other hand, plant maintenance and amortization of capital are not counted as part of national income. In fact, they are items of outlay rather than income for the manufacturers and do not represent a new value created in the course of manufacturing. The gap between the value added by manufacturing and the income originated in manufacturing in the United States is illustrated by the following figures (in millions): [29]

	Value Added by Manufacturing	Income Originated in Manufacturing
1929	$30,591	$22,012
1933	14,008	7,563
1937	25,174	19,304
1947	74,426	59,459

Thus, the share of manufacturing in national income is 20–25 per cent less than the net value of manufacturing.[30]

If our estimate of $152.8 billion as the net value of the world's manufacturing output in 1947 is valid, the figure for 1948 must have been close to $185 billion, at current U.S. prices.[31] The corresponding amount of income originated

---

28. The index number for the whole world was 119 in 1947 and 156 in 1950 (1937 = 100). For the world without the United States and the USSR, the rise was from 83 to 121, or 46 per cent.

29. Computed from **14**, 1950, p. 753; and **15**, July 1950, p. 15.

30. The relative gap is bound to increase in depressions, when production declines more rapidly than maintenance costs.

31. Allowing for an increase of 11 per cent in the physical volume of output and 9.2 per cent in wholesale prices of manufactured goods.

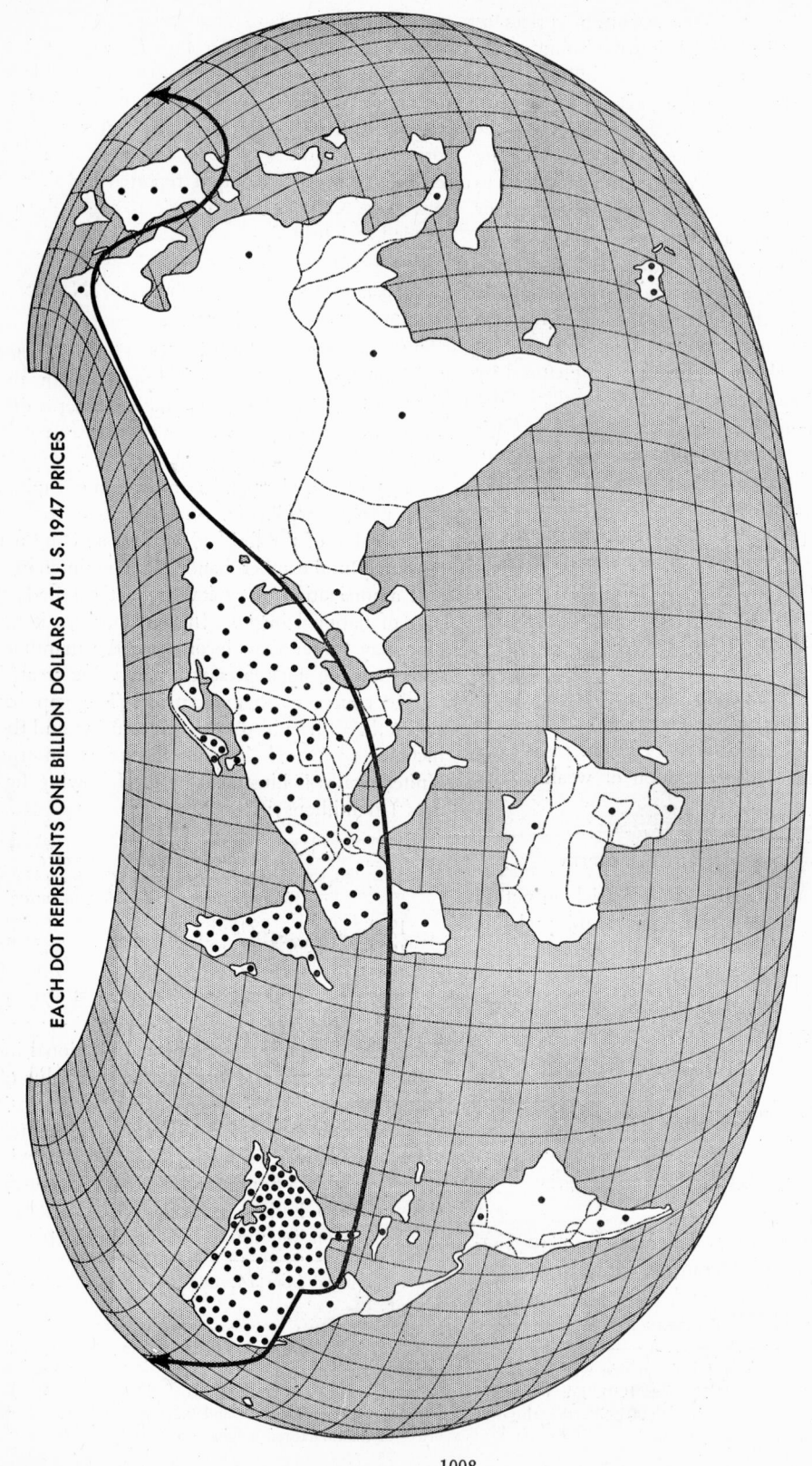

EACH DOT REPRESENTS ONE BILLION DOLLARS AT U. S. 1947 PRICES

FIGURE 290. INDUSTRIAL PRODUCTION: GEOGRAPHIC DISTRIBUTION IN THE WORLD IN RELATION TO POPULATION, 1950

Continents, geographic regions and individual countries are shown on this map on the scale of their population. The density of the dots indicates the value of industrial output per capita of population in each area. The black line shows the rough demarcation between the industrialized areas and those in which agriculture and a subsistence economy prevail.

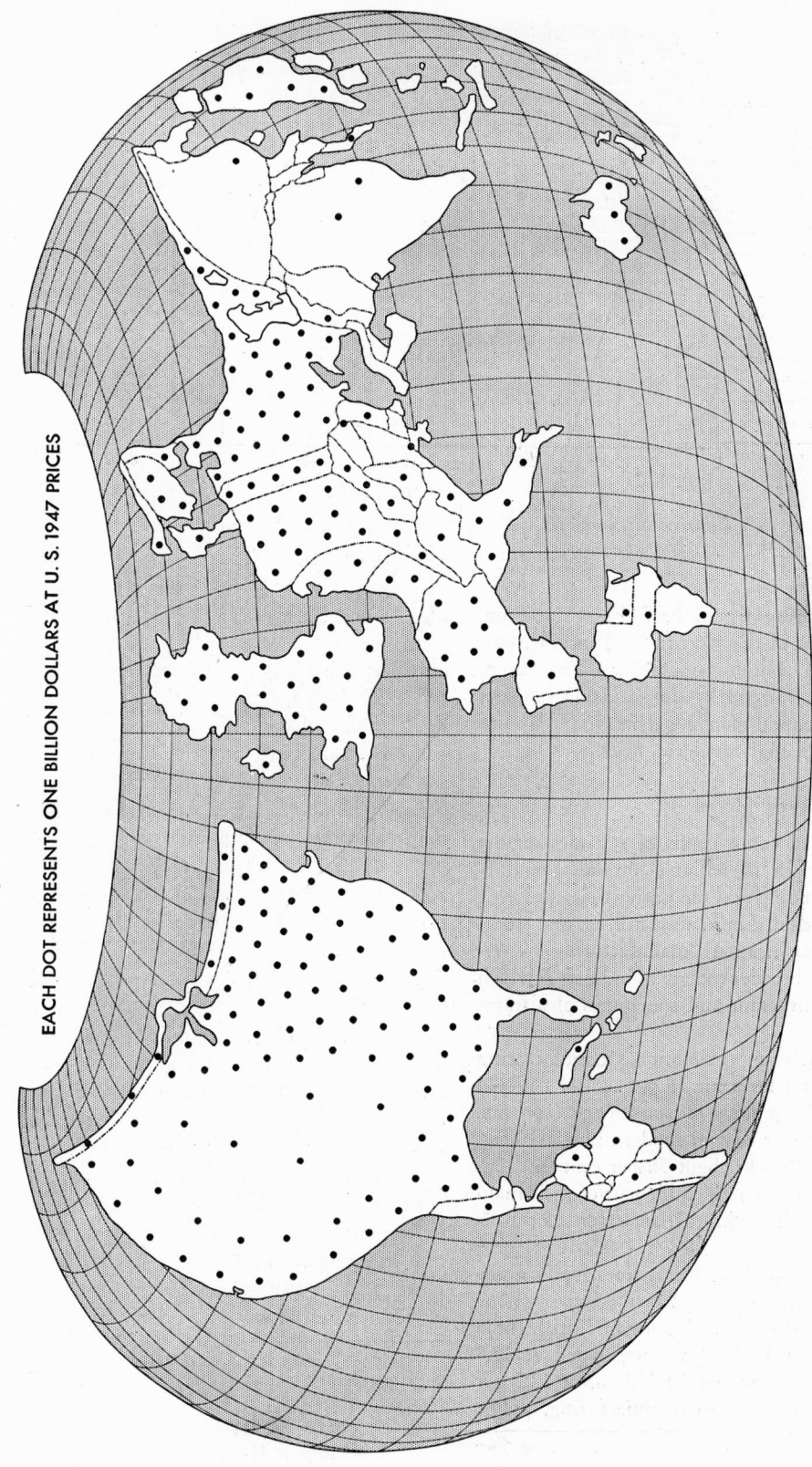

EACH DOT REPRESENTS ONE BILLION DOLLARS AT U. S. 1947 PRICES

FIGURE 291. INDUSTRIAL PRODUCTION: GEOGRAPHIC DISTRIBUTION IN RELATION TO NATIONAL INCOME, 1950

Like Figure 290, this is a distorted map: it shows continents, geographic regions and individual countries on the scale of their estimated national income in 1949. The density of the dots indicates the relationship of the value of industrial output to national income or of per capita industrial output to per capita income in each area. The comparatively even dispersion of dots over the map suggests a close correlation between the two values.

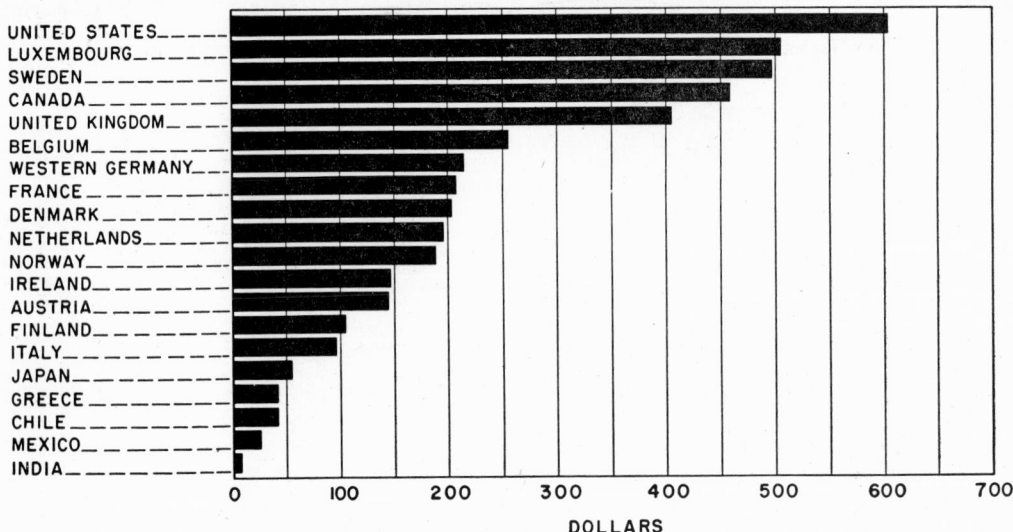

FIGURE 292. INDUSTRIAL PRODUCTION: PER CAPITA VALUE IN SELECTED COUNTRIES, 1950
(Value estimated at 1947 prices)

in manufacturing would be $140–$145 billion, or 26 per cent of the world's 1948 income, estimated at $549 billion U.S. dollars. This rough estimate is confirmed by the available statistics on the distribution of national income by industrial origin in individual countries.

National Patterns

International comparisons of statistics on the industrial origin of national income are difficult. Often mining and the production of electric power are included in manufacturing, and sometimes the classification "manufacturing" is replaced by the broader category "industry," which includes construction and sometimes also transportation.[32]

At a rough approximation, manufacturing proper accounts for some 10 per cent of national income in the regions of subsistence economy, more than 30 per cent in modern industrialized countries, and up to about 50 per cent in countries that export a considerable part of their manufactured products in exchange for foodstuffs and raw materials.

India, China and the Philippines typify a primarily agricultural subsistence economy. The home-produced national income of British India and Burma in 1931–32 was estimated at 17.3 billion rupees, of which 2.1 billion, or 12.2 per cent was attributable to manufacturing, public

utilities and construction.[33] The share of manufacturing proper was hardly more than 10 per cent, but it is likely to have increased since that time. For China, the estimate cited by the Statistical Office of the United Nations sets the net national product in 1936 at 25.7 billion yuan and the income originated by manufacturing at 2.5 billion yuan, or 9.6 per cent.[34] The share of manufacturing had been increasing: in 1931, 7.8 per cent; in 1932, 8.1 per cent; in 1933, 9.3 per cent; in 1934, 9.4 per cent; in 1935 and 1936, 9.6 per cent. In the Philippines, industrial production, including mining and building construction, accounted for 6–7 per cent of national income in 1947–48.[35]

In the Dominican Republic and Colombia, manufacturing industries and mining account for a somewhat larger share of national income. The ratio is still larger — close to 25 per cent — in such primarily agricultural countries as Peru, Argentina, Bulgaria and Greece.[36]

In Ireland, one of the most prosperous primarily agricultural countries in the world, 19 per cent of national income originated in industrial production in 1942–44.[37] Similar rates were recorded before the war in Turkey: 17.3 per cent

32. See **5**, *passim.*

33. **26.**
34. **25.**
35. **2**, 1949–50, p. 413.
36. **2**, 1949–50, pp. 411–13.
37. **2**, 1949–50, p. 412.

TABLE 429

NET VALUE OF INDUSTRIAL PRODUCTION: RELATION TO TOTAL NATIONAL INCOME,
IN EUROPEAN COUNTRIES, 1938 AND 1948

(Dollar Figures in Millions, at 1938 Prices)

Country	National Income		Net Value of Industrial Production		Net Value of Industrial Production as Percentage of National Income	
	1938	1948	1938	1948	1938	1948
Europe, total	$84,720	$73,740	$28,243	$26,317	33.3	35.6
United Kingdom	18,020	20,040	6,696	8,102	37.1	40.4
Ireland	730	860	125	171	17.1	19.9
France	9,860	9,550	3,155	3,407	31.9	35.7
Belgium–Luxembourg	2,390	2,450	830	955	34.7	38.9
Netherlands	2,810	2,450	665	745	23.6	30.4
Denmark	1,200	1,290	324	421	27.0	32.6
Sweden	2,310	2,850	771	1,102	33.4	38.6
Norway	740	810	219	258	29.5	31.8
Finland	660	690	137	196	20.7	28.4
Germany	23,140	10,840	9,066	4,129	39.2	38.1
Poland	3,600	3,390	711	946	19.7	27.9
Czechoslovakia	2,690	2,400	875	892	32.5	37.2
Switzerland	1,540	2,030	536	805	34.8	40.0
Austria	1,220	910	400	296	32.7	32.5
Hungary	1,020	890	241	243	23.6	27.3
Italy	6,230	6,500	1,798	1,564	28.8	24.0
Romania	a	a	234	190	—	—
Bulgaria	430	470	65	111	15.1	23.6
Greece	570	480	a	a	—	—
Other European countries	6,230	6,500	1,395	1,784	22.4	27.4

Source: **7**, 1948, pp. 21 and 235.   a. Included in other European countries.

in 1933–34, 17.9 per cent in 1934–35, 18.1 per cent in 1935–36.[38]

For postwar years the following percentages have been recorded: [39]

Chile, 1946–48	32–33
Italy, 1947–49	32–34
Union of South Africa, 1946–48	33
Denmark, 1947–49	34–36
France, 1946–48	34–38
United States, 1947–49	36–37
Netherlands, 1946–48	35–39
Canada, 1946–48	35–39
Finland, 1946–48	36–39
Hungary, 1946	46
Norway, 1947–49	48–52
Western Germany, 1948–49	49–52
United Kingdom, 1948–49	53

Industrial income, in these computations, includes manufacturing, mining and quarrying, building construction and electric utilities. The United Nations Economic Commission for Europe in its estimate of the net value of industrial production in selected European countries in 1938 and 1948 does not include building construction. Its data are not strictly comparable with those derived from national income statistics.[40] (See Table 429.)

Assuming that the income originated in manufacturing is about 20–25 per cent less than that derived from all industrial activities, it appears that in 1948 manufacturing, in the narrow sense, accounted for more than 30 per cent of national income in the United Kingdom, Sweden, Bel-

38. **27**, Chapter 11.

39. **2**, 1949–50, pp. 411–13. Countries are arrayed by increasing share of industrial production in national income. Construction is included.

40. To ensure comparability between the prewar and postwar data, the Commission developed a special procedure, which cannot be discussed here but does not substantially affect the ratios in the last two columns in Table 429.

TABLE 430

INCOME FROM MANUFACTURING: RELATION TO TOTAL NATIONAL INCOME
IN THE UNITED STATES, 1929–50

(*Dollar Figures in Millions*)

Year	National Income	Income from Manufacturing	Income from Manufacturing as Percentage of National Income	Year	National Income	Income from Manufacturing	Income from Manufacturing as Percentage of National Income
1929	$87,355	$22,012	25.2	1940	$ 81,347	$22,368	27.4
1930	75,003	18,217	24.2	1941	103,834	32,897	31.7
1931	58,873	12,434	21.1	1942	137,119	45,239	32.9
1932	41,690	7,196	17.3	1943	169,686	58,104	34.2
1933	39,584	7,563	19.1	1944	183,838	60,456	32.9
1934	48,613	10,922	22.5	1945	182,691	51,918	28.4
1935	56,789	13,336	23.4	1946	180,286	48,905	27.1
1936	64,719	16,183	25.0	1947	198,688	59,459	29.9
1937	73,627	19,304	26.2	1948	223,469	67,215	30.1
1938	67,375	14,997	22.2	1949	216,716	63,157	29.1
1939	72,532	17,936	23.8	1950	238,963	74,075	31.0

Sources: Computed from **15**, July 1947, p. 26; **16**, p. 159.

gium-Luxembourg, Germany and Switzerland, and for 25–30 per cent in France, Denmark, Austria, Norway and the Netherlands. Applying the same rough yardstick to other countries, the following general pattern for the share of manufacturing in national income is found:

Countries in which a subsistence economy prevails   Less than 10 per cent

Most of the primarily agricultural countries with a prevailing money economy   10–15 per cent

Primarily agricultural countries with developed mining, forestry and so on   15–25 per cent

Agricultural-industrial countries   25–30 per cent

Highly industrialized countries with comparatively weak agriculture   30–40 per cent

In the USSR, in striking contrast to this pattern, industry (including mining, lumbering and fishing) accounted for 53.5 per cent of national income in 1937, and agriculture for only 15.4 per cent. The disproportionately large percentage for industry is due partly to the method of computing national income and partly to the Soviet government's practice of compulsory expropriation of agricultural produce at nominal prices.

The United States

The relative share of manufactures in national income in the United States has varied from year to year in the past two decades. It amounted to 25.2 per cent in 1929, dropped to 17.3 per cent at the depth of the depression in 1932, rose to 26.2 per cent in 1937, fell back under the impact of the recession of 1938, jumped to 34.2 per cent during the war, and returned to about 30 per cent after demobilization. (See Table 430.) These shifts were due partly to changes in the distribution of economic activities, partly to divergent trends in prices. The general trend in the share of manufactures in national income since 1929 has been slightly upward.

PRODUCTIVITY OF LABOR IN MANUFACTURING

A comparison of the labor force in manufacturing and the income originated there reveals striking contrasts among countries in the value of the output per worker. (See Figure 293.)

At a rough approximation, the net income originated per worker in manufactures and handicrafts in 1948 is estimated as follows: [41]

World	$ 910
United States	4,110
Australia	3,600

41. These figures relate the estimated income originated in manufactures and handicrafts (excluding so far as possible mining, building construction, etc.) to the estimated number of persons engaged, without distinction between employers and employees and without allowance for unemployment.

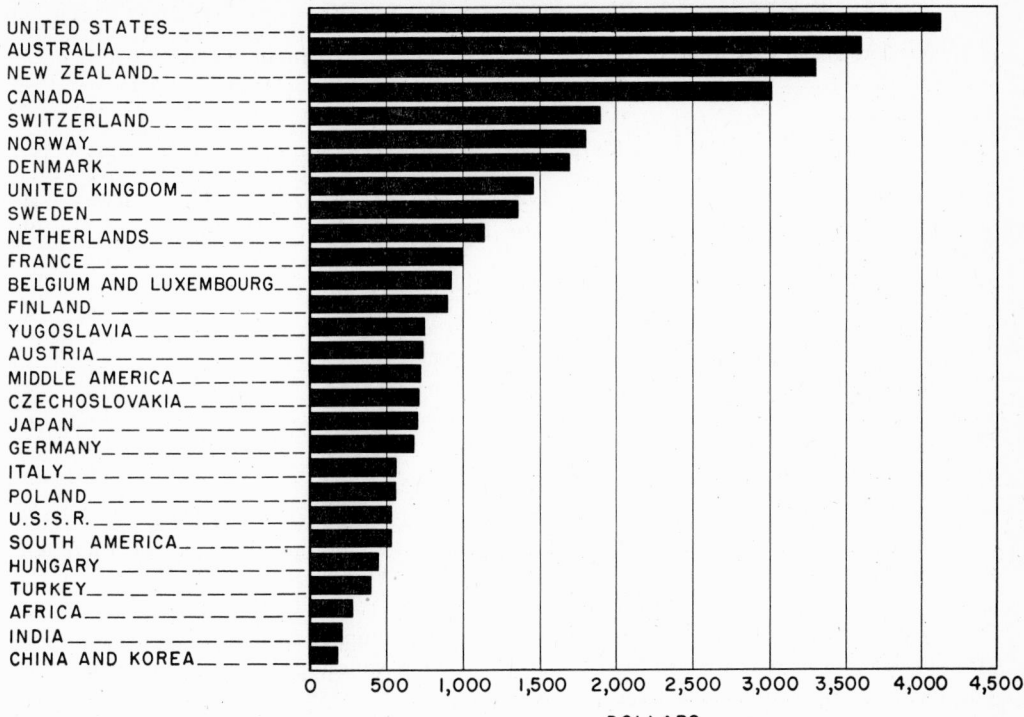

FIGURE 293. INDUSTRIAL PRODUCTION: VALUE PER WORKER IN SELECTED COUNTRIES, 1948

New Zealand	$3,300
Canada	3,000
Switzerland	1,900
Norway	1,800
Denmark	1,700
United Kingdom	1,450
Sweden	1,380
Netherlands	1,150
France	1,000
Belgium-Luxembourg	900
Finland	890
Yugoslavia	750
Austria	750
Middle America	720
Czechoslovakia	700
Japan	700
Germany	650
Italy	550
Poland	540
USSR	520
South America	520
Hungary	440
Turkey	400
Africa	265
India	200
China and Korea	175

These figures make no claim to precision. The ranking of individual countries may change if

corrections are made for differences in classification, purchasing power of currency, and so on, but such adjustments would hardly alter the general picture.

The United States and young, sparsely populated countries — Australia, New Zealand and Canada — head the list of nations in the ranking according to the efficiency of the industrial plant. In these countries output per worker in the manufacturing industries is three or four times the world average.

Next come the industrial nations of northwestern Europe, where output per worker ranges from the world average to double that amount — the United Kingdom, France, Belgium, Switzerland and the Scandinavian countries. Normally, this group would include Germany and probably also Austria and Czechoslovakia.[42]

The third group of countries—where output per worker in manufactures is below the world average but not less than two thirds of this amount—includes, among others, Japan, Mexico

42. The relative position of particular countries in this group and the relation between their output per worker and that in the United States, Australia and Canada cannot be ascertained with precision. The figures suggest only the order of magnitude.

TABLE 431

INDUSTRY GROUPS: DISTRIBUTION OF FACTORY WORKERS IN THE UNITED STATES, 1880–1947

Industry	Number, in Thousands				Per Cent			
	1880	1900	1919	1947	1880	1900	1919	1947
Total	2,553	4,749	9,096	14,294	100.0	100.0	100.0	100.0
Food and kindred products	212	377	740	1,442	8.3	7.9	8.1	10.1
Tobacco	88	142	157	112	3.4	3.0	1.7	0.8
Textiles, apparel and related products	710	1,030	1,611	2,315	27.8	21.7	17.7	16.2
Leather	182	238	349	383	7.1	5.0	3.8	2.7
Lumber, furniture and fixtures	320	547	839	958	12.5	11.5	9.2	6.7
Stone, clay and glass products	133	245	299	462	5.2	5.2	3.3	3.2
Paper, printing and publishing	119	298	510	1,165	4.7	6.3	5.6	8.1
Chemicals and allied products [a]	45	102	427	1,103	1.8	2.1	4.7	7.7
Iron, steel and other metal industries [b]	465	925	1,925	4,709	18.2	19.5	21.2	32.9
Transportation equipment	90	363	1,012	1,182	3.5	7.6	11.1	8.3
Miscellaneous	189	483	1,227	464	7.4	10.2	13.5	3.2

Sources: **28**, Vol. IV, pp. 30–31; **10**, p. cxliv; **12**, Vol. II, p. 24.

a. Includes petroleum and coal products, and rubber.
b. Includes machinery, electrical and other.

and Yugoslavia. In the early postwar years Czechoslovakia and Austria were in this class.

The fourth group comprises a large part of South America, the least prosperous European countries — Italy, Spain, Portugal, Poland, Hungary, Romania and Bulgaria — the USSR and Turkey. In these countries, output per worker in manufacturing industries is about half the world average.

In Asia and Africa the productivity of labor is still lower.

The contrasts among countries in the productivity of labor are smaller if the comparison is limited to establishments covered by industrial censuses, subject to special regulations, or registered as factories. Such limitation eliminates handicrafts and home work and, for the underdeveloped areas, restricts the coverage to "modern" establishments, often owned by foreigners. The fragmentary information of this type provided by industrial censuses in Argentina (1943), Brazil (1939), Mexico (1944) and other countries (see Table 423), suggests that the net value of output per worker in modern factories in underdeveloped countries was fairly high — only 20–30 per cent less than that in the United Kingdom.

Such industrial establishments, however, are not typical of underdeveloped countries. Advanced industrial techniques are often transplanted directly into premechanized civilizations. Most of the "modern" establishments in such

areas are equipped with imported machinery and employ technical personnel trained abroad. To justify the investment of capital, such plants must yield a substantial profit and make liberal allowance for amortization. The price of their products is often protected by high tariffs or by a monopolistic position. In brief, the net value of output per worker in modern industrial establishments in underdeveloped areas has to be and is appreciably higher than the average for workers in local manufactures and handicrafts.

DISTRIBUTION BY INDUSTRY GROUP

The distribution of the manufacturing labor force and output among the broad subgroups of the industry is governed mainly by three factors: (1) the relationship between the subsistence and market economy in the area; (2) the income level; (3) local conditions favorable to the development of particular types of production for the domestic market or export.

National Patterns

The contrast in patterns of distribution of manufacturing activities (including handicrafts) between underdeveloped and highly industrialized areas is illustrated by the following comparison of the distribution of the industrial labor force in India and the United States: [43]

43. **22**, 1944, pp. 66–67; **14**, 1950, p. 191. For both countries, data are from population censuses.

	British India, 1931		United States,[a] 1940	
	Number, in Thousands	Per Cent	Number, in Thousands	Per Cent
Total	15,259	100.0	11,756	100.0
Food, drink and tobacco	1,665	10.9	1,337	11.4
Textiles	4,512	29.6	1,293	11.0
Apparel	3,916	25.7	959	8.2
Hide, skins, leather	360	2.4	407	3.5
Wood and furniture	1,997	13.1	1,070	9.1
Metals	845	5.5	2,863	24.3
Transportation equipment	33	0.2	962	8.2
Stone, clay, glass, ceramics	1,196	7.8	373	3.2
Chemicals and similar products	735	4.8	679	5.8
Other	—	—	1,813	15.4

a. Experienced labor force only.

More than half the labor force in manufacturing in India is employed in the production of textiles and apparel, while these industries absorb less than 20 per cent of the manufacturing labor force in the United States. Wood, stone and clay products account for more than 20 per cent of the manufacturing employment in India and only 12 per cent in the United States. On the other hand, the share of metal products and transportation equipment in industrial employment is less than 6 per cent in India and more than 32 per cent in the United States.

A similar contrast exists in the distribution of employees of manufacturing establishments in the United States in 1880 and 1947. (See Table 431.) During the intervening sixty-seven years, all industry groups increased their work force, but the chemical and metal industries — including rubber, petroleum and coal products, machinery, electrical equipment, transportation equipment and instruments — expanded much more than other industries. They employed nearly half of all factory workers in 1947 as compared with slightly less than a fourth in 1880; the change came after the turn of the century.

The chemical and metal industries are, indeed, the token of an advanced phase of industrial development.[44] Their predominance is particularly clear among export industries in highly industrialized countries. In Great Britain in 1946, for example, metals and engineering factories employed 36 per cent of all workers engaged in production for the home market and 49 per cent

of factory workers in export industries. (See Table 432.)

Despite differences in classification, a fairly plausible general pattern is evident. Textiles and articles of clothing are the main manufactured products in the primarily agricultural areas. Next comes the processing of such readily available raw materials as wood and clay. Not until a much higher level of industrial development is reached does manufacturing shift to metals, machinery and mechanical transportation equipment.

In a highly developed industrial economy, iron and steel and engineering industries dominate the scene, supplying other industries with equipment that enables them to expand production without increasing the number of workers.

Peru is a typical example of the composition of manufacturing in an underdeveloped country. The 1940 census of population enumerated 380,000 persons in manufacturing, among whom 191,000 were engaged in the production of textiles and 90,000 in the clothing industries. Only 18,400 were counted in the food, drink and tobacco industries, and only 14,800 in the fabrication of metals. This situation is characteristic of a phase of economic development in which the textile and clothing industries have become differentiated from the economy of farm and home, while food processing still remains a domestic activity. The picture changes, of course, if small craftshops are excluded and the enumeration is limited to "manufacturing establishments"; but even with this limitation, food and textile industries predominate in manufacturing in primarily agricultural countries.

In Latin America, for example, the food and beverage industries (including the tobacco indus-

44. In *Das Kapital,* which purported to give a generalized picture of a capitalist system that had passed its climax and was approaching maturity, Karl Marx did not so much as mention metal mills. To him a cotton mill epitomized industrial production.

TABLE 432

INDUSTRY GROUPS: DISTRIBUTION OF FACTORY WORKERS
IN GREAT BRITAIN, 1939 AND 1946

(Thousands)

Industry	1939			1946		
	Total	For the Home Market	For Export	Total	For the Home Market	For Export
All manufactures	5,645	4,655	990	6,042	4,732	1,310
Metals and engineering	1,590	1,200	390	2,326	1,684	642
Building materials		545		547	478	69
Food, drink and tobacco		604		521	500	21
Textiles and clothing	4,055	1,334	600	1,211	973	238
Chemicals		140		265	204	61
Other manufactures		832		1,072	793	279

Source: **21,** 1935–46, p. 105.

try) accounted for more than 35 per cent of the gross value of manufacturing production in Mexico, Brazil, Chile and Argentina; more than 50 per cent in Colombia; and more than 55 per cent in Guatemala, Venezuela, Bolivia and Uruguay. (See Table 433.)

At the other extreme are such countries as Great Britain, Germany, Belgium, the United States. Manufacturing labor in prewar Germany was distributed very much as in the United States. According to the census of 1933, 16.7 million workers were attached to manufacturing pursuits (including handicrafts). Of these, 24 per cent were employed in the textile and clothing industries; 15 per cent in processing food, drink and tobacco; and 35 per cent in iron, steel and other metals industries, including machinery and transportation equipment.

The World

Considering the distribution of the manufacturing labor force of India and the United States as typical of the two extreme patterns of existing economic systems, and using the fragmentary information available for the countries with an intermediate type of economy, the distribution of the world labor force in manufactures and handicrafts among broad industry groups may be estimated as follows:

The food, drink and tobacco industries, excluding workers engaged mainly in selling foodstuffs and prepared food, may employ approximately 20 million.

Textile industries and clothing, counted together because of the considerable differences between underdeveloped and industrialized countries in delimiting the two, may employ 50 million workers.[45]

The metals and machinery industries, ranging from primitive ironsmith shops to modern shipyards and automobile and aircraft factories, employ about 37 million workers, of whom approximately 60 per cent are in North America and Europe. (See Table 434.)

LONG-RANGE TRENDS

The progress of the modern industrial nations has been marked by a gradual shift of the labor force from agricultural to nonagricultural pursuits and a rise in the share of manufacturing in employment and national output. This change has not always been accompanied by more rapid increase in factory employment than in other nonagricultural pursuits.[46]

As industrialization progresses, the role of manufactures in the national economy increases under the impact of three factors: the contraction of production for own consumption (domestic economy), the mechanization of agriculture, and a continual growth of needs and demands for

45. In industrial countries, textile mills usually employ more workers than the clothing trades, while the opposite is usually true in underdeveloped countries. In the world as a whole, the clothing industries probably employ more hands than textiles, even when home weavers are included.

46. Cf. Chapter 13.

TABLE 433

INDUSTRY GROUPS: PERCENTAGE DISTRIBUTION OF FACTORY WORKERS AND OUTPUT
IN LATIN AMERICAN COUNTRIES

(*Per Cent*)

Country and Year [a]	All Manufacturing	Food and Beverages	Tobacco	Textiles and Clothing	Lumber [b]	Leather	Chemicals	Metals	Miscellaneous
			Factory Workers						
Mexico, 1941	100.0	26.1	1.4	35.1	3.8	1.0	4.5	13.1	15.0
Guatemala, 1946	100.0	26.5	4.4	32.3	8.8	2.2	3.1	4.0	18.6
Venezuela, 1936	100.0	55.8	4.8	12.2	3.9	8.7	4.6	0.1	9.6
Colombia, 1945	100.0	27.2	5.6	28.4	6.1	6.6	4.0	6.3	15.8
Brazil, 1940	100.0	24.9	c	34.7	8.1	1.8	4.4	10.7	15.3
Bolivia, 1942	100.0	33.6	1.5	24.6	3.7	9.0	2.2	0.7	24.6
Chile, 1945	100.0	27.2	5.6	28.4	6.1	6.6	4.0	6.3	15.8
Uruguay, 1936	100.0	37.0	1.7	17.3	5.0	6.7	3.2	15.5	13.8
Argentina, 1943	100.0	23.0	c	17.7	9.3	4.3	4.3	19.6	21.9
			Output (Gross Value)						
Mexico, 1941	100.0	31.9	3.5	28.3	1.9	1.3	7.5	10.0	15.5
Guatemala, 1946	100.0	47.4	8.6	21.9	4.3	1.9	4.0	2.4	9.5
Venezuela, 1936	100.0	45.4	12.8	9.6	3.9	7.0	9.5	1.8	9.9
Colombia, 1945	100.0	49.3	2.5	18.7	3.0	4.4	4.4	3.4	14.4
Brazil, 1940	100.0	35.8	c	27.8	4.4	2.0	7.5	11.3	11.2
Bolivia, 1942	100.0	52.3	6.0	23.2	1.6	6.1	5.0	0.5	5.2
Chile, 1945	100.0	35.6	3.5	18.5	4.5	8.8	9.3	9.4	10.3
Uruguay, 1936	100.0	54.2	2.7	14.2	2.8	5.0	3.9	8.7	8.4
Argentina, 1943	100.0	37.3	1.5	19.3	4.8	4.3	6.1	14.6	11.9

Source: **4**, 1948, p. 17.

a. Most recent data available.

b. Includes furniture and fixtures.

c. Included in food and beverages.

TABLE 434

INDUSTRY GROUPS: DISTRIBUTION OF MANUFACTURING LABOR FORCE, IN THE WORLD
AND EACH CONTINENT, 1950

(*Millions*)

Region	All Manufacturing	Food, Beverages and Tobacco	Textiles and Clothing	Metals, Machinery, Transportation Equipment	Other
World	165.0	20.0	50.0	37.0	58.0
North America	18.2	2.2	3.6	6.1	6.3
Middle and South America	6.3	0.7	3.3	0.5	1.8
Europe	54.0	6.5	12.0	16.5	19.0
USSR	20.0	2.8	4.0	7.0	6.2
Asia	58.5	7.0	23.5	6.0	22.0
Africa	7.0	0.7	3.4	0.5	2.4
Oceania	1.0	0.1	0.2	0.4	0.3

Source: Estimated by the authors.

manufactured consumer goods. Thus manufacturing not only meets new needs but also takes over functions that are performed on farms and in homes in earlier phases of economic development.

Within the industrialized sector of the economy, the long-range trend is toward an increase in output per worker. Progress depends on expansion of the use of mechanical power, specialization and standardization of production, and new methods of management.

Historically, industrialization has often been stimulated by military considerations and spearheaded by munitions factories. The ultimate goal of industrialization, however, is to raise the level of consumption and standard of living of the population.

The geographic distribution of manufacturing output contrasts with the distribution of the input of labor in industrial production. Of the net value of approximately $182 billion of industrial output in 1950, about 90 per cent originated in the Northern Hemisphere. More specifically, North America and Europe accounted for 75 per cent. (See Figure 289.)

If our industrial civilization is to become a universal pattern of the world economy, this concentration of manufacturing in the hands of a minority of mankind will cease. The probable trend is toward geographic dispersion of manufacturing as handicrafts in Asia, Africa and South America yield to modern methods of production.

Such a trend implies appreciable shifts in the composition of manufacturing production from the Indian pattern — predominance of the textile and clothing industries — toward the patterns in the United States, Great Britain, Germany and Belgium — predominance of industries producing metals, machinery and transportation equipment. However, as industrialization advances, the predominance of the metals and capital goods industries throughout the world will probably be less than it now is in the industrial exporting countries.

This general trend is sometimes obscured by the vicissitudes of business cycles and political clashes. A depression not only curtails industrial output but also changes its distribution: production of capital goods suffers more severely than consumer goods industries. An international political crisis acts in the opposite direction. Its approach is heralded by a race in armaments and disproportionate expansion of heavy industries. On the other hand, a major war is usually accompanied by wholesale destruction of capital goods and, as a result of this destruction, the postwar economy calls for expansion of capital goods industries. In the world as a whole, and especially in leading industrial countries, the development of manufacturing represents a succession of advances and setbacks, which result, in the long run, in the development of new techniques and their application on a steadily growing scale, in an expanding territory, among a growing number of nations.

CHAPTER 27

THE FOOD, DRINK AND TOBACCO INDUSTRIES

COMMERCIAL PROCESSING of foodstuffs on a large scale is relatively new on the economic scene, having developed much later than other major industries, such as textiles and iron and steel.

THE DEVELOPMENT OF FOOD PROCESSING

In a predominantly agricultural, premechanized economy, most foodstuffs are processed at home. Farm families themselves bake bread, churn butter, slaughter livestock, dry or smoke meat for the winter, make cheese and cider, and dry fruit or vegetables, employing techniques more or less like those used thousands of years ago in ancient Egypt or Babylon. In such an economy, town families also process much food for themselves.

With industrialization and the growth of cities, food processing shifted from the farm and kitchen to the factory. Life in crowded city quarters, employment of women outside the home, the absence of home-grown raw materials, and the rising standard of living contributed to the development of specialized food industries. Thus grain mills, bakeries, dairies, meat-packing houses and canneries emerged to satisfy the demands of town people, and new methods of production, based on the use of mechanical power, gradually replaced the old domestic techniques. Some branches of food production, such as grain milling, were modernized in the latter part of the nineteenth century; others, like canning, developed considerably later. In time, food factories found customers in rural as well as urban areas.

In the United States, the per capita production of manufactured foods has been expanding faster than the total output of foodstuffs at the farm level, as the following indexes show:[1]

	All Food-stuffs	Manufactured Foods
1909	100	100
1919	102	127
1929	95	168
1939	96	174
1948	109	228

In less industrialized countries, much food processing is still done at home, but the cities are becoming more and more dependent on factory products. Large modern plants usually penetrate into underdeveloped areas to work primarily for export, like the meat packing houses in Uruguay and the sugar factories in Cuba.

Since the use of manufactured food implies the transfer of household work to factories at extra cost, the demand for manufactured foodstuffs declines during business slumps, more severely for some food-processing industries than for others. Canning, for example, is more affected by adverse economic conditions than bread baking or slaughtering.

Along with the differentiation of food processing from farming and the home economy, there has been a shift from small local shops, such as neighborhood bakeries or butcheries, to large mechanized plants, often concentrated in the hands of a few companies. In the United States, for example, three companies accounted for 43 per cent of all meat packing and three companies for 30 per cent of all commercial canning before World War II. One firm produced 33 per cent of all the cheese made in the country.[2] Nevertheless, in the food industries a few "big" firms cannot discount the competition from the many small enterprises nor can they, as in heavy industry, control nearly all the national output.

In the industrialized countries, the various branches of the food industry are often highly concentrated geographically. In the United States, for example, Illinois leads in meat packing, California and Florida in fruit canning, New York in bread and bakery products. Canning of fish, brewing, production of wine, and processing of tobacco are also highly localized.

ESTABLISHMENTS AND EMPLOYMENT

Establishments

The reported number and average size of food-processing plants depend not only on the structure of this industry in a country, but also

---

1. **38,** November 1950, p. 50.

2. **15,** p. 90.

largely on the method of classification used in its census. In some countries, all enterprises engaged in processing food, drink and tobacco are recorded as industrial establishments; in others, only the larger plants or those using motive power.

In 1947 the United States reported 41,000 food- and tobacco-processing plants with a total of more than 1.5 million employees.[3] Before the war Italy had about 134,000 enterprises with nearly 0.5 million employees; Colombia, 500 establishments with 13,000 employees. (See Table 435.) These figures seem to indicate an average of 38 employees per establishment in the United States, 26 in Colombia and little more than 3 in Italy. The contrasts, however, are due not so much to differences in the degree of concentration within the industry as to the fact that small family enterprises are included in the census in Italy but excluded in the United States and Colombia.

The reported number of food-processing establishments is thus less significant than the proportion of such enterprises among all the manufacturing establishments in a country. The ratios range from about 12 to 20 per cent in the United States, Sweden, Norway, Denmark, Finland, Germany, Austria, Australia and New Zealand, and from 20 to 30 per cent in Belgium, the Netherlands, Poland, Czechoslovakia, Hungary, Romania, Bulgaria, Argentina, Uruguay and Canada. The percentage is much higher in Italy and in many Latin American countries, including Venezuela, Bolivia and Mexico.

Employment

How many of the world's workers are in industries that process food, drink and tobacco as distinguished from home processing and the final processing in eating places? Because of the fragmentary information available for Latin America and the lack of data for the USSR, Asia and most African countries, only a rough estimate can be made.

The thirty-six countries listed in Table 435 have reported about 8 million employees in food, drink and tobacco industries—about 9 employees per 1,000 inhabitants. The rate is approximately

10–11 in the United States, France, Italy, Germany,[4] Belgium and the United Kingdom. The proportion is higher in Canada, Cuba, the Netherlands, Australia and New Zealand. It is lower in Mexico, Colombia, Brazil and many other primarily agricultural countries, and probably less than one per 1,000 in China, India, Korea, the Near East, Africa and some other areas not enumerated in Table 435.

In some countries for which only prewar data are available, the present ratio is probably above that indicated by the table; for example, while the 1935 census in the United Kingdom recorded 520,600 employees in these industries, the official estimate for December 1950 indicated 773,000. For other countries, the reverse may be true; Italy employed 474,000 persons in this industrial group in 1937–39 and only 405,000 in 1948.[5] If we apply the ratios observed in economically similar countries to those areas for which no statistics are available, it appears that the food industries may employ up to 20 million persons, or about 4 per cent of the world's nonagricultural labor force.[6]

On the basis of the most recent data available, the share of food industries in industrial employment ranges from 10 to 15 per cent in the United States (10.9 per cent), Czechoslovakia (11.1), Hungary (11.6) and Australia (13.8) — areas differing widely in economic structure. In only a few countries, mostly in Latin America, does the ratio exceed 30 per cent.

In the food industries as a group, the average plant is generally smaller than in other industries. In most countries, accordingly, the food industries account for a smaller proportion of all industrial employment than of all industrial establishments. The respective ratios in the United States are 10.9 and 17.0 per cent; in Canada, 15.8 and 27.6; in Belgium, 11.6 and 22.7; in Poland, 15.6 and 27.0; in Italy, 16.0 and 64.3; in Australia, 13.8 and 19.2. The various branches of the food industries, however, differ greatly in the average size of establishments. The average in the United States, for example, ranges from 14 employees per establishment in the soft-drink industry to 695 in cane sugar refining and 988 in the cigarette industry. In Canada, the average

---

3. The U.S. Bureau of the Census conducted annual surveys of manufactures in 1949 and 1950, using the sampling method. The 1950 data are given in each table, but the analysis in the text refers throughout to the 1947 Census of Manufactures, since the 1950 survey does not report, in most cases, the number of establishments. Cf. **3,** *passim.*

4. The total employment in these industries in Germany (1937 boundaries) exceeded 1.5 million persons. More than half the employed were in establishments averaging 3 employees. **18,** p. 242.

5. **21,** February 1951, p. 10; and **30,** 1949, p. 162.

6. Cf. Chapter 26, pp. 1016–18.

TABLE 435

FOOD PROCESSING ESTABLISHMENTS: NUMBER, EMPLOYMENT AND VALUE OF
OUTPUT IN SELECTED COUNTRIES

Country and Year	Number, in Thousands		Value of Output, in Millions		Percentage of All Manufacturing			
	Establish-ments	Per-sons Em-ployed	Gross	Net	Establish-ments	Per-sons Em-ployed	Gross Value	Net Value
United States, 1947 (*Census*)	41.0	1,554	...	$9,666	17.0	10.9	...	13.0
1950 (*Annual Survey*)	(38.5 ª)	(1,573)	...	(10,901)	...	(11.0)	...	(12.2)
Canada, 1947	9.0	179	$2,531	744	27.6	15.8	25.1	17.4
Mexico, 1940	8.1	64	110	49	67.6	26.7	39.0	37.2
Cuba, 1943	...	81	...	...	...	...	...	...
Dominican Republic, 1941	...	8	...	...	...	56.6	...	...
Venezuela, 1936	4.7	28	41	...	60.0	61.4	58.2	...
Colombia, 1940	0.5	13	49	...	35.6	31.5	45.4	...
Brazil, 1940	16.6	203	538	...	40.6	25.0	35.8	...
Bolivia, 1939	0.4	3	57	24	53.6	39.0	57.5	54.2
Chile, 1940	1.5	29	72	...	35.9	25.2	44.4	...
Uruguay, 1936	3.0	26	72	23	29.2	37.7	56.9	46.0
Argentina,ᵇ 1941	4.4	153	456	89	26.7	23.6	39.6	25.3
United Kingdom,ᶜ 1935	6.8	521	3,252	987	...	10.1	23.4	17.0
Ireland, 1946	...	34	307	71	...	28.5	56.5	41.2
France, 1946	...	478	...	...	...	10.3	...	...
Belgium, 1937	12.0	83	...	...	22.7	11.6	...	...
Netherlands, 1930	23.7	193	...	...	23.0	23.8	...	...
Denmark,ᵇ 1948	1.4	37	419	...	19.5	16.6	26.9	...
Sweden,ᵇ 1947	2.8	54	1,093	...	17.6	8.8	22.8	...
Norway,ᵈ 1948	0.7	21	248	161	12.1	9.3	19.8	24.2
Finland, 1947	0.8	18	229	...	14.0	6.5	13.4	...
Germany,ᵉ 1939	14.3	656	...	...	15.1	8.0	...	...
Poland, 1947	46.5	216	...	...	27.0	15.6	...	...
Czechoslovakia, 1946	3.6	110	...	...	20.2	11.1	...	...
Switzerland,ᵇ 1949	0.8	33	...	...	7.0	6.6	...	...
Austria,ᵇ 1949	0.5	35	...	...	11.8	8.9	...	...
Hungary, 1939	1.2	39	297	100	29.5	11.6	29.7	23.8
Portugal, 1948	0.8	32	...	...	...	...	...	...
Italy,ᶠ 1937–39	133.8	474	...	...	64.3	16.0	...	18.9
Yugoslavia, 1938	1.5	...	...	...	37.6	...	...	...
Romania, 1937	1.0	35	...	...	28.2	12.4	...	...
Bulgaria, 1934	19.3	41	...	...	22.2	19.3	...	...
USSR,ᵍ 1938	8.5	1,100	...	...	...	...	...	...
Union of So. Africa, 1945–46	2.1	72	397	127	...	15.8	26.7	18.7
Australia, 1946–47	5.9 ʰ	110	814	223	19.2 ʰ	13.8	25.7	17.9
New Zealand,ⁱ 1946–47	0.9	35	292	65	11.8	18.6	42.8	25.2

Sources: Censuses and statistical yearbooks. Free-market exchange rates are used in converting foreign currencies into dollars for countries where official and free rates differ. For Denmark: persons employed include wage earners only.

a. Excludes tobacco factories (1947: 1,086).
b. Establishments with 5 or more workers.
c. Establishments with more than 10 employees.
d. Establishments in which total employment amounted to at least 12,000 hours during the year.
e. 1939 census data adjusted to 1937 territory. Estab-lishments with 11 or more employees.
f. "Industrial establishments" according to the census. Excludes some 165,000 small enterprises without employees.
g. Excludes many small enterprises operated by cooperatives or subordinated to the Commissariat of Domestic Trade, which represented about 37 per cent of all food processing in 1938.
h. 1945–46.
i. Establishments with 2 or more workers or with motor power, not including bakeries and butcheries.

ranges from 10–11 employees in flour mills to about 300 in sugar factories; in Italy, from 2 in bakeries to 671 in sugar factories and 825 in tobacco factories.

Value of Output

Food, drink and tobacco manufactures account for 20–30 per cent of the gross value of the national industrial output in most industrialized countries, and for 30–40 per cent in predominantly agricultural areas, like Latin America. The ratio is also very high in New Zealand, where the food industries work largely for export.

These industries account for 13 per cent of the total value added in manufacturing in the United States, 17 per cent in the United Kingdom, and more than 17 per cent in Canada. The importance of the food industries in agricultural countries like Ireland or Uruguay is shown by their share in the value added in all industrial output — 41 and 46 per cent, respectively. (See Table 435.)

PRINCIPAL BRANCHES

The most important branches of the modern food, drink and tobacco industries are grain milling, baking, meat packing, sugar refining, canning and preserving, and processing of dairy products, beverages and tobacco.[7] (See Table 436.)

The relative importance of these and other branches differs from country to country, depending on climatic conditions, the national diet, the extent of export trade in certain foods, and so on. In countries that depend primarily on cereals for their daily diet, grain mills and bakeries dominate the food-processing industries. Where consumption of meat is high, as in the United States, Canada and Argentina, meat packing is particularly important.[8] Similarly, in Uruguay, which exports as much as half the meat it produces, the meat industry leads all other food-processing industries.

GRAIN MILLING

Until late in the nineteenth century, grain was handled all over the world by methods fundamentally the same as those used in biblical times.

In many places these practices still persist, along with modern methods. People in Asia, Africa and South America grind wheat, corn or rice by hand with such crude crushing devices as the saddle stone, mortar and pestle, or quern. Mills using stones and powered by water, wind or horses or cattle still exist, even in countries familiar with modern methods of milling grain.

Development

It took mankind almost 8,000 years to shift from grinding grain by hand to steam-powered milling. Water mills were introduced a few hundred years before the Christian era; windmills did not appear in western Europe until the twelfth century.

The peasants in medieval times usually did their own milling. About A.D. 1000 some French landlords built mills and ordered their tenants to use them and pay in grain. This system of so-called *banalité* spread to many parts of Europe, against the peasants' violent resistance. It died out in various parts of France and Germany, but the English lords won their fight. Monasteries, too, ran mills on a commercial basis.[9]

In the United States, the first mills were horse-driven. The earliest water mill was built in Virginia in 1621. In 1643, Boston offered the exclusive right to grind corn to anyone who would build a water mill.[10] By the end of the seventeenth century, water mills were common in New England, and a hundred years later almost every village in the country had one.

Changing the source of power did not affect the milling method; grain was crushed and ground between millstones as before. Husks and extraneous matter in the grain — dirt, chaff, seeds and stones — were crushed and mixed with the flour. Flour was sieved through linen, wool, horsehair and other materials to eliminate the impurities, but as long as millstones ground the grain, the husk could not be fully separated from the kernel.

Until the end of the sixteenth century, it was customary to pass the grain between the millstones only once. Then a French miller, Pigeaud, invented a new technique, which was kept secret until 1760. It consisted in passing the grain between the millstones three or four times and sifting it repeatedly. This system of gradual grain reduction, called "repeated milling" or "reduc-

---

7. For production of sugar, see Chapter 16, pp. 566–75; of dairy products, Chapter 18, pp. 669–75.

8. In the United Kingdom meat consumption is high under normal conditions but is covered largely by imports.

9. **40**, p. 96.

10. **62**, p. 197.

TABLE 436

FOOD PROCESSING ESTABLISHMENTS: NUMBER, EMPLOYMENT AND VALUE OF OUTPUT,
BY INDUSTRY, IN SELECTED COUNTRIES

Country, Year and Industry	Number, in Thousands		Value of Output, in Millions		Percentage Distribution, by Industry			
	Establishments	Persons Employed	Gross	Net	Establishments	Persons Employed	Value of Output Gross	Value of Output Net
United States,[a] 1947	41.0	1,554	$5,227	$9,666	100.0	100.0	100.0	100.0
Grain mill products	4.2	113	2,957	1,002	10.2	7.3	...	10.4
Bakery products	7.1	279	...	1,366	17.3	18.0	...	14.1
Meat products	4.0	274	...	1,281	9.8	17.6	...	13.2
Dairy products	5.4	93	5,365	595	13.2	6.0	...	6.2
Canned, preserved and frozen foods	3.8	202	2,469	917	9.3	13.0	...	9.5
Sugar	0.2	35	1,141	234	0.5	2.3	...	2.4
Confectionery and related products	1.8	92	1,443	587	4.4	5.9	...	6.1
Beverages	6.8	203	3,193[b]	1,851	16.1	13.0	...	19.1
Miscellaneous food products	6.7	151	3,889	1,193	16.3	9.7	...	12.3
Tobacco	1.1	112	2,541	641	2.7	7.2	...	6.6
Canada, 1947	9.0	179	2,531	744	100.0	100.0	100.0	100.0
Grain mill products	1.3	14	460	67	14.4	7.8	18.2	9.0
Bread, bakery	3.0	36	206	101	33.3	20.1	8.1	13.6
Fruit and vegetable processing	0.5	17	153	61	5.6	9.5	6.0	8.2
Meat products	0.2	23	496	80	2.2	12.9	19.6	10.8
Dairy products	2.2	24	382	85	24.4	13.4	15.1	11.4
Fish curing and packing	0.6	12	105	41	6.7	6.7	4.2	5.5
Sugar refineries	0.01	3	80	14	...	1.7	3.2	1.9
Confectionery, cocoa	0.2	9	77	35	2.2	5.0	3.0	4.7
Beverages	0.6	20	251	166	6.7	11.2	9.9	22.3
Miscellaneous foodstuffs	0.3	10	174	45	3.3	5.6	6.9	6.0
Tobacco	0.1	11	147	49	1.1	6.2	5.8	6.6
United Kingdom,[c] 1935	6.8	521	3,252	987	100.0	100.0	100.0	100.0
Grain milling	0.5	30	319	59	7.3	5.8	9.8	6.0
Bakery products	2.7	155	396	184	40.1	29.7	12.2	18.6
Sugar, confectionery, cocoa	0.4	74	180	86	5.3	14.2	5.5	8.7
Preserved foods	0.4	50	180	77	6.3	9.6	5.5	7.8
Bacon and fish curing, sausage	0.6	25	191	48	9.1	4.9	5.8	4.8
Dairy	0.2	15	141	34	2.7	2.9	4.3	3.4
Brewing and malting	0.6	56	600	216	8.7	10.7	18.4	21.8
Other beverages	1.0	45	372	109	14.9	8.7	11.4	11.1
Tobacco	0.1	43	598	139	1.7	8.2	18.4	14.1
Other	0.3	27	275	36	3.9	5.3	8.5	3.6

(Continued on page 1024)

TABLE 436—continued

Country, Year and Industry	Number, in Thousands		Value of Output, in Millions		Percentage Distribution, by Industry			
	Establishments	Persons Employed	Gross	Net	Establishments	Persons Employed	Value of Output	
							Gross	Net
Germany,[a] 1939	14.3	655.5	...	...	100.0	100.0	...	...
Grain mills	1.1	31.3	...	...	7.7	4.8	...	...
Bakeries	2.8	66.1	...	...	19.6	10.1	...	...
Sugar	0.2	30.6	...	...	1.4	4.7	...	...
Chocolate, candy, cocoa	0.5	55.9	...	...	3.5	8.5	...	...
Meats	2.1	58.0	...	...	14.7	8.9	...	...
Fish	0.3	14.6	...	...	2.1	2.2	...	...
Milk products	1.2	35.8	...	...	8.4	5.5	...	...
Margarine, vegetable oils	0.2	19.9	...	...	1.4	3.0	...	...
Fruit and vegetable canning	0.5	22.0	...	...	3.5	3.4	...	...
Brewing, malting	1.5	85.3	...	...	10.5	13.0	...	...
Wine, brandy, other	0.5	17.1	...	...	3.5	2.6	...	...
Other foodstuffs and foods	1.6	82.7	...	...	11.2	12.6	...	...
Tobacco	1.8	136.2	...	...	12.6	20.8	...	...
Italy, 1937–40	133.8	474	...	...	100.0	100.0	...	...
Milling	22.5	52	...	...	16.8	11.0	...	...
Bakeries	51.1	102	...	...	38.1	21.5	...	...
Macaroni, biscuits, etc.	10.1	45	...	...	7.5	9.5	...	...
Dairy products	18.5	43	...	...	13.8	9.1	...	...
Public slaughtering	2.4	4	...	...	1.8	0.8	...	...
Meat products	0.7	8	...	...	0.5	1.6	...	...
Fish products	0.9	9	...	...	0.7	1.9	...	...
Sugar, honey	0.1	41	...	...	0.1	8.6	...	...
Fruit conserves	3.2	39	...	...	2.4	8.2	...	...
Pressing of olives	8.6	37	...	...	6.4	8.0	...	...
Beverages	12.3	42	...	...	9.4	8.9	...	...
Cocoa, chocolate, etc.	0.6	14	...	...	0.5	3.0	...	...
Vegetable oils	0.2	9	...	...	0.1	1.9	...	...
Tobacco	0.03	21	...	...	...	4.4	...	...
Other	2.6	8	...	...	2.0	1.7	...	...

Sources: 4, Vol. I, pp. 24–25, and Vol. II, passim; 17, 1951, p. 589; 20, Part III, pp. 1–2; 18, p. 242; 23, 1941, pp. 101–06.

a. Data for gross value of output represent the value of products shipped.
b. Excludes wine and brandy.
c. Only establishments with more than 10 employees. In December 1950, the food, drink and tobacco industries employed (in thousands): in all branches, 773; grain milling, 42; bread, biscuits and flour confectionery, 235; dairy products, 44; cocoa, chocolate and sugar confectionery, 79; beverages, 151; tobacco, 47; other branches 174. (21, February 1951, p. 10.)
d. 1939 census data adapted to 1937 territory. Establishments with 11 or more employees.

1024

tion milling," was accepted in most countries soon after it became known.[11]

Modern Methods

In Hungary, where hard wheat is grown, the flour was discolored by the heat generated in milling and suffered in quality and taste. In 1874 a way was found to preserve the excellent quality of the Hungarian grain and release the endosperm particles from the husk by replacing millstones with rollers with a finely toothed surface. Great Britain, which had some 10,000 mills with about 18,000 millstones in 1880, soon adopted the new technique. By 1890 British milling had been completely reorganized, although millstones are still used in a few establishments for flour and quite extensively for milling grains for animal feed.[12]

Millers in the midwestern region of the United States, particularly in Minnesota, were also handicapped by the hardness of their spring wheat. They pioneered in introducing the new methods, importing machinery and hiring foremen from Hungary. The imported machinery did not quite fit the American grain, however, and the foreign millers could not handle the American workers. Moreover, the Hungarian technique was designed to produce eleven grades of flour, while only four were in demand in the United States.[13] Failing in their attempt to transplant the Hungarian process lock, stock and barrel, the Minnesota millers adapted the new process to domestic conditions. The use of rollers — first of porcelain, then of chilled corrugated iron — spread from Minnesota to other states and revolutionized the American milling industry. By 1890 most American "merchant" mills — mills purchasing grain for grinding and selling their products — were roller mills.[14] In time, better methods were introduced to clean, sift and gradually reduce the grain between successive pairs of fluted rollers.

The next important step was the introduction of the airblast purifier. While previously the outer layers of the grain had been removed from the flour by sifting it through cloth ("bolting"), the purifier removed the bran by currents of air. Invented in France in 1860, the first air purifier

was built in Minneapolis in 1870,[15] and soon thereafter purifiers were in common use.

Today most of the operations in a modern mill are almost wholly automatic. While grain and flour once were handled constantly, wheat is ground to flour in modern mills without being touched by human hands.[16] Automatic milling has become general in Great Britain and the United States, but Hungary did not accept it and gradually lost its commanding position.[17]

A modern mill is a complex establishment representing a large investment. (See Figure 294.) Modern European mills are often more elaborate than those in the United States. Since European bakeries demand many kinds of flour, each kind uniform, the mills are designed to process blended wheats, whereas most mills in the United States use only one type.[18] On the other hand, ancient millstones are still in use in some small mills, even in France.[19]

Establishments and Employment

In the United States, the 1947 census reported 4,206 grain mills with 113,217 employees, or 27 employees per mill, as compared with an average of 10–11 per mill in Canada. Grain milling is a billion-dollar industry in the United States, standing fourth among the food industries in value added by production and fifth in number of employees.

In Great Britain, the gross output of milling was close to half a billion dollars in 1948, and the ratio of value added to gross value approximated 20 per cent, as it does in the United States. The average mill in Great Britain has 94 employees and in the United Kingdom (including Northern Ireland), 60; in Czechoslovakia, 20; and in Poland, Italy and the Netherlands, from 2 to 4. (See Table 437.) Since these latter countries have some large and many middle-sized mills, their averages point to the predominance of "one-man" mills in small localities.

Location of Mills

The first milling centers in the United States were at Philadelphia, Richmond and Baltimore.

---

11. **55**, pp. 176–78.
12. **47**, pp. 281-83; and **55**, p. 177.
13. **46**, p. 123.
14. **15**, p. 136.

15. **15**, p. 137.
16. Other grains, such as rye or corn (dry milling), are processed in about the same way as wheat. Rice is first freed of the husk and cuticle; the kernel is then polished and treated for whiteness and luster.
17. **47**, p. 284.
18. **57**, p. 9.
19. **27**, p. 8.

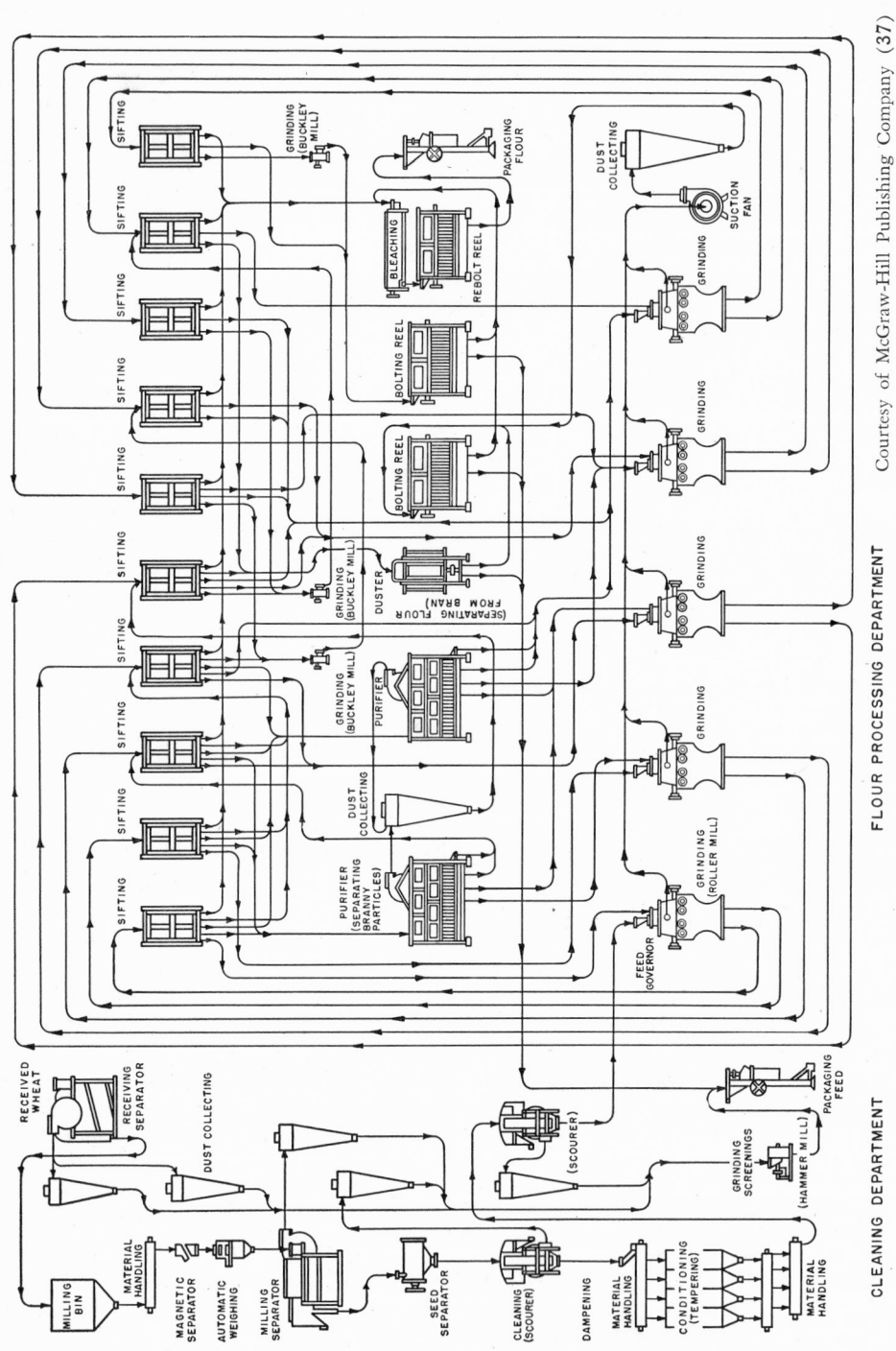

CLEANING DEPARTMENT   FLOUR PROCESSING DEPARTMENT   Courtesy of McGraw-Hill Publishing Company (37)

FIGURE 294. GRAIN MILLS: FLOW SHEET OF FACTORY OPERATIONS IN THE UNITED STATES

From the receiving separator (upper left), wheat is transferred to the milling bin, automatically weighed, separated from impurities and seeds, cleaned and conditioned (dampened and tempered). At all stages dust is eliminated. Then cleaned wheat is directed through a scourer to the roller mill (lower row). Flour is transferred to the sifter (upper row). Sifted flour is further purified, bolted (sifted through cloth) and bleached before it reaches the final stage of packaging (middle right).

TABLE 437

GRAIN MILLS: ESTABLISHMENTS, EMPLOYMENT AND VALUE OF OUTPUT ·
IN SELECTED COUNTRIES

Country and Year	*Number, in Thousands*		*Value of Output, in Millions*	
	Establishments	*Persons Employed*	*Gross*	*Net*
United States, 1947 (*Census*)	4.2	113.2	$5,227	$1,002
1950 (*Annual Survey*)	. . .	(115.0)	. . .	(1,111)
Canada, 1947	1.3	13.9	460	67
Mexico, 1944	0.3	3.9	38	. . .
Argentina, 1941	0.2	7.0	. . .	. . .
United Kingdom,[a] 1935	0.5	30.1	319	59
Ireland, 1946	. . .	4.0	58	6
Netherlands, 1930	2.2	8.6	—	. . .
Denmark,[b] 1948	0.1	1.3	40	. . .
Sweden,[b] 1947	0.08	2.4	64	. . .
Norway,[c] 1948	0.2	2.2	15	4
Finland, 1947	0.1	1.3	26	4
Germany,[d] 1939	1.1	31.1	. . .	. . .
Poland, 1946	9.7	36.0	. . .	. . .
Czechoslovakia, 1946	0.4	8.0	. . .	. . .
Switzerland,[b] 1949	0.1	1.9	. . .	. . .
Hungary, 1939	0.7	8.6	133	19
Italy, 1937–40	22.5	51.9	. . .	. . .
Union of So. Africa, 1945–46	0.8	8.8	98	13
Australia, 1946–47	. . .	4.4	68	10
New Zealand, 1946–47	0.05	0.7	9	2

Sources: Statistical yearbooks and censuses. For Denmark: persons employed include wage earners only.

    a. Establishments with more than 10 employees.
    b. Establishments with 5 or more workers.
    c. Establishments that employed workers for at least 12,000 hours during the year.
    d. Establishments with 11 or more employees. 1939 census data adjusted to 1937 territory.

In the middle of the nineteenth century, Rochester took the lead but later, with the westward expansion of agriculture, this city yielded supremacy to Chicago and St. Louis. By the turn of the century, Minnesota's star began to rise. At that time this state led in milling techniques, turning its hard spring wheat into the finest bread flour. Minneapolis gradually became the leading milling center of the world. Other midwestern cities, such as Oklahoma City and Kansas City, also became important. In the 1920's, however, the Midwest's supremacy in milling was challenged by Buffalo, which had cheap hydroelectric power from Niagara Falls, cheap water transportation, and a strategic location between Canada's wheat areas and export markets. Since 1930, Buffalo has been producing more wheat flour than any other milling center in the country.[20] (See Table 438.)

Besides the grain mills crossing the Great Plains in a broad belt from the Great Lakes to Texas and in the East (in Buffalo and elsewhere), the industry has western centers for processing the wheat of the Columbia Plateau and California. (See Figure 295.)

The location of large mills in western Europe is considerably influenced by the fact that most European wheat, while of good milling quality, is "weak" in baking and has to be blended with "strong" imported wheat, preferably Canadian wheat and the hard winter wheat of the United States.[21] Consequently, most of the efficient modern European mills are located at seaports where foreign wheat arrives. In South America and

cline was the decrease in quantity and quality of the northwestern wheat. Farmers diversified their production, lowering their output of spring wheat and began to grow durum wheat, suitable for macaroni and similar products but not for bread. **62,** p. 444.

    20. One of the important causes of Minneapolis' de-

    21. **57,** p. 2.

TABLE 438

GRAIN MILLS: OUTPUT OF WHEAT FLOUR IN CHIEF CENTERS IN THE UNITED STATES, 1913–50

(*Millions of Sacks*)

Year	Total [a]	Minne- apolis	Kansas City	Buffalo	Toledo	St. Louis	Wichita	Salina	Seattle	Tacoma	Port- land
1913	. . .	34.6	4.5	10.0	2.6	2.0	. . .	. . .	. . .	. . .	. . .
1921	217.3	29.1	7.8	13.1	2.4	3.0	. . .	3.3	2.1	2.9	3.2
1925	203.4	23.6	10.6	18.5	3.4	2.4	3.2	2.6	2.4	2.3	2.6
1929	226.0	21.2	15.5	19.9	4.5	3.9	3.7	3.9	2.9	4.4	2.6
1934	191.6	14.9	11.5	18.9	3.8	2.0	3.5	3.5	2.4	3.6	2.2
1939	206.5	10.9	14.2	20.0	3.9	1.7	4.0	5.2	2.8	3.9	4.2
1944	236.4	14.8	12.8	24.8	6.1	2.3	4.6	4.7	3.5	4.0	3.4
1949	234.4	13.1	15.7	26.6	5.8	2.4	4.4	4.4	3.6	2.6	2.5
1950	225.7	13.4	15.5	25.1	5.8	2.3	4.5	4.4	3.6	2.4	2.2

Source: **52**, 1951, p. 27.

a. Based on reports from mills producing 98 per cent of wheat flour.

Australia, likewise, most of the large mills that operate for export are located at ports. The small mills that produce for local markets and handle domestic grain are widely scattered.

Concentration of the Industry

Concentration of the milling industry of the United States began after World War I. The number of merchant mills with output of $5,000 or more has declined and the average output per mill has greatly increased: [22]

	Number of Mills	Average Output of Flour Per Mill, in Barrels
1899	9,476	10,528
1909	11,691	9,046
1919	10,708	12,371
1929	4,022	29,859
1939	2,143	80,728
1947	1,243	198,149

In 1909, the United States had about one flour mill per 8,000 inhabitants; in 1947, about one per 115,000.

However, financial concentration has been less in flour milling than in some other industries. The six largest flour-milling companies, each with many mills, accounted for some 27 per cent of the total milling capacity in 1945 and the next thirty companies for 23.3 per cent; the remaining milling capacity, half of the total, was distributed among thousands of small plants.[23] The largest

company, General Mills, accounted for less than 10 per cent of the capacity. Concentration has consisted not so much in the expansion of a few leading plants as in the acquisition by single companies of many small scattered mills and many grain elevators. In 1944, General Mills had mills in 17 states, owned and operated 140 grain elevators with a storage capacity of 47.5 million bushels, and was engaged in wholesale and retail trade in flour and feeds in many communities.[24] (See Figure 295.)

In Canada, the United Kingdom and Sweden, concentration is much greater. Seven flour and feed mills account for 80 per cent of Canada's flour production. In the United Kingdom, three milling companies produce two thirds of the flour and in Sweden one company accounts for a fourth of the grain milling.[25]

In the USSR, the largest mills are at railroad junctions, to which grain is transported from the producing areas, often over great distances. Mills in Baku, for example, obtain grain by rail from the North Caucasus and the Ukraine and by water (Caspian Sea) from the Volga region, and supply flour to the greater part of the Transcaucasus. Tashkent, receiving grain from Kazakhstan and the Volga region, furnishes flour to the central Asiatic part of the USSR.[26]

THE BAKING INDUSTRY

People must have baked in the Stone Age, since flat burnt cakes have been found in Swiss

22. **15**, p. 39; and **4**, Vol. 1, p. 24.
23. **8**, pp. 1–2.

24. **8**, p. 13.
25. **52**, April 27, 1938, p. 8.
26. **25**, pp. 325–26.

U.S. Federal Trade Commission

FIGURE 295. GRAIN MILLS: LOCATION OF PLANTS OF THE FIVE LARGEST COMPANIES IN THE UNITED STATES, 1947

lake dwellings.[27] These were baked against the hot inside walls of stone ovens, a practice still common in Turkish villages.

Development

Commercial baking existed on a small scale as early as the sixth century B.C., and bakeries appeared in Italy some centuries later.[28] In time, commercial baking spread throughout Europe. A bakers' guild in London was mentioned in 1156.[29] Bakers' guilds in western Europe were among the oldest and strongest trade organizations of the Middle Ages. The tradition of bread making in small establishments still persists in many countries, notably France.[30] Bread baking moved first from the home to small neighborhood shops in the towns, and then, with the growth of cities, to larger establishments.

Technical progress in bread making was very slow. Throughout the Middle Ages molds, kneading tables and hearth ovens were of about the same type as those in ancient Egypt.[31] (See Figure 296.) Although machinery for mixing dough was invented in France in the second half of the eighteenth century, kneading with the feet continued in some plants in Scotland, Russia and other countries.[32] The first loaf-making machine was invented only half a century ago. Many other types of mechanical equipment have followed: blenders and sifters of flour, dough-mixers, loaf makers (dividers, rounders, molders), swinging traveling trays and so on.

Since World War I, the baking process has been mechanized in most industrial countries (see Figure 297) and homemade bread has become practically obsolete. In the United States, for example, automatic bakeries produce 85 per cent of the bread and 35 per cent of the cake.[33] A modern automatic oven produces from 2,000 to 2,500 loaves of bread an hour.

Automatic operation is particularly important in countries where night work is forbidden, as in

---

27. **56**, p. 107.
28. **60**, p. 64.
29. **56**, p. 107.
30. **27**, p. 12.
31. **49**, p. 9.

32. Herodotus described the use of this method in ancient Egypt not without humor: "Dough they knead with feet, but they mix mud, and even take up dirt, with their hands." (**41**, Second Book, 36, p. 130.) Maxim Gorki tells in his autobiography of working in a Russian bakery where dough was kneaded with the feet.
33. **9**, Part II, p. 1.

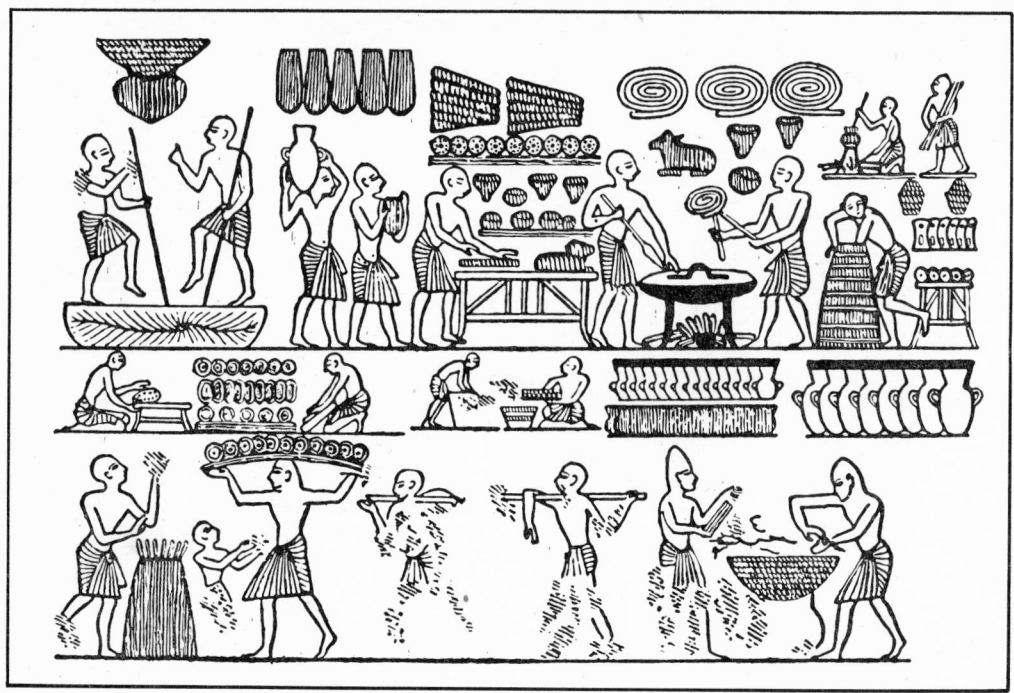

FIGURE 296. BAKING TECHNIQUES IN THE THIRTEENTH CENTURY B.C.

(Egyptian Tomb Painting)

We see first two men with long poles energetically tramping the dough. They seem to be dancing; probably they are working in rhythm, using the poles partly to keep their balance upon the yielding dough, partly to jump higher. Next we see waterbearers carrying amphorae to a table where an apprentice begins tumbling the dough back and forth with his hands. The bottom of a baking dish is heated and molded dough is placed upon the dish with the aid of large tongs. Next, another assistant arranges or turns the dough in the pan with the aid of a shovel-like tool. Near by a large oven is being filled with fresh fuel. This serves for the smaller molds, which are not handled as carefully as the large ones. The next picture shows that care is taken to make the small breads of equal size so that all will be thoroughly baked.

the Netherlands, Scandinavia and Germany. During the night, automatic dough mixers, operating in dark factories, prepare the batch and have it ready when the workers arrive early in the morning. In a short time, fresh buns are ready for delivery to the breakfast table, just as milk is delivered in the United States.

The geographic distribution of bakeries is determined by the nature of their products, fresh supplies of which are needed daily everywhere, even in the smallest towns. Hence the multiplicity of small bakeries in every country.

Establishments and Employment

In many countries — among them Canada and Italy — bakeries comprise a third or more of the establishments in the food, drink and tobacco industries. The proportion is even higher in Finland and Switzerland.

The baking industry includes several types of specialized establishments. The baking of bread and cake is often separated from the production of less perishable products, such as biscuits, crackers and pretzels.

Bakeries employ more people than any other branch of food processing: almost 280,000 workers in the United States; about 155,000 in the United Kingdom; 102,000 in Italy. (See Table 439.)

The average baking plant in the United States in 1947 employed 39 workers. The companies producing biscuits, crackers and pretzels, which distribute their products all over the country, operate large plants, averaging 141 employees, or more than four times as many as the average bread bakery (34 employees).

The gross value of the output of the baking industry is smaller than that of some other divi-

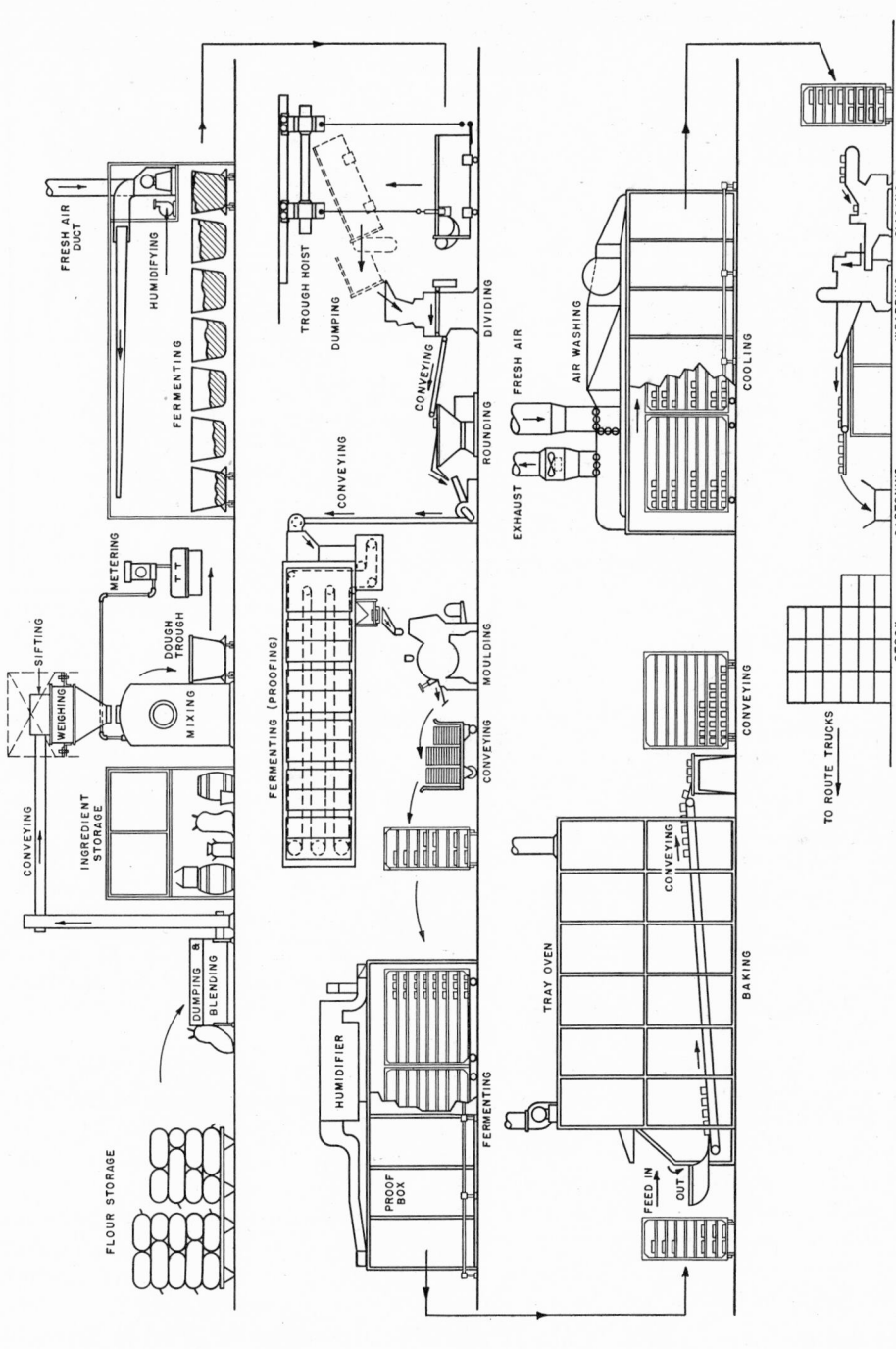

FIGURE 297. BAKING: FLOW SHEET OF OPERATIONS IN BREAD BAKING IN THE UNITED STATES

Courtesy of McGraw-Hill Publishing Company (37)

TABLE 439

BAKING: ESTABLISHMENTS, EMPLOYMENT AND VALUE OF OUTPUT
IN SELECTED COUNTRIES

Country and Year	Number, in Thousands		Value of Output, in Millions	
	Establishments	Employed Persons	Gross	Net
United States, 1947 (*Census*)	7.1	279.4	$2,957	$1,366
1950 (*Annual Survey*)	. . .	(293.7)	. . .	(1,639)
Canada, 1947	3.0	36.4	206	101
Mexico, 1944	4.1	19.1	73	. . .
United Kingdom,[a] 1935	2.7	154.6	396	184
Ireland, 1946	. . .	8.5	38	13
France, 1948	42.0	. . .	. . .	. . .
Netherlands, 1930	14.0	65.7	. . .	. . .
Denmark,[b] 1948	0.1	1.9	15	. . .
Sweden,[b] 1947	0.8	13.5	94	. . .
Finland, 1947	0.3	4.7	16	7
Germany,[c] 1939	2.8	66.1	. . .	. . .
Poland, 1946	13.5	36.4	. . .	. . .
Switzerland,[b, d] 1949	0.2	5.8	. . .	. . .
Hungary, 1939	0.1	2.0	8	2
Italy, 1937–40	51.1	101.8	11	3
Union of So. Africa, 1945–46	0.4	10.2	46	17
Australia, 1946–47	2.2[e]	15.5	64	25
New Zealand, 1946–47	0.1	2.5	12	5

Sources: Censuses and statistical yearbooks. For Denmark: persons employed include wage earners only.

  a. Establishments with more than 10 employees.
  b. Establishments with 5 or more workers.
  c. Establishments with 11 or more employees. 1939 census data adjusted to 1937 territory.
  d. Including confectionery.
  e. 1943–44. A large number of bakehouses are omitted from the production statistics. Includes plants producing cakes and pastry.

sions of the food industry (for example, meat packing), but the ratio of value added to the gross value is among the highest in food processing.

Concentration of the Industry

The perishability of the product and the costs of transportation militate against the concentration of bread baking on the scale found in some other food industries, such as meat packing. In Great Britain, 40 per cent of the bread is baked in establishments with fewer than 10 workers. In Denmark, Switzerland and Italy, bakeries average only 2–4 workers, as they did also in prewar Germany.

In the United States, decentralization of production in the baking industry is combined with a considerable degree of financial and managerial concentration. A few firms control a large part of the total output, each operating many plants located close to consuming centers. At the end of 1944, the Big Four multiple-plant companies (Continental Baking, General Baking, Ward Baking Company and Purity Bakers) had 192 plants in 98 cities in 34 states and the District of Columbia. Ten other companies controlled 160 plants.[34]

The location of baking establishments is beginning to be affected by the postwar introduction of the use of chemicals to keep bread soft for a longer period. The big chain stores now have large centralized baking establishments that serve their units within an entire region.

THE MEAT INDUSTRY

Meat packing ranks first among food-processing industries in the gross value of output

---

34. **9,** Part I, p. 7.

TABLE 440

MEAT PACKING: ESTABLISHMENTS, EMPLOYMENT AND VALUE OF OUTPUT
IN SELECTED COUNTRIES

| | Number, in Thousands | | Value of Output, in Millions | |
Country and Year	Establishments	Persons Employed	Gross	Net
United States, 1947 (*Census*)	4.0	274.4	. . .	$1,281
1950 (*Annual Survey*)	. . .	(282.3)	. . .	(1,506)
Canada, 1947	0.2	22.6	$496	80
United Kingdom,[a] 1935	0.4	19.7	170	31
Ireland,[a] 1946	. . .	2.0	24	3
Netherlands,[b] 1930	0.2	4.4	. . .	. . .
Denmark,[c] 1948	0.2	3.1	43	. . .
Sweden, 1947	0.3	9.7	199	. . .
Germany,[d] 1939	2.1	58.0	. . .	. . .
Poland, 1946	11.1	24.6	. . .	. . .
Switzerland,[e] 1949	0.1	2.2	. . .	. . .
Hungary,[e] 1939	0.05	3.2	21	5
Italy, 1937–40	0.7	8.0	. . .	. . .
Australia,[e] 1943–44	0.1	10.9	93	19
New Zealand,[f] 1946–47	0.1	11.3	131	27

Sources: Censuses and statistical yearbooks. For Denmark: persons employed include wage earners only.

a. Bacon curing and sausage; for Ireland, bacon curing only.
b. Meat for export and canned meat.
c. Establishments with more than 5 workers.
d. Establishments with 11 or more employees. 1939 census data adjusted to 1937 territory.
e. Meat and fish freezing and preserving, and bacon curing; chilled meat mostly for export.
f. Meat freezing and preserving, ham and bacon curing.

though the ratio of value added to gross value is lower than that in some other branches of food processing, for example, the beverage industry.[35]

Establishments and Employment

While every country has some small slaughter-houses, the average number of employees per establishment in the meat industry is larger than in many other food industries. In the United States the average meat-packing plant had 69 employees in 1947; in Canada (1947), 113; in New Zealand (1946–47), 113. In Europe, small plants, averaging 10–20 employees, are usual. (See Table 440.)

Even in industrialized countries, meat-packing plants do not produce all the nation's output. In the United States, for example, about 30 per cent of the cattle and 40–45 per cent of the hogs are slaughtered on farms or by retail butchers not subject to federal inspection.[36] In many other

countries, packing houses have a considerably smaller share in meat production.

The complexity of meat production in a modern plant is illustrated by the flow sheet of operations in a hog-packing house, as shown in Figure 298.

Despite the development of cold storage, the perishability of fresh meat remains one of the greatest difficulties of the meat industry. Speed is essential in all operations. Within three or four weeks after the livestock reach the stockyards, the animals have been slaughtered and dressed and the meat shipped to warehouses, distributed among retail stores and sold to the consumer.[37] Indeed, beef is sold at retail in the United States within ten or twelve days after the animal has been slaughtered.

Location

The location of the industry is determined

35. For production of meat, see Chapter 18.
36. These percentages have remained about the same in recent decades. **5,** p. 102. In 1949, only about 85 mil-

lion head of meat animals out of 119 million were slaughtered under federal inspection. **6,** 1950, p. 645.
37. **48,** p. 67.

HOG PACKING HOUSE

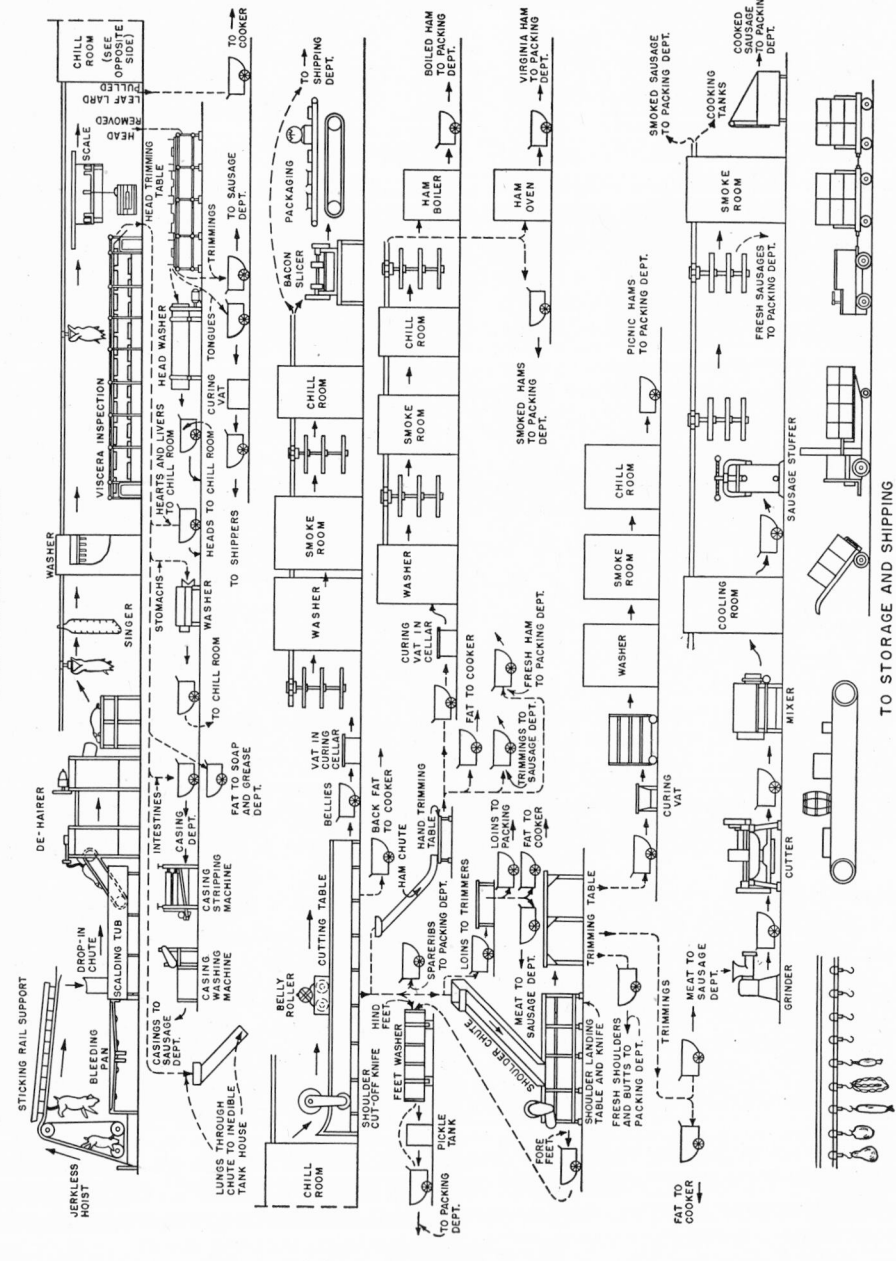

Figure 298. Meat Packing: Flow Sheet of Operations in a Hog-Packing House in the United States

Courtesy of McGraw-Hill Publishing Company (37)

1034

largely by the need to handle meat quickly. The problem is not so serious in small countries as in the United States and Canada, where grazing grounds are remote from the principal consuming centers. In the United States, for example, 63 per cent of the cattle, 50 per cent of the hogs and 78 per cent of the sheep are raised west of the Mississippi, while 70 per cent of the meat is consumed east of it. Thus beef travels about 1,000 miles, on the average, from producer to consumer. To shorten the distance, the packing plants have been located at railroad junctions at the borders of livestock-producing regions — Chicago, Kansas City, Omaha, St. Paul, Fort Worth and St. Louis. In Canada, meat packing is concentrated, for the same reason, on a line from Alberta in the west to Montreal in the east, and in the St. Lawrence lowlands.

In Argentina, which exports vast quantities of chilled meat, the large packing plants are located at seaports that lie comparatively near the grazing grounds. In contrast, the many small municipal and private slaughterhouses that produce the domestic supply are scattered throughout the country.

Some 70 per cent of Brazil's meat packing is concentrated in the three most populous states (Rio Grande do Sul, Minas Gerais and São Paulo), where about half the country's livestock is raised and to which neighboring states send their cattle on the hoof to be "finished." Brazil's big meat-packing plants (American- and British-owned) are thus in the unique position of having their raw materials and consumers close together.[38]

In continental Europe, where distances are small and large cities are not far from livestock-raising areas, meat packing is less centralized. In the USSR, the largest meat-packing houses are in Moscow and Leningrad; others are found in various parts of the country.

Concentration of the Industry

Meat packing is highly concentrated financially in the world's chief centers of production. In the United States the "Big Four"[39] had 88 slaughterhouses before World War II and processed, under federal inspection, 65 per cent of all the cattle, 52 per cent of all the hogs and 80 per cent of all the sheep and lambs slaughtered

in packing houses.[40] In Canada, the two largest companies[41] control about 85 per cent of the packing. It is believed that no other single firm handles as great a part of national output (60 per cent) as Canada Packers.[42] In Uruguay, four packing plants handle 95 per cent of the output;[43] in the USSR, seven modern packing plants accounted for a third of the meat produced in 1936.[44]

By-Products

Large packing plants increasingly utilize parts of dressed animals that, before the invention of refrigeration, used to be dumped into rivers or thrown away as waste and that are still discarded in small local slaughterhouses or on farms. Almost everything is found to be worth processing.

Blood and bones are converted into fertilizer, horns and hoofs are used for combs and brush handles, gut for musical instruments and sutures, hair for brushes. Various organs are used for pharmaceutical preparations (liver extract and red bone marrow for the treatment of anemia; pituitary and other substances for making insulin, adrenalin and so on). Hides and skins and wool, of course, have always been the most valuable by-products. On the whole, about 40 per cent of the weight of a steer, 50 per cent of a sheep and 25 per cent of a hog must go into by-products or be lost entirely.[45] Receipts from the sale of by-products often cover the costs of processing the animals for meat.[46] It has been estimated that in Canada by-products account for about 15 per cent of the total value of products derived from cattle, 20 per cent from sheep, and 3.5 per cent from hogs.[47]

Meat packers produce other foodstuffs as well as meat. In the 1930's, ten packing houses in the United States accounted for nearly half the nation's cheese output (about as much as eleven big dairy companies produced together), nearly a fifth of the butter, a tenth of the condensed and evaporated milk, and a third of the oleomargarine and shortening.[48]

---

38. **43**, pp. 166 and 289.
39. The Armour, Swift, Cudahy Packing and Wilson companies.
40. **34**, pp. 74–75.
41. Canada Packers and Swift, a subsidiary of the Swift Company in the United States.
42. **35**, p. 18.
43. **14**, p. 12.
44. **24**, p. 113.
45. **29**, 1948, p. 332.
46. **31**, p. 179.
47. **35**, p. 19.
48. **7**, p. 228.

Meat Packing in the United States

Commercial meat packing in the United States began in New England in the 1660's. Meat was salted and smoked. The first meat "packed" was pork, which was consumed domestically and exported to England and also to the West Indies, in exchange for sugar.[49]

As the population moved westward, Cincinnati, then the center of corn production, became the main center of pork packing as well; pork packed in brine was shipped in barrels to near-by areas and to the East.[50] By 1850, Cincinnati accounted for 27 per cent of all meat products of the West.[51] Until the 1870's, the cities of the United States obtained most of their meat from animals that were driven there for slaughter and often arrived exhausted or sick.[52]

Most slaughtering was done in winter; in the smaller communities, by itinerant butchers. Salted and smoked beef was less popular than pork. Before refrigeration was introduced, only about a tenth of all beef was packed as compared to one half to two thirds of all pork.[53]

With the development of railroads and refrigeration, slaughtering became a year-round industry and began to cater to a nation-wide market. It was not practicable to drive livestock over long distances for slaughtering when meat could be shipped in refrigerated cars to all parts of the country. Stockyards and meat-packing houses sprang up near the border of the Great Plains at railroad junctions close to the supply of livestock, especially Chicago, a transportation center near the hog-raising states and grazing grounds.

The shift in meat packing from local butchering to centralized production in a few vast packing houses was not accomplished without a struggle. Railroads that had invested in boxcars for livestock shipment were reluctant to build refrigerated cars for meat. Owners of feeding centers along the trails over which livestock were driven, and companies in charge of moving livestock, fought the extinction of their business. Moreover, eastern consumers were at first disinclined to accept "western dressed" instead of "city dressed" meat.[54]

It was a losing fight, however. Packing plants built their own refrigerated cars and agreed to pay higher freight rates for dressed meat than for live animals. In 1865, nine railroads established the Union Stockyards at Chicago to handle livestock. These yards, extending over 300 acres and able to load 500 cars at a time, became the model for later stockyards.[55] Chicago became the chief packing center of the United States and has held the lead despite the development of large centers at Kansas City, St. Louis, Omaha, South St. Paul, Fort Worth, Sioux City and so on. Its share in the number of animals received by stockyards is continually declining, however — from 18 per cent in 1921–25 to 9.5 per cent in 1951 — as a result of increasing decentralization.[56]

THE CANNING INDUSTRY

Since very early times, people have preserved food by drying it in the sun and by the use of salt and cold. Commercial canning, however, is a development of the last century and a half, largely under the stimulus of wars.

Development

The canning industry was born during the Napoleonic wars out of the armies' demand for food that would not spoil. The French government sponsored a contest in 1795 for the best method of preserving food for its far-flung armies. The prize was won in 1809 by Nicolas Appert, an unknown baker, who is considered to be the inventor of canning. His method consisted in packing foodstuffs in jars, filling the jars to the brim, keeping them for at least six hours in boiling water, then sealing them with cork and wax, and again boiling for some time.[57] This process, with some improvements, has been used all over the world for more than a century and is still used in home canning in most countries.

Almost as soon as Appert's method became known, the idea of using tins instead of bottles was conceived in England, which was concerned with provisioning its sailors. Peter Durand was granted a patent for a tin can in 1810, and production in England began with sardines and peas.[58]

---

49. **31**, pp. 36–37.

50. The first packing house in the United States was established in Cincinnati in 1830, and soon barreled pork was so closely associated with Cincinnati that the city was called Porkopolis. **56**, p. 237.

51. **36**, p. 265.

52. **31**, p. 38.

53. **62**, p. 433.

54. **34**, pp. 59–60.

55. **62**, p. 433.

56. **6**, 1940, p. 681, and 1952, p. 646.

57. **63**, p. 3.

58. **22**, p. 2. In the United States canning of fish started in 1819, of fruit and berries in 1822, and of oysters about 1840. (**32**, pp. 33-34; and **28**, p. 31.)

During the American Civil War, the demand of the northern armies for canned foodstuffs gave an impetus to the industry in the United States. Similarly, wars with China in the 1890's and with Russia in 1904–05 forced a rapid development of canning in Japan.[59] Extensive use of canned foods in the Crimean War, the British colonial wars and the two world wars stimulated the growth of the industry in all belligerent countries.

Modern Techniques

The growing demand for commercially canned foodstuffs could not be met, however, until three main technical difficulties had been overcome: the time used for processing food in boiling water had to be shortened; the crude and unreliable cans, in which food often spoiled, needed improvement; and cleaning, peeling, sorting and grading had to be mechanized.

The first problem was solved in 1861 by Isaac Solomon of Baltimore, who found that the addition of calcium chloride to the cooking bath raised the temperature of the water and shortened the process from 5 or 6 hours to about 25 or 30 minutes. Since that time, great strides have been made in the study of heat treatment suitable for different kinds of food and for cans of different size.[60] The second problem was solved about 1885, when containers cut, soldered and closed by hand were replaced by machine-made, open-topped tin cans, lacquer-lined and automatically sealed. Eventually a great variety of machinery was introduced for every process in canning, together with conveyors to speed up the handling of products and cans. On modern processing lines, 150 cans can be filled, 240 sealed and 1,500 labeled in a minute, and can-making machines can turn out 300 cans a minute.[61]

The problem of mechanization of the various phases of processing has also been solved. Many products are canned today without being touched by human hands.[62] The efficiency of modern canning is exemplified by the operation of a Hawaiian pineapple plant. The entire operation takes only fifteen minutes from the time the fresh fruit enters the factory until the can of trimmed and sliced pineapple — sealed, processed, cooled and labeled — is ready for the market. On one record day, 3.5 million cans were packed, some 2,776 a minute.[63]

With the development of mechanization and heat treatment and the improvement of containers, canning has become a mass production industry, particularly in the United States. From packing primarily the more expensive foods, such as meat, fish or dessert fruit, it has extended to almost every kind of food. There is now virtually no vegetable so lowly that it is not worth canning, and almost every product traditionally prepared at home is now canned commercially.

Establishments and Employment

This comparatively young branch of the food-processing industry has found its greatest opportunities in the United States, where, in 1947, nearly 202,000 persons on the average were engaged in commercial canning, preserving and freezing. (See Table 441.) At the peak season, employment is much higher. The added value of output in 1947 was close to a billion dollars.

The industry has also developed in Canada, where fruit and vegetable preserving alone occupies 17,000 persons. Before the war, Italy had 39,000 workers in fruit canning; the United Kingdom and France each employed 50,000 in canning establishments.

Canning is a highly seasonal industry, and its various branches have their peaks at different times. Fruits and vegetables must be packed as soon as they are harvested. Plants canning salmon in the United States and Canada and herring in Norway work day and night during the run of the fish; some fish are even canned at sea in floating factories. During the fruit and vegetable canning season, employment in this industry in the United States may be as high as 350,000; in the off season, it drops to 100,000.

---

59. **42**, pp. 4 and 9.

60. In cans containing solid foodstuffs, heat penetrates from the outside to the center; in those containing liquids, it moves with the currents of the expanding liquid. Non-acid foodstuffs, such as meat, sea food and most vegetables, require processing at temperatures much higher than boiling water to destroy the bacteria that cause spoilage. Large cans require longer processing than small containers, and so on.

61. **51**, p. 4, and **22**, p. 3.

62. Peas, for example, are so handled through all operations from the field to the can except for the pick-ing-out of defective peas on the sorting belt. Machines separate the peas from the pods, wash them and grade them by size, fill and seal the cans, convey them to the cookers, process, cool, label and crate them. On the Pacific Coast, the "iron chink" has replaced Chinese laborers in salmon canning; it automatically cleans the fish, cuts off head, tail and fins, and removes the entrails. **50**, p. 14.

63. **22**, p. 44.

TABLE 441

CANNING: ESTABLISHMENTS, EMPLOYMENT AND VALUE OF OUTPUT
IN SELECTED COUNTRIES

Country and Year	Number, in Thousands		Value of Output, in Millions	
	Establishments	Persons Employed	Gross	Net
United States, 1947 (*Census*)	3.8	201.6	$2,469	$917
1950 (*Annual Survey*)	...	(203.4)	...	(1,118)
Canada,ᵃ 1947	1.1	29.0	258	102
United Kingdom,ᵇ 1935	0.4	50.0	180	77
France, 1938	1.4	50.1	...	...
Netherlands,ᵃ 1930	0.1	4.1	...	...
Denmark,ᶜ 1948	0.1	3.4	24	...
Sweden,ᵉ 1947	0.1	3.9	23	...
Norway,ᵈ 1948	0.2	8.2	19	...
Germany,ᵉ 1939	0.5	22.0	...	...
Switzerland,ᵉ 1949	0.1	4.0	...	...
Portugal,ᶠ 1948	0.2	1.0	...	...
Italy,ᵍ 1937–40	3.2	39.2	3	0.4
Union of So. Africa,ʰ 1945–46	0.03	7.9	24	8
Australia,ⁱ 1946–47	...	14.8	48	15
New Zealand,ⁱ 1946–47	0.03	0.9	5	2

Sources: Statistical yearbooks and censuses. For Denmark: persons employed include wage earners only.

a. Fruit, vegetable and fish processing.
b. Establishments with more than 10 employees.
c. Establishments with 5 or more workers.
d. Establishments employing workers for at least 12,000 hours during the year.
e. Establishments with 11 or more workers. Canning of fruit and vegetables. 1939 census data adjusted to 1937 territory.
f. Fish preparation.
g. Fruit canning.
h. Fruit preserves, jams, jellies, pickles.
i. Fruit and vegetable preserves and jams.

Dehydration and Freezing

Dehydration as a method of preserving food has been of minor commercial importance except in wartime. During World War II, the critical shortage of tonnage stimulated the production of dehydrated foodstuffs in the United States for the armed forces overseas and for the Allies. New techniques were developed, and the products were more satisfactory than in past wars. The output of dehydrated vegetables rose from 5.4 million pounds in 1940 to 115 million in 1943.[64] Plants were scattered all over the country to handle local surpluses. Canada, likewise, increased its output of dried vegetables, from 70,000 pounds in 1939 to 13 million pounds in 1943.

Germany, the Netherlands and Switzerland produced various dehydrated foodstuffs before World War II and developed new kinds in wartime.[65] Argentina dehydrates meat for export; all its packing houses have the necessary equipment.[66]

Recently a new branch of the food-processing industry — freezing — has begun to compete with canning. The principle itself is not new. For example, "weather freezing" of fish on ice was practiced in the Great Lakes area in the middle of the nineteenth century and still is to a small extent.[67] Freezing of vegetables dates from 1929, but the production before World War II was insignificant. During the war, this branch attained considerable importance, and it is now expanding rapidly. The 1949 pack of quick-frozen foods in the United States amounted to 1,834 million pounds avoirdupois; that of 1950,

64. **11**, p. 11.

65. **27**, p. 94.
66. **13**, p. 46.
67. **59**, p. 1.

to 2,173 million. Production of frozen juice concentrates started in 1945–46, with Florida the single producer of about a quarter million gallons. In 1949–50, the United States output of citrus fruit concentrates was just under 30 million gallons.[68] Florida remains the ranking producer of frozen juices. It accounted in 1949–50 for 21.6 million gallons of orange juice out of 25.1 million and for 1.6 million gallons of grapefruit juice out of 1.7 million.[69] Consumption of frozen orange juice in the United States doubled from 1950 to 1952.

In the beginning, lack of storage space at zero temperature and lack of facilities for low-temperature transportation were serious obstacles to the development of the industry. Further difficulties were experienced in finding outlets for frozen foods, since thousands of small grocers could not afford the large investment required for display freezers. Some large food-freezing companies supplied their own cabinets at relatively low rentals, but smaller companies could not do so. Few retailers invested in display cabinets until 1940; the supermarkets were the first outlets for frozen products in the United States. Today almost every food store in urban centers has a cabinet for frozen goods.

The transportation of frozen products from plants to retailers involves special problems. Ordinary refrigerator cars are not cold enough for quick-frozen foodstuffs, which are affected by changes in temperature during loading and transport. Some technicians have suggested that refrigerator tunnels be built from the door of the plant to freight cars made especially for these products.

Industrial distinctions between the preservation of food by heat and by low temperature are gradually disappearing. Some companies engage in both processes, while frozen-food packers have adopted cans for some products, such as fruit juices. It costs little more to freeze food than to can it, but considerably more to store, transport and market frozen products.[70] Another difference is that fruit and vegetables are harvested half-ripe so as to reach the canning factory fully ripe, but they must be harvested at their prime for quick-freezing.

World Output of Canned Food

Before World War II, the world's annual output of canned food approached 400 million cases.[71] In 1937, it was distributed as follows: [72]

	Millions of Cases	Per Cent
Total	391.6	100.0
Vegetables	202.5	51.7
Fruit	72.2	18.4
Meat and dairy products	76.7	19.6
Sea food	40.3	10.3

The world's output of canned milk, which exceeds that of any other single product, totaled 3 billion cans or more in 1935.[73] The United States accounted for 60 per cent, with Canada, the United Kingdom and the Netherlands next in line. Production of evaporated and condensed milk is expanding in Argentina.

While commercial canning has been introduced in many areas and the number of products processed in canning plants is rising continually, the industry is still concentrated in a few countries, pre-eminently the United States. In 1937, for example, according to one estimate, eight countries produced 97.5 per cent of all canned fruit as follows: [74]

	Millions of Cases	Per Cent
World	72.5	100.0
United States	46.8	64.5
Hawaii	10.5	14.5
Canada	1.5	2.1
United Kingdom	1.2	1.6
Germany	2.7	3.7
Japan	2.5	3.4
British Malaya	3.1	4.3
Australia	2.5	3.4
Other countries	1.8	2.5

Output in the United States

The United States is the world's largest producer and consumer of canned food. In a typical prewar year it produced more than 290 million cases of canned food (about 10 billion cans) a

---

68. **61,** May 25, 1951, pp. 65–66 and 175.
69. **61,** May 25, 1951, p. 175.
70. **59,** p. 20.

71. Although cans are of different size and cases may contain from 6 to 96 cans, the case is the universally accepted unit for measuring the output of this industry.
72. **42,** p. 28.
73. **63,** p. 82.
74. **26,** p. 3.

year, or more than seven tenths of the world's output of the following products: [75]

	Millions of Cases	Percentage of World Output
Total	299	76.3
Vegetables	165	81.5
Fruit, excluding juices	55	76.2
Meat and dairy products	62	80.8
Sea food	17	42.2

During the war, the canning industry of the United States expanded very considerably to meet requirements for the armed forces and exports to the Allies. The average annual pack in 1936–40 and 1941–45 was as follows (in millions of cases of various sizes): [76]

	1936–40	1941–45
Total	344.8	512.7
Seasonal vegetables	105.7	161.9
Nonseasonal vegetables	41.1	35.9
Fruit	48.6	55.2
Juices	41.2	79.1
Meat	7.7	40.5
Poultry	—	0.6
Fish	19.0	18.9
Milk	49.4	81.1
Baby food	1.7	8.4
Other products	30.4	31.1

The peak output was reached in 1946; since that year production of some products, such as green peas and orange and tomato juice, has declined somewhat, largely because of the competition of frozen foods, while output of some others, including beans and beets, has increased. Canned baby food, unknown in the United States at the turn of the century and representing only a small branch of the industry in the 1930's is now being produced in increasing quantities, with California the leading producer. In 1950, some 17 million cases (about 263,000 short tons) were packed.[77]

Altogether, the pack of processed foodstuffs (canned, frozen and dried) in the United States in 1950 amounted to more than 16 million short tons.

Canning is widely dispersed in the United States. Beans are packed commercially in 40 states, tomatoes in 37, corn in 29, peas in 27.[78]

Canneries are in operation in 45 states, but there is considerable regional specialization. Maine is known for its canning of sweet corn, Wisconsin for peas. The Pacific Coast is the center of fruit canning, while Florida and Texas lead in canning grapefruit juice. California normally accounts for some 95 per cent of the national pack of canned apricots; in 1950 it was the only producing state, with 4.1 million cases. In that year it produced 17.4 million cases of canned peaches out of the total of 18 million. Florida and Texas accounted for 7.9 and 2.7 million, respectively, of the 11.8 million cases of grapefruit juice, and Florida alone produced 17.4 million cases of orange juice out of the total of 19.3 million.[79]

Except for pineapples, produced largely in Hawaii, peaches are by far the most popular canned fruit. Nearly a fourth of the fresh peach crop is canned, and California usually accounts for about 95 per cent of the output. The United States as a whole supplied about 85 per cent of the world total.[80] Canned pears follow, at a distance, with one third the peach output. The United States accounts for about 75 per cent of the world total; the Pacific Coast, for 85 per cent of the domestic output.[81]

Production of canned tomatoes in the United States is about double that in the rest of the world and takes about three fourths of the country's commercial tomato crop. Much of the rest of the crop is canned by housewives. Tomatoes are canned commercially in 42 states, but for the most part near the 39th parallel — from New Jersey through Maryland, Virginia, Indiana, Arkansas, Colorado and Utah to California. California and Maryland lead.[82]

To assure an adequate supply of fruit and vegetables of standard quality, the canning industry in the United States contracts for an extensive acreage and controls the selection of seed and the cultivation of the crop. For some products, the acreage planted for canning exceeds that for fresh marketing. For example, 430,000 acres of sweet corn, 331,000 acres of green peas and 442,000 acres of tomatoes were grown in 1937 for canning, as compared with 24,000, 118,000 and 199,000, respectively, for fresh marketing.[83] Packers of frozen foods also engage in farming, since success in freezing depends on the uniform

75. **51**, p. 8.
76. **61**, April 25, 1948, *passim*.
77. **61**, May 25, 1951, pp. 63 and 78.
78. **50**, p. 6.

79. **61**, May 25, 1951, pp. 61–63.
80. **10**, Part 4, p. 133.
81. **10**, Part 4, p. 163.
82. **10**, Part 6, p. 77.
83. **50**, p. 8.

excellence of the produce.[84] In 1950 the western packers controlled 1.9 million out of 2.4 million acres in vegetables (except potatoes) in the West. They also had 850,000 acres for growing fruit.[85]

Production in Other Countries

In the Western Hemisphere, Canada is second only to the United States in production of canned foods. Its large and diversified canning industry packs vegetables, fish, meats, milk and fruit, the last partly imported from the United States.[86]

In Latin America, the canning industry is in its infancy, although World War II gave a strong impetus to the canning of meat and fruit, particularly peaches and pears, in Argentina.

The United Kingdom has many modern plants, equipped with American machinery, for packing vegetables, fruit, fish and milk products. While domestic fruit is used largely, the United Kingdom also imports canned fruit for repacking in fruit salads or cocktails, mostly during the off season to reduce overhead costs in local canneries.

The French canning industry is dispersed throughout the country. The Loire Valley specializes in asparagus, Provence and the Garonne Valley in tomatoes, Brittany and the northern and southwestern regions in peas, the Saône Valley and Paris in spinach.[87]

The Netherlands specializes in canned milk, condensed or evaporated; Portugal, in packing sardines. Spain prepares apricot pulp in large cans of 11 or 22 pounds and is second only to Portugal in sardine exports from Europe. Norway cans fish, especially herring. Prewar Germany had a considerable output of canned vegetables, about 100 million cans a year. Italy is second to the United States in canning tomatoes and exports about 70 per cent of the pack, as against less than 0.5 per cent for the United States.[88]

In Japan, canning of sea food and fruit is particularly important; of 15.2 million cases packed in 1938, sea food accounted for 6.7 million and fruit for 4.6 million.[89] Hawaii accounts for more than two thirds of the world's pineapple pack: 10.5 million cases out of 15.6 million

in 1936–41 and 14.5 million out of 20 million in 1950–51. The Philippines has a growing pineapple industry; its average pack in 1936–41 was 662,000 cases; in 1950, 2 million.[90] Malaya also cans pineapples, which were first grown as a "catch crop" in rubber groves but are now raised for their own value. Unlike the Hawaiian plants, Malayan canneries use largely manual labor, and before the war the industry was almost entirely in Chinese hands. During the war, the industry was nearly ruined; its installations were either destroyed or dismantled by the Japanese. A slow recovery began in 1947; modern automatic canning units were introduced and great efforts made to regain old, and capture new, markets. The pack, however, is still less than a fourth of the prewar: 500,000 cases in 1950, in comparison with an average of 2.3 million in 1936–41.

The canning industry of the USSR reportedly produced close to a billion cans of various foodstuffs in 1940.[91] More recent data are not available.

In Australia, canning of fruit, especially peaches, pears and pineapples, has developed largely within the "closer settlements," which the government fostered by granting land to exservicemen and other groups for colonization. The enterprises born of these efforts are mostly cooperative in character, but so-called proprietary, or private, canneries are also developing.[92]

THE BEVERAGE INDUSTRY

Production of distilled liquors, wine, malt and soft drinks is a multibillion dollar industry in the United States and an important branch of the economy in many other countries. In most countries, this industry has been a substantial source of tax revenue for many hundreds of years. In probably no other industry is there as much illegal, and therefore unrecorded, production.

The chief branches of the beverage industry are brewery products, wine, distilled spirits and soft drinks.[93]

Development

Beer from crushed barley was made in Babylon 5,000 or more years ago. The Babylonians and the Egyptians used beer as a drink and for

84. **44**, 1948, p. 181.
85. **61**, May 25, 1951, p. 91.
86. **26**, p. 12.
87. **27**, pp. 87–88.
88. **10**, Part 6, p. 77.
89. **42**, p. 13.

90. **61**, May 25, 1951, p. 119.
91. **24**, p. 9.
92. **22**, pp. 60–65.
93. For lack of international statistics, distilled spirits and soft drinks are not discussed here.

medicinal purposes. From Egypt, the art of brewing spread to Greece. According to Tacitus, beer was a common drink in Germany in his time.

In medieval Europe, brewing was commonly practiced in monasteries, which began to produce on a commercial scale as the cities grew. Most manors had their own breweries, and farm families made beer for themselves. In the Western Hemisphere, Indians knew the art of brewing.

As in other fields of food processing, home brewing was gradually displaced by commercial production. Most important in its development was Pasteur's discovery that many of the diseases caused by beer originated from bacteria in the yeast. He showed the role of yeast in fermentation and proved that yeast organisms could be controlled. Pure yeast was introduced late in the nineteenth century.

Invention of machinery for automatic bottling and labeling gave a powerful fillip to the entire beverage industry and to beer in particular. With the growth of the canning industry, use of cans has been widely adopted, especially in the United States.

Wine. Viticulture has flourished in the Near East and the Mediterranean since very early times. Decorations on ancient Egyptian tombs reconstruct grape-gathering and wine-making by people who lived as long ago as 4000 B.C.

In Greece, the Balkans, the Iberian Peninsula, France and other European countries, viticulture and wine-making became common long before our era. Missionaries introduced grape and wine production at early dates wherever they settled — in Germany, for example, and, in more recent times, along the Pacific Coast, in California, Mexico and Chile.[94] The Romans imported wine from the continent to Britain, where wine-drinking became an established custom before the Norman Conquest.

The development of wine-making in Europe in the Middle Ages was stimulated by the fact that drinking water was not safe and often caused digestive troubles. Home-produced "ordinary," or country, wine was served at every meal to grownups and children alike.

Wine-making, like other industries, has been mechanized, but primitive methods persist in small wineries. In some wineries in Bordeaux, for example, grapes are crushed by hand and rubbed through screens. Grapes are still trodden in some small wineries — in Portugal with the bare feet, in Spain with shoes made for the purpose.[95]

The quality and specifications of wine depend on soil and climatic conditions, altitude, and even the very position of the vineyard, as well as on the care and skill with which the grapes are raised and processed. Practically all the best wines come from grapes grown on hillsides terraced in such a way that each plant receives sun and air.[96]

While most of the world's wines are of ordinary types, highly specialized kinds are produced in some places where the physical conditions are peculiar and the methods of wine-making are adapted to specialized varieties of grapes.[97] Methods differ, for example, among the various wine-producing departments of France.

Establishments and Employment

The manufacture of beverages occupies more than a million people in the world. The industry engaged 202,600 persons in the United States in 1947; 135,000 persons in Germany (all establishments) in 1939; 101,100 in the United Kingdom in 1935; and 77,500 in Japan in 1938. (See Table 442.)

The relative importance of the various branches of the industry differs from country to country. In the United States, the net value of all beverages produced in 1947, taxes excluded, was close to $1.9 billion and comprised: malt liquors, $809 million; soft drinks, $421 million; distilled liquors, $472 million; wines and brandy, $95 million; malt (from barley and other grains), $54 million.[98]

In the United Kingdom, beer and whisky are the most important products, while wine predominates in the Mediterranean and Danubian countries and Chile. Beer accounted for the largest part of Germany's output of beverages before World War II. (See Table 436.)

Since raw materials cost much less in the beverage industry than, for example, in the meat industry, the ratio of value added to gross value of output is therefore high: 66 per cent in Canada, 50–60 per cent or more in Ireland, the Union of South Africa, Australia and New Zealand.

---

95. **33**, p. 121.

96. **54**, p. 7.

97. In France alone there are more than 2,000 distinct varieties of *Vitis vinifera,* the wine grape grown throughout the world. **54**, p. 5.

98. **4**, Vol II, p. 129. Malt liquors include ale, beer, porter, stout and malt extract.

94. **54**, pp. 2–3.

TABLE 442

THE BEVERAGE INDUSTRY: ESTABLISHMENTS, EMPLOYMENT AND VALUE OF OUTPUT
IN SELECTED COUNTRIES

Country and Year	Number, in Thousands		Value of Output, in Millions	
	Establishments	Persons Employed	Gross	Net
United States, 1947 (*Census*)	6.8	202.6	$3,193 [a]	$1,851
1950 (*Annual Survey*)	...	(210.8)	...	(2,019)
Canada, 1947	0.6	20.0	251	166
Mexico, 1944	1.6	16.7	54	...
United Kingdom,[b] 1935	1.6	101.1	972	325
Ireland, 1946	...	4.2	37	24
France, 1948	1.6	34.0	...	...
Denmark,[c] 1948	0.4	9.2	84	...
Sweden,[c] 1947	0.4	8.9	93	...
Norway,[d] 1948	0.3	2.4	22	18
Germany,[b, e] 1939	2.0	102.5	...	...
Poland, 1946	3.8	29.5	...	...
Czechoslovakia, 1930	1.5	25.9	...	...
Switzerland,[c] 1949	0.1	3.2	...	...
Hungary, 1939	0.1	4.0	24	12
Italy, 1937–40	12.3	42.1	...	...
Japan, 1938	6.8	77.5	...	...
Union of So. Africa,[f] 1945–46	...	2.8	21	13
Australia, 1946–47	...	4.5	40	22
New Zealand, 1946–47	0.2	2.5	11	6

Sources: Statistical yearbooks and censuses. For Denmark: persons employed include wage earners
    only.

    a. Excludes wine and brandy.
    b. Establishments with 11 or more employees.
    c. Establishments with 5 or more workers.
    d. Establishments that employed workers for at least 12,000 hours during the year.
    e. 1939 census data adjusted to 1937 territory.
    f. Brewing and malting.

Output of Beer

In 1939 the beer output of the world (excluding the USSR) totaled 6.1 billion gallons, of which the three largest producers — the United States, Germany and the United Kingdom — together accounted for more than two thirds.

In 1950, the world produced somewhat more beer, and the share of the United States rose from about 27 per cent to 40 per cent. Production barely reached the prewar level in the United Kingdom, and fell considerably in Germany, France and Japan. Between 1939 and 1950, Mexico tripled its beer output, and Canada and Argentina more than doubled theirs. (See Table 443.)

The most important beer-producing areas in the United States and their 1940 output are as follows: [99]

	Millions of Barrels	Per Cent
United States	54.9	100.0
New York	8.9	16.2
Pennsylvania	6.2	11.3
Wisconsin	5.7	10.4
Missouri	4.3	7.8
Illinois	3.7	6.7
Ohio	3.7	6.7

Output of Wine

Both before and since World War II, Europe, the wine continent, has accounted for three

99. **53**, pp. 12–13.

TABLE 443

BEER: OUTPUT IN SELECTED COUNTRIES, 1929–50

(*Millions of U.S. Gallons* [a])

Country	1929	1939	1949	1950
World [b]	5,204	6,132	6,594	6,684
United States	[c]	1,670	2,782	2,753
Canada	76	80	217	214
Mexico	19	42	107	131
Brazil	47	55	. . .	. . .
Chile	13	18	24	24
Argentina	56	41	99	103
United Kingdom	1,076	1,104	1,136	1,088
Ireland	93	62	78	81
France	798	610 [d]	230	207
Belgium	406	341	277	. . .
Netherlands	61	40	35	37
Denmark	39	46	71	75
Sweden	40	46	45	46
Norway	13	14	15	16
Finland	[c]	10	19	20
Germany	1,562	1,354	354 [e]	451 [e]
Poland	74	40 [d]	67	. . .
Czechoslovakia	307	220 [f]	216	. . .
Switzerland	67	58	50	53
Austria	138	71 [f]	59	76
USSR	72	234	. . .	. . .
Japan	39	70	37	45
Union of South Africa [g]	8	12	27	. . .
Australia	89	107	175	209
New Zealand	16	21	38	42

Source: **1**, 1948, pp. 187–89, and 1951, pp. 196–98.

  a. Conversion factor: one U.S. gallon = 3.8 liters.
  b. Excludes the USSR.
  c. Prohibition in effect.
  d. 1938.
  e. Western Germany.
  f. 1937.
  g. Excludes beer made by natives.

fourths of the world's annual output, as is evident from the following figures (in millions of gallons): [100]

	1935–39 Average	1949
World (excluding the USSR)	4,497	4,658
North America	197	336
South America	308	362
Europe	3,396	3,459
Asia	35	15
Africa	540	441
Oceania	21	48

100. **2**, December 12, 1949, pp. 7–8.

Most wine is ordinary in grade and is consumed in the producing areas. International trade accounts for only 3–4 per cent of the total output and is limited to high-priced wines.[101]

France leads in production, accounting for more than a third of the world total before World War II and now about a third. Next in line among European countries are Italy, Spain and Portugal, which together produce some 35 per cent. The United States, Argentina and Chile are the chief wine producers in the Western Hemisphere. Argentina's output is considerable but its wine is much lower in quality than the Chilean product. Algeria ranks first in Africa. (See Table 444.)

France is outstanding in the quality and variety, as well as the quantity, of its wines. Most of its output, however, is of the ordinary type and is bottled by grocers. Of the 1.5 million vineyard owners, about a third make wine only for their households. The department of Gironde, in which Bordeaux lies, is outstanding for its fine wine, which it exports to many countries. The custom of taking wine with every meal is so well established in France that this chief wine-making country imports common wine, usually from Algeria, to counterbalance the export of its finest grades.

Except for a few well-known types, Italy produces ordinary "beverage" wine for domestic consumption. Some excellent wines of Spain and Portugal have a world-wide reputation.

All these countries have luxuriant vineyards in almost all parts of their territory, but Germany can grow wine grapes in only a comparatively small area in the south, along the Rhine and the Moselle. The German output is therefore small, but its quality is high. Germany imported grapes before the war to make "must" for lower-priced wines, and even imported some for wine-processing, exporting the wines as "made in Germany."

In the United States, California accounts for about 93 per cent of the grape crop and nearly the same percentage of the wine output.[102] The Great Lakes region, especially New York State, is also an important producing area. The country's wine industry has developed slowly because of dietary customs, the traditional preference for imported European wines, and distrust of the domestic product. Since physical conditions are

101. **12**, p. 16. Excludes export of wine from Algeria to France, which is classified as domestic trade.
102. **12**, p. 19.

TABLE 444

WINE: OUTPUT IN SELECTED COUNTRIES, 1935–39
ANNUAL AVERAGE AND 1948–50

(*Millions of U.S. Gallons* [a])

Country	1935–39	1948	1949	1950
World [b]	4,497	4,542	4,413	5,236
United States	193	435	298	426
Canada	4	7	5	7
Brazil	21	24	16	26
Peru	3	5	4	4
Chile	85	98	95	89
Uruguay	16	23	19	20
Argentina	184	180	330	264
France	1,603	1,253	1,054	1,620
Germany	81	47	36	86
Czechoslovakia	11	9	...	...
Switzerland	17	21	17	15
Austria	29	32	26	34
Hungary	102	91	...	...
Portugal	192	192	209	230
Spain	491	398	247	357
Italy	473	940	945	1,051
Yugoslavia	125	68	106	86
Romania	120	89	...	...
Bulgaria	49	41	...	...
Greece	99	98	119	113
Turkey	29	3	4	5
Cyprus	4	4	6	6
Lebanon	1	2	2	2
Israel	1	2	2	2
Syria	1	2	3	3
French Morocco	15	9	13	19
Algeria	451	334	382	378
Tunisia	42	20	23	20
Union of South Africa	33	70	56	63
Australia	21	48	41	30

Sources: **2,** December 12, 1949, pp. 7–8; *Foreign Crops and Markets,* October 1952.

a. Conversion factor: one U.S. gallon = 3.8 liters.
b. Excludes the USSR.

favorable for growing all types of grapes, the industry has gradually established itself. It has more than doubled its output since World War II.

THE TOBACCO INDUSTRY

Tobacco, like beer and wine, plays a significant role in the tax system of most countries, but its illicit production must be far less common, for one reason because of the lengthy and compli-cated operations required in processing the leaf.[103]

Before tobacco is shipped to the factory, the leaf is cured by air, sun or flue. Then the manufacturer must store it to mellow or age for one to three years. Because of slight differences between successive crops in aroma, color, flavor and strength, it is necessary to blend crops of two or three seasons to assure a standard quality in manufactured tobacco. A tobacco manufacturer must maintain considerable stocks of tobacco for this purpose; the leaf inventory of one of the three big companies in the United States has been estimated at $100 million.[104]

After aging in hogsheads, tobacco is unpacked and steamed, to prevent crumbling. The midrib is then removed and the tobacco is stemmed, flavored, blended, moistened again and left to mellow for a day or two. Next, the blend is shredded, and the manufacture of cigars or cigarettes follows.

Development

The first Europeans to disembark in the Western Hemisphere found the Indians consuming tobacco in various ways — smoking pipes, cigars (among the Caribs) and a kind of cigarette; chewing and snuffing. When Europe adopted tobacco, the various countries developed different tastes; cigars were in favor in Spain, pipes in England and France and later in central Europe and Scandinavia. By the middle of the seventeenth century, Spain had developed a kind of cigarette, the *papelete,* which found its way to the Levant and southern Russia. In the following century, tobacco users in France shifted to snuff. In the nineteenth century, pipes and cigars came to the fore. Cigarettes were accepted slowly — in France and the United States after the middle of the nineteenth century, in England even later. The opposition to cigarette smoking was very strong, particularly in the United States. Its ill effects on health were emphasized. As recently as 1914, Thomas Edison wrote to Henry Ford that cigarette smoking caused the brain cells to degenerate and that he employed no person who indulged in it.[105]

The use of cigarettes continued to spread in many countries, nonetheless. By 1913, per capita

103. For production of tobacco leaf, see Chapter 17, pp. 626–28.
104. **48,** p. 371.
105. **58,** pp. 128–35.

TABLE 445

TOBACCO MANUFACTURE: ESTABLISHMENTS, EMPLOYMENT AND
VALUE OF OUTPUT IN SELECTED COUNTRIES

Country and Year	Establishments	Persons Employed, in Thousands	Value of Output, in Millions	
			Gross	Net
United States, 1947 (*Census*)	1,086	111.8	$2,541	$641
1950 (*Annual Survey*)	. . .	(92.3)	. . .	(806)
Canada, 1947	91	10.9	147	49
United Kingdom,[a] 1935	118	42.9	598	139
Ireland, 1946	. . .	2.6	64	6
Netherlands, 1930	2,520	30.1	. . .	. . .
Denmark,[b] 1948	379	9.6	117	. . .
Sweden, 1947	7	1.9	96	. . .
Norway,[c] 1948	36	2.4	58	43
Finland, 1947	6	1.7	11	4
Germany,[d] 1939	1,845	136.2	. . .	. . .
Switzerland,[b] 1949	117	7.0	. . .	. . .
Hungary, 1939	13	5.7	42	36
Italy, 1937	25	21.5	. . .	. . .
Union of So. Africa, 1945–46	. . .	5.1	29	12
Australia, 1946–47	. . .	5.6	53	8
New Zealand, 1946–47	6	1.0	10	3

Sources: Censuses and statistical yearbooks. For Denmark: persons employed include wage earners only.

    a. Establishments with more than 10 employees.
    b. Establishments with 5 or more workers.
    c. Establishments employing workers for at least 12,000 hours during the year.
    d. Establishments with 11 or more employees. 1939 census data adjusted to 1937 territory.

consumption was a third greater in Finland than in the United States. Despite the spectacular increase in cigarette consumption in the United States before World War II its per capita consumption was 40 per cent less than in the United Kingdom.[106]

Until the turn of the century — and in many countries much later — cigarettes were customarily made at home from purchased tobacco. The first cigarette-making machine was patented in the 1870's, and the first satisfactory machine, capable of producing 200–220 cigarettes a minute, was introduced in the mid-1880's. The producers of the machines usually rented them out on a royalty basis.[107] Yet, mechanization of the industry was slow until World War I. When a machine was built that turned out 1,500 cigarettes a minute, mass production became feasible. It was particularly stimulated by the additional consumption when women took up smoking.

106. **58**, pp. 141–42.
107. **58**, pp. 18–19.

Mechanization of cigar-making came much later. The first efficient machine for this purpose did not appear in the United States until 1917. Even today, hand labor is customary in many countries, especially for high-priced cigars.

Establishments and Employment

Establishments in the tobacco-fabricating industry are ordinarily large and relatively few in number. In 1947 the United States had 1,086 tobacco factories. Characteristically, only 28 of them manufactured cigarettes, while 822 produced cigars. The manufacture of cigars, however, took only about one eighth as much tobacco leaf as was used in making cigarettes. Canada has some 90 tobacco-fabricating establishments; Sweden, 7; Finland, 6; New Zealand, 6. (See Table 445.) The average tobacco factory in the United Kingdom has 362 employees; in the United States, 103; in Canada, 120; in New Zealand, about 170. In Germany, one-family or one-person "establishments" predominate, especially in cigar-making. The work is done mostly for large plants, a system once common in the clothing industry in the United States.

In countries with a government monopoly of tobacco manufacture, the industry was highly concentrated even in the nineteenth century. Thus tobacco manufacture was carried on in 20 government factories in France, 28 in Austria and 21 in Hungary and was similarly concentrated in Italy, Spain, Portugal, Turkey, Russia and Romania.

In the United States, concentration was furthered when mechanization entailed large capital investments. It has progressed considerably since the 1920's, particularly in the production of cigars and cigarettes. Cigar plants decreased from 14,578 in 1921 to 822 in 1947; cigarette factories, from 381 in 1914 to 28 in 1947. Small cigar plants either closed or merged with others, and the number of very large plants producing upwards of 40 million cigars a year more than doubled. In the cigarette industry, one of the most highly concentrated major industries in the United States, the six largest companies accounted for 98 per cent of the total output in 1949, the remaining 2 per cent being distributed among many small producers. The three largest cigarette companies together produced 78 per cent of the total.[108]

In prewar Germany, too, cigarette production was more concentrated than other branches of tobacco manufacturing. In 1938–39 there were 95 cigarette plants as compared with 3,571 cigar establishments.[109]

Output

The United States and Germany lead in tobacco manufacture; before World War II, Germany produced considerably more cigars than the United States but only about one fourth as many cigarettes. During recent decades, cigarette manufacture has increased tremendously while the production of cigars and other tobacco products has been declining in some countries and fluctuating mildly in others. The output of cigarettes in the United States rose from 122 billion in 1929 to 393 billion in 1950; in Canada from 5 billion to 17 billion; in Denmark, from 1.1 billion to 4.4 billion. (See Table 446.) The output in Germany dropped sharply as a consequence of the war; the prewar upward trend in this country will probably be resumed soon. The

output of manufactured tobacco (plug, twist, smoking, chewing and snuff) has fallen in many countries, while more or less maintaining its 1929 level in others. There has been a slight increase in Norway, Spain, Australia and a few other countries.

In the United States the manufacture of cigarettes has grown at the expense of other tobacco products. Less than 3 per cent of the tobacco leaf was used for cigarettes in 1900–1905, nearly 80 per cent in 1950. (See Table 447.) The industry has specialized increasingly in the production of "small" cigarettes, the annual output of which has grown from 50 million in 1875 to 700 million in the early 1880's, 2.5 billion in 1890 and 392 billion in 1950:[110]

Annual Average or Year	*Millions of Cigarettes*	
	Small	*Large*
1901–05	3,227.6	7.1
1911–15	14,802.4	15.7
1921–25	65,904.0	16.7
1931–35	121,702.7	20.4
1941–45	285,675.8	23.8
1945	332,164.7	82.4
1946	350,038.1	1.7
1947	369,682.8	0.5
1948	386,825.7	0.6
1949	384,961.7	0.7
1950	391,955.7	0.7

In contrast to European producers, each company in the United States produces only one type of cigarette.

North Carolina is the leading state of the United States in the manufacture of cigarettes, accounting for 64 per cent of the national output in 1930 and 54 per cent in 1950. Virginia follows, with 23.5 and 27 per cent in the respective years. (See Table 448.) North Carolina's position has been unchallenged from the beginning, while Virginia did not move into second place until the late 1920's, when its output increased almost fivefold and its rival, New York State, cut down its production by nearly 90 per cent. Kentucky's share is increasing.

OUTLOOK

Although a latecomer to the realm of manufacturing, food processing in industrialized countries has acquired most of the characteris-

---

108. **58**, pp. 4–5.
109. **19**, 1939–40, p. 192.

110. **39**, p. 468; **6**, 1950, p. 788; **16**, 1951, p. 152. Small cigarettes weigh not more than 3 pounds per thousand.

TABLE 446

TOBACCO MANUFACTURE: OUTPUT IN SELECTED COUNTRIES, BY TYPE OF PRODUCT, 1929–50

Country	Cigars, in Millions				Cigarettes, in Billions				Tobacco,[a] in Thousands of Tons			
	1929	1939	1949	1950	1929	1939	1949	1950	1929	1939	1949	1950
United States[b]	6,938	5,355	5,453	5,468	122.4	180.8	385.7	392.6	172.9	155.7	108.4	106.7
Canada	191	136	207	201	5.0	7.2	17.1	17.4	13.5	12.8	13.2	13.3
Cuba	283	155	367	350	5.7	5.0	8.0	8.2	0.2[e]	[d]	0.1	0.1
Brazil	177	160	130	130	9.6	12.8	29.0	29.5	2.7	1.5	…	…
Chile	5	6	4	4	2.6	3.8	7.0	7.7	—	—	—	—
United Kingdom	204	211	148	150	63.0	81.7	102.6	103.0	24.2	22.5	20.0	20.0
Ireland	—	—	—	—	1.9	3.2	5.0	5.7	2.1	1.7	1.5	1.3
France	…	87	80	106	…	57.3	51.3	51.1	…	2.3	1.4	1.3
Netherlands[e]	1,402	1,713	1,020	880	3.0	4.7	6.6	8.2	15.4	12.9	12.1	13.5
Denmark	263	488	392	401	1.1	2.1	3.9	4.4	3.5	3.8	3.6	3.5
Sweden	36	25	20	18	1.8	2.2	3.5	4.0	6.0	5.4	4.8	4.4
Norway	12	25	20	16[e]	0.5	0.9	1.4	1.3	2.5	2.7	3.3	3.3
Finland	22	19	8	10	3.7	4.0	4.2	4.6	0.6	0.5	0.7	0.9
Germany[f]	6,973	9,110[g]	2,229[e]	3,588	32.9	47.3[g]	22.3	23.6	39.5	33.6[g]	20.6	19.9
Poland[e]	77	34[g]	23	23	10.7	9.4[g]	21.3	20.6	13.7	11.5[g]	1.0	…
Switzerland	511	476	440	442	…	2.4	6.2	6.8	2.6	2.5	2.3	2.4
Austria	274	131	73	74	5.1	6.3	4.3	6.0	5.2	3.9	1.4	1.5
Hungary	155	44[g]	25[h]	…	2.4	2.3[g]	6.3	…	4.7	4.5[g]	0.9[h]	…
Spain	—	—	—	—	7.4	6.8[i]	9.5	9.8	18.2	11.8[i]	18.9	19.3
Italy	—	—	—	—	14.7	20.0	28.4	29.9	9.9	7.3	6.0	6.2
Yugoslavia	…	17	11	…	…	5.6	22.2	…	3.6[e]	6.0	0.5	…
Greece	—	—	—	—	4.5[j]	5.8	9.2	…	—	—	—	—
Korea	—	—	—	—	3.9	7.1	6.0[k]	…	11.9	11.6	7.6[k]	…
Japan	2	—	—	—	32.3[j]	53.1	53.0	62.4	24.1[j]	18.2	14.4	10.3
Turkey	—	—	—	—	…	10.6	15.7[h]	…	…	4.5	2.5[h]	…
India	—	—	—	—	…	…	21.9	23.6	—	—	—	—
Algeria	…	17	6[h]	…	…	2.3	…	…	…	1.9	…	…
Union of South Africa	4	7	5[h]	…	2.4	4.2	9.4	…	4.6	6.6	7.9	…
Australia	33	29	19	21	2.4	3.1	4.5	4.8	7.1	7.4	8.7	9.1
New Zealand	—	—	—	—	0.2	0.5	1.5	…	…	1.6	2.1	…

Sources: **1**, 1948, pp. 190–94, and 1951, pp. 199–204; for the United Kingdom: *Tobacco* (Bulletin No. 20), Food and Agriculture Organization, Rome, October 1952, pp. 44–46.

a. Snuff, smoking and chewing tobacco; for France, snuff and chewing tobacco; for Switzerland and the United Kingdom, smoking tobacco.

b. Cigars weighing three pounds or more per thousand and excluding cigars manufactured in custom bonded manufacturing warehouses (in 1949, 150 million large cigars). Cigarettes include cigars weighing less than three pounds per thousand.

c. 1931.
d. Negligible production.
e. Cigarillos counted with cigars.
f. In 1949 and 1950, Western Germany.
g. 1938.
h. 1947.
i. 1940.
j. 1930.
k. South Korea.

tics of modern industry: mechanization of production, assembly line operation, utilization of by-products, search for new products and processes, study of markets, and so on. Food chemistry and research in nutritive values of various products have become a necessary part of every large-scale establishment in the food industries.

Factors that have supported the transfer of food processing from home to factory in advanced countries — industrialization, urbanization, increased employment of women, and so on — must have the same effect in underdevel-

TABLE 447

TOBACCO MANUFACTURE: CONSUMPTION OF LEAF, BY TYPE OF PRODUCT, IN THE UNITED STATES, 1896–1950

Annual Average or Year	Total	Tobacco[a] and Snuff	Cigars[b]	Cigarettes[c]
Millions of Pounds				
1896–1900	359	255	88	16
1901–05	451	315	124	12
1906–10	524	363	139	22
1911–15	578	374	152	52
1916–20	650	365	155	130
1921–25	672	323	151	199
1926–30	763	301	149	313
1931–35	741	283	112	346
1936–40	879	262	125	492
1941–45	1,183	228	133	821
1945	1,291	218	128	944
1946	1,307	168	137	1,001
1947	1,355	164	135	1,056
1948	1,400	161	139	1,099
1949	1,382	161	125	1,096
1950	1,393	160	127	1,106
Percentage Distribution				
1896–1900	100.0	71.0	24.5	4.5
1901–05	100.0	69.8	27.5	2.7
1906–10	100.0	69.3	26.5	4.2
1911–15	100.0	64.7	26.3	9.0
1916–20	100.0	56.2	23.8	20.0
1921–25	100.0	48.1	22.3	29.6
1926–30	100.0	39.4	19.5	41.0
1931–35	100.0	38.2	15.1	46.7
1936–40	100.0	29.8	14.2	56.0
1941–45	100.0	19.3	11.4	69.4
1945	100.0	16.9	9.9	73.1
1946	100.0	12.9	10.5	76.6
1947	100.0	12.1	10.0	77.9
1948	100.0	11.5	9.9	78.5
1949	100.0	11.6	9.0	79.3
1950	100.0	11.5	9.1	79.4

Sources: **6**, 1951, p. 776; **16**, 1951, p. 151.

a. Plug, twist, fine cut and smoking. b. Large. c. Small.

oped areas, once the spiral of industrialization begins to operate. This is a one-way road, and there is no way back to grinding grain and making flour at home once this traditional field of home economy has been invaded by factory production.

Poverty and custom have so far checked the penetration of fabricated foodstuffs into under-developed areas: manufactured food is, on the whole, more expensive than that prepared at home, and the saving of time in its preparation is generally of little importance in such areas. Industrialization changes this pattern of life, as rising incomes enable consumers to shift to more expensive foodstuffs and the time factor gains in importance. When a country enters on the path of industrialization, the development of food manufacturing becomes inevitable. The drive to industrialization in India, Pakistan, Indonesia, all of Latin America, and many other

TABLE 448

TOBACCO MANUFACTURE: OUTPUT OF SMALL CIGARETTES IN THE
UNITED STATES, BY STATE, 1920–50

State [a]	Number, in Billions					Percentage of Total				
	1920	1930	1941	1949	1950	1920	1930	1941	1949	1950
Total	47.4	123.8	217.9	385.0	392.0	100.0	100.0	100.0	100.0	100.0
North Carolina	24.1	79.0	105.0	209.9	211.0	50.8	63.8	48.2	54.5	53.8
Virginia	5.2	29.1	78.2	104.7	105.5	11.1	23.5	35.9	27.2	26.9
Kentucky	. . .	4.4	13.0	50.5	57.9	. . .	3.6	5.9	13.0	14.8
New Jersey	3.1	5.2	10.9	9.7	9.9	6.6	4.2	5.0	2.5	2.5
California	1.1	4.8	4.4	5.9	3.8	2.4	3.8	2.0	1.5	1.0
New York	10.8	1.2	0.9	1.8	2.0	22.9	0.9	0.4	0.5	0.5
Pennsylvania	1.9	0.1	5.6	2.3	1.5	4.0	0.1	2.6	0.6	0.4
Other	1.1	0.1	—	—	0.3	2.2	0.1	—	—	0.1

Source: **16,** various years.

a. States arrayed by declining output of small cigarettes in 1950.

countries is concomitant, therefore, with the shrinkage of the home and subsistence economy and the shift to consumption of fabricated foods.

A rising standard of living fosters the growth of food manufacturing, and depression affects it unfavorably. But economic conditions and changes in nutritional concepts affect the various branches of the food-processing industry differently. Bread bakeries may count on a stable de-

mand even in depression, as compared with factories producing chocolate and candy. New nutritional patterns calling for a more diversified diet and year-round consumption of vegetables and fruit promote the development of canning and preserving. The increasing awareness of the importance of "protective foods" is fostering the growth of the dairy and meat-packing industries.

CHAPTER 28

THE TEXTILE INDUSTRY

TEXTILE MANUFACTURE, with some 25 million workers and an output valued at about $47 billion in 1947–48, is one of the world's leading industries. The spearhead of industrialization in western Europe and North America, it is playing the same role today in the economic growth of underdeveloped areas in Asia, Latin America and Africa. Indeed, "the world-wide diffusion of industrial technique of textile manufacturing shows no signs of having reached its end. Today, as in the past, most countries tend to take their first plunge into the Industrial Revolution by establishing a ' domestic textile manufacturing industry." [1]

No longer, however, need a country undergo decades of experimentation with various types of machinery as England did two centuries ago. It can adopt modern techniques immediately, bridging in one leap the gap between primitive hand tools and highly mechanized modern manufacturing. Some textile mills in India, in fact, are more up to date in equipment and layout than many English factories built before 1900.[2]

The textile industry is highly international. Spread over all parts of the world, it processes raw materials from every part of the globe and sells its products to the most backward and the most advanced countries.

DEVELOPMENT OF THE TEXTILE INDUSTRY

Spinning must have been invented during the Stone Age, some twenty-five thousand years ago. Weaving, probably suggested to man by birds' nests and bees' hives, is believed to be still older. Linen and woolen cloth was produced in northern and western Europe two millenniums before the Romans appeared there. The Romans ordered the weavers of Gaul to supply 60,000 blankets for their army, and in Winchester, England, they established an army factory for woolen cloth.[3]

The highest degree of perfection in early cloth-making, however, was achieved in Asia and northern Africa. India produced cobweblike cotton fabrics, which modern mechanized mills cannot duplicate.[4] India was the home of resist and mordant dyeing, and of printed cotton cloth (calico). Nearly 6,000 years ago, the Egyptians excelled in making exquisite linen fabrics.[5] Long before the Christian era, silk was customarily worn in southeastern Asia, whence the craft of silk weaving was introduced into the Middle East.

Medieval Handicrafts

Hand production of wool and linen cloth was widespread in medieval Europe. The Flemish wool weavers, renowned for their skill, imported raw wool from England and exported wool fabrics to England and other European countries. In England, the wool industry was the most widespread — there was not a town, village or hamlet where woolens were not produced. Because of its wide dispersion, this industry combined national importance with the fortunes of every community.[6]

In the fourteenth century, England made great efforts to expand its wool industry. A Parliamentary act of 1337 promised most liberal franchises to foreign craftsmen who would migrate to England: "All the cloth-workers of strange lands, of whatsoever country they be . . . shall be in the king's protection and safe-conduct." The simultaneous prohibition of the exportation of raw wool was perhaps even more effective. Thousands of unemployed Flemish workers migrated to England and established centers for manufacturing wool fabrics.[7] British wool, then considered the finest in the world, and the excellent craftsmanship of the newcomers soon raised England's industry to prominence in Europe. It

---

1. **12**, Vol. I, p. 44.
2. When visiting cotton mills in Lancashire in 1931, Gandhi remarked that they were behind the modern installations in Bombay. **58**, p. 154.
3. **74**, pp. 3–6.

4. **74**; and **53**, p. 67.
5. One piece of cloth found on an Egyptian mummy had 540 threads to the inch, while the finest European linen has 350 threads. **55**, p. 163.
6. **71**, p. 6.
7. **71**, pp. 13–15.

became so important to the country's economy that in 1350 Edward III ordered the Lord Chancellor to "sit on a woolsack," as a symbol of the great national industry.

The other milestone in the history of England's wool industry was the sixteenth-century immigration of Dutch and Walloon weavers fleeing the Alvan regime of terror in their homeland. They introduced a new branch, known as "fine drapery," [8] which grew until it not only met domestic requirements but dominated the international textile trade. Wool, wrote Defoe, "is an exclusive grant from Heaven to Great Britain, 'tis peculiar to this Country and no other nation has it or anything equal to it in the world . . . all the world wears it, and all the world desires it and all the world almost envies us the Glory and Advantage of it." [9]

Europe's Cotton Manufacture

Europe's cotton industry began later.[10] While wool and flax were produced in almost all European countries, and silk in Italy and France, cotton had to be imported from distant areas, mainly from India. Transportation was so difficult and dangerous that each arrival of a shipment represented a major achievement. Consequently, Indian fabrics long were highly prized luxuries on the continent and in England.

This trade was interrupted for a long time after the capture of Constantinople in 1453 by the Turks, who cut off the old trade routes. Indian cotton fabrics did not reappear on European markets until the sixteenth century, after Vasco da Gama had discovered a new passage to India around the Cape of Good Hope in his "search for Christians and spices." The Portuguese and Spaniards then revived and monopolized the commerce with India, selling Indian cotton goods to the Dutch, who re-exported them to various European countries. The defeat of the Spanish Armada by the British in 1588 enabled northwestern Europe to trade with India directly.

English, French and Dutch East India Companies were formed, and regular commercial relations with India developed.[11]

Small-scale production of fustian, half-cotton and half-linen, began in Spain around the middle of the fifteenth century. Toward the end of that century Switzerland became known for its pure cotton textiles. England began much later to import Indian yarn for fustian; its industry was firmly established by the end of the seventeenth century. Competition between domestic fustian and imported cotton goods then became so intense that the home producers managed to have the wearing or other use of Indian cotton fabrics prohibited (acts of 1700 and 1721). To safeguard the interests of England's foreign trade, such goods could be imported, but only for re-export to the American colonies and European countries. The growing popularity of cotton fabrics, particularly Indian calicoes, led to widespread disregard of the prohibition. According to Defoe, calicoes were used for curtains, cushions and sheets. Persons of distinction wore Indian cotton shawls, and even the Queen appeared in calicoes. Meanwhile, the English producers strove to imitate Indian calico, though with little success at first.[12]

In 1736, the Manchester Act finally legalized the production and sale of cotton cloth. The British cotton industry actually dates from this act, which some textile experts consider the beginning of cotton manufacture in Western civilization.[13]

Tools of the Industrial Revolution

The eighteenth century brought a series of important innovations in the techniques of making textiles — the invention of the fly shuttle by John Kay (1733),[14] the spinning jenny by Hargreaves (1770), the water frame by Arkwright (1769), the spinning mule for fine yarn by Crompton (1779), the power loom by Cartwright (1785), and copper cylinders for calico printing by Bell (1770).

Until Kay's invention of the fly shuttle, two persons worked at the handloom, throwing the

---

8. **70**, p. 494.

9. As quoted in **69**, p. 38. It is interesting to note that Adam Smith mentions the wool industry many times in *The Wealth of Nations* but never alludes to the cotton industry.

10. In the Western Hemisphere, the Incas of Peru were skilled in making cotton cloth and printing it with wooden blocks before the discovery of America. Columbus' diary records that Indians brought skeins of cotton thread to his ship, and cotton fabrics were among the presents sent by Cortes to Charles V. **74**, p. 151.

11. **53**, p. 85.

12. **91**, pp. 117–18; **57**, pp. 290–91; **25**, p. 594.

13. **76**, p. 15.

14. The great painter of the Italian Renaissance, Leonardo da Vinci, left in his papers a sketch of a similar device he had made, but his invention was never applied commercially. **58**, p. 125.

shuttle from one end to the other, each pressing one of the treadles. The fly shuttle permitted one person to work the loom and send the shuttle across by pulling a cord. Although invented for woolen manufacture, it was more readily accepted by the young cotton industry.[15] Output per weaver rose fourfold, and wider cloth could be made.

As the weaving process was speeded up, the shortage of yarn became acute. This was eased when the spinning jenny, with eight spindles, appeared on the market.[16] Use of the jenny was so simple that children could operate it, and soon the balance between the supply of yarn and weaving capacity was restored. The Arkwright water frame could make both warp and woof yarn. Thus, for the first time, pure cotton goods could be produced in England. The legislation prohibiting the wearing of cotton cloth was repealed in 1774.[17] While the jenny could be used in workers' homes, Arkwright's machine, based on the use of water power, required a factory.

Crompton's mule (so called because it was essentially a cross between the jenny and the water frame) and Cartwright's power loom finally provided the young cotton industry with all its basic equipment. About the same time, an advance was made in bleaching "gray" (unfinished) cotton. As a substitute for the practice of bleaching by sunlight which was time-consuming and beyond the bleachers' control and required large areas for "bleaching walks," Berthollet, the French chemist, introduced the use of chlorine, thereby shortening the whitening from six months to a few days, irrespective of the weather.[18] Bell's cylinders, replacing the hand blocks used for printing calico, permitted one man to do the work of a hundred.[19] In 1804, Jacquard's adaptation of the loom made it possible to weave patterned fabrics.[20]

England's Cotton Industry

These inventions tremendously stimulated all branches of England's textile industry, especially cotton. The new machinery was the more welcome because of the insufficiency of workers to satisfy the increasing demand for cotton piece goods.[21] The cotton industry soon met all domestic requirements and began to supply the rest of the world. Textiles, particularly cotton, became the foundation of England's rapid industrialization and economic supremacy. So important did the industry become that it was said: "The nation's bread hangs by a thread."

British textile production benefited not only from technical progress but also from plentiful reserves of skilled domestic labor and abundant supplies of raw cotton from the United States. British imports of cotton soared from half a million pounds in 1793 to 6.3 million in 1795 and 17.8 million in 1800.[22] In addition, the humid climate of the British Isles proved a great advantage in the manufacture of textiles.[23]

Beginnings in the United States

England's efforts to maintain its monopoly by prohibiting exports of textile machinery, whole or in parts, and even the emigration of skilled textile workers, retarded the development of the textile industry in America. In 1770, nevertheless, American producers secured the designs of some English textile machines and obtained a few carding machines and spinning jennies. They were not able, however, to obtain the model or the design of Arkwright's frame [24] until Samuel Slater, an English textile worker, attracted by Philadelphia's offer of a prize, brought them the needed information. Emigrating to the United States, he built Arkwright's machine from memory and, moving to Rhode Island in 1790, engaged in cotton manufacturing.

The American cotton industry gradually began to expand, especially after 1793, when Eli Whitney invented the gin for separating cotton lint from the seed [25] — America's first epoch-making invention.[26] Since water was essential for bleach-

---

15. **91**, pp. 450 and 471.
16. The number of spindles was gradually increased to 16 and ultimately to 120.
17. **69**, p. 48.
18. **61**, pp. 140–41.
19. **82**, p. 23.
20. **62**, p. 491.

21. **69**, p. 16.
22. **58**, p. 144.
23. The rubbing of yarn creates frictional electricity, which tangles the strands. Humid air carries off the electricity. Damp yarn is also less likely to snap or curl. Modern cotton mills use special equipment to humidify the air.
24. **75**, 1949, p. 3.
25. The lint of the hairy upland cotton clings tenaciously to the seed, and cleaning by hand was slow and costly.
26. The charkha gin, similar to the roller gin, was used in India for centuries, but it worked well only on smooth-seeded types of cotton, such as the Sea Island or Egyptian varieties.

ing unfinished cotton textiles, the New England mills were built on streams and lakes. Labor was chiefly recruited among women and children.[27] The English machinery, designed for skilled workers and found to be too elaborate,[28] was simplified.

The Nineteenth-Century Industry

Workers, guilds and sometimes public authorities fought the use of the inventions that ushered in the Industrial Revolution in England. The textile industry was long "the first battleground of machine technology against hand tools," and public authorities frequently forbade the use of labor-saving devices and imprisoned the inventors.[29] Spinners and weavers, fearing unemployment, often destroyed the machines, burned the factories and harried the inventors, some of whom, including Kay, had to flee their native land and ended life in poverty abroad. But the use of machinery continued to spread. Although the British cotton industry, in particular, was receptive to the new technology, the power loom did not gain a firm position in the industry until the 1830's.[30] In the United States, the mule was not introduced until 1830, for lack of skilled male labor; [31] the power loom, not until 1850.

In the first half of the nineteenth century, cotton mills began to mushroom in France, Belgium, Germany and Switzerland. The inventory of spindles and looms increased. Cotton was imported from the United States and cotton yarn from England. In Russia, the young cotton industry was developing rapidly, although it had less support from the czarist government than any other; in 1840 it was the only Russian industry that employed free labor exclusively.[32] At

first, Russia imported English yarn, but after 1842, when England lifted the ban on the exportation of spinning machinery, it began to produce its own. In a few decades Russia completely reorganized its cotton mills in line with English techniques.[33]

Over the course of time, many improvements have been made in textile machinery. Ring spindles, of which a worker can tend a greater number than mule spindles, were invented in the United States in 1831. The Noble combing machine for separating long wool fibers ("tops") from the rest ("noil") was introduced in the early 1850's in England. In 1894, Northrop invented the battery loom, considered the most important single invention in textile machinery since Arkwright's water frame. A special attachment on this loom throws out an empty bobbin from the shuttle and inserts a fresh one, without interruption of work, thus permitting the weaver to tend many more looms than before. British manufacturers were slow to shift to battery looms, but Northrop's invention was readily accepted by the southern cotton mills of the United States and later in Japan, India and Latin America.

Although no major improvements in spinning and weaving machinery were introduced during the following decades, every branch and section of the textile industry exhibited a continuous trend toward modernization. Semiautomatic machines have, over the years, been made fully automatic; automatic processes have been simplified and extended. Increasing emphasis has been placed on the use of mechanical aids and labor-saving devices. This has been particularly true in the United States, where such features as traveling overhead ceiling blowers in card rooms, overhead cleaners in ring rooms, beam trucks for carrying the warp to the looms, application of mechanical power at the point of use, comprehensive mill conditioning and so on have become common. All advanced mills have installed equipment for better handling of materials and control of quality. Continuous processing in bleaching, dyeing and printing has been developed and applied in the United States. The speed and efficiency of production have been increased. Human labor in modern mills is confined chiefly to the supervision of complex high-speed machinery that must be watched constantly; threads, for example, may break in the spinning and warping

---

27. The first nine workers hired by Slater, seven boys and two girls, were all under 12 years of age. **67**, p. 305; and **63**, p. 170.

28. **58**, p. 151.

29. **26**, pp. 55–56.

30. In 1835, England had about 117,000 power looms, all but a few thousand of which were in the cotton factories. **82**, p. 22.

31. **67**, p. 156.

32. **44**, p. 301; and **72**, Vol. I, p. 536. One of the most difficult problems in Russia's industrial development at that time was labor supply. Skilled artisans were not numerous, and serfdom tied large masses of the population to the landowners. The government ran state factories and the landowners "manorial factories" with serf labor. Private factories employed some *obrok* serfs, who were permitted to move freely and work for wages against specified annual payments to their lords, and some free labor.

---

33. **44**, p. 302.

frames, and most repairs have to be done by hand.[34]

Recent Developments

The most important recent innovation in the textile industry has been the use of man-made raw materials, a development that may have far-reaching repercussions in agriculture and in international commerce in textile fibers and manufactured goods. Man-made fibers have already made heavy inroads upon the kingdom of natural fibers, and their use is increasing.

Compared with this revolution in the supply of raw materials for the industry, recent innovations in machinery, though very important, are less impressive. Many new types of machinery, some of radically new design, have been invented, and several of them are being used commercially with outstanding success. Many textile engineers believe that the industry is on the threshold of great technological changes.

One new development is the ring spinning frame for the woolen industry. Ring frames are displacing mule spindles in the United States; nearly 260,000 were in use in 1943. The advantages of the ring frame are productivity two to four times greater than that of the mule spindle, ability to handle larger packages, reduction in floor space requirements by 60 per cent, and savings in labor costs. Frame yarn is claimed to be stronger and more uniform than mule yarn. It is also claimed that frame spinning is suitable for all grades of wool and for mixtures of wool with some other fibers.[35]

Among the most important innovations in textile machinery in the United States are the Pacific converter, the pin drafter and the new (Warner-Swasey) weaving machine. The converter can process two or more types of tow simultaneously and blend natural and synthetic fibers in proper proportion. In a single operation it converts any continuous filament into a sliver of the desired fiber length. The pin drafter, a precision-built machine, about halves the number of drawing operations in the worsted industry and performs better work. It is expected that new systems for producing worsted yarn will supplant large portions of the English (Bradford) and French (continental) systems, now used to a great extent in the United States. It is claimed that new systems can handle natural and man-made fibers

in most combinations, if the fibers are not longer than seven inches.[36]

A new loom using an entirely new principle for weaving cloth has been demonstrated and tested and is producing cloth. A 100-pot spinning frame has been invented that can spin worsted fibers, synthetics and jute. It promises high yarn yield along with savings in labor and reduction in waste.[37]

Many other innovations in textile machinery were demonstrated at a 1951 international exhibition in Lille, France, by English, French, Swiss and German firms. The goal of all innovations is greater speed, more uniform products and savings in labor at every stage of factory operation. Some of them may reveal faults, some may claim more than they can deliver, but on the whole it can reasonably be expected that the entire field of textile technology will be overhauled in the near future. Within the past decade, some engineering experts have maintained that much textile machinery is cumbersome and obsolete, and now the industry generally expects radical innovations.[38]

While in advanced countries the industry is engaged in technological changes, in other areas of the world it still is using a good deal of antiquated equipment. In Brazil, for example, about three fourths of the cotton spindleage and more than nine tenths of the looms are of old types.

The spinning wheel and hand loom are still important in many countries. Some 2 million looms, operated by 2.4 million workers, provide about a fourth of India's total output of cloth. Almost 78 per cent of the cotton yarn consumed in China in 1930 was woven on hand looms, which are used not only in small rural mills but also in some city plants.[39] Hand looms account for a considerable part of the textiles used in Latin American countries. While in color and design some handspun fabrics are reminiscent of the exquisite tissues of ancient times and bespeak great skill and craftsmanship, the slowness of production on hand looms condemns the weavers to poverty. In the long run most

---

34. **14**, 1950, pp. 63–68; **15**, p. 11.
35. **90**, p. 491.

36. **86**, December 1951, p. 112.
37. **86**, December 1951, pp. 110–12; **41**, April 26, 1951, p. 12.
38. For example, a 1945 survey on the postwar plans of textile manufacturers reported the experts of the South Cotton Mill as saying that the present loom "is about the crudest thing to perform the highest precision work there is." (**87**, p. 13.)
39. **14**, 1948, p. 111; and **12**, Vol. I, p. 42.

hand work will have to capitulate to mechanized production.

The Textile Industry in the World Economy

The textile industry is one of the largest in the world in terms of the number of persons it employs, the gross value of its output and its share in international trade.

EMPLOYMENT AND ESTABLISHMENTS

Employment in the World

According to the International Labor Organization (ILO), about 14 million people were gainfully occupied in the world's textile industry in the early 1930's, distributed as follows (in thousands):[40]

United States	1,217
Canada	55
Mexico	88
Brazil	88
United Kingdom	1,443
France	920
Belgium	257
Netherlands	88
Sweden	63
Germany	1,118
Poland	147
Czechoslovakia	368
Switzerland	107
Austria	84
Hungary	53
Portugal	56
Spain	207
Italy	731
USSR	893
Japan	1,489
India	3,845
Other countries, including China	800

This estimate is extremely conservative. China, with a larger population and a colder climate than India, must have had at least as many textile workers as India's 3.8 million instead of the 600,000 here included. The remainder of about 200,000 for all the countries for which data were not estimated separately is far below the number actually employed at the time in Indonesia, Indochina, Turkey, the Middle East, other Latin American countries, Africa and Oceania, and a number of European countries.

Considering these discrepancies and also the widespread production on hand looms, the present writers estimated in an earlier publication that 20 million persons were gainfully occupied in the world's textile industry in the 1920's.[41] Increase in population may have caused the number to rise about 10 per cent, to 22 million by 1938–39.

Employment fell considerably during World War II in Germany, Japan, the USSR and many other countries but has regained its prewar level in recent years in some countries and exceeded it in others. Taking into account the growth of the world's population, it may be roughly estimated that the world textile industry now employs approximately 25 million people. About the same number may be engaged in the clothing trades.

Employment in the Various Branches

The cotton branch of the textile industry accounts for the largest share of the workers: in the 1930's, about 75 per cent in India; about 58 per cent in the USSR; 40 per cent in the United Kingdom; and 35 per cent in the United States. The proportion of workers in the wool branch ranged between 3 per cent in India and 20 per cent in France. The silk and rayon industry accounted for about 50 per cent of all textile employment in Japan; about 30 per cent in Switzerland; 17 per cent in the United States; 14 per cent in France; and 3 per cent in the USSR and India. (See Table 449.)

In the world as a whole, the cotton industry may now employ some 15 million persons; the wool branch hardly more than 2 million; the rayon and silk industry as many or somewhat more; and some 6 million persons may be engaged in processing flax, hemp, jute, hard and mixed fibers.

Skilled and Unskilled Labor

The textile industry has a great variety of job requirements. Some jobs, such as bale breaking or picker feeding, require no experience and only a day's training, but others may call for half a year or even a year or two of experience, as, for example, loom fixing.

Semiskilled workers constitute the largest group in many countries — 43 per cent in the Netherlands; 50 per cent in Belgium; about 56

---

40. **12**, Vol. I, p. 220; and **13**, p. 6. Data for Brazil and Spain are for 1920; data for the USSR include only wage earners.

41. **92**, p. 290.

TABLE 449

TEXTILES: EMPLOYMENT IN SELECTED COUNTRIES IN THE EARLY 1930's

(*Thousands*)

Country	*Total*	*Cotton*	*Wool*	*Silk and Rayon* [a]	*Other*
Total for countries listed	10,880	5,365	1,080	1,210	3,225
United States	1,217	422	145	205	446
Canada	55	18	8	9	19
United Kingdom [b]	1,443	585	244	71	542
France [b]	818	189	163	118	348
Netherlands	88	37	12	9	31
Germany [b]	856	215	166	61	414
Czechoslovakia [b]	339	115	51	22	151
Switzerland [b]	107	35	8	34	30
Austria	84	21	12	4	46
Hungary	53	—	7	4	43
USSR [b]	893	517	85	26	265
Japan [b]	1,081	326	70	531	154
India	3,845	2,884	109	115	737

Source: **12**, Vol. I, p. 229.

a. The rayon industry alone employed (in thousands) in the United States, 34; in the United Kingdom, 21; in the Netherlands, 9; in Switzerland, 6; in Japan, 113.

b. Wage earners only. Classification of all gainful workers by branch not available.

per cent in the United States; 70 per cent in Italy; and nearly 87 per cent in Switzerland.[42] They are also in the majority in France, Denmark, Australia and some other countries. The proportion of skilled workers ranges from 10 per cent to 38 per cent in different branches of the industry. In France, for example, relatively more skilled workers are employed in the silk branch than in either the wool or the cotton.[43]

Factory Employment

Textile mills vary from country to country in average size, according to the degree of specialization, the efficiency of labor, the extent of the "farming out" system and the use of machinery, and so on. Statistics on textile establishments also depend on whether or not the census count of "establishments" includes small shops and individuals working on their own account or on contract for a factory.

According to the ILO, *factory* employment in the world's textile industry before World War II included about 10.8 million workers, of whom two thirds were in eight countries. The United States, the United Kingdom, Germany, India and Japan each had about a million or more; the USSR had about 900,000; France and Italy from 600,000 to 700,000.[44] This estimate seems reasonable if "factory" is used in a narrow sense to represent mills with modern equipment. Allowing for the growth of population and changes in employment in various countries, the labor force in textile factories may now be close to 12 million.

Mills and Workers in Various Countries

In 1947 the United States had 8,185 textile mills with 1.2 million employees; France had 23,000 mills employing 580,000 persons. Thus, the average plant in the United States had about 150 employees and the average French plant 25. Brazil reported employment of 106 persons per plant in 1940; Uruguay (1940) and Venezuela (1936), averages of 23 and 6, respectively. (See Table 450.)

Germany has always tended to have small textile enterprises that mushroom in many parts of the country. In 1875 its first industrial census reported an average of less than 3 employees per plant, as compared with 200 in Britain at that

42. **13**, p. 21.
43. **13**, p. 94.

44. **13**, pp. 6–7.

TABLE 450

TEXTILES: ESTABLISHMENTS, EMPLOYMENT AND VALUE OF OUTPUT IN SELECTED COUNTRIES

Country and Year	Establishments, in Thousands	Employment, in Thousands	Value of Output, in Millions		Percentage of All Manufacturing		Value of Output	
			Gross	Net	Establishments	Employment	Gross	Net
United States, 1947 Census	8.2	1,233	...	$5,341	3.4	8.6	...	7.2
1950 (Annual Survey)	...	1,239	...	5,624	...	8.6	...	6.3
Canada, 1947	0.7	73	$509	213	2.2	6.4	5.1	5.0
Mexico, 1944	2.5	106	197	...	7.8	31.2	38.7	...
Venezuela, 1936	0.9	6	7	...	11.4	12.0	10.1	...
Brazil, 1940	2.2	233	181	71	5.4	28.7	23.3	22.0
Chile, 1940	0.4	19	22	...	8.4	16.2	13.6	...
Uruguay, 1940	0.3	7	17	6	3.3	10.8	9.0	8.0
Argentina, 1941	2.0	112	199	60	11.8	17.3	17.3	17.0
United Kingdom,[a] 1935	7.0	1,055	2,198	776	14.3	20.5	15.8	13.3
Ireland, 1946	...	13	40	16	...	12.8	7.4	9.1
France, 1947	23.0	580	2,520	...	...	...	...	...
Belgium, 1937	8.9	165	...	...	5.8	17.6	...	...
Netherlands,[b] 1947-48	0.4	79	356	...	...	...	...	...
Denmark,[c] 1948	1.2	31	140[d]	...	16.2	11.6	...	...
Sweden,[e] 1947	0.6	58	312	...	3.7	7.6	6.5	...

(Continued on facing page)

Table 450—*continued*

Country and Year	Establishments, in Thousands	Employment, in Thousands	Value of Output, in Millions		Percentage of All Manufacturing			
			Gross	Net	Establishments	Employment	Value of Output Gross	Value of Output Net
Norway,[f] 1948	0.3	18	90	36	5.2	8.4	6.7	5.7
Finland, 1947	0.4	32	78	...	6.9	11.4	7.0	...
Germany,[g] 1939	9.8	1,076	...	...	10.4	13.1	...	...
Poland,[h] 1947	5.6	283	...	...	19.3	20.4	...	...
Czechoslovakia, 1947	2.4[i]	184	...	...	2.6	12.2	...	...
Switzerland, 1949	1.0	62	...	...	8.1	12.6	...	...
Austria, 1949	0.5	62	...	...	10.6	15.9	...	...
Hungary, 1939	0.4	70	...	...	9.4	16.8	...	...
Italy, 1937–40	9.2	591	...	...	...	...	...	...
USSR, 1941	...	1,243	...	...	...	...	...	...
Japan, 1938	28.1	977	1,117	365	25.1	30.5	20.3	16.8
India,[j] 1948	...	996	...	...	...	...	...	...
Union of South Africa, 1945–46	...	5	23	10	...	1.1	1.5	1.3
Australia, 1946–47	0.8	60	210	87	2.3	7.6	6.6	6.8
New Zealand,[k] 1946–47	0.1	5	15	10	1.3	3.9	2.3	4.2

Sources: Statistical yearbooks; for the United States: **21**, 1947, Vol. II, p. 23 and **20**, p. 24; for Germany, **30**, pp. 240–41; for France, **28**, p. 13; for Japan, **79**, pp. 241–42; **66**, *passim*; for the USSR, **38**, p. 522; for the Netherlands, **37**, 1949, p. 70. As far as possible, mining and utilities are excluded.

a. Establishments with 11 or more employees.
b. Establishments with 25 or more workers.
c. Establishments with 6 or more wage earners.
d. 1947.

e. Establishments with 5 or more employees.
f. Establishments in which total employment amounted to at least 12,000 hours during the year.
g. Territory of 1937. Establishments with 11 or more employees.
h. Industrial enterprises and crafts.
i. 1946.
j. As reported to the ILO.
k. Woolen mills, hosiery and knitted goods.

time. The last German census, in 1939, enumerated 143,078 establishments with nearly 1.3 million employees, or 8–9 employees per establishment.[45] Germany then had 114 plants averaging nearly 1,700 workers each but characteristically had none with as many as 5,000 employees. Brazil, in contrast, had six plants in which employment exceeded 5,000 and one with more than 10,000 workers.[46]

Russia had very large textile establishments even before the turn of the century. In 1894 it had 494 cotton mills with a total of about 242,000 workers, or about 500 workers per mill; among these were eight mills averaging 7,000 workers.[47] Before World War I Russia had, along with some small mills, the largest textile establishment in the world, with nearly 60,000 workers.

Production of textiles absorbs a larger proportion of the industrial labor force in primarily agricultural countries than in primarily industrial countries.[48] This is also the situation in factory employment; textile mills accounted for 8.6 per cent of all factory employment in the United States (1947) and 13.1 per cent in Germany (1939), as compared with 28.7 per cent in Brazil (1940) and 31.2 per cent in Mexico (1944). The relatively large share in employment in the underdeveloped areas is explained by the fact that these areas generally have few industries and that textile factories are among the first plants introduced.

A United Nations survey of the cotton industry in Latin America found that in Brazil and Mexico, as in other countries, employment of superfluous labor is more or less general, even in new mills with up-to-date equipment. An abundant supply of labor, low wages, the traditional tendency to keep the worker's family attached to the mill and engage all its members, inadequate organization of work by management, the relative unimportance of the average wage level in comparison with the average prices the industry can charge, and various other factors result in a disproportionate level of employment in textile mills in such areas.[49]

Production of textiles accounts for 5–8 per cent of the total value of manufacturing output in Canada, in many countries of western Europe, and in Australia, and for 20–40 per cent in some Latin American countries — for example, Brazil and Mexico.

The cotton branch now generally employs, as in the 1930's, the greatest part of the labor force in textile mills, although there are exceptions, such as Japan (rayon and silk) and Australia (wool). In Brazil, cotton textiles account for eight or nine times as many workers as all other textile branches together; in the United States, the Netherlands, Poland and Italy, for twice or more than twice as many workers as either the wool or the rayon branch. In the United Kingdom, the cotton branch has half again as many workers as the wool branch and more than three times as many as are engaged in the production of silk and synthetic fibers. (See Table 451.)

Specialization in Manufacture

The textile industry is highly specialized in terms of processing stages and type and quality of products. There are spinning, weaving and finishing mills. Some spinning mills produce yarn for cloth, others for hosiery or rubber tires. Mills manufacturing cotton gray goods tend to specialize either in standard construction cloths, industrial fabrics or fancy weaves. Some mills specialize in low-priced products, others in fine-quality goods. Each stage in finishing — bleaching, dyeing and printing — may be performed in a special mill.

Specialization, while generally characteristic of the industry, differs in degree from country to country. The classic example of specialization is the cotton industry of Great Britain, in which four fifths of all the spindles are in spinning mills without weaving departments, while an almost equal proportion of all the looms are in weaving factories that do not engage in spinning.[50] The textile industry of the United States, though specialized, is more highly integrated and standardized than the British. Most mills in the United States both spin and weave.

Location of the Industry

While the production of natural fibers of one kind or another is dispersed all over the globe,

---

45. **30**, pp. 240–41.
46. **94**, p. 162.
47. **88**, p. 353.
48. Cf. Chapter 26, pp. 989 ff.
49. **3**, *passim*.

50. **32**, p. 48.

TABLE 451

TEXTILES: ESTABLISHMENTS AND EMPLOYMENT IN SELECTED COUNTRIES,
BY MAJOR INDUSTRY BRANCH

Country, Year and Major Branch	Establish-ments	Employ-ment, in Thousands	Country, Year and Major Branch	Establish-ments	Employ-ment, in Thousands
United States, 1947			France, 1948 (continued)		
Total	8,185	1,233	Knitted goods	3,095	65
Cotton	1,006	450	Other	3,592	152
Wool	828	180	Netherlands,[b] 1948		
Rayon and related fabrics	507	98	Total	...	71
Silk	43	2	Cotton	...	33
Knitted goods	3,126	231	Wool	...	14
Other [a]	2,675	272	Rayon	...	5
Canada, 1947			Other	...	19
Total	735	73			
Cotton	211	28	Sweden, 1947		
Wool	206	19	Total	584	58
Rayon, silk	40	15	Cotton	68	18
Flax	37	1	Wool	105	15
Other	241	11	Rayon, silk	24	3
			Knitted goods	216	12
Mexico, 1939–43			Other	171	10
Total	941	98			
Cotton	225	49	Germany,[c] 1939		
Wool	55	11	Total	9,813	1,076
Rayon	252	13	Cotton and wool spinning	470	136
Other	409	25	Cotton, wool and silk		
			weaving	1,245	264
United Kingdom, end of 1950			Knitted goods	2,106	161
Total	...	1,023	Coarse yarns	892	110
Cotton	...	330	Yarns, threads	259	37
Wool	...	217	Rayon	28	47
Silk, rayon, nylon	...	98	Other	4,813	321
Knitted goods	...	124			
Other	...	254	Poland, 1946		
			Total	899	199
France, 1948			Cotton	125	81
Total	11,108	539	Wool	194	42
Cotton	1,268	141	Rayon, silk	75	29
Wool	1,237	125	Other	505	47
Silk	1,916	56			

(*Continued on page 1062*)

their large-scale commercial conversion into fabrics and other textile products is concentrated in a comparatively few industrialized countries. This concentration is not nearly so great as in some other industries, in which one or two leading countries may control half or more of the world output. Moreover, the trend is decidedly away from the pattern of the nineteenth century, when England was the world's textile workshop.

Even so, before World War II from 70 to 75 per cent of all cotton yarn and cloth was manufactured in six leading countries — the United States, India, the United Kingdom, the USSR, Japan and Germany.[51] The United States, the United Kingdom and France together accounted for the largest part of the world's manufacture of woolens. In the rayon industry, Germany and Japan produced more than half the total output before World War II, while in the postwar years the United States alone has accounted for about the same proportion of the world's rayon production. The prewar output of silk in the United

51. **12**, Vol. I, pp. 57–58.

TABLE 451—*continued*

Country, Year and Major Branch	Establishments	Employment, in Thousands	Country, Year and Major Branch	Establishments	Employment, in Thousands
Switzerland, 1949			Japan,[b] 1947		
Total	1,038	62	Total	. . .	735
Cotton	303	21	Cotton	. . .	158
Wool	105	10	Wool	. . .	41
Rayon, silk	115	13	Rayon, silk	. . .	211
Knitted goods	203	2	Other	. . .	325
Flax	54	2	India,[b] 1948		
Other	258	14	Total	. . .	996
Italy, 1948			Cotton	. . .	633
Total	. . .	666	Jute	. . .	319
Cotton	. . .	260	Other	. . .	43
Wool	. . .	134	Australia,[d] 1946–47		
Rayon, silk	. . .	125	Total	. . .	60
Other	. . .	147	Cotton	78	8
USSR, 1936			Wool	114	23
Total	. . .	893	Knitted goods, hosiery	376	19
Cotton	. . .	517	Other	. . .	10
Wool	. . .	85			
Other	. . .	291			

Sources: Statistical yearbooks; for the United States, **21**, 1947, Vol. II, p. 23; for France, **89**, pp. 1 and 4; for Italy, **49**, 1949, p. 162.

a. Includes 641 finishing mills (except wool) with 78,000 employees; 296 carpet and rug factories with 57,200 employees; 479 narrow-fabric mills with 27,700 employees, and so on.

b. As reported to the ILO (**14**, 1950, pp. 155–59). Not necessarily full employment in the industry.

c. Territory of 1937. Establishments with 11 or more employees.

d. Data for establishments: 1945–46.

States was three times that in the rest of the world.

The trend toward geographic dispersion of the textile industry began after World War I. New centers of textile manufacturing appeared in Asia, particularly in Japan, India and China, to challenge the traditional supremacy of Great Britain. Brazil began to develop textile production. During World War II, many countries increased their textile capacity; further expansion is planned in almost all the Latin American countries, the Middle East, India and Africa. For example, until a very few years ago the textile industry of Africa was confined almost exclusively to Egypt; today, besides 62 mills in Egypt, there are 13 in other parts of the continent — five in the Union of South Africa, three in the Belgian Congo, the rest in North Africa, Southern Rhodesia, Ethiopia and so on — and five additional mills are planned.[52] Most of these mills are small, but they are likely to grow. In less than a decade, between 1938 and 1948, a score of countries in underdeveloped areas raised their mill consumption of cotton by more than 50 per cent.[53]

OUTPUT AND USE OF TEXTILES [54]

Output before World War II

The output of the world's textile industry in 1928 was valued at $20–$21 billion by Germany's Institute for the Study of Business Conditions (Institut für Konjunkturforschung). Eight countries accounted for about 85 per cent of the total: the United States for 25 per cent; the United Kingdom for 18 per cent; Germany for 11 per cent; France for 9 per cent; India, Japan and the USSR each for 5–6 per cent; and Italy for 4 per cent.

The total value of the output on the eve of World War II may have been about the same, roughly $20–$22 billion. Prices were lower at this time, but industrial consumption of fibers, a sure indicator of the volume of production, was

52. **56**, p. 18.

53. **4**, 1948, p. 19.

54. For production of natural textile fibers, see Chapter 17, pp. 597–618.

about 16 per cent greater than in 1928. On the whole, the world's mill consumption of fibers, while rising, has been highly stable except for silk and rayon, the consumption of which has soared, as is shown by the following estimates (in thousands of tons): [55]

	1913	1928	1938
Total	9,445	9,703	11,251
Cotton	5,583	5,658	6,300
Wool, greasy	1,429	1,480	1,690
Raw silk	27	65	54
Rayon	14	174	874
Flax	577	608	458
Jute	1,815	1,718	1,875

These estimates relate only to textile manufacture in mills. Spinning and weaving in the villages of underdeveloped regions, which account for a great part of the consumption of fibers, are not registered anywhere. Inclusion of the value of yarn and cloth produced on hand spindles and looms would raise the total value of the world's textile output by at least 15 per cent, to about $25 billion in 1938.

Output after World War II

In the United States, the Census of Manufactures found that the value added in textile manufacturing in 1947 amounted to $5,341 million, as compared with $1,818 million in 1939.[56] The gross value of output was not reported for 1947 but in 1939 amounted to $3,931 million, or more than twice the value added. Use of the same ratio between gross and net value for 1947 indicates that the gross value of textile output in 1947 was about $11.5 billion, which agrees fairly well with the current reports of the Department of Commerce on manufacturers' sales. The corresponding figure for 1948 would be about $13.6 billion.

Strictly comparable data for other countries are not available, but there are fairly reliable estimates of the consumption of various fibers by textile industries in various parts of the world.

The consumption of fibers in 1947–48 was distributed among the continents as follows (per cent): [57]

World	100
North America	30
United States	29
Middle and South America	5
Europe	28
USSR	7
Asia	28
Africa	1
Oceania	1

Thus in 1947–48 the United States consumed more fibers than Europe or Asia and four times as much as the USSR. (See Figure 299.) For purposes of a very rough approximation, it may be assumed that the share of the United States and of other parts of the world in the output of textiles about equals their share in the consumption of fibers. Consequently, the value of the world's textile output may have been in the neighborhood of $47 billion at current U.S. prices and without adjustment for differences in the quality of products.[58]

Use of Textiles

The textile industry provides fabrics for wearing apparel and household furnishings and various products for use in industry and agriculture. The United States normally uses about two fifths of all its textiles for clothing; an equal amount for agricultural and industrial purposes; and one fifth for furnishings.[59] In prewar Germany, on the other hand, 71 per cent went into apparel; only 5 per cent was used by industry and agriculture; and 21 per cent went for household necessities.[60] In Great Britain, 38.5 per cent of the cotton textiles produced for domestic consumption was used for clothing; 24.5 per cent for furnishings; and the rest for industrial and agricultural needs.[61]

Changing patterns of consumption, rising standards of living and fluctuations in fashion greatly affect the use of textiles in apparel and household furnishings. In the United States, men's suits have been reduced 30 per cent in

---

55. **68**, p. xvii; **60**, p. 10. Data for 1913 represent output.

56. **21**, 1947, Vol. II, p. 23.

57. **9**, p. 8.

58. This aggregate includes the value of fibers, maintenance costs, amortization of invested capital and many other items that do not constitute net income originated by manufacturing. There is no significance, therefore, in comparing it with the total net value of the world's manufacturing output (estimated at $185 billion for 1948). The net value of the world's textile manufacturing may have amounted to $18–$19 billion.

59. **16**, p. 86.

60. The rest was unclassified. **29**, No. 30–31, August 1935.

61. **32**, p. 18.

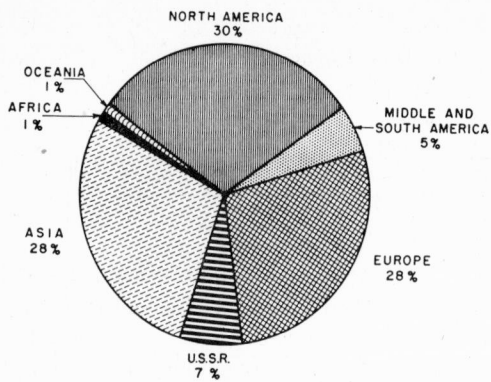

FIGURE 299. TEXTILE FIBERS: PERCENTAGE DISTRIBU-
TION OF WORLD CONSUMPTION BY CONTINENT,
1947–48

weight during recent decades and women's and
children's clothing even more.[62] The yardage in
women's apparel is only about a fourth of what
it was a few decades ago. In furnishings, higher
incomes and hygienic standards have doubled
the demand of the average household for sheets,
pillowcases, towels, tablecloths. The influence of
fashion is greatest in women's apparel and is
spreading into furnishings, but it does not affect
gray goods.

Recently, man-made fibers have begun to replace the old natural fibers — cotton, wool and
silk — which had satisfied textile requirements
for thousands of years. Cotton must compete
with rayon,[63] silk with nylon, wool with acrylic
fibers. Textile mills have felt this competition;
many have passed out of existence, while many
others have shifted to the processing of mixed
fibers.

COTTON MANUFACTURE

The durability, washability and cheapness of
cotton cloth account for the fact that about three
fourths of all the fabrics produced in the world
are of cotton. In the United States, the cotton
industry supplies 93 per cent of the country's
industrial requirements for textiles and 82 per
cent of its household requirements. In men's and
boys' apparel, it represents 73 per cent of the
total; in women's and children's wear, 49 per
cent.[64] Between 1919 and 1939, about 37–38 per

---

62. **63**, pp. 217–18.

63. Cotton and rayon, for example, are interchangeable for all but three of a hundred and sixty-five uses.
16, p. 88.

64. **81**, December 1939, p. 178.

cent of all cotton was used for clothing; about
an equal amount for industrial and agricultural
purposes; and 25 per cent for furnishings. In
1949, manufacture of apparel consumed the same
proportion of all cotton (37.6 per cent); and the
other uses accounted for 33.5 and 28.9 per cent,
respectively.[65]

The automobile industry is an important consumer, an average passenger car requiring about
90 pounds of cotton.[66] In 1949, more than 8 per
cent of the cotton consumed in the United States
went into motor vehicles. Prewar Germany used
more cotton for furnishings (54 per cent) than
for any other purpose and only 3 per cent for
industry and agriculture.

CONSUMPTION OF RAW COTTON

Throughout the nineteenth century the cotton industry grew with modern cities and the
industrial system. The world consumed 43,000
tons of cotton in 1800, an average of 215,000
tons a year in 1831–35, 1.1 million tons in 1871–
75, and 4.5 million tons in 1900 — a hundredfold
expansion in a century. Since 1900, the rate of
increase has slowed down: 4.6 million tons in
1913, 5.9 million in 1938. After a sharp drop in
consumption during and just after World War
II, mill output again increased. In 1950 world
consumption of cotton was about 14 per cent
higher than in 1938. (See Table 452.)

In the United States, mill consumption of cotton grew from 51,000 tons in 1840 to 793,000 in
1900 and 1.8 million in 1940, reached its peak in
1942 with 2.5 million tons, declined in postwar
years and is now again close to 2.5 million tons
a year.

In contrast, consumption of cotton in Great
Britain declined from 867,000 tons in 1913 to
583,000 in 1938 and 438,000 in 1948. In 1950 it
increased to 466,000 tons. The rapid upward
trend in Japan was broken during World War
II because of the shortage of cotton and the scrapping of machinery; Japan's defeat caused a further decline. In the USSR, mills consumed 70
per cent more cotton in 1938 than in 1929, but in
1950 only about two thirds as much as in 1938.
India's consumption of cotton rose rapidly between 1929 and 1938 and is now considerably
higher than that of the United Kingdom. In 1929,
1938 and 1950, eight major cotton-consuming

---

65. **64**, pp. 11–18; **80**, p. 30; and **78**, p. 4.
66. **51**, p. 23.

TABLE 452

COTTON MANUFACTURE: CONSUMPTION OF RAW COTTON IN
SELECTED COUNTRIES, 1913–51

(*Thousands of Metric Tons*[a])

Country	1913	1929	1938–39	1948–49	1949–50	**1950–51**
World [b]	4,627	5,870	5,860	5,745	5,950	6,660
United States	1,244	1,595	1,555	1,768	2,007	2,427
Canada	24	52	57	83	91	105
Mexico	34	37	53	65	65	67
Cuba	...	...	2	5	6	7
Colombia	...	...	11	27	28	28
Brazil	109	107	139	179	179	184
Peru	...	...	7	14	13	12
Chile	...	...	4	15	17	20
Uruguay	...	...	c	4	5	5
Argentina	...	...	33	87	90	92
United Kingdom	867	635	583	438	454	466
France	224	278	281	226	244	260
Belgium	58	103	70	78	87	103
Netherlands	19	43	56	54	62	64
Denmark	6	5	8	7	9	10
Sweden	19	22	34	25	28	29
Norway	2	2	3	4	5	5
Finland	8	8	13	12	10	11
Germany	386	313	249	151	215	255
Poland	70	57	76	85	87	87
Czechoslovakia	—	112	43	60	60	60
Switzerland	20	24	30	29	30	33
Austria	...	34	39	15	20	20
Hungary	...	5	28	30	30	30
Portugal	17	20	19	33	35	33
Spain	75	92	30	91	65	65
Italy	169	236	144	205	203	206
Yugoslavia	...	...	20	30	28	28
Romania	...	...	20	20	22	20
Bulgaria	...	...	19	14	14	13
Greece	...	...	17	18	21	24
USSR [d]	362	488	825	455	...	516
China [e]	...	444	714	640	488	585
Korea [f]	...	...	46	30	37	11
Japan	359	627	581	160	224	336
Turkey	...	...	29	42	40	42
Iran	...	...	21	17	15	12
Pakistan	}385	453	745{	20	26	30
India				809	705	672
Egypt	...	...	26	51	50	54
Union of South Africa	...	...	c	5	7	9
Australia	...	...	7	15	15	17

Sources: **92**, p. 292; **31**, 1931, p. 40 *; **1**, 1951, p. 297; **65**, July–August 1951, pp. 276–78.

a. Conversion factors: one metric ton = 1.1023 short tons = 2,204.6 pounds.
b. From 1938–39: excludes the USSR.
c. Negligible amount.
d. The FAO estimates the USSR consumption of raw cotton, in thousands of metric tons, at 600 in 1938, 410 in 1948, 480 in 1949 and 500 in 1950 (**7**, p. 10).
e. Includes Manchuria.
f. From 1938–39: South Korea.

countries acounted for the following percentages of the world's total consumption:

	1929	1938	1950
United States	27.2	26.5	36.4
United Kingdom	10.8	9.9	7.0
France	4.7	4.8	3.9
Germany	5.3	4.2	3.8
USSR	8.3	...	...
China	7.6	12.2	8.8
Japan	10.7	9.9	5.0
India	7.7	12.7	10.1
Other countries	17.7	19.8	24.9

In the world as a whole, cotton is trying to hold its own against rayon and other raw materials, such as paper used for tablecloths, napkins, towels and handkerchiefs. The cotton industry has tempered the threat of rayon, the chief rival, by adjusting many mills for the processing of mixtures of the two fibers.

In an analysis of potential inroads by competitive fibers, the Association of Cotton Textile Merchants of New York surveyed thirty principal fields representing more than three fourths of all cotton consumption in the United States. Competition was found to be greatest in the manufacture of piece goods, trousers, women's dresses and underwear, men's hosiery, blankets, draperies, upholstery, rugs, carpets and similar items. This group of commodities accounted for almost two thirds of the cotton consumption in the fields surveyed. Moderate competition was reported by manufacturers of shirts, men's underwear and bedspreads — products representing one tenth of the cotton consumption. The threat was negligible to the rest of the surveyed mills, which produced men's work gloves, bed tickings, oilcloth and so on.[67]

MILL EQUIPMENT

Spindles

The number of the world's cotton spindles increased rapidly throughout the nineteenth century and until 1929. In 1913 there were 143 million spindles; in 1929, 164 million. Between 1929 and 1938, spindleage declined in the United States and the United Kingdom, remained about the same in Germany and France, and almost doubled in Japan. In the USSR, China and India the number of spindles also rose, but in the

67. **81,** June 1945, p. 96.

world as a whole, the decline was, nevertheless, considerable — some 17 million. Though spindleage has increased in recent years in Japan, several Latin American countries, Africa and the Near East, the downward trend continues: in January 1951 the world's total was 124.9 million spindles, as compared with 147.2 million in 1938. (See Table 453.) Despite this reduction of some 15 per cent, the present number of spindles proved fully capable of consuming the all-time high of nearly 7 million tons of cotton in 1950.[68]

Cotton spindleage is of two types — mule and ring. It has been held that mule spindles produce a finer yarn than ring, but this is not true of the latest model of ring spindles. While mule spindles previously produced yarn finer than 60's, ring spindles are now used for yarn finer than 100's (the higher the count, the finer the yarn).[69] In the world at large, ring spindles, invented much later than the mule, constituted three fourths of the total in 1938, and more than eight tenths in January 1951 (101,452,000 out of 124,894,000). In Great Britain, known for the fineness of its yarn, the relation was almost exactly the reverse: in 1938, 71.5 per cent of the spindles were of the mule type, 28.5 per cent of the ring; in 1951, 64.1 and 35.9 per cent, respectively. Ring spindles represented the following percentages of the total in 1951: [70]

World	81.2
United States, Brazil, Chile, Argentina, Denmark, Turkey, China, Japan	100.0
Canada, Mexico, Italy	98.0–100.0
Belgium, Sweden, Western Germany, Switzerland, Portugal, India	93.0–98.0
USSR, Netherlands	85.0–90.0
France, Czechoslovakia, Spain	80.0–85.0
United Kingdom	35.9

The number of spindles alone does not indicate a country's spinning capacity. Of the two types, ring spindles are much the faster in operation, and six may produce as much yarn as ten mule spindles. The major textile-producing countries ranked as follows in 1951 in number of spindles and in spinning capacity in terms of

68. **50,** December 1951, p. 13.
69. **32,** p. 66.
70. Computed from **65,** July–August 1951, pp. 273–75.

TABLE 453

Cotton Manufacture: Number of Spindles in Selected Countries, 1913–51

(*Thousands*)

Country	1913	1929	1938	1949	January 1951
World	143,453	164,211	147,153	129,138 [a]	124,894
United States	31,520	34,829	26,376	23,500	23,007
Canada	855	1,240	1,137	1,088	1,120
Mexico	700	751	830	1,000	988
Brazil	1,200	2,750	2,725	3,100 [a]	3,288
United Kingdom	55,653	55,917	36,879	35,310	28,968
France	7,400	9,880	9,794	8,230	8,110
Belgium	1,492	2,156	1,986	2,300 [a]	1,844
Netherlands	475	1,160	1,209	1,200 [a]	1,170
Sweden	534	626	557	562	542
Germany	11,186	11,250	11,074 [b]	6,200	6,168 [c]
Poland	1,322	1,557	1,748	1,600 [a]	1,085 [a]
Czechoslovakia	4,909 [a]	3,673	3,330	2,200	2,340 [a]
Switzerland	1,398	1,504	1,241	1,134 [a]	1,162
Portugal	480	503	490	700 [a]	782
Spain	2,000	1,875	2,000	2,500	2,210
Italy	4,600	5,210	5,350	5,450	5,661
Russia (USSR)	7,668	7,465	10,050 [a]	10,000 [a]	9,750 [a]
China	1,000 [a]	3,602	4,300	4,600	4,000
Japan	2,300	6,530	12,550	3,319	4,468
Turkey	. . .	. . .	. . .	250 [d]	289 [a]
India [e]	6,084	8,704	9,731	10,350	10,849
Other countries	677	3,029	3,796	4,795	7,093

Sources: **65,** September 1923; November 1929, pp. 226–27; October 1938, pp. 80–81; July–August 1951, pp. 273–75; **52,** 1949, p. 110.

a. Estimate.
b. Includes Austria.
c. Western Germany. Eastern Germany: 850,000 spindles.
d. 1946.
e. Excludes Pakistan in 1949 and 1951.

the mechanical equivalent of ring spindles (figures in millions):[71]

	Spindles in Place	Equivalent in Ring Spindles
United States	23.0	23.0
United Kingdom	29.0	21.5
India	10.8	10.7
USSR	9.8	9.3
France	8.1	7.6
Western Germany	6.2	6.1
Japan	4.5	4.5
China	4.0	4.0

71. **12,** Vol. I, pp. 52–53. Conversion factor: ring spindle = 1.0 and mule spindle = 0.6, as used by the International Labor Organization for illustrative purposes only.

The United States, with less than eight tenths of the spindleage of the United Kingdom, has a greater spinning capacity. India, with a little more than a third of the spindles in the British cotton industry, has half its capacity.

Utilization of available spindleage varies from country to country, depending on number of working hours per week, number of shifts, and economic factors such as the availability of raw materials and market demand for yarn.

This rough conversion overlooks the relative age of spindles, variations in average yarn counts produced by different countries, relative machine speed and other factors, but it still provides some comparison of spindleage in various areas.

TABLE 454

COTTON MANUFACTURE: NUMBER OF LOOMS IN SELECTED COUNTRIES, 1913–36

(*Thousands*)

Country	Looms, in Thousands			Percentage of Automatic Looms, December 1936
	1913 or 1914	1928 or 1929	December 1936	
World	2,807	3,115	3,070.4	23.7
United States	696	736	573.5	68.6
Canada	31	27	24.8	92.0
Mexico	27	30	29.9	0.3
Brazil	50	79	80.9	8.3
Peru	...	...	4.4	27.3
Argentina	...	...	3.6	55.6
United Kingdom	805	740	504.8	4.1
France	108	193	193.9	21.2
Belgium	24	54	52.0	...
Netherlands	40	52	51.2	10.3
Denmark	...	...	4.0	20.0
Sweden	12	16	15.8	58.0
Norway	...	...	3.0	23.3
Finland	6	7	7.9	22.8
Germany	230	250	200.5	20.3
Poland	31	42	36.3	29.8
Czechoslovakia	...	110 [a]	104.2	3.2
Switzerland	22	27	21.2	28.8
Austria	}170 [b]{	27	11.1	23.4
Hungary		...	14.0	17.9
Portugal	12	22	16.1	6.8
Spain	55	71	66.6 [c]	7.8 [c]
Italy	140	150	146.5 [c]	27.5 [c]
Yugoslavia	...	...	11.6	—
Romania	...	...	14.5	—
Bulgaria	...	...	3.5	—
Greece	...	...	5.3	6.7
USSR [d]	213	159	250.0	13.6
China	6	30	56.2	31.3
Manchukuo	...	...	3.6	...
Korea	...	...	4.5	—
Japan	21	82	332.6	12.0
India and Ceylon	94	167	201.5	21.8
Egypt	...	...	3.3	—
Other countries	...	...	17.6	11.4

Sources: **60**, p. 15; and **65**, July 1937, pp. 4–5.

  a. Including Hungary.
  b. Including Czechoslovakia.
  c. 1933.
  d. Estimate.

Looms

The world's prewar inventory of cotton looms was about 3 million. Of these, Europe had about 48 per cent, North America about 20 per cent and Latin America 4 per cent; Asia had some 20 per cent, and the USSR 8 per cent. The United Kingdom and the United States together had more than a third of the world's looms; next in line were Japan, the USSR, India and Germany. (See Table 454.) The weaving capacity of Japan,

China and India, however, is substantially greater than the data in Table 454 would indicate, because hand looms, widely used in these countries, are not included.

More than seven tenths of the world's looms were nonautomatic. The remainder were either automatic or were provided with automatic attachments. Mills equipped with one or the other type of loom differ greatly in speed of operation and in number of weavers needed. A weaver can tend sixty or more automatic looms but usually only four of the older type.

The percentage of automatic looms has undoubtedly increased in many countries since 1936, but international data are not available. For the United States, the 1947 Census of Manufactures reported 386,521 cotton and cotton-type looms, of which only 8,945, or less than 3 per cent, were nonautomatic.[72] In the United Kingdom, in contrast, only 5 per cent of the looms were automatic before World War II. Generally, countries with an old cotton industry have a higher percentage of nonautomatic looms than those where the industry has been largely established after World War I.

OUTPUT OF COTTON PRODUCTS

About 5 million tons of yarn and from 25 to 30 billion meters of cotton fabrics were produced annually in the world's mills before World War II.[73] The United States accounted for about a fourth of both products. The next largest producers were India, the United Kingdom, the USSR, Japan and Germany.

In 1950 the world's output, after the wartime drop, was approaching the prewar level. The United States produced in that year almost as much cotton cloth as India, the USSR and the United Kingdom together: 9,041 billion meters as against 9,116 billion. The share of the United States increased to about a third of the total. India's output of cotton textiles declined in 1950, because of a shortage of cotton, the closure of some obsolete mills, and labor difficulties. Japanese cotton manufacture is gradually recovering, but the 1950 output was still less than half that of 1938. (See Table 455 and Figure 300.)

The United States

The cotton industry of the United States began to grow in 1812, when war cut off the British market for both exports of raw cotton and imports of cotton cloth. With the return of normal trade, the British flooded the American market with cheap textiles and the United States erected a high tariff wall to protect its young industry.

Behind this wall, the industry continued to develop. By 1850 the United States had more than a thousand mills. With some ups and downs, this number has persisted for a century. Between 1850 and 1900 the value of the output quintupled. The peak in active spindleage (34.9 million) was reached in 1919; since that time, the number has declined considerably. (See Table 456.) A large number of old spindles have been scrapped and replaced by fewer but more efficient spindles. New equipment and longer hours of operation, with two, and sometimes three, shifts, have resulted in the production of equal or larger amounts of yarn.[74]

The number of wage earners has also been increasing, and mechanization has more than doubled the output per worker. Between 1909 and 1939, employment rose from 379,000 to 409,000 and it has been estimated that 237 workers in 1936 could do as much as 600 did in 1910.[75]

Cotton has been and remains the chief fiber in the United States, although mill consumption is smaller than at the peak in 1942. The United States still fabricates twice as much cotton as all other fibers combined. (See Figure 301, A.) Cotton's share in fibers available for use by ultimate consumers is somewhat smaller, because of exports, but it has declined only slightly, to the advantage of rayon.[76] (See Figure 301, B.) The all-time high in per capita consumption was in 1942, with 40.2 pounds; the figure dropped to 28 pounds in 1947, but this was still 3 pounds more than the average in 1935–39.

New England's lead in cotton manufacture was challenged after the turn of the century, and around 1925 the South became the chief center of the industry. The southward movement continued through the depression years and during World War II. Between 1940 and 1945, consumption of cotton by the southern mills increased some 27 per cent, while that of the New England mills declined. (See Table 457 and

---

72. **21**, 1947, Vol. II, p. 169.
73. **14**, 1948, p. 73.

74. In 1925, active spindles averaged 2,599 hours of operation during the year; in 1942, 5,556 hours. **42**, p. 25.
75. **13**, p. 13.
76. **19**, pp. 5 and 14. Imports of manufactured cotton are included.

TABLE 455

COTTON MANUFACTURE: OUTPUT OF COTTON YARN AND FABRICS
IN SELECTED COUNTRIES, 1929–50

Country	Cotton Yarn,[a] in Thousands of Metric Tons					Cotton Fabrics,[b] in Millions of Meters				
	1929	*1938*	*1948*	*1949*	*1950*	*1929*	*1938*	*1948*	*1949*	*1950*
United States [c]	...	1,108 [d]	1,763 [e]	...	...	...	7,578 [d]	8,815	7,686	9,041
Canada	...	54	82	81	96	204	200	229	250	291
Mexico	...	8	6	5	7	...	313	392	347	367
Colombia	...	...	2	1	2	...	74 [f]	166	164	160
Brazil	...	...	168 [e]	...	...	478	846	1,120	...	...
Chile	...	4	3	...	...	...	13	45	52	...
Argentina	...	24	70	70	76	...	...	...	...	...
United Kingdom	...	432	366	373	387	2,958	3,328 [d]	1,768	1,833	1,941
France	...	250	224	228	251	...	1,320	1,253	1,287	1,394
Belgium	69	75	80	84	98	506	407	520	493	610
Netherlands	50	52	55	62	60	...	495	364 [e]	...	...
Sweden	21	28	24	26	28	124	166	155	169	194
Germany [g]	...	369 [f]	119	228	282	...	1,820	631	1,201	1,570
Poland	51	64	82	91	92	301	427 [h]	489	560	573
Czechoslovakia	...	89 [f]	68	76	...	...	462 [h]	495	319	...
Hungary	...	21	23	31	35	...	148	126 [e]	...	...
Portugal	51	64	31	30	36	...	139	214	205	231
Italy	220	178	177	182	183	1,170	1,087	935	911	980
Yugoslavia	...	11 [e]	29	29	29	...	115	162	170	144
USSR [i]	...	699 [h]	...	...	...	2,742 [j]	3,442 [h]	3,098	3,532	3,815
China	...	394	336	200 [k]	...	...	942	...	...	...
Korea [l]	...	27	6	13	10	145	198	26	58	...
Japan	507	554	125	158	238	2,214	2,757	773	823	1,289
Turkey	12	20	29	30	30	...	135	165	177	187
India [m]	378	585	660	603	536	2,212	3,937	4,044	3,480	3,360
Egypt [n]	...	21	33	34	32	...	66	156	152	158
Australia	...	5	12	11	12	...	7 [f]	14	14	17

Sources: **1**, 1948, pp. 195–98; and 1951, pp. 205–08; **14**, 1948, *passim;* **5**, 1949, p. 44 and 1950, p. 249.

a. Includes mixed yarn for France, Belgium, the Netherlands, Sweden, Italy and Japan.

b. Includes mixed fabrics for Belgium, Germany, Yugoslavia, Chile, Brazil, India and Japan. Square meters (one square meter = 1.196 square yards) for Yugoslavia, Japan, Egypt and Australia, Mexico, France, Belgium, Germany, Poland, Portugal, Turkey, Sweden and Italy. For countries reporting output of cotton fabrics in tons, conversion to square meters is made on the basis of 1 ton = 8,300 square meters. Cf. **9**, 1949, Table R in the Appendix.

c. For cotton yarn, total production; data available for census years only. For cotton fabrics, woven goods 12 or more inches in width.

d. 1939.

e. 1947.

f. 1940.

g. Western Germany since 1948.

h. 1937.

i. Estimate (**6**, 1951, p. 128).

j. 1928.

k. Estimate.

l. 1948–50: South Korea.

m. Excludes Pakistan in 1948–50.

n. Excludes fabrics produced on hand looms.

Figure 302.) The South now dominates the industry as New England never did, even in its heyday, accounting for 90 per cent of the country's consumption of cotton, as compared with New England's peak of about 70 per cent.

More than eight tenths of the 21.8 million active cotton spindles in the United States are in cotton-growing states, and almost all the rest are in New England. The Carolinas lead — North Carolina with 6.0 million spindles in place in 1950 and South Carolina with 5.7 million. Georgia and Alabama have recently begun to

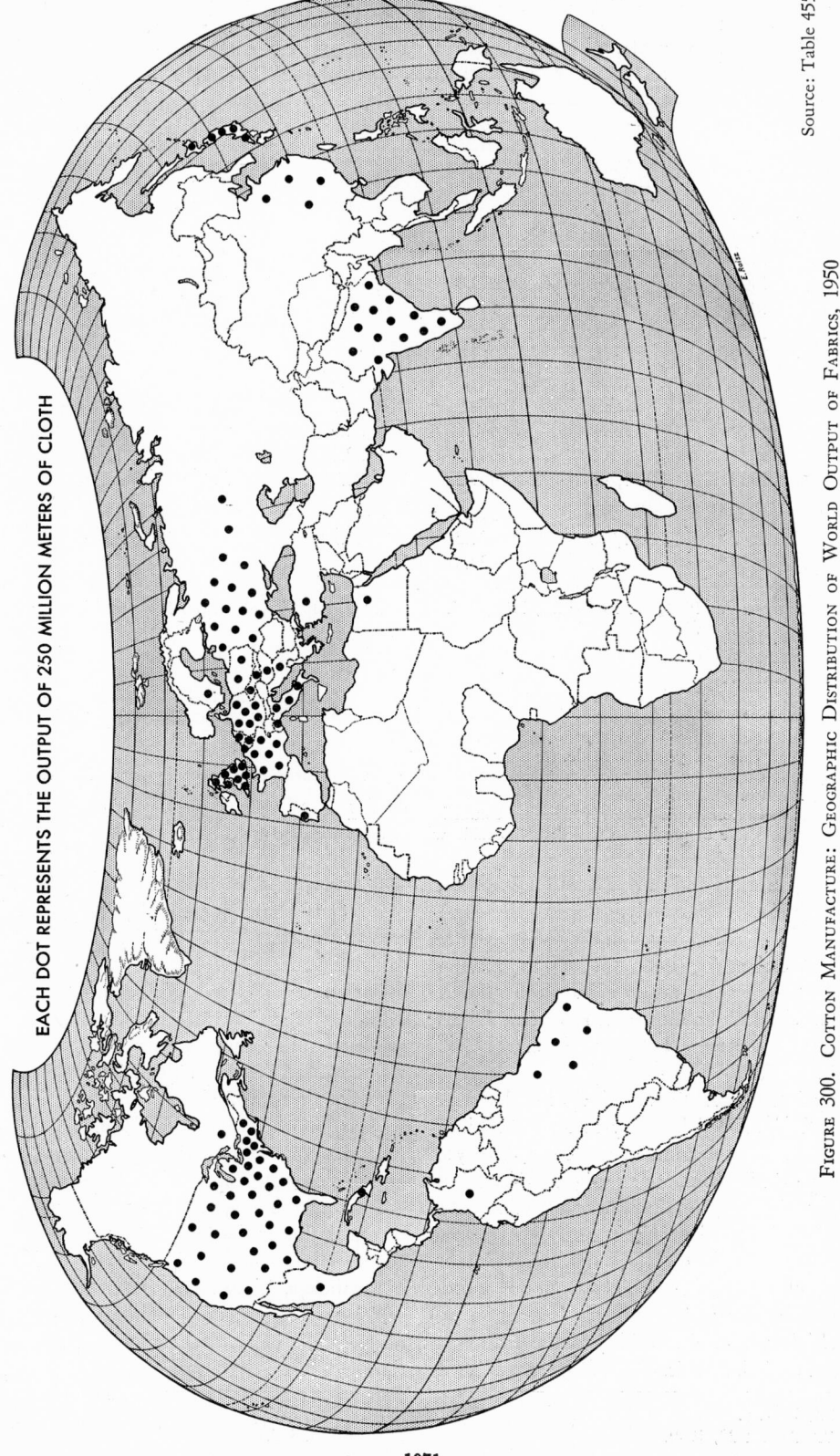

EACH DOT REPRESENTS THE OUTPUT OF 250 MILLION METERS OF CLOTH

Source: Table 455

FIGURE 300. COTTON MANUFACTURE: GEOGRAPHIC DISTRIBUTION OF WORLD OUTPUT OF FABRICS, 1950

TABLE 456

COTTON MANUFACTURE: ESTABLISHMENTS, EMPLOYMENT, EQUIPMENT
AND VALUE OF OUTPUT IN THE UNITED STATES, 1831–1950

Year	Mills	Wage Earners, in Thousands	Active Spindles, in Millions	Looms, in Thousands	Gross Value of Output, in Millions
1831	795	...	1.2	...	$ 32
1840	1,240	...	2.3	...	46
1850	1,094	92.3	4.0	—	66
1860	1,091	122.0	5.2	126	116
1870	956	135.4	7.1	157	177
1880	756	172.5	10.7	226	192
1889	905	218.9	14.4 [a]	325	268
1899	1,055	302.9	19.5 [b]	451	339
1909	1,324	378.9	28.0	633	628
1919	1,452	440.4	34.9	692	2,166
1929	1,502	441.0	32.4	654	1,596
1939	1,248	409.3	23.7	504 [c]	1,168
1939 [d]	986	398.5	...	...	1,061 [e]
1947 [d]	1,006	431.2	22.7 [f]	260 [g]	4,064 [h]
1950 [d]	...	428.8	...	...	...

Sources: **75,** 1941, pp. 16–29; **21,** 1929, Vol. II, *passim* and 1947, Vol. II, pp. 155 and 169.

a. 1890.
b. 1900.
c. 1937.
d. Cotton broad woven fabrics and yarn mills, cotton-system only. The 1947 Census of Manufactures gives no breakdown for other cotton products. 1939 data retabulated on this basis by the Census Bureau are included for comparison.
e. Value of products made.
f. Cotton-system-spinning spindles, although the yarn produced may be made of wool, silk, rayon or synthetic fibers.
g. Cotton looms primarily weaving cotton broad goods.
h. Value of products shipped; comparable with gross value of output.

attract cotton mills and have 3.2 and 1.7 million spindles in place, respectively.[77] (See Figure 303.) Of the 378,767 cotton looms in the United States as of December 31, 1949, the cotton-growing states had 298,678, or nearly eight tenths. South Carolina alone had almost twice as many looms as all the New England states together: 117,382 as against 67,717.[78]

Many factors account for this spectacular shift of a well-established industry to a new region: lower wages, longer hours of work per employee and per spindle (because of night shifts), less difficulty with labor unions, lower taxes and costs of construction, and proximity to raw materials and a large supply of labor. These and other factors have outweighed the advantages of manufacturers in New England: an earlier start, trained labor, natural humidity of the air, availability of capital, technical knowledge, established

outlets for their products, and the concentration of auxiliary plants, such as bleaching or finishing establishments, in the vicinity of the weaving mills.

Only a small number of spindles, about 1.5 million, were shipped from New England to the southern mills; most of the latter's equipment was new.[79] As early as 1929, 80 per cent of the plain looms and 67 per cent of the fancy looms, such as Jacquard and dobby looms, in the southern mills were automatic, as compared with 59 and 33 per cent, respectively, in New England.[80]

Some of the advantages the South offered the cotton industry have been lessened in recent years — for example, relative wage differentials. Nevertheless, it seems clear that New England will never regain its old position and will follow the example of Great Britain in specializing in finer products.

77. **23,** 1951, p. 778.
78. **22,** August 23, 1950.

79. **42,** p. 25.
80. **40,** p. 317.

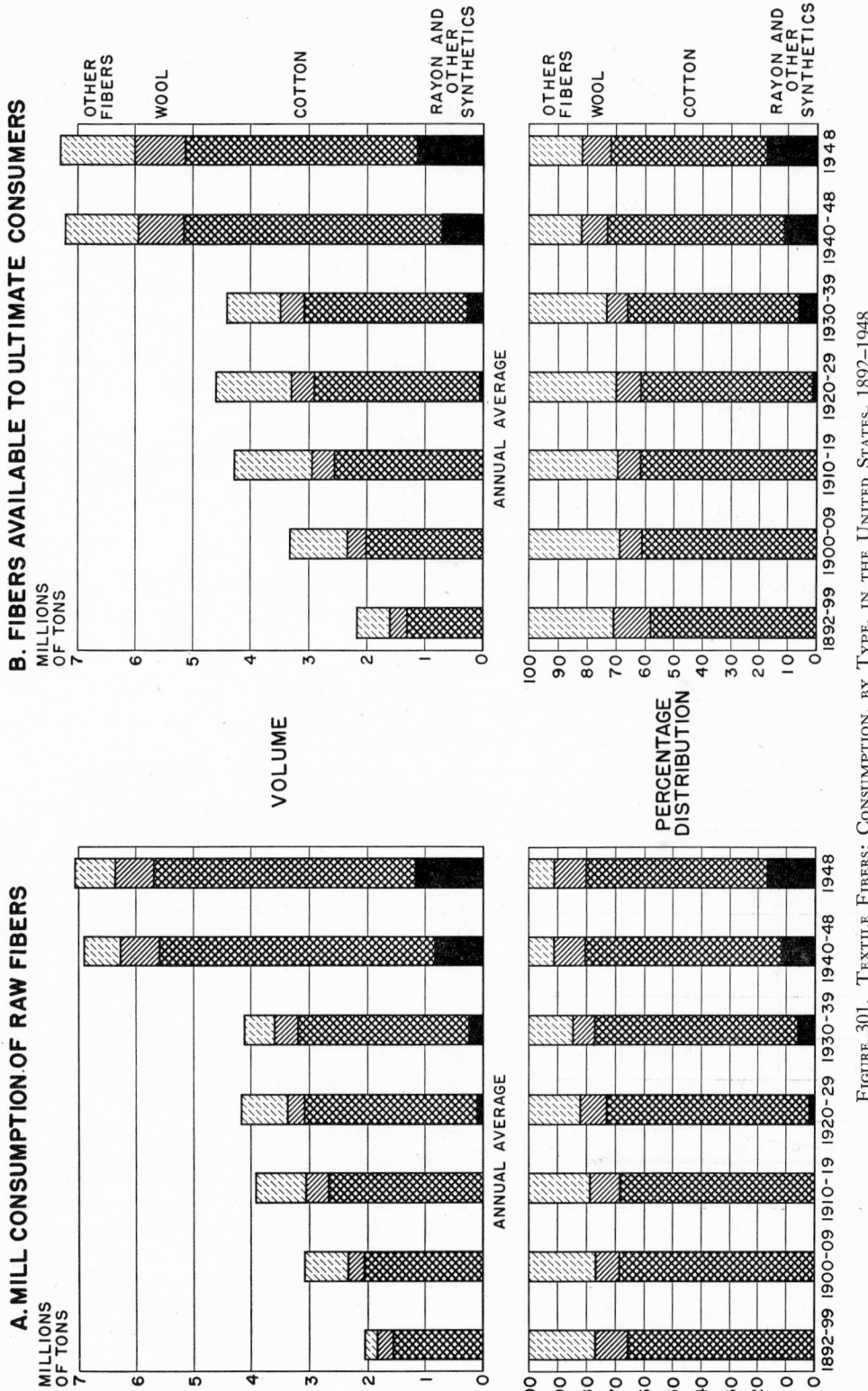

FIGURE 301. TEXTILE FIBERS: CONSUMPTION, BY TYPE, IN THE UNITED STATES, 1892–1948

TABLE 457

COTTON MANUFACTURE: REGIONAL DISTRIBUTION OF ACTIVE SPINDLES AND
MILL CONSUMPTION IN THE UNITED STATES, 1840–1950

	Active Spindles,[a] in Thousands				Mill Consumption of Raw Cotton,[b] in Thousands of Bales			
Year	Total	New England	Cotton-Growing States	Other States	Total	New England	Cotton-Growing States	Other States
1840	2,285	1,597	181	506	237	159	71	7
1860	5,236	3,859	324	1,053	845	567	94	184
1880	10,653	8,632	561	1,460	1,570	1,129	189	252
1900	19,472	13,171	4,308	1,933	3,873	1,909	1,523	440
1910	28,267	15,735	10,494	2,038	4,622	1,995	2,234	393
1920	35,481	18,287	15,231	1,963	6,420	2,397	3,583	440
1930	31,245	11,351	18,586	1,308	6,106	1,143	4,749	214
1940	23,586	5,279	17,641	666	7,784	918	6,647	219
1945	22,675	4,511	17,610	554	9,568	891	8,455	222
1948	22,675	4,429	17,807	439	9,354	887	8,254	213
1949	20,134	3,276	16,491	367	7,795	644	6,986	165
1950	21,790	3,739	17,673	378	8,851	664	8,030	157

Source: **23**, 1951, p. 777.

a. Until 1948, cotton spindles active at any time during the year; later, all cotton-system spindles active on the last day of the year, regardless of type of fiber spun.

b. After 1900, excludes linters.

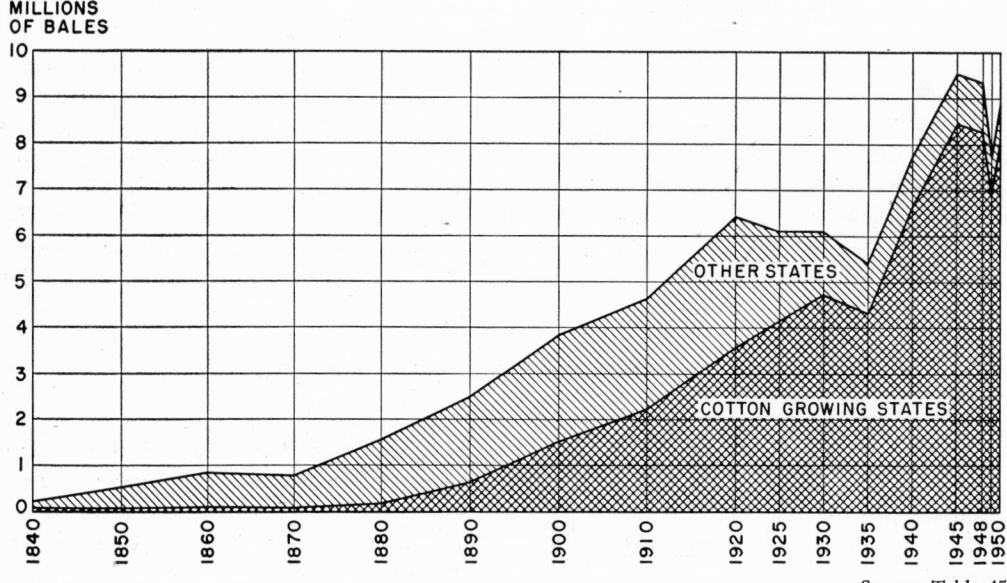

Source: Table 457

FIGURE 302. COTTON MANUFACTURE: MILL CONSUMPTION OF RAW COTTON IN THE UNITED STATES, BY
REGION, IN SELECTED YEARS, 1840–1950

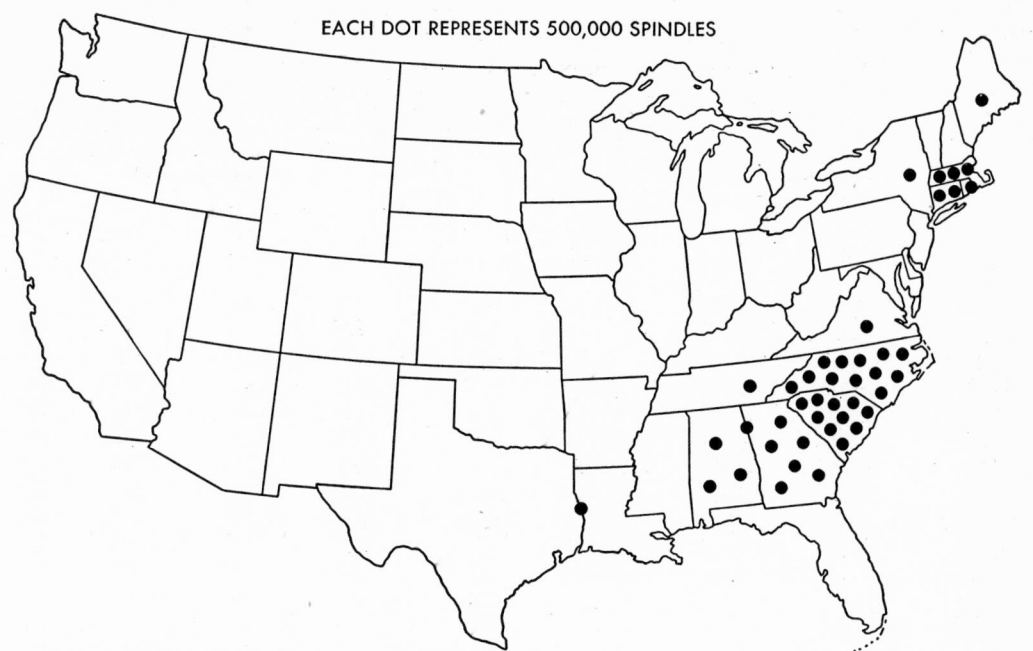

EACH DOT REPRESENTS 500,000 SPINDLES

FIGURE 303. COTTON MANUFACTURE: GEOGRAPHIC DISTRIBUTION OF ACTIVE SPINDLES IN THE UNITED STATES, 1950

New England's mills are larger, on the whole, than those in the South. Among the integrated mills, with both spinning and weaving departments, an average northern mill has 80,000 spindles and 2,000 looms, as against 30,000 spindles and 700 looms in an average southern mill.[81] In textile manufacturing, however, efficiency does not generally entail large-scale operation. Though a factory with less than 25,000 spindles is considered small, a mill with some 10,000 spindles may be efficient.[82]

Taken as a whole, the cotton industry of the United States is among the least concentrated of the country's manufacturing industries: in 1935 the four largest firms accounted for only 8.4 per cent of the total value of the industry's output.[83] The four largest cotton manufacturers had only 4.9 per cent of the industry's total spindleage in 1937.[84]

World War II, however, accelerated the consolidation of ownership and control of production. On the one hand, the federal government awarded many contracts to large plants capable of producing great quantities of needed commodities according to specifications and time schedules. On the other, many sellers of textiles pressed for integration so as to be assured of a supply in times of scarcity and price ceilings. A firm desiring to expand production had to buy existing mills: shortages of equipment and labor, difficulties in obtaining allocations of materials for construction, and high costs of new construction were among the obstacles to building new plants.[85]

The United Kingdom

From the first decades of the eighteenth century until World War I, Great Britain's cotton center, Lancashire, dominated world trade in cotton goods. The English cotton industry provided hundreds of millions of people all over the world with all kinds of cotton goods — yarns and unbleached cloth; bleached, dyed and printed fabrics; and various manufactured products, such as sheets, towels and pillowcases.

In 1850, when the cotton mills in the United States had only 4 million spindles and 92,000 workers, the British cotton industry had 21 mil-

81. **76**, p. 85.
82. **76**, p. 93; **51**, p. 3. Manufacture of synthetic fibers is an exception, since it requires large financial investments, costly equipment, extensive experimental facilities, and high technical and managerial skill.
83. **18**, p. 276.
84. **17**, p. 255.
85. **43**, pp. 401–02.

lion spindles and more than 330,000 workers. It continued to grow, with some fluctuations, until the turn of the century:

	1861	1881	1903
Number of workers, in thousands	451.6	488.7	523.0 [a]
Number of spindles, in millions	30.4	40.4	43.9
Power looms, in thousands	298.8 [b]	550.0	683.6

a. 1904.
b. 1856.

In 1913 the British industry had more than 55 million spindles and more than 800,000 looms. Its output exceeded 12 billion square yards of cloth, of which five sixths were exported. Two thirds of the world's imports of cotton goods then came from the United Kingdom.[86]

Even when the British cotton industry seemed to be at its highest point, it felt the threat of growing competition from the Far East — Japan, India and China. The dislocations resulting from World War I were a severe blow, one from which it has never recovered. Between 1920 and 1938, threats to the Lancashire mills cumulated. Some of Britain's steadiest customers developed cotton manufacture; exports to India, for example, dropped from more than 3 billion yards in 1913 to less than 300 million in 1938. Japan entered into fierce competition, and high tariff walls barred British products from the United States and Brazil. The resulting contraction was of an order and rapidity almost unparalleled in major industry.

In the early 1920's, Lancashire tended to consider the difficulties temporary, a natural aftermath of war. When the world's consumption of cotton began to rise, however, while British exports continued to decline (by 1937 to less than a fifth of the 1913 volume), Lancashire realized that the foundation of its world supremacy had been undermined beyond repair. Many attempts were made to revitalize the sick industry by such measures as price-fixing, elimination of surplus capacity through scrapping and mergers, government subsidies and the Ottawa Agreement on preferential custom rates. Between 1918 and 1940, 800 cotton mills were shut down, 21 million spindles destroyed and 360,000 looms abandoned. These and other measures occasionally

brought some relief, but they did not reverse the trend. To top its difficulties, Lancashire lacked capital to modernize its mills so they could compete effectively with the new mills in younger industrial countries. In 1939, Parliament passed the Cotton Industry Reorganisation Act, designed to create machinery for orderly competition within the industry, but the outbreak of World War II made the act ineffective.[87]

Although World War II subdued its most powerful rival, Japan, at least temporarily, Lancashire's cotton industry now ranks behind that of both the United States and India. Much of the British equipment is obsolete. The mule spindles that made Lancashire famous for the fine quality of its yarn are losing their superiority, and the makers of textile machinery have almost ceased to manufacture them, for lack of demand. Lancashire's looms are predominantly nonautomatic. A substantial part of its machinery is not only old, but actually past working efficiency.

Productivity of labor is much lower than in the United States. The Productivity Team of the British cotton industry found, during its recent visit to America, that operative hours per 100 pounds of yarn produced are 138 per cent higher in the average English mill, and 93 per cent higher in the most efficient mill, than in the United States. The number of spindles per spinner in the United States is 82 per cent greater than in England.[88] The difference in the weaving department is no less striking: a weaver in the United States tends as many as 104 automatic looms, as compared with 16–24 looms in Lancashire. Even considering the variation in types of looms and job assignments, this differential is very great.

The need for modernization is urgent, but the postwar foreign-exchange position of the United Kingdom makes the requisite outlay particularly difficult. Moreover, modernization requires time as well as dollars. The British machinery industry could not provide the 120,000 automatic looms needed in the industry in five years. According to a government investigating committee, it could hardly produce even half that number within twice that time.[89] The cotton industry, moreover, is reluctant to invest in new equipment, which costs two or three times as

---

86. **54**, p. 339.

87. **32**, p. 5; **25**, p. 596.
88. **10**, pp. 58 and 68.
89. **36**, pp. 4–5.

much as it did before the war, while future economies to be obtained from modernization are not too certain.[90]

Germany

The German cotton industry did not begin to grow until the 1870's after Germany captured the mills in Alsace-Lorraine, which had produced France's finest yarn.[91] It counted 4.9 million spindles in 1883, 7.9 million in 1898 and 11.2 million in 1913. The annual consumption of cotton rose from an average of 68,000 metric tons in 1866–90 to 386,000 tons in 1913.

After World War I, Germany had to return Alsace-Lorraine and its mills to France; during the depression of the 1930's its textile capacity declined further. By 1938, German spindleage was at about its 1913 level. Although the output of yarn was greater in 1938, a large part of it was mixed yarn — two parts cotton and one part rayon. Some additional yarn was imported. The German output of cotton fabrics more than met domestic requirements, and a considerable part was exported.

During World War II, many German cotton mills were badly damaged; about a third of the equipment in the Allied zone was destroyed and probably more in the Soviet zone. Much of the machinery has now been repaired or reassembled and many mills are again in operation. Some mill equipment not subjected to air attack was found to be in surprisingly good condition.[92]

Great difficulties have been caused, however, by the division of Germany into two separate economies and the consequent necessity for Western Germany to rebuild its cotton industry on an entirely new basis. Before the war, two thirds of all the cotton workers in Germany were in that area — nearly half of them in the southwestern mills (Bavaria, Württemberg and Baden) and a fifth in Rheinland-Westphalia. Mills in Western Germany, particularly in Rheinland-Westphalia, were heavily bombed and lost a great deal of equipment. The industry suffers also from the loss of many markets that were neglected even in Hitler's time, when the drive to self-sufficiency was at its height. Germany is now trying to regain some of its former markets by producing cotton goods especially designed for them.[93]

Japan

A latecomer, the Japanese cotton industry built its first mill, with 6,000 spindles, in 1866. It had 1.3 million spindles by the turn of the century and the number rose steadily in following decades: 1910, 2.1 million; 1920, 3.8 million; 1930, 7.2 million; and in 1938, the peak year, 12.6 million. In 1934–38 Japan ranked second only to the United States in consumption of raw cotton and third, after the United Kingdom and the United States, in cotton spindleage. On the eve of World War II, it was the largest exporter of cotton goods:[94]

	Exports, in Millions of Square Yards		Percentage of World Exports of Cotton Cloth	
	1912	*1938*	*1912*	*1938*
Japan	210	2,181	2	41
United Kingdom	6,913	1,386	65	30

The main factors in the spectacular rise of the Japanese cotton industry were the abundance of skilled and cheap labor, long hours of work, the practice of the double shift seven days a week, modern machinery, and a tight commercial organization. The industry was controlled to a considerable extent by a few large companies. During World War II, the Big Ten controlled almost the entire industry in all its branches — spinning, weaving, dyeing, finishing.[95]

The ILO has estimated that the labor cost per unit in Japan was not more than a fourth of that in any major cotton-manufacturing country of Europe.[96] Hence, Japan could produce large quantities of inexpensive cotton goods for export to traditional British markets in Asia. The impact on Lancashire was stronger as the lower prices of Japanese goods exerted a general pressure on prices on world markets.

When World War II cut off sources of raw materials and markets for textile goods, Japan decided to scrap its textile equipment and thus obtain metal and floor space for its war industries. Almost 8 million spindles were scrapped, about half a million were sent to occupied areas, and somewhat less than a million were stored.[97] Bombing damaged about as many spindles as Japan put in storage. This was of little concern to

---

90. **14**, 1950, p. 70.
91. **47**, pp. 246 and 296.
92. **34**, p. 2.
93. **11**, September–October 1950, *passim*.

94. **14**, 1948, p. 161.
95. **85**, pp. 9 and 22.
96. **12**, Vol. I, p. 215.
97. **48**, p. 392.

Japan while the war lasted, since all but 44 of 271 mills were converted to munitions factories.[98]

The war radically changed Japan's position in the world's cotton industry. Losses in equipment at home and in China (some 2 million spindles) wiped out almost half a century of development. But despite innumerable difficulties — shortages of cotton, metals and fuel, lack of foreign exchange and loss of prewar outlets — the industry is slowly recovering. Its spindleage increased from 2.2 million in 1946 to 4.5 million early in 1951 and passed the 6 million mark during October of that year. Plans for the immediate future indicated a target of 6.5 million spindles.[99] Moreover, some of the new machinery is more efficient than that used before the war. All the new spindles are of the long-draft type, and some mills have even introduced super-high-draft spinning.[100] Even so, Japan's cotton mills in 1949–50 were only approaching half of the prewar output.

India

India's cotton industry, once world famous for its light and fine hand-made cloth capitulated in the nineteenth century to cheap machine-made fabrics produced elsewhere. The country became dependent on Great Britain for most of its clothing. Before World War I, it imported as much as 60 per cent of the cotton cloth it required. Of the rest, about half was produced in domestic mills and the remainder was home-woven. Between the two world wars, however, India's factory production increased, so that it was able to supply 96 per cent of the country's requirements for cotton yarn and 77 per cent of its cloth.[101]

Long before the establishment of the Indian Union in 1947, cotton manufacture was shifting from its old center in Bombay to up-country areas — Ahmadabad, Nagpur, Delhi. The textile industry had established itself early in Bombay, which offered cheap transportation facilities and benefited from the nearness to sources of raw materials, the existence of big cotton cloth markets in China and Japan, the availability of trained labor, better banking facilities and a humid climate. When, before the end of the nineteenth century, the Chinese and Japanese

markets began to shrink and in the course of a few decades were lost, Bombay's supremacy was undermined. The domestic market grew in importance, and the new mills in up-country areas, more modern and efficient, profited from their location in the center of the consuming area.[102] Ahmadabad, in particular, resembles in geographic situation the great English textile center of the Lancashire region and is therefore often called the "Bolton of the East." Differentials in wages, the cost of fuel and taxes encouraged the industry's shift from Bombay, just as they influenced the move from New England in the United States. Bombay produces cloth mainly of light texture from medium- and high-count yarn, which compares fairly well with the imported British textiles, and is trying to shift to the manufacture of superior types. The mills in Delhi and other up-country centers concentrate on coarser cloth from short-staple cotton.[103]

During World War II, India's cotton industry, freed from Japanese competition, grew rapidly despite the shortage of machinery. Annual cotton consumption in 1940–45 was 40 per cent greater than in 1938–39, and exports of cotton goods rose from 177 million yards a year in the earlier period to 819 million in the later. At the same time, imports fell from 647 million yards to 13 million, and in 1945–46 to 3 million. All in all, India emerged after the war as the second largest producer of cotton goods, exceeded only by the United States.[104] In 1948 the Indian Union had 400 cotton mills, more than 10 million spindles, 265,000 looms and nearly a million workers. In addition, about 1.5 million hand looms were used in the cotton industry.[105]

Immediately after World War II, the output of cotton goods declined, partly because of unsettled political conditions but mostly because of obsolescence of equipment and difficulties in replacing machinery. The domestic demand for textiles has been so great that the government has restricted exports of cotton goods and even arranged to import some 100 million yards of cotton gray goods from Japan. In 1948, mill production of cotton cloth slightly exceeded the 1938 level, but in 1950 was again below that line, be-

98. **85**, p. 10.
99. **50**, December 1951, p. 11.
100. **14**, 1948, p. 23.
101. **12**, Vol. I, p. 175.

102. **59**, pp. 24–25 and 60–61.
103. **59**; **83**, pp. 55–57; **12**, Vol. I, pp. 112–13.
104. **14**, 1948, p. 147. According to the Economic Commission for Europe, the USSR ranked second in cotton manufacture in 1950. Cf. Table 455.
105. **14**, 1950, p. 155.

cause of a shortage of cotton, the closing of some old mills and labor disturbances.[106]

With independence, the Union has become a net importer of raw cotton and relies on Pakistan for a large share of its supply. Second only to the United States in both output and exports of raw cotton before World War II, the subcontinent of India is now divided into two separate economies.[107] India's domestic supply is insufficient in quantity and of a short-staple variety suitable for coarse spinning only. In contrast, Pakistan's cotton has a highly valued long fiber. When difficulties between India and Pakistan arose in 1948–49, India increased its imports of cotton from Egypt and tried to prevent exportation of the domestic crop by increasing export duties.[108] Nevertheless, India's postwar plan has set, as a target, the addition of 4.8 million spindles, construction of scores of new mills, increase in the output of yarn to about 750,000 metric tons (536,000 in 1950) and of cotton cloth, to 8 million meters (output equaled 3.4 million in 1950).[109]

Pakistan

Pakistan inherited fourteen mills with 165,884 spindles and 4,441 looms. It has built four new mills and increased the number of spindles by about 135,000, and the number of looms by some 800. Production in 1950 at full capacity for yarn and 85 per cent of capacity for cloth met only about a tenth of the domestic requirements. The target set for 1954–55 is 24 mills with one million spindles and production of 550 million yards, instead of the current 75 million.[110]

China

China's first cotton mill was built in 1890. In 1913, although foreign capital had been admitted into the industry, China had fewer than a million spindles and only 6,000 looms. As in India and Japan, the cotton industry began to grow after World War I; by 1938, Chinese mills had 4.3 million spindles and nearly 60,000 looms. About half were owned and operated by the Japanese but changed hands after World War II. In 1948 the Chinese cotton industry had 4.4 million op-

erable spindles in 240 mills.[111] China's output of cotton yarn in that year was about 85 per cent of the prewar and in 1949 it dropped by about 40 per cent. Some improvement has been noticeable since the middle of 1950, particularly in the government-owned mills in Shanghai, which account for three fifths of that city's output.

The main centers of the industry are Shanghai, which has half the spindles, Tientsin, Tsingtao and Hankow. They are located in the cotton-producing area of China but ordinarily import part of the raw cotton and cotton yarn they use because the domestic fiber has a very short staple. The coastal blockade and ban on exports to China may affect the industry.[112]

The Chinese cotton industry has always suffered from serious handicaps. Although home-grown, cotton is expensive because of the poor marketing and transportation systems. Management and labor are inefficient and labor costs per unit are high even though wages are low. The Chinese Cotton Control Committee found in 1935 that a bale of 20's yarn produced in a Chinese-owned mill cost $16, as against $7.46 in the Japanese-owned plants, although the latter paid somewhat higher wages.[113]

Russia (USSR)

At the turn of the century, Russia had 6 million cotton spindles. Raw cotton and cotton yarn were imported, but the value of exported cotton cloth was double that of the imports. Supplies of domestic cotton from Turkistan were increasing, and large irrigation works were in progress to expand cotton growing. By 1913, the Russian cotton industry (not including the Polish and Finnish provinces) ranked fourth in the world and consumed about 1.5 million bales of raw cotton, as much as the German mills. Russia produced 14.9 per cent of Europe's output of cotton goods, as compared with Britain's 28.6 per cent and France's 10.0 per cent.[114]

The greatly increased military requirements for cotton goods during World War I encouraged further development of the industry. In 1917, it counted 9.6 million spindles and 213,179 looms and its cotton consumption had risen to 1.9 mil-

---

106. **5**, 1950, p. 249.

107. Cf. Chapter 17, pp. 601–02.

108. **5**, 1949, pp. 45–46.

109. **85**, p. 64; **39**, pp. 238–39.

110. **5**, 1950, p. 249; **65**, April-May 1951, p. 153.

111. **85**, p. 58.

112. **5**, 1949, pp. 44–45.

113. Production costs of textile mills in Japan amounted, before World War II, to about a third of those in India, according to the findings of the Indian Tariff Board.

114. **68**, p. 37; and **44**, p. 608.

lion bales. By that time most of the cotton used was domestic, from Turkistan and the Transcaucasus. During the civil war that followed, the cotton industry, like others, waned. Of about 7.2 million spindles in 1924, only 2.7 million were active.[115]

The industry resumed its progress in the 1930's. Both raw cotton and yarn were produced domestically. By 1938, the output of the mills totaled 3.5 billion square meters of gray cloth. During World War II, the USSR is reported to have lost more than 3 million spindles, of which a large part must have been in cotton mills. The output of cotton goods declined 60 per cent from 1940 to 1945, more because of shortages of manpower and fuel than because of military destruction. The output in 1947 was about 72 per cent of that in 1938.[116]

The 1950 target set by the fourth Five-Year Plan was 4.7 billion square meters of cotton fabric. If this goal had been achieved,[117] the USSR would have had about the same per capita output as Russia had in 1899 — 4.7 billion square meters for a population of more than 190 million, as compared to 3.4 billion meters for a population of 130 million.[118]

France

The French cotton industry dates from the second half of the eighteenth century, when its main branch was the printing of imported calico (*indienne*). The development of other branches was retarded by the French Revolution and the Napoleonic wars. Spinning and weaving did not begin until the second quarter of the nineteenth century. By 1847, France had some 3.5 million spindles; by 1867, 6.8 million spindles and 80,000 power looms. Even the loss of the Alsatian mills did not stop the growth of the industry. From 124,000 tons in 1869, cotton consumption rose to 216,000 metric tons in 1897 and 319,000 in 1909. On the eve of World War I, the northeastern area, including Lille, Roubaix and Tourcoing, had complete modern equipment and operated a third of France's 7.6 million spindles and more than half of its 113,300 looms.[119] The return of Alsace in 1918 at once increased the capacity

of the industry, and before World War II it was second only to the German in continental Europe. It ranked first after the war, but returned to second place after the recovery of the textile industry in Western Germany.

Latin America

In many Latin American countries — Argentina, Brazil, Mexico, Chile, Peru and so on — the cotton industry is now able to meet all domestic requirements for at least the popular types of fabrics. In many of them, the beginnings of the industry go back to the late decades of the nineteenth century or the early years of the twentieth. With some exceptions, little progress has been achieved since that period in modernizing equipment. Most of the machinery is obsolete, techniques of production are antiquated, and productivity is low.

Brazil has the largest industry, with more spindles than all the other Latin American countries combined: in 1913, 1.2 million spindles; in 1938, 2.7 million spindles and more than 80,000 looms; in 1951, 3.3 million and 100,000, respectively. Until recently, 91 and 95 per cent, respectively, of this equipment was of old types. Lately, replacement of some old spindles has lowered the proportion of obsolete spindles to 73 per cent.[120] Only 5 per cent of the looms are automatic; most of these are in São Paulo, which is notable for the modernity of its equipment.[121] The remaining looms are of the hand shuttle-change type, so that a weaver normally tends only two or three looms. In 1949 it was reported that a new mill with a fully modern layout and 80,000 spindles was nearing completion and would be one of the largest in South America.[122]

Brazil's output of cotton goods in 1948 was about a third greater than in 1938 (1.1 billion meters of cloth as compared with 0.8 billion). Exports rose in this period from 7 million yards to 160 million. Yarn, previously imported, is now produced by domestic mills.[123] This industry is protected by high tariffs.

Brazil is planning to increase its spindleage to 6 million and to more than double its output of cotton textiles. Half the projected output is assigned to export.

115. **65**, September 1924, pp. 54-55; and October 1925, pp. 26–27.

116. **14**, 1948, p. 127.

117. The 1950 output was almost 20 per cent below it. (See Table 455.)

118. **72**, Vol. II, pp. 132–33.

119. **47**, pp. 245–48.

120. **2**, p. 255.

121. **3**, p. 3.

122. **94**, p. 162; see also **93**.

123. **14**, 1948, p. 157.

Mexico's cotton industry is second to that of Brazil. The condition of its machinery is about the same as that of Brazil: 85 per cent of its spindles are old and 95 per cent of its looms non-automatic. Most of the mills produce manta, a heavy cotton cloth made from coarse yarn used by the native population. The sellers' market for textiles during and after World War II sent prices up and encouraged the building of fifteen new modern plants and the re-equipment of many old ones. This was possible only because the new mills, established at a time of great demand for labor, have not been subjected to the rigid labor legislation applied to the old mills. To give one example of the type of legislation: since 1912, it has been stipulated that a tender in the carding section may attend no more than eight machines and must be paid in proportion to output. A Mexican manufacturer who installed a few attachments and reorganized the work load to forty cards, as in other countries, would have to pay the carding-tender five times his normal wage and compensate the four surplus tenders.[124] Under such conditions, speedy modernization can hardly be expected.

In contrast, Chile's young cotton industry benefits from its later establishment. About three fourths of the country's spinning capacity and nearly half its weaving capacity were installed after 1938 and are entirely modern. The industry is favored by restriction on imports, except for the raw material, cotton, which is not grown in Chile. In 1938, six tenths of the textiles were imported, but in one decade the industry developed so vigorously as to meet domestic demand almost fully. It is concentrated in three areas: Santiago (79 per cent), Concepción (12 per cent) and Valparaíso (9 per cent).[125] Nevertheless, the productivity of Chile's modern industry is 30 per cent below the maximum productivity that can be obtained with old equipment. In fact, in many old mills in other Latin American countries productivity is higher than the average achieved by Chile's modern establishments.[126]

Argentina's cotton industry dates from long before World War I, but it developed so slowly that in 1930 it supplied only about 9 per cent of the country's textile requirements. Rapid progress coincided with the depression and was accentuated by World War II. In 1940 the in-

dustry's output met 57 per cent of domestic consumption; in 1945, 86 per cent; and in 1950 it satisfied the entire national demand for textiles except for certain fine fabrics. The industry has no problem of obsolete equipment, since 90 per cent of the spindles were installed after 1930. About half the spinning mills are small (with fewer than 10,000 spindles each) and account for about 18 per cent of the total output; more than 97 per cent of the weaving mills are small establishments, together contributing only about a third of the national output. Many of the small mills work for large establishments.[127]

Peru has a small cotton industry, about the same size as Chile's. It differs from the industry in other Latin American countries in that nearly every degree of modernity of machinery can be found in its mills. Manufacturers in neighboring countries have generally built new mills while old mills continued in operation, but Peruvian producers have modernized their old mills by installing new equipment gradually. Most of the technical personnel have come from the United States and England, and the industry has been granted less protection than in other Latin American countries, a situation that has encouraged competition and better management.[128] Domestic cotton is of excellent quality.

According to a United Nations mission to Latin America, output in the cotton industry in all the countries surveyed is considerably lower than is warranted by the number of employees. The two main causes, about equally significant, are obsolescence of equipment and inadequate organization of work. The second category includes excessive employment, antiquated working methods, poor layout of rooms, inadequate or no control of humidity, lack of cleanliness, poor quality control or none at all, lack of training facilities, lack of technical personnel, and so on. There are some efficiently managed mills, of course, but considering the cotton industry as a whole, the mission's conclusions point to the need for thorough reorganization. Unless an intensive effort is made to change the entire operational system within the industry, even modernization of its equipment will not produce the desired results. Moreover, Latin American countries have little foreign currency for the purchase of new equipment and must often divert the available capital to more pressing needs. The mission

124. **3**, pp. 81–84.
125. **3**, p. 3.
126. **3**, p. 51.

127. **2**, 1949, pp. 176–77.
128. **3**, p. 105.

therefore gave priority in its recommendations to the importance of administrative reorganization, which would increase productivity without requiring substantial investments.[129]

WOOL MANUFACTURE

In contrast to the cotton industry, the development of woolen manufacture in almost all countries has been based on domestic raw materials. Long before the Industrial Revolution, the wool industry was a flourishing handicraft in England, Germany, France, Belgium and the Netherlands. Continental countries imported fine English wool, and "all Europe was clothed in English wool bought in Flanders." [130]

The wool industry, older and more prosperous than the cotton industry, proved less receptive to technical progress, but its growth was stimulated after 1830 by the increasing imports of wool from Australia and later also from South America and South Africa.[131] Before World War I, two thirds of the wool processed by European mills came from overseas. In England, the domestic clip provided some two thirds of the wool consumed in 1850–51 but only 10 per cent in 1936.[132]

In the United States, the domestic clip met 70–75 per cent of the mill requirements for apparel wool in the nineteenth century. The proportion dropped to 53 per cent in the 1920's, and about 26 per cent in 1950.[133] Most carpet wool is imported.

CONSUMPTION OF RAW WOOL

In prewar years, the world (without the USSR) consumed 855,000 tons of clean raw wool annually. The United Kingdom was the largest consumer, followed by the United States, France and Germany. In 1950, world consumption was about 30 per cent greater. The United States, having almost doubled its consumption, accounted for about half the increase. Consumption of wool by British mills rose approximately 20 per cent; French mill consumption remained about the same; and Japan used about half the prewar amount. Argentina, Italy, Turkey, New Zealand and Australia doubled their consumption of wool, while the Netherlands, Ireland, Denmark, Sweden and Uruguay showed even greater increases. Consumption of wool in Western Germany was rising steadily. (See Table 458.)

The two main branches of wool manufacture, worsteds and woolens, use different processes and different kinds of wool. In making worsteds, wool goes through a series of processes, with tops as an intermediate product, before yarn is produced. In making woolens, it is spun directly into yarn. The longer fibers, kept parallel to one another, are preferred for worsted yarn, while woolen yarn is made of fibers of all lengths and wool of various grades. Woolen cloth permits greater variety in dyeing and finishing than worsted and takes brighter colors.

Wool is used predominantly for apparel. The United States uses 78 per cent of all its wool products for this purpose; Germany, 71 per cent. The use of wool for clothing has been declining, however, particularly in the United States, because of better heating of homes and offices and the heating of automobiles.

MILL EQUIPMENT

The equipment for wool manufacturing is much more complex than that for cotton. Both the drawing and the combing of wool, for example, require nine operations by different machines. It is expected, however, that recent inventions will simplify the processing of woolen and worsted fibers and bring it closer to operations in the cotton industry. Adjustments must often be made in wool machinery to meet changes in style, which frequently call for a different grade of wool or a new weave. Fashion is much more important in the manufacture of wool than of cotton, for most style changes affect only the finishing of cotton — for example, the printing.[134]

Before World War II, nearly three fourths of all wool machinery was concentrated in the factories of five leading countries — the United States, the United Kingdom, France, Germany and Japan. (See Table 459.)

In the United States, much machinery was scrapped or replaced between the two world wars. Nearly all narrow looms were discarded because of the growing preference for wider cloth; the number was reduced from 18,984 in

---

129. **3**, *passim*.

130. **74**, p. 2; **25**, p. 616.

131. Cf. Chapter 18, pp. 643–47; **69**, p. 56.

132. From a third to a half of the home-produced wool is exported, but now British sheep are generally raised for mutton and lamb, rather than for wool. **33**, p. 35.

133. **23**, 1951, p. 644.

---

134. **76**, pp. 219–20.

TABLE 458

WOOL MANUFACTURE: CONSUMPTION OF WOOL IN SELECTED COUNTRIES,
1934–38 ANNUAL AVERAGE AND 1948–50

(*Thousands of Metric Tons* [a])

Country	1934–38	1948	1949	1950
World [b]	855.0	1,080.0	1,020.0	1,120.0
United States	149.7	319.8	231.8	288.9
Canada	9.1	18.1	15.4	13.2
Uruguay	1.4	3.6	4.5	4.5
Argentina	16.3	27.2	31.8	29.5
Other Latin American countries	14.1	19.5	24.0	23.1
United Kingdom	197.3	219.1	223.2	235.0
Ireland	0.9	3.6	3.2	3.2
France	105.2	116.1	118.8	110.7
Belgium	27.2	27.7	26.8	33.1
Netherlands	4.5	17.7	18.1	16.8
Denmark	0.9	2.7	3.6	3.6
Sweden	5.0	12.2	13.2	13.6
Germany [c]	81.6	21.3	41.3	58.1
Poland	15.9	15.4	15.9	15.9
Czechoslovakia	10.9	9.1	6.4	4.5
Switzerland	5.4	8.2	6.8	8.2
Austria	5.9	5.4	5.9	9.1
Portugal	4.5	5.9	4.5	3.6
Spain	15.9	20.4	21.8	19.5
Italy	25.9	61.7	54.0	57.2
USSR [d]	70.0	75.0	90.0	90.0
China	18.0	20.0	20.0	20.0
Japan	49.0	4.5	7.3	23.1
Turkey	9.1	18.1	18.1	18.1
Other Asiatic countries	34.0	33.1	31.8	32.7
Union of South Africa	0.5	4.1	5.0	5.4
Other African countries	5.4	10.0	9.5	10.0
Australia	15.9	36.3	34.0	31.8
New Zealand	1.8	3.2	3.6	3.6

Sources: **1**, 1951, p. 298; for China and the USSR, estimates of the FAO (**9**, 1949, p. 91; and
7, pp. 16–17).

    a. Conversion factors: one metric ton = 1.1023 short tons = 2,204.6 pounds. Clean wool.
    b. Excludes the USSR.
    c. 1948–50: Western Germany.
    d. Includes the Baltic states.

1919 to 1,776 in 1946.[135] Automatic broad looms largely replaced the nonautomatic type. The number of spindles dropped from 2.4 million in 1919 to 1.6 million in 1946 and declined likewise in the United Kingdom.

OUTPUT OF WOOL PRODUCTS

International data on wool manufacture are even less satisfactory than for cotton. Some countries report the output of all yarn made of wool, others of worsted yarn only, still others of wool yarn mixed with other fibers or made of waste. The data on woolen fabrics are even more heterogeneous. Reported in tons, meters and square meters, they relate either to all-wool fabrics or include all cloth containing a given percentage of wool — 25 per cent or more, 50 per cent or more, and so on.

135. **90**, pp. 45–49.

TABLE 459

WOOL MANUFACTURE: MILL EQUIPMENT IN SELECTED COUNTRIES, 1937–38

Country	Combs	Spindles, in Thousands			Looms
		Total	Woolen	Worsted	
United States [a]	2,494	3,492	1,536	1,956	41,465
Canada [b]	23	94	77	17	1,997
Mexico [c]	32	. . .	. . .	. . .	1,485
Argentina [b]	60	150	85	65	2,800
United Kingdom	2,800	5,600	2,600	3,000	98,000
France	3,000	2,742	626	2,116	40,000
Belgium	700	826	376	450	7,500
Netherlands [b]	. . .	250	. . .	. . .	5,758
Denmark	. . .	100	85	15	1,100
Sweden [d]	. . .	277	. . .	. . .	3,900
Norway	12	93	85	8	1,444
Germany [b]	3,553	5,637	2,426	3,211	96,313
Poland	458	799	325	474	13,700
Czechoslovakia	100	857	. . .	. . .	7,400
Switzerland	160	210	60	150	3,600
Hungary	28	103	71	32	2,100
Portugal	92	165	99	66	2,156
Spain [c]	365	391	265	126	11,900
Italy	946	1,171	624	547	19,500
Yugoslavia	106	81	63	18	1,445
Romania	20	129	90	39	4,300
Bulgaria [b]	161	44	. . .	. . .	1,254
Greece [b]	. . .	42	17	25	1,350
USSR [c]	199	434	259	175	11,917
Turkey [d]	44	46	30	16	1,000
Japan	1,355	1,249	121	1,128	29,421
India [a]	. . .	75	41	34	1,595
Australia	319	393	. . .	. . .	4,332

Source: **74,** p. 505.

a. 1941.   b. 1936.   c. 1934.   d. 1935.

In 1937–38 the world's output of wool yarn was about 1.3 million tons.[136] The United States, the United Kingdom and Germany accounted for almost half the total. In 1950 the total output was somewhat smaller: the increase in the United States, the USSR and in a few other countries was more than offset by the sharp decline in Germany and Japan.

The world's prewar output of woolen fabrics totaled some 1.3–1.5 billion meters. The United States and the United Kingdom were the largest producers, followed by France and Japan. In 1950 the United States accounted for about a third of the total, and the United Kingdom for somewhat more than a fifth. The output in Japan had dropped to 30 per cent of that in 1938, but many European countries were producing more than before the war. (See Table 460 and Figure 304.)

The United States

Manufacture of wool in the United States began late in the eighteenth century. The American Indians had no sheep, and the few animals brought to the country in the early days suffered from the cold New England winters. Exportation of sheep from England was forbidden in 1660, and the ban was not lifted until 1765. Im-

136. The output of wool yarn exceeds the consumption of clean new wool in countries where reclaimed wool is used, as in Germany and the United Kingdom (see Chapter 17, pp. 609, 611), or where yarn is produced from mixed fibers.

TABLE 460

WOOL MANUFACTURE: OUTPUT OF YARN AND FABRIC IN SELECTED COUNTRIES, 1938–50

Country	Yarn,[a] in Thousands of Tons				Fabric,[b] in Millions of Meters			
	1938	1948	1949	1950	1938	1948	1949	1950
United States	262.2 [c]	361.8	312.0	363.7	301.0	455.0	379.0	408.0
Canada	4.1	8.4	7.1	7.2	13.1	24.3	22.0	20.7
Brazil	...	...	...	...	6.4	13.6 [d]	...	...
Chile	...	1.3	...	...	3.4	7.9	...	...
United Kingdom	101.7 [c]	227.5	239.7	252.1	290.0	244.0	258.0	264.0
Ireland	1.4	4.5	4.0	...	2.6	5.1	4.7	5.5
France	118.0	133.0	123.0	127.0	260.5	277.2	263.8	261.4
Belgium	25.8	34.1	35.6	40.2	50.9	63.3	69.8	86.2
Netherlands	9.7	21.9	23.5	...	...	...	...	...
Denmark	4.9	10.7	11.7	...	7.6	13.9	14.9	...
Sweden	10.5	17.5	17.8	17.3	31.1	46.2	47.0	45.7
Norway	4.2	6.7	7.4	...	9.2	13.7	14.9	...
Finland	1.5	1.7	1.8	...	7.2	14.5	15.5	...
Germany [e]	170.2 [c]	38.3	65.1	85.0	...	83.8	141.7	196.7
Poland	34.2 [c]	33.2	38.6	41.9	68.2 [c]	76.5	91.7	...
Czechoslovakia	27.2 [c]	32.0	35.4	...	39.5 [c]	...	47.8	...
Austria	13.5 [c]	6.8	8.4	11.0	35.3 [c]	14.1	20.7	23.4
Hungary	11.6	7.7	8.0	12.0	20.0	9.8 [f]	...	...
Portugal	2.5 [g]	5.8	4.5	3.9	5.3 [g]	7.3	6.2	2.1
Spain	14.7 [h]	13.6	8.8	10.0	...	...	...	...
Yugoslavia	6.0 [g]	13.0	13.3	13.1	9.8 [g]	26.0	27.9	24.4
Greece	1.6	2.7	3.8	...	9.0	7.7	10.9	...
USSR	6.5	...	...	...	105.0 [c]	136.0	162.0	167.0
Japan	53.7	11.0	16.5	32.5	222.0	21.2	28.7	66.0
Turkey	4.5	7.5	7.9	7.5	10.3	21.0	20.4	14.3
India	...	...	...	...	...	29.7	31.0	26.7
Australia	13.7	23.4	23.0	21.9	24.8	34.4	34.1	32.5
New Zealand	0.3	0.6	0.9	...	1.7	2.6	2.5	...

Sources: **1**, 1951, pp. 209–11; **6**, 1951, p. 28.

a. Includes mixed yarn for Norway, Denmark, the Netherlands, Ireland and Hungary; mixed and carpet yarn for the United States; mixed yarn and yarn made from waste for France and Sweden; worsted yarn for Canada.

b. Includes fabrics with various percentages of wool: 25 per cent or more for the United States; 50 per cent or more for Austria, Denmark, France, Norway, Sweden, Poland, Canada and Brazil; 15 per cent of wool or other animal hair for the United Kingdom. Square meters (one square meter = 1.196 square yards) for Austria, Belgium, Czechoslovakia, Norway, Denmark, Finland, France, Germany, Ireland, Poland, Sweden, Yugoslavia, Turkey, Japan and Australia. For countries reporting output in tons, conversion to square meters was made by the coefficient of the FAO (UN): 2.56 tons = 10,000 square yards. (**9**, p. 113.)

c. 1937.

d. 1946.

e. Includes the Saar in 1938; for 1948–50: Western Germany.

f. 1947.

g. 1939.

h. 1940.

migrant English combers and carders made cloth in the new country from British wool.[137] The first mills in the United States were soon closed; they could not compete with imported British fabrics because of the poor quality of the domestic wool and the lack of skilled labor.

In the nineteenth century, the importation of

sheep of the best breeds from France, Spain and England contributed to the domestic supply of wool, although the finest grades had to be imported from Germany and Spain. At the same time, equipment was improved. Spinning was made semiautomatic, power looms were introduced and the finishing of woolen cloth was improved. Consumption of raw wool grew from 15 million pounds in 1830 to 189 million in 1869.

137. **90**, p. 2.

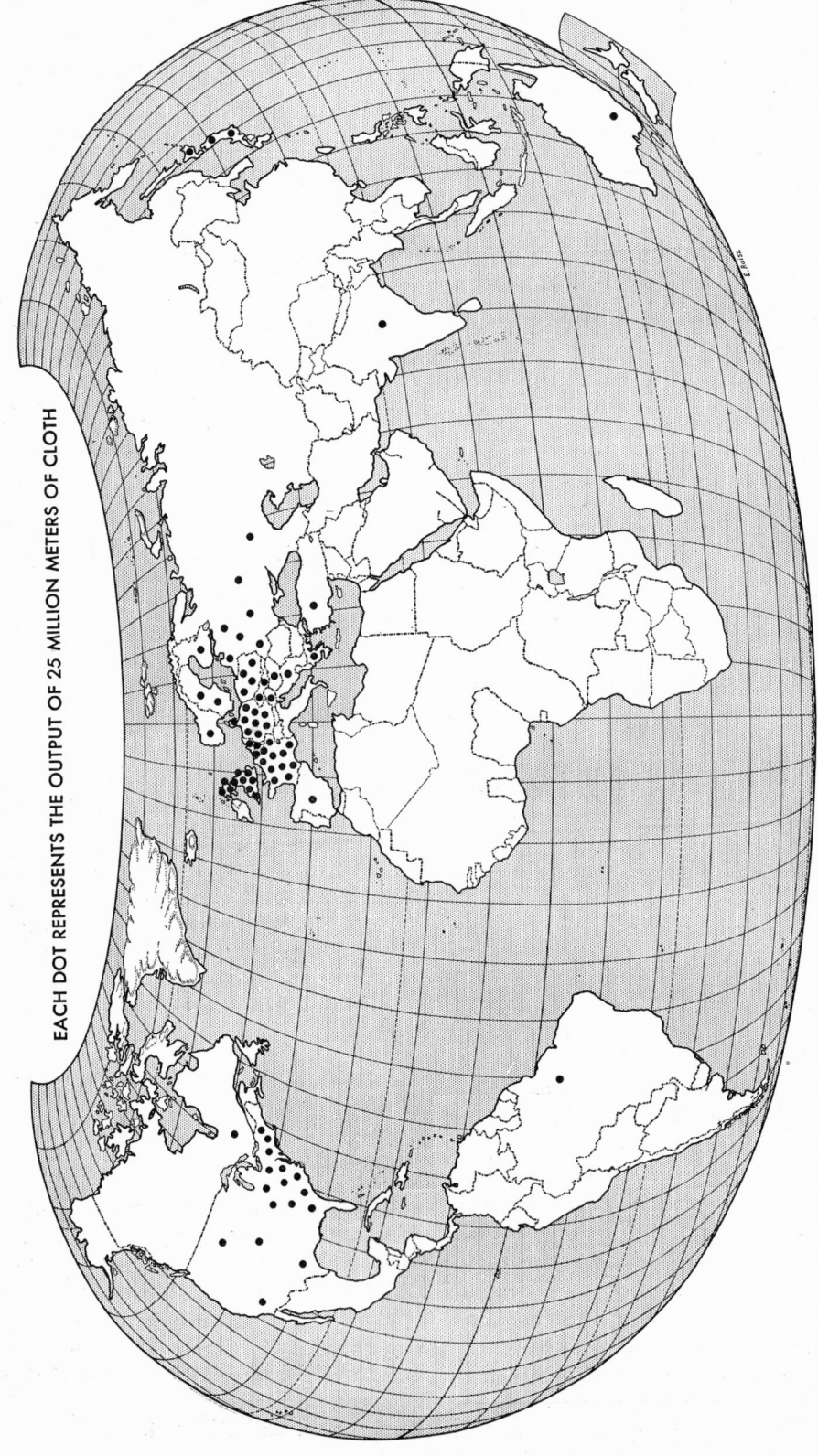

EACH DOT REPRESENTS THE OUTPUT OF 25 MILLION METERS OF CLOTH

Figure 304. Wool Manufacture: Geographic Distribution of World Output of Fabrics, 1950

TABLE 461

WOOL MANUFACTURE: SUPPLY OF WOOL IN THE
UNITED STATES, 1871–1950

(Millions of Pounds)

Annual Average, or Year	Total Supply	Domestic Production	Net Imports [a]
1871–1880	249.9	186.3	63.6
1881–1890	371.9	280.7	91.2
1891–1895	460.8	309.4	151.4
1896–1900	435.5	271.8	163.7
1901–1905	476.6	298.5	178.1
1906–1910	520.0	321.1	198.9
1911–1915	543.8	309.2	234.6
1916–1920	686.7	294.5	392.1
1921–1925	603.7	283.1	320.7
1926–1930	606.1	364.3	241.8
1931–1935	569.5	431.1	138.3
1936–1940	680.8	425.3	255.5
1941–1945	1,375.0	428.5	740.9
1946	1,391.0	341.8	1,049.2
1947	937.0	309.4	627.6
1948	1,036.5	280.5	755.9
1949	671.3	252.5	418.8
1950	962.3	252.5	709.8

Source: **23**, 1950, p. 656, and 1951, p. 644.

a. Until 1934, general imports; thereafter, imports for consumption.

Manufacture of worsteds did not begin until 1850. The 1860 census reported three worsted mills. By 1870, factory production of both woolen and worsted cloth was well established, under the protection of high tariffs.

Technical progress was rapid and resulted in an almost complete mechanization of manufacturing processes. In particular, the mechanization of combing, previously performed by hand and almost prohibitive in cost, stimulated the development of the worsted branch. The domestic supply of raw wool was insufficient to satisfy the increasing demand, and imports increased decade by decade, particularly during and immediately after the two world wars. (See Table 461.)

In 1939 the output of wool products in the United States was valued at nearly a billion dollars — $736 million in woolens and worsteds, $160 million in wool carpets, rugs and carpet yarns, and the remainder in felt hat bodies and hats, processed wool waste and the like. The value of woolen and worsted fabrics alone rose from $536 million in 1939 to $1,355 million in 1947. As the following figures show, the output of the woolen branch once greatly exceeded that of the worsted in value, but since 1909 worsteds have been in the lead (figures in millions):[138]

	Woolen Mills	Worsted Mills
1859	$ 61.8	$ 3.7
1869	155.5	22.0
1879	160.6	33.5
1889	133.5	79.1
1899	118.4	120.3
1909	107.1	312.6
1919	364.9	700.5
1929	285.9	515.4
1933	150.2	307.7

The woolen and worsted industry of the United States is concentrated in New England and the Middle Atlantic states, where four fifths of the country's 495 mills as of 1947 were located. Massachusetts leads in production. Boston in particular and Philadelphia, Chicago and New York are the main wool markets. Boston has the country's largest wool warehouse, which can store about a third of the nation's clip. New England's

138. **46**, p. 2; **23**, 1938, p. 758. No comparable data are available for later years.

TABLE 462

WOOL MANUFACTURE: MILL EQUIPMENT IN THE UNITED STATES,
BY REGION, 1949

Region	Woolen and Worsted Looms	Wool Carpet and Rug Looms	Spindles,[a] in Thousands	Worsted Combs
United States	37,493	5,208	3,260	2,720
New England	21,695	880	2,017	1,915
Middle Atlantic states	8,090	3,909	754	671
Southern states	4,654	[b]	262	[b]
North Central states	2,532	[b]	185	[b]
Western states	522	[b]	44	[b]

Source: **24**, p. 2.

    a. Excludes American System spindles operated in cotton mills.
    b. Data for southern, north central and western states cannot be shown separately without disclosing the equipment of individual companies, but are included in the total.

mills have about two thirds of all the looms, combs and spindles; the Middle Atlantic states, some 20–25 per cent. (See Table 462 and Figure 305.)

Production of woolen and worsteds, although more highly concentrated in ownership than that of cotton, includes many small independent firms. In 1935 the four largest producers accounted for 24.2 per cent of the total output; in 1947, for 28.1 per cent.[139]

The United Kingdom

From 1700 until very recent times, the United Kingdom was the largest producer and exporter of woolens. Mechanization of the industry proceeded slowly, however, and in 1850 only about half its 250,000 workers were employed in factories.[140] The number of employees remained almost constant until World War II, while output rose with the increase in mechanization; the same number of workers processed 240 million pounds of wool in 1851 and 850 million pounds in 1911. In 1944–45 only about 126,000 workers were employed, half as many as in 1850, but employment had almost regained its prewar level by 1950.

West Riding is as representative of the British woolen and worsted industry as Lancashire is of the cotton.[141] It accounts for more than nine

tenths of all the mills in the worsted branch and two thirds in the woolen; the remaining mills are widely scattered, in Scotland, western England and Lancashire.

The total value of woolen and worsted goods produced in the United Kingdom was $636 million in 1924, $438 million in 1930 and $476 million in 1935. About 70 per cent of these amounts represented finished goods, some 15 per cent semifinished, and the rest yarns.

Since the beginning of this century, output has declined, on the whole, as follows (in millions of square yards):[142]

	Woven Tissues	Flannels and Delaines
1907	530	76
1912	573	68
1924	440	26
1930	324	16
1937	426	20

British exports of woolen and worsted goods likewise declined between 1912 and 1938, from 63 million pounds of yarn to 28 million, and from 235 million square yards of cloth to 61 million.[143]

Germany once furnished the largest single market for British yarn and tops, but after 1918 it began to develop its own wool industry and cut down imports. In the last two decades, British

---

    139. **18**, p. 281; **23**, 1951, p. 745.
    140. **33**, pp. 1 and 3.
    141. These two textile centers differ in that one district in West Riding processes all worsteds (Bradford and Halifax) and other woolens (Leeds), while in Lancashire some districts (such as Manchester) spin fine

yarns, others (such as Oldham) coarse yarns, and still others (such as Blackburn) engage in weaving. **57**, p. 299.
    142. **33**, pp. 23–24.
    143. **33**, *passim*.

FIGURE 305. WOOL MANUFACTURE: GEOGRAPHIC DISTRIBUTION OF WOOLEN AND WORSTED SPINDLES IN THE UNITED STATES, 1949

exports of woolen and worsted goods have become more and more dispersed and increasingly dependent on non-European markets. At the same time, a greater share of the total output has been consumed domestically.

On the whole, British exports of woolens have declined not so much because of the competition of other exporters, as was the case with cotton goods, but because more and more countries themselves manufacture what they require. Before World War II, Great Britain maintained its proportion of the diminishing international trade, and even increased it occasionally, but nevertheless felt the pinch of the declining demand for its wool products. Moreover, the equipment of the wool mills in the United Kingdom is about as obsolete as that in the cotton branch. Some of the carding machines have been in use for more than eighty years. Nearly a fourth of all the worsted spindles, and an even higher proportion of the woolen spindles, date from the nineteenth century, and many looms are at least fifty years old.[144]

SILK MANUFACTURE

Silk manufacture has always been a luxury industry, with a small physical output of comparatively high value. Originated in China, silk

manufacture spread very early to Japan and much later to Europe. Sicily produced silk textiles in the twelfth century; from there production spread to northern Italian cities — Venice, Milan, Genoa and Florence — and later to France.

The United Kingdom

The silk industry, like the wool industry, gained much impetus in Great Britain from the immigration of skilled workers from continental Europe — Flemish weavers in the sixteenth century, and French, German and Swiss craftsmen late in the seventeenth century. At that time England had to import thrown [145] silk from the continent to make silk cloth. In 1718 an Englishman succeeded in doing about what Slater [146] did for the United States: he became a worker in an Italian throwing mill and prepared drawings of the machinery, which, on his return to England, were used to build the first English throwing mill. In 1860 England eliminated tariffs on silk manufactures and allowed imports from France, previously banned. This change resulted in a rush of French silk textiles into Eng-

144. **33**, p. 76.

145. Raw silk (the continuous thread obtained from the cocoon) must be twisted, or thrown, to make it stronger.

146. See pp. 1053–54.

land and virtually destroyed the British industry, forcing many English throwsters and weavers to join the throngs of emigrants to the New World. Most of them settled in Paterson, New Jersey, where they established the American silk industry.

The United States

In contrast to Great Britain, the United States authorized free importation of raw silk in 1863 but introduced high custom duties on manufactured silk. The silk industry reacted quickly, the more so because Japan, opened to the western world in 1854, began to export raw silk to the United States: 21,600 pounds a year in 1873–74, 5.3 million in 1897–98.[147] The silk power loom, which appeared in Switzerland in the middle of the century, was soon adopted by silk manufacturers in the United States.[148]

By the turn of the century, the United States ranked second only to Japan in silk manufacturing. Its consumption of raw silk reached 29.3 million pounds in 1920 and 81.3 million in the peak year 1929. Since the silk industry of the United States depended on foreign raw materials, it was of great importance to it that, paralleling the growth of its demand and largely because of it, Japan, its chief supplier, effectively expanded production of raw silk.[149] In the 1930's the United States was the chief consumer of raw silk and the chief producer of manufactured silk.

Suddenly, the silk industry in the United States was hit from two sides — Pearl Harbor cut off the supply of raw silk, and nylon destroyed much of the demand for silk products. Ninety per cent of the country's raw silk consumption used to go into women's hosiery, for which nylon displaced silk most effectively.[150] The industry could have recovered from the first blow after the war, but the second was fatal.

The only solution was to convert silk-weaving mills to the use of nylon and other synthetic fibers. This the manufacturers did, finding that a given number of employees could produce eight to ten times as much fabric as they had previously made from natural silk.[151] While the silk

mills have adjusted to the situation, the silk industry as such has almost passed out of existence. It has been merged with the manufacture of broad goods from synthetic fibers and has lost its own distinct features.[152]

The prosperous silk industry of Japan was also seriously affected by the war. More than eight tenths of its equipment was scrapped during the war by government action, in contrast to less than 2 per cent damaged by bombing. The greater part of the mulberry acreage was converted to the production of soybeans and potatoes, which deprived the industry of its raw material. The slow recovery that began after the war was interrupted by the 1948 earthquake, which destroyed 16 per cent of the country's silk looms.[153]

MAN-MADE FIBERS

The range of fibers used by man for thousands of years has recently been greatly widened by the discovery of ways to produce new textile materials. The most important among them is rayon; others are discussed under the general heading of synthetic fibers.

Rayon, a continuous-filament yarn, was introduced in the 1890's, but the staple rayon fiber, of short lengths that can be spun on cotton, woolen and other textile spindles, did not appear on the market until the late 1920's. Today, rayon of both types is vastly superior to the original products, having been improved in elasticity, tenacity, appearance, dyeing properties and resistance to shrinkage. The main advantages of these man-made fibers are uniformity, versatility and absence of waste, except when the filament breaks during its manipulation.

The spectacular success of rayon stimulated experimentation in making other artificial fibers. In the last ten or fifteen years many different new materials have been produced commercially, among them synthesized polymeric fibers — nylon, vinyon, dacron, dynel; glass and aluminum fibers; protein fibers made from skim milk, soybeans, peanuts, corn or hair. Some of these are superior in certain respects to natural fibers and to rayon, which, however, remains the most important of all man-made fibers.

Moreover, materials are being developed that affect the entire textile industry, regardless of the fiber used. Traditional textile products are being

---

147. **73**, p. 64.
148. The first large silk mill, with power looms, was built in Switzerland in 1860; other European countries used hand looms until 1900. **73**, pp. 30–34.
149. Cf. Chapter 17, pp. 612–13.
150. See Chapter 31.
151. **8**, pp. 165 and 176.

---

152. **76**, p. 231.
153. **48**, pp. 400 and 482.

replaced by plastic fiber and sheeting and by paper. Together, such products have replaced an estimated textile fiber consumption of some 300 million pounds.[154]

RAYON

Rayon is made from cotton linters and, most of all, from wood pulp, both of which have an extremely high cellulose content and are available in large quantities at relatively low cost.

The possibility of making artificial fibers by imitating the spinning processes of the silkworm was envisaged by Robert Hooke, the English scientist, as early as 1664, and was again predicted by René de Réaumur, the French scientist, in 1734. About a century and a half passed, however, before their vision became a reality. The four processes now in use for making rayon were patented in rapid succession: nitrocellulose in 1884, cuprammonium in 1891, viscose in 1892–1902 and acetate in 1894–99. The principle common to all four is the preparation of a solution that when pressed through the tiny holes of nozzles ("spinnerettes") reappears in the form of threads. The viscose process uses wood pulp primarily, and cotton linters for special grades only; the other processes use cotton linters. The raw material is treated with great amounts of chemicals and water. About 1,000 gallons of water are needed, for example, to prepare a pound of acetate yarn. Abundance of water and its purity are therefore among the decisive factors in the choice of a location for a rayon plant.

Processes

The nitrocellulose process, which gave the world its first artificial fiber, was invented by Count H. De Chardonnet, the "father of the rayon industry." The present technique is to convert purified cotton linters, through the action of nitric and sulfuric acids, into nitrocellulose, which is then subjected to various treatments, such as repeated washing, boiling in a special solution, and then dissolving in a mixture of ether and alcohol. The resulting substance is freed of air bubbles, filtered and finally forced through special glass tubes. The yarn then drawn out is denitrated by special treatments, washed, bleached and dried. The process is now used only in Brazil and Hungary.

The cuprammonium process is much more complicated and requires careful chemical control of all operations. Purified cotton linters are combined with copper compounds, then freed of salts, mixed with a solution of ammonia and other chemicals, filtered and stored in tanks for deaeration. This mixture is then pressed through spinnerettes into a container with water to remove part of the copper and most of the ammonia, placed in a sulfuric acid bath to remove more of the copper, and subjected to repeated washing in soap baths and drying, until a fine, soft yarn is obtained.

The viscose process, the most widely used today, starts with bleached sulfite wood pulp, which is steeped in a caustic soda solution. After the excess soda is removed, the wet cellulose must weigh three times as much as the original raw material if the proper relationship with the caustic soda has been obtained. The mass is then shredded, left to age in special receptacles, treated with carbon disulfide and dissolved in another solution. The resulting mixture is filtered repeatedly to remove all impurities and stored to ripen for a couple of days. Later, this solution is pressed through spinnerettes into a warm bath of sulfuric acid and other chemical compounds. The yarn coming through the spinnerettes is washed free of all chemicals in the last bath, desulfurized, again washed, softened by the application of oil or soap, and finally dried.

To make rayon by the acetate process, purified cotton linters are soaked in acetic acid and treated with other acids at carefully controlled temperatures. The transparent mixture thus obtained is diluted in a solution of water and acetic acid and subsequently undergoes various treatments at rising temperatures and repeated washing to remove the acids. Then the acetate cellulose flakes are dried, again dissolved in acetone in a mixer until the solution has the proper percentage of cellulose acetate, blended with other batches in large tanks to assure uniformity, filtered and freed of bubbles. The resulting spinning solution is pressed through spinnerettes into a spinning chamber, where a current of warm air removes the rest of the acetone.

In 1939, 81 per cent of the world's rayon was made by the viscose process and 15 per cent by the acetate. Of the 29 rayon-producing countries, all had viscose plants; 9 also had acetate plants and 6, cuprammonium plants.[155] Of the 187

154. **14**, 1950, p. 144.

155. **35**, p. 125.

rayon filament and the 93 staple-fiber plants in the world in 1948, 155 and 83, respectively, used the viscose process. Projects in various countries for 29 plants — of which 18 were in operation in 1951 and 11 were to be completed by December 1952 — are, with one exception, based on this process.[156] About a third of all plants make more than one product — for example, viscose and acetate filament yarn.

Filament rayon can be woven on looms used in cotton mills. In 1935, 43,471 looms, or more than half the looms weaving rayon in the United States, were cotton looms. For staple fiber, the cotton industry uses the same cards, spindles and looms as in processing cotton.[157]

Output

In less than half a century, the rayon industry has become one of the major branches of the world's textile manufacture. Growth in the production of rayon filament has been phenomenal — from 13 metric tons produced by a single company in 1890 to 1,000 tons in 1900, 205,000 tons in 1930, and 519,000 tons in 1939.[158] The world output of staple fiber increased even more rapidly (figures in thousands of metric tons):[159]

	Total	Filament Yarn	Staple Fiber
1929	200	197	3
1935	487	424	63
1939	1,016	519	497
1941	1,275	572	703
1945	637	409	228
1949	1,225	743	482
1950	1,585	875	710

At the end of World War II, production of both types of rayon dropped sharply, but the output of filament yarn soon increased and in 1950 was at the highest level in its history, while the output of the staple fiber barely exceeded that of 1941.

Twenty-nine countries produced rayon in 1939. By the end of 1948, there were six more: Mexico,

Cuba, Colombia, Chile, Peru and Egypt. Australia, China, India and Israel are building rayon plants.[160]

In 1938, Japan was the largest producer of rayon, followed by Germany. The war crippled the industry in both countries; the German is recovering faster than the Japanese. At present, the United States ranks first and accounts for half the world output of rayon filament. The United Kingdom, Italy, Germany, Japan and France are next in order. The USSR output is estimated as about equal to that of the Netherlands. In contrast to the United States, production of staple rayon is more developed in many European countries than that of filament yarn, as for example in Germany, Austria, Czechoslovakia and all the Scandinavian countries. (See Table 463 and Figures 306 and 307.)

The capacity of the rayon industry is substantially greater than its present output. In the world as a whole it is about one and a half times as much; for filament yarn, capacity is 1.2 million tons as against an output of 0.9 million tons; for staple rayon, 1.1 and 0.7 million tons, respectively. In some countries — Japan and the USSR, for example — capacity is twice or more than twice the current output. Estimates for 1952 show the capacity of the industry in the most important countries to be as follows (in thousands of metric tons):[161]

	Total	Filament Yarn
United States	707	503
Japan	218	75
Italy	200	80
United Kingdom	195	111
Western Germany	181	56
France	138	72
USSR	54	27
Austria	45	2
Poland	42	13
Netherlands	41	29
Brazil	38	25
Spain	36	17
Canada	33	22
Belgium	25	10

The world's consumption of rayon, in terms of yardage, increased from 2 per cent of all tex-

156. **81**, June 1948, p. 91, and June 1951. Eighteen plants in the USSR, Korea and Manchuria are not included in these figures.

157. **27**, pp. 12–13.

158. **74**, p. 742; **81**, June 1939, p. 91; **1**, 1949–50, p. 216.

159. **1**, 1948, pp. 202–04; and 1949–50, pp. 216–18; **81**, January 1952, pp. 23–25.

160. **81**, June 1948, p. 91.

161. **81**, January 1952, pp. 23–25. Countries are arrayed by total capacity.

TABLE 463

RAYON: OUTPUT IN SELECTED COUNTRIES, 1929–50

(*Thousands of Metric Tons* [a])

Country	Filament					Staple				
	1929	1939	1948	1949	1950	1929	1939	1948	1949	1950
World	197	519	704	743	875	3	497	410	482	710
United States	55	149	388	363	433	b	23	122	88	139
Canada	2	6	14	15	17	—	—	1	2	7
Mexico	—	—	4	8	10	—	—	b	2	b
Cuba	—	—	b	3	4	—	—	—	1	3
Brazil	b	7	11	13	17	—	b	1	2	3
Argentina	—	3	5	6	8	—	—	—	1	b
United Kingdom	24	50	67	76	86	1	27	39	53	78
France	19	26	44	46	45	—	7	30	26	36
Belgium	6	6	10	9	10	—	1	11	10	13
Netherlands	8	11	16	20	22	—	—	10	10	11
Sweden	b	1	2	2	2	—	2	10	11	12
Norway	—	b	b	1	1	—	—	7	11	13
Finland	—	b	1	1	1	—	b	5	5	6
Germany c	27	73	30	45	49	1	200	40	82	111
Poland	3	4	7	9	10	—	5	11	11	9
Czechoslovakia	2	2	5	5	5	—	1	18	20	21
Switzerland	5	6	9	9	9	—	—	9	8	8
Austria	1	1	1	1	2	—	5	10	15	31
Spain	1	1	7	6	9	—	—	10	6	9
Italy	32	54	48	50	50	1	86	18	36	53
USSR	b	8	10	14	18	—	5	9	11	16
Japan	12	109	16	30	47	—	137	16	27	68

Sources: **81**, January 1952, pp. 23–25; **7**, pp. 20–21.

a. Conversion factors: one metric ton = 1.1023 short tons = 2,204.6 pounds.

b. Less than 500 metric tons.

c. 1948–50: Western Germany; the output of Eastern Germany in these years is estimated (in thousands of metric tons) as follows: filament, 4, 5 and 10, respectively; staple, 34, 36 and 54, respectively.

tile consumption in 1926–28 to 15 per cent in 1936–38 and nearly 20 per cent in 1948.[162]

Production in the United States

The rayon industry was taken from Europe to the United States, where British, French, Italian and Belgian concerns participated in establishing and operating the plants. They supplied their patents, skilled personnel and even a large part of the machinery. Commercial production of rayon by purely American firms did not develop successfully until after the 1930's.

In 1911, the United States produced less than 200 tons of rayon, or about 2 per cent of the world total; in 1936, 137,696 tons, or 27 per cent ; in 1946, 387,333 tons, or 51.1 per cent. The country produces a larger percentage of the world's output of filament yarn than of staple fiber:[163]

	Filament Yarn	Staple Fiber
1931	33.4	11.0
1941	35.4	7.9
1946	61.4	31.0
1948	55.1	29.8
1949	48.8	18.1
1950	49.5	19.6

The United States has led in the production of filament yarn since 1919, but was far behind Germany, Japan and Italy in the output of staple yarn even in 1939. During and since the war, however, its output of staple fiber has continued

162. **14**, 1950, p. 62.

163. **9**, Table 54; see also Table 463 above.

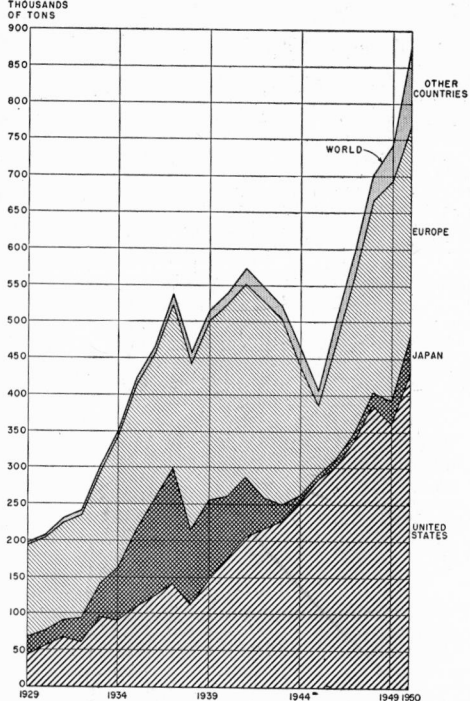

FIGURE 306. RAYON: OUTPUT OF FILAMENT YARN IN
THE WORLD AND SELECTED COUNTRIES, 1929–50

SYNTHETIC FIBERS

All synthetic fibers are made by a series of steps that yield a polymer consisting of extremely long chain-like molecules. These are entangled with each other and form a viscous mass. This viscous polymer is pumped through a multitude of small holes in a spinnerette, and then solidified. The next step is to orient the molecules. By the control of their orientation and crystallinity, a single polymer can be used to make several fibers with different mechanical properties; some may be weak and stretchable, others strong and rigid. The range of a single polymer is limited, however, and several must be used to cover the entire field.[167]

Nylon

Nylon, which has a protein-like chemical structure and is made of coal, air and water, is the most important of the recently created synthetic fibers. In contrast to rayon, it "sprang mature and full fledged into the textile world," after ten years of research. It can be spun on cotton, wool or worsted machines.[168]

Nylon differs from rayon in composition and properties. It can be drawn cold to four to six times its original length into fibers stronger than those of wool, silk or rayon; it dries faster than cotton, silk or rayon and has a high resistance to abrasion, mildew and moth damage. Made both as filament yarn and staple, this fiber can be manufactured in any form to meet any technical requirement.[169] It is used chiefly for hosiery, for which it displaced silk in a few years,[170] but its use for cloth is growing steadily.

Nylon was introduced by the Du Pont Company. The first commercial plant began operating in 1939 and produced 4 million pounds. The total output of nylon in the United States rose to 20 million pounds in 1942 and 24 million in 1945. The popularity of nylon and the demand for it grew so fast that Du Pont raised output and expanded capacity from year to year. The 1948 output amounted to 60 million pounds.[171] The capacity of the company reached 100 million

to grow and has assured its lead in this sector of the industry as well.

Rayon accounted for one per cent of the mill consumption of all fibers in the United States in 1924 and 16.4 per cent in 1948. (See Figure 301, A.) It constituted 0.6 per cent of the ultimate consumption of all fibers in 1920–24 and 14.7 per cent in 1948.[164]

The rayon industry is concentrated in the southern Appalachian and Middle Atlantic states (see Figure 308), which produce about 60 and 32 per cent, respectively, of the nation's output. The location of the plants has been determined by the industry's main requirements — an abundance of water, the availability of cheap power,[165] an adequate labor supply, proximity to textile plants that use the rayon, and access to raw materials.[166] Virginia, West Virginia and Tennessee produced more than 40 per cent of the national output in 1947. Pennsylvania, the cradle of the rayon industry in the United States, now has only a small output.

164. **19**, pp. 5 and 15.

165. Power must be supplied twenty-four hours a day for the continuous operation of spinning.

166. Wood pulp comes from Canada, Sweden and the Appalachian forests, and cotton linters from the South.

167. **45**, August 1951, p. 125.

168. **77**, p. 8; **80**, p. 50.

169. **74**, p. 868; and **77**, p. 9.

170. One pound of nylon makes twenty pairs of stockings.

171. **95**, p. 373.

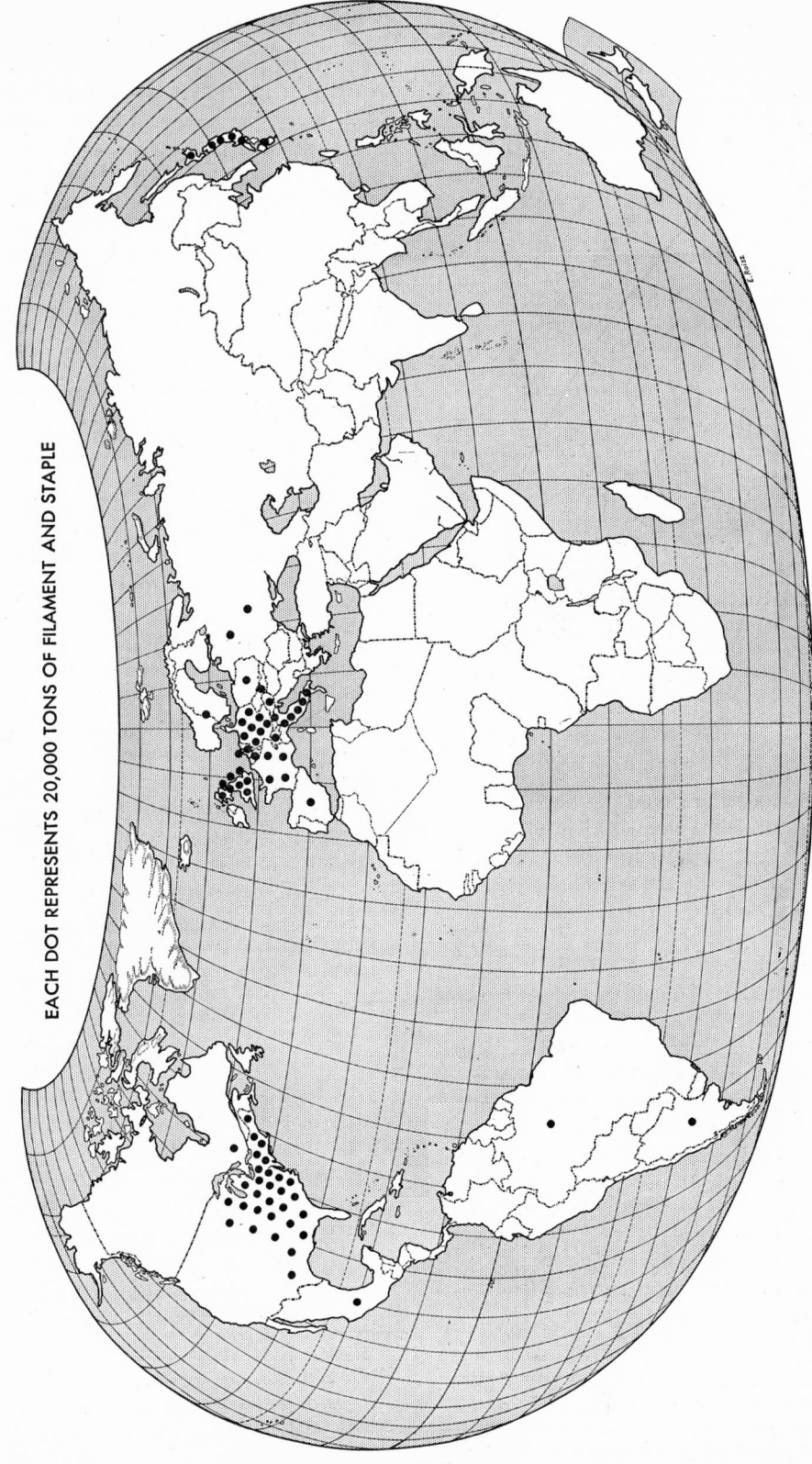

EACH DOT REPRESENTS 20,000 TONS OF FILAMENT AND STAPLE

FIGURE 307. RAYON: GEOGRAPHIC DISTRIBUTION OF WORLD OUTPUT, 1950

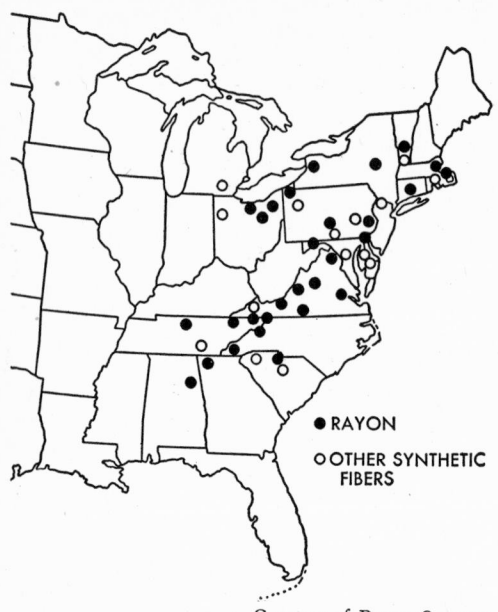

● RAYON

○ OTHER SYNTHETIC FIBERS

Courtesy of *Rayon Organon*

FIGURE 308. MAN-MADE FIBERS: LOCATION OF PLANTS
IN THE UNITED STATES, 1950

pounds in 1950, 170 million in 1951 and 190 million in 1952.[172]

Other Synthetic Fibers

A number of other synthetic fibers have appeared in the United States. Orlon was released by the Du Pont Company in 1948. Because of its strength and resistance to sunlight, it is used for awnings, sailcloth, tent material, rainwear and increasingly for apparel. The output in 1952 was estimated at 37 million pounds.[173]

Dynel, a product of Union Carbide, is resistant to acids, alkalis, salts and bleaches and does not shrink. The 1952 output is estimated at 35 million pounds. Vinyl, also a Union Carbide product, is a predominantly industrial fiber used for filter cloth, fish nets and lines, protective clothing and the like. It is exceptionally resistant to chemical corrosion, sunlight and mildew, but its heat resistance is low. It has a high tensile strength, wet or dry. One fiber of the vinyl family, Vinyon N, consists of five types, each with distinct characteristics.[174]

Glass fiber, entirely fireproof, is used industrially when heat resistance and electrical insulation

are important. Few chemicals attack it. The output in 1939 was valued at $3 million; in 1944, at $44 million.[175]

Vicara, a corn-protein fiber, produced in a single plant in Connecticut, is less promising. The plant's capacity is estimated at 25 million pounds a year.[176]

The output of all man-made fibers, exclusive of rayon, in the United States increased from 5 million pounds in 1940 to 49 million in 1944, 75 million in 1948 and 145 million in 1950.[177]

Italy began producing a wool-like fiber, lanital, from casein in the middle 1930's. The output rose from 0.7 million pounds in 1936 to about 3 million in 1937. On the eve of World War II, the Italian capacity was 33 million pounds a year. A similar fiber from the same source, aralac, is being produced in the United States. The output in 1943 amounted to about 9 million pounds, but has not gained ground subsequently, partly because of the price.[178]

Japan started production of vinylon in 1951; the United Kingdom, of terylene. Aluminum yarn is being made experimentally; it is said that one pound of aluminum can be stretched into six miles of gleaming yarn.[179]

Many companies in various countries are very active in the field of synthetic fibers and are carrying on intensive research and experimentation with products made from synthetic resins and proteins. Many of the new synthetics are more expensive than cotton or rayon and so far are used only for special purposes for which they are considered superior to natural fibers. Their commercial success and wider application will depend, to a considerable degree, on their ability to compete in price with other fibers.

OUTLOOK

With the end of the war, the world textile industry entered a period of reconstruction. Shortages of raw material, manpower, machinery and parts have been acute in almost all the textile-producing countries. Lack of maintenance during the war and obsolescence of machinery have considerably lowered the capacity of many mills. The alleviating factors have been the existence of excess capacity in some areas and the

172. **45**, August 1951, p. 128.
173. **45**, August 1951, pp. 129–31.
174. **66**, p. 389; **80**, pp. 64–65.

175. **84**, pp. 3–4; **80**, pp. 70–71.
176. **45**, August 1951, pp. 129–31.
177. **81**, January 1952, pp. 34 and 40.
178. **74**, pp. 877–85.
179. **45**, August 1951, p. 131; **77**, pp. 14–15.

TABLE 464

TRENDS IN THE TEXTILE INDUSTRY: INDEXES OF OUTPUT
IN SELECTED COUNTRIES, 1938–50

(1937 = 100)

Country	1938	1948	1949	1950	Country	1938	1948	1949	1950
United States	80	160	139	173	Finland [c]	107	118	140	155
Canada	85	158	. . .	. . .	Germany [d]	100	44	75	98
Mexico	94	100	92	98	Poland	104	114	133	150
Chile	100	142	143	143	Czechoslovakia [c]	. . .	77	81	89
Argentina	109 [a]	238	248	240	Austria	. . .	50	77	94
United Kingdom [b]	100	95	102	112	Hungary [b]	100	88	111	129
Ireland [b]	100	148	160	185	Spain [e]	. . .	153	145	163
France	95	97	96	104	Italy [b]	100	96	99	102
Belgium	80	93	96	114	Greece	111	86	97	132
Netherlands	95	100	116	130					
Denmark	98	132	149	170	Japan	93	15	20	33
Sweden	98	147	151	147	Turkey [b]	100	133	. . .	. . .
Norway [b]	100	144	168	180	India [f]	109	112	. . .	. . .

Sources: **1**, 1951, pp. 122–34; **6**, 1951, p. 178.

a. 1939.
b. 1938 = 100.

c. Includes ready-made clothing.
d. Western Germany; 1938 = 100.
e. 1940 = 100.
f. Cotton textiles only; 1948–50, without Pakistan.

possibility of working double shifts wherever manpower was available. Rebuilding and modernization of textile mills is going forward in many countries, and further recovery is to be expected. Reassembly of parts has restored many mills to production. UNRRA shipped large quantities of cotton and wool to Europe, the USSR and China, and machinery and parts were also supplied, first by UNRRA and later through the Marshall Plan. Through their own efforts and with the help of the United States, many countries have succeeded in effecting a considerable recovery.

The output of textiles, stimulated by pent-up demand, has risen to the prewar level in some European countries, in others beyond it. In Austria, Czechoslovakia and Germany, however, recovery has been very slow. The indexes of textile production in Austria and Czechoslovakia in 1950 were still below the 1937 level. Japan's output was the lowest — only about a third the prewar figure. (See Table 464.)

A few long-range lines of development of the world textile industry can be foreseen with reasonable certainty.

In the underdeveloped countries household spinning and weaving will gradually yield to mechanized factory production, as is happening in India, Gandhi's efforts to the contrary. The financial outlay necessary for the erection of a textile mill is not prohibitive, and skill requirements are less exacting than, say, in the chemical industry. Domestic markets will absorb the simpler types of fabrics, and the infant industry will probably be protected almost everywhere by tariffs and other measures. Underdeveloped countries able to supply their young textile industries with domestic raw materials will be in a particularly favorable position. The textile industry will thus become more and more decentralized.

Some division of work between the old textile industries and the newcomers may be worked out. The former will probably orient their production toward goods of finer quality, while the latter will concentrate on staple products.

Man-made fibers will continue to grow in importance. Rayon output in 1950 was equivalent to 8 million bales of cotton, and the estimated capacity of rayon plants by the end of 1952 (5 billion pounds) is equivalent to about 11 million bales. The output of synthetics is increasing steadily, resembling the early days of rayon. Blends will also be used increasingly.

Cotton will probably lose some ground. Wool,

the more expensive fiber, will be used more and more in blends to make it accessible to larger groups of consumers. The prospects for silk are gloomy.

In the world as a whole, the textile industry will remain one of the leading branches of manufacturing, although it may have a decreasing share in the world's industrial labor force, the total value of industrial output and especially in international trade.

CHAPTER 29

THE IRON AND STEEL INDUSTRY [1]

IRON AND STEEL are the backbone of our industrial civilization. Almost every article we use in our daily life is made of ferrous metal or with tools and machinery of such metal. The food we eat, the clothes we wear, our kitchen utensils, drugs, paper and books are manufactured or processed in factories where the structure and equipment contain a great deal of iron and steel. Raw and finished products are delivered largely by means of trains, ships, trucks or planes made of steel. The oil consumed by trains, ships and trucks is drilled with steel machinery and moved in steel pipes. Coal and other minerals are dug from the earth and carried to the surface by steel machinery. The amount of iron and steel available in the world is steadily increasing, since every year's production is added to the quantities already in use in buildings, machinery, railroads, telephone lines, radio stations, automobiles and the like.

The annual per capita consumption of ferrous products is one of the best single indicators of the industrial development of a country. The difference between the per capita output of 1,155 pounds in the United States or 656 pounds in the United Kingdom and the 58 pounds per capita in Spain or 8 pounds in India illustrates the gulf between these countries in extent of industrialization. In vast areas of the world, the direct consumption of iron and steel by much of the population is only two or three pounds per capita — a mattock for field work, a can to carry water, a knife, a few nails. Even in such countries, however, railways are laid and goods are moved to trade centers in vehicles put together by means of nails and screws, bolts and hammers.

Doubtless, a country can reach a high level of economic development and wealth without having a strong iron and steel industry within its borders; Switzerland and Norway have done so. But to grow and prosper such countries must import large quantities of ferrous products, as those countries do.

Of all the metal produced in the world, 93

per cent is iron and steel.[2] The output of the world's iron and steel industry in 1949 was valued at $12.8 billion (at U.S. prices). Before the war, the industry employed about 2 million people.[3]

DEVELOPMENT OF THE INDUSTRY

Archaeologists date the Iron Age, when men melted ore and made weapons and other articles of iron, from about 1400–1500 B.C., but iron was worked in India some eight hundred years earlier. Wrought-iron beams similar in size and appearance to those in modern buildings have been found in the ruins of Indian temples. How these blocks of iron were forged without tools or machinery remains a mystery to metallurgists.[4] At Hyderabad and Trichinopoly, India produced the famous wootz steel that was traded to Syria and, later, to Spain. The reputation of Damascus and Toledo swords, which could be bent from hilt to tip and at the same time take a cutting edge that has never been surpassed by modern techniques, was due to the strength and flexibility of wootz.[5]

Another ancient center of iron production developed on the northern coast of the Black Sea, whence iron was introduced to western Europe. Iron was also known to the ancient Hebrews and Assyrians, but the earliest date at which the ore was smelted in Egypt is now considered to have been the sixth century B.C.[6] Because of its softness, iron was not particularly valued for weapons until at least the third century B.C.[7] Although Caesar found iron in use in Britain, the Romans are believed to have installed the first extensive

2. **24**, p. 329.
3. **11**, p. 23. See Chapter 21, pp. 762 ff.
4. **70**, p. 6. The earliest remains of iron articles, in the form of ornaments, were found in Egypt and date from 5000–6000 B.C., when iron was considered a precious metal. About 3000 B.C., iron, probably of meteoric origin, was used for other than ornamental purposes. (**57**, p. 2.)
5. **57**, p. 2. Aristotle described the process of making wootz.
6. **61**, pp. 273–74.
7. **57**, p. 3.

---

1. For iron ore and ferroalloys see Chapter 22, pp. 776–91.

iron works there; at least, the remains of iron works have been discovered only among Roman ruins.[8] Spain was known for its iron for hundreds of years after the Roman occupation (192 B.C.), and its Catalan forges, developed in the latter part of the thirteenth century, were used in every iron-making country.[9]

In these flat-bottomed forges, iron was made by the direct reduction of ore heated with charcoal. The air to fan the fire was obtained by natural draft or by hand-operated bellows. The hot, pasty metal, mixed with slag from ore impurities, was then drawn out and hammered into shape, while as much slag as possible was eliminated. The resulting iron was soft and malleable. If heated for a long time, it would take more carbon from the charcoal and harden but would then become brittle, and break rather than bend.

Not until 1350 did the iron makers of medieval Europe discover how to cast iron. In this process, which had become common by the beginning of the fifteenth century, the hot metal was run into sand molds with lateral channels. Because of the mold's resemblance to a sow with suckling pigs, the product was called pig iron. The English under Henry VII and the Spaniards under Philip II used cast-iron guns.[10]

THE SEVENTEENTH AND EIGHTEENTH CENTURIES

Early in the seventeenth century, a process for steel manufacture (cementation), very similar to India's wootz process, was invented in Europe, either in Germany or in the Low Countries. England imported this high-quality but expensive steel and used it for weapons and knives.[11]

Somewhat later, England introduced a new blast furnace that was economical in the use of fuel and permitted the withdrawal of iron in essentially pure form. Built of masonry, the furnace consisted of two truncated cones placed end to end. Ore, charcoal and flux were charged at the top, and air was blown at the bottom. The process of iron reduction was carried out before the raw materials entered the bottom of the furnace. This generated sufficient heat there to sep-arate the gangue in the ore from the molten iron.[12]

The Problem of Fuel

England made more and better iron in these furnaces than in the Catalan forges until the overcutting of forest stands for charcoal became a limiting factor. "Green" Sweden, however, had abundant supplies of charcoal and produced some 30,000 tons of pig iron a year.[13] The largest part of its output was exported to England. But in Sweden, too, concern over the destruction of the forests by the iron makers finally became so great that, in 1633, the country prohibited the erection of new furnaces and the indiscriminate expansion of production from the existing ones.[14]

The demand for iron increased slowly. As late as the middle of the eighteenth century, England made only some 7,000 tons of pig iron a year. Fuel was the bottleneck, the cost of charcoal amounting in some places to almost three fourths of the total cost of production.[15] In 1770, England produced only about as much iron as Belgium — 20,000 tons. France and Austria-Hungary were about equal in output.[16] In 1796, Russia matched the English output of 125,000 tons and shipped about a third of its product to England.[17] The American colonies also exported some pig iron to England, but most of England's imports came from Sweden — more than 82 per cent around 1720 and 40 per cent in the later part of that century.[18]

The Rise of England

England, though only one of many small iron producers in the eighteenth century, laid the foundation for its world leadership slowly but surely during the next century. The use of coal in iron ore smelting, developed by Abraham Darby, freed England's industry from its worst handicap — the shortage of fuel.[19] The Watt steam engine provided the strong blast of hot air to remove, by burning coke, the oxygen from the

---

8. **63**, p. 12; and **44**, p. 33. Slag abandoned in Roman furnaces was used in the sixteenth century for making iron in England. (**46**, p. 115.)

9. **26**, p. 44.

10. **26**, p. 206.

11. **57**, p. 3.

12. **39**, 1948, p. 315.

13. **60**, p. 41.

14. This law remained on the books throughout the eighteenth century. (**48**, p. 499.)

15. **48**, pp. 498–99.

16. **53**, pp. 781–88.

17. **71**, p. 64; **70**, p. 40.

18. **60**, p. 64.

19. Incidentally, this was a serious blow to the Swedish iron industry, developed with the use of charcoal.

iron ore. Henry Cort introduced rolling of sheet iron and later patented grooved rollers for shaping iron. He also originated the first fundamental change in iron making for many centuries, the puddling process.[20] The crucible process, the basis of the steel industry, was developed in the eighteenth century through an invention by Benjamin Huntsman, whose contemporaries hailed it as the greatest discovery of all time.[21]

THE NINETEENTH CENTURY

With raw materials assured and technology improved, England's iron and steel industry was ready to meet the increasing demand. When machine tools were invented in England in the 1820's, it was called upon to provide iron for building machinery with the greater precision and speed required by all branches of manufacturing. Before long, the railroads appeared, absorbing ever greater quantities of metal. Iron began to displace lumber in bridges and ships.

The Iron Era was about to begin — arriving so quietly and inconspicuously, however, that even the keenest observers hardly noticed it. The founder of economic science, Adam Smith, did not so much as mention iron in his *The Wealth of Nations*, published in 1776. To understand this omission, it should be remembered that at this time all iron-making countries together produced less pig iron in a year than one modern blast furnace now turns out.

The Iron Era

In the nineteenth century, production of iron began to grow rapidly. World output rose from less than 400,000 metric tons in 1800 to 1.7 million in 1820, 3.3 million in 1840, 7.4 million in 1860. England's unchallenged lead, with about a fourth the total in 1820 and more than half in 1860 is shown in the following figures (in thousands of tons): [22]

	1820	1840	1860
World	1,650	3,300	7,360
United States	20	289	821
England	400	1,396	3,827
France	...	348	898
Belgium	...	...	320
Sweden	...	...	205
Germany	...	143	529
Russia	163 [a]	184	296

a. 1826.

Railroads, shipbuilding and the machinery industries needed ever growing quantities of iron, and much was consumed in the Napoleonic wars. With this insatiable demand, the industry enlarged its capacity, built larger blast furnaces, improved techniques.

Even when the Iron Era was in full force, its importance escaped the notice of many economists. For example, the capitalist world portrayed by Karl Marx was a world practically without iron. None of Marx's writings discussed the significance of railroads, steamships, or the iron and steel industry in general, for the development of our civilization. In contrast, Friedrich List, writing at about the same time, was fully aware of the economic role that iron production and the railroads were to play.

The Iron Era soon reached its zenith. Its weakness was that the products were not sufficiently durable. Rails had to be replaced every four months though traffic was not heavy at that time; [23] iron bridges sagged under their loads or collapsed.

The Steel Age

The way to satisfy the growing need for a more durable and resistant metal was found soon after the middle of the century. The Steel Age is held officially to date from 1856, when Henry Bessemer announced his process of making steel from pig iron.[24]

Bessemer Steel

In the Bessemer process, molten iron is poured into a pear-shaped tilting converter. A strong air blast is then introduced through the openings at the bottom. The oxygen burns out the impurities in the pig iron — carbon, silicon and manganese. This reaction generates enough heat for the operation, and no fuel is required. The whole process takes about ten minutes, at the end of

20. **63**, p. 15.
21. **57**, pp. 3–4.
22. **53**, pp. 781–91; and **20**, p. 149.
23. **57**, p. 5.
24. Credit for this invention was a matter of litigation between William Kelly, an iron maker from Kentucky, and Bessemer. The American courts sustained the claim of Kelly, and the United States could not start steel production until the inventors reached a settlement in favor of Bessemer after eight years of litigation. (**54**, pp. 187–88.)

which time the molten iron is concentrated at the bottom of the converter, under a layer of slag. Both iron and slag are tapped at regular intervals. Only minute quantities of the carbon, silicon and manganese remain in the molten iron. Since the air blast generates compounds of gases, an alloy of manganese, iron and other elements is added to the molten charge to remove them. The purified metal is steel.

Bessemer steel was lower in quality than the steel made in Huntsman crucibles, yet it was satisfactory for most purposes. The main advantage of the process was its rapidity, which made it possible to produce large quantities in a short time. Though the response to Bessemer's invention was not immediate, it eventually came into general use, particularly after a test of iron and steel rails, made in 1861. A rail of each kind was used on opposite sides of the same track: the iron rail had to be changed twenty-three times before the steel rail needed replacement.[25]

Open-Hearth Process

A few years later, a rival method of making steel was invented almost simultaneously by William Siemens in England and the Martin brothers in France (1864–67). As raw materials, Siemens used pig iron and ore; the Martins, pig and scrap.[26]

In this process, a furnace of the reverberatory type burns gas as the source of heat; oil is now used in the United States. The charge — pig iron, scrap, flux — is heated on a shallow hearth by the gas flame. The furnace has an opening at each end; gas and air enter at one end and the products of combustion escape through the other, with reversal of the flow every fifteen to twenty minutes. Two regenerative chambers below the furnace, one at each end, are alternately heated by exhaust gases from the open hearth and cooled by giving off the heat to air and gas, which pass through them before they enter the furnace. The molten steel and slag in the open hearth are discharged at various levels. The whole operation takes up to fifteen hours.

The open-hearth process has several advantages over the Bessemer. Because of the longer period of operation and the slower combustion of carbon, it permits better control over the com-

position of the steel. Samples for analysis can be taken at any time. Also, the use of scrap considerably increases the supply of raw materials for steel production. A greater amount of finished steel can be obtained from the same quantity of pig iron, and fewer blast furnaces are required for a given tonnage of steel. While Bessemer steel is satisfactory for certain products, such as wire, pipes, bolts, nuts, small structural shapes and many classes of sheets, and also has excellent machinability and is readily welded, open-hearth steel is generally of higher quality and is used for many purposes for which Bessemer steel is not considered fit.[27]

Facilitated by these new processes, steel output rose rapidly, while prices for steel dropped about 50 per cent between 1856 and 1870.[28] One difficulty, however, was still unsolved. Pig iron made of iron ore rich in phosphorus, such as the English or French ore, produced brittle steel.[29] Iron ore and pig iron with little or no phosphorus were therefore required, but such materials were rare in Europe and costly. England imported suitable pig iron from Sweden and Spain, but it was essential for the industry to find a way to eliminate phosphorus from the domestic ores.

"Basic" Steel

In 1878, Sidney Thomas, a London police clerk who studied chemistry in his evening hours, announced that he and his cousin, Gilchrist, had worked out a solution: the Bessemer converter should be lined with a basic material, dolomite. The reaction between phosphorus, oxygen and lime during the blast would keep the phosphorus from entering the steel and it would be deposited in the slag.[30]

The Thomas process, called "basic," in contrast to the "acid" process introduced by Bessemer, has been widely adopted in Europe. One of history's ironies is that while Thomas' objective was to benefit his own country, he actually opened the way for the triumphant advance of German steel production. In fact, his invention enabled Germany to utilize the enormous reserves of iron ores in Lorraine, captured from

25. **57**, p. 5.
26. **44**, p. 381.

27. **44**, pp. 356 and 380; **55**, p. 183.
28. **48**, p. 500.
29. Phosphorus has little affinity with oxygen and is actually the only material entering the blast furnace over which the metallurgist has no control. Thus all phosphorus is retained in the metal. (**44**, p. 233.)
30. This slag, known as Thomas slag, makes an excellent phosphate fertilizer.

France a few years earlier, which were high in phosphorus and therefore useless until that time.

Thomas' invention also had consequences for the Siemens-Martin process. Previously the entire furnace — open-hearth, roof and walls — was lined with highly siliceous materials since only slag that was acid would not corrode it; as in the acid Bessemer process, pig iron and scrap had to be low in phosphorus. Thomas' discovery of the basic process suggested its use for open-hearth production. The first basic open-hearth furnace lined with dolomite was built in 1884 in England, where, as in the United States, the Siemens-Martin method proved in time to be the most suitable for domestic ores.

One of the most important features of the basic open-hearth process in the United States has been that it eliminates the phosphorus before the carbon. This permits the use of pig iron of any phosphorus content up to one per cent, thus making it possible to smelt vast quantities of iron ore that otherwise would have been useless. In contrast, the basic Bessemer process removes the carbon and phosphorus simultaneously, and therefore requires pig iron with 2 per cent phosphorus to maintain a temperature sufficient for the afterblow of the carbon.[31]

With the establishment of techniques for large-scale production, steel, formerly a costly product used mostly for ordnance, became available in large quantities for railroads, ships and machines. Stronger and more resistant to wear than pig iron, it began to displace iron most effectively. The production of iron rails, still flourishing in 1870, was a dying industry by 1890, as the following figures show (in thousands of tons): [32]

	Iron Rails		*Steel Rails*	
	1870	*1890*	*1870*	*1890*
United States	523	14	31	1,871
France	171	0.4	54	176

The first steel ship was built in England in 1865, but even in 1878 shipbuilders used more than a hundred times as much iron as steel. In 1888, however, 90 per cent of the ships classed by Lloyd's were built of steel.[33]

THE TWENTIETH CENTURY

World output of steel had risen with each decade, from 700,000 tons in 1870 to 4.4 million in 1880, 12.4 million in 1890 and 28.3 million in 1900. On the eve of World War I, it amounted to 76.5 million tons.[34] In the twentieth century, progress was measured by the quality and diversity, as well as the quantity, of the output.

The Age of Super-Steel

While minute quantities of alloy steels were produced earlier, the age of alloy steels began only a few decades ago. Some alloy steels were introduced in the second half of the nineteenth century, such as tungsten steel for tools by Mushet (1850) and manganese steels for points of heavy wear by Hadfield (1888). But the structural changes caused in making such steels were not fully understood.

The actual development of alloy steels began at the end of the nineteenth century, with the advent of the metallurgical microscope, thermal and, later, X-ray analysis, and other devices, such as tests of hardness.[35] What had been to a considerable extent craftsmanship or an art became a science. Alloy-steel metallurgy no longer consists in the simple addition of one alloying element, since we now know that no single element will endow the metal with all the desired qualities — strength, resistance to corrosion or abrasion, ductility, toughness and so on.[36]

Types of Furnaces

Two types of steel furnaces have been chiefly used for alloy steels: crucible and electric. The crucible process produces a thoroughly homogeneous steel and consists in remelting wrought iron in crucibles for several hours and then adding the necessary amounts of carbon. Because of the high cost of the product, made in small quantities, only the finest tools have been manufactured from crucible steel. The electric furnace, originated by Héroult in France in 1899 and still the most successful of those of the direct arc type, is used to produce alloy, stainless and tool steels. The other type of electric furnace, high-frequency induction, was invented by Northrop in 1916 and supplements the arc furnace. The crucible process has been displaced by the electric,

31. **44**, p. 380.
32. **53**, pp. 793–94.
33. **57**, pp. 5–7.

34. **47**, p. 251.
35. **56**, p. 301.
36. Specific properties of alloying elements used in making steel are discussed in Chapter 22, pp. 787 ff.

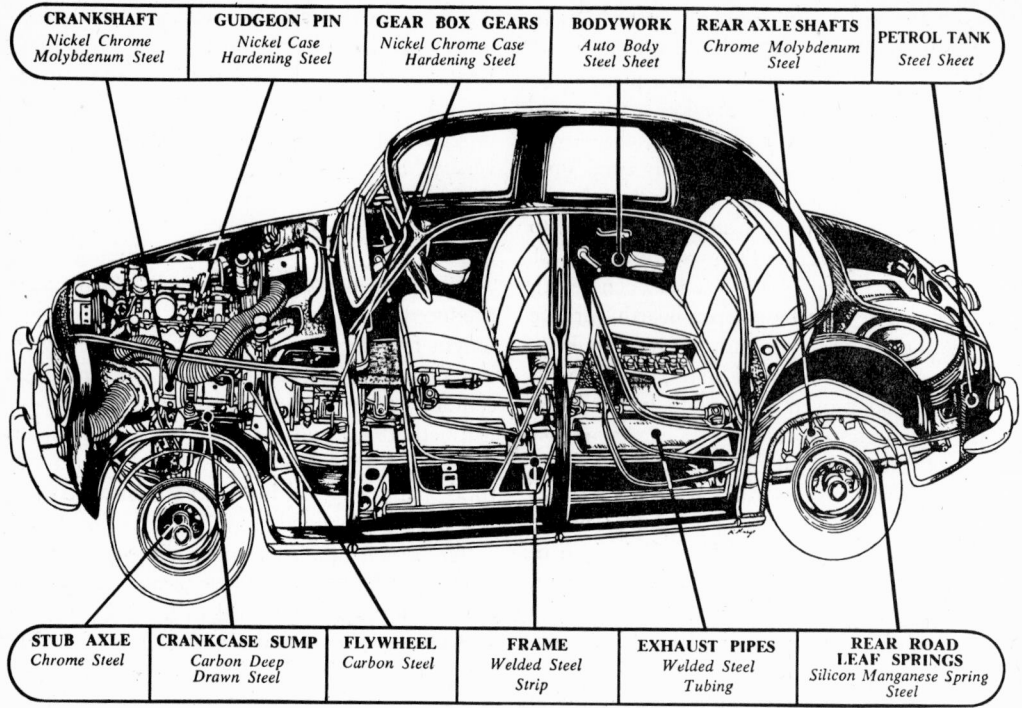

| CRANKSHAFT Nickel Chrome Molybdenum Steel | GUDGEON PIN Nickel Case Hardening Steel | GEAR BOX GEARS Nickel Chrome Case Hardening Steel | BODYWORK Auto Body Steel Sheet | REAR AXLE SHAFTS Chrome Molybdenum Steel | PETROL TANK Steel Sheet |

| STUB AXLE Chrome Steel | CRANKCASE SUMP Carbon Deep Drawn Steel | FLYWHEEL Carbon Steel | FRAME Welded Steel Strip | EXHAUST PIPES Welded Steel Tubing | REAR ROAD LEAF SPRINGS Silicon Manganese Spring Steel |

British Iron and Steel Federation

FIGURE 309. ALLOY STEELS: MAJOR TYPES USED IN A BRITISH AUTOMOBILE

One of the principal factors that have made possible improvements in design, strength and lightness of the modern car has been the production of new kinds of special and alloy steels. A car contains, on the average, about one ton of finished steel, ranging from sheet to wire.

This diagram (from the "Autocar" and the Rover Car Company) indicates some of the many different kinds of steel used in a car.

which is cheaper in operation, produces as good a steel, and has many metallurgical advantages.[37]

Making Steel to Specifications

The metallurgist's aim is to alter the microstructure of the steel by using a combination of different alloys, a specified heat schedule and various other procedures, such as quenching or tempering. Once he has the specifications for a certain type of steel, he can select the needed alloying elements as "building blocks" and, "noting and balancing the effect of each," can "synthesize a steel having all the required properties."[38] The variety of alloy steels that a single industrial product may now require was unheard of even a decade or two ago. The American automobile, for example, now contains 125 different steel alloys as well as many nonferrous alloys.[39]

The British distinguish a dozen principal types of steel that go into a car. (See Figure 309.)

Although alloy steels at first constituted only a small fraction of the total steel output (about 6 per cent in the United States), their economic importance was relatively much greater. Introduction of high-speed-tool steels at the beginning of this century raised the efficiency of all industries in the United States by about 15 per cent.[40] Important as they are in a peacetime economy, alloy steels are still more important in modern warfare. "A country whose plants could produce only carbon steel and whose ammunition, tanks and aircraft contained no alloy, could not resist indefinitely an enemy equipped with tools and weapons made of alloy steel."[41] The demand for alloy steels during World War II rose to such heights that by the end of 1942, one out of every six tons of steel produced in the

37. **44,** p. 334.
38. **44,** p. 306.
39. **56,** p. 294.

40. **24,** p. 354.
41. **23,** p. 2.

United States was of this type, in contrast to one ton in fourteen in 1929.[42]

Stretching Alloying Elements

To overcome the shortage of various alloying elements during World War II, special war steels were developed in the United States and elsewhere.[43] They were based on the combined effect of small amounts of two or more available alloys, and of alloys contained in the scrap. Alloying elements were frequently interchanged to provide substitutes for those that were scarce or lacking. Low-alloy steels of high strength were produced, and super-alloy steels were created for special ordnance.

Recently the steel industry has developed new types of steel that permit the stretching of short supplies of some of the critical alloys. For example, laboratory research revealed that small additions of boron, which is abundant in Death Valley, California, reduce the required amounts of nickel, chromium and molybdenum in certain steels about 50 per cent. The action of boron is as yet unexplained, but it has been proved that it increases the hardenability and strength of steel without reducing its toughness.[44]

The Modern Plant

While the basic principles of pig iron and steel production have remained unchanged in this century,[45] many improvements have been made in the design, size and arrangement of plants and machinery.

Once a comparatively simple unit, the blast-furnace plant today is enormously complex and, including the blast furnace itself, of incomparably greater proportions: four cylindrical stoves to heat air, which are nearly as high as the furnace itself; the boiler house, power plant, pumping station, turboblower, stockyard, ore bridge, car dumper, raw-material bins and so on.[46] In 1880, the capacity of the most efficient blast furnace was 100 tons a day; in 1940, up to 1,200 tons. In 1948, the world record was achieved in Pittsburgh by a blast furnace with a capacity of 1,910 tons a day. Capacity of 2,000 tons is near at hand.

The world's largest furnace for making steel, with a capacity of 550 tons per heat (of 12 to 16 hours), was recently lighted at a midwestern plant in the United States.[47]

Continuous-Strip Mills

The introduction of the continuous-strip mill has been the most important single technological development in steel production in recent times. Synchronization of the rolling process — from ingot to finished sheet — has made it possible to turn out a substantially improved product in a fraction of the time previously required. Before the introduction of such a mill, semifinished steel (in billets or slabs) was cooled after leaving the open hearth, to be reheated later and guided by manual force through steam-powered rollers until it acquired the desired shape. In a continuous-strip mill, the hot metal passes from the hearth through several sets of rollers, is first elongated into a strip, then reduced to the desired thickness and cut to the desired length. The entire process is controlled electrically from a switchboard.[48]

In 1939 the annual capacity of the 28 continuous-strip mills in the United States amounted to about 12.5 million tons of steel;[49] it now exceeds 25 million tons. Rolling mills are rapidly increasing in size. In 1936, an annual capacity of 600,000 tons of finished flat-rolled steel was record-breaking. Two years later a mill with a capacity of almost a million tons was opened in Ohio.[50]

Development in other countries has been much slower: only two continuous-strip mills were operated in the United Kingdom in 1947, while a third was planned. Germany and Soviet Russia each had one mill before World War II; the Russian mill was destroyed by the Germans, and the German mill was transferred to the USSR after the end of the war. Canada is introducing one mill of this type,[51] and India has a modern continuous mill. France is completing one hot and cold continuous-strip mill under the Monnet Plan.

A parallel continuous-casting process was introduced in 1948 at Beaver Falls, Pennsylvania,

42. **63**, p. 188.
43. National Emergency (NE) Steels in the United States.
44. **37**, April 1951, p. 5. Cf. Chapter 22, p. 787.
45. **55**, p. 180.
46. **17**, p. 13901.

47. **37**, February 1950, p. 2.
48. **16**, p. 111.
49. **44**, p. 1209.
50. **17**, p. 13901.
51. **11**, p. 45.

to convert molten metal into usable shapes, by-passing the ingot mold, soaking pit and blooming mill.[52] The molten steel is poured into an electric induction ladle and then passes through water-cooled dies.[53]

New Techniques

A very recent development in the manufacture of steel, although still in controversy, seems to affect the entire process in blast, open-hearth and electric furnaces. This is the use of oxygen, which, in the opinion of some metallurgical experts in the United States, opens a new vista for the industry.[54] According to them, it reduces the amount of coke needed for the blast and makes the entire operation smoother. It may widen the range of utilizable ore and yield more iron from a given quantity of ore. In steel furnaces of all types, it raises the output while lowering the quantity of fuel or electricity required.[55] Some blast furnaces of the USSR have also introduced the use of oxygen,[56] and promising experiments have been conducted in the United Kingdom, at Leeds.[57]

Equally controversial is the new method of high-top pressure recently applied in some blast furnaces by the Republic Steel Corporation. The purpose is to reduce the iron ore to pig iron in a shorter time by a more rapid blast of air. A fast current of air ordinarily blows many fine particles of ore out at the top of the furnace, along with carbon gases. The high-top pressure forces the gas to move more evenly and slowly, with comparatively little loss of ore dust. This method has resulted in an 11 to 20 per cent increase in output, a 15 per cent cut in coke consumption, a 30 per cent decrease in flue dust, and a decrease in heat requirements per ton of pig iron. Experiments at other plants have given various results, differing even from furnace to furnace. Nevertheless, the new blast furnaces built in the United Kingdom are designed to be readily adaptable to this novel process if it should prove desirable.[58]

Sponge Iron

Sweden, famous for the quality of the steel it produced from charcoal pig iron, finds it more and more difficult to meet the rise in charcoal prices and compete with the improved and less expensive grades of steel from coke pig iron made elsewhere, in the United States in particular. The search for ways to reduce fuel costs coincided with the long-standing desire of the Swedish industry to obtain malleable iron directly from the ore, instead of via pig iron. After much research and experimentation, the solution seems to have been found in the shift to sponge iron, a base material that can be produced more cheaply than pig iron without sacrificing the quality of the steel.

Sponge iron is obtained through the reduction of iron ore at a low temperature. It contains some impurities, which must be removed by smelting. The basic metallurgical requirements for the production of sponge iron have long been known, but the practical application had been unsuccessful until recently.[59] Germany and Japan produced something like sponge iron before World War II, and the United States operated a plant during the war but later closed it.[60]

Various processes have been worked out in Sweden, two of which are in commercial use. The Wiberg process seems to be the choice of the Swedish steelworks as the less costly in terms of fuel, manpower and plant construction. Two leading Swedish steel plants are building sponge-iron furnaces, and others plan to follow suit.[61]

Technological Leadership

The knowledge of steel processing has improved so much in the last decade that the properties of a given lot of metal can now be controlled with an accuracy unknown even in the 1930's. Alloy steels can be made at different times in different mills and under varying conditions to meet the same specifications precisely; before such control was achieved, extra alloy content or heavier weight was used to provide a comparatively wide margin of safety.[62] Testing standards have been so tightened that steel products acceptable fifteen years ago are rejected today.

The United States is the unquestioned leader in metallurgical technology. Germany, which

52. **68**, p. 140.
53. **51**, August 19, 1948.
54. **69**, pp. 212–48.
55. **69**, *passim.*
56. **40**, p. 253.
57. **12**, p. 16.
58. **12**, pp. 24–25.

59. **60**, pp. 105 and 118.
60. **50**, p. 56.
61. **50**, p. 52.
62. **17**, p. 14115.

spared no efforts to create its "national" technology in the continuous rolling of sheet and strip, had to admit in 1942 that it could not even approach the performance of American metallurgy.[63]

LOCATION OF THE INDUSTRY

Two regions dominate the production of iron and steel. Facing each other across the three-thousand-mile span of the North Atlantic, they extend back from the sea coast in each continent into the hinterland.

World Centers

On the western shore of the Atlantic, the main realm of iron and steel stretches to the southern edge of Lake Michigan (Gary–Chicago). The Eastern Hemisphere has two distinct areas: Great Britain, and a group of industrial countries on the continent — Germany, France, Belgium and Luxembourg. (See Figure 310.)

On the eve of World War I, the two North Atlantic regions accounted for 90 per cent of the world's output of pig iron and steel. Even today, after many other countries have built blast furnaces and steel mills, they produce 80 per cent of the total.

In northwestern and central Europe as a whole, the pattern of iron ore, coal and waterways is somewhat similar to that in the United States, but with the difference that in America all the requirements for large-scale iron production lie within one nation, while in Europe they are scattered over half a dozen separate countries.

The political demarcation between the iron deposits in Lorraine and the coal fields in the Ruhr has been of decisive importance for the iron economy of Europe and fatal for Europe's political life. This line existed for thousands of years before the peoples on both sides of it learned how to convert iron ore and coal into steel. Since that time, the most intricate international cooperation has been developed and the most destructive wars have been fought in the region between Lorraine and the Ruhr.

In peacetime, the iron and steel industry in northwestern and central Europe was based on the combination of Lorraine minette and Swedish iron ore with the coal of Germany, Belgium–Luxembourg and the United Kingdom. Condi-

tions in the iron and steel industry in this troubled corner of the world are similar to what might have existed in the Western Hemisphere if Minnesota, Pennsylvania, West Virginia, Illinois, Kentucky and Ohio were independent nations. The Schuman Plan — a bold and imaginative project — promises to reconcile European conflicts of interest.[64]

Factors in a Nation's Industry

The location of the iron and steel industry in individual countries has been determined chiefly by three factors: the site of the deposits of iron ore or coal or both; favorable transportation facilities; and the proximity of industrial centers that serve both as markets for steel and suppliers of scrap. The best location is a place where iron ore and coal meet economically and from which delivery of steel products to the market is cheapest. The physical distance of raw materials is of less importance than the economic distance — the cost and ease of transportation or so-called assembly cost.[65]

An abundant supply of water is also important. Steel plants require large quantities of water for cooling furnaces and rolling equipment. A steel plant in the Pittsburgh district has been reported to use 250 million gallons a day, largely for cooling, while a near-by city with a population of 25,000 used only one million gallons a day.[66]

In the early days of the industry, plants were usually established near iron deposits, and charcoal was obtained from near-by forests. When coking coal became the chief fuel, its availability and quality and the freight costs had to be weighed against those of the iron ore. The higher the grade of iron ore, the greater the advantage of shipping it to the coal beds instead of moving the coal to the iron mines. Moreover, iron ore is transported more easily and cheaply than coal or coke. On the other hand, there has been a steady decline in the coal equivalent of coke used per ton of pig iron: in the United States, from 2.1 tons in 1879 to 1.27 tons in 1938; in the United Kingdom, from 2.55 tons in 1873 to 1.67 tons in 1938.[67] Since the recovery of coke from coal has increased some 13–15 per cent in the meantime, consumption of coke per ton of pig iron

63. **65,** March 18, 1943, pp. 221–25.

64. See pp. 1140 ff.
65. **45,** Vol. I, pp. 28–32.
66. **25,** p. 182.
67. **52,** pp. 205–06.

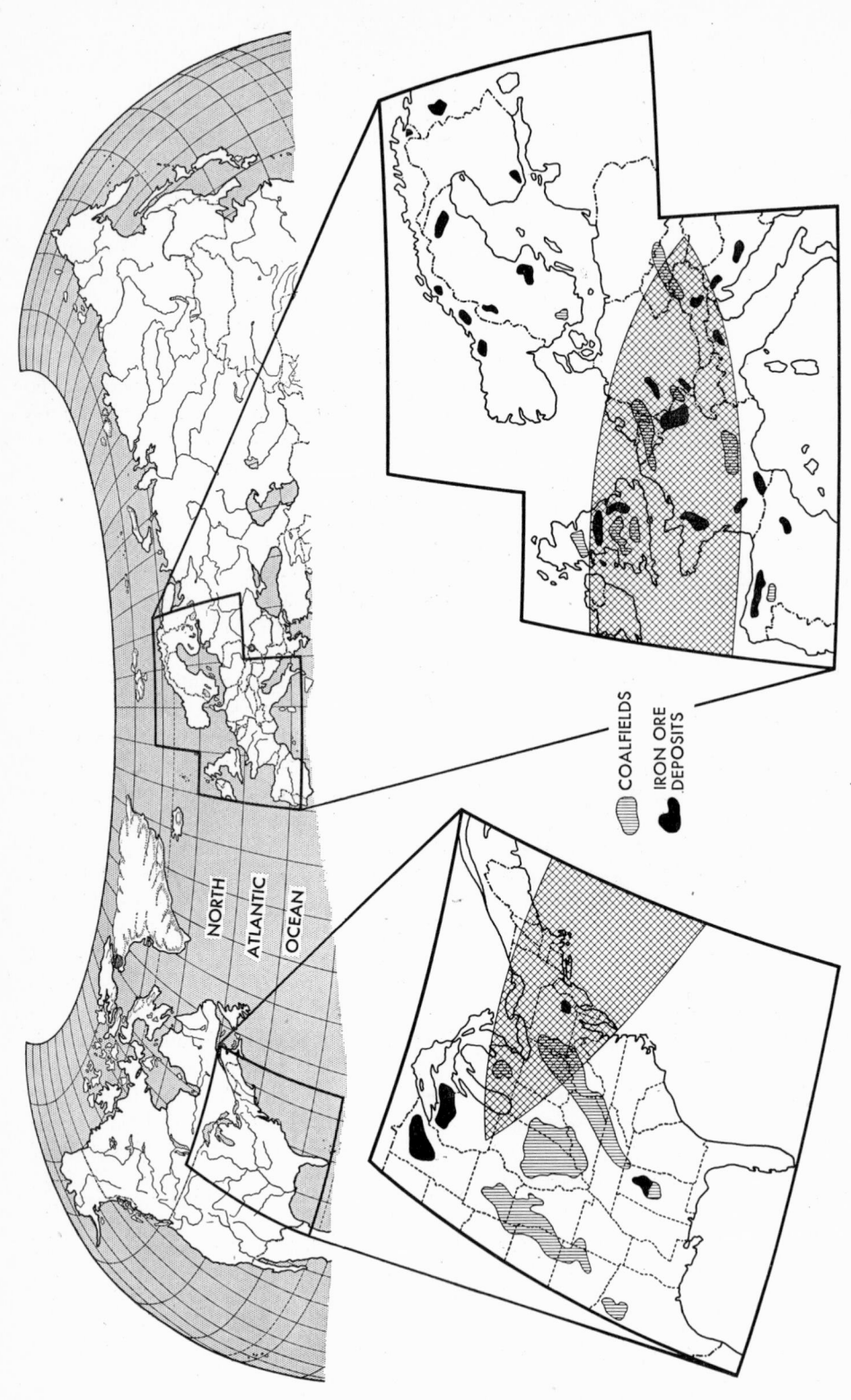

Figure 310. The Steel Industry: World Centers Facing the North Atlantic

The world's iron and steel industry is heavily concentrated in two areas that face each other across the North Atlantic: the northeastern region of the United States and the northwestern corner of Europe. Both areas are rich in iron ore and coal and have accessible waterways for shipping these bulky raw materials.

NORTH ATLANTIC OCEAN

COALFIELDS

IRON ORE DEPOSITS

has declined somewhat less than its coal equivalent. The blast furnace now uses about seven tenths of a ton of coke to each ton of pig iron.

The largest iron and steel center in the United States is near the coal beds in Pennsylvania, to which iron ore is hauled over a long distance from the head of the Great Lakes. Similarly, in Germany the industry is centered in the coke-rich Ruhr, while the ore was largely imported before World War II from France and Sweden. In France, on the other hand, the steel industry is concentrated near the ore deposits and uses imported coke to a considerable extent. In all these countries, the plants are in the neighborhood of the chief markets for steel.

The steel industry, however, may shift from one location to another because of changes in technology or other factors. Between 1927 and 1937 the biggest steel corporation in the United States dismantled plants with a capacity of about 5 million tons and built new mills capable of producing some 6 million tons in other areas to achieve greater efficiency.[68]

The United States

The location of the industry in the United States was predetermined by the vast iron ore deposits of the Lake Superior region,[69] the position of Pittsburgh in the center of the finest metallurgical coking coals, and the great demand of the industrial East for steel. (Cf. Figure 118.)

The Great Lakes area has plants as far apart as Duluth and Buffalo, a distance of some nine hundred miles. Its two main centers are Chicago and Cleveland. The mills in this region are close to the ore fields but are less favorably located than Pittsburgh with respect to coal.

The steel district at Birmingham, Alabama, is exceptionally favored by the low assembly costs of raw materials: iron ore, coal and flux are all close at hand. These advantages are offset to some

extent by the comparatively low grade of the raw materials and the remoteness of major markets.

The fourth center is at Sparrows Point, Maryland. While the industry there normally works with high-grade imported ores, it is so strategically located that ore costs have been estimated to be lower than at the Pittsburgh plants. Large markets are near by on the eastern seaboard, and the West Coast markets can be reached by all-water transportation.

The fifth area in which costs for assembly, production and delivery permit integrated steel production on a commercial basis is the Colorado–Utah region. Iron ore, coking coal and limestone are available in adequate quantities and at reasonable distances from one another. However, the plants must depend mostly on local and West Coast demand for their products.[70] During the war, fully integrated plants were built at Geneva, Utah, and Fontana, California, mainly with government money. They almost tripled the capacity of the Far West to produce pig iron and doubled its steel capacity.[71]

A new steel center may emerge as a part of the Chesapeake Bay–Delaware River area. The United States Steel Corporation has begun construction of an integrated steel mill of 2 million tons capacity at Trenton, New Jersey, for processing iron ore from its recently acquired concession in Venezuela. The deposit, a mountain eleven miles long and a mile wide, is believed to contain the world's greatest single reserve of high-purity ore. Some experts believe that by the mid-1960's another South Chicago will have sprung up at Trenton on the basis of this ore, brought from the interior of Venezuela to the ocean ports.[72] (See Figure 311.)

The United Kingdom

One of Britain's leading iron and steel districts is on the northeastern coast, in the vicinity of abundant supplies of excellent coke and limestone. Although the local economic reserves of iron ore are depleted and those of the Midlands are at some distance, this area benefits from proximity to ports where high-grade ore, largely from Sweden, Spain and North Africa, is unloaded at the furnaces, and from transportation

68. **35,** p. 66.
69. The Canada–United States boundary established by the Paris treaty of 1783 was agreed upon by the Americans and British with complete unawareness on either side that the most extensive iron ore reserves of the world in the Lake Superior region were turned over to the United States and the greatest known world deposits of nickel to Canada (**63,** pp. 97–98; **58,** p. 191). "A change in a line on the inaccurate map would have placed practically the whole Lake Superior region within the Canadian border." **38,** 1951, pp. 37–38.

70. **17,** pp. 13898–900.
71. **67,** June 14, 1945, pp. 80–94.
72. **58,** p. 192; cf. Chapter 22, pp. 776–78.

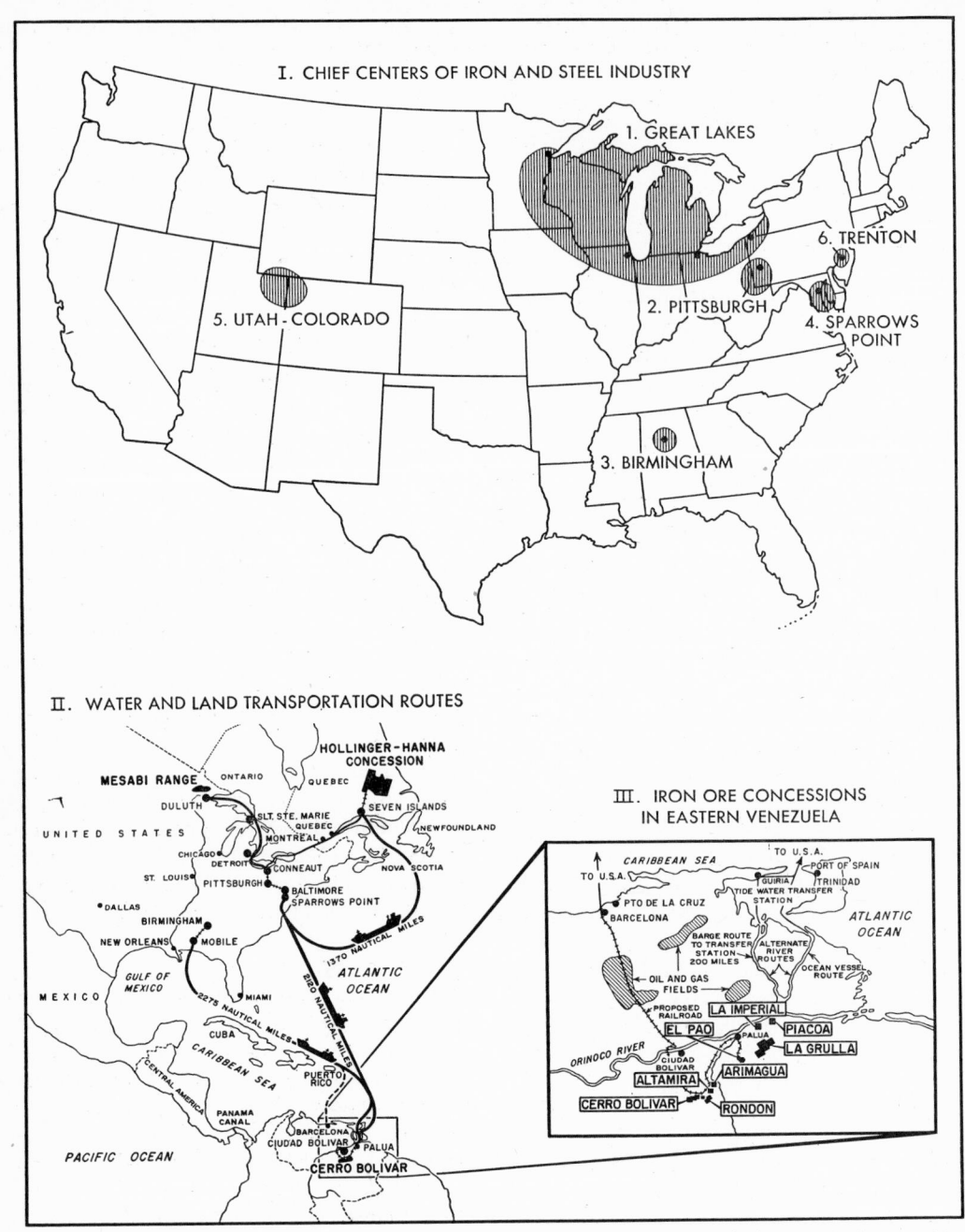

I. CHIEF CENTERS OF IRON AND STEEL INDUSTRY

1. GREAT LAKES
6. TRENTON
5. UTAH - COLORADO
2. PITTSBURGH
4. SPARROWS POINT
3. BIRMINGHAM

II. WATER AND LAND TRANSPORTATION ROUTES

HOLLINGER-HANNA CONCESSION

III. IRON ORE CONCESSIONS IN EASTERN VENEZUELA

FIGURE 311. THE STEEL INDUSTRY: CHIEF CENTERS IN THE UNITED STATES; ORE TRANSPORTATION ROUTES; IRON ORE CONCESSIONS IN EASTERN VENEZUELA

facilities to all parts of the country, coupled with the advantage of the seaboard for export of finished products.

The South Wales center is located near high-grade coal fields and also has the advantages of a seaboard position.

The third district is in Scotland, along the Clyde. While coal supplies come from extensive deposits near by, iron ore has to be imported.

The Midlands, with Sheffield, famous for its cutlery since the eighteenth century, and Lincolnshire, Staffordshire and other districts, is the fourth important center. It, too, works with near-by domestic ores and imported ore and with scrap. Markets for its products are economically located.

These four districts together accounted for 81 per cent of the British steel output in 1913 and for 70 per cent in 1937. (See Figure 312.)[73]

Germany

The dominant center of the German iron and steel industry is the Ruhr, a small valley with tremendous reserves of excellent coking coal. Smaller than the Chicago metropolitan district and with a population of 4.2 million, the Ruhr accounted for more than 70 per cent of the output of pig iron and steel in Germany in 1938.[74] First-class transportation facilities of all kinds — railways, rivers and canals — connect this area with supplies of iron ore in Sweden, France, Spain and other countries. Near-by industrial cities provide most of the market scrap.

Germany lost, at least temporarily, two other important centers of iron and steel, Upper Silesia and the Saar, after World War II. (See Figure 313.)

France

The French industry is concentrated in Lorraine, in the vicinity of deposits that supplied almost 94 per cent of the country's iron ore in 1938. This district accounted for 77 per cent of France's pig iron and 67 per cent of its steel.[75] The other important center is in the Nord Department, which produces 13 per cent of France's pig iron and 19 per cent of its steel. The industry

imports coal, mostly from the Ruhr. (See Figure 314.)

Sweden

Iron and steel works are heavily concentrated in the east central part of Sweden, near the ore fields. Coal and coke are imported, mostly from the United Kingdom and Germany, but machine shops and other metalworks are near by. Shortage of labor causes some difficulties.

The USSR

The principal centers of the iron and steel industry of the USSR are in the southern Ukraine, in the center (Moscow and Leningrad) and in the east (Ural-Siberia). (See Figure 315.) The southern district, the oldest metallurgical center in Russia, has been built up on the combination of coal and fluxes from the Donets Basin, iron ore of Krivoi Rog, and manganese of Nikopol, at a comparatively short distance from one another. Most of the furnaces are near the coal deposits. On the eve of World War II this district accounted for about two thirds of the pig iron and more than half the steel produced in the USSR.

The central district includes the blast-furnace plants for pig iron at Tula and Lipetsk and open-hearth mills in Moscow and near-by areas, which obtain most of their scrap from local metalworking plants. The district is important for its production of high-grade steels and foundry-cast iron.

The most recently developed center of iron and steel, the Kuznetsk Basin, consists of two great combines — Magnitogorsk in the Urals and Kuznetsk in Siberia — fourteen hundred miles apart. Iron ore is shipped from the Urals to Siberia, and the returning trains carry coal to the Magnitogorsk mills. The Ural iron and steel mills also obtain coal from Karaganda, only five hundred miles away.[76] Manganese and limestone deposits are comparatively near. The abundance of forests in the Urals has encouraged the use of charcoal in a number of metallurgical plants, the largest of which, at Serov, has a capacity of 400,000 tons of pig iron a year. The largest center for the production of ferroalloys is Chelyabinsk, where metallurgy is well developed in an area centrally located in relation to other

73. **43**, p. 484; and **27**, pp. 13–23.
74. **66**, p. 10.
75. **73**, pp. 42–43.

76. **41**, p. 24; and **62**, pp. 83–88.

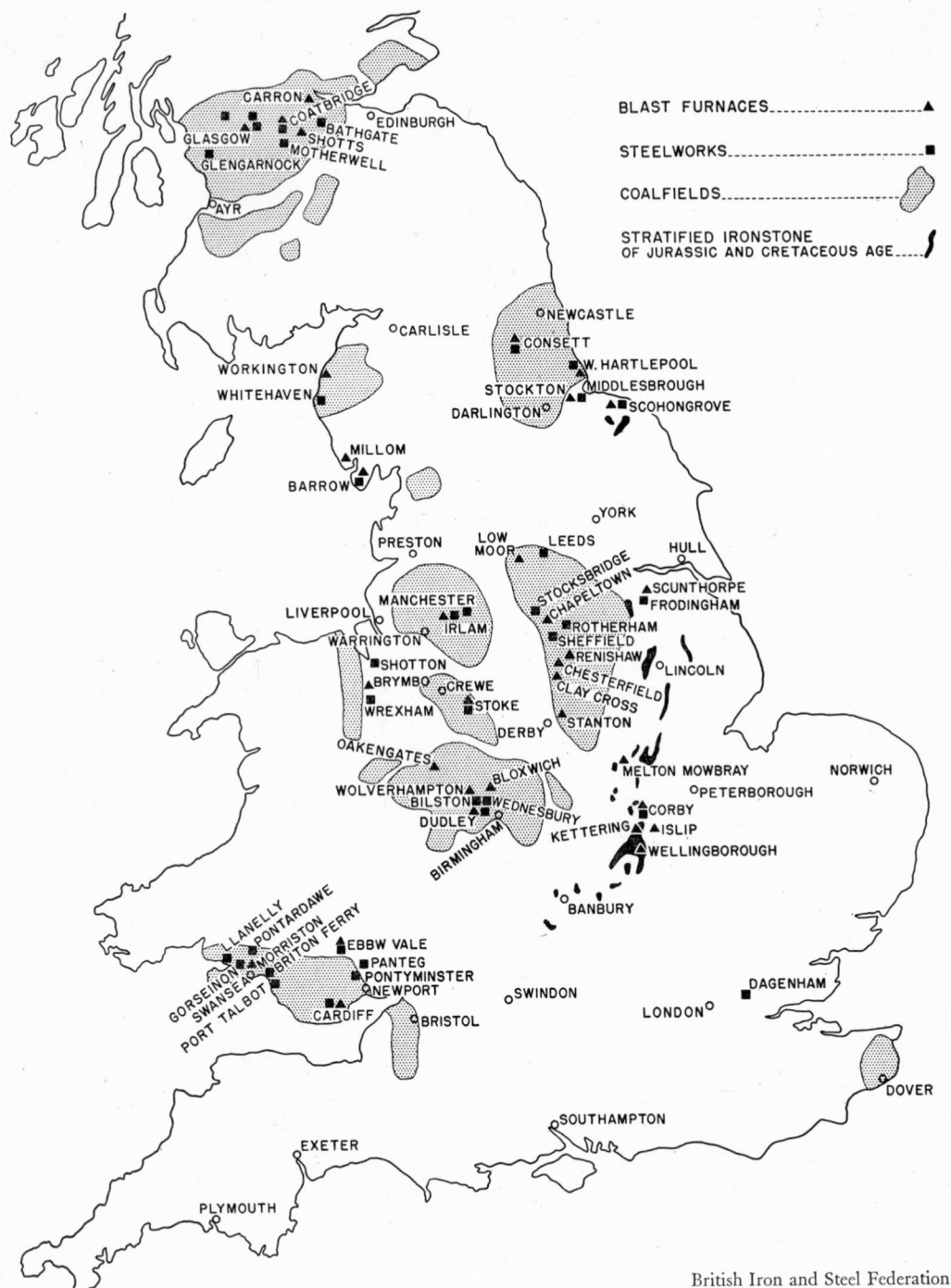

BLAST FURNACES.....................▲

STEELWORKS..........................■

COALFIELDS..........................⬭

STRATIFIED IRONSTONE
OF JURASSIC AND CRETACEOUS AGE.....

CARRON
COATBRIDGE
EDINBURGH
GLASGOW
BATHGATE
SHOTTS
MOTHERWELL
GLENGARNOCK
AYR

CARLISLE
NEWCASTLE
CONSETT
WORKINGTON
W. HARTLEPOOL
WHITEHAVEN
STOCKTON
MIDDLESBROUGH
DARLINGTON
SCOHONGROVE

MILLOM
BARROW

YORK
PRESTON
LOW MOOR
LEEDS
HULL

STOCKSBRIDGE
CHAPELTOWN
SCUNTHORPE
MANCHESTER
FRODINGHAM
LIVERPOOL
IRLAM
ROTHERHAM
WARRINGTON
SHEFFIELD
SHOTTON
RENISHAW
BRYMBO
CREWE
LINCOLN
CHESTERFIELD
WREXHAM
STOKE
CLAY CROSS
DERBY
STANTON

OAKENGATES
BLOXWICH
MELTON MOWBRAY
NORWICH
WOLVERHAMPTON
PETERBOROUGH
BILSTON
WEDNESBURY
DUDLEY
CORBY
BIRMINGHAM
KETTERING
ISLIP
WELLINGBOROUGH

BANBURY

LLANELLY
PONTARDAWE
GORSEINON
MORRISTON
EBBW VALE
SWANSEA
BRITON FERRY
PANTEG
PORT TALBOT
PONTYMINSTER
NEWPORT
SWINDON
DAGENHAM
CARDIFF
LONDON
BRISTOL

DOVER

SOUTHAMPTON
EXETER

PLYMOUTH

British Iron and Steel Federation

FIGURE 312. THE STEEL INDUSTRY: CHIEF CENTERS IN THE UNITED KINGDOM

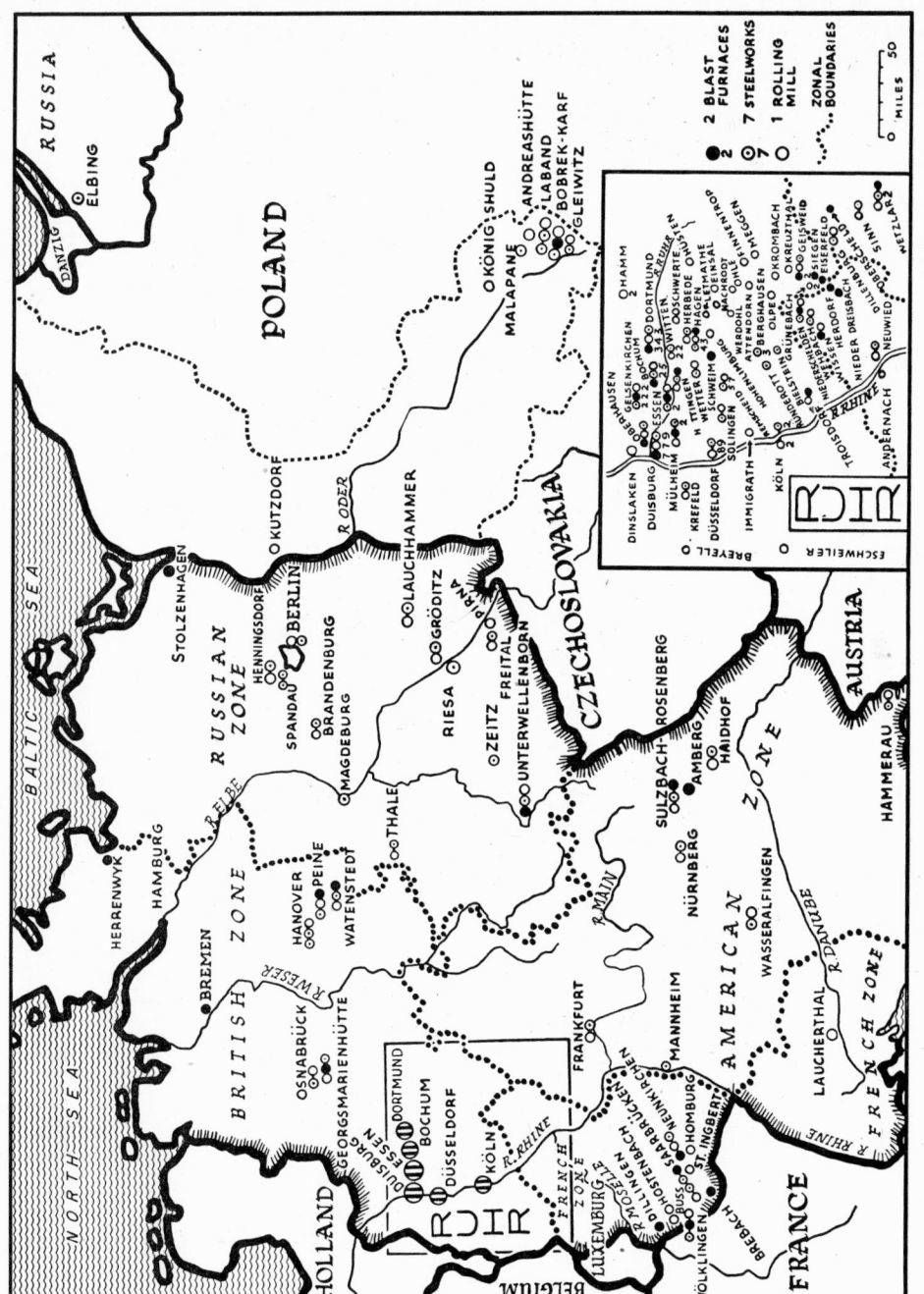

FIGURE 313. THE STEEL INDUSTRY: CHIEF CENTERS IN GERMANY

British Iron and Steel Federation

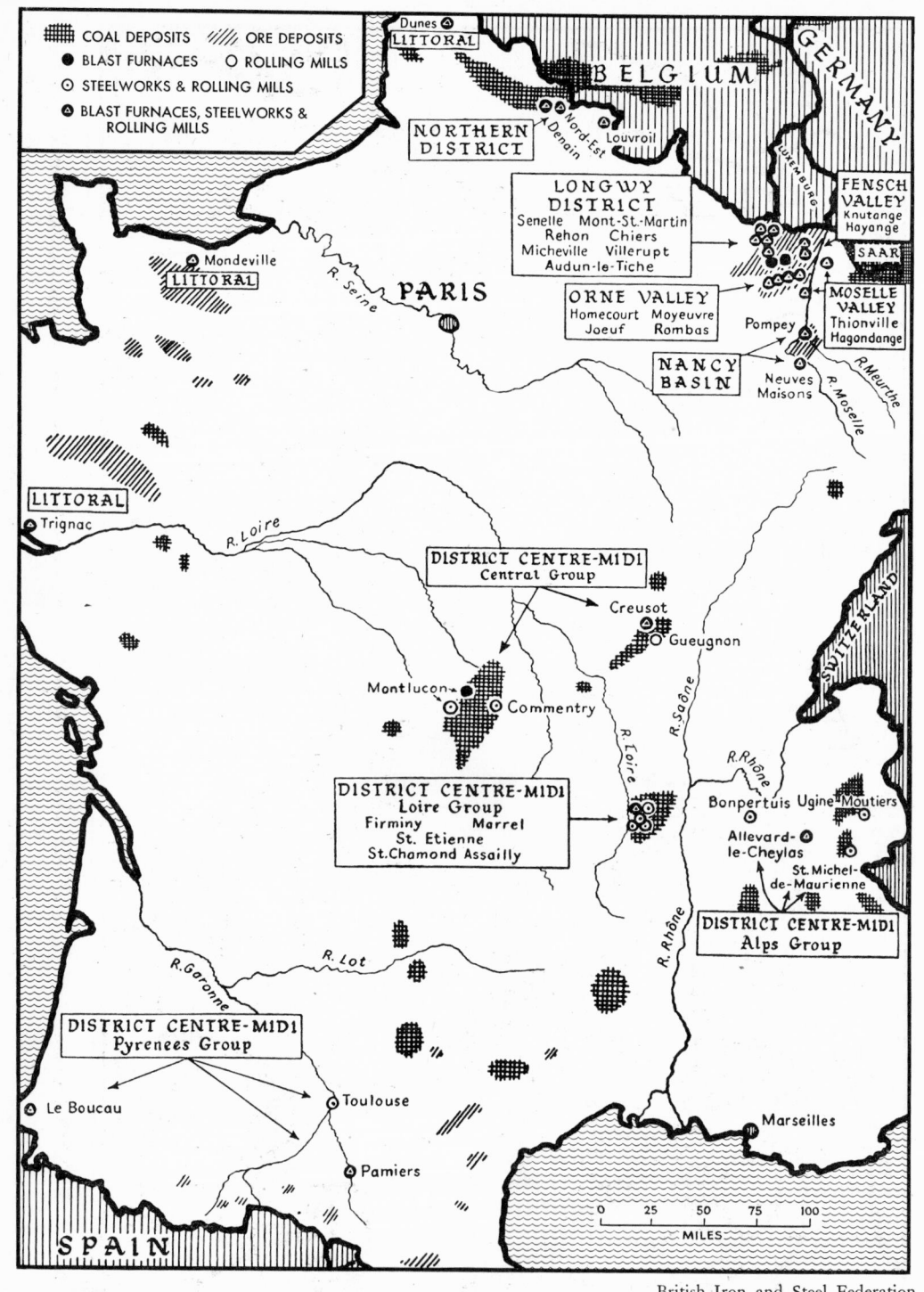

FIGURE 314. THE STEEL INDUSTRY: CHIEF CENTERS IN FRANCE

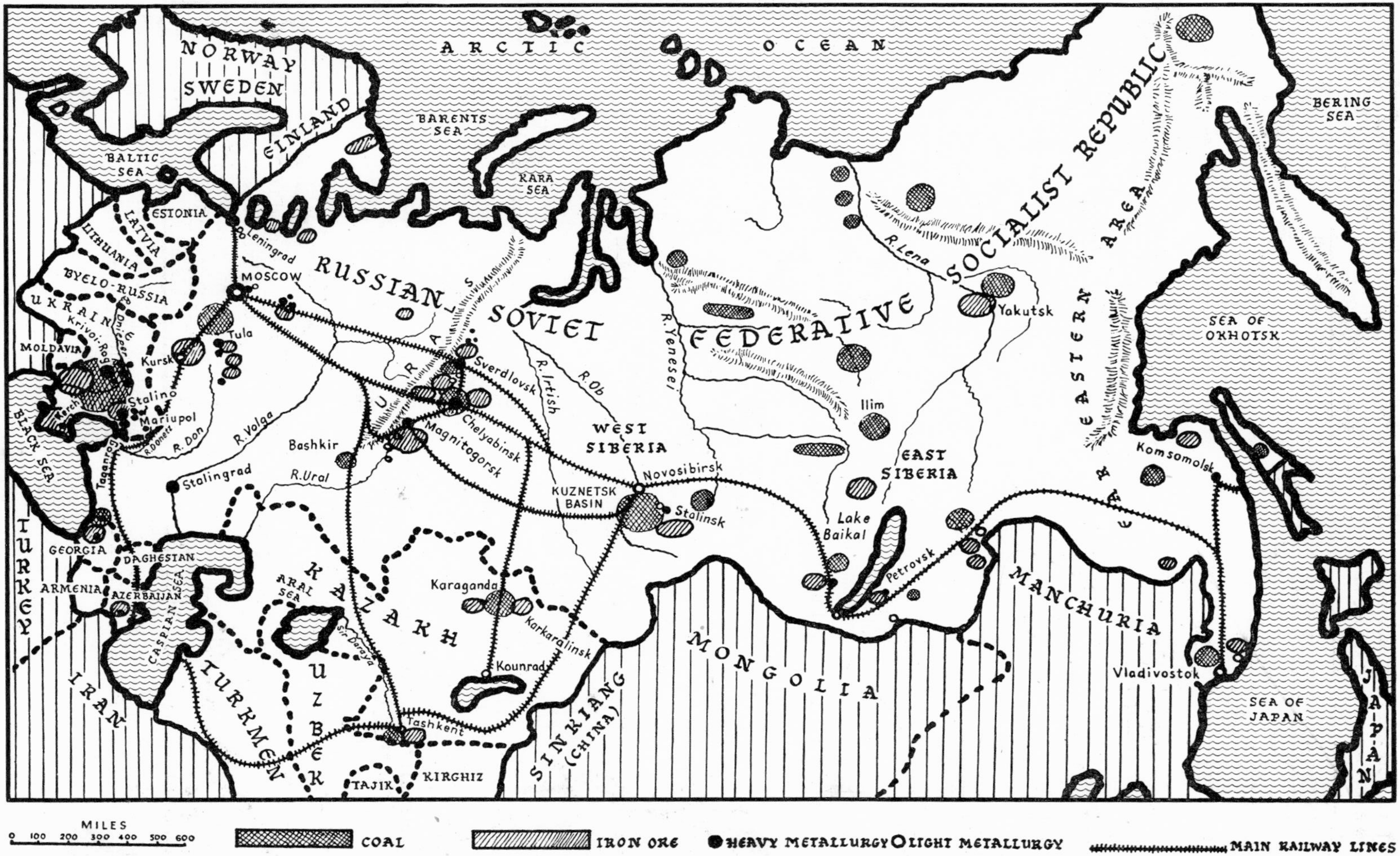

FIGURE 315. THE STEEL INDUSTRY: CHIEF CENTERS IN THE USSR

COAL   IRON ORE   ● HEAVY METALLURGY ○ LIGHT METALLURGY   MAIN RAILWAY LINES

British Iron and Steel Federation

MILLIONS
OF TONS

MILLIONS
OF TONS

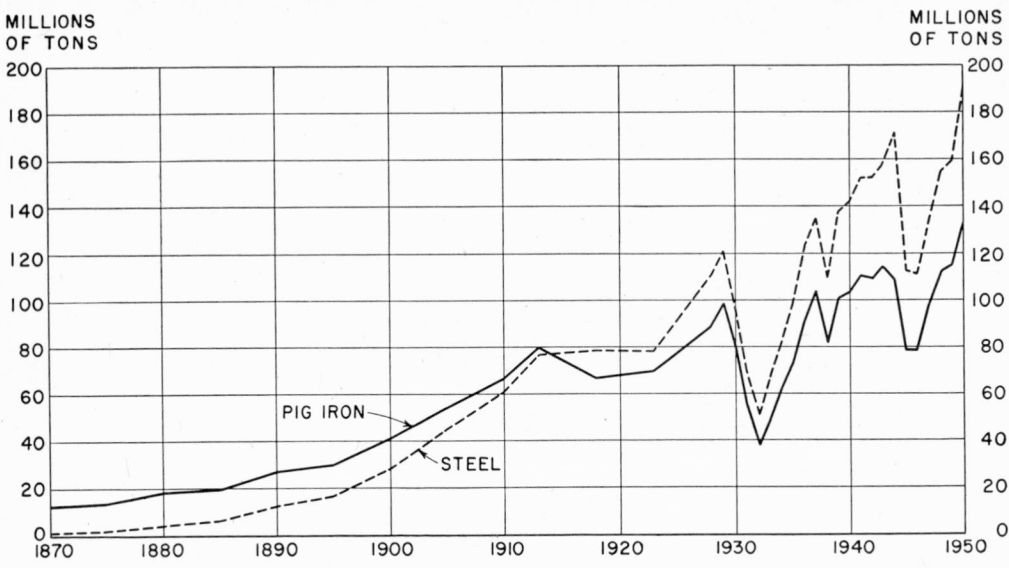

FIGURE 316. PIG IRON AND STEEL: WORLD OUTPUT, 1870–1950

metallurgical regions and far from the country's borders.[77]

Japan

Japan, which has only insignificant supplies of domestic raw materials to produce iron and steel, has built its industry mostly along the seaboard, where supplies from abroad can be delivered readily. The most important combine, the old Imperial Steel Works at Yawata, is in the northern part of the island of Kyushu, near the coal deposits. In 1936 it produced more than 90 per cent of Japan's output of pig iron and 50 per cent of its steel.[78]

PRODUCTION OF PIG IRON AND STEEL OUTPUT

Since pig iron was produced before steel and the latter was made mostly of pig iron (in Bessemer converters),[79] the world used to make more pig iron than steel. After World War I the spread of the open-hearth process and the growing use of scrap reversed this relationship. (See Figure 316.)

In 1870 the world produced 12.5 million tons of pig iron and only 700,000 tons of steel. In

77. **40,** pp. 249–53.

78. **26,** p. 280.

79. In the Bessemer converter, pig iron constitutes almost the entire metallic charge; in the open-hearth furnace, normally about half.

1914 the amounts were equal. In 1939 the output of steel was 138 million tons, that of pig iron, about 100 million tons; in 1950, 188 and 132 million tons, respectively. The lead of steel may increase further.

From 1870 to World War II

Between 1870 and 1939–40, production of pig iron and steel fluctuated considerably. The world's output of pig iron amounted to 41 million tons in 1900, rose to 80 million tons in 1913 and nearly 100 million tons in 1929, sank to about 38 million tons in 1932, and exceeded 100 million in 1939–40. (See Table 465; cf. Figure 316.)

Fluctuations in steel output have been even greater, from 28.3 million tons in 1900 to 76.5 million in 1913, 120.5 million in 1929, 50.7 million in 1932 and 142 million in 1940. (See Table 466; cf. Figure 316.)

Until 1885 the United Kingdom produced more than 40 per cent of the world output of pig iron. Since 1890 the United States has been the largest producer, even during the worst depression year, 1932. In 1939 the United States accounted for 32 per cent of all the pig iron and about 35 per cent of all the steel produced in the world.

In contrast, the share of the United Kingdom in the world's pig iron output declined from 29.0 per cent in 1890 to 22.0 per cent in 1900 and 8.0 per cent in 1939; in that of steel, from

TABLE 465

Pig Iron:[a] Output in the World and Major Producing Countries, 1870–1950

(*Millions of Metric Tons* [b])

Year	World [c]	United States	United Kingdom	France	Belgium	Luxem- bourg	Germany [d]	Russia (USSR) [e]	Japan [f]
1870	12.5	1.7	6.1	1.2	0.6	0.1	1.4	0.4	—
1875	14.0	2.1	6.5	1.4	0.5	0.3	2.0	0.4	—
1880	18.5	3.9	7.9	1.7	0.6	0.3	2.7	0.4	—
1885	19.8	4.1	7.5	1.6	0.7	0.4	3.7	0.5	—
1890	27.6	9.4	8.0	2.0	0.8	0.6	4.6	0.9	—
1895	29.9	9.6	7.8	2.0	0.8	0.7	5.5	1.5	—
1900	41.0	14.0	9.1	2.7	1.0	1.0	8.5	2.9	—
1905	54.5	23.4	9.8	3.1	1.3	1.4	10.9	2.7	—
1910	66.3	27.7	10.2	4.0	1.9	1.7	14.8	3.0	—
1913	80.0	31.5	10.4	5.2	2.5	2.5	19.3	4.6	0.2
1918	67.0	39.7	9.2	1.3	...	1.3	11.9	0.5	0.7
1923	69.8	41.0	7.6	5.5	2.1	1.4	4.9	0.3	0.8
1928	88.8	38.8	6.7	10.1	3.9	2.8	11.8	3.3	1.5
1929	98.9	43.2	7.7	10.4	4.0	2.9	13.4	4.0	1.6
1930	79.6	32.3	6.3	10.1	3.4	2.5	9.7	5.0	1.7
1931	55.1	18.7	3.8	8.2	3.2	2.1	6.1	4.9	1.4
1932	38.4	8.9	3.6	5.5	2.7	2.0	3.9	6.2	1.6
1933	48.8	13.6	4.2	6.4	2.7	1.9	5.3	7.1	2.1
1934	62.4	16.4	6.1	6.1	3.0	2.0	8.7	10.5	2.5
1935	73.5	21.7	6.5	5.8	3.1	1.9	12.8	12.6	2.8
1936	90.7	31.5	7.8	6.2	3.2	2.0	15.3	14.3	2.9
1937	103.6	37.8	8.6	7.9	3.8	2.5	16.0	14.5	3.1
1938	81.6	19.3	6.8	6.0	2.4	1.5	18.0	14.6	3.8
1939	100.5	32.2	8.0	7.3	3.0	1.8	17.4	15.2	4.6
1940	103.2	43.0	8.3	3.7	1.8	1.0	13.9	15.2	5.4
1941	110.1	51.5	7.5	3.3	1.4	1.2	15.3	13.1	6.4
1942	109.1	55.3	7.9	3.8	1.3	1.7	15.3	7.1	6.9
1943	114.5	57.0	7.3	4.9	1.6	2.3	15.8	7.5	6.3
1944	108.6	57.1	6.8	2.9	0.7	1.2	15.3	8.6	5.7
1945	79.0	49.9	7.2	1.2	0.7	0.3	...	9.2	1.0
1946	78.9	42.0	7.9	3.4	2.2	1.3	2.1	10.3	0.2
1947	98.3	54.6	7.9	4.9	2.8	1.8	2.3	11.4	0.4
1948	112.8	56.2	9.4	6.6	3.9	2.6	4.7	14.0	0.8
1949	115.1	49.8	9.7	8.4	3.7	2.4	7.1	16.6	1.6
1950	132.2	60.0	9.8	7.8	3.7	2.5	9.5	19.4	2.3

Sources: **47**, p. 251; **21**, various years; **51**, January 6, 1949, p. 194; **2**, 1951, pp. 251–52; **4**, December 1951, pp. 48–49.

a. Includes ferroalloys.

b. Conversion factor: one metric ton = 1.1023 short tons.

c. Excludes China and, from 1945, Manchuria.

d. Since 1946, Western Germany.

e. For 1947–50: estimates of the Economic Commission for Europe (**6**, 1950, p. 39).

f. Includes Korea up to 1945 and, 1935–45, Manchuria.

29.0 per cent to 17.7 and 9.6 per cent, respectively.

After 1895, Germany ranked second in steel output. Just before World War I, it accounted for 24–25 per cent of the world output of pig iron and steel; before World War II, for 16.2 per cent of the steel and 17.3 per cent of the pig iron. (See Table 467 and Figure 317.)

In continental Europe, France was second only to Germany; its share in both pig iron and steel has ordinarily been more than double that of Belgium, next in line. Russia's output nearly equaled that of France in 1913 and increased further during World War I. The revolution and civil war almost destroyed the industry, but in the 1930's the old plants were rehabilitated and new ones were built. By 1939, the USSR

TABLE 466

STEEL: OUTPUT IN THE WORLD AND MAJOR PRODUCING COUNTRIES, 1870–1950

(Millions of Metric Tons [a]*)*

Year	World [b]	United States	United Kingdom	France	Belgium	Germany [c]	Russia (USSR) [d]	Japan [e]
1870	0.7	[f]	0.2	[f]	[f]	0.2	[f]	—
1875	1.9	0.4	0.7	0.2	[f]	0.3	[f]	—
1880	4.4	1.3	1.3	0.4	0.1	0.7	0.3	—
1885	6.3	1.7	1.9	0.5	0.2	1.2	0.2	—
1890	12.4	4.3	3.6	0.7	0.2	2.2	0.4	—
1895	16.9	6.2	3.3	0.9	0.5	4.0	0.9	—
1900	28.3	10.4	5.0	1.6	0.7	6.6	2.2	—
1905	45.2	20.3	5.9	2.3	1.2	10.1	2.5	—
1910	60.5	26.5	6.5	3.4	1.9	13.7	3.5	—
1913	76.5	31.8	7.8	4.7	2.5	18.9	4.8	0.2
1918	78.6	45.2	9.7	1.8	[f]	15.0	0.4	0.8
1923	78.5	45.7	8.6	5.3	2.3	6.3	0.6	1.0
1928	110.5	52.4	8.7	9.5	3.9	14.5	4.3	1.9
1929	120.5	57.3	9.8	9.7	4.1	16.2	4.9	2.3
1930	95.0	41.4	7.4	9.4	3.4	11.5	5.8	2.3
1931	69.5	26.4	5.3	7.8	3.1	8.3	5.6	1.9
1932	50.7	13.9	5.3	5.6	2.8	5.7	5.9	2.4
1933	68.0	23.6	7.1	6.6	2.7	7.6	6.8	3.2
1934	82.4	26.5	9.0	6.2	2.9	11.9	9.7	3.9
1935	99.3	34.6	10.0	6.3	3.0	16.4	12.5	4.9
1936	123.7	48.5	12.0	6.7	3.2	19.2	16.2	5.7
1937	135.1	51.1	13.1	7.9	3.9	19.3	17.7	6.3
1938	109.4	28.8	10.6	6.1	2.3	22.7	18.0	7.0
1939	137.9	47.9	13.3	7.9	3.1	22.4	18.6	7.3
1940	142.0	60.8	13.4	4.4	1.9	19.0	18.0	7.5
1941	151.9	75.2	12.4	4.3	1.6	20.7	14.9	7.6
1942	152.0	78.0	13.0	4.6	1.4	20.3	11.0	7.9
1943	158.0	80.6	13.1	5.1	1.7	19.8	12.0	9.1
1944	170.2	81.3	12.3	3.1	0.6	18.0	13.9	7.4
1945	112.5	72.3	12.0	1.7	0.7	0.3	12.0	2.1
1946	110.8	60.4	12.9	4.4	2.3	2.6	13.0	0.6
1947	134.7	77.0	12.9	5.7	2.9	3.1	13.4	0.9
1948	155.1	80.4	15.1	7.2	3.9	5.6	18.6	1.7
1949	159.7	70.7	15.8	9.2	3.8	9.2	23.3	3.2
1950	188.2	87.6	16.6	8.7	3.8	12.1	27.3	4.5

Sources: **47**, p. 253; **36**, 1948, pp. 190–91; **51**, January 6, 1949, p. 195; for 1947–50: **2**, 1951, pp. 253–54; **4**, December 1951, pp. 50–51.

a. Conversion factor: one metric ton = 1.1023 short tons.

b. Excludes China and, from 1945, Manchuria.

c. Since 1946, Western Germany.

d. For 1947–49: estimates of the Economic Commission for Europe (**6**, 1950, p. 39).

e. Includes Korea up to 1945 and, 1935–45, Manchuria.

f. Less than 100,000 tons.

was again among the world's leading producers. In Japan and India, each of which produced less than 200,000 tons of iron and steel in 1910, the industry began to expand in the 1920's. With the occupation of Manchuria, Japan's output increased substantially and in 1940 totaled 7.5 million tons of steel; that of India tripled between 1923 and 1939.

Czechoslovakia, Italy and Australia each produced more than a million tons of pig iron in 1939; Czechoslovakia and Italy each produced 2.3 million tons of steel and Australia 1.2 million. The industry took root in many other countries. In Mexico, for example, 49,000 tons of pig iron were produced in 1928 and four times that amount in 1949. In the Union of South Africa,

TABLE 467

PIG IRON AND STEEL: DISTRIBUTION OF WORLD OUTPUT,
BY MAJOR PRODUCING COUNTRY, 1880–1950

(Per Cent)

Country	1880	1890	1900	1910	1913	1918	1923	1929	1934	1939	1944	1949	1950
Pig Iron [a]													
World	100.0	100.0	100.0	100.0	100.0	100.0	100.0	100.0	100.0	100.0	100.0	100.0	100.0
United States	21.1	34.1	34.1	41.8	39.4	59.3	58.8	43.7	26.3	32.0	52.6	43.3	45.4
United Kingdom	42.7	29.0	22.2	15.4	13.0	13.7	10.9	7.8	9.8	8.0	6.3	8.4	7.4
France	9.2	7.2	6.6	6.0	6.5	1.9	7.9	10.5	9.8	7.3	2.7	7.3	5.9
Belgium	3.2	2.9	2.4	2.9	3.1	—	3.0	4.0	4.8	3.0	0.6	3.2	2.8
Germany	14.6	16.7	20.7	22.3	24.1	17.8	7.0	13.5	13.9	17.3	14.1	6.2	7.2
Russia (USSR)	2.2	3.3	7.1	4.5	5.8	0.8	0.4	4.0	16.8	15.1	7.9	14.8	14.7
Other	7.0	6.8	6.8	7.1	8.1	6.6	12.0	16.5	18.6	17.3	15.8	16.8	16.6
Steel													
World	100.0	100.0	100.0	100.0	100.0	100.0	100.0	100.0	100.0	100.0	100.0	100.0	100.0
United States	29.5	34.7	36.7	43.8	41.6	57.5	58.2	47.6	32.2	34.7	47.8	44.3	46.6
United Kingdom	29.5	29.0	17.7	10.7	10.2	12.3	11.0	8.1	10.9	9.6	7.2	9.3	8.9
France	9.1	5.6	5.7	5.6	6.1	2.3	6.8	8.0	7.5	5.7	1.8	5.8	4.6
Belgium	2.3	1.6	2.5	3.1	3.3	—	2.9	3.4	3.5	2.2	0.4	2.4	2.0
Germany	16.1	17.7	23.3	22.6	24.7	19.3	8.0	13.4	14.4	16.2	10.6	5.8	6.5
Russia (USSR)	6.8	4.6	7.8	5.8	6.3	0.5	0.8	4.1	11.8	13.5	8.2	14.5	14.5
Japan [b]	—	—	—	—	0.02	1.0	1.3	1.9	4.1	5.3	4.3	2.0	2.4
Other	6.8	6.9	6.4	8.3	7.7	7.2	11.1	13.4	15.6	12.8	19.7	15.9	14.5

Sources: Tables 465 and 466.

a. Includes ferroalloys. b. Includes Korea up to 1945 and, 1935–1945, Manchuria.

1119

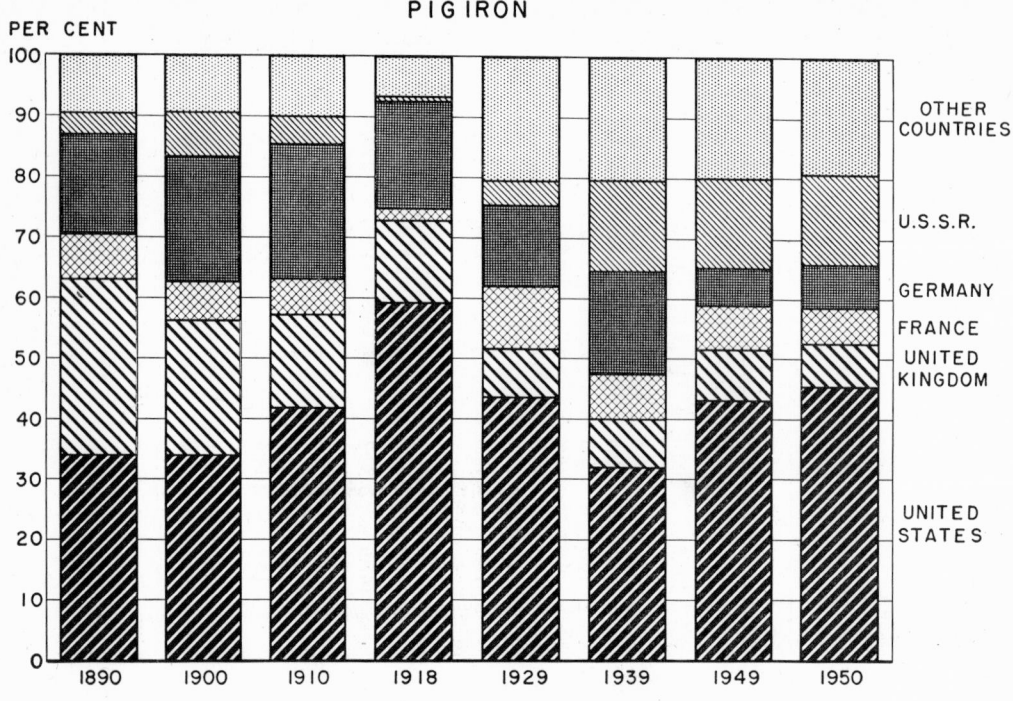

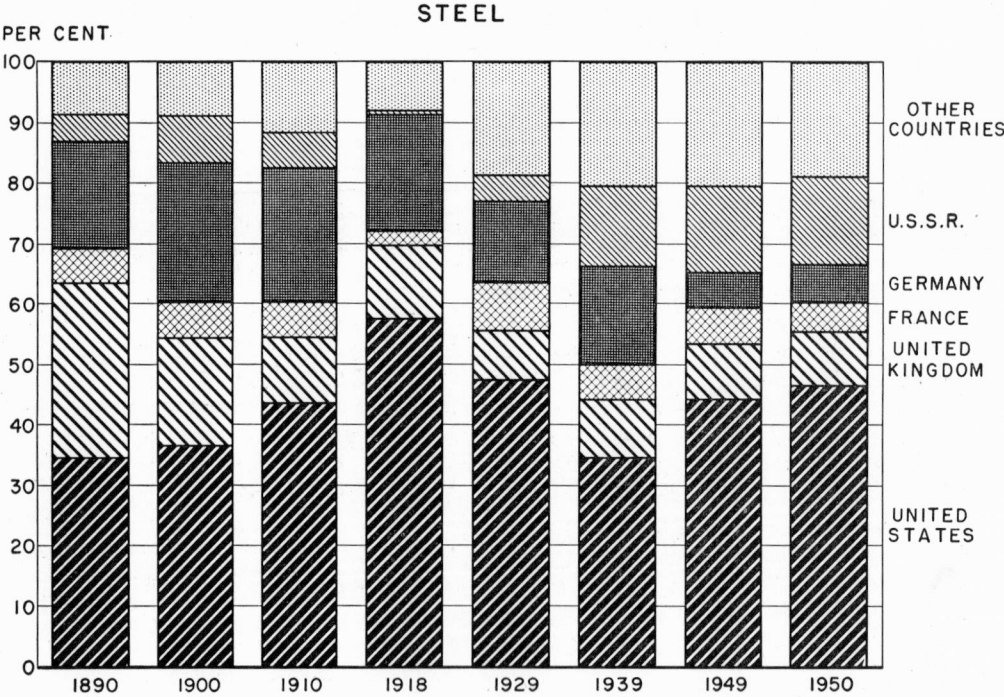

FIGURE 317. PIG IRON AND STEEL: DISTRIBUTION OF WORLD OUTPUT, BY MAJOR PRODUCING COUNTRY, 1890–1950

TABLE 468

PIG IRON AND STEEL: OUTPUT IN LESSER PRODUCING COUNTRIES, 1929–50

(*Thousands of Metric Tons* [a])

Country	Pig Iron				Steel			
	1929	1939	1949	1950	1929	1939	1949	1950
Canada	1,188	845	2,148	2,256	1,400	1,407	2,892	3,072
Mexico	60	141	206	228	114 [b]	77	331	218
Brazil	36	160	511	704	27	114	616	788
Luxembourg	2,906	1,838	2,376	2,496	2,702	1,758	2,268	2,448
Netherlands	254	284	434	454	—	110	428	490
Sweden [c]	524	691	811	785	694	1,152	1,368	1,440
Saar	2,105	1,896	1,584	1,692	2,210	2,028	1,752	1,896
Poland	706	880 [d]	. . .	. . .	1,377	1,441 [d]	2,304	2,520
Czechoslovakia	1,645	1,608	1,875	1,883	2,204	2,293	2,700	2,900
Austria	459	732	838	883	644	796	834	943
Hungary	368	409	428	500	514	733	890	1,000
Spain	753	482	629	671	1,003	584	720	818
Italy	727	1,099	445	572	2,122	2,283	2,052	2,364
China	444	. . .	11 [e]	. . .	20	. . .	44 [e]	. . .
India	1,395	1,867	1,632	1,704	584	1,219	1,380	1,464
Union of South Africa	18	300	708	733	39	368	636	816
Australia	469	1,123	1,056	1,104	440	1,223	1,200	1,212

Sources: **2**, 1948, pp. 236–39; **4**, December 1951, pp. 48–51; **6**, 1950, p. 63; data for China: **5**, 1949, p. 37.

a. Conversion factor: one metric ton = 1.1023 short tons.

b. 1930.
c. Excludes ferroalloys in 1949 and 1950.
d. 1938.
e. 1948.

the output of iron rose from 18,000 tons in 1929 to 733,000 tons in 1950 and steel production increased from 39,000 to 816,000 tons. China proper had a negligible production; Manchuria's output was also small and insufficient to meet the domestic demand. By 1948, as a result of war, internal and international, the removal of plant equipment from Manchuria by Russia, and the shortage of coal and iron ore, production had dropped catastrophically: to 11,000 tons of pig iron and 44,000 tons of steel. (See Table 468.) In 1949 Manchuria produced 94,000 tons of pig iron and 89,000 tons of steel.[80]

During and after World War II

During the war the United States raised its output of pig iron and steel to unprecedented heights, in 1944 producing slightly more than all the rest of the world combined. The output in Germany and the USSR declined considerably;

in the former, primarily because Germany could use the producing capacity of occupied countries — France, Czechoslovakia, Belgium and Luxembourg — while reserving its own manpower for service on the battlefields. In the USSR the chief center of the industry fell into German hands, and the available plants and labor, transferred to the east, could not maintain the prewar level of operation. Production in the United Kingdom also declined, but less sharply — by 15 per cent for pig iron and about 8 per cent for steel in the worst year, 1944, as compared with 1939. Japan was able to increase its output to an all-time high of 6.9 million tons of pig iron and 9.1 million tons of steel, meeting part of the shortage of raw materials by scrapping machinery in civilian industries.

In the postwar years the steel industry of the United States has continued to operate, with some fluctuations, at the wartime level, and in 1950 it exceeded that level. The United Kingdom is producing about 20–25 per cent more than be-

80. **5**, 1949, p. 37.

fore the war. Substantial recovery has also been achieved in other Marshall Plan countries. In Western Germany rapid progress in reconstruction, stimulated by the currency reform in 1948 and ECA aid, brought output in October 1951 to an annual rate of 15 million tons of steel, or about two thirds the prewar amount.

In Europe as a whole, the prewar level (1936–38 average) in pig iron was reached in 1950, while steel production was 4–5 per cent above that level as early as 1949.[81]

In the USSR, recovery of iron and steel production began slowly, but in 1949 output exceeded the prewar level and continued to increase thereafter.

Thirty countries report steel production, but only sixteen of these produced more than a million tons in 1950. As in earlier periods, the two North Atlantic regions dominated production. (See Figure 318.)

PER CAPITA OUTPUT AND CONSUMPTION

Belgium–Luxembourg produce more steel per capita of population than any other area in the world — 1,393 metric pounds in 1950. Luxembourg, taken alone, towers above all other countries with the extraordinary figure of 16,484 pounds. The United States produces 1,155 pounds per capita, and the United Kingdom follows, though at a great distance, with 656 pounds. Canada's output per capita rose considerably between 1937 and 1950 — from 269 to 444 pounds; that of the Union of South Africa, from 58 to 132 pounds.

The steel output of the USSR was 171 pounds per capita in 1939 and 250 to 300 pounds in 1950. The insignificant position of the steel industry in the economy of Latin America is emphasized by the 1950 per capita output in the two major producing countries: Brazil, 30 pounds and Mexico, 17 pounds. India's per capita output in 1950 was only 8 pounds.

The target for steel output in China, including Manchuria, is 800,000 tons a year. This would mean less than 4 pounds per capita, but production has not reached this level so far.[82]

Consumption of steel per capita of population reflects the industrial development of a region or country. It rose substantially in many regions between 1925–29 and 1950, particularly in the USSR, from 50 metric pounds to 278. The corresponding figures for Latin America are 42.0 and 48.2; for the Middle East, 13.2 and 37.6; for the Far East, 15.0 and 17.0; for Africa, 16.6 and 31.4.[83]

In countries for which data are available, per capita consumption of steel varies widely, though within a narrower range than per capita output. The United States leads, with 1,130 metric pounds in 1950. In prewar years the United Kingdom was next in line but now Canada is second, and Sweden is third. In continental Europe, per capita consumption was abnormally low in the immediate postwar years. It is gradually rising, however, and in some countries is now higher than before the war. The stagnation of Spain's economy is indicated by the same per capita consumption of steel — 52 pounds — in 1949 as in 1935. (See Table 469.)

TYPES AND PRODUCTS OF IRON AND STEEL

Since pig iron is the basic raw material for all ferrous products and primarily for steel, it is produced in types requested by steel mills.[84] More than 80 per cent of the world output of steel, and about 90 per cent of the output of the United States, the United Kingdom and the USSR, is made by the open-hearth process. Bessemer steel dominates in production in France and Belgium–Luxembourg and is important in Germany. (See Table 470.)

About 80 per cent of the output of pig iron in the United States and 70 per cent in the United Kingdom is of the basic open-hearth type.[85] Basic Bessemer pig iron constitutes about 80 per cent of the German and French output, more than 95 per cent of the Belgian, and all of that of Luxembourg.[86] In Sweden about half the pig iron is of the basic type, mostly for open-hearth furnaces, but the purity of the raw materials permits a very high proportion (about a third) to be made by the acid process. The rest is largely foundry pig iron.[87] Most of the pig iron made in India is of the basic open-hearth type and is of excellent quality.

---

81. **8,** December 1950, pp. 12–15.
82. **9,** p. 25.

83. **9,** pp. 19–23. The 1950 figure for the Far East excludes China, Manchuria and Korea.
84. About 86 per cent of all the pig iron produced in the United States in 1936–40 went into steel. (**51,** December 11, 1941.) The remainder was used in castings and in manufacturing wrought iron.
85. **21,** 1948, p. 666; and **33,** 1938–48, p. 134.
86. **8,** December 1950, *passim.*
87. **26,** p. 170.

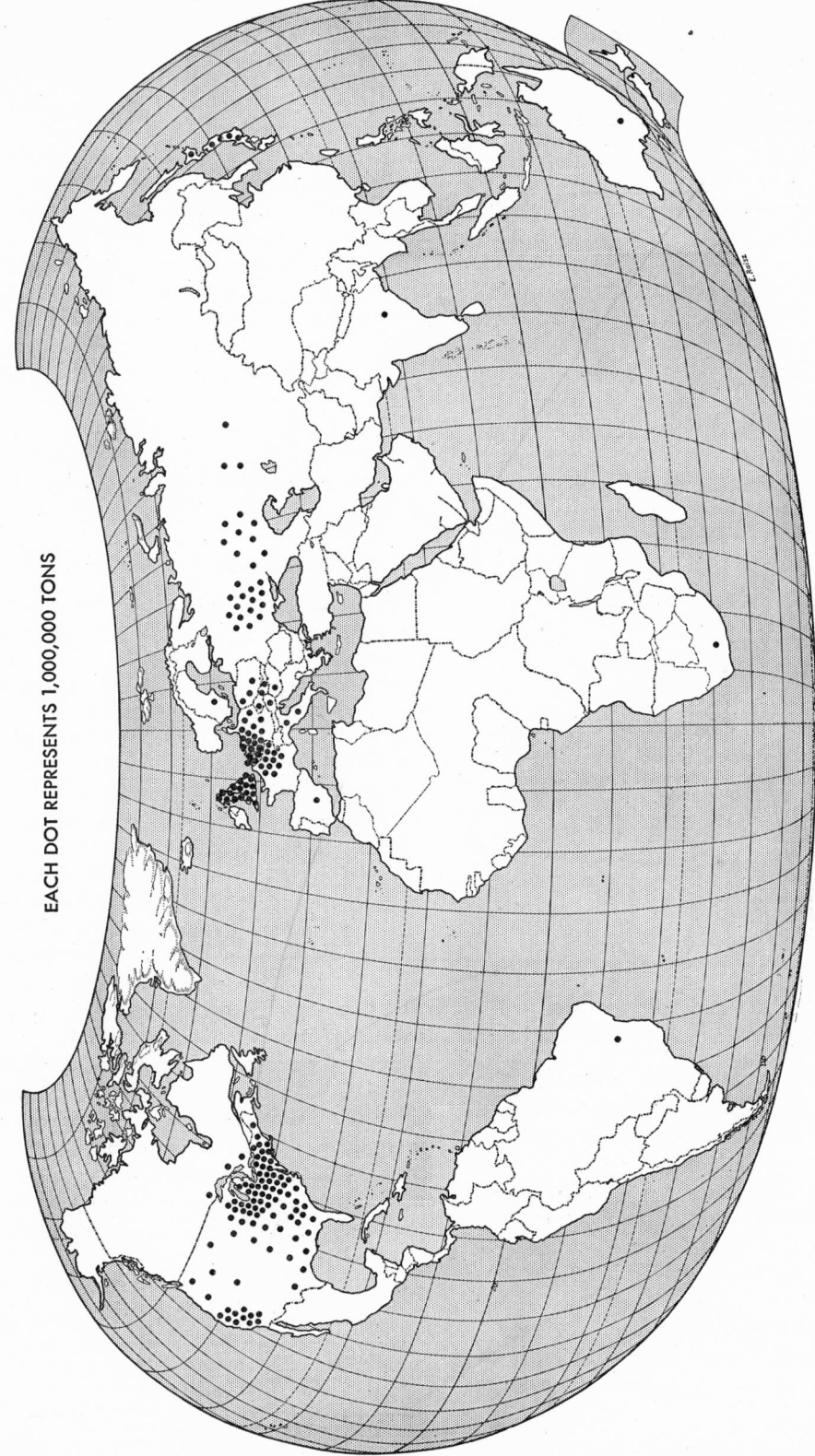

EACH DOT REPRESENTS 1,000,000 TONS

FIGURE 318. STEEL: GEOGRAPHIC DISTRIBUTION OF WORLD OUTPUT, 1950

Table 469

STEEL: OUTPUT AND CONSUMPTION PER CAPITA OF POPULATION
IN SELECTED COUNTRIES, 1937 AND 1950

(*Metric Pounds* [a])

Country [b]	Output		Consumption	
	1937	*1950*	*1937*	*1950*
Belgium–Luxembourg	1,446	1,393	502	420
United States	793	1,155	624 [c]	1,130
United Kingdom	558	656	520	556
Germany	478	508 [d]	504	408 [d]
France	383	492 [e]	302	300 [e]
Czechoslovakia	319	461	162 [f]	390 [g]
Canada	269	444	280 [c]	750
Sweden	352	410	492	584
Australia	324	296	. . .	. . .
USSR	171 [h]	283	196 [c]	278
Austria	194	267	70	108
Hungary	136	215	. . .	. . .
Poland	85	202	52 [f]	142 [g]
Union of South Africa	58	132	. . .	. . .
Japan	165	109	145 [f]	111
Italy	99	102	104	126
Spain	13	58	52 [i]	52 [j]
Brazil	4	30	24 [k]	44
Mexico	8 [h]	17	37 [k]	62
India	. . .	9	8 [k]	11

Sources: **2**, 1951, pp. 253–54; **9**, *passim*; **1**, 1951, pp. 91–101.

    a. Conversion factor: one metric pound = 1.1023 avoirdupois pounds.
    b. Countries are arrayed by declining output of steel per capita of population in 1950.
    c. 1935–39 average.
    d. Western Germany.
    e. Includes the Saar.
    f. 1936.
    g. 1948.
    h. 1939.
    i. 1935.
    j. 1949.
    k. 1936–38.

It is likely that more and more steel will be produced by the open-hearth process, and therefore that the world's blast furnaces will continue to increase their proportionate pig iron output for this purpose.

Electric steel constitutes about 6 per cent of the total steel output in the United States and 5 per cent in the USSR and the United Kingdom but nearly 40 per cent in Sweden. (See Table 470.)

Scrap

About 5 billion tons of metallic iron, in one form or another, have been produced since the manufacture of pig iron began. It has been estimated that about 35 per cent of all iron and steel is irretrievably lost by rusting or burial or is abandoned as worthless. The other 65 per cent returns to the steel mills for remelting and re-use — about 20–25 per cent in a short time, the rest within thirty years or more.[88] At any given time the world uses a steel tonnage roughly equivalent to the output of the past thirty years. The amount at mankind's disposal today may range between 3 and 3.5 billion tons, somewhat more than one ton per capita.

This tremendous amount of steel is used on railroads and in their rolling stock; in bridges, harbor installations, ships, buildings, factories and machinery; in automobiles and trucks, arms and other ordnance, household utensils and so

88. **17**, p. 349.

TABLE 470

STEEL: OUTPUT, BY TYPE, IN SELECTED COUNTRIES
BEFORE AND AFTER WORLD WAR II

(*Thousands of Metric Tons* [a])

Country and Year		Total	Open-Hearth	Bessemer		Electric	Crucible and Other
				Basic	Acid		
United States	1939	52,799	48,410	3,359		1,029	0.9
	1950	87,581	78,090	4,114		5,377	—
United Kingdom	1938	10,565	9,616	437	167	226	119
	1949	15,803	13,815	832	230	752	174
France	1938	6,221	2,074	3,735	49	359	4
	1949	9,152	2,759	5,651	105	634	3
Luxembourg	1938	1,437	—	1,390	—	47	—
	1949	2,272	—	2,226	—	46	—
Belgium	1938	2,296	323	1,906	32	34	—
	1949	3,865	469	3,271	37	88	—
Sweden	1938	987	633	106	12	236	—
	1949	1,391	691	136	28	536	—
Germany	1938	22,656	12,266	9,309	170	881	30
	1949 [b]	9,156	4,868	4,057	34	163	34
USSR	1936	16,400	14,056	291	1,187	862	5
Japan	1939	6,696 [c]	5,634 [d]	152		655	1
	1949	3,157 [c]	2,350	78		614	—

Sources: Statistical yearbooks of each country; **8,** December 1950, *passim;* **42,** 1949, Part II, p. 230; for the USSR: **73,** p. 66. Slight deviations in some totals from Table 466 are explained by different sources used.

a. Conversion factor: one metric ton = 1.1023 short tons.
b. Western Germany.
c. Includes steel not classified by type.
d. Includes castings, other than electric.

on. Each year, some of it becomes obsolete or deteriorates or is wrecked and finds its way back to steel mills in the form of scrap. The steel mills also use their own "home scrap" — cut-off ends of ingots, spattered metal, rolling-mill croppings, clippings and the like. From the fabricators comes the waste from stamping, grinding, punching and other machining operations.

Market scrap and home or intraplant scrap together constitute about half the metal used in making steel in the United States. In 1948 the industry consumed about 28 million tons of market scrap. To replace this amount with pig iron would have required the mining and transporting of some 50 million tons of iron ore, 35 million tons of coal, 10 million tons of limestone, and the construction of scores of additional furnaces.[89]

Various countries use different proportions of scrap and pig iron in the charge. Where the open-hearth process predominates, scrap constitutes half or more; in countries producing Besse-

mer steel, the mills use more pig iron than scrap. In 1936 the percentages were as follows:[90]

	Scrap	Pig Iron
United States	52	48
United Kingdom	55	45
Germany	35	65
France	28	72
Belgium (1935)	12	88
Luxembourg	9	91

These ratios have remained about the same. In 1949, for example, the steel-furnace melt comprised 50 per cent scrap in the United States and 56 per cent in the United Kingdom.[91] This considerable use of scrap in open-hearth furnaces and the full charging of electric furnaces with scrap have enabled some countries deficient in iron ore, such as Italy and Japan, to develop a steel industry.

Some American metallurgists believe that the proportion of home scrap for melting operations

89. **49,** p. 347.

90. **26,** p. 62.
91. **21,** 1949, p. 652; and **33,** 1938–48, p. 134.

may decline because of the increase in the relative amount of usable products leaving the steel plants. They also expect that less scrap will be returned to the mills because of greater efficiency in metal utilization. The protective coating given to much steel today increases its resistance to corrosion and thus prolongs its life cycle. All in all, it is considered quite possible that the proportion of scrap used in making steel may decline, particularly in the United States, which exported about 20 million tons of scrap in the years just preceding World War II and nearly 150 million tons of steel in munitions during the war.[92]

Vast quantities of steel products that would ultimately have become scrap were destroyed on battlefields during World War II and additional amounts were sent to the bottom of the sea. The expectation that rubble scrap from bombed areas would be a considerable source of supply has proved to be mistaken. Such scrap, estimated for Germany at as much as 10 million tons, is often difficult to gather. Europe, which relied on imported scrap before the war, felt the shortage in 1947–48.[93] In 1949, Western Germany exported 3 million tons of scrap, of which two thirds were shipped to the United Kingdom. The supplies from this source are declining, however, because of the rise in German steel production, and in 1951 total scrap exports from Western Germany were not expected to exceed a million tons.[94]

Finished Products

A steel ingot is not marketable as such. It has to be rolled, forged or pressed to the desired shape before it is finally converted into structural shapes, rails, sheets, plates, wire rods and other finished products. These operations are performed in rolling mills, in which the ingot is moved through sets of grooved rollers, each succeeding set nearer the required width, length and shape than the preceding one. Some rolling mills specialize in only one finished product, while others produce a long list. The steel industry as a whole manufactures some 500 separate types of products in as many as 100,000 different sizes, shapes and finishes.[95] A large part of its output is "tailor-made," and the specifications tend to become increasingly precise as to the

physical properties of both the ingot and the finished product.[96]

Most of the products of rolling mills serve as raw materials for other industries — machine and tool manufacture, shipbuilding, automobile and aircraft industries, mining, construction and so on. Some products are used by one or a few industries, others by many. Rails and crossties are taken by railroads; pipes and tubes mostly by gas, oil and water companies. Sheets, strip and bars constitute from 75 to 90 per cent of all the steel products used in the automobile industry. Tin plate and black plate are important in the container industry; heavy structural shapes, in building construction. Plates, bars and wires have a variety of customers in practically all industries.

A thousand tons of steel ingots yield, on the average, 700 to 800 tons of finished products. The output of rolling mills therefore usually approximates seven tenths of that of steel ingots. In 1950, for example, the United States produced 87.6 million tons of steel ingots and 67.9 million tons of rolled and other finished steel products. (See Table 471; cf. Figure 319.) Most products of rolling mills require further processing: sheets must be coated, wire drawn, pipes made from tube rounds, and so on. Some steel mills have special departments for such operations; others turn them over to their subsidiaries or sell their products to specialized plants. In the United States, half the tonnage of finished products in 1939 was processed in such special plants.

Sheets, plates and bars make up the largest group of rolling-mill products in most countries — more than half of all finished steel in 1949. Railroad material represents about 5–8 per cent of the total in the United Kingdom and France; about 3 per cent in Belgium; and one per cent in Sweden. Heavy sections range from 12 to 13 per cent of the total in the United Kingdom; they constitute some 9 per cent in Germany and 7 per cent in France and Italy. (See Table 472.)

Various finished products represent a larger or smaller proportion of the total output of finished steel at various times and in various countries. In the United States, plates, strips and sheets made up 33 and 47 per cent of the total in 1925 and 1935, respectively, 44 per cent in 1945, and 53 per cent in 1950. (See Table 473.)

When a country is engaged in intensive shipbuilding, as the United States was during the

---

92. **49,** pp. 339 and 352.
93. **7,** 1949, p. 42.
94. **6,** 1950, p. 75.
95. **17,** p. 350.

96. **11,** p. 37; and **63,** p. 145.

TABLE 471

FINISHED STEEL PRODUCTS: OUTPUT IN SELECTED COUNTRIES, 1913–50

(*Millions of Metric Tons* [a])

Country	1913	1929	1935	1938	1947	1949	1950
United States	25.2	41.7	24.1	21.2	60.0	55.2	67.9
Canada	...	1.1	0.8	0.8	2.1	2.4	2.6
United Kingdom	8.1	8.0	7.4	7.7	10.2	12.2	...
France	3.9	6.7	4.2	4.4	4.6	6.5	6.0
Luxembourg	1.2	1.9	1.3	1.2	1.4	1.8	...
Belgium	2.3	3.3	2.4	1.9	2.5	3.3	...
Saar	...	...	...	2.1	1.0	1.4	1.3
Sweden	0.5	0.5	0.6	0.7	0.8	1.0	...
Germany	19.6	11.3	11.7 [b]	17.0	2.5 [c]	7.0 [c]	...
Poland	...	1.0	0.7	1.1 [d]	0.9	1.0 [e]	...
Czechoslovakia	...	...	...	1.6 [d]	1.6	1.8 [e]	...
Austria	...	0.5	0.3	0.5	0.3	0.7	...
Italy	...	2.0	1.9	1.8	1.4	1.7	...
USSR [f]	3.5	3.9	9.3	13.1 [g]	10.9	17.8	20.8
Japan	0.3	2.0	4.1	5.0	0.6	2.2	3.5
India	...	0.4	0.6	0.7	0.9	0.9	1.0
Union of South Africa	...	...	...	0.2	0.4	0.5	...
Australia	...	...	...	1.2	1.1	1.1	...

Sources: **72**, Vol. IV, p. 173; **32**, 1938, p. 77*; statistical yearbooks of each country; **42**, 1947, Part II, *passim,* and 1949, Part II, *passim;* **8**, December 1950, *passim.*

a. Conversion factor: one metric ton = 1.1023 short tons.

b. Includes the Saar.
c. Western Germany.
d. 1937.
e. 1948.
f. For 1947–50: estimate of the Economic Commission for Europe (**6**, 1951, p. 127).
g. 1940.

two world wars, heavy sections are produced in larger quantities than ordinarily. The automobile industry requires sheets, plates and strips, the output of which is affected substantially by the ups and downs in this industry. Aircraft, building construction and the production of containers also require these articles, and the present trend in the United States is toward an increase in sheets, plates and strips.[97] (See Table 474 and Figure 320.)

The output of these products is making rapid strides in Europe also, and it is expected that the completion of continuous-strip mills now under way in various countries will stimulate the upward trend in flat products, particularly thin sheets. In Europe as a whole, mechanical and electrical engineering and the railroads are the largest consumers of finished steel — in 1948, 26.9 and 16.1 per cent, respectively; coal mining, the building trades and industries manufacturing household products (furniture, hardware, containers and so on) each account for 8–9 per cent; agriculture for 7 per cent.[98]

STRUCTURE OF THE INDUSTRY IN SELECTED COUNTRIES

Blast and steel furnaces in different countries vary greatly in size, equipment and efficiency and in the quality of their products. Even greater are the differences in the structure of the iron and steel industry and its interrelation with the rest of the economy.

The United States

The iron and steel industry of the United States has been favored by an exceptional combination of circumstances. The essential raw materials — iron ore, coking coal and limestone — are all available domestically, and the ore

97. See discussion of the consumption of finished steel products by various industries in **10**, pp. 99 ff.

98. **7**, 1949, p. 37.

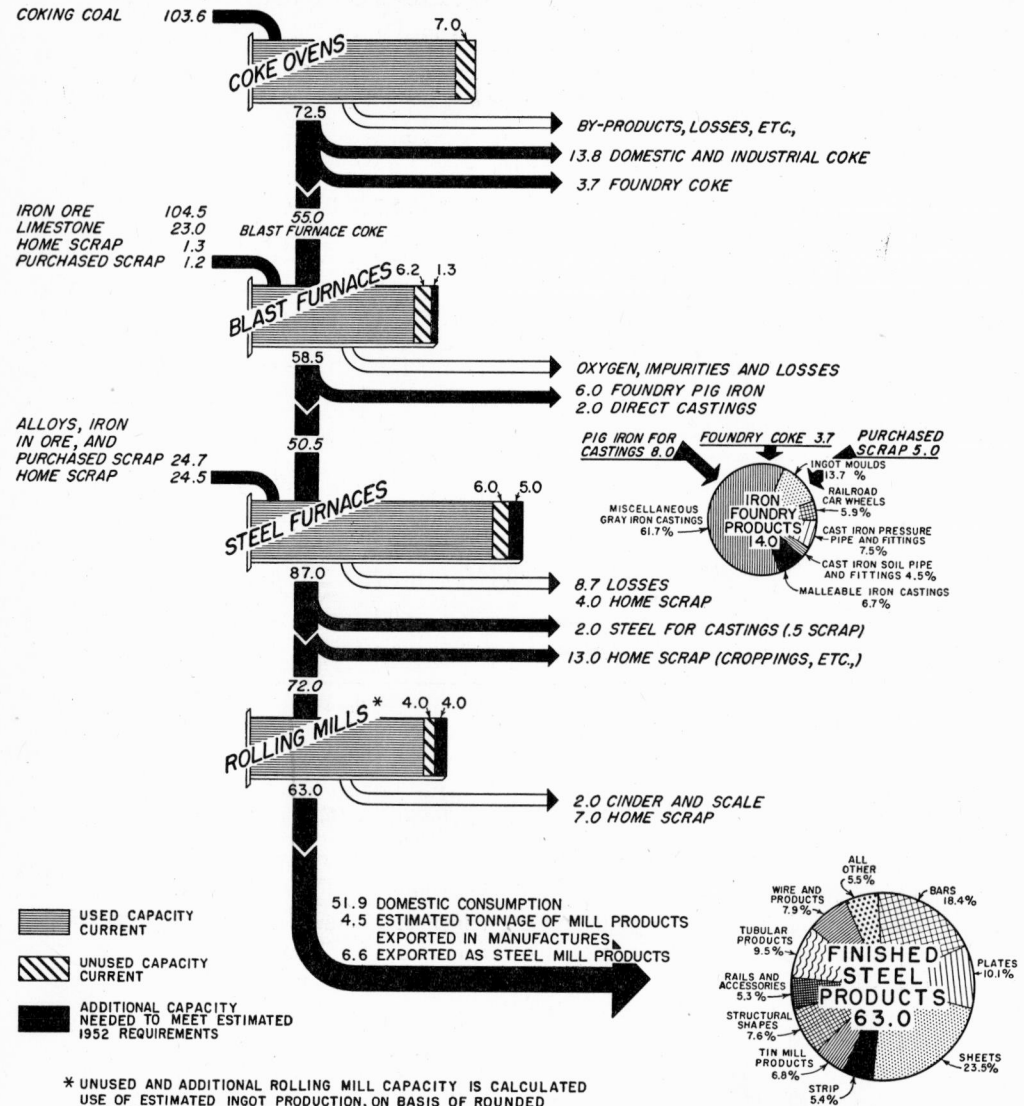

FIGURE 319. STEEL: FLOW FROM RAW MATERIALS TO FINISHED PRODUCTS IN THE UNITED STATES, 1947

The flow from raw materials to finished steel portrayed in this chart is typical of a steel industry where the open-hearth process predominates.

The flow begins with the raw materials used by blast furnaces — coking coal, iron ore, limestone. In 1947, as estimated on the basis of the first six months, the blast furnaces delivered 58.5 million tons of pig iron, of which 50.5 million tons were used in making steel. To the pig iron were added 24.7 million tons of purchased scrap and 24.5 million tons of home scrap. From these 99.7 million tons of iron, 87.0 million tons of steel ingots were produced and processed into 63.0 million tons of rolling-mill products. The waste in steel and rolling mills is returned to steel furnaces as home scrap. Sheets, bars and plates together accounted for 52 per cent of all finished products, tubular goods for 9.5 per cent, structural shapes for 7.6 per cent, and wire and wire products for 7.9 per cent.

TABLE 472

FINISHED STEEL PRODUCTS: OUTPUT, BY TYPE, IN SELECTED COUNTRIES, 1938 AND 1949

(Thousands of Metric Tons[a])

Country	1938						1949					
	Plates and Sheets	Strip	Bars	Wire Rods	Railway Material[b]	Heavy Sections	Plates and Sheets	Strip	Bars	Wire Rods	Railway Material[b]	Heavy Sections
United Kingdom	2,941	478	1,322	446	540	1,470	4,417	913	2,356	813	599	1,535
France	1,046	190	1,482	395	419	346	1,566	347	2,284	596	477	475
Saar	357	189	718	185	139	261	360	92	419	96	26	177
Luxembourg	62	57	427	56	95	328	142	75	622	156	135	293
Belgium	508	122	711	127	112	120	848	218	1,130	354	108	202
Sweden	139	34	241	104	12	17	219	62	332	116	30	11
Germany[c]	4,234	924	5,070	1,379	1,170	1,179	1,839	609	1,860	645	285	612
Poland[d]	215	48	308	135	152	99	237	34	255	114	196	112
Czechoslovakia[e]	294	...	607	169	183	71	...	...	...	...	...	...
Austria	88	27	159	62	45	58	176	27	182	96	21	25
Italy	467	...	493	170	92	68	362	...	632	216	24	116
Japan[f]	1,801	...	1,315	401	283	664	176	...	94	91	37	12
Australia[f]	88	60	379	122	48	172	132	92	329	94	43	98

Sources: **42,** 1947, Part II, pp. 11 and 183; **8,** December 1950, *passim.*

a. Conversion factor: one metric ton = 1.1023 short tons.

b. Rails, crossties, fishplates.

c. 1949: Western Germany.

d. 1937 and 1947. Data for 1947 are estimated.

e. 1937.

f. 1938 and 1947.

TABLE 473

FINISHED STEEL PRODUCTS: OUTPUT, BY TYPE, IN THE UNITED STATES, 1925–50

(*Thousands of Short Tons*)

Hot-Rolled Product	1925	1935	1940	1945	1948	1949	1950
Total	37,393	26,840	48,660	59,812	69,192	60,882	74,823
Plates	4,204	1,630	4,323	7,246	7,612	6,547	7,386
Sheets	4,588	5,797	11,706	12,067	17,925	16,814	22,325
Black plate	2,192	2,307	522	1	158	110	153
Strip	1,398	2,965	2,078	2,543	3,185	2,838	3,904
Strip and sheets for cold reduced black plate and tin plate	a	a	3,104	4,437	5,722	5,250	5,991
Bars							
Merchant	6,388	4,143	6,459	9,649	9,590	7,390	9,353
Concrete	918	624	1,426	835	1,561	1,664	1,833
Rails	3,119	797	1,679	2,418	2,208	1,901	1,850
Skelp	3,617	1,514	2,709	2,894	3,618	3,639	4,164
Wire rods	3,186	2,734	4,352	4,531	5,431	4,388	5,820
Structural shapes	4,036	1,951	4,232	4,467	5,456	4,672	5,442
Other	...	...	6,070	8,724	6,726	5,669	6,602

Sources: **19**, 1951, p. 796; **36**, 1950, pp. 38–39. a. Data not available.

TABLE 474

FINISHED STEEL PRODUCTS: DISTRIBUTION OF CONSUMPTION, BY INDUSTRY IN THE
UNITED STATES, 1929–51

(*Per Cent*)

Consuming Industry	1929	1934	1939	1944	1947	1949	1950	1951
Total	100.0	100.0	100.0	100.0	100.0	100.0	100.0	100.0
Automobile	18.0	21.3	15.1	7.4 a	16.3	18.8	20.5	16.7
Construction and maintenance	16.5	13.3	15.6	9.8	16.0	12.1	12.2	12.3
Container	4.9	9.6	7.6	6.1	8.9	8.0	8.3	8.4
Machinery, tools	3.0	4.8	3.7	5.1	9.2	6.7	7.4	8.1
Oil, gas, mining	10.6	7.4	4.7	3.9	5.9	7.7	1.3 b	1.6
Railroads	17.0	10.6	8.3	9.6	9.6	6.3	6.1	7.4
Shipbuilding	c	c	1.3	18.8	0.6	1.1	0.5	1.1
Agriculture	5.7	7.4	3.6	3.1	3.8	2.5	2.1	2.1
Exports	5.4	4.2	7.2	8.0	7.3	6.0	3.6	3.6
All other	19.0	21.3	32.9	28.2	22.4	30.8	38.0	38.7

Sources: Adapted from **51**, January 7, 1937, p. 75; January 4, 1945, p. 59; **37**, April 1950, p. 8, and April 1952, p. 3.

a. Includes aircraft.

b. Much additional steel was shipped for the oil and gas industry to the steel warehouses, but the breakdown of their receipts (18.9 per cent) is not available.
c. Included in "all other."

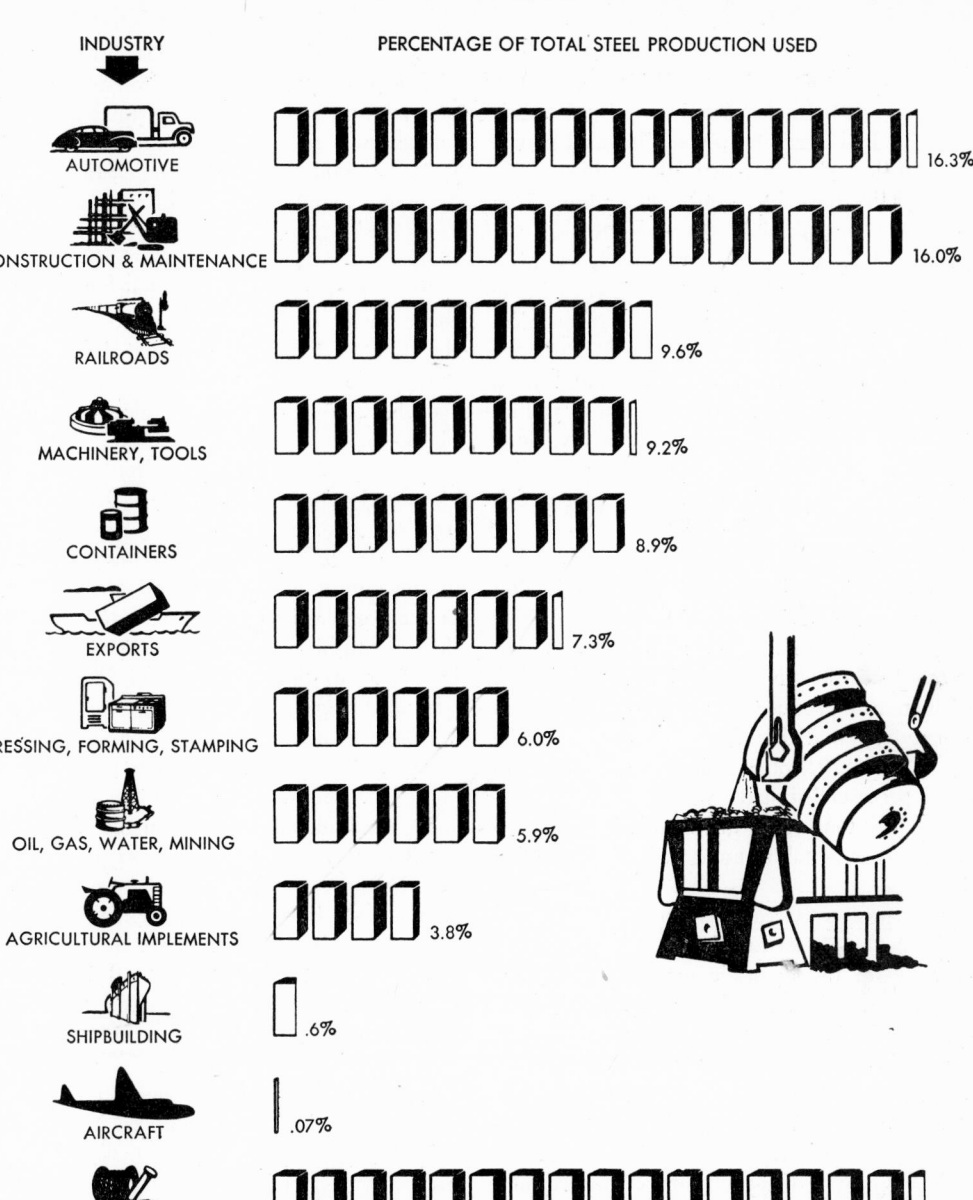

INDUSTRY

PERCENTAGE OF TOTAL STEEL PRODUCTION USED

AUTOMOTIVE — 16.3%

CONSTRUCTION & MAINTENANCE — 16.0%

RAILROADS — 9.6%

MACHINERY, TOOLS — 9.2%

CONTAINERS — 8.9%

EXPORTS — 7.3%

PRESSING, FORMING, STAMPING — 6.0%

OIL, GAS, WATER, MINING — 5.9%

AGRICULTURAL IMPLEMENTS — 3.8%

SHIPBUILDING — .6%

AIRCRAFT — .07%

ALL OTHERS — 16.4%

Prepared by Dun & Bradstreet, Inc.; estimate by *Iron Age;* basic data by American Iron and Steel Institute

FIGURE 320. FINISHED STEEL PRODUCTS: DISTRIBUTION OF CONSUMPTION, BY INDUSTRY, IN THE UNITED STATES, 1947

and coking coal are of high quality.[99] The country's dense network of railroads and waterways, its great financial resources, large domestic market and advanced technology have all played a part in the rapid growth of this industry.

While the basic principles of making iron and steel were inherited from the British, the American industry incorporated many technical improvements that have vastly increased the efficiency and speed of all operations. Mechanical charging of blast and open-hearth furnaces, mechanical shoveling, changes in plant layout, and the mechanical handling of metal in rolling mills were introduced in the last century. Such innovations were characterized by an English steelmaker as "engineering common sense which amounts almost to genius." [100]

The size of furnaces and other equipment has been increased continually and new laborsaving and fuel-saving devices have been adopted. The speed at which rolling mills operate has been increased steadily. In the continuous-strip mills, 130 men can produce as many steel sheets as formerly required the labor of more than 4,000 men.[101] In 1879, some 220 workers were employed per establishment, with an average output of 6,700 tons of unrolled steel; in 1935, 908 workers per establishment averaged 87,000 tons.[102]

In contrast to Great Britain, Germany and Belgium, the American industry has worked primarily for the domestic market. Only some 5–7 per cent of the steel output has been exported, not counting indirect export in the form of machinery, automobiles and other manufactured products.

During World War II the industry modernized its equipment, partly with government funds.[103] Growth of capacity has continued, and the industry will have an annual capacity of more than 120.5 million short tons of steel by the end of 1953.[104]

The industry is highly integrated, both vertically and horizontally. Vertical integration begins with the ownership of iron ore and often of coal mines and limestone quarries as well, and extends throughout production, from blast furnaces to rolling mills. In some cases, it reaches even into manufacturing and construction, such as the building of ships, bridges and prefabricated houses.

As of January 1947 more than 88 per cent of the capacity of the iron and steel industry in the United States was owned by wholly or partially integrated companies. The Big Three, completely integrated, owned almost 56 per cent of the nation's capacity.[105]

The largest concern, the United States Steel Corporation, owns about half the high-grade iron ore reserves in the Lake Superior region. In January 1945 it accounted for 36.6 per cent of the output of pig iron and ferroalloys, 33.8 per cent of the steel output, and 31.1 per cent of that of finished hot-rolled products.[106] There is less concentration of ownership in the more advanced stages of production.

About 85 or more per cent of the iron ore is shipped directly from the mines to the large integrated concerns. Similarly, these concerns consume the bulk of the pig iron, ingot and semifinished steel in their own works, while a small part is sold to semi-integrated or nonintegrated companies, without capacity for making pig iron or steel, for further processing. In 1939, 6.8 per cent of the semifinished steel and 51.7 per cent of the finished steel were produced for sale — to rolling mills, wire mills, foundries and forges for further manufacturing.[107]

Pennsylvania and Ohio together account for about half the pig iron produced in the United States. Indiana, Illinois and Michigan are next in line, with about a fourth of the total, and the rest is distributed among seventeen states. Since most pig iron is converted into steel in the mill in which it is produced, the distribution of the steel output by state is similar.

In finished steel products, Pennsylvania (Pittsburgh) has traditionally been the leader and is still ahead, but Ohio, Indiana, Illinois and other midwestern states are gaining importance. (See Table 475; cf. Figure 321.)

---

99. The United States is less well endowed with alloying elements, being self-sufficient only in molybdenum and tungsten. Others, such as manganese, chromium and nickel, are either lacking or of such low grade that it is more economical to import high-grade foreign ores than to exploit the domestic deposits. (See Chapter 22, *passim*.)

100. **43**, p. 184.

101. **16**, p. 238.

102. **26**, p. 86.

103. **27**, p. 16.

104. **37**, April 1952, p. 7.

105. United States Steel, Bethlehem Steel and Republic Steel. (**22**, p. 14.)

106. **27**, pp. 42–44.

107. **18**, 1939, Vol. II, Part 2, p. 187. Some of the finished products, such as rails, are sold directly to consumers.

TABLE 475

PIG IRON AND STEEL: OUTPUT IN THE UNITED STATES, BY STATE, 1929–50

(Millions of Short Tons)

State	1929	1939	1948	1949	1950
			Pig Iron		
Total	46.8	34.8	60.1	53.4	64.6
Pennsylvania	15.7	9.8	17.7	15.0	18.2
Ohio	10.9	8.0	12.5	10.6	12.5
Indiana, Michigan [a]	5.7	4.8	8.6	8.0	9.8
Illinois	4.9	3.0	5.5	4.9	6.0
Alabama	3.0	3.0	4.0	3.7	4.3
New York, Massachusetts	3.1	2.4	3.9	3.5	4.3
Maryland, West Virginia, Kentucky, Tennessee [b]	2.4	3.1	5.5	5.5	6.7
Other	1.1	0.7	2.4	2.2	2.8
		Ingots and Steel for Castings			
Total	63.2	52.8	88.6	78.0	96.8
Pennsylvania	22.6	15.0	26.2	21.8	27.3
Ohio	14.8	11.7	17.7	15.1	18.8
Indiana	7.5	6.7	10.8	9.4	11.4
Illinois	5.4	4.1	7.4	6.8	8.2
Alabama, Georgia [c]	1.9	2.4	3.7	3.3	4.0
New York [d]	2.8	2.7	4.3	4.0	4.8
Michigan, Minnesota	1.0	3.0	4.1	3.9	5.5
Maryland, New Jersey, Delaware [e]	2.1	3.1	5.0	4.8	5.7
Virginia, West Virginia, Kentucky, Tennessee	2.5	2.3	3.3	3.3	3.9
California			2.0	1.9	2.4
Missouri, Oklahoma, Texas, Colorado	2.6	1.8	2.2	2.0	2.7
Utah, Washington, Oregon			1.5	1.3	1.7
Other			0.4	0.4	0.4
		Finished Iron and Steel Products			
Total	46.0	39.0	69.2	60.9	75.2
Pennsylvania	16.6	11.0	18.9	15.8	18.9
Ohio	9.9	8.6	14.2	12.0	14.7
Indiana	5.8	5.0	9.3	8.2	10.0
Illinois	3.6	2.7	5.2	4.9	5.9
Alabama	1.4	1.7	2.6	2.3	3.1
New York	2.1	1.9	3.4	3.1	3.7
Michigan	0.9	2.1	3.0	2.8	4.2
Maryland, Delaware [f]	1.4	2.2	4.3	4.2	5.4
West Virginia	1.5	1.4	2.4	2.4	2.4
California			1.6	1.5	1.8
Missouri, Oklahoma, Texas, Colorado	2.8	2.4	1.8	1.6	2.1
Washington, Oregon, Utah			1.0	0.9	1.3
Other			1.5	1.2	1.7

Source: **36**, various years, *passim*.

a. 1948–50: includes Minnesota.
b. 1929: includes Virginia; 1948–50: includes Texas.
c. 1929: includes Florida.
d. 1939: includes New Jersey.
e. 1929 and 1939: Maryland, Virginia and Delaware.
f. 1929 and 1939: includes Virginia.

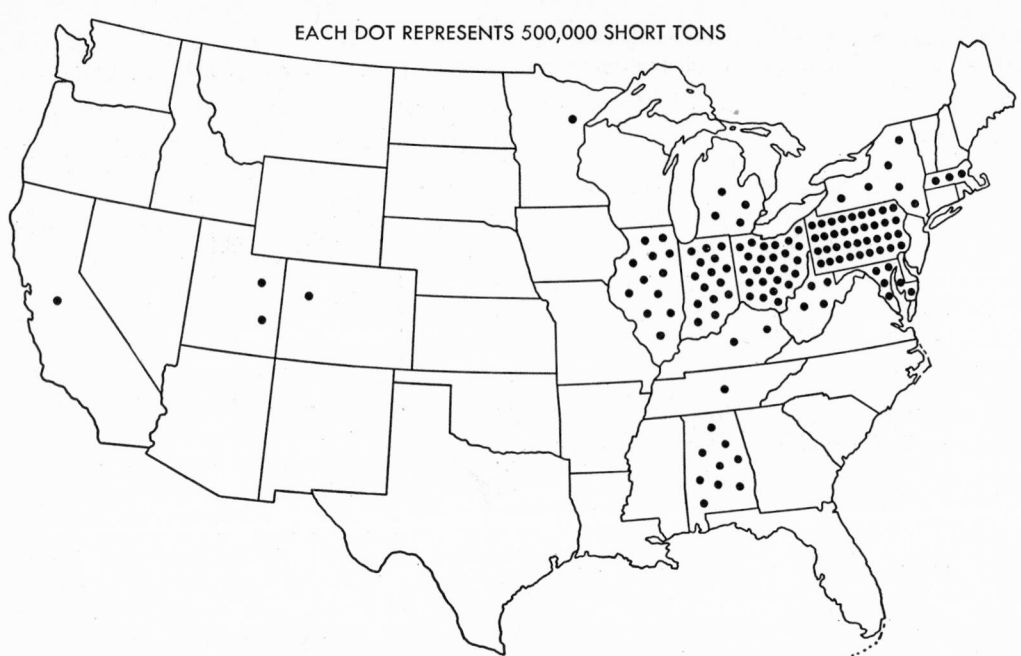

EACH DOT REPRESENTS 500,000 SHORT TONS

FIGURE 321. PIG IRON: GEOGRAPHIC DISTRIBUTION OF OUTPUT IN THE UNITED STATES, BY STATE, 1950

The United Kingdom

The British industry is favored with domestic coke of excellent quality but its iron ore is mostly of low grade, though self-fluxing. To supplement the domestic supplies, the United Kingdom imports high-grades ores from Sweden, Norway, Spain, North Africa and other areas. It is estimated that, in general, imports of iron ore, pig iron and scrap accounted for about 40 per cent of the metallic iron used in the British steel industry before World War II.[108] Since the war the United Kingdom has imported 45 per cent of the iron content in the ore it consumes, 10 per cent of the scrap, all alloy ores and a varying percentage of the pig iron.[109]

Even before the turn of the century, the British industry lagged behind the American and the German in technology and operational practices. It was slow in adopting mechanical handling of material and equipment and in improving the design and capacity of blast furnaces and rolling mills.[110] Before World War II, however, some old blast furnaces were replaced by new and larger ones, better control practices in furnaces were introduced, and fuel consumption per ton

of pig iron was lowered. New plants have been installed at Corby and Ebbw Vale, South Wales. In particular, the Corby plant, producing basic Bessemer steel, applies an entirely new principle in using soda ash to enable it to use iron ore high in sulfur. Two continuous-strip mills have been installed, at Ebbw Vale and Shotton.

In 1946 the British Iron and Steel Federation prepared a seven-and-a-half-year plan for reorganizing and modernizing the industry. Ingot capacity was to be raised to 16 million tons; hand-charged blast furnaces were to be replaced by larger mechanical ones; 26 blast furnaces and additional continuous-strip mills were to be erected and the capacity of the existing ones increased; outdated steel mills were to be eliminated. The capacity of rolling mills was to be correspondingly increased.[111] Under the threat of impending nationalization the plan was shelved.

By 1948, steel output in Great Britain had reached the target of 15 million tons set by the Economic Cooperation Administration for 1951. In 1949 it rose to nearly 16 million tons and in 1950 to 16.6 million, exceeding the target set in the plan of the British Iron and Steel Federation. Yet productivity, in terms of man-hours, is still considerably lower than in the United States. Productivity teams, organized to visit the steel plants

108. **73**, p. 25.
109. **7**, 1949, p. 43.
110. **43**, pp. 183–218.

111. **34**, pp. 36–37.

in the United States and familiarize themselves with American techniques, found, for example, that productivity per man-hour in foundries is 50–90 per cent higher in the United States than in Britain.[112]

Early in 1951, the industry was nationalized, but in 1952 the new British government introduced in Parliament a bill for its denationalization.

France

In contrast to the United Kingdom, France relies exclusively on domestic iron ore for its steel industry but must import a substantial part of its coking coal from England and Germany.[113]

During World War I, many plants were destroyed, and much of the best equipment — electric motors and cranes, gas engines and so on — was removed to Germany. When the war ended, the French steel industry underwent a process of modernization, financed by reparations and government loans.

During World War II, the damage to plants was smaller, and output went down mainly because Germany did not supply enough coking coal and had mobilized the French workers for its own purposes.

The Monnet Plan, adopted soon after the end of the war, aims at expanding the capacity of the French steel industry to 12 million tons of ingots, largely by technological improvements in existing plants, patterned after practices in the United States. Finishing capacity is to be increased by the establishment of continuous-strip mills. By the end of 1949, two large blast furnaces had been built and many old ones remodeled, three open-hearth furnaces and one continuous-strip mill had been constructed, and various other improvements had been introduced.[114]

Vertical integration is characteristic of the French iron and steel industry, especially in the east, which has coal and iron ore beds, blast furnaces, steelworks and rolling mills under one financial roof.

Germany

After the loss of Lorraine in World War I, the German steel industry was handicapped by the inadequate supply of domestic iron ore, but a new basis for its development was worked out. Germany imported French minette, and in the returning trains shipped coking coal to the steel mills of France. Minette was used for Bessemer steel, which represented a sizable proportion of the total output. For the high-grade iron ore needed in the open-hearth process, Germany turned to Sweden. Boats carrying iron ore from Sweden went back with coal, with which Sweden is poorly endowed. Scrap for open-hearth and electric steel was supplied by rolling mills and numerous steel-consuming factories in near-by cities.[115] On this broad foundation, the efficiently organized German iron and steel industry staged its comeback. After the incorporation of the Saar in 1935, its annual output exceeded the combined production of Great Britain and France.

Preparing for the second world war and envisaging the possible loss of French and Swedish sources of iron ore, Germany began to build an immense and wholly modern steelworks south of Brunswick to utilize local low-grade domestic ore (Salzgitter deposit). Soda ash was to be used to eliminate impurities, as at the Corby plant in Britain. The works were to have thirty-two blast furnaces, several steel furnaces and rolling-mill installations. An annual capacity of 4 to 5 million tons of steel was planned. The war began before the plant was completed, and only units with about half the planned capacity were operable.[116]

After its conquest of Austria, Germany initiated another ambitious project — the steelworks at Linz — to utilize Erzberg ore and Silesian coal.

Germany's iron and steel industry was closer to the United States in technological practices than that of any other country. Production was standardized and highly mechanized, with extensive use of electric power. The first continuous-strip mill outside the United States was installed in 1937.

The main features of the prewar organization of the German industry were geographical centralization in the Ruhr, the Saar and Silesia

---

112. **13**, p. 34.

113. The annual output of iron ore, the largest in Europe, by far exceeds the nation's requirements, and more than half was exported before the war. France led the world in iron ore exports by a wide margin. In addition, North Africa also has extensive ore deposits, which supply France with higher-grade ore. Cf. Chapter 22, pp. 778 and 785–86.

114. **31**, *passim;* and **30**, pp. 72–73.

---

115. Germany also imported ore from Spain, North Africa and other countries.

116. **11**, p. 106.

and complete vertical integration — from production of coal to manufacture of machinery and tools and construction of ships and bridges. The twelve largest combines owned mines producing two thirds of all the coal and accounted for more than 90 per cent of the total steel output. Their coking plants owned two thirds of the nation's total capacity and provided basic raw materials to the chemical industry, with which the steel combines were closely interrelated. Moreover, the steel magnates extended their power over various sectors of the economy — over agriculture, through Thomas slag for fertilizer; over the building trade, through slag-cement; over many industries as well as municipal gas works, through their surplus coke-oven gas.

After World War II, Germany lost the Saar, Silesia and Alsace-Lorraine, and the Allies imposed limitations on the remaining capacity and output of the German industry. The country was split into two parts, and Western Germany had to reconstruct the entire system. The industry suffered from shortages of raw materials and labor, destruction of many plants during the war and dismantling thereafter, and general disorganization.

In view of these and other difficulties, its recovery is impressive. The leaders of the industry succeeded in preventing the dismantling of some plants and in having the limitations on capacity relaxed. After long negotiations, Western Germany obtained the consent of the Allies in 1947 to an output of 11.1 million tons of steel and a capacity of 11.5 million, and in 1949, to an output of 13 million tons. In 1950, the German output exceeded 12 million tons, and its trend is upward. All limitations on steel output were removed in 1952.

The Benelux Countries

The Belgium–Luxembourg Union was sixth among the world's prewar iron and steel producers, but ranked first as an exporter except in a few years when Germany held the lead. The Belgian export prices for iron and steel were the world prices, and Brussels was the center of the European export market.[117] Iron and steel constitutes one of the key industries in Belgium, and in Luxembourg it is *the* industry, employing about two thirds of all industrial workers.

Belgium has to supplement its domestic supplies of coal, and Luxembourg of iron ore, by imports. In contrast to other countries, both produce more pig iron than steel. Almost all the pig iron is basic, made for Thomas steel plants, which produce more than 85 per cent of the steel.

In both countries the industry is vertically integrated. The Belgian centers, Liége and Charleroi, form a single economic unit. The two largest concerns in Luxembourg, Arbed and Hadir, own mineral deposits both within the country and in Lorraine and France, and also have plants outside Luxembourg.

In the postwar years, efforts have been made to expand output and capacity. Belgium is also endeavoring to enlarge the production of open-hearth and electric steel. Both countries have been modernizing and re-equipping their plants.

The Netherlands has a small iron and steel industry, wholly dependent on foreign ore but supplied with domestic fuel. It produces less than half a million tons each of pig iron and steel per year. About 80 per cent of the steel is of the open-hearth type.

Italy

Italy has none of the raw materials needed for a sizable iron and steel industry. Iron ore, coking coal, all alloying elements, and even a large part of the scrap, have to be imported. Hydroelectric power and electric furnaces are used as much as possible. In 1939, output amounted to 1.1 million tons of pig iron and 2.3 million of steel. This quantity was more or less maintained during the first war years, but in 1945 only 75,000 tons of pig iron and 400,000 tons of steel were produced. The postwar recovery has been much greater in steel than in pig iron; and in 1950 steel production had regained its 1938 volume. The rate of production in the first three quarters of 1951 indicated an output of 3 million tons.[118]

Czechoslovakia and Poland

The bases of the Czechoslovakian industry are large deposits of coking coal and iron ore, coupled with skilled labor. Domestic supplies of ore and coke were supplemented by imports before the war.

The open-hearth process is used for about 80

---

117. **11**, p. 95.

118. **6**, 1951, p. 181.

per cent of all production, predominantly in the steel mills of Moravia (Ostrava basin). Before the war, British capital controlled the fully integrated plant at Vítkovice, the largest in the country, which had 35,000 workers. Besides a full line of steel articles, it also produced machinery, bridges, rolling mills and mining equipment.[119] The famous steel-manufacturing Skoda works near Pilsen were controlled by French capital. The industry has a high technological standard and was a large exporter before World War II.

The industry was nationalized after the war. In 1950 the output of pig iron, and particularly of steel (1.9 and 2.9 million tons, respectively), exceeded the prewar level.

The prewar capacity of Poland's steel industry has been increased by a million tons through the incorporation of German Silesia. In 1939, Poland produced less than 1.5 million tons of steel; in 1950, 2.5 million. It is reported that the USSR intends to establish a "little Ruhr" between Katowice, the center of the industry in the southwest corner of Poland, and Ostrava, in Moravia, across the border in Czechoslovakia. It is planned to develop an annual output of 10 million tons in about twelve years.[120]

Sweden

Sweden has one of the largest high-grade iron ore deposits in the world but lacks coking coal. Hence it is the largest iron ore exporter after France and imports considerable quantities of coal, largely from Germany and the United Kingdom. It also uses charcoal from the "green coal" of the country, and water power. As long as pig iron was universally made with charcoal, Sweden led in its production. Use of coke and the puddling process shifted the supremacy to coal-rich countries.[121]

About 50 per cent of Sweden's steel output is of the open-hearth type. A very high proportion of the steel (40 per cent or more) and about 10 per cent of the pig iron are made in electric furnaces.

The products of the centuries-old Swedish industry, particularly its special and tool steels, have always enjoyed the highest reputation and brought top prices in world markets. Sweden is

also unique in making considerable quantities of sponge iron.

The highly integrated industry extends into the manufacturing of diversified machinery and precision instruments. Owning large forest areas, the industry also holds interests in timber, pulp and paper production.

Austria and Other European Countries

Before its occupation by Germany in 1938, Austria produced about 500,000 tons of pig iron and 650,000 tons of steel a year. A single company, the Alpine Montana, accounted for more than nine tenths of the pig iron, two thirds of the crude steel, and three fourths of the rolled and forged products. After invading Austria, Germany began to build a completely integrated plant at Linz, which was to produce 2 million tons each of pig iron and steel. Only half that capacity for pig iron was built, however, and none for steel.

In 1950, Austria produced almost 0.9 million tons of pig iron and nearly a million tons of steel.

Spain, Hungary, Norway and Yugoslavia also produce either pig iron or steel or both. Spain has a good grade of ore, but half the ore output is usually exported, since the industry is small and not developing. In 1950 the output was somewhat higher than before World War II, but below the level of 1928–29. Exports and imports of iron and steel are negligible.

Hungary, with an output of about the same size, increased the production of steel immediately before and during the war, when it exceeded its previous high — half a million tons in 1929 — by 40–50 per cent. Production dropped immediately after the war, but gained momentum afterwards and reached the million mark in 1950.

The USSR

The USSR is self-sufficient in all raw materials basic to the production of iron and steel, and its industry is practically isolated from the rest of the world. Exports and imports of raw materials, pig iron, steel and finished products are negligible. The only significant import, mostly from the United States and Germany, has been in the field of technology — machinery, tools and consulting engineers. The industry is highly integrated and is organized in combines. Many

---

119. **73**, pp. 28–32.
120. **51**, January 1949, p. 196.
121. **26**, p. 164.

plants are completely mechanized and modern.

The production plan for 1942 was set at 28 million tons of steel,[122] but the mills suffered heavy damage during the war. Many furnaces were destroyed, coal mines were flooded, and the power plant at Dneprostroi was greatly damaged. Intensive reconstruction was carried out after 1945, but the Five-Year Plan set a more modest goal — 19.5 million tons of pig iron and 25.4 million tons of steel in 1950 — less than a third the annual output of the United States. The 1950 output exceeded the target for steel by about 2 million tons, and in 1951 the USSR produced about 30 million metric tons.[123]

There are several reasons for this relatively small output in a country that has a population of nearly 200 million and is as richly endowed as the United States with most raw materials for the steel industry and better provided with some of them. The most important and obvious are the relatively low productivity of labor, the inefficiency of management, and limited transportation facilities. Moreover, coal, iron ore, manganese and flux are favorably located in relation to one another only in the Donets Basin, which has always been Russia's chief center of pig iron and steel. Military considerations, however, have stimulated the development of new Siberian centers, which are rich in ore but depend on long hauls of coal. This dependence is gradually being lessened, however, by coal deliveries from the Karaganda region in Kazakhstan.[124] According to the latest Five-Year Plan, the share of the eastern mills in the total output was to be increased from 29 per cent to 44 per cent for pig iron and from 34 to 51 per cent for steel.[125]

Nevertheless, Russia's progress has been considerable in recent years, particularly in view of the great damage to the steel industry during the war: the Germans destroyed 62 blast furnaces and 213 open-hearth furnaces in the occupied territory. The newly built plants have the most modern equipment and installations at all stages of production. The size of furnaces has been greatly increased. Large steel plants are being built in Georgia in the Transcaucasus, and efforts are being made to develop an iron and steel industry in Leningrad, which will be provided with coal from the Pechora basin.[126]

Canada

The Canadian iron and steel industry is based on imported raw materials. The country has considerable deposits of coal and iron ore, but they are located so far from consuming centers that it has been more economical to import iron ore (80 per cent or more was imported), coal (85 per cent) and coke (95 per cent) from the United States.[127] Iron ore was also imported from Newfoundland, which became the tenth province of Canada in 1949.

In recent years, Canada has been rapidly increasing its capacity for making iron and steel. The discovery of iron ore deposits at Steep Rock in western Ontario has increased the domestic supply. Canadian and American companies are now developing the Labrador deposit, which is high-grade and suitable for open-pit mining.[128]

The two world wars stimulated the growth of the Canadian industry. Steel output rose from 0.7 million tons in 1910 to 1.7 million in 1918, and again from 1.2 million tons in 1938 to 2.8 million in 1942. Technologically, the industry has much in common with that in the United States, and it does not produce Bessemer steel.

Despite the growth in output, the industry cannot meet national requirements for iron and steel products. Canada imports these commodities, chiefly from the United States and the United Kingdom.

Latin America

Mexico, Brazil, Peru, Argentina and Chile together produce about a million tons of steel a year, Mexico and Brazil accounting for the largest part.

Mexico has one fully integrated plant at Monterrey, with blast furnaces, Bessemer converters, open-hearth and electric furnaces, and a large rolling mill. Until 1941, this plant was the largest iron and steel producer south of Alabama, but Brazil now has a plant at Volta Redonda with a greater capacity.[129] The Monterrey plant produces most of Mexico's output, which exceeded 200,000 tons each of pig iron and steel in 1950. Two other mills, at Mexico City and Piedras Negras, which belong to an American

---

122. **40**, p. 253.
123. **37**, February 1952, p. 2.
124. Cf. Chapter 23.
125. **59**, p. 59.
126. **64**, pp. 227–30.

127. For about thirty years a bounty was paid for each ton of pig iron produced from native ore. The bounty was discontinued in 1911 and no ore was produced domestically until 1939. (**29**, 1947, p. 459.)
128. **37**, April 1951, p. 3.
129. **74**, p. 27.

company, operate largely with scrap and use, in part, natural gas piped from Texas. The plant at Mexico City has a rolling mill with an extensive list of products. A new plant, at Monclova, not far from the Texas border, financed by an American steel company, has a 350-ton blast furnace, coke ovens, three open-hearth furnaces, a hot-plate mill with a capacity of 70,000 tons, and two cold-strip mills. There are also a few steel mills with electric furnaces.[130]

Brazil produced 160,000 tons of pig iron and around 115,000 tons of steel ingots in 1939. It has huge reserves of iron ore at Itabira that have never been adequately explored. Only some of the Minas Gerais reserves have been mined, yielding about 0.7–0.8 million tons of ore a year. Coal deposits are poor in quality and costly to exploit. Pig iron is made, therefore, in twenty-eight charcoal blast furnaces, some with a daily output of only 10 or 20 tons. Minas Gerais leads in the production of pig iron, steel and finished products, but there are also important mills in the states of São Paulo and Rio de Janeiro.

The newly built steel plant at Volta Redonda is the only coke-using plant in Brazil. Designed for an eventual capacity of a million tons a year, it so far produces only 200,000.[131] It is unfavorably located with respect to coal supplies, which have to be transported five hundred miles, first by rail, then by water and then again by rail. The Export-Import Bank of the United States financed about 50 per cent of the cost of the project, the rest coming from the Brazilian government and private investors.[132] The plant employs 8,000 workers, housed in a model village built on the surrounding slopes. Schools for technical training have also been erected on the site. The plant consists of a blast furnace with a daily capacity of 1,200–1,300 tons; three open-hearth furnaces, each with a capacity of 150 tons; rolling mills; and a continuous hot- and cold-strip mill with a capacity of about 100,000 tons. The layout is designed for expansion.[133]

Argentina has no coking coal and only low-quality iron ore. It produces small quantities of pig iron but has a substantial foundry output and several rolling mills. The nation imports most of the steel products it requires. The Five-Year Plan aimed at production of 315,000 tons of steel in 1951.[134] In recent years the output has averaged 160,000 tons. Part of the pig iron is imported, and local scrap is used in open-hearth and electric furnaces.[135]

Chile has a small iron and steel industry, with its oldest plant at Valdivia and a new integrated plant near Concepción. The capacity of the latter was planned initially for 100,000 tons of steel a year. Domestic iron ore from the El Tofo deposit (450 miles to the north) is of high grade, and power is derived from a plant ninety miles away. Total production capacity now exceeds 250,000 tons a year.[136] A few small mills equipped with electric furnaces use scrap and pig iron to manufacture various steel products.

Peru, Colombia and Uruguay have steel mills that use local or imported scrap. Peru is planning to establish an integrated steel plant near Chimbote, and Colombia has a plant under construction at Belencito.[137]

There are no iron and steel mills in other Latin American countries except for a few small foundries here and there.

Japan

Before World War II, Japan accounted for about 80 per cent of Asia's output of iron and steel. The growth of its industry was spectacular, steel output rising nearly thirtyfold between 1913 and 1936 despite the fact that all basic raw materials — iron ore, metallurgical coke, pig iron and scrap — had to be imported. Foreign ships were frequently purchased for scrapping.[138]

More than 95 per cent of Japan's steel was of the open-hearth type, the rest electric. The production of pig iron was almost wholly in the hands of the government, while that of steel was about equally divided between private capital and the state.

Japan's defeat in World War II almost crushed the industry. The annual output of steel fell from 9.1 million tons to 0.6 million. A gradual comeback is under way; in 1950 the industry produced 2.3 million tons of pig iron and 4.5 million tons of steel. Today Japan depends on increased home production of iron ore and pig iron

130. **74,** pp. 309–10.
131. **74,** p. 27.
132. **28,** pp. 41–42; **75,** pp. 137–38 and 171–72; **74,** p. 27 and pp. 176–78.
133. **12,** pp. 117–18.

134. **3,** p. 20.
135. **74,** p. 118.
136. **9,** p. 27; and **74,** pp. 206–08.
137. **9,** p. 27.
138. **26,** p. 293.

and on imports of coking coal from the United States.[139]

India

India ranks second to Japan in Asia's production of pig iron and crude steel. Raw materials are available, and the industry is growing. The Tata Works at Jamshedpur, the largest single steel plant within the British Commonwealth, has modern equipment in all departments and an excellent laboratory. India has a continuous-strip mill of the latest design and is building new rolling mills as a part of its industrialization program. The other large plant is at Asansol. Together they account for 80 per cent of India's steel output. Increased steel output absorbs more pig iron than before the war, and less is exported.[140]

In 1950 the Indian Union produced 1.7 million tons of pig iron and 1.5 million tons of steel, approximately 9 pounds of steel per capita of the population. Thus it may take a long time before India's per capita consumption of steel approaches that in western Europe.

The Union of South Africa

The Union of South Africa, the only producer of iron and steel on that vast continent, is abundantly supplied with domestic raw materials. Production of steel did not start until the second quarter of this century but was greatly stimulated by World War II. In 1950 the output of pig iron amounted to 733,000 tons and of steel, to 816,000 tons. The large integrated plant of the South African Iron and Steel Corporation at Pretoria is completely modern and produces a wide range of rolled, forged, cast and special steel products. The same corporation is building new steelworks at Vanderbijl Park with an ingot capacity of 320,000–350,000 a year and designed for extension of capacity to about a million tons.[141]

Australia

Endowed with all raw materials, including the essential alloying elements, Australia has developed a sizable iron and steel industry during this century. Its annual output of about 1.2 million tons each of pig iron and steel meets do-

mestic requirements. In time Australia may become an exporter to southeastern Asia and New Zealand. The industry produces all types of finished steel, including high-alloy and tool steels. The open-hearth process predominates; electric furnaces are used for the remainder.

A single concern owns the main steel mills as well as a string of subsidiaries. It is the largest single employer of labor in the country. Australia is considered the lowest-cost producer of iron and steel in the world.[142]

THE SCHUMAN PLAN

None of the countries in western Europe is self-sufficient in raw materials for its steel industry, though together they possess enough coal, ore and scrap to produce iron and steel for their own needs and for export. France has abundant supplies of low-grade iron ore but must import coke from Germany and scrap from various sources. Germany is well provided with excellent coking coal but depends on imports of iron ore from Sweden and France. Belgium has developed its steel industry on French iron ore and domestic coal, part of which is exchanged for foreign coking coal. Luxembourg has no coking coal and, although it produces iron ore, must also import ore from France and Sweden. Italy has no coal and little iron ore. It imports coal from Germany, Poland, the United Kingdom and, in recent years, from the United States.

This interdependence on basic raw materials — coal and iron ore — has been the source of much friction. Various countries have subsidized the industry by means of tariffs and restrictions on import or export and other measures. Labor has often been forced to accept low wages to meet competition. Consumers in countries with a less efficient industry, such as Italy, have had to pay high prices for domestic products because of the restrictions placed on foreign supplies.

The European steel cartel tried to solve the problem in the interest of producers by setting production and export quotas, but the interests involved were too powerful to submit to regulation. The Schuman Plan, submitted in May 1950 and ratified by France, Germany, Belgium, the Netherlands, Luxembourg and Italy by 1952, is a new attempt to find a solution in the interest of consumers as well as producers. Two impor-

139. **5**, 1950, p. 244.
140. **12**, 135; **5**, 1950, p. 244.
141. **12**, pp. 143–44.

142. **11**, p. 92; and **12**, p. 113.

tant steel-producing countries, the United Kingdom and Sweden, do not participate directly in this organization,[143] although they, too, depend on foreign raw materials — the United Kingdom on imports of iron ore, chiefly from Sweden and North Africa, and Sweden on imports of coal from Germany and the United Kingdom.

Objectives of the Plan

The basic idea of the Plan is to create a single market out of the territories of the member countries, in which all producers will have free and equal access to raw materials at the same prices, except for the difference in transportation costs, and in which all consumers will have equal access to supplies. Customs duties and quantitative restrictions are to be abolished within this area. In case of shortages, all available basic raw materials, regardless of their place of origin, are to be allocated among member countries in accordance with their needs. Subsidies and any other governmental aid to coal and steel industries, unfair competition through intentional lowering of prices or wages for the purpose of capturing the market, and cartels among various members of the group are forbidden. Also forbidden are measures — such as export quotas — that tend to allocate foreign markets among producers.

This European Coal and Steel Community must strive, through its institutions, to establish the lowest possible prices that will permit necessary amortization and normal profits. The basis of price calculations must be made public. The High Authority, the central body of the Community, will be empowered to order a rise or a cut within the common market of the Community if it considers that prices are too low or too high. Disregard or violation of such a decision is to be penalized by fines.[144]

The purpose of the Coal and Steel Community is also to encourage the development of the productive capacities of coal and steel industries and efficient exploitation of natural resources so as to prevent their premature exhaustion. To this

effect, the High Authority is to facilitate investment programs through loans to enterprises or guarantees of their loans. It may finance projects that aim at increasing the output, lowering the production costs or facilitating the distribution of products under its jurisdiction. If it finds that a project implies either subventions or discriminations forbidden by the treaty, it will prohibit the enterprise concerned from resort to resources other than its own funds and may fine the violator the full amount spent unduly.

If introduction of new techniques or machinery results in a considerable displacement of workers, the High Authority may assist governments in the respective countries in financing economically sound programs either in industries under its jurisdiction or in any other industry capable of reabsorbing the idle manpower productively. It may provide nonreimbursable grants on at least a fifty-fifty basis to pay benefits to displaced workers and finance their reinstallation and technical retraining.[145]

The Community is to promote improvement and equalization of living and working conditions of workers in the coal and steel industries. Discrimination between nationals and immigrants in pay or other working conditions is forbidden.

Importing or exporting countries of the Community may not discriminate in freight rates for coal and steel products. The Community may establish maximum and minimum tariffs for its products in commerce with nonmembers. Within the limits fixed by such decision, each government will set its tariffs according to its national procedure.

During a business setback, the High Authority may set production quotas for each member country on an equitable basis, and may fine violators up to the maximum value of the excess output. It will allocate supplies of coal and steel among industries under its jurisdiction, exports and other consumption.

The treaty will come into full force when a single market for coal and steel is established among the six member countries. The organization envisages the gradual adaptation of the industry to new conditions during two preliminary stages: "preparatory" and "transition" periods. The first began with the ratification of the treaty

---

143. Great Britain agreed to the establishment of representation at the High Authority.

144. These decisions shall not prevent members from aligning their quotations with prices offered by enterprises outside the Community, provided such transactions are reported to the High Authority. In case of abuse, the latter may limit or eliminate the right of the respective enterprises to benefit from this exception. (Chapter V, Article 60, of the treaty.)

145. A two-thirds majority of the Community's Council may authorize an exception of the fifty-fifty basis for the grant.

by all member governments and will end when a common market is established. The second is to last five years thereafter.

The European Coal and Steel Community

The Community has four central institutions: the High Authority, assisted by a consultative committee; a Common Assembly; a Special Council of Ministers; and a Court of Justice.

The High Authority consists of nine members, eight of whom are nominated, in common accord, by the governments; the ninth is elected by a majority vote of the first eight members. The members of the High Authority are responsible only to the Community, not to their respective governments. They may not participate in any activities, paid or unpaid, nor acquire or hold, directly or indirectly, any interest in any business related to coal and steel during their six-year term and for three years thereafter.

The Consultative Committee consists of not less than thirty and not more than fifty-one members, appointed by the Special Council and representing three groups, in equal numbers — producers, workers, and consumers and dealers. Representatives of the first two groups, unlike the rest, are not nominated personally but are chosen from lists drawn up by their central organizations. Each list contains twice as many names as the number of seats allocated to each group. No Committee member is to be bound by any instructions from his organization. The High Authority must consult the Committee in all cases prescribed by the treaty and may call on it for advice at any time.

The Common Assembly, elected by the legislative bodies of the six countries from their members, will meet once a year to vote on the report of the High Authority. If two thirds of the votes and the majority within the Assembly disapprove the report, the High Authority must resign collectively and be replaced. The member countries send the following number of delegates to the Assembly: France (including the Saar), Italy and Germany, eighteen each; Belgium and the Netherlands, ten each; Luxembourg, four.

The Council of Ministers, established for the purpose of liaison between the High Authority and the member governments, and for coordination of measures promulgated by the High Authority, consists of six members. Each country designates to the Council one of the members of its government.

The Court of Justice, consisting of seven members, is nominated for six years by a common agreement and handles appeals of member states concerning violations of the treaty, or decisions and recommendations of the High Authority on the ground of lack of legal competence, abuse of power, substantial procedural violation and so on. It is not to rule, however, on the economic premises of decisions of the High Authority.

Germany signed the treaty with the reservation that its signature did not imply recognition of the present status of the Saar as final. The German declaration to this effect is attached to the treaty, together with the formal French answer that while the Saar is now incorporated in the territory of France, the international position of the Saar will be settled in a peace treaty with Germany.

An additional convention contains various provisions tending to facilitate, for certain countries, the transition from a national to a common market in coal and steel. For example, it was recognized that the Italian coking plants are in a special position and need tariff protection. Italy is permitted to maintain customs duties on coke coming from other member countries during the transition period but must reduce them by 10 per cent the second year, by 25, 45 and 70 per cent, respectively, the third, fourth and fifth years, and abolish them entirely by the end of the transition period.

Concessions were also made to France and Belgium to ease the adjustment of their coal industries, and consideration was promised to the iron and steel industry of Luxembourg, in view of its exceptional importance in that nation's economy.[146]

Outlook

The world output of steel may be expected to grow. Per capita consumption of steel has not reached its limits even in the United States. In Europe it averages less than a fourth of that in the United States, in the USSR less than a sixth, and in the Far East about one hundredth.[147] Thus the world as a whole could use many times more steel than it produces currently. More agricultural implements, machinery, transportation equipment, household appliances —

---

146. **15**, *passim;* **14**, *passim.*
147. **7**, 1951, Appendix Table; and **37**, April 1951, pp. 2–3.

more of all products made of steel — are needed everywhere. The growth of world population and of industrialization are also bound to raise the demand for steel. Armament programs and threats of war increase it further.

Steel production can be expected to spread gradually to many areas that have traditionally been consumers of steel products imported from the industrialized parts of the world. Although more capital is required to build a steel plant than, for example, a textile mill, there can be no doubt that steel mills will be established in underdeveloped areas that possess at least one of the two essential raw materials — iron ore or an adequate type of coal. The fact that the domestic product may be costlier and possibly of lower quality will not deter the young nations from starting their own steel production as a part of their drive toward economic independence.

Important as such production will be for these countries, their combined output will, however, represent only a fraction of the world output for some decades to come. The firmly established steel industry on both sides of the Atlantic will retain its dominant position for a long time and has a good chance of keeping its markets, not so much for ordinary steel as for machinery, special tools, electrical and other equipment. Demand for such products made of high-grade steel will grow as underdeveloped countries enter the path of industrialization and raise their standard of living. India, which exports ordinary textiles to neighboring countries, may become an exporter of ordinary steel products, but the growth of India's steel industry will multiply the country's demand for higher-quality imported steel products many times.

In the long run, the steel industry is likely to become more decentralized geographically, but there are no indications that such a dispersion will undermine the old centers of steel manufacture.

The current annual demand for steel will continue to depend on changes in business conditions, rising in times of prosperity and declining in depression. In the near future the industry will probably operate at capacity, to meet the combined military and civilian demand.

CHAPTER 30

THE MACHINERY AND TRANSPORTATION EQUIPMENT
INDUSTRIES

PRODUCTION OF MACHINERY and transportation equipment is a highly dynamic and progressive industry and holds a leading place in both peace and war. Though it covers a wide range of products, from machine tools to aircraft, it can be considered as one broad sector of manufacturing, since it is epitomized by engines. A locomotive, an airplane, even an automobile, is primarily an engine, a machine.

In some countries, censuses include this sector of manufacturing in one category as "engineering" or the "mechanical industry." Some censuses, including the American and the German, distinguish electrical, optical and other machinery but classify production of electric bulbs, for example, with that of electrical machinery. Until recently, others, such as the Swiss, have reported production of watches under "metals and machines." Still others lump together not only all "engineering" products but also other products made of metal under one broad heading as metal industries.

This chapter deals with five subdivisions of the engineering industry as the term is used in Europe: production of all machinery (both electrical and nonelectrical), railroad equipment, ships, automobiles and aircraft.

EMPLOYMENT AND VALUE OF OUTPUT

In 1948 the manufacture of machinery and transportation equipment employed some 20–22 million people in the world (including the USSR), or about a seventh of all factory workers. The United States and the United Kingdom employed 3.7 and 3.1 million persons in this field, respectively, and together accounted for more than a third of all the workers in these industries. Western Germany had 1.3 million workers,[1] France 1.2 million and Italy 0.7 million. (See Figure 322.) Since then employment has risen in most countries. The United States, for ex-

ample, counted more than 5 million employees in these industries in 1951, and the United Kingdom more than 4 million. The number in Western Germany, Canada and Australia has also increased greatly.

Recent data on the gross value of output are available for the United States only. Sales effected by manufacturers in the country in 1950 amounted to nearly $50 billion, of which nonelectrical machinery accounted for $11.4 billion, electrical machinery and equipment for $16.4 billion, motor vehicles and equipment for $17.6 billion, and other transportation equipment for $4.3 billion. Thus machinery represented 56 per cent and transportation equipment 44 per cent of the total sales in these industries.[2] In the United Kingdom, in contrast, transportation equipment represents less than 33 per cent of the total, despite the considerable shipbuilding industry.

According to a recent estimate of the United Nations Economic Commission for Europe, the gross value of the output of machinery and transportation equipment industries in 1948 was $5.7 billion in the United Kingdom, $2.8 billion in France, $1.7 billion in Western Germany, and $1.1 billion in Italy. In Belgium–Luxembourg, the Netherlands and Czechoslovakia, it slightly exceeded half a billion dollars.

In Western Germany, Czechoslovakia, Switzerland and Australia, production of nonelectrical machinery is the most important sector within this group of industries; in France and Italy, production of nonelectrical machinery and of transportation equipment account for approximately equal shares of the total gross value of output. (See Table 476 and Figure 323.)

Before World War II, Germany's output exceeded that of any other European country and represented about a third of the total value of machinery and transportation equipment produced in Europe. In 1950, the United Kingdom accounted for the largest percentage of the Eu-

1. In 1939 Germany had, within the territory of 1937, about 2.5 million employees in establishments with 11 or more workers. 28, pp. 238–41.

2. 19, March 1951, p. S–3.

1144

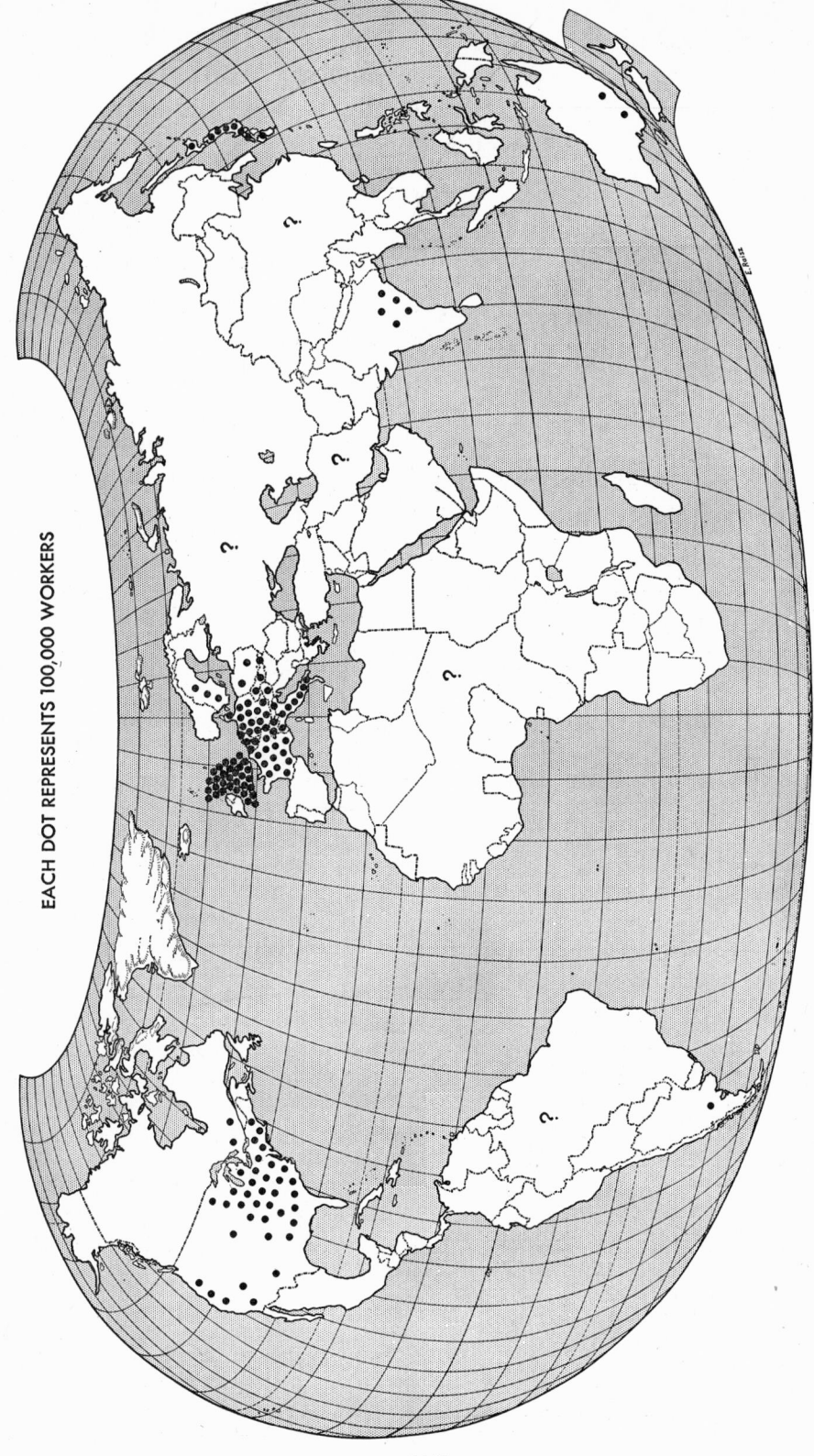

EACH DOT REPRESENTS 100,000 WORKERS

Figure 322. Machinery and Transportation Equipment: Geographic Distribution of Employment in the World, Around 1948

1145

TABLE 476

MACHINERY AND TRANSPORTATION EQUIPMENT: EMPLOYMENT AND VALUE OF OUTPUT

IN SELECTED COUNTRIES, 1948

Country	Employment, in Thousands	Gross Value, in Millions			
		Total	Nonelectrical Machinery	Electrical Machinery and Equipment	Transportation Equipment
United States	3,688	$43,457 [a]	$15,278	$9,493	$18,686
Canada (1947)	193	1,394	224	367	804
Argentina (1950)	117	...	...	...	...
United Kingdom	3,134	5,699	2,330	1,557	1,812
France	1,248	2,787	1,149	609	1,030
Belgium–Luxembourg	233	567	182	173	212
Netherlands	221	551	168	182	200
Denmark	68	269	113	74	81
Sweden	314	962	477	214	271
Norway (1947)	53	110	57	32	22
Finland	84	296	...	...	...
Western Germany	1,309	1,731	1,038	386	307
Poland	245	410	98	146	166
Czechoslovakia	347	549	356	57	136
Switzerland	186	436	254	118	64
Austria	...	135	64	43	28
Hungary	88	195 [b]	103	47	45
Italy	680	1,094	506	161	428
Japan (1947)	836	...	...	...	...
India (1944)	545	...	...	...	...
Australia (1945–46)	141	190 [c]	107	31	53
New Zealand (1946–47)	27	84	36	12	36

Sources: **8**, pp. 1, 6 and 170; **9**, 1949, *passim,* and 1952, p. 38; **19**, October 1949, p. 15, and July 1950, p. 21; statistical yearbooks.

a. Manufacturers' sales. This total, like the gross value of output, includes duplications resulting from transactions among enterprises (sales of semifinished products, accessories and so on).

b. 1947–48.

c. Value added.

ropean output, and France was third, with almost exactly the same percentage it had had in 1938:[3]

	1938	1950
United Kingdom	26.5	34.5
Germany	32.4	...
Western Germany	...	22.4
France	15.2	15.3
Italy	7.8	6.6
Sweden	3.9	5.1
Netherlands	2.8	3.7
Czechoslovakia	2.3	3.6
Poland	1.5	3.2
Belgium–Luxembourg	2.6	2.6
Denmark	1.5	1.6
Switzerland	1.6	...
Austria	1.0	1.4
Hungary	0.9	...

3. **8**, p. 69.

THE MACHINERY INDUSTRY

Besides supplying mechanical equipment, the machinery industry develops new machines and often leads other industries to change their production methods and the layout of their plants.

Production of machine tools — machines to make machines — is the foundation of the modern machinery industry. Machine tools are indispensable for the manufacture of any engine or mechanism. Practically every manufactured product is made either by a machine tool or by a mechanism made by such tools.

Machine Tools

For millenniums, metal was cut and shaped by hand. The making of even a comparatively simple instrument — a pump, a water wheel, a hand loom — was a slow and tedious process.

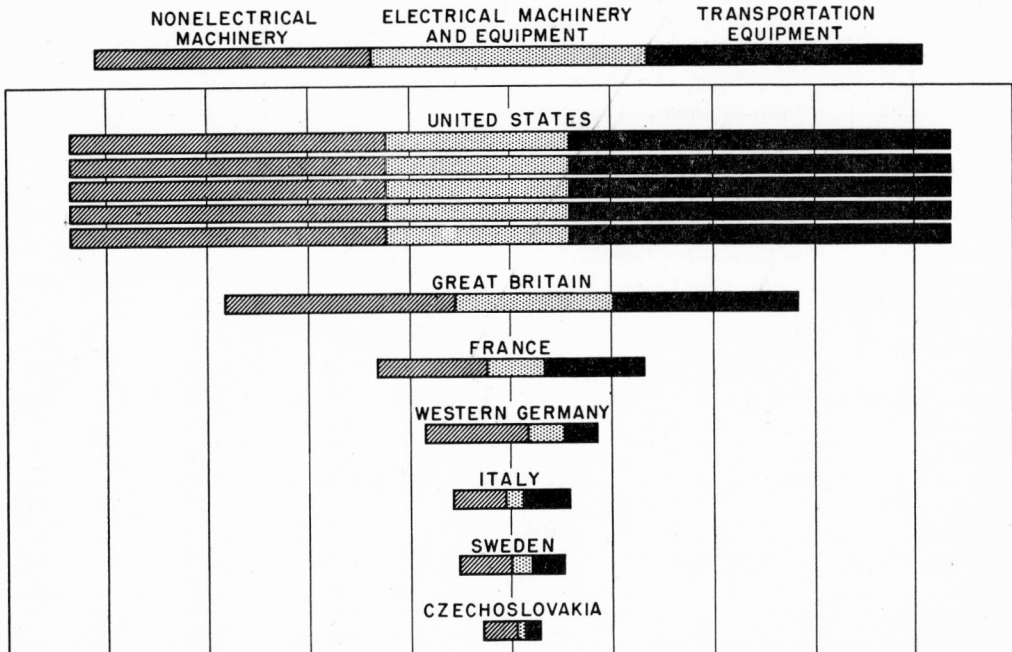

NONELECTRICAL MACHINERY ELECTRICAL MACHINERY AND EQUIPMENT TRANSPORTATION EQUIPMENT

UNITED STATES

GREAT BRITAIN

FRANCE

WESTERN GERMANY

ITALY

SWEDEN

CZECHOSLOVAKIA

A SECTION OF A BAR BETWEEN TWO VERTICAL LINES REPRESENTS A GROSS VALUE OF $1 BILLION

FIGURE 323. MACHINERY AND TRANSPORTATION EQUIPMENT: GROSS VALUE OF OUTPUT IN SELECTED COUNTRIES, BY MAJOR INDUSTRY GROUP, AROUND 1948

The few metal parts were fashioned laboriously with the aid of hand tools. When large metal parts were required, they were cast and fitted by hammering, scraping and filing.

As late as the 1770's, the construction of Watt's steam engine presented such difficulties that Smeaton, the famous English engineer, had to inform the inventor that "neither tools nor workmen existed that could manufacture so complex a machine with sufficient precision." [4] For ten years, from 1765 to 1774, the Watt machine existed only on paper because there were no machines to produce the cylinders according to the inventor's specifications.[5] Even when built, the early machines required continual adjustment during operation. A foreman practically lived beside them for weeks after they were first set up until smooth functioning was more or less assured.[6]

In 1751 the first practical lathe was invented in France.[7] Various machine tools — borers, shapers and planers — were built in England at about that time. Then, at the close of the eighteenth century, came the first all-metal lathe, the parent of all machine tools. The English inventors, Henry Maudslay and Joseph Bramah, assured precision work to the thousandth of an inch, and for a long time the lathe was used for all drilling, boring, grinding and milling. Gradually, various machine tools were designed for special operations. Jigs, fixtures, gauges — devices for holding the work, guiding the tool, checking the dimensions of cuts, and so on — were designed and redesigned to fit a particular purpose. The basic features were so well established that, with all their subsequent improvements and refinements, these devices remain essentially the same as they were a century and a half ago.[8]

The early machine tools were crude and slow, however, and could perform only single operations. The motor operated outside the machine tool. Sufficient precision was still lacking. It took nearly a century of adjustments and redesigning of parts before machine tools acquired the speed and accuracy common today.[9] Progress has

4. **48**, p. 494.
5. **35**, July 3, 1935, p. 491.
6. **53**, p. 74.
7. **35**, June 11, 1951, p. 156.

8. **47**, p. 654.
9. For the role that the invention of tool steels and the improvement of lubricating oils have played in the development of the machinery industry, see Chapter 24, p. 882 and Chapter 29, p. 1104.

been greatest in the twentieth century, when parts have been standardized, tolerances have become strictly limited, and methods of machining and testing have been improved. The motor was made an integral part of the machine tool, and separate motors were established within the machine for special functions. Electrical control of various operations was introduced and centralized. Automatic lathes have been developed, in many cases served by automatic loaders feeding work into the machine so that the operator has only to fill the loader.

Besides such general-purpose machine tools, special-purpose tools have been devised, to make mass production possible. Such machines perform multiple operations — boring, turning, drilling, grooving; others drill more than a hundred holes simultaneously, finish top and side surfaces at one time, and so on. Many modern machine tools are automatic, resuming their cycle of work without action on the part of the operator.

In recent years, combination or "transfer" machine tools have been built. These, operating as a single unit, may consist of as many as ten single machines connected by conveyors. An automobile cylinder block, for example, placed at one end of such a machine tool is subjected automatically to a series of operations and reappears at the other end in the desired form.

Modern machine tools have considerably greater productive capacity than those designed earlier — 9 to 14 times as great as those built in 1900, and 33 to 50 per cent more than those designed in 1936.[10]

The precision work that may be required today for the construction of an especially complex and efficient machine tool is illustrated by the following description of a Swiss jig-boring machine:

All its machine surfaces are scraped to an accuracy of less than a millionth of an inch in surface smoothness. Bearings for its spindles are ground to within one three-millionth of an inch of accuracy. . . . Workmen . . . who built the machine made some of the parts in controlled-temperature rooms three stories underground. The delicate work was done on automatic machines, which were set to begin operating 18 hours after workers left the room — so the parts could recover from any expansion due to heat from workers' bodies. Workers did not enter the room again until 8 hours after the cutting operations were completed. A seismo-

graph beside the cutting machine recorded any earth tremor that may have affected the accuracy of the work.[11]

Interchangeability of Parts

The era of modern machining began when standard measurements for each part of a machine were established and held within very close limits. Achievement of the goal of interchangeability of parts paved the way to mass production.

Craftsmanship has been built into the machine, and the operator, by merely pushing a button or turning a wheel, can reproduce this superior skill as many times as are required. Any specimen of the same kind, once off the machine, can be fitted snugly into the place for which it was designed. Indeed, each part fits much more accurately than it could possibly be fitted by human hands.

The first known attempts to produce interchangeable parts were made by French gunsmiths in the 1780's. When Thomas Jefferson, then Minister to France, heard of this novel process, he went to see the performance and reported about it to John Jay, in a letter of August 30, 1795:

. . . the workman . . . presented me the parts of fifty locks taken to pieces, and arranged in compartments. I put several together myself, taking pieces at hazard as they came to hand, and they fitted in the most perfect manner. The advantages of this, when arms need repair, are evident.[12]

Interchangeability of parts, also for the production of firearms, was introduced into the United States a few years later by Eli Whitney, inventor of the cotton gin. Whitney not only designed and made all the jigs, fixtures and gauges for the manufacture of firearms, but also designed and built machine tools for making these parts.[13]

This was the beginning of what is known the world over as the "American" system of interchangeable parts. This system has gradually substituted the automatism of machine work for individual craftsmanship, and mass production for custom manufacturing. It made possible assembly operations, first introduced in some small industries and now epitomized by the automobile industry.

10. **44,** p. 13; **41,** pp. 360–61.

11. **36,** December 1949, p. 7.
12. **47,** p. 657.
13. **14,** p. 3.

Location of the Industry

The machinery industry tends to follow the geographic pattern of the manufacturing industries, for which it supplies equipment. Plants producing textile machinery, for example, are usually near the centers of textile manufacturing.

In the United States, machinery production is concentrated in the eastern and east north central states. New England and the Middle Atlantic states are the home of the textile machinery industry. Ohio, Michigan, southern New England, the Philadelphia district and Illinois are the machine-tool makers of the nation; Ohio leads the states in value of output of metalworking machinery; Michigan specializes in cutting tools, jigs and fixtures. Diesel engines are produced chiefly in the area between the Great Lakes and the east coast and in California; internal combustion engines in the northeastern and north central manufacturing states and on the Pacific Coast; woodworking machinery in Cincinnati.

In the United Kingdom, the manufacture of textile machinery is concentrated in Lancashire and the West Riding of Yorkshire, the two centers of the textile industry. Cotton-manufacturing machinery is produced mostly in Lancashire, the very symbol of the British cotton industry; woolen and worsted machinery, in the West Riding, the heart of the woolen and worsted industry. Machine tools are made in Birmingham and Coventry, Manchester, northeast Yorkshire, Glasgow and London. Glasgow, in particular, leads the world in the production of machine tools for marine engines.[14] Heavy electrical equipment is produced in Manchester, Rugby, Birmingham and a few other centers.

In Germany, the chief centers of machinery production are the Ruhr, Berlin and Saxony. The Ruhr produces much of the equipment for steel mills; Berlin, Saxony and Württemberg, most of the machine tools. Berlin has also specialized in electrical machinery and precision instruments and Saxony in textile machinery.

In France, the machinery industry is concentrated around Paris, in central France (Lyons, Grenoble and Saint-Étienne), in Alsace-Lorraine and in the north, near the iron and steel mills.

Italy's machinery industry is concentrated in the north, which accounts for more than eight

tenths of all the establishments and an even higher proportion of the value of output. The most important centers are Lombardy, Piedmont and Liguria.[15]

In the USSR, plants producing metallurgical machinery are located in the Ukraine and the Urals. Mining equipment is manufactured in the principal coal areas, near the Donets Basin and in Siberia. Baku and Grozny are the chief producers of equipment for the oil industry. Moscow, Leningrad, Gorki, the Urals and the Ukraine have machine-tool plants. The main textile machinery plants are at textile centers — Moscow, Leningrad, Ivanovo, Shuya and others. Tractor and combine plants are at Stalingrad and Kharkov, in the middle of the two largest agricultural areas — the Ukraine and the Volga region — and in Chelyabinsk.[16]

MAJOR BRANCHES OF THE MACHINERY INDUSTRY

Machine Tools

The value of the total output of machine tools in the United States was $348 million in 1947; $278 million in 1948 and $241 million in 1949, as compared with $1.5 billion in 1943. The comparatively small output in the later years reflected the fact that many industries had retooled only a few years earlier. The index of machine-tool output (1939 = 100) in the United States was 448.4 in 1943 and 326.5 even in 1945.[17]

The postwar defense program stimulated demand for new machine tools; in 1950 the orders placed for such tools increased more than fourfold — from 90,000 units in January to 410,000 in December.[18] In January 1951 more orders were placed than at any time since the middle of 1942, when war production of machine tools was at its peak, and the number in February was even larger by almost 30 per cent.[19]

Capacity of the industry in the United States, however, had been markedly reduced after the war, and rapid expansion was confronted with various difficulties: shortages of necessary machine tools, various raw materials and manpower. Three out of eight workers in this industry are skilled, and such skills normally re-

---

14. **59**, p. 407; **45**, pp. 15–22.

15. **51**, pp. 41–43.
16. **38**, pp. 273–77.
17. **35**, January 22, 1951, pp. 143–45; **16**, Vol. I, p. 29.
18. **50**, February 1, 1951, p. 35. Presses and forging machines are not included.
19. **19**, March 1951, p. 3, and April 1951, p. S–34.

quire a three-year training period. Although the number of production workers increased from 38,000 in June 1950 to 60,000 in July 1951, an additional rise of 50 per cent was required in 1952.[20]

Europe's machine-tool industry is concentrated in the west, which accounted for $470 million in 1949, or 85 per cent of the value of Europe's total output ($552 million).[21] Czechoslovakia, Hungary and Poland manufactured the remainder. About two thirds of the machine tools made in Europe are general-purpose tools of varying complexity. The remainder consists of specialized tools of particular importance in the development of modern industry: boring and milling machines, center lathes and planing machines, automatic lathes, gear-cutting and grinding machines. The percentage share of western countries in Europe's total output of such specialized machine tools in 1938 and 1947 and in the projected output for 1952–53 is as follows:[22]

	1938	1947	1952–53 Estimate
Western Germany	44.6	2.9	22.9
United Kingdom	19.0	26.4	20.0
Italy	11.0	15.1	13.4
France	9.0	15.0	11.0
Switzerland	9.0	16.4	10.4
Sweden	3.5	11.3	7.0
Belgium	2.1	10.1	8.0
Other	1.8	2.8	7.3

Actually, by the end of 1948, German production had increased more than had been anticipated, hence its share for 1952–53 is likely to be greater than the estimate shown here.

Textile Machinery

Since the end of World War II, the demand for automatic textile machinery has risen in many countries because of the shortage of labor, the factor that stimulated the introduction of such machinery in the United States. The United Kingdom has become the leading European manufacturer of automatic looms and other specialized textile machinery. France produces most types of textile equipment; Belgium specializes in machinery for the wool industry; Italy,

in machinery for cotton and wool manufacturing and cotton dyeing and finishing.

Over the war years Germany lost its position as the chief European producer; the value of the output of textile machinery in Western Germany dropped from $140 million in 1936 to $16.6 million in 1948 (both figures in terms of 1948 prices). Meanwhile, the United States more than doubled the value of its output, from $193 million in 1939 to $442 million in 1947, and its share of the total production in major countries increased from 34.1 per cent to 47.0 per cent. Though the United Kingdom nearly doubled the value of its output, from $131 million in 1937 to $233 million in 1948, its share in the considerably larger total value in 1948 was only slightly larger: 23.2 per cent in 1937; 24.8 per cent in 1948. (See Table 477.) From 1948 to 1950, Germany tripled its output of textile machinery, and the increase is continuing.

Agricultural Machinery

The value of all agricultural machinery, including tractors, produced in the United States in 1937 amounted to $485 million; in 1949, to $1.8 billion. Data on the value of the output of the European industry are available only for farm machinery exclusive of tractors: $521 million (at 1948 prices) in 1936 and $465 million in 1948.[23]

In recent years, tractors have become the symbol of agricultural mechanization, and they are the chief type of farm machinery for which international statistics are available.

Until 1920, the United States was practically the only producer of tractors. The first European tractor plant was built in Germany in 1920.[24] The USSR started tractor production in 1923, using machinery imported chiefly from the United States. Until the early 1930's the USSR output was small. Most of the tractors used in its agriculture were imported from the United States.[25] When production increased, imports were suspended and a few tractors were exported to neighboring countries.

During 1937 the world produced about 364,000 tractors, the United States accounting for 272,-500, or about 75 per cent. Next in line were the USSR, with 51,000 units (almost 14 per cent),

---

20. **19,** October 1951, pp. 4–5.

21. **8,** p. 55.

22. **11,** p. 21. Countries are arrayed by their percentage share in 1938.

23. **18,** 1951, p. 806; **8,** p. 63.

24. The Ford Motor Company set up a tractor factory in Ireland in 1917.

25. Cf. Chapter 15, p. 522.

TABLE 477

TEXTILE MACHINERY: VALUE OF OUTPUT IN SELECTED COUNTRIES, 1938 AND 1948

Country	Value, in Millions, at 1948 Prices		Percentage of Total	
	1938	1948	1938	1948
Total	$565.5	$939.0	100.0	100.0
United States	193.0 [a]	442.0 [b]	34.1 [a]	47.0 [b]
United Kingdom	131.1 [c]	232.8	23.2 [c]	24.8
France	30.9	61.1	5.5	6.5
Belgium–Luxembourg	5.7	19.0	1.0	2.0
Netherlands	...	2.6	...	0.3
Denmark	2.1	4.0	0.4	0.4
Sweden	3.9	11.2	0.7	1.2
Western Germany	140.0 [d]	16.6	24.8 [d]	1.8
Poland	4.0	10.4	0.7	1.1
Switzerland	20.0	52.0	3.5	5.5
Austria	1.5	0.8	0.3	0.1
Italy	33.3	86.5	5.9	9.2

Source: **8,** p. 64.

  a. 1939.
  b. 1947.
  c. 1937.
  d. 1936. The output of Germany as a whole in that year amounted to $310 million.

and the United Kingdom, with 17,900 (nearly 5 per cent), followed by Germany, with 16,000 units. Seven other European producers manufactured the remainder.

The growing world demand for tractors after World War II gave the industry a powerful fillip, and production expanded rapidly in many countries. In the course of a few years, the world's output more than doubled, as compared with 1937. The United States still ranked first, but its share in the total fell from 75 to 60 per cent between 1937 and 1950, while the share of European countries (not including the USSR) rose from 11 to 27 per cent. Moreover, the tractor industry of Europe is young, equipped with machinery of the latest design, largely American, and its production methods are, on the whole, comparable with those in the United States. It has a considerable unused capacity and is able to produce about half again as many tractors as in 1950. The United Kingdom has become the second largest manufacturer in the world; the USSR now ranks third, followed by Western Germany. (See Table 478.)

The United States produces more than sixty types of wheeled tractors and about thirty types of track-laying tractors. The all-purpose wheeled tractor, representing 80 per cent of the tractor output in 1950, is the mainstay of the industry. This type is also gaining popularity in Europe, where few were manufactured before the war. Now about half of Europe's total output is of the all-purpose type.[26]

In the United States, the United Kingdom and Western Germany, the bulk of the tractor production is concentrated in the hands of a few firms. Thus eight manufacturers in the United States produced about three fourths of all the wheeled tractors in 1950; three of them produced more than half. In the United Kingdom three producers accounted for about eight tenths of the output in 1950. In Western Germany five producers accounted for an even larger percentage.[27]

The Economic Commission for Europe estimated the 1951 world output of tractors at 991,000 units, with the Big Three — the United States, the United Kingdom and the USSR — together accounting for 828,000 (600,000, 138,-000 and 90,000, respectively), or more than four fifths. The United States and the United King-

26. In prewar years tractors were used chiefly for heavy plowing and for driving threshing machines, while lighter work was performed manually or by horses. **7,** pp. 17 and 55.

27. **7,** pp. 40 and 51.

Table 478

Tractors: [a] Output in Selected Countries, 1937–50

(*Thousands of Units*)

Country	1937	1948	1949	1950
World	363.7	801.7	860.7	908.6
United States	272.5	569.3	589.2	544.2
Canada	. . .	15.0	15.0	16.0
United Kingdom	17.9	117.0	90.4	120.2
France	1.7 [b]	12.4	17.3	14.2
Sweden	0.3 [c]	3.9	5.4	7.0
Germany				
Western	12.0	8.1	26.7	57.6
Eastern	4.0	—	0.6	5.0
Poland	—	1.2	2.3	3.7
Czechoslovakia	0.2	9.1	9.7	12.0
Switzerland	1.3	2.9	1.8	1.2
Austria	0.1	4.1	4.2	5.7
Hungary	0.7	1.5	3.4	5.1
Italy	2.0 [c]	3.4	7.5	8.0
Romania	—	0.8	2.2	3.7
USSR [d]	51.0	51.0	79.0	97.0
Australia	—	2.0	6.0	8.0

Sources: **18**, 1938, p. 795, and 1951, p. 807; **8**, pp. 61–62; **30**, April 1951, p. 52; **6**, 1950, p. 185; **7**, p. 13.

  a. Excludes garden tractors.
  b. 1938.
  c. 1934–38 annual average.
  d. Data for 1948–50 are estimates of the Economic Commission for Europe, on the basis of official statements. In terms of units of 15 horsepower, the 1937 output amounted to 79,000 tractors. The output target for 1950 was 112,000 tractors.

dom are expected to continue providing the world's agriculture with this machinery, while the USSR's chief aim is to meet domestic needs. The United States, too, produces tractors principally for its domestic market; nevertheless, it ships a considerable number abroad — about one out of every six in 1950. The United Kingdom's tractor industry works primarily for foreign markets, exporting up to 70 per cent in 1949 and 1950. The largest single importer of tractors is Canada, followed by Australia.[28]

In Latin America, the production of agricultural machinery is very limited and is concentrated in Argentina, Brazil, Chile, Mexico and Peru. Only the simpler agricultural tools are produced, and spare parts for some types of machinery.[29]

MACHINERY PRODUCTION IN SELECTED COUNTRIES

Production of machinery is more concentrated

geographically than many other industries. The United States, the United Kingdom and Germany together accounted for almost 85 per cent of the world's prewar output.[30] France, Italy, Czechoslovakia, Belgium, Switzerland, Sweden, the USSR and Japan shared the larger part of the remainder. Many other countries make agricultural machinery, small steam engines or the more easily built light machine tools. Many countries not in a position to manufacture heavy machinery or precision instruments have plants for assembling imported parts. Argentina, for example, imports motors for domestically made electric railway cars.[31] Imported automobile parts are assembled in many Latin American countries — Argentina, Brazil, Mexico, Chile and Uruguay. Bus bodies are made locally, and production of various parts and accessories is increasing.[32]

28. **7**, pp. 54–55.
29. **9**, 1952, p. 7.

30. **39**, p. 438.
31. **25**, p. 59.
32. **63**, p. 16.

Although the industrially developed countries produce almost every kind of machinery, there is some specialization. Even the United States imports some special types of machinery that are of outstanding quality or too costly to manufacture domestically — for example, marine chronometers and certain textile machines (for cordage, embroidery, lacemaking) from the United Kingdom, and watchmaking machinery from Switzerland. The Swiss jig-borer mentioned earlier would probably cost its weight in gold if manufactured in the United States. On the other hand, the United States exports combustion engines, mining machinery and other types of machinery to European countries with a highly developed machinery industry.

The United Kingdom is becoming the major European producer of specialized mining and quarrying machinery (cutting, loading and conveying equipment) and specialized equipment for making iron and steel. Its position in world markets is well established in electrical and textile machinery. Germany specialized in electrical machinery before World War II. Sweden has no rival in the quality of its cream separators and is one of the principal producers of ball bearings. Switzerland is known for its specialized electrical machinery, precision instruments and machinery tools. Denmark is the chief European producer of cement-making equipment.[33]

The United States

The United States produces more machinery than all the rest of the world together and is the leading producer of almost every kind. Many factories specialize in a particular type of machine for a single industry. Thus textile machinery plants usually concentrate on a single line, such as cotton yarn machinery, looms or finishing equipment. Some plants produce complete machines, others only parts and accessories. Some specialize in one type of machine tool and depend on other producers for their operating equipment.[34]

In 1949–51, production of electrical machinery occupied somewhat more than a third of the total labor force employed in the machinery industry in the United States.[35]

The main branches of the nonelectrical machinery industry are general industrial machinery, metalworking machinery, special industrial machinery, and household and service-industry machines. In 1947 each of the first three branches employed 215,000–217,000 persons and accounted for about 10 per cent of the total value of output. (See Table 479.)

World War II necessitated the retooling of a large part of the industrial plant of the United States and consequently the renovation of metalworking equipment. More than 700,000 new metalworking units were installed in various industries, and the proportion of machine tools more than ten years old dropped from 70 per cent in 1940 to 38 per cent in 1945.[36] The largest single beneficiary was the industry that supplied machinery for aircraft production, which increased its equipment from 9,000 units in 1940 to 276,466 in 1945.[37] In 1940, 28 per cent of the equipment of this industry was at least ten years old; in 1945, only 2 per cent.

The trend was similar, though less pronounced, in all branches of the machinery industry. Between 1940 and 1945, the proportion of old metalworking equipment was reduced from 60 per cent to 36 per cent in the precision mechanisms industry; from 71 per cent to 25 in the engine, turbine and water wheel industry; from 82 to 42 in the railroad equipment industry, and so on, all along the line.

The most urgent wartime needs for machine tools were met by the end of 1943; by that year the value of the annual output had risen from an average of $280 million in 1937–39 to $1.5 billion. It has been estimated that in less than four years the machine-tool industry produced tools equivalent to more than twenty years' production at the prewar rate: production from 1920 to 1940 was valued at about $2 billion; from 1940 through September 1944, at more than $4 billion.[38]

The value of the output of other metalworking equipment rose also, from $125 million before the war to $460 million in 1943, partly because of the rise in prices. The entire machinery industry of the United States was much larger and more efficiently equipped at the end of the war than before it.

---

33. **62**, p. 232; **8**, pp. 104–07.
34. **19**, October 1951, p. 4.
35. **19**, 1949–1951, *passim.*

36. It is generally considered that a machine tool can perform precision work for about ten years, after which it is no longer fit for such work although still capable of functioning in other manufacturing departments.
37. **35**, July 5, 1945, p. 98.
38. **24**, Part 4, p. 113; **13**, p. 143.

TABLE 479

MACHINERY: ESTABLISHMENTS, EMPLOYMENT AND VALUE OF OUTPUT IN THE UNITED STATES, BY INDUSTRY BRANCH, 1939 AND 1947

| Industry | Establishments | | Employment, in Thousands | | | | Value of Output, in Millions | | | |
| | | | Production Workers | | All Employees[a] | | Gross[b] | | Added | |
	1939	1947	1939	1947	1939	1947	1939	1947	1939	1947
All machinery[c]	11,520	21,879	779	1,883		2,347	$4,982	$18,123	$2,969	$11,707
General industrial	1,616	2,191	102	164		217	664	2,067	420	1,189
Metalworking	1,332	4,293	78	173		215	443	1,646	313	1,131
Special industrial	1,346	4,106	65	174		216	350	1,777	228	1,096
Tractors and farm machinery	347	1,102	59	140		171	422	1,779	207	754
Engines and turbines	92	151	19	72		93	135	813	72	408
Construction, mining and related machinery	487	747	35	89		114	263	1,216	153	641
Office and store machines	230	357	43	84		98	188	678	143	504
Service-industry and household machines	472	1,088	53	181		220	392	1,050[d]	188	1,106
Machine shops and parts	3,584	3,871	70	168		201	399	1,529	246	984
Electrical machinery	2,014	3,973	256	639		801	1,727	5,568	1,000	3,894

Sources: **18**, 1948, pp. 846–48; **16**, Vol. II, *passim.*

a. Total number of employees was not reported in 1939 census.
b. In 1947: value of products shipped.
c. Includes electrical and nonelectrical.
d. Excludes refrigerators and radios, for lack of data.

The wartime renovation of machine tools and other metalworking equipment was largely supported by the federal government through direct financing and by allowing rapid amortization for income tax purposes. When the war ended, the government owned some 600,000 units of such equipment, most of which, except that reserved for military needs, was sold to private firms. In 1949 the United States had 2,224,665 machine tools: 1,762,165 in private factories; 259,000 in government plants; and 193,500 in maintenance shops.[39]

The United Kingdom

The United Kingdom, birthplace of the machinery industry, completely dominated the world's machinery market until the latter part of the nineteenth century. At the turn of the century it still ranked first in exports of machinery but exported less than its two chief competitors, the United States and Germany, taken together. On the eve of World War I, British and German exports of machinery were about equal in value. After that time the exports of the United Kingdom lagged increasingly behind those of the United States and Germany.

The industry employs more than one third of the nation's total manufacturing labor force. It accounted for 28 per cent of the net value of output of all manufacturing, mining and building construction in 1946, as compared with 17 per cent in 1935.[40] Its products represent about two fifths of all the exports of finished goods from the United Kingdom, and the share is increasing from year to year. Targets set for this industry for 1952–53 were attained in 1950, and the defense program is a further stimulus to utilization of its full capacity. Since supplies of raw materials — special alloy steels and imported scrap and iron ore — may set a limit to further expansion, the rearmament program will probably affect both civilian consumption and exports of machinery.

The British machinery industry is highly diversified and much less standardized in production methods than that of the United States. The assignment of a large part of the output to export hinders the urgently needed re-equipment and modernization of domestic plants. Produc-

tivity per worker is lower than in the United States, partly because the average American worker has two to three time as much electric power at his disposal as the British worker.[41] The quality of the products is high.

Germany

The machinery industry occupies a prominent position in manufacturing in Germany and stood first in value of exports before World War II. Its equipment was almost completely renovated in the 1920's after much of the obsolescent machinery had been delivered as reparations or sold abroad in the period of currency depreciation. The new equipment was largely patterned after American models.

The German machinery industry is closely associated with the iron and steel industry; in fact, a large proportion of its demand for steel and castings ordinarily is met by steel mills owned by machinery manufacturers. Research and training of personnel have been kept at a high level, and there has been less traditionalism than in Great Britain.

Considerable proportions of the industry's products were exported before World War II: 47 per cent of the output of textile machinery, 41 per cent of that of paper-making machinery, and 27 per cent of the optical and precision instruments.[42]

In 1938, Germany had 1.6 million metalworking machines; in 1945, between 2.1 and 2.6 million units. Of the total, Western Germany had one million in 1938 and 1.3–1.6 million in 1945. The extent of dismantling after the war cannot be estimated precisely, but it is believed to be in the neighborhood of 20–25 per cent for the country as a whole.[43]

Dismantling, the requisitioning of entire plants by the Russians, bomb damage, and the split between east and west have slowed down postwar recovery. German industry has, however, shown great vitality in staging a rapid comeback after this reverse, as it did after World War I and after the depression in the early 1930's. In 1950 the output of many branches was well above the 1936 level, the main exceptions being shipbuilding and rolling stock. German machinery and motor vehicles reappeared in quantity on world markets in 1950.

---

39. **35**, January 23, 1950, pp. 118–19. Total includes 10,000 units in college shops.

40. **8**, p. 80; **21**, p. 186.

41. See Table 419, p. 978.

42. **29**, p. 201.

43. **8**, pp. 75–76.

The USSR

Concentrated efforts have been made by the Soviet government to achieve a rapid growth in the machinery industry. Much equipment of various types was purchased abroad, and a number of Russian plants were planned and built by American firms and technicians. During World War II many plants were destroyed or damaged but some of the equipment was moved to the east. The United States and the United Kingdom supplied large quantities of machinery of various types to enable the USSR to open new plants and convert some of the old ones to the production of tanks, planes and arms.

The USSR produced 36,000 machine tools in 1937 and 50,000 in 1940. The target for 1942 was set at 70,000, but World War II interrupted the production. After the war, destroyed plants were rebuilt, and many units were seized in Germany and brought to the USSR, together with skilled workers and technicians. The goal for 1950 was to produce 74,000 machine tools. Some reports indicate that the annual productive capacity at the end of that year was 95,000. Assembly-line techniques are reported to cause difficulties of a serious order, and the geographic distribution of specialized plants producing parts and semifabricated products often necessitates shipment over long distances.[44]

The industry has nevertheless made considerable strides in the last years, since Czech and German machinery of superior quality has become freely available to the USSR. The technical "know-how" of the many specialists from these countries, who now service Russia's industry, must also have borne fruit.

Great efforts are being made to increase the production of tractors. In 1947, 29,000 tractors were made; in 1948, 51,000; in 1949, 79,000; and in 1950, 97,000 — as against the target for that year of 112,000. Even the 1950 target, however, was less than the reported 1936 output of 116,000.[45]

The postwar Five-Year Plan provided for the erection of four steam turbine plants in the regions of Sverdlovsk, Ufa, Novosibirsk and Kaluga. A milling-machine plant has been built at Gorki and an automatic machine-tool plant at Kiev. Along with the rehabilitation of the old machinery centers in the central and western parts of the USSR and in the Ukraine, duplicate plants are planned in the eastern Urals, the Volga region and Siberia.[46]

France

The French machinery industry, third in size in Europe, is distributed over the entire country. Plants are generally of medium size. Most of them are in or near cities, especially Paris, where the railways join and demand is at hand. While the industry is diversified, certain types of machine tools and precision instruments, as well as tractors and agricultural machinery, were imported before World War II. With the aid of the Marshall Plan, France acquired large amounts of equipment to modernize old plants and erect new ones.

Comparable data on the weight of machinery produced are available only for two branches of the industry: 26,000 tons of machine tools in 1938 and 36,700 tons in 1947–48; and, in the same periods, 163,000 and 175,660 tons of agricultural machinery.[47] Output is on the upgrade in other sectors of the industry as well. It is expected that increased capacity will enable the industry to handle the demand of the rearmament program without undue strain.[48]

Italy

Production of machinery occupies an important position in Italy, where the industry has a considerable tradition as well as skilled labor.

Before World War II this industry ranked first in industrial employment and value of output and was third in value of exports, following the textile and food industries.[49] It employed 675,000 persons in about 2,500 industrial establishments and 172,000 in more than 95,000 machine and repair shops.[50] Its share in all manufacturing, calculated in relation to employment, horsepower installed and capital investment, was estimated at 18.8 per cent. Electrical equipment, agricultural and textile machinery, and machine tools are the main branches.

In 1939 the country counted about 207,000 machine tools. Of these, some 52 per cent were

44. **6**, 1951, p. 127; **8**, p. 93; **60**, January 3, 1949, pp. 156–57; **58**, pp. 240–45.

45. **8**, p. 61.

46. **38**, pp. 282–83.
47. **26**, 1949, pp. 88 and 95.
48. **8**, pp. 71–73.
49. **51**, p. 12.
50. **20**, p. 66.

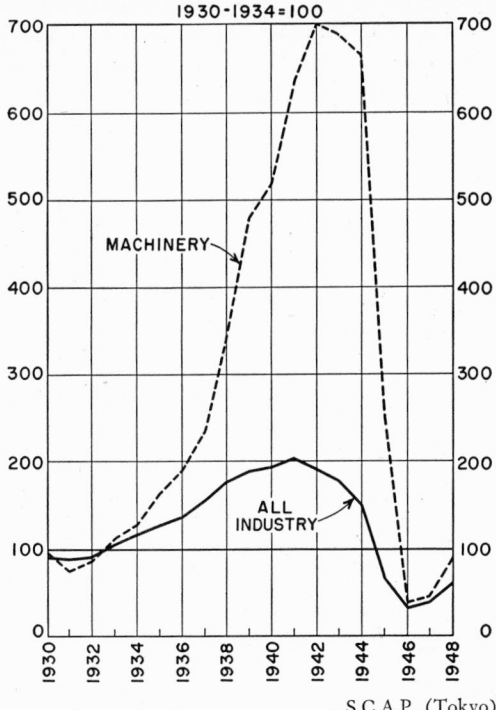

S.C.A.P. (Tokyo)

FIGURE 324. MACHINERY INDUSTRY: CHANGES IN
PRODUCTION IN JAPAN, 1930–48

manufactured before 1925, 26 per cent between
1925 and 1934, and the remaining 22 per cent
in later years. Ordinary types of machine tools
were almost exclusively of domestic production,
while most special types were imported.[51]

In the first years of World War II the industry
increased its capacity, which had never been fully
utilized, by 60–80 per cent. Today Italy accounts for about 7 per cent of Europe's total output of machinery and for a higher percentage
in some branches of the industry, but only about
60 per cent of its capacity is utilized. The capacity
of the machine-tool industry is particularly underutilized. Italy now has some 300,000 machine
tools. The industry works largely for export,
since domestic outlets are rather limited.[52]

Japan

Production of machinery was the most important industry in prewar Japan. In 1938 it employed more than a fourth of all the industrial
workers and accounted for about a fifth of the

total value of manufacturing output. Its growth
after 1929 was as follows:[53]

	Establish-ments	Workers, in Thou-sands	Value of Output, in Millions
1929	5,296	190	$ 396
1933	7,850	249	256
1937	14,636	602	738
1938	17,570	860	1,089
1942	25,097	1,683	...

While the index for all manufacturing almost
doubled between 1930–34 and 1940–42, that for
the machinery industry rose phenomenally, increasing sevenfold.[54] Production of machine tools
is particularly important in a war-geared economy. Japan raised its output from 22,000 in 1937
to more than 67,000 in 1938. For the most part
general-purpose tools were produced; special
types were largely imported. Output of machine
tools was maintained at a comparatively high
level throughout the war until the collapse in
1945 (figures in thousands of units): [55]

1941	46
1942	51
1943	60
1944	54
1945, January–July	7

By the end of 1941 Japan had a total of
700,000 units, about two thirds as much equipment as the United States. Because of shortages
of raw materials and manpower, however, the
available tools were not fully utilized. With allowance for obsolescence, and for bomb destruction of some 200,000 machine tools, Japan found
itself at the close of the war with about 600,000,
about a third of the vastly expanded equipment
in the United States at that time.[56]

The decline of production in the machinery
industry as a whole was equally sharp. The index of machinery production (702.6 in 1942 and
659.2 in 1944, on a 1930–34 base) fell to 38.0 in
1946. (See Figure 324.) After Japan's defeat,
the industry faced a bleak future. The general
economic position of the country was changed
radically; coal, steel and other raw materials
were in very short supply; inflation was rampant;
export outlets were lost. A slow recovery has
begun, but output of machine tools remains be-

51. **51,** p. 53.
52. **20,** pp. 16–17; **8,** pp. 8–88; **31,** 1949, p. 72.

53. **46,** pp. 501–02a; **56,** p. 241; **9,** 1949, p. 226.
54. **12,** March 1949, p. 6.
55. **42,** p. 204.
56. **42,** pp. 201–07.

low the 1936 level. In 1951, for example, only 9,127 units were produced, as compared with 16,624 in 1936. Production of equipment for the iron and steel, the chemical, textile and food–processing industries has shown a much steadier improvement.[57]

THE TRANSPORTATION EQUIPMENT INDUSTRIES

Transportation equipment is made by four distinct industries — the shipbuilding, railroad equipment, motor-vehicle and aircraft industries. Not including workers in the USSR, these industries employ 4–5 million persons, of whom 1.2 million are in the United States and more than 900,000 in the United Kingdom.

SHIPBUILDING

From the dawn of civilization to the beginning of the nineteenth century, practically every vessel, whether crude raft, canoe or ocean-going ship, was made of wood. The other important material of the shipbuilding industry was naval stores (resin and turpentine).[58] Oars or sails supplied the propelling power.

Shortage of timber, particularly for warships, began to be felt in England and other seafaring European nations in the Middle Ages.[59] It was an increasing problem for several centuries, until iron began to be used in shipbuilding. The first iron vessel was classed by Lloyd's Register in 1837.[60] This new raw material was greeted with great skepticism, since it was generally believed that, while wood floats, iron would necessarily go to the bottom. When the principle of flotation by displacement was established and experience showed the superiority of iron over wooden ships, iron became the basic material for shipbuilding.

Late in the eighteenth century, the steam engine began to be used in small ships plying the English Channel. The first steamboat for travel on the Hudson River was constructed in 1807. Sailing vessels continued to dominate long-distance navigation, however, and transoceanic ships used the steam engine only as an auxiliary to sails. With each decade, the advantages of steam over sails became more widely recognized: arrival on time; independence of the whims of the weather; greater safety for passengers, crew and cargo; less risk for shipowners. The leading shipbuilding companies began to concentrate on steamships in the 1870's, but even in 1880 as much sailing as steam-powered tonnage was built. The United States lagged behind Europe; as late as 1900, sailing vessels accounted for about half its merchant fleet.[61]

When the steam turbine was introduced in 1891, the victory of steam over sails became clear. Growing ocean traffic called for larger ships, and the need for greater speed raised new engineering problems. Iron could no longer satisfy the requirements of the shipbuilding industry and had to yield to steel, which by 1900 had almost wholly displaced it.

These radical changes in basic raw materials and propelling power transformed the structure of the shipbuilding industry, which became more and more dependent on steel production. As time went on, the association of shipbuilding and steelmaking became closer, and many of the largest steel firms in the United States, the United Kingdom, Germany and Japan installed their own shipbuilding departments.[62]

Modern shipbuilding depends on many other industries, primarily on the machinery and electrical equipment industries but also on industries producing paints and varnishes; woodwork; marine cables; fire-fighting, heating and refrigerating equipment; navigation instruments and so on.

During this century, the shipbuilding industry has developed new types of vessels, such as tankers and refrigerated ships, and has greatly increased the size of both passenger and cargo vessels.

Development of Shipbuilding

Before World War I the world's production of merchant ships fluctuated widely from year to year, ranging between 1.5 million tons launched in 1909 and 3.3 million in 1913. Early in World War I, shipbuilding dropped to less than half the prewar tonnage (1.2 million tons in 1915). Later it increased when German submarines opened their destructive offensive against merchant ships in the Atlantic and the United States, after having entered the war, launched a large shipbuilding program.

57. **5**, 1951, p. 318.
58. See Chapter 19, pp. 708–11.
59. See Chapter 19, p. 687.
60. So-called composite ships made of wood and iron plates, were built late in the eighteenth century.

61. **47**, p. 745.
62. In the United Kingdom about a third of the total steel output is used to build ships. **59**, p. 391.

TABLE 480

SHIPBUILDING: TONNAGE OF MERCHANT SHIPS LAUNCHED
IN THE WORLD, 1900–50 [a]

(Thousands of Gross Registered Tons)

Year	Tonnage	Year	Tonnage	Year	Tonnage	Year	Tonnage	Year	Tonnage
1900	2,158	1910	1,792	1920	5,705	1930	2,835	1940	1,707
1901	2,441	1911	2,570	1921	4,320	1931	1,604	1941	2,491
1902	2,336	1912	2,802	1922	2,436	1932	724	1942	7,815
1903	1,961	1913	3,263	1923	1,563	1933	480	1943	13,885
1904	1,935	1914	2,790	1924	2,184	1934	955	1944	11,170
1905	2,316	1915	1,173	1925	2,129	1935	1,291	1945	7,193
1906	2,638	1916	1,560	1926	1,629	1936	2,080	1946	2,115
1907	2,496	1917	2,733	1927	2,221	1937	2,643	1947	2,103
1908	1,678	1918	4,967	1928	2,635	1938	2,976	1948	2,310
1909	1,472	1919	6,589	1929	2,740	1939	2,474	1949	3,132
								1950	3,493

Sources: **40**, 1920–1921, p. 156, and 1947–1948, p. 142; **2**, 1951, p. 263.

a. Excludes ships of less than 100 gross tons, and vessels built on the Great Lakes. Excludes the USSR from 1928.

Tremendous losses during 1914–18 — about 13 million tons — were offset by launchings in these years — some 13.2 million tons. Many ships (almost 17 million tons) were built in the three following years, largely by the United States.[63] In fact, the increase in the tonnage of the world's merchant fleet during those years outran the demand for many years ahead; less shipping was built in 1925–27 than in 1910–12 — an annual average of 2 million tons as compared with 2.4 million. During the depression in the early 1930's shipbuilding almost ceased, falling to 480,000 tons in 1933. Despite the ensuing recovery, the tonnage launched in 1938, the highest year in that decade, was less than in 1913. (See Table 480; cf. Figure 325.)

During World War II the industry expanded to an unprecedented extent as a result of the race between ship construction in the United States and the activities of German submarines. In 1943, 13.9 million tons of shipping were launched, an all-time record.

Perhaps the most important changes in construction methods in the history of shipbuilding were introduced during World War II. To meet the emergency, multiple-construction design was used in many shipyards, heavy lifting cranes facilitated preassembly, welding was used on a large scale, and so on. As a result, the time from the laying of the keel to the launching of the vessel was greatly reduced. For the first time in history, a commercial ship of 10,000 tons was

built in two weeks, largely from prefabricated parts.

As soon as the war ceased, the world's shipbuilding contracted as it had after World War I. Although it revived in Europe, and the shipyards of the United Kingdom, Sweden and the Netherlands had a backlog of orders, the tonnage of ships launched in the world in 1949 was again smaller than in 1913 and in 1950 exceeded the 1913 level only slightly. (See Table 481; cf. Figure 326.)

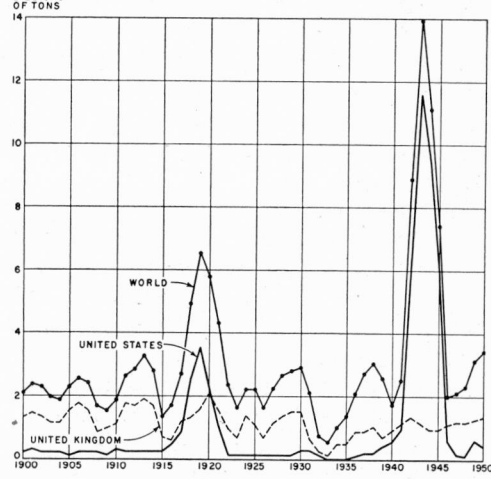

FIGURE 325. SHIPBUILDING: TONNAGE OF MERCHANT VESSELS LAUNCHED IN THE WORLD, THE UNITED STATES AND THE UNITED KINGDOM, 1900–50

(Vessels of 100 Gross Tons and Over)

63. **62**, p. 248.

TABLE 481

SHIPBUILDING: TONNAGE OF MERCHANT VESSELS LAUNCHED IN THE WORLD
AND SELECTED COUNTRIES, 1900–50 [a]

(Thousands of Gross Registered Tons)

Country	1900	1913	1919	1929	1938	1943	1947	1948	1949	1950
World [b]	2,158	3,263	6,589	2,740	2,976	13,885	2,103	2,310	3,132	3,493
United States	191	228	3,580	101	163	11,580	165	126	633	437
Canada	...	...	...	11	11	996	104	102	70	40
United Kingdom	1,442	1,932	1,620	1,523	1,030	1,137	1,192	1,176	1,267	1,325
France	117	176	33	82	47	...	92	138	155	181
Belgium	...	...	...	...	30	...	26	53	45	66
Netherlands	45	104	137	187	240	...	88	143	169	228
Denmark	11	41	38	111	159	...	61	99	86	126
Sweden	6	19	51	107	166	146	223	246	323	348
Norway	33	51	58	40	55	...	37	47	59	53
Germany	205	465	135	249	479	...	—	—	—	156
Poland	—	—	—	...	25	—	—	5	...	...
Italy	68	50	83	71	94	...	62	112	99	108
Japan	5	65	612	164	441	...	—	—	148	348
Australia	—	—	—	...	1	10	25	9	20	16

Sources: **62**, pp. 246–47; **40**, 1920–21, p. 156, 1947–48, p. 142, and 1950–51, p. 109; **2**, 1951, p. 263; **6**, 1950, p. 179.

a. Excludes ships of less than 100 gross tons, and vessels built on the Great Lakes.
b. From 1929: excludes the USSR.

On the whole, two factors have largely determined the ups and downs in shipbuilding in this century: fluctuations, caused by changes in business conditions, in the tonnage launched by the United Kingdom; and the tremendous increase in shipbuilding in the United States during both world wars. Germany has also been important, with two peak periods, in 1913 and 1938, on the eve of war. Canada constructed few ships before World War II, but then suddenly became a large-scale builder of merchant ships, increasing the tonnage launched from 4,100 in 1940 to 707,000 in 1942 and 996,000 in 1943. In contrast, shipbuilding in Japan had its heyday in the late 1930's, before World War II, but broke down in wartime.

The United Kingdom

Great Britain has ruled not only the waves but also the world's shipbuilding. This supremacy was secured by the combination of British resources and assets — vast coal deposits, an early start in iron and steel production, advanced mechanical industries, a seafaring tradition and a large overseas trade. In the 1890's the United Kingdom launched more than 80 per cent of

the world's merchant tonnage. Then the development of shipbuilding in the United States, Germany, France and Sweden and the slow decline in Britain began to cut down this share in two ways. In 1913, the United Kingdom accounted for about 60 per cent of the tonnage launched in the world; in 1929, for about 56 per cent; in 1938, for about 34 per cent.

The greatest shipbuilding center in the United Kingdom, and probably in the world, is the Clyde, where the largest ocean liners and warships are built. Its waterway, however, has the great drawback of shallowness and requires constant dredging. The other important centers are the Tyne on the northeast coast, where most of the warships and tankers are built, and Barrow, which concentrates on submarine construction.[64]

The United States

Shipbuilding in the United States has grown to world importance only in wartime. The industry's greatest asset is its capacity for phenomenal expansion when the necessity arises. In 1916, 22 shipyards were active in building seagoing

64. **59**, pp. 385–88.

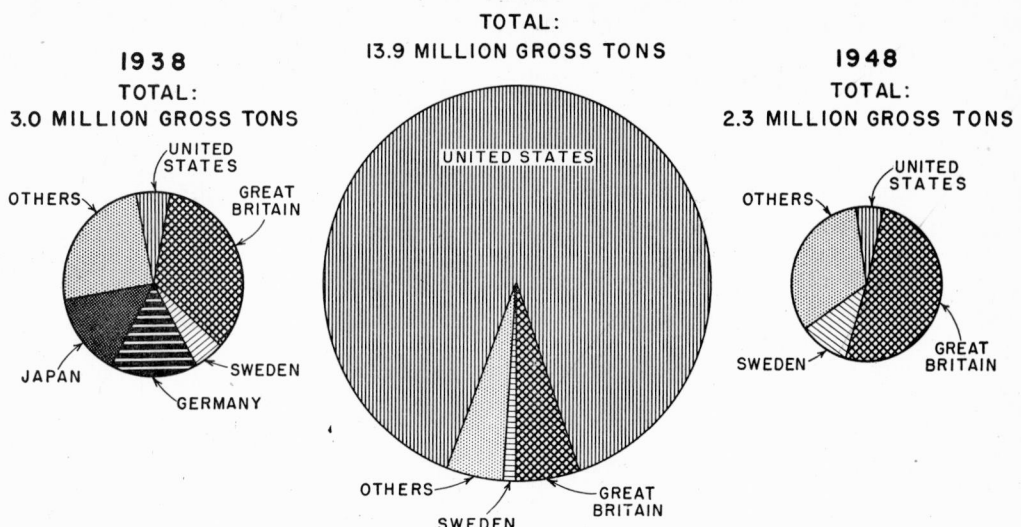

FIGURE 326. SHIPBUILDING: DISTRIBUTION OF TONNAGE OF MERCHANT VESSELS LAUNCHED IN THE WORLD IN WAR AND PEACE

vessels; in 1918, 211 were at work. The corresponding figures for 1939 and 1944 are 22 and 325. In 1939 about 67,000 workers were employed in private shipbuilding; by the end of 1943, 1.9 million were employed,[65] for the most part in plants and shipyards financed by the government. The merchant tonnage launched in the United States fluctuated widely. It rose from an average of 311,000 gross tons in 1936–40 to 5.7 million in 1942 and reached an all-time high of 11.6 million in 1943. During the last two war years, 1944 and 1945, the tonnage launched was gradually declining. The level in 1947 and 1948 was as low as in 1926–30, and in 1950 was lower than in 1940. (See Table 482.)

Sweden

Sweden moved into third place in shipbuilding after 1938. The tonnage launched by its shipyards has doubled since that year, and at the beginning of 1950 orders for 209 ships were booked. Four out of five of these had been ordered by foreign countries — Norway, Denmark, the Netherlands, France, Greece, Portugal, Argentina and Brazil.

During World War II, when business was slow, Swedish shipyards were completely modernized. When the war ended, they stood ready to resume activities. All-welded ship construction,

in which Sweden pioneered with a tanker in 1940 after eight years of experimentation, has now become standard. Swedish shipbuilders consider this process the most revolutionary change

TABLE 482

SHIPBUILDING: TONNAGE OF MERCHANT VESSELS LAUNCHED IN THE UNITED STATES, 1910–50

Annual Average or Year	*Thousands of Gross Tons*	*Percentage of World Total* [a]
1910–1914	253	11.1
1915–1920	1,877	47.5
1926–1930	159	4.4
1931–1935	83	8.1
1936–1940	311	12.8
1940	579	33.3
1941	1,035	41.4
1942	5,671	72.4
1943	11,580	83.5
1944	9,339	83.5
1945	5,968	82.9
1946	501	23.6
1947	165	7.8
1948	126	5.4
1949	633	20.1
1950	437	12.5

Source: **18**, 1951, p. 534.

a. The percentages for the years of World War I relate to shipbuilding in allied and neutral countries; for the years of World War II, enemy and enemy-occupied countries and the USSR are excluded.

65. **13**, p. 157.

in building techniques in recent years and have been quick to recognize the economies it offers in space and weight and in amount of steel needed. A welded ship can carry 10 per cent more cargo than a riveted ship of the same size, and nine welded ships use no more steel plates than eight riveted ones. Labor costs are also lower. Prefabricated parts are used extensively.

Two thirds of the ships built in Sweden today are tankers. Recently, Sweden designed and built two combined oil and iron ore carriers, the first of their kind. (See Figure 327.) They carry Swedish iron ore to Baltimore and Philadelphia and bring back oil from the Dutch West Indies and the Gulf of Mexico.[66]

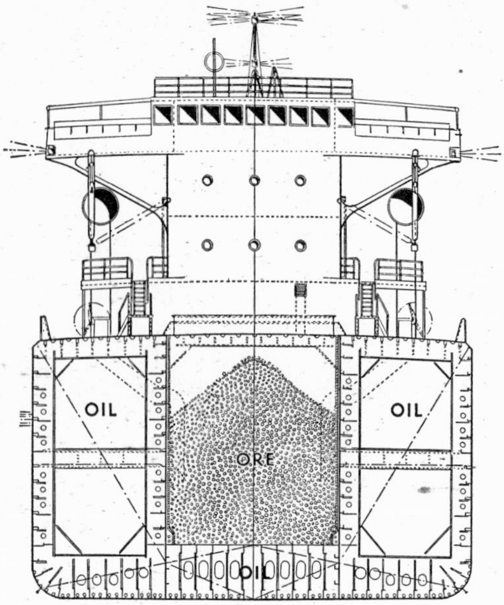

THE RAILROAD EQUIPMENT INDUSTRY

The railroad equipment industry has three main products — locomotives, passenger cars and freight cars. Production of locomotives presents the greatest engineering problems. Locomotives have been redesigned repeatedly to provide greater carrying power, speed and smoothness of motion. Passenger cars have also been improved considerably in size, arrangement of space, dining and sleeping facilities, lighting, heating, air conditioning and so on. Freight cars are also larger and heavier than before, and various types have been developed for perishable goods and other special purposes.

The mere number of units built therefore does not reveal all the progress in this industry or the relative importance of production in different countries. Moreover, many countries report the output of passenger and freight cars together, without indicating differences in the size or quality of the units built. Table 483 shows the output of rolling stock in the main producing countries.

Output in Major Countries

The United States is the largest producer of locomotives and freight cars, followed by the United Kingdom, which, however, is first in output of passenger cars.

Production in the United States continued at a high level after World War II; in 1947, 32,000 freight cars, about a third of the output, were shipped to Europe, mainly to France.[67] In 1948 the United States exceeded the production goal

Industria (**49**)

FIGURE 327. SHIPBUILDING: SWEDISH COMBINED OIL AND IRON ORE CARRIER

This cross section of a new type of carrier, launched in Gothenburg, Sweden, in 1950, shows how oil and ore hauling are combined by the ingenious construction of the holds. The ship, about 15,000 gross tons, will haul ore from, and oil to, Sweden.

of 10,000 freight cars a month. In 1950 and 1951, production was at a lower rate; the backlog of unfilled orders at the end of 1951 exceeded 100,000.[68]

Almost every country in western Europe produces locomotives and other rolling stock. The total annual capacity of the fourteen chief European producers is estimated, as of 1949, at about 3,300 locomotives, 7,200 passenger cars and 225,000 freight cars.[69] The United Kingdom's capacity represented a fourth of the total in locomotives, about three tenths in passenger cars and a fifth in freight cars. The capacity of the British industry is underutilized, however, partly because of the financial difficulties of most European railways, partly because of labor shortages; the output in 1950 was slightly smaller than in 1949. Western Germany, France, Belgium and Italy are also important producers of rolling stock.

Demand for railway equipment was high in the first postwar years, but by 1950 it leveled off. On the one hand, the most urgently needed re-

---

66. **49,** pp. 38–39 and 61–63.
67. **4,** 1948, p. 23.

68. **19,** January 1952, p. S–40.
69. **8,** p. 44.

TABLE 483

RAILROAD EQUIPMENT: OUTPUT IN SELECTED COUNTRIES, 1929–50

Country	Locomotives				Passenger Cars				Freight Cars			
	Around 1929	Around 1939	1949	1950	Around 1929	Around 1939	1949	1950	Around 1929	Around 1939	1949	1950
United States	1,065	354	1,920 [a]	4,669 [a]	2,202	276	1,045	964	85,038	25,513	95,172	44,209
Canada [b]	98	1	319	146	...	...	...	...	13,242	2,423	10,798	4,738
Brazil (State of São Paulo) [b]	6 [c]	4	—	...	...	...	...	...	11	265	625	277
United Kingdom	932 [c]	356 [d]	826	808	2,007 [a]	235 [d]	2,089	3,320	33,132	21,304 [d]	38,379	33,155
France	266 [e]	51 [f]	131	73	688 [e]	412 [f]	305	360	7,922 [e]	234 [f]	12,608	10,376
Belgium	56 [g]	39	...	...	56 [g]	25 [f]	...	...	...	2,765 [f]	...	...
Sweden	39	83	96	...	73 [g]	125	...	...	737 [g]	771	4,935 [h]	...
Finland [b]	36	15	112	90	...	...	129 [h]	...	1,142	376	1,752	534
Western Germany [b]	...	28 [f]	200	143	...	...	...	...	3,583 [g]	579 [f]	13,263	2,732
Poland [b]	130 [g]	74 [i]	215 [h]	...	...	...	...	...	...	1,648 [f]	12,177 [h]	...
Czechoslovakia [b]	...	...	...	...	...	...	...	...	...	...	...	...
Spain [b]	...	...	2	46	...	...	...	...	...	...	846	873
Italy	...	299	66	36	...	618	660	586	...	2,198	3,689	1,454
Japan	93	740	100	85	355 [g]	1,048	808	865	1,217 [g]	8,542	2,166	2,373
Union of South Africa	...	179	...	...	...	...	...	...	...	1,492	...	...
Australia [b]	...	39	71 [h]	...	...	...	...	...	...	1,382	1,330	...

Source: 2, 1948, pp. 249–50, and 1951, pp. 264–65.

a. On order.
b. Passenger and freight cars reported together.
c. 1930.
d. 1940.
e. 1926–32 average.
f. 1938.
g. 1931.
h. 1948.
i. 1937.

placements in rolling stock had already been effected in many countries, and, on the other, financial outlays for more pressing needs led to a reduction in investments in this sector of public expenditures.[70]

Canada increased its production considerably during the war. Brazil makes no locomotives but assembles a few and has a small output of other rolling stock. Japan's production of passenger cars in 1950 was about 83 per cent of that in 1939, and of freight cars, 28 per cent. Australia is expanding its industry and builds more locomotives than before the war. (See Table 483.) The USSR's plan called for 2,700 locomotives, 2,600 passenger cars and 146,000 freight cars in 1950.[71]

THE AUTOMOBILE INDUSTRY

Automobile production is an American industry par excellence. In no other country does the automobile play so decisive a role in everyday life or the automobile industry so outstanding a role in the national economy. About 10 per cent of the national income is spent in the United States each year for the purchase and operation of automobiles, including expenditures for gasoline, repairs, insurance and taxes. Sales of motor vehicles and equipment by manufacturers in 1950 totaled $17.6 billion.[72]

Nearly a million workers are employed in the United States in the direct production of motor vehicles and parts, including tires. As many more are engaged in producing the raw materials that go into cars. The automobile industry is the chief consumer of steel, rubber, plate glass, gasoline and many other products. In 1937 it absorbed 20 per cent of all the steel produced in the country, 54 per cent of the malleable iron, 31 per cent of the nation's consumption of lead and 28 per cent of that of nickel, 67 per cent of the upholstery leather, 73 per cent of the plate glass, 80 per cent of the rubber, and 90 per cent of the gasoline. The modern automobile is made up of approximately 6,500 parts and 15,000 pieces, all of which must be designed, manufactured and assembled.[73]

The manufacture of a typical American passenger car (1942 model, with accessories) consumes 3,385 pounds of steel, 697 pounds of iron,

171 pounds of rubber, 81 pounds of safety glass, 25 pounds of other glass, 81 pounds of paint, 66 pounds of cotton, 18 pounds of jute and 9 pounds of wool, 61 pounds of paper products, 54 pounds of copper, and much other material.[74]

The automobile industry is growing rapidly in half a dozen other countries — Canada, the United Kingdom, France, Germany, Italy and the USSR. While still an outgrowth of the pattern of life in the United States, it is tending increasingly to become one of the leading world industries.

Origin of the Industry

The automobile, that most American of products, was born in Europe, with French, German and British inventors in attendance.

The development of a self-propelled road vehicle, with a steam engine, began in France in the latter part of the eighteenth century. After years of experimentation, the English improved the French vehicle. Early in the nineteenth century they put steam coaches, with metal or metal-rimmed wheels, on the road. The coaches, however, had to compete with the railroads, which appeared about the same time; the noise they made frightened people as well as cattle and horses; and they damaged the roads considerably. In 1831 Parliament passed the Red Flag Law and imposed discriminatory taxes upon coach companies.[75] In 1860 the French invented the gas engine, and in 1876 the Germans developed the four-stroke cycle, which is most generally used in motor vehicles and can thus be considered the prototype of the automobile engine.[76]

Further improvements came in 1885, when an internal combustion engine, mounted in a crude frame, appeared on the streets of Mannheim, Germany. In 1892 the combined efforts of French and German inventors brought forth a motor vehicle so sound in principle that there has been no radical subsequent change in either the theory or the practice of automobile construction.[77] In the meantime, the new process of rubber vulcanization made it possible to manufacture rubber tires, which quickly displaced metal-rimmed

---

70. **8**, p. 45; **6**, 1950, p. 48. Most European railways are either publicly owned or under public control.

71. **8**, p. 44.

72. **19**, March 1951, p. S–3; **47**, p. 802.

73. **37**, 1938, p. 47; **47**, p. 807.

74. **37**, 1943, p. 60.

75. To warn people of the approaching vehicle, a man had to precede the coach with a red flag by day and a lighted lantern by night. The restrictions of the 1831 act were not lifted until 1896.

76. **47**, p. 804.

77. **47**, p. 805.

wheels and greatly improved the comfort of riding.

In the United States, electric automobiles were developed around this time, but because they required smooth roads and recharging every three hundred miles, they could not be used outside cities. Moreover, they were so expensive as to be actually a "rich man's toy." [78] In 1895 there were 300 cars in the United States, but only 4 of them were of domestic manufacture. In 1900 about 4,200 cars were built in the United States, mostly with steam or electric engines, though about a fourth had internal-combustion engines. The following decade was a period of experimentation. Cars of every conceivable design were produced, with the motor under the rear seat, the front seat or the hood, with from one to sixteen cylinders, two- or four-cycle engines, bar or wheel steering, and so on.

Cars were still not "manufactured," but were built one at a time with such hand tools as were available. After the turn of the century, particularly after the establishment of the Ford Company in 1903, factory production really began. Since that time the industry has been fertilized by American inventiveness, the chief contributions of which have been methods of mass production and continued improvements in existing models of cars.

Around 1908–10 the internal-combustion engine finally won recognition as the motor best suited to the automobile. Ford produced 10,000 cars in 1908, and other companies were running a close race. Although the automobile was still a luxury, the industry began to expand rapidly. Parts and methods were gradually standardized, and prices were cut drastically. Highways were built, gasoline stations began to mushroom, and installment payment and the trade-in system for used cars developed. Two decades later the car had become an almost universal means of transportation in the United States.

The Beginning of Mass Production

The American automobile industry was the first to make full use of the principle of interchangeability of parts. As early as 1903 an American manufacturer took three cars of domestic make to England, drove in them around race tracks and then took them apart and reassembled them, before the spellbound crowd,

from the parts mixed indiscriminately.[79] The system of interchangeable parts was soon adopted throughout the industry.

The further step of standardization of parts was taken after 1912, when automobile manufacturers concluded a cross-licensing agreement on the exchange of patents. This agreement, covering more than a thousand patents on various auto parts, put an end to many uneconomical practices, such as the use by different firms of 135 grades of steel and 1,600 sizes of steel tubing. The agreement has been renewed every five years, according to the statutory requirement, and has given all car manufacturers free use of improvements and inventions made since 1915.

While some companies produce parts, others obtain various parts from special manufacturers. The assembly of parts has been completely mechanized throughout the industry. Since the introduction of the man-high moving assembly line, the time for assembling a chassis has been reduced from the twelve and a half hours required in stationary assembly to one and a half hours.[80] The production of automobiles has achieved such a degree of synchronization in all operations and such efficiency in mass production methods that two weeks after the raw material is purchased, a completed car leaves the assembly line.

Thus the motor vehicle, invented in Europe, started its triumphal march as an article of mass production and mass consumption in the United States and then traveled back to Europe and around the world, as the very symbol of America's superior technology. The modern automobile industry in all parts of the globe largely uses methods developed in the United States. In some countries, as in the United Kingdom, France, Germany and Italy, American methods are combined with distinctly original ideas of local inventors and engineers; in others, as in the USSR, they are simply duplicated, often with the use of American dies.

World Output of Motor Vehicles

In 1913 the world produced some 600,000 motor vehicles, of which the United States accounted for 485,000 units; in 1928, 5.3 and 4.4 million, respectively, were manufactured. In 1938, when the output in the United States fell to 2.5 million vehicles, the world total shrank to

78. **52**, p. 216.

79. **47**, p. 810.
80. **34**, p. 119.

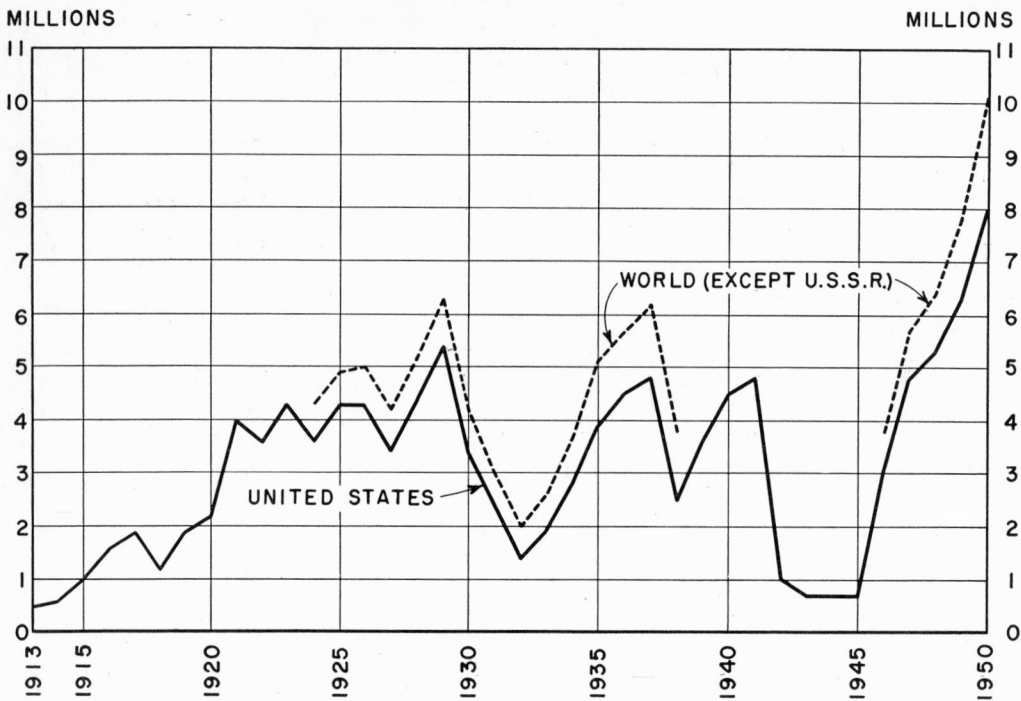

FIGURE 328. MOTOR VEHICLES: OUTPUT IN THE WORLD AND THE UNITED STATES, 1913–50

3.8 million. In 1950, the world put about 10.1 million new motor vehicles on the road, of which 8 million were built in the United States.[81] (See Figure 328.)

The United Kingdom is the second largest producer, with an output of about 800,000 vehicles in 1950. Before World War II, Germany was next in line, but now (except possibly for the USSR) Canada holds third place, producing nearly 400,000 vehicles a year. France follows Canada closely. Western Germany, although behind France, manufactures more vehicles than this part of Germany produced before the war: 301,000 vehicles in 1950 as against 217,000 in 1936.[82] Italy's ouput of 128,000 vehicles in 1950 greatly exceeded that in 1938 (71,000). (See Table 484.)

The USSR produced 211,000 vehicles in 1938. The target for 1950 was 500,000; of these, 428,-000 were to be trucks, 65,000 passenger cars, and the remainder buses.

Automobile Production in the United States

From 1900 through 1950 the United States produced more than 116 million motor vehicles

— 94.7 million passenger cars and 21.6 million commercial vehicles — with a total value of more than $100 billion. The output of passenger cars rose from 4,192 in 1900 to 181,000 in 1910, nearly 2 million in 1920, and 4.6 million in 1929. After a setback during the early 1930's, output increased rapidly to 3.8 million in 1941. Production of passenger cars was prohibited after Pearl Harbor; only 139 cars were made in 1943, 610 in 1944.

During the war, the industry shifted to the manufacture of various products for the armed forces. It is estimated that it accounted for a sixth of the nation's war production. Among the 1,000 or more products that came from its plants were 26,669 bombers, fighters and gliders; nearly 50,000 tanks; 2.6 million military trucks; 6 million guns and cannon; 1.2 million rocket motors; and tremendous quantities of bombs, small-arms ammunition, aircraft propellers, mines, shells and so on.[83]

Under the stimulus of pent-up demand, the output of passenger cars rose after the war from 70,000 in 1945 to 3.9 million in 1948 and 6.7 million in 1950. (See Table 485.) The interruption in private-car production during the war,

---

81. Cf. **1**, various years; **2**, 1951, p. 266.
82. **3**, May 1951, p. 58.

83. **47**, pp. 830–31.

TABLE 484

MOTOR VEHICLES: OUTPUT IN SELECTED COUNTRIES, 1928–50

(*Thousands*)

Country	1928		1938		1949		1950	
	Passen-ger	Commer-cial	Passen-ger	Commer-cial	Passen-ger	Commer-cial	Passen-ger	Commer-cial
United States	3,815	543	2,001	488	5,119	1,134	6,666	1,337
Canada	198	44	124	42	194	99	285	106
United Kingdom	182 [a]	57 [a]	341	104	412	216	522	261
France	211 [a]	42 [a]	190	25	188	97	257	99
Sweden	[b]	[b]	2	5	5	6	10	8
Germany [c]	108	32	275	63	104	57	216	85
Poland	...	...	2	1	—	—	—	—
Czechoslovakia	15 [a]		11	2	21	6	22	8
Italy [d]	54 [a]	...	59	12	78	7	115	13
USSR	2 [a]		27	184	375		28	376
Japan [e]	...	...	9	16	1	28	2	30
Australia	...	...	66 [f]	17 [f]	8	—	19	2

Sources: **10**, p. 68; **2**, 1948, p. 251, and 1951, p. 266; **37**, 1949, p. 13, 1951, p. 12, and 1952, p. 27; **3**, May 1951, pp. 59.

a. 1929.
b. Assembled from imported parts: 13,777 vehicles.
c. Western Germany in 1949 and 1950; in 1928 and 1938, includes vehicles assembled from imported parts (5–25 per cent of the total).
d. **6** (p. 181) reports output of 20,700 commercial vehicles in 1949 and 26,500 in 1950.
e. Excludes cars assembled from imported parts.
f. Assembled from imported parts.

coupled with the difficulty in obtaining new cars and their higher cost, curtailed the widespread peacetime practice of replacing a car after a year or two. As the following data and Figure 329 show, the average age of vehicles, from time of purchase to scrapping, and the mileage of cars scrapped after the war were much greater than in earlier years: [84]

	1925	1930	1949
Average age of scrapped vehicles, in years	6.5	7.0	14.0
Average lifetime mileage of scrapped vehicles, in thousands	25.8	41.5	120.5

In 1950–51, however, the fear that production of passenger cars would be cut down or even discontinued induced many owners of two- or three-year-old cars to exchange them for new ones.

Production of commercial vehicles — trucks and buses — began in 1904 with 700 units and increased to 74,000 in 1915, 322,000 in 1920, and 771,000 in 1929. The depression had less effect on this branch of the industry than on the production of passenger cars, and the 1937 output exceeded the peak in 1929. Production continued at a high level throughout the war. Moreover, wartime production concentrated on heavy-duty trucks, which require twice as much material, facilities and labor as ordinary commercial vehicles.[85] After the war, production continued to increase and reached an all-time high in 1948, with about 1.4 million units.

The automobile industry is concentrated in Michigan, Ohio and Indiana, with its major center in Detroit. Other plants are in operation in New York, New Jersey, Pennsylvania, Wisconsin and California. The industry also owns plants abroad — in Canada, Belgium, the Netherlands, various Latin American countries and the Union of South Africa.

In terms of production, the automobile industry is more highly concentrated than any other major manufacturing industry in the United States. Giant corporations are typical, and three firms ordinarily account for about 80 per cent of all the passenger cars produced and a

84. **37**, 1951, p. 20.

85. **13**, p. 152.

Table 485

MOTOR VEHICLES: OUTPUT IN THE UNITED STATES, 1900–51

(*Thousands*)

Year	Total	Passenger Cars	Trucks and Buses	Year	Total	Passenger Cars	Trucks and Buses
1900	4	4	—	1926	4,301	3,784	517
1901	7	7	—	1927	3,401	2,937	465
1902	9	9	—	1928	4,359	3,815	543
1903	11	11	—	1929	5,358	4,587	771
1904	23	22	1	1930	3,356	2,785	571
1905	25	24	1	1931	2,390	1,973	417
1906	34	33	1	1932	1,371	1,135	235
1907	44	43	1	1933	1,920	1,574	347
1908	65	64	2	1934	2,753	2,178	575
1909	127	124	3	1935	3,947	3,252	695
1910	187	181	6	1936	4,454	3,670	785
1911	210	199	11	1937	4,809	3,916	893
1912	378	356	22	1938	2,489	2,001	488
1913	485	462	24	1939	3,577	2,867	710
1914	573	548	25	1940	4,472	3,717	755
1915	970	896	74	1941	4,841	3,780	1,061
1916	1,618	1,526	92	1942	1,042	223	819
1917	1,874	1,746	128	1943	700	—	700
1918	1,171	943	227	1944	738	1	738
1919	1,876	1,652	225	1945	725	70	656
1920	2,227	1,906	322	1946	3,090	2,149	941
1921	1,616	1,468	148	1947	4,798	3,558	1,240
1922	2,544	2,274	270	1948	5,285	3,909	1,376
1923	4,034	3,625	409	1949	6,253	5,119	1,134
1924	3,603	3,186	417	1950	8,003	6,666	1,337
1925	4,266	3,735	531	1951	6,765	5,337	1,428

Source: **37,** 1952, p. 3.

large percentage of the trucks.[86] Concerns with assets of more than $50 million did almost 70 per cent of the business in 1939. Three companies sold more than 90 per cent of the new passenger cars registered in 1938.[87] The Ford Motor Company is the most highly integrated of all corporations, with its own coal and iron ore mines, steel plants, glass and tire factories, and other plants.[88]

The Automobile Industry in Other Countries

The British automobile industry produces both very small cars with eight-horsepower engines and very expensive, practically handmade cars. Since automobiles were taxed until recently on the basis of their horsepower, most passenger cars were built with from eight to twelve horsepower.[89] This fact put a premium on extracting the maximum performance from low horsepower; hence the engines were built to develop two or three times their rated power. The models announced in 1948, after the removal of the tax, had larger engines and an increased ratio of power to weight.[90]

The British motor vehicle industry is located in four main areas: Coventry and Birmingham, London, the shires of Bedford, Oxford, Northampton, and Lancashire. The heaviest concentration and almost half the total working force are in Coventry and Birmingham. Most firms installed new machinery during World War II for the production of military vehicles,

86. **24,** Part IV, p. 3.
87. **22,** p. 19.
88. **13,** p. 146.

89. In the early 1930's every new model of low horsepower was advertised by the producers as a "tax-dodger." (**57,** p. 65.)
90. **57,** p. 66.

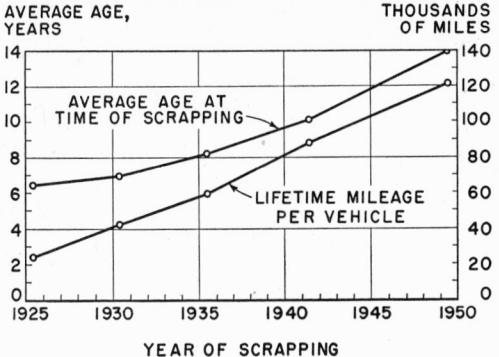

AVERAGE AGE, YEARS

THOUSANDS OF MILES

YEAR OF SCRAPPING

Automobile Facts and Figures, 1951 (37)

FIGURE 329. MOTOR VEHICLES: AVERAGE AGE AND LIFETIME MILEAGE OF VEHICLES SCRAPPED IN THE UNITED STATES, 1925–50

Since 1925 the average life of scrapped vehicles has more than doubled, and the average lifetime mileage has increased nearly fivefold.

but after the war many firms, particularly the smaller ones, found it difficult to obtain new machine tools. Some of these special-purpose machines are produced in the United Kingdom, but it is considered unlikely that the British machine-tool industry will find it practicable to produce all the types of special-purpose machine tools needed in automobile production.

While the Big Six manufacturers, accounting for 85 per cent of the total output, use large-scale methods of production, smaller firms rely more on craftsmanship and turn out higher-priced cars. Heavier transport vehicles are not, for the most part, standard products, but are "tailored" to customers' specifications. Production of such vehicles is largely in the hands of smaller firms, which prefer to use skilled labor rather than expensive special-purpose equipment.[91]

In 1929 France was the second largest producer of motor vehicles, but it ranked fourth in 1938, with the United Kingdom and Germany occupying the second and third places, respectively. Progress in the industry was delayed by the comparatively low demand of the domestic market, because of heavy taxation on gasoline, insufficient income of the population and slow replacement rate of cars in use. While sales in North Africa were substantial, they were not large enough to offset the resistance of the domestic market.[92]

After the war, the French industry had to

make a new start. Its equipment had been transferred to Germany, and the installations had suffered from Allied bombing. Nevertheless, the 1950 output exceeded that in 1938 by nearly 66 per cent, though its composition differed. France is now producing about four times as many commercial vehicles as before the war but less than twice as many passenger cars. The change is due both to the growing domestic demand for trucks and buses and to increased exports of such vehicles.[93] The increase in output is continuing, but France did not reach the 1951 target for passenger cars that was set by the Monnet Plan (511,000 motor vehicles: 390,-000 passenger cars and 121,000 commercial vehicles).[94]

Germany's motor vehicle industry developed slowly until the early 1930's, when, under the strong encouragement of the Nazi government, it began to expand rapidly. The industry had close affiliations with the American producers.[95] This made the latest techniques available to it, and continuous production methods were used. The more important German producers of component parts had licenses for the use of American designs. Production on the eve of the war and during it was concentrated on trucks and military vehicles. War damage and the dismantling of plants have greatly reduced the capacity of the industry. In the Soviet Zone, only one plant, in Eisenach, has been left in operation by the Russians. Recovery in Western Germany has been comparatively rapid since 1948; in 1950 Western Germany produced some 300,000 vehicles. Exports are increasing, and the low-priced *Volkswagen* (people's car) is making inroads into British and French exports.

Canada has a substantial production of motor vehicles, built mostly by United States firms. In 1947, Ford, General Motors and Chrysler accounted for 95 per cent of Canada's ouput. Components and accessories come mostly from the United States.

Czechoslovakia's industry has recovered its prewar position, and output is rising. Italy in 1950 reached an all-time high in the production of motor vehicles.

91. **57,** *passim.*
92. **57,** pp. 118–19.

93. **9,** 1949, p. 125.
94. **27,** Appendix, Table I.
95. A subsidiary of General Motors, Opel A.G., accounted for 40 per cent of the passenger cars and 30 per cent of the commercial vehicles; Ford-Werke accounted for another 10 per cent of the cars and 20 per cent of the commercial vehicles. **57,** p. 116.

India recently began the assembly of the *Hindustan* car, and Australia entered automobile production with a standard-type passenger car, the "Holden," and an expensive car constructed largely of light alloys and based on a French design. Mexico is trying to establish domestic production of a three-seater car, the *Nacional,* designed along European lines, which first appeared on the market in 1950; the engine, differential and gear box are imported.[96]

THE AIRCRAFT INDUSTRY

The aircraft industry is the youngest and most dynamic of all the transportation equipment industries. The tendency to outload and outspeed existing aircraft models is so strong that often before a new aircraft leaves the factory the designers are already at work on an improved model.

The early development of the industry, following the first flight of a heavier-than-air machine in 1903, was anything but rapid. Production gained momentum in the latter part of World War I but broke down completely at its close. The industry did not begin to expand again until the 1930's, and progress was rather slow. World War II changed the situation radically. In a few years, aircraft production in the United States advanced to the first place among all manufacturing industries in value of output.

Although ouput declined after 1944, the experience after World War I was not repeated. Development of commercial and civil aviation has kept the plants busy. Unquestionably, the cold war has also had an effect. All indications are that aviation has become incorporated into our civilization, in peace as well as in war, and that the industry will maintain its place in our economic system.

Beginnings of the Industry

The first flight in an airplane, by the Wright brothers in North Carolina in 1903, lasted 12 seconds and covered a distance of 120 feet.[97]

This event did not arouse any great interest in aviation. Although there was some "backyard" production of a few hundred planes for record flights, experimental flying or even mere display, the aircraft industry as such did not exist in the United States until World War I. The United States government ordered its first military plane in 1909. Great Britain, Germany and France had a somewhat greater awareness of the possibilities of aircraft for military use and had a few planes in operation from the beginning of World War I.

Development during the Two World Wars

When the United States entered World War I, its aircraft industry was immediately swamped with orders. Although it was poorly equipped for such an emergency and had to start from scratch, its facilities expanded rapidly. In the two years 1917–18, more than 16,000 planes were produced. With the Armistice and the ensuing cancellation of military orders, production in the United States, as in Europe, nearly ceased. But the "air-mindedness" created in the war years did not vanish completely, and with the establishment of airmail service and commercial airlines, a limited demand for aircraft production remained. Research and experimentation were continued in some aircraft plants to make planes safer and faster, but the demand was too limited for mass production to develop.

In contrast, the aircraft industry was growing in Germany, the USSR and Japan, all of which were preparing for war. After the outbreak of World War II and the Battle of Britain, orders for various types of planes began to flow into the United States so fast that in the latter part of 1941 the factories had a backlog representing thirty years' output at the 1939 rate.[98] The industry expanded rapidly in the United States, the United Kingdom, Germany and the USSR. The call everywhere was for more and more planes, with greater speed and safety, larger carrying capacity, greater resistance to changes in temperature and atmospheric pressure.

The output in the United States rose phenomenally. Even the production statistics fail to tell the whole story, since a small civilian airplane and a heavy bomber are each counted as a unit, though they involve vastly different

---

96. **54,** January 21, 1950, p. 146; **35,** February 6, 1950.

97. Attempts to fly in lighter-than-air aircraft began in the latter part of the eighteenth century, when the Montgolfiers made a successful flight in a balloon in France. Experiments continued throughout the following century in France and Germany and were crowned by the completion of an airship by Zeppelin in 1900. A few Zeppelins were built and flown, but several met with dis-

aster. Development of this type of aircraft has ceased, at least for the time being.

98. **34,** p. 171.

TABLE 486

AIRCRAFT: OUTPUT IN THE UNITED STATES, 1910–51

(*Units*)

Year	Total	For United States Military Services	Other	Year	Total	For United States Military Services	Other
1910	1	1	—	1936	3,010	858	2,152
1913	43	14	29	1937	3,773	858	2,915
1914	49	15	34	1938	3,623	925	2,698
1917	2,148	2,013	135	1939	5,856	921	4,935
1918	14,020	13,991	29	1940	12,804	6,019 [a]	6,785 [b]
1919	780	682	98	1941	26,277 [c]	19,433 [a]	6,844 [b]
1920	328	256	72	1942	47,836 [c]	47,836 [a]	—
1926	1,186	478	708	1943	85,898 [c]	85,898 [a]	—
1928	4,346	847	3,499	1944	96,318 [c]	96,318 [a]	—
1929	6,193	779	5,414	1945	49,761 [c]	47,714 [a]	2,047
1930	3,437	836	2,601	1946	36,670	1,669	35,001
1931	2,800	853	1,947	1947	17,717	2,100	15,617
1932	1,396	500	896	1948	9,791	2,489	7,302
1933	1,324	331	993	1949	...	...	3,545
1934	1,615	393	1,222	1950	...	...	3,520
1935	1,710	336	1,374	1951	...	...	2,477

Sources: **18**, 1952, p. 531; **15**, 1950, p. 41.

a. Includes military aircraft for Lend-Lease shipments.

b. Excludes production of aircraft for export.

c. Includes United States–financed aircraft manufactured in Canada.

amounts of work and material.[99] For some types, 500,000 hours of designing and 100,000 hours of testing were required before the plane could be built for passenger transport or military service. In the peak month of 1944 the rate of production in units was more than seventeen times that in 1939; in terms of weight of output, it was fifty times the 1939 rate.[100]

This feat was achieved largely through the application of mass production methods similar to those used in making automobiles and by the efficient use of subcontracting. Semiassembly is used, the line remaining stationary for several hours as the work proceeds. The contrast in the speed of production in the automobile and aircraft industries is illustrated by the fact that while two or three motor vehicles drive off the assembly line every minute, only one to six planes a day come down the semiassembly line.[101]

Production in the United States

During World War II the United States became the largest producer of aircraft. From fewer than 6,000 planes, worth $248 million, in 1939, its output rose to nearly 100,000 units, valued at more than $16 billion, in 1944. In the three years 1942–44, more than 230,000 aircraft left the factories for service. About 90 per cent of this expansion was financed by the government; contracts awarded to the industry before June 1945 exceeded $62 billion.[102] After 1945, production slowed down considerably, but output in 1947 was still three times that in 1939. (See Table 486.)

Employment in the aircraft industry, which stood at only 168 in 1914, rose to 3,543 in 1919, 14,710 in 1929, and 48,638 in 1939.[103] In 1944, more than 2 million persons, or 12.4 per cent of all factory workers, were employed in aircraft production. For 1947, the Census of Manufactures reported 220,000 employees in this industry. In December 1950, employment amounted to 282,200.[104]

Sixteen concerns in the United States produce

---

99. The bomber consists of some 60,000 parts, many of which are manufactured to close tolerances, and has hundreds of precision instruments that must perform perfectly in temperatures ranging from 65° F. below zero to 160°F. above and at altitudes up to 40,000 feet. **32**, 1948, p. 79.

100. **43**, p. 778.

101. Trainer planes can be produced at the rate of one every two and a half hours. **34**, pp. 166–67 and 173.

102. **23**, p. 1; **13**, p. 155.

103. **17**, Vol. II, Part I, p. 540.

104. **33**, p. 22; **18**, 1950, p. 769; **15**, p. 48.

complete aircraft, and many firms manufacture component materials and parts. Production of engines is in the hands of three companies; two dominate the output of high-power engines and one specializes in low-power engines for small civilian planes. One concern accounts for three fourths of the national output of propellers. In 1940, eight firms produced 95.5 per cent of all air frames.[105] The sixteen largest companies obtained nearly two thirds of the wartime government contracts, and eight of them received more than half the orders.[106]

California, New York, Ohio and Pennsylvania lead in aircraft production. During the war the industry was dispersed to some extent for security reasons and also to tap new sources of labor. Since the end of the war, it has shown a definite tendency to return to prewar locations on the east and west coasts. Recently, some of the more important plants for military aircraft have been moved inland.[107]

Production in Other Countries

During the war the United Kingdom produced almost half as many planes as the United States. Its output of military aircraft was as follows (in units): [108]

1939, September–December	2,924
1940	15,049
1941	20,093
1942	23,671
1943	26,263
1944, January–June	14,609

Production declined after the war, although government orders and intensive research still provide the industry with considerable work. At present, Britain is running the United States a close race in the development of large commercial high-speed aircraft and in the field of military aircraft.[109]

France produced nearly 1,400 planes in 1938, but only 780 in 1948. The country's four-year plan projected an even lower rate: 480 planes in 1949, 230 in 1950, and 441 in 1951.[110]

In Germany, output increased from 13 planes in 1931 to 8,295 in 1939. During the war more

than 102,000 were built. The shortage of gasoline forced Germany to stop production of aircraft in January 1945. After the war all aircraft plants in the Allied zones were dismantled.[111]

In the USSR the aircraft industry is integrated and most plants are large. During World War II the assembly line was introduced, and machine-tool shops were established in most plants. The annual output increased from 10,000 units to 40,000, including many small planes, such as attack craft and fighters. After the war, production shifted to large transport aircraft and heavy bombers. It is estimated that 1,000 bombers of the B-29 type and about 2,400 jet craft were produced in 1948.

Moscow was the main center of the Soviet aircraft industry before the war, but many plants were later moved to the Volga area. Today the three most important centers are Moscow, Ufa and Molotov, on the Kama River.[112]

CURRENT TRENDS AND OUTLOOK

Current Trends

The machinery and transportation equipment industries in many countries have increased greatly in capacity and output in recent years. The United States has nearly tripled its 1938 output. According to the United Nations Economic Commission for Europe, the United Kingdom, the Netherlands and Sweden increased their production by about 60 to 70 per cent. Austria, Poland and Finland show even greater increases, but their progress has less significance for the European economy than the relatively smaller rise in the output of the United Kingdom, now the largest European exporter of machinery. (See Table 487.) [113]

Western Germany's index of output in these industries shows 1950 below the level of 1936, mostly because there was very little shipbuilding and no aircraft building; its 1950 index for non-

---

105. **24,** Part 4, p. 13; **23,** p. 11.
106. **13,** p. 156.
107. **47,** p. 842.
108. **33,** p. 160.
109. **9,** 1949, p. 135.
110. **61,** 1948, p. 313.

111. **61,** 1948, p. 336.
112. **61,** 1948, p. 500.
113. Another publication of the Commission (**6,** 1951), which appeared almost simultaneously with that used in Table 487, gives substantially different figures for various countries, mostly on the higher side. The discrepancy is accounted for by differences in sources and methods used. For example, metal goods and aircraft are included in one publication and excluded in the other. However, the indexes for the engineering production of Europe as a whole in 1949 and 1950 are about the same in both publications: 124 and 139, respectively, in **6,** 1951, p. 177; 117 and 135, respectively, in **8,** p. 8.

TABLE 487

MACHINERY AND TRANSPORTATION EQUIPMENT:
INDEXES OF OUTPUT IN SELECTED COUNTRIES,
1948–50

(*1938=100*)

Country	1948	1949	1950
United States [a]	277	234	270
United Kingdom	151	164	182
Ireland	190	218	251
France	120	141	131
Belgium	126	122	115
Netherlands	122	143	159
Denmark	156	161	179
Sweden	164	168	171
Norway	148	160	162
Finland	211	230	186
Western Germany	47	79	109
Poland [b]	193	240	. . .
Czechoslovakia [b]	120	131	156
Switzerland	139	117	121
Austria [b]	98	152	188
Italy	92	101	108
USSR [c]	154	. . .	. . .
Japan [d]	67	79	77

Sources: **6**, 1951, p. 177; **9**, 1952, p. 14; for the United States, **18**, 1951, p. 741, for Japan, **12**, January 1951.

  a. Machinery. 1935–39 = 100.
  b. 1937 = 100.
  c. 1940 = 100.
  d. 1936 = 100.

electrical machinery was 120.7 (1936 = 100); for electrical machinery, 236.3; and for transportation equipment (motor vehicles, motorcycles and so on), 153.8.[114]

Japan's industries, which grew spectacularly during World War II, were severely disrupted by bombing and dismantling and have a long way to go before they return to the high level of 1938. In 1950, the output was about three fourths of the considerably smaller production of 1936. (See Table 487 and Figure 330.) Certain branches are recovering more rapidly, among them production of textile machinery and communication and transportation equipment.[115]

World War II gave many countries a strong incentive to establish domestic production of various types of machinery. Mexico, which until recently manufactured only the simplest agricultural implements, has built a large plant in Mexico City for the production and assembly of tractors and is building a plant near Saltillo for making and assembling other heavy agricultural machines.[116] The Union of South Africa has entered the world market as an exporter of agricultural machinery and produces a considerable range of electrical equipment. India aims at establishing machine-tool production and is building the locomotives for its railroads. The first large Indian-built vessel, an 8,000-ton steamer, was completed in 1948, and the government is actively supporting further development of shipbuilding. Productive capacity has been achieved in making automatic looms, spinning-ring frames, power transformers, diesel engines and other equipment. Australia, where only the less accurate types of machine tools were made before the war, is now producing all types; agricultural machinery and earth-moving equipment are also manufactured and shipbuilding has become an important industry.[117] The list of developments in these industries could be continued to include nearly every country in the world.

Outlook

The machinery and transportation equipment industries have every prospect of growing in old-established strongholds and of taking root in many other parts of the world. Underdeveloped countries regard our mechanized civilization as the symbol of the higher living standards of the West, and they yearn to reach these standards. The drive to industrialization, noticeable almost everywhere, is therefore bound to gain in strength and speed.

Although the machinery and transportation equipment industries are among the most complicated branches of manufacturing, they can reasonably be expected to grow and spread throughout the world. Supported by governments eager to achieve self-sufficiency, or at least greater economic independence for their awakening nations, these industries will be financed partly from public funds and partly by private capital, mostly of foreign origin but including domestic investment as well. Technical skill and knowledge, now articles of export, are available; moreover, these countries are striving to train their nationals. Insofar as the growth of the machinery and transportation equipment industries in underdeveloped areas contributes to

114. **55**, April 1951, p. 90.
115. **9**, 1949, p. 218; **5**, 1951, pp. 67 and 318.

116. **9**, 1949, pp. 242–43.
117. **9**, 1949, pp. 230–38; **5**, 1951, p. 68.

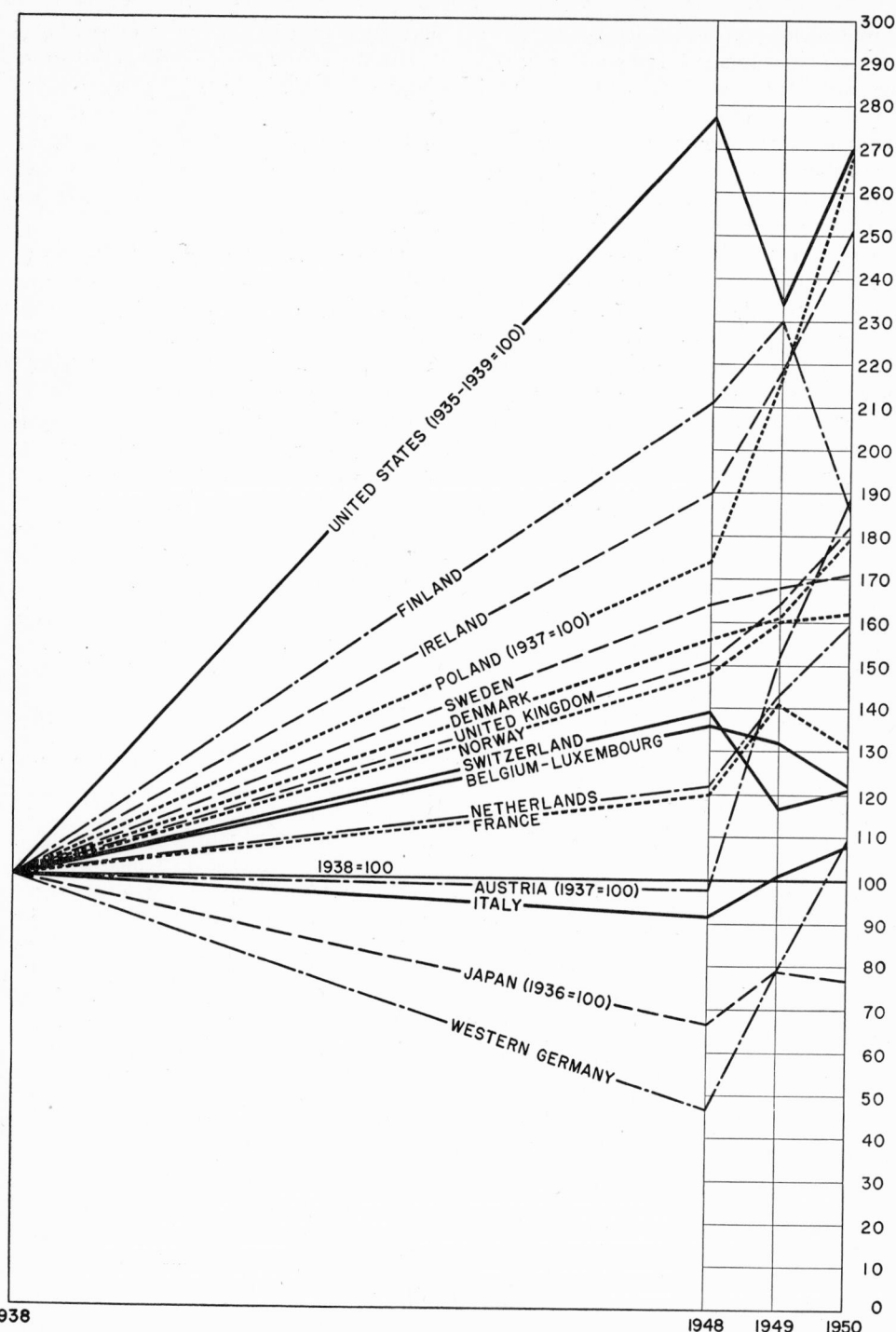

FIGURE 330. MACHINERY AND TRANSPORTATION EQUIPMENT: INDEXES OF PRODUCTION IN SELECTED
COUNTRIES, 1948–50

(*1938 = 100*)

their welfare and economic independence, it will also contribute to economic and political stability in the world. While old industrialized countries will be deprived of some outlets for the products of these industries, they will benefit from this greater stability and feel easier as dissatisfied and hungry neighbors become fewer. In the long run, such development may even be advantageous to the old strongholds of these industries, because of the demand abroad for machinery and transportation equipment of more exacting types. At the same time, rising standards of living in the West should continue to increase the demand for a greater variety of goods that must be produced and delivered by means of machinery and transportation equipment.

The growth of these industries will create new difficulties, however: there will be a steadily increasing demand for raw materials, much of which comes from the underdeveloped areas, and possibly a decline in the willingness of such areas to export the necessary raw materials to the industrialized countries. Increased competition will tend to change the structure of prices of raw materials, and some of them may be in limited supply.

The solution of these difficulties lies not in trying to keep the bulk of machinery and transportation equipment industries within their present confines and to prevent them from spreading throughout the world, but in further technological progress, more economical extraction of raw materials, greater efficiency in their consumption, and progress in the industries that can create new raw materials, as, for example, the chemical industry.

CHAPTER 31

THE CHEMICAL INDUSTRY

CHEMISTRY HAS BEEN AN ART, a science and an industry. It was practiced as an art thousands of years ago. As a science, it dates from the middle of the seventeenth century. Its beginnings as an industry go back to the early years of the nineteenth century, but it did not come of age until the twentieth.

The development of industrial chemistry and the chemical industry is a salient feature of our times. The range of chemical products has become so wide, and the application of chemical processes in various industries so extensive, that it has become increasingly difficult to define the scope of the industry as such.

Some experts define it as an industry that produces commodities different in their molecular structure from the raw materials from which they were made.[1] Yet such a definition, if consistently applied, would necessarily include all metallurgy, petroleum refining, production of artificial fibers, and so on. Indeed, the manuals on chemical technology deal with the smelting of iron, petroleum refining and coal carbonization. A definition of the chemical industry that included these would be too broad, however, and at variance with the widely accepted industrial classification.

The common usage in the United States is to distinguish the chemical industry, which produces chemicals, from "chemical-process" industries, in which chemical processes play a preponderant role, as in the production of paper, or in petroleum refining. The Chemical Industries Committee of the International Labor Organization tried for two years to work out a definition that would be acceptable to the various member countries but ended with only a list of commodities that are considered chemical products in most countries.[2] Thus, it returned to the definition of the chemical industry in accordance with the common use of the word "chemicals."

The Census of Manufactures in the United States classifies the following groups of products under "chemicals and allied products": industrial inorganic chemicals; industrial organic chemicals (coal-tar crudes, plastics, synthetic rubber, synthetic fibers, explosives and others); drugs and medicines; soap and related products; paints and allied products; gum and wood chemicals; fertilizers; vegetable and animal oils; miscellaneous chemical products (printing ink, toilet preparations, glue and gelatin, insecticides and fungicides, salt and so on). That classification is used in this chapter in the analysis of employment and value of output in the chemical industry. More detailed information is given in later sections on the most important chemicals, including a few heavy chemicals (sulfuric acid, soda ash, caustic soda and nitric acid); some organic chemicals derived from coal, natural gas, petroleum and oils; dyestuffs; synthetic rubber; plastics and fertilizers (superphosphates and synthetic nitrogen).[3]

DEVELOPMENT OF THE CHEMICAL INDUSTRY

The ancients made a few medicines, some animal and vegetable colors, glass and some metals. The Tyrians produced their famous purple dye from shellfish about 1500 B.C.,[4] and the Chinese made gunpowder. Geber (a Latin scholar who lived in the twelfth or thirteenth century) was the first to describe the preparation of mineral acids, and was familiar with salts and some alkalies (neutralizers of acids).[5] Theophilus, who lived in the eleventh century, described methods of making pigments and glass.

In the Middle Ages, the chief industrial acid in Europe was vinegar, easily and cheaply obtained but too weak for most chemical reactions. The lactic acid of buttermilk was used in bleaching textiles. Manufacture of alum was introduced into Europe from Arabia and became a monopoly of the popes ("Roman alum"). Dung was the

---

1. **40**, pp. 1–2; **38**, p. 11.
2. **7**, 1950, pp. 8–29.

3. Synthetic fibers are discussed in Chapter 28; naval stores and tanning materials in Chapter 19; vegetable and animal oils in Chapters 16, 18 and 20; salt, sulfur, potassium, phosphate rock and nitrates in Chapter 22.
4. **57**, Vol. I, p. 14.
5. **24**, p. 609.

industrial source of ammonia.[6] Sulfuric acid, blue cobalt pigment and iron pigments were produced in small quantities. These early beginnings of chemical production were empirical in character, stemming from incidental discoveries and based on the rule of thumb. Despite the small scale of production, monopolistic practices were common; knowledge of a process was often jealously guarded and kept for generations within a single family.

Even in the eighteenth century, chemical production was limited to a few dyes, pigments, drugs, and small quantities of sulfuric acid and gunpowder.[7] Larger-scale production was made possible in 1746 by the discovery in England of means of producing sulfuric acid in lead chambers and, in 1790, by the discovery in France of a method of producing soda ash.

New Products

The two products — sulfuric acid and soda ash — spearheaded the growth of the chemical industry in the early nineteenth century and are still the first chemicals to be produced in countries beginning the manufacture of chemicals.[8]

Soda ash, needed to make glass, soap and bleaching material, had been obtained previously from burning a sea plant, saltwort, and from trona deposits of dry lakes in Egypt.[9] Supplies were limited, but demand grew, particularly because of the growth of the textile industry. France felt the pinch especially, since, then at war with England, it was cut off from seaborne Spanish alkali and Egyptian trona. In 1782, the French Academy offered a prize for the best method of producing soda ash from domestic raw materials, and eight years later Nicolas Leblanc won the award by synthesizing sulfuric acid with common salt and limestone. The first step in this method was to form salt cake and hydrochloric acid.

The first Leblanc plant for making soda ash was founded in France in 1791, the second in 1806, and in time the industry assumed considerable proportions. Production of soda ash by the Leblanc method was not taken up in England until the 1820's. Here also production grew,

and since it required large quantities of sulfuric acid, which were used also in the textile and other industries, it stimulated the production of the acid. Production of superphosphates, stimulated by Liebig's discovery of the importance of fertilizers for the productivity of the soil,[10] began in England in the 1840's. In the next decade, the incidental discovery of a chemical dye by W. H. Perkin, in England in 1856, gave origin to an important new branch of the chemical industry, dyestuffs. The following decade saw the commercial production of explosive nitroglycerine (Nobel, 1862) and an essential improvement in the manufacture of soda ash (the Solvay method, Belgium, 1863), which was already a sizable industry.

New Methods

In the latter part of the century, inventions in the field of chemistry followed one another rapidly. Methods were found to utilize light oils distilled from coal tar. Pharmaceuticals, perfumes and paints appeared on the market in increasing quantities. The use of cellulose for explosives was introduced. The chemical industry branched out in various directions. New processes and products were developed, one line of production supporting another. Machinery and equipment became increasingly elaborate in line with the growing complexity of chemical engineering.

It was reserved to the twentieth century, however, to integrate all these branches of chemical production through systematic research in industrial laboratories and to strengthen the ties between the chemical industry and other branches of manufacturing. The two world wars greatly stimulated chemical production. They brought an immense and urgent demand for all kinds of chemicals, from explosives to fertilizers, from drugs to dyestuffs. This demand, in turn, stimulated that most potent of catalysts, the human brain. The many processes invented not only met an emergency but have proved even more widely applicable in peacetime.

Progress in the United States

Development of the chemical industry in the United States was slow at first. While potash to make soap and candles was produced in colonial times, the first sulfuric acid plant, in Philadel-

---

6. **38**, pp. 24–25.
7. In the United States, the manufacture of gunpowder was begun in 1801 by du Pont in Wilmington, on the advice of Thomas Jefferson. **40**, p. 20.
8. **37**, Vol. III, p. 3.
9. **44**, p. 84.

10. Cf. Chapter 15, pp. 526 ff.

phia, was not built until 1792. For the next hundred years American manufacturers of chemicals imported processes, and often equipment, from England, France and Germany. But the European equipment was largely designed for skilled workers, then scarce in the United States, and was not large enough to handle the output desired. Independent development of the chemical industry in the United States dates from the beginning of this century. Since that time, the country has made many important contributions, and today it leads not only in volume of chemical production but also in technical knowledge. Among other techniques it has been instrumental in introducing the continuous process and automatic control of chemical reactions.

The shift from batch jobs to a continuous process has played much the same role in chemical production as the introduction of interchangeable parts played in the machinery and transportation equipment industries. While requiring more complex equipment, the continuous process has effected a great saving in time and labor and has assured a more uniform product. No longer must each single chemical reaction be carried out separately: here in a kettle, there in a filter or autoclave. Instead, the raw material travels from one piece of apparatus to another by means of a conveyor or through a series of pipes, until the finished product appears at the end of the system.

Automatic controls assure greater precision in all processes, guarding against the smallest differences in pressure, temperature, density, humidity and so on, all along the line. As a result, a fair-sized plant for alcohol distillation, for example, can now operate with one man per shift.[11]

CHARACTERISTICS OF THE CHEMICAL INDUSTRY

The chemical industry differs from other manufacturing industries in its methods of production, the range and the nature of the raw materials it uses, the character of its products, the role that research plays in its development and many other features.

Methods of Production

Among the great variety of chemical reactions and physical processes used industrially to change the molecular structure of raw materials, some of the most frequently employed are: [12]

Chemical Reactions	Physical Processes
Combustion	Fluid flow
Oxidation	Heat transfer
Neutralization	Evaporation
Causticization	Humidification or
Electrolysis	dehumidification
Double decomposition	Gas absorption
Calcination	Solvent extraction
Nitration	Adsorption
Reduction	Distillation
Ammonolysis	Drying
Halogenation	Mixing
Sulfonation	Filtration
Hydrogenation	Screening
Alkylation	Crystallization
Condensation	Centrifugation
Polymerization	Disintegration
Fermentation	
Pyrolysis	

The chemical industry has made more frequent changes in its processes and equipment than most other industries. Textile mills use spindles and looms as they did a hundred years ago, with differences in operating speed and the arrangement of the machinery but not in the principles of spinning and weaving. Iron and steel have been produced in Bessemer, open-hearth or electric furnaces since the second half of the past century, and the principle of steelmaking remains the same despite changes in the quality of the steel and the construction of the furnaces. But the chemical industry has frequently worked out new optional processes, based on essentially different principles and requiring entirely new machinery and equipment. Obsolescence of equipment is therefore a much more serious problem in this industry than in most other branches of manufacturing.

Raw Materials

While other industries must have specific raw materials — hides and skins to make leather, iron ore and scrap to make iron and steel, textile fibers to make fabrics, and so on — the chemical industry, because of its ability to change the structure of materials, can produce an identical finished commodity from various raw materials and many products from the same raw materials. In woodworking, for example, the same raw

---

11. **42**, pp. 293–94.

12. **53**, p. 10.

TABLE 488

THE CHEMICAL INDUSTRY: RAW MATERIALS USED IN PRODUCING THE 150 MOST IMPORTANT
CHEMICALS IN THE UNITED STATES

Raw Material	Number of Products	Raw Material	Number of Products
Water	99	Iron ores	6
Air	96	Phosphate rock	6
Coal	91	Sea water	5
Sulfur	88	Copper ores	4
Mineral salt	75	Fluorine minerals	4
Limestone	63	Arsenic minerals	3
Sulfide ores	32	Magnesium minerals	3
Brines	24	Mercury ores	3
Petroleum	23	Zinc ores	3
Natural gas	16	Antimony minerals	2
Saltpeter	13	Barium minerals	2
Potassium minerals	11	Boron minerals	2
Gypsum	10	Manganese ores	2
Lead ores	9	Tin ores	2
Sand	9	Bismuth minerals	1
Aluminum minerals	8	Silver ores	1
Chromium ores	7	Titanium ores	1

Source: **53**, p. 6.

material is used throughout the fabricating process, and the by-products — scrap, sawdust, shavings — are also wood. But when a chemical plant subjects the same wood to destructive distillation, it produces charcoal, crude pyroligneous acid, wood tar and gas. Each of these is used for a variety of products: charcoal in smelting some metals, in the manufacture of some grades of gunpowder, in sugar and oil refining and so on; acid in making methanol, acetic acid, acetone and many other products; wood tar, apart from its use as fuel or as a binder of briquettes from waste charcoal dust, in the recovery of creosote and other wood preservatives.[13] "From the same raw materials the chemist can produce fuels, fertilizers, beverages, drugs, and explosives."[14]

Sulfuric acid is an example of a product that may be made from various raw materials. It may be obtained from sulfur (brimstone), pyrites, iron, sulfides, copper and zinc; from sulfur waste in refining petroleum and manufacturing fuel gas; or from gypsum, as in Germany and France.[15]

The chemical industry, moreover, makes wide use of abundantly available and almost universally cheap raw materials, such as salt, lime and coal. It has been estimated that about three dozen raw materials are used in making the hundred and fifty most important chemicals in the United States. (See Table 488.) Some of these are used only in producing one or two of these commodities, but each of six raw materials — water, air, coal, sulfur, mineral salt and limestone — is needed for from 63 to 99 of these chemicals. Chemical-process industries also use many of the raw materials enumerated in Table 488 and many others, such as wood pulp (the rayon and paper industries), corn (starch industry), cotton linters (the synthetic fibers and explosives industries). Even complex chemical compounds such as synthetic nitrogen (ammonium sulfate or cyanamide) require such ordinary raw materials as air, water or coal, and lime. The techniques are so intricate, however, and require such precision and skill that only a few industrialized countries can avail themselves of them. Every state in the United States produces some raw materials used in the manufacture of chemicals or in chemical-process industries. (See Figure 331.)

Products

The manufacture of chemicals is an industry

---

13. **38**, pp. 36–37.
14. **56**, p. 380.
15. **45**, p. 54; and **35**, Vol. I, p. 250.

Chemical Facts and Figures, 1940 (**30**)

FIGURE 331. THE CHEMICAL INDUSTRY: GEOGRAPHIC DISTRIBUTION OF PRINCIPAL RAW MATERIALS REQUIRED BY THE CHEMICAL AND CHEMICAL–PROCESS INDUSTRIES IN THE UNITED STATES

of many products, extremely heterogeneous and complex. The production of almost any chemical results in one or more by-products: glycerin is produced with soap, hydrogen with chlorine or electrolytic caustic soda, and so on. Often the by-product proves to be more important than the primary product. Calculation of the cost of producing any commodity therefore usually takes into account the value of its by-products.

The chemical industry produces both raw materials and finished products. It makes nitrocellulose, for example, which becomes a raw material for the manufacture of synthetic fibers, photographic materials, lacquers and explosives. The industry is its own best customer, since products of one branch serve as raw materials for others. Phenol, for example, is made from benzene but is used, in turn, as a raw material for lacquers and plastics. In the United States the chemical and chemical-process industries consume more than three fourths of the chemical industry's total output: nearly 80 per cent of sulfuric acid; more than 85 per cent of soda ash and chlorine; more than 90 per cent of caustic soda, hydrochloric, nitric and acetic acids, ammonia and sodium sulfates.[16] (See Figure 332.)

16. **29,** September 1939, p. 545.

Industrial Research

There is a saying that technical brains are the most important raw material of the chemical industry. Research is its lifeblood; its birth, existence and development have depended on patient work in numerous laboratories. From these laboratories has flowed a constant stream of new products — plastics, dyes, nitrogen compounds, synthetic fibers and rubber. Discovery of one product is usually the starting point for further research.

A country that does not have the raw materials for certain chemical products but does have trained personnel, mechanical power and capital can readily develop an important chemical industry. Thus Switzerland has become one of the principal European producers of dyestuffs, although it has to import the raw material, coal. On the other hand, Brazil, with almost all the raw materials needed in the chemical industry, until recently produced practically no chemicals.

Because of constant changes in methods of production, raw materials and products, the industry is particularly dependent on laboratory experiments, tests and discoveries. Every chemical plant must be constantly on the watch for new procedures, devices and products.

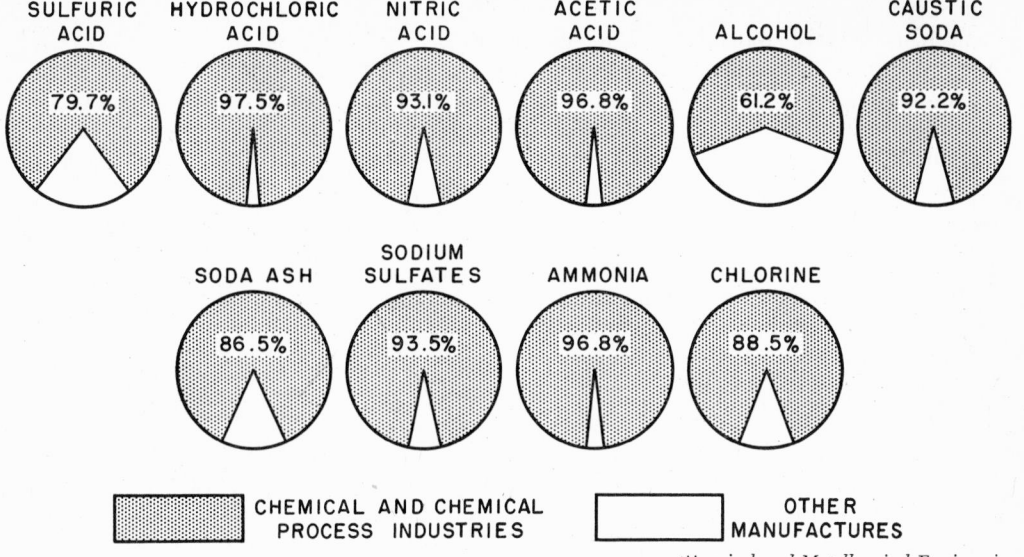

FIGURE 332. DISTRIBUTION OF CONSUMPTION OF SELECTED CHEMICALS BETWEEN THE CHEMICAL AND CHEMICAL–PROCESS INDUSTRIES AND OTHER MANUFACTURES IN THE UNITED STATES

In 1920 the United States had 350 chemical laboratories; in 1937 nearly 2,000, with some 40,000 trained chemists and a budget of $300 million; in 1947 the industry employed 133,500 researchers and spent $600 million for this purpose.[17] The ratio of specialists to workers is higher in chemical plants than in any other industry except petroleum refining — 303 researchers for every 10,000 production workers in 1937, as compared with 41 in automobile production, 28 in paper and pulp manufacture, 16 in food processing, 15 in the manufacture of iron and steel, and 2 in textile industries. In 1938 the chemical industry accounted for 21.5 per cent of all research employment in manufacturing.[18] In prewar Germany the ratio of trained chemists and engineers to workers was even higher than in the United States. In the USSR the industry employs at least 50,000 chemists.[19]

The concomitants of the new processes and techniques developed by chemical research are higher capital investment per worker than in other industries and more rapid obsolescence of equipment.

Location

With some exceptions, chemical plants seek proximity to their industrial outlets. Proximity to raw materials is less important than in many other industries; only plants that use bulky and cheap raw materials need to be near their sources of supply. Thus a soda plant is usually built in the vicinity of solid salt or brine and at a place where limestone is available at low cost. A plentiful supply of fuel and power is essential for electrochemical plants (caustic soda, chlorine, calcium carbide and so on). The danger connected with the production of explosives does not permit operation of such plants near other factories or in densely populated areas.[20] Usually, many factors are considered in selecting the site of a chemical plant.

In the United States the chief centers of the chemical industry have traditionally been New York, Philadelphia, Pittsburgh and Chicago. Cheap natural gas in West Virginia and cheap electricity in Tennessee have attracted many plants to those states. California is a chemical empire in itself, and many important chemical plants operate in Texas.

In the USSR about half the chemical output before World War II came from the northwestern part and some 42 per cent from the central area. Even then, however, it was planned to shift the plants eastward so that by 1942 only 15 per cent of the chemicals would be produced

17. **58**, p. 26; **7**, 1950, p. 66.
18. **30**, 1940, pp. 43–44.
19. **7**, 1950, p. 70.

20. **58**, pp. 72–74.

in the northwest, 46 per cent in the central region, 10 per cent in the Ukraine, and most of the rest in the Urals, Siberia and the Volga-Vyatka area. The war halted this plan, but the eastward movement of the Soviet industry is continuing.[21]

Concentration

The chemical industry is among the most highly concentrated branches of manufacturing. In the United States, the four largest firms control from 50 to 75 per cent of the production of many essential chemicals and more than 80 per cent of that of ammunition and explosives. The eight largest companies account for 99 per cent of the production of essential oils.[22] In 1939, 40 major chemical companies in the United States had total assets of more than $2 billion. The du Pont and the Union Carbide companies together accounted for 52 per cent of the total.[23]

Each of the three largest dye manufacturers in the United States represents an almost complete vertical combination in the field of coal-tar products. These manufacturers also produce acids, alkalies, salts, ammonia and synthetic nitrates.[24] Moreover, the largest producers have substantial interests in foreign chemical production. The du Pont company, for example, owns plants in Mexico, Chile, Germany, France, Uruguay, two plants in Argentina and England, and a 47 per cent interest in Canadian Industries, Ltd.[25] Even more important is the close partnership between du Pont and Imperial Chemical Industries, of England.

In 1939 the German dye trust, I.G. Farben, controlled 85 per cent of the German chemical industry. It had a virtual monopoly (nearly 98 per cent) of Germany's output of dye and an equally strong position in the manufacture of nitrogen, explosives, synthetic rubber and fuels. Moreover, it owned or controlled plants in almost every principal dye-producing country, including the United States.[26] It produced almost all the raw materials it needed within its own organization, and its plants, with a total employment of 220,000 workers, were self-contained manufacturing units. In 1943, employment in

I.G. and plants connected with it amounted to 333,000.[27]

In the United Kingdom, Imperial Chemical Industries, Ltd. (ICI), controls the dye industry and many other branches of chemical production. Its position in the chemical economy of the country is similar to that of I.G. in prewar Germany. Before the war ICI controlled sales agencies in each of its principal foreign markets, including China, India, Japan, Malaya, the Levant, Egypt, Chile, Peru, South Africa. It also had interests in chemical plants in South Africa, Argentina, Brazil, Canada, Chile, Australia and New Zealand. At the end of 1948, this company employed nearly 100,000 persons.[28]

The Swiss I.G. (Basler Interessen Gemeinschaft) has a virtual monopoly of Switzerland's organic chemical industry and owns plants in many countries, including the United States and the United Kingdom. Before the war, its worldwide sales network was second only to that of the German firms.[29]

In France, Établissements Kuhlmann occupies a position roughly parallel to the du Pont empire in the United States in the production of dyes, lacquers, rayon, fertilizers and many other chemicals.

The firm of Montecatini in Italy carries a full line of heavy chemicals and produces fertilizers, plastics and rayon. It uses a tenth of all the electric power consumed in the country and accounts for about 90 per cent of Italy's output of pyrites; 80–90 per cent of the nitrate fertilizers; 70 per cent of the sulfuric acid and insecticides; 60–70 per cent of the phosphate fertilizers; and 60 per cent of the coloring matter.[30]

In prewar Czechoslovakia, the Aussiger Verein controlled more than 60 per cent of the chemical output.[31]

Control of World Markets

These industrial giants have differed in international policy. Du Pont and Imperial Chemical Industries have been actual partners in many fields; for example, they operate in Canada, Argentina and Brazil as a single concern through jointly owned local companies. In turn, du Pont

21. **29,** February 1948, pp. 129–31 and 141.
22. **9,** p. 183.
23. **56,** p. 381.
24. **16,** p. 62.
25. **40,** p. 233.
26. **16,** pp. 80–83.

27. **29,** January 1948, p. 98; **36,** Appendix I, p. 4.
28. **16,** pp. 89–90; **7,** 1950, p. 59.
29. One of the five largest dye producers in the United States is owned by Swiss interests. **16,** pp. 17 and 87.
30. **7,** 1950, p. 95.
31. **39,** pp. 103–04.

recognizes the British Empire as the territory of ICI, just as the latter considers the market of the United States to belong to du Pont. I. G. Farben preferred to operate alone, and when engaging in joint operations, tried to retain control in one way or another. It even re-entered the American market lost in World War I and made agreements to this effect with various concerns in the United States.

All the combinations and arrangements among the few major concerns of the United States, Germany, the United Kingdom, France and other countries cannot be mentioned here in detail. Generally speaking, these firms have divided a considerable part of the world market among themselves by a network of arrangements, which have sometimes covered single products, sometimes the whole line. The legal form of such arrangements has differed from case to case — and occasionally has been merely an informal "gentlemen's agreement." [32]

THE CHEMICAL INDUSTRY IN THE WORLD ECONOMY

The chemical industry is increasingly important in the world economy. It enables farmers to increase the fertility of their soil and to protect plants and cattle from pests and diseases. It provides medicine with new weapons in the struggle against disease and infection and enables it to cure many maladies previously incurable. It supplies mining and manufacturing with new tools: modern manufacturing uses some 3,000 chemical products, and practically all industries depend, directly or indirectly, on chemical products or on processes developed by the chemical industry. Indeed, all manufacturing in countries like the United States and the United Kingdom has been "chemicalized" in the past two or three decades.

The chemical industry has enabled man to extract metals from the earth and to build tunnels through mountains. Without explosives, the construction of Boulder Dam or the Holland Tunnel under the Hudson River might have taken hundreds of years. Similarly, the draining of swampland by methods other than ditch blasting would have been prohibitively expensive and time-consuming. [33]

By utilizing waste from various manufactures, the chemical industry cuts down their costs of production. It contributes to the conservation of natural resources by producing substitutes for raw materials that are becoming scarce. It has helped to neutralize or destroy useless waste that once polluted the water or poisoned the air. Until methods for utilization, or at least disposal, of waste were found, alkali plants ran their waste into the nearest stream; wool factories threw away the fertilizing scourings of raw wool; iron works illuminated the air with open-top furnaces; coke beehives fumed away potentially valuable gases, and so on. [34]

The chemical industry has created synthetic products equal and sometimes superior to such natural products as textile fibers, dyes, rubber, camphor. In industrially developed countries, chemicalization and mechanization of production keep pace, both being aspects of the increasing application of modern science to economic activities.

Spearheading technical progress in recent decades, the chemical industry has tended to grow more rapidly than manufacturing as a whole. In the United States, for example, chemical output tripled in volume from 1929 to 1950, while the output of manufacturing as a whole only doubled. The chemical industry was among the leading military industries during World War II. (See Figure 333.[35])

Employment

Because of lack of statistics and wide differences in the classifications used in various countries, it is extremely difficult to estimate precisely the number of workers employed in the world's chemical industries. At a rough approximation, it amounted to 400,000 in 1875; 850,000 in 1907; a million in 1913; and 2 million in 1929. Depression years caused a smaller drop in employment in the chemical industries than in other branches of manufacturing — only about 12.5 per cent in 1933. About 2.1 million workers were employed in 1936, slightly more than in 1929.[36]

In recent years, employment in the chemical industries has increased considerably and may

32. For a detailed description of the international interrelationships in chemical production, see **56**, pp. 363–517.

33. Eighty-five million acres of muck and swampland have been drained by ditch blasting in the United States **53**, p. 439.

34. **33**, p. 238.

35. Cf. **10**, 1950, p. 755 and 1951, p. 741.

36. **41**, p. 257.

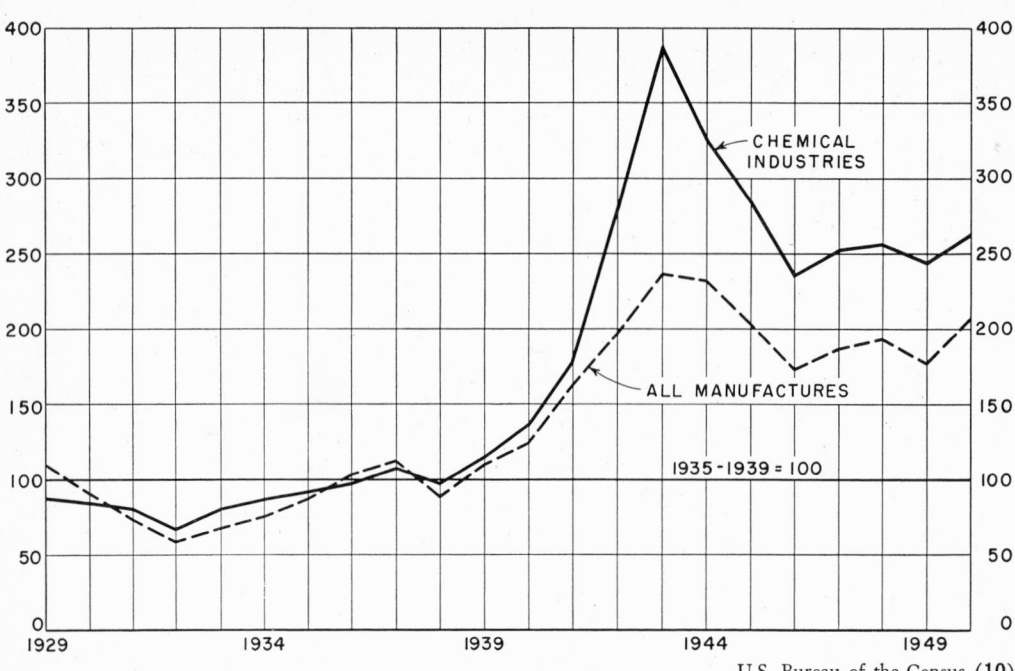

FIGURE 333. VARIATIONS IN ANNUAL OUTPUT OF CHEMICAL INDUSTRIES IN RELATION TO ALL MANUFACTURES
IN THE UNITED STATES, 1929–50

now approach 3.5 million workers. There are more than 630,000 in the United States and about 150,000 in other countries of the Western Hemisphere; about 500,000 in the United Kingdom; more than 250,000 in France; about 330,000 in Western Germany and 180,000 in Italy; about 400,000 or more in other European countries (Czechoslovakia, Switzerland, Poland, Scandinavia and so on). (See Table 489 and Figure 334.) There are now more than 320,000 in the USSR, some 400,000 in Asia, and perhaps 100,000 or more in Oceania and Africa.

	Millions	*Per Cent*
Total	$7,500	100.0
Sulfuric acid	1,607	21.4
Fixation of nitrogen	536	7.1
Other fertilizers	357	4.8
Tar dyes	321	4.3
Paints, varnishes, lacquers, mineral dyes	1,250	16.7
Explosives	250	3.3
Rayon	464	6.2
Drugs	857	11.4
Perfumes, toilet preparations, etc.	571	7.6
Other chemicals	1,286	17.1

Value of Output

The gross value of the world output of chemicals, without duplications resulting from the purchase of semifinished products by one chemical plant from another, has been estimated at $800–$850 million for 1875 and about $1.7 billion for 1907. The figure rose to $2.5 billion in 1913 and to nearly three times that amount in 1929 ($7.2 billion), decreased to $4.3 billion in 1933, and was about $7.5 billion in 1939. Sulfuric acid ranked first in value of output in 1939; paints, varnishes, lacquers and mineral dyes were in second place and drugs, in third: [37]

Of the world output of chemicals in 1938–39, estimated at about $8 billion, the United States accounted for 47 per cent, Germany for 19–20 per cent, and the United Kingdom for 12 per cent.[38] The rest was distributed among some two dozen countries.

The United States may now produce about 55 per cent of the world output, while Germany's share has shrunk drastically. The value added by production of chemicals in the United States in 1947 totaled $5.4 billion, and the gross value (without duplication) may have been around $7 billion. Thus the gross value of the world

37. **41**, p. 257; and **59**, p. 29.

38. **51**, p. 28.

TABLE 489

THE CHEMICAL INDUSTRY: ESTABLISHMENTS AND EMPLOYMENT IN SELECTED COUNTRIES

Country and Year [a]	Establish-ments	Employees, in Thou-sands	Country and Year [a]	Establish-ments	Employees, in Thou-sands
United States, 1947	10,073	632	Western Germany, 1951	...	323
Canada, 1947	1,046	39	Poland, 1946	976	76
Mexico, 1940	410	9	Czechoslovakia, 1948	...	82
Venezuela, 1936	284	2	Switzerland,[b] 1949	384	23
Chile, 1940	307	7	Austria, 1949	401	27
Uruguay, 1936	291	2	Italy, 1948	...	172
Argentina,[b] 1941	1,402	27	USSR, 1938	...	280
United Kingdom, 1951	...	486	Japan, 1938	6,146	322
France, 1946	...	256	India, 1939	708	70
Belgium, 1948	...	67	Union of South		
Netherlands, 1942	2,417	41	Africa, 1945–46	302	23
Denmark,[b] 1948	402	9	Australia, 1946–47	929	31
Sweden,[b] 1947	508	29	New Zealand, 1943–44	261	4
Norway, 1948	156	9			
Finland, 1948	191	8			

Sources: Statistical yearbooks and censuses; for the USSR, **7**, 1950, p. 60; for Italy, **23**, 1949, p. 163; for Germany, **21**, May 1951, p. 558.

a. Most recent data available.
b. Establishments with more than 5 workers.

output of chemicals must have been close to $13 billion. In 1950, the volume of the output of chemicals in the United States was, on the average, about 5 per cent greater than in 1947, and prices were about 5–6 per cent lower.[39] The value of the chemical output in the United States consequently was about the same as in 1947, as was also that in the world.

BASIC CHEMICALS

In the last quarter century, the number of chemical products marketed in the United States increased by 6,500–7,000 items, or an average of 270 products a year. A new chemical appears on the market almost every day.[40]

The two most important industrial chemicals, which have innumerable uses and enter into the production of a great many very different commodities, are sulfuric acid and soda.

SULFURIC ACID

If the art of making sulfuric acid were to be lost tomorrow, our world would become hardly recognizable:

. . . we should be without steel and all other metals and products of the metallurgical industry; rail-

roads, airplanes, automobiles, telephones, radios, reinforced concrete, all would go because the metals are taken from the earth by using dynamite made with sulfuric acid; and for the same reason construction work of all kinds, road and bridge building, canals, tunnels, and sanitary construction work would cease . . . The textile industry would be crippled . . . We should find ourselves without accumulators, tin cans, galvanized iron, radio outfits, white paper, quick-acting phosphate fertilizers, celluloid, artificial leather, dyestuffs, a great many medicines, and numberless other things into the making of which this acid enters at some stage.[41]

The output of sulfuric acid has always been considered a good business indicator, "the grandfather of all indicators," since the acid is used in so many industries, and the hazard of storing it in quantity keeps the inventory of producers low and forces them to respond rapidly to changes in demand.[42]

Methods of Production

Sulfuric acid was known to the alchemists and, according to Geber, was produced in the twelfth or thirteenth century by distillation from alum. In the seventeenth century, small quantities were produced in wet receptacles. Salt was first added

39. **10**, 1950, pp. 280 and 755; **11**, March 1951, p. S–5.
40. **7**, 1950, p. 66.

41. **43**, Vol. I, pp. 8–9.
42. **34**, p. 601.

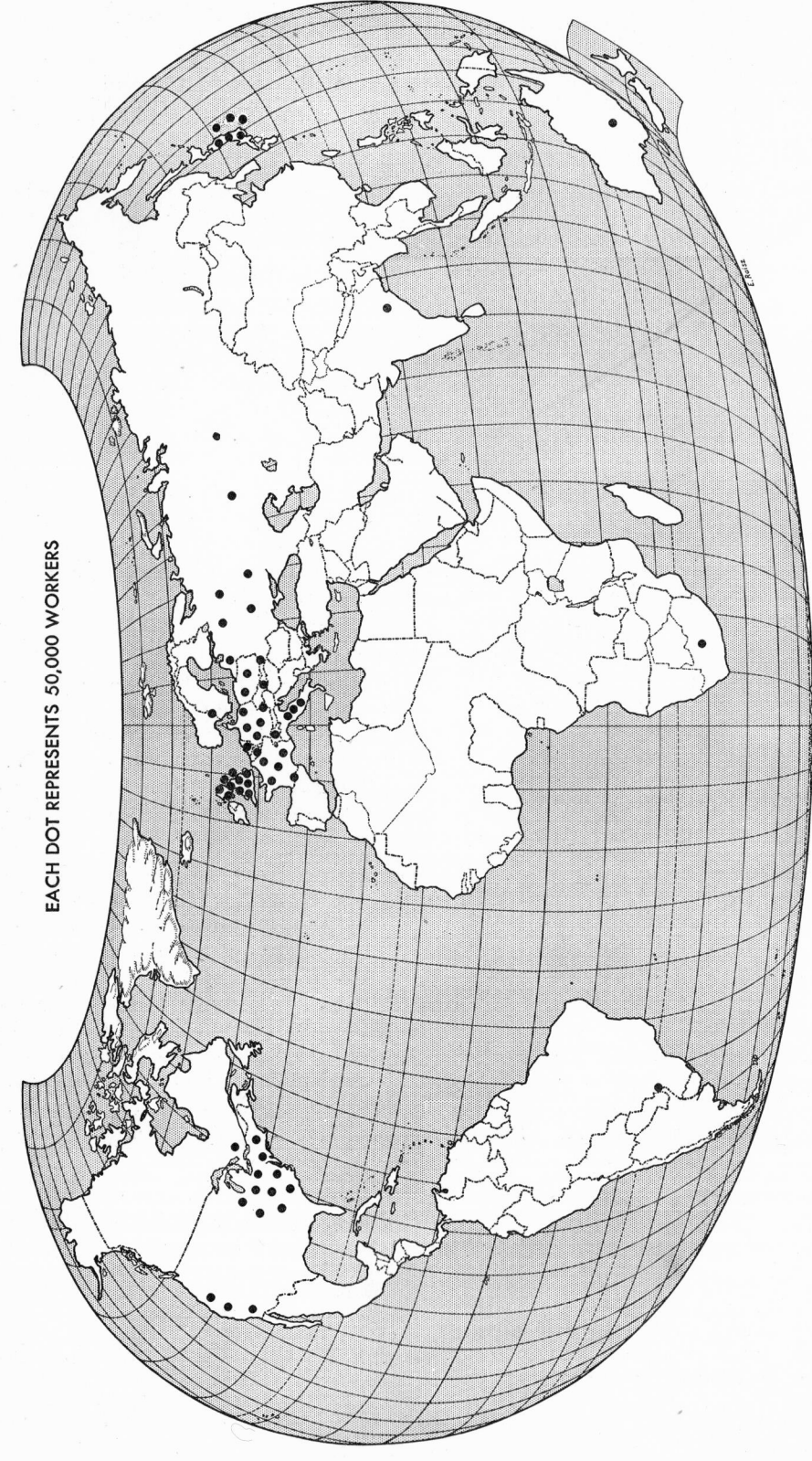

EACH DOT REPRESENTS 50,000 WORKERS

FIGURE 334. EMPLOYMENT IN THE CHEMICAL INDUSTRY: GEOGRAPHIC DISTRIBUTION IN THE WORLD
(Latest Available Data)

to burn sulfur in 1666. The acid, however, remained an expensive product until 1746, when the use of lead chambers was introduced in England. Then it began to be produced and marketed by tons.[43]

The so-called contact process, with the use of a catalyst, was invented later, also in England, to produce fuming sulfuric acid. Actually discovered by P. Philips in 1831, the process was not applied commercially for more than forty years, until, in the 1870's, the invention of a synthetic dye, alizarin, created a demand for concentrated acid. This process employed a platinum catalyst and produced a stronger sulfuric acid than the lead-chamber process, then in universal use. Though the contact process had become widespread in Europe by 1900, the United States had no contact plants until that year.[44]

Around that time, the Frasch process for extracting sulfur from deep deposits in Louisiana, invented in 1894, began to provide the United States with domestic supplies of sulfur for manufacturing the acid.[45] Since the 1920's, the country has led in manufacturing techniques, simplifying the contact process and shifting from the use of platinum as a catalyst to vanadium, which has now become of equal, or greater, importance. In 1936, more than 50 per cent of the sulfuric acid produced in the United States was made by the contact process, and in 1944, about 65 per cent. Most plants built in the country during World War II used this process, and all postwar plants are equipped for contact operation.[46] In 1949, this process accounted for about 74 per cent of the output, and the chamber process for the rest.[47]

Opinion still differs, however, as to which catalyst is preferable. Vanadium is less sensitive to the impurities present in burner gases; even minute quantities of such impurities render the platinum catalyst inefficient. Whatever the catalyst, the contact process yields sulfuric acid of any required strength and of great purity.

Output

Although many industries were using sulfuric acid increasingly in the nineteenth century, in 1867 the output was only half a million tons, of which Great Britain and France were the major producers (115,000 and 125,000 tons, respectively). The United States produced only 40,000 tons that year.[48] With the rise in demand, the world output rose to 1.4 million tons in 1880, 2.2 million in 1890, and 4.2 million in 1900.[49]

By the turn of the century, the United States was one of the leading producers of the acid, which was consumed chiefly by the petroleum and fertilizer industries. On the eve of World War I, the United States ranked first, with an annual output of 2.3 million tons, or nearly 30 per cent of the world's total. Between 1913 and 1929, output of sulfuric acid in the United States more than doubled. During World War II, it rose to the record height of 8.6 million tons, and even this amount has been considerably exceeded in recent years.

Prewar Germany was second only to the United States in production of sulfuric acid, but in the late 1930's it began to feel the competition of Japan, which had raised its output from 210,-000 tons in 1925 to 2.4 million tons in 1937. There was some subsequent decline in Japan, but its output exceeded that of any European country except Germany throughout World War II.

In the postwar years the United States, with 10–12 million tons a year, has accounted for half or more of the world output of sulfuric acid;[50] the United Kingdom (1.7–1.8 million tons) for about 8 per cent; and France (1.2 million tons) for 5–6 per cent. Production in Italy is slightly below the prewar level; Western Germany produced in 1950 almost as much as all of prewar Germany in 1939. Canada built three new plants during the war and almost tripled its output. (See Table 490 and Figure 335.)

Uses

The industrial uses of sulfuric acid are highly

---

43. **44**, pp. 166–67.

44. **53**, p. 359.

45. The Frasch process consists in melting sulfur underground, sometimes 2,000 feet down, by hot water and pumping it to the surface into storage vats, each containing about half a million tons of sulfur. The sulfur is kept in the vats from 6 to 12 months, until it solidifies. **44**, p. 170.

46. **44**, pp. 200–01; **34**, p. 602.

47. **30**, 1950, p. 32.

48. **45**, p. 45.

49. **59**, p. 17.

50. Excluding the production of the USSR and Czechoslovakia, for which reliable information is not available. Reportedly the USSR's capacity for producing sulfuric acid was reduced by 77 per cent during the war. Its output in 1935 amounted to about 900,000 metric tons. **29**, February 1948, pp. 129–31, and December 1951, p. 344.

TABLE 490

SULFURIC ACID: OUTPUT IN SELECTED COUNTRIES, 1900–50

(Thousands of Metric Tons [a] *)*

Country	1900	1913	1929	1939	1943	1948	1949	1950
World [b]	4,200	7,946	11,300	15,200	15,500	20,100	21,200	23,600
United States	940	2,250	4,790	4,350	7,658	10,393	10,371	11,907
Canada	...	40	100	232	509	616	642	684
United Kingdom	1,000	1,082	930	1,086	1,271	1,577	1,687	1,832
Ireland	...	...	58	55 [c]	...	53	53	...
France	500	900	1,032	1,272 [c]	342	1,275	1,151	1,215
Belgium	165	420	496	749 [c]	...	829	826	...
Netherlands	—	320	360 [d]	515	92	370	396	438
Sweden	—	77	129	171	185	280	302	329
Finland	...	...	18	25	24	62	89	94
Germany [e]	950	1,686	1,475 [d]	1,491	2,543	...	1,139	1,446
Poland	—	—	233	180 [c]	...	222	276	...
Czechoslovakia	—	—	...	166 [f]	...	215	...	...
Portugal	...	...	...	85	60	141	145	153
Spain	...	...	110	118 [g]	74	440	465	540
Italy	200	600	834	1,284	547	975	1,160	1,211
Yugoslavia	...	...	21	25	...	46	45	40
Greece	...	...	28 [d]	44	...	30	38	32
Russia (USSR)	...	110	265	1,208 [h]	...	...	...	...
Japan	50	70	698	1,919	1,571	1,217	1,613	2,030
India [i]	—	—	27	31	43	26	84	101
Australia	...	...	191	497	224	493	595	617

Sources: **2**, p. 81; **3**, 1948, pp. 212–13, and 1951, pp. 223–24; **5**, 1950, p. 175.

a. In terms of pure (monohydrate) sulfuric acid, 100 per cent H₂SO₄. Conversion factor: one metric ton = 1.1023 short tons.
b. Excludes the USSR and Czechoslovakia.
c. 1938.

d. 1930.
e. For 1948–50, Western Germany. The output of that part of Germany amounted to 1,254,000 tons in 1936.
f. 1937.
g. Excludes production in superphosphate plants.
h. 1936.
i. For 1948–50, without Pakistan.

diversified, and the distribution of industrial consumption varies from country to country. In the United States, consumption in 1949 was distributed as follows: [51]

	Thousands of Short Tons	*Per Cent*
Total	10,100	100.0
Fertilizer	3,470	34.4
Chemicals	2,060	20.4
Petroleum refining	1,210	12.0
Coal	620	6.1
Iron and steel	520	5.1
Other metallurgy	325	3.2
Paints, pigments	670	6.6
Industrial explosives	123	1.2
Rayon, cellulose film	650	6.4
Textiles	75	0.8
Miscellaneous	377	3.7

51. **29**, December 1950, p. 34.

SODA ASH AND CAUSTIC SODA

Soda is as important among the alkalies as sulfuric acid among the acids. Soda ash is used in the glass, pulp and paper, soap and textile industries, among others, and in the manufacture of caustic soda, sodium bicarbonate and sodium phosphates. Caustic soda is essential in the production of rayon, explosives and water softeners and in many other chemicals.

Methods of Production

Commercial production of soda ash by the Leblanc method predominated for more than three quarters of a century despite the great difficulties that manufacturers encountered because of the large amounts of evil-smelling waste that this process created around the plants. For each ton of soda almost two tons of waste, containing nearly all the sulfuric acid used in

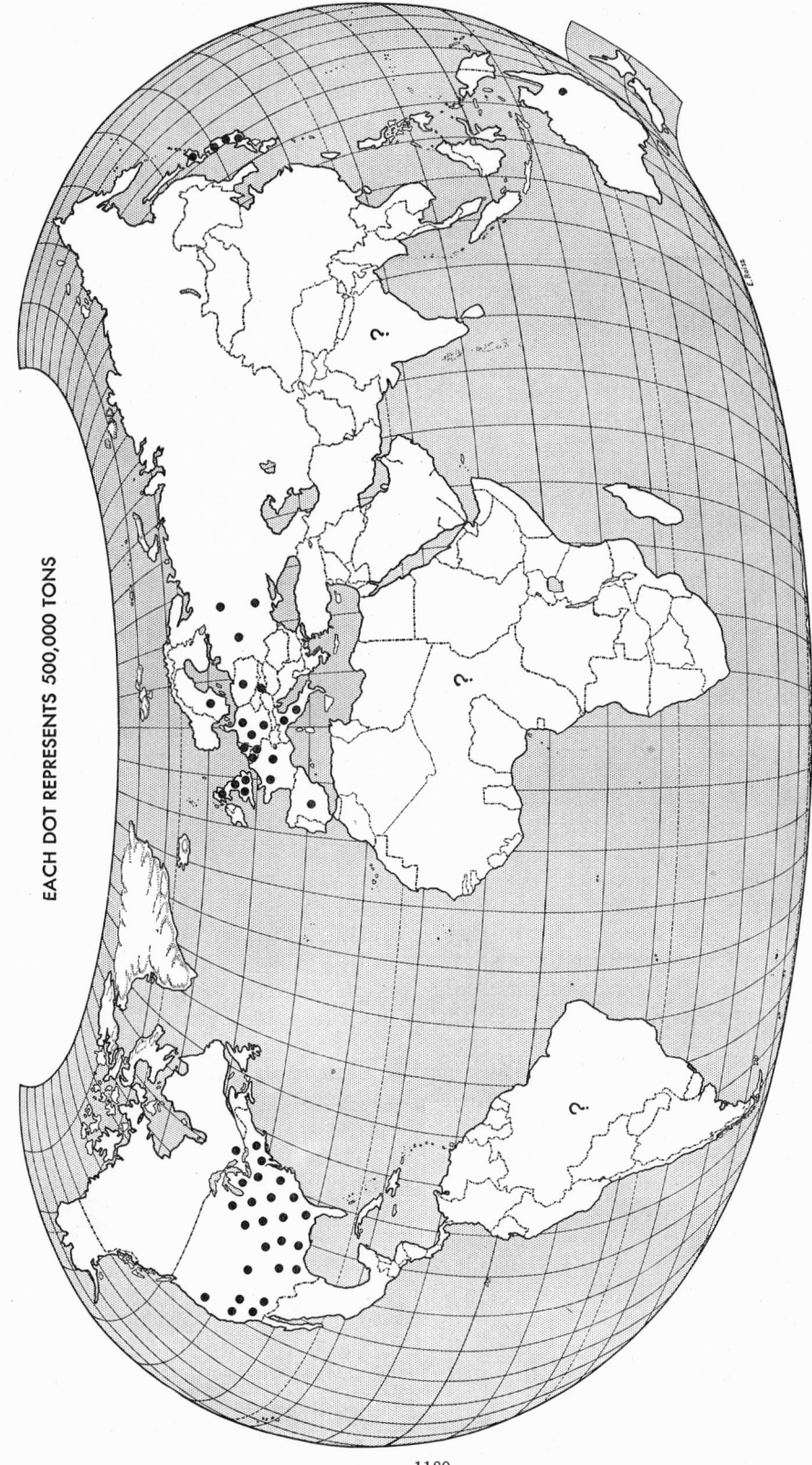

EACH DOT REPRESENTS 500,000 TONS

FIGURE 335. SULFURIC ACID: GEOGRAPHIC DISTRIBUTION OF WORLD OUTPUT, 1950

the process, were produced. The hydrogen chloride, carried out of the furnaces by combustion gases, spread over the neighboring area and destroyed vegetation. When England prohibited this diffusion, the manufacturers dissolved the gas in water, converting it to hydrochloric acid, and dumped the waste into rivers, killing all aquatic life. Prohibited from disposing of the waste in this way also, and searching for methods to utilize it, they produced bleaching powder, for which there was a great demand from the textile industry, and also recovered sulfur from the waste.[52]

In 1863, the Solvay brothers, Belgians, introduced a simpler and considerably cheaper process for making soda from salt and limestone. The limestone, which must be of good quality, serves two purposes, providing carbon dioxide gas (which is used, in combination with sodium of the salt for production of sodium bicarbonate) and lime with which ammonia is recovered, to be used again and again in the cycle of operations. The Solvay (or ammonia) process does not result in any by-product, but the final product, soda ash, is of high purity, averaging 98 per cent sodium carbonate. Plants for the Solvay process were soon built in Belgium, England, Germany, Austria, Russia and the United States. In the last, where no Leblanc plant was ever built, the first Solvay plant was established in 1884, in New York State.[53]

A long struggle took place between producers of soda ash by these two processes. Those using the Leblanc process had the advantage of marketable by-products, which somewhat lowered their production costs. On the other hand, they had to use large quantities of sulfuric acid and fuel and the purity of their product was not satisfactory in operations in which purity was important. Moreover, the handling of by-products required complex installations and became less attractive when cheaper and often superior products for the same purposes came on the market.[54]

After nearly forty years of struggle, the Solvay process almost wholly supplanted the Leblanc method and reduced the price of soda by about two thirds. As the following figures show, the world output of soda ash rose many times in a few decades (figures in thousands of tons): [55]

	Leblanc Process	*Solvay Process*
1863	300	—
1874	495	30
1885	435	365
1902	150	1,650

The final blow struck the Leblanc factories during World War I, when England, their stronghold, forbade them to use sulfuric acid, which was needed for making explosives.

The historic significance of the Leblanc method remains, nevertheless, great: the first process for producing alkali, it stimulated the manufacture of glass, soap and also sulfuric acid. Its by-products, chlorine and bleaching powder, created a new chemical industry, and its equipment later served in the design of the equipment for new processes.

An electrolytic process for manufacturing soda was invented late in the nineteenth century and by 1900 was in use in some plants, but it did not replace the Solvay process. In 1947, for example, the United States made about 94 per cent of its soda ash by the Solvay ammonia process, 6 per cent from lake brine in California, and one per cent by electrolysis. On the other hand, the country is using the electrolytic method increasingly in the production of caustic soda: for 29 per cent of the total output in 1925, 44 per cent in 1935, and 70 per cent in 1948.[56]

Output

The world's output of soda ash in the early 1930's exceeded 3 million metric tons and that of caustic soda a million tons. Production expanded considerably just before World War II and amounted to more than 6 and 2.5 million metric tons, respectively — exclusive of the United Kingdom and the USSR, for which data are not available. The United States leads by a wide margin, producing more than all the other countries listed in Table 491 together. In postwar years output rose considerably above the 1939 level in all countries except Japan and Italy. Western Germany produces more than twice as much of both chemicals as was produced in the same area in 1936. (See Table 491.)

The USSR produced about 0.5 million tons of soda ash in 1938 and more than twice as much in 1942. Its current output is estimated to be about half that of the United States.[57]

---

52. **44**, p. 91; **49**, p. 4.
53. **53**, p. 271.
54. **44**, pp. 93–94.
55. **59**, pp. 13–14; and **55**, pp. 520–21.

---

56. **53**, pp. 273–74; and **34**, pp. 543 and 564.
57. **29**, December 1951, p. 344.

TABLE 491

SODA ASH AND CAUSTIC SODA: OUTPUT IN SELECTED COUNTRIES, 1929–50

(*Thousands of Metric Tons* [a])

Country	Soda Ash					Caustic Soda				
	1929	1939	1948	1949	1950	1929	1939	1948	1949	1950
United States	2,433	2,564	4,151	3,553	3,621	691	948	2,156	2,017	2,278
France	...	483 [b]	715	582	717	...	126 [b]	196	215	242
Sweden	...	...	1	...	...	4	18	58	61	72
Germany [c]	...	1,256	381	568	735	...	422 [b]	155	251	336
Poland	100	89 [d]	77	...	...	17	30 [b]	48	56	65
Czechoslovakia	...	166 [b]	102	...	...	...	...	...	...	...
Austria	...	42 [d]	72	92	106	6	8	14	22	31
Spain	49	...	77	77	79	34	30 [d]	56	57	68
Italy	200	406	385	391	351	77	200	211	195	162
USSR	231	532 [b]	...	...	...	64	102 [e]	...	...	...
Japan	44	635	142	201	267	34	455	106	146	198
Kenya	...	42	118	68	106	...	55	108	148	...

Sources: **22**, 1938, p. 86 *; **3**, 1948, p. 215, and 1951, pp. 226–27; **5**, 1950, p. 175; for Kenya, **12**, June 18, 1951, p. 17.

a. Conversion factors: one metric ton = 1.1023 short tons = 2,204.6 pounds.

b. 1938.

c. For 1948, Bizone; for 1949–50, Western Germany; 1939 includes Austria and Sudeten.

d. 1937.

e. 1935.

Uses

Before World War II, leading industries consumed the following percentages of the world output of soda ash and caustic soda: [58]

	Soda Ash	Caustic Soda
Total	100.0	100.0
Glass	25.0	—
Soap	25.0	16.0–17.0
Textiles		
Rayon	16.0–17.0 {	33.0
Other	}	16.0–17.0
General chemicals	10.0	—
Paper	5.0	12.0–13.0
Miscellaneous	17.0–18.0	20.0–22.0

The percentage distribution of the industrial consumption of these two chemicals in the United States in 1948 was somewhat different: [59]

	Soda Ash	Caustic Soda
Total	100.0	100.0
Glass	28.0	—
Soap	3.0	5.2
Petroleum refining	0.5	7.7
Pulp, paper	4.5	6.3
Textiles		
Rayon	1.5 {	22.0
Other	}	5.0
Chemicals	45.0	22.0
Rubber reclaiming	—	1.3
Water softeners, cleansers	4.5	5.8
Exports and miscellaneous	13.0	24.7

NITRIC ACID

Nitric acid, a strong oxidizing agent, is used extensively in the production of sulfuric acid, various coal-tar dyes, explosives, and many of the nitrates required in various chemical branches. Geber mentioned nitric acid in his essay "De Inventione Veritatis seu Perfectionis Metallorum," but not until 1785 was it demonstrated, by H. Cavendish, that this acid could be synthesized by passing an electric current through moist air. Small quantities of nitric acid were produced experimentally in 1839 in France in the Kuhlmann plants, but there was no subsequent development of this field for about seventy years, since it was considered more advantageous to extract nitric acid from Chilean saltpeter.

58. **49**, p. 10. The figure for consumption of caustic soda by the paper industry includes consumption in petroleum refining.

59. **29**, January 1951, p. 286; and **34**, pp. 542 and 563.

TABLE 492

NITRIC ACID: OUTPUT IN SELECTED COUNTRIES, 1929–50

(*Thousands of Metric Tons* [a])

Country	1929	1935	1939	1948	1949	1950
United States	130	87	152	1,028	1,025	1,212
United Kingdom	...	...	...	244	245	258
France	...	...	297 [b]	385	427	487
Sweden	1	6	12	35	38	38
Norway	11	4	9	8	7	10
Italy	21	121	203	115	144	207
Japan	6 [c]	24	85	30	33	38

Source: **3**, 1948, p. 214, and 1951, p. 225.

a. Conversion factor: one metric ton = 1.1023 short tons.   b. 1938.   c. 1931.

In 1909 commercial production of nitric acid by the Kuhlmann process (oxidation of ammonia in the air over a platinum catalyst) began on a small scale. World War I stimulated production, and in 1916 the United States built its first plant for making nitric acid by this process.[60]

The chief producers of nitric acid are the United States, France, the United Kingdom and Italy. Exclusive of the USSR, for which data are not available, the world output in 1950 was somewhat more than 2 million tons. In that year, the United States produced 1,212,000 tons — nearly eight times as much as in 1939. Output in France in 1950 considerably exceeded the prewar level. (See Table 492.)

CHEMICAL FERTILIZERS

The chemical industry provides agriculture with various fertilizers, among them ammonium salts, calcium cyanamide and urea as a source of nitrogen; phosphatic fertilizers such as superphosphates and phosphate of ammonia; and potassium salts — potassium sulphate, potassium chloride and so on.[61]

SUPERPHOSPHATES

Superphosphates are produced in larger quantities than any other chemical except sulfuric acid. Manufacture was begun in England in 1842, by Sir John Bennet Lawes. The process first consisted of dissolving ground bones in sulfuric acid. In about a decade, coprolite deposits from which mineral "superphosphates" could be produced

were discovered in Suffolk. Now practically all superphosphate is made from phosphate rock.[62]

The industry grew rapidly, first in Great Britain, Germany and France, and later in the United States. Before World War I, world output increased each year. By 1913, the total was 11.5 million tons, of which the United States produced more than 28 per cent and France and Germany 17 and 16 per cent, respectively.

World output continued to grow after World War I, but at a much slower pace. In the peak peacetime year, 1929, it amounted to 15.6 million tons. The United States and France still led, but Germany ranked seventh, behind Italy, Spain, Japan and Australia. The USSR became an important producer of superphosphates by 1935.

During World War II, production of superphosphates collapsed in most European countries. France produced 5,000 tons in 1944 and Germany 14,000. Production broke down in Italy, Czechoslovakia, the Netherlands and many other countries. In contrast, output in the United States increased from 3.8 million tons in 1939 to 6.8 million in 1944 and 9.5–9.3 million in 1948–50. An upward trend has been noticeable also in various European countries; output in the United Kingdom in 1950 was more than double the prewar amount. (See Table 493.)

SYNTHETIC NITROGEN

The only sources of nitrogenous fertilizers before World War I were minerals — Chilean nitrates and, later, coal, from which by-product

---

60. **44**, p. 276; **53**, p. 407.
61. For fertilizers, see also Chapters 15 and 22.

62. **2**, p. 83. Cf. Chapter 22, pp. 834–36.

TABLE 493

SUPERPHOSPHATES: OUTPUT IN SELECTED COUNTRIES, 1913–50

(*Thousands of Metric Tons* [a])

Country	1913	1929	1935	1939	1948	1949	1950
World	11,500 [b]	15,610	13,330	...	...	...	...
United States [c]	3,248	3,939	2,680	3,821	9,574	9,505	9,258
Canada	...	1	55	80	250	250	438
United Kingdom	830 [d]	444	444	457	1,063	1,127	1,156
Ireland [e]	—	163	105	155	...	119	124
France	1,920	2,430	1,084	1,186	1,680	1,201	1,056
Belgium	450	433	229	208	652	826	451
Netherlands	346	633	529	545	845	947	843
Denmark	90	289	343	388	421	420	430
Sweden	184	236	247	261	355	404	433
Finland	...	30	51	53	129	154	64
Germany [f]	1,819	843	700	1,118 [g]	200	313	350
Poland	196	316	71	228 [g]	...	...	...
Czechoslovakia	—	245	186	128 [g]	200	198	...
Portugal	126	227	284	215	303	228	300
Spain	225	973	1,076	420	710	750	850
Italy	972	1,314	1,049	1,653	...	1,138	1,474
USSR	158	204	1,168	1,571 [g]	...	...	...
Japan	514	947	1,316	1,488	874	1,041	1,353
Union of South Africa	...	88 [e]	143	142	295	360	500
Australia	37	914	823	1,219	1,287	1,423	1,505
New Zealand	—	269	328	424	569	580	636

Sources: **2**, p. 84; **22**, 1927, p. 56 *, and 1938, p. 81 *; **1**, 1938–39, p. 168; **3**, 1951, pp. 228–29. The figures refer to superphosphates obtained by mixing phosphate rock with either sulfuric acid or phosphoric acid or with both.

a. Conversion factor: one metric ton = 1.1023 short tons.

b. Estimate.
c. Until 1935: fertilizer industry only; 1935–50: all grades converted to a basis of 18 per cent available phosphoric acid.
d. Fertilizer establishments only.
e. Until 1948, includes compound manures.
f. For 1948, Bizone; for 1949–50, Western Germany.
g. 1938.

ammonia was obtained during the manufacture of coke and coal gas. By that time these sources were becoming inadequate to meet the growing demand by agriculture, although Chile's production was expanding and an increasing amount of nitrogen (ammonium sulphate) was obtained through the shift of European coke manufacturers from beehives to by-product coke ovens.[63] Concern over the situation prompted Sir William Crookes, the well-known English chemist, to urge scientists to search for ways to produce nitrogen synthetically, lest "the great Caucasian race will cease to be foremost in the world, and will be squeezed out of existence by races to whom wheaten bread is not the staff of life." [64]

Methods of Production

In 1905, Norway became the first country to make synthetic nitrogen on a commercial scale, using the arc process, which requires an abundant supply of water power. About the same time, Germany began the manufacture of nitrogen as cyanamide, a process which, in recovering calcium carbide from limestone and coke, requires high temperatures attainable only in

63. Cf Chapter 22, pp. 837–38, and Chapter 23, pp. 876–77.

64. **37**, Vol. II, p. 56.

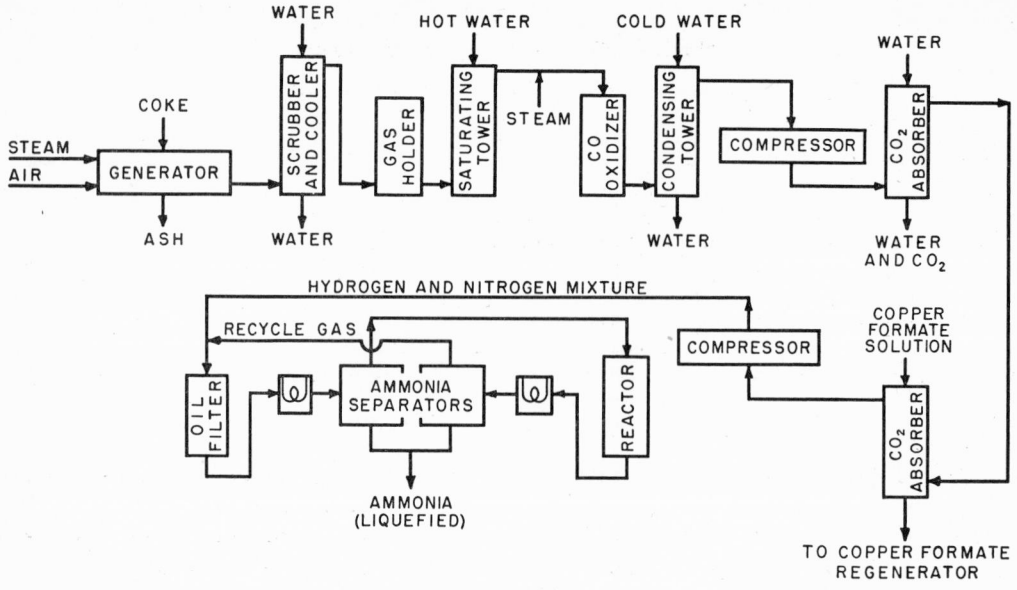

Courtesy of John Wiley and Sons

FIGURE 336. SYNTHETIC NITROGEN: FLOW SHEET OF OPERATIONS IN PRODUCTION OF AMMONIA BY SYNTHESIS
OF NITROGEN AND HYDROGEN

Nitrogen and hydrogen in a 1 to 3 ratio react catalytically at high temperatures and pressures to produce ammonia. The nitrogen is derived from the air by means of liquefaction, the producer gas reaction, or by burning out the oxygen in air with hydrogen. Hydrogen is obtained from many sources, such as water gas or natural gas, or by the electrolysis of water or brine.

electric furnaces and consumes large quantities of electricity. In 1913, Germany inaugurated the Haber-Bosch process for producing nitrogen from the air, and thus laid the foundation for a great new world industry.

In this process, three parts of hydrogen and one of nitrogen are combined to form ammonia by a series of chemical reactions and the use of catalysts. Both the nitrogen and the hydrogen must be highly purified because of the sensitivity of the catalyst, and the production of them in a pure state represents about three fourths of the total cost of producing ammonia; the preparation of hydrogen accounts for the largest part of this amount.[65] (See Figure 336.)

Great Britain's first plant for nitrogen fixation, at Billingham, began operating in 1921; the first in the United States began operating in 1927–28. The Haber-Bosch process has been so extensively modified in the United States that the present technique is known as the "American process."

In the United States the cheapest long-term source of hydrogen for ammonia synthesis is the reactions of water gas and producer gas on coke, with further catalytic conversion. Before

World War II, almost all the synthetic-ammonia hydrogen was obtained from coke and coal, but now about 40 per cent comes from natural gas, mostly in parts of the country where natural gas is abundant and cheap.[66] Some other countries utilize hydrogen that was previously wasted as a by-product from brine electrolysis. Electrolysis of water provides the necessary elements in Norway and Italy. In the world as a whole, about 57 per cent of the hydrogen for ammonia synthesis was obtained before the war from water gas, 25 per cent from coke oven gas, 16 per cent from electrolysis of water, and the rest from other sources.[67]

In time, the arc process was abandoned because of the large investment it required and its high operating costs. The drawbacks of the cyanamide process are its high consumption of electric power and complicated operations, but it produces a solid nitrogenous fertilizer directly and its product can also be used to make ammonia, urea, cyanides and some organic chemicals not otherwise obtainable. In 1934 there were fifty-two cyanamide plants in the world, the largest

65. **35,** Vol. I, p. 326; and **46,** pp. 79–80.

66. **34,** p. 78.
67. **53,** p. 397.

TABLE 494

NITROGEN: OUTPUT IN THE WORLD, 1900–37

(*Thousands of Metric Tons of Contained Nitrogen* [a])

Product	1900	1910	1913	1918	1929	1934	1937
Total	300	591	766	1,044	2,164	1,925	2,766
By-product nitrogen	100	205	281	362	448	358	467
Cyanamide nitrogen	—	4	38	88	226	213	296
Synthetic nitrogen [b]	—	5	22	155	992	1,223	1,790
Chilean nitrogen	200	378	426	439	500	131	213

Source: **15**, p. 66.

a. Conversion factor: one metric ton = 1.1023 short tons.

b. By arc and cyanamide processes.

at Niagara Falls. No additional plants have been built for this process.[68]

The importance of the Haber-Bosch process for world agriculture can hardly be exaggerated. It has provided farmers with a synthetic fertilizer identical with natural nitrogen yet so low in price that it has banished the specter of a possible nitrogen famine in tilled soil.

During World War I this process played an immense role in Germany, when the Allied blockade cut off the Chilean nitrates needed for both explosives and fertilizers. Germany expanded production and built a large plant at Leuna in 1916. The new plant was producing 1,000 tons of ammonia a day in 1917; until the close of World War II it was the world's largest plant for nitrogen fixation.[69]

Output

Before World War II, synthetic nitrogen accounted for three fourths of the total output of nitrogen, and Chilean nitrates were used for only 7 per cent. Some 10 per cent of the output was obtained by the cyanamide process. (See Table 494.)

In 1938–39 Germany ranked first in nitrogen, with a third of the total output, Japan was second, and the United States, Chile and France were next in line. In 1950–51, the United States accounted for more than 25 per cent of the world's output and produced about as much as Western Germany and Japan together. The United Kingdom, Chile and France were about equal, each accounting for approximately 6–7 per cent. (See Table 495.)

Production of chemical nitrogen in the United States did not drop after World War II, like that of many other commodities used extensively for military purposes, but increased because of the growing use of nitrogen in agriculture. Consumption of nitrogenous fertilizers in 1949–50 was at least two and a half times as much as before the war, and is still increasing.[70]

In the world at large, more than 85 per cent of the output of chemical nitrogen is consumed as fertilizer; in the Western Hemisphere, 74 per cent; in Europe, 89 per cent; and in Asia, 95 per cent.[71]

Capacity

In 1937, the capacity of the German plants to produce synthetic nitrogen about equaled the combined capacity of plants in the United States, the United Kingdom, France, Italy and Japan, as the following figures show (in thousands of tons):[72]

Germany	1,366
United States	293
United Kingdom	233
France	244
Italy	147
Japan	490

World War II changed these relationships. The United States increased its capacity almost fourfold, mostly through government financing. In 1939, the nitrogen fixation capacity of private plants totaled 380,000 tons and in 1944, about 704,000 tons, while government plants, built

68. **44**, pp. 242–43.
69. **51**, p. 317; and **15**, p. 124.

70. **34**, pp. 78–79.
71. **26**, 1948–49, p. 1.
72. **51**, p. 320.

TABLE 495

NITROGEN (N): OUTPUT IN SELECTED COUNTRIES, 1913–51

(*Thousands of Metric Tons* [a])

Country	1913	1929	1938–39	1948–49	1949–50	1950–51
World [b]	766	2,164	2,565	3,320	3,735	3,955
United States	35	287	240 [c]	975	1,050	1,021
Canada	5	57	49	175	181	144
Peru	. . .	. . .	21	22	25	35
Chile	429	500	224	275	277	253
United Kingdom	90	196	124	281	271	262
France	17	94	196	188	214	238
Belgium [d]	10	40	93	152	160	171
Netherlands	1	12	99	86	120	189
Sweden	4	7	8	22	21	26
Norway	20	67	90	108	148	160
Germany [e]	119	680	832	328	426	612
Poland	3	49	52	55	. . .	. . .
Czechoslovakia	—	21	25 [f]	30	30	30
Switzerland	2	6	10	11	13	14
Austria	—	—	2 [g]	59	66	75
Spain	—	—	4	3	9	7
Italy	6	50	109	104	130	169
Yugoslavia	2	7	8	2	3	3
USSR	3	5	. . .	. . .	. . .	. . .
China [h]	. . .	. . .	18	9	. . .	. . .
Japan	4	82	256	274	343	434
India	—	4	5	13	11	9
Australia	1	4	5	9	9	11

Sources: **20**, 1934, p. 71 *; **6**, p. 45; **3**, 1951, p. 230.

a. Estimated nitrogen content of nitrogenous fertilizers. Conversion factor: one metric ton = 1.1023 short tons. For 1938–39 to 1950–51, years ending June 30.
  b. Excludes the USSR.
  c. Excludes ordnance production.

d. From 1938–39 on, Belgium–Luxembourg.
  e. From 1948–49 on, Western Germany. The output of that part of Germany in 1938–39 was 354,000 tons.
  f. 1937–38.
  g. 1936.
  h. 22 provinces and Formosa.

from scratch during the war, had a capacity of 606,000 tons in 1944.[73] The German plants, on the other hand, suffered from bombing during the war and from postwar dismantling, and their capacity has been reduced by about 60 per cent.

For 1950–51, the capacity of the world (except for the USSR and the Soviet Zone in Germany) and of major countries was estimated as follows: [74]

73. **14**, p. 39.
74. **29**, February 1948, p. 109; and **7**, 1950, p. 85. The Leuna factory is located in the Soviet Zone of Germany; its capacity exceeded half a million tons before the war. Its output in 1949–50 was estimated at 180,000 tons.

	Thousands of Tons	*Per Cent*
World	4,130	100.0
United States	1,158	28.0
Canada	204	4.9
United Kingdom	294	7.1
France	315	7.6
Italy	275	6.7
Western Germany	461	11.2
Japan, Korea, Formosa	332	8.0
Other	1,091	26.4

DYESTUFFS

Dyestuffs are the foundation of the organic

chemical industry. The raw material and the basic technology of dye manufacture are common to the manufacture of a great variety of products — such as synthetic pharmaceuticals, rubber, plastics, resins, camphor, insecticides, flavoring, perfumes, explosives and many others. Many synthetic products could not have been made except for the experience acquired in the large-scale production of dyes.[75] Moreover, the dye industry can be easily converted in wartime to the production of explosives, smoke screens, poison gases and so on. This characteristic has been a chief reason for the high tariff protection and other support the industry enjoys in all major producing countries, as well as for the secretiveness about its size, capacity and output.

Early Development

The first chemical dye, mauve, was produced less than a hundred years ago when an 18-year-old British student, W. H. Perkin, stumbled on a brilliant mauve solution with remarkable dyeing properties during the course of an unsuccessful attempt to obtain quinine from aniline. He immediately began the commercial production of mauve for dyeing silk. His purified mauve became worth its weight in platinum,[76] and for almost two decades he was *the* dye industry of Great Britain.[77]

While the cradle of the industry was the Thames valley, the initiative for further discoveries soon shifted to France, which produced a magenta dye in 1862, and then to Germany, which developed alizarin in 1869. Alizarin was the first synthetic dye, and manufacture started immediately in Germany and Great Britain. After seventeen years of research, Germany began to market blue (indigo) pigment, first synthesized in 1880, in commercial quantities. This was a fatal blow to planters of indigo in India and of woad in England — herbs until then irreplaceable for their blue coloring and highly valued for thousands of years.[78]

In 1901 Germany introduced "vat," or indan-threne, dyes, the only unalterably fast colors mankind has ever known. In contrast to other dyes, these are insoluble in water and are applied in a strong chemical solution or "vat." Fabrics are dipped into the vat and then ex-posed to air; the insoluble dye becomes a permanent part of the fabric. Until very recently, vat dyes were used almost exclusively on cotton goods, but new processes now permit their use on rayon, wool gabardines and some other fabrics.[79]

Beginning with the late 1870's Germany led in the manufacture of dyes and in research in this field. By the turn of the century, it had achieved unchallenged supremacy and almost monopolized the world market. The United States and the United Kingdom imported nearly 90 per cent of the dyes they used from Germany. Even the remaining dyes were not fully produced at home, since as much as 90 per cent of the "intermediates" used in their manufacture was imported from Germany.[80] In Germany's many laboratories, thousands of trained chemists experimented with ever new products extracted from tar. The vast German coke industry supplied abundant raw materials. In 1913, Germany produced 135,000 tons of dyes out of the world's total of 162,000, or nearly 85 per cent. At that time, the United States had seven small dye plants, with a total ouput of only 3,000 tons, and production in the United Kingdom was only slightly larger.

The United Kingdom

The outbreak of World War I caused a virtual dye famine in all countries cut off from Germany. In the United Kingdom, the world's largest textile manufacturer and exporter, the situation was critical. The great British textile industry, spoon-fed by the German plants suddenly found itself without dyes at a time when the demand for fabrics on the part of the armed forces was urgent.[81] Within a year, the pressure of circumstances had forced the British to overcome their deficiencies in materials, trained personnel and equipment and, despite German predictions to the contrary, Britain had an efficient dyestuffs industry.[82]

---

75. **16**, p. 69.
76. **49**, p. 266.
77. **53**, p. 875.
78. **47**, p. 91.

79. **16**, p. 25.
80. Intermediates are chemicals advanced by manufacturing processes beyond the crude state and are either sold as such for further processing or converted to finished products, in this case, dyes. They are derived chiefly from the distillation of coal, and in recent years increasingly from the processing of petroleum and natural gas.
81. **49**, pp. 272–73.
82. German experts had predicted that no British firm would produce vat colors on a manufacturing scale within ten years. **49**, p. 274.

The United States

In the United States, also, World War I evoked great efforts to develop a dyestuffs industry. Backwardness in technology and lack of scientific research were the most serious handicaps. Domestic colors, inferior in quality and limited in range, were from two to four times as costly as imported German products. Moreover, raw materials for dyes, the tar crudes, were needed for explosives, smoke screens and other war materials. Not until 1919, and then largely on the basis of German patents seized by the government and under the protection of high tariffs,[83] did the dye industry take root in the United States.

By 1920–22, both the United States and the United Kingdom could produce 90 per cent of the dyes they required, but Germany remained the world's largest producer until the outbreak of World War II. (See Table 496.)

Other Countries

The USSR, which before 1930 had virtually no dye industry and imported its dyestuffs primarily from Germany, gradually developed an industry, but it produces mainly the cheaper sulfur colors.[84] Japan likewise started its production with cheap and easily made sulfur colors, but in the 1930's it became one of the largest producers of dyes.[85] These countries together with Germany, England and the United States produced all but a few thousand tons of the world's annual output of dyes before World War II. Most countries were wholly dependent on imports.

Recent Developments

Defeat in World War II disrupted the German and Japanese dye industries and encouraged production in other countries.

Today the United States is the largest producer, with 95,000 tons of dyes in 1947, as compared with 37,000 in 1938. Output decreased in 1948, however, and again in 1949 but began to expand in 1950 (about 89,000 tons). The industry is located principally in New York, New Jersey, Pennsylvania and Ohio. In 1942 the nine

TABLE 496

DYESTUFFS: OUTPUT IN THE WORLD AND SELECTED COUNTRIES, 1913–49

(*Thousands of Metric Tons* [a])

Country	1913	1924	1938	1947	1949
World	162	154	. . .	. . .	188
United States	3	30	37	95	65
United Kingdom	5	15	21	34	20
France	7	17	9	16	12
Germany	135	70	61	8 [b]	18 [b]
Switzerland	10	13	7	15	10
Italy	—	5	11	9	9
Russia (USSR)	4	13 [c]	35	. . .	40
Japan	—	2	28	. . .	5

Sources: **2**, p. 84; **16**, p. 10; **8**, p. 37; **29**, July 1951, pp. 138–39.

a. Conversion factor: one metric ton = 1.1023 short tons.   b. Western Germany.   c. 1929.

largest producers accounted for 94 per cent of the entire output.[86]

The United Kingdom, France and Switzerland had also increased production by 1947, and had invaded some of the markets previously dominated by Germany. Their 1949 output, however, was considerably smaller. The output in Western Germany, on the other hand, shrank to 8,000 tons in 1947, rose to 18,000 in 1949 and the ECA expected that it would more than double by 1952–53. All important European producers planned to achieve higher levels of production by that time. (See Table 496.)

Consumption

The demand for dyes in different countries depends largely on the volume of their textile output. It has been roughly estimated that the United States and China together consumed some 30 per cent of all the dyestuffs produced in prewar years; the United Kingdom, 13 per cent; Germany 10 per cent; and France and the USSR, 6 per cent each. India, Japan, Italy and Switzerland together may have taken from 15 to 20 per cent, and all other countries, the remaining 15–20 per cent.[87]

In the United States, textiles account for about

---

83. After the war, the importation of dyes was prohibited except for types that could not be produced domestically.
84. **16**, p. 105.
85. **16**, pp. 93–95.

86. **19**, Part II, p. 98; **10**, 1952, p. 801.
87. **51**, p. 112.

80 per cent of the consumption of dyes, and the paper and leather industries for an additional 9 per cent. Other customers include the industries producing drugs, cosmetics, photographic materials, plastics, water colors, polishes and so on. During World War II, dyestuffs were used for many special military purposes, such as camouflage and coloring for smoke.[88]

Uses

At present, several thousand different dyes are produced for use on various types of material. More than two hundred and fifty varieties of blue, for example, are on the market. Dyes vary greatly in chemical structure, methods of application, fastness, concentration and, accordingly, in price. They are sold in paste, lump and powdered form.[89] Synthetic dyes have almost completely displaced the natural dyes of vegetable and animal origin that people used for millenniums to brighten their surroundings with colorful fabrics, pottery or glass.[90] Many thousands of acres that were planted to indigo or woad, or to madder for the red coloring obtainable from its root, have been turned over to food crops.

PLASTICS

The first plastic material was created in 1868, when a prize was offered for a substitute for ivory, then becoming scarce, for making billiard balls.[91] Using cotton linters, nitric acid, camphor and paper pulp, J. W. Hyatt (United States) prepared a new material, which he called celluloid. This was widely used for various small articles of everyday life — combs, brushes, cuff buttons and so on. Later it was also used in the manufacture of photographic film. In 1890, Adolph Spitteler, in Germany discovered casein, a protein plastic.[92] Two decades passed before the third type of plastic material, bakelite, was introduced (1909) by L. H. Baekeland in the United States. Bakelite was a more versatile product than celluloid and could be molded; once hardened and molded, it would not soften when

heated. The basic raw material for bakelite was phenol-formaldehyde, which still leads in the plastics industry.

In the 1920's and, particularly, the 1930's, many plastic materials were discovered in rapid succession. Today the plastics industry uses literally hundreds of materials. A new molding technology adaptable to mass production has been introduced, and facilities for molding plastics have been expanded in many countries. The manufacture of plastics has become an important branch of the chemical industry.

Although plastics cost more per pound than competitive nonplastic materials, a greater volume of goods can be produced from a pound of plastics than from most other substances. Moreover, plastics offer the manufacturer various advantages that offset the basic difference in price; the built-in color, for example, eliminates painting.

Plastics differ in their reaction to heat during processing, the chemical origin of the materials from which they are made, the form in which they are prepared for further manufacturing, and in their uses.

Types of Plastics

Plastic materials are divided into two basic groups, thermoplastics and thermosetting plastics, according to the way they are affected by heat during processing. Thermoplastics soften under the action of heat and solidify on cooling; they can be reheated, resoftened and reworked into other shapes. Thermosetting plastics are shaped when soft from the first heating, but subsequent heating produces chemical changes (polymerization[93]) and hardens them permanently. Thermosetting plastics are usually improved in their mechanical properties by the addition of "fillers" such as wood flour, mica, cellulose fibers and asbestos. For example, phenolic plastics can be made resistant to heat, moisture or shock, depending on the filler used. Cotton fillers lend additional strength to thermosetting plastics; mica is added to make the plastic material suitable for electrical insulation; asbestos, to make the product more resistant to fire. Fillers, moreover, increase the volume of plastic material and, being cheap, reduce the cost per unit of weight.

---

88. **16**, p. 26.

89. **19**, Part II, p. 94.

90. Only the logwood dye from Central America has survived the competition of synthetic dyes and is still extensively used for black and blue-black colors on wool and silk. A few natural dyes — catechu, cochineal, fustic — are used in smaller quantities. **53**, p. 900.

91. **32**, p. 9; and **50**, p. 3.

92. **27**, p. 2.

93. Polymerization consists in combining small molecules with larger ones with the same chemical structure but different physical properties.

Materials for Plastics

Plastics are made from four groups of materials: natural resins, synthetic resins, cellulose derivatives and protein compounds.

Natural resins, of which shellac is the most important, are used less and less.

Synthetic resins constitute nearly 90 per cent of the total quantity of plastics used in the United States.[94] Coal, petroleum and natural gas are the chief raw materials from which they are produced. The most-used synthetic resin has been phenol-formaldehyde. Vinyl resins, of small importance until 1941, are used now in increasing quantities and have become volume leaders since 1950. In 1951 they accounted for 28 per cent of all the synthetic resins used in manufacturing plastics, and the capacity of plants producing vinyl resin is growing steadily.[95] Polysterene and polyamides are also important. The manufacture of synthetic resins involves many complex processes.

Cellulose derivatives rank second to synthetic resins but are used in much smaller quantities, particularly in the United States, where they represent about 9 per cent of the total. In the United Kingdom, cellulose compounds constituted about 15 per cent of all the plastic materials used in 1947; in France, some 30 per cent.[96]

The most important cellulose plastics are cellulose nitrate and cellulose acetate. The main difference between them is that the first is inflammable and the second is not. They are produced from cotton linters or wood, combined in the first case with sulfuric and nitric acids and in the second with acetic acid, acetic anhydride and sulfuric acid.

Protein compounds, which are relatively unimportant as a source of plastic materials, are derived from animal or vegetable sources. Casein, the most-used type, is derived from skim milk; soybean plastic material, from soybean meal; lignin, from the sulfite liquor resulting from processing paper pulp and so on.

Forms in Which Plastic Materials Are Used

In manufacturing, plastic materials are used in the form of powders, granules and pellets; sheets, rods, tubes and blocks; and laminates.

The form selected depends on the method of manufacture and the type of article to be made. Plastic products are molded, extruded and cast or are fabricated. Molders and extruders generally use dry powders, granules and pellets, employing a compression machine for thermosetting plastics and an injection machine for thermoplastics. In the first case, dry powders or similar materials are placed in the mold and then pressed into its cavities so it shapes the product. For thermoplastics, such materials are injected into the mold through a nozzle. Ordinarily, compression molding makes one product at a time while injection molding turns out many products of the same kind in one operation. Powdered plastics can also be extruded by forcing them through the apertures of a die. Extrusion is a continuous process and is used, for example, to make rods or tubes, which can then be cut to any desired length. Cast plastics can also be shaped from such materials, without pressure, in molds.

Fabricated plastics are made (in the form of sheets, rods, tubes or blocks) from molded, extruded or cast materials or from laminates. Laminated plastics, made by bonding layers of resin-impregnated paper, textiles, asbestos, or glass fibers, have excellent mechanical properties — durability, resistance to moisture and chemicals, and great strength.

Plastic Products

Plastics are used for an endless variety of products in both civilian and military fields because of the great range in properties of the different types resulting from different materials and processes. For example, shellac plastics are used chiefly for phonograph records; casein plastics, for buttons, insignia and novelties. The uses of cellulose (nitrate) plastics range from piano keys, fountain pens and toys to tool handles, photographic film and range-finder parts. Cellulose (acetate) plastics enter into automotive parts and containers and were used in wartime for gunsight lenses, gas-mask parts, bomber visors and so on.

Among synthetic types, some, like polysterene plastics, are outstanding in electrical qualities and hydroscopicity. These are widely used in refrigerator parts, instrument panels, battery boxes and chemical containers. Other types are particularly fitted for use in clock, radio and scale housings or in electrical and ignition parts

94. **17**, p. 13.
95. **48**, January 1952, pp. 76 and 83.
96. **8**, p. 37.

because of their colorability and their electrical properties. Still others, excelling in transparency and optical qualities, are used in lenses, reflectors, dials and surgical instruments. Typical uses for polyamides (nylon) are in fibers, filaments and molded tableware. A battleship may have more than a thousand plastic parts of various types, an airplane more than two hundred.[97]

Output in the United States

The United States accounts for 75–80 per cent of the world output of plastics. Its production increased from 21,000 short tons in 1933 to 106,500 in 1939, 360,000 in 1944, and 405,000 in 1945.[98] During the war, more than 85 per cent of the total went for military purposes; during one nine-month period plastics were produced only for military use. Output continued to rise after the war and amounted to 671,000 tons in 1949.[99] The largest single use for plastics and resin materials in 1949 was for protective coating, which accounted for about 225,000 tons. Molding and extrusion were next in importance.

The plastics industry was first established in the New England and the Middle Atlantic states but has recently spread into the North Central states and California. Ohio and Pennsylvania hold the lead.

Output in Other Countries

Before World War II, Germany was second in the production of plastics, manufacturing about half as much as the United States. Other important producers were the United Kingdom, Italy, France, the USSR and Japan. Germany led in research on synthetic resins and was endeavoring to find substitutes for materials not available at home. Other countries were producing chiefly thermoplastics from cellulose acetate and casein; Japan, from cellulose nitrate.

The British plastics industry is now the largest outside the United States. France, Sweden, Italy, Switzerland and other countries still produce thermoplastics chiefly. The 1947 output and the annual output planned for 1952–53 by the main European producers are as follows (in thousands of metric tons): [100]

	1947	*Planned for* 1952–53
United Kingdom	67.7	186.6
France	23.1	86.4
Benelux	18.2	50.4
Norway	0.4	6.3
Western Germany	22.8	99.4
Italy	8.8	32.0
Switzerland	10.3	15.5

Japan had a considerable output of plastics before the war, made chiefly of cellulose nitrate with a great deal of hand labor. Trinkets, toys and various other articles fashioned from this inflammable material were exported to all parts of the world. Camphor, used as a plasticizer for cellulose nitrate, came only from Formosa; Japan, controlling its production, thus had a substantial advantage over other producing countries. Recently, a synthetic camphor has been developed in the United States and in some European countries, and use of highly automatic injection machinery has deprived Japan of its other asset, cheap labor.

The USSR now has a substantial production of plastics, but many of its products are of asphalt and similar cheaper types. The value of its output, on a dollar basis, is smaller than that of the United Kingdom.[101] The Canadian industry is developing rapidly.

American equipment for molding plastics is in great demand in the world today. Some Latin American countries (Cuba, Mexico) and Sweden, France, Italy, India and Australia are trying to establish or expand production of plastics. In many countries, the latest American machinery is displacing obsolete equipment of German, Italian and Swiss design.[102]

SYNTHETIC RUBBER

Since the beginning of this century, some thirty synthetic materials have been developed that possess many of the physical properties of natural rubber.[103] Some of these are produced in very small quantities and used only for special purposes.

97. **17**, pp. 6–7; and **32**, p. 12.

98. **17**, pp. 20–21; and **32**, p. 11.

99. **20**, 1949, pp. 38–41. Excludes the output of cellulose plastics, about 40,000 tons.

100. **8**, p. 37.

101. **54**, p. 1292.

102. **17**, p. 58.

103. Synthetic rubber is defined as a vulcanizable material that will stretch repeatedly at least 150 per cent and return immediately and with force to its approximate original shape. Natural rubber is discussed in Chapter 17, pp. 618–22.

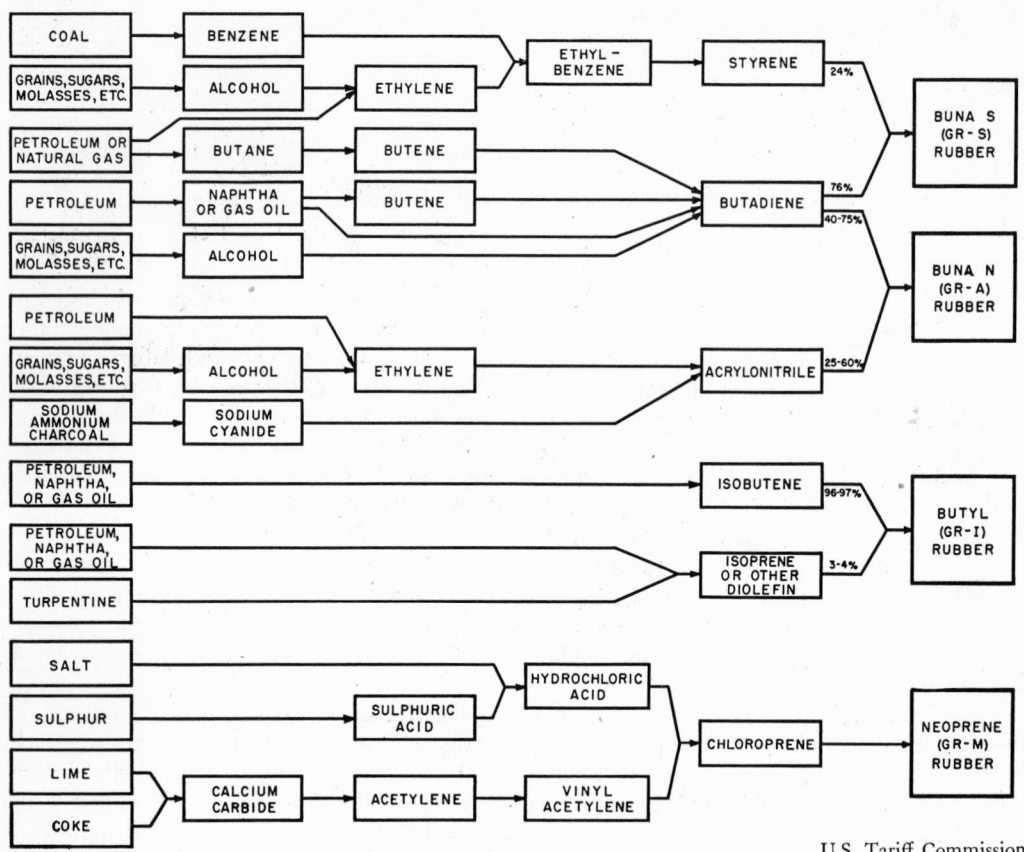

U.S. Tariff Commission

FIGURE 337. SYNTHETIC RUBBER: FLOW SHEET OF OPERATIONS FROM RAW MATERIALS TO FINISHED PRODUCTS

Types of Synthetic Rubber

The five chief types of synthetic rubber are buna S, butyl, neoprene, buna N and thiokol. The first is an all-purpose material; the others are used for special purposes. Actually, butyl and neoprene could be used for general purposes but are made in limited quantities.

The raw materials are largely petroleum and petroleum gases, but molasses, alcohol and grain sugars can also be used for certain types. (See Figure 337.) In the manufacture of synthetic rubber, the raw materials are first processed to extract the necessary chemicals.

For example, buna S is made from two principal chemicals, butadiene and styrene, and smaller amounts of other chemicals, all of which are obtained from petroleum, natural gas or alcohol. About three parts of butadiene, by weight, to one of styrene are then fed into a soapy water solution, emulsified by vigorous action, and polymerized with the aid of a catalyst and high temperature. The resulting latex is placed in an-

other tank with a sulfuric-acid and salt solution, where it coagulates and rises to the surface.

One of the plants producing synthetic rubber recently introduced a low-temperature process (just above the freezing point of water). Its output of "cold" rubber in 1950 was at the annual rate of 300,000 tons.[104]

Output

Germany once led in synthesizing rubber. It manufactured several thousand tons during World War I, when the Allied blockade cut off its supplies of natural rubber. Production ceased after the war but experimentation continued, and in 1926 a method to synthesize rubber from butadiene was established, though manufacturing on a commercial scale did not begin until 1936.[105]

The USSR started production of synthetic

104. **29**, November 1951, pp. 148–49.
105. **51**, p. 540.

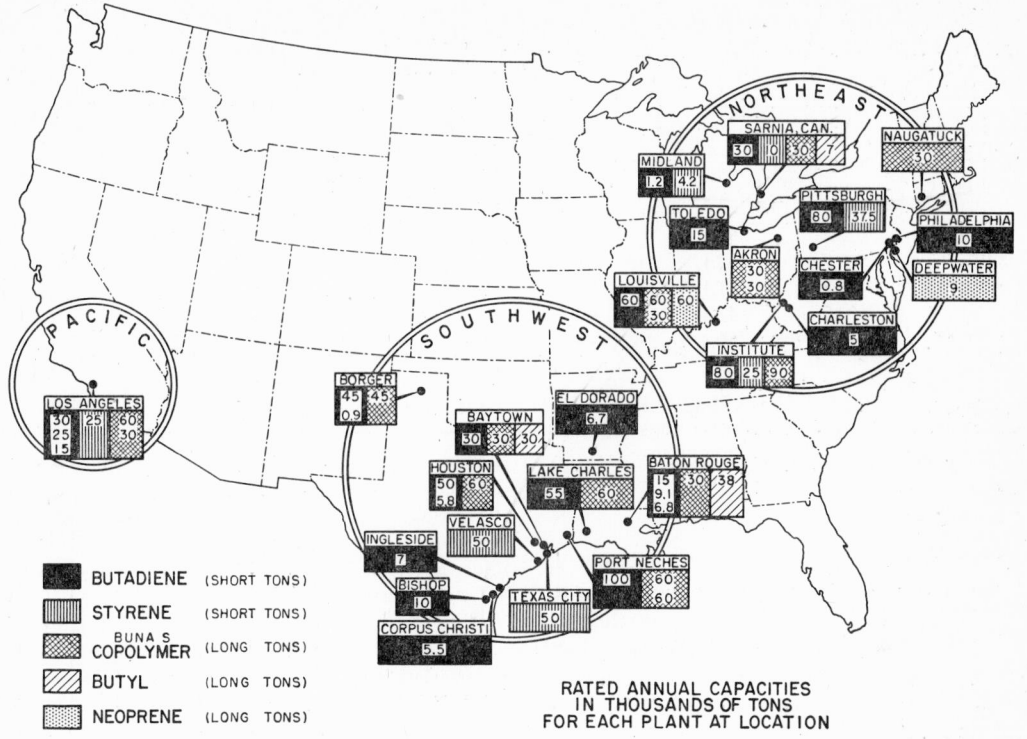

BUTADIENE (SHORT TONS)
STYRENE (SHORT TONS)
BUNA S COPOLYMER (LONG TONS)
BUTYL (LONG TONS)
NEOPRENE (LONG TONS)

RATED ANNUAL CAPACITIES
IN THOUSANDS OF TONS
FOR EACH PLANT AT LOCATION

U.S. Tariff Commission

FIGURE 338. SYNTHETIC RUBBER: LOCATION OF PLANTS IN THE UNITED STATES AND CANADA

rubber in 1932 and by 1938–39 could make enough to meet most of its small requirements for rubber. Alcohol from potatoes and limestones are used as raw materials. Most of the plants are in the potato-growing areas (Jaroslaw, Voronezh, Kazan and Yerevan) and near the limestone deposits of Yerevan, in Transcaucasus.[106]

The world output of synthetic rubber in 1935 was estimated at 10,000 tons; in 1939, at 72,000 tons, of which Germany and the USSR together produced 70,000 tons and the United States, the rest.[107]

The United States began to produce a little synthetic rubber in 1934, mostly of types superior to natural rubber and suitable for specific purposes. After the attack on Pearl Harbor, development of production became vitally important. In the ensuing struggle, rubber's role was second only to that of steel and oil. Just when tremendous quantities of rubber were needed for tanks, airplanes, military trucks and so on, natural rubber, normally used, was suddenly cut off. Existing stocks were inadequate,

and it would have required several years to develop new plantations in Latin America. The only solution was immediate production of synthetic rubber in the quantities and of the types urgently needed.

To meet this need, the United States government financed the erection of plants with an aggregate capacity of as much as 1,250,000 tons a year and also built one plant in Canada. The major centers are in the northeastern industrial section, from Canada and Connecticut to Kentucky; in the Southwest, mostly in Louisiana and Texas; and near Los Angeles. (See Figure 338.) The plants were never utilized to their full capacity during the war. The peak output in 1945 was nearly 835,000 tons.

When the war ended and supplies of natural rubber began to arrive from Asia, production of synthetic rubber declined. It was not discontinued, however, partly because of a desire to maintain plants for an emergency and partly because a mixture of natural and synthetic rubber proved to be superior in some respects to natural rubber.

Data on production, available only for the

106. **25**, pp. 289–90.
107. **18**, pp. 32 and 93; **31**, p. 778; **52**, p. 236.

United States, Canada and Germany, are as follows (in thousands of metric tons): [108]

	United States	Canada	Germany
1937	0.5	—	2.5
1939	1.8	—	22.4
1941	8.2	—	70.5
1943	235.5	2.6	117.6
1945	820.4	46.4	...
1947	508.7	43.1	8.4
1948	488.3	41.1	3.4
1949	393.7	47.4	—
1950	476.2	59.4	—

The USSR's output at the beginning of 1950 was estimated at 200,000 metric tons or more; that of Eastern Germany, at 30,000.[109]

OUTLOOK

Of all industries, the chemical industry appears to have the brightest outlook. Many industries may be expected to grow in their old centers and develop in new ones but none holds such mysterious promise as chemical manufacturing, which can, so to speak, pull rabbits out of hats.

Moreover, the chemical industry has unlimited fields, and its "rabbit" may be a new drug today, and tomorrow a new fiber or some new material stronger than steel and lighter than down. No one, not even the chemists themselves, knows of all the substances turned out in the thousands of laboratories. But there can be no doubt that countless new products will enter the market.

More than half a million organic compounds have been described in the technical literature, but only about 7,000, or one per cent, have so far been produced commercially.[110] Many of the others may be shelved forever, but a great many new commercial products can be expected. Some experts believe that 3,000–4,000 inventions now in an experimental stage may command large markets in the next few years.

In addition, existing chemicals continue to lend themselves to new uses, while new and more efficient processes are being developed to make chemicals now in common use.

The chemical industry was a major branch of manufacturing before World War II, and the war enhanced its importance. The end of hostili-

108. **3,** 1951, p. 231; and **10,** 1951, p. 790.
109. **29,** July 1951, pp. 138–39 and November 1951, p. 152; **52,** p. 237.
110. **7,** 1949, p. 65; 1950, p. 66.

TABLE 497

INDEXES OF PRODUCTION IN CHEMICAL AND ALL MANUFACTURING INDUSTRIES, IN SELECTED COUNTRIES, 1950 AND 1951

(1937 = 100)

Country	Chemical Industry 1950	Chemical Industry 1951, First Six Months	All Manufacturing, 1951, First Six Months
United States	236	264	204
Canada	182	198	207
Chile	119	127	...
Argentina	248	...	177
United Kingdom	192	214	141
France	118	138	130
Belgium	152	178	116
Netherlands	133	...	152
Denmark	139	152	158
Sweden	174 [a]	...	161 [b]
Norway	192	198	156
Western Germany	104	124	109 [c]
Poland	480	...	236
Czechoslovakia	140	162	...
Switzerland	169	...	...
Austria	191	220	157
Hungary	174	...	...
Spain	122	...	...
Italy	121	159	131
Greece	120	143	109 [c]
Japan	71	95	88
India	209	...	...

Sources: **4,** January 1952, pp. 18–21; **29,** December 1951, p. 349.

a. 1947. b. 1950. c. 1938 = 100

ties, which brought a setback to many industries, did not check chemical production. On the contrary, output increased in most of its branches — fertilizers, pharmaceuticals, plastics and so on. As in the United States, the index of chemical production is higher in most other countries than that for all manufacturing. Even in Germany and Japan, chemical production increased more rapidly than all manufacturing, despite the restrictions imposed by the occupying powers. The Italian chemical industry is overcoming the consequences of war damage and the shortage of coal and is topping all manufacturing in recovery.

The rapid increase in chemical production between the end of 1950 and July 1951 is reflected in the indexes of the United States, 236 and 264, respectively; the United Kingdom, 192 and 214; Belgium, 152 and 178, and so on. (See Table 497.) In Canada also, although the index of this industry is somewhat lower than that for all manufacturing, chemical production expanded greatly during and after the war. Poland, too, has grown in importance as a producer of chemicals and now ranks next to the United Kingdom and Western Germany among the European producers, accounting for some 12.5 per cent of Europe's chemical output.[111]

Along with increased production of chemicals in the old strongholds of the industry, new plants have appeared in many countries that relied exclusively on imports before the war. India, for example, now has eighty plants for manufacturing plastics, with 10,000 workers. Its chemical plant at Bihar, built by the government, is the largest in Asia.[112] Many chemical plants were established during or after the war in practically every republic of Latin America. Argentina, which used to import chemicals for mixing, bottling and packaging — just as it imports automobile parts for assembly — is now producing solvents, acids and other basic chemicals.

Brazil is no longer satisfied to import coal-tar dyes and is manufacturing them from imported intermediates. It also produces paints and varnishes, pharmaceuticals, insecticides and various other chemicals. While most of the plants are branches of foreign firms and their technicians come from abroad, Brazil is trying to train its own chemists to make increasing use of domestic raw materials. Ecuador is planning to build plants to produce sulfuric acid and caustic soda. El Salvador, Costa Rica, Guatemala and some other countries in Central America now produce various acids, insecticides and pharmaceuticals. Mexico opened a large new plant in 1948 for manufacturing caustic soda; Colombia completed a plant at Bogota in 1944 for the production of chlorine and caustic soda.[113]

Australia produced few chemicals before World War II and manufactured them largely from imported materials. Today it is self-sufficient in numerous chemicals and exports many.[114] Many chemical plants have been built in Egypt since 1942, and British East Africa now produces caustic soda, sulfuric acid and paints.[115]

These are only beginnings, often on a very modest scale. But the tendency is unmistakable, and further development of chemical production can be expected. As the manufacture of chemicals progresses, industry and agriculture throughout the world will become more and more "chemicalized."

111. **29,** December 1951, p. 349
112. **12,** June 25, 1951.

113. **60,** *passim;* and **13,** Part II, *passim.*
114. **13,** Part I, pp. 92–93.
115. **13,** Part II, p. 3.

SOURCE REFERENCES

PART I. MAN AND HIS ENVIRONMENT

CHAPTER 1

THE EARTH

1. League of Nations, *Statistical Year-Book, 1942–44,* Geneva, 1945.

UNITED STATES

2. Department of Agriculture, *Climate and Man (Yearbook of Agriculture, 1941),* 1941.
3. Department of Commerce, Bureau of the Census, *Statistical Abstract of the United States.*
4. Department of Defense, Lake Survey Office, *Survey of Northern and Northwestern Lakes, April 1951* (Bulletin No. 60, Great Lakes Pilot), 1951.

---

5. Finch, Vernor C., and Trewartha, Glenn T., *Elements of Geography, Physical and Cultural,* McGraw-Hill Book Company, New York, 1942.
6. *Hübner's Geographisch Statistische Tabellen Aller Länder der Erde,* 71st edition, L. W. Seidel und Sohn, Vienna, 1932.
7. Huntington, Ellsworth, *Civilization and Climate,* 3d edition, Yale University Press, New Haven, 1939.
8. ———, *Mainsprings of Civilization,* J. Wiley and Sons, New York, 1945.
9. ———, *Principles of Economic Geography,* J. Wiley and Sons, New York, 1940.
10. ———, and Cushing, Sumner W., *Principles of Human Geography,* 5th edition, J. Wiley and Sons, New York, 1940.
11. Koeppen, W., *Grundrisse der Klimakunde,* 2d edition, Gebrüder Bornträger, Berlin, 1931.
12. ———, "Das Geographische System der Klimate," in *Handbuch der Klimatologie,* Vol. I, Part C, Gebrüder Bornträger, Berlin, 1936.
13. Kossinna, Erwin, *Die Tiefen des Weltmeeres* (Institut für Meereskunde an der Universität Berlin. Neue Folge, A: Geographisch-Naturwissenschaftliche Reihe, No. 9), E. S. Mittler und Sohn, Berlin, 1921.
14. Markham, S. F., *Climate and the Energy of Nations,* revised edition, Oxford University Press, London and New York, 1944.
15. Pearl, Raymond, "A Comparative Examination of Certain Aspects of the Population of the New World," *Human Biology,* September 1940.
16. Raisz, Erwin J., *Atlas of Global Geography,* Global Press, New York, 1944.
17. Ratzel, Friedrich, *Politische Geographie,* R. Oldenbourg, Munich, 1897.
18. Renen, Albrecht, *Morphologie der Erdoberfläche,* Part I, Verlag von J. Engelhorn, Stuttgart, 1894.
19. Scobel, Albert, *Geographisches Handbuch zu Andrees Handatlas,* Velhagen und Klasing, Bielfeld, 1909.
20. Supan, Alexander, *Grundzüge der Physischen Erdkunde,* 5th edition, Veit, Leipzig, 1911.
21. Sverdrup, H. U., Johnson, Martin W., and Fleming, Richard H., *The Oceans, Their Physics, Chemistry and General Biology,* Prentice-Hall, New York, 1942.
22. Templeman, Thomas, *A New Survey of the Globe: or an Accurate Mensuration of all the Empires, Kingdoms, Countries, States, Principal Provinces, Counties and Islands in the World,* London, 1729.
23. Thornthwaite, C. Warren, "The Climates of Northern America According to a New Classification," *The Geographical Review,* October 1931.
24. ———, "The Climates of the Earth," *The Geographical Review,* July 1933.
25. Vidal de la Blache, J. M. C., *Atlas Général,* A. Colin, Paris, 1909.
26. Woytinsky, Wl. (W.S.), *Die Welt in Zahlen,* Vol. I: *Die Erde—Die Bevölkerung—Der Volksreichtum,* Rudolf Mosse, Berlin, 1925.

CHAPTER 2

PEOPLES OF THE WORLD

1. League of Nations, *Statistical Year-Book, 1942–44,* Geneva, 1945.
2. United Nations, *Demographic Yearbook,* New York.
3. ———, *Statistical Yearbook,* New York.
4. ———, *World Population Trends, 1920–1947,* New York, 1949.
5. ———, *Population and Vital Statistics Reports.*
6. ———, *Economic Bulletin for Europe.*
7. *Inter-American Statistical Yearbook, 1942,* Macmillan Company, New York; El Ateneo, Buenos Aires; Freitas Bastos, Rio de Janeiro, 1942.
8. International Institute of Statistics, *Aperçu de la Démographie des Divers Pays du Monde,* The Hague, 1925.

UNITED STATES

9. Department of Agriculture, *Climate and Man (Yearbook of Agriculture, 1941),* 1941.
10. Department of Commerce, Bureau of the Census, *Sixteenth Census of the United States (1940), Population,* Vol. II, 1943.
11. ———, ———, *Statistical Abstract of the United States.*
12. National Resources Committee, *The Problems of a Changing Population,* Report of the Committee on Population Problems, May 1938.

13. CHINA. National Government, Directorate General of Budgets, Accounts and Statistics, *Statistical Abstract of the Republic of China,* Nanking, 1947.

14. FRANCE. Statistique Générale, *Annuaire Statistique,* Paris.

GREAT BRITAIN

15. Registrar-General, *Reports on the Census of Population of England and Wales,* London.
16. *Royal Commission on Population Report,* London, 1949.

---

17. Beloch, Julius, *Die Bevölkerung der Griechisch-Römischen Welt* (Historische Beiträge zur

Bevölkerungslehre, Vol. I), Duncker und Humblott, Leipzig, 1886.

18. Carr-Saunders, Alexander M., *World Population: Past Growth and Present Trends*, Oxford University Press, London, 1936.

19. Condliffe, J. B., *The Economic Pattern of World Population* (Planning Pamphlet No. 18), National Planning Association, Washington, 1943.

20. Embree, Edwin R., *Indians of the Americas*, Houghton Mifflin Company, Boston, 1939.

21. Friis, Herman R., *A Series of Population Maps of the Colonies and the United States, 1625–1790* (Mimeographed Publication No. 3), American Geographical Society, New York, 1940.

22. Haddon, A. C., *The Races of Man and Their Distribution*, Macmillan Company, New York, 1925.

23. Kuczynski, Robert R., *Colonial Population*, Oxford University Press, London, 1937.

24. ———, *Population Movements*, Oxford University Press, London, 1936.

25. Meyer, Eduard, *Die Bevölkerung des Altertums* (Handwörterbuch der Staatswissenschaften, Vol. II), Gustav Fischer, Jena, 1909.

26. Pearl, Raymond, "A Comparative Examination of Certain Aspects of the Population of the New World," *Human Biology*, September 1940.

27. Pearson, Frank A., and Harper, Floyd A., *The World's Hunger*, Cornell University Press, Ithaca, 1945.

28. *Population Index*, Office of Population Research, Princeton University, and Population Association of America, July 1950.

29. Raisz, Erwin, *Atlas of Global Geography*, Harper, New York, 1944.

30. Sauer, Carl O., "The Prospect of Redistribution of Population," in *Limits of Land Settlement*, Isaiah Bowman (Ed.), Council on Foreign Relations, New York, 1937.

31. Shapiro, Leon, and Sapir, Boris, "Jewish Population of the World," *American Jewish Yearbook, 1948–49*, Jewish Publication Society of America, Philadelphia, 1949.

32. Ta Chen, "Population in Modern China," *American Journal of Sociology*, July 1946 Supplement.

33. Thompson, Warren S., and Whelpton, P. K., *Estimates of Future Population of the United States, 1940–2000*, National Resources Planning Board, Washington, 1943.

34. Toynbee, Arnold J., *A Study of History*, abridgment of Volumes I–VI by D. C. Somervell, Oxford University Press, New York and London, 1947.

35. Wander, Hilde, *Die Bedeutung der Auswanderung für die Lösung Europäischer Flüchtlings- und Bevölkerungsprobleme*, Kieler Studien, Kiel, 1951.

36. Wilcox, Walter F. (Ed.), *International Migrations*, Vol. II: *Interpretations*, National Bureau of Economic Research, New York, 1931.

37. Woytinsky, E. S. and W. S., "Progress of Agricultural Statistics in the World," *Journal of Farm Economics*, November 1939.

38. Woytinsky, Wl. (W.S.), *Die Welt in Zahlen*, Vol. I: *Die Erde—Die Bevölkerung—Der Volksreichtum*, Rudolf Mosse, Berlin, 1925.

CHAPTER 3

MIGRATION

1. United Nations, *Demographic Yearbook*, New York.

2. ———, Conciliation Commission for Palestine, *Final Report of the United Nations Economic Survey Mission for the Middle East*, Part I, Final Report and Appendices, New York, December 1949.

3. International Labor Office, *Year Book of Labour Statistics*, Montreal.

4. ———, *International Labour Review*, Geneva.

5. ———, Preliminary Migration Conference, Geneva, April–May 1950, *Organization of Migration Movements and Obstacles to the International Mobility of Manpower*, Working Paper submitted by the Italian Government.

6. International Union for the Scientific Study of Population, "Cultural Assimilation of Immigration," supplement to *Population Studies*, Vol. III, Cambridge University Press, London, 1950.

UNITED STATES

7. Department of Commerce, Bureau of the Census, Fifteenth Census of the United States (1930), *Population*, Vol. II, 1933.

8. ———, ———, Sixteenth Census of the United States (1940), *Population*, Vol. II, 1943.

9. ———, ———, Sixteenth Census of the United States (1940), *Population, Internal Migration, 1935–1940*, 1946.

10. ———, ———, *Statistical Abstract of the United States*.

11. ———, ———, *Current Population Reports—Population Characteristics*, "Internal Migration in the United States, April 1940 to April 1947," Series P-20, No. 14, April 15, 1948.

12. ———, ———, *Interstate Migration and Other Population Changes, 1940 to 1943*, Series P-44, No. 17, August 28, 1944.

13. Department of Justice, Immigration and Naturalization Service, *Annual Reports*.

14. National Resources Committee, *The Problems of a Changing Population*, Report of the Committee on Population Problems, May 1938.

15. CHINA. National Government, *Crop Reports*, National Agricultural Research Bureau, Nanking.

16. FRANCE. Statistique Générale, *Mouvements Migratoires entre la France et l'Étranger*, by Henri Bunle, Paris, 1943.

GERMANY

17. Deutsches Institut für Wirtschaftsforschung, *Die Deutsche Wirtschaft. Zwei Jahre nach dem Zusammenbruch*, Berlin, 1947.

18. Länderrat des Amerikanischen Besetzungsgebiets, *Statistisches Handbuch von Deutschland, 1928–1944*, Munich, 1949.

19. INDIA. *Indian Year-Book*, a Statistical and Historical Annual of the Indian Empire, 1944–1945, Times of India Press, Bombay.

20. Bowman, Isaiah, *The Pioneer Fringe* (Special Publication No. 13), American Geographical Society, New York, 1931.

21. Carr-Saunders, Alexander M., *World Population: Past Growth and Present Trends,* Oxford University Press, London, 1936.

22. Edding, Friedrich, Hornschu, Hans-Erich, and Wander, Hilde, *Das Deutsche Flüchtlingsproblem,* Institut für Weltwirtschaft an der Universität Kiel, 1949.

23. Ferenczi, Irme, "International Migration Statistics," in *International Migrations,* Vol. I, *Statistics,* Walter F. Wilcox (Ed.), National Bureau of Economic Research, New York, 1929.

24. Forsyth, William D., *The Myth of the Open Spaces,* Melbourne University Press, Melbourne, 1942.

25. Friis, Herman R., *A Series of Population Maps of the Colonies and the United States, 1625–1790* (Mimeographed Publication No. 3), American Geographical Society, New York, 1940.

26. Hutchinson, Edward P., *Current Problems of Immigration Policy,* American Enterprise Association, Washington, 1949.

27. ———, "The Present Status of Our Immigration Laws and Policy," *Milbank Memorial Fund Quarterly,* April 1947.

28. Isaac, Julius, "European Migration Potential and Prospects," *Population Studies,* March 1949.

29. Joerg, W. L. G. (Ed.), *Pioneer Settlement,* American Geographical Society, New York, 1932.

30. Kimble, George H. T., *The World's Open Spaces,* T. Nelson and Sons, New York and London, 1939.

31. Kirk, Dudley, "European Migrations: Prewar Trends and Future Prospects," *Milbank Memorial Fund Quarterly,* April 1947.

32. Kulischer, Eugene M., *The Displacement of Population in Europe,* International Labor Office, Montreal, 1943.

33. ———, *Europe on the Move: War and Population Changes, 1917–1947,* Columbia University Press, New York, 1948.

34. Myrdal, Gunnar, *An American Dilemma: The Negro Problem and Modern Democracy,* 2d edition, Harper and Brothers, New York, 1944.

35. Pelzer, Karl J., *Population and Land Utilization (An Economic Survey of the Pacific Area,* Part I), Institute of Pacific Relations, New York, 1942.

36. Revusky, Abraham, *Jews in Palestine,* Vanguard Press, New York, 1945.

37. Sauer, Carl O., "The Prospect of a Redistribution of Population," in *Limits of Land Settlement,* Isaiah Bowman (Ed.), Council on Foreign Relations, New York, 1937.

38. ———, "The Settlement of the Humid East," *Climate and Man (Yearbook of Agriculture, 1941),* U. S. Department of Agriculture, 1941.

39. Schechtman, Joseph B., *European Population Transfers, 1939–1945,* Oxford University Press, New York, 1946.

40. Sutherland, Stella U., *Population Distribution in Colonial America,* Columbia University Press, New York, 1936.

41. Thompson, Warren S., *Population Problems,* 3d edition, McGraw-Hill Book Company, New York, 1942.

42. Thornthwaite, C. Warren, and Slentz, H. I., *Internal Migration in the United States,* University of Pennsylvania Press, Philadelphia, 1934.

43. Thucydides, *The Peloponnesian War* (R. Crawley, trans.), Modern Library, New York, 1934.

44. Trewartha, Glenn T., "Climate and Settlement of the Sub-humid Land," in *Climate and Man (Yearbook of Agriculture, 1941),* U. S. Department of Agriculture, 1941.

45. Vidal de la Blache, J. M. C., *Principes de Géographie Humaine,* A. Colin, Paris, 1922.

46. Wander, Hilde, *The Importance of Emigration for the Solution of Population Problems in Western Europe* (Research Group for European Migration Problems, Publication No. 1), Martinus Nijhoff, The Hague, 1951.

47. Wilcox, Walter F. (Ed.), *International Migrations,* Vol. I, *Statistics,* 1929; Vol. II, *Interpretations,* 1931, National Bureau of Economic Research, New York.

48. Woytinsky, Wl. (W.S.), *Die Welt in Zahlen,* Vol. I: *Die Erde—Die Bevölkerung—Der Volksreichtum,* Rudolf Mosse, Berlin, 1925.

49. Woytinsky, W. S., "Interstate Migration during the War," *State Government,* March 1946.

50. ———, "Internal Migration during the War," Special Report, Social Security Board, November 1944 (mimeographed).

CHAPTER 4

CITIES

1. United Nations, *Demographic Yearbook,* New York.

2. ———, *Data on Urban and Rural Population in Recent Censuses,* New York, 1950.

3. ———, Economic Commission for Europe, *The European Housing Problem, a Preliminary Review,* Geneva, 1949.

4. International Institute of Statistics, *Bulletin.*

UNITED STATES

5. Department of Commerce, Bureau of the Census, Fifteenth Census of the United States (1930), *Population,* Vol. II, 1933.

6. ———, ———, Sixteenth Census of the United States (1940), *Population,* Vol. II, 1943.

7. ———, ———, *Statistical Abstract of the United States.*

8. ———, ———, *Current Population Reports—Population Characteristics,* "The Development of the Urban-Rural Classification in the United States, 1874–1949," Series P-23, No. 1, August 1949.

9. National Resources Committee, *Our Cities: Their Role in the National Economy,* June 1939.

10. FRANCE. Ministère de la Reconstruction et de l'Urbanisme, *Pour un Plan National de l'Aménagement du Territoire,* Paris, 1950.

11. GERMANY. Statistisches Reichsamt, *Statistisches Jahrbuch für das Deutsche Reich,* Berlin.

GREAT BRITAIN

12. *General Reports of the Census of England and Wales.*

13. London County Council, *L.C.C. Post-War Housing, 1945–49,* London, 1949.

14. THE NETHERLANDS. *Some Facts about Housing and Town Planning in the Netherlands,* The Hague, 1949.

15. NORWAY. *Reconstruction of Norway,* Housing Directorate, Oslo, 1947.

SWEDEN

16. *Swedish Housing,* Swedish Institute, Stockholm, 1949.

17. *Swedish Town Planning, 1949–1950,* Plan, No. 1-2, 1950, Vol. IV, Stockholm.

18. Aristotle, *Politics* (Benjamin Jowett, trans.), Oxford University Press, New York, 1943.

19. Baker, O. E., "Rural-Urban Migration and the National Welfare," *Annals of the Association of American Geographers,* June 1933.

20. Dickinson, Robert E., *City Region and Regionalism, a Geographical Contribution to Human Ecology,* Oxford University Press, London, 1947.

21. Hoyt, Homer, *The Structure and Growth of Residential Neighborhoods in American Cities,* Federal Housing Administration, Washington, 1939.

22. Jefferson, Mark, "Distribution of the World's City Folks, a Study in Comparative Civilization," *Geographical Review,* July 1931.

23. McKenzie, Roderick D., *The Metropolitan Community,* McGraw-Hill Book Company, New York, 1933.

24. Mitchell, R. B. (Ed.), "Building the Future City," *Annals of the American Academy of Political and Social Science,* November 1945.

25. Morley, Sylvanus Griswold, *The Ancient Maya,* Stanford University Press, Stanford University, 1946.

26. Mumford, Lewis, *The Culture of Cities,* Harcourt, Brace and Company, New York, 1938.

27. Petty, William, *Essays on Mankind and Political Arithmetic,* Cassell and Company, New York, 1888.

28. Prescott, W. H., *History of the Conquest of Mexico* [and] *History of the Conquest of Peru,* Modern Library, New York, 1936.

29. Renner, George T., and Associates, *Global Geography,* Thomas Y. Crowell Company, New York, 1944.

30. Rist, Charles, "Urbanisation-Desurbanisation," *Urbanisation et Desurbanisation, Problème de l'Heure,* Librairie Plon, Paris, 1945.

31. Rostovzeff, Michael, "Cities in the Ancient World," in *Urban Land Economics,* Institute for Research in Land Economics, Ann Arbor, 1922.

32. Shine, Mary L., "Urban Land in the Middle Ages," in *Urban Land Economics,* Institute for Research in Land Economics, Ann Arbor, 1922.

33. Suetonius, *The Lives of the Twelve Caesars,* Modern Library, New York, 1931.

34. Sulkevich, S. I., *Territoriiā i naselenie SSSR,* Politizdat, Moscow, 1940.

35. Thompson, Warren S., *Population Problems,* 3d edition, McGraw-Hill Book Company, New York, 1942.

36. Weber, Adna Ferrin, *The Growth of Cities in the Nineteenth Century, a Study in Statistics,* Columbia University Press, New York, 1899.

37. Woytinsky, Wl. (W.S.), *Die Welt in Zahlen,* Vol. I: *Die Erde—Die Bevölkerung—Der Volksreichtum,* Rudolf Mosse, Berlin, 1925.

CHAPTER 5

BIRTHS, DEATHS, MARRIAGE AND DIVORCE

1. League of Nations, *Statistical Yearbook, 1942–44,* Geneva, 1945.

2. United Nations, *Demographic Yearbook,* New York.

3. ——, *Fertility Data in Population Censuses,* New York, 1949.

4. ——, *Population and Vital Statistics Reports,* New York.

5. ——, *Monthly Bulletin of Statistics,* New York.

6. ——, World Health Organization, *Epidemiological and Vital Statistics Report,* Monthly Supplement to the *Weekly Epidemiological Record,* Geneva.

UNITED STATES

7. Department of Commerce, Bureau of the Census, Sixteenth Census of the United States (1940), *Population: Differential Fertility, 1940 and 1910, Women by Number of Children ever Born,* 1945.

8. ——, ——, *Statistical Abstract of the United States.*

9. Federal Security Agency, U.S. Public Health Service, *United States Life Tables and Actuarial Tables, 1939–41,* 1946.

10. ——, ——, *Summary of International Vital Statistics, 1937–1944,* 1947.

11. ——, ——, *Vital Statistics Rates in the United States, 1900–1940,* 1947.

FRANCE

12. Statistique Générale, *Annuaire Statistique,* Paris.

13. ——, *Statistique des Familles en 1906,* Paris, 1912.

GREAT BRITAIN

14. Registrar-General, *Mortality of Men in Certain Occupations in Three Years, 1910, 1911 and 1912,* Supplement to the Seventy-fifth Annual Report of the Registrar-General of England and Wales, Part IV, London, 1912.

15. ——, *Decennial Supplement, England and Wales, 1931,* London, 1936.

16. ——, *Statistical Review of England and Wales for the Year 1938,* London, 1939.

17. *Family Limitation and Its Influence on Human Fertility during the Last Fifty Years,* Papers of the Royal Commission on Population, Vol. I, London, 1949.

18. *Royal Commission on Population Report,* London, 1949.

19. Bertillon, Jacques, *La Dépopulation de la France, ses Conséquences, ses Causes, Mesures à Prendre pour la Combattre,* Les Presses Universitaires de France, Paris, 1911.

20. Bonar, James, *Theories of Population from Raleigh to Arthur Young,* Allen and Unwin, London, 1931.

21. Buck, John Lossing, *Land Utilization in China,* University of Chicago Press, Chicago, 1937.

22. Davis, Kingsley, and Casis, Ana, "Urbanization in Latin America," *Milbank Memorial Fund Quarterly,* Part I, April 1946; Part II, July 1946.

23. Dublin, Louis I., *Health and Wealth: a Survey of the Economics of World Health,* Harper and Brothers, New York, 1928.

24. ———, "Longevity in Retrospect and in Prospect," in *Problems of Ageing,* 2d edition, E. V. Cowdry (Ed.), Williams and Wilkins Company, Baltimore, 1942.

25. ———, and Lotka, Alfred J., *Length of Life, a Study of the Life Table,* Ronald Press Company, New York, 1936.

26. ———, and ———, "On the True Rate of Natural Increase," *Journal of the American Statistical Association,* September 1925.

27. Gini, Corrado, *Eccerzióni Apparenti ed Eccerzióni Reali alla Norma del Minore Accréscimento Naturale delle Classi Elevati,* XII Congrès de l'Institut International de Sociologie, Rome, 1935.

28. ———, *Les Facteurs de la Decroissance de la Natalité à l'Époque Contemporaine* (Extracto dos Actas do Congresso Nacional de Ciêncas da Populacão, Vol. I.), Imprensa Portugesa, Pôrto, 1940.

29. ———, "Vecchie e Nuove Osservazióni sulle Cause della Natálita Differenziale e sulla Misura della Fecondità Naturale delle Confugate," *Metron,* July 1949.

30. Grotjahn, A., *Die Verschiedenheit der Geburtenhäufigkeit in Deutschland,* Congrès Mondial de la Population, Rome, 1927.

31. Hersch, Liebman, *L'Inégalité devant la Mort, d'après les Statistiques de la Ville de Paris: Effets de la Situation Sociale sur la Mortalité,* Recueil Sirey, Paris, 1920.

32. Ichok, G., *La Mortalité à Paris et dans le Département de la Seine,* Union de Caisses d'Assurance Sociales de la Région Parisienne, Paris, 1937.

33. Innes, J. W., "Class Birth Rates in England and Wales, 1921–1931," *Milbank Memorial Fund Quarterly,* January 1941.

34. Jacobson, Paul H., "The Trend of the Birth Rate among Persons on Different Economic Levels, City of New York, 1929–1942," *Milbank Memorial Fund Quarterly,* April 1944.

35. Karpinos, Bernard D., and Kiser, Clyde V., "The Differential Fertility and Potential Rates of Growth of Various Income and Educational Classes of Urban Population in the United States," *Milbank Memorial Fund Quarterly,* October 1939.

36. Knibbs, G. H., *On the Influence of Infantile Mortality on Birth Rate* (Melbourne Professional Papers), Commonwealth Bureau of Census and Statistics, Sydney, 1908.

37. Kuczynski, Robert R., *The Balance of Births and Deaths,* The Brookings Institution, Washington, Vol. I, 1928; Vol. II, 1931.

38. Lamson, Herbert D., "Differential Reproduction in China," *Quarterly Review of Biology,* September 1935.

39. Landry, Adolphe, *Traité de Démographie,* Payot, Paris, 1945.

40. Lewis, C. J., and Lewis, J. Norman, *Natality and Fecundity: a Contribution to National Demography,* Oliver and Boyd, Edinburgh, 1906.

41. Livi, Livio, *Trattato di Demografia, Le Leggi Naturali della Popolazione,* Cedam, Padua, 1940.

42. March, Lucien, "Some Researches Concerning the Factors of Mortality," *Journal of the Royal Statistical Society,* April 1912.

43. Methorst, H. W., "Differential Fertility, Birth Rates and Infantile Mortality in the Netherlands" (Special Memoire to the International Union for the Scientific Investigation of Population Problems), in *Population,* Allen and Unwin, London, April 1935.

44. Newsholme, Arthur, *Elements of Vital Statistics in Their Bearing on Social and Public Health Problems,* Allen and Unwin, London, 1943.

45. Notestein, Frank W., and others, *The Future Population of Europe and the Soviet Union, Population Projections, 1940–1970,* League of Nations, Geneva, 1944.

46. Panunzio, Constantine, "Are More Males Born in Wartime?" *Milbank Memorial Fund Quarterly,* July 1943.

47. Pearl, Raymond, *The Natural History of Population,* Oxford University Press, London, 1939.

48. *Population Index,* Office of Population Research, Princeton University, and Population Association of America.

49. Sauvy, Alfred, *Richesse et Population,* Payot, Paris, 1943.

50. ———, "La Reprise de la Natalité dans le Monde, Ses Causes, Ses Chances de Durée," *Population,* Paris, April-June 1948.

51. *Statistical Bulletin,* Metropolitan Life Insurance Company, New York, July 1947.

52. Stevenson, J. H. C., "The Fertility of Various Social Classes in England and Wales from the Middle of the Nineteenth Century to 1911," *Journal of the Royal Statistical Society,* London, May 1940.

53. Süssmilch, Johann Peter, *Die Göttliche Ordnung,* Berlin, 1742.

54. Thompson, Warren S., *Population Problems,* 3d edition, McGraw-Hill Book Company, New York, 1942.

55. Tietze, Christopher, "Differential Reproduction in England," *Milbank Memorial Fund Quarterly,* July 1939.

56. ———, "Life Tables for Social Classes in England," *Milbank Memorial Fund Quarterly,* April 1943.

57. Whelpton, P. K., and Kiser, Clyde V., "Social and Psychological Factors Affecting Fertility," *Milbank Memorial Fund Quarterly,* July 1943; January 1944; July 1945; January 1946; January 1947; October 1947; April 1948.

58. Whitney, Jessamine, *Death Rates by Occupation, Based on Data of the Census Bureau, 1930*, National Tuberculosis Association, New York, 1934.

59. Zingali, Gaetano, "Demografia," in *Demografia, Antropometria, Státistica Sanitaria, Dinamica delle Popolazioni*, by Corrado Gini, Marcello Boldrini, Luigi de Berardinis and Gaetano Zingali (Trattato Italiano di Igiene, Monografia 18A), Unione Tipografico-Editrice Torinese, Turin, 1930.

CHAPTER 6

HEALTH

1. League of Nations, Health Organization, *Annual Epidemiological Reports*, Geneva.
2. United Nations, *Demographic Yearbook*, New York.
3. ———, *Statistical Yearbook*, New York.
4. ———, World Health Organization, *Annual Epidemiological and Vital Statistics, 1939–1946*, Part I, *Vital Statistics and Causes of Death*, Geneva, 1951.
5. ———, ———, *Epidemiological and Vital Statistics Report*, Monthly Supplement to the *Weekly Epidemiological Record*, Geneva.

UNITED STATES

6. Department of Commerce, Bureau of the Census, *Statistical Abstract of the United States*.
7. Department of Labor, Bureau of Labor Statistics, *Money Disbursements of Wage Earners and Clerical Workers, 1934–36*, Summary Volume, Bulletin No. 638, 1941.
8. Federal Security Agency, *The Nation's Health, a Ten-Year Program*, Report to the President by Oscar R. Ewing, September 1948.
9. ———, Social Security Board, *Disability among Gainfully Occupied Persons*, Bureau Memorandum No. 61, June 1945.
10. ———, ———, *Medical Care and Costs in Relation to Family Income*, Statistical Handbook, March 1943.
11. ———, ———, *Need for Medical-Care Insurance*, Bureau Memorandum No. 57, April 1944.
12. ———, ———, *Social Security Legislation Throughout the World*, Bureau Report No. 16, 1949.
13. ———, U. S. Public Health Service, *Summary of International Vital Statistics, 1937–44*, 1947.
14. ———, ———, *Vital Statistics Rates in the United States, 1900–1940*, 1947.
15. ———, ———, *United States Summary of Vital Statistics, 1948*, June 1950.
16. National Resources Committee, *The Problems of a Changing Population*, Report of the Committee on Population Problems, May 1938.
17. National Resources Planning Board, *Family Expenditures in the United States*, Statistical Tables and Appendixes, June 1941.
18. Office of Price Administration, *Civilian Spending and Saving, 1941 and 1942*, March 1943.

19. CHINA. National Government, Directorate General of Budgets, Accounts and Statistics, *Statistical Abstract of the Republic of China*, Nanking, 1947.

20. FRANCE. Statistique Générale, *Annuaire Statistique*, Paris.

21. GERMANY. Statistisches Reichsamt, *Statistisches Jahrbuch für das Deutsche Reich*, Berlin.

GREAT BRITAIN

22. Central Statistical Office, *Annual Abstract of Statistics, 1938–1948*, London, 1949.
23. ———, *Monthly Digest of Statistics*, Central Statistical Office, London.
24. *Report of the Ministry of Health for the Year Ended 31st March, 1949*, London, 1950.

25. INDIA. *Statistical Abstract for British India*, London.

26. SWEDEN. Central Bureau of Statistics, *Statistisk Årsbok för Sverige*, Stockholm.

27. American Medical Association, Bureau of Medical Economics, *Factual Data on Medical Economics*, Chicago, 1940.
28. Bowles, Gordon T., *New Types of Old Americans at Harvard and at Eastern Women's Colleges*, Harvard University Press, Cambridge, 1932.
29. Dublin, Louis I., and Lotka, Alfred J., *Length of Life: a Study of the Life Table*, Ronald Press Company, New York, 1936.
30. ———, and ———, *Twenty-Five Years of Health Progress*, Metropolitan Life Insurance Company, New York, 1937.
31. Falk, Isidore S., Klem, Margaret C., and Sinai, Nathan, *The Incidence of Illness and the Receipt and Costs of Medical Care among Representative Families* (Committee on the Costs of Medical Care, Publication No. 26), University of Chicago Press, Chicago 1933.
32. Herodotus, *History* (Everyman's Library), E. P. Dutton and Company, New York.
33. *Journal of the American Medical Association*.
34. Klem, Margaret C., and Hollingsworth, Helen, "Medical Care," in *America's Needs and Resources*, by J. Frederic Dewhurst and Associates, Twentieth Century Fund, New York, 1947.
35. Mustard, Harry S., *Summary of Vital Statistics, 1948*, Department of Health, City of New York, New York, 1949.
36. Prinzing, Friedrich, *Handbuch der Medizinischen Statistik*, G. Fischer, Jena, 1906.
37. Propper-Grashchenkov, N., *Public Health Protection in the USSR*, Foreign Languages Publishing House, Moscow, 1939.
38. Raisz, Erwin J., *Atlas of Global Geography*, Global Press, New York, 1944.
39. ———, *The Nine Miseries of Mankind* (unpublished article).
40. Research Council for Economic Security, *Compulsory Social Security in Latin America* (Publication No. 29), Chicago, 1947.
41. ———, *Our National Health Problem* (Publication No. 15), Chicago, 1946.
42. ———, *The Extent and Economic Cost of Disability* (Publication No. 23), Chicago, 1947.
43. ———, *Health Legislative Developments, 1947: Compulsory Cash Sickness and Related Bills in*

1947 State Legislatures (Publication No. 53), Chicago, 1948.

44. ———, *The National Health and S. 545* (Publication No. 51), Chicago, 1948.

45. ———, *Sick Pay in Industry* (Publication No. 43), Chicago, 1948.

46. ———, *Toward Better Health* (Publication No. 36), Chicago, 1947.

47. Sanders, Barkev S., *Environment and Growth*, Warwick and York, Baltimore, 1934.

48. Sigerist, Henry E., *Medicine and Human Welfare*, Yale University Press, New Haven, 1941.

49. Simmons, James S., and Associates, *Global Epidemiology, a Geography of Disease and Sanitation*, Vol. I, J. B. Lippincott Company, Philadelphia, 1944.

50. *Statistical Bulletin*, Metropolitan Life Insurance Company, New York.

51. Stern, Bernhard J., *Society and Medical Progress*, Princeton University Press, Princeton, 1941.

52. Stieglitz, Edward J., *A Future for Preventive Medicine*, Commonwealth Fund, New York, 1945.

53. Thomas, Lowell, Jr., *Out of This World: Across the Himalayas to Forbidden Tibet*, Greystone Press, New York, 1950.

54. Woytinsky, Wl. (W.S.), *Die Welt in Zahlen*, Vol. VII: *Daten der Politischen und der Moralstatistik*, Rudolf Mosse, Berlin, 1928.

55. ———, and Woytinsky, E. S., "Die Offentliche Gesundheitspflege in Zahlen," in *Ergebnisse der Sozialen Hygiene und Gesundheitsfürsorge*, Vol. I, George Thieme Verlag, Leipzig, 1929.

56. Woytinsky, W. S. and Associates, *Employment and Wages in the United States*, Twentieth Century Fund, New York, 1953.

CHAPTER 7

THE FUTURE OF WORLD POPULATION

1. United Nations, *Demographic Yearbook*, New York.
2. ———, *Population and Vital Statistics Reports*.
3. ———, *Monthly Bulletin of Statistics*.

UNITED STATES

4. Department of Commerce, Bureau of the Census, *Forecasts of the Population of the United States, 1945–1975*, 1948.

5. ———, ———, *Current Population Reports—Population Estimates*, "Illustrative Projections of the Population of the United States, 1950 to 1960," Series P-25, No. 43, August 1950.

6. National Resources Committee, *Population Statistics*, No. 1, National Data, October 1937.

7. National Resources Planning Board, *Estimates of Future Population of the United States, 1940–2000*, August 1943.

8. FRANCE. Statistique Générale, *Prévisions Conditionnelles pour la Population Française jusqu'en 2005*, by M. J. Grot, Études Démographiques, No. 6, Paris, 1946.

9. GERMANY. Deutsches Institut für Wirtschaftsforschung, *Die Deutsche Wirtschaft. Zwei Jahre nach dem Zusammenbruch*, Berlin, 1947.

10. GREAT BRITAIN. *Royal Commission on Population Report*, London, 1949.

11. Bonynge, Francis, *The Future Wealth of America: Being a Glance at the Resources of the United States and the Commercial and Agricultural Advantages of Cultivating Tea, Coffee and Indigo, the Date, Mango, Jack, Leechee, Guava, and Orange Trees, etc., with a Review of the China Trade*, New York, 1852.

12. Bürgdorfer, Friedrich, *Volk ohne Jugend*, Kurt Vowinckel Verlag, Berlin Grunewald, 1939.

13. Carr-Saunders, Alexander M., *World Population: Past Growth and Present Trends*, Oxford University Press, London, 1936.

14. Davis, Joseph S., *The Population Upsurge in the United States* (Food Research Institute, War–Peace Pamphlets, No. 12), Stanford University Press, Stanford University, 1949.

15. Gini, Corrado, *Teorie della Popolazióne*, Casa Editrice Castellani, Rome, 1945.

16. Glass, David V., *The Struggle for Population*, Oxford University Press, London, 1936.

17. ———, "Estimates of Future Population of Various Countries," *Eugenics Review*, October 1943.

18. Landry, Adolphe, *Traité de Démographie*, Payot, Paris, 1945.

19. Malthus, T. R., *An Essay on the Principle of Population, or a View on Its Past and Present Effects on Human Happiness* (reprinted from the 6th edition, 1826), Ward, Lock and Company, London, 1932.

20. Notestein, Frank W., "Population—The Long View," in *Food for the World*, Theodore W. Schultz (Ed.), University of Chicago Press, Chicago, 1945.

21. ———, and Associates, *The Future Population of Europe and the Soviet Union: Population Projections, 1940–1970*, League of Nations, Geneva, 1944.

22. Pearl, Raymond, *The Biology of Population Growth*, Alfred A. Knopf, New York, 1930.

23. ———, *The Natural History of Population*, Oxford University Press, London, 1939.

24. ———, and Reed, Lowell J., "On the Rate of Growth of the Population of the United States since 1790 and Its Mathematical Representation," *Proceedings of the National Academy of Sciences*.

25. Petty, William, *Economic Writings*, The University Press, Cambridge, 1899.

26. Political and Economic Planning, *Population Policy in Great Britain*, London, 1948.

27. Pritchett, H. S., *A Formula for Predicting the Population of the United States* (reprinted from *Transactions* of the Academy of Science of St. Louis), December 1890.

28. Reed, Lowell J., and Berkson, Joseph, "The Application of the Logistic Function to Experimental Data," *Journal of Physical Chemistry*, May 1929.

29. ———, and Pearl, Raymond, "On the Summation of Logistic Curves," *Journal of the Royal Statistical Society*, 1927, Part IV.

30. Taeuber, Irene B., "Literature on Future Populations, 1943–48," *Population Index*, January 1949.

31. Ta Chen, "Population in Modern China," *American Journal of Sociology,* July 1946 Supplement.

32. Thompson, Warren S., *Population Problems,* Mc-Graw-Hill Book Company, New York, 1942.

33. Verhulst, P. F., "Notice sur la Loi que la Population suit dans son Accroissement," in *Correspondance Mathématique et Physique,* A. Quetelet, Brussels, 1838.

34. Whelpton, P. K., "Calculation of Future Development of Population," *Verhandlungen des Internationalen Kongresses für Bevölkerungsforschung,* Vol. VII, Rome, 1934.

35. Woytinsky, Wl. (W.S.), "Bevölkerung und Ökonomie der Menschlichen Arbeitskraft," *Verhandlungen des Internationalen Kongresses für Bevölkerungsforschung,* Vol. IX, Rome, 1933.

PART II. WORLD NEEDS AND RESOURCES

CHAPTER 8

CONSUMER NEEDS AND OUTLAYS

1. International Labor Office, *International Labour Review*, Geneva.

UNITED STATES

2. Department of Agriculture, *Studies of Family Living in the United States and Other Countries: an Analysis of Material and Method*, by Faith M. Williams and Carle C. Zimmerman, Miscellaneous Publication No. 223, 1935.
3. Department of Commerce, Bureau of Foreign and Domestic Commerce, *Survey of Current Business*.
4. ———, ———, *National Income*, 1947 Edition, Supplement to *Survey of Current Business*.
5. ———, ———, *National Income*, 1951 Edition, Supplement to *Survey of Current Business*.
6. Department of Labor, Bureau of Labor Statistics, *Money Disbursements of Wage Earners and Clerical Workers, 1934–36*, Summary Volume, Bulletin No. 638, 1941.
7. ———, ———, *Monthly Labor Review*.
8. National Resources Committee, *Consumer Expenditures in the United States, Estimates for 1935–36*, 1939.
9. ———, *Consumer Incomes in the United States, Their Distribution in 1935–36*, August 1938.
10. National Resources Planning Board, *Family Expenditures in the United States*, Statistical Tables and Appendices, June 1941.

11. GERMANY. Statistisches Reichsamt, *Statistisches Jahrbuch für das Deutsche Reich*, Berlin.

---

12. Aristotle, *Politics* (Benjamin Jowett, trans.), Oxford University Press, New York, 1943.
13. Bücher, Carl, *Industrial Evolution* (trans. from 3d German ed.), Henry Holt and Company, New York, 1901.
14. Davies, David, *The Case of Labourers in Husbandry stated and considered in three parts, with an Appendix containing a Collection of Accounts, showing the earnings and Expenses of Labouring Families, In Different Parts of the Kingdom*, Dublin, 1796.
15. Dewhurst, J. Frederic, and Associates, *America's Needs and Resources*, Twentieth Century Fund, New York, 1947.
16. Drummond, Henry, *Tropical Africa*, John B. Alden, New York, 1890.
17. Eden, Frederick M., *The State of the Poor or an History of the Laboring Classes in England, from the Conquest to the present period, in which are particularly considered their domestic economy, with respect to Diet, Dress, Fuel and Habitation, etc.*, London, 1797. (Reprinted and abridged edition, George Routledge and Sons, London, 1928.)
18. Engel, E., *Die Lebenskosten Belgischer Arbeiter Familien, Früher und Jetzt*, Dresden, 1895.

19. Gordon, Leland J., *Economics for Consumers*, 2d edition, American Book Company, 1944.
20. King, Gregory, *Two Tracts* (edited, with an introduction by George E. Barnett), Johns Hopkins University Press, Baltimore, 1936.
21. Kyrk, Hazel, *Economic Problems of the Family*, Harper and Brothers, New York, 1933.
22. LePlay, M. F., *Les Ouvriers Européens, études sur les travaux, la vie domestique, et la condition morale des populations ouvrières de l'Europe précédées d'un exposé de la methode d'observation*, Imprimerie Impériale, Paris, 1855.
23. Marx, Karl, *Capital*, Modern Library, New York, 1936.
24. Sydenstricker, E., King, W. T., and Wiehl, D., *The Income Cycle in the Life of the Wage Earner*, U. S. Public Health Service, Washington, 1924.
25. Thorp, Willard L. (Ed.), *Economic Problems in a Changing World*, Farrar and Rinehart, New York, 1939.
26. Woytinsky, W. S., *Earnings and Social Security in the United States*, Committee on Social Security, Social Science Research Council, Washington, 1943.
27. Zimmerman, Carle C., *Consumption and Standards of Living*, D. Van Nostrand Company, New York, 1936.

CHAPTER 9

CONSUMPTION AND STANDARDS OF LIVING

1. League of Nations, *Nutrition*, Final Report of the Mixed Committee on the Relation of Nutrition to Health, Agriculture and Economic Policy, Geneva, 1937.
2. ———, *Problems of Nutrition* (prepared by the International Institute of Agriculture in Rome), Geneva, 1930.
3. United Nations, *Statistical Yearbook*, New York.
4. ———, *World Iron Ore Resources and Their Utilization*, New York, 1950.
5. United Nations, Food and Agriculture Organization (FAO), *Commodity Series*, Washington.
6. ———, ———, *Forestry and Forest Products: World Situation, 1937–1946*, Washington, 1946.
7. ———, ———, *The State of Food and Agriculture, 1948*, Washington, September 1948.
8. ———, ———, *World Fiber Review, 1949*, Washington, 1949.
9. ———, ———, *World Food Survey*, Washington, 1946.
10. ———, ———, *Yearbook of Forest Products Statistics*, Washington.
11. International Institute of Agriculture, *Agricultural Commodities and Raw Materials*, Rome, 1944.
12. ———, *Les Grands Produits Agricoles*, Rome, 1944.

UNITED STATES

13. Department of Agriculture, *Agricultural Production and Trade by Countries*, 1945.
14. ———, *Consumption of Food in the United States, 1909–48*, 1949.

15. Department of Labor, Bureau of Labor Statistics, *Monthly Labor Review*.

16. ——, ——, *Workers' Budgets in the United States, City Families and Single Persons, 1946 and 1947*, Bulletin No. 927, 1948.

17. GREAT BRITAIN. *The Colonial Territories (1948–1949)*, Cmd. 7715, H.M.S.O., 1949.

18. Bennett, M. K., "Wheat in National Diets," *Wheat Studies* (Food Research Institute, Stanford University), October 1941.

19. Davies, David, *The Case of Labourers in Husbandry, stated and considered in three parts, with an Appendix containing a Collection of Accounts, showing the earnings and Expenses of Labouring Families, in Different Parts of the Kingdom*, Dublin, 1796.

20. Gandhi, M. K., *The Story of My Experiment with Truth*, Navajavan Press, Ahmadabad, 1927.

21. Herodotus, *History* (Everyman's Library), E. P. Dutton and Company, New York, and J. M. Dent and Sons, London, 1936.

22. Kellog, Lester S., and Brady, Dorothy S., *The City Worker's Family Budget* (Originally appeared in *Monthly Labor Review*, February 1948; reprinted in **16**).

23. Malthus, Thomas Robert, *An Essay on the Principle of Population or a View of Its Past and Present Effects on Human Happiness*, new edition, London, 1803.

24. Osborn, Fairfield, *Our Plundered Planet*, Little, Brown and Company, Boston, 1948.

25. Raushenbush, Stephen, *People, Food, Machines* (Bold New Program Series, No. 5), Public Affairs Institute, Washington, 1950.

26. Vogt, William, *Road to Survival*, William Sloan Associates, New York, 1948.

27. Woytinsky, Wl. (W. S.), *Die Welt in Zahlen*, Vol. II: *Die Arbeit*, Rudolf Mosse, Berlin, 1926.

28. Woytinsky, W. S., *Earnings and Social Security in the United States*, Committee on Social Security, Social Science Research Council, Washington, 1943.

CHAPTER 10

NATURAL RESOURCES

1. League of Nations, *World Production and Prices, 1938–39*, Geneva, 1939.

2. United Nations, *Proceedings of the United Nations Scientific Conference on the Conservation and Utilization of Resources, 1949*, New York, 1950:
    a. Clapp, Gordon R., "The Experience of the Tennessee Valley Authority in the Comprehensive Development of a River Basin," in Vol. I, *Plenary Meetings*.
    b. Levorsen, A. I., "Estimates of Undiscovered Petroleum Reserves," in Vol. I.
    c. Shelton, Barrett, "The Decatur Story," in Vol. I.
    d. Woodward, F. N., "Creatable Resources: The Development of New Resources by Applied Technology," in Vol. I.

    e. Miller, H. J., "The Supply and Industrial Application of Scrap Volumes," in Vol. II, *Mineral Resources*.
    f. Pehrson, Elmer W., "Tables to Accompany Discussion of Estimates of Selected World Mineral Supplies by Cost Range," in Vol. II.
    g. Raver, P. J., "Power for Industrial and Agricultural Development," in Vol. III, *Fuel and Energy Resources*.

3. United Nations, Food and Agriculture Organization (FAO), *Forestry and Forest Products: World Situation, 1937–1946*, Stockholm, 1946.

4. ——, ——, *Soil Conservation, an International Survey*, Washington, 1948.

5. ——, ——, *Yearbook of Forest Products Statistics*, Washington.

6. ——, ——, *Unasylva* (a journal published by the Division of Forestry and Forest Products of the FAO), Washington.

7. International Institute of Agriculture, *Agricultural Commodities and Raw Materials*, Rome, 1944.

UNITED STATES

8. Department of Agriculture, Soil Conservation Service and Forest Service, *Headwaters Control and Use*, 1937.

9. Department of Commerce, Bureau of the Census, *Reports of Census of Mineral Industries, 1939*, 1943.

10. ——, ——, *Statistical Abstract of the United States*.

11. Geological Survey, *The Composition of the Earth's Crust*, by Frank Wigglesworth Clarke and Henry Stephen Washington (Professional Paper No. 127), 1924.

12. National Resources Planning Board, *Industrial Location and Natural Resources*, December 1942.

13. Tennessee Valley Authority, *Annual Report*.

14. ——, *Tennessee Valley Resources, Their Development and Use*, 1947 (mimeographed).

15. ——, *TVA, 1950*, 1950.

16. ——, *TVA Power, 1949*, 1949.

17. *A Water Policy for the American People*, Report of the President's Water Resources Policy Commission, 1950.

18. Agricola, Georgius, *De Re Metallica* (trans. from the first Latin edition of 1556 by Herbert Clark Hoover and Lou Henry Hoover), Dover Publications, New York, 1950.

19. American Iron and Steel Institute, *Steel Facts*, October 1951.

20. Baker, O. E., "Land Utilization in the United States," *Geographical Review*, January 1923.

21. Baudhuin, F., *Économique Agraire*, 4th edition, Institut de Récherches Économiques et Sociales, Louvain, 1945.

22. Leith, C. K., Furness, J. W., and Lewis, Cleona, *World Minerals and World Peace*, Brookings Institution, Washington, 1943.

23. Lippert, T. W., "Cerro Bolivar, Saga of an Iron Ore Crisis Averted," *Journal of Metals*, February 1950 and *Mining Engineering*, February 1950.

24. Osborn, Fairfield, *Our Plundered Planet*, Little, Brown and Company, Boston, 1948.
25. Pearson, Frank, and Harper, Floyd A., *The World's Hunger*, Cornell University Press, Ithaca, 1945.
26. Plato, *Works* (B. Jowett, Trans.), Tudor Publishing Company, New York, 1937.
27. Raushenbush, Stephen, *People, Food, Machines* (Bold New Program Series, No. 5), Public Affairs Institute, Washington, 1950.
28. Renner, George T., and Associates, *Global Geography*, Thomas Y. Crowell Company, New York, 1944.
29. Schurr, Sam H., and Marschak, Jacob, *Economic Aspects of Atomic Power* (Cowles Commission for Research in Economics), Princeton University Press, Princeton, 1950.
30. Terrall, Rufus, *The Missouri Valley, Land of Drought, Flood and Promise*, Yale University Press, New Haven, 1947.
31. Toynbee, Arnold J., *A Study of History* (abridgment of Volumes I-VI by D. C. Somervell), Oxford University Press, New York and London, 1947.
32. Vogt, William, *Road to Survival*, William Sloane Associates, New York, 1948.
33. Watts, Lyle F., "Timber Shortage or Timber Abundance in the USA," *Unasylva*, July–August 1947.

CHAPTER 11

HUMAN RESOURCES

1. League of Nations, *World Production and Prices, 1938–39*, Geneva, 1939.
2. United Nations, *Demographic Yearbook*, New York.
3. ———, *Statistical Yearbook*, New York.
4. ———, *National Income Statistics of Various Countries, 1938–1948*, New York, 1950.
5. ———, *World Economic Report, 1948*, New York, 1949.
6. ———, *Proceedings of the United Nations Scientific Conference on the Conservation and Utilization of Resources*, Vol. I, *Plenary Meetings*, New York, 1950.
7. International Labor Office, *Yearbook of Labour Statistics*, Geneva.
8. ———, *International Labour Review*.

UNITED STATES

9. Department of Commerce, Bureau of the Census, *Sixteenth Census of the United States (1940), Population*, Vols. I-V, 1943.
10. ———, ———, *Population, Comparative Occupation Statistics for the United States, 1870 to 1940*, 1943.
11. ———, ———, *Statistical Abstract of the United States*.
12. ———, ———, *Historical Statistics of the United States, 1789–1945*, 1949.
13. ———, ———, *Current Population Reports, Labor Force*, Series P-57.
14. ———, Bureau of Foreign and Domestic Commerce, *Survey of Current Business*.

15. GERMANY. Statistisches Reichsamt, *Statistisches Jahrbuch für das Deutsche Reich*, Berlin.

16. SWEDEN. Central Bureau of Statistics, *Statistisk Årsbok för Sverige*, Stockholm.

17. Clark, Colin, *National Income and Outlays*, Macmillan Company, London, 1937.
18. ———, *The Conditions of Economic Progress* (1st ed., 1940; 2d ed., 1951), St. Martin's Press, New York; Macmillan Company, London.
19. Daric, Jean, *L'Activité Professionelle des Femmes en France* (Institut National d'Études Démographique, Travaux et Documents, Cahier No. 5), Presses Universitaires de France, Paris, 1947.
20. ———, *Vieillessement de la Population et Prolongation de la Vie Active* (Institut National d'Études Démographiques, Travaux et Documents, Cahier No. 7), Presses Universitaires de France, Paris, 1948.
21. Dewhurst, J. Frederic, and Associates, *America's Needs and Resources*, Twentieth Century Fund, New York, 1947.
22. Dublin, Louis I., and Lotka, Alfred J., *The Money Value of a Man*, revised edition, Ronald Press, New York, 1946.
23. Dugé de Bernonville, L., "Les Révénues Privés," *Revue d'Economie Politique*, May–June 1937; "Les Révénues Privés et les Consommations," *Revue d'Economie Politique*, May–August 1939.
24. Durand, John D., *The Labor Force in the United States, 1890–1960*, Social Science Research Council, New York, 1948.
25. Gini, Corrado, "Apparent and Real Causes of American Prosperity," *Banca Nazionale del Lavoro Quarterly Review*, 1948.
26. Martin, Robert F., *National Income in the United States, 1799–1938*, National Industrial Conference Board, New York, 1939.
27. Petty, Sir William, *Political arithmetik, or A discourse concerning the . . . value of lands, people buildings. . . . As the same relates to every country in general, but more particularly to the territories of His Majesty of Great Britain, and his neighbours of Holland, Zealand and France*, published by R. Cavel, London, 1691.
28. President's Research Committee on Social Trends, *Recent Social Trends in the United States*, McGraw-Hill Book Company, New York, 1933.
29. Simon, Raúl, *Determinacion de la Entrada Nacional de Chile*, Imprenta Nascimentó, Santiago, 1935.
30. Woytinsky, Wl. (W. S.), *Die Welt in Zahlen*, Vol. II: *Die Arbeit*, Rudolf Mosse, Berlin, 1926.
31. ———, "Hours of Labor," *Encyclopaedia of the Social Sciences*, Vol. VII, Macmillan Company, New York, 1935.
32. Woytinsky, W. S., and Associates, *Employment and Wages in the United States*, Twentieth Century Fund, New York, 1953.

CHAPTER 12

ABUNDANCE AND SCARCITY

1. United Nations, *Statistical Yearbook*, New York.
2. ———, *Demographic Yearbook*, New York.
3. ———, *Measurement of National Income and the Construction of Social Accounts*, Report of Sub-Committee on National Income Statistics of the

League of Nations Committee of Statistical Experts, Geneva, 1947.

4. ———, *National and Per Capita Incomes, Seventy Countries — 1949,* New York, October 1950.

5. ———, *National Income Statistics of Various Countries, 1938–1947,* New York, 1948.

6. ———, *National Income Statistics of Various Countries, 1938–1948,* New York, 1950.

7. ———, *National Income Statistics and Its Distribution in Underdeveloped Countries,* New York, 1951.

UNITED STATES

8. Eighty-first Congress, Second Session, *Act to Provide Foreign Economic Assistance* (Point 4 Program), 1950.

9. The President, *The Economic Report of the President to the Congress.*

10. Department of Commerce, Bureau of the Census, *Historical Statistics of the United States, 1789–1945,* 1949.

11. ———, Bureau of Foreign and Domestic Commerce, *National Income,* 1951 Edition, Supplement to *Survey of Current Business.*

12. ———, ———, *Survey of Current Business.*

13. National Resources Committee, *Consumer Incomes in the United States: Their Distribution in 1935–36,* August 1938.

14. AUSTRALIA. Census and Statistics Bureau, *Official Yearbook,* Melbourne.

CANADA

15. Statistics Bureau, *National Accounts — Income and Expenditures, 1938–1945,* Ottawa, 1946.

16. ———, *National Income of Canada,* Ottawa, 1941.

GERMANY

17. Statistisches Reichsamt, *Wirtschaft und Statistik,* Berlin, 1939.

18. ———, *Das Deutsche Volkseinkommen vor und nach dem Kriege,* Berlin, 1932.

GREAT BRITAIN

19. Central Statistical Office, *Annual Abstract of Statistics, 1938–1948,* London, 1949.

20. ———, *National Income and Expenditure of the United Kingdom, 1946 to 1948,* London, 1949.

21. NEW ZEALAND. Census and Statistics Office, *New Zealand Official Year Book,* Wellington.

22. Bowley, Arthur L., *Wages and Income in the United Kingdom since 1860,* Cambridge University Press, Cambridge, 1937.

23. Brochier, Hubert, *Finances Publiques et Redistribution des Revenus* (Cahiers de la Fondation Nationale des Sciences Politiques, No. 15), Libraire Armand Colin, Paris, 1950.

24. Clark, Colin, *The Conditions of Economic Progress* (1st ed., 1940; 2d ed., 1951), St. Martin's Press, New York; Macmillan Company, London.

25. ———, *National Income and Outlay,* Macmillan Company, London, 1937.

26. Copeland, Morris A., Jacobson, Jerome, and Clyman, Bernard, "Problems of International Comparisons of Income and Product," in *Studies in Income and Wealth,* Vol. X, National Bureau of Economic Research, New York, 1947.

27. Derksen, J. B. D., "Measurement of National Income and Related Aggregates" (paper presented to the first Conference of the International Association for Research in Income and Wealth, September 1949), in *Income and Wealth* (Series 1), Editor, Erik Lundberg, Bowes and Bowes, Cambridge, 1951.

28. Gini, Corrado, "National Income Estimates," reprint from Nos. 3, 4 of *Review of the International Statistical Institute,* 1949.

29. King, Willford I., and Huntley, K. E., *National Income and Its Purchasing Power,* National Bureau of Economic Research, New York, 1930.

30. Klarman, Herbert E., "A Statistical Study of Income Differences among Communities," in *Studies in Income and Wealth,* Vol. VI, National Bureau of Economic Research, New York, 1943.

31. Kuznets, Simon, *Long Term Changes in the National Product of the United States* (paper presented to the second Conference of the International Association for Research in Income and Wealth held in Royaumont, France, August 25–September 1, 1951).

32. ———, "National Income and Industrial Structure," in *Proceedings of the International Statistical Conference,* Vol. V, Calcutta, 1950.

33. ———, *National Product since 1869,* National Bureau of Economic Research, New York, 1946.

34. Lorenz, M. O., "Methods of Measuring the Concentration of Wealth," *Quarterly Publications of the American Statistical Association,* June 1905.

35. Martin, Robert F., *National Income in the United States, 1799–1938,* National Industrial Conference Board, New York, 1939.

36. Mendershausen, Horst, *Changes in Income Distribution during the Great Depression,* National Bureau of Economic Research, New York, 1946.

37. Miller, Herman P., "Changes in Income Distribution in the United States," *Journal of the American Statistical Association,* December 1951.

38. Pareto, Vilfredo, *Cours d'Economie Politique,* Vol. II, F. Rouge, Lausanne, 1897.

39. Prest, A. R., "National Income in the United Kingdom, 1870–1946," *Economic Journal,* March 1948.

40. Schmoller, Gustav, "Die Einkommensverteilung in Alter und Neuer Zeit," *Jahrbuch für Gesetzgebung, Verwaltung und Volkswirtschaft im Deutschen Reich,* 4th Issue, 1895, Duncker and Humblot, Leipzig.

41. Staehle, Hans, "The International Comparison of Real National Income: a Note on Method," in *Studies in Income and Wealth,* Vol. XI, National Bureau of Economic Research, New York, 1949.

42. Studenski, Paul, and Wyler, Julius, *International Survey of National Income,* National Bureau of Economic Research, New York. (Unpublished study.)

43. Tucker, Rufus S., "Distribution of Tax Burden in 1948," *National Tax Journal,* September 1951.

44. Wisniewski, Jan, *Rozklad Dochodow Wedlug Wisokosci,* Institute of Economic Research, Warsaw, 1939.

45. Woytinsky, Wl. (W. S.), *Die Welt in Zahlen,* Vol. I: *Die Erde—Die Bevölkerung—Der Volksreichtum,* Rudolf Mosse, Berlin, 1925.

46. Woytinsky, W. S., *Earnings and Social Security in the United States,* Committee on Social Security, Social Science Research Council, Washington, 1943.

CHAPTER 13

ECONOMIC PATTERNS

1. League of Nations, *Industrialization and Foreign Trade,* Geneva, 1945.

2. United Nations, *Demographic Yearbook,* New York.

3. ———, *Statistical Yearbook,* New York.

4. ———, *National Income Statistics of Various Countries,* New York.

5. ———, *National Income Statistics, Supplement 1938–1950,* New York, 1951.

6. ———, *National and Per Capita Incomes, Seventy Countries — 1949,* New York, October 1950.

7. ———, *Population and Vital Statistics Reports,* New York.

8. ———, *Statistics of National Income and Expenditure,* New York, 1952.

9. International Labor Office, *Year Book of Labour Statistics,* Montreal.

UNITED STATES

10. Eighty-first Congress, Second Session, *Act to Provide Foreign Economic Assistance* (Point 4 Program), 1950.

11. Department of Agriculture, *Foreign Agriculture.*

12. Department of Commerce, Bureau of the Census, Sixteenth Census of the United States (1940), *Population,* Vols. I-V, 1943.

13. ———, ———, *Historical Statistics of the United States, 1789–1945,* 1949.

14. ———, Bureau of Foreign and Domestic Commerce, *National Income and Product of the United States, 1929–1950,* 1951.

15. ———, ———, *Survey of Current Business.*

16. Department of the Interior, Bureau of Mines, Releases and memoranda.

17. Ayres, Clarence E., *The Theory of Economic Progress,* University of North Carolina Press, Chapel Hill, 1944.

18. Bean, Louis H., "International Industrialization and Per Capita Income," in *Studies in Income and Wealth,* Vol. VIII, National Bureau of Economic Research, New York, 1946.

19. Bücher, Carl, *Industrial Evolution* (trans. from 3d. German ed.), Henry Holt and Company, New York, 1901.

20. Clark, Colin, *The Conditions of Economic Progress* (1st ed., 1940; 2d ed., 1951), St. Martin's Press, New York; Macmillan Company, London.

21. Deane, Phyllis, *The Measurement of Colonial National Incomes* (National Institute of Economic and Social Research, Occasional Papers, No. 12), Cambridge University Press, London, 1948.

22, Gini, Corrado, *La Popolázione Mondiale, il suo Sviluppo, il suo Sistema di Redditi e di Consumi,* Cedam-Casa Editrice Dott. A. Milani, Padua, 1951.

23. Hahn, Eduard, *Die Entstehung der Pflugkultur (unseres Ackerbaus),* Carl Winter's Universitätsbuchhandlung, Heidelberg, 1909.

24. ———, *Die Haustiere und ihre Beziehungen zur Wirtschaft des Menschen,* Duncker and Humblot, Leipzig, 1896.

25. Hildebrand, Bruno, *Die Nationalökonomie der Gegenwart und Zukunst und Andere Gesammelte Schriften,* Vol. I, Gustav Fischer, Jena, 1922.

26. Hoffmann, Walther, *Stadien und Typen der Industrialisierung,* Gustav Fischer, Jena, 1931.

27. List, Friedrich, *Das Nationale System der Politischen Ökonomie,* 1844 (reprinted in Vol. VI of *Friedrich List Schriften, Reden, Briefe,* Reimar Hobbing, Berlin, 1930).

28. Liu, Ta-chung, *China's National Income, 1931–1936, An Exploratory Study,* The Brookings Institution, Washington, 1946.

29. Martin, Robert F., *National Income and Its Elements,* National Industrial Conference Board, New York, 1930.

30. National Bureau of Economic Research (Universities-National Bureau Committee on Economic Research), *Problems in the Study of Economic Growth,* New York, July 1949 (mimeographed).

31. Raisz, Erwin J., *Atlas of Global Geography,* Global Press, New York, 1944.

32. Rostás, L., *Comparative Productivity in British and American Industry,* Cambridge University Press, London, 1948.

33. Schumpeter, Joseph, *Theorie der Wirtschaftlichen Entwicklung,* Duncker and Humblot, Leipzig, 1912.

34. Sombart, Werner, *Der Moderne Kapitalismus,* Duncker and Humblot, Leipzig, 1902.

35. ———, *The Quintessence of Capitalism, a Study of the History and Psychology of the Modern Business Man,* T. Fischer Unwin, London, 1915.

36. Studenski, Paul, and Wyler, Julius, *International Survey of National Income,* National Bureau of Economic Research, New York. (Unpublished study.)

37. Wagemann, Ernest F., *Economic Rhythm, a Theory of Business Cycles* (trans. from the German by D. H. Blelloch), McGraw-Hill Book Company, New York, 1930.

38. Whittlesey, Derwent S., "Major Agricultural Regions of the Earth," *Annals of the Association of American Geographers,* December 1936.

PART III. AGRICULTURE

CHAPTER 14

AGRICULTURE IN THE WORLD ECONOMY

1. League of Nations, *Industrialization and Foreign Trade*, Geneva, 1945.
2. ———, *World Production and Prices, 1938–39*, Geneva, 1939.
3. United Nations, *Statistical Yearbook*, New York.
4. ———, *National Income Statistics*, New York.
5. ———, Food and Agriculture Organization (FAO), *Yearbook of Food and Agricultural Statistics*, Washington.
6. ———, ———, *Monthly Bulletin of Food and Agricultural Statistics*, Washington.
7. International Labor Office, *Yearbook of Labour Statistics*, Geneva.
8. International Institute of Agriculture, *Agricultural Commodities and Raw Materials*, Rome, 1944.

UNITED STATES

9. Department of Agriculture, *Yearbook of Agriculture*.
10. Department of Commerce, Bureau of the Census, *Sixteenth Census of the United States (1940), Population*, Vol. II, Part 1, 1943.
11. ———, ———, *Statistical Abstract of the United States*.
12. ———, ———, *Sixteenth Census of the United States (1940), Population, Comparative Occupation Statistics for the United States, 1870 to 1940*, 1943.
13. ———, Bureau of Foreign and Domestic Commerce, *Survey of Current Business*.
14. Tariff Commission, *Agricultural, Pastoral and Forest Industries in Brazil*, 1946.

15. DENMARK. *Report from the Danish National FAO Committee to the Food and Agriculture Organization of the United Nations*, Copenhagen, 1949.

16. Baudhuin, Fernand, *Économique Agraire*, 4th edition, Institut de Recherches Économiques et Sociales, Louvain, 1945.
17. Chuprov, A. Y., *Melkoe Zemledelie i ego Osnovnye Nuzhdy*, Slovo, Berlin, 1921.
18. Cohen, Ruth L., *The Economics of Agriculture* (Cambridge Economic Handbooks), James Nisbet and Company, London, 1940.
19. Corey, Lewis, *Meat and Man: a study of Monopoly, Unionism and Food Policy*, Viking Press, New York, 1950.
20. Kautsky, Karl, *Die Agrarfrage*, J. H. W. Dietz Nachf., Stuttgart, 1899.
21. Moore, Wilbert E., *Economic Demography of Eastern and Southern Europe*, League of Nations, Geneva, 1945.
22. Royal Institute of International Affairs, *World Agriculture*, Oxford University Press, London, 1932.
23. Whittlesey, Derwent, "Major Agricultural Regions of the Earth," *Annals of the Association of American Geographers*, December 1936.
24. Wythe, George, Wight, Royce A., and Midkiff, Harold M., *Brazil: an Expanding Economy*, Twentieth Century Fund, New York, 1949.
25. Yates, Paul L., *Commodity Control: a Study of Primary Products*, Jonathan Cape, London, 1943.

CHAPTER 15

LAND, FARMS AND FARMING

1. United Nations, *Economic Report: Salient Features of the World Economic Situation, 1945–47*, New York, 1948.
2. ———, *Land Reform, Defects in Agrarian Structure as Obstacles to Economic Development*, New York, 1951.
3. ———, *Proceedings of the United Nations Scientific Conference on the Conservation and Utilization of Resources, 1949*, Vol. I, *Plenary Meetings*, New York, 1950.
4. ———, *Review of Economic Conditions in the Middle East*, New York, 1951.
5. ———, Conciliation Commission for Palestine, *Final Report of the United Nations Economic Survey Mission for the Middle East*, New York, 1949.
6. ———, Economic Commission for Asia and the Far East, *Economic Survey of Asia and the Far East*, New York.
7. ———, Economic Commission for Europe, *The European Tractor Industry in the Setting of the World Market*, Geneva, 1952.
8. ———, ———, *Possibilities of Increasing Production and Trade in Fertilizers, Tractors and Farm Machinery*, Geneva, 1949.
9. ———, ———, (E/ECE. SR. 5/16), Geneva, June 30, 1950.
10. ———, Food and Agriculture Organization (FAO), *Agriculture in Latin America, Its Development and Outlook*, Washington, 1951.
11. ———, ———, *Fertilizer* (Commodity Reports), Washington, 1950.
12. ———, ———, *Fertilizers* (Commodity Series, No. 17), Washington, 1949.
13. ———, ———, *Progress and Economic Problems in Farm Mechanization*, Washington, 1950.
14. ———, ———, *Report of the FAO Mission for Poland*, Washington, 1948.
15. ———, ———, *Rice Bulletin* (Commodity Series, No. 11), Washington, 1949.
16. ———, ———, *Soil Conservation: an International Survey*, Washington, 1948.
17. ———, ———, *Storing and Drying Grain in Canada, the United States and the United Kingdom*, Washington, 1948.
18. ———, ———, *World Food Survey*, Washington, 1946.
19. ———, ———, *Yearbook of Food and Agricultural Statistics*, Washington.
20. ———, ———, *Monthly Bulletin of Food and Agricultural Statistics*, Washington.
21. Inter-American Development Commission, *Agricultural Resources of Mexico*, Washington, 1946.

22. International Institute of Agriculture, *Documentation for the European Conference on Rural Life, 1939*, Rome, 1939.

23. ——, *The First World Agricultural Census* (5 volumes), Rome, 1939.

24. ——, *The First World Agricultural Census; Bulletins: Chile* (No. 3); *Australia* (No. 6), Rome, 1932–36.

UNITED STATES

25. Eightieth Congress, Second Session, Committee on Agriculture of the House of Representatives, *Long-Range Agricultural Policy, a Study of Selected Trends and Factors Relating to the Long-Range Prospect for American Agriculture*, 1948.

26. Department of Agriculture, *Agricultural Geography of Europe and the Near East* (Miscellaneous Publication No. 665), 1948.

27. ——, *Agricultural Outlook Charts, 1950*, 1951.

28. ——, *The Agricultural Situation*.

29. ——, *Agricultural Statistics*.

30. ——, *The Agriculture of Burma*, 1950.

31. ——, *The Agriculture of French Indo-China*, 1950.

32. ——, *Foreign Agriculture*.

33. ——, *Our Food Potential*, 1944.

34. ——, *Prewar World Production and Consumption of Plant Foods in Fertilizers* (Miscellaneous Publication No. 593), 1946.

35. ——, *Report of the Administrator of the Rural Electrification Administration*.

36. ——, *Report of the Chief of the Soil Conservation Service*.

37. ——, *Report of the China-United States Agricultural Mission* (Report No. 2), 1947.

38. ——, *Soil Conservation*.

39. ——, *Teamwork in World Agriculture*, 1950.

40. ——, *Technology on the Farm*, (Special Report), 1940.

41. ——, *Yearbook of Agriculture*.

42. Department of Commerce, Bureau of the Census, *Fifteenth Census of the United States* (1930), *Drainage of Agricultural Lands*, 1932.

43. ——, ——, *Sixteenth Census of the United States* (1940), *Irrigation of Agricultural Land*, 1942.

44. ——, ——, *Census of Agriculture 1945*, Special Report, *Farms and Farm Characteristics by Type of Farm*, 1948.

45. ——, ——, *Statistical Abstract of the United States*.

46. Department of Labor, *Productivity in Agriculture*, 1948.

47. Department of the Interior, *National Resources and Foreign Aid*, Report by J. A. Krug, 1947.

48. Economic Cooperation Administration, *Report of the ECA Mission to the United Kingdom*, London, 1948.

49. ——, Technical Assistance Commission, *The Integration of Refugees into German Life*, Bonn, 1951.

50. Federal Trade Commission, *Report on Agricultural Implements and Machinery*, 1938.

51. National Resources Committee, *Technological Trends and National Policy*, 1937.

52. Tariff Commission, *Agricultural, Pastoral and Forest Industries in Chile*, 1945.

53. ——, *Agricultural, Pastoral and Forest Industries in Mexico*, 1948.

54. *Annual Report of the Government of the United States to FAO*, 1948.

55. *European Recovery and American Aid*, A Report by the President's Committee on Foreign Aid, 1947.

56. *Farm Tenancy*, Report of the President's Committee, 1937.

57. *A Water Policy for the American People*, Report of the President's Water Resources Policy Commission, 1950.

58. AUSTRALIA. Census and Statistics Bureau, *Official Yearbook*, Melbourne.

CANADA

59. Department of Agriculture, *Agriculture Abroad*, Ottawa.

60. Dominion Bureau of Statistics, *The Canada Year Book*, Ottawa.

CHINA

61. National Government, Directorate General of Budgets, Accounts and Statistics, *Statistical Abstract of the Republic of China*, Nanking, 1947.

62. ——, National Agricultural Research Bureau, *Crop Reports* (No. 12), Nanking, December 15, 1936.

63. DENMARK. *Memorandum on the Aims of the Danish Agricultural Organizations in the Development of Danish Agriculture up to 1952–53*, Copenhagen, 1950.

FRANCE

64. Comité Interministériel de l'Alimentation et de l'Agriculture, Sous-Comité de la Conservation des Sols, *La Conservation du Sol, Le Problème Français*, Paris, 1950.

65. Présidence du Conseil, *État des Operations du Plan de Modernisation et d'Équipment, France Métropolitaine*, Paris, 1949.

66. GERMANY. Statistisches Amt des Vereinigten Wirtschaftsgebietes, *Statistische Berichte*, Wiesbaden-Biebrich.

67. GREAT BRITAIN. *National Farm Survey of England and Wales, 1941–43*, A Summary Report, London, 1946.

68. GREECE. Statistikon Grapheion, *Annuaire Statistique de la Grèce*, Athens.

INDIA

69. Commercial Intelligence and Statistics Department, *Statistical Abstract for British India*, Calcutta.

70. National Planning Committee, *Soil Conservation and Afforestation*, Bombay, 1948.

71. ITALY. Central Statistical Office, *Annuario Statistico Italiano*, Rome.

72. JAPAN. Ministry of Agriculture and Forestry, *Statistical Abstract, 1935–36,* Tokyo.

73. THE NETHERLANDS. Ministry of Agriculture, Fisheries and Foods, *Dutch Agriculture—Facts,* The Hague, 1947.

74. SWITZERLAND. Eidgenoessisches Statistiches Amt, *Statistisches Jahrbuch der Schweiz,* Bern.

USSR

75. *Electrifica Selskogo Khosîâstva Zaporozhtsîâ,* Moscow, 1939.

76. Ministry of Agriculture, *Sotsialisticheskoe Zemldelie,* Moscow.

77. *Opyt Raboty, MTS* (Working Experiences of the Motor-Tractor Stations), Selchosguiz, Moscow.

78. POLAND. Central Statistical Office, *Statistical Year Book of Poland,* Warsaw.

---

79. Abbott, J. C., "The Regrouping of Holdings in France," *The Farm Economist,* April 1949.

80. Ahlgren, Gilbert H., Klingman, Glenn C., and Wolf, Dale E., *Principles of Weed Control,* John Wiley and Sons, New York, 1951.

81. Ayres, Quincy Claude, and Scoates, Daniels, *Land Drainage and Reclamation,* McGraw-Hill Book Company, New York, 1939.

82. Azevedo, P., "Agriculture and the Civil Code," *Food and Agriculture, International Law Journal* (FAO), January–June 1947.

83. Balzac, S. S., Vasyutin, V. F., and Feigin, Y. G., *Economic Geography of the USSR* (Translated from the Russian by the American Council of Learned Societies), Macmillan Company, New York, 1949.

84. Baudhuin, Fernand, *Économique Agraire,* 4th edition, Institut de Recherches Économiques et Sociales, Louvain, 1945.

85. Bennett, Hugh Hammond, *Soil Conservation,* McGraw-Hill Book Company, New York, 1939.

86. ———, "Development of National Resources," *Science,* January 3, 1947.

87. Bittard, D. W., "Settlement Possibilities of Canada," *Journal of Farm Economics,* May 1945.

88. Bonadonna, T., "Artificial Insemination of Animals," *Food and Agriculture, International Law Journal* (FAO), August–September 1947.

89. Bowman, Isaiah, *The Pioneer Fringe* (Special Publication No. 13), American Geographical Society, New York, 1931.

90. Brandt, Karl, *The Reconstruction of World Agriculture,* Norton and Company, New York, 1945.

91. Brasse-Brossard, Lucien, *Le Bétail,* 2d edition, La Maison Rustique, Paris, 1947.

92. Buck, John Lossing, *Land Utilization in China,* University of Chicago Press, Chicago, 1937.

93. Ciaska, Raffaele, *"Rievocazioni in Tema di Bonifiche nel Mezzogiorno," L'Agricoltura Italiana,* June 15, 1950.

94. Cohen, Ruth L., *The Economics of Agriculture* (Cambridge Economic Handbooks), James Nisbet and Company, London, 1940.

95. Cooper, Martin B., and Associates, *Progress of Farm Mechanization* (Miscellaneous Publication No. 630), U. S. Department of Agriculture, 1947.

96. Cumberland, K. B., *Soil Erosion in New Zealand; a Geographic Reconnaisance,* 2d edition, Whitcombe and Tombs, Christchurch, New Zealand, 1947.

97. Demolon, Albert, *Dynamique du Sol, Principes d'Agronomie,* 4th edition, Vol. I, Dunod, Paris, 1948.

98. Ely, R. T., and Wehrwein, G. S., *Land Economics,* Macmillan Company, New York, 1940.

99. *Family Farm Policy* (edited by Joseph Ackerman and Marshall Harris), Proceedings of a Conference on Family Farm Policy, February 1946, University of Chicago Press, Chicago, 1947.

100. Gorrie, R. Maclagen, *Soil and Water Conservation in the Punjab,* Simla, India, 1948.

101. Gras, N. S. B., *A History of Agriculture in Europe and America,* 2d edition, F. S. Crofts and Company, New York, 1940.

102. Hainsworth, Reginald G., *A Graphic Summary of World Agriculture* (Miscellaneous Publication No. 705), U. S. Department of Agriculture, 1949.

103. ———, and Moyer, Raymond T., *Agricultural Geography of the Philippine Islands,* U. S. Department of Agriculture, 1945.

104. Hall, Sir Alfred D., *Fertilizers and Manure,* 4th edition, John Murray, London, 1947.

105. Hecht, Reuben W., and Barton, Glen T., *Gains in Productivity of Farm Labor,* U. S. Department of Agriculture, 1950.

106. Hertz, Friedrich O., *The Economic Problem of the Danubian States,* Gollancz, London, 1947.

107. Hollman, A. H., "Die Agrarreform in Rumanien," in *Berichte über Landwirtschaft* (New Series, No. 1), P. Parey, Berlin, 1923.

108. ———, "Agrarverfassung und Landwirtschaft Yugoslaviens," in *Berichte über Landwirtschaft* (New Series, No. 30), P. Parey, Berlin, 1931.

109. Hopkins, John A., *Changing Technology and Employment in Agriculture,* U. S. Department of Agriculture, 1941.

110. ———, *Mexican Farm Wages and Farm Labor Productivity,* U. S. Department of Agriculture, 1950.

111. Howard, Sir H., "India's Forest Organization," *Journal of Forestry,* August 1948.

112. Huntington, Ellsworth, and Associates, *Business Geography,* 2d edition, John Wiley and Sons, New York, 1926.

113. Jacks, G. V., and Whyte, R. O., *Vanishing Lands, a World Survey of Soil Erosion,* Doubleday, Doran and Company, New York, 1939.

114. Jasny, Naum, *The Socialized Agriculture of the USSR: Plans and Performance,* Stanford University Press, Stanford University, 1949.

115. Kellogg, Charles E., *Food, Soil and People, a Unesco Project,* Manhattan Publishing Company, New York, 1950.

116. Klatt, W., *Food and Farming in Germany,* Vol. 1, Weltwirtschaftliches Archiv, Kiel, 1950.

117. Kolesnev, Samuil G., *Organizatsia Sotsialisticheskich Sel'sko-Khozyaystvennykh Predprîâtiî* Selchsoguiz, Moscow, 1947.

118. Kramer, Matthias, "Die Landwirtschaft in der Sowjetischen Besatzungszone," *Bonner Berichte aus Mittel- und Ostdeutschland,* Bundesministerium für Gesamtdeutsche Fragen, Bonn, 1951.

119. Long, H. C., and Benchley, Winifred E., *Suppression of Weeds by Fertilizers and Chemicals,* 4th edition, Crosby, Lockwood and Son, London, 1950.

120. Moore, Wilbert E., *Economic Demography of Eastern and Southern Europe,* League of Nations, Geneva, 1945.

121. *The Orient Yearbook, 1942,* Asia Statistics Co., Tokyo, 1942. (Republished by the Interdepartmental Committee for the Acquisition of Foreign Publications.)

122. Osborn, Fairfield, *Our Plundered Planet,* Little, Brown and Company, Boston, 1948.

123. Parkins, A. E., and Whitaker, J. R., *Our National Resources and Their Conservation,* John Wiley and Sons, New York, 1936.

124. Pearson, Frank A., and Paarlberg, Don, *Food,* Alfred A. Knopf, New York, 1944.

125. Pelzer, Karl J., *Population and Land Utilization* (An Economic Survey of the Pacific Area, Part I), Institute of Pacific Relations, New York, 1942.

126. Rama Rao, D. V., *Land Reforms,* Padmaja, Baroda, India, 1948.

127. Reithinger, Anton, *Das Wirtschaftliche Gesicht Europas,* Deutsche Verlags-Anstalt, Stuttgart, 1936.

128. Roger, Sir Thomas, *Drainage and Reclamation of Irrigated Lands,* Karachi, Pakistan, 1949.

129. Royal Institute of International Affairs, *World Agriculture,* Oxford University Press, London, 1932.

130. Sakoff, A., "Recent Agrarian Reforms," *Food and Agriculture, International Law Journal* (FAO), January–June 1947.

131. Salter, Robert M., "World Soil and Fertilizer Resources in Relation to Food Needs," *Science,* September 1947.

132. Schubring, Walter, "Hauptergebnisse des Ersten Landwirtschaftlichen Welt Zensus," in *Berichte über Landwirtschaft* (New Series, No. 147), P. Parey, Berlin, 1939.

133. Sering, Max, *Die Agrarischen Umwalzungen im Ausserrussischen Osteuropa,* W. de Gruyter and Company, Berlin, 1930.

134. Stewart, Alexander B., *Report on Soil Fertility, Investigations in India with Special Reference to Manuring,* Army Press, Delhi, 1947.

135. Taylor, Henry C., *Outlines of Agricultural Economics,* revised edition, Macmillan Company, New York, 1949.

136. Thompson, Warren S., *Population Problems,* 3d edition, McGraw-Hill Book Company, New York, 1942.

137. Van der Post, A. P., *Economics of Agriculture,* Central News Agency, Johannesburg, South Africa, 1937.

138. Volin, Lazar, "Agricultural Development in USSR," in *USSR; a Concise Handbook,* E. J. Simmons (Ed.), Cornell University Press, Ithaca, 1947.

139. ———, *A Survey of Soviet Russian Agriculture,* U. S. Department of Agriculture, 1951.

140. Warriner, Doreen, *Land and Poverty in the Middle East,* Royal Institute of International Affairs, London, 1948.

141. Weir, Wilbert Walter, *Soil Science, Its Principles and Practice,* revised edition, J. B. Lippincott Company, Philadelphia, 1949.

142. Whetten, Nathan L., *Rural Mexico,* University of Chicago Press, Chicago, 1948.

143. Whitney, Milton, *Soil and Civilization,* D. Van Nostrand and Company, New York, 1925.

144. Wickizer, V. D., and Bennett, M. K., *The Rice Economy of Monsoon Asia,* Food Research Institute, Stanford University Press, Stanford University, 1941.

145. Wilcox, W. W., *The Farmer in the Second World War,* Iowa State College Press, Ames, 1947.

146. *Wirtschaftsdienst,* Hamburg.

147. Woytinsky, Wl. (W. S.), *Die Welt in Zahlen,* Vol. III: *Die Landwirtschaft,* Rudolf Mosse, Berlin, 1926.

148. Wythe, George, Wight, Royce A., and Midkiff, Harold M., *Brazil: an Expanding Economy,* Twentieth Century Fund, New York, 1949.

149. Yates, Paul L., *Food Production in Western Europe,* Longman's Green and Company, New York, 1940.

150. ———, and Warriner, Doreen, *Food and Farming in Postwar Europe,* Oxford University Press, London and New York, 1943.

151. Yoder, Fred R., *Introduction to Agricultural Economics,* Thomas Y. Crowell Company, New York, 1938.

CHAPTER 16

FOOD CROPS

1. League of Nations, *World Economic Survey, 1942–44,* Geneva, 1945.

2. ———, *World Production and Prices, 1938–39,* Geneva, 1939.

3. United Nations, Food and Agriculture Organization (FAO), *Agriculture in Latin America, Its Development and Outlook,* Washington, 1951.

4. ———, ———, *The State of Food and Agriculture,* Washington.

5. ———, ———, Commodity Reports:
   a. *Rice,* December 1950.
   b. *Cocoa,* June 1950.
   c. *Sugar,* November 1950.

6. ———, ———, *Grain* (Commodity Series, No. 18), Washington, May 1950.

7. ———, ———, *Vegetables and Fruits Bulletin* (Commodity Series, No. 6), Washington, May 1948.

8. ———, ———, *Yearbook of Food and Agricultural Statistics,* Washington.

9. ———, ———, *Monthly Bulletin of Food and Agricultural Statistics,* Washington.

10. International Institute of Agriculture, *Agricultural Commodities and Raw Materials,* Rome, 1944.

11. ———, *Les Grands Produits Agricoles,* Rome, 1944.

12. ———, *International Yearbook of Agricultural Statistics,* Rome.

UNITED STATES

13. Department of Agriculture, *Agricultural Geography of Europe and the Near East* (Miscellaneous Publication No. 665), 1948.
14. ———, *Agricultural Outlook Charts.*
15. ———, *The Agricultural Situation.*
16. ———, *Agricultural Statistics.*
17. ———, *Crops and Markets,* 1950 edition.
18. ———, *Fats and Oils, World Production and Trade,* (Foreign Agricultural Report No. 11), August 1946.
19. ———, *Foreign Agricultural Circular.*
20. ———, *Foreign Agricultural Report* (No. 40), October 1949.
21. ———, *Foreign Agriculture.*
22. ———, *Foreign Crops and Markets.*
23. ———, *A Graphic Summary of Farm Crops* (No. 512), February 1943.
24. ———, *World Food Situation.*
25. ———, *Yearbook of Agriculture.*
26. Department of Commerce, Bureau of the Census, *Statistical Abstract of the United States.*
27. Tariff Commission, *Agricultural, Pastoral and Forest Industries in Brazil,* 1946.
28. ———, *Agricultural Products and Provisions* (Summaries of Tariff Information, Vol. VII, 6 Parts), 1948.

29. GREAT BRITAIN. Imperial Economic Committee, *Oils and Fats: Production and International Trade,* London, 1934.

---

30. Baker, O. E., "Land Utilization in the United States," *Geographical Review,* January 1923.
31. ———, "The Potential Supply of Wheat," *Economic Geography,* March 1925.
32. Balzac, S. S., Vasyutin, V. F., and Feigin, Y. G., *Economic Geography of the USSR* (Translated from the Russian by the American Council of Learned Societies), Macmillan Company, New York, 1949.
33. Bennett, M. K., "Wheat in National Diets," *Wheat Studies* (Food Research Institute, Stanford University), October 1941.
34. ———, and Farnsworth, H. C., "World Wheat Acreage, Yields and Climates," *Wheat Studies* (Food Research Institute, Stanford University), March 1937.
35. Crickman, C. W., *Feed Grains and Meat Animals in War and Peace,* U. S. Department of Agriculture, 1945.
36. Finch, V. C., and Baker, O. E., *Geography of the World's Agriculture,* U. S. Department of Agriculture, 1917.
37. Geerligs, H. C. Prinsen, Licht, F. O., and Milkush, Gustav, *Sugar,* Memoranda prepared for the Economic Committee of the League of Nations, World Peace Foundation, Boston, 1929.
38. Gericke, S., *Voraussetzungen und Möglichkeiten einer Ertragsteigerung im Deutschen Hackfruchtbau,* Limes, Wiesbaden, 1947.
39. Hansen, Peter L., *World Trends in Major Oil Crops,* U. S. Department of Agriculture, 1946.
40. Hunnicut, Benjamin H., *Brazil Looks Forward,* Instituto Brasileiro de Geografia e Estatistica, Rio de Janeiro, 1945.
41. *Indian Sugar Supplement,* Indian Sugar Syndicate, Kanpur, 1948.
42. Jasny, Naum, *Competition among Grains* (Grain Economics Series, No. 2), Food Research Institute, Stanford University, 1940.
43. Johnson, Sherman E., "Agricultural Production after the War," *Journal of Farm Economics,* May 1945.
44. Klages, Karl H. W., *Ecological Crop Geography,* Macmillan Company, New York, 1942.
45. Licht, F. O., *World Sugar Statistics,* F. O. Licht, Magdeburg, 1938–39.
46. Moyer, Raymond T., and Hainsworth, Reginald G., *Agricultural Geography of the Philippine Islands,* U. S. Department of Agriculture, 1945.
47. Purves, C. M., *Wartime Changes in World Food Production,* U. S. Department of Agriculture, 1944.
48. ———, "Major Shifts in World Agriculture," *Journal of Farm Economics,* May 1945.
49. Rogers, James E. T., *A History of Agriculture and Prices in England,* Vol. IV, Clarendon Press, Oxford, 1866.
50. Smith, Charles W., and Tucker, R. G., *World Citrus Production and Trade,* U. S. Department of Agriculture, 1945.
51. Stamp, L. Dudley, *Asia: a Regional and Economic Geography,* 3d edition, E. P. Dutton and Company, New York, 1936.
52. Stuart, William, *The Potato, Its Culture, Uses, History and Classification,* J. B. Lippincott, Philadephia, 1937.
53. Taylor, Henry C., *Outlines of Agricultural Economics,* revised edition, Macmillan Company, New York, 1949.
54. Varro, M. T., *Rerum Rusticarum* (L. Storr-Best, trans.), Macmillan Company, London, 1912.
55. Volin, Lazar, *A Survey of Soviet Russian Agriculture,* U. S. Department of Agriculture, 1951.
56. Wickizer, V. D., "Rice and Wheat in World Agriculture and Consumption," *Wheat Studies* (Food Research Institute, Stanford University), March 1941.
57. ———, and Bennett, M. K., *The Rice Economy of Monsoon Asia,* Food Research Institute, Stanford University Press, Stanford University, 1941.
58. Woytinsky, Wl. (W. S.), *Die Welt in Zahlen,* Vol. III: *Die Landwirtschaft,* Rudolf Mosse, Berlin, 1926.
59. Wylie, Kathrin H., *Production, Consumption and Price Trends of Coffee,* U. S. Department of Agriculture, December 1948.
60. Wythe, George, Wight, Royce A., and Midkiff, Harold M., *Brazil: an Expanding Economy,* Twentieth Century Fund, New York, 1949.
61. Yates, Paul L., *Commodity Control: a Study of Primary Products,* Jonathan Cape, London, 1943.

CHAPTER 17

TECHNICAL CROPS

1. League of Nations, *Statistical Year-Book,* Geneva.
2. ———, *The Network of World Trade,* Geneva, 1942.

3. ———, *World Production and Prices 1938–39,* Geneva, 1939.

4. United Nations, Economic Commission for Asia and the Far East, *Economic Survey of Asia and the Far East,* New York.

5. ———, Food and Agriculture Organization (FAO), *Fats and Oils* (Commodity Reports), Washington.

6. ———, ———, *Hard Fibers* (Commodity Reports), Washington, May 1950.

7. ———, ———, *Jute* (Commodity Reports), Washington, June 1950.

8. ———, ———, *Wool* (Commodity Reports), Washington, March 1950.

9. ———, ———, *The State of Food and Agriculture: Review and Outlook,* Rome, 1951.

10. ———, ———, *World Fiber Survey,* Washington.

11. ———, ———, *Yearbook of Food and Agricultural Statistics,* Washington.

12. ———, ———, *Monthly Bulletin of Food and Agricultural Statistics,* Washington.

13. International Institute of Agriculture, *Agricultural Commodities and Raw Materials,* Rome, 1944.

14. ———, *International Yearbook of Agricultural Statistics, 1941–42 to 1945–46,* 3 vols., Rome, 1947.

15. ———, *Sericulture in the World* (Studies of the Principal Agricultural Products on the World Market, No. 8), Rome, 1947.

UNITED STATES

16. Department of Agriculture, *Agricultural Statistics.*

17. ———, *Crops and Markets.*

18. ———, *Foreign Agriculture.*

19. ———, *Foreign Agriculture Circular.*

20. ———, *Foreign Crops and Markets.*

21. ———, *Report of the China-United States Agricultural Mission* (Report No. 2), 1947.

22. ———, *Yearbook of Agriculture.*

23. Tariff Commission, *Agricultural Products and Provisions* (Summaries of Tariff Information, Vol. VII, 6 Parts), 1948.

24. ———, *Burlap* (War Changes in Industry Series, Report No. 26), 1947.

25. ———, *Cotton Cloth* (War Changes in Industry Series, Report No. 27), 1947.

26. ———, *Raw Wool* (War Changes in Industry Series, Report No. 1), 1943.

27. ———, *Rubber* (War Changes in Industry Series, Report No. 6), 1945.

28. Statement of the United States Delegation to the Annual Meeting of the International Cotton Advisory Committee (a. Cairo, 1948; b. Brussels, April 1949; Washington, June 1949).

29. CANADA. Department of Agriculture, *Agriculture Abroad,* Ottawa.

GREAT BRITAIN

30. Imperial Economic Committee, *Industrial Fibres,* London, 1939.

31. ———, *Plantation Crops,* London, 1938.

32. ———, *World Consumption of Wool,* London, 1937.

33. Secretariat of the Rubber Study Group, *Rubber Statistical Bulletin,* London.

34. Bailey, A. E., *Cottonseed and Cottonseed Products; Their Chemistry and Chemical Technology,* Interscience Publishers, New York, 1948.

35. Bauer, P. T., *The Rubber Industry; a Study in Competition and Monopoly,* Harvard University Press, Cambridge, 1948.

36. Bobkov, P. K., *Proizvodstvo Kautchuka iz Kok-Sagyza,* State Scientific and Technical Printing Office, Moscow, 1948.

37. Carleton, M., *Wool, the Raw Material,* Boston Wool Trade Association, Boston, 1947.

38. *China Economist,* Shanghai.

39. Crane, Julian C., "Kenaf—Fiber Plant Rival of Jute," *Economic Botany,* September 1947.

40. *La Culture du Coton en Égypte,* Société d'Enterprises Commerciales en Égypte, Alexandria, 1950.

41. Dunn, Read P., Jr., *Cotton in Africa,* National Cotton Council of America, Memphis, 1950.

42. ———, *Cotton in British East Africa,* National Cotton Council of America, Memphis, 1949.

43. Faulkner, Harold U., *American Economic History,* 5th edition, Harper and Brothers, New York, 1943.

44. Fourteenth International Wool Conference, London, 1938.

45. Frazer, Allan, *Sheep Husbandry,* Crosby Lockwood and Son, London, 1951.

46. Herodotus, *History* (Everyman's Library), E. P. Dutton and Company, New York and J. M. Dent and Sons, London, 1936.

47. Hunnicutt, Benjamin H., *Brazil Looks Forward,* Instituto Brasileiro de Geografia e Estatistica, Rio de Janeiro, 1945.

48. Klages, Karl H. W., *Ecological Crop Geography,* Macmillan Company, New York, 1942.

49. Leroy, André Max, "Le Mouton: Races, Élevage, Viande, Laine," in *Encyclopédie des Connaissances Agricoles,* Hachette, Paris, 1948.

50. McFadyean, Sir Arthur (Editor), *The History of Rubber Regulation, 1934–1943,* International Rubber Regulation Committee, W. W. Norton and Company, New York, and George Allen and Unwin, London, 1944.

51. Malott, Deane W. and Martin, Boyce F., *The Agricultural Industries,* McGraw-Hill Book Company, New York, 1939.

52. Martin, F., *Principes d'Agriculture et d'Économie Rurale Appliqués aux Pays Tropicaux,* Imprimerie des Orphelins–Apprentis d'Auteuil, Paris, 1935.

53. Polo, Marco, *Travels,* Modern Library, New York, 1931.

54. Rice, Victor Arthur, and Andrews, Frederick Newcomb, *Breeding and Improvement of Farm Animals,* 4th edition, McGraw-Hill Book Company, New York, 1951.

55. Stamp, L. Dudley, *Asia: a Regional and Economic Geography,* 3d edition, E. P. Dutton and Company, New York, 1936.

56. Tilley, Nannie May, *The Bright-Tobacco Industry, 1860–1929,* University of North Carolina Press, Chapel Hill, 1948.

57. Volin, Lazar, *A Survey of Soviet Russian Agriculture,* U. S. Department of Agriculture, 1951.

58. Wythe, George, Wight, Royce A., and Midkiff, Harold M., *Brazil: an Expanding Economy,* Twentieth Century Fund, New York, 1949.

CHAPTER 18

LIVESTOCK AND ANIMAL PRODUCTS

1. League of Nations, *Statistical Year-Book*, Geneva.
2. United Nations, Food and Agriculture Organization (FAO), *Animal Feedstuffs* (Commodity Series, No. 15), 1949.
3. ——, ——, *Dairy Products* (Commodity Series, No. 4), 1948.
4. ——, ——, *Dairy Products* (Commodity Series, No. 16), 1949.
5. ——, ——, *Meat and Livestock* (Commodity Reports), December 1950.
6. ——, ——, *Poultry and Eggs* (Commodity Reports), September 1950.
7. ——, ——, *Yearbook of Food and Agricultural Statistics*, Washington.
8. ——, ——, *Monthly Bulletin of Food and Agricultural Statistics*.
9. International Institute of Agriculture, *Agricultural Commodities and Raw Materials*, Rome, 1944.
10. ——, *L'Agriculture dans le Monde*, Rome, 1933.
11. ——, *Les Grands Produits Agricoles*, Rome, 1944.
12. ——, *International Yearbook of Agricultural Statistics*, Rome.
13. ——, *World Meat Production*, Rome, 1938.

UNITED STATES

14. Department of Agriculture, *Agricultural Geography of Europe and the Near East* (Miscellaneous Publication No. 665), 1948.
15. ——, *The Agricultural Situation*.
16. ——, *Agricultural Statistics*.
17. ——, *Crops and Markets*.
18. ——, *Changes in the Dairy Industry of the United States, 1920–1950*, 1950.
19. ——, *Foreign Agriculture Circulars*.
20. ——, *Foreign Agricultural Outlook, 1952*, October 1951.
21. ——, *Foreign Agriculture*.
22. ——, *Foreign Crops and Markets*.
23. ——, *Our Food Potential*, 1944.
24. ——, *Yearbook of Agriculture*.
25. Department of Commerce, Bureau of the Census, *1945 Sample Census of Agriculture*, Special Report, 1947.
26. ——, ——, *Statistical Abstract of the United States*.
27. ——, ——, *Land Utilization in the United States* (Cooperative Report with the Department of Agriculture), 1947.
28. ——, Bureau of Foreign and Domestic Commerce, *World Trade in Commodities*, Part 7, Leather and Its Products.
29. Tariff Commission, *Agricultural, Pastoral, and Forest Industries in Argentina*, 1947.
30. ——, *Agricultural, Pastoral, and Forest Industries in Brazil*, 1946.
31. ——, *Hides and Skins and Leather* (War Changes in Industry Series, Report No. 13), 1946.

32. CANADA. Department of Agriculture, *Agriculture Abroad*, Ottawa.

DENMARK
33. Agricultural Council, *Agriculture*, Copenhagen, 1935.

34. *Memorandum on the Aims of the Danish Agricultural Organizations in the Development of Danish Agriculture up to 1952–53*, Copenhagen, 1950.

GREAT BRITAIN
35. Central Statistical Office, *Annual Abstract of Statistics*, London.
36. Imperial Economic Committee, *Cattle and Beef Survey*, London, 1934.

37. GREECE. *Statistique Annuelle Agricole et d'Élevage des Bestiaux de la Grèce*, Athens.

38. INDIA. Famine Inquiry Commission, *Final Report*, Government Press, Madras, 1945.

39. NEW ZEALAND. Census and Statistics Office, *New Zealand Official Year Book*, Wellington.

USSR
40. *Bol'shaĭa Sovetskaĭa Entsiklopediĭa*, Moscow, 1947.
41. *Special Supplement on the Fourth Five-Year Plan*, Embassy of the USSR, Washington, June 1946.

---

42. Anderson, Arthur L., *Introductory Animal Husbandry*, Macmillan Company, New York, 1943.
43. Balzac, S. S., Vasyutin, V. F., and Feigin, Y. G., *Economic Geography of the USSR* (Translated from the Russian by the American Council of Learned Societies), Macmillan Company, New York, 1949.
44. Behnsen, Henry, and Genzmer, W., *Weltwirtschaft der Wolle*, J. Springer, Berlin, 1932.
45. Brasse-Brossard, Lucien, *Le Bétail*, 2d edition, La Maison Rustique, Paris, 1947.
46. Buck, John L., *Land Utilization in China*, University of Chicago Press, Chicago, 1937.
47. Dowell, Austin A., and Bjorka, Knute, *Livestock Marketing*, McGraw-Hill Book Company, New York, 1941.
48. Duckham, A. N., *Animal Industry in the British Empire*, Oxford University Press, London, 1932.
49. Ensminger, M. E., *Beef Cattle Husbandry*, Interstate Printers and Publishers, Danville, 1951.
50. Frazer, Allan, *Sheep Husbandry*, Crosby Lockwood and Son, London, 1951.
51. Fredericsen, Johan D., *The Story of Milk*, Macmillan Company, New York, 1919.
52. Hall, Sir Alfred D., *Our Daily Bread: a Geography of Production*, John Murray, London, 1938.
53. Kelavkar, S. K., *Our Food Problem*, Padma Publications, Bombay, 1946.
54. Kolesnev, Samuil G., *Organizatsia Sotsialisticheskich Sel'sko-Khozyaystvennykh Predpriĭatiĭ*, Selchsoguiz, Moscow, 1947.
55. Leroy, André Max, "Le Mouton: Races, Élevage, Viande, Laine," in *Encyclopédie des Connaissances Agricoles*, Hachette, Paris, 1948.
56. McFall, R. J., *The World's Meat*, D. Appleton and Company, New York, 1927.
57. Malott, Deane W., and Martin, Boyce F., *The Agricultural Industries*, McGraw-Hill Book Company, New York, 1939.

58. Moore, Oscar K., *Argentine Farming and Farm Trade*, U. S. Department of Agriculture, 1948.

59. National Research Council, Food and Nutrition Board, *The Food Situation*, Washington, 1947.

60. Pearson, Frank A., and Paarlberg, Don, *Food*, Alfred A. Knopf, New York, 1944.

61. Philipps, Ralph W., Johnson, Ray G., and Moyer, Raymond T., *The Livestock of China*, U. S. Government Printing Office, 1945.

62. Rossiter, Fred Y., *Fats and Oils: World Production and Trade*, U. S. Department of Agriculture, 1946.

63. Royal Institute of International Affairs, *World Agriculture*, Oxford University Press, London, 1932.

64. Schnitzer, Julius G., *Hide and Skin Developments and Trends in Brazil, Panama and Venezuela*, (Industrial Reference Service), U. S. Department of Commerce, July 1945.

65. Smith, Charles, *Britain's Food Supplies in Peace and War*, George Routledge and Sons, London, 1940.

66. Taylor, A. E., *Corn and Hog Surplus of the Corn Belt* (Miscellaneous Publications, No. 6, Food Research Institute), Stanford University, 1932.

67. Tyler, John M., *The New Stone Age in Northern Europe*, Charles Scribner's Sons, New York, 1921.

68. Volin, Lazar, *A Survey of Soviet Russian Agriculture*, U. S. Department of Agriculture, 1951.

69. Wythe, George, Wight, Royce A., and Midkiff, Harold M., *Brazil: an Expanding Economy*, Twentieth Century Fund, New York, 1949.

CHAPTER 19

FORESTS AND FOREST PRODUCTS

1. United Nations, *Proceedings of the United Nations Scientific Conference on the Conservation and Utilization of Resources, 1949*, Vol. I, *Plenary Meetings*, New York, 1950.

2. ——, Food and Agriculture Organization (FAO), *Forest Resources of the World*, Washington, 1948.

3. ——, ——, *Forestry and Forest Products*, Stockholm, 1946.

4. ——, ——, *Forestry and Primary Forest Products* (Five Technical Reports on Food and Agriculture), Washington, 1945.

5. ——, ——, *Report of the Preparatory Conference on World Pulp Problems*, Montreal, 1949.

6. ——, ——, *Yearbook of Forest Products Statistics*, Washington.

7. ——, ——, *Unasylva*.

8. International Institute of Agriculture, *Cork Production and International Cork Trade*, Rome, 1947.

9. ——, *International Yearbook of Forestry Statistics*, Rome, 1938.

UNITED STATES

10. Department of Agriculture, *Agricultural Statistics*.

11. ——, *Headwaters Control and Use* (Upstream Engineering Conference), 1937.

12. ——, *Yearbook of Agriculture*.

13. ——, Forest Service, *Forests and National Prosperity* (Miscellaneous Publication, No. 668), 1948.

14. ——, ——, *Living Forests and Human Needs*, 1939.

15. ——, ——, *Report of the Chief of the Forest Service*.

16. Department of Commerce, Bureau of the Census, *Historical Statistics of the United States, 1789–1945*, 1949.

17. ——, Bureau of Foreign and Domestic Commerce, *Leather and Products* (World Trade in Commodities, Part II), 1950.

18. Tariff Commission, *Agricultural, Pastoral and Forest Industries in Argentina*, 1947.

19. USSR. *Les*, Glavsnables (Forest Resources Board), Moscow.

20. Allen, Shirley W., *An Introduction to American Forestry*, McGraw-Hill Book Company, New York, 1938.

21. Anderson, Mark L., *State Control of Private Forestry Under European Democracies* (Oxford Forestry Memoirs No. 22), Oxford University Press, London, 1950.

22. Bruère, Martha S., *Here Are Forests* (prepared for the Third World Power Conference), U. S. Department of Agriculture, Forest Service, 1936.

23. ——, *Your Forests*, J. B. Lippincott and Company, Philadelphia, 1945.

24. Cooke, Giles B., *Cork and Cork Products*, Crown Cork and Seal Company, Baltimore, 1942.

25. Deffontaines, P., *L'Homme et la Forêt*, Gallimard, Paris, 1933.

26. Fernow, Bernhard E., *A Brief History of Forestry*, 2d edition, University Press, Toronto, 1911.

27. Glesinger, Egon, *The Coming Age of Wood*, Simon and Schuster, New York, 1949.

28. Gurney, Robert, *Our Trees and Woodlands*, Medici Society, London, 1947.

29. Hall, J. Alfred, "Forest Utilization," *Unasylva*, July–August, 1947.

30. ——, and Mosley, T. Y., *Products of American Forests*, U. S. Department of Agriculture, Forest Service, 1946.

31. Hunnicut, Benjamin H., *Brazil Looks Forward*, Instituto Brasileiro de Geografia e Estatistica, Rio de Janeiro, 1945.

32. Illick, Joseph S., *An Outline of General Forestry*, 3d edition, Barnes and Noble, New York, 1939.

33. Lowdermilk, Walter C., *The Conquest of the Land through Seven Thousand Years*, U. S. Department of Agriculture, Soil Conservation Service, 1948.

34. *Naval Stores Review International Yearbook* (formerly *Gambel's*), H. L. Peace Publications, New Orleans.

35. Pack, Charles Lathrop, and Gill, Tom, *Forests and Mankind*, Macmillan Company, New York, 1929.

36. Panshin, A. J., and Associates, *Forest Products, Their Sources, Production and Utilization*, McGraw-Hill Book Company, New York, 1950.

37. Parde, Leon, and Parde, Maurice, *Arbres et Forêts*, A. Colin, Paris, 1938.

38. Pinchot, Gifford, *Breaking New Ground*, Harcourt, Brace and Company, New York, 1950.

39. Reynolds, R. V., and Pierson, Albert H., *Fuel Wood Used in the United States, 1630–1930* (Circular No. 641), U. S. Department of Agriculture, 1942.

40. Rowe, W. H., *Our Forests,* Faber and Faber, London, 1947.
41. Steer, Henry B., *Lumber Production in the United States, 1799–1946,* U. S. Department of Agriculture, Forest Service, 1948.
42. Streyffert, Thorsten, *The Forests of Sweden* (W. Wayne Lobdell, trans.), Bonnier, Stockholm, 1938.
43. Taylor, Norman, *Cinchona in Java,* Greenberg, New York, 1945.
44. Taylor, William L., *Forests and Forestry in Great Britain,* Crosby Lockwood and Son, London, 1945.
45. Troup, Robert S., *Forestry and State Control,* Oxford University Press, London, 1938.
46. Watts, Lyle F., "Timber Shortage or Timber Abundance in the USA," *Unasylva,* July–August 1947.
47. Winters, Harold F., *Cinchona Propagation* (Bulletin No. 47), U. S. Department of Agriculture, 1950.
48. Wythe, George, Wight, Royce A., and Midkiff, Harold M., *Brazil: an Expanding Economy,* Twentieth Century Fund, New York, 1949.
49. Zon, Raphael, and Sparhawk, William N., *Forest Resources of the World,* McGraw-Hill Book Company, New York, 1923.

CHAPTER 20

FISHERIES

1. United Nations, *Proceedings of the United Nations Scientific Conference on the Conservation and Utilization of Resources, 1949,* Vols. I-VIII, New York, 1950–52.
2. ———, Economic Commission for Asia and the Far East, *Economic Survey of Asia and the Far East,* New York.
3. ———, Food and Agriculture Organization (FAO), *Fisheries* (Five Technical Reports on Food and Agriculture), Washington, 1945.
4. ———, ———, *Yearbook of Fisheries Statistics,* Washington, 1948.
5. ———, ———, *Fisheries Bulletin.*
6. International Commission on Whaling, *First Report of the Commission,* London, 1950.

UNITED STATES

7. Seventy-ninth Congress, First Session, *Fishery Resources of the United States* (Senate Document No. 51), 1945.
8. Eighty-first Congress, First Session, Committee on Merchant Marine and Fisheries of the House of Representatives, *Problems of the Fishing Industry,* 1949.
9. Department of Agriculture, *Foreign Agriculture.*
10. ———, *Foreign Crops and Markets.*
11. Department of Commerce, Bureau of the Census, *Statistical Abstract of the United States.*
12. Department of the Interior, *Fisheries of the United States and Alaska.*
13. ———, *Fishery Statistics of the United States, 1946,* Washington, 1950.
14. ———, *Fishing Industry in Brazil* (Fishery Leaflet 329), 1948.
15. ———, *Growth of South African Fisheries* (Fishery Leaflet 347), 1948.
16. ———, *Japanese Fishing Industry* (Fishery Leaflet 157), 1945.
17. ———, *Natural Resources of Japan* (Fishery Leaflet 249), 1947.
18. Department of State, *Northwest Atlantic Fisheries* (Treaties and Other International Acts Series, No. 2089), 1950.
19. Tariff Commission, *Agricultural, Pastoral, and Forest Industries in Brazil,* 1946.
20. ———, *Products and Provisions* (Summaries of Tariff Information, Vol. VII, 6 parts), 1948.

21. CANADA. Department of Fisheries, *Canada's Fisheries,* Ottawa, 1937.

22. GREAT BRITAIN. Central Statistical Office, *Annual Abstract of Statistics, 1938–1948,* London, 1949.

23. Balzac, S. S., Vasyutin, V. F., and Feigin, Y. G., *Economic Geography of the USSR* (Translated from the Russian by the American Council of Learned Societies), Macmillan Company, New York, 1949.
24. Bigelow, Henry B., *Oceanography, Its Scope, Problems and Economic Importance,* Houghton Mifflin Company, Boston, 1931.
25. Brandt, Karl, *Whale Oil, An Economic Analysis* (Fats and Oils Studies No. 7), Food Research Institute, Stanford University, 1940.
26. ———, *Whaling and Whale Oil During and After World War II* (War-Peace Pamphlets No. 11), Food Research Institute, Stanford University, 1948.
27. Carson, Rachel L., *The Sea Around Us,* Oxford University Press, New York, 1951.
28. Committee of International Whaling Statistics, *International Whaling Statistics,* Sandefjord.
29. Dardel, Eric, *Les Pêches Maritimes,* Presses Universitaires de France, Paris, 1946.
30. Grant, Ruth Fulton, *The Canadian Atlantic Fishery,* Ryerson Press, Toronto, 1934.
31. Lebret, L. J., and Sauvée, J., *Pêcheries Mondiales et Marché du Poisson,* Institut National de la Statistique, Paris, 1950.
32. Legendre, René, *La Vie dans les Mers,* Presses Universitaires de France, Paris, 1942.
33. Loture, Robert de, *Les Pêches Maritimes Modernes,* Société d'Éditions Géographiques, Maritimes et Coloniales, Paris, 1946.
34. Meehean, Lloyd P., "Cultivation of Fish in Ponds and Its Relation to Soil Conservation" (Paper presented to the United Nations Scientific Conference on the Conservation and Utilization of Resources), New York, 1950.
35. Minville, Esdras (Editor), *Pêche et Chasse,* Éditions Fides, Montreal, 1946.
36. *Norway Fisheries and Fish Processing,* Norwegian Export Council, Oslo, 1949.
37. *Norway's Export Trade,* Blix Publishing Company, Oslo, 1939.
38. *Norwegian Export Review, 1949,* The Mercantile Publishing, Oslo, 1950.
39. Peters, Nicolaus (Editor), *Der Neue Deutsche Walfang,* Verlag Hansa, Hamburg, 1938.

40. Raleigh, Sir Walter, *Observations Touching Trade and Commerce with the Hollander, and other Nations,* Printed for M. Sheares, London, 1664.

41. Rass, T. S., *Mirovoĭ Promisel Vodnuch Zhivotnuch,* Gosisdat, Moscow, 1948.

42. Rudolph, Willi, *Nahrung und Reichtum aus dem Meer,* Wissenschaftliche Verlagsgesellschaft, Stuttgart, 1946.

43. Salzman, L. F., *English Industries of the Middle Ages,* new edition, Oxford University Press, London, 1924.

44. Schultz, Leonard P., and Stern, E. M., *The Ways of Fishes,* D. Van Nostrand Company, New York, 1948.

45. Smith, Guy-Harold (Editor), *Conservation of Natural Resources,* John Wiley and Sons, New York, 1950.

46. Sverdrup, H. U., Johnson, Martin W., and Fleming, Richard H., *The Oceans, Their Physics, Chemistry and General Biology,* Prentice-Hall, New York, 1942.

47. Taylor, Harden F., and Associates, *Survey of Marine Fisheries of North Carolina,* University of North Carolina Press, Chapel Hill, 1951.

48. Thomazi, A., *Histoire de la Pêche,* Payot, Paris, 1947.

49. Thomasevich, Jozo, *International Agreements on Conservation of Marine Resources; with Special Reference to the North Pacific* (Commodity Policy Studies), Food Research Institute, Stanford University, 1943.

50. Tressler, Donald K., *The Wealth of the Sea,* The Century Company, New York, 1927.

51. ———, and Lemon, James M., *Marine Products of Commerce,* Reinhold Publishing Corporation, New York, 1951.

52. Tysser, Harry F. (Editor), *World Fisheries Yearbook and Directory,* British-Continental Trade Press, London.

53. Woytinsky, Wl. (W. S.), *Die Welt in Zahlen,* Vol. III: *Die Landwirtschaft,* Rudolf Mosse, Berlin, 1926.

PART IV. ENERGY AND MINING

CHAPTER 21

MINING IN THE WORLD ECONOMY

1. League of Nations, *The Network of World Trade*, Geneva, 1942.
2. ———, *World Production and Prices, 1938–39*, Geneva, 1939.
3. United Nations, *Demographic Yearbook*, New York.
4. ———, *Statistical Yearbook*, New York.
5. ———, *National Income Statistics of Various Countries, 1938–1948*, New York, 1950.
6. ———, *Proceedings of the United Nations Scientific Conference on the Conservation and Utilization of Resources, 1949*, Vol. I, *Plenary Meetings*, New York, 1950.

UNITED STATES

7. Department of Commerce, Bureau of the Census, Sixteenth Census of the United States (1940), *Population*, Vol. II, 1943.
8. ———, ———, *Historical Statistics of the United States, 1789–1945*, 1949.
9. ———, Bureau of Foreign and Domestic Commerce, *National Income*, 1951 Edition, Supplement to *Survey of Current Business*.
10. ———, ———, *Survey of Current Business*.
11. Department of the Interior, Bureau of Mines, *Minerals Yearbook*.
12. ———, ———, Releases and Memoranda.
13. Department of State, *Energy Resources of the World*, 1949.

---

14. Agricola, Georgius, *De Re Metallica* (trans. from the first Latin edition of 1556 by Herbert C. Hoover and Lou H. Hoover), Dover Publications, New York, 1950.
15. Aristotle, *Politics* (Benjamin Jowett, trans.), Oxford University Press, New York, 1943.
16. Leith, C. K., Furness, J. W., and Lewis, Cleona, *World Minerals and World Peace*, Brookings Institution, Washington, 1943.
17. Meisner, M., "Die Versorgung der Weltwirtschaft mit Bergwerkerzeugnissen," in *Weltmontanstatistik*, Part I, Die Preussische Geologische Landesanstalt, Stuttgart, 1925.
18. Treptow, E., "Der Älteste Bergbau und Seine Hilfsmittel," in *Beiträge zur Geschichte der Technik und Industrie, Verein Deutscher Ingenieure*, Berlin, 1918.
19. Woytinsky, Wl. (W.S.), *Internationale Hebung der Preise als Ausweg aus der Krise*, Die Frankfurter Gesellschaft für Konjunkturforschung, Hans Buske, Leipzig, 1931.
20. ———, *Die Welt in Zahlen*, Vol. IV: *Das Gewerbe*, Rudolf Mosse, Berlin, 1926.

CHAPTER 22

METALLIC AND NONMETALLIC MINERALS

1. League of Nations, *Statistical Year-Book*, Geneva.
2. United Nations, *Statistical Yearbook*, New York.

3. ———, *Proceedings of the United Nations Scientific Conference on the Conservation and Utilization of Resources, 1949*, Vol. I, *Plenary Meetings*, 1950; Vol. II, *Mineral Resources*, New York, 1951:
   a. Pehrson, Elmer Walter, "Estimates of Selected World Mineral Supplies by Cost Range," in Vol. II.
   b. Sutton, H., "The Future of Light Metals," in Vol. II.
   c. Teed, P. Litherland, "Magnesia and Magnesium from Sea Water," in Vol. II.
4. ———, *World Iron Ore Resources and Their Utilization*, New York, 1950.
5. ———, Economic Commission for Asia and the Far East, *Economic Survey of Asia and the Far East*, New York.
6. ———, Economic Commission for Europe, *Economic Survey of Europe*, Geneva.
7. International Tin Study Group, *Statistical Bulletin*, The Hague, 1949.
8. ———, *Tin, 1949–50*, The Hague, 1951.

UNITED STATES

9. Seventy-ninth Congress, Senate, *Economic Concentration and World War II* (Document No. 206), 1946.
10. Eightieth Congress, Senate, Subcommittee of the Committee on Public Lands, *Investigation of National Resources* (Hearings, May 15–20, 1947), 1947.
11. Department of Commerce, Bureau of the Census, *Historical Statistics of the United States, 1789–1945*, 1949.
12. Department of the Interior, Bureau of Mines, *Asbestos*, by Oliver Bowles (Bulletin No. 403), 1937.
13. ———, ———, *Economic Relations of Silver to Other Metals in Argentiferous Ores*, by Charles White Merrill (Economic Paper No. 10), 1930.
14. ———, ———, *Gypsum and Anhydrite*, by Forrest T. Moyer (Information Circular No. 7049), 1939.
15. ———, ———, *Metal-Mining Practice*, by C. F. Jackson and J. H. Hedges (Bulletin No. 419), 1939.
16. ———, ———, *Mica*, by W. M. Myers (Information Circular No. 6205), 1929.
17. ———, ———, *Mineral Trade Notes*.
18. ———, ———, *Minerals Yearbook*.
19. ———, ———, *1950 Materials Survey, Zinc* (with the cooperation of the Geological Survey), 1951.
20. ———, ———, *Summarized Data on Copper Production*, by C. E. Julihn (Economic Paper No. I), 1928.
21. ———, ———, *Summarized Data on Gold Production*, by Robert H. Ridgeway (Economic Paper No. 6), 1929.
22. ———, ———, *Summarized Data on Lead Production*, by Lewis A. Smith (Economic Paper No. 5), 1929.
23. ———, ———, *Summarized Data on Tin Production*, by John B. Umhau (Economic Paper No. 13), 1932.

24. ——, ——, *Summarized Data on Zinc Production*, by Elmer W. Pehrson, 1929.
25. ——, Geological Survey, *Mineral Resources of the United States*.
26. Federal Trade Commission, *The Copper Industry*, 1947.
27. President's Materials Policy Commission, *Resources for Freedom*, 5 volumes, 1952.
28. Tariff Commission, *Aluminum* (War Changes in Industry Series, No. 14), 1946.
29. ——, *Magnesium* (War Changes in Industry Series, No. 10), 1945.
30. ——, *Mining and Manufacturing Industries in Bolivia*, 1945.
31. ——, *Mining and Manufacturing Industries in Chile*, 1945.
32. ——, *Mining and Manufacturing Industries in Venezuela*, 1945.
33. ——, *Unmanufactured Copper, Lead and Zinc* (Summaries), 1949.

34. CANADA. Bureau of Mines, *The Canadian Mineral Industry, 1945*, Ottawa, 1946.

35. USSR. Fersman, A. E., and Kogan, B. I., *Mineral' noe Sur'e Zarubezhnykh Stran*, Academy of Sciences of the USSR, Moscow–Leningrad, 1947.

36. Agricola, Georgius, *De Re Metallica* (trans. from the first Latin edition of 1556 by Herbert C. Hoover and Lou H. Hoover), Dover Publications, New York, 1950.
37. Alderfer, E. B., and Michl, H. E., *Economics of American Industry*, McGraw-Hill Book Company, New York, 1942.
38. American Bureau of Metal Statistics, *Year Book*, New York.
39. American Institute of Mining and Metallurgical Engineers, *Seventy-five Years of Progress in the Mineral Industry, 1871–1946*, New York, 1947.
40. Balzac, S. S., Vasyutin, V. F., and Feigin, Y. G., *Economic Geography of the USSR*, Macmillan Company, New York, 1949.
41. Bateman, Alan M., *Economic Mineral Deposits*, 2d edition, John Wiley and Sons, New York. 1950.
42. Bureau of Mines and Geological Survey, Department of the Interior, *Mineral Resources of the United States*, Public Affairs Press, Washington, 1948.
43. *Chemical Engineering*.
44. D'Arcy, George, *Mineralogy of Uranium and Thorium-Bearing Minerals*, revised, U.S. Atomic Energy Commission (RMO-563), 1949.
45. Déribéré, Maurice, *L'Uranium; La Clef et la Source des Energies Nucléaires*, Elzévir, Paris, 1946.
46. Engle, Nathanael H., and Associates, *Aluminum: an Industrial Marketing Appraisal*, Richard D. Irwin, Chicago, 1944.
47. Friedensburg, Ferdinand, *Die Bergwirtschaft der Erde*, F. Enke, Stuttgart (1st ed., 1938; 2d ed., 1948).
48. Furness, J. W., "History of the Development of the Copper Industry of the World," in *Copper Resources of the World*, Vol. I (Sixteenth International Geological Congress), George Banta Publishing Company, Menasha, 1935.

49. *Gemeinfassliche Darstellung des Eisenhüttenwesens*, Verein Deutscher Eisenhüttenleute in Düsseldorf, 1937.
50. Holland, Sir Thomas H., *Minerals and International Relations: the International Relationship of Minerals and International Movement of Mineral Products in Peace and War* (International Conciliation, No. 266), Carnegie Endowment for International Peace, New York, 1931.
51. *International Control in the Non-Ferrous Metals*, by William Y. Elliott and Associates, Macmillan Company, New York, 1937.
52. International Geological Congress (Fifteenth: South Africa, 1929), *Gold Resources of the World*, Wallachs' P. & P. Company, Pretoria, 1931.
53. ——, (Sixteenth: Washington, 1933), *Copper Resources of the World*, 2 vols., George Banta Publishing Company, Menasha, 1935.
54. Jones, W. R., and Williams, David, *Minerals and Mineral Deposits*, Oxford University Press, London, 1948.
55. Ladoo, Raymond B., and Myers, W. M., *Nonmetallic Minerals*, 2d edition, McGraw-Hill Book Company, New York, 1951.
56. Leith, C. K., *World Minerals and World Politics*, McGraw-Hill Book Company, New York, 1931.
57. ——, Furness, J. W., and Lewis, Cleona, *World Minerals and World Peace*, Brookings Institution, Washington, 1943.
58. *Light Metal Age*.
59. Lilley, Ernest R., *Economic Geology of Mineral Deposits*, Henry Holt and Company, New York, 1936.
60. Lippert, T. W., "Cerro Bolivar, Saga of an Iron Ore Crisis Averted," *Journal of Metals* and *Mining Engineering*, February 1950.
61. Lovering, T. S., *Minerals in World Affairs*, Prentice-Hall, New York, 1943.
62. *Metal Bulletin* (London).
63. *Metal Statistics*.
64. Mikami, Harry M., "World Iron-Ore Map," *Economic Geology*, January 1944.
65. *The Mineral Industry, Its Statistics, Technology and Trade During 1941*, G. A. Roush (Editor), Vol. 50, McGraw-Hill Book Company, New York, 1942.
66. *Mines Magazine*.
67. *Mining Journal* (London).
68. *Modern Uses of Nonferrous Metals*, C. H. Mathewson (Editor), American Institute of Mining and Metallurgical Engineers, New York, 1935.
69. Notman, Arthur, "Estimated World Reserves of Copper," in *Copper Resources of the World*, Vol. I (Sixteenth International Geological Congress), George Banta Publishing Company, Menasha, 1935.
70. "The Outlook for Platinum," *South African Mining and Engineering Journal*, April 6, 1946.
71. Roush, G. A., *Strategic Mineral Supplies*, McGraw-Hill Book Company, New York, 1939.
72. Schmidt, Albrecht, and Fischbeck, Kurt, *Die Industrielle Chemie in Ihrer Bedeutung im Weltbild*, 2d edition, Walter de Gruyter and Company, Berlin, 1943.

73. Spence, Hugh S., "Mica," in *Industrial Minerals and Rocks*, American Institute of Mining and Metallurgical Engineers, New York, 1937.

74. Tarr, William Arthur, *Introductory Economic Geology*, 2d edition, McGraw-Hill Book Company, New York, 1938.

75. Woytinsky, Wl. (W. S.), *Die Welt in Zahlen*, Vol. IV: *Das Gewerbe*, Rudolf Mosse, Berlin, 1926.

CHAPTER 23

COAL

1. League of Nations, *Statistical Year-Book*, Geneva.

2. United Nations, *Statistical Yearbook*, New York.

3. ———, Economic Commission for Asia and the Far East, *Economic Survey of Asia and the Far East*, New York.

4. International Labor Office, *The World Coal Mining Industry*, 2 vols., Geneva, 1938.

5. ———, *Technical Tripartite Meeting of the Coal Mining Industry*, 2 vols., Geneva, 1938.

6. ———, Coal Mines Committee, *Report of the First Session*, Geneva, 1947.

7. International Geological Congress (Twelfth: Toronto, 1913), *The Coal Resources of the World*, 3 vols., Morang and Company, Toronto, 1913.

8. ——— (Seventeenth: Moscow and Leningrad, 1937), *The Coal Resources of the USSR* (M. M. Prigorovsky, Editor), Chief Editorial Office of the Mining-Fuel and Geological-Prospecting Literature, Leningrad, 1937.

9. World Power Conference, *Statistical Year-Book*, London.

10. ———, International Executive Council, *Power Resources of the World (Potential and Developed)*, London, 1929.

11. ——— (Fourth: London, 1950), Reports and Papers:
    a. "Energy Resources of the United States."
    b. "Energy Resources and Power Development in the United Kingdom."
    c. "Energy Resources of Canada and Their Development."
    d. "Trends in Mechanical Mining and Preparation of Coal for Steam Generation."

UNITED STATES

12. Sixty-eighth Congress, Second Session, Senate, *Report of the United States Coal Commission* (Document No. 195, Part 2), 1925.

13. Eightieth Congress, Senate, Subcommittee of the Committee on Public Lands, *Investigation of National Resources* (Hearings, May 15–20, 1947), 1947.

14. Department of Commerce, Bureau of the Census, *Historical Statistics of the United States, 1789–1945*, 1949.

15. Department of the Interior, Bureau of Mines, *Minerals Yearbook*.

16. ———, Geological Survey, *World Atlas of Commercial Geography*, Part 1, Distribution of Mineral Production, 1921.

17. Economic Cooperation Administration, *Coal and Related Solid Fuels, Commodity Study*, 1949.

18. National Resources Committee, *Energy Resources and National Policy*, 1939.

19. National Resources Planning Board, *Industrial Location and National Resources*, 1943.

20. CANADA. *Report of the Royal Commission on Coal*, Ottawa, 1947.

21. FRANCE. Statistique Générale, *Annuaire Statistique*, Paris.

GERMANY

22. Reichskohlenrat, *Statistische Übersichten über die Kohlenwirtschaft*, Berlin.

23. Statistisches Reichsamt, *Statistisches Jahrbuch für das Deutsche Reich*, Berlin.

GREAT BRITAIN

24. Central Statistical Office, *Annual Abstract of Statistics, 1938–1948*, London, 1949.

25. Ministry of Fuel and Power, *Coal Mining: Report of the Technical Advisory Committee*, Cmd. 6610, H.M.S.O., 1945.

26. National Coal Board, *Annual Report and Statement of Accounts*, H.M.S.O.

27. *Report of the Royal Commission on the Coal Industry (1925)*, Vol. I, H.M.S.O., 1926.

28. Agricola, Georgius, *De Re Metallica* (trans. from the first Latin edition of 1556 by Herbert C. Hoover and Lou H. Hoover), Dover Publications, New York, 1950.

29. American Institute of Mining and Metallurgical Engineers, *Seventy-five Years of Progress in the Mineral Industry, 1871–1946*, New York, 1947.

30. Ashton, Thomas Southcliffe, and Sykes, Joseph, *The Coal Industry of the Eighteenth Century*, Manchester University Press, Manchester, 1929.

31. Averitt, Paul, and Berryhill, Louise R., *Coal Resources of the United States* (Circular 94), U.S. Geological Survey, 1950.

32. Balzac, S. S., Vasyutin, V. F., and Feigin, Y. G., *Economic Geography of the USSR*, Macmillan Company, New York, 1949.

33. Bateman, Alan M., *Economic Mineral Deposits*, 2d edition, John Wiley and Sons, New York, 1950.

34. Bituminous Coal Institute, *Bituminous Coal Annual*, Washington.

35. ———, *Bituminous Coal, Facts and Figures*, Washington.

36. Bone, William A., and Himus, Godfrey W., *Coal, Its Constitution and Uses*, Longmans, Green and Company, London, 1936.

37. Campbell, Maurius R., *The Coal Fields of the United States, General Introduction* (Professional Paper No. 100), U.S. Geological Survey, 1929.

38. Crichton, Andrew B., "How Much Coal Do We Really Have?" *Coal Technology*, August 1948, and in *Transactions* (Vol. 177), *Coal Division*, 1948, American Institute of Mining and Metallurgical Engineers, New York, 1949.

39. Dunstan, A. E. (Editor), *The Science of Petroleum*, 5 vols., Oxford University Press, London, 1938–1950.

40. Eavenson, Howard N., *Coal Through the Ages*, American Institute of Mining and Metallurgical Engineers, New York, 1935.

41. ———, *The First Century and a Quarter of American Coal Industry*, privately printed, Pittsburgh, 1942.

42. ———, "Where Can Coal Go from Here?" *Mining Engineering*, February 1950.

43. Fanning, Leonard M., *The Rise of American Oil*, revised edition, Harper and Brothers, New York, 1948.

44. Fieldner, Arno C., "Solid Fuels," *Oil and Gas Journal*, March 17, 1949.

45. *Glückauf, Berg- und Hüttenmannisch Zeitschrift*, Gelsenkirchen.

46. Ickes, Harold L., "Coal's New Horizons," *Coal Age*, April 1943.

47. *International Industry Yearbook, the Encyclopedia of Industrial Progress*, Kristen-Browne Publishing Company, New York.

48. Mining Association of Great Britain, *Historical Review of Coal Mining*, Fleetway Press, London, 1924.

49. *Mining Journal* (London).

50. Moore, Elwood S., *Coal: Its Properties, Analysis, Classification, Geology, Extraction, Uses and Distribution*, John Wiley and Sons, New York, 1922.

51. Nef, J. U., *The Rise of the British Coal Industry*, 2 vols., George Routledge and Sons, London, 1932.

52. Political and Economic Planning (PEP), *Report on the British Coal Industry*, London, 1936.

53. Polo, Marco, *Travels*, Modern Library, New York, 1931.

54. Regul, R., and Mahnke, K. G., *Energiequellen der Welt* (Institut für Konjunkturforschung, Vol. IV, Part 44), Hanseatische Verlagsanstalt, Hamburg–Berlin, 1937.

55. *Reviews of Petroleum Technology*, Vol. IX (1947), The Institute of Petroleum, London, 1950.

56. Rice, George S., and Hartmann, Irving, *Coal Mining in Europe* (Bulletin No. 414), U.S. Bureau of Mines, 1939.

57. Roy, Andrew, *The Coal Mines*, Robison, Savage and Company, Cleveland, 1876.

58. Schneider, Eugène, *Le Charbon, Son Histoire, Son Destin*, Plon, Paris, 1945.

59. Schwartz, Harry, *Russia's Soviet Economy*, Prentice-Hall, New York, 1950.

60. Shermann, Allan, and MacMurphy, Allen B., *Facts about Coal*, U.S. Bureau of Mines, 1948.

61. Shurick, A. T., *The Coal Industry*, Little, Brown and Company, Boston, 1924.

62. Stine, Charles M. A., "Today's Efficiencies, Tomorrow's Wastes," *Chemical Industries*, No. 5, 1946.

63. Thiessen, Reinhardt, *What Is Coal?* (Information Circular, No. 7397), U.S. Bureau of Mines, 1947.

64. Thom, W. T., Jr., *Petroleum and Coal: the Keys to the Future*, Princeton University Press, Princeton, 1929.

65. *Übersichten der Weltwirtschaft, 1885–1889*, J. Maier, Berlin, 1896.

66. *World Petroleum*.

67. Woytinsky, Wl. (W.S.), *Die Welt in Zahlen*, Vol. IV: *Das Gewerbe*, Rudolf Mosse, Berlin, 1926.

CHAPTER 24

PETROLEUM AND NATURAL GAS

1. League of Nations, *Statistical Year-Book*, Geneva.

2. United Nations, *Statistical Yearbook*, New York.

3. ———, *Monthly Bulletin of Statistics*, New York.

4. ———, Economic Commission for Asia and the Far East, *Economic Survey of Asia and the Far East*, New York.

5. ———, Economic Commission for Europe, *Economic Survey of Europe*, Geneva.

6. World Power Conference (Fourth: London, 1950), Reports and Papers:
   a. "Advances in Petroleum Refining."
   b. "Energy Resources of the United States."

UNITED STATES

7. Eightieth Congress, Senate, Subcommittee of the Committee on Public Lands, *Investigation of National Resources* (Hearings, May 15–20, 1947), 1947.

8. Department of Commerce, Bureau of the Census, *Statistical Abstract of the United States*.

9. ———, *Historical Statistics of the United States, 1789–1945*, 1949.

10. Department of the Interior, Bureau of Mines, *Petroleum Refinery Statistics, 1930*, by G. R. Hopkins (Bulletin No. 367), 1932.

11. ———, ———, *International Petroleum Trade*.

12. ———, ———, *Minerals Yearbook*.

13. Tariff Commission, *Petroleum* (War Changes in Industry Series, Report No. 17), 1946.

14. USSR. Gosudarstvennyĭ Plan Razvitiiā Narodnogo Khoziāstva SSSR na 1941 god. Prilozheniiā k Postanovleniiū SHK SSSR i ZK VKP (b), No. 127 ot Janvariiā 1941 goda. [Moscow, 1941.]

15. Alderfer, E. B., and Michl, H. E., *Economics of American Industry*, McGraw-Hill Book Company, New York, 1942.

16. American Gas Association, *Gas Facts*, New York.

17. American Institute of Mining and Metallurgical Engineers, *Seventy-five Years of Progress in the Mineral Industry, 1871–1946*, New York, 1947.

18. American Petroleum Institute, *Petroleum Facts and Figures*, New York.

19. Ball, Max W., *This Fascinating Oil Business*, Bobbs-Merrill Company, Indianapolis, 1940.

20. Balzac, S. S., Vasyutin, V. F., and Feigin, Y. G., *Economic Geography of the USSR* (Translated from the Russian by the American Council of Learned Societies), Macmillan Company, New York, 1949.

21. Baranskiĭ, N. N., *Economicheskaiā Geografiā SSSR* Uchpegdiz, Moscow, 1947.

22. Bell, Harold S., *Oil Shale and Shale Oils*, D. Van Nostrand Company, New York, 1948.

23. Crowther, James G., *About Petroleum*, Oxford University Press, London, 1938.

24. DeGolyer, E. L. (Editor), *Elements of the Petroleum Industry*, American Institute of Mining and Metallurgical Engineers, New York, 1940.

25. Dunstan, A. E. (Editor), *The Science of Petroleum*, 5 vols., Oxford University Press, London, 1938–1950.

26. Fanning, Leonard M., *The Rise of American Oil,* revised edition, Harper and Brothers, New York, 1948.

27. —— (Editor), *Our Oil Resources* (1st edition, 1945), 2d edition, McGraw-Hill Book Company, New York, 1950.

28. Hager, Dorsey, *Fundamentals of the Petroleum Industry,* McGraw-Hill Book Company, New York, 1939.

29. ——, *Practical Oil Geology,* 6th edition, McGraw-Hill Book Company, New York, 1951.

30. Institute of Petroleum, *Modern Petroleum Technology, London,* 1946.

31. *Journal of Petroleum Technology.*

32. Lalicker, Cecil G., *Principles of Petroleum Geology,* Appleton-Century-Crofts, New York, 1949.

33. Leven, David D., *Petroleum Encyclopaedia; Done in Oil,* edited and revised by Sylvain J. Pirson, Philosophical Library, New York, 1942.

34. Levorsen, A. I., "Estimates of Undiscovered Petroleum Reserves," in *Proceedings of the United Nations Scientific Conference on the Conservation and Utilization of Resources, 1949,* Vol. I, New York, 1950.

35. *Mines Magazine.*

36. *Oil and Gas Journal.*

37. *Petroleum Times.*

38. Pogue, Joseph S., *Economics of the Petroleum Industry,* Chase National Bank, New York, 1939.

39. ——, *Oil in Canada,* Chase National Bank, New York, 1949.

40. ——, *Oil in Venezuela,* Chase National Bank, New York, 1949.

41. Pratt, Wallace E., *Oil in the Earth,* University of Kansas Press, Lawrence, 1942.

42. ——, and Good, Dorothy (Editors), *World Geography of Petroleum* (American Geographical Society, Special Publication No. 31), Princeton University Press, Princeton, 1950.

43. Redwood, Sir Boverton, *Petroleum,* 3 vols., 4th edition, Charles Griffin and Company, London, 1922.

44. Richards, Ralph W., "Natural Gas Reserves," in *Energy Resources and National Policy,* National Resources Committee, 1939.

45. Schwartz, Harry, *Russia's Soviet Economy,* Prentice-Hall, New York, 1950.

46. Uren, Lester C., *Petroleum Production Engineering —Petroleum Production Economics,* McGraw-Hill Book Company, New York, 1950.

47. Volin, Lazar, "Machine-Tractor-Stations in the Soviet Union," *Foreign Agriculture,* April 1948.

48. Winchester, Dean E., *The Oil Possibilities of the Oil Shales of the United States,* Appendix I, Report No. 2 of the Federal Oil Conservation Board to the President, 1928.

49. *World Oil.*

CHAPTER 25

THE ECONOMICS OF ENERGY AND POWER

1. League of Nations, *Statistical Year-Book,* Geneva.

2. United Nations, *Statistical Yearbook,* New York.

3. ——, *Economic Bulletin for Europe,* Geneva.

4. ——, *Monthly Bulletin of Statistics,* New York.

5. ——, *Proceedings of the United Nations Scientific Conference on the Conservation of Resources, 1949,* Vol. I, *Plenary Meetings,* New York, 1950.

6. ——, Economic Commission for Asia and the Far East, *Economic Survey of Asia and the Far East,* New York.

7. ——, Economic Commission for Europe, *Economic Survey of Europe,* Geneva.

8. *Inter-American Statistical Yearbook, 1942,* Macmillan Company, New York; El Ateneo, Buenos Aires; Freitas Bastos, Rio de Janeiro, 1942.

9. World Power Conference, *Statistical Year-Book,* London.

10. —— (Fourth: London, 1950), "Atomic Energy" (General Report, Section J).

11. ——, ——, "Development of Power from Nuclear Energy."

12. ——, ——, "Energy Resources and Power Development in Norway."

13. ——, ——, "Energy Resources and Power Development since 1924" (General Report, Section A).

14. ——, ——, "Energy Resources of the United States."

15. ——, ——, "Exploitation et Utilisation du Gaz Naturel en France."

16. ——, ——, "Nuclear Energy for Power Production."

17. ——, ——, "Other Sources of Energy" (General Report, Section K).

18. ——, ——, "Projected Hydro-Electric Power Development in India, and Studies from the Point of View of Economic Planning of Power Transmission and Interconnection of Power Systems in this Development."

19. ——, ——, "Recent Developments in Large-Scale Wind Power Generation in Great Britain."

20. ——, ——, "Recursos de Energia de Chile."

21. ——, ——, "State of Hydro-Electric Power Development in the United States."

22. ——, ——, "Statistics of all Existing Water Power Resources."

23. ——, ——, "Utilisation du Gaz Naturel dans la Vallée du Po."

24. ——, ——, "Water Power Resources of Egypt."

25. ——, ——, "Water Power Resources of Greece and Their Development."

UNITED STATES

26. Department of Commerce, Bureau of the Census, *Statistical Abstract of the United States.*

27. Department of the Interior, *Energy Uses and Supplies, 1939, 1947, 1965* (Information Circular 7582), 1950.

28. ——, Bureau of Mines, *Minerals Yearbook.*

29. Department of State, *Energy Resources of the World,* 1949.

30. Federal Power Commission, *Consumption of Fuel for Production of Electric Energy, 1947,* 1948.

31. ——, *Production of Electric Energy and Capacity of Generating Plants, 1946,* 1948.

32. ——, *Summary of Industrial Electric Power in the United States, 1939–46,* 1946.

33. President's Materials Policy Commission, *Resources for Freedom,* 5 volumes, 1952.

34. CANADA. *Report of the Royal Commission on Coal,* Ottawa, 1947.

GERMANY

35. Institut für Konjunkturforschung, *Die Energiewirtschaft der Welt in Zahlen,* Vierteljahrshefte zur Konjunkturforschung, Sonderheft 19, Reimar Hobbing, Berlin, 1930.
36. Statistisches Reichsamt, *Statistisches Jahrbuch für das Deutsche Reich,* Berlin.

---

37. Ayres, Eugene, "Major Sources of Energy," in *Proceedings* (Vol. 28), American Petroleum Institute, New York, 1948.
38. Beard, James R., "Power, Its Production and Distribution," *Advancement of Science,* March 1951.
39. Dewhurst, J. Frederic, "Relation of Energy Output to Production in the United States," *Social Science,* October 1948.
40. Edison Electric Institute, *Annual Statistical Bulletin,* New York.
41. Egerton, Sir Alfred, "Civilisation and the Use of Energy," *Advancement of Science,* March 1951.
42. Hartley, Sir Harold, "Man's Use of Energy," *Advancement of Science,* September 1950.

43. Hünecke, Günter, *Gestaltungskräfte der Energiewirtschaft,* Verlag von Felix Meiner, Leipzig, 1937.
44. Laemmel, Rudolf, *Energie der Welt,* A. Stutz, Wädenswil, Switzerland, 1947.
45. Murphy, E. J., "Development of Atomic Energy," *Chemical and Engineering News,* January 25, 1946.
46. Pratt, Wallace E., and Good, Dorothy (Editors), *World Geography of Petroleum* (American Geographical Society, Special Publication No. 31), Princeton University Press, Princeton, 1950.
47. Schurr, Sam H., and Marschak, Jacob, *Economic Aspects of Atomic Power* (Cowles Commission for Research in Economics), Princeton University Press, Princeton, 1950.
48. Thomas, Percy H., *Electric Power from the Wind,* Federal Power Commission, 1945.
49. ——, *The Wind Power Aerogenerator, Twin Wheel Type,* Federal Power Commission, 1946.
50. Woytinsky, Wl. (W. S.), *Die Welt in Zahlen,* Vol. IV: *Das Gewerbe,* Rudolf Mosse, Berlin, 1926.
51. Zolotarev, T. L., *Energetika Budusshchego,* Gosudarstvennoe Izdatelstvo Culturno-Prosvetitel'noi Literaturi, Moscow, 1948.

PART V. MANUFACTURES

CHAPTER 26

MANUFACTURES IN THE WORLD ECONOMY

1. League of Nations, *Statistical Year-Book,* Geneva.
2. United Nations, *Statistical Yearbook,* New York.
3. ———, *Demographic Yearbook,* New York.
4. ———, *Economic Survey of Latin America,* New York.
5. ———, *National Income Statistics of Various Countries, 1938–1948,* New York, 1950.
6. ———, *Monthly Bulletin of Statistics,* New York.
7. ———, Economic Commission for Europe, *Economic Survey of Europe,* Geneva.
8. International Labor Office, *Yearbook of Labour Statistics,* Geneva.
9. *Inter-American Statistical Yearbook, 1942,* Macmillan Company, New York; El Ateneo, Buenos Aires; Freitas Bastos, Rio de Janeiro, 1942.

UNITED STATES

10. Department of Commerce, Bureau of the Census, Twelfth Census of the United States (1900), *Manufactures,* Vol. VII, 1902.
11. ———, ———, Sixteenth Census of the United States (1940), *Manufactures,* Vol. I, 1942.
12. ———, ———, *Census of Manufactures, 1947,* Vol. I: *General Summary,* 1950.
13. ———, ———, Population, Second Series, *Characteristics of the Population,* United States Summary, 1943.
14. ———, ———, *Statistical Abstract of the United States.*
15. ———, Bureau of Foreign and Domestic Commerce, *Survey of Current Business.*
16. ———, ———, *National Income,* 1951 Edition, Supplement to *Survey of Current Business.*
17. The President's Materials Policy Commission, *Resources for Freedom,* 5 volumes, 1952.

18. CHINA. National Government, Directorate General of Budgets, Accounts and Statistics, *Statistical Abstract of the Republic of China,* Nanking, 1947.

GERMANY

19. Institut für Konjunkturforschung, *Die Industriewirtschaft,* Vierteljahrshefte zur Konjunkturforschung, Sonderheft 31, Reimar Hobbing, Berlin, 1933.
20. Länderrat des Amerikanischen Besatzungsgebiets, *Statistisches Handbuch von Deutschland, 1928–1944,* Munich, 1949.

21. GREAT BRITAIN. Central Statistical Office, *Annual Abstract of Statistics,* London.

22. INDIA. Commercial Intelligence and Statistics Department, *Statistical Abstract for British India,* Calcutta.

23. USSR. Gosudarstvennyĭ Plan Razvitii︠a︡ Narodnogo Khozi︠a︡stva SSSR na 1941 god. Prilozhenii︠a︡ k Postanovlenii︠u︡ SHK SSSR i ZK VKP (b), No. 127 ot ĭanvari︠a︡ 1941 goda. [Moscow, 1941.]

24. Mulhall, M., *The Dictionary of Statistics,* 4th edition, London, 1889.
25. Pao-San Ou, *National Income of China, 1933, 1936 and 1946,* Institute of Social Sciences, Academia Sinica, Nanking.
26. Rao, V. K. R. V., *The National Income of British India, 1931–1932,* Macmillan, London, 1940.
27. Studenski, Paul, and Wyler, Julius, *International Survey of National Income,* National Bureau of Economic Research, New York (unpublished study).
28. Woytinsky, Wl. (W. S.), *Die Welt in Zahlen,* Rudolf Mosse, Berlin, 1924–28.

CHAPTER 27

THE FOOD, DRINK AND TOBACCO INDUSTRIES

1. United Nations, *Statistical Yearbook,* New York.

UNITED STATES

2. Department of Agriculture, *Foreign Agricultural Circular.*
3. Department of Commerce, Bureau of the Census, *Annual Survey of Manufactures 1949 and 1950,* 1952.
4. ———, ———, *Census of Manufactures, 1947,* 1950.
5. ———, ———, *Historical Statistics of the United States, 1789–1945,* 1949.
6. ———, ———, *Statistical Abstract of the United States.*
7. Federal Trade Commission, *Agricultural Income Inquiry,* 1938.
8. ———, *Growth and Concentration in the Flour Milling Industry,* 1947.
9. ———, *Wholesale Baking Industry,* Report to the 79th Congress, Parts 1 and 2, 1946.
10. Tariff Commission, *Agricultural Products and Provisions* (Summaries of Tariff Information, Vol. 7, 6 parts), 1948.
11. ———, *Dehydrated Vegetables* (War Changes in Industry Series, Report No. 5), 1944.
12. ———, *Grapes and Grape Products* (War Changes in Industry Series, Report No. 24), 1947.
13. ———, *Mining and Manufacturing Industries in Argentina,* Washington, 1945.
14. ———, *Mining and Manufacturing Industries in Uruguay,* 1945.
15. Temporary National Economic Committee, *Large-Scale Organization in the Food Industries* (Monograph No. 35, 76th Congress, 3d sess.), 1940.
16. Treasury Department, Bureau of Internal Revenue, *Annual Report of the Commissioner.*

17. CANADA. Statistics Bureau, General Statistics Branch, *The Canada Yearbook,* Ottawa.

GERMANY

18. Länderrat des Amerikanischen Besatzungsgebiets, *Statistisches Handbuch von Deutschland, 1928–1944,* Munich, 1949.
19. Statistisches Reichsamt, *Statistisches Jahrbuch für das Deutsche Reich,* Berlin.

Great Britain

20. Board of Trade, *Final Report on the Fifth Census of Production and the Import Duties Act Inquiry,* 3 parts, London, 1938–40.

21. Central Statistical Office, *Monthly Digest of Statistics,* London.

22. Imperial Economic Committee, *A Survey of the Trade in Canned Food* (Report No. 32), London, 1939.

23. Italy. Instituto Centrale di Statistica, *Compendio Statistice Italiano, 1941,* Vol. 20, Rome, 1941.

24. USSR. *Kalendar-Spravochnik, 1948,* Ogiz, Moscow, 1948.

---

25. Balzac, S. S., Vasyutin, V. F., and Feigin, Y. G., *Economic Geography of the USSR* (Translated from the Russian by the American Council of Learned Societies), Macmillan Company, New York, 1949.

26. Birgfeld, Clarence E., *Fruit Canners of the World,* U.S. Department of Commerce, 1939.

27. Brunerie, Georges, *Les Industries Alimentaires et Leur Organisation Rationelle,* Dunod, Paris, 1949.

28. Collins, James H., *The Story of Canned Foods,* Dutton and Company, New York, 1924.

29. Commodity Research Bureau, *Commodity Year Book,* New York.

30. Confederazione Generale del' Industria Italiana, *Annuario,* Rome.

31. Corey, Lewis, *Meat and Man: a Study of Monopoly, Unionism and Food Policy,* Viking Press, New York, 1950.

32. Cruess, William V., *Commercial Fruit and Vegetable Products,* 2d edition, McGraw-Hill Book Company, New York, 1938.

33. ———, *The Principles and Practice of Wine Making,* 2d edition, Avi Publishing Company, New York, 1946.

34. Dowell, Austin A., and Bjorka, Knute, *Livestock Marketing,* McGraw-Hill Book Company, New York, 1941.

35. Drummond, W. M., *The Impact of War Controls on the Meat Packing Industry, and the Implications for Postwar Policy,* Department of Reconstruction and Supply, Ottawa, 1943.

36. Faulkner, Harold U., *American Economic History,* 5th edition, Harper and Brothers, New York, 1943.

37. *Flow-Sheets of the Food Processing Industries,* 2d edition, McGraw-Hill Publishing Company, New York, 1947.

38. *Food Industries.*

39. Garner, Wrightman Wells, *The Production of Tobacco,* Blakiston Company, Philadelphia, 1946.

40. Heaton, Herbert, *Economic History of Europe,* revised edition, Harper and Brothers, New York, 1948.

41. Herodotus, *History* (Everyman's Library), E. P. Dutton and Company, New York, and J. M. Dent and Sons, London, 1936.

42. Hoshino, Saki, *The Canning Industry of Japan,* Japan Economic Federation, Tokyo, 1940.

43. Hunnicut, Benjamin H., *Brazil Looks Forward,* Instituto Brasileiro de Geografia e Estatística, Rio de Janeiro, 1945.

44. *International Industry Yearbook, the Encyclopaedia of Industrial Progress,* Kristen-Browne Publishing Company, New York.

45. Jacob, H. E., *Six Thousand Years of Bread,* Doubleday, Doran and Company, New York, 1944.

46. Kuhlmann, Charles Byron, *The Development of the Flour-Milling Industry in the United States,* Houghton Mifflin and Company, Boston, 1929.

47. Lockwood, J. F. and Simon, Anthony, *Flour Milling,* Northern Publishing Company, Liverpool, 1946.

48. Malott, Deane W. and Martin, Boyce F., *The Agricultural Industries,* McGraw-Hill Book Company, New York, 1939.

49. Moore, Mary Kinnavey, *The Baking Industry,* American Institute of Baking, Bellman Publishing Company, Boston, 1946.

50. National Canners Association, *The Canning Industry,* Washington, 1939.

51. ———, *The Story of the Canning Industry,* Washington, 1940.

52. *Northwestern Miller* (Almanack number).

53. Persons, Warren Milton, *Beer and Brewing in America; an Economic Study,* 3d edition, United Brewers Industrial Foundation, New York, 1940.

54. Simon, Andre L., *Wine and the Wine Trade,* Sir Isaac Pitman and Sons, London, 1921.

55. Smith, Leslie, *Flour Milling Technology,* 3d revised edition, Northern Publishing Company, Liverpool, 1944.

56. Stewart, Jean J., and Edwards, Alice L., *Foods: Production, Marketing, Consumption,* 2d edition, Prentice-Hall, New York, 1948.

57. Swanson, C. O., *European Milling and Baking Practices and the Demand for American Wheat and Flour,* U.S. Department of Agriculture, 1930.

58. Tennant, Richard B., *The American Cigarette Industry,* Yale University Press, New Haven, 1950.

59. Tressler, D. B., and Evers, C. F., *The Freezing Preservation of Foods,* 2d ed. revised and enlarged, Avi Publishing Company, New York, 1946.

60. Wahl, Arnold Spencer, *Bread Production under Scientific Management,* Baker's Helper, Chicago, 1930.

61. *Western Canner and Packer* (Statistical Review and Yearbook issue).

62. Williamson, Harold F. (Editor), *The Growth of the American Economy,* Prentice-Hall, New York, 1944.

63. Woodcock, F. Huntley, and Lewis, W. R., *Canned Foods and the Canning Industry,* Sir Isaac Pitman and Sons, London, 1938.

Chapter 28

The Textile Industry

1. United Nations, *Statistical Yearbook,* New York.

2. ———, *Economic Survey of Latin America,* New York.

3. ———, *Labour Productivity of the Cotton Textile Industry in Five Latin-American Countries,* New York, 1951.

4. ———, *World Economic Report*, New York.

5. ———, Economic Commission for Asia and the Far East, *Economic Survey of Asia and the Far East*, New York.

6. ———, Economic Commission for Europe, *Economic Survey of Europe*, Geneva.

7. ———, Food and Agriculture Organization (FAO), *Per Caput Fiber Consumption Levels* (Commodity Series, Bulletin No. 21), Rome, 1952.

8. ———, ———, *Report of the China-United States Agricultural Mission*, Washington, 1947.

9. ———, ———, *World Fiber Review*.

10. Anglo-American Council on Productivity, *Cotton Spinning* (Productivity Team Report), London and New York, 1950.

11. International Labor Organization, *Revue Internationale du Travail.*

12. ———, *The World Textile Industry, Economic and Social Problems*, 2 volumes, Geneva, 1937.

13. ———, Textile Committee, *Employment Problems*, Geneva, 1948.

14. ———, ———, *General Report*, Geneva.

15. ———, ———, *Reduction of Hours of Work in the Textile Industry*, Geneva, 1946.

UNITED STATES

16. Seventy-fourth Congress, First Session, *Cotton Textile Industry* (Senate Document, No. 126), 1935.

17. Seventy-sixth Congress, Third Session, Temporary National Economic Committee, *The Structure of Industry*, Monograph No. 27), 1941.

18. ———, ———, ———, *Technology in our Economy* (Monograph No. 22), 1941.

19. Department of Agriculture, *Trends in the Consumption of Fibers in the United States, 1892–1948* (Statistical Bulletin No. 89), 1950.

20. Department of Commerce, Bureau of the Census, *Annual Survey of Manufactures, 1949 and 1950*, 1952.

21. ———, ———, *Census of Manufactures.*

22. ———, ———, *Facts for Industry* (MI5A-C-09-Suppl.).

23. ———, ———, *Statistical Abstract of the United States.*

24. ———, ———, *Woolen and Worsted Machinery by Region: 1949* (Census, Industry No. 882).

25. Economic Cooperation Administration, Special Mission to the United Kingdom, *The Sterling Area, an American Analysis*, London, 1951.

26. National Resources Committee, *Technological Trends and National Policy*, 1937.

27. Tariff Commission, *Cotton Cloth* (War Changes in Industry Series, Report No. 27), 1947.

28. FRANCE. Commissariat Général du Plan de Modernisation et d'Équipement, *Rapport Définitif d'ensemble de la Commission de Modernisation du Textile*, Paris, 1948.

GERMANY

29. Institut für Konjunkturforschung, *Wöchentliche Berichte*, Reimar Hobbing, Berlin.

30. Länderrat des Amerikanischen Besatzungsgebiets, *Statistisches Handbuch von Deutschland, 1928–1944*, Munich, 1949.

31. Statistisches Reichsamt, *Statistisches Jahrbuch für das Deutsche Reich*, Berlin.

GREAT BRITAIN

32. Board of Trade, *Working Party Reports: Cotton*, London, 1946.

33. ———, *Working Party Reports: Wool*, London, 1947.

34. ———, British Intelligence Objectives Sub-Committee, *A Survey of the German Cotton, Rayon and Silk Industries*, London, 1947.

35. Commonwealth Economic Committee, Intelligence Branch, *Industrial Fibres*, London, 1948.

36. Ministry of Supply, Committee of Investigation into the Cotton Textile Machinery Industry, *Second and Final Report*, London, 1947.

37. THE NETHERLANDS. Central Bureau voor de Statistiek, *Statistisch Zakboek*, Utrecht.

38. USSR. Gosudarstvennyĭ Plan Razvitiſa Narodnogo Khozſastva SSSR na 1941 god. Prilozheniſa k Postanovleniſu SHK SSSR i ZK VKP (b), No. 127 ot Janvarſa 1941 goda. [Moscow, 1941.]

39. Akhtar, Sardar M., and Associates, *Indian Economics*, 3d edition, Premier Publishing Company, Delhi, 1941.

40. Alderfer, E. B., and Michl, H. E., *Economics of American Industry*, McGraw-Hill Book Company, New York, 1942.

41. *The American Wool and Cotton Reporter.*

42. Backman, Jules, and Gainsbrugh, M. R., *Economics of the Cotton Textile Industry*, National Industrial Conference Board, New York, 1946.

43. Barkin, Solomon, "The Regional Significance of the Integration Movement in the Southern Textile Industry," *The Southern Economic Journal*, April 1949.

44. Bowden, Witt, Karpovich, Michael, and Usher, Abbott P., *An Economic History of Europe since 1750*, American Book Company, New York, 1937.

45. *Chemical Engineering.*

46. Cherington, Paul T., *The Commercial Problems of the Woolen and Worsted Industries*, Textile Foundation, Washington, 1932.

47. Clapham, J. H., *The Economic Development of France and Germany*, 4th edition, Cambridge University Press, Cambridge, 1937.

48. Cohen, Jerome B., *Japan's Economy in War and Reconstruction*, University of Minnesota Press, Minneapolis, 1949.

49. Confederazione Generale dell' Industria Italiana, *Annuario*, Rome.

50. *Cotton.*

51. Cotton Textile Institute, *Cotton from Raw Material to Finished Product*, New York, 1947.

52. *Cotton Year Book*, New York Cotton Exchange, New York.

53. Crawford, Morris De Camp, *The Heritage of Cotton*, Fairchild Publications, New York, 1948.

54. Daniels, G. W., and Campion, H., "The Cotton Industry and Trade," in *Britain in Depression* (British Association for the Advancement of Science), Sir Isaac Pitman and Sons, London, 1935.

55. Dooley, William H., *Economics of Clothing and Textiles,* D. C. Heath and Company, Boston, 1934.

56. Dunn, Read P., Jr., *Cotton in Africa,* National Cotton Council of America, Memphis, 1950.

57. Fay, C. R., *Great Britain from Adam Smith to the Present Day,* Longmans, Green and Company, London, 1928.

58. Glover, John G., Cornell, William B., and Collins, G. Rowland (Editors), *The Development of American Industries,* 3d edition, Prentice-Hall, New York, 1951.

59. Govil, K. L., *Cotton Industry of India,* Hind Kitabs, Bombay, 1945.

60. Grünbaum, Heinz, *Die Welttextilkrise* (Institut für Konjunkturforschung, Sonderheft 24), Reimar Hobbing, Berlin, 1931.

61. Haynes, Williams, *Chemical Economics,* Van Nostrand Company, New York, 1933.

62. Heaton, Herbert, *Economic History of Europe,* revised edition, Harper and Brothers, New York, 1948.

63. Hess, Katharine P., *Textile Fibers and Their Use,* 4th edition, J. B. Lippincott Company, Philadelphia, 1948.

64. Horne, McDonald K., and McCord, F. A., *Cotton Counts Its Customers,* National Cotton Council of America, Memphis, 1942.

65. *International Cotton Bulletin.*

66. *International Industry Yearbook, The Encyclopaedia of Industrial Progress,* Kristen-Browne Publishing Company, New York.

67. Keir, Robert Malcolm, *Manufacturing* (Industries of America Series), Ronald Press Company, New York, 1928.

68. Kertesz, Adolf, *Die Textilindustrien Sämtlicher Staaten,* F. Vieweg und Sohn, Brunswick, 1917.

69. Knowles, Lillian C. A., *The Industrial and Commercial Revolutions in Great Britain during the Nineteenth Century,* E. P. Dutton and Company, New York, 1921.

70. Lipson, Ephraim, *The Economic History of England,* 7th edition, Macmillan Company, New York, 1937.

71. ———, *The History of the Woolen and Worsted Industries,* Macmillan Company, London, 1921.

72. Liashchenko, Peter, *Istoriia Narodnogo Khoziaistva SSSR,* 2 volumes, Moscow, 1948.

73. Matsui, Shichiro, *History of the Silk Industry in the United States,* Howes Publishing Company, New York, 1930.

74. *Matthews' Textile Fibers,* 5th edition (edited by Herbert R. Mauersberger), John Wiley and Sons, New York, 1947.

75. Merrill, Gilbert R., Macormac, Alfred R., and Mauersberger, Herbert R., *American Cotton Handbook,* American Cotton Handbook Company, New York.

76. Michl, Herman E., *The Textile Industries: an Economic Analysis,* Textile Foundation, Washington, 1938.

77. National Cotton Council of America, *The Age of Textiles,* Memphis, 1945.

78. ———, *Cotton Counts Its Customers,* Memphis, 1950.

79. *The Orient Yearbook, 1942,* Asia Statistics Co., Tokyo, 1942. (Republished by the Interdepartmental Committee for the Acquisition of Foreign Publications.)

80. Parsons, L. E., and Stearns, John K., *Textile Fibers,* International Textbook Company, Scranton, 1951.

81. *Rayon Organon* (since 1952: *Textile Organon*).

82. Redford, Arthur, *Economic History of England (1760–1860),* Longmans, Green and Company, New York, 1931.

83. Sharma, Tulsi Ram, *Location of Industries in India,* 2d edition, Hind Kitabs, Bombay, 1948.

84. Sherman, Joseph V., and Sherman, Signe Lidfeldt, *The New Fibers,* D. Van Nostrand Company, New York, 1946.

85. Stewart, John R., *Japan's Textile Industry,* Institute of Pacific Relations, New York, 1946.

86. *Textile World.*

87. *Textiles Plan for Postwar* (an interview conducted by *Cotton*), W. R. Smith Publication, Atlanta, 1945.

88. Tugan-Baranovskiĭ, M. I., *Russkaia Fabrika v Proshlom i Nastoiashchem,* St. Petersburg, 1898.

89. Union des Industries Textiles, *Bilan Statistique Résumé de l'Industrie Textile Française 1938–1948,* Paris, 1950.

90. Von Bergen, Werner, and Mauersberger, Herbert R., *American Wool Handbook,* 2d edition, Textile Book Publishers, New York, 1948.

91. Wadsworth, Alfred P., and Mann, Julia de Lacy, *The Cotton Trade and Industrial Lancashire, 1600–1780,* Manchester University Press, Manchester, 1931.

92. Woytinsky, Wl. (W. S.), *Die Welt in Zahlen,* Vol. IV: *Das Gewerbe,* Rudolf Mosse, Berlin, 1926.

93. Wythe, George, *Industry in Latin America,* Columbia University Press, New York, 1945.

94. ———, Wight, Royce A., and Midkiff, Harold M., *Brazil: an Expanding Economy,* Twentieth Century Fund, New York, 1949.

95. Zimmerman, E. W., *World Resources and Industries,* 2d edition, Harper and Brothers, New York, 1951.

CHAPTER 29

THE IRON AND STEEL INDUSTRY

1. United Nations, *Demographic Yearbook,* New York.

2. ———, *Statistical Yearbook,* New York.

3. ———, *Economic Development in Selected Countries,* New York, 1947.

4. ———, *Monthly Bulletin of Statistics,* New York.

5. ———, Economic Commission for Asia and the Far East, *Economic Survey of Asia and the Far East.* New York.

6. ———, Economic Commission for Europe, *Economic Survey of Europe,* Geneva.

7. ———, ———, *European Steel Trends in the Setting of the World Market,* Geneva.

8. ———, ———, *Quarterly Bulletin of Steel Statistics for Europe.*

9. ———, ———, *Steel Production and Consumption Trends in Europe and the World,* Geneva, 1952.

10. International Labor Organization, Iron and Steel Committee, *General Report,* Geneva, 1949.

11. ———, ———, *Report of the First Session,* Geneva, 1947.

12. ———, ———, *Technological Improvements in the Iron and Steel Industry and Their Effects on Employment*, Geneva, 1949.

13. Anglo-American Council on Productivity, *Steel Founding* (Productivity Team Report), London, 1949.

14. Communauté Européenne du Charbon et de l'Acier (European Coal and Steel Community), *Convention Relative aux Dispositions Transitoires*, Paris, 1951.

15. ———, *Traité Instituant la Communauté Européenne du Charbon et de l'Acier*, Paris, 1951.

UNITED STATES

16. Seventy-sixth Congress, Third Session, Temporary National Economic Committee, *Technology in our Economy* (Monograph No. 22), 1941.

17. ———, ———, ———, *Iron and Steel Industry* (Investigation of Concentration of Economic Power, Part 26), 1940.

18. Department of Commerce, Bureau of the Census, *Census of Manufactures.*

19. ———, ———, *Statistical Abstract of the United States.*

20. ———, ———, *Historical Statistics of the United States, 1789–1945*, 1949.

21. Department of the Interior, Bureau of Mines, *Minerals Yearbook.*

22. Federal Trade Commission, *Report on International Steel Cartels*, 1948.

23. Foreign Economic Administration, *Ferro-Alloys in the German Steel Economy*, 1944.

24. National Resources Committee, *Technological Trends and National Policy*, 1937.

25. National Resources Planning Board, *Industrial Location and National Resources*, 1943.

26. Tariff Commission, *Iron and Steel* (Report No. 128, Second Series), 1938.

27. ———, *Iron and Steel* (War Changes in Industry Series, Report No. 15), 1946.

28. ———, *Mining and Manufacturing Industries in Brazil*, 1945.

29. CANADA. Statistics Bureau, General Statistics Branch, *The Canada Yearbook*, Ottawa.

FRANCE

30. Présidence du Conseil, *Rapport du Commissaire Général sur le Plan de Modernisation et d'Équipement de l'Union Française*, Paris, 1949.

31. Présidence du Gouvernment, *Premier Rapport de la Commission de Modernisation de la Sidérurgie*, Paris, 1946.

32. GERMANY. Statistisches Reichsamt, *Statistisches Jahrbuch für das Deutsche Reich*, Berlin.

GREAT BRITAIN

33. Central Statistical Office, *Annual Abstract of Statistics*, London.

34. *Iron and Steel Industry* (Reports by the British Iron and Steel Federation and the Joint Iron Council to the Ministry of Supply), London, 1946.

35. Alderfer, E. B., and Michl, H. E., *Economics of American Industry*, McGraw-Hill Book Company, New York, 1942.

36. American Iron and Steel Institute, *Annual Statistical Report*, New York.

37. ———, *Steel Facts*, New York.

38. ———, *Year Book*, New York.

39. American Society for Metals, *Metals Handbook*, Cleveland.

40. Balzac, S. S., Vasyutin, V. F., and Feigin, Y. G., *Economic Geography of the USSR*, Macmillan Company, New York, 1949.

41. Baranskiĭ, N. N., *Ekonomicheskaia Geografiia SSSR*, Uchpegdiz, Moscow, 1947.

42. British Iron and Steel Federation, *Statistical Year Book*, 2 Parts, London.

43. Burn, Duncan L., *The Economic History of Steelmaking, 1867–1939: a Study in Competition*, Cambridge University Press, Cambridge, 1940.

44. Camp, J. M., and Francis, C. B., *The Making, Shaping and Treating of Steel*, 5th edition, Carnegie-Illinois Steel Corporation, Pittsburgh, 1940.

45. Daugherty, C. R., De Chazeau, M. G., and Stratton, S. S., *The Economics of the Iron and Steel Industry*, 2 vols., McGraw-Hill Book Company, New York, 1937.

46. Friend, J. Newton, *Iron in Antiquity*, Charles Griffin and Company, London, 1926.

47. *Gemeinfassliche Darstellung des Eisenhüttenwesens*, Verein Deutscher Eisenhüttenleute in Düsseldorf, 1937.

48. Heaton, Herbert, *Economic History of Europe*, revised edition, Harper and Brothers, New York, 1948.

49. Holton, C. R., "The Future Sources of Iron Units in Scrap," in *Year Book of the American Iron and Steel Institute, 1948*, New York, 1949.

50. *Industria* (International edition, 1950).

51. *Iron Age.*

52. Isard, W., "Some Locational Factors in the Iron and Steel Industry Since the Early Nineteenth Century," *Journal of Political Economy*, June 1948.

53. Juraschek, F., von, "Eisen und Eisenindustrie," in *Handwörterbuch der Staatswissenschaften*, 3d edition, Vol. III, Jena, 1909.

54. Keir, Robert M., *Manufacturing* (Industries of America Series), Ronald Press Company, New York, 1928.

55. King, C. D., "Seventy-five Years of Progress in Iron and Steel," in *Seventy-five Years of Progress in the Mineral Industry*, American Institute of Mining and Metallurgical Engineers, New York, 1947.

56. Kinzel, A. B., "Progress in Metallurgy: the Science of Alloys," *Journal of the Franklin Institute*, September 1939.

57. Larke, Sir William, "Address to the British Iron and Steel Federation," *Monthly Statistical Bulletin*, London, February 1949.

58. Lippert, T. W., "Cerro Bolivar, Saga of an Iron Ore Crisis Averted," *Journal of Metals* and *Mining Engineering*, February 1950.

59. Lokshin, E., *Promyshlennost' SSSR v Novoĭ Stalinskoĭ Piatiletke*, Ogiz, Moscow, 1946.

60. Löwegren, Gunnar, *Swedish Iron and Steel*, Svenska Handelsbanken, Stockholm, 1948.

61. Lucas, A., *Ancient Egyptian Materials and Industries,* 3d edition, Longmans, Green and Company, New York, 1948.
62. Mikhaïlov, N. N., *Nad Kartoĭ Rodiny,* Molodaîa Gvardiîa, Moscow, 1947.
63. Parker, Charles M., *Steel in Action,* Jacques Cattell Press, Lancaster, Pennsylvania, 1943.
64. Schwartz, Harry, *Russia's Soviet Economy,* Prentice-Hall, New York, 1950.
65. *Stahl und Eisen.*
66. *Statistisches Heft,* Verein für die Bergbaulichen Interessen, Essen, 1939.
67. *Steel.*
68. *Steel (Yearbook* issue), January 3, 1949.
69. Strassburger, Julius H., "Tonnage Oxygen for Increased Iron and Steel Production," in *Year Book of the American Iron and Steel Institute, 1948,* New York, 1949.
70. Swank, James M., *History of the Manufacture of Iron in All Ages,* published by the author, Philadelphia, 1884.
71. Tugan-Baranovskiĭ, M., *Russkaîa Fabrika,* 6th edition, Gossudarstvennoîe Sotsialisticheskoîe Ekonomicheskoie Izdatelstvo, Moscow, 1934.
72. Woytinsky, Wl. (W. S.), *Die Welt in Zahlen,* Vol. IV: *Das Gewerbe,* Rudolf Mosse, Berlin, 1926.
73. Wright, Charles Will, *The Iron and Steel Industries of Europe* (Economic Paper No. 19), U.S. Bureau of Mines, 1939.
74. Wythe, George, *Industry in Latin America,* 2d edition, Columbia University Press, New York, 1949.
75. ———, Wight, Royce A., and Midkiff, Harold M., *Brazil: an Expanding Economy,* Twentieth Century Fund, New York, 1949.

CHAPTER 30

THE MACHINERY AND TRANSPORTATION EQUIPMENT INDUSTRIES

1. League of Nations, *Statistical Year-Book,* Geneva.
2. United Nations, *Statistical Yearbook,* New York.
3. ———, *Monthly Bulletin of Statistics,* New York.
4. ———, *World Economic Report,* New York.
5. ———, Economic Commission for Asia and the Far East, *Economic Survey of Asia and the Far East,* New York.
6. ———, Economic Commission for Europe, *Economic Survey of Europe,* Geneva.
7. ———, ———, *The European Tractor Industry in the Setting of the World Market,* Geneva, 1952.
8. ———, ———, *A General Survey of the European Engineering Industry,* Geneva, 1951.
9. International Labor Organization, Metal Trades Committee, *General Report,* Geneva.
10. ———, ———, *Regularization of Production and Employment at a High Level,* The Automobile Industry, Geneva, 1947.
11. Organisation for European Economic Cooperation, *Machine Tools,* Paris, 1949.
12. Supreme Command Allied Powers, General Headquarters, *Japanese Economic Statistics,* Tokyo.

UNITED STATES
13. Seventy-ninth Congress, Senate, *Economic Concentration and World War II* (Document No. 206), 1946.
14. Department of Commerce, *Review of the American Machinery Industries,* 1936.
15. ———, *Statistical Handbook of Civil Aviation 1950.*
16. ———, Bureau of the Census, *Census of Manufactures, 1947,* 1950.
17. ———, ———, *Census of Manufactures, 1939,* 1942.
18. ———, ———, *Statistical Abstract of the United States.*
19. ———, Bureau of Foreign and Domestic Commerce, *Survey of Current Business.*
20. Economic Cooperation Administration, *Italy: Country Study,* 1949.
21. ———, Special Mission to the United Kingdom, *The Sterling Area: an American Analysis,* London, 1951.
22. Federal Trade Commission, *Motor Vehicles Industry, Summary and Conclusions,* 1939.
23. Surplus Property Administration, *Aircraft Plants and Facilities,* 1946.
24. Tariff Commission, *Metals and Manufactures* (Summaries of Tariff Information, Vol. 3, 5 parts), 1948.
25. ———, *Mining and Manufacturing Industries in Argentina,* 1945.

FRANCE
26. Bureau Central de Statistique Industrielle, *Annuaire de Statistique Industrielle,* Paris, 1949.
27. Commissariat Général du Plan de Modernisation et d'Équipement, *Rapport de la Commission de Modernisation de l'Automobile,* Paris, 1948.

GERMANY
28. Länderrat des Amerikanischen Besatzungsgebiets, *Statistisches Handbuch von Deutschland, 1928–1944,* Munich, 1949.
29. Reichsamt für Wehrwirtschaftliche Planung, *Die Deutsche Industrie,* Vol. I, Berlin, 1939.

30. GREAT BRITAIN. Central Statistical Office, *Monthly Digest of Statistics,* London.

31. ITALY. Confederazione Generale dell' Industria Italiana, *Annuario,* Rome.

32. Aeronautical Chamber of Commerce of America, *The Aircraft Year Book,* New York.
33. Aircraft Industries Association of America, *Aviation Facts and Figures,* McGraw-Hill Book Company, New York, 1945.
34. Alderfer, E. B., and Michl, H. E., *Economics of American Industry,* McGraw-Hill Book Company, New York, 1942.
35. *American Machinist.*
36. Automobile Manufacturers Association, *Automobile Facts,* Detroit.
37. ———, *Automobile Facts and Figures,* Detroit.
38. Balzac, S. S., Vasyutin, V. F., and Feigin, Y. G., *Economic Geography of the USSR,* Macmillan Company, New York, 1949.
39. Bogart, Ernest L., and Landon, Charles E., *Modern Industry,* 2d edition, Longmans, Green and Company, New York, 1936.

40. Chamber of Shipping of the United Kingdom, *Annual Report,* Witherby and Company, London.

41. Clark, Victor S., *History of Manufactures in the United States,* Carnegie Institution of Washington, 1929.

42. Cohen, Jerome B., *Japan's Economy in War and Reconstruction,* University of Minnesota Press, Minneapolis, 1949.

43. Dewhurst, J. Frederic, and Associates, *America's Needs and Resources,* Twentieth Century Fund, New York, 1947.

44. *The Machine Tool Industry* (An Engineering Interpretation of the Economic and Financial Aspects of American Industry, Vol. 2), George S. Armstrong and Company, New York, 1941.

45. Ferney, L. A., "The British Machine Tool Industry," *Fabian Quarterly,* April 1945.

46. Foreign Press Association of Japan, *The Japan Year Book, 1940–41,* Japan Press Times, Tokyo.

47. Glover, John G., Cornell, William B., and Collins, G. Rowland (Editors), *The Development of American Industries,* 3d edition, Prentice-Hall, New York, 1951.

48. Heaton, Herbert, *Economic History of Europe,* revised edition, Harper and Brothers, New York, 1948.

49. *Industria* (International edition, 1950), Stockholm.

50. *Iron Age.*

51. Jacoboni, Attilo, *L'Industria Meccanica Italiana,* Centro di Studi a Piani Tecnico-Economici, Rome, 1949.

52. Keir, Robert M., *Manufacturing* (Industries of America Series), Ronald Press Company, New York, 1928.

53. Knowles, Lillian C. A., *The Industrial and Commercial Revolutions in Great Britain during the Nineteenth Century,* E. P. Dutton and Company, New York, 1921.

54. *Machinery Lloyd* (Overseas edition), London.

55. *Monatsberichte der Bank Deutscher Länder,* Frankfurt.

56. *The Orient Yearbook, 1942,* Asia Statistics Co., Tokyo, 1942. (Republished by the Interdepartmental Committee for the Acquisition of Foreign Publications.)

57. Political and Economic Planning (PEP), *Motor Vehicles,* London, 1949.

58. Schwartz, Harry, *Russia's Soviet Economy,* Prentice-Hall, New York, 1950.

59. Stamp, L. Dudley, and Beaver, Stanley H., *The British Isles,* 3d revised edition, Longmans, Green and Company, New York, 1941.

60. *Steel.*

61. *World Aviation Annual, 1948,* Aviation Research Institute, Washington, D. C., and James Jackson Cabot Professorship of Air Transportation of Norwich University, Northfield, Vermont.

62. Woytinsky, Wl. (W. S.), *Die Welt in Zahlen,* Vol. IV: *Das Gewerbe,* Rudolf Mosse, Berlin, 1926.

63. Wythe, George, *Industry in Latin America,* 2d edition, Columbia University Press, New York, 1949.

CHAPTER 31

THE CHEMICAL INDUSTRY

1. League of Nations, *Statistical Year-Book,* Geneva.

2. ———, International Economic Conference, *The Chemical Industry* (Documentation), Geneva, 1927.

3. United Nations, *Statistical Yearbook,* New York.

4. ———, *Monthly Bulletin of Statistics,* New York.

5. ———, Economic Commission for Europe, *Economic Survey of Europe,* Geneva.

6. ———, Food and Agriculture Organization (FAO), *Fertilizers* (Commodity Series, No. 17), Washington, September 1949.

7. International Labor Organization, Chemical Industries Committee, *General Report,* Geneva.

8. Organisation for European Economic Cooperation, *Report of the Chemical Products Committee,* Paris, 1949.

UNITED STATES

9. Seventy-ninth Congress, Senate, *Economic Concentration and World War II* (Document No. 206), 1946.

10. Department of Commerce, Bureau of the Census, *Statistical Abstract of the United States.*

11. ———, Bureau of Foreign and Domestic Commerce, *Survey of Current Business.*

12. ———, *Foreign Commerce Weekly.*

13. ———, *World Chemical Developments, 1940–46,* 2 parts, 1947–48.

14. Surplus Property Administration, *Chemical Plants and Facilities,* 1945.

15. Tariff Commission, *Chemical Nitrogen* (Report No. 114), 1937.

16. ———, *Dyes* (War Changes in Industry Series, Report No. 19), 1946.

17. ———, *Plastic Products* (War Changes in Industry Series, Report No. 28), 1948.

18. ———, *Rubber* (War Changes in Industry Series, Report No. 6), 1945.

19. ———, *Summaries of Tariff Information,* Vol. I, 6 parts, 1948.

20. ———, *Synthetic Organic Chemicals, United States Production and Sales* (Report No. 169, Second Series), 1950.

GERMANY

21. Statistisches Amt des Vereinigten Wirtschaftsgebietes, *Wirtschaft und Statistik,* Stuttgart.

22. Statistisches Reichsamt, *Statistisches Jahrbuch für das Deutsche Reich,* Berlin.

23. ITALY. Confederazione Generale dell' Industria Italiana, *Annuario,* Rome.

24. Agricola, Georgius, *De Re Metallica* (trans. from the first Latin edition of 1556 by Herbert C. Hoover and Lou H. Hoover), Dover Publications, New York, 1950.

25. Balzac, S. S., Vasyutin, V. F., and Feigin, Y. G., *Economic Geography of the USSR,* Macmillan Company, New York, 1949.

26. British Sulphate of Ammonia Federation, *Annual Report,* London.

27. Brown, Derek W., *Handbook of Engineering Plastics,* George Newnes, London, 1943.

28. ——, and Harris, Wilbur T., *An Introduction to Engineering Plastics,* Murray Hill Books, New York, 1947.

29. *Chemical and Metallurgical Engineering.*

30. *Chemical Facts and Figures,* Manufacturing Chemists' Association, Inc., Washington, D. C.

31. Clough, Shepard B., and Cole, Charles W., *Economic History of Europe,* D. C. Heath and Company, Boston, 1946.

32. Crandall, Barrett L., *The Plastics Industry* (American Industries Series, No. 5), Bellman Publishing Company, New York, 1946.

33. Croome, Honor M., and Hammond, R. J., *The Economy of Britain: a History,* Christophers, London, 1938.

34. Faith, W. L., Keyes, Donald B., and Clark, Ronald L., *Industrial Chemicals,* John Wiley and Sons, New York, 1950.

35. Furnas, C. C. (Editor), *Rogers' Industrial Chemistry,* 6th edition, 2 volumes, D. Van Nostrand Company, New York, 1942.

36. Gross, Hermann, *Material zur Aufteilung der I. G. Farbenindustrie Aktiengesellschaft,* Institut für Weltwirtschaft, Kiel, 1950.

37. Haynes, Williams, *American Chemical Industry,* 3 volumes, D. Van Nostrand Company, New York, 1945.

38. ——, *Chemical Economics,* D. Van Nostrand Company, New York, 1933.

39. ——, *Men, Money and Molecules,* Doubleday, Doran and Company, New York, 1936.

40. Hempel, Edward H., *The Economics of Chemical Industries,* John Wiley and Sons, New York, 1939.

41. Henglein, F. A., *Grundriss der Chemischen Technik,* 5th edition, Verlag Chemie, Berlin, 1949.

42. Howe, Harrison E., "The Chemical Industries," in *Technological Trends and National Policy,* National Resources Committee, 1937.

43. —— (Editor), *Chemistry in Industry,* 2 volumes, Chemical Foundation, New York, 1924.

44. Kobe, Kenneth A., *Inorganic Process Industries,* Macmillan Company, New York, 1948.

45. Kreps, Theodore J., *The Economics of the Sulfuric Acid Industry,* Stanford University Press, Stanford, 1938.

46. Landis, Walter S., *Your Servant the Molecule,* Macmillan Company, New York, 1944.

47. Miall, Stephen, *A History of the British Chemical Industry,* Ernest Benn, London, 1931.

48. *Modern Plastics.*

49. Morgan, Sir Gilbert T., and Pratt, David D., *British Chemical Industry, Its Rise and Development,* Longmans, Green and Company, New York, and Edward Arnold and Company, London, 1938.

50. Robinson, Clark N., *Meet the Plastics,* Macmillan Company, New York, 1949.

51. Schmidt, Albrecht, and Fischbeck, Kurt, *Die Industrielle Chemie in Ihrer Bedeutung im Weltbild,* 2d edition, Walter de Gruyter and Company, Berlin, 1943.

52. Schwartz, Harry, *Russia's Soviet Economy,* Prentice-Hall, New York, 1950.

53. Shreve, Randolph Norris, *The Chemical Process Industries,* McGraw-Hill Book Company, New York, 1945.

54. Simonds, Herbert R., Weith, Archie J., and Bigelow, M. H., *Handbook of Plastics,* 2d edition, D. Van Nostrand Company, New York, 1949.

55. Stamp, L. Dudley, and Beaver, Stanley H., *The British Isles,* 3d revised edition, Longmans, Green and Company, New York, 1941.

56. Stocking, George W., and Watkins, Myron W., *Cartels in Action,* Twentieth Century Fund, New York, 1946.

57. Thorp, Sir Thomas Edward, *History of Chemistry,* 2 volumes, G. P. Putnam's Sons, New York, 1909–10.

58. Tyler, Chaplin (Editor), *Chemical Engineering Economics,* McGraw-Hill Book Company, 3d edition, New York, 1948.

59. Ungewitter, Claus, *Chemie in Deutschland,* Junker und Dünnhaupt Verlag, Berlin, 1939.

60. Wythe, George, *Industry in Latin America,* 2d edition, Columbia University Press, New York, 1949.

ALPHABETICAL LIST OF AUTHORS

(Page references to full citations in the Source Reference section)

Francis, C. B., *see* Camp, J. M., 1242
Frazer, Allan, 1227, 1228
Fredericsen, Johan D., 1228
Friedensburg, Ferdinand, 1233
Friend, J. Newton, 1242
Friis, Herman R., 1210, 1211
Furnas, C. C., 1245
Furness, J. W., 1233; *see also* Leith, C. K., 1218, 1232

GAINSBRUGH, M. R., *see* Backman, Jules, 1240
Gandhi, M. K., 1218
Garner, Wrightman Wells, 1239
Geerligs, H. C. Prinsen, 1226
Genzmer, W., *see* Behnsen, Henry, 1228
Gericke, S., 1226
Gill, Tom, *see* Pack, Charles L., 1229
Gini, Corrado, 1213, 1215, 1219, 1220, 1221
Glass, David V., 1215
Glesinger, Egon, 1229
Glover, John G., 1241, 1244
Good, Dorothy, *see* Pratt, Wallace E., 1236, 1237
Gordon, Leland J., 1217
Gorrie, R. Maclagen, 1224
Govil, K. L., 1241
Grant, Ruth Fulton, 1230
Gras, N. S. B., 1224
Gross, Hermann, 1245
Grotjahn, A., 1213
Grünbaum, Heinz, 1241
Gurney, Robert, 1229

HADDON, A. C., 1210
Hager, Dorsey, 1236
Hahn, Eduard, 1221
Hainsworth, Reginald G., 1224; *see also* Moyer, Raymond T., 1226
Hall, Sir Alfred D., 1224, 1228
Hall, J. Alfred, 1229
Hammond, R. J., *see* Croome, Honor M., 1245
Hansen, Peter L., 1226
Harper, Floyd A., *see* Pearson, Frank A., 1210, 1219
Harris, Wilbur T., *see* Brown, Derek W., 1245
Hartley, Sir Harold, 1237
Hartmann, Irving, *see* Rice, George S., 1235
Haynes, Williams, 1241, 1245
Heaton, Herbert, 1239, 1241, 1242, 1244
Hecht, Reuben W., 1224
Hempel, Edward H., 1245
Henglein, F. A., 1245
Herodotus, 1214, 1218, 1227, 1239
Hersch, Liebman, 1213
Hertz, Friedrich O., 1224
Hess, Katharine P., 1241
Hildebrand, Bruno, 1221
Himus, Godfrey W., *see* Bone, William A., 1234
Hoffmann, Walther, 1221
Holland, Sir Thomas H., 1233
Hollingsworth, Helen, *see* Klem, Margaret C., 1214
Hollman, A. H., 1224
Holton, C. R., 1242

Hopkins, John A., 1224
Horne, McDonald K., 1241
Hornschu, Hans-Erich, *see* Edding, Friedrich, 1211
Hoshino, Saki, 1239
Howard, Sir H., 1224
Howe, Harrison E., 1245
Hoyt, Homer, 1212
Hünecke, Günter, 1237
Hunnicut, Benjamin H., 1226, 1227, 1229, 1239
Huntington, Ellsworth, 1209, 1224
Huntley, K. E., *see* King, Willford I., 1220
Hutchinson, Edward P., 1211

ICHOK, G., 1213
Ickes, Harold L., 1235
Illick, Joseph S., 1229
Innes, J. W., 1213
Isaac, Julius, 1211
Isard, W., 1242

JACKS, G. V., 1224
Jacob, H. E., 1239
Jacoboni, Attilo, 1244
Jacobson, Jerome, *see* Copeland, Morris A., 1220
Jacobson, Paul H., 1213
Jasny, Naum, 1224, 1226
Jefferson, Mark, 1212
Joerg, W. L. G., 1211
Johnson, Martin W., *see* Sverdrup, H. U., 1209, 1231
Johnson, Ray G., *see* Philipps, Ralph W., 1229
Johnson, Sherman E., 1226
Jones, W. R., 1233
Juraschek, F., von, 1242

KARPINOS, Bernard D., 1213
Karpovich, Michael, *see* Bowden, Witt, 1240
Kautsky, Karl, 1222
Keir, Robert Malcolm, 1241, 1242, 1244
Kelaukar, S. K., 1228
Kellog, Lester S., 1218
Kellogg, Charles E., 1224
Kertesz, Adolf, 1241
Keyes, Donald B., *see* Faith, W. L., 1245
Kimble, George H. T., 1211
King, C. D., 1242
King, Gregory, 1217
King, W. T., *see* Sydenstricker, E., 1217
King, Willford I., 1220
Kinzel, A. B., 1242
Kirk, Dudley, 1211
Kiser, Clyde V., *see* Karpinos, Bernard D., 1213; *see also* Whelpton, P. K., 1213
Klages, Karl H. W., 1226, 1227
Klarman, Herbert E., 1220
Klatt, W., 1224
Klem, Margaret C., 1214
Klingman, Glenn C., *see* Ahlgren, Gilbert H., 1224
Knibbs, G. H., 1213
Knowles, Lillian C. A., 1241, 1244
Kobe, Kenneth A., 1245
Koeppen, W., 1209
Kolesnev, Samuil G., 1224, 1228

Kossinna, Erwin, 1209
Kramer, Matthias, 1225
Kreps, Theodore J., 1245
Kuczynski, Robert R., 1210, 1213
Kuhlmann, Charles Byron, 1239
Kulischer, Eugene M., 1211
Kuznets, Simon, 1220
Kyrk, Hazel, 1217

LADOO, Raymond B., 1233
Laemmel, Rudolf, 1237
Lalicker, Cecil G., 1236
Lamson, Herbert D., 1213
Landis, Walter S., 1245
Landon, Charles E., *see* Bogart, Ernest L., 1243
Landry, Adolphe, 1213, 1215
Larke, Sir William, 1242
Lebret, L. J., 1230
Legendre, René, 1230
Leith, C. K., 1218, 1232, 1233
Lemon, James M., *see* Tressler, Donald K., 1231
LePlay, M. F., 1217
Leroy, André Max, 1227, 1228
Leven, David D., 1236
Levorsen, A. I., 1236
Lewis, C. J., 1213
Lewis, Cleona, *see* Leith, C. K., 1218, 1232, 1233
Lewis, J. Norman, *see* Lewis, C. J., 1213
Lewis, W. R., *see* Woodcock, F. Huntley, 1239
Liashchenko, Peter, 1241
Licht, F. O., 1226
Lilley, Ernest R., 1233
Lippert, T. W., 1218, 1233, 1242
Lipson, Ephraim, 1241
List, Friedrich, 1221
Liu, Ta-chung, 1221
Livi, Livio, 1213
Lockwood, J. F., 1239
Lokshin, E., 1242
Long, H. C., 1225
Lorenz, M. O., 1220
Lotka, Alfred J., *see* Dublin, Louis I., 1213, 1214, 1219
Loture, Robert de, 1230
Lovering, T. S., 1233
Lowdermilk, Walter C., 1229
Löwegren, Gunnar, 1242
Lucas, A., 1243

McCORD, F. A., *see* Horne, McDonald K., 1241
McFadyean, Sir Arthur, 1227
McFall, R. J., 1228
McKenzie, Roderick D., 1212
MacMurphy, Allen B., *see* Shermann, Allan, 1235
Macormac, Alfred R., *see* Merrill, Gilbert R., 1241
Mahnke, K. G., *see* Regul, R., 1235
Malott, Deane W., 1227, 1228, 1239
Malthus, Thomas Robert, 1215, 1218
Mann, Julia de Lacy, *see* Wadsworth, Alfred P., 1241
March, Lucien, 1213
Markham, S. F., 1209
Marschak, Jacob, *see* Schurr, Sam H., 1219, 1237
Martin, Boyce F., *see* Malott, Deane W., 1227, 1228, 1239

INDEX

INDEX

BECAUSE THIS BOOK is principally concerned with the whole world rather than its separate nations, states and cities, as such, this is essentially a subject index rather than a geographical one. It gives the location of information on the main topics and subtopics covered by the study — population, natural resources, specific products, income, consumer expenditures, etc. References to particular regions, continents, countries and cities are included only when there is extended or special discussion of them.

The book contains a vast quantity of information about geographical areas — mainly in the form of comparative statistics under each subject division. The reader wanting information about India, for example, will find it by referring first to the heading "India" for special discussions of the country and then to the various subject headings under "World, *data for selected countries.*" The same is true for continents and cities, for which information can be found by referring to the subject headings listed under "World, *data by continent*" and "Cities." The United States is an exception to this rule and is more fully indexed than any other country under "United States, *data by state,*" "United States, *totals,*" and by important subjects under these headings.

Personal entries include only the names of persons specifically mentioned or quoted in the text or footnotes. A separate Alphabetical List of Authors appears on pages 1247–1250 and a complete chapter-by-chapter listing of authors and source materials in the Source References section on pages 1209–1245.

An extensive Table of Contents is shown on pages ix–xxix and detailed lists of the statistical tables and figures (maps, graphs and charts) on pages xxxi–lviii in the front of the book.

The designation (t) following a page number in the index indicates a reference to a table; the designation (f) to a map, graph or chart.